REVOLUTIONARY WAR PENSIONS

Awarded by State Governments 1775 - 1874,
the General and Federal Governments Prior to 1814,
and by Private Acts of Congress to 1905

REVOLUTIONARY WAR PENSIONS

Awarded by State Governments 1775 - 1874,
the General and Federal Governments Prior to 1814,
and by Private Acts of Congress to 1905

By
Lloyd de Witt Bockstruck, FNGS

Published by Genealogical Publishing Company
3600 Clipper Mill Road, Suite 260
Baltimore, Maryland 21211-1953
Library of Congress Catalogue Card Number 2011921428
ISBN 978-0-8063-1869-1
Made in the United States of America

Contents

Introduction

This compilation is an attempt to identify and recreate the Revolutionary War pension files generated prior to the disastrous conflagration in the War Department on 8 November 1800, which destroyed nearly a quarter of a century of records. Despite the best efforts on the part of the War and Treasury Departments to reconstruct the files and to prevent any future such tragedies, a second and even more disastrous fire occurred during the War of 1812 on 24 August 1814 with the British invasion of Washington, D.C. The second fire effectively eliminated all of the pension files from 1776 to 1814. Despite the tragic loss of nearly four decades of pension records at the national level, it has been possible not only to identify many of those pensioners whose files are commonly believed to have been irretrievably lost but also to reconstitute in varying degrees their contents. More than 16,500 pensioners are featured in this work.

Among the largely overlooked sources used to do so were the pension records generated by the governments of each of the Thirteen Original States. The state governments had their own programs and in varying degrees preserved many of their pension files. The private acts of Congress are another major source utilized to recreate the missing pension files. Both of these sources may supplement or complement the records in the regular Revolutionary War pension series, micro-publication M804, *Revolutionary War Pension and Bounty-Land-Warrant Applications Files*, 2,360 rolls.

The earliest authorization for Revolutionary War pension files was by the resolution of 26 August 1776 of the Continental Congress. Because the Continental Congress was without money and any real executive power, it had to rely upon the individual states to implement and fund the pension programs. Congress could do no more than make the recommendation. Each state was responsible for determining eligibility and for granting final approval of each applicant from within its borders. The amount of the pension was either half-pay for life or during the disability of the officer, soldier, or sailor who had lost a limb or had been disabled in the service so as to be rendered incapable of earning a livelihood.

At the national level *The Papers of the Continental Congress, 1774–1789*, micro-publication M247, 204 rolls, and *Miscellaneous Papers of the Continental Congress, 1774–1789*, micro-publication M332, 10 rolls, include a significant amount of material pertaining to individual pensioners. John P. Butler's five-volume *Index, The Papers of the*

Introduction

Continental Congress, 1774–1789 (Washington, D.C.: National Archives and Records Service, General Services Administration, 1978) provides access to these records. In addition the thirty-four volume set, the *Journals of the Continental Congress 1774–1789* (Washington, D.C.: Government Printing Office, 1904–37) is equally valuable. Access to the latter is provided by Kenneth E. Harris and Stevens D. Tilley's *Index: Journals of the Continental Congress 1774–1789* (Washington, D.C.: National Archives and Records Service, General Services Administration, 1976).

Central Treasury Records of the Continental and Confederation Governments Relating to Military Affairs, 1775–1789, micro-publication T1015, 7 rolls, contains important financial records anent Revolutionary War pensioners. On the last roll are the ledgers of pension payments made to Revolutionary War invalids, widows, and orphans of Pennsylvania for the period 1785–1804.

The eight-volume set *Documentary History of the First Federal Congress of the United States of America, March 4, 1789–March 3, 1791* (Baltimore: The Johns Hopkins University Press, 1972 ff.) is also useful. *The Public Statutes at Large of the United States of America* (Boston: Charles C. Little and James Brown, 1848) I, 454–58, giving the names, ranks, and percentage of pensioners paid by the Secretary of War in 1796 expands the list of identifiable pensioners.

Veterans and their next of kin unable to qualify under statutory authorized pensions resorted to private acts by Congress. *Unbound Records of the U.S. House of Representatives, 10th Congress, 1807–1809,* micro-publication M1711, 10 rolls, contains a number of petitions of that ilk.

Supplementing the published sources is the online database *Papers of the War Department, 1784–1800,* created by the Center for History and New Media at George Mason University by bringing together 55,000 documents from more than 200 depositories and 3,000 collections. The documents have been digitized. It does suffer from some misinterpretations of forenames and surnames.

There were a number of pension acts after the one of 1776. The next was that of 15 May 1778, which authorized half-pay for seven years to all officers who remained in Continental service to the end of the war. It did not apply to foreign officers or officers above the rank of colonel. It also provided a gratuity of $80 to every enlisted man who served to the end of the war. The states were to make the payments on account with the United States. The act of 24 August 1780 extended the half-pay provision to widows or orphan children of officers who had died or would die in the service.

Following the resignation of 160 officers between January and October 1780, Congress addressed the problem of a lack of pensions. By the Resolve of 21 October

Introduction

1780, all officers who continued to the end of the war should be entitled to half-pay for life. Congress did not, however, make any funds available to implement the program. On 23 April 1782 soldiers who were sick or wounded and were reported unfit for duty in the field or garrison were to be pensioned at the rate of $5 per month. The states were to dispense the funds annually and to draw upon the Superintendent of Finance for the money advanced. On 22 March 1783 Congress authorized full-pay for invalid officers for no more than five years or half-pay for life.

After the war, on 7 June 1785, Congress provided half-pay pensions for commissioned officers so disabled as to be wholly incapable of earning a livelihood. Non-commissioned officers and privates were to receive $5 per month. Each state was to appoint officers to examine the evidence of the claimants, admit claims, and make the pension payments. The amounts expended were to be deducted from each state's quota. Each state was to transmit annually to the Secretary of War a listing of each invalid, pay, age, service, and disability. On 11 June 1788 Congress imposed a time limit of six months for people to apply and produce the requisite certificates and evidence.

With the creation of the federal government in 1789, Congress provided that the federal government–rather than the individual states–should bear the responsibility of paying the pensions under the Resolve of 26 August 1776. The law was valid for a year, but it was later extended. It should be noted that there was not a complete transfer of pensions from the states to the federal roll. On 23 March 1792 applicants for invalid pensions could submit their requests directly to the federal government except for the state of South Carolina. The Palmetto State's position was unique. It was not until 1803 that the federal government paid pensions to South Carolinians. There were 1,472 invalid pensioners of whom 1,358 were noncommissioned officers and privates.

On 3 March 1805 Congress extended benefits to those with wounds received in military service and who had become and continued to be disabled and unable to procure a subsistence by manual labor. This was the first time that disabilities and ills later in life were the result of wounds claimants received in the service. The most generous pension legislation came on 10 April 1806 when Congress repealed all previous acts and extended coverage to all classes of claimants including volunteers, militia, and state troops. Disability had to be due to wounds received in the line of duty and must have rendered the applicant wholly or partially unable to procure a subsistence by manual labor. Desertion was a bar to a claim.

On 25 April 1808 Congress directed the Secretary of War to place all persons on the federal pension list who remained on the pension lists of any of the states in consequence of wounds received in the war. It was not possible for someone to claim a pension from both a state and the federal government. Recognition of this situation is indicated by the oath required of every applicant that "He hereby relinquishes every claim whatever to a pension or annuity, except the present, and he declares that his name is not on the Pension Roll of any Agency in any State, or (if any) only that of the Agency in the State of _____." Federal pensions were larger than those paid by the states so any informed veteran sought to be transferred to the federal roll when he could demonstrate eligibility. A number of those who transferred to the federal rolls were later stricken from the rolls. Finding themselves in much distress, they were forced to reapply to their home states for the resumption of their state pensions. The states were seemingly more understanding of their plight and were less stringent about the burden of proof on the part of the applicant.

Due to the 8 November 1800 fire in the War Department in Washington, D.C., which destroyed almost all of the pension files submitted before that date, there are pension files bearing the notation "Dis. No. Papers" that were created from pension claims submitted for approval to Congress between 1792 and 1795. They are listed in the *American State Papers, Class 9, Claims.* There was a second fire in the War Department 24 August 1814, which destroyed the pension files submitted within the first fourteen years of the nineteenth century. Some of those pension files were also partially recreated and also bear the notation "Dis. No Papers." Such files contain the name of the veteran, unit, date of enlistment, nature of disability, residence, and amount of pension. In the micro-publication *Letters Received by the Secretary of War, Main Series, 1801–1870,* M221, are some letters of inquiry about eligibility for pensions, replacement of lost pension certificates, &c.

Army and Navy Pension Laws, and Bounty Land Laws of the United States, Including Sundry Resolutions of Congress, from 1776 to 1852: Executed at the Department of the Interior with an Appendix, Containing the Opinions of Attorneys General of the United States, with the Decisions, Rules, and Regulations Adopted by Different Secretaries Relative to the Execution of Those Laws (Washington, D.C.: Printed by Jno. T. Towers, 1852) by Robert Mayo and Ferdinand Moulton remains an important source for ascertaining the existence of pension files before the two fires. Another one is *Resolutions, Laws, and Ordinances Relating to the Pay, Half Pay, Commutation of Half Pay, Bounty Lands, and Promises Made by Congress* (Baltimore: Genealogical Publishing Company, 1998).

At various times Congress requested lists of pensioners, and these reports have been printed. These lists augment the other fragmentary records and provide data not available elsewhere. The pension report for the year 1792 is the second volume of House

Introduction

publication *Reports War Department 1ˢᵗ Congress, 3ʳᵈ Session to 2ⁿᵈ Congress 2ⁿᵈ Session.* It contains the names of 1,358 pensioners. Seven reports between 1794 and 1795 are in Senate publication *War Office Returns to Invalid Claims.* The 1796 report first appeared in print in Mary Govier Ainswoth's "Recently Discovered Records Relating to Revolutionary War Veterans Who Applied for Pensions under the Act of 1792," *National Genealogical Society Quarterly,* XLVI (1958) 8–13, 73–78.

    A Transcript of the Pension List of the United States of 1813 (Baltimore: Genealogical Publishing Company, 1959) is extremely significant because it was the last one to appear prior to the fire of 1814. It contains the names of 1,766 pensioners, not all of whom, however, were Revolutionary War veterans. Of course, many pensioners were already deceased by 1813. The U.S. War Department's *Pension List of 1820* (Baltimore: Genealogical Publishing Company, 1991) contains the names of more than 15,000 pensioners. In order to replace the papers and applications submitted after 1800 but destroyed in the fire of 1814, Congress issued *The Pension List of 1835* (Baltimore: Genealogical Publishing Company, 1835, 1968). The four-volume set has been greatly enhanced by the addition of indexes.

    A Census of Pensioners for Revolutionary or Military Services; with Their Names, Ages, and Places of Residence, under the Act for Taking the Sixth Census, Bound with a General Index (Baltimore: Genealogical Publishing Company, 1974) contains the names of pensioners—both veterans and their widows at the time of the 1840 census. Some of these pensioners had been on the rolls prior to the fire of 1814. Others were state pensioners. By no means, however, were all of these individuals veterans of the Revolutionary War. Other pension lists include *Letter from the Secretary of War, Communicating a Transcript of the Pension List of the United States* (1817). It contains the names of about 1,000 pensioners and 300 half-pay pensioners. *Pensioners of the United States, 1818* (Baltimore: Southern Book Company, 1959) has 5,900 pensioners and *The Pension List of 1820* (Baltimore: Genealogical Publishing Company, 1991) has 17,000 pensioners.

    The final payment vouchers found in Record Group 217 of the Treasury Department include a few invalid pensioners approved prior to 1814. The vouchers for the states of Georgia and Delaware have been microfilmed. Those for the District of Columbia, Louisiana, Maryland, Mississippi, New Jersey, Pennsylvania, Rhode Island, South Carolina, and Virginia have been published.

    Perhaps as many as a few hundred state bounty land recipients who do not appear in *Revolutionary War Bounty Land Grants Awarded by State Governments* (Baltimore: Genealogical Publishing Company, 1996) are also featured in this work.

Introduction

African American pensioners include Scipio, John Busby, John Cary, Edward Chambers, Daniel Chavis, William Couch, Austin Dabney, John Francis, Pearson Freeman, Primus Hall, Peter Harris, Nero Hawley, William Jones, Valentine Locus, George McCoy, Paul Meacham, Richard Nicken, Stephen Philips, Cato Quasha, David Scott, Jeremith Smith, Caesar Thompson, John Tranus, Benjamin Vicary, Aaron Weaver, and Stacy Williams.

Women whose service qualified them for pensions were Elizabeth Bergen, Margaret Corbin, Rachel Fox, Deborah Gannett, Anna Maria Lamb, Sarah Sherwood, Elizabeth Thompson, Hannah Weston, and Rumah Williams.

American Indians include Daniel Eldridge; William Henry Kilbuck, a Delaware chief; and Peter Harris, a Catawba.

Pensioners identified as original members of the Society of the Cincinnati include Louis Baury, Robert Coltman, John Craig, John Davis, Bartlett Hinds, John Jordan, Seth Lewis, Peter Nestell, Gassaway Watkins, and William Williams.

Veterans who were in the Battle of King's Mountain include Benoni Benning, William Campbell, William Carson, John Clark, Alexander Dennis, William Dudly, David Duff, James Dysart, Samuel Espey, Frederick Fisher, John Gribey, William Guest, John Hambright, Martin Hammond, Samuel Hammond, John Hicks, Peter Hilton, John Hollis, Pendleton Isbell, Samuel Johnson, John Kenseller, David Kerr, John Loggin, Stephen McElheney, James Merritt, Robert Miller, Thomas Moore, William Moore, John S. Polereczsky, Joseph Read, Benjamin Rowan, Robert Sevier, William Shaw, David Shipes, John Skeggs, Jonathan Tipton, Thomas Toms, Robert Walker, John Wilfong, and James Williams.

Although it was not legal for males under the age of 16 to serve in the war, there are a number of examples of service performed by boys younger than the minimum age. Examples include William Brown age 14, Christopher Cary, John W. Hunter age 13, Daniel Ingalls age 15, Samuel Jenkins age 15, Josiah King age 14, Thomas King age 15, Elizur Kirtland age 14, Robert Lorimore age 15, Hampton Lovegrove age 11, Leslie Malone age 14 or 15, Judah Mandingo age 15, Michael Seitsinger age 14, George Seigler age 15, Josias Sessions age 12, James Shanks age 14, George Singly age 15 or 16, Jonathan Smith age 15, Roger Strong age 13, James Tinsley age 15, Gershom Van Voast age 14, Bartholomew Vorman under 15, Josias Vorman age 11, Conrad Widrig age 15, and Theophilus Wilson, who was born *ca.* 1767.

Revolutionaries born outside of the Thirteen Colonies include Robert Simmons from Great Britain; Alexander Dow, Daniel Sellers, and Arthur St. Clair from Scotland; John Brown, Richard Canfield, Charles Dowd, Henry Dugan, Patrick Dunn, Joseph

Ferguson, Kinley Hazlet, Patrick Leonard, Daniel McCarthy, John McCormack, John McMullen, Charles Proud, Robert Orr, James Scott, Alexander Tennant, Charles Teulon, and Henderson Wright from Ireland; and William Birchmore, John Jackson, Peter Robertson, and John White from England.

Charles Brimline, George Grau, Charles Fiere, John Lockmann, Anthony Shoppe, Nicholas Ferdinand Westphal, and Frederick Weissenfels were from Germany. John Baury was from Santo Domingo. From France were Lewis Ansart, John Anthony, Louis Joseph de Beaulieu, Philip Beccannan, John Brown, Maximin Claistrier, Francis Suzor Debever, Joseph Gowden, John H. Genther, John Hagie, Marc Antonie Fouquet, Nicolas Fouquet, Charles LeHoux, and Frederick Wolf. John Polereczsky came with the French troops.

The last Revolutionary War pensioner was Esther S. Damon, widow of Noah Damon, who received an increase in her pension by an act of Congress in February 1905. She died the following year.

Each entry contains the name of the veteran, the state of his or her service or residence, and details of service and family data consolidated from various sources. In some instances the evidence was insufficient for differentiating between individuals of the same name, or variations in spelling were so different that it was impossible to determine if there was a single pensioner. In such instances entries were left unconsolidated.

The sources for the individual states are treated alphabetically by the Thirteen Original States plus the Green Mountain and Pine Tree states–Vermont and Maine. Kentucky and Tennessee also provided relief to selected Revolutionary War veterans living within their borders. The resources are discussed in alphabetical order for each locality.

Connecticut

The richest sources of the Nutmeg State's Revolutionary War pensions are found in Sylvester Judd's *Connecticut Archives: Revolutionary War (Selected Papers)*, 2nd Series, volume V, XIV. XV, XVI, XVII, and LV, 3rd Series, volume III. There is a partial pension list for the period 5 September 1791 to 4 March 1792. A complete one survives for the period 5 March to 4 September 1795. Henry Phelps Johnston's *Records of Connecticut Men in the I. War of the Revolution, II. War of 1812, III. Mexican War* (Reprint, Baltimore: Clearfield Company, 1997), 647–49, lists invalid pensioners in Connecticut.

Introduction

Delaware

Two pension lists exist for Delaware: 1792 and 1802. These have been printed in *Delaware Archives* (Wilmington, Del.: Charles L. Story Company Press, 1919) v. III, pp. 1212–1214.

Georgia

Georgia provided for annual pensions ranging from £5 for the loss of one eye to £30 for the loss of both hands or both eyes, or for those who were otherwise maimed so as to be rendered incapable of self-support. Georgia granted widows £10 a year plus four shillings for each child under the age of fourteen. Coverage extended to both Continental and State Troops under the Act of 10 January 1782. By the Act of 13 February 1786, Georgia granted half-pay to totally disabled Continental officers living in Georgia. Disabled noncommissioned officers and soldiers were to receive $5 per month, and those partially disabled were to receive amounts proportional to their disabilities. *The Georgia Military Record Book* contains the 1789 list of pensioners.

Examples of local records containing Revolutionary War pensions in Georgia include Michal Martin Farmer's *Elbert County, Georgia Deed Books K-R 1806–1819* (Dallas: the author, 1998), 241–43. In the *Southern Sentinel & Universal Gazette* issue of 4 February 1796, Judge Nathaniel Pendleton published the remarks of the Secretary of War about the proofs of the claimants which the judge had forwarded to Congress in 1795.

Maine

Virtually all of the pensioners, the veterans or their widows, who received the one-time cash payment from Maine proved their eligibility by using the same paperwork that had been submitted for their federal pension applications. Accordingly, abstracts of the applications have been omitted from this work. Instead, the name of the pensioner, town of residence, and the amount of payment are given. These are noted in Charles J. House's *Names of Soldiers of the American Revolution Who Applied for State Bounty under Resolves of March 17, 1835, March 24, 1836, and March 30, 1836, as Appears of Record in Land Office* (Augusta, Me.: Burleigh & Flynt, Printers to the State, 1893). The

Introduction

Resolve of 24 March 1836 granted $50 to more than 300 individuals who had not qualified for bounty land under earlier resolves. Since Maine was a district of Massachusetts until 1802, Massachusetts was the state of service of veterans from Maine.

Maryland

Maryland first granted pensions under the act of October 1778, which provided relief for disabled and maimed officers, soldiers, marines, and sailors. Relief came at the local level in county orphan courts. Some references appear in *Muster Rolls and Other Records of Service of Maryland Troops in the American Revolution 1775–1783* (Baltimore: Clearfield Company, 1996). Additional references appear in the *Journal and Correspondence of the Council of Maryland,* a sub-series of the *Archives of Maryland* (Baltimore: Maryland Historical Society, 1883–1972), in volumes XLIII, LXV, LXVII, LXVIII, LXXI, and LXXIII. Later there were additional acts. The most complete treatment of Maryland pensioners appears in Gaius Marcus Brumbaugh's *Maryland Records: Colonial, Revolutionary, County, and Church from Original Sources* (Baltimore: Genealogical Publishing Company), vol. II, 314–41, and in *Westward of Fort Cumberland, Military Lots Set off for Maryland's Revolutionary Soldiers Granted Pensions by the State of Maryland* (Finksburg, Md.: Pine Creek Publications, 1933) by Mary K. Meyer. The latter also includes *A List of the Names of Persons Who Are Entitled to Receive a Pension from the State of Maryland December Session 1822* (Annapolis, Md., 1822). Both works, however, are incomplete. The proceedings of the county orphan courts contain numerous references to pensions to veterans and widows.

Massachusetts

On 15 March 1777 Massachusetts provided for a Commissary of Pensions. John Lucas became Commissary. Commissioned officers, noncommissioned officers, private soldiers, and seamen wounded in the service of the United States from 19 April 1775 were entitled to pensions according to the Resolve of the Continental Congress of 26 August 1776. *Muster Rolls of the Pensioners of the Navy of the United States of America from 31ˢᵗ December 1786 to 31 December 1787 Inclusive,* and *Muster Rolls of the Pensioners of the Army of the United States of America Made up to 31 Dec. 1787 Conformably to a Resolve of Congress of 11ᵗʰ June 1788* exist for Massachusetts. Nearly three dozen Revolutionary War pensioners are identified in the seventeen-volume set *Massachusetts Soldiers and Sailors of the Revolutionary War* (Boston: Wright and Potter Printing Company, 1896–1908).

The Commonwealth of Massachusetts provided for one-time cash payments under the Resolve of 5 March 1801, which provided for the awarding of $20 in lieu of the 200 acres offered to noncommissioned officers and soldiers who had served three years and had been honorably discharged. If the veteran was dead, the children were the heirs. If there were no children, the widow was the heir. Applications had to be made within six years of the passage of the act.

In the manuscript collections of the New England Historic Genealogical Society are the Massachusetts Revolutionary Pensioners' Receipts 1799–1807, 1829–1837, giving the name of each pensioner, the amount of the pension, and the period for which payment was received. These financial records contain few biographical details.

At the Massachusetts State Archives is the finding aid *Pensions*, arranged by surname, forename, rank, regiment, residence, dollar amount of bounty, and remarks showing the lot number and location as well as the name of the widow of the veteran receiving the said land. It is a good finding aid.

New Hampshire

The New Hampshire legislature appointed John Taylor Gilman of Exeter as pension agent on 12 April 1777. He was to register all New Hampshire men who had been disabled in the Continental Army and to examine their claims and certificates. Disability pensions continued throughout the Confederation period. Under the act of 23 June 1786 ex-veterans who could produce certificates of disabilities were entitled to compensation. Continental officers received half-pay, and noncommissioned officers and privates received $5 per month. The widows of officers received the half-pay of their deceased husbands. Joseph Pearson, Secretary of State, was paymaster of pensions, and his invalids' accounts ledger is at the New Hampshire State Archives.

The list of invalids on the New Hampshire pension roll of 23 June 1786 is in the *Papers of the Continental Congress*, roll 88, item 74, page 41. In 1789 there were eighty-three invalid pensioners and fifteen pensions to widows and orphans of the Granite State.

The two-reel microfilm set *New Hampshire French and Indian War and Revolutionary Papers Index* also has relevant documents. An every-name index appears in *The New Hampshire Genealogical Record*, XVIII (2001), 51–78, 113–40.

Introduction

In *Rolls and Documents Relating to Soldiers in the Revolutionary War*, III, 320–406, are rich and varied collections of pension documents. Isaac W. Hammond edited the three-volume set *Documents Relating to Towns in New Hampshire* (Concord, N.H.: Parsons B. Cogswell, State Printer, 1882–1884), in which appear a number of pension-related petitions. The towns are treated in alphabetical order.

New Jersey

Names of New Jersey pensioners taken from the accounts of Isaac Southard, State Treasurer from 1837 to 1843, appear in the *Proceedings of the New Jersey Historical Society*, New Series, XVI, 28–29. In "Revolutionary Pension Records of Morris County," *Proceedings of the New Jersey Historical Society*, New Series, I (1916), 89–99, 49–59, and II (1917), 27–32, 98–177, are thirty-nine state pensions.

State Pension Payments, Books A, B, & C are three manuscript volumes containing accounts of payments made to Revolutionary War pensioners, veterans and/or their next of kin authorized by the state legislature between the years 1821 and 1870. Veterans of other wars are interspersed in the records. Russell Bruce Rankin prepared an index of abstracts from the legislative acts in his article "Revolutionary Soldiers Pensioned by the State of New Jersey," *The Genealogical Magazine of New Jersey*, VIII (1932–33), 74–81 and a correction, IX (1936), 136. He based his work on the *Index of Colonial and State Laws: Between the Years 1663 and 1903 Inclusive*, by John Hood (Camden, N.J.: Sinnickson Chew & Sons Company, 1905), 818–1820. His abstracts were limited to the name of the pensioner, county of residence, and the amount of the pension. He included three one-time relief payments. *New Jersey State Archives–Revolutionary War*, microfilm reel 187, contains pension accounts for the years 1777–1783 by John Stevens, Jr., State Treasurer.

"Half-pay to Hunterdon County Families of the Revolution, 1780–1796," *Proceedings of the New Jersey Historical Society*, XIII (1928), 190–99, and "Essex County Half Pay Applications for Revolutionary War Soldiers," *Proceedings of the New Jersey Historical Society*, LXVI (1948), 183–93, are early pension records authorized by the New Jersey legislature on 10 June 1779 in compliance with the 26 August 1776 Resolve of the Continental Congress.

Three very valuable micro-publications for New Jersey state pensions are *Registers of Payments, 1821-1870 Including Books B & C of State Pensions, 1837-1870*, Archives Reel 1-0236, *State Treasurer's Accounts, 1777-1783 Adjutant General's*

Compiled Rosters, New Jersey Militia & Continental Line, ca. 1776-1814, Archives Reel 187, and the *Revolutionary War Manuscripts, New Jersey Numbers 1-10811,* Family History Library—particularly reels 10289, 10290, 10292, and 10293.

New York

New York passed its first pension law in 1779. An applicant had to submit certificates from his commanding officer and a surgeon verifying that he had been wounded or disabled in the service. The certificates were forwarded to the Auditor General who recorded the certificates and authorized the state treasurer to pay the pension. Other acts followed in 1783 and 1786 authorizing payments to invalid veterans who had been disabled due to military service. By the latter act claimants had to submit their applications to examiners at either New York City or Albany. The second edition of *New York in the Revolution as Colony and State,* by James A. Roberts, and bound with the supplement by Frederic G. Mather (Baltimore: Genealogical Publishing Company, 1996), preserves many of the New York records. *Certificates Submitted by Disabled Revolutionary War Veterans Claiming Pensions and Audited Accounts of Pensions, 1779–1789,* Series A0174, are contained on three rolls of microfilm. These records survived the fire at the state capitol; others were lost or badly damaged by the flames. *Revolutionary War Accounts and Claims, 1775–1808,* Series A0200, has two important sub-series. One is for aid given to the families of soldiers and the other for pension applications. There are also lists of pensioners. There are two ledgers of accounts of the New York State Auditor in which entries pertaining to invalid pensioners appear.

North Carolina

The General Assembly of North Carolina passed a pension act in 1781. A second act followed in April 1784 and was amended in October following. It provided that at the first county court in the new year the justices were to receive pension applications and determine the sum necessary for relief for one year. The justices had the power to levy taxes for the funds needed to underwrite the cost of the pensions. The justices were required to submit triennial reports of their receipts and expenditures to the public treasurer, who in turn was to lay the accounts before the General Assembly. The amount of a pension was based upon rank, length of service, and severity of wounds. On 21

Introduction

November 1800 the General Assembly passed a resolution to maintain those pensioners who had been unable to transfer to the pension rolls of the United States.

Many of the records of North Carolina are included in the *Treasurer's and Comptroller's Papers, Military Papers, State Pensions to Invalids and Widows, 1784–1808,* which are contained on three rolls of microfilm in alphabetical order with appropriate references to applications pertaining to two or more veterans. State pension accounts, 1802–1829, are in book 69. Others appear in the legislative papers and in courts of pleas and quarter sessions minutes of individual counties.

A list of those receiving pensions from North Carolina first appeared in *North Carolina Genealogy,* pp. 679–84. It represented those who were transferred to the United States pension rolls the following year. Another version is that by Mark Vopelak, "Revolutionary War Pension Records at the North Carolina State Archives," *The North Carolina Genealogical Society Journal,* XXVIII (2001), 295–300. Ransom McBride's "Revolutionary War Gems from the N.C. General Assembly Papers to 1800," *The North Carolina Genealogical Society Journal,* XXVIII (2002), 76–81, includes some state pension petitions. Jo White Linn and B. R. McBride prepared abstracts from the Delamar transcripts of entries from the North Carolina legislative papers for economic relief, land, and pensions following the Revolutionary War. Their series, "Private Petitions in the North Carolina Legislative Papers: Revolutionary War Service-Related Benefits," provides details for reconstructing and supplementing the state pension files. The abstracts appear in *The North Carolina Genealogical Society Journal,* I (1975), 141–68; II (1976), 39–47, 108–16, 148–53, 198–203; III (1977), 84–89, 160–65, 222–28; IV (1978), 40–45, 102–7, 171–76; V (1979), 24–30, 100–04, 158–64; VI (1980), 9–16, 100–06, 175–77, 236–40. Ransom McBride's "Revolutionary War Gems from the General Assembly Papers up to 1800," *The North Carolina Genealogical Society Journal,* XXVIII (2002), 76–81, featured abstracts from the legislative session records that had not been previously published.

Pennsylvania

Under the act of 22 September 1785 Pennsylvania provided for state pensions. Veterans or their widows could apply to county Orphans' Courts or the State Supreme Court. At the local level such records may appear in the minutes of the county orphans' courts and the deed books. The next act was 11 March 1790. For those unable to qualify for federal pensions the act of 14 April 1834 expanded coverage for veterans and their

Introduction

widows. There are probably more Revolutionary War pensions from Pennsylvania than any other state. *List of Pensioner Names on the Pennsylvania List Taken from the Pension Book of the United States Commencing on the 4th of March 1789* contains two versions of the same list. *Abstracts of Pension Applications on File in the Division of Public Records, Pennsylvania State Library* appear in the *Pennsylvania Archives,* Fifth Series, IV, 497–596. Some of those who qualified under the act of 25 February 1813 appear on the *List of Officers and Soldiers of the Revolutionary War, Placed on the Pension List of Pennsylvania, by Especial Acts, & by the Board Instituted for the Granting of Pensions to Officers and Soldiers of the Pennsyl'a Line.* The list was probably made about the year 1820. It is found in the *Pennsylvania Archives,* Second Series, XI, 796–807. In the same series, XV, 763–771, is a list of soldiers who were applicants for state annuities taken from the journals of the Assembly, giving the name of the pensioner, county of residence, military unit, rank, and other data.

Harry E. Cope was the first to recognize the importance of Pennsylvania's private acts. His work, *Soldiers and Widows of Soldiers of the Revolutionary War Granted Pensions by the Commonwealth of Pennsylvania,* contains a great number of errors and should not be regarded as authoritative. *The Name Index to Revolutionary Pensioners from Series in Records Groups: 2, 4, 7, & 33* serves as a most authoritative finding aid to the records. *The Statutes at Large of Pennsylvania from 1682 to 1801* and *Acts of the General Assembly of the Commonwealth of Pennsylvania* (*Laws of Pennsylvania*) are two of the best sources of pensions awarded by the Commonwealth.

The Pennsylvania statutes frequently include several names of veterans and widows. Unfortunately, eligibility rested on both the Revolutionary War and later Indian campaigns. In many instances—especially from the 1830s—there was no distinction between the two categories. The Appendix contains Pennsylvania pensioners with unidentified war service. Accordingly, it is especially important to determine if the pensioner was indeed a Revolutionary War veteran or if his widow was being pensioned for Revolutionary War service.

Petitions submitted for pensions were also submitted to the State Supreme Court, Eastern District, and include additional data for pensioners as well as the names of individuals not included in other series.

Rhode Island and Providence Plantations

The 1786 invalid pension report from the General Assembly appears in the *Papers of the Continental Congress,* roll 88, item 75, folio 31. John Russell Bartlett's *Records of the Colony of Rhode Island and Providence Plantations in New England 1784–1792* (reprint, New York: AMS Press, 1968) contains sundry invalid pension entries.

South Carolina

Because there were more battles during the Revolutionary War in the Palmetto State than in other states, and because of the British occupation of the capital, Charleston, in 1780, the records of benefits to Revolutionary veterans and their families in South Carolina are somewhat more complex due to the lack of an official bureaucracy to deal with the situation and the large number of casualties. Laurence K. Wells in two articles, "Compensation for Revolutionary Service," *The South Carolina Magazine of Ancestral Research,* I (1973), 59–70 and 156–60, and "State Pensions to Revolutionary Survivors," IV (1976), 3–8, treated Revolutionary War pensioners and annuitants. *The Accounts Audited of Claims Growing out of the Revolution in South Carolina* is a sixty-five-roll micro-publication containing the records for the latter period of the war and for decades thereafter. South Carolina had its own program of state pensions and annuities. These claims appear as a supplement to the audited accounts at the end of the last roll of the series. Interspersed among the series are several files pertaining to post-Revolutionary War service, so care should be exercised in interpreting the records. Another micro-publication, *Revolutionary War Annuitant Lists 1799–1857,* contains two lists of pensioners representing those claimants paid out of the offices at Charleston in the low country and Columbia in the up country. Some of the names on these lists no longer have state pension files extant. While most of the audited accounts contain the applicant's affidavits, proof of service, and net worth, some have nothing more than a receipt of payment. Private acts of the legislature for individual pensions also provide rich details. Tony Draine's *Guide to South Carolina Pensions and Annuities 1783–1869* (Columbia, S.C.: Draban Publications, 1991) lists more than 800 pensions awarded by the state to veterans of not only the Revolutionary War but also of the War of 1812 and the Mexican War. South Carolina's legislative petitions are also rich in details and in some instances are the only records remaining for Revolutionary pensioners. The petitions are included in *Petitions to the General Assembly* on this 109-roll micro-publication. Annuitants and pensioners also appear in the five-volume set *Journals of the House of Representatives 1783–1794* (Columbia, S.C.: Published for the South Carolina Department of Archives and History by the University of South Carolina, 1977 ff.).

Introduction

Tennessee

The Tennessee Legislative Petitions, 1799–1865 are contained on twenty-two rolls of microfilm. Residents of the Volunteer State filed petitions regarding their bounty lands and various other types of relief.

Vermont

The Records of the Governor and Council of the State of Vermont (New York: AMS Press, 1973) for the period 1777 to 1796 and *The State Papers of Vermont* (Montpelier, Vt.: Published by the Secretary of State, 1918 ff.) in the reports of committees to the General Assembly submitted between 1778 to 1801 contain some references to Revolutionary War pensions. They also contain many general petitions from 1778 to 1799, in volumes VIII–XI, from citizens seeking invalid pensions. Mary Greene Nye created a personal name card file index at the Vermont State Archives. It covers all eighteenth-century records and includes references to Revolutionary War pensions.

Virginia

In the October 1777 session the General Assembly of Virginia authorized the payment of pensions to soldiers who had become disabled and to the widows of men who had been killed in the war. The Commonwealth depended upon the clerks of the county and hustings courts to verify the lists of pensioners that the auditor of public accounts maintained. The latter also issued the warrants for the disbursements of funds. The files are arranged in alphabetical order and contain correspondence, powers of attorney, medical evaluations, and receipts. Abstracts of the records first appeared in *Virginia Revolutionary War State Pensions* (Richmond: Virginia Genealogical Society, 1980). Included within the series are also pensions granted to veterans of the French and Indian War, Pontiac's Conspiracy, and Dunmore's War so a careful reading is necessary to differentiate between colonial and Revolutionary military service. A number of the applicants derived eligibility in both categories. *The Virginia State Pensions, 1777–1784* is a fifteen-roll micro-publication of the original documents. It is by no means complete.

There are two volumes of Virginia pension rolls, 1786–1851, with the names of pensioners, dates of payments, and additional data such as county of residence, rank, unit, amount of payment, and nature of service. These records are on *Miscellaneous Reel 990*.

    Miscellaneous Reel 986 has a ledger of military accounts for the French and Indian and the Revolutionary wars. Entries for the latter pertain to disabled veterans and their widows. There is an additional ledger for the years 1778–1788 containing accounts of Revolutionary War pensioners giving their names, disabilities, dates, and amounts of warrants issued.

    Randolph W. Church's *Virginia Legislative Petitions: Bibliography, Calendar, and Abstracts from Original Sources 6 May 1776–21 June 1782* (Richmond: Virginia State Library, 1984) provides access to an extremely valuable record group.

    The thirteenth volume of William Waller Hening's *The Statutes at Large: Being a Collection of All the Laws of Virginia, from the First Session of the Legislature, in the Year 1619* (Charlottesville, Va.: University Press of Virginia, 1969) and Samuel Shepherd's supplement, *The Statutes at Large of Virginia, from October Session 1792 to December Session 1806, Inclusive, in Three Volumes, (New Series) Being a Continuation of Hening* (reprint, New York: Kraus Reprint Corporation, 1968) also abound in references to Revolutionary War pensioners. The fourth and sixth volumes of the *Calendar of Virginia State Papers and Other Manuscripts* (reprint, New York: AMS Press, 1970) likewise identify pensioners. *The Journals of the Council of the State of Virginia* (Richmond: Commonwealth of Virginia Division of Purchase & Printing, 1949), volumes III–V, provide comprehensive coverage for the years involved. There are also *passim* references in *The Journal of the Senate of Virginia* for the sessions 1791–1802/03 (Richmond: Virginia State Library, 1949 ff.).

    The 1785, 1786, and 1787 lists of Virginia pensioners appear in *Virginia Military Records from the Virginia Magazine of History and Biography, the William and Mary College Quarterly, and Tyler's Quarterly* (Baltimore: Genealogical Publishing Company, 1983), 710–22. The 1799 and 1800 pension lists appear in Joan W. Peters' *Neglected & Forgotten: Fauquier County, Virginia, French & Indian War, Revolutionary War, & War of 1812 Veterans* (Bowie, Md.: Heritage Books, 2004), 15–17. The 1802 pension list appears in Joan W. Peters' *Fauquier County, Virginia's Clerk's Loose Papers: A Guide to the Records 1759–1919* (Westminster, Md.: Willow Bend Books, 2001), 84. William H. Dumont discovered in the old loan records of the Treasury Department several Virginia pension lists, which appeared in his article "Virginia Pensioners 1790–1800," *National Genealogical Society Quarterly*, XLIV (1956), 47–51.

*   *   *

Introduction

I would like to acknowledge the assistance of Dr. Frank C. Mevers, Director and State Archivist of the State of New Hampshire in Concord; Conley Edwards, Archivist of the Commonwealth of Virginia at the Library of Virginia in Richmond; Charles Sherrill of Brentwood, Tennessee; Brent H. Holcomb of Columbia, South Carolina; James Hansen, FASG, of the State Historical Society of Wisconsin, Madison, Wisconsin; Robert Scott Davis of Wallace State Community College, Hanceville, Alabama; Patricia Law Hatcher, FASG, of Dallas, Texas; and Marian Hoffman, Editor of the Genealogical Publishing Company.

Having used so many sources in compiling the entries, I could not always be certain about the names of people and places. Such figures as Nathaniel Greene, George Rogers Clark, and Thomas Sumter appeared with a host of spellings. Battles and skirmishes such as Stoney Robby. i.e., Stone Arabia, were not always apparent in the course of compiling this work and will appear under their phonetic variant spellings. All of the mistakes are mine alone, and I look forward to having them pointed out.

Dallas, Texas
A.D. MMX

Revolutionary War Pensions Awarded by State Governments 1775-1874, the General and Federal Governments Prior to 1814, and by Private Acts of Congress to 1905

[no name] —. —. His daughter, Lucinda Allen, sought a pension on his service. Her grandfather was also a Revolutionary War veteran, and two of her brothers were veterans of the War of 1812. She was 91 years old when she petitioned Congress 10 June 1890 and was granted a pension.

[no name]—. —. Lt. He served in the Continental Line to the end of the war. He lost an arm at Savannah and died in 1812. He drew his half-pay. His daughter, Rebecca Frances Bailey, had her petition for a pension rejected by Congress 27 Mar. 1876.

[no name] —. —. Congress refused to approve the request of Bethia Black who sought a pension for her mother 30 June 1854.

[no name]. —. —. Maria L. Carbee was the sister of two veterans in the Civil War and of another who was a veteran of the Mexican War. Her two great-grandfathers and her paternal grandfather were veterans of the American Revolution. She was 63 years old. Congress rejected her petition for a pension 25 Feb. 1896.

[no name] —. —. Esther Jackson sought a pension on the basis of her father's service in the Revolutionary War. Congress rejected her petition 17 May 1898.

[no name]. —. —. Mary E. Woodworth sought a pension on the basis of her father's service in the Revolutionary War. Congress rejected her petition 17 May 1898.

[no name] —. Conn. —. He married Elizabeth ----- in New Fairfield, Conn. in 1784. Because of his adulteries they were divorced. He married again and was deceased. Congress granted Elizabeth Rowe a pension based on his service on 6 Feb. 1839. She had been married three times.

[no name] —. S.C. —. Mrs. Mary Alexander sought compensation for maintaining a Revolutionary pauper, but her application was rejected 29 Nov. 1844.

[no surname] Scipio. S.C. —. He was a colored man and received an annuity 2 Mar. 1842.

Abagast, Ludwick. Pa. Pvt. He was in Philadelphia County 12 Dec. 1785. He was in the Invalids. He lost his right leg in action with the enemy and was discharged 28 Mar. 1783. He was 28 years old. He served as a matross. He appeared on the 1813 pension list as Ludwig Arbigust and also as Ludwig Arbogast.

Abbott, Aaron. Mass. Pvt. He served under Col. Samuel McNabb and Capt. John Hinckley. He was disabled by sundry wounds on his head, both thumbs, back, and left breast. His shoulder was dislocated, and he had been stabbed in the back. He was pensioned 24 Apr. 1786 in Middlesex County and was 59 years old. He was on the 1813 pension list.

Abbott, George. Md. Pvt. He pensioned at the rate of half-pay of a private on 2 Jan. 1813.

Abbott, Isaac. Mass. Lt. He was pensioned 8 Apr. 1809 in Essex County. He was on the 1813 pension list.

Abbott, James. Mass. Pvt. He served in the 8th Regiment. He resided in Gloucester and his widow, Martha Abbott, was paid $50.

Abbott, Matthew. S.C. —. He served in 1780 and 1781 under Gen. Pickens in the Cherokee Nation. His brother, Samuel Abbott], served with him. He applied 12 Nov. 1850.

Abbott, Thomas. Pa. —. He was awarded a $40 gratuity in Adams Co., Pa. 23 Apr. 1829. He was awarded a $40 gratuity and a $40 annuity in Adams Co., Pa. 24 Mar. 1832, 20 Feb. 1833, and 18 Mar. 1834.

Abeel, Garret. N.Y. Pvt. He served under Lt. Daniel Beeker in Capt. William Snuyder's Company in Col. Anthony Vroman's Regiment and was wounded in his right shoulder by a musket ball on 22 Jul. 1778. He was pensioned 17 Sep. 1780. He was born 15 Mar. 1755. A merchant, he lived in Catskill, Albany Co., N.Y. on 1 Aug. 1788. He later lived in Greene County. He was on the 1813 pension list and died 23 Oct. 1829.

Abel, John. —. —. He served for two months. He was then attached to a militia company much longer and held himself in readiness. He died 21 Nov. 1838. He married Catherine ----- 21 June 1783. She sought a pension but was rejected 4 Jan. 1848 by Congress.

Able, William. Pa. —. He was awarded a $40 gratuity in Montgomery Co., Pa. 21 Feb. 1834.

Abney, Samuel. S.C. —. He was killed by Cunningham. His widow, Martha Abney, was paid 15 Aug. 1785. She had two children in 1791.

Abrams, Gabriel. Pa. —. He was awarded a $40 gratuity and a $40 annuity in Fayette County 4 May 1832. He died 7 Oct. 1841.

Absalom, —. Va. Mrs. Absalom was granted support in King William County in 1779.

Absalom, Edmund. Va. Pvt. He enlisted 13 Dec. 1776 for three years in the 15th Virginia Regiment under Lt. Giles Raines and Maj. Robert Richeson. He was taken prisoner at Charleston and there capitulated. He was wounded at Fort Putnam by falling timber being carried for repairs of the garrison and was worn out on a fatigue on the day it happened. He died 1 Nov. 1787 at the home of Henry Slaughter. He was about 35 years old in 1786 and applied from King William County. There was one of his name on the 1813 pension list.

Acker, Christian. Pa. —. He was awarded a $40 gratuity and a $40 annuity in Lehigh Co., Pa. 17 Mar. 1835. He died 18 Aug. 1843.

Acker, Jacob. N.Y. Pvt. He served in Capt. Daniel Martling's Company under Col. James Hammond in the Westchester County militia. He had one wound in his chin, another near his gullet, and another in his right shoulder. At another time he had three more wounds in his left shoulder by a broadsword. He was pensioned 10 June 1786. He lived in Westchester Co., N.Y. on 27 Apr. 1789 and later in New York City. He was aged 24 in 1786. He had a wife and two children. He was on the 1813 pension list. He died 5 Nov. 1832.

Acklin, —. Pa. —. His widow, Nancy Acklin, was granted a $40 annuity in Fayette Co., Pa. 4 May 1852 for his Revolutionary service. She died 6 June 1859.

Adair, —. —. —. His widow, Catharine Adair, sought a pension from 1841 to 1843 which had not been provided by law. Congress denied her claim 11 Apr. 1850.

Adair, Benjamin. S.C. —. He was killed 20 March 1781. His widow, Catharine Adair, was paid 10 June 1785.

Adair, Isaac. S.C. —. He was killed in Apr. 1781. His widow, Ruth Adair, was paid 21 Sep. 1785. She had one child in 1791.

Adair, John. —. —. His widow, Catharine Adair, had her petition for a pension rejected by Congress because they were married subsequent to 1 Jan. 1794.

Adair, John. S.C. —. He was killed in 1782. His widow, Sarah Adair, was paid 24 May 1785. There were two children in 1791.

Adair, Robert. S.C. —. He was killed by the Indians. His widow, Elizabeth Adair, was paid 7 Feb. 1785 in Pendleton District. One Elizabeth Adair received an annuity 7 Dec. 1819.

Adams, —. Va. —. His wife, Nancy Adams, was granted £12 support in Fauquier Co., Va. in May 1778.

Adams, Abijah. R.I. Pvt. He was pensioned in 1788. He was on the 1813 pension list.

Adams, Adam. Md. Pvt. He was pensioned at the rate of the half-pay of a private on 23 Jan. 1816.

Adams, Albert. Pa. QM. He served in the 7th Battalion of the Cumberland County militia and was killed in the service on 1 May 1778 at the Crooked Billet in Bucks County. He left a widow Agnes Adams. She married ------ Murray upwards of a year later. The children were James Adams born 8 Dec. 1771, Robert Adams born 23 Dec. 1775, and Ephraim Adams born 29 Apr. 1777. Their guardian was their uncle, Ephraim Blaine, who applied for their pension 10 Sep. 1795 in Cumberland County.

Adams, Andrew. S.C. —. He served in the 2nd S.C. Regiment and was maimed in the service by the loss of an arm. He was paid 19 May 1785 until 1791 after which he received nothing from S.C. or the U.S.A. On 1 Dec. 1798 he sought restoration of aid and was placed on the pension roll with an annuity of $22 per annum. He was last paid in 1808. He was from Spartanburgh District, S.C.

Adams, Andrew. S.C. —. He was being pensioned in Orangeburg District in 1798.

Adams, Francis. S.C. —. He was from Lancaster District. He applied 3 Dec. 1825. His petition was rejected in 1829. He joined the army at a very early age and was in most of the principal battles in South Carolina. He was severely wounded in one of them. He was pensioned 25 Nov. 1830. In 1831 he had a wife and three young children. He was nearly 70 years old. His camp mate, William Woody, attested to his service. The state rejected his plea for his arrearage but did grant him a $60 annuity per annum 4 Jan. 1831. He was last paid in 1834.

Adams, Gabriel. Pa. —. He was awarded a $40 gratuity and a $40 annuity in Fayette Co., Pa. 11 June 1832. Some accounts have incorrectly rendered him as Gabriel Abrams.

Adams, Henry. Mass. —. He served as a surgeon's mate from 1 Jan. 1777 to 14 May 1782. He married Sarah Pelton 11 Nov. 1786. She married secondly William Besley. Her second husband had been dead eight or ten years when she applied to Congress for a pension. Congress granted her petition.

Adams, Jacob. —. —. He enlisted in July 1780 for six months. The rolls indicated that he was discharged 7 Dec. 1780 and given 12 days to return home. He was credited with having fulfilled the six-month tour and was approved for a pension 5 Mar. 1840.

Adams, James. N.Y. Sgt. He served in Capt. Bleeker's Company under Col. Goose Van Schaick. His sight was much impaired. He lived in Albany, Albany Co., N.Y. in 1786 and on 6 June 1789. He was 52 years old in 1786. He was on the 1813 pension list.

Adams, James. Pa. —. He was pensioned 28 Feb. 1795.

Adams, Jeremiah. N.C. He enlisted for eighteen months 1 Aug. 1782 and was discharged in 1783. Congress granted him a pension 17 Mar. 1832 even though he did not have sufficient service to qualify under the law.

Adams, John. Mass. Pvt. He served under Col. William Prescott in Capt. John Nutting's Company. He lost his left arm and was wounded in his left leg. He was pensioned 16 Nov. 1786. He was 34 years old. He was on the 1813 pension list and died 4 Feb. 1835 in Middlesex County.

Adams, John. Pa. —. He was awarded a $40 gratuity and a $40 annuity in Northumberland County 28 Mar. 1820. He died 30 Sep. 1824.

Adams, John. Pa. —. He was awarded a $40 gratuity and a $40 annuity in Huntingdon Co., Pa. 21 Mar. 1837. He served three tours. The first was about 1778 when he was 15 years of age. He was at

Brandywine. Between 1778 and 1782 he served two other tours. Since he had a state pension, Congress credited him with at least six months of service and granted him a federal pension 14 June 1850.

Adams, John Carroll. S.C. Sgt. He served in McKenzie's Troops in Hill's Regiment in the brigade of Gen. Sumter. He was a regular soldier in the 3rd S.C. Regiment under Col. William Thompson in Capt. Joseph Wailey's Company. He served three years and was discharged at Charleston. He applied 3 Apr. 1819. Morgan Griffin and Gideon Griffin attested to his service. He was in the battle of Savannah and other engagements. He had great poverty and a large family. He had neither land nor Negroes, an aged wife to support, and for more than five years had suffered from a stroke of the dead palsy. His relatives and friends had left him. He was approved at the rate of $60 per annum 7 Dec. 1825. He was paid to 1833. His widow, Sarah Adams, stated that he served seven years on 30 Nov. 1837. He was from Richland District.

Adams, Jonas. N.H. Pvt. He served in the 1st Regiment. He was wounded by a musket ball which passed through his leg in Oct. 1777 at Bemis Heights. He lived in Jeffrey, N.H. in 1794. He enlisted 1 Feb. 1777 for three years and was discharged 1 Feb. 1780. He transferred to Vermont. He was granted one-third of a pension 20 April 1796. He died 19 Feb. 1813. He was on the 1813 pension list.

Adams, Joseph. Me. —. He was from Jay. He was paid $50 under the resolve of 1836.

Adams, Joseph. Pa. —. His widow, Priscilla Adams, was awarded a $40 gratuity in Northumberland Co., Pa. 12 Feb. 1829.

Adams, Joshua. Mass. —. He served in the 8th Regiment. He was paid $20 and lived in Alfred.

Adams, Matthew. N.Y. Pvt. He served in Col. Van Schaick's Regiment. He received several wounds. He lived in Goshen, Orange Co., N.Y. 3 June 1789. He was pensioned 10 June 1786. He was on the 1813 pension list. He died 12 Feb. 1832.

Adams, Matthew. Pa. Pvt. He applied 20 Mar. 1818 from Dauphin County. He served one year or more under Capt. William Rippey. He died 10 Jan. 1822. His widow, Priscilla Adams, was granted a $40 gratuity 12 Feb. 1829. She applied 15 June 1830.

Adams, Moses. —. —. He was from Portage County, Ohio and applied to Congress 11 May 1830 for his arrearage because his paperwork had been mislaid for upwards of two years. He was rejected.

Adams, Nathan. Del. Capt. He died at Long Island 27 Mar. 1778. His heirs were awarded his seven years' half-pay of $1,680. His bounty land warrant was placed in the hands of Samuel White who had died. The warrant was not found amongst his papers. Congress authorized a duplicate of warrant #573 on 22 Dec. 1837.

Adams, Peter. Md. Col. His bounty land warrant was issued 15 Dec. 1807 and placed in the hands of Samuel White. After White's death, the warrant could not be found. Congress authorized warrant #571 to be reissued.

Adams, Peter. Mass. Pvt. He served in the 1st Regiment. He lived in Taunton and was paid $50.

Adams, Solomon. Pa. —. He was awarded a $40 gratuity and a $40 annuity in Bedford County on 30 Mar. 1822.

Adams, Thomas. S.C. —. He served under Col. William ------- and was wounded. He was paid an annuity 27 Jan. 1780.

Adams, William. Md. Lt. His bounty land warrant #572 was issued 15 Dec. 1807, but it could not be found among the papers of Samuel White when he died. Congress authorized a duplicate on 22 Dec. 1837.

Adams, William. Pa. —. He was awarded a $40 gratuity and a $40 annuity in Greene Co., Pa. 15 Apr. 1834. He died 14 Oct. 1848.

Adams, William. S.C. Lt. He served under Capt. Joseph Calhoun. He was pensioned 25 Apr.1808. He was deceased by 2 Nov. 1818 in Abbeville District when Arthur Gray and Samuel Adams were his administrators.

Adams, William. Va. —. His wife, Catherine Adams, was awarded £12 support in Cumberland Co., Va. 24 Aug. 1778. She was granted additional support for herself and her eight children, the eldest of whom was a daughter in her fourteenth year on 25 Jan. 1779. He was in Continental service.

Adams, Winborn. N.H. Lt. Col. He was killed at the battle of Bemis Heights on 19 Sep. 1777. His widow, Sarah Adams, was in Portsmouth, N.H. in 1784. Her son was also in the service. She married ------- Hobart secondly.

Adare, Bozeman. Ga. Pvt. He was awarded 640 acres of bounty land on 13 Dec. 1811 by legislative act.

Adkins, Jehu. S.C. Pvt. He applied 16 Nov. 1831 in Anderson District. He was formerly of Abbeville District. He was 71 years old, and his family of children had left him. His property did not exceed the value of $100. He served under Gen. Muhlenburg and Gen. Washington. He was at Little York when Lord Cornwallis and Tarleton surrendered. John Bowen, age 68, stated that he was with him at the battle of Little York.

Adkinson, William. Va. Pvt. He was pensioned at the rate of £12 per year 20 Feb. 1786. He was on the 1791 national pension list. He was also on the 1813 pension list.

Adson, Charles. Va. —. His wife, Mary Adson, and children were granted £40 relief on 2 Oct. 1778 in Chesterfield Co., Va. while he was away in Continental service.

Aggings, Hugh. N.J. —. He was pensioned 27 Jan. 1831 at the rate of $60 per annum. He was 86 years old in 1840.

Agnew, John. U.S. —. He was granted an annuity for furnishing clothing to the son of Chittaway by Congress for the year 1782.

Aiken, John. Va. Pvt. He was disabled. He was continued on the pension roll 28 June 1786 for £12 per annum. He was on the 1791 pension list. He was on the 1813 pension list.

Aikin, Andrew. N.H. Sgt.-Maj. He served under Col. Stickney. He was wounded by a musket ball shot through his right breast in Aug. 1777 at Bennington. He lived in Deering, N.H. in 1794. He was in the militia. He was granted three-fourths of a pension 10 Apr. 1796. He was on the 1813 pension list.

Ailey, Michael. Pa. —. He applied 28 Mar. 1814. He served under Col. Maxfield in 1775, Col. Noakley in the 10th Pa. Regiment in 1776, and aboard the *Holkar* commanded by Decatur. He was removed to the *South Carolina* and was taken prisoner by the British. He also appeared as Michael Ealy.

Aimes, Henry. Va. Capt. He lived in Henry County when he entered the service in the spring of 1776. He was promoted to colonel. He later lived in Rowan Co., N.C., Wilkes Co., Ga., and Liberty Co., Ga. where he died in 1789. His heirs were his children Samuel Aimes and Fisher Aimes as proved by John Nail of Franklin Co., Ga. 17 Oct. 1814.

Airs, George. —. Matross. He served in Col. Crane's Artillery. He was hurt by the sudden discharge of a cannon to which he was stationed and lost the sight of his right eye Sep. 1777 at the battle of Brandywine. He enlisted 5 May 1777 and continued to the end of the war. He resided in Arundel, Me. in 1792. He was on the 1813 pension list. He also appeared as George Ayres.

Akeley, John. Pa. —. He was in Mifflin County on 19 Mar. 1814. He enlisted in Mar. 1778 in Capt. Plunkett's Company in the 4th Regiment of Dragoons. He was discharged by Capt. Pike. He sold his donation land of 200 acres in Mercer County to John White. He fell from his horse while in the service. He had 100 acres of federal bounty land in Ohio.

Akerman, Peter. N.H. Pvt. He was wounded in his right arm on 19 Sep. 1777 at Bemis Heights. He was in Capt. Beel's Company in the 3rd N.H. Regiment under Col. Scammel. He was aged 39 when he was pensioned 7 Nov. 1787. He was on the 1813 pension list. He was from Rye, N.H. He also appeared as Peter Ackerman.

Akin, John. Va. Pvt. He served in Capt. Wallace's Company under Col. Buford when he was wounded in his head. He had a large open ulcer on his left leg. He lost all he had by fire. He applied from Nansemond County in 1786. He was aged about 28 years in 1786.

Akley, Samuel. Me. —. He was from Rumford and was paid $50 under the resolve of 1836.

Albee, Jabez. N.J. —. He served in the 1st Regiment. His wife was Phebe Bedannah.

Albert, —. Pa. —. His widow, Mary Albert, was awarded a $40 gratuity and a $40 annuity in Washington Co., Md. 4 Apr. 1831.

Albert, Jacob. Pa. —. He was in Dauphin County, Pa. and in Washington Co., Md. 24 Mar. 1825. He was taken prisoner at Fort Washington and sent to New York where he was paroled. He again enlisted in the Pa. Line. He was in the company of Capt. John Spoon in the Battalion in 1776 from Berks County. He was on the payrolls of the 1st and 6th Regiments. He married Mariah Benner in 1778. He died 4 May 1830.

Albertson, Levi. N.J. —. He served under Capt. Samuel Hugg and Lt. David Moore in the artillery. He died at Princeton 30 Apr. 1777. His widow, Keziah Albertson, was granted a half-pay pension in Gloucester County. He married Keziah Roberts 26 Apr. 1756 in Gloucester Co.

Albrecht, Martin. Pa. Pvt. His widow, Sophia Albrecht, sought a pension from Congress but her evidence did not prove that he served six months. His first tour was calculated at two months but his second tour was less than four months. Her petition was rejected 9 Jam. 1847. There was a Sophia Albrecht of Lebanon Co., Pa. who was granted a $40 gratuity and a $40 annuity on 11 Apr 1844. She died 11 Sep. 1855.

Albright, George. Pa. —. He received a $40 gratuity and a $40 annuity 6 Apr. 1838. He was from Lancaster County.

Albrittain, Matthew. S.C. —. He served 13 months under Capt. Benjamin Coleman, Col. Little, and Gen. Greene after which he was discharged. He was 63 years old, but his application was rejected 19 Nov. 1824 due to a lack of being sufficiently vouchered.

Albro, Clarke. R.I. Pvt. He was wounded by a musket ball in his left arm at Newport on 9 Aug. 1778. He served in the Kingston Reds under Col. John Wait. He lived in Newport, R.I. in 1794. He was granted one-fourth of a pension 20 Apr. 1796.

Alcock, Robert. Md. Pvt. He was pensioned in Anne Arundel County at the rate of half-pay of a private on 30 Jan. 1829.

Alcorn, James. Pa. —. He was wounded and pensioned 10 May 1783.

Alcorn, James. S.C. —. His widow, Catherine Alcorn, was granted an annuity 27 Sep. 1784 in York District. He also appeared as James Allcorn.

Alden, Ebenezer. Mass. Pvt. He served in the 1st Regiment. He lived at Adams and was paid $50.

Aldred, William. Va. —. His widow, Ann Aldred, was granted £10 support in Frederick Co., Va. on 2 Mar. 1779. It was certified that he died in the service and that his widow was Ann Aldred in Frederick Co., Va. on 8 Mar. 1780.

Aldrich, —. —. —. His widow, Susan Aldrich, had her petition for a pension rejected by Congress 27 Mar. 1846 because they married subsequent to 1 Jan. 1794.

Aldrich, Caleb. N.H. & R.I. Pvt. He served in the Continental Line under Col. George Reed and Capt. Ellis. He was disabled in the joint of his left hip by a fall on board a small vessel in the North River in 1781. He was from Westmoreland, N.H. He was granted a full pension 20 Apr. 1796. He was on the 1813 pension list. He died 4 Jan. 1828. His widow, Lovey Aldrich, was granted an increase in her pension from $12 per month by Congress 24 May 1890. She was 90 years of age. His son was Edwin O. Aldrich.

Aldrich, Clark. —. Pvt. He served under Capt. Fenner and Col. Christopher Lippett. He was the son of Andrew Aldrich and brother of Richard Aldrich. He lived in Johnston, R.I. in the war and then moved to N.H. His widow was Polly Aldrich. Congress granted the widow relief 26 Apr. 1848.

Aldrich, Gustavus. Mass. Sgt. He was pensioned 24 Feb. 1806. He was on the 1813 pension list and died 3 Aug. 1822 in Worcester County.

Aldrich, Henry. Mass. —. He served in the 6th Regiment. He was paid $20. He also appeared as Henry Aldrick.

Aldrick, —. Va. —. He served in the Continental Line. His wife, Barbara Aldrick, was allowed £20 relief in Berkeley County, Va. 21 Sep. 1779.

Aldridge, Esek. R.I. Drummer. He was disabled by disease. He lived in Smithfield, R.I. in 1794.

Aldridge, Luke. Mass. Pvt. He served in Col. Thomas Marshall's Regiment and Capt. William Warner and lost the sight in his left eye. He was pensioned at the rate of one-eighth pay of a soldier from 7 Dec. 1779 on 23 Feb. 1785. He was 31 years old in 1787. He was on the 1813 pension list as Luke Aldrich.

Alexander, —. S.C. —. His widow, Ann Alexander, lived in Chesterfield in 1791.

Alexander, Alexander. Pa. Pvt. His widow, Catherine Alexander, was in Philadelphia County 26 Nov.1790. He was in Capt. William McCalla's company and Col. James Irwin in the Bucks County militia when he was wounded and captured in 1777 at Guelph Mills. He languished and died in jail in Philadelphia on 31 Dec. 1777. He served under Gen. Lacey. She died 9 Apr. 1814.

Alexander, Dan. N.C. Pvt. He served for three months in 1778 under Capt. Alexander and six weeks under Capt. Pettis, Capt. Martin Fifer, and Maj. William R. Davie. He was born in Mecklenburg Co., N.C. in Mar. 1757. He was in Hardeman Co., Tenn. and was 76 years old.

Alexander, Jacob. Md. Sgt. His widow, Mary Alexander, was pensioned at the rate of half-pay of a sergeant on 13 Feb. 1835.

Alexander, James. Va. —. His wife, Dorcas Alexander, was granted £20 support on 8 Feb. 1779 in Northumberland Co., Va.

Alexander, John. Va. —. His wife, Judith Alexander, and children were granted £8 support 13 on July 1778 and £50 on 13 Apr. 1779 in Northumberland County.

Alexander, Morgan. Va. Col. He enlisted 1 Jan. 1777 in the 2nd Virginia Regiment. He was at the battle of Monmouth. He died in 1783. His representatives were entitled to his half-pay. They applied to Congress 27 June 1838.

Alexander, Thomas. Mass. Capt. He had a hip dislocated and his thigh bone broken in a fall about20 January 1777 between Peekskill and King's Ferry. He served under Col. Vose. He lived in Northfield, Mass. in 1795. He received half-pay as a captain from Mass. from 1 Jan. 1778 to 11 Feb. 1783 when his pension was discontinued. A resolve of Mass. of 8 Feb. 1792 declared that he ought not to have been discontinued and ought to be placed on the list again. He was granted half a pension 20 Apr. 1796. On 24 Sep. 1796 he was awarded $300 and recommended to

Congress as a fit subject for a pension. He died 23 Mar. 1801.

Alexander, William. N.J. Brig. Gen. He was Lord Sterling and died 15 Jan. 1783. His widow, Sarah Alexander, died in 1804. Her trustees were William A. Deur, John Deur, and Beverly Robinson. They received £1607.4.6 3/4 for her. His seven years' half-pay was made 30 June 1834.

Alexander, William. N.C. Capt. He applied in Mecklenburg County in 1819. He served in the militia and in the state troops. He was aged about 70 years and had an infirm wife. He was awarded a $75 annuity.

Alexander, William. Va. —. His widow, Dorcas Alexander, was granted support 8 Feb. 1779 in Northumberland County 8 Feb. 1779 and 13 Apr. 1779.

Alexander, William. Va. —. His wife, Rachel Alexander, was granted £6 support in York Co., Va. on 15 June 1778.

Alford, Benedict. —. —. He applied but was rejected because he failed to specify the length of his service, his different grades, or the names of officers. He enlisted 1 Feb. 1776 under Capt. A. Prior for six months. Two months later he procured a substitute. In June 1776 he enlisted under Capt. Jonathan Farret and Col. Samuel Safford of Pittsford, Vt. and served six months. On 1 Apr. 1777 he served under Capt. Simeon Wright and Col. James Mead in the militia. His next tour was under Capt. James Sawyer and Col. Herrick for six months being discharged in December. He volunteered and took command to guard and escort prisoners from Bennington to Hartford for three months. In Apr. 1778 he was a minute man near Rutland under Col. Thomas Sawyer and then under Col. Warner and Capt. Branson. He was discharged six months later. In 1780 he volunteered in the militia under Capt. Samuel Clark from Williamstown, Mass. and went to New York. He was discharged a month later. His service amounted to six months as a sergeant and the rest of a private. His brother was George Alford. He was upwards of 75 years of age. Congress granted him a pension 15 Jan. 1834 for his service as a private.

Alford, George. Conn. —. He was struck from the pension roll in Dec. 1843 for insufficient proof of service. He could not be found on the roll of Capt. Josiah Elliott in 1775 in the 3rd Conn. Regiment. He sought restoration to the rolls and his arrearage. Congress did not approve his petition 9 Jan. 1847.

Alford, Jacob. Va. Pvt. He served in the 7th Va. Regiment from 1 Jan. 1777 until his discharge on 15 Nov. 1779. He was wounded at Brandywine by a musket ball in the joint of his left ankle which was never extracted. It remained ulcerated. Capt. Mayo Carrington certified that he served in the 5th Va. Regiment. He resided in Albemarle County in 1787. He was continued at the rate of £8 per annum on 28 Feb. 1787. He did 23 June 1803.

Alger, Archibald. N.J. —. He was pensioned in Middlesex County on 3 Feb. 1839 at the rate of $60.

Algier, Joseph. Pa. —. He was awarded a $40 gratuity on 7 Apr. 1830 in Lancaster Co., Pa.

Alhouse, David. Pa. Pvt. He served in the 2nd Pa. Regiment. He was disabled by a fall from one of the ramparts at West Point in 1780. He lived in Northampton Co., Pa. in 1794. He enlisted for the war. He appeared on the 1813 pension list as Daniel Aleshouse and David Alshouse.

Allday, John. Va. —. His wife, Mary Allday, was furnished 1 barrel of grain in Charlotte Co., Va. 2 Aug. 1779; 3 barrels of corn, 150 pounds of pork, and ½ bushel of salt on 1 Nov. 1779; £185 on 6 Mar. 1780; 4 barrels of corn and 250 pounds of pork for her and her five children on 6 Nov. 1780, and £995 for her and her five children on 5 Feb. 1781.

Allen, —. Va. —. His mother, Mary Allen, was granted financial support in Caroline Co., Va. 8 May 1781.

Allen, —. Va. —. His father, Joseph Allen, was granted £10 in Caroline Co., Va. on 9 Apr. 1778.

Allen, Abraham. —. —. He served about three years. He died 4 June 1820 and his widow died 12 Dec. 1832. His son, Stephen Allen, sought relief for himself and his brother and sister, but Congress denied their claim 9 May 1850.

Allen, Andrew. Pa. Pvt. He served in the Marines. He was afflicted with a rupture which he received at the fort of New Providence in dragging a large cannon through the sally port. The cannon rolled over and the drag rope took him by the belly and occasioned the rupture. The accident occurred in Nov. 1775 on the ship, *Columbus*. He lived in Berks Co., Pa. in 1794.

Allen, David. N.C. —. He was killed in the service. His widow, Susannah Allen, of Granville County was being pensioned in 1784. He also appeared as David Allin.

Allen, Edward. N.J. —. He was pensioned in Burlington County 4 Mar. 1839 at the rate of $60 per annum.

Allen, Ethan. Vt. Col. He set out to capture Ticonderoga and Crown Point. He was captured when trying to capture Montreal in 1775 and held captive until 6 May 1778 when he was exchanged. His heirs sought his pay to the time of his death 12 Feb. 1789. Congress rejected their claim 21 Jan. 1857.

Allen, Henry. Va. —. He enlisted in Culpeper Co., Va. and went north. He was at Stoney Point 1 July 1779 under Gen. Wayne. He returned on furlough in Dec. 1781. In Jan. 1782 he transferred to the U.S. Manufactory of arms at Fredericksburg until the factory was broken up. He was discharged in 1783. He died in 1831. He married Catherine ----- in Dec. 1781. She sought a pension from Congress on 4 Jan. 1841 and 8 Mar. 1842.

Allen, Hooper. Mass. —. He served in the 5th Regiment and resided at Manchester. His widow, Sarah Allen, was paid $50 in 1833.

Allen, Jacob. Md. Pvt. He was pensioned at the rate of half-pay of a private on 2 Jan. 1813.

Allen, Jacob. Me. —. He was from Scarboro. He was paid $50 under the resolve of 1836.

Allen, Jacob. Mass. Capt. He died 19 Sep. 1777. His seven years' half-pay of $1,680 was paid to his heirs.

Allen, James. Mass. Pvt. He served under Capt. Hill in the Invalids. He was disabled due to old age and lived in Concord, Mass. He was 61 years old in 1786. He died 13 Dec. 1809.

Allen, Job. Me. —. He was from Pownal. He was paid $50 under the resolve of 1836.

Allen, John. —. —. He was at Sandy Point, Me. In 1779. His shoulder was dislocated by the recoil of his gun with a double load. The injury healed and was calloused. He could use his arm but not for hard labor. His brother was William Allen. He sought relief from Congress in 1838.

Allen, John. Mass. —. He was paid $20.

Allen, John. Pa. —. He was from Butler County. He served in Col. Potter's Regiment. He was at Trenton, Princeton, and skirmishes at Piscataway and Quibbletown. He served under Col. Antes at Big Island. One of his name received a $40 gratuity and a $40 annuity in Butler County in 1840. He was 85 years old in 1840.

Allen, John. Pa. —. He served in the 1st Regiment upwards of three years. He was wounded at Yorktown and was discharged 22 Jan. 1782. He was awarded 200 acres of donation land 7   Apr. 1897. He was late of Morris Co., N.J.

Allen, Judah. Mass. Capt. He served in 2nd Regiment. About thirty years ago he applied for and obtained a bounty warrant for 300 acres but he lost it. The War Office burned in 1800. There was no record of the warrant and no evidence of location. Congress granted him a replacement 13 Jan. 1830.

Allen, Lathrop. N.Y. Capt. He enlisted in May 1775 and served as a sergeant in Capt. Baldwin's Company under G. Van Schaick in the expedition against Canada. In Dec. 1775 he was appointed a lieutenant under Capt. Roswell Beebe. In Feb. 1776 he served under Col. Samuel Elmore and on 15 Apr. 1776 received his commission. He was at Bennington, Saratoga, and the capture of Burgoyne. His widow was Abigail Allen. Henrietta Barnes petitioned for his five years' pay 19 Jan. 1836. Congress denied the claim from the heirs 10 June 1842 and again on 27 Jan. 1846.

Allen, Malachi. Mass. Pvt. He served under Col. Ebenezer Bridges in Capt. Benjamin Parker's Company. He was disabled by a musket ball which took part of the small bone above his right eye. He was 33 years old when he was pensioned in Mar. 1786. He was on the 1813 pension list. He served in the 27th Regiment.

Allen, Nathan. Md. Pvt. He was pensioned in Queen Anne's County at the rate of half-pay of a private on 1 Feb. 1834.

Allen, Peter. Pa. —. He was awarded a $40 gratuity 10 Jan. 1823. He was from Huntingdon County. He served in Col. Watts' Flying Camp and subsequently in Capt. Thomas Alexander's Company under Col. Piper. He was stationed in Sinking Valley to protect the lead mines.

Allen, Richard. N.C. —. He died 10 Oct. 1832. He left no widow. His son and executor, Richard Allen, sought his arrearage to be paid to the children and requested a special act to that effect. They were numerous and far removed from each other. Powers of attorney would have been of great difficulty to obtain. His petition was rejected 7 Jan. 1837 by Congress.

Allen, Robert. N.J. —. He was pensioned in Somerset County on 11 Nov. 1841 at the rate of $60 per annum.

Allen, Samuel. N.H. Pvt. He served in Cilley's Regiment. He was pensioned 24 Nov. 1812 in Rockingham County. He was on the 1813 pension list at the rate of $60 per annum.

Allen, Samuel. N.J. Pvt. He served in the 4th Regiment and lost a leg. He was 54 years old and was from Somerset County. He was on the 1791 pension roll.

Allender, George. Pa. Pvt. He was on the 1798 pension roll.

Alley, —. Va. —. His widow, Elizabeth Alley, applied for a pension from Henrico Co., Va. 30 Oct. 1793.

Alling, Stephen. N.Y. —. He was granted 200 acres bounty land 11 Apr. 1808.

Allison, —. Pa. —. His widow, Catharine Allison, was awarded a $40 gratuity and a $40 annuity in Franklin County 21 Mar. 1837.

Allison, Andrew. N.C. —. He was in Continental service, was wounded on 4 April 1779, and taken prisoner. He received a bayonet through his body on the left side. He was exchanged in Aug. 1779 and discharged due to his wound. He married a widow with a life estate to 400 or 500 acres, 3 adult slaves, and 4 Negro children. He was in Rowan County in 1807. He was transferred to the U.S. pension roll 4 Sep. 1808. He was on the 1813 pension list in Kentucky.

Allison, Andrew. Pa. —. He applied in Aug. 1826. He served in the 3rd Regiment under Col. Shay. He enlisted for one year in Philadelphia in 1777 in Capt. West's Company under Col. Helsymer. He was discharged at Valley Forge. He was in battle at White Plains, Trenton, and Princeton.

Allison, David. N.C. Pvt. He served in Capt. William Douglas's Company and was wounded at Lindley's Mills. He was crippled in both hands having two fingers on his left hand shot off and two fingers on his right hand withered and useless. A musket ball entered his left arm and came out at his back bone. He was 82 years old in 1815 and had a wife who had been bedridden for six years. He lived in Orange County.

Allison, John. Pa. Sgt.-Maj. He served in the 4ᵗʰ Pa. Line under Lt. Col. William Butler. He was in Adams County on 21 Apr. 1813.

Allison, John. Pa. —. He was awarded a $40 gratuity in Chester Co., Pa. 11 June 1832.

Allison, Richard. N.Y. Pvt. He enlisted in May 1778. He was disabled by a cutlass wound on his head, another on his neck, one on his right arm and a third on his right shoulder at the battle of Monmouth. He was in captivity about six weeks. After he was exchanged, he was put in hospital. He served under Col. Henry B. Livingstone and Capt. Israel Smith. He was a farmer. He lived at Bethlehem, Orange Co., N.Y. On 17 May 1789 he was 29 years old. He was on the 1813 pension list.

Allison, Robert. Pa. Lt. He was pensioned in June 1813. He served in the 3ʳᵈ Regiment to the close of the war. He received warrant #43 on 6 Apr. 1799. William Steel located it on 10 Feb. 1800, but Allison never assigned it. It was a forgery so Congress awarded him a duplicate for 200 acres of bounty land 13 Feb. 1835. He was from Franklin County. He was dead by Jan. 1837.

Allison, Thomas. Pa. —. He was awarded a $40 gratuity and a $40 annuity in Indiana County 29 Mar. 1824. He served in Col. Watts' Regiment of Flying Camp and afterwards was wagon master in the light dragoons until June 1778.

Allison, William. Pa. —. He was granted relief in Greene County in 1865.

Allman, Lawrence. Pa. Capt. Lt. He served in the Pennsylvania Line. His widow was Hannah Allman, and she was executrix of his will.

Allsop, Thomas. Va. —. He was away in Continental service and his wife, Mary Allsop, was awarded support of beef and grain in the amount of £15 in Botetourt Co., Va. on 15 Apr. 1778.

Allsworth, Andrew. Pa. —. He was awarded a $40 gratuity and a $40 annuity in Butler County on 9 Feb. 1824. He was in the Flying Camp.

Alrick, Adam. Pa. —. He was pensioned.

Alsop, John. Md. Pvt. He served in the 7ᵗʰ Regiment and was wounded at the Barges. He was pensioned in Frederick County 4 Mar. 1789. He died 2 May 1805.

Alsop, Samuel. Pa. Matross. He was in Philadelphia County 10 Apr. 1787. He was in Proctor's Regiment in Capt. Porter's Company of Artillery. He was wounded in the leg and suffered   from other disabilities sustained in the service. He served from 1776 to the end of the war. He enlisted in the Marine Dept. for one year in 1776. He was 67 years old. Capt. James McClure of the Artillery recommended him for a pension. He was paid to Sep. 1802. He was made a corporal a little later after his enlistment.

Altigh, Michael. Pa. Pvt. He was awarded a $40 gratuity and a $40 annuity in Washington Co., Maryland 15 Mar. 1826. He served in the Pennsylvania line.

Altman, James. S.C. —. He was from Horry District and applied 15 Oct. 1832. He served in the militia under Francis Marion, was of advanced age, and experienced all the ills and imbecility of old age. Harmon Flowers stated he was personally acquainted with him during the war. His claim was rejected 4 Dec. 1832.

Alverson, John. Va. Pvt. He served in Capt. Smith's Company in the 10ᵗʰ Va. Regiment. He was wounded in his left hand at the battle of Brandywine. He had two of his fingers shot off and was wounded in his right thigh by a musket ball. He lived in Va. in 1794. He later transferred to North Carolina. He was on the 1813 pension list.

Alvey, Josias. Md. Pvt. He was pensioned in St. Mary's County at the rate of half-pay of a private on 23 Jan. 1816.

Alvey, Thomas Green. Md. Corp. He served in the 3ʳᵈ Maryland Regiment. He was pensioned in

St. Mary's County in 1785. He was on the 1813 pension list of Maryland. He later moved to Perry Co., Ind. and died 12 Feb. 1824.

Alvis, Emanuel. Va. —. His wife, Mildred Alvis, was granted £6 support on 15 June 1778 and £25 on 21 June 1779 in York County.

Alvis, John. Va. —. His wife was granted £6 support in Hanover County 20 Dec. 1779.

Alvord, John. Mass. —. He was paid $20 and resided in New York.

Alvord, Job. Mass. Capt. He served one year as a lieutenant and in Jan. 1777 became a captain under Col. William Shepherd. He was deranged in 1779. He received no bounty land warrant in his lifetime. On or about 1 Apr. 1798 warrant #21 for 300 acres was issued to Justin Alvord who used it in partial payment for land in Ohio. Yet, Justin Alvord made no such application. He and his sister, Lucina Lyman of Bolton, N.Y. were the only heirs. Congress granted them relief 10 Jan. 1830. Job Alvord was from South Hadley, Mass.

Amack, Matthew. Va. Pvt. He served in Capt. Henry Pawling's Company of Botetourt County militia under Col. Crocket. He was wounded in his left arm at the battle of Guilford in 1781. His elbow was stiffened and the sinews of his hand were contracted. He was a farmer and had a large family. He was granted an annuity of half-pay for life in Botetourt County 3 June 1782. He was aged about 35 years in 1788. He was continued on the roll at the rate of £9 per annum on 16 June 1788. He later transferred from Botetourt County to Kentucky. He also appeared as Matthew Amicks, Matthew Amock, and Matthew Amox.

Ambler, Squire. —. —. He married Elizabeth Picket 5 Feb. 1784. They were divorced. He married secondly in 1820 and died 14 Jan. 1829. Elizabeth Ambler married secondly Thomas Bearse 21 Aug. 1801. He died 29 Dec. 1813. She married thirdly Abel Rowe 6 Feb. 1819. He died in 1824. Congress granted her pension. She died 23 Feb. 1842. *Vide* also page one.

Ames, James. N.C. Pvt. He applied in Halifax County. In 1789 he was 38 years and five feet eleven inches tall. He served as a private in the 2nd N.C. Regiment of the Continental Line. He lost his right arm. He was aged 35 in 1785. He was on the 1813 pension list. He died 8 Jan. 1828 in Wake County. He also appeared as James Amos.

Ames, Prince. Mass. —. He served in the 5th Regiment. He was paid $20.

Ames, Robert. Mass. Pvt. He was pensioned 21 Mar. 1807. He was on the 1813 pension list and died 12 Feb. 1821 in Suffolk County.

Ames, Smith. Conn. Pvt. He was pensioned 24 Aug. 1805. He was on the 1813 pension list. He died 21 Mar. 1823 in Hartford Co., Conn.

Ames, Spafford. Mass. Pvt. He served under Col. Frye in Capt. Farnum's Company. He was wounded by a musket ball in his right thigh and another in his right hand which injured two fingers at the battle of Bunker Hill in June 1775. He resided in Andover, Mass. in 1792. He was in the militia. He was on the 1813 pension list.

Amesbury, John. R.I. Pvt. He lost one joint from the toes of his right foot and one joint from the toes on his left foot by severe frost bite on the Oswego Expedition under Col. Willet in Feb. 1783. He served under Col. Jeremiah Olney. He applied 12 Jan. 1786 and was aged 21. He was listed as John Armsbury on the 1813 pension list. He died in Kent Co., R.I. 30 May 1821.

Ammons, Joshua. S.C. —. His application was rejected 21 Dec. 1822.

Ammonds, —. Va. —. His wife, Ann Ammonds, was granted £40 support in Fauquier Co., Va. in Nov. 1778 and Nov. 1779. She also appeared as Ann Amonds.

Amos, —. Md. Capt. His widow, Elizabeth Amos, was pensioned in Baltimore at the rate of half-pay of a captain 4 Mar. 1834. Her arrearage was paid to her heir, Samuel B. Hugo of Baltimore,

16 Mar. 1840.

Amsden, John. Mass. Sgt. He served in the 4th Regiment. He resided in Southboro. His widow, Louisa Amsden, was paid $50.

Amsden, Silas. Mass. Pvt. He served in the 2nd Mass. Regiment. He was wounded in the left knee by a sled load of wood running over it which he was drawing for the garrison at West Point in 1783. He was discharged 17 Sep. 1783. He resided at South Borough in 1794. He also appeared as Silas Ansden.

Ander, —. Pa. —. His widow, Catherine Ander, received a $40 gratuity and a $40 annuity in Lancaster County 13 Apr. 1838.

Anders, Richard. N.C. Lt. Congress rejected the claim of his heirs because there were funds unaccounted for but charged to him on 12 Feb. 1835. He also appeared as Richard Andrews.

Anderson, —. S.C. —. His widow, Lucy Anderson, resided in Spartanburg in 1791.

Anderson, —. Va. —. His wife, Anne Anderson, was granted 150 pounds of pork and 1 barrel of corn in Berkeley County, Va. on 21 Nov. 1780.

Anderson, —. Va. —. His mother, Nancy Anderson, was granted £20 in Caroline Co., Va. 8 Apr. 1779 while he was away in the service. There were three in her family 8 May 1781.

Anderson, —. Va. —. His mother, Mary Anderson was granted £30 in Caroline Co., Va. 10 June 1779 while he was away in the service.

Anderson, —. Pa. —. His widow, Phoebe Anderson, was awarded a $40 gratuity and a $40 annuity in Philadelphia County 12 Feb. 1825. She died 4 Dec. 1829.

Anderson, —. Pa. —. His widow, Elizabeth Anderson, was awarded a $40 gratuity and a $40 annuity in Cumberland County 11 Apr. 1844 for his Revolutionary service.

Anderson, —. Pa.—. His widow, Margaret Anderson, was granted a 40 gratuity and a $40 annuity in Allegheny County 22 Dec. 1834.

Anderson, Adam. Pa. —. He was pensioned with a $40 gratuity and a $40 annuity by the act of 24 Mar. 1818 in Westmoreland County.

Anderson, Amariah. N.J. Pvt. He served under Capt. William Faulkner and Lt. James Dillon and died at Fort George in Aug. 1776. He married Joyce Cargill 4 June 1775 in Philadelphia. She married secondly Henry Miles 4 June 1779. Her brother was William Cargill, a Quaker. She also appeared as Joyce Cowgill and was from Gloucester County.

Anderson, Daniel. Va. —. He was wounded in the breast and left arm at Quebec on 31 Dec. 1775. He was pensioned at the rate of $80 per annum on 3 Feb. 1814. He was in Shenandoah County in 1815 and in Page County in 1831. He died 6 Nov. 1840, and his heir was Catherine Wood on 5 Aug. 1841.

Anderson, David. N.C. Pvt. He served in Capt. William Douglas's Company. He was severely wounded at Lindley's Mill. Two fingers on his left hand were shot off and two fingers on his right hand were withered so that he was crippled in both hands. A musket ball entered his left arm and came out at his back bone. He was 82 years old, and his wife had been bedridden for six years. He applied in Orange Co., N.C. in 1815. He was awarded a £25 annuity.

Anderson, Elijah. N.J. —. He was pensioned in Monmouth County 23 Feb. 1841 at the rate of $60 per annum. He died 24 Nov. 1844. His children were Tina Anderson, Ezekiel Anderson, and Anna Staff.

Anderson, Ephraim. N.J. Capt. He served in the 2nd N.J. Regiment under Col. Israel Shreve and was killed at the battle at Short Hills on 26 June 1777. His widow, Rezine Anderson, married secondly Ephraim Harris of Cumberland County on 15 Aug. 1780. She was entitled to half-pay for the term of her widowhood. The Hunterdon County court approved her application in Feb. 1780.

Anderson, George. Pa. —. He enlisted in the nine months Rangers under Capt. Thomas Campbell and marched up the Allegheny on the Muncey campaign. He re-enlisted and served to the end of the war He applied 17 Mar. 1814 in Westmoreland County. He died 18 June 1848.

Anderson, George. S.C. —. He was killed in 1781. His widow, Margaret Ingram, was paid 19 Aug. 1785. There were four children in 1786.

Anderson, Henry. S.C. —. He was killed in Oct. 1781. His widow, Ruth Anderson, was paid 27 Feb. 1785. There were three children in 1791.

Anderson, Jacob. S.C. —. His widow, Rebecca Anderson, was paid 10 Jan. 1786 and was from Spartanburgh.

Anderson, James. —. Capt. His heirs sought five years' full pay 10 Jan. 1834. Congress rejected their petition because payment had already been made.

Anderson, James. Pa. —. He was granted a $40 gratuity and a $40 annuity 2 Apr. 1822. One James Anderson died 1 Nov. 1823.

Anderson, James. S.C. —. He had one child in 1791.

Anderson, John. Md. Pvt. He was on the 1791 pension roll.

Anderson, John. Md. Pvt. He was pensioned at the rate of half-pay of a private on 13 Feb. 1817.

Anderson, John. Mass. Sgt. He served in the 7th Regiment and resided in Boston. He was paid $20.

Anderson, John. Pa. Pvt. He was in Philadelphia County 14 Nov. 1785. He transferred from the 3rd Pa. Regiment to the Invalids. He was wounded in his knee and ankle in the service. He was 30 years old. He died 2 Mar. 1787. He was from York County.

Anderson, John. Pa.—. He was pensioned 2 Apr. 1822.

Anderson, John. S.C. —. He was killed in 1780. Two of his sons were also lost in the war. His widow, Sarah Anderson, was paid 13 Jan. 1787 in Greenville in 1786. She had one child in 1791. She collected her annuity until she was compelled to follow her other children and leave the state. She sought what she would have drawn on 11 Aug. 1809 from Livingston Co., Ky.

Anderson, Joseph. Va. —. He was wounded in the service on way to guarding prisoners from York to Winchester. He sought compensation for his loss of time and for the expenses in getting himself cured on 14 Feb. 1786 in Botetourt County.

Anderson, Joseph. Va. —. His wife, Mary Anderson, and two children were furnished 3 barrels of corn and 100 pounds of pork in Louisa Co., Va. on 12 Mar. 1781.

Anderson, Joseph. Va. —. His application was rejected 7 June 1787.

Anderson, Matthew. Va. —. He was disabled by infirmities. He received £5 per annum for two years on 27 May 1784.

Anderson, Michael. Pa. —. He was pensioned in Armstrong County 13 Apr. 1858.

Anderson, Richard. Md. Capt. He was pensioned at the rate of half-pay of a captain in Nov. 1785. He was on the 1813 pension list. Congress granted him payment of a pension between 3 Mar. 1826 and 31 May 1830. He died 22 June 1835 in Frederick Co., Md.

Anderson, Robert. Pa. Pvt. He was in Philadelphia County 12 Dec. 1785. He was transferred from the 12th Pa. Regiment to the Invalids. He lost his hand by a wound in the service. He was 33 years old. He was dead by March 1795.

Anderson, Robert. Pa. —. He applied from Franklin County 3 Oct. 1820. He enlisted at New London cross roads in Chester County in 1776 in Capt. James McClelland's Company in the 2nd Pa. Regiment. He also served under Capt. Watkins in the regiment of Col. Stewart. He was discharged at Downings Town, Pa. He was 66 years old. His family included his wife and four children: Alexander Anderson aged 25, Ann Anderson age 23, Mary Anderson age 21, and Charlotte Anderson age 19. He was in battle at Brandywine, Germantown, and Monmouth.

Anderson, Robert. Pa. —. He was granted relief in Cumberland County 11 Apr. 1825.

Anderson, Thomas. Mass. Capt. He received a fall which dislocated his hip bone in 1778. He was a cripple and lived in Northfield, Mass. He was pensioned at the rate of half-pay on 24 Sep. 1779. He was pensioned at the rate of £5 per annum from 1 Jan. 1775 in Monson, N.H. 14 Mar. 1786.

Anderson, Thomas. Pa. —. He was in Bucks County 9 Sep. 1813. He served in Capt. Bower's Company in the 2nd Pa. Regiment. Henry Wilhelm saw him in the winter of 1782-83 as an orderly sergeant in the military hospital at Lancaster. Jacob Leipcap found him in the Philadelphia Hospital in 1783 sick and lame in his arms and leg.

Anderson, Thomas. Pa. —. He was awarded a $40 gratuity and a $40 annuity in Washington County 14 Mar. 1818. He was paid to 19 Oct. 1832.

Anderson, Thomas. Pa. —. He was pensioned 14 Mar. 1838 in Westmoreland County.

Anderson, William. —. Capt. His widow, Elizabeth Anderson, sought pay for life. Congress rejected her claim 24 Feb. 1830 since she was not covered by law.

Anderson, William. Conn. Corp. He served in the 5th Bradley Invalids. He was debilitated by the hardships in the battle of Monmouth. He resided in East Hartford, Conn. in 1792. He was transferred to the invalids 29 Oct. 1780.

Anderson, William. Mass. —. He served in the artillery and was paid $20.

Anderson, William. S.C. —. He was killed 1 Sep. 1780. His orphans were paid 24 May 1785.

Andrews, Daniel. N.Y. —. He served as a levy and volunteer in the militia. He died 9 Aug. 1840. He had been rejected as a pensioner because he did not serve at least six months. His son, Henry Andrews, had maintained him and sought the pension due his father. Since he submitted no evidence of his father's death, his claim was rejected 12 Feb. 1841 by Congress.

Andrews, Edward. S.C. Pvt. He served under Col. Thomas Taylor. He sought compensation 5 Dec. 1811 and was from Fairfield District.

Andrews, Humphrey. Pa. —. He was awarded a $40 gratuity and a $40 annuity in York Co., Pa. 8 Apr. 1826.

Andrews, Israel. S.C. —. He entered the service at the very commencement of the war and was in the first engagement of Bloody Point in repelling a British cruiser that made an attack for plunder. He was at Parker's Ferry, Brier Creek, Coosawhatchie Bridge, and was one of the party of thirty-six under Lt. Ervin who attacked the jail in Beaufort and captured eleven officers and sixty-nine privates. In 1787 he was ordered out to suppress an insurrection and in a conflict with a party of Negroes was wounded in the hand. He was 62 years old and had a large family. His application of 5 Nov. 1821 was rejected.

Andrews, John. —. —. He served 3 months and 8 days. His widow, Mary Andrews, had her claim for a pension rejected 9 Jan. 1847 by Congress due to the length of his service.

Andrews, John. Pa. —. *Vide* entry in appendix for man of his name.

Andrews, Joseph. Mass. Lt. He served in the artillery and died 11 Sep. 1780. His seven years' half-pay of $1,400 was paid to his heirs.

Andrews, Reuben. Mass. Corp. He served in Crane's Artillery. He resided in Raynham. His widow, Olive Andrews, was paid $50.

Andrews, Samuel. —. —. He served one year on Continental establishment. He was pensioned under the act of 1818 but stricken from the rolls in 1820 because he had made payment to his son without a written contract. He was recommended for restoration of his pension by Congress on 7 Mar. 1832.

Andrews, Samuel. Conn. Corp. He served under Capt. Asa Bray in Gen. Wolcott's brigade of militia and was wounded by a musket ball in the wrist of his hand by an accidental discharge of the gun of his father while on their march. His hand was amputated on 21 Oct. 1777 in New York. He also served in Latimer's and Mason's Regiments. He resided in Southington, Conn. in 1792. He was in the militia. He was granted half of a pension 20 Apr. 1796. He was on the 1813 pension list. He died 6 Aug. 1832. He also appeared as Samuel Andrus.

Andrews, William. —. —. He was pensioned in 1833 at the rate of $80 per annum. His rate was reduced to $30.88 because his service was recalculated at 9 months and 8 days rather than two years. He was granted relief for 18 months service by Congress 5 Mar. 1840.

Andrews, William. Va. Sgt. He was wounded by a musket ball through his thigh at Brandywine in Sep. 1777 and in his loins at Stoney Point on 26 July 1779. He lost the use of his lower parts and had to travel on crutches. He served in the 5th Va. Regiment. He was awarded a gratuity of £500 and a full set of clothes 25 Nov. 1780. In 1783 he had no visible estate except a tract of 200 acres. He resided in Cumberland County in 1787 and was aged about 30 years. He was continued on the pension list at the rate of £15 per annum on 17 Apr. 1787. He removed to Georgia and was there on the 1813 pension list. He died 3 May 1821.

Andrus, Clement. Conn. Pvt. He served in the 1st Regiment. He was wounded in the leg by a stick of timber which produced an open ulcer on his leg. He resided in Farmington, Conn. in 1792. He enlisted 20 Dec. 1780 and was discharged 17 May 1783.

Andrus, Theodore. Conn. Pvt. He served in Col. S. B. Webb's Regiment He was wounded by falling on a rock while in the line of duty at Tiverton, R.I. in Oct. 1779. It injured his left hip so as to produce a carious ulcer which totally disabled him. He resided at New Hartford, Conn. in 1796. He enlisted 11 Apr. 1777 for three years and was discharged 11 Apr. 1780. He was granted a full pension 20 Apr. 1796. He died 4 Sep. 1806 [?] in Hartford Co., Conn. His name was on the 1813 pension list.

Andruss, Abner. Conn. Pvt. He served in Jeduthan Baldwin's Regiment of Artificers. He was pensioned 6 Sep. 1787. He was from Wallingford and aged 28 years on 6 Sep. 1787. He was affected with palsy. His right arm and leg were ulcerated. He also served under Capt. William Mills and Lt. Jarius Willcocks. His father was Dennison Andruss. He was on the 1813 pension list. He died 23 Dec. 1825 in Middlesex Co., Conn.

Angel, John. Va. Pvt. He enlisted in Jan. 1781 for the war under Col. Green. He was wounded by a musket ball through his right arm breaking the bone in May 1781 near Camden. He was put on the pension list on 19 June 1784. Lt. Col. S. Hawes and Maj. T. Meriwether attested to his service. He was aged about 30 years and applied from Chesterfield County in 1787. He was continued on the roll at the rate of £12 per annum on 2 Aug. 1787. He served in the 2nd State Regiment. He was on the 1813 pension list.

Angevine, Lewis. Conn. Pvt. He enlisted in Capt. Joseph Walker's Company under Col. Samuel B. Webb in 1777 and served to 1780 when he was transferred to the Invalids. He was disabled by having the main bone of his right leg broken and other disorders. He was pensioned at the age of 57 in Stratford, Conn. on 1 Dec. 1788. He died in 1803.

Angier, Samuel. Mass. Pvt. He served in Capt. Aaron Gardner's Company under Col. Moses Brooks. He was wounded by a musket ball which entered the left side of his neck and passed through his right shoulder. He was pensioned at one-third the pay of a soldier from Nov. 1776 on 20 Mar. 1786. He was 49 years old. He also appeared as Samuel Anger.

Angst, Michael. Pa. —. He was granted relief.

Angst, Nicholas. Pa. —. He was awarded a $40 gratuity and a $40 annuity in Schuylkill County 24 Mar. 1817. He died 20 June 1826.

Angus, Jacob. Pa. —. He was awarded a $40 gratuity and a $40 annuity in Lancaster Co., Pa. 10 Apr. 1835. He died 20 Nov. 1848. His daughter, Elizabeth Leebrick, of Quincy, Illinois had met with a severe accident while assisting in the transfer of the sick and wounded after Shiloh to Quincy, Ill. and lost sight in one eye. Her husband had been totally blind for eight years. She had spent more than $700 of her money in charity relief. She was granted a pension by Congress 22 July 1882. She was 82 years old.

Annis, Phineas. —. —. His widow was Hannah Annis. Congress acted on the claim of the daughter, Caty Burnham, on 18 May 1848.

Ansart, Lewis. Mass. Col. His name was Lewis Ansart de Maresquille, and he was a captain in the French Army. He entered the service in Massachusetts as Superintendent of Casting of Cannon for the state. He was to be paid $1,000 a year and $666.66 2/3 pension for life. He was Colonel of Artillery and Inspector General of Foundry. He also performed military duties not connected with the foundry to the close of the war. He married Catherine Wimple 9 Sep. 1781. He died in 1804. His widow had her name changed by act of the legislature of Massachusetts to Ansart. She applied in 1836 but was rejected because he was not a military officer. On 31 Aug. 1778 he was directed to perform the duty of engineer when Count D'Estaign arrived with the French fleet. He received a staff appointment of colonel without command in the Line. His widow died 27 Jan. 1849. Congress approved her heirs' petition for a pension 25 May 1860. The surviving children were Atis Ansart, Julia A. Varnum, Abel Ansart, Felix Ansart, and Sophia Spaulding.

Anthony, —. Pa. —. His widow, Wilhelmina Anthony, received a $40 gratuity and a $40 annuity in Philadelphia 23 Mar. 1858.

Anthony, John. R.I. Pvt. He had a fever sore on his neck contracted in Feb. 1781 when he was sick in hospital. It rendered his neck stiff and his shoulders much deformed. He served under Col. Jeremiah Olney. He was aged 23 in 1785. He lived in Providence County.

Anthony, John. S.C. Pvt. He was born in France and came to Charleston, S.C. in 1764. He served in the artillery under Capt. Edward Rutledge and Col. Daniel Stevens. He was a harness maker. He was wounded at Beaufort but continued to the end of the war. He died intestate in 1818. His widow, Mary Anthony, was a native of Charleston. Under the law she was entitled to one-third of his realty. He had no children and no heirs in America. The act of 1826 entitled her to all of his reality. She sought a ruling of her situation 31 Oct. 1826.

Anthony, Nathaniel. Va. —. His wife, Mary Anthony, and two children were furnished 3 barrels of corn and 75 pounds of bacon in Louisa Co., Va. on 12 Aug. 1782.

Antil, Edward. N.J. Maj. He received half-pay. He resided in Goshen, Orange Co., N.Y. in 1811.

Anyan, —. Va. —. John Anyan was granted financial assistance while his sons were away in the service in Amelia Co., Va. 25 June 1778.

App, —. Pa. —. His wife, Sophia App, was awarded a $40 gratuity and a $40 annuity in Lancaster, Pa. 1 Apr. 1830.

Apperson, Peter. Va. —. He was pensioned in Spotsylvania County 1 Jan. 1820 at the rate of $60 per annum. He was in Orange County in 1832.

Apperson, Richard. Va. Capt. He was commissioned lieutenant 11 Mar. 1777 and captain in the

6th Regiment 26 Sep. 1777. He became supernumerary 30 Sep. 1778 at White Plains. He was not entitled to commutation. Because he did not serve three years, he was rejected for bounty land from Virginia at the close of the war. In Jan. 1807 he was allowed 4,666 acres for seven years of service.

Appleby, Stephen. —. —. He never applied to the Pension Office so Congress declined to act on his petition 29 June 1840.

Applegate, Andrew. N.J. —. His widow, Elizabeth Applegate, was pensioned in Middlesex County on 9 Apr. 1847 at the rate of $100 per annum.

Applegate, Joseph. N.J. —. His widow, Ann Applegate, was pensioned in Middlesex County on 9 Apr. 1847 at the rate of $100 per annum.

Applegate,. N.J. —. His widow, Elizabeth Applegate, was pensioned in Burlington County on 9 Mar. 1868 at the rate of $100 per annum.

Applegate, William. N.J. —. His widow, Hannah Applegate, was pensioned in Monmouth County on 13 Mar. 1844 at the rate of $40 per annum.

Appleton, Thomas. Mass. Sgt. He was disabled by a rupture and fits. He was pensioned 4 Jan. 1783.

Apply, Jacob. N.Y. Pvt. He served under Col. Klock and was slain 20 Apr. 1779. His children, Margaret Apply, Dorothy Apply, Jacob Apply, and Elizabeth Apply, received a seven year half-pay pension.

Arbuckle, Samuel. Mass. Pvt. He served in the 3rd Company and resided at Salem. His widow, Abigail Roberts, was paid $50.

Archer, —. Pa. —. His widow, Hannah Archer, was granted a $40 gratuity 8 Apr. 1826. She resided in Philadelphia, Pa.

Archer, Jacob. N.Y. Pvt. He served under Col. Ann Hawkes Hay and was slain 29 Dec. 1779. His widow, Mary Archer, received a half-pay pension.

Archy, John. Pa. —. He was pensioned by the act of 14 Mar.1818. He also appeared as John Harachy.

Arcules, James. Mass. —. He served in the 4th Regiment and was paid $20.

Ardman, Andrew. Pa. —. He was granted a $40 gratuity and a $40 annuity in Montgomery Co., Pa. in 1836. He died 16 Dec. 1843.

Arell, David. Va. Capt. He served in the infantry. He was appointed 7 Oct. 1776 and resigned 14 Feb. 1778. His children, Christina Lowe and Richard Arell, unsuccessfully sought his commutation 1 Mar. 1838. A bounty land warrant for 4,000 acres had been issued 12 Apr.1778.

Argubrite, Jacob. Va. Soldier. He was born in Lancaster Co., Penn. and moved as a boy to Rockingham County. He volunteered in May 1778 under Capt. Cravens for three months. He assisted in building Fort Laurens. He was under Capt Sullivan of Berkeley County in the cavalry. He was in the rifle company of Capt. Coker and was at Yorktown at the surrender of Cornwallis. After the war he located in Albemarle County. He applied from Monroe Co., Va. at the age of 71 on 15 Oct. 1832.

Arkenson, John. Mass. Gunner. He served in Crane's Artillery. He resided in Somerset. His widow, Mary Neal, was paid $50.

Armand, Tuffin. Brig. Gen. Congress awarded bounty land to his heirs 19 Jan; 1841 even though the time for such had expired.

Armbruster, Matthias. Pa. —. He was awarded a $40 gratuity and a $40 annuity in Philadelphia 22 Mar. 1814. He was paid $300 in full for his claim to donation land 18 Feb. 1819.

Armistead, Thomas. Va. Capt. His heirs received his commutation of full pay for five years in lieu of half-pay for life as a captain of infantry in the Virginia Line with no interest on 25 Feb.

1826. He died in King William County 1 Sep. 1809 leaving five daughters.

Armistead, William. Va. Capt. His heirs received his commutation of full pay for five years in lieu of half-pay for life as captain of cavalry in the Virginia Line with no interest on 27 Feb. 1827.

Armor, James. Pa. —. His lineal heirs in Chester Co., Pa. were awarded $200 for his right to donation land on 23 Apr. 1829.

Armstrong, —. Pa. —. His widow, Margaret Armstrong, was awarded a $40 gratuity and a $40 annuity in Allegheny Co., Pa. 14 Jan. 1835. She died 7 June 1854.

Armstrong, Edward. Del. Lt. He was pensioned in 1778. He lived in New Castle County and died 14 May 1824.

Armstrong, Edward. N.Y. Pvt. He served in Capt. Richard Sackett's company under Col. Thomas Thomas in the Westchester County militia. He was wounded in his back by a musket ball and his left arm stiffened. He was 29 years old on 8 Dec. 1787. He was pensioned 12 Apr. 1788 and lived in New York County. He was on the 1813 pension list. He died 9 June 1830.

Armstrong, Elijah R.I. His widow, Mercy Armstrong, of Gloucester Co., R.I. sought arrearage of her pension from 4 Mar. 1848 to 3 Feb. 1853 on 23 Feb. 1857. Congress allowed same.

Armstrong, George. Va. —. His widow, Jane Armstrong, and four children were granted financial support in Yohogania Co., Va. 25 Aug. 1778.

Armstrong, James. Pa. —. He was pensioned in Lycoming County 16 June 1836.

Armstrong, James. S.C. —. He was greatly wounded by the enemy and was far advanced in age. He was paid 19 Jan. 1785 and was from Abbeville District. He applied in Pendleton District 4 Dec. 1802. He had no slaves, and owned a small tract of land. He was on the 1813 pension list.

Armstrong, James. Va. Sgt. He served in the 3rd Va. Regiment and died in the service. He left a considerable family of small children. A son was 11 years old in 1792. His widow, Mary Anne Armstrong, applied from King George County in 1786. She was continued at the rate of £15 per annum on 31 May 1790.

Armstrong, James. Va. —. The statements in the declaration were in conflict. He was probably in the militia. He probably did not perform the service mentioned in the certificate from the Secretary of the Commonwealth of Virginia. His widow, Nancy Armstrong, had her petition rejected 9 Jan. 1847.

Armstrong, John. —. Pvt. He lived in Kent Co., R.I. and died 30 May 1821.

Armstrong, Robert. Pa. —. He was awarded a $40 gratuity in Columbia Co., Pa. 12 Apr. 1828.

Armstrong, William. Conn. Sgt. He was on the 1795 pension list.

Armstrong, William. Pa. Sgt. He was on the 1798 pension list.

Armstrong, William. S.C. Pvt. He served under Capt. Benjamin Kilgore in a company of militia cavalry in Gen. Williamson's Brigade. He was on the Cherokee Expedition in 1776. One of the three hard fought battles was the Ring Fight. He then joined Capt. Porter's Company of N.C. militia and was at the battle of Ramsour's Mill where he was wounded twice. One ball shattered his right leg; the other entered his right shoulder and broke his collar bone. He served a total of three years. He was promised a bounty of 640 acres when he entered the Cherokee Expedition, but he never got a cent for his service or suffering. He was in his 69th year and sought a commutation of his bounty land and to be placed on the pension roll. He applied in Richland District 30 Nov. 1818. He was allowed a pension of $60 per annum, but his bounty land was denied on 14 Dec. 1818. He was paid to 1 Mar. 1823. He died insolvent in Oct. 1823. His widow, Elizabeth Armstrong, nearly 70 years of age, sought his arrearage which was paid on 3 Dec. 1825. She was pensioned at the rate of $30 per annum for her widowhood. She was paid as late as 1834.

Armstrong, William. S.C. —. He was pensioned 6 Dec. 1828 and was paid from 1829 to 1834. He again applied from Pendleton District on 8 Nov. 1836. He served under Gen. Andrew Pickens and Gen. Thomas Sumter in Capt. John McCall's and Capt. John McClure's companies. He was in the battles of Hanging Rock, Rocky Mount, Col. Bratton's, and Tarleton's defeat. After passage of the Act of Congress of 1832 he applied and was approved as a federal pensioner. After a few years his pension was suspended for further detailed proof of his service. He could not document same. All he had was his bed and wearing apparel. He sought to be restored to his former $60 per annum South Carolina pension. He was paid his annuity in 1834.

Armstrong, William. S.C. —. He was pensioned on 7 Dec. 1836.

Arnold, Thomas. R.I. Capt. He lost his right leg in the battle of Monmouth on 28 June 1778. He served under Col. C. Greene. After his leg was amputated, he served in the Invalid Corps. He was aged 44 in 1786. He was on the 1813 pension list. He sought the restoration of his commutation from Congress 21 Dec. 1818 as a gratuity but was rejected. He died 8 May 1821 in East Greenwich, Kent Co., R.I.

Arthur, John. Va. —. He applied from Bedford County on 28 Jan. 1825 and was pensioned at the rate of $60 per annum. He was also granted $40 immediate relief. He received several severe wounds in battle. He seemingly died in 1850 when reference to the pension of Mrs. Sally Arthur was made.

Artis, —. Va. —. He died in Continental service. His widow, Margaret Artis, was allowed £30 in Berkeley County 17 Nov. 1779.

Ashburn, William Graves. —. His wife, Frances Ashburn, and family were granted financial support in Caroline Co., Va. 8 Jan. 1778 and on 12 Nov. 1778.

Ashby, —. Va. —. His mother, Sarah Ashby, was furnished £12 support on 15 June 1778, £50 on 21 June 1779, and the same on 17 July 1780 in York County.

Ashby, John. Va. Pvt. He served in the 3rd Va. Regiment. His widow, Sarah Ashby, lived in Stafford County 1787. She was put on the pension roll at the rate of £12 per annum on 14 Apr.1787.

Ashby, Peter. —. —. His widow was Winifred Ashby. She was dead when Congress denied any arrearage to the heirs on 6 Mar. 1850 because they failed to prove the marriage.

Ashe, John Baptiste. —. Lt. Col. He entered as a captain in Apr. 1776, was promoted to Lt. Col., and commissioned major in the 1st N.C. Regiment effect from 28 Jan. 1777 in 1779. Congress authorized that his executor or administrator receive his commutation 19 Feb. 1836. On 8 Nov. 1838 his legal representative was allowed $3,600. That figure did not allow for interest so Congress awarded same 27 June 1890 to his heir Samuel P. Ashe.

Asher, Gad. Conn. Pvt. He was disabled by blindness. He was transferred to the Invalid Corps. He was pensioned 10 Apr. 1783. He lived in New Haven Co., Conn. He was on the 1813 pension list.

Asher, John Baptiste. —. Maj. He served under the command of John Jay in the 1st N.C., having entered the service as a captain in Apr. 1776. He was entitled to his commutation 22 Dec. 1837.

Asher, Kennedy. Mass. —. He served in the 4th Regiment. He was paid $50.

Ashley, John. Pa. —. He was pensioned 20 Mar. 1814.

Ashley, Moses. Mass. Lt. He received his commutation for five years in lieu of half-pay for life. He died 25 Aug. 1791.

Ashlock, —. Va. —. He was slain in the service. His father, John Ashlock, was granted relief on 15 June 1780. His father had another son in Continental service at that time.

Ashton, James. Pa. —. He was in Philadelphia County 9 June 1813. He served in the 3ʳᵈ Pa. Regiment from Jan. 1777 to Jan. 1783 when he was discharged. He was 71 years old.

Askew, James. Va. Pvt. He enlisted 1 Dec. 1780 and served under Lt. John White until discharged on 23 July 1783. He was a prisoner in Charleston and fell out of a house while in confinement. He lost one of his eyes due to a fever. He was upwards of 65 years of age in 1787. Capt. Mayo Carrington stated he served in the 5ᵗʰ Va. Regiment, and Brig. Gen. James Wood stated he served in the 7ᵗʰ Va. Regiment. He applied from Fluvanna County 1787. He was continued on the roll of £8 per annum on 21 Oct. 1787. His pension was increased to £12 per year on 19 Nov. 1787. He was continued on the roll at the rate of £8 per annum on 12 Feb. 1789. He was issued a duplicate certificate on 22 June 1790. He was on the 1813 pension list.

Atherton, Caleb. Mass. Pvt. He served in Capt. Moses Adams' Company under Col. Brooks. He was deprived of his eyesight. He was pensioned at the rate of half-pay of a soldier from 1 May 1778 on 6 July 1784. In 1786 he was 20 years old. He lived in Bristol County. He was on the 1813 pension list.

Atherton, Joel. Me. —. He was from Waterford. He was paid $50 under the resolve of 1836.

Atkins, Bartlett. Va. —. His wife was granted support in Pittsylvania Co., Va. 25 Feb. 1779.

Atkins, David. Conn. Pvt. He served in the 4ᵗʰ Regiment. He was disabled with a withered leg. He was pensioned 1 Sep. 1782. He lived in Litchfield Co., Conn. and was on the 1813 pension list.

Atkins, James. Va. —. His wife, Sarah Atkins, was granted £3 per annum on 7 Aug. 1777 in Isle of Wight Co., Va. while her husband was away in the service.

Atkins, Moses. Va. —. His wife, Sarah Atkins, was granted £3 support in Isle of Wight County on 7 Aug. 1777. She later married Thomas Addison.

Atkinson, —. Va. —. His wife was granted support in Cumberland Co., Va. 17 Aug. 1779.

Atkinson, —. N.J. —. His widow, Anna Atkinson, was pensioned 7 Mar. 1872 at the rate of $50.

Atkinson, Isaac. N.J. —. His widow, Anna Atkinson, was pensioned in Cape May County 14 Feb. 1847 at the rate of $50 per annum.

Atkinson, James. N.C. —. He enlisted in Jan. 1781 in Edgecombe County under Lt. Thomas Partin, Capt. Peter Benet, and Col. Archibald Lyttle in the 2ⁿᵈ Regiment. He was at Cowpens, Guilford Court House, and Eutaw Springs. He was wounded by a bayonet through his thigh. He died in 1782 in Halifax County.

Atkinson, William. Me. —. He was from Lewiston. He was paid $50 under the resolve of 1836.

Atkinson, William. Pa. Pvt. He lived in Philadelphia County. He was on the 1789 and 1813 pension lists.

Atkinson, William. Va. Pvt. He served under Lt. Col. Lee from 20 Mar. 1781 to 31 Dec. 1781 when he was disabled by a number of wounds at the High Hills of Santee. His left hand was nearly cut off at the wrist, and he was wounded in the elbow of the same arm. He served in Col. Michael Rodolph's Company of Infantry. He was presumed dead and omitted from the returns given to Col. Meriwether. Maj. Joseph Eggleston stated he served in Col. Campbell's Regiment and was annexed to the legion. He applied from Henrico Co. in 1786. He was aged about 27 years of age in 1786. His pension was increased from $40 to $60 per annum 25 Jan. 1813. He died 14 Feb. 1814 in Caroline Co., Va. leaving a widow Sarah Atkinson and a daughter Sarah Atkinson.

Attender, George. Pa. Pvt. He was on the 1813 pension list.

Atwood, —. Va. —. His wife, Betty Atwood, was granted support in Prince Edward Co., Va. on 15 Mar. 1779 while he was away in Continental service.

Atwood, Jesse. Me. —. He was from Wilton.

Aubel, Conrad. Pa. —. He was awarded a $40 annuity and a $40 gratuity in Union County 11 Apr. 1825. He died 21 Aug. 1832.

Auber, John. Md. Sgt. He served in the 2nd Regiment and was disabled at Eutaw Springs. He was pensioned in Frederick County in 1789. He also appeared as John Ober.

Auchmuty, Samuel. Pa. —. He was awarded a $40 gratuity and a $40 annuity in Dauphin Co., Pa. 14 Apr. 1834.

Audebert, Philip. Mass. Marine. He served aboard the armed frigate *Hazard* under Foster Williams and was wounded 17 July 1779 at Penobscot by a ball in the vertebrae of his loins. He was discharged 14 Aug. 1779. He was pensioned at the rate of half-pay from that date on 19 Apr. 1781.

Augur, Felix. N.Y. Pvt. He served four tours. The first was under Capt. Higgins and Col. Douglas for six months in 1776 (but known to be but five months), as a substitute for his father under Capt. Butrous at Saybrook in Mar. and Apr. 1776 for two months, for eight months under Capt. Plumer and Col. Elly, and for twelve months under Capt. Chapman and Col. McClellan in 1778. He died in Murray, Orleans Co., N.Y. 21 July 1839. He married 8 Dec. 1784. Congress granted his widow, Esther Augur, a pension based on nineteenth months of service on 21 July 1842.

Auld, Daniel. Md. Pvt. He was pensioned at the rate of half-pay of a private on 9 Mar. 1826. He was wounded at Eutaw Springs. His widow, Sarah Auld, was awarded his unpaid pension in Feb. 1832. She was pensioned on 9 Mar. 1832 in Talbot County during her widowhood. She died 28 June 1847. Her arrearage was paid to Philip Pasterfield, her surviving brother, in Talbot County 19 Jan. 1848.

Ault, James. Pa. —. He was awarded a $40 gratuity and a $40 annuity in Chester Co., Pa. 6 Apr. 1833. He died 23 Dec. 1840.

Aurand, John Detrick. Pa. —. He applied 19 Feb. 1813. He enlisted for three years in the 2nd Pa. Regiment in 1778 at Valley Forge in Capt. Bankson's Company under Col. Walter Stewart. He was acquainted with Hugh Mulholan, an orderly sergeant, who left him in the service at Trenton. He was a minister of the gospel.

Austin, —. Va. —. Fanny Austin was granted support in King William County in 1778.

Austin, Benjamin. Me. —. His widow was Abigail Austin of York. She was paid $50 under the resolve of 1836.

Austin, Caleb. N.H. Pvt. He served under Col. Brooks in the militia. He was wounded by a musket ball in his right ankle in Oct. 1776 at White Plains. He lived in Bow, N.H. in 1794. He was granted one-third of a pension 20 Apr. 1796. He was on the 1813 pension list.

Austin, David. Me. —. He died 18 Mar. 1833 at Dresden. His widow was Judith Austin of Alna. She was paid $50 under the resolve of 1836.

Austin, Isaac. N.Y. Pvt. He enlisted in New York City under Capt. Forbish and Col. McDougal. He was in the battles of Long Island, White Plains, Trenton, and several other skirmishes. He served three years. The War Department found that Forbish did not continue in the service after 1776 and was not in McDougal's regiment. His enlistment for three years was not in accordance with the history of service at that time. He was stricken from the rolls. Congress restored his pension 5 Mar. 1840.

Austin, John. Va. —. He served in both the French and Indian War and the Revolutionary War. His application was rejected on 27 May 1784.

Austin, Nathaniel. Conn. Pvt. He served in Thaddeus Cook's Regiment. He was disabled at the battle of Stillwater. He was pensioned 25 Mar. 1778 in Suffield, Conn. He was on the 1813 pension list. He died 20 Nov. 1829 in Hartford Co., Conn.

Austin, Richard. Conn. —. He served two years and two months under Capt. Hanchett and Col. Butler in the Connecticut Line. He was listed on the roll as a deserter in Aug. 1780. The same record showed his settlement for pay 29 Mar. 1782. He was formerly of Suffield, Conn. and married there on 7 Dec. 1767 Mary ----. He died in May 1783, and she married secondly Joseph Phelps who died in 1794. She was allowed a pension by Congress on 27 Mar. 1846 of $96 per annum beginning 17 Feb. 1848.

Austin, Samuel. Pa. —. He was granted a $40 gratuity and a $40 annuity in Armstrong Co., Pa. 1 Apr. 1836. He was 84 years old in 1840.

Austin, Valentine. Ct. —. He served in Cook's Regiment and was disabled at Stillwater. He died 20 Nov. 1829.

Averett, —. N.C. —. He was killed in service. His widow, Ann Averett, was paid in 1784.

Avery, Amos. Conn. Pvt. He served in the militia. He was pensioned 26 Sep. 1788. He lived in Groton, New London Co., Conn. and was 30 years old. He had been wounded by a musket ball in his left arm. He was on the 1813 pension list.

Avery, Daniel. Conn. Pvt. He served in the militia under Col. Lattimer in Capt. Nathaniel Wales' Company. He was disabled in Oct. 1777 at the capture of Gen. Burgoyne in New York when he was wounded in the side by a stick of timber. He lived in Tolland Co., Conn. He lived in Coventry, Conn. and was 27 years old when he was pensioned 3 Dec. 1788. He was on the 1813 pension list.

Avery, David. —. Chaplain. His children sought a pension for five years or the amount of wages plus interest due him on the grounds that he was paid in Continental money of little or no value. Congress rejected their claim on 4 May 1846.

Avery, Ebenezer. Conn. Corp. He was in the militia opposing the British troops under Gen. Arnold who landed at New London. He was wounded in the head and body in several places by a bayonet on 6 Sep. 1781 at Fort Griswold. He served under Capt. William Latham in the Artillery. Dr. Amos Prentice attended him at the fort. He resided at Groton and was 42 years old when he was pensioned 28 Sep. 1788. He was on the 1813 pension list. He died 10 Jan. 1827 in New London Co., Conn.

Avery, Park. Conn. Lt. He served in the 8th Conn. Regiment of militia. He was disabled at Groton in opposing the British troops under Gen. Arnold who had landed at New London. He was wounded in the head on 6 Sep. 1781 at Fort Griswold and had his right eye taken out by a bayonet. He received a musket ball in his left side. He was pensioned 26 Sep. 1788 when he was 46 years old. He was on the 1813 pension list. He died 20 Dec. 1821 in New London Co., Conn.

Avery, Thomas. Conn. Lt. He served in the 1st Conn. Regiment and was wounded by grape shot in his neck, shoulder, and back on 27 Aug. 1777 on Long Island. He was attended by Dr. Philip Turner, Surgeon in the General Continental Hospital. He was first pensioned 31 Aug. 1777. He lived in Groton, Conn. and was 40 years old when he was pensioned 30 Nov. 1786. He was on the 1813 pension list. He died 4 May 1825 in Franklin Co., Mass. He was a blacksmith.

Avis, William. N.C. —. He never drew any money.

Axe, Frederick. Pa. —. He was awarded a $40 gratuity and a $40 annuity in Philadelphia Co., Pa.18 Mar. 1834.

Axson, Samuel Jacob. S.C. Surgeon's Mate. He came to the army after the battle of Eutaw and served in the 1ˢᵗ S.C. Regiment to the end of the war. He had the entire care of the regiment when Dr. Flagg, the surgeon, was employed as Apothecary General to the Hospital. He lived in the country when the other surgeon mates received their commutation. He sought his commutation of five years' pay in 1789. It was paid to his legal representative 15 June 1832.

Ayer, Benjamin. Me. —. He was from Winthrop. He was paid $50 under the resolve of 1836.

Ayers, —. N.Y. —. Mary Ayers was granted relief during the war.

Aylett, William. Va. Col. He died in the service about 1780 at Yorktown; his widow, Mary Aylett, married secondly Callohill Minnis and died about 1787. His heirs received 6,666 acres of bounty land in 1809. His heirs sought his seven years' half-pay, but they were ineligible because his rank was not a military one. They were rejected in 1842.

Ayott, Pierre. —. Capt. He served under Col. Moses Hazen. He died intestate in Clinton Co., N.Y. 15 Oct. 1814. His widow, Marie Ayott, also died there. Her daughter, Mary, married Pierre Vincelet. Congress denied relief to the soldier's administrator, Francis Picard, 15 Dec. 1857. New York gave him three lots of 333 1/3 acres as a Canadian refugee. He was the son of William Aillot and Marie Anne Levasseur. His wife was Marie Monty. They were married 25 Jan. 1769.

Ayres, Ebenezer. —. —. He died 29 May 1832. His widow, Achas Ayres, sought to be paid a pension before she qualified from his death to 4 Mar. 1848. Congress denied her claim 21 July 1854.

Ayres, James. S.C. —. He applied from Pickens District 8 Nov. 1830. He was in his 70ᵗʰ year. In 1781 in Kershaw District he volunteered under Capt. William Nettles for nine months and returned home. His father was then drafted. He volunteered under Capt. William Deason and joined Gen. Marion and Col. Richeson. He was in the battles of Orangeburg and Eutaw. He owned 28 acres in the mountains, had 5 cattle, 3 hogs, 1 mare, 2 beds and furniture, a few farming tools, and a little parcel of household and kitchen furniture. The total value was less than $20. Benjamin O'Bannon served with him under Capt. William Nettles in 1781 and attested to his service. He was pensioned 25 Nov. 1830. He was paid as late as 1834.

Ayres, Reuben. —. —. He was pensioned due to his disability from wounds received in the Revolutionary War 26 Feb. 1813.

Ayres, Samuel. Mass. Capt. He served in the 5ᵗʰ Regiment and lived at Manchester. His widow, Lydia Ayres, was paid $50.

Ayres, Thomas. Md. Pvt. His widow, Elizabeth Ayres, was pensioned at the rate of half-pay of a private on 26 Jan. 1837.

Babbidge, Courtney. Me. —. He died at Vinalhaven 9 Oct. 1834. His widow was Catherine Babbidge of Winalhaven. She was paid $50 under the resolve of 1836.

Babbs, William. Pa.—. He was pensioned.

Babcock, Joseph. Mass. —. He served in the 5ᵗʰ Regiment and lived at Manchester. His widow, Mary Babcock, was paid $50.

Babcock, Phineas. N.Y. —. He resided at Queensburg in 1777 and owned a store of goods at Lake George. The troops of Gen. Schuyler took his goods. Congress declined to reimburse him on 15 Jan. 1821.

Babcock, Robert. —. —. Congress denied his claim for a pension 30 June 1854.

Babcock, Seth. Mass. —. He was from Weston. His widow, Abigail Babcock, was pensioned in June 1839.

Baber, William. Va. Pvt. He served under Col. Lewis Burwell in the militia in 1782. He was at the siege of York in Gloucester County. He was blinded in both eyes by sickness. He received half-pay from 1 Nov. 1781 to 27 Nov. 1783 when he was put on the pension list. He had no property other than two small Negroes. He was a resident of Mecklenburg County on 26 Mar. 1787. He was continued at the rate of £12 per annum on 25 Aug. 1788. He was on the 1813 pension list.

Bacher, Jacob. Pa. —. He was awarded a $40 annuity in Schulykill County 5 Feb. 1836. He also appeared as Jacob Backer.

Backer, Daniel. N.Y. Pvt. He served under Col. Thomas Thomas in the Westchester County militia and was slain 25 Nov. 1781. His widow, Jemima Backer, received a seven year half-pay pension.

Backus, Clark. Mass. Pvt. He served in the 1st Regiment and resided at Barnstable. His widow, Elizabeth Backus, was paid $50.

Bacon, Ebenezer. —. —. He was killed at Saratoga. His widow was Phebe Bacon. She married (2) Lt. Col. Andrew Colburn and (3) ------ Root. Congress rejected relief to the heirs, Elizabeth Root, Ebenezer Bacon, and Amena Robson, on 7 June 1842.

Bacon, George. Mass. Marine. He served aboard the continental ship *Warren* under Dudley Saltonstall, Commander, and was wounded in the right arm at Penobscot in July 1779. He was pensioned at the rate of one-third of his pay from 14 Aug. 1779, the date of his discharge, on 19 Apr. 1781. He resided in Tisbury, Mass. in 1788 and was 29 years old. He was on the 1813 pension list. He transferred from Berkshire Co., Mass. to Huron Co., Ohio 4 Sep. 1822.

Bacon, Nathaniel. S.C. Capt. In 1779 he served under Capt. John Harris, Col. John Hammond, and Col. Leroy Hammond. He was at the siege of Augusta and served to the end of the war. He received no compensation. His heirs at law were Lyddall Bacon, Elizabeth Darby, and Joseph Wood. Their application was rejected 19 Dec. 1837.

Bacon, Samuel. —. —. He was pensioned in 1818 and stricken in 1820. His property was worth $566.50. Congress granted him a pension 13 Mar. 1832.

Bacon, Timothy. Me. —. He was from Gorham. He was paid $50 under the resolve of 1836.

Badcock, Seth. Mass. —. He served in Nichols' Artificers and resided at Weston. His widow, Abigail Badcock, was paid $50.

Badger, ——. Pa. —. His widow, Nancy Badger, was awarded a $40 gratuity and a $40 annuity in Fayette Co., Pa. 8 Apr. 1833.

Baggerly, David. —. —. He served six months. He was at Yorktown in 1781. Congress awarded his widow, Rebecca Baggerly, a pension 23 June 1854.

Baggs, John. R.I. Sgt. He was wounded in the left hand by the splitting of his musket which discharged while he was cleaning it at South Kingston. He served in the militia under Col. Dyer. He lived in Richmond, R.I. in 1794. He was granted one-third of a pension 20 Apr. 1796.

Baer, Jacob. Pa. —. He was awarded a $40 gratuity and a $40 annuity in Westmoreland County 1 Apr. 1836.

Bagley, Benjamin. Mass. —. His widow, Sarah Bagley, was allowed his gratuity on 16 Nov. 1777. He was retained in captivity.

Bailey, Anselm. Va. Pvt. He entered the service in 1775 under Col. Patrick Henry at the age of 16 and marched to Williamsburg against Lord Dunmore. Afterwards he was attached to the 1st Va. Regt. He was at Germantown. He was made a prisoner and put in jail in Philadelphia for three months. He made his escape and joined the army at Valley Forge. At Monmouth he was wounded in his leg by a ball which he still carried. He was also at Paulus Hook, Stoney Point, and Yorktown. He was pensioned and stricken from the rolls in 1819. He was restored. He sought his pension from the time he was stricken. He was 83 years old. He received the arrearage of his pension without interest 9 Feb. 1842. He had been stricken initially because he served under Col. George Gibson whose unit was not accepted as qualifying Continental service.

Bailey, Daniel. Me. —. He died 13 Mar. 1817. His widow, Susannah Bailey, was from Woolwich. She was paid $50 under the resolve of 1836.

Bailey, Ephraim. Mass. Pvt. He served under Col. Nixon in the 6th Regiment. He was wounded by a musket ball through his right ankle on 28 Apr. 1777 at Crump's Hill. He lived in Brookfield, Mass. in 1795. He enlisted 10 Mar. 1777 and was on the rolls in 1780. He was granted a half pension 20 Apr. 1796. He was on the 1813 pension list.

Bailey, George. Pa. —. He was awarded a $40 gratuity and a $40 annuity in York Co., Pa. 18 Feb. 1834. He was 90 years old in 1840. He died 23 Nov. 1843.

Bailey, Hezekiah. Conn. Ens. He lived in Fairfield Co., Conn. He was on the 1813 pension list.

Bailey, Israel. Me. —. He died 20 May 1830 at Brookfield. His widow, Lucy Bailey, was from Minot. She was paid $50 under the resolve of 1836.

Bailey, James. —. —. He served in the Revolutionary War and in the War of 1812. He was injured by a bullet in his elbow. He was 86 years old. Congress rejected his request to be restored to his invalid pension 12 Feb. 1841.

Bailey, James. Pa. —. He applied in Chester County 4 Dec. 1813.

Bailey, John. Conn. Pvt. He served in Oliver Coit's Company under Col. John Ely. At White Plains in Nov. 1776 he was taken with a mortification of his feet by a fever and lost all toes on his right foot and some on his left. He was pensioned at the age of 30 in Groton, Conn. on 6 Dec. 1788. He was attended by Amos Prentice, Surgeon. He died in 1791.

Bailey, John. Me. —. He died 19 July 1833. His widow, Lucy Bailey, was from Turner. She was paid $50 under the resolve of 1836.

Bailey, John. Mass. —. He served in the 5th Regiment and resided in Ipswich. He was paid $20.

Bailey, John. Mass. Pvt. He served in Col. Porter's 3rd Regiment. He was wounded in Apr. 1776 in Quebec and lost the sight of his left eye. His other eye was considerably weakened due to smallpox. He lived in Greenwich, Mass. in 1795. He served in the militia.

Bailey, John. S.C. —. He applied in Chester District 24 Nov. 1827. He volunteered under Capt. John Nixon in the Snowy Campaign against the Indians and Tories in 1775. He was at Reedy River when many of the enemy were taken. He caught cold. He next served under Capt. Andrew Hemphill and Col. Joseph Brown when the British were expected to invade Charleston. He was taken sick with the flux at the Quarter House and was hauled home in a wagon before the campaign was over. He then served in the Augusta campaign under Capt. Nixon and Col. Winn. His next tour was to Charleston, but he could not go because his family were ill. He hired a substitute and gave him a good horse and a guinea. He later served under Lt. Col. McGriff to collect and carry provisions to Gen. Gates' army. He went across the Wateree River with the wagons when they heard of his defeat and had to return. He was at the taking of the Congaree Fort under Capt. Samuel Adams in Col. Lacy's Regiment on the fatigue party and labored all night the fort was taken in making the entrenchment and raising the platforms for the cannon. He was under Gen. Sumter at the taking of Biggen Church near Monk's Corner on the Santee River after which he was discharged. He was 77 years old. He had no slaves. His son and three daughters were all of age. His youngest child was 30 years old. John McDill stated that he served with him under John Nixon and Col. John Winn at Stono, the taking of Granby Fort, and the burning of Biggen Church near Waddrel's Point. James Harbison stated he was with him in Augusta Camp under Gen. Williamson, at the taking of Friday's Fort, and Biggam Church when it burnt. John Brown was with him in the Snowy Camp and at the Quarter House. He had a tract of land for which he paid $500, 2 old horses, a small stock of cattle, a few young hogs, and a few kitchen utensils. He owned about $200. He was pensioned 25 Nov. 1830. His pension was $60 per annum. It was last paid in 1834. He died 25 Feb. 1836. Robert Jamieson was executor. His heirs sought his arrearage of $59.83, but their petition was rejected since there was actually nothing due the decedent.

Bailey, Joseph. Mass. —. He served in the 3rd Regiment. He was paid $20.

Bailey, Joseph. —. —. He was from Pelham, Mass. and enlisted at Windham, N.H. in June 1781 and served six months under Capt. Cherry and Col. George. He went to Amherst where he passed muster and was allowed one week to return home to prepare his clothing, arms, and accoutrements after which he returned to the service. He was stationed most of the time at Saratoga until discharged in December. He reached home at Pelham on the 7th or 8th of Jan. 1782. Congress granted him a pension for six months and ten days of service on 5 Mar. 1840.

Bailey, Josiah. Me. —. He died 5 Feb. 1836. His widow, Mary Bailey, was from Woolwich. She was paid $50 under the resolve of 1836.

Bailey, Mountjoy. Md. Capt. He received five years' full pay free from interest in Nov. 1808. He received a warrant for 200 acres of bounty land as a donation on 3 Feb. 1826 in Allegany Co. He also appeared as Mountjoy Bayly. He was approved for commutation of his five years' full pay 26 May 1830.

Bailey, Noah. Mass. —. He served in the 5th Regiment and was paid $20.

Bailey, Robert. Conn. Pvt. He served in the Connecticut militia and was wounded by a musket ball in the palm of his hand which injured the tendons of his two middle fingers on 19 Sep. 1777 near Stillwater. He resided in Chatham, Conn. in 1796. He was granted one-fourth of a pension 20 Apr. 1796. He was on the 1813 pension list.

Bailey, Thomas. Md. Pvt. He was pensioned at the rate of half-pay of a private on 19 Feb. 1819.

Bailey, William. Conn. Pvt. He served in the Connecticut militia and was wounded by a musket ball and three buck shot in his hip in Jan. 1779 at Redding. In 1796 he resided at Haddam, Conn. He was granted one-fourth of a pension 20 Apr. 1796. He was on the 1813 pension list.

Bailie, James. Pa. —. He was granted assistance by the Court of Enquiry 3 Dec. 1817.

Baily, Samuel. —. —. He did not serve in the regular army so Congress declined to pass a special act for his relief on 23 Feb. 1820.

Bain, John. —. —. He sought an increase in his pension. Congress denied him relief 14 June 1850 because he was already being paid at the highest rate. He was 113 years old.

Bain, John. Pa. —. He was awarded a $40 gratuity and a $40 annuity in Lancaster County 9 Mar. 1826. He was 103 years old in 1840. He died 1 July 1850.

Baird, Absalom. Pa. Surgeon. He served in a regiment of artificers under Col. Jeduthan Baldwin. He removed to western Pennsylvania in 1786 and died in Washington Co., Pa. in Oct. 1805. His five years' full pay commutation was paid to his legal representatives in 1836. They were allowed the back interest 13 Mar. 1838. His son, Thomas H. Baird, upon coming of age, took out letters of administration of his father's estate. Their were five children: John Baird, the eldest son, whose widow was Mrs. N. Baird; George Baird; ----- Baird who married a Hodge and was the mother of George B. Hodge; William Baird, deceased; and Thomas H. Baird.

Baird, Adam. Pa. —. He was awarded a $40 gratuity and a $40 annuity in Berks County 29 Mar. 1824. His widow, Catharine Baird, was awarded a $40 gratuity and a $40 annuity in Berks Co., Pa. 14 Apr. 1828.

Bakehorn, Jeremiah. N.Y. Pvt. His wife, Margaret Bakehorn, was granted support 1 May 1779 while he was away in the service. He died in the spring of 1781. His widow and three children lived in Dutchess County 3 Nov. 1781.

Baker, Amos. Me. —. He died 7 Oct. 1814 in Buffalo, N.Y. His widow, Elizabeth Baker, was from China. She was paid $50 under the resolve of 1836.

Baker, Andrew. Mass. He served aboard the *Independence* and was wounded. He was paid £4 for two months pension from 19 Dec. 1777 to 19 Feb. 1778.

Baker, Benjamin. S.C. —. He lived in Liberty Co., Marlboro District in 1791. He was paid his annuity from 1799 to 1806.

Baker, Daniel. Pa. Pvt. He served in the 2nd Regiment of Pa. Levies. He was pensioned 28 Sep. 1791. He lived in Delaware County. He transferred to Delaware Co., N.Y. 4 Mar. 1829. He was on the 1813 pension list.

Baker, Edmund. Mass. —. He served in Crane's Artillery. He was paid $20.

Baker, Henry Cleland. Md. Lt. He was deprived of the use of his limbs in South Carolina. He served in the 3rd Md. Regiment. He had a wife and children. He was granted half-pay in 1791.

Baker, Isaac. R.I. Pvt. He lived on a farm in Middletown, R.I. when the British took possession. All communication with the mainland was shut off. In Apr. or May 1777 there was a British regiment stationed near his farm. He maintained communication by a system of signals with Lt. Chaffee for fourteen months from Aug. 1778. He was 81 years old. Congress granted him a pension for fourteen months of service as a private 4 Feb. 1834.

Baker, Jacob. Pa. —. He served in the Pa. Line. He was in the Invalid Corps from June 1777 to 15 Nov. 1784. He was awarded a $40 gratuity and a $40 annuity on 30 Mar. 1811, He was from Philadelphia County. He was on the 1813 pension list. He died 2 Aug. 1815.

Baker, Jacob. Pa. Artificer. He served in Rockfountain's Regiment. He transferred to New York, New York 5 Sep. 1817.

Baker, James. Pa. —. He applied in Adams County 18 Feb. 1814. He was in Capt. Coran's Company in 1777 in the 4th Regiment under Col. Proctor. He served six or seven years and was discharged by Col. Humpton. William Waugh swore that Baker was a servant to his father in July 1777 and went to Carlisle and enlisted. He applied to Coran to have him given up, but Coran refused. James Baker died 5 Oct. 1822.

Baker, John. Pa. —. He was awarded a $40 gratuity and a $40 annuity in York Co., Pa. 14 Apr. 1834. He died 11 Sep. 1840.

Baker, Moses. S.C. Pvt. He served in the 1st S.C. Regiment. Charles Cotesworth Pinckney verified his service. He was disabled in the service by the breech of a cannon falling on him at Fort Johnston on 15 Sep. 1775. He recovered and returned to service. He joined Gen. Greene before the battle of Guilford. He was also kicked by a horse. He applied 13 Oct. 1788. He died 9 Apr. 1791. His children were Ann Baker born 20 Feb. 1777, Elizabeth Baker born 23 Feb. 1779, Moses Baker born 20 Sep. 1782, and Zilpha Baker born 5 Jan. 1784. His widow, Susannah Baker, was paid the arrears of his annuity on 14 June 1792 for herself and the children.

Baker, Nathaniel. Mass. Pvt. He served in Capt. Nathaniel Wade's Company under Col. Moses Little. He was wounded on the heights of Charlestown on 12 June 1775. The gun shot fractured the bones of his left leg. He was pensioned at the rate of one-quarter pay of a soldier from 1 Jan. 1776 on 2 Mar. 1778 and on 15 Mar. 1784. He was 33 years old in 1789. He resided in Suffolk Co., Mass. He was on the 1813 pension list.

Baker, Rowland. Va. Pvt. He was wounded in Continental service. He was on the 1785 pension roll.

Baker, Samuel. Me. —. He died 3 Aug. 1826. His widow, Mary Baker, was from North Yarmouth. She was paid $50 under the resolve of 1836.

Baker, Samuel. Mass. —. He served in Crane's Regiment. He resided at Dorchester and was paid $20.

Baker, Thomas. —. Capt. He served as a post captain in the Navy and commanded the sloop of war, *Delaware*. He was injured in his constitution and was incapable of further service. He drew a pension for $450 per annum. His widow, Jane Baker, and one child were in penury and sought relief. Their application was not covered by law so the claim was rejected 28 Feb. 1821. He had entered the service at the age of 16 as an apprentice to Capt. Gustavus Conyngham. His widow had her request for relief rejected by Congress 7 Feb. 1845 since there was no law to provide such.

Baker, Thomas. Md. Pvt. He was pensioned 4 Mar. 1789. He was on the 1813 pension list.

Baker, Thomas. N.J. Pvt. He served in the 3rd Regiment and was worn out in the service. He was 58 years old and lived at Trenton. He was on the 1791 pension roll in the latter.

Baker, Thomas. Pa. —. He was on the 1789 pension list.

Baker, Thomas. Va. —. He lived in Fincastle. He was on the 1785 pension roll.

Baker, Thomas Marshall. Mass. Capt. He died 14 Nov. 1809.

Balcolm, Joseph. Mass. Eng. He received his commutation for five years in lieu of half-pay. He died 11 Nov. 1827. He also appeared as Joseph Bolcomb.

Balding, Moses. Pa. Pvt. He was in the company of Capt. John Haling in the 3rd Pa. Regiment. He was 26 years old in 1777.

Baldridge, John. —. Capt. He served several tours for a total of two years and two months. He died 17 Oct. 1823. He married 21 Aug. 1780. His widow, Isabella Baldridge, was allowed a pension by Congress 3 Jan. 1846.

Baldy, Paul. Pa. —. He was pensioned.

Baldwin, Daniel. N.J. Capt. He was wounded in his left leg at Germantown 4 Oct. 1777, and it was amputated in April following. He served in the 1st New Jersey Regiment under Col. Matthias Ogden. He received half-pay pension in Essex Co., N. J. in 1781. He had neither house nor settlement and sought the small place offered to Baron Steuben in return for declining his half-pay pension 12 Nov. 1784. He was 33 years old 2 June 1786. He was granted half a pension 20 Apr. 1796. He lived in Brooklyn, Kings Co., N.Y. and received a New York pension. He was on the 1813 pension list.

Baldwin, Henry. Md. Lt. His widow, Mary Gambrill, was pensioned at the rate of half-pay of a lieutenant on 18 Feb. 1830. Her son, William H. Baldwin, in Anne Arundel County in Jan.1835 claimed the two months of the pension due his mother, Mary Gambrill.

Baldwin, James. Va. —. His wife, Elizabeth Baldwin, was allowed £15 on 23 Mar. 1778 in Bedford Co., Va. at which time there was a correction to the record. The name of her husband had been mistakenly given as James Boyd on 23 Feb. 1778.

Baldwin, Moses. Pa. —. He was granted relief in Crawford County 28 Mar. 1836.

Baldwin, Nathan. Conn. Pvt. He was drafted into the militia in 1779 under Capt. Diamond Perry, Col. Hooker, and Gen. Meade for one and a half months. He was at Horse Neck and Quaker Bridge. He was drafted in 1780 for three months under Lt. Dexter and Col. Canfield. He was a substitute for his brother under Capt. Sizer for six months at West Point. He also served at various other times. Congress granted him a pension for six months of service on 12 Feb. 1841.

Baldwin, Samuel. Md. Pvt. He was pensioned at the rate of half-pay of a private on 25 Feb. 1836.

Baldwin, Silas. Conn. Pvt. He served in Col. R. J. Meigs' Regiment. He was inoculated for smallpox and lost one of his eyes. He lived in Derby, Conn. in 1792. He enlisted 27 Mar. 1777 and deserted Aug. 1779.

Baldwin, Thomas. N.Y. Sgt. He was wounded in an engagement with the Indians with a ball which fractured the knee pan in 1779; another wound in the forehead in a scouting party the following year; and another wound by a ball which passed through his left hand in 1780. He received his wounds on the Western Expedition and Susquehannah. He resided in Newton, N.Y. in 1796. He joined an independent company in Jan. 1781 and was discharged 17 Jul. 1781. He was on the 1813 pension list.

Baldwin, Waterman. Conn. Pvt. He was pensioned from 25 Oct. 1807 at the rate of $5 per month. He was on the 1813 pension list of New York.

Bale, Abraham. Pa. Corp. He was in Philadelphia 11 Sep. 1786. He served in the 10th Pa. Regiment and was wounded in one leg by an ax and in the other at Brandywine. He was 50 years old.

Balfour, Andrew. N.C. Col. Margaret and Eliza Balfour received an annuity for five years for Andrew Balfour, a minor, beginning in 1788. Col. Balfour was killed 10 Mar. 1782 and was from Randolph Co., N.C. His son was 18 in 1787 and needed money for his education. He was granted a small sum in 1793.

Ball, Benjamin. Mass. Sgt. He served in the 4th Regiment and was paid $20.

Ball, Daniel. Va. Ens. He served in Campbell's Regiment. He resided in Chesterfield County. He was on the 1813 pension list.

Ball, Jonathan. Mass. Sgt. He served under Col. Christopher Green and Capt. Jonas Hubbard. He contracted a scorbutic habit. He was on the 1813 pension list.

Ball, Josiah. Mass. Pvt. He was disabled by a broken right arm and a broken left arm. He was pensioned 17 Mar. 1786. He died 1 July 1811. One of his name was on the 1813 pension list.

Ball, Samuel. N.J. Pvt. He served under Capt. Isaac Gilman and Col. Philip Van Courtland in the Essex County militia. He was wounded in action at Connecticut Farms 7 June 1780. He died six days later. His widow, Hannah Ball, applied for half-pay in June 1782 in Essex County.

Ball, Samuel. Vt. Pvt. Marlboro. He lost his health in the service and was subject to epileptic fits being overcome with heat and fatigue at the battle of Monmouth. He also lost the use of his right eye. His sight in the other eye had been greatly injured due to smallpox. He served in the 10th Mass. Regiment. He lived in Windsor, Vt. in 1792 and in Marlborough, Vt. on 10 Oct. 1795. He was in the militia.

Ballance, —. Va. —. His wife, Patty Ballance, was granted financial assistance in Fauquier Co., Va. in Sep. 1778, Oct. 1779, Nov. 1780, and 2 barrels of corn and 20 pounds of bacon in July 1782.

Ballard, Ebenezer. Mass. —. He served in the 2nd Regiment and resided at Haverhill. He was paid $20.

Balmer, Jacob. Pa. —. He was pensioned 3 June 1813. He died 27 Feb. 1821.

Balsle, John. N.Y. Pvt. He was in Capt. Hous' militia. He was wounded in thirteen places on 20 May 1781 at Fort Hous. He lived in Connajoharrie, N.Y. in 1794. He was in the militia.

Baltzel, Charles. Md. Capt. He was granted relief.

Bancroft, Ebenezer. Mass. Capt. He served under Col. Ebenezer Bridge and was wounded in the battle on the heights of Charlestown on 17 June 1775. He lost his forefinger on his left hand and his thumb was injured. He was pensioned at the rate of half-pay from 1 Jan. 1776 on 26 Jan. 1778. He was on the 1813 pension list. He died 22 Sep.1827 in Norfolk Co., Mass.

Bancroft, Jonathan. Mass. Sgt. He served in the 5th Regiment and resided at Pepperell. He was paid $20.

Bancroft, Robert. Mass. Pvt. He was wounded in his right foot with the stroke of an axe. He also lost his forefinger on his left hand and had his thumb injured. He was 48 years old in 1786. He lived in Middleton, Mass. in 1794. He enlisted 10 May 1778. He was granted one-fourth of a pension 20 Apr. 1796. He was on the 1813 pension list. He received $20 from the Commonwealth.

Baney, Peter. Pa. —.He was awarded a $40 gratuity and a $40 annuity in Lebanon County 18 June 1836. He was dead by Jan. 1839.

Bange, Joshua. Me. —. He died 23 Apr. 1823. His widow, Anna Woodbury, was from Auburn. She was paid $50 under the resolve of 1836.

Banks, Andrew. Pa. —. He was awarded a $40 annuity in Schuylkill County 5 Feb. 1836. He died 1 Jan. 1845.

Banks, John. Va. Pvt. He was disabled by an accidental injury. He was crippled by the fall of a log across his back. He was awarded a £300 gratuity on 13 Nov. 1780. He was in Continental service and enlisted in Albemarle County.

Banks, Obediah. Conn. Pvt. He served in Capt. Isaac Howe's Company in the Connecticut militia under Col. John Mead. He was a laborer. He was serving under Capt. Elnathan Close on Long Island in Oct. 1779 when he was wounded in his shoulder, arm, and back. He received a musket ball in his left arm and body. He lived in New York City, N.Y. on 10 Dec. 1788 when he was pensioned. He was on the 1813 pension list.

Banks, Reuben. —. —. He served under Col. Livingston in 1777, Capt. Knowles Sears and Col. Waterbury in 1777, Capt. Pierce and Col. Drake, and Capt. Hunt and Col. Weisenfeld.

Banks, Vincent. S.C. Pvt. He applied from Darlington District 10 Nov. 1825. He was over 80 years old and since February had been helpless with dead palsy. His application was rejected.

Bankers, —. Pa. —. His widow, Barbara Bankers, was awarded a $40 gratuity and a $40 annuity in Lancaster County 21 Mar. 1840 for his Revolutionary service. She died 26 Aug. 1840.

Bankstone, Elijah. Ga. —. He served under Col. Elijah Clarke for two years and nine months. He was late of Butts County and died 22 Feb. 1849. His application for a pension had been lost in the mails and Lt. David Madden died after certifying his service for a pension. Congress granted his widow, Elizabeth Bankstone, relief 3 Mar. 1855.

Bannen, Jeremiah. Pa. —. He was awarded a $40 gratuity and a $40 annuity in Beaver County 30 Mar. 1822. His widow, Agnes Bannen, was awarded a $40 gratuity and a $40 annuity in Beaver Co., Pa. 1 Apr. 1834. He also appeared as Jeremiah Bannon.

Banon, Robert. Pa. —. He was on the 1789 pension list.

Banquit, William. Pa. Sgt. He was in Philadelphia County on 13 Oct. 1785. He was in the 5th Pa. Regiment under Col. Butler and was transferred to the 3rd. He was wounded in the head and transferred to the Invalids. His widow was mentioned 7 Aug. 1788.

Bansall, Benjamin. Pa. —. He was granted relief in Perry County 3 Apr. 1841.

Bantham, Peregrine. Md. Pvt. He was pensioned at the rate of half-pay of a private in Kent County on 3 Feb. 1816.

Bantley, —. Va. —. His wife, Elizabeth Bantley, was granted £70 relief in Brunswick Co., Va. while her husband was away in Continental service.

Barace, Christopher. Pa. Pvt. He was in Philadelphia County on 30 Sep. 1785. He was transferred from the 10th Pa. Regiment to the Invalids. He was wounded by the stroke of a broad ax in 1778. He died 19 Mar. 1786.

Barber, Benjamin. Va. Pvt. He served in the 4th Va. Regiment. Col. James Williams certified that he lost his toes on both feet in Nov. 1778 by frost bite. He lived in Culpeper County on 26 July 1786. He was continued at the rate of £12 per annum on 25 Aug. 1788. He was on the 1813 pension list. He also appeared as Benjamin Barbee.

Barber, Francis. N.J. Lt. Col. He was Lt. Col. and Commandant of the 2nd N.J. Regiment and was killed in the service 11 Feb. 1783. His widow, Ann Barber, received his half-pay in 1783 in Essex Co. She also appeared as Nancy Barber.

Barber, John. N.H. Sgt. He served in the 2nd N.H. Regiment. He was wounded by a musket ball which passed through his thigh on 17 Sep. 1777 at Bemis Heights. He resided at New Market, N.H. in 1796. He enlisted 11 Nov. 1776 for the war and was promoted to corporal on 6 Jun. 1780 and sergeant in Jan. 1783.

Barber, Joseph. S.C. —. He was taken prisoner by the British in Sep. 1780 and died in captivity. His widow, Mary Barber, was paid 8 June 1785 and was from Chester.

Barber, Silas. Mass. Sgt. He served in the 3rd Regiment of Artillery under Col. John Crane in Capt. Nathaniel Donnel's Company. He had four of his ribs on his right side fractured when he was putting out a fire in the barracks at West Point when he fell into the story below and landed on a beam. He was disabled due to rheumatism and other complaints. He was pensioned 17 Sep. 1783. He was 32 years old in 1787 and lived in Massachusetts. He lived in New York City, N.Y. on 17 Apr. 1789. He was a carpenter. He was on the 1813 pension list.

Barber, Timothy. N.Y. —. Pvt. He served in the Ulster County militia under Col. James McClaughrey and was slain 22 July 1779. His son, Timothy Barber, sought his seven years' half pay. His widow, Reuben [?] Barber, was 104 years old in 1855.

Barber, William. N.Y. Pvt. His only heir and daughter, Jane Ann Mancius, wife of Jacob Mancius, was awarded his 500 acres of bounty land 11 Apr. 1808.

Barber, William. Va. —. He was on the 1785 pension roll.

Barber, Zacheriah. N.Y. He served under Capt. Amos Ellis, Capt. John Lincoln, and Col. Joseph Webb. He was 86 years old and was from DePeyster, N.Y. His service amounted to four months and seven days. Congress rejected his claim for a pension 13 Feb. 1850 because he had not served the minimum of six months.

Barberick, John. Mass. Corp. He served in Capt. Child's Company under Col. John Greaton and suffered from a dislocation of his left shoulder. He was pensioned at the rate of one-third pay of a corporal on 21 Oct. 1783. He was 39 years old in 1789. He transferred to Lincoln Co., Me. in 1818. He was on the 1813 pension list and died 22 June 1827. His service was in the 3rd Regiment, and he was from Weston, Mass. His widow, Mary Barberick, was paid $50. She died 30 Apr. 1836 but drew no pension. His daughter, Hannah W. Vreeland, petitioned Congress for a special bill 16 Jan. 1874. He also appeared as Jonathan Barbrick.

Barclay, Robert. Pa. —. He was awarded a $40 gratuity 27 Feb. 1834 in Cumberland Co., Pa. He also appeared as Robert Barkley.

Barclo, Harmanus. N.Y. —. His family was granted support 27 Nov. 1780.

Barden, Elijah. —. —. He was pensioned under the act of 1818 but stricken in 1820 on account of his property. He was restored in 1832. He sought his arrearage 24 Jan. 1837 which Congress allowed.

Bardt, Christian. N.Y. —. He served under Lt. Col. Samuel Clyde in the militia and was slain 6 Aug. 1779. His widow, Catharine Bardt, received a half-pay pension.

Bardt, Nicholas. N.Y. Lt. He served under Col. Samuel Clyde in Capt. Jacob Difendorff in the militia. He was wounded in his breast at Johnstown on 25 Oct. 1781. He was pensioned 7 Oct. 1786. He was 42 years old in 1786. He lived in Montgomery Co., N.Y. 15 June 1789. He was on the 1813 pension list and died 17 May 1824. He also appeared as Nicholas Bradt and Nicholas Barth.

Barhyt, Daniel. N.J. Pvt. He served in Capt. Morrell's Company of five month men. He was taken prisoner at the battle of Long Island in 1776 and thrown into a prison ship. He was later taken to N.Y. and imprisoned in a church. He took a fit of sickness which terminated in an ulcerated leg. He was a shoemaker and lived in Elizabeth, N.J. in 1794.

Barkelow, James. Pa. —. He served in the Flying Camp. He was from Union County.

Barker, —. Va. —. Lucy Barker was being pensioned on his service 13 Aug. 1778.

Barker, Isaac. R.I. —. He lived on a farm in Middleton three and half miles from Newport when the British took possession of Rhode Island. He was permitted to stay on his farm and maintained constant communications with the American Army by means of signals mutually agreed upon between himself and Lt. Cheffee. He continued in the service for fourteen months. His widow, Wealthy Barker, was 81 years old when Congress granted her a pension for his fourteen months of service on 5 Mar. 1840.

Barker, James. Mass. Pvt. He enlisted 24 Feb. 1777 for three years under Capt. Joshua Browne and Col. Timothy Bigelow in the 15th Regiment. He was wounded in one of his legs with fever and ague and returned home to Stow. He was noted as a deserter on 9 July 1778. He was able to produce the pass granted him at Valley Forge on 12 Mar. 1778. Congress granted him a pension 31 Jan. 1825.

Barker, Jesse. Mass. —. He served in the 2nd Regiment. He was paid $20.

Barker, John. Mass. Sgt. He served in the 7th Regiment. He was paid $20.

Barker, Michael. Pa. Pvt. He served in the 15th Battalion under Col. John Patterson and Capt. James Noble. He enlisted 10 June 1776 and was taken prisoner 18 June 1776. Afterwards he was carried to New York. He was from Philadelphia County.

Barker, Samuel. Mass. —. He served in the 8th Regiment. He lived at Methuen and was paid $20.

Barker, William. Mass. Capt. He served in the 2nd Regiment under Col. John Cushing and Gen. Joseph Cushing in the 2nd Plymouth County. He served from 1775 to 1783. He died 19 Feb. 1819. His grand-daughters were Sarah S. Spring and Harriet Spring. Congress awarded his half-pay 2 Apr. 1872.

Barker, William. N.Y. Pvt. He served under Col. Benjamin Allison in the militia and was slain 22 July 1779. His orphans, Mary Barker, William Barker, Icabud Barker, Susanna Barker, and John Barker, sought a gratuity 3 July 1784.

Barker, William. Va. —. He was pensioned.

Barker, Zacheriah. R.I. Pvt. He served under Capt. Amos Ellis in from 3 to 17 Mar. 1781. He also served under Capt. John Lincoln and Col. Joseph Webb from 20 Aug. to 29 Nov. 1781 for three months and twenty-two days. Congress accepted service for four months and seven days and denied him relief 13 Feb. 1850. He resided in DePeyster, N.Y. and was in his 86th year.

Barksdale, Peter. Va. —. He was disabled by illness and was awarded a £90 gratuity on 4 Nov. 1779.

Barksdale, Richard. S.C. —. He was from Abbeville in 1793.

Barksdale, Thomas. S.C. —. He was killed at the siege of Augusta. He left five orphans. Maj. Uel Hill and William Pettigrew deposed about his service. His son, John Barksdale, had his application rejected 11 Sep. 1821.

Barlet, John. Pa. —. He was pensioned 16 Apr. 1827 in Armstrong County.

Barlet, Paul. Pa. —. He was awarded a $40 gratuity in Berks Co., Pa. 4 May 1832 and on 18 Mar. 1834. He died 27 Oct. 1840. He also appeared as Paul Berlet.

Barlow, John. Va. —. His widow, Kitty Barlow, was placed on the roll by act of 6 Feb. 1807 at the rate of $40 per annum and given $40 relief.

Barnard, John. Pa. —. He was granted a $40 annuity on 15 Mar. 1826 but died 2 Mar. 1826 before the passage of the act. His widow, Elizabeth Barnard, was paid the money. She lived in Philadelphia Co., Pa. 21 Dec. 1827. She was pensioned 21 Feb. 1838.

Barnard, Jonathan. Mass. Pvt. He served in the 15th Regiment and resided at Bolton. His widow, Anna Barnard, was paid $50.

Barnard, Joseph. Mass. Pvt. He served in Alden's Regiment and resided at Plainfield. He was paid $50.

Barnard, Richard. Mass. —. He served in the 1st Regiment and was paid $20.

Barnes, —. Va. Pvt. He was in Continental service and died shortly after he marched to the northward. His widow, Delia Barnes, was on the 1785 pension list.

Barnes, Amos. —. —. He was on the 1794 pension roll.

Barnes, Caesar. Pa. Pvt. He was on the 1798 pension list in New Hampshire.

Barnes, Charles. S.C. —. He served in the 2nd S.C. Regiment. He was paid an annuity in 1787. He was also paid from 1804 to 1813.

Barnes, Daniel. Conn. Capt. He served in the 8th Regiment. He suffered from bodily infirmities brought on through excessive fatigue at the battle of Monmouth on 21 Aug. 1780. He resided in Bristol, Conn. in 1796. He was appointed lieutenant 1 Jan. 1777, was promoted to captain 20 Apr. 1779, and resigned 21 Aug. 1780.

Barnes, David. Conn. Pvt. He served under Col. Livingston. He lost his right eye occasioned by the bursting of a musket belonging to a soldier who stood at his right hand as he fired at the enemy in 1777 at Bemis Heights. He lived in Cheshire, Conn. in 1795. He enlisted 1 Jan. 1777 for the war and was on the rolls in 1781.

Barnes, Elijah. Mass. Pvt. He served in the 9th Regiment. He lost the tops of three fingers of his left hand occasioned by a cut with an axe in 1780 at New Windsor. He lived in Bernard, Vt. in 1795. He enlisted in Feb. 1779 and was on the rolls in 1781. He was granted one-fourth of a pension 20 Apr. 1796. He was on the 1813 pension list. He died 14 July 1816.

Barnes, George. S.C. —. He served in the 1st Regiment. He was wounded in the service. His children were paid 14 Jun. 1786.

Barnes, Isaiah. Va. —. He served in the 4th Virginia Regiment in Capt. Matthews' Company. He was disabled by illness in the service in 1776. He was awarded a £30 gratuity on 12 Oct. 1778.

Barnes, Job. Md. —. He enlisted in 1775 or 1776 for five years or the war. He was from Talbot County.

He was at White Plains and Long Island. He became separated from the rest of the army and fell in with some discharged soldiers after Long Island. He returned home. It was rumored that he had deserted so he purchased his discharge for £100. His son, Ford Barnes, sought reimbursement for the amount, but Congress rejected his claim 31 May 1860.

Barnes, John. —. Lt. He enlisted as a private in 1776 and was promoted to ensign, lieutenant, and quartermaster respectively. He returned home after the surrender of Cornwallis. His heirs were paid five years' pay.

Barnes, John. Va. QM. He entered the service as a private and rose from ensign and lieutenant to quartermaster. Congress allowed his representatives his commutation of five years plus interest 21 Dec. 1838.

Barnes, Joseph. Me. —. He died 28 May 1838. His widow, Lydia Barnes, was from Lubec. She was paid $50 under the resolve of 1836.

Barnes, Richard. Mass. —. He served in the 1st Regiment.

Barnes, Theophilus. S.C. —. He was in Beaufort District when he applied 16 Sep. 1830. He was in his 81st year and served under Gen. Marion. He had 200 acres in dispute worth about $200, a horse worth $40, 12 head of small hogs $20, 1 bed and some household furniture $25, some plantation tools $20, and seven head of sheep $10.50. He was in battle at Georgetown in the first year of the war under Gen. Marion when his nephew was killed. He was at Santee near Linch's Causeway under Col. McDonald when Maj. Benson was killed. He was at Eutaw under Gen. Marion. He was drafted near the mouth of Sparrow's Swamp and served under Robert Ellison. John Stone stated he served with him. He was pensioned at the rate of $60 per annum on 25 Nov. 1830. In 1834 he resided in Prince William Parish.

Barnes, Thomas. —. Conn. He was from Middletown, Conn. and served three years. He died in 1806 or 1807. He married Sibel ----- 17 Feb. 1772. She was unable to make a declaration because she was deaf and infirm. The children applied in behalf of their mother in Ohio 2 Jan. 1839. She was granted a pension by Congress.

Barnes, William. Pa. —. He was pensioned by the court of enquiry 15 Jan. 1815. He died 26 Dec. 1821.

Barnet, John. S.C. —. His widow, Margaret Clendening, and a number of small children drew a pension.

Barnet, Robert. Md. Pvt. He was pensioned in Frederick County 4 Mar. 1789. He was on the 1813 pension list.

Barnett, —. Pa. —. His widow, Anne Barnett, was granted a $40 gratuity and a $40 annuity in Fayette County 15 June 1836.

Barnett, —. Va. —. Ann Barnett was granted additional relief in Fauquier County in Nov. 1776.

Barnett, —. Va. —. His mother, Mary Barnett, was furnished support in Feb. 1781 and Mar. 1782 in Westmoreland County. Her sons were away in the service.

Barnett, Isaac. S.C. —. He sought a pension.

Barnett, Jacob. S.C. —. He was wounded at Rocky Mount. He was paid 8 Jan. 1785.

Barnett, James. —. Lt. He served in the Infantry in the Continental Line from 1776 to the end of the war. He was at Trenton, Princeton, Germantown, and Monmouth. After the war he removed to Kentucky. He received 3,444 acres of bounty land in 1809. He received his five years' full pay commutation in lieu of half-pay for life 26 May 1830. He was paid the interest on same 2 Mar. 1833. He died in 1835. His only daughter married Alexander Miller, aged 91, who alleged that his father-in-law served as a captain and sought the difference. Congress rejected his petition

4 May 1876 because the claim was not supported by the records.

Barnett, James. N.Y. Pvt. He served under Col. Goose Van Schaick and died in Aug. 1778. His widow, Mary Barnett, received a seven year half-pay pension.

Barnett, Joseph. Pa. —. He was awarded a $40 gratuity and a $40 annuity in Fayette County 15 June 1836.

Barnett, Robert. N.H. Lt. He served in Capt. Reid's Company in Gen. John Stark's Regiment first as a ensign until being promoted to a lieutenant in the spring in 1775. Due to disease he lost the greater part of his upper jaw and upper lip due to black scurvy. He also contracted smallpox on the retreat from Canada. His constitution was broken in the service. He was transferred to the Invalids Corps. He was from Londonderry in 1783. He was aged 38 in 1787. He was from Pownal.

Barnett, Robert. Pa. —. He was awarded a $40 annuity and a $40 gratuity in Westmoreland Co, Pa. 5 Apr. 1826. He was 78 years old in 1840.

Barney, Nathaniel. Mass. Corp. He was wounded by a bayonet which entered his left breast and passed through his back at Yorktown, Virginia in 1781. The wound was still open in 1791. He served under Col. H. Jackson.

Barney, Samuel. Conn. —. He enlisted under Capt. Caleb Trowbridge in May 1775 at New Haven, Conn. and went to Lexington. He entered under Capt. Oliver Hanchett to go with Gen. Arnold to Canada. He suffered from the severity of the climate and was in the battle of Quebec and helped convey his wounded general from the field. He married Sarah Bassett 20 Aug. 1778 in the First Church in New Haven. In Mar. 1779 he sailed to the West Indies. He was taken prisoner and confined on the prison ship, *Jersey*. He was exchanged in Aug. 1779. His wife was pregnant and had to fly place to place while he was away. He died in 1805. She was pensioned for one year of service 18 Jan. 1838.

Barnhardt, Henry. Pa. —. He was awarded a $40 gratuity and a $40 annuity in Montgomery Co., Pa. 18 Mar. 1834. His widow, Sophia Barnhardt, was awarded a $40 gratuity and a $40 annuity 17 Mar. 1835 in Montgomery Co., Pa. She also appeared as Sophia Barnhart and he as Henry Barnhart.

Barnhart, —. Pa. —. His widow, Catharine Barnhart was awarded a $40 gratuity and a $40 annuity in York County 12 Mar. 1836. She was dead by July 1838.

Barnhart, Daniel. Pa.—. He was pensioned in 1813. He was from Berks County

Barnhart, Philip. Pa. —. He was awarded a $40 gratuity and a $40 annuity in Centre Co., Pa. 6 Apr. 1833. He was 82 years old in 1840. He died 3 Apr. 1844.

Barnheiser, John. Pa. —. He was awarded a $40 annuity in Franklin County 12 Jan. 1836. He died 2 June 1849.

Barnitz, Jacob. Pa. Ensign. He enlisted at age 18 in July 1776 and went with the militia to New Jersey. He was in York County 1 Dec. 1785. He was wounded in both legs and taken prisoner at Fort Washington 16 Nov. 1776. He served in the Flying Camp under Capt. Christian Stakes and Col. Swope. He was 26 years old. He was on the 1813 pension list.

Barns, —. Va. —. His mother, Sarah Barns, was granted financial assistance while he was away in the service in Caroline Co., Va. 14 May 1778.

Barns, Amos. Conn. Pvt. He served in the 1ˢᵗ Regiment. He was ruptured in his right groin while on duty at Ridgefield, Conn. in 1777. He resided at Farmington, Conn. in 1796. He enlisted 1 Mar. 1777 for the war. He was also listed as being in the Invalids 3ʳᵈ Regiment.

Barns, Daniel. —. Capt. He served in the 8ᵗʰ Regiment. He was disabled by heat and fatigue at the battle of Monmouth. He resided in Conn. in 1792.

Barns, Hartwell. Conn. Pvt. He served in 3rd Regiment. He lost his hearing and incurred disability. He resided in Farmington, Conn. in 1792. He enlisted 1 Mar. 1777. He was a clergyman.

Barns, Lemuel. Mass. Pvt. He served in the 1st Mass. Regiment under Capt. J. Parsons, Maj. Cady, and afterwards under Capt. Moses Ashley. He lost one of his eyes due to smallpox on the retreat from Canada. He also suffered from heat and fatigue four days before the battle of Monmouth. He resided at Stockbridge, Mass. in 1792 and 1796. He enlisted 20 Feb. 1777 and was discharged 20 Feb. 1780.

Barns, William. Pa. —. He was granted $40 per annum 1 Feb. 1815.

Barnum, Joshua. N.Y. Capt. He served in Cornelius Humphrey's Regiment in the Dutchess County militia. He was disabled by a musket ball wound in his right arm below the elbow. He was taken prisoner in Mar. 1777 and lost the sight in his right eye. He returned from captivity in Sep. 1778. He had a family of five children. He was pensioned 26 June 1786. He lived in South East Town, Dutchess Co., N.Y. on 22 Apr. 1789. He was aged 49 years in Dec. 1785. He later lived in Putnam County. He was on the 1813 pension list.

Barnum, Stephen. Conn. Pvt. He served in Col. Gemott's Regiment. He was wounded by a musket ball in the shoulder in action near Jamestown, Va. at Green Springs in Jul. 1782. He resided at Danbury, Conn. in 1794. He was on the 1813 pension list. He transferred to Berkshire Co., Mass. 4 Mar. 1826.

Barnum, Stephen. Conn. Sgt. He served in the 7th Conn. He had a fistula in ano by straining and excessive exertions and being overheated at the battle of Monmouth in 1778. He resided in Monkton, Vt. in 1794. He enlisted 21 Apr. 1777 and was discharged 5 Apr. 1781.

Barrackman, —. Pa. —. His widow, Margaret Barrackman, was granted relief 1 Apr. 1836 in Luzerne County.

Barr, Alexander. N.H. Pvt. He was pensioned 18 Apr. 1814.

Barr, John. Pa. —. He was awarded a $40 gratuity and a $40 annuity in Washington County in 1815.

Barr, Nathan. S.C. Lt. He was in Lancaster District on 25 Nov. 1820. His first tour was under Gen. Richardson in the snow camps at Reedy River. He entered the militia under Capt. John Barkley. He next served under Col. Thomas and Capt. James Adams against the Cherokee. He was with Gen. Lincoln at Purrysburg on the Savannah River. His fourth tour was under Col. Joseph Kershaw and Capt. Robert Montgomery at the battle of Stono with his five brothers. There his brother, Silas Barr, was mortally wounded. He was in service to the fall of Charleston in 1780. He next served under Gen. Davidson in the company of Capt. Stephen Alexander and was with Davidson when he was killed crossing the Catawba River in North Carolina. He contracted smallpox and returned home. He was never wounded. He was 77 years old and afflicted with palsy. He received a few hundred dollars in old currency but had been unable to pass it away. His household included two females. He was approved 8 Dec. 1820 at the rate of $60 per annum and was pensioned 10 Dec. 1821. He died 11 Feb. 1824. His executrix, Jean Barr, and executor, James Kirkpatrick, were paid $56.66 for eleven and a half months' arrearage on 7 Dec. 1824. She also appeared as Jane Barr.

Barr, Robert. Pa. Pvt. —. He was awarded a $40 gratuity and a $40 annuity in Harrisburg, Pa. 29 Mar. 1824.

Barr, Samuel. Pa. —. He was granted relief in Washington County 5 Feb. 1836.

Barr, William. Pa. —. He was awarded a $40 gratuity and a $40 annuity in Allegheny County 3 Apr. 1837. He was 95 years old in 1840.

Barren, Oliver. Mass. Pvt. He served in the 7th Regiment and resided at Boston. His widow, Mary Davenport, was paid $50. He also appeared as Oliver Barron.

Barrett, —. Va. —. Ann Barrett, was granted financial assistance in Fauquier Co., Va. in May 1777 and in May 1778.

Barrett, —. Va. Lt. He served aboard an armed brig. He was taken prisoner to New York where he died leaving a widow and two children. His widow, Amy Barrett, sought support and his pay arrearage 3 Dec. 1784.

Barrett, Beatty. Va. —. He was in Nansemond County on 28 Feb. 1816. He died there 27 May 1817. His mother was Mourning Peck. He was wounded at Petersburg in 1780. He was pensioned on 21 Feb. 1817 at the rate of $60 per annum. He also received $70 relief on that date.

Barrett, James. —. —. He was in the war from 1776 to the close and served as a recruiting officer. He was at Trenton, Princeton, Germantown, and Monmouth. He was with Gen. LaFayette against Cornwallis. He moved to Kentucky after the war. He was granted his commutation pay 26 Jan. 1830.

Barrett, James. Pa. —. He was awarded a $40 gratuity and a $40 annuity in Columbia County 30 Mar. 1822.

Barrett, Jonathan. Va. Sailing Master. He served aboard the brig *Raleigh*. He died as a prisoner of war in New York aboard the *Jersey*. His widow, Amy Barrett, applied 3 Nov. 1778. She had two small children. She was on the pension roll of 27 Oct. 1792.

Barrett, Joseph. S.C. —. He was killed by Tories in 1781. His widow, Elizabeth Barrett, was paid 30 May 1785.

Barrett, Joshua. Md. Sgt. He was pensioned at the rate of half-pay of a sergeant Nov. 1804.

Barrett, Nathaniel. S.C. —. His widow, Abigail Barrett, was receiving relief in 1791 and had children. On 18 Dec. 1794 she received £15 and £2 for one child. She was in Newberry District.

Barrett, Stephen. Mass. Sgt. He served in the 6th Regiment and resided at Billerica. His widow, Olive Barrett, was paid $50.

Barrett, William. Va. Capt. He served in the 3rd Regiment of the Light Dragoons under Col. Baylor and was wounded through the ilium on the left side at the battle of Guilford. He was aged *ca.* 32 on 11 Nov. 1786 . He was from Henrico County and received a pension of half-pay allowance. He was continued on the roll on 7 June 1790 and was in Fairfax Co. He died 13 Jan. 1792 and John Barrett was administrator of his estate.

Barrick, Nicholas. Pa. —. He was awarded a $40 gratuity and a $40 annuity in Perry County 1 Apr. 1836. He was dead by 1844.

Barritt, Zalmon. —. —. He did not serve in the regular army so Congress rejected his application 23 Feb. 1820.

Barron, —. S.C. —. His widow, Mary Barron, had two children in 1791. She was from Union District.

Barron, Benjamin. Mass. —. He served in the 8th Regiment. He was paid $20.

Barron, Elias. Mass. Pvt. He served in Col. Elisha Sheldon's Regiment of Dragoons under Capt. Webb and was wounded in the action with the enemy on his head and on his left and right shoulders. He lost the use of one hand. He was pensioned at the rate of one-third pay from 20 Sep. 1780, the date of his discharge, on 19 Apr. 1781. In 1786 he was 30 years old. He was on the 1813 pension list. He died 9 Mar. 1822 in Middlesex Co., Mass.

Barron, George. Mass. Marine. He was disabled by the gravel and was pensioned 1 Sep. 1782.

Barron, Jonathan. Me. —. He died 21 Mar. 1815 at Minot. His widow, Mehitable Barron, was from Topsham. She was paid $50 under the resolve of 1836.

Barron, Robert. Pa. —. He was pensioned.

Barron, Robert. —. Sgt. He was pensioned 12 Oct. 1792. He was on the 1813 pension list of Kentucky. He later removed to Perry Co., Ohio. He died 31 Sec. 1831 in Perry Co., Ohio. His widow was Sophia Barron.

Barron, William. Va. 1st Lt. He served aboard the frigate, *Boston,* under the command of Capt. Tucker. He was killed in the service 26 or 27 Mar. 1778 on the voyage conveying John Adams to France. His seven years' half-pay was to be paid to his daughter, Ann Mortimer Barron of Norfolk, 30 June 1834.

Barrott, Solomon. Md. Fifer. He was pensioned at the rate of half-pay of a fifer on 23 Jan. 1816. His widow, Susan Barrott, was pensioned at the same rate on 31 May 1852 in Talbot County.

Barrous, Abraham. Me. —. He died 24 Oct. 1819. His widow, Margaret Barrous, was from Cornish. She was paid $50 under the resolve of 1836.

Barrows, Malachi. Mass. Pvt. He served in the 2nd Regiment under Col. John Bailey and Capt. Jude Alden. He was disabled by a musket ball in his left shoulder and collar bone. He was 30 years old in 1789. He was pensioned at the rate of one-quarter pay of a soldier from 21 Feb. 1780 on 20 Mar. 1786.

Barrows, Peter. R.I. Pvt. His jaw was fractured in a wound received at the storming of a British redoubt at Yorktown, Va. on 14 Oct. 1781. He served under Col. Jeremiah Olney. He applied 12 Jan. 1786 and was aged 30. He was probably the one of that name who lived in Waldo Co., Maine. He was on the 1813 pension list.

Barry, James. Pa. —. He was pensioned 15 Nov. 1816.

Barry, Michael. Pa. Pvt. He served in the 2nd Pa. Regt. and was transferred to the Invalids. He was discharged unfit for duty 10 Apr. 1783. He was from Philadelphia County.

Barter, John. N.H. Sgt. He served under Capt. Samuel Blodget. He was wounded in the thigh by a musket ball on 17 Sep. 1777 at Bemis Heights. He served in the 2nd N.H. Regiment. He was from Middleton, N.H. in 1783. He lived in New Market, N.H. in 1796. He was granted a half pension 20 Apr. 1796.

Barth, Nicholas. N.Y. Lt. He served under Col. Clyde and was pensioned 7 Oct. 1786.

Bartin, John Duglass. Mass. —. He served in the 14th Regiment. He resided at Duxbury. He also appeared as John Dublass Barton.

Bartle, Andrew. Pa. Pvt. He lived in Philadelphia County. He was on the 1813 pension list.

Bartlet, Benjamin. Pa. —. He transferred to New Hampshire in or by Sep. 1795.

Bartlet, Zadock. —. Pvt. He enlisted under Capt. Wood and Col. Ward and served from May 1775 to Feb. 1776. He was not in Continental service. Congress granted him a pension 10 Jan. 1832.

Bartlett, —. Va. —. He served in the 11th Virginia Regiment in Capt. Bruin's Company. His wife, Sarah Bartlett, and three children were granted £8 support in Frederick Co., Va. on 4 Nov. 1777.

Bartlett, Aaron. Mass. —. He was pensioned under the act of 1818 in Eaton, Madison Co., N.Y. He married at Shutesbury, Mass. 25 Nov. 1777 Joanna -----. He died 22 Apr. 1823. Her sister, Lydia Peck, proved the marriage. Their marriage was announced in Amherst and Leverett, but they had to go to Shutesbury where there was a minister, the Rev. M. Hill, to be married. His widow was pensioned 6 Feb. 1839 by Congress.

Bartlett, Benjamin. —. Sgt. He was on the 1813 pension list in New York. He died in 1825 in York Co., Me.

Bartlett, John. Mass. Sgt. He served under Lt. Col. Ebenezer Sprout and Col. Edward Wigglesworth in the 13th Mass. Regiment. He was wounded in his right hip by a musket ball at the battle of Rhode Island on 29 Aug. 1778. He lived in Albany Co., N.Y. on 16 June 1789. He was 25 years old on 15 Sep. 1785. He was a school teacher. He died *ante* 5 Sep. 1807.

Bartlett, John. Pa. —. He was awarded a $40 gratuity and a $40 annuity in Huntingdon Co., Pa. 16 Apr. 1827.

Bartlett, Jonas. —. —. He married Abigail Dale, daughter of Jeremiah Dale, who was a non-commissioned officer slain at Saratoga. His heirs were not eligible for seven years' half-pay 6 Feb. 1838.

Bartlett, Joseph. Mass. Sgt. He served in the 7th Regiment. He was paid $20.

Bartlett, Samuel. Mass. Capt. He served under Col. Weston. He was disabled during the defense of Fort Stanwix, alias Fort Schuyler, by the British in 1777. He lived in Bennington, Vt. in 1792.

Bartlett, Scipio. Mass. Pvt. He served in Crane's Regiment and resided at Salem. His widow, Catherine Gilbert, was paid $50.

Bartlett, Solomon. Mass. —. He resided at Plymouth and was paid $20.

Bartlett, William. Mass. Sgt. He was at the siege of Boston for about eight months. From Feb. to Nov. 1776 he was a member of the seacoast guard. He was also in the naval service as a gunner and privateersman and was wounded. He died more than forty years ago. His widow died as a pensioner in Apr. 1838. His son, Devereaux D. Bartlett, of Marblehead, Mass. for himself and the other children sought relief. Congress denied them a pension 3 Mar. 1851.

Bartlett, Zacheus. Mass. —. He served in the 1st Regiment and was paid $20.

Bartley, John. N.J. —. He was pensioned in Somerset County 28 Feb. 1837 at the rate of $60 per annum.

Barton, —. Va. —. Ann Barton was furnished support in Loudoun County 8 Mar. 1779, May 1779, and in Sep. 1780.

Barton, Douglas. Mass. —. He served in the 14th Regiment and was from Duxbury. He was paid $20.

Barton, John. Va. —. He was drafted into the militia. His wife, Ann Barton, and four children were granted £2.10 support in Frederick Co., Va. on 4 Nov. 1777.

Barton, Thomas. S.C. —. He was killed in the service. His widow, Amey Barton, was paid 24 May 1785. She was from Orangeburg/Lewisburg and had one child in 1791.

Barton, William. R.I. Sgt. While commanding a party of militia in R.I. in May 1778, he received a wound which was incurable. He was also in the Continental Army. He was on the 1791 pension roll. John B. Barton and the other surviving children sought relief from Congress 16 Jan. 1850.

Bartram, Job. Conn. Capt. He served in the 4th Regiment of militia. He was wounded by a musket ball which entered his right breast and penetrated nearly to his shoulder on 7 July 1779 at Fairfield. He lived in Norwalk, Conn. in 1792. Thaddeus Betts and Samuel Willman, justices of the peace, and four selectmen of the town forwarded affidavits from Sally Gregory, John Sanders, Timothy Fitch, and two others setting forth that Bartram never appeared to them nor ever complained of being wounded. In his affidavit Capt. Jabez Gregory stated that in 1784 Job Bartram was brought into his house in great pain due to a dislocated shoulder from the oversetting of a sled. He transferred to New York. He was granted half a pension 20 Apr. 1796. He was on the 1813 pension list. He died 19 July 1813.

Bartze, Michael. S.C. —. He was paid an annuity 6 Mar. 1829.

Bascom, Samuel. Mass. —. He served in Nixon's Western Regiment and was paid $20.

Bass, Edward. Mass. —. He served in the 8th Regiment and was paid $20.

Bass, Edward. Pa. —. He was pensioned 16 Dec. 1813, He died 17 July 1822.

Bass, Hardy. Va. —. His wife, Ann Bass, and their two children were granted £20 support in Southampton County 9 July 1779.

Bassett, Benjamin. Mass. —. He served in the 4th Regiment and was paid $20.

Bassett, Edward. Conn. Pvt. He served in Col. Sheldon's Regiment of Light Dragoons and was wounded by two musket balls and buck shot. One passed through his side, and the other lodged in his shoulder blade. The buck shot lodged in his ham. He was pensioned 2 Apr. 1788 at Derby, Conn. at the age of 32. He was on the 1813 pension list.

Bassett, Timothy. Conn. —. He served in the 2nd Regiment of Militia under Capt. Moses Gilbert and Lt. Moses Ford. He and James Bassett were wounded at New Haven on 5 July 1779. He was wounded through the chest by a musket ball. He was pensioned 17 Oct. 1779.

Bastian, Jacob. Pa. —. He was awarded a $40 gratuity and a $40 annuity in Lycoming Co., Pa. 5 Feb. 1833.

Bastow, William. Mass. Sgt. He lost the use of his left arm due to a fever sore on the elbow in Oct. 1779 causing his arm and hand to wither. He served under Col. William Shepherd in the 4th Mass. Regiment. He applied at age 32 on 5 Jan. 1786 in Rhode Island. He was paid $20 from the Commonwealth. He appeared on the 1813 pension list as William Barton. He died 26 May 1818 in R.I.

Batchelder, Archelaus. N.H. Lt. He was from Wilton in 1784. He was wounded at the battle of Bennington on 16 Aug. 1777 by a ball entering his left side under his arm and exiting near his back bone. He did duty as an orderly sergeant in Capt. John Goss's Company under Col. Nichols in Stark's Brigade. He was from Milford. He was granted half a pension 20 Apr. 1796. He was on the 1813 pension list. He died 18 Dec. 1823. He also appeared as Archelaus Bacheldor. His widow, Betty Batchelder, died in 1829. His daughter, Elizabeth Grinnell, sought a pension from the time of the death of her father to the time of death of her mother. Congress rejected her petition for a special act 27 Mar. 1846.

Batchelder, James. Mass. Pvt. He was blown up into the air while drilling a rock and received a violent contusion on his shoulder in July 1779 at Fort Putnam at West Point. He was from Beverley. He was granted one-fourth of a pension 20 Apr. 1796 and was paid as late as Sep. 1799.

Bate, Abraham. Pa. Corp. He was in Philadelphia County 11 Sep. 1786. He served in the 10th Pa. Regiment and was wounded in the leg by an axe when cutting wood. He was also wounded at Brandywine in the other leg. He was 50 years old. He was dead by Mar. 1791.

Bateman, George. Md. Corp. He was pensioned at the rate of half-pay of a corporal on 23 Jan. 1816.

Bates, —. Mass. —. He was from Weymouth. His widow, Ruth Bates, was paid $50.

Bates, Daniel. Va. —. He was in Pendleton District, S.C. 7 Nov. 1825. At the outbreak of the war he lived in Virginia. He served under Col. George Boyd of Halifax Co., Va. and served three weeks against the British troops near Norfolk. He was called into the service under Col. Charles Philemon, a supernumerary Continental officer. He next served under Col. George Tucker against Lord Cornwallis. He was nearly 70 years old; his wife was 67 and was almost helpless. He had no children and was trying to earn a living as a constable. He was rejected since he did not serve from South Carolina.

Bates, Edward. Mass. Pvt. He served in the 7th Mass. Regiment under Col. John Brooks and Capt. Luke Day. He was deprived of the use of his hips. He was pensioned at the rate of three quarters pay of a soldier from 1 Jan. 1780 on 20 Feb. 1786.

Bates, Edward. N.Y. Pvt. He was on the 1813 pension list. He died 30 Apr. 1830. Compare with the entry *supra*.

Bates, Elisha. Mass. —. He was from Cohasset. His widow, Ruth Bates, was paid $50.

Bates, Isaac. N.C. Pvt.. He applied in Co., N.C. in 1806. He served under Col. James Robinson. He also served under Col. John Sevier and was wounded in the right arm by the Cherokee. His arm was amputated by Dr. Vance. On 1 Sep. 1802 he was about 53 years old and had a large family. By 1808 he had located in Clay Co., Ky. He was on the 1813 pension list in North Carolina. He also appeared as John Baits.

Bates, John. Mass. —. He was from Plymouth and was paid $20. He also appeared as John Rates.

Bates, John. Va. Drummer. He was in the 3rd Va. Regiment and died in the service. His widow, Catharine Bates, was from Louisa County on 1 Jan. 1787. She was put on the pension list at the rate of £6 per annum on 20 Nov. 1787.

Bates, Joseph. Mass. Pvt. He served in Sheldon's Regiment. He received a rupture in the side from fatigue at Brookfield. He lived in Egremont, Mass. in 1792. He enlisted 3 Dec. 1779.

Bates, Joshua. Mass. Sgt. He served under Capt. Lincoln in Revere's Regiment and resided at Weymouth. His widow was Tirza Bates. They married in Weymouth, Mass. 7 Oct. 1804. He died in 1808. She had married secondly Ebenezer Hunt who was a pensioner. She then claimed a pension on the service of her first husband. Congress granted same 12 Apr. 1842. She was paid $50.

Bates, Mowry. R.I. —. He served more than six months. Congress awarded him a pension 25 May 1860.

Bates, Nathaniel. N.H. Pvt. He was killed at Stillwater. He widow, Abigail Bates, and two small children sought relief. She was left a new lot of 41 acres of which only 5 acres were improved. She sought permission to sell same on 28 Oct. 1778.

Bates, William. S.C. —. There were children in 1791.

Bathurst, Lawrence. Pa. —. He was awarded a $40 gratuity and a $40 annuity in Centre Co., Pa. 6 Apr. 1833. He was 83 years old in 1840. He died 17 Feb. 1845.

Batson, James. Va. Pvt. He was on the 1813 pension list.

Batt, Eden. S.C. —. He first served in the North Carolina militia and then in the South Carolina militia. He was paid $100 in order to return to North Carolina on 5 Mar. 1779.

Battersby, John. Pa. Pvt. He was in Philadelphia County 13 Mar. 1786. He was in the 2nd Pa. Regiment and was wounded in the service.

Baugh, Jacob. Va. —. He volunteered in Apr. 1776 under Capt. Robert Davis and served three months and two weeks. In Nov. 1776 he served under Capt. Stevens for three months against the Cherokee Indians. He served two months under Capt. James Montgomery from Sep. 1779. He also served two tours of two months each under Capt. John Stevens in 1778 and 1779. In 1776 he marched from Wythe County to North Carolina and was stationed at Middletown. In the fall of 1776 he marched to Long Island. In 1777 he was in the expedition against the Shawnee. He served under Col. James Robertson and Col. Walter Crockett from Wythe County. He resided in Pulaski Co., Ky. when Congress granted him a pension on 4 Apr. 1840.

Baum, Frederick. Pa. —. He was awarded a $40 gratuity in Mifflin Co., Pa. 4 May 1832 and again on 25 Mar. 1833. He was dead by July 1833.

Baumgartner, George. Pa. Capt. He was awarded a $40 gratuity in Westmoreland County on 29 Mar. 1813. He also appeared as George Bumgarten.

Baun, John George. N.Y. —. He served under Col. Jacob Klock in the Montgomery County militia and was slain 6 Aug. 1777. His widow received a half-pay pension.

Baury, Louis. —. —. He was a native of St. Domingo. He served from 1779 to 1783. He was aide-de-camp to Maj. Gen. Lincoln and in 1787 was in Shay's Rebellion. Two of his sons were later officers in the U.S. Navy. He married in 1784. He died 20 Sep. 1807 in Middletown, Conn. His widow, Mary Baury, of Boston, Mass., furnished no evidence of her marriage, his rank, his service, or his death. Congress denied her a pension 3 Mar. 1851. He was an original member of the Society of the Cincinnati. His son was the Rev. Alfred L. Baury who said his father was wounded in the war.

Bause, John. Pa. —. He was awarded a $40 gratuity and a $40 annuity in Berks Co., Pa. 16 Feb. 1835. He died 18 Jan. 1835.

Bausher, Philip. Pa. —. He was awarded a $40 gratuity and a $40 annuity in Berks County 11 Apr. 1844 for his Revolutionary service. He died 27 Apr.

Bausman, —. Pa. —. His widow, Elizabeth Bausman, was awarded a $40 gratuity and a $40 annuity in Lancaster County 16 Apr. 1838. Her name was mistakenly given as Elizabeth Bainman. The act was corrected in 1839, and she was given a $80 gratuity and a $40 annuity. She died 12 Nov. 18–.

Baxter, —. Va. —. His wife, Milly Baxter, was granted financial support in Fauquier Co., Va. in Nov. 1780.

Baxter, Francis. Conn. Pvt. He served in the militia under Capt. B. Wright and Col. Meade. He was wounded by a broad sword in his left arm, and the outer bone was entirely cut between the wrist and elbow. He also had a wound in each leg injuring the muscles on 23 May 1780 at Greenwich, Conn. He resided at East Windsor, Conn. in 1796. He enlisted 18 Feb. 1777 and was discharged 2 Feb. 1780. He was granted one-third of a pension 20 Apr. 1796. He died 25 July 1807.

Baxter, John. N.Y. Pvt. He served in Col. Thaddeus Crane's Regiment in Capt. Jesse Trusdale's Company of the Westchester County militia. He was disabled by a wound in his shoulder and another in his left elbow on 27 June 1779. He was pensioned 16 Nov. 1786. He lived in Westchester Co., N.Y. on 24 Apr. 1789. He later lived in Alleghany County. He was on the 1813 pension list.

Baxter, John. N.C. —. He applied in Mecklenburg Co., N.C. He was of York District, S.C. in 1807. Near the end of 1780 he was in a scouting party of militia commanded by Capt. William Barnett when he was wounded in the head and both arms by some of Tarleton's calvary. He was in the regiment of Robert Ervin under Gen. Davidson. He was on the 1813 pension list in North Carolina.

Baxter, Malachi. Mass. —. His widow, Rhoda Baxter, was paid $50.

Baxter, William. —. —. He and his widow died before pension legislation covered their situations. His daughter, Mary Bird, sought a pension, but Congress ruled against same 4 May 1860.

Baxter, William. Pa. Col. His widow, Elizabeth Baxter, was in Bucks County 11 Sep. 1786. He fell in the service at Fort Washington 16 Nov. 1776. He was in the Flying Camp.

Baxton, John. Pa. Pvt. He was in Montgomery County 5 Aug. 1786. He served in the 3rd Pa. Regiment. He was disabled by rheumatism contracted in the service. He was 53 years old.

Bayard, John. Pa. —. He was in Berks County 9 Feb. 1814. He served under Col. Stephen Bayard. His father-in-law, George Adams, left his children property, but it could not be sold while his widow, Mary Adams, was alive. She was 75 years old. His son was George Bayard. On

6 Feb. 1821 he deposed that he was the indentured servant of Joseph Wood who was appointed Major of one of the Pennsylvania regiments in 1776. He went with him to Canada as a waiter. When Col. William Allen resigned command of the regiment, Wood took his place. He was in Capt. Craig's troop of horse. Bayard enlisted in Capt. Strong's Company under Col. Arthur St. Clair and was wounded in the arm and was disabled at Strawberry Hill. He spent nearly two years in Canada and New Jersey. He was 67 years old. He was in battle at Three Rivers in May 1776 in Canada, Ticonderoga on 6 July 1777, Bird Brook, Strawberry Hill, Trenton, and Stoney Point.

Bayard, Stephen. Pa. Lt. Col. He applied in Allegheny County on 23 Sep. 1813. He served in the 8th Pa. Regiment. John Crawford, aged 80, was Lieutenant and Adjutant and was present at Brandywine when Col. Bayard was wounded by a rifle gun being struck by a cannon ball. He was 70 years old.

Bayles, —. Ga. —. Ann Bayles and five children were furnished assistance 25 Jan. 1782.

Bayles, David. Pa. —. He entered the service in 1781 under Col. Zackael Morgan and Gen. George Rogers Clark. Six months later he was taken sick and was ill for another sick months. Since the militia in Pennsylvania did not serve six month tours, Congress denied his claim 23 Feb. 1855.

Bayley, —. Va. —. He died in the service in the Continental Army. His widow, Catherine Bayley, was paid £6 in Aug. 1781 and furnished necessaries in Sep. 1782. She was from Fauquier County. She also appeared as Catherine Bailey.

Bayley, William. —. Maj. He served in Col. Swoop's Regiment called the Flying Camp. His heirs had their application for commutation rejected 16 Feb. 1838.

Baylor, —. Pa.—. His widow was Sarah Baylor. She lived in Lancaster County 11 Apr. 1825. She died 23 May 1834.

Baylor, George. —. Col. He served in the cavalry. He died in 1784 from wounds received at Tappan, N.J. His five years' full pay instead of half-pay for life was issued to the widow Ann D. Baylor as trustee for his only son and heir at law, John Walker Baylor, 25 May 1832. The claim included 4% interest. On 1 Apr. 1842 his legal representative sought interest of 6%, but Congress rejected the claim.

Baylor, Walker. Va. Capt. He was 26 years old when he applied on 27 Nov. 1786 from Caroline County. He served in the 3rd Va. Regiment and was wounded by a cannon ball at Germantown. His left ankle and foot were injured. He suffered from the loss of bone and a violent inflamation and manifest withering of his leg from the hip down. His brother was John Baylor. His pension was at the rate of £45 per annum. He was on the 1813 pension list in Pennsylvania. He died in 1823.

Baynton, Abriel. —. —. He had a scar on his left side occasioned by some external force or instrument. He resided in Massachusetts in 1796. He also appeared as Abiel Baynton.

Baytop, Thomas. Va. Capt. His heirs were rejected in their claim for seven years' half-pay 25 Jan. 1838. He served from 1776 to 1783. His sister married Col. Philip Taliaferro, and her son, Dr. William Taliaferro, deposed that Baytop lived with them prior to entering the service. The heirs sought relief from Congress 18 Feb. 1836. They sought half-pay for life 25 Jan. 1838 but Congress rejected their claim. He was captain lieutenant from 13 Jan. 1777 to 5 Feb. 1778 and captain from 5 Feb. 1778 to 11 Dec. 1779.

Beach, Israel. Conn. Pvt. He enlisted for one year under Capt. Titus Watson from Norfolk in the winter of 1776. He served two two-month tours in 1777 and one year under Col. Burwell in the expedition against Quebec. He disposed of all his property to his children before the pension law was passed. He had lived with one of his children for the last five years. He applied to Congress 22 Dec. 1831.

Beach, Nathaniel. Conn. Pvt. He served in the 3rd Regiment under Col. Samuel Webb in Capt. Barber's Company. He was wounded in his right foot by cutting it with an ax and lost his great toe in 1778 at Fredericksburg. He resided in Weston, Conn. in 1792. He enlisted 25 Apr. 1777 and continued to the end of the war.

Beach, Robert. —. —. He served more than two years. His feet were frozen, and he was injured in his right hand by burning of a cartridge. He was lame and nearly helpless. He was 87 years old. Congress denied his request for an increase in his pension 29 Jan. 1850 because his injuries were not the result of Revolutionary service.

Beach, Samuel. —. Maj. He sought commutation of five years' full pay. Congress rejected his claim 11 Apr. 1846.

Beach, Samuel. N.H. Ens. He served under Col. Warner until he was deranged in 1781. He sought a stay of demands against him for his debts 15 Sep. 1792.

Beal, Joseph. Mass. —. He served in the 1st Regiment and was from Frankfort. He was paid $20.

Beal, Zacheriah. N.H. Capt. He served in the Continental Army under Col. Scammell and died 27 Oct. 1777 or 6 Nov. 1777 leaving a widow and three children who lived in Newmarket in 1784. His widow, Abigail Beal, married William Badger on 24 May 1779 in Portsmouth, N.H. He became guardian to the children. She sought his half-pay for the time of her widowhood and then for her children. He also appeared as Zacheriah Beall and Zacheriah Bell.

Beall, Lawson. Md. Pvt. His widow, Henrietta Beall, was pensioned at the rate of half-pay of a private 3 Mar. 1840.

Beall, Lloyd. Md. Capt. He was pensioned in 1815. His widow, Elizabeth Beall, was pensioned at the rate of half-pay of a captain 31 Jan. 1817.

Beall, Thomas. Md. Capt. He entered in Apr. 1776 and served under Col. Moses Rawlings. He was in battle at Fort Washington and made a prisoner. He was sent to Long Island on parole and made his escape. His son, Isaac Beall, received his commutation from Congress 28 Feb. 1849.

Beall, William Dent. Md. Maj. He was pensioned at the rate of half-pay of a major in Nov. 1808.

Bealle, Robert. Va. Capt. There were two men of the name one of whom was from Westmoreland Co., Va. who was pensioned under the act of 1832.

Bealle, Robert. Va. Capt. He served in the 13th Virginia Regiment as a lieutenant under Capt. John Stephenson. He was in the battle of Germantown and was in the 9th Regiment. At the close of the war he was in the 7th Regiment. He became supernumerary in 1781. He married Elizabeth Stephenson, a widow. In 1789 she resided in Fayette Co., Penn. She was in Shelbyville, Ky. 17 June 1808. There were two children–Betsey Brooke Bealle, who married Adam Steele, and Robert Bealle. The grandson of one Robert Bealle had his claim for commutation rejected since his grandfather resigned 31 Dec. 1780. His two children had Revolutionary War bounty warrant #263 on 16 Sep. 1808.

Beam, Daniel. S.C. —. He entered the service in his 16th year under Capt. Lewis Hoy in Newberry District in 1779. He was detached to guard the wagons at Eutaw Srping. He was 75 years old. Sgt. Thomas Ressenger, aged 73-74, deposed anent his service. He resided in Abbeville District in 1829. He was paid his annuity as late as 1834.

Beaman, Jonas. Mass. —. His widow, Rebecka Beaman, was paid $50.

Bean, —. Pa. —. His widow, Eleanor Bean, was awarded a $40 gratuity in Montgomery County 10 Apr. 1833. She, was awarded a $40 gratuity in Montgomery Co., Pa. 28 Feb. 1834. She was awarded a $40 gratuity and a $40 annuity in Montgomery Co., Pa. 15 Apr. 1835.

Bean, Ebenezer. N.H. Pvt. He served in the 2nd New Hampshire Regiment. He was wounded in the foot by a musket ball on 19 Sep. 1777 at Bemis Heights. He resided at Pittsfield, N.H. in 1796. He enlisted 15 Nov. 1776 for three years and was discharged 18 Nov. 1779. He was granted one-third of a pension 20 Apr. 1796. He was on the 1813 pension list.

Bean, Jacob. Pa. —. He was granted relief in Westmoreland County 1 Apr. 1836.

Bean, James. Pa. —. He was awarded a $40 gratuity and a $40 annuity in Philadelphia Co., Pa. 18 Feb. 1834. He was dead by Nov. 1838.

Bean, John. Me.—. He was pensioned 7 June 1794.

Bean, John. Md. Pvt. He enlisted 9 Jan. 1779 in the 3rd Regiment. He was wounded at Camden in his left arm in 1780. In 1794 the rolls indicated that he deserted on 13 Jan. 1782. He cleared himself of the charge of desertion by producing his discharge certificate of 22 Nov. 1781 signed by Henry Clagett, Captain in the Maryland line, in 1795. His pension was approved. He was in Prince George's Co., Md. in 1785. He was granted half a pension 20 Apr. 1796. He was on the 1813 pension list.

Bean, John. N.H. Corp. He was from Poplin in 1784. He served in the 3rd N.H. Regiment and was wounded in the left arm at Newton on 29 Aug. 1779 in the Indian expedition under Gen. Sullivan. He resided in the Washington, District of Maine in 1792. He enlisted 15 Feb. 1777 and was discharged 15 Feb. 1780. He was on the 1813 pension list.

Bean, John. N.Y. Pvt. He was on the pension roll of 23 June 1786.

Bean, Leonard. Md. Pvt. He was pensioned at the rate of half-pay of a private in Mason Co., Ky. 2 Mar. 1832.

Bean, William. Pa. —. He served in the Flying Camp.

Bean, William. Pa. —. He was awarded a $40 gratuity in Mercer Co., Pa. 25 Mar. 1831, 4 May 1832, and 6 Apr. 1833.

Beard, —. Pa. —. His widow, Elizabeth Beard, was awarded a $40 gratuity and a $40 annuity in Wayne Co., N.Y. 20 Feb. 1833.

Beard, Adam. Pa. Lt. He served in the associators in May 1777. He was in service 1 Mar. 1778.

Beard, David. S.C. —. He was taken prisoner by a party of Tories and delivered to the Indians who killed him. He left a widow and two children, one of whom was under the age of twelve. His widow and executrix, Elizabeth Beard, was paid 23 Dec. 1784 in Abbeville District. She had one child in 1791.

Beard, James. S.C. —. He applied from Abbeville District on 15 Dec. 1792. About Dec. 1781 he was in command of the wagons to bring provisions to Gen. Andrew Pickens' block house. He, his father, and several others were taken by a party of Tories and carried prisoners to the Cherokee Nation where his father fell victim to the Indians. He was seemingly spared since he was so young. He was stripped of his clothing except for an old hunting shirt. He suffered from the inclement weather and was disabled in his ankle from exposure.

Beard, John. Va. —. He was away in the service. His wife and children were granted £50 of pork and a barrel of corn for each person in Montgomery Co., Va. 9 Nov. 1780.

Beard, William. S.C. —. He was pensioned by South Carolina on 4 Dec. 1832. He was paid as late as 1844. He removed to Tennessee and applied to Congress for a special bill for a federal pension for having served 484 days. He could no longer collect his state pension. Congress granted him a pension of $53 from 1 Mar. 1844 on 17 Feb. 1846.

Beardt, Henry. Pa. —. He was receiving a pension in 1811. He received a $40 gratuity and a $40 annuity. He was a native of York County. He served in Capt. Fred Kurtz's Company in Col. John Andrews' Regiment under Gen. Potter. He was wounded in Dec. 1777. He resided in New York. He also appeared as Henry Bardt.

Beardsley, Ichabod. Conn. —. He enlisted in the coast guard in Fairfield and served about two years. Congress granted him a pension for eighteen months of service on 5 Mar. 1840.

Beardsley, John. Conn. Pvt. He served in the 8th Conn. Regiment under Col. John Chandler. He enlisted 8 Apr. 1777 for three years and suffered from deafness at Germantown and Fort Mifflin. He was 30 years old and a resident of Stratford, Conn. when he was pensioned 5 Sep. 1787. He was pensioned at the rate of $5 per month from 13 Nov. 1807. He died 22 Apr. 1822 in Fairfield Co., Conn. He was on the 1813 pension list. He also appeared as John Beardslee.

Beardt, Henry. Pa. —. He was granted a gratuity of $40 and an annuity of $40 on 30 Mar. 1811.

Bears, James. —. Pvt. He served under Col. Warner. He was disabled by the inoculation of smallpox which fell into his right leg and ankle and withered his leg in 1777. He resided in Conn. in 1792.

Beatley, James. Va. He served in the 11th Virginia Regiment in Capt. Bruins' Company. His wife, Margaret Beatley, and two children were granted £9 support in Frederick Co., Va. on 4 Nov. 1777, £16 on 2 Mar. 1779, 3 barrels of corn and 50 pounds of bacon for herself and her three children on 7 Mar. 1780, 4 barrels of corn and 150 pounds of bacon for herself and her three children on 6 Mar.1781, £4.5 support for herself and three children on 7 May 1782, 200 pounds of pork and 4 barrels of corn on 2 Oct. 1782, and 200 pounds of pork and 4 barrels of corn on 7 May 1783 for herself and her three children.

Beatty, —. Va. —. His wife, Mary Beatty, was granted 5 bushels of corn and 50 pounds of bacon for her support and her three children in Frederick Co., Va. 8 Mar. 1780.

Beatty, John. Pa. —. He was awarded a $40 gratuity and a $40 annuity in Beaver County 29 Mar. 1824.

Beatty, John. Pa. —. He was granted relief in Cumberland County 18 Feb. 1839.

Beatty, Reading. —. Surgeon. He served in the artillery to the close of the war and drew a pension. He died 29 Oct. 1831. His son, C. C. Beatty, sought the difference of $120 per annum from 1828 to 1831. Congress rejected his petition 25 Apr. 1854.

Beatty, Samuel. Pa. —. He was awarded a $40 gratuity and a $40 annuity 14 Apr. 1827. He lived in Cecil Co., Md. He died 14 Oct. 1833.

Beatty, Thomas. Md. Lt. His widow, Anne Semmes, was pensioned at the rate of half-pay of a lieutenant in Georgetown, D.C. 21 Mar. 1833.

Beatty, Thomas. N.J. Corp. He served in the 3rd N.J. Regiment. He was pensioned 4 Sep. 1794.

Beatty, Thomas. Pa. —. He applied from Westmoreland County in May 1813. He served three years in the Pa. Line. He was wounded and abused by the British while a prisoner. He died 3 Apr. 1822.

Beatty, William. Md. Capt. He was killed at Hobkirk's Hill 24 Apr. 1781. His widow, Jane Beatty, was pensioned at the rate of half-pay of captain in Pittsburgh, Pa. 12 Mar. 1827. Congress rejected a claim 12 Feb. 1855.

Beaty, Hugh. Pa. —. He was awarded a $40 gratuity in Union Co., Pa. 4 May 1832. He also appeared as Hugh Beatty.

Beaty, John. N.C. Pvt. He applied from Mecklenburg County in 1807. He was a soldier in Capt. Richard Spring's Company of militia and was wounded in the head and right wrist at the battle of Camden. He died before 15 Dec. 1813 when his widow, Leah Beaty, indicated that her son was also dead. She was pensioned in that year.

Beaty, John. Pa. —. His widow, Jane Beaty, received a $40 annuity in Beaver County 19 Apr. 1853.

Beaulieu, Louis Joseph de. —. Capt. He was pensioned by the act of 5 Aug. 1782 by which he received $100 per annum for life. He was a brave officer in the legion of Count Pulaski. He was wounded four times near Charleston, S.C. 14 May 1780. One was on his forehead near his left eye. He lost the use of the eye. The other was in his left arm which injured the tendons in three of his fingers. He was wounded fourteen times at Little Egg Harbor, Monk's Corner, and in the sieges of Charleston and Savannah. He was blind in one eye and lost the use of one arm. Washington honored him with the rank of brevet captain. He was pensioned at the rate of $100 per annum. Subsequently his service was adjusted, and he was allowed half-pay for life with interest on the arrears. He lived on his pension and from pay earned from teaching the French language. He was 68 years old and had a wife and child to support. The disorders in France forced him to repair to the United States. Congress granted him relief 14 Dec. 1819.

Beaumont, Isaiah. Conn. Pvt. He served in Col. Durkee's Regiment. He as wounded in his arm at the battle of Princeton on 3 Jan. 1777. He lived in Lebanon, Conn. in 1794. He was on the 1813 pension list.

Beaumont, William. —. —. He received his commutation and was to receive half-pay for life by deducting same.

Beauthifer, Adam. Pa. —. He applied 18 Aug. 1821.

Beaven, Charles. Md. Lt. He was pensioned at the rate of half-pay in Harford County 23 Jan. 1816. He also appeared as Charles Beaver.

Beaver, Benjamin. Pa. —. He was paid $200 for his right to donation land 3 Apr. 1829. The money was to be paid to Ezra Blythe in Adams Co., Pa. for his use.

Beaver, Daniel. S.C. —. He served under Capt. William Ross. He was pensioned in Lancaster District 7 Dec. 1824 and was paid as late as 1833. His widow, Catherine Beaver, whom he married about 1784, had her claim rejected 28 Oct. 1836.

Beccannan, Philip. France. —. He served under the Marquis de La Fayette. His widow, Jane Beccannan, had her claim rejected by Congress 25 Apr. 1854 because he was a foreign soldier.

Bechgy, —. Pa. —. His widow, Catharine Bechgy, was awarded a $40 gratuity and a $40 annuity in Northampton County 27 Jan. 1835. She was dead by July 1838. She also appeared as Catharine Beckgy.

Bechtel, Borick. Pa. —. He was pensioned in Chester County 3 Apr. 1837. He was dead by Dec. 1842.

Beck, —. Pa. —. His widow, Agnes Beck, was granted a $40 gratuity and a $40 annuity in York County 18 Feb. 1834. She died 31 Jan. 1843.

Beck, George. Pa. —. He was awarded a $40 gratuity and a $40 annuity in Berks County 5 Feb. 1836. He died 11 Nov. 1850.

Beck, Jacob. —. —. He was pensioned 8 Jan. 1796.

Beck, James. Va. —. He was pensioned at the rate of $100 per annum on 10 Jan. 1811. He died 24 Aug. 1821, and his widow, Elizabeth Beck, was granted administration of his estate on 11 Oct. 1821 in the Hustings Court of Fredericksburg, Va.

Beck, John. N.C. —. He was pensioned under the act of 1832 and was then stricken from the rolls because he was in a voluntary unit wholly unconnected with the military organization of the state. He served six months in the militia under Capt. Hendrick in 1778. He served twelve months from the spring of 1780 to May 1781. He was restored to his pension 9 Feb. 1843 by Congress.

Beck, Simon. Md. —. He was pensioned.

Beck, Thomas. Pa. —. He was awarded a $40 gratuity and a $40 annuity in Philadelphia, Pa. 4 May 1832.

Becker, Jacob. N.Y. —. He was pensioned under the act of 1832 at the rate of $30 per annum and was suspended 4 Mar. 1836. He showed payment of two periods of service of less altogether than one month as being paid. He claimed seven months additional service to the nine months under Lt. Deitz and Col. Vroman in 1778. His service was in and about Schoharie opposing the British and the Indians. He was 84 years old. He was pensioned for nine months 23 Feb. 1838. He proved an additional seven months of service 5 Mar. 1840.

Becker, John P. N.Y. Pvt. He resided in Schoharie Co., N.Y. and served Capt. Ryghtman and Col. Peter Vroman in the militia until the close of the war. In 1777 he was in a company of scouts. He was born 9 May 1762. He was pensioned 1 Jan. 1835 at the rank of private rather than a sergeant which he also claimed.

Becket, Humphrey. —. —. He was pensioned 25 Apr. 1808 at the rate of $2.50 per month from 8 Jan. 1808.

Beckham, Robert. Va. Pvt. He was aged 45 years when he applied from Chesterfield County on 1 Jan. 1786. He served in the 12th Va. Regiment and was wounded at Brandywine in the right side of his head and lost an eye. He was pensioned at the rate of £12 per annum. He was on the 1813 pension list.

Beckham, Thomas. S.C. Lt. His son, William Beckham, applied from Barnwell District on 19 June 1841. His father was from Edgefield District and in the winter of 1778-79 was a lieutenant in Col. Leroy Hammond's Regiment of the militia. He was at the siege of Savannah and was made a prisoner at Charleston in May 1780. Captain John Martin and Lt. Thomas Beckham were in the regiment of Col. Samuel Hammond at the siege of Augusta and the surrender of Brown and Glacerson's forts. He was in the service until after the battle of Eutaw Springs. Col. Samuel Hammond attested to much of his service. David Beckham proved that William Beckham was the son of Thomas Beckham. His father never received a pension, and his son sought what his father would have received. His petition was rejected.

Beckland, Robert. Va. Pvt. He served in the 12th Virginia Regiment. He was being pensioned 12 Sep. 1780.

Becktel, Borick. Pa. —. He received a $40 gratuity and a $40 annuity 3 Apr. 1837. He died 2 Oct. 1841. He also appeared as Borick Bechtel.

Beckwith, Benjamin. —. —. He applied for his pension 25 Apr. 1808.

Beckwith, Nehemiah. Md. Pvt. He was pensioned at the rate of half-pay of a private in Dorchester County 2 Mar. 1827.

Becroft, John. Md. Pvt. He was pensioned at the rate of half-pay of a private in Baltimore County 27 Jan. 1816.

Bedinger, Daniel. Va. Lt. He enlisted at the age of 16 and was promoted to the 4th Regiment. He served under Capt. Abraham Shepherd from 1 July 1776 to 1 Jan. 1779. He was made a prisoner 16 Nov. 1776. He died 17 Mar. 1818. His administrator was Edmund J. Lee. His children received his commutation pay plus interest from Congress 16 Feb. 1854. His daughter, Henrietta B. Lee, received a pension from Congress 4 June 1896. She was his only surviving child and was past

86 years of age.

Bedinger, George Michael. Va. Capt. He served from 1775 to 1781. He was also an Indian spy at Boonesborough. He was also a captain and did duty as adjutant for five months before the siege of Yorktown. His service at Boonesborough was not accepted. Congress granted him a pension for one year as a private and five months as a captain on 25 Apr. 1840. He was allowed an additional three months as a private on 9 Feb. 1842.

Bedinger, Henry. Va. Capt. He entered the service in July 1775 in a volunteer corps of riflemen under Capt. Hugh Stevenson in Virginia for one year. He marched to Boston and was a lieutenant in Stevenson's Regiment attached to Capt. Shepherd's Company. He marched to Bergen, New Jersey. After Stevenson's death, he served under Lt. Col. Moses Rawlings. He was captured at Fort Washington on York Island and held as a prisoner until exchanged 1 Nov.1780. He was promoted to captain 21 May 1781. He served 8 years, 3 months, and 26 days. He had accepted a commutation certificate for five years of full pay instead of half-pay for life, but he was not consulted about the difference between the two. His certificate was greatly depreciated before he could use it. His application for commutation pay was not allowed 28 Jan. 1820.

Bedolph, Jasper. Va. Pvt. He was a soldier under Capt. Moody in the artillery and died in service. His widow, Margaret Bedolph, had no children to support when she applied from Surry County in July 1786. She was continued at the rate of £5 per annum on 7 Mar. 1787. She was upwards of 80 years of age in 1804.

Bedon, William. Conn. Corp. He enlisted in 1777 from Stratford and in 1780 was transferred to the Invalids. He served in Capt. Joseph Walker's Company under Col. Samuel B. Webb. At the battle of Rhode Island he was wounded by a piece of rail broken by a cannon ball and thrown against his body. It occasioned a rupture. He was pensioned 10 Dec. 1788 at Washington, Conn. He transferred to Vermont in 1793, but he never appeared on that state's roll. He was, however, on the 1813 pension list of that state.

Bedworth, William. Pa. Pvt. He was in Philadelphia County 12 Dec. 1785. He was in the 12th Pa. Regiment in Capt. Matthew McConnell's Company and was transferred to the Invalids. He was disabled by rheumatism and consumption contracted in the service. He was 53 years old. He died 26 Apr. 1787.

Beebe, Jason. —. —. He was pensioned 28 Feb. 1804. His widow was also pensioned.

Beebe, Paul. Conn. Pvt. He was pensioned 2 Aug. 1813 and was 74 years old.

Beebe, Thaddeus. Conn. Pvt. He served under Col. Huntington in the 1st Regiment. He lost his right eye due to smallpox after being inoculated in 1777 at New London, Conn. He resided at New London, Conn. in 1796. He enlisted 27 Jan. 1777 for the war and was discharged 21 Apr. 1778. He also appeared as Thaddeus Bube.

Beebe, William C.. Conn. Corp. He served in Tyler's Regiment. He was pensioned 8 Feb. 1811. He resided in New London Co., Conn. He was on the 1813 pension list.

Beecher, John. Pa. —. He was awarded a $40 gratuity in Adams Co., Pa. 17 Mar. 1835.

Beekes, Benjamin. —. —. His widow, Sally Beekes, had her petition for a pension rejected by Congress 4 May 1846.

Beekins, William. N.Y. —. His wife and children were granted relief 3 Nov. 1781 in Dutchess Co. His name may have been William Beckins.

Beem, John. N.J. —. He was pensioned in Hunterdon County 22 Feb. 1843 at the rate of $50 per annum.

Beers, James. Conn. Pvt. He served in Col. Warren's Regiment. He had a withered leg occasioned by smallpox in Apr. 1777 in Canada. He lived in Fairfield, Conn. in 1792. He was on the 1813 pension list in New York.

Beeson, Mercer. Va. —. He died in Continental service. His widow, Mary Beeson, was granted support in Frederick Co., Va. on 3 May 1780.

Beetam, Jacob. Pa. Pvt. He was in Berks County 27 Feb. 1786. He served in the 9th Pa. Regiment and was transferred to the Invalids. In Aug. 1778 he was drafted into the Light Infantry under Col. Richard Butler. On 20 Aug. 1778 he was under Maj. Stewart when they were surprised by Emrick's Corps. He was wounded in the head and hands by stabs of a bayonet by the enemy near Valentine's Hill between Tuckahoe and King's Bridge. His head and hand were cut by sword. He was stabbed in four places by a bayonet, had his skull fractured, and was taken prisoner. He was discharged from the Invalids as unfit for duty on 18 July 1781. He had been enlisted by Capt. Witman. James Mahony and William Thomas served with him. He was 24 years old when he enlisted. He later lived in Union County. He also appeared as Jacob Beatum and Jacob Bectum. He was on the 1813 pension list.

Behan, James. Va. —. His wife and three children were granted financial support while he was away in the service in Yohogania Co., Va. 28 Apr. 1778.

Beickel, Jacob. Pa. —. He was awarded a $40 gratuity and a $40 annuity in Union Co., Pa. 3 May 1832.

Beilor, George. Pa. —. He applied from Lancaster County 22 Feb. 1814. He served under Capt. James Ross in 1776. He enlisted at Long Island for the war and was discharged by General Arthur St. Clair at Philadelphia. He was wounded by a musket ball in his leg at White Plains and by a bayonet in his shoulder at Paoli. His sight had almost failed him.

Beisel, John. Pa. —. His heirs were awarded $300 for his tract of donation land on 27 Mar. 1819. The heirs of one John Beisel received $250 for donation land 9 Apr. 1852.

Beitenman, —. Pa. —. His widow, Catharine Beitenman, was awarded a $40 gratuity and a $40 annuity in Montgomery County in Apr. 1837. She died 16 Sep. 1841.

Belcher, —. Va. —. Isabella Belcher and two children were provided necessaries in Amelia Co., Va. 23 Nov. 1780 while her two sons were away in Continental service.

Belcher, Benjamin. Md. —. He served in the 4th Regiment under Capt. David Lyn and Gen. William Smallwood. He applied for a pension in Patrick Co., Va. 17 Dec. 1818.

Belcher, John. Va. —. His family was granted support in Amelia County 25 Feb. 1780,

Belcher, John. Va. Pvt. His wife, Mary Belcher, and family were provided necessaries 25 June 1779, 25 Feb., and 23 Nov. 1780 while he was in the service. He was a soldier under Col. Heath and died a prisoner at Charlestown, S.C. in 1780 according to the oath of John Miles in Chesterfield County on 21 Aug. 1781. His widow and five children resided in Amelia County in 1786. She was put on the pension list at the rate of £12 per annum on 13 Jan. 1787.

Belcher, Samuel. Mass. Pvt. He served in Crane's Regiment and resided at Randolph. He was paid $50.

Belknap, Isaac. —. —. His widow, Susan Belknap, had her petition for a pension which her husband ought to have been granted rejected by Congress 27 Mar. 1846.

Belknap, Jonas. Mass. —. He served in the 7th Regiment and resided at Belchertown. He was paid $20.

Belknap, Jonas. N.Y. Sgt. He served in Col. J. Brook's Regiment. He was wounded in the left side in action with the Indians on 30 May 1778 at Cobuskill. He was pensioned 4 Sep. 1793. He resided in Cherry Valley, Otsego Co., N.Y., in 1794 and later in Ontario County. He was on the 1813 pension list.

Bell, Archibald. Ga. —. He was on the 1796 list.

Bell, David. Pa. —. His widow, Mary Bell, was awarded a $40 gratuity and a $40 annuity in York County on 26 Mar. 1813. She died 29 July 1829.

Bell, David. Pa. —. His lineal heirs were paid $300 for a tract of donation land 12 Apr. 1828. The heirs were Mary Klein, Eliza Wright, John Bell, and the children of Rachel Morrison.

Bell, Frederick Mordant. N.H. Capt. He was wounded on 19 Sep. 1777 and left a widow, Elizabeth Bell, and orphans at his death on 8 Oct. 1777. He served under Col. Reid. Benjamin Bennett who was the guardian of the children. His heirs were paid his seven years' half-pay $1,680. They were pensioned in Dover in 1784.

Bell, Fredrich. N.Y. Pvt. He served under Col. Bellinger in the militia and was slain 13 July 1778. His children were Dederick Bell, Adam Bell, Frederick Bell, and Magdalen Bell.

Bell, George. Pa. —. He was granted relief in Westmoreland County 21 July 1842.

Bell, George. S.C. Lt. He applied from Lancaster District 4 Nov. 1824, and he was pensioned 7 Dec. 1824. He volunteered in the militia in 1776 for five months in the Flying Camps in New York under Capt. John Reed. He was in the battles of Long Island, White Plains, Five Miles Square with the Hessians, Brandywine, and Germantown. At White March Church he was shot through his right hand while taking ammunition from his cartridge box and lost the use of two forefingers. In 1777 he was a lieutenant under Capt. James Murray in the 3rd Battalion of Lancaster Co., Penn. militia. He was in battle against the Indians under Capt. William Johnston. His brother, William Bell, stated that he believed that George Bell brought his commission as lieutenant with him when they came to South Carolina from Pennsylvania. He died 3 Nov. 1825. His widow was Sarah Bell. All of her sons had left her. She had a very delicate constitution and was often sick and unable to work. She was pensioned in Dec. 1826 and received $30 per annum plus $60 in arrearage. She died 22 Jan. 1849. Her unpaid annuity in the amount of $26.50 was paid to her son, Nelson Bell, of Lancaster District.

Bell, George H. N.Y. Pvt. He served in Capt. Michael Edy's Company under Col. Peter Bellinger in the militia. He was wounded in the thigh on 6 Aug. 1777 at Oriskany. He lived at German Flatts, Montgomery Co., N.Y. 29 Sep. 1788. He was 58 years old. He was on the 1813 pension list.

Bell, Hugh. Ga. —. He received $50 per annum as an invalid soldier. Payments were made to him as early as 1796. He was still being paid in 1803.

Bell, Jabez. N.J. Corp. He served under Capt. Nathan Luse and Col. John Starkes and was killed at an alarm in Bergen County on 30 Sep. 1778. He married Mary Heaton. Mary Bell married secondly Samuel Case 19 Sep. 1780. Mary Case was granted a half-pay pension in 1786 in Morris County during her widowhood from 30 Sep. 1778 to 19 Sep. 1780.

Bell, Jacob. N.Y. Pvt. He served under Col. Bellinger and was slain 6 Aug. 1777. His widow, Mary Bell, received a seven years half-pay pension.

Bell, James. —. —. He led the assault on Fort Chambly having equipped the troops at his own expense. He was wounded and taken prisoner. Friends in Scotland sought to have him released. He died in 1814 in Chambly, Lower Canada. His son was William Bell. His daughter, Margaret Bell, married Daniel Cameron. She made her will 11 July 1844, and it was proved 11 Sep. 1844. Her executor was Ralph Richardson. Congress rejected his claim for relief 10 Dec. 1857. Ralph Richardson was the husband of the Caroline M., nee Bell, Richardson, the daughter of the veteran.

Bell, James N. Pa. —. He was granted relief in Columbia County 17 Mar. 1838.

Bell, James. S.C. —. He was wounded at Musgrove. He was paid 18 Jan. 1785 and was from Union District. There were two children in 1791.

Bell, James. S.C. —. He was wounded in the Revolution and received an annuity of $21.42. He died 18 January 1801. He was paid his annuity to March 1792. His widow, Mary Bell, was in Pickens District on 21 Nov. 1813 when she sought the arrearage of his annuity. She was paid for three years and ten months. She received all of the arrears of her husband on 15 Dec. 1818. She was paid as late as 1820.

Bell, John. Pa. —. He was awarded a $40 gratuity and a $40 annuity in Clearfield County 8 Feb. 1825. He died 31 July 1835.

Bell, John. Pa. —. He was granted support in Dauphin County 1 Apr. 1823.

Bell, John. S.C. —. He was in Chester District on 11 July 1827. He served in the expedition to Florida in Capt. Nixon's Company in Col. Jack's Regiment. He was discharged at Midway, Georgia. He was in the tour against the Creek Indians as a volunteer and rescued the women and children hostages. He helped cover the retreat of Gen. Ashe when he was defeated at Briar Creek near the Savannah River. He joined the scouting parties under the Polks in North and South Carolina. He went with Major Davie to join Gen. Gates but arrived after the latter's defeat. He was with Gen. Greene under Capt. Alexander at Batey's Fort on the Catawba River. He was stationed at Tuckasegee Ford and pursued the British toward Haw River. After the battle of Guilford Courthouse, he was discharged. He next served under Col. Richard Winn and went down to Edistoe to keep off the Tories and relieve Gen. Greene. He was 69 or 70 years old and had a large family. Only two girls were at home, and one was unhealthly. His wife was lame. He had one colt, some cattle, and house stuff. Revolutionary soldiers Francis Wylie, William Lewis, and James McCaw endorsed his application. It was approved at the rate of $60 per annum. He was paid as late as 1835.

Bell, John. Va. Lt. He served in the 6th Regiment. He was wounded at the battle of Brandywine in 1777 in the knee by a musket ball. He lost the use of his leg. He lived in Va. in 1794. He was commissioned 28 Dec. 1776 and rendered supernumerary on 30 Sep. 1778. He was granted one-third of a pension 20 Apr. 1796. He was on the 1813 pension list. He died 9 Nov. 1840.

Bell, John Sprigg. Md. Capt. He was pensioned at the rate of $125 per annum. He received a pension at the rate of half-pay of a captain in 1811 and again on 23 Jan. 1816. He also appeared as John Sprigg Belt.

Bell, Joshua. N.H. Pvt. He served in Capt. Livermore's Company in the 3rd N. H. Regiment under Col. Scammel and was disabled. He was from Goffstown and was aged 35 in 1789. He was insane, and his unnamed father was still alive.

Bell, Thomas. Va. —. His family was granted support in Prince Edward County on 16 Aug. 1779. His wife and family were granted support again 20 Nov. 1780. In Jan. 1781 when she was granted support, he was a prisoner in Charles Town. On 17 Sep. 1781 there were seven in the family.

Bell, William. S.C. —. He was pensioned in Abbeville District 4 Dec. 1828. He was upwards of 70 years old and had served under Capt. Weems and Capt. Joseph Pickens. He was in action at Cambridge, Kettle's Creek in Georgia, and Saint Mary's River. He had been pensioned by virtue of certificates from Maj. John Hodges and Maj. Alexander Hamilton. They were dead by 1835 so he could not qualify for a federal pension. He was to draw $60 for one year while his claim for a resumption of his South Carolina pension was being investigated on 15

Dec. 1835. He died in Laurens District, S.C. 17 Dec. 1838. His son, William Bell, Jr., was the administrator of the estate and collected his arrearage of $120.

Bell, William. S.C. —. He was from Lancaster District in 1839.

Bellinger, Fredrik. N.Y. Pvt. He served under Col. Klock in the Montgomery County militia and was slain 12 July 1781. His children, John Bellinger, and Elizabeth Bellinger, received a half-pay pension.

Bellinger, Johannes Frederick. N.Y. Ens. He served under Col. Peter Bellinger in the Montgomery County militia and was slain 6 Aug. 1777 at Oriskany. His son, Johannes Bellinger, was granted a half-pay pension for seven years. His daughter, Elizabeth Bellinger, also received the half-pay pension.

Bellinger, Peter. N.Y. Pvt. He served under Col. Peter Bellinger and was slain 29 June 1779. His widow, Elizabeth Bellinger, received a half-pay pension.

Bellinger, Peter. N.Y. Col. He died in 1823.

Bellington, Francis. Mass. Pvt. He was on the 1791 pension roll.

Bellington, James. N.Y. Pvt. He served under Col. Jacob Klock and was slain 6 Aug. 1777. His widow, Elizabeth Bellington, received a half-pay pension.

Bellows, Elihu. Mass. —. He served in the 2nd Dragoons and resided at South Hadley. He was paid $20.

Bellows, Ezra. Vt. Pvt. He served under Col. Brewer. He was wounded in his left hand by the accidental discharge of his gun in 1776 at Mount Hope. He lived in Springfield, Vt. in 1795. He was in the militia. There was no evidence to prove that he was wounded in the line of duty or when he left the service.

Bellows, Isaac. Mass. Pvt. He served under Col. Nixon in the 6th Regiment. He sprained his hip by slipping on some timber when fording Schuyler's Creek on 12 Oct. 1777. His disability increased by the hardships he endured afterwards by having to sleep for several successive nights with damp clothes on. He resided in Hubbardston and received a two-thirds pension.

Belote, Esme. Va. —. His child was allowed £14 in Northampton Co., Va. It was increased to £25 on 8 Dec. 1778

Belote, William. Va. —. His widow, Amy Belote, was allowed £12.6 for herself and her children on 24 Feb. 1778 in Accomack Co., Va.

Belsiah, Thomas. N.C. —. He applied in Caswell County in 1807. At the age of 16 or 17 he entered the Continental Army under Capt. Daugharty. He marched to Wilmington under the command of Gen. Nash. He was at the battles of Brandywine and Germantown where he was taken prisoner. He spent the winter in jail in Pennsylvania and the following spring was transferred by sea to New York. He was exchanged and returned to North Carolina. He was taken prisoner again at Charleston, S.C. but escaped. He was wounded by a musket ball through his body and fell at Camden. He was put in a prison ship but made his escape and sailed to Boston. Twenty-two years later he sailed back to Charleston, S.C. and came overland to Caswell Co., N.C. He served under Capt. Oldham and Capt. John Graves. Robert Clark was a platoon officer. He was on the 1813 pension list.

Beltzhoover, Jacob. —. —. He was pensioned 27 Feb. 1795.

Belvin, Lewis. Va. Pvt. He served in the Light Dragoons of the 1st Va. Calvary Regiment. He received several wounds in his head, body, and other parts of his body. He lost an eye. He applied from Gloucester County on 1 Jan. 1786 aged *ca.* 35 years. He was continued at the rate of £15 per annum on 7 June 1787. He was on the 1813 pension list.

Bement, Ebenezer. Mass. Brigade Maj. He served under Brig. Gen. J. Patterson. He was wounded in the shoulder by a musket ball at the retreat from Ticonderoga at Hubbardston. He was also a prisoner. He resided in Lenox, Mass. in 1792. He appeared to be an aide-de-camp in the records.

Bemis, Jonas. Mass. Pvt. He served at the Castle and resided at Royalston. His widow, Mary Bemis, was paid $50.

Bender, Lewis. Pa. —. He applied in Philadelphia County on 22 Feb. 1819. He served in Capt. Caleb North's Company in General Wayne's Brigade and served at least one year. Capt. John Christy took command when North was promoted to major. Maj. Thomas Bower sent him from Egg Harbor to Philadelphia to James McClure. He was 77 years old. He died 25 Dec. 1840.

Bender, Christian. Pa. —. He was granted relief in Philadelphia 17 Mar. 1838.

Bender, Ludwig. Pa. —. He was awarded a $40 gratuity in Montgomery Co., Pa. 14 Apr. 1834.

Benedict, —. Pa. —. His widow, Dorothea Benedict, received a $40 gratuity and a $40 annuity in Lancaster County 27 Mar. 1837. The act had her name incorrectly given as Sophia Benedict but a correction was enacted 12 Jan. 1838. She died 4 May 1843.

Benedict, George. Pa. Pvt. He was on the 1813 pension list. He died in York County 27 July 1817.

Benetin, David. N.Y. Pvt. He served under Col. James McClaghry in the Ulster County militia and was slain at Fort Montgomery 6 Oct. 1777. His children, Catharine Benetin and Sarah Benetin, received a half-pay pension for seven years.

Benge, Obediah. —. —. His widow was Sarah Benge of DeKalb Co., Alabama. She filed no paperwork with her memorial so Congress rejected her claim 9 Apr. 1856.

Benjamin, Benjamin. N.Y. Pvt. He was on the 1813 pension list of New York. He moved to Baltimore Co., Md. 4 Sep. 1821. He died in 1822.

Benjamin, Ebenezer. —. —. He became blind in the service due to sickness. He was 88 years old and resided in Oneida Co., N.Y. He sought an increase of his pension, but Congress denied his claim 23 Feb. 1855.

Benjamin, William. Mass. Pvt. He served in the 2nd Regiment. He resided at Lincoln. His widow, Beulah Benjamin, was paid $50.

Benner, —. Pa. —. His widow, Agnes Benner, was pensioned in Beaver County 1 Apr. 1834.

Benner, Christopher Peter. Pa. —. His heirs were awarded £5.4 due on certificate with interest 19 Mar. 1816.

Benner, Peter. Mass. —. He served in the 2nd Regiment and resided at Bridgewater. He was paid $20.

Bennet, Andrew. Mass. —. He served in the 8th Regiment and was paid $20.

Bennet, Isaac. N.J. Sgt. He served in the 2nd N. J. militia. He was wounded by a musket ball which lodged in his right arm just above the elbow when he was with a detachment to remove a boat from Rahway to Elizabethtown at Rahway Creek on 30 Sep. 1777. He lived in Somerset Co., N. J. in 1794.

Bennet, James. S.C. —. There were two children in 1791.

Bennet, John. Md. Pvt. He was pensioned 4 Mar. 1789.

Bennet, John. N.Y. Pvt. He served under Col. Philip Van Cortland in the 2nd N.Y. Regiment. He was wounded in his right knee at Stillwater and had his leg amputated. He lived in New York City, N.Y. on 12 June 1788.

Bennet, Rowland. Mass. —. He served in the 6th Regiment. He was paid $20.

Bennet, Rufus. Pa. —. He received a $40 gratuity and a $40 annuity 13 Apr. 1835. His widow, Martha Bennet, was in Luzerne County 4 Mar. 1844. She was 78 years old. They married 1 June

1783 in Wilkesbarre Township. Mrs. Cornelius Cortright of Pittstown and Mrs. Comfort Carey of Susquehanna County were present at the wedding. He also appeared as Rufus Bennett. He died 20 Apr. 1842.

Bennet, Samuel. Conn. Fifer. He served under Col. P. Bradley in Capt. E. Abel's Company and lost his toes on both feet due to frost bite while aboard a prison ship at New York on 19 Feb. 1776. He lived in Stratford, Conn. in 1792 and Weston, Conn. in 1795. He was in the militia.

Bennett, —. Va. —. Mrs. Bennett was granted support while her "friend" was away in Continental service in Prince Edward County 16 Aug. 1779. [The use of the term "friend" was seemingly as a label for one who was supporting the American cause. The only other instance where this term was used in the county was for a husband who was away in the service.]

Bennett, —. Va. —. His father, Richard Bennett, was granted support in Prince Edward County 18 Oct. 1779 while he was away in Continental service.

Bennett, Benjamin. Conn. Pvt. He served in the 5th Conn. Regiment under Capt. Josiah Lacy and had his feet frozen in the winter of 1778-79. His toes came off. He was pensioned in Stratford, Conn. 8 Dec. 1788 at the age of 30. He lived in Fairfield Co., Conn. He was on the 1813 pension list.

Bennett, Charles. Va. Sail maker. He was disabled by the loss of use of his right arm. He received half-pay from 1 Apr. 1781 to 10 Nov. 1783 and was put on the pension list on 12 Nov. 1783. He was on the 1785 pension list.

Bennett, Edward. R.I. Pvt. He lost his left arm above the elbow at Harlem Heights on Fort Island 16 Sep. 1776. He served under Col. Daniel Hitchcock. He applied at age 35 on 29 Dec. 1785. He was on the 1813 pension list. He died 12 May 1825.

Bennett, Elijah. Vt. Pvt. He served under Col. Israel Putnam. He was wounded in his right arm by a musket ball on 17 June 1775 at Bunker Hill. He lived in Orwil, Rutland Co., Vt. in 1794. He was in the militia. He was granted half a pension 20 Apr. 1796. He was on the 1813 pension list.

Bennett, Frederick. Md. Corp. He was pensioned at the rate of half-pay of a corporal in Dorchester County on 6 Jan. 1812.

Bennett, George. S.C. —. He served to the end of the war. He was in battle at Capt. Edward Hampton's on North Pacolet, Musgrove's Mill, and the taking of Anderson's Fort on Thickety Creek in 1780. He applied 17 Nov. 1827. Daniel Bennett of Hall Co., Ga. attested to his service. John McClure did duty with him near the end of the war.

Bennett, Isaac. N.J. Pvt. He served in the N. J. militia. He was on the 1813 pension list.

Bennett, John. Md. Pvt. He served in the 2nd Maryland Regiment and was wounded at the battle of Camden. He was in Baltimore Co. in 1787. He was on the 1791 pension list. He was on the 1813 pension list. He was pensioned at the rate of half-pay of a private on 27 Jan. 1816.

Bennett, John. N.Y. Pvt. He was wounded in his right knee and lost his leg at Stillwater. He was 28 years old on 1 Jan. 1786. He was on the 1791 and 1813 pension lists.

Bennett, Nehemiah. N.C. —. His widow, Sarah Bennett, applied in Wayne County in Dec. 1793. He was in the militia. He was made a prisoner 19 Aug. 1781 and died in captivity. He left eight children. She was paid £40 for ten years of her pension.

Bennett, Oliver. Pa. Pvt. He was on the 1791 pension roll. He was on the 1813 pension list of the District of Columbia. He transferred from Pennsylvania to Connecticut.

Bennett, Reuben. S.C. —. He was at the battle of Eutaw Springs under Gen. Greene. He served twelve months under Capt. Robert Raford in a volunteer company. He was 68 years old. Stephen

Crain of Chester District, S.C. served in the same regiment for twelve months after the battle
of Guilford. They served under Gen. Jethro Sumner and Col. John B. Ashe until the regiment
was divided and Bennett served under Col. Win Dickson and Capt. Robert Reford. They were
together at High Hills, the Round O, and Bacon & Bridge. He was pensioned 7 Dec. 1825 in
Lancaster District. On 10 Nov. 1836 Bennett stated that he served under Gen. Greene, Maj.
Blunt, and Capt. Robert Rayford. He was 76 years old and was at the battle of Eutaw Springs.
He did not apply for a federal pension because he had no living witness who could prove his
service. He knew others had tried and had been unsuccessful. He was pensioned at the rate of
$60 per annum and died 14 Nov. 1847. His administrator was James Bennett who sought his
arrearage from 1 Mar. 1847 to his death.

Bennett, Samuel. Mass. Corp. He served under Col. Gamaliel Bradford and Capt. Redding. He was
disabled by a musket ball through his right leg. He was 33 years old in 1787.

Bennett, Stephen. Conn. —. He entered the service 1 May 1775 at Canterbury under Capt. Noulton
and Col. Parsons. He was in the vicinity of Boston till the evacuation 17 Mar. 1776. He arrived
in New York in Apr. and was under Gen. Washington on Long Island. He was at White
Plains in 1776. He crossed the Delaware at Princeton and Trenton. In 1777 he enlisted for
three years under Capt. Webb and Col. Durkee and went to Peekskill. He was at Brandywine.
He was at the siege of Fort Mifflin and wintered at Valley Forge. He was under Lafayette in
1778 and was at the evacuation of Philadelphia and at Monmouth. He was at Stoney Point in
1779 under Col. Meigs. In 1781 he enlisted for another three years under Col. Durkee. His
officers were Captains Hart, Comstock, and Clift. He was at the battle of Montgomery Farms
under Gen. Lincoln, Col. Scammell, and Col. Huntington. He was at Yorktown in 1781. He
was discharged at New York City by Gen. Knox. Congress reported that he had no claim to
bounty land because he had entered the service for the war on 21 Apr. 1836. He was from
Plainfield, Windham Co., Conn. and was 72 years old on 28 Nov. 1828. His wife had been
deranged for more than twenty years, and his only daughter was in a similar unhappy condition.

Bennett, Stephen. Mass. Pvt. He served in the 2nd Regiment and resided at Middleborough. He was
paid $50.

Bennett, Thomas. —. —. He was pensioned at the rate of $80 per annum under the act of 1832, but
was suspended in 1836 on the grounds that his service was not recognized by the law. He had
his pension restored for nine months but no more by Congress 5 Mar. 1840.

Benning, Benoni. Va. —. He was wounded at King's Mountain. He was in Washington Co., Va.
15 Apr. 1783.

Bennington, Jacob. Pa. —. He applied 10 Sep. 1813 in Crawford County.

Bennington, Job. Pa. —. He applied 14 Sep. 1813.

Bennington, William Pa. —. He was awarded a $40 gratuity in York County 31 Mar. 1836.

Bensell, George. Pa. Adjt. He also served as aide-de-camp to Gen. Lacy. His widow, Mary Bensell,
submitted evidence that was very vague and unsatisfactory. Congress denied her claim 23
Feb. 1855.

Bensinger, Frederick, Pa. —. He was awarded a $40 annuity in Schulykill County 5 Feb. 1836. He
was 80 years old in 1840.

Benson, Abel. Mass. Pvt. He served in the 3rd Regiment and was from Framingham. He was paid
$50.

Benson, Joseph. Md. Pvt. He was pensioned at the rate of $40 per annum on 6 Mar. 1856.

Benson, Perry Md. Capt. He was pensioned in 1785. He was on the 1813 pension list. His widow,

Mary Benson, was pensioned at the rate of half-pay of a captain 24 Feb. 1831.

Benston, George. Va. —. His wife, Elizabeth Benston, was allowed 10 bushels of corn on 28 May 1782 in Accomack Co., Va.

Bentley, —. —. His widow, Mary Bentley, had her petition for a pension by a special act of Congress refused because she married the veteran subsequent to 1 Jan. 1794.

Bentley, Elisha. Ct. —. He enlisted in June 1776 at Norwich under Capt. Joshua Huntington for nine months. He joined Col. Selden in New York and on Long Island served under Maj. Gen. Putnam. The Americans retreated when the British landed at Flat Bush. He was at Turtle Bay and White Plains. In 1777 he entered at Terringham, Berkshire Co., Mass. under Capt. Herrick for three months. He was at Fort Edwards where he joined Col. Nixon. He was at Kingsbury, Fort Miller, Saratoga, and the taking of Burgoyne. In June 1778 at Woodberry, Conn. he enlisted under Capt. Ezra Chatman for three years but was returned by the enlisting officer as doing so for the war. He was at Horse Neck and joined Col. Meigs and Gen. Huntington. In June 1779 he was involved in preventing refugees and Tories from plundering the inhabitants on the north side of the East River. He was discharged in 1783. He was granted a full pension 21 Mar. 1838.

Bentley, Gideon. —. —. He served as a minuteman for a year and a half. He was very old. His pension was $50 per annum, and he sought further relief. Congress rejected his claim 7 Feb. 1850.

Bentley, Henry. Pa. —. He applied 6 May 1812. He died 21 Aug. 1819.

Benton, —. Va. —. His wife, Ann Benton, was granted support for necessaries in Fauquier Co., Va. 12 Sep. 1780.

Benton, Edward. Conn. Pvt. He was disabled by fits. He was pensioned in Conn. 6 Jan. 1783. He was on the 1813 pension list of New York.

Benton, John. N.C. Pvt. He was wounded in his hip at Eutaw Springs in 1781. He lived in Wake County in 1783 and in 1794. He enlisted in 1781 and was discharged 17 Feb. 1782. He was granted a full pension 20 Apr. 1795.

Benton, ---. Va. —. Lazarus Benton was awarded a £20 annuity on 2 Dec. 1777. Four of his sons and a son-in-law had been killed by the Indians. He had a widowed daughter and a little girl.

Benton, Selah. N.Y. Capt. Although he was not wounded in the war, he had a disability from disease and exposure in the service. He had scorbutic ulcers. He was pensioned 31 Jan. 1812. He died 12 May 1812. He was on the 1813 pension list as Silas [sic] Benton. His widow was Mary E. Benton. Congress did not grant her relief 11 Dec. 1824. He had also served in the French and Indian War under Col. P. Lyman in Connecticut.

Beoler, George. Pa. —. He was pensioned 26 Feb. 1814.

Beran, Nicholas. Pa. Pvt. He was pensioned.

Bergen, Elizabeth. —. N.Y. She was pensioned by the act of 24 Aug. 1781 of Congress. She had three children. She assisted the American prisoners in New York with not only necessaries but also with making their escapes.

Berger, Yost. Pa. Pvt. He enlisted in 1777 under Col. Thompson in the 1st Regiment. About fifteen months later he and about a hundred others were detached under Gen. Gates. He applied in Lehigh County 1 Feb. 1817. He was discharged at Trenton in 1781.

Bergerhoff, William. —. —. He served in the 4th Regiment. He applied 8 Feb. 1816. He also appeared as William Bergenhoff and William Burgenhoff. He died 18 Mar. 1820.

Bergy, George. Pa. —. He was awarded a $40 gratuity and a $40 annuity in Northampton County

6 Apr. 1833. He was dead by Feb. 1839.

Berlin, Isaac. Pa. —. He applied from Crawford County 3 Jan. 1819. On 27 Apr. 1821 he filed his application again indicating that he had never followed up on his initial application. He had received but had been stricken from his U.S. pension so he reapplied to Pennsylvania. His widow, Mary Berlin, was awarded a $40 gratuity and a $40 annuity in Crawford Co., Pa. 11 June 1832.

Bernard, John. Pa. —. He was awarded a $40 gratuity and a $40 annuity 15 Mar. 1826. He was from Philadelphia County. He died 21 Dec. 1828. The final payment was made to his widow, Elizabeth Bernard.

Bernhart, Daniel. Pa. —. He applied in Berks County 1 June 1813. He also appeared as Daniel Barnhart.

Berns, William. Pa —. He served under Capt. Stake in the Penn. Line. He was from Berks County.

Berrien, John. Ga. Capt. He was wounded at Monmouth. He was paid $465.634 3/4 in 1802.

Berry, —. Pa. —. His widow was Agnes Berry.

Berry, —. Mass. —. His widow, Betty Berry, was paid $50.

Berry, Benjamin. Mass. Pvt. He served in Col. Jonathan Reed's Regiment in Capt. Asahel Wheeler's Company. He lost his arm in the battle of Lake Champlain on 11 Oct. 1776. He was pensioned at the rate of half-pay on 25 Sep. 1777. He was on the 1813 pension list. He was paid $20 and was from Andover. He served in the 5th Regiment.

Berry, Benjamin. Mass. Pvt. He served in the 11th Regiment and was from Andover, Mass. His widow, Hannah Berry, was paid $50.

Berry, Benjamin. Mass. —. He served in the 5th Regiment and was paid $20. He was from Andover.

Berry, Benjamin. N.H. —. He served three months and fourteen days under Capt. Moses Leavitt in the militia. He suffered a gun shot wound in his knee from the accidental discharge of a musket. Congress granted him a pension 26 Feb. 1856.

Berry, George. Pa. —. He was awarded a $40 gratuity and a $40 annuity in Northampton Co., Pa. 6 Apr. 1833.

Berry, George. Va. —. He was wounded in his leg by the Indians. His petition was rejected 16 June 1777 for insufficient proof.

Berry, James. Pa. Sgt. He was in York County 2 Dec. 1785. He served in the Pa. Line and was wounded in the leg by a bayonet on the night of 19 Sep. 1777 under the command of Lt. Col. David Grier of the 7th Pa. Regiment. He was 35 years old. He also appeared as James Barry. He later applied in Cumberland County on 2 Mar. 1815 and stated that he was in the 1st Pa. Regiment. He died 17 Nov. 1821.

Berry, James. Va. Pvt. He served in Capt. Harrod's Company of militia. He was wounded 11 Sep. 1777 on the Indian expedition. He had six children. He was awarded a £30 gratuity and one year's pay of a soldier in Washington Co., Va. 9 Oct. 1778.

Berry, John. Mass. Pvt. He was pensioned 21 Mar. 1807 in Suffolk Co., Mass. He was on the 1813 pension list.

Berry, John. Pa. —. He was pensioned.

Berry, John. Va. Pvt. He served in the 9th Va. Regiment. He was on the 1813 pension list. He resided in Shenandoah County and died 2 Oct. 1826.

Berry, Joseph. Me. —. He was from York. He was paid $50 under the resolve of 1836.

Berry, Michael. Pa. Pvt. He was in Philadelphia County 13 Oct. 1785. He served under Col. Walter Stewart in the 2nd Pa Regiment and was transferred to the Invalids. He was wounded and disabled. He was discharged 10 Apr. 1783. He was 30 years old. On 25 July 1792 he lived in Queen Anne's Co., Md.

Berry, Peter. Pa. —. He was awarded a $40 gratuity in Lebanon Co., Pa. 4 May 1832 and again 5 Feb. 1833. He was dead by Nov. 1835.

Berry, Thomas. S.C. —. He was 82 years old and served two years as a drafted militia man and as a substitute. He served under Gen. Francis Marion and Capt. Wetherspoon in Col. Giles' Regiment and under Capt. Renue in Col. Horry's Regiment. He saw action at Watboo and Eutaw Springs. Joseph Davis swore that Berry was a Continental soldier. John Boothe swore that they were in Col. Peter Horry's Regiment. He was pensioned in Barnwell District 30 Nov. 1827. He was a member of the Baptist Church.

Berry, Thomas. Va. —. He was wounded in the breast 4 Sep. 1776 by a shot from Indians while in the service and continued ill to 1 June 1777. He was granted support in Washington Co., Virginia 26 Feb. 1777. He served under Capt. Benjamin Gray.

Berryman, Benjamin. Va. —. He died in the service. His widow, Sarah Berryman, was awarded a gratuity of £11.6.8 in King George County 9 Nov. 1779. The churchwardens of Washington Parish were ordered to look into her circumstances 29 July 1777 in Westmoreland County.

Berryman, John. Md. Gunner. He served aboard the *Defense* and lost his right arm in 1777. He was awarded £250 on 26 July 1780.

Besaw, Nicholas. Pa. Pvt. He was in Philadelphia County 13 Oct. 1785 and 9 Jan. 1786. He was in the 3rd Pa. Regiment, was wounded, and transferred to the Invalids. He was discharged 3 Sep. 1782. He was 66 years old. He also appeared as Nicholas Beatro and Nicholas Beaso. He was dead by Mar. 1791.

Beshaw, Thomas. Va. Pvt.

Beskins[?], **William**. N.Y. —. His wife and three children were granted support in Dutchess County 3 Nov. 1781.

Bess, Edward. Pa. —. He applied from Washington County 3 Nov. 1813. He served in the 8th Pa. Regiment under Capt. Van Swearingen for three years. He was discharged and volunteered for service on the frontier. He was at Crawford's defeat in 1782. His son aged 18 was hired out.

Best, Abraham. Pa. Pvt. He was in Philadelphia County 12 Dec. 1785. He was in the 6th Pa. Regiment and lost his leg by a cannon ball at Germantown 4 Oct. 1777. He was 33 years old. His officers were Lt. James Glentworth and Capt. John Savidge.

Best, Henry. S.C. —. His widow, Mary Best, was paid an annuity 29 July 1786 and was from Winton. There was one child in 1791.

Bettlmoyer, Martin. Pa. —. He was granted relief in 1839.

Betts, Hezekiah. Conn. —. He served under Capt. Stephen Betts in the Connecticut volunteers having enlisted for three years in July 1779 under Col. Butler and Col. Webb. He died in 1837 and his widow, Grace Betts, in 1840. His daughter and only surviving child, Juliette Betts, aged 91, received a pension from Congress 12 May 1896. All of the officers in the Norwalk, Conn. DAR corroborated her statements as to paternity, age, and her dependency.

Betts, James. N.Y. —. His wife and nine children were granted relief in Dutchess County 3 Nov. 1781.

Betts, Preserved. N.Y. —. —. His widow, Elizabeth Betts, sought a pension by a special act of Congress. His sister, Lydia Parmlee, proved that he was a wounded by a ball and was disabled for five years. He was on the pay roll for five months excluding the time of his sickness. Another payroll proved he served seven months. Congress credited him with one year and 3 months of service and awarded her a pension by special act for $60 per annum commencing 25 Dec. 1843 on 27 Mar. 1846.

Betz, George. Pa. —. He was granted a gratuity in 1823.

Betz, Peter. Pa. —. He was awarded a $40 gratuity and a $40 annuity in Dauphin County 19 Feb. 1823. His widow, Elizabeth Betz, received a $40 gratuity and a $40 annuity in Harrisburg 9 Apr. 1856.

Bevan, Matthew. N.J. Pvt. He served in the 1st Regiment and lost the use of his arm. He resided in Northampton, Burlington Co., N.J. He was 55 years old.

Bevans, Wilder. Pa. Lt. He was dead by 3 Aug. 1809.

Bevins, Ebenezer. Conn. Pvt. He served in the 1st Regiment. He was disabled by rheumatism. He resided in Conn. in 1792. He was transferred to the Invalids 1 May 1781.

Bewley, George. Md. Pvt. His widow, Grace Bewley, was paid the $200 arrearage of his pension and was pensioned at the rate of $40 per annum on 5 Mar. 1858.

Beyer, —. Pa. —. His widow, Catherine Beyer, was awarded relief in Montgomery County 14 Mar. 1835.

Beyers, George. Pa. —. He was awarded a $40 gratuity and a $40 annuity 24 Feb. 1812 in Armstrong County.

Beyers, Samuel. Pa. —. He was pensioned 24 Mar. 1837 in Mercer County. He died 10 Mar. 1839.

Beyles, John. Pa. —. He was pensioned by the act of 28 Mar. 1809.

Bichard, Thomas. Pa. —. He was granted relief.

Bickel, Jacob. Pa. —. He received a $40 gratuity and a $40 annuity in Union County 3 May 1832. He also appeared as Jacob Bickle.

Biddle, Robert. Pa. —. He was pensioned.

Bidwell, Richard. Md. Pvt. He was pensioned at the rate of half-pay of a private in Baltimore 27 Jan. 1816.

Bieghy, George. Pa. —. He was awarded a $40 gratuity in Northampton County on 14 Mar. 1814.

Bigelow, Samuel. Mass. —. He served in the 8th Regiment and was from Newton. He was paid $20.

Bigelow, William. Mass. Pvt. He served in the 5th Regiment and was from Littleton. His widow, Hannah Bigelow, was paid $50.

Biggs, John, Jr. Va. —. His wife, Mary Biggs, and three children were granted financial support in Amherst Co., Va. in Sep. 1781 while he was away in the service.

Biggs, Joseph. Pa. Pvt. He transferred to Virginia in or by Mar. 1796. He was on the 1813 pension list

Biggs, William. —. Lt. He served under Col. George Rogers Clark and was taken prisoner by the Wabash Indians. By 1785 he moved from Ohio Co., Va. to the Illinois country. He sought 2,000 acres in the Illinois country. Congress ruled that his claim was not a valid one against the United States. Congress reversed itself 8 May 1826.

Bill, Benjamin. Conn. Pvt. He served in the militia in the 2nd Company of the 8th Regiment. He was wounded in the ankle by a musket ball at Fort Griswold on 6 Sep. 1781 in opposing the British under Gen. Arnold who had landed at New London. He was pensioned 26 Sep. 1788 at Groton, Conn. at the age of 25.

Bill, Daniel. Conn. Pvt. He served in the 8th Conn. Regiment of militia in Capt. William Stanton's Company in 1776. He was at Morrisana, Kingsbridge, and White Plains under Col. Oliver Smith. He took sick with dysentery which settled in his limbs and rendered him a cripple.

He was pensioned 28 Nov. 1788. He resided in New London having previously lived in Stonington. He was 33 years old. He was on the 1813 pension list. He died 6 Aug. 1818 in New London Co., Conn.

Bill, Ebenezer. Mass. Matross. He served in Crane's Artillery and resided at Roxbury. His widow, Hannah Bill, was paid $50.

Bill, Nathaniel. Mass. Matross. He served in Crane's Artillery and resided at Dedham. He was paid $50.

Billings, John S. —. —. He served six months as a privateer in Dec. 1778. He was wounded in his left leg by a musket ball. He served as a common sailor and then a mate. [The later service may have been after the Revolution.] He was pensioned at the rate of $4 per month. He sought an increase in his pension of $8 per month from 30 June 1837 on 10 July 1840. He was 80 years old. Congress rejected his request.

Billings, Robert. Mass. —. He served in the 7th Regiment and was paid $20.

Billings, Samuel. Mass. —. He served in the 1st Regiment and was paid $20.

Billington, Francis. Mass. Pvt. He served in the 6th Regiment under Capt. Taylor and Col. Benjamin Tupper. He was disabled by fractured ribs. He also suffered from gravel and epilepsy. He was pensioned 4 Jan. 1783 and was 25 years old in 1786. He was a resident of New York.

Bills, —. Pa. —. His widow, Elizabeth Bills, was awarded a $40 gratuity and a $40 annuity in Philadelphia County 15 Feb. 1825.

Bindow, Joseph. N.Y. Commissary of Clothing. He served two years and died 29 May 1832 in Champlain, N.Y. His death was just before passage of the act of 7 June 1832. His son, Joseph Bindow, on 8 Aug. 1856 was awarded the arrearage. He also appeared as Joseph Bendon. He received half-pay for life.

Bingham, Ralph. Conn. Sgt. He served in the artillery and was disabled at Bunker Hill on 17 June 1775 by severe duty in the heat of the day. He did not eat or drink the whole day of the battle. He lived in Windham, Conn. and was 33 years old when he was pensioned 20 Sep. 1788. He died 16 July 1801.

Bingham, Warren. Mass. —. His widow, Lucy Bingham, sought an increase in her pension, but Congress rejected her claim 31 Mar. 1856.

Binkley, Adam. N.C. —. He used his horses and wagons and received bounty land warrant no. 1314 and entered 5,000 acres in Tennessee. He was defrauded of his land and sought a new warrant from Tennessee which he desired to locate in the western district of Tennessee. He was 90 years old and indigent in 1807.

Birch, Thomas. Pa. —. He was awarded a $40 gratuity and a $40 annuity in Fayette County 15 June 1836. He died 17 Apr. 1844.

Birchett, Edward. Va. Corp. He served in the cavalry. He lost the use of his right arm in action. He was on the 1785 pension roll.

Birchmore, William. S.C. —. He was an Englishman by birth and came to America before the Revolutionary War. He was 88 years old. He served under Gen. Francis Marion, Col. Richard Richardson, and Capt. Dukes. He had a large family. He lost three sons in the service under Capt. R. J. Manning and a valuable Negro to the British. He was present at the taking of Fletchers at the Snowy Camp and was under Gen. Williamson at Augusta. He was pensioned in Clarendon in Dec. 1826. Richard Richardson, the son of the late Richard Richardson, swore that he had heard his father state that Birchmore was in the service.

Bird, Andrew. Pa. Pvt. He was in Cumberland County on 2 May 1818. He entered the service in the summer of 1777 and served under Ens. Shanks and Lt. Benjamin Carpenter in the 10th Regiment until the revolt. He was discharged at Trenton. He reenlisted at Philadelphia in the same regiment and was transferred to the 1st Regiment. He served to the end of the war in Capt. Irwin's Company. He died 3 May 1851 in Perry County.

Bird, Edmund. Mass. —. He served in the 1st Regiment and was paid $20.

Bird, Frederick. Pa. —. He was awarded a $40 gratuity and a $40 annuity in Philadelphia County 26 Mar. 1822.

Bird, Herman. Ga. Pvt. He served in the Burke County Militia and was wounded in the right side of his back, in his right arm, and his right foot at Burke jail on 25 Jan. 1779. He resided in Burke Co., Ga. in 1796. He was on the 1813 pension list.

Bird, Joseph. Mass. Pvt. He was pensioned at the rate of $4 per month from 29 Jan. 1808. He was on the 1813 pension list of Vermont. He lived in Addison Co., Vt.

Bird, Nathaniel. —. —. He was pensioned in 1818 but stricken in 1820. He was restored effective 26 Apr. 1832. He sought a pension for the period it was suspended. Congress rejected his claim 10 Feb. 1846.

Birmingham, James. S.C. —. He was wounded through the body on 19 Nov. 1775 and died 22 Nov. 1775. He left a widow and a large family very poor. He was paid £100. The same amount per annum from 1 Apr. 1776 was paid to his widow during her widowhood and afterwards to the children or child under the age of twelve.

Birmingham, Patrick. Va. Pvt. He applied from Berkeley Co., Va. in Oct. 1788. He served in the 2nd Va. Regiment and was twice wounded at Ninety Six, S.C. One musket ball entered his body and another broke his wrist. William Eskridge, late of the 2nd Va. Regiment, attested to his service. He also appeared as Patrick Brummagem and Patrick Bremagen. He was continued on the pension roll on 13 Nov. 1788 at the rate of £12 per annum.

Biscoe, Josiah. Md. —. He served under Capt. John Ham Abell in 1776 and guarded the shores of the Potomac and the Chesapeake. In 1779 he was on the schooner *Harford* of Baltimore. It was a private armed vessel. He was taken prisoner and held in New York. After he was released, he shipped himself on board a privateer in 1782. He was again taken prisoner and carried to Little York and was there when Lord Cornwallis surrendered. He was rejected as a pensioner because he was not in Continental service on 12 Feb. 1841.

Bishop, Benjamin. N.J. Pvt. He served under Col. Crane in the Essex County militia. He lost his forefinger and was shot through the thigh. He was 24 years old and was from Woodbridge. He was on the 1791 pension roll and on the 1813 pension list. He later moved to Montgomery Co., Ind.

Bishop, Benoni. —. —.He enlisted 13 Jan. 1777 and was reported deserted in Nov. 1779. His record also revealed that on 6 Jan. 1783 he received a furlough which became a discharge. He married in Mar. 1781. His widow, Elizabeth Bishop, was allowed a pension 12 Feb. 1841 on the interpretation that his record showing him as a deserter was an error since he was later in the service.

Bishop, Charles. N.Y. Pvt. He served under General Herkimer. He was wounded in the left arm by buck shot in Aug. 1777 in Oriskie. He lived in Montgomery Co., N.Y. in 1794.

Bishop, Comfort. R.I. Pvt. He lost the use of his left wrist and hand after his inoculation for smallpox in May 1782 at the hospital in Philadelphia. He served under Col. Jeremiah Olney. He was aged 29 in 1785. He was on the 1813 pension list. He died 28 Jan. 1816.

Bishop, Henry. S.C. —. He was wounded by the British 1 Aug. 1780 and lost his life. His widow,

Elizabeth Bishop, was paid 21 Jan. 1785 and was from Spartanburgh District. There were two children in 1791.

Bishop, Joshua. N.Y. Matross. He served in Capt. Gershom Mott's Company in the 2nd N.Y. Regiment under Col. John Lamb. He was disabled in his right breast in 1781 at Morristown by falling on the stump of a tree. He lived in Westchester Co., N.Y. on 21 Apr. 1789. He was on the 1813 pension list.

Bishop, Paul. Pa. —. He was awarded a $40 gratuity and a $40 annuity in Philadelphia Co., Pa. 20 Feb. 1833. His widow, Sarah Bishop, of the 22nd Ward received a $40 gratuity and a $40 annuity 1 May 1857.

Bishop, Simeon. Conn. Pvt. He served in Butler's Regiment. He was disabled by deafness in the service. He was pensioned 1 Sep. 1782. He was on the 1813 pension list. He died 15 Oct.1825 in New Haven Co., Conn.

Bishop, Squire. Me. Pvt. He was wounded by a musket ball near the back bone in the expedition against Penobscot in 1779. He served under Col. S. Webb. He also served under Col. McCobb. He was pensioned 5 Apr. 1793. He lived at Washington, Me. in 1792. He was on the 1813 pension list.

Bishop, Thomas. Md. Pvt. He was pensioned in Frederick County in 1789. He was wounded at Guilford Court House. He served in the 2nd Regiment. He was on the 1813 pension list.

Bishop, Thomas. Va. —. His wife, Catherine Bishop, was granted £10 support while he was away in Continental service in Berkeley County on 17 Nov. 1778.

Bissell, Samuel. —. —. His widow, Anna Bissell, had her application for a pension rejected by Congress on 27 Mar. 1846 because their marriage was subsequent to 1 Jan. 1794.

Bisson, Charles. Pa. —. He was awarded a $40 gratuity and a $40 annuity on 16 Feb. 1813. He applied from Center Square, Pa. 3 July 1815. His widow, Elizabeth Bisson, was awarded a $40 gratuity and a $40 annuity in Montgomery Co., Pa. 13 Apr. 1827.

Bitler, John. Pa. —. He received a $40 gratuity in Schuylkill County 16 June 1836.

Bittenbender, Conrad. Pa. —. He was taken prisoner at Fort Washington and was released in Feb. 1777. He was from Northampton County.

Bitting, Adam. Pa. Capt. He was from Philadelphia County. He served in the 4th Pa. Regiment of Foot under Lt. Col. William Butler and was killed near Morristown, N.J. His children were John Bitting aged 12 on 8 Jan. 1792, James Bitting aged 13 on 21 Jan. 1784, and Margaret Bitting aged 11 on 14 Feb. 1784. His widow, Deborah Bitting, married secondly Robert Connelly 8 Nov. 1783. He also appeared as Adam Bitten.

Bitting, Joseph. Pa. —. He was awarded a $40 gratuity and a $40 annuity in Union Co., Pa. 15 Apr. 1835. He died 6 Dec. 1844

Bittle, Samuel. Pa. —. He was pensioned in Montgomery County 18 Jan. 1838.

Black, —. Pa.—. His widow, Lydia Black, received a $40 annuity in Greene County 8 May 1854. She died in May 1863.

Black, —. S.C. —. His widow was Mary Black. The balance of her annuity, $60, was paid to her executor, John B. Black, 8 Dec. 1826.

Black, —. Pa. —. His widow, Sarah Black, was awarded a $40 gratuity and a $40 annuity 15 Apr. 1834 in Adams County. She died 9 June 1842.

Black, David. —. —. He sought an increase in his pension, but Congress rejected his claim 14 Mar. 1848

Black, George. Va. Pvt. He served in the 12th Va. Regiment. He was shot through his thigh which broke the bone at Brandywine. He was a prisoner for a considerable time. Capt. Joseph Swearingen attested to his service on 17 June 1788. He was aged *ca.* 30 in 1788. He applied from Berkeley Co., Va. on 19 Apr. 1787. He was continued at the rate of £10 per annum on 1 July 1788. He was later in Frederick County. He was on the 1813 pension list.

Black, Henry. Me. —. He was from Kittery. He was paid $50 under the resolve of 1836.

Black, Henry. Pa. —. He was awarded a $40 gratuity and a $40 annuity in Adams Co., Pa. 31 Jan. 1831.

Black, James. Pa. Sgt. His widow, Ruth Black, was in Westmoreland County 4 May 1791. He was in the Westmoreland County militia in Col. Archibald Lockrey's Battalion on the expedition down the Ohio River. He was tomahawked and killed by Indians 24 Aug. 1781. He left six small children.

Black, James. Pa. —. He was awarded a $40 gratuity and a $40 annuity in Dauphin County 28 Mar. 1836.

Black, John. N.C. Pvt. He entered the service as a militiaman under Capt. John Brumfield and Col. Irwin in Dec. 1779. Later he was detached and placed in an armory with Isaac Price to repair arms and make swords for the horse troops. He was dropped as pensioner because he had served 2 months and 26 days in the militia and 7 months in the smith's shop. The latter was embraced by the law. Congress restored him to his pension for six months of service on 12 Feb. 1841. He was then a resident of Georgia.

Black, John. S.C. Pvt. He was a Whig soldier in the militia. He served six weeks as a private in 1776 against the Cherokee under Col. Neil, Poag, and Capt. Kirkpatrick. He next served two months at Briar Creek in Georgia. His third tour was under Capt. Black before the fall of Charleston. His last tour of two months was just before the peace under Capt. Hillhouse near Four Holes. He became a federal pensioner and received $35.67 per annum for four years under the act of 1832. He was then stricken from the roll. He applied from York District 19 Nov. 1836 when he was 82 years old and his wife was 76. He had previously made a deed of gift to his three daughters reserving a life estate for himself and his wife. His brother, Jacob Black, of York District stated that they were together at Briar Creek.

Black, Joseph. Mass. Drummer. He served in the 2nd Regiment and resided at Kittery. He was paid $20.

Black, Matthew. Pa. —. He was awarded a $40 gratuity and a $40 annuity in Adams Co., Pa. 15 Apr. 1834. He was dead by May 1838.

Black, Robert. S.C. —. He lost his life in action with the British. His widow, Eleanor Black, was paid 27 Feb. 1785 an annuity and was from Pendleton District. She had two children in 1791. She was paid her annuity 7 June 1820 in Abbeville District.

Black, Samuel. R.I. Ens. He had a bad rupture in his groin contracted in 1775. He served under Col. Daniel Hitchcock. He was aged 48 in 1786. He lived in Providence Co., R.I.

Black, William. Mass. —. He volunteered at Lexington 19 Apr. 1775 for a few weeks of service. He enlisted in the regular army in 1778 and served eight months at Roxbury. He next enlisted for five months in New York. He was at Fort Washington, White Plains, and Howland's Ferry. He was in an engagement with a row galley. He also served three months under Gen. Sullivan in Rhode Island. Congress granted him a pension 21 Dec. 1831.

Black, William. Pa. —. He applied in Franklin County 10 Feb. 1815. He enlisted under Col. Irwin in the Pa. Line in 1776 for one year. He was wounded in his left hand aboard a gunboat on Lake Champlain and was sent to hospital at Fort George. He was discharged at Carlisle. He reenlisted under Gen. Hazen and Maj. James Read at Albany, N.Y. and marched to Philadelphia to join the regiment under Col. Entle. He served six years and six months. John Chamberlain, Quartermaster, issued provisions to him in 1776.

Blackburn, Arthur. Va. —. He served in Capt. William Cocke's Company of militia. He was wounded in his side. He was scalped twice in defending crops from the Indians. He was granted a £20 gratuity and a £6 annuity on 7 June 1777.

Blackburn, John. Pa. Pvt. He was on the 1789 pension list.

Blackburne, John. Va. —. His pension of $50 year was discontinued 23 Jan. 1799 since he had removed to Tennessee.

Blackerby, Nathaniel. Va. —. He served in the 3rd Va. Regiment and died in the service on 24 Apr. 1777. His widow, Beheathland Blackerby, and two small children were granted support 14 July 1777, £5 on 11 May 1778, and £10 on 10 May 1779. She received his half-pay from May 1779 to 15 May 1782. She received 2 barrels of corn on 8 July 1781. Lt. Col. Thomas Gaskins certified his service on 12 Apr. 1785. His widow lived in Northumberland County. She also appeared as Hetty Blackerby.

Blackford, David. Mass. —. He was paid $20.

Blackford, Jacob. Pa. —. He received a $40 gratuity and a $40 annuity in Adams County 9 Feb. 1837 He later lived in Fayette County. He was 81 years old in 1840. His widow, Margaret Blackford, received a $40 annuity 27 Apr. 1852.

Blackington, James. Me. —. He died 25 Oct. 1835. His widow, Elizabeth Blackington, was from Thomaston. She was paid $50 under the resolve of 1836.

Blackley, Richard. Va. —. His widow, Frances Blackley, was granted £12 support in Middlesex Co., Va. on 28 June 1779. There was one child on 22 Feb. 1779.

Blackman, David. Conn. Pvt. He served in guarding the seacoast. He was badly wounded by a British sloop of war and so cut to pieces that his entrails came out at his wounds on 10 Sep. 1781. He served in Capt. Fitch's Company. He resided in Huntington, Conn. in 1792. He enlisted 11 May 1777 and was discharged 30 Apr. 1780. He was granted two-thirds of a pension 20 Apr. 1796. He was on the 1813 pension list.

Blackman, Elisha. Pa. —. He was awarded a $40 gratuity and a $40 annuity in Luzerne County 28 Mar. 1836. He was 80 years old in 1840. He died 4 Dec. 1845.

Blackemore, George. —. Pvt. & Drummer. He was pensioned at the rate of $46.22 per annum under the act of 1832. He died in Aug. 1837. His service was in the militia. His widow, Sarah Blackmore, applied under the act of 1838 but was rejected since his service was not acceptable. Congress awarded her a pension 7 Mar. 1844.

Blackney, John. S.C. —. His application was rejected in Dec. 1826.

Blackshire, Ebenezer. —. —. His widow sought a pension. Congress rejected her petition 12 Feb. 1841. She furnished no evidence of his service and had married the veteran after 1794.

Blacksley, Enos. Conn. Pvt. He died 10 July 1812.

Blackstone, Prideaux. Va. —. His widow, Bridget Blackston, was granted financial support in Yohogania Co., Va. 24 June 1778. His widow, Bedy Shilling, was awarded a $40 gratuity and a $40 annuity in Mercer Co., Pa. 14 Apr. 1834.

Blackwell, —. —. —. The heirs of Ann Blackwell had their application rejected 4 May 1846. They were from Maine.

Blackwell, Joseph. Va. Lt. He was commissioned in the 3rd Regiment early in 1776. About two years later he became supernumerary. In 1780 he was appointed quartermaster. There was no proof that he served to the end of the war. Congress rejected the claim of the heirs 27 Apr. 1836.

Blackwell, Thomas. Va. Capt. He served in the 10th Regiment and received bounty warrant #2493 on 25 Feb. 1793. He received his five years' full pay commutation in lieu of half-pay for life 29 May 1830. His legal representatives sought 6% interest 27 May 1892.

Blackwell, William. Va. Capt. He was appointed I July 1776. Two years later he became supernumerary with the consolidation of his unit and another. Congress found that he resigned and rejected the claim of Elizabeth Scott for relief on 11 Jan. 1834.

Blain, —. Va. —. His wife, Sarah Blain, was allowed £10.10 relief in Halifax Co., Va. on 17 Sep. 1778.

Blain, John. Pa. —. He was awarded a $40 gratuity and a $40 annuity in Venango County 26 Mar. 1813.

Blair, —. Pa. —. His widow, Eleanor Blair, was awarded a $40 gratuity and a $40 annuity in Westmoreland County 31 Mar. 1836. She was dead by July 1838.

Blair, Edward. S.C. —. He served in the militia under Capt. John Allison, Robert Allison, Col. Winn, and Col. Kirkpatrick for two full tours. He was at the battle of Eutaw Springs with Gen. Williamson. He applied in Fairfield District 15 Dec. 1828.

Blair, James. Pa. —. He was awarded a $40 gratuity and a $40 annuity in Westmoreland Co., Pa. 15 Apr. 1834. He died in Mar. 1843.

Blair, John. Md. Pvt. He was pensioned in Montgomery County 4 Mar. 1789. He died in either 1792 or 1794.

Blair, John. Md. Pvt. He died in either 1792 or 1794. [second of the name]

Blair, John. Pa. —. He enlisted with Capt. Bush of Wilmington, Del. at New London cross roads when he was 22 years old. He marched to Lancaster and was put under the command of Capt. Stake. The major was Butler and the adjutant was Butler. They were brothers. Archibald McVicar, Thomas Ivory, and James Davis enlisted with him. He was 60 years old on 27 Jan. 1817 and lived in Lancaster County having located there five years ago from Chester County. He also served a tour in the Western Expedition under Capt. Andrews in Major Hartman's Battalion in the regiment of Col. Harris of Little Britain Township, Lancaster County.

Blair, John. S.C. —. His application was rejected in Dec. 1826.

Blair, John. Va. —. His wife, Elizabeth Blair, and three children were furnished £8 support in Louisa Co., Va. on 11 Aug. 1777.

Blair, Joseph. Va. —. His wife, Alice Blair, was granted £12 support while he was away in the service in Henry Co., Va. 28 Oct. 1779.

Blair, Robert. Va. —. He was in Continental service. His wife, Sarah Blair, was furnished 1 barrel of corn and 50 pounds of pork in Frederick Co., Va. on 2 Aug. 1780.

Blair, Samuel. Pa. —. He was awarded a $40 gratuity and a $40 annuity in Northumberland County 28 Feb. 1822.

Blair, Samuel. Va. Sgt. He enlisted under Capt. Thomas Bowyer in 1777 in the 12th Va. Regiment for three years or the duration of the war. He died in 1778. His widow, Florence Blair, had three helpless children on 10 Apr. 1788 in Botetourt County. She was pensioned on 9 June 1788 at the rate of £10 per annum. She lived in Jefferson County. Tennessee from 1819 to 1830.

Blair, Thomas. Pa. Lt. He was in Philadelphia County 22 Jan. 1788. He was in the 5th Battalion of Foot in the Cumberland County militia under Capt. Henry Taylor and was wounded in the shoulder by a musket ball in a skirmish with the enemy at Gulph Mills 11 Dec. 1777. He lost the use of his right arm. He was attended by Dr. Richard Brownson who was surgeon in the 3ʳᵈ Battalion. He took out several bones. Thomas Tarbell swore that he saw Blair after he was wounded. Col. William Chambers also attested to his service. He was 33 years old. He was on the 1813 pension list. He died in 1814.

Blair, William. Va. Pvt. He served in the state militia. He was being pensioned 31 Mar. 1783. He was continued at the rate of £10 per annum on 24 June 1788. He was from Randolph Co.

Blair, William R. —. —. Congress denied his claim for relief 1 Aug. 1850.

Blaisdell, Daniel. Me. —. He died 4 Feb. 1829 at Phippsburg. His widow was Phebe Howard of Mexico, Maine. She was paid $50 under the resolve of 1836.

Blake, Ebenezer. Mass. —. He served in the 4ᵗʰ Regiment and was from Stoddard, N.H. He was paid $20.

Blake, Eleazer. Mass. Sgt. He served in the 4ᵗʰ Regiment and was paid $20.

Blake, James. Mass. Pvt. He served in Crane's Regiment and resided at Charleston. His widow, Margra Rogers, was paid $50.

Blake, John. —. —. He served as an officer in the army. He was pensioned under the act of 1818 but stricken under the act of 1820. His son was George Blake. He had a broken arm and a wife aged 70. Congress restored his pension 1 Mar. 1832.

Blake, John. Me. —. He drowned 14 July 1806. His widow was Jane Blake from Brunswick. She was paid $50 under the resolve of 1836.

Blake, John. Md. Pvt. He was pensioned at the rate of half-pay of a private on 1 Mar. 1826. His widow, Patsy Blake, was pensioned at the same rate in Worcester County on 7 Mar. 1834.

Blake, John. Pa. —. He was awarded $100 in Philadelphia County on 3 Feb. 1824.

Blake, Robert. Va. —. He served in the militia and was absent in Georgia. His widow was granted support in Mecklenburg Co., Va. 11 May 1779.

Blake, William. Pa. Sgt. He applied 26 May 1817. He served in the 8ᵗʰ Regiment.

Blake, Willing. Me. —. He was from Warren. He was paid $50 under the resolve of 1836.

Blakely, David. Pa. —. He was awarded a $40 gratuity in Northampton Co., Pa. 7 Apr. 1830.

Blakely, George. Pa. Pvt. He applied in Washington County 4 Apr. 1809. He enlisted in the rifle company of Capt. Moses McClain in the 6ᵗʰ Pa. Regiment on 22 Jan. 1776. He went to Canada and was in the battle of Three Rivers under Gen. Thompson. He later enlisted in the company of Capt. Hupps or Upps and was attached to Col. Hartley's Regiment. In 1777 he was transferred to Capt. McDowell's Company and was discharged in 1781. He was in the battle of Paoli where he received three stabs by bayonet in his body and several wounds in his head by a musket. He was a prisoner. He was granted a gratuity of $40 and an annuity of $40. He died 31 June 1818. He also appeared as George Blackely.

Blakeney, —. —. —. His widow, Mary Blakeney, sought an increase in her pension. Congress denied her claim 10 June 1854..

Blakeney, Abel. —. —. He was a pensioned and was late of Baltimore. His widow, Mary Blakeney, had her application refused by Congress 14 Mar. 1848. She had married the veteran in 1805.

Blakeney, Dionysius. S.C. —. He was from Lexington District in 1791.

Blakeney, Gabriel. Pa. Lt. He was awarded a $80 gratuity and a $80 annuity in Washington County on 10 Feb. 1817. He was dead by Feb. 1828.

Blakeney, John. S.C. —. He was wounded at Sumter's surprise. He was paid 6 Dec. 1785 and was from York District. His pension was revoked in 1795 because he was in fact wounded as a prisoner of the Americans. He also appeared as John Blackney.

Blakeney, William. Pa. —. He lived in Beaver County 6 Feb. 1811 and was awarded $300.

Blakesle, Abel. —. —. He died in 1833. Congress rejected the claim for a pension from his widow, Mary Blakesle, on 1 Mar. 1845. She married too late to be qualified.

Blakey, William. Va. —. He applied 25 Sep. 1796.

Blaksley, Enos. Conn. Pvt. He served in Col. Huntington's Regiment and in the 4th Regiment under Col. Webb. He was wounded in his back by a bayonet of a fellow soldier who, while behind him fell, having his bayonet fixed. He had infirmity and was a cripple, being cut for the stone in 1782 in hospital. He lived in North Haven, Conn. in 1792. He enlisted 5 June 1777 for the war and was discharged in 1783. He also appeared as Enos Blacksley. He was granted a full pension 20 Apr. 1796. He was reported dead on the 1813 pension list.

Blaksley, Obed.—. Pvt. He served in Col. Sheldon's Regiment He was wounded in his left wrist by a stroke of a cutlass and a fall from his horse in May 1779 at Durham and Poundridge. Several pieces of bone had to be removed. He resided at Watertown, Conn. in 1796. He enlisted 9 Mar. 1777 for three years and was discharged 1 Mar. 1780.

Blanck, Peter. Pa. —. He was awarded a $40 gratuity and a $40 annuity in Columbia County 31 Mar. 1836. He was 84 years old in 1840. He died 13 Dec. 1840.

Blanchard, Amos. Mass. Musician. He served in the 10th Regiment and was from Lynn. He was paid $50.

Blanchard, Francis. Mass. —. He served in the 3rd Regiment and was paid $20.

Blanchard, Jeremiah. Mass. —. Matross. He served in Revere's Regiment and was from Newburyport. He was paid $50.

Blanchard, Joseph. Pa. —. He applied at Ballston Springs, N.Y. 10 July 1818. He enlisted in Oct. 1777 at the forks of the Delaware in Capt. Samuel Craig's Company in the 1st Pa. Regiment under Col. James Chambers for three years. He was discharged at Little York in 1780.

Blanchard, Nathaniel. Mass. Pvt. He served in the 13th Regiment and was from Dunstable. He was paid $50.

Blanchard, Simeon. Mass. Pvt. He served at the Castle and was from Plainfield. His widow, Leah Blanchard, was paid $50.

Blanchard, William. Conn. Pvt. He served in the militia in the new levies in 1776 under Capt. William Belcher and Lt. Col. Jonathan Latimer. He was dangerously wounded in his shoulder and breast near Westchester by the falling of a tree. He was aged 63 and a resident of Windham Co., Conn. when he was pensioned 22 Feb. 1787. He was a carpenter by trade. He was on the 1795 pension list.

Blanchard, William. Mass. Pvt. He served in the 10th Regiment and was from Boston. He died in 1791. His widow, Elizabeth Blanchard, was paid $50.

Blanchard, William. N.H. Pvt. He transferred to Worcester County, Mass. 4 Sep. 1816.

Blaney, John. Del. Pvt. He was pensioned in 1783. He was on the 1791 pension list.

Blank, George. Va. Pvt. He was pensioned.

Blankenship, George. Va. —. His mother, Mary Blankenship, and her three children were granted 2 ½ bushels of corn and 150 pounds of bacon in Chesterfield Co., Va. on 3 Mar. 1780 while he was away in Continental service.

Blankenship, Henry. Va. Pvt. He enlisted in Bedford Co., Va. in 1779 or 1780 under Capt. John Rogers in Continental Service. He marched to Illinois and was placed under the command of Col. George Rogers Clark. He served two years. He did not prove that he was in the Continental Army, and Col. Clark's Regiment was not on Continental establishment. He was granted relief by Congress 20 Dec. 1831.

Blanks, David. Va. Sgt. He served in the artillery under Capt. Lawrence House. He was accidentally wounded in his right hand while getting timbers for gun carriages. He was awarded a £30 gratuity and half-pay of an artificer for three years on 22 Oct. 1778. He was discharged due to his hands being injured by a cannon. He applied 12 Sep. 1792.

Blanton, Burwell. N.C. —. He served under Col. John Earle in the militia. He died 14 May 1861 at 99 years of age. His widow was Mary Blanton. They were married 13 Oct. 1833. She was allowed a land warrant for three months of service in 1812. Congress did not allow her a pension 9 Apr. 1894.

Blasdell, Henry. Mass. Pvt. He served in the 2nd Regiment and was from Charlestown. His widow, Mary Blasdell, was paid $50.

Blatt, Andrew. Pa. Lt. He was pensioned.

Blattenberger, Daniel. Pa. —. His widow, Margaret Blattenberger, was awarded a $40 gratuity and a $40 annuity in Lancaster Co., Pa. 17 Feb. 1827.

Blauvelt, —. —. —. Congress rejected the application for a pension for his son, Isaac Blauvelt, 2 Feb. 1858.

Blauvelt, Abraham. N.Y. Pvt. He served in Lt. Col. Cooper's militia in Capt. Eckorson's Company. He was wounded by a bayonet in his breast and by a ball in his left thigh in Oct. 1778 at Orangetown. He lived in Orange Co., N.Y. in 1794. He was granted a full pension 20 Apr. 1796.

Bledsoe, Berryman. S.C. —. He, Capt. Starling , Capt. Turner, and Capt. James Butler were killed by Maj.William Cunningham and his party. His widow, Amelia Bledsoe, was paid 24 Feb. 1785. She was from Edgefield District. There was one child in 1791. She was pensioned on 13 Dec. 1815 and allowed her arrearage from 1785 to date on 13 Dec. 1815. Her brother-in-law was Barkley Bledsoe. She also appeared as Milly Bledsoe.

Bledsoe, George. N.C. Pvt. He was granted a full pension 20 Apr. 1796. He was pensioned in 1807. He was on the pension list of 1813. He died in Montgomery County 1 July 1831.

Bledsoe, George. Ga. Sgt. He served in the Georgia Dragoons. He was wounded in his left leg by a musket ball on 19 Apr. 1779. He lived in Franklin Co., N.C. in 1795.

Bleeker, Leonard. N.Y. Capt. He was pensioned under the act of 1828 at the rate of $40 per month. At the close of the war he received a commission of brevet major on 30 Sep. 1783 and considered himself entitled to the highest pay of a captain. A captain of artillery was entitled to $50 per month. Congress rejected his claim 19 Jan. 1836.

Blever, John. Md. Pvt. He lived in Frederick County and was pensioned 4 Mar. 1789.

Blevin, James. R.I. Forage Master. He received a contusion in his right leg while removing hay from the island of Prudence to the mainland in 1779 by order of Col. C. Greene. He lived in Newport, R.I. in 1794.

Blevin, Samuel. R.I. Deputy Forage-master. He was in Col. C. Greene's Brigade. He was hurt by a fall from a horse at East Greenwich, R.I. in Apr. 1779 while removing hay. He lived in Westerly, R.I. in 1792.

Blew, David. Pa. Pvt. He served in the 1st Regiment of Levies under Wayne. He was pensioned 6 Sep. 1792. He transferred to Virginia. He was on the 1800 and 1813 pension lists. He later transferred to Kentucky.

Blie, John Christian. N.Y. Pvt. He served under Capt. Parson and Col. Goose VanSchaick and was slain 23 July 1781. His widow, Dorothy Blie, received a half-pay pension.

Blimline, Charles. —. —. He was one of the soldiers from Ansbach who deserted from the British and joined the American forces. He was receiving a pension in 1807.

Blintzinger, George Michael. Pa. —. He was granted a $40 gratuity in York Co., Pa. 25 June 1839 for his Revolutionary service.

Bliss, Elijah. Mass. Pvt. He had a tumor on the right side of the scrotum due to an external blow or injury. He resided in Mass. in 1796. He served in the 7th Regiment and later lived in Vermont. He was paid $20. *Vide* also Frederick Wolf.

Bliss, Samuel. Mass. Sgt. He served in the 16th Regiment and was from Rehoboth. His widow, Rebecca Carpenter, was paid $50.

Bliss, Samuel. —. —. He enlisted in 1776 for one year and served under Col. Andrew Ward and Capt. James Stedman. He was pensioned after the war but struck from the roll because of the value of his real estate. He sold his land to Charles Bliss for $2,000 to pay off his debts. He lived in Columbia, Tolland Co., Conn. Congress granted him relief on 10 Jan. 1832.

Blizard, John. S.C. —. He was a soldier about 1779 or 1780 and came home on furlough. He had been a prisoner but had been retaken by the Americans. He returned to the service leaving his wife and two children. He died in camp. His widow, Celia Blizard, was 80 years old when she applied from Fairfield District on 21 Nov. 1840.

Blodget, Elijah. Conn. —. He was wounded in 1781 near New London. He served under Capt. Amasa Loomis, Lt. Williams, and Col. McClellan. He did not show that he was wounded in the line of duty, and he produced no certificates from two physicians as required. On 23 Dec. 1844 Congress approved his claim by accepting that he was wounded by ball in his shin bone of his left leg on the line of duty below the light house in New London. He had been lame for fifty years. He was approved for $4 per month from 1 Jan. 1833. He also appeared as Elisha Blodget.

Blodget, Jonas. Mass. Pvt. He served in the 4th Mass. Regiment under Col. Henry Jackson and Capt. Caleb Clap. He was pensioned at the rate of half-pay of a soldier from 10 Apr. 1783 on 17 June 1784. In 1786 he was 28 years old. He was disabled by swelling in his right knee. He transferred from Middlesex Co., Mass. to N.H. He was on the 1813 pension list.

Blood, Caleb. Mass. Pvt. He served in the 15th Regiment and was from Groton. His widow, Mary Ann Blood, was paid $50.

Blood, Francis. N.H. Pvt. He served in Griswold's Regiment. He was pensioned at the rate of $5 per month from 16 Dec. 1806. He was pensioned 4 Oct. 1808 in Merrimack Co., N.H. He was on the 1813 pension list.

Blood, Moses. Mass. —. He was from Pepperell. He was paid $50.

Bloom, Solomon. Mass. —. He served in Vose's Regiment and was paid $20.

Bloomfield, Thomas. —. —. He was pensioned in Mar. 1830 by special act of Congress. His widow, Ann Bloomfield, who had married him during the war, sought the benefits of the law of 1836. Congress granted her a pension on 16 Feb. 1837 from his date of death.

Blose, —. Pa. —. His widow, Elizabeth Blose, received a $40 gratuity and a $40 annuity in Northampton County 16 June 1836.

Bloser, Peter. Pa. —. He received a $40 gratuity and a $40 annuity in Cumberland County 15 June 1836. He was dead by Jan. 1840.

Bloss, Henry. Pa. —. He was awarded a $40 gratuity in Northampton Co., Pa. 1 Mar. 1833 and a $40 gratuity and a $40 annuity 1 Apr. 1834.

Blount, John. —. —. His widow, Sarah Blount, proved three months of service and obtained a land warrant. She sought a pension but failed to prove six months of service. Congress rejected her claim 5 May 1856.

Bloxom, Charles. Va. Pvt. He died in the service. His widow, Comfort Bloxom, was allowed 30 shillings per month for herself and her child 26 Nov. 1777. His widow applied from Accomack County on 30 Nov. 1790 and was continued at the rate of £8 per annum. He was also known as Stewart Bloxom. He served in the 9th Virginia Regiment. She also appeared as Comfort Blonton.

Bloxom, Scarbrough. Va. —. He applied from Norfolk County on 13 Apr. 1819. He served 17 months as a midshipman on the row galley, *Accomac*, and retired in ill health. He was pensioned at the rate of $80 per annum and was granted $60 immediate relief on 3 Mar. 1819.

Bluer, James. Md. Pvt. He was pensioned in Frederick County 4 Mar. 1789. He was pensioned at the rate of half-pay of a private in Frederick County on 10 Mar. 1832. He also appeared as James Blewer.

Blume, John. S.C. —. He was from Winton. There were children in 1791.

Blundell, —. Va. —. His father, Thomas Blundell, was furnished support 27 Apr. 1779 in Westmoreland County.

Blunt, John. Mass. Capt. He served in Col. Hitchcock's Regiment and was wounded on Long Island 27 Aug. 1776. He was also wounded at the landing at Majorbigwaduce in Aug. 1779 when he was a captain in Gen. Lovell's corps. He was wounded in his right shoulder and in his right arm. His right arm was rendered in great measure useless. On 30 Oct. 1781 he was pensioned at the rate of one-quarter pay of a captain from 6 Sep. 1780. He was 50 years o l d in 1787. He died 18 May 1804.

Blythe, Benjamin. Pa. —. He was paid $200 for his donation tract 3 Apr. 1829. He was from Adams Co., Pa. Ezra Blythe received the money.

Blythe, Samuel. Pa. Capt. He was paid $375 for his donation land in Franklin Co., Pa. 7 Apr. 1828. He was from Franklin County and served in the Rangers. He was awarded a $60 gratuity and a $60 annuity 25 Mar. 1825.

Boal, George F.. Pa. —. He was granted relief 1 July 1841. He also appeared as George F. Boul.

Board, Cornelius D. N.J. —. He was pensioned in Passaic County 2 Mar. 1841 at the rate of $60 per annum.

Boardman, Elijah. Conn. Sgt. He served in Col. S. Webb's Regiment. He was severely wounded by a stick of wood falling on him when assisting in building a hut in Mar.1782. He resided in Wethersfield, Conn. in 1792. He enlisted 22 Apr. 1777 for three years and was promoted 20 Nov. 1777. He was granted one-third of a pension 20 Apr. 1796.

Boardman, Moses. Conn. Pvt. He served under Col. S. B. Webb. He was disabled by rheumatism. He resided in Bristol, Conn. in 1792. He enlisted 22 Apr. 1777 and was invalided 5 Apr. 1781.

Boardman, Seth. Conn. Pvt. He was enrolled by Lt. Stephen Gould in Col Thaddeus Cook's Regiment on 19 Sep. 1777. He was wounded at Bemis Heights and lost his thumb. He was a shoemaker. He was pensioned 24 Dec. 1777. He lived in Hartford Co., Conn. He was on the 1813 pension list.

Boardman, Seth. Pa. Pvt. He was on the 1791 pension roll. He transferred to N.H. in or after Sep. 1798.

Boardman, Thomas. Mass. Corp. He served in Capt. Benjamin Curtis' Company under Col. Moses Little. He lost many bones from his skull and the use of his right hand. He was wounded in thirteen parts of his frame. He was pensioned at the rate of half-pay from 31 Jan. 1777 on 24 June 1777. He was 32 years old in 1788.

Boardman, William. Mass. —. He served in the 1ˢᵗ Regiment and was from Milton. He was paid $20.

Boaz, James. Pa. —. He was awarded a $40 gratuity in Bedford Co., Pa. 12 Apr. 1828.

Boaz, James. Me. —. He was from Portland. He was paid $50 under the resolve of 1836.

Boaze, John. Va. —. His wife, Catharine Boaze, was granted relief in May 1777, £15 on 11 Dec. 1777 and £60.10 on 9 Oct. 1778 in Lunenburg Co., Va.

Bobbitt, William. S.C. —. He applied from York District 20 Nov. 1821. He was wounded at Guilford, N.C. He had lived in S.C. twenty-four years and had an aged wife and large family. He was confined to bed. Spell Kimbrell proved that he was wounded but his affidavit was not in the file. He also appeared as William Boblet. The claim was rejected.

Bobo, Solomon. S.C. He was from Pendleton District 1831. He was paid his annuity as late as 2 June 1834.

Bobst, Michael. Pa. Maj. He was from Lehigh County. He was also a veteran of the French and Indian War in 1758-59.

Bock, George. Pa. Pvt. He was pensioned under the act of 1832 at the rate of $40 per annum. His pension was suspended. He has served twelve tours of militia service as a substitute from Lehigh County. He was rejected 20 June 1848.

Boden, James. Pa. Pvt. He served in Capt. Joab Houston's Company of Foot under Col. Johnson in the militia. He lived in Burlington Co., N.J. from 1797. He was on the 1813 pension list and died 4 Mar. 1828.

Bodfish, —. —. —. His widow, Abigail Bodfish, had her petition for a pension by a special act of Congress rejected because she married subsequent 1 Jan. 1794.

Bodine, Frederick. Pa. —. He served in Capt. Calhoun's Company under Col. Hunter. He was awarded a $40 gratuity in Lycoming Co., Pa. 3 Mar. 1829, in Niagara Co., N.Y. 17 Jan. 1831, in Lycoming Co., Pa. 1 Mar. 1832, and 21 Mar. 1832. He was awarded a $40 gratuity and a $40 annuity in Niagara Co., New York 17 Mar. 1835.

Bodle, Abraham. Pa. —. He was granted a $40 gratuity and a $40 annuity in Westmoreland County 1 Mar. 1811. He served in Capt. Boyd's Company of Rangers and was wounded in his right thigh at Frankstown in pursuit of Indians.

Bodle, Alexander. Pa. —. He was pensioned 1 Mar. 1813 by the Court of Enquiry.

Bodley, Thomas. Pa. —. He was awarded a $40 gratuity in Chester Co., Pa. 14 Apr. 1828 and 23 Mar. 1829. He was 81 years old in 1840.

Bodwell, Ebenezer. Mass. Corp. He transferred to Maine 4 Mar. 1817.

Boeler, George. Pa. —. He was granted relief 21 Jan. 1814. He died in Apr. 1822.

Bogan, —. Va. —. His mother, Jane Bogan, was granted £15 support in Frederick Co., Va. on 1 June 1779.

Bogardus, Lewis. N.Y. Sgt. His wife, Anna Bogardus, was granted assistance 29 June 1779 while her husband was away in the service.

Bogart, Gilbert. N.Y. —. He enlisted in Col. Schaick's Regiment and served to June 1779 when he was taken prisoner by the Indians. He married about the end of the war and had two daughters, Catharine Bogart and Elizabeth Bogart. His only heir was his daughter Catherine Bogart who married Zacharias Flageler. She received his 200 acres of bounty land 9 Apr. 1804.

Bogart, Nicholas N.. N.Y. Surgeon's Mate. He served to the end of the war. Congress rejected the claim from his daughter, Catherine VanRensselaer of Albany County, on 28 March 1850 because there was no evidence accompanying her petition.

Bogart, Tunis. N.C. —. He served in Capt. Fenner's 10ᵗʰ N.C. Regiment and died about the close of the war. He left one son, William Bogart. He was in Warren County, Ky. in 1820.

Boger, Christian. Pa. —. He received a gratuity in Lehigh County 5 Feb. 1836.

Bogge, John. N.Y. Pvt. He also appeared as John Bogue. He was on the 1813 pension list.

Boggs, Aaron. S.C. Lt. He served as a volunteer under Capt. Wallis and Col. Neil. He was in a tour against the Cherokee at Snow Camps on Rabuns Creek where Cunningham was routed. He later served under Gen. Sumter in Capt. Hannah's Company. He was in several skirmishes at Congaree Fort, the mouth of Fishing Creek, and at Wright's Bluff where he lost his horse worth about $60, his saddle, accouterments, and clothes. He served upwards of four years. In his last three month tour he used his wagon and team from Charleston to Edisto, Orangeburg &c. He was upwards of 75 years old and his wife, Elizabeth Boggs, was about 65 years old when he applied 15 Nov. 1825. He was pensioned 6 Dec. 1825. He was paid as late as 1832.

Boggs, Daniel. Pa. —. He applied at Germantown, Pa. 16 May 1819. In the spring of 1777 he enlisted under Capt. Irish in Col. Gurney's 6th Regiment of Infantry for one year. He was discharged at Carlisle. William Vanhorn, aged 65, was a fellow soldier.

Boggs, John. N.C. Pvt. He served in the Continental Army from 15 July 1776 to July 1778. He married in Orange County while he was in the service. His widow, Eve Boggs, stated that she was married 8 May 1776 on one occasion. On another occasion she stated that she married 8 May 1781 after the battle of Guilford. She lived in Davidson County. She had the testimony of two individuals who were at the wedding. Congress acknowledged that there was no doubt that she was his widow even though she was mistaken about the date. She was granted a pension 19 July 1848.

Boggs, William. Pa. —. He was awarded a $40 gratuity and a $40 annuity in Franklin Co., Pa. 15 Apr. 1835. He also appeared as William Boogs. He died 22 June 1841.

Bogle, Archibald. N.C. Sgt. He served under Capt. Allen. He died in the service and left a son, Robert Bogle.

Bogs, Samuel. Me. —. He died 1 Oct. 1834. His widow, Susanna Bogs, was from Warren. She was paid $50 under the resolve of 1836.

Bohannon, —. Va. —. His wife, Margaret Bohannon, was provided necessaries in Lunenburg Co., Va. in May 1777 and 11 Dec. 1777.

Boice, William. Mass.. —. He was from Milton. He was paid $20.

Bole, Peter. Pa. Pvt. He was in Dauphin County on 26 June 1786. He served in the Lancaster County militia in Capt. James Collier's Company in Col. Elder's Battalion. He was wounded at Fort Muncy in Northumberland County on 20 Aug. 1778. His was wounded in his right thigh, his right leg was broken, and he was scalped and otherwise wounded in his head by a tomahawk. He was 27 years old. He was dead by Sep. 1791.

Boley, —. Va. —. His wife, Elizabeth Boley, was granted financial support in Nov. 1777 in Fauquier Co., Va.

Bolling, John. Va. —. His wife, Elizabeth Bolling, was granted £5 support while he was away in Continental service in Berkeley County 17 Mar. 1778. She received 100 pounds of pork and 3 barrels of corn on 22 Nov. 1780. He also appeared as John Bowland. There were three children.

Bollinger, Emanuel. Pa. Pvt. He and Valentine Weirick were in Capt. Matthew Smith's Company in the1st Pa. Regiment and marched from Lancaster County to Boston and on to Quebec under Benedict Arnold. They had to support themselves for seven months without compensation. He was granted $40 in Dauphin County 27 Mar. 1812.

Bolon, Antoine Marie. Va. Interpreter. His wife was Margaret. The couple were interpreters to the

Virginia troops at Post Vincennes. Gabriel Bolon, Amable Bolon, and the other heirs sought relief. They sought confirmation of the 400 acre grant at which they claimed for their parents' service. Congress rejected the claim 27 Mar. 1810.

Bolton, David. Me. —. He died 4 Feb. 1828. His widow was Hannah Bolton from Augusta. She was paid $50 under the resolve of 1836.

Bolton, John. Md. Pvt. He was pensioned at the rate of half-pay of a private on 2 Jan. 1812 in Hardy Co., Va.

Bolton, John. Mass. —. He served in the 2nd Regiment and was paid $20.

Bolton, Richard. Va. Pvt. He lived in Hardy County on 8 Oct. 1787.

Boltz, John J.. N.Y. —. His family was granted relief during the war.

Boltzley, Jacob. Pa. —. He enlisted 1 Aug. 1780 in the militia and served seven months. He applied from Monongalia County, Virginia.

Bomgardner, William. Md. Pvt. He was pensioned at the rate of half-pay of a private in Washington County 16 Feb. 1821. His widow, Margaret Bomgardner, was pensioned at the same rate on 2 Mar. 1827.

Bond, John. Md. Sgt. He was pensioned at the rate of half-pay of a sergeant in Hampshire County, Virginia 1 Mar. 1826.

Bond, Moses. S.C. Capt. His widow, Usley Bond, was allowed an annuity 17 Oct. 1786 and was from Chester.

Bond, Thomas. Pa. Pvt. He was in Philadelphia County on 14 Nov. 1785. He was in Capt. Deprey's Company of Infantry in General Pulaski's Legion. He was wounded in the belly at Egg Harbor in 1778. He was 46 years old. His wife, Ann Bond, applied for his pension when he did not return from Maryland where he had gone to get some money coming to him. He had returned and she did not know what had happened to him. He did in fact return and collected his pension. He died 5 Nov. 1790.

Bond, William. Mass. Col. He was commissioned in the 25th Regiment of Foot 1 Jan. 1776 and died at Ticonderoga on 31 Aug. 1776. His widow, Lucy Bond, and nine children sought his seven years' half-pay in 1791. His half-pay was to be paid to her legal representative 30 June 1834.

Bone, James. S.C. —. He was pensioned from Williamsburgh on 7 Dec. 1825. He served under Daniel Horry and was at Sullivan's Island in June 1776. In 1778 and 1779 he served under Capt. John Alston and Gen. Pulaski. After the fall of Charleston in 1780, he joined Gen. Francis Marion. He was in action at Jacksonborough, Stono, fork of Black River with a party of Tories where he was wounded by buck shot, lower bridge opposing Col. Watson, Camden, and Tidimons old field. He was between 67 and 70 years and had a wife of the same age. He died 1 Jan. 1834. His administrator, William J. Bone, was paid $50 on 8 Dec. 1818. Sarah Bone, his widow, applied 10 Nov. 1838 at the age of 73 years.

Bonham, William. Pa. —. He was in Northumberland County 24 Nov. 1797.

Bonnel, Paul. Pa. —. His children were paid $200 for their father's donation land 1 Apr. 1830. The money was to be paid to Dr. Daniel Milliken in Hamilton Co., Ohio.

Bonnell, John. N.J. —. He entered the service in May 1777 under Capt. Stephen Chandler and Col. Samuel Potter. He guarded the shore line opposite Staten Island to July 1781. He was in the state troops in 1781 under Capt. Henry Van Blorcom and Col. Seely at Morristown. He was at Dobb's Ferry, Connecticut Farms, and Springfield. His next tour was in the militia under Capt. Littell in the artillery to the close of the war. He was born 21 Apr. 1761. He was allowed a pension for eighteen months by Congress 31 Jan. 1844.

Bonnell, Joseph. N.J. Pvt. He was drafted in the militia under Col. Samuel Potter and Capt. Stephen Chandler in May 1777. He guarded the shore opposite Staten Island to July 1781 when he enlisted in the state troops for three months under Capt. Henry Van Blorcom and Col. Seely at Morristown, N.J. He served one month at Dobb's Ferry under Gen. Elias Dayton. He was in battle at Connecticut Farms and Springfield. He was under Capt. Heniman at Springfield in the taking of the baggage of Col. Fox. He next served three months in the militia under Capt. Littell in the artillery to the close of the war. He was born 21 Apr. 1761. He lived in Elizabeth, Essex Co., N.J. He was pensioned for one year of service on 12 Apr. 1842 and for eighteen months of service 31 Jan. 1844.

Bonner, Thomas. Pa. —. He served under Capt. Orbison in the 5th Battalion of the York County Associators. He resided in Adams County.

Bonney, Alexander. Va. Pvt. In 1779 he marched to Charleston, S.C. and continued to Camden under Lt. Col. Wallace. The wheel of a wagon ran over his right leg at Charleston. He was aged *ca.* 60 years old on 23 July 1787 when he applied from Henrico County. Col. William Heth and Major William Lewis were his officers. He was continued at the rate of £10 per annum on 30 July 1787. He also appeared as Alexander Bonnell and Alexander Bawney. He was on the 1813 pension list.

Bonnicks, —. Pa. —. His widow, Catherine Bonnicks, was awarded a $40 gratuity and a $40 annuity in York Co., Pa. 7 May 1832.

Bonny, John. N.Y. —. He enlisted for nine months in May 1782 under Col. Marinus Willet and served all but two weeks. Congress granted him relief 15 Mar. 1832.

Bonsall, Benjamin. Pa. —. He received a $40 gratuity and a $40 annuity in 1841 in Perry County. His widow, Catherine Bonsall, received a $40 annuity in Perry County 18 Mar. 1852.

Bonsall, Evan. Pa. —. His widow, Charlotte Bonsall, applied 22 Feb. 1816. He was a volunteer in Capt. Serrill's Company in Delaware County. They were married by John L. Reason, J.P.

Booker, Lewis. —. —, He received his commutation and, by deducting same, half-pay for life.

Booker, Richard. Va. Pvt. His wife, Sarah Booker, and her three children were furnished a barrel of corn and 50 pounds of bacon 12 June 1780. They were paid £237 on 11 Dec. 1780. He served in the 3rd Va. Regiment and died at Petersburg. His widow applied from Mecklenburg County in Sep. 1788 at which time she had three small children.

Boomer, Ephraim. Mass. Pvt. He served in the 3rd Regiment and was from Fall River. He was paid $50.

Boon, Hawkins. Pa. Capt. He died in the service 29 July 1779 leaving a widow, Jane Boon, who remained such for more than seven years. She married secondly Philip Fortenbaugh. She received a $60 gratuity and a $60 annuity in Dauphin County 19 Jan. 1825. Her second husband died in 1821. Congress rejected her claim for seven years' half-pay but later reversed itself. The half-pay due the widow was granted to her heirs 23 June 1840 by Congress. He also appeared as Hawkins Boone.

Boon, Ralph. Pa. —. He was granted relief in Fayette County 18 Apr. 1843. His name may have been Ralph Roon.

Boone, —. S.C. —. His widow, Sarah Boone, had three children in 1791.

Boone, Elisha. N.C. —. He enlisted for nine months in May 1778 under Capt. Isaac Horne in the 10th Regiment. He next served under Capt. John Baker. He re-enlisted and was in South Carolina under Capt. Tilman Dixon and Col. Loony. His third tour was in 1781 for twelve months under Capt. Dixon. He was at Eutaw Springs. He next took a militiaman's place for six months. He served to the end of the war. He had a wife Aysley and children Eliza aged 2, Anderson aged 7, and Josiah aged 4 when he applied in Stokes County 21 Apr. 1825.

Boone, John. Md. Lt. He was pensioned in Charles County on 7 Jan. 1812 at the rate of $125 per annum. He was subsequently pensioned at the rate of half-pay of a lieutenant in lieu of the previous amount on 23 Jan. 1816. He applied for a federal pension in 1828 but was rejected because he did not prove that he served to the end of the war. He reapplied in 1829 and received commutation certificates amounting to five years' full pay instead of half-pay for life. He was not put on the pension roll. In 1832 he stated he entered in 1776 in Capt. Brock's Company. In 1777 he entered the Continental Army and served to 14 Mar. 1780 when he was appointed ensign in the Maryland line. He was promoted to lieutenant in Aug. 1780 and served to 1 Jan. 1782. On 21 Mar. 1836 he was pensioned for one year and 5 months' service at the level of lieutenant.

Booth, Isaiah. —. —. His widow, Polly Booth of Madison Co., N.Y. received the arrearage of his pension from 4 Mar. 1848 to 3 Feb. 1853 as authorized by Congress 15 Dec. 1857.

Booth, James. Va. Capt. He served in a company of Rangers or Indian Spies for 13 months. His son-in-law and daughter, Alexander and Bathsheba McCleland, received $130 on 4 Apr. 1838. Similar warrants went to the other children, James Booth, John Booth, and Sarah Evans.

Booth, John. Pa. —. He applied in Lancaster County 19 Apr. 1813.

Booth, John. S.C. —. He served in the 3rd South Carolina Regiment and was killed 6 June 1779. His widow, Mary Booth, was paid an annuity 23 Dec. 1785. There were three children in 1791.

Booth, John. S.C. —. He served under Gen. Francis Marion and was thrice wounded in the abdomen at Black Mingo, in the thigh at Scotts Lake or Watson's Ford, and in the leg at Congaree. He was upwards of 70 years old. He was pensioned in Marion District 30 Nov. 1827. He was paid as late as 1833.

Booth, Matthew. S.C. —. He resided in Marlboro District in 1791.

Booth, Thomas. Va. Pvt. He enlisted on 15 Feb. 1776 in the 5th Va. Regiment. He was wounded in the middle finger of his right hand and his forefingers were much confined in motion. He served under Capt. Gross Scruggs. He applied from Franklin County on 28 Oct. 1786. He was on the 1813 pension list.

Booth, William. Mass. —. He served in Crane's Regiment. He was paid $20.

Booz, Jacob. Pa. —. He was awarded a $40 gratuity in Montgomery Co., Pa. 22 Apr. 1829, 14 Mar. 1831, and 1 Mar. 1833.

Boraliace, Amable. —. —. He had half-pay for life.

Borckert, Christian. Pa. —. He was awarded a $40 gratuity and a $40 annuity in Berks Co., Pa. 6 Apr. 1833. He died 12 June 1840. He also appeared as Christian Barchart. His executor was Solomon Barchart.

Bordner, Jacob. Pa. —. He was awarded a $40 gratuity and a $40 annuity in Berks County 31 Mar. 1836. He was dead by Dec. 1837.

Boreman, John. —. —. He married Anna Park, the widow of Jonathan Park. She was unable to prove that he had served six months so Congress rejected her petition for a pension. She was the widow Anna Yarrington.

Borral, Jacob. Pa. —. He was awarded a $40 gratuity and a $40 annuity in Berks County 29 Mar. 1824.

Boss, Edward. Pa. —. He was pensioned.

Bossard, Jacob. Pa. —. He was awarded a $40 gratuity and a $40 annuity in Northampton Co., Pa.

6 Apr. 1833.

Bost, Johannes. N.Y. Pvt. He served under Col. Samuel Clyde in the Montgomery County militia and was slain 11 Oct. 1780. His widow received a half-pay pension.

Bostwick, Oliver. Conn. Ens. He served in Col. Beebe's Regiment. He was wounded in his left shoulder by a musket ball on 2 July 1780 at Kingstreet, New York. He resided in New Milford, Conn. in 1794. He was on the 1813 pension list. He died 30 July 1815.

Bosworth, Daniel. Me. —. He was from Dennysville. He was paid $50 under the resolve of 1836.

Bosworth, Ichabod. Mass. —. He served in the 6th Regiment and was paid $20.

Bosworth, Samuel. —. Pvt. He served under Capt. Billings in the militia for six months and one year in the state troops. He was at several places in Rhode Island. He was drafted in 1776 for the expedition to Long Island and went off in whaleboats. They took a body of refugees. He was wounded in his thigh while on guard in Sullivan's expedition. He was discharged at Saratoga in 1783. He married in Mar. 1782. He died in 1827. His widow was Tabitha Bosworth. Her brother was Allen Wardwell and her brother-in-law was Jonathan Fales. Congress granted his widow relief 20 Jan. 1837.

Bosworth, Samuel. Va. —. He enlisted in 1780 under Capt. Overton in the 3rd Regiment and then under Capt. Lamb and Col. Gaskings. He was at the siege of York. His service was for eighteen months. He was in the militia under Capt. Threadlile at Wilmington, N.C. for three months. He also served three months under Capt. Goodrich and Col. Watson in Virginia. Congress accepted eighteenth months of his service but ruled that the remaining six months were not proved. He applied 11 May 1836.

Bottomer, Jacob. Pa. —. He applied in 30 Apr. 1813 in Washington County. He served under Lt. Bernard Hubley in Col. Hand's 2nd Regiment upwards of four years. He was ordered by Gen. Washington to prevent the enemy from crossing Maidenhead Bridge in New Jersey. The enemy forced a retreat, and he was wounded in the streets of Trenton on the left side of his body by a musket ball which broke two ribs. He fell down at the bridge and was run over by at least 54 soldiers. He managed to cross the bridge and was ordered to the care of the surgeon. Conrad Hill saw him wounded at Trenton. His captain was Peter Boyer. His sons supported him. He was awarded 200 acres of donation land 7 Apr. 1807. He died 26 Aug. 1818. He also appeared as Jacob Bottimore and Jacob Baltimore. Compare with Jacob Buttmore.

Botts, Joseph. Md. Pvt. He was pensioned 4 Mar. 1789. He died in 1801.

Bouce, Henry. N.Y. Pvt. He served in Col. Willett's Regiment. He was wounded in the side in an engagement with the Indians in June 1781 at Tourlock. He resided at Watervliet, Albany Co., N.Y. in 1794. He was on the 1813 pension list.

Bouck, Abraham. —. —. He was taken prisoner by the Indians and held in captivity for two years. Congress rejected his application for a pension because he was not a soldier at the time of his capture on 27 Mar. 1846.

Boude, Samuel. Pa. Lt. He was killed at Brandywine 11 Sep. 1777.

Bough, John. Pa. —. His widow, Elizabeth Bough, was awarded a $40 gratuity in Lancaster, Pa. 7 Mar. 1829 and 7 Apr. 1830. She was awarded a $40 gratuity and a $40 annuity in Lancaster Co., Pa. 14 Apr. 1834. She died 11 Oct. 1845.

Boughner, John. Pa. —. He received a $40 gratuity in Centre County 27 Apr. 1852. He was a soldier in the Revolutionary and Indian Wars. He was granted a $40 annuity 27 Apr. 1852. He died 8 Oct. 1858.

Boughner, Sebastian. N.J. —. He was pensioned in Hunterdon County 2 Mar. 1842 at the rate of $60 per annum.

Boughter, Mathias. Pa. —. He served under Capt. Edward Sewell and Lt. William Henderson. He was from Berks County 6 Mar. 1818.

Boughum, Paul. Del. Sgt. He also appeared as Paul Boughman. He was on the 1813 pension list.

Boulware, Elias. Va. —. His wife, Ann Boulware, and five children were furnished £30 in Essex Co., Va. on 17 Aug. 1779. She was furnished 3 barrels of corn and 150 pounds of meat on 15 May 1780 for herself and three children.

Boulware, Samuel. Va. —. His child, Davis Boulware, was furnished £12 per annum while the father was away in Continental service in Essex Co., Va. on 19 Apr. 1779.

Bourke, William. Mass. Pvt. He was disabled by the loss of his right thumb and wounds. He was pensioned 1 Sep. 1782 and resided in Plymouth, Mass. in 1788.

Boush, Goodrich. Va. Capt. He served in the state navy as the captain of an armed vessel and died in the service. His widow, Mary Boush, received three years' half-pay of on 24 Dec. 1790 and half-pay annually for seven years on 24 Dec. 1791. She applied from Norfolk on 1 Jan. 1791. There were four children.. Her pension was continued for life on 20 Dec. 1796. She died 3 Jan. 1805.

Boush, Robert. —. Ens. His commutation was paid 26 Apr. 1791. He may have been the one of the name who was killed at Savannah 9 Oct. 1779.

Bouton, Daniel. Conn. Capt. He served in the 9th Conn. Militia. He was wounded in the shoulder when he came to the aid of Brig. Gen. David Waterbury at Compo in Fairfield Bounds on 30 May 1781. He lived at Stamford, Conn. and was 48 yeas old when he was pensioned 24 Nov. 1788. He was on the 1813 pension list. He died 12 Feb. 1821 in Fairfield Co., Conn.

Bovie, Nicholas. N.Y. Pvt. He served in Capt. Oston's Company in the 2nd N.Y. Regiment under Col. Peter Gansevoort. He was wounded in his left arm and scalped. He was 29 years old in 1786. He lived in Montgomery Co., N.Y. on 6 June 1789. He was on the 1813 pension list. He also appeared as Nicholas Bovier.

Bowden, Amos. Me. —. He died 20 Dec. 1820. His widow, Lucy Bowden, was from Castine. She was paid $50 under the resolve of 1836.

Bowden, John. S.C. —. He served aboard the *South Carolina* under Commodore Alexander Gillon. His administratrix, Mary Bowden, was granted his compensation 18 Nov. 1808.

Bowden, Theodore. Me. He was from York and was paid $50 under the resolve of 1836.

Bowditch, —. Va. —. His wife, Eve Bowditch, was granted financial support in Fauquier Co., Va. in July 1779.

Bowen, Archibald. S.C. —. His application was rejected in 1828.

Bowen, Benjamin. S.C. —. He was pensioned in Anderson District 23 Nov. 1829.

Bowen, Jehu. Md. —. He was wounded at Germantown.

Bowen, John. Md. Lt. He was pensioned in Nov. 1788.

Bowen, Nathaniel. Mass. Sgt. He served in the Artillery under Col. John Crane and Capt. Eustis. He was disabled by a musket ball shot through his right hand. He was 63 years old and resided in Kittery, Me. He was pensioned 1 Sep. 1782. He was on the 1813 pension list.

Bowen, Stephen. Mass. Pvt. He served in the 4th Regiment and was from Rehoboth. His widow, Priscilla Bowen, was paid $50.

Bowen, Sterling. S.C. —. He served two or three years and was at Eutaw Springs and Camden. He had been dead 17 years. Susan Bowen, his widow, stated that they were married about 58 years ago. She was 78 years old. She had a widowed daughter with two children. He was from Virginia and joined with William Mize for a reward in the state draught. They served under Col. William Moore. Her application from Abbeville District in Nov. 1839 was rejected.

Bowen, Timothy. N.Y. Pvt. He served under Col. John Harper in Capt. John Shemerhorn's Company. He also served in Capt. Walter Vroman's Company. He was taken prisoner along with Capt. Walter Vroman on 23 Oct. 1780 near Oneida. He was made a prisoner in Montreal, Canada. He was wounded in his body by the muzzle of a musket when trying to escape. His hands were tied behind his back; they were frost bitten. He lost the upper joints of six of his fingers. He also had a hernia. He was 45 years old in 1786. He lived in Phillipstown, East District, Rensslearwyck, Albany County in 1785 and on 22 Apr. 1789. His name also appeared as Timothy Brown. He was on the 1813 pension list.

Bower, —. Pa. —. His widow, Jane Bower, was awarded a $40 gratuity and a $40 annuity in Lancaster County 29 Mar. 1824.

Bower, Adam. Pa. Maj. He was from Somerset County and served in the militia. He died about 1813. His widow, Sophia Elizabeth Bowers, was in Somerset County 25 Jan. 1814. They were married before the war. He also appeared as Adam Bowers.

Bower, Benjamin. S.C. —. He served six years. His captain was Arthur F------. He fought at Guilford. He was paid for the Cherokee Expedition and nothing else. His wife was upwards of 64 years of age. Philip Evans, John Wilson, and Andrew Hughes served with him. He was paid as late as 1834.

Bower, David. Pa. Commissary of Provisions. He was awarded a $40 gratuity and a $40 annuity in Lancaster County 14 Jan.1823. He died later that year.

Bower, Jacob. Pa. —. He was granted relief in Mifflin County 15 Apr. 1834. He died 16 Feb. 1842.

Bower, Jacob. Pa. Capt. He applied in Berks County 8 Feb. 1814. He was granted an annuity equal to one-quarter of his pay on 8 Mar. 1815. He died 3 Aug. 1818. His widow, Rebecca Bower, was granted a $60 gratuity and a $60 annuity in Lebanon County 29 Mar. 1823. She died 12 June 1843.

Bower, John Brittain. Va. —. He enlisted in Southampton County under Capt. Edwards and Col. Blount. He was at Guilford Court House under Capt. Hart and was at Yorktown in 1781 at the surrender of Cornwallis. He had a wife and five children. His youngest was born 15 Dec. 1823. He was 65 years old when he applied in Orange Co., N.C. on 22 Sep. 1824.

Bower, John Jacob. Pa. —. He received a $40 gratuity and a $40 annuity. He was dead by Dec. 1827.

Bower, John. Conn. —. He was pensioned 2 July 1778.

Bowers, Baalam. Va. —. He enlisted in 1780 in Capt. Overton's Company in the 3rd Virginia Regiment on Continental establishment. He went south and was under Capt. Lamb and Col. Gaskins until the siege of York and surrender of Cornwallis. He served eighteen months. In 1777 he was in the militia under Capt. Threadlile at Wilmington, N.C. for three months. He returned to Virginia and marched under Capt. Goodrich to James River. He served three months under Col. Watson. Congress approved his first eighteen months of service but the other six months could not be approved on 11 May 1836.

Bowers, George. Md. Pvt. He was pensioned at the rate of half-pay of a private on 2 Mar. 1837.

Bowers, Jonathan. Conn. Corp. He served in the 1st Regiment of Militia under Col. Cook. He was wounded by a musket ball passing through his right arm near the shoulder and breaking the bone on 19 Oct. 1777 near Stillwater. He was pensioned 2 July 1778. He resided at Chatham, Conn. in 1792. He was granted half a pension 20 Apr. 1796. He transferred to Washington Co., N.Y. He was on the 1813 pension list.

Bowger, Laban. Pa. Corp. He served in the 4th Regiment. He lost the use of his right hand in the service. He was 39 years old in 1791 on the New Jersey pension roll. He lived in Northampton, Burlington County.

Bowie, John. S.C. Capt. On 17 Dec. 1821 he was paid $4,416 as computation for his Revolutionary service as an officer on Continental establishment in the infantry. He was detached and placed on state service for protection of the frontier of S.C.

Bowker, Ishmael. Mass. Pvt. He served in the 14th Regiment and was from Palmer. He was paid $50.

Bowker, Levi. Me. —. He was from Machias. He was paid $50 under the resolve of 1836.

Bowl, Peter. Pa. —. He served in the 4th Battalion of the Lancaster County militia and went to Northumberland to fight the Indians. He served under Capt. James Collier. He was wounded, his skull was punctured, his leg and thighbones were broken, and he was scalped. He was brought to his father's home in Paxton Township. He was pensioned in Lancaster County 5 Feb. 1779.

Bowland, John. Va. —. His wife, Margaret Bowland, was granted £30 relief in Berkeley County on 17 Nov. 1779.

Bowler, —. Va. —. His father, James Bowler, was granted financial assistance while he was away in the service in Caroline Co., Va. 8 Jan. 1778.

Bowles, John. Va. Pvt. He served in the Va. Line and died in service in 1778. His two children were granted £15 support in York Co., Va. on 16 Nov. 1778. His children were Clara Bowles and Joseph Bowles; they were in York County in 1787. They were put on the roll at the rate of £6 per annum on 22 Nov. 1787. The daughter was *ca.* 20 years of age in 1790. Rebecca Baker was their guardian. Their pension was renewed on 27 Aug. 1791.

Bowles, Jonathan. Mass. Corp. He served in the 11th Regiment and was from Beverly. His widow, Tabitha Bowles, was paid $50.

Bowles, Stephen. Mass. —. He was pensioned.

Bowling, Thomas. Mass. Gunner. He served on the sloop *Tyrancide* and lost his left hand by a swivel gun on 5 July 1777. He was pensioned at the rate of one-third of a gunner from 20 Feb. 1777 on 30 Sep. 1783.

Bowman, Abraham. Va. Lt. Col. He served in the 8th Va. Regiment. from Jan. 1776 to June 1778. He was at the battle of Charleston, S.C. and was in New Jersey and Pennsylvania. His application for half-pay from 1778 was rejected in 1834.

Bowman, Albert. Conn. Pvt. He served in the 5th Conn. Regiment. He was disabled by his sight being impaired and from old age and long service. He was pensioned 3 Nov. 1782. He died in 1807.

Bowman, Charles. Mass. —. He served in the Artillery and was paid $20.

Bowman, Charles. Pa. —. He was awarded a $100 gratuity and a $40 annuity in Philadelphia County on 21 Dec. 1818.

Bowman, Isaac. Va. Lt. He served under Col. George Rogers Clark in the Illinois Regiment. He was wounded four times in his body and limbs by leaden balls from the Chickasaw Indians. He was made a prisoner. The Indians sold him to one Trumbull who took him to New Orleans He was taken to Cuba, Philadelphia, and Virginia. He never resigned. He died 9 Sep. 1824 in Shenandoah Co., Va. His brother was Abraham Bowman. His will named his sons Philip Bowman, Abraham Bowman, Joseph Bowman, and John Bowman; daughters Susanna the wife of William H. Richardson, and Eliza B. the wife of Joseph Fauntleroy; and other children Isaac Bowman, George Bowman, Robert Bowman, Washington Bowman, Mary Bowman, and Rebecca Bowman. He also named his nephew George Brinker. Congress ruled that he had no right to half-pay 7 Dec. 1850. Congress granted his son, Issac Bowman, his father's half-pay 30 June 1854.

Bowman, Michael. Pa. Pvt. He was on the 1813 pension list. He died 4 Sep. 1813.

Bowman, Paul. —. —. He was pensioned.

Bowman, Samuel. Va. —. He was pensioned in 1824 at the rate of $8 per month. He was stricken from the rolls upon fraudulent service. The government filed a suit against him in the U.S. District Court in Western Virginia to recover the pension money. He proved that he was improperly stricken. Counsel moved for a new trial, but the court overruled the motion and rendered judgment. He applied for reinstatement. His name was found on the rolls of Col. Lamb as Samuel Bauman. He died about that time in Marshall Co., Va. His widow, Dorothy Bowman, applied but was denied so she appealed to Congress who approved she should have the money from 1825 to the time of her husband's death on 9 Feb. 1842.

Bowmann, John. N.Y. Pvt. He served under Col. Fisher in the Montgomery County militia and was slain 23 Oct. 1781. His children were John Bowman, Lewis Bowman, Catharine Bowman, and Cornelia Bowman. They received a half-pay pension for seven years..

Bowyer, Laban. N.J. Corp. He was pensioned 4 Mar. 1789.

Box, Daniel. R.I. Brig. Major. His left arm was rendered useless due to a fall from his horse in Dec. 1776 when the army was quartered at Neshamany Ferry in Pennsylvania. He fractured his arm; several pieces of bone had been extracted and the wound was still open. His hand was entirely useless. He served under Gen. Varnum. He applied 23 Feb. 1786 at the age of 51 in 1786. He lived in Providence Co., R.I.

Boyanton, Moses. S.C. —. He had one child in 1791.

Boyce, Thomas. N.Y. Ens. He served under Capt. George Comb and Col. Joseph Drake and later under Capt. James Hammond in the Westchester County militiia. In 1782 he was sent out under Capt. Israel Honeywell. He was overtaken by the enemy and taken prisoner. He was released 6 June 1782. He suffered from two wounds by a cutlass–once in the left side of his neck and other in his left arm. He was pensioned 24 June 1786. He lived in Westchester Co., N.Y. on 5 June 1787. He was on the 1791 pension roll as Thomas Buyce. He was on the 1810 pension list. He died 7 June 1826. He also appeared as Thomas Boyes.

Boyce, William. S.C. —. His widow was Elizabeth Boyce. They were married about the middle of the war and lived in North Carolina until his death in 1805 or 1806. Shortly after their marriage he served three months under Capt. William Kimbrell from N.C., three months under Capt. Samuel Lewis from N.C., and six months under Gen. Francis Marion from South Carolina. He was discharged at Round O. Drury Boyce swore that he had seen the discharge from Gen. Marion as did John F. Coker. His widow removed to South Carolina after his death. She applied in Laurens District 6 Dec. 1845.

Boyce, William. Va. Lt. He served in the 4th Regiment and became supernumerary 30 sep. 1778. Yet, he acted as adjutant at Guilford Court House in 1781 and was at Gates' defeat and the siege of York. His heirs sought his commutation. Congress rejected their claim 3 Mar. 1836.

Boyd, —. —. —. His widow, Rebecca Boyd, sought a pension. Her marriage took place after 1 Jan. 1792 so her application was rejected 30 Mar. 1818. It was again rejected 27 Mar. 1846.

Boyd, —. S.C. —. His widow, Usley Boyd, had one child in 1791.

Boyd, Alexander. Pa. Pvt. He was pensioned.

Boyd, Ebenezer. N.Y. Capt. He served in the Westchester militia under Col. Samuel Drake. His frightened horse threw him, and he hurt his back and hip. He suffered the same fate a second time, and he injured his leg. He lived in Frederickburg, Dutchess Co., N.Y. on 15 Dec. 1788. He was aged [?]7 on 4 June 1788.

Boyd, Francis. Va. Pvt. He served in the 7th Va. Regiment under Maj. William Moseley and was wounded in his left knee at Brandywine on 24 June 1788. He was taken prisoner. He was aged *ca.* 28 on 24 June 1788. He was put on the roll at the rate of £10 per annum on 24 June 1788. He was on the 1813 pension list. He later transferred to Ohio.

Boyd, Frederick. Pa. —. He received an annuity. He was from York County 29 Mar. 1824.

Boyd, Isaac. —. —. He alleged he had been wounded, but the rolls did not sustain his claim. His petition was rejected 12 Apr. 1842.

Boyd, James. —. —. He was pensioned by the special act of 7 July 1838 at the rate of $40 per annum. He died 23 Apr. 1846. His widow, Flora Boyd, had married him 27 July 1789. She was allowed a pension 24 Feb. 1847. She moved from Cecil Co., Md. to Virginia.

Boyd, James. Pa. He served under Capt. Williams in the Chester County militia. He enlisted in Feb. 1777 under Capt. Richard Dobson in the 7th Maryland Regiment. He was at Brandywine, Germantown, Monmouth, White Plains, King's Bridge, and Mud Island when the fort was attacked. In 1779 he was at Three Rivers, N.Y.; in 1780 most of the time in N.J. and Conn. and in 1782 in R.I. He was discharged in 1782 at Trenton. Congress granted him relief 18 Jan. 1838.

Boyd, James. S.C. —. He was killed by the enemy. James Norton was paid for the children on 8 Feb. 1785.

Boyd, James. Va. —. His wife, Elizabeth Boyd, and children were granted assistance in Bedford County 23 Feb. 1778. The order was set aside 23 Mar. 1778.

Boyd, John. Va. —. His wife, Elizabeth Boyd, and three children were furnished £10 support on 13 Oct. 1777 in Louisa Co., Va. His wife and four children were furnished 5 barrels of corn and 250 pounds of pork on 12 June 1780.

Boyd, John. —. —. His widow was Mary Boyd. He could not be identified as her husband so Congress denied her claim for a pension 23 June 1854.

Boyd, John. S.C. —. He served in the 6th Regiment and died in the service. Esther Buchanan was paid for his children 30 Nov. 1785.

Boyd, Robert. Pa. —. He was awarded relief in Mercer County 12 Mar. 1836.

Boyd, Robert. Pa. —. He was awarded relief in Indiana County 14 Feb. 1835.

Boyd, Robert. S.C. —. He died on board a prison ship. His widow, Mary Boyd, was paid 7 May 1785. She was from Abbeville District. She had two children in 1791.

Boyd, Robert. S.C. —. He was wounded in his foot at Rocky Mount in 1780. He was from Chester District in 1811. He died in Mar. 1812, and his arrearage was paid to his administrator, John Boyd.

Boyd, Samuel. N.H. Pvt. He served in Col. Dearborn's Regiment and was an invalid. His constitution was worn out in service. He was discharged 23 Apr. 1782. He was aged 59 in 1787. He also appeared as Samuel Boid. He was from New Boston, N.H.

Boyd, Samuel S.C. —. He was wounded in battle in Newberry District on Broad River. His eye was shot out. After the war he removed to the west. He was pensioned at the rate of $60 per annum for life on 21 Dec. 1822. He lived in Indiana and on 16 Nov. 1825 sought his arrearage. His widow was Isabella Boyd.

Boyd, Thomas. —. —. He was pensioned.

Boyd, William. Pa. —. His widow, Margaret Boyd, was granted relief in Beaver County 19 Mar. 1816.

He was on the 1813 pension list.

Boyd, William. Pa. —. He was awarded a $40 gratuity and a $40 annuity in Chester County 27 Mar. 1837.

Boyd, William. Pa. —. He was awarded a $40 gratuity in Washington Co., Pa. 23 Apr. 1829.

Boyden, Amos. Mass. Pvt. He served in the 3rd Company and was from Orange. He was paid $20.

Boyer, —. Pa. —. His widow, Elizabeth Boyer, was awarded a $40 gratuity and a $40 annuity in Berks County 1 Apr. 1836.

Boyer, Christian. Pa. —. He was awarded a $40 gratuity in Lehigh County 5 Feb. 1836.

Boyer, Jacob. Pa. —. He was from Dauphin County.

Boyer, Frederick. Pa. —. He was awarded a $40 gratuity and a $40 annuity in York County 29 Mar. 1824. He died 4 Dec. 1840.

Boyer, Michael. Md. Capt. He was pensioned at the rate of half-pay of a captain on 27 Jan. 1816.

Boyers, Samuel. Pa. —. He was awarded a $40 gratuity in Mercer County 31 Mar. 1836.

Boyet, Samuel. S.C. —. There were children in 1791.

Boykin, Bias. —. Capt. His widow was Sarah Boykin who died after she had applied for a pension but before she received it. He was a refugee from Georgia to North Carolina where he was a good soldier. He received bounty land from Georgia. His son, John Boykin, sought bounty land, but Congress rejected his claim 14 Mar. 185-. [His name was Tobias Boykin.]

Boylan, James. N.J. Pvt. He served in the militia from Apr. 1776 to the fall of 1777 under Capt. Logan, Capt. McCoy, Capt. Van Zuyl, and Capt. Seabon. He was born 4 June 1755 in Barnardstown, Somerset Co., N.J. When he was drafted in Mar. or Apr. in 1776, he served under Capt. Jacob Ten Eyck and Col. Quick. He was later under Col. Meddick. He was on guard duty every third day at Elizabethtown. He stayed one month longer as a substitute for his uncle, James Kerr, who had been drafted but refused since he was a Tory in principle. He was at Newark, Hackensack, and Amboy. He was verbally discharged and was confident he had served more than one year. He enlisted in the fall of 1777 for three years. He was under Sgt. Scott, Capt. McCoy, Lt. Crawford, and Ens. Finley. He was attached to Catteneau's Battalion from Fort Plitt. He spent the summer at Millstone. In the fall of 1779 he was in winter quarters at Middle Brook until he was taken prisoner by the British cavalry in Christmas. He was carried to Brunswick for two months when he was suffered to return home. When he applied in 1832, he was rejected because he had no credible witnesses to prove his claim. He later procured witnesses who proved his service. He was granted a pension for two years' service 23 June 1836. He was born in 1755 in New Jersey.

Boyle, Daniel. Pa. Sgt. He applied from Armstrong County. He enlisted in 1776 in Cumberland County under Capt. William Peoples and served to 1 Jan.1778 in Capt. Matthew Scott's Company in the 2nd Pa. Regiment under Col. Walter Stewart. He was at Germantown and Brandywine. He was 73 years old when he applied. He was pensioned 19 Feb. 1824.

Boyle, James. N.Y. —. Aaron Perkinson of Onondaga, N.Y. was born in the same neighborhood and proved they served together 9 Jan. 1838.

Boyle, John. Pa. Pvt. He transferred to Maryland in or by Mar. 1795. He was on the 1813 pension list.

Boyle, John. Pa. —. His widow, Elizabeth Boyle, received a $40 gratuity and a $40 annuity 2 Apr. 1822.

Boyle, Robert. Pa. —. He was awarded a $40 gratuity and a $40 annuity in Indiana Co., Pa. 16 Feb. 1835.

Boyle, Thomas H. Pa. Maj. He was mortally wounded at Paramus in Dec. 1779 and died shortly thereafter. His wife was Jane Simpson. His heir, his daughter Sarah Withirs, was paid $300 for his donation land on 24 Mar. 1828. She also appeared as Sarah Weathers. She was late of Bullitt Co., Ky. Sarah Weathers received his seven years' half-pay 7 July 1838.

Boyles, Daniel. Del. Pvt. He was on the 1798 roll and on the 1802 pension list but died later that year.

Boyles, Daniel. Md. Pvt. He was paid 1 Dec. 1787. He was on the 1791 pension list. He was from Charles County.

Boyls, John. Pa. Sgt. He was enlisted by Capt. Thomas Campbell in 1777 for the war. He lost his eyesight eight years ago. He was awarded a $40 gratuity and a $40 annuity in Huntingdon County 29 Mar. 1809. One Elizabeth Boyles, widow of John Boyles, received a $40 gratuity and a $40 annuity 2 Apr. 1822.

Boylston, William. Mass. —. He served in the Artificers and was from Tewksbury. He was paid $50.

Boynton, —. Mass. —. He was wounded at the battle of Bunker Hill and died. His widow, Mary Boynton, and children sought a pension 4 Oct. 1775.

Boynton, Daniel. —. —. His widow, Hannah Severance, proved her marriage but failed to prove sufficient service. Congress rejected her claim for a pension 21 May 1846.

Bozworth, Ichabod. Mass. —. He served in the 6th Regiment and was from Bellingham. He was paid $20.

Brabstone, William. Va. —. He served in the 12th Virginia Regiment. His wife, Mary Brabstone, and child were furnished £5 support in Frederick Co., Va. on 1 Sep. 1778, £30 on 7 Sep. 1779, and 150 pounds of pork and three barrels of corn on 1 Oct. 1782. He was placed on the pension roll 5 Jan. 1798 at the rate of $40 per annum and given $40 immediate relief. He was wounded in his shoulder at Brandywine having entered the service in 1776.

Bracco, Bennett. Md. Capt. His heir at law, Bennett Bracco of Talbot County, received $250 in lieu of his 200 acres of bounty land on 28 Mar. 1839.

Brackett, John. Me. —. He was from Harrison. He was paid $50 under the resolve of 1836.

Brackett, William. —. —. He served under Col. Plimney and strained the cords of his right leg. He was lame and had a tumor on the inner side of his right leg. It weighed five pounds. Congress granted him a pension 3 Apr. 1832.

Brackett, William. Mass. —. He served in Crane's Artillery. He was paid $20.

Bracon, William. Pa. —. He was granted relief.

Bradbich, John. N.Y. Capt. He served in the militia under Col. Jacob Klock. He was wounded in his right shoulder by a musket ball on 6 Aug. 1777 at Fort Schuyler. He lived in Palatine, Montgomery Co., N.Y. on 12 May 1789. He was aged 45 in 1786. He also appeared as John Bradpick.

Bradbury, —. N.H. Sgt. He enlisted in the service and died on his return from a march to the Indian country under Gen. Sullivan in 1779. He was also a veteran of the French and Indian War. He left a widow, Sarah Bradbury, and a large family of small children, of Nottingham. She sought relief 10 Feb. 1780.

Bradbury, Daniel. Mass. —. He served in the 1st Regiment and was from York. He was paid $20.

Bradenberg, Baltus. N.Y. Pvt. He served in the militia under Col. Peter Bellinger in Capt. Staining's Company. He was wounded in his left thigh at New Petersburg in 1780. He was aged 42 in 1788. He was from Montgomery County. He was pensioned 21 Apr. 1788. He lived in Herkimer, N.Y. 20 Aug. 1789. He was on the 1813 pension list. He also appeared as Balthus

Briedenbucher and Balthus Brandenburg.

Bradford, —. Va. Pvt. He died in Continental service. His widow, Elizabeth Bradford, resided in Charlotte Co. on 2 Jan. 1786. She also appeared as Elizabeth Brafford. *Vide* also John Brafford.

Bradford, —. Pa. —. His widow, Mary Bradford, was awarded a $40 gratuity and a $40 annuity in Montgomery Co., Pa. 17 Mar. 1835.

Bradford, Alden. —. —. He was an officer and sought half-pay for life on 15 Dec. 1827.

Bradford, Charles Darnell. S.C. Dep. QM Gen. He was born in Maryland and had been a resident of S.C. fifty-five years. He was made a prisoner of war at Gen. Sumter's defeat at Fishing Creek, placed in jail at Camden, and condemned to death. He was reprieved but witnessed the execution of many of his compatriots. He was 83 years old and his wife was Mary Bradford. He applied from Fairfield District 20 Nov. 1818. He was paid as late as 1821.

Bradford, George. R.I. Pvt. His arm became lame by a wound received at the battle of Monmouth on 28 June 1778. He served under Col. Israel Angell. He was aged 28 in 1786. He was on the 1813 pension list. He died 12 May 1823 in Providence Co., R.I.

Bradford, John Lemon. S.C. —. He was pensioned in Fairfield District 23 Nov. 1829 at the age of 68 years. He entered the service at the age of 16. He was at Sumter's defeat at Fishing Creek and made a prisoner with his father by Cornwallis. They were consigned to Camden. He was paroled after savage confinement of four months and rejoined the army. He was at the capture of Fort Congaree under Capt. John Gray in the cavalry. He served to the end of the war. He was paid as late as 1834.

Bradford, Peabody. Me. —. He was from Minot. He was paid $50 under the resolve of 1836.

Bradford, Perez. Mass. Sgt. He served in Capt. William Croel Cotton's Company under Col. Josiah Whitney. He was wounded by a musket ball in his left knee in Rhode Island in 1778. He left thigh was broken. He was pensioned at the rate of one-quarter pay of a sergeant on 15 Mar. 1783. He was 33 years old in 1786. He resided in Plymouth Co., Mass. He was on the 1813 pension list. He was not granted an increase in his pension by petition to Congress 25 June 1818.

Bradford, William. N.H. Lt. He served in Capt. Jason Watt's Company in Col. Cilley's Regiment to 24 Apr. 1778. He was from Amherst. He sought his depreciation pay 14 Oct. 1780.

Bradish, Samuel. Mass. Pvt. He served in Capt. Abraham Wilder's Company under Col. Ephraim Doolittle. He was wounded in the head on the heights of Charlestown on 12 June 1775 and lost his left eye due to a musket ball through his head. He was pensioned at the rate of one-third of his pay from 4 Apr. 1779, the time of his discharge, on 26 Sep. 1782. He was 30 years old in 1786. He transferred to Vermont where he was on the 1813 pension list. He also appeared as Samuel Braddish.

Bradley, Abner. Conn. Sgt. He was wounded by a musket ball which entered his back and broke one of his ribs at Campo in Apr. 1777. He served in the militia. He resided at Watertown, Conn. in 1794. He was granted a half pension 20 Apr. 1796. He was on the 1813 pension list. He died 13 Mar. 1824. He also appeared as Aner [sic] Bradley.

Bradley, Edward. Pa. Sgt. He was in Cumberland County 23 Feb. 1786 and had previously been in Lancaster County. He was wounded in the elbow at Germantown. He was discharged from the Penn. Line in Gen. Hazen's Regiment. He died 7 Feb.1786. His widow was Sarah Bradley.

Bradley, James. N.Y. He was awarded 200 acres of bounty land 13 Apr. 1813.

Bradley, Joseph. —. —. He died in Oct. 1847. His children sought the amount due him at the time of his death. Congress did not grant them relief 27 May 1852 because the evidence was insufficient.

Bradley, Joseph. N.C. —. He was a native of Halifax Co., N.C. and served a three year enlistment as a private. He died en route home after his discharge. His widow, Ruth Bradley, was aged 106 years on 4 July 1860 and resided in Owen Co., Ind.

Bradley, Nathan. Conn. Pvt. He served in Col. Webb's Regiment. He was struck in the heel and leg and badly wounded in the storming of Stony Point in jumping over the abatis. He lived in Fairfield, Conn. in 1794. He enlisted 1 Aug. 1777 for the war and was discharged 24 Apr. 1780. He transferred to New York. He was on the 1813 pension list. He also appeared as Nathaniel Bradley. His pension was $5 per month from 26 Jan. 1808.

Bradley, Richard. Va. —. His wife, Jane Bradley, and family were furnished a barrel of corn in Prince William Co., Va. 1 May 1780.

Bradley, Robert. Pa. Sgt. He was in Philadelphia County on 25 Sep. 1787. He was in the 1st Pa. Regiment and was wounded in his right foot and ankle in the campaign in 1780 near Elizabeth Town, N.J. His leg was ulcerated. He was 56 years old. His wife was Mary Bradley.

Bradley, Thomas Wilson. Pa. —. He was awarded a $40 gratuity and a $40 annuity in Adams County 29 Mar. 1824.

Bradley, William. Pa. Sgt. He was in Cumberland County 26 Oct. 1786. He served in the 4th Pa. Regiment and was wounded in the leg and in the thigh. He removed to Ga. by Mar. 1790. He was on the 1791 pension list.

Bradley, William. Pa. —. He served in the Flying Camp and was taken prisoner at Fort Washington. He was confined on the prison ship, *Jersey*. He was from Allegheny County.

Bradley, William. Va. Sgt. He enlisted a second time on 10 Dec. 1777 for three years in the 7th Va. Regiment and was discharged 10 Dec. 1780 by Col. A. Buford. He was wounded at the defeat of Col. Buford at Waxsaws. He had several cuts on his head, two of which injured his skull. He had a number of wounds on his left hand and lost a finger. He had a severe cut on his wrist and had a fractured rib on his right side. He was aged 36 years and resided in Rockbridge County on 13 June 1786. He was on the 1813 pension list. In Jan. 1816 he received a $60 increase in his pension. He died 5 Feb. 1819.

Bracon, William. Pa. —. He was pensioned.

Bradston, William. Va. —. He entered the service in 1776 and served to the end of the war. He was wounded in the shoulder at Brandywine. He was granted $40 relief and an annual pension of $40 on 5 Jan. 1798. He lived in Wythe County on 5 Jan. 1798. He also appeared as William Brabstone.

Bradstreet, Dudley. Me. Pvt. He served in Col. Francis's Regiment. He was hurt by an unlucky blow on his breast at Ticonderoga in 1777 while at work on a bridge. He was wounded by a musket ball in the jugular artery on 19 Sept. 1777 and was also wounded in his thumb aboard a guard ship at Boston. He was in the Invalids in 1778 and was discharged 14 Dec. 1779. He resided at Portland, Me. in 1792.

Bradt, Henry. N.Y. Pvt. He served under Col. Goose Van Schaick and died in the service in Aug. 1778. His widow, Maria Barbara Bradt, sought his seven years' half-pay in 1781.

Bradt, James. N.Y. —. His widow received his seven years' half-pay in 1782.

Brady, —. Va. —. His wife, Mildred Brady, was granted financial support in Fauquier Co., Va. in Nov. 1777.

Brady, Abner. —. —. He was pensioned in 1796.

Brady, John. —. —. His widow, Roseman Porter, was refused a pension by Congress on 6 Mar. 1850.

Brady, John. Pa. Capt. His heirs were granted his donation land 19 Mar. 1804. He served in the 12th Pa. Regiment under Col. William Cooke. In 1778 he took a leave of absence to assist in defending his family against the Indians. While returning from a scout to a small fort where he had placed his family, he fell. His heirs in Northumberland County were awarded $750 to release their claim to the tract of donation land on 27 Mar. 1819.

Brady, John. Pa. —. He was granted relief in Indiana County 18 Jan. 1838. He was 64 years old in 1840. He was the son of James Brady. He died 25 Sep. 1855.

Brady, John. Va. —. His wife, Catherine Brady, was granted relief on 12 June 1777 and 11 Dec. 1777 in Lunenburg Co., Va.

Brady, Robert. Pa. Sgt. He was pensioned.

Brady, Roger. Pa. Pvt. He was pensioned.

Brady, Samuel. Pa. —. He was in Indiana County 4 Apr. 1809 when he was awarded a $40 gratuity and a $40 annuity.

Brafford, John. Va. —. His wife, Elizabeth Brafford, was furnished 5 barrels of corn in Charlotte County 5 May 1777; 150 pounds of pork, 100 pounds of beef, and 1 peck of salt on 3 Nov. 1777; 1 peck of salt on 4 May 1778; 3 barrels of corn and a peck of salt on 4 July 1778; £4.10 on 5 Oct. 1778; 8 barrels of corn, 500 pounds of pork, and 3 pecks of salt on 2 Nov. 1778; and £143.11 provisions on 3 May 1779. *Vide* also — Bradford.

Bragdon, John. Me. —. He was from New Gloucester. He was paid $50 under the resolve of 1836.

Bragdon, Josiah. Mass. Lt. He died 30 Apr. 1778. His heirs were paid his seven years' half-pay of $1,120.

Bragdon, Warren. Mass. —. He served in the 2nd Regiment. He was paid $20.

Brailler, Emanuel. Pa. —. He was granted relief in Somerset County 5 Apr. 1842.

Braidfoote, John. Va. Chaplain. He died in the service in 1778. His grandchildren sought his seven years' half-pay. They had received his bounty land from Virginia. Congress found that he never left his residence in the neighborhood of Norfolk and was in the state troops. They were due nothing on 19 Jan. 1836 because his service was not Continental.

Brainard, Elijah. Mass. Pvt. He served under Col. Sage. He was on the 1813 pension list. He moved to Warren Co., N.C. where he died 23 May 1828.

Bramen, Benjamin. —. —. He resided in Mass. in 1796. He enlisted 22 Nov. 1776 for the war.

Branan, Thomas. Va. Sgt. He was on the 1785 pension roll.

Branch, Elijah. —. —. He served three years and was pensioned. He married Hannah ----- before 1 Jan. 1794. The Supreme Court of Vermont granted her a divorce in 1811. He died in 1831. Congress denied her a pension 11 Feb. 1846 because her divorce did not entitle her to any benefits as his widow.

Brandon, John. Pa. —. He was awarded a $40 gratuity and a $40 annuity in Indiana County 2 Apr. 1821. He died 27 Dec. 1823.

Brandon, John. S.C. Capt. He was killed by the Indians. His widow, Jane Brandon, was paid 18 Jan. 1785.

Brandon, Richard. S.C. Sgt. He was killed in Aug. 1781. His widow, Agnes Brandon, was paid an annuity 18 Jan. 1785. She had four children on 12 Feb. 1787. There were two children in 1791. She was from Union District. She was also paid an annuity from 1819 to 1834.

Brandon, William. Pa. —. He was awarded a $40 gratuity and a $40 annuity in Butler County 11 Apr. 1825. He served on the frontiers until 1779.

Brandon, William. Va. Pvt. He was disabled in the service. He lost the use of his left side due to a disorder he contracted as an artificer in Continental service. He was being pensioned 9 Dec. 1784. He also appeared as William Brannon.

Brandt, Henry. N.Y. Lt. He served in Col. Cox's Regiment. He had two wounds on his head and under his left eye on 7 Aug. 1777 at the battle of Herkimer. He resided at Cherry Valley, Otsego Co., N.Y. in 1794.

Brandt, Henry. Pa. —. He was pensioned 30 Mar. 1811.

Brandt, Joachim Jacob. Pa. Marine. In moving a cannon, he was struck by an iron bar and wounded in the lower part of the belly which brought on a rupture. It happened in the taking of New Providence in Mar. 1776. He lived in Philadelphia, Pa. in 1794. The arrears of his pension were paid to his administrator 27 Feb. 1795.

Branen, William. Va. Artificer. He lost the use of one side by hard labor and applied for relief 31 May 1783. He also appeared as William Bronan.

Brannon, James. Pa. Pvt. He was in Philadelphia County 19 Dec. 1785. He was wounded in the groin at Block House on Bergen Point in July 1780. He was discharged in Feb. 1783. He was 35 years old. He was on the 1813 pension list. He served in the 2nd Pennsylvania Regiment.

Brannon, John. Pa. Pvt. He served in the 3rd Regiment and was transferred to the Invalids. He was discharged in Feb. 1783. He was from Philadelphia County 14 Nov. 1785 and was 32 years old. He had lost his sight. He was on the 1791 pension roll.

Brannon, John. Pa. —. His heirs in Westmoreland County were granted $300 in lieu of his donation land 28 Mar. 1820.

Branson, John B. Md. Pvt. He was pensioned at the rate of half-pay of a private in St. Mary's County 2 Jan. 1813. His widow, Mary Branson, collected the $12.11 due him at his death and was pensioned at the same rate he was on 3 Mar. 1840.

Brant, Jacob. Pa. Marine. He was granted relief.

Brantley, —. Va. —. His widow, Elizabeth Brantley, was granted support in Southampton County 9 July 1778.

Brashears, Ignatius. Md. Pvt. He was pensioned at the rate of half-pay of a private in Prince George's County on 7 Feb. 1817.

Brasswell, Henry. S.C. —. He was from Marion District in 1838 and was upwards of 80 years of age.

Brawn, Daniel. Mass. Pvt. He served in Col. Edmund Phinney's Regiment. He was wounded by a musket ball which impaired his hearing and injured his understanding in Oct. 1777 at Bemis Heights. He lived in York, Me. in 1794. He was in the militia. He was granted two-thirds of a pension 20 Apr. 1796.

Braxton, James. Va. Pvt. He served in the 3rd Troop of Dragoons. He lived in Henrico County. He was on the 1813 pension list.

Bray, Joseph. Me. —. He was from Anson. He was paid $50 under the resolve of 1836.

Braynan, John. Pa. —. He was from Philadelphia County.

Brechall, Martin. Pa. Pvt. He served in Capt. Seely's Company. He was discharged in June 1783. He was a native of Pennsylvania and was awarded a $40 gratuity and a $40 annuity in Northampton County 11 Mar. 1815. He also appeared as Martin Brechel.

Breech, Thomas. Pa. —. He was pensioned.

Breiner, Philip. Pa. Pvt. He was in Berks County 12 May 1786. He served in Col. Peter Racklein's Regiment of the Northampton County militia. He was in Capt. Hagenbrook's Company and was wounded in battle on Long Island in 1776 in his right wrist by a musket ball. He was aged 40. He was on the 1813 pension list.

Breitigam, John. Pa. —. He was awarded a $40 gratuity and a $40 annuity in Berks Co., Pa. 23 Nov. 1829. His name was also reported as John Breitzgarns.

Breland, Amos. S.C. —. He applied from Beaufort District 25 Sep. 1827. Nathan Johnston swore that he served with him. His application was rejected.

Breneman, —. Pa. —. His widow, Barbara Breneman, received a $40 gratuity and a $40 annuity in York County 24 Mar. 1837. She died 29 June 1841.

Breneman, Benjamin. Pa. —. He was awarded a $40 gratuity and a $40 annuity 1 Mar. 1836. He lived in Baltimore, Md. His residence was at one time York County.

Breneman, Henry. Pa. —. He was awarded $100 in Westmoreland County 14 Mar. 1814.

Brent, George. Va. Lt. He served in the cavalry. His administrator was A. H. Mason of Stafford County. No commutation was due because he was not in Continental Establishment.

Brent, Willoughby. Va. —. He died in Continental service. His widow, Ann Brent, was granted a barrel of corn in Prince William Co., Va. on 1 May 1780.

Bressler, Nicholas. Pa. —. He was awarded a $40 gratuity and a $40 annuity in Centre Co., Pa. 15 Apr. 1835. He was 86 years old in 1840. He died 20 Apr. 1843.

Brevard, Joseph. N.C. —. He served as an officer in the Continental Army from North Carolina from which state he received his bounty land along the Tennessee River. He was an associate judge in South Carolina and was forbidden by state law to quit the state without the permission of the governor. He was in danger of losing his bounty land and needed to travel to Tennessee to attend to the matter. He sought permission from the House to leave the state of South Carolina between May and October.

Brewer, Caleb. N.H. Lt. He was pensioned at half-pay from 3 Nov. 1783.

Brewer, Elijah. Mass. —. He served in the 7th Regiment and was from Northampton. He was paid $20.

Brewer, James. S.C. —. He served in the state dragoons under Lt. Col. Samuel Hammond until 8 Sep. 1781 when he was dangerously wounded at Eutaw Springs in his right arm which limb was useless. He applied from Edgefield District 27 Mar. 1795.

Brewer, Thomas S. Md. Sgt. He was pensioned at the rate of half-pay of a sergeant in Annapolis 30 Dec. 1812. His widow, Susannah Brewer, was pensioned 24 Feb. 1823 at the same rate.

Brewer, William. S.C. —. He served under Gen. Sumter and was wounded 18 Aug. 1780. He was paid 26 Mar. 1785. He was from Kershaw District. There were two children in 1791.

Brewster, Caleb. Pa. Lt. He served in the artillery on an armed boat and was wounded in action against the enemy in Dec. 1782. He was pensioned 5 Dec. 1785. He was on the 1813 pension list in New York. He also appeared as Caleb Breuster.

Brewster, Henry. N.Y. Lt. He served in the Orange County militia in William Allison's Regiment and was wounded by bayonets at Fort Montgomery 6 Oct. 1777. He was in a redoubt under the command of James McClaughrey. He also suffered from a violent bruise on the head from the butt of a firelock. He was also wounded by a bayonet in his right side near the small of his back. He was made a prisoner aboard the *Archer*. He was pensioned 17 Apr. 1786 in Orange County. He was on the 1813 pension list. He died 15 Mar. 1830. He was awarded 200 acres of bounty land 19 June 1812.

Briant, Jacob. N.J. —. He sought assistance 18 June 1781 in Gloucester County.

Brice, —. Md. Lt. His widow, Julianna Brice, was pensioned at the rate of half-pay of a lieutenant in Mar. 1833.

Brice, Daniel. S.C. —. His widow was Rachel Brice. There were two children in 1791.

Brice, Robert. —. Seaman. He served aboard the frigate *Constitution* and was killed in action with the *Guerriere*. His widow, Nancy Brice, married secondly Aaron Bowen who died in 1848. Congress granted her a renewal of her pension 25 Apr. 1854.

Brice, William. Mass. —. He was pensioned.

Brice, William. Md. Capt. He was pensioned at the rate of half-pay of a captain on 30 Dec. 1812.

Bricker, Peter. Pa. Pvt. He applied from Franklin County 26 Dec. 1814. He enlisted in 1776 in the 6th Regiment under Col. North in Capt. William Findley's Company. He was discharged in 1778.

Bridges, Edmund. Me. —. He was from Castine. He was paid $50 under the resolve of 1836.

Bridget, James. Va. Pvt. He was wounded by a musket ball in the leg at the battle of Guilford Court House. It broke the bone. He served three years at the commencement of the war after which he enlisted again under Col. Blewford and Capt. Thomas Bowyer. He was in the 6th Regiment. John Sweet swore that he saw him the morning of the battle of Guilford. He resided in Rockbridge County on 9 June 1808. He was on the 1813 pension list.

Briggs, Abner. Mass. Pvt. He served in the 16th Regiment under Col. Henry Jackson and Nathaniel Jarvis. He was wounded 6 June 1779 at Point Judith, R.I. and lost his right leg. He was pensioned at the rate of half-pay of a soldier from 30 Sep. 1780, the time of his discharge, on 27 June 1781. He lived in Bristol Co., Mass. He was on the 1813 pension list. He also appeared as Abner Brigs. He was paid $50 by the Commonwealth.

Briggs, Adin. Me. —. He died 26 Feb. 1828 at Anson. His widow was Abigail Seavey from Starkes. She was paid $50 under the resolve of 1836.

Briggs, Arnold. Mass. —. He served in the 2nd Regiment and was from Rochester. He was paid $20.

Briggs, Burton. R.I. Pvt. He served under Col. C. Greene. He was disabled by disease. He lived in Coventry, R.I. in 1794.

Briggs, Jacob. R.I. Pvt. He was pensioned in 1788. He lived in Washington Co., R.I. He was on the 1813 pension list.

Briggs, James. Mass. Pvt. He served in the 16th Regiment and was from Dighton. His widow, Sarah Briggs, was paid $50.

Briggs, James. Mass. —. His widow, Sarah Briggs, was paid $50.

Briggs, John. R.I. Sgt. He lived in Providence Co., R.I.

Briggs, Joseph. —. —. He applied 29 Jan. 1797. His application was not approved..

Briggs, Joseph. Va. Eng. He served in the Rangers and was a pensioner in Brooke County 29 June 1796. He removed to Ohio.

Briggs, Richard. S.C. Surgeon First Mate. He served aboard the frigate, *South Carolina*, under Commodore Gillon. He was paid $77.55 on 19 Apr. 1808.

Bright, William. Md. Sgt. He served in the militia and died in the service. His widow, Sarah Bright, was pensioned in 1782 in Frederick County.

Brighton, Andrew. S.C. —. His family was furnished 20 bushels of corn on 2 June 1782 by Capt. J. Waring.

Brim, Henry. Pa. Sgt. He applied from Franklin County on 26 Mar. 1819. He enlisted in 1777 in Capt. Baker's Company under Col. Potter. He was transferred to Capt. Joseph Prowell's Company and was appointed sergeant. He served for nearly three years. He was in the battles of Burlington, Brandywine, Germantown, and Monmouth. He also served three years in Capt. Luis' Company in the Md. Line under the command of Gen. Wayne against the Indians. He was discharged at Green Vale. He died 3 Jan. 1835.

Brimigion, Thomas. Mass. —. He was paid $20.

Brinck, Aaron. N.J. Pvt. He was pensioned 27 Apr. 1810. He was on the 1813 pension list of New York. He lived in Otsego County. He also appeared as Aaron Brink. He later removed to Michigan.

Briner, Frederick, Pa. —. He received a $40 gratuity and a $40 annuity in Montgomery County 18 Feb. 1834.

Briney, Kilian. Pa. —. He was awarded a $40 gratuity in Westmoreland County 5 Feb. 1836. He was in Armstrong County in 1840 and was 73 years old.

Briney, William. Pa. He was pensioned in Westmoreland County 18 Jan. 1838. He died 24 Feb. 1848.

Brinkerhoff, John. Pa. —. He was awarded a $40 gratuity in Adams Co., Pa. Feb. 1834. He was dead by July 1838.

Brinkley, William. N.C. Capt. He served in the 3rd Regiment. The proof was lacking to show that he was entitled to commutation 27 June 1838 so Congress rejected the claim of the heirs.

Brinsfield, William. Md. —. He had ulcers in his left shoulder occasioned by a wound received on a scouting party in Oct. 1777 near Crooked Billet, Pa. He lived in Talbot Co., Md. in 1795.

Brisbin, John. Pa. Capt. He was from Dauphin County. He was commissioned in Mar. 1776 and marched under Col. Arthur St. Clair to Canada. He was wounded in his left leg at Three Rivers in June 1776. He reentered the service that fall under Col. Wood and Gen. Conway. He received a furlough to visit his family in Lancaster County. His wound made him unfit for duty, but he was placed in the Wagon Master and Foraging Departments. His application was not approved on 20 Apr.1796. He also appeared as John Brisban and John Brisben.

Briscoe, —. His widow, Eliza Briscoe, had her petition for a pension rejected by Congress 4 May 1846.

Brison, Daniel. S.C. —. He was pensioned 15 Dec. 1818.

Bristol, Thomas. Conn. Pvt. He served in the militia in 1776 under Col. Thaddeus Cook. He was wounded on 5 July 1779 at New Haven by a musket ball in his left thigh and suffered from a running sore. He was pensioned 14 Sep. 1787 at Cheshire, Conn. at the age of 46 years. He was pensioned at the rate of $5 per month from 22 Oct. 1807. He died in 1809.

Bristow, William. Va. —. He served in Capt. George Nichols' Company and lost the use of his leg. He was granted £20 relief 26 Nov. 1777. His entry included the date of 2 Aug. 1783 and the notation "expired."

Britain, Nathan. Va. —. He died in Continental service. His widow, Elizabeth Britain, and child were furnished support in Frederick Co., Va. on 4 Apr. 1780.

Britenman, —. Pa. —. His widow was Catharine Britenman.

Britt, Edmund. Mass. Pvt. He served in Capt. Abel Holden's Company under Col. Thomas Nixon. He was wounded 19 Sep. 1777 by a musket ball in his right hip. He was pensioned at the rate of half-pay of a soldier in 1785. He was 26 years old in 1786.

Britt, Richard. S.C. —. He was on the 1791 pension list. He served in the 3rd Regiment of the S.C. Continental Line under Lt. James Mayson, Col. Thompson, and Capt. Baker. He enlisted at Orangeburg. He was made a prisoner of war at the fall of Charleston. He was exchanged by Washington in Virginia. His application was rejected in Oct. 1819 since he was entitled to a federal pension.

Britt, Robert. Md. —. He was pensioned.

Brittain, Samuel. Va. —. His wife, Mary Brittain, was granted £5 support in Berkeley County on 21 May 1778 while he was away in Continental service. She had two children. She received

£8 on 20 Apr. 1779.

Britton, Job. N.H. Pvt. He served under Col. Reid. He was wounded in his right shoulder by a musket ball on 17 June 1775 at Bennington. He lived in Westmoreland, N.H. in 1795. He was granted one-third of a pension 20 Apr. 1796.

Britton, Jonathan. Mass. Pvt. He served under Capt. Miller and Col. Vose from 10 Feb. 1778 to 31 Dec. 1779 for 22 months and 11 days. From 1 Jan 1778 to 30 Sept. 1780 he served 9 months under Col. Vose from Lanesboro for a total of 2 years, 7 months, and 11 days. He deserted 30 Sep. 1780 but returned in Jan. 1781. He applied from Otisfield, Cumberland Co., Maine and was pensioned 27 Dec. 1842.

Britton, Joseph. Md. Lt. He was pensioned at the rate of half-pay of a lieutenant in Hawkins Co., Tenn. 19 Jan. 1830. His name was also given as George Britton.

Britton, Joseph. Pa. —. He applied 9 Jan. 1822. He served under Caleb North in Col. Anthony Wayne's Regiment. He served more than a year.

Britton, Samuel. Va. Pvt. He served under Capt. Clough Sheldon in the 1ˢᵗ Regt. and died in Richmond, Virginia. His widow, Mary Britton, was from Philadelphia County, Penn.

Broadhead, Luke. Pa. Capt. He was in Philadelphia County 2 Jan. 1788. He served in the Pennsylvania Rifle Regiment. He was disabled by a wound in his side received in the battle of Long Island 27 Aug. 1776. Col. Samuel Miles attested to his service. He also appeared as Luke Brodhead. His widow, Elizabeth Broadhead, was awarded a $40 gratuity and a $40 annuity in Northhampton County 27 Mar. 1819. He was on the 1813 pension list. She died 17 Dec. 1837.

Broadus, —. Va. —. His wife, Elizabeth Broadus, was granted financial support in Fauquier Co., Va. in June 1778.

Broadus, James. Va. Ens. He enlisted in 1776 as a private and acted as sergeant. He was commissioned ensign in the 2ⁿᵈ Virginia Regiment 7 Jan. 1780 effective from 25 Sep. 1779. He was at Yorktown after which he returned home but never resigned his commission. He served to the end of 1781. His son received his five years' full pay 13 Mar. 1838. His widow, Susannah Broadus, was not entitled to his commutation 6 Mar 1850. He had received 2,666 2/3 acres of bounty land 19 Feb. 1784. He sought his commutation of five years pay. Congress approved the claim 6 Mar. 1850.

Broadus, Robert. Va. —. He was approved under the act of 6 Feb. 1808 at the rate of $40 per annum and given $40 relief.

Broadus, William. Va. Lt. He was from Jefferson County. He received his commutation of full pay for five years in lieu of half-pay for life as a lieutenant of infantry in the Virginia Line on 5 Feb. 1825.

Brock, John. Mass. Gunner. He was wounded at Castle William and was pensioned for one year to 20 Dec. 1778.

Broderick, William. N.J. Sgt. He served in the 3ʳᵈ Regiment and was wounded in the leg. He was 32 years old. He lived at Mansfield. He was on the 1791 pension roll. He was on the 1813 pension list. He removed to Belmont Co., Ohio and died 17 May 1815. He also appeared as William Brodrick.

Brodie, Lodowick. Va. Surgeon. His commutation was paid 14 May 1792.

Brodnox, Thomas. Pa. —. He was awarded a $40 gratuity in Bucks County on 28 Mar. 1814.

Brodock, Bartholomew. N.Y. Pvt. He served in the militia or state troops under Capt. Campbell and Gen. Bellinger for four months. He died upwards of 29 years ago. His wife had died before him. His three lawful heirs had their petition rejected by Congress on 13 Jan. 1846.

Brogan, John. Va. —. His wife, Agnes Brogan, and young child were provided necessaries in Amelia Co., Va. 26 Feb. 1778, 25 June 1778, 25 Feb. 1779, and 28 Feb. 1780.

Brognard, John. —. Sgt. He served in the grenadiers in the allied French troops under Duc de Lauzan from 13 Nov. 1778. He was discharged at Wilmington 1 May 1783. He died at Burlington, N.J. 17 Apr. 1823. He married secondly 27 Feb. 1791. His widow, Mary Brognard, had been denied a pension in Feb. 1847. She proved that Peter Cleer of Baltimore, Md. who had belonged to the same corps had been granted a pension by a special act of Congress. Congress awarded her a pension from 4 Mar. 1852 at the rate of $8 per month on 2 Feb. 1853.

Brohes, William. Pa. Pvt. He was in Philadelphia 13 Mar. 1786. He served in the 9th Pa. Regiment and was wounded in his right leg at White Marsh.

Brokaw, John. N.J. Lt. He served under Capt. Jacob Ten Eyck. He was killed at Germantown 4 Oct. 1777. He was from Somerset County. His widow, Mary Brokaw, remarried four years and one month later William Lane. She was granted a half-pay pension for her widowhood.

Broker, George. Va. —. He was killed in the service. His widow was granted assistance in Loudoun Co., Va. on 14 Apr. 1778.

Bronan, Thomas. Va. Sgt. He received several wounds in the French and Indian and the Revolutionary Wars. He was pensioned 14 June 1784.

Bronson, Isaac. Conn. Surgeon's Mate. He served in the 2nd Regiment of Light Dragoons under Col. Elisha Sheldon from 14 Nov,. 1779. Congress granted his commutation 26 Dec. 1836.

Brook, John. Mass. —. $45 was paid to Maj. John Philips for the use of John Brook for one year's pension ending 20 Dec. 1780 on 16 Apr. 1781.

Brooke, Charles. Pa. —. His place of residence was incorrectly given as Fayette County. The law was corrected to Allegheny County for his residence. It did not indicate in which war he served in the act of 16 Apr. 1840. He was 79 years old in 1840. His widow, Malinda Brooke, of Ohio Township, Allegheny County was granted a $40 gratuity 16 Apr. 1857. He also appeared as Charles Brooks.

Brooke, Edmund. Va. 1st Lt. He served in the 1st Regiment of Virginia Artillery on Continental establishment under Col. Charles Harrison. He was appointed in Feb. 1781 and continued in the service till the siege of Yorktown when he was extremely ill and was compelled to ask for a furlough for a few weeks. He was not due any depreciation of pay since he was not engaged for three years. He was not entitled to commutation since he had not served to the end of the war. He applied 29 Jan. 1787. He was paid his five years' full pay in lieu of half-pay for life 25 May 1832. He had warrant #2541 for 2,666 2/3 acres from Virginia. He also received 200 acres of federal bounty land.

Brooke, Lawrence. —. Surgeon. His heir, Lucy Alexander, sought relief from Congress 20 Apr. 1842. He served on board John Paul Jones' squadron.

Brookhouser, —. Pa. —. His widow, Mary Brookhouser, received a $40 gratuity and a $40 annuity in Crawford County in 1836. She died 22 Dec. 1839.

Brookins, Artemas. Mass. —. He served in the 1st Regiment and was from Lenox. He was paid $20.

Brooks, —. —. —. He was pensioned at the rate of $320 per annum and died Aug. 1838. His widow, Maria M. Brooks, sought a pension which Congress awarded her on 26 May 1842.

Brooks, —. Pa. Sgt. He was pensioned 8 Jan. 1787.

Brooks, —. Va. —. His widow, Sarah Brooks, was put on the pension roll at the rate of £8 per annum on 28 July 1789.

Brooks, —. Va. —. His father, John Brooks, was granted support in Carolina County 12 Aug. 1779.

Brooks, David. —. Lt. He entered the service in 1776 and was taken prisoner at Fort Washington, N.Y. He was exchanged in May 1778. He next served as Assistant Clothier General to the close of the war. The Treasury Department rejected his application for a pension because he was not in the Continental Line at the close of the war. Congress awarded him a pension 6 Feb. 1832. It was retroactive to 3 Mar. 1826 instead of 1 Jan. 1830.

Brooks, Ebenezer. Vt. Pvt. He served under Col. Reed in Capt. Hind's Company. He caught smallpox in the service and lost his right eye in July 1776 at Crown Point. He lived in Windham, Vt. in 1795. He was in the militia.

Brooks, Edward. —. —. He failed to show that he acquired his disability in the service. He was from Marblehead, Mass. Congress rejected his request for a pension 10 Aug. 1842.

Brooks, John. Mass. Col. He served in the 7th Regiment to the end of the war. He was elected governor of the state after the war. His surviving executor, Dudley Hall, sought his commutation pay. Congress rejected the claim on 22 May 1850 since Brooks had claimed it in his own lifetime.

Brooks, John. N.Y. Pvt. He served in Col. Rudolphus Ritzma's Regiment under Capt. Cornelius Hardenburgh. He was disabled by a musket ball in his right arm at White Plains on 28 Oct. He later served in Capt. Abraham Cuddeback's Company under Col. James McClaughery in the Ulster County militia and received three wounds in the same arm above the elbow. He lived in Ulster Co., N.Y. on 16 Apr. 1789. He was aged 31 years on 4 Dec. 1786. Job Rockwell testified that he saw Brooks when he was wounded. He was on the 1813 pension list.

Brooks, John. Pa. 2nd Lt. He was commissioned 9 Jan. 1776 and went to Canada under Gen. Montgomery. He was returned supernumerary as early as 1778. In Apr. 1778 Gen. Horatio Gates appointed him major. He was made assistant commissary of issues in July 1779 and served to July 1781. He held the rank of captain. Congress rejected his petition 8 Feb. 1842.

Brooks, Joseph. S.C. —. There were two children in 1791.

Brooks, Lawrence. Pa. —. He lived in Philadelphia County 9 Jan. 1786. He suffered from divers wounds received in the service. He was 30 years old. On 18 July 1786 his widow drew his pension. He was quartermaster sergeant of the Invalids.

Brooks, Micajah. S.C. & Ga. Pvt. He served as much as two years. He received 160 acres of bounty land from South Carolina. He was nearly 100 years of age. Congress allowed him if alive or his surviving children a pension for $48 per annum from 1 Jan. 1850 on 26 Mar. 1858.

Brooks, Michael. N.Y. Pvt. He served in Capt. Abijah Gilbert's Company under Col. Thomas Thomas. On 24 Dec. 1776 John Brooks, a private in the same company, wounded him by a musket ball through his right leg below the knee. He was 33 years old on 4 Aug. 1787. He was pensioned 13 Nov. 1787. He was a tailor and lived in Salem, Westchester Co., N.Y. on 18 June 1788. He later lived in Greene County. He was on the 1813 pension list.

Brooks, Nathaniel. Mass. —. He served in the 1st Regiment and was from West Springfield. He was paid $20.

Brooks, Reuben. Va. —. His father, John Brooks, was granted £20 support in Caroline Co., Va. 12 Aug. 1779.

Brooks, Thomas. N.Y. Pvt. He served in Col. Van Cortland's Regiment. He was wounded in his right knee by a musket ball on 7 Sep. 1777 at Bemis Heights. He lived in Westchester Co., N.Y. in 1794. He enlisted 2 Jan. 1777 for the war. He was on the rolls in 1782. He was granted three-fourths of a pension 20 Apr. 1796. He was on the 1813 pension list.

Brooks, Thomas. Va. Pvt. He served under Col. Buford and died 3 May 1779. His widow, Mary Brooks, also lost two sons in the service. She and five children resided in Prince Edward County in Nov.

1784. The oldest was 17 years and the youngest 7 years. She was put on the pension roll on 17 Nov. 1788 at the rate of £10 per annum. Administration on her estate was granted 9 Nov. 1829 in Buckingham County to Arthur Conner. She died 16 Oct. 1829.

Brooks, William. Pa. Pvt. He was in Philadelphia County 13 Mar. 1786. He served in the 9th Pa. Regiment. He was wounded at White Marsh in his right leg. He also appeared as William Brols. He was dead by Sep. 1798.

Brougher, Christian. Pa. —. He was born in 1758 in Weisenberg Township, Northampton County, Penn. He was in his twentieth year of age and was a tailor's apprentice when he was drafted into the militia. He served under Capt. Meyer, Col. Brinich, and Gen. Irvin in 1778 and spent two months at Allentown and Farmer's Mills near Germantown. In 1779 he was drafted for the same service and was under Capt. Stahler and Col. Heavener. In 1780 he was again drafted under Capt. Meyer. He was sick and could not go. He followed a week later and had a certificate from his physician. He received pay for the full term when he was discharged. He lived in Hartley Township, Union Co., Pa. when Congress granted him a pension 5 Mar. 1840. He was credited with the few days which he was short in order to qualify due to sickness.

Broughton, John —. —. He was allowed £16 in 1797 and in 1798. He applied in Caswell Co., N.C. in Oct. 1832.

Broughton, William. Va. Sgt.-Maj. He served in the 11th Va. Regiment. At Brandywine he received a bayonet wound through the fleshy part of his arm. It penetrated his thorax thereby damaging his lungs. He lived in Hardy County 1 Jan. 1786 and was aged *ca.* 52 years. He was continued at the rate of £12 per annum on 1 Dec. 1787. He was on the 1791 pension list.

Brower, Jacob. Pa. —. He was awarded a $40 gratuity in Mifflin Co., Pa. 15 Apr. 1834. He applied from Mifflin County 27 Aug. 1838. He was dead by Jan. 1843.

Brown, —. —. —. His widow, Phoebe Brown, produced no testimony to support the facts set forth in her petition for relief so Congress did not approve her request 9 Feb. 1848.

Brown, —. N.Y. —. His widow was granted relief during the war.

Brown, —. Pa. —. His widow, Catherine Brown, was awarded a $40 gratuity and a $40 annuity in Lancaster, Pa. in 1836. She died 24 Oct. 1841.

Brown, —. Pa. —. His widow, Barbara Brown, was awarded a $40 gratuity and a $40 annuity 8 Apr. 1826. She resided in York Co., Pa. She died 2 May 145.

Brown, —. S.C. —. His widow, Betsey Brown, was from Union. There was one child in 1791.

Brown, —. S.C. —. His widow, Betsey Brown, was being pensioned in 1819. She was paid as late as 1829.

Brown, —. S.C. —. His widow, Eliza J. Brown, was from Charleston in 1844. She also appeared as Elizabeth J. Brown and was paid as late as 1845.

Brown, —. Pa. —. His widow, Isabella Brown, was awarded a $40 gratuity and a $40 annuity 8 Apr. 1826. She resided in Perry Co., Pa.

Brown, —. Pa. —. His widow, Mary Brown, was granted a $40 gratuity and $46 annuity in Franklin County 29 Mar. 1823.

Brown, —. Pa. —. His widow, Phebe Brown, received a $40 annuity in Fayette County 8 May 1854.

Brown, —. S.C. —. His widow, Sarah Brown, was designated "not entitled" on the 1791 list.

Brown, —. Va. —. He and his three brothers were in the service in Capt. Boone's Company of militia. Two of them were taken prisoner at Salt Springs. Their mother, Sarah Brown, an ancient widow, sought relief and was granted £30 on 26 Nov. 1778.

Brown, Alexander. Pa. —. He applied from Bedford County 5 Jan. 1811. With him in Canada were

Daniel Bloom, James Porter, Charles Tepper, and Jacob Bowers in 1776. He was wounded. He had eight children. He was awarded a $40 gratuity and a $40 annuity on 31 Mar. 1812.

Brown, Archibald. S.C. —. He sought a pension 28 Nov. 1827. His application was rejected.

Brown, Bazell. Va. Pvt. He served under Col. David Rogers and was wounded on 4 Oct. 1779 by the Indians. He was pensioned 21 Nov. 1785 at the rate of half-pay for his disability and £25 relief. He lived in Ohio Co., Va. on 6 July 1789 and was continued at the rate of £9 per annum on 28 July 1789. He was on the 1813 pension list of Virginia. He later transferred to Pennsylvania from Fayette County.

Brown, Barron. Mass. —. He served in the 4th Regiment and was from Westminister. He was paid $20.

Brown, Charles. Va. Pvt. He enlisted for two years in the 7th Virginia Regiment on Continental establishment under Capt. Joseph Spencer and Col. Woodford. He was discharged at White Marsh Camp, Pennsylvania. Until 1827 he was able to labor when he was attacked by paralysis. He was totally unable to work, in need, and 76 years old. He resided in Hopkins Co., Ky. when he was pensioned 18 Jan. 1830.

Brown, Daniel. N.H. Pvt. He served in Capt. Kimball Carlton's Company in Col. Nichol's Regiment and was wounded at Bennington on 16 Aug. 1777. He was from Westmoreland, N.H. on 20 Aug. 1778.

Brown, Daniel. Pa. Pvt. He transferred to Vermont by Sep. 1793. He was on the 1813 pension list.

Brown, Daniel. S.C. —. He was pensioned on 23 Nov. 1829. He was paid as late as 1830.

Brown, David. Conn. Lt. He served in Capt. Benjamin Green's Company under Col. John Mead in the Fairfield Co., Conn. militia. He was wounded by a musket ball in the lower part of his belly. On 11 Oct. 1786 he was 29 years old. He lived in Salem, Westchester Co., N.Y. in 1788. He was on the 1813 pension list.

Brown, David. Mass. —. He served in the 3rd Regiment. He was paid $20.

Brown, David. N.Y. Ens. He was wounded at Horse Neck 26 Feb. 1779. He was pensioned 5 Dec. 1785. He lived in New York County.

Brown, David. S.C. —. He was paid in 1830, 1831, and 1832.

Brown, Ebenezer. —. Lt. He died in 1844. His widow, Abigail Brown, sought to have his pension continued. Congress denied her claim 20 Feb. 1852.

Brown, Ebenezer. Mass. Pvt. He lived in Middlesex County. He served in the 2nd Regiment. He was paid $20 by the Commonwealth. He was on the 1813 pension list.

Brown, Edward. Conn. Pvt. He was disabled by old age and from being worn out in the service. He was pensioned 4 Jan. 1783. He died in 1801.

Brown, Edward. Mass. —. He served in Crane's Regiment and was paid $20.

Brown, Gabriel. S.C. —. He was killed at Sumter's defeat by Tarleton at the Blackstocks. His widow was paid 18 Jan. 1785. There was a Mary Brown with three children on the 1791 pension list.

Brown, George. N.Y. Pvt. He served under Col. Goose Van Schaick and was slain 25 July 1779. His widow received a half-pay pension.

Brown, George. Va. Pvt. He was wounded in Continental service. He was put on the pension list on 19 June 1784. He was on the 1785 pension roll.

Brown, Henry. Pa. —. He was awarded a $80 gratuity and a $40 annuity in Northampton County from 5 February 1835. He was 85 years old in 1840.

Brown, Jacob. —. —. He was sick and infirm the last thirteen years of his life. He died in Oct. 1845 in his 83rd year. His widow, Mary Brown, of Clarksburg, Mass. was 74 years when she applied for relief. Her step-son, Jacob Brown, was killed in the Mexican War at Fort Brown on the Rio Grande. She was granted relief by Congress 20 Dec. 1847.

Brown, Jacob. Me. —. He died in Dec. 1831. His widow, Rhoda Brown, was from Hiram. She was paid $50 under the resolve of 1836.

Brown, Jacob. Pa. —. He was awarded a $40 gratuity and a $40 annuity in Lancaster County 15 Mar. 1826. He died 27 Nov. 1842.

Brown, James. Mass. Pvt. He served under Capt. Eustis in the 4th Regiment under Col. William Sheppard. He was disabled with palsy and resided in Westfield, Mass. in 1787 at which time he was 54 years old.

Brown, James. Pa. —. He applied in Armstrong County 10 Dec. 1812. He served as a non-commissioned officer in the company of Capt. Alexander Patterson in 1776 in the 12th Pa. Regiment under Col. William Cook until it was reduced. He was then drafted into the 3rd Pa. Regiment under Capt. Thomas Butler and Col. Thomas Craig. He was discharged 1 Apr. 1780.

Brown, James. S.C. —. His annuity in 1787 was £47.2.3.

Brown, James. S.C. —. He served in 1776 under Gen. Williamson and Gen. Lincoln. He was also under Col. Lacy and Col. Niel. He fought at Stono, Rocky Mount, Hanging Rock, and Friday's Ferry. In his 69th year he had a wife and one infant. He was pensioned in Anderson District on 23 Nov. 1828 and was paid as late as 1834.

Brown, James. Va. Pvt. He served in the expedition against the Indians under Capt. James Booth for thirteen months. He was paid $104 on 13 Mar. 1834.

Brown, Jedediah. Conn. Sgt. He enlisted in Dec. 1776. He served under Capt. U. Raymond in the 9th Regiment of militia under Col. Durkee. He was under the command of Capt. Colefax of Gen. Washington's Guards when he was wounded at Kingsbridge by a musket ball in his right arm which disjointed his shoulder. He was wounded in his right hand by the bursting of his musket 19 Feb. 1779. Dr. David Adams, Surgeon of the 4th Conn. Regt., attended him. He was pensioned in Dec. 1787 in Brooklyn, New York. He resided in Norwalk, Ct. in 1792. He was 30 years old. He was granted one-fourth of a pension 20 Apr. 1796. He was on the 1813 pension list.

Brown, Jesse. Me. —. He died 10 Dec. 1831. His widow, Elee Brown, was from Raymond. She was paid $50 under the resolve of 1836.

Brown, John. —. —. He enlisted in Paris, France in the French Army and served to the end of the war. He was wounded at Yorktown. Congress did not grant him a pension 2 Dec. 1818.

Brown, John. —. —. He was wounded in the right hand by a bayonet. He resided in Mass. in 1796.

Brown, John. Conn. Lt. He was on the 1795 pension list.

Brown, John. Del. Pvt. He was born in Ireland, was single, and was wounded in the hip at the battle of Eutaw on 28 Sep. 1781. He was pensioned in 1783.

Brown, John. Md. Sgt. He was pensioned in Washington County in 1786. He was wounded at Camden. He served in the 6th Regiment. He was on the 1813 pension list.

Brown, John. Mass. Sgt. He served in Capt. Seth Washburn's Company under Col. Jonathan Ward. He was wounded at Bunker Hill on 17 June 1775 by a musket ball in his right foot and left thigh. He was pensioned at the rate of 20 shillings per month from 1 Aug. 1776 on 17 Apr. 1777. He was pensioned 27 Sep. 1786 and was 51 years old. He transferred to Pennsylvania in 1803.

Brown, John. Mass. Col. He went to Canada in Feb. 1775 and helped take Fort Ticonderoga in May. He was promoted to major. He was at Montreal and Quebec. In July 1776 the Continental

Congress commissioned him a Lieutenant Colonel. He resigned due to a controversy he had with Benedict Arnold but continued in militia service. He left home in Pittsfield, Mass. for Albany, New York on private business. Col. Ashley prevailed upon him to take command of his regiment on an expedition up the Mohawk River. The force was betrayed by a traitor and ambushed at Stone Arabia where he lost his life 19 Oct. 1780 at the age of 36. He left a widow and children. His only surviving child was Huldah Butler who died 12 Nov. 1857 in Northampton, Mass. at the age of 84. Her widowed daughters, Sarah Whitney and Mary Huggerford, sought relief from Congress on 18 May 1860 and on 4 Mar. 1864.

Brown, John. N.Y. Pvt. He was pensioned.

Brown, John. Pa. Lt. He was in the marines.

Brown, John. Pa. Pvt. He was in York County 31 May 1786. He served in the 7th Pa. Regiment in Capt. Andrew Irwin's Company. He was wounded by a musket ball through both legs at Brandywine on 11 Sep. 1776. He was 36 years old. He served under Lt. Col. David Grier. He was dead by Mar. 1801.

Brown, John. Pa. —. He was awarded a $40 gratuity and a $40 annuity 15 Apr. 1835 in Armstrong County. He was 80 years old in 1840. He died 27 Nov. 1842.

Brown, John. Pa. Sgt.

Brown, John. Pa. Pvt. He served under Capt. Robert Kirkwood in the Delaware Regiment and in the Pennsylvania Associators. He was from Philadelphia.

Brown, John. S.C. —. He was killed 20 Apr. 1781. His widow, Frances Brown, was paid 30 May 1785. She was from Abbeville District.

Brown, John. S.C. —. He was called out at the time of the Snowy Camps under Capt. John Nickson and Col. Richison. He was at Charleston and at the battle of Sullivan's Island under Capt. Adams. In 1778 he was at Purysburg. He returned home for fifteen days and was drafted to go to Augusta under Gen. Williamson for three months. After the fall of Charleston he was under Gen. Sumter and Capt. John McClure at Rocky Mount. He was also in action at Hanging Rock and Carey's Old Field where they took 75 Scots grenadiers and 32 wagons loaded with provisions. He was at Sumter's defeat and made a prisoner of war by a party of Tories. He was carried to Camden and then to Charleston where he was confined in a prison ship with William Hambleton. Due to the interference of some friends he was liberated. After his release he joined Gen. Henderson. He was at Four Holes, Laurance's Ferry on the Santee, and Orangeburgh. He was 77 years old and had two daughters. He was pensioned in Chester District on 17 Dec. 1831.

Brown, John. S.C. —. He enlisted in Capt. Thomas Pinkney's Company in 1776 and served in the 1st S.C. Regiment under Col. Gadsden. He was also in Capt. Cottle's Company and was discharged in 1778. He reenlisted at Boston on the frigate *Dean* and later transferred to the frigate *Alliance*. He served to the end of the war. He was 67 years old. His application bore no date.

Brown, John. S.C. —. He was killed in a skirmish with the enemy in Georgia. His widow, Sarah Brown, was paid 23 Apr. 1779.

Brown, John. Va. —. He served in the 9th Virginia Regiment in Col. Morgan's Riflemen. He was wounded by a ball in his left arm at the battle of Saratoga. He was awarded a £30 gratuity on 20 May 1778.

Brown, Jonathan. N.Y. —. He entered the service at the age of 14 in the spring of 1777 as a drummer boy in the company of his father and continued in the service as a volunteer. In 1778 he was appointed conductor of ordnance at Fishkill, N.Y. and served 20 months. He was 85 years old and a resident of the poor house in Sullivan Co., N.Y. He had been refused a pension in 1845 because he was too young to be deemed a soldier and he did not produce any evidence of his appointment of conductor or ordnance. Congress accepted him as having served twenty months in that capacity in 1779 and 1780 and granted him a pension 24 Feb. 1847. On 27 Mar. 1846 he was 85 years of age and a resident of the poor house in Sullivan Co., N.Y.

Brown, Joseph. Mass. Sgt. He served in Capt. Samuel Patch's Company under Col. William Prescott. He was 33 years old. He was disabled by a musket ball which passed through both thighs. He was pensioned 7 Nov. 1786. He resided in Suffolk Co., Mass. He was on the 1813 pension list.

Brown, Joseph Chandler. S.C. —. His widow, Major Brown, and her four children were pensioned 20 Dec. 1800. She received $21.30 per annum during her widowhood and $9 per child to the age of 12. She was paid as late as 1829.

Brown, Levi. Mass. Corp. He served in the 5th Regiment and was from Brownsfield, Vt. He was paid $20.

Brown, Moody. Me. —. He was from Waterboro. He was paid $50 under the resolve of 1836.

Brown, Nehemiah. N.H. Pvt. He was from Westmoreland in 1785. He was drafted for two months in 1777 in Capt. Kimbal Carleton's Company. On 16 Aug. 1777 at Saratoga he was wounded by a musket ball which passed through his leg which cut off the cord of his leg.

Brown, Nicholas. N.Y. Pvt. He served in Capt. Parsons's Company in Col. Gose Van Schaick's Regiment. He was wounded in his left side on 23 May 1779 at Fort Schuyler. He was discharged 8 June 1783. He lived in Montgomery Co., N.Y. on 13 July 1789. He also appeared as Nicholas Braun. He was on the 1813 pension list.

Brown, Obadiah. N.Y. Pvt. He served in Col. Notton's Rangers. He was wounded in his left arm at Harlem Heights on 6 Sep. 1776. He lived in Cambridge, N.Y. in 1794. He was in the militia. He was on the 1813 pension list.

Brown, Obadiah. N.Y. Pvt. He served in Col. Dudley's Regiment. He was pensioned 4 Mar. 1797. He lived in Washington County.

Brown, Paul. Mass. Pvt. He served in the 7th Regiment under Col. Brooks and Capt. Coburn. He had his right arm broken in the service. He was pensioned at the rate of one-quarter pay of a soldier from 20 June 1783 on 10 June 1785. He was also under Capt. Mainard and Col. Alden.

Brown, Reuben. S.C. —. He was pensioned 6 Dec. 1828. He was paid as late as 1834.

Brown, Richard. N.H. QM. He served in the 2nd N.H. Regiment and was from Unity. His widow, Mary Tuttle, wife of Oliver Tuttle, sought his depreciation pay 14 Nov. 1791. She was his sole administratrix and was from Claremont.

Brown, Richard. Pa. —. He was awarded a $40 gratuity and a $40 annuity in Adams Co., Pa. 27 Feb. 1834.

Brown, Robert. N.C. —. He served a few days under Capt. Martin in the Cavalry. He hired a substitute and perhaps lost his horse. He was rejected in 1838. He was from Lincoln County.

Brown, Robert. S.C. —. He served under Col. Bratton and was at Blackstocks and Briar Creek. He was pensioned in Chester District on 30 Nov. 1827. He was paid as late as 1834.

Brown, Sampson. Mass. Pvt. He served in Col. T. Bigelow's Regiment. He was injured in his right hip by a cannon ball in his thigh bone at the capture of General Burgoyne and was also ruptured. He resided in Boston, Mass. in 1792. He enlisted 20 May 1777 for three years.

Brown, Samuel. —. Pvt. He served from 1781 to Dec. 1783. He was injured in his leg in constructing a fort at West Point. His leg was broken in several places by a rock which fell from the fort.

Two physicians proved that he was two-thirds disabled and was recommended for relief at half-pay 5 Mar. 1840.

Brown, Samuel. Me. —. He was from Oxford. He was paid $50 under the resolve of 1836.

Brown, Samuel. Mass. Pvt. He served in Crane's Regiment. He moved to New York and was paid $20.

Brown, Samuel. Mass. Pvt. He served in the 8th Regiment and lived at Malden. His widow, Lois Brown, was paid $50.

Brown, Samuel. Mass. 2nd Lt. He served in Capt. Ebenezer Bancroft's Company under Col. Ebenezer Bridges and was wounded on the heights of Charlestown in his left shoulder 17 June 1775 by a musket ball. He was discharged 3 Jan. 1777. He was pensioned at the rate of one-third pay of a lieutenant on 27 Oct. 1783. He was 46 years old age in 1786.

Brown, Samuel. Va. —. His wife, Mary Brown, was allowed £10 relief on 18 Nov. 1777 and 10 bushels of corn and 44 pounds of pork on 16 Aug. 1780 in Berkeley County.

Brown, Stark. —. —. He applied for a Revolutionary War pension.

Brown, Thomas. N.J. —. He was born 16 Mar. 1759. He was wounded in his right hand at Brandywine. He was also wounded at Great Bridge between his knee and ankle and by a ball in his right breast which came out his back. He died 3 Dec. 1833. His widow died 3 Feb 1834. He was from Monmouth County.

Brown, Thomas. Pa. —. He was granted relief.

Brown, Thomas. Pa. —. He received a $40 gratuity and a $40 annuity in Rutland, Ohio 1 Apr. 1858.

Brown, Thomas. S.C. —. He was killed in the service. His widow, Mary Brown, was paid 29 Apr. 1785.

Brown, Thomas. Va. Pvt. He enlisted in Feb. 1776 in the 9th Va. Regiment under Capt. Samuel Woodson. He was taken prisoner at Germantown. He suffered from frost bite while confined in the new British jail in Philadelphia, Pa. and lost both of his legs. J. Payne, Ensign, attested to his service. His left leg was greatly enlarged and ulcerated in 1789. He was awarded a £30 gratuity and an annuity of full pay of a private on 9 Oct. 1778. He was 32 years of age in 1789. He was continued at the rate of £12 per annum on 8 Sep. 1789. He applied from Goochland County on 21 Dec. 1785. He lived later in Fluvanna County. He was on the 1813 pension list and died 24 Sep. 1817.

Brown, Valentine. Pa. —. He was awarded a $40 gratuity and a $40 annuity in Berks County 5 Feb. 1836.

Brown, William. Pa. —. He applied in Chester County 27 Dec. 1813. Thomas Minor of Cecil Co., Md. served with him in the militia of Pennsylvania in 1778 and 1779. He wore the uniform of a regular. He was discharged by Col. Walter Stewart. He was arrested as a deserter but produced his discharge and was liberated. He was under Capt. Shannon at McCartney's Station and also under Capt. Craig.

Brown, William. Pa. —. He was awarded a $40 gratuity on 30 Mar. 1812. He died 12 Mar. 1820.

Brown, William. Pa. —. He was granted relief in Mercer County.

Brown, William. Pa. —. He was awarded a $40 gratuity and a $40 annuity in Westmoreland County 12 Feb. 1825.

Brown, William. Pa. —. He was awarded a $40 gratuity and a $40 annuity in Venango Co., Pa. 16 Feb. 1835.

Brown, William. S.C. Maj. He served in the 6th S. C. Regiment and was at Fort Moultrie. He died in Feb. 1782. His son, Elijah Brown, sought the pay due his father and a pension for his sister, Mary Ann Hannah, 2 Nov. 1827. Willey S. Brown joined Elijah Brown in seeking their father's pay. Elijah Brown had eighteen children.

Brown, William. S.C. —. He entered the service at the age of 14. He served in 1781 and 1782 under Gen. Francis Marion and was at the jail Long Bluff on the Pee Dee. He was a blacksmith. He was from Sumter District in 1827. His sons, William D. Brown and Haston Brown, sought his arrearage in 1856. He died 27 July 1832.

Brown, Windsor. Va. Capt. & Paymaster. His commutation pay was issued 13 May 1791.

Browne, John. Pa. 1ˢᵗ Lt. He was wounded in his hip and the small of his back by a large chest giving way out of a wardroom on 28 May 1777 on the frigate *Boston*. He lived in Philadelphia, Pa. in 1794.

Brownfield, Robert. —. —. "He is a democrat of the first water" and knew Vice President R. M. Johnson in Kentucky when he resided there. He resided in Champaign Co., Ill. He served nine months on the western frontier in Pennsylvania. His pension had been suspended. He appeared in court in Vermillion Co., Ill. 4 June 1835 and gave his age as 75. He entered the service as a major in May or June 1780 under Capt. Thomas Campbell, Lt. Armstrong, Lt. Josiah Glass, and Col. Gibson in Cumberland Co., Penn. He served nine months and was discharged at Hanorstown, Penn. In 1836 he was in Warren Co., Indiana. Col. Gibson was the commandant at Fort Pitt. He sought his arrearage but was not approved because he failed to adduce the corroborative testimony for granting same on 25 Apr. 1840.

Browning, —. N.Y. —. Elizabeth Browning was granted relief during the war.

Brownlee, Alexander. —. Ens. He was slain at Guilford, North Carolina. His seven years' half-pay was issued to his widow to be paid to his sole heir, James Brownlee, 9 Feb. 1833.

Brownlee, John. Pa. —. He applied in Washington County 18 Jan. 1811. He enlisted in Capt. Joseph Erwin's Company under Col. Samuel Miles 1 April 1776. He was discharged the last of Jan. 1778 at Valley Forge. He was in the battles of Long Island, White Plains, Brandywine, Trenton, Princeton, Germantown, and Quebec. Andrew Brison was his messmate. Capt. John Marshall stated that Brownlee served 1 year and 10 months. He was 70 years old.

Brownlee, William. Va. QM. He received his commutation.

Brownlow, John. S.C. —. He and his helpless wife were both near 80 years of age. He was literally covered with scars from sword wounds. He was pensioned in Pendleton District on 7 Dec. 1824. He was paid as late as 1831.

Brownson, Abraham. Conn. Sgt. At the age of 17 he entered the service in Apr. 1776 under Capt. Thaddeus Lacy and Col. Heman Swift and was discharged at Mount Independence in Dec. 1776. In Sept. 1777 he entered under Capt. Gideon Brownson and Col. Seth Warner for three years. He served until 1778 when Congress offered $80 bounty to those who would enlist for the war. He was appointed a sergeant. He procured Gideon Benedict as his substitute. He later served under Col. Allen. He was granted a pension 6 Apr. 1830.

Brownson, Gideon. N.H. Maj. He served under Seth Warner. He received thirteen gunshot wounds-- one in his left shoulder at the battle of Bennington in Aug. 1777 and the others on Fourteen Mile Island in Lake George in action with the savages in different parts of his body in July 1779. He was granted a full pension 29 Apr. 1796. He lived in Vt. in 1794. He died in Oct. 1796, and his widow in June 1818. His only surviving child, Mary Everts, sought a pension, but Congress ruled that neither her father nor her mother was entitled one in his or her lifetime so they denied her request 23 Jan. 1860.

Broyles, —. Pa. Maj. He died in Dec. 1779. His seven years' half pay was paid in 1838.

Bruce, Charles. S.C. —. He was paid $60 for a horse lost in the Revolutionary War 18 Dec. 1818.

Bruce, Daniel. Mass. —. He served in the 15th Regiment and was from Marlborough. He was paid $20.

Bruce, Robert. Md. Trooper. He was pensioned at the rate of half-pay of a private in Charles County 27 Jan. 1816. He was pensioned at the rate of half-pay of a trooper retroactively on 7 Feb. 1817.

Bruce, William. Md. Capt. He was pensioned at the rate of half-pay of a captain 30 Nov. 1812.

Bruen, Caleb. —. Spy. He was pensioned by the act of 7 Sep. 1786. He was a double agent.

Bruff, James. Md. Capt. He served in the 4th and 6th Md. Regiments. He was pensioned in 1785 for a disability contracted in the service. He was pensioned at the rate of $20 per month from 17 Aug. 1807. He was on the 1813 pension list. His widow, Margaret Bruff, was pensioned at the rate of half-pay of a captain in Queen Anne's County 20 Jan. 1820.

Bruner, Frederick. Pa. —. He was awarded a $40 gratuity in Montgomery Co., Pa. 6 Mar. 1833 and again on 18 Feb. 1834.

Bruner, Peter. Pa. —. He was awarded a $40 gratuity and a $40 annuity in Lancaster County 28 Mar. 1836. He was 77 years old in 1840. He died 15 Feb. 1852.

Brunot, Felix. Pa. Surgeon. He served in the army and was at Brandywine, Germantown, and the Barges near Annapolis for at least twelve months in the Pennsylvania Line in 1778. He died 23 May 1838. He married 17 Dec. 1789 Elizabeth Kreider. She died 5 Sep. 1845. The administrator of her estate was Hilary Brunot, a son of Dr. Brunot. She had applied for a pension 15 Mar. 1841 in Pittsburgh, Penn. and was upwards of 75 years. The committee ruled that the approved pension should go to the children of the veteran and not to the administrator of the widow's estate on 18 May 1848.

Brunson, Alexander. S.C. —. He was killed by Tories at the close of the war. His daughter, Elizabeth Brunson, married George Polan and had eight children, six of whom were still alive. She married secondly Benjamin Carter on 18 Jan. 1820 by whom she had a child. Benjamin Carter died 9 July 1826 as a pensioner. She married thirdly Jacob Hess. She had a ten year old child and a four year child to maintain. Her third husband was city guard with a salary of $16 per month. She supplemented their income by what she could earn with her needle. She sought the arrearage of her second husband 10 Nov. 1827. She was paid $21.48.

Brunson, Daniel. Pa. —. He served under Capt. John Reed in the Flying Camp and was taken prisoner at Long Island. He applied from Dauphin County.

Brunson, John. Pa. —. He was pensioned.

Brunson, William R. S.C. —. He served under Gen. Francis Marion and was a prisoner of war. He was confined on a British prison ship near Charleston for nine months. Jesse Hilton served with him. He was pensioned in Clarendon County, Sumter District 23 Nov. 1829.

Brush, Robert. —. —. He entered the service in Mar. or Apr. 1776 for nine months under Capt. John Weeks and Col. Josiah Smith. He served until the evacuation of Long Island. He went to Dutchess Co., N.Y. and served five months. In 1777 he volunteered under Lt. Delavan in the militia. He was on the expedition to Peekskill two or three weeks. He also volunteered when the British burned Danbury in the battle of Ridgefield when Gen. Wooster fell. He moved to Norfolk where he guarded the coast, repelled invasions, and carried expresses. He went under Lt. Caleb Brewster to gather military intelligence for at least two months each in 1778, 1779, 1780, and 1781. He did so for a month in 1782 for a total of one year and two months. The committee approved a bill for his relief.

Brush, Thomas. —. Pvt. He was wounded in the ankle at Ridgefield in Apr. 1777. He resided at St. Albans, Vt. in 1796. He was granted one-fourth of a pension 20 Apr. 1796. He was on the 1813 pension list.

Brussels, Joseph. —. Seaman. He served aboard the *Bon Homme Richard* under Capt. John Paul Jones in action on 23 Sep. 1779. He was disabled by loss of limb and was being pensioned by the act of 15 Sep. 1783.

Bruster, —. S.C. —. His widow was Levicy Bruster. There were children in 1791.

Bruton, —. S.C. —. His widow was Izabel Bruton. There were three children in 1791.

Bruton, Joseph. Pa. —. He was wounded in the service. His widow, Bridget Bruton, of Bristol, Pa. was awarded a $40 gratuity and a $20 annuity on 3 Feb. 1812.

Bryan, Charles. Md. Pvt. He was pensioned at the rate of half-pay of a private in Lycoming Co., Pa. 2 Mar. 1827.

Bryan, Charles. Pa. Sgt. He applied 14 Mar. 1815.

Bryan, David. Pa. —. He applied from Allegheny County. He served in the 8th Pa. Regiment in Capt. Riggs' [?Pigget] Company for three years. He served with Sgt. Forbes in New Jersey in 1776 and 1777. In the spring 1778 he was ordered out against the Indians. He helped build Fort McIntosh on the Ohio and Fort Laurence on the Muskingham River. In 1779 he was one of the volunteers who was wounded in the hand in the expedition against the Indians to the Muncy towns.

Bryan, John. S.C. —. He was taken prisoner and confined in Charleston where he died. His widow, Mary Bryan, was paid 28 Jan. 1785.

Bryant, Billy. Mass. Pvt. He served in the 3rd Regiment and was from Rochester. He was paid $50.

Bryant, Charles. Pa. —. He was granted relief.

Bryant, David. Mass. Capt. He died 11 Sep. 1777. His seven years' half-pay of $2,100 was paid to his heirs.

Bryant, Edward. —. —. He was pensioned 4 Jan. 1796.

Bryant, James. Md. Pvt. He was pensioned at the rate of half-pay of a private in Queen Anne's County 4 Mar. 1841.

Bryant, John. Mass. Lt. He served in the artillery under Col. John Crane. He was 38 years old and lost his right arm in the service. He was pensioned 1 Jan. 1789. He resided in Hampden Co., Mass. He was on the 1813 pension list.

Bryant, John. Va. —. His wife, Millener Bryant, was paid £4.11.6 on 5 Jan. 1778. He was discharged on account of bad health. He sought relief in Charlotte Co., Va. on 6 Oct. 1778. He was directed to apply to Dr. Hopkins and Dr. Brodie at their hospital in Mecklenburg Co., Va.

Bryant, Randolph. N.J. Pvt. He served in the 2nd Regiment and was wounded in his left shoulder. He was 39 years old and was from Woolwich. He was on the 1791 pension roll at the rate of $20 per annum. He also appeared as Randolph Briant.

Brydia, David. R.I. Pvt. He served in Col. Herrick's Regiment. He was wounded in the thigh by a musket ball which entered near the knee. He was also wounded by a ball entering the right breast coming out his armpit on 16 Aug. 1777 near Bennington, Vt. He resided at Ferrisburgh, Vt. in 1796. He was granted half a pension 20 Apr. 1796. He was on the 1813 pension list. He died in June 1831.

Bryson, Andrew. Pa. Pvt. He applied from Bucks County. He enlisted in 1776 in Capt. Erwin's Company of riflemen under Col. Samuel Miles. When Miles was taken prisoner at Long Island, Col. Broadhead took command. Later Col. Stewart took command. He also served under Capt.

Cornelius. He was in the battles of Long Island, the taking of the Hessians at Trenton, Brandywine, and Princeton. He served 1 year and 9 months. He died 5 June 1824.

Bryson, Daniel. S.C. —. He was pensioned in South Carolina in 1819. In 1830 he was 74 years old and lived in Macon Co., N.C. On 25 Nov. 1830 he sought a one-time payment of $120 in return for having his name erased from the roll.

Buch, John. Pa. ---. He served several five months tours. He was in Capt. Jacob Livenguth's Rifle Company in the winter of 1781-1782. His widow, Elizabeth Buch, of Lancaster County was granted $40 on 26 Mar. 1808. She also appeared as Elizabeth Pugh.

Buchanan, —. Pa. General. He applied 18 Jan. 1811.

Buchanan, David. Pa. —. He was granted relief 20 Mar. 1838 in Fayette County. He died 13 May 1841.

Buchanan, James. Pa. —. He was granted relief 15 Jan. 1815 in Fayette County.

Buchanan, James. Pa. Sgt. He applied in Butler County 28 June 1817. He served three years in the 12th Pa. Regiment under Capt. Brady and the 3rd Pa. Regiment under Capts. Moore and Buddams from 1776 to Jan. 1780 or 1781. He was ruptured in trying to lift a cannon in the fall of 1777.

Buchanan, James. Va. —. He was killed in the service. His widow, Sarah Buchanan, was allowed 75 pounds of bacon and 10 bushels of wheat for her support of her two children 21 May 1782 in Augusta Co., Va.

Buchanan, John. N.Y. Capt. He was wounded at Tarry Town by a musket ball in his right arm and shoulder in Jan. 1778. He was aged 41 years on 5 Jan. 1783. He lived in New York City, N.Y. on 13 Apr. 1788.

Buchanan, John. Pa. —. He received relief in Butler County from the Board of Inquiry 15 Jan. 1815.

Buchanan, John. —. —. He was an officer and was a resident of South Carolina. He sought to have his bounty land located in Alabama Territory which was much nearer than Ohio. Congress rejected his request 8 Jan. 1819.

Buchanan, Robert. Pa. —. He was in Cumberland County in Dec. 1812. He served three years under Capt. Samuel Kearsly. He was discharged in 1780 and reenlisted. He took a wife after the war. He became blind and lame and could not work. He died 10 Aug. 1825.

Buchanan, Thomas. Pa. Capt. He applied in Cumberland County 13 Jan. 1811. He was in the 1st Pa. Regiment of Riflemen under Col. Thompson and marched to Boston. He resigned in 1779 chiefly due to the depreciation of his pay. He resigned his commission under the belief of an appointment in a corps of horse under Thompson, but Thompson was not exchanged. Matthew McConnel was his lieutenant. His service was proved by Col. Andrew Porter, Capt. Robert Patton, and Capt. Thomas Boude [Major by Brevet]. Col. Francis Johnston, Capt. John Steele, Maj. D. Lenox, and Lt. Col. Thomas Robinson. Superintendent of Military Stores Callender Ivins also confirmed his service. He was at White Plains, the taking of the Hessians at Trenton, Princeton, Brandywine, Paoli, Germantown, and Monmouth.

Buchanan, William. Va. —. He entered the service in 1776 at Richmond, Va. In the same year he was commissioned a lieutenant at Philadelphia. Later he was Adjutant Major or Lieutenant. He was wounded at Guilford and lost his horse. He served to the close of the war. He was at Long Island, Flatbush, Trenton, White Plains, Sandy Hook, Cowpens, Eutaw Springs, and Yorktown. On 10 Apr. 1841 he stated he was in the calvary. There was a man of his name in the infantry. On 3 Feb. 1844 he was 96 years old, poor, and a resident of Georgia. He stated that he entered the service in 1775 for nine months in North Carolina. His evidence was entirely parol. Congress rejected his claim for a pension 19 Feb. 1845.

Buchlup, Charles. Md. Pvt. He served in the 1st Regiment and was wounded at Eutaw Springs. He was pensioned in Frederick County in 1783. He was on the 1813 pension list as Charles Bucklup.

Buchter, Matthias. Pa. —. He was pensioned 9 Mar. 1818.

Buck, —. Va. —. He served under Capt. Thomas Nelson and died in the northward in Feb. 1777. His widow, Jane Buck, was granted an annuity on 7 Jan. 1778 of £ 20.

Buck, Daniel. Mass. Pvt. He served in Capt. David Wheeler's Company under Col. Benjamin Simonds. He was wounded in battle at Wallumsuck near Bennington and lost the use of his left arm. He was pensioned at the rate of half-pay from 16 Aug. 1777 on 1 Mar. 1779. He was 32 years old and lived out of state when he was pensioned. He resided in Norwich, Vermont 16 Nov. 1807.

Buck, Daniel. Pa. Pvt. He was on the 1789 and 1813 pension lists.

Buck, Ebenezer. Mass. Capt. He served as a lieutenant and a captain in the militia under Col. Allen, Gen. Lovell, and Gen. Wardsworth. He served under Capt. Buck in 1777 for 1 month and 10 days and Col. Brewer for 2 months and 22 days. He died in 1824. His widow, Mary Buck, whom he married 25 Mar. 1781, was approved for a pension of $10 a month for at least six months of service on 20 June 1848. She had been rejected 10 Jan. 1846 because of insufficient service.

Buck, John. Va. —. He served under Capt. Thomas Nelson and died in the service in Feb. 1777 in the north. His widow, Diana Buck, was granted a £20 gratuity on 10 Dec. 1777.

Buckhannan, John. Md. Drummer. He was from Charles County in 1783. He served under Col. John H. Stone and was wounded in his knee.

Buckley, Job. Va. —. He served in Capt. Berry's Company. His wife, Catharine Buckley, and child were furnished £20 support in Frederick Co., Va. on 4 May 1779.

Buckman, Benjamin. —. —. His widow, Eunice Buckman, had her petition for a pension rejected by Congress on 27 Mar. 1846 because they married subsequent to 1 Jan. 1794.

Buckminister, William. Mass. Lt. Col. He was wounded on 17 June 1775 on the heights of Charlestown in his right shoulder and in great measure lost the use of it. On 7 Feb. 1777 he forfeited all claim to a place in the list of pensioners as a wounded officer. He was put under bond for good behavior for a year. The selectmen of Barre attested to same. He was forgiven. He was pensioned at the rate of one-eighth the pay of a lieutenant colonel from 22 Feb. 1782 on 23 Feb. 1784.

Buckner, Thomas. —. —. He received his commutation and was to receive half-pay for life upon deducting same.

Budd, George. N.J. —. His widow, Mary Budd, was pensioned in Camden County 26 Feb. 1846 at the rate of $30 per annum.

Budding, —. Pa. —. His widow, Elizabeth Budding, was granted a $40 gratuity and a $40 annuity in York County.

Buel, Ezra. N.Y. Lt. He enlisted in Apr. 1775. He was appointed a 2nd Lieutenant and set out for Fort Ticonderoga. He took prisoners to Albany and returned in May to Ticonderoga. He was in a party of forty volunteers and was paid by the Massachusetts Committee of Charlestown. In Jan. 1776 he was in the expedition to disarm Tories about Johnstown, Montgomery Co., N.Y. for ten days. He was called out on an alarm for 12 days in Apr. 1776. He took the place of Isaac Wright and served nine months. He served two weeks under Col. Warner in Mar. or Apr. 1777. He was a guard and was wounded in Aug. 1777 at Stillwater. In Apr. 1780 he served under Capt. Harrison and Col. John Harper. He was commissioned as 1st Lieutenant and was discharged in Dec. 1780. He was 86 years old when he applied to Congress 12 Nov. 1830.

Buell, Isaac. Conn. Pvt. He served in Col. Baldwin's Artificers. He was ruptured in the scrotum in removing a stick of timber. He lived in Lebanon, Conn. in 1792. He enlisted 17 Feb. 1778 for three years and was omitted in 1780. He was granted one-third of a pension 20 Apr. 1796. He was on the 1813 pension list.

Buell, Salmon. Conn. Pvt. He served in the 17th Regiment of militia under Col. Ephaphras Sheldon. He was wounded in the thigh on 27 Apr. 1777 at the battle of Compo. He lived at Litchfield, Conn. and was 46 years old on 3 Jan. 1787. He died 14 Dec. 1812. He was listed as dead on the 1813 pension list.

Burford, Abraham. Va. —. He was in South Carolina in 1779 under Gen. Charles Scott. He was in Scott Co., Ky. He received his commutation of five years' full pay.

Buford, John. S.C. Capt. He applied from Barnwell District 25 Nov. 1826. He was in the service in 1780 under Gen. Francis Marion, Capt. James, Capt. Leseur, and Capt. Witherspoon. He was at Stono, Eutaw Springs, and Wambabridge at Marion's defeat. He was 66 years old, lame in one limb, blind in one eye, and deaf in one ear. He had fourteen children. His application was rejected.

Bugbee, Timothy. Conn. —. He served under Lt. Col. Ephraim Stores and was wounded by a musket ball through his viscera at Bunker Hill on 17 June 1775. He arrived home 4 Aug.1775. He was pensioned in Mansfield, Conn. 16 Sep. 1775.

Buice, Abraham. N.Y. Pvt. He served under Lt. Col. James Hammond in the Ulster County militia and was slain 10 Dec. 1780. His widow, Ann Buice, received a half-pay pension.

Buice, James. N.Y. —. His wife and two children were granted relief 3 Nov. 1781 in Dutchess Co.

Buken, —. Pa. —. His widow was Elizabeth Buken.

Buker, Israel. Mass. Sgt. He served in the 3rd Regiment and was paid $20.

Bulfinch, Samuel. S.C. Seaman. He served aboard the frigate, *South Carolina,* under Commodore Gillon and was paid $514.27 on 25 May 1808.

Bull, Epaphras. Conn. Maj. He died of wounds in Oct. 1781 at Yorktown, Va. He left three children but no widow. His father, Aaron Bull, of Hartord sought to determine the benefits due his grandchildren on 1 June 1786.

Bull, John. —. —. He died at New Lebanon, New York 14 Nov. 1839. His son, John Bull, Jr., sought his arrearage of $77.80 on 11 Jan. 1844. Congress determined there was no need of a special act because his situation was covered by legislation.

Bullard, Joel. Mass. Pvt. He served in Capt. John Black's Company under Col. Jonathan Brewer. He was wounded 17 June 1775. He was disabled by a musket ball in his left hip and another through his body. He was pensioned at the rate of one-third of a soldier from 1 Jan. 1776 on 30 Jan. 1784. He was 30 years old in 1786.

Bullard, John. Mass. Corp. He served in the 13th Regiment and was from Westhampton. His widow, Ruth Bullard, was paid $50.

Bullion, Thomas. S.C. —. There were children in 1791.

Bulloch, Daniel. N.C. —. He was drafted into the militia for nine months under Capt. Quinn and Col. Hogan and served about a year. He died in Jan. 1821. He married Mary ---- 14 Jan. 1777 in N.C. In 1843 she applied but was rejected. She died 29 May 1845. There were several children and grandchildren. Letters of administration were granted to Robert S. Lanier. Congress awarded the pension to his children 30 Mar. 1860.

Bullock, Jesse. Md. Pvt. He was pensioned at the rate of half-pay of a private on 1 Jan. 1813.

Bullock, Simeon. —. Pvt. He enlisted in 1776 under Capt. S. Peck and Col. Lippit for one year. He marched from R.I. to N.Y. He was in battle at Haerlem Heights and White Plains. He next served fifteen months in the R.I. Line under Col. Craig. Congress accepted his more than nine months of Continental service, and he was approved for a pension 3 Jan. 1832.

Bumgarden, George. Pa. —. He was granted a gratuity 29 Mar. 1813. He also appeared as George Bumgarten.

Bumpus, Asa. Mass. —. He served in the 5th Regiment and was from Wareham. He was paid $20.

Bunce, Asa. Conn. Corp. He served in the 3rd Regiment. He was overheated on the march on the day of the battle of Monmouth. He resided in Hartford, Conn. in 1792. He enlisted 27 Apr. 1777 and was discharged 24 Apr. 1780.

Bunce, Daniel. Mass. —. He served in the 1st Regiment and was from Richmond. He was paid $20.

Bunce, Isaiah. Conn. Pvt. He served in the 7th Regiment under Col. Swift. He was wounded in the leg resulting in ulcers and lameness on 27 Apr. 1777 at New Milford. He resided in Washington, Conn. in 1792. He enlisted 26 Mar. 1777 and was discharged 31 Mar. 1780. He died in 1804. His name was on the 1813 pension list.

Bunch, —. S.C. —. His widow was Mary Bunch from Richland. There were children in 1791.

Bunch, James. Va. —. He was in Capt. Joseph Martin's Company of militia. He was wounded several times in 1777 in Washington Co., Va. in an engagement with the Indians. He was awarded a £30 gratuity and half-pay of a soldier on 20 Nov. 1778.

Buncombe, Edward. N.C. Col. His heirs, his daughters Elisabeth Buncombe and Hester Buncombe, received half-pay of £180 for seven years in 1784. They were from Tyrrell County.

Bunckam [?], Isaac. Pa. —. He was granted relief.

Bunker, Benjamin. Mass. —. He was from Nantucket and was paid $50.

Bunn, Barnes. N.J. Pvt. He served in Col. Lamb's Artillery. He was wounded through his shoulder before Quebec. He was pensioned 31 Dec. 1775. He was 36 years old and was from Woodbridge. He was on the 1813 pension list. He later moved from Sussex Co., N.J. to Montgomery Co., Ind.

Bunting, Ritchie. Va. —. His wife, Esther Bunting, was allowed 30 shillings per month for her support and maintenance in Accomack County in 1777.

Bunting, William B. Va. Ens. He served in the 9th Virginia Regiment under Capt. John Cropper and died in the service in hospital at Philadelphia 1 Apr. 1777. He had been appointed lieutenant 31 Aug. 1776. His grandchildren were William Core, Edward Core, and Margaret Core of Accomack Co., Va. They were granted his seven years' half pay 22 Dec. 1837 by Congress.

Bunton, Alexander, Va. Pvt. He was wounded in his right knee at the battle of Guilford. He served under Col. Samuel McDowell in the militia. He was awarded a gratuity of one year's pay and an annuity of half-pay on 21 Nov. 1781 in Rockbridge County. He was aged *ca.* 28 years in 1786. He resided in Rockbridge County on 4 Apr. 1787. He had a wife and one or two children. He was continued at the rate of £12 per annum on 23 Apr. 1787. He was pensioned 21 Jan. 1809 at the rate of $20 per annum. He was on the 1813 pension list. He also appeared as Alexander Buntain.

Burbank, Ebenezer. Mass. —. He was pensioned.

Burbridge, Thomas. —. —. He was pensioned.

Burch, Benjamin. Md. Pvt. He was pensioned at the rate of half-pay of a private in Kentucky 11 Mar. 1828.

Burch, Benjamin. Md. Sgt. He served as a sergeant in the Maryland Line for several years to the close of the war. He was eligible under the act of 1818. In 1828 he was serving as Principal Doorkeeper of the House of Representatives. He died in May 1832 and did not esteem he should seek a pension. He married a few months after the termination of his enlistment. His widow,

Rebecca Burch, sought the pension he would have received had he applied for the same on 31 May 1838.

Burcham, John. —. —. He guarded McGee's Station against the Indians and joined the army of Wayne. Congress rejected his claim for a pension 5 Mar. 1840 since his type of service was not qualifying.

Burchard, Samuel. Del. Corp. He also appeared as Samuel Burchure. He was on the 1802 and 1813 pension lists.

Burcher, John. Va. He died in the service. His widow, Lucy Burcher, was granted £8 support in York Co., Va. on 20 July 1778 and £12 on 21 June 1779.

Burchett, Robert. Va. Pvt. He served in the 1st Va. Regiment. He lost his left leg and thigh and was wounded in his hip and right leg at the siege of Ninety Six. He was *ca.* 30 years old on 28 Oct. 1786. He resided in Halifax County in June 1786. He was continued at the rate of £18 per annum. He was on the 1813 pension list.

Burchfield, Thomas. Pa. —. He was granted relief in Juniata County 28 Mar. 1836. He was 85 years old in 1840. He died 17 Dec 1842.

Burdan, Henry. N.J. —. He was pensioned in Bergen County 25 Feb. 1847 at the rate of $60 per annum.

Burdeen, Timothy. Mass. —. He was granted relief.

Burden, —. Va. —. His mother, Sarah Burden, was granted £30 support in Caroline Co., Va. 12 July 1779.

Burden, James. Va. —. He was granted financial assistance while his three sons were away in the service in Caroline Co., Va. 12 Mar. 1778.

Burdick, Walter. Conn. Pvt. He served in the 1st Alarm List of the 8th Conn. Regiment of militia. He was disabled by a musket ball which lodged in his back at Bristol, R.I. 25 May 1778. He was a volunteer. He was pensioned 8 Dec. 1788 at Groton, Conn. at the age of 33. He was on the 1813 pension list. He died 1 Sep. 1831 in Tolland Co., Conn.

Burdwin, Samuel. Conn. Pvt. He served in the 5th Regiment under Col. Sherman. He was wounded by a musket ball in and through his right side and intestines on 29 Aug. 1782 near Fishkill. He resided in Tolland, Conn. in 1794. He enlisted 27 Apr. 1781 for three years and transferred to the Invalids Corps 27 June 1782. He was on the 1813 pension list. He died 23 July 1823. He also appeared as Samuel Bardwin and Samuel Baldwin.

Burg, Conrad. Pa. Pvt. He was in Lancaster County 11 May 1787. He was a soldier in an independent company of foot in 1777 under Capt. Jacob Weaver which was annexed to the 10th Pa. Regiment and renamed the 6th Regiment. He was wounded in his left thigh by a musket ball on 21 July 1780 at the Block House near New York City. He was discharged 26 Mar. 1781. He was 33 years old. Lt. Col. Adam Hubley and Lt. William Feltman attested to his service. He was dead by Sep. 1799. He also appeared as Conrad Burgh and Conrad Burk. He was a saddler by trade.

Burgain, Thomas. Va. —. He was killed in the service. His widow, Margaret Burgain, and four children resided in Greenbrier County, Va. on 17 Aug. 1779.

Burgenhoff, William. Pa. —. He was granted relief.

Burger, Michael. S.C. —. He served in the Wagon Department in the 2nd Regiment. He was captured at the fall of Charleston and put on a prison ship. His widow, Mary Magdalen Burger, sought a pension 10 Oct. 1808. Her application was rejected because she did not prove his death.

Burges, Bangs. Mass. —. He served in the 4th Regiment and was paid $20.

Burges, Ichabod. Mass. —. He served in the 1st Regiment and was from Rochester. He was paid $20.

Burges, John. N.Y. Pvt. He served under Col. Ann Hawkes Hay and was slain 29 Dec. 1778. His widow, Susanna Burges, received a half-pay pension.

Burges, Jonathan. Mass. —. He served in the 4th Regiment and was from Vassalboro. He was paid $20.

Burgess, Basil. Md. Lt. He was pensioned at the rate of half-pay of a lieutenant on 27 Jan. 1816.

Burgess, James. N.Y. Quarter Master Sgt. He was in Capt. William Britton's Co. under Col. Oliver Spencer. He was wounded by cannon shot at Germantown on 4 Oct. in his left hip. He lived at Fredericktown, Dutchess Co., N.Y. on 13 June 1788. Gilbert Groseclose, stone cutter, and Barnet Mooney, hatter, attested his service. He was on the 1813 pension list.

Burgess, Joshua. Md. Lt. He was pensioned at the rate of half-pay of a lieutenant in Mason Co., Ky. 19 Jan. 1830. His heirs were paid his arrearage of $46.67 in Feb. 1836.

Burgess, Thomas. Mass. Pvt. He was in the 7th Regiment in Capt. Benjamin Warren's Company under Col. Alden. He lost his right thumb and was wounded in his left leg in Rhode Island. In 1788 he was 39 years and resided in Boston, Mass. He died 22 Nov. 1809. His widow, Jemima Muscum, was paid $50 from the Commonwealth and was from Plymouth.

Burgess, Vachel. Md. Capt. He received four years of full pay free from interest in 1810.

Burgher, Jeremiah. N.Y. He applied in Hudson, Columbia County, N.Y. under the act of 1832. He was a native of Stattsburgh, Dutchess County, N.Y. His father was a contractor for supplies for the army. He drove teams in 1777 when Esopus was burnt but did not claim that service. He served three days afterwards. In Apr. 1778 he volunteered in Capt. Wood's Company under Col. Van Bentschoten in the militia for nine months. He was discharged after six months of service 1 Jan. 1779. From May to Nov. 1780 he served six months under Capt. Cornelius Paulding. From Apr. to Oct. 1781 he was in Capt. Connel's Company. He claimed service for one year, nine months, and three days but only proved nine months. He furnished additional proof in 1836 and died 9 May 1854. He married in 1792 in Stattsburgh. Hannah Gibbs was at the wedding and proved it. His widow, Maria Burgher, had her claim approved 19 July 1856 by Congress.

Burk, —. Pa. —. His widow, Catharine Burk, was granted relief 12 Feb. 1829 in Northampton County.

Burk, —. Pa. —. His widow, Mary Burk, was awarded a $40 annuity in York County 27 Apr. 1852 for his Revolutionary service.

Burk, —. Va. —. His father, William Burk, was granted £12 assistance in Caroline Co., Va. in Sep. 1777.

Burk, Francis. Pa. —. He was awarded a $40 gratuity in Cumberland Co., Pa. 23 Jan. 1830.

Burk, James. Md. Pvt. He served in the 2nd Regiment and was wounded at Cowpens. He was pensioned in Frederick County in 1788. He died 3 Dec. 1817.

Burk, James. Pa. —. He was awarded a $40 annuity and a $40 gratuity in Northumberland Co., Pa. 13 Apr. 1826.

Burk, John. Va. Pvt. He was killed in the service at Brandywine. His widow, Elizabeth Burk, resided in Culpeper County on 17 July 1786. She was aged more than 60 years on 28 Feb. 1787. She was continued on the roll at the rate of £6 per annum. She lived in Madison County on 24 Sep. 1801.

Burk, Matthew. Va. Pvt. He served in the 4th Va. Regiment and was shot through the body at Trenton in 1777. Capt. William Cherry attested to his service. He resided in Berkeley County, Va. on 20 Feb. 1787. He was continued on the roll at the rate of £12 per annum on 22 Oct. 1787.

Burk, Michael. Va. —. His wife, Rachel Burk, was granted £10 support in Berkeley County on 18

Aug. 1778 while he was away in Continental service.

Burk, Nathaniel. Md. Pvt. He was pensioned at the rate of half-pay of a private in Baltimore 13 Mar. 1829. His widow, Elizabeth Burk, was pensioned at the same rate on 7 Mar. 1838.

Burk, Patrick. Pa. —. He received a $40 gratuity and a $40 annuity in Washington County 3 Mar. 1837. He was dead by Apr. 1838.

Burk, Thomas. Md. Pvt. He was pensioned 7 June 1785.

Burk, Thomas. Pa. —. He was awarded a $40 gratuity and a $40 annuity in York County 18 Mar. 1833.

Burk, William. Va. —. He served in Capt. Bruin's Company in the 11ᵗʰ Virginia Regiment. His mother, Ann Burk, was furnished £5 support in Frederick Co., Va. on 2 Dec. 1777 and £15 support on 1 June 1779. She also appeared as Ann Berk.

Burke, James. Pa. —. He was pensioned 13 Apr. 1827 and died 29 Aug. 1828. His widow, Catharine Burke, was awarded a $40 gratuity in Northumberland Co., Pa. 12 Feb. 1829.

Burke, Martin. Md. —. He served under Capt. James Morris and Col. Uriah Forest for five years. He was at Bunker Hill, Brandywine, and Eutaw Springs. He was discharged at Annapolis. Congress rejected his application for relief 27 Apr. 1840 because there was no evidence of his service.

Burke, Thomas. N.C. —. He was a prisoner. His acting executor, James Hogg, was allowed £120 in compensation for his expense in 1784.

Burke, William. Va. Pvt. He was disabled and was pensioned in 1808. He resided in Frederick County. He was on the 1813 pension list. He died 23 Jan. 1826.

Burke, William. Va. Pvt. He resided in Culpeper Co., Va. He was on the 1813 pension list.

Burket, Christopher. Pa. —. He was granted relief in Somerset County 21 June 1839. He was 93 years old in 1840. His widow was Mary Ann Burket in 1849. His surname appeared as Burkel.

Burkett, John. S.C. —. He was pensioned in Marlboro District 23 Nov. 1829. He served in the militia under Capt. James Thompson. He was on the Savannah River with Gen. Lee and was in Georgia three years. He was in the battle on the Savannah River at Briar Creek. He returned to the Pee Dee and joined Capt. Standard's militia. He was ordered to Charleston under Capt. Stackhouse where he was taken prisoner and paroled. He then joined Gen. Francis Marion and served until he was discharged. He was 88 years old. He also appeared as John Burkitt. He was paid as late as 1833.

Burkett, Moses. N.C. —. He was wounded in the service. His application in 1800 from Wayne County was rejected. He applied again in 1807. He was a shoemaker. He died 20 Feb. 1815.

Burkhalter, David. S.C. —. He was from Barnwell District. There was one child in 1791. He was pensioned 19 Dec. 1809. He served under Gen. Andrew Pickens at Liberty Hill in 1781 and was wounded by a ball through his arm in the elbow joint at the siege of Augusta. He was pensioned until 1791. Lt. John Adams of Col. Hammond's Regiment was at the siege of Augusta in 1781 with him. John Burkhalter on 25 Oct. 1808 stated that he knew David Burkhalter was wounded in the elbow. Because he had been stricken from the roll by some misrepresentation, he was paid his arrearage of $64.29 on 9 Dec. 1809. He was paid as late as 1838.

Burkhalter, John. —. —. Congress denied his application for a pension because of evidence of his service on 9 Apr. 1856.

Burkhart, Frederick. Pa. —. He was awarded a $40 gratuity 1 Apr. 1830 in Philadelphia, Pa., 4 May 1832, and 23 Jan. 1833. On the latter date he was granted a $40 gratuity and a $40 annuity. He was 79 years of age in 1840.

Burkher, George. Pa. —. The act of 15 June 1836 providing for his pension reported his name as Joseph Burkher. It was corrected by the act of 27 Jan. 1837. He resided in Fayette County and received a $40 gratuity and a $40 annuity. He died 25 Mar. 1844.

Burks, George. Va. Soldier. He served in Crocket's Regiment and received bounty land from Virginia. He was not in Continental service so Congress rejected the claim for bounty land 5 Jan. 1843.

Burn, Joseph. Va. Sailor. He died in the service. His widow resided in Lancaster County on 3 Nov. 1785. His widow, Jane Burn, was aged 50 years in Apr. 1788 and had two sons, aged 14 and 12 years, on 27 Oct. 1788. She was continued at the rate of £6 per annum on 9 June 1790. She resided in Middlesex County where she died about the first week of June 1799. She also appeared as Jane Burns.

Burnall, John. Mass. —. He served in the 12th Regiment and was from Gorham. He was paid $20.

Burnes, James. N.J. Pvt. He was on the 1791 pension roll at the rate of $60 per annum.

Burnes, Peter. R.I. —. He was on the roll in 1788.

Burnet, Josiah. N.J. Ens. He was wounded in the leg in action near Second River in Sep. 1777. He was pensioned in Morris County 21 Dec. 1779. He was on the 1791 pension roll at the rate of $120 per annum. He was on the 1813 pension list. He died 3 Dec. 1812.

Burnett, John. Va. —. His wife, Mary Burnett, was awarded a gratuity of £30.10 in Amherst County 1 Dec. 1779. He died in Continental service. She had been furnished provisions in Oct. 1778 and Feb. 1779.

Burnett, Oliver. Pa. —. He was pensioned.

Burnett, Samuel. Pa. Capt. He was granted relief.

Burnham, David. Mass. Pvt. He served in the 1st Regiment and was from Gloucester. His widow, Martha Burnham, was paid $50.

Burnham, Isaac. Mass. —. He was in the 5th Regiment. He was paid $20.

Burnham, Isaac. Pa. Pvt. He lived in D.C. after the war. He was on the 1813 pension list in Kentucky.

Burnham, Joseph. Mass. —. He served in the 8th Regiment and was from Ipswich. He was paid $20.

Burnham, Joseph. Me. —. He died at sea about 1793. His widow was Susanna Stone from Kennebunkport. She was paid $50 under the resolve of 1836.

Burnham, Oliver. Conn. Sgt. He served under Col. Beebee in Capt. Chapman's Company. He dislocated his ankle in pursuit of the enemy in 1777 at West Chester. He lived in Cornwall, Conn. in 1795. He was in the militia. He was granted one-fourth a pension 20 Apr. 1796. He was on the 1813 pension list.

Burnham, Thomas. Mass. —. He served in the 8th Regiment and was from Ipswich. He was paid $20.

Burnham, Walcott. —. —. He had been pensioned under the act of 1818, was suspended in 1820, and restored in 1829. He asked to be paid from 4 March 1820 to 9 May 1829. His petition to Congress was not granted 20 June 1848.

Burnie, John. Pa. —. He was awarded a $40 gratuity and a $40 annuity in Crawford County 21 Mar. 1825.

Burnley, Garland. Va. Capt. He entered the service as a minute man and saw hard action at Norfolk. In 1776 he was a lieutenant in Capt. Spencer's Company of Regulars. In 1778 he was captain in Col. Francis Taylor's Regiment. He served to June 1781 when he became supernumerary. He was from Orange County. His grandchildren received his five years' full pay 4 Jan. 1838. Congress found that there was not sufficient proof for commutation pay 5 Mar. 1840.

Burns, Alexander. Pa. —. He was awarded a $40 gratuity and a $40 annuity in Washington County

5 Mar. 1819.

Burns, Francis. Pa. —. He was awarded a $40 gratuity and a $40 annuity in York Co., Pa. 14 Apr. 1834.

Burns, John. Md. Pvt. He was pensioned at the rate of half-pay of a private on 19 Feb. 1819.

Burns, John. S.C. —. His widow, Mary Burns, was paid 11 Feb. 1786 and was from Greenville District. There were two children in 1791.

Burns, Luke. Md. Pvt. He was pensioned 4 Mar. 1789 at $40 per annum. He died in 1794.

Burns, Matthew. Va. —. He served in the 11th Virginia Regiment. His widow, Hannah Burns and child were granted financial support in Yohogania Co., Va. 24 June 1778.

Burns, Pierce. Pa. Pvt. He was from Philadelphia County.

Burns, Samuel. Pa. Sgt. He applied from Montgomery County 2 Feb. 1813. He enlisted in 1777 in Capt. John Pugh's Company under Col. Stewart. He was at Brandywine, Germantown, Monmouth, and Stoney Point. He was seized with violent rheumatism and discharged in 1781. He was awarded a $40 gratuity 22 Mar. 1813. He died 21 Oct. 1818.

Burns, Samuel. S.C. —. He was a pensioner of the U.S. at the rate of $30 per annum. He died 1 Dec. 1837. He was married in Aug. 1781. His widow, Mary Burns, applied for a federal pension 27 Mar. 1845 in York District. Her application was rejected because of no record of service of her husband. He served three months under Capt. Neal and Gen. Williamson in 1778, three months under Capt. Moffit and Gen. Sumter in 1780, and three months under Capt. Byers in 1781. He was wounded in Sep. 1780. He was a wagoner for some time. She was pensioned by S.C. at the rate of $30 per annum in 1846. She died 2 Feb. 1848. Her administrator was Amos Burns, and he sought her arrearage. He was paid $27.50.

Burnside, James. Pa. —. He was awarded a $40 gratuity and a $40 annuity in Butler Co., Pa. 19 Feb. 1828. He died 10 May 1833.

Burpe, Jacob. N.Y. —. He was pensioned.

Burr, Daniel. —. —. He was pensioned under the act of 1818 and stricken from the rolls in 1820. Congress granted him a pension 2 Mar. 1832.

Burr, Nathan. —. Pvt. He served in Col. Fletcher's Regiment. He was wounded by a musket ball through his right shoulder in Jul. 1781 at Crown Point. He resided in Rockingham, Vt. in 1796. He was granted half a pension 20 Apr. 1796.

Burr, Salmon. Conn. Pvt. He served in Col. Eno's Regiment. He was wounded in the great toe of each foot by walking in a cold storm while on duty at Crumpond, N.Y. near the Hudson River in Oct. 1777. Several pieces of bone were removed from a running sore on one of his toes. He resided at Farmington, Conn. in 1792.

Burr, Semo. Mass. Pvt. He served in the 4th Regiment and was from Canton. He was paid $50.

Burr, Simeon. Mass. Pvt. He served in the 5th Regiment and was from Freetown. His widow, Elizabeth Burr, was paid $50.

Burridge, John. Mass. Pvt. He served in the 9th Regiment and was from Medford. His widow, Lois Burridge, was paid $50.

Burril, Noah. Mass. Sgt. He served in the 2nd Regiment and was from Eastward. He was paid $20.

Burrill, Benoni. Me. —. He died 8 Apr. 1814 at Clinton. His widow was Lydia Burrill from Fairfield. She was paid $50 under the resolve of 1836.

Burritt, William. Conn. Pvt. He served under Col. Waterbury in Capt. Reed's Company. He was wounded by a musket ball in his left arm; it passed through his shoulder blade. He also had two buck shot lodged in the back part of his neck in Sep. 1775 at Lake Champlain. He lived in Washington Co., N.Y. in 1795. He served in the militia. He was granted one-fourth of a pension 20 Apr. 1796. He was on the 1813 pension list. .

Burroughs, Norman. Md. Pvt. His widow, Esther Turner Burroughs, was pensioned at the rate of half-pay of a private in St. Mary's County on 19 Mar. 1839.

Burrows, Elisha. Conn. Pvt. He served in Col. John Ely's Conn. Regiment in Capt. Oliver Coit's company. He was wounded at White Plains by a musket ball through his neck. He was pensioned 14 Nov. 1788. He was from Groton and was 32 years old. He was on the 1813 pension list. He transferred to Washington Co., N.Y. 4 Mar. 1826.

Burrows, Joseph. Pa. Pvt. He served in Col. Cook's 12th Regiment. He was wounded by a musket ball in the elbow joint at Short Hills in Jersey. He was discharged at Valley Forge. He enlisted 1 Nov. 1776 for the war and joined the Invalids Jan. 1778. He died 8 Feb. 1797.

Burrows, William. Conn. Pvt. He served in the 3rd Conn. Regiment. He was disabled in Dec. 1782 while on a wooding party by being wounded in the knee near West Point. He served under Col. Samuel B. Webb. Dr. Eneas Munson was the Assistant Surgeon. He was discharged 10 Apr. 1783. Dr. Albigence Waldo amputated his leg 29 Feb. 1784. He was born 17 Sep. 1761. He lived in Killingsley, Conn. He was pensioned 19 Sep. 1788. He was on the 1813 pension list.

Burt, Benjamin. —. —. He died 1 Mar. 1849. Congress awarded his widow, Mary Burt, of Scioto Co., Ohio, the arrearage of her pension from 4 Mar. 1848 to 3 Feb. 1853 on 23 Feb. 1857. Congress granted it to her.

Burton, Charles. S.C. —. He applied in Pendleton District 30 Nov. 1827. He had previously lived in Newberry District. He served two tours against the Cherokee Indians in Col. Lyles' Regiment under Capt. Houzeal. He was in the Florida Expedition under Capt. Kyser. He then served under Maj. Thomas Gordon and was wounded in the right leg at Stono. He was nearly 87 years old and his wife was five years younger. She had fallen and received a dislocated collar bone. James McNure of Newberry District saw him in the service. David Boyd said he was with him on a tour in Georgia at least forty days. Edward Wade of Anderson District stated he heard Charles Burton state that he served in the King's Army at Briar Creek and boasted about chasing the American Army that night. Solomon Geer related the same as did Lesly Brown. William Brown stated that Burton fought in three engagements against the British. James Wardlaw stated that Burton was at Musgrove's Mill on the side of the British and was wounded there. Andrew McAllaster of Pickens District swore that Burton was in the Florida Expedition in Col. John Lisle's Regiment in Capt. William Houzeal's Company. Burton's pension application was rejected since he was in the King's service.

Burton, George. Pa. Pvt. He was on the pension list of 1813.

Burton, James. Va. Capt. & Adjt. He served in the infantry. His widow was Elizabeth Burton. He was commissioned an ensign early in 1776 and saw active service until 1778 when he was sent out on recruiting service. In 1779 he was appointed a captain under Col. Francis Taylor until disbanded in 1781 when he became supernumerary. He was at the barracks in Albemarle County guarding the convention army of Burgoyne. His legal representative was allowed his commutation pay 4 Jan. 1838. He was from Orange County. Virginia issued bounty land warrants #6053 for 2,666 2/3 acres and #7650 for 2,055 acres. Congress granted 300 acres bounty to his devisees on 8 Mar. 1833. They received five years' full pay 4 Jan. 1838.

Burton, John. N.J. Pvt. He was wounded through the wrist and lost the use of his hand. He was 47 years old and was from Hardwick. He was on the 1791 pension roll. He was on the pension list of 1813. He lived in Sussex County and died 15 Feb. 1815.

Burton, John. Va. Sgt. He served in the 5th Regiment. He was wounded at Germantown on 4 Oct. 1777 in the head by a musket ball which fractured the skull and in one of his hips. He lived in Augusta Co., Va. in 1794. He was taken prisoner 4 Oct. 1777 and was exchanged 30 Apr. 1778. He was continued on the roll at the rate of £5 per annum on 15 Nov. 1787. He was on the 1813 pension list. He resided in Henrico County. He died 27 Dec. 1828.

Burton, Samuel. Va. Pvt. He served in the Va. Line. He lived in Amelia County. He was on the 1813 pension list.

Burtz, Michael. S.C. —. He was pensioned in Barnwell District 30 Nov. 1827. He served under Capt. Jacob Wanamaker and Col. Jacob Rumph for five to six years in the state militia. He pursued the Tories while serving in scouting parties protecting Orangeburg District. He was about 75 years old and was married. All of his children were married off. He died 1 Aug. 18[–]. His widow, Hannah Burtz, had a little assistance from his nephew and was 60 to 70 years of age when she applied. The date of her application is lacking. He was paid in 1828 and again in 1830.

Burwell, Jonathan. Pa. Pvt. He was pensioned 7 June 1794. He was on the 1813 pension list.

Bury, Conrad. Pa. Pvt. He was granted relief.

Bury, John. Pa. —. He served under Capt. Jacob Glotz and Col. Cunningham in the Flying Camp. He was from Lancaster County. He also appeared as John Berry.

Bury, John. S.C. —. His annuity in 1787 was £7.

Burzette, Charles. —. —. He served for the war. He married in 1803 and died in 1825. His legal representatives were entitled to his bounty land. His widow was not known, and the names of his heirs were not known according to Congress on 11 May 1838.

Busby, John. S.C. —. He was pensioned in Barnwell District 23 Nov. 1829. He was a free man of color. He entered the service in 1779 on the Savannah River under Capt. Daniel Green. He also served under Capt. Benjamin Matthews, John Sapp, ------ Ferguson, and Joseph Johnson. They suppressed the Tories in South Carolina and Georgia. He was at the siege of Augusta and was never wounded.

Bush, —. Va. —. His father, William Bush, was awarded £20 relief in Caroline Co., Va. in Sep. 1779 while he was away in Continental service.

Bush, Adam. Va. —. He served 13 months under Capt. James Booth in an expedition against the Indians. His widow, Margaret Bush, was paid $104 on 28 Feb. 1835.

Bush, Henry. Pa. —. He was awarded a $40 gratuity and a $40 annuity in Pike County 9 Feb. 1824. His widow, Eve Bush, was awarded a $40 gratuity and a $40 annuity in Pike Co., Pa. 18 Mar. 1834. He served in the Associators and Flying Camp.

Bush, Henry. Pa. —. He failed to prove his service under Pulaski and Capt. Orran. Abraham Bloom of Lansing, Tompkins County, proved his service of seven months under Capt. John Van Etter in 1837. He was a solider from Easton, Northampton County, to protect the settlements from the Indians in either 1778 or 1779. He could not recall if his service was that of a private or ensign. He applied 6 Apr. 1838.

Bush, Joseph. Md. Pvt. He was pensioned 12 Feb. 1820 in Talbot County at the rate of half-pay.

Bush, John. S.C. Lt. He served in the 2nd South Carolina Regiment. He was killed at Savannah 9 Oct. 1779. His widow remarried. His three daughters sought a pension in 1791.

Bush, Joseph. Md. Pvt. He was pensioned at the rate of half-pay of a private in Talbot County 12 Feb. 1820.

Bush, Prescott. S.C. —. He was pensioned in Barnwell District 23 Nov. 1829. He went into the service at the age of sixteen. He served under Capt. Turner, Capt. Mitchell, and Capt. William Butler. He was 62 years old in 1827. He was paid as late as 1845.

Bush, Solomon. Pa. Deputy Adjutant General of Militia with rank of Lt. Col. He was in Philadelphia County 24 Oct. 1785. He was wounded in the thigh in action in Chester County 16 Sep. 1777. He served under Brig. Gen. James Potter. He was 32 years old. His father was alive 11 Feb. 1789. The veteran was dead by Mar. 1795.

Bush, William. Pa. Pvt. He was on the 1813 pension list.

Bushnell, Daniel. Conn. Pvt. He served in the 3rd Conn. Regiment. He was disabled by old age and infirmity. He was pensioned 6 Jan. 1783. He was on the 1813 pension list. He died 12 Dec. 1818 in Litchfield Co., Conn.

Buskell, John. Pa. Pvt. He was on the 1813 pension list in Pennsylvania. He also appeared as John Buskill.

Bussell, Daniel. N.H. Pvt. He was under Capt. John Wentworth in Continental service on 1 Jan. 1776. He had to have his leg amputated after a skirmish at Ticonderoga in Aug. 1776. He also had smallpox. He was aged 40 in 1787 and 45 in 1789. He was on the 1813 pension list. He died 4 May 1821. He also appeared as Daniel Buzzle and Daniel Buswell. He was from Barrington, N.H.

Butcher, John. Md. Pvt. He was pensioned 4 Mar. 1789.

Butcher, Matthias. Pa. —. He was pensioned.

Butcher, Paulsen. Va. Pvt. He served under Capt. James Booth in the expedition against the Indians for thirteen months. His widow, Elizabeth Butcher, was paid $104 on 7 Feb. 1835.

Butler, —. Va. —. His wife, Frances Butler, was granted financial support in Fauquier Co., Va. in Apr. 1779 and May 1780.

Butler, Charles. N.C. —. He applied in Craven County in 1800. He was a cordwainer and a shoemaker. He was wounded by a musket ball at Ramsey's Mills. The ball entered his cheek near his nose. A soldier fired his gun accidentally, and the surgeon could not remove the ball. He served in the militia. He was on the 1813 pension list.

Butler, Daniel. Ga. Pvt. He served under Col. Clarke. He was wounded in his right hip, right arm, and testicles by musket balls in 1780 in South Carolina. He lived in Ga. in 1795. He was in the militia.

Butler, James. Pa. —. He was in Lycoming County. He was the son of Richard Butler. He served in Capt. Thomas Robertson's Company. He was first in the Pa. Rangers. Andrew Flatt served six months under him. William Saxton was granted letters of administration on the estate of Stephen James Butler, cordwainer, in Philadelphia on 14 June 1815.

Butler, James. S.C. —. He was killed in the service. His widow, Mary Butler, was paid 3 Feb. 1785. His orphans were paid 21 Mar. 1786.

Butler, James. S.C. —. His orphans were paid 29 Apr. 1786.

Butler, James. Va. Pvt. He served in the 4th Va. Regiment. His wife was granted £5 support on 11 May 1778 and £30 support on 13 Apr. 1779. He died in Dec. 1780. His widow, Mary Butler, resided in Northumberland County on 12 June 1786. She was pensioned at the rate of £8 per annum on 14 Dec. 1786. He also appeared as James Butoler.

Butler, John. Mass. Pvt. He served in the 8th Regiment and was from Essex. His widow, Abigail Butler, was paid $50.

Butler, John. N.Y. Pvt. He served under Col. Goose Van Schaick in Capt. John H. Wendell's Company.

He was wounded twice, once in his left hand and the other in his right leg. He lost an eye. He was discharged 15 Sep. 1782. He lived in New York City, N.Y. on 14 June 1788. He was late of Albany. He was on the 1813 pension list.

Butler, Patrick. Pa. —. He applied in Dauphin County on 11 Mar. 1813. He died 3 Apr. 1819.

Butler, Patrick. Pa. Corp. He served in the 7th Regiment until the army was disbanded. He applied from Philadelphia County but was a resident of Augusta Co.,Va.

Butler, Patrick. Pa. —. He enlisted at Carlisle in Mar. 1778 under Col. Irwin. After the battle of Green Springs, he was put in the 2nd Regiment under Col. Hermir. He was discharged 19 Oct. 1783 at Philadelphia. He was from York County.

Butler, Phineas. Mass. Pvt. He served in the 6th Regiment under Col. Calvin Smith and Capt. Smith and was disabled by rheumatism and other complaints. He suffered from the gravel. He was pensioned 1 Sep. 1782. He was 57 years old in 1787. He was on the 1813 pension list.

Butler, Reuben. —. Capt. He served under Col. Grayson. He was paid from 25 Feb. 1777 to 1 Oct. 1781. Congress rejected the claim from the heirs 13 Jan. `1837.

Butler, Richard. Pa. Maj. He was commissioned 20 July 1779 and was promoted to Lieutenant Colonel. He was killed in battle after the war 4 Nov. 1791. His widow, Ann W. Butler, of Allegheny County had her claim rejected by Congress 15 Dec. 1857.

Butler, Robert. S.C. —. His widow had one child in 1791.

Butler, Robert. Va. —. His wife, Mary Butler, was furnished assistance on 8 Sep. 1777, 14 Apr. 1778, and 11 Feb. 1782 in Loudoun County. Her pension was continued on 28 Oct. 1791.

Butler, William. Pa. Pvt. He transferred to Virginia where he was on the 1813 pension list.

Butler, William. Pa. —. He applied from Crawford County 28 June 1813. He enlisted in 1775 in Capt. Henry Christ's Company under Col. Samuel Miles for 1 year and 9 months. He reenlisted for three years in Capt. Marshall's Company in the 2nd Pa. Regiment under Col. Walter Stewart. He also served in the artillery under Col. Proctor in Capt. Duffy's Company. He was in the battles of Long Island, the taking of the Hessians at Trenton, Brandywine, Monmouth, Green Springs, and Yorktown. He was twice wounded but not severely. John Burnie served with him at the skirmish at the Block House. He was 88 years old in 1822. In that year he stated that Capt. Benjamin Davis enlisted him in 1776 and that he served to 1783 when he was discharged by Col. Francis Johnston.

Butler, William. Pa. —. He was awarded a $40 gratuity and a $40 annuity in Philadelphia, Pa. 8 Apr. 1833.

Butt, Edward. Md. —. He was pensioned.

Buttemore, Jacob. Pa. —. His administrator, George Buttemore, was paid $229 for his right to donation land 11 Apr. 1825. Compare with Jacob Bottomore.

Buttolph, George. Conn. Pvt. He served under Gen. Parsons. He lost his eyesight almost entirely at the battle of Monmouth in June 1778 in consequence of the heat of the day. He lived in Stonington, Conn. in 1794. He enlisted 10 Jan. 1777 for the war and was invalided 7 Apr. 1781.

Button, Joseph. R.I. Pvt. He lost his left leg and part of his thigh in action on 28 Aug. 1778 in Rhode Island. He served Col. Topham. He was aged 26 in 1786. He was on the 1813 pension list in Connecticut. He was transferred from Connecticut to Chenango Co., N.Y. in Sep. 1826.

Buttrick, Amos. Mass. Pvt. He served in the Invalids under Col. Lewis Nichola. He was 32 years in 1790. He was worn out in the service. He also appeared as Amos Butterick.

Butts, Thomas. Pa. —. He was awarded a $40 gratuity and a $40 annuity in Cumberland County 14 Mar. 1814. He may be the Thomas Butz who claimed to be in Hazen's Regiment but had his application rejected 14 Dec. 1813.

Buxton, James. Va. Lt. He served in the 4th Va. Regiment. He lived in Nansemond Co., Va. He was on the 1813 pension list.

Buxton, John. Pa. Pvt. He was in Montgomery County 5 Aug. 1786. He was 54 years old. He served in the 3rd Pa. Regiment for 7 years and 11 months. He suffered from rheumatism, fatigue, and hardships. Col. Thomas Craig and Capt. Richard Fullerton attested to his service. He died 11 Aug. 1811. He was still on the 1813 pension list. He was also from Philadelphia Co.

Buxton, Peter. —. —. He entered the service in the summer of 1775 under Capt. Knapp and Col. Mead for two months. He then entered as a volunteer for one year under the same officers. He next had a two-month tour and a tour of six months under Capt. Amos Smith. He was approved for a pension for a little less than three years of service by Congress 20 Dec. 1831.

Buys, Jacob. N.Y. Pvt. He served in the Westchester County militia under Col. James Hammond. He was wounded in his right knee by a musket ball on 22 June 1780 near Tarry Town. He had a wife and five children. He died 1 Oct. 1785. He also appeared as Jacob Buyse.

Buzley, William. —. Fife Major. He was a resident of Pennsylvania.

Byas, William. Md. Lt. He applied from Dorchester County. He was pensioned at the rate of half-pay of a boatswain on 14 Feb. 1820. His rate was amended to that of half-pay of a lieutenant on 16 Feb. 1821. He also appeared as William Byus. Benjamin F. Byus of Dorchester County on behalf of himself and the other legal heirs received the $320 arrearage of the pensioner on 2 Mar. 1858.

Bybee, Joseph. Va. —. He served in the 7th Virginia Regiment in Capt. Jorutt's [sic] Company. He was wounded by a ball through his leg at the battle of Brandywine and was awarded a £30 gratuity and half-pay of a soldier for a year on 3 Nov. 1778.

Byers, Ebenezer. Pa. —. He was awarded a $40 gratuity in Mercer Co., Pa. 5 Feb. 1833. He was awarded a $40 gratuity and a $40 annuity in Mercer Co., Pa. 17 Mar. 1835.

Byers, George. Pa. —. He was awarded a $40 gratuity and a $40 annuity in Armstrong County 20 Mar. 1812. He also appeared as George Buyers. He served under Capt. William Scott in the Lancaster County Associators.

Byers, John. Pa. —. He was awarded a $40 gratuity and a $40 annuity in York Co., Pa. 4 Apr. 1831. He died 12 Jan. 1842.

Byington, John. Conn. Pvt. He was 76 years old in 1818.

Byram, Seth. Mass. —. He served in the 2nd Regiment. He was paid $20.

Byrd, Baylor. Va. —. He served in the calvary for at least two years in the Virginia Line prior to 1 Jan. 1782. He died in 1830. His widow, Nancy Byrd, applied under the act of 1838 but was rejected because of unsatisfactory proof of service and no proof of her marriage. The family record gave the date of their marriage as 4 Oct. 1785. They lived together more than forty years. Congress accepted him as identical as the man of that name who served and that she was his widow and awarded her relief 12 Apr. 1842. She lived in Williamson Co., Tenn.

Byrne, John. Md. Pvt. He transferred to Loudoun Co., Va. 4 Mar. 1793. He was on the 1813 pension list of Maryland.

Byxbe, Samuel. —. —. He used his wagon and team in transporting military stores on several occasions. That class of service was not embraced in the pension laws so Congress rejected his petition 6 Feb. 1838.

Cabot, Aaron. Mass. Seaman. He served aboard the continental ship *Queen of France* under J. P. Rathbone and lost the sight of both eyes due to sickness on 27 June 1779. He was pensioned from that date at the rate of half-pay on 20 Nov. 1780.

Cadwell, Matthew. Conn. Pvt. He served in Webb's Regiment. He was disabled by a rupture and by being worn out in the service. He was pensioned 16 Sep. 1782. He lived in Hartford Co., Conn. He was on the 1813 pension list.

Cade, John. N.J. Pvt. He served in the 2nd N.J. Regiment under Capt. Joseph Brearley. In 1776 he took ill with smallpox in Canada and died 15 June 1776 in hospital. His widow, Mary Cade, was allowed his half-pay in Hunterdon Co., N.J. in 1780.

Cady, Abijah. Conn. Pvt. He served in the 4th Regiment. He was incapacitated by lameness and infirmity caught by severe cold in 1777. He resided in Canterbury, Conn. in 1792. He enlisted 11 June 1777 and was discharged 26 Aug. 1779.

Cady, David. N.Y. Pvt. He served in Capt. Woodworth's Company under Col. Willett. He was wounded in his left arm at Fort Herkimer. He was 24 years old in 1788. He resided in Montgomery Co., N.Y. when he was pensioned 27 May 1788. He was on the 1813 pension list. He also appeared as David Cadey.

Cady, David. N.Y. —. He served under Capt. Steiner [?Skinner] and Col. Marinus Willet. He was a pensioner from King's District, Albany County. [second of the name]

Cady, Phineas. Mass. —. He served in the 8th Regiment and was from Berkshire. He was paid $20.

Cahill, James. —. —. He was wounded in the service and suffered from great disabilities. He sought an increase in his pension. He was 104 years old. Congress granted him relief on 3 Mar. 1851. He was from Brown Co., Ohio.

Cahoe, Thomas. Md. Pvt. He was pensioned at the rate of half-pay of a private in Charles County 2 Jan. 1813.

Cain, —. Pa. —. His widow, Mary Cain, was awarded a $40 gratuity and a $40 annuity in Philadelphia, Pa. 15 Feb. 1825. She also appeared as Mary Kain.

Cain, Edward. Md. Pvt. He was pensioned 4 Mar. 1789. He was on the 1813 pension list.

Cain, Henry. Pa. Sgt. He was on the 1789 pension list.

Cain, James. Pa. Pvt. He was in Philadelphia County on 12 Dec. 1785. He served in the 11th Pa. Regiment and was wounded in the back at Brandywine in 1777. He was 26 years old. He died 23 Jan. 1800.

Cain, Michael. S.C. —. He was from Abbeville District in 1798.

Cain, Patrick. S.C. —. There were three children in 1791. [His widow may have been Rhoda Cain.]

Cain, Robert. S.C. Legionnaire. He served aboard the *South Carolina* under Commodore Alexander Gillon. He was paid 21 Oct. 1809.

Caine, Patrick. Pa. Drummer. He served as a marine on the galley *Ranger* from Aug. 1775 to June 1777. He served with James Montgomery. He lost his right leg by amputation after having it shot off when he was aboard the *Hope*. He enlisted as a drummer in Col. B. Flowers' Regiment of Artillery and Artificers on 1 Sep. 1779 and was turned over to Capt. Young on the *Saratoga*. Capt. Lt. Alexander Dow was in the same regiment. He also appeared as Patrick Kain.

Cairns, —. Pa.—. His widow, Elizabeth Cairns, was granted relief 19 Mar. 1816.

Cairns, Andrew. Pa. —. He served in the 138th militia regiment. His children were granted relief by the court of enquiry 28 June 1817.

Cakely, Benjamin. Va. Pvt. He was a soldier in the army. His widow, Catherine Cakely, was on the 1785 pension list.

Calahan, —. Pa. —. His widow, Rebecca Calahan, was awarded a $40 gratuity and a $40 annuity in Lycoming Co., Pa. 14 Apr. 1834.

Caldwell, James. N.J. Chaplain/Commissary of Supplies. The British shot his wife as she sat in her home in the midst of the children. They burned and plundered his home at Connecticut Farms. He was shot by a sentinel at Elizabethtown Point 24 Nov. 1781. His heirs sought compensation, but Congress rejected their petition 15 May 1838.

Caldwell, James. S.C. —. He was 75 years old when he applied from Anderson District on 8 Oct. 1832. He lived near Saluda in Lexington District in the war and served under Capt. John Kinslee and Col. Charles H–ckly for a month before the fall of Charleston. His second tour was under Capt. Godfrey Fryer, Maj. Hart, and Col. William Thompson. His third tour was under Capt. Jonathan Owens and Capt. Friday. His brother, Joseph Caldwell, attested to his service as did his brother, John Caldwell of Newberry District. His application was rejected.

Caldwell, John. —. —. Congress denied his claim for relief 9 May 1850.

Caldwell, John. Va. Pvt. He served in the Rockbridge County militia under Col. William McKee and was wounded at Cowpens by a ball through his right arm near the middle of his biceps. He was awarded one year's pay as a gratuity and an annuity of half-pay on 21 Nov. 1781. He was aged *ca.* 24 years on 28 Nov. 1786 and resided in Rockbridge County. He served under Brig. Gen. Morgan. He was continued at the rate of £12 per annum. He was on the 1813 pension list. He transferred to Knox Co., Tenn. 24 Apr. 1816. He died 25 Feb. 1829.

Caldwell, John. Va. —. He served in the militia and was wounded at Guilford. He was pensioned in 1784.

Caldwell, Joseph. S.C. —. He was pensioned in Anderson District 4 Dec. 1832. He was 70 years old when he applied 8 Oct. 1832. He served three months under Capt. Godfrey Fryer, Maj. Hart, and Col. William Thompson. He marched under Capt. Owens to Four Holes. He guarded the wagons at Orangeburg under Capt. Friday. His brother, James Caldwell, testified as to his service. He was paid as late as 1851.

Caldwell, Nicholas. Pa. Carpenter Yeoman. He was in Philadelphia Co. 14 Nov. 1785. He served aboard the frigate *Trumbull*. He was wounded on 9 Aug. 1781 in action with the ships of war, *Iris* and *Monk*. He was 33 years old. His wife was Mary Caldwell. He died 11 Dec. 1813.

Caldwell, William. S.C. Capt. He was a prisoner of war and did not receive Continental or state pay. He applied in 1792.

Caldwell, —. S.C. —. His widow was Mary Caldwell. There was one child in 1791.

Calhoun, —. Pa. —. His widow, Mary Calhoun, was awarded a $40 gratuity and a $40 annuity in Fayette County 15 June 1836.

Calhoun, James. Pa. —. He was wounded and taken prisoner at Crooked Billet in the militia under Capt. Robert McCoy and Col. Watt in May 1778. He was in Westmoreland County on 29 Mar. 1802. His annuity was $40.

Calhoun, John. Pa. —. He was awarded a $40 gratuity in Bucks County 25 June 1839 for his Revolutionary service.

Calhoun, John. S.C. —. He died in the service. His orphans were allowed an annuity 10 June 1785.

Calhoun, John. S.C. Capt. He was wounded at Tarleton's defeat and had to pay £10 for the cost of care while he lay wounded. On 23 Nov. 1798 he fell and hurt his knee and could not walk without the aid of crutches. His sister, Martha Anderson of Pendleton District, had become his security. He gave her order on the treasury for a note to draw his two years' annuity as a pensioner. She had to pay the note. She did not know that she would not be allowed to give a satisfactory receipt for same. Martha Anderson's husband was killed in the service and left her with four small children. He left the state and went westward in 1808 apparently fearful of punishment. He was pensioned by the U.S. in 1811. He was on the 1813 pension list. He died in 1823. His widow, Violet Calhoun, had married him in 1790 or 1791. Her son, John Gaw by her first husband, was four years old when she remarried. She was granted a pension by a private act 28 Feb. 1844.

Califfe, Stephen. Pa. Pvt. He was pensioned 11 Aug. 1790. He later lived in New York.

Callaghan, Edward. N.Y. Pvt. He lost his sight by the strain of over lifting in removing cannon from the battery in New York City. He served under Col. Alexander McDougall in Capt. William Goforth's Company in the 1st N.Y. Regiment. He lived in New York City, N.Y. on 13 June 1788. He also appeared as Edward Callahan. He was on the 1791 pension and the 1813 pension lists.

Callahan, Daniel. Pa. Pvt. He served in the 1st Pa Regiment. He was wounded in the right arm near the shoulder by a musket ball at Green Springs, Va. He lived in Northumberland, Pa. in 1794. He enlisted 1 July 1776 for two years and was discharged 16 May 1778. He was on the 1813 pension list. He later lived in Lycoming County.

Callahan, Joel. —. Pvt. & Capt. He was pensioned at the rank of a private at $40 per annum. His only child, Catharine Compton, sought his arrears because he served as a captain. Congress denied her petition because he swore "he was in no battle of any importance."

Callahan, John. Md. 1st Lt. His widow, Sarah Callahan, was pensioned at the rate of half-pay of a first lieutenant in Annapolis 18 Mar. 1839.

Callahan, Patrick. Pa. Pvt. He was in Northumberland County on 28 Mar. 1786. He was in Col. Potter's Battalion of the Northumberland County militia in Capt. John Clark's company. He was wounded by a musket ball in the right thigh on 1 Feb. 1777 at Piscataway. Joseph Green was the surgeon's mate who assisted Dr. Benjamin Allison who dressed the wound. Lt. Col. James Murray was also mentioned. He was 40 years old.

Callaway, Richard. N.C. —. He applied in Ashe County in 1816. He served in the Wilkes County militia and was wounded in the hands, arms, and shoulders by swords in Sumter's defeat. He was also wounded in the thigh by a ball from a rifle. He died 5 Mar. 1829 as proved by Elijah Callaway, administrator of his estate.

Callender, William. Mass. —. He served more than two years under Col. Craft in the artillery. He died 24 Mar. 1839. Congress granted his widow, Catherine W. Callender, a pension 8 Mar. 1842.

Calliham, Morris. S.C. —. He was 85 years old when he applied and had lived in the state sixty-five years. He had been a pilot to Gen. Grant in 1759 in the war against the Cherokee. In 1779 he and his son entered the service. The Indians attacked, burnt his house, murdered his wife, children, and seven Negroes. He remarried and had four small children. His application was undated.

Cameron, Alexander. Ga. Pvt. He was paid $50 as an invalid soldier in 1803. He was on the 1813 pension list.

Cameron, John. Pa. —. He was awarded a $40 gratuity and a $40 annuity in Huntingdon County 5 Feb. 1836.

Cameron, John. Va. Pvt. He served in the 14th Virginia Regiment. His widow, Catherine Cameron, was granted a pension in Hanover County 3 Nov. 1779. She was on the pension list in 1787.

Cames, Nicholas. N.Y. Pvt. He served under Col. Peter Bellinger in the Montgomery County militia and was slain 15 June 1778. His children, John Cames, Nicholas Cames, Christopher Cames, and Mary Catharine Cames received his half-pay pension.

Camfield, Aaron. Va. Capt. He entered the service as ensign from Bedford County and served under Capt. Henry Terrell, 1st Lt. Thomas McReynolds, and 2nd Lt. John Gaggin in the 5th Regiment. He became a captain due to the illness of Capt. McReynolds. In 1783 he removed to Hancock Co., Ga. and in 1785 married Miss Jones. He died in 1786 leaving a son, Richard Camfield, as proved by the oath of John Nail 17 Oct. 1814.

Cammack, William. Va. Pvt. He enlisted for 18 months and served under Col. Campbell. He was wounded by a ball in the right knee on 15 Mar. 1781 at Guilford Court House, N.C. He resided in Caroline Co., Va. in 1786 and in 1796. Lt. Col. S. Hawes, formerly Lt. Col. of the 1st Va. Regiment, attested to his service. He was continued at the rate of £6 per annum on 28 Dec. 1786.

Cammell, George. Mass. —. He was pensioned at the rate of $15 per annum and collected payments to March 1804.

Cammock, Henry. Va. —. He was accidentally wounded when his own gun discharged the load through his right hand. His application was rejected on 28 Nov. 1777 since he was fit for duty.

Camp, —. Pa. —. His widow, Christina Camp, received a $40 gratuity and a $40 annuity 3 Apr. 1837 in Crawford County. She died 6 June 1844.

Camp, Aaron. N.J. —. He was pensioned in Essex County 10 Mar. 1842 at the rate of $40 per annum.

Camp, Amos. N.H. Pvt. He served in Col. Hale's Regiment. He was wounded in the left arm and belly by a musket ball on 19 Sep. 1777 at Bemis Heights. He resided in Columbia Co., N.Y. in 1794. He enlisted 14 Apr. 1777 and was discharged 1 May 1780. He was on the 1813 pension list of New York.

Camp, Caspar. Pa. —. He received a $40 gratuity in Crawford County 22 Mar. 1825.

Camp, David. Pa. —. He was awarded a $40 gratuity and a $40 annuity in Berks Co., Pa. 6 Apr. 1830.

Camp, Joel. Conn. Pvt. He served in Col. Patterson's Regiment. He was wounded aboard a batteau when crossing Lake Champlain in June 1778; the wound caused an ulcer. He resided in Litchfield, Conn. in 1794. He died in 1807.

Camp, William. N.J. —. He was pensioned from 29 May 1781.

Campbell, —. S.C. His widow, Agnes Campbell, was from York District in 1799.

Campbell, —. Pa. —. His widow, Mary Campbell, was awarded a $40 gratuity and a $40 annuity in Philadelphia, Pa. 30 Jan. 1832.

Campbell, —. Pa. —. His widow, Elizabeth Campbell, received a $40 gratuity and a $40 annuity in Lycoming County 18 Mar. 1834.

Campbell, —. Pa. —. His widow, Mary Campbell, was awarded a $40 gratuity and a $40 annuity in Northumberland County 31 Mar. 1836. She was 77 years old in 1840.

Campbell, Alexander. Me. —. He died 15 Feb. 1827. His widow, Mary Campbell, was from Minot. She was paid $50 under the resolve of 1836.

Campbell, Alexander. Pa. Mariner. He was in Philadelphia County 9 Jan. 1786. He served aboard the frigate *Trumbull*. He was wounded in the knee in an engagement with the British frigate *Iris* off the capes of Delaware. He was 23 years old. He was on the 1813 pension list.

Campbell, Andrew. S.C. —. He applied 8 Nov. 1836 from Spartanburg District. He was 76 years old and was blind. He had been a school teacher. He served three months under Gen. Henderson, Col. Bratton, and Capt. William Davis. His application was rejected.

Campbell, Archibald. N.J. —. He was pensioned in Atlantic County on 28 Feb. 1839 at the rate of

$60 per annum.

Campbell, Archibald. S.C. —. He applied from Williamsburg District 14 Nov. 1829. At the age of 16 he entered the service under Gen. Francis Marion in 1778 and served under Capt. John McCauly. He was 70 years old and had lately been disabled by a fall from his horse. Robert Davis swore that he saw him in the service. His application was rejected. On 18 Nov. 1833 at the age of 74 he again applied. He was finally approved 20 Nov. 1837. He was paid as late as 1846.

Campbell, Daniel. N.C. —. He applied in Lincoln County in Oct. 1799. He was wounded at Adam Torrence's in Rowan County by Tarleton's Corps of Dragoons on 1 Feb. 1781. He had five saber wounds on his head which penetrated his skull, one on his chin, two on his left hand which cut off his forefinger, and one on his right hand. He was 30 years old in 1781. In 1790 he was stricken with palsy. His wife died in 1796. He had a family of children.

Campbell, Donald. N.Y. Col. & Brig. Gen. by brevet. He was granted 5,000 acres bounty land 9 Apr. 1795.

Campbell, Duncan. N.Y. Lt. He served under Col. Livingston. He was wounded in his right leg in an engagement with the British troops in Oct. or Nov. 1777 at Bemis Heights. He lived in New York in 1794. He was sick in Albany from 20 July 1777 to Feb. 1779. He was granted half a pension 20 Apr. 1796. He died 4 Jan. 1807.

Campbell, George. Md. Pvt. He was pensioned at the rate of $50 per annum in Nov. 1800.

Campbell, Hugh. Pa. —. He was awarded a $40 gratuity and a $40 annuity in Chester County on 16 Mar. 1819.

Campbell, James. Pa. —. He was paid $200 20 May 1839 for the donation land which he was due which had been granted by patent 24 Aug. 1787. The land was in New York.

Campbell, Jacob. R.I. —. He enlisted in 1780 for one year under Capt. William Potter and Col. Christopher Green. He was discharged at Newport in Feb. 1781 at which time he was ill. He was granted relief by Congress 10 Jan. 1832. He lived in Chenango Co., N.Y.

Campbell, James. R.I. Pvt. He served in Col. Topham's R.I. Regiment. He was wounded by a musket ball which broke the main bones of his right leg on 29 Aug. 1778 in R.I. He resided in Voluntown, Conn. in 1792 and in Middleburg, Vt. in 1796. He was granted half a pension 20 Apr. 1796.

Campbell, James. —. Pvt. He served in the Volunteers. He was wounded in both legs by a musket ball and another ball in the hip at Ticonderoga, N.Y. in May 1775. He resided at Chester, Mass. in 1796. He was granted one-fourth of a pension 20 Apr. 1796. He was on the 1813 pension list.

Campbell, James. Me. —. He was from Monmouth. He was paid $50 under the resolve of 1836.

Campbell, James. N.H. Pvt. He was from Acworth in 1780. He served in Col. Cilley's Regiment and was wounded through his thigh. He was aged 27 in 1787. He was on the 1813 pension list.

Campbell, James. N.C. Capt. He applied in Cumberland County in 1811. He was in the Continental Line under Col. John Paisley. He was sent home ill. He had a family of small children and was upwards of 60 years of age. He was dead by 18 Dec. 1813. Another record indicated a pension being paid to him in 1816. His widow was Isabella Campbell.

Campbell, James. Pa. Lt. His heirs received $200 in lieu of donation land on 29 May 1839. The tract, #249, had fallen into New York.

Campbell, James. Pa. —. He received a $40 gratuity in Westmoreland County 13 Mar. 1839.

Campbell, James. Vt. Pvt. He received a half pension in 1796.

Campbell, James. Va. Lt. He served in Capt. George Scott's Company of Volunteers under Col. Charles M. Thurston. He was wounded in his left arm and had the bone fractured in action near Piscataway, N.J. on 1 Mar. 1777. He was awarded a £30 gratuity and half-pay for life from 15 Apr. 1777 on 22 Oct. 1778. He resided in Berkeley County on 28 Oct. 1788. He was on the 1813 pension list.

Campbell, John. —. Maj. He served as assistant deputy quartermaster. On 13 Mar. 1838 he was allowed the interest on his commutation pay.

Campbell, John. Del. Pvt. He served under Capt. George Latimer having entered the service in 1776 at Wilmington for nine months. He next volunteered for a two year tour of duty and lastly for a third tour to the end of the war. He was at Staten Island when the Americans under Gen. Messer attacked the Hessians. He married in 1771. His widow, Mary Campbell, of Philadelphia, Pa. was placed on the pension roll by Congress 14 Mar. 1846 at the rate of $30 per annum from 9 Feb. 1842.

Campbell, John. N.J. Pvt. He served in the 2nd Regiment. He was disabled with a rupture. He was 38 years old and was from Greenwich. He was on the 1791 pension roll.

Campbell, John. N.Y. Maj. He served as barracks and foragemaster from 25 Dec. 1776 to 25 July 1783 under Col. Adney Hay, Deputy Quartermaster General, and Gen. Greene. He received federal bounty land warrant #397 for 200 acres for service as lieutenant of artillery. He died in 1798 in New York City. His daughter, Sarah Campbell, married Thomas Kirk. She died 29 Dec. 1855 and her husband 10 Oct. 1851. They were buried in Greenwood Cemetery in Brooklyn. Their son, Asbury W. Kirk, for himself and Julia A. Kirk, James Van Antwerp, Salina Van Antwerp (daughter of the veteran), Sarah Cooper, William Cooper, and Thomas Cooper, applied to Congress for relief on 11 Feb. 1860. Margaret Cooper was a daughter of the veteran, and Peter Cooper was a grandson.

Campbell, John. Pa. —. He was pensioned 8 Dec. 1817 at the rate of $40 per annum.

Campbell, John. Pa. —. He was awarded a $40 gratuity and a $40 annuity in Franklin Co., Pa. 29 Mar. 1824. He served under Capt. Samuel Blythe in a company of rangers in 1780.

Campbell, John. Pa. —. He received a $40 gratuity in Cumberland County 27 Mar. 1824.

Campbell, John. Pa. —. He was placed on the pension by the Court of Enquiry 3 Dec. 1817. He died 28 May 1822.

Campbell, John. Pa. —. He applied from Northumberland County 19 Nov. 1817. His cousin was Daniel Campbell. He enlisted in Capt. Thomas Comb's N.J. Rangers under Col. Ebenezer Pike until he was transferred to the 17th Pa. Regiment under Col. Cook. He was wounded in the left arm at Piscataway and lay sick five or six months. Cook's unit was annexed to the 3rd Regiment under Col. Thomas Craig. Capt. Nicholas Miller signed his discharge.

Campbell, John. Pa. Pvt. He was in the Washington County militia under Col. William Crawford and was killed by Indians 4 June 1782 in the expedition against the Sandusky towns. His widow was Rosanna Campbell.

Campbell, John W. —. —. Congress denied his claim for relief 1 Aug. 1850.

Campbell, Joseph. Pa. —. He received a $40 gratuity and a $40 annuity in Mercer County 1 Apr. 1836.

Campbell, Lewis. N.J. Pvt. He served in the 1st Jersey Regiment and was shot through his body. He was 30 years old and was from Woodbridge. He was on the 1791 pension roll at the rate of $60 per annum.

Campbell, Michael. Pa. Pvt. He was in Lancaster County on 5 Dec. 1787. He served in the 3rd Battalion of the Northumberland County militia and was killed by savages in actual service 13 June 1778.

His widow, Sarah Campbell, married second William Ferguson who was guardian of his children. They were Margaret Campbell about 12 years old and Sarah Campbell about 9 years old. Margaret Campbell was indisposed by a gunshot wound. The allowance to his daughter, Sarah Campbell, ceased 26 Mar. 1791.

Campbell, Patrick. —. Col. He died 10 July 1818. His widow, Catharine Campbell, died in Mar. 1824. Congress denied his son, Adam P. Campbell, and the other children relief on 26 Apr. 1848 and on 14 June 1850.

Campbell, Richard. Va. Col. He was wounded at Camden 25 Apr. 1781. He was slain leading the charge upon the British line at Eutaw Springs 8 Sep. 1781. His widow, Rebecca Campbell, married secondly Joseph Pugh on 3 Jan. 1785. Jacob Fetter performed the marriage. She lived in Shenandoah County on 13 Apr. 1789. The children were allowed the balance due them 22 Dec. 1837.

Campbell, Robert. N.Y. Lt. He served in the Montgomery County militia. He was killed at Oriskany 6 Aug. 1777. His children, Sarah Campbell, Jennet Campbell, and Samuel Campbell, received a seven year half-pay pension.

Campbell, Robert. Pa. —. He was awarded a $40 gratuity and a $40 annuity in Perry Co., Pa. 25 Mar. 1833.

Campbell, Robert. Pa. Capt. His widow, Mary Fullerton, was in Philadelphia County on 12 May 1787. He died in the service 5 Oct. 1779. She collected his pension to 31 Dec. 1780. It was probably the date of her remarriage.

Campbell, Robert. S.C. Capt. He was killed by the enemy's galleys in Savannah River. His widow was allowed an annuity 24 May 1785.

Campbell, Robert. Va. —. He served in Capt. James Thompson's Company and was wounded by accident in the service of the country. He was granted support in Washington Co., Va. 30 Sep. 1777.

Campbell, Samuel. —. —. He applied for a pension in 1837 but was rejected because his service war for only four months. Other service he claimed was not covered by the act of 1832. He applied for private relief, but Congress denied his petition 12 Feb. 1841.

Campbell, Samuel. Pa. —. He was awarded a $40 gratuity and a $40 annuity 1 Apr. 1834 in Allegheny County, Pa. He died 18 Dec. 1849.

Campbell, Thomas. Pa. Capt. He enlisted in the Pennsylvania Rifle Regiment under Gen. Thompson in June 1775 and served until Jan. 1777. He was promoted from 3rd to 1st Lieutenant in the 4th Pennsylvania Regiment under Col. Lambert Cadwallader. He applied firstly at the age of 32 on 9 Jan. 1786 from York County and again on 31 Dec. 1812. He was wounded in battle at Germantown by a musket ball through his left wrist and body on 4 Oct. 1777. His widow, Isabella Campbell, was awarded a $60 gratuity and a $60 annuity in York County on 27 Mar. 1819. He had five children. He was on the pension list of 1813.

Campbell, Thomas. Pa. —. He was awarded a $40 gratuity and a $40 annuity in Westmoreland Co., Pa. on 29 Mar. 1824 and again on 22 Dec. 1834. He was a ranger on the frontiers. He was 85 years old in 1840. He died in May 1846 in Allegheny County.

Campbell, William. Md. —. He served in the 3rd Md. Regiment under Capt. Samuel Griffiths. He was wounded in his right leg at the battle of Germantown in 1777. He was awarded £100 on 27 July1780.

Campbell, William. N.J. Sgt. He applied in Penn. 14 Apr. 1789. He served in Col. Sylvanus Seeley's Regiment in Capt. John Davis's Company in N.J. and was wounded in the service. He lost an arm. He was 46 years and lived at Milford. He lived in Pennsylvania when he was pensioned from 1 Sep. 1779 to 1 May 1787.

Campbell, William. Pa. Sgt. He was on the 1791 pension roll. He was on the pension list of 1813. He removed to Bourbon Co., Ky. He was from Hopkins Co., Ky. at another time.

Campbell, William. Pa. Pvt. He was in Dauphin County on 21 June 1786. He was in the Flying Camp from Lancaster County and marched to New York. In October 1776 he was taken sick at Delancey's Mill and left in the hospital. He was taken prisoner. He was disabled by sickness contracted in the service. He had a certificate from Capt. Robert Clark regarding his service. He was 46 years old. He was on the pension list of 1813.

Campbell, William. Pa. —. His widow, Rachel Campbell, was awarded a $40 gratuity and a $40 annuity on 18 Mar. 1834 in Lycoming Co., Pa. She was 76 years old in 1840. She applied 13 May 1847. He was in Capt. Montgomery's Company and served seven months in 1780. He was pensioned in 1832 for 13 months of service. He had three tours of two months each in the militia and seven months as a draft. Her pension was refused unless she could prove that Capt. Montgomery and Col. Harmar were in the Line in 1780. The return of men enlisted for seven months in the Pa. Line in Capt. Montgomery's Company included Henry Shafer, William Barnes, William Campbell, and Nicholas Eastman. The latter was supposed to be a deserter. Capt. Binion's Company included Peter Sinck. Capt. Doyle's Company included Isaac Davis and Henry Sharp. Rachel Campbell was in Marshall, Clark Co., Ill. She died 19 Aug. 1842.

Campbell, William. Va. —. He served under Col. Patrick Henry. He was created a brigadier general in the Virginia militia in Dec. 1780. He was at King's Mountain and died 22 Aug. 1781 at Yorktown. On 19 Dec. 1783 his heirs were awarded 5,000 acres. His son, Charles Campbell, died as a minor. His daughter married Francis Preston who petitioned to have the land located in Ohio between the Scioto and Miami Rivers. Congress approved the request 25 Feb. 1830.

Campbell, William. S.C. —. He was killed in Dec. 1782. His widow, Jane Campbell, was allowed an annuity 22 Feb. 1786. There were two children in 1791.

Campbell, William. Va. Col. His heirs, Susan Campbell and others, sought his commutation pay. He served in Gibson's Regiment until Oct. 1780. They alleged that the U.S. had granted bounty land for his service, but there was no proof of same. Congress rejected the claim on 17 Feb. 1846 from the heirs for bounty land or commutation since he resigned. It did so again 26 Apr. 1848.

Camperlane, Jacob. —. Capt. He was wounded in his right knee at Stono. He applied in Stokes Co., N.C. in Sep. 1788;

Campfield, —. S.C. —. His widow, Elizabeth Campfield, was being pensioned in 1830.

Campfield, Asahel. N.J. —. He served in the 1st Regiment and died of smallpox at Fort George on 15 July 1776. He married Electa Riggs 23 Nov. 1772. She married secondly Mathias Campfield 15 Dec. 1783.

Campin, James. N.C. Lt. He was pensioned in 1809..

Campton, Archibald. Va. Pvt. He served in the 2nd Va. Regiment. He resided in Pittsylvania County.

Camron, —. Va. Pvt. His widow, Martha Camron, was pensioned 17 Dec. 1778.

Camron, John. Va. Pvt. He enlisted for three years in the 14th Va. Regiment under Capt. John Winston on 5 Jan. 1779. He died in the service on 7 Mar. 1779. He left a widow, Catharine Camron, and several children who were very poor on 6 Nov. 1784. His heir at law was William Camron. His widow also appeared as Catherine Cameron. The family lived in Hanover County.

Canada, Asher. Mass. —. He was paid $20.

Canavan, James. Va. —. His wife, Mary Canavan, was granted £30 for support of her and her family while her husband was away in the service in Rockbridge Co., Va. 3 Aug. 1779.

Canfield, David. N.J. —. He enlisted 26 Nov. 1776 and served under Capt. Benoni Hathaway. He was wounded in his leg in Dec. 1776 at Springfield. Both of the bones were broken. His father cared for him. He had a wife and seven children on 6 Nov. 1797 in Essex County. He was paid 13 May 1800.

Canfield, Philo. Conn. Sgt. He served in Capt. James Stoddard's Company in the Conn. State Troops under Lt. Col. Samuel Canfield. He was ordered out by Lt. Josiah Smith on 24 May 1782. All in his party were either killed, wounded, or taken prisoner. He was disabled by a musket shot through the right side of his right knee. He was aged 26 years on 13 June 1788. He lived in Kent Parish, South East Precinct, Dutchess Co., N.Y. on 5 May 1789. He was a farmer. He was on the 1813 pension list. He died 11 Mar. 1827.

Canfield, Richard. Del. Pvt. He was pensioned in 1784. He was born in Ireland, was married, and was wounded accidentally in the arm on duty at Camden on 10 Dec. 1780. He also appeared as Richard Cawfield.

Canfield, Thomas. Md. Pvt. He was granted relief.

Cannady, —. Va. —. He died in the service. His father, James Cannady, and seven children were granted support in Westmoreland County. The father lost his sons in Continental service.

Cannady, George. Va. —. He died in the service. His widow was Mildred Cannady in Westmoreland County.

Cannears, —. Va. —. Ambrose Cannears was granted support in King William County in 1778.

Cannius, John. Pa. —. He was from Berks County and was pensioned 26 June 1823. He also appeared as John Conius.

Cannon, —. Va. —. His widow, Catherine Cannon, was continued on the roll at the rate of £10 per annum on 15 Nov. 1787.

Cannon, John. Del. —. He was receiving a pension in 1787.

Cannon, [Joseph]. Va. —. He died in Continental service. His widow, Obedience Cannon, was granted support in Brunswick County 22 Jan. and 27 July 1781. His orphans were John Cannon and William Cannon.

Cannon, Luke. Va. Lt. Since he received his commutation in his lifetime, his heirs were rejected 17 Jan. 1838.

Cannon, Matthew. N.Y. Pvt. He served in the militia under Capt. James Wilson in Col. Samuel Campbell's Regiment. He was wounded by a musket ball through his thigh by the Indians at Cherry Valley 11 Nov. 1778. He was 70 years old in 1788. He lived in Montgomery Co., N.Y. on 15 July 1789. He died in 1794.

Cannon, Peter. Pa. —. He was granted relief.

Cannon, William. S.C. —. He was killed in July 1781 by Tories. His widow, Ann Cannon, was from Pendleton District and was paid £15 in May 1794.

Canterberry, Joseph. Va. —. His wife, Ruth Canterberry, was provided financial support for necessaries while her husband was away in the service in Amherst Co., Va. in Aug. and Oct. 1778.

Cantine, George. Mass. —. He served in the 3rd Artillery and was from Philadelphia. He was paid $20.

Cantley, Roger. S.C. Pvt. He served under Capt. Daniel Conyers in the calvary. He was 60 years of age and had a considerable family. He applied from Williamsburg District, S.C. 5 Dec. 1821, but he was rejected.

Capen, James. Mass. —. He was granted relief.

Capen, James. —. —. He served five months and 12 days. Congress credited him with six months of service by including the time of his going and returning from his place of muster. He was pensioned at the rate of $8 per month from 4 Mar. 1851 but died before he received any payment. His administrator sought the pension. Congress did not concur in making money available to his creditors or indifferent heirs on 25 Jan. 1855.

Capes, —. Va. Pvt. His widow, Mary Capes, was pensioned 14 Oct. 1778.

Capp, Ebenezer. —. Sgt. He served in Col. Reed's Regiment. He was wounded by a cannon ball which fractured his ribs and forced on him an incurable rupture on 17 June 1775 at Bunker Hill. He resided at Hampstead, N.H. in 1796.

Cappel, Charles. Pa. —. He was pensioned 4 Feb. 1813 in Bucks County. His widow, Margaret Cappel, was granted a $40 gratuity on 28 Mar. 1820. She was awarded a $40 annuity in Bucks County 29 Mar. 1822. He also appeared as Charles Capple and Charles Copple..

Capps, William. N.C. Pvt. He applied in Craven County in 1785. He was in Continental service and was disabled in his left knee. He was aged 37 in 1785.

Capron, Elisha. Vt. Pvt. He was pensioned 3 Mar. 1811. He was on the 1813 pension list.

Caps, John. S.C. —. He served in the 6th S.C. Regiment. He was taken prisoner at Charleston and died in confinement. His widow, Mary Caps, was allowed an annuity 5 Aug. 1785.

Car, Christopher. Pa. —. He was awarded a $40 gratuity in Montgomery Co., Pa. 25 Mar. 1831, 4 May 1832, and 6 Apr. 1833. He also appeared as Christopher Carr.

Carber, Henry. Va. —. His wife, Margaret Carber, was granted 1 barrel of corn and 50 pounds of pork on 18 Sep. 1781 in Berkeley County. There were two children. He served in Col. Crocket's Regiment of State Troops.

Carberry, Henry. Md. Capt. He was on the 1813 pension list of the District of Columbia. He died 26 May 1822.

Carbury, Peter. Md. Pvt. He was pensioned 4 Mar. 1789. He was on the 1813 pension list.

Cardiff, John. Pa. Pvt. He served in Col. Hartley's 16th Additional. He lost the use of his left arm by the bursting of a musket in July 1778 in Philadelphia. He lived in Pa. in 1795. He was in hospital in Feb. 1779 and omitted from the rolls in May 1779. He was granted a full pension 20 Apr. 1796. He was on the 1813 pension list.

Cardiff, Miles. Va. Pvt. He served in the 10th Va. Regiment. He was wounded in the arm which withered. He was discharged from the Invalid Corps by Col. Walter Stewart, Inspector of the Northern Army, on 15 Sep. 1782. He was aged 36 on 8 May 1787. He lived in Rockbridge County. He was continued at the rate of £10 per annum. He was on the 1813 pension list.

Cardwell, —. Va. —. His mother, Agnes Cardwell, was granted £10 support on 15 June 1778 in York Co., Va. She was also paid for maintaining the infant daughter of William White, a deceased soldier. She was paid £40 on 21 June 1779 as the mother of a veteran and for maintaining two children of William White, deceased.

Cardwell, John. Va. Pvt. He served in the militia. He was being pensioned 27 Dec. 1781.

Cardwell, Lewis. Va. —. His mother, Agatha Cardwell, was granted £10 support in York Co., Va. on 17 Aug. 1778 for supporting her son's two children. [Compare with the unnamed Cardwell *supra* with a mother named Agnes Cardwell.]

Careton, John. Mass. Pvt. He was on the 1813 pension list.

Carey, —. —. —. His son, Arnold Carey, had his petition for a pension rejected by Congress 15 Apr. 1886.

Carey, Clarke. —. —. He entered the service on Long Island in 1775. He fought at Bunker Hill, Long Island, White Plains, Trenton, and Princeton. He was present at the capture of Lord Cornwallis and Gen. Prescott. In 1777 he was appointed lieutenant of infantry. In 1803 he was appointed 1st Lieutenant in the Artillery and served three years. He had yellow fever twice and lost his eyesight. Congress granted him an increase in his pension 19 Jan. 1832.

Carey, John. Pa. —. He was pensioned by the act of 24 Mar. 1818 with a $40 gratuity and a $40 annuity. He was from Northampton County. He died 20 Nov. 1839.

Carey, Samuel. Pa. —. He was awarded a $40 gratuity and a $40 annuity in Luzerne Co., Pa. 29 Mar. 1824. He was 77 years old in 1840. He died 23 Apr. 1843.

Carey, Simon. Pa. —. He applied 18 Sep. 1792. He also appeared as Simon Karney.

Carhart, Thomas. N.J. Corp. He served under Capt. T. Patterson in the 3rd N.J. Regiment. He was wounded by a ball in his knee on 31 July 1778 at Elizabethtown Point. He lived in Bernard's Town, Somerset Co., N.J. He enlisted 12 Jan. 1777, was a prisoner 23 Aug. 1778, and was discharged 1 June 1779. He was on the 1813 pension list. He died 19 Feb. 1825.

Carithers, John. Pa. 1st Lt. He served in the 12th Pa. Regiment under Col. William Cooke and was killed at Germantown 4 Oct. 1777. His widow, Mary Carithers, died 13 July 1788. His son, Thomas Walter Carithers, was born 9 Feb. 1770, and the child's grandmother was Martha Stevenson who supported him. He was granted support 2 Dec. 1791.

Carle, Ebenezer. Mass. —. He was from Phillipsburgh and was paid $20.

Carle, John. Mass. He was from Lyman and was paid $20.

Carleton, Ebenezer. N.H. Pvt. He served in the 1st Regiment. He fell from his horse and was badly ruptured in his groin when he was acting as surveyor to General Washington's family in June 1782. He lived in Alexandria, N.H. in 1794. He was granted one-third of a pension 20 Apr. 1796. He was on the 1813 pension list.

Carleton, Edward, Pa. —. He was pensioned 2 May 1814 at the rate of $40 per annum.

Carleton, John. Pa. —. He was awarded a $40 gratuity and a $40 annuity in York County 29 Apr. 1829.

Carleton, Moses —. —. He marched from Bedford 25 June 1780 and was discharged 10 Dec. 1780. He was short three days of the minimum time of service. Congress granted his widow, Mary Carleton, a pension of $24 per annum on the presumption that he enlisted three days before he marched.

Carley, Jonathan. Mass. —. He served in the 3rd Artillery and was from Greenfield. He was paid $20.

Carlin, William. Md. Pvt. His widow, Mary Carlin, was pensioned at the rate of half-pay of a private 21 Mar. 1837.

Carlisle, —. S.C. —. His widow, Margaret Carlisle, was pensioned 16 Dec. 1835.

Carlton, Ezra. Me. —. He was from Letter E Plantation. He was paid $50 under the resolve of 1836.

Carlton, John. Me. —. He was from Frankfort. He was paid $50 under the resolve of 1836.

Carlton, John. Ma. Pvt. He was pensioned from 4 Mar. 1801.

Carlton, John. Pa. —. He was awarded a $40 gratuity and a $40 annuity in York Co., Pa. 20 Apr. 1829.

Carmack, John. —. —. The five months of service in 1774-75 against the Indians was not Revolutionary service. In 1777 and 1778 he served as a captain of a brigade of packhorses to provision Gen. McIntosh on the Ohio River below Fort Pitt. That service was not embraced in the act of 1832. Of the 17 months and 26 days he claimed as service, only 5 months and 26 days counted. He sought relief by a special act of Congress. The committee credited him with

12 months and 26 days of service and gave him a pension 11 Feb. 1834.

Carman, Andrew. Pa. —. He applied in Lancaster County on 13 Dec. 1813. He was a cooper. He was dead by May 1826.

Carman, Henry. N.Y. Ens. He served in Col. S. Drake's militia. He was wounded by a ball from a pistol that went off by accident which entered the left part of his neck and lodged in his shoulder and caused his left arm to perish. He was wounded 3 Nov. 1780 at Crumpond, now Yorktown. He lived in Yorktown, Chester Co., N.Y. in 1794.

Carman, Moses. N.J. Pvt. He served under Col. Oliver Spencer and Capt. Jonas Ward and died at Valley Forge 20 Feb. 1778. He married Abigail Dean. His widow, Abigail Carman, was granted a half-pay pension in Morris County in 1781 and 25 Sep. 1792.

Carmany, John. Pa. —. He served in a Lancaster County Battalion of the Flying Camp on Long Island. He was from Lancaster County.

Carmichael, James. Md. Pvt. He served in the 1st Regiment. He was pensioned from Kent County in 1781. He died in 1785.

Carmichael, John. Va. Pvt. He was pensioned in Ohio County. He later moved to the state of Ohio. He was on the 1813 pension list.

Carmine, William. Pa. —. His widow, Elizabeth Carmine, received a $40 gratuity and a $40 annuity 27 Jan. 1819.

Carmondy, John. Pa. —. He was awarded a $40 gratuity and a $40 annuity in Columbiana Co., Ohio. 17 Jan. 1831.

Carn, John. Va. —. He served under Col. Gibson and was pensioned before being dropped. Congress granted his children relief.

Carnall, —. Va. —. His wife, Mason Carnall, was granted £20 support 12 Nov. 1778 , £30 on 8 Apr. 1779, and £50 on 11 May 1780 in Caroline Co., Va.

Carne, John. S.C. —. He served as apothecary in the Continental Hospital. He was held as a prisoner for fourteen months before he was exchanged and sent to Virginia. He repaired to Philadelphia and eventually returned to South Carolina. He had a large family and sought his commutation pay. It was allowed in 1789.

Carney, John. Pa. Pvt. He was in Chester County 20 June 1786. He served in the 9th Pa. Regiment and lost his sight by severe duty. He was 35 years old. He was dead in or by 1798.

Carney, Patrick. Va. —. His wife died while he was away in the service. The Manchester Parish church wardens of Chesterfield County were ordered to sell the perishable part of his estate to care for his child on 7 Feb. 1777.

Carney, Thomas. Md. Pvt. He was pensioned at the rate of half-pay of a private on 2 Jan. 1812.

Carney, Thomas. Mass. —. He transferred to Alleghany County, Pennsylvania 5 Sep. 1808. He was on the 1813 pension list.

Carothers, —. Pa. —. His widow, Ann Carothers, was awarded a $40 gratuity and a $40 annuity in Chester Co., Pa. 6 Mar. 1833.

Carothers, James. Pa. Pvt. He was in Chester County on 21 Dec. 1785. He was in the 5th Pa. Regiment and was wounded at Green Springs in 1781. He was 42 years old. He died 18 Feb. 1801. He also appeared as James Caruthers.

Carothers, John. Pa. —. He applied from Butler County in 1819. He enlisted in Capt. William Butler's Company under Col. St. Clair in 1775 and was discharged in 1778 by Maj. Woods. He received a slight wood in his hand at Three Rivers. He was 96 years old in 1840. He died 18 Feb. 1841.

Carpenter, Abel. R.I. Sgt. He served in the R.I. Continental Line under Col. Hitchcock and Jeremiah

Olney. He was disabled by a musket ball which entered his body on the left side of his back bone and lodged therein. He was 32 years old in 1786 and was pensioned by Massachusetts. He was on the 1813 pension list of Massachusetts. He later moved to Caledonia, Vt.

Carpenter, Benajah. R.I. Capt. He served in the Light Artillery and was killed in the battle of Long Island 27 Aug. 1776. His heirs were paid his seven years' half-pay of $1,120. His widow had her application rejected 8 Jan.1796.

Carpenter, Thomas. N.Y. Lt. He served under Col. Thomas Thomas in Capt. John Thomas's Company in the Westchester County militia. He was wounded by a bayonet in his left side through his body. He had four other wounds in the left side of his neck and one through his right hand by thrusts of a bayonet. He was 37 years old on 21 Nov. 1786. He lived in Harrison Purchase, Westchester Co., N.Y. in 1787. He was on the 1813 pension list.

Carr, David. Va. —. His wife, Ally Carr, was awarded 50 pounds of pork and 6 barrels of corn in Bedford County in Nov. 1780. There were six in her family. She was awarded 2 barrels of corn and 50 pounds of pork on 28 May 1781 and again on 25 Feb. 1782.

Carr, Hezekiah. Md. Drummer. He was pensioned at the rate of half-pay of a drummer in May 1812.

Carr, Ingram. Md. Pvt. He was pensioned at the rate of half-pay of a private 2 Jan. 1813.

Carr, John. —. —. He was at Philip Baregais' fort in Montgomery County in the spring of 1776. He served under Capt. Floyd, Lt. Christian Snidow, and Ens. John Chapman for various tours in 1777 and 1780. He sought relief from Congress 7 Jan. 1841

Carr, John. Del. Pvt. He was disabled by a stroke received across his loins by a log in the execution of his duty. He was unable to support himself and was pensioned in 1783. Afterwards he was struck off the roll on the supposition that his disability had ceased. That was not the case so in 1794 he reapplied. He lived in Wilmington, Del. in 1792. He enlisted in Oct. 1777 for three years and was discharged 6 Oct. 1779.

Carr, John. Md. Lt. He served in the 3rd Maryland Regiment. He was a native of Anne Arundel Co., Md. He entered the service in the spring of 1776 to the spring of 1777 when he received a commission as an ensign. Soon after he was promoted to 2nd Lieutenant. When the number of officers was reduced, he was appointed Lieutenant in the 3rd Md. Regiment with his rank back dated from 13 Nov. 1779. He continued on duty to Oct. 1780. He was reduced by disease and was unable to perform his duty and was never able to rejoin the army. His name was left out of the muster rolls. He never resigned his commission, and he never received his commutation. In June 1778 he was obliged to serve as forage master very much against his inclination. He lost all of his papers and baggage at the battle of Camden. He was dreadfully afflicted with chronic rheumatism. He received five years' full pay without interest in 1810.

Carr, John. Md. Pvt. His widow, Margaret Long, was pensioned at the rate of half-pay of a private in Baltimore County on 9 Mar. 1846. The name of his widow was corrected from Margaret Loney to Margaret Long on 20 Jan. 1847.

Carr, John. Pa. —. He married Elizabeth Abbot 16 Dec. 1809 in St. Paul's Church in Philadelphia.

Carr, John. Va. Pvt. He served under Col. George Gibson. He applied under the act of 1818 and was rejected because his service was state rather than Continental. He was restored to his pension in 1831. He died in 1833 of cancer of the face. Elizabeth Jones and the other children were to be paid the arrearage due him to the time of his death 19 Jan. 1844 by private act of Congress. On 19 July 1848 they were instructed to apply to the proper office for the arrearage of their father. He was from Prince William County and had been confined to the poor house. Congress granted Elizabeth Jones relief 29 Dec. 1841.

Carr, Joseph. Va. He was killed in the service near Camden 11 May 1781. His widow, Elizabeth Carr, had two in her family. Se was pensioned and was receiving £8 per annum in 1786. She was continued at the same rate per annum on 3 Apr. 1787 and lived in Caroline County.

Carr, Richard. Va. —. He died in Continental service. His widow, Margaret Carr, and three children were furnished 4 barrels of corn and 200 pounds of pork in Rockbridge Co., Va. on 1 Oct. 1782. She was pensioned 20 Dec. 1792 at the rate of £12 per annum. On 14 Jan. 1817 she lived in Warren Co., Ohio. She also appeared as Margaret Karr.

Carr, Robert. R.I. Pvt. He was wounded by a musket ball entering his left cheek; it passed through his upper jaw and came out his mouth at a skirmish near Kingsbridge, N.Y. on 2 July 1781. He had difficulty in chewing and had a constant discharge of saliva from outside his cheek. He served under Col. J. Olney. He lived in Providence, R.I. in 1794. He enlisted 10 Aug. 1780 and was on the rolls in 1782. He was granted half a pension 20 Apr. 1796. He died 13 Sep. 1806. He also appeared as Robert Cars.

Carr, Thomas. Va. —. He was in the service. The Manchester Parish church wardens bound out his sons, Ezekiel Carr and Richard Carr, and appropriated £6 for his wife and eldest son, John Carr, who was a cripple, in Chesterfield County 7 Mar. 1777.

Carr, William. Mass. —. He served in the 8th Regiment and was from Prospect. He was paid $20.

Carragan, Thomas. Pa. Pvt. He was in Philadelphia County on 13 Feb. 1786. He served in the Chester County militia under Capt. Denning the in the 7th Battalion and was wounded the night before Brandywine on a detachment surprised by the enemy light horse. He was trampled under foot and miserably bruised. He was 61 years old. His wife was mentioned 1 Aug. 1787. He was dead by 1798.

Carrell, Isaac. Del. Pvt. He was on the 1813 pension roll. He was from New Castle County.

Carrent, James. Md. Pvt. He was pensioned in Montgomery County in 1783. He was pensioned again in Mar. 1789. He was on the 1791 pension list. He was on the 1813 pension roll as James Current. He died 4 Sep. 1822.

Carrick, Adam. S.C. —. He was pensioned in St. Matthews on 6 Dec. 1828. He was paid as late as 1834. He also appeared as Adam Garrick [sic].

Carrier, Joseph. Mass. —. He was from Haverhill. He was paid $20.

Carrigan, Gilbert. N.Y. Pvt. He served in Capt. Comfort Ludenton's Company in the Dutchess County militia under Col. Henry Ludenton. He was accidentally disabled in the back of his right hand by a shot from his own musket when he was attempting to fix a bayonet on 24 Oct. 1777. He lived in Fredericktown, Dutchess County on 16 Apr. 1789. His name also appeared as Gilbert Carrington. He was a shoemaker. He was aged about 25 years when he was pensioned 5 Apr. 1788. He lived in Putnam County. He was on the 1813 pension roll He was a shoemaker.

Carrigan, James. N.C. —. He applied in Iredell County in 1801. He was a soldier in the company of Capt. Andrew Petree and Lt. James Todd in the 1st N.C. Regiment under Col. Alexander. He was wounded in his right shoulder by two large musket balls at Camden in 1780 where he was taken prisoner for twelve months until he was exchanged. He died in the spring of 1808. His name was, however, on the 1813 pension list.

Carroll, —. S.C. —. His widow was Martha Carroll from York District in 1843.

Carroll, Charles. Md. —. A resolution for a full length likeness to be painted was passed 11 Mar. 1833.

Carroll, Dennis. Pa. Sgt. He applied 18 Dec. 1825. He was awarded a $40 gratuity and a $40 annuity in Erie County 6 Mar. 1822. He died 21 Mar. 1841.

Carroll, Isaac. Del. Pvt. He was on the 1798 roll.

Carroll, John. —. —. He was killed in the war. His widow received a pension.

Carroll, William. Mass. —. He served in the 7th Regiment and was from Salem. His widow, Hannah Carroll, was paid $50.

Carrollton, Edward. Pa. —. He was granted relief by the Court of Enquiry 9 Mar. 1814.

Carruth, Thomas. —. —. He was wounded in the war.

Carson, Benjamin. Pa. Sgt. He applied from Centre County on 13 Jan. 1813. David Lamb was a soldier in Capt. William Hendrick's Company of Rifleman under Col. William Thompson and marched to Boston in 1775. He knew Benjamin Carson was a private in Capt. James Chambers's Company in 1776. He left him in the service in 1776. Samuel Leonard of the 1st Pa. Regiment under Col. James Chambers knew Benjamin Carson was wounded in his right thigh at Brandywine. Sgt. Timothy O'Neill was in Capt. Miller's Company in the 7th Regiment and knew Carson from 1776 to 1781. David Davidson thought Carson was at Paoli and Germantown. James Brady knew Carson was a private upwards of six years. William Morris knew Carson was in Capt. David Ziegler's Company from 1778 to 1781. He was also in Dauphin County.

Carson, —. S.C. —. His widow, Elizabeth Carson, and children were being paid an annuity in 1819 and 1820.

Carson, James. Pa. He served under Capt. Clark and Capt. Sanderson. He was from Mifflin County.

Carson, John. S.C. —. His remarried widow, Martha Brock, was allowed an annuity 21 Mar. 1786. There was one child in 1791.

Carson, Robert. N.J. —. He was pensioned in Mercer County at the rate of $60 per annum. He also received a $40 gratuity. He was 77 in 1840.

Carson, Samuel. S.C. —. As Jean Moore, the former widow of Samuel Carson of old Ninety Six District, she applied 3 Dec. 1810. He had a claim for £56.0.6 certified in 1784 and died shortly thereafter after his return from the siege of Augusta. He was ill when he returned home and lingered some time before he died. Nearly all of his property had been taken by the Tories. She married secondly John Moore. Her pension was approved in Oct. 1817. She was paid as late as 1833. She also appeared as Jane Moore.

Carson, Thomas. S.C. —. He served under Col. William Bratton and fought at Rocky Mount and Hanging Rock. John Kidd and Capt. James Wallace verified his military service. He was pensioned in York District 30 Nov. 1827.

Carson, William. S.C. —. He applied from York District on 22 Sep. 1821. He entered the militia and served under Gen. Sumter, Col. Neal, and Col. Graham. He was at Congaree, Hook's defeat, and King's Mountain. He was severely wounded at Friday's Fort on the Congaree. He was shot through the wrist of his right arm and much disabled. He suffered from a broken left arm some years back. He had a large family. Capt. James Martin attested that Carson was in his company and was wounded in his right arm at Friday's Fort. He assisted in dressing his wound. He was paid as late as 1849.

Carte, John. Pa. Matross. He applied 25 Sep. 1787. He served in the artillery as an artificer and was wounded in the head in pursuit of a deserter. He was 45 years old.

Carter, —. Ga. —. His widow, Abigail Carter, was granted assistance 15 Mar. 1782. She was from Wilkes County.

Carter, —. Va. —. His wife, Judith Carter, was awarded £5 while her husband was away in the service on 16 June 1777. He died in the service. She was awarded £10 on 10 Oct. 1777 and £50 on 20

Sep. 1779 in Goochland Co., Va.

Carter, —. Va. —. His widow, Mary Carter, was being pensioned 20 July 1785.

Carter, Benjamin. S.C. —. He was wounded at Stono in his right arm and sought the two year arrearage of his pension in Richland District on 2 Dec. 1824. He served under Capt. Richard Brown and Col. Thompson in the 3rd Regiment. John Joyner, Absalom Joyner, Berry Harris, and Allen Jeffry certified his service 29 Nov. 1824. He married Elizabeth Polan, widow of George Polan, on 18 Jan. 1820. He died 1 July 1826. His wife had eight children by George Polan and six were alive when she applied for her pension. Her father, Alexander Brunson, was killed by Tories at the close of the war. Her only child by Benjamin Carter was four years old. Elizabeth Carter married thirdly Jacob Hess. He was a member of the city guard and earned $16 per month. She was able to earn a little with her needle. They sought the arrearage of Benjamin Carter's pension from 1 Mar. 1826 to 9 July 1826. They were paid $21.48 on 10 Nov. 1827.

Carter, Charles. S.C. —. He applied in Edgefield District on 18 Nov. 1840 and was nearing the age of 78. He had been denied a federal pension due to the lack of living evidence. All of his compatriots were dead. He entered the service in North Carolina in Capt. Sharp's Company in 1781 or 1782. He made a trip to Salisbury guarding prisoners and was on various scouting parties. He was under Capt. Reed at Frowhank's Old Field. He was in Continental service under Capt. Daves, Maj. Hogg, and Col. Bull. He came to South Carolina under Lt. Lamb and joined Gen. Greene at James Island. He was attached to Capt. Robert Rayford and Lt. Campain in the N.C. Light Infantry. He served under Maj. Bynum and Col. Lightly to the close of the war. He was paid in 1842.

Carter, Charles. Va. Pvt. He enlisted early in the war and died shortly after leaving the service. He left a widow, Judith Carter, and several children. His widow was pensioned at the rate of £12 per annum on 20 Dec. 1792. She resided in Goochland County on 28 Dec. 1792.

Carter, Charles. Va. Capt. He served in the state navy from 1776. He resigned 17 Aug. 1776. Congress granted the claim of his heirs for half-pay 8 Mar. 1842. He was not supernumerary.

Carter, David. S.C. —. He was pensioned from Pendleton District on 12 Dec. 1823. He had been a resident of the state for 37 years. He lived in Wilkes Co., N.C. and volunteered at the age of 16 in Virginia to serve against the Shawnee Indians for five to six months four consecutive summers. He was in the N.C. militia under Col. Benjamin Cleveland and Capt. Salathiel Martin. He was in action at Shallow Ford on the Yadkin River and Bryan's settlement. He was also under Capt. Bostick and joined Gen. Gates at Colson on the Pee Dee River. He was at Camden and taken to Charleston as a prisoner of war. He was on a prison ship for eleven months and exchanged at Jamestown, Va. He was 65 years old and his wife was 63. Pendleton Isbell served two terms with him. Marmaduke Maples of Lincoln Co., N.C. was a prisoner at Charleston. While he did not remember David Carter, they later became acquainted and Carter related such small incidental occurrences that Maples believed that Carter was also there. Daniel Green of Greene Co., Tenn. also testified as to Carter's service. He was paid as late as 1833.

Carter, Jerias. Conn. Pvt. He served in Swift's Conn. Regiment. He lost one of his feet by a fever. He was pensioned 1 Sep. 1782. He was on the pension list of 1813. He transferred to Otsego Co., N.Y. on 4 Sep. 1826.

Carter, John. N.J. Pvt. & Guide. He was pensioned in Burlington County 9 Feb. 1843 at the rate of $40 per annum. He received a supplement on 5 Feb. 1853. His widow, Mary Carter, was pensioned 29 Mar. 1855.

Carter, John. Va. —. He was pensioned 2 Jan. 1807 at the rate of $50 per annum which was an increase in his pension. He was wounded while guarding the frontiers of the state against inroads by the Indians. He lived in Kanawha County on 7 Nov. 1808. His will was probated in Cabell County on 24 Sep. 1838. The executors were S. Thornbury and John Samuels. [**N.B.** There is no indication whether the service was performed during the Revolutionary War or at a later time.]

Carter, John Jarret. Va. Sgt. Maj. He enlisted in January in 1776 in the 5th Virginia Regiment under Capt. Ball. He was disabled by hard duty in 1776. He was awarded a £15 gratuity on 10 May 1777.

Carter, Joseph. Va. Pvt. He was drafted for six months under Capt. Charles Patterson and Col. Peters in either 1780 or 1781. He sought relief 25 Feb. 1845 from Congress. He moved to Kentucky. Congress rejected a bill for his private relief because his application was not properly authenticated and because he had not ever applied to the proper agency in government on 12 Jan. 1848. Congress did so again 1 Aug. 1850.

Carter, Josiah. Conn. —. He served in the 2nd Regiment and was disabled by the loss of his foot. He was pensioned 29 Aug. 1782.

Carter, Richard. N.J. Pvt. He was on the 1791 pension roll at the rate of $60 per annum.

Carter, Samuel. N.C. —. He applied in Anson County in 1803. He was in Continental service under Capt. John Pugh Williams and was disabled at Germantown by a ball in his ankle. He was on the 1813 pension list.

Carter, Stephen. Pa. Sgt. He was awarded a $40 gratuity and a $40 annuity in Northumberland County 28 Mar. 1820. He was on the 1813 pension list. He died 25 June 1822.

Carter, Stephen. S.C. —. His pension was to be paid to William Carter, a pensioner, of the state and at the time of his death to his administrator and administratrix. It was granted 25 Nov. 1830.

Carter, Thomas. Pa. Spy. He served under Lt. Hunter and subsequently under Capt. Clark in 1777. He was from Venango County and was granted relief 3 Mar. 1837. He was 88 years old in 1840. His widow, Margaret Carter, received a $40 gratuity and a $40 annuity 12 Mar. 1856.

Carter, Thomas. Va. Surgeon. He served under Col. Dabney. His heirs received his commutation of full pay for five years in lieu of half-pay for life as a surgeon on state establishment with no interest on 23 Feb.1826. His heirs were James Broadnax Carter, John Mitchell Carter, Rebecca Broadnax (Carter) Stanard , Jane Maria Carter, and William Boyd in right of his wife Lucy Gray Edmonds (Carter) Boyd. The heirs were allowed half pay 25 May 1838. The heirs sought interest on the pay 1 Mar. 1842.

Carter, William. —. Surgeon. He was appointed in July 1776 and was at the Continental Hospital at Williamsburg to the close of the war. His heirs were paid his five years' full pay in commutation of his half-pay 25 May 1832. They were James H. Carter, Joseph Jackson, Harriet Rebecca Jackson, and Elizabeth W. Spencer.

Carter, William. S.C. —. He was paid $257.14 for twelve years of his pension from 1786 to 1798 on 29 June 1808.

Carter, William. S.C. —. He was paid his pension from 1785 to 1793 from which time he has already drawn on 19 Dec. 1812. One William Carter was paid his arrearage of $171.42 on 8 Dec. 1814.

Carter, William. S.C. Pvt. He served under Capt. Robert Thornley and Col. John Ervin in Britton's Neck Regiment of militia. He was wounded by a musket ball through his breast and hip at Eutaw Springs while in Gen. Greene's army. He also served under Gen. Francis Marion.

He had a wife and three children to support when he applied 20 Nov. 1797 in Liberty County in Georgetown District, S.C. On 21 Oct. 1807 he was in Williamsburg District. He died 16 January 1827. His widow, Feraby Carter, aged 60, applied for his arrearage on 24 Oct. 1827. She suffered from rheumatism. She was paid $52.50. His son, Stephen Carter, was administrator of his estate.

Carter, William. Va. —. He served in Col. Baylor's Regiment of Calvary. He received a very severe cut on each wrist at Lenews Ferry in May 1780. He applied 9 Dec. 1780. He resided in Caroline Co., Va. in 1796.

Carter, Zacheriah. N.C. —. He served under Capt. John Pugh Williams and Col. Buncombe in the 5th Regiment. He resided in Bertie County. He had smallpox in the service. He applied at the age of 78 from Duplin County 28 Aug. 1832.

Carther, Robert. Pa. —. He received relief in Greene County in 1843.

Cartwright, Gideon. Pa. —. He was pensioned in Tioga County 13 Apr. 1838.

Cartwright, Thomas. N.J. Pvt. He served in the 1st Regiment. He was wounded and disabled with piles. He was 49 years old. He was on the 1790 pension roll at the rate of $60 per annum and died 10 Feb. 1790.

Carty, John. Pa. Pvt. He was in Philadelphia County 27 Sep. 1787. He was a soldier in Capt. Thomas Wiley's Company under Col. Benjamin Flowers. He was badly wounded in the head in pursuit of a deserter from the Philadelphia barracks. His wife cared for him. He was 45 years old. Lt. John Sprowl attested to his service. He also appeared as John Carter. He was on the 1789 pension roll but was dead by 1802.

Caruthers, James. Pa. —. He served under Capt. Thomas Boud in the 5th Regiment. He was 42 years old. He was wounded by a musket ball in both heels at Green Springs, Va. and received his half-pay pension 2 Sep. 1784.

Carvell, Isaac. Del. Pvt. He was pensioned in 1783. He was on the 1791 pension list as well as the 1813 pension list.

Carver, Henry. Mass. Pvt. He was pensioned 16 Oct. 1806. He was on the 1813 pension list. He died 12 July 1823 in Bristol Co., Mass.

Carver, Henry. Va. Pvt. He served in the 8th Va. Regiment and died in the service. His widow, Mary Carver, and four children were granted £25 support on 2 Mar. 1779. She lived in Frederick County in Aug. 1784. She was pensioned 23 Jan. 1786 at the rate of £18 per annum. Her pension was continued 28 Oct. 1791.

Carvell, Isaac. Del. Pvt. He was pensioned in 1783. He was on the 1791 pension list.

Carvill, Henry. Me. —. He died 12 July 1823. His widow, Mercy Carvill, was from Lewiston. She was paid $50 under the resolve of 1836.

Carvin, James. Md. Pvt. He was granted relief.

Carwile, Zachariah. S.C. —. He was pensioned 6 Dec. 1828. He suffered from palsy which prevented him from walking several years before his death. He died 4 Aug. 1841. His son, Zachariah Carwile of Abbeville District, sought his father's arrearage 26 Aug. 1850. Another son, James Carwile, had not been heard from for the last twenty years. A daughter, Rebecca Hanna, had not been heard from for thirty years. Both had removed to the west.

Cary, Christopher. Vt. —. He was an underage soldier who did guard duty on the frontier Capt. Charles Nelson and Col. Wait where he was taken prisoner and held captive in Canada. His father, Samuel Cary, sought relief 16 Jan. 1782

Cary, John. Pa. Pvt. He served under Capt. Spalding. He was wounded in his right arm by a musket ball which fractured the bone. It was in 1778 when he was on command down the Susquennah from Wyoming. He lived in Luzerne, Pa. in 1794. The time of his enlistment was unknown, but he was in service in 1781.

Cary, John. Va. —. He was a free man of color and served as a body servant of George Washington at Braddock's defeat in 1755 in the French and Indian War and at the surrender of Cornwallis in 1781. He was a native of Westmoreland Co., Va. and a resident of Washington, D.C. when he was awarded a pension by a private act of Congress on 3 Feb. 1843. He was 112 years of age. He was without relatives.

Cary, Samuel. Pa. He was taken prisoner by the Indians 8 July 1778 at Wyoming. He was from Luzerne County. He was also in the battle on Abraham's Plains.

Casady, Thomas. Va. —. He died in Continental service. His widow, Masa Casady, and her six children were granted £20 support in Prince William Co., Va. in Aug. 1778.

Casbolt, Robert. Pa. —. He was awarded a $40 gratuity and a $40 annuity in Greene Co., Ohio. 7 May 1832. He died 9 Apr. 1840 in Indiana. His widow was paid in June 1840.

Case, James. —. —. He was a pensioner under the act of 1832 for five months service as a corporal and nineteen months as a private. He married 29 May 1778. His widow, Elizabeth Case, was allowed a pension by Congress by a private act at the same rate he had been allowed on 5 Mar. 1840.

Case, John. N.Y. —.

Case, William. Conn. Sgt. He served in Col. Mott's Regiment. He became ill and developed an ulcerous sore on his right leg from diseases contracted in the service. He resided in Berkhamstead, Conn. in 1792.

Casey, Archibald. Va. —. He was pensioned 19 Feb. 1816 at the rate of $50 per annum and lived in Powhatan County. The Richmond Hustings Court granted administration of his estate on 18 Oct. 1820 to William Caulfield. He died 16 Mar. 1820.

Casey, Henry. Va. —. His widow, Martha Casey, was furnished £6 support in Isle of Wight County 7 Aug. 1777. His orphans were Francis Casey and Thomas Casey.

Casey, John. —. Pvt. He served under Capt. Joseph Porter and Col. Frank Taylor in 1777. He had both arms broken and one shoulder dislocated. In 1778 enlisted in the dragoons under Col. William Washington and served to the close of the war. He was at Guilford Court House, Camden, and Eutaw Springs. He was pensioned at the rate of $96 per year. He was wounded at Cowpens by a ball and a sword. He sought an invalid pension. Physicians proved he was totally disabled and that his left leg was still diseased. Congress granted him the additional invalid pension 16 Feb. 1836. He was allowed an increase 25 Jan. 1838.

Casey, John. Pa. Pvt. He lived in Luzerne County.

Casey, John. Va. Pvt. He served in Capt. Peter Bryan Bruin's Company in the 11th Va. Regiment under Col. Morgan. Maj. Charles Magill and Robert White, officers, proved his service. He was wounded in his right arm by a musket ball at Brandywine. It was broken in two places. He was aged *ca.* 38 in June 1786 in Frederick Co. He was in Hampshire County on 14 June 1786.

Casey, Morris. Pa. Pvt. He was in Lancaster County on 6 Sep. 1786. He was in the 3rd Pa. Regiment. He received sundry wounds, one of which was in the left breast at Horseneck, N.Y. He also received a musket ball in his left arm. He was in Capt. William West's Company. Col. Shee enlisted him in Nov. 1778. He served eight years. He was 28 years old.

Casey, Patrick. Pa. Pvt. He was on the 1789 pension list.

Cash, John. Va. —. His wife, Rachael Cash, and two children were granted £30 support in Rockingham Co., Va. 23 Mar. 1779.

Caskey, Samuel. S.C. —. He served under Col. Simons, Col. Hampton, and Gen. Sumter. He was at Charleston, Fort Bluff, and Eutaw Springs. He would have been 76 years of age in four or five months when he was pensioned 11 Dec. 1824 in Lancaster District. James Hood served with him. He was paid as late as 1833.

Casler, Peter. N.Y. Pvt. He served under Col. Samuel Clyde in the Montgomery County militia and was slain 18 July 1781. His widow, Margaret Casler, received a half-pay pension.

Casper, John. Pa. —. He applied 31 Jan. 1814. He served in the militia and was discharged by Gen. Wayne 17 Jan. 1781.

Cass, Moses. N.H. Pvt. He was from Raymond in 1783. He enlisted in the spring in 1777 for three years and served in the 3rd N.H. Regiment. He was inoculated for smallpox at Valley Forge which produced an ulcer on his right arm and left him disabled. The regimental surgeon, Edmund Chadwick, attended him. He was wounded in his right arm and hand. He lived in Hallowell, Maine in 1792. He was on the 1813 pension list.

Cassidy, William. Pa. —. He was awarded a $40 gratuity and a $40 annuity in Beaver Co., Pa. 12 Apr. 1828.

Cassity, Thomas. S.C. —. He was pensioned 6 Dec. 1828. He was paid as late as 1834.

Casson, Philip. Md. Lt. He served in the 5th Md. Regiment. He was wounded by a ball in his right knee on 4 Oct. 1777 at Germantown. He resided in Caroline Co., Md. in 1796.

Castor, Jacob. Pa. —. His widow, Catharine Castor, was awarded a $40 annuity in Philadelphia Co., Pa. 5 May 1852 for his Revolutionary service.

Castor, Vincent. Va. —. He was granted necessaries in Fauquier Co., Va. 8 Oct. 1781. He had three sons in the Continental Army. He was also granted the same in Loudoun County on the same date.

Caswell, Abraham. Mass. Pvt. He served in the 4th Regiment and was from Middleborough. His widow, Celia Caswell, was paid $50.

Caswell, Job. Mass. Pvt. He served in the Mass. Continental Line in the 2nd Regiment under Capt. Luther Bailey and Col. John Bailey. His sight had been injured. He was disabled by rheumatism. He was 61 years old in 1786. He was paid $20 by the Commonwealth. He was on the 1813 pension list. He moved to Baltimore Co., Md. from South Carolina on 4 Mar. 1820. He died 30 Oct. 1820.

Caswell, Job, Jr. Mass. —. He was paid $20.

Caswell, Jonathan. Mass. Pvt. He served in the 1st Regiment and was from Middleborough. His widow, Mary Caswell, was paid $50.

Catlet, John. Va. —. He was struck off the roll 10 Jan. 1787 since he had no further need.

Cato, George. Md. Pvt. He was pensioned at the rate of half-pay of a private on 19 Feb. 1819.

Cato, William. S.C. —. He served under Capt. Thomas Woodward, Col. Richard Richardson, Capt. William Kirkland, Col. Goodwyn, Col. Joseph Kirkland, Col. Wade Hampton, Winn, and Col. John Pearson. He was in battle at Stono. He was taken prisoner at Camden but broke his parole. He rejoined and was in the battle of Juniper. Capt. Charnel Durham proved his service as did Thomas Parrott, aged 72. He died in 1831. His widow, Susan Cato, was from Fairfield District and had her application rejected in 1831. She had a daughter about 40 years. The name of the latter was Betsey [?].

Caul, Alexander. Pa. Pvt. He was in Washington County on 7 Apr. 1788. He served in the 2nd Pa.

Regiment and was disabled in the service. He lost the use of his limbs. He was 40 years old. He had a wife and four small children. He was on the 1813 pension list.

Caustin, Samuel. Capt. —. He served in Delaware row galleys. Because of insufficient evidence, Congress denied his only surviving child, Elizabeth McDougall, relief 13 Apr. 1848.

Cavenaugh, Edward. Pa. Pvt. He enlisted in Capt. Matthew Smith's company of riflemen in the 7th Pa. Regiment for one year. He marched to Boston in 1775 and thence to Quebec. He served under Col. Edward Hand. He was discharged after two years due to rheumatism. He was wounded by a musket ball in the shoulder on 11 Sep. 1777 at Brandywine. He lived at Managhan, Pa. in 1794. He was in hospital in Oct. 1777. He was granted a $40 gratuity and a $40 annuity in 1808 in York County. He was granted supplementary relief on 19 Mar. 1816. He was 89 years old in 1840. He died 14 Dec. 1842.

Cavenaugh, Philip. Pa. —. He applied from Allegheny County 14 Aug. 1812. He served under Capt. Michael Huffnagh in the 8th Pa. Regiment.

Cavenough, John. Pa. Pvt. He applied in York County on 28 Mar. 1808. He was wounded at Brandywine by a musket ball in his left shoulder. He was awarded a $40 gratuity and a $40 annuity. He was on the 1813 pension list.

Cavenough, Patrick. Pa. —. He also appeared as Patrick Caveny.

Caviner, James. Va. —. His wife, Susanna Caviner, was granted £50 support in Northumberland County on 10 May 1779.

Cawthorn, —. Va. —. His widowed mother was granted £27.15 support in Hanover County in 1779.

Ceasar, Timothy. Conn. Pvt. He was disabled by a rupture and pensioned 4 Jan. 1783. He was on the 1813 pension list. He died 28 Mar. 1832 in New Haven County. He also appeared as Timothy Caesar.

Cesar, Levi. R.I. Pvt. He lost all of his toes on his left foot, and those on his right foot were damaged by frost bite in Feb. 1783 on the Oswego Expedition. He served under Col. Jeremiah Olney. He was aged 24 in 1785. He was on the 1813 pension list.

Chace, Ezra. R.I. Pvt. He lost all of his fingers on both hands by the accidental discharge of a field piece when ramming the cartridge on a field day at Tiverton on 7 Nov. 1777. He served under Col. R. Elliott. He was aged 27 in 1786. He was listed as Ezra Chase on the 1813 pension list.

Chace, John. N.Y. Pvt. He served in Capt. Henry Tiebout's Company under Col. Goose Van Schaick in the 1st N.Y. Regiment. He was injured by falling timber across his loins at West Point in Oct. 1782 and was incapable of walking. He lived in New York City, N.Y. in June 1786. He was on the 1791 pension roll. His widow was Ann Chace. He also appeared as John Chase.

Chace, Richard. Mass. Pvt. He served in Col. Babcock's Regiment. He had a contused wound on the large bone of his leg, and the bone was rotten. He resided in Stockbridge, Mass. in 1796. He was on the 1813 pension list as Richard Chase.

Chadbourn, Levi. Me. Pvt. He was from Parsonfield. He served under Col. Edward Wigglesworth. He was wounded through the trunk of his body by a musket ball which entered near the spine of the back and came out through the breast bone between the ribs in Aug. 1778 in Rhode Island. He enlisted 21 May 1777 and was discharged 21 May 1780. He lived in York Co., Me. in 1792. He was on the 1813 pension list.

Chadsey, Rowland. Pa. Pvt. He later lived in Washington Co., R.I. He was on the 1813 pension list. He died in North Kingston; his widow was Mary Chadsey.

Chadwick, —. Pa. —. His widow, Sarah Chadwick, was awarded a $40 gratuity and a $40 annuity in Philadelphia Co., Pa. 8 Apr. 1826. She died 18 Oct. 1829.

Chadwick, Abijah. Mass. —. He served in the 7th Regiment. He was paid $20.

Chadwick, Caleb. Mass. Pvt. He was wounded in his right thigh by a musket ball which lodged against the hip bone at Tyringham on 20 June 1775. The musket had been accidentally discharged. He served under Col. J. Patterson. He resided in Tyringham, Mass. in 1792 and in Great Barrington, Mass. in 1796. He was granted one-fourth of a pension 20 Apr. 1796. He was on the 1813 pension list.

Chadwick, Elihu. N.J. Lt. He served in the 2nd Regiment of the Hunterdon Co., N.J. militia first as an ensign and then as a lieutenant. He was transferred to the 1st Regiment of the Monmouth Co., N.J. militia. His daughter, Susannah Chadwick, was 78 and pensioned by Congress 15 Mar. 1892.

Chadwick, John. S.C. —. He was killed 17 July 1781. His orphans were allowed an annuity 26 Oct. 1785.

Chadwick, Levi. N.J. —. He sought a duplicate of bounty land warrant #716 for 100 acres on 1 June 1836. Congress authorized same. He also appeared as Levi Shadwick.

Chaise, Eseck. Mass. Pvt. He served under Col. William Sheppard and Capt. Fisher. He lost his left leg and thigh. He was discharged from the Invalids on 2 Feb. 1780. He was pensioned from that date on 14 Apr. 1780. He was 28 years old in 1786. He also appeared as Eseck Chace.

Chalant, Peter. —. Sgt. He enlisted in Boston, was wounded, and taken prisoner. He returned to the service under Gen. Hazen. He carried letters to and from Canada and was wounded by a ball in his body, another through his left hand, and three in his skull depriving him of the use of his left eye. He was pensioned in May 1792 at Boston at the rate of $5 per month. He was entitled to half-pay and $200 arrearage. He moved from Canada to New York in 1820 and died 3 Mar. the same year. His widow was buried 12 Mar. 1838 in St. John Parish, Dorchester, Lower Canada. His only surviving child was Jacques Chalant of St. Athenos, Iberville Co., Canada East who sought the $200 plus interest. Congress approved the claim 8 Aug. 1856. He also appeared as Peter Charlant. New York granted bounty land warrant #12889 for 100 acres to his assignee Benjamin Moore. The bounty land warrant was in the name of Peter Charlong.

Challer, Henry. Mass. Pvt. He removed to New York Co., N.Y. 2 Mar. 1806. He was on the 1813 pension list.

Chalmus, Robert. Pa. Capt. He was on the 1789 pension list.

Chamberlain, Jacob. N.C. Capt. He applied in Stokes County in Nov. 1799. He was a militia captain and was wounded at the Battle of Stono. He also appeared as Jacob Camlin, Jacob Champerlin, and Jacob Champlain. He was still alive in 1819.

Chamberlain, Jeremiah. Me. —. He died 24 Oct. 1831. His widow was Sarah Chamberlain from Nobleboro. She was paid $50 under the resolve of 1836.

Chamberlain, Joshua. Mass. Capt. He served three years having enlisted in 1777 for three years under Capt. Miller and Col. Vose. He was discharged in 1780. He reentered the service and was promoted to captain. He had also lived in Richmond Co., N.Y. He died in 1812; his widow died in 1826. His heirs claimed his bounty land and half-pay. Congress ruled that his heir had no claim against the U.S. on 15 Dec. 1857 since no record of his service was produced. He might have been in the militia. The claim was filed by E. B. Chamberlain. His daughter-in-law was Amy B. Chamberlain. His son, Pierce Chamberlain, was 14 years of age at the end of the war. Congress granted relief to the heirs 12 July 1870.

Chamberlain, Moses. Me. —. He died 9 Dec. 1833 in Moscow. His widow was Anna Chamberlain from Norridgewock. She was paid $50 under the resolve of 1836.

Chamberlain, Richard. Conn. Pvt. He was drafted in a party of rangers under Col. Knowlton. He was captivated by the enemy at Fort Washington on 16 Nov. 1776. He endured cruel and hard usage in captivity and was confined to a sugar house in New York. He also served under Col. Samuel Wyllys. He was pensioned at Glastenbury, Conn. on 5 Sep. 1788 at age 29. He was on the 1813 pension list.

Chamberlain, Uriah. N.J. Pvt. He served under Capt. John Polhemus in the 1ˢᵗ N.J. Regiment. He was taken prisoner on Staten Island on 27 Aug. 1777 and died the following winter. His widow, Mary Chamberlain, was allowed his half-pay in Hunterdon County from 1 Jan. 1778 for her widowhood in 1783.

Chambers, —. Pa. —. His widow, Sarah Chambers, was awarded a $40 gratuity and a $40 annuity 27 Mar. 1837.

Chambers, Edward. Md. Pvt. He was pensioned at the rate of half-pay of a private in Anne Arundel County on 16 Feb. 1821. He was a man of color.

Chambers, George. Pa. —. He was awarded a $40 gratuity and a $40 annuity in Westmoreland County 1 Apr. 1837.

Chambers, James. Va. Pvt. He served in the 3ʳᵈ Va. Regiment in Capt. Thomas Catlet's Company under Col. Buford. He was wounded at Buford's defeat near Hanging Rock in South Carolina. He lost his right arm and part of his left hand. He also had a bad wound on his neck. He was awarded a £500 gratuity on 20 Nov. 1780. He was pensioned again on 18 Feb. 1786 in Louisa County. In Mar. 1786 he was 23 years old. He was continued on the pension roll at the rate of £18 per annum on 5 Feb. 1789. He was on the 1813 pension list. He died 10 Jan. 1833.

Chambers, Matthew. Mass. Capt. He was paid $52 per annum from 27 Feb. 1794. He was from Chelmsford.

Chambers, Matthew. N.H. Pvt. He was pensioned.

Chambers, Robert. Pa. Corp. He was in Lancaster County 11 Nov. 1786. He served in Col. Proctor's Regiment in Capt. Robert Jones's company of artillery. He was wounded by a musket ball at Brandywine Sep. 1777. Dr. John Kuhn removed it. He was 35 years old and had a wife and six small children. He died 15 Feb. 1815 about 60 years of age.

Chambless, —. Va. —. His wife, Millicent Chambless, was granted relief in May 1777 in Lunenburg Co., Va.

Champ, John. —. Ens. His son, Nathaniel Champ, was due 100 acres of bounty land. The warrant was delivered to W. W. Petree who died soon after and was never located. Congress agreed that a duplicate warrant should be reissued on 13 Feb. 1850. The widow had been pensioned from 4 Mar. 1831 and had been allowed commutation pay of an ensign 3 Mar. 1847.

Champe, John. Va. Sgt. At the age of 23 or 24 he enlisted in 1776 and was attached to Lee's Legion as a corporal. In 1779 he was promoted to sergeant and continued in the service until 20 Oct. 1780. He was a native of Loudoun Co., Va. He married Phebe ------ in July 1782. The heirs represented by William Champe of Franklin Co., Ohio indicated that their mother had received 300 acres from Virginia and commutation pay equal to that of an ensign. John Champe had been detained on a British transport. The heirs sought the reward which Gen. Washington himself had promised. Congress granted her a pension 17 Feb. 1838. The heirs sought relief from Congress 1 Apr. 1842.

Champion, Reuben. Ct. Assistant Commissary. He served under Israel Champion and Col. Henry Champion from 1779 to 22 Mar. 1783. He was unsuccessful in applying for a pension on the basis that he was a civil agent. He married Rhoda Hyde Jewett 12 Nov. 1782. He died

26 Apr. 1838 in Hartford, Conn. She died 3 Jan. 1852. Their son, Reuben J. Champion, was granted relief 10 Jan. 1857. Congress allowed a pension to the veteran and his widow retroactively 19 Mar. 1860.

Champlin, Jack. R.I. Pvt. He lost his toes by frost bite on the Oswego expedition under Col. Willet. He served under Jeremiah Olney in Feb. 1783. He applied 29 Dec. at the age of 25. He lived in Providence Co., R.I.

Chandler, —. Va. —. His mother, Frances Chandler, was granted support in Caroline Co., Va. 8 Apr. 1779.

Chandler, —. Va. —. His mother, Grace Chandler, was granted financial support in Caroline Co., Va. 8 May 1781. There were three in her family.

Chandler, —. Va. —. His mother, Sarah Chandler, was granted financial support in Caroline Co., Va. 8 May 1781. She had a family of five.

Chandler, —. Va. —. His father, Thomas Chandler, was granted £10 support on 12 Feb. 1778 and £20 in May 1779 while his son was away in the service in Caroline Co., Va.

Chandler, —. Va. —. His widow, Mary Chandler, was granted £20 support in Caroline Co.,Va. Apr. 1779.

Chandler, Carter B.. Va. Pvt. He served in the militia as a substitute for Barnett Mitchell who had been drafted. His second tour was for three months in 1781. In the winter after the defeat of Cornwallis he was a substitute for John Gunter of Louisa County and served eighteen months. Congress granted him a pension for eighteen months of service on 12 Apr. 1842.

Chandler, Daniel. N.C. Lt./Pvt. He served under Col. Cleveland. His widow, Frances Chandler, gave evidence for twelve months of service in 1780 and 1781 as a volunteer. She alleged three years of service. Congress credited him with twelve months of service as a private and awarded her a pension 8 Feb. 1838. She was from Kentucky.

Chandler, Isaac. N.Y. —. He served in Capt. Westfall's Company under Col. Wiesenfelt. Betsey Dure inquired about his service 13 Nov. 1855.

Chandler, Jere[miah]. Va. —. His family was granted £5 assistance in Orange Co., Va. on 26 Mar. 1778 while he was away in the service.

Chandler, Joel. Me. —. He died 29 Apr. 1794. His widow was Deborah Glidden from Winthrop. She was paid $50 under the resolve of 1836.

Chandler, John. Conn. Col. He contracted various infirmities with nephritic disorders and a chronic hydrocele. He resided in Newton, Conn. in 1792. He was commissioned 1 Jan. 1777 and resigned 5 Mar. 1778.

Chandler, John. S.C. —. He served eight years under Capt. Nathaniel Moore, Robert Fullwood, James Burgess, and John Nelson. He was at Stono, Eutaw, Tyne's defeat, and two skirmishes in Georgia until he was taken prisoner. On 15 Sep. 1780 he received several deep wounds at Tyne's defeat. His right eye was shot out. He had a bullet through his nose, another through his chin, and another lodged in his right shoulder. His fifth wound was a deep one in his right hip. He also had been shot through his right hand. Duke Adkinson deposed that he had heard Stephen Mitchell state that he had taken Chandler prisoner and delivered him to Col. Tyne. George Yates came to Steward Dickey's house and saw Chandler there as a prisoner. R. Richardson deposed that Chandler was not in Tyne's camp by choice but as a prisoner. Since his wounds made him unfit for militia duty except for patrol and alarm duty he had been discharged. He was 60 years old in 1791. He was from Darlington District. In 1808 Richard Richardson, John Nelson, David Nelson, William Dinkins, William Richburgh, Capt. Little, and Samuel Nelson deposed that they knew him in the service. His application was rejected 14 Dec. 1814.

Chandler, Martin. —. —. He was a pensioner from 1826 to 1836. His widow, Meribah Chandler, sought his pension from 1818 to 1826. Congress rejected her claim 7 Feb. 1850. She was receiving a pension at the time.

Chandler, Meshack. S.C. —. He applied in the fall of 1828 and was paid one year. He sought his arrearage in Union District on 25 Nov. 1830. He was paid as late as 1834.

Chandolet, Francis. —. Lt. He served in Hazen's Regiment. He died 6 Apr. 1810 in Chazy, N.Y. His administrator, Augustin Demers, nephew and nearest of kin, sought his commutation. Congress rejected the claim 10 Dec. 1857 because it was barred by the statute of limitation.

Chaney, John. —. —. He was pensioned under the act of 1818. He was stricken from the roll in 1820 bur was restored from 14 Nov. 1826. He sought his pension from 4 Mar. 1820 to 15 Nov. 1826. Congress rejected his petition 4 May 1846.

Channel, John. N.J. —. He served under Capt. David Lyon and Col. Oliver Spencer. He was taken prisoner between Boundbrook and Brunswick on 1 June 1777. He was said to have remained a prisoner a full year in New York. He married Rachel Hulbard. His widow, Rachel Channel, was granted a half-pay pension in Morris County in Dec. 1783.

Chanpenois, William. N.Y. Pvt. He served in Col. Thomas' militia. He was wounded by a ball in his forehead. He was on a march when ambushed in 1781 at King Street. He was pensioned 4 Sep. 1793. He lived in Westchester Co., N.Y. in 1794. He was granted one-third of a pension 20 Apr. 1796. He also appeared as William Chapenous, William Champenois, and William Champennis. He later lived in New York County. He was on the 1813 pension list as William Champernois.

Chapanard, Simon. N.Y. Pvt. He served in Capt. Gabriel Requea's Company under Col. James Hammond in the Westchester County militia. He was twice wounded, once in the back part of his head and neck and the other in his left hand by a sword. He was taken prisoner on 17 Dec. 1779. He lived in Westchester Co., N.Y. on 18 June 1788.

Chapel, James. R.I. Pvt. He was wounded in the lower part of his belly at the battle of Harlem Heights on 16 Sep. 1776. He was in Capt. Cole's company under Col. Varnum. He was aged 32 in 1786. He was on the 1813 pension list. He died 13 Dec. 1829 in Newport Co., R.I. He also appeared as James Chappell. His widow was Abigail Chappell.

Chapin, Benjamin. —. Surgeon. He was appointed in 1776 and served to 1778. He lost his health and died while absent on leave. His seven years' half-pay was paid to his orphan children 17 Apr. 1858 by Congress.

Chapin, Joel. Mass. —. He served in the 4th Regiment and was paid $20.

Chapin, Joseph. Mass. —. He served in the 3rd Regiment and was from Springfield. He was paid $20.

Chapin, Seth. R. I. Lt. He served under Capt. Samuel Cragin and Col. Ezra Wood. He was commissioned 9 July in 1776. He performed vidette or boat service for about twelve months in carrying and bringing intelligence to Gen. Cornell in 1779. Congress accepted five months of service for him, but was not satisfied that his service in 1779 was military. It was special and secret service, and he was paid at that time. His son, Seth Chapin, presented the petition on behalf of all the heirs. Congress recommended a bill for a pension 25 Apr. 1840. Congress rejected the heirs' claim 10 Feb. 1846.

Chaplin, Philip. —. —. He sought a disability pension.

Chapman, Albert. —. Capt. He received $10 per month from 17 Oct. 1807. He was on the 1813 pension list of New York. He lived in New York County and died 26 Dec. 1819.

Chapman, Barnabas. Mass. Pvt. He served in Col. Bailey's Regiment. He was wounded by a ball shot through his right hand at Bemis Heights on 19 Sep. 1777. He resided in Mass. in 1796. He enlisted 15 Apr. 1777 and was transferred to the Invalids when he was wounded. He was granted one-third of a pension 20 Apr. 1796. He was on the 1813 pension list. He was paid $20 by the Commonwealth.

Chapman, Benjamin. —. —. He was pensioned under the act of 1832 and dropped from the rolls 13 June 1839 because his service under Capt. Benjamin Plummer in 1779 did not appear on the rolls. Congress accepted two months and eighteen days of service under Capt. Plummer and three months and fourteen days under Capt. Crosby. That did not meet the minimum of six months. Chapman proved seven months and fourteen days of service and was pensioned by Congress on 10 July 1840.

Chapman, Ezra. Conn. Ens. He served under Capt. Horton and Col. Baldwin until his death. His widow married (2) Elihu Marvin and died in 1788. His son, Ezra Chapman, died leaving a widow, Abigail Chapman, and seven children. She and Sherman Chapman, administrators, received relief from Congress 10 June 1854.

Chapman, George. Pa. Pvt. He applied from Lycoming County 16 Aug. 1805. He served 1 year and 9 months as a foot soldier in Capt. Peter Grubbs' Company under Col. Miles. He also served under Col. John Bull and Col. Walter Stewart in Capt. James Cannoughen's Company. He was discharged by Dr. Tomson at the Turks Head at the battle of Brandywine. Michael Wheeland deposed that Chapman served under Col. Stewart in Capt. James Kernohan and was discharged at Valley Forge in 1778. He was awarded a $40 gratuity and a $40 annuity in Lycoming Co., Pa. 19 Jan. 1825.

Chapman, Henry H. Md. Lt. He was pensioned at the rate of half-pay of a lieutenant in Georgetown, D.C. on 16 Feb. 1821. His widow, Mary Chapman, was pensioned at the same rate 12 Mar. 1833.

Chapman, John. Mass. —. He served in the 4th Regiment and was from Foxborough. He was paid $20.

Chapman, Jonathan. N.H. Pvt. He served in under Lt. Michael McClary in Capt. Morrill's Company under Col. Stark. He lost the use of one of his legs. He resided at Epsom. He was pensioned in 1776 and left sick in hospital at Cambridge. He was aged 60 in 1787.

Chapman, Peter. Mass. Pvt. He was in the 4th Regiment and was from Mansfield. He was paid $50.

Chapman, Reuben. Conn. Pvt. He served under Col. P. B. Bradley. He contracted sickness and consumption while a prisoner in New York in 1776. He lived in Derby, Conn. in 1792.

Chapman, Thomas. Md. Pvt. He was pensioned at the rate of half-pay of a private in Dorchester County on 25 Feb. 1824.

Chapman, Thomas. S.C. —. He served under Col. Manning. He gave his papers to his gallant commander in order to obtain a federal pension who died before making the application. He was unable to recover them. His widow, Nancy Chapman, had been married to him before the end of war and was 80 years old. She was from Sumter District in 1846 when she had her application rejected.

Chapman, William. Mass. Corp. He served in the 4th Regiment and was from Belchertown. His widow, Anna Chapman, was paid $50.

Chapman, William. Va. —. He was a soldier in the Continental service. His wife, Mary Chapman, and her five children were granted £20 in Botetourt Co., Va. 13 Aug. 1779.

Chappell, Amaziah. Pvt. Conn. He served in Col. Samuel Webb's Regiment. He enlisted 8 May 1777 for three years and was discharged 8 May 1780. He served under Lt. Col. Ebenezer Huntington. He was disabled by extraordinary exertions resulting in an inguinal hernia. He was pensioned 14 Aug. 1788 and was 34 years old. He lived in Litchfield Co., Conn. He was on the 1813 pension list.

Chappell, James. R.I.. Pvt. He served in Varnum's Regiment. He lived in Newport, R.I. and died 13 Dec. 1839.

Chappell, Russell. Conn. Pvt. He served in the 1st Regiment. He broke the bone of his left thigh by getting a cannon carriage into a boat in order to cross the North River in 1782 at King's Ferry. He lived in Schenectady, N.Y. in 1795. He enlisted 10 Feb. 1781 and was on the rolls in Jan. 1783. He was granted half a pension 20 Apr. 1796. He died 3 Apr. 1807. He was on the 1813 pension list of New York.

Chappell, William. Pa. —. He was pensioned 19 Mar. 1853 in Butler County and died 25 Mar. 1854.

Chapple, John. Conn. Pvt. He served in the 6th Regiment under Col. R. Parsons. He was wounded by two balls in his shoulder and side which fractured his shoulder blade and greatly disabled his arm at the battle of Bunker Hill on 17 June 1775. He resided in Montville, Conn. in 1792. He was in the militia. He was granted one-third of a pension 20 Apr. 1796. He died in 1797. He also appeared as John Chappell.

Chardavoyne, Anthony. N.J. —. He was pensioned in Sussex County on 16 Feb. 1844 at the rate of $60 per annum.

Charles, Leonard. Pa. —. He served as a ranger on the frontiers. He was from Bedford County.

Charlesworth, John M. N.Y. Sgt. He served in Col. Van Cortland's Regiment. He developed an ulcer in his left knee from disease in 1780. He lived in Connajorharrie, N.Y. in 1794.

Charlton, John Usher. Md. Paymaster. He was granted relief.

Chase, Asa. Mass. Pvt. He served in the 7th Regiment and was from Douglass. He was paid $50.

Chase, Benjamin. Mass. Pvt. He served in the 9th Regiment and was from Haverhill. His widow, Phebe Chase, was paid $50.

Chase, Elijah. Mass. —. He was granted relief.

Chase, Enoch. N.H. Capt. Lt. His widow, Joanna Chase, had a large family of small children and sought relief 24 June 1779. She was from Dover.

Chase, Eseck. Mass. Pvt. He served in the 4th Regiment and was from Charlton. His widow, Lois Belknap, was paid $50. He also appeared as Eseck Chaise. *Vide* that entry also.

Chase, Ezra. R.I. Pvt. He lost all the fingers from both hands occasioned by the accidental discharge of a field piece while ramming home the cartridge on a field day at Tiverton on 7 Nov. 1777. He was pensioned 4 Mar. 1789. He was on the 1813 pension list. He transferred to Bristol Co., Mass. 4 Mar. 1825.

Chase, James. Mass. Fifer. He served in the 5th Regiment and was from Harwich. His widow, Mercy Chase, was paid $50.

Chase, James. Va. —. His wife, Annis Chase, and three children were furnished £8 support in Louisa Co., Va. on 11 Aug. 1777.

Chase, John. N.Y. Pvt. He was granted relief.

Chase, Moses. Mass. Pvt. He served in the 16th Regiment and was from Groton. He was paid $50.

Chase, Richard. Mass. Pvt. He was granted half of a pension 20 Apr. 1796.

Chase, Simeon. —. —. He enlisted for one year under Capt. Sawyer and Col. Elliott. His property was worth no more than $300. Congress granted him relief 3 Jan. 1832.

Chase, Solomon. —. Capt. His widow, Sarah Chase, had her petition for a pension rejected by Congress because it was not satisfied that he had served six months and rejected her petition 25 Apr. 1840. It was claimed that he was a doctor or chaplain.

Chase, Timothy. Mass. Pvt. He served in the 9th Regiment under Col. Henry Jackson and Capt. John Blanchard. He broke his right arm, and his back was injured by the falling of a tree. He was pensioned 30 Sep. 1786. He was on the 1813 pension list. He also appeared as Timothy Chaise.

Chase, Timothy. Mass. —. He served in the 4th Regiment and was from Belchertown. He was paid $20.

Chatfield, Joel. —. —. His widow, Charity Chatfield, had her petition for a pension rejected by Congress on 27 Mar. 1846 because they were married subsequent to 1 Jan. 1794.

Chatham, John. Va. —. He enlisted in Feb. 1777 under Capt. Thomas West and Col. Stephens and in Dec. 1777 enlisted under Capt. Nathan Lamme. He was at Brandywine, Germantown, and sundry others. He was discharged 19 July 1783. He applied from Person Co., N.C. 12 Sep. 1820 at the age of 62.

Chatlin, William. Md. Corp. He was on the 1791 pension list.

Chaudolet, Francis. —. Lt. He served in Hazen's Regiment and died 6 Apr. 1810. He received half-pay for life. His administrator and nephew was Augustin Demers, of Rouse's Point, Clinton Co., N.Y. Congress ruled that he was entitled to commutation pay 15 Dec. 1857 and on 2 Mar. 1860. The veteran drew bounty land from New York for his service to the end of the war.

Chavis, Daniel. S.C. —. In 1780 he served under Capt. Mattocks, Capt. Cronicle, Col. Tomson, and Gen. Lincoln. He was wounded many times in the engagement with the Tories at Ramsour's Mill in North Carolina. Jacob Salter of Effingham Co., Ga. knew him. He was pensioned in 1823. He was a free man of color. He was denied any payment because he had not had a guardian appointed. He was killed by the fall of a tree before he obtained one. Joseph Streadle, who had cared for him, sought $110 for doing so on 25 Nov. 1825.

Cherry, Robert. Pa. Pvt. He was in Chester County on 21 Mar. 1786. He was in the Flying Camp under Capt. Matthew Henderson and was wounded in his left hip by a musket ball at Fort Lee. He was 67 years old. He was dead in or by 1798.

Cherry, William. Va. Capt. In Sep. 1778 he was arranged out of service as supernumerary. His heirs had received his half-pay. They had no right to one year's pay which was a gratuity intended for officers in the Continental Line and not in state regiments so Congress rejected the claim of the heirs on 8 Aug. 1848. They had tried earlier on 5 Mar. 1846.

Chesley, —. —. —. Congress declined to change the pension rate of his widow, Sarah Chesley, on 10 June 1854.

Chesley, Robert. Md. Capt. His heirs in St. Mary's County were awarded 200 acres bounty land on 11 Mar. 1828. They forewent payment of composition money.

Chestin, —. Va. —. His widow, Franny Chestin, was granted support in Prince William County in 1778.

Chevis, James. Va. Capt. He entered the service from either Pittsylvania or Halifax Co., Va. in the spring of 1776. He died in 1781. He left a wife and one or two children. His widow married secondly Mr. Jones of Albemarle Co., Va. as proved 17 Oct. 1814 by John Nail of Franklin Co., Ga.

Chew, John. Va. Lt. He resided in Spotsylvania County on 28 Mar. 1786. He was born 5 Aug. 1753 in the same county according to the family Bible entry of his birth. He was appointed a lieutenant in the summer of 1780. He was wounded in his left arm at Camden, S.C. on 16 Aug. 1780. His arm had to be amputated. He served in the 2nd Regiment of Va. Militia under Col. George Stubblefield. He was awarded a gratuity of one year's pay and an annuity of half-pay on 29 Nov. 1781. He died 12 Feb. 1806.

Child, Edward. Pvt. Va. He was pensioned from May 1781.

Child, Jonathan. Vt. —. He was from Willston, Vt and applied 30 Sep. 1789. He was a commissary for New Hampshire and incurred numerous debts in furnishing the troops. He was almost 60 years old and had a family to support. He sought an act of insolvency.

Child, Jonas. Mass. Pvt. He served in the 16th Regiment under Capt. Nicola. He was disabled by the loss of his right leg and part of his thigh in action at Rhode Island 29 Aug. 1779. He also suffered a rupture and a broken left arm. He was 24 years old in 1782 and resided in Shrewsbury, Mass. in 1788.

Child, Moses. —. —. He served in the French and Indian War and held the same rank under George Washington. He was at the capture of Burgoyne. His grandson, Albert D. Spatler, sought a gratuity from Congress 11 Dec. 1889.

Child, Timothy. —. —. His widow, Nancy Child, sought a pension. Congress ruled that her claim was based entirely on hearsay evidence and rejected her claim 10 Feb. 1846.

Childress, Alexander. Va. —. Congress awarded his widow, Temperance Childress, the arrearage of her pension from 4 Mar. 1848 to 3 Feb. 1853 on 15 Dec. 1857.

Childress, Benjamin. Va. —. His wife, Susan Childress, was granted support in Charlotte County on 3 Nov. 1777. He was in Continental service in the state of Georgia. She also received support on 5 Oct. 1778 and £97.5 on 4 Jan. 1779. He died in the service, and she received his half-pay on 3 Apr. 1780 and 5 June 1780.

Childress, Henry. Va. —. His wife, Elizabeth Childress, was granted £10 on 24 Nov. 1777 while he was away in Georgia, £6 on 24 Aug. 1778, £20 on 23 Nov. 1778, £50 on 27 Apr. 1779 and £50 on 27 Sep. 1779 in Bedford County. She was supplied 2 barrels of corn and 100 pounds of pork on 28 Feb. 1780. He also appeared as Henry Childers.

Childs, Amos. Me. —. He was from Vassalboro. He was paid $50 under the resolve of 1836.

Childs, John. Mass. Matross. He served in the 5th Regiment and was from Charlton. His widow, Susannah Childs, was paid $50.

Childs, Nathan. S.C. —. His annuity in 1787 was £8.3.4.

Chiles, Thomas. N.C. Capt. He was in the militia and was wounded in the middle finger of his left hand and in his right arm in an engagement with Tories at Musk's Ferry on 10 Sep. 1780. He resided in Montgomery Co., N.C. in 1796. He was granted two-thirds of a pension 20 Apr. 1796. He was on the 1813 pension list. He died in Anson County 15 Sep. 1820.

Chilson, John. Conn. Pvt. He served in Capt. Nathaniel Tuttle's Company under Col. Charles Webb. On 28 Oct. 1776 at White Plains he was wounded in his left arm. It was amputated near the shoulder. Samuel Orton, Surgeon, dressed the stump. He was pensioned 5 Mar. 1787 and resided in Woodbury [?Southbury], Conn.

Chilton, John. Va. Capt. He served in 3rd Virginia Regiment. He was killed at Brandywine 11 Sep. 1779. There was no widow, only orphans. They were allowed his seven years' half pay 22 Dec. 1831. They had already received bounty land.

Chime, George. S.C. —. He was wounded in action at Savannah 9 Oct. 1779. He suffered the use of his right arm and was paid an annuity 15 Oct. 1779.

China, John. S.C. Pvt. He entered the service in the calvary in 1781 and was discharged in Aug. 1782. Thomas Wilson, William McIntosh, Reden McCoy, and William Brown served with him. He was pensioned in Sumter District 4 Dec. 1828. He was paid as late as 1834.

Chipman, William. Me. —. He was from Oxford. He was paid $50 under the resolve of 1836.

Chisseldon, Edward. Pa. —. He served in the 8th Pa. Regiment and received his donation land 7 Apr. 1807. Peter Benson redeemed the certificate on 8 June 1785. John Malone received fraudulent letters of administration on his estate. Chisseldon brought suit against him in Dec. 1789 in Philadelphia, but Malone could not be found. He was blind and without relations. He was granted $512. He resided in Washington County.

Chivitty, David. Pa. —. He was pensioned.

Choate, Ebenezer. Me. —. He was from Bridgton. He was paid $50 under the resolve of 1836.

Chote, Benjamin. N.H. —. He serve under Col. Poor and later under Capt. Edward Burbank. He and his widow, Abigail Chote, received pensions. His daughter, Plumy E. Marden, was the widow of David N. Marden who died thirteen years ago. She lived in West Epping, N.H. and suffered from neuralgia, heart trouble, and light shock. She was allowed a pension by Congress 14 Apr. 1896.

Chowning, —. Va. —. His father, Robert Chowning, was granted £16 support in Dec. 1777 and £60 support in Caroline Co., Va. 14 Apr. 1780.

Chowning, John. Va. Pvt. He enlisted in Jan. 1776 in the 7th Va. Regiment for two years; he reenlisted in Apr. 1777 for three years and died in the fall of 1778. Maj. Thomas Hill certified his service. His widow, Priscilla Chowning, and her child received £50 support on 28 June 1779. She was aged *ca.* 40 years on 1 June 1787 and had a son aged *ca.* 9 years. She lived in Middlesex County. She was put on the pension list at the rate of £6 per annum on 18 Aug. 1789 and continued on 9 June 1790 at the same rate.

Chrisman, Felix. Pa. —. He received a $40 gratuity and a $40 annuity in Chester County 3 Apr. 1837.

Christ, Adam. Pa. Sgt. He was in Northumberland County on 3 Mar. 1786. He was in the State Regiment in Capt. Anderson's Company under Maj. John Murray. He was wounded in the breast at Brandywine on 11 Sep. 1777 by a musket ball which went through his body. He signed in German. He was on the 1813 pension list. He also appeared as Adam Crist.

Christ, Henry. Pa. —. He was awarded a $40 gratuity and a $40 annuity in Lancaster, Pa. 15 June 1836. He died 23 Sep. 1848.

Christian, —. —. —. His widow, Jemima Christian, sought a pension. Both her father and her husband were Revolutionary War veterans. Congress rejected her claim 1 Mar. 1860.

Christian, Daniel. Pa. —. He applied in Hagarstown, Md. 11 June 1818. He served in the 6th Regiment of the Pa. Line under Maj. Talbot. He was discharged in 1781 by Capt. Doyle.

Christian, James. N.C. Pvt. He was disabled by a broken arm in Continental service. He was aged 35 when he was pensioned in Dec. 1785 at the rate of £2 per month. He was on the 1813 pension list. He died in Cumberland County 11 Oct. 1826.

Christian, James. N.C. Pvt. He was pensioned in Chatham County in 1785. He was in the 2nd N.C. He was wounded by a musket ball which broke the bone of his right arm and occasioned two of his fingers to be contracted into the palm of his hand in May 1780 in Charleston. He was aged 39 in 1785. He enlisted 19 May 1777 for three years. He was granted half a pension 20 Apr. 1796. He was on the 1813 pension list. He died 28 Mar. 1815.

Christian, John. Mass. —. He served in the 15th Regiment and was paid $20.

Christian, William. —. —. Congress rejected the request from the heirs for commutation 25 July 1850.

Christie, John. N.Y. Corp. His wife and three children were granted support 3 Nov. 1781 in Dutchess

County. He also appeared as John Christy. He died 28 July 1781. His widow, Eleanor Christie, received a half-pay pension.

Christine, —. Pa. —. His widow, Magdalena Christine, was awarded a $40 gratuity and a $40 annuity in Berks Co., Pa. 1 Mar. 1832.

Christman, Charles. Pa. —. He was awarded a $40 gratuity and a $40 annuity in Schuylkill County on 14 Mar. 1818.

Christman, Henry. Pa. —. He received a $40 gratuity and a $40 annuity in Northampton County 18 Feb. 1834.

Christmas, Robert. N.C. —. He was pensioned in 1784. He was wounded in the service.

Christy, Alexander. Pa. Pvt. He was on the pension lists of 1789 and 1813.

Chubbuck, Levi. Mass. Fifer. He served under Col. Prescott. He was wounded in his left knee by a musket ball on 14 Oct. 1776 at Frog's Point. He lived at Bartlett, N.H. in 1794. He was in the militia. He was granted one-fourth of a pension 20 Apr. 1796. His rate was $3.75 per month from 20 July 1807. He was on the 1813 pension list. He died 18 Mar. 1818.

Chubbs, William. Pa. Artificer. He was granted relief.

Church, —. —. —. His widow, Abigail Church, had her petition for a pension rejected by Congress on 27 Mar. 1846 because they were married subsequent to 1 Jan. 1794.

Church, Asa. Mass. QM Sgt. He served in the 6th Regiment and was from Hubbardston. He was paid $20.

Church, Caleb. R.I. —. He enlisted for one year in Apr. 1780 under Capt. William Potter and Col. Christopher Green. He resided in Chenango Co., N.Y. when Congress awarded him a pension by private act 10 Jan. 1832.

Church, Charles. Me. —. He was from Phillips. He was paid $50 under the resolve of 1836.

Church, Jabez. N.H. Pvt. He served in Hubbard's Regiment. He was pensioned 25 Apr. 1808 in Grafton Co., N.H. at the rate of $2.50 per month. He was on the 1813 pension list.

Church, John. Pa. —. He was granted $40 per annum 17 May 1813.

Church, Nathaniel. Conn. Pvt. He served in Capt. Nathan Hurd's Company and was wounded at White Plains, New York 28 Oct. 1776 by grape shot in his right shoulder. He was pensioned 23 Aug. 1780. His pension was suspended 10 Jan. 1788 until he produced new and satisfactory evidence that he ought to receive it. He was on the 1813 pension list.

Church, Nathaniel. N.H. Pvt. He was from Barrington in 1784. He lost his right leg and part of his thigh by a cannon ball on 29 Aug. 1778 in the retreat from R.I. He was in Capt. Peter Drown's Company under Col. Stephen Peabody. He was aged 36 in 1787. His rate was $5 per month from 8 Oct. 1807. He was on the 1813 pension list. He died 18 Feb. 1826.

Church, Robert. Va. —. He was in the Bedford County militia and was wounded at Guilford in 1781. He was pensioned 22 June 1784.

Church, Stephen. Mass. —. He served in the 6th Regiment and was from Hubbardston. He was paid $20.

Churchfield, John. Pa. —. He applied in Westmoreland County 2 Apr. 1813. He served in the 8th Pa. Regiment. He enlisted in June or July 1776 to the end of the war. He was wounded in his leg at Germantown. Lt. Gabriel Peterson and Lt. Col. S. Bayard were officers in his regiment.

Churchill, Ephraim. Mass. —. He was paid $20.

Churchill, Charles. Va. —. He served in the 12th Virginia Regiment. His wife, Christiana Churchill, and her two children were granted financial support in Yohogania Co., Va. 24 June 1778.

Churchill, Isaac. Mass. —. He was granted relief.

Chute, Josiah. Mass. Sgt. He served in Richard Maybre's Company under Col. Benjamin Tupper in the militia. He was disabled by a musket ball and buck shot in his right shoulder. He was pensioned 11 July 1776. He lived in Cumberland Co., Me. He was on the 1813 pension list.

Cissel, —. Va. —. His mother, Catherine Cissel, was furnished support in Mar. 1779 and Feb. 1780 in Westmoreland County.

Clagett, Samuel. Md. Surgeon's Mate. His widow, Amie Clagget, was pensioned at the rate of half-pay of a surgeon's mate 7 Mar. 1834. His half-brother was William Horner who was in his 70th year in 1837. She did not receive commutation because his service ended in 1780 as ruled by Congress 2 Jan. 1837.

Claiborne, Buller. Va. Capt. He entered in 1775 as a lieutenant and was promoted to captain. He was an aide to Gen. Lincoln and was at Valley Forge. His five years' full pay commutation was paid to his legal representative, Starling Claiborne his administrator, 30 June 1834.

Claiborne, Richard. —. Maj. He died in 1819. His widow, Catharine S. Claiborne, sought a pension but furnished no evidence of his service or their marriage. Congress denied her claim 7 Feb. 1850.

Clandince, —. S.C. —. His widow, Elizabeth Clandince, was a pensioner in 1791.

Clapp, Daniel. —. Lt. He served from 1776 to 1780. He married in 1788 and died in 1817. His widow, Mary Clapp, died 11 Nov, 1839. Their children were Betsy Clapp and Daniel Clapp of Royalston, Vt. They asked for the pension which was due their mother. Congress awarded them that amount 28 Feb. 1844.

Clapp, Jonathan. —. —. His widow, Lydia Clapp, of Washington Co., N.Y. was allowed the arrearage of her pension from 4 Mar. 1853 to 3 Feb. 1853 by Congress on 15 Dec. 1857. Her husband's name was also reported as Stephen Clapp.

Clapp, Joshua. Mass. 1st Lt. He served in the 8th Regiment under Col. Michael Jackson and Capt. Amos Cogswell. He was wounded at Bemis Heights on 19 Sep. 1777. The gun shot fractured the bones of his left leg. He was pensioned at the rate of one-third pay from 1 Jan. 1783 in Nov. 1783 and had to show he had not received his commutation pay. He was pensioned at the rate of half-pay on 28 Jan. 1790. He was 38 years old in 1790. He was listed as dead on the 1813 pension list. He had died 4 Nov. 1810.

Clapper, George. —. Pvt. He married about 1780 and died 24 Dec. 1836. Congress approved a pension for his widow, Elizabeth Clapper, 4 Jan. 1848.

Clapsadle, Augustin. N.Y. Maj. He served under Col. Peter Bellinger in the Montgomery County militia. He was killed at Oriskany 7 Aug. 1777. His widow, Maria Barbila Clapsadle, received a half-pay pension.

Clapsadle, Michael. Pa. —. He was awarded a $40 gratuity and a $40 annuity 14 Apr. 1834 in Adams County. He was 91 years old in 1840. He died 23 Aug. 1843.

Clarage, Henry. Md. Pvt. 1785. He was wounded in his left arm. He served under Col. Otho Williams in the 2nd Md. Regiment. He lived in Dorchester Co., Md.

Clark, —. —. —. His widow, Agnes Clark, sought a pension. Congress reported that it had already reported a bill for her relief 29 Feb. 1848.

Clark, —. —. —. His widow was Eunice Clark. Congress rejected her claim 18 May 1848. There was "not a shadow of foundation upon which her claim can rest."

Clark, —. —. His widow was Jane Clark. Both her husband and her father were killed by Indians.

Clark, —. Pa. —. His widow, Nancy Clark, was awarded a $40 gratuity in Guernsey Co., Ohio 24 Jan. 1832.

Clark, —. Pa. —. His widow, Catharine Clark was awarded a $40 gratuity in Warren County 12 Apr. 1851 for his Revolutionary service.

Clark, Alexander. N.J. —. He was killed 13 Feb. 1777 on the Navesinck Highlands. He was from Monmouth County. His widow, Ann Clark, received a half-pay pension.

Clark, Ambrose. N.J. —. He was pensioned in Cumberland County on 18 Feb. 1841 at the rate of $60 per annum.

Clark, Asa. Mass. Pvt. He served in 3rd Regiment and was from Sherburne. He was paid $50.

Clark, Benjamin. Mass. —. He served in the 6th Regiment and was paid $20.

Clark, Benjamin. Pa. —. He was in Greene County on 16 Sep. 1805 but previously had been in Washington County. He enlisted for three years in the 8th Pa. Regiment in Capt. Kilgore's Company. In 1778 he was wounded in the thigh and in the hand in the march to Fort McIntosh. He served under Col. John Clark. His hearing and vision were much impaired. He was deceased by Aug. 1831.

Clark, Benjamin. S.C. —. He was wounded by the enemy. He was allowed an annuity 28 May 1785.

Clark, Charles. Pa. 1st Lt. He was in Northumberland County on 24 Aug. 1786. He served in the Northumberland County militia in the 2nd Battalion in Capt. Arthur Taggart's Company in the Regiment of James Morrow. He received four wounds in an engagement near Gulph Mills, three in his left arm, and a fractured skull. He was a prisoner three years and one month. He was aged 37 years. He was on the 1813 pension list.

Clark, Charles Morris. Pa. Sgt. He was granted relief.

Clark, Daniel. Mass. Pvt. He served in the 6th Regiment and was from Ashburnham. He was paid $50.

Clark, David. Mass. —. He served in the 3rd Regiment and was from Bridgton. He was paid $20.

Clark, Edward. N.H. Sgt. He served under Col. Hazen in Capt. Frye's Company. He was wounded in his leg by a shell in Oct. 1781 at Yorktown. He lived in Haverhill, N.H. in 1795. He was on the rolls in 1780 and continued thereon to Jan. 1782. He was granted one-fourth of a pension 20 Apr. 1796.

Clark, Elisha. —. —. He was a pensioned and died 16 May 1835. Congress approved a bill for his widow, Martha Clark, to draw his arrearage 10 Feb. 1846.

Clark, Elisha. Conn. Artificer. He served under Capt. E. Boilstone. He lost all his toes except the great toe of his right foot in erecting a carriage for public service in 1777 in the laboratory at Springfield. He resided in Southington, Conn. in 1792. He enlisted 9 Mar. 1778 and was discharged 7 Mar. 1781. He was granted one-fourth of a pension 20 Apr. 1796. He was on the 1813 pension list. He was 77 years old in 1818.

Clark, Francis. N.J. Pvt. He served under Col. Newcomb. His widow was Ann Clark, and she received his half-pay pension.

Clark, George. Pa. —. His heirs were awarded his donation land 2 Apr. 1811.

Clark, George. Pa. —. He was awarded a $40 gratuity and a $40 annuity in Cumberland Co., Pa. 1 Apr. 1823. His widow, Margaret Armstrong, was awarded a $40 gratuity in Cumberland Co., Pa. 14 Apr. 1834.

Clark, Gershom. R.I. Pvt. He served in Col. Putnam's Regiment. He was wounded in the body at the battle of Bunker Hill in June 1775. He resided in Vt. in 1794. His rate was $5 per month from 1 Jan. 1808. He was on the 1813 pension list. He died in 1816.

Clark, Greenleaf. Mass. Capt. He first served as a non-commissioned officer until the latter part of 1778. He married in 1770. He died 4 Dec. 1836 in Newburyport, Mass. Congress granted his widow, Eleanor Clark, a pension 25 Apr. 1840. She was 87 years old.

Clark, Hezekiah. Va. Pvt. He served in the 13th Virginia Regiment. His widow, Sarah Clark, was allowed £15 for her support and her two children in Ohio County, Va. in June 1778.

Clark, Jesse. N.C. —. He applied in Mecklenburg County in 1787. He died 25 Sep. 1832. His widow was Hannah Clark.

Clark, Job. Pa. He was awarded a $40 gratuity and a $40 annuity in Fayette County 15 June 1836. He was 88 years old in 1840. He died 28 Oct. 1841.

Clark, John. —. —. He was paid in 1779 and 1781 as a soldier, but his service did not amount to two months. Congress rejected his claim 15 Feb. 1841.

Clark, John. —. Pvt. His widow, Lucy Clark, sought an increase in her pension based upon her husband having been a colonel. Her claim was unsupported by any testimony. Congress rejected her claim 20 June 1848.

Clark, John. —. Maj. He entered the service at the commencement of the war and served until 10 Jan. 1779. He acted as aide-de-camp to Gen. Greene. He received an accidental wound when his servant was taking his pistol to put it into his holster and became ineligible for active duty. On 10 Jan. 1779 he was appointed auditor of accounts but resigned 1 Nov. 1779 due to feebleness of health. He was pensioned at the rate of $8 per month from 15 Dec. 1807. He applied for assistance 12 Jan. 1819. He had no claim to commutation pay, but he did have the right to bounty land.

Clark, John. Conn. Pvt. He served in the 5th Conn. Regiment. He lost a leg. He was pensioned 29 Aug. 1792 and was on the 1813 pension list. He died 5 Feb. 1818 in Windham Co., Conn.

Clark, John. Me. —. He died 9 Nov. 1810. His widow, Lydia Clark, was from Whitefield. She was paid $50 under the resolve of 1836.

Clark, John. Mass. —. He served in the 1st Regiment and was paid $20.

Clark, John. Pa. Capt. He commanded a sub-legion under St. Clair and was wounded at the Miami. He was pensioned 27 Mar. 1813 at $120 per annum.

Clark, John. Pa. —. He served under Col. James Murray and was wounded in his hand. He was from Northumberland County.

Clark, John. Pa. Sgt. He was drafted out of the 1st Pa. Regiment and was wounded at the taking of Burgoyne. He served under Col. Morgan, Capt. Pear, and Lt. Boyd. He had so many wounds that he was discharged. Angus McKeann [?] of Berkeley Co., Va. stated he was in the 3rd Pa. Regiment, that John Clark was in the 1st Pa. Regiment under Col. Harmar, and that Clark was discharged in 1783. He died 10 Dec. 1819.

Clark, John. Pa. —. Maj. His widow, Margaret Clark, was awarded a $60 annuity in York, Pa. 19 Mar. 1828.

Clark, John. S.C. —. He was badly wounded in his shoulder and deprived of the use of his arm at King's Mountain. He was 70 years old. He was from Union District in 1820 when he had his application rejected for want of paper vouchers.

Clark, John. Va. Lt. He enlisted as a private under Capt. Burgess Ball in the 4th Regiment for two years in Oct. 1775 and acted as sergeant.. He was discharged at White Marsh, Pennsylvania. He next served for three years under Capt. Colston for three years in the 9th Regiment under Col. Parks. He acted as sergeant major and was appointed ensign at Valley Forge. He resigned and was appointed cornet in Ashe's Company of Cavalry on North Carolina. He was at Pittsburgh and Beaver Creek until 1780 He was ordered to North Carolina to recruit. He became sick en route to Halifax and took furlough back home. He did return. He received a furlough after Yorktown. He became ill again and was furloughed. He had been commissioned at a lieutenant in May 1778 under Capt. Colston which he exchanged for that of cornet in a North Carolina company of dragoons until disbanded in 1781. He received 2,666 acres of bounty land from Virginia.. He received his half-pay commutation 22 Dec. 1837. His name did not appear on Colston's rolls. The Continental troops were not disbanded until 1783. His widow was Lucy Clark. Congress rejected her claim 9 Jan. 1847.

Clark, John. Va. Pvt. He served in the 15th Va. Regiment and died in the service. His widow, Eve Clark, resided in Sussex County on 16 Mar. 1786 and was aged *ca.* 35 years. She had four children. She was pensioned 18 Jan. 1787. She was continued at the rate of £8 per annum on 29 May 1790. In June 1791 she was aged *ca.* 46 years. Her arm had been broken, and she had a child aged *ca.* 14 years. Her pension was continued 12 Oct. 1791.The children were Edey Clark, Thomas Clark, Becky Clark, Richard Clark, Littleberry Clark, William Clark, and Lucy Clark.

Clark, Jonas. —. —. His widow, Ann Clark of Madison Co., Tenn., was granted his arrearage from 4 Mar. 1848 to 3 Feb. 1853 as allowed by Congress 23 Feb. 1857.

Clark, Jones. —. —. Congress awarded his widow, Ann Clark, of Madison Co., Tenn. the arrearage of his pension from 4 Mar. 1848 to 3 Feb. 1853 on 21 Feb. 1857.

Clark, Joseph. Me. —. He was from Wiscasset. He was paid $50 under the resolve of 1836.

Clark, Josiah. R.I. Pvt. He served from July to Dec. 1779 under Capt. Ezekiel Worthen. Congress granted him a pension 11 Jan. and 22 Dec. 1837.

Clark, Moses. Mass. —. He served in the 5th Regiment and was paid $20.

Clark, Nathaniel. S.C. —. He entered the service in 1775. Hugh McCain deposed he saw him enlist. Sarah Croxton deposed that she lived with him at the time of his enlistment. He was pensioned 7 Dec. 1824 in Lancaster District. He was paid as late as 1834.

Clark, Noah. —. —. He served as a teamster during considerable part of the war. Since teamsters were not entitled to pensions, Congress rejected his application 27 Mar. 1846 and on 30 Mar. 1848.

Clark, Parker. N.J. —. He was pensioned in Gloucester County on 6 Mar. 1837 at the rate of $60 per annum.

Clark, Peter. Mass. Pvt. He was in the 6th Regiment and was from Beverly. He was paid $50.

Clark, Peter. Pa. Gunner. He was in Philadelphia County 14 Nov. 1785. He served aboard the vessel *Vulture* and lost the use of his limbs and his speech. He was 53 years old. He died 4 Sep. 1805.

Clark, Reuben. N.J. —. He was pensioned in Atlantic County on 28 Feb. 1847 at the rate of $60 per annum.

Clark, Robert. Va. Pvt. He was pensioned 4 Sep. 1789. He resided in Fairfax County and died 11 1806.

Clark, Rufus. Mass. —. He served in the 5th Regiment. He was paid $20.

Clark, Samuel. —. —. He served nine months under Capt. Caleb Carr, Col. Archibald Cary, and Gen. Sullivan. Congress granted him relief in 1832.

Clark, Samuel. Mass. Capt. He was wounded at Johnstown. He was on the roll in 1791. He died 26 Nov. 1801.

Clark, Samuel. Pa. —. He was awarded a $40 annuity in Berks County 28 Jan. 1836. He died 16 Feb. 1846.

Clark, Samuel. S.C. —. He served under Gen. Nathaniel Green for nine months and for seven years in the west under Col. Crafford and Maj. Stenson against the Shawnee. He had lived in Sumter District, South Carolina for the last twenty years. He had been blind for fourteen years. He sought to be placed on the pension list 14 Dec. 1814 in South Carolina.

Clark, Silas. Mass. Capt. He served under Col. Benjamin Tupper. He was wounded at the battle of Monmouth. He was pensioned at the rate of half-pay of a captain from 1 Jan. 1782 on 4 Nov. 1785 on the condition that he return his commutation pay to the United States. He was 43 years old in 1788. He transferred to Pennsylvania 4 Sep. 1791. He died there 13 Aug. 1800.

Clark, Thomas. N.H. —. He enlisted in the 1st N.H. Regiment and was wounded in 1777. He was discharged 16 June 1781. He was from Hanover.

Clark, Thomas. Pa. —. He was awarded a $40 gratuity and a $40 annuity in Butler Co., Pa. 11 Mar. 1833. He was 90 years old in 1840. He died 3 Sep. 1842 in Allegheny County.

Clark, William. —. —. His widow, Rosa Clark of Crittenden Co., Ky., sought a pension. Congress denied her claim on 6 Mar. 1850 because she furnished no proof of marriage.

Clark, William. —. —. He received an invalid pension 19 Jan. 1797 in Mississippi.

Clark, William. Mass. Pvt. He was pensioned 20 Dec. 1805. He resided in Essex Co., Mass.

Clark, William. Mass. Pvt. He served in the 2nd Regiment and was from Rochester and was paid $20 by the Commonwealth.

Clark, William. N.J. Sgt. He served under Lt. John Van Dyke, Capt. Daniel Niel, and Capt. Thomas Clark in the artillery and was wounded in the leg at Short Hills in the spring of 1777. He was allowed his half-pay in Essex County in 1801.

Clark, William. Pa. —. He was granted relief in Columbia County 21 Mar. 1837. He was 84 years old in 1840. He died 1 Jan. 1841.

Clark, William. Pa. —. He was awarded a $40 gratuity and a $40 annuity in Bedford Co., Pa. 21 Mar. 1833. He was 80 years old in 1840. He died 2 Apr. 1842.

Clark, William. S.C. —. He served in the 2nd S.C. Regiment and lost his arm. He was allowed an annuity 17 Feb. 1787.

Clarke, Alexander. Pa. —. He was awarded a $40 gratuity and a $40 annuity in Adams Co., Pa. 14 Apr. 1834.

Clarke, Carey. —. —. He enlisted on Long Island in 1775. He was at Bunker Hill, White Plains, Trenton, Princeton, and Yorktown. He served three years. He had yellow fever twice. He lost his eyesight. Congress granted him a pension 19 Jan. 1832.

Clarke, George. Pa. —. His widow, Margaret Clarke, was in Chillicothe, Ohio 28 Aug. 1822. He was in Capt. Campbell's Company of the 6th Pa. Regiment in 1776 and was in Canada under Col. W. Irwine. He was under Gen. Wayne in the south and was at Ashley Hills, S.C.

Clarke, George Rogers. Va. Gen. He was pensioned at the rate of $4,000 per annum with $400 relief on 20 Feb. 1812. He also received a sword. He was from Jefferson Co., Ky. He was awarded $400 per annum and $400 immediate relief on 14 Mar. 1812 as half-pay as Colonel of the Illinois Regiment.

Clarke, James. —. —. He served nine months and was pensioned under the act of 1818. He was stricken under the act of 1820 because he had conveyed property to his son. Congress restored his pension 12 Mar. 1823.

Clarke, James. Md. Matross. He was pensioned at the rate of half-pay of a matross on 2 Jan. 1813. His widow, Barbara McMahon, was pensioned at rate of a private 6 Mar. 1850. She was also granted his arrearage of $21.66.

Clarke, James Sampson. Va. —. He died in the service. His widow and five children were granted support in Surry County 26 July 1778. The orphans were William Clarke, Mary Clarke, James Clarke, Sarah Clarke, and Anne Clarke.

Clarke, Norman. —. —. He was wounded by a musket ball in his left thigh. He resided in Mass. in 1796.

Clarke, Samuel. Mass. Capt. He was wounded. He was pensioned at the rate of one-eighth pay from 27 Nov. 1781 on 30 June 1784.

Clarke, Richard. R.I. —. He served three months in 1776. In 1778 he served one year under Capt. Sawyer and Col. Elliott. He had $200 property. He was more than 70 years old. Congress granted him a pension 3 Jan. 1832.

Clarke, Richard. Va. Lt. He served in the Illinois Regiment under Maj. George Wells to the end of the war. He was entitled to commutation of five years in the amount of $6,757.33.

Clarke, Thomas. Va. Sgt. He was wounded in his arm at Brandywine and lost the use of it. He served in the 10th Va. Regiment in Capt. Thomas West's Company having enlisted in the spring of 1777 for three years. After being wounded, he was discharged. He was continued at the rate of £18 per annum on 17 Mar. 1787. He was awarded a £30 gratuity and an annuity of full pay on 20 Nov. 1778. He was aged 26 years and lived in Fairfax County on 5 Mar. 1787. He was on the 1813 pension list. He later removed to Kentucky. He also appeared as Thomas Clark.

Clarke, William. Va. Lt. He served in the Illinois Regiment under Col. George R. Clark to the end of the war. He was entitled to five years' pay plus interest in the amount of $5,454.38.

Clarkson, Randolph. N.J. Pvt. He served in the militia. He lived in Middlesex Co., N.J. and was on the 1813 pension list.

Clastrier, Maximin. S.C. —. He was born in France and arrived in 1778 at Beaufort. He was a merchant and volunteered for the artillery in Charleston when Gen. Lincoln ordered all the French citizens to enroll themselves in a district corps under the Marquis of Brittany. He was taken prisoner and fourteen months later was released. S. Clement, the widow of William Clement and the mother of William Clement late treasurer, said Clastrier gave her mother $1.50 every week for the care of sick American soldiers. Clastrier had Lt. Gorget of the Continental Artillery who was wounded at Haddrell Point brought to his home where he cared for him until his death when he buried him at his own expense. He had been ruined by depreciation of the Continental dollar. His application from Charleston was rejected in 1815.

Claubaugh, —. Pa. —. His widow, Margaret Claubaugh, was awarded a $40 gratuity and a $40 annuity in Huntingdon Co., Pa. 12 Feb. 1825. She died 3 Mar. 1848.

Clayes, Elijah. N.H. Capt. He served in the 2nd N.H. Line under Col. Reid and died of wounds in 1779. He left a widow, Abigail Clayes, and a family of small children of Fitzwilliam, N.H. in 1784. She sought his half-pay.

Clayton, Henry. —. Lt. His widow, Ann Clayton, was pensioned at the level of a private. She sought an increase as the level of a lieutenant. Congress granted her a pension at the higher grade 17 June 1846.

Clayton, Isham. S.C. —. There were children in 1791.

Cleaveland, Enoch. Mass. —. He served in the 7th Regiment and was from Randolph. He was paid $20.

Cleaver, —. Pa. —. His widow, Catharine Cleaver, was awarded a $40 gratuity and a $40 annuity in Berks County 25 Mar. 1837. She died 14 Sep. 1841.

Cleft, Willis. Conn. Maj. He married in 1792. His widow was Mary Cleft who died without any children or grandchildren on 12 Mar. 1847. John V. S. Hazard was her administrator. Congress granted her heirs at law her pension from 4 Mar. 1841 to 4 Mar. 1843.

Clemence, Christian. Pa. —. He was awarded a $40 gratuity and a $40 annuity in Berks County 23 Jan. 1833. He was dead by Feb. 1856.

Clement, Isaac. Mass. —. He served in the 8th Regiment and was paid $20.

Clements, Charles. Va. —. He received several wounds and was pensioned at the rate of $40 per annum plus $40 relief on 22 Jan. 1795. He was in Fluvanna County on 29 Nov. 1798. His pension was increased to $60 per annum on 15 Jan. 1829. He died 25 June 1848 in the same county leaving no widow and five children, Harris K. Clements, Hesekiah Clements, Mecha Clements, Ransom Clements, and Ezekiah Clements. His son, Harris K. Clements, was executor.

Clements, Clement. S.C. Pvt. He served under Capt. Lemuel Benton, Capt. Andrew Dubois, and Lt. Peter Dubois from 1780 to 1782. He was at Watboo, Hanging Rock where he was wounded in his leg,. He was again wounded in his head and hand in a scrimmage in Darlington District in 1781. He had a wife and four children to support. Capt. Gabriel Clements attested his service. He was paid $148 for his Revolutionary service on 20 Dec. 1820. He was twice severely wounded. He was pensioned in Richland District with one year arrearage on 15 Dec. 1821.

Clements, Gabriel. S.C. Capt. He had his house burned twice by Tories. He served in the Snow Camp. He was under Capt. Dubois and Col. Benton. Afterwards he was elected a captain in the militia, and Peter Dubois was his lieutenant. Charles Spears deposed that his father was an ensign under Clements. He was 80 years old. He was pensioned with one year arrearage in lieu of all claims for his Revolutionary services on 4 Dec. 1823. He was paid as late as 1825.

Clements, John. Va. Pvt. He served in the 3rd Regiment of Dragoons. He was wounded by a ball which passed a little above his right ham at the battle of Eutaw. He was en route to Bertie Co., N.C. He received half-pay for his disability 22 Dec. 1785 and £5 relief. Maj. Richard Call certified his service on 26 Feb. 1789.

Clendenin, James. Pa. —. He was awarded a $40 gratuity and a $40 annuity in Lancaster Co., Pa. 13 Apr. 1827.

Clendenin, John. Pa. —. He was awarded a $40 gratuity and a $40 annuity in Lancaster Co., Pa. 30 Mar. 1824.

Clendenin, Robert. Va. Pvt. He served in the militia and was wounded in 1776. He lived in Greenbrier County in 1788. He was continued on the roll at the rate of £10 per annum on 22 Dec. 1788. He also appeared as Robert Clendinnen.

Clerk, George. Va. —. His widow, Scarborough Clerk, was allowed £3 per month from 1 Jan. 1779 in Accomack Co., Va. on 27 Apr. 1779.

Clever, Anthony. Mass. Pvt. He served in the 1st Regiment under Col. Joseph Vose and Capt. Jeremiah Miller. He was disabled by a rupture. He was 40 years old in 1789. He died 16 May 1803.

Clewley, Isaac. Mass. —. He served in Crane's Artillery.

Clewley, Isaac. Mass. —. He served in the 3rd Regiment and was from Barrington. He was paid $20.

Clewley, Joseph. Md. Pvt. He was pensioned at the rate of half-pay of a private in Montgomery County 23 Jan. 1816. His arrearage of $11.11 was paid to Henry Harding for Mary Whelan, the legal heir of Joseph Clewley, 2 Feb. 1830.

Cliborn, —. S.C. —. His widow, Frances Cliborn, was from Edgefield District. There was a child in 1791. She was paid her annuity in 1819 and 1820. She died 28 Feb. 1821. James Falkner as administrator of the estate received $60 arrearage on 7 Dec. 1824. He had furnished her clothing and provisions for several years. She also appeared as Frances Claiborne.

Cliff, Samuel. —. —. He received commutation and upon deducting same half-pay for life.

Clift, Benjamin. Pa. —. He was awarded a $40 gratuity and a $40 annuity in Philadelphia Co., Pa. 15 Apr. 1835. He was dead by Nov. 1838.

Clift, Jonathan. Pa. —. He was awarded a $40 gratuity in Philadelphia Co., Pa. in Feb. 1834. He did so again in 1847.

Clift, Lemuel. Conn. Capt. He served in the 4th Conn. Regiment from 20 May 1779 to the end of the war. He died in 1821 but left no widow. His children sought his half-pay from 4 Mar. 1818 to 1821. Congress denied their claim 6 Mar. 1850 because his service terminated before the end of the war.

Clift, Wells. —. —. He received his commutation and upon deducting same, half-pay for life.

Clifton, —. Ga. —. Elizabeth Clifton was on the 1796 list.

Clifton, John. Del. Pvt. He was wounded in his right arm in May 1777 in Maryland, and his eyes were hurt by the flash of a gun on 16 Aug. 1780. He served under Col. John Hazlet and David Hall. He was discharged at Camden, South Carolina. He was aged 37 in 1783 and lived in Sussex County. He was listed as dead on the 1796 roll. He was on the 1813 pension list.

Clindeinst, —. Pa. —. His widow, Elizabeth Clindeinst, was awarded a $40 gratuity and a $40 annuity in York Co., Pa. 4 May 1832.

Cline, Conrad. Pa. —. He applied 21 Mar. 1825 from Dauphin County. He had an aged wife; his son-in-law was Joab Moats. He served in the 2nd Pa. Regiment and was a mechanic.

Cline, William. Pa. —. He was awarded a $40 gratuity and a $40 annuity in York Co., Pa. 29 Mar. 1824.

Clinesmith, Baltzer. Pa. —. His widow, Mary Clinesmith, was in Northumberland County 27 Aug. 1788. He served in the Northumberland County militia under Capt. Joseph Green and was killed by Indians 15 July 1780. Two of his daughters were wounded at the same time. He also appeared as Baltzer Cline Smith.

Clinton, James. —. —. He received his commutation and upon deducting same, he was to receive half-pay for life.

Clinton, Matthew. Pa. Pvt. He applied 4 Apr. 1788 in Cumberland County. He served in the 3rd Pa. Regiment in Capt. McCully's Company. He was wounded and taken prisoner 6 July 1780 at Paramus at the time Maj. Biles was killed. He contracted several ulcers in his right arm. He was 31 years old. Lt. James Glentworth of the 6th Pa. Regiment attested to his service.

Clinton, Peter. N.J. Pvt. He served in the 3rd Regiment and was disabled with a dislocated thigh. He was 64 years old. He was on the 1791 pension roll at the rate of $40 per annum.

Clinton, Thomas. Md. Fife Major. He was pensioned at the rate of half-pay of fife major on 2 Jan. 1813.

Cliver, —. Pa. —. His widow, Catharine Cliver, was granted a $40 gratuity in Berks County 31 Mar. 1836.

Close, Benjamin. Conn. Pvt. He served in the Independent Volunteer Company of Capt. Jabez Fitch. He enlisted for one year on 26 Feb. 1781. In March 1781 he was wounded in his left hand, left arm, and right arm at Eastchester by a party of Delancey's Light Horse. Sgt. Abner Ogden was killed at that time. He drew his pay until 26 Feb. 1782. He was first pensioned 17 Feb. 1785. He resided in Greenwich, Conn. when he was pensioned 13 Nov. 1788. He was on the 1813 pension list.

Closson, Zacheriah. Pa. —. He was awarded a $40 gratuity in Montgomery Co., Pa. 3 Mar. 1829 and 11 June 1832. He was awarded a $40 gratuity and a $40 annuity in Montgomery Co., Pa.

1 Mar. 1833.

Cloudas, Abraham. Va. —. His wife, Ann Cloudas, and four children were granted £100 support in Middlesex Co., Va. 28 June 1779.

Cloudas, Richard. Va. —. He and his brother, Thomas Cloudas, were in Continental service. Their mother, Jedidah Cloudas, was granted £40 support in Middlesex Co., Va. on 28 June 1779.

Cloudas, Thomas. Va. —. He and his brother, Richard Cloudas, were in Continental service. Their mother, Jedidah Cloudas, was granted £40 support in Middlesex Co., Va. on 28 June 1779.

Clough, Benjamin. Me. —. He was from Monmouth. He was paid $50 under the resolve of 1836.

Clough, John. N.H. Pvt. He was wounded in his legs and hip at Highlands in 1779. He was in the 2nd Regiment. He lived at Claremont, N.H. in 1783 and Henniker in 1792. He enlisted 21 Apr. 1777 and was discharged 21 Apr. 1780.

Clough, John. Va. —. His wife, Frances Clough, and two children were granted 3 barrels of corn and 150 pounds of pork in Rockingham Co., Va. 28 Nov. 1780.

Clough, Noah. Mass. Pvt. He served in Col. B. Arnold's Regiment. He was wounded by a musket ball through his right leg which broke and scattered both bones and carried away some portion of them. His wounded leg was about an inch and a quarter shorter than the other. The upper end of one of the bones on the left leg was out of socket. He was wounded on 31 Dec. 1775 at the siege of Quebec. He resided at Arundel, Me. in 1794. There was no way to confirm his story. He was on the 1813 pension list.

Clowes, Thomas. Mass. Pvt. He served in the 6th Regiment under Col. Calvin Smith and Capt. Phelps. He was disabled by a rupture and a broken left arm. He was pensioned 10 July 1783. He was 62 years and resided in Boston, Mass. in 1787.

Clugage, Thomas. Pa. Capt. He was awarded $200 on 3 Feb. 1817.

Clum, Philip P. N.Y. Pvt. He served under Capt. Rockfellow and Col. Livingston. He was at the taking of Burgoyne at Saratoga. He married Helen Hamm in July 1775. About eighteen months after his death in 1798, she married secondly Jacob Millar. He died about thirty years ago. She was 84 years old in 1837. Congress granted her relief 14 Apr. 1838.

Clutter, Simeon. Md. —. His name could not be found by Maryland of those who were entitled to bounty land for having served in the Continental Line. Congress rejected his petition for a pension 15 Apr. 1836.

Clutterbook, Henry. Pa. Pvt. He also appeared as Henry Clutterback and Henry Kusterback. He died 21 July 1790.

Clutterbook, Joseph. Pa. Pvt. He was in Philadelphia County 13 Feb. 1786. He served in the 5th Pa. Regiment in Capt. Miller's Company and was wounded at Fort Washington on York Island. He had two fingers of his hand shot off. He was 36 years old. He died 21 July 1790. He also appeared as Joseph Clutterback.

Coal, Jacob. Pa. —. He received a gratuity in Berks County in Dec. 1843.

Coates, John. Pa. Capt. He served in the 11th Penn. Regiment. He was wounded in his right hand by a musket ball which rendered his middle finger useless in May 1777 at Piscataway, New Jersey. He lived in Easton, Md. in 1794.

Coats, Thomas. Va. —. His mother was granted £30 support while her son was away in the service on 7 June 1779 in Richmond County.

Cob, Eber. Mass. —. He served in the 7th Regiment. He was paid $20.

Cobb, Daniel. —. —. He was put on the pension rolls in 1832. In 1834 he learned that his pension had been suspended since it was unclear if he served in a corps of soldiers or in a company of minutemen. Congress decided in his favor and restored him to his pension 7 June 1836.

Cobb, Isaac. —. —. He was a native of Plymouth, Mass. He served two months on the expedition to Rhode Island, three months under Capt. Benjamin Rider in 1780 at Tiverton, R.I., and was on the payroll of Capt. Jesse Sturtevant under Col. John Jacob for service in R.I. from 21 July to 1 Nov. 1780 for three months and 12 days. Congress gave him a pension 30 Jan. 1852. He resided in Abbott, Maine.

Cobb, Stratton. Va. —. His widow, Bridget Cobb, and three children were allowed £4.10 per month on 23 Feb. 1779 in Accomack Co., Va.

Cobb, Thomas. N.J. —. His widow, Clara R. Cobb, was pensioned in Hudson County on 18 Mar. 1846 at the rate of $30 per annum.

Cobby, James. Mass. Pvt. He served in the 27th Regiment in Capt. Bancroft's Company and Col. Ebenezer Bridge. He was wounded by a musket ball which entered the rim of his belly and passed through his right hip at the battle on the heights of Charlestown 17 June 1775. He was pensioned at the rate of half-pay from 31 Dec. 1775 on 26 Jan. 1776. He was 44 years old in 1787. He transferred to New Hampshire and lived in Newmarket, N.H. in 1789. He died 12 Nov. 1811 in New Hampshire. He was listed on the 1813 pension roll as dead. He also appeared as James Colby.

Coburn, Morrel. N.H. Pvt. He served under Col. John Stark in Capt. Woodbury's Company. He was wounded in his left hand by a musket ball in June 1775 at Boston Harbor. He lived in Cornish, N.H. in 1795. He was in the militia. He was granted one-fourth of a pension 20 Apr. 1796. He was on the 1813 pension list.

Coburn, Moses. Me. —. He was from Newry. He was paid $50 under the resolve of 1836.

Coburn, Saul. Mass. —. He served in the 3rd Regiment and was from Dracutt. He was paid $50.

Cochlin, John. Pa. Pvt. He was in Philadelphia County on 13 Feb. 1786. He served in the 10th Pa. Regiment under Col. Nagel. He was in the hospital in Lancaster in 1778 with inflammatory fever and totally lost the sight in one of his eyes.. He was in the Invalids under Col. Nicola and was under the care of Dr. Fred Phile. He was unfit for duty on account of the loss of his eyesight and old age. He was 71 years old. He was in New Castle, Del. in 1796 when he collected his pension. He died 14 July 1806. He also appeared as John Cocklin and John Coghlan.

Cochran, Blaney. Pa. —. He was in Schuylkill and Berks Counties. He was pensioned 5 Aug. 1814. He died 22 Jan. 1829.

Cochran, James. Md. Capt. He was paid $200 in Cecil County on 24 Feb. 1823.

Cochran, James. Md. Pvt. He was pensioned at the rate of half-pay of a private 13 Feb. 1837. His widow, Ann Mary Cochran, was pensioned at the same rate in Frederick County on 18 Jan. 1847. She also appeared as Ann Mary Cockrane.

Cochran, John. Pa. Pvt. William McCaulister deposed that he was enlisted by Sgt. John O'Neal in the 9th Pa. Regiment and was transferred to the Invalids by Col. North. He swore that John Cochran was enlisted by Sgt. Southerland in the same regiment and was transferred to the Invalids at the same time. Lewis Nicola discharged Cochran from the Invalids on 14 Nov. 1777.

Cochran, John. Pa. —. He applied 5 Nov. 1832. He was in the artillery artificers corps.

Cochran, Robert. Pa. —. He applied 18 July 1814 from Allegheny County. He enlisted 7 May 1777 in the 5th Pa. Regiment under Col. Francis Johnston in Capt. Frederick Varnum's Company. He was discharged by Gen. Wayne at Trenton, N.J. 26 Jan. 1781. James Boogs of Brooke Co., Va. deposed that Cochran served under Lt. Levi Griffith in the 5th Pa. Regiment. He was

73 years old in 1840. He died 23 Feb. 1844.

Cochran, Robert. Pa. —. He was granted relief 3 Mar. 1837 in Butler County. He was dead by May 1842.

Cochran, Robert. S.C. Marine Capt. He served under Commodore Alexander Gillon on the *South Carolina*. He was allowed his share of prize money 12 Jan. 1791.

Cochran, Samuel. Va. —. He died in Continental service. His widow, Elenor Cochran, was allowed £15 for her support and her young children 19 May 1778 in Augusta Co., Va. She was allowed £40 as his widow 19 May 1779.

Cochran, Thomas. S.C. —. His claim was rejected 8 Dec. 1831.

Cocke, —. Va. —. He served in Col. Wood's Regiment. His wife, Mary Cocke, and four children were furnished £30 pounds support in Frederick Co., Va. on 3 Aug. 1779. They were furnished 4 barrels of corn and 200 pounds of pork on 5 Sep. 1780 and 5 barrels of corn and 250 pounds of pork on 5 Feb. 1782.

Cockley, Rirchard. Pa. —, He was granted a pension 27 Mar. 1812.

Cockrall, William. S.C. —. He served three years in the 3rd S.C. Regiment under Col. William Thompson. John Hague was paymaster. Capt. David Hopkins enlisted him in 1775 for three years. John Stone was with him under Col. John Winn. John Smith was with him when they were taken prisoner at the fall of Charleston. They were put on a British man of war and held there for eleven months and four days when they were taken to Jamaica. They were freed when peace was concluded. He applied 10 Nov. 1815 in Chester District. He had a large and helpless family.

Cockrell, —. Va. —. He served in the state artillery. His wife, Mary Cockrell, was granted £25 support in Fauquier Co., Va. in Apr. 1779.

Coddington, Robert. N.J. Fifer. He served in the 4th Regt. He resided in Middlesex County. He was disabled with an ulcerated leg. He was on the 1791 pension roll. He was on the 1813 pension list. He died in Woodbridge Township 15 Aug. 1833. His widow was Margaret Coddington.

Coddrington, Benjamin. Md. Pvt. He was pensioned in Allegany County on 25 Apr. 1812. He was on the 1813 pension list. He also appeared as Benjamin Coddington.

Coden, David. N.Y. Pvt. He served under Capt. Marshall and Col. Philip Van Cortland and was slain 19 June 1780. His son, William Coden, received a half-pay pension.

Coderman, Conrad. Pa. —. His heirs were paid $300 in full for his tract of donation land 23 Mar. 1819. He also appeared as Conrad Catterman.

Codwise, Christopher. N.Y. —. His wife and three children were granted support on 3 Nov. 1781 in Dutchess County.

Coe, Ebenezer. Conn. Capt. He served in the 4th Conn. Militia under Col. Samuel Whiting. Joseph Walker was lieutenant. Gen. Arnold ordered him to attack the enemy on their retreat from Danbury through Ridgefield. He was obliged to retreat and was wounded by a musket ball which entered his head near his right ear and came out his right eye in 1777. He was a carpenter and wheelwright. He was pensioned 25 Nov. 1788 at Stratford, Conn. at the age of 53. He was pensioned 25 Nov. 1788. He was on the 1813 pension list. He died 1 Aug. 1820 in Fairfield Co., Conn.

Coe, Richard. Md. Sgt. He was pensioned in Prince George's County at the rate of half-pay of a sergeant 20 Feb. 1830. He received a warrant for his 50 acres of bounty land in Allegany County in 1832. His son, George G. Coe, was paid the arrearage 2 Mar. 1844.

Coe, William. Md. Matross. He was pensioned at the rate of half-pay of a private on 12 Feb. 1820. That rate was rescinded, and he was pensioned at the rate of half-pay of a matross in Annapolis, formerly of Baltimore, 16 Feb. 1821. His widow, Mary Coe, received the arrearage of $12.50 of his pension 17 Feb. 1834. She was pensioned at his rate on 4 Mar. 1834. Her arrearage of $50.00 was paid to Alexander Benson Coe 12 Jan. 1836.

Coffee, —. Va. —. He was killed while in the Continental Army. His widow, Mary Coffee, was paid £6 in Nov. 1780 in Fauquier County.

Coffee, Hugh. S.C. —. He lost his knives, forks, stock, crops, and household furniture at Blackstocks on Tiger River. He was at Camden and lay with Marion in the swamps. He was drafted at Fort Moultrie under Col. Marshall. Alexander Montgomery and William Nelson served with him. He was pensioned from Lancaster District 9 Dec. 1825. His executors, Alexander Coffee and Nancy Coffee, sought his arrearage but were rejected.

Coffee, John. Va. Pvt. He served in the 11th Va. Regiment. He was 37 years in 1786 and resided in Hampshire County.

Coffield, Owen. Md. Pvt. He was from Prince George's County and was pensioned in 1783. He served under Col. Grayson. He died in 1792.

Coffill, Hugh. Del. —. He received his half-pay pension in 1784.

Coffin, James Josiah. —. —. Early in 1776 he engaged to go on the schooner *William* under Capt. Joshua Bunker to sail to Europe for a cargo of warlike stores and arms for the government. They sailed to Bordeaux, France where they obtained powder, arms, and woolen clothes. En route back near Bermuda they were taken by the *Galatea* under Thomas Jordan. Coffin and Bunker were taken on board, abused, and ill treated. They were put on the prison ship *Whitby* at New York until Feb. 1778 when he was exchanged. He made his way to Nantucket. Timothy Bunker served with him. Even though his type of service was not covered by law, Congress awarded him a pension of $40 per annum 3 Jan. 1837.

Coffin, John. Mass. —. He served in Washington's Dragoons and was from Newbury. His widow, Mary Moores [?], was paid $50.

Coffin, Lemuel. Mass. —. He served in Washington's Dragoons and was from Newburyport. He was paid $50.

Coffin, Obed. Mass. Pvt. He was in the 1st Regiment and was from Barnstable. He was paid $50.

Coffroth, Conrad. Md. Fifer. He was pensioned in Franklin Co., Pa. at the rate of half-pay of a fifer on 3 Mar. 1826. His widow, Magdalena Coffroth, was pensioned at the rate of half-pay of a fifer in Washington Co., Md. 28 Feb. 1832.

Cogan, John. Del. Pvt. He was pensioned in 1784.

Cogan, Richard. Del. Pvt. He was on the 1791 pension list.

Coggeshall, James. Mass. Pvt. He served in the 14th Regiment and was from Middleborough. His widow, Zilpha Hackett, was paid $50..

Cogswell, Ashael. Mass. Corp. He served in Capt. Aaron Rowley's Company under Col. John Ashley. He was wounded at or near Fort Edward 22 July 1777 by a musket ball which passed through his left shoulder. He was pensioned at the rate of half-pay of a corporal from 1 Apr. 1782 on 17 Mar. 1784. In 1786 he was 46 years of age.

Cogswell, Jonathan. Mass. Sail Maker. He served aboard the continental ship of war *Alfred* under Hinman. He was wounded and lost his right eye in an engagement with two British frigates, the *Arcade* and the *Ceres*, in Mar. 1777. He died 20 Mar. 1782 in Halifax prison. His widow received one-third pay from the time of his being wounded to his death which according to another source was on 24 Mar. 1783.

Cogswell, Joseph. —. —. Congress rejected his claim 20 June 1848 due to insufficient proof.

Cogswell, William. —. —. He lived in Upper Canada and served two months under the British before he took protection of the American forces. He gave information where British public property was secreted. The Americans took it. He fled Canada and remained in service with the Americans. Congress rejected his petition 18 Feb. 1820.

Cogswell, William. N.H. Surgeon's Mate in military hospital. He fell in walking to the hospital and was rendered lame in 1783 at New Windsor. He lived in Atkinson, N.H. in 1794. His heirs received his commutation pay 13 June 1838.

Cohen, Jacob. Va. Capt. He served in the cavalry to the end of the war. Virginia awarded 4,000 acres of bounty land based on his three years of service. Congress did not allow his heirs their claim of commutation 8 Mar. 1842. He had served in the militia, but the amount of time was uncertain. He did not serve to the end of the war and did not become supernumerary.

Coil, Burnet. S.C. —. His widow, Martha Coil, was made a prisoner by the Tories 7 Dec. 1781 and murdered by the Indians. She was granted an annuity 29 Mar. 1785 in Abbeville. He also appeared as Barney Coil.

Coil, John. S.C. —. He died in the service in Dec. 1781. His widow, Mary Coil, was granted an annuity 21 Feb. 1785.

Coit, Benjamin. Conn. —. He served nearly three months in the militia under Capt. Benjamin Leffingwell in 1776. In the spring of 1778 he was under Capt. Robert Niles the commander of the state vessel *Spy*. He was ordered to go to France with dispatches for Benjamin Franklin. He sailed from Stoughton and reached Brest in twenty-two days. He sailed home in Sept. Two or three days out they were captured by a privateer and carried to the island of Jersey. He was put on board a ship from Bremen bound to Bordeaux where he arrived in Oct. or Nov. He took passage to Baltimore. He was again taken prisoner and carried to Jersey Island where he went on board a vessel from Sweden to Spain. Ninety days later he arrived and found a privateer belonging to Newburyport which he reached in the summer in 1779. He sought relief from Congress 29 Mar. 1836. He died 28 Dec. 1841. He married in 1788. Congress rejected the petition of his widow, Sarah Coit, because he did not serve.

Coit, Daniel. Mass. —. He served six months under Capt. Nobles in 1776 and was at the battle of White Plains. In the fall of 1776 he served in an independent company of artillery raised at Sheffield. In the next season his company left the artillery and were mounted on horseback with small arms and went to Vermont under Col. Seth Warner to oppose Gen. Burgoyne who capitulated 17 Oct. 1777. He returned home. He was drafted in 1779 and went to Fairfield which was burnt by the British. He served two years but not nine continuous months. He died 4 July 1832. His widow died a few weeks later. Congress awarded his four surviving children his arrears 23 Mar. 1860.

Colbey, John Christopher. —. —. He enlisted in 1778 under Capt. Shaffer for the war. He was wounded at the defeat of Gen. Gates. He partially recovered and rejoined his regiment. His dwelling house burned in 1783. He received a pension. On 12 Apr. 1838 Congress ruled that he was not entitled to bounty land because he was discharged before the end of the war.

Colburn, Andrew. N.H. Lt. Col. He was killed at the battle of Stillwater 19 Sep. 1777. His heirs were paid his seven years' half-pay of $2,520. His widow, Phebe Colburn, lived in Marlborough in 1785 when she was pensioned. She next married Ephraim Root. She was a native of Coventry, Conn.

Colburn, John. N.H. Sgt. He served under Col. Cilley in Capt. House's Company. He caught a violent cold in fording the Mohawk River having little clothing to cover himself. He lived in Hanover, N.H. in 1795.

Colburn, Lewis. Mass. —. He was paid $50.

Colby, Samuel. Me. —. He was from Portland. He was paid $50 under the resolve of 1850.

Colby, Samuel. Mass. —. He served in the 8th Regiment and was from Edgecomb [Maine]. He was paid $20.

Colby, Sylvanus. Mass. Pvt. He served in the 6th Regiment and was paid $20.

Colding, John. S.C. —. He was killed 26 May 1780. His orphans were granted an annuity 23 Dec. 1785. He also appeared as John Colden. There were two children in 1791.

Coldwater, Philip. Pa. —. His widow, Margaret Coldwater, received a $40 gratuity and a $40 annuity in Philadelphia 14 Apr. 1859.

Coldwell, Robert. Va. Pvt. He served under Col. Campbell. He was wounded in his right wrist and in his groin in 1781 at the siege of Ninety Six.

Cole, —. Va. —. His wife, Happy Cole, was granted support in Prince Edward County in Feb. 1778.

Cole, Alexander. Va. —. His wife, Mary Cole, and family were granted support in Prince Edward County on 16 Mar. 1778 and 29 Apr. 1779.

Cole, Benjamin. —. —. He married in 1786 and died in 1834. His widow, Rachel Cole, married secondly James McMurphy in May 1838. Congress denied her claim 3 Mar. 1851.

Cole, Benjamin. Mass. —. He served in the 3rd Artillery Regiment and was from New Marlboro. He was paid $20.

Cole, Benjamin. N.Y. Matross. He served under Col. John Lamb and was slain 23 Jan. 1782. His widow, Phebe Cole, received a half-pay pension.

Cole, Daniel. Pa. —. He was granted relief in Fayette County 16 June 1836. He was 84 years old in 1840. He died 24 Mar. 1841.

Cole, Ebenezer. Mass. —. He served in the 7th Regiment and was from Chesterfield. He was paid $20.

Cole, Eli. Me. —. He died 16 Dec. 1832. His widow, Olive Cole, was from Buxton. She was paid $50 under the resolve of 1836.

Cole, Henry. N.Y. Pvt. He served in the 2nd N.Y. Regiment and was slain 19 Oct. 1777. His widow, Christine Cole, received a half-pay pension. He also appeared as Henry Coal.

Cole, Isaiah. Me. —. He was from Waldoboro. He was paid $50 under the resolve of 1836.

Cole, Jacob. Mass. Pvt. His widow was Huldah Cole of New Medord who was paid 4 Mar. 1835.

Cole, James. N.Y. Sailor. He served on the sloop *Mechias Liberty*. He was wounded in the leg in action with a British tender in June 1775. He lived in Westfield, N.Y. in 1794.

Cole, John. —. —. He suffered from a rupture caused by lifting and carrying grapeshot in the service. He was 93 years old. Congress granted him a pension of $8 per month on 30 June 1854.

Cole, John. N.J. —. He was pensioned in Hunterdon County on 26 Feb. 1840 at the rate of $60 per annum.

Cole, John. Penn. —. He left the service without leave and was considered a deserter. His mother, Mary Moore, and John Moore were administrators of his estate. The arrearage of his wages was denied.

Cole, Joseph. Mass. Pvt. He served in the 16th Regiment and was from Freetown. He was paid $50.

Cole, Joseph. Mass. Pvt. He served in the 16th Regiment and was from New Ashford. His widow, Huldah Cole, was paid $50.

Cole, Levi. —. —. He applied for a pension in 1818 at which time he had a wife, a child 15, and a girl in school. He married (2) Elizabeth Simmons 6 Apr. 1830. He died in Annapolis, Md. 8 June 1846. Congress gave his widow a pension 23 May 1860.

Cole, Richard. Va. —. He was away in the service. His wife, Patsy Cole, was allowed 1 bushel of corn, 100 pounds of pork, and 124 pounds of beef as provisions in Augusta Co., Va. for her support and that of her children on 19 Dec. 1781.

Cole, Solomon. Mass. Pvt. He served in the 2ⁿᵈ Regiment under Col. Reed and Capt. Caleb Robinson. He was disabled by a musket ball in his right arm on 19 Sep. 1777 at Bemis Heights. He was from Salem in 1785. He was pensioned 5 May 1788 and was 45 years old. He lived in Hampden Co., Mass. He was on the 1813 pension list.

Cole, Thomas. N.C. Sgt. He was in Richmond Co., N.C. and Kershaw District, S.C. He applied in 1810. He served six months and did duty as a captain under Col. Caswell and fought at Moore's Creek. He served in the 5ᵗʰ Regiment under Col. Buncombe. He was at Brandywine, Germantown, and Monmouth Court House. He also served in the 2ⁿᵈ Regiment under Col. Patten in Capt. Robert Fenner's Company. He received a $200 gratuity. He had a wife and two children. He was disabled in Continental service. He marched from West Point to Charleston, S.C. He was receiving a pension of $30 per annum in 1822 and sought a two or three year advance due to the difficulty of returning to Raleigh, North Carolina to collect it annually. He was a native of North Carolina and had been reared in Newbern. His children were poor, he was worn out with age, and had walked from Columbia, S.C. tottering on his staff. He was granted a $50 pension with one year in advance. He had moved to Camden, S.C. to be near his wife's relatives. His son-in-law was Edward Cobb of Kershaw Dist., S.C.

Cole, William. N.J. Pvt. —. He served under Col. Scudder in the militia. He died a prisoner 15 Mar. 1778. His widow was Elizabeth Cole of Monmouth County who received a half-pay pension.

Colegate, Asaph. Md. Pvt. He was pensioned at the rate of half-pay of a private 10 Mar. 1842.

Coleman, —. Va. —. His wife, Mary Coleman, was granted £25 support in Fauquier Co., Va. in Apr. 1779.

Coleman, Benjamin. Pa. —. He was pensioned 16 June 1836 in Columbia County.

Coleman, Daniel. —. Pvt. He served as a musician. Congress denied his widow, Mary Coleman, relief 19 July 1848.

Coleman, James. Va. Pvt. He served under Col. Buford and was inhumanely wounded and taken prisoner at the Waxsaws. He was paroled. He was recommended for £150 gratuity on 7 Nov. 1780. He was on the 1791 pension list.

Coleman, Joel. Va. —. His wife, Jemima Coleman, was furnished support in Loudoun County in Aug. 1779, Mar. 1780, and July 1780.

Coleman, John. N.Y. —. He served under Col. Dubois. His wife, Sarah Coleman, was granted support while her husband was away in the service 10 May 1779.

Coleman, John. Pa. —. He was awarded a $40 gratuity and a $40 annuity in Indiana County 16 Feb. 1813. He was paid to 5 Dec. 1831. He also appeared as John Colman.

Coleman, Patten. Md. —. He was from Baltimore County.

Coleman, Patrick. Pa. Pvt. He lived in Lancaster County. One of his name was on the 1813 pension list in Delaware.

Coleman, Thomas. Pa. —. He lived in Bedford County in 1777 and led the settlers in an attack on the Indians. He acted as guide.

Coleman, Thomas. Pa. —. He was awarded a $40 gratuity in Huntingdon Co., Pa. 27 Mar. 1830.

Coleman, Thomas. Va. —. His child in the care of Archelaus Harris was awarded £6.10 in Louisa

Co., Va. on 13 Oct. 1777. The same amount was paid to Bartelot Smith for another child on the same date. William Smith was paid the same amount for another child on 8 Dec. 1777. William Smith was paid £30 for three children, and Archelaus Harris was paid £10 for one child in 1778.

Coleman, William. N.J. —. He was pensioned in Mercer County on 12 Feb. 1841 at the rate of $60 per annum.

Coleman, Wyatt. Va. Lt. & Adj. He was issued his commutation pay in Apr. 1791.

Coles, Daniel. Pa. —. He received a $40 gratuity and a $40 annuity in Fayette County 16 June 1836. He was dead by July 1841.

Coles, William. N.Y. —. He enlisted at Shawangunk in Apr. 1778 under Col. Wisenfels and served his full nine-month term. He served two years in the war. Congress granted him relief 18 May 1832.

Colfax, Jonathan. Conn. Sgt. He served three years in the Connecticut Line for three years. He served under Col. Josiah Starr from 20 Jan. 1777 to 1 Jan. 1780 for two years, eleven months, and eleven days. He was one of the forlorn hope on 15 July 1779 at the storming of Stony Point. He married Elizabeth Wilson, daughter of Thomas Wilson, in New London, Conn. Rev. Mr. Tyler officiated. He died in Jan. 1790. His widow, Elizabeth Colfax, married secondly his brother, Robert Colfax, in June 1803. Robert Colfax served as a private for three years in the 9th Regiment under Col. Samuel B. Webb from 9 Apr. 1777 to 1 Jan. 1780. Both husbands entered the sea service after they left the army. Both of them were lieutenants on the brig *Minerva* when she captured the *Hannah*. Her second husband was appointed to command an American privateer and was captured off Sandy Hook, carried to New York, and imprisoned on "*Old Jersey.*" He died in Sep. 1825 as a pensioner. She married too late to qualify on the service of her second husband. Congress granted her a pension for five years at the highest rate of a sergeant on 8 Mar. 1842.

Colfax, Robert. Conn. Pvt. *Vide* Jonathan Colfax.

Colhoun, John. S.C. —. He was from Abbeville District in 1786.

Colkins, Jonathan. Mass. —. He served in the 1st Regiment. He was paid $20.

Collamore, Benjamin. Mass. Pvt. He had served in the Invalids under Capt. McFarland. He was disabled by an ulcerated leg. He also lost his right eye. He was pensioned 1 Sep. 1782. He was 66 years old in 1786. He died 1 July 1803. He also appeared as Benjamin Killmore.

Collember, Thomas. Md. Pvt. He was pensioned 4 Mar. 1789. He was on the 1813 pension list. He also appeared as Thomas Colember.

Collings, John. Va. Pvt. He was on the 1813 pension list.

Collins, —. Va. —. He died in the service. His widow, Martha Collins, was pensioned in 1783 in Westmoreland County..

Collins, Balthus. Pa. Sgt. He was in Philadelphia County 13 Feb. 1786. He served in the 4th Regiment of Artillery in Capt. Gibbs Jones' Company in Col. Proctor's Battalion of Artillery. He was wounded at Monmouth in his left leg and discharged unfit for duty on 10 May 1779. He was 38 years old.

Collins, Benjamin. Mass. —. He was pensioned.

Collins, Charles. Va. Pvt. He served in the 2nd Regiment of militia under Col. George Stubblefield and was wounded at Camden, S.C. in 1780. He had several wounds in his body and extremities. He suffered almost the total loss of the use of his left arm. He was put on the roll on 14 Apr. 1788 at the rate of £12 per annum. He was aged *ca.* 42 years in 1791. He resided in Spotsylvania

County.

Collins, Daniel. S.C. —. An annuity was paid to his two children 1 Apr. 1825. In 1826 it was paid to Mary Matilda Collins, his heir, in care of her guardian Robert Gamble.

Collins, Jabez. —. Sgt. He served as an orderly sergeant for two months in 1775, another tour of enlistment for two and a half months in the winter of 1776, and three months in the summer of 1776 as a drafted militiaman. He was at Harlaem Heights. He was born in Somers, Conn. He was dismissed in New York. He was an invalid and unable to return home to R.I. His brother went home and returned with a horse for the 150 mile journey. He was put on the pension roll and drew his arrears for six months' service. When he learned he was due a larger amount for his service as an orderly sergeant, he was told he was not entitled to any pension. Congress granted him a pension for seven and a half months of service at the higher rank 4 Jan. 1841.

Collins, James. Md. Sgt. He was wounded at the siege of York in Virginia. He was in Baltimore County in 1787. He was pensioned 4 Mar. 1789. He died in 1795.

Collins, John. Pa. —. He applied from Delaware County on 25 July 1815.

Collins, John. —. —. He served as 1st Mate on the schooner *Sally* under Capt. Gamaliel Smith and sailed from Plymouth to Baltimore where they took on a load of flour and returned to Boston 20 June 1776. He reentered the service in Nov. 1778. He was master of the schooner *Starke* from Boston and sailed to Charleston for provisions for the Board of War. He was taken prisoner off Wilmington, N.C. by the British ship *Jason*. He was carried to New York City and put on the prison ship, *Good Hope*. He was discharged the last of May 1779 and arrived in Boston the 10th or 15th of June. He was born 15 June 1753. Congress granted him a pension for six months of service on 4 Feb. 1846.

Collins, John. Va. —. His widow was furnished assistance in Loudoun Co., Va. on 14 Apr. 1778.

Collins, John. Va. —. He was wounded in the expedition against the Indians in 1777. He was granted £40 relief 1 Jan. 1799.

Collins, Joseph. Va. —. His widow, Isabel Collins, was granted support in Loudoun County 8 Mar. 1779. His widow was furnished necessaries in Fauquier Co., Va. 12 Sep. 1780. He had died in the service.

Collins, Matthew. N.C. —. He served under Gen. Ashe. He was hacked and almost cut to pieces. He was allowed money to cover expenses on his return to North Carolina on 9 July 1779. He was blind in 1789.

Collins, Patrick. Pa. Pvt. He was on the 1813 pension list.

Collins, Peter. Va. Pvt. He was a disabled Continental soldier. He was on the 1785 pension list.

Collins, Reuben. S.C. Lt. He served twelve months in the militia under Capt. Petty, Capt. Dunlap, Col. Marshall, and Capt. John Grimes. He fought at Rocky Mount, Hanging Rock, Parker's Ferry, and Eutaw. He had been compelled to use crutches for the past twenty years. He lost his documents when his dwelling house was destroyed by fire. William Nettle served with him. He was pensioned in Kershaw District on 14 Dec. 1826. He was paid as late as 1830.

Collins, Robert. Va. —. His wife, Mary Collins, was granted 200 pounds of pork and 4 barrels of corn for her support and her three children in Berkeley County on 16 Oct. 1781. She was furnished 100 pounds of bacon and 4 barrels of corn on 20 Aug. 1782.

Collins, William. Pa. —. He was granted relief.

Collins, William D.. S.C. —. He served under Capt. Jacob Barnett and Col. Mayham for 18 months. He was a waiting man for Capt. Barnett and Lt. Minor Winn. He was pensioned in Kershaw

District on 23 Nov. 1829. He was paid as late as 1834.

Colony, George. Va. —. His wife, Elizabeth Colony, and two children were allowed 2 barrels of corn and 100 weight of pork on 31 Jan. 1783 in Accomack Co., Va.

Colony, Richard. N.H. Pvt. He served in the 2nd Regiment under Capt. Frederick Bell and Col. George Reid. He was wounded by a musket ball which passed through his thigh and by a small ball which lodged in his hip on 19 Sep. 1777 at Stillwater. He lived in New Durham, N.H. in 1794. He enlisted 20 Mar. 1777 for three years and was discharged 26 May 1780. He was granted half a pension 20 Apr. 1796. He also appeared as Richard Colamy.

Colson, David. Me. —. He died 17 Mar. 1834 at Thomaston. His widow, Mary Colson, was from Bath. She was paid $50 under the resolve of 1850.

Colson, Joseph. Mass. —. He served in the 5th Regiment and was from Plainfield. He was paid $20.

Coltman, Robert. Pa. Capt. He served under Col. Proctor in 1779 and 1780 in the Artillery. He was a member of the Society of the Cincinnati and died in 1816. His widow died many years ago. His illegitimate son, John Coltman, aged 82, had his petition rejected by Congress 17 Mar. 1876 because it was believed that the father had received his commutation.

Columber, John. Va. —. His wife was furnished assistance in Loudoun Co., Va. on 14 Apr. 1778.

Colver, Dan. Mass. Pvt. He served in Capt. Bradley's Company under Col. Brown and lost his left leg near Fort Ann. He was pensioned at the rate of half-pay from 8 July 1777 on 29 Sep. 1779.

Colwell, Medford. Mass. —. He served in the 6th Regiment and was from Williamsburg. He was paid $20.

Colwise, Christopher. N.Y. —. His wife and three children were granted support in Dutchess County 3 Nov. 1781. His name may have been Christopher Colwire.

Combs, —. S.C. —. His widow was Winnefred Combs. There was one child in 1791.

Combs, Francis. Va. Pvt. He served in the 10th Va. Regiment. He was 30 years old and resided in Caroline County in 1786. He was on the 1813 pension list. He lost an arm in the service.

Combs, John. Pa. —. He was on the 1789 pension list.

Combs, Thomas. N.J. Capt. He served under Gen. Maxwell in the militia. He was wounded in one of his feet when he was ordered to take off a picquet of the enemy. He was from Middlesex County 2 May 1786. He was 39 years old. He was on the 1791 pension roll at the rate of $96per annum.

Combs, Uriel. N.Y. Sgt. He served in the Montgomery County militia. He was killed at Oriska on 6 Aug. 1777. His widow, Christina Combs, sought a pension 20 Mar. 1785.

Comins, Josias. —. —. He entered the service in 1779 and served three months that year and in 1781. He served out his full enlistment and was permitted to return home after 2 ½ months due to the scarcity of provisions. In the summer of 1779 he was on an alarm and marched from Massachusetts to Rhode Island and did duty for a fortnight. He served a total of 5 months and 29 days. He was one day short of qualifying for a pension. Congress granted him a pension 25 Mar. 1836.

Commack, William. Va. Pvt. He served in Col. Campbell's Detachment. He was being pensioned in 1785.

Commoding, Nicholas. N.Y. —. He applied in Oct. 1786.

Compton, Abraham. Va. —. He was a soldier in the Continental Army. His widow, Mary Compton, and her three children were granted £100 in Botetourt Co., Va. 10 Feb. 1780.

Compton, Archibald. Va. Pvt. He served in the 2nd Va. Regiment and was wounded at Germantown by a ball through the joint of his right knee. He was enlisted by E. Meade. He was awarded a £30 gratuity and a annuity of half-pay. He was awarded a £100 gratuity on 13 May 1780 because of depreciation of the currency. He was in Amelia County on 1 Jan. 1786. Later he was in Pittsylvania County. He died in Nov. 1810. He was on the 1813 pension list.

Compton, George. N.J. Corp. He served in the 1ˢᵗ N.J. Regiment under Capt. Jeremiah Chadwick. He lived in Middlesex County. He was on the 1813 pension list. He died 22 Nov. 1828 in Perth Amboy. He left no widow or children.

Con, Martin. Pa. —. He was granted relief.

Conant, Bartholomew. Mass. Pvt. He served under Col. Ebenezer Frances and Capt. Richard Murray. He was disabled by a rupture. He age was not given on the roll in 1790. He died 14 Jan. 1803.

Conant, Ebenezer. Conn. Pvt. He enlisted for six months in 1776 and served under Capt. John Barnard and Col. Willys. He served another five months in the fall of that year. On 1 Apr. 1780 he served under Lt. Peleg Heath, and Col. Willys for nine months. He applied from Jefferson Co., N.Y. and Congress approved a special bill for his relief 17 Feb. 1846. He had made an earlier attempt on 30 Dec. 1836 when he stated that he served under Col. Parsons for several tours. He was a substitute and answered to the name of Bibbens at roll calls. He was in no battle or skirmish. There was no evidence that the one for whom he substituted was dead so Congress rejected his petition. Congress did grant him a pension for nine months of service on 17 Feb. 1846.

Conant, Luther. Mass. Sgt. He served in the 7ᵗʰ Regiment and was from Shutesbury. His widow, Susanna Conant, was paid $50.

Conant, Solomon. Mass.—. He was granted relief.

Conant, William. Mass. Pvt. He served in the 14ᵗʰ Regiment under Col. Gamaliel Bradford and Capt. Joshua Eddy. He was disabled by a musket ball in his right arm and leg. He also suffered from a rupture. He was 40 years old. He was pensioned 27 Oct. 1786. He resided in Plymouth Co., Mass. He was on the 1813 pension list.

Cone, Henry. Conn. Pvt. He served in 3ʳᵈ Regiment. He lost the sight of one of his eyes by smallpox in 1777. Later in battle he received several cuts in the head and was taken prisoner in July 1781 at Horse Neck. He lived in Lyme, Conn. in 1794. He enlisted 24 Nov. 1776 for three years and was discharged 1 Dec. 1779. He was granted one-fourth of a pension 20 Apr. 1796. He was on the 1813 pension list. He died 15 Feb. 1827.

Cone, Jared. Conn. —. He enlisted under Lt. Olmstead and joined Col. Sherman's Regiment in Conn. He was then transferred to Capt. Bett's Company under Col. Scammel. He was at Yorktown as the surrender of Cornwallis. He served more than ten months. Congress granted him a pension 20 Dec. 1831. He married 22 Dec. 1800. Congress denied his widow, Caroline W. Cone, a pension 9 Feb. 1848.

Cone, Phineas. Conn. Corp. He served in Gen. Spencer's Regiment. He was disabled by accumulated disorders. At Roxbury in 1775 he suffered a severe fit of sickness and came home sick with bilious fever. He was a shop joiner by trade. He was pensioned at Eastham, Conn. on 10 Dec. 1788.

Conely, James. N.Y. Pvt. He served under Col. Philip van Cortland and Capt. Israel Smith in the 2ⁿᵈ N.Y. Regiment. He was wounded in his loins and left leg on fatigue duty at West Point in Oct. 1780. He was 42 years old on 28 Dec. 1785. He lived in New York City, N.Y. 13 June 1788. He was a shoemaker. He also appeared as James Connoly and James Connelly. He died 15 Dec. 1807.

Congleton, Moses. —. —. He was pensioned as a musician for two years. He died 6 Nov. 1838 in

Brooke Co., Va. Congress granted his widow, Mary Congleton, a full pension of $88 per year for the residue of five years unexpired at the time of death of her husband on 9 Feb. 1842.

Congleton, William. Pa. Pvt. He was in Northampton County 25 Mar. 1786. He served in the First Battalion of the Northampton County militia and was wounded in Sep. 1777 at Brandywine. Col. Stephen Balliet appointed him to drive off one of the wagons. When the horses took fright, he was thrown down and suffered from a contusion in his right shoulder. He was 50 years old. His wife, Mary Congleton, was mentioned 18 June 1788. He also appeared as William Congelton. He was on the 1813 pension list.

Conkell, Henry. Pa. Matross. He was in Philadelphia County on 9 Jan. 1786. He was in Col. Proctor's Regiment of Artillery. He was wounded in his leg at Brandywine in Sep. 1777. He was 47 years old. He also appeared as Henry Conkle.

Conklin, John. Pa. Pvt. He was on the 1789 pension list. He was dead by Sep. 1806.

Conklin, Samuel. N.Y. —. He served under Col. Lewis Dubois. His 200 acres of bounty land were awarded to Edward Conklin in trust for himself and the other children 19 June 1812.

Conkling, Joseph. Pa. Pvt. He served in the Somerset Co., Pa. militia. He was wounded in his left thigh and hip by two musket balls at Springfield in June 1780. He resided in Somerset Co., Pa. in 1795. He was granted half a pension 20 Apr. 1796. He also appeared as Josiah Conkling and Josiah Conckling. He was on the 1813 pension list.

Conley, Patrick. Va. —. He was in Continental service. His wife, Mary Conley, was granted 10 bushels of corn and 44 pounds of pork in Berkeley County on 16 Aug. 1780.

Conn, George. S.C. —. He served from 1779 to the end of the war under Capt. Thomas Robins, Lt. James Anderson, and Col. Winn. He was in his 78th year. John R. Love was with him at Sumter's defeat at Fish Dam on Broad River. Robert Cowley also served with him. He was pensioned in Chester District 17 Nov. 1831. He was paid as late as 1834.

Connell, —. Va. —. His wife, Ann Connell, was granted relief in May 1777 in Lunenburg Co., Va.

Connell, Benoni. Conn. Pvt. He was disabled by an internal ulcer. He was pensioned in 1782. He was on the 1813 pension list.

Connell, John. Va. —. His widow, Esther Connell, and small child were granted £15 support in Frederick Co., Va. on 7 Apr. 1779. They were given support again on 9 Mar. 1780. He also appeared as John Conner.

Connelly, Henry. —. —. Congress awarded his widow, Tempey Connelly of Johnson Co., Ky., the arrearage of her pension from 4 Mar. 1848 to 3 Feb. 1853 on 23 Feb. 1857.

Connelly, Hugh. Md. Pvt. He was pensioned at the rate of half-pay of a private in Washington County 27 Jan. 1816.

Connelly, Thomas. Pa. —. He was awarded a $40 gratuity in Washington Co., Pa. 23 Jan. 1833.

Connelly, William. Md. Pvt. His widow, Priscilla Connelly, was pensioned at the rate of half-pay of a private on 28 Feb. 1832. Her arrearage of $54.45 due for 1 year, 1 month, and 10 days at the time of her death was paid to Elizabeth Rich, the only surviving child, on 10 Mar. 1854 in Worcester County.

Conner, —. Pa. —. His widow, Eleanor Conner, was awarded a $40 gratuity and a $40 annuity in Westmoreland Co., Pa. 15 Apr. 1835.

Conner, Ambrose. Pa. —. He applied from Westmoreland County on 7 Jan. 1815. He enlisted in Philadelphia in 1777. Barney McGuire became acquainted with him soon after the battle of Monmouth. Conner was in the 9th Pa. Regiment under Col. Richard Butler in Capt.

Bartholomew Bowen's Company. They separated in 1781 when Conner marched to the south. He served to 1783 when he was discharged.

Conner, Daniel. Ga. Lt. He was on the 1813 pension list.

Conner, Daniel. Va. —. His wife, Susannah Conner, was granted financial support while he was away in Continental service in Amherst Co., Va. in Oct.1778 and Mar. 1779.

Conner, David. Pa. —. He was granted relief in Union County 21 Mar. 1837. He died 8 Feb. 1840.

Conner, David. Md. Pvt. He was pensioned in Frederick County in 1784. He was disabled by sickness. He served in the 7th Regiment.

Conner, Edmund. Pa. Steward. He served aboard the *Sky Rocket* under William Burk. He was disabled 23 Dec. 1782. He was wounded by a musket ball through his testicles into his right thigh at Penobscot. He was 36 years old in 1788 and resided in Pennsylvania. He later removed to Massachusetts.

Conner, John. Pa. —. He served in Capt. David Wilson's Company in the Flying Camp. He was made a prisoner at Fort Washington. He was liberated in a state of indisposition and never received any compensation. He was granted $100 on 10 Mar. 1810.

Conner, John. Pa. —. His widow, Elizabeth Conner, received a $40 gratuity and a $40 annuity in Cincinnati, Ohio 12 Mar. 1856.

Conner, John. Va. —. He was wounded at Camden, S.C. He received a gratuity of one year's pay and an annuity of half-pay on 7 Dec. 1781. He sought the arrearage of his pension, but a decision was postponed on 9 Dec. 1788.

Conner, Lawrence. Va. Pvt. He served three years in the 8th Va. Regiment under Capt. Wallace, was wounded at Brandywine or Germantown, and was discharged by Col. Febiger. He lived in Botetourt County on 14 June 1786. He was continued on the list at the rate of £6 per annum on 22 Oct. 1787. His pension was increased to £12 per annum on 25 Apr. 1789. He was on the 1813 pension list as Lawrence Corner.

Conner, Matthew. Pa. Pvt. He applied from Indiana County 27 Nov. 1813. He served in the 5th Pa. Regiment in Capt. Christy's Company under Col. Johnston in 1777 until the Pa. Line revolted. He served from Jan. 1776 to 1783 when he was discharged. He died 10 May 1816.

Conner, William. Va. —. His wife, Ursly Conner, was awarded £10 relief in Bedford Co., Va. on 27 July 1778, £25 on 22 Feb. 1779, and £50 on 27 Sep. 1779.

Conner, William. Va. Ens. He served under Col. John Gibson in the Virginia Continental Line. His son, John Conner, sought his five years' full pay. Since his father resigned, the son was not eligible and was refused 29 Mar. 1838.

Connolly, Robert. Pa. Quartermaster Sergeant. He served in Col. McDougall's Regiment in Canada in 1775 and later in New York. He was taken prisoner 16 Sep. 1776 when the British occupied the city. He became blind and sought a disability pension. It was found that he was discharged in May 1776 but did not fall blind until 1787 well after 1775 when he was injured by a cartridge and camp fever in the storming of Quebec. His pension was rejected in 1792 and again 1795. He was in the service when he was taken prisoner. He also appeared as Robert Condly.

Connor, John. Del. Pvt. He was on the 1791 pension list. He died 18 Feb. 1805.

Connor, John. Pa. —. He served under Capt. David Wilson in the Flying Camp. He was taken prisoner at Fort Washington and confined on the prison ship *Jersey*.

Connor, Matthew. N.Y. He was granted relief.

Connor, Owen. Va. —. His wife, Hannah Connor, was granted relief on 14 Aug. 1777, 11 Dec. 1777, 9 July 1778, and 10 Dec. 1778 in Lunenburg Co., Va.

Connor, Peter. Pa. —. He was pensioned 2 Apr. 1822. He died 14 Nov. 1829.

Conrad, Jacob. Pa. —. He was granted relief in Berks County 18 Jan. 1838. He died 21 June 1853.

Conrad, John. Pa. Matross. He served under Capt. Derrick in the 4th Regiment of Artillery under Col. Thomas Proctor. He was wounded in his left knee by a musket ball at Brandywine on 11 Sep. 1777. In the afternoon of the same day at the breast works above Chadsforde one of the gun carriages ran over his wounded knee. He was discharged 6 May 1779. He was from Philadelphia County.

Consolver, John. Va. Pvt. He enlisted 25 Apr. 1779 for 18 months. He served under Col. A. Buford until his defeat on 29 May 1780 at the Waxsaws. He was wounded in that battle. He lost both of his arms. He was awarded a £150 gratuity on 7 Nov. 1780. He was aged 27 years on 23 Feb. 1786 and lived in Henrico County. His pension of £18 per annum was continued on 23 Feb. 1786. On 17 Jan. 1798 he was pensioned at the rate of $80 per annum. His pension was increased $30 on 31 Dec. 1798.

Constantine, Cornelius. S.C. —. He served in the 2nd S.C. Regiment. His widow, Jane Constantine, was allowed an annuity 29 May 1786.

Converse, Josiah. Mass. Ens. He served in the 3rd Mass. Regiment under Col. John Greaton in Capt. James Tisdol's Company. He was disabled by a rupture. He was pensioned at the rate of one-third pay of an ensign from 30 Nov. 1782 on 28 Oct. 1785. He was 35 years old in 1786. His widow, Elizabeth Converse, was from Danvers and was paid $50 by the Commonwealth. Congress ruled that his widow and heirs were entitled to bounty land on 29 Feb. 1848.

Conway, —. Va. —. His widow, Anne Conway, was granted £6 support in Northumberland County on 11 May 1778.

Conway, James. Va. —. His wife, Rachel Conway, and three children were furnished £4.10 support in Frederick Co., Va. on 5 June 1782.

Conway, James. Va. Lt. He served in the 6th Virginia Regiment and died in the service near Trenton 28 Dec. 1776. He left a widow and four children. His heirs were not allowed his seven years' half-pay 22 May 1850.

Conye, Peter. —. Adjutant. He was pensioned 4 Aug. 1810. He was on the 1813 pension list of New York. He lived in Montgomery County.

Cook, —. Pa. —. His widow, Ann Cook, was awarded a $40 gratuity and a $40 annuity in York County 27 Mar. 1837.

Cook, —. S.C. —. Mary Cook had her application rejected 20 Dec. 1823.

Cook, —. Va. —. His wife, Eleanor Cook, was granted £10 support in Shenandoah Co., Va. on 28 May 1778. He was in Continental service.

Cook, —. Va. —. His widow, Elizabeth Cook, was aged *ca.* 35 years of age and had four children. She was in Sussex County on 16 Mar. 1786.

Cook, —. Va. Pvt. His widow, Nancy Cook, was awarded a £12 gratuity on 6 Nov. 1779. She was from King William County.

Cook, Aaron. Conn. Pvt. He served under Col. Ebenezer Learned and Col. Shepherd. He had a large callous ulcer on the small of his left leg occasioned by a wound in the ankle by means of some timber received on a dark night while on guard at Roxbury in 1776. He resided in Granby, Conn. in 1792.

Cook, Adam. N.Y. —. He served under Gen. Schuyler in 1775 and 1776. He with his two horses, wagon, and sleigh was pressed into service. He then went into regular service until the close of the war. He lived in Nassau, Rensselaer County. His deceased widow was entitled to a pension five years before her death. N. Pease of Lennox, Mass. sought a certificate of his service 17 Nov. 1855.

Cook, Daniel. S.C. —. He served under Capt. Pagan until Pagan's death at Sumter's defeat at Fishing Creek. He was also under Capt. Mills, Capt. Cooper, and Col. Lacey. He was at Ramsour's, Hook's defeat, Rocky Mount, Hanging Rock, Fishing Creek, Fish Dam Ford, and Blackstocks. He was above 60 years of age and had a wife and four children. At Fishing Creek he received a severe wound in his hand and had his skull fractured by a British dragoon. He received his back pay for his Revolutionary War services on 18 Dec. 1812 amounting to $18.93 3/4 on 18 Dec. 1812. He was from Chester District. He received $645 in arrears for his pension on 18 Dec. 1817. He was pensioned at $60 per annum on 10 Dec. 1817 and was paid his pension from 1 Dec. 1787 to 1 Dec. 1817 at the rate of £5 per annum. He was almost deaf. He died 31 Oct. 1823. His widow, Delila Cook, and five children were pensioned at the same rate since the receipt of his pension last March on 12 Dec. 1823. She was from York District.

Cook, Daniel. N.J. Capt. He served in the artillery. He was shot through the body at Monmouth. He sought two thirds of his commutation of half-pay in 1790.

Cook, David. —. —. He sought the arrears of his pension 12 Oct. 1795 in Vermont.

Cook, David. Pa. —. He transferred to Maryland.

Cook, Elihu. Mass. —. He was paid $20.

Cook, George. Pa. —. He was awarded a $40 gratuity and a $40 annuity in Greene County 18 Mar. 1833.

Cook, Henry. Md. Pvt. He was pensioned at the rate of half-pay of a private 19 Feb. 1835.

Cook, Henry. Pa. —. He was awarded relief in Lebanon County 5 Feb. 1836.

Cook, Jacob. Pa. Pvt. He was in Philadelphia County 26 Sep. 1787. He was in the 11th Pa. Regiment under Col. John Patton and Lt. John Redman. He was wounded in his right leg by a musket ball at Brandywine. He was 28 years old.

Cook, James. N.J. Col. He was pensioned in Morris County on 11 Mar. 1836 at the rate of $60 per annum. His widow, Susan Cook, was pensioned 6 Feb. 1844 at the rate of $40 per annum.

Cook, James. N.Y. —. He volunteered under Col. Samuel Drake in 1775. He served as adjutant at Horn's Hock for nine months. He was at White Plains. He was appointed assistant commissary of the army by Gen. Washington at Red Mills, Dutchess Co., N.Y. to the close of the war. He married 19 Feb. 1767 and died 21 Oct. 1801. His widow, Hannah Cook, died 15 July 1845. Congress directed the heirs to apply in the regular manner on 3 Mar. 1851.

Cook, James. N.C. Pvt. He applied in Rutherford County in 1823. He enlisted in the spring in 1781 in Capt. Thomas Price's Volunteer Company. He was wounded in his hip. His claim was rejected.

Cook, James. Pa. —. He was awarded a $40 gratuity in Chester Co., Pa. 1 Mar. 1832. He received a $40 annuity 28 Jan. 1836. He died 22 Mar. 1841.

Cook, James. Va. Pvt. His widow, Elizabeth Cook, was pensioned 15 Mar. 1784. Her pension was not renewed in Sussex County on 16 Mar. 1786 because she was able bodied, about 35, and had four children. They were Rebecca Cook, Sarah Cook, Faith Cook, and James Cook.

Cook, John. Mass. —. He was paid $50.

Cook, John. N.Y. Pvt. He served under Col. Goos Van Schaick in Capt. Charles Parsons' Company. He was disabled by the fall of a bomb shell on his left leg near Slaughter's Landing in Virginia in Sep. 1781. He was rendered unfit for his livelihood. He was 47 years old in May 1786. and lived in Orange County.

Cook, John. S.C. —. Michael Finney received $45 for arrearage of his pension 17 Dec. 1819 due his estate.

Cook, John. Va. —. His grandfather, John Mullin, was granted £10 support in Caroline Co., Va. on 9 Apr. 1778 and £30 on 11 Mar. 1779.

Cook, Jonah. Conn. Pvt. He served in the 5th Regiment under Col. Isaac Sherman. By an accidental fall on a cedar stump, he broke the rim of his belly which produced a serious scrotal rupture in Aug. 1781 at Peekskill, N.Y. He resided in Watertown, Conn. in 1794. He enlisted 5 Jan. 1781 for six months. He was on the rolls in 1782. He was granted half a pension 20 Apr. 1796. His rate was $5 per month from 22 Jan. 1808. He was on the 1813 pension list. He died 6 Sep. 1825 in Litchfield Co., Conn.

Cook, Moses. —. Capt. He served in the artificers. His heirs sought his commutation. Congress ruled that he was not entitled to it and rejected their claim 4 May 1846.

Cook, Nathan. Mass. Pvt. He served under Col. Rufus Putnam and Capt. Joshua Benson. The main cord of his right knee was cut. He was 37 years old. He was pensioned 26 Oct. 1786. He resided in Worcester Co., Mass. He was on the 1813 pension list.

Cook, Nathaniel. Pa. Sgt. He served under Col. Bradley. He was wounded by a musket or rifle ball through the back part of the arm near the shoulder. It entered his side. It was in Aug. 177[?] at Chemung. He lived in Luzerne, Pa. in 1794. He enlisted 1 Jan. 1777 and was discharged 11 Jan. 1780. He died 21 Oct. 1801.

Cook, Rains. Ga. Capt. Since his heirs were allowed his five years' full pay at the end of the war, Congress found there was, therefore, nothing further due them 17 May 1836.

Cook, Reuben. Pa. —. He was awarded a $40 gratuity and a $40 annuity in Tigoa Co., Pa. 16 Jan. 1823. He was a minute man in the regiment of Col. Stroud.

Cook, Rudolph. N.Y. Capt. He served in Col. Klock's Regiment. He lost the sight of an eye which was struck out when he was assisting some women to draw water out of a well at Stone Arabia fort in July 1780. He resided in New York in 1794.

Cook, Stephen. Pa. He died in 1785 or 1786 in Morristown, N.J. His widow, Susannah Cook, applied 17 Mar. 1794 in Morris Co., N.J.

Cook, Sylvanus. —. —. He sought an increase in his pension but was not successful 11 Jan. 1796.

Cook, Thomas. N.H. Pvt. He served in the 2nd N.H. Regiment. He was wounded by a musket ball in his side. It broke a rib and remained in his body at the battle of Bemis Heights on 19 Sep. 1777. He resided in Salisbury, Mass. in 1792. He enlisted 28 Jan. 1777 and continued to the end of the war.

Cook, William. Mass. —. He served in the 2nd Regiment and was from Wrentham. He was paid $20.

Cook, William. Va. Pvt. He served in the 8th Va. Regiment under Col. Woods. His wife, Mary Cook, and four children were granted £30 relief in Frederick Co., Va. on 3 Aug. 1779 and £105 for 4 barrels of corn and 200 pounds of pork on 5 Sep. 1780. He died in the service. His widow with either two or three children resided in Frederick Co., Va. in June 1786. She was continued at the rate of £12 per annum on 22 Feb. 1787. She was in Knox Co., Tenn. on 14 Jan. 1823.

Cooke, Phineas. Mass. Capt. He served under Col. Bond and lost the sight of one eye due to smallpox in 1776. He was pensioned at the rate of one-quarter pay from 12 Jan. 1777 on 19 Apr. 1781.

Cooke, Samuel. N.Y. Surgeon. His wife, Temperance Cooke, was granted support 28 May 1779 while he was away in the service. She was from Poughkeepsie.

Cooke, Thomas. Pa. Capt. He served in the 8th Pennsylvania Regiment for the whole of the war. He never received his commutation of five years full pay. He had received his bounty land from the United States and was a pensioner under the act of 1828. Congress awarded his commutation to his heirs 26 Jan. 1836 and on 21 Dec. 1838.

Coolidge, Samuel. Mass. Pvt. He served in the 3rd Regiment and was from Watertown. His widow, Mary Carnan [?], was paid $50.

Coolidge, William. Mass. Pvt. He served in the 1st Regiment and was from Bolton. His widow, Anna Coolidge, was paid $50.

Coombs, Francis. Va. Pvt. He served in the 10th Va. Regiment. In 1776 he enlisted for three years and then reenlisted for the duration of the war. He served under Capt. Thomas Fox. He was a prisoner at Hadroul's Point. Lt. Col. Gust. B. Wallace certified that his last pay was in Dec. 1779. He was wounded at the siege of Charleston. He lived in Caroline County on 1 Jan. 1786. He also appeared as Francis Combs and Francis Coms.

Coombs, John. Pa. —. He was granted a $40 gratuity and a $40 annuity in Fayette County 28 Mar. 1836. He was 87 years old in 1840. He died 1 Nov. 1844.

Coomer, William. Mass. —. He was in the 14th Regiment and was from Duxboro. He was paid $20.

Coon, Jacob. Pa. —, He was granted relief 12 June 1840 in Greene County.

Coon, James. —. Fifer. He was from Hopkintown. He served under Col. Warner in Conn. having enlisted for three years. He had married as early as 1790 in New York. He died in 1799. His widow, Sarah Coon, married secondly Jasper Crandall. There were two James Coons in Warner's regiment. When she applied for her husband's service, she received the record of the one who was the lieutenant who was actually from Salisbury. She had married in New York and was unacquainted with the details of his service. Congress granted Sarah Crandall a pension 20 Feb. 1849.

Cooney, James. Pa. Pvt. He served under Capt. Twine. He was wounded at the battle of Brandywine in his leg on 11 Sep. 1777. He lived in Middleton, Pa. in 1794. He enlisted Nov. 1776 for the war and deserted 8 Dec. 1777. He was on the 1813 pension list. He died 25 May 1818 in Cumberland County.

Cooney, John. Pa. Pvt. He was in Philadelphia County 14 Nov. 1785. He was transferred from the 4th Pa. Regiment of Artillery to the Invalids. He was disabled by a wound and discharged 1 Nov. 1783. He was 27 years old. He also appeared as John Conney. He was dead by June 1792.

Coonley, John. Pa. —. He was from Philadelphia County.

Cooper, —. —. —. He died in the service. His daughter, Mary Cooper, received his half-pay.

Cooper, —. —. —. He died in the service. His son, Jacob Cooper, received his half-pay.

Cooper, —. Pa. —. His widow, Hester Cooper, received a $40 gratuity and a $40 annuity in Delaware County 3 Apr. 1837.

Cooper, —. Va. —. Lucretia Cooper was granted £10 relief on 9 July 1778 while her two sons were away in Continental service in Lunenburg Co., Va.

Cooper, Apollos. Va. Lt. He was killed at Brandywine and left a widow and three children. His two surviving children were allowed his half-pay 22 Dec. 1837.

Cooper, Charles. Pa. —. He applied from Delaware County in Dec. 1817. He served from Jan. 1777 to the close of the war. He was discharged by Benjamin Lincoln, Secretary of War.

Cooper, James. —. —. He died in the service. His children received relief.

Cooper, James. N.J. —. He served in Lee's Legion of Partisan Light Dragoons. He lost his bounty land warrant. Congress granted him a duplicate 4 Jan. 1838.

Cooper, John. N.J. Pvt. He was approved in 1795.

Cooper, John. N.Y. Pvt. He was in Capt. Robert Johnson's Company under Col. John Nicholson. He was disabled by the rolling of a log by which he received a rupture in 1776. He lived in Orange Co., N.Y. on 19 May 1789. He was 45 years old in 1786. He was a farmer. He reportedly died in 1794. One of his name was on the 1813 pension list.

Cooper, John. N.Y. Pvt. He was in the militia in 1776 and 1777. He hired a substitute so he could fulfill his engagement to marry for $60 under Col. Dubois. The substitute served in his name to the end of the war and received a pension. In 1778 he accepted a commission as 2nd Lieutenant under Capt. VanWyck and Col. Brinckerhof. He was not in Continental service. He lived in New York City. Congress rejected his application 21 Apr. 1838.

Cooper, John. S.C. —. He served under Capt. John Nixon, Lt. Adams, Col. Winn, and Col. Lacey. He was 76 years old. William McGerrety, John McDill, and George Oliver served with him. He applied from Chester District in 1827. He was rejected.

Cooper, Leonard. Va. Capt. In the campaign of 1779 he was involved in a dispute on parade with fellow officer, Capt. Abraham Kirkpatrick, at Pompton Plains, New Jersey. Kirkpatrick much abused him and heaped ill language upon him. Many of the officers in Cooper's own company indicated that they would have to leave the regiment if he did not stand up to Kirkpatrick. Capt. Kirkpatrick struck him many times with a cane, and Cooper reluctantly challenged him to a duel with pistols. He was wounded in his leg, and it had to be amputated above the right knee. He served in the 4th Va. Regiment and the Invalid Corps in Philadelphia. He continued in the latter from 3 Nov. 1785 to 7 June 1787. He was an officer of great merit and was put on the pension list 24 Dec. 1787. He was aged *ca.* 38 years and resided in Frederick County on 5 Apr. 1787. He was in Shenandoah County on 26 Feb. 1789. He was continued at the rate of £50 per annum on 14 May 1789. He was on the 1813 pension list. He also appeared as Leonard Cowper.

Cooper, Sion. N.C. —. He enlisted at the age of 16 and served eighteen months. He was drafted from Wake Co., N.C. He served under Capt. Lane, Capt. Bryant, and Maj. John Humphries. He spent about half of the time in South Carolina. He moved to South Carolina about 1799 and was 66 years old. He was pensioned in Pendleton District, South Carolina 7 Dec. 1826. He died 6 Mar. 1831. His widow, Mary Cooper, was pensioned on 17 Dec. 1831 and given her husband's arrearage. She was paid as late as 1850.

Cooper, Thomas. Pa. —. He was from Delaware County.

Cooper, William. Md. Pvt. He received a warrant for 50 acres of bounty land in Allegany Co., Md. 12 Mar. 1832. He resided in Ohio Co., Ky. He was pensioned at the rate of half-pay of a private on the same date.

Cooper, William. Pa. —. Corrective measures were to be taken to resolve the difficulties in overlapping surveys and claims in his donation land with that of John Gill on 28 Mar. 1806.

Copeland, —. S.C. —. His widow, Ann Copeland, was from Chesterfield in 1791. She also appeared as Ann Copelin.

Copeland, Charles. N.C. —. He was in the militia and was in the battle of Guilford. He was 65 years, married, and much afflicted with rheumatism. He had an infirm wife. He applied in 1824.

Copeland, Christian. Pa. —. Corp. He was on the 1789 pension list.

Copenhaefer, Michael. Pa. —. He was awarded a $40 gratuity and a $40 annuity in York Co., Pa. 25 Mar. 1831.

Copes, Solomon. Va. —. His widow, Molly Copes, was allowed £3 per month from 28 Jan. 1778 in Accomack Co., Va. on 28 Apr. 1779.

Copp, Aaron. N.H. Sgt. He was in Capt. Stone's Company in Col. Scammel's Regiment and was wounded in his left wrist on 7 Oct. 1777 at Bemis Heights. He was on the roll in 1779. He was aged 42 in 1787. He was from Salem, N.H.

Copp, Ebenezer. N.H. Sgt. He was badly wounded in the back, side, and groin at the battle of Bunker Hill on 17 Jun. 1775. He served under Col. Read. He resided at Hampstead, N.H. in 1796. He was granted a full pension 20 Apr. 1796.

Coppernoll, Adam. N.Y. Pvt. He served in Capt. Blackbus's Company under Col. Goose Van Schaick in Continental service. He received several wounds in Virginia. He was pensioned 14 Sep. 1786. He was from Montgomery County. He later lived in Herkimer County. He was on the 1813 pension list and died 17 Aug. 1826.

Copple, Nicholas. Pa. Matross. He was in Philadelphia County 13 Feb. 1786. He served in the 4th Regiment of Artillery under Col. Proctor. He was wounded at Germantown and lost his eyesight. He was discharged 3 Nov. 1783 unfit for duty. He was 54 years old. He was dead by Sep. 1799.

Copps, David. N.H. He was shot in the knee in action on Lake Champlain. He was under Benedict Arnold. He had a wife and two children on 7 June 1777 and was from Durham.

Corbett, John. Md. Pvt. He was pensioned 1 Jan. 1803. He was on the 1813 pension list.

Corbett, John. Va. Pvt. He enlisted for the war and served five years and nine months. He was wounded on the back of his head and in his left groin by a musket ball at the battle of Monmouth. He was discharged on furlough on 11 June 1783 by George Washington effective with the ratification of the definitive treaty. He lived in Henrico County on 13 Jan. 1787 and was aged 43 years. He was continued at the rate of £6 per annum. His request for an increase in his pension was denied 4 Oct. 1788. He was on the 1813 pension list.

Corbett, John. Va. Pvt. [He was the second of the name.]

Corbett, Joseph. S.C. —. He was wounded and never recovered. He was being paid on 15 Nov. 1798.

Corbett, Richard. Va. —. He was in the Invalid Corps. He lived in Henrico County in June 1787.

Corbin, Margaret. —. —. She was wounded and disabled in the attack on Fort Washington in heroically defending the post of her husband who had been killed by her side serving a piece of artillery. She was to receive during the time of her disability or for life the one-half of the monthly pay of a soldier. She was also to receive a suit of clothes or the value thereof by resolve of the Continental Congress on 6 July 1779. She was the first woman to be pensioned by the United States. On 24 July 1780 she was still in deplorable condition due to her wound and was deprived of the use of one arm. She was likely to be a cripple during her life. Accordingly, she was to receive a complete suit of clothes, or the value thereof in money, every year for the rest of her life.

Corbin, Isaiah. Va. Pvt. He lived in Culpeper County. He was on the 1813 pension list. He died 1 May 1822.

Corblin, —. Va. —. His wife, Mary Corblin, was granted £30 support in Fauquier Co., Va. in July 1780, 8 barrels of corn in Aug. 1781, 8 barrels of corn and 40 pounds of bacon in Aug. 1781, and 6 barrels of corn and 100 pounds of bacon in Aug. 1782.

Corey, Joseph. N.J. —. Capt. Daniel Smith Wood of Col. Moses Jacquis' Regiment of Essex County militia certified his service. He was wounded in the right leg near Elizabeth Town. The Essex County court ruled that he was entitled to £25 in Sep. 1781.

Corey, Nathan. —. —. Congress denied his claim for a pension 29 Jan. 1850. He did not even sign his petition.

Corlew, Daniel. Mass. —. He was in the 10th Regiment and was from Scituate. He was paid $20.

Corley, Abner. S.C. —. He served under Capt. William Butler. He was upwards of 70 years of age.

He applied 2 Nov. 1831 but was rejected.

Corley, John. S.C. —. He served under Capt. James Butler and fought at Augusta, Cambridge, and Eutaw Springs. He was between 80 and 90. He was pensioned at the rate of $60 per annum in Edgefield District 6 Dec.1826.

Corn, —. Pa. —. His widow, Elizabeth Corn, was pensioned 13 Apr. 1838 in Lancaster County.

Cornelius, Josiah. Va. —. His wife, Jane Cornelius, and four children were granted £100 support in Middlesex Co., Va. on 28 June 1779.

Cornell, Thurston. Mass. Pvt. He served three and a half months under Capt. Lucas and Gen. Sullivan and was at the battle of Rhode Island. He was then discharged at Boston 20 Nov. 1778. His next tour was for eight months under Capt. Borden in the militia. He then served nine months under Lt. Dunham from Dec. 1780 to Sep. 1781. He was quartered at Bunton's Neck and the north battery in Newport. He lived in Tiverton, R.I. Congress approved him for six months of service and granted him a pension 5 Mar. 1840.

Cornhill, John. Va. Pvt. He died in the service. His widow, Mary Cornhill, was pensioned at the rate of $40 per annum and was given $40 relief on 23 Dec. 1795 in Prince William County and again on 12 Oct. 1796.

Corning, Benjamin. Mass. —. He was in the 11th Regiment and was from Beverly. His widow, Anna Corning, was paid $50.

Cornwall, Amos. N.Y. Pvt. He enlisted in Mar or Apr. 1781 and served about nine out of his sixteen months. He was at Middletown, Conn. in the town guards under Capt. Meigs and Lt. Gilbert. His brother was Daniel Cornwall. Congress rejected his application for a pension 11 May 1838.

Cornwell, John. Va. —. He died in Continental service. His widow, Ann Cornwell, and two small children were granted £12 support in Prince William Co., Va. in July 1778.

Correll, Christian. Pa. —. He was awarded a $40 gratuity 15 Jan. 1829 in Lancaster Co., Pa.

Correll, Nicholas. Pa. —. He was awarded a $40 gratuity and a $40 annuity in Columbia County 27 Mar. 1837.

Cort, Peter. Pa. —. He was awarded a $40 gratuity and a $40 annuity in Columbia Co., Pa. 15 Mar. 1824. His act was repealed 30 Mar. 1824.

Cort, William. Pa. —. He was awarded a $40 gratuity and a $40 annuity in Columbia Co., Pa. 30 Mar. 1824.

Cortwright, William Ennis. Pa. Pvt. He served in the Northampton County militia under Henry Shoemaker and Col. Jacob Stroud in June 1781. On 18 June he was taken prisoner by a party of hostile Indians but was retaken on the 19th. He was wounded by the Indians and his right thigh was broken. He applied 12 Mar. 1793.

Corvin, James. Pa. —. He was pensioned in Westmoreland County 21 Mar. 1837.

Corwin, Gershom. N.Y. Pvt. He served under Col. Henry B. Livingston in Capt. Jonathan Titus's Company in the 4th N.Y. Regiment. He was disabled due to sickness at Valley Forge by a malignant fever followed by jaundice and dropsy. He lost the sight of his right eye, and his left eye was much impaired. He was 31 years old on 7 May 1788. He lived in Ulster Co., N.Y. on 2 June 1789. His widow, Margaret Corwin, had her petition for a pension rejected by Congress on 27 Mar. 1846 because they married subsequent to 1 Jan. 1794. He also appeared as Gershom Curvan. He was listed as Gershom Curvin on the 1813 pension list.

Corwin, Jedediah. —. Sgt. Congress denied his widow a pension 4 Jan. 1848 because she furnished no proof of his military service or of her marriage.

Corwine, George. N.J. Corp. He served in the Jersey Battalion and was disabled by dysentery in his body. He was from Amwell, Hunterdon County and was 28 years old.

Cosat, David. N.Y. Pvt. He served under Col. Volkert Veeder in the Montgomery County militia and was killed 18 Dec. 1780. His widow, Jennie Cosat, received a half-pay pension.

Cosby, Robert. S.C. Sgt. He was wounded through the knee 20 Nov. 1775 at Ninety Six. He was paid an annuity 17 July 1779. He served under Capt. Thomas Langdon and Gen. Andrew Williamson. He was from Abbeville District. He was in Knox Co., Tenn. 5 Aug. 1797. James Cosby testified as to his service.

Cosner, John. Pa. —. He was awarded a $40 gratuity and a $40 annuity in Bucks Co., Pa. 18 Mar. 1834.

Coston, Henry. S.C. —. He was crippled. He had a wife and four small children. He was from St. Bartholomew Parish, Colleton District and was on the roll in 1797. He was paid as late as 1806. He also appeared as Henry Casten.

Cotheal, Isaac. N.J. Pvt. He was wounded in the head. He was from Woodbridge and was 46 years old. He was on the 1791 pension roll. He was on the 1813 pension list even though he died in May 1812.

Cott, Richard. Pa. —. He applied from Bucks County on 17 Feb. 1813.

Cotteneau, —. —. —. His widow was Lucy Cotteneau. She failed to submit any affidavits to substantiate her claim so Congress rejected her application 2 Dec. 1818.

Cotter, John. Pa. Pvt. His name may have been John Cotten.

Cotterel, Samuel. Va. —. His wife, Susannah Cotterel, and child were furnished 2 barrels of corn and 100 pounds of meat in Essex Co., Va. on 21 Mar. 1780 and on 26 July 1781.

Cottle, Robert. Mass. Sgt. He was in the 7th Regiment and was paid $20.

Cottman, James. Va. Pvt. He served in the New Kent County militia and was drafted to serve in the Continental Army for 18 months. He lost his eyesight. He lived in Charles City County on 10 Nov. 1787. He had no property. He was put on the pension roll at the rate of £10 per annum on 13 Apr. 1789. He was on the 1813 pension list.

Cotton, Benjamin. N.H. Pvt. He served in Cilley's Regiment. He was pensioned 4 Aug. 1810. He lived in Grafton County. He was on the 1813 pension list.

Couch, —. Conn. —. He served three years. His daughter, Rebecca Couch, was baptized 25 Mar. 1781 in the Congregational Church in New Milford, Conn. Congress granted his widow, Prudence Couch, a pension 26 May 1842.

Couch, John. N.J. Pvt. He served under Capt. William Smith and Col. Benjamin Holmes. He was killed at Quinton's Bridge 18 Mar. 1778 in a skirmish with the British. His widow was Esther Couch of Salem County.

Couch, John. S.C. —. He sought his arrearage, but it was rejected 7 Dec. 1839.

Couch, William. Conn. —. He was a man of color and a former slave. He was wounded by a musket ball in the head at Ridgefield. He was totally blind. Congress granted him a pension 7 Feb. 1845.

Coughey, James. Pa. Pvt. He was on the 1789 pension list.

Cougleton, William. Pa. Pvt. He served under Col. Stephen Balliet in the militia. He was thrown drown from the wagon when his horse took fright at the battle of Brandywine. He received a contusion in his right shoulder. His arm was dislocated. He was from Northampton County. He received a half-pay pension.

Coulter, Nathaniel. Pa. —. He applied from Lycoming County on 15 Feb. 1808. He served in Col. Hubley's Regiment. John Barr knew him one year in the service. He enlisted in 1777 for three years in Capt. John Steele's Company. He was discharged at Trenton from the 11th Pa. Regiment in Jan. 1781 and reenlisted in the Rangers under Maj. McPherron. He lived in Union County 18 Mar. 1822. He was dead by July 1839.

Coulter, Nathaniel. Pa. —. He applied from Washington County 15 Feb. 1808. He served in 1781, 1782, and 1783 in several tours in the militia on the western frontier against the Indians. He was granted $60.

Coun, George. S.C. —. He was about to apply for a federal pension and applied for a certificate showing that he had been a pensioner of South Carolina on 16 Nov. 1840.

Countryman, Frederick. N.Y. Pvt. He served under Col. Samuel Clyde in the Montgomery County militia and was slain 31 July 1780. His children, John Countryman, Frederick Countryman, Henry Countryman, Adam Countryman, Abraham Countryman, Eve Countryman, Margaret Countryman, Catharine Countryman, and Leah Countryman, received a half-pay pension for seven years.

Counts, William. Mass. Pvt. He served in the 8th Regiment under Col. Henry Jackson and Capt. Cogswell. He was disabled by a rupture. He was injured in his sight. He lived in Hanover, Mass. in 1788. He was 42 years old in 1790. He also appeared as William Counes.

Couper, Leonard. Va.. Capt. He was granted relief. He also appeared as Leonard Cowper. *Vide* also Leonard Cooper.

Coupland, Christian. Pa. Corp. He was in Chester County on 20 Dec. 1785. He served in the 5th Pa. Regiment in Capt. John Cristy's Company. He was wounded at Brandywine by a musket cousball through his left arm on 11 Sep. 1777. He was 35 years old. He also appeared as Christian Cowpland. He died 2 June 1808.

Courter, William. N.J. —. He was pensioned in Bergen County on 19 Feb. 1838 at the rate of $60 per annum.

Courtney, Francis. N.Y. Pvt. He served in the 1st N.Y. Regiment under Col. McDougall. He lost his sight at Quebec on 7 Jan. 1776. He resided in Montgomery, Ulster Co., N.Y. He enlisted 24 Dec. 1776. He was pensioned 9 June 1794. He was on the 1813 pension list.

Courtney, William. Va. Pvt. He was wounded at Jamestown. He was pensioned at the rate of £12 annually on 14 Dec.1790. He was in the Virginia Line. He lived in Stafford County on 17 Dec. 1790.

Courts, Richard Hanley. Md. Surgeon's Mate. His widow, Eleanor Courts, was pensioned in Prince George's County at the rate of half-pay of a surgeon's mate on 16 Feb. 1821. She received his five years' commutation 2 Mar. 1833

Courtwright, William Ennis. Pa. Pvt. He served in the Northampton County militia under Henry Shoemaker and Col. Jacob Stroud. He was taken prisoner on 18 June by the Indians but retaken on the 19th by his own party. He was wounded and his thigh was broken. He was rendered a total cripple. He was 36 years old. He also appeared as William Ennis Cortwright.

Cousins, —. Pa. —. His widow, Mary Ann Cousins, was awarded a $40 gratuity and a $40 annuity in Venango County 28 Mar. 1836.

Cousins, Samuel. Me. —. He died 6 Aug. 1835. His widow, Pamelia Cousins, was from Sedgwick. She was paid $50 under the resolve of 1836.

Covenhaven, Abraham. N.J. He served in the 4th Regiment of the Hunterdon County militia. He was deprived of the use of his right hand and his eyesight above five years. He had had an operation on his right eye. He could not travel without spectacles. He sought a law for him to have an annuity to be raised by the town of Readington 28 Oct 1803.

Covenhaven, Peter. N.Y. Sgt. He enlisted in Aug. 1777 and served in the militia under Capt. Jacob Gardiner and Col. Fisher. He was wounded by a musket ball in his right knee which was shot to pieces on 6 Aug. 1777 at Fort Schuyler when Gen. Herkimer was wounded. He was unable to walk for twenty-six months. In Feb. 1787 the wound broke open. His leg had to be amputated in Nov. 1790. He was left a cripple. He was on the 1791 pension list in New Jersey. He petitioned for assistance with his medical bills in 1793. He was from Montgomery County. He was pensioned again on 26 May 1808. He was on the 1813 pension list. He also appeared as Peter Covenhover and Peter Cowenhoven.

Coverly, Thomas. Va. Ens. He served in the 9th Va. Regiment and was taken prisoner at Germantown 4 Oct. 1777. He resided in Amelia County. He was on the 1813 pension list and died 22 Sep. 1827. His executor was William Vaughan. The $7.01 due him was paid to Jno. A. Hillsman.

Covey, Daniel. Vt. —. He was an underage soldier under Capt. Charles Nelson and Col. Wait. He was taken captive while on guard duty on the frontier and held captive in Canada. His father, Samuel Covey, sought relief 26 Jan. 1782.

Cowan, James. Pa. —. He was granted relief in Westmoreland County 21 Mar. 1837. He died 20 Feb. 1846. His widow, Mary Cowan, received a $40 gratuity 10 Apr. 1849.

Cowan, William. Pa. Capt. He was from Westmoreland County and served on the frontiers.

Coward, Samuel. N.J. —. His widow, Elizabeth Coward, was pensioned in Monmouth County on 9 Apr. 1846 at the rate of $40 per annum. He died in 1811.

Coward, William. Md. Lt. His widow, Nancy Coward, was pensioned at the rate of half-pay of a lieutenant in Baltimore 26 May 1852.

Cowden, John. S.C. —. His widow, Elizabeth Cowden, was allowed an annuity 3 Oct. 1786.

Cowell, Isaac. Pa. —. He was awarded a $40 gratuity and a $40 annuity in Greene Co., Pa. 4 May 1832. He died 27 Oct. 1841.

Cowell, Joseph. Mass. —. He served in the 1st Regiment and was from Boston. He was paid $20.

Cowen, William. Pa. —. He was awarded a $40 gratuity and a $40 annuity in Westmoreland Co., Pa. 29 Mar. 1824.

Cowhick, Daniel. Pa. —. He applied from Lycoming County on 3 May 1824. He enlisted at Lancaster in 1781 before the capture of Cornwallis. Sgt. Bennet enlisted him; he was in Capt. Price's Company in Col. Proctor's Artillery. He marched to Yorktown and was at the taking of Cornwallis. He continued to Ashley Hill near Charleston, S.C. until the British evacuated where he was discharged. He continued to draw provisions until he reached Lancaster, Pa. He was 67 years old. Joseph Hogendobler of Northumberland Co., Pa., 67, deposed that he enlisted in 1776 in Capt. Joseph Work's Company as a drummer attached to the 1st Regiment under Col. Cunningham. He knew Cowhick at the battle of White Plains and at several skirmishes. He died 18 Sep. 1825

Cowley, —. Va. Pvt. His widow was Sarah Cowley. She was pensioned 1 Sep. 1778.

Cowling, John. Mass. —. He served in the 7th Regiment and was from Boston. He was paid $20.

Cowsert, —. S.C. —. His widow, Ann Cowsert, and three children were paid an annuity in 1826. Another record indicated that she and two children were paid in 1826. She alone was paid an annuity in 1830.

Cox, —. Pa. —. His widow, Mary Cox, was awarded a $40 gratuity and a $40 annuity in Mifflin Co., Pa. 8 Apr. 1826. She was 93 years old in 1840. She died 10 July 1844 in Juniata County.

Cox, —. Va. —. His mother, Mary Cox, was granted £24 support in Caroline Co., Va. 12 Aug. 1779.

Cox, Bartlett. Va. Pvt. He served in the Mecklenburg County militia under Col. Robert Munford and was wounded in 1781 at Guilford Courthouse in N.C. He lost his leg. He had 30 acres of land and a horse. He resided in Mecklenburg County in Dec. 1787. He was continued at the rate of £18 per annum on 25 Aug. 1788. He was on the 1813 pension list. He also appeared as Barclay Cox.

Cox, Ebenezer. N.Y. Lt. Col. He served in the Montgomery County militia. He was killed at Oriskany 6 Aug. 1777. His children, Ebenezer Cox, George Cox, and Anna Cox received a half-pay pension.

Cox, James. Md. Maj. He served in the Baltimore militia and was killed at Germantown. His widow, Mary Cox, received half-pay of major in 1788.

Cox, James. S.C. —. He was killed by Indians. His widow, Rachel Cox, was allowed an annuity 6 Sep. 1785.

Cox, John. Mass. —. He served in the Artillery and was from Springfield. He was paid $20.

Cox, John. S.C.—. He was in the militia for three years under Capt. Samuel Price, John Warden, and Thomas Livingston. He had an aged companion. He was pensioned in All Saints Parish, Horry District 23 Nov. 1829. He died 3 Feb. 1830 without receiving any part of his pension. His widow, was Sarah Cox, and they had eight children. She was upwards of 60 years of age when she was pensioned at the rate of $30 per annum on 25 Nov. 1830. Her claim for drawing any arrearage due her husband was rejected. She was pensioned as late as 1834.

Cox, Joseph. Mass. Sgt. He lost his right leg at the battle of Monmouth by a wound from a musket ball in June 1778. He served in Col. Bigelow's Regiment. He lived in Cambridge, Mass. in 1792 and 1794. He enlisted 10 Mar. 1777 for three years. He was on the rolls in 1780. He was granted two thirds of a pension 20 Apr. 1796. He was on the 1813 pension.

Cox, Martin. Pa. —. He served in the 6th Regiment. He was from Lancaster County. He was receiving a pension 7 Sep. 1784.

Cox, Matthew. —. —. Gov. Alexander Martin of N.C. believed he was entitled to an invalid pension 12 June 1790.

Cox, Phineas. N.Y. Pvt. He was ruptured in stretching a chain across the North River in Oct. 1776 at Fort Montgomery. He resided in New York in 1794. He was on the 1813 pension list.

Cox, Samuel. Pa. Pvt. His widow, Ann Cox, of Dunbar Township, Fayette County, received a $40 gratuity and a $40 annuity 20 Feb. 1857.

Cox, Thomas. —. —. He was wounded in the service. He sought relief from Congress 4 Feb. 1824.

Cox, Thomas. Pa. —. He was in Bucks County on 6 Jan. 1809. He enlisted in 1777 and was wounded in the thigh at Germantown. He was discharged in 1781. He was given a $40 gratuity and a $40 annuity 4 Feb. 1808. He died 7 Jan. 1815.

Cox, William. Md. Pvt. He was pensioned at the rate of half-pay of a private in 1803.

Cox, William. Pa. Capt. He applied from Mifflin County on 1 Aug. 1814. He was discharged as supernumerary on half-pay by Anthony Wayne. He was between 70 and 80 years old.

Coy, Willis. Mass. Corp. He served in the American Regiment and was from Amherst. He was paid $50.

Coyle, Manassah. Pa. —. In 1781 he was in Capt. Orr's Company on the expedition down the Ohio River and was taken prisoner by the Indians on 24 Aug. He was from Fayette County.

Coyn, Dominick. Md. Pvt. His widow, Mary Coyn, was pensioned at the rate of half-pay of a private in Harford County on 25 Feb. 1824.

Cozier, Benjamin. N.J. —. He was pensioned in Cumberland County on 15 Mar. 1837 at the rate of $60 per annum.

Crabb, James. N.J. Pvt. He was on the 1791 pension roll at the rate of $60 per annum.

Craddock, Thomas. Va. —. He died in the service. His widow, Lilly Craddock, was awarded £6 on 17 Nov. 1777, £10 on 17 Aug. 1778, and £30 on 20 Sep. 1779 in Goochland Co., Va.

Craddock, William. N.Y. Pvt. He served in the New York Artillery and was worn out in the service. He was pensioned in Connecticut 10 Apr. 1783. He was on the 1791 pension roll in Connecticut.

Craft, —. S.C. —. His widow, Rachel Craft, was being pensioned in 1791.

Crafton, Bennet. S.C. —. His annuity was £3 in 1787.

Crafts, Jacob. N.Y. —. He was awarded 200 acres of bounty land 13 Apr. 1813.

Cragwall, James. Va. —. His wife, Anne Cragwall, was awarded £8 in Goochland Co., Va. 17 Nov. 1777.

Craig, James. S.C. —. His widow, Hannah Craig, was allowed an annuity 12 Nov. 1784. One child was being supported in 1791.

Craig, James. S.C. —. He died in the service on 1 Feb. 1781. His widow, Rhoda Craig, was allowed an annuity 11 Jan. 1785. She was from Abbeville District. One of their children in 1791 was being supported.

Craig, James. Va. —. He was a clergyman from Lunenburg County. He had a large mill on Flat Rock Creek, a house for drying cloth, a blacksmith's shop, and a granary. The British under Carleton took him prisoner, carried off his Negroes, and destroyed the whole establishment. His grandchildren, James Craig, Edward C. Craig, Ann (Craig) Organ the wife of John A. Organ, Martha Carter and her husband, Rebecca Gregory, George E. Gregory, Richard Gregory, and James Gregory sought relief. Congress granted the heirs same 6 Mar. 1858.

Craig, Jerard. Pa. Pvt. He was in Philadelphia County on 12 Dec. 1785. He was in the Invalids, having been wounded in the service, and was discharged 10 July 1783. He was 45 years old. He also appeared as Garrard Craig. He was on the 1791 pension roll.

Craig, John. Md. Pvt. He was on the 1813 pension list of Maryland. He lived in Harford County and died 29 Sep. 1821.

Craig, John. Pa. —. He served in Capt. Church's Rifle Company in the 5th Pa. Regiment under Col. Anthony Wayne and was wounded. He was granted a $40 gratuity and a $40 annuity in Butler County 4 Apr. 1809. He died 6 Mar. 1813.

Craig, John. Pa. Capt. He entered the service in 1775 and remained until the end of the war. He was promoted to captain in the Light Dragoons in Dec. 1778. His constitution was much impaired, and he had lost the use of his third finger on his right hand. He received a $1,000 gratuity from the federal government on 24 Jan. 1811. He applied for a state pension from Northampton County on 26 Feb. 1813. He had been unable to get to Lancaster in 1810 or 1811 until Charles Biddle, treasurer of the Society of the Cincinnati, advanced the money to do so. He was paid to 29 Nov. 1829.

Craig, John. S.C. —. His claim was rejected 7 Dec. 1825.

Craig, Joshua. Pa. —. He applied from Cumberland County on 12 May 1820. His first enlistment was in Capt. Cluggage's Company from Bedford County and marched to Boston. He next served a year under Capt. Rippy and marched to Quebec where he was taken prisoner, paroled, and exchanged. He enlisted the third time in New York in Capt. Thomas Campbell's Company. He never received his donation land or his U.S. federal land. He was in the battles of Bunker Hill, Quebec, Long Island, Trenton, Brandywine, Germantown, and Yorktown. He died 6 Oct. 1823.

Craig, Moses. Mass. —. He served in the 3rd Artillery and was from New Castle. He was paid $20.

Craig, Samuel. S.C. —. He was killed at the Hanging Rock. His widow, Ann Craig, was allowed an annuity 12 Nov. 1784 in York District. There was one child in 1791.

Craig, Thomas. Pa. Col. He applied from Northampton County on 20 Apr. 1781. He enlisted as a captain and left as a colonel. He was passed 78 years of age. He died 14 Jan. 1832.

Craigue, William. Mass. —. He served in the 1st Regiment and was from Weathersfield, Vt. He was paid $20.

Crain, —. Va. —. His wife, Sarah Crain, was granted £730 support in Fauquier Co., Va. in Apr. 1781.

Craine, James. Va. Capt. He entered as a private in 1775, was commissioned a lieutenant, and lastly a captain. He died in Dec. 1788 in Lancaster County. His five years' full pay commutation was paid to his child, Maria Brown, the wife of Edwin C. Brown, 30 June 1834. Virginia bounty land warrant #5524 for 1,500 acres was issued.

Craine, William. S.C. —. He served ten months under Col. William Fare against the Cherokee. John Farmer served with him. He applied from Greenville District. His application was rejected in 1831.

Cram, Smith. —. —. He enlisted for six months and served all but nine days when he was discharged. The pay roll showed his service was five months and eleven days. Congress rejected his claim for a pension 1 Mar. 1845.

Cramer, Jacob. Pa. Lt. He was awarded a $40 gratuity and a $40 annuity in York, Pa. 3 Apr. 1829. Congress refused the request for 200 acres of bounty land to his heirs 26 Feb. 1878. He had received 200 acres from Pennsylvania and was from Westmoreland County. He died 19 May 1832.

Cramer, John. N.Y. Pvt. He was pensioned in 1807. He was on the 1813 pension list.

Cramling, Adam. Pa. —. He was awarded a $40 gratuity and a $40 annuity in Berks Co., Pa. 31 Mar. 1831. He died 30 Apr. 1841.

Crampton, Thomas. Md. Pvt. He was pensioned at the rate of half-pay of a private 16 Mar. 1835.

Cranberry, Francis. N.Y. Pvt. He served in the 3rd Regiment. He died 15 Sep. 1780. His former widow, Mary Hibbon, had her application rejected 27 Jan. 1797.

Crane, Aaron. N.J. He served under Capt. Peter Dickerson and Col. Elias Dayton near the end of 1776. He took sick in 1777 and died at Mount Independence near Ticondergoa. He married Mary Hathaway 27 Jan. 1774 in Morris Town. His widow, Mary Crane, married secondly David Porter 6 Apr. 1780. She was pensioned in Morris County.

Crane, Aaron. N.Y. Sgt. He was pensioned 25 Apr. 1808 at the rate of $2.50 per month. He was on the 1813 pension list.

Crane, Abel. Mass. —. He served in the 2nd Artillery and was from Becket. He was paid $20.

Crane, Abijah. —. —. He served three years. He was pensioned under the act of 1818 and was stricken from the rolls in 1820. He had a crippled son as a dependent. Congress ruled that he should not have been stricken and restored him on 1 Mar. 1832.

Crane, David. Mass. —. He served in the 6th Artillery and was from Sandisfield. He was paid $20.

Crane, Henry. N.Y. Maj. He died in Aug. 1808.

Crane, Henry. Pa. Sgt. He was on the 1791 pension roll. Compare with the entry for Henry Cain.

Crane, Jacobus. N.Y. —. His children were granted support.

Crane, John. Conn. —. He served in Capt. Samuel Camp's Company under Col. Thaddeus Cook in the militia. He was wounded by a musket ball through his right shoulder at Compo on 28 Apr. 1777. He was pensioned 22 May 1778.

Crane, John. Mass. Maj. & Lt. Col. He was wounded in the foot by a cannon ball from the British sloop commanded by Capt. Wallace in 1776. He had received his commutation which was not returned. He resided in Boston, Mass. in 1794. He died 21 Aug. 1805.

Crane, Jonas. N.J. Pvt. He served in the Essex County militia and received a wound in a skirmish with the enemy of which he died 4 Apr. 1782. His widow, Sarah Crane, was allowed half-pay in 1784 in Essex County. Rebeckah Hawley took out letters of administration on her mother's estate 26 Oct. 1819. She sought the arrearage of $40 per annum for nearly 34 years.

Crane, Joshua. N.J. Pvt. He was on the 1791 pension roll at the rate of $60 per annum.

Crane, Noah. —. —. He was deaf, blind, and deprived of his mental faculties. His son was William Crane. A petition from sundry inhabitants of Wabash Co, Ill. sought a pension for him. Congress rejected the petition because there was only hearsay proof of service on 20 Apr. 1836.

Crane, Richard. Mass. Pvt. He was pensioned 4 Mar. 1795. He resided in Berkshire Co., Mass.

Crane, Samuel. N.J. Pvt. He served in the Essex County militia under Capt. Thomas Williams and Col. Philip Van Courtland. In an attack on 20 Sep. 1777 with the musketeers near Second River he was killed. He received a musket ball in his body and was bayoneted in his heart. His widow, Mary Crane, married Jedediah Mills 27 Sep. 1786. Joseph Tomkins and Zadoc Hedden served with him. His widow was allowed half-pay until her remarriage in Essex County on 10 Nov. 1792.

Crane, Thaddeus. N.Y. Maj. He served in the Westchester County militia under Col. Thomas Thomas. He was wounded in his left hip on the expedition to Danbury on 27 Apr. 1777. He was on the 1791 pension roll.

Crane, William. N.Y. Lt. He served in the 4th N.Y. Regiment under Col. Philip Van Courtland. He was wounded in his left leg by the bursting of a shell at the siege of St. John's in Canada in 1775. He lived in Elizabethtown, N.J. in 1794. He was granted a full pension 20 Apr. 1796. He was on the 1813 pension list of New Jersey. He died in Aug. 1803 [There is a conflict in the dates.]

Crank, Peleg. Mass. —. He served in the 8th Regiment and was paid $20.

Crans, Jacobus. N.Y. Pvt. He served in the Ulster County militia and was killed 6 Oct. 1777 at Fort Montgomery. A pension was paid to his children in 1781. They were Elizabeth Crans, Susanna Crans, Johannes Crans, Mary Crans, and Catharine Crans.

Cranston, Abner. Mass. Maj. He was killed 29 May 1777. His heirs were paid his seven years half-pay of $2,100.

Crary, Archibald. R.I. Col. He served from 16 Dec. 1777 to 16 Mar. 1780. His son, Archibald Crary, asked Congress to pay the balance due his father 30 June 1863. He was paid $1,256.44.

Craswell, —. Pa. —. His widow, Ann Craswell, was awarded a $40 gratuity and a $40 annuity 17 Mar. 1835 in Crawford County.

Craven, John. Pa. —. He received a $40 gratuity and a $40 annuity in Westmoreland County 1 Apr. 1825. He died in Feb. 1840.

Craven, John. Pa. —. He applied 23 Feb. 1830 in Indiana County. He enlisted in Capt. Benjamin Bartholomew's Company under Col. Francis Johnston in 1777. He spent six months in prison under the British in 1781 in Philadelphia. He was a volunteer under Capt. Jamison in 1776. While out, he enlisted under Capt. Samuel Hinds in the Flying Camp at Amboy. He was present at the battles of Trenton, Princeton, and Germantown. He served in Capt. Zephaniah Lott's Company in 1777.

Craven, Thomas. Pa. —. He was awarded a $40 gratuity and a $40 annuity in Indiana Co., Pa. 6

Apr. 1830.

Crawford, —. Pa. —. His widow, Leah Crawford, received a $40 gratuity and a $40 annuity in Montgomery County 3 Mar. 1837.

Crawford, —. S.C. —. His widow, Elizabeth Crawford, was being pensioned in 1791.

Crawford, Andrew. S.C. —. He was killed in action by the Tories. His widow, Jane Crawford, was allowed an annuity 21 Apr. 1785. She was from Abbeville District. She was paid her arrearage of $65 on 21 Dec. 1804.

Crawford, Henry. N.Y. Dragoon. He served under Col. Sheldon. He was wounded by a musket ball in the thigh in Nov. 1777 at Mile Square. He resided in Washington, N.Y. He enlisted 7 May 1777 and was discharged 15 Nov. 1780. He died 9 Oct. 1801.

Crawford, James. N.J. —. He served under Capt. Samuel Carhart and Col. Nathaniel Scudder in the 1st Battalion of the Monmouth County militia. He was killed at the Highlands of Neversink on 23 Feb. 1777. He left a widow, Margaret Crawford, and seven children, the youngest of whom was five. They were granted a half-pay pension 17 June 1780.

Crawford, James. N.Y. —. He served as a private, corporal, and sergeant in 1780, 1781, and 1782. Congress granted him a pension 7 Mar. 1844.

Crawford, James. Pa. Maj. He served in the 12th Pa. Regiment and was awarded a $60 gratuity and a $60 annuity 29 Mar. 1813 in Lycoming County. His widow, Agnes Crawford, was awarded an additional $20 per annum to the $40 she was receiving 18 Feb. 1824.

Crawford, James. Pa. —. He was pensioned in Mercer County 21 Feb. 1838.

Crawford, James. S.C. —. He was from Lancaster District in 1791.

Crawford, John. Mass. —. He was in the 7th Regiment and was from Bennington. He was paid $20.

Crawford, John. Pa. Capt. He was on the 1813 pension list. He may been the one who was pensioned under the act of 3 Mar. 1805 and was from Delaware.

Crawford, Jonathan. N.H. Pvt. He did not state if he was disabled by wounds. Congress believed that he served in the militia and not in the Continental Line and rejected his petition for a pension 9 Feb. 1820. He was from Bridgewater.

Crawford, Nehemiah. Md. Sgt. He was pensioned at the rate of half-pay of a sergeant on 23 Jan. 1816.

Crawford, Patrick. S.C. —. He died in the service in 1781. His widow, Mary Crawford, was allowed an annuity 21 Jan. 1785.

Crawford, Peter. Pa. —. He was awarded a $40 gratuity and a $40 annuity in Berks Co. 28 Feb. 1822.

Crawford, Robert. Pa. —. He was awarded a $40 gratuity and a $40 annuity in Westmoreland County on 28 Feb. 1822.

Crawford, Robert. Pa. —. He received assistance in Venango County 22 Mar. 1825. He died 28 June 1841.

Crawford, Robert. Va. —. His wife and three children were granted financial support in Yohogania Co., Va. on 26 Mar. 1778 and 28 May 1779.

Crawford, Thomas. N.Y. Bombardier. He enlisted in July 1775 and served under Col. James Holmes in Capt. Ambrose Horton's Company. He was wounded in his throat by a musket ball. Later he served under Col. John Lamb in the Artillery as a matross. He was wounded and lost part of his right hand on 6 Aug. 1777. He lived in New York City, N.Y. on 14 June 1788. He was on the 1813 pension list.

Crawford, Thomas. Pa. Pvt. He was on the 1789 pension list.

Crawford, William. Me. —. He was from Gardiner. He was paid $50 under the resolve of 1836.

Crawford, William. Pa. Capt. He applied from Bucks County on 3 Apr. 1813. He served in the 5th Pa. Regiment where he was appointed lieutenant in Jan. 1776. He was promoted to captain in the same year. He had a brother and mother alive. He was made a prisoner at Fort Washington in 1776 and held four years. He lost his 250 acres while a prisoner. He got his thumb injured in laying a platform at Fort Washington. He was also from Philadelphia County.

Crawford, William. Va./Pa. Col. He served in the militia. He was killed in the expedition against the Indians at the Sandusky towns in June 1782. His widow, Hannah Crawford, applied 9 June 1783. She lived in Frederick Co., Va. on 11 Jan. 1787. She had her pension continued on 28 Oct. 1791. She was in Fayette Co., Pa. 3 Mar. 1794. He also appeared as William Crafford.

Crawl, Samuel. Pa. —. He received a $40 gratuity and a $40 annuity in Allegheny County 1 Apr. 1837. He was 81 years old in 1840. He died 3 May 1843.

Crawl, William. Pa. —. He was awarded a $40 gratuity and a $40 annuity in York County 1 Apr. 1836. He died 21 Mar. 1840. His widow, Sally Crawl, received a $40 gratuity and a $40 annuity 6 Feb. 1856.

Crawley, —. Va. —. Elizabeth Crawley was on the 1785 pension list. She may be identical with the Elizabeth Crawley granted support in King William County 23 June 1779.

Crayton, William. Va. —. He was wounded seven times at Buford's defeat. One cut the leaders of his left arm. He served three years and six months. He had a wife and four children. He was awarded a £300 gratuity on 29 Nov. 1780.

Creamer, George. —. —. He was pensioned 9 June 1794.

Creamer, John. N.Y. Pvt. He served under Col. Fisher and was wounded in his left hip at Fort Clyde in July 1782. He was pensioned 18 Apr. 1796. He lived at Connajorharrie.

Cree, Asa. Me. —. His widow, Love Cree, was from Canaan. She was paid $50 under the resolve of 1836.

Creech, Stephen. S.C. —. He served under Maj. Richard Creech. He was pensioned in Barnwell District on 23 Nov. 1829 and was paid as late as 1834. He also appeared as Stephen Creach.

Creedle, William. Va. —. His father, Benjamin Creedle, was granted £10 support in York County on 14 Jan. 1778 and £20 on 15 Feb. 1779.

Cresap, Joseph. Md. Lt. He was pensioned at the rate of half-pay of a lieutenant 19 Feb. 1819. His pension was rescinded in Feb. 1822 in Allegany County since he was wealthy. He sustained losses in consequence of endorsing for others in the Cumberland Bank of Allegany. He was greatly embarrassed and had a large family to support. Accordingly, his pension was restored 3 Mar. 1826.

Cress, George. Va. Pvt. He lived in Rockbridge County. He was on the 1813 pension list and later removed to Ohio.

Cresswell, Charles. Pa. —. His widow, Isabella Cresswell, was awarded a $40 gratuity and a $40 annuity in Chester Co., Pa. 8 Feb. 1823. He also appeared as Charles Creswell.

Criddle, William. Va. Pvt. He served in the 2nd Va. Regiment. He lost his right arm at Norfolk in Jan. 1776. He was awarded a £10 gratuity and a £10 annuity on 7 May 1776. He was awarded a £8 gratuity and a £2 annuity on 15 May 1778. He was aged about 30 in 1787 and resided in Cumberland County. He also appeared as William Creedle and William Creddle. He was continued at the rate of £18 per annum on 17 Apr. 1787. He gave his age as about 30 years in 1787. He was continued at the rate of £15 per annum on 6 Apr. 1789. He died in or about 1791 or 1792. He was in Cumberland Co., Va. 29 Apr. 1783.

Cripps, John. —. —. Due to insufficient proof, Congress rejected his claim 20 June 1848.

Criswell, Robert. Pa. —. He applied from York County on 28 Feb. 1833. He served two months in 1777 or 1778. He was awarded a $40 gratuity and a $40 annuity in York Co., Pa. 6 Apr. 1833. He received the same 28 Mar. 1836.

Critchlow, James. Pa. —. He enlisted in 1776 in the 8th Regiment under Capt. Moses Carson. He subsequently served under Col. Brodhead. He was at Saratoga and the taking of Burgoyne. He was also in Col. Monzan's Riflemen. He applied from Butler County on 10 Dec. 1817. He died 2 Mar. 1833. His widow, Mary Critchlow, was awarded a $40 gratuity and a $40 annuity in Butler Co., Pa. 15 Apr. 1835. He also appeared as James Crutchlow. His widow was dead by May 1842.

Crittendon, —. Va. —. His widow, Eleanor Crittendon, lived in New Kent County on 27 Dec. 1792. Her husband died in the service. She was pensioned at the rate of £12 per annum on 20 Dec. 1792. She also appeared as Eleanor Crittenden.

Crittendon —. Va. Pvt. His widow, Frances Crittendon, was awarded a £12 gratuity 6 Nov. 1779 in King William County.

Crocker, Ansel. Mass. —. He was paid $50 by resolution of 15 Apr. 1836.

Crocker, Benjamin. Mass. Pvt. He was wounded in Dec. 1782 at Newburg. He lived in Shaftesbury, Mass. in 1794. He was in the militia.

Crocker, Josiah. Mass. Pvt. He served in the 3rd Regiment. His widow, Thankful Crocker, was paid $50 and was from Barnstable.

Crocker, Tilden. Mass. —. His widow, Priscilla Crocker, was paid $50.

Crockett, Joseph. —. Capt. He was rendered supernumerary. His half-pay was $1,415.33.

Crofoot, Benjamin. N.Y. —. He enlisted in Dutchess Co., N.Y. in 1776 as a militiaman for nine months. A week after his discharge he entered the service again and marched to White Plains, Westchester Co. for four months. He enlisted for the third time at Saratoga when Burgoyne surrendered. He was 71 years old, lame in both feet, and indigent. Congress granted him a pension 22 Dec. 1831.

Croft, William. Md. Corp. His widow, Catharine Croft, was pensioned at the rate of half-pay of a corporal 4 Mar. 1835.

Crofts, Daniel. S.C. —. He was taken prisoner at Briar Creek in 1779 and died on board a prison ship. His widow, Mary Crofts, was allowed an annuity 25 Feb. 1785. She was from Abbeville District. She had two children on 26 Jan. 1787 and in 1791.

Crofts, Edward. S.C. —. He was wounded at Wrights Bluff in Feb. 1781, was taken prisoner, and died in confinement. His orphans were allowed an annuity 26 Nov. 1784. There was one child in 1791.

Crofts, Joseph. S.C. —. He was wounded at Eutaw Springs. He applied 2 Dec. 1793 and lived in Winton County. He had a wife and six small children.

Crombie, James. N.H. 1st Lt. He served in Capt. Samuel Blodget's Company under Col. Hale. He had a rupture in his groin by being thrown from his horse shortly after the evacuation of Ticonderoga in July 1777. He was riding to purchase supplies for the army. He lived in Rindge, N.H. in 1778 and in 1795. He was mustered on furlough in Dec. 1777 and omitted in Nov. 1778. He was pensioned by N.H. receiving half-pay as a lieutenant from 1 Sep. 1778 to 20 Mar. 1782. He was granted a full pension 20 Apr. 1796.

Crome, Christian. —. —. He was granted relief for wounds he received in the war.

Crommit, James. N.H. Pvt. He served in the 2nd N.H. Regiment. He was pensioned 4 Mar. 1804 in

Stafford Co., N.H.

Crone, Henry. Pa. Sgt. He was in Philadelphia County on 12 Dec. 1785. He served in the 1st Pa. Regiment and was wounded in the knee at the storming of Stoney Point. He was also disabled by sickness contracted in the service. He was 35 years old. He also appeared as Harry Crone.

Cronhart, George. N.Y. —. His family was granted support during the Revolutionary War.

Cronk, John. —. —. He died in 1816. He married Lois Gifford in 1782. Her brother was Benjamin Gifford, and her brother-in-law was Joseph Lewis. There were eleven children. Hannah Cronk was the eldest daughter and died in 1816. The daughter, Patsey Cronk, married John Wilson. Their fourth child, John Cronk, was born in 1794. Congress granted a pension to the widow 15 Feb. 1844. John Cronk also appeared as John Cronkhite.

Crook, —. Va. —. His wife, Hannah Crook, was granted £6 support in Fauquier Co., Va. in July 1778 and £240 in Apr. 1781.

Crook, —. Va. —. He and his brother died in Continental service. Their father, John Crook, was granted £5 support in Prince William Co., Va. on 5 Oct. 1778.

Crook, Charles. Va. —. He was pensioned in Loudoun County on 21 Jan. 1809 at the rate of $40 per annum. He was been wounded at the battle of Jamestown in 1781.

Crook, Henry. Md. Pvt. He was pensioned in Frederick County. He served under Capt. Archibald Golden in Col. Adams' Regiment. He was wounded at Guilford Courthouse. He moved from Frederick Co., Md. to Washington Co., Va. where he had lived for thirty years on 13 Apr. 1818. He was on the 1813 pension list of Virginia. His pension was increased to $60 per annum on 10 Feb. 1817. He died 18 Mar. 1819. His widow, Chrischany Crook, was the executrix of his will.

Crookshanks, John. Va. Pvt. He served in Lt. Col. Lee's Legion. He was pensioned on 7 Dec. 1782. He lived in Augusta County. He was on the 1813 pension list.

Crookshanks, Robert. Va. —. He served under Lt. Col. Lee. He was a spy for six months and was wounded. He applied on 7 Dec. 1782.

Cropper, John. Va. Lt. Col. He entered as lieutenant to 1 Sep. 1779 in the 7th Virginia Regiment. His family was in distressed condition because the enemy had destroyed most of his property so he resigned. Congress refused to let him resign, but he was never recalled. He died 15 Jan. 1821. His heirs were allowed his commutation 6 Mar. 1838.

Crosby, Jesse. Pa. Lt. He was on the 1791 pension roll.

Crosby, Joel. Mass. —. He served in the 6th Regiment and was from Leominster. He was paid $50.

Crosby, Joseph. Mass. —. He served in the 6th Regiment and was paid $50.

Crosby, Joshua. Mass. —. He enlisted under Capt. Newell and Col. Keyes in June 1777 for six months. He next served three months. He served under Capt. Cutler and Col. Wade to Feb. 1779. He was under Col. Putnam for six months in 1780. He was a preacher from Enfield. Congress granted him a pension 3 Jan. 1832.

Crosby, Nathan. Mass. —. He served in the 2nd Artillery and was from Ware. He was paid $20.

Crosby, Simon. Conn. Pvt. He served in the 2nd Regt. of Dragoons under Col. Sheldon. He was badly wounded by a broad sword in the wrist of his right hand in Jul. 1779 at Poundridge, N.Y. He resided at East Windsor, Conn. in 1792. He enlisted 7 May 1777 for the war and was discharged 1 Aug. 1780. He was granted half a pension 20 Apr. 1796. He was on the 1813 pension list. He died 4 Jan. 1827 in Hampden Co., Mass. where he had removed in 1826.

Cross, —. S.C. —. He was killed in the service. His widow, Mary Cross, was allowed an annuity 6 Feb. 1786.

Cross, —. Pa. —. His widow, Sarah Cross, was awarded a $40 gratuity in Philadelphia Co., Pa. on

20 Feb. 1833.

Cross, Elisha. Mass. —. He was in Crane's Regiment and was paid $20.

Cross, Robert. Md. Fifer. His widow was Mary Cross.

Cross, Samuel. S.C. —. He served under Col. William Thompson. He spent four months in prison and five months on a prison ship. He was granted 200 acres of bounty land, but due to the scarcity of land he could not take advantage of that benefit. He was pensioned in Abbeville District 30 Nov. 1827. His widow, Elizabeth Cross, was pensioned at the rate of $30 per annum on 4 Dec. 1828. She was paid as late as 1833.

Cross, Thomas. N.H. —. He enlisted for one year under Col. Enoch Poor in the New Hampshire Line in 1775. He applied from Fort Covington. Congress granted him a pension 22 Dec. 1831 from 24 Sep. 1831.

Crosset, James. N.Y. Pvt. He served under Col. Willet. He was slain in battle, and his widow, Jane Crosset, was granted seven and a half years' pay. She was paid £112 on 9 Apr. 1792.

Crossland, John. S.C. —. He enlisted in March 1779 and served under Capt. John Bowie. He was made a prisoner at the storming of Savannah. He was put on a prison ship and obligated to enlist. He made his escape at Charleston and returned home. He was taken prisoner by the Tories and given over to the British at Camden who took him to Petersburg, Va. about May 1781. He escaped once more and was under Capt. William Kirkland and Col. Taylor. He was never in action with Americans while he was in the British army. He was paid $83.72 for his nine months of duty as a soldier in the Revolution on 16 Dec. 1816. His family included a son crippled from infancy. There were four other children. He suffered from a wound in his leg at Savannah. He was pensioned in Fairfield District on 17 Dec. 1819. He also appeared as John Croslin. He was paid as late as 1843 and died 13 Sep. 1845. His widow was Sarah Crossland who was 77 years old in 1845. They had married during the war. Their son was Abram Crossland.

Crossley, James. N.Y. Pvt. He was pensioned in 1809. He was on the 1813 pension list.

Crossley, Jesse. Pa. Lt. He applied 12 Feb 1787 in Philadelphia County. He served in the 4th Pa. Regiment of Artillery and was wounded in his hip and groin by a musket ball at Green Springs, Va. 6 July 1781. He was dead by Sep. 1792. He also appeared as Jesse Crosley.

Crossman, Samuel. —. —. He never applied for a pension before his death on 31 Oct. 1831. His widow, Lydia Crossman, died 17 Aug. 1855 without applying. Congress did not grant relief to the heirs on 4 May 1860.

Crossman, William. —. Lt. He served 36 months. He married in Dec. 1792. Congress granted his widow, Eunice Crossman, a pension 20 June 1848.

Crosson, John. Pa. —. He applied from Bedford County on 4 Aug. 1815. He served in the 3rd Pa. Regiment under Capt. William West, 1st Lt. W. Bickers, Ens. D. Steddiford, and Col. John Shay. He also appeared as John Crossin.

Crouch, Richard. Mass. Cooper. He served aboard the continental frigate *Dean* under Samuel Nicholson. He was disabled by a fever which settled in his legs. He suffered from lameness. He was pensioned at the rate of half-pay from 1 June 1782 on 25 Jan. 1785. He lived in Boston, Mass. in 1787 and was 32 years old. He was on the 1813 pension list. He was a cooper.

Crouch, Robert. Md. Pvt. He was pensioned at the rate of half-pay of a private on 1 Jan. 1813 in Cecil County. He died 12 Oct. 1823. His widow, Hannah Crouch, was paid his arrearage of $11.33 on 19 Feb. 1845.

Crout, Matthais. Pa. —. He applied 7 Mar. 1821.

Crow, George. Pa. Pvt. He was on the 1789 pension list.

Crow, William. Va. —. He was pensioned in Essex County on 2 Feb. 1811 at the rate of $40 per annum. He had been wounded in the war.

Crowell, Thomas. Mass. Pvt. He served under Col. Holman in Capt. Warner's Company. He was wounded by a musket ball passing through his right foot on 28 Oct. 1776 at White Plains. He lived in Harwich, Mass. in 1795. He was in the militia. He was granted a full pension 20 Apr. 1796. He was on the 1813 pension list.

Crowley, —. Va. —. Eleath Crowley was granted support in Prince William County in 1778.

Crowley, —. N.Y. —. Elizabeth Crowley was granted support during the war.

Crowley, —. Va. —. He was killed in the service. His widow, Elizabeth Crowley, was awarded a £500 gratuity due to depreciation in Henry Co., Va. on 23 Nov. 1780. She had five small children. She was on the 1785 pension list.

Crowley, David. Pa. Pvt. He was in Philadelphia County on 14 Nov. 1785. He was transferred from the 2nd Pa. Regiment to the Invalids. He was wounded in his wrist and discharged 1 Nov. 1783. He was 38 years old.

Crowley, Miles. Pa. —. He was awarded a $40 gratuity and a $40 annuity 17 Jan. 1812.

Crox, Barclay. Va. —. He was on the 1785 pension list.

Croxall, Charles. Md. Capt. He was pensioned at the rate of half-pay of a captain of dragoons in Baltimore 12 Mar. 1827. At his death the sum due him of $31.67 was paid to Claudius Legrande.

Crozer, —. Pa. —. His widow, Elizabeth Crozer, was awarded a $40 gratuity in Juniata County 12 Mar. 1836.

Crozer, —. Pa. —. His widow, Catharine Crozer, was granted a $40 gratuity and a $40 annuity in Delaware County 14 Mar. 1835.

Crozier, Matthew. Pa. —. He was pensioned 15 Dec. 1815.

Cruduck, William. N.Y. Matross. He served in the 2nd N.Y. Regiment in Capt. William Stephens's Company under Col. John Lamb. He was disabled by rheumatism and a hernia. He was aged 50 years on 1 Apr. 1787. He lived in N.Y. in June 1788. He was a laborer. He also appeared as William Crudock.

Crum, Harmanus. N.Y. —. He served under Col. Lewis Dubois. His 200 acres of bounty land were awarded to Agnes Youmans in trust for herself and other heirs 19 June 1812.

Crumb, John. N.Y. Pvt. He served in Capt. Pell's Company under Col. Philip Van Cortlandt. He suffered from frost bite in his private parts. He lived in Albany, N.Y. on 17 July 1789. He was 42 years old in 1787. He also appeared as John Crum. He was on the 1813 pension list.

Crumlow, Caleb. Pa. —. He was awarded a $40 gratuity and a $40 annuity in Fayette County in 1836. He was 82 years old in 1840.

Crummitt, James. Mass. Pvt. He served in the 2nd Regiment. He was wounded in action at Fort Ann on the retreat from Ticonderoga by a ball which entered his left shoulder and came out the back of his neck on 7 July 1777. He resided at Washington, Me. in 1794. He was in New Hampshire on the 1813 pension list.

Crump, Abner. Va. Capt. His commutation was paid 23 Apr. 1791.

Crutcher, John. Pa. —. He was awarded a $40 gratuity and a $40 annuity in Chester Co., Pa. 14 Apr. 1834.

Crute, John. Va. Lt. He was taken prisoner at the fall of Charleston. He was wounded at the battle of Hanging Rock. He was pensioned 3 Mar. 1809 at the rate of $13 per month. He lived in

Prince Edward Co., Va. and was on the 1813 pension list.

Cryder, —. Pa. —. His widow, Catherine Cryder, was granted relief in Cumberland County 23 Mar. 1830.

Crysall, Jeremiah. —. —. His widow, Mary Crysall, sought the pension due him from 1830 to 1837. Congress rejected her claim on 17 June 1846. He could have applied and been restored. The law did not cover widows.

Cubbeback, William A. N.Y. —. He served several tours in the last three years of the war for a total of eighteen months to two years. He was at Gunear's and DeWitt's forts in Ulster and Orange Counties after Deer Park was destroyed by the Indians at the end of 1777 or the beginning of 1778. He was also at Fort Montgomery on the Hudson. Congress granted him a pension for six months of service at the rate of $20 per year on 5 Mar. 1840.

Cuddle, William. Va. Pvt. He was granted relief.

Culbertson, John. Pa. —. He was granted relief in Crawford County in 1839.

Culley, Barney. Pa. Pvt. He was on the 1789 pension list.

Culliatt, Adam. S.C. —. His widow, Ava Culliatt, and her child were pensioned 20 Dec. 1800. She received $21.30 per annum during her widowhood and $12 per annum until the age of 12 for her child.

Cullins, John. Va. —. He volunteered in Capt. William Forman's company of militia. He was wounded in his right leg by a shot from the enemy in 1777. It broke and shattered the bone. He was in danger of losing his leg. He then took the smallpox. He was awarded a £30 gratuity in Hampshire County on 21 May 1778. He was in Hampshire County 22 Jan. 1799 and in Muskingham Co., Ohio in 1809. He was wounded in 1777 by the Indians.

Culp, —. Pa. —. His widow, Mary Culp, was granted relief in Philadelphia County 12 Mar. 1836.

Culp, Abraham. Pa. —. He was granted relief 5 Apr. 1842 in Lycoming County.

Culver, Daniel. Mass. Pvt. He served in Col. John Brown's Mass. Regiment under Capt. Bradley. He was 32 years old and was disabled by the loss of his left leg. He was pensioned 7 Nov. 1788. He transferred to Broome Co., N.Y. He was on the 1791 pension roll of New York. He was on the 1813 pension list and died 7 Dec. 1833.

Cumbis, John. Pa. Pvt. He was on the 1813 pension list as John Cambis.

Cumbo, Stephen. S.C. —. He served under Col. Samuel Hammond, Capt. Thomas Harvey, and Capt. Jesse Johnson. He was at the siege of Savannah, Eutaw, and fought the Cherokee. He was pensioned in Edgefield District 30 Nov. 1827. He was paid as late as 1834.

Cummins, George. Va. —. His wife, Isabel Cummins, was given £20 and £30 for support for her and her family in Rockbridge Co., Va. while he was away in the service on 2 Feb. 1779 and 1 Feb. 1780.

Cummins, Matthew. Va. —. His wife, Elizabeth Cummins, was furnished 4 barrels of corn and 100 pounds of bacon for her support and her three children on 4 Mar. 1782. He was a prisoner of the British in Charleston, S.C. She was furnished 200 pounds of pork and 3 barrels of corn on 2 Sep. 1782 in Charlotte Co., Va.

Cummings, Gershom. Mass. Pvt. He served in the 13th Regiment and was from Leverett. His widow, Rhoda Cummings, was paid $50.

Cummings, James. Vt. —. Congress granted him a pension for twelve months of service on 25 Mar. 1836.

Cummings, John. Mass. —. He served in the 5th Regiment and was from Vermont. He was paid $20.

Cummings, John. S.C. —. He entered the service in 1776 and was between the ages of 16 and 18.

He served to the end of the war under Capt. Oliver Towls, Capt. Lockley Leonard, Lt. Angus Campbell, Col. Joseph Hays, Capt. John Wallace, and Capt. Pollard. William Watson served with him. He was pensioned in Abbeville District 17 Dec. 1831. He was paid as late as 1838.

Cummings, Samuel. —. —. He resided in Mass. in 1796.

Cummins, —. Va. —. Her mother, Bridget Cummins, was furnished assistance in Loudoun Co., Va. on 10 Mar. 1778.

Cummins, Jeremiah. S.C. —. He was killed 8 July 1781. His widow, Mary Cummins, was allowed an annuity 6 Sep. 1785. His orphans were allowed an annuity 3 Oct. 1786 to be paid to Josiah Patterson. There was one child in 1791.

Cumpton, Archibald. Va. Pvt. He served in the 2nd Virginia Regiment. He was on the 1785 pension list. He was continued at the pension rate of £12 per annum on 23 Dec. 1786.

Cundiff, John. Pa. Pvt. He was granted relief.

Cunias, John. Pa. —. He applied from Berks County on 27 June 1823. He served in the 2nd Pa. Regiment under Col. Walter Stewart and was discharged 3 Nov. 1783.

Cunningham, —. S.C. —. His widow, Ann Cunningham, was on the 1791 list.

Cunningham, Andrew. N.Y. Sgt. He served under Col. Bellinger in the Montgomery County militia and was slain 6 Aug. 1777. His widow, Barbara Cunningham, received a half-pay pension.

Cunningham, Bartlett. Va. Pvt. He served in the militia from Cumberland Company under Col. Ballow in the south. On the night of the day of the beginning of the engagement with General Gates he was out in a detached party with Col. Porterfield at Camden. He never returned. Charles Ballow and Benjamin Harrison proved his service. He left three children, the eldest about 11 years on 18 Oct. 1787 when his widow, Elizabeth Cunningham, was 40 years old. She was put on the roll at the rate of £12 per annum.

Cunningham, James. Va. —. He was in the Augusta County militia and was wounded in both thighs at Guilford Courthouse. He was awarded a gratuity of one year's pay and an annuity of half-pay in Augusta County on 22 Nov. 1781.

Cunningham, John. Va. Pvt. He served in the 3rd Va. Regiment and died in the service. His widow, Elizabeth Cunningham, and three small children lived in Fauquier County on 25 Sep. 1786. She was put on the roll at the rate of £10 per annum on 9 June 1788. She was continued on the roll on 22 Dec. 1790 at the rate of £12 per annum.

Cunningham, Joseph. Pa. Sgt. He applied from Mifflin County on 13 Jan. 1817. He was dead by Dec. 1838.

Cunningham, Peter. Md. Pvt. He was pensioned in Frederick County in 1784. He was wounded in South Carolina. He served in the 7th Maryland Regiment.

Cunningham, Peter. Pa. Pvt. He transferred to Delaware by Sep. 1796. He was on the 1813 pension list.

Cunningham, Robert. Pa. Sgt. He was in Lancaster County 19 Dec. 1785. He served in Capt. Matthew Smith's Company in William Thompson's 2nd Continental Regiment styled the 1st Rifle Regiment and marched to Quebec. He was in a detachment under Benedict Arnold when he was wounded on 31 Dec. 1775 by a bayonet in his right thigh at the storming of Quebec. He was taken prisoner. He suffered from disorders contracted in the service, namely asthma. He was 36 years old.

Cunningham, Thomas. Va. Pvt. He served in the company of Capt. James Booth in the expedition against the Indians for thirteen months. His widow, Phebe Cunningham, was paid $104 on 13 Mar. 1834.

Cunningham, William. S.C. —. He was hurt at Ninety Six. He was 81 years old. He was pensioned in 1812. He was paid as late as 1820.

Cupples, James. Pa. —. He was awarded a $40 gratuity and a $40 annuity in Mifflin Co., Pa. 14 Apr. 1834. He was 84 years old in 1840.

Cureland, James. Va. Pvt. He served in the 1ˢᵗ Virginia Regiment. He was pensioned 5 Nov. 1778.

Cureton, James. Va. —. He was wounded in his hand and breast near Amboy, N.J. He was awarded a £30 gratuity and an annuity of half-pay of a soldier on 29 Oct. 1778. He served in the 1ˢᵗ Regiment of Light Dragoons under Col. Bland.

Curran, William. Pa. —. He received a $40 gratuity in 1811.

Currier, Henry. N.H. Pvt. He served under Col. Stark. He lost his right eye by smallpox in July 1776 at Crown Point. He lived in Hopkinton, N.H. in 1794. He was in the militia.

Currier, Joseph. Mass. —. He was from Haverhill and was paid $20.

Curry, —. Pa. —. His widow, Catherine Curry, was awarded a $40 gratuity in Allegheny Co., Pa. 11 Jan. 1832 and 11 Mar. 1833. She was awarded a $40 gratuity and a $40 annuity in Allegheny Co., Pa. 23 Jan. 1834. She was dead by July 1838.

Curry, Charles. S.C. —. His widow was Prudence Curry from York District in 1827. Her application was rejected.

Curry, James. Pa. —. He was awarded a $40 gratuity and a $40 annuity in Delaware Co., Pa. 11 Mar. 1833.

Curry, James. Va. —. He lived in Franklin Co., Ohio. 22 Dec. 1819. He served in Lord Dunmore's War in Capt. Moffett's Company from Augusta. He was shot through his right elbow at Point Pleasant in 1774. In Sept. 1775 he was allowed £20 and a pension of £5 per annum. He drew it one year and then entered the army again and served to the end of the Revolutionary War. In 1816 he came from Ohio and sought to resume his benefits but was disappointed. The legislature authorized the back payment of his pension and placed him on the pension roll at the rate of £5 per annum.

Curry, Robert. Mass. —. He was in the 4ᵗʰ Regiment and was from Blanford. He was paid $20.

Curtain, John. Pa. —. He was from Philadelphia County.

Curtis, Ebenezer. Conn. Pvt. He served in the 1ˢᵗ Regiment. He lost the use of both arms by inoculation of smallpox. He resided in Canterbury, Conn. in 1792.

Curtis, George. Mass. —. He was granted a pension 30 Apr. 1776.

Curtis, John. Md. Matross. He was pensioned in Baltimore at the rate of half-pay of a matross in the artillery on 23 Feb. 1829.

Curtis, John. N.J. Sgt. He served in the Jersey Battalion. He lost two fingers and was hurt in his back. He was 33 years old and lived in Elizabeth, Essex County. He was on the 1791 pension roll at the rate of $24 per annum.

Curtis, John. Pa. —. He was awarded a $40 gratuity and a $40 annuity in Fayette Co., Pa. 8 Apr. 1833. He removed to Ohio.

Curtis, Joseph. Mass. —. He was from Quincy and was paid $20.

Curtis, Joshua. Mass. —. He served at the Castle and was from Abington. His widow, Nancy Curtis, was paid $50.

Curtis, Jotham. —. Pvt. He served under Capt. Bake and Col. Meigs for five years. He served from Mar. 1778 to Feb. 1779. He had no claim to bounty land because he had not served for the war according to Congress 10 June 1842. He was pensioned under the act of 1818.

Curtis, Marmaduke. Pa. Lt. He was in the militia in 1776.

Curtis, Stephen. Mass. —. He served in the 13th Regiment and was from Hanover. He was paid $20.

Curtis, Thomas. Pa. Sgt. He applied from Berks County on 22 Nov. 1814. He enlisted 21 Jan. 1776 under Walter Stewart and served one year. He enlisted again 13 Mar. 1777 in Capt. Walter Bricker's Company in the 11th Pa. Regiment as an orderly sergeant. He was 62 years old. He was awarded £69.5.8 as adjusted depreciation pay 29 Jan. 1816. He died 26 Sep. 1823.

Curtis, William. N.H. Pvt. He served under Col. Whiting. He was wounded by a musket ball in the fleshy part of his left thigh in Apr. 1777 at Ridgefield, Conn. He lived in Stratford, N.H. in 1795. He served in the militia. He was granted half a pension 20 Apr. 1796. He was on the 1813 pension list.

Curwin, Theophilus. N.Y. Pvt. He served under Col. McClaghry and was slain 6 Oct. 1777. His widow, Anne Curwin, received a half-pay pension for seven years.

Curwin, Timothy. N.Y. Sgt. He served under Col. James McClaghry in the Ulster County militia. His children, David Curwin and Mary Curwin, received a half-pay pension.

Cushing, Abel. Mass. Corp. He served in the 4th Regiment and was from Hingham. He was paid $50.

Cushing, William. Mass. Lt. He resided in Plymouth Co., Mass. He was on the 1813 pension list. He died 4 Jan. 1825.

Cushman, Andrew. —. —. He was pensioned under the act of 1818 and stricken from the roll in 1820. He was refused restoration because the real estate he conveyed to his son was not by a written contract. He was restored to his pension effective from 28 Mar. 1829 on 12 Mar. 1832.

Cushman, Daniel. Conn. Corp. He served in Col. Elisha Sheldon's Conn. Regiment of Light Dragoons six years and two months. He was discharged 12 June 1783. He was wounded at Tarrytown on 20 Nov. 1780. He was under the command of Lt. Elijah Janes. He was wounded near the elbow in his right arm. He was a blacksmith. He was 30 years old in June 1786. He was pensioned 17 Mar. 1790. He transferred to Vermont in 1797. He moved to Essex Co., N.Y. from Vermont. He was on the 1813 pension list in New York.

Cushman, Joshua. Me. —. He died 26 Jan. 1834 at Augusta. His widow, Lucy Cushman, was from Winslow. She was paid $50 under the resolve of 1836.

Cushman, Simeon. S.C. Pvt. He entered in the fall of 1778 in Edgefield and served two years in the militia. The British burned his dwelling house in the war, and he lost the whole of his property. He was a prisoner of Col. Brown, the British commandant at Augusta. He was also at Stono. He served under Capt. John Hammond, Col. Leroy Hammond, and Capt. Bacon. He was 77 years. He died about 1825. John Randall served with him. His widow, Judith Cushman, was from Barnwell District in 1839.

Cusick, John. Pa. —. He was in Philadelphia County on 11 Sep. 1786. He served in the 2nd Pa. Regiment and was wounded by a musket ball at Three Rivers in Canada near the articulation of his lower jaw. He also served in the 3rd and 12th Pa. Regiments. He was 53 years old.

Cusick, John. Va. —. He served in the Washington County militia under Col. William Campbell en route to reinforce Gen. Greene before the battle of Guilford. He was wounded. He was awarded a gratuity of two years' pay in Washington County on 21 Nov. 1781.

Custis, Thomas. Va. Lt. He was in the 9th Regiment. He was made a prisoner at Germantown but escaped to Virginia. His regiment had been broken up. He never resigned. His son, William R. Custis, had his claim for commutation rejected by Congress 4 Feb. 1837.

Cutlar, —. Va. —. His widow, Betty Cutlar, was granted a pension in Northumberland Co., Va. 11 May 1788.

Cutler, —. Mass. —. His widow, Elizabeth Cutler, was paid $50 for her late husband's service.

Cutler, Davis. Mass. Pvt. He served in Capt. Moses Knap's Company under Col. Shepard and lost his hand. He was pensioned at the rate of half-pay of a soldier on 21 Mar. 1783. He also appeared as David Cutler.

Cutler, Henry. N.Y. —. His wife and three children were granted support 3 Nov. 1781 in Dutchess County.

Cutler, Joseph. Conn. Ens. He was in Capt. James Stoddard's Co. of Conn. Troops. under Col. Samuel Campbell. He also served under Col. Philo Canfield. He was wounded in his right thigh by a bayonet on 27 May 1782. He also was wounded by a musket ball through his thigh at White Plains. The enemy under Col. James DeLancy left him at Dr. Bailey's at New Rochelle on parole. He was born at Plainfield, Conn. and was a farmer. Since he could no longer farm, He moved to New York City, N.Y. in 1787 where he kept a lodging house. He also bought a sloop which he loaded and sent to Virginia. Both the vessel and its cargo were lost. He was later defrauded by one John Fuller and William Campbell. He was in Westchester Co., N.Y. in June 1788. He was aged 28 years on 15 Apr. 1787. He was on the 1791 and the 1813 pension lists of New York. His rank also appeared as ensign.

Cutright, John. Va. Pvt. He served in a company of rangers under Capt. James Booth for 13 months. He was awarded $104 in Lewis County 9 Feb. 1833.

Cutter, Benjamin. Mass. —. He served in the 6th Regiment and was from Princeton. He was paid $20.

Cutting, Earl. Mass. Pvt. He served in the 9th Regiment and was from Phillipston. He was paid $50.

Cutting, Hezekiah. Mass. —. He served in the 7th Regiment and was from Brookfield. He was paid $20.

Cutting, Silas. Mass. —. His widow, Sarah Cutting, of Royalston received a gratuity 21 June 1779.

Cutting, Silas. Mass. Pvt. He died 18 Feb. 1824 in Middlesex Co., Mass.

Cuyper, John. N.Y. Pvt. He was disabled by a rupture. He served under Col. Goose Van Schaick. He lived in N.Y. 8 July 1788.

Cycencider, —. Pa. —. His widow, Rachel Cycencider, was awarded a $40 gratuity and a $40 annuity in Crawford County in June 1836. She was dead by Feb. 1842.

Dabney, Austin. Ga. Pvt. He was pensioned in 1782 in Burke County. He was on the 1813 pension list. By act of 14 Aug. 1786 he was granted an annuity as a wounded and disabled soldier for serving under the command of Col. Elijah Clarke. In one engagement he was severely wounded and rendered incapable of hard servitude. On 16 May 1821 he was granted 112 acres in Walton Co., Ga. which was number 284 in the first district for his natural life. He was a free man of color.

Dabney, Charles. Va. Lt. Col. His commutation was issued 21 Apr. 1791.

Dabney, James. Va. —. The petition to furnish his wife and children necessaries was rejected on 19 Nov. 1779.

Dabney, John Q. —. —. His widow, Sarah Dabney, had per petition for an increase in her pension from $12 to $30 per month approved by Congress 17 Mar. 1890. She was from Pike Co., Ill. and was past 90 years of age.

Daboll, John. Conn. Pvt. He served in Ledyard's Conn. Militia. He was disabled at Groton. He was on the 1813 pension list. He died 7 May 1825 in New London Co., Conn.

Dager, Peter. Pa. —. He was awarded a $40 gratuity in Montgomery Co., Pa. 14 Jan. 1835.

Daggett, Nathan. —. —. Congress rejected relief for his heirs 25 Apr. 1854.

Daggett, Tristram. Mass. —. He served in the 7th Regiment and was from New Vineyard. He was paid $20.

Dailey, Alexander. S.C. —. He was killed in the service. His widow, Elizabeth Dailey, was from Newberry District *ca.* 1796. She sold her certificate to James Halliday. She also appeared as Elizabeth Daly.

Dailey, John. Pa. Pvt. He served in the 5th Regiment and was discharged at Trenton by Anthony Wayne. He was from Crawford County.

Dailey, John. Pa. —. He was awarded a $40 gratuity and a $40 annuity in Warren Co., N.J. 7 Feb. 1831. He died 12 July 1842.

Dailly, Dennis. Pa. —. He was awarded a $40 gratuity and a $40 annuity in Washington Co., Pa. 26 Mar. 1812. He also appeared as Dennis Daley.

Daily, —. Va. —. His wife, Sarah Daily, was granted £50 support in Caroline Co., Va. in June 1780.

Dal, John. Mass. —. He enlisted at Boston 8 June 1779 for nine months. He went to West Point about the 10th of July. On 27 Dec. 1779 he was ordered to cross the Hudson River with clothing for the soldiers. His party was detained on the river for three days due to the drifting of ice which broke their boat to pieces. He eventually got ashore. His feet and legs were badly frostbitten. He was unable to do duty and was discharged 8 Jan. 1780. He was allowed pay for seven months. Congress granted him a pension 20 Jan. 1836.

Dalby, William. Va. Corp. He served under Col. Innis. He was wounded at the battle of Germantown by a musket ball on 4 Oct. 1777. He lived in Norfolk, Va. in 1794.

Dale, Andrew. Pa. Sgt. He was in Philadelphia County on 3 Apr. 1788. He served in the German Regiment in Capt. Bunnen's Company before being transferred to the Invalids under Col. Lewis Nicola. On the western expedition at Wyoming he received a fall which gave him a rupture. He was discharged 11 June 1783. He was 64 years old.

Dale, Samuel. Conn. Pvt. He died 22 Dec. 1804.

Dale, Samuel. Pa. —. He was on the 1789 pension list.

Dallas, Archibald. N.J. Capt. He served under Col. Spencer and fell in a skirmish with the enemy near Christian Bridge in Delaware 5 Sep. 1777. He married Rachel Frost in 1772. She married secondly David Cory, Sr. of Persippany 28 Jan. 1779. Archibald Dallas, Jr. was born 22 Sep. 1777. The widow received a half-pay pension from 5 Sep. 1777 to 28 Jan. 1779. Her son drew a pension from 28 Jan. 1779. It was to terminate 22 Sep. 1785. They were from Morris Co., N.J.

Dallas, Dennis. Pa. —. His application was submitted 27 Feb. 1813.

Dalley, John. N.C. Pvt. He served under Capt. Samuel House, Col. William Lewis, and Maj. Joel Lewis for three months. He next served six months under Capt. George Hodge, Lt. McAdams, Col. Tinnen, and Robert Mebane. His third tour was under Capt. Gwin and Col. William O'Neal. His last tour was under Capt. Jamison, Lt. William Riley, Maj. Ab. Tatum, and Col. Thaxton. He was born in Pennsylvania 3 Jan. 1755 and moved to Orange Co., N.C. at the age of three. He was 79 when he applied there on 26 Feb. 1838.

Dallinor, Richard. Del. Capt. He served in the militia and was commissioned 18 Dec. 1775. He had been dead about thirty years. His two living children and grandchildren sought five years' pay and bounty land. Congress denied their petition 18 Mar. 1844.

Dalton, Isaac. —. —. He served fifteen months in 1777, 1778, and 1779 and was at Stillwater at the capture of Burgoyne. He served under Capt. Scott and Col. Cilley from Mar. 1780 to Dec. 1780. His wife was ill, and he had lost the use of one eye. Congress granted him a pension 23 Dec. 1831.

Dalton, Thomas. N.Y. Corp. He served in Capt. Jacob Wright's Company under Col. Philip Van Cortland in the 2nd New York Regiment. He was wounded at Stillwater on 19 Sep. 1777 in his right knee. He was transferred to the Invalid Corps. He lived in New York City, N.Y. in June 1788. He was a cooper. He died 2 Jan. 1791. He was pensioned as a private. He also appeared as Thomas Dolton.

Dalton, Valentine Thomas. Va. 2nd Lt. He served under Capt. Robert George in the Illinois Regiment under Col. Crockett. His commutation of five years in the amount of $4,456.89 was paid to his administrator *d.b.n.c.t.a.*

Damans, Abiah. Me. —. He died 9 Apr. 1836. His widow, Lucretia Damans, was from Charlotte. She was paid $50 under the resolve of 1836.

Damon, Noah. Mass. —. He served as early as 19 Apr. 1775 for 6 days under Capt. Tucker; 25 days from 17 Apr. 1777 under Capt. Seth Sumner and Col. Benjamin Gill; 2 months and 5 days under Capt. Moses French and Col. Jonathan Titcomb from 15 May 1777; 2 months and 22 days under Capt. Thomas White and Col. Edward Proctor from 10 Dec. 1777; 2 months and 25 days under Capt. Benjamin Lapham and Col. Jonathan Clapp from 9 Apr. 1778; 1 month and 7 days under Capt. Nathaniel Clapp and Col. Benjamin Howe from 26 July 1778; 9 days under Capt. Abner Crane from 5 Feb. 1779; 1 month and 1 day under Capt. Joseph Richard and Col. Gill from 14 Aug. 1779; and 8 months under Capt. Caleb Champney from 11 May 1780. His widow, Esther Damon, of Plymouth, Union Co., Vt., aged 91, sought an increase in her pension. She had no means. She had received a little aid from the Daughters of the American Revolution. Congress approved her petition 20 Feb. 1905. She was the only surviving pensioner at the rate of $12 per month.

Damon, Stephen. —. —. He died in 1846 without applying for a pension. Congress rejected the petition from his heirs 4 May 1860.

Dampsey, Patrick. Pa. —. He was from Philadelphia.

Damron, Charles. Ga. Pvt. He was pensioned in 1779. He was on the 1813 pension list. He died in Oct. 1829 in Jackson Co., Ga. He had been wounded at the battle of Briar Creek in Georgia. He married prior to 1 Jan. 1794. His widow, Polly Damron, was pensioned by Congress who reasoned that he must have served more than six months since he entered in Virginia and marched to Georgia. Congress approved her pension 27 Mar. 1846.

Dana, Joseph. N.Y. Pvt. He enlisted for one year 1 Apr. 1782 and served under Col. Allen and Col. Campfield in the infantry. He did garrison duty at Horse Neck, Conn. and served several times on patrol duty. He was discharged 1 Apr. 1783. Born 10 June 1766, he was the second son of Maj. James Dana. Congress granted him a pension 19 July 1848.

Danally, —. Va. Pvt. His widow was Elizabeth Danally. Her husband was killed in Continental service. She was on the pension roll of 1785. The auditor was left to his discretion to pay her arrears on 5 Jan. 1787. She also appeared as Elizabeth Danley.

Dandridge, Peter. Va. Capt. He served in the artillery for more than six years until returned supernumerary. Congress granted his widow, Elizabeth Dandridge, his commutation 10 Feb. 1830.

Danforth, Abner. Me. —. He was from Litchfield. He was paid $50 under the resolve of 1836.

Danforth, Henry, N.H. Pvt. He served under Col. Reed. He was wounded by a musket ball which lodged in his left shoulder in 1782 near Mohawk River. He lived in Northfield, N.H. in 1794. He enlisted 5 Feb. 1777 for the war. He was on the rolls in 1783. He was granted half of a pension 20 Apr. 1796. He was on the 1813 pension list.

Danforth, Jesse. Mass. Pvt. He served in the Invalids and was from Templeton. He was paid $20. He was indicated as dead on the list of 1801.

Danforth, John. Mass. Pvt. He served in the 8th Regiment and was from Tewksbury. He was paid $50.

Danforth, John. Mass. Pvt. He was paid 4 May 1819.

Danforth, Joseph. Mass. —. He served five months and thirteen days under Col. Michael Jackson. He was allowed to return home before the expiration of his enlistment of six months. Congress granted him a pension 21 Mar. 1836

Danforth, Joshua. —. —. He received his commutation. Upon deducting same, he was to receive half-pay for life.

Daniel, —. Va. —. His wife, Mary Daniel, was granted £24 support in Caroline Co., Va. 9 Sep. 1779.

Daniel, Charles. Pa. Pvt. He also appeared as Charles Daniels. He was on the 1813 pension list.

Daniel, James. S.C. Pvt. He served under Gen. Marion in 1780, 1781 and 1782. He was paid $77.12 ½ on 10 Dec. 1823. He applied 29 Nov. 1824 in Williamsburg District at the age of 77. He had a wife, a daughter, and two helpless grandchildren. He was pensioned 3 Dec. 1825. His widow, Martha Daniel, was pensioned 7 Dec. 1826. She was 69 years old. She was paid as late as 1838.

Danielly, Daniel. Ga. —. The only evidence he produced was a certificate signed by Gov. George Matthews of Ga. stating that he had been wounded and that he had been on the pension roll of Ga. from 12 July 1782. He was granted a two year gratuity of £30 on 30 Nov. 1784.

Danielly, Daniel. N.J. Pvt. He served six years and two months. He was awarded the badge of merit. He applied for assistance in Burlington County 30 July 1791.

Daniels, James. Mass. Pvt. He was pensioned from 3 Oct. 1816 for life on 12 June 1818. He served from the town of Lunenburg and was 17 years old when he enlisted in 1780.

Daniels, Job. N.J. Fifer. He sought a pension 26 Mar. 1836 from Congress. He stated that he was one of two dozen men who were taught the martial arts at Morristown, N.J. in 1775. Twelve were drummers, and twelve were fifers. They were taught by Fife Major Joseph Rodgers and Drum Major Jabez Bigelow. In Apr. 1776 he entered the service and was under Capts. Losey, Gordon, Bigelow, Jackson, Salmon, Stephens, Dickerson, Starke, Crane, Wade, and Hathaway until 1778 for a total of 2 ½ years in the militia. He also served as a private in the State Troops as a substitute for Elijah Leonard in 1781 under Capt. Wade.

Daniels, John. —. —. His application was laid on the table 18 Dec. 1798.

Danley, John. Mass. Sgt. He served in the 4th Regiment and was from Tyngsborough. He was paid $50.

Dannehower, George. Pa. —. He was granted a $40 gratuity and a $40 annuity in Philadelphia County 1 Apr. 1836.

Dansby, Isham. S.C. —. His widow was Martha Dansby. There was one child in 1791.

Darcy, John. N.C. —. He was the son of Joseph Darcy and was born in 1764 or 1765. He served under Capt. William Young, John Whitaker, Abner Beckham, Col. James Twiggs, Elijah Clarke, Col. Sumter, Morgan, Wayne, and Col. John Twiggs. He was at Augusta, Ga. He was a prisoner at Savannah until Feb. 1779. His brothers were Lt. James Darcy, Joseph Darcy who died on a prison ship in Charleston in 1780 or 1781, William Darcy who died in Laurens Co., Ga., Benjamin Darcy who died in Laurens Co., Ga., and Joel Darcy who settled in Burke Co., Ga. after the war. John Darcy moved to Decatur Co., Ga. and applied 11 Dec. 1845.

Darling, Benjamin. Mass. —. He was in the 6th Regiment and was paid $20.

Darling, Oliver. Vt. Pvt. He served under Col. Brooks in Capt. G. Reed's Militia Company. He had a dislocated right hip due to a fall while carrying provisions to supply the company to which he belonged in 1780. He lived in Grafton, Vt. in 1795. He was granted five-eights of a pension 20 Apr. 1796. His evidence was incomplete. He was on the 1813 pension list.

Darling, Zelek. Mass. Pvt. He was in the 1st Regiment and was from Mendon. He was paid $50.

Darnell, John. Pa. Pvt. He lived in Delaware County. He was on the 1813 pension list as John Durnall.

Darr, Leonard. Pa. Pvt. His widow, Elizabeth Darr, was in Lancaster County on 10 Jan. 1787. She was married on 11 Apr. 1771 at Trinity Church in Lancaster by Henry Muhlenberg. She was the former Elizabeth Wolf. Her husband served in the militia in Capt. Abraham Forrey's [?Torrey's] Company under Col. Curtis Grubbs. He enlisted in the Flying Camp in Capt. Daniel Oldenbrook's Company at Bergen, N.J. He was wounded at Paoli, taken to hospital at Bergen and then to Perth where he died a prisoner. Major Christian Herr proved his service. Jacob Shaffer saw him in camp after he was wounded.

Darrah, Archiblad. Pa. —. He received a $40 gratuity and a $40 annuity in Bucks County 16 June 1836.

Darrow, John. Va. —. His wife, Hannah Darrow, was granted £40 relief in Berkeley County on 17 Aug. 1779. She also received 150 pounds of pork and 3 barrels of corn for her support and her three children on 22 Nov. 1780. He also appeared as John Darrough.

Dasher, Christian. Ga. —. He died in the line of duty. His orphan child sought assistance 13 Jan. 1783.

Datamar, John. Pa. —. He was awarded a $40 gratuity and a $40 annuity in York, Pa. 23 Apr. 1829.

Daub, Dillman. Pa. —. He was awarded a $40 gratuity and a $40 annuity in Lebanon Co., Pa. 18 Feb. 1834. He died in 1849. His widow, Nancy Daub, was awarded a $40 gratuity 8 May 1850. She received a $40 gratuity and a $40 annuity in Lebanon County 24 Feb. 1860.

Daub, William. Pa. —. He was granted relief in Lebanon County 18 Feb. 1834.

Daubert, Peter. Pa. Pvt. He was in Berks County on 12 Aug. 1786. He served in the 3rd Pa. Regiment in Capt. Bile's Company under Col. Shee in 1776. He was taken prisoner at Fort Washington and carried to New York where he was confined in the French Church. His left leg ulcerated and never healed. He was lame. Lt. Daniel Brodhead proved his service. He was 49 years old.

Daugherty, Daniel. Pa. —. He was awarded a $40 gratuity and a $40 annuity in Butler Co. 10 Mar. 1812.

Daugherty, Henry. Pa. Pvt. He was in Northumberland County 25 Aug. 1786. He served in the Northumberland County militia and was wounded at Piscataway, N.J. in an engagement with the British. He also appeared as Henry Dougherty.

Davenport, Hezekiah. Conn. Lt. He was killed 27 Apr. 1777. His heirs were paid his seven-years' half-pay of $1,120.

Davenport, James. Mass. —. He served in the 8th Regiment and was from Dorchester. He was paid $20.

Davenport, James. Va. Pvt. He served in the 7th Va. Regiment under Capt. Matthew Jouett from 15 Feb. 1776 until discharged 3 Feb. 1778 on account of being wounded in his left ankle at Brandywine in Sept. 1777. His leg was somewhat withered, and his foot was impaired. He had enlisted in 1776 for three years from Hanover County. He was awarded a £30 gratuity and an annuity of full pay on 21 May 1778. He was 28 years old and lived in Louisa County on 15 Mar. 1787 when he was continued at the rate of £6 per annum. He had an aged indigent father and mother upon whom he depended in Jan. 1789. He was on the 1813 pension list. He was in the 7th Virginia Regiment. He was first pensioned at the rate of $20 per annum and later at $40 per annum. He had empowered his brother, William Davenport, until the latter's death and then his brother, Jesse Davenport, to draw his pension to 4 Sep. 1818. For four years there was no application for his stipend. Congress approved that his heirs be allowed arrearage from 4 Sep. 1818 to the time of his death at the rate of $40 per annum 23 Apr. 1828.

Davenport, Jonathan. R.I. Pvt. He served in Col. Thomas Church's Regiment. He was hurt while throwing up works near Penny Ferry near Charlestown. The end of an handbarrow struck the rim of his belly and produced an inguinal rupture in 1775. He resided in Portsmouth, Newport Co., R.I. in 1794. He later lived in Providence Co., R.I. He was granted one twenty-fourth of a pension 20 Apr. 1796. He was on the 1815 pension list.

Davenport, Joseph. —. —. Congress found that his heirs were not entitled to relief 4 May 1846. They were Sally Beekes the widow of Benjamin Beekes, William Pratt, Eliza Briscoe, and Ann O. Wright.

Davenport, Joseph. —. —. He died of smallpox at Crown Point in 1776. Congress rejected a pension for his son, Isaac Davenport, on 22 Feb. 1847.

Davenport, Joseph. Va. —. His wife, Mary Davenport, was awarded relief in the amount of £10 on 22 Dec. 1777 in Bedford Co., Va.

Davenport, Philip. Me. —. He died in Apr. 1820 in Hallowell. His widow, Jerusha Davenport, was from Augusta. She was paid $50 under the resolve of 1836.

Davenport, Thomas. —. Capt. He received his five years' full pay commutation 14 July 1832.

Davenport, William. Va. Capt. He served first as a lieutenant and was appointed captain in Feb. 1776. He resigned in Dec. 1779. He received warrant #4,019 for 4,000 acres on 3 Dec. 1785. Congress rejected the claim of his heirs on 28 Mar. 1850. He was not entitled to half-pay.

Davidson, —. S.C. —. His widow was of Aikin County. There were three children in 1791. She was paid as late as 1826.

Davidson, Alexander. Pa. —. He applied 9 May 1818.

Davidson, David. Pa. —. He was awarded a $40 gratuity and a $40 annuity on 13 Mar. 1812 in Armstrong County. He died 26 Dec. 1839.

Davidson, Edward. Pa. —. He was pensioned 10 Nov. 1813. He was from Lancaster County. He also appeared as Edward Davison.

Davidson, Francis. N.H. Pvt. He served in Bridge's Regiment. He was pensioned 25 Aug. 1808 in Rockingham Co., N.H. He was pensioned at the rate of $4 per month from 16 Jan. 1808. He was on the 1813 pension list.

Davidson, Francis. Pa. —. He was awarded a $40 gratuity in Westmoreland Co., Pa. 23 Apr. 1829. He died 8 Nov. 1845

Davidson, James. Md. Pvt. He was pensioned at the rate of half-pay of a private 27 Jan. 1816.

Davidson, John. S.C. —. He was killed at the Hanging Rock. His widow, Sarah Davidson, was allowed an annuity 21 Feb. 1785 in Union County.

Davidson, John. Va. Dragoon. He served in Lee's Legion. He lived in Prince Edward County.

Davidson, Joshua. Va. Dragoon. He was wounded in the right arm and in the shoulder on 15 Mar. 1781 at Guilford. He lost the use of his arm. He lived in Prince Edward Co., Va. in 1794. He was on the 1813 pension list.

Davidson, Josiah. Mass. —. He was in the 2nd Regiment and was from Charlemont. He was paid $20.

Davidson, Thomas. S.C. —. He served under Capt. Stephen Buckner and Col. William Heath and was wounded. He was pensioned and died in 1807. His widow, Rosanna Davidson, was from Colleton District and had five children to support. Her application was rejected.

Davidson, Thomas. Va. Pvt. He was disabled by the total loss of sight in his right eye and a partial loss of sight in his left due to smallpox while in Continental service. He was awarded a £30 gratuity and an annuity of half-pay for six years on 16 Oct. 1778. He was in the 4th Virginia Regiment. He also appeared as Thomas Davison.

Davidson, William. Pa. Sgt. He applied from Erie County on 29 Jan. 1817. He served in the 11th Pa.

Regiment under Col. Hubley in Capt. Lawrance King's Company. He enlisted in Apr. 1777 at Carlisle in Capt. Matthew Irvine's Company and was discharged at Trenton, N.J. in Jan. 1781. He lost his eye from injury received by the fall of a tree.

Davidson, William Lee. N.C. Lt. Col. He died in the service. His widow, Mary Davidson, applied in 1789. She lived in Tennessee.

Davies, Daniel. Pa. —. He was awarded a $40 gratuity and a $40 annuity 27 Mar. 1837.

Davies, John. Va. —. His wife, Sarah Davies, was granted 4 barrels of corn and 100 pounds of pork in Bedford Co., Va. on 23 Oct. 1780.

Davis, —. N.Y. —. His widow, Catharine Davis, of Montgomery County, N.Y. gave a power of attorney to Daniel Paris to collect her annual pension of £30 due her by the act of 14 Feb. 1793. John Frey had her power of attorney on another occasion.

Davis, —. S.C. —. He died in the service. His widow, Christiana Davis, sought an annuity 2 Dec.1796,

Davis, —. Pa. —. His widow, Sarah Davis, was awarded a $40 gratuity and a $40 annuity in Westmoreland County 31 Mar. 1836.

Davis, —. S.C. —. His widow, Eleanor Davis, and child received an annuity 25 Sep. 1791.

Davis, —. Va. —. Their mother was granted financial support in Caroline Co., Va. 11 June 1778.

Davis, —. Va. —. Ann Davis was granted £30 support while her son was away in the service in Caroline Co., Va. 12 July 1779.

Davis, —. Va. Pvt. He was in Continental service. His widow, Martha Davis, was on the pension roll of 1785.

Davis, Aaron. Me. —. He was from Warren. He was paid $50 under the resolve of 1836.

Davis, Aaron. Mass. —. He served in the 6th Regiment and was from Mendon. He was paid $20.

Davis, Abraham. Mass. Pvt. He served in the 6th Regiment and was from Phillipston. His widow, Grace Davis, was paid $50.

Davis, Abraham. Va. Pvt. He died in the service. His widow, Ann Davis, with two small children lived in Essex County in 1787. She was continued on the pension list at the rate of £10 per annum on 12 Nov. 1787. Administration on her estate was granted to Edmund Davis in King and Queen Co., Va. 13 May 1812.

Davis, Abraham. Va. Pvt. He was awarded a gratuity of £500 on 29 Nov. 1780. He was aged 35 and lived in Louisa County in Mar. 1786. He had no trade. He served in the 3rd Regiment of new levies in Capt. Thomas Catlet's Company under Col. Buford. He was wounded at Buford's defeat near Hanging Rock in S.C. He had two wounds in his left arm near his elbow and suffered from a rupture in assisting with the artillery. He was continued at the rate of £12 per annum on 4 Mar. 1789. He was on the 1813 pension list.

Davis, Amon. N.J. —. He enlisted at Crosswicks 10 Jan. 1777. He took sick out on a scout into Monmouth County under Maj. Davis of the Pennsylvania militia and died at Shrewsbury. He was from Cumberland County. His widow, Abigail Davis, married secondly ----- Lupton and received a half-pay pension from 31 Jan. 1777 to 25 Dec. 1780 on 16 June 1797.

Davis, Amos. Mass. —. He served in the 8th Regiment and was from Gloucester. He was paid $20.

Davis, Benjamin. S.C. —. He was killed at the siege of Ninety Six in 1781. His widow, Ann Davis, was granted an annuity 3 Oct. 1785.

Davis, Caleb. N.J. Pvt. He served in Oliver Spencer's Regiment under Capt. Jonathan Peirson. He was wounded in the leg at Germantown 4 Oct. 1777 and disabled. He spent two years in the hospital in Pennsylvania and was discharged as an invalid. He applied for half-pay in Essex County. He was 31 in 1791.

Davis, Cato. Mass. —. He was in the 5th Regiment and was from Worcester. He was paid $20.

Davis, Charles. Va. Pvt. He was awarded a £500 gratuity 9 Nov. 1780. He was in Albemarle County in Oct. 1785. He was pensioned at the rate of £6 per annum during his disability on 27 Oct. 1785. He was 30 years old and in Culpeper County on 4 Nov. 1786 when he was continued on the roll at the rate of £16 per annum. He had been wounded in his forearm and served in the 1st Light Dragoons at Col. Buford's defeat. He died 1 Feb. 1807.

Davis, Daniel. Mass. —. He served in the artillery under Capt. David Strout in the Massachusetts Line in Mar. 1781 to defend Cape Elizabeth, Maine. He received pay and rations from Joseph Noyes, commissary and paymaster. He was 71 years old. He was pensioned for 18 months of service 22 Dec. 1837.

Davis, Daniel. Pa. —. He enlisted in 1776 under Capt. Wilkins. He was wounded in the wrist at Brandywine. He was taken prisoner and put in the provo in the jail in Philadelphia. He was exchanged and discharged as incapable of military duty. He was from Mifflin County. He was paid to 25 Dec. 1829.

Davis, Daniel. Pa. —. He was pensioned in Armstrong County 27 Mar. 1837.

Davis, Elisha. —. —. He enlisted for six months and was discharged a few days before the expiration of his enlistment. Congress granted him a pension for six months of service 20 Mar. 1838.

Davis, Francis. N.Y. —. He was wounded. He was on the 1785 list.

Davis, Francis. Va. Pvt. He removed to Pennsylvania and was on the pension list there in 1789. He died 15 Feb. 1805.

Davis, George. S.C. —. His remarried widow, Elizabeth Hutson, and three children were granted an annuity 17 Jan. 1787.

Davis, Henry. Pa. —. He was granted relief 3 Apr. 1837 in Armstrong County. He was 73 years old in 1840.

Davis, Hezekiah. Pa. —. He was pensioned 2 Apr. 1822.

Davis, Hugh. —. Sgt. He served in the Continental Line. He was pensioned in 1818 at the rank of a private. He was pensioned in 1832 as a sergeant. He asked for the difference between the two. Congress granted him such a pension 5 Mar. 1840.

Davis, Isaac. N.Y. Sgt. He served under Col. Fisher. He suffered from lameness and inflamation. He resided in Conewaga, N.Y. in 1794.

Davis, Isaac. Pa. —. His heirs applied from Bedford County on 26 Feb. 1820. Mary Davis was their guardian.

Davis, Isham. S. C. Pvt. He served under Col. John Purvis and Capt. John Martin. He was at Eutaw Springs and the siege of Ninety Six. Thomas Williams served with him. He lived in Macon Co., N.C. in 1829 when his application was rejected.

Davis, Ismael. Va. —. His wife, Martha Davis, was provided necessaries in Amelia Co., Va. 22 Jan. 1778 while he was absent in the service.

Davis, Jacob. Pa. —. He was pensioned in Philadelphia 16 June 1836.

Davis, Jacob. Va. —. His wife, Sarah Davis, and three children were furnished £30 on 25 June 1779.

Davis, James. Va. —. He died in the service. His widow, Ruth Davis, and three children were granted financial support in Yohogania Co., Va. 28 Dec. 1779.

Davis, James. Pa. —. He was granted relief in Fayette County 14 Mar. 1835. He was 79 years old in 1840.

Davis, James. Va. Capt. He became supernumerary in Sep. 1778. He was from Stafford County. Congress rejected the claim of the heirs for his commutation 2 Feb. 1836.

Davis, Jesse. —. —. He served longer than six months per certificate from Capt. Armistead Shelton of N.C. He married 29 Oct. 1836. He died in South Carolina 22 Dec. 1851. Congress allowed his widow, Rebecca Davis, a pension of $20 per annum 6 Apr. 1860.

Davis, Jesse. Va. Capt. He served from 1775 to 1779 or 1780 when he became supernumerary. He was at Monmouth in June 1778. Congress did not grant his widow, Nancy Davis, any commutation on 22 Mar. 1830.

Davis, John. —. Pvt. He served three months as a substitute for his brother in 1776. He also served six days under Capt. Israel Heald and Col. Eleazer Brook. From 16 Aug. to 30 Nov. 1777 he served under Capt. George Minott and Col. Ballard. His service amounted to 3 months and 25 days. Congress denied his widow, Abigail Davis, a pension 1 Aug. 1850. She furnished no proof of her marriage.

Davis, John. Conn. —. He had a land warrant for his service from 10 June 1779 to the end of the war. His widow was Nancy Davis.

Davis, John. Md. Sgt. He was pensioned in Charles County at the rate of half-pay of a sergeant 2 Jan.1813.

Davis, John. Md. Pvt. He was pensioned in Kent County in 1781. He lived "down" in the county. He died in 1790.

Davis, John. Md. Pvt. He served in the 6th Regiment. He was pensioned in Kent County in 1785. He lived "up" in the county.

Davis, John. Md. Pvt. His heirs sought his commutation and bounty land. He was a private and was not entitled to the former. Congress directed the heirs to apply to the Bounty Land Office of the War Department on 6 Jan. 1837.

Davis, John. Mass. —. He served in the 1st Regiment and was from St. Georges. He was paid $20.

Davis, John. N.Y. Capt. He was killed at Oriskany 6 Aug. 1777. He served under Col. Frederick Fisher. His children, Mart---- Davis, John Davis, Mary Davis, Catharine Davis, and Sarah Davis received a half-pay pension for seven years.

Davis, John. N.C. Corp. He applied in Lincoln County in 1828. He served in the N.C. Continental Line from May 1778 to Aug. 1779. He was disabled by rheumatism. He was awarded an annuity of $60. He was about 70 years old.

Davis, John. Pa. Capt. He was from Chester County. He was commissioned in the 9th Regiment in Nov. 1776. He was a member of the Society of the Cincinnati and married a daughter of John Morton, signer of the Declaration of Independence. He died 1 Sep. 1827. His administrator, Charles J. Davis, sought what was due on 25 July 1850. He was allowed half-pay with interest.

Davis, John. Pa. —. He was awarded a $40 gratuity and a $40 annuity in Armstrong Co., Pa. 7 Mar. 1827. He was 79 years old in 1840.

Davis, John. Pa. Gunner. He was on the 1791 pension roll.

Davis, John. Pa. Pvt. He was in Philadelphia County on 30 Sep. 1785. He was a gunner in the 4th Pa. Regiment of Artillery and was transferred to the Invalids. He was wounded in S.C. by Refugees while he was cutting wood. He was 30 years old. His mother was living 1 Sep.1787.

Davis, John. Pa. Pvt. He applied from Westmoreland County 25 Aug. 1815. He was enlisted for three years or the war by Lt. Forbes in Middletown, Pa. and marched to Valley Forge where he was put in the company of Capt. Smith in Col. Francis Johnston's Regiment. He was furloughed at Morristown to see his friends at Harrisburg. He then returned home where one of his legs became sore and very much ulcerated. He was never able to return to duty. He was 70 years old. He was in Capt. McLellan's Company of Light Infantry under Col. Butler. He was wounded in the foot at the Block House near Fort Lee on the Hudson River. He was discharged in 1780. He was pensioned 3 Jan. 1824 in Wayne Co., Ohio. He was in Franklin Co., Ohio in 1829. He served to 1780. His widow was mentioned on 13 Mar. 1846. He was also wounded in the hand by a British dragoon sword. His widow was in Hendersonville, Kentucky.

Davis, John. Pa. —. He was pensioned in Franklin County 21 Oct. 1829.

Davis, John. S.C. —. His children were allowed an annuity 17 Mar. 1786. It was paid to Andrew Baskins.

Davis, John. S.C. Sgt. He served in the 2nd S.C. Regiment. He was wounded 28 Sep. 1780. He was awarded an annuity 15 Oct. 1785. On 4 Sep. 1789 he transferred to Monroe Co., Va. He later removed to Alabama.

Davis, John. S.C. —. He served for ten months under Capt. James Giles and Col. William Hill. He was 69 years old and had a wife aged 68. All of his children were gone from home. He was pensioned in Abbeville District 25 Nov. 1830. Henry Livingstone, aged 68, served with him. He died 1 Sep. 1831. His widow was Elizabeth Davis. She gave her age as 67. She had no children of her own or any relation in the country. She was pensioned at the rate of $30 per annum on 17 Dec. 1831 and was paid as late as 1833.

Davis, John. Va. Capt. He served from 10 June 1779 to the end of the war and received bounty land. Congress granted his remarried widow, Nancy Terry, relief on 30 Apr. 1840. She was from Norfolk County.

Davis, John. Va. —. He was on the 1813 pension list.

Davis, John. Va. —. His wife, Sarah Davis, and four children were furnished 5 barrels of corn and 250 pounds of pork in Essex Co., Va. on 25 May 1781 and on 17 Mar. 1783.

Davis, John. Va. —. His wife, Ann Davis, was furnished 1 barrel of corn and 50 pounds of pork in Essex Co., Va. on 25 May 1781, 2 barrels of corn and 100 pounds of pork on 20 May 1782, and 3 barrels of corn and 150 pounds of pork for herself and her children on 17 Mar. 1783.

Davis, John. Va. —. His wife, Ann Davis, and two children were furnished £8 support in Louisa Co., on 11 Aug. 1777 and £10 on 10 Aug. 1778.

Davis, John. Va. Pvt. He served in the 10th Va. Regiment and died in Continental service. His widow, Catherine Davis, aged 55, and one son lived in Essex County on 15 Oct. 1787. She died *ante* May 1789; her legal representative was John Davis of Essex County. On 3 Mar. 1787 Mark Davis of Caroline County swore that he was present at the marriage of John and Catherine. She was put on the pension list at the rate of £8 per annum on 12 Nov. 1787.

Davis, John. Va. —. He lived in Harrison Co., Va. when he was pensioned in 1832 but was later stricken. The commissioner of pensions agreed to restore him to the rolls if he would return what he had overdrawn. Congress ruled that he should have to return the money and gave him a pension 5 Mar. 1840 at the rate of $44 per annum. He had previously received $88 per annum.

Davis, Jonathan. Mass. Pvt. He lived in Shirley, Mass. and served in Capt. Silvanus Smith's Company under Col. Timothy Bigelow in the 15th Regiment. He was wounded 3 Feb. 1780 by a musket ball through his left arm. He was 40 years old. He was pensioned 15 Jan. 1789. He resided in Norfolk Co., Mass. He was on the 1813 pension list.

Davis, Jonathan. Va. —. His wife, Eliza Davis, was granted £18 support while he was away in the service in Yohogania Co., Va. 24 May 1779.

Davis, Joseph. N.J. Pvt. He served under Col. Scudder in the militia. He was taken prisoner and died 11 Mar. 1777 in New York. He was from Monmouth County. His widow, Penelope Davis, received a half-pay pension.

Davis, Joseph. S.C. —. He served under Col. Baxter. He was from Marion District in 1826. His application was rejected.

Davis, Joshua. S.C. —. He was drafted at the age of 16 and served to 21. He was in Col. Maham's Regiment of Calvary. His application was rejected in 1825.

Davis, Lathrop. Conn. Sgt. He served in Starr's Regiment. At Stony Point on 15 July 1779 a musket ball destroyed his left eye, passed through his head, and came out the opposite cheek. He suffered from dizziness and was scarcely able to stoop or bend. He was 33 years old and resided in Lebanon, Conn. He was pensioned 5 May 1788. He was on the 1813 pension list. He also appeared as Lothrop Davis. Congress rejected his request for an increase in his pension 21 Jan. 1820.

Davis, Levi. Pa. Sgt. He applied from Chester County on 9 Sep. 1813. He was in Capt. John Pugh's Company. Later he served under Capt. Robb and Capt. Samuel Tolbert in Col. Walter Stewart's Regiment. He enlisted in the spring of 1776 and was discharged in Jan. 1781. Joseph Harris served with him as did Joseph Madden. Capt. John Davis was his captain. He was paid to 18 Mar. 1834.

Davis, Micah. Me. —. He died 7 Jan. 1832 in Fairfield. His widow was Lydia Davis from Gardner. She was paid $50 under the resolve of 1836.

Davis, Moses. Pa. —. He was awarded a $40 gratuity and a $40 annuity in Columbia Co., Pa. 22 Dec. 1834.

Davis, Nathan. Mass. —. He served in the 6th Regiment and was from Rutland. He was paid $20.

Davis, Nathan. N.Y. Sgt. He served under Col. Gansevoort. He was wounded by accident in his leg by an axe while scouting timber at Fort Stanwix in 1778. He resided in New Galloway, Saratoga Co., N.Y. in 1794. He enlisted 1 Jan. 1777, was returned sick, and omitted Sep. 1778. He was pensioned 3 Mar. 1792. He later lived in Onondaga County. He was on the 1813 pension list as a private.

Davis, Nathaniel. Mass. —. He served in the 1st Regiment and was from Arundell. He was paid $20.

Davis, Nathaniel, Jr. Mass. —. He served in the 11th Regiment and was from Arundell. He was paid $20.

Davis, Nicholas. Me. —. He died 14 Jan. 1832. His widow was Abigail Davis from Hollis. She was paid $50 under the resolve of 1836.

Davis, Paul. Mass. —. He served in the 5th Regiment and was paid $20.

Davis, Phineas. Pa. Pvt. He was in Philadelphia County on 12 Dec. 1785. He was in the Invalids and was discharged 15 Sep. 1782 unfit for duty on account of rheumatism and other complaints. He was 55 years old. He was dead by Sep. 1794.

Davis, Samuel. —. —. He served six months and eight days and was receiving a pension of $20.90. Congress denied him an increase 7 Feb. 1849.

Davis, Samuel. Pa. Lt. He served as 1st Lt. in the 9th Regiment in 1776 and was deranged in 1778. He was disabled by bodily infirmities and did not have enough property to maintain himself. He was 65 years in March 1815 and was from Whitemarsh Twp., Montgomery County.

Davis, Robert. S.C. —. He served in Col. Mayham's Calvary Regiment. Lt. Theus enlisted him for twelve months after which he was enlisted by Maj. James Conyers for the war. After eight months he was discharged. John McClary served with him. He was pensioned in Williamsburg District 25 Nov. 1830.

Davis, Samuel. Me. —. He was from Standish. He was paid $50 under the resolve of 1836.

Davis, Samuel. Md. Pvt. His widow, Margaret Davis, was pensioned at the rate of half-pay of a private in Mar. 1835.

Davis, Samuel. Md. Fifer. He was pensioned in Kent County at the rate of half-pay of a fifer 12 Feb. 1820. He was stricken from the pension roll 24 Feb. 1822 because he was never in the service of the state or the United States. On 9 Mar. 1826 he was restored to the pension roll and his pension was made retroactive to the time he was stricken. He lived in Baltimore at that time and pensioned at the rate of half-pay of a sergeant.

Davis, Samuel. Mass. —. He served in the 2nd Regiment and was from Great Barrington. He was paid $20. He was pensioned 8 Feb. 1812 for life from 5 Sept. 1810.

Davis, Samuel. Pa. Lt. He applied from Montgomery County on 10 Jan. 1815. He served in the 9th Pa. Regiment in 1776 and was discharged in 1778. He was deranged in 1778 with bodily infirmities. He was 67 years old. In 1819 he did not have enough property to maintain himself.

Davis, Samuel D. —. —. He served six months and eight months. Congress rejected his request for an increase of his pension of $20.90 on 7 Feb. 1849.

Davis, Thomas. Md. Pvt. He was pensioned at the rate of half-pay of a private in Ohio 12 Feb. 1820.

Davis, Thomas. —. He received a $40 gratuity and a $40 annuity in Chester County 16 June 1836.

Davis, Thomas. S.C. —. His officers included Col. Hicks, Capt. Thomas Ellerbee, C. Pegues, D. Sparks, and L. Benton. He was made a prisoner at the fall of Charleston and paroled. He served five years but was not wounded. He suffered from rheumatism. He was pensioned 6 Dec. 1828. He was paid as late as 1834.

Davis, Thomas. Va. Pvt. He was continued on the pension list on 10 Mar. 1789. He was on the 1790 pension roll.

Davis, Thomas. Va. —. His wife, Nancy Davis, and four children were granted £20 support in Prince William Co., Va. on 6 July 1778.

Davis, Thomas Lamar. S.C. —. He was pensioned in 1791. He received $2.50 per month from 17 Oct. 1807. He was on the 1813 pension list in Georgia and died there 19 Oct. 1816.

Davis, Thompson. Va. Pvt. He applied for his pension 12 July 1786 from Louisa County and was 40 years old. He served in the 3rd Regiment of Light Dragoons under Col. Baylor. He enlisted to the end of the war. He was granted a pension of half-pay during his disability and £8 relief on 5 May 1785. He was wounded about the head in Aug. 1778 at the surprise of the regiment in the Jerseys as proved by the oath of William Barret on 11 July 1786. He was continued on the list 12 July 1786.

Davis, William. —. —. He was pensioned in 1818 and stricken because he was discharged ten days prior to the expiration of his nine months at Saratoga. He had served eight months and twenty-two days. He was a considerable distance from his home in Rhode Island. His discharge did not specify that his term of service had expired but that his service was no longer required. Congress granted him relief because he had been improperly stricken on 7 Feb. 1845. His widow, Lucy Davis, sought his pension for the time he had been refused. Congress rejected a special act for her relief since she could apply under the act of 1838 on 27 Mar. 1846.

Davis, William. Md. Pvt. He was pensioned at the rate of half-pay of a private on 27 Jan. 1816.

Davis, William. N.Y. Pvt. He was wounded by musket balls and bayonets in July 1779 near Verplanck Point. He served in Col. Hamman's Regiment.

Davis, William. R.I. —. He was pensioned under the act of 1818 but stricken in 1820 because his discharge was dated ten days before the expiration of his nine month enlistment. He was discharged at Saratoga. Congress ruled that he had served the nine month tour. His papers stated that his services were no longer required rather than his service had expired. Congress granted him his pension of $966.92 for the ten years he had not been paid on 3 Mar. 1836.

Davis, William. Va. Pvt. He served in the 15th Va. Regiment and died in the service. His widow, Judith Davis, with three young children lived in King William County in July 1786. Thomas Smith was administrator of the estate in June 1789.

Davis, William Royal. S.C. —. He was killed near Dorchester in Feb. 1782. His widow, Eleanor Davis was left with a large family three of whom were under twelve when he died. One child was under twelve years of age when an annuity was paid to her 25 Oct. 1791. She was paid as late as 1811.

Davis, Winthrop. N.H. —. He entered the service 16 Aug. 1782 for three years and was under Capt. Frye in the 2nd N.H. Regiment. He was discharged 30 June 1783. Congress ruled that the peace was ratified before the end of his term and granted him relief on 3 Jan. 1832.

Davis, Zacheriah. S.C. —. He was killed in the service in Nov. 1781. His widow, Christiana Davis, was allowed an annuity 20 Aug. 1785. Her application from Colleton District in 1786 was rejected.

Davison, Benjamin. N.Y. —. His family was granted support 18 Feb. 1779 while he was away in the service.

Davison, John. Mass. Pvt. He served in the Invalids and was from Gloucester. He was paid $20.

Davison, Joseph. S.C. —. He was paid his annuity in 1802.

Davy, Thomas. N.Y. Pvt. He served under Col. Samuel Clyde in the militia and was slain 6 Aug. 1777. His children, Henry Davy and Ann Davy, received a half-pay pension.

Daw, John. N.H. —. He enlisted in the summer of 1780 for six months. He marched to Rhode Island and was discharged there in Dec. 1780 having served five months and twenty-seven days. Congress credited him with six months of service and granted him a pension 12 Apr. 1836.

Dawkins, Charles. Md. Sgt. He entered the service on 25 Apr. 1778 for three years. He was discharged 5 Apr. 1781. His widow, Elizabeth Dawkins, was pensioned at the rate of half-pay of a sergeant in Calvert County on 24 Feb. 1830. Congress granted her a pension 12 Apr. 1842 for two years of service.

Dawkins, John. S.C. —. He served under Col. John Lyles and went out from Newberry District to Georgia. He was also under Col. Glenn and Maj. Gordon. He was in the battle of Stono. He was 69 years old when he was pensioned in 1829 in Abbeville District. He was paid as late as 1834. Thomas Low, aged 76, saw him in the service. He died in 1838. His widow, Margaret Dawkins, whom he married in 1800 had her application rejected in 1847.

Dawkins, William. S.C. —. He had his arm broken at Eutaw. He was granted an annuity 20 Nov. 1784.

Dawson, —. Pa. —. His widow, Mary Dawson, was awarded a $40 gratuity and a $40 annuity in Philadelphia Co., Pa. 8 Apr. 1826.

Dawson, —. Pa. —. His widow, Jane Dawson, was awarded a $40 gratuity in Juniata Co., Pa. 15 Apr. 1834.

Dawson, Anthony. Pa. Pvt. He was in Cumberland County 16 Aug. 1786. He served in the 6th Pa. Regiment under Col. William Irwin. He was wounded at the battle of Three Rivers in Canada on 7 June 1776. He was 32 years old. He later lived in Philadelphia County. He was on the 1813 pension list.

Dawson, Joseph. Md. Capt. He served in the 5th Maryland Regiment. He was being pensioned in 1791. He was wounded at the battle of Eutaw Springs.

Dawson, Joseph. Md. Pvt. He was being pensioned in 1791.

Dawson, Levi. N.C. Col. He died in 1803 in Charleston, S.C. His heirs were Matthew A. Outlen,

Elizabeth Marshall, Ann Sparrow the wife of Gideon Sparrow, Margaret Smaw the wife of John D. Smaw, Eunice Smaw, Caroline Smaw, Frances Fulford the wife of Absalom Fulford, William Dawson, Fanny Dawson, and Martha Dawson. They were from Craven Co., N.C. in Feb. 1838 except for the first three who were from Pasquotank Co., N.C.

Dawson, Matthew. Pa. Sgt. He applied 21 Nov. 1785. He was in the Invalids.

Dawson, Peter P. Pa. —. His widow, Jane Dawson, was awarded a $40 gratuity in Juniata Co., Pa. 15 Apr. 1835. She was dead by Jan. 1840.

Dawson, William. Md. Pvt. He was pensioned in Cecil County at the rate of half-pay of a private in 1810.

Dawson, William. S.C. —. He was at the battles of Stono, Eutaw, Augusta, Cambridge, and the expedition against the Cherokee. He served under Capt. Benjamin Tutt. Matthew Barrett, Elias Gibson, and William Robinson were fellow soldiers. He was pensioned from Edgefield District 12 Dec. 1823. It was to be paid from Dec. 1822 by act of 18 Dec. 1823 as late as 1834.

Day, Asa. —. —. He sought that his pension be increased at the rank of a sergeant for more than two years. He did not prove his claim by any record of positive testimony. Congress rejected the claim 20 June 1848.

Day, Benjamin. —. —. He was from Limington, Maine. He was pensioned in 1818 and stricken from the roll in 1820. His request to be restored was rejected 2 Feb. 1825.

Day, James. Va. —. He was wounded in Col. Buford's Regiment. He was to be allowed to remain in hospital until the cure of his leg was effected. He was also awarded a full set of clothes on 5 Dec. 1780. He served three and half years in Continental service.

Day, Jedediah. Mass. Pvt. He served in the 4th Regiment and was from West Springfield and was paid $50.

Day, John. Pa. Pvt. He was granted the arrears of his pension 16 Jan. 1797. He was on the 1813 pension list. He died 26 Apr. 1821 in Dearborn Co., Ind.

Day, Joseph. Ga. Capt. He served in the 4th Regiment. His administrator, Thomas N. Box, sought his commutation plus interest, but Congress rejected the claim 16 Feb. 1836.

Day, Nathaniel. Me. —. He applied from Lovell. He was paid $50 under the resolve of 1836.

Day, Samuel. Mass. Ens. He enlisted 1 Apr. 1777 under Capt. Rapp in the 4th Regiment. He was promoted to sergeant 1 June 1778 and to ensign 18 Aug. 1779. He married 1 Jan. 1794 in Mansfield, Mass. He died before Mar. 1818. Congress granted his widow, Sally Day, a pension 8 Mar. 1842.

Deagle, Michael. Mass. —. He served in the 4th Regiment and was paid $20. His alias was Michael Noagle.

Deagles, —. Va. —. His mother, Ann Deagles, was granted £10 relief while in Lunenburg Co., Va. while he was away in Continental service on 13 Jan. 1778 and £40 on 11 Mar. 1779.

Deal, Andrew. Pa. Sgt. He was on the 1791 pension roll.

Deal, George. Md. Capt. After his death, his arrearage was paid to Richard Thomas 7 Feb. 1843.

Dealty, James. —. Pvt. He was allowed a pension for six months but claimed twelve months. Congress granted him a pension 5 Mar. 1840 for the longer period of service.

Dean, —. Va. Pvt. Elizabeth Dean was pensioned 1 Jan. 1778. She was awarded 1 ½ barrels of corn in Southampton Co., Va. on 10 June 1779.

Dean, —. Pa. —. His widow, Mary Dean, was awarded a $40 gratuity and a $40 annuity in Bucks Co., Pa. 30 Mar. 1824. She died 17 June 1839.

Dean, —. Pa. —. Martha Dean of Indiana County received relief.

Dean, —. Va. —. Rebeckah Dean had three sons in Continental service and was granted support in Halifax Co., Va. on 18 June 1778.

Dean, Ebenezer. Me. —. He was from Madison. He was paid $50 under the resolve of 1836.

Dean, Enos. Mass. Sgt. He served in the 14th Regiment and was from Taunton. His widow, Lydia Wilde, was paid $50.

Dean, Gilbert. —. —. He died in 1825 before any law to claim a pension applied to his situation. Congress rejected the petition of his daughter, Emma Delaney, for a pension 7 Jan. 1859.

Dean, James. N.H. Pvt. He served under Col. Nichols in Capt. Stone's Company. He was wounded by a musket ball which passed through his thigh in 1777 at Bennington. He lived in Marlborough, N.H. in 1795. He served in the militia. He was granted one-fourth of a pension 20 Apr. 1796. He was on the 1813 pension list.

Dean, Lemuel. N.H. Pvt. He served under Col. Cilley. He was wounded in his neck by a musket ball and lost his hearing in his right ear. He had difficulty in speaking and a great debility. He was wounded on 20 June 1778 at Monmouth. He lived at Claremont, N.H. in 1795. He enlisted 3 Mar. 1777 for three years and was discharged 31 Mar. 1780. He was granted half a pension 20 Apr. 1796. His rate was $5 per month from 8 Oct. 1807. He was on the 1813 pension list.

Dean, Matthew. Va. His widow, Elizabeth Dean, was granted support in Southampton County 11 June 1778.

Dean, Michael. Va. —. His wife, Mary Dean, was furnished £8 for support in Frederick Co., Va. on 6 May 1777. He served in the 8th Virginia Regiment.

Dean, Moses. N.C. —. He applied in 1807 from Washington Co., Ga. He served from Pitt Co., N.C. He was wounded at Eutaw Springs with a broken leg on 8 Sep. 1781. His application was rejected.

Dean, Samuel. Pa. Capt. He applied from Bucks County. In 1775 he served as a lieutenant in Col. Thomson's Regiment and marched to Boston in 1776. He was in the Flying Camp until he was discharged. He next entered the 11th Pa. Regt. under Col. Richard Humpton. He served to 1778 when he became supernumerary. Upon his return home, he was elected colonel of the militia which he commanded to the end of the war. He was on the 1813 pension list as Samuel Doane [sic].

Dean, Samuel. S.C. —. He was paid from 1829 to 1834. He died in 1840. His widow, Milly Dean aged 77, was from Edgefield District in 1842. She was paid as late as 1850.

Dean, Silas. Mass. Lt. He served in the Mass. Infantry. He was wounded by a ball in his right arm on 7 Oct. 1777 at Bemis Heights. He resided at Dublin, N.H. in 1796.

Dean, William. Pa. Pvt. His widow, Martha Dean, was in Franklin County on 19 June 1788. He was in the Franklin County militia and was killed 1 May 1778 at Crooked Billet. He left five children.

Dearman, Joseph. Pa. —. He was awarded a $100 gratuity in Philadelphia Co., Pa. 3 Feb. 1824.

Dearmond, Michael. Pa. —. He was awarded a $40 gratuity and a $40 annuity in Northumberland County on 22 Dec. 1817. He was dead by Dec. 1835.

Deas, —. S.C. —. His widow was Elizabeth Deas. There were children in 1791.

Deatley, James. —. Pvt. He was at Yorktown under Capt. Killis. He had been pensioned for six months of service. He claimed twelve months of service. Congress approved his pension for an additional six months on 29 Dec. 1841. His brother was Christopher Deatley.

Deaver, Aquilla. Md. Pvt. He was pensioned at the rate of half-pay of a private in Harford County on 2 Mar. 1827. The arrearage of his pension was to be paid to William B. Stephenson for the widow, Sarah Deaver, in Jan. 1836. She was pensioned at the same rate in 13 Feb. 1836. She died 24 Nov. 1850. Julia Ann Harwood was the only surviving child, and she requested that the arrearage of $15.85 be paid to John H. Mitchell who had furnished indispensable articles to her mother. It was so done on 26 May 1852.

Deaver, William. Md. Pvt. He was pensioned at the rate of half-pay of a private in Mason Co., Ky. 7 Mar. 1826.

Deaver, William. Pa. Pvt. He was on the 1813 pension list.

Deavy, John. N.Y. Sgt. He served in Col. Bellinger's Regiment of the Montgomery County militia. He was slain 25 Oct. 1780. His widow, Margaret Deavy, received a half-pay pension for seven years. He also appeared as John Davy.

Debever, Francis Suzor. Mass. Surgeon's Mate. He served in the 7th Massachusetts Regiment from 20 Aug. 1778 to 10 Nov. 1778 when he was taken prisoner and held until 3 Nov. 1783. He then embarked from Canada to return to France, his place of nativity. He applied in 1791.

Decamp, Matthew. N.Y. Pvt. He served in Capt. Parsons's Company in Col. Goose Van Schaick's Regiment. He received a burst between his breast at Fort Stanwix and was disabled. He lived in the West District, Rennselaerwyck, Albany Co., N.Y. on 2 June 1789. As Mathias DeCamp he received his 200 acres of bounty land 11 Apr. 1808. He was on the 1813 pension list. He died 1 July 1813. His widow was Molly Decamp.

Decamp, Morris. Conn. Sgt. He served in the Conn. Line in the 2nd Cavalry. He was wounded in his foot. He was on the 1791 pension roll of New Jersey. He was on the 1813 pension list of New Jersey.

Deck, Wilhelm. –. —. He was pensioned as an invalid 24 May 1790.

Decker, —. Pa. —. His widow, Elizabeth Decker, was awarded a $40 gratuity and a $40 annuity in Montgomery Co., Pa. 18 Mar. 1834.

Decker, Samuel. N.J. Pvt. He served in the 2nd N.J. Regiment. He was pensioned in 1786. He lived in New York County, N.Y. He was on the 1791 pension roll of New Jersey. He was on the 1813 pension list and died 7 Sep. 1829 in New York City. He lost an arm by a canon ball. He married 4 July 1782. Congress allowed his widow, Sarah Decker, a pension 12 Feb. 1841. He was from Hardy, N.J.

Dedier, John. Pa. Wagon Master. He applied from Germantown, Philadelphia County on 24 Apr. 1820. He enlisted in 1778 in the Pa. Line under Col. Thomas Craig in Capt. John McDay's Company. He was honorably discharged and had been blind eleven years. He died 4 July 1824. He also appeared as John Derdier.

Deeds, Thomas. Pa. —. He was awarded a $40 gratuity in Montgomery Co., Pa. 21 Mar. 1833, 18 Mar. 1834, and 28 Jan. 1836.

Deem, Jacob. Pa. —. He was granted relief 7 Feb. 1812. He died 18 Dec. 1817.

Deem, Samuel. S.C. —. He was pensioned 6 Dec. 1828.

Deemer, Philip. Pa. —. He was awarded a $40 gratuity and a $40 annuity in Northampton Co., Pa. 6 Apr. 1833. He was 80 years old in 1840. He died 27 July 1842.

Deeter, —. Pa. —. His widow, Magdalena Deeter, received a $40 gratuity and a $40 annuity in Northumberland County 3 Apr. 1837.

Deffenderfer, Jacob. Pa. —. He resided in New Holland, Lancaster County and received a $40 gratuity and a $40 annuity 7 May 1855.

Defrance, John. Pa. —. His widow, Martha Defrance, was awarded a $40 annuity in Washington County 27 Mar. 1852 for his Revolutionary service. She died 4 May 1856.

Defrance, Peter. Pa. —. He was granted relief in Berks County 14 Jan. 1835.

DeForrest, Ebenezer. —. —. He served two terms of nine months each in 1775 and 1776. He was wounded in one skirmish and confined several months. He was 82 years old. Congress granted him a pension 20 Dec. 1831.

Defrene, Peter. Pa. —. He was awarded a $40 gratuity and a $40 annuity in Berks Co., Pa. 14 Jan. 1835.

DeGraff, —. —. —. He served as an officer. His widow, Jane DeGraff, applied for a pension in 1836 but never was able to make her claim. She died 6 Mar. 1843. Their daughter, Sarah Allen, had her claim rejected by Congress 20 Jan. 1847.

DeGraffenreidt, Tscharner. Va. Sgt. In 1787 he was aged 34 as based on a register in the hands of Col. Christopher Billups. William Porter of Prince Edward County., formerly a lieutenant under Col. Abraham Buford, testified that DeGraffenreidt of Lunenburg County acted as sergeant. Near Hanging Rock in the Waxsaw settlement in action against Col. Bannister Tarleton in 1780, DeGraffenreidt received 17 wounds in his body with sword, ball, and bayonet. His head and hands were cut most shockingly, and he suffered a bayonet wound in his side. John Wokes, late Captain of the 2nd Va. Regiment also confirmed the service. Lt. John Crute of Prince Edward County was with him at Buford's defeat on 29 May 1780 when they were paroled. James Johnson, Captain of the 6th Va. Regiment, certified that he was a soldier in 1776. He was put on the roll at the rate of £18 per annum on 16 June 1788. He was on the 1813 pension list.

DeGrasse, Admiral. Fr. —. His daughters, Amelie deGrasse, Adelaide deGrasse, Melanie deGrasse, and Silvie deGrasse, had to flee St. Domingo and seek refuge in the United States. They lost their property there. They were awarded financial assistance 18 Feb. 1795. The four daughters received 5,000 francs from the U.S. in 1795 and an annual pension of 2,000 francs for five years in 1798. His daughter, Adelaide, the widow of Grochamps, sought assistance from Congress 16 Feb. 1835. His son, Count Alexandre Francois Auguste de Grasse, sought pecuinary relief for his father. Congress rejected his request 27 Aug. 1848.

Dehm, William. Pa. —. He was awarded a $40 gratuity and a $40 annuity in Berks County 5 Feb. 1836. He died 14 Sep. 1845.

Dedier, Henry. Pa. —. He was from Westmoreland County and was granted relief 21 Mar. 1837. He also appeared as Henry Dieder.

Deihl, George. Pa. —. His widow, Eve Deihl, was awarded a $40 gratuity in York Co., Pa. 16 Feb. 1835.

Deilcord, Jacob. Pa. —. He received a $40 gratuity and a $40 annuity in Lehigh County 9 Feb. 1837. He also appeared as Jacob Dilcord. He died 11 Oct. 1843.

Deily, George. Pa. —. He was awarded a $40 gratuity and a $40 annuity in Lehigh Co., Pa. 15 Apr. 1835. He also appeared as George Deiley.

Deitrich, John. Pa. —. He was granted relief.

Deitz, John Joset. N.Y. Fifer. He served under Col. Vroman in 1778, 1779, 1780, 1781, and 1782 and was discharged 15 Sep. 1782. He was pensioned in 1834 at the rate of $80 per annum. His pension was stopped in 1836 because his name was not on Col. Vroman's roll. Congress granted him a pension retroactively on 25 Jan. 1838. He was from Albany Co., New York.

DeKalb, John, Baron. —. Maj. Gen. He was killed on the field of honor at Camden, S.C. in Aug. 1780. His heirs, Elie Baron of Kalb and Knight of the Royal Order of Military Merit and Maria Anna Caroline of Kalb, widow of Geymuller, sought their father's back pay and five years' pay or bounty land due the widow and families of officers killed in the war on 10 Dec. 1819. They had been unable to apply earlier due to political conditions in France. The heirs had received eleven tracts of land in Ohio. They did not know that they had to pay taxes. The land was alienated and sold. They sought compensation. His grandsons were Rodolphe Theophile Geymuller and Luc Geymuller.

DeKlyn, Barnt. —. —. He and his wife were late of Mercer County, N.J. Congress granted his daughter, Catharine Beatty, relief 23 Mar. 1860.

DeLaColombe, P. Maj. Congress awarded his heirs bounty land on 19 Jan. 1841 even though the time had expired.

Delaney, Thomas. Va. —. His wife, Ann Delaney, was granted £20 support in York Co., Va. on 20 Sep. 1779. He also appeared as Thomas Laney.

Delano, Alpheus. Me. —. He died 9 Mar. 1826. His widow, Margaret Delano, was from Friendship. She was paid $50 under the resolve of 1836.

Delano, Seth. Mass. Sgt. He served in the 10th Mass. Regiment. He was wounded in the head at Tarrytown in 1779 and suffered from dizziness. He enlisted 8 Jan. 1777 and returned a prisoner on 21 Jan. 1779. He lived in Winthrop, Me. in 1792. He was on the 1813 pension list.

Delapt, Richard. Pa. Pvt. His heirs were in Bedford County on 14 Feb. 1786. He was in the Bedford County militia under Capt. John Boyd and was killed in the engagement with Indians near Frankstown on 3 June 1781. His heirs were his widow, Jane Delapt, and child. The child was 6 years old in 1786. He also appeared as Richard Dunlapt.

Delavan, —. Pa. —. His widow, Barbara Delavan, was awarded a $40 gratuity and a $40 annuity in Philadelphia 21 Mar. 1837. She died 1 May 1840.

Delazenne, Christopher. —.—. He sought the commutation of five years' full pay. Congress rejected his claim 11 Apr. 1846.

DeLesdernier, Lewis Frederick. Mass. 1st Lt. He served under Capt. John Preble and Col. John Allen from 1777 to 3 June 1783. He was discharged in Philadelphia. All of his property amounted to only a few articles of trifling value. Congress granted him a pension 10 Jan.1832.

Delian, —. N.Y. —. Agnes Delian was granted a gratuity of a cow.

DeLisselene, Francis G. S.C. Pvt. He was born in South Carolina and was a resident of St. Mary's, Ga. and was aged 82. He enlisted in 1778 at the age of 14. He was at Cat Island near Georgetown to protect from English privateers. He captured 14 horses, was wounded, and made a prisoner. He served under Capt. Barnet and Capt. McGregor from St. James Parish Santee attached to Col. Maybank's Regiment with Marion's Brigade. He was at Lenud's Ferry. Later he fled to North Carolina and worked in a manufactory of arms. He was in the volunteer horse attached to Col. Washington's Legion. He fought at Quinby's Bridge, Monk's Corner, Wambaw, and Scott's Lake. His grandfather and great-grandfather were Huguenots. Congress did not grant him a pension 9 Feb. 1848 because of insufficient proof of his military service.

Delong, Francis. N.Y. Lt. He served in Capt. Hogeboom's County under Col. Peter Van Ness in the militia. He was wounded through his breast and shoulder in 1780. He was pensioned 20 Dec. 1787. He was 48 years old. He lived at Hills Dale, Columbia Co., N.Y. on 6 July 1789. He later lived in Otsego County. He was on the 1813 pension list. He also appeared as Francis DeLong.

Demarest, Peter. N.J. Pvt. He was pensioned 3 Mar. 1807. He was on the 1813 pension list of New York. He died 16 June 1832.

Demming, Lemuel. Conn. Pvt. He served in Huntington's Regiment under Capt. Ozias Bessell. On 27 Aug. 1776 he was wounded in the elbow by a broad sword and taken prisoner at Flat Bush on Long Island. He was pensioned on 7 Sep. 1788 at East Hartford, Conn. at the age of 30. He was on the 1791 and 1813 pension lists as Lemuel Denning. He died 26 Dec. 1815.

Demon, Edward. N.J. Maj. He served in the militia under Col. Aaron Hankinson and died in the service at Amboy 1 Sept. 1776. His widow, Hannah (Thornel) Demon, married secondly Arthur Henry 4 Jan. 1780. She was allowed his half-pay in Hunterdon County from the time of his death to the date of her remarriage in 1796. He also appeared as Edward Dumont.

Demoth, Hans Marcus. N.Y. Capt. He served under Col. Lewis Dubois. He was wounded in the joint of his left elbow on 29 Oct. 1780 at German Flatts and was made a prisoner. He was 57 years old in 1786. He lived at Herkimer, Montgomery Co., N.Y. 10 July 1789. He also appeared as Mark Demond and Hans Marx DeMuth. He was on the 1813 pension list.

Dempsey, —. S.C. —. His widow was Elizabeth Dempsey. There was one child in 1791.

Dempsey, —. Pa. —. His widow, Nancy Dempsey, was awarded a $40 gratuity and a $40 annuity in Cumberland Co., Pa. 19 Mar. 1824.

Dempsey, —. Pa. —. His widow, Margaret Dempsey, of Ross County, Ohio was awarded a $40 gratuity 4 May 1832.

Dempsey, Charles. Pa. Pvt. He applied from Cumberland County. He enlisted 1 Oct. 1776 and was discharged in Aug. 1783. He died about ten days after being pensioned.

Dempsey, Patrick. Pa. Pvt. He was in Philadelphia County on 12 Dec. 1785. He was transferred from the 4th Pa. Regiment to the Invalids. He was discharged 6 Jan. 1783 on account of wounds received in service. He was 55 years old. He was on the 1813 pension list.

Dempsey, Sampson. Pa. —. He applied 17 Dec. 1812 in Hartford Co., Conn. He died 2 May 1826.

Dempsey, Thomas. Va. —. His wife, Alice Dempsey, was granted 100 pounds of pork and 2 barrels of corn in Berkeley County on 21 Nov. 1780. There was one child. She also received 2 barrels of corn and 100 pounds of pork on 19 Mar. 1782.

Dener, George Frederick. S.C. Lt. He served in the German Fusileers for one year prior to the taking of Charleston by the British on 12 May 1780. He was held prisoner for twelve months. He escaped and served under Gen. Francis Marion. On the reorganization of the German Fusileers he became captain and served from Sep. 1782 to Sep. 1783. He married Christiana Speidel 15 Mar. 1787. He died in 1795 and was buried in the Lutheran Church cemetery. He was at Port Royal, Stono, and Savanna. His widow, Christiana Dener, sought an increase in her pension. Congress denied her request because she had no claim against the United States on 10 Dec. 1857. She died 31 Mar. 1856.

Denman, James. Pa. —. He was granted relief.

Dennett, Andrew. Mass. —. He was granted relief.

Denning, James. Pa. —. He received a $40 gratuity 20 Mar. 1838 in Westmoreland County. The war of his service was not indicated.

Denning, William. Pa. Sgt. He applied 24 Mar. 1815. He was in Nathaniel Irish's Company of Artillery Artificers in Col. Benjamin Flowers' Regiment. He was 70 years old. He died 19 Dec. 1830.

Dennis, Alexander. N.C. Pvt. He applied in Rutherford County in 1832. He was drafted in 1779 and served three months under Capt. William Porter. He volunteered for three months on 15 Nov. 1779 under Capt. Gilky. In May 1780 he was in a volunteer troop of cavalry under Captain Adam Hampton. He was in the battle of King's Mountain and served to 1782.

Dennis, Andrew. Pa. —. He was paid $200 for his donation land 25 Feb. 1834. He lived in Ohio. He was awarded a $40 gratuity and a $40 annuity in Washington Co., Ohio 14 Mar. 1842.

Dennis, Edward. Md. Pvt. He was pensioned at the rate of half-pay of a private 25 Mar. 1836.

Dennis, John. Mass. Pvt. He was granted a full pension 5 Apr. 1777. He was in the Invalids under

Capt. Nicola. He was disabled by a musket ball through his right shoulder in 1776 while serving under Col. Arnold. He was 30 years old in 1782. He lost one hand and was wounded in the other.

Dennis, John. N.J. Capt. He served in the 3rd Regiment of the Monmouth County militia under Col. Moses Holmes. He was wounded 3 Oct. 1777 at Shrewsbury. He was made a prisoner and carried to New York where he died 15 Jan. 1778. His widow was Rebeckah Dennis who was granted a pension 26 Jan. 1786. Her maiden name was Rebecca West.

Dennis, John. N.Y. —. He was discharged in May 1781. He, his wife, and four children were granted support 3 Nov. 1781 in Dutchess County.

Dennis, Sumril. S.C. —. His widow was Nancy Dennis of York District in 1827. Her application was rejected.

Dennison, Andrew. Pa. —. He was awarded a $40 gratuity and a $40 annuity in Bucks Co., Pa. 4 May 1832. He died 25 Feb. 1847.

Dennison, Christopher. —. Sgt. He resided at Spencertown, N.Y. at the time of Lexington and repaired to Boston and served as a volunteer some months every year until the end of 1781. He was credited with nine months. Congress allowed him a pension 8 Feb. 1837.

Dennison, David. Me. —. He applied from Freeport. He was paid $50 under the resolve of 1836.

Dennison, James. Mass. Corp. He was in the 7th Regiment and was from Freetown. He was paid $20.

Dennison, James. N.Y. Capt. He served in the 6th Regiment raised in the manor of Van Rensselaerwick. He was attacked with smallpox and died leaving a widow and five children. Nancy Hammond was the sole survivor. Congress rejected her claim 13 Apr. 1858 because militia service was not covered.

Dennison, Prince. Conn. Pvt. He served under Col. Huntington. He was wounded in his arm by a musket ball at Yorktown. He lived in Stonington, Conn. in 1794. He was in the militia. He was granted half a pension 20 Apr. 1796. He died in 1810.

Denniston, John. N.J. Pvt. He was on the 1791 pension roll at the rate of $60 per annum.

Denny, James. Pa. —. He was awarded a $40 gratuity and a $40 annuity in Greene Co., Pa. 4 May 1832.

Denny, Robert. Md. Capt. His widow, Augusta Denny, was pensioned at the rate of half-pay of a captain 2 Feb. 1815.

Denny, Walter. Pa. Capt. His widow, Mary Denny, was in Cumberland County on 6 Dec. 1787. He was in the militia and was killed on 1 May 1778 at the Crooked Billet. He served under Col. Frederick Watts. The administrators of the estate of Mary Denny were Daniel Denny and John Denny on or before 24 July 1805.

Denoon, John. Md. Drummer. He was pensioned at the rate of half-pay of a drummer on 26 Feb. 1829 in Ohio.

Denslow, Benjamin. Conn. Pvt. He served in Col. Thaddeus Cook's Regiment in Capt. Wadsworth's Company. He was wounded by a musket ball in the wrist at the capture of Gen. Burgoyne in New York in Oct. 1777. He was first pensioned 29 Dec. 1778. He was pensioned again on 4 Sep. 1788 at Suffield, Hartford Co., Conn. at the age of 28 years. He later lived in Herkimer Co., N.Y. He was on the 1813 pension list.

Denson, Thomas. S.C. —. He served under Col. Casey, Capt. Stark, and Capt. Irby. He was in the Cherokee Expedition. Thomas Entrekin served with him. He was in Newberry District when he was pensioned on 30 Nov. 1829 in Laurens District. He was confined to bed with palsy for two or three years before he died 1 Nov. 1849. His daughter, Sarah Galligly, sought his arrearage, but had her application rejected.

Dent, George. Md. Pvt. He was pensioned at the rate of half-pay of a private in St. Mary's County in Jan. 1829.

Dent, John. Md. Corp. He was pensioned 4 Mar. 1789. He died 26 Mar. 1803.

Dent, John. Md. Pvt. He served in the 3rd Md. Line. His widow, Eleanor Dent, was pensioned at the rate of half-pay of a private 17 Mar.1835.

Dentlinger, —. Pa. —. His widow, Barbara Dentlinger, was awarded a $40 gratuity and a $40 annuity in York Co., Pa. 15 Apr. 1834. She died 20 Dec. 1834.

Dentzler, —. Pa. —. His widow, Margaret Dentzler, was awarded a $40 gratuity and a $40 annuity in Lebanon Co., Pa. 25 Mar. 1833. She also appeared as Margaret Denstler. She died 4 Dec. 1840.

DePue, William. N.Y. Pvt. He served under Col. Thomas Thomas in the Westchester County militia and was slain 28 Oct. 1781. His widow received a half-pay pension.

Depugh, John. Va. —. His wife, Elizabeth Depugh, and three children were granted financial support in Yohogania Co., Va. 28 Apr. 1778.

Depuy, Benjamin. —. —. He was pensioned.

Derby, Joseph. Mass. Sgt. He was in Crane's Artillery and was from Boston. His widow, Elizabeth Derby, was paid $50.

Derham, —. Va. —. His wife, Mary Derham, was granted £10 support in Fauquier Co., Va. in Aug. 1776.

Derr, —. Pa. —. His widow, Elizabeth Derr, was awarded a $40 gratuity and a $40 annuity in Lancaster County 3 Mar. 1837. The place of her residence was corrected to Lebanon County 3 Apr. 1837.

Derr, Mathias. Pa. —. He was awarded a $40 gratuity and a $40 annuity in Lebanon Co., Pa. 15 Apr. 1835.

Derrah, Archibald. Pa. —. He was awarded a $40 gratuity in Bucks Co., Pa. 6 Apr. 1833 and on 30 Jan. 1834.

Derrick, James. —. —. He received a Revolutionary War pension.

Derrick, Joseph. Mass. Sgt. He served in the 4th Regiment under Col. William Shepard and Capt. D. Holbrook. He was wounded by a musket ball through his right shoulder. He was disabled by the hedick [?headache]. He resided in Plympton, Mass. in 1787 and was 55 years old.

Derumple, Robert. Pa. —. He enlisted in 1781 under Capt. Combie at Carlisle. His second tour was under Harmane. He was 71 years old and had a small family. He was from Beaver County. He also appeared as Robert Dalrymple.

Derusia, Anthony. N.Y. Pvt. He served in 2nd N.Y. Regiment under Capt. Wilkens and Col. Philip van Courtland. His widow, Mary Derusia, received a seven year half-pay pension.

Desdevens, Maurice. —. —. He was pensioned under the act of 6 May 1782.

Deshon, James. Me. —. He was from Waterboro. He was paid $50 under the resolve of 1836.

Dessausure, Lewis. S.C. Lt. He was killed 1 Nov. 1779. His heirs received settlement from the state.

Deter, Jacob. Pa. —. He applied 17 Feb. 1787. He also appeared as Jacob Teter.

Dether, —. Pa. —. Hid widow, Eve Dether, was awarded a $40 gratuity and a $40 annuity in Lehigh County in 8 Apr. 1826.

Detman, —. Pa. —. His widow, Dorothy Detman, was awarded a $40 gratuity and a $40 annuity in York County 12 Mar. 1836. She died 7 Jan. 1845. She also appeared as Dorothy Dataman.

DeTreville, John. S.C. Capt. He served in the 4th Regiment. He died in 1790. His two surviving children were Robert De Treville and Harriet De Treville. Both children died in 1817. The children of his son, Richard De Treville, Ellis De Treville, Caroline De Treville, Elizabeth De Treville, and Harriet De Treville, and the son of his daughter, Samuel Lawrance, were due their grandfather's five years' half pay 22 Dec. 1837.

Detrick, —. Pa. —. His widow, Hannah Detrick, received a $40 gratuity in Crawford County 17 Jan. 1837.

Devaney, Aaron. —. —. He applied in Oct. 1834 in Rutherford Co., N.C. at the age of 87.

Develin, James. S.C. —. He served under Col. William Thompson, Col. Andrew Pickens, and Capt. Joseph Dawson. He received a bounty land warrant for 200 acres. The warrant laid on land previously granted, and he lost his land in a suit at law plus court costs of $50 in 1810. He was pensioned in 1820 in Abbeville District and died 26 Mar. 1825. John Develin sought his arrearage 21 Nov. 1826. He also appeared as James Devlin.

Develin, Henry. Va. Pvt. His widow, Eleanor Develin, lived in Berkeley County in Sep. 1786 and in Monongalia County in 1803. He served in the 12th Va. Regt. in 1778 and died in hospital in N.J. She was put on the roll at the rate of £8 per annum on 14 Dec. 1786.

Deveny, Daniel. Pa. —. He was awarded a $40 gratuity and a $40 annuity in Juniata Co., Pa. 27 Jan. 1835. He died 1 May 1835.

Deveny, John. Pa. —. He applied from York County on 7 Feb. 1821. He enlisted in the 4th Pa. Regiment in the fall of 1775 under Capt. Robison and Col. Anthony Wayne. He was 64 years old.

Devinney, James. Pa. —. He was awarded a $40 gratuity and a $40 annuity in Juniata Co., Pa. 10 Apr. 1835. He was 104 years of age in 1840. He died 22 Aug. 1840.

DeVoe, John. N.Y. Pvt. He was pensioned in Aug. 1806 in New York County. His pension was increased to the rate of $5 per month from 30 Jan. 1808. He was on the 1813 pension list.

DeVoe, Moses. N.Y. Pvt. He was pensioned in 1807.

Dewalt, Michael. Pa. —. He applied from Franklin County. In 1781 he was at Ashley Hills about four miles from Charleston, S.C. and had been in the service better than four years as a regular soldier in the 1st Pa. Regiment. He enlisted in the spring of 1778 in Capt. Joseph Prowl's Company in Col. John Patton's Regiment. After two years he was transferred to the Va. Line in Capt. Oldham's Company under Col. Campbell upon whose death Col. Green replaced him. He was discharged by General Morgan at Shenandoah, Va. but he lost his discharge. Daniel Welker saw him in the service in the spring of 1778. Henry Br---- enlisted him.

Dewberry, John. Va. —. His mother, Mary Dewberry, was granted £6.10 support on 20 Oct. 1777 and £10 support in York County on 16 Nov. 1778.

Dewees, —. Pa. —. His widow, Mary Dewees, was awarded a $40 annuity in Montgomery County 5 Feb. 1836. She died 20 Nov. 1845.

Dewees, Samuel. Pa. —. He was awarded a $40 gratuity and a $40 annuity in Baltimore, Md. 7 Apr. 1830.

Dewees, William. Pa. —. He owned the estate of Valley Forge in Chester County. When the British landed at the head of Elk River and marched to Philadelphia, Quartermaster Gen. Mifflin ordered the greater portion of provisions and military stores. While Gen. Washington and the army remained there in the winter of 1777 and 1778, they totally destroyed the timber. Congress did not grant relief. His widow was Sarah Dewees.

Dewey, Ebenezer. N.H. Pvt. He volunteered in Oct. 1779 under Capt. Elias Mack and Col. Timothy Ellis to guard the frontier at Haverhill, New Hampshire and Newburg, Vermont and served one year. He was a resident of Gilsum, N.H. In June 1781 he enlisted for three months under Capt. Peter Page and Col. Ebenezer Walbridge and did duty at Lake Champlain. After the burning of Royalton by the Indians in the fall of 1780, he returned home. Congress granted him a pension for twelve months of service on 4 Jan. 1841.

Dewey, Martin. —. —. Congress rejected his claim because it was not sustained by proof on 30 Mar. 1848.

Dewey, Samuel. N.Y. —. He enlisted in Apr. 1780 in Washington County. He served under Capt. Sherwood and Col. DuBois in July 1780. He was taken prisoner 15 Oct. 1780 by Maj. Carleton under Sir John Johnson and taken to St. Johns, Canada and then to Caughnawaga where he was detained for two years by Indians. He was sent to Quebec and confined to the end of the war. Congress awarded him a pension 7 Feb. 1850.

Dewire, James. Md. —. He was retired from the Invalids on pension 1 Sep. 1782.

Dewitt, —. S.C. —. Martha Dewitt was paid an annuity.

Dewitt, Jacob. Pa. —. He was awarded a $50 gratuity in Pike County on 19 Mar. 1816.

Dewitt, Martin. S.C. —. He served two years in the militia. He was in his 65th year and had a wife and four young children. Kindred Holloman was acquainted with him in the army. He was pensioned in Darlington District on 4 Dec. 1828. He was paid to 1834. He applied to the federal government, but failed in being approved. He prayed to be restored in South Carolina and was pensioned 7 Dec. 1836.

DeWitt, William. Pa. Pvt. He served in Col. Proctor's Regiment. He was wounded by a musket ball shot through his left thigh in 1777 at Short Hills. He resided at Luzerne, Penn. in 1796. He was granted half a pension 20 Apr. 1796. He was on the 1813 pension list.

Dews, —. Ga. —. His wife, Mary Dews, and three children were granted assistance 20 Aug. 1782.

Deyer, Emanuel. Pa. —. He was awarded a $40 gratuity and a $40 annuity in Lancaster County in 1836.

Deygart, John. N.Y. Capt. He served under Col. Klock in the Montgomery County militia and was slain 6 Aug. 1777. His children, Zaphrimus Deygart, Warner Deygart, Rudolph Deygart, Elizabeth Deygart, Catharine Deygart, and Gertrite Deygart, received a half-pay pension for seven years.

Dibble, Israel. Conn. Pvt. He served under Col. Whitney in Capt. Griswold's Company. He received seven wounds by a bayonet in different parts of his body in 1777 at West Chester. He lived in Cornwall, Conn. in 1795. He was in the militia. He was granted one-third of a pension 20 Apr. 1796. He was on the 1813 pension list.

Dickerson, Henry. Pa. —. He applied from Washington County on 11 June 1823. He enlisted in Aug. 1776 in the 8th Pa. Regiment in Capt. Van Swearingen's Company. Thomas Stokely was in the same regiment. He served three years and was honorably discharged by Col. Bayard. He was elected a captain back in Washington County and later a major. He was in the battles of Piscataway, Chestnut Ridge, and two battles near Saratoga with Gen. Burgoyne where he took two prisoners. His horse died after being wounded by Indians. He had a crippled wife.

Dickerson, John. —. —. He was at Brandywine, Germantown, Monmouth, and Stony Point. He served more than four years and died 9 July 1833. His widow, Catharine Dickerson, was ignorant and did not apply until 1853. She could not prove her marriage so her request was rejected. She was granted five years' pension from 1836 on 22 June 1854. The Iowa legislature by a joint resolution recommended the widow for relief from Congress 16 Apr. 1858. She was granted same 11 May 1858. She was probably over 80 years old. Her first child was born in 1796 three years after their marriage.

Dickerson, Robert. Va. —. His heirs received bounty land from Virginia. Congress rejected the claim of the heirs for U.S. bounty land on 30 July 1842.

Dickerson, William. Va. Pvt. He applied from Hanover County on 6 Jan. 1787 at the age of 27. He enlisted in Feb. 1776 and served two years under Lt. Col. O. Towles in the 6th Virginia Regiment. He was wounded at Brandywine and had his right arm amputated above the elbow. He was awarded a £30 gratuity and an annuity of full pay on 18 May 1778. He was awarded an increase of £26 to his gratuity on 29 Oct. 1779. On 23 May 1780 due to depreciation his gratuity was set at £150. He was continued at the rate of £18 per annum on 5 Jan. 1787. He died 5 Feb. 1803. He also appeared as William Dickinson.

Dickey, Anthony. Ga. —, He served as a liberty man in Richmond Co., Ga. under Capt. George Dickey, Lt. William Green, and Col. Candler. The British drove them out of Georgia in 1777. He next served under Capt. James McFadden and Col. Andrew Hampton. He was at Ninety Six under Capt. John McClain. He was born in Chester Co., Penn. 29 Nov. 1745 and went to Georgia in 1771. His brother was George Dickey. He was 87 years of age when he applied in Rutherford Co., N.C. 10 Sep. 1832.

Dickey, Charles. Pa. —. He applied 15 Oct. 1813 because his family could not support him. He was 53 years old. He applied from Montgomery County on 3 June 1822. He died 20 Aug. 1823. He served in the 11th Regiment.

Dickhaut, Francis. Pa. —. He was granted relief.

Dickinson, John. Va. Capt. He was on the 1785 pension list. He may have been the one of that name from Augusta County. He was continued on the pension list at the rate of £50 per annum on 15 Nov. 1787.

Dickinson, Seth. Mass. —. He served ten months in 1776 in the militia. Congress granted him a pension 22 Dec. 1831.

Dickinson, Varsal. N.Y. Pvt. He served under Col. Dubois. His wife, Catherine Dickinson, was granted support while her husband was away in the service 18 Oct. 1778. There were six children on 3 Nov. 1781 in Dutchess County. His name may have been Vestal Dickinson.

Dickman, John. —. —. He died 6 Mar. 1833. His widow was Phebe Dickman. Congress allowed her a pension 5 Mar. 1840.

Dickson, —. S.C. —. His widow, Ann Dickson, had one child in 1791. She also appeared as Ann Dixon. She was from Salem.

Dickson, —. S.C. —. His widow, Margaret Dickson, was being pensioned in 1791.

Dickson, —. Pa. —. His widow, Miriam Dickson, was awarded a $40 gratuity and a $40 annuity in Perry Co., Pa. 24 Mar. 1828. She was 84 years old in 1840.

Dickson, John. Pa. Sgt. He was in Philadelphia County on 2 Apr. 1788. He served in the Pa. Artillery and was disabled by sickness contracted in the service while a prisoner. He suffered from a great weakness in his urinary passage and involuntary discharge of urine. He entered the service in June 1776 in Capt. Magaw's Regiment. He was taken prisoner at Fort Washington 1 Nov. 1776. Following his release on 5 Jan. 1777, he joined Capt. Gibbs Jones' Company of Artillery on 23 Jan. 1777. He served 7 years, 3 months, and 28 days. He also served under Capt. Lt. David Fink. He was 34 years old. He also appeared as John Dixon. He died 22 June 1804.

Dickson, Marshal. N.Y. Pvt. He served in Capt. Samuel Lawrence's Company in the Westchester County militia under Col. Thaddeus Crane. He and Lt. Nathaniel Reynolds went to Crompond to join the troops. He was wounded in the upper part of his thigh through the lower part of his hip at Crompond on 22 June 1779. He was under the command of Lt. Isaac Keeler. He was 25 years old on 26 Apr. 1788. He lived in Lower Salem, Westchester Co., N.Y. on 17 June 1788. He also appeared as Marshall Dixon. He was on the 1813 pension list.

Dickson, Matthew. S.C. Pvt. He was about 95 years old and had resided in the state about 35 years. His captain, James Martin, proved his service. He was blind. He was pensioned in Pendleton District 30 Nov. 1827. He died 10 July 1830. His arrears were granted to his executor, Hugh Gaston, on 25 Nov. 1830.

Dickson, Patrick. Pa. —. He received a $40 gratuity and a $40 annuity in Beaver County 14 Apr. 1827.

Didson, Seth. Mass. Pvt. He served in the 3rd Regiment and was from Dracut. His widow, Bridget Didson, was pensioned.

Dieffendorph, Jacob. N.Y. Lt. He served in Capt. Henry Dieffendorph's Company. He was wounded in his left foot by the accidental discharge of a musket in 1775. He lived in Connajoharrie, N.Y. in 1794. He served in the militia.

Diffendorf, Henry. N.Y. Capt. He was slain 6 Aug. 1777 at Oriskany. His widow, Rosina Diffendorff, received a half-pay pension for seven years. He also appeared as Henry Dittendorf.

Dietrich, George. Pa. —. He was pensioned 21 Aug. 1819. He died 10 Aug. 1826.

Digges, Dudley. Va. Lt. He served in the cavalry from 1779 to 1783. He was in state service and joined the Southern Army in 1780. He was pensioned 8 Jan.1820 in Louisa County at the rate of $90 per annum and $100 immediate relief. He had sons named Cole C. Digges, Robert N. Digges, and Seneca T. P. Digges. He received his commutation of full pay for five years in lieu of half-pay for life as a lieutenant of cavalry in the Virginia line with no interest on 27 Feb. 1827 at which time his pension was discontinued.

Dike, Daniel. Mass. —. He was from Bethel, Vt. He also appeared as Daniel Dyke, *quo vide*.

Dike, Daniel, Jr. Mass. —. He served in the 1st Regiment and was from Pittsfield. He was paid $20.

Dill, John. S.C. —. His widow, Elizabeth Dill, was pensioned in Greenville District on 25 Nov. 1830 for her widowhood at the rate of $30. Her children were Runnels G. Dill born 28 Dec. 1819, Hiram W. Dill born 15 May 1822, and Manly F. Dill born 15 Aug. 1825. She was to receive $20 per annum for each child until they arrived at the age of 12. Her pension was revoked on 17 Dec. 1831 from a petition of sundry citizens of Greenville District stating that her husband did not die from an illness contracted in the war. It was a scheme which David Jackson, justice of the quorum, arranged with her for receiving half of the pension.

Dill, Lemuel. Mass. —. He served in the 3rd Regiment and was from Hingham. He was paid $20.

Dill, Reynolds. S.C. —. He was pensioned in Greenville District on 17 Dec. 1831. He also appeared as Runnels Dill. He married Evaline Hooper 6 July 1830. Jacob Jackson performed the marriage. He died 27 Oct. 1844 and James Odam was administrator of his estate. He sought the arrearage of $39.50. His widow had her application rejected in 1852 because she was not married to the soldier at the time of his service.

Dill, Samuel. Mass. —. He served in the 3rd Regiment and was from Hingham. He was paid $20.

Dillard, James. Va. Capt. He served in the 10th Regiment and was from Amherst County. His heirs sought his commutation. Congress rejected their claim because he had received it in his life-time on 2 July 1836.

Dillard, William. Va. Pvt. He was killed in the service and his widow, Mary Dillard, lived in Culpeper County in 1792. She was pensioned at the rate of £12 per annum on 20 Dec. 1792.

Dillenbach, Andrew. N.Y. Capt. He served in the Montgomery County militia under Col. Jacob Klock and was killed at Oriskany 6 Aug. 1777. His children, Margaret Dillenbach, Mary Dillenbach, Andrew Dillenbach, and Magdalen Dillenbach, received a half-pay pension for seven years.

Dillon, Thomas. Va. —. His two children were awarded £15 in Northampton Co., Va. on 8 Dec.

1778.

Dimick, Peter. —. —. He served seven months as a substitute for Joseph Dimick and had had his application for his pension rejected because the rolls bore his name as Joseph rather than Peter Dimick. Frederick Pearl corroborated his service. Congress granted him a pension 27 Jan. 1836.

Dimm, —. **Pa.** —. His widow, Margaret Dimm, was awarded a $40 gratuity in Lycoming County 20 May 1839, 5 May 1841 for his Revolutionary service. She received a $40 gratuity 18 Apr. 1843 and in Apr. 1846.

Dimon, David. Conn. Lt. Col. He was killed 17 Sep. 1777. His seven years' half-pay of $2,520 was paid to his heirs.

Dimon, Thomas. R.I. —. He served in the militia and provided clothing and supplies for the troops. Congress rejected the petition of his grand-daughter, Deborah Chaffee, for compensation 26 Feb. 1856.

Dimond, Moses. N.Y. Pvt. He served under Capt. Pawling and Col. Van Cortlandt. He was slain 10 Dec. 1781. His widow was granted a half-pay pension.

Dinges, —. N.Y. —. His widow was granted support during the war.

Dingman, Gerardus. N.Y. Pvt. He was pensioned 15 Jan. 1810 in Oneida Co., N.Y. He was on the 1813 pension list.

Dismire, Joseph. S.C. —. Legionnaire. He served aboard the frigate *South Carolina* under Commodore Alexander Gillon and was paid $126.41 on 20 Sep. 1808.

Ditcher, Robert. Pa. —. He was awarded a $40 gratuity and a $40 annuity in York, Pa. 22 Apr. 1829.

Ditlow, John. Pa. —. He was awarded a $40 gratuity in Berks Co., Pa. 6 Apr. 1833. He was awarded a $40 gratuity and a $40 annuity in Berks Co., Pa. 1 Apr. 1834. He died 4 May 1842.

Dixon, —. **Pa.** —. His widow, Mary Dixon, was awarded a $40 gratuity and a $40 annuity in Cumberland Co., Pa. 31 Jan. 1825.

Dixon, —. **S.C.** —. His widow, Ann Dixon, was paid an annuity between 1814 and 1821. [Compare with Dickson, — with widow Ann].

Dixon, George. Conn. Pvt. He served in the 2nd Regiment of Artillery. He was wounded in the service. He was pensioned in Mar. 1783. He died in 1803. He was on the 1813 pension list.

Dixon, Harry. N.C. Col. His heirs sought his commutation of five years' full pay. They did not establish same by testimony and did not prove that he died in the war. In Apr. 1793 $360 was paid to him as a pension or to his widow and children for seven years' half-pay. In neither case, however, could he have been entitled to commutation. It would seem that the payment was as a pension, but his name was not on the list of pensioners. Congress rendered its decision 18 Jan. 1835. [It is apparent that his record was overlooked because his record was under Henry Dixon rather than his diminutive Harry Dixon as indicated by the next entry.]

Dixon, Henry. N.C. Lt. Col. His widow, Martha Dixon, applied in Caswell County in 1786. He died in the service on 17 July 1782 leaving a widow and seven children, viz. Wynne Dixon. Roger Dixon, Elizabeth Dixon, Robert Dixon, Frances Dixon, Henry Dixon, and Susannah Dixon.

Dixon, James. Pa. —. He was granted relief.

Dixon, Jared. —. Pvt. He served under Col. Chandler. He was wounded at Germantown in 1777 by a ventral rupture. He lived in Chittenden, Vt. in 1792.

Dixon, John. Pa. Pvt. He was on the 1789 pension list. Compare with John Dickson.

Dixon, William. Md. Pvt. He was pensioned at the rate of half-pay of a private 19 Feb. 1819.

Doan, Samuel. Pa. Lt. He served under Col. Thomas in 1775 and marched to Boston in 1776. He was appointed to the Flying Camp until the unit was discharged. He next served in the 11th Regiment under Col. Hampton to 1778 when he became supernumerary. He returned home and was elected colonel of the Bucks County militia which he commanded to the end of the war.

Dobson, Thomas. Pa. —. He was awarded a $40 gratuity and a $40 annuity in Northumberland Co., Pa. 3 Feb. 1824. He died 13 Feb. 1829.

Doby, John. S.C. —. He was killed 18 Aug. 1780. His widow, Elizabeth Doby, was allowed an annuity 22 Nov. 1785. She was in Lancaster District in 1796.

Docherty, John. N.J. Pvt. He served in the 1st Regiment. He was wounded in both thighs and suffered from a rupture. He was 57 years old and was from Maidenhead. He was on the 1791 pension roll at the rate of $60 per annum.

Dodd, Abijah. N.J. —. He was pensioned in Essex County on 4 Mar. 1836 at the rate of $50 per annum.

Dodd, Daniel. N.Y. Pvt. He was pensioned 18 Apr. 1814 and died 3 Sep. 1822.

Dodd, Guy. —. Conn. He served under Capt. Phineas Bradley in the artillery at New Haven from 6 June 1780 to 1 Jan. 1781 for six months and 25 days. He next served from 9 Apr. 1781 to 1 Jan. 1782 under Capt. William Vandusen and Capt. John Warner for eight months and twenty-two days. He married Hannah Heaton 4 Oct. 1784 in the Congregational Church, Cheshire, Conn. He died 7 Apr. 1795. His widow married secondly Jeremiah Carrier on 18 May 1814. He died 18 June 1837. His widow, Hannah Carrier, of Oneida, New York was granted a pension by private act of Congress on 8 Mar. 1842 for 15 months and 17 days of service for five years at the rate of $51.75 per annum from 4 Mar. 1836 on 8 Mar. 1842.

Dodd, John. Va. —. His wife, Mary Dodd, was granted £10 support in Caroline Co., Va. 8 Jan. 1778.

Dodd, William. Va. —. His mother, Ann Dodd, and her children were granted two barrels of corn for their support in Chesterfield Co., Va. 7 July 1780 while he was away in Continental service.

Doddridge, John. Pa. —. He was wounded twice in the arm. He was awarded a $40 gratuity and a $40 annuity in Berks Co., Pa. 3 Feb. 1812.

Dodge, William. Mass. —. He was paid $20.

Dodridge, Jacob. Pa. —. He received a $40 gratuity and a $40 annuity 23 Jan. 1813. He was from Berks County.

Dodridge, John. Pa. —. He received a $40 annuity and a $40 gratuity 22 Jan. 1811.

Dodson, Benjamin. Me. —. He was from Starks.

Dodson, George. Va. —. He was wounded at Guilford Courthouse and applied from Pittsylvania County. He was pensioned on 10 Feb. 1830 at the rate of $60 per annum with $30 immediate relief. He died 27 June 1848.

Doebler, Abraham. Pa. —. He was awarded a $40 gratuity and a $40 annuity in Lebanon County 1 Apr. 1836.

Doerr, —. Pa. —. His widow was Catharine Doerr.

Doggett, George. Va. —. He served in the militia and was accidentally wounded at headquarters in Pennsylvania by a gun which went off. The ball entered his thigh above the knee and came out the small part of his leg. He applied 20 May 1778.

Dogherty, Patrick. Va. Pvt. He served in Capt. Mims' Co., 1st Va. Regiment. He was wounded in the neck by a musket ball passing through at Charleston, S.C. He lived in Va. in 1794.

Dohrman, Arnold Henry. —. —. He aided American seamen through captives on the shores of Portugal in the Revolution in 1780. He died in Steubenville, Ohio in 1813 leaving a widow, Rachel Dohrman, and eleven minor children. She was granted an annuity of $3,000 for her widowhood and each child was granted a $100 annuity per year until age 21. He had a brother, Jacob

Dohrman. His heirs applied 27 Jan. 1817.

Dolbear, Benjamin. Me. —. He was from Freeman. He was paid $50 under the resolve of 1836.

Dolby, John. S.C. —. His widow was Elizabeth Dolby in 1786. There was one child in 1791.

Dolby, William. Del. Sgt. He served in Fanning's Artillery. He was on the 1813 pension list. He transferred to Maryland 4 Sep. 1819. He died 19 May 1822.

Dole, Enoch. —. Surgeon's Mate. He entered the service 27 Apr. 1775 and was killed at Dorchester 9 Mar. 1776. His widow was Eunice Dole, and she died 23 Sep. 1822. His only child, Barent W. Dole, sought a pension from Congress 5 Mar. 1860. He was not entitled to any benefits.

Dole, James. N.Y. Sgt. He served under Col. Elisha Sheldon in the Cavalry. He was wounded in his left hip by a gun shot on 17 Aug. 1780 at Kingstreet, N.Y. He resided in Lansingburg, N.Y. in 1794 and had been in Pennsylvania. He enlisted 7 May 1777 as a sergeant in Capt. Epaphrus Sheldon's Co. and was promoted to lieutenant. He received the commutation which had not been returned. He was aged 37 in 1 June 1788. He lived in Albany Co., N.Y. in Nov. 1788. He was on the 1813 pension list.

Dole, Lemuel. Mass. —. He was from Concord. His widow, Rebecca Dole, was paid $50.

Dole, Samuel. Pa. Lt. He was on the 1789 pension list.

Dole, William. N.Y. —. He was granted relief.

Doll, Henry. Pa. —. He was awarded a $40 gratuity and a $40 annuity in York Co., Pa. 5 Apr. 1826.

Doll, John. Pa. —. He was awarded a $40 gratuity and a $40 annuity in Lehigh Co., Pa. 5 Mar. 1828.

Doll, Martin. Pa. —. He was awarded a $40 gratuity in York Co., Pa. 23 Apr. 1829.

Dollar, Reuben. S.C. Sgt. He served under Capt. William Miles of Spartanburgh, Col. Thomas, and Capt. Abraham Allen. Walker [?] Williamson was a fellow soldier. He applied from Anderson District in 1831. It was rejected.

Dollinger, John. Pa. —. He was awarded a $40 gratuity and a $40 annuity in Schuylkill County 1 Apr. 1836. He also appeared as John Dolinger. He was 91 years old in 1840. He died 21 Nov. 1843.

Dollins, —. Va. —. His wife, Dice Dollins, was allowed assistance in Caroline County in 1778.

Dollins, William. Va. —. His wife, Ann Dollins, and three children were granted support in Oct. 1780 in Westmoreland County.

Dollison, John. Mass. —. He served in the 6th Regiment and was paid $20.

Dolten, —. Va. Pvt. He was in Continental Service. His widow, Mary Dolten, was pensioned 1 Mar. 1779. [Compare with the entry *infra*.]

Dolton, John. Va. Pvt. He enlisted as a soldier in the 1st State Troops under Lt. Joseph Selden and died in Nov. 1777 at the home of William Crawley. He left a widow and seven children, the oldest 12 years of age. His widow, Mary Dalton, applied for a pension from Henrico County on 6 Nov. 1786. She was put on the roll at the rate of £8 per annum on 27 Dec. 1788. He also appeared as John Dorton. She had broken her arm and had three children with her. [Compare with the entry *supra*.]

Dominey, Andrew. S.C. —. He served under Col. Godwyn and Thompson. Benjamin Hodge served with him. His widow, Margaret Dominey, was pensioned in Fairfield District 7 Dec. 1835. She was paid as late as 1842.

Donald, William. Pa. —. He was granted relief 31 Mar. 1835. He was 89 years old in 1840. He died 31 Mar. 1842 in Westmoreland County.

Donaldson, John. Pa. Sgt. He applied from Lycoming County 14 Feb. 1817. He was in the 6th Pa. Regiment under Col. Robert Magaw. He was discharged at West Point 24 July 1779. He was lame and had been unable to walk above five years. He was between 66 and 70 years old.

His son was John Donaldson, Jr. His children were grown and were mixing in strange families.

Donaldson, Lothario. Mass. —. He enlisted for three years in Mar. 1781 under Col. Henry Jackson and served to Feb. 1784. He moved from Medfield to Rochester, N.Y. in 1827. Congress granted him a pension 15 Mar. 1832. His son-in-law was Walter H. Johnson of Philadelphia.

Donally, James. N.Y. Pvt. He served in Capt. Parsons's Company in the 1ˢᵗ N.Y. Regiment under Col. Goose Van Schaick. He was worn out by long and faithful service. He was 86 years old in 1786. He lived in New York City, N.Y. in 1787. He also appeared as James Donely.

Donally, Patrick. Md. Pvt. He was pensioned at the rate of half-pay of a private in Frederick County on 25 Jan. 1816. His widow, Elizabeth Donally, received the arrearage of his pension 20 Feb. 1829. She was pensioned at the same rate 6 Mar. 1832. She also appeared as Elizabeth Donnelly.

Done, Thomas. N.Y. Matross. He served in the artillery under Capt. Isaiah Wool in Col. John Lamb's Regiment and was wounded in the eye by a flash of a cannon before Quebec. He lost his sight. He was in Newburgh, Ulster Co., N.Y. in 1785 and 28 May 1789. He was aged 3- in Feb. 1786. He later lived in Rensselaer County. He was on the 1813 pension list.

Donley, David. Pa. —. He was awarded a $40 gratuity in Washington Co., Pa. 1 Mar. 1832.

Donlin, William. Pa. —. He was disabled at Stoney Point and received a pension. He set out from Westmoreland Co. into the wilderness to Kentucky and was murdered before he arrived. He left orphaned children. His widow, Thomsy Donlin, was of Post St. Vincent on 4 May 1787.

Donnel, William. Pa. —. He received assistance in Westmoreland County 31 Mar. 1825.

Donnell, John. —. —. He was a pensioner and died in 1830. His widow died in 1840. Mary B. Perry and the other heirs sought pension for five years. Congress approved same 18 Mar. 1844.

Donnelly, Francis. Pa. Sgt. He applied at Harrisburg 17 May 1813. He enlisted in the Pa. Regiment of Artillery in 177- and served until discharged in March 1781. Col. Andrew Porter proved his service.

Donoehy, James. Pa. Pvt. He served under Capt. George Graff and Col. James Cunningham in the Flying Camp. He was killed at Long Island 27 Aug. 1776. His widow, Jane Donoehy, was pensioned 28 Mar. 1787. He also appeared as James Donahy and James Donahay.

Donnom, William. S.C. Lt. He was killed 9 Nov. 1779.

Donovan, John. Pa. Pvt. He was in Philadelphia County on 12 June 1786. He served in the 3ʳᵈ Pa. Regiment and was wounded in the leg at Brandywine. He was 35 years old. On 26 Oct.1786 he sought an advance to help with the expenses of burial of his stepson, Thomas, who died the day before. He died 31 Jan. 1803.

Dooley, —. S.C. —. His widow, Mary Dooley, was from Richland District. There were children in 1791.

Doolittle, Hackaliah. N.Y. Pvt. He was on the 1813 pension list.

Doran, James. Pa. Pvt. He was in Philadelphia County on 8 Jan. 1787. He served in the 1ˢᵗ Pa. Regiment. He was in Capt. Thomas Boude's Company in Col. Daniel Brodhead's Regiment. He lost a leg by a wound on James Island, S.C. He was 53 years old. He had lived in Maryland but returned to Pennsylvania.

Doran, Miles. Mass. —. He served in the 6ᵗʰ Regiment and was from Boston. He was paid $20.

Dornbach, John. Pa. —. His widow, Anna Maria Dornbach, was awarded a $40 gratuity and a $40 annuity in Columbia Co., Pa. 15 Jan. 1829. She was 67 years old in 1840.

Dorgan, John. Md. Pvt. He was pensioned in Talbot County at the rate of half-pay of a private 26

Jan. 1828.

Dorman, Gershom. Conn. Pvt. He served in the 2nd Dragoons under Col. Sheldon. He was wounded in the arm by a stroke of a broadsword in June 1779 at Poundridge. He enlisted 16 Apr. 1777 for the war. He lived at Sharon, Conn. in 1794. He was granted one-third of a pension 20 Apr. 1796. He resided some time in Berkshire Co., Mass. and died 1 June 1820 in Windham Co., Conn. He was on the 1813 pension list.

Dorrent, John. Md. —. He was granted relief.

Dorsey, Ely. Md. —. He was paid $960 in Frederick County on 19 Feb. 1819.

Dorsey, James. Mass. —. He served in the Artillery and was from New York. He was paid $20.

Dorsey, Richard. Md. Capt. He was wounded at the battle of Camden, S.C. He was pensioned at the rate of half-pay of a captain in Nov. 1791. He served in the artillery to the end of the war. His representatives sought his commutation of five years of full pay, but Congress rejected their claim 10 Feb. 1835 since he had already received it.

Dorsey, William. S.C. —. He was paid $192.66 for service in the S.C. Continental Line on 20 Dec. 1810.

Dorsius, John. S.C. —. His annuity was £50 in 1787.

Dosh, —. Pa. —. His widow, Catharine Dosh, was awarded a $40 gratuity and a $40 annuity in Lancaster Co., Pa. 15 Apr. 1834.

Doss, John. Va. —. His wife, Judith Doss, and one child were granted £14 support in Cumberland Co., Va. 24 Nov. 1777.

Dotrow, John. Md. Pvt. He was pensioned in Frederick County at the rate of half-pay of a private 12 Mar. 1828.

Doty, Isaac. N.J. Sgt. He served under Capt. Peter Baley and Capt. Jeremiah Dunn. He was mortally wounded on Long Island. He had two musket balls shot through both thighs and one through his hand. He died about 29 Aug. 1776. He married in 1758. His widow, Mary Doty, married secondly Joseph Stewart 20 June 1779. She received a half-pay pension in Somerset County 15 Apr. 1799.

Doty, Jarathmeel. Mass. Marine. He served aboard the continental frigate *Alliance* under John Barry and was shot through the body by a musket ball. It entered near his back bone and came out his right side. He was pensioned at the rate of one-third pay from 1 Apr. 1783 on 18 Mar. 1785. He resided in Swansey, Mass. in 1788 and was 24 years old. He was on the 1813 pension list as Jonathan [sic] Doty. He transferred from Berkshire Co., Mass. to Rutland Co., Vt. 4 Mar. 1819.

Doty, Thomas. Mass. Quarter Master Sgt. He served in the 2nd Regiment under Capt. Seth Drew and Col. Ebenezer Sprout. He was disabled by a hectic habit. He resided in Gloucester, Mass. in 1788 and was 40 years old. He was from Carver, Mass. when he was paid $20 by the Commonwealth. He was on the 1813 pension list. He died 22 Apr. 1818 in Plymouth Co., Mass.

Dougan, John. Pa. —. He married Mary Evans in the English church in Reading, Berks Co., Pa. The minister, Alexander Murray, thought it was about the beginning of 1770; his records had been lost in the Revolutionary War.

Dougherty, —. Pa. —. His widow, Elizabeth Dougherty, was awarded a $40 gratuity and a $40 annuity in Washington Co., Pa. 9 Mar. 1825.

Dougherty, Andrew. Pa. —. He was pensioned in Armstrong County 21 Feb. 1838. He was 71 years old in 1840.

Dougherty, Barnabas. Md. Pvt. He was pensioned 4 Mar. 1789. He was on the 1813 pension list.

Dougherty, Daniel. Pa. —. He was awarded a $40 gratuity and a $40 annuity in Butler County on

20 Mar. 1812.

Dougherty, Henry. Pa. Pvt. He was in Northumberland County on 25 Aug. 1786. He served in Capt. Cookson Long's Company of the 2nd Battalion of the Northumberland County militia under Col. James Potter. He was wounded at Piscataway, N.J. He marched under Lt. Col. John Morrow and was wounded by a musket ball in the joint of his right shoulder as proved by a certificate from James Davidson, surgeon in the 5th Pa. Regiment. He was born 24 Mar. 1760. He received $16 per annum from the United States and had a large family. He was awarded donation land on 28 Mar. 1806. He was on the 1813 pension list. He received a $40 gratuity and a $40 annuity in Lycoming County.

Dougherty, James. Pa. —. He enlisted under Capt. Matthew Smith and Col. Jameson in Lancaster County in July 1775 and marched to Boston under Col. Benedict Arnold. He went to Quebec in Nov. 1775. Henry McEwen saw him at Quebec under Lt. Sted. He was taken prisoner 5 Jan. 1776 and sent to New York where he was paroled in Aug. 1776. After being liberated, he enlisted under Capt. John Brady and Col. William Cook in the 12th Battalion. He was taken into Gen. Washington's Life Guard under Capt. Colfax where he remained to the end of the war. Maj. James Crawford proved his service as did Atchison Mellon. He applied from Lycoming County 21 July 1809. He was 60 years old and was from Centre County 22 Nov. 1813.

Dougherty, James. Pa. —. He enlisted in the fall of 1776 under Capt. Taylor under Col. Walter Stewart and Col. Harmar. He was at Germantown and in skirmishes in Virginia, North Carolina, and South Carolina. He lost an eye at Brandywine. He was furloughed at Charleston, S.C. He was from Chester County.

Dougherty, James. Pa. —. He was pensioned 14 Dec. 1814 and resided in Venango County. He was 89 years old in 1840.

Dougherty, James. Pa. —. He was from Westmoreland or Allegheny County.

Dougherty, John. N.Y. Pvt. He served under Col. Goose Van Schaick and Capt. Charles Parson. He was disabled in his left leg by the fall of a barrel of pork. He was transferred to the Invalids Corps and discharged 15 Sep. 1782. He was 37 years old in 1786. He lived in New York City 23 Apr. 1787. He also appeared as John Doughty.

Dougherty, John. Pa. —. He was awarded a $40 gratuity and a $40 annuity in Somerset County on 14 Mar. 1818. He died in May 1836.

Dougherty, Patrick. Pa. —. His widow, Eve Dougherty, was awarded a $40 gratuity and a $40 annuity in Armstrong County to her death or the termination of her widowhood and then to the guardian of the minor heirs.

Dougherty, Patrick. Va. Pvt. He was on the 1813 pension list.

Dougherty, William. N.Y. —. He was granted relief.

Dougherty, William. Pa. —. He was from Mercer County 11 Apr. 1825 when he received assistance.

Doughty, James. Me. —. He was from Harpswell. He was paid $50 under the resolve of 1836.

Doughty, John. Me. —. He died 5 Oct. 1827. His widow was Dorcas Doughty from Freeport. She was paid $50 under the resolve of 1836.

Doughty, Nathaniel. Me. —. He was from Portland. He was paid $50 under the resolve of 1836.

Douglas, Elisha. Mass. —. He was pensioned 12 June 1815 for four years. He was pensioned for another four years 23 June 1818.

Douglas, John. Pa. —. He was awarded a $40 gratuity and a $40 annuity in Lancaster Co., Pa. 12 Apr. 1828.

Douglas, Robert. Pa. —. He was awarded a $40 gratuity and a $40 annuity in Lancaster Co., Pa. 14

Apr. 1834. He was 76 years old in 1840. He also appeared as Robert Dugless.

Douglas, Thomas. Va. —. His wife, Winifred Douglas, was furnished support in Feb. 1779 in Westmoreland County.

Douglass, Alexander. S.C. —. He enlisted in 1775 for 16 months and served under Capt. Eli Kershaw and Col. William Thompson. He next served under Capt. Bivens in the 2nd Battalion of Minutemen under Col. John Stewart of Georgia. He had five motherless children, four of whom were females. He was 65 years old. John Neely was a mess mate. He was pensioned from Richland District on 17 Dec. 1819. He was paid as late as 1825.

Douglass, James. Conn. Pvt. He served in the 5th Conn. Regiment and was disabled by a rupture in 1781. He was pensioned at New London, Conn. at the age of 50 years on 26 Sep. 1788.

Douglass, John. Me. —. He was from Denmark, Maine. He was paid $50 under the resolve of 1836.

Douglass, Jonathan. Va. —. He lost an eye and was wounded in the hand by an accidental shot from his gun while preparing to pursue a party of Indians under Capt. Benjamin Gray, although he was not regularly enlisted. He was recommended for support in Washington Co., Va. 26 Feb. 1777.

Douglass, Samuel. S.C. —. He enrolled at the age of 16 at Kingstree in Williamsburg District under Capt. James Witherspoon. He was at Scots Lake and Eutaw Springs. He was pensioned in Williamsburg District 24 Nov. 1825. He was paid as late as 1837. On 8 Dec. 1838 his administrator, Thomas S. Thompson, was paid his arrearage of $68.33.

Douglass, Samuel. Va. —. He was accidentally wounded in his thigh by a knife when he lay down in his tent. He was granted £10 on 16 June 1777. He served under Capt. Aaron Lewis.

Douglass, William. Conn. Col. His widow, Hannah Douglass, sought seven years half-pay from 15 May 1777 (the time of his death) in Mar. 1791. He was appointed 11 Oct. 1776 and served in the Continental Army.

Douglass, William. N.Y. Matross. He enlisted 28 May 1776 and was disabled by the loss of his right arm on 12 June 1776 by the explosion of a cannon on the battery in New York City. He served in Capt. Alexander Hamilton's Company under Col. John Lamb in the artillery. He was 48 years old on 19 Jan. 1786. He lived in New York City, N.Y. on 13 June 1788. He died 9 July 1791. His half-pay was issued to the representative of his widow 30 June 1834.

Douglass, William. S.C. —. He worked with Maj. James Campbell and William Stretch making swords and shoes for the troops. He was from Williamsburg District in 1843. He had two daughters one of whom was married and had a large family. He had one-third of a 160 acre tract in Arkansas to which his deceased son, William A. Douglass, was entitled as his bounty in the War of 1812. The son had died at Columbia. Peter Mouzon saw him making swords for the troops during the war. He died 15 Sep. 1844, and his only surviving child, Eliza M. Poulden, sought his arrearage.

Doush, —. Pa. —. His widow, Ann Catherine Doush, was pensioned 14 Apr. 1834 in Lancaster County.

Douthard, Thomas. Va. —. His wife, Mary Douthard, and six children were granted financial support while he was away in the service in Yohogania County 20 Oct. 1777 and in Caroline Co., Va. 23 May 1782.

Dover, Andrew. Pa. Lt. He served in the 5th Regiment. He chose his five years' full pay rather than half-pay for life 16 Nov. 1794.

Dow, Alexander. Pa. 1st Lt. He came to America in 1773 from Scotland. He enlisted 13 Apr. 1777 and served in Malcolm's Regiment. His widow sought one year's full pay from Congress 20 Jan. 1794.

Dow, John. Mass. Sgt. He served in the 9th Regiment and was from Malden. His widow, Mehitable

Hancock, was paid $50.

Dow, Jonathan. —. —. He served under Capt. Perryman and Col. Dearborn from 28 June 1780 to 17 Dec. 1780. Congress allowed him thirteen days for returning home and granted him a pension for six months of service 21 Mar. 1836.

Dow, Reubin. Mass. Capt. He was wounded on 17 June 1775 in the battle of Bunker Hill. A bullet broke and shattered the bones in his right ankle. He served in Col. Prescott's Regiment. He was aged 56 in 1787. He was from Hollis, New Hampshire when he sought relief in 1778.

Dow, Samuel. Mass. —. He served in the Artificers. He was from Boston and was paid $50.

Dowd, Charles. Del. Corp. He was pensioned in 1783. He was born in Ireland, was disabled by a rupture at the battle of Camden, and was married. He was on the 1813 pension list of Maryland.

Dowd, Michael. Pa. Pvt. He was discharged from the Invalids. He was from Philadelphia County. He was disabled by infirmities. He was 36 years old and in the almshouse 12 Dec. 1785. He died 12 Feb. 1791. He also appeared as Michael Doud.

Dowdney, Samuel. N.J. Sgt. He was pensioned 3 Mar. 1807 at the rate of $30 per annum.

Dowling, James. Pa. Pvt. He was on the 1789 and 1813 pension lists.

Dowling, Thomas. Pa. Pvt. He served under Col. Richardson. He was discharged unfit for duty in January 1782. He was from Philadelphia County.

Dowman, Speakman. N.C. —. He served three years in the 10th N.C. Regiment under Col. Abraham Sheppard. He received a broken thigh at Georgetown, Md. He had a wife and six children. His application was rejected in 1802.

Downer, Avery. Conn. —. He was born in Preston, Conn. 17 Nov. 1762. He was 16 years of age when he was in the militia and did duty as a private to 15 July 1781 when he became surgeon's mate in the 8th Regiment of militia. He was at Fort Griswold and the massacre on Gorton Heights. He cared for forty wounded soldiers for seven months after 6 Sep. 1781. Congress granted him a pension 7 Feb. 1850 since Conn. regarded his as public service. Congress reconsidered his claim 23 Mar. 1852.

Downer, Eliphalet. Mass. Surgeon. He served under Capt. Nicholson. The strength and motions of his left arm were impaired due to a wound by grape shot in Sep. 1777 on board the brig *Lexington* in action with the cutter *Alert* in the English Channel. He lived in Roxbury, Mass. in 1795. He entered on board the *Dolphin* in Apr. 1777, but the roll did not show how long he served. He entered on the *Lexington* as a passenger only. Nathan Dorsey, surgeon of the Continental armed brig *Lexington,* stated that he was a volunteer on board when he was wounded. His pension, therefore, would be for whatever capacity he volunteered and not for his profession as surgeon. He died 4 Apr. 1806. He also appeared as Eliphalet Donner.

Downes, Jesse. Mass. Pvt. He served in the 4th Regiment and was from Canton. His widow, Naomi Downes, was paid $50.

Downey, James. Pa. —. He applied 13 Jan. 1809 from Strongstown.

Downey, John. Pa. Pvt. He sold his donation land on 1 Mar. 1796 to James Gordon. The land was since found to be in New York; therefore, the heirs of James Gordon were to be granted 200 acres of donation land 28 Jan. 1812.

Downing, Butler. Md. Pvt. He died 18 Nov. 1829. His widow, Elizabeth Downing, was paid his arrearage of $24.24 by the act of 18 Feb. 1833. She was pensioned 5 Mar. 1835.

Downing, James. Pa. —. He was pensioned in Venango County 20 Mar. 1838 and died 26 Apr. 1840.

Downing, John. Me. —. He was from Minot. He was paid $50 under the resolve of 1836.

Downing, Lemuel. Conn. Pvt. He served under Capt. Ozias Bissell. He was wounded in his elbow and taken prisoner at Flatbush 27 Aug. 1776. He was from East Hartford.

Downing, Nathaniel. Md. Pvt. He was pensioned in Prince George's County at the rate of half-pay of a private 7 Feb. 1817.

Downing, Palfrey. Mass. Sgt. He served in the 4th Regiment and was paid $50.

Downing, Samuel. Me. —. He was from Minot. He was paid $50 under the resolve of 1836.

Downs, James. N.Y. —. He was awarded 200 acres bounty land 13 Apr. 1813.

Downs, John. Conn. Orderly Sgt. He served in the 3rd Regiment under Col. Samuel B. Webb. He suffered from weakness in his breast, blood spitting, ulcerated lungs, and general disability in consequence of a strain by drawing of cannon and of a violent shock he sustained by falling or leaping over a redoubt at Yorktown in 1781. He resided in Huntington, Conn. in 1792. He enlisted 20 Mar. 1777 and continued to the end of the war. It was stated he also enlisted in Aug. 1780 and was on the rolls in 1782.

Downs, John. Pa. —. He was awarded a $40 gratuity in Huntingdon County on 29 Mar. 1813.

Downs, John. Pa. —. He was in Carroll Co., Ohio 8 Feb. 1842.

Doxator, Peter. N.Y. —. He served in the militia under Col. Frederick Bellinger and Capt. Henry Horton. He resided at German Flats. Congress granted him a pension for three years of service 25 Mar. 1834 and 5 Jan. 1836.

Doyle, Henry. Pa. Pvt. He was in Montgomery County 14 Jan. 1786. He served in the 3rd Pa. Regiment and was disabled by a wound in the ankle on 11 Sep. 1777 at Brandywine. He was 28 years old. He was on the 1813 pension list.

Doyle, Jonathan. Me. —. He died in 1789 at Harpswell. His widow was Huldah Doyle from Bowdoin. She was paid $50 under the resolve of 1836.

Doyle, Jonathan. Pa. —. He was granted a $40 gratuity 13 Apr. 1841. One of his name was awarded a $40 gratuity and a $40 annuity in Bucks county 21 July 1842.

Doyle, John. Pa. —. He was awarded a $40 gratuity in Bucks County 13 Apr. 1841 as a Revolutionary veteran.

Doyle, Thomas. Pa. 1st Lt. He served from 1776 to the end of the war. He was a captain by brevet. Maj. J. Moore of the 1st Pa. Regiment attested to his service. He died 6 Feb. 1802.

Doyley, Daniel. Pa. —. He enlisted from Lehigh County on 15 Sep. 1817. He enlisted in the 3rd Pa. Regiment in Jan. 1776 and marched to Canada and was honorably discharged by Col. Thomas Craig. He served three months in the militia and was stationed at Germantown. He served three months against the Indians north of the Blue Mountains. Abraham Rinker and Leonard Nagle served with him. He also appeared as Daniel Daili and Daniel Dayley. He died 12 Feb. 1826.

Dozier, John. S.C. —. He was pensioned 6 Dec. 1828. He was granted one year of his pension in advance on condition of acquitting the state from any other claims on 25 Nov. 1830. He was then stricken from the pension roll.

Drake, John Z. N.J. —. He was pensioned 13 Feb. 1834 at the rate of $60 per annum.

Drake, Samuel. N.Y. —. He was granted relief.

Draper, Simeon. Mass. Sgt. He served in the 4th Regiment and was from Brookfield. He was paid $50.

Drebs, —. Pa. —. His widow, Catharine Drebs, was awarded a $40 gratuity and a $40 annuity 15 Apr. 1835 in Montgomery County. She died 8 Oct. 1844. Her name may have been Catharine Drehs.

Dreher, Godfreid Pa. —. He was awarded a $40 gratuity in Schuylkill County 12 Jan. 1836. He also appeared as Godfrey Dreher.

Drehs, George. Pa. —. He was awarded a $40 gratuity and a $40 annuity in Montgomery Co., Pa. 17

Mar. 1835.

Drench, Jacob. Mass. —. He served in the 7th Regiment and was from Jay. He was paid $20.

Drenin, James. Pa. —. He received a $40 gratuity and a $40 annuity in Chester County 6 Apr. 1830.

Drennan, James. Pa. —. He was awarded a $40 gratuity in Chester Co., Pa. 6 Apr. 1830. He was awarded a $40 gratuity and a $40 annuity 4 May 1832. He died 25 Feb. 1841.

Drennan, William. Pa. —. He was awarded a $40 gratuity and a $40 annuity in Allegheny Co., Pa. 30 Mar. 1824.

Drenning, William. Pa. —. He was awarded a $40 gratuity and a $40 annuity in Bedford Co., Pa. 6 Apr. 1833. He was 77 years old in 1840.

Drew, Daniel. Mass. —. He was pensioned at the rate of £4 per annum for three years from 2 June 1776 on 27 Dec. 1776. As Daniel Druce of Grafton, Mass. on 17 Nov. 1780, he was allowed £4 due him for the year beginning 1 June 1780 when his last pension ceased.

Drew, Samuel. Mass. —. He served in the 7th Regiment and was from Plymouth. He was paid $20.

Drew, William. N.Y. Corp. He served under Col. Morris Graham in Capt. John Drake's Company and was accidentally wounded by a fellow soldier with a knife in the calf of his left leg. He lived in Fredericktown, Dutchess Co., N.Y. on 13 Apr. 1789. He was pensioned 13 Apr. 1787. He later lived in Putnam County. He was on the 1813 pension list.

Drinkhouse, Jacob. Pa. —. He entered the service from Philadelphia County as assistant to his father, Adam Drinkhouse, wagonmaster, to 1778 when his father was appointed Deputy Assistant Quartermaster General. He was with his father to 1780 at Amboy and Brandywine. His father was taken prisoner at Red Bank. He was at Reading with the hospital department after Brandywine and Germantown. Pennsylvania granted him an annuity of $40 in 1848. He was later elected representative from Montgomery County, postmaster at Pottstown, and justice of the peace by appointment and election. He was 90 years old. Congress granted him a pension 13 Feb. 1850.

Driscoll, Jeremiah. Mass. Corp. He served in the 6th Regiment and was from Gloucester. He was paid $20.

Driver, Gaspar. Pa. —. He applied 4 Mar. 1807. He served as a soldier in Col. Wayne's Regiment and was wounded at the battle of Three Rivers by a ball through his arm and a bayonet in his thigh. He was taken prisoner and exchanged. He then served under Col. Humpton to the end of the war. He lived in Allegheny County and was awarded a $40 annuity and a $40 gratuity.

Drury, John. S.C. Legionnaire. He served aboard the frigate *South Carolina* under Commodore Gillon. He was paid $118.31 on 18 Apr. 1809.

Drury, Michael. Pa. Pvt. He applied 28 Mar. 1808 in Somerset County. He served in Capt. John Christy's Company. He was hurt in his head and became deaf. He was granted a $40 gratuity and a $40 annuity. He was on the 1813 pension list. He died 25 Aug. 1817. His name has also been interpreted as Michel Drivey.

Dubberly, Sacher. N.C. He was drafted twice into the militia. In 1779 he served three months under Capt. Jesse Bryan. He took sick and hired William Wennan as his substitute for £100 and some stock. In 1781 he served under Capt. Hardy Gatlin and Col. John Herritage. He was discharged at Ramsey's Mills. He was in no battle. He was 76 years of age when he applied in Craven Co, N.C. 12 Nov. 1832.

Dubbs, Leonrd. Pa. —. He was pensioned 7 Mar. 1834. He also appeared as Leonard Dupps. He died 23 Feb. 1840.

230 Revolutionary War Pensions

Dubois, Lewis. N.Y. Col. He was a deranged officer and received his commutation of half-pay 4 June 1794. He was granted his bounty land on 28 Mar. 1805.

Dubois, Martin. —. —. He was a pensioner. He stated that he rode as an express for some time before he enlisted. Congress ruled that even if the evidence were sufficient, no special act was warranted and rejected an increase in his pension 19 Sep. 1850.

Duck, Jacob. Pa. —. He was awarded a $40 gratuity and a $40 annuity in Centre Co., Pa. 15 Apr. 1835. He was dead by May 1836.

Duck, John. Pa. —. He was pensioned 21 Mar. 1837 in Union County and died 15 Mar. 1840.

Duck, Philip. Pa. Sgt. He was pensioned 21 Aug. 1820. He was paid to 15 July 1830.

Duckwall, Henry. Va. —. He sought relief 24 June 1780.

Duckworth, John. N.C. —. He applied in 1825 in Mecklenburg County. He was in his 80s. He was disabled at the battle of Stono. He served under Gen. Lincoln. He had been blind for two years. All of his children had removed to the western country except a daughter whose circumstances were too humble to render him any relief.

Dudley, Banks. Va. Sgt. He lived in King and Queen County and was 25 years old on 1 Apr. 1787. He served in the 7th Va. Regiment. He was wounded in the face at Brandywine by a ball through his upper jaw. He could not speak and swallowed with great difficulty. The wound remained open, and he had to wear a tent. Maj. Thomas Hill certified his service. He was continued at the rate of £18 per annum on 3 Apr. 1787. He died 11 Nov. 1802.

Dudley, James. Ga. —. He had an aged wife and was perfectly blind. On 6 Dec. 1822 he was vested in section 34 in district 9 in Henry County for his natural life and at his death to revert to the state. He could not sell the tract, and it could not be taken for debt.

Dudley, Joseph. Mass. Pvt. He served in the 1st Regiment and was from Concord. His widow, Mary Dudley, was paid $50.

Dudley, William. N.C. —. He served 18 months in the militia and was drafted in Wilkes Co., N.C. He fought at King's Mountain. He next enlisted in Continental service for six months. He was 100 years old and had not applied for a regular pension because he had sufficient means. Congress allowed his relief 18 May 1860. He was from Adair Co., Ky.

Due, James. Md. Pvt. He was pensioned at the rate of half-pay of a private 19 Feb. 1819.

Duesto, Jesse. S.C. Pvt. He served in Capt. Isaac Ross's Company under Col. Charles Middleton. His administrator was paid $1,418.78 for his service and that of Thomas Tatum on 20 Dec. 1810.

Duey, Emanuel. Pa. —. He was awarded a $40 gratuity and a $40 annuity in Dauphin Co., Pa. 15 Apr. 1834. He was paid to 20 July 1834.

Duff, David. S.C. —. He was killed at the battle of King's Mountain at Ferguson's defeat. His remarried widow, Agnes Campbell, was allowed an annuity 11 Nov. 1784.

Duff, James. Pa. —. He served three years under Capt. James Christy in the 3rd Regiment under Col. Thomas Craig. He was discharged at Trenton 15 Jan. 1781. He lost the power of his arm. He was from Washington County.

Duff, Joseph. Pa. —. He was granted relief.

Duffee, Taurence. Pa. —. He was awarded a $40 gratuity and a $40 annuity in Tioga Co., Pa. 6 Apr. 1830. He served under Capt. Moser, Col. Crawford in New York, and Gen. Roberdeau. He was from Tioga County. He also appeared as Terrins Duffy and Torrence Duffee.

Duffee, Thomas. Md. Sgt. He was pensioned in Harford County at the rate of half-pay of a sergeant on 12 Feb. 1820. His widow, Bridget Duffee, was pensioned at the same rate 10 Mar. 1835.

His arrearage of $7.50 was to be paid to James Moore for her.

Duffield, Thomas. Pa. —. He was awarded a $40 gratuity and a $40 annuity in Philadelphia Co., Pa. 21 Mar. 1825.

Duffy, Michael. Pa. Pvt. He applied in Philadelphia 13 Feb. 1786. He served in Capt. Righley's Company in the 5th Pa. Regiment and was transferred to the Invalids. He was discharged on account of his wounds. He was 33 years old. He was in Maryland 1 Mar. 1786 and was on the 1791 pension list there. He was on the 1813 pension list.

Duffy, Patrick. S.C. —. He served under Col. Edward Lacy and Gen. Sumter and was killed in Nov. 1780 at Fish Dam. His widow died a short time after her son, Hugh Duffy, was bound out. He was from Chester District and made his application for the arrearage 22 Nov. 1800.

Dugan, George. Pa. Pvt. He served under Gen. Wayne. He lived in Westmoreland County. He died 16 Aug. 1834 having been a resident of the county for 40 years and of Washington County before that.

Dugan, Henry. Pa. Sgt. He applied from Hamilton Co., Ohio 3 June 1818. He came from Ireland about 1760 and lived in Cumberland County. His wife and three children were killed after they moved to Monongalia County. In 1774 he went to Kentucky to improve land but was driven off by Indians. He returned home and joined the army under Col. Andrew Lewis. After they beat the Indians at the mouth of Kanawha River, he crossed the Ohio River and joined Lord Dunmore at Chillicothe. The next spring or summer he enlisted with Capt. Michael Cresap in Old Town, Md. in a company of riflemen for one year. He marched to Boston and was discharged at Staten Island. He reenlisted in Col. Malcomb's Regiment of N.Y. troops for a short time and was discharged. In 1780 or 1781 he enlisted with John Boyd in a company of Pa. Rangers. At the battle of Franks Town he and Capt. John Boyd were taken prisoner. He went to New York in 1782 and was discharged in 1783. He was 82 years old.

Dugan, Nathan. N.J. Pvt. He served under Capt. Stiles and Col. Johnstone in the militia. He was killed at Long Island in Aug. 1776. He married Elizabeth Channel. His widow sought a pension 8 Oct. 1795 in Somerset County.

Dugart, John. N.Y. Capt.

Duggan, Jeremiah. N.Y. Maj. He was an inhabitant of Canada and left with his family when the army of the U.S. retreated in 1776. He obtained a commission of a major and died in the service. His name was not inserted on the list of refugees who were entitled to bounty land. His eldest son, James Duggan, and his second son, William Duggan, were each granted 500 acres 24 Feb. 1795.

Duggins, William. Mass. Corp. He served in the 7th Regiment and was paid $20.

Duiguid, John. Pa. Lt, He was granted relief 23 Sep. 1783.

Duke, Henry. Ga. —. His widow, Lettice Duke, and three children were granted assistance 26 Nov. 1784.

Dull, William. Pa. —. He died 4 Dec. 1816.

Dullin, Matthew. Va. —. His widow, Elizabeth Dullin, was granted £6 support on 11 May 1778 and £25 on 10 May 1779 in Northumberland County.

Dulph, William. S.C. —. He was wounded at Ninety Six. He was allowed an annuity 23 May 1778.

Dumison, Pierre. —. —. He received an invalid pension 20 Apr. 1796.

Dummer, Nathaniel. —. —. He applied for a pension on 30 May 1796.

Dumont, John. N.J. —. He was pensioned 1 Dec. 1834 at the rate of $60 per annum.

Dunbar, — . Va. —. He was away in the service. His wife, Frances Dunbar, was allowed 10 bushels of corn valued at £100 in Augusta Co., Va. 18 May 1780.

Dunbar, Joseph. Conn. Corp. He served in the 2nd Regiment of Dragoons under Col. Sheldon. He was injured in his private parts by the leaping of his horse which caused a rupture. He was wounded through his right leg by a shot and by another through his mouth at the battle of Germantown. He was wounded at Whitemarsh by having his sword shot out of his hand and his thumb broken in 1777. He lived in Watertown, Conn. in 1792. He enlisted 1 Mar. 1777 and was discharged 1 July 1780. He was granted one-third of a pension 20 Apr. 1796. He was on the 1813 pension list. He died 2 Feb.1813.

Duncan, —. Pa. —. His widow, Esther Duncan, was awarded a $40 annuity in Cambria County 27 Apr. 1852 for his Revolutionary service.

Duncan, David. N.H. Corp. He had a disease in one of his testicles. He was in Col. Scammel's Regiment. He was discharged from the Invalids Corps. He was from Portsmouth and was aged 45 in 1787. He was on the 1813 pension list. He also appeared as David Dunking.

Duncan, Jared. Conn. Pvt. He was pensioned 28 Apr. 1810. He was on the 1813 pension list of New York. He lived in Columbia Co., N.Y.

Duncan, John. Mass. Pvt. He served in Capt. Adam Wheeler's company under Col. Doolittle. He was wounded in his right arm by a musket ball which passed under his collar bone at Bunker Hill on 17 June 1775. He was pensioned at one-third pay from 1 Jan. 1776 until he was fit for service on 22 June 1782. He was pensioned 17 Mar. 1786. He was 36 years old. He was on the 1813 pension list and transferred to Herkimer Co., N.Y. 4 Mar. 1827.

Duncan, John. N.Y. Capt. He served under Col. Allison in the militia. He was killed at Minisink 22 July 1779. His widow, Abigail Duncan, received a half-pay pension for seven years.

Duncan, John. Pa. —. His heirs received $200 in lieu of donation land 25 Mar. 1822.

Duncan, John. S.C. —. He served under Col. Henry at Williamsburg, Va., Long Island, New York, Brandywine, and Little York. He was at the capture of Burgoyne in Pennsylvania [sic]. His officers included Capt. Thomas, Maj. Thomas Martin, Capt. Dick Knapper, and Col. Daniel Gaines. He saw Lafayette. He was wounded. He was from Fairfield District and had his application rejected in 1826.

Duncan, John. Va. —. He died in service about the last of May 1779. His widow, Mary Duncan, and two children were furnished £20 support in Frederick Co., Va. on 5 Sep. 1780. She was on the pension list in 1785.

Duncan, Samuel. Va. —. He died in the service. His widow, Mary Duncan, and two children were furnished £20 support in Frederick Co.,Va. on 7 Sep. 1779 and on 5 June 1782.

Duncan, Thomas. N.Y. Pvt. He served in the 2nd N.Y. Regiment under Col. Philip Van Cortland and acted as sergeant in Capt. Jonathan Hallet's Company in the latter part of the war. He was disabled by rheumatism and siatica on his right side. He was discharged in 1783. He was of the alms house in New York City, N.Y. on 8 May 1787. He was on the 1813 pension list.

Duncanson, James. Va. Lt. He was on the 1785 pension list.

Duncom, —. Va. —. He served under Capt. Jacob Womack and died in the Cherokee expedition. His widow, Elizabeth Duncom, was crippled and had five children. She was awarded a £20 gratuity and a £10 annuity for five years in 1777.

Dungan, Henry. N.H. He served in Capt. Fogg's Company and was wounded in one of his feet. He was from Durham and applied for relief 30 Jan. 1786.

Dungan, James. Pa. —. He was awarded a $40 gratuity in Philadelphia Co., Pa. 4 Apr. 1831. He was awarded a $40 gratuity and a $40 annuity 4 May 1832.

Dunham, Ammi. Me. —. He was from Freeport. He was paid $50 under the resolve of 1836.

Dunham, Cornelius. N.Y. Pvt. He served in Capt. Judd's Company under Col. Samuel Wells. He also served in Capt. Asa Bray's Company under Col. Cook. He was aged 30 years in 1787. He was disabled by a cannon ball in his left leg which caused a contusion of blood in Feb. 1777. He lived in Saratoga, Albany Co., N.Y. in 1788 and in New Lebanon, Columbia Co., N.Y. on 17 Apr. 1789. He died 2 Aug. 1802.

Dunham, Manassah. Mass. —. He served in the 1ˢᵗ Regiment and was from Sandisfield. He was paid $20.

Dunham, Philemon. Mass. —. He served in the 4ᵗʰ Regiment and was paid $20.

Dunham, Samuel. Conn. Pvt. His widow, Asenath Turner, was 84 years old. She had an invalid son. Congress allowed her an increase 21 Apr. 1890.

Dunham, Stephen. Conn. Pvt. He served under Capt. John Shumway in Col. Jedediah Huntington's Regiment. He lost the sight of his right eye due to smallpox in June 1777. He lived in Tolland, Conn. in 1794. He enlisted 12 Apr. 1777 and was discharged 12 Apr. 1780. Congress granted him a pension 22 Dec. 1831. Congress rejected his request for an increase 27 Apr. 1840.

Dunkill, George. N.Y. Pvt. He served under Col. Samuel Clyde. He was wounded in his right eye 10 June 1781 in action near Torlach. He was pensioned 22 Sep. 1786. He lived in Montgomery Co., N.Y. 2 June 1789. He was aged 27 years in 1787. He was on the 1813 pension list.

Dunlap, —. Pa. —. His widow, Sarah Dunlap of Philadelphia County, received a $40 gratuity and a $40 annuity 3 Apr. 1837.

Dunlap, Andrew. N.Y. Sgt. He served under Col. Philip VanCortland. He lost his sight and the use of his left arm. He was discharged 15 Mar. 1782. He was in Montgomery Co., N.Y. in 1787 and in Albany Co., N.Y. on 17 Apr. 1789. He was on the 1813 pension list. He later transferred to Vermont.

Dunlap, James. N.Y. Pvt. He served in Capt. Read's Company under Col. John Lamb in the Continental Line. He lost his eye sight. He lived in New York City in May 1788.

Dunlap, John. Pa. —. His widow was in Dauphin County on 20 Sep. 1787. He was in the militia in Capt. James Crouch's Company. He was killed at Chestnut Hill in 1777. He left a widow and two children: a son aged 12 and a daughter aged 10. His widow, Robina Dunlap, was in Mifflin County in 1804. She also appeared as Veney Dunlap. She was awarded $53.33 per month on 2 Mar. 1805.

Dunlap, John. S.C. —. He died in the service in May 1781 or 1782. His widow, Margaret Dunlap, was allowed an annuity 3 Feb. 1785.

Dunlap. Joseph. Pa. —. His heirs were awarded $300 in lieu of his donation land on 27 Mar. 1819.

Dunlap, Robert. Pa. —. He served under Capt. Willard and Col. William Montgomery. He was taken prisoner at Fort Washington.

Dunlap, William. S.C. Pvt. He lost a leg on 19 Nov. 1775. He had a wife and two children. He was paid an annuity of £90 from 1 Mar. 1776 during his life. He was pensioned in 1791 in Abbeville District. He had one child in 1791. He was on the 1813 pension list.

Dunlop, Robert. S.C. —. He was pensioned 3 Dec. 1825. He was paid as late as 1830.

Dunn, —. Va. —. His wife, Ann Dunn, was granted £30 support in Caroline Co., Va. 8 Apr. 1779.

Dunn, James. Pa. —. He lost his eye trying to remove a table at Germantown 4 Oct. 1777. He served under Capt. Rupert in the Artillery under Col. John Eyre.

Dunn, Jacob. N.J. —. He moved to Virginia after the war. His administrator and son, Ephraim Dunn, sought his commutation for life, but Congress rejected the claim.

Dunn, John. Pa. —. His heirs were awarded $200 in full for his tract of donation land on 25 Mar. 1822.

Dunn, John. Va. —. His wife, Elizabeth Dunn, was granted £10 support for herself and two children on 20 July 1778, £15 support on 21 Dec. 1778, and £40 support in York County on 19 July 1779.

Dunn, Jonathan. —. —. He sought relief for wounds he received in the war 28 Mar. 1796. He was allowed to withdraw his petition.

Dunn, Joshua. Me. —. He was from Dixfield. He was paid $50 under the resolve of 1836.

Dunn, Patrick. Del. Sgt. He was wounded in the leg near Camden on 16 Aug. 1780. He was born in Ireland and was single. He was pensioned in 1783. He was on the 1791 pension list.

Dunn, Robert. —. —. He entered in 1776 and served to the close of the war. He was an express rider attached to the QM General Department under Gen. Green. He was at Princeton and Yorktown. Col. Pickering gave him a commission as Captain of Express Riders. In 1782 when the express service was discontinued, he entered a troop of horse under Capt. Walker and acted as QM Sergeant for the defense of the N.J. coast. He was 72 years old. Congress granted him a pension 21 Dec. 1832.

Dunn, Robert. Pa. —. He was awarded a $40 gratuity in Franklin Co., Pa. 8 Apr. 1833 and on 1 Apr. 1834.

Dunn, Thomas. Va. —. His wife, Jane Dunn, and four children were granted financial support while he was away in the service in Yohogania Co., Va. 28 Apr. 1778.

Dunne, John. Va. —. His wife, Dorcas Dunne, and family were furnished necessaries in Amelia Co., Va. 28 Aug. 1777 and 26 Feb. 1778.

Dunning, Benjamin. N.Y. Pvt. He served in the Orange County militia and was slain 22 July 1779. His son, July Dunning, received a half-pay pension.

Dunning, Butler. Md. Pvt. He was pensioned at the rate of half-pay of a private in Charles County on 16 Feb. 1821. He died 18 Nov. 1829. His widow, Elizabeth Dunning, collected his arrearage of $24.24 in Feb. 1833. She was pensioned at the same rate in Mar. 1833. He also appeared as Butler Downing and she as Elizabeth Downing.

Dunscomb, —. —. —. He died in 1814. He married 14 June 1786. Congress rejected a pension for his widow, Mary Dunscomb, 9 Aug. 1842.

Dunston, —. Va. —. Martha Dunston was the mother of two and was granted £80 support in York Co., Va. on 21 Aug. 1780.

Duntlin, Nathaniel. Mass. —. He served in Crane's Artillery and was paid $20.

Dunton, James. Mass. —. He was paid $50.

Dunton, Levi. Mass. Pvt. He served in the 15th Regiment and was from Southboro. His widow, Salley Dunton, was paid $50.

Dunton, William. Pa. 2nd Lt. He applied 22 Apr. 1795. He served on the ship of war *Hyder Alley* and was wounded in action with the British warship *General Monk* on 8 Apr. 1782. He lived in Philadelphia Co., Pa. in 1794. There was no proof that he left the service. He was a sailing master in the marines. His ship captain was Joshua Barney.

Dunway, Joseph. Va. —. His widow, Judith Dunway, was granted £12 support in Northumberland Co., Va. on 9 Aug. 1779.

Duportail, Louis Lebique. Maj. Gen. Congress authorized a bounty land warrant to be issued to the heirs on 19 Jan. 1841 even though the time had expired to do so.

Durand, Ebenezer. Conn. Pvt. He served in the 4th Conn. Regiment. He was disabled by a contracted arm and other complaints. He was pensioned in 1783. He died 31 Jan. 1826 in Middlesex Co., Conn. He also appeared as Ebenezer Duran. He was on the 1813 pension list.

Durand, Isaac. Conn. Pvt. He served in Cook's Regiment. He lived in Fairfield County. He was on the 1813 pension list. He died 15 Dec. 1825.

Durant, George. S.C. —. He served in Gov. Rutledge's Life Guard under Capt. John Alston. Other officers were Lt. Withers, Lt. Coachman, Col. Daniel Horry, Capt. John Tomplitt, Col. McDaniels, and Col. Peter Horry. He was 67 years old. John Green served with him. He was in Horry District in 1826. He was paid as late as 1831.

Durant, Isaac. Mass. Pvt. He served in the 4th Regiment and was from Pepperell. He was paid $50.

Durant, Thomas. Mass. Commissary. He served at Charleston from Oct. 1777 to Oct. 1778. He married 23 July 1777 in Newton. He died 2 Aug. 1831 in Middlefield, Mass. Congress granted his widow, Elizabeth Durant, a pension 21 Dec. 1838.

Durant, Thomas. S.C. —. He served in Gov. Rutledge's Life Guard under Capt. John Alston. He was also under Lt. Withers, Lt. Coachman, Col. Daniel Horry, Col. McDonald, and Maj. Hugh Horry. He was in the battles of Parker's Ferry near Charleston and Waccamaw. He was 72 years old. He was pensioned from Horry District 10 Dec. 1825. He died 27 Feb. 1827. His arrearage was paid to Sarah Durant, Margaret Durant, and David Durant, administrator, on 30 Nov. 1827. His daughter, Frances Graham, sought his arrearage for herself and her two sisters 29 Oct. 1858.

Durfree, Benjamin. Mass. Pvt. He served two and a half years. He did duty under Capt. Joseph Durfree to guard towns on the Taunton River in 1775 and 1776. He was under Gen. Sullivan in May 1778. He did duty in R. I. when the British evacuated the island. Congress granted him a pension for nine months of service 11 May 1838. He was from Fall River.

Durfree, Joseph. Mass. & R.I. Capt. He was advanced to the rank of major or colonel. Records revealed that he was in the state troops. He was helpless and compelled to use crutches. Congress granted him a pension 13 Mar. 1832.

Durham, James. Va. Pvt. He applied from Hanover County in 1786. He served in the 1st Va. Regiment under Capt. Holman Winnes. He was wounded in the shoulder and lost part of his shoulder blade bone at Paulus Hook on 17 Aug. 1779. He was pensioned 30 Apr. 1785 at the rate of half-pay. He was on the 1813 pension list. He transferred to Lincoln Co., Kentucky.

Durkee, Benjamin. —. —. He sought his commutation of five years' full pay. Congress rejected his claim 11 Apr. 1846.

Durkee, John. Conn. Col. He was wounded and died at Bean Hill 21 Mar. 1782. His widow was entitled to seven years' half pay. She was dead when his daughter, Anna Young, received his seven years' half-pay 30 Mar. 1812.

Durkee, Nathan. —. —. He volunteered under Col. Seth Warner and served more than one year. While on a scout, he was poisoned and suffered much sickness. Congress granted him a pension 10 Jan. 1832.

Durkee, Nathaniel. —. QM. Congress awarded his widow, Melinda Durkee, the arrearage of her pension from 4 Mar. 1848 to 3 Feb. 1853 on 18 Dec. 1857.

Durnal, John. —. —. He was pensioned 25 Apr. 1808.

Dutton, Timothy. Mass. —. He was paid $20.

Dutton, William. Mass. Sgt. He served in the 7th Regiment and was from Charlemont. He was paid $20.

Dutville, John. S.C. —. His application was rejected in 1810. He was a subordinate officer on the frigate *South Carolina* under Commodore Alexander Gillon. He sought interest on his unpaid balance. He and George Redevault were paid $130.30 on 20 Dec. 1810. He also appeared as John Dutille.

Duval, Daniel. —. —. His legal representatives were allowed his commutation 13 June 1838.

Duvall, Benjamin. Md. Pvt. He was pensioned at the rate of half-pay of a private on 18 Feb. 1831. He was the son of Elisha Duvall. He died 13 Jan.1830. His arrearage of $33.22 was paid to Benjamin L. Ganntt, executor, for the use of Benjamin L. Duvall, Jr., of Prince George's County.

Duvall, Joseph. Md. Pvt. He was pensioned at the rate of half-pay of a private 16 Feb. 1821 in Montgomery County.

Dwelley, Allen. Me. —. He was from Springfield. He was paid $50 under the resolve of 1836.

Dwelley, Joseph. Mass. Pvt. He served in the 2nd Regiment and was from Holden. He was paid $50.

Dych, Peter. Pa. —. He was pensioned in Westmoreland County 27 Mar. 1837. He died 27 Dec. 1839.

Dye, Jonathan. Va. Lt. His widow, Sarah Ann Dye, lived in Lancaster County when she was pensioned on 21 Jan. 1809 at the rate of $40 per annum. He was killed at the battle of Brandywine. His daughter, Nancy Dye, died unmarried in her mother's lifetime. The widow died 31 Dec. 1813, and administration of her estate was granted to Sarah C. Davis on 31 Oct. 1814. The daughter and her husband, Richard Davis, was allowed the seven years' half pay due her mother. He also appeared as John Dye. Congress granted half-pay to the administrator of the widow 23 May 1855.

Dyer, Benjamin. Mass. Pvt. He served at the Castle and was from Weymouth. His widow, Hannah Dyer, was paid $50.

Dyer, Jonathan. Md. Pvt. He served in the 1st Regiment in Capt. Paroll's Company. He lost his leg at the battle of Eutaw on 9 Sep. 1781. He lived in Pittsylvania Co., Va. in 1795. He enlisted 22 Mar. 17[--] for the war, was wounded 9 Sep. 1781, and sent to hospital. He was on the 1813 pension list. He died 5 Mar. 1829.

Dyer, Joseph. Mass. —. He served in the 4th Regiment and was paid $20.

Dyer, Walter. Md. Lt. He was pensioned at the rate of half-pay of a lieutenant in Jan. 1816.

Dygert, Warner.—. Capt. He served in the militia and was killed by the Indians in 1782. His children sought relief. One son was Honjost Dugert.

Dyke, Daniel. Mass. Pvt. He served in the 4th Regiment. He lost his left arm and his right thumb in action at Lake Champlain. He lived in Boston, Mass. in 1788. He also appeared as Daniel Dike and Daniel Dykes. He was paid $20 and was from Bethel, Vt. *Vide* also Daniel Dike.

Dysart, James. Va. Capt. He was on the 1813 pension list. He later removed to Rockcastle Co., Ky. He served from 1780 to 1783 and was wounded in his left arm at King's Mountain. He served under Col. William Campbell. He died in 1817. His widow died about a decade later. His heirs, Charles C. Carson, Elizabeth Carson, and John B. Dysort, sought relief, but Congress rejected their claim 3 Mar. 1851.

Eaches, William. Pa. —. He was awarded a $40 gratuity in Crawford County 31 Mar. 1836.

Eagan, —. Pa. —. His widow, Mary Eagan, was awarded a $40 gratuity and a $40 annuity in Cumberland Co., Pa. 19 Mar. 1824.

Eagan, Thomas. Pa. Matross. He served under Col. Proctor. He was wounded in both legs in mounting heavy ordnance in 1778 at Fort Mifflin. He resided in Chester Co., Pa. in 1796. He enlisted for the war and was transferred to the Invalids in June 1778 and was discharged 24 Sep. 1778. He was granted half a pension 20 Apr. 1796.

Eager, Haran. Mass. Pvt. He was from Lancaster. His widow, Betsey Eager, was paid $50.

Eager, John. Va. —. He was wounded 19 Sep. 1777 at Stillwater. He brought a certificate from Col. John Posey and sought certification in order to receive payment from the Commissioner of

Loans.

Eager, Peter. Pa. Pvt. He was in Philadelphia County 30 Sep. 1785. He was transferred from the 9th Pa. Regiment to the Invalids. He was wounded at Brandywine. He was 30 years old. He transferred to Connecticut in or by Mar. 1799 and to New York 4 Mar. 1805. He was on the 1813 pension list. He also appeared as Peter Egar.

Ealey, John. Va. —. He died in the service. His widow, Hannah Ealey, and child were granted support in Surry Co., Va. 28 Dec. 1778.

Ealy, Michael. Pa. —. He was pensioned by the Court of Enquiry 28 Mar. 1814. He also appeared as Michael Ealey.

Ealy, Thomas. Va. —. His wife, Jane Ealy, was granted 200 pounds of pork in Bedford Co., Va. on 27 Mar. 1780. There were eight in her family on 25 July 1780 when she was furnished four barrels of corn.

Eames, Luther. Mass. Pvt. He served in the 6th Regiment and was from Boston. His widow, Eliza Eames, was paid $50.

Eanes, Arthur. Va. —. He was pensioned from Pittsylvania County on 27 Jan. 1814 at the rate of $80 per annum. He had been wounded in the service at Guilford Courthouse. He died 27 Jan. 1819. Joseph H. Eanes was executor of his will.

Eanoff, Samuel. Pa.—. He was pensioned 1 July 1787.

Earden, —. Pa. —. His widow, Elizabeth Earden, received a $40 gratuity and a $40 annuity in Lancaster, Pa. 28 Feb. 1856.

Earl, William. Mass. Seaman. He served on the continental ship *Alliance* under John Paul Jones, Esq., and lost his right leg in service at Penobscot. He was pensioned at the rate of half-pay from 6 Sep. 1780, the date of his discharge, on 11 May 1781. He was 22 years old in 1787 and resided in Worcester Co., Mass. He later resided in Norfolk Co., Mass. He was on the 1813 pension list as William Earle. Another record indicated that he served on the *Bon Homme Richard.*

Earle, —. Pa. —. His widow, Sarah Earle, was awarded a $40 gratuity and a $40 annuity in Allegheny County in 1841 for his Revolutionary service. She died 9 Feb. 1849.

Earle, Samuel. S.C. —. He received $1,800 plus interest of 3% from 1793 as commutation in lieu of half-pay for life on 11 Dec. 1820.

Earns, —. Va. —. He and his two brothers were away in the service. Their mother, Jane Earns, was granted £30 support on 19 July 1779 in York County.

Earthen, Reuben. Va. Pvt. He applied from Culpeper County on 4 Jan. 1788. He was 40 years old. He enlisted 5 Feb. 1776 in the 3rd Va. Regiment. He received several severe wounds in his head and was ridden over by a dragoon at Col. Buford's defeat. He was discharged 9 Dec. 1780 at the expiration of his term of enlistment. Capt. John Blackwell and Col. John Greene of the 6th Va. Regiment corroborated his service. He was put on the roll at the rate of £8 per annum on 4 Jan. 1788. He was on the 1813 pension list.

Easley, —. S.C. —. His widow was Ann Easley of Spartanburg in 1791.

East, David. Va. —. He was wounded at Lenew's ferry on the Santee River. He served under Col. Washington. He applied in Isle of Wight Co., Va. 15 De. 1780.

Easterly, George. Pa. —. He was awarded a $40 gratuity and a $40 annuity 30 Mar. 1824. He resided in Baltimore, Md.

Eastforth, Samuel. —. —. Capt. Benjamin Fry testified that Eastforth served from 22 Apr. 1776 to 2 Oct. 1776. Capt. Waller succeeded Capt. Fry. Maj. Tallman swore that Col. Richmond's

Regiment disbanded in Nov. 1776 and those remaining in the service transferred to Col. Cook's Regiment and completed their time of service. Congress ruled that he did serve his term and awarded him a pension 15 Mar. 1832.

Eastman, Edmund. Me. —. He died 19 Dec. 1812. His widow was Hannah Eastman of Limerick. She was paid $50 under the resolve of 1836.

Eastman, Eli. Conn. Sgt. He enlisted in 1776 under Capt. Bradley and Col. Gay. He was at White Plains and Long Island. At Flatbush he was wounded in his head by a musket ball. In 1777-1778 he served under Capt. Leavenworth and Col. Meigs. He was pensioned in 1831 and paid to 1834. He had used R. Temple as his agent. Later the government learned that Temple defrauded the government by forging certificates and perjured witnesses and cancelled all pensions processed by him. For the past twelve year he was *non compos mentes*. His son and guardian was Elisha Eastman. Congress restored him as a pensioner 12 Jan. 1838. He utilized the service of R. Temple who had defrauded the government by forged certificates and perjured witnesses so that Eastman was the innocent included with the guilty.

Eastman, Thomas. N.H. Pvt. He was wounded in the head by a musket ball at the battle of Bemis Heights on 19 Sep. 1777. He served under Col. Cilley in Capt. Hutchins's Company. He lived at Hopkinton, N.H. in 1792. He enlisted 16 July 1777 and was discharged 16 July 1780. He was granted one-third of a pension 20 Apr. 1796. He was on the 1813 pension list. He was subject to convulsions and derangement in his mind.

Eastman, Zacheriah. Mass. —. He served in the 9th Regiment and was paid $20.

Easton, Eliphalet. Conn. Pvt. He served under Col. Chandler. He was wounded in his left hand in removing casks of salt and lost the use of two fingers. He lost the use of both hands in 1778. He resided in Conn. in 1792. He enlisted 21 May 1777 and was discharged 23 May 1780. He was on the 1813 pension list. He died 22 July 1816.

Easton, James. Mass. Col. He was much debilitated by rheumatic pains by an operation for a fistula in 1775 in Canada. He resided at Pittsfield, Mass. in 1796.

Easton, Richard. Pa. —. He was awarded a $40 gratuity and a $40 annuity in Allegheny County 1 Apr. 1837. He was 88 years old in 1840.

Easton, Samuel. Conn. Sgt. He served in 3rd Regiment. He was disabled by excessive fatigues and hardships in 1780. He resided in East Hartford, Conn. in 1792. He enlisted 12 Apr. 1777 for the war but did not continue to the end.

Easton, William. —. Pvt. He served under Col. Bayley. He was wounded in his right hand at the battle of Bemis Heights on 19 Sep. 1777.

Eaton, Eliab. Me. —. He was from Strong. He was paid $50 under the resolve of 1836.

Eaton, John. Pa. —. He was granted relief in Armstrong County 8 Apr. 1840.

Eaton, Joseph. Mass. Pvt. He served in the 11th Regiment and was from Ashby. His widow, Betsey Eaton, was paid $50.

Eaton, Nathaniel. Mass. Pvt. He served in the 1st Regiment and was from West Springfield. His widow, Susan Eaton, was paid $50.

Eaton, Noah. Mass. Pvt. He served in the 7th Regiment under Capt. Rufus Lincoln and Col. John Brooks. He was disabled by sundry wounds and had become deaf. He was 54 years old in 1788.

Eaton, William. Mass. Sgt. He served in the 8th Regiment. He lost the sight of his left eye by an accidental wound in 1779 at Tarrytown. He lived in Boston, Mass. in 1792. He enlisted 17 Mar. 1777 and was discharged 17 Mar. 1780. He was paid $50 by the Commonwealth and was from Reading. His widow, Sarah Eaton, received the arrearage from 4 Mar. 1848 to 3 Feb. 1853 as determined by Congress 10 Dec. 1857. He was from Worcester, Mass.

Eaton, William. N.C. —. He filed a property schedule 26 Nov. 1821 in Stokes Co., N.C.

Eaton, William. Va. —. His wife was furnished necessaries in Loudoun Co., Va. on 8 Mar. 1779.

Eaves, William. S.C. —. He was born in 1748 in Maryland and apprenticed to tailoring. He was wounded by a sword in his head and by a musket ball in his left knee. He was in the battles of Guilford and Camden. He was in the calvary under Col. Lee. He was nearly blind in his left eye, deaf, and had lost the use of his left side. He had lived in South Carolina more than fifty years. He applied from Union District. His application was rejected in 1828.

Ebbs, Emanuel. Md. Pvt. He was pensioned at the rate of half-pay of a private 23 Jan. 1816. There was one of his name in Juniata Co., Pa. in 1840 aged 106. [There is a 10 year discrepancy in their ages.]

Eberman, —. Pa. —. His widow, Elizabeth Eberman, was awarded a $40 gratuity and a $40 annuity in Lancaster, Pa. 10 Apr. 1826. She died 1 Apr. 1836 in Lancaster County and her arrearage was paid to her kinswoman.

Ebetts, William. Mass. —. He served in the 3rd Regiment and was paid $20.

Eckles, Arthur. Pa. —. He was awarded a $40 gratuity and a $40 annuity in Beaver Co., Pa. 6 Apr. 1830.

Edelin, John. Md. —. His arrearage of $12 was paid to his administrator, Walter H. S. Mitchell, 24 Feb. 1838.

Eddy, —. Pa. —. His widow, Ann Eddy, was awarded a $40 gratuity and a $40 annuity in Chester Co., Pa. 9 Mar. 1825.

Eddy, Comfort. R.I. Pvt. He lost the use of right arm, foot, and leg; he also had a lame back received in removing a cannon at the head of the Elk in Sep. 1781. He served under Col. Jeremiah Olney. He was aged 41 when he applied 29 Dec. 1785. He was on the 1813 pension list. He died 22 Feb. 1819 in Providence Co., R.I.

Eddy, Ebenezer. Mass. Sgt. He served in the 2nd Regiment and was from Colerain. He was paid $20.

Eddy, Josiah. Mass. —. He served in the 4th Regiment and was from Sturbridge. He was paid $20.

Eddy, Joshua. Mass. Capt. He served as lieutenant in 1777 and captain in 1778. He received a furlough from Gen. Washington and requested to be supernumerary. He was pensioned under the act of 1818. He died in 1833 aged 85. His widow was pensioned and died in 1838. He received federal bounty land warrant #656 for 300 acres which he assigned to Samuel Emery. His sons, Joshua Eddy (aged 69 in 1848), Zechariah Eddy (aged 67 in 1848), Nathaniel Eddy, and William S. Eddy were from Middleborough, Mass. They sought their father's five year pay plus interest allowed a supernumerary officer. Congress refused their request 1 Mar. 1860

Edegh, Jacob. N.Y. Pvt. He served in Col. Bellenger's Regiment. He was wounded in the back by a tomahawk by the Indians at Thompson's place in Sep. 1779. He lived in Schuyler, New York in 1794.

Edes, Thomas. Mass. —. He served in the 9th Regiment and was from Gloucester. $20 was paid to Martha McKnight *et al.*

Edgar, David. Pa. —. He was granted a $40 gratuity in Bucks County 24 Mar. 1812. He also appeared as David Edgen. One David Eagar received $40 on 17 Mar. 1813.

Edgar, James. Pa. —. His widow, Elizabeth Edgar, received a $40 gratuity and a $40 annuity in Chester County 1 May 1857.

Edgar, John. U.S. —. He was granted support by Congress for the year 1782.

Edgecomb, Samuel. Conn. Pvt. He lost part of his forefinger of his right hand on 6 Sept. 1781 at

New London. He had volunteered about the time of the attack on Fort Griswold in Groton. He was made a prisoner and was sent home in confinement where he suffered for another four months. He lived in Groton, Conn. in 1794. He was in the militia. He lacked one month to qualify under the pension act of 1832. Congress allowed him service of six months and granted him a pension 1 Feb. and 22 Dec. 1837 and on 9 Feb. 1842.

Edger, John. Va. —. His wife, Margaret Edger, was awarded £10 support in Bedford Co., Va. on 23 Mar. 1778.

Edgerly, —, —. —. His widow, Abigail Edgerly, sought an increase in her pension and arrearage. Congress refused her claim 19 July 1848.

Edgerly, Edward. Md. Capt. He died in the service and left no legal representative. He had a natural son whom he acknowledged and who was to be named Edward Edgerly. He was to receive the interest from the amount due to the decedent until the age of 21 or his marriage when he was to receive the full amount. Daniel Ramsey was appointed his guardian in 1782.

Edgerly, John. Mass. Pvt. He served in the Invalids under Col. Lewis Nichola and Capt. Moses McFarland. He was wounded in his right hip and leg. He was disabled by epileptic fits. He was from Buxton, Mass. and was pensioned 6 Sep. 1780. He was 62 years old. He lived in Scarboro, Me. in 1788. He was on the 1813 pension list as John Elgerly [sic].

Edison, Thomas. U.S. —. He was granted support by Congress in 1782.

Edmester, Noah. Me. —. He was from Newburg. He was paid $50 under the resolve of 1836. He also appeared as Noah Edminster.

Edminston, Samuel. Pa Surgeon. In 1777 he attended the sick and wounded on board armed vessels. He was ordered to accompany the Flying Camp and then to attend the general hospital. He served to the end of the war. He was awarded donation land. He also appeared as Samuel Edmiston.

Edmonds, David. S.C. Lt. He died 1 Aug. 1778.

Edmonds, Daniel. Va. Pvt. He served in a corps of state marines in Capt. Gabriel Jones' Company. He died in the service. His widow, Sarah Edmonds, lived in Shenandoah County on 1 Jan. 1787 with her son and his five children. She was aged 75. Compare *infra*.

Edmonds, David. Va. Pvt. He served as a sailor and died in the service. His widow, Sarah Edmonds, applied on 1 Jan. 1793. Compare *supra*.

Edmonds, Elias. Va. Lt. Col. His heirs received his commutation of full pay for five years in lieu of half-pay for life as lieutenant of artillery in the Virginia Line on 14 Jan. 1829.

Edmonds, James. Va. Sailor. He died in the service. His widow was Sarah Edmonds. She was put on the pension list 15 Aug. 1787 at the rate of £8 per annum. She was on the pension list of 1798.

Edmonds, William. Conn. Pvt. He served in Increase Moseley's Regiment under Brig. Gen. Wooster in the 12th Company of the 13th Conn. Regiment. On 27 Apr 1777 at Ridgefield, he was wounded in the thigh by a musket ball leaving three running sores. He lived in New Town, Conn. and was 33 years old when he was pensioned 4 Dec. 1788. He had previously resided in Woodbury, Conn. He was on the 1813 pension list.

Edmondson, James Powell. Va. Pvt. He was recommended for a pension from Caroline Co., Va. in May 1778. He was awarded a £30 gratuity and an annuity of full pay on 23 May 1778. He applied from Franklin County on 10 Sep. 1787. He was 34 years old in Mar. 1789. He served in the 9th Va. Regiment detached in a corps of riflemen under Col. Morgan. In an engagement at Somerset Courthouse he lost one of his legs. He was continued on the roll at the rate of £15 per annum on 25 May 1789. He also appeared as James Powell Edminston. He was on the 1813 pension list of Georgia. He died 18 Mar. 1820 in Chatham Co.,Georgia.

Edmondson, John. S.C. Pvt. He entered the service at Fort Rutledge or Fort Seneca about 1 Mar. 1777 under Capt. Benjamin Tutt and Col. Leroy Hammond to the last of Oct. 1779. He next served for three years. He was taken prisoner when his captain surrendered to the British under Capt. Smith. He escaped eight days later and joined Capt. Robert Maxwell as a volunteer for eighteen months. The company was disbanded the last of Apr. 1781. He also saved the camp of Col. Robert Armstrong from a surprise in the dead of night at Norwood's Mill by giving them intelligence of the approach of a band of Tories. He did wagon service in 1780 and 1781. He had an aged wife. Congress granted him a pension for two years 18 Mar. 1844.

Edmondson, Joseph. Va. —. He was granted assistance in Orange Co., Va. in 1778.

Edmondston, William. Va. Col. He was commissioned captain by Patrick Henry in 1777 and advanced to major in 1780. He was made colonel of the Washington County militia in 1783 from 17 Apr. 1782.

Edmons, John. Mass. Corp. He served in the 8th Regiment and was from Malden. He was paid $50.

Edson, Samuel. Mass. Sgt. He served in the 3rd Regiment and was paid $20.

Edwards, —. Va. —. Nelly Edwards was granted support in Prince William County in 1778.

Edwards, Evan. Pa. —. Bounty land warrant #1205 for 400 acres was issued to his son Charles Lee Edwards 9 Feb. 1827.

Edwards, Gideon. Conn. Pvt. He resided in Litchfield Co., Conn. He was on the 1813 pension list. He died 13 Dec. 1817.

Edwards, Henry. S.C. —. He escaped capture at the fall of Charleston. He was wounded at both Quimby and Eutaw. He received two wounds: one in the lower part of his abdomen and the other by a ball in his breast which had never been extracted. He was 73 years old and suffered from rheumatism. Robert Polk knew him in the militia. He was pensioned in Chesterfield District on 4 Dec.1828. He was paid as late as 1834.

Edwards, Jonathan. Mass. —. He served in the 5th Regiment and was paid $20.

Edwards, Pumfret. —. —. He served under Capt. John Dickerson and was in the service two and a half years. He had a wife but no children at home. He applied at age 80 in Wake Co., N.C.

Edwards, Robert. Mass. —. He served in the 5th Regiment and was paid $20.

Edwards, Samuel. —. Sgt. He entered the service in 1775 and served seven months under Capt. Samuel Whiting as a private. He was a 1st sergeant in 1776 under Capt. Elijah Beach for six months. He took sick and died at the end of the tour. His only surviving child was Betsey Booth. Congress ruled that it was inexpedient to grant her relief 30 Jan. 1840.

Edwards, William. Va. Pvt. He served in the 15th Va. Regiment and died in the service. His widow, Elizabeth Edwards, received a £12 gratuity on 6 Nov. 1779. His widow lived in King William County in July 1786. There were four children. She was pensioned 18 Jan. 1787. She died 18 Aug. 1795. Administration on her estate was granted to Garland Madison on 24 July 1809.

Edwards, William. Va. Pvt. He died in the service in 1781. His widow, Mary Ann Edwards, lived in Northumberland County on 13 Feb. 1787. She was put on the pension list at the rate of £6 per annum on 7 Apr. 1787. On 10 Aug. 1791 she had two children, one aged 14 and the other aged 9. She died 10 July 1832, and administration of her estate was granted to Isaac Edwards 13 May 1833.

Eells, —. —. —. He and his widow died before they were covered by pension legislation. Their son was James T. Eells. Congress decided against awarding him a pension 14 June 1852.

Egan, Thomas. Pa. Matross. He was pensioned 20 Apr. 1796.

Eggleston, John. Mass. Corp. He served in the 3ʳᵈ Regiment and was from West Springfield. He was paid $50.

Egleston, Jehial. Mass. —. He served in the 4ᵗʰ Regiment and was paid $20.

Egner, —. Pa. —. His widow, Mary Egner, received relief in York County 11 Apr. 1844.

Egner, Peter. Pa. —. He was awarded a $40 gratuity and a $40 annuity in Northumberland County 24 Mar. 1837. He was 76 years old in 1840.

Egolf, Henry. Pa. —. He was awarded a $40 gratuity and a $40 annuity in Perry Co., Pa. 15 Mar. 1826.

Ehler, —. Pa. —. His widow, Margaret Ehler, was awarded a $40 gratuity and a $40 annuity in Lancaster County in 1837. She died 19 Sep. 1851.

Ehney, Frederick. S.C. —. He was killed in the service. His widow, Catherine Ehney, was paid an annuity from 1793 to 1823. Her daughter, Christina Starns, received payment from 1805.

Ehnick, Frederick. S.C. Corp. He served in the 1ˢᵗ S.C. Regiment and was killed at Stono. His widow, Ann Ehnick, and child were allowed an annuity 7 Sep. 1786. There were three children in 1791.

Eichelberger, George. Pa. —. He served in the Flying Camp and was from Dauphin County. He was awarded a $40 gratuity and a $40 annuity in Lancaster Co., Pa. 14 Apr. 1828. He died 19 Dec.1832.

Eichelberger, John. Pa. —. His widow, Mary Eichelberger, of Washington Co., Md. was awarded a $40 gratuity and a $40 annuity 19 Feb. 1828. She died 22 Feb. 1848.

Eichholtz, George. Pa. Pvt. He served in the Pa. Line in Capt. Dehuff's Company under Col. Atlee. He was wounded in the groin at Flatbush, Long Island by a musket ball. He died 15 Jan.1786, but hc was in Lancaster County 5 Mar. 1804 when he was granted an annuity of $60.

Eicholtz, John. Pa. —. He applied from Lancaster County 16 Sep. 1813. He died 21 May 1821.

Eidson, James. S.C. —. He enlisted for eighteen months. His captain, Michael Watson, was killed. He was under Capt. William Butler until the latter was paroled. He next served under Starling Turner and Tolls. He was from Edgefield District in 1828. He was paid until 1834 when the pension act was repealed in Dec. 1835 so he sought a federal pension and was approved. He sought to collect his credit of $240 in the pension office in Charleston but was denied it because it was unlawful to collect from two governments. He also appeared as James Edson.

Eighler, John. N.Y. Corp. He served under Col. Fisher in the militia and died 4 Dec. 1781 of wounds. His widow, Susannah Eighler, received his half-pay pension. He may be the John Eckler whose family was granted support in the Revolutionary War.

Eirich, Michael. Pa. Pvt. He was in York County 1 May 1786. He served under Col. Butler. His feet were frost bitten in 1780. He was 40 years old. He also appeared as Michael Erick. He was dead by Mar. 1791.

Eisell, John. Md. Pvt. He was pensioned at the rate of half-pay of a private in Baltimore 9 Mar.1832.

Eisenlord, John. N.Y. Maj. He served under Col. Peter Bellinger in the Montgomery County militia and was killed at Oriskany 6 Aug. 1777. His children, John Eisenlord, Peter Eisenlord, Mary Eisenlord, and Catharine [?] Eisenlord, received a half-pay pension for seven years.

Elam, —. Va. —. Jane Elam was awarded 4 barrels of corn and 200 pounds of pork for support in Bedford Co., Va. on 28 Feb. 1780.

Elam, William. Va. —. His widow, Elizabeth Elam, and four children were granted 300 pounds of bacon and 6 barrels of corn for support in Chesterfield Co., Va. on 2 Aug. 1782.

Elbert, Samuel. Ga. Col. Congress rejected the claim of the representatives for his commutation on

15 Feb. 1836. He had received it in 1785.

Elbertson, William. N.Y. Pvt. He served in Capt. David Van Ness's Company under Col. Goose Van Schaick. He was wounded in his left leg on 28 June 1778 at Monmouth. One wound was from a musket ball and the other from grape shot. He was 64 years old in 1786. He lived in Albany Co., N.Y. on 13 June 1788. He was aged 64 in Feb. 1785. He was on the 1813 pension list. He also appeared as William Albertson.

Elbums, Charles. N.C. —. He served under Capt. Jacob Turner and lost an eye in the service. He was from Rowan County.

Elder, John. Pa. —. He served several tours in the militia for eight and a half months and was pensioned for same. When his widow, Mary Elder, applied, she was refused because he had been called out for self-defense and not on the authority of the state. Congress, however, granted her a pension on 26 May 1842.

Elder, Robert. S.C. Pvt. He was being pensioned in 1791. He was on the 1813 pension list. He was paid his arrearage from 19 July 1811 to the time he became a U.S. pensioner on 18 Dec. 1818.

Eldridge, Charles. Conn. Ens. He served in the 1st Company of the 8th Regiment of militia under Capt. William Latham. In opposing the British under Gen. Arnold who had landed at New London, he was wounded by a picket in his right knee at Fort Griswold at Groton 6 Sep. 1781. He resided at Groton, Conn. and was 45 years old when he was pensioned on 1 Oct. 1788. He died in 1798.

Eldridge, Daniel. Conn. Sgt. He served in the 2nd Alarm List in the 8th Regiment. He was wounded by a musket ball in his right arm at Groton 6 Sep. 1781. He served under William Latham in the Artillery. Amos Prentice, surgeon, cared for him. He was pensioned 24 Nov. 1788 while a resident of Groton, Conn. at the age of 49. He lived at New Shoreham, R.I. in 1794. He was an Indian.

Eldridge, Heber. —. —. He served three months in the war and seven years as privateersman. He had received $1,000 in Continental bills which became worthless. He married 18 Apr. 1782. He was taken prisoner and confined at Brooklyn. He returned to privateering, was captured again, carried to the West Indies, and eventually escaped. His widow, Mary Eldridge, sought relief. Congress declined her any relief 6 Mar. 1850. His son was Edmund Eldridge.

Eldridge, James. N.Y. —. He retreated with his family from Fort Miller near Saratoga to Williamstown, Mass. due to the incursion of Indians and Tories. His property went to the use of the American army. His son was James Eldridge. Congress did not grant him relief 12 Feb. 1822.

Elland, John. —. —. He was in Orange Co., N.C. in Oct. 1832.

Ellcock, —. Va. —. His wife, Hannah Ellcock, was granted £6 support in Fauquier Co., Va. in Mar. 1778 while he was away in the service.

Eller, Leonard. Pa. —. He served in the Lancaster County militia in the Flying Camp. He was taken prisoner at Long Island 27 Aug. 1776 and died in captivity. His widow, Catherine Eller was pensioned 30 Sep. 1786.

Ellett, —. Va. —. His wife, Winney Ellett, was granted £5 support in Fauquier Co., Va. in Feb. 1778.

Elliot, Arthur. S.C. Pvt. He served 357 days in the militia. He married 4 July 1784. He died in Habersham Co., Ga. in Nov. 1837. His widow, Mary Elliot, died 10 Oct. 1855. He had applied for a pension but died before its adjudication. Her application was pending at the time of her death. Congress approved the heirs to receive what their mother would have been allowed 6 Apr. 1860.

Elliot, Bernard. S.C. Lt. Col. He served in the artillery. He was on Continental Establishment and died 25 Oct. 1778. His widow remarried. His only son sought his seven years' half-pay in 1791.

Elliot, Jacob. N.H. —. He was from Chester when he was pensioned in 1777. He was wounded at the battle of Bennington.

Elliott, Francis. Mass. —. He served in the 5th Regiment.

Elliott, George. Mass. —. He served in the 2nd Regiment and was from Scipio. He was paid $20.

Elliott, John. —. —. He served in the militia and the Continental Army for about 25 months. He had enlisted for eight months under Col. Marshall and Col. Putnam. Congress granted him a pension 20 Dec. 1831.

Elliott, John. Md. Wagoner. He was pensioned in Baltimore County on 26 Dec. 1811. He was on the 1813 pension list.

Elliott, John. R.I. Pvt. He had a broken hip occasioned by a fall in Dec. 1777. He served under Col. Israel Angell. He was aged 39 in 1785. He lived in Providence Co., R.I. He was on the 1813 pension list. He died in Scituate 6 Dec. 1829; his widow was Nancy Elliott.

Elliott, Joseph. Pa. Pvt. He was on the 1813 pension list.

Elliott, Richard. N.Y. —. In the spring of 1780 he enlisted at Verplank Point, N.Y. He was born in 1764 and was not quite 16 years of age when he joined. Two or three weeks later he was moved across the river and set his date of enlistment as May 1780. He enlisted 27 June 1780 for six months and was discharged 3 Dec. 1780. He was short of 23 days for the six months minimum of service. His residence was Killingsworth, Conn. Congress took the position that his early discharge might have been due to allow him time to reach home. Congress allowed him six months of service and granted him a pension 21 June 1836.

Elliott, Robert. Md. Pvt. He was wounded in the service. He was pensioned in Harford County at the rate of half-pay of a private 4 Jan. 1812.

Eliott, Robert. S.C. —. He was wounded in the service at Eutaw Springs. His officers were Lt. John Daniel, Capt. George Gavins, and Col. Benjamin Garden. He lived in St. Peter's Parish, Beaufort District. His annuity was effective from 1 Oct. 1779. He sought an increase from Congress in his pension for his wound when he was 90 years old in 1846. Even though the law had been repealed in 1834, Congress granted him relief 10 Aug. 1846.

Elliott, Samuel. Mass. —. He served in the 2nd Dragoons. He was paid $20.

Elliott, Thomas. Md. Pvt. He was pensioned at the rate of half-pay in Baltimore 2 Mar. 1827.

Elliott, Thomas. Md. Pvt. He was pensioned at the rate of half-pay of a private 2 Jan. 1813.

Elliott, Thomas. N.C. —. He applied in Mecklenburg County in 1819. He served in the militia under Maj. William R. Davis and was wounded en route from Charlotte to Camden. He was awarded a £25 annuity. He was upwards of 60 years of age.

Elliott, William. Mass. —. He served in the 2nd Dragoons and was from New Hampden. He was paid $20.

Elliott, William. Pa. —. He was awarded a $40 gratuity in Butler Co., Pa. 24 Mar. 1828 and again on 23 Mar. 1829.

Elliott, William. Pa. —. He was awarded a $40 gratuity and a $40 annuity in Philadelphia, Pa. 16 Feb. 1835. He died 12 Feb. 1841.

Elliott, William. Pa. —. He was granted a $40 annuity 10 Apr. 1849 for his Revolutionary service. He lived in Washington County.

Ellis, —. Va. —. Their father, Thomas Ellis, was granted financial support in Greenbrier Co., Va. 23 May 1782. He had been killed in the service.

Ellis, Atkins. Mass. —. He was granted relief.

Ellis, Daniel. Va. —. His widow, Ann Ellis, was granted support in Southampton County 14 May 1778 and £101.16 on 11 Mar. 1779. She had two children.

Ellis, Edmund. S.C. —. His remarried widow, Rebecca Barton, had the restraining order on the issue of the indent repealed on 5 Dec. 1792.

Ellis, Joseph. Pa. —. He was awarded a $40 gratuity and a $40 annuity in Columbia County 12 Mar. 1836.

Ellis, Michael. Md. Fifer. He was pensioned in Craven Co., N.C. at the rate of half-pay as a fifer on 9 Mar. 1826.

Ellis, Nathan. Conn. Pvt. He served in the 1st Conn. Regiment. He was disabled with consumption. He was pensioned 1 Sep. 1782. He lived in New York County, N.Y. He was on the 1813 pension list and died 5 July 1826.

Ellis, Robert. —. —. He was wounded at Eutaw Springs and had never recovered. He was upwards of 90 years of age. Congress granted him a pension 10 Aug. 1846 and an increase 25 Jan. 1848 for his wounds.

Ellis, Thomas. Md. Pvt. He was pensioned at the rate of half-pay of a private in Harford County 16 Feb. 1820.

Ellis, William. Pa. —. His widow, Mary Ellis, applied 10 Oct. 1792. He served one year under Capt. Samuel Hugg in the Artillery and then under Capt. Lee. His daughter was Martha Ellis.

Ellison, John. —. —. He was in Rutherford Co., N.C. in Oct. 1832.

Ellsworth, William. Mass. —. He served in the 8th Regiment and was from Rowley. He was paid $20.

Ellums, Charles. N.C. —. He applied in Mecklenburg County in 1802. He served in the Continental Line; at the battle of Eutaw he was disabled by a musket ball in his left eye on 8 Sep. 1781. He was in Capt. Turner's Company. He was on the 1813 pension list as Charles Ellam.

Ellwood, Isaac. N.Y. Corp. He served in the militia under Col. Gooke and Capt. Henry Diefendorff and was wounded in his right shoulder at Oriskany on 6 Aug. 1777. He lived in Montgomery Co., N.Y. 15 June 1789. He was on the 1813 pension list. He died in 1813. He also appeared as Isaac Elwood.

Elmer, Moses. N.J. Surgeon's Mate. He served in the 2nd Regiment from fall of 1778 to the end of the war. Congress allowed his heirs commutation 21 Jan. 1839.

Elmer, Nathan. N.J. —. He was pensioned in Essex County on 22 Feb. 1838 at the rate of $60 per annum.

Elmore, —. Pa. —. His widow, Hannah Elmore, was awarded a $40 gratuity and a $40 annuity in Philadelphia Co., Pa. 30 Mar. 1824.

Elton, Thomas. Pa. —. He was awarded a $40 gratuity and a $40 annuity in Bucks Co., Pa. 21 Jan. 1828.

Elwell, Robert. Mass. Bombardier. He served in the artillery under Col. John Crain and Capt. Benjamin Frothingham. He had been entirely worn out. He was disabled by deafness. He lived in Plympton, Mass. in 1786 and was 65 years old. He died 27 Mar. 1805. He was on the 1813 pension list as Robert Elvell.

Ely, Elisha. —. Capt. He was commissioned 16 Mar 1779 and resigned 28 Apr. 1780. He was taken prisoner and paroled 6 Oct. 1781. He was exchanged. Congress rejected the claim for commutation on 28 Jan. 1837 because if he did service, it was in the state troops.

Ely, Henry. —. —. His petition for a pension was rejected 12 Mar. 1798.

Ely, John. Conn. Col. He was taken prisoner 9 Dec. 1777 and was paroled 25 Dec. 1780 on Long Island and exchanged. He served as physician to the American prisoners. He applied in 1790.

Ely, Michael. Pa. —. He was granted relief.

Emerick, Michael. Pa. —. He was awarded a $40 gratuity and a $40 annuity in Centre Co., Pa. 5 Mar. 1828. He also appeared as Michael Emerich. His widow, Margaret Emerich, was granted a $40 gratuity and a $40 annuity in Centre County 10 Apr. 1837. He also appeared as Michael Emrich.

Emerson, —. Va. —. His widow was Martha Emerson. Her husband was slain in Continental service. She was granted £15 support in Caroline Co., Va. 8 Oct. 1778 and £12 14 Oct. 1779.

Emerson, John. Va. Lt. He served in the infantry in the 13th Regiment under Col. William Russell and received his five years' full pay commutation 30 June 1834. He was allowed interest on his pay 13 Mar. 1838. He also appeared as John Emmerson.

Emerson, Jonathan. N.H. Lt. He was wounded by a musket ball through his arm and body on 19 Sep. 1779 at the battle of Stillwater. He served under Col. Cilley. He later lived in Dunstable, Mass,

Emerson, Nathaniel. Mass. —. He served in the 5th Regiment. He was paid $20. He was in the family of Lucy Emerson.

Emerson, Nathaniel. N.H. —. In 1776 he served one month in the militia as a private under Capt. Joseph Parker and Col. Enoch Hale. In May or June 1776 he then enlisted and served under Capt. Lindsay and Col. Baldwin in the artificers. He was assigned to take command by the chief engineer and was discharged 4 June 1777 due to sickness at Ticonderoga. He had been a lieutenant under Capt. Jedediah Thayer. His application under the act of 1818 was rejected because his service was not Continental. He proved additional service as a lieutenant colonel under Col. Thomas Stickney and Gen. Starke from 23 July to 28 Sep. 1777. He died at Solon, Courtland Co., N.Y. 20 Sep. 1828. He married Dolly Dearborn at Cheshire, N.H. 24 May 1769. She died 17 May 1835. Their children were Joseph Emerson, Samuel Emerson, and Wilder Emerson. After the death of the son, Joseph Emerson, Congress approved twelve months of a pension from 4 Mar. 1818 to 20 Sep. 1818 and the amount due the widow between 4 Mar. 1831 and 17 Mary 1835 to the children.

Emerson, Parker. Mass. Sgt. He served in the 7th Regiment and was from Boston. His widow, Rebecca Emerson, was paid $50.

Emerson, William. R.I. Pvt. He lost all the toes on his left foot; his toes on his right foot were much injured by frost bite on the Oswego Expedition. He served under Col. Jeremiah Olney. He was aged 28 in 1785.

Emery, David. Me. —. He died 18 Nov. 1830. His widow, Abigail Emery, from Fairfield. She was paid $50 under the resolve of 1836.

Emes, Charles. Mass. Pvt. He served in the 6th Regiment and was from Leverett. He was paid $50.

Emmes, Nathaniel. Mass. —. He was from Boston and was paid $50 per annum.

Emory, Charles. Md. Bargeman. He was paid £7 for his services in Nov. 1801.

Empie, Jacob. N.Y. Pvt. He served under Col. Klock in the Montgomery County militia and was slain 6 Aug. 1777. His son, Jacob Empie, received a half-pay pension for seven years.

Ende, Philip. Pa. —. He was awarded a $40 annuity in Lycoming County 12 Jan. 1836. He also appeared as Philip End. He died 29 Nov. 1840.

England, John. —. —. His petition for a pension was rejected by Congress on 25 Feb. 1846 because he did not prove service of six months.

England, John. Va. Artificer. He was drafted from Stafford County and was detailed for making firearms about a mile above Falmouth in 1781 under Gen. Weedon. He was 80 years old. Congress granted him a pension 27 June 1846. A bill had been reported earlier on 5 Mar.

1840, 22 Dec. 1840, and 29 Dec. 1841.

Engle, —. Pa. —. His widow, Catharine Engle, was awarded relief in Montgomery County 10 Apr. 1833.

Englebright, John. Pa. —. He was granted a $40 gratuity and a $40 annuity in Baltimore, Md. 31 Mar. 1836. He was dead by Jan. 1839.

Englehaupt, John. Pa. —. He was awarded a $40 gratuity and a $40 annuity in Crawford Co. Pa. 15 Mar. 1826. He died 25 Dec. 1833.

English, George. Pa. Pvt. He was in Philadelphia County on 9 Jan. 1786. He served in the 4th Pa. Regiment and was wounded in the head, shoulder, arm, and one hand at Paoli. He was 26 years old.

English, James. Pa. —. He was in Lycoming County 16 Apr. 1813. James Davidson knew him as a soldier in S.C. prior to the peace.

English, James. Pa. —. He was granted a $40 gratuity and a $40 annuity on 10 Mar. 1818. He died in Georgia 15 Feb. 1824.

English, James. Pa. Sgt. He was in Berks County 28 Jan. 1786. He served in the 6th Pa. Regiment in Capt. John Nyce's Company. He then did duty in Capt. Bower's Company of Light Artillery. He was under Lt. James Gibbons and was wounded at Stoney Point by a musket ball passing through his body. Capt. John Seely proved his service. He was 27 years old. Later he was in Sussex Co., N.J. and Dauphin Co., Pa. He was on the 1813 pension list. His widow was Jane English on 28 June 1813. They married in March 1779. His nephew was Claudius English. She may have been the Jane English who was pensioned in Lycoming County 15 Mar. 1834.

English, John. Pa. —. He was awarded a $40 gratuity and a $40 annuity in Lycoming Co., Pa. 20 Feb. 1833. He was 87 years old in 1840.

English, Joseph. N.J. —. His widow, Mary English, was pensioned in Atlantic County on 9 Mar. 1848 at the rate of $50 per annum.

Enloe, John. S.C. —. He enlisted in the spring of 1778 in Capt. David Hopkins' 3rd S.C. Regiment under Col. Thompson. He was drafted into Capt. William Caldwell's company. He served three years. He was in the militia under Col. Thomas Brandon and wounded at Ninety Six. He applied for a pension in 1797 and was paid from 1792. He sought to be paid from 1781 to 1792 on 3 Dec. 1821. His claim was rejected. He had been pensioned by the United States but had been suspended in 1818. He reapplied in South Carolina and was paid from 1819 to his death in 1830. His widow, Lucy P. Enloe, had her application for his arrearage rejected in 1821. He also appeared as John Inlow.

Ennes, Benjamin. Pa. Lt. He was slain by the Indians and his widow, Magdalena Ennes, was awarded a $40 gratuity and a $40 annuity on 20 Mar. 1812. She died 4 Apr. 1819. He also appeared as Benjamin Ennis.

Ennis, Leonard. Md. Pvt. His widow, Jane Bishop, was pensioned at the rate of half-pay of a private 23 Feb. 1838.

Ennis, Richard. —. —. His widow sought a pension.

Ensley, —. Pa. —. His widow, Elizabeth Ensley, was granted relief in Bedford County 20 May 1839.

Ensminger, John. Pa. —. He served in the 3rd Regiment and was wounded at Monmouth. He was granted a pension in Lancaster County.

Ent, Daniel. Pa. —. He was awarded a $40 gratuity and a $40 annuity in Bucks Co., Pa. 12 Apr. 1828.

Entrekin, Thomas. S.C. —. He was pensioned in Laurens District 30 Nov. 1827. He was paid as late as 1834.

Epperson, David. Va. —. He died in Continental service. His widow, Judith Epperson, was awarded a gratuity of £164 in Albemarle Co., Va. 14 Dec. 1780.

Epperson, Richard. Va. —. He was wounded at the battle of Boonesborough. He was granted relief 18 Nov. 1777. He applied 26 Nov. 1778.

Eppes, Francis. Va. Lt. Col. He served as major until 18 Mar. 1776 when he was promoted to Lieutenant Colonel in the 1st Virginia Regiment. He died in 1776 leaving no widow and one child, Elizabeth Kell Eppes. The daughter married Thomas Woodliff, and they were the parents of Francis Eppes Woodliff. Thomas Woodliff married again and was the father of Martha Woodliff. Francis Eppes Woodliff died unmarried and devised his property to his half-sister, Martha Woodliff who married Robert Lancer. She in turn died survived by her husband and two children. The latter were allowed the half-pay of Francis Eppes 4 June 1838.

Erb, Henry. Pa. —. He was awarded a $40 gratuity and a $40 annuity in Montgomery Co., Pa. 6 Apr. 1833.

Erb, Jacob. Pa. —. He was awarded a $40 gratuity and a $40 annuity in Northampton Co., Pa. 6 Mar.1833. He entered the service in 1777 under Capt. Brooks, Col. Reed, and Gen. Porter in the militia. He was in scouting parties two months. He was at Brandywine. In Dec. 1777 he served another two months. In 1778 he enlisted for three months under Capt. Gibson and guarded the powder wagons at Philadelphia for seven months. His brother was Henry Erb. Congress granted him relief 25 Jan. 1838. He was from Montgomery Co., Pa. He received a $40 annuity and a $40 gratuity from Pennsylvania 15 Mar. 1838. He died 15 Nov. 1841.

Erick, Michael. Pa. Pvt. He was on the 1789 pension list.

Erdman, Andrew. Pa. —. He was granted relief in Montgomery County 12 Mar. 1836.

Erickson, Thomas. N.J. —. He was pensioned in Gloucester County on 17 Mar. 1846 at the rate of $40 per annum.

Erisman, George. Pa. —. He was awarded a $40 gratuity in Lancaster Co., Pa. 7 Mar. 1829.

Erskine, George. Me. —. He was lost at sea on the privateer *Dart* in Oct. 1812. His widow was Huldah Erskine from Portland. She was paid $50 under the resolve of 1836.

Erwin, Jacob. Pa. Pvt. He was in Philadelphia County 13 Feb. 1786. He served in the 9th Pa. Regiment in Capt. Erwin's Company under Col. Scammel, late Adjutant General. He was wounded once through his body and another through his right hand. He was 34 years old.

Erwin, John. Pa. Lt. He served from 9 July 1776. He was taken prisoner 16 Nov. 1776 and was exchanged 25 Feb. 1781. He was disabled by many distempers and bodily infirmities and was incapable of employment. He was pensioned 20 Dec. 1781. He lived in Tinicum Township.

Erwin, Joseph. Pa. Capt. Bounty land warrant #1161 for 300 acres was issued to James Erwin and other heirs. Congress authorized a duplicate 23 June 1840. His son, William Erwin, for himself and the other heirs received $200 for the donation land due them from Pennsylvania 19 Apr. 1853.

Erwin, —. Pa. —. His widow, Margaret Erwin, was awarded a $40 gratuity and a $40 annuity in Philadelphia Co., Pa. 4 May 1832.

Erwin, William. —. —. His application was rejected 13 Dec. 1797.

Erwine, Henry. Pa. —. He was awarded a $40 gratuity and a $40 annuity in Columbia Co., Pa. 3 Mar. 1829. He was 88 years old in 1840.

Eshelman, Abraham. Pa. —. He was awarded a $40 gratuity and a $40 annuity in Lancaster Co., Pa. 3 Mar. 1825. He was 82 years old in 1840.

Eskins, —. Va. —. Elenor Eskins was allowed £5 for her support and her young children in Augusta

Co., Va. 19 May 1778.

Eskridge, Burdid. S.C. —. He was killed at the battle at Carter's house. His widow, Hannah Eskridge, was granted an annuity 24 Dec. 1784.

Espey, Samuel. N.C. —. He applied in Lincoln County in 1803. He served under Capt. William Graham and Lt. Col. Frederick Hamright. He was wounded in the right arm at the battle of King's Mountain on 6 Oct. 1780. He was on the 1813 pension list.

Esterbrooks, Nehemiah. Mass. —. He served in the 15th Regiment and was from Scipio. He was paid $20.

Esterly, George. Pa. —. He was awarded a $40 gratuity and a $40 annuity in Baltimore, Md. 30 Mar. 1824. He also appeared as George Easterly.

Estes, Elijah. Va. Pvt. He served in the 6th Va. Regiment under Lt. Col. Oliver Towles. He was wounded three times at Brandywine. One was in his left arm by a musket ball and his hand ulcerated. Another wound was in his left thigh by a musket ball, and the third was in his left leg. He was awarded a £30 gratuity and an annuity of half-pay for three years in 1778. He lived in Caroline County in Dec. 1783 and was 25 years old. He was put on the roll at the rate of £12 per annum on 6 Nov. 1786. He later lived in Spotsylvania County. He was on the 1813 pension list.

Estes, Lydal. —. —. He produced no witnesses or documents. Congress rejected his petition 9 Jan. 1847.

Estes, Moses. Va. —. He was pensioned in Spotsylvania County 5 Jan. 1820 at the rate of $60 per annum. He died 26 Oct. 1826. Richard Estes was granted probate of his estate on 5 Feb. 1827. He also appeared as Moses Estis.

Estill, William. N.J. —. He was pensioned. His son, William Estill served in the War of 1812 in Capt. Gooden's Company in the Kentucky militia. His grandson, William J. Estill, was a private in Co. A, 16th U.S. Infantry in the Mexican War and was wounded at Shiloh having served as a captain in Co. F, 28th Illinois Volunteers in the Civil War and pensioned to his death in 1891. His great-grandson, William C. Estill, lost both arms at the elbow as well as his left eye at a public celebration by the premature discharge of a cannon at Petersburg, Ill. in 1868. He was 34 years old and had to be fed and waited on by a attendant. William J. Estill's brother was in Co. F, 4th U.S. Infantry in the Civil War and was wounded at Hatchie, Tenn. and died at Bolivar, Tenn. in Dec. 1861. Another brother, David F. Estill, served in Co. K., 114th Illinois Volunteers and died at Camp Sherman, Miss. in 1863. Another brother, Samuel Estill, served as a captain in Co. K., 114th Illinois Volunteers. There was no relation to support the great-grandson so Congress granted him a pension 9 Apr. 1896.

Etheridge, —. S.C. —. His widow, Drucilla Etheridge, was being pensioned in 1791.

Eurich, —. Pa. —. His widow, Catharine Eurich, was awarded a $40 gratuity and a $40 annuity in York Co., Pa. 29 Mar. 1824.

Eustis, William. —. Surgeon. His widow, Caroline Langdon Eustis, sought the arrearage, but Congress rejected her petition on 24 Feb. 1830 and again on 12 Dec. 1850.

Evans, —. Pa. —. His widow, Ruth Evans, was awarded a $40 gratuity and a $40 annuity in Montgomery Co., Pa. 6 Apr. 1833. She died 27 Oct. 1852.

Evans, Cotton. —. —. He was pensioned in 1832. It was suspended. He was from Brookline, Vt. Congress granted him a pension effective from the time of his suspension on 25 Apr. 1840.

Evans, Daniel. Conn. He served in the Conn. Line. He lived in Bennington, Vt. He was on the 1813 pension list.

Evans, David. S.C. —. He was wounded in the service on 4 Sep. 1780 in action with Tories. His thigh bone was broken. He was granted an annuity 4 Feb. 1785 and was paid as late as 1799.

He was from Georgetown District.

Evans, Edward. N.H. Pvt. He served in the 1st N.H. Regiment and was wounded in the ankle. He was aged 41 in 1787. He was from N. Plymouth. He was on the 1813 pension list.

Evans, Evan. Pa. —. In the service he marched from Montgomery Township under Capt. George Smith to Amboy, N.J. in the militia and served out his term. He then enlisted in the Flying Camp and served another term. His term of service was for three years in the 6th Pa. Regiment. He was discharged at Trenton. He was in battle at Stoney Point where he was wounded in the arm by a bayonet, Brandywine, Germantown, and Monmouth. He was awarded a $40 gratuity and a $40 annuity 3 Apr. 1837. He was 82 years old in 1840. He died 5 July 1845.

Evans, George. Va. Surgeon. He served under Col. Baylor in the cavalry. He suffered a severe wound in Sept. 1778 and resigned from the service. His served two years and nine months. His executor was William R. Johnson. Congress ruled that there was no valid claim to any commutation 8 Feb. 1836.

Evans, Jacobus. N.Y. —. He was granted relief.

Evans, James. Va. —. He served in the militia and was wounded in 1777. He applied but was rejected 21 Nov. 1777.

Evans, Jenkins. Del. Sgt. He was pensioned in 1783. He was on the 1813 pension list.

Evans, John. Pa. Gunner. He served in the 4th Regiment of Artillery for six years, five months, and twenty-five days. He was discharged by Isaac Craig. He was from Philadelphia County.

Evans, John. Pa. —. He was pensioned 21 Mar. 1837 in Indiana County. He died 9 Nov. 1844.

Evans, John. Va. —. He was away in the service in Capt. Heth's Company. His three children were granted financial support in Yohogania Co., Va. 23 June 1778.

Evans, Leonard. Mass. Sgt. He served in the 14th Regiment and was from Freetown. His widow, Levina Evans, was paid $50.

Evans, Moses. Conn. Pvt. He served in Col. Huntington's Regiment. He lost the sight of one of his eyes due to inoculation of smallpox at New London. On an expedition to Staten Island he had his feet frozen in Feb. 1777. He resided at East Hartford, Conn. in 1792. He enlisted 15 Feb. 1777 for the war and continued to the end. He also served under S. B. Webb.

Evans, Philip. Va. —. He was pensioned at the rate of £10 per annum from 30 Dec. 1791. He resided in Essex County on 17 Nov. 1794. He was wounded in the service.

Evans, Sherebiah. Mass. Pvt. He served in Crane's Artillery and was from Vermont. He was paid $20.

Evans, Thomas. Md. Pvt. He was pensioned at the rate of half-pay of a private in Frederick County on 1 Mar. 1830. He was also issued a warrant for 50 acres of bounty land in Allegany County at the same time. His widow, Eleanor Evans, was pensioned at the same rate on 4 Mar. 1834.

Evans, Thomas. N.J. Sgt. He served in the 1st Regiment and was disabled with an ulcerated leg from a bruise. He was from Morris County. He was on the 1791 pension roll at the rate of $40 per annum. He was 53 years old.

Evans, William. Md. Pvt. He was pensioned 4 Mar. 1789. He was on the 1813 pension list.

Evans, William. Pa. —. He was awarded a $40 gratuity and a $40 annuity in Montgomery Co., Pa. 19 Jan. 1825.

Evans, William. S.C. —. He served in the 5th S.C. Regiment and was disabled. He was granted an annuity 18 Mar. 1778.

Evans, William. Va. Lt. He was wounded at the battle of Brandywine. He was pensioned in 1808. He lived in Cumberland and Buckingham Cos., Va. He was on the 1813 pension list. He was probably the one of the name and rank whose heirs were due his invalid pension of $9.06

2/3 from 3 Mar. 1826 to 3 Nov. 1836 which Congress awarded on 13 Jan. 1846.

Eveleth, Aaron. Mass. Sgt. He served in the 8ᵗʰ Regiment and was from Essex.

Eveleth, Zimri. Mass. —. He served in the 6ᵗʰ Regiment and was paid $20.

Everett, Jeremiah. N.Y. Mariner. He served aboard the frigate *Confederacy*. He had his right leg fractured by the carriage wheel of a cannon in 1779 on the Delaware River near Chester. He lived in Hudson, N.Y. in 1795. He served from 22 Feb. to 20 Aug. 1779 when he was discharged. He was granted half a pension 20 Apr. 1796. He was on the 1813 pension list.

Everhart, John. Pa. —. He was awarded a $40 gratuity and a $40 annuity in Berks Co., Pa. 15 Apr. 1834. He was 81 years old in 1840. He died 29 May 1850.

Everhart, Lawrence. Md. Sgt. He was on the 1813 pension list. He lived in Frederick Co., Md.

Everly, John. —. —. Congress granted him a pension 1 Mar. 1843 for six months of service. He was from Tennessee.

Everly, Michael. Pa. Lt. He died 17 Mar. 1827. His widow, Sarah Everly, died in July 1836. His son, Michael Everly, and the other heirs sought what their father would have been due from 3 Mar. 1826 to 17 Mar. 1827. Congress granted their request 9 Jan. 1854.

Everton, Benjamin. Mass. Pvt. He served in the 14ᵗʰ Regiment and was from Medway. His widow, Lucinda Everton, was paid $50.

Everts, Stephen. Conn. Pvt. He served in Seth Warner's Conn. Regiment when he was wounded in the shoulder on 7 July 1777 at Hubberton. He was taken prisoner and held for three months. He returned to the army and was sent into the country to recover after the capture of Gen. Burgoyne. The troops then moved into winter quarters. He rejoined the regiment and did duty as an officer's servant. The disorder in his ankle persisted, and he lost the use of one arm. He also served under Capt. John Chapman and William Moulton who were in the same engagement. He resided in Salisbury, Conn. and was 29 years old when he was pensioned 3 Dec. 1788. He was on the 1813 pension list. He moved to Dutchess Co., N.Y. 4 Sep. 1827.

Evitt, John. S.C. —. He served in the 5ᵗʰ S.C. Regiment and died in General Hospital 17 May 1779. His widow, Eleanor Evitt, was allowed an annuity 1 Apr. 1785. She was paid as late as 1807.

Ewell, Charles. Va. Capt. He was from Prince William County. He received his commutation of full pay for five years in lieu of half-pay for life as captain of infantry in the Virginia Line on 3 Feb. 1825. He died 1 Apr. 1830 in McCracken Co., Ky.

Ewell, Thomas. N.C. —. He was from Craven County.

Ewell, Thomas Winder. Va. Capt. He served under Col. Charles Dabney and Col. George Gibson to the end of the war. He was entitled to half-pay for life or commutation of five years in the amount of $10,136.

Ewer, Jonathan. Me. —. He died 29 Jan. 1829. His widow, Betsey Ewer, was from Vassalboro. She was paid $50 under the resolve of 1836.

Ewing, —. Pa. —. His widow, Jane Ewing, was granted a $40 gratuity and a $40 annuity in Armstrong County 1 Apr. 1836.

Ewing, Alexander. Pa. —. He was pensioned in Mercer County 24 Mar. 1837.

Ewing, Bennington. N.J. Pvt. He was pensioned 4 Mar. 1789.

Ewing, Charles. —. —. He served in several Indian campaigns and was wounded by being thrown from his horse. He served four months. Congress refused him a pension 5 Mar. 1840 because he furnished nothing other than his own oath to show that he was disabled in consequence of his injury in the service.

Ewing, James. Md. Capt. He was pensioned in 1785.

Ewing, James. Pa. —. He was pensioned in Indiana County 18 Jan. 1838. He was 73 years old in 1840. He died 25 Feb. 1851.

Ewing, James. Pa. —. He received a $40 gratuity in Huntingdon County 24 May 1832.

Ewing, John. Pa. —. He was from Huntingdon County and received a $40 gratuity and a $40 annuity 6 Apr. 1833.

Ewing, John. Pa. He was from Indiana County and was pensioned 6 Apr. 1833 [or 1838]. He was 75 years old in 1840. He died 25 Jan. 1842.

Ewing, Remington. N.J. Pvt. He served in the 2nd Regiment and lost his leg at Yorktown in 1781. He resided in Greenwich, Cumberland County. He was 42 years old. He was on the 1791 pension roll at the rate of $60 per annum. He also appeared as Bennington Ewing.

Ewing, Samuel. Pa. Ens. He was in Chester County on 1 Mar. 1787. He was in the Chester County militia in Capt. Ephraim Blackburn's Company in the 4th Battalion under Col. William Montgomery. He was disabled in some degree by wounds in the right thumb and arm received in 1776 by the discharge of a musket. He was 30 years old. He died 8 Apr. 1804. He was, however, on the 1813 pension list.

Eyen, Frederick. Md. Pvt. He was pensioned 4 Mar. 1789.

Eyler, Jacob. Pa. —. He was awarded a $40 gratuity in Cumberland Co., Pa. 24 Mar. 1828, 23 Mar. 1829, 4 May 1832, and 20 Feb. 1833. He died 17 Aug. 1833.

Eyres, Samuel. Vt. Pvt. He served under Col. Stark in G. Reed's Company of militia. He was wounded in his left arm by a musket ball which fractured the bone at Bunker Hill on 17 June 1775. He lived in Windham, Vt. in 1792 and Londonderry, Vt. in 1795. He was granted one-fourth of a pension 20 Apr. 1796. He was on the 1813 pension list. He died 20 Dec. 1823.

Eyster, George. Pa. —. He was awarded a $40 gratuity and a $40 annuity in Adams Co., Pa. 14 Feb. 1833. He was dead by Dec. 1836.

Fabian, John. S.C. Pvt. He served under Col. William Hardin and was wounded in both arms at Savannah in Aug. 1781. He applied 19 Feb. 1793. His widow, Mary Ann Fabian, sought relief.

Fabricius, John Christian. Del. Pvt. He was on the 1813 pension list.

Fagain, John. Pa. —. He applied from Dauphin County on 6 July 1820. He enlisted in the spring of 1776 for three years in Capt. Chambers' Company in Col. Butler's Regiment and then fell under Capt. Irvin's command first followed by Capt. Jonathan Morris. He was wounded in the cheek by a bayonet at Paoli. He was also wounded in the leg. He was taken prisoner to Philadelphia until April 1778 when he returned home unfit for service. His discharge from Capt. Irvin was burned in James Moor's house in Chester County. He received no pay, deprecation pay, or lands from either Pa. or the U.S. His uncle, William Fagain, was in the service the whole time and died soon after the war without issue. Joshua Craig knew he was at the battle of Germantown. He was also at Brandywine. He also appeared as John Fagan.

Fagan, William. N.Y. Pvt. He served in Capt. Robert ------'s Co. under Col. James Livingstone. He was transferred to the Invalids under Col. Lewis Nichola. He was disabled by rheumatism and a rupture in his right groin. He lived in Johnstown, N.Y. 3 June 1789. He also appeared as William Feagan. He was 54 years old in 1788. He was on the 1813 pension list.

Fagas, John. Pa. Matross. He was on the 1813 pension list.

Fahner, Jacob. Pa. —. He was awarded a $40 gratuity and a $40 annuity in Bedford Co., Pa. 7 Mar. 1827.

Fair, John. Pa. —. He was granted relief.

Fair, Jonathan. —. —. He had been a pensioner but was dropped from the rolls when he did not submit a property schedule under the act of 1818. He was restored in 1830. His heir, J. S. Fair, sought his arrearage with interest from 1820 to 1830, but Congress did not approve his request 20 June 1848.

Fair, Robert. S.C. —. He was at Paoli, Pennsylvania and Cowpens. He had been thrice wounded. His wife was older than himself. He was 80 years old. He was from Pendleton District in 1827.

Fairbanks, Benjamin. Mass. —. He served in the 9th Regiment and was from Enfield. He was paid $50.

Fairbanks, John. Mass. Pvt. He served in the 5th Regiment and was from Union, Maine. He was paid $20.

Fairbanks, William. Mass. —. He was paid $50.

Fairbrother, Francis. Md. Pvt. He was pensioned in 1806. His widow, Patience Fairbrother, was pensioned in Anne Arundel County at the rate of half-pay of a private 6 Mar. 1832.

Fairbrother, Richard. Mass. Pvt. He was in the 4th Regiment and was paid $20 by the Commonwealth. He transferred to Windham Co., Vt. He was on the 1813 pension list.

Fairweather, John. —. —. His widow, Abigail Fairweather, had her application laid on the table.

Fairy, John. S.C. —. He was killed at Hanging Rock. His widow, Elizabeth Fairy, was allowed an annuity 10 Aug. 1785. There was one child in 1791.

Faith, Abraham. Pa. —. He applied from Somerset County on 4 June 1812. He enlisted for three years and was discharged.

Falls, Samuel. Mass. Pvt. He served in the 7th Regiment and was from Berwick. He was paid $20.

Falls, Samuel. N.Y. Pvt. He served under Col. James McClaughry in the Ulster County militia and died of wounds 5 Jan. 1778. His widow received a half-pay pension.

Fambrough, John. Va. —. His widow, Jean Fambrough, was granted relief in Halifax Co., Va. on 15 June 1780. He died in Continental service.

Fancher, James. —. —. He enlisted 19 Dec. 1777 under Capt. David Waggoner and was transferred to Capt. William Morgan. He marched to Guilford Court House. He was in Capt. Thomas Bowyer's Company in the battle there. He was wounded in his knee and was furloughed. Congress granted him a pension 14 Jan. 1837. He resided in Overton Co., Tennessee.

Fancher, John. —. Pvt. He served under Capt. Jonathan Platt for nine months in 1775. He was under Col. Holmes and was at St. John's in Canada. He was discharged at Philadelphia. Congress granted him a pension 23 Dec. 1831.

Fanell, William. Pa. —. He served under Col. William Butler for nearly five years. He then joined the artillery under Col. Porter from 10 Sep. 1781 to 30 July 1783. He was at Trenton, Germantown, and Paoli. He was wounded at the latter. He was 63 years old. He was from Franklin County.

Fann, John. Mass. —. He served in 2nd Regiment. He was paid $20.

Fanning, John. —. Surgeon's Mate. He served from June 1775 to the spring 1781 and was pensioned in 1818. Stricken in 1820, he died 21 Aug. 1830. He married 15 Oct. 1795. His widow was Abigail Fanning. She bore the burden of supporting a crippled child. There were four other children. She sought arrearage as though he had not been stricken and her own arrearage from the time of his death. Congress refused her claim 29 Jan. 1850.

Fanning, Alexander. Mass. —. He was pensioned 28 Feb. 1809 from 4 Oct. 1808 for life.

Fanning, Elisha. N.Y. Sgt.-Maj. He was on the 1813 pension list. He lived in New York County. He died 29 Jan. 1818.

Fanning, Jehu. Va. —. His wife was granted 500 pounds of pork, 300 pounds of beef, 6 barrels of corn, and 1 bushel of salt in Halifax Co., Va. on 21 Oct. 1779.

Fanning, Joshua. —. Lt. He served under Capt. Biddle as early as 1776 on the *Randolph*. He sailed on the last cruise of the vessel from Charleston 9 Mar. 1778. The *Randolph* was engaged with the British man-of-war *Yarmouth* off Barbados and was blown up and 350 perished. A brother served on the frigate *Trumbull*. Another brother also served. All three were lost. The father was on a British prison ship. The mother died of a broken heart two years later. Her daughter was four years old at that time. The children of his daughter, Mary Fanning Hibbs, sought the seven years' half-pay due their grandfather 22 Dec. 1837.

Fansher, Squire. N.Y. Pvt. He had his skull fractured on 18 Mar. 1781 and his arms and hands were cut to pieces. He served in Capt. Samuel Lewis's Company under Col. Thaddeus Crane. He was 22 years old 6 July 1786. He lived in Poundridge, Westchester Co., N.Y. in June 1788. He appeared on the 1813 pension list as Squire Fancher. He also appeared as Squire Foucher.

Fansher, William. N.Y. Pvt. He was disabled by a musket ball in both feet by the accidental firing of a gun on 10 June 1781. He was in Capt. Daniel Bouton's Company of Westchester County Militia under Col. Thaddeus Crane. He lived in Poundridge, Westchester Co., N.Y. on 18 June 1788. He also appeared as William Fancher. He was on the 1813 pension list.

Farbis, Andrew. N.Y. —. His family was granted relief during the war.

Farble, David. Mass. —. He served in the 5th Regiment and was from Pepperill. He was paid $20.

Faree, Ephraim. N.C. Capt. He was in the militia and was taken prisoner in 1781 at Hillsboro and held on a prison ship at Charleston, S.C. for twelve months. He was exchanged for Capt. Isaac Nicholson in the N.C. Loyalist forces. His children were David Faree, Rachel Faree, Ann Faree, Joseph Faree, Catherine Faree, and John Faree. His widow, Hester Faree, had her application rejected in 1823.

Faree, William. Pa. —. He was pensioned.

Farell, Denis. Va. —. He served in the 11th Virginia Regiment. His wife, Ann Farell, and two children were furnished £8 support in Frederick Co., Va. on 7 Oct. 1777.

Fargo, Zaccheus. Conn. Pvt. He served in the 3rd Regiment of militia under Capt. Jabez Bebee and Col. Jonathan Latimer. On an alarm of a British fleet off the harbor of New London, he was sent to Millstone Point. In loading his piece, he was wounded in his right hand by the accidental discharge on 8 July 1779. He was 30 years old and lived in New London when he was pensioned 26 Sep. 1788. He was on the 1813 pension list.

Faris, Thomas. S.C. —. He was wounded by a pistol ball in his right shoulder in 1781 near Edisto. He served under Capt. Patton and Col. Lacy. He was paid an annuity 1 Feb. 1785 in Chester District. He was pensioned 14 Dec. 1820. He died 28 Aug. 1825. He left a small family. His widow, Margaret Faris, was paid $60 arrearage on 8 Dec. 1826. He also appeared as Thomas Faires.

Faris, William. —. —. He was pensioned under the act of 1818 at the rate of $8 per month but was dropped because he was able to support himself. In 1832 he was again pensioned at the rate of $6 per month. Congress restored the amount of his pension to $8 per month on 3 Mar. 1836. It was retroactive to the time he had been restored to the pension rolls.

Farmer, —. S.C. —. His widow, Nancy Farmer, applied at the last session of the legislature, but the paper work did not get through the Senate. She reapplied from Richland District in 1825.

Farmer, Aaron. Mass. Pvt. He served in the 8th Regiment under Col. Michael Jackson and Capt. Wait. He was wounded in his right shoulder and was disabled with lameness in his right side. He was pensioned 1 Sep. 1782, and in 1788 he was 30 years old. He was on the 1813 pension list. He died 13 May 1831 in Tolland Co., Conn.

Farmer, Thomas. S.C. —. He served under Col. John Baxter, Capt. Robert Baxter, and Capt. Coffee. He was at Bluford's defeat. He applied from Richland District 8 Nov. 1825. He was to be 86 years old in Jan. 1826. John Hill of Darlington District served with him. His son, James Farmer, served with him. He was paid as late as 1831. He had his hip put out of place for five or six years before his death so he could not go to the Treasurer's Office to collect his pension. He died 30 June 1832. His son, William Farmer of Harris Co., Ga., sought the arrearage for the heirs some of whom resided in South Carolina on 7 Aug. 1851. James Kelly swore that his son, John Kelly, was born 31 May 1832 and that Thomas Farmer died a month later. Mary Kelly was the wife of the said James Kelly. William Farmer's sister lived in Georgia. Their brother had remained behind in Richland District, and they believed that he would have sought their father's arrearage. The brother died in 1837. James Kelly's wife was a grand-daughter of the pensioner, Thomas Farmer, and was present when he was buried. Her father died a few years after her grandfather. The pensioner's surviving children were the Rev. William Farmer and Sarah Honeycut. They were paid the arrearage of $250 jointly.

Farnham, Benjamin. —. —. He served under Col. Knowlton and was at Harlem in 1776 when Col. Knowlton was killed. He also served under Col. Sheldon in the dragoons for nearly two years. He also was a substitute at other times. He married 28 Mar. 1781. He resided at Ashford, Conn. He died 5 May 1807. His widow, Anna Farnham, married John Giffin, and he died 13 May 1821. Congress granted her a pension on 4 May 1846 from 25 May 1845 at $8 per month. Compare with Benjamin Farnum.

Farnham, Elisha. N.Y. Pvt. His name was on the 1813 pension list.

Farnham, Thomas. Conn. Sgt. He served in the 2nd Conn. Regiment. He was wounded in his right arm by a musket ball at Edge Hill near White Marsh on 7 Dec. 1777. The ball was extracted 23 Aug. 1781 by John Brewster. He served under Col. Charles Webb and Lt. Col. Isaac Sherman. He was pensioned at Windham, Conn. at the age of 34 years on 21 Sep. 1788. He also appeared as Thomas Farnum. He was on the 1813 pension list.

Farnsworth, John. Va. —. His widow was furnished assistance in Loudoun Co., Va. on 14 Apr. 1778.

Farnsworth, Jonas. Mass. Capt. He resided in Essex Co., Mass. in 1807. He was on the 1813 pension list.

Farnsworth, Levi. Mass. Pvt. He served in Col. Thomas Bigelow's Regiment. He was wounded in the arm by a musket ball which fractured the bone. It happened in battle with the army of Gen. Burgoyne in Sep. 1777 near Stillwater. He enlisted 14 Apr. 1777 for three years, was invalided 26 Jan. 1779, and was discharged 14 Apr. 1780. He lived in Shirley, Mass. in 1792. He was granted half a pension 20 Apr. 1796. He was on the 1813 pension list.

Farnsworth, William. Mass. Sgt. He served in the 3rd Regiment and was from Hanley. He was paid $20.

Farnum, Benjamin. Mass. Capt. He served under Col. J. Fry. He was wounded by musket balls in his left leg and near the right hip in the battle of Bunker Hill on 17 June 1775. The latter remained lodged in his body. He resided in Andover, Mass. in 1795. He served in the militia. He was granted one-third of a pension 20 Apr. 1796. He was on the 1813 pension list as Benjamin Farnham. He died 4 Dec. 1833.

Farr, John. N.J. Pvt. He served under Capt. Joseph Huddy in Feb. 1782. He was killed at the Block House at Toms River 24 Mar. 1782. His heirs were his widow and posthumous child in Monmouth County. He married Sarah Bown 10 Mar. 1782.

Farr, John. Pa. —. He was granted relief in Fayette County 21 June 1839. He died 21 Nov. 1844.

Farrar, —. —. Chaplain. His widow, Mary Farrar, was refused a pension by Congress on 20 May 1850 because no evidence of his service had been furnished.

Farrar, Samuel. Mass. Pvt. He served in the 2nd Regiment under Col. John Bailey in Capt. Samuel Danby's Company. He was disabled by a rupture. He was 50 years old in 1786.

Farrell, William. Pa. Pvt. He applied from Franklin County 15 Apr. 1813. He served in the 4th Pa. Regiment for nearly five years under Col. William Butler. After his discharge he joined the artillery under Col. Potter from 10 Sep. 1781 to 30 July 1783. He was in the battles of Trenton, Brandywine, Germantown, and Paoli. He was wounded in the head by a sword and in the left arm by a bayonet at the latter. He belonged to Capt. Mears' Company. He was 63 years old.

Farrill, James. N.J. —. He was pensioned in Gloucester County 8 Nov. 1837 at the rate of $60 per annum. His widow, Elizabeth Farrill, was pensioned there 4 Feb. 1845 at the rate of $30 per annum. She also appeared as Elizabeth Ferrell, widow of James Ferrell.

Farrin, John. Me. —. He applied from Bath. He was paid $50 under the resolve of 1836.

Farrington, Aaron. Mass. Pvt. He served in the 1st Regiment and was from Bellingham. He was paid $50.

Farrington, Eliphalet. Mass. —. He was in the 1st Regiment and was paid $20.

Farrington, Joseph. Mass. He served in the 1st Regiment and was paid $20.

Farrington, Josiah. Mass. —. He served in the 7th Regiment and was from Wrentham. He was paid $20.

Farrington, March. —. —. He sought relief, but Congress rejected his claim 28 Mar. 1850.

Farrington, William. Mass. Drum Major. He served in the 3rd Regiment and was from Malden. He was paid $20.

Farrow, Thomas. S.C. Lt. He was wounded in the service. He was allowed an annuity 3 Sep. 1784. He received his commutation of full pay for five years in the amount of $3,417.31 on 16 Dec. 1818. He also appeared as Thomas Farrar.

Farster, Martinus. N.Y. Pvt. He served under Col. Peter Vroman in the militia and was slain 30 May 1778 His widow, Annatye Farster, was granted a half-pay pension..

Farwell, Henry. Mass. Capt. He served in Col. William Prescot's Regiment. He was shot through his body by a musket ball on the hills of Charlestown on 17 June 1775. His pay ceased 1 Jan. 1776. He was pensioned at the rate of one-eighth pay from 1 Jan. 1776 on 17 Mar. 1784. He was 64 years old in 1788. He was on the 1813 pension list.

Faulkner, Ammi. Mass. —. He served in the 6th Regiment and was from Royalston. He was paid $50.

Faulkner, William. N.Y. Capt. He served under Col. James McClaughery in the Ulster County militia. He received four bayonet wounds, one in the pit of his stomach, at Fort Montgomery on 6 Oct. 1777. He also had a bruised testicle. He lived in Wallkill, Ulster Co., N.Y. on 21 May 1789. He was aged 39 years in 1787. He was pensioned 1 Dec. 1777. He later lived in Orange County. He was on the 1813 pension list.

Fauntleroy, Robert. Va. Ens. He served in the 5th Virginia Regiment. He was appointed 10 May 1777 and was borne on the roll to May 1778. His devisee, Henry Fauntleroy, sought his commutation, but Congress rejected his petition 15 June 1838.

Fausey, John. Pa. —. He was awarded a $40 gratuity and a $40 annuity in Columbia Co., Pa. 15 Apr.1835.

Faust, John. —. —. He was pensioned under the act of 1818 but discontinued in 1820. He died 10 Apr. 1820, and his widow, Mary Faust, died 31 Mar. 1835. His son, Anthony P. Faust, had his claim rejected by Congress 16 Feb. 1865.

Faust, John. Pa. —. He was pensioned 24 Mar. 1812. He received a $40 gratuity and a $40 annuity. He was from Cumberland County. He died 28 Apr. 1822.

Faxon, Elisha. Mass. Sgt. He served in the 14th Regiment and was from Halifax. His widow, Sarah Faxon, was paid $50.

Fay, Joseph. N.H. Ens. He was in Capt. Ellis's Company in Col. Scammel's Regiment. He died of wounds 19 Sep. 1777. He left a widow, Lucy Fay, and small children in Nov. 1777. They were paid his seven years' half-pay of $840. They lived in Walpole in 1786.

Fay, Levi. Mass. —. He served in the 6th Regiment and was from Brimfield. His widow, Abigail Fay, was paid $50.

Fayris, —. S.C. —. His widow, Elizabeth Fayris, sought the arrearage 6 Dec. 1791.

Feagan, William. N.Y. Pvt. He served under Col. John Livingstone in Capt. Robert Wright's Company. He was disabled by rheumatism and a rupture in his right groin. He was transferred to Capt. Moses McFarlin's Company in the Invalids Corps under Col. Lewis Nichola. He was 54 years old in 1788 and lived in Montgomery County. He was on the 1791 pension roll. He also appeared as William Fagan.

Feagart, William. Pa. Pvt. He was on the 1791 pension roll. He was on the 1813 pension list as William Fegart.

Fealls, Samuel. N.Y. Pvt. His widow was granted relief according to an undated roster. He also appeared as Samuel Falls.

Fear, Hamner. Va. —. He was wounded in the heel of his left foot accidentally by a guard in Mar. 1776. He was discharged by Gen. Lewis. He was awarded a £20 gratuity on 17 May 1777.

Fearson, Joseph. Md. Pvt. He was pensioned at the rate of half-pay of a private 23 Jan. 1816.

Feaster, Henry. N.J. —. He was pensioned in Cumberland County on 7 Mar. 1837 at the rate of $60 per annum.

Feather, —. Pa. —. His widow, Elizabeth Feather, was granted a $40 gratuity and a $40 annuity in Montgomery County 28 Mar. 1836. She was dead by Jan. 1838.

Feather, Isaac. Pa. —. He was awarded a $40 gratuity and a $40 annuity in Montgomery Co., Pa. 4 May 1832.

Feathergill, Joseph. Mass. —. He was paid $20.

Fee, Michael. Pa. —. He was awarded a $40 gratuity and a $40 annuity in Fayette Co., Pa. 8 Apr. 1833. He was 81 years old in 1840. He died 26 Nov. 1847. His widow, Rebecca Fee, was awarded a $40 gratuity 8 May 1850.

Feeks, Robert. N.Y. Corp. He served in the Westchester County militia under Col. Thomas Thomas in Capt. Gilbert Lyons' Company. He was wounded by a musket ball in his left eye which came out the left side of his head at White Plains in Dec. 1780. He lost the use of his eye and several bones of his skull. While Dr. Isaac Smith was dressing his wound, a party of the enemy took him to New York and held him as a prisoner until he was exchanged 3 Sept. 1781. He resided in North Castle, Westchester Co., N.Y. in 1787 and in Ballstown, Albany Co., N.Y. on 15 May 1789. He was a shoemaker. He was aged 38 years on 18 Oct. 1786. He also appeared as Robert Feak. He was on the 1813 pension list.

Feely, Timothy. Va. Lt. He served as ensign in the 11th Virginia Regiment and as lieutenant in the 7th Virginia Regiment and was paid from 10 Dec. 1776 to 31 Dec. 1781. His heirs were allowed five years' full-pay 22 Dec. 1837.

Fegan, John. Pa. —. He applied from Cumberland County on 14 July 1802. He served in the Pa.

Line.

Feikle, Peter. Pa. —. His widow, Mary Feikle, was awarded a $40 gratuity in Lancaster Co., Pa. 8 Apr. 1829.

Felker, George. Pa. Pvt. He served under Capt. Leech and Col. McVeaugh. He was killed at Germantown in Oct 1777. His widow, Agnes Felker, applied 17 Jan. 1780. She had to provide for a daughter.

Felker, George Godfrey. —. —. He died in Mar. 1827. His son, George Felker, sought his father's arrearage, but Congress denied his claim 25 Jan. 1855.

Felix, Peter. Pa. Pvt. He applied from Schuylkill County on 25 Apr. 1816.

Fell, —. Pa. —. His widow, Catherine Fell, was awarded a $40 gratuity and a $40 annuity in Luzerne Co., Pa. 17 Mar. 1835.

Fell, Henry. Pa. —. He was awarded a $40 gratuity in Northampton Co., Pa. 17 Jan. 1831. He was awarded a $40 gratuity and a $40 annuity 1 Mar. 1832. He was dead by July 1832.

Fell, Josiah. Pa. —. He was granted relief in Luzerne County 1 Apr. 1836.

Fellows, Stephen. Conn. Sgt. He served in Capt. Stevens' Company under Col. Charles Burrell on the Canada Expedition in 1776. He contracted a disorder which fell into his limbs and left him crippled. He was unable to walk. He was pensioned 24 Jan. 1780. In 1788 he was 30 years old on 29 Nov. and was from Canaan. He was on the 1813 pension list. He had died in 1812.

Felter, Peter. N.Y. Guide. He led that part of the army at the storming of Stony Point. He was wounded in one of his legs and claimed the gratuity promised by Gen. Wayne. He was wounded in Apr. 1782 at Princeton, N.J. He lived in Westchester Co., N.Y. in 1794.

Felter, Tunis. N.J. —. He was pensioned in Morris County on 28 Feb. 1838 at the rate of $60 per annum. His widow, Rachel Felter, was pensioned on 2 Apr. 1845 at the rate of $30 per annum.

Felton, Daniel. Mass. —. He served under Capt. Mills in the 5th Regiment for three years. He was stricken from the pension roll so he applied to Congress 3 Jan. 1832.

Felton, Robert. Mass. & N.Y. —. He served in the 5th Mass. Regiment under Capt. Mills for three years. He also served a tour of one month and another of one year in the New York Line. He was pensioned in 1818 but stricken because of his property. Congress approved him for a pension 3 Jan. 1832 from the time of his being stricken.

Felty, Henry. Pa. —. His widow, Nancy Felty, was awarded a $40 gratuity in Philadelphia County on 28 Mar. 1820.

Fenn, Thomas. Va. Capt. Lt. He applied from Elizabeth City County on 28 Feb. 1787. He was aged 37. He served in the 1st Regiment of Va. Artillery under Col. Charles Harrison from 1776 to the end of the war. He was wounded at Eutaw, and the ball stuck in the joint of his left shoulder. He was continued on the roll at the rate of £50 per annum on 28 Feb. 1787. He was continued on the roll on 27 June 1790. He was paid at the rate of £75 per annum on 20 Dec. 1792. He was seemingly still alive to 15 Nov. 1805 but was dead by 27 Feb. 1806 when John Shepherd refused to qualify as his executor. The next day Rosa Fenn and Frances Frazier, the legal representatives, refused to qualify as administrators. His name was on the 1813 pension list. He also appeared as Thomas Finn.

Fennell, Stephen. Md. Pvt. He was pensioned in Brown Co., Ohio at the rate of half-pay of a private 13 Feb. 1833.

Fenns, Oliver. Mass. —. He served in the 16th Regiment. He was paid $20. He also appeared as Oliver Fenno.

Fenton, Frederick. Va. —. He was continued on the pension list at the rate of £8 per annum on 23 July 1787.

Feree, Jacob. Pa. —. He was awarded a $40 gratuity and a $40 annuity in Adams Co., Pa. 18 Apr. 1834. He died 28 Aug. 1835. His widow, Mary Feree, was awarded a $40 gratuity and a $40 annuity 14 Jan. 1835. He also appeared as Jacob Ferre.

Fergus, John. Pa. Pvt. He served in the Pa. Line. He lived in Hunterdon Co., N.J. He was on the 1813 pension list. He died 2 Jan. 1829.

Ferguson, —. Va. —. His widowed mother was granted £22.5 for necessaries in Halifax Co., Va. on 17 Dec. 1778.

Ferguson, —. Va. —. John Ferguson was granted £10 support because his two sons were away in the service in Caroline Co., Va. 14 May 1778 and £20 on 8 Apr.1779.

Ferguson, David. Pa. —. He applied from Butler County on 4 Apr. 1820. He was 75 years old. He served in Capt. Miller's Co. under Col. McCoy in the 8th Pa. Regiment for three years. He was in battle at Brunswick and at the taking of Burgoyne.

Ferguson, Edward. Va. —. His wife, Lucy Ferguson, was provided necessaries in Amelia Co., Va. 27 May 1777 and 26 Feb. 1778 while he was away in the service.

Ferguson, James. Pa. —. He was granted relief in Westmoreland County 16 Apr. 1845. He died 22 Mar. 1846.

Ferguson, John. —. —. His son and heir, Samuel Ferguson, sought relief. Congress rejected his request 20 Jan. 1847.

Ferguson, John. —. —. He was a native of New Hampshire and enlisted in 1775 for nine months under Capt. William Scott. He was at Bunker Hill and was discharged after having served nine months. He enlisted for eight months in 1778 under Capt. Drury in the Massachusetts Line. He was discharged at West Point. Both of his discharges were lost in the burning of his step-father's house. He served a total of 17 months. He applied from Washington Co., Penn. He had a wife and children and was unable to work. Congress granted him a pension 22 Dec. 1831.

Ferguson, John. Md. Pvt. He was pensioned 1 Jan. 1803. He was on the 1813 pension list.

Ferguson, John. Pa. —. He was awarded a $50 gratuity and a $40 annuity in Indiana Co., Pa. 22 Dec. 1834.

Ferguson, John. Va. —. His wife, Lucy Ferguson, and seven children were furnished necessaries while he was absent in the service 27 May 1777 and 26 Feb. 1778 in Amelia Co.,Va.

Ferguson, John. Va. —. His wife, Elizabeth Ferguson, was granted 10 bushels of corn and 64 pounds of pork in Berkeley County on 15 Aug. 1780. She received 200 pounds of pork and 3 barrels of corn for herself and three children on 21 May 1782.

Ferguson, John. Va. —. His wife, Esther Ferguson, was furnished 200 pounds of pork and three barrels of corn for the support of her and her three children on 10 Mar. 1782 in Berkeley County.

Ferguson, Joseph. Del. Pvt. He was pensioned in 1783. He was born in Ireland and lost his hearing. He was single. He was on the 1813 pension list. He also appeared as Joseph Forguson.

Ferguson, Robert. Va. —. His wife, Lucy Ferguson, was provided necessaries in Amelia Co., Va. 22 Jan. 1778.

Ferguson, Robert. Va. Pvt. He was in Richmond County on 8 Feb. 1791. He served in Lt. Col. Lee's Legion of Horse and was wounded in 1781 at Camden. He received £12 relief and was pensioned at the same rate on 24 Dec. 1791. He died 25 Dec. 1814. His administrator was

Martin Sisson.

Ferguson, William. —. Pvt. He served nine months under Capt. Daniel McKean and Col. Harper in 1777, four months under Capt. Demond in 1778; and nine months in 1783 under Capt. Phelps and Col. Willet. One witness stated he was under Lt. Walter Vroman and Col. Harper in 1779. His name was not on the roll of Capt. Vance or of Capt. Mark Demond in 1780 for two months and four days. He could not have been a nine month man in 1779 or 1780 so Congress rejected his claim 21 May 1840.

Fernald, Joshua. Mass. —. He served in the 7th Regiment and was from Jay. He was paid $20.

Fernald, Simeon. N.H. Carpenter. He served aboard the *Hampton*, was captured, escaped, and returned home sick. Confined to bed, he died in Feb. 1780. His widow, Margery Fernald, and six children sought relief 12 Feb. 1780.

Ferrara, Emmanuel. Md. Pvt. He was pensioned 4 Mar. 1789.

Ferrell, —. S.C. —. His widow, Elizabeth Ferrell, received the arrearage due her from 1821 and was continued on the pension roll on 20 Dec. 1823.

Ferrell, James. N.J. —. His widow, Elizabeth Ferrell, was pensioned in Gloucester County 4 Feb. 1845.

Ferrill, Dennis. Va. —. He was recommended for a pension 24 Apr. 1783 in Shenandoah Co., Va. He was on the 1785 pension list. He was wounded in his foot at Brandywine in Continental service. He served in the 11th Virginia Regiment.

Ferris, John. —. —. He became a pensioner in 1829. He sought to have his pension made retroactive to 1820, but Congress denied his claim 1 Aug. 1850.

Ferris, John. N.Y. Sgt. He served in Capt. Daniel Miller's Company under Col. Goose Van Schaick. He was inoculated for smallpox and lost the sight of his right eye. He was discharged from hospital at Fort George on 15 Aug. 1776. He was 54 years old on 24 Feb. 1787. He was a shoemaker and lived at Poundridge, Westchester Co., N.Y. in 1787. He was pensioned 29 Mar. 1787. He was on the 1813 pension list.

Ferris, Ransford Avery. Conn. Pvt. He served in a company of coast guards under Capt. Jesse Bell. He was wounded in his right elbow by a ball at Danbury when under the command of Gen. Gould S. Silliman. He was first pensioned at Stamford, Conn. on 19 May 1779. He was again pensioned at the age of 35 on 24 Nov. 1788. He was on the 1813 pension list. He died 2 Jan. 1824 in Fairfield Co., Conn.

Ferris, Silvanus. N.Y. Pvt. He served in Capt. Richard Sackett's Company under Lt. Col. Albert Paulding. He was disabled by a musket ball which entered his cheek, broke his jaw bone, and lodged under his left ear on 5 Sep. 1781. It was removed in May 1784. He was aged 24 years on 6 Aug. 1786. He lived in Columbia, Albany Co., N.Y. on 27 Apr. 1789 but had previously lived in Bedford, Westchester Co., N.Y. He was pensioned 29 Mar. 1787. He was on the 1813 pension list and died 13 Oct. 1827.

Ferris, Squire. —. —. He and his father were taken prisoners by the British on 11 Oct. 1778 and confined to 26 July 1782. He was no more than 11 or 12. Congress rejected him for a pension on 11 Jan. 1838 because he was not in military service.

Ferst, John Adam. Pa. —. He was awarded a $40 gratuity and a $40 annuity in Lancaster County 5 Feb. 1836. He also appeared as John Adam First.

Fertenbaugh, —. Pa. —. His widow, Jane Fertenbaugh, received a $40 annuity in Dauphin County 19 Jan. 1825.

Fessenden, John. Mass. —. He served in the 6th Regiment. He was paid $20.

Feston, John. Va. —. He was injured in his side when a wagon overturned on him. He was in

Continental service. He was awarded a £15 gratuity and an annuity of half-pay of a soldier for two years on 24 Oct. 1778.

Fetner, Aberhard. S.C. Musician. He enlisted in 1777 in the 3ʳᵈ S.C. Regiment under Col. William Thompson for three years. He was taken prisoner at Briar Creek and confined on a prison ship at Savannah until retaken by Capt. Rudolph and Col. Lee. He was 67 years old and had been compensated for three months out of the sixty he served. William Taylor knew him in Capt. Derrill Hart's Company. He was from Richland District in 1826. He was paid as late as 1847.

Fetterhoff, Matthias. Pa. —. He was awarded a $40 gratuity in Adams Co., Pa. 15 Apr. 1835. He also appeared as Mathias Featherhoof. He died 26 May 1840.

Fickle, Benjamin. Md. Lt. He was on the 1813 pension list. He was pensioned at the rate of half-pay of a lieutenant in Muskingum Co., Ohio 2 Mar. 1827.

Fides, George. N.J. Pvt. He served in the 1ˢᵗ Regiment and wounded in his left knee. He was 30 years old. He was on the 1791 pension roll at the rate of $60 per annum.

Field, Abraham. Va. Pvt. He served in the state militia and was wounded in 1775. He was being pensioned 5 Mar. 1785. He was continued on the pension list at the rate of £10 per annum on 20 Nov. 1788.

Field, Henry. —. Lt. He died in the service at the close of 1777 or the beginning of 1778. He left two infant daughters, Judith Field and Elizabeth Field. His wife had predeceased him. Elizabeth Field died unmarried in 1795. His seven years' half-pay was paid to his daughter, Judith Taylor, wife of Francis Taylor, 30 June 1834.

Fielding, Ebenezer. N.H. Pvt. He lost his left eye due to smallpox in the retreat from Canada in 1776. He served under Col. James Read in Capt. Oliver's Company. He lived in Cheshire Co., N.H. in 1792 and in Claremont, N.H. in 1795.

Fields, John. S.C. —. He received an annuity on 13 Mar. 1820.

Fields, William. N.C. —. He was in Rockingham County in 1796 and 1803. He was in Russell Co., Va. in 1809. He was in the battle of Stone Ferry, S.C. where he was disabled by a bullet wound in his right arm. He was on the 1813 pension list of North Carolina as William Fireds [sic]. He later lived in Scott Co., Va.

Fields, William. Pa. —. He applied from Huntingdon County on 2 June 1815. He enlisted at Carlisle in Capt. Waugh's Company in the 6ᵗʰ Pa. Regiment under Col. Irwin. He served nearly two years. He was wounded by a musket ball through his right hand and lost two fingers at the battle of Monmouth in the detachment under Gen. Wayne. He was discharged unfit for service. He lost his discharge when his house was consumed by fire. He was 74 years old. He was generally called Feely, and he did not know how his name was entered on the muster rolls.

Fields, William. Va. Pvt. He lived in Scott County and was pensioned 4 Mar. 1809.

Fierer, Charles. Va. Capt. He was a Hessian officer who resigned his commission and was appointed captain in Nelson's Corps of Cavalry in Dabney's State Legion in the Continental Line. He served to the end of the war. He sustained an injury by a fall from his horse. His estate in Hesse Cassel was confiscated. He was also denounced as guilty of treason. He received 2,000 acres of bounty land from Virginia. His heirs received his commutation in 1836. His administratrix, Caroline Fierer, sought his commutation 2 Feb. 1855. Congress awarded the heirs five years' full pay plus 5% interest from the close of the war to the time of payment on account of half-pay 3 Mar. 1879.

Fifield, John. Me. —. He was from Fryeburg. He was paid $50 under the resolve of 1836.

Figg, —. Va. —. His widow, Mary Figg, was granted £20 on 7 Jan. 1778. Her husband served in Capt. Thomas Nelson's Company and died in the northward in Feb. 1777.

Figg, James. Va. Pvt. He died in the service. His widow, Sarah Figg, was awarded a £20 gratuity 10 Dec. 1777, £10 on 21 Dec. 1778, £12 on 19 July 1779, and £400 on 21 Aug. 1780. She had four children in 1780. She was in York County on 16 Oct. 1786. She had three children: a son aged 16 bound an apprentice, a daughter aged 14, and a son aged 9. She was put on the roll at the rate of £6 per annum on 16 June 1787.

Filer, Thomas. N.Y. —. He served in the 4th Regiment and was killed in battle. His widow was Zephaniah Filer of Rensselaer.

Files, Jeremiah. S.C. —. He was wounded in his left arm and right hand on 17 Jan. 1781 at Tarleton's defeat. His widow, Mary Files, was in Lancaster/Laurens District in 1794. She was paid as late as 1834.

Files, John. S.C. —. He was killed in May 1781. His widow, Mary Files, was allowed an annuity 31 Oct. 1785.

Files, Thomas. N.Y. —. He was wounded in the service. He was on the 1785 pension list.

Fillingsby, —. Pa. —. His widow, Olive Fillingsby, was awarded a $40 gratuity and a $40 annuity in Philadelphia Co., Pa. 28 Feb. 1834. In 1840 Olive was 88 years old. She also appeared as Olive Fulllingsby.

Filmore, George. Mass. Pvt. He served in the 5th Regiment and was from New Salem. His widow, Sarah Filmore, was paid $50.

Filmore, Henry. Conn. Pvt. He served under Col. Whitney in Capt. Griswold's Company. He was wounded in his thigh by a bayonet, in his leg by buck shot, and in his left arm and left hip by musket balls in 1777 at West Chester. He was pensioned in Mar. 1793. He lived in Cornwall, Conn. in 1795. He was granted half a pension 20 Apr. 1796. He was on the 1813 pension list. He transferred to Saratoga Co., N.Y. on 4 Mar. 1826.

Filp, —. Pa. —. His widow was Catherine Filp.

Filson, David. Pa. 1st Lt. His widow, Catherine Filson, was in Montgomery Co. 4 Oct. 1790. He served in the Philadelphia County militia in the 6th Battalion in a company of foot. He died at Pottstown of wounds received in the service a few days before 30 Mar. 1778.

Filson, George. Pa. Pvt. He was in Chester County on 20 Dec. 1785. He served in the 1st Pa. Regiment in Capt. Willson's Company and was wounded in his left leg by a musket ball near Trenton, N.J. in Jan. 1777. He was sent to general hospital at Bethlehem and then to one at Lititz on 20 Mar. 1777. He was transferred to Yellow Springs on 28 Aug. 1778 by Francis Alison, Surgeon and Physician. His brother, Benjamin Filson, was mentioned 7 July 1788. He was 30 years old.

Finch, Christian. N.Y. Corp. His child was granted assistance according to an undated list. He also appeared as Christian Finck.

Finch, Isaac. Conn. Pvt. He served under Col. Samuel Blackley Webb and was discharged in 1783. He was disabled by smallpox and in large measure lost his right eye. He was pensioned in Stratford, Conn. 9 Nov. 1787. He was 21 on 30 Oct. 1787. He appeared as Isaac Finck on the 1791 pension roll. He was on the 1813 pension list as Isaac Frink.

Finch, Jonathan. N.Y. Pvt. He served under Col. Thomas Thomas in the Westchester County militia in Capt. Marcus Moseman's Company. He was disabled by a musket ball in his right arm when on patrol under Lt. Abraham Hyatt at Cortland Manor. He also served under Charles Webb and was pensioned 21 Apr. 1781 from Saratoga County. He lived in Albany Co., N.Y. on 28 May 1789. He also appeared as Jonathan Fink. He was aged 2[?] on 31 Mar. 1786. He was on the 1813 pension list.

Finch, Nathaniel. N.Y. Adjutant. He served under Col. John Hathorn in the Orange County militia and was killed at Minnisink 22 July 1779. His widow, Keziah Finch, was granted a half-pay pension for seven years.

Finchley, George. Conn. Pvt. He was from Stamford, Fairfield Co., Conn. He enlisted in 1775 in Capt. Joseph Hoit's Company under Col. Charles Webb. He was also in Capt. Stephen Bell's Company. At the battle of Harlem Heights he was on a wagon when he was ordered to make his escape. His left arm was caught on one of the wheels. Both of his wrists were broken. He lost the use of his left hand. He applied for his disability pension in New York. He was 37 years old on 4 Aug. 1788. He was on the 1791 pension list. He was also on the 1813 pension list. He also appeared as George Finckley.

Finck, Andrew. —. —. He received his commutation and was to receive half-pay for life by surrendering same.

Finder, Frederick. Va. Pvt. He was in Shenandoah County on 24 May 1783 when he was recommended for a pension and on 27 Apr. 1787. He served under Col. Abraham Buford and was wounded in the elbow at Guilford Courthouse. He was aged 26. His pension was increased to £8 per annum on 14 May 1789. On 1 Feb. 1817 his pension was increased by $60 per annum being added to £8. He was on the 1813 pension list. He lived in Rockbridge County in 1818. He signed his name in German script. He died 9 June 1836, and letters of administration were issued to Robert White 4 Oct. 1836. His widow was Rachel Finder. He also appeared as Frederick Fender.

Findley, Joseph L. —. Capt. He died 23 May 1839. His widow died 1 July 1840. His son, John Blair Findley, sought what was due his mother from the death of his father to the time of her death. Congress rejected his claim

Findley, Kellock. Mass. —. He served as a substitute for Joseph Robinson who was in the militia under Capt. Plummer in guarding the seacoast. He served from 20 Mar. to 10 Dec. 1776. Robinson was deceased. Congress granted him a pension 15 Apr. 1836.

Fink, Christian. N.Y. Corp. He served under Col. Jacob Klock in the Montgomery County militia and was slain 6 Aug. 1777. His children, Ann Fink and Christina Fink, received a half-pay pension for seven years.

Fink, George. Pa. —. He was awarded a $40 gratuity and a $40 annuity in York County 1 Apr. 1836.

Fink, Jacob. Pa. —. He was pensioned in Westmoreland County 13 Apr. 1838.

Finley, Andrew. Pa. —. He resided in Westmoreland County and was awarded 400 acres of donation land 26 Mar. 1813. He served in the 8th Penn. Regiment and was deranged or supernumerary in 1778 or 1779. Congress granted his heirs relief 14 July 1854.

Finley, John. Va. —. He was wounded in the thigh by Cherokee Indians near Long Island on the Holstein River on 20 July 1776. He was awarded a £10 gratuity on 20 June 1777. He was from Washington Co., Va.

Finley, William. N.J. Pvt. He served in the militia under Capt. Sheppard and Maj. Henry Sparks in Salem County. He suffered 19 bayonet stabs in his body and limbs on 21 Mar. 1778 in the neighborhood of Hancock's Bridge. He applied 7 Oct. 1800 in Gloucester County. He also appeared as William Finlow. He was receiving a half-pay pension 10 Feb. 1801 as William Findley.

Finleyson, George. Md. Pvt. He was pensioned 4 Mar. 1789. He was on the 1813 pension list.

Finney, —. S.C. —. His widow, Elizabeth Finney, was granted an annuity 29 Nov. 1785.

Finney, John. S.C. —. There were two children in 1791.

Finney, John L. Pa. Sgt. Maj. He was on the 1813 pension list. He died 10 Oct. 1823 in Northumberland County.

Finney, Michael. S.C. Pvt. He served three years under Col. William Thompson. He was wounded thrice on 9 Oct. 1779 at Savannah. He lost two fingers on his left hand, had 18 pieces of bones extracted from his right arm, and suffered a slight wound in his left ankle. He was pensioned at the rate of $21.30 per annum for life on 20 Dec. 1800. He died 15 Dec. 1818. John Cook of Laurens District was administrator of his estate and sought his arrearage in 1819.

Finney, Richard. Conn. Pvt. He served in the 3rd Regiment. He lost his right arm. He was pensioned in 1783. He was on the 1791 pension roll.

Finney, Richard. Mass. Pvt. He died 12 Mar. 1805.

Fipps, John. Mass. Soldier. He served in the 1st Regiment and was from Ipswich. He was paid $50.

Fischer, John. Va. —. His wife, Elizabeth Fischer, and two children were granted support in Westmoreland County in Feb. 1779 and Mar. 1781.

Fiscus, Abraham. Pa. —. He was awarded a $40 gratuity in Armstrong Co., Pa. 7 Apr. 1828. He was awarded a $40 gratuity and a $40 annuity 8 Apr. 1833. He was from Montgomery County.

Fisher, —. Pa. —. His widow, Catharine Fisher, was awarded relief 31 Mar. 1812.

Fisher, —. Pa. —. His widow, Mary Fisher, was awarded a $40 gratuity and a $40 annuity in Beaver Co., Pa. 15 Apr. 1835. She died 20 Sep. 1843.

Fisher, Adam. Pa. —. He applied from Philadelphia County on 11 Feb. 1823. He was 67 years old. He enlisted in 1776 in Capt. John Douglass' Company in Col. Atlee's Regiment. He served a year in the Pa. Line and was at Long Island, Fort Lee, and White Plains.

Fisher, Cyrus. Mass. Pvt. He served in the 5th Regiment and was from Wrentham. He was paid $50.

Fisher, Frederick. N.Y. Col. He served in the Montgomery County militia and was scalped on 22 May 1780 by a party of Indians at Caughnawaga. He lived in Montgomery Co., N.Y. on 1 July 1789. He died 9 June 1809. He was on the 1813 pension list.

Fisher, Frederick. Va. Pvt. He was awarded a gratuity of one year's pay and an annuity of half-pay for three years on 24 Dec. 1781. He had been wounded at King's Mountain. He was in Washington Co., Va. 15 Apr. 1783. He was pensioned at the rate of £12 per annum on 30 Dec. 1791. His pension was made retroactive from 24 Dec. 1784 since his physical condition was the same. He was in Mecklenburg Co., N.C. on 19 Jan. 1792. He was the son of Charles Fisher. On 3 Apr. 1809 he was in Rowan Co., N.C. He was disabled by a severe wound in his right leg at King's Mountain. He was in the militia and served under Col. William Campbell. He was in Bedford Co., Tenn. in 1820, Maury Co., Tenn. 1830-1836, and Marshall Co., Tenn. in 1839.

Fisher, George. Pa. —. He was awarded a $40 gratuity 22 Dec. 1828 in Lehigh Co., Pa. He was awarded relief again 14 Mar. 1835. He died 22 Sep. 1842.

Fisher, George. S.C. Captain's Steward. He served on the frigate *South Carolina.* He joined the crew at Amsterdam the last of June 1780 and continued in the service to June 1782 when he left the ship in Philadelphia. He served under Commodore Alexander Gillon and Capt. Joiner. He was entitled to prize money from the ship *Venus* and her cargo which was captured and sent to Spain. Lt. John Mayrant was an officer on board. He was 66 years old, nearly blind, and afflicted with palsy. His wife was as aged as himself and incompetent to any labor. Richard Wall confirmed his service. He was from Barnwell District in 1823.

Fisher, Jacob. Pa. —. He was pensioned in Lehigh County 16 June 1836.

Fisher, James. Pa. Pvt. He died 1 Feb. 1798.

Fisher, John. N.J. —. He served under Capt. Paterson in the 3rd Regiment and lost his life 28 June 1778 at the time of the enemy's marching from Philadelphia to New York through New Jersey. He married Louis Duryee 24 Sec. 1777. His widow, Louis Fisher, received a half-pay pension in Morris County in July 1780.

Fisher, John. Pa. —. He was pensioned in Lancaster County 15 June 1836.

Fisher, John. Va. —. His wife, Joyce Fisher, was furnished £20 in Essex Co., Va. on 21 Dec. 1778.

Fisher, John. Va. —. His wife and two children were allowed assistance in Westmoreland County in 1779.

Fisher, Leonard. Mass. —. He was paid $50.

Fisher, Peter. —. —. He lived in Frederick Co., Md.

Fisher, Peter. Pa. —. He was awarded a $40 annuity in Columbia County 5 Feb. 1836.

Fisher, Philip. Md. Pvt. He was pensioned in Frederick County 1789. He was wounded at Guilford Court House. He served in the 1st Regiment. He was on the 1813 pension list.

Fisher, Richard. Va. —. His wife, Elizabeth Fisher, and child were paid £5 support in Louisa Co., Va. on 9 Mar. 1778, £10 in the autumn of 1778, and £45 on 14 June 1779.

Fisher, Samuel. Pa. Capt. He was commissioned 21 May 1777 in the Northumberland County battalion and was made prisoner at Guelph Mills in Chester County. He was held in captivity three years.

Fisher, Stephen. Va. —. He served as pack-horse master in a detachment of militia sent to Kentucky under Col. Bowman. He was wounded in his right shoulder by Indians. He had a large family and was incapable of getting subsistence. He was awarded a £30 gratuity and an annuity of three shillings *per diem* for three years from 25 Oct. 1777 on 14 Oct. 1778.

Fisher, Thomas. Mass. Pvt. He was in the 1st Regiment and was from Taunton. His widow, Jane Fisher, was paid $50.

Fisher, Thomas. Va. —. His wife, Naomi Fisher, and three children were awarded 3 barrels of corn and 150 weight of pork in Accomack Co., Va. 31 Jan. 1783.

Fisher, William. Mass. Pvt. He served in the 10th Regiment under Capt. Emmons and Col. Benjamin Tupper. He was disabled by rheumatism. He was 53 years old in 1786.

Fismire, —. Pa. —. His widow, Catherine Fismire, was granted relief in Philadelphia County 12 Mar. 1836.

Fisk, Robert. Mass. —. He was in the 3rd Regiment and was paid $20.

Fiske, Abijah. —. —. In 1779 he entered on the vessel *Oliver Cromwell* belonging to Connecticut. He was taken prisoner three months later by the British ship *Daphne*. He was wounded severely in his collar bone and right arm. His shoulder was broken and dislocated. He was 76 years old when he applied 18 Jan. 1832. Congress granted him a pension of three-quarters of a disability from 1 Jan. 1825.

Fitch, James. Conn. —. He enlisted in 1777 when he was 15 years old and served under Capt. William Burrall, Lt. Dibble, Ens. Luke Camp, and Col. Porter. In 1779 he was under Capt. Joshua Stanton and Col. Matthew Mead. He was under Capt. Ebenezer Fletcher and Col. Campfield in 1780. In the spring of 1781 he was in the Vermont State Troops under Capt. John Spafford and in the summer was at the fort at Castleton. Congress rejected his petition for a pension because the evidence was not sufficient to prove his service on 27 Jan. 1836.

Fitch, Moses. Mass. Pvt. He served under Col. E. Brooks. He was wounded by a cannon ball and had part of his right shoulder blade carried away at White Plains in 1776. He resided in Bedford, Mass. in 1792. He was in the militia. He was granted one-fifth of a pension 20 Apr. 1796. He was on the 1813 pension list. He died 12 Oct. 1825 in Middlesex Co., Mass.

Fitch, William. —. —. He served as assistant surgeon in the Continental Army for at least seven months and a surgeon in the navy. He attended prisoners at the capture of Gen. Burgoyne. He was appointed doctor on the sloop *Guilford* of Connecticut on 5 Apr. 1779. He was from Stamford, Conn. He married 12 Oct. 1781 Elizabeth Holly. She lived in Richmond Co., N.Y. when Congress granted her a pension 13 July 1846.

Fithian, Aaron. N.J. Pvt. He served under Col. Newcomb. His widow, Mary Fithian, received a half-pay pension.

Fithian, Philip Vickers. N.J. Chaplain. He served under Col. Newcomb and died at Fort Washington in Oct. 1776. His widow, Elizabeth Fithian, was from Cumberland County.

Fitten, Isaiah. S.C. —. He served under Gen. Sumter and was mortally wounded at Eutaw Springs. Administration on his estate was granted to his widow and her father, Roger Cunningham, in Mecklenburg Co., N.C. On 29 Nov. 1805 his only son, Isaiah Cunningham Fitten, sought his deceased father's compensation and was granted £86.10.8 plus interest from 26 Mar.1784. He had turned 21 years old in 1801. Isaiah Cunningham Fitten was paid $352.50 with interest on 20 Dec. 1806. James Martin swore that Isaiah Fitten was the name of a man on his roll. George Alexander saw him killed at Eutaw. Nathaniel Alexander, Surgeon's Mate in the General Hospital of the Southern Department, had twenty-five of the worst cases at Eutaw Springs under his care. Fitten's thigh had been broken by a musket ball and he died in a few days. Mary (Cunningham) Fitten had become Mary Sharp by 10 Nov. 1801.

Fitter, Jacob. Pa. —. He was in Philadelphia County on 8 Jan. 1787. He was in Capt. Dawson's Company in the 10th Pa. Regiment under Col. Richard Humpton. He was afterwards drafted as a blacksmith into the artificers. He was bruised in the breast while shoeing a Continental horse. He was 33 years old.

Fitzgerald, —. Pa. —. His widow, Susanna Fitzgerald, was granted a $40 gratuity and a $40 annuity in Montgomery County 12 Mar. 1836.

Fitzgerald, Benjamin. Md. QM Sgt. He was pensioned at the rate of half-pay of a quartermaster sergeant in Kentucky 7 Mar. 1834.

Fitzgerald, Charles. —. —. He was a pensioner on the Indiana roll when he died. His administrator sought to have the arrearage paid to him. The heirs were so numerous and so dispersed that the amount would be absorbed in fees to prepare and authenticate their claim. Congress allowed his petition 25 Apr. 1840.

Fitzgerald, John. Pa. —. His heirs were paid $200 for his bounty land on 24 Mar. 1832. The money was to be paid in trust to Jacob Drumkeller for the heirs.

Fitzgerald, Nicholas. Md. Pvt. He was pensioned in Washington County at the rate of half-pay of a private 16 Feb. 1821.

Fitzgerald, Thomas. S.C. Legionnaire. He served aboard the frigate *South Carolina* under Commodore Alexander Gillon. His administrator was granted his pay 28 Feb. 1808.

Fitzgerald, William. Md. Pvt. He served from 1777 to the end of the war. A man of his name was paid from 1 Aug. 1780 to 5 Nov. 1783 and awarded a gratuity of $80. Congress acted on his petition 18 Jan. 1837. He claimed to have served under Capt. Richard Andrews of Newton, Md. in the 2nd Regiment. He went south to South Carolina. After the battle of Eutaw in 1781, he went to James Island and eight or nine months later shipped to Annapolis, Md. He was under Greene and Capt. Hugo. Congress found that there was a Capt. Richard Anderson and a Capt. Hugo from Maryland. He was 91 years old in 1835. Congress indefinitely postponed any action 6 Aug. 1847. On 9 Feb. 1842 he claimed service under Capt. Shepperd and Col. Stewart and sought a bill for a pension from 3 Mar. 1826 to 4 Mar. 1832.

Fitzhugh, Peregrine. —. —. His application made 23 Feb. 1810 was rejected.

Fitzhugh, William. Md. Capt. He was pensioned at the rate of half-pay of a captain on the British establishment in Calvert County in Nov. 1791.

Fitzpatrick, Nathan. Md. Pvt. He was pensioned at the rate of half-pay of a private 11 Mar. 1840.

Fitzsimmons, John. Pa. Pvt. He was in Northumberland County 5 Aug. 1786. He was in the militia and was wounded in the right hand by a musket ball at Piscataway, N.J. 1 Feb. 1777. He served in Capt. Cookson Long's Company. He was 60 years old. Lt. Col. James Murray was an officer.

Fitzsimmons, William. Pa. —. He was awarded at $40 gratuity and a $40 annuity in Northumberland Co., Pa. 5 Mar. 1828.

Fladger, Charles. S.C. —. His annuity was £100 in 1787.

Flagg, Jonathan. Conn. Artificer. He served under Col. Baldwin. He suffered from weakness in his breast and the spitting of blood. He resided in Hartford, Conn. in 1792. He enlisted 1 Apr. 1777 and returned sick in Aug. 1780.

Flagler, —. S.C. —. He lost his life at Haddrel's Point. His widow, Elizabeth Flagler, and her four children of Sumter District received payment from 1819 to 1833. [The war was not identified.]

Flanagan, Dennis. Md. Pvt. He was on the 1791 pension list.

Flanagan, James. Pa. —. He was pensioned 12 Apr. 1856 in Philadelphia.

Flanders, Daniel. Mass. —. He was paid $50.

Flannegan, Daniel. N.Y. Pvt. He served under Col. Dubois. He was wounded in the knee while quelling a riot in winter quarters on 12 Dec. 1777 at Newburgh. He lived in Warwick, N.Y. in 1794.

Flatt, Andrew. Pa. —. He was awarded a $40 annuity in Lycoming County 12 Jan. 1836. He was 83 years old in 1840.

Flaugherty, James. Va. —. His wife, Frances Flaugherty, and two children were furnished £40 support in Frederick Co., Va. on 1 June 1779.

Fleck, John. Pa. —. He was awarded relief in Montgomery County 5 Feb. 1836.

Fleck, Peter. Pa. —. He was awarded a $40 gratuity and a $40 annuity in Centre Co., Pa. 20 Mar. 1827.

Fleet, John. Va. Lt. His heirs received his commutation of full pay for five years in lieu of half-pay for life as lieutenant of infantry in the Virginia Line on 15 Feb. 1829.

Fleisher, Jacob. Pa. —. He was awarded a $40 gratuity and a $40 annuity in Berks Co., Pa. 27 Jan. 1835. He served on the *South Carolina*, was captured, and sent to a prison ship in New York. Eleven months later he was discharged. He was pensioned under the act of 1818 but was stricken because his service was not on Continental Establishment. Congress granted him a pension 14 May 1832. He died 10 Dec. 1845.

Fleming, —. —. Va. His wife, Ann Fleming, was granted £25 support in Ohio Co., Va. 3 May 1779. Her husband was away in the service.

Fleming, James. Mass. —. He served in the 1st Regiment and was from Hallowell. He was paid $20.

Fleming, John. N.Y. Pvt. He was on the 1813 pension list.

Fleming, John. S.C. —. He served under Col. Joseph Taylor and Capt. Nathaniel Waller for three months in 1781. James Godfrey, who was between 70 and 80, and Rawleigh Hammon proved his service. The latter saw him under his captain, William Gilliam, in 1780. He also served under Col. William Moore. William Owens served with him. He was at the capture of Fort Ridgely. He was pensioned in Lancaster District 23 Nov. 1829. He was paid as late as 1834.

Fleming, Richard. Pa. —. His widow, Elizabeth Williams, was awarded 200 acres of donation land on

30 Mar. 1812.

Fleming, Robert. Pa. —. He was granted relief 20 May 1839 in Fayette County. He was 71 in 1840. He died 20 Dec. 1845. His widow, Mary Fleming, was awarded a $40 annuity in Allegheny County 10 Apr. 1849 for his Revolutionary service. She died 30 July 1849.

Flenniken, David. N.C. Ens. He applied in Mecklenburg County in 1800. He was wounded in his right side at the battle of Hanging Rock. He was in the militia. He was rejected in 1802. He appeared on the 1813 pension list as David Flannagan. He died 25 Sep. 1826.

Fletcher, —. Va. —. Robert Fletcher was granted financial support because his sons were away in the service in Caroline Co., Va. 8 Jan. 1778 and again on 8 Apr. 1779. He had three sons in the service 9 Aug. 1781 and a family of five.

Fletcher, Benjamin. N.H. Fifer. He served in the 2nd Regiment. He was wounded by a bullet which passed through the small of his back in July 1777 at Hubbardstown. He lived in New Ipswich, N.H. in 1794. He enlisted 5 Mar. 1777 and was discharged 1 Apr. 1780.

Fletcher, Ebenezer. N.H. Fifer. He served in Hale's Regiment. He was pensioned 22 Aug. 1794 in Hillsborough Co., N.H. He was granted one-fourth of a pension 20 Apr. 1796. He was on the 1813 pension list.

Fletcher, John. N.Y. Corp. He served under Col. Seth Warner and was slain 11 Oct. 1780. His widow, Fanny Fletcher, was granted a half-pay pension for seven years.

Fletcher, Patrick. —. —. His widow received an annuity 29 Apr. 1802.

Fletcher, Simon. Pa. QM. He applied from Butler County on 26 Oct. 1820. He enlisted in Capt. John Findley's Company in the 8th Pa. Regiment under Col. Broadhead in 1777 and served to the end of the war. He died 1 Aug. 1824.

Flicker, Christian. Pa. —. He was granted relief.

Fling, James. —. —. He was pensioned under the act of 1818 but was dropped in 1820 because he did not exhibit a property schedule. He was restored in 1832 retroactively from 4 Mar. 1831. He sought his pension from 4 Mar. 1820 to 4 Mar. 1831. Congress rejected his petition 25 Mar. 1836.

Fling, James. Md. Sgt. He was pensioned at the rate of half-pay of a sergeant in Montgomery County 24 Feb. 1824. His arrearage of $7.00 was paid to his executor, Henry Harding, in Jan. 1837.

Flint, Ebenezer. Mass. —. He served in the 8th Regiment and was paid $20.

Flint, John. Mass. —. His widow, Betty Flint, was paid $50.

Flint, Jonathan. —. —. He was granted a pension in 1832 and then stricken due to being listed as a deserter on the roll. He performed the duties of a sergeant under Col. Durkee and was promised to be appointed an ensign when one became available. After Monmouth he became displeased and refused to serve longer. He had a sixty day furlough. The colonel sent a sergeant after him. He was told he could have an honorable discharge if he found a substitute. He got his brother, Daniel Flint, to serve out his time. Congress granted him a pension 7 June 1836.

Flint, Thomas. —. —. His application made 7 May 1796 was rejected.

Flonagan, Dennis. Md. Pvt. He was pensioned 4 Mar. 1789. He was on the 1813 pension list as Dennis Flannaghan.

Flood, —. Pa. —. His widow, Jane Flood, received a $40 gratuity and a $40 annuity in Westmoreland County 22 Apr. 1857.

Flood, Stephen. Mass. —. He served in the 1st Regiment and was paid $20.

Floyd, Ebenezer. —. —. He received his bounty land. His daughter, Betsey A. Faulkner, sought to receive his pension 30 June 1854. Congress refused her claim.

Floyd, Henry. —. Pvt. He was pensioned. Congress rejected the claim of his widow, Jemima Floyd, for relief because she married in 1800 on 18 Mar. 1846.

Fluck, John. Pa. —. He was pensioned in Bedford County 24 Mar. 1837. He died 23 Aug. 1840.

Flue, William. Pa. —.He was pensioned in Philadelphia 3 Mar. 1837.

Fluelling, —. Va. —. He died in the service. His widow, Ann Fluelling, was awarded £10 in Goochland Co., Va. 20 Oct. 1777.

Fly, Isaac. Pa. —. He applied in Berks County on 10 Feb. 1807. He enlisted 8 Aug. 1776 for the war and served in Capt. Andrew Redheffer's Company under Col. John Moore in the Flying Camp. On 18 Nov. 1776 he was taken prisoner at Fort Lee and held to Feb. 1777 when he was permitted to go home on parole. He was exchanged in May 1780 having served three years, nine months, and some days. He was awarded donation land.

Flynn, Samuel. Pa. —. He was granted $40 per annum 18 Apr. 1814.

Flynn, Simon. Pa. —. He was pensioned 18 Apr. 1814. He died 12 Sep. 1821.

Foendenmiller, —. Pa. —. His widow, Catherine Foendenmiller, was awarded a $40 gratuity and a $40 annuity in York Co., Pa. 15 Apr. 1835. She died 1 Feb. 1840..

Fogas, John. Pa. Matross. He was on the 1813 pension list.

Fogg, Charles. Me. —. He was from Brownfield. He was paid $50 under the resolve of 1836.

Fogg, George. Me. —. He was from Wales, Maine. He was paid $50 under the resolve of 1836.

Fogg, Jonathan. —. —. He enlisted in May 1775 for three months under Capt. Daniel Moore and Col. John Stark. He was at Bunker Hill. He left the service in July 1775. At the end of the month he enlisted under Capt. Henry Dearborn and marched from Cambridge under Benedict Arnold to the mouth of Kennebeck to the Plains of Abraham. On that march he was forced to eat the flesh of the dogs. He was wounded in the assault on Quebec and confined in prison. Nine months later he was exchanged and discharged in Oct. 1776. He applied for a pension 4 Apr. 1828 but his time of imprisonment was not construed as military service. Congress granted him a pension 3 Jan. 1832 effective from 4 Apr. 1828.

Foggett, Richard. Md. Pvt. He was pensioned in Anne Arundel County at the rate of half-pay of a private 12 Feb. 1820. His widow, Artridge Foggett, received her arrearage 17 Mar. 1835 and was pensioned at the same rate 30 Mar. 1835. Her arrearage was to be paid to her legal representative on 6 Feb. 1850. It was paid to Gassaway Owens, her legal representative, 14 Feb. 1850.

Fogler, Simon. Md. Pvt. He served in the German Regiment. He was wounded by a cannon ball or grape shot in his hip in 1777 at Germantown. He lived in Md. in 1794. He mustered, was wounded in Nov. 1777, and was discharged in Apr. 1778. He was on the 1813 pension list.

Foins, —. S.C. —. Edith Foins received her annuity of $30 per annum 19 Dec. 1832. *Vide* — Forns.

Folk, Simon. Pa. —. He was awarded a $40 gratuity and a $40 annuity in Cumberland Co., Pa. 18 Feb. 1834. He also appeared as Simon Foulk.

Folkson, Charles. Ga. —. His family was granted assistance 8 Feb. 1782.

Follett, Frederick. Mass. Pvt. He served under Capt. Spaulding. He was scalped, wounded by a musket ball in the right shoulder blade and by another in his left arm, and was stabbed nine times at Susquehanna in 1779. He resided at Dalton, Mass. in 1779. He enlisted in Sept. 1776 for the war. He was granted half a pension 20 Apr. 1796. He was on the 1813 pension list.

Folley, John. S.C. —. He served in Col. Lytle's Regiment. He was unable to earn a living so he applied to the Fairfield District Court for financial assistance. Receiving none, he applied to the legislature 11 Dec. 1798. He was again rejected because there was no provision for such a case.

Follingsby, James. —. —. His widow, Sarah Foster, sought a pension in 1838 but was rejected because he served but five months and 18 days. Congress declined to award her a pension 1 Aug. 1850.

Foltz, Hans Jost. N.Y. Pvt. He was wounded in his right shoulder and arm by a musket ball at German Flatts on 9 July 1779. He served in Capt. Henry Herter's Company under Col. Peter Bellinger. He was pensioned 14 Sep. 1786 at the age of 44. He lived in Kingsland, Montgomery Co., N.Y. on 28 July 1789. He also appeared as Hans Jost Fults and John Jose Foltz. He later lived in Rensselaer County. He was on the 1813 pension list.

Foltz, Peter. N.Y. Pvt. He served under Col. Peter Bellinger and was slain in the service. His sons, Peter Foltz and Conrad Foltz, were granted a half-pay pension.

Fonda, Jellis A.. N.Y.. —. He served as an officer from 1777 to 1783. He was not pensioned in 1828 because he was not on Continental Establishment. Congress granted him a pension on 22 Dec. 1831 from 1 Jan. 1830. He was agent for the purchase of supplies for the troops but had no special appointment by N.Y. or the U.S. His dwelling house, barn, and outhouses in Tryon Co., N.Y. were destroyed while he was serving as commissary. His heirs, grand-daughter Jane VanHorne and Abraham VanHorne, had their claim rejected by Congress 9 Feb. 1842.

Fontaine, William. Va. Lt. Col. His regiment guarded the convention troops until disbanded in May 1781 under Maj. Robert Roberts. There was no evidence of his resignation. Congress gave the heirs his commutation 21 Dec. 1838.

Fonter, White. Pa. —. He was granted relief in Philadelphia 10 Apr. 1849.

Fontonwhite, Jacob. Pa. —. His widow, Mary Ann Fontonwhite, was awarded a $40 gratuity in Philadelphia County 10 Apr. 1849 for his Revolutionary service.

Foochee, Elijah. —. Pvt. He served eight months as a drafted militia man in 1780 and six months as a captain of a volunteer troop of horse. Congress did not find that his latter service was satisfactorily made out and granted him a pension for eight months service as a private on 5 Mar. 1840.

Foos, Matthias. Pa. —. His widow, Hannah Foos, was awarded a $40 gratuity and a $40 annuity in Chester Co., Pa. 1 Mar. 1832.

Foot, —. —. —. His widow, Mary M. Foot, was refused a pension by Congress on 29 Feb. 1848 because she did not sustain her claim with proof.

Foot, Samuel. Mass. —. He served in the 6th Regiment and was from Londonderry. He was paid $20.

Foote, Thomas. Mass. Pvt. He served under Col. Ebenezer Frances and Capt. George White. He was 64 years in 1787. He was wounded on the retreat from Ticonderoga. He was pensioned at the rate of half-pay from 23 Dec. 1778 on 25 Jan. 1779. He was disabled by the loss of his eye sight and sundry wounds in his breast and right arm. He was on the 1813 pension list. He also appeared as Thomas Foot and Thomas Fool [sic].

Forbes, Alexander. N.Y. Pvt. He served in Capt. James Grigg's Company in the 3rd N.Y. Regiment under Col. Peter Gansevoart. In 1778 he was transferred to Capt. Leonard Bleeker's Company. The bones in his left leg were fractured. He was then transferred to Capt. Aaron Arson's company of the 1st N.Y. Regiment under Col. Goose Van Schaick. He had enlisted 1 May 1778 and served to the end of the war. He was also under Capt. Howson. He was about 56 years old in 1788. He was a painter in New York City, N.Y. in June 1788. He died 10 Mar. 1790.

Forbes, Daniel. Pa. Sgt. He served in 4th Penn. Regiment of Artillery. He was hurt by the oversetting of a six pound cannon which broke his left arm and much bruised his head on 18 May 1780 at Short Hills, N.J. He lived in Philadelphia Co., Pa. in 1794. He was a corporal 31 Aug. 1777 and was promoted to sergeant on 1 Mar. 1778.

Forbes, Elisha. Conn. Pvt. He served in Major Ball's Conn. Regiment. He lived in Warren Co., N.Y. He was on the 1813 pension list and died 26 Sep. 1831.

Forbes, James. Mass. Sgt. He served in the 3rd Regiment and was paid $20. He also appeared as James Fobs.

Forbes, John. S.C. —. He was wounded by the British under Col. Hook and was literally cut to pieces. He served under Col. Neal. His brother, Joseph Forbes of York District, and Joseph McCorkle proved his service. He was pensioned 4 Dec. 1819. He received one year's arrearage. His executors were paid his arrearage on 25 Nov. 1830.

Forbes, William. S.C. Pvt. He enlisted for three years and served under Capt. John Caldwell and Col. Thompson. He was discharged after 17 or 18 months because of white swelling which rendered him incapable of duty. He partially recovered and returned to serve under Capt. Francis Logan and Col. Pickens against the Cherokee. He was pensioned 7 Dec. 1819 in Pendleton District. His widow, Margaret Forbes, received his arrears of $60 on 18 Dec. 1820. She was placed on the pension roll on 20 Dec. 1821. She was 56 years old. Her daughter Cynthia Forbes was about 21, her daughter Eliza Forbes about 16, and her son Alanson Forbes was about 11 and very sickly. She was paid as late as 1834.

Forbis, Arthur. N.C. Capt. His widow, Elizabeth Forbis, applied in Guilford County in 1833. He was wounded in the battle of Guilford and died soon afterwards. He also appeared as Arthur Forbes. She and her numerous family had been granted assistance in 1782 and 1783.

Forbus, William. Pa. —. He was from Allegheny County.

Forbush, David. Mass. Corp. He served in the 9th Regiment and was from Royalston. His widow, Dorcus Forbush, was paid $50.

Force, Joseph. —. He served as an officer and was disabled by wounds received at Brandywine. He died in 1812; his widow in 1837. The children sought what their mother might have claimed. She never applied so Congress decided nothing was due them on 14 June 1852.

Ford, Dennis. Pa. —. He was in the Pennsylvania Hospital from 25 Jan. 1782 and was paid 9 June 1788 after which there were references to his funeral charges.

Ford, Hezekiah. Md. Lt. He was pensioned in Cecil County at the rate of half-pay of a lieutenant 9 Feb. 1822.

Ford, Jacob. N.J. Col. He served in the 1st Regiment of Foot of the Morris County militia. He contracted a cold on the retreat from the Mud-rounds to Morristown. He was struck with pleurisy. He died 10 Jan. 1777. His widow, Theodosia Ford, applied in Morris County 18 Dec. 1795.

Ford, James. N.H. Capt. He served under Col. Moses Nichols in Gen. Stark's Brigade and was badly wounded on 6 Aug. 1777 by two musket balls which passed through his two thighs in the battle of Walloomsuck Hill near Bennington. He lived in West Nottingham, N.H. in 1794. He was in the militia. He was granted half a pension 20 Apr. 1796.

Ford, John. Va. —. His pension of £6 per annum was continued 12 May 1787.

Ford, Joseph. —. —. He was disabled at Brandywine. He died in 1812, and his widow died in 1837. Congress rejected the claim from his children for a pension 14 June 1852.

Ford, Joseph. Md. Capt. He died in Dec. 1812.

Ford, Joseph. Md. 2nd Lt. His widow, Mary Ford, was pensioned at the rate of half-pay of a second lieutenant 4 Mar. 1837.

Ford, Mahlon. N.J. Capt. His pension was approved 5 July 1812. He transferred to New York City and died 14 June 1820.

Ford, Nathan. Vt. Pvt. His pension was approved 5 July 1812. He was on the 1813 pension list.

Ford, Simon. Pa. —. He was the servant of Rudolph Spangler of York County. He enlisted in 1777 in Col. Thomas Hartley's Regiment for one year and eleven months agreeable to the terms of his indenture. Spangler was to be paid $50.33 plus interest in satisfaction for his loss of Ford's service on 31 Mar. 1806.

Ford, Theodosius. —. —. He applied for a Revolutionary War pension.

Ford, William. —. —. He served under Col. Edmonds. He was under Capt. Jennings for six months, Capt. Bailiss for six months, and on three other tours. He was at the surrender of Cornwallis at Yorktown. He was pensioned in 1832 but stricken from the roll. Congress granted him a pension 2 Jan. 1839 for $20 per annum.

Forehand, Darby. Va. —. His widow, Elenore Forehand, was allowed £40 in Augusta Co., Va. 19 May 1779.

Foreman, —. Pa. —. His widow, Esther Foreman, was granted relief 18 Apr. 1843 in Columbia County. She died 5 May 1843.

Foreman, Jacob. S.C. —. There were two children in 1791.

Foreman, Peter. Pa. —. He was awarded a $40 gratuity and a $40 annuity in Franklin Co., Pa. 15 Mar. 1826. He was 87 years old in 1840

Forns, Edmund. S.C. —. His widow, Edith Forns, was in Fairfield District in 1791. *Vice* — Foins.

Forrest, Andrew. Pa. Capt. He applied from Danville 7 Aug. 1813. He was appointed lieutenant in 1776, was made a prisoner at the reduction of Fort Washington 16 Nov. 1776, and held a captive for nearly two years. He then rose to the rank of captain and was given a commission in the Pa. Line. Capt. Alexander Graydon of the 3rd Battalion proved his service. He was from Milton, Northumerland Co., Pa. 28 May 1813. He died 22 Jan. 1818.

Forrest, John. Mass. —. He served in the 4th Regiment and was paid $20.

Forrest, Uriah. Md. Lt. Col. He was commissioned a major 1 Jan. 1777 and a lieutenant colonel 17 Apr. 1777. He lost his leg in battle at Germantown. He resigned 23 Feb. 1781. He died 8 July 1805. His widow was Rebecca Forrest. The arrearage of her pension was paid to her daughters, Ann Green and Maria Bohrer, on 12 Feb. 1844. Congress allowed his daughters his five years' full pay 5 Feb. 1873. Osceola C. Green was administratrix *de bonis non*.

Forrest, William. Mass. —. He served in the 4th Regiment and was from Suffield. He was paid $20.

Forrester, John. S.C. —. He served 10 months under Capt. William Alexander in the Light Dragoons and Col. Wade Hampton. He applied for a pension, but there was a delay. He died in Georgia. Congress allowed his surviving children relief 19 Mar. 1860.

Forschthe, James. Pa. —. He was granted a $40 gratuity and a $40 annuity in Allegheny County in June 1840.,

Forsman, Alexander. Pa. Capt. He was on the 1813 pension list. His name may have been Alexander Foreman.

Forster, James. N.Y. —. His wife and five children were granted support in Dutchess County on 3 Nov. 1781. [This entry is very faint in the manuscript.]

Forster, Thomas. Pa. —. He was pensioned 8 Apr. 1815.

Forsyth, Robert. —. —. His heirs sought a pension.

Fort, Sherwood. N.C. Pvt. He applied in Cumberland County in 1827. He fought at Brandywine, Guilford Court House, Briar Creek, Long Bridge, &c. Nazary Mitchell of Robeson County served as drum major with him and confirmed his service. He was deaf. His pension was $50 per annum.

Fortner, Charles. S.C. —. His widow and two children were on the pension roll in 1791.

Fortune, —. Va. —. Frances Fortune was granted £5 support because her sons were away in the service in Caroline County 11 June 1778.

Fortune, Richard. —. —. His heirs, Lucy Knowles and Margaret Williams, sought bounty land. Congress rejected their claim 9 June 1838.

Foss, David. Mass. Pvt. He served in the 1st Regiment under Capt. Philip Thomas and Col. Thomas Marshall. He was disabled by epileptic fits. He was 25 years old in 1788.

Foss, Elias. Me. —. He was from Limington. He was pensioned in 1818 but stricken from the rolls in 1820. His petition to be restored was rejected 2 Feb. 1825. He was paid $50 under the resolve of 1836.

Foss, Joseph. Me. —. He was from Buckfield. He was paid $50 under the resolve of 1836.

Foster, —. S.C. —. Martha Foster and her children received an annuity 8 Jan. 1820.

Foster, Anthony. R.I. Pvt. He was wounded in the hip by the bursting of a shell at Red Bank, N.J. on 22 Oct. 1777; wounded in the ankle at Springfield, N.J. 23 June 1780; and received a broken shoulder on a march to Virginia in Sept. 1781. He served under Col. Jeremiah Olney. He was aged 66 in 1785. He resided in Providence Co., R.I.

Foster, Benner. Me. —. He was from Portland. He was paid $50 under the resolve of 1836.

Foster, Cato. Mass. —. He was in the 1st Regiment and was from Salem. He was paid $20.

Foster, Cosby. Va. Pvt. He was in Louisa County on 7 Apr. 1787. He was aged 26. He enlisted in July 1778 in the 3rd Regiment of Baylor's Light Dragoons. He was disabled by a wound in his right thigh. The bone was shattered. That limb was several inches shorter than the other. His captain was William Barrett. He was continued on the pension list on 3 Apr. 1787 at the rate of £15 per annum. It was continued on 10 Mar. 1789. He was on the 1813 pension list.

Foster, Daniel. Mass. —. He was allowed £8 in full to June next on 19 Jan. 1780. He was paid £12 in full for his pension to 7 June 1781. One of his name sought an increase of his pension 25 Sep. 1793 from Pembroke, Mass.

Foster, Elisha. Mass. Ens. He received his commutation for five years in lieu of half-pay. He was from Brookfield.

Foster, Haekaliah. Mass. Sgt. He served in Col. Shepherd's Regiment. He was wounded by a musket ball in his right hand on 29 Aug. 1779 in R.I. He lived in Saratoga, N.Y. in 1794. He enlisted 1 Mar. 1777. He was pensioned in Sep. 1793. He was on the 1813 pension list of New York and died 4 Sep. 1820.

Foster, James. Mass. Pvt. He served under Col. John Mixon and Capt. Joseph Butler. He was 55 years old in 1787. He was disabled by the loss of his left eye.

Foster, John. N.Y. Pvt. He served in Jonathan Hallett's Company under Col. Philip Van Schaick. He was wounded in his left knee by a musket ball. He once lived in New Jersey. He lived in New York City, N.Y. in 1788 and in Marlborough, N.Y. on 10 June 1789. He was aged -----ty-nine years on 15 Aug. 1785. He was on the 1813 pension list.

Foster, John. Va. —. He was fatally wounded by a canon ball at Gwyn's Island in opposing the forces of Lord Dunmore. His widow, Elizabeth Foster, was awarded a £20 gratuity in Gloucester Co., Va. 7 Nov. 1776.

Foster, Jude. Mass. Corp. He served under Col. Asa Whitcomb and Capt. Jonathan Danforth. He was wounded by musket balls which broke his left hip. He was 27 years old in 1787. He was pensioned 30 Oct. 1784. He died 28 Mar. 1789.

Foster, Levi. —. —. He was drafted to serve under Col. Benjamin Foster and Maj. George Stillman and marched to Machias, Me. He did duty as a soldier for a year followed by two years in a breastwork. He was in the engagement with the brig *Dawson*. He was also drafted to go to St. Johns to take a British vessel. His brother, Samuel Foster, was about five years younger. His total service was about a third of the time for four years. Congress declined to give him a pension 9 May 1850.

Foster, Moses. Mass. Pvt. He served in the 8th Regiment and was from Essex. His widow, Mary Foster, was paid $50.

Foster, Parker. Me. —. He was from Eliot. He was paid $50 under the resolve of 1836.

Foster, Peter. Va. Lt. He served in the infantry. He received his five years' full pay commutation 2 Mar. 1833.

Foster, Robert. Va. Lt. He served under his brother, Capt. James Foster, in the 15th Virginia Regt. His brother died in 1779. Robert Foster marched from Amelia Co., Va. He was wounded and taken prisoner in 1778. His children, Elizabeth Robert Foster, who married Edmund Booker, and James B. Foster sought their father's and uncle's commutation pay. Their claims were rejected in 1820.

Foster, Samuel. N.H. Sgt. He served in Cilley's Regiment. He was pensioned 18 Aug. 1796 in Merrimack Co., N.H.

Foster, Samuel. S.C. —. He served in Capt. Dawson's Company in Col. Pickens' Regiment. James Devlin affirmed his service. He was from Abbeville District 11 Nov. 1823.

Foster, Thomas. Mass. Pvt. He served in the 7th Regiment and was from Middleborough. He was paid $20.

Foster, Thomas. Mass. Sgt. He served in the 1st Regiment and was from Essex. His widow, Susannah Foster, was paid $20.

Foster, Thomas. Pa. —. He applied from Cumberland County in Feb. 1816. He enlisted in Mar. 1777 in Capt. Ulrick Ming's Company in the Pa. Line and was transferred to Capt. Alexander Dow's Company as an orderly sergeant and foreman of matross artificers in Col. Benjamin Flowers' Regiment. He was discharged in 1781. He died 24 Nov. 1818.

Foster, William. Mass. Sgt. He served in Col. E. Bridge's Regiment. He was wounded in his left wrist by a musket ball at Bunker Hill on 17 July 1775. In 1794 he resided in Bristol, Lincoln Co., Me. He was on the 1813 pension list.

Foster, William. N.Y. Pvt. He served in Capt. Salisbury's Company under Col. William B. Whiting in the Albany County militia. He lost his right eye in battle. He was taken captive and carried to Fort Edward. He lived in Upper Salem, Westchester Co., N.Y. He was aged 25 years old on 8 Apr. 1787. Compare with William Foster from Pa. *infra.*

Foster, William. N.Y. Pvt. He served in Col. Van Schaick's Regiment. He transferred to Pennsylvania by Mar. 1810.

Foster, William. Pa. Pvt. He served under Col. William B. Whiting. He was on the 1789 pension list. He later transferred to New York. Compare with William Foster from N.Y. *supra.*

Fotte, —. Pa. —. His widow was Hannah Fotte of Chester County who was pensioned 3 Mar. 1829 and was deceased by Apr. 1839.

Fouchee, Isaac. N.C. —. There were no terms of continuous service in North Carolina. He claimed eight months. He also served six months in a troop of horse. Congress rejected him for relief 23 June 1840.

Fought, Frederick. Pa. —. He was awarded a $40 gratuity and a $40 annuity in Perry Co., Pa. 22 Dec. 1834. He died 16 Dec. 1853.

Foulk, John. Penn. Drummer. He and his father were at Trenton when the Hessians were taken at

Trenton in 1776. He was in the militia. He was also at Germantown. He was taken prisoner and was on a prison ship in New York for seven months. Congress rejected him for a pension on 1 Mar 1842 because he had not served the minimum of six months.

Fountain, John. Conn. Pvt. He served in the 5th Conn. Regiment and was wounded in both legs. He was pensioned 29 Aug. 1782 and was on the 1813 pension list.

Fountain, William. —. Lt. Col. He guarded the convention troops until disbanded in May 1781. His legal representative was allowed his commutation 17 May 1836.

Fouquet, Nicolas. Mass. Capt. He and his son, **Marc Antoine Fouquet**, came with Gen. LaFayette to New England to instruct the people how to make gunpowder. They were paid as captain and lieutenant artillery officers. The father was not heard from after he reached Bordeaux, France. Marc Antonie Fouquet married Lydia Giddings in Aug. 1780 in Brentwood, N.H. and had two children Marie Jeanne Fouquet born 14 Apr. 1782 and Henrietta Marie Fouquet born 13 Oct. 1784. The latter died unmarried at the age of 26. He went to Tobago, W.I. in 1784 and died of a fever in 1786. His widow died in 1813. Marie Jeanne Fouquet married Robert Jenkins and had Mary Jane (Jenkins) Marston, Elizabeth Jenkins, James Fouquet Jenkins, William Jenkins, and Sarah Jenkins. They were granted relief 24 Feb. 1882.

Foust, Jasper. S.C. Physician. He was pensioned in Dec. 1846 and died 25 Oct. 1849. His widow, Esther Foust, was from Richland District in 1850. She was 77 or 78 years of age. They had married in Feb. 1791. He also appeared as Jasper Faust and Casper Faust.

Foust, John. Pa. —. He was granted a $40 gratuity in Cumberland County 1 Mar. 1811.

Foust, John. Pa. —. He was granted relief in Columbia County 27 Jan. 1837. He was 84 years old in 1840.

Fowe, William. Pa. —. He received a $40 gratuity and a $40 annuity in Philadelphia County 1 Apr. 1836.

Fowle, Curtis. Mass. —. He served in the 6th Regiment and was paid $20.

Fowle, Jeremiah. N.H. Corp. He served in the 1st N.H. Regiment of the militia. He was pensioned 31 July 1796 in Rockingham Co., N.H.

Fowler, Alexander. Pa. Brig. Gen. His widow and executrix, Sarah Fowler, applied 19 Dec. 1811.

Fowler, Benjamin. R.I. Pvt. He served in the R.I. Regiment. He lost the use of his eyes by smallpox. He served under Col. Benedict Arnold in Quebec. He had a leg amputated after the war. He resided in Providence, R.I. in 1794. He enlisted 15 Mar. 1777 and continued to the end of the war. He served in Col. Angel's Regiment.

Fowler, Israel. S.C. —. He returned home from the service and died of disease. His widow, Martha Fowler, and two children (who were under the age of twelve) received an annuity 3 June 1819 in Horry District. Payment was made as late as 1824.

Fowler, John. Va. —. His wife, Bridget Fowler, and children were granted £20 support in Rockingham Co., Va. 26 May 1778. She and the three children were granted £50 relief on 23 Aug. 1779.

Fowler, Joseph. Va. —. His widow, Anne Fowler, and children were granted £15 relief in Powhatan Co., Va. on 19 Feb. 1778. She and the three children were awarded £100 on 10 Feb. 1779.

Fowler, Nehemiah. Conn. Pvt. He served in the 5th Conn. Regiment. On 4 Oct. 1777 at Germantown, he was under the command of Capt. Josiah Lacy and was in the rear guard on the retreat from the enemy. He was wounded by a ball in both legs. He was 33 years old and resided in Fairfield when he was pensioned 16 Aug. 1788.

Fowler, Patrick. Pa. Matross. He was on the 1813 pension list.

Fowler, Thedosius. Capt. N.Y. He was in the service in 1776 and was promoted in Apr. 1778. He served to the end of the war and died 16 Oct. 1841. He married in Sept. 1784. Congress granted his widow, Maria Fowler, a pension 9 Feb 1842.

Fowler, William. Va. —. His heirs were continued on the pension roll in Washington County 15 April 1783. The auditor was left at his discretion to pay the arrears due to the heirs on 5 Jan. 1787.

Fowles, Benjamin. Mass. —. He served in the 1ˢᵗ Regiment and was paid $20.

Fowles, Samuel. Mass. Pvt. He served in Capt. Benjamin Farnum's Company under Col. James Frye. He was wounded on the heights of Charlestown and was pensioned at the rate of half-pay from 31 Dec. 1775 on 22 Sep. 1777. He was on the 1813 pension roll. He also appeared as Samuel Fowle.

Fox, —. Pa. —. His widow, Catharine Fox, was awarded a $40 gratuity and a $40 annuity in Berks Co., Pa. 10 Apr. 1835. She died 2 Oct. 1843.

Fox, —. Pa. —. His widow, Elizabeth Fox, was awarded relief in Berks County 5 Feb. 1836.

Fox, —. Pa. —. His widow, Elsie Fox, received a $40 annuity in Greene County 8 May 1854.

Fox, —. Pa. —. His widow, Mary Fox, was awarded a $40 gratuity and a $40 annuity in Montgomery Co., Pa. 3 Mar. 1829.

Fox, —. Pa. —. His widow, Rachel Fox, was granted relief 12 Mar. 1836. She died in Lancaster Co . 6 Nov. 1846.

Fox, Andrew. Pa. —. He received a $40 gratuity and a $40 annuity 2 Apr. 1822.

Fox, Anthony. Md. Pvt. He was pensioned at the rate of half-pay of a private in Anne Arundel County in Nov. 1806.

Fox, Christopher William. N.Y. Capt. He served in the militia under Col. Jacob Klock. He was wounded in his right arm in 1777 by a musket ball at Oriskany at Fort Schuyler. He was 39 years old in 1786. He lived in Palatine in 1787 and in German Flatts, Montgomery Co., N.Y. 15 June 1789. He also appeared as Christian W. Fox. He was on the 1813 pension list.

Fox, George. Pa. —. He was awarded a $40 gratuity and a $40 annuity in Philadelphia Co., Pa. 4 May 1832.

Fox, Jacob. Pa. Pvt. He served in the Flying Camp. He was wounded at or near Cuckold's town, N.J. in his right hand. The ball lodged therein. He was a weaver. He lived in Pa. in 1794. He was granted one-third of a pension 20 Apr. 1796. He was on the 1813 pension list. He received a $40 gratuity and a $40 annuity in Greene County 4 Jan. 1823. He died in Berks County 29 Sep. 1826.

Fox, Joel. Conn. Pvt. He served under Col. Durkee in the 4ᵗʰ Regiment. He lost the use of his right eye by smallpox and was wounded in the battle of Germantown 4 Oct. 1777. He resided in Hebron, Conn. in 1792. He enlisted 24 Apr. 1777 and was discharged 24 Apr. 1780. He was on the 1813 pension list. He transferred to Monroe County, N.Y. 4 Sep. 1832.

Fox, John. S.C. —. He was taken prisoner by the Tories in 1781 and turned over to the Indians. He was put to death by the Cherokee. His widow, Mary Fox, was awarded an annuity 4 Jan. She was a resident of Abbeville District in 1785. There were two children in 1791. She was from Horry District. She was paid from 1819 to 1828.

Fox, John. S.C. —. He served aboard the *South Carolina*. He was put on a prison ship in New York and was discharged about 11 months later. He was pensioned under the act of 1818 but was stricken because his service was not on Continental Establishment. Congress granted him a pension 14 May 1832.

Fox, Joseph. Pa. —. He was awarded a $40 gratuity and a $40 annuity in Greene Co., Pa. 14 Jan.

1823. He was 84 years old in 1840. He died 13 Dec. 1847.

Fox, Joseph. Pa. —. He died in Montgomery Co., Pa. 29 Sep. 1826.

Fox, Nathaniel. Va. Capt. He was wounded at Brandywine. At the reduction of the Virginia Line at White Plains in Aug. 1778, he was left out of the line on account of being badly wounded. He was not expected to be able to take the field for a long time if ever again. He had served from Feb. 1776. He wanted to resign but was refused by George Washington who gave him permission to retire until called for. P. Muhlenberg, Brig. Gen.; Daniel Morgan, Brig. Gen.; C. Anderson, Brig. Gen.; George Weedon, Brig. Gen.; William Heath, Col.; A. Buford, Col.; Burgess Ball, Com.; Richard C. Anderson, Lt. Col.; Jona: Clark, Lt. Col., Gust B. Wallace, Lt; O. Towles, Lt. Col.; and William Croghan, Maj., attested to his service. He was pensioned at the rate of £40 per annum on 26 Nov. 1785. He received his commutation 1 July 1796. He died in 1820. His son, Richard Fox, was two years old at that time and was the only surviving child of the second wife. The first wife was Mary Carver King, and his second wife was Susan Prosser. Both left issue. The heirs sought relief from Congress 19 Jan. 1899.

Fox, Simon. Pa. —. He was pensioned in Huntingdon County 21 Mar. 1837. His widow, Eve Fox, received a $40 annuity 11 Apr. 1848. She died 9 Sep. 1850.

Fox, William. —. —. His only evidence furnished was his own statement. Congress refused him a pension 11 Jan. 1838.

Fox, William P. N.Y. —. He broke his left thigh by the oversetting of a sleigh in carrying flour to Fort Schuyler in 1777. His only evidence was the depositions of two witnesses to prove the accident.

Fox, William. Pa. Pvt. He served as a drafted militia man or as a substitute under Capt. Humphrey Williams and Capt. William Renshaw. He was at Brandywine, Paoli, Germantown, Elizabethtown, Princeton, and New Brunswick. He died at the age of 84 without bounty land. His widow was Rachel Fox. She resided with the family of her uncle, Col. George Miller, in Germantown, Philadelphia Co., Pa. At the battle of Germantown a wounded American officer and faint due to the loss of blood appeared at the door. He staggered in and besought a drink of water. She held the pitcher to his lips since he could not do so. A gigantic Scotchman arrived and attempted to insult her. He drew his broadsword and struck her across the shoulder about half-way between it and her elbow. The wound was deep and dangerous. A passing British officer saw the attack, ordered the Scotchman away under guard, and summoned a British surgeon to dress the wound. Ultimately her arm became paralyzed. She was crippled for life. She was placed on the pension roll of the United States 30 Jan. 1857.

Foxworthy, William. —. —. He served two tours for twenty-one months. He was under Capt. Hugh Brent of Prince William County, Capt. Kirkpatrick, Maj. Willis, and Col. Posey. He had lived in Kentucky more than forty years. Congress granted him a pension 16 Feb. 1836.

Foy, Peter. S.C. —. He was killed at the battle of Carters House. His widow, Hamutel Foy, was granted an annuity 24 Dec. 1784. She had six children in 1787.

Frales, —. Va. Sgt. His widow, Sukey Frales, was awarded a gratuity of £12 in King William Co., Va. 6 Nov. 1779. She also appeared as Suckey Frayle and Sukey Frailes.

Frances, James. Pa. —. He was awarded a $40 gratuity in Fayette Co., Pa. 5 Mar. 1828 and again on 22 Dec. 1828. He also appeared as James Francis.

Francher, James. Va. —. He enlisted 19 Dec. 1771 under Capt. David Waggoner and transferred to Capt. William Morgan. He went to Guilford, N.C. and was attached to Capt. Thomas Bowyer's Company. He was wounded there in his knee and was furloughed. He claimed to have enlisted for three years and served two years and three months. He applied in Overton Co., Tenn. Congress granted him a pension 5 Mar. 1840.

Francis, Charles. Pa. —. He applied in Philadelphia County on 9 Mar. 1819. He and John Burkheater with their team of horses were impressed into service in Sep. 1777. They loaded the cannon at the state house yard to haul them to Brandywine but changed their route to Valley Forge when they were told that the British were approaching. There Col. Thomas Proctor impressed them into the artillery and Francis remained until the end of the war. He was 72 years old. He was rejected since he was already on the U.S. pension roll.

Francis, Christopher. Va. —. His wife and children were granted £20 support in York County on 16 Nov. 1778.

Francis, Ebenezer. Mass. Col. He was killed 7 July 1777 at the battle of Hubardtown. His heirs were paid his seven years' half-pay of $3,150.

Francis, James. Conn. Pvt. He enlisted 24 Nov. 1776. On 9 June 1778 he served under Capt. Starr and Col. R. J. Meigs in the 6th Regiment. He was at West Point and Morristown. A year or two after the war he went to sea and was never heard from. Congress granted his widow, Mary Francis, a pension 9 Feb. 1842.

Francis, James. Pa. —. He was granted a $40 gratuity in Fayette County 5 Mar. 1828.

Francis, John. Mass. Capt. He served in the 11th Mass. Regiment under Col. Benjamin Tupper and Capt. Richard Maybre. He lost one finger of his left hand and the use of another by a shot. He was pensioned at the rate of one-eighth pay from 19 Mar. 1780 on 17 Mar. 1785. He was on the 1813 pension list. He died 30 July 1822 in Essex Co., Mass.

Francis, John. Mass. Pvt. He served in the 13th Regiment and was from Barnstable. He served through the war and was discharged at Newburgh, N.Y. His widow, Patience Francis, married secondly Scipio Allen. Patience Allen was paid $50. He was a mulatto and was from Marshpee Plantation.

Francis, John. Pa. Pvt. He was in Bucks County on 21 May 1787. He served in the 3rd Pa. Regiment in Capt. Henry Epple's Company under Col. Craig. Both of his legs were much shattered by grape shot and musket balls at Brandywine 11 Sep. 1777. He was taken prisoner and paroled. He was discharged from the hospital at Lancaster by Dr. Fred Phile. He had a wife and three small children. He was 50 years. He later lived in Philadelphia County. He was a free man of color.

Francis, John. Pa. —. He received a $40 gratuity and a $40 annuity in Philadelphia County in 1836.

Francis, Roswell. Conn. Pvt. He served in Capt. Blagg's Company under Col. Thaddeus Cook. He was wounded in his left leg on 19 Sep. 1777 near Saratoga and was discharged. He was pensioned 6 May 1778 in Killingworth.

Francis, William. Va. Pvt. He was in Augusta County on 19 Apr. 1786 at age 48. He was wounded in 1778. He was discharged as unfit for duty. He served in the 16th Va. Regiment under Capt. John McGuire and Col. William Grayson. Capt. William Brownslee proved his service. He was granted a £30 gratuity and half-pay for two years on 14 Nov. 1778. He was put on the pension list at the rate of £18 per annum on 18 Jan. 1787. He was on the 1813 pension list.

Francisco, Peter. Va. —. He served in the Virginia Line and received several wounds. He distinguished himself by several acts of bravery and intrepidity. He was also in the cavalry to the southward under Col. William Washington. He purchased at his own expense a very valuable horse which was worn down by hardship and died in the service. He was from Charlotte County on 20 Dec. 1790 when he received £75. He was wounded at Guildford Court House. Congress rejected his request for a special pension law for him 29 Jan. 1819. He died in 1830 or 1831. He married in

July 1823. Congress declined to grant a pension to his widow, Mary B. Francisco, 11 Apr. 1850.

Frank, Andrew. N.Y. Pvt. He served in Capt. Robert Yates' Company under Col. Frederick Fisher. He was wounded in the thigh at Oriskany on 6 Aug. 1777. He was 38 years on 25 Oct. 1786. He lived in Mohawk, Montgomery Co., N.Y. 12 June 1789. He was on the 1813 pension list.

Frank, George. Pa. —. He was awarded a $40 gratuity and a $40 annuity in the District of Columbia 14 Apr. 1834.

Frank, Henry. N.Y. —. He was slain in battle with the Indians in 1779. Henry Frank and his other children petitioned for relief.

Frank, Jacob. N.Y. Pvt. He served under Col. Frederick Fisher in the Montgomery County militia. His son, John Frank, received a half-pay pension.

Frank, John. N.Y. Pvt. He served under Col. Fisher in the Montgomery County militia and was slain 6 Aug. 1777. His child, Susannah Frank, received a half-pay pension for seven years.

Frank, John Henry. N.Y. —. He was granted a gratuity.

Frankenberg, Lewis. Pa. —. His widow, Margaret Frankenberg, was awarded a $40 gratuity and a $40 annuity in Fayette Co., Pa. 14 Apr. 1834.

Frankford, Henry. Pa. —. He was granted relief in Dauphin County 5 Feb. 1836. He died 1 Apr. 1840.

Franklin, John. S.C. —. He served under Col. Carruth, Col. Far, Col. Crawford, and Col. John Thomas. He was in the Cherokee War, Downing Creek in North Carolina, Wilmington, and Savannah. He was pensioned in Chester District 4 Dec. 1834.

Franklin, Thomas P.. —. —. He sought an increase to his pension due to disability and wounds received in the war. Congress rejected his petition 10 Feb. 1846 because the law had expired.

Franks, —. N.Y. —. Mary Franks was granted support during the Revolutionary War.

Franks, Henry. N.Y. —. His family was granted support during the Revolutionary War.

Franks, Henry. —. —. His application made 22 Apr. 1794 was not approved.

Franks, John Henry. N.Y. —. His family was granted relief during the Revolutionary War.

Frantz, —. Pa. —. His widow, Mary Frantz, received a $40 gratuity and a $40 annuity in Westmoreland County 22 Feb. 1856.

Fraser, Andrew. S.C. —. He was at Orangeburg, Biggens Church, and other tours in 1781 and 1782. William Thompson proved his service. He served under his brother, Capt. Fraser. He was pensioned in Fairfield District 23 Nov. 1829. He was paid as late as 1834.

Frauncis, Samuel. N.Y. —. He was granted relief by the act of 4 Apr. 1785. He was paid $1,625 for the use of his house for two years as rent and to discharge the mortgage on same. For his singular services and advances to American prisoners he received the sum of $2,000 on account of the loan office certificates in his hands.

Frazer, Bernard. Pa. —. His widow, Elizabeth Frazer, was awarded a $40 annuity for his service in the Revolution on 21 Apr. 1852. She was from Lancaster County.

Frazer, Samuel. —. Pvt. A warrant for his bounty land was issued to William Thomas on 24 Jan. 1792, but he had not authorized the same. He sought a new one 12 Jan. 1803, but Congress declined to do so.

Frazier, —. Va. —. His wife was granted support in Prince Edward Co., Va. on 19 Oct. 1778 while he was away in Continental service.

Frazier, —. Va. —. Ann Frazier was granted £20 support while her two sons were away in the service in Fauquier Co., Va. in Nov. 1778.

Frazier, Charles. Mass. —. He served in Crane's Artillery. He was paid $20.

Frazier, David. Pa. —. He was granted relief.

Frazier, Duncan. N.Y. Pvt. He served in Capt. Charles Parson's Company in the 1ˢᵗ N.Y. Regiment under Col. Goose Van Schaick. He was ruptured by hard labor on fatigue and was worn out. He was 55 years old in Mar. 1786. He lived in Albany, N.Y. 4 June 1789. He was on the 1813 pension list. He also appeared as Duncan Frazer.

Frazier, James. Md. Pvt. He was pensioned in Dorchester County at the rate of half-pay of a private on 14 Feb. 1820. His widow, Susan Frazier, was paid his arrearage and was pensioned 9 Mar. 1847.

Frazier, Levin. Md. 1ˢᵗ Lt. He was pensioned at the rate of half-pay of a lieutenant in Dorchester County on 12 Feb. 1820. His widow, Elizabeth Frazier, received his arrearage and was pensioned at the same rate on 10 Jan. 1843. Priscilla Jackson, her legal representative, was paid the balance of her pension. Her arrearage of $8.22 was paid to Samuel Harrington, trustee, 4 Mar. 1850.

Frazier, Robert. Pa. Marine/Sailor. He was in Philadelphia County on 14 July 1788. He enlisted with Obadiah Gore in 1777 and served in the 3ʳᵈ Regiment from Connecticut. He next served aboard the Continental frigate, *Confederacy*, for one year. He served on the Continental frigate *Alliance* under Capt. Berry. He was wounded in his arm in engagement with a British frigate. He was 58 years old. He died 15 Mar. 1790.

Frazier, Samuel. Md. Pvt. He was pensioned in Harford County at the rate of half-pay of a private 7 Jan. 1816. His widow, Penelope Frazier, was pensioned at the same rate 16 Mar. 1836. She died 2 Dec. 1848, and her arrearage was paid to her executrix, Priscilla Frazier, in Baltimore County on 29 Jan. 1850.

Frazier, Solomon. Md. Capt. He was pensioned at the rate of half-pay of a captain 19 Feb. 1819. He was paid $337.50 plus interest 9 Feb. 1822.

Frazier, William. Md. Lt. His widow, Henrietta M. Frazier, was pensioned in Baltimore at the rate of half-pay of a lieutenant 7 Feb. 1840.

Frazier, William. Pa. —. He was pensioned in Bedford County 1 Jan. 1836.

Fream, Thomas. Pa. Sgt. He was on the 1813 pension list.

Freas, Martin. Pa. —. He was pensioned in Montgomery County 27 Mar. 1837. He died 7 July 1843.

Frederic, Michael. Pa. —. He was awarded a $40 gratuity and a $40 annuity in Schuylkill Co., Pa. 15 Apr. 1835. He died 23 Apr. 1845 in Franklin County.

Frederick, —. Pa. —. His widow, Mary Frederick was granted relief in Washington County 27 Mar. 1852.

Free, John. Pa. —. He was granted relief 15 June 1836 in Huntingdon County. He died 22 Aug. 1845.

Freelove, David. Mass. —. He served under Capt. Thomas Elsbue and Col. Livingston from 11 July to 24 Sep. 1779. He joined again in Freetown and served from 15 Aug. 1780 to 21 Jan. 1781. He enlisted 2 Dec. 1780 under Capt. Brightman from Bristol Co., Mass. He was also in service from 21 Mar 1781 to the latter part of 1783. Congress granted him a pension 25 May 1840.

Freeman, —. Va. —. His widow, Frances Freeman, was allowed relief in King William County 23 June 1779.

Freeman, Benjamin. Pa. Sgt. He was in Philadelphia County on 8 Jan. 1787. He was in the Philadelphia militia in Capt. Alexander Boyd's company under Col. Bayard. He was 31 years old. He was wounded in his right thigh at Amboy in 1776. A daughter was mentioned. He was on the 1813 pension list. He died 16 Dec. 1820.

Freeman, Doss. Mass. —. He served in the 8ᵗʰ Regiment. He was paid $20.

Freeman, Elijah. —. —. He was a pensioner up to 4 Mar. 1820 and soon after he became deranged and unable to provide for himself. He lived in Queensburg, Warren Co., N.Y. His brother,

Stephen Freeman, lived in Erie Co., N.Y. He spent $80 on his brother. He sought the arrearage due his brother from 4 Mar. 1820 to 4 Mar. 1832. He took Elijah Freeman away from the poor house in Saratoga. Congress did not approve his petition 20 Mar. 1838.

Freeman, Fortune. Mass. —. He served in the 10th Regiment and was from Salem. He was paid $20.

Freeman, Henry. N.J. Pvt. At age 16 he enrolled in the New Jersey militia and was on guard duty and patrol between Amboy and Woodbridge at night for 22 months over six years. His officers were Capt. W. Freeman and Col. Webster. Congress granted him a pension 12 Apr. 1842. He did not state if he enlisted or was drafted. Congress did not approve his application on 26 Apr. 1848.

Freeman, Henry. S.C. —. He served in the 5th S.C. Regiment. His widow, Lucretia Freeman, was from Marlborough District but late of Darlington District in 1791.

Freeman, Jacob. Pa. —. He was granted relief in Westmoreland County 8 Jan. 1838. He was dead by Aug. 1840. He died 14 Feb. 1840.

Freeman, John. Mass. —. He served in the 1st Regiment and was from New Marlborough. He was paid $20.

Freeman, John. Mass. —. He was in the 5th Regiment and was paid $20.

Freeman, Pearson. —. —. He had been a pensioner and died 27 Jan. 1847. He married 26 July 1790 in the First Congregational Church in the towns of Washington and Milford in Conn. He was a colored man and was detailed as a waiter to Capt. Ransom and to Maj. Cogswell in the Wagon Department. He was 71 years old in 1832. He was pensioned and died 27 Jan. 1841. His widow, Rebecca Freeman, had her claim for a pension approved by Congress 11 Apr. 1850. She received 160 acres of bounty land 27 Mar. 1856 at which time she was in her 90th year.

Freeman, Samuel. Me. —. He died 10 Dec. 1786. His widow, Hannah Bradford, was from Minot in 1807. She was paid $50 under the resolve of 1836.

Freeman, Samuel. N.C. Pvt. He applied in Beaufort County in 1805. He served in the 1st N.C. Regiment at the age of 15 or 16; he was wounded in the leg by a splinter at the fort in Charleston, S.C. His leg was ulcerated. He was aged 46 or 47 in 1805. He was on the 1813 pension list.

Freemont, —. Va. Pvt. His widow, Fanny Freemont, was pensioned 23 June 1778.

Freer, —. N.Y. —. Sarah Freer was granted support in 1779.

French, —. —. —. His widow, Joanna French, had her petition for a pension to Congress rejected 27 Mar. 1846 because they were married subsequent 1 Jan. 1794.

French, Cummell. —. —. He enlisted for nine months and served under Capt. Elijah Brent and Col. Heman Swift and died in the service. Congress awarded his widow, Elizabeth French, a pension 12 Jan. 1838 and on 5 Mar. 1840.

French, Daniel. Pa. —. He applied 5 Aug. 1822. He was in the army in Boston. His companion was a good deal helpless and sickly, and his eldest son died the previous fall. He was 68 years old and blind.

French, David. Mass. —. He served in the 7th Regiment and was paid $20.

French, Eleazer. Mass. Pvt. He served in Capt. Gilbert's Company under Col. William Prescott and lost his arm in the battle of Charlestown on 17 June 1775. He died 26 Oct. 1776. His heirs were entitled to half-pay from 1 Jan. to 26 Oct. 1776. His mother, Abigail French, was paid £13.4.8. for tending to her son on 2 Mar. 1778.

French, Jacob. Mass. —. He served in the 1st Regiment and was from Jay. He was paid $20.

French, John. Md. Matross. He was on the 1813 pension list. He lived in Baltimore Co., Md.

French, John. Mass. Sgt. He served in the 3rd Regiment and was paid $20.

French, Jonathan. Mass. —. He served in the 2nd Regiment and was from Vermont. He was paid $20.

French, Lemuel. Mass. —. He served in the 9th Regiment and was from Hardwick. He was paid $20.

French, Nathaniel. Mass. Matross. He served in Crane's Artillery and was from Canton. He was paid $50.

French, Samuel. Conn. Pvt. He served in Col. John Chandler's Regiment. He was wounded by a stick of timber falling on his breast in building huts for the army on the Shuylkill River. He resided at Weston, Conn. in 1796. He enlisted 24 Apr. 1777 for the war and was discharged 20 Apr. 1778. He was granted half a pension 20 Apr. 1796. He was on the 1813 pension list. He died 24 Nov. 1814.

French, Samuel. Mass. Pvt. He served at the Castle and was from Braintree. He was paid $50.

Fretwell, Richard. Va. —. His wife, Lucy Fretwell, and two small children were awarded £14 support in Cumberland Co., Va. 22 Sep. 1777.

Fretz, Abraham. Pa. —. He was paid in July 1841.

Frew, Alexander. He served in the 3rd Company, 8th Battalion, York County militia in 1781. He was from Beaver County.

Frey, —. Pa. —. His widow, Catherine Frey, was awarded a $40 gratuity in Lancaster Co., Pa. 15 Apr. 1834.

Frey, Conrad. Pa. —. He applied from Northampton County on 7 May 1818. He enlisted in Capt. Charles Craig's Company of Riflemen in Col. Hand's Regiment. A year later he was transferred to Capt. Samuel Craig's Company of Infantry under Col. Chambers where he continued one year longer before he was discharged.

Frey, Jacob. Pa. —. He applied from Northampton County on 13 Nov. 1818. He was in Capt. Jost Dreispack's Company of Riflemen in 1777 for two years after which he enlisted in Capt. Seeling's Company until he was discharged. He also appeared as Jacob Fry. He died 3 Apr. 1851.

Frey, John. N.Y. Brigade Major. He served under Col. Jacob Klock and Brig. Gen. Herkimer in the militia. He was wounded in his right arm at Oriskany on 6 Aug. 1777 by a musket ball. He lived in Palatine, Montgomery Co., N.Y. 15 June 1789. He also appeared as John Fry. He was pensioned 14 Sep. 1786. He was on the 1813 pension list.

Fricker, Peter. Pa. —. He was awarded a $40 gratuity and a $40 annuity in Reading, Pa. 24 Mar. 1817. He died in Jan. 1828.

Friedley, Ludwig. Pa. —. He was awarded a $40 annuity in Centre County 5 Feb. 1836.

Frigner, George. Pa. He was granted relief.

Frink, John. —. —. He served three years in the Continental Line and was discharged. He was in his 89th year and was in a deranged state of mind. His son, Luther Frink, had supported him the last twenty years. Congress granted him a pension 24 Dec. 1818.

Frisbee, Philemon. —. —. He died in 1797. He married 1 Jan. 1790. His brother was Abraham Frisbee. The veteran's widow, Rhoda Frisbee, was refused a pension by Congress 2 Feb. 1853.

Frisbie, Israel. Conn. Pvt. He entered the service in the spring of 1776 under Capt. Phineas Porter and Gen. Wooster at Waterbury and served eight months. He enlisted again in the spring under Capt. John Lewis and Col. Douglas for eight months and was discharged in Dec. 1776. He married Esther Tyler in Feb 1793. He died 8 Feb. 1825 at Spafford, Onondaga Co., N.Y. His widow died 16 June 1842. He applied but was never pensioned. Jerusha Johnson and the other heirs sought the five years of pension to which the widow was entitled. She had applied in 1840. She could produce but one witness to prove her marriage so her application was denied.

Congress allowed the heirs $480 for the five years of the pension to which the widow was entitled on 23 Dec. 1861.

Frisbie, Jacob. Conn. Pvt. He served in Col. Silliman's Regiment. He was disabled by a fall from the top of a house from whence he was watching the enemy then on Long Island on 30 Aug. 1776 in New York. He resided in Litchfield, Conn. in 1794. He died in 1785.

Frizzle, Elisha. N.Y. Pvt. He served under Col. M. Jackson. He was wounded in the shoulder at Bemis Heights on 7 Oct. 1777. He lived at Salem, Washington Co., N.Y. in 1794. He enlisted 1 May 1777, invalided 14 Feb. 1779, and was discharged 1 Jan. 1780. He was on the 1813 pension list.

Frost, Abijah. Mass. —. He was paid £25 in full for his pension for two years which became due on 5 Apr. 1781 on 17 Apr. 1781.

Frost, George P.. N.H. Capt. He served in the 1ˢᵗ Regiment under Col. Cilley. He was entitled to 300 acres of bounty land. He received the warrant and put in the hands of a friend who lost it in New York City. It was #673. It had never been presented so Congress authorized a duplicate to be issued on 31 Dec. 1828. He lived in Rochester, Ulster Co., N.Y.

Frost, Jacob. Mass. Pvt. He served in the militia under Col. Ebenezer Bridge and Capt. Benjamin Walker. He was disabled by a musket ball through his left hip bone. He was 35 years old in 1788. He lived in Oxford Co., Me. He was on the 1813 pension list.

Frost, John. N.Y. Pvt. He was granted relief.

Frost, Joseph. Mass. Pvt. He served in the militia under Col. Williams and Capt. Ferry. He was wounded in the left arm by a musket ball on 16 Aug. 1777 at Bennington. He lived in Tewkesbury, Mass. in 1795.

Frost, Joseph. Mass. Pvt. He served in the 6ᵗʰ Regiment under Capt. Jackson and Col. Benjamin Tupper. He was disabled by rheumatism and gravel. He was 49 years old in 1787. He was granted one-eighth of a pension 20 Apr. 1796. He was on the 1813 pension list.

Frost, Mark. Me. —. He died 5 Oct. 1835. His widow, Hannah Frost, was from Belgrade. She was paid $50 under the resolve of 1836.

Frost, Nathaniel. Mass. Sgt. He served in the 2ⁿᵈ Regiment and was from Kittery. He was paid $20.

Frost, Richard. Mass. Drummer. He served in the 10ᵗʰ Regiment and was from Marblehead. He was paid $50.

Frost, Samuel. Mass. Capt. He received his commutation for five years rather than half-pay. He died 1 Nov. 1817.

Frost, Simon. Me. —. He died 1 Oct. 1803 in Kittery. His widow was Jane Morrill from Cornville. She was paid $50 under the resolve of 1836.

Frothingham, Samuel. —. —. He enlisted in 1776 under Capt. Churchill and Col. Comfort Sage for six months. He next served under Col. Return J. Meigs and served until 1781. Congress granted him a pension 3 Jan. 1832. He sought an increase in his pension but furnished no evidence for his claim. He had served as a mechanic in the war. Congress rejected his petition for a special act 20 Jan. 1846.

Frothingham, Samuel. Mass. Pvt. He was in the 8ᵗʰ Regiment and was from Boston. His widow, Lydia Rowe, was paid $50.

Frotter, Robert. Pa. —. He was granted relief.

Fry, —. Pa. —. His widow, Catharine Fry, was awarded relief in York County 6 Apr. 1833.

Fry, Benjamin. Va. Sgt. He was wounded in the battle of Brandywine and lost the use of his left arm. He was awarded a £30 gratuity and an annuity of full pay for life on 15 May 1778. One of his name was struck from the roll because he was capable of procuring a livelihood

21 June 1786.

Fry, Benjamin. —. Pvt. He lived in Jasper Co., Ga. He was on the 1813 pension list. He died in Sep.1823.

Fry, Conrad. Pa. —. He was awarded a $40 gratuity and a $40 annuity in Berks Co., Pa. 18 Mar. 1834. He was 85 years old in 1840. He died 30 Apr. 1841.

Fry, Conrad. Pa. —. He was granted relief 15 May 1818. He died in Mercer County 24 Sep. 1842.

Fry, John. N.Y. Corp. He served in Capt. Green's Company of Albany County militia. He was wounded at Saratoga on 15 Oct. by a musket ball in his arm.

Fry, John. N.Y. Maj. He received a half-pay pension.

Fry, Lawrence. Pa. —. He was from Cumberland County when he received assistance 1 Apr. 1825.

Fry, Lawrence. Pa. —. His widow, Mary Fry, received a $40 gratuity and a $40 annuity in Dauphin County 13 Apr. 1854.

Fry, Peter. Pa. —. He was granted relief 15 Mar. 1838. He died in Chester County 10 June 1842.

Fry, Phillip Martin. S.C. Drummer. He was wounded in the Revolutionary War. He subsequently lost his eyesight. He was pensioned 17 Dec. 1812 in Lexington District. He died in June 1833. His widow, Nancy Fry, who lived with her son, sought his arrearage. He also appeared as Phillip Martin Frey.

Fugard, Samuel. N.H. Pvt. He was in the 1st N.H. Regiment. He had asthma and was worn out in the service. He was from Bedford and was aged 57 in 1787. He was deceased by Dec. 1791 and left a widow and children.

Fulford, John. —. Maj. He was killed in Oct. 1780 by the bursting of the cannon he was testing. His heirs sought his half-pay. Congress rejected the claim 4 Mar. 1846 because the service was state and not Continental.

Fulfords, John. Conn. Sgt. He served in Col. Meigs' Regiment. He was wounded in service in July 1779 at Stony Point. He resided at Watertown, Conn. in 1794. He died in 1807.

Fulham, George. Md. Sgt. He served in the 7th Regiment in Capt. Anderson's Company. He was wounded in his leg at the battle of Germantown on 4 Oct. 1777 and invalided in Jan. 1782. He was in Delaware in 1795 when his pension application was pending. He died 28 Mar. 1802.

Fulis, —. S.C. —. His widow, Susannah Fulis, and her only child received an annuity 3 June 1819.

Fulks, —. —. —. His son, John B. Fulks, furnished no proof of his father's service. He said he volunteered in 1780 and was at Guilford Court House and Eutaw Springs in 1781. He died in 1820. The son claimed a pension from 1780 to 1820 for his father. Congress rejected his petition 12 Feb. 1841.

Fuller, —. Pa. —. His widow, Ruth Fuller, was awarded relief in Susquehanna County 5 Feb. 1836.

Fuller, —. Pa. —. His widow was Susannah Fuller who was from Fayette County when she received assistance 11 Apr. 1825.

Fuller, Andrew. Mass. —. He served in the 7th Regiment and was from Warren. He was paid $20.

Fuller, Azariah. Mass. Pvt. He served in the 2nd Regiment and was from Fitchburg. He was paid $50.

Fuller, Barzilla. Mass. —. He served in the 4th Regiment and was from Hebron. He was paid $20. He died 8 Aug. 1833 in Hebron, Me. His widow, Polly Fuller, was paid $50 under the resolve of 1836.

Fuller, Benjamin. Mass. Pvt. He served in the Invalids under Col. Lewis Nichola and Capt. Moses McFarland. He was disabled by a wound in his right shoulder. He resided in Essex Co., Mass. He was pensioned 6 Jan. 1783. He was 50 years old. His widow was from Hebron, Maine.

Fuller, Eliphalet. Mass. Drummer. He served in the 2nd Regiment and was from Richmond. He was paid $20.

Fuller, Jedediah. Mass. Pvt. He served in the 13th Regiment under Col. Edward Wigglesworth and Capt. John K. Smith. He was disabled by the loss of his right hand. He was 31 years old in 1788. He resided in Norfolk Co., Mass. He was on the 1813 pension list.

Fuller, Joseph. Mass. Pvt. He was in the Invalids under Capt. McFarland. He was disabled by the gravel and was 50 years old in 1788. He served in the 3rd Regiment and was from Sandwich. He was paid $20 by the Commonwealth.

Fuller, Josiah. Mass. Pvt. He served in the 1st Regiment and was from Barnstable. He was paid $50.

Fuller, Lemuel. Mass. —. He served in the 4th Regiment and was paid $20.

Fuller, Meshack. S.C. Sgt. He served under Col. George Hicks, Capt. Edward Irby, and Capt. Thomas Cochran. He was paroled at Charleston. He was a pensioner of the United States and died in May 1829. His widow, Bethany Fuller, was left with three daughters to support. Her application for a state pension was rejected in 1829.

Fuller, Oliver. Mass. —. He was pensioned.

Fuller, Robert. Mass. —. He served in the 3rd Regiment and was from Hebron. He was paid $20.

Fuller, Stephen. N.H. Pvt. He served under Col. Benjamin Howe. He lost his right thumb in 1777. He lived in Francistown, N.H. in 1794. He served in the militia. He was granted one-third of a pension 20 Apr. 1796. He was on the 1813 pension list.

Fuller, Stephen. Ga. —. He was a private and an officer. He served in the militia and was also a regular soldier. He enlisted in 1776 in Georgia in Capt. Colson's Company under Col. Habersham. He also served under Maj. Gardner and Gen. McIntosh. He was discharged in 1777. He was at Fort Barrington on the Altemaha River and the Snow Camp. He moved to South Carolina after the war. He was 71 years old; his wife was 60. Congress rejected his petition for a special bill of relief for an increase in his pension but instructed him to follow the existing laws on 4 Dec. 1818. He was pensioned by the state of South Carolina 6 Dec. 1825. He was a resident of Pendleton District in 1824. He was paid as late as 1833.

Fuller, Zacheus. Mass. —. He was paid $50.

Fullerton, —. Pa. —. His widow, Hannah Fullerton, was awarded a $40 gratuity and a $40 annuity in Crawford County in 1836.

Fullerton, Edward. Pa. Surgeon. He went with Gen. Thompson to Cambridge. He was appointed one of the Hospital Surgeons. He came to New York after the evacuation of Boston. He was appointed surgeon in the Flying Camp and was taken prisoner at Fort Washington on 16 Dec. 1776. He returned to Yorktown 14 Apr. 1778. He was unexchanged and died 5 May 1781 leaving a wife, Ann Fullerton, and child. She married secondly ------ McKnight on 9 Jan. 1786. Her brother was Joseph Chambers. She was in Philadelphia County 18 Feb. 1788. The child later died.

Fullerton, George. Pa. Pvt. He served in the 1st Philadelphia Volunteer Troop of militia. His widow, Margaret Fullerton, was in Philadelphia County on 8 Dec. 1781. He was in the light horse militia and was killed 5 Aug. 1776. He was shot accidentally by a ball through his leg from the pistol of Mr. Hull near Brunswick, New Jersey.

Fullerton, James. S.C. —. His annuity was £39.2.4 in 1787.

Fullerton, Thomas. Pa. —. He was awarded a $40 gratuity and a $40 annuity in Crawford Co., Pa. 1 Apr. 1823.

Fulmer, —. Pa. —. His widow, Mary Fulmer, was awarded a $40 gratuity and a $40 annuity in Philadelphia County 31 Mar. 1836.

Revolutionary War Pensions

Fulton, —. Pa. —. His widow, Mary Fulton, was awarded a $40 gratuity and a $40 annuity in Fayette County 31 Mar. 1836.

Fulton, David. S.C. —. His application was rejected 14 Dec. 1829.

Fulton, James. Pa. —. He was awarded a $40 gratuity and a $40 annuity in Chester Co., Pa. 4 May 1832.

Fulton, Jesse. Pa. —. He was awarded a $40 annuity in Armstrong County 5 Feb. 1836.

Fulton, Joseph. Pa. —. He received a $40 gratuity and a $40 annuity in Columbia County 3 Apr. 1837. He was 87 years old in 1840. He died 10 Mar. 1843.

Fulton, Robert. Mass. —. He served in Crane's Artillery and was paid $20. He was from Hebron.

Fulton, Samuel. —. —. He offered no evidence to sustain his claim. Congress rejected his claim 4 May 1846.

Fulton, Samuel. Pa. Capt. He served in the militia and was wounded. He was at Long Island, Brandywine, and Staten Island. He was also wounded in his knee when out in the Indian wars on the Susquehanna. He was also a captain in the York County militia in 1781. He married 5 May 1785. He died 13 May 1821. His widow, Catharine Fulton, was granted a pension by Congress 4 May 1846.

Fultz, Frederick. Pa. Pvt. He was in Philadelphia County on 10 Apr. 1786. He enlisted 12 Feb. 1777 in Capt. John Ennis' Company under Col. John Patton. He was taken prisoner 25 Apr. 1777 and held captive in a New York sugar house nearly three years. He was wounded in the head and body and lost an eye in the service. He was 36 years old. He was awarded $33.33 per month 25 Mar. 1805 at which time he resided in Chester County. He was on the 1813 pension list. He died 21 Feb. 1815. He also appeared as Frederick Foltz.

Funk, George. Pa. —. He was awarded a $40 gratuity and a $40 annuity 24 Mar. 1812 in Lancaster Co.

Furman, Alexander. N.Y. Lt. He died a prisoner in the provost in New York City. His widow was Rebecca Furman who was rejected for assistance from New York because she had received payment from the federal government.

Furniville, Richard. N.C. Pvt. He applied in Cabarrus Co., N.C. in 1821. He served 18 months. He was directed to apply to the wardens of the poor in his county.

Furguson, John. —. —. His heir, Samuel Furguson, did not receive a pension from Congress on 26 Apr. 1848 because the evidence did not warrant it.

Furguson, William. —. —. He served two years. He was pensioned, but his name was erased from the rolls due to some misnomers of the names of his officers. Congress granted him a pension for nine months of service 23 Mar. 1838.

Gabeau, Anthony. S.C. —. He served under Capt. William Greenwood in the True Blues. He was at the siege of Savannah in Oct. 1779. He had a family of grandchildren to maintain who were left by his sons who were deceased. He sought remuneration for his Revolutionary War services. He was from Charleston District. The Comptroller General was to investigate to determine what sums, if any, were due on 20 Dec. 1823.

Gaby, —. Va. —. His widow, Molly Gaby, was awarded a £12 gratuity in King William Co., Va. 6 Nov. 1779. He also appeared as — Gabey.

Gadd, Thomas. Md. Pvt. He was pensioned at the rate of half-pay of a private 16 Nov. 1811.

Gaffrey, John. N.J. —. He died at Crown Point, N.J. in June 1776. His widow, Hannah Gaffrey, sought a half-pay pension. There were four children.

Gage, Abner. N.H. Pvt. He was wounded in his right foot at Bunker Hill 17 June 1775. He was in Pelham in 1783. He was in Capt. Elisha Woodberry's Company in Col. Stark's Regiment.

He was aged 34 in 1787. He was from Andover. His rate was $5 per month from 26 Jan. 1808. He was on the 1813 pension list.

Gage, George. N.Y. Pvt. Her served in the Montgomery County militia under Col. Jacob Klock and was slain 6 Aug. 1777. His widow, Mary Gage, received his half-pay pension.

Gage, James. N.Y. Pvt. He served in the militia under Col. McClagrey in he Ulster County militia and was slain 6 Oct. 1777 at Fort Clinton. His widow was Mary Gage received a half-pay pension.

Gaghby, James. Pa. —. He was awarded a $40 gratuity and a $40 annuity in Westmoreland Co., Pa. 30 Mar. 1824.

Gaile, Asa. Mass. —. He served in the 1st Regiment and was paid $20.

Gain, —. N.Y. —. Elenor Gain was granted support in Feb. 1779.

Gains, William. Mass. Pvt. He served in the 2nd Regiment under Col. Ebenezer Sprout and Capt. Ames. He was wounded in his right knee. He was disabled by the involuntary release of urine. He was pensioned 3 Jan. 1783. He resided in Boston, Mass. in 1788 and was 29 years old.

Galaspie, Charles. Pa. —. His widow, Margaret Galaspie, was awarded $200 on 7 Apr. 1828 in Lycoming Co., Pa.

Galbraith, —. Pa. —. His widow was Catharine Galbraith.

Galbraith, Alexander. Pa. —. He was pensioned 3 Jan. 1817.

Galbreath, James. Pa. Pvt. He was in Cumberland County on 7 Dec. 1784. He served in the 4th Pa. Regiment and was wounded through his body under his right breast in battle with the enemy at Green Springs, Va. He was 56 years old. He died 23 Feb. 1805.

Gale, Jonathan. Mass. Pvt. He served in the 3rd Regiment and was from Royalston. His widow, Susannah Gale, was paid $50.

Galentine, Jacob. Pa. —. He was awarded a $40 gratuity and a $40 annuity in Fayette Co., Pa. 2 Apr. 1831. He was a wagoner in the Flying Camp at Amboy. He also appeared as Jacob Gallendin.

Galford, Thomas. Va. —. He was pensioned in Bath County on 10 Jan. 1811 at the rate of $50 per annum.

Gallagher, Francis. Pa. —. He transferred to New York by Sep. 1806. He was on the 1813 pension list as Francis Gallaher.

Gallagher, George. Pa. Corp. He was on the 1789 pension list.

Gallagher, Thomas. Pa. —. He was cut and mangled by the British at Crooked Billet. He was from Mifflin County.

Gallaher, John. Md. —. He was in the 6th Md. Regiment and was allowed £61.1.5 depreciation pay in Nov. 1798.

Gallant, James. Pa. Pvt. He was in Philadelphia County on 9 Jan. 1786. He served in the 12th Pa. Regiment and was wounded at Germantown 4 Oct. 1777. He lost his right arm. He was 34 years old. He was dead by Sep. 1793.

Gallart, James. Conn. Pvt. He served under Col. Swift in Capt. Durkee's Company. He was wounded in his knee at Jamestown, Virginia on 6 July 1781. He was 44 years old in 1788 and lived in Albany Co., N.Y. He later lived in Worcester Co., Mass. He was on the 1813 pension list. He also appeared as James Gallut.

Gallaspy, James. N.Y. Pvt. He was granted relief.

Gallaway, John. Va. 2nd Lt. He served in the 12th Regiment and two years later became supernumerary. In 1779 or 1780 he engaged in militia service. Congress rejected the claim of the heirs for commutation 29 May 1838.

Gallentine, Abraham. Pa.—. He was pensioned in Fayette County 16 June 1836. He also appeared as Abraham Gallantine.

Gallentine, Jacob. Pa. —. He received a $40 gratuity and a $40 annuity in Fayette County 2 Apr. 1831.

Galligan, Thomas. Mass. —. He served in the 6th Regiment and was paid $50.

Galloway, —. Va. Pvt. Milly Galloway was granted £8 support in Northumberland County on 11 May 1778. She received £30 relief on 17 Dec. 1778 in Lancaster County .

Galloway, John. N.C. —. His widow, Sarah Galloway, was from Wayne Co., N.C. In 1784 she received a stipend of £15 per annum for three years. He had enlisted for twelve months in the Continental Line and died in camp. She had four helpless children

Gallup, Andrew. Conn. Pvt. He served in the militia. He was wounded in the thigh near the groin by a musket ball and was crippled for life. It happened at Fort Griswold on 6 Sep. 1781 in opposing the British troops under Gen. Arnold who had landed at New London. He served under Capt. William Latham in the artillery. He was pensioned in Groton at age 24 on 26 Sep. 1788. He was on the 1813 pension list.

Gallup, Robert. Conn. Pvt. He served in Ledyard's Conn. Regiment. He was at Fort Griswold and was wounded by a bayonet under his right breast which passed through his body and entered his lungs. He also received a musket ball in his left knee. He was pensioned 1 Dec. 1788 at Groton at the age of 26 years. He was on the 1813 pension list. He moved to Chenango County, N.Y. 4 Mar. 1822.

Galworth, Gabriel. Md. Pvt. He was pensioned at the rate of half-pay of a private in Montgomery County 27 Jan. 1816.

Gambare, John. Md. Pvt. He was pensioned in Montgomery County on 4 Mar. 1789. He served in the Flying Camps. He was on the 1813 pension list. [Compare with John Gomber.]

Gambell, Abraham. Md. Pvt. He was wounded in his shoulder at the battle of Camden 25 Apr. 1781. He was about 30 years old in 1789. Capt. Perry Benson certified same. He lived in Dorchester Co., Md. 23 June 1785. He was on the 1813 pension list.

Gambell, George. Mass. —. He was paid $20. He also appeared as George Gambol.

Gamble, James. Va. Pvt. He served under Capt. Thomas Nelson in the 1st Va. Regiment and went to Philadelphia. He died in the service. His widow, Margaret Gamble, was awarded a £30 gratuity on 1 Nov. 1777. She was in Warwick County on 9 Nov. 1786 and had two infants. She was put on the pension list at the rate of £12 per annum on 12 Dec. 1786. She was in Nansemond County in 1788 and Warwick County in 1790.

Gamble, John. S.C. Drummer. He moved from Pennsylvania to South Carolina before the war. He was a refugee from the British in North Carolina. In 1776 he was on the Cherokee Expedition under Capt. Josiah Greer and Col. James Williams. He was at Seneca Fort that winter. In 1778 he was in East Florida. In 1779 he was under Capt. Joseph Rammage and Capt. George Davis. The latter was mortally wounded at Savannah. He also served in Capt. James Dillard's Company. He was between 68 and 70 years of age. Robert Long was a fellow soldier. He was pensioned from Laurens District 4 Dec. 1828. He was paid in 1829.

Gamble, Stephen. S.C. —. He received his annuity 14 June 1828.

Gambrel, Gideon. Md. Pvt. He was pensioned at the rate of half-pay of a private in Caroline County on 2 Mar. 1827.

Gamwell, James. Mass. —. He served in the 7th Regiment and was from Middlefield. He was paid $20.

Gandy, Brinkley. N.C. —. He served from Nash Co., N.C. under Maj. Griffin, Maj. Gandy, and Capt. Elling. Noah Wheddon proved his service. His application from Darlington District, South

Carolina in 1827 was rejected.

Gangawer, Andrew. Pa. —. He was awarded a $40 gratuity in Lehigh Co., Pa. 6 Apr. 1830. He was awarded a $40 gratuity and a $40 annuity 10 Apr. 1835. He also appeared as Andrew Gangwer.

Gannett, Deborah. Mass. Pvt. She resided in Norfolk Co., Mass. She enlisted under the name of Robert Shurtliff in Capt. George Webb's Company in the 4th Mass. Regiment. She served from 20 May 1782 to 23 Oct. 1783. She was injured at Tarrytown by a musket ball through her body. She was granted £34 on 20 Jan. 1792 with interest from the time of her discharge. She was on the 1813 pension list. She married Benjamin Gannett 7 Apr. 1784 in Sharon. She died 29 Apr. 1827. He was 83 years old. He had two daughters and was dependent on charity for support. Congress granted him a pension 22 Dec. 1837.

Gannon, Joseph. Pa. —. He was awarded a $40 gratuity and a $40 annuity in Tioga Co., N.Y. 15 Apr. 1835.

Gano, Daniel. N.Y. Capt. He served under Capt. Andrew Moodie in the 2nd Regiment of Artillery from July 1777 to Nov. 1778. He resigned 12 Oct. 1778. His grand-daughter was Mary E. Gano. In 1822 she married firstly Lewis H. Bryan or Bryant who was a veteran of the War of 1812 from Kentucky under Capt. Isaac Cunningham and Col. Donaldson. He died in 1834 and she married secondly Elisha Cobb. An account of the celebration of her 96th birthday in the *New York Herald* of 5 Feb. 1899 reported that she was one of the last eight surviving daughters of the Revolution. Her father and grandfather were both veterans. Francis Gerneaux founded the family in America. He came as a Huguenot refugee from the Isle of Guernsey to New Rochelle, N.Y. in 1686. His son was born at Hopewell, N.J. 27 July 1727 and in 1762 became the pastor of the first Baptist Church in New York City. When the British arrived, he sheltered his family at Horseneck. He accepted a chaplaincy in the Continental Army and was the last to leave Fort Montgomery when it fell. He moved to Kentucky where his children had already located and died there 10 Aug. 1804. His son Daniel Gano served as captain of artillery. He was desperately wounded at the siege of Ninety Six. Mary E. (Gano) Cobb of Kokomo, Ind. was granted a pension by Congress for both her father's and her husband's service. Congress rejected a claim for bounty land from the heirs because he had not served to the end of the war on 25 Jan. 1828.

Gansvort, Peter. —. —. He received his commutation. He also appeared as Peter Gansworth.

Gapen, Stephen. Pa. —. He was awarded a $40 gratuity and a $40 annuity in Greene Co., Pa. 11 June 1832.

Garanger, Charles. —. —. He and Lewis Garanger had their applications made 26 Apr. 1792 rejected.

Garanger, Lewis. Pa. —. He sought to replace a lost certificate of registered debt granted to him for service in the Revolutionary War for £737.12.6. He and Charles Garanger had their applications made 26 Apr. 1792 rejected.

Garden, Alexander. —. Lt. He served in Lee's Legion and as aide-de-camp to Gen. Greene shortly after the evacuation of Charleston. He received his five years' full pay in commutation of his half-pay 23 May 1828. His executor was H. D. DeSaussure who sought and obtained interest of same 8 Apr. 1832.

Gardiner, Jacob. N.Y. Capt. He served under Col. Frederick Fisher in the militia. He was wounded in his left groin, right thigh, and right leg at Oriskany on 6 Aug. 1777. He lived in Mohawk, Montgomery County in 1787 and on 28 Sep. 1789. He was aged 57 years of age on 31 Jan. 1787. He died 9 May 1808. He was on the 1813 pension list. He was a blacksmith. He also appeared as Jacob Gardinier.

Gardiner, Samuel. N.Y. Pvt. He served in the militia under Col. Frederick Fisher. He was wounded in his left groin, right thigh, and right leg on 6 Aug. 1777 at Oriskany. He lived in Mohawk, Montgomery Co., N.Y. 14 Oct. 1788. He was 56 years of age on 1 Jan. 1786. He died 31 Dec. 1806. He was on the 1813 pension list. He also appeared as Samuel Gardinier.

Gardner, Andrew. —. Capt. Congress rejected relief for his heirs 9 May 1836.

Gardner, Andrew. Mass. Pvt. He served in the 3rd Regiment and was from Chelsea. His widow, Elizabeth Wheeden, was paid $50.

Gardner, Andrew. Pa. —. He was awarded a $40 gratuity and a $40 annuity in Fayette County in Apr. 1837. He was 65 years old in 1840.

Gardner, Calvin. Mass. —. He served in the 4th Regiment and was from Passamaquiddy. He was paid $20.

Gardner, Isaac. Mass. Pvt. He served in the 1st Regiment and was from Hingham. His widow, Sarah Gardner, was paid $50.

Gardner, Jack. Mass. Pvt. He served in the 4th Regiment and was from Worcester. He was paid $50.

Gardner, Jacob. Mass. —. He served in the 3rd Regiment and was from Fayette. He was paid $20.

Gardner, Jacob. Mass. —. He served in Revere's Regiment and was from Plainfield. His widow, Deborah Gardner, was paid $50.

Gardner, John. Pa. —. He was awarded a $40 gratuity in Adams Co., Pa. 15 Apr. 1835.

Gardner, John. S.C. —. He was in North Carolina in 1781 and 1782 and served a tour in South Carolina. He was in Lancaster District and was pensioned 30 Nov. 1827. He also appeared as John Gardiner. He died 8 Apr. 1836. He left no wife, children, father, or mother. Mary Cook was his sister. There was $6.31 due his administrator and brother, William Gardener, on 7 Dec. 1837.

Gardner, Joseph. Va. Pvt. He was in Fauquier County in 1788. He enlisted in the 1st Va. Regiment on 5 Sep.1775 and was wounded the next spring. Col. John Grisen certified that he was wounded in the arm. On 25 Oct. 1788 he was 36 years old. He was wounded in the joint of his left arm in an accident on duty at Williamsburg. He was continued at the rate of £10 per annum on 27 Oct. 1788. He was on the 1813 pension list of Virginia. He transferred to Georgia. He also appeared as Joseph Garner.

Gardner, Perez. Mass. Pvt. He served in the 1st Regiment and was from Hingham. He was paid $50.

Gardner, Samuel. Mass. Pvt. He served in the 4th Regiment and was from Duxbury. He was paid $50.

Gardner, Sherman. Conn. Pvt. He was disabled with consumption. He was pensioned in Nov. 1786. He was on the 1813 pension list. He transferred to Hampshire Co., Mass. 4 Sep. 1825 and died 21 Dec. 1826.

Gardner, Thomas. Mass. Col. He was wounded in the battle of Charlestown on 17 June 1775 and died 3 July 1775. He left three small children. His widow, Joanna Gardner, sought his seven years' half-pay in 1793.

Gardner, Thomas. Mass. Col. He served in the 4th Regiment and was from Northampton. He was paid $20.

Garland, George. N.Y. —. His wife was granted support in Dutchess County on 3 Nov. 1781.

Garland, James. N.H. —. He enlisted in the spring of 1775 under Capt. Clough and Col. Poor. He was discharged in Feb. 1777. He married at Sanborton, N.H. 13 May 1776. His sister, Susannah Tolford, was at the wedding. She was 79 years old in 1847. His wife was Abigail Tilton. He was born 25 Aug. 1754 and his wife 3 Aug.. 1761. Their children were John Garland 16 Sep. 1776, Deborah Garland 21 Sep. 1778, Ruth Garland 13 Sep. 1780, Jacob Garland 21 Feb. 1783, Abigail Garland born 9 May 1785, Sally Garland 19 May 1787, Naby Garland 2 Nov. 1788,

Jacob Garland born 7 July 1790, Nathiel Garland 30 Sep. 1792, Sally Garland 6 June 1794, George W. Garland 16 June 1796, Martha Garland 11 June 1799, and Statira Garland 4 June 1805. Congress granted the widow a pension 6 Feb. 1874.

Garland, Peter. Va. Capt. He served in the 6th Regiment as lieutenant and was promoted. He was made a prisoner in Sep. 1778. He never resigned his commission. His children sought five years' full pay, but Congress rejected their claim 13 Jan. 1836.

Garlock, Adam. N.Y. —. He served under Col. Willett in 1779, 1780, and 1781. He had his leg broken. He was 84 years old when Congress granted him a pension from 4 Mar. 1846 on 11 Apr. 1850. He had been refused a pension 26 Apr. 1848 because his name was not on the rolls.

Garlock, Charles. N.Y. Sgt. He served under Col. Samuel Clyde in the Montgomery County militia and was slain 6 Aug. 1777. His children, Jacob Garlock, Adam Garlock, Elias Garlock, and Elizabeth Garlock received a half-pay pension.

Garner, —. Va. —. His wife, Lettice Garner, was granted support in Westmoreland County in Feb. 1779 and Aug. 1779.

Garner, Charles. He served three years in the Revolutionary War and was unable to make a living. He petitioned for relief from taxes in Fauquier Co., Va. in 1783.

Garner, John. —. Pvt. He was on the 1813 pension list of Georgia. He moved to Butler Co., Ala. 4 Mar. 1824.

Garner, Joseph. Va. —. He served under Capt. John Green. He was wounded in the arm by a musket ball from a fellow soldier. He lost the use of his arm. He was granted £5 for life on 19 May 1777.

Garner, Samuel. S.C. —. He served under Capt. Benjamin Tutt, Col. Huger, and Lt. Thomas Farrow. He was a resident of Greenville District in 1827. He was paid as late as 1832. He also appeared as Samuel Gardner.

Garnet, John. N.Y. Pvt. He served in the artillery. He was wounded and lost two fingers at the taking of Fort Montgomery on 6 Oct. 1777. He lived in Goshen, N.Y. in 1794. He continued to the end of the war. He was on the 1813 pension list.

Garon, Uriah. N.J. —. His widow, Mary Garon, was pensioned in Burlington County on 27 Feb. 1847 at the rate of $30 per annum.

Garrabrants, Garrabrants N. —. —. He died as a pensioner in 1833. He married *ca.* 1788 Elizabeth -----. Congress rejected her request for a pension because of insufficient evidence of her marriage 21 May 1840.

Garrell, James. S.C. —. His annuity was £75 in 1787.

Garrell, Solomon. Va. —. His family was granted £15 support in Orange Co., Va. on 28 Jan. 1779 while he was away in the service. He also appeared as Solomon Garrett.

Garret, Andrew. Mass. Lt. He received his commutation for five years in lieu of half-pay for life.

Garret, Samuel. N.Y. Pvt. He served under Col. Goose Van Schaick in the 1st Regiment and was slain 28 June 1778. His widow, Molly Garret, received his half-pay pension.

Garretson, Isaac. Pa. —. He was granted a $40 annuity and a $40 gratuity in York Borough 31 Mar. 1836. He died 18 Apr. 1842.

Garretson, Samuel. N.J. Pvt. He was pensioned 11 Aug. 1790 at the rate of $60 per annum.

Garrett, Alexander. Pa. Pvt. He served in the 4th Regiment under Col. Johnston. He was wounded by a musket ball in his left leg in Sep. 1777 at Brandywine. He lived in Lancaster Co., Pa. in 1795. He enlisted 22 Apr. 1777 for the war and was on the rolls in 1780. He was granted one-third of a pension 20 Apr. 17967. He was on the 1813 pension list.

Garriott, —. Va. —. He died in the service. His widow, Catherine Garriott, was awarded £73.1.4.

in Culpeper Co., Va. 1 Dec. 1779 for 150 pounds of bacon and 4 barrels of corn.

Garrison, Benjamin. Pa. —. He received a $40 gratuity and a $40 annuity in Washington County 9 Feb. 1837.

Garrison, Jeremiah. Va. —. His widow, Priscilla Garrison, was granted £30 support for her and her family in Rockbridge Co., Va. on 6 Oct. 1778 and 7 Sep. 1779. Her husband died in the service.

Garrison, Richard. N.Y. Qr. Mr. Sgt. He served under Col. Joseph Drake in the militia. He was disabled by a musket ball in his right side on 7 July 1779 at Saratoga. His sixth and seventh ribs were fractured. He was 41 years old in 1786. He lived in Westchester Co., N.Y. on 22 Apr. 1789. He was a carpenter. He was on the 1813 pension list.

Garrison, Samuel. N.Y. —. He served under Col. Lewis Dubois. His 200 acres of bounty land were awarded to his heirs, John Garrison and Samuel Garrison.

Garrott, —. Va. —. His wife, Mary Garrott, was granted support in Prince Edward County 19 July 1779 and 16 Aug. 1779 while he was away in Continental service.

Garth, James. Md. Pvt. He served in the 4th Regiment. He was pensioned in Frederick County 1789. He was wounded at Ninety Six. He was on the 1813 pension list.

Garvey, —. Pa. —. His widow, Eleanor Garvey, was awarded a $40 gratuity and a $40 annuity in Butler Co., Pa. 23 Apr. 1829.

Garvin, Henry. Pa. —. He applied 17 Feb. 1814. He served from 1776 to the end of the war.

Garvin, Hugh. Va. —. His wife, Susannah Garvin, was allowed 4 barrels of corn and 200 pounds of pork for a family of four in Bedford Co., Va. in Nov. 1780.

Gary, —. Pa. —. His widow, Mary Gary, was awarded a $40 gratuity in Westmoreland County in 1847 for his Revolutionary service.

Gary, Joshua. Mass. Sgt. He served in the 7th Regiment and was from Boston. His widow, Sarah Gary, was paid $50.

Gary, Moses. —. —. He was wounded by a musket ball in his right leg. He resided in Mass. in 1796.

Gaskill, Budd. Pa. —. He was granted relief.

Gaskin, Job. —. —. His petition was rejected 17 Apr. 1798.

Gaskins, Herman. N.C. Pvt. He lived in Craven Co., N.C. He was on the 1813 pension list.

Gaskins, Thomas. Pa. Lt. He was in Northumberland County on 12 Sep. 1787. He was in Capt. Hugh White's Company in the Northumberland County militia under Col. James Potter and was wounded in his left hand at Piscataway, N.J. on 1 Feb. 1777. He was aged 40 years. He was on the 1813 pension list.

Gassaway, Henry. Md. Lt. He was pensioned at the rate of half-pay of a lieutenant in Anne Arundel County in Nov. 1804.

Gassaway, John. Md. Capt. He was pensioned at the rate of half-pay of a captain 23 Jan. 1816. His widow, Elizabeth Lane Gassaway, was pensioned at the same rate 10 Feb. 1821. She was paid his arrearage of $38 on 19 Dec. 1821 and died 1856. Their daughter, Louisa Gassaway, sought to have the pension continued to her, but Congress rejected her petition 29 Jan. 1884. She should be provided for a pension by the general law.

Gasser, John. Pa. —. He was granted a $40 gratuity and a $40 annuity in Lebanon County 31 Mar. 1836.

Gasten, Harman. N.C. —. He served in the 2nd N.C. Regiment and lost his thumb. He was awarded a gratuity of £18.3.4 in 1777.

Gaston, Joseph. —. —. His widow, Jane Gaston, sought an increase in her pension. Congress denied her claim 23 Feb. 1855.

Gaston, Robert. S.C. Lt. He was killed 16 Nov. 1779.

Gates, Benjamin. Mass. Capt. He received a rupture in the line of duty on 16 Aug. 1776 in New York. He resided at Bane, Mass. in 1796. He was appointed 2 Apr. 1777 and resigned 15 Jan. 1778. He served in the 5th Regiment.

Gates, Ezra. —. Pvt. He served under Col. Moses Hazen in 1780. He was wounded in his arm in action at Gen. Bayley's house.. He transferred to New Hampshire. He was from Oxford in 1786. He transferred to Vermont and was at Newbury in 1792. He was on the 1813 pension list.

Gates, Henry. Mass. Pvt. He served under Col. John Nixon and Capt. Thomas Drury. He was wounded by a ball which entered his cheek and was taken out of the back part of his head. He was 29 years old in 1786. He lived in Framingham, Mass. in 1792. His rate was $5 per month from 9 Mar. 1807. He was on the 1813 pension list.

Gates, Stephen. Vt. Sgt. He served under Col. Selden. He was disabled near White Plains by a wound in his left leg in Oct. 1776. He resided in Windham, Vt. in 1792.

Gates, William. Md. Pvt. He was pensioned at the rate of half-pay of a private 23 Jan. 1816.

Gaul, —. Pa. —. His widow, Sabina Gaul, was awarded a $40 gratuity and a $40 annuity in Philadelphia Co., Pa. 23 Apr. 1829.

Gavet, Edward. R.I. Pvt. 1786. He lost the use of his right leg and thigh when a ball passed through his knee and knee pan. His leg and thigh had withered. He served under Col. Christopher Lippit. He was aged 38 in 1786. He resided in Providence Co., R.I. He was on the 1813 pension list.

Gay, Thomas. Mass. Pvt. He served in Crane's Regiment and was from Franklin. He was paid $50.

Gay, Thomas. Pa. —. He was awarded a $40 gratuity and a $40 annuity in Pike County on 2 Apr. 1821.

Geddis, Joseph. Pa. —. He was awarded a $40 gratuity and a $40 annuity in Huntingdon County on 27 Mar. 1819.

Geddis, Samuel. Pa. Pvt. He applied 30 May 1788. He served in Capt. Laird's Company in the Cumberland County militia. He was wounded in the head by a broad sword by the British 11 Dec. 1777 at Gulph Mills and taken prisoner. He was released in July 1778. He also served under Col. William Chambers. He was 48 years old. He also appeared as Samuel Gaddis.

Gedenberger, Adam. Pa. —. He was granted relief.

Gee, Henry. Va. —. His wife was granted £7.18.9 in Halifax Co.,Va. on 19 Mar. 1778 and on 17 Feb. 1780.

Gee, Moses. N.Y. —. His wife and two children were granted support in Dutchess County 3 Nov. 1781.

Geer, Benajah. N.Y. Pvt. He served under Capt. Experience Storr in Col. Israel Putnam's Regiment. He was disabled by a ball in his right shoulder at Bunker Hill 17 June 1775. He was 34 years old in 1788. He lived at Kinderhook, Columbia Co., N.Y. on 22 Apr. 1789. He was on the 1813 pension list.

Geese, —. Pa. —. His widow, Elizabeth Geese, was awarded a $40 gratuity and a $40 annuity in Lebanon Co., Pa. 27 Jan. 1835. She was dead by Oct. 1837.

Geese, Ernst. Pa. —. He was granted $30 per annum 10 June 1814.

Geesey, Jacob. Pa. —. His widow was Catharine Geesey.

Gehret, —. Pa. —. His widow, Elizabeth Gehret, was awarded a $40 gratuity in Berks Co., Pa. 6 Apr. 1833. She was awarded a $40 gratuity and a $40 annuity 15 Apr. 1835. She died 4 Apr. 1841.

Geiger, Jacob. Pa. —. He was awarded a $40 gratuity and a $40 annuity in Lebanon County on 28 Mar. 1820. He died 9 Aug. 1822.

Geiger, John L. Pa. —. He was awarded a $40 gratuity and a $40 annuity in Northampton Co., Pa. 15 Apr. 1835.

Geiger, Peter. Pa. —. He enlisted at Hannah's Town in the Rifle Company of Capt. Joshua Irwin. His son, Jacob Geiger, enlisted as a drummer in the same company and lost his life in the battle of Germantown. He was from Berks County.

Geip, Henry. Pa.—. His widow, Ann Catharine Geip, received a $40 gratuity and a $40 annuity 30 Mar. 1860.

Gelder, Jacob. S.C. —. He was killed 10 Feb. 1781. His widow, Frances Gelder, was allowed an annuity 1 Apr. 1785.

Gellis, Henry. Pa. —. He was granted relief.

Gellon, John. N.C. Pvt. He lived in Cabarrus County.

Gelwicks, George. Pa. Ens. He was in Capt. Eichelberger's Company in the York County Associators in 1776 and marched to Amboy to guard the prisoners captured with Burgoyne. He was later under Capt. Foreman in the York County militia and marched to Guelph Mills. He was from Mifflin County.

Gemmel, —. Va. —. He served in the 1st Virginia Regiment. His father, James Gemmel, was granted £12 support in York County on 16 Feb. 1778. James Gemmel was granted £30 support on 15 Feb. 1779 while his two sons were away in the service.

Gen, Thomas. Va. —. He was on the 1785 pension roll.

Gendell, John. Mass. —. He served in the 10th Regiment and was paid $20.

Gensimer, —. Pa. —. His widow, Eve Gensimer, was awarded a $40 gratuity and a $40 annuity in Lancaster County 31 Mar. 1836. She died 12 Nov. 1841.

Gensimer, John. Pa. —. His widow, Eve Gensimer, was awarded a $40 gratuity in Washington Co., Pa. 23 Jan. 1833.

Gensler, Conrad. Pa. —. His widow, Eve Gensler, was awarded a $40 gratuity 8 Apr. 1833 in York Co., Pa.

Gensler, George. Pa. —. His widow, Magdalena Gensler, was awarded a $40 gratuity and a $40 annuity in York Co., Pa. 6 Apr. 1833. She also appeared as Magdalena Gentsler. She was paid to 11 Oct. 1835.

Gentsel, John Adam. Pa. —. He was granted a $40 gratuity in Columbia County 12 Jan. 1836.

Genther, John H. France. —. He volunteered at Paris, France in 1778 and served under Capt. Mescotzay. He sailed to America in 1780. He was at Rhode Island, White Plains, Yorktown, North River, Fort Washington, and Yorktown. He was naturalized in 1790. He was upwards of seventy years of age when he sought a pension from Congress on 23 Dec. 1831. Congress granted him one 5 Mar. 1840.

Gentry, Marshal. —. —. He resided in Tennessee but did not sign his petition to Congress. He gave no declaration or evidence. Congress rejected the claim 25 Jan. 1848.

Gentzel, Michael. Pa. —. He was awarded a $40 gratuity and a $40 annuity in Columbia Co., Pa. 15 Apr. 1835.

Gentzler, Conrad. Pa. Ens. He was from York County and was killed near Perth Amboy in 1776.

Genung, Isaac. N.J. or N.Y. Pvt. He was on the 1823 pension list of New York. His widow, Mary Genung, was pensioned in Chatham, Morris Co., N.J. 3 Feb. 1847 at the rate of $25 per annum.

George, —. S.C. —. His widow was Bethiah George. There were children in 1791.

George, Bartholomew. N.H. Pvt. He served in June 1782 when he was taken prisoner by the Indians and carried to Canada where he remained until Sep. 1783. It was supposed that he had been killed so he was returned dead on the roll and payment had ceased. He was awarded £30 plus interest. He was from Dublin on 12 June 1792.

George, Francis. Me. —. He was from Leeds. He was paid $50 under the resolve of 1836.

George, Matthew. Pa. —. He was awarded a $40 gratuity in Montgomery Co., Pa. 1 Mar. 1832. He was awarded a $40 gratuity and a $40 annuity 23 Jan. 1833.

George, Moses Swett. N.H. Pvt. He served under Col. Hale in Capt. Cloyce's Company. He was wounded by a musket ball in his right elbow which broke the bone and rendered the limb crooked and stiff on 7 July 1777 at Hubbardstown. He had a pension in 1786. He lived in Lyman, N.H. in 1795. He enlisted 10 Apr. 1777 for three years and was discharged 10 Apr. 1780. He was granted half a pension 20 Apr. 1796. He was on the 1813 pension list.

George, Robert. Va. Capt. He served in the artillery in the Illinois Regiment from 4 June 1779 to 15 Feb. 1784. He died intestate and his commutation of $8,071.44 was paid to his administrator.

George. William. —. Sailing Master. He served aboard the *Sachem* and died in the service. His widow, Christian George, sought his half-pay. He was not covered by the law

Geortner, George. N.Y. Pvt. He entered the service in 1777 for three years. He returned to his family in Herkimer Co., N.Y. in 1780. He died in Montgomery Co., N.Y. in 1813. Congress rejected the petition of his son, Peter Geortner, on 26 Jan. 1837.

Gerhart, Peter. Pa. —. He was awarded a $40 gratuity and a $40 annuity in Columbia Co., Pa. 23 Jan. 1834. He also appeared as Peter Gearhart.

Gerlack, George. Pa. Pvt. He was on the 1791 pension roll. He was on the 1813 pension list. He lived in Columbia County. He also appeared as George Gerloch.

Gerlock, John. Pa. Pvt. He was in Philadelphia County on 14 Nov. 1785. He was in the Invalids. He was disabled by a broken leg and was discharged 4 Feb. 1783. He was aged 45 years. His wife was Elizabeth Gerlock. He died 5 Mar. 1790. He also appeared as John Gerloch.

German, John. Pa. —. He was awarded a $40 gratuity and a $40 annuity in Berks Co., Pa. 21 Mar. 1833.

Gerrish, Edward. Md. Pvt. He was pensioned at the rate of half-pay of a private 2 Jan. 1813.

Gerry, Reuben. Mass. Bombardier. He served in the 3rd Artillery Battalion and was from South Reading. His widow, Joanna Green, was paid $50.

Gervis, James. Va. —. He served in the 9th Virginia Regiment. His widow, Margaret Gervis, was granted £10 maintenance in Washington Co., Va. 19 Mar. 1778.

Gervis, John. S.C. —. He was from Fairfield. There were four children in 1791.

Gettig, Christopher. Pa. 1st Lt. He was in Northumberland County on 30 Aug. 1786. He was in the 12th Pa. Regiment under Col. William Cook. He was wounded by a musket ball in his right leg which he lost at Piscataway, N. J. He was 42 years old. Frederick Gettig was his son. He died 2 July 1790. His widow, Ann Dorothy Gettig, was granted a $40 gratuity and a $40 annuity.

Getz, John. Pa. —. He was awarded a $40 gratuity and a $40 annuity in Lancaster County 12 Mar. 1836.

Geyer, James. Mass. —. He served in the 1st Regiment. He was paid $20.

Geyer, John. Pa. —. He served under Capt. Irwin and Col. Miles in the 4th Regiment. He was under Capt. Carnauhan. He was also under Col. Butt and Col. Stewart. He was at Long Island, Fort Washington, Trenton, and Germantown. He was wounded at the latter. He was from Franklin County. He died 29 May 1854.

Geyer, Peter. Pa. —. His widow, Mary Geyer, was awarded a $40 gratuity and a $40 annuity in Franklin Co., Pa. 10 Apr. 1826.

Gher, Jacob. Pa. —. He was awarded a $40 gratuity in Crawford Co., Pa. 21 Feb. 1834. He also appeared as Jacob Gehr.

Gibb, Robert. Pa. Pvt. He was in Westmoreland County. He served in Capt. Samuel McKane's Company in Col. Frederick Watts' Battalion in the Pa. Line. He was in the Flying Camp for six months in 1776. He was awarded a $40 gratuity and a $40 annuity 11 Apr. 1825.

Gibbart, Peter. Md. —. He was awarded $200 on 23 Jan. 1816. He also appeared as Peter Gibhart.

Gibbon, James. —. Capt. He resigned in Mar 1781 as a lieutenant and was promoted to brevet rank of captain and aid to Gen Irwin. Congress found that he was not entitled to any arrearage of pay but was entitled to commutation on 2 Mar. 1830. He served in the army and received five years' full pay commutation 2 Mar. 1833.

Gibbons, Phillip. Pa. Pvt. He served in the 4th Pa. Regiment of Infantry. He was on the 1813 pension list. He lived in Chester County. He died 17 May 1823. His administratrix was Catharine Gibbons, single woman, of Lancaster County.

Gibbs, Churchill. Va. Pvt. He served in the 1st Va. State Regiment in 1775 and rose by promotion to lieutenant. He served to the close of the war. He served under Col. George Gibson and was taken prisoner at Petersburg. Congress refused him relief 28 Feb. 1849. He received his commutation 7 May 1792. On 3 Mar. 1847 Congress rejected his claim for five years' full pay.

Gibbs, Frederick. —. —. He applied for a pension in 1819 but omitted to give the correct names of his officers. He was successful in 1831. He applied and asked that he be allowed a pension from 1819 to 1831, but Congress refused to approve a special act 27 Mar. 1846. It was his mistake and not that of the government.

Gibbs, James. Mass. —. He served in the 1st Regiment and was paid $20.

Gibbs, Rufus. —. —. He enlisted 20 Apr. 1779 under Capt. Warner and Col. Wyllis and was discharged at Morristown 18 Feb. 1780. Congress granted him a pension 3 Jan. 1832.

Gibbs, Samuel. Conn. Lt. He served in Capt. Daniel Allen's Company in the 3rd Conn. Regiment under Col. Samuel B. Wyllys. He was disabled by a gun shot wound in his right arm above the elbow at Norwalk on 11 July 1779. He lived in New York City, N.Y. on 5 May 1789. He was aged 30 years on 1 Aug. 1786. He was on the 1813 pension list.

Gibbs, Simeon. N.Y. Corp. He was pensioned 28 Mar. 1808 in Ontario Co., N.Y. He was on the 1813 pension list.

Gibbs, Thomas. Mass. Pvt. He served in the 4th Regiment and was from Sandwich. His widow, Temperance Gibbs, was paid $50.

Gibbs, Thomas. S.C. —. He served seven years. He had an old and blind consort. He was pensioned 2 Dec. 1819. He died 6 Apr. 1821.

Gibbs, William. Va. —. His wife, Mary Gibbs, and child were furnished 1 barrel of corn and 50 pounds of pork in Frederick Co., Va. on 6 June 1780.

Gibson, Abraham. Ga. —. He applied unsuccessfully for a pension from South Carolina since he did not serve from that state.

Gibson, Alexander. N.Y. —. He was pensioned 20 Mar. 1834 from 4 Mar. 1831. His pension was suspended in Apr 1835. He should not have been dropped. Congress restored him 1 June 1836. He lived in Bracken Co., Ky.

Gibson, Elias. S.C. Pvt. He was in the militia under Capt. Robert Bryan, Capt. Cain, and Capt. Davison. He was at Ninety Six, Stono, and the Cherokee Expedition. James Shanks, William Dawson, and Samuel Stalnaker were fellow soldiers. He was pensioned in Abbeville District 6 Dec. 1826. He was paid as late as 1834.

Gibson, George. —. —. He married 15 Mar. 1786 in Spartanburgh Co., S.C. He died 20 May 1841. Congress granted his widow, Abigail Gibson, a pension 28 Feb. 1844.

Gibson, George. Va. Col. He enlisted 100 men at Pittsburgh and marched to Williamsburg. He was commissioned captain in the Virginia Line and sent to negotiate a secret treaty with the Spanish for powder and lead. He engaged Oliver Pollock to ship the cargo. On his return to Virginia he was appointed colonel in the 1st Virginia Regiment. He was at Germantown in 1781. He became supernumerary. He marched prisoners with Cornwallis to York until they were returned to England. His legal representative was granted his commutation 22 Dec. 1837.

Gibson, Isaac. Pa. —. He was awarded a $40 gratuity and a $40 annuity in Lancaster, Pa. 15 Jan. 1829.

Gibson, James. —. —. He received his five years' commutation 2 Mar. 1833.

Gibson, James. Va. —. He was pensioned in Scott County on 5 Feb. 1823. He enlisted in 1776 and served two years. He lost his eyesight by disease. He received $60 per annum and $50 in relief.

Gibson, Nathaniel. Mass. —. He served in the 4th Regiment and was from Pepperell. He was paid $20.

Gibson, Samuel. Ga. —. He was granted $100 relief to enable him to be placed on the pension list of the United States in Nov./Dec. 1817. The act did not specify that the military service was Revolutionary.

Gibson, Samuel. Pa. —. He was awarded a $40 gratuity and a $40 annuity in Chester Co., Pa. 15 Apr. 1834

Gier, George. Mass. —. He served in the 4th Regiment and was from Boston. He was paid $20.

Giffin, —. —. —. Congress granted his widow, Anna Giffin of Wyoming Co., N.Y. a pension from 4 Mar. 1845 on 13 Feb. 1850. He was John Giffin. *Vide* also Benjamin Farnham.

Gilbert, Allen. N.Y. Pvt. He served under Col. Sheldon. He was wounded in the head, hand, and leg but to no great consequence on 2 July 1779 at Poundridge. He lived in Otsego Co., N.Y. in 1794. He enlisted 1 Apr. 1778 and continued to the end of the war. He was on the 1813 pension list.

Gilbert, Burr. Conn. Sgt. He served in the 1st Regiment under Col. Butler in Capt. Eel's Company. He was overheated at the battle of Monmouth. He was wounded in his legs, arms, and hands by a cannon ball being fired into a pile of bricks several of which were forced against him on 28 June 1778 at Fort Mifflin. He resided in Weston, Conn. in 1792. He enlisted 12 Apr. 1777 for the war. He was granted two-thirds of a pension 20 Apr. 1796. He transferred to New York in 1806. He was on the 1813 pension list. His rank was given as corporal in 1796. Congress granted his widow, Clarissa Turney, a pension 9 Feb. 1842.

Gilbert, Ebenezer. Conn. Pvt. He served in the 1st Regiment. He was ruptured in 1780. He resided in Brooklyn, Conn. in 1792. He enlisted 29 Apr. 1777 and continued to the end of the war.

Gilbert, Joel. Mass. Pvt. He served in the 5th Regiment and was from Brookfield. He was paid $50.

Gilbert, John. N.Y. Pvt. He served under Capt. Allen and Col. Elmar of Watertown on 18 Apr. 1776 for one year. In June 1777 he served under Capt. Elisha Gilbert and Col. Whiting. He was taken sick at Stillwater with measles and went home on furlough where he recovered and rejoined his company. He had short tours in 1778 and 1780. He married Anna Eaton in 1778. He died 12 Apr. 1852 at Lansdown and his widow died 6 Dec. 1827 [sic]. His children applied for his arrears. They were Jerusha Napp aged 76, Ira Gilbert aged 72, William Gilbert aged 68, John

Gilbert aged 67, Lydia Taylor aged 60, and Enos Gilbert aged 63. Ira Gilbert lived in Elgin County, Canada West in 1856. His nephew was Elisha Gilbert, the son of Elisha Gilbert. He had served under Capt. Elisha Gilbert from Oct. 1777 to 10 July 1779. The heirs were recommended to receive the arrearage 19 July 1856.

Gilbert, John. Pa. —. He was awarded $100 in Westmoreland County on 14 Mar. 1814.

Gilbert, Joseph. Va. —. He served under Col. George Gibson not less than nine months. He had been suspended from his pension because his service was not Continental. He was restored in 1830 when it was determined the unit was in Continental service. Congress granted him the arrears of his pension 13 May 1834.

Gilbert, Lewis. Mass. —. He enlisted in 1776 for eight months. He next enlisted for a year under Capt. Crocker and Col. Bailey. He was transferred to Col. Brewer in New York. He lived at Easton and was pensioned by Congress 22 Dec. 1831. He was 77 years old.

Gilbert, Stephen. Pa. —. His heirs were paid $200 in lieu of his donation land because the land had fallen into New York. They were from Berks County 12 Apr. 1851.

Gilbert, Thomas. Mass. —. He served in the 5th Regiment and was paid $20.

Gilbraith, John. Pa. —. He was granted relief.

Gilchrist, John. Pa. Lt. He was in Dauphin County on 22 Mar. 1786. He served in the Lancaster County militia and was drafted into the Flying Camp. He was wounded in his right arm below the elbow in Aug. 1776 at Elizabethtown, N.J. when he was on the march from Perth Amboy by the accidental discharge of a gun. Capt. Timothy Green of the 6th Company, Capt. James Weaver of the 2nd Company, 1st Lt. James Collier of the 1st Company, and 1st Lt. William Allen of the 6th Company attested his service. He served under Capt. John Read. He was 35 years old. He was granted $50 annuity for life 20 Feb. 1804. He died 27 Dec. 1805 in Westmoreland County. His widow was Eleanor Gilchrist. She was granted relief in 1840. She died 10 May 1844.

Gilder, Jacob. S.C. —. His widow, Frances Gilder, was on the roll in 1786. There were two children in 1791.

Gildersleeve, Daniel. N.Y. —. He was granted relief.

Giles, John. S.C. —. He was taken prisoner 27 Feb. 1781 and died in confinement. His widow, Abigail Giles, was awarded an annuity 24 Sep. 1785.

Giles, Aquilla. —. —. He resided in New York City. Congress rejected his petition for relief because he was a debtor to the United States on 23 Feb. 1820.

Giles, Thomas. Mass. —. He enlisted for three years in the 13th Regiment and was honorably discharged. He reentered as a sailmaker and served to the close of the war. He died 18 Nov. 1795. He married 22 June 1780. His widow died 22 Sep. 1822. Neither received a pension or bounty land. His father, Thomas Giles, Sr., was a combatant at Bunker Hill and died the day after the battle. The grandchildren of Thomas Giles, Sr., were granted 100 acres of bounty land 12 Dec. 1856 and 160 acres for the service of their father.

Gill, —. Va. —. His widow, Nancy Gill, was granted £6 support in Northumberland County 11 May 1778.

Gill, James. S.C. —. He was at Purysburg, Black Swamp, Charleston, Friday's Ferry, Belville, and Wright's Bluff. He was shot through the arm at the latter. William Lewis and David Morrow were fellow soldier. He was 60 years old. He gave a power of attorney to George Gill of Chester District, S.C. He was from Greene Co., Ala. when his application in 1827 was rejected.

Gill, John. Pa. Pvt. He was in Philadelphia County on 14 Nov. 1785. He was transferred from the

8th Pa. Regiment to the Invalids. He was wounded in both hands and one leg. He was 46 years old. He also appeared at John McGill. His wife was alive 1 Aug. 1787.

Gill, John. Pa. —. He and William Cooper had donation tracts which were in part covered by surveys and overlapping claims and these problems were to be corrected by act of 28 Mar. 1806.

Gill, Joshua. Mass. —. He served in the 4th Regiment and was paid $20.

Gill, Robert. S.C. Smith/Cutler. He served under Capt. Alexander Pagan. He was at Fishing Creek. He died shortly after the war was over leaving a widow and five small children. He died in 1786. His widow was Elizabeth Gill from Chester District in 1828. She was 75 years old. Her application was rejected.

Gill, Silas. N.H. Pvt. He served in the 1st N.H. Regiment under Col. Sille and was wounded by two musket balls in his right thigh at the battle of Bemis Heights 19 Sep. 1777 and left at Albany. He was in Capt. Isaac Farewell's Company. He was pensioned in Massachusetts. He resided in New Ipswich and was 31 years old in 1788. He was on the 1813 pension list.

Gill, Thomas. S.C. Capt. He served in the militia from Camden District from Dec. 1778 under Capt. Philip Walker for three months. His next tour was under Col. Lawrence until Aug. 1779. His third tour was under Capt. Alexander Pagan at Ramsour's Mill in North Carolina. He was attached to Col. Sumter and marched to Rocky Mount. In Aug. 1780 he was elected lieutenant. When Capt. Pagan was killed at Old Fields and most of the company was cut to pieces, the remnant reorganized and elected him captain. He was at Congaree, Biggin Church, and Engro's Quarters. His heirs were due five years' full pay from Congress on 8 July 1856.

Gill, William. Pa. —. He was awarded a $40 gratuity and a $40 annuity 28 Jan. 1813. He applied 15 Jan. 1822. He was from Mercer County.

Gill, William. Pa. —. He was awarded a $40 gratuity and a $40 annuity 27 Mar. 1837 in Crawford County. He died 9 Nov. 1845.

Gillam, Nathaniel. N.J. —. He enlisted in the beginning of 1775, sickened, and died 15 Aug. 1775 in the service. His widow, Martha Gillam, married secondly Isaac Shipman. Rev. Jacob Van Arsdalen performed the marriage on 4 Apr. 1782 at the First Presbyterian Church in Springfield. She applied for his half-pay 13 Mar. 1793 in Essex County.

Gilleland, Philip. Pa. —. He was awarded a $40 gratuity in Bedford Co., Pa. 12 Apr. 1828.

Gillespie, —. Pa. —. His widow, Margaret Gillespie, was awarded a $40 gratuity and a $40 annuity in Union Co., Pa. 5 Feb. 1829.

Gillespie, Daniel. S.C. —. He married and reared a family of nine children. The four youngest were with him. His wife was dead. He was pensioned from Abbeville District on 23 Nov. 1829. He was paid as late as 1833. He was incorrectly reported as David Gillespie.

Gillespie, James. Pa. —. He was wounded on the Sandusky Expedition.

Gillespie, John. S.C. —. He was wounded by a musket ball at the Cherokee Ford of the Savannah River a few days before Kettle Creek in Georgia by a party of Tories under Col. Boyd. One of his leg bones was broken. He was from Abbeville District and was pensioned 8 Dec. 1826. He was paid as late as 1834.

Gillet, Benjamin. N.Y. —. His 200 acres of bounty land were awarded to his heirs 19 June 1812.

Gillet, Joel. Conn. Ens. He served under Col. Jed. Huntington. He was disabled while a prisoner on board a prison ship. He resided in Harwinton, Conn. in 1792.

Gillett, Aaron. S.C. Surgeon. When the British took the state, he and his son fled to North Carolina with a party of militia and joined the Continental Army. He was appointed Senior Surgeon in the General Hospital. He was later deranged. His son, Elijah Gillett, sought their commutation pay.

Gillett, Elijah. S.C. Surgeon's Mate. When the British took the state, he and his father fled to North Carolina with a party of militia and joined the Continental Army. He was appointed Surgeon's Mate in the General Hospital. He was later deranged. His father was Aaron Gillett. He sought their commutation pay.

Gilligan, Thomas. Mass. —. He served in the 6th Regiment. He was paid $20.

Gillion, John. N.C. —. He was in Lancaster District, S.C. in 1803. He served in the militia. He was wounded in the head and body by Tarleton's troops between Charlotte and Salisbury at the Sassafras Fields in Mecklenburg County. He was on the 1813 pension list. He also appeared as John Gillon.

Gillis, Alexander. N.Y. —. He was commissioned to command a company of rangers in June 1777. He was at Bennington and Stillwater. His second tour was from May to Oct. 1778. His third tour was from Apr. to Oct. 1779. He served six months in 1780. He was also called out in 1782. Congress granted him a pension at the rank of a private 23 June 1836. He was from Argyle, Washington Co., N.Y.

Gillison, James. S.C. —. He died in 1813. His widow was Jane Gillison from Pendleton District in 1846. Their children were James Gillison, Israel Gillison, Jonathan Gillison, Elijah Gillison, and Esther Gillison. Her application was rejected 30 Nov. 1846.

Gillman, Philip. Pa. Pvt. He was in Philadelphia County on 3 Apr. 1787. He served in the German Regiment under Capt. Rice and was wounded through his left breast at Germantown on 4 Oct. 1777. He was under the command of Col. Weltner. He was on the 1813 pension list.

Gilman, Jeremiah. —. Col. He resigned in Mar. 1780. His grandchildren, John Mason and others, sought relief from Congress 7 Mar. 1858. Congress rejected the petition because he resigned before the half-pay resolution.

Gilman, John. Pa. —. He was granted relief in 1813.

Gilman, Joshua. N.H. Pvt. He was in Capt. Christopher Webb's Company under Col. David Hobart and was wounded on 16 Aug. 1777 by a musket ball in the battle of Bennington. The ball entered one side of his breast and came out above his left elbow breaking his arm. He lived in Walpole and received a state pension until 31 Dec. 1779 when he was struck off the roll by order of the court. He lived in Alstead, N.H. in 1792. He was in the militia. He was granted two-thirds of a pension 20 Apr. 1796. He was on the 1813 pension list. He transferred to Orleans Co., Vt.

Gilman, Samuel. Pa. Pvt. He served in the 7th Regiment. He was wounded in his left hand in Sep. 1777 near Paoli. He lived in Washington Co., Pa. in 1795. He was omitted on the rolls in May 1778. His son-in-law was John Reynolds. He was granted half a pension 20 Apr. 1796. He was on the 1813 pension list. He applied again 4 Sep. 1814. His widow, Nancy Gilman, was awarded a $40 gratuity and a $40 annuity in Fayette Co., Pa. 23 Apr. 1829. He also appeared as Samuel Gilmore. His application for a pension was rejected in 1814 because he was on the roll of the United States.

Gilmer, George. Va. Surgeon. He served in the battalion of guards of the Convention troops at the barracks in Charlottesville, Va. From 21 June 1781. His executor sought five years' commutation, but Congress rejected the claim 19 Jan. 1835.

Gilmer, Henry. Conn. Pvt. He served in Hazen's Regiment. He was disabled with a rupture. He was pensioned 3 Nov. 1782. He was on the 1791 and 1813 pension lists as Henry Gilner. He died 12 Feb. 1822 in New London Co., Conn.

Gilmer, Samuel. Va. —. He was on the 1785 list. His application was rejected 9 Jan. 1786 because he was capable of getting a livelihood by labor.

Gilmore, —. Va. —. His father, William Gilmore, was furnished support in Loudoun County 15 Nov. 1778.

Gilmore, —. Va. —. His mother, Sarah Gilmore, was furnished support in Loudoun County in Apr. 1779. She was the wife of William Gilmore.

Gilmore, James. S.C. —. He had a bounty land warrant for 180 acres located in York District. After his death it was discovered that the said tract was part of a survey to the Rev. Thomas Harris McCally and Thomas Black. His widow, Elizabeth Gilmore, was a resident of Chester District in 1824. She died 22 Dec. 1828. Jonathan Hinkle sought her arrearage, but his claim was rejected. He also appeared as James Gilmon.

Gilmore, Joseph. S.C. Pvt. He transferred to Davidson Co., Tenn. 5 July 1812, but he was on the 1813 pension list in South Carolina. He died 23 Feb. 1825.

Gilmore, Robert. Pa. —. He was pensioned 29 Mar. 1813.

Gilmore, Samuel. Va. —. He was on the pension roll of 1785. He was pensioned in Rockingham County 10 Jan. 1812 at the rate of $80 per annum with $60 immediate relief. He was wounded at the defeat of Gen. Buford in S.C. in 1780. He was in Bath County in 1830.

Gilmore, Toby. Mass. Pvt. He served in the 16th Regiment and was from Raynham. His widow, Rose Gilmore, was paid $50.

Gilpin, William. Md. Pvt. He was pensioned in Jefferson Co., Va. at the rate of half-pay of a private 2 Mar. 1827.

Gimbo, Thomas. Va. —. His wife and children were granted £6.5 support in Halifax Co., Va. on 21 Aug. 1777.

Gire, George. Mass. —. He was allowed £4 for one year's pension commencing in June 1779 to be paid by the selectmen of Grafton on 20 Feb. 1781.

Gissendanner, Daniel. S.C. —. He served ten months in Col. Myddleton's Regiment. He died about 1793. His widow, Elizabeth Gissendanner, who had five small children, sought compensation. 28 Nov. 1796.

Gist, Thomas. Va. —. He was being pensioned in Mar. 1781. Ann Gist, his administratrix, had her request for the arrearage of his pension rejected since she submitted no proof of his death or of the vouchers required by laws on 7 Nov. 1789.

Gist, William. S.C. —. He was from Pendleton District in 1836.

Githins, Joseph. Pvt. N.J. He served under Capt. Benjamin Whitall and Col. Newcomb. He was killed 13 Sep. 1776 on the retreat from Long Island. He married Sarah Stoy 14 Apr. 1776. She was granted a half-pay pension 4 Oct. 1795 for her widowhood. She married secondly John Dorum 3 May 1790.

Givens, Robert. S.C. —. He was pensioned 25 Nov. 1830.

Gladhill, Ely. N.J. Pvt. He served in the 2nd N.J. Regiment. He was wounded in the left leg on 31 Dec. 1775 at Quebec. He lived in N.Y. in 1794.

Glantz, James. Pa. —. He was granted relief in Centre County 21 Feb. 1838.

Glasgow, —. Pa.—. His widow, Jane Glasgow, received a $40 gratuity and a $40 annuity in Huntingdon County 19 Mar. 1855.

Glasgow, James. Pa. —. He was awarded a $40 gratuity and a $40 annuity in Mifflin Co., Pa. 1 Apr. 1834. He was 77 years old in 1840. He died 12 Oct. 1840.

Glasgow, John. S.C. —. His horse was shot out from under him. He was wounded in his hip. He served under Capt. John Bowie in the 5th Regiment under Col. Isaac Huger. He was from Abbeville District and was pensioned 6 Dec. 1826.

Glason, Patrick. Va. Pvt. He was in King and Queen County on 1 Jan. 1786 when he was aged 28. He served in the 3rd Regiment of Light Dragoons. He enlisted in Baylor's Dragoons on 18 Dec. 1779. He was wounded by a ball through his right hand and rendered unfit as a soldier at Cowpens. Capt. William Barret confirmed his service. He was pensioned at the rate of £12 per annum for life on 24 Jan. 1785. His pension was continued on 24 May 1787. He was on the 1813 pension list as Patrick Glasson.

Glass, ——. Va. —. His wife, Elizabeth Glass, was granted £14.16.9 for necessaries in Halifax Co., Va. on 15 Jan. 1778.

Glass, Consider. Me. —. He was from Guilford. He was paid $50 under the resolve of 1836.

Glass, Robert. Pa. Pvt. He served in the 5th Regiment.. He was pensioned 20 Jan. 1813.

Glassmyer, Jacob. Pa. Pvt. He applied from Berks County on 15 Jan. 1810. He was in Capt. Jacob Mouser's Company under Col. Robert Megan. He enlisted in Feb. or Mar. 1777. John Kerner was the sergeant in Oct. 1777 and was wounded by the accidental discharge of a musket in his hand and lost the second finger of his left hand. Kerner served three years and lost his finger while he was in Capt. George Nagle's Company raised in Berks Co. Glassmyer died 7 Nov. 1822.

Glaze, Frederick. Pa. —. He was awarded a $40 gratuity and a $40 annuity in Berks County 28 Mar. 1836. He died 28 Feb. 1841.

Glazier, Aaron. Mass. —. He served in the 6th Regiment and was paid $20.

Gleason, John. Mass. Pvt. He served in the 5th Regiment and was from Worcester. He was paid $50.

Gleason, Jonathan. Mass. Pvt. He served in the 6th Regiment under Capt. Ebenezer Smith and Col. Calvin Smith. He was wounded in the breast and back. He was worn out in the service. He was pensioned 1 Sep. 1782. In 1786 he was aged 65 and resided in Waltham, Mass. He was on the 1813 pension list.

Gleason, Thomas. Mass. Pvt. He lost one of his thumbs, and much of his hand was injured by the bursting of a gun on 19 Apr. 1775 at Lexington and Concord. He was in the militia. He lived in Woburn, Mass. in 1792.

Gleason, William. Mass. —. He served in the 5th Regiment and was from Chester. He was paid $20.

Gleason, Windsor. N.H. Pvt. He served under Col. Cilley in Capt. Farwell's Company. He was wounded in his right side in the Indian expedition under Gen. Sullivan at Newtown. He lived in Langdon, N.H. in 1795. He enlisted 1 Feb. 1779 and was discharged in Feb. 1780. He was granted one-fourth of a pension 20 Apr. 1796. He was on the 1813 pension list. He died 8 Aug. 1816.

Gleim, Philip. Pa. Sgt. He was awarded a $40 gratuity and a $48 annuity in Dauphin County on 4 Mar. 1813. He died 29 Aug. 1813.

Glen, John. Pa. —. He served in the militia and was disabled.

Glendy, William. Pa. —. He was granted a $40 gratuity in Beaver County on 1 Mar. 1811. He applied 2 Jan. 1813.

Glenn, ——. Va. —. He served in Col. Morgan's Virginia Regiment. His wife, Elizabeth Glenn, and child were furnished £20 support in Frederick Co., Va. on 4 May 1779.

Glenn, ——. Va. —. His wife, Mary Glenn, was granted £60 support while her husband was away in the service in Fauquier Co., Va. in Nov. 1779.

Glenn, Bernard. Va. —. Lt. He applied for a grant of land on the north side of the Ohio River to satisfy a Virginia land warrant. Congress rejected his claim 11 Feb. 1803.

Glenn, William. S.C. —. He was killed in Sep. 1781. His widow, Hannah Glenn, was granted an annuity 10 Feb. 1785. She was from Laurens District. There were three children in 1791.

Glenn, William. S.C. —. He served under Maj. Ross and Col. Neal in the militia. He was taken prisoner at Briar Creek in 1779 and died in confinement. He left six small children and a widow. His widow, Jennet Glenn, was granted an annuity 15 Oct. 1785. On 3 December 1794 she received the £5 due her for her pension of 1793. She was from York District. All of her children were grown. She was paid as late as 1834.

Glenny, Isaac. Mass. —. He served in the 7th Regiment and was from Tyngsborough. He was paid $20.

Glentworth, James. Pa. Lt. He was on the 1813 pension list. He lived in Philadelphia County.

Glentzer, John. Pa. —. He received a $40 gratuity and a $40 annuity in Berks County 1 Apr. 1837. He was dead by Aug. 1838.

Glidden, William. N.H. —. He was in the Regiment of Col. Hazen and honorably discharged. He sought his depreciation pay on 17 Oct. 1785. He was from Northwood, Rockingham County.

Glover, —. Ga. —. Sarah Glover and her two children were granted assistance 25 Jan. 1782.

Glover, Alexander. Mass. Pvt. He served in the 9th Regiment and was from Dorchester. His widow, Nancy Glover, was paid $50.

Glover, Ezekiel. —. Drummer. He enlisted in 1776 under Col. Drake and Gen. Scott. He was taken ill at Greenwich. His constitution was broken in the service. His claim was not sustained by any proof other than his own statement. Congress rejected his petition 27 June 1838. He lived in New York.

Glover, James. Pa. Corp. He was in Philadelphia County on 9 Jan. 1786. He was in the 2nd Pa. Regiment and was wounded in his side. He was discharged 1 Jan. 1781. He was 41 years old. He was dead by Mar. 1801.

Glover, Samuel. N.C. Sgt. He served in Capt. Charles Allen's Company of the 2nd N.C. Continental Regiment under Col. Robert Howe. He fought at Brandywine, Germantown, and Stony Point. He was executed 23 Feb. 1780. His widow, Ann Glover, and two children sought a pension in Apr. or May 1780. No action was ever taken until 10 June 1780 when the legislature granted her an allowance of £15 per annum.

Glover, William. —. —. He did not apply to the Pension Office so Congress rejected his claim for relief 29 June 1840.

Goashorn, George. Pa. —. He was awarded a $40 gratuity 12 Feb. 1829 in Beaver County.

Gobey, —. Va. —. Molly Gobey was granted support in Prince William County in 1778.

Goddard, Edward. —. —. His application was rejected 25 Feb. 1795.

Goddard, John. Md. Pvt. He was pensioned in Prince George's County at the rate of half-pay of a private 23 Feb. 1829. He died 2 Sep. 1832. The arrearage of $16.89 was paid to Raphael C. Edelen for the use of his only son, Benjamin Goddard, on 17 Jan. 1833.

Goddard, Samuel. Mass. Artificer. He was from Hopkinton and was paid $20.

Godenberger, Adam. Pa. Pvt. He was granted one-fourth of a pension 20 Apr. 1796.

Godfrey, William E. Pa. Capt. He served in the artillery. He went on board a public vessel. He was taken prisoner and carried to New York where he was held for seven months. From 1 July to 11 Nov. 1777 he served under Col. Fowler. He was paid by Pennsylvania to 1 Jan. 1820. He claimed that he was supernumerary. He was from Cumberland County. His widow, Jane Godfrey, was awarded a gratuity of $60 and a annuity of $60 on 17 Feb. 1820 in lieu of donation land. Empson Hamilton sought bounty land from Congress but was rejected 20 Aug. 1842.

Godman, Samuel. Md. Capt. His heirs were issued a warrant for 200 acres in Allegany County on 10 Mar. 1856.

Godown, John. N.J. —. His widow, Mary Godown, was pensioned 13 Mar. 1845 at the rate of $30 per annum.

Goff, Israel. Mass. Pvt. He served in the 6th Regiment and was from Rehoboth. He was paid $50.

Goff, James. Mass. —. He served in the 2nd Regiment and was from Minot. He was paid $20.

Goff, Joshua. Conn. —. He was inoculated for smallpox and lost his left eye in Apr. 1777 at Norwich. He resided at Chatham, Conn. in 1796. He enlisted 24 Mar. 1777 for three years and was discharged 27 Mar. 1780.

Goff, Nathan. N.J. Pvt. He served under Col. Patton and was wounded in his thigh at Brandywine. He was from Hopewell. He was on the 1791 pension roll.

Goff, William. —. —. He applied in 1837, but there was no evidence on the roll of his service. On 31 Jan. 1855 Congress rejected his claim again because his only proof was his own declaration.

Goggans, William. S.C. —. He was from Newberry District and was pensioned 30 Nov. 1827. He received his annuity as late as 1833. He also appeared as William Goggins.

Gohn, Philip. Pa. —. He was awarded a $40 gratuity and a $40 annuity in York Co., Pa. 15 Apr. 1835. He was dead by July 1839.

Going, Frederick. S.C. —. He was killed at the siege of Charleston. His widow, Mary Going, was a resident of Claremont County in 1797. She appeared as Mary Gowen in 1799. Her brother was Thomas Burbridge. She was paid as late as 1819. He also appeared as Frederick Gowning.

Going, William. Va. —. His wife, Jemima Going, was awarded £10 relief in Bedford Co., Va. on 24 Nov. 1777. While she was to be paid £8 on 27 July 1778, that amount was reduced to £5 on 29 Sep. 1778 because her husband had returned from the service.

Golden, Walter. Md. Pvt. He was pensioned in Baltimore County on 10 Nov. 1814.

Goldsborough, —. Md. Pvt. His widow, Ann Goldsborough, was pensioned in St. Mary's County at the rate of half-pay of a private 11 Mar. 1834.

Goldsborough, Charles. Md. Pvt. He was pensioned at the rate of half-pay of a private 23 Jan. 1815.

Goldsmith, Ezra. N.Y. —. His 200 acres of bounty land were issued to Issac Goldsmith in trust for himself and the other heirs on 19 June 1812.

Goldsmith, Jeremiah. —. Pvt. He served nine months. His guardian was Jeremiah Goldsmith, Jr. He was *non compos mentes*. Congress granted him a pension 3 Mar. 1836.

Goldsmith, Thomas. Md. —. His heirs, James Mills, Thomas Mills, Elizabeth Mills, Sarah Campfield, and Harriet Goldsmith, received a warrant for 200 acres of bounty land in Allegany County in Feb. 1836.

Goldthwait, Philip. Mass. —. He served in the 2nd Dragoons and was paid $20.

Goldthwait, Timothy. Me. —. He was from Augusta. He was paid $50 under the resolve of 1836.

Goltrey, Thomas. N.J. —. He was pensioned in Somerset County on 6 Feb. 1846 at the rate of $60 per annum.

Gomber, John. Md. Pvt. He was pensioned in Frederick County in 1789. He was wounded at York Island. He was pensioned again in Frederick County at the rate of half-pay of a private 18 Feb. 1825. He served in the Flying Camp. He also appeared as John Gombare. [Compare with John Gambare.]

Gonter, George. Pa. —. He was pensioned in Franklin County 14 Mar. 1835.

Gonter, John. Pa. —. He received a $40 gratuity in Berks County 1 Apr. 1837. He was in Lancaster County afterwards. He was 79 years old in 1840. His widow, Elizabeth Gonter, applied 25 Jan.

1879 and indicated that he had applied twenty or thirty years before. The state of Pennsylvania had awarded Elizabeth Gonter a $40 annuity in Lancaster County 27 Feb. 1851.

Good, John. Mass. —. He served in Crane's Artillery and was paid $20.

Good, John. Pa. —. He was granted a $40 annuity in Ohio 12 Apr. 1845. The act was repealed 11 Apr. 1848. He died 17 Jan. 1851.

Good, Joseph. Pa. Pvt. He applied from Philadelphia County 6 Apr. 1819. He served in Capt. David Lenox's Company in the Pa. Line for one year or more. One of his name received a $40 gratuity and a $40 annuity 2 Apr. 1822.

Goode, Archibald. Va. —. He served in the 10th Virginia Regiment and was disabled by a rheumatic disorder. He was on the 1785 pension roll.

Goodel, William. Mass. Pvt. He served in the 8th Regiment and was from Marlborough. He was paid $50.

Goodell, —. —. —. His widow, Eunice Goodell, sought a pension for life 4 Jan. 1848 because hers was to expire 4 Mar. 1848. Congress did not grant her relief by a special act. She also appeared as Eunice Goddell.

Gooden, Christopher. N.C. Capt. He was killed in Continental service on 8 Sep. 1781 at Eutaw Springs. His heirs were pensioned in Bladen County in 1784.

Goodenough, Adino. N.H. Sgt. Maj. He was appointed in June 1777 under Col. Scammel and was taken prisoner and held about seven months. He was discharged by Brig. Gen. Poor on 18 Dec. 1778 in consequence of bad health contracted while he was a prisoner. His son, John B. Goodenough, sought bounty land for himself and the heirs. Congress declined to issue same because he had not enlisted for the war on 27 Mar. 1846.

Goodheart, Henry. Pa. —. He was pensioned by the act of 14 Mar. 1815. He died 25 Nov. 1818.

Goodman, Ansel. Va. —. His wife, Edith Goodman, was paid £18 on 26 Oct. 1778 in Bedford Co., Va. Her husband was being held captive in Kentucky by the Indians.

Goodman, Christian. Pa. —. He was granted relief in Columbia County under the act of 18 Mar. 1839.

Goodman, Joseph. S.C. Quartermaster. He served 322 days. Although his claim was not properly vouched, he was able to do so on 18 Dec. 1792 and received £103.10.0 at 45 shillings old money per diem.

Goodman, Peter. Pa.—. His widow, Christiana Goodman, received a $40 gratuity in Columbia County 18 Feb. 1839.

Goodrich, Noah. Mass. —. He served in the 1st Regiment and was from Vermont. He was paid $20.

Goodridge, Ezekiel. Mass. Lt. He served from Almsbury in Col. Edward Wigglesworth's Regiment and was killed at Saratoga on 7 Oct. 1777. His seven years' half-pay of $1,120 was paid to his heirs. On 22 June 1793 his brother, Bernard Goodridge, sought the balance of his half-pay for the children which their mother received until her marriage to Henry Trussell on 20 May 1780.

Goodridge, Joseph. Mass. Pvt. He was wounded by a stroke from the muzzle of a musket of another soldier in 1775 and lost his right eye. He served under Col. Gerrish. He lived in Boston, Mass. in 1792. At the time of his enlistment he was a school master and had received a good education. By the loss of his eye and the pain he suffered, he had to leave the business and also that of studying physic and go to labor. He was wounded in July 1775 near Chelsea. He lived in Lebanon, N.H. in 1794. He served in the militia. He also appeared as Joseph Goodrich.

Goodrum, Thomas. —. —. He was pensioned 27 Apr. 1810.

Goodson, James. S.C. —. He served a hundred days in Marion's Brigade. His officers included Capt. King, Col. Coles, Capt. Windham, and Col. Braxton. He was 71 years old. Thomas Merser and James Sanders were fellow soldiers. He was pensioned from Orangeburg District 23 Nov. 1829. He was paid as late as 1834.

Goodwin, —. Mass. —. Esther Goodwin was paid $50 for her husband's services.

Goodwin, Amaziah. N.H. —. He volunteered in 1776 or 1777 at Somersworth in the militia under Capt. Moses Yeaton. He spent three months at Portsmouth and erected works for the defense of Kittery. His next tour was under Capt. Samuel Emerson and Col. Bartlett and went to West Point. He was drafted or "voluntarily enlisted" under Ens. Sinclair and went to Stony Point where he repaired the works and remounted the cannon which Gen. Arnold had previously dismounted. He was discharged five months later. He served eleven and a half months. Congress granted him a pension 18 Mar. 1844.

Goodwin, Francis LeBaron. Mass. Surgeon's Mate. He served in the 9th Regiment of the Mass. Line under James Thatcher, M.D. His son, William B. Goodwin, sought his father's half-pay. Congress rejected his claim on 1 Aug. 1850 because that grade was not covered.

Goodwin, George. Me. —. He was from Avon. He was paid $50 under the resolve of 1836.

Goodwin, Joseph. N.Y. Pvt. He served under Capt. Bauman and was slain 16 Oct. 1778. His widow, Elizabeth Goodwin, received a half-pay pension. He also appeared as Joseph Godwin.

Goodwin, Nathaniel. Conn. Capt. He died in the service on 1 May 1777 from wounds received at Crompo Hill. His seven years' half-pay was to be paid to the legal representative of his widow, Elizabeth Goodwin, 30 June 1834. The heirs were allowed interest 18 Jan. 1836.

Goodwin, Ozias. Conn. Pvt. He served in Capt. Archibald McNeal's Company and was wounded in his right arm by a musket ball at Wilton in Norwalk. Dr. Abel Catlin dressed his wound. He was pensioned 3 Feb. 1778 in Litchfield, Conn.

Goodwin, Reuben. Me. —. His widow, Ruth Goodwin, was also from Lebanon. She was paid $50 by the resolve of 1836.

Goodwin, Simeon. Me. —. He died 21 Apr. 1836. His widow, Mary Goodwin, was from Lebanon. She was paid $50 under the resolve of 1836.

Goodwin, Uriah. Mass. Pvt. He served in the 15th Regiment under Col. Bigelow in Capt. Houdin's Company. He was wounded by a musket ball which passed through his body from his left breast and out near the spine at White Plains in Jan. 1780. He lived in Bedford, Mass. in 1792. He enlisted 19 July 1779 for nine months and was discharged in Apr. 1780. He was granted one-fourth of a pension 20 Apr. 1796. He was on the 1813 pension list. He died 13 Mar. 1832 in Middlesex Co., Mass.

Goodwin, William. Mass. Pvt. He collected pension payment of $30 from March 1803 to March 1840.

Goodyear, George. Pa. —. He was awarded a $40 gratuity and a $40 annuity in York Co., Pa. 20 Mar. 1834. He was dead by July 1837.

Goodyear, Theophilus. Conn. Corp. He served in Col. Meigs' Regiment. He was wounded by a musket ball in the back in Oct. 1778 at White Plains. He enlisted 1 Apr. 1777 for the war. He resided at Reading, Conn. in 1794. He died in Sept. 1803.

Gookin, Daniel. N.H. Ens. He served as a sergeant from 1777 to 19 Mar. 1779 . He was breveted as ensign. He was commissioned at that rank 1 June 1779. He was from North Hampton. He sought his depreciation pay and his wages as a sergeant and ensign.

Gooshorn, Nicholas. Pa. —. He was awarded a $40 gratuity in Juniata Co., Pa. 10 Apr. 1835. His widow was paid in Oct. 1836.

Goothery, Adam. Mass. Pvt. He served in the 6th Regiment under Col. Calvin Smith and Capt. Pillsbury. He was wounded in the knee. He was 61 years old in 1786.

Gorden, William. N.J. Capt. He served in the 3rd Regiment and died 30 Apr. 1777. His widow, Jemima Gorden, was granted a half-pay pension in Morris Co., N.J. 19 Dec. 1781.

Gordon, Albion. Va. QM Sgt. He was in King William County on 3 Mar. 1787. He was 28 years old. He served in the 1st Regiment of Light Dragoons under Col. Anthony White. He was disabled by inflamation in both eyes due to repeated colds in the Continental Army. He was continued on the roll at the rate of £18 per annum on 25 Nov. 1786. He was on the 1813 pension list. In 1819 he was in Nelson County.

Gordon, Archibald. Md. Pvt. He was a resident of Cecil County in 1807. He was paid at the rate of half-pay of a private.

Gordon, Charles C. Va. —. He enlisted for eighteen months in Mar. 1778 in Chesterfield County and served under Capt. Tarlton Paine and Col. Richard Parker. He applied from Guilford County, N.C. 21 Aug. 1826. He was to become age 66 in Oct. 1826.

Gordon, Daniel. —. Corp. He served under Capt. Ambrose and Col. Johnson. He applied in 1833 but was rejected in 1836 because he did not serve six months. His widow, Susannah Gordon, died 23 July 1838 without applying. His daughter, Elizabeth Gordon, sought a pension. Congress rejected her petition 29 Jan. 1884.

Gordon, James. Pa. He died in Westmoreland County. His heirs were granted donation land upon their releasing the tract in New York.

Gordon, John. Md. Pvt. His widow, Elizabeth Gordon, was pensioned at the rate of half-pay of a private 16 Feb. 1821.

Gordon, John. Pa. Surgeon. He was in the militia and was wounded in the service. He was on the roll 21 Apr. 1795.

Gordon, John. S.C. —. He received his annuity 8 June 1829.

Gordon, Joshua. N.C. Pvt. He applied in Franklin County in 1799. He was in Rutherford County in 1804. He served in the Franklin County militia and was wounded in the thigh at Sumter's defeat in Sep. 1799. He served under Col. Isaacs, Lt. Samuel Jones, and Lt. Col. William Briskell. He had a wife and seven children. He was on the 1813 pension list. He died 7 Aug. 1816.

Gordon, Peter. Pa. —. He was awarded a $40 gratuity and a $40 annuity in Philadelphia County on 24 Feb. 1820.

Gordon, Robert. Pa. —. He applied from Indiana County on 21 Dec. 1812. He served six years in the Pa. Line under Col. Moses Hazen and was discharged at Pompton Plains, N.J. in June 1783. He had a family of small children. He died 10 Apr. 1826.

Gordon, Thomas. Pa. —. His widow, Mary Gordon, was awarded a $40 gratuity and a $40 annuity in Bedford County on 24 Mar. 1812. One Mary Gordon was 92 years old in 1840 in Bedford County.

Gordon, William. —. —. He was pensioned in 1818 but died in October in Strafford Co. N.H. without drawing any money. He married Hannah ----- in Mar. 1784. Congress rejected her claim 14 Jan. 1837.

Gore, —. —. —. He served as an officer and died soon after the war. His son, Isaac Gore, and the other heirs sought a pension. Congress rejected the claim 26 Apr. 1848.

Gore, Simeon. Pa. Pvt. He was in Philadelphia 30 Nov. 1785. He was in the 5th Battalion of the Philadelphia Militia under Capt. Thomas Palmer of the Rifle militia.. He was wounded in the thigh at Perth Amboy in July 1776 in the service by a ball through both thighs.. He was 37 years old. He was in jail in Philadelphia in Dec. 1786. His wife was Sarah Gore. He was dead by Mar. 1790. He also appeared as Simon Gore.

Gorham, John. Mass. —. He served in the 7th Regiment and was from Barre. He was paid $20.

Gorham, Josias. Mass. —. He served in the 7th Regiment and was paid $20.

Gorman, James. N.Y. Matross. He was on the 1813 pension list.

Gorman, John. —. —. He was not provided for by any act so Congress rejected his claim 29 Feb. 1848.

Gorman, John. Del. Pvt. He was pensioned in 1782. He died in June 1812.

Gorman, William. Pa. —. He served under Wayne in the campaign against the Indians. He was from Franklin County.

Gorman, William. Va. —. He was wounded in transporting gunpowder and military stores from New Orleans to Pittsburgh in Apr. 1777. He was awarded a £40 gratuity on 10 Nov. 1777.

Gosline, Clement. —. —. He received his commutation. Upon deducting same, he was to receive half-pay for life.

Gosline, Louis. —. —. He was allowed half-pay for life.

Gosnell, —. Pa. —. His widow, Eleanor Gosnell, was awarded a $40 gratuity and a $40 annuity in Philadelphia, Pa. 4 May 1832.

Goss, Abraham. Pa. —.He was pensioned 31 Mar. 1837 in Clearfield County.

Goss, Zachariah. S.C. —. He was being pensioned in 1791.

Gossler, John. Pa. —. He was granted a $40 gratuity in Adams County 3 Mar. 1829.

Gossling, George. S.C. —. He served in the 2nd Regiment of S.C. State Troops under Col. Middleton. He was wounded in his left arm at Eutaw by a musket ball. It began to mortify about seven months later and had to be amputated by Dr. Martin. He was a school teacher. He was awarded an annuity 19 July 1785. He was from St. Peter's Parish, Beaufort District. He died 9 July 1822. His widow was Elizabeth Powers. They were married by the Rev. John Youmans, a Baptist, on 10 Aug. 1816. She married secondly — Powers on 3 Apr. 1826. Rev. John Brooker, a Baptist, performed the marriage. He was a cabinet worker and died in 1829 as a journey worker. She was 73 years old when she sought her first husband's arrearage on 12 Oct. 1855.

Gould, Asa. Mass. Pvt. He served in the 6th Regiment. He was wounded in his head by a musket ball and in several parts of his body with a bayonet in May 1777 at Green Farm. He lived in Bethel, Vt. in 1795. He was granted half a pension 20 Apr. 1796. He enlisted 1 Mar. 1777 and was discharged 1 Mar. 1780. He was on the 1813 pension list.

Gould, Benjamin. Mass. Pvt. He served in the Invalids under Capt. Moses McFarland and Col. Seth Warner. He was wounded in his right knee by a musket ball at Bennington in Aug. 1777. He was disabled by the gravel. He was on the roll in 1779. He was pensioned 4 Jan. 1783. He was 47 years old in 1788. He lived in Brattleboro, Vt. in 1794. He was granted half a pension 20 Apr. 1796. He died 13 Dec. 1800. There was one of his name on the 1813 pension roll.

Gould, Camaralyaman. Mass. Pvt. He served in the 2nd Regiment and was from Cambridge. He was paid $50.

Gould, David. Va. Surgeon. He was appointed a surgeon 11 Oct. 1779 and served in the Hospital Department in Virginia and died en route to Philadelphia 12 July 1781. His widow, Hannah Gould, was awarded his half-pay of seven years amounting to $3,150 on 21 Jann. 1790. His son was also mentioned.

Gould, James. N.H. Lt. He served in Col. Joseph Cilley's Regiment and was wounded on 19 Sep.

1777 at the battle of Bemis Heights by a musket ball which passed through his body. He was aged 44 in 1787 and was from Hanover. He was on the 1813 pension list.

Gould, John. Mass. Pvt. He served in the 3rd Regiment under Col. William Hull and Capt. Hobby. He was disabled by gravel and was 37 years old in 1790. He was pensioned 13 Apr. 1783. He was on the 1813 pension list. He transferred to New Haven, Ct. 4 Mar. 1826.

Gould, John. —. Pvt. He served in Cilley's Regiment. He was pensioned 4 Mar. 1789. He transferred from Mass. to Strafford Co., N.H. where he died 4 Aug. 1828.

Gould, John. N.Y. —. He was wounded in his nose and third finger of his left hand in 1777.

Gould, William. Md. Pvt. His widow, Sarah Gould, was pensioned in Dorchester County at the rate of half-pay of a private 10 Feb. 1830.

Goulding, William T. Va. —. He was wounded at the battle of Guilford Courthouse. He was pensioned at the rate of $40 per annum on 17 Jan. 1798. He was in Richmond, Va. on 14 Mar. 1799 and in Pittsylvania County on 15 Nov. 1813. He also appeared as William Gauldon and William Golding.

Gove, Jacob. Me. —. He died 9 Apr. 1823. His widow, Martha Gove, was from Lubec. She was paid $50 under the resolve of 1836.

Gove, Nathaniel. Pa. Lt. He was pensioned 11 Aug. 1790. He transferred to New York by Mar. 1791. He was on the 1813 pension list.

Gove, Nathaniel. Vt. —. He applied from Rutland on 15 Oct. 1790. He was a prisoner of the British. He was employed as a purchaser for the army. He was put on half-pay. He was confined for debt and sought to be liberated and to be allowed to discharge his debt.

Gowan, Hugh. Pa. Sgt. He enlisted in 1776 in the 12th Pa. Regiment under Col. William Cook to 1778 when he was annexed to the 3rd Pa. Regiment under Col. Thomas Craig to the end of the war. He was discharged at Lancaster in 1783. John Boyd, an officer in both regiments, proved his service.

Gowden, Joseph. Mass. —. He was a Frenchman and was wounded by a musket ball in his right leg. He was pensioned. He married under the name of Joseph Cushing afterwards, and his widow, Sally Gowden, had to prove that her late husband Joseph Cushing was identical with Joseph Gowden on 1 Dec. 1785. He also appeared as Joseph Gowgen and as Joseph Guzan *quo vide.*

Gower, John. Me. —. He died 28 June 1810. His widow, Mary Gower, was from Wells. She was paid $50 under the resolve of 1836.

Gowin, Charles. Mass. Pvt. He resided in Suffolk Co., Mass. He was on the 1813 pension list as Charles Gowen.

Graaf, John. Pa. Pvt. He served under Col. Hampton. He was wounded in his left leg with a musket ball on 17 Sep. 1777 at Brandywine. He lived in Bucks Co., Pa. in 1794. One John Grove served in the regiment. He enlisted 27 Apr. 1777 and was transferred to the invalids in Aug. 1778. He was on the 1813 pension list.

Grace, Aaron. Pa. Pvt. He applied from Philadelphia 16 Feb. 1819. He served in Capt. Gill's Company in the 4th Troop of Light Dragoons in Col. Miles' Regiment. He was 66 years old. He died 16 Jan. 1823.

Grace, Adam. Pa. Pvt. He served under Capt. Gill and Col. Miles in the Light Dragoons. He was from Philadelphia County.

Grace, George. Pa. Pvt. He was in Philadelphia County 13 Mar. 1786. He served in the 4th Pa. Regiment and was wounded at Fort Washington in his left arm. He was dead by Sep. 1793.

Grace, John. Mass. Lt. He was injured by great exertions and excessive heat at the battle of Monmouth.

He served in the 1ˢᵗ Mass. Regiment. He was appointed ensign 1 Jan. 1777 and was promoted to lieutenant 4 Nov. 1777. He resigned in 1782. He resided at Lenox, Mass. in 1792 and 1796.

Gracey, Joseph. S.C. Pvt. He was killed 8 Sep. 1782. His widow, Sidney Gracey, was allowed an annuity 8 Sep. 1786 in Lancaster County. There were three children in 1791. She was paid $60 per annum in 1819, 1820, 1821, and 1825. Her annuity for 1825 was issued 7 Mar. 1825, but she died before she received any of it. On 19 Dec. 1825 her daughter, Elizabeth Gracey, was granted administration on her mother's estate. She sought what was due her late mother. She was paid her mother's arrearage 15 Nov. 1825. The paperwork in the file contains the confused statement that the veteran was named Sidney Gracey and that his widow was Elizabeth Gracey who was actually his daughter.

Gradey, —. Va. —. His wife, Catharine Gradey, had her request for assistance rejected in Nov. 1779. She was from Lunenburg County.

Grady, —. Va. —. Ann Grady was granted £6 relief in Caroline Co., Va. 11 June 1778 while her sons were away in the service.

Grady, David. Pa. —. He was in the Pennsylvania Hospital and was pensioned from 25 Jan. 1782.

Grady, John. Va. —. His wife, Catherine Grady, was granted relief on 12 June 1777 and £30 on 10 Dec. 1778 in Lunenburg Co., Va.

Grady, Younger. Pa. Pvt. He was on the pension list in 1789. He removed to Virginia and then to Ohio by Mar. 1796.

Graeff, Garret. Pa. Capt. He served in the Flying Camp and was taken prisoner at Fort Washington. He died in captivity. He was from York County. His widow, Catherine Fisher, was awarded a $40 gratuity and a $40 annuity 31 May 1812. He also appeared as Garret Graff.

Graeff, Martin. Pa. —. He was granted relief in Berks County 20 May 1839.

Graff, Samuel. Pa. —. He was awarded a $40 gratuity and a $40 annuity in Crawford Co., Pa. 7 Mar. 1827. He was 82 years old in 1840. He died 27 June 1848.

Graham, —. Pa. —. Nancy Graham of Butler County received relief in 1816. She died 6 Feb. 1816.

Graham, —. S.C. —. His widow, Elizabeth Graham, had her application approved in Dec. 1826. She also appeared as Elizabeth Grimes.

Graham, Daniel. Pa. —. He was from Allegheny County. He enlisted in the spring of 1777 under Capt. Nichols for three years. He served under Capt. Nichols, Maj. Thomas Moore, and Col. Richard Butler. He strained his back at West Point in assisting to lift a cannon.

Graham, Francis, Pa. —. He was awarded a $40 gratuity and a $40 annuity 14 Mar. 1835 in Franklin County.

Graham, George. Pa. Pvt. He applied from Butler County and was late of Cumberland County on 22 Apr. 1817. He served in Capt. John Morrow's Company under Col. Walter Stewart for one year and nine months. He was in the 1ˢᵗ Artillery and mustered in Jan. 1779. He had been blind for three years. He died 1 Feb. 1818.

Graham, James. Pa. —. He served as a ranger on the frontiers and was from Mifflin County.

Graham, James. S.C. —. He served under Capt. Turner, Col. Winn, Maj. Wallace, and Capt. John Mills. He was 65 years old when he applied 17 Nov. 1827 in Chester District. James McCaw and John McDill served with him. He was at Purysburg, Orangeburg, Black Swamp, Friday's Fort, Edisto, the Indian Expedition, High Hills of Santee, Congaree Fort, and Wright's Bluff. His application was rejected.

Graham, James. Va. —. His wife, Deborah Graham, was allowed 2 barrels of corn and 100 pounds of pork in Bedford Co., Va. on 24 Apr. 1780 and 1 barrel of corn and 150 pounds of pork on 26 June 1781 at which time there were four in the family.

Graham, John. N.Y. Lt. He served under Col. McClaughry in the Ulster County militia and was killed at Westchester 6 Sept. 1778. His widow, Catharine Graham, received a half-pay pension. He also appeared as John Grahan.

Graham, John. Pa. —. He applied from Beaver County on 7 May 1812. He enlisted in the spring in 1775 in Capt. McDonald's Company in Col. Hartley's Regiment. He served until the fall of 1776 when he was taken prisoner by the British at Fort Washington. He was detained eleven weeks and three days when he was set at liberty and given a full discharge. In the fall of 1780 he enlisted in Capt. Humphrey's Company in Col. Coxe's Regiment and served to the end of the war. He was a stone mason.

Graham, John. S.C. —. His annuity was £57 in 1787.

Graham, Joseph. Conn. Pvt. He was disabled by a wound and abscess. He was pensioned 15 Sep. 1782. He died 29 Sep. 1807.

Graham, Richard. S.C. Master's Mate. He was wounded in his right arm aboard the frigate *South Carolina* under Commodore Gillon and Capt. Joiner. They took a brigatine from Newfoundland laden with codfish and carried her away. Augustine Buyck purchased her in Teneriffe and sent her to Cadiz. They took three ships and two brigatines from Glasgow in Jamaica. They sold them in Havana. His administrator sought his principal and interest as well as the same for seamen William Lardner, Richard Cain, and John Callaghanon 30 Nov. 1801. The claim was rejected.

Graham, Samuel. Pa. —. His wife was Nancy Graham. She was granted relief 19 Mar. 1816 and died 6 Feb. 1821. Their minor children were granted relief in Sep. 1822.

Gramlin, Adam. —. —. He was pensioned under the act of 1818 but was excluded due to his property in 1820. He was 80 years old with a wife not much younger, a deaf and dumb son, and a paralytic and helpless daughter. Congress granted him a pension 14 May 1832.

Grandy, Asa. Mass. —. He served in the 8th Regiment and was from Whiting, Vermont. He was paid $20.

Grandy, Reuben. Mass. —. He served in the 6th Regiment and was paid $20.

Granger, Daniel. Mass. Pvt. He served as a drummer for 2 ½ months in 1775, 4 months in 1777, 4 months in 1778, and 6 months in 1780 in the militia. He failed to qualify in 1832 because he was short a few days of service. His brother, Joseph Granger, proved that he entered as a substitute in 1775 for an older brother. Congress credited him with six months of service and granted him a pension 7 June 1836.

Granger, Frederick. Mass. —. He served in Crane's Regiment and was paid $20.

Granger, Frederick. Mass. Musician. He served in the artillery under Col. John Crane. He married in 1815. His widow, Charlotte Granger, had her petition for a pension rejected by Congress 3 Mar. 1851.

Granger, Thomas. Mass. —. He served in the 2nd Regiment and was from Sandisfield. He was paid $20.

Grannis, Enos. Conn. Lt. His first tour was under Capt. David Smith and Col. Porter in 1776 as a private. He reentered 13 Apr. 1777 as a sergeant under Capt. Daniel Pendleton and Col. Jeduthan Baldwin in the artillery for the war. He was promoted to lieutenant 12 Nov. 1779. He received bounty land warrant #2336 for 200 acres. He died in Mar. or Apr. 1824. His widow was Margaret Grannis. His five years' full pay commutation was paid to his legal representative 30 June 1834. His heirs were Mary Adams, Elizabeth Sipe, Thankful Naugle, and Lucinda Nicholas. Palmer Grannis was a son. Congress declined any further relief to the heirs 5 Feb. 1861.

Grant, —. Va. —. His wife, Sarah Grant, was granted £5 support in Prince William Co., Va. on 5 Oct. 1778.

Grant, David. N.C. —. He served in the 2nd N.C. Regiment. He was disabled by pain and weakness in his joints due to a cold he caught in camp. He was in Wake County in 1795. He left his wife and child, a cripple, to be cared for by his mother-in-law, Mary Thompson, and departed the state. He was last paid his pension in 1800. Mary Thompson's request to have his pension paid to her was rejected in 1803 because he forfeited his rights when he left the state.

Grant, David. Va. —. His wife, Faith Grant, was granted £100.15.10 support in Halifax Co., Va. on 17 June 1779 and £511.14 on 19 Oct. 1780. Both her husband and her son died in the service.

Grant, Deskin. —. —. He was near the age of three score and ten in Montgomery County, Tennessee when he sought assistance from the state on 10 August 1825.

Grant, Edmund. N.H. Pvt. He was on the 1813 pension list of Massachusetts as Edward [sic] Grant. He lived in Essex County. He moved to York Co., Me. 4 Mar. 1819.

Grant, Edward. R.I. Pvt. He lived in Providence.

Grant, Jesse. Conn. Capt. He had a double inguinal rupture occasioned by a cannon ball which passed near the lower part of his body before he was made a prisoner at Fort Washington. He lived in Litchfield, Conn. in 1794. On 30 Dec. 1794 four depositions from witnesses proved that Grant, when a child, had a rupture in his abdomen.

Grant, Joshua. Me. —. He died in June 1825. His widow, Abigail Grant, was from York. She was paid $50 under the resolve of 1836.

Grant, Richard. R.I. Pvt. He lost all of the toes on his left foot, and his toes on his right foot were severely injured on the Oswego Expedition in Feb. 1783 under Col. Willett. He served under Col. Jeremiah Olney. He was aged 36 in 1786. He lived in Providence Co., R.I.

Grant, Samuel. Pa. Pvt. He died 1 Apr. 1803.

Grant, William. S.C. Lt. Congress granted his widow, Mary Grant, her arrearage from 4 Mar. 1848 to 3 Feb. 1853 on 15 Dec. 1857.

Grantham, Jesse. S.C. —. He served five years. He was at Cape Fear, Bluford Bridge, Charleston, Briar Creek, and Guilford. One of his officers was Capt. John Grantham. He was pensioned from Darlington District 23 Nov. 1829. He was 74 years old. He died in 1835. His widow, Levicy Grantham, was pensioned 7 Dec. 1837 at the rate of $30 per annum. She collected $60 arrearage from her late husband's pension.

Grau, George. —. —. He was among the soldiers from Anspach who deserted and joined the American forces. He was receiving a pension in 1807.

Graul, Jacob. Pa. —. He was awarded a $40 gratuity and a $40 annuity in Berks County 28 Mar. 1836. He died 17 Mar. 1848. His widow, Susanna Graul, was awarded a $40 annuity 10 Apr. 1849.

Gravel, John. Pa. —. He was awarded a $40 gratuity in Montgomery Co., Pa. 14 Apr. 1834.

Graver, Henry. Pa. —. He was granted relief in Schuylkill County 1 July 1845.

Graver, Philip. Pa. —. He received a $40 gratuity and a $40 annuity in Lancaster County 3 Mar. 1837.

Graves, Edmond. Va. —. His wife and children were furnished necessaries while he was absent in Continental service in Amelia Co., Va. 28 Oct. 1779.

Graves, Gideon. Mass. —. He served in the 3rd Artillery and was from Palmer. He was paid $20.

Graves, Obediah. Va. —. His wife, Milly Graves, was granted relief on 13 Nov. 1777 in Lunenburg Co., Va.

Graves, Ralph. Va. Cornet. He served in the cavalry under Maj. John Nelson to the end of the war. He was entitled to commutation of $6,562.40.

Graves, Richard. Md. Maj. He was on the roll in 1822.

Graves, Samuel. —. —. His widow, Sarah Graves, failed to show six months of service for her husband. Congress rejected her claim 4 Jan. 1841.

Graves, William. Va. —. He was in Charlotte County 5 Jan. 1820. He received $60 relief and a $60 per annum pension.

Graves, William. Va. Cornet. His widow and heirs received his commutation of five years' full pay in lieu of his half-pay for life as a cornet of calvary and quartermaster of the Virginia line on 16 Jan. 1829.

Gravett, John. Va. —. His wife, Milly Gravett, was granted relief 10 July 1777 and £50 on 8 Oct. 1778 in Lunenburg Co., Va.

Gray, Alexander. Pa. Pvt. He was on the 1813 pension list.

Gray, Amos. Conn. Pvt. He served in the 4th Regiment of militia. He was wounded by a musket ball on 27 Apr. 1777 at Compo Hill. The shot broke the trunk of his body. There was a considerable discharge of blood from the lungs. The ball exited through one of his arms. Dr. Ebenezer Joseph and Dr. Jos: Chapman dressed the wound. He served under Capt. John Andrews and Ens. Jesse Bennett. He resided in Fairfield, Conn. in 1792.

Gray, Andrew. Pa. —. He enlisted in 1776 and served under Capt. Whitsall, and Col. Meigs as a rifleman. He was at the battle of Long Island and taken prisoner. In the winter he was exchanged and returned to his regiment which had been reorganized as the 13th under Col. Walter Stewart. He was permitted to go home on furlough. He joined the regiment at Valley Forge and was at Monmouth. His unit became the 2nd Regiment. He was discharged in 1780. Congress granted him a full pension 12 Apr. 1836.

Gray, Ebenezer. Conn. Lt. Col. His bounty land was in Ohio. He died soon after the close of the war. His widow was also deceased. He left three children. His son, Ebenezer Gray, died unmarried. His son, Samuel Gray, left a widow, Ann C. Gray, and children John S. Gray, Charlotte Tracy, Anne Fales, Sarah LeRoy, and Mary Gray. The veteran's daughter, Charlotte Gray, married Patrick Lynch and had been granted relief as the only surviving child. The other heirs sought relief from Congress 3 Mar. 1851. They were not entitled to their grandfather's bounty land. It belonged to his only surviving child and daughter Charlotte Lynch.

Gray, Francis. Va. Pvt. He was in Caroline County on 27 Feb. 1787 and was 29 years old. He enlisted in Dec. 1776 under Capt. Thomas Fox in the 10th Va. Regiment. He was discharged due to his inability to serve. He lost the use of his left eye totally and was almost blind in his right ruined by smallpox while in the army. Lt. Col. Samuel Hawes attested to his service. He was continued on the pension list at the rate of £15 per annum on 27 Feb. 1787.

Gray, George. Md. Pvt. He was pensioned in Charles County at the rate of half-pay of a private 12 Feb. 1820.

Gray, Jacob. Md. Pvt. He lost his arm at the storming of Henry Point. He was pensioned in Somerset County 24 June 1783.

Gray, Jacob. Pa. —. He was granted relief.

Gray, James. Pa. —. He enlisted in June 1775 at Little York for one year in Capt. Michael Doodle's or Dowdel's Company in Col. Thompson's Regiment of Riflemen on Continental establishment. Capt. Doodle or Dowdel was arrested and returned home. Lt. Miller took command. Gray's time expired on Long Island in July 1776 at which time Col. Hand had command of the regiment.

He had lost his discharge. He applied from Ohio.

Gray, Joel. Pa. Pvt. He applied from York County on 18 Sep. 1812. He was in Col. Hartley's Regiment in the 11th Regiment of the Pa. Line. Andrew Johnston was lieutenant. He died 24 June 1819.

Gray, Joshua. Mass. —. On 4 June 1781 he was pensioned at the rate of ten shillings per month from 11 Oct. 1776 the time he was wounded until 11 Apr. 1781 when he was fit for military duty again.

Gray, Joshua. Mass. Sgt. He served in the 7th Regiment. His widow, Sarah Gray, was from Boston and received a pension in Sep. 1838.

Gray, Robert. Pa. —. He served in the 13th Pa. Regiment under Lt. Col. Lewis Farmer and Capt. Stephen Stevenson. He was wounded in the leg at Brandywine on 11 Sep. 1777.

Gray, Robert. R.I. —. He was an officer in the navy in the Revolutionary War and subsequently served in the merchant marine. He married 3 Feb. 1794 and died in the summer of 1806. He discovered the Columbia River in 1792. He was born in Tiverton, R.I. in May 1757. Congress granted his widow, Martha Gray, a pension for $500 a year 27 Mar. 1846. She had been able to obtain a pension earlier because of the time of their marriage. There were four daughters.

Gray, Robert. S.C. —. He was being pensioned in 1791.

Gray, Samuel. Va. —. He served three years in the Virginia Line and was pensioned at the rate of $96 per annum. He died in 1832. He married Leah ---- in Sep. 1793 in Wilkes Co., N.C. Justice of the Peace Mitchell performed the ceremony. He moved to South Carolina and eventually to Kentucky. Robert Lisk was present at the wedding, but he was illiterate so the Pension Office rejected his testimony. Congress approved a pension for the widow 14 Mar. 1846. The widow lived in Hopkins Co., Ky. 13 Feb. 1844. Her first child in the family Bible record was Hiram Gray born 16 June 1794.

Graydon, Alexander. Pa. Capt. He applied 1 Apr. 1813. He was taken prisoner at Fort Washington 16 Nov. 1776 and was rendered supernumerary when his men's one year enlistment expired before his exchange leaving him without a command in the former 3rd Battalion. He was 61 years old.

Grayson, Presly. Va. Pvt. He volunteered in 1781 in Fairfax Co., Va. and served under Maj. Dennis Ramsey, Capt. Charles Little, Lt. Edward Sanford, and Ens. James Doneal for six months. He was discharged a short time before the expiration of his tour. He lived in Kentucky afterwards. Congress granted him a pension for six months of service as a private because his other service as a captain was after the peace.

Grayson, William. Va. Col. He was appointed 1 Jan. 1777 and became supernumerary or was deranged 1 Jan. 1781. Congress appointed him to the Board of War and Ordnance 8 Dec. 1778. He resigned 10 Sept. 1781. He died in May 1790. All of his children were dead by 1828. Congress awarded his heirs his commutation pay 9 Feb. 1848. Virginia allowed him land bounty on 23 June 1783 for three years of service. On 12 Sep. 1809 Virginia allowed 926 acres of bounty land for ten months of service over six years as a reduced officer at the end of the war.

Greaves, —. S.C. —. His widow was Agnes Greaves. There were children in 1791.

Greech, —. S.C. —. His widow, Elizabeth Greech, was from Orangeburg.

Greeley, Joseph. N.H. Pvt. He served in the militia under Col. James Reed. He was wounded in his right leg by a ball on 17 June 1775 at Bunker Hill. He lived in West Nottingham, N.H. in 1794. He was granted one-fourth of a pension 20 Apr. 1796. He was on the 1813 pension list.

Green, —. Va. —. His mother, Jane Green, was granted £20 support in Caroline Co., Va. 8 Apr. 1779 and £50 on 11 May 1780.

Green, —. Va. —. He died in the service. His mother, Ann Green, was furnished support in Westmoreland County in Apr. 1779 and Oct. 1780.

Green, Andrew. Va. Pvt. He was in Cameron Parish, Loudoun County in May 1785. He served in the Western Battalion under Col. Joseph Crockett. He was disabled by a fracture in his right leg. He received £12 per annum which was discontinued in 1785. He was readmitted, and his arrearage was paid on 29 Nov. 1793. He was in Fairfax County on 31 Jan. 1801.

Green, Benjamin. Ga. Pvt. He was pensioned in 1780 as Benjamin Greer. He was on the 1791 pension list.

Green, Daniel. Me. —. He was from Durham. He was paid $50 under the resolve of 1836.

Green, Elijah. —. Pvt. He was pensioned under the act of 1818 but was stricken in 1819 because his regiment commanded by Col. George Gibson belonged to the state troops rather than the Continental Line. In 1828 or 1829 he entered the poor house. The Secretary of War reversed the decision and restored him to the rolls 23 Aug. 1831. Congress awarded his arrearage from 4 March 1819 to 4 Mar. 1829 to his heirs, Peggy Abel, Sally Rolls, and Elijah Green on 14 Jan. 1832.

Green, Henry. Md. Pvt. His widow, Elizabeth Green, was pensioned at the rate of half-pay of a private in Montgomery County on 6 Mar. 1850.

Green, Isaac. Mass. Pvt. He served in the Mass. Line under Col. William Prescott and Capt. Joshua Perkins. He was 31 years old in 1786 and was disabled by the loss of the middle finger of his right hand. He was on the 1813 pension list as Isaac Greer [sic]. He later removed to Windsor Co., Vt. He died 25 July 1822.

Green, James. Mass. Pvt. He served under Col. M. Jackson. He was pensioned 21 Sep. 1808. He died in Hillsborough Co., N.H. 3 June 1827.

Green, James. Va. —. He was pensioned under the act of 1832 as a midshipman and strickened on 15 June 1840. He lived in Fauquier Co., Va. He was known as George Green in his neighborhood. That man was in receipt of a pension to which he was not entitled. Congress reinstated him 17 June 1846. Congress rejected his claim 9 Jan. 1847.

Green, John. Ga. Lt. He was on the 1791 pension list.

Green, John. Mass. —. He served in the 4th Regiment and was from Upton. He was paid $20.

Green, John. Pa. Pvt. He was in Philadelphia County 13 Feb. 1786. He served in the 10th Pa. Regiment and was disabled by fatigues and ruptures. He was discharged from his regiment about 1782. He had been wounded in his hand and leg while on duty. He was 55 years old. He was dead by Sep. 1793.

Green, John. Pa. Pvt. He applied from Butler County 3 Apr. 1819. He enlisted in Capt. Hopps's Company under Col. Hartley in the Pa. Line in the fall of 1776 for six years. After the death of Col. Hopps at the battle of Brandywine, Capt. Walker took command. He was in the battles of Brandywine, Paoli, Germantown, and Trenton. He was in two skirmishes with the Indians up the Susquehannah. He had lost his discharge. Lydia Green, widow of John Green, was awarded a $40 annuity in Butler County 27 Mar. 1852.

Green, John. Va. Col. He was in Culpeper Company 11 June 1784. He served in the 6th Va. Regiment and was disabled by two balls which passed through the head of his right shoulder. He was wounded at Marrow Neck in New York in 1776. He had a large family and sought half-pay for life in June 1784. He was continued on the pension list at the rate of £100 per annum on 29 Nov. 1786. He died 18 Nov. 1793. Moses Green was executor.

Green, John Thompson. S.C. Maj. He was awarded $1,368 pay for his service in the Revolution on

25 Dec. 1820.

Green, Jonas. Mass. Pvt. He was wounded by a musket ball which passed through his body at Ticonderoga in 1777. He served under Col. M. Jackson. He enlisted 4 Feb. 1777 and was discharged 24 Oct. 1779. He lived in Pepperell, Mass. in 1792. He was pensioned at the rate of $5 per month from 8 Oct. 1807. There was a man of his name on the 1813 pension list in New Hampshire.

Green, Joseph. —. —. Congress rejected his claim 4 May 1846 since his application was not sustained by necessary proof.

Green, Joseph. Mass. Pvt. He served in the 2nd Regiment and was from East Brookfield. His widow, Sarah Green, was paid $50.

Green, Joseph. N.H. Pvt. He served under Col. Webb in Capt. Wallbridge's Company. He was wounded in his left shoulder by a musket ball 7 Dec. 1777 at White Marsh. He lived in Hanover, N.H. in 1795. He was in the militia. He was granted half a pension 20 Apr. 1796. He was on the 1813 pension list.

Green, Josiah. Conn. Pvt. He served in the 3rd Conn. under Lt. Col. Isaac -----man. He was wounded in his left shoulder on 28 Apr. 1777. Capt. Daniel Duncan was with him. He was from Montgomery County. He lived in Dutchess Co., N.Y. on 2 June 1787. He died 19 Feb. 1812. He was on the 1813 pension list.

Green, Lemuel. Mass. Pvt. He served under Col. Jonathan Holman in Capt. Loring Lincoln's Company and was wounded by a musket ball in action at White Plains on 28 Oct. 1776. He lost the use of his right hand in great measure due to a musket ball through his arm. He was pensioned at the rate of a quarter of pay from 30 Nov. 1776 on 26 Jan. 1778. He lived in Worcester Co., Mass. He was on the 1813 pension list as Samuel [sic] Green.

Green, Moses. Va. —. He was pensioned in Caroline County on 4 Feb. 1827 at the rate of $60 per annum with $30 relief. He was in Spotsylvania County 4 Feb. 1828. He died 27 May 1829.

Green, Nathan. S.C. —. His widow, Elizabeth Green, and her two children were granted an annuity 30 Jan. 1787 and were from Winton.

Green, Prince. R.I. Pvt. He lost all his toes by frost bite on the Oswego Expedition in Feb. 1783. He served under Col. Jeremiah Olney. He was aged 39 in 1785. He lived in Kent Co., R.I. He was on the 1815 pension list. He died 21 Jan. 1828.

Green, Robert. Md. Fifer. His widow, Mary Green, was pensioned at the rate of half-pay of a musician for five years on 10 Mar. 1854.

Green, Robert. Va. Lt. He was the son of Col. John Green of Culpeper County. He was a cadet at Williamsburg in 1776 and was with Col. Slaughter on the Ohio in 1779 or 1780. He returned to Virginia and was at Camden. He received bounty land from Virginia for his three years of service. His brother was Moses Green. He married Frances Edmonds, daughter of William Edmonds of Fauquier County in Aug. 1787. He died in June 1791. She went to Kentucky about sixteen years ago and settled near the Blue Lick. Their daughter, Susanna Eliza Green, was born 9 Jan. 1789 and married ------ Payne. Congress granted her a pension.

Green, Thomas. Ga. Pvt. He was on the 1813 pension list.

Green, Thomas. N.H. Pvt. He enlisted in Capt. Scott's Company in Col. John Stark's Regiment. He was wounded by a musket ball at Bunker Hill on 17 June 1775. It passed through his left shoulder. He was from Swanzey in 1778. He was aged 35 in 1787. He transferred to Vermont. He was on the 1813 pension list.

Green, Wardwell. R.I. Sgt. He served under Col. Green. He was wounded in the throat and shoulder at Province Island in Penn. in Oct. 1777. He resided in Mass. in Lanesborough in 1792.

Green, William. Md. Pvt. He was pensioned in Charles County in 1780. He was disabled and served under Col. John H. Stone. He was pensioned at the rate of $8 per month from 7 Feb. 1807. He was on the 1813 pension list. He died in 1822.

Green, William. N.H. Adjutant. He served in Col. Cilley's Regiment.

Green, William. N.Y. Lt. He served in the 14th Regiment of the Albany County militia and served under Lt. Col. Knickerbaker He was killed 26 July 1777. His sons, William Green and John Green, received a half-pay pension.

Green, Zachariah. Conn. Corp. He served in Capt. Amos Walbridge's Company in the 2nd Conn. Regiment under Col. Charles Webb. He was wounded in his left shoulder by a musket ball which broke his shoulder blade at White Marsh, Pa. on 7 Dec. 1777. He was pensioned 26 Feb. 1779. Dr. Coleman attended him. He lived in Suffolk Co., N.Y. on 16 May 1789. He was a clergyman. He was on the 1813 pension list.

Greenamoyer, Edward. Pa. —. He was awarded a $40 gratuity and a $40 annuity in Northampton Co., Pa. 18 Feb. 1834. He died 2 Mar. 1840.

Greene, Christopher. R.I. Lt. Col. He was killed at Point Bridge in Westchester Co., New York 14 May 1781 by Col. Delancy's Tories.

Greene, John. Pa. —. He was pensioned.

Greenelsh, Edward. Va. —. While her husband was away in the service, Elizabeth Greenelsh and her child were granted 2 barrels of corn and 100 pounds of pork for support in Shenandoah Co., Va. 29 Mar. 1781.

Greenland, James. Pa. —. He served under Capt. Brady in the 8th Regiment under Col. Broadhead and Gen. Irwin. He guarded the military stores until the Maryland troops arrived. He received 200 acres of donation land. He was from Westmoreland County. He died 10 Mar. 1821.

Greenleaf, Enoch. Mass. —. He was paid $20.

Greenlow, John. Me. —. He was from Brownfield. He was paid $50 under the resolve of 1836.

Greenman, Job. R.I. Pvt. He lost the use of his left knee and leg by a wound in Jan. 1776 on the island of Prudence under Col. William Barton. He served under Col. William Richmond. He was aged 43 when he applied 12 Jan. 1786. He resided in Providence Co., R.I. He was on the 1813 pension list.

Greentree, Benjamin. Md. Pvt. He was pensioned at the rate of half-pay of a private in Montgomery County 12 Feb. 1820. His widow, Mary Greentree, received his $10 arrearage and was pensioned at the same rate 3 Mar. 1840 in Frederick County. Her arrearage was paid to Elizabeth Beal 20 Jan. 1848.

Greenwalt, Nicholas. Pa. —. He applied from Cumberland County on 30 Mar. 1819. He enlisted in the spring of 1776 in Capt. Shade's Company and served until the battle of Long Island when the troops were cut to pieces. He was put in Capt. Moor's Company. He served one year and nine months until discharged by Col. Stewart. He reenlisted under Col. Stewart for three years. He was home on furlough for two months when he was kicked by a horse and rendered a cripple. He recovered and returned to the army at West Point in 1778. In Jan. 1779 he was unfit for duty and Maj. Murray permitted him to go home. He was in the battles of Long Island, White Plains, Germantown, and Brandywine. He knew Thomas Suloven, a sergeant in Capt. Farmer's Company; Balser Meeze in the same unit; Luis Houzer who formerly lived near Strassburg, Franklin County; and Benjamin Beaver a private in the same regiment. He died 28 Sep. 1831. He also appeared as Nicholas Greenawalt.

Greer, Daniel. Me. —. He was from Readfield.

Greer, David. Pa. Lt. Col. He was commissioned by the Continental Congress 12 Jan. 1777 and served in the 7th Regiment. He was wounded by a bayonet at Paoli and rendered unfit for service in 1777. He continued as paymaster at York to the close of the war. He died in 1790 survived by his widow and four daughters. Three had died. His sole heir was Margaret Barnitz, the wife of Charles A. Barnitz. She was granted his commutation in lieu of half-pay in 1848. Congress awarded her the half-pay due her father for his lifetime 25 Apr. 1854. She died in 1857. D. G. Barnitz was her son. The veteran also appeared as David Grier.

Greer, John. Ga. Pvt. He was pensioned in 1780.

Greer, Joseph. Md. —. He was pensioned from Prince George's County in 1783. He lost a leg at Ninety Six.

Greer, Thomas. Ga. Pvt. He served in a Volunteer Company of Refugees. He was wounded several times in the head on 11 Dec. 1780 near Long Canes. He resided in Columbia Co., Ga. in 1796.

Gregg, James. N.Y. Capt. He was wounded by a musket ball through his body. He was scalped by Indians near Kingston, N.Y. at Fort Schuyler 13 Oct. 1777. He lived in Montgomery County in June 1788. He was permitted to return his commutation pay for an invalid pension from Congress 14 Sep. 1786. He also appeared as James Grigg.

Gregg, John. Pa. Sgt. He was in Bucks County 13 Mar. 1786. He was in the 3rd Pa. Regiment in Capt. Graydon's Company and was disabled in 1776 and 1777 by disease contracted in the service. He lost the use of his left arm. He was 32 years old. Lambert Cadwallader and Hugh Hodge, Surgeon, of the 3rd Pa. Regiment proved his service. He was 32 years old in 1787. He also appeared as John Greeg. He was from Philadelphia County. He gave a power of attorney to Francis Gregg to collect his pension in 1787. He was on the 1791 pension list.

Gregory, —. Va. —. Mary Gregory was granted £7 support while her husband was away in the service in Fauquier Co., Va. in Aug. 1776

Gregory, Charles. Va. Sgt. His widow, Hannah Gregory, lived in Hanover County 7 May 1785. Her husband, Charles Gregory, and their son, William Gregory, enlisted under Capt. John Winston in the 14th Va. Regiment of Infantry in Jan. 1777 for three years. Both died at Valley Forge, Pa. in Mar. or Apr. 1778. There was a large family of eight children. In Jan. 1794 one child aged 15 was left. Capt. John Overton of the 14th Va. Regiment certified the service. She was pensioned 19 Jan. 1786 at the rate of £18 per annum.

Gregory, John. —. Lt. He was slain in the service. His seven years' half pay was to be paid to his sole heir, John M. Gregory, whose children received their grandfather's half-pay 30 June 1834.

Gregory, John. N.J. —. He was pensioned in Monmouth County on 26 Mar. 1846 at the rate of $60 per annum.

Gregory, John. N.C. —. He was drafted in Brunswick Co., N.C. and went to South Carolina and Georgia. He served under Capt. Sharp. He received two severe sword cuts–one from his eyelid to the crown of his head and other in the same place and direction. He applied in Craven Co., N.C. 15 Aug. 1832.

Gregory, Samuel. N.Y. —. He served in the militia from May 1776 to the close of the war under Capt. Scribner and Capt. Waterbury. Because of the lack of sufficient proof, Congress rejected his petition 9 Feb. 1848.

Gregory, Thomas. S.C. —. He enlisted in Capt. Rose's Company in Gen. Sumter's Brigade for a ten month tour and was promised a Negro. He was dead by 24 Oct. 1785 when his mother, Crecy Gregory, of Brunswick Co., Va. sought the benefits due her deceased son. She was

Crecy Scout shortly thereafter.

Gregory, William. Capt. Va. He was from Charles City County and died in the service in 1776. His only child, William H. Gregory, died in 1829. The latter gave his estate to his wife Frances Gregory. His half-brother, Edmund Christian, and his half-sister, Nancy (Christian) Hilliard, of New Kent Co., Va. received his seven years' half-pay 4 Jan. 1838.

Grenell, William. Conn. —. He enlisted at Derby under Col. Wooster in 1775 for seven months. He marched to Boston. In July 1778 he was in Capt. Sperry's Company. He was at Danbury, Fairfield, Norwalk, and New Haven. He was made an ensign in 1779 and a captain in 1780. He sought relief from Congress 21 Dec. 1831.

Gresham, George. —. Capt. He married 3 July 1792 and died in Oct. 1837. Congress granted his widow, Elizabeth Gresham, a pension 10 Jan. 1843.

Gresham, Joseph. Va. —. His wife, Mary Gresham, and two children were paid £10 support in Louisa Co., Va. on 13 Oct. 1777 and £14 in 1778. He died in Continental service, and his widow and child were furnished 2 barrels of corn and 100 pounds of pork on 10 Dec. 1781.

Gress, Ernest. Pa. Ens. He received a $40 gratuity 1 Mar. 1811. He was from Berks County on 21 May 1814. He served in the 6th Pa. Regiment. He was commissioned in 1777 and in June 1778 became supernumerary. Jacob Bower, captain and a breveted major, proved his service. He also appeared as Ernst Greese. He died 15 Apr. 1816

Gress, Mathias. Pa. —. He was granted a $40 gratuity and a $40 annuity in Northampton County 14 Mar. 1835.

Grett, —. Pa. —. His widow, Elizabeth Grett, received a $40 gratuity and a $40 annuity in Berks County 15 June 1836.

Grey, Jonathan. Pa. —. He was granted relief 28 Mar. 1808. He died 10 Oct. 1823.

Gribey, John. S.C. —. He was wounded at King's Mountain. He was allowed an annuity 9 May 1785.

Grice, Thomas. S.C. —. He had been blind for twenty-three years. He was from Marion District in 1827. He received $60 per annum from 1828 to 1837.

Gridley, Daniel. Pa. —. He served in Capt. Thomas Robinson's Company of rangers. He was awarded a $40 gratuity and a $40 annuity in Luzerne County on 28 Mar. 1820.

Gridley, Richard. Mass. Col. He was pensioned at the rate of £121.13.4 annually. He was pensioned by the Continental Congress by the act of 26 Feb. 1781.

Grieger, Cato. Mass. —. He served in the 1st Regiment and was paid $20.

Grien, George. Pa. —. He was granted relief and was paid in Aug. 1839.

Gries, —. Pa. —. His widow, Magdalena Gries, was awarded a $40 gratuity and a $40 annuity in Berks County for her husband's Revolutionary service 12 June 1839. She died 23 Oct. 1841.

Griff, —. Pa. —. His widow, Margaret Griff, was awarded relief in Berks County 20 May 1839.

Griffen, Moses. N.C. —. He was from Craven County.

Griffin, Amos. S.C. —. He was being pensioned in 1791.

Griffin, Corbin. Va. Surgeon. He served at the hospital at Yorktown to the end of the war. He received no bounty land from Virginia. His son and heir was Thomas Griffin whose executor was Robert P. Waller. Congress rejected his claim for bounty land on 24 Apr. 1840 and 12 Feb. 1842.

Griffin, Edward. S.C. —. He was being pensioned in 1791.

Griffin, Edward. Va. Pvt. He was granted relief.

Griffin, George. Del. Pvt. He was pensioned in 1782. He was on the 1813 pension list.

Griffin, Gideon. S.C. —. He was pensioned in Richland District 12 Dec. 1826. He served under Col. William Thompson in the 3rd S.C. State Troops for two years. Other officers were Capt. Richard

Brown and Capt. Little. He was discharged at Charleston. Morgan Griffin served with him He had a large family. He was last paid his annuity in 1834.

Griffin, James. S.C. —. He lost his life in the service. His widow, Frances Griffin, was awarded an annuity 16 Sep. 1785.

Griffin, John. Pa. Corp. He was pensioned 23 Mar. 1796. He was dead by Mar. 1802.

Griffin, Joseph. S.C. Pvt. He was pensioned from Pendleton District 6 Dec. 1828. He was paid his annuity from 1829 to 1833.

Griffin, Lewis. S.C. —. He served in the 3rd S.C. Regiment, was taken prisoner 29 Dec. 1778, and died on board a prison ship. His children were granted an annuity 9 July 1785. His remarried widow, Mary Blakeman, was granted an annuity 11 July 1786.

Griffin, Martin. Va. Pvt. He was in Shenandoah County on 29 June 1786 and was aged 46. He served in the 12th Va. Regiment under Col. Abraham Buford. He was wounded at Guilford Courthouse in 1781 by a musket ball in his right arm near the elbow and another on the same arm. He also appeared as Martin Griffith. He was in Fauquier County in July 1783. He was continued on the pension roll at the rate of £15 per annum on 5 Jan. 1787 and on 14 May 1789. He was on the 1813 pension list.

Griffin, Morgan. S.C. —. He was from Richland District when his claim for Revolutionary services was referred to the Comptroller on 3 Dec. 1817. He served three years in the 3rd Regiment under Col. William Thompson in Capt. Little's Company. He also served under Capt. Richard Brown. He was taken prisoner at Sullivan's Island after the fall of Charleston. He received four wounds at the siege of Savannah. He was pensioned 3 Dec. 1819 and received his annuity from 1821 to 1831.

Griffin, Nathan. Md. Pvt. He was pensioned at the rate of half-pay of a private in Dorchester County on 27 Jan. 1816.

Griffin, William. S.C. —. He was on the pension list in 1791. On 8 Dec. 1813 he was paid to the year 1794. He was from Sumter District when he was put on the pension roll on 2 Dec. 1813. He served under Col. Owen Roberts in the Artillery and was injured at Stono by the explosion of an ammunition chest occasioned by the bursting of a shell from the British. He was discharged by Col. Richard Richardson. He became blind about 1806. His son, Dempsey Griffin, collected his pension in 1814.

Griffis, Henry. Va. —. His widow, Mary Griffis, was granted 5 barrels of corn and 100 pounds of bacon in Northumberland Co., Va. on 12 Aug. 1782.

Griffith, —. S.C. —. His widow, Barbara Griffith, was on the roll in 1791.

Griffith, Abraham. Pa. —. He applied 4 Mar. 1807. He served three years as a soldier and was awarded $100.

Griffith, Barney. N.Y. Pvt. He served under Col. Goose Van Schaick in Capt. Parson's Company and was disabled by infirmity. He was wounded in his left shoulder at Crompo 28 Apr. 1777. He was 75 years old. He applied 15 Sep. 1786. He lived in Fredericksburg, N.Y. and was a weaver.

Griffith, Benjamin. Pa. Lt. He died 17 Mar. 1778. His widow, Margaret Griffith, sought his half-pay 18 May 1787. She was from Berks County.

Griffith, David. Pa. —. He was granted a gratuity of $40 in Indiana County 28 Mar. 1836.

Griffith, Evan. Pa. —. He was awarded a $40 gratuity in Baltimore, Md. 28 Mar. 1836.

Griffith, Griffin. Va. Pvt. He was recommended for a pension in Halifax Co., Va. on 15 May 1783. He was in Henry County 24 July 1786. He enlisted in the 6th Va. Regiment for two years.

He was wounded at Guilford Courthouse by a ball in his thigh. He was on the 1813 pension list. He resided in Henry County. He died 14 Mar. 1816.

Griffith, John. Pa. Corp. He enlisted in 1776 under Capt. Anderson and Col. Atley and served one year and nine months. He reenlisted in 1778 under Capt. Taylor and Col. Johnson. He was at Long Island, Fort Washington, Brandywine, Germantown, and Monmouth. He was from Chester County. One John Griffith died 19 Aug. 1821 after having been put on the pension roll 17 Feb. 1818. He was in the 5th Regiment.

Griffith, Levi. Pa. —. He applied from Mifflin County on 21 May 1832. He served three years and six months in the Pa. Line under Col. Chambers. He was in Capt. Boyd's Company and later in Capt. Ziegler's Company. He was honorably discharged by Lt. Col. Robison at Trenton at the end of the war. He was awarded a $40 gratuity and a $40 annuity in Fayette County on 24 Mar. 1812.

Griffith, Philemon. Md. Maj. He was pensioned at the rate of half-pay of a major 19 Feb. 1819.

Griffith, Samuel. Md. Capt. He was pensioned in Montgomery County at the rate of half-pay of a captain 19 Feb. 1819. His arrearage was paid to his widow, Ruth Griffith, 10 Feb. 1834.

Grigg, James. N.Y. Capt. He was to return his commutation to the U.S. 4 Sep. 1786.

Griggs, Gideon. —. Pvt. He transferred from New Hampshire to Vermont. He was on the 1813 pension list. He lived in Orleans Co., Vt.

Griggs, John. N.J. Sgt. He lived in Middlesex Co., N.J. and was on the 1813 pension list. He died 29 Aug. 1815.

Griggs, Simon. N.Y. Sgt. He served on several alarms in 1775 and 1776 from Watertown, Saratoga County. In 1777 he volunteered and served under Capt. Joshua Taylor and Col. John Van Schoonhorn in the militia. He was discharged having served as private, corporal, and sergeant. He was at Saratoga at the surrender of Gen. Burgoyne. In the spring of 1778 he volunteered and served another six months in the same company. His federal pension under the act of 1832 was suspended for further proof, and he died before doing so. In 1855 his widow, Letty Griggs, obtained 160 acres of bounty land. She proved further service for him in 1779, 1780, and 1781. She was granted approval 19 July 1856. They were married 8 Jan. 1784. He also appeared as Simeon Griggs.

Griggs, William. Mass. —. He served in the 3rd Regiment and was paid $20.

Grigsby, —. Va. —. While her husband was away in the service, Ann Grigsby was granted £10 support in Caroline Co., Va. in Nov. 1777. After he was slain, she was awarded £15 relief on 8 Oct. 1778.

Grimes, John. Pa. —. He served three and a half years under Col. Chambers. He was under Capt. Boyd and later Capt. Ziegler and others. He was discharged at Trenton by Lt. Col. Robison. He was from Mifflin County 30 May 1832.

Grimm, John. —. —. Congress rejected his claim because there was no evidence on file on 4 Apr. 1840.

Grinder, Martin. Pa. —. He was 90 years old in 1840. Anne Grinder, his widow, was awarded a $40 annuity in Mercer Co., Pa. 5 May 1852 for his Revolutionary service.

Grinding, Jesse. Pa. —. He was awarded a $40 gratuity and a $40 annuity in Greene County on 14 Mar. 1818. He died 2 Oct. 1829.

Grinnall, James. N.Y. Lt. He served under Col. Samuel Clyde in the Montgomery County militia and was slain 6 Aug. 1777. His children, Albert Grinnall, Jane Grinnall, Wyntie Grinnall, and Cornelia Grinnall, received a half-pay pension.

Grisham, Joseph. Mass. Pvt. He was on the 1791 pension roll.

Grissum, Richard. N.C. Pvt. He applied in Granville County in 1803. He served under Capt. Bennett and was wounded on 16 Aug. 1780. He was on the 1813 pension list. He also appeared as Richard Grisham and Richard Gresham.

Grist, Jacob. Pa. —. He entered the service as a substitute for his father in the 22nd Regiment of the militia under Col. Thompson. He served three months. In 1780 he served another two months for his father. In July 1781 he entered for eighteen months in the 4th Regiment under Col. Craig. He sailed from Baltimore under the convoy of the privateer *Washington* to the mouth of James River in Virginia. He was at Yorktown and Cypress Hills. He marched in Dec. 1782 home to Carlisle under Capt. Studsbury. He was discharged by Col. Hampton. Congress ruled that there was no proof for his first tour and granted him a pension for eighteen months 13 Feb. 1838. There was a Jacob Grist of Westmoreland County who received a $40 gratuity and a $40 annuity from Westmoreland 17 Mar. 1838. He died 1 July 1847.

Griswold, Andrew. Conn. Lt. He served under Col. Durkee. He was from Norwich and was 33 years old on 25 Nov. 1788. He was badly wounded at Germantown. He was on the 1791 and 1813 pension lists.

Groet, Petrur. N.Y. Pvt. He served in the Montgomery County militia under Col. Frederick Fisher and was slain 6 Aug. 1777. His children, Philip Groet and Annatie Groet, received his half-pay pension.

Grof, George. Pa. —. He was awarded a $40 gratuity and a $40 annuity in Dauphin County 1 Apr. 1836. He was dead by July 1838. He also appeared as George Groff.

Grogerty, Thomas. Va. —. Biddy Grogerty was awarded £10 in Goochland Co., Va. 17 Sep. 1781 while he was away in the service. He was killed in the service. His widow, Bridget Groggotty, was on the pension roll of 1785.

Groh, Nicholas. Pa. —. He was awarded a $40 gratuity and a $40 annuity in Berks Co., Pa. 27 Jan. 1835. He died 13 Mar. 1854.

Groom, John. Va. Pvt. He was in Orange County on 13 May 1787 and was aged 39. He was a militia man from Orange County in Capt. Robert Stubblefield's Company annexed to Col. Darke's Regiment. He was detached under Maj. Nathaniel Welch in the teamsters before Yorktown on 15 Oct. 1781 when he was wounded by a shot from the enemy and lost his right leg. He was continued on the pension list at the rate of £15 per annum on 13 June 1787.

Grooms, —. S.C. —. His widow was Rachel Grooms. There were children in 1791.

Groos, George. Mass. Pvt. He served in the 11th Regiment. His widow was Elizabeth Groos from Beverly and was paid $50. He also appeared as George Groce.

Grosh, Michael. Md. Lt. He was killed at Germantown. His two children were pensioned from 18 Oct. 1778 to 18 Oct. 1783 in Frederick County.

Grose, Samuel. Conn. Pvt. He served in Col. Chandler's Regiment. He suffered from epileptic fits contracted in 1778 at Valley Forge. He lived in Lebanon, Conn. in 1794. He enlisted 29 Apr. 1777 for three years and was discharged 7 Mar. 1779.

Gross, Abraham. Pa. —. He was granted relief in Clearfield County 21 Mar. 1837.

Gross, Elisha. Mass. —. He served in Crane's Artillery and was paid $20.

Gross, John. Mass. —. Pvt. He served in the 11th Regiment and was from Beverly. His widow, Elizabeth Gross, was paid $50. He also appeared as John Groce.

Gross, John. N.Y. Pvt. He served under Col. Van Schaick and was killed at Fort Schuyler 23 July 1779. His son, John Gross, received a half-pay pension for seven years.

Gross, John. Pa. —. He was awarded a $40 gratuity and a $40 annuity in Adams Co., Pa. 15 Apr. 1834.

Grosscup, —. Pa. —. His widow, Sybilla Grosscup, was awarded a $40 gratuity and a $40 annuity 18 Mar. 1834. She died 25 July 1842.

Grostcrost, John. Pa. —. He was awarded a $40 gratuity and a $40 annuity in Beaver Co., Pa. 15 Mar. 1826. He died 4 Nov. 1843. He also appeared as John Grostcost.

Groteclass, Gilbert. N.Y. —. He was granted relief.

Groten, John. Va. Pvt. His widow, Margery Groten, lived in Accomack County 28 Dec. 1792 when she was pensioned at the rate of £12 per annum. He served in the 9th Va. Regiment and died in the service.

Grotin, —. Va. —. His widow, Mary Grotin, was on the pension roll of 1798.

Grout, Nathan. Mass. Artificer. He was from Sherburn. His widow, Mary Grout, was paid $50.

Grove, David. Md. Pvt. He was pensioned in Washington County at the rate of half-pay of a private 17 Feb. 1820. His widow, Catharine Grove, was pensioned at the same rate 1 Mar. 1832. His arrearage was paid to David Brookhart 3 Mar. 1832.

Grove, George. Pa. —. He was awarded a $40 gratuity and a $40 annuity in Huntingdon County 28 Mar. 1836.

Grove, Peter. Pa. Capt. His widow, Sarah Grove, was awarded a $40 gratuity and a $40 annuity in Lycoming Co., Pa. 2 Apr. 1826.

Grove, William. Md. Pvt. He was pensioned in Allegany County in Feb. 1820. His widow, Mary Grove, was pensioned at the same rate 1 Mar. 1850. He also appeared as William Grover and William Groves.

Grover, Amasa. Conn. Pvt. He served under Col. Grosvenor. He was wounded in the neck by a musket ball on 3 Mar. 1782 at Morrisiana. He lived in Bethel, Vt. in 1795. He was granted one-third of a pension 20 Apr. 1796. He was in the militia. He was on the 1813 pension list.

Grubb, —. Pa. —. His widow, Elsy Grubb, was awarded a $40 gratuity and a $40 annuity in Allegheny County 27 Mar. 1837. She was 75 years old in 1840. She died 12 Mar. 1849.

Grubb, Jacob. Pa. —. He applied from Lancaster County 13 July 1826. His son-in-law was John Brown. He was inclined to tippling. He was out as a rifleman under Capt. James Ross in 1775 to Boston and was discharged in July 1776 at Long Island. He rejoined the army and was under Capt. App at the battle of Germantown. He enlisted in Capt. John Craig's Company of Cavalry for the duration of the war. Jacob Danck, alias Tank, was his lieutenant. He died 12 July 1829.

Grubb, Philip. Pa. —. He was awarded relief in Allegheny County 14 Mar. 1835. He was dead by Nov. 1837.

Gruber, George. Pa. —. He was awarded a $40 gratuity and a $40 annuity in Delaware Co., Pa. 1 Apr. 1834.

Gruber, John. Pa. —. He was awarded a $40 gratuity and a $40 annuity in Luzerne County 28 Mar. 1836. He died 3 Apr. 1839. His widow may have been the Mary Gruber who was pensioned there 21 Mar. 1840.

Gruber, Valentine. Pa. —. He was awarded a $40 annuity in Bedford County 5 Feb. 1836.

Grugg, Conrad. Pa. —. He was in the Invalids and was due but £2.13.4 in 1790.

Grumble, Jacob. Pa. —. He was granted relief.

Grymes, George. Va. —. His wife, Elizabeth Grymes, was granted £40 support in York Co., Va. on 15 Nov. 1779.

Grymes, William. Va. Capt. He served as captain in the 15th Virginia Regiment and died shortly after the battle of Germantown 1 Aug. 1777. He was reportedly promoted to major before his death but the evidence was insufficient to prove same. His wife died in 1789. His seven years' half-pay was to be paid to his daughter, Nancy Haggard, 2 July 1836. She was allowed interest on same 4 Jan. 1838. He also appeared as William Grimes.

Guard, Daniel. N.J. Pvt. He served in the N.J. Line. He lived in Morris County. He was on the 1813 pension list and died 18 June 1824.

Gudgeon, William. Md. Pvt. He was pensioned in Kent County at the rate of half-pay of a private 19 Feb. 1819. His pension was suspended because he was never in the service of Maryland or of the United States in Kent County in Feb. 1823. He also appeared as William Gudgington. He was pensioned at the rate of half-pay of a private in Kent County on 17 Feb. 1824. His arrearage was to be paid to his representative 11 Mar. 1828. One of the heirs, Benjamin Gudgeon of Kent County, was paid the arrearage 20 Feb. 1829.

Guechen, Peter. Pa. Pvt. He was in Philadelphia County 13 Feb. 1786. He served in the 11th Pa. Regiment in Capt. Bush's Company. He was wounded in an engagement with the savages near Tioga and discharged in 1780. He was 28 years old. He also appeared as Peter Guhen.

Guen, Thomas. Va. —. While he was away in Continental service, his wife, Mary Guen, and child were granted 40 shillings per month support in Yohogania Co., Va. 28 Sep. 1779.

Guenall, James. N.Y. Lt. He was granted relief.

Guerard, Godin. S.C. —. His annuity was £100 in 1787.

Guerney, Francis. Pa. Capt. He served as a captain in 1775 and Lt. Col. in the 11th Battalion of Continental Troops in Oct. 1776. No evidence could be found of a galley, *Flora*, in service in 1782.

Guest, William. S.C. —. He volunteered in 1779 and served to the evacuation of Charleston. He later served as a spy on the frontier when the Indians were doing mischief. He was pensioned 19 Dec. 1826 from Pendleton District where he had resided since 1785. Capt. John Barton, Sr., of Franklin Co., Georgia swore that Guest served in his company and was at the battle of King's Mountain. After drawing his pension for seven years, he became a federal pensioner. After two semi-annual draws he was stricken from the rolls and forced to reapply to South Carolina. He died 8 July 1841 in his 80th year in Pickens District, S.C. His widow, Anna Guest, was pensioned in 1842. She was last paid 1851. He also appeared as William Gist.

Guffin, John. Pa. Pvt. He died 10 Feb. 1812.

Guild, Jesse. —. —. He was stricken from the pension roll and sought to be restored. He had sold his property to his son, Calvin Guild, for $500. He did not have any written contract so Congress rejected his restoration to the roll 10 Jan. 1832.

Guild, Joseph. Mass. Sgt. He served in the 7th Regiment and was paid $20.

Guiles, Abraham. —. Pvt. He served under Capt. Hart and Col. Ebenezer Huntington. He married 5 Feb. 1795. He died 17 Mar. 1835. His widow was Deborah Guiles who was born 10 July 1779. She sought relief from Congress 6 Feb. 1844.

Guilford, John. Me. —. He was from Hollis. He was paid $50 under the resolve of 1836.

Guillow, Francis. Mass. Pvt. He served in the 4th Regiment and was from Norton. He was paid $20. He also appeared as Francis Gillon.

Guinn, John. Pa. —. He was granted relief in Huntingdon County 17 Mar. 1838.

Guleck, John. —. —. He sought a radical change in the manner of paying Revolutionary pensions. Congress laid his petition on the table 7 Feb. 1850.

Gullock, Richard. Va. —. He was away in the service. His wife and children were granted support in the amount of £50 of pork and a barrel of corn for each person in Montgomery Co., Va. 9 Nov. 1780.

Gum, Claypole. Va. —. His was granted £40 support in Rockingham Co., Va. on 24 Aug. 1779. He subsequently died in Continental service. His widow and two orphan children were recommended for relief on 23 Oct.1780.

Gump, Frederick. Pa. —. He was awarded a $40 gratuity and a $40 annuity in Greene Co., Pa. 7 Apr. 1830. He served in the Chester County militia under Capt. Culbertson in the Flying Camp. He also appeared as Frederick Gumpf.

Gumpf, Christopher. Pa. —. He was awarded a $40 gratuity and a $40 annuity in Lancaster County 28 Mar. 1836. He was 80 years old in 1840

Gumpf, Michael. Pa. —. He received benefits 27 Mar. 1837. He died 8 Sep. 1843. His widow, Margaret Gumpf, was awarded a $40 annuity in Lancaster Co. 27 Apr. 1852. He also appeared as Michael Gompf and Gump.

Gunby, John. —. Officer. He received a bounty land warrant for 500 acres. In 1839 he had located 340 acres in Coshocton Co., Ohio. His heirs sought a further grant, but Congress rejected their claim 30 July 1842.

Gundy, Jacob. Pa. —. He was awarded a $40 gratuity and a $40 annuity in Hamilton Co., Ill. 14 Jan. 1835. He died in Sep. 1845.

Gunn, —. Pa. —. His widow, Ann Gunn, was awarded a $40 gratuity and a $40 annuity in Washington Co., Pa. 8 Apr. 1826.

Gunn, Alexander. N.C. Sgt. He served in the 6th Regiment and enlisted in 1776. He served three and a half years. He had a family of small children and sought relief in 1788.

Gunn, Jeremiah. Pa. Pvt. He was on the 1813 pension list.

Gunn, William. Pa. —. He was awarded a $40 gratuity and a $40 annuity in Washington Co., Pa. Mar. 1824.

Gunter, George. Pa. —. He was awarded a $40 gratuity and a $40 annuity 14 Mar. 1835 in Franklin County. He was 83 years old in 1840.

Gunter, John. Pa. —. His wife was Elizabeth Gunter.

Gunter, William. S.C. Sgt. He served in the 2nd S.C. Regiment. His widow, Mary Gunter, was granted an annuity 4 Oct. 1786.

Gunther, Needham. S.C. —. He was from Horry District when he was pensioned 23 Nov. 1829 at which time he was aged 98 years. His son, John Gunter, administrator of his estate, was paid his arrearage for eighteen months on 7 Dec. 1836. He also appeared as Needham Gunter.

Gunyon, John. Va. —. He died in Continental service. His two children were granted £40 support in Prince William Co., Va. on 8 Feb. 1779.

Guralt, John. —. —. He applied in Person Co., N.C. in Sep. 1833.

Gurganus, Wiley. N.C. Sgt. He was drafted and served to 2 Aug. 1782. He moved his family to South Carolina where he remained about ten yeas. He returned to N.C. He had a large family and applied 8 Dec. 1810. He was from Bladen County. He furnished a substitute and was discharged before his twelve month tour was completed. He was rejected in Anson County.

Gusham, Joseph. Mass. Pvt. He was on list of pensioners who had not been paid by Benjamin Lincoln in 1790. His pension was $5 per month. He also appeared as Joseph Guzan. Vide also Joseph Gowden.

Gushart, Isaac. Pa. —. He received a $40 gratuity in Franklin County 24 Mar. 1837.

Guthard, Henry. Pa. —. He was awarded a $40 gratuity and a $40 annuity in Northumberland County 14 Mar. 1818. He also appeared as Henry Guthardt.

Guthrie, —. S.C. —. His widow, Sarah Guthrie, was pensioned from Pendleton District on 4 Dec. 1832 at the rate of $30 per annum. She was last paid in 1834.

Guthrie, Benjamin. —. —. Congress rejected his application 4 May 1846 because it was not sustained by necessary proof.

Guthrie, Francis. S.C. —. He was pensioned on 25 Nov. 1830. He was a horseman under Capt. Robert Thomson in Gen. Sumter's Brigade. He also appeared as Francis Guthry.

Guthrie, Henry. —. —. He served in the militia as a volunteer and draftee for two years. He was mostly an armorer at military posts. There was no proof that he was a soldier. He presented no evidence other than his testimony so Congress rejected his claim 24 Mar. 1836.

Guthrie, John. N.C. Pvt. He served in the Twelve Month Men. He was wounded by a ball entering his spine in May 1781 at Halifax, N.C. He resided in Augusta, Ga. in 1796. He was on the 1813 pension list.

Guthrie, Joseph. Mass. —. He served in the 1st Regiment. His widow, Betsey Guthrie, was paid $50.

Guthrie, William. Pa. —. He applied from Westmoreland County on 11 May 1814. He enlisted in Capt. Joseph Irvin's Company for one year and nine months. He was a prisoner for eighteen weeks on Long Island. He was sick about two months in Philadelphia after he was discharged at Valley Forge 1 Jan. 1778. He also served under Capt. James Carnahan in the 2nd Regiment under Col. Broadhead. He was transferred to the 13th Regiment under Col. Walter Stewart. He was in the battles of Germantown and Brandywine. He also served two months in the Cumberland County militia under Col. Culbertson. He was 73 years old. William Waddle was a sergeant in the company and confirmed his service.

Guthrie, William. Pa. —. He was awarded a $40 gratuity and a $40 annuity in Armstrong County 30 Mar. 1822.

Guthrie, William. Pa. Capt. His widow, Elizabeth Guthrie, was awarded a $60 gratuity and a $60 annuity 23 Mar. 1829 in Armstrong Co., Pa.

Guy, —. Pa. —. His widow was Barbara Guy. She was from Montgomery County 11 Apr. 1825. She died 13 Dec. 1831.

Guy, Jonathan. Pa. Sgt. He was in Montgomery County 28 Mar. 1808. He served in Capt. Van Zant's Company in the 5th Pa. Regiment under Col. Robert McGaw and was wounded on the night before the capture of Fort Washington. He served in Col. Walter Stewart's Regiment from 29 Apr. 1778 to 16 Jan. 1781. He was awarded a $40 gratuity and a $40 annuity. He died 10 Oct. 1823.

Guyant, Luke. Conn. Pvt. He lived in New London Co., Conn. He was on the 1813 pension list.

Guyer, Peter. Pa. —. He enlisted under Capt. Irwin near Fort Pitt for one year and nine months in the spring of 1776. His wife, Mary Guyer, went along as wash woman. His son, John Guyer, aged about eleven, was drummer. He and his son were both wounded at the battle of Germantown. He was from Franklin County. His widow and son were from Cumberland County. She died 4 Feb. 1830.

Guzard, Valentine. Pa. —. He was awarded a $40 gratuity and a $40 annuity in Ohio on 9 Mar. 1825. He served in the Flying Camp.

Gwinn, John. Md. Sgt. His widow, Julia Gwinn, was pensioned at the rate of half-pay of a sergeant 21 Mar. 1837. He also appeared as John Gwyn and John Gwynn. He served in the 4th Regiment under Col. Carvill Hall. He died in Baltimore, Md. in 1800. He was entitled to 100 acres of bounty land. On 14 July 1795 warrant #11, 262 was issued to William Marbury who posed as his administrator five years before Gwynn's death. Congress authorized the widow and children, Catherine Gwynn and Susannah Gwynn, relief 28 Jan. 1828.

Gwinnup, George. —. —. He was a pensioner and died 16 Aug. 1840. His widow, Margaret Gwinnup of Hamilton Co., Ohio sought a pension, but Congress rejected a special act for her relief 5 Mar. 1846. The couple were married 7 Feb. 1783.

Gwyne, Joseph. Pa. —. He lived in Bucks County. He enlisted in 1777 and was wounded in the thigh at Germantown. He was discharged in 1781. He was granted a $40 gratuity and a $40 annuity 4 Feb. 1808.

Gwyne, Joseph. Pa. —. He was in Greene County. He served in the 8th Pa. Regiment for three years and was granted $150 for depreciation pay 15 Feb. 1808.

Haas, Peter. Pa. —. He was awarded a $40 gratuity and a $40 annuity in Northumberland Co., Pa. 3 Apr. 1829. He was probably identical with the one of that name who served as a corporal in the 2nd Pennsylvania Regiment and sought any sums that might be due him. He died 13 Mar. 1835.

Hackathorn, David. Pa. —. He was awarded relief in Juniata County 5 Feb. 1836.

Hacker, James. Pa. —. He was paid a $40 gratuity in Berks County in Apr. 1835. He also appeared as John Hacher.

Hacker, John. Va. —. He served as a ranger or Indian spy for thirteen months under Capt. James Booth. His heirs, Jonathan Hacker, Absalom Hacker, Thomas S. Hacker, and Sarah (Hacker) Smith, were paid $104 on 23 Mar. 1839.

Hackett, Benjamin. Mass. —. He served in the 7th Regiment and was paid $20.

Hackley, James. —. Lt. He served to the end of the war. His heirs, Asa Winsett and Amos Winsett sought his commutation pay 18 May 1838.

Hackley, Richard. Pa.—. He served under Lt. William Jack and Capt. Moorhead in the 8th Regiment. He was from Westmoreland County.

Haddock, Isaac. S.C. —. He served in the 3rd S.C. Regiment and was killed at the siege of Charleston. His widow, Sarah Haddock, was granted an annuity 8 June 1785. There were three children in 1791.

Haden, Josiah. —. Capt. His heirs sought his seven years' half-pay. Because he served in the militia, Congress rejected their claim 17 Jan. 1837.

Haden, Peleg. Mass. —. He served in the 6th Regiment and was paid $20.

Hadley, James. Pa. —. He was awarded $200 on 15 Mar. 1826. He lived in Steuben Co., N.Y.

Hafferman, —. Pa. —. His widow, Catharine Hafferman, was awarded a $40 gratuity and a $40 annuity in Crawford Co., Pa. 20 Feb. 1833.

Hafferman, Hugh. Pa. —. He applied in Crawford County in Feb. 1813. He enlisted in Apr. 1776 under Col. Samuel J. Atlee in Capt. Joseph McClelland's Company. He was in battle at Long Island and was taken prisoner at Fort Washington. He was paroled in Apr. 1777. He enlisted again in June 1777 in the 9th Pa. Regiment under Col. George Nagel and later under Col. Richard Butler. He was in the battle of Brandywine and was wounded in his leg in action under Gen. Wayne. He was at Monmouth in June 1778. In 1779 he was drafted into the company of Capt. George Grant at the storming of Stoney Point and wounded in the breast by a bayonet. He returned to Capt. McClelland's Company. The 5th and 9th Pa. Regiments were merged into the 2nd Regt. under Col. Richard Butler. He was at Yorktown in 1781. Afterwards he was commanded by Col. Josiah Harmer and marched to S.C. to join Gen. Greene. He was in Capt.

Thomas B------'s Company to Oct. 1782 when he returned to Pa. and was transferred to the 4th Pa. Regt. under Col. Humpton in Capt. --------ley's Company. He was discharged in June 1783 in Philadelphia. He was a sergeant from 14 June 1779 to the end of the war. Jacob Beetham who served with him proved his service. Adam Hill was with him at Stoney Point. James Mitchell swore he enlisted Hafferman in 1776. He suffered from rheumatism and piles. He was 65 years old. He also appeared as Hugh Hefferman.

Hafley, Stephen. Md. Pvt. He was pensioned at the rate of half-pay of a private in Frederick County 18 Feb. 1830. His arrearage of $31.22 for 9 months and 11 day to the time of his death was paid to John H. Boyle for the widow, Mary Magdalena Hafley, on 9 Feb. 1839. She was pensioned at the same rate on 15 Feb. 1839.

Hagan, Henry. Pa. —. He was granted a $40 gratuity and a $40 annuity in Mercer County 28 Mar. 1836.

Hagan, John. Pa. —. He was pensioned 18 July 1820.

Hagarty, Nicholas. Va. —. His children were awarded an allowance in Yohogania Co., Va. 28 May 1779 while he was away in the service.

Hagarty, Paul. Md. Pvt. He was pensioned in 1789 in Frederick County. He was wounded at Brandywine. He served in the 1st Regiment.

Hagedorn, John. N.Y. —. He was wounded. He was on the 1785 pension list.

Hagens, —. S.C. —. His widow, Fearby Hagens, was from Liberty in 1791. She was paid an annuity from 25 Feb. 1808 to 1814. She also appeared as Phereby Hagins and Fearby Heagins.

Hager, Joseph. N.Y. Pvt. He served under Col. Vrooman. He was wounded in action with the Indians with a musket ball on 10 Nov. 1781 at the head of the Delaware. He was pensioned in Sep. 1793. He lived in Schoharie, N.Y. in 1794 and later in Seneca County. He was on the 1813 pension list. He also appeared as Joseph Hagan.

Hagerman, James. Pa. —. He was pensioned 1 Apr. 1814. He died 24 Apr. 1819.

Hagerty, Andrew. Md. —. He was pensioned.

Hagerty, Enos. N.Y. Matross. He served under Col. Lamb and was slain 19 Feb. 1781. His widow, Mary Hagarty, received a half-pay pension..

Hagerty, John. Pa —. He was on the 1789 pension list. He also appeared as John Hoagarty.

Hagerty, Morter. N.Y. Pvt. He served in the Dutchess County militia under Col. Henry Luddington and was slain 31 Jan. 1777. His widow was granted his half-pay pension.

Hagerty, Paul. Va. Pvt. He was on the 1813 pension list.

Hagerty, William. Pa. Pvt. He was pensioned.

Haggard, James. Va. —. He was disabled by a violent cold before he recovered from smallpox following his inoculation. He sought relief on 3 Dec. 1784. His claim was rejected 13 Dec. 1784.

Hagie, John. —. —. He came over to America in the French Army with Gen. LaFayette and was paid by the French government. He served under Capt. Escaline and Polish Col. Polovoleki in the French light horse calvary. He was at White Plains, Little York, and was discharged in New York. His discharge was destroyed in a house fire in Knoxville, Tenn. He applied for a pension in Davidson Co., Tenn. Lafayette recognized him when he returned to America. Congress entertained a bill for a pension 5 Mar. 1840. Congress denied his widow, Catharine Hagie, a pension 8 May 1860.

Hahn, —. Pa. —. His widow, Catherine Hahn, received a $$0 gratuity in Berks County 25 Feb. 1854.

Hahn, Conrad. N.Y. —. He served in the Montgomery County militia and was slain 6 Aug. 1777. His orphan children received a half-pay pension for seven years.

Hahn, Daniel. Pa. —. He was awarded a $40 gratuity in Lancaster County 14 Mar. 1835.

Hahn, Samuel. Pa. —. He was granted a $40 gratuity in Northumberland County 1 Apr. 1836.

Haigler, Jacob. S.C. —. He had served in the last Old Indian War before the Revolutionary War. He was born in 1743 and served ten months under Capt. Isaac Ross and Gen. Thomas Sumter. He also served under Capt. Grissett. While serving under Col. Charles Middleton, he was taken prisoner and left sick. He eventually rejoined his unit and was legally discharged. George Osman testified that he was present at the latter. He was from Orangeburg District in 1825. His application was rejected because none of his vouchers were certified.

Hailes, Silas. S.C. —. He was pensioned from Darlington District on 6 Dec. 1828.

Hailey, Daniel. Mass. —. He served in the 4th Regiment. He was paid $20 in July 1804.

Haines, Joshua. N.H. Pvt. He served under Col. Nixon in a minute company. He was wounded by a musket ball in his right shoulder in Apr. 1775 at Lexington. He lived in Washington, N.H. in 1794. He was pensioned 21 June 1796. He was on the 1813 pension list as Joshua Haynes. He died 30 Dec. 1821 in Hillsborough Co., N.H.

Haines, Thomas. N.H. Pvt. He was wounded through his jaws at Bemis Heights on 19 Sep. 1777. He was from Exeter in 1782. He served in Col. Cilley's Regiment. He was aged 27 in 1787.

Haines, William. Va. Pvt. He served in the artillery. His widow, Sarah Haines, was being pensioned 1 June 1784.

Hains, John. Pa. —. He was awarded a $40 gratuity and a $40 annuity in Berks Co., Pa. 6 Apr. 1830. He also appeared as John Haines. He died 2 Sep. 1843.

Hair, John. Mass. —. He was granted relief.

Hait, Joel. Conn. Pvt. He served from 1777 to the peace in Col. Samuel B. Webb's Regiment. He was disabled by a rupture. He was pensioned 24 Nov. 1788 as a resident of Stamford, Conn. and was aged 31 years. He died 6 June 1805.

Hait, Joice. Conn. Pvt. He was on the 1813 pension list as Isee [sic] Hayt.

Halbert, Richard. Va. Pvt. His widow, Mary Halbert, lived in Spotsylvania County 5 Sep. 1786. He served in the militia and died in the service in S.C. She was continued on the pension roll on 14 Apr. 1791. She was dead by 3 Mar. 1797.

Halcum, —. S.C. —. His widow, Lucy Halcum, was on the roll in 1791.

Halcum, Joseph. S.C. —. There were children in 1791.

Haldeman, Christian. Pa. —. He received a $40 annuity in Lancaster County 28 Mar. 1854. He received a $40 gratuity 17 Apr. 1854.

Hale, Benjamin. Me. —. He was from Waterford. He was paid $50 under the resolve of 1836.

Hale, Daniel. N.J. Sgt. He served under Capt. Silas Howell in the 1st Regiment and was killed at Germantown on 4 Oct. 1777. He married Sarah Lacey 21 Dec. 1772 in Morristown. His widow, Sarah Hale, married secondly Henry Frazee 3 Dec. 1778. She was granted a half-pay pension in Morris County in 1792. He also appeared as Daniel Hall.

Hale, Joseph. Mass. Pvt. He served under Col. Lee in Capt. Lyman's Company. He was wounded by a musket ball passing through his right arm on 29 Aug. 1778 at Newport, R.I. He lived in Harwich, Mass. in 1795. He served in the militia. He was granted half a pension 20 Apr. 1796. He was listed as dead in the 1813 pension roll.

Hale, Mordecai. N.Y. Surgeon's Mate. He was wounded in his private parts. He suffered from a hernia and rupture. He could no longer ride. He served in 2nd N.Y. Regiment of Artillery under Col. John Lamb. He was pensioned 7 June 1786 and was 23 years old. He lived in Westchester Co., N.Y. on 12 June 1788. He also appeared as Mordecia Haile. He was on the 1813 pension list as

Mordecai Hall [sic].

Hale, Nathan. N.H. Col. He commanded the 2nd Regiment. He died a prisoner of the British on Long Island on 23 Sept. 1780. His widow, Abigail Hale, was from Rindge, N.H. in 1787. His son sought a monument at the sepulcher 27 July 1834.

Hale, Silas. S.C. —. He was a soldier in 1781 and 1782 under Col. Benton and Col. Murphy. Capt. Peter Dubose testified that Hale served under him. He applied 29 Oct. 1827 in Darlington District. He was last paid his annuity in 1838.

Hale, William. —. Pvt. He served under Col. Meade. He resided in West Springfield, Mass. in 1796.

Haley, Barnbas. —. —. He served three years. His name was not on the rolls, and he furnished no proof other than his testimony so Congress rejected his claim 13 Feb. 1836. He was receiving an annual pension of $20 and sought an increase 25 Oct. 1846. Congress rejected his petition.

Haley, John. Pa. Corp. He was granted one-third of a pension 20 Apr. 1796. He was on the 1813 pension list. He lived in Philadelphia County and died 21 or 22 July 1823.

Haley, Joseph. —. —. He was granted a pension 20 Apr. 1796.

Halfpenny, John. Va. Pvt. His wife, Sarah Halfpenny, and two children were furnished £35 support on 5 Oct. 1779 in Frederick Co., Va. He lived in Frederick County 22 Feb. 1787 and was aged 47. He served in the 11th Va. Regiment. He received a number of wounds in the service; one was in his right hand. He was in Capt. Bruin's Company at Buford's defeat. He was granted £12 relief and half-pay during his disability. He also appeared as John Halfpane. He was on the 1813 pension list.

Halkerstone, Robert. Md. Lt. He was pensioned in Charles County at the rate of half-pay of a lieutenant 7 Feb. 1817. He also appeared as Robert Halkerson.

Hall, —. Va. —. His wife, Eleanor Hall, was granted £10 in Fauquier Co., Va. in May 1778 while her husband was away in the service.

Hall, Abner. Mass. —. He served in the 2nd Regiment and was from Kingston. He was paid $20.

Hall, Agrippa. Mass. —. He served in the 2nd Regiment and was from Stockbridge. He was paid $20.

Hall, David. Conn. Sgt. He served in the Sappers & Miners Regt. under Capt. D. Bushell. He was knocked off the breast work by the wind of a cannon ball and fell on a sharp stake which ran into his back. The injury brought on the spitting of blood followed by epileptic fits. He was shot in the knee by two buck shot in 1781 near Yorktown. He suffered from internal bleeding. He resided in Weston, Conn. in 1792. He served to the end of the war. He was pensioned 4 Sep. 1794. He was granted half a pension 20 Apr. 1796. His rate was $5 per month from 12 Feb. 1808. He moved to Ontario Co., N.Y. 3 May 1808. He was on the 1813 pension list. He died 25 Aug. 1824.

Hall, Ebenezer. Mass. Sgt. He was in the 13th Regiment and was from New Marlboro. His widow, Mary Hall, was paid $50.

Hall, Elisha. Mass. Sgt. He served in the 14th Regiment and was from Plymouth. His widow, Asenath Hall, was paid $50.

Hall, Enoch. Me. —. He died 10 Dec. 1835. His widow, Miriam Hall, was from Buckfield. She was paid $50 under the resolve of 1836.

Hall, George A. S.C. —. His annuity was £26.2.6 in 1787.

Hall, Hugh. Pa. —. He received a $40 gratuity and a $40 annuity in Clearfield County 15 June 1836.

Hall, Jabez. Me. —. He was from Readfield. He was paid $50 under the resolve of 1836.

Hall, Jacob. N.H. Surgeon. He served in the 3rd Regiment. It was claimed that he was reduced as supernumerary, but Congress ruled that he had resigned at the consolidation and rejected the claim of his representative for his bounty land and commutation.

Hall, Jacob. N.J. Pvt. He served in the N.J. Line and was wounded in his shoulder. He was 29 years old. He was pensioned in Burlington County in 1786. He was on the 1813 pension list.

Hall, James. S.C. —. He was wounded at the Eutaw. He was granted an annuity 12 Feb. 1785. He was from Union District. There were two children in 1791.

Hall, John. Pa. —. He was awarded a $40 gratuity in Allegheny County 1 Apr. 1837.

Hall, John. Va. —. His wife was granted support in Pittsylvania Co., Va. on 26 Mar. 1778, 28 May 1778, and on 25 Feb. 1779.

Hall, John. Va. —. His wife, Agnes Hall, and two children were granted £8 support in Louisa Co., Va. on 11 Aug. 1777. He died in Continental service. She was pensioned 8 May 1778. His widow and two children were paid £30 support on 8 Mar. 1779. They received 3 barrels of corn and 150 pounds of pork on 11 Dec. 1780, 4 barrels of corn and 200 pounds of pork on 10 Dec. 1781, and 4 barrels of corn and 100 pounds of bacon on 8 July 1782.

Hall, Joseph. Mass. Pvt. He died 10 Mar. 1807.

Hall, Lott. —. —. He entered the service in May 1776 as lieutenant of marines under Lt. Elijah Freeman Payne of the *Randolph*, twenty guns, lying in Charleston, S.C. Robert Cochran was the captain. He enlisted 29 men and a boy in Massachusetts and sailed to S.C. in June 1776 on the *Eagle*. They took four prizes en route, and he was put on board the last one taken. He was ordered to take the prize to Boston and was retaken by the British and carried to Glasgow, Scotland. He was detailed a year and took passage to Va. on the *Duke of Grafton* and was taken prisoner at Hampton Roads on 1 Jan. 1778 by the sixty-four gun *St. Albans* commanded by Robert Onslow. He was exchanged. En route home to Mass. he stopped in Philadelphia and made a petition to Congress. He asked subsistence and pay while a prisoner as well as his share of the prize money with interest. He died shortly after petitioning Congress in 1808 on 17 May 1809. He married 13 Feb. 1786. His son, while trying to collect the evidence for his mother's pension found the claim of his father. Congress did not allow him the claim of the veteran's being an exchanged Continental supernumeray officer, but he was entitled to his share of prize money and his pay and support while a prisoner without interest. Congress approved same to the heirs 27 Mar. 1846. His executrix was Polly Hall of Westminister, Windham Co., Vt. The veteran resided in Barnstable Co., Mass. when he entered the service. In 1839 the children were Daniel Hall aged 51, Mary Parrott Lyman the wife of John Lyman aged 44, and Timothy Hillard Hall aged 35. Elizabeth Price Hall aged 19, a grand-daughter, was the only child of Benjamin Homer Hall, deceased.

Hall, Primus. Mass. Pvt. He was a man of color. He enlisted at Cambridge in Feb. 1776 under Capt. Joseph Butler in the 5th Regiment for one year. He was at Winter Hill, New York City, White Plains, Trenton, and Princeton. He was discharged at Morristown. His second tour in 1777 was under Capt. Samuel Flint and Col. Johnson. He was in the engagement with Burgoyne and was discharged. He served three months under Capt. Woodbury in 1778 and twenty-two months under Col. Timothy Pickering as a steward in 1781-1782. He was discharged in Dec. 1782 at Newbury, N.J. His pocket book was stolen in 1782 at Dumfries, Va. He lost his discharges. He did not apply in 1818 because he had too much property. He was also known as Primus Trask. He applied to Congress 2 Jan. 1832.

Hall, Richard. Md. Pvt. He was pensioned at the rate of half-pay of a private in Anne Arundel County on 2 Feb. 1832. His arrearage of $17.60 was paid to Mrs. Anne Cadle, his legal representative, 5 Jan. 1841.

Hall, Robert. Mass. —. He served in the 5th Regiment and was paid $20.

Hall, Samuel. Mass. —. He served in the 3rd Artillery under Col. Crane and was from Raynham. He was paid $20.

Hall, Talmadge. Conn. Lt. He served under Col. Haman Swift in the 7th Connecticut Regiment. He was wounded in his left wrist and his left groin at Stoney Point on 16 Aug. 1779. He was transferred to the Invalids Corps. He was 32 years old 24 Jan. 1786. He resided in New York City, N.Y. in May 1787. He was an innkeeper.

Hall, Thomas. N.C. Lt. He died in the service and was in the Continental Line. His siblings, Frances Bain, John Hall, William Hall, and Roger Hall of Brunswick County sought his seven years' half-pay. They were all minors at the time of his death and had recently come of age in 1790.

Hall, Thomas. Pa. —. He was awarded a $40 annuity in Beaver County 5 Feb. 1836.

Hall, Thomas. Pa. —. He served more than three months as a officer against the Indians on the frontier. He was not under the requisition of the state for militia forces. His service was not strictly military and was not embraced by the law. Congress rejected his claim for a pension 6 May 1846.

Hall, Thomas. S.C. —. His annuity was £164.3.1 in 1787.

Hall, William. Mass. Fifer. He served in Crane's Artillery and was from Stoughton. He was paid $20.

Hall, William. N.J. Pvt. He served under Col. Forman in the militia and lost his forefinger. He was 44 years old and was from Shrewsbury. He was on the 1791 pension roll.

Hall, William. N.C. Capt. He applied in Nash County in 1804. He was in the militia under Col. James Keneon and was wounded 13 times in the head and elbow at the battle of Rockfish. He was a captive from 2 Aug. to 13 Nov. He was on the 1813 pension list. He died 3 June 1825.

Hall, William. Pa. Pvt. His widow, Frances Allison, was in Dauphin County 18 Mar. 1787. He served in Capt. Green's Flying Camp in the militia from Lancaster Co. He was killed and left a widow and child of eight months. Lt. Col. William Hay and Lt. William McCullough attested to his service. His widow married secondly George Allison. John Rodgers was the guardian of the soldier's daughter, Margaret Hall. His widow's application was rejected on 18 May 1787 since her husband belonged to the Flying Camp.

Hall, William. Pa. —. He was granted relief in Washington County 9 Feb. 1837. His name may have been William Hull.

Hallet, William. Pa. Pvt. He was pensioned.

Halliday, David. N.Y. Pvt. He served under Col. McClaghry in the Ulster County militia and was slain 6 Oct. 1777. His children, William Halliday and Samuel Halliday, were granted a half-pay pension for seven years.

Hallman, George. Pa. —. He enlisted under Capt. Henderson in the 9th Regiment. He served from 1776 to the revolt in New Jersey. He re-enlisted under Capt. Stake under Col. Butler. He was from Montgomery County.

Hallman, John. Pa. —. He was awarded a $40 gratuity and a $40 annuity in Montgomery Co., Pa. 15 Apr. 1835.

Hallow, Richard P. Conn. Sgt. He served in Durkee's Regiment. He was in the Invalids Corps and was worn down in the service. He was pensioned 4 Jan. 1783. He was on the 1813 pension list. He died in Sep. 1817 in Tolland Co., Conn.

Halloway, William. Mass. —. He was paid $20.

Hallowell, Henry. Mass. Pvt. He served in the 5th Regiment and was from Lynn. He was paid $50.

Halsey, Job. —. —. He volunteered for 6 months 20 June 1776 and served under Col. Josiah Smith and Capt. Zephaniah Rogers. He was at Sag Harbor, Brooklyn, and Long Island until it was given up to the enemy. He was discharged at Stonington, Conn. from Col. Livingston's Regiment in January for he recalled having a "high time" in "New year's." Congress gave him credit for six months of service and awarded him a pension 5 Mar. 1840.

Halsey, John. Pa. Corp. He was on the 1813 pension list.

Halsey, Malachi. N.C. —. He applied in Chowan County in 1810. In retreating from the enemy at the battle of Briar Creek, he was considerably hurt. He had a very large family. His application was rejected.

Halsey, Zephaniah. —. Lt. He served three or four years as assistant superintendent of horse yard. He served under Capt. Alexander Church for three and a half years and was discharged at Newburgh in 1783. He could not qualify for a pension because his service did not qualify as military. His widow, Rebecca Halsey, sought a pension from 4 Mar. 1831 to 6 Aug. 1847 and as a widow. Congress approved her claim 24 Mar. 1856.

Halson, Levy. N.Y. —. His wife and nine children were granted support in Dutchess County on 3 Nov. 1781. His name may have been Levy Hatson.

Halsted, Elbert H. Pa. —. He received a donation tract of land for 200 acres, It was number 750 and located in Mercer County. He died intestate and without issue. He left a living father, John Halsted, who had a life estate to the property. The siblings of Elbert H. Halsted were John J. Halsted, Andrew Halsted, Susan Halsted who married Edward J. Ball and was the mother of John Halsted Ball, Mathias Halsted, Aletta Halsted who married Thoms McKean Thompson, Elizabeth Halsted who married Alexander Caldwell, and Joanna W. Halsted. Thomas McK. Thompson by the act of 24 June 1809 received authorization to sell the interest of his nephews John J. Halsted, Andrew Halsted, and Edward J. Ball. The latter three were minors.

Ham, Joseph. Me. —. He died 3 Jun 1800. His widow, Margaret Staples, was from Kennebunkport. She was paid $50 under the resolve of 1836.

Hamblen, Prince. Me. —. He died 17 Apr. 1836. His widow, Bethia Hamblen, was from Gorham. She was paid $50 under the resolve of 1836.

Hambleton, —. S.C. —. His widow, Jane Hambleton, was paid pensioned 4 Dec. 1832 at $30 per annum.

Hambleton, David. Va. —. He served in Capt. Francis Willis's Company in Col. Grayson's Regiment. He was slain at Brandywine. His widow was Margaret Hambleton. There were five small children. She was granted support 10 Sep. 1781 in Loudoun County. She sought relief on 10 Dec. 1777. She was put on the pension list at the rate of £8 per annum on 15 Nov. 1787. He also appeared as David Hamilton.

Hambleton, John. Va. Capt. His orphan, Patty Hambleton, aged 12, was in King William County on 5 Feb. 1791. Her guardian was her step-father, Bennett Tuck, who had married the widow of the veteran. He was probably the John Hambleton who was awarded a £30 gratuity on 21 May 1778.

Hambleton, John. Va. —. He was a soldier in the 15th Virginia Regiment. His health was much impaired, and he was unable to labor. He was granted £30 on 23 May 1778.

Hambleton, William. S.C. —. On 1 Nov. 1823 John Brown of Chester District stated he was confined in prison in the same mess with him and that Hambleton had been wounded in the war.

Hambright, John. N.C. Capt. He served in the light horse and was elected captain at the age of eighteen in the fall of 1779 from Lincoln County for a year. He was at King's Mountain. He elected to serve again for three years. At the time of Tarleton's defeat by Gen. Morgan at Cowpens, he was en route to join Gen. Morgan when news was received of the defeat of the British. He followed the British and took several prisoners. He served eighteen months and died in 1830. Congress granted his widow, Nancy Hambright, a pension 12 Aug;. 1842.

Hamerick, Henry. Pa. —. He was from Philadelphia County.

Hamil, Hugh. Pa. —. He was from Westmoreland County 1 Apr. 1825 when he received assistance. He served in the 8th Regiment. He also appeared as Hugh Hammill.

Hamilton, —. Pa. —. His widow, Catharine Hamilton, was awarded a $40 gratuity and a $40 annuity in Dauphin County 3 Apr. 1837. She died 22 May 1840.

Hamilton, —. Pa. —. His widow, Deborah Hamilton, was awarded a $40 gratuity and a $40 annuity in Huntingdon Co., Pa. 8 Apr. 1826.

Hamilton, Alexander. N.Y. Col. He was in Congress when the resolution passed granting half-pay to officers. He relinquished his claim to avoid any conflict of interest. He was promoted to the rank of colonel by brevet on 28 Oct. 1783 so he served to the end of the war. His widow, Elizabeth Hamilton, was denied his commutation pay 11 Jan. 1810. She did receive his five years' full pay 29 Apr. 1816.

Hamilton, Barton. S.C. —. He served under Col. William Washington and was wounded in his right ankle by a ball at Camden. He had a large family of females. On 12 Nov. 1811 he sought to bring a few Negroes into the state to support him. He was from Barnwell District.

Hamilton, Daniel. Pa. —. He was awarded a $40 gratuity and a $40 annuity in Washington Co., Pa. 15 Apr. He was dead by Apr. 1837.

Hamilton, David. Va. —. He died at Brandywine. His widow, Margaret Hamilton, had her application rejected 10 Dec. 1777.

Hamilton, David. Va. —. He was killed in the service. His widow was granted support in Fauquier Co., Va. 8 Oct. 1781.

Hamilton, Eliakim. Mass. Corp. He served in the 5th Regiment and was from West Stockbridge. He was paid $50.

Hamilton, Eliphalet. —. —. His petition was rejected 7 May 1796.

Hamilton, James. S.C. Capt. In 1780 he was ordered to the frontier and was wounded in his left shoulder in action with the Cherokee. He lost the use of his hand. He was from Anderson District when he was pensioned 3 Dec. 1819. He was paid to 1831. His widow, Jane Hamilton, was paid in 1833 and 1834. They had two or three children at the time of the war.

Hamilton, James. Va. Pvt. He lived in Augusta County on 22 Mar. 1786 and was 30 years old. He served in the militia in Capt. Patrick Buchanan's Company in Col. Sampson Matthews' Regiment. He was wounded in the leg at the battle of Hot Water near Williamsburg in opposing Lord Cornwallis's army on 26 June 1781. He was put on the pension list on 13 Nov. 1786 at the rate of £10 per annum. He was on the 1813 pension list.

Hamilton, John. Pa.—. He was awarded $200 in Crawford Co., Pa. 15 Mar. 1826.

Hamilton, John. Va. —. His wife, Judith Hamilton, and children were granted support while he was in the service on 8 Sep. 1777 in Mecklenburg Co., Va.

Hamilton, John. Va. Lt. He served in the navy. His widow, Nancy Hamilton, was being pensioned 30 Dec. 1785.

Hamilton, John A. Md. Capt. His widow, Margaret Hamilton, was pensioned in Baltimore at the rate of half-pay of a captain 25 Feb. 1824.

Hamilton, Joseph. Mass. Sgt. He served in the 3rd Regiment and was from Belchertown. His widow,

Martha Hamilton, was paid $50.

Hamilton, Richard. Pa. —. He was awarded a $40 gratuity in Chester Co., Pa. 1 Mar. 1832.

Hamilton, Richard. Pa. —. He was awarded a $40 gratuity and a $40 annuity in Lancaster Co., Pa. 15 Apr. 1834.

Hamilton, Robert. Pa. —. He was awarded 200 acres of donation land 26 Mar. 1813.

Hamilton, Robert. Pa. —. He was paid $200 in Lycoming Co., Pa. 8 Feb. 1823.

Hamilton, Thomas. N.C. —. He served on land and sea. He was almost three score and ten years of age. He asked for the privilege of retailing spirituous liquors free from duty in 1818. His petition was postponed indefinitely.

Hamilton, Thomas. Pa. —. He was awarded a $40 gratuity and a $40 annuity in Dauphin Co., Pa. 6 Apr. 1833.

Hamilton, Thomas. S.C. —. He was from Pendleton District and was pensioned 7 Dec. 1824. He was last paid his annuity in 1834.

Hamilton, William. Pa. —. He served under Capt. Samuel McCune in the Flying Camp. He took sick at Fort Lee. He was from Indiana County.

Hamilton, William. Pa. —. He was pensioned 20 Mar. 1838 in Allegheny County and died 7 May 1849.

Hamilton, William. S.C. —. He died in hospital. His widow, Mary Hamilton, was awarded an annuity 10 Apr. 1786.

Hamilton, William. S.C. —. He entered the service in 1776 in the militia in the Snow Campaign. He was wounded in his leg by a bayonet from a British soldier before he could dismount his horse in action at the house of John Stevenson. He was in Col. Patton's Regiment. He was at Hanging Rock and was taken prisoner on 18 Aug. 1780 at the defeat on the Catawba River above the mouth of Fishing Creek. He was confined in a prison ship in Charleston harbor for nearly a year. He was removed to Jamestown, Va. where he was exchanged. John Walker and his son Thomas Walker were fellow prisoners. He was 72 years old and his wife was about 65 years old when he applied in Nov. 1823 in Chester District. They still had one son at home. He died 19 Aug. 1824. His widow, Elizabeth Hamilton, the mother of ten children, was from Chester District when she was pensioned 6 Dec. 1825 at the rate of $30 per annum. She was last paid in 1826.

Hamlen, Cornelius. Conn. Corp. He served in the 7th Regiment. He was in Col. Swift's Invalids. He was disabled by epileptic fits and internal bleeding in 1780. He resided in Washington, Conn. in 1792. He was transferred to the invalids 23 Oct. 1780.

Hamlet, Hezekiah. —. —. He served under Col. Wingate at Ticonderoga for five months. He was at Bennington and Saratoga under Capt. Clark. His record showed he served four months and twenty-five days so Congress rejected his petition 1 Apr. 1844. He was 87 years old.

Hamlin, Bezaleel. Mass. —. He served in the 6th Regiment and was from Boston. He was paid $20. He also appeared as Bezaleel Hamblen.

Hamlin, Reuben. Mass. —. He served in the 2nd Regiment and was paid $20.

Hamman, Staats. N.Y. Sgt. He served in Capt. Gabriel Requea's Company of Westchester County militia. He was wounded in his left leg. He lived in Westchester Co., N.Y. on 5 June 1787.

Hammer, George. Pa. —. He was pensioned in Lancaster County 18 Feb. 1839. He died 9 Nov. 1846.

Hammer, Jacob. Pa. —. He was awarded a $40 gratuity and a $40 annuity in Lancaster Co., Pa. 30 Jan. 1834. He was dead by Dec. 1838.

Hammer, Peter. Pa. —. He received a $40 gratuity and a $40 annuity in Fayette County in 1836.

Hammerick, Henry. Pa. —. He applied from Philadelphia County on 24 Apr. 1819. He enlisted in

1776 under Daniel Vinsant for one year at Philadelphia in the 5th Regiment and afterwards under Col. Ludwick Weldner in the German Regiment and was attached to Gen. Muhlenberg's Brigade. He served three years and was discharged by Capt. Jacob Burner. Sgt. Henry Moser and Corp. Philip Shrader proved his service. David Boggs and William Anhorn were mentioned as having served in the 4th Pa. Line under Col. Gurney. He was wounded in the left shoulder at Germantown. He was 82 years old.

Hammill, John. N.J. —. He was pensioned in Burlington County on 9 Mar. 1844 at the rate of $50 per annum.

Hammon, Peter. Mass. —. He served in the 4th Regiment and was from Westfield. He was paid $20 in 1804.

Hammond, —. —. —. His widow, Sarah Hammond, had her application for a pension rejected by Congress 27 Mar. 1846 because they were married subsequent to 1 Jan. 1794.

Hammond, —. Md. Pvt. His widow, Elizabeth Hammond, was pensioned at the rate of half-pay of a private in Frederick County on 5 Mar. 1844.

Hammond, David. Pa. 1st Lt. He was in Northumberland County 25 Aug. 1786. He was in the 1st Pa. Regiment under Capt. William Wilson. He was wounded in his right shoulder by a musket ball at the Block House at Bergen Neck in 1780. He was 33 years old.

Hammond, Elijah. Mass. —. He served in the 5th Regiment and was paid $20.

Hammond, Elisha. Mass. Lt. He served from 1 Jan. 1777 and was appointed ensign 10 May 1780. He was made a lieutenant 14 Oct. 1780 and served to May 1782. Due to severe indisposition he had to leave the army and did not rejoin. Congress granted him a pension 13 Mar. 1832.

Hammond, Martin. S.C. —. He was wounded at King's Mountain. He was granted an annuity 2 Sep. 1785. He was from Union District.

Hammond, Samuel. Va. & S.C. Col. He was engaged in several military expeditions and battles in Virginia until 1779 when he removed to S.C. where he fought at the battles of Savannah, Cowpens, King's Mountain, Guilford, Ninety-Six, and Eutaw. He served as captain, major, and colonel in the militia and never received any remuneration except a pension of $600 per annum under the act of 1832. He died in 1842. His children sought to be put on the same footing as the children of officers of the Continental Line and to be paid the amount their father would have been entitled to receive if he had been in the regular army. Congress rejected their request 17 Mar. 1858.

Hammonds, Staats. N.Y. Sgt. He served in Col. James Hammond's N.Y. Regiment. He was disabled by a musket ball in his left leg just below his knee in action near Sinksing. He was 39 years old in Aug. 1785. He was pensioned 8 June 1786. He was on the 1813 pension list and died in Westchester County 26 July 1820.

Hampstead, Stephen. Conn. Pvt. He was on the 1791 pension roll.

Hampston, William. Md. —. In 1834 his son was Nathan T. Hampston of Montgomery County.

Hampton, —. Va. —. Leah Hampton was granted £10 relief while her two sons were away in the service in Caroline Co., Va. 12 Nov. 1778. She was granted £24 in 11 Nov. 1779 and support again on 8 May 1781.

Hampton, Edward. S.C. Col. He was killed in action with the Tories near Fairforest. His reputed and acknowledged daughter, Mary Ellen Hampton, married John Cook of Georgia. She had inherited two slaves from her maternal grandfather, George Dawkins, in 1780 or 1781. They were Ellis and his sister Easter or Hester. Ellis was mistaken as a white Tory and accidentally killed by an American party of militia under Col. James Lyles. Ellis was valued between $500 and $600. John Cook sought compensation for his wife in 1815.

Hampton, Joel. —. —. He died 20 Aug. 1832. His widow, Hannah Hampton, sought a pension, but was rejected by Congress on 14 Mar. 1848. She was uncertain about his service and presented vague and inconclusive testimony.

Hampton, John. N.J. Ens. He served in the militia and lived in Middlesex County under Col. Webster. He was disabled in his hand. He was 45 years and was on the 1791 and the 1813 pension lists. His pension was $6 per month from 17 Feb. 1808. He died 30 Aug. 1822. His daughter was Mary Ann Wheaton.

Hampton, Preston. S.C. —. He was killed and his goods taken by the Indians in 1776. John Hampton was granted an annuity for the estate 27 Feb. 1778 from South Carolina. His widow, Eliza Hampton, was able to prove their marriage but not the service of her husband so Congress denied her a pension 21 July 1842.

Hamsher, Adam. Pa. —. He was awarded a $40 gratuity and a $40 annuity in Montgomery Co., Pa. 18 Feb. 1834.

Hamson, William. Pa. —. He was awarded a $40 gratuity and a $40 annuity in Lebanon County on 24 Mar. 1817. He died 4 Sep. 1820.

Hanar, Daniel. Pa. —. He was granted relief in Montgomery County 18 Mar. 1834.

Hancock, —. S.C. —. His widow was Isabella Hancock of Laurens District.

Hancock, Clement. S.C. —. He fell in defense of the state 18 Nov. 1781. His widow, Elizabeth Hancock, was granted an annuity 3 Feb. 1785. There were two children in 1791.

Hancock, Joseph John. S.C. —. He entered the service at the age of 16 and served under Col. Culp and Col. Hicks. He was 72 years old and his wife was nearly as old in 1826. He was pensioned from Chesterfield District on 25 Nov. 1830. He died in 1834. His widow was Elizabeth Hancock.

Hancock, Thomas. Mass. Corp. He served in the 4th Regiment and was from Braintree. He was paid $50.

Hand, Jeremiah. N.J. —. He was pensioned in Cape May County on 27 Jan. 1844 at the rate of $50 per annum.

Hand, Jonathan. N.J. —. He was pensioned in Cumberland County on 4 Mar. 1839 at the rate of $60 per annum.

Hand, Recompence. N.J. —. He was pensioned in Cape May County on 27 Jan. 1844 at the rate of $50 per annum.

Handlier, Stephen. —. —. He applied 11 Dec. 1828. He also appeared as Stephen Hanlia and Stephen Hanlier.

Handy, Gamaliel. Mass. Pvt. He was wounded in his breast and back with a bayonet in Aug. 1778 in Rhode Island. He lived in Mass. in 1795. He was in the militia. He was granted two-thirds of a pension 20 Apr. 1796. He was on the 1813 pension list. He died 28 July 1823 in Bristol Co.

Handy, George. Md. Capt. His widow, Elizabeth Handy, was pensioned in Somerset County at the rate of half-pay of a captain 9 Feb. 1821. Her arrearage of $54 was paid to her executrix, Anne G. Handy, 19 Feb. 1838.

Handy, Isaac. Md. Pvt. His widow, Priscilla Woolford, was pensioned at the rate of half-pay of a private in Somerset County on 28 Jan. 1838.

Handy, Joseph. Mass. Pvt. He served in the 1st Regiment under Col. Joseph Vose and Capt. Orange Stoddard. He was disabled by the loss of his right eye. He was 28 years old in 1787. He was from Lee and was paid $50 by the Commonwealth.

Handy, Levin. Md. Capt. His widow, Nancy Handy, was pensioned at the rate of half-pay of a captain

9 Feb. 1822 in Somerset County.

Hanefield, James. Va. —. He died in the service on 3 May 1779 at Fort Bennington. He served under Col. Elbert in Georgia. His widow, Agnes Hanefield, and five children, the eldest being a son aged 14, were granted support in Prince Edward County in Sep. 1779 and in Sep. 1784. *Vide* also James Harefield.

Haney, David. Pa. Pvt. He was on the 1813 pension list.

Haney, William. Md. Pvt. His widow, Susanna Haney, was paid at the rate of half-pay of a private in Baltimore 1 Apr. 1839.

Hanford, Ozias. Conn. Pvt. He served in Capt. Albert Chapman's Company in the 2nd Conn. Regiment under Col. Haman Swift. He was disabled at Germantown, Penn. by a musket ball in his right thigh. He lived in Bedford, Westchester Co., N.Y. on 21 Apr. 1789. He was 25 years old on 9 July 1787. He was a shoemaker. He also appeared as Ozias Handford. He died in Jan.1806. He was on the 1813 pension list.

Haning, Christian. Pa. He was granted relief in Bedford County 27 Mar. 1830.

Haning, John. Pa. —. He was granted relief 18 Feb. 1839 and died 4 Feb. 1845 in Fayette County.

Hanisey, John. Pa. —. He applied from Franklin County on 24 Jan. 1815. He served in the Pa. Line and had an aged wife and infirm daughter.

Hankey, John. N.Y. Pvt. He was disabled by a rupture, piles, and other infirmities.

Hanley, Matthew. R.I. Pvt. He died 26 May 1804 in Providence Co., R.I.

Hanley, Russell. Mass. —. He served in the 2nd Regiment and was from Swanzey. He was paid $20.

Hanline, James. Va. —. His wife, Elizabeth Hanline, was granted 10 bushels of corn and 44 pounds of pork in Berkeley County on 16 Aug. 1780. She received 150 pounds of pork and 3 barrels of corn on 21 May 1782. He also appeared as James Handline.

Hanna, Robert. Pa. —. He was pensioned 17 Mar. 1814.

Hanna, Robert. Pa. —. He was granted relief in Westmoreland County 5 May 1841.

Hanna, Robert. S.C. —. He served in the expedition against the Indians under Capt. Leard [?] and Col. Killgore. He also served under Capt. William Harris and Col. Hays. He was at the siege of Ninety Six under Gen. Levi Casey. He was from Laurens District in 1826. He was paid his annuity in 1832.

Hanna, Robert. Va. —. His mother, Jeane Hanna, was granted support in Charlotte Co., Va. on 5 Oct. 1778, 2 barrels of corn and 200 pounds of bacon on 7 Dec. 1778, and 2 barrels of corn and 100 pounds of pork on 6 Mar. 1780.

Hanna, Thomas. S.C. —. He sought a pension 16 Dec. 1841. His application was rejected.

Hanna, Thomas. S.C. Lt. & Capt. He was pensioned under the act of 1832 at $320 per annum. He died in Mar. 1837. His widow, Catherine Hanna, never applied. They were married in Jan. 1794. She died 29 Oct. 1839. His son-in-law, A. J. Hindman, who married Jane H. Hanna, for all of the heirs applied for the arrears which would have been due their mother. Congress rejected their petition 18 May 1860.

Hannah, Archibald. Pa. Matross. He was in Philadelphia County on 13 Feb. 1786. He served in the 4th Regiment of Artillery. He was discharged from the Invalids on account of a wound received at the Block House at Bergen Neck, N.J. in the service. He was 29 years old.

Hannah, James. S.C. —. He entered the service at the age of 16 and served under Capt. Sadler and Col. Neil. He was in an engagement in York District where Capt. Hook was defeated. He was also at Hanging Rock, Rocky Mount, Sumter's defeat on Fishing Creek, Fishdam, and Blackstock. He acted as lieutenant at the latter two. He was in his 70th year. He was pensioned from York District on 4 Dec. 1832.

Hannah, John. Pa. —. He was granted relief.

Hannah, Robert. Pa. —. He resided in Jefferson County rather than in Venango as the act for him stated. The correction was made 20 May 1839. The war in which he served was not specified.

Hannon, —. Pa. —. His widow, Hannah Hannon, was awarded a $40 gratuity and a $40 annuity in Philadelphia Co., Pa. 6 Apr. 1830.

Hannon, Matthew. Pa. —. He was granted relief in Green County 1 Mar. 1832.

Hannon, Peter. Mass. —. He served in the 4th Regiment and was from Westfield. He was paid $20.

Hannon, William. Pa. Sgt. He applied 25 Sep. 1787 in Philadelphia. He was in the Pa. Artillery and was disabled by a wound in his thigh in the attack on the Block House on the North River under the command of General Wayne. He was under the care of Michael Dietrich, Mate in the General Hospital. He was 30 years old.

Hanoll, Thomas. Pa. —. He was dead by Sep. 1793.

Hans, James. Me. —. He died 6 Oct. 1825. His widow was Hannah Hans from Portland. She was paid $50 under the resolve of 1836.

Hanscom, John. Me. —. He died 27 Apr. 1827. His widow was Catherine Hanscom from Litchfield. She was paid $50 under the resolve of 1836.

Hanse, Isaac. Pa. —. He was awarded a $40 gratuity in Delaware Co., Pa. 6 Apr. 1830.

Hanse, Leonard. Pa. —. He was awarded a $40 gratuity and a $40 annuity in Northampton Co., Pa. 1 Apr. 1825.

Hansel, George. N.Y. Pvt.. He served in Klock's Regiment. He was pensioned 22 Sep. 1786. He lived in Onondaga County.

Hansel, George. Pa. Pvt. He served in Capt. Rudolph Bonner's Company in Col. Arthur St. Clair's Regiment. On the retreat from Canada he was injured in the lower part of his belly and ruptured by the crash of a batteau. On 7 May 1788 he was 67 years old. He was pensioned 22 Sep. 1786 in Ulster Co., N.Y. He was later in Onondaga Co., N.Y. He was on the 1813 pension list.

Hansen, Henry. N.Y. Lt. He served in Wemppell's Regiment and was killed 2 May 1780. His widow was granted a pension.

Hansford, Cary. —. Surgeon's Mate. Congress rejected the claim of his heirs for commutation 24 June 1834.

Hanshaw, Thomas. Ga. Pvt. He was on the roll in 1778. He served in the 2nd Regiment.

Hanson, —. —. —. His widow, Margaret Hanson, was put on the pension list 13 June 1853. She sought payment from the time of her husband's death, but Congress denied her claim 31 Mar. 1856.

Hanson, —. Va. —. His wife, M. J. Hanson, was granted £50 relief while her husband and her two sons were away in Continental service in Bedford Co., Va. on 28 June 1779.

Hanson, Henry. N.Y. Lt. He served under Col. Jacob Klock in the militia and was slain 2 May 1780. His widow received a half-pay pension.

Hanson, Isaac. Md. Lt. He was pensioned at the rate of half-pay of a lieutenant in Nov. 1785.

Hanspan, John Codlep. Md. Pvt. He was pensioned in Anne Arundel County at the rate of half-pay of a private 7 Feb. 1817.

Hantz, John. Pa. —. He was pensioned in Dauphin County 27 Mar. 1837.

Hany, John. R.I. Pvt. He was wounded in the ankle and groin in May 1780 and in July 1781; both of his heels were frost bitten in the Oswego Expedition in Feb. 1783. He served under Col. Jeremiah Olney. He was aged 59 in 1786. He also appeared as John Haney.

Harbison, David. Pa. —. He was awarded a $40 gratuity and a $40 annuity in Wilmington, Del. 15 Apr. 1834.

Harbison, James. S.C. —. He served under Capt. Samuel Adams and Col. Lacey. He was severely wounded by the British at Wright's Bluff and taken prisoner. Other officers he mentioned were Capt. John Nixon, Col. John Wilson, and Capt. McClure. He was awarded an annuity 12 Feb. 1785. He was from York District. He was paid the arrears of his annuity in the amount of $440 on 21 Dec. 1804. He was 64 years old and had an eleven year old son still at home in Chester District on 23 Nov. 1826. He was last paid his annuity in 1834.

Harbison, Patrick. S.C. —. He was pensioned 30 Nov. 1827.

Harbison, William. Pa. —. He was awarded a $40 gratuity and a $40 annuity in Butler Co. 28 Feb. 1822. He died 24 Oct. 1839.

Hardaway, Joel. S.C. Lt. He served in the 4th Regiment. He sought five years' full pay 4 Jan. 1838 but was rejected. There was no evidence of the commencement or termination of his service.

Hardchy, John. Pa. —. He was awarded a $40 gratuity and a $40 annuity in Philadelphia 14 Mar. 1818.

Hardee, Joseph. S.C. —. In 1776 he served under Capt. Armstrong and Col. Caswell. He was at Gates' defeat and Guilford. He was wounded in his leg on 8 Sep. and had it amputated at the knee on 28 Jan. following. He was from Horry District on 2 Dec. 1826. He was last paid an annuity in 1831. He also appeared as Joseph Hardy.

Harden, Francis. Va. —. The pensioner was dead by 16 Mar. 1786 in Sussex Co., Va. He also appeared as Francis Hardin and was marked dead in the 1785 pension roll.

Harden, Richard. Pa. Sgt. He served in the 10th Pa. Regiment. He was wounded by a shot in his left arm in 1777 at Germantown. He was mustered and wounded in Oct. 1777. He lived in Md. in 1794. He was on the 1813 pension list.

Harden, Peter. Pa. —. He was pensioned in Columbia County 3 Apr. 1837.

Hardenburgh, John L. N.Y. —. He was issued duplicate certificates of depreciation of pay 30 Mar. 1782. He had lost the originals.

Hardesty, Obediah. —. —. Congress rejected the petition from his heirs 13 Apr. 1860. They submitted no evidence.

Harding, Fielding. Va. Sgt. He was on the 1800 and 1813 pension lists.

Harding, Israel. —. —. He was at the battle of Eutaw and died about May 1824. His sons were Henry Harding, Israel Harding, and Nathaniel Harding in Beafort Co., N.C. in Nov. 1827.

Harding, John. Pa. —. He was awarded a $40 gratuity and a $40 annuity in Fayette County 28 Mar. 1836. He also appeared as John Hardin.

Harding, Robert. —. —. He employed a substitute to serve for him. Congress denied his heirs bounty land 2 Mar. 1839.

Harding, Robert. Md. Pvt. He was on the 1791 pension roll of Pennsylvania and had transferred from Maryland.

Harding, Samuel. —. —. He served from Feb. 1783 to Dec. 1783. He had been rejected because the war had terminated in Apr. 1783; yet, some troops were not disbanded until Nov. 1783. Congress granted him a pension 10 Jan. 1832.

Harding, Seth. —. Capt. He served in the navy and was pensioned at the rate of $360 per annum in 1808.

Hardy, Christopher. S.C. Lt. He was killed 18 Nov. 1781. His widow, Jane Hardy, was granted an annuity 3 Feb. 1785. There were three children in 1791.

Hardy, Joshua. Mass. Drummer. He served in Crane's Regiment and was from Boston. His widow,

Lucy Hardy, was paid $50.

Hardy, Joshua. Mass. Pvt. He served in the 1st Regim3nt and was paid $20. He was from Lee.

Hardy, William. Me. —. He was from Wilton. He was paid $50 under the resolve of 1836.

Harefield, James. Va. Pvt. His widow, Agnes Harefield, was granted assistance on 18 May 1778 and 20 Sep. 1779. He died in Continental service 3 May 1779 at Fort Barrington. He was under Col. Elbert in Georgia. She was on the 1785 pension list and was from Prince Edward Co. There were five children, the eldest of whom was 14. *Vide* also James Hanefield.

Harford, Peter. —. Sgt. He was pensioned 8 Mar. 1810. He was on the 1813 pension list of New York. He lived in Orange County.

Hargrave, Michael. Va. Pvt. His widow, Ann Hargrave, was granted £15.16.4 relief on 11 Mar. 1779. She lived in Southampton County 1 Jan. 1786. He served in the 4th Va. Regiment and died in the service. He also appeared as Michael Hargrove.

Hargus, John. Va. Ens. He served in the 13th Regiment and was discharged at the end of the war. He was pensioned in 1818. He stated he resigned at Pittsburgh in July 1778. He was 90 years old and sought half-pay for life or commutation pay. Congress rejected his claim 12 Apr. 1836.

Harker, Joseph. N.J. Capt. He served in the militia under Col. Hankinson. He was shot through his arm at Laxawaxon, Pa. 22 July 1779. He was on the 1791 pension roll. He was 48 years old. He was from Sussex County. He was on the 1813 pension list. He lived in New York later.

Harkins, —. Pa. —. His widow, Ellen Harkins, of Lancaster, Pa. war awarded a $40 gratuity and a $40 annuity 21 June 1839 for her husband's Revolutionary service.

Harleson, John. Pa. —.

Harlin, —. Pa. —. His widow, Elizabeth Harlin, was granted support in Mercer County 21 July 1842.

Harlin, Jonathan. Pa. —. He was granted relief in Mercer County 27 Mar. 1837.

Harlow, James. Mass. Bombardier. He served in Crane's Artillery and was from Plymouth. His widow, Hannah Bartlett, was paid $50.

Harlow, Lewis. Mass. —. He served in the 5th Regiment and was paid $20.

Harman, —. Pa. —. His widow, Elizabeth Harman, was awarded a $40 gratuity and a $40 annuity in Columbia County 24 Mar. 1837. She died 10 June 1841.

Harman, George. Pa. —. He was awarded a $40 gratuity in Northampton Co., Pa. 14 Apr. 1828. He also appeared as George Harmon.

Harman, John. Pa. —. He was awarded a $40 gratuity in Fayette Co., Pa. 4 Apr. 1831.

Harmanie, John. Pa. —. He was awarded a $40 gratuity in Franklin Co., Pa. 3 Mar. 1829. He also appeared as John Harmony.

Harmon, Christian. Pa. —. He served in the Pennsylvania Line.

Harmon, Lazarus. Md. Pvt. He was pensioned in Apr. 1792.

Harmon, William. Pa. Sgt. He served in the Artillery and was wounded in an attack on the Block House on the North River under Gen. Wayne. He was from Philadelphia County.

Harmontree, John. Va. —. His wife, Sarah Harmontree, was granted £7.10 support in Cumberland Co., Va. 25 Aug. 1777. He was dead by 24 Aug. 1778.

Harper, —. Pa.—. His widow, Eve Harper, received a $40 annuity in Washington County 13 Apr. 1854.

Harper, —. S.C. —. His widow was Alice Harper from Marlboro. There were children in 1791.

Harper, —. S.C. —. His widow was Mary Harper from Darlington. There was one child in 1791.

Harper, Alexander. N.Y. Capt. He served in the rangers on the frontier under Gen. Sullivan. He was taken prisoner by the Indian Chief Brandt and held until 1782. When he returned home, he found his property in ruins. He was paid from 7 Apr. 1780 to 28 Nov. 1782. Congress rejected the petition of the heirs for relief 12 Feb. 1855.

Harper, James. Va. Capt. Lt. His commutation was made 15 May 1791.

Harper, Jethro. N.C. Pvt. He was drafted and served for 18 months under Lt. Robert Bell and Col. Hogg in July 1782. He was under Col. Archibald Lytle, Capt. Bacotes, and Lt. John Ford in South Carolina. He applied in Halifax Co., N.C. in Aug. 1832 aged 66.

Harper, John. Va. —. He lived in Hampton, Va. when he was pensioned on 29 Dec. 1809 at the rate of $50 per annum. He served in the 1st Va. Regiment and was wounded in the thigh at Stony Point. He died in April 1817 in Elizabeth City Co., Va. Letters of administration were granted to James Gammell on 22 Jan. 1835.

Harper, Joseph. N.Y. Lt. He served under Col. John Harper in the militia. He was wounded in his left shoulder by a musket ball on 19 Oct. 1780. He lost the use of his left arm. Surgeon Peter Osborn and his father attended him. He was aged 43 on 12 Feb. 1787. He lived in Harpersfield, Montgomery Co., N.Y. on 6 May 1789. He died 17 May 1805.

Harper, Joseph. N.Y. Maj. He was on the 1786 pension list with the rank of lieutenant.

Harper, Lewis Lyttleton. S.C. —. He served under Col. Murphy after Gates' defeat in 1780. In 1781 he served six months in the Cheraw militia. Afterwards he was under Col. Harding in Marion's Brigade. He was at Eutaw Springs. Congress rejected his claim 8 May 1840.

Harper, Samuel. Md. Pvt. His widow, Elizabeth Harper, was pensioned at the rate of half-pay of a private 28 Feb. 1832.

Harper, Samuel. Pa. —. He was granted a $40 gratuity in Greene County 28 Mar. 1836.

Harper, William. Md. Pvt. He was pensioned at the rate of half-pay of a private 2 Jan. 1813. His widow, Bethula Harper, was pensioned at the same rate 18 Feb. 1846 in Dorchester County.

Harper, William. N.Y. —. He was granted relief.

Harper, William. N.C. —. He was born in Delaware 23 Nov. 1758 and at the age of 12 moved to N.C. He enlisted in 1775 at Hillsborough, N.C. under Capt. Tinnen, Col. Sexton, and Maj Sexton. They took 40 prisoners at Cross Creek. He served several other short tours. In 1780 he served six months in the rangers. When the British marched into his neighborhood after Gates' defeat, he joined Capt. Gwin's light horse at the battle of Guilford. He was credited with twelve months of service. He was from Anderson Co., S.C. 13 June 1837. Congress granted him a pension 8 Feb. 1842.

Harple, —. Pa. —. His widow, Mary Harple, was awarded a $40 gratuity and a $40 annuity in Philadelphia Co., Pa. 20 Feb. 1833. She was from Montgomery County. She died 4 Dec. 1843.

Harple, John. Pa. —. He was awarded a $40 gratuity and a $40 annuity in Montgomery Co., Pa. 25 Mar. 1831. He died 22 June 1832.

Harrall, Thomas. Pa. Pvt. He was disabled at West Point in 1779 on fatigue at Fort Constitution Island. Timber fell on him and broke the rim of his belly. He suffered from an ulcerated leg and a rupture. He was in the 5th Pa. Regiment.

Harrar, Daniel. Pa. —. He was awarded a $40 gratuity and a $40 annuity in Montgomery Co., Pa. 18 Mar. 1834.

Harrell, Elisha. S.C. —. He served under Gen. Caswell and Col. Jarvis. He was in Darlington District on 3 Nov. 1830. His petition for a pension was not granted.

Harrellson, Jeremiah. S.C. —. He was pensioned from Marion District 4 Dec. 1832.

Harrington, Ammi. Mass. —. He served in the 6th Regiment and was from Pepperill. He was paid $20.

Harrington, Asa. Mass. —. He was in the 5th Regiment and was from Uxbridge. He was paid $20.

Harrington, Charles. Va. —. He was away in Continental service. His wife, Ann Harrington, was allowed two barrels of corn valued at £70 and 100 pounds of pork valued at £120 for her support and that of her child in Augusta Co., Va. 19 Dec. 1780.

Harrington, Jacob. Pa. —. He died 15 Oct. 1817.

Harris, —. Pa. —. His widow, Eleanor Harris, was awarded a $40 gratuity and a $40 annuity in Cumberland Co., Pa. 14 Apr. 1834.

Harris, —. Va. —. His wife, Mary Harris, was granted £15 support while he was away in the service in Fauquier Co., Va. in May 1778 and £20 in Feb. 1779. She also appeared as Mary Harriss.

Harris, Arthur. Md. —. He was granted relief in 1786.

Harris, Benjamin. S.C. —. He served under Capt. Richard Taylor and Gen. Rutherford. He was at the battle of Guilford. He was 72 years old, afflicted with palsy, and nearly blind. He was pensioned from Anderson District 23 Nov. 1828. He was last paid in 1832. His widow, Karon Harris, was pensioned 4 Dec. 1832. She was last paid her annuity in 1834.

Harris, Burwell. N.C. —. His widow, Elizabeth Harris, applied in Warren County in 1826. He died in militia service. She received a $15 increase to her annuity of $75 in 1826. She was blind and without property.

Harris, Charles. Va. —. He was wounded on the Shawnee Expedition and was paid 17 May 1777.

Harris, Daniel. N.J. —. He was pensioned in Cumberland County 18 Feb. 1841 at the rate of $60 per annum.

Harris, Daniel. Va. —. His wife, Elizabeth Harris, was granted £18 support in Berkeley County on 16 Mar. 1779. He was away in Continental service.

Harris, David. S.C. —. He was paid the arrearage of his pension in the amount of $107.50 on 18 Dec. 1810.

Harris, Drury. S.C. —. He served in the 3rd Regiment under Col. William Thompson. He was wounded by a bayonet in the arm and a shot in his thigh at the battle of Savannah. An officer was Capt. George Little. His sergeant was John Davis who was living in Anson Co., N.C. when he attested to his service. Richard Brown, formerly his captain, and fellow soldier, Benjamin Carter, did likewise. He was from Richland District when he was pensioned 11 Dec. 1817 at the rate of $60 per annum for life with £5 sterling arrearage for five years. He moved to Alabama. He was last paid his annuity in 1834.

Harris, Ezekiel. —. —. His widow was Elizabeth Harris. She stated that he served in 1781 under Capt. Vermillea and Col. Thomas in 1781 and 1782. The records indicated that Col. Thomas went out of the service in 1780. Vermillea was not a captain until 1786. He was a cornet and a lieutenant in the war. His rolls do not bear the name of Harris. He did command a company of militia in Westchester Co., N.Y. Congress postponed action 17 Feb. 1843.

Harris, James. Pa. Drummer. He was dead by Mar. 1794.

Harris, James. Pa. —. He was granted a pension by the Court of Inquiry in 1813.

Harris, John. —. Capt. He served to the close of the war. Congress rejected the claim of the heirs on 30 Dec. 1833 for five years' full pay instead of half-pay for life.

Harris, John. Conn. 1st Lt. He served in the 2nd Connecticut Regiment. He was killed in action 7 Dec. 1777 at White Marsh, Pennsylvania. His widow died shortly thereafter. His orphans, Josiah Harris, John Harris, and Polly Lee the wife of Stephen Lee, sought his seven years' half-pay in 1790. His children were paid $1,120.

Harris, John. Me. —. He was from Litchfield. He was paid $50 under the resolve of 1836.

Harris, John. Pa. —. He was awarded a $40 gratuity and a $40 annuity in Lancaster County on 26

Mar. 1813.

Harris, John. Pa. —. He applied from Northumberland County on 17 May 1813.

Harris, John. Pa. —. He was from Lancaster County and was pensioned 26 Mar. 1816.

Harris, John. Pa. Drummer. He was granted relief.

Harris, Joseph. Mass. Sgt. He served under Capt. Stephen Pearl [?] and Col. Woodbridge. He was wounded in his left leg in 1775. Sickness settled in both of his legs, and he was discharged unfit for duty due to lameness in 1776. He married a sister of Increase Bennet in Oct. 1773. He was nearly 39 years old in 1788. He lived in Columbia Co., N.Y. on 25 June 1788. He was on the 1813 pension list.

Harris, Joseph. Pa. Sgt. He was pensioned 19 May 1813. He died 25 Oct. 1815.

Harris, Luda. Mass. Pvt. He served in the 4th Regiment and was from Newton. His widow, Elizabeth Harris, was paid $50.

Harris, Moses. N.Y. —. He was awarded 200 acres bounty land 5 Apr. 1810.

Harris, Nathaniel. Va. —. His application was rejected 22 Oct. 1787.

Harris, Peter. S.C. —. He was from York District and was pensioned 12 Dec. 1822 at the rate of $60 per annum. He received one year arrearage. He was a Catawba Indian warrior and his pension was to be paid to the agent of the Catawba Nation. "The strength of his arm decays, his feet fall in the chase, and the hand, which fought for the liberties of the country, is now open for relief." He served under Col. Thompson. He died 6 Dec. 1823.

Harris, Richard. Mass. Matross. He served in Capt. Phillips's Company under Col. Thomas Croaft. He lost his arm by an accident of a cannon going off when it was loaded. He was pensioned at the rate of half-pay from 9 May 1780 when his pay ceased on 18 Apr. 1781.

Harris, Richard. Md. —. He was granted depreciation pay of £77.6. ½ in 1797. He had not applied previously because he had lived outside of the state.

Harris, Robert. N.C. Pvt. He served in the Mecklenburg County militia. His right hand was cut off at the wrist joint, and his right arm was nearly half cut off. He received several strokes of a sword on his head in Mar. 1781 at Guilford. He resided in Cabarrus Co., N.C. in 1796. He was granted a full pension 20 Apr. 1796. He died 16 Mar. 1804.

Harris, Robert. Pa. Lt. He was in Philadelphia County 12 Dec. 1785. He served on the sloop of war, *Reprisal*, commanded by Lambert Weeks and was wounded in an engagement with the packet, the *Swallow*, on 5 Feb. 1777 and lost his left arm by an accidental explosion of his own gun. He lived in New York City, N.Y. in 1787 and was 54 years old. He died in 1805.

Harris, Robert. Va. —. His four youngest children were granted £15 for their maintenance in Chesterfield Co., Va. on 4 Apr. 1777 while he was away in the service.

Harris, Samuel. Md. Matross. He was pensioned in Montgomery County on 26 Oct. 1810. He was on the 1813 pension list. He died 19 Sep. 1826.

Harris, Solomon. Md. Pvt. He was pensioned at the rate of half-pay of a private in Dorchester County on 2 Jan. 1813.

Harris, Stephen. Mass. —. He served in the 8th Regiment. He was paid $20.

Harris, Thomas. Ga. Capt. He served in the artillery. He died of smallpox in Matthews Co., Va. in 1781. Congress paid his heirs half-pay 30 Jan. 1855.

Harris, Thomas. N.J. Pvt. He under Col. Potter in the Cumberland County militia and was wounded through his arm. He was 28 years old and was from Hopewell. He was on the 1791 pension roll at the rate of $40 per annum.

Harris, Thomas. N.C. Maj. He was on the 1813 pension list. He died 31 Aug. 1826. He lived in Iredell

County.

Harris, Thomas. Va. Armorer. He lived in Fluvanna County on 6 Dec. 1793. He received several wounds in defending the armory at Williamsburg in a mutiny of American soldiers and then acted as armorer. He was pensioned at the rate of £12 per annum and received the same amount for relief on 2 Dec. 1793. His pension was increased from $40 to $100 per annum on 24 Feb. 1818. His son was Lewis Harris. Probate was granted to his executors, Elizabeth Harris, his daughter, and Eleanor Humphrey, 26 Oct. 1818 in Fluvanna County.

Harris, William, 3rd . Mass. —. He was in the 1st Regiment and was from Leyden. He was paid $20.

Harris, William. Pa. Pvt. He was in Philadelphia County on 10 Apr. 1786. He was wounded at Stoney Point in his body, leg, and arm. He was 51 years old. He died 1 Oct. 1786.

Harrison, Archibald. Pa. —. He was from Philadelphia County.

Harrison, Benjamin. Va. Capt. He was commissioned a captain in the Virginia Line on Continental Establishment 16 Dec. 1776. He equipped a company of men principally at his own expense. He was at the surrender of Cornwallis and was disbanded at New York in 1783. He was from Fauquier County not far from Prince William County. He died in 1798. His heirs received Virginia land warrant #6016 for 4,000 acres on 20 Sep. 1812. Congress refused to grant his heirs either commutation or federal bounty land 9 Feb. 1849. His son, Russell B. Harrison, married Mary Eliza Wagoner. She died in 1849 Their children were William B. Harrison, Mary F. E. Harrison who married William F. Purcell, Margaret P. Harrison who married Bertrand E. Hays, and Julia Harrison who married Thomas J. Murray.

Harrison, Higgins. N.J. —. He was pensioned in Hunterdon County on 12 Dec. 1823 at the rate of $40 per annum. He served in Capt. Job Houghton's Company of militia and was wounded.

Harrison, John P. —. Capt. He became supernumerary 27 Oct. 1780 and sought his five years' full pay. It was granted to his heirs 29 May 1838.

Harrison, Kinsey. Md. Pvt. He was pensioned at the rate of half-pay of a private in Anne Arundel Co. on 22 Jan. 1816.

Harrison, Pate. Va. He died in the service. There were two children 20 July 1778. His son, Edward Harrison, received support 15 Feb. 1779. Richard Harrison was paid for maintaining a child of the solider 21 Feb. 1780 in York County. He also appeared as Pate Harris. His widow was Mary Wade.

Harrison, Robert Hanson. Md. Aide-de-Camp & Lt. Col. He entered the service in Oct. 1775 and served as aide-de-camp to Gen. Washington. Due to ill health he retired on furlough in 1781 and died in Mar. 1790. His wife had died two years before. He had been appointed a justice of the Supreme Court. His daughters, Sarah Easton and Dorothy Storer, were to receive his bounty land and depreciation pay from Virginia in the same manner as did Lt. Col. Richard Kidder on 9 Feb. 1814. His two daughters received his five years' full pay and land warrant for 20 acres on 29 May 1830. His two daughters received his half-pay at the rate of an aide-de-camp to General George Washington in Maryland 11 Mar. 1840. The amount in Maryland precluded them from making any claim for bounty land in that state.

Harrison, William. Md. Lt. He served from Jan. 1776 as 1st Lt. under Capt. Edward Veazey and Col. William Smallwood. When Veazey was killed in the battle of Long Island, Harrison became captain by appointment. He was not commissioned by Congress. He died from wounds in 1777. His nephews and nieces, Samuel T. Harrison, Charlotte A. Meredith, Jane Harrison, and Washington Harrison of Queen Anne Co., Md. sought his commutation pay. Congress denied their claim 1 Aug. 1850. There was no evidence that he had been commissioned by Congress.

Harrison, William. Pa. Maj. His widow, Sarah Springer, was in Fayette County on 17 Mar. 1794. His daughter was Mary Harrison. He went out under Col. William Crawford in 1782 against the Indians at the Sandusky towns. He was killed in June 1782 and left a widow and five children. The oldest was 10 ½ and the youngest was 9 months. His widow married secondly ------ Springer who was the guardian of Mary Harrison, the only child under the age of 14.

Harrod, Noah. Mass. —. He served under Capt. George Webb and Col. Shephard in 1782, 1783, and 1784. He was pensioned in 1818 and died in 1820. His widow, Eusebia Howard, was pensioned in 1836. His daughter, Hannah Newell Barrett, was about 96 years of age and seriously crippled as a result of a fall. Congress granted her a pension of $12 per month 22 May 1896. He also appeared as Noah Harwood.

Harroff, Ludwig. Pa. —. He was awarded a $40 gratuity and a $40 annuity in Lancaster Co., Pa. 6 Apr. 1833.

Harron, David. Pa. —. He was granted relief.

Harrup, —. Va. —. He served in the 15th Virginia Regiment in Capt. Mason's Company. He died at Brandywine. His widow, Elizabeth Harrup, had two sons in the service and three small children at home. She was awarded a £30 gratuity in Brunswick Co., Va. 4 Nov. 1778.

Harrup, Joseph. Conn. Pvt. He served in the 2nd Conn. Regiment in Capt. Mills' Company having enlisted 7 Dec. 1778. He was wounded in his leg by a musket ball. He served to the end of the war. He was pensioned 25 Nov. 1788. His rate was $5 per month from 15 Sep. 1807. He lived in Stratford, Conn. He was on the 1813 pension list. He died 7 Aug. 1820. He also appeared as Joseph Harrop.

Hart, —. —. —. His widow, Sally Hart, had her petition for a petition rejected by Congress because she had married the veteran in 1797.

Hart, —. Va. —. His widow, Lucy Hart, was pensioned 6 Aug. 1778.

Hart, —. Pa. —. His widow, Magdalena Hart, was awarded a $40 gratuity and a $40 annuity in Tioga Co., Pa. 14 Apr. 1834.

Hart, Adam. Pa. —. He was awarded a $40 gratuity and a $40 annuity in Lancaster, Pa. on 29 Mar. 1824.

Hart, Asher. N.J. —. He was pensioned in Mercer County 14 Feb. 1846 at the rate of $60 per annum.

Hart, Barnabas. Pa. —. He received a $40 gratuity and a $40 annuity in Lancaster County 21 Feb. 1838.

Hart, Daniel. —. —. Congress rejected the claim of his heirs 25 July 1850 because it was not covered by any legislation.

Hart, George. Pa. —. He applied from Tioga County on 28 May 1813. He served seven or eight years. He was gone about five years, returned home on furlough, tarried a few days, and then returned for another two and a half years according to the testimony of his brother, Aaron Hart. He was paid to 28 Feb. 1833.

Hart, Henry. N.Y. Pvt. He served in the Montgomery County militia under Col. Klock and was slain 20 Apr. 1776. His widow, Mary Christina Hart, received his half-pay pension for seven years.

Hart, Jacob. S.C. —. He was killed in Nov. or 1 Dec. 1781. His widow, Ann Hart, was allowed an annuity 13 Aug. 1785. She was from Chester.

Hart, John. —. —. His widow, Hannah Hart, married Jonathan Wightman. Hannah Wightman failed to provide sufficient proof so Congress rejected her prayer for relief 29 Feb. 1848.

Hart, John. —. —. By act of the Kentucky legislature of 22 Dec. 1831 John Hart, an aged and infirm solider in indigent circumstances, who had settled on a tract of poor vacant land supposedly containing 150 acres, the Register of the Land Office was authorized to issue a warrant without charge. Upon a survey being returned, a patent was to be issued. The veteran had only a daughter living with him.

Hart, John. Mass. Surgeon. He received warrant #937 for 400 acres on 23 Apr. 1797. It was never located so Congress authorized a duplicate to be issued to Thaddeus Spalding, one of the executors, on 10 Apr. 1844.

Hart, Joseph. Conn. Pvt. He was on the 1791 pension roll.

Hart, Patrick. N.J. Pvt. He was on the 1813 pension list. He later removed to Philadelphia Co., Pa.

Hart, Robert. Va. Drum Major. He served in Col. Harrison's Artillery in the 1ˢᵗ Va. Regiment. He lost the sight of his left eye by a cartridge taking fire. He lived in Chesterfield Co., Va. in 1794. He was on the 1813 pension list.

Hart, Samuel. Conn. Lt. He served in Col. Cook's Regiment. He was wounded in his right breast by a musket ball which came out near the shoulder blade on 18 Sep. 1777. He resided in Durham, Conn. in 1794. He died 13 Jan. 1805.

Hart, Thomas. Va. —. His widow, Lucy Hart, was granted £12 support in Middlesex Co., Va. on 28 June 1779. She had two children on 22 Feb. 1779.

Hartchy, —. Pa. —. His widow, Catharine Hartchy, was awarded relief in Philadelphia County 6 Apr. 1833.

Hartman, — Pa. —. His widow, Margaret Hartman was awarded a $40 gratuity and a $40 annuity in Lancaster County 3 Apr. 1837. She died 2 Jan. 1843.

Hartman, Adam. N.Y. Pvt. He served in Capt. Marcus Demoth's Company under Col. Lewis Dubois. He was wounded through the joint of his shoulder in Oct. 1780 at Fort Dayton at German Flatts. He lived at Kingsland, Montgomery Co., N.Y. 10 July 1789. He also appeared as Adam Hardman. He was on the 1813 pension list.

Hartman, Adam. Pa. —. He was awarded a $40 gratuity and a $40 annuity in Franklin Co., Pa. 5 Apr. 1826. He was 77 years old in 1840.

Hartman, Jacob. Pa. Pvt. He was in Philadelphia County 13 Feb. 1786. He served in the 11ᵗʰ Pa. Regiment. He was wounded in the leg above the knee at Brandywine in 1777 and was disabled. He was 35 years old. His wife was Mary Hartman. He was on the 1813 pension list.

Hartman, John. Pa. —. His widow, Magdalena Hartman, received a $40 gratuity and a $40 annuity in Adams County 30 Apr. 1855.

Hartman, Michael. Pa. —. He was awarded a $40 gratuity in Berks Co., Pa. 11 June 1832.

Hartman, Philip. Pa. —. He entered the service at Reading, Pa. in the latter part of 1779 or the beginning of 1780 as a drafted militiaman under Capt. Strough. He was discharged two months later. His next tour was for six months under Capt. Hill. His third tour was for twenty days. In the spring of 1781 he was in the artillery under Capt. Feisch at Reading. He joined in with the French artillery in New Jersey and went to Williamsburg, and Yorktown. He was stricken from the pension roll. Congress accepted the first year of his service and granted him a pension 5 Mar. 1840. He was from Rockingham County, Va.

Hartney, Patrick. Pa. Pvt. He was on the 1813 pension list. He died 9 Nov. 1819 in Philadelphia County.

Harton, Howell. N.C. Pvt. He applied in Warren County in 1801. He was disabled in militia duty by a wound in his right leg. He had a wife and nine children and was a planter. He had 112 ½ acres of poor land. He was on the 1813 pension list. He also appeared as Howell Hathorn.

Hartraulft, Abraham. Pa. —. He was awarded a $40 gratuity in Montgomery Co., Pa. 4 May 1832.

Hartrauft, Leonard. Pa. —. He was awarded a $40 gratuity and a $40 annuity in Montgomery Co., Pa. 15 Apr. 1835. He died 28 Aug. 1842.

Hartshog, Valentine. Pa. Pvt. He was in Philadelphia County 19 Dec. 1785. He served in the 5th Pa. Regiment and was wounded at Green Springs, Va. 7 July 1781. He was 42 years old.

Hartshill, Peter. Pa. Pvt. He was on the 1813 pension list. He lived in Philadelphia County.

Hartshorn, John. Md. Lt. His widow, Nancy Williams, was pensioned at the rate of half-pay of a lieutenant 13 Feb. 1836.

Hartwell, —. Va. —. His wife, Mary Hartwell, was granted support in Prince Edward County in July 1779 while he was away in Continental service.

Hartwell, Oliver. Me. —. He was from Stetson. He was paid $50 under the resolve of 1836.

Hartwick, Neilley. Va. —. His wife was granted support in Pittsylvania Co., Va. 16 Nov. 1779.

Harvey, Benjamin. —. —. He died before the end of the war. Congress denied the claim of the heirs for bounty land on 2 Mar. 1839.

Harvey, John. Pa. —. His surviving heirs, George Harvey, Joseph Harvey, William Harvey, and Jane Rankin, were paid $200 in lieu of his donation land 18 Apr. 1843.

Harvey, Samuel. Pa. Pvt. He was in Philadelphia County 12 Dec. 1785. He was in the Invalids and was discharged 14 Dec. 1782 unfit for duty due to his arm being withered and sickness. He was 35 years old.

Harvey, Thomas. —. Soldier & Wagonmaster. He served longer than twelve months in 1780 and 1781. The evidence did not support his claim so Congress rejected his claim 12 Feb. 1846.

Harvey, Zadoc. Md. Pvt. He was pensioned in Dorchester County at the rate of half-pay of a private 6 Jan. 1812.

Harvy, Robert. —. —. He was in Rutherford Co., N.C. in Sep. 1832. He was 75 years old.

Harwood, Benjamin. —. —. He was pensioned.

Harwood, Jonathan. Mass. —. He was in the 5th Regiment and was from Danvers. His widow, Thankful Harwood, was paid $50.

Harwood, Joseph. S.C. —. Hid widow, Mary Harwood, was awarded an annuity for her two children 29 July 1791.

Hascall, Jonathan. N.Y. Pvt. He served under Col. McClaghry in the Ulster County militia and was slain 22 July 1779. His widow, Anna Hascall, received a half-pay pension for seven years.

Hase, William. S.C. —. There were children in 1791.

Haskell, Andrew. Mass. —. His widow, Lois Haskell, was paid $50.

Haskell, Josiah. Me. —. He was from Thomaston. He was paid $50 under the resolve of 1836.

Haskell, Stephen. Me. —. He died 3 Dec. 1830 in Levant. His widow was Rebecca Haskell from Topsham. She was paid $50 under the resolve of 1836.

Haskell, William. Me. —. He died 15 Sep. 1827. His widow was Rhoda Haskell from China. She was paid $50 under the resolve of 1836.

Haskew, John. S.C. —. He applied and received a federal pension 11 Mar. 1833. He sought a supplemental pension from Marlboro District 12 Oct. 1837. His application was rejected.

Haskins, Benjamin. Pvt. Conn. & Mass. He served as a private under Capt. Hubbell and Col. Charles Webb from 12 July to 19 Dec. 1775; as a private under Capt. Jabez Cottle and Col. Ebenezer Sproat in the Massachusetts militia for 15 days and 1 day for travel for 35 miles; as a private under Capt. Joseph Parker and Col. Sproat from 1 Jan. 1778 for three months; as a private under Capt. Barnabas Doty and Col. Sproat from 5 Sep. 1778 for 6 days on the Dartmouth alarm; as a private in Capt. Job Pierce and Col. Theophilus Cotton for 14 days in Oct. 1778; and as a private under Capt. Joseph Norton and Col. John Hathaway for 4 days from 4 Aug. 1780. He resided at Rochester, Mass. and in 1775 went to Conn. to work on a farm where he enlisted. He applied under the act of 1832, but his mind was so afflicted that he was unable to make known his service satisfactorily. He died 18 Aug. 1834 in Candor, N.Y. His widow, Mary Haskins, whom he married 15 Dec. 1781 in Rochester, Mass., applied under the act of 1838. Her application was rejected for insufficient evidence. She died 8 Sep. 1859 and devised her claim to her daughter, Mrs. Friend Barron, with whom she lived her last sixteen years. Her daughter received her mother's pension from 4 Mar. 1831 to 8 Sep. 1859 from Congress at the rate of $30 per annum 25 May 1860.

Haskins, William. Mass. —. Pvt. He was in the 5th Regiment and was from New Salem. His widow, Joanna Eddy, was paid $50.

Hasock, David. Pa. —. He was pensioned.

Hassen, Barney. Pa. —. He was pensioned 14 Feb. 1814 by the Court of Enquiry.

Hassler, Stephen. Pa. —. He was awarded a $40 gratuity and a $40 annuity in Lancaster Co., Pa. 5 Apr. 1826. He died 7 Apr.1833.

Hasson, Barney. Pa. —. He enlisted in 1776 under Capt. H. McKinley and Col. William Cook. His unit was destroyed at Monmouth, and he was drafted into Capt. James Christie's Company under Col. Thomas Craig. After he was discharged, he entered the naval service, was taken prisoner, and carried to Halifax. He was from Centre County. He was in the 12th Regiment.

Hastings, Theophilus. Mass. Pvt. He served in the 7th Regiment and was from Hardwick. He was paid $50.

Hastings, William. N.H. Pvt. He was from Amherst. He served under Lt. Col. Stephen Peabody in the militia and was wounded in the leg on 29 Aug. 1778 by a cannon ball in Rhode Island. He was aged 30 in 1787. His pension rate was $5 per month from 11 Feb. 1807. He was on the 1813 pension list. He died 20 Apr. 1832.

Hatch, Asa. Me. —. He died 25 Dec. 1798 in Gorham. His widow was Jane Hatch from Westbrook. She was paid $50 under the resolve of 1836.

Hatch, Joseph. Mass. —. He was paid $20.

Hatch, Lewis. Mass. —. He served sixteen months but could only document four months and twenty days. Congress rejected his claim for a pension 14 Jan. 1837. He was from Granville, Washington Co., N.Y. and was 71 years old when he proved four months and twenty days of service. Congress granted him a pension of $20 per annum 25 Jan. 1838 for six months of service.

Hatch, Robert. S.C. —. He served in the Revolutionary War. Afterwards he was employed for several years in the West Indian trade. He volunteered as pilot and sailing master on the U.S. *Alligator* during the War of 1812. He was wounded below the temple and lost both eyes in action with the British near the mouth of Stono River. He remained on deck cheering and encouraging his comrades and died six days later on 14 Feb. 1814. He left a widow and several children. His widow was Mary M. Hatch, upwards of 80 years, applied for a pension from Charleston on 27 Nov. 1845. She was last paid in 1851.

Hatcher, Benjamin. S.C. Capt. He was killed in the service. His widow, Lucy Hatcher, was granted an annuity 25 Apr. 1785.

Hatcher, Jeremiah. S.C. —. He lost his leg in the service. He was granted an annuity 16 Feb. 1785. He was from Edgefield.

Hatcher, William. Va. —. He was in the naval service and died about Mar. 1776. He left a widow and two children in Lancaster County 20 Apr. 1780. She was Hannah Hatcher in 1786.

Hatfield, Samuel. S.C. Sgt. He served under Lt. Robert Miscampbell and was killed in the service. His sister, Mary Darnald, a widow with small children, sought any benefits due her 16 Aug. 1784.

Hathaway, Benoni. N.J. Capt. He served in the New Jersey militia. He lived in Morris Co., N.J. He was on the 1813 pension list.

Hathaway, Job. Mass. —. He served in the 4th Regiment. He was paid $20.

Hathaway, Joseph. N.J. Matross. He served under Capt. Lt. John Doughty in the Artillery under Capt. Daniel Neil. About Aug. 1776 he was seized with a dysentery and died. He married Sarah Lyon 15 Nov. 1753. Sarah Hathaway received a half-pay pension in Morris County in 1784. She died 3 Feb. 1793. His legatees sought her arrearage in Morris County 19 Mar. 1793.

Hathaway, Shadrack. N.J. Sgt. He enlisted 23 Nov. 1776 in the 4th Regiment under Capt. Noadiah Wait and Col. Ephraim Martin. He was wounded at Germantown and died four days later. His widow was Martha Hathaway. She was granted a half-pay pension in Morris County in Mar. 1780.

Hathaway, Theophilus. N.J. Pvt. He served in 2nd Regiment and was wounded in his ankle at Springfield. He was 30 years old and was pensioned in 1786 in Morris County. He was on the 1813 pension list.

Hathers, Thomas. N.Y. Pvt..He was granted relief.

Hathorn, John. N.Y. —. He was disabled.

Hatman, Ludwick. Pa. —. He was from Westmoreland County in 1781.

Haton, —. Pa. —. His widow, Elizabeth Haton, was granted relief.

Hatrick, —. Pa. —. His widow, Ruth Hatrick, received a $50 gratuity 10 Mar. 1817.

Hatt, John. S.C. —. He served in the Continental Army. His widow, Sylvia Hatt, was allowed an annuity 13 Dec. 1786.

Hatton, John. Pa. —. He was pensioned 8 Mar. 1813 at the rate of $40 per annum.

Hatton, Samuel. Va. —. He was drafted as a militia man from Loudoun Co., Va. under Col. Christopher Greenup. He served three months and was discharged at Gloucester. His second tour was for three months. He served again and was discharged after the surrender of Cornwallis. Congress granted him a pension of $20 per annum 2 Jan. 1839. He was 101 years old in 1838.

Hatz, John. Pa. —. He was awarded a $40 gratuity and a $40 annuity in Lancaster Co., Pa. 16 Feb. 1835.

Haughpaugh, Philip. S.C. —. His application for a pension was not approved, but he was allowed $450 on 11 Dec. 1806.

Havart, John. N.Y. —. He was granted relief

Haven, Elias. Mass. —. He was from Wrentham and was paid $20.

Haven, James. Mass. —. He served in the 4th[?] Regiment and was paid $20.

Haven, John. Mass. Sgt. He was in the 3rd Regiment and was from Attleboro. He was paid $20.

Havens, Daniel. Vt. Pvt. He served two months in the spring of 1777 under Capt. Timothy Bush and Col. Joseph Marsh in the militia. In the summer of 1778 he served a month in scouting and took a British spy named Airs whom he delivered to Capt. Benjamin in Windsor. In 1779 he served a year under Capt. Elias Stearns. In 1780 he volunteered under Capt. Joseph Parkhurst and Col. Marsh. In July he pursued the Indians. In Oct. 1780 the Indians burned Royalton and destroyed his property. He was ordered into the service and served two months. Congress granted him a pension 25 Mar. 1836.

Haviland, Ebenezer. N.Y. Surgeon. He served under Col. Philip Van Cortland and died 21 June 1780. His widow, Tamar Haviland, received a half-pay pension for seven years.

Hawbrand, Thomas. Pa. —. He applied from Zanesville 23 Aug. 1819. He had previously lived in Bucks Co., Pa.

Hawes, Jabez. —. —. He served one month at Roxbury in 1775. He next enlisted in the artillery under Capt. Smith for eight months. He subsequently served four months under Capt. Whipple. He sought relief from Congress 3 Jan. 1832.

Hawes, Pelatiah. Mass. —. He was paid $20.

Hawgerdon, John. N.Y. Pvt. He served under Col. Vrooman. He was wounded by a musket ball in the left hip on 10 June 1780 near Delaware. He lived in Otsego Co., N.Y. in 1794.

Hawkey, Richard P.. N.Y. Sgt. He served in the 2nd N.Y. Regiment and was disabled. He was on the 1785 pension list.

Hawkins, Bartlett. Va. Pvt. He was aged 23 when he applied on 5 Dec. 1786. He served in the 3rd Regiment of Light Dragoons. He lived in Nelson County. He was pensioned at the rate of £5 per annum on 4 Nov. 1786. He was on the 1813 pension list.

Hawkins, Job. Mass. —. He was pensioned under the act of 1828 and paid from 1830 to 3 Mar. 1838 when he was stricken from the roll because he was listed on the muster roll as having deserted 26 May 1783. He was a musician. Congress ruled that since he had served three years and was not likely to have deserted three months after the peace that he merited a pension. Congress recommended him for a pension to include any portion which had been unpaid 19 Feb. 1846.

Hawkins, John. Va. Capt. He served in the 3rd Regiment. His heirs sought commutation of five years full pay as captain. He was an adjutant 28 Dec. 1776, a lieutenant 11 Sep. 1777, and on the rolls to Nov. 1779. Congress rejected the petition of the heirs because their claim was not sustained by the evidence on 23 Jan. 1832.

Hawkins, Joshua. Va. Pvt. He served in the 6th Virginia Regiment. He was wounded and taken prisoner, but the British did not attend to his wound. He had a broken leg. He was awarded a £30 gratuity on 15 Oct. 1778. He served in the Virginia Line. He removed to Spartanburgh District, S.C. He was on the 1813 pension list.

Hawkins, Moses. Va. Capt. He was killed at Germantown 4 Oct. 1777. His heirs were paid his seven years' half-pay of $1,680. His widow, Lucy Hawkins, married Thomas Coleman 26 June 1784. His children were William Hawkins, Moses Strother Hawkins, Sarah Hawkins, and Lucy Hawkins. They were being pensioned 2 Sep. 1784. On the 1785 pension roll it was noted that their pension had expired. His widow's application was rejected on 13 Nov. 1786 due to her remarriage..

Hawkins, Stephen. N.Y. —. He enlisted for six months in Washington Co., N.Y. under Capt. Adial Sherwood in the summer of 1780. He was taken prisoner at Fort Ann by Maj. Carleton, taken to Montreal, and confined in prison a year. Part of the time he was in irons. Congress granted him a pension 10 Jan. 1832.

Hawkley, James. N.H. Pvt. He served in Cilley's Regiment. He was pensioned 13 Sep. 1808 at the rate of $5 per month from 6 Jan. 1808. He died 27 June 1816 in Hillsborough Co., N.H. He was on the 1813 pension list.

Hawks, Henry. Mass. Pvt. He served under Col. M. Jackson in the 8th Regiment. He lost the use of his arms and one of his legs. He resided in Newton, Mass. in 1792. He enlisted 30 Apr. 1777 and was discharged 30 Apr. 1780.

Hawley, David. Conn. Maj. He was wounded in his shoulder by a musket ball on 8 July 1777 at Sasco

Hill at Fairfield at the time the British burned the town. He served under Col. Samuel Whiting in the 4th Brigade of the militia. He was pensioned 5 Dec. 1788 and lived at Stratford, Conn. He died in 1807.

Hawley, Nathan. Conn. Corp. & Pvt. He served under Col. Webb. He was wounded by a musket ball in his thigh in 1777 at White Marsh. He lived in Stratford, Conn. in 1795. He enlisted 28 Mar. 1777 for the war and was on the rolls in 1781. He was granted one-third of a pension 20 Apr. 1796. He was on the 1813 pension list.

Hawley, Nero. Conn. Pvt. He served in the 3rd Conn. Regiment. He was discharged 12 Apr. 1781 as an invalid. He was pensioned 2 Apr. 1788 as a resident of Stratford, Conn. and was aged 47 in 1789. He was on the 1813 pension list. He died 30 Jan. 1817 in Fairfield Co., Conn. He was a Negro.

Hawley, Talcott. Conn. Pvt. He served in Col. Heman Swift's Regiment. He was disabled by small pox and had a number of ulcers on his arms, shoulders, and neck. He was pensioned 1 May 1788 at Ridgefield. He died 11 Sep. 1807.

Hawman, —. Md. —. His widow was Elizabeth Hawman. Her arrearage of $10 was paid to her heirs, Philip Hawman and Frederick Hawman, 1 Mar. 1850.

Hawn, Samuel. Pa. —. He was granted a gratuity in Northumberland County 1 Apr. 1836.

Hawth, —. Va. —. Mary Hawth was granted support in Prince William County in 1778.

Hay, —. S.C. —. Sarah Hay was paid an annuity in 1830 for three years. She was last paid in 1832.

Hayburn, William. Pa. —. He applied in 1792.

Hayden, Peleg. Mass. Sgt. He was in the 6th Regiment and was from Scituate. He was paid $20.

Hayden, William. Mass. Matross. He served in Crane's Artillery and was from Boston. His widow, Elizabeth Hayden, was paid $50.

Hayes, John. S.C. —. His application was rejected in Dec. 1831.

Hayes, John. Va. —. He and his wife, Nancy Hayes, were pensioned on 6 Feb. 1808 at the rate of $40 per annum. She was dead by 9 Jan. 1810. They also appeared as John and Nancy Hays.

Haymore, Britain J. Va. He enlisted for two years in 1776 in Brunswick County under Capt. James Lucas and Col. Stephens in the 4th Regiment. He was discharged at Hanover, Va. He applied from Davidson Co., N.C. 28 Jan. 1824.

Haynes, Aaron. Mass. —. He served in the 6th Regiment and was from Sudbury. He was paid $20.

Haynes, Alexander. N.C. Pvt. He applied from York District, S.C. in 1802. He was wounded in his eye at Rocky Mount on the Wateree. John L. Davis served with him under General Sumter and Capt. Brownfield when he was wounded in July 1780. William Alexander saw him receive the wound. He had a small helpless family. He had once lived in Mecklenburg Co., N.C. He was on the 1813 pension list. He died 2 Feb. 1828.

Haynes, John. S.C. —. He was wounded in the knee. He was awarded an annuity 15 Oct. 1785.

Haynes, Jonathan. Vt. Pvt. He was wounded in the battle of Bennington 16 Aug. 1777 by a ball which passed through his breast. He served under Col. Moses Robinson and Capt. Samuel Robinson. For about two years afterwards he could not feed himself with his right hand. He lived in Middletown, Vt. in 1785 and 1794. He served in the militia. He was granted two-thirds of a pension 20 Apr. 1796. He was on the 1813 pension list. He died 18 May 1814. He also appeared as Jonathan Hayes.

Haynes, Joshua. N.H. Pvt. He served in Nixon's minute company. He was wounded by a musket ball in his right shoulder in Apr. 1775 at Lexington. He was granted half a pension 20 Apr. 1796. He lived at Washington.

Haynes, Reuben. Mass. Sgt. He was in the 6th Regiment and was from Gardiner. He was paid $50.

Haynie, —. Va. —. His widow, Sinah Haynie, was granted £8 support in Northumberland County 11 May 1778.

Haynie, William. —. —. He served three years: one as adjutant and two as a private, ensign, and lieutenant. He died 25 Aug. 1825. His widow died 10 Nov. 1843. Ann Haynie, sought the difference of the pension as a lieutenant and an adjutant. Congress allowed relief from 4 Mar. 1831 to the time of decease from $159 per annum to $380 per annum on 25 May 1860.

Hays, Daniel. Va. Pvt. He was in the 8th Virginia Regiment in Capt. Anthony Singleton's Company and died in the service. His widow, Ann Hays, was recommended for a £20 gratuity and a £25 annuity for three years on 24 Nov. 1777. There were six children the eldest of whom was not more than ten. She lived in James City County 15 May 1787. There were five children at a later date. She was continued on the pension list at the rate of £12 per annum on 1 Dec. 1787. She was 60 years old in 1789 and lived in New Kent County. Robert Hays was administrator of her estate on 7 Oct. 1795. He also appeared as Daniel Hayes.

Hays, Dudley. —. —. He was from Granby, Hartford Co., Conn. and was wounded at Stillwater by a shot through his groin which crippled him for life. His wife cared for him for 39 years. He married Beda ------ in 1805. Congress allowed her a pension based on 15 months of service on 30 Mar. 1860. He also appeared as Dudley Hayes.

Hays, George. Va. —. He served in the Western Battalion. In his absence his wife, Cassandra Hays, was granted financial support in Amherst Co., Va. in Aug. 1780, Feb. 1781, and June 1781. She had four children.

Hays, John. Md. Pvt. He was pensioned at the rate of half-pay of a private 9 Mar. 1836.

Hays, John H. Md. Pvt. He was pensioned at the rate of half-pay of a private in St. Mary's County 2 Feb. 1828. His arrearage was paid to Joseph F. Shaw for his widow, Theresa Hays, on 18 Jan. 1839 to the time of his death on 29 Sep. 1838 She was pensioned at the same rate 8 Mar. 1850.

Hays, Thomas. S.C. —. He received a $60 annuity in 1825. His petition for a pension was approved in Dec. 1826 but rejected in Dec. 1827. He was pensioned from Pendleton District 6 Dec. 1828. He died in Anderson in 1839. He was a well digger. His widow was Margaret Hays. On 7 Dec. 1840 she was to be paid the $60 due her late husband at the time of his death.

Hays, Thomas. S.C. —. He was pensioned 4 Dec. 1832.

Hayward, Barzilla. Mass. —. He was paid $20.

Hayward, Caleb. Mass. —. He served in the 2nd Regiment and was paid $20.

Hayward, Samuel. Conn. —. He served one year and four months under Capt. Bliss and Capt. Dana. He died 22 Mar. 1837. His widow was Sarah Hayward who was pensioned 12 Mar. 1869. His daughter, Jerusha Brown, aged 71, a Daughter of the American Revolution, suffered from rheumatism, and resided in South Dakota. She had married Edward M. Brown. She received a pension from Congress 20 Aug. 1894. Her husband served as Lt. Col. in the 8th Regiment of Vermont Infantry in the Civil War. He was pensioned for chronic diarrhea and disease of the rectum. They were married 2 May 1846. He died 31 July 1903. She ceased to collect her $12 a month pension as a daughter of a Revolutionary soldier and opted to collect her $30 a month pension as the widow of a Union Civil War veteran. 27 Feb. 1906.

Hayward, Simeon. Mass. —. He served in the 2nd Regiment and was from Lenox. He was paid $20.

Haywood, John. Mass. Pvt. He served in Capt. Robins' Company under Col. Timothy Bigelow. He was wounded in his left arm and lost the use of it. He was pensioned at one third pay from

1 June 1780 on 20 Feb. 1781.

Haywood, Solomon. Mass. Sgt. He served in Capt. Hugh Maxwell's Company under Col. John Bailey and was wounded at Bemis Heights 19 Sep. 1777. He suffered from a musket ball which entered his neck and settled down by the back of his wind pipe. He was granted half-pay 7 July 1780. He was 39 years old in 1786. He was on the 1813 pension list as Solomon Hayward.

Haywood, Thomas. Md. Pvt. St. He was pensioned at the rate of half-pay of a private in St. Mary's County 10 Mar. 1832.

Hazard, Thomas. Mass. Pvt. He served in the 12th Regiment and was from Boxborough. He was paid $50.

Hazelberger, Philip. Pa. —. He was pensioned. His name was probably Philip Hortleberger, *quo vide*.

Hazele, George. Va. —. His widow, Mary Hazele, was granted £10 support in Shenandoah Co., Va. on 28 May 1778. He died in Continental service. [Compare with — Hazle with widow Mary.]

Hazelip, Richard. Md. Pvt. He was pensioned in Washington County at the rate of half-pay of a private 16 Feb. 1821.

Hazeltine, Prince. Mass. —. He served in the 2nd Regiment and was from Worcester. He was paid $20.

Hazeltine, William. N.H. Pvt. He was from Westmoreland in 1778. He served in Capt. Kimball Carlton's Company under Col. Nichols. He was wounded on 16 Aug. 1777 at the battle of Bennington by a shot which broke his left arm. He was under the care of John Young, Regimental Surgeon. He lived in Rockingham, Vt. in 1795 and in Windham, Vt. in 1796. He was granted half a pension 20 Apr. 1795. He was on the 1813 pension list. He also appeared as William Haseltine.

Hazen, Jacob. Me. —. He was from Bridgton. He was paid $50 under the resolve of 1836.

Hazen, Moses. Canada. Brig. Gen. Congress appointed him colonel 22 Jan. 1776. At that time he was lieutenant on British establishment for half-pay. The British struck him off their roll 25 Dec. 1781. He was colonel in the 2nd Canadian Regiment. His widow, Charlotte Hazen, was pensioned 23 Jan. 1805 at the rate of $200 per annum for life. On 23 Apr. 1812 she received 960 acres of bounty land. She was on the 1813 pension list in New York. She died 28 Feb. 1827. His executor, Moses White, sought to received his indemnity but was rejected 28 Feb. 1820

Hazerman, George. Pa. —. He applied from Northumberland County on 13 Sep. 1819. He enlisted in 1775 in Capt. Charles Craig's 1st Pa. Regiment under Col. Hand. He served two years and was discharged at Valley Forge. Conrad Fry was his mess mate.

Hazerman, James. Pa. He served in the 3rd Regiment. He applied 10 Jan. 1814 from Lehigh Gap.

Hazle, —. Va. —. He served in the 8th Virginia Regiment. His widow, Mary Hazle, and child were furnished £25 support in Frederick Co., Va. on 3 Nov. 1779. [Compare with George Hazele.]

Hazlet, John. Del. Col. He served from Jan. 1776 to 3 Jan. 1777. He was killed at Princeton and left a widow and five children, John Hazlet, Mary Hazlet, Ann Hazlet, Joseph Hazlet, and Jemima Hazlet. His widow lived but a short time. John, Mary, and Ann died without issue. Joseph married and died in 1813 with no surviving issue. Jemima Hazlet married George Monro and died in 1821. She left five children: Lydia the wife of E. W. Gilbert, Mary Ann the wife of Thomas J. Boyd, Margaretta the wife of William Darrach, George Monro, and Susan E. Monro. Her son George Monro died without issue. The surviving heirs were to be paid whatever they were due 2 July 1836.

Hazlet, Kinley. Del. Pvt. He was born in Ireland, was single, and was wounded in the body at the battle of Ninety Six on 15 June 1781. He was on the 1813 pension list in Washington Co., Tennessee. He also appeared as Kenly Hazler and Kenley Hazlett.

Head, James. S.C. —. He was being pensioned in 1843. He was paid 1849, 1850, and 1851. He died 28 Oct. 1851. His grandson, George W. Dorn, had maintained him during the last years of his life. Dorn lived in Edgefield District, S.C. and sought the unpaid balance of his grandfather's pension. He received $40.

Head, John. Md. Pvt. He was pensioned at the rate of half-pay of a private 19 Feb. 1819.

Headley, William. —. —. He enlisted in Jan. 1776 under Capt. Gordon and Col. Lippet for a year and was discharged at Chatham, N.J. 20 June 1777. He was rejected for a pension in 1818 because his service was not Continental. He was 82 when Congress granted him a pension 22 Dec. 1831.

Headly, Joseph. S.C. —. He was wounded in his shoulder and body. He was granted an annuity 10 Sep. 1785.

Healey, George. Conn. —. He served under Col. Heman Swift. He married in the autumn of 1784. He was from Stratford. Congress granted his widow, Bethia Healey, a pension for six months of service 28 Feb. 1844.

Healey, Eliphas. Mass. —. He volunteered at Lexington 19 Apr. 1775. He enlisted in the regular army in the same year and served eight months at Roxbury. He again enlisted and served three months at Howland's ferry. In the spring of 1776 he served five months in New York. He was at Fort Washington and White Plains. He spent another three months at Howland's ferry and was in an engagement with a row galley. He also served three months under Gen. Sullivan in Rhode Island. He was put on the pension list 20 Dec. 1831.

Healy, Lemuel. Mass. Corp. He served in the 4th Regiment and was from Dudley. He was paid $50.

Heard, John. N.J. Capt.. Congress rejected the petition of his son, William V. Heard, 10 June 1854.

Heard, Nathaniel. N.J. Gen. Congress rejected the petition of his grandson, William V. Heard, 10 June 1854. He was in the militia and used his home as headquarters. The British burned it. He was late of Woodbridge, N.J. His heirs sought relief from Congress 26 Mar. 1858.

Hearn, Drury. S.C. He received a federal pension and died in Oct. 1840. His widow was Keron H. Hearn, aged about 60 years, and mother of six daughters. Her two eldest sons had left the state. She sought a state pension 15 Oct. 1845.

Heaslet, Andrew. Pa. —. He was awarded a $40 gratuity and a $40 annuity in Westmoreland Co., Pa. 5 Apr. 1826.

Heath, —. Va. —. Anne Heath and her children were awarded £15 in Northampton Co., Va. on 8 Dec. 1778.

Heath, Benjamin. N.H. —. He enlisted in 1775 in Capt. Osgood's Company and went to Canada. He next served in Capt. Nelson's Company for the winter. In the spring he served a year in Capt. Sartel's Company in Col. Cilley's Regiment. His next enlistment was in Capt. Sartel's Company in Col. Hazen's Regiment. He was honorably discharged after six years and six months. He suffered from the fatigue of long service. He was almost deprived of his sight in one eye. He discovered that Daniel Cook had forged orders for his pay.

Heath, John. Mass. Corp. He was ruptured by the rolling of a log on his breast in Dec. 1780 when he was cutting wood for huts for the troops. He served in the 6th Regiment. He resided in Sandisfield, Mass. in 1792 and in Berkshire, Mass. in 1796. He enlisted 22 Apr. 1777 for the war. He was transferred to the Invalids 10 Apr. 1781 and was dead by 1796.

Heath, Nathaniel. N.Y. Lt. He served in the Montgomery County militia under Col. Samuel Clyde. His children, Amelia Heath, Jacob Heath, and Josiah Heath, received his half-pay pension.

Heath, Phineas. —. —. He was granted relief.

Heath, William. Va. —. His two children were awarded £60 in Northampton Co., Va. on 8 Dec. 1778.

Heaton, James. Md. Pvt. His widow, Elizabeth Heaton, was pensioned at the rate of half-pay of a private in Berks Co., Pa. 9 Mar. 1827.

Heaton, —. Pa. —. His widow, Elizabeth Heaton, was awarded a $40 gratuity and a $40 annuity in Berks County in 1836. She died 25 Oct. 1840.

Heaton, John. Va. —. Anne Heaton was awarded £15.10 in Charlotte Co., Va. on 5 Oct. 1778. She was awarded a gratuity of £52.10 on 3 Nov. 1779 for provisions in Charlotte Co., Va. The widow, Anne Heaton, was furnished 2 barrels of corn and 100 pounds of bacon on 1 Mar. 1779.

Heaton, Salathiel. S.C. —. He served as a Whig on a two month tour at the siege of Ninety Six under Capt. George Anderson of Newberry District, a three month tour to Ashley Ferry and Bacon's Bridge towards Charleston under Lt. William Adanton in Capt. William Young's Company from Union District. He was 69 years old and had an aged wife to support. He applied 31 Oct. 1829. He was pensioned in Anderson District 23 Nov. 1829. He was paid in 1830, 1831, 1832, 1833, and 1834.

Heaton, William. Pa. —. He served under Capt. John Thomson and Col. John Lacey in the Bucks County militia. He was taken prisoner in Dec. 1777 and died in Provost Prison in Philadelphia. His widow, Catharine Heaton, was pensioned 12 June 1786.

Heavner, Charles. Me. —. He was from Waldoboro. He was paid $50 under the resolve of 1836.

Hebbird, John. Mass. —. He served under Lt. Col. Brooks. He enlisted in May 1777 in Capt. John Wiley's Regiment in Col. Michael Jackson's Regiment in Col. Learned's Brigade. He was furloughed for 60 days after which he was discharged as unfit for duty by Gen. Glover. His application was returned because it had been reported that he had deserted 15 Apr. 1779.

Hebron, William. N.Y. Sgt. He served in the 2nd N.Y. Regiment. He was hurt by a branch of a crooked tree on the brink of Hudson River on his passage from West Point to Dobb's ferry. The branch struck him in his eye, and he became blind. In 1794 he lived in Philadelphia Co., Pa. in 1794. He enlisted 10 May 1777 and continued to the end of the war. He was on the 1813 pension list.

Heckman, —. Pa. —. His widow, Margaret Heckman, received a $40 gratuity and a $40 annuity in Northampton County 3 Mar. 1837. She died 30 Dec. 1845.

Heckman, George. Pa. —. He enlisted in 1775 under Capt. Charles Craig in the 1st Regiment under Col. Hand and served two years. He was discharged at Valley Forge. He applied 13 Sep. 1819 in Montgomery County.

Heckman, Jefferson K. Pa. —. He was granted relief 3 Apr. 1841.

Heckman, Ulrich. Pa. —. He was awarded a $40 gratuity and a $40 annuity in Northampton Co., Pa. 20 Feb. 1832.

Hector, Edward. Pa. —. He was awarded a $40 gratuity in Montgomery Co., Pa. 5 Feb. 1833.

Hector, Monday. Mass. Pvt. He served in the 4th Regiment and was from Grafton. His widow, Lucy Hector, was paid $50.

Hedges, Elijah. Pa. —. There was a man of his name on the 1790 and 1813 pension lists of Virginia in Brooke County. He served in the Frontier Rangers and later removed to Ohio.

Hedrick, Peter. N.C. —. He entered in Rowan Co., N.C. for two years under Capt. Hedrick if his services were required. He served twelve months. He fought against the Tories at Back Creek in Orange Co. to the Raft River. He was dismissed in Sept. 1779. He then substituted for Philip Garner for three months in the militia under Capt. Enoch and Col. McDowell. He was at Monk's Corner in South Carolina in 1780. Congress granted him a pension 5 Mar. 1840.

Heedson, Elijah. Mass. Sgt. He served in Capt. Barnes's Company under Col. Ward. He was pensioned at the rate of half-pay from 31 Dec. 1776 on 20 June 1777.

Heffener, Thomas. Pa. Sgt. He applied 19 July 1814.

Heffer, Andrew. Pa. Pvt. He was in Northumberland County 14 Nov. 1787. He served in Capt. Michael Weaver's Company in the militia of Northumberland County under Col. Hugh White. He was wounded in his right arm and lost his thumb and forefinger of his right hand on 20 Nov. 1777 by the bursting of his gun. He was 50 years old.

Hefferman, John. Pa. —. He applied 15 July 1814. Proof of his discharge was wanting.

Hefferman, Thomas. Pa. Sgt. He applied in Lancaster County on 16 July 1814. He was a schoolmaster and taught in Rockingham Co., Va. and had one daughter. He enlisted in Capt. Thomas Church's Rifle Company in the 4th Pa. Regiment under Col. Anthony Wayne in 1776. He was in battle at Three Rivers in Canada under Gen. Sullivan. At the expiration of his one year enlistment, he reenlisted at Ticonderoga for three years or the war. He was soon appointed sergeant in Capt. John Bankson's Company in the 12th Pa. Regiment. Capt. Thomas Boude, Major by brevet, in the 1st Pa. Regiment left him on James Island in S.C. on 8 June 1783. Hefferman sailed for Philadelphia and soon after was discharged. He also appeared as Thomas Hafferman.

Hefflebower, Jacob. Pa. —. He was awarded a $40 gratuity in Delaware Co., Pa. 14 Apr. 1834. He was awarded a $40 gratuity and a $40 annuity in Lancaster Co., Pa. 15 Apr. 1835. He was 85 years old in 1840. He died 24 Oct. 1842 in Cumberland County.

Heflin, —. Va. —. His wife, Sibby Heflin, was granted £5 support in Fauquier Co., Va. in May 1778 and £40 in June 1779 while he was away in the service.

Hefflinger, George. Pa. —. He applied from York County. He served in the 9th Pa. Regiment under Col. Richard Butler and was at the battle of Green Springs 5 July 1781 and at the taking of Cornwallis at Yorktown. Afterwards he served in S.C. He was paid to 2 Nov. 1831. He also appeared as George Heffinger.

Hefser, John. Pa. —. He was pensioned.

Heft, Henry. Pa. —. He was awarded a $40 gratuity and a $40 annuity in Bucks Co., Pa. 15 Apr. 1834. He was 82 years old in 1840. He died 13 Jan. 1841.

Hegarman, James. Pa. —. He applied in Jan. 1814 from Upper Merion. He served in the 3rd Pa. Regiment under Col. Joseph Wood having enlisted 20 May 1777. His discharge did not specify his length of service.

Heidler, Joshua. Pa. —. He was awarded a $40 gratuity and a $40 annuity in Adams Co., Pa. 15 Apr. 1835. He was aged 77 in 1840.

Heidler, Josiah. Pa. —. He was awarded a $40 gratuity and a $40 annuity in Adams County 28 Mar. 1836. The act was repealed 15 June 1836.

Heimer, John. Pa. —. He was pensioned 11 May 1826 in Philadelphia.

Heindall, —. Pa. —. His widow, Elizabeth Heindall, was awarded a $80 gratuity and a $40 annuity for her husband's Revolutionary service. Her name had been misspelled in the act as Elizabeth Kendall necessitating a corrected new law. She was from York County in 1839.

Heintzelman, Andrew. Pa. —. He was awarded a $40 gratuity and a $40 annuity in Adams Co., Pa. 18 Feb. 1834.

Heiny, Christian. Pa. —. He was awarded a $40 gratuity and a $40 annuity in Northampton Co., Pa. 22 Dec. 1834. He died 15 Oct. 1841. He also appeared as Christian Heiney.

Heitler, —. Pa. —. His widow, Susannah Heitler, was awarded a $40 annuity in 1845 in Lancaster

County for his Revolutionary service.

Heller, George. Pa. —. He was granted relief in Philadelphia 11 Mar. 1833. He died 1 Jan. 1836.

Heller, Jacob. Pa. —. He was pensioned.

Heller, John. Pa. —. He enlisted at Germantown under Lt. Cole in the company of Capt. Calhoun a short time before the battle of Trenton. He was in the Continental Line under Capt. John Steel, Col. Hubley, and Col. Humpton for four years and seven months. He was from Luzerne County.

Heller, John. Pa. —. He applied from Northampton County on 25 Jan. 1818. He was 60 years old and suffered from a rupture. He enlisted in the 3rd Regiment in Capt. Henry Alles's Company and served one year and four months. He was honorably discharged at Philadelphia by Col. Stewart. He had a family of 15 children.

Helm, Samuel. Pa. —. He was granted assistance in Pike County 5 Apr. 1842. He died 3 Apr. 1848.

Helm, Thomas. Va. Lt. He served in the 8th Regiment from 23 Mar. 1776 to his resignation 27 Nov. 1777. His heirs sought five years' full pay 15 June 1831. Congress rejected their claim.

Helmer, Frederick. N.Y. Pvt. He served under Col. Bellinger in the Montgomery County militia and was slain 6 Aug. 1777. His widow received a half-pay pension.

Helmer, George. N.Y. Lt. He served in Capt. Small's Company under Col. Peter Bellinger. He was wounded in his left arm at Oriskany. He lived in German Flatts, Montgomery Co., N.Y. on 24 July 1789. He also appeared as George Halmer. He was pensioned 14 Sep. 1786. He later lived in Herkimer County. He was on the 1813 pension list.

Helmer, John G. N.Y. Corp. He suffered from bruises and debility. He lived in Palatine, N.Y. in 1794. He enlisted 25 Oct. 1776 and continued to the end of the war. His claim was rejected in 1795 because he was not wounded in the service.

Helmer, John L. N.Y. Corp. He served in Capt. Fink's Company under Col. Goose Van Schaick. He was aged 37 and sought a pension 14 Sep. 1786 for wounds received in 1777. He died 26 Oct. 1786. He was either killed by Indians or drowned.

Helms, Job. Pa. —. He was awarded a $40 gratuity in Delaware Co., Pa. 25 Mar. 1833, 1834, and in 1838. He also appeared as Job Helmes.

Helphinstone, Peter. Va. Maj. His widow, Catharine Helphinstone, lived in Frederick County in Apr. 1786. He entered the service in 1776 in the 8th Va. Regiment. He went to S.C. After the battle of Sullivan's Island he contracted an indisposition which compelled him to be furloughed. He died in Winchester, Va. in the service. She was on the 1785 pension roll as Catharine Hilpenstone. She was continued on the pension roll at the rate of £20 per annum on 12 Nov. 1789. He left four children all of whom by 1795 were gone from home. She died about 13 Feb. 1796 and Conrad Kremer of Winchester was administrator of her estate. His heirs were allowed seven years' half-pay 12 June 1838.

Helton, Jesse. S.C. Pvt. He was from Sumter District in 1826. He served under Capt. John James and was in the party that captured the Tory, Col. Fletcher, and took him to Charleston. He was at Charleston in 1776 when Sir Peter Parker led the British attack. He was at Stono, Eutaw, and was discharged at Watboo near Big Church.

Hemingway, James. Mass. —. He was granted relief.

Hemingway, Rufus. Mass. —. He served in the 4th Regiment. He was paid $20.

Hemmenway, Daniel. Mass. Sgt. He served in the 9th Regiment and was from Hubbardston. He collected his pension of $10 from Sep. 1806 to Mar. 1807. His widow, Polly Hemmenway, was paid $50. [His name may have been David Hemmenway.]

Hemmenway, Peter. Mass. Pvt. He served under Col. Proctor. He was wounded by the bursting of his gun and had his arm amputated at Saratoga in 1777. He served in the militia. He lived in Boston, Mass. in 1792. He was granted half a pension 20 Apr. 1786. He was on the 1813 pension list. He died 18 Feb. 1830 in Norfolk Co., Mass.

Hemmerer, Frederick. Pa. —. He was pensioned 13 June 1817.

Hemmingway, Daniel. Mass. Pvt. He served under Col. Peirce and Capt. Simon Edge. He was disabled by a musket ball in his right thumb and right side. He was pensioned 18 July 1786. He resided in Norfolk County., Mass. He was on the 1813 pension list. He also appeared as David Hemmenway, *quo vide*.

Hemp, Samuel. Md. Pvt. He was wounded in his head and was granted relief 20 Sep. 1780. He was from Frederick County.

Hempstead, Samuel B.. Conn. 1ˢᵗ Lt. He served in the marines aboard the frigate *Deane* under Capt. Nicholson. He was wounded in his hip by a musket ball which remained lodged there while on furlough in Sept. 1781 in New London. He lived in New London, Conn. in 1794. His account was settled in 1787 by the late commissioner for the marine department and a certificate issued for the balance found due to him.

Hempstead, Stephen. Conn. Sgt. He served in the militia. He had two ribs broken by grape shot at Harlem Heights on 27 Oct. 1776. He was in Capt. Wales' Company in Col. Webb's Regiment. He was wounded by a musket ball which broke his arm and by a bayonet which pierced his hip at New London on 6 Sep. 1781 at Fort Griswold. He was in Capt. Shapley's Company. He was pensioned 8 Nov. 1788 at the age of 35. He was on the 1813 pension list.

Hempston, William. Md. Pvt. He was pensioned in Montgomery County at the rate of half-pay of a private 19 Feb. 1819. His arrearage was paid to his son, Nathan T. Hempston, 7 Mar. 1834 in Montgomery County.

Henage, —. Va. —. His wife, Jane Henage, was granted support in Feb. 1779 and Aug. 1779 in Westmoreland County.

Hendershot, Abraham. Pa. —. He received a $40 gratuity and a $40 annuity in Huntingdon Co., Pa.16 Feb. 1830.

Henderson —. S.C. —. His widow, Margaret Henderson, was pensioned 2 Dec. 1824. James Anderson or James Jamieson of Chester District was to draw the pension. She was last paid in 1832.

Henderson, Adam. Va. —. His widow, Catherine Henderson, was granted assistance in Loudoun County in Sep. 1780. She was granted 4 barrels of corn and 200 pounds for support in Fauquier Co., Va. 12 Sep. 1780. Her husband had died in the service.

Henderson, Elisha. N.Y. Pvt. He served under Col. Goose Van Schaick in the militia. He died 1 Dec. 1778. His widow, Mary Henderson, received his half-pay pension.

Henderson, Hezekiah. —. —. His daughter, Lucinda Peters the wife of Barton Peters, had her claim for a pension rejected by Congress 9 Apr. 1856.

Henderson, Hugh. Va. —. His wife was furnished assistance in Loudoun County 8 Feb. 1779.

Henderson, John. S.C. —. He was paid $441 for his Revolutionary services on 20 Dec. 1810.

Henderson, Sampson. Va. —. He was wounded in the thigh at the storming of Savannah. He was pensioned on 19 Jan. 1810 at the rate of $50 per annum and $40 relief. He lived in Hampshire County 8 May 1810. He died 7 July 1820; administration of his estate was granted to James M. Offutt in Aug. 1820.

Henderson, Samuel. Pa. —. He was awarded a $40 gratuity in Indiana County 12 Jan. 1836.

Henderson, Samuel. S.C. —. He served in the 2ⁿᵈ S.C. Regiment. His widow, Rebecca Henderson, was granted an annuity 26 Oct. 1785.

Henderson, Thomas. Pa. —. He was awarded a $40 gratuity and a $40 annuity in York Co., Pa. 11 Mar. 1833. His widow, Mary Henderson, was awarded a $40 gratuity 8 May 1850.

Henderson, William. Mass. —. He served in Nixon's Regiment. He was paid $20.

Henderson, William. N.Y. Pvt. He served in the 1st N.Y. Regiment under Col. Goose Van Schaick. He was wounded in his right knee. He was disabled by the fall of a load of timber which bruised the small of his back. He suffered from a continued discharge of urine. He lived in Armenius, Dutchess Co., N.Y. 4 June 1787. He was aged 56 in 1786. He died in 1797.

Hendricks, Baker. N.J. Capt. He served in the Essex County militia under Maj. William Crane and Col. Moses Jaquis. He was wounded in the arm on 7 June 1780. He lost the use of his fingers which prevented him from following his trade. The wound was unhealed in Sep. 1781. The legislature disallowed his award because of irregularity in entering it so the Essex County court revised the certificate in Apr. 1782.

Hendricks, Moses. S.C. —. He applied 8 Dec. 1827; his application was rejected.

Hendricks, William. Pa. Capt. He marched from the Kennebec River in the depth of winter to Quebec and was slain in the unsuccessful attempt to storm the fortress. His niece, Elizabeth Hunt, sought his seven years' half pay and bounty land. She was ineligible for the former but was eligible for the latter 22 Dec. 1837.

Hendrickson, —. N.Y. —. Bethia Hendrickson was granted support 7 Aug. 1779 while her husband was away in the service under Col. Dubois.

Hendrickson, Garret. N.J. Lt. He served in the Monmouth County militia. He was wounded in 1780 and lost the use of his right arm. He was on the 1791 pension roll at the rate of $120 per annum. He was 55 years old. He died 21 Dec. 1801. He also appeared as Garretson Hendrickson.

Henesy, John. Pa. —. He was pensioned 10 Feb. 1815.

Hening, Henry. Pa. —. He was granted relief 7 Mar. 1827. He was 87 years old in 1840. He died in Centre County 1 Dec. 1840.

Henley, Matthew. R.I. Pvt. He had a very bad rupture in his groin in Mar. 1782 which rendered him incapable of obtaining a livelihood by labor occasioned when on fatigue in backing wood from the public magazine to the barracks in Pennsylvania. He served under Col. Jeremiah Olney. He was aged 36 when he applied on 5 Jan. 1786. He died 26 May 1804.

Hennen, Matthew. Pa. —. He was awarded a $40 gratuity and a $40 annuity in Greene Co., Pa. 1 Mar. 1832. He died 31 Dec. 1839.

Henner, John. Pa. —. He was granted relief 13 Jan. 1818.

Henner, Peter. N.Y. Pvt. He served in the militia under Col. Klock and died in 1777. His widow was granted his half-pay pension.

Hennion, Cornelius. N.J. Capt. He served in the 3rd Regiment. He was wounded at Short Hills, and his right arm was broken. He lost the use of his left elbow. He was from Bergen County in 1789. He was 34 years old. He was on the 1791 pension roll at the rate of $120 per annum. He died 28 Mar. 1800.

Hennis, Samuel. Md. Pvt. He was pensioned in Frederick County in 1783. He was wounded in his hand at White Horse.

Henry, —. Pa. —. His widow, Elizabeth Henry, was awarded a $40 gratuity and a $40 annuity in Lancaster Co., Pa. 1 Mar. 1833. She died 3 Sep. 1833.

Henry, —. Va. —. His mother, Lydia Henry, was granted £10 support while her son was away in the service in Fauquier Co., Va. in Apr. 1779.

Henry, Francis. Va. —. His wife was granted support in Pittsylvania Co., Va. 27 Nov. 1777, 26 Mar. 1778, and 25 Feb. 1779.

Henry, James. Pa. Pvt. His heirs were in Bedford County 14 Feb. 1786. He served in the Bedford County militia under Capt. John Boyd and was killed in an engagement with Indians near Frankstown on 3 June 1781. His heirs were his widow, Elizabeth Henry, and children. Two of the children were under the age of 9 in 1786, and the youngest was in a state of insanity.

Henry, John. Pa. —He was pensioned 10 Feb. 1815. He died 10 June 1819.

Henry, Philip. Pa. Pvt. He was in Philadelphia County 14 Nov. 1785. He was transferred from the 1st Pa. Regiment to the Invalids. He was wounded in his thigh and leg. He was 35 years old. He was on the 1813 pension list.

Henry, William. —. Gen. He died in 1824. His widow, Hester L. Henry, neglected to prove the extent of his service. Congress did not grant her a pension on 10 Feb. 1851.

Henshaw, Thomas. Ga. Pvt. He was on the 1813 pension list as Thomas Henshaid. He died 24 Jan. 1814.

Hensley, —. Va. —. Jane Hensley was granted assistance in Orange Co., Va. in 1778 while her son was away in the service.

Hensley, Samuel. S.C. Pvt. His widow, Mary Hensley, was allowed an annuity 31 Dec. 1785. She was from Newberry District. She was paid her annuity in 1821.

Henson, John. S.C. —. He served under Capt. Patrick Stewart and Col. Hawkins. The Tories stripped him of his property. He was wounded at the battle of Collins Creek. He was 75 years old. He was from Lancaster District in 1823. He died 26 Feb. 1845. Richmond R. Terrell was the administrator with the will annexed.

Hentz, Conrad. Pa. —. He was pensioned.

Hentzel, William. Pa. —. He was pensioned 15 June 1836 in Lancaster County. He was 90 years old in 1840.

Hepner, Valentine. Pa. —.He was pensioned in Huntingdon County 13 Apr. 1838.

Hepworth, Daniel. N.Y. Pvt. He enlisted as matross and served in Capt. Thomas Seward's Company under Col. John Crane in the 3rd Artillery on 17 Oct. 1778. He was wounded in the joint of his elbow of his right arm which cut the tendons by the discharge of a piece of field artillery in Danbury, Conn. He lost the sight of his right eye, and the vision in his left eye was very dim. He was 48 years of age on 5 May 1788. He lived in Fredericksburg, Dutchess Co., N.Y. on 8 July 1789. He died *ante* 5 Sep. 1807. He also appeared as Daniel Hipworth.

Herbert, Peter. N.Y. Pvt. He served under Capt. Lawrence Olivie and Col. Hazen. He was carried on the roll as dead in Jan. 1783. He received 500 acres which he released to Benjamin Morris who was adjutant of the regiment. Capt. Clement Goselline confirmed Herbert's service. He died 9 Apr. 1853 at the age of 100 years at St. John's, Canada. He had married three times but left no widow. The children were Marie Joseph Herbert the widow of Pierre Picard aged 74, Pierre Herbert aged 66, Francois Herbert aged 56, Jean B. Herbert aged 30. Congress granted the heirs relief 2 Aug. 1856. He received bounty land from New York.

Herbert, Thomas. Va. —. His widow, Mary Herbert, applied 23 Dec. 1794.

Herbold, Adam. Pa. —. He was awarded a $40 gratuity and a $40 annuity in Bedford Co., Pa. 1 Apr. 1823. He also appeared as Adam Harbold.

Herbst, Conrad. Pa. —. He received a $40 gratuity in Berks County 27 Jan. 1837.

Herbst, Peter. Pa. —. He was pensioned 3 Mar. 1837 in Lancaster County. His widow, Theresia Herbst received a $40 annuity 11 Apr. 1848.

Hereford, Jesse. N.Y. Pvt. He appeared as Jesse Hedsford on the 1791 pension roll. He died in Sep. 1805.

Hergerer, Andrew. Pa. —. He was awarded a $40 gratuity and a $40 annuity in Columbia Co., Pa. 18 Feb. 1834. He was dead by Sep. 1836. He also appeared as Andrew Hergener.

Hering, Henry. Pa. —. He was pensioned.

Herkimer, Nicholas. N.Y. Brig. Gen. He died of wounds received at Oriskany 16 Aug. 1777. His widow, Maria Herkimer, sought relief.

Herkley, Richard. Pa. —. He was pensioned.

Herman, —. Pa. —. His widow, Susannah Herman, was awarded a $40 gratuity and a $40 annuity in York Co., Pa. 6 Apr. 1833. She died 6 June 1833.

Herman, John. Pa. —. He and Maria Gentzel were married by J. Friedrich Schmidt, minister of the Lutheran Congregation in Philadelphia, 18 Oct. 1801. He was seemingly dead by 4 June 1816.

Hermanies, John. Pa. —. He served three tours in the militia. He was from Franklin County.

Hermitty, Henry. Pa. Pvt. He was in Lancaster County 12 May 1788. He served in the 3rd Pa. Regiment under Col. Samuel Atlee in Capt. Abraham Dehuff's Company. He was wounded by a musket ball in his right arm at Fort Washington in on 7 Nov. 1776. His left foot had also been frozen. He was 63 years old and had two small children, the older not exceeding 9 years. He died 18 Nov. 1804.

Herndon, Edward. Va. —. He enlisted for two years in 1776 under Capt. Woodson and Col. Thomas Fleming. Afterwards he was under Col. Matthews. He was made a prisoner at Germantown. He later was appointed lieutenant in the regiment of guards at Albemarle guarding Burgoyne's men. He then received a commission as a captain. Congress granted him a pension 19 Mar. 1832.

Herndon, Joseph. —. —. He sought an increase in his pension due to bodily infirmity and a helpless family. Congress denied his claim 1 Aug. 1850.

Herner, John. Pa. —. He was pensioned.

Herod, Ezra. Mass. —. He served in the 3rd Regiment and was paid $20.

Herrar, Daniel. Pa. —. He was granted relief in Montgomery County 18 Mar. 1834.

Herrell, Thomas. Pa. Pvt. He was in Philadelphia County on 2 July 1787. He was in the 5th Pa. Regiment and was disabled by a rupture and other disorders contracted in his service. In 1779 he was injured by the fall of heavy timber on his body at West Point. He was 39 years old.

Herrick, Andrew. Mass. Pvt. He served in the 11th Regiment and was from Beverly. He was paid $50.

Herrick, Zebulon. Mass. —. He served in the 7th Regiment. His widow, Mary Herrick, was paid $50.

Herring, —. Pa. —. His widow, Anna Maria Herring, was awarded a $40 gratuity and a $40 annuity in Venango County 3 Mar. 1837. She was 79 years old in 1840. She died 30 Aug. 1846.

Herring, Christian. Pa. —. He was awarded a $40 gratuity in Bedford Co., Pa. 27 Mar. 1830. He was awarded a $40 gratuity and a $40 annuity 1 Mar. 1832.

Herring, Ebenezer. Mass. —. He served in Revere's Regiment and was from Malden. He was paid $50.

Herring, Henry. Pa. —. He was awarded a $40 gratuity and a $40 annuity in Centre Co., Pa. 7 Mar. 1827.

Herring, John. Pa. —. He served in the Bucks County militia under was wounded 11 Dec. 1777. He was taken prisoner and died in Philadelphia 4 Jan. 1778. His widow was Sarah Herring.

Herring, Thomas. Mass. —. He served in the 3rd Regiment and was from Cape Ann. He was paid $20.

Herrington, —. S.C. —. His widow was Sarah Herrington of Liberty in 1791.

Herrington, Ammi. Mass. —. He served in the 6th Regiment and was from Pepperill.

Herrington, Jacob. Pa. —. He was awarded a $40 gratuity and a $40 annuity in Crawford County on 13 Mar. 1817.

Herron, James. Md. Pvt. He was pensioned in Baltimore County on 8 Aug. 1814. He died 4 Sep. 1818.

Herron, John. Conn. Pvt. He enlisted in the 1st Conn. Regiment under Capt. Eliphalet Holmes for three years in Jan. 1777. He was at Valley Forge in the spring of 1778 when he was wounded by the accidental fall of some boards on the small of his back and hip. He came home on furlough. His urine was nearly half blood. He returned to camp but was unfit for duty. He returned home again. He lived in Lyme, Conn. and was 39 years old when he was pensioned 9 Dec. 1788. He was pensioned at the rate of $2.50 per month from 26 Jan. 1808. He was on the 1813 pension list.

Herrur, Daniel. Pa. —. He was pensioned in Montgomery County 18 Mar. 1834.

Hertzhog, Valentine. Pa. Pvt. He was on the 1791 pension roll. He was on the 1813 pension list. He died 26 Sep. 1825 in Philadelphia County.

Hervey, Samuel. Pa. Pvt. He was discharged from the Invalids due to this arm being withered and sickness. He was from Philadelphia County.

Hess, Andrew. Pa. —. He was awarded a $40 gratuity and a $40 annuity in Berks Co., Pa. 18 Mar. 1840.

Hess, Augustinus. N.Y. Pvt. He served under Col. Peter Bellinger in the Montgomery County militia and was slain 15 July 1782. His widow, Agnes Hess, was granted a half-pay pension.

Hess, George. Pa. —. He was awarded a $40 gratuity and a $40 annuity in Lebanon Co., Pa. 18 Feb. 1834. He died 22 June 1844. His widow, Barbara Hess, received a $40 gratuity 8 May 1850. She died 1 June 1850.

Hess, Henry. Pa. —. He was granted a $40 gratuity and a $40 annuity 28 Mar. 1835 in Berks County.

Hess, Johannes. N.Y. Pvt. He served under Col. Peter Bellinger. He was wounded in his right arm at Oriskany on 7 Aug. 1777. He was 38 years old in 1786. He lived in German Flatts, Montgomery Co., N.Y. in Nov. 1788. He was on the 1813 pension list as John Hess.

Hesser, Frederick. Pa. —. He was awarded a $40 gratuity and a $40 annuity in Schuylkill Co., Pa. 27 Mar. 1830. He was 78 years old in 1840. He died 22 June 1846.

Hesser, John. Pa. —. He was awarded a $40 gratuity and a $40 annuity in Schuylkill Co., Pa. 12 Feb. 1825.

Heston, Thomas. Pa. Col. He served under Capt. Copperthwait at Trenton and was promoted to lieutenant. He was at Princeton. His brother was Jacob Heston who was 80 years old. The soldier married in Sept. 1785 Hannah ------ and died in Oct. 1802. He had been dismissed from the Society of Friends 26 Jan. 1776 for his military service. Congress rejected the claim of his widow 23 Feb. 1842 because the requisite time of service had not been met.

Hetfield, Moses. —. —. He received the arrears of his pension 31 May 1796.

Hetherling, Jacob. Pa. Capt. in the Pa. Line. His heirs applied 25 Mar. 1789. He served in the Flying Camp and died while a prisoner of the British. His children were under the guardianship of Thomas Bull and Jonathan Pugh. His youngest daughter, Hannah Hetherling, married Andrew Leenam. He was from Chester County.

Hettick, Christian. Pa. —. His widow, Agnes Morrison, was in Northumberland County. She married secondly 8 May 1787 Ephraim Morrison. He was a private in Capt. Samuel McGrady's Company of militia. He was killed by Indians about a mile from Gundy's mill on 6 Oct.1781. He was tomahawked and scalped. His children were Andrew Hettick born 1 May 1775, Catherine Hettick born 15 Mar. 1777, Elizabeth Hettick born 15 June 1779, and Polly Hettick born 16 Oct. 1781. He also appeared as Christian Hettig.

Hewes, William. N.H. —. He enlisted for six months in 1780 but served only five months and nineteen days. Congress allowed him credit for the time to travel home and granted him a pension 1 Jan. 1835.

Hewett, Daniel. Conn. Sgt. He served in Col. Dennison's Regiment. He was wounded in his hand and wrist by a musket ball in Jul. 1778 at Wyoming. He was pensioned 4 Mar. 1792. He lived at Tolland, Conn. in 1794. He was on the 1813 pension list. He moved to Oswego Co., N.Y. after 4 Sep. 1823.

Hewett, Daniel. Conn. Pvt. He served under Col. Dennison. He was granted one-third of a pension 20 Apr. 1796. He later lived in Orleans Co., Vt. He was on the 1813 pension list as Daniel Hewitt.

Hewins, Joseph. Mass. Pvt. He served three months and fourteen days in the Continental Line in 1781 and one year and eight months from Apr. 1782 to Jan. 1784. Congress granted him a pension for twenty-two months of service 10 July 1840.

Hewitt, James. Md. Pvt. He was pensioned at the rate of half-pay of a private 19 Feb. 1819.

Hewitt, James. Va. —. Ann Hewitt was aged *ca.* 35 years of age. She had one child, Ann Hewitt, and was encumbered with several small Negro children on 16 Mar. 1786 in Sussex County.

Heydt, George. Pa. —. He was awarded a $40 gratuity and a $40 annuity in Berks Co., Pa. 16 Feb. 1835. He was dead by Dec. 1837. He also appeared as George Haydt.

Heylman, Martin. Pa. —. He was from Chester County and served under Capt. McKissack and Col. Baxter. He was taken prisoner at Fort Washington. After his release he served under Capt. Thomson and Col. Lacey. He was wounded in the head near Burned Mill. He was pensioned 19 Mar. 1810. He also appeared as Martin Hyleman.

Hibbets, James. N.J. —. He was made a prisoner and died in New York. He was from Monmouth County and served under Col. Scudder in the militia. His widow, Isabella Hibbits, received a half-pay pension.

Hickey, Daniel. Mass. Pvt. He served under Col. Wadsworth. He was wounded 17 Feb. 1781 and lost the use of his right arm. He was also wounded in his left leg. He was pensioned at the rate of half-pay from 25 Aug. 1781 on 28 Sep. 1782. He was 46 years old in 1788. He was on the 1813 pension list. He was paid $20 by the Commonwealth.

Hickey, Daniel. Va. —. His wife, Mary Hickey, was furnished support in Berkeley County 18 Oct. 1780. She received 4 barrels of corn and 160 pounds of pork.

Hickey, David. Pa. Pvt. He served under Col. Hartley. He was wounded in the head, collar, arm, and throat in Oct. 1777 at Paoli. He mustered in Sep. 1777 and was wounded on 21 Sep. 1777. He lived in Pa. in 1794. He was granted a full pension 20 Apr. 1796. He was on the 1813 pension list.

Hickley, James. Va. Lt. Congress allowed his heirs commutation 18 May 1838.

Hickman, —. Pa. —. His widow, Margaret Hickman, was awarded a $40 gratuity and a $40 annuity in Fayette County 16 June 1836. She died 1 Dec. 1842.

Hickman, George. Pa. —. He enlisted in 1775 under Capt. Charles Craig and Col. Hand in the 1st Regiment. He was discharged at Valley Forge two years later. Conrad Frey was his mess mate. He was from Northampton County.

Hickman, John. —. —. He died in Georgia before submitting his proof under the act of 1832. His widow, Elizabeth Hickman, died 17 Oct. 1852. Her son and administrator, Lewis G. Hickman, proved that his parents were married prior to 1 Jan. 1794. Congress allowed him the benefits his parents were entitled for the heirs under the act of 1838 on 25 May 1860.

Hicks, —. Pa. —. His widow, Hannah Hicks, was pensioned in Fayette County 16 July 1836. She died 1 Oct. 1837.

Hicks, Isaac. Ga. Capt. He was commissioned captain in the 3rd Battalion of the Georgia Continental Line and served to the end of the war. He also served as paymaster. He died in Brunswick Co., Va. 20 June 1817. On 12 Mar. 1794 he received federal bounty land warrant #1113 for 300 acres which David Galbreath and Thomas Elms patented in Licking Co., Ohio. His surviving executor, Thomas Hicks, sought the balance of his half-pay plus interest, but Congress rejected the claim 4 Dec. 1861.

Hicks, Jesse. S.C. —. He was about 88 years old and was nearly blind and deaf. His application was rejected in 1848.

Hicks, John. Conn. Pvt. He served in the 6th Regiment under Col. Lamb and Capt. John Hunniwell. He was disabled by the loss of his left leg and all of the knee joint. He was pensioned 8 Nov. 1786 and was 27 years old. He resided in Plymouth Co., Mass. He was on the 1813 pension list.

Hicks, John. S.C. —. He served more than seven years and was at Black Stocks and was wounded by a ball at the battle of King's Mountain. He served under Col. Sumter and Col. Pickens. He was nearly 70 years old. He lived in Barnwell District when he was pensioned on 7 Dec. 1825. He was last paid his annuity in 1832. His widow was Sarah Hicks. She was nearly 82 years old and lived with her widowed daughter and her four children. She applied 13 Nov. 1841. Temperance Long swore that she was present at their marriage, and Tarlton Brown had known them for fifty years and stated that John Hicks had been dead eight years. She died at the home of her daughter, Frances Reeves, who on 18 Dec. 1844 sought the arrearage due her mother. He also appeared as John Hix.

Hicks, Thomas. Ga. Cpt. He was commissioned 4 Dec. 1776 in the 3rd Battalion. He was from Brunswick Co., Va. Bounty land warrant #1113 for 300 acres was issued 12 Mar. 1795. His executor was Isaac Hicks. Congress ruled that he was not entitled to relief 4 Dec. 1861.

Hicks, William. —. —. He was pensioned to 4 Mar. 1841. His widow Mary Hicks sought his pension from 4 Mar. 1841 to 4 Mar. 1843. Congress rejected her request 20 Jan. 1841.

Hickworth, Daniel. N.Y. Pvt. He died 24 June 1809.

Hiebner, George. Pa. —. He was awarded a $40 gratuity 1 Apr. 1834 in Schuylkill Co., Pa.

Hier, Walter. N.J. Pvt. He was the son of Peter Hier. He served in the state troops and was wounded in his right wrist or forearm from a sword or cutlass at Pleasant Valley in Monmouth County. He lost part of the bone, and his hand was rendered almost entirely useless. He was 44 years and from Middletown.

Higbee, Elnathan. —. —. He served two years. His widow, Abigail Higbee, sought an increase in her pension 20 June 1848. Congress rejected her petition.

Higgins, Benjamin. Mass. —. He served in the 4th Regiment and was from Partridgefield. He was paid $20.

Higgins, Isaac. Conn. Fifer. He served under Col. Webb in the 3rd Regiment. He was ruptured about his abdomen by falling with a log of wood on his shoulder which he was carrying to the barracks. He resided in Weston, Conn. in 1792. He enlisted 5 July 1779 and was on the rolls in Mar. 1782. He was granted half a pension 20 Apr. 1796. His pension rate was $3.33 1/3 from 29 Sep. 1807. He died in 1812. He was listed on the 1813 pension list as dead.

Higgins, Jonathan. N.Y. Pvt. He served under Peter Gansevoort in Capt. Abraham Swartwout's Company at Fort Schuyler. He was wounded in his left shoulder by a bomb shell on 8 Aug. 1777. His left arm was amputated. He was 45 years old in 1785. He lived in New York City, N.Y. in 1787.

Higgins, Moses. N.Y. —. He enlisted in 1775 for nine months under Capt. Mills and Col. James Holmes. He marched to Canada and was at St. John's and Montreal. He was discharged at White Plains. He was 84 years old. Congress granted him a pension 3 Jan. 1832.

Higgins, Timothy. Mass. Pvt. He served in the 8ᵗʰ Regiment and was from Wenham. He was paid $50.

Higginson, William. Pa. Pvt. He was on the 1813 pension list.

High, George. Pa. —. He was awarded a $40 gratuity and a $40 annuity in Union County 1 Apr. 1836. He was dead by Feb. 1838.

Highland, Furguson. Va. —. He was on the pension roll of 1796 at the rate of £10 per annum.

Hightower, —. Va. —. His wife, Elizabeth Hightower, was granted relief in May 1777 in Lunenburg Co., Va.

Hightower, Thomas. Va. Pvt. He lived in Amelia County 6 Dec. 1787 and was 37 years old. He served in the Chesterfield County militia under Col. Goode. He received several wounds on his head and was cut across his hand in 1781. On 28 Nov. 1784 he sought to have his pension made retroactive to the time he was wounded; his request was rejected. He was continued on the pension list at the rate of £12 per annum on 7 Dec. 1787. He also appeared as Thomas Hightour.

Higins, James. S.C. —. His application was rejected in Dec. 1825.

Hiland, William. Pa. —. He applied from Allegheny County on 28 Apr. 1826. He was 70 years old. He enlisted for three years or the war in the spring of 1776 in Capt. John Hays' Company in the 9ᵗʰ Pa. Regiment under Col. Matthis and later under Col. Muhlenberg. In the summer of 1777 he was put under Capt. Morgan and so served until 1779. Afterwards he was in the 4ᵗʰ Pa. Regiment of Light Dragoons under Maj. Washington and was discharged at the conclusion of the war by Col. Milin.

Hilands, —. Pa. —. His widow, Mary Hilands, was granted a gratuity and a annuity of $40 each in Fayette County 4 Apr. 1837.

Hilands, Nathan. Pa. —. He was awarded a $40 gratuity and a $40 annuity in Indiana Co., Pa. 15 Mar. 1824.

Hilard, — Pa. —. His widow, Mary Hilard, received a $40 gratuity and a $40 annuity in Fayette County 4 Apr. 1837. She also appeared as Mary Hillard.

Hildreth, John. —. —. Joseph Grey was guardian of the heirs. His son, John T. Hildreth, claimed that by fraud Grey was paid the five years' half-pay without the knowledge or consent of the widow. Congress found that the records of the judge of probate of Montpelier, Vt. proved that the payment was properly made. Congress rejected the claim 9 May 1854.

Hileman, —. Pa. —. His widow, Dorothy Hileman, was awarded a $40 gratuity and a $40 annuity in York Co., Pa. 14 Apr. 1834.

Hilgard, —. Pa. —. His widow was Mary Hilgard.

Hill, Adam. Pa. —. He was awarded a $40 gratuity 4 Mar. 1815. He was awarded a $40 gratuity and a $40 annuity in Mercer County on 19 Mar. 1816. He died 3 Dec. 1817.

Hill, Amos. Va. —. His widow, Ann Hill, applied 29 Nov. 1794. He served in the 1ˢᵗ State Regiment and fell at the siege of York. She was pensioned at the rate of £12 per annum and received the same amount in relief on 2 Dec. 1793.

Hill, Asa. N.Y. Pvt. He served in Capt. Gross's Company under Col. Willet. He was disabled by a fall from his horse and dislocated his foot at Fort Rensselaer. He was discharged in Nov. 1781. He was 27 years old in 1788. He lived in Hillsdale, Columbia Co., N.Y. 10 July 1789. He was on the 1813 pension list.

Hill, Daniel. Me. —. He died 10 Mar. 1835. His widow was Phebe Hill from Buxton. She was paid $50 under the resolve of 1836.

Hill, Edward. S.C. —. He was wounded in the shoulder at the battle of Hanging Rock. He was allowed an annuity 8 June 1785. It was paid to William Hill. There were four children in 1791.

Hill, Ezekiel. Va. —. His widow, Mary Hill, was granted £25 support on 8 Feb. 1779. She lived in Northumberland County 16 Nov. 1785. She married William Baylis in Apr. 1785. Her first husband died in Apr. 1777 in the service.

Hill, Frederick. Pa. —. He applied from Lycoming County on 10 Jan. 1815. He served in the 4th Pa. Regiment. He died 8 May 1833.

Hill, Frederick, Pa. Pvt. He applied from Bedford County. He served more than fifteen months but had no proof other than his own declaration. He served in 1780 and 1781. Congress granted him a pension 22 Dec. 1837. Pennsylvania had granted him relief 12 Mar. 1836.

Hill, George. Va. Pvt. He served in the 3rd Regiment of Virginia Dragoons. He lived in Hampshire County.

Hill, Henry. Md. Capt. He served in the Flying Camp under Col. Luke Marbury and Gen. Smallwood in 1777. He was appointed a captain 1 Sep. 1777. He married 24 Apr. 1781 in Prince George's County Hetta Brooke. He died 27 Apr. 1822. His nephew was Daniel Carroll. Congress rejected her claim for relief 28 Apr. 1840. His widow also appeared as Hester Hill.

Hill, Ichabod. —. Artificer. Congress awarded his widow, Anna Hill, of Monroe Co., N.Y. the arrearage of her pension from 4 Mar. 1848 to 3 Feb. 1853 on 10 Dec. 1853.

Hill, Ichabod. Mass. —. He served in the 4th Regiment and was paid $20.

Hill, Jacob. Pa. —. He enlisted in 1776 for one year and then re-enlisted for the war. He was from Lycoming County.

Hill, John. —.—. He applied in 1833. He died in 1838 without ever being put on the rolls. Congress denied his heirs any claim because he served only about three months on 9 May 1850.

Hill, John. Md. Pvt. He was pensioned at the rate of half-pay of a private 2 Jan. 1813. He died 5 Feb. 1828. His arrearage was paid to his son, George Hill, in Anne Arundel County 5 Feb. 1828.

Hill, John. Mass. —. He served in Crane's Artillery. He was from Andover and was paid $20.

Hill, John. S.C. —. He was wounded in his body, right arm, left wrist, and thigh. After the war he removed to North Carolina but returned to Darlington District, South Carolina three years later. He served under Lt. John Stewart and Col. Samuel Benton. He was pensioned from Darlington District 11 Dec. 1816. He was last paid in 1834.

Hill, Jonathan. Mass. —. He served in the 3rd Regiment and was paid $20.

Hill, Martin. Va. Marine. His widow, Rachel Hill, lived in Lancaster County on 21 Nov. 1782. He served in the dragoons of a ship of war and was drowned 13 Aug. 1777.

Hill, Richard. Md. Pvt. His heirs, Lydia Brown and Ann Hill, of St. Mary's County received a warrant for 50 acres for bounty land in Allegany County in 1832 without any compensation money.

Hill, Richard. Mass. —. He served in the 7th Regiment. He was paid $20.

Hill, Richard. Mass. Pvt. He served in the Invalids. He was paid $20.

Hill, Richard. Va. —. His wife, Margaret Hill, was furnished assistance in Loudoun Co., Va. on 9 Mar. 1778.

Hill, Samuel. Va. —. He was pensioned in Louisa County on 25 Feb. 1818 at the rate of $60 per annum. He received $100 relief. He had been wounded. His will was proved 13 Apr. 1818; his executor was Daniel Lipscomb.

Hill, Thomas. Mass. —. He served in the 4th Regiment. He was from Brookfield. He was paid $20.

Hill, Thomas. N.Y. Pvt. He served under Col. Livingstone. He was wounded by a musket ball at Bemis Heights on 19 Sep. 1777. He lived in Rensselaerville, N.Y. in 1794. He enlisted 1 Jan. 1777 and continued to Jan. 1782. He was on the 1813 pension list.

Hill, Thomas. Pa. —. He served in the Pa. Line and was injured in his knee. He was granted a $40 gratuity in York County on 20 Mar. 1811.

Hill, William. Va. —. His widow and orphans lived in Princess Anne County on 20 Sep. 1787. He died testate 27 Feb. 1784; Nathan Douger was his executor.

Hill, William. Va. —. He was a wounded militia man and was being pensioned 25 Mar. 1784. He lost his right arm at Norfolk in a skirmish with the British. He served in Capt. Amos Weeks' Company and was from Princess Anne County.

Hill, Zimri. —. Pvt. He served in the 5th Regiment under Col. Starr in the militia. He was disabled by a wound in the right hand by a broadsword at Horse Neck which deprived him of the use of two forefingers in Aug. 1779. He was pensioned in Sep. 1793. He lived in Chittenden or Charlotte, Vt. in 1795. He was granted half a pension 20 Apr. 1795. He was on the 1813 pension list in Vermont. He transferred from Vt. to Chautauqua Co., N.Y. 4 Mar. 1823. He also appeared as Zimri Hills and as Limri Hill.

Hillary, Rignal. Md. Lt. He died in service. His widow, Mary Hillary, was pensioned at the rate of £60 per annum in Nov. 1785. She married Samuel Magruder of Prince George's County and asked that her pension be continued to her two children [Reginald Hillary and Elizabeth Magruder]. She requested that the £62.10 half-pay from 16 Jan. 1792 to 1 Feb. be paid to Samuel Magruder on 20 Mar. 1793. Elizabeth Magruder received his bounty land warrant for 200 acres 20 July 1830. She was granted five years' full pay commutation 25 May 1832. Elizabeth Magruder claimed to be the sole heir. Her brother, Reginald alias Nick Hillary, died in Georgetown, D.C. and left a widow. His children were John Bruno Hillary born 12 July 1811 and George Thomas Hillary born 22 Mar. 1822. His widow was Mary Ellen Hillary, and she married Francis Kellenberger. Upon obtaining their majority, they brought suit against their aunt for half of their grandfather's commutation which they were granted 15 May 1836. Elizabeth Magruder was utterly insolvent. He also appeared as Raynold Hillary and Reginald Hillary.

Hiller, George. Pa. —. He received a $40 gratuity and a $40 annuity in Lebanon County 1 Apr. 1823. He died 18 Nov. 1834.

Hiller, Jacob. N.Y. Ens. He served under Col. Bellinger and was slain 6 Aug. 1777 at Oriskany. His widow, Elizabeth Hiller, received his half-pay pension.

Hillers, —. N.Y. —. His widow was granted support during the war.

Hillery, Ozborn. Pa. —. He was awarded a $40 gratuity and a $40 annuity in Fayette Co., Pa. 8 Apr. 1833.

Hillhouse, John. S.C. —. He served under Col. Neale in the Cherokee Expedition. Later he served under Col. Bratton. He was 82 years old. He was from Pendleton District when he was pensioned 7 Dec. 1826. He was last paid in 1833.

Hilliard, Thurston. Conn. Artificer. He served under Capt. F. Pattin. He was wounded by a piece of timber which fractured his breastbone at Yorktown. He lived in Reading, Conn. in 1792 and

Weston, Conn. in 1795. He enlisted in Mar. 1778 for the war and was on the rolls in 1782. He was granted one-third of a pension 20 Apr. 1796. He was on the 1813 pension list.

Hillier, David. Pa. Pvt. He was in Philadelphia 30 Sep. 1785. He served in the 2nd Pa. Regiment and was transferred to the Invalids. In Jan. 1783 he lost the use of both of his legs due to frost some time in the preceding year. He was 22 years old. He was dead by Sep. 1795.

Hillion, John. Va. Pvt. His widow, Selby Hillion, lived in Frederick County on 12 Apr. 1786. He served in the 3rd Va. Regiment in Capt. Blackwell's Company and died in the service. She was put on the pension list at the rate of £8 per annum on 14 Dec. 1786. She was continued on 14 Nov. 1791. She died 17 Sep. 1821 in Fayette Co., Pa. Administration of her estate was granted to William Hilling 8 June 1825. She also appeared as Sibby Hillion and he as John Hellion.

Hillman, Benjamin. —. —. He was pensioned 25 Apr. 1808. He died 21 Aug. 1821 in Delaware Co., Ohio.

Hillman, James. Pa. Pvt. He was a boatman in Sullivan's Expedition for five months. He served one year in the commissary department and was with the French army in the spring after the defeat of Cornwallis in the Revolutionary War. He was also under Gen. Harmar in 1784 and 1785. He also served seven months in the War of 1812. His service under Sullivan was deemed not sufficiently military to qualify and his service under Gen. Harmar did not qualify him for a pension. In the spring after the defeat of Cornwallis he enlisted at Easton, Penn. and took a number of horses to Williamsburg for the army. He served out his term. Congress rejected his application for a pension 12 Jan. 1848. He was from Trumbull Co., Ohio.

Hillman, John. —. —. He was granted relief.

Hillman, William. Md. Pvt. He was pensioned at the rate of half-pay of a private 2 Jan. 1813. His widow, Sally Hillman, was pensioned at the same rate 1 Mar. 1833 in Somerset County. Her arrearage was paid to Constant D. Stanford for her children Nancy Stanford, Elizabeth Smith, and Biddy Hillman 5 Feb. 1846.

Hillmer, Jonathan. Mass. —. He served in the 5th Regiment. He was from Kingston and was paid $20.

Hillock, Robert. Mass. —. He served in the 1st Regiment and was paid $20.

Hills, Frederick. N.Y. Pvt. He served in the 1st New York Regiment. He was suffered from disease contracted in the service. He lived in Herkimer Co., N.Y. in 1794. He enlisted 29 Mar. 1777.

Hills, William. Mass. —. He served in the 10th Regiment and was from Andover. He was paid $20.

Hillsman, —. —. —. He served under Capt. William Johnson, Col. Morgan, and Maj. Gen. William Heath for three years. He died in Aug. 1818 in Ala. Congress granted his widow, Elizabeth Hillsman, of Madison Co., Ala. a pension 21 July 1842.

Hillsman, Benjamin. Pa. Lt. He was on the 1813 pension list. He also appeared as Benjamin Hillman.

Hilt, John. Pa. Pvt. He was in Philadelphia County on 30 Sep. 1785. He was transferred from the 2nd Pa. Regiment to the Invalids. He lost the use of both legs in 1783 due to frost bite.

Hiltebrick, George. Md. —. He was allowed his half-pay in Frederick County.

Hilton, Edward. Me. —. He died 26 Apr. 1833. His widow was Mary Hilton from Wells. She was paid $50 under the resolve of 1836.

Hilton, Isaac. —. Drummer. He enlisted in the spring of 1777 under Sgt. Peter Merrell and Col. Peter Noyes. He was a guard at Falmouth. He next served under Lt. McLelland. He erected and repaired fortifications around Portland. He was under Capt. Abner Lowel, Ens. Enoch Moody, and Lt. Dudley Garnett for fourteen months. In Oct. 1778 he enlisted on the *Cumberland* under

Capt. Collins. Later he was on the *Monmouth* and the *Effingham.* Congress granted him a pension 24 Jan. 1837.

Hilton, John. N.H. Sgt. He served in the 2nd New Hampshire Regiment under Col. Hale in Capt. Robinson's Company. He was wounded by a musket ball through his right leg at Bemis Heights. He lived in Montgomery Co., N.Y. on 15 June 1789. He died in 1807. He was on the 1813 pension list.

Hilton, John. Pa. —. He was awarded a $40 gratuity and a $40 annuity in Philadelphia Co., Pa. 6 Apr. 1833.

Hilton, Joseph. N.H. Lt. He was wounded in his left side by a musket shot on 7 Oct. 1777 near Stillwater. He also had an injury in his left ankle. He served in the 3rd N.H. Regiment. He resided at Deerfield, N.H. in 1796. He was granted half a pension 20 Apr. 1796. He was on the 1813 pension list. He died 26 Nov. 1826.

Hilton, Peter. —. —. He served under Gen. Greene, Capt. Dorley, and Francis Marion as 1st Sgt. and 2nd Lt. He was at Eutaw Springs and King's Mountain. He was 105 years old. Congress denied his claim for a pension because he submitted no record evidence 14 June 1850.

Himer, John. Pa. —. He applied in Philadelphia County 22 Apr. 1826. He was 64 years and 8 months of age. He enlisted 7 Apr. 1776 in the Col. Cadwalder's Regiment. He was taken prisoner by the British at Fort Washington. He was wounded in the leg by a musket ball which lodged in his leg. He escaped and made his way to Philadelphia where in the spring of 1777 he enlisted in the German Regiment under Col. Hoonaker in Capt. Farman's Company for one year and six months. He was discharged by Col. Stewart in Va. the morning before the surrender of Cornwallis. His wife was old and feeble, and his daughter was *non compes mentis.* He also appeared as John Himes.

Hinckley, Jared. Conn. Pvt. He transferred to Vermont. He was on the 1813 pension list.

Hinckley, West. Pa. Pvt. He was pensioned.

Hinckley, Wait. Conn. Pvt. He served in Gen. Waterbury's Brigade in Capt. Charles Miels's Company. He was wounded in both arms by the stroke of a cutlass in action at Horse Neck near Greenwich on 24 June 1781 and lost the use of both hands. He was taken captive and carried to New York. He was pensioned 24 June 1787 at Stonington, Conn. He was 25 years old. He was on the 1813 pension list in North Carolina. He also appeared as Wiatt Hinkley.

Hindman, Matthew. Va. —. While he was away in Continental service, his two children were granted support at the rate of 20 shillings per month in Yohogania Co., Va. 24 May 1779.

Hinds, Abijah. Mass. Pvt. He served under Col. Aaron Willard. He had a preternatural hardness and humor in his navel which became ulcerous occasioned by lifting a wagon wheel in Aug. 1776 at Number Four Woods. He lived in Scituate, Mass. in 1794. He served in the militia.

Hinds, Bartlett. Mass. Lt. He served in the 10th Mass. Regiment under Capt. Amasa Soper and Col. Thomas Marshall. He was wounded by a ball passing through his lungs at Still Water 19 Sep. 1777. He was pensioned at one-quarter pay from 12 Sep. 1780 on 17 Mar. 1784. He was on the 1813 pension list of New York. He was a member of the Society of the Cincinnati. His heirs sought relief from Congress 29 Jan. 1852. He also appeared as Bartlett Hines.

Hinds, David. Mass. —. He served in the 1st Regiment and was paid $20.

Hinds, Owen. S.C. —. He was wounded at Fort Moultrie 28 June 1776. He was granted an annuity 14 Dec. 1778.

Hinds, Samuel. Me. —. He was from St. George and was paid $50 under the resolve of 1836.

Hinds, Thomas. N.Y. Pvt. He served in Capt. Peter Ten Broeck's Company under Col. Goose Van

Schaick. He was disabled by a rupture in May 1777. He lived in Albany, N.Y. on 21 Apr. 1789. He was on the 1813 pension list. He died 22 Apr. 1813. He also appeared as Thomas Hines.

Hinds, William. Va. —. He served under Col. Clark in Kentucky and was wounded twice in his right arm by the Indians. He applied 5 Dec. 1783. He was pensioned in Prince Edward County in July 1786.

Hineman, —. Pa. —. His widow, Charity Hineman, of Roane Co., Va. Received a $40 gratuity and a $40 annuity 20 May 1857.

Hines, Thomas. Va. —. He was in Continental service. His wife and child were granted £10 support in Prince William Co., Va. on 8 Feb. 1779.

Hines, William. Va. —. He was in the militia and was disabled. He was on the 1785 pension list.

Hink, John. Pa. Pvt. He was in Philadelphia County 10 Apr. 1786. He served in Capt. Isaac Seely's Company in the 5th Pa. Regiment under Col. Richard Butler. He was wounded by a musket ball in his left groin at Green Springs, Va. in 1781. He lived in Orange Co., N.Y. in June 1788. He died 27 Dec. 1808. He was on the 1813 pension list.

Hinkle, Nathan. Pa. —. He applied 20 Jan. 1845. He served in the company of Capt. Christ or Crist in Philadelphia and belonged to a rifle regiment under Col. Miles. He thought his lieutenant was one Broadhead and his major one Pifer of Fifer.

Hinkley, Nehemiah. Me. —. He applied from Bluehill. He was paid $50 under the resolve of 1836.

Hinley, William. Md. Pvt. He was on the 1791 pension list.

Hinman, Joel. Conn. Pvt. He was on the 1813 pension list. He died in 1813.

Hinnis, Samuel. Md. Pvt. He was pensioned 4 Mar. 1789. He was on the 1813 pension list.

Hinsley, Samuel. S.C. —. His widow was Mary Hinsley from Laurens District in 1786. There were children in 1791.

Hinson, Edmund. S.C. —. There were children in 1791.

Hinson, John. S.C. —. He was pensioned at the rate of $60 per annum for life on 12 Dec. 1823.

Hinton, William. Pa. —. He was awarded a $40 gratuity and a $40 annuity in Centre Co., Pa. 27 Mar. 1824.

Hiott, Arthur. S.C. —. He served under Capt. Hogen, Col. Isaac Huger, and Capt. Henry Council. He was taken prisoner by the Tories and was severely castigated. He was in his 78th year, and his wife was nearly the same age. He suffered from a rupture. Joel Hiott and Abraham Garrett served with him. He was from Colleton District on 3 Dec.1825 when he was pensioned.

Hiott, Joel. S.C. Drummer. He enlisted at the age of 15 in the winter before the defeat of Gen. Gates at Camden. He served under Col. Issac Huger in the company of Capt. Hogan in the 5th S.C. Regiment. He was at the siege of Savannah. After he returned home, he was out plowing when he was captured by a party of Tories. They left him helpless with wounds in his leg and arm and saber wounds in his head. His brother, Arthur Hiott, served with him. Abraham Garret swore that he saw him at Fort Johnston in Charleston Harbor as a drummer. He was from Colleton District when he was pensioned 6 Dec. 1826. He was last paid in 1832.

Hipkins, William. Va. —. His wife was Judith Hipkins. They were in Richmond, Va. 13 Feb. 1808, and both were pensioners. Under the act of 6 Feb. 1808 they received $40 per annum. He died 17 Jan. 1813.

Hipple, Lawrence. Pa. Pvt. He served in the 4th Battalion of Pa. Militia. He was wounded by a musket shot which passed through his body in the fall of 1777 near Derby, Chester Co., Pa. He lived at Pikeland, Chester Co., Pa. in 1794. He was granted half a pension 20 Apr. 1796.

He was on the 1813 pension list. He died 10 Mar. 1821.

Hirley, William. Pa. Pvt. He was pensioned 4 Mar. 1789. Compare with William Hinley. He was a pensioner in Maryland.

Hitchcock, —. —. —. His widow, Mary Hitchcock, sought a continuance of her husband's pension. Congress rejected her petition because they were not married until her husband's service had ended on 12 Feb. 1841.

Hitchcock, Abraham. N.Y. —. He was attached to the Quartermaster Department under Col. Hewes and was stationed at King's Ferry as a ferryman. He served to the close of the war. He was 67 years old. Congress granted him a pension 3 Jan. 1832.

Hitchcock, Elias. Mass. —. He served in the 1st Regiment and was paid $20.

Hitchcock, Platt. Pa. —. He was granted support 3 Apr. 1841.

Hitchman, Salisbury. Mass. —. He served in the 14th Regiment and was from Wareham. He was paid $20.

Hite, Conrad. Pa. —. He was awarded a $40 gratuity and a $40 annuity in Somerset County on 7 Mar. 1821.

Hite, George. Va. Lt. He lived in Berkeley County in June 1786 and was aged 25. He served in the 1st Regiment of Light Dragoons and was wounded 8 Dec. 1781 near Orangeburg, S.C. in his right arm a little below the elbow. His pension was continued at the rate of £40 in Frederick Co., Va. on 29 Nov. 1786. He was continued on the pension list at the same rate. He was in Jefferson County in 1799.

Hite, Isaac. Va. —. He served in the militia under Capt. John Todd at Boonesborough. He was wounded in his right shoulder in action with the Indians. He was unable to earn a living. He was given £40 on 14 June 1779.

Hitt, John. Pa. —. He was pensioned in Delaware County 20 Feb. 1833.

Hix, James. Va. —. His wife, Nancy Hix, and two small children were granted £8 for necessaries in Fluvanna Co., Va. 6 Nov. 1777.

Hix, John. Va. —. His wife, Elizabeth Hix, was granted £10 support in York Co., Va. on 16 Nov. 1778 and £40 on 21 June 1779.

Hixt, William. S.C. Capt. His heirs sought relief from Congress 28 Mar. 1850. Congress rejected their claim for commutation pay because they submitted no evidence.

Hoagland, John. N.Y. Deputy Commissary. He served two years and upwards. Congress granted his widow, Susannah Hoagland, a pension of $80 per annum on 6 Apr. 1838.

Hoar, Edmund. Mass. —. He served in the 4th Regiment and was from Monson. He was paid $20.

Hoard, David. Mass. Pvt. He served in the 16th Regiment and was from Norton. His widow, Prudence Carpenter, was paid $50.

Hoard, David. N.Y. —. He entered the service in 1776 under Col. Wynkoope. He served under Capt. Harrison in 1777, Lt. Hubbs in 1778, and Capt. Chapman and Col. Harper in 1780. He was pensioned for only six months and seventeen days due to insufficient proof. Congress accepted nine additional months in 1780 and one month in 1778 and granted him a pension 12 Feb. 1841.

Hoast, —. Pa. —. His widow, Elizabeth Hoast, was pensioned in Lancaster County 3 Apr. 1837.

Hobart, Daniel. —. —. He was killed at White Plains in Sep. 1776. He left a son and a daughter aged 4 and 18 months respectively. His widow was Keziah Hobart. He was late of Ashburnham, Worcester Co., Mass. His widow was more than 80 years old in 1834. Congress rejected her application because of the lack of proof on 27 Mar. 1846. He also appeared as David Hobart.

Hobbs, John. S.C. —. He enlisted and served under Capt. Pinckney and Col. Gadson in 1775 for three years. He was 70 years of age when he applied in Orange Co., N.C. 29 Aug. 1821.

Hobart, Jonas. N.H. Pvt. He was on the 1813 pension list of Vermont. He moved to Schuyler Co., Ill. He died 15 Dec. 1833.

Hobbs, Josiah. N.H. —. He served eight months from July to Nov. 1775 under Capt. Nathaniel Hobbs. He applied under the act of 1832. He died 23 Apr. 1849. He married in 1785 Mary W. ---- who was 97 years old. Congress granted her a pension 25 May 1860.

Hobbs, Thomas. Va. —. He was wounded on the Cherokee Expedition. He was in Washington County on 15 Apr. 1783.

Hobby, Thomas. Conn. Major. He served under Col. Waterbury. He was wounded by a musket ball which passed through his hip at the siege of St. John on Lake Champlain in 1775. He resided in Greenwich, Conn. in 1792. He became supernumerary after his release from captivity. He was in the militia. He was granted one-eighth of a pension 20 Apr. 1796.

Hobdy, William. Va. Pvt. He served under Capt. Henry Young and Col. Alexander M. McLenachen in the 7th Regiment. He helped drive Dunmore from Gwyn's Island. He was at Brandwine, Germantown, and was discharged at Valley Forge. He re-enlisted in Bland's Corps of Dragons for three years under Capt. Thomas Pendleton. He was at Savannah, Monks Corner, and Lenew's Ferry. He was a prisoner on a ship in the Stono River, was exchanged, and was at Yorktown. He was born in Gloucester Co., Va. 12 Apr. 1754. He applied from New Hanover Co., N.C. 10 May 1818.

Hobson, Joseph. Va. Lt. He served in the 7th Regiment for more than three years from 1776. He was entitled to bounty land. He was commissioned 7 Mar. 1776 and resigned 26 May 1778. Congress ruled that he was due no bounty land on 12 Feb. 1841.

Hobson, William. Pa. Sgt. He was on the 1789 pension list.

Hockley, Richard. Pa. Pvt. He applied 19 Oct. 1812 in Westmoreland County. Lt. William Jack in 1777 or 1778 enlisted him in Capt. Moorhead's Company attached to the 8th Pa. Regiment for a two year term. He was discharged at Pittsburgh by Gen. Irwin. Capt. John Clark of the 8th Pa. Regiment under Col. Broadhead proved his service. He was old and had an infirm wife. He died 9 Apr. 1818.

Hockman, George. Pa. —. He was pensioned 29 Oct. 1820.

Hodge, Benjamin. S.C. —. He was a soldier in 1775 in the Little River Regiment and died in the service. His widow, Sarah Hodge, of Laurens County was granted relief 10 Nov 1798.

Hodge, John. N.J. Capt. He entered the service in July or August 1776 in the Volunteers. He was badly wounded in both hands by the explosion of powder at the cannon he was managing at the fort in New York. He resided in New Brunswick, New Jersey in 1792. He was pensioned at the rate of £40 per annum.

Hodge, John. S.C. —. His widow was Mary Hodge of Montgomery Co., Ala. in 1814. She sought her arrearage on 9 Dec. 1825. She was not on the state roll but on the roll of the general government from 1815 to 28 Dec. 1823. She was paid $60 and was pensioned at the rate of $30 per annum for her widowhood. He died 28 Dec. 1814 at Hadrell's Point. He had served under James Bennett.

Hodge, Thomas. S.C. —. He served in the militia and was in the Florida Expedition, at Gates' defeat near Camden, and at the Congaree near Granby under Col. Taylor. Jeremiah Taylor served with him under Capt. Murphey and Col. Robert Goodwyn. His widow, Ann Hodge, was pensioned from Fairfield District on 7 Dec.1837.

Hodge, William. Conn. —. He served in Capt. Samuel Bronson's County under Col. Noadiah Hooker in the militia. He was wounded at Horse Neck on 29 June 1779. His skull was badly fractured.

Hodge, William. S.C. —. He was not paid for his services and property lost in the Revolutionary War due to the lack of vouchers, but he was pensioned on 18 Dec. 1818. At the time of the Revolution he had a wife and three children. He had migrated from Pennsylvania and bought a tract on the Pacolet. On the second day after the battle of Blackstocks, his wife and children were driven from home, and he was carried to Camden jail. He and sixteen others later escaped. He served 53 months under Capt. John Thompson, Maj. Samuel Otterson, and Col. Thomas Brandon. He was also at Eutaw Springs, the Siege of Ninety Six, Snow Camps, and at the fort on Congaree. He was 85 years old when he applied 29 Nov. 1817.

Hodges, —. S.C. —. His widow was Sarah Hodges from Laurens District.

Hodges, —. Va. —. His father, Robert Hodges, was granted £13 support in Henry Co., Va. 28 Oct. 1779.

Hodges, Benjamin. S.C. Lt. He died 18 Oct. 1778.

Hodges, Ezra. Me. —. He was from Hallowell. He was paid $50 under the resolve of 1836.

Hodges, Elijah. Pa. Pvt. He was granted relief.

Hodges, Joseph. Va. Pvt. He was wounded by a musket ball in his leg. He was pensioned at the rate of £12 a year on 8 Sep. 1791. He lived in Norfolk, Va. 2 Sep. 1791. He died 17 Aug. 1800.

Hodgkins, John. Mass. —. He was in the 8th Regiment and was from Gloucester. He was paid $20. He also appeared as John Hodgins.

Hodgkins, Timothy. Mass. Pvt. He was in the 9th Regiment and was from Gloucester. His widow, Eunice Hodgkins, was paid $50.

Hodgman, John. Me. —. He died 24 Feb. 1834 in Wales., Maine. His widow was Mehitable Hodgman from Plymouth.

Hoff, Charles. N.J. —. His widow, Hannah Hoff, was pensioned in Morris County on 26 Mar. 1846 at the rate of $40 per annum.

Hoff, Nicholas. N.J. Pvt. He was pensioned 22 Feb. 1803. He was pensioned at the rate of $5 per month from 22 Feb. 1808. He was on the 1813 pension list. He moved to Seneca Co., N.Y. 4 Mar. 1825.

Hoffer, Andrew. Pa. Pvt. He applied 14 Nov. 1787. He was in Capt. Weaver's Company in the Northumberland County militia. He was wounded in his right arm 20 Nov. 1777 and lost his thumb and finger. He was aged 50. He was dead by Mar. 1791.

Hoffman, Christian. Pa. —. He was pensioned in Westmoreland County 16 Apr. 1840.

Hoffman, Cornelius. Pa. Pvt. He applied from Schuylkill County on 2 Jan. 1815. He was 68 years old.

Hoffman, George. Pa. —. He was pensioned.

Hoffman, Henry. Pa. —. He enlisted 5 Sep. 1782 in the 2nd Regiment under Capt. Striker. His heirs sought the $80 reward he should have received for enlisting on 6 Feb. 1839. Congress declined their claim 31 Jan. 1855.

Hoffman, Nicholas. Pa. —. He served in the 10th Pennsylvania Regiment under Col. Humpton. He was discharged due to old age and infirmities. He was recommended for half-pay for life from Pennsylvania. He sought a pension.

Hoffman, Philip. Pa. —. He served several tours in the militia in 1776 and 1777. He was from Lancaster County. He was pensioned 28 Jan. 1833.

Hoffman, Thomas. Pa. Sgt. He was pensioned 19 July 1814.

Hoffman, William. Pa. —. He served on the frontier under Col. Thomas Hartley. He was awarded

$200 on 20 Feb. 1819 in Northumberland County.

Hofley, Stephen. Md. —. His widow, Mary Magdalene Hofley, was paid the amount due him at the time of his death and was granted his half-pay in 1839.

Hofstider, Christian. N.Y. He was granted support during the war. He also appeared as Christian Hofstelar.

Hog, James. S.C. —. There were two children in 1791.

Hogaboom, Peter. N.Y. Pvt. He served under Col. Harker. He hurt his leg by a fall from a rock on a scout in the woods in June 1780. He lived in Mohawk, N.Y. in 1794. He was on the 1813 pension list. He died 14 July 1820 in Montgomery Co., N.Y.

Hogan, David. Va. Pvt. His widow, Mary Hogan, lived in Hanover County 7 Sep. 1786. He served in the 5th Va. Regiment under Capt. Richard C. Anderson and died in the service. She was put on the pension list at the rate of £5 per annum on 26 Oct. 1787.

Hogan, James. —. Gen. He was taken prisoner at the capture of Charleston and died in captivity. His heirs received seven years' half pay. Congress refused them bounty land on 6 Feb. 1838 because there was no law embracing his situation.

Hogan, James. Pa. —. He was awarded a $40 gratuity and a $40 annuity in Delaware Co., Pa. 3 Mar. 1825.

Hogan, Patrick. N.Y. Pvt. He served in the 1st N.Y. Regiment under Goose Van Schaick. He was wounded in his left hip and discharged 3 Nov. 1782. He lived at Fishkill, Dutchess Co., N.Y. on 9 July 1789. He was aged 31 years in 1786.

Hogan, William. S.C. Lt. He served under Capt. John Woodward, Capt. John Miles, Capt. Jacob Bethany. He was on the expedition against the Tories in Georgia. He was pensioned from Richland District on 23 Nov. 1829. Capt. John Smith of Fairfield District swore he saw him in the service. He was last paid an annuity in 1834.

Hogan, William. Va. Pvt. He lived in Goochland County 22 Dec. 1786 and was 26 years old. He enlisted for 18 months on 25 Apr. 1779 and was discharged 25 Nov. 1783 by Col. A. Buford. He received a number of wounds and lost his left arm a little below the shoulder. He was in the 3rd Virginia Regiment. He was continued on the pension list on 22 Dec. 1786 with an additional allowance of £6 per annum.

Hogart, —. Va. —. His widow, Mary Hogart, was allowed an additional 20 shillings per annum on 8 Sep. 1789. Compare with David Hogan.

Hogeland, John. Pa. Capt. His widow, Jane Hogeland, was in Allegheny County in Mar. 1797. He served in the militia under Col. William Crawford in the expedition against the Sandusky villages and was killed 5 June 1782.

Hogeland, Joseph. Pa. —. He was awarded a $40 gratuity and a $40 annuity in Berks County 1 Apr. 1834. He died 30 Apr. 1840. He also appeared as Joseph Hogland.

Hogge, James. Pa. —. He was awarded a $40 gratuity and a $40 annuity in Bucks Co., Pa. 1 Feb. 1834. He also appeared as James Hoggs.

Hogshire, Robert. Va. Pvt. His wife, Agnes Hogshire, and three children were granted 30 shillings per month on 25 Sep. 1777. His widow lived in Accomack County 28 Nov. 1787. He served in the 9th Va. Regiment and died in the service. He left four children. She was put on the roll at the rate of £8 per annum on 1 Jan. 1788. His widow died 1 Oct. 1805.

Hohns, Job. Pa. —. He was paid a $40 gratuity in Delaware County in Apr. 1833.

Hoklar, John. —. —. He was granted relief without interest 12 July 1854.

Holbrook, Ebenezer. Mass. —. He served in Burbeck's Artillery. He was from Randolph, and his widow, Elizabeth French, was paid $50.

Holcomb, John Va. Capt. He served in the 4th Va. Regiment. He lived in Campbell County. He was pensioned at the rate of $15 per month from 1 Dec. 1807. He was on the 1813 pension list.

Holcombe, —. Va. —. His wife was furnished support in Prince Edward County in Apr. 1779.

Holcombe, John. —. Capt. He served in the infantry. His heirs petitioned for his five years' full pay. His services terminated 25 Mar. 1779. His petition was rejected because he was in the militia service and not in the Continental Line 25 Jan. 1838.

Hold, Luis. Pa. —. He was a servant of Robert McConnell and enlisted in the 8th Regiment under Col. Robert McKay and Capt. James McGomery. His indenture stated he promised to serve Robert McConnell from 19 Oct. 1774 to 19 Oct. 1778. Hold enlisted about 22 Aug; 1776 and served two years. McConnell received £45.7.6. He was from Westmoreland County.

Holden, Beniah. Pa. —. He was granted relief in Bucks County under the act of 18 Feb. 1839. He died 14 Oct. 1844.

Holden, John. Mass. Capt. He received his commutation for five years in lieu of half-pay for life.

Holden, Joseph. Mass. Sgt. He served in the 7th Regiment. He was paid $20.

Holden, Nehemiah. Mass. Pvt. He served in the 3rd Regiment. He was from Charlestown and was paid $50. He asked Congress for an increase in his federal pension. Congress denied his claim 11 Apr. 1850.

Holden, Samuel. Mass. —. He served in the 6th Regiment and was from Sedgwick. He was paid $20.

Holder, Jacob. Pa. —. He was pensioned 30 Jan. 1818.

Holder, Jesse. Va. —. His wife was granted support in Pittsylvania Co., Va. on 24 July 1777.

Holder, William. Va.—. His wife was granted support in Pittsylvania Co., Va. on 24 July 1777.

Holdren, —. Pa. —. His widow, Elizabeth Holdren, was granted a $40 annuity in Bucks County 6 Apr. 1845 for his Revolutionary service.

Holdridge, John. Mass. Sgt. He served in the 3rd Mass. Regiment. He received violent contusions in a fall from a precipice in the night in July 1777 at Kingsbury. He lived in Hillsdale, N.Y. in 1794. He was promoted to an ensign. He had received commutation.

Holdston, Thomas. Del. Pvt. He served in the Delaware Continental Line. He was wounded in the arm by a musket ball at the battle of Cowpens 17 Jan. 1781. He served under Col. John Hazlet and David Hall. He was married and aged 33 in 1783. He lived in Sussex County. He was on the 1791 pension list. He was on the 1813 pension list as Thomas Heldston. He lived in Kent County and died 24 Apr. 1828. He also appeared as Thomas Holston.

Hole, James. —. —. His application was rejected 17 Apr. 1798.

Holefield, Daniel. Va. —. He served in the 3rd Virginia Regiment. His widow, Ruth Holefield, and child were granted £10 support in Prince William Co., Va. on 6 July 1778.

Holgate, —. Pa. —. His widow, Mary Elizabeth Holgate, was awarded a $40 gratuity and a $40 annuity in Philadelphia Co., Pa. 15 Apr. 1835.

Holgate, William. Pa. —. He received a $40 gratuity and a $40 annuity in Montgomery County 1 Apr. 1823. He died 12 May 1843.

Holkar, John. Va. —. His widow, Nancy Holkar, sought relief from Congress for payment of supplies he furnished. Congress granted same 3 Feb. 1858. She was of Clarke County.

Holladay, —. Va. —. He commanded a company of militia from Spotsylvania County and was ordered to South Carolina where he was killed at the defeat of Gen. Gates. His widow was Mildred Holladay who sought relief on 9 June 1784. Her claim was rejected.

Holladay, Thomas [?]. Va. —. His wife, Elizabeth Holladay, was furnished support in Westmoreland

Co. in Feb. 1779.

Holland, —. Pa. —. His widow, Ann Holland, was awarded a $40 gratuity in Lycoming County 3 Mar. 1829.

Holland, —. Va. —. His wife, Mary Holland, was granted £8 relief in Amelia Co., Va. 26 Feb. 1778.

Holland, Edward. Md. Drummer. His widow, Mary Holland, was pensioned at the rate of half-pay of a drummer 22 Jan. 1836.

Holland, Francis. Va. —. While he was away in Continental service, his wife and child were granted support in Yohogania Co., Va. 29 Sep. 1779.

Holland, Henry. S.C. —. He was from Edgefield District in 1828.

Holland, Jacob. Md. Corp. He was pensioned at the rate of half-pay of a corporal of dragoons 19 Feb. 1819.

Holland, Jacob. S.C. —. He was wounded in the knee by a ball from a party of Tories on 11 Feb. 1778 three days before the battle of Kettle Creek. He had a wife and six children. Robert Anderson of Pendleton District swore that Holland fought under his orders. Elizabeth Steel nursed him the night he was wounded. He was from Abbeville District in 1809. He was paid his annuity as late as 1833.

Holland, James. Md. Pvt. He was pensioned at the rate of half-pay of a private 19 Feb. 1819.

Holland, John. Md. Pvt. He was pensioned at the rate of half-pay of a private 13 Mar. 1837.

Holland, John. Pa. —. He was granted a $40 gratuity in Bedford County 12 Apr. 1828.

Holland, Joseph. Md. Pvt. He was pensioned at the rate of half-pay of a private 19 Feb. 1819.

Holland, Thomas. Del. Capt. He was killed at Germantown 4 Oct. 1777. His widow, Joanna Holland, of New Castle sought his arrearage 28 Oct. 1782. His heirs were paid his seven years' half-pay of $1,680.

Holland, Thomas. Pa. —. The act of 12 Apr. 1828 mistakenly authorized the $40 gratuity to be paid to John Holland in Bedford Co., Pa. The act was amended on 3 Mar. 1829 to be paid to Ann Holland, the mother of John Holland.

Holliday, John. Pa. —. His widow, Dorcas Holliday, received a $40 gratuity and a $40 annuity in Huntingdon County 1 Apr. 1823.

Hollidayoke, Daniel. Md. Pvt. He served in the artificers. He presented no evidence that he enlisted for the war so Congress refused bounty land on 12 Apr. 1842.

Holliman, Edmund. S.C. —. He sought his commutation pay as full pay for five years rather than half-pay for life.

Holliman, James. S.C. —. He lived near the North Carolina line and served from the state. He died in Lancaster District 8 May 1836. His daughters, Sarah Holliman and Elizabeth Parker, sought his arrearage 11 Nov. 1854. Their claim was rejected since he was a federal pensioner.

Hollingshead, Benjamin. S.C. Pvt. He served 13 months under Capt. Sharp, Col. Little, and Gen. Green and was discharged at Ten Mile Springs. He was upwards of 60 years of age on 19 Nov. 1824 and applied from Newberry District. His application was rejected because it was not vouchered.

Hollingshead, James. —. His name was incorrectly reported as William Hollingshead of Bedford County. The correction was made by act of 21 June 1839. The war in which he served was not indicated. He was 84 years old in 1840.

Hollingsworth, Elias. S.C. —. He served under Col. Thomas Brannon. He was from Pickens District in 1843. He was pensioned. He died 22 Nov. 1848 and William S. Williams, administrator, sought his arrearage and was paid $42.50 on 18 Dec. 1849.

Hollingsworth, John W. Pa. —. He received relief in 1837 in Montgomery County.

Hollis, Barnabas. Mass. Sgt. He served in Sheldon's Regiment from 15 Mar. 1777 and was from Abington. He was killed by the British 1 Nov. 1781. His widow, Huldah Pennyman, was paid $50. Congress rejected her claim for a pension 16 Feb. 1837.

Hollis, Elijah. S.C. —. He was pensioned on 6 Dec. 1828. He was last paid in 1832.

Hollis, Isaac. Mass. Pvt. He served in the 10th Regiment and was from Braintree. His widow, Dolly Hollis, was paid his pension.

Hollis, James. S.C. —. He was from Fairfield District and was pensioned 30 Nov. 1827. He was still living 5 May 1844.

Hollis, John. S.C. Capt. He served from 1774 to the end of the war. He served under Capt. Samuel Boykin and Capt. William Ransom Davis. He was taken prisoner in the back part of Georgia or Florida and later paroled. He was at Sullivan's Island, Orangeburg, the fort below Granby, St. Illis fort, Barry's fort, Rocky Mount, and King's Mountain. He was wounded by a musket ball. He was born 3 Dec. 1750. He was nearly 80 years of age; his wife was between 65 and 70. He had four daughters and four grandchildren, three of whom were under ten years of age, living with him. There were also two younger sons, but they worked for themselves. He was from Fairfield District 10 Nov. 1830. Elijah Hollis was his younger brother and served under him at the end of the war in Col. Lacey's Regiment. His application was not granted.

Hollis, Samuel. Mass. —. He served in the 4th Regiment and was from Hanover. He was paid $20.

Hollman, Anthony. Pa. —. His widow, Mary Hollman, was awarded a $40 gratuity and a $40 annuity in Montgomery Co., Pa. 27 Dec. 1826.

Hollman, John. Pa. —. He was awarded a $40 gratuity in Montgomery County 15 Apr. 1834.

Holloway, Hind. Va. —. His wife, Elizabeth Holloway, was granted £3 support on 19 May 1777 in York Co., Va.

Holloway, John. Pa. Pvt. He served in the 9th Pa. Regiment. He was wounded in the eye by a stake which projected into the road on a march in the night to camp in June 1777 the use of which, together with the other eye, he was nearly deprived. He lived in Sunbury, Pa. in 1794. He enlisted 13 Apr. 1777 and was discharged 3 Aug. 1777.

Hollowell, Samuel. N.C. —. He was born in Virginia and moved to N.C. about 1777. He died in 1791. He married Maria Palin. His daughter, Nancy Hollowell, married Wilson Aydlett and was from Pasquotank County in Mar. 1834.

Hollums, —. S.C. —. His widow, Ann Hollums, was a resident of Union District in 1786. There was one child in 1791. She also appeared as Ann Hollems.

Holly, John. Va. —. His wife, Judith Holly, was allowed support in the amount of £50 while he was a prisoner in Kentucky on 27 July 1778 She was allowed 4 barrels of corn and 200 pounds of pork on 29 Feb. 1790.

Hollydyoak, John. Md. Pvt. His widow, Ann Hollydyoak, was pensioned in Annapolis at the rate of half-pay of a private 9 Mar. 1827.

Holman, George. Pa. —. He applied in Montgomery County on 19 Oct. 1812. He served in Capt. Henderson's Company in the 9th Pa. Regiment in 1776 or in the beginning of 1777. He was discharged in New Jersey. He then enlisted in Capt. Stake's Company under Col. Butler. He also appeared as George Hollman.

Holman, Samuel. Mass. —. He served in the 7th Regiment and was paid $20.

Holmes, —. S.C. —. His widow, Ann Holmes, was granted an annuity 20 Mar. 1786.

Holmes, Abijah. —. —. He served nine and a half months. His first tour was under Capt. Samuel

Delavan, the second under Capt. John Thomas, and the third under Capt. Richard Sackett. He was 74 years old. Congress granted him a pension 3 Jan. 1832.

Holmes, Gershom. Me. —. He was from Minot. He was paid $50 under the resolve of 1836.

Holmes, Isaac. Mass. —. He served in the 4th Regiment. He was from Hanover and was paid $20.

Holmes, Isaac. Va. Lt. & Paymaster. His commutation was paid 10 July 1792.

Holmes, James. Pa. —. He applied in Cumberland County in Dec. 1817. He enlisted in the 11th Pa. Regiment under Col. Hubley in Capt. Jackson's Company at the commencement of the war. He was discharged in 1781. James Hutton swore that he saw him as a drummer in the Pa. Line. He died 27 Aug. 1839.

Holmes, James. S.C. —. There were children in 1791.

Holmes, John. N.Y. Pvt. He served in Capt. Theodosius Fowler's Company in the 2nd N.Y. Regiment under Col. Philip Van Cortland. He was wounded by a musket ball in his right hip storming a redoubt at the siege of Yorktown, Virginia. He lived at Little Britain, Ulster Co., N.Y. in June 1787. He died in July 1803.

Holmes, Jonathan. Me. —. He died 16 Oct. 1836. His widow was Mercy Holmes from Hartford. She was paid $50 under the resolve of 1836.

Holmes, Jonathan. Mass. —. He served in the 5th Regiment and was from Kingston. He was paid $20.

Holmes, Nathaniel. —. —. He was pensioned in 1818 and dropped in 1820 since he was not indigent. He was restored in 1828. He sought his arrearage and bounty land. Congress rejected his claim 14 Jan. 1837. He resided in New York City, N.Y.

Holmes, Phillips. Mass. —. He served in the 3rd Regiment. He was paid $20.

Holmes, Robert. Mass. Drummer. He served in the 5th Regiment and was from Taunton. He was paid $50.

Holmes, Samuel. Conn. Pvt. He served in Col. Samuel Wyllys's Regiment. In 1777 he was wounded in his right leg near Tarrytown. He served under Capt. Buchannen and Capt. Lt. Peleg Heath. He was pensioned at Hartford, Conn. on 11 Dec. 1788. He died in 1791.

Holmes, Samuel. Pa. —. He served under Capt. John Van Etter and Col. Stroud. He was wounded 20 Apr. 1780 in battle with the Indians on the frontiers. He was from Berks County.

Holmes, Sylvester. Mass. Sgt. He served in the 4th Regiment and was paid $50.

Holmes, Thomas. —. —. His application for relief for wounds received in the Revolutionary War on 28 Mar. 1806 was not approved.

Holmes, Thomas. S.C. —. He was from Pendleton District and was pensioned 21 Dec. 1823 at the rate of $60 per annum for life. He was 78 years old and was without any relation in America. He was so afflicted with palsy that he could not carve or cut his food when he applied in May 1825. He sought his bounty land on 14 Dec. 1825, but his claim was rejected. He was paid two years' arrearage on that date. Thomas Farrar, former officer in the 1st Independent Company under Capt. Benjamin Tutt, swore that Holmes had never applied for bounty land since he lived in the Cherokee Nation or in Georgia. Holmes last received his annuity in 1834.

Holmes, Zacheus. Mass. —. He served in the 2nd Regiment and was paid $20.

Holaday, William. Pa. —.He was pensioned in Indiana County 1 Apr. 1837.

Holsey, Zephaniah. —. —. He was assistant keeper of Continental horse guards to 1783 when he was discharged at Newburgh, N.Y. His service was not military. His widow, Rebecca Holsey, had her application for a pension rejected by Congress 26 Mar. 1858.

Holstein, Peter. Pa. —. He received a $40 gratuity and a $40 annuity in Philadelphia 1 Apr. 1823.

Holston, Jacob. Pa. —. He was awarded a $40 gratuity and a $40 annuity in Northumberland Co., Pa. 4 May 1832.

Holt, —. Va. —. Mary Holt was granted support in Prince Edward County in Apr. 1779, 19 July 1779, and 19 Oct. 1779. On the last date there were five children. They were also granted support in Mar. 1780.

Holt, Daniel. Mass. Pvt. He served in the 2nd Regiment and was from Townsend. His widow, Mary Carle, was paid $50.

Holt, Darius. Me. —. He was from Norway, Maine. He was paid $50 under the resolve of 1836.

Holt, Evan. Pa. —. He was paid $200 for his donation land 6 Apr. 1830 and was a resident of Knox Co., Ohio.

Holt, Jesse. Mass. Corp. He served under Col. Bridge. He was wounded in his left shoulder on 17 June 1775 at Bunker Hill. He lived in Tewkesbury, Mass. in 1795. He was in the militia. He was granted one-eighth of a pension 20 Apr. 1796. He was on the 1813 pension list.

Holt, John. Me. —. He died 16 July 1830. His widow was Lydia Holt from Bethel. She was paid $50 under the resolve of 1836.

Holt, Nathan. N.H. Pvt. He served under Col. Stark. He was wounded by a musket ball which passed through his right thigh in June 1775 at Bunker Hill. He lived in Pembroke, N.H. in 1794. He was granted one-fourth of a pension 20 Apr. 1796. He was on the 1813 pension list.

Holt, Nicholas. Conn. Pvt. He was the son of Capt. Nicholas Holt. He served in Capt. Titus Watson's Company under Charles Burrall. He was inoculated in the summer of 1776 and took sick with smallpox. It fell into an incurable sore on one of his hips. He was from Norwalk. He was on the 1791 pension roll.

Holt, Thomas. Pa. —. He was pensioned 31 Mar. 1837 in Mifflin County. He was 76 years old in 1840.

Holt, Thomas. Va. —. His wife, Sarah Holt, was granted 10 bushels of corn and 64 pounds of pork in Berkeley County 15 Aug. 1780.

Holtsman, Jacob. Pa. —. He was granted relief in Northumberland County 4 May 1832.

Holton, John. Pa. Lt. He served in the 8th Pa. Regiment. Andrew Finley was his lieutenant and proved his service in 1776 and 1777. John Clark proved that Holton was in his company formerly commanded by Capt. Miller and was at the battle of Fort Lawrence on 4 Jan. 1779. Lt. Col. S. Bayard swore that he gave Holton a discharge in 1779. He died 21 Apr. 1830.

Holton, Jonathan. N.H. Lt. He served under Col. Stark in Capt. Carlton's Company under Col. Nichols. He was wounded by a musket ball through his upper jaw bone under his nose and by a small shot in his cheek at the battle of Bennington 16 Aug. 1777. He was pensioned from 24 Sep. 1777 to 24 Jan. 1780. He lived in Charleston, N.H. in 1795. He was in the militia. He was granted half a pension 20 Apr. 1796. He was on the 1813 pension list.

Holton, Peter. Pa. —. He served in the 8th Regiment from 1776 for three years. He was in the battle of St. Lawrence under Maj. Richard Butler, at Banbrook under Gen. Lincoln, and at Brandywine and Paoli under Gen. Wayne. He was wounded in his thigh at Brandywine and was struck with a bayonet at Paoli. He was also at Germantown. He lost the use of his right arm. He was also due nine months pay and also for a lost rifle. He was from Westmoreland County.

Homan, Ambrose. Mass. Pvt. He was pensioned at the rate of $2.50 per month from 15 Dec. 1806. He was on the 1813 pension list.

Homan, Joseph. N.H. —. He enlisted 5 Apr. 1781 for three years in the 1st N.H. Regiment. He was lame by the time he reached home, and his left leg had to be amputated in 1788. He was granted relief on 28 Nov. 1789.

Honey, John. R.I. Pvt. He resided in Providence Co., R.I.

Honeyman, William. Pa. Lt. He served in the 2nd Penn. Regiment. He applied at Philadelphia 13 Feb. 1786 at 27 years of age. He was wounded in his chin and right shoulder in action with the British troops in 1777 at Iron Hill. He died 25 June 1788; his executor was Alexander Fullerton.

Honkins, James. —. —. He was present when Cornwallis surrendered. His "head was whitened by the frost of seventy winters." His youngest son had died in the War of 1812. He sought a 100 acres tract of bounty land in Roane County, Tennessee 11 Oct. 1823.

Hood, —. Pa. —. His widow, Catherine Hood, received a $40 gratuity and a $40 annuity in Philadelphia County 3 Apr. 1837.

Hood, Edward. Md. Pvt. He was on the 1791 pension list. He was on the 1813 pension list. He was pensioned at the rate of half-pay of a private in Anne Arundel County on 23 Feb. 1822.

Hoobler, John. Pa. —. He was granted a $40 gratuity and a $40 annuity in Beaver County 14 Mar. 1835.

Hood, George. Pa. —. He was awarded a $40 gratuity and a $40 annuity in Philadelphia Co., Pa. 17 Jan. 1834.

Hood, James. Md. Asst. Commissary. He was pensioned in Anne Arundel County at the rate of assistant commissary on 6 Feb. 1817. His widow, Kitty Hood, was pensioned 28 Mar. 1832 at the rate of half-pay of a lieutenant. Her arrearage was paid to Isaiah Hood 5 Feb. 1847.

Hood, James. S.C. —. He served under Col. Kershaw. He was at Purysburgh, Rocky Mount, Hanging Rock, Sumter's defeat on the Catawba where he guarded the baggage, Friday's Ferry, Parker's Ferry on the Edisto River, and Eutaw. He was nearly 70 years old with a wife about the same age. William Wood of Lancaster District swore he knew him in the service. He was pensioned 19 Dec. 1825. He was last paid in 1826. His arrearage of $60 was paid to his sons, Allen Hood and James Hood, on 30 Nov. 1827.

Hood, William. Pa. —. He received relief in Erie Co. In 1839 and died 28 Apr. 1840.

Hoog, George. Pa.—. He was pensioned.

Hook, James. Pa. —. He was pensioned.

Hook, Joseph. Md. Corp. He was pensioned at the rate of half-pay of a corporal 23 Jan. 1816.

Hook, Martin. S.C. —. In 1781 he enlisted under Capt. Alexander of North Carolina. He was in the calvary under Wade Hampton. He next served in the Clothing Department under Frederick Class and was discharged at Orangeburg in 1782. He was a recent immigrant to the country and was not acquainted with the language. James Fridig was his captain and swore to his service. He was pensioned 19 Dec. 1825.

Hooker, James. Conn. —. He was at Monmouth, Princeton, and Trenton. He died the 9th or 19th Aug. 1844 in Vermont. He was pensioned in 1818, dropped in 1820, and restored in 1828. The heirs of his widow, Mary Hooker, were granted relief by Congress 2 Aug. 1856. The heirs at law, the Rev. Herman Hooker, Maria Goodspeed, Emily Ranson, James C. Hooker, and Mary J. Mann sought the balance to which he was entitled under the act of 1828 from 1 May 1820 to 19 Aug. 1844. Congress rejected their claim 3 Feb. 1859.

Hoomes, Benjamin. Va. Capt. He lived in King and Queen County 9 Aug. 1795. He served in the 2nd Va. Regiment. He enlisted as an ensign under Col. Woodford and then under Col. Febiger. He was promoted to captain at the Great Bridge near Norfolk. He was at Brandywine, Germantown, and Monmouth. He was wounded in his ankle by a musket ball and another in the head at the latter on 28 June 1778. He was taken prisoner. He was also wounded in his forehead with a sword, and his body was run through with a bayonet. He was disabled by epilepsy and general debility of his body. His son was Thomas Hoomes. He was continued on the pension roll on 18 Mar. 1791. He also appeared as Benjamin Holmes. He was on the 1813 pension list.

Hooper, —. Va. —. His wife, Esther Hooper, was granted £20 support in Caroline Co., Va. on 11 Mar. 1779. *Vide* also Hopper, — with wife Esther.

Hooper, Abraham. Md. Pvt. He was pensioned at the rate of half-pay of a private in Harford County on 27 Jan. 1816.

Hooper, Absalom. S.C. —. He served under Capt. Richard Doggett in the 6th S.C. Regiment under Col. William Henderson. He lived in Georgia after the war and served in the Indian War. He was paid $192.66 for service in the South Carolina Continental Line on 20 Dec. 1810. He was aged 55 in 1819. Capt. Jesse Baker attested to his service. He was 5'8" tall with dark brown eyes. He was from Greenville District and was pensioned 12 Dec. 1820. He was granted one year's arrearage. He had previously lived in Buncombe Co., N.C. He was last paid his annuity in 1834.

Hooper, James. —. —. Congress awarded his widow, Mary Ann Hooper of Virginia, the arrearage of her pension 4 Mar. 1848 to 3 Feb. 1853 on 10 Dec. 1857.

Hooper, John A. N.J. Capt. He served more than two years. The British destroyed his property at Hoppertown, N.J. due to the efficiency and zeal in the American cause. He married 11 Sep. 1779 and died in 1824. His widow, Mary Hooper, received a pension from Congress 13 Apr. 1860. *Vide* John A. Hopper.

Hoops, Adam. Md. Capt. He was pensioned at the rate of half-pay of a captain in Watervleit, Albany Co., N.Y. 13 Feb. 1833.

Hoose, Hendrick. Mass. —. He served in the 9th Regiment and was paid $20.

Hooten, Thomas. Va. —. His wife, Susannah Hooten, was awarded £5 on 16 June 1777, £10 on 20 Oct. 1777, and £10 on 21 Sep. 1778 in Goochland Co., Va.

Hoover, Henry. Pa. —. He applied from Mifflin County on 4 Aug. 1812. He served in the 5th Pa. Regiment and was discharged at Trenton 20 Feb. 1781. He had enlisted in Capt. Cristy's Company in 1777 and served four years. He was wounded in his leg at Germantown. He died 13 Nov. 1823.

Hoover, Henry. Pa. —. He was pensioned 16 June 1836 in Franklin County.

Hoover, Jacob. Pa. —. He was awarded a $40 gratuity and a $40 annuity in Lancaster Co., Pa. 15 Apr. 1835. He died 31 July 1848.

Hoover, John. —. —. Congress rejected his petition because there was no evidence filed on 4 Apr 1849.

Hope, Thomas. N.Y. Pvt. He was granted relief.

Hopkins, Benjamin. Vt. Capt. He served under Col. Seth Warner until he was killed by the enemy. His widow sought a half-pay pension on 15 Oct. 1790. Stephen Hopkins was administrator of his estate.

Hopkins, David. Md. Capt. He was pensioned at the rate of half-pay of a captain of horse in Nov. 1805. He had a wife and five children.

Hopkins, David. S.C. Capt. He entered the service in 1776. He was in battle at the Fish Dam in 1780 and was promoted to colonel. He commanded the 3rd Regiment to the end of the war. Sarah Hopkins, was granted his half-pay 8 Feb. 1836. His son was Ferdinand Hopkins whose children were Wade Hopkins, George W. Hopkins, and John A. Hopkins. His heirs received $2,400 for his service as a captain but not as Lt. Col. They also received his 300 acres of bounty land. Congress determined that his heirs were due an additional 450 acres and the half-pay for his higher rank and awarded same 2 Mar. 1861.

Revolutionary War Pensions 383

Hopkins, Frederick. — . Pvt. He volunteered as a cadet under Capt. E. B. Hopkins and Col. Samuel B. Webb in the spring of 1781 and served to the spring of 1783. He claimed to have been an ensign. He was granted a pension as a private by a special act of Congress 10 Feb. 1846 from 1 Jan. 1844 for two years of service.

Hopkins, Peter. Mass. Pvt. He contracted an ulcer or fever sore which settled in his left leg in 1776. He served under Col. Hitchcock. He lived in Winthrop, Me. in 1792. He was on the 1813 pension list.

Hopkins, Peter. Mass. Pvt. He was pensioned 5 Apr. 1793. He resided in Middlesex Co., Mass.

Hopkins, Richard. R.I. Pvt. He was lame in his left leg which was broken by a musket ball at the battle of Springfield, N.J. on 25 June 1780. He served under Col. Israel Angell. He was aged 25 when he applied 16 Feb. in 1786. He resided in Providence Co., R.I. He was on the 1813 pension list.

Hopkins, Thomas. S.C. — . He enlisted in 1780 and served two years and six months under Generals Green, DeKalb, and Smallwood. He was at Gates' defeat, Camden, Fort Thompson, Fort Friday, Ninety Six, and Eutaw Springs. He was pensioned 7 Dec. 1824. He was from Lancaster District in 1836. He was 74 years old and could not get a federal pension because he had no witnesses to prove his service.

Hopkins, Wait. Vt. Maj. He served under Col. Seth Warner until he was killed by the enemy near Stony Point 15 July 1779. His orphans sought a half-pay pension on 15 Oct. 1790.

Hoplin, John. Pa. — . He was pensioned.

Hopper, —. Va. — . While he was away in the service, his wife, Esther Hopper, was granted £15 support in Caroline Co., Va. 11 June 1778. *Vide* also Hooper, — with wife Esther.

Hopper, Henry. N.Y. Pvt. He served in Capt. James Spencer's Company under Col. Cornelius Van Dyck. He was wounded in the breast and had two ribs broken. He lived at Hilldale, Columbia Co., N.Y. on 11 May 1789. He was 57 years old in 1788. He was on the 1813 pension list.

Hopper, John. — . — . He sought relief for his disability and sufferings in the Revolutionary War. He was allowed to withdraw his petition 28 Mar. 1806.

Hopper, John. N.Y. Pvt. He served under Col. Hammon in the Westchester County militia and was slain 10 June 1782. His widow, Sukey Hopper, received a half-pay pension,

Hopper, John A. N.J. Capt. He served more than two years. He and his six brothers were active Whigs. The American troops occupied his home and storeroom when the British from Staten Island attacked, captured the son, and killed the commanding officer on 16 Apr. 1780. He was wounded in twenty places. His son was killed in the attack. His grand-daughter, Charity (Hopper) Van Vorhees sought compensation from Congress on 22 Jan. 1858. He was late of Hopperstown, Bergen Co., N.J. when Congress granted his widow, Mary Hopper, a pension 13 Apr. 1860. His daughter was Rachel Yelverton. *Vide* John A. Hooper.

Hopseker, Powles. N.J. Pvt. His feet and legs were frosted on an expedition at Staten Island in 1782. Later at White Plains his feet and legs were again injured. He lived in Somerset, N.J. in 1794.

Horder, Peter. Pa. — . He was awarded a $40 gratuity and a $40 annuity in Columbia Co., Pa. 15 Apr. 1835.

Horn, —. Ga. — . His wife, Emily Horn, was granted support 21 Nov. 1781.

Horn, —. Ga. — . His wife, Milly Horn, and four children were furnished assistance 25 Jan. 1782.

Horn, —. Pa. — . His widow, Magdalena Horn, was awarded a $40 gratuity and a $40 annuity in York Co., Pa.

Horn, Abraham. Pa. — . He was awarded a $48 gratuity and a $48 annuity on 14 Mar.1818 in

Northampton County. He died in 1826.

Horn, Daniel. N.H. Sgt. He served in the 2nd N.H. Regiment. He was wounded in the arm in battle at Hubbardtown and was taken prisoner back to Ticonderoga where he remained fifteen months. The surgeon removed fourteen pieces of bone there. After he returned home, he had another piece of bone removed. He was wounded on 7 July 1777. He resided in Shapley, Me. in 1794. He was on the 1813 pension list.

Horn, Thomas. S.C. —. He died in Continental service. His widow, Elizabeth Horn, was awarded an annuity 2 Feb. 1792 and was paid as late as 1803. She was from Prince William Parish, Beaufort District.

Hornbeck, John D. N.Y. Ens. He served in the militia and died 9 May 1835. Congress granted his widow, Maria Hornbeck, a pension 27 June 1838.

Hornbecker, Philip. Pa. —. He was awarded a $40 gratuity and a $40 annuity in Lycoming County on 20 Mar. 1812.

Horner, Gustavus B. Md. Surgeon's Mate. His widow, Frances Horner, was pensioned at the rate of half-pay of a surgeon's mate 4 Mar. 1834 by the state of Maryland. His legal representatives claimed five years' full-pay or half-pay for life as surgeon's mate. He had retired as supernumerary. Congress allowed his heirs relief 19 Mar. 1860. They had been rejected 27 Jan. 1846.

Horney, William. Md. Pvt. He was pensioned in Talbot County at the rate of half-pay of a private in 1810.

Horral, James. Pa. —. He was awarded a $40 gratuity and a $40 annuity in Mifflin Co., Pa. 30 Mar. 1824.

Horsford, Jesse. N.Y. Pvt. He served in Capt. Person's Company under Col. Goose Van Schaick. He was disabled with epilepsy. He was 37 years old in 1786.

Horsford, John. Conn. Pvt. He served in Capt. Buel's Militia Company. He was wounded in the fourth finger on his left hand by a shot which broke the bone in Aug. 1776 at Harlem Heights. He lived in Litchfield, Conn. in 1794. He was granted one-eighth of a pension 20 Apr. 1796. He was reported dead on the 1813 pension roll. He also appeared as John Horseford.

Hortendorf, Henry. Pa. —. He was awarded a $40 gratuity and a $40 annuity in York Co., Pa. 14 Apr. 1834. He also appeared as Henry Horlendorf.

Hortigle, John. N.Y. —. His family was granted support 2 June 1779.

Hortleberger, Philip. Pa. Pvt. He applied 24 Sep. 1787. He was 26 years old. He served in the 11th Regiment. under Capt. Adam Hubley. He was wounded in his breast by a musket ball. The forefinger of his left hand was shot off in a skirmish with the Indians near Fort Jenkins on the Susquehannah. He was under Capt. George Bush. He was aged 26. He also appeared as Philip Hoselberger and Philip Hostleback. He was dead by Sep. 1793.

Horton, —. Va. —. His mother, Elizabeth Horton, was granted £80 support while her son was away in the service in Fauquier Co., Va. in July 1780.

Horton, Barnabas. Mass. Pvt. He was from Bridgewater. His widow, Mary Horton, was paid $50.

Horton, Elisha. Mass. Ens. He received his commutation for five years in lieu of half-pay.

Horton, Enoch. Mass. Pvt. He served in the 8th Regiment and was from Medfield. His widow, Bathsheba Horton, was paid $50.

Horton, Jonathan. N.J. Surgeon. He served as assistant to Dr. Isaac Spafford and died 24 May 1777. His widow was Elizabeth Horton who applied in Morris County in Sep. 1779. His widow married secondly ------ Dunham.

Horwood, Joseph. S.C. Pvt. He served under Capt. Benjamin Waring and Francis Marion. He was killed at the surprise of Gen. Marion on the Santee. Mary Horwood of St. Philip and St. Michael Parish, Charleston District was his widow. She had a daughter under the age of 12 in 1793. In 1795 a son and a daughter were under the age of 12. She collected her last pension in 1822. In 1821 her daughter was Mary Eddy Clark. He also appeared as Joseph Harwood.

Hosford, Jesse. N.Y. Pvt. He served in Capt. Parsons's Company under Col. Goose Van Schaick. He was disabled by epilepsy or falling sickness. He was aged 37 in 1787. He lived in Columbia Co., N.Y. in 1787. He also appeared as Jesse Horsford.

Hoskins, Benjamin. —. Pvt. He served fourteen months from Mass. and Conn. in the city of New York. His service amounted to a total of three years. He married in 1780 in Rochester, Plymouth Co., Mass. He died in 1834. His widow, Mary Hoskins, was aged 86. She failed to prove his service except for 26 days, her marriage, or his death so Congress denied her claim for a pension 3 Mar. 1851.

Hoskins, John. Pa. —. He was awarded a $40 gratuity and a $40 annuity in Allegheny County on 20 Mar. 1812. He was granted £42.3.9 for three months of half-pay on 12 Aug. 1789.

Hoskins, Noah. Mass. —. He was in the 4th Regiment and was paid $20.

Hoskins, Randall. Md. Pvt. He was pensioned at the rate of half-pay of a private in Washington Co., Ky. 7 Mar. 1829. He also appeared as Randolph Hoskins.

Hossack, David. Pa. —. He was granted a $40 gratuity in Westmoreland County 5 Feb. 1836.

Hosmer, Ashbel. Conn. Corp. He served under Gen. Waterbury. He was wounded in the back by a musket ball in July 1781 at Frog's Neck. He lived in Wallingford, Conn. in 1794. He died in 1812. He was listed as dead on the 1813 pension list.

Hotleeling, —. Pa. Capt. He served in the Pa. Line. His widow and children were his heirs.

Hotton, John. Pa. Pvt. He was granted $40 per annum 8 Mar. 1813.

Houchins, Edward. Va. Pvt. He resided in Spotsylvania County 4 Feb. 1806. He served in the 4th Va. Regiment under Col. Lucas and was badly wounded at the defeat of Gen. Gates at Camden, S.C. In 1787 he gathered the necessary documents and placed them in the hands of his representative in Goochland County. They were mislaid. When they were later located, he was pensioned on 15 Jan. 1806 at $40 per annum and $300 in relief. He was in Louisa Co., Va. in 1808 and Mercer Co., Ky. in 1823. His pension was increased from $40 to $80 per annum on 5 Jan. 1819 when he was of Louisa Co, Va.

Houck, Peter. Pa. —. He was awarded a $40 gratuity in Lehigh Co., Pa. 10 Apr. 1835. He also appeared as Peter Hauck, Peter Houk, and Peter Hauk. He was dead by Jan. 1843.

Houets, Philip. N.Y. Pvt. He served in the Montgomery County militia under Col. Fisher and was slain 6 Aug. 1777. His widow, Mary Houets, received a half-pay pension for seven years.

Houghton, Abijah. —. —. He was injured in his left ankle. He resided in Mass. in 1796.

Houghton, Jonathan. Vt. Pvt. He served under Col. Williams in the militia. He was wounded in the right hand by a musket ball which deprived him of two of his fingers on 16 Aug. 1777 at Bennington. He lived in Windham, Vt. in 1795.

Hous, Michael. Pa. —. He applied 3 Jan. 1815 in Harrisburg.

House, Conrad. N.Y. Pvt. He was slain 6 Aug. 1777. His widow, Catharine House, received a half-pay pension for seven years.

House, Elias. N.C. Pvt. He applied in Cabarrus County on 9 Aug. 1793. He served in the militia from Mecklenburg County under Col. Harrington and was disabled at the siege of Charleston, S.C. in 1780 by a cannon ball which took off his left arm. He served under Capt. James Osburn. His father had died in Jan. 1789 so he had two families to support. He was on the 1813 pension list.

House, Henry.. N.Y. Pvt. He served under Lt. Col. Samuel Clyde and was slain 6 Aug. 1777. His widow, Eve House, received a half-pay pension..

House, Johannes. N.Y. Pvt. He served under Col. Goose Van Schaick. His family was granted assistance in May & June 1779 while he was away in the service. He died 17 Jan. 1783. His widow, Ann House, received a half-pay pension for seven years.

House, Joseph. N.Y. Pvt. Indians attacked his house and destroyed everything in and about the property. His wife, Elizabeth, and two children were taken prisoner. They were taken from Montgomery County to Fort Niagara about 300 miles away. The Indians murdered the eldest child on the march. She took fever at Niagara and two months later was taken to Detroit. Back in Niagara, she suffered another attack of fever for four months. She recovered and was sold to Col. Johnson of the British army. Four years later her husband brought her home. Congress rejected her claim for relief 15 Jan. 1822.

House, Michael. Pa. Pvt. He was pensioned in Washington County, Md. at the rate of half-pay of a private 23 Feb. 1822. His widow, Christina House, was pensioned at the same rate on 12 Mar. 1827. He also received a pension from the Commonwealth of Pennsylvania. He died 20 Dec. 1828 and his pension in the amount of $40 was continued to his widow.

Houseman, Jacob. Pa. He was awarded a $40 gratuity in Westmoreland County for his Revolutionary service 12 Apr. 1851. He also appeared as Jacob Housman.

Houser, Albright. Pa. —. He was awarded a $40 annuity in Montgomery County 5 Feb. 1836.

Houser, John. N.Y. —. His family was granted support 20 Feb. 1779. He also appeared as John Howser.

Houser, Peter. N.Y. Sgt. He served under Col. Klock in the Montgomery County militia and was slain 19 Oct. 1780. His widow, Mary Houser, received a half-pay pension for seven years. He also appeared as Peter House.

Houstain, Henry. N.C. —. He applied in Mecklenburg County in 1827 at the age of 76.

Houston, Daniel. N.C. Pvt. He was in Iredell and Robeson Counties. He applied in 1794. He served under Col. Francis Lock and Capt. David Caldwell in the Rowan County militia. He was wounded in his left hand by the British when they marched out of Salisbury on 8 Feb. 1781. He was taken prisoner. Dr. Jeremiah Nelson cured his wound. He sought an increase in 1795. He was on the 1813 pension list. He also appeared as David Houston.

Houston, James. Ga. Surgeon. Congress found that his commutation had already been allowed. Warrant #1231 had been issued 4 Mar. 1827. Congress rejected the claim of the heirs 16 Feb. 1836.

Houston, James. N.C. Capt. He was wounded at Ramsour's Mill 20 June 1778. He was on the 1813 pension list. He died 2 Aug. 1819.

Houston, Leonard. —. —. He served on an armed vessel. He was captured three times by the British and pressed into their service–once for ten months. He escaped. Congress granted him a pension 3 Jan. 1832.

Houston, Peter. N.C. Pvt. He served in the militia under Gen. Rutherford and under Col. Brevard at Ramsour's Mill. He was robbed of $300 worth of money and clothing by the enemy. For his services and sacrifices Congress awarded him bounty land lying east of the Indianapolis State Road leading from Indianapolis to Bloomington on the east side of Beanblossom Creek which land remained unsold for twenty years. He was from Monroe County, Indiana 13 Feb. 1840.

Hout, Jacob. Pa. —. He applied in Westmoreland County on 3 Oct. 1812. He enlisted in Capt. Kelly's Company in Col. Hartley's Regiment. He was wounded in his knee by a bullet at the battle of Germantown. Capt. James Kerny enlisted him at Sheppards Town, Va. He was at Martinsburg,

Berkeley Co., Va. 20 Feb. 1787. He died 7 Mar. 1820. He also appeared as Jacob Houte.

Houzer, Louis. Pa. —. He was formerly of Franklin County.

Hover, Manuel. —. —. He was taken prisoner at the age of 16 in the French and Indian War, held one year by the Indians, escaped, and joined a detachment of regulars under Sir William Johnson. He served as a pilot. En route to reenforce the garrison at Detroit, he was beset by a violent storm on Lake Erie. The provisions and stores were lost. Col. Butler appointed him a captain on scouting parties. During the Revolutionary War he was at the battle of Princeton. He lived on a farm a hundred miles above Philadelphia on the Delaware River in Sussex Co., N.J. where he had a fortified house. He removed to Trumbull Co., Ohio where he died 9 Aug. 1824 at the age of 76. His heirs were Hannah Nicholls, Caty Clark, Sarah Holladay, and Nancy Adgate. His son-in-law was William Nicholls. Congress denied the heirs any relief 28 Mar. 1848.

How, Richard. N.H. Pvt. Portsmouth. 1787. He was in Capt. Caleb Robinson's Company. He was inoculated for smallpox and was blinded. He was aged 43 in 1787.

Howard, —. Va. —. Sarah Howard was awarded a £12 gratuity in King William Co., Va. 6 Nov. 1779.

Howard, Andrew. Mass. Pvt. He served in the 8th Regiment. He was from Belchertown and was paid $50.

Howard, Benjamin. —. —. His widow, Susan Howard, had her petition rejected by Congress because she furnished no proof of her marriage or of his service on 4 May 1846.

Howard, Benjamin. Md. Pvt. His heirs were awarded a warrant for 50 acres for his bounty land in Allegany County 17 Feb. 1832.

Howard, Benjamin. N.J. Pvt. He enlisted for twelve months under Capt. Commandant John Scudder at Elizabeth Town in 1781. He fell among the enemy and received a bayonet wound in his body. He shot his opponent dead. In his attempt to escape over a board fence he received a blow from the end of a musket. He managed to hobble to the burying ground two or three hundred yards. He found 15 or 10 comrades. He asked them for a replacement of the musket he had lost so he could go back and attack the enemy. Two of them went with him to aid him in his escape so he could find some relief. The British had sentinels on both bridges so he had to wade the creek and walk another three miles. He was recommended for half-pay in June 1788. He was 33 years old. He was on the 1791 pension roll at the rate of $40 per annum.

Howard, Edward. Mass. —. He served in Crane's Regiment and was paid $20.

Howard, Edward. Mass. —. He served in the artillery and was paid $20. [second of the name]

Howard, Hiram. N.J. Pvt. He served under Capt. Hall and Col. Spencer. He was wounded in his ankle at Ash Swamp on 23 Feb. 1777. He received a half-pay pension in Morris County in Dec. 1782. He was on the 1791 pension roll at the rate of $32 per annum.

Howard, Ignatius. Va. Pvt. His widow, Sarah Howard, lived in Greenbrier County 15 Nov. 1786 when her pension was continued at the rate of £12 per annum. He served in the company of Capt. Matthew Arbuckle and died in 1777 of smallpox. She was 60 years old and had a son and two daughters. The son had left her by 1786. The auditor was authorized to issue at his own discretion the arrears due her on 3 Jan. 1787.

Howard, Isaac. Mass. Pvt. He served in the 12th Regiment under Col. Moses Little and Capt. Benjamin Perkins. He was disabled by the loss of a finger on his left hand. He was 37 years old in 1789.

Howard, James. Conn. Deputy or Assistant Commissary. He was appointed by Dr. Joshua Elderkin, Commissary. He married Sarah ------ 4 Dec. 1779. He died 8 Jan. 1811. Congress allowed his children relief 13 Apr. 1860 because it was not important whether his service was volunteer or otherwise.

Howard, James. S.C. —. He was born in Virginia and served under Gen. Nelson, Col. F. Maclin, and Capt. John McLin. At the age of 18 or 19 he removed to South Carolina where he served under Capt. Joseph McJunkin at Jimison's Fort and at Ten Mile Springs. Other officers included James Steen, Col. Brandon, Lt. Col. Capt. William Young, Lt. Bishop, Lt. Burges, Lt. Addington, Winn, and Capt. John Watts. He had three daughters one of whom was a cripple. He was in his 70th year. Isaac Barnett of Union District served with him in the Cherokee Expedition. He was pensioned 25 Nov. 1830. He was in Marion District in 1836. He died 24 Nov. 1843 in Union District. His daughters, Martha Howard and Sarah Howard, sought his arrearage. They did not state that they were his only heirs so their application was rejected. His administrator was the proper one to be paid the arrearage.

Howard, James. Va. Pvt. He was wounded at the battle of Guilford. He lived in Hanover Co., Va. He was on the 1813 pension list.

Howard, John. Md. Pvt. He was pensioned 4 Mar. 1789. He was on the 1813 pension list.

Howard, John. Md. Pvt. He was pensioned at the rate of half-pay of a private 6 Mar. 1839 in Mason Co., Ky.

Howard, John D. —. —. He served one year in 1777 on the U.S. schooner, *Gen. Lee*. He had his leg broken twice. He next served for a year on the U.S. brig, *Gen. Gates*. He transferred to the *Queen of France*. It was sunk by order of Gen. Lincoln in Charleston Harbor so he transferred to land service. Congress granted him a pension 3 Jan. 1832.

Howard, John Eager. Md. Col. He was a native of Maryland and one of the most distinguished officers. His portrait was to be painted and placed in the House of Delegates by resolution in 1823 following his death.

Howard, Jonathan. —. Pvt. He served under Capt. Bentley and Col. Humphrey. He was discharged at Fort Constitution 1 Dec. 1776. He died in Oct. 1828 about 75 years of age. He never was pensioned. His widow died about a year later. His son, Stephen Howard, sought any bounty land due his father. Congress rejected the claim 14 June 1850.

Howard, Josiah. Mass. Pvt. He served under Col. Timothy Bigelow and Capt. Brown. He was 30 years old in 1787. He was disabled by a musket ball through his left arm and a ball which entered the rim of his belly. He was pensioned 27 May 1787. He was on the 1813 pension list of Massachusetts. He transferred to Essex Co., Mass. 4 Mar. 1819.

Howard, Nehemiah. Va. —. His wife, Susannah Howard, and two children were awarded £3 per month in Accomack Co., Va. on 23 Feb. 1779.

Howard, Peter. Va. Pvt. He served in 5th Regiment from Mar. to Sep. 1778 and was on furlough when he entered the 3rd Va. Regiment. He was wounded in several places at the defeat of Col. Abraham Buford on 29 May 1780 in S.C. He lived in Va. in 1794. He was on the 1813 pension list.

Howard, Samuel. Pa. —. He was granted relief 15 Mar. 1838. He was 84 years old in 1840. He died 30 June 1842 in Mercer Co.

Howard, Solomon. Mass. —. He served in the 2nd Regiment and was paid $20.

Howard, Thomas. Mass. —. He served in the 13th Regiment and was from Milton. He was paid $20.

Howard, Thomas. Va. Pvt. He served in Campbell's Regiment. He lived in Hanover County.

Howard, Timothy. Mass. Pvt. He served in the 1st Regiment and was from Milton. He was paid $20.

Howd, Benjamin. Conn. Pvt. He served in the 3rd Regiment of Militia. He was wounded by a musket ball in his thigh on 5 July 1779 at East Haven. He resided at Branford, Conn. in 1794. He was granted one-third of a pension 20 Apr. 1796. He was on the 1813 pension list.

Howe, Baxter. N.Y. Lt. He served under Col. John Lamb and died 22 Sep. 1781. His widow, Mary Howe, received his half-pay pension.

Howe, Cato. Mass. —. He was from Plymouth.

Howe, Ebenezer. Conn. —. He was wounded in his hip at Compo on 28 Apr. 1777. He was pensioned at Stamford, Conn. 27 Sep. 1777.

Howe, Jazaniah. Conn. Sgt. He served in the 5th Conn. Regiment. He lost his sight. He was pensioned 10 July 1783. He was on the 1813 pension list. He died in Mar. 1817 in Litchfield Co., Conn. His name may have been Jeremiah Howe.

Howe, Joseph. Mass. Sgt. He served in the 7th Regiment and was paid $20.

Howe, Richard. N.H. Pvt. He served under Capt. Caleb Robinson in Col. Hale's Regiment in Gen. Poor's Brigade. He was inoculated for smallpox and became blind. He was from Portsmouth in 1787. He was disabled.

Howe, Silas. N.H. Pvt. He served four years. He died in 1840. His widow, Elizabeth Howe, of Avon, Livingston Co., N.Y. received a pension from Congress 9 Feb. 1842.

Howe, Simeon. Mass. —. He served in the 3rd Regiment and was paid $20.

Howell, Benjamin. Conn. Pvt. He served in Russell's Regiment.

Howell, Charles. Va. —. His wife, Elizabeth Howell, was granted support for necessaries in Amelia Co., Va. 26 Feb. 1778 and 28 Jan. 1779 while he was away in the service.

Howell, Edward. N.J. Sgt. He served in the 1st Regiment and was wounded through his body and his arm. He was from Morris County. He was on the 1791 pension roll at the rate of $60 per annum. He was 43 years old. He died 9 June 1804.

Howell, George. Va. Pvt. His widow, Jemima Howell, lived in Fauquier County on 25 Sep. 1786. He served in the Va. Regiment and died in Continental service at Buford's defeat leaving her with three children to maintain. She was put on the pension roll at the rate of £10 per annum on 25 Jan. 1787. On 10 July 1788 in Hampshire County one was aged 9 and another aged 8, and the latter was blind. She died 2 Sept. 1830 in Hampshire Co., W. Va. Her children were Hannah Anderson, Lucreasy Anderson, and Anna Johnson. Grandchildren included Anna Anderson and Jemima Anderson. Her grandson, George Warfield, was her executor. She made her will 5 May 1828. She was granted £60 support in Fauquier Co., Va. in Aug. 1779 while her husband was away in the service.

Howell, Richard. Pa. —. He applied in Westmoreland County in Nov. 1814. He enlisted in Capt. James Calderwood's Company in Col. Morgan's Regiment in Frederick, Md. He went to New Jersey. He was drafted into Col. Malcom's N.Y. Regiment. He was drafted a second time in Col. Spencer's N.J. Regiment. He was last drafted in Hubley's 11th Pa. Regiment. He was discharged at Trenton 28 Jan. 1781 by Gen. Anthony Wayne. He settled in Morris Co., N.J. and made a record of his discharge in the docket of Jonathan Staples, Justice of the Peace. He was in battle at Brandywine, Germantown, Springfield, Connecticut Farms in N.J. and various other skirmishes.

Howell, William. N.J. Pvt. He served in the 11th Regiment. He was wounded through his body. He was 35 years old and was from Morris County. He was on the 1791 pension roll. He was on the 1813 pension list. He died 21 Jan. 1824.

Howell, William. Pa. —. He enlisted 9 Apr. 1777 under Capt. Calderwood and Col. Morgan in Frederick, Md. He was drafted into Col. Malcolm's Regiment and later into Hubley's Pennsylvania's Regiment from which he was discharged 28 Jan. 1781 He was at Brandywine,

Germantown, Springfield, and Connecticut Farms in New Jersey. After his discharge he settled in Morris Co., N.J. He was from Westmoreland County. He died 11 Feb. 1827.

Howell, William. S.C. —. He served in Col. Eaton's Regiment. He was discharged 26 Mar. 1779 by Maj. John Paynter. He then served in Col. Laurens' Regiment and was discharged 25 Mar.1780 by Capt. Richard Ransom. He was pensioned at the rate of $60 per annum for life from Dec. 1822 on 23 Dec. 1823. He was deaf and upwards of 90 years. He was last paid in 1831.

Howell, William. Va. —. He enlisted for three years under Capt. Abiel Wishfall of Hampshire. He was at Germantown and served six months under Capt. Oakley and Col. McIntosh. He served one month under Gen. Morgan in Hardy and Pendleton Counties against the Tories. Congress granted him a pension 3 Jan. 1832.

Howell, Zephaniah. N.Y. Pvt. He served under Col. Woodhull in the Orange County militia and was slain 6 Oct. 1777. His widow, Elizabeth Howell, received a half-pay pension.

Howes, Asa. Mass. —. He served in the 5th Regiment and was from Vermont. He was paid $20.

Howes, Abner. Mass. Pvt. He served in the 4th Regiment under Col. Shepard and died in the service 28 Feb. 1782. His heirs, represented by Solomon L. Howes, sought relief from Congress 12 Apr. 1842.

Howes, Cato. Mass. —. He was from Plymouth and was paid $20.

Howes, William. Mass. —. He served in the 6th Regiment and was from Bristol. He was paid $20.

Hoxie, John. —. Seaman. He sought to have his pension of half-pay for life in the amount of $8.50 per month converted to a lump sum payment, but Congress rejected his request 16 Dec. 1801.

Hoy, Alexander. Va. —. His wife, Barbara Hoy, was granted £12 support for herself and her children in York Co., Va. on 15 Dec. 1777 and £40 on 21 June 1779.

Hoy, James. S.C. —. He was paid an annuity in 1832.

Hoy, John. Va. Sgt. He served in the 8th Virginia Regiment and died 3 Nov. 1776. His widow, Catherine Hoy, was on the 1785 pension list. He was from Shenandoah County.

Hoyd, —. Pa. —. His widow, Elizabeth Hoyd, was awarded a $40 gratuity and a $40 annuity in Montgomery County 13 Mar.1836. She died 19 Aug. 1851.

Hoyer, Jacob. Pa. —. He was awarded a $40 gratuity and a $40 annuity in Bedford Co., Pa. 10 Apr. 1826.

Hoyt, David. Mass. —. He was in the 8th Regiment and was from Boscaven. He was paid $20.

Hoyt, Elijah. Mass. Pvt. He served in the 13th Regiment under Col. Wigglesworth. He was wounded by a bayonet which entered his right side near the lower ribs and came out on the left side near his back at Monmouth. He resided at New Milford, Conn. in 1794. He enlisted 1 Mar. 1777 and was discharged 7 Mar. 1780. He was granted half a pension 20 Apr. 1796. He was on the 1813 pension list.

Hoyt, Elisha. Mass. Sgt. He served in Crane's Artillery. He was from Groton. His widow, Hanna Hoyt, was paid $50. He also appeared as Elisha Hoit.

Hoyt, Robert. Mass. —. He was in the 5th Regiment and was from New Braintree. He was paid $50.

Hoyt, Stephen. —. Lt. He served at Lexington and Bunker Hill from Apr. 1775 to Feb. 1776. In July 1776 he hired a man named Putney to serve as his substitute to Dec. 1776. His heirs submitted no evidence so Congress rejected the claim 25 July 1850.

Hubbard, Christian. Pa. —. He was awarded a $40 gratuity and a $40 annuity in Philadelphia 14 Mar. 1818. He also appeared as Christian Hubbert. He died 21 June 1840.

Hubbard, Elisha. —. —. He died 28 Jan. 1837. His administrator, Chauncey Wetmore, sought the arrears of his pension from 4 Sep. 1836. Congress rejected the claim because it was barred by the statute of limitations.

Hubbard, George. —. —. He married in 1806. Congress did not approve a pension for his widow, Emily Hubbard, on 20 June 1848.

Hubbard, John. N.Y. —. His wife and child were granted support in Dutchess County on 3 Nov. 1781.

Hubbard, John. N.Y. Ens. He served under Col. James Livingston from 8 Dec. 1776 to 1 Feb. 1779 when he was transferred to a regiment of the Rhode Island troops. He was granted a certificate of depreciation of pay 10 May 1784. He was on the 1813 pension list.

Hubbard, Joshua. Mass. —. He was granted relief.

Hubbard, Moral. N.H. Pvt. He served in Stark's Regiment. He lived in Sullivan Co., N.H.

Hubbard, Nathaniel. Mass. Artificer. He was from Randolph. His widow, Hannah Hubbard, was paid $50.

Hubbard, Nathaniel. Mass. —. He served in Knox's Artillery and was from N. Bridgewater. He was paid $50.

Hubbard, Silas. Conn. Pvt. He served in Col. Chandler's Regiment. He was disabled by a fit of sickness at White Marsh in 1777. He enlisted 28 Apr. 1777 for eight months and was discharged 1 Jan. 1778. He resided at Tolland, Conn. in 1794. His pension was denied because his disability was do to sickness and not by wounds.

Hubbard, William. Mass. Seaman. He served aboard the continental ship *Warren* under Capt. Saltonstall and was wounded through the knee by a musket ball on 29 July 1779 at Majorbigwaduce. He lost the use of his knee. He was discharged 2 Sep. 1779 and was pensioned at the rate of half-pay from that date on 20 Apr. 1781. He resided in Brownfield, Worcester Co., Mass. He was 42 years old in 1788. He was on the 1813 pension list.

Hubbard, William. Va. Sgt. He was put on the pension list at the rate of £18 per annum on 2 Jan. 1786. He lived in Prince Edward County in Apr. 1787. He served three years in the 9th Va. Regiment. He was wounded in the leg at the battle of Germantown. He was discharged by Brig. Gen. Scott. He later lived in Campbell County.

Hubbel, Isaac. —. Maj. He was at West Point when Benedict Arnold tried to betray his country. He died leaving an eight year old daughter. She was Frances Munson who was aged 82 and blind when Congress gave her pension 8 June 1864.

Hubbell, David. Conn. Pvt. He served under Col. Sherman in Capt. Sill's Company. He strained himself by lifting a log while building a hut at the Highlands. He lived in Huntingdon, Conn. in 1795. He enlisted 12 April 1777 and was on the rolls in 1781. He was granted half a pension 20 Apr. 1796. He was pensioned at the rate of $5 per month from 19 Mar. 1808. He was on the pension roll in 1813 and died 6 Apr. 1820.

Hubble, Abijah. Conn. Corp. He served in the 2nd Regiment. He was disabled by violent fits of sickness. He had weakness in his breast and eyes due to sickness in Dec. 1782. He resided in Stratford, Conn. in 1792. He enlisted 19 May 1777 for the war but did not continue to the end.

Hubble, Nathaniel. Pa. Maj. He was granted two-thirds of a pension 20 Apr. 1796. He was dead by Mar. 1802.

Hubble, William. N.Y. Lt. He served under Col. Lane. Congress rejected the claim for bounty land because he had not served to the end of the war on 25 Jan. 1828.

Huber, Andrew. Pa. —. He applied in Lebanon County on 11 Aug. 1832. He enlisted as a fifer in Capt. Henry Buckler's Company under Col. Philip Greenewalt. Christopher Way was Lt.

Col. He was in the volunteer militia in the first part of 1776 in what was then Somerset County. He marched from Lebanon to Reading, Easton, Bethlehem, and Amboy to Paulus Hook near New York. He enlisted in Capt. Andrew Fricker's Company of the Flying Camp in the summer of 1776 for six months in Newark, N.J. His officers were Lt. John ------, 2nd Lt. Peter Horter, Ens. John -----, Col. Jacob Klotz, and Maj. Boyd. In 1777 he entered as a substitute for his brother, John Adam Huber, and guarded British prisoners. He also was a substitute for Christian Becker. He was born in Lebanon Township in May 1762. He was awarded a $40 gratuity and a $40 annuity in Lebanon Co., Pa. 14 Apr. 1834.

Huber, Casper. Pa. —. He was granted a $40 gratuity and a $40 annuity in Lancaster County in 1836. He died 10 Apr. 1842. He also appeared as Casper Hubert.

Huber, Conrad. Pa. —. He was awarded a $40 gratuity and a $40 annuity in Lehigh Co., Pa. 27 Jan. 1835.

Huber, George. Pa. Pvt. He with Michael Zeller served in Capt. Deckert's Company in the 5th Pa. Regiment. They were made prisoners at the surrender of Fort Washington. He applied in Dauphin County 31 Mar. 1807 and was awarded 200 acres of donation land in common with Zeller.

Huber, Peter. Pa. —. He was awarded a $40 gratuity in Philadelphia County 5 Feb. 1836. There was no record of any payment ever made.

Hubert, —. Pa. —. His widow, Mary Hubert, was awarded a $40 gratuity and a $40 annuity in Philadelphia County 31 Mar. 1836. She died 6 July 1842 She also appeared as Mary Huber.

Hubler, John. Pa. —. His widow, Catharine Hubler, received a $40 gratuity and a $40 annuity in Mercer County 13 Apr. 1854.

Hubley, —. Pa. —. His widow, Anna Maria Hubley, was awarded a $60 gratuity and a $60 annuity in Dauphin Co., Pa. 29 Mar. 1823. She died 23 June 1825. She also appeared as Anna Maria Hubler.

Hubley, Bernard. Pa. —. He was an officer in the Northumberland County militia. He used his certificate of pay to purchase part of the estate of William Rankin, an attainted traitor. Thomas Campbell had a title paramount to 74 of the 140 acres and 76 perches. Hubley brought an ejectment. He had also bought a tract and ferry house known as Niblet's Ferry. The sale and title were not confirmed; his money was not returned. He was awarded $3,478.58 for the loss of the 74 acres and Niblet's Ferry because he was a Revolutionary War veteran on 31 Mar. 1807.

Hubner, George. Pa. —. He was paid a $40 gratuity 1 Apr. 1834 in Schuylkill County.

Huchingson, John. Conn. Corp. He was wounded at Kings Bridge in July 1781. A musket ball broke one of his ribs and entered the trunk of his body. It passed out through his shoulder blade. He was taken to the hospital at West Point. He served in Capt. Comstock's Company in the 5th Conn. Regiment.

Hudders, —. Pa. —. His widow, Ann Hudders, was awarded a $40 gratuity in Chester Co., Pa. 6 Apr. 1833.

Huddleston, John. N.C. Pvt. He applied in Rutherford County in 1807. He served in the militia under Capt. Adam Hampton and was wounded in the right thigh. He was unable to support his small family. He was on the 1813 pension list.

Huddy, Joshua.. N.J. Capt. He was from Monmouth County and was in the militia in 1776. He had command of a company of artillery in 1777. He commanded a post at Tom's River in 1781. He was taken prisoner in 1782 and put on a vessel at New York City. He was hanged in Apr. 1782. His daughter, Martha Piatt of Cincinnati, Ohio, sought relief from Congress on 14 Feb. 1837 for having her father treated as a Continental officer. She was 70 years old. Her mother and her sister, Elizabeth Green, were dead. She was awarded seven years' half-pay of a captain of artillery. She was also given scrip for 300 acres in the public domain at the cost of $1.25 per acre.

Hudgens, Ambrose. S.C. Capt. He served with Col. William Thompson, Col. Williams, Lt. Robert Long, and Col. Purvis. He was 68 years old and his wife was about the same age. William Millwee of Anderson District swore that Hudgens served under him. James Dillard of Laurens District served with him under Capt. Bround. He was from Laurens District when he was pensioned 23 Nov. 1829. He was last paid in 1842.

Hudnut, Richard. N.J. —. He served in Dayton's Regiment in 1778 but his name could not be found on the rolls. His widow was Grace Hudnut. She failed to set forth proof of her marriage or his service. Congress rejected her petition 9 Jan. 1847.

Hudson, —. N.C. —. He died in militia service. His widow, Mary Hudson, later married ----- Jones. She was from Warren County in 1805.

Hudson, —. Va. —. His wife, Sarah Hudson, was granted £10 support while her husband was away in the service in Fauquier Co., Va. in Nov. 1776.

Hudson, Benjamin. Va. —. His wife, Mary Hudson, was granted £6 support on 15 June 1778, £25 support on 21 Dec. 1778, and £20 on 21 June 1779 in York County.

Hudson, Eleazer. Conn. Pvt. He served in the 1st Conn. Regiment. He enlisted in Capt. William Richards' Company in Jan. 1777 for three years. He had both bones of his leg broken in an accident at Germantown on 12 Oct. 1777. He served under Lt. Col. David F. Sill. He was pensioned 30 Sep. 1788. He lived in Lyme, Conn. and was 50 years old. He was on the 1813 pension list. He died 14 Mar. 1814 in New London Co., Conn.

Hudson, Elijah. Mass. Sgt. He served under Capt. Barnes and Col. Jonathan Ward and was thrice wounded. He was pensioned in 1786. He was on the 1813 pension list. He died 30 Aug. 1823 in Worcester Co., Mass.

Hudson, Enos. Mass. —. He was in the 7th Regiment and was paid $20.

Hudson, John. —. —. He was on the pension roll and asked for certain arrearage. Congress rejected his petition 4 May 1846.

Hudson, John. Md. Pvt. He was pensioned in Caroline County at the rate of half-pay of a private 7 Feb. 1817. He also appeared as John Hutson. His widow, Elizabeth Hudson, was pensioned at the same rate 11 Mar. 1828.

Hudson, John. Mass. —. He was paid $20.

Hudson, Samuel. Mass. —. He served in the 6th Regiment. He was paid $20.

Hudson, Timothy. Me. —. He died 4 Apr. 1834. His widow was Jane Hudson of Clinton. She was paid $50 under the resolve of 1836.

Hudson, William. —. —. He enlisted for seven years. He died or was killed in the service. He never married. His father never sought any relief. The family was from Huntington Co., Penn. His heirs were his half-brothers, John Hudson and Matthew Hudson, of Portage Co., Ohio who sought his bounty land. His name was not on the rolls. Congress denied them relief 28 Mar. 1848.

Hueston, William. S.C. —. He was wounded at the Hanging Rock in Aug. 1780. His widow, Eleanor Hueston, was granted an annuity 17 Nov. 1784.

Huey, James. S.C. Sgt. He was pensioned 7 Dec. 1824 by South Carolina. His last annuity payment was in 1834. He was in the service for 176 days under Capt. R. Frost and Capt. Anderson

Thomas which was six or seven days less than the time necessary for a federal pension. He
served under Capt. Robert Montgomery as a private in 1780 for four months. The soldier died
on 6 Apr. 1836 in Lancaster Dist., S.C. and his widow, Jane Huey, died 23 Dec. 1841 in
Mecklenburg Co., N.C. The widow was survived by James Huey, Thomas W. Huey, Jane B.
Walkup, and Alexander B. Huey. The son, Thomas W. Huey, served in the South Carolina
legislature and was executor of his father's will. The last surviving child was Alexander B.
Huey. The veteran served under Col. Kershaw and went to Purisburg. He was also under Col.
Kimball at Camden. He also served under Gen. Thomas Sumter and Maj. Davis at Walkup's
Mills where he shot the first bullet. He was in a skirmish at Waxhaw's and at Hobkirk Hill. The
veteran married Jane Walker on 8 Feb. 1787 in Mecklenburg Co., N.C. The Rev. Brice Miller,
a Presbyterian minister, performed the service. The record could not be found in the courthouse
in Charlotte. James Huey was born 29 May 1759. Jane Walker Huey was born 22 Mar. 1760.
The children of James and Jane Huey were: Alexander B. Huey born 22 Dec. 1787, Elizabeth
Boyd Huey, born 8 Dec. 1789 and died 9 Aug. 1791, Robert Davis Huey born 21 or 22 Feb.
1792, John Huey born 5 Apr. 1794, James Huey born 4 Oct. 1796, Thomas Walker Huey born
27 Nov. 1798, and Jane Boyd Huey born 18 Dec. 1801. The children of Alexander B. Huey were:
Alonzo Legrand Huey born 5 Apr. 1812, James Grandison Leroy Huey born 28 June 1813,
William Frierson Johnston Huey born 23 Feb. 1816, Robert Walker Huey born 14 Apr. 1818,
Alexander Harvey Huey born 19 May 1820, John Boyd Huey born 4 Dec. 1822, Jane Josephine
Clarissa Huey born 24 July 182[?], Margaret Florentine Huey born 12 Oct. 1827, George [?------]
Huey born 23 Jan. 1830, and Thomas Calvin Huey born 9 May 1832. The children of Robert D.
Huey were: Alexander Sinclair Huey born 30 Dec. 1814, Jane Adeline Huey born 3 Nov. 1816,
Nelly Lavina Johnston Huey born 26 Dec. 1818, Juliet Editha Huey born 25 Dec. 1820, and
Sarah Elizabeth Huey born 16 Feb. 1823. The children of John B. Huey were: Jane Clementine
Huey born 8 Mar. 1819, Louisa Clarissa Huey born 4 Oct. 1821, Caroline Elizabeth Huey
born 26 Nov. 1825, Albertine Elizabeth Huey born 26 Nov. 1825 and married 27 Jan. 1848,
James Alexander Huey born and died 9 Mar. 1828, Emily Florentine Huey born 1 Mar. 1829
and died 2 Mar. 1829, Frances Ruth Huey born 20 June 1830, and John Thomas Huey born
22 May 1833. The children of Thomas W. Huey were: Jane Minerva Huey born 4 Mar. 1822,
Sarah Cynthia Huey born 24 Oct. 1823, Elizabeth Clementine Huey born 27 Oct. 1825, Martha
Floret Huey born 14 Nov. 1828, and Margaret Ann Huey born 14 Nov. 1828. Alexander B. Huey
was the administrator of the estate of his mother, Jane Walker Huey, in Harris Co., Ga. Congress
awarded the sum of an annual rate of $37.50 per annum from 4 Mar. 1831 to 23 Dec. 1841 to
the heirs on 2 Aug. 1856.

Huff, John. Pa. —. He was awarded a $40 gratuity and a $40 annuity in Northampton Co., Pa. 9 Feb.
1824.

Huffman, George. Pa. —. He was awarded $200 in Frederick, Md. 17 Feb. 1827.

Huffman, Michael. Pa. —. He was awarded a $40 gratuity and a $40 annuity in Westmoreland Co.,
Pa. 10 Apr. 1835. He was dead by Jan. 1839.

Huffnagell, Christian. N.Y. Pvt. He served under Col. Jacob Klock in the militia. His children, Ann
Huffnagell and Christian Huffnagell, were granted a half-pay pension.

Huger, Benjamin. S.C. Maj. He served in the 5th S.C. Regiment on Continental Establishment and
died at Charleston 11 May 1779. His widow and three children sought his seven years' half-
pay 23 Nov. 1791.

Huggins, Samuel. Md. Pvt. He was pensioned in Cecil County on 12 Aug. 1788. He was on the 1813
pension list. He died 24 Aug. 1818.

Huggins, William. S.C. Pvt. He served under Brig. Gen. Charles Cotesworth Pinckney and was disabled by the falling of a cannon which crushed his hip and left hand. He was discharged unfit for duty. He was allowed an annuity from 1786. He wife was 40 to 50 years of age. His children were Nancy, Harry an idiot aged 18 or 19, Polly aged 12 or 13, Daniel aged 10 or 11, George aged 8, Hariot, and Jenny. He was from Richland District and was paid $450 for his pension from 1786 to 1808 on 29 June 1808. He received his annuity in 1819. His widow, Nancy Huggins, was placed on the pension roll on 16 Dec. 1823 as Nancy Higgins. He had died about two years earlier. She was about 60 years old. Due to the misspelling of her surname, the treasurer refused to pay her. Her name was corrected 7 Dec. 1824, and she was given the unpaid amount. She was last paid in 1834.

Hughes, —. S.C. —. His widow was Sarah Hughes. There were two children in 1791. She sought to be placed on the pension list on 14 Dec. 1814 but was rejected.

Hughes, Andrew. S.C. —. He fought against the Cherokee and was as Cross Creek where the Scots were defeated, Camden, and Briar Creek. His officers included Gen. Rutherford, Gen. Nash, Capt. Waddy Tate and Capt. Jameson. He was from Pendleton District and was pensioned 7 Dec. 1826. He was 71 and his wife was about 61. He had lived in the district 39 years. John Wilson swore he served with him. He was last paid in 1834.

Hughes, Elias. Va. —. He was a ranger or Indian spy for thirteen months under Capt. James Booth. He received $104 on 23 Mar. 1839.

Hughes, George. Pa. —. He received a $40 gratuity and a $40 annuity in Mercer County 3 Apr. 1837.

Hughes, Henry. —. —. He received his commutation.

Hughes, Hugh. —. QM. He entered the service in 1776 and was appointed Commissary of Military Stores and was promoted to Assistant Quartermaster General and served to the Spring 1778. He was appointed Quartermaster General and served to 1783. He died in New York City. Congress ruled that his heirs, Jasper W. Hughes, Charles Hughes, Harriette M. Hughes, grand-daughter Ruth M. Gamble, and Philemon Dickerson whose wife was a grand-daughter, had no cause for action 10 Dec. 1857.

Hughes, James. Va. Sgt. He lived in Fairfax County 17 Sep. 1787 and was 39 years old. He served in Col. Joseph Crockett's Western Battalion. He drew no pay from 1 Dec. 1780 until the regiment was discharged 22 Dec. 1782. He was disabled in guarding the convention troops at Albemarle barracks. His right leg had to be amputated. Capt. William Cherry, paymaster, certified his service on 17 July 1787. He was put on the pension list on 1 Oct. 1787 at the rate of £15 per annum. William Hickman was appointed administrator of his estate on 15 Sep. 1788 in Fairfax County.

Hughes, John. Pa. Capt. He applied in Washington County. He was confined to prison for debt on 3 Mar. 1813. Col. Andrew Porter of the Pa. Regiment of Artillery proved his service. His claim was to be paid in full on 19 Mar. 1816. He died 15 Sep. 1818. He also appeared as John Hughs.

Hughes, John. Pa. —. He served under Capt. Simon Cole and Col. Antes in June 1778. In 1779 he was scouting in the Buffalo Valley. He was from Lycoming County.

Hughes, John. S.C. —. He was killed in service. His widow, Elizabeth Hughes, was granted an annuity 20 Feb. 1786.

Hughes, John. Va. Sgt. He was awarded a £70 gratuity on 18 Oct. 1779 and a £500 gratuity on 8 Dec. 1780. He resided in Fluvanna County 25 Jan. 1787 and was 32 years old. He served in Col. Charles Harrison's Regiment of Artillery. In 1777 he enlisted in the Old Company of Artillery under Col. Innis. In the spring of 1778 he was inoculated for smallpox at Cealey's prior to the march of the regiment to the northward. He became blind from that disorder. Capt. Lt. Samuel Coleman attested to his service. He was continued at the rate of £18 per annum on 25 Jan. 1787. He died 6 Dec. 1788 and George Moody qualified as administrator of his estate in Bedford County in July 1790. One of the same name and rank was on the 1813 pension list.

Hughes, Joseph. Va. —. His wife, Anne Hughes, was granted £6 support on 19 May 1777 in York Co., Va.

Hughes, Joseph. Va. —. His wife, Jane Hughes, was granted £25 support on 15 June 1778 in York Co.

Hughes, Pratt. Va. Lt. His commutation was made 1 Nov. 1793.

Hughes, Thomas. N.Y. —. He served in Capt. Cap's Company in Col. Van Schaick. He was awarded 200 acres of bounty land 11 Apr. 1804.

Hughes, William. S.C. —. He served 20 months in Capt. John Burke's Company of Georgia Minutemen and later from South Carolina. He was at Eutaw and Stono. He was upwards of 70 years and his family consisted mostly of females. He was 66 years old; his wife was about the same age. He was almost blind. He was also in the Florida Campaign. His officers included Capt. Dugan, Capt. Casey, Capt. Starks, and Capt. McCracken. He was from Pendleton District when he was pensioned 7 Dec. 1826. He had lived in the state 60 years and 20 years in the District. Benjamin Nabours stated he served with him in the Florida Campaign under Gen. Andrew Williamson and Col. McCrary. He was last paid in 1834.

Hughs, Dempsey. S.C. —. He was killed in battle. His widow was Sarah Hughs. She removed to Georgia and was prevented from collecting the money due her. She suffered from rheumatism and in 1812 sought her arrearage. Her claim was rejected.

Hughs, George W. S.C. —. He served in the state troops. He was from Newberry District when he was pensioned 30 Nov. 1827. He was paid in 1828. He also appeared as George W. Hughes.

Hughs, Richard. S.C. —. He died in prison. His widow, Mary Hughs, was granted an annuity 17 Feb. 1786.

Hughs, William. S.C. —. He was killed in the service. His children were granted an annuity 17 Feb. 1786.

Hulet, William. Pa. Pvt. He was in Philadelphia County on 12 Dec. 1785. He was in the 2nd Pa. Regiment under Col. St. Clair and was transferred to the Invalids. He was discharged 14 Dec. 1782 on account of loss of his eyesight in his right eye and the sight in the other being greatly impaired. He also suffered from rheumatism. His wife was Keziah Hulet. He was 45 years old in 1785 and 51 years old in 1787. He also appeared as William Hullet.

Hull, —. Mass. —. His widow was Ruth Hull. She was paid 4 Feb. 1834.

Hull, Agrippa. Mass. —. He served in the 2nd Regiment. He was paid $20.

Hull, Henry. Va. Pvt. He was on the 1813 pension list as Henry Hall.

Hull, Samuel. N.J. Sgt. He was pensioned 2 Feb. 1798. He was on the 1813 pension list.

Hull, Samuel. N.Y. Corp. He served in Col. J. Clinton's Regiment. He was wounded by a musket ball in the breast in action in Canada in 1776 at St. Pierre. He volunteered again in 1777 and served as a recruiting sergeant. He was taken prisoner 15 Jan. 1779 and held to the end of the war. He lived in Poughkeepsie, N.Y. in 1794.

Hull, Samuel. N.Y. —. He enlisted for the war and was taken prisoner. He was carried to the West Indies and in consequence was returned a deserter on the rolls. He could not, therefore, obtain his bounty land. He was an invalid and desired his bounty land to be issued to his brother David

Hull, saddler, and Samuel Sayre, mason, of Newark, N.J. as trustees to dispose of same 18 Mar. 1796.

Hull, Stephen. Conn. Corp. He served in Capt. Sanford's Company under Col. Chandler. On 11 Jan. 1778 he was taken with bilious fever which fell into his leg. He lost the leg. He was pensioned 4 May 1787. He lived in Woodbury, Conn. and was aged 55 years. He was on the 1813 pension list.

Hull, Thomas. Mass. —. He served in the 4th Regiment and was from Brookfield. He was paid $50.

Hull, Thomas. Va. —. His wife, Sarah Hull, was granted £25 support in Berkeley County on 19 Aug. 1779. She received 10 bushels of corn and 64 pounds of pork on 15 Aug. 1780.

Hull, William. Mass. Lt. Col. He received his commutation for five years in lieu of half-pay for life. He died 29 Nov. 1825.

Hull, William. Pa. —. He was granted $40 per annum 27 Jan. 1814. [The entry is smeared and the surname may be misinterpreted.]

Hulm, Bell. Va. —. His wife, Mary Hulm, was granted relief 11 Dec. 1777 and £40 on 11 Mar. 1779 in Lunenburg Co., Va. He also appeared as Bell Halm.

Hulme, John. Pa. —. He was awarded a $40 gratuity and a $40 annuity in Dauphin Co., Pa. 14 Apr. 1834.

Hulsey, Jesse. N.C. —. He applied from Hall Co., Ga. in 1822. He was wounded in his left arm by Indians in an attack on Wafford's Fort in Turkey Cove, Burke Co., N.C. He was a member of Capt. William Johnson's company under Col. Benjamin Cleveland. He had a wife and seven children. He was awarded a $25 gratuity and a $50 annuity in 1824.

Hultz, William. Pa. —. He was granted a $40 gratuity and a $40 annuity in Lancaster County 13 Apr. 1841. He died 7 Apr. 1844.

Hume, William. Va. —. He served in the militia and was wounded in 1781 near Williamsburg. He was in the Fauquier County militia. He was pensioned 19 Dec. 1783. He was on the 1785 pension list.

Hummel, Christopher. Pa. —. He was awarded a $40 gratuity and a $40 annuity in Venango Co., Pa. 16 Feb. 1835. He died 17 Dec. 1835.

Hummel, John George. Pa. —. He was granted relief in Northumberland Co. 13 Mar. 1839 and died 23 Sep. 1853..

Hummel, Henry. Pa. —. He was pensioned in 1813.

Humphrey, John. Va. —. His mother, Secilia Humphrey, was furnished 1 barrel of corn and 50 pounds of pork in Louisa Co., Va. on 12 June 1780.

Humphrey, William. Va. Pvt. He served 17 months in 1780 and 1781 under Capt. Holt Richardson and Col. Dabney in the 3rd Regiment and was discharged after the surrender of Lord Cornwallis at Yorktown in Oct. 1781. He applied 23 Aug. 1833 but died in Mar. 1850. His children sought his arrearage 16 Feb. 1871, and Congress granted same. They had tried earlier on 16 Jan. 1857 and 6 Apr. 1860.

Humphreys, John. Va. Lt. He was killed at Quebec 31 Dec. 1775. His heirs were paid his seven years' half-pay of $1,120. His widow, Sarah Humphreys, was awarded a £200 gratuity on 18 Nov. 1778. She was being pensioned in 1783. Her helpless infant was an idiot. He also appeared as John Humphries.

Humphries, Robert. —. —. His widow, Esther Humphries, had her petition for a pension rejected by Congress on 27 Mar. 1846 because they were married subsequent to 1 Jan. 1794.

Hundley, George. Va. —. His wife was granted support in Pittsylvania Co., Va. 23 Jan. 1778 and on 26 Feb. 1778.

Hungarius, Gabriel. Pa. Pvt. He was in Philadelphia County 13 Oct. 1785. He was transferred from the 6th Pa. Regiment to the Invalids. He was stabbed in his side. He served under Col. Richard Humpton. He was 30 years old. He was dead by Mar. 1797. He also appeared as Gabriel Hungarie.

Hungerford, —. Va. —. George Hungerford was granted £10 relief while his two sons were away in Continental service on 11 Dec. 1777 in Lunenburg Co., Va.

Hunnewell, John. Mass. Pvt. He was in the Invalids under Capt. Fox and Col. Henry Jackson. He was disabled by a consumptive habit and was 41 years old in 1786. He suffered from involuntary discharge of urine. He resided in Rhode Island. He died 15 Oct. 1790. He also appeared as John Hunawell.

Hunnewell, Jonathan. Mass. Artificer. He served in Mason's Regiment and was from Roxbury. He was paid $50.

Hunt, —. Pa. —. His widow, Anna Hunt, was granted relief in Fayette County 16 Apr. 1840.

Hunt, Benjamin. Mass. —. He served in Crane's Regiment. He was paid $20.

Hunt, Caleb. N.H. Pvt. He served under Col. Hale in Capt. Blodgett's Company. He was wounded in both thighs by musket balls in July 1777 at Hubbardstown. He lived in Marlow, N.H. in 1795. He was on the rolls in 1780 and continued thereon to Jan. 1782. He was granted half a pension 20 Apr. 1796. His rate was $5 per month from 5 Mar. 1808.

Hunt, Eden. N.Y. Qr. Mr. He served under Col. Graham in the militia. He was badly wounded by a musket ball through his lungs near Pine Ridge in Mar. 1781. It entered to the left of his spine below the scapula and came out of his body under his right arm. It fractured a rib. He lived in Westchester Co., N.Y. on 22 June 1787 and in New York City, N.Y. on 21 June 1788.

Hunt, Elisha. N.C. Pvt. He applied in Northampton County in 1785. He was in Continental service and lost an arm. He was aged 27 in 1785. He was on the 1813 pension list. He lived in Lenoir County.

Hunt, Ephraim. Mass. —. He was from Canton and was paid $50.

Hunt, Francis. N.Y. Pvt.. He died in Sep. 1805.

Hunt, Humphrey. —. Matross. He was pensioned 4 Sep. 1793. He transferred from Conn. to Cayuga Co., N.Y. 4 Mar. 1832.

Hunt, Humphrey. N.H. Pvt. He served under Col. Scammel. He was wounded by a musket ball shot through his left hand in Aug. 1779 at Newtown. He lived in Sanbornton, N.H. in 1794. He enlisted 27 Jan. 1778 for two years and was discharged 27 Jan. 1780. He was granted a fourth of a pension 20 Apr. 1796. He was on the 1813 pension list.

Hunt, Jesse. Va. —. His wife was allowed assistance in Lancaster County in 1778.

Hunt, Josiah. N.J. —. He received $268.03 for the 14 years of interest on his depreciation pay 15 Feb. 1838. He may be identical with the one of the name who served under Col. Spencer in 1776 to the end of the war and received several wounds.

Hunt, Nathaniel. Mass. —. He served in Burbeck's Artillery. He was from Randolph. His widow, Hannah Linfield, was paid $50.

Hunt, Noah. Mass. —. He served in the 2nd Regiment and was from Tewksbury. He was paid $50.

Hunt, Peter. N.Y. Pvt. He served under Capt. Frank and Col. Peter Bellinger in the Montgomery County militia and was slain 6 Aug. 1777. His widow, Cartret Hunt, received his half-pay pension.

Hunt, Samuel. —. —. He was a guard over prisoners taken from Burgoyne's Army. When the roof of the barracks took fire, he ascended to the roof to extinguish the flames. He was injured in one of his knees. His leg had to be amputated near the hip. Congress granted him a pension 24 Jan. 1824. He received further relief 21 Jan. 1836. He was from Rutland, Worcester County, Vermont.

Hunt, Samuel. Mass. Pvt. He served at the Castle and was from Weymouth. His widow, Phebe Hunt, was paid $50.

Hunt, Samuel. Va. Pvt. He lived in Cumberland County in 1787 and was 33 years old. He served in the 2nd Va. Regiment of Dragoons from 1 Jan. 1777 to 29 May 1780. He was disabled by wounds and lost the use of both of his hands at the Waxsaws. Capt. Thomas Parker attested to his service. He was continued at the rate of £18 per annum on 11 Jan. 1787. He later lived in Monroe County. He was on the 1813 pension list.

Hunt, William. Vt. Pvt. or Corp. He served under Col. Warner in Capt. Woolcot's Company. He was wounded by a ball which passed through his right thigh on 16 Aug. 1777 near Bennington. He lived in Middlebury, Vt. in 1795. He enlisted 16 Jan. 1777 and was on the rolls in 1780. He was granted half a pension 20 Apr. 1796.

Hunter, —. Pa. —. His widow, Jane Hunter, was awarded a $40 gratuity in Adams Co., Pa. 17 Mar. 1835.

Hunter, Andrew. Pa. —. He was awarded a $40 gratuity and a $40 annuity in Indiana Co., Pa. 16 Feb. 1835.

Hunter, Benjamin. Pa. —. He was awarded a $40 gratuity and a $40 annuity in Philadelphia Co., Pa. 21 Jan. 1828. He died 3 Aug. 1834.

Hunter, James. S.C. —. He was in action with the Negro Dragoons at Watboo. His officers were Francis Marion and Capt. Jackson (called "Killing Steve"). He was about 70 years old and suffered from rheumatism. Two daughters still lived with him. Peter Aarant stated he served with him. He was pensioned from Lancaster District on 23 Nov. 1829. He was last paid in 1848. He died 26 May 1849. M. D. Duren sought reimbursement of $30 for burial expenses. Titus Long had maintained him and sought his arrearage. Duren was paid $10 but Long was not awarded anything.

Hunter, John. Mass. Pvt. He served under Col. Learned. He had ulcerated sores on his left leg occasioned by a fever in the service in Sept. 1775 at Roxbury. He lived in Brookfield, Mass. in 1795. He was in the militia.

Hunter, John. Pa. Pvt. He served in the 4th Company, 2nd Regiment, Westmoreland County militia and was wounded in the service.

Hunter, John W. S.C. —. He enlisted in 1781 as a trumpeter at the age of 13 under Gen. Sumter. He was with Maj. Moore in Georgia. He served from 1791-1794 in the Georgia troops on the frontier. In 1795 he removed to Pennsylvania. In 1822 he moved to Augusta, Georgia. His claim for compensation was rejected 26 Nov. 1830 because he had already been paid.

Hunter, Robert. Pa. Pvt. He was in Westmoreland County in 28 Jan. 1808. He served in Capt. John Findley's Company under Col. McCoy. At Boundbrook he was wounded in the leg which became incurable. He was ruptured in crossing a fence at Paoli in the retreat. He was awarded a $40 gratuity and a $40 annuity by Pennsylvania. He married 5 Sep. 1792 in Westmoreland County and died 26 May 1839. He was granted donation land by Pennsylvania in 1808. Congress granted his widow, Ann Hunter, a pension 28 Feb. 1844. Robert Hunter was paid $209 by Pennsylvania in the right of his wife, Ann Hunter, formerly Ann Sloan, in 1827.

Hunter, Robert. Pa. —. He was awarded a $40 gratuity and a $40 annuity 27 Mar. 1837 in

Westmoreland County.

Hunter, Samuel. S.C. —. He was granted an annuity 7 Feb. 1787.

Hunting, Amos. Mass. —. He resided in Shutesburg, Mass. when Congress granted him a pension 9 Feb. 1842.

Huntingdon, Jedediah. Conn. Brig. Gen. He received his commutation.

Huntingdon, William. —. —. He enlisted for three years. He had been rejected for a pension because of his inability to state the changes in his property since 1818. Congress granted him a pension 15 Mar. 1832.

Huntley, —. —. —. His widow, Abigail Huntley, sought an increase in her pension. Congress rejected her petition 13 Apr. 1860.

Huntley, Zadock. —. —. Since his name could not be found on the rolls, Congress rejected his claim for a pension 21 Jan. 1846.

Huntoon, Charles. N.H. Pvt. He served under Col. Doolittle in Capt. Stearn's Company. He had his right knee fractured by a cannon ball from the British entrenchments while in the line of duty in Sep. 1775 at Plough Hill. He lived in Grantham, N.H. in 1795. He served in the militia. He was granted one-third of a pension 20 Apr. 1796. He died 21 Nov. 1829.

Huntoon, Joseph. N.H. Lt. He was from Unity. He was wounded in his right arm at the battle of Stillwater on 7 Oct. 1777. He was in Capt. Grey's Company under Col. Scammell in the 3rd N.H. Regiment. He was pensioned 25 June 1779. He petitioned for arrearage 7 Jan. 1790. His dwelling house was burnt 16 Feb. 1781. He was aged 53 in 1787. He was on the 1813 pension list. He had a large family.

Huntsman, John. Va. —. He served two tours as a volunteer and was drafted for a third. In 1780 he left Charlotte Co., Va. for six more months. He married in 1796. His widow was Elizabeth Huntsman. Congress denied her claim 14 June 1850.

Hurd, David. Conn. Pvt. He served in the 3rd Conn. Regiment. He was pensioned 23 June 1808. He lived in Fairfield Co., Conn. He was on the 1813 pension list. He died 28 Jan. 1829.

Hurd, Lewis. Conn. Sgt. He served in the 3rd Conn. Regiment and was wounded. He was pensioned 29 Aug. 1782. He was on the 1813 pension list in Vermont.

Hurd, Zadock. N.H. Pvt. He served under Col. Scammel. He was wounded by a ball passing through his thigh on 19 Sep. 1777 at Bemis Heights. He lived in Gilsum, N.H. in 1794. He was sick in Albany in Sep. 1777. He was granted one-third of a pension 20 Apr. 1796. He was on the 1813 pension list.

Hurdle, Lawrence. Md. Pvt. He was pensioned at the rate of half-pay of a private 27 Jan. 1816.

Hurlburt, George. Conn. Capt. He served in Col. Sheldon's Regiment of Light Dragoons and was wounded at Tarrytown in the summer of 1781. Gen. Washington requested that he swim to a transport laden with supplies. It had been set on fire by rockets by the enemy from the opposite bank. He received a gun shot wound and died 8 May 1783 having languished from his wounds. His executrix, his sister Anna Welsh, sought his commutation and land warrant. She applied 7 Feb. 1797. His service did not qualify her for seven years of half-pay. She was also rejected in 1816 and again 1 Apr. 1818. His five years' full pay was issued 30 June 1834.

Hurlbutt, Stephen. Conn. Drum Major. He served in the 5th Conn. Regiment under Col. Philip Burr Bradley in Capt. Ezekiel Sandford's Company. Job Smith was the paymaster. He was taken ill in 1777 and was disabled by a fever sore in his right leg. He was discharged unfit for duty. He was a weaver. On 5 Feb. 1788 he was 40 years old. He was pensioned 10 May 1788. He lived in Fredericktown, Dutchess Co., N.Y. in 1789 and later in Seneca County. He was on the 1813 pension list. He died 4 May 1822.

Hurley, Daniel. Mass. —. He served in the 4th Regiment. He was paid $20.

Hurley, William. Md. Pvt. He was pensioned in Montgomery County in 1784. He was on the 1813 pension list. He may be identical with the William Hirley pensioned in Pennsylvania.

Hurdle, Lawrence. Md. Sgt. He was pensioned in 1816.

Hurst, Henry. Va. Pvt. He was on the 1813 pension list.

Hurst, Samuel. Md. Pvt. He was pensioned at the rate of half-pay of a private in Dorchester County on 7 Feb. 1817.

Hurston, Thomas. S.C. —. There was one child in 1791.

Hurt, James. Va. —. His wife, Ann Hurt, was allowed 50 pounds of pork and 2 barrels of corn for relief in Bedford Co., Va. in Nov. 1780. There were six in her family.

Hurt, Zacheriah. Va. —. He was pensioned on 7 Jan. 1824 at the rate of $60 per annum with $40 immediate relief. He was wounded at Guilford Courthouse. He lived in Wythe County on 11 Jan. 1824.

Hustler, Thomas. N.Y. Sgt. He was pensioned in Sep. 1803 in Niagara Co., N.Y. He was on the 1813 pension list. He died 13 Dec. 1821.

Huston, —. Pa. —. His widow, Ann Huston, received a $40 gratuity and a $40 annuity in Washington County 27 Apr. 1844. She died 21 Mar. 1848.

Huston, —. S.C. —. His widow was Eleanor Huston. There was one child in 1791.

Huston, James. Pa. —. He was awarded a $40 gratuity and a $40 annuity in Washington Co., Pa. 21 Feb. 1834. His widow was paid in Dec. 1834.

Huston, John. Me. —. He was from Sanford. He was paid $50 under the resolve of 1836.

Huston, Robert. Va. Pvt. He was wounded by the Indians at Fort Henry. He was being pensioned 20 Jan. 1786.

Huston, William. Pa. 1st Lt. His widow, Susanna Huston, was in Lancaster County 28 July 1787. He was commissioned 8 Nov. 1780 and was in the Invalids. She was granted a pension. It was later proved that since he died after the war, his widow was not entitled to a pension and had to return £225. He also appeared as William Houston.

Hutchens, Jonathan. —. —. His service did not exceed four months so Congress denied his claim 11 Apr. 1850.

Hutchings, Joseph. Va. Col. His widow, Sarah Hutchings, lived in Norfolk County 19 Dec. 1787. He entered the service and was appointed commander of a regiment of minutemen. He was taken by Lord Dunmore and confined on board a prison ship where he contracted a dreadful disease. He was paroled but died before he could be exchanged. He left a widow and six children, ranging in age from 19 to 12. She was pensioned at the rate of £75 per annum.

Hutchins, Benjamin. Me. —. He died 4 Sep. 1810. His widow was Nancy Hutchins from Minot. She was paid $50 under the resolve of 1836.

Hutchins, Burkley. N.H. —. He served nine months under Capt. Moody Dustin and Col. H. Dearborn in the militia as a substitute for his brother, Simon Hutchins, from Jan. or 1 Feb. 1782 to Nov. 1782. His record, however, showed 1 Mar. 1782 to 1 Nov. 1782 which was eight months. Congress ruled that there was no need for further action 14 June 1850 since the pension he was receiving was the correct amount.

Hutchins, James. N.H. Pvt. He served under Col. Nixon. He suffered a universal debility due to a fever in the service which terminated in an ague and sore in his leg in Jan. 1777 at Chatham. He lived in Sutton, N.H. in 1794.

Hutchins, Joseph. Me. —. He was from Hartford. He was paid $50 under the resolve of 1836.

Hutchins, Thomas. Me. —. He died 14 June 1803. His widow was Abigail Hutchins from Waterboro. She was paid $50 under the resolve of 1836.

Hutchinson, —. Pa. —. His widow, Jane Hutchinson, was awarded a $40 gratuity in Union Co., Pa. 28 Feb. 1834.

Hutchinson, Cornelius. Pa. —. He applied on 28 Feb. 1816 in Huntingdon County but resided in Indiana County. He formerly lived in Cumberland County. He was 84 years old in 1840. He served in Capt. Matthew Scott's Company under Col. Walter Stewart for three years He died 10 Mar. 1843.

Hutchinson, James. S.C. —. He lost his life in the service. His widow, Agnes Hutchinson, was granted an annuity 3 Oct. 1785 in Abbeville District. There was one child in 1791.

Hutchinson, John. Conn. Corp., He was wounded at King's Bridge in July 1781. He served under Capt. Comstock. A musket ball entered his trunk, broke one of his ribs, and came out his shoulder blade. He received half-pay in 1783.

Hutchinson, John. N.Y. Pvt. He enlisted in 1776 in Capt. John Hyatt. He was wounded near Brooklyn, Long Island by a musket ball in his left arm below the elbow and another through his body over the stomach. He reenlisted in Capt. Samuel Sackett in the 4th N.Y. Regiment under Col. Henry B. Livingstone. Capt. Theodosius Fowler replaced Sackett upon his death. He was transferred to the 2nd N.Y. Regiment under Col. Philip Van Cortland. He lived in Crumpond, Westchester Co., N.Y. He was a laborer and was born on 27 Sep. 17--.

Hutchinson, John. Pa. Pvt. He was in Philadelphia County 14 Nov. 1785. He served in the 2nd Pa. Regiment and was wounded in his leg in the battle of Green Springs. He was discharged in Nov. 1783. He was 31 years old. One of his name was dead by Sep. 1798.

Hutchinson, John. Pa. —. [second of the name].

Hutchinson, Peter. Va. —. His wife, Elizabeth Hutchinson, was granted support in Pittsylvania Co., Va. on 27 Aug. 1778 and on 25 Feb. 1779.

Hutchinson, Samuel. —. —. He entered the service as a substitute for his father who had been drafted on 1 May 1780. In Apr. 1781 he was drafted for six months under Capt. Daniel White. In Oct. 1781 he enlisted for a year under Capt. Buel and Col. Durkee. He guarded the coast around New London. He furnished no additional proof so Congress denied him a pension 29 Feb. 1848.

Hutchinson, Thomas. —. —. He served in Gibson's Regiment. He had been pensioned in 1818 and then stricken from the rolls. His son, Thompson Hutchinson, had to support him and proved that he had been erroneously stricken and sought his father's arrearage. Congress granted same by special act on 31 Dec. 1845 having authorized same 5 Mar. 1840.

Hutchinson, William. Pa. —. He was pensioned 24 Mar. 1837 in Chester County.

Hutinack, Francis. —. —. He served three years in the Continental Line. He had not applied under the act of 1832 because he mistakenly believed that he needed to prove his service by two witnesses and was unaware that his name was to be found on the muster rolls. Congress approved his pension by special act 27 Mar. 1846.

Hutson, John. Va. —. He was a guide for Col. Shelby. He was drown on duty in the Indian country. His widow, Eleanor Hutson, was awarded a £24 gratuity and a £12 annuity for her widowhood on 21 Oct. 1779. She had five small children.

Hutton, James E. Pa. —. He was granted relief.

Hutton, James. Pa. Corp. He applied in Cumberland County on 20 July 1813. He enlisted in the spring of 1778 in the 11th Regiment under Col. Hubley and Capt. Jackson. He served to the year 1781 or to the end of the war in 1783. William Alexander enlisted him. He was encumbered with a large family. He died 24 Feb. 1843.

Hutton, John. Pa. —. He was wounded in the leg at Roundabouts on the Raritan River in 1777. He was awarded a $40 gratuity and a $40 annuity in Cumberland County on 29 Mar. 1809.

Hutts, Jacob. Va. —. His wife, Torah [?] Hutts, and children were granted relief in Bedford Co., Va. on 28 July 1777. She was granted £20 on 23 Nov. 1778.

Hyde, Jedediah. Conn. Capt. He served in the Conn. Line. He was pensioned 25 Apr. 1808. He was on the 1813 pension list of Vermont. He lived in Orleans Co., Vt.

Hyden, Daniel. Va. —. He was pensioned in Lee County on 3 Jan. 1818 at the rate of $120 per annum with $50 immediate relief. He had been wounded in the service. He died 12 Nov. 1837. His widow, Polly Hyden, was administratrix of the estate.

Hyer, Conrad. —. —. The citizens of Waldoboro, Me. asked that his pension be continued to his grandson. Congress rejected their request 19 May 1852.

Hyer, Walter. N.J. Pvt. He was on the 1791 pension roll at the rate of $26.66 2/3 per annum.

Hyland, Ferguson. Va. Pvt. He was pensioned at the rate of £10 per annum on 30 Dec. 1791. He lived in Berkeley Co. in Apr. 1793. He served in the Va. Line and was disabled in service. He lived in Jefferson Co. in 1806. He also appeared as Ferguson Hiland and Ferguson Highland.

Hylier, David. Pa. Pvt. He was in Philadelphia County 12 Dec. 1785. He was in the Invalids and was discharged 1 Nov. 1783 unfit for duty on account of a wound in one of his legs.

Hynes, Thomas. Va. —. He was in Continental service. His wife, Mary Hynes, was allowed £15 for her support and her two small children in Augusta Co., Va. 18 Nov. 1777 while he was in the service.

Hyre, Philip. Conn. Pvt. He was transferred to the Invalids Corps. He was from Fairfield on 28 May 1789. He died in 1792.

Ickes, Peter. Pa. Capt. He served in the militia. He was from York County.

Iddings, William. Pa. —. He was awarded a $40 gratuity 23 Apr. 1829 in Beaver County and a $40 gratuity and a $40 annuity 16 Feb. 1830. He died 21 Oct. 1833.

Ide, Nathan. Mass. —. He served in the 16th Regiment. He was from Dighton and was paid $50.

Illich, Marks. N.Y. Pvt. He served under Col. Bellinger in the militia and was slain 2 Sep. 1779. His children, Jacob Illich, Mary Illich, Catharine Illich, Elizabeth Illich, Marks Illich, Henry Illich, and Peter Illich, received his half-pay pension.

Ilwane, —. Pa. —. His widow was Mary Ilwane.

Imeson, John. Md. Pvt. He was pensioned at the rate of £15 per annum in Nov. 1803.

Imfelt, Vincent. Pa. —. He was awarded a $40 gratuity in York Co., Pa. 10 Apr. 1828 and again on 8 Apr. 1829.

Impson, Henry. N.Y. —. He was awarded 200 acres of bounty land 13 Apr. 1813.

Impson, Henry. Pa. Pvt. He served in the 4th Regiment of Light Dragoons under Col. Stephen Maylen. He was discharged in 1783. Robert Shepard was Quartermaster Sergeant in the unit.

Ingalls, Daniel. —. —. He was not actually a private but a waiter. He enlisted at the age of 15 in 1775 under Capt Poor. He was a waiter in 1777, 1778, and 1779 to Col. Stephen Moyland of the 4th Regiment of Light Dragoons. He was then employed as an assistant in the clothing department for the rest of the war. Congress rejected him 13 May 1844. Since he did not come within any of the existing laws for a pension, Congress approved a special act 13 Jan. 1846.

Ingalls, Israel. —. —. He served five months and twenty-three days in 1776 and 1778. His widow was Betsey Ingalls. Congress granted him a pension by special act and extended the same to her on 25 Apr. 1840.

Ingersoll. Samuel. Mass. —. He was paid $20.

Ingersoll, Zebulon. Mass. Pvt. He served in the 9th Regiment and was from Haverhill. His widow, Mary Woodbury, was paid $50.

Ingram, Samuel. Va. —. He served in Capt. Buchanan's Company under Col. Bowman. He was ambushed and wounded in the breast by Indians in July 1777. He was awarded a £30 gratuity and an annuity of half-pay of a soldier for four years on 21 Oct. 1778.

Ingram, Thomas. N.Y. Pvt. He served in the 5th Regiment under Col. Lewis duBois and died 18 Feb. 1777. His child, John [?] Ingram, received his half-pay pension.

Inglirth, George. Pa. —. He served in the 4th Pa. Regiment and was wounded in the hand, shoulder, arm, and head on picket at Paoli. He served under Capt. John McGowan and was under the command of Edward Randolph when he was wounded.

Ingraham, Francis. —. —. He failed to provide sufficient proof of his service. Congress rejected his petition 20 June 1848.

Inlow, John. S.C. —. He enlisted for three years and served under Capt. David Hopkins in the 3rd S.C. Regiment under Col. William Thompson. He also served under Capt. William Caldwell and Col. Thomas Brandon. He was wounded in the thigh by a musket ball at Ninety Six. He was from Union District in 1795. His annuity was backdated to 1792. He was reinstated on the pension list on 19 Dec. 1818 and was granted his arrearage.

Innis, James. Pa. —. His widow, Isabella Innis, received a $40 gratuity and a $40 annuity in Adams County 18 Apr. 1855.

Irby, Joseph. S.C. —. He was killed 19 Nov. 1781. His widow, Frances Irby, was granted an annuity 26 Oct. 1785 in Laurens District.

Ireland, George. Md. Lt. His widow, Mary Ireland, was pensioned at the rate of half-pay of a lieutenant in Calvert County on 14 Mar. 1828. His legal representatives received a warrant for 200 acres of bounty land in Allegany County on 12 Mar. 1829. In 1832 the bounty land location was clarified as to be located west of Fort Cumberland. His heirs were paid $250 for his warrant on 13 Mar. 1839 because there was no vacant land left.

Ireland, John. Pa. —. He was awarded relief in Columbia County 6 Apr. 1833.

Irick, Michael. Pa. —. His heirs were granted his donation land 29 Mar. 1804. He enlisted in 1777 in Col. Hartley's Regiment for three years or the war. He was on command at Wyoming in 1780 and had his feet nearly frozen off. He could not provide for his family. He was from York County. He also appeared as Michael Irig.

Irine, —. N.Y. —. Elizabeth Irine was granted support during the war. She also appeared as Elizabeth Iren.

Irish, Nathaniel. —. Capt. He served under Col. Flower in the Regiment of Artillery Artificers. He left the regiment in Aug. 1780 and transferred to a command in the South where he served as Commissary of Military Stores. He was entitled to commutation 23 Mar. 1838.

Irvin, James. Pa. Brigadier General. He was in Philadelphia on 3 Oct. 1785 at which time he was 49 years of age. He was wounded in the neck and hand at the battle of Germantown and was disabled 5 Dec. 1777. He was on the 1813 pension list. He died 28 Apr. 1819. He also appeared as James Irwin.

Irvine, Abraham. Va. —. He served under Capt. George Lambert and died from cold settling in his lungs and smallpox in May 1777. His widow, Margaret Irvine, and her four children were awarded a £35 gratuity in York Co., Va. 10 Nov. 1777. She was on the 1785 pension roll.

He also appeared as Abraham Irwin.

Irvine, Alexander. Ga. Lt. He served in the Burke Co., Ga. militia. He was wounded in the left arm which fractured one of the bones in May 1781 in Burke County. He resided at Great Ogeechee, Ga. in 1796. He died in 1799.

Irvine, J. S.C. Officer. He served aboard the *South Carolina* under Commodore Alexander Gillon and was paid 28 May 1811.

Irvine, John. Pa. Lt. He was in Philadelphia County 30 Sep. 1785. He was wounded at Germantown in the neck and hand. He was 49 years old. He died 5 May 1808.

Irwin, Henry. N.C. Lt. Col. He was commissioned 15 Apr. 1776 and killed 4 Oct. 1777 at the battle of Germantown. He left a widow and five children. His heirs were pensioned in Edgecombe County in 1789. They were allowed his bounty land 13 Apr. 1810. They were entitled to his seven years' full pay 22 Dec. 1837.

Irwin, Henry. Pa. —. He was granted relief 3 Mar. 1829 in Columbia County. He died 11 May 1844.

Irwin, James. Pa. —. He was awarded a $40 gratuity and a $40 annuity in Franklin Co., Pa. 14 Apr. 1834. He was 82 years old in 1840.

Irwin, James. Pa. Capt. He served two tours in the militia. He was from Philadelphia and died *ante* 1825. His widow, Margaret Irwin, was granted a $40 gratuity in Philadelphia County 7 Apr. 1830.

Irwin, Jared. Ga. Capt. He served as a lieutenant or captain and was at Camden, Briar Creek, Black Swamp, and Augusta. He received bounty land from Georgia. His daughter, Jane Irwin, received half-pay of a captain from the end of the war to his death from Congress 25 Feb.1851.

Irwin, John. Pa. —. He was pensioned 23 Apr. 1818.

Irwin, Nathaniel. Pa. —. He was granted a $40 gratuity in Chester County 7 Apr. 1830.

Irwin, William. —. —. His warrant was issued to a person he did not authorize to obtain it. Congress ruled it could not re-grant same on 27 Feb. 1809.

Irwine, Alexander. Pa. Pvt. He was on the 1789 pension list.

Isaacs, James. Md. Pvt. He was pensioned 4 Mar. 1789. He was on the 1813 pension list.

Isabell, —. Md. Sgt. His widow, Elizabeth Isabell, was pensioned at the rate of half-pay of a sergeant at Annapolis 20 Feb. 1822.

Isbell, Pendleton. S.C. Capt. He suffered from rheumatism and was 71 years old. He had lived in the district about 40 years. His wife was 69 years old. John Burton, Sr., of Franklin Co., Ga. swore that he was in the battle of King's Mountain. He was pensioned 30 Nov. 1827. He was paid in 1828 and 1829.

Iszard, Henry. N.J. —. He was pensioned in Cape May County on 27 Jan. 1844 at the rate of $50 per annum.

Ittig, Conrad. —. —. Congress awarded his widow, Nancy Ittig of Herkimer Co., N.Y. , the arrearage of her pension from 4 Mar. 1848 to 3 Feb. 1853 on 15 Dec. 1857.

Iver, Frederick. N.Y. Corp. He served under Col. Bellinger and was slain 6 Aug. 1777. His widow received a half-pay pension.

Ivers, Samuel. Mass. —. He served in the 1st Regiment and was paid $20.

Ivery, James. N.Y. Pvt. He was wounded in his right elbow and in his neck. He served in Capt. Hamtrammak's Company under Col. Philip Van Cortland in 1781. He lived in Ulster Co., N.Y. on 29 Apr. 1789. He was 28 years of age in Nov. 1785. He was awarded 200 acres of bounty land 19 June 1812. He was on the 1813 pension list. He also appeared as James Ivory. He was a shoemaker.

Ives, Joel. Conn. Pvt. He enlisted in 1776 in Col. Andrew Ward's Regiment in Capt. Isaac Cox's company. While on guard duty at Frogs Point in Westchester County, he was wounded by a musket ball in his right arm and lost the use of it up to his shoulder. It was from an accidental shot from a fellow soldier on guard duty. He was pensioned 2 May 1778 in Wallingford. He died in 1808.

Ives, Lent. Conn. Pvt. He served under Col. Matthew Mead in Capt. John Yates' Company. He was wounded in his left arm by a cutlass near Morrisena, N.Y. on 18 Jan. 1780. He was taken prisoner. He was pensioned in Bristol, Conn. at the age of 34 on 2 Sep. 1788. He was on the 1813 pension list.

Ivins, Abel. N.J. —. He served in the 4th Regiment from 11 Sep. 1777 under Lt. Wessel T. Stout. He was killed at Brandywine 11 Sep. 1777. He married Valeriah Compton. His widow, Valeria Ivins Coussons, sought a pension 26 Oct. 1788. She had married secondly Charles Cussons in 1783 or 1784.

Izard, Harrison. S.C. —. He was killed in the service in Nov. 1781 at Pauls Creek. His widow, Ferribe Izard, was allowed an annuity 18 Mar. 1786. There were two children in 1791.

Jack, Matthew. Pa. Lt. He was in Westmoreland County 24 Nov. 1785. He was in the 8th Pa. Regiment and was wounded and disabled at Bound Brook in N.J. on 13 Apr. 1777 by loss of his left hand due to the bursting of his rifle gun. He was in Capt. Samuel Wilson's Company. He was 38 [?30] years old. He was on the 1813 pension list. Congress rejected commutation sought by his heirs 11 Jan. 1851. He was rendered supernumerary in 1779 and discharged at Pittsburgh. Congress granted his heirs relief 10 June 1854.

Jack, Stephen. S.C. —. He was pensioned 6 Dec. 1828.

Jackaway, Samuel. Va. —. His wife, Elizabeth Jackaway, was granted support in Halifax Co., Va. on 19 Feb. 1778.

Jackson, —. Md. Pvt. His widow, Ann Jackson, was pensioned at the rate of half-pay of a private in Annapolis 23 Feb. 1822.

Jackson, Anthony. Md. Pvt. He was on the 1791 pension roll in Pennsylvania and had been transferred from Maryland. He died 24 Feb. 1804.

Jackson, David. Mass. —. He served in the 9th Regiment and was from Uxbridge. He was paid $20.

Jackson, David. N.J. —. He lost an arm. He received his half-pay pension 1 June 1785.

Jackson, David. Pa. Pvt. He was in Chester County 20 June 1786. He was in the militia in Capt. David Hayes' Company under Col. Evan Evans and had his left hand shot off by a cannon ball at the battle of Trenton on 2 Jan. 1777. He was 50 [?59] years old. He had a U.S. pension of $48 per annum and a state pension of $12 per annum. He was in Lancaster County. He was on the 1813 pension list.

Jackson, David. S.C. —. He was wounded and left for dead at the defeat of Brig. Gen. Sumter near Fishing Creek in 1780. His skull was fractured, and he lost the use of his arm. He was a resident of York District. He had a wife and 10 children in 1795.

Jackson, Elijah. Conn. Pvt. He served under Col. Charles Burrall in Capt. David Downs' Company. He took sick at Ticonderoga in 1776 and was discharged the following Oct. He was 32 years old and a resident of Sharon, Conn. when he was pensioned 28 Apr. 1787.

Jackson, Ephraim. Mass. Lt. Col. He died 19 Dec. 1777. His heirs were paid his seven years' half-pay of $2,520.

Jackson, George. S.C. —. His application was rejected in Dec. 1840.

Jackson, Grant. —. —. He served under Col. Heman Swift and was disabled by a rheumatic disorder in 1782. In 1783 he developed a sore on one of his legs. He died 8 Aug. 1788.

Jackson, Henry. —. —. Congress denied his claim for a pension 30 Jan. 1852.

Jackson, John. —. —. In Sept. 1779 he resided in Yorkshire, Eng. and was decoyed aboard the *Bon Homme Richard* under John Paul Jones on 22 September and acted as pilot of the fleet. In the battle with the *Serapis* and *Countess of Scarborough* he had his arm shot off. Jones promised him $300 and a pension for life. He died in 1815. His three children, James Jackson, John Jackson, and Mary Jackson, sought to obtain what was due their father. His only surviving son, James Jackson, came to America to pursue the claim. James Jackson was born 20 Feb. 1787 and baptized 29 Dec. 1790 at Holy Trinity, Kingston-upon-Hull. On 2 Feb. 1835 James submitted his memorial to Congress. Congress granted relief to James Jackson, who was a resident of the navy yard in Washington, D.C., on 14 June 1850 and 13 Jan. 1854.

Jackson, John. —. —. His widow, Catherine Jackson, had her petition for a pension rejected by Congress 27 Mar. 1846 because they were married subsequent to 1 Jan. 1794.

Jackson, John. Pa. —. He was granted relief in 1841.

Jackson, Jonathan. Mass. Matross. He served in Crane's Artillery and was from Medford. His widow, Abigail Burrill, was paid $50.

Jackson, Joseph. N.Y. Pvt. He served under Lt. Col. Samuel Clyde and was slain 6 Aug. 1777. His children, James Jackson, Mary Jackson, and Elizabeth Jackson, received a half-pay pension.

Jackson, Michael. —. Col. He was wounded by a musket ball in the leg which fractured the bone and injured the muscles on 24 Sep. 1776 on Montressor's Island. He had received his commutation which was not returned. He resided in Newton, Middlesex Co., Mass. in 1794.

Jackson, Reuben. Va. —. He was granted $50 relief and an annual pension of $80 on 22 Feb. 1817. He lived in Henrico County 10 Mar. 1817.

Jackson, Simon. Mass. Capt. He received his commutation for five years in lieu of half-pay for life. He died 17 Oct. 1818.

Jackson, Stephen. —. —. He entered the service in the spring of 1777 in the South Carolina militia under a draft and served three months. He had a second tour that year and was at Charleston. He returned home after the defeat of Gen. Gates at Camden, (but that battle was not in 1777 but on 16 Aug. 1780). He returned home and was in pursuit of Tories and served until Christmas. In 1778 Capt. Joseph Griffy became disabled, and he was elected in his place. He served until the surrender of Cornwallis. His testimony was incoherent and contradictory. It was impossible to determine if he was in the N.C. or S.C. militia. He said he fought at Ramsour's Mills on 22 June 1778, but everyone there was in the N.C. militia. There were three Stephen Jacksons who served from South Carolina. Congress rejected the claim of his heirs 31 Mar. 1856.

Jackson, Stephen. S.C. Capt. He was 78 years old. He was on the roll in 1828.

Jackson, Thomas. N.C. —. He married Deborah Gallop and died in 1821. His children were Thomas Jackson, Sarah Jackson, and Bailey Jackson. He applied in Pasquotank Co., N.C. in Dec. 1833.

Jackson, Thomas. S.C. —. His claim for arrears of his pension was approved.

Jackson, William. —. —. Congress rejected the claim of the heirs 1 Mar. 1838. It had done so in Feb. 1819, Feb. 1820, and Jan. 1826.

Jackson, Zebulon. Conn. Pvt. He served under Col. Philip B. Bradley in the 5th Conn. Regiment. At Germantown on 4 Oct. 1777 he was hurt in one of his eyes and lost the same. He was left totally blinded since he had but one eye when he entered the service. His brother was Daniel Jackson. He was pensioned in Norwalk, Conn. at age 30 years on 16 Aug. 1788.

Jackways, Robert. Conn. Pvt. He served in the 5th Regiment under Col. Bradley. He enlisted 22 Feb. 1777 and was invalided 29 Oct. 1780. He lived in Stonington, Conn. in 1794. His surname also appeared as Jacway.

Jacobs, —. Pa. —. His widow, Eliza Jacobs, was awarded a $40 gratuity and a $40 annuity in Luzerne Co., Pa. 17 Mar. 1835. She died 7 Dec. 1843.

Jacobs, —. Va. —. His wife, Ann Jacobs, and child were furnished £20 support in Frederick Co., Va. on 2 Mar. 1779.

Jacobs, —. Va. —. His wife, Lucy Jacobs, was granted support in Prince William County in 1779.

Jacobs, Enoch. Conn. Pvt. He served in the militia. He was wounded by the British at their return from Danbury by a bayonet which passed through his right arm six or seven times in Apr. 1777 at Green's farm and also near Campo. He resided at New Haven, Conn. in 1796. He was granted one-third of a pension 20 Apr. 1796.

Jacobs, Esop. Mass. —. He was from Hanover. He was paid $20.

Jacobs, Francis. —. Waiter/Guide/Spy. He was a waiter to Gen. Washington and was wounded the night of Brandywine when crossing the fields and woodland. He was rejected under the act of 1832 because his type of service was not covered. He was pensioned by special act of 30 June 1834. He died 27 Dec. 1844. His widow, Catherine Jacobs, failed in her attempt to receive a pension from Congress 7 Jan. 1859.

Jacobs, Isaac. Mass. —. He served in the 8th Regiment and was from Gloucester. He was paid $20. He was deceased by 24 Aug. 1818. His son was Abram T. Jacobs.

Jacobs, John. Me. —. Mt. He was from Vernon. He was paid $50 under the resolve of 1836.

Jacobs, John. Mass. —. He served in the 3rd Regiment and was from Lynn. He was paid $20.

Jacobs, John J. Md. 1st Lt. He was awarded a sum of money in addition to that received in Nov. 1811 equal to that of half-pay of a lieutenant on 27 Jan. 1816. He received a warrant for 200 acres of bounty land in Allegany County 17 Feb. 1830. He was paid $22.12 in 1832 for the composition money he paid for the tract of bounty land which was found to have escheated and been patented by Edward Norwood. On 17 Feb. 1832 the portion of bounty land resolution requiring the 200 acres of bounty land to be located west of Fort Cumberland was repealed. He received his half-pay commutation in 1832.

Jacobs, John. Pa. —. He was awarded a $40 gratuity and a $40 annuity in York Co., Pa. 7 Apr. 1832.

Jacobs, Jonathan. Pa. —. He was awarded a $40 gratuity and a $40 annuity in York Co., Pa. 6 Mar. 1833. He was 84 years old in 1840. He died 11 Apr. 1843.

Jacobs, Peter. Pa. —. He was in Cumberland County 25 Feb. 1818. He lived in Chester County and was a servant of John Lawback. He left his master and enlisted before the battle of Brandywine.

Jacobs, Primus. Mass. Pvt. He served in the 11th Regiment and was from Boston. His widow, Dinah Jacobs, was paid $50.

Jacobs, Whitman. Mass. Pvt. He served under Col. Hutchinson in Capt. Richardson's Company. He suffered from great debility and contraction of his limbs occasioned by a disorder called the ground itch in Sept. 1776. He lived in Croydon, N.H. in 1795. His claim was not allowed under the law.

Jacobs, William. Conn. Sgt. He enlisted in the militia in Capt. Odel Close's Company under Col. John Mead. On 26 June 1780 at Greenwich, Conn. he was wounded by a broadsword in his left arm and lost the use thereof. He was 45 years old 21 Aug. 1788. He lived in New York City, N.Y. in 1788. He was on the 1791 pension roll and died 21 Aug. 1805.

Jacobs, William. Md. Pvt. He was pensioned at the rate of half-pay of a private in Hampshire Co.,

Va. on 2 Mar. 1827.

Jacobs, William. Mass. Pvt. He served in the Invalids under Col. Lewis Nichola. He was 61 years old in 1780. He was disabled with rheumatism. He was pensioned 4 Jan. 1783. He was on the 1813 pension list.

Jacobson, George. Pa. —. He enlisted in 1776 under Capt. Sealey in the 5th Regiment and served five years. He was discharged by Col. Butler. He was from Lehigh County.

Jacoby, Philip. Pa. —. He served in the 3rd Regiment and applied in Lehigh County 27 Dec. 1819. He enlisted in 1781 under Capt. John Craig for the war. He had served previously in the militia. He resided with a son who was a poor man with a large family. He had been on the pension list of the U.S. but was not retained. He was pensioned 13 Dec. 1821 and died 7 Nov. 1823. He also appeared as Philip Jacobi.

Jacques, Nathan. —. —. He was pensioned 20 Apr. 1796.

Jacquet, John D. Md. Sgt. He was pensioned at the rate of half-pay of a sergeant in Dec. 1815.

Jacquet, Joseph. Pa. Lt. His widow, Susannah Jacquet, was in Philadelphia County 20 May 1791. He served in Col. Miles' Rifle Regiment in the Pa. Line. He was killed at Long Island on 27 Aug. 1776. His widow married secondly Hance Jacquet 28 Oct. 1783. He was also dead. She was paid from 27 Aug. 1776 to 28 Oct. 1783.

Jaines, Richard. Va. —. While he was away in Continental service, his wife and three children were granted support at the rate of £4 per month in Yohogania Co. Va. 20 Oct. 1777.

Jamerson, Alexander. Pa. Pvt. He was on the 1789 pension list.

James, —. Va. —. He and his brother were in the service. Their mother, Mary James, was granted £25 support in York County on 15 Feb. 1779.

James, —. S.C. —. His widow, Elizabeth James, was paid three years of arrearage and put on the pension roll 3 Dec. 1819.

James, Catlett. Va. —. He served in the 1st Regiment from 1 Aug. 1776 to 1 Aug. 1779. He was wounded in his right arm by Indians in Kentucky in Mar. 1777. He was in Capt. Boone's Company. He was pensioned at the rate of £12 per annum on 15 Oct. 1778. He was discontinued on 10 Jan. 1787 by order of the executive because he had no further need. His mother, Mildred James, received the same amount from that date to 22 May 1788 by act of 30 Dec. 1791. His mother lived in Orange County 23 Apr. 1792. He also appeared as Catlett Jones.

James, Elisha. S.C. Capt. He enlisted for 18 months before Charleston and served under Capt. James Milliken and Col. Sheppard. He was taken prisoner at Charleston. His children were Franky aged 8, Sally aged 1, and Emma aged 2, when he applied at age 65 in Halifax Co., N.C. on 16 Nov. 1824.

James, James. S.C. —. He served under Col. Wade, Col. Crawford, Col. Love, Capt. Wall, Capt. Speed, and Capt. William Easterling. He was at Bettis Bridge on Drowning Creek and Ashpole. He was 81 years old. He was from Chesterfield District in 1829. Israel Watkins of Richmond Co., N.C. served with him as did Joseph Black. His name was incorrectly entered as James Jones, and he was unable to draw his pension until the legislature corrected the mistake.

James, John. S.C. Capt. He died in 1789 in possession of an indent. He named William McConnico, Thomas Jones, and his son Matthew James executors. Jones declined to serve and the son was under age. When McConnico died, the indent was discovered among his papers. On 22 Nov. 1798 Mary Johnson, Elizabeth James, Clarence James, and Matthew James, children of the John James, sought compensation.

James, John. S.C. Pvt. He also acted as adjutant in Col. McDonald's Regiment from 1779 to 1782.

He was taken prisoner and paroled. He was awarded $75.50 in 1823. He was 66 years old. He also served under Gen. Richard Richardson at the Snowy Camps when Col. Fletcher was captured. He was under the Captain of the Guard, William Davis, at Statesburg. He also served under his father, Capt. John James. He was at Mossy Camps, Purysburg, Augusta, Georgetown, and Fort Wats on Scots Lake. William Birchmore swore that he was at the taking of Fort Watson.

James, Jordan. Pa. —. He was pensioned.

James, Leonard. Md. Pvt. He was pensioned at the rate of half-pay of a private in Cecil County on 7 Feb. 1817.

James, Nathan. Pa. —. He was awarded relief in Bucks County 18 Feb. 1834. He was 85 years of age in 1840. He died 11 May 1845.

James, Nicholas. Pa. —. He was awarded a $40 gratuity and a $40 annuity in York Co., Pa. 14 Apr. 1834. He died in June 1850.

James, Peter. Va. —. His mother, Mary James, was granted £12 support on 15 Dec. 1777 and £25 support in York Co., Va. on 15 Feb. 1779. His brother, Elisha James, was also away in the service.

James, Samuel. Mass. —. He was pensioned.

James, Thomas. Pa. Lt. —. He was pensioned.

James, William. N.Y. Pvt. He was on the 1791 pension roll and on the 1813 pension list.

James, William. N.Y. Sgt. He served under Col. Goose Van Schaick in Capt. Barent Ten Eyck's Company. He was wounded in his knee at St. Johns, Canada. He was 45 years old in 178-. He lived in Schnectady, Albany Co., N.Y. 7 Oct. 1789. He died 26 Nov. 1800.

Jameson, —. Va. —. His widow, Eliza Jameson, was alive 7 Feb. 1798. Her nephew was Charles Johnson. She died 6 Jan. 1800.

Jameson, Alexander. Va. —. His widow, Elizabeth Jameson, was awarded $200 relief and a pension for the same amount per annum on 22 Jan. 1798. She was in Prince George County.

Jameson, Dennis. Pa. —. He was granted relief.

Jameson, John. Pa. Pvt. He was in Philadelphia County 12 Dec. 1785. He served in the 3rd Pa. Regiment and was disabled by a wound and rheumatic complaint contracted in the service. He was 27 years old. He also appeared as John Jemmison and John Jamison. He died 6 June 1787.

Jamison, —. Pa. —. His widow, Elizabeth Jamison, received relief in Westmoreland County 21 June 1839.

Jamison, —. Pa. —. His widow, Margaret Jamison, received a $40 gratuity and a $40 annuity in Lancaster County 16 June 1836.

Jamieson, James. S.C. Capt. He served under Col. Bratton and was wounded in his right hip at the battle of Hanging Rock in 1780. He was from Chester District. He was awarded a one year pension of $21.42 to 1 June 1808 on 19 Dec.1807. He was granted $171.43 1/4 arrearage on 17 Dec. 1808. He received his annuity as late as 1834.

Jamieson, John. Va. Sgt. He lived in Rockbridge County. He was continued on the pension list at the rate of £15 per annum on 7 May 1787. He enlisted for 18 months on 1 Apr. 1779 in Col. Buford's Regiment. He was captured at the latter's defeat. Lt. Henry Bowyer of the 1st Regiment of Light Dragoons attested to his service. He was wounded by a broad sword and bayonet, twice on the left side of his head and twice on the back of his head, once in his belly resulting in a partial rupture, and another in his right arm. He was aged 35 in 1787. He was in Henrico County later. He was dead by 10 Aug. 1792.

Jamison, Francis. Pa. —. He applied in Somerset County 28 Jan. 1818. He served in the Robert Cluggage's Company in the 1st Rifle Regiment under Col. William Thomson from Lancaster County. He was under James Grier the next year and afterwards Col. Edward Hand. He marched to Boston where he arrived 3 Sep. 1775 and went to New York in 1776. Daniel Stoy served with him.

Jamison, James. S.C. —. He applied from Sumter District in 1830.

Jamison, John. Pa. —. He was granted relief in Butler County 24 Mar. 1818. He died 10 June 1839.

Jamison, Thomas. Pa. —. He was pensioned.

Janes, Elijah. Pa. Lt. He served under Col. Sheldon. He was wounded by a horseman's sword on the right wrist on 20 Nov. 1780. He lived in Lansingburg, N.Y. in 1794. He was commissioned 16 Nov. 1779. He had received the commutation which had not been returned. He was transferred to New York by Mar. 1795. He was on the 1813 pension list.

Jansen, Cornelius. N.Y. Capt. He served from 21 Nov. 1776 to the end of the war. He died in 1796. His widow, Christiana Jansen, married secondly Cornelius Low. He was also deceased. Congress granted her a pension 8 Mar. 1842.

Jansen, Matthew. N.Y. Capt. He was disabled in the lower part of his back by jumping over the rampart of the redoubt of Fort Montgomery in the escape on the night of 6 Oct. 1777. He also had an injury to his left eye by a musket shot. Jonathan Harden helped him. He served under Col. William Allison. He was 49 years old on 2 Apr. 1787. He lived in Ulster Co., N.Y. on 11 May 1789. He died in 1796. He also appeared as Matthew Janson.

Jarrell, —. S.C. —. Rebecca Jarrell's claim was not granted in Nov. 1827.

Jarvis, Nathaniel. N.Y. Corp. He served under Capt. Jonathan Titus in the 4th N.Y. Regiment and was slain 12 May 1775. His widow received a half-pay pension.

Jasper, William. S.C. Sgt. He served in the 2nd S.C. Regiment. His widow, Elizabeth Jasper, was granted an annuity for her children 31 Jan. 1783. She was Elizabeth Wagner when she was granted an annuity for her children 9 May 1785.

Jaques, Nathan. R.I. Pvt. He was wounded by a musket ball in the breast which came out near his left scapula in July 1781 near Kingsbridge. He served under Col. Olney. He lived in South Kingston, R.I. in 1794. He enlisted 5 Jul. 1780 and was on the rolls in 1782. He was granted one-third of a pension 20 Apr. 1796. He transferred to Addison Co., Vt. 4 Mar. 1801. He was on the 1813 pension list. He also appeared as Nathan Jaquay and Nathan Jacques.

Jaquet, John D. Md. Sgt. He was pensioned at the rate of half-pay of sergeant 23 Jan. 1816.

Jeane, David. Va. —. His wife, Elizabeth Jeane, was awarded assistance in Charlotte Co., Va. on 2 June 1777 consisting of 2 barrels of corn and meat, provisions on 4 Aug. 1777, and £18.4.3 on 4 May 1778.

Jeffers, Francis. N.J. Pvt. He lived in Monmouth County. He was wounded by a musket bullet in his right arm at Shrewsbury. He was on the 1791 pension roll. He was 26 years old. He was on the 1813 pension list. He was from Shrewsbury and was the son of Richard Jeffers.

Jeffries, Jacob. Md. Pvt. He was pensioned in Queen Anne's County at the rate of half-pay of a private 4 Feb. 1816.

Jeffries, James. Pa. —. He was pensioned in Allegheny County 13 Apr. 1838.

Jeffries, John. Del. Pvt. He was in Cumberland Co., Pa. 2 Feb. 1786. He was wounded at Germantown and had his finger shot off. He served in Capt. Enoch Anderson's Company of the Delaware Regiment of Foot. He was sent home from hospital in 1777. He was 41 years old. He transferred to Franklin Co., Virginia in or by Sep. 1800. He was on the 1813 pension list of Virginia. He also appeared as John Jeffers.

Jeffrys, Allen. S.C. Pvt. He served in the State Troops and received a draw for one Negro. The Negro was taken from him as the estate of Andrew Lord. He sought relief, but his claim was rejected 19 Dec. 1832.

Jeffs, Thomas. Mass. Corp. He served in the 3rd Regiment. He was from Essex and was paid $20.

Jeffs, Thomas. Va. —. He served in the 11th Virginia Regiment. His wife, Mary Jeffs, and three children were furnished £10 support in Frederick Co., Va. on 7 Oct. 1777 and £10 on 7 Oct. 1778.

Jemison, John. Pa. —. He was from Butler County and was pensioned 24Mar.1833.

Jenckes, Oliver. R.I. Lt. He died of fever at Philadelphia, Pa. 3 Feb. 1782.

Jenckes, Prince. R.I. Pvt. He was on the roll in 1788. He died 5 Jan. 1801 in Providence Co., R.I.

Jenkins, —. Pa. —. His widow, Bethia Jenkins, was awarded a $40 gratuity and a $40 annuity in Luzerne County 1 Apr. 1836.

Jenkins, —. Va. —. His father, William Jenkins, was granted support in Westmoreland County in Feb. 1779.

Jenkins, —. Va. —. He served in Capt. Bruin's Company in the 11th Virginia Regiment. His wife, Margaret Jenkins, and two children were furnished £8 support in Frederick Co., Va. on 4 Nov. 1777.

Jenkins, Absalom. Va. —. He was pensioned in Hanover County 28 Feb. 1832 at the rate of $60 per annum with $30 immediate relief. He died 5 Apr.1836. Burwell Jenkins was his administrator.

Jenkins, Benjamin. N.H. Sgt. He served in Goodman's Regiment. He was pensioned at the rate of $2.50 per month from 12 Mar. 1807. He was on the 1813 pension list. He moved to Montgomery Co., N.Y. 4 Sep. 1822.

Jenkins, James. N.J. —. He served in Capt. Sharp's Company in the 3rd Regiment from 7 Jan. 1777 to 28 Apr. 1777 when he deserted. He rejoined 1 Jan. 1783 and served to 6 June. He also served under Capt. Outwater for six months and four days. Congress granted his widow, Hannah Jenkins, a pension 3 Feb. 1843.

Jenkins, James. S.C. —. He served under Capt. John Rodgers and Gen. Marion. He was blind with a wife and children to support. Loftus Munnerlyn confirmed his service.

Jenkins, Job. Va. —. He wife, Elizabeth Jenkins, was afflicted with rheumatism. She and their child were granted £10 support on 6 Oct. 1778 and £40 on 5 Oct. 1779 in Frederick Co., Va.

Jenkins, John. Conn. Maj. He served from 17 Sep. 1776 to 6 July 1778 and was commissioned 1st Lieutenant 6 July 1777. He resigned in Mar. 1782. He was appointed major to protect the frontier from Indian depredations. Congress rejected the claim of the heirs since they were not entitled to anything.

Jenkins, Jonathan. Mass. —. He served in the 2nd Regiment. He was paid $20.

Jenkins, Josiah. Va. Pvt. His widow, Anne Jenkins, lived in Fauquier County in Sep. 1787. Ennis Combs swore that he served with Jenkins in 1775 and that he enlisted in the 3rd Va. Regiment under Capt. John Ashby and died soon after in Philadelphia, Pa. in December 1776. He left a widow and a small child. She was granted £15 support in May 1778. She was granted 8 barrels of Indian corn for support in Aug. 1781. She was put on the pension list at the rate of £8 per annum on 1 Oct. 1787. He also appeared as Josiah Jinkins.

Jenkins, Lemuel. Me. —. He was from Bowdoin. He was paid $50 under the resolve of 1836.

Jenkins, Philip. Md. Pvt. His widow, Sarah Jenkins, was pensioned at the rate of half-pay of a private 13 Feb. 1837.

Jenkins, Robert. Md. Matross. He was pensioned 18 Sep. 1812. He was on the 1813 pension list. He lived in Washington Co., Md.

Jenkins, Samuel. Me. —. He died 15 Nov. 1832. His widow, Thankful Jenkins, was from Buckfield. She was paid $50 under the resolve of 1836.

Jenkins, Samuel. S.C. —. At the age of 15 he entered the service in 1779 under Col. Hugh Horry and Gen. Marion as a militiaman. He also served under Col. Morris Simons. He was not wounded and never received any compensation. He was at Fort Watson, Eutaw, and Quinby where his brother fell. He was from Williamsburg District in 1821. He was granted $240 on 21 Dec. 1825. Officers who attested to his service were Maj. John — of Baxter's Regiment, Capt. Richard Green, William Carter, William J. James, Gavin Witherspoon, 1st Lt. Francis Green in Col. Horry's Regiment, and 1st Lt. James Green.

Jenkins, Thomas. Md. Pvt. He was pensioned at the rate of half-pay of a private in the District of Columbia 19 Jan. 1830.

Jenkinson, William. Pa. —. He was born in Cumberland Co., Pa. in 1755. He entered the service in 1776 under Capt. Gilbert McCoy for seven months. He served two months in 1777 as a substitute for Hugh McClelland in the militia under Capt. Wilson. In June 1781 he served eighteen months under Col. Craig and Thomas Campbell. He went to Baltimore and sailed under the convoy of the *Washington* to the mouth of James River before Yorktown. He was under Capt. Ferguson, Col. Proctor, and Lt. Col. Tarlton at Yorktown. He marched with the troops to South Carolina and joined Gen. Greene on Christmas in 1781. He was taken prisoner but escaped. He marched to Lancaster, Penn. under Capt. Studsburry and was discharged by Col. Hampton. He was awarded a $40 gratuity in Westmoreland County 29 Apr. 1829. He received a $40 gratuity and a $40 annuity 18 Feb. 1834.. Congress granted him a pension 24 Jan. 1837. He also appeared as William Jinkinson.

Jenks, Thomas. Mass. —. He served in the 1st Regiment and was paid $20.

Jennett, —. Va. —. His mother, Jane Jennett, was granted support in Halifax Co., Va. on 17 June 1779 while he was away in Continental service. She was given £26 on 18 Sep. 1779.

Jennings, —. Ga. —. His widow, Priscilla Jennings, and four children were granted an allowance of £72 for four years on 26 Nov. 1784.

Jennings, Benjamin. Pa. —. He was awarded $40 for his losses in the service on 18 Mar. 1816.

Jennings, Charles. Conn. Corp. He served in Capt. Parmerly's Company under Col. Burrell. In Canada in 1776 he took smallpox and a fever set in. His constitution was broken, and he was subject to fits of falling sickness. He lived in Woodbury, Conn. and was 37 years old when he was pensioned 25 Apr. 1787. He was from Sharon in 1789. He died in 1797. His rank was given as captain on the 1791 roll.

Jennings, Daniel. Mass. Pvt. He served in the 3rd Regiment under Col. John Greaton and Capt. Thomas Prichard. He was disabled by a musket ball in his left shoulder. He was 31 years old in 1786.

Jennings, Ebenezer. N.H. Sgt. He served under Col. Reid in Capt. Potter's Company. He was wounded in his left leg by a musket ball in the Indian expedition against Gen. Sullivan in 1779 at Newton. He lived in Marlborough, N.H. in 1795. He enlisted 20 June 1778 for two years and was discharged 1 Apr. 1780. He was granted one-fourth of a pension 20 Apr. 1796. He was on the 1813 pension list.

Jennings, Eliphalet. Me. —. He was from Framington. He was paid $50 under the resolve of 1836.

Jennings, John. Mass. —. He was granted relief.

Jennings, John. Pa. —. He was allowed bounty land from the state. Congress ruled that there was no evidence that he was entitled to federal bounty land on 22 Feb. 1843 and rejected the claim from his heirs. John S. Jennings was paid $200 for himself and the other heirs for the donation land due their father 14 Mar. 1842.

Jennings, John. Va. Sailing Master. He served in the State Navy. He was on the schooners *Liberty* and *Patriot*. He received a state bounty land warrant for 2,666 1/3 acres for three years of service from 1776 to 1779. Congress rejected the claim of the heirs for commutation 28 June 1836 since he did not serve to the end of the war.

Jennings, Jonathan. Mass. —. He served in the Dragoons. He was paid $20.

Jennings, Justus. Conn. Pvt. He entered on the brig *Defense* 10 Mar. 1776 as a clerk to Capt. Seth Harding. On 16 June 1776 he was wounded in one of his legs by the recoiling of the gun he was assisting in firing in an engagement with two Scottish vessels, the ship *George* and the brig *Annebella*, armed and loaded with soldiers. His leg had to be amputated. Gideon Wells was the surgeon. He was pensioned 28 July 1782. He was from Sharon.

Jennings, Nathaniel B. Pa. —. He was awarded a $40 gratuity and a $40 annuity in Schuylkill Co., Pa. 14 Apr. 1834. He was 91 years old in 1840. He died 12 May 1841. He also appeared as Nathan B. Jennings.

Jennings, Stephen. Mass. Bombardier. He served in Capt. Thomas Pierce's Company under Col. Henry Knox. He lost his right hand and his thumb near Dorchester heights. He was pensioned at the rate of half-pay from 31 Dec. 1776 on 18 Oct. 1777. It was continued on 28 Apr. 1779. He was 44 years old in 1786.

Jennings, Thomas. Pa. Drummer. He was in Philadelphia County 2 Jan. 1788. He served in the 4th Regiment of Artillery under Col. Proctor. He contracted rheumatism in the service; he was also afflicted with the stone. He was 34 years old. He died 14 Mar. 1790.

Jennings, William. Mass. —. He was pensioned 3 Mar. 1792 for life at the rate of $50 per annum.

Jenny, Thomas. Pa. Lt. He served in the Old 5th Pa. Regiment. He sought five years' full commutation pay in lieu of half-pay for life in 1794.

Jero, Baptiste. Canada. Sgt. He served under Gen. Hazen for more than two years. He died 20 Nov. 1837 in Canada. He married 27 July 1795. He died 20 Nov. 1837. His widow, Hippolite Jero, was granted a pension which was suspended. She died 18 May 1854 before she could furnish the additional evidence. Their son, Jacob Jero, sought the arrearage of his parents 16 Jan. 1857, but Congress did not approve same..

Jerolman, James. N.J. Lt. He served in the 4th Regiment of the Essex County militia under Capt. Harry Jeroleman in Philip Van Cortland's Regiment. He was wounded in the arm at Springfield 7 June 1780. He sought his half-pay in Essex Co., N.J. He then lived in Bergen Co., N.J. He was on the 1791 pension roll in New Jersey. He was also on the 1813 pension list of New Jersey.

Jerome, Isaac. Mass. Pvt. He served under Capt. Enos Parker. He was disabled by a complicated disorder. Some of his blood vessels in his breast and lungs were ruptured and threatened internal decay. He was 23 years old in 1786. He died 17 Feb. 1790.

Jerome, Robert. Conn. Fifer. He served in the New Levies under Col. Douglass. He broke the bones in his left knee when he fell in the retreat from New York in 1776 which left his leg stiff. He resided in Watertown, Conn. in 1792. He was in the militia. He was granted one-fourth of a pension 20 Apr. 1796. He also appeared as Robert Jeroin.

Jervin, Robert. Conn. Fifer. He died in 1802.

Jervis, John. N.Y. Sgt. He served in Capt. Daniel Miller's Company under Col. Goose Van Schaick. He was disabled by being inoculated for smallpox by which he lost the sight in his right eye.

He lived in Pounds Ridge, N.Y. on 21 Apr. 1789.

Jeter, James. S.C. Pvt. His officers included Col. William Thompson, Capt. Richard Winn, and Capt. David Hopkins. He was at Fort McIntosh. James McClure and Capt. Dan McDuff testified about his service. He had his horse, bridle, saddle, gun, and accouterments taken by the enemy. He was from Union District in 1820.

Jett, William S. Va. Lt. He served under Capt. Harper first as a private and then as a lieutenant having enlisted in Sep. 1779. He drew a pension from 1832 to about 1840 when he died. There were 13 loan certificates for $600 each issued to Thomas Jett, the father of William Jett, on 4 Mar. 1779 which were still unpaid. Congress granted Jane Christian Marye, the daughter of William S. Jett, relief 30 Apr. 1896. She was 76 years of age and resided in Alexandria, Va.

Jewel, David. Mass. —. He served in the 1st Regiment. He was paid $20.

Jewel, Hubbard. N.J. He served in 1st N.J. Regiment and was killed at Germantown 4 Oct. 1777. His widow, Mary Jewel, married Joseph Badcock, Jr. 14 Feb. 1779. She was awarded his half-pay from the time of his death to the date of remarriage. She applied in Essex County in Sep. 1785. She had three children by Jewel.

Jewett, Caleb. Conn. Pvt. He served in Burrell's Regiment in Capt. David Downs' Company in Canada in 1776 where he took smallpox and lost sight in one eye. He was pensioned 3 Apr. 1787 while a resident of Sharon, Conn. He was 47 years old. He was on the 1813 pension list. He died 8 Feb. 1820 in Litchfield Co., Conn.

Jewett, David. Mass. —. He married 24 Dec. 1772. He died 21 Nov. 1825. His widow, Ruth Jewett, died 14 Jan. 1838. Neither applied for a pension. Solomon Jewett and other representatives sought relief. Congress rejected their claim for the pension due their mother at her death on 14 Mar. 1848.

Jewett, Gibbons. Conn. Surgeon. In the summer of 1776 he did duty under Col. Samuel Selden in New York in the Continental Army. He was taken sick with bilious fever. His nerves were much affected, and he suffered partial paralysis of his lower parts. He served under Brig. Gen. James Wadsworth. He was pensioned 1 May 1787 at East Haddam, Conn. A complaint to have his pension revoked was rejected 26 Nov. 1788. He died in 1789.

Jewett, Jonathan. Me. —. He died 19 Nov. 1806 in Pittstown. His widow was Hannah Crooker from Bath. She was paid $50 under the resolve of 1836.

Jewett, Joseph. Conn. Capt. He was from Lyme and was slain 31 Aug. 1776. He marched to Roxbury at the time of the Lexington alarm. He was in the 8th Regiment under Col. Jedediah Huntington. He was taken prisoner at Long Island 27 Aug. 1776. He refused to deliver up his watch and was mortally shot by a British solider on 31 Aug. 1776 who ran his sword through him. He left a widow and nine children. He married Lucretia Rogers 18 May 1758 in Norwich, Conn. She married secondly Capt Abner Lee and died 18 Jan. 1836. His nephew was Nathan Jewett. Joshua R. Jewett and Josiah Jewett, his sons, sought half-pay and bounty land. Congress ruled that their claim was barred on 10 Dec. 1857. The children of Joseph and Lucretia Jewett were recorded in Lyme; they were: Lucy Jewett born 12 May 1759, Mary Jewett born 25 Mar. 1761, Joseph Jewett born 7 June 1763, Zabadiah Jewett born 20 Apr. 1765, Lucretia Jewett born 24 Apr. 1767, twins Elizabeth Jewett and Deborah Jewett born 27 Aug. 1769, Joshua Jewett born 14 Aug. 1771, and George Washington Jewett born 10 Mar. 1776. George Washington Jewett lived in Ann Arbor, Michigan. Samuel Jewett, a grandson, lived in Washtenaw Co., Michigan. Joseph Jewett lived in Moravia, Cayuga Co., N.Y. The veteran's brother was Gibbon Jewett.

Jinkins, Samuel. S.C. —. He was paid $240 as compensation for his Revolutionary service on 19 Dec.

1825.

Jobs, William. N.J. —, He served in the 2nd Regiment and lost his right arm. He was on the 1791 pension roll at the rate of $60 per annum. He was 43 years old. He was on the 1813 pension list.

Joel, Richard. Mass. —. He served in the 2nd Regiment and was paid $20.

Johnnot, William. —. Apothecary. His legal representatives sought 6% interest on his five years' full pay 27 May 1893.

Johns, James. Va. —. His wife, Mary Johns, was awarded £12 in Goochland Co., Va. on 21 Dec. 1778.

Johnson, —. —. —. Congress denied his widow, Lucy Johnson, a pension 9 Feb. 1848.

Johnson, —. N.Y. —. Amey Johnson was granted support in 1779 while he was away in the service under Col. Dubois.

Johnson, —. S.C. —. His widow was Elizabeth Johnson. There were three children in 1791.

Johnson, —. S.C. —. He died in the service. His widow was Jane Johnson. She was granted an annuity 21 Feb. 1786.

Johnson, —. Pa. —. His widow, Mary Johnson, was awarded a $40 gratuity and a $40 annuity in Fayette Co., Pa. 15 Apr. 1835.

Johnson, —. S.C. —. His widow was Mary Johnson from Abbeville.

Johnson, —. S.C. —. His widow was Mary Johnson from Darlington.

Johnson, —. S.C. —. His widow, Caroline Johnson, was paid in 1828, 1829, 1830,1 1831, 1832, 1833, and 1834.

Johnson, —. Va. —. His mother, Ann Johnson, was granted support in Westmoreland County in Mar. 1779 and Mar. 1780.

Johnson, Abraham. S.C. —. He served in the 3rd Regiment under Col. William Thompson. He was wounded in one of his thighs in 1779. He was on the roll in 1798.

Johnson, Andrew. Va. Capt. He served under Col. Spotswood and resigned in 1778. Four witnesses testified he served to the close of the war. If so, the service must have been in the militia. He died in Scott Co., Ky. Congress refused relief to his devisee, Robert McCauley, 30 Apr. 1830.

Johnson, Archibald. Md. Sgt. He was pensioned in Charles County at the rate of half-pay of a sergeant on 2 Jan. 1813.

Johnson, Artemas. Conn. Pvt. He served in Capt. Douglass' Company in Wooster's Regiment. He was wounded on Lake Champlain on 8 Sep. 1775 when a soldier's gun accidentally discharged behind him and hit his left arm. It was amputated 17 Sep. 1777. He had a large family of children. He was pensioned 8 Jan. 1783 at Bradford, Conn. He died 13 Aug. 1784.

Johnson, Benedict. Md. Pvt. He was pensioned 4 Mar. 1789. He was on the 1813 pension list.

Johnson, Burrell. S.C. —. He served under Col. Pickney as a spy. He was a saddler in Col. Samuel Hammond's Regiment of Calvary. He was an artificer and was under Capt. Cowen. He was 68 years old and was greatly afflicted by a stroke. His application in Dec.1823 was rejected.

Johnson, Christopher. S.C. —. He was on the roll in 1791.

Johnson, Daniel. Pa. —.He received a $40 gratuity and a $40 annuity in Northampton County 18 Mar. 1834.

Johnson, David. —. —. He was on the expedition against Quebec from the fall of 1775 to May 1776. There was some evidence that he was present at the surrender of Cornwallis. There was insufficient testimony that he was an officer. He married 15 Dec. 1784. Congress granted his widow, Mary Johnson, a pension for six months of service on 30 Apr. 1840.

Johnson, David. N.H. Pvt. He was from Westmoreland. He was in Capt. Wait's Company in Col. Bedel's Regiment. He lost his gun.

Johnson, David. Pa. —. His widow, Catherine Johnson, was awarded a $40 annuity in Beaver Co. for his Revolutionary War service 1 Apr. 1851. She was paid $640 on 19 Apr. 1853 for the period of 6 Apr.1837, the time of his death, to 9 Mar. 1852.

Johnson, David. R.I. Lt. He died of fever on Rhode Island 22 Nov. 1780.

Johnson, Dennis. Me. —. He was from Waterboro. He was paid $50 under the resolve of 1836.

Johnson, Ebenezer. Mass. —. He served in the 8th Regiment and was from Andover. He was paid $20.

Johnson, Edward. Mass. —. He served in the 1st Regiment and was paid $20.

Johnson, Frederick. N.C. Pvt. He married in 1783 Edy -----. He died 15 May 1831. His widow applied at age 72 in 1840 in Rutherford Co., N.C. His son was Willis Johnson.

Johnson, George. S.C. —. He served under Lt. Isaac Morgan, Capt. Wadlington, Col. John Liles, Capt. Thomas Jones, Gen. Pickens, Gen. Sumter, Capt. James Kelly, and Lt. (later Capt.) Lewis Hogg. He fought at Blackstocks, Sumter's defeat, and Hanging Rock. He was about 60 years old and suffered from rheumatism. He had no home and was forced to live among friends and neighbors. He was from Newberry District in 1823. He died 16 Apr. 1826. His children were Thomas Johnson, Edward Johnson, Bartholomew Johnson, Stephen Johnson, and Mary McGatha. Mary McGatha sought the arrears of his pension in Nov. 1826.

Johnson, George. Va. —. His family was granted support while he was away in the service in Amelia Co., Va. 24 July 1777.

Johnson, Grant. Conn. —. He served in the 2nd Conn. Regiment under Col. Heman Swift. He enlisted in 1778 for the war. He was much exercised with rheumatic disorders, and his illness was due to fatigue and hardships. He was born 27 June 1762. He was pensioned 7 Aug. 1787 in Stratford, Conn.

Johnson, Henry. —. —. He lived in Ohio. Congress denied him relief 26 Apr. 1848.

Johnson, Henry. —. —. Congress denied him relief 30 Jan. 1852.

Johnson, Henry. Mass. Pvt. He served in the 4th Regiment under Capt. Haskell and Col. Henry Jackson. He was disabled by a musket ball injury to his left hand. He was worn out in the service and was 31 years old in 1788. He also appeared as Henry Johnston.

Johnson, Ira. Mass. —. He served in the 7th Regiment and was from Brookfield. He was paid $20. At the age of 16 he went with his father, Ira Johnson, to the battle of Lexington. His father was killed or died of wounds. The son enlisted and fought in several other battles until he was wounded and taken prisoner by the Indians. He was held for 14 months. He was then appointed a sergeant in the 7th Mass. Regiment under Lt. Col. John Brooks. He died 31 Mar. 1812 and his widow in 1833. Congress allowed his children what was due them 16 Jan. 1857.

Johnson, Isaac. N.J. Corp. He served under Capt. Shute and Col. William Maxwell in Canada. His next tour was under Col. Israel Shrieve in the 2nd Regiment. He was wounded at Brandywine by a musket ball in his left breast. He had a wife and child. He applied 13 Feb. 1798.

Johnson, Jacob. Mass. Corp. He served in the 7th Regiment and was from Newburg, New York. He was paid $20.

Johnson, Jacob. Pa. —. He was granted relief 23 Jan. 1830. He was 85 years old in 1840. He died in Columbia County 23 July 1841.

Johnson, Jacob. Pa. —. He was awarded a $40 gratuity and a $40 annuity in Columbia Co., Pa. 16

Feb. 1830.

Johnson, Jacob. Pa. —. He was awarded a $40 gratuity in Montgomery Co., Pa. 17 Jan. 1831 and again on 4 May 1832. He was awarded a $40 gratuity and a $40 annuity 23 Jan. 1833. He was dead by Dec. 1833. He also appeared as Jacob Johnston.

Johnson, Jacob. Va. Pvt. He served in Capt. Smallwood's Company. He was wounded in the head at the Waxsaw. He lived in Va. in 1794.

Johnson, James. Pa. Pvt. He was on the 1813 pension list.

Johnson, James. Pa. —. He was awarded a $40 annuity in Adams County 1 Apr. 1851 for his Revolutionary service. His widow, Sarah Johnson, received a $40 annuity in Adams County 20 Apr. 1854.

Johnson, John. Mass. —. He was in the 5th Regiment and was paid $20.

Johnson, John. Mass. —. He was in the 5th Regiment and was paid $50.

Johnson, John. N.Y. Pvt. He enlisted 1 Apr. 1781 in Capt. Cummings's Company in Col. Willet's Regiment for nine months. He reenlisted 1 Apr. 1782 and was discharged at Fort Stanwix at the close of the war. He died at Stockbridge, Oneida Co., N.Y. 12 May 1833. His widow was Caty Johnson of Augusta, N.Y. They were married 1 Nov. 1781 in Kinderhook, Hudson Co., N.Y. The Rev. White performed the ceremony. Anna Johnson, aged 79, and George Johnson, aged 76, deposed for her.

Johnson, John. Pa. —. He was granted relief 7 Mar. 1838 in Mercer County. He died 15 Mar. 1844.

Johnson, John. S.C. —. His widow, Mary Barron, was paid an annuity from 1785 to 1792. She had two children in 1791 and one child in 1792.

Johnson, John. Va. —. He died of frost bite in the Jerseys. His mother, Winniford Johnson, was granted relief 10 June 1779.

Johnson, Joseph. Mass. Pvt. He served in Capt. Baker's company under Col. Benjamin House. He was wounded by a musket ball in his right knee in Rhode Island on 29 Aug. 1778. It could not be extracted. He was crippled. He was pensioned at the rate of half-pay on 15 Apr. 1780. He was 26 years old in 1787. He was on the 1813 pension list. He died 21 Mar. 1826.

Johnson, Joseph. Pa. Pvt. He was dead by Mar. 1793.

Johnson, Joseph. Pa. Sgt. He was in Philadelphia County 14 Nov. 1785. He was transferred from the 4th Pa. Regiment to the Invalids. He was disabled by the loss of his left hand in service and was discharged 1 Nov. 1783. He was 47 years old. He also appeared as Joseph Johnston.

Johnson, Joseph. Pa. —. He was awarded $40 gratuity and $40 annuity plus 200 acres of donation land on 10 Mar. 1812 in Butler County.

Johnson, Joseph. Va. —. He served in the calvary under Col. White. He married in 1786 and came to Lynchburg in 1788. He died 1802. His widow, Elizabeth Johnson, married Nathan Williamson. Congress granted her a pension 26 Apr. 1848.

Johnson, Justus. Conn. Pvt. He served in Capt. David Hinman's Company in the 13th Regiment under Col. Increase Moseley. He was wounded in his left arm by the splitting of his gun at Chestnut Hill near Norwalk on 28 Apr. 1777. His left hand had to be amputated. He was pensioned 10 Apr. 1787 while a resident of Woodbury, Conn. He was aged 36 years. He was on the 1813 pension list. He died 5 Dec. 1814 in New Haven Co., Conn.

Johnson, Lambert. N.J. Pvt. He was taken prisoner at the Highlands 13 Feb. 1777 and died in captivity in New York 25 Mar. 1777. He was from Monmouth County. His widow was Charity Johnson. He also appeared as Lambert Johnston.

Johnson, Martin. Mass. —. He was granted relief.

Johnson, Nicholas. Md. Pvt. His widow, Rebecca Johnson, was pensioned at the rate of half-pay in Queen Anne's County on 4 Mar. 1835.

Johnson, Obediah. Mass. —. He served in the 13ᵗʰ Regiment and was from Windsor. His widow, Azubah Johnson, was paid $50.

Johnson, Peter. N.H. Pvt. He was wounded in the right arm by a musket ball on 17 June 1775 at Bunker Hill. He received a pension of 15 shillings per month from N.H. from 7 June 1783 to 31 July 1786. He lived at Enfield, N.H. in 1789 and 1794. He served under Col. John Stark. He was granted one-fourth of a pension 20 Apr. 1796. He was on the 1813 pension list.

Johnson, Peter. Va. Lt. He served in the cavalry. His widow, Ann B. Johnson, of Henrico Co., Va. sought arrearage of the pension from 4 Mar. 1848 to 3 Feb. 1853 on 10 Dec. 1857.

Johnson, Philip. N.J. Col. He served under Brig. Gen. Nathaniel Beard. He died 27 Aug. 1776 at the battle of Long Island. He left three daughters one of whom was born 9 Jan. 1774. His widow was Rachel B. Johnson. His daughter, Elizabeth Johnson, was allowed half-pay from 27 Aug. 1776 to 9 Jan. 1782. He was from Hunterdon County. His widow died intestate in Alleghany Co., Pa. Her administrator was William H. Johnson. Congress rejected the claim of his heirs for seven years' half-pay 23 Jan. 1837 because he was appointed by New Jersey and not by Congress. Congress reversed its decision and paid the heirs $1,537.33 on 2 Mar. 1860. He also appeared as Philip Johnston.

Johnson, Richard. Mass. Pvt. He served in the 2ⁿᵈ Regiment and was from Kingston. He was paid $50.

Johnson, Richard. Pa. Lt. He served under Col. Hazlett from Delaware and was discharged in Dec. 1776. He subsequently went to Carlisle and served under Col. Watt. He was in the service on the frontiers of Cumberland, Northumberland, Bedford, and Westmoreland Counties. He was ensign in 1780 and was promoted to lieutenant. He was from Mifflin County.

Johnson, Robert. N.Y. Pvt. He was wounded at the capture of Fort Montgomery on 6 Oct. 1777. He resided in New Windsor, N.Y. in 1794. He died 26 Nov. 1800.

Johnson, Robert. Pa. Surgeon. He served in the 6ᵗʰ Pa. Regiment from the beginning to 1781 when Gen. Greene ordered him to leave the regimental service to care for officers and soldiers who were then prisoners at Charleston, S.C.. He was, therefore, granted donation land 25 Mar. 1803.

Johnson, Samuel. Mass. —. He served in the 10ᵗʰ Regiment and was from Hallowell. He was paid $20.

Johnson, Samuel. N.C. Pvt. He applied in Wilkes County in 1806. He served under Col. Benjamin Cleveland and was wounded through the belly at the battle of King's Mountain. He was on the 1813 pension list.

Johnson, Samuel. Va. Pvt. He was pensioned in Essex County on 25 Feb. 1818 at the rate of $50 per annum. He entered the service in 1776 and served two years. He was disabled by a dislocated ankle joint. He died 11 Feb. 1830, and his widow, Patsey Johnson, was administratrix of his estate.

Johnson, Seth. Conn. —. He was pensioned 23 May 1778.

Johnson, Shepherd. N.Y. Pvt. He served in Col. McDougal's Regiment. He was wounded and had his arm broken by a musket shot in May 1777 in Bergen Co., N.J. He lived in Orange Co., N.Y. in 1794.

Johnson, Simon. Mass. Pvt. He lost his health in the service. He served under Col. Lewis Nichola and afterwards was in the Invalids under Capt. Moses McFarland. He was wounded by a musket ball in his left hand. He was disabled with a consumptive habit. He was pensioned 1 Sep. 1782. He was aged 51 in 1786. He was on the 1791 roll in Rhode Island. He died 23 July 1808 in Providence Co., R.I.

Johnson, Thomas. Pa. 2nd Lt. He served in Col. Cunningham's Flying Camp. He was wounded by a musket ball in the thigh in Aug. 1776 at Flatbush, Long Island. He lived in Managhan, Pa. in 1794. His rate was $5 per month from 17 Apr. 1807. He was on the 1813 pension list.

Johnson, Thomas. Va. Capt. His heirs received a bounty land warrant for 2,666 1/3 acres from Virginia for three years of service from 1776 to 1779. Congress rejected the claim of the heirs for commutation 9 Jan. 1838. They were from Louisa County.

Johnson, William. —. Capt. Congress granted his heirs commutation 17 Jan. 1838.

Johnson, William. —. —. He served under Capt. Elisha Woodward and Col. John Starke. He was at Bunker Hill. He transferred to a company under Capt. Henry Dearborn. He went to Quebec and fought with Gen. Montgomery. He transferred to the riflemen under Capt. Smith. He served nine months to 1 June 1776. Congress rejected the petition 29 Jan. 1822.

Johnson, William. Conn. Pvt. He lived in Fairfield Co., Conn. He was on the 1813 pension list. He was 83 years old in 1818.

Johnson, William. Mass. —. He served in Hazen's Regiment and was paid $20.

Johnson, William. Mass. —. He served in Hazen's Regiment and was paid $20. [second of the name]

Johnson, William. Pa. —. He received a $40 annuity 2 Apr. 1822.

Johnson, William. R.I. He served three months under Capt. Whitman and Col. Cooke, three months in the militia, and ten months in 1777 under Capt. Hammett and Col. Stanton. He was 78 years old. Congress granted him a pension 3 Jan. 1832.

Johnston, —. Pa. —. His widow, Barbara Johnston, was awarded a $40 gratuity and a $40 annuity in York Co., Pa.

Johnston, —. Pa. —. His widow, Ann Johnston, was granted relief in Huntingdon County 21 July 1842. She died 18 Nov. 1842.

Johnston, —. S.C. —. His widow, Mary Johnston, was a resident of Abbeville District in 1791.

Johnston, Abraham. Pa. —. He was awarded a $40 gratuity in Bucks Co., Pa. 12 Apr. 1828.

Johnston, Andrew. Pa. Lt. He enlisted in the 1st Regiment and marched to Boston. He received a stab by a bayonet in his right hip in 1777 at Paoli. He had a contusion on his left leg caused by a musket ball at Monmouth. He applied in York County 3 Jan. 1812. He was on the 1813 pension list as Andrew Johnson. He died 15 Dec. 1815.

Johnston, Crawford. —. —. He received bounty land warrant #1294 for 100 acres on 2 Apr. 1828. It has been lost so a duplicate was issued 22 Dec. 1837.

Johnston, Daniel. Pa. —. He was awarded a $40 gratuity and a $40 annuity in Northampton Co., Pa. 18 Mar. 1834. He died 24 Aug. 1841.

Johnston, David. N.C. Pvt. He applied in 1784. He was wounded in militia service in action on the Tiger River in South Carolina in 1780. He lost his left arm. He served under Col. Robert Erwin. He lived in Ashe County. He was on the 1813 pension list. He died 18 Feb. 1829. He also appeared as David Johnson.

Johnston, David. Pa. Pvt. He was granted relief.

Johnston, Francis. N.C. Pvt. He applied in Iredell County in 1799. He was hired as a substitute for Joseph Chambers for three months. He served in the militia under Col. Malmudy. He was disabled by a wound in his left arm at the battle of Eutaw. Robert Wasson who served with him attested to his service. He was on the 1813 pension list as Francis Johnson. James Chambers proved that his brother, Joseph Chambers, was dead by 1801.

Johnston, Francis. S.C. —. He lost his life in the service. His widow, Margaret Johnston, was granted an annuity 31 Dec. 1784.There were two children in 1791.

Johnston, Gideon. Va. Capt. He enlisted at Yorktown and was promoted to lieutenant, a brigade quartermaster, and lastly a captain. The British destroyed his house in the battle of Yorktown. Congress rejected his claim for compensation because it was barred by statute on 2 Jan. 1822.

Johnston, Hugh. Pa. —. He applied in Cumberland County on 13 Dec. 1814. He was in the 4th Pa. Regiment in Capt. Thomas Campbell's Company under Col. William Butler and served from 1 Jan. 1781 to the end of the war. He was also in the German Regiment under Maj. Selling for four years before serving in the 4th. He was discharged at Carlisle Barracks in Dec. 1783. He had a small family. He died in or about Apr. 1826. He also appeared as Hugh Johnson. His heirs were paid $200 in lieu of his donation land 16 June 1836. The heirs were Crowell Farrell and Lucinda Farrell.

Johnston, James. S.C. —. His annuity was £3.4.10 in 1787.

Johnston, John. Pa. —. He was granted relief 1 Apr. 1825 in Westmoreland County. He was 93 years old in 1840.

Johnston, John. Pa. —. He was awarded a $40 gratuity and a $40 annuity in Greene Co., Pa. 8 Apr. 1833.

Johnston, John. S.C. —. He was killed at Black Rock. His widow, Mary Johnston, was on the roll in 1785.

Johnston, John. Va. —. His wife, Mary Johnston, was allowed 3 bushels of corn valued at £15 while her husband was away in the service in Augusta Co., Va. 21 Mar. 1780.

Johnston, John. S.C. —. He was killed at Black Rock. His widow, Sarah Johnston, was granted an annuity 8 June 1785.

Johnston, Joseph. Pa. —. He was pensioned 10 Mar. 1812.

Johnston, Matthew. S.C. —. He was killed 18 Aug. 1780 in action with the British troops. His widow, Jennet Johnston, was granted an annuity 15 Nov. 1784. There were children in 1791.

Johnston, Michael. Pa. 1st Lt. His widow, Ruth Johnston, was in Lancaster County. He served in the Flying Camp, was taken prisoner at Fort Washington, and made his escape from New York. He took sick, came to Philadelphia where he got some better, and returned home. He died 12 Oct. 1779 in captivity. He left a widow, Ruth Johnston, and two small children. She was no longer eligible for a pension after 29 Aug. 1792. He also appeared as Michael Johnson. One Ruth Johnson was paid in Jan. 1814.

Johnston, Philip. Pa. —. When Morrison, Darlington, and he were called to return to captivity in 1779, he was cradling oats for one Clemson and was in good health. Clemson asked him if he were going back. He replied that he had been there once, got away, and that he would be damned if he were to return again. His widow was receiving a pension 20 Aug. 1789.

Johnston, Richard. Pa. —. He was a ranger. He was awarded a $40 gratuity and a $40 annuity on 17 Jan. 1812. He was paid to Apr. 1832.

Johnston, Robert. Pa. Surgeon. He served in the 6th Regiment to 1781. Gen. Greene ordered him to leave the regiment in order to attend the wounded of the American Army held as prisoners in a British hospital at Charleston. He was issued bounty land.

Johnston, Samuel. Pa. —. He applied in Cumberland County on 6 Jan. 1819. He enlisted in 1776 in Capt. Taylor's Company in the 5th Pa. Regiment under Col. Francis Johnston. He also served in Capt. Thomas Bond's Company under Col. Richard Butler and was discharged in 1782. He was paid $300 in lieu of his donation land 28 Mar. 1820.

Johnston, Thomas. Ga. —. He was on the 1796 list.

Johnston, Thomas. S.C. —. He was hanged by the enemy. His children were granted an annuity 8 Oct. 1785. There were two children in 1791.

Johnston, William. —. Capt. He received five years' full pay in his lifetime. The application on the part of his heirs for same on 17 Jan. 1838 was, therefore, rejected

Johnston, William. —. —. He was pensioned at the rate of $2.50 per month from 1 Apr. 1807.

Johnston, William. Md. Pvt. He was pensioned at the rate of half-pay of a private in Harford County on 2 Mar. 1827.

Johnston, William. Pa.—. He received assistance 1 Apr. 1823 and was from Westmoreland Co.

Johnston, William. Pa. —. He was awarded a $40 gratuity and a $40 annuity in Adams Co., Pa. 15 Apr. 1835.

Johnston, William. Pa. —. He was awarded a $40 gratuity and a $40 annuity 27 Mar. 1812 in Chester County. He was on the 1813 pension list.

Johnston, William. Pa. —. He was granted relief in Huntingdon County 14 Mar. 1835. He died 14 May 1841.

Johnston, William. S.C. —. He served in the 3rd S.C. Regiment and died in Charleston in May 1780. His widow, Mary Johnston, was awarded an annuity 21 May 1783. There were five children in 1791.

Johnston, William. S.C. —. He had a large family most of whom were females. He was 73 years old. He served under Capt. Charles Louis and Lt. John Hollis. He was from Fairfield District when he was pensioned 25 Nov. 1830. He was still being paid in 1834.

Johonnot, William. Mass. Apothecary. He was late of Boston, Mass. and was apothecary of hospitals in the eastern district 7 Apr. 1777. With the reorganization of the army on 30 Sep. 1780 he became apothecary general. He and his wife died at the close of the war. His heirs received his commutation pay 28 Jan. 1836.

Joice, James. N.Y. Sgt. He served in 2nd N.Y. Regiment under Capt. Benjamin ---- and was slain 30 Aug. 1778, His children, Charles Joice, James Joice, Sarah Joice, and Stephen Joice, received a half-pay pension.

Joiner, Matthew. N.C. —. He served in the 3rd Regiment and enlisted for 2 ½ years under Capt. Gray and Col. Sumner. He was at the battle of Sullivan's Fort. He was born 19 June 1757. He had a wife Lucy Joiner aged about 70, daughter Polly Joiner aged about 30, and grandson Nathaniel Joiner aged about 9. He applied in Wake Co., N.C. 10 May 1828.

Joliff, John. Va. Lt. He died 5 Apr. 1777. His widow, Mary Joliff, was being pensioned 20 June 1783. The names of the orphans were not given.

Jolly, John. S.C. Lt. His widow was Sarah Jolly. There were two children in 1791.

Jolly, Joseph. Va. Pvt. He served in the 1st Va. Regiment and died in service leaving a widow, Mary Anne Jolly, and three small children. She and her three children were furnished 4 barrels of corn and 200 pounds of pork for 1781 and 1782 in Henrico Co., Va. on 7 Jan. 1782. She lived in Henrico County in Mar. 1786. She died in Nov. 1797.

Jolly, Wilson. S.C. —. He was from Pendleton District and was pensioned 30 Nov. 1827. He died 10 June 1829. His widow, Mary Jolly, was pensioned at the rate of $30 per annum on 23 Nov. 1829 and was from Anderson District. She was still being paid in 1834.

Jonas, John. Md. Pvt. He was wounded in four places near Woodbridge, N.J. in Sep. 1782. He lived in Allegany County. He was on the 1813 pension list.

Joneman, —. Va. —. Francis Joneman was granted support in Prince William County in 1778.

Jones, —. Md. Pvt. His widow, Nancy Jones, was pensioned at the rate of half-pay of a private in Worcester County on 4 Mar. 1834.

Jones, —. S.C. —. His widow was Elizabeth Jones. There was one child in 1791.

Jones, —. Pa. —. His widow, Elizabeth Jones, was granted a $100 gratuity for five years 18 Mar. 1851.

Jones, —. Pa. —. His widow, Margaret Jones, was awarded relief in Fayette County 5 Feb. 1836.

Jones, —. S.C. —. His widow was Mary Jones of Edgefield in 1791.

Jones, Aaron. Md. Pvt. He was pensioned in Dorchester County at the rate of half-pay of a private 23 Jan. 1816.

Jones, Abraham. N.J. —. He was pensioned in Gloucester County on 11 Feb. 1839 at the rate of $60 per annum.

Jones, Abraham P. Ga. Lt. He was paid a gratuity in 1801. He died 28 Jan. 1831.

Jones, Alexander. Va. Pvt. He was wounded at Ninety Six 18 June 1781. He was on the 1785 pension roll. He was in Continental service and was wounded in his knee. He was from Prince William Co., Va. on 5 May 1783. He was pensioned at the rate of $3.33 1/3 cents from 19 June 1784 on 25 Apr. 1808.

Jones, Amos. Conn. Pvt. He served for two months. He was past 90 years of age, and his home had burned. Congress denied his claim 23 Feb. 1855 because he had not served the minimum time.

Jones, Bartly. S.C. —. He was killed in the service. His widow, Mary Jones, received an annuity in 1819, 1820, and 1821. She died at the home of her son-in-law James Carroll, the husband of her daughter Kesiah Carroll. Kesiah Carroll and Patsey Carroll sought her arrearage. Burrell Evans swore that Kesiah Carroll was a daughter.

Jones, Benjamin. Pa. —. He was awarded a $40 gratuity and a $40 annuity in York Co., Pa. 14 Feb. 1833. He was 90 years old in 1840. He died 23 Feb. 1848.

Jones, Catlett. Va. —. He was given relief having been wounded 5 Dec. 1778. His pension was discontinued by order of the executive 10 Jan. 1787. His widow, Mildred Jones of Orange County, was paid what he was due at the time of death on 23 Apr. 1792. He also appeared as Catlett James.

Jones, Charles. Conn. Pvt. He was on the 1795 and the 1813 pension lists.

Jones, Cotter. Md. Pvt. He was pensioned at the rate of half-pay of a private 12 Mar. 1827 in Somerset County.

Jones, Daniel. N.J. Corp. He served under Capt. Samuel Ogden. His widow was Mary Jones who married secondly Jeremiah Usted or Husted and was his widow by 9 Mar. 1798 when she sought a pension.

Jones, Daniel. N.Y. Sgt. He served in Capt. John Craig's Company in the New Jersey Regiment. He was wounded with a musket ball above his left knee and had his left leg amputated at Newark, N.J. He was formerly of Elizabethtown, N.J. but was a schoolmaster in New York City, N.Y. on 12 July 1786.

Jones, Harrison. Va. Pvt. He lived in Cumberland County 1 Jan. 1786 and was aged 30 years. He served in the Cumberland County militia and was wounded at the battle of Guilford on 15 Mar. 1781 where he lost a leg a little below the knee. He served in the regiment under Beverley Randolph. He was pensioned 13 Jan. 1785 at half-pay for life and was continued at the rate of £15 per annum on 25 Jan. 1787. He was on the 1813 pension list of Georgia.

Jones, Isaac. Pa. —. He was awarded a $40 gratuity and a $40 annuity in York Co., Pa. 8 Apr. 1833. He was 85 years old in 1840. He died 16 Nov. 1841.

Jones, Hugh. N.J. Pvt. He served under Capt. John Stokes and Col. Joseph Ellis and was wounded in Nov. 1777 by a ball in his left side which was never extracted. He was granted a half-pay pension in Gloucester County 8 Feb. 1798.

Jones, James. Ga. —. He was paid $50 in 1796. His widow, Amy Jones, and orphans were receiving $30 per annum in 1797. They were granted $50 18 Feb. 1799. They were still being paid in 1803.

Jones, James. S.C. —. He was taken prisoner at Briar Creek and died in confinement. His widow, Jane Jones, was awarded an annuity 15 Mar. 1785.

Jones, James. S.C. —. He was pensioned 25 Nov. 1830.

Jones, James Morris. Pa. Lt. $400 was paid to his daughter, Martha Levi Adams of Philadelphia, Pa., for his donation land 18 Mar. 1834.

Jones, Jeremiah. S.C. —. He lived in Orangeburg District and applied 27 Nov. 1828. His claim was rejected in Nov. 1830.

Jones, John. Pa. —. He was wounded at Fort Washington.

Jones, John. Pa. —. His widow, Margaret Jones, was alive 27 Dec. 1806.

Jones, John. Va. —. His wife, Sarah Jones, and two children were awarded £3 per month in Accomack Co., Va. 23 Feb. 1779.

Jones, John. Va. —. He was pensioned in Essex County on 10 Feb. 1812 at the rate of $40 per annum. He was disabled by a wound in a half moon battery when Charleston was attacked.

Jones, John. Va. —. He enlisted in Sep. 1776 under Capt. Arbuckle and was stationed at Point Pleasant until he was discharged in 1777. He returned home to Greenbrier Co., Va. In 1778 he was employed as a spy and was paid $1 per diem until he was discharged. Congress granted his widow, Frances Jones, relief 9 Jan. 1839.

Jones, John Paul. —. Capt. He commanded a squadron and took many valuable prizes. He sent these vessels to Bergen, Norway. They were given to prize masters by orders of Capt. Peter Landais. The King of Denmark ordered them seized and returned to England. His heir was his niece, Jeanette Taylor, who sought relief from Congress 20 Aug. 1842.

Jones, Jonathan. S.C. —. David Neely served two tours, one at Congaree and the other at Orangeburg, with him. He was also in battle at Hook's defeat and Sumter's defeat. William Knox and David Morrow served with him. James McClure also confirmed his service. He was from Chester District and was pensioned 8 Dec. 1826. He died 4 Aug. 1835. His widow was Elizabeth Jones. Most of her children had left her.

Jones, Joshua. —. —. He was a pensioner. Two of his children, Isaac Jones and Polly Jones, sought the arrearage due their father as a pensioner by virtue of their father's last will and testament. There were seven other children. Congress rejected their petition 4 May 1846.

Jones, Joshua. Va. —. He was wounded near Long Island on the Holstein River. He was awarded a £10 gratuity on 16 June 1777.

Jones, Josiah. Mass. Pvt. He was wounded and pensioned at half-pay from 10 June 1784 on 21 Jan. 1785. He served in the 10th Mass. Regiment and transferred to Bergen Co., N.J.

Jones, Josiah. Mass. Pvt. He was pensioned 21 Mar. 1807. He was on the 1813 pension list and died 23 Feb. 1826 in Barnstable Co., Mass.

Jones, Josiah. Mass. —. He served in the sappers and miners in the 7th Regiment under Capt. King and Col. Brooks. He was 25 years old in 1786.

Jones, Josiah. Va. & N.C. —. He served in the 6th Va. Regiment before moving to North Carolina where he served under Gen. Charles McDowell. He was a blacksmith by trade and made swords and shoed horses. He suffered from an almost entire loss of sight. He was in his 79th year of age. He also served under Andrew Hampton of Rutherford Co., N.C. He applied from Anderson District, South Carolina 13 Oct. 1830. His application was rejected. He also appeared as Joshua Jones.

Jones, Nathaniel. S. C. Sgt. He served under Capt. McFarlane on the frontier of Georgia. He also served under Capt. John Land, Col. John Winn, Maj. Brown, Capt. John Watts. He was at Rocky Mount, Orangeburg, and Charleston. At the latter he was wounded in his shoulder. He had previously been wounded in the leg near Altamaha in Georgia. He was a cripple. He was in his 80th year and lived in Kershaw District. Isham Powell attested to his service. His application was rejected in 1831.

Jones, Neale. Md. Pvt. He was pensioned at the rate of half-pay of a private 2 Jan. 1813.

Jones, Nehemiah. —. Pvt. He was a pensioner. He married in 1785. His widow, Anna Jones, was disallowed under the act of 7 July 1838 because she was not a widow at its passage. She sought relief from Congress 26 May 1842.

Jones, Nelce. Md. Corp. He served in the 2nd Regiment. He was wounded in the front of his ankle through the bone by which he was disabled in Sept. 1781 at Eutaw Springs. He lived in Kent Co., Del. in 1795. He enlisted in Feb. 1778 for the war and was on the rolls in 1783. He was on the 1813 pension list in Delaware.

Jones, Philip. Pa. —. He enlisted in 1776 and served four years and eight months. His feet were severely frozen and his eye was much injured on the night of the attack on the Block House. He had since lost his sight. He was awarded a $40 gratuity and an annuity of $40 in Chester County on 19 Mar. 1810. He applied from Chester County on 31 Dec. 1812. He died 20 Sep. 1820.

Jones, Richard. N.J. Pvt. He served under Lt. Thomas in the Burlington County militia and was wounded in both legs. He was 53 years old and resided at Williamsburg. He was on the 1791 pension roll at the rate of $40 per annum. He was on the 1813 pension list.

Jones, Richard. S.C. Lt. He died 2 July 1779.

Jones, Richard. S.C. Capt. He served in the militia from South Carolina and Georgia in the Light Horse. His grandchildren sought the pension due him on 4 May 1860. He was credited with twenty-five months of service.

Jones, Richard. Va. Pvt. His widow, Elizabeth Jones, lived in Norfolk County 18 Jan. 1787. She was 50 years old and had one child 10 years old. He served in the Norfolk County militia and was killed. She was continued on the pension list at the rate of £8 per annum on 24 Feb. 1787. Their daughter was 18 years on 16 May 1791.

Jones, Richard. Va. Pvt. He was pensioned in Louisa County 8 Feb. 1817 at the rate of $70 per annum. He also received $80 relief. He was wounded in the leg at Brandywine. He served in the 6th Virginia Regiment under Capt. Oliver Towles.

Jones, Robert. —. —. He sought relief for wounds received in the Revolutionary War.

Jones, Russell. Ga. —. He was on the 1796 list.

Jones, Samuel. Mass. —. He served in the 10th Regiment and was from Hallowell. He was paid $20.

Jones, Samuel. Md. Capt. His daughter, Lillias M. Jones, received a warrant for 200 acres of bounty land in Allegany County in Mar. 1828.

Jones, Samuel. N.J. Sgt. He served in Capt. John Craig's Company from New Jersey. He was wounded above the left knee by a musket ball at Newark by a party of refugees and had his leg amputated. He was awarded his half-pay in Essex County in June 1783. He was 27 years old in 1786. He lived in New York City, N.Y. on 13 June 1788 when he was pensioned. He was a school teacher.

He was on the 1791 pension roll in New Jersey at the rate of $60 per annum. He was on the 1813 pension list.

Jones, Samuel. N.Y. Capt. He served in the Orange County militia and was slain 22 July 1779. His widow, Hannah Jones, received his half-pay pension.

Jones, Samuel. Va. Lt. There were two men of the name and same rank. One acted as paymaster of the 15th Virginia Regiment. The other was the paymaster of the 11th Virginia Regiment. Samuel Jones was paid from early 1777 to Jan. 1780 and from Jan. 1780 to 1 Feb. 1781 when he was paid as captain and became supernumerary. He never resigned. He died in 1784. His posthumous son, Samuel Jones, was not granted his commutation 22 Feb. 1843. The son was allowed relief from Congress 5 Mar. 1858 for the service of the one in the 11th Regiment until 1779 when he became supernumerary.

Jones, Silas. S.C. —. He was on the roll in 1791.

Jones, Solomon. Md. —. He was from Dorchester County.

Jones, Strother. —. Capt. He served under Col. Gist. Commutation of five years' full pay in lieu of half pay during life was paid to his estate in 1791.

Jones, Thomas. Md. Pvt. He was pensioned at the rate of half-pay of a private in Anne Arundel Co. on 11 Mar. 1834.

Jones, Thomas. S.C. Capt. He was killed 3 Apr. 1781. His widow, Catharine Jones, was awarded an annuity 17 Nov. 1784. There were two children in 1791.

Jones, Thomas. Va. —. His wife was provided financial support while he was in Continental service in Amherst Co., Va. in Oct. 1778.

Jones, Uriah. R.I. Pvt. He enlisted in the R.I. Line under Capt. Humphrey and Col. Israel Angel and served to Sep. 1782. He was at the battles of Springfield, Red Bank, and Yorktown. He was wounded several times and had two balls in his body when he died. His two maiden daughters supported him. He was unable to get a pension under the act of 1832 because he was carried on the roll as deserted. Toward the end of the war, Capt. Allen took command, and the company did not like him because he was arbitrary and unjust. Eight to ten soldiers left the company at the same time. He had no idea his action was deserting. His daughters sought a pension for the period 4 Mar. 1831 to Dec. 1845 when he died. They did so 26 Mar. 1852. Congress granted the heirs relief 21 June 1854.

Jones, William. Conn. Marine. He served aboard the ship *Oliver Cromwell* with 20 guns under Capt. Timothy Parker. He was wounded by a grape shot which entered his thigh and discharged itself at the hip in an engagement with the British ship *Admiral Keppell* on 15 Apr. 1778 at sea about 60 leagues from the island of Antigua. After landing at Charleston, S.C., he was sent to hospital. Thirteen months later, finding little or no benefit, he returned to Connecticut. He was first pensioned 16 Sep. 1779. He was 23 years old, five foot ten inches tall, and had a brown complexion. He lived in Norwich, Conn. in 1794. His ship was not a Continental vessel. He resided in Nova Scotia from the close of the war until lately [*i.e.* 1794]. There was no evidence of his disability during this time. Since he was not in the service of the United States, he had no claim to a pension.

Jones, William. Md. Pvt. He was pensioned at the rate of half-pay of a private on 14 Feb. 1820. He lived in Virginia but was formerly of Prince George's Co., Md.

Jones, William. Md. Pvt. He was pensioned at the rate of half-pay of a private in Caroline County on 8 Mar. 1833.

Jones, William. Mass. —. He served in the 8th Regiment and was worn out in the service. He was pensioned 1 Sep. 1782.

Jones, William. Mass. —. He served under Col. Crary and Col. Topham of R.I. for more than eighteen months. He was promoted from sergeant to quartermaster. His heirs sought his pension from 16 Aug. 1819 to the time of his death 22 June 1829. Congress did not grant their petition 26 Mar. 1852.

Jones, William. Va. Capt. He was killed at the battle of Guilford Courthouse. His son and heir, David Jones, of Campbell Co. received $120 for his father's three months of service from Bedford Co. on 12 Mar. 1835.

Jones, William. Va. Pvt. He was awarded a £15 gratuity and an annuity of full pay on 12 Oct 1778. He lived in Berkeley County 4 June 1787. He served in the 8th Va. Regiment in Capt. Kirkpatrick's Company. He was wounded in his left knee at Brandywine in Sep. 1777 and was discharged in May 1778. Lt. Col. William Darke of the Va. State Line attested to his service. He was 40 years old in 1787. He was conditioned on the pension list at the rate of £12 per annum on 4 June 1787. He was disabled by a musket ball through his knee which broke the bone. He was on the 1813 pension list.

Jones, William. Va. Pvt. He lived in Fredericksburg, Spotsylvania County on 29 Mar. 1826. He was pensioned 24 Feb. 1826 at the rate of $60 per annum with $30 immediate relief. He enlisted in 1776 and served to 1780. He served in the 8th Va. Regiment. He was a free man of color.

Jones, William. Va. —. He was the sole support of his grandmother, Mary Jones, who was granted £30 support on 3 May 1779 in Richmond County while he was away in the service.

Jonet, Robert. Va. Lt. He became supernumerary and was discharged at Charleston. Congress granted his representative commutation 13 Jan. 1835.

Jor, Gabriel. —. Maj. He served in a regiment of Canadian Refugees. He joined in Canada and served five months before retreating in the summer of 1776. After spending five months at or near Ticonderoga, he was dismissed due to sickness. He married 4 Oct. 1783. His widow sought relief. He also appeared as Gabriel Shor and Gabriel Ghor.

Jordan, Abner. Me. —. He died 26 Sep. 1819 in Lisbon. His widow was Hannah Jordan from Auburn. She was paid $50 under the resolve of 1836.

Jordan, Abraham. Me. —. He died 18 Apr. 1835. His widow was Lydia Jordan from Durham. She was paid $50 under the resolve of 1836.

Jordan, Edmond. Va. —. He served in the 4th Regiment under Capt. Lucas from about Mar. 1776 for two years. He applied from Northampton Co., N.C.

Jordan, Hugh. Pa. —. He received a $40 gratuity and a $40 annuity in Clearfield County 15 June 1836. He was 84 years old in 1840. He died 18 July 1840.

Jordan, Jesse. Mass. —. His widow, Hannah Jordan, was paid $50.

Jordan, Jesse. S.C. —. He served under Col. George Hicks and Col. Kolb. He was from Darlington District when he was pensioned on 25 Nov. 1830. His unnamed grandson sought a warrant for the payment of the pension on 4 Mar. 1844. Joel Jordan confirmed his service.

Jordan, John. —. Seaman. He was disabled by the loss of a limb in action with the British on 23 Sep. 1779 aboard the *Bon Homme Richard* under Capt. John Paul Jones. He was pensioned under the act of 15 Sep. 1783.

Jordan, John. Md. Capt. His widow, Sarah Easton, was pensioned at the rate of half-pay of a captain in Jan. 1836.

Jordan, John. Mass. —. He was in the 12th Regiment and was paid $20.

Jordan, John. Pa. —. He was in Westmoreland County on 21 Nov. 1789.

Jordan, John. Pa. Capt. He entered the service in Philadelphia as lieutenant of artillery in Feb. 1777 and was promoted to captain in 1778. He also served under Col. Benjamin Fowler. He moved to Botetourt Co., Va. in 1795 and died 4 May 1835. His executor and son-in-law, James Paxton, sought the half-pay to which he had been entitled. The heirs were the children of his daughter Mary Steinberger, viz. Eliza Lewis, Mary E. McCullock, Catharine B. Neal, Sarah A. Couch, Cornelia S. Menager. Susan V. Spencer, Rhoda Steinberger, Ellen Steinberger, John W. Steinberger, and Maria L. Menager; the grandchildren of his daughter, Elizabeth Rowland, viz. Rutherford R. Houston, Thomas Gilmore, Elizabeth Gilmore, Henry Gilmore, R. Rowland Echols, John J. Echols, and Fannie Echols. He died 4 May 1835. All of the children of Elizabeth Rowland were dead. His widow was Catherine Jordan. Bounty land warrant #1165 for 300 acres was issued 19 Feb. 1792. He was an original member of the Society of the Cincinnati. Congress did not allow the heirs relief 5 Feb. 1861.

Jordan, John. Pa. Capt. He served in the artillery in 1779. He sought his half-pay or commutation in 1790, but he was not qualified to receive same. His legal representatives did likewise, and Congress granted same 21 Jan. 1839.

Jordan, John. Va. Lt. He lived in Albemarle County. He was pensioned in 1811 and had been wounded in the battle of Edge Hill. He was on the 1813 pension list.

Jordan, Johnson. R.I. ——. He enlisted 1 June 1778 under Capt. Traffin and Col. Tappan and served to Mar. 1779. He had applied in 1818 but had been refused because his service was not in the Continental Line. Congress granted him a pension 10 Jan. 1832.

Jordan, Martin. Mass. Pvt. He served under Capt. Allen and Col. Joseph Vose. He was disabled with a rupture and other bodily infirmities. He was 59 years old in 1786. He was from Oxford and was paid $20 by the Commonwealth.

Jordan, Michael. Va. ——. He was pensioned at the rate of $40 per annum and received $50 relief on 4 Dec. 1795. He lived in Fluvanna County on 2 July 1796. He was wounded in the thigh in the battle of Eutaw. He died 16 Sep. 1806 and left a widow and 4 children, the youngest of whom was 6 months old.

Jordan, Thomas. Va. Pvt. He was awarded a £30 gratuity and an annuity of half-pay on 26 Nov. 1778. He lived in Culpeper County in Feb. 1788. He enlisted 20 Apr. 1776 under Col. Mercer. He served in Capt. John Thornton's Company of the 3rd Va. Regiment. He lost nearly all of his toes on his right foot, his left foot was considerably drawn inward, and his toes were greatly contracted. He was discharged unfit for duty 12 Dec. 1778. He was granted a £30 gratuity and half-pay for life on 11 Dec. 1778. He was aged 38 years in 1788. He was continued at the rate of £12 per annum on 10 Nov. 1788. He was on the 1813 pension list. He died 24 July 1827 in Fauquier Co., Va.

Jordan, Timothy. Mass. ——. He enlisted at Gorham, Me. in Apr. 1781 for three years. He was at West Point under Capt. McDonald and Col. Hand. He acted as a servant for one year and three months. He was discharged at his own request. Congress ruled that his service was military and granted him a pension for one year's service 31 May 1834.

Jorden, Samuel. ——. ——. He served thirteen months in 1782 and 1783 as a volunteer in scouting parties against the Indians and in protecting the frontier settlements. Congress accepted nine months of service for him and granted him a pension of $30 a year from 1 Jan. 1844 on 16 Jan. 1846.

Jordon, Henry. Pa. ——. His name was mistakenly entered as Henry Gordon of Mercer County in the act of 27 Mar. 1837 so the act was corrected 20 May 1839.

Jouett, Robert. Va. Lt. He served in the Virginia Line. His five years' full pay commutation was paid to his representative, James W. Bouldin, 20 Mar. 1836.

Joy, Ebenezer. Mass. Pvt. He served in the American Regiment and was from Weymouth. His widow, Anna Joy, was paid $50.

Joy, Nehemiah. Mass. Sgt. He was in Revere's Regiment and was from Buckland. His widow, Hannah Joy, was paid $50.

Joy, Richard. Va. Pvt. He lived in Henrico County on 15 June 1787 and was 33 years old. He enlisted at Chesterfield Courthouse in Aug. 1780. He was badly wounded at Eutaw Springs by a ball in his right thigh. His leg ulcerated and became nearly useless. He was in Capt. William L. Lovely's Company in the 1st Va. Regiment. He was continued on the pension list at the rate of £15 per annum on 21 June 1787. He also appeared as Richard Joyce. He was on the 1813 pension list.

Joy, Samuel. Mass. Pvt. He served in Col. Willett's Regiment. His feet were frozen on the expedition from Fort Plain on the Mohawk River to Oswego, N.Y. in Feb. 1783. He resided at Egremont, Mass. in 1796. He enlisted 5 May 1778 for nine months. He reenlisted and was omitted June 1780.

Joyal, John Baptiste. Canada. —. He joined the regiment of Col. James Livingston and was in Capt. Antoine Paulent's Company. He was with Col. Ethan Allen at Montreal and was taken prisoner. He escaped, rejoined, marched to Quebec, and was present when Montgomery was killed in battle. He was made a prisoner at Three Rivers on the retreat. He was tried by court martial, condemned to hard labor, and was to be shot if he were to be found in arms again. He worked on fortifications for upwards of two years at Isle aux Noix. He was let out on parole to go home to Belisle. In 1792 he moved with his son to Vermont and was pensioned 7 June 1832. He died 23 Dec. 1848 at Swanton aged 108 or 113. Congress allowed 100 acres bounty land and New York 500 acres to the Canadian and Nova Scotian refugees. No more land remained in New York, and his name was omitted from the list of veterans. His son, Joseph B. Joyal, had his request for 600 acres of bounty land. Congress did not allow the son a pension 21 Jan. 1858.

Judd, Jehiel. Conn. Pvt. He was disabled in Fort Griswold 6 Sep. 17--. He was on the 1813 pension list. He died 23 Aug. 1826 in Middlesex Co., Conn.

Judd, Ozias. Mass. Sgt. He was in Col. Porter's Regiment. He had an interruption in the circulation of the blood occasioned, it was supposed, by a violent strain in lifting in 1776 in Canada. He resided at West Stockbridge, Mass. in 1796. His widow, Sarah Taylor, was paid $50 by the Commonwealth.

Jump, William. N.Y. Pvt. He served under Col. Thaddeus Crane in Capt. Ephraim Lockwood's Company in the Westchester County militia. He was wounded by a cutlass in his head and deprived of part of his skull. He was also wounded in right shoulder on 24 June 1779 at Crumpond under Lt. Isaac Keeler and taken prisoner. He was pensioned 19 Dec. 1786. He lived in Fredericktown, Dutchess Co., N.Y. on 20 Apr. 1789 and later in Schoharie County. He was on the 1813 pension list.

Jumper, Daniel. Me. —. He was from Harrison. He was paid $50 under the resolve of 1836.

Junkin, Joseph. Pa. —. He was awarded a $40 gratuity and a $40 annuity in Mercer Co., Pa. 5 Mar. 1828.

Jurden, Edmund. Mass. Pvt. He was in the 1st Regiment and was from Florida. He was paid $50.

Justice, Jacob. Pa. —. He was awarded a $40 gratuity and a $40 annuity in Beaver Co., Pa. 15 Mar. 1826.

Justice, Peter. Pa. —. He was awarded a $40 gratuity and a $40 annuity in Indiana Co., Pa. 15 Mar. 1826. He served in Capt. Stokeley's Company of Rangers.

Justice, Robert. Pa. —. He applied in Franklin Co., Ohio 15 Sep. 1829. He was in the Pa. Line in Capt. Scott's Company under Col. Stewart. He was transferred to Capt. Copeley's Company under Col. Craig. He later served under Capt. Campbell in the same regiment. He was 77 years old. On 18 Dec. 1834 at the age of 88 he stated that he served six years and named his officers at Ens. LaRoy, Col. Stewart, Lt. Farmer, and Maj. Morrow. He was in the battles of Brandywine, Germantown, and Yorktown. He said that Thomas Moore of Franklin Co., Ohio could verify his service. He also appeared as Robert Justus.

Kaisey, —. Pa. —. His widow, Catharine Kaisey, was awarded a $40 gratuity and a $40 annuity in Berks Co., Pa. 8 Apr. 1826.

Kalb, Andrew. Pa. —. He was awarded a $40 gratuity and a $40 annuity in Montgomery Co., Pa. 14 Apr. 1834.

Kaler, Isaac. N.Y. Lt. He was on the 1791 pension roll.

Kame, Edward. Md. —. He lived in Harford County in Apr. 1790. He appeared as Edward Kane on the 1813 pension list. He died 10 Dec. 1832.

Kamp, Andrew. Pa. —. He was awarded a $40 gratuity and a $40 annuity in Berks Co., Pa. 7 Mar. 1829.

Kamp, David. Pa. —. He was granted relief

Kane, Charles. Pa. —. His widow, Ann Kane, was awarded a $40 gratuity on 28 Mar. 1820 in Washington County. She died 20 Dec. 1825.

Kane, William. Pa. —. He applied in Armstrong County on 13 Jan 1814. He served in Capt. Samuel Millan's Company in the 8th Pa. Regiment for three years in 1776. He was 57 years old and had a wife and eight children.

Kantner, Nicholas. Pa. —. He was awarded a $40 gratuity and a $40 annuity in Berks Co., Pa. 17 Mar. 1835. He died 18 June 1840.

Karmony, John. Pa. —. He was awarded a $40 annuity in Lebanon County 28 Mar. 1836. He died 19 May 1840. His widow, Barbara Karmony, was awarded a $40 gratuity 11 Apr.1848.

Karr, Henry. Ga. Capt. He served under Col. Clarke. The motion of his left shoulder was considerably impaired and that of his whole arm much weakened in consequence of a wound from a musket ball in Oct. 1780 in South Carolina. He lived in Greene Co., Ga. in 1795. He served in the militia.

Karr, James. Pa. —. He was awarded a $40 gratuity and a $40 annuity in Washington County 19 Mar. 1816..

Kautz, Daniel. Pa. —. He was awarded a $40 gratuity in Perry Co., Pa. 14 Apr. 1834 and again on 15 Apr. 1835.

Kautz, Thomas. Pa. —. He was awarded a $40 gratuity 23 Mar. 1829 in Lancaster County. He was awarded a $40 gratuity and a $40 annuity in Lancaster Co., Pa. 6 Apr. 1833. He was dead by Dec. 1837.

Kean, Charles. Pa. —. He was granted relief.

Kean, Dennis. Pa. —. He applied 1 July 1819. He enlisted in 1776 for a year in Capt. John Brisbane's Company in the 2nd Pa. Regiment under Col. Arthur St. Clair.

Kean, James. Pa. —. He was awarded a $40 gratuity and a $40 annuity in Westmoreland Co. 13 Mar. 1815. He died 1 Nov. 1845.

Kean, Manus. —. —. His application made 2 Mar. 1795 was not approved.

Kean, Robert. — Lt. He served as commander of a private armed vessel, the *Holkar*, fitted out in Philadelphia. His children were Jane McKean, Mary A. Reynolds, and Catharine Kean. Congress rejected their claim 17 Mar. 1858.

Keane, Charles. Pa. —. He was pensioned 24 Mar. 1818. He received a $40 gratuity and an $40 annuity.

Kearnes, Samuel. Md. Sgt. He served in the 12th Regiment. He was transferred to the Invalids. He was pensioned 4 Mar. 1789.

Kearnes, Robert. Pa. Sgt. He was in Philadelphia County 30 Sep. 1785. He was transferred from the 12th Pa. Regiment to the Invalids. He was disabled in the service. He was on the 1813 pension list. He later resided in Maryland. Compare with Robert Kerns.

Kearney, Edward. —. —. He was pensioned in 1833 but stricken from the roll after a year. His claim was deemed fraudulent by the attorney of the U.S. for the Western District of Va. Congress refused to act on the petition 24 Feb. 1837.

Kearney, Thomas. Md. Pvt. He served under Col. John Gunby in Dec. 1776 from Md. in Capt. Mountjoy Bailey's Company in the 7th Md. Regiment. In 1779 he was drafted into Capt. Hardy's Company of Foot under Maj. Henry Lee. He was wounded in the left side of his breast by a musket ball at Paulus Hook 9 Aug. 1779. Dr. Samuel Bradshaw attended him. He was a weaver. He was pensioned in New York. He was of Poundridge, Westchester Co., N.Y. He was 47 years old in 1786. He was on the 1791 pension roll. He also appeared as Thomas Kerney.

Kearney, Thomas. N.Y. Matross. He served under Col. John Lamb and Capt. Gershom Mott in the 2nd N.Y. Artillery as a matross. He lost his sight in both eyes when he was wounded in the battle of Springfield. He resided in the almshouse in New York City, N.Y. in 1786. He was 47 years old on 24 Aug.178[?]. He also appeared as Thomas Kerney. By trade he was a ship carpenter.

Kearsley, Samuel. Pa. Capt. He was awarded a $50 gratuity and a $50 annuity in Cumberland Co. on 11 Mar. 1815.

Kearslick, Abraham. S.C. Sgt. He was on the roll in 1791.

Keasy, —. Pa. —. His widow, Catherine Keasy, was awarded a $40 gratuity and a $40 annuity in Butler Co., Pa. 29 Mar. 1824.

Keasy, John. Pa. —. He was awarded a $40 annuity in Lancaster County on 30 Mar. 1812.

Keating, Edward. Pa. Pvt. He applied 10 Nov. 1787. He was in Capt. Nicholas Miller's Company in the 12th Pa. Regiment. On 10 May 1777 at Piscataway, N.J. he was disabled by the burning of some powder. He served under Col. William Cook and Maj. James Crawford. [There is a possibility that a clerical error exists in his forename and that Ignatius Keating was intended.]

Keating, Ignatius. Pa. Pvt. He was in Philadelphia County in 16 Nov. 1787. He served in the 12th Pa. Regiment under Col. William Cook in Capt. Nicholas Miller's Company. He was greatly injured by the burning of some powder in an engagement with the British at Piscataway, N.J. He was aged 45 and lived in Northumberland County.

Keatley, Christopher. Pa. —. He applied in Centre County on 26 Jan. 1826. He enlisted in June 1776 in Capt. William Hays's Company and marched to Long Island where he was attached to the Flying Camp. The regiment was reformed under Lt. Col. Hays, and he was discharged at Philadelphia. He reenlisted in the summer of 1777 and marched under Capt. Thomas Robinson in the brigade of Gen. Potter. He was in the battle of Brandywine and was discharged in October. Five or six weeks later he enlisted in Capt. Patrick Hays' Company under Col. Clotz for seven months. He was wounded by a bayonet in the arm at Germantown. He was discharged the following April. When Gen. Sullivan marched to Wyoming, he belonged to the militia and served three months. He was 75 years old and had a wife advanced in years. Robert Moore served with him and left him at Brunswick, N.J. Keatley died 18 Oct. 1831. He resided in Lancaster County when he enlisted. He was married in Centre County in the fall of 1790 to

Esther ------. She survived him. He was awarded a $40 gratuity and a $40 annuity.

Keaton, William. N.C. —. He was born in Pasquotank Co., N.C. and married Mary Snowden. He died in 1814. His children were Mary Keaton who married Evan Sanders, Nancy Keaton who married Henry Luton, and Anthony Keaton. They were in Pasquotank Co., N.C. in Dec. 1833.

Kechley, —. Pa. —. His widow, Eve Kechly, was awarded a $40 gratuity in Lebanon County 12 Mar. 1836.

Keefer, —. Pa. —. His widow, Anna Maria Keefer, was awarded a $40 gratuity and a $40 annuity in Northmuberland County 1 Apr. 183.

Keefer, Frederick. Pa. —. He received relief in Harrisburg, Pa. 29 Mar. 1824.

Keefer, Frederick. Pa. —. He received relief in Franklin county 3 Apr. 1837.

Keefer, Frederick. Pa. —. He was awarded a $40 gratuity and a $40 annuity in Harrisburg, Pa. 29 Mar. 1824. His daughter, Angelina Keefer, sought a pension 21 Jan. 1890, but Congress rejected her petition.

Keel, Charles. N.C. —. He married Elizabeth Lewis. He died in 1803. His daughter, Sarah Keel, married Hugh Raper who sought relief in Pasquotank Co., N.C. in Dec. 1833.

Keel, Philip. Pa. —. On 23 June 1847 he gave an order to Jacob Rohm to draw his pension since he did not expect to live many more days. He died 29 June 1847 in Bedford County. [His name has been misinterpreted as Philip Steel.]

Keeler, Aaron. Conn. —. He served in 1776 in the militia under Capt. David Olmstead for six months at Norwalk, Conn. He also served in the artillery under Capt. Ebenezer Whitney for six months. He was 15 years old at the end of his service. Congress denied his claim 7 Feb. 1850 because there was no proof accompanying the petition.

Keeler, Isaac. N.Y. Lt. He served in Capt. Ephraim Lockwood's Company under Col. Thaddeus Crane in the Westchester County militia. He and William Jump were captured on 24 June 1779. He was wounded in the neck by a cutlass and in the hand. He was aged 4- years on 8 Aug. 1786. He lived in Westchester Co., N.Y. on 24 Apr. 1789. He died 26 Aug. 1808.

Keeling, Robert. Mass. —. He was in the 3rd Regiment and was paid $20.

Keen, Andrew. Pa. —. He was pensioned in Philadelphia 17 Mar. 1838.

Keen, Isaac. Me. —. He was from Clinton.

Keene, Samuel Y. Md. Surgeon's Mate. He served two years and five months prior to January 1783 when he became supernumerary. He was paid to 15 Nov. 1783. His five years' full pay was paid to his heir 11 May 1838.

Keener, George. Pa. —. He was awarded a $40 gratuity and a $40 annuity in York Co., Pa. 6 Apr. 1833. He was 87 years old in 1840. He died 11 Mar. 1841.

Keener, John. Pa. Sgt. He served in the 6th Regiment. He was pensioned 10 Feb. 1818.

Keenile, John. —. —. His application was not approved.

Keepharte, Martin. —. —. He was granted relief.

Keesey, Philip. Pa. —. He was awarded a $40 gratuity in Montgomery Co., Pa. 17 Mar. 1835. He was dead by Jan. 1840.

Keeter, —. Va. —. His wife, Sarah Keeter, was granted support in Brunswick Co., Va. on 26 July 1779 while he was away in Continental service.

Keeter, James. Mass. —. He was in the 13th Regiment and was from Marshpee. His widow, Mercy Keeter, was paid $50.

Keezer, David. Me. —. He was from Calais.

Kehley, Peter. Pa. —. He was granted a $40 gratuity in Schuylkill County 12 Mar. 1836.

Keibler, George. Pa. —. He applied in Northampton County on 12 Jan. 1822. He served in Capt. Henry Shade's Company of Infantry in the Pa. Line in the spring of 1776. He was taken prisoner at Long Island and held at Halifax until October 1778. He was struck off the U.S. pension roll because he had too much property. Frederick Nagle was a prisoner with him. He was pensioned 27 Feb. 1822. He also appeared as George Kibler. He died 18 May 1841.

Keidler, Jacob. Pa. —. He was awarded a $40 gratuity in Philadelphia Co., Pa. 1 Apr. 1830.

Keiffer, Henry. Pa. —. He was awarded a $40 gratuity and a $40 annuity in Indiana County 31 Mar. 1836.

Keighley, —. Pa. —. His widow, Barbara Keighley, was awarded a $40 gratuity and a $40 annuity in Cumberland County 15 Apr. 1835. Her name was mistakenly given as Barbara Reighley. The correction was made 13 Jan. 1836. She died 12 July 1841.

Keiler, William. Pa. —.

Keims, John. Pa. —. He was awarded a $40 gratuity and a $40 annuity in Adams Co., Pa. 14 Apr. 1834.

Keiner, John. Pa. Sgt. He was granted relief 10 Feb. 1818.

Keirnes, —. Va. —. His wife, Ann Keirnes, was granted £80 support while her husband was away in the service in Fauquier Co., Va. in Oct. 1779.

Keiser, Henry. Pa. —. He was granted relief in Montgomery County.

Keiser, —. Pa. —. His widow, Ann Elizabeth Keiser, was awarded relief in Berks County 5 Feb. 1836. She died 2 Feb. 1842.

Keiser, Jacob. Pa. —. He was awarded a $40 gratuity and a $40 annuity in Northampton Co., Pa. 14 Apr. 1834.

Keisey, —. Pa. —. His widow, Catharine Keisey, was awarded a $40 gratuity and a $40 annuity in York Co., Pa. 6 Mar. 1833. She was dead by Dec. 1839.

Keist, Frederick. Pa. —. He enlisted under Capt. John Murray in the 2nd Penn. Riflemen under Col. Daniel Brodhead. He was from Dauphin County.

Keith, Ichabod. N.H. —. He was from Sullivan. He enlisted in July 1779 under Capt. Webb in Col. Shepherd's Regiment of the Massachusetts Line on Continental establishment for nine months. At Fishkill he was out on a fatigue party to procure wood. He received a severe wound in his left leg when the log he was carrying on his shoulder, fell, and struck his leg. It tore the flesh away from the bone for six or seven inches. He served to 21 Apr. 1780. He applied 2 Jan. 1822 from Sullivan, New Hampshire. He had not done so earlier because he had been able to earn his livelihood. He did not qualify for a pension.

Keith, Isaac. Mass. Sgt. He served in the 8th Regiment and was from East Bridgewater. His widow, Betty Keith, was paid $50.

Keith, Japhet. Mass. —. He was in the 2nd Regiment and was from Chesterfield. He was paid $20.

Keith, John. Mass. Sgt. He enlisted on or about 1 May 1775 for nine months under Capt. Mace Williams. He did so again in Feb. 1776 for two months under Capt. Matthew Randall, in Apr. 1776 for six months under Capt. Dana Hodges, in Aug. 1778 for three months under Capt. Matthew Randall. He served one day under Capt. Isaac Hodges for one day in Nov. 1776 for a total of two years and eight months. He had also served as a private. He was from Easton, Mass. Later he resided in Madison Co., N.Y. Congress accepted six months of his service and granted him relief 15 Apr. 1846 having recommended same as early as 25 Apr. 1840.

Keith, Simeon. —. —. He was granted relief.

Keith, Thomas. Va. —. He served as a captain and then a commissary in the Virginia Continental

Line to the surrender of Cornwallis. His widow, Judith Keith, sought a pension from Congress, but that body directed her to apply through normal channels 4 May 1846.

Kelchner, Matthias. Pa. —. His widow, Maria Kelchner, was awarded a $40 gratuity and a $30 annuity in Berks County on 27 Mar. 1819. Her annuity was increased to $40 per annum 27 Feb. 1834.

Kelheffer, Frederick. Pa. —. He was awarded a $40 gratuity and a $40 annuity in Columbia Co., Pa. 10 Mar. 1835.

Kell, Robert. Pa. Pvt. He was granted relief.

Kellar, Abraham. Va. Capt. His widow, Mary Kellar, lived in Jefferson Co., Ky. 3 May 1788. He served in the Illinois Regiment and died in the service.

Kellen, Edward. Pa. Pvt. He was in Philadelphia Company 11 Sep. 1786. He served in the 5th Pa. Regiment under Col. Robert McGaw in Capt. Vansant's Company. He was wounded at Fort Washington in his thigh, hand, right foot, and testicle. He was 37 years old. He died 11 Mar. 1786. He was on the 1813 pension list. He also appeared as Edward Kellon.

Keller, —. Pa. —. His widow, Catharine Keller, was granted relief in Lancaster County 13 Apr. 1841.

Keller, —. Pa. —. His widow, Margareta Keller, was granted relief in Philadelphia 3 Apr. 1841.

Keller, Conrad. Pa. —. He served under Col. Broadhead. He died in the 1820s. His widow, Catharine Keller, had her claim rejected by Congress 7 Apr. 1858 because of insufficient proof of his service. She may be identical with the Catharine Keller who received a $40 gratuity and a $40 annuity 14 Apr. 1859 in Mansfield Twp., Warren Co., New Jersey.

Keller, Frederick. Pa. —. He was pensioned 3 Mar. 1837 in Juniata County. He was 83 years old in 1840.

Keller, George. Pa. —. He was drawing a half-pay pension in 1790.

Keller, George. —. Pa. He was pensioned in Berks County 3 Apr. 1837.

Keller, Jacob. Pa. —. He was granted relief in Lancaster County 12 Mar. 1836. He died 8 June 1840. He was 78 years old in 1840.

Keller, Jacob. Pa. —. He was granted a $40 gratuity and a $40 annuity in Dauphin County in 1836. He died 27 Jan. 1847.

Keller, James. Pa. —. His widow, Elizabeth Keller, received a $40 gratuity and a $40 annuity in Dauphin County 15 Apr. 1856.

Keller, John. —. —. His widow, Catherine Keller, sought a pension 16 Jan. 1846, but Congress denied her a special act because she furnished no proof of her marriage. He had been dead seven years. Because she married since 1794, Congress rejected her again 14 Mar. 1848.

Keller, John. Pa. —. He was awarded a $40 gratuity and a $40 annuity in Lehigh County on 14 Mar. 1818. He died 28 Jan. 1819.

Keller, John. Pa. —. He received a $40 gratuity and a $40 annuity in Washington County 4 Apr. 1837.

Keller, John. Pa. —. He was pensioned in Berks County 21 Feb. 1838. He died 29 July 1841.

Keller, Solomon. N.Y. —. He was granted relief.

Keller, William. Pa. —. He was awarded a $40 gratuity 15 Apr. 1834. He was from Northampton Co.

Kellers, —. N.Y. —. Margaret Kellers was granted support during the war.

Kelley, Hugh. Md. Pvt. He was pensioned 4 Mar. 1789.

Kelley, James. Pa. —. He was granted a $40 annuity in Allegheny County 7 Apr. 1846 for his Revolutionary service.

Kelley, John. S.C. —. In 1776 he was in the Cherokee Expedition. He served under Col. Thomas guarding stores. He was at Whitehall and Ninety Six under Capt. James Steven [?]. He was also under Capt. Lusk and Capt. Moses Wood in Roebuck's Regiment. He was from Greenville District and was pensioned 14 Dec. 1820. He died 2 Apr. 1824. His widow, Martha Kelley, was granted the balance of the pension due her husband on 8 Dec. 1824. She also appeared as Martha Kelly.

Kelley, William. Md. Capt. He served under Lt. Col. Stevenson and Col. Rawlins in 9 July 1776. He escaped when Fort Washington fell on 16 Nov. 1776 and returned to Virginia. In 1779 he was ordered to Pittsburgh. One William Kelley was a tailor. His wife died early. He made his will 9 Sep. 1777; it was proved 16 Sep. 1777. He named his son John Kelley and his sister Susannah Kelley. Congress ruled that it was probable that the William Kelley of Boundbrook, New Jersey and later of Virginia was the one who received the commission in Hartley's Regiment. Lt. Parker was appointed his successor on 9 Sep. 1777. His son, John Kelley, moved to New York and was last heard of four years ago. Congress rejected seven years' half-pay 22 Mar. 1842.

Kelley, William. Pa. Capt. He died in Sept. 1777 before the resolution of half-pay was in effect. Neither he nor his children were entitled to half-pay. His child's claim was rejected 16 July 1842 by Congress.

Kellogg, Stephen. Conn. Pvt. He served in the 3rd Regiment. He was wounded in his left leg by an accidental stroke of an axe in 1781 near West Point. He lived at Whitestown, N.Y. in 1795. He enlisted 22 Apr. 1777 for the war and was discharged 5 Jan. 1783. He was on the 1813 pension list. He died 23 Jan. 1813.

Kelly, —. Va. —. He served in Capt. Bruin's Company of the 11th Virginia Regiment. His wife, Bridget Kelly, who was ill, was furnished £8 support in Frederick Co., Va. on 4 Nov. 1777 and £16 on 3 Mar. 1779.

Kelly, —. S.C. —. His widow, Elizabeth Kelly, wad paid an annuity in 1818. In 1821 she and her children were paid. In 1824 and 1825 she and one child were paid. She received an annuity as late as 1833.

Kelly, Charles. Pa. —. His heirs, John Kelly and Jane Matthews, in Cumberland Co., Pa. were paid $300 for his donation land on 15 Mar. 1826.

Kelly, David. N.J. —. His widow, Sarah Kelly, was pensioned in Somerset County on 13 Feb. 1849 at the rate of $100 per annum.

Kelly, Edmund. S.C. —. In 1775 he served in the Snow Camps under Col. Richardson. He was also in Capt. Taylor's Company in Col. Thompson's Regiment. He was at Charleston and Camden. He was 71 years old in 1825. He was in Capt. Boykin's Company at Eutaw Springs, Solomon's Island. He went to North Carolina after the fall of Charleston where he volunteered under Capt. Farrow. He later transferred to Col. Dixon's Regiment. He would have been 73 on Christmas 1827. He was pensioned from Newberry District 30 Nov. 1827. One James Kelly confirmed his service before he died. He was paid to 1834. On 7 Oct. 1836 he petitioned to be reinstated since he could not qualify for a federal pension because he had no living officer who could confirm his service. He died 2 Oct. 1842. His only child was Jane E. Mansfield, and her son, James D. Mansfield, was administrator of his estate.

Kelly, Edward. Pa. Pvt. He applied in Beaver County on 6 Dec. 1815. He enlisted 1 Jan. 1779 for four years and eight months in Capt. William Wilson's Company under Lt. Col. Robertson. He was furloughed by Maj. Moore. He was more than 70 years old, very deaf, and had palsy. He had a large scar between his neck and shoulder at least two feet and eight inches in circumference.

Kelly, Emanuel. Va. His wife, Jemima Kelly, was granted support in Rockingham County 27 Mar. 1780 while he was away in the service.

Kelly, John. Conn. Pvt. He was disabled by rheumatism. He was pensioned 29 Aug. 1782 and died post 23 Sep. 1788.

Kelly, John. S.C. —. He served in the militia under Col. Water. His widow, Mary Kelly, had to prove which man of her husband's name was the soldier 6 Jan. 1840.

Kelly, John Hugh. S.C. Sgt. He served in the 5th Continental Regiment under Gen. Isaac Huger. His widow was Joanna Kelly. There was one child in 1791. His widow received an annuity from 1795 to 1806 and was from Charleston District.

Kelly, Matthew. N.J. Pvt. He was on the 1791 pension roll at the rate of $60 per annum.

Kelly, Matthew. Pa. Pvt. He was from Philadelphia County.

Kelly, Michael. Va. —. His wife, Mary Kelly, was allowed £10 support in Bedford Co., Va. on 24 Aug. 1778.

Kelly, Patrick. Md. —. He was pensioned.

Kelly, Patrick. Pa. —. He served in the militia from Lancaster County for six months. He was under Capt. Cowdeir and Col. Grubb. He was sent to Philadelphia in the spring of 1778 for two months. He was under Col. Mason for two months in the fall of 1778. He was drafted in the spring of 1780 and served two months guarding stores and prisoners. Congress granted him a pension 10 Feb. 1846. He was from Indiana Co., Pa. and died 16 July 1848.

Kelly, Peter. Mass. Pvt. He was disabled by the loss of his right hand. He was 52 years old in 1786. He was in the Invalids under Col. Lewis Nichola.

Kelly, Samuel. Pa. —. He received a $40 gratuity and a $40 annuity 2 Apr. 1822 in Armstrong County. He was dead by Nov. 1838. There was an imposter who continued to collect his benefits.

Kelly, Thomas. Pa. Pvt. He applied 5 Apr. 1788 in Philadelphia County. He served in the 1st Pa. Rifle Regiment under Col. Thompson. He was wounded in the head by a shell on Long Island in 1776. He suffered from dizziness. He served 8 years, 4 months, and 4 days. He was on the 1813 pension list.

Kelly, Thomas. Pa. —. Bounty land warrant #959 for 100 acres was issued 3 Feb. 1821. The warrant was lost in a flood of Bear Grass Creek in Kentucky. Congress issued a duplicate to his daughter, Ann Haskett, 13 Feb. 1846.

Kelly, Thomas E. S.C. —. His arrears were paid to James D. Mansfield 10 Dec. 1852.

Kelly, William. Md. Capt. His widow, Martha Kelly, was pensioned at the rate of half-pay of a captain in Carroll County on 15 Feb. 1839.

Kelly, William. Pa. —. He was awarded a $40 gratuity and a $40 annuity in Center Co., Pa. 15 Apr. 1835.

Kelly, William. Va. —. His wife, Mary Kelly, was awarded 5 bushels of corn in Accomack Co., Va. 28 May 1782.

Kelser, Joseph. N.Y. —. His family was granted support during the war.

Kelsey, Aaron. Conn. Lt. He served in the militia in Capt. Shipman's Company under Col. Thaddeus Cook. He was wounded by two buck shot entering the upper part of the calf of his leg which were extracted from the lower part on the opposite side on 19 Sep. 1777 near Stillwater at Bemis Heights. He resided at Killingsworth, Conn. in 1796. He was granted one-fourth of a pension 20 Apr. 1796.

Kelsey, Giles. N.H. Pvt. He served under Col. Warner. He lost an eye and his constitution was impaired due to smallpox in the service in Canada. He lived in Newport, N.H. in 1795. Since he was not wounded, his claim was not allowed.

Kelsey, Joel. —. —. Congress denied his claim for relief because there was no evidence to prove same on 14 July 1854.

Kemmell, Jacob. Pa. —. His widow, Hannah Margaret Kemmell, was awarded a $40 gratuity and a $40 annuity in Westmoreland Co., Pa. 8 Jan. 1827.

Kemmerer, Frederick. Pa. Pvt. He applied in Lehigh County on 9 June 1817. He enlisted 5 Jan. 1776 in Capt. John Miller's Company under Col. Robert Magaw and went to New York. He helped erect Fort Washington and was taken prisoner there. After he was paroled and permitted to return home, he received notice of having been duly exchanged. He was wounded at the battle of Long Island and was at Brandywine. He served to the end of the war. He was under Lt. Andrew Dover in the 5th Pa. Regiment. He later lived in Schuylkill County. He died 1 Dec. 1843 in Lehigh County.

Kemp, —. Pa. —. His widow, Mary Kemp, was pensioned in 1811.

Kemp, Benjamin. Mass. Pvt. He served in Hall's [?] Regiment and was from Fitchburg. His widow, Abigail Davis, was paid $50.

Kemp, Dudley. Mass. —. He served in the 5th Regiment and was from Pepperell. He was paid $20.

Kemp, William. Mass. Sgt. He served in the 5th Regiment and was from Skeensboro, Vermont. He was paid $20.

Kemplin, Thomas. Pa. Capt. He and his eldest son fell in the service at the hands of the savages. They were scalped and butchered. His widow, Mary Kemplin, was pensioned 1 Apr. 1788. There were eight small children.

Kemplin, William. Pa. —. He applied in Franklin County on 2 Dec. 1811. He was in the 11th Pa. Regiment which was later the 10th under Col. Richard Humpton in Capt. William Coats' Company. He was blind.

Kempton, Oliver. Mass. —. He served in the 7th Regiment and was paid $20.

Kempton, Rufus. Pvt. He served under Col. Nicholas in Capt. Stevens's Company. He had a weakness in his right shoulder due to a cold caught when on guard at West Point. He lived in Croydon, N.H. in 1795. He was in the militia.

Kendall, —. Pa. —. His widow, Elizabeth Kendall, was awarded a $40 gratuity and a $40 annuity in York County 21 June 1839 for her husband's Revolutionary service.

Kendall, Reuben. Mass. —. He served in the 5th Regiment and was paid $20.

Kendren, William. Va. —. He was away in the service when his wife, Priscilla Kendren, was granted 3 barrels of corn and 60 pounds of bacon for her support and that of their five children in Richmond County on 6 Aug. 1782.

Kendrick, Benjamin. Pa. Pvt. He was on the 1813 pension list.

Kendrick, Benjamin. Va. Pvt. He served in Capt. Gilliem's Company in the 10th Va. Regiment. He was wounded in his left hip. He had an open ulcer in the left groin which he said was produced by a musket ball which had not been extracted. He was wounded at Brandywine. He lived in Va. in 1785 and 1794. He enlisted 17 Jan. 1777 for three years. He was pensioned at the rate of $3.33 1/3 cents from 1 Jan. 1786.

Kendrick, John. N.C. Lt. He applied in Chatham County in 1785. He was in the militia under Gen. Butler and was wounded at Brown Marsh in 1781. He was aged 24 in 1785. He died 14 Dec. 1802 in Ga.

Kenedy, Thomas. Pa. —. He applied 4 Jan. 1814 and was aged 66 years.

Kenley, William. S.C. —. He was granted relief.

Kenmore, John. S.C. —. At the age of 16 or slightly older, he served under Lt. Walker, Capt. David Patton, Lt. Prince, Lt. William Brocket, Commissary Kilbreth, and Lt. Quin. After Camden he went to North Carolina and joined Sumter. He had suffered from consumption for the last four years and had spent most of the last two confined to bed. He was from York District in 1827 and was 67 years old. James Anderson and Capt. David Patton knew him in the service. His claim was not granted.

Kennedy, Archelas. Mass. —. He was from Rochester and was paid $20.

Kennedy, Daniel. Pa. —. He was in Bucks County 12 Sep. 1786. He died 11 Mar. 178-.

Kennedy, David. Pa. Capt. He was in Berks County 25 Nov. 1789. He served in the 6th Pa. Regiment. He suffered from disabilities, fatigues, and exposures in the campaign of 1777 and by capture by the enemy. His arrearage was paid to William McIlvaine and S. Kinney, administrators.

Kennedy, Isaac. N.C. Pvt. He applied in Robeson County in 1801. He was in the militia under Capt. John Willis. He was shot by a ball in his breast and right shoulder in 1780 in Bladen County and lost the use of his right hand. He was on the 1813 pension list. He also appeared as Isaac Kanedy.

Kennedy, James. Va. Lt. & Adjt. He was commissioned 8 June 1778 having previously served as a private and lieutenant. His administrator was John G. Mosby of Henrico Co. His son was Granville Kennedy. He was supernumerary and received his half-pay 13 Apr. 1782.

Kennedy, John. Pa. —. He was awarded a $40 gratuity and a $40 annuity in Butler Co., Pa. 18 Feb. 1824. He served in the Flying Camp.

Kennedy, Patrick. Pa. —. He was granted a $40 gratuity in Centre County.

Kennedy, Samuel. Pa. Surgeon. He served in Col. Anthony Wayne's Regiment in 1776. His widow, Sarah Kennedy, applied in Jonesboro, Tenn. She was formerly of Chester Co., Pa. He had died in the service prior to 28 June 1778 in the military hospital at Yellow Springs, Chester Co., Pa. John Kennedy was his only surviving son. His seven years' half-pay was approved 25 May 1832. Congress ruled that no bounty land was due the heirs on 25 Mar. 1836.

Kennedy, Thomas. Pa. —. He was a disabled soldier from the Pennsylvania Line. He was granted £30 half-pay in Washington County 5 Nov. 1782.

Kennedy, William. S.C. —. He was wounded in the service and was granted an annuity 18 Jan. 1785 in Union District. He later lived in Blount and Marion Cos., Ala. and Tenn. He was granted his arrearage since the year 1809 and the increase due him from the previous year under the act of 1815 on 11 Dec. 1817. He was granted $210.50 in arrearage of his pension on 18 Dec. 1818. Since he lived 580 miles away, it was inconvenient for him to draw a pension. Accordingly, in exchange for $120 on 23 Nov. 1829, he acquitted the state from any further claim.

Kennedy, William. Va. —. His wife, Frances Kennedy, was granted £6 on 17 Aug. 1778 and £25 on 21 June 1779 in York Co., Va.

Kenney, Benjamin. Me. —. His widow was Lydia Kenney. She was paid $50 under the resolve of 1836.

Kenney, David. Mass. —. He served in the 7th Regiment and was paid $20.

Kenney, Lyman. Conn. Pvt. He served in Col. Webb's Regiment. He was wounded by a musket ball in the right leg. The musket was accidentally discharged in the lower room of the guard house while he was lying in the upper room on 9 Jan. 1786 [sic]. He enlisted 27 May 1777 and was discharged 9 Jan. 1778.

Kenney, Thomas. Me. —. He died 11 Apr. 1825 in Hallowell. His widow was Hannah Kenney from Pittston. She was paid $50 under the resolve of 1836.

Kennon, Ambrose. Va. —. He was granted relief in King William County 23 June 1779. He also appeared as Ambrose Cannon. *Vide* also Ambrose Cannears.

Kenny, Archeleus. Mass. Pvt. He was on the 1791 pension roll. He collected his pension as late as September 1803.

Kenny, Hance. Va. Corp. He was on the 1800 pension list.

Kenny, Richard. Va. —. His wife, Elizabeth Kenny, was granted £5 support in Berkeley County on 15 Sep. 1778 while he was away in Continental service. She was granted 5 bushels of corn and 22 pounds of pork on 15 Aug. 1780.

Kenny, Thomas. N.Y. Matross. He was disabled by blindness. He lived in N.Y. in 1788.

Kenseler, John. S.C. —. He enlisted in 1775 and served under Capt. Ezekiel Polk and Col. William Thompson in the Rangers. He fought at King's Mountain, Hanging Rock, Rocky Mount, Fish Dam Ford, Black Stock, and Sumter's defeat. He was 72 years old. Maj. Thomas Henderson corroborated some of his service as did Col. John Moffett. He applied in Nov. 1820. He was paid his annuity as last as 1831. He also appeared as John Kanseler.

Kensey, James. N.J. Pvt. He was on the 1791 pension roll at the rate of $60 per annum. He died 19 Jan. 1798.

Kent, Abner. Mass. Pvt. He served under Col. William Prescott and Capt. Abijah Wayman. He was disabled by a ball in his right side which broke his right arm. He was pensioned 16 Nov. 1786 and was 49 years old. He resided in Essex Co., Mass. He was on the 1813 pension list.

Kent, Ebenezer. Mass. Ens. He served under Col. Henry Jackson. He injured his constitution particularly at the battle of Monmouth. He resided in Watertown, Mass. in 1792. He was mustered out as a sergeant major. He was paid $20 by the Commonwealth.

Kent, Isaac. Md. Pvt. He was pensioned at the rate of half-pay of a private in Ohio 12 Feb. 1820.

Kent, Jesse. Va. —. He died *ca.* May 1779. He was in the naval service. He left a widow and five children. The Lancaster Co., Va. court certified same on 20 Apr. 1780.

Kent, Peter. —. —. On 11 Oct. 1841 in Greene Co., Tenn. he was aged 82 years and had an aged wife and two orphan children. He sought the right from Tennessee to vend articles without a license or paying taxes.

Kentfield, Erastus. Mass. Pvt. He served in the 7th Regiment and was from Granby. He was paid $50.

Keough, William. Md. Pvt. He was pensioned 3 Mar. 1809. He was on the 1813 pension list.

Keplin, John. Pa. —. His widow, Susannah Keplin, was awarded a $40 gratuity and a $40 annuity in Chester Co., Pa. 12 Apr. 1828.

Keplinger, Peter. Pa. —. He served in the 9th Pa. Regiment under Capt. George Grant for three years. Sgt. Andrew Nelson enlisted him in the spring of 1777. He was in the battles of Shorthills, Brandywine, and Germantown. He was discharged and enlisted again for nine months. He suffered from rheumatism. He received an additional annuity of $12 on 19 Mar. 1804.

Kepner, Bernard. Pa. —. He was awarded a $40 annuity in Schuylkill County 12 Jan. 1836. He was 76 years old in 1840.

Kerbaugh, David. Pa. —. He was awarded a $40 gratuity and a $40 annuity in Montgomery Co., Pa. 12 Feb. 1825. Mary Kerbaugh was granted a $40 gratuity and a $40 annuity 15 June 1836. She was dead by Apr. 1837.

Kerby, Patrick. Va. —. His wife, Mary Kerby, was granted £45 support in Berkeley County on 17 May 1780.

Kerly, James. Pa. —. He was granted relief.

Kermer, John. —. —. He was pensioned 9 June 1794.

Kernachan, William. Pa. —. He served in the 1ˢᵗ Pa. Regiment and was wounded in the face. He applied 1 Jan. 1813 in Bucks County. He received a $40 gratuity and a $40 annuity. He also appeared as William Kernichon. He died 1 Apr. 1841.

Kerner, John. Pa. Pvt. He applied from Union County 6 Feb. 1818. He enlisted at Reading, Pa. in Capt. George Nagle's Company of Riflemen and marched to Boston in 1775. He belonged to the regiment of Col. Thompson. He was wounded at Bunker Hill and lost two of his fingers on his left hand in 1775. He served fourteen months and was discharged. He reenlisted in Capt. Mousher's Company for three years or the war. He served in 6ᵗʰ Pa. Regiment under Col. Harmar. Afterwards Capt. Finney commanded the company. After five years he received his discharge from Gen. Anthony Wayne. His leg was broken.

Kerner, John. Pa. Sgt. He was from Berks County in 1810. He had a large family.

Kerns, Charles. N.Y. —. He was granted support during the war.

Kerns, Robert. Md. Sgt. He was pensioned in Frederick County in 1789. He was wounded at York. He served in the 2ⁿᵈ Regiment. Compare with Robert Kearnes.

Kerr, David. S.C. —. He served under Col. Williams. He was wounded in his left arm by a rifle ball at King's Mountain on 7 Oct. 1780. The bullet remained lodged in his body. He had a wife and family. He was a resident of Abbeville District in 1796. He was 72 years old and sought his arrears 9 Dec. 1829. He was paid his annuity as late as 1834.

Kerr, Henry. Ga. Capt. He was pensioned 2 Feb. 1798. He was on the 1813 pension list.

Kerr, Hugh H.. —. —. He was pensioned 2 Feb. 1798.

Kerr, James. Pa. —. He was pensioned 19 Mar. 1816. He died 25 Dec. 1833. His name has been incorrectly rendered as James Kern.

Kerr, James. Pa. —. He was awarded a $40 gratuity and a $40 annuity in York Co., Pa. 8 Apr. 1833.

Kerr, Joseph. N.C. Pvt. He was disabled in militia service. He was aged 32 in 1785. He was on the 1813 pension list in North Carolina. He transferred to South Carolina 4 Sep. 1813.

Kerr, Joseph. S.C. Maj. He served in the 1ˢᵗ S.C. Regiment. He went as a volunteer to Florida. Afterwards he returned to his abode in North Carolina. When Gen. Provost invaded South Carolina, he returned to the service and was in action at Stono. Later he again turned out as a volunteer and was in a detachment under Brig. Gen. Huger when he was shockingly cut and mangled by a body of British Cavalry. He was totally maimed and disabled. He applied 10 Feb 1783 from York District. He was granted an increase to $200 per annum on 10 Dec. 1817 at which time he was three score years of age. He served five years in the war and was wounded seventeen times. He died 4 Jan. 1822. The administrator with the will annexed was Daniel H. Kerr who sought his arrears on 21 Nov. 1822.

Kerr, Robert. Pa. —. He served under Capt. Robert Craig in the 3ʳᵈ Battalion of the Lancaster County militia. He went to Philadelphia in 1776, took sick with flux, and got better. He went aboard a shallop to go to Trenton to join the army at Amboy. He fell overboard and drowned in Aug. 1776. His widow, Martha Kerr, was pensioned 30 June 1786.

Kerr, Samuel. S.C. —. He was killed in 1781. His widow, Mary Kerr, was granted an annuity 19 May 1785. She and her two children were granted an annuity 5 Feb. 1787 in Abbeville District.

Kerr, Thomas. Pa. —. He served under Capt. Robert Clark in the Flying Camp. He was taken prisoner at Long Island and died in captivity.

Kerr, William. Pa. —. He enlisted in 1776 under Capt. Samuel Miller in the 8ᵗʰ Regiment and served three years. He had a wife and eight children. He was from Armstrong County.

Kerr, William. Pa. —. He served three years and upwards. He was from Cumberland County.

Kerr, William. Pa. —. He served seven months under Col. Potter. He was from Perry County.

Kersey, —. S.C. —. His widow, Nancy Kersey, had her claim rejected in Dec. 1836. She also appeared as Nancy Casey.

Kersey, William. N.C. Pvt. He was pensioned.

Kershner, Michael. Md. Pvt. He was pensioned at the rate of half-pay of a private in Allegany County 23 Jan. 1816. His widow, Mary Ann Kershner, was pensioned at the same rate 2 Mar. 1827. Her arrearage was paid to Jacob Lantz for the use of Mrs. Mary C. Shryer of Allegany County as the next and dear friend of Mary A. Kershner 6 Mar. 1832.

Kersteller, George. Pa. Pvt. He served in the German Regiment under Col. Ludwig Wendle. He was from Union County and was pensioned 12 Dec. 1821. He died 31 Dec. 1843.

Kesler, John. N.J. —. He was pensioned in Gloucester County 28 Jan. 1836 at the rate of $100 per annum.

Kesler, John. Pa. Midshipman. He served in the Marines. He lost the use of the middle finger of his left hand in 1781 on the frigate *Alliance*. He lived in Philadelphia, Pa. in 1794. He was on the 1813 pension list.

Kesselbach, Oswald. Pa. Pvt. He served in Pulaski's Legion. He was wounded at Little Egg Harbor in 1778 with three bayonet wounds in his private parts and five in his back. He was put in the military hospital at Trenton and afterwards discharged as unfit for duty on 15 Mar. 1779. He then entered the corps of artillery artificers of Penn. and served 4 years, 2 months, and 7 days to the end of the war when he was discharged by Gen. R. Humpton on 31 Oct. 1783. He lived in Philadelphia, Pa. in 1794.

Kessler, John. —. —. He was pensioned 9 June 1794.

Kesslinger, Peter. Pa. —. He was pensioned by the act of 19 Mar. 1804.

Kester, Jacob. Pa. —. He received a $40 gratuity and a $40 annuity in Columbia County 15 June 1836. He died 5 Apr. 1842.

Ketcham, John. N.J. Pvt. He served in the 1st Regiment and was disabled with lameness due to smallpox. He was 49 years old. He was on the 1791 pension roll at the rate of $60 per annum. He was on the 1813 pension list.

Ketcham, Solomon. —. —. He served six months on the armed vessel, *Montgomery*, fitted out by New York. He was pensioned and later strickened because he had deserted. Congress restored him to his pension 22 Dec. 1837 because he was able to explain his situation satisfactorily.

Ketchum, John. N.Y. Pvt. He served under Capt. John Hyatt and Col. Samuel Drake and was wounded through his body and left arm below the elbow by a musket ball on 27 Aug. 1776 in the battle of Long Island. He also served in the 2nd N.Y. Regiment under Col. Philip Van Cortlandt. He also served under Capt. Samuel Sackett and Col. Henry B. Livingstone in the 4th Regiment. He was disabled. He was pensioned 14 Apr. 1787. He lived in Dutchess Co., N.Y. He was on the 1813 pension list.

Ketchum, John. Pa. —. He applied in Lancaster County on 7 Feb. 1818. He enlisted for three years. He also appeared as John Ketcham.

Ketslaugh, Jacob. Va. —. His widow, Patience Ketslaugh, and two children were awarded £3 per month in Accomack Co., Va. 27 Jan. 1779.

Kettle, Andrew. Mass. —. He was granted relief.

Kettle, George. Pa. Pvt. He was in Philadelphia County 30 Sep. 1785. He was transferred from the 2nd Pa. Regiment to the Invalids. He was disabled at West Point in 1776 by a stone rolling on him. He was 63 years old. He was on the 1813 pension list.

Ketterage, Thomas. Mass. Pvt. He died 26 Mar. 1804.

Keyes, Daniel. Mass. —. He served in the 4th Regiment.

Keyes, Eli. Mass. —. He served in the 6th Regiment and was paid $20.

Keyes, Ephraim. —. Pvt. He served five months and twenty-seven days. He married Sally Gerry. Congress rejected her claim for a pension 11 July 1856 because her husband had not served the minimum six months.

Keyes, Stephen. —. —. He entered the service in 1775 for two years, took ill, and was obliged to return home. He moved to Vermont in 1783. He sought financial assistance 1 Oct. 1793 from Burlington, Chittenden Co., Vt.

Keyher, Frederick. Va. —. While he was away in the service, his wife, Elizabeth Keyher, and four children were granted £15 support per month in Yohogania Co., Va. 28 Dec. 1779.

Keyser, —. Pa. —. His widow, Christiana Keyser, was awarded a $40 gratuity and a $40 annuity in York Co., Pa. 20 Mar. 1834.

Keze, Malcolm. S.C. Pvt. He was a resident of Abbeville District in 1791. He died 26 May 1820. He also appeared as Malcolm Keys in the 1813 U.S. pension list.

Khun, Christian. Pa. Pvt. He served in Moylan's Light Dragoons. He was pensioned in Sep. 1791 and transferred to Orange Co., N.Y. 4 Mar. 1791. He was on the 1791 pension roll of New Jersey.

Kidd, John. N.C. —. He enlisted for eighteen months 1 Aug. 1782 and was discharged in 1783. Congress granted him a pension even though he could not qualify under the law because of his length of service.

Kidd, John. S.C. —. He served under Col. Richardson, Col. Neel, Col. Winn, and Col. Bratton. He was in the Snowy Camps, Charleston, Hanging Rock, Camden, Bingham's Church, and Rocky Mount. He was pensioned from York District 25 Nov. 1830. Fellow soldiers who corroborated his service were Samuel McElhenney, Stephen McElhenney, Thomas Carson, and James Wallace. He was paid as late as 1834.

Kidd, Peter. Pa. —. He was paid a $40 gratuity and a $40 annuity in Washington County on 21 Feb. 1822.

Kidwell, Elijah. N.C. Pvt. He was disabled in Continental service. He was aged 31 in 1785. He lived in Rutherford County. He was on the 1813 pension list and died 19 Nov. 1831.

Kieffer, Henry. Pa. —. He received a $40 gratuity and a $40 annuity in Indiana County 31 Mar. 1836.

Kighler, John. Pa. —. He was awarded a $40 gratuity and a $40 annuity in Philadelphia Co., Pa. 27 Mar. 1824.

Kihn, George. Pa. —. He was pensioned in Allegheny County 21 Feb. 1838.

Kilbourn, Ashbal. Conn. Pvt. He served in Col. Charles Webb's Regiment. His feet were frozen, and he lost several of the joints of his toes at Philadelphia, Pa. on 17 Dec. 1777. He resided at East Hartford, Conn. in 1796. He enlisted 27 May 1777 for eight months. He was taken prisoner 7 Dec. 1777.

Kilbuck, William Henry. Pa. —. He was a chief of the Delaware tribe. He was awarded a $40 gratuity and a $40 annuity and three rifles for his sons John Henry Kilbuck, Charles Henry Kilbuck, and Christian Gotlieb Kilbuck on 28 Mar. 1811.

Kilburn, Jacob. —. —. He was wounded by some pointed instrument between the ribs. He resided in Mass. in 1796.

Kilburn, Jno. —. —. He was wounded by a cutting instrument in his great toe and lost one-half of his second toe. He resided in Mass. in 1796.

Kilby, John. Va. Mariner. He was alive on 18 Mar. 1818. He served on the frigate *Bon Homme Richard*.

Kilgo, Linsfield. N.C. —. He was on the roll in 1784. He was wounded in the service at Eutaw.

Kilgore, Charles. Va. Pvt. He served in Campbell's Regiment. He was pensioned in Virginia. He was on the 1813 pension list of Tennessee. He lived in Greene Co., Tenn.

Kilgore, James. Me. —. He was from Lovell. He was paid $50 under the resolve of 1836.

Kilgore, John. Me. —. He was from Newry. He was paid $50 under the resolve of 1836.

Killen, Edward. Pa. —. He served under Col. Robert McGaw and Capt. Nathaniel Vansant in the 5th Battalion. He was wounded in his thigh, hand, right foot, and testicles at the capture of Fort Washington. He was pensioned 11 Sep. 1786 in Philadelphia.

Kilpatrick, Spencer. S.C. —. He served in the artillery. He was in advanced years and had a family of a wife, son, and seven daughters. He was paid $100 in lieu of his 100 acres of bounty land in Dec. 1816.

Kilton, Jonathan. Mass. —. He was in the 9th Regiment and was from Boston. His widow, Margaret Kilton, was paid $50.

Kilty, John. Md. Capt. His widow, Catharine Kilty, was pensioned at the rate of half-pay of a captain 4 Jan. 1822.

Kimball, Abraham. N.H. Pvt. He was in Capt. Joshua Bailey's Company of militia under Col. Stickney. He was wounded in the thigh of his right leg at the battle of Bennington on 16 Aug. 1777. He was in Hillsborough Co., N.H. in 1792 and in Hopkinton, N.H. in 1795. He was granted half a pension 25 Apr. 1796. He was on the 1813 pension list. He died 12 May 1828.

Kimball, Benjamin. Mass. —. He was from Ipswich, married 25 Feb. 1802, and died 20 June 1822. Congress denied his widow, Susannah Kimball, a pension 19 July 1848.

Kimball, Benjamin. N.H. Capt. He was in Capt. Joseph Cilley's Regiment and engaged as a lieutenant; he was appointed a captain on 1 Sep. 1776 and made paymaster of the regiment. He was accidentally killed 23 Aug. 1779 leaving a widow with a large family of young children. His widow, Sarah Poor, lived in Plastow, Rockingham Co., N.H. in 1785. She married second Jonathan Poor on 2 June 1785.

Kimball, David. Me. —. He was from Harmony. He was paid $50 under the resolve of 1836.

Kimball, Hezekiah. Mass. —. He served in the 4th Regiment and was paid $20.

Kimball, James. Mass. Lt. He served under Col. Thomas Nixon and Micajah Gleason. He was disabled by a musket ball which entered the center of his left cheek and passed through his neck. He was 36 years old in 1786.

Kimball, Samuel. Mass. Pvt. He served in the 11th Regiment and was from Dracut. His widow, Polly Kimball, was paid $50.

Kimball, Thomas. N.H. Pvt. He was wounded by a musket ball in the arm at Chemung in action with some Indians in 1779. He served under Col. Read. He lived in Hillsborough, N.H. in 1792 and in Amherst, N.H. in 1794. He enlisted 3 June 1778 and continued to the end of the war. He was granted one-fifth of a pension 20 Apr. 1796.

Kincade, John. Pa. Pvt. He was on the 1813 pension list.

Kindle, William. Md. Pvt. He was pensioned at the rate of half-pay of a private in Washington Co. on 7 Feb. 1817.

King, —. —. —. Congress rejected a pension to his widow, Olive King, 18 May 1848 because the evidence did not support her claim.

King, —. S.C. —. His widow was Ann King. There were two children in 1791.

King, —. S.C. —. His widow, Rebecca King, had her claim rejected in Dec. 1844.

King, —. Va. —. Mary King was granted support in King William County in 1778.

King, —. Va. —. His widow, Hannah King, was granted £12.8.0 in Hanover County in 1779.

King, —. Va. —. He and his brother were in Continental service. Their father, Samuel King, was granted £5 support in Prince William Co.,Va. on 5 Oct. 1778.

King, Aaron. N.J. Pvt. He served in Capt. Abraham Spier's Company under Col. Philip Van Courtland of the 2nd Regiment of Essex County militia. He was wounded by a canon ball at Elizabeth Town on 8 June 1780. He lost three fingers on his right hand. He was allowed half-pay in Apr. 1783. He was 26 years old. He was on the 1791 pension roll. He lived in Essex Co., N.J. He was on the 1813 pension list.

King, Alexander. Pa. Sgt. He applied in Huntingdon County. He enlisted with Capt. Henry Darby at New London Crossroads in Chester County in the Delaware Regiment for one year in Jan. 1776. He was in the battle of Long Island and at the taking of the Hessians at Trenton. He enlisted again early in 1777 in Capt. Benjamin Fishburn's Company in the 4th Pa. Regiment. He was promoted to sergeant. He was discharged by Lt. Col. William Butler in Jan. 1781. He was wounded in the hand by a Hessian's bayonet and afterwards in the foot. He had a wife to support. John Boyle served with him and was first sergeant when King acted as a corporal. In 1777 King became master tailor for the regiment and made clothing until he was discharged. His officers were Maj. William Henderson, Lt. Andrew Henderson, and Capt. Benjamin Burd. He was 63 years old. Agnes King, his wife, went with him in 1780 and continued with him in the camp. After the revolt of the troops, she applied to Col. William Butler and stated to him the situation of herself and her small child who had met with an unfortunate accident. Col. Butler then gave her husband a discharge. They returned home to Chester County. He died 8 Aug. 1826.

King, Andrew. Va. —. His wife, Mary Hammond King, was awarded assistance in Charlotte Co., Va. on 4 May 1778 and £32.1.4 for provisions on 5 Apr. 1779.

King, Charles. —. —. His application was laid on the table.

King, Christian. Pa. —. He was awarded a $40 gratuity in Bedford Co., Pa. 25 Mar. 1831.

King, Francis. Pa. —. His widow, Barbara King, was awarded a $40 gratuity and a $40 annuity in Berks Co., Pa. 22 Dec. 1828.

King, George. Md. Pvt. He was pensioned at the rate of half-pay of a private 19 Feb. 1819.

King, George. Pa. —. He was awarded a $40 gratuity in Franklin Co., Pa. 16 Feb. 1835.

King, Henry. Md. Commissary. He was pensioned at the rate of half-pay of a commissary 13 Feb. 1817. He entered the service as a sergeant 30 May 1778 and continued to Oct. 1778. He was a commissary clerk from 1778 to 1780, and assistant commissary 1780 to 1781. His brother was Jeremiah King. He died in Kentucky in 1820. Congress granted relief 24 Apr. 1854.

King, Jacob. —. —. His widow, Elizabeth King, sought the arrearage from 4 Mar. 1848 to 3 Feb. 1853 from Congress 15 Dec. 1857.

King, James. Va. —. He was pensioned in Rockbridge County on 30 Jan. 1819. He enlisted in Sept. 1781 at the age of 16 and joined the army at Yorktown. He was detached to Capt. Charles Callaway's Company of militia and remained in the service until the capture of the British. He had his thigh broken. He was awarded $80 in relief and $100 per annum. He died 20 Feb. 1828. William King was administrator of his estate.

King, John. —. Pvt. He was a pensioner and sought to be paid from 4 Mar. 1818 to 11 Oct. 1824. Congress denied his claim 30 Jan. 1852.

King, John. Pa. Lt. He transferred to New York by Mar. 1795.

King, John. Pa. Pvt. He was in Capt. Spear's Company under Col. Stewart. He was from Armstrong County. He was on the 1813 pension list.

King, John. Va. Pvt. He enlisted in 1777 in Capt. Charles West's Company. His wife, Mary King, was allowed support in King William County in 1779. He was awarded a £500 gratuity on 7 Nov. 1780. He was awarded a gratuity of two years' pay and an annuity of half-pay on 12 Dec. 1781. He lived in Prince William County in 1788. He enlisted for three years in the 3rd Va. Regiment. He lost both of his arms at Buford's defeat. Brig. Gen. W. Smallwood issued a military pass for John King to return to Virginia with his father, Samuel King. They were to be issued forage for their horses and rations and ferriage. Gen. Horatio Gates gave Samuel King a certificate to allow forage for both horses. Maj. Charles West also attested to John King's service. Samuel King received his son on 22 Aug. 1780 from Gen. Smallwood and Dr. Clements at Salisbury, N.C. He was continued at the rate of £18 per annum on 31 Mar. 1788. He was issued a duplicate certificate on 26 June 1790. He died 20 Nov. 1804.

King, John S. Pa. —. He received a gratuity 5 May 1841.

King, Jonathan. Pa. —. He was awarded relief 6 Apr. 1833 in Armstrong County. He was dead by Jan. 1841.

King, Joseph. —. Paymaster & Clothier. He served in the artificers. Congress rejected the claim from his heirs for bounty land on 16 Feb. 1843.

King, Joseph. N.J. Adjutant. He served in the 4th Regiment and was wounded in the thigh 26 June 1777 at Short Hills and made a prisoner. He was deranged in 1779. He was granted half-pay in Morris County in 1782. He was on the 1791 pension roll in New York.

King, Joseph. Pa. Pvt. He applied in Crawford County on 10 June 1820. He enlisted in the Pa. Line in 1776 in Capt. Hawkins Boone's Company in the 12th Pa. Regiment under Col. William Cook. In May or June 1777 he was drafted into Capt. Michael Simpson's Company under Col. Daniel Morgan. He served in the Rifle Regiment until it was reduced, and he was transferred to Capt. George McCally's Company in the 3rd Pa. Regiment under Col. Thomas Craig. He served six or eight months. He was then drafted into a rifle corps under Maj. James Parr until he was discharged in Jan. 1781. He served 4 years and 5 months. He received a U.S. pension 26 May 1818. He was awarded a $40 gratuity and a $40 annuity in Crawford County on 7 Mar. 1821. He was 68 years old in 1820. He married Mrs. Sally Hays 6 Feb. 1827. She applied for her pension 31 Mar. 1869.

King, Joseph. S.C. Chaplain. He served three months under Col. John Carter. He lived in All Saints Parish. He was pensioned from Horry District 30 Nov. 1827. He was last paid in 1834.

King, Joseph. S.C. —. His widow was Nancy King. He died six or seven years before she applied 10 Dec. 1825. She was 80 years old. Her application was rejected since no record could be found for him.

King, Josiah. Mass. —. He served in the 7th and 9th Regiments and was from Norton. He was paid $20.

King, Josiah. Mass. Pvt. He entered the service when he was fourteen years of age with his father, Josiah King, Sr. before the battle of Bunker Hill. His father was a captain in the 9th Regiment. Congress rejected his petition for benefits as a refugee 10 June 1842. He was already a pensioner.

King, Lemuel. Conn. Pvt. He served in Webb's Regiment. He was wounded 10 Dec. 1780 at Horse Neck. He received three wounds from a cutlass in his head, one wound on his shoulder blade, one wound in his upper arm, another in his lower arm, and one in his knee. He was pensioned 17 Mar. 1783 in North Bolton. He was pensioned at the rate of $5 per month from 23 Dec. 1807.

He was on the 1813 pension list. He died 17 Nov. 1827 in Tolland Co., Conn.

King, Lemuel. Mass. Pvt. He served in the 9th Regiment and was from Cambridge. He was paid $50.

King, Leonard. N.Y. —. He was wounded. He was on the 1785 pension list.

King, Levin. Md. Ens. His widow, Margaret King, was pensioned at the rate of half-pay of an ensign in Somerset County in Mar. 1832. She died 12 Sep. 1839, and the arrearage of her pension was paid to her heirs 5 Apr. 1841.

King, Miles. Va. Surgeon's Mate. Congress rejected the claim of the heirs for commutation 14 Jan. 1837.

King, Moses. Mass. Pvt. He served in the 6th Regiment under Col. Thomas Nixon in the Invalids under Capt. Spurr. He was disabled by a rupture and loss of his right hand on 25 Sep. 1775 at Pownalborough and was pensioned 1 Sep. 1782. He died 24 Aug. 1804.

King, Nathan. S.C. Capt. His heirs sought commutation with six per cent interest. In 1832 he swore he served eighteen months. Congress ruled that the proof was not there and rejected their claim 25 Jan. 1851.

King, Philip. Pa. —. He enlisted in the dragoons under Capt. Van Hare and was encamped at White Plains, New York. He was wounded by a saber in his left arm. He had a family. He was from Berks County. His widow was the Mary Ann King who was awarded a $40 gratuity and a $40 annuity 12 Apr. 1828.

King, Reuben. N.Y. Pvt. He served in Col. Goose Van Schaick's Regiment under Capt. George White. He was detached to Montreal under Col. Ethan Allen. He was wounded by the bursting of his musket on 25 Sep. 1775. He had his left arm amputated. He lived in New Lebanon, Columbia Co., N.Y. in 1786. He was 28 years old on 21 July 1786. He was in Kinderhook, Columbia Co., N.Y. on 2 June 1789. He had a wife and two children. He was on the 1813 pension list and died 28 May 1823.

King, Robert. Pa. —. He was awarded a $40 gratuity and a $40 annuity in Lycoming County 1 Apr. 1836. He was 88 years old in 1840. He died 29 Mar. 1848.

King, Robert. Pa. Lt. He served in the 3rd Regiment. He was paid $64 on 4 Apr. 1792.

King, Robert. Pa. —. He was awarded a $40 gratuity and a $40 annuity in Erie Co., Pa. 15 Mar. 1826. His widow, Elizabeth King, was awarded a $40 gratuity and a $40 annuity in Erie County 1 Apr. 1825. He died 20 Dec. 1826. His widow died 3 Dec. 1840.

King, Stephen. Mass. Pvt. He served in the 14th Regiment and was from Dana. His widow, Mehitable King, was paid $50.

King, Stephen. Mass. Pvt. He served in the 16th Regiment and was from Raynham. His widow, Hannah King, was paid $50.

King, Thomas. Md. Sgt. He was pensioned in 1809. His pension was paid to his widow, Mary King, at the rate of half-pay of a sergeant 16 Nov. 1811. He belonged to the artillery of Baltimore and was wounded on 10 June by the firing of a cannon and lost his right hand.

King, Thomas. S.C. —. He entered the service at the age of 15 and served under Col. Jonah Clarke, Capt. Morrell, and Capt. William Alston. He was in the battle of Quinby Bridge. He was in his 62nd year on 1 Dec. 1826. His claim was rejected in Dec. 1827. He was 65 years old on 28 Oct. 1830 and had his claim approved in Dec. He died 17 Nov. 1842. His widow was Ann King of All Saints Parish, Horry District who was in her 81st year on 6 Nov. 1843. She married him in 1789.

King, Walter. N.Y. Pvt. He served under Col. James McClaughery in Capt. James Humphrey's Company in the Orange County militia. He was wounded by a musket ball in his groin and right hip at Fort Clinton 6 Oct. 1777. He lived in New York City, N.Y. on 13 June 1788. He had a wife and three children. He was aged 26 on 15 Oct. 1785. He died in 1796.

Kingham, Joshua. Del. —. He was pensioned in 1783.

Kingman, Benjamin. Mass. —. He served in the 2ⁿᵈ Regiment and was from West Bridgewater. His widow, Martha Kingman, was paid $50.

Kingman, Edward. Mass. Ens. He died of wounds received at Saratoga on 1 Oct. 1777. His heirs were paid his seven years' half-pay of $840.

Kingman, Loring. Mass. —. He served in the 7ᵗʰ Regiment and was paid $20.

Kingman, Peter. Pa. —. He was pensioned 14 Mar. 1834 in Union County.

Kingsbury, Aaron. Mass. —. He served in the 3ʳᵈ Regiment and was paid $20.

Kingsley, Asahel. —. Pvt. He served two years in guarding the powder mill at Windham, Conn., but that service was not covered by the pension legislation. He enlisted for seven months 1 June 1780 under Capt. Douglas and Col. Starr. He was discharged after five months and nine days of service. Congress granted him a pension 25 Apr. 1840 by allowing him to count the time for his coming and going to and from the service.

Kinne, Lyman. Conn. Pvt. He served under Col. C. Webb. He was wounded by a musket ball which passed through his thigh which cut the cords of his thigh in 1776. He resided in Washington, Conn. in 1792. He enlisted 27 May 1777 for eight months and was discharged 9 Jan. 1778.

Kinney, Amos. N.Y. —. He served about seven months in the N.Y. levies under Col. Willet. He then enlisted for the war and was discharged in the winter or spring of 1784. He died in 1813. He married 9 Dec. 1784. His widow, Hannah Kinney, aged 80 years, was pensioned by Congress 19 July 1848. His sister, Lois Waldo, was at their wedding.

Kinney, Archelaus. Mass. Pvt. He served in the 5ᵗʰ Regiment under Capt. Joseph Kilham and Col. Rufus Putnam. He was worn out in the service and was 55 years old in 1786.

Kinney, David. Mass. —. He was a pensioner. He married in March 1782. His eldest son, John Kinney, was 65 years old when the widow Elizabeth Kinney was pensioned by Congress 20 June 1848.

Kinney, Peter. Pa. —. He was pensioned by the court of inquiry 17 Apr. 1819.

Kinsell, Lewis. Va. —. His wife, Mary Kinsell, was granted £30 support in Berkeley County on 16 Nov. 1779.

Kinney, Peter. Pa. —. He was pensioned by the court of enquiry 17 Apr. 1819.

Kinser, George. Pa. —. He was granted relief 4 Apr. 1837. He died in Allegheny County by 30 Apr. 1842. His service was in the Indian Wars.

Kinser, Michael. Va. Pvt. He lived in Montgomery County 28 Nov. 1786. He served in the 1ˢᵗ Va. Regiment in Capt. B-------'s Co. He was drafted as an 18 month soldier. All of the fingers on his right hand were cut off except the forefinger which appeared stiff and of little use at the battle of Camden. He was aged 27. He later lived in Wythe Co., Va. He was continued on the pension list at the rate of £12 per annum of 28 Apr. 1787. He was on the 1813 pension list as Michael Kinson [sic]. His unit of service was also given as the 2ⁿᵈ Virginia Detachment. He also appeared as Michael Kinsier.

Kinsey, —. Pa. —. His widow, Catherine Kinsey, was awarded a $40 gratuity and a $40 annuity in Bucks Co., Pa. 8 Apr. 1833. She died 27 Nov. 1848.

Kinsey, James. N.J. Pvt. He served in the 2ⁿᵈ Regiment. He was worn out by seven years of faithful service. He was 68 years old and was from Salem.

Kinsey, William. Pa. —. He served under Capt. Thompson in 1776. He was at White Marsh, Germantown, Chestnut Hill, and the taking of the Hessians at Trenton. He was 69 years old in 1824. He was awarded a $40 gratuity in Bucks Co., Pa. 14 Apr. 1828 and a $40 gratuity and a $40 annuity 1 Mar. 1832. He died 9 Dec. 1832.

Kinsley, James. N.J. Pvt. He served under Capt. Huddy and died of a wound received from a British soldier 22 Mar. 1782 at the Block House at Tom River. He was shot through the head. He was from Monmouth County. His widow was Elizabeth Kinsley.

Kintell, Michael. Pa. —. He was paid a $40 gratuity in Berks County in 1835.

Kinter, John. Pa. —. He was awarded a $40 gratuity in Indiana County 5 Feb. 1836.

Kip, James. N.Y. Lt. He served from 6 Feb. 1777 to Jan. 1782. He was appointed a sergeant in Oct. 1778. His application under the act of 1832 was rejected since his service as an artificer in the armory was civil rather than military. For his prompt and efficient service in preventing the surprise and capture of Gen. Baron de Steuben, he was promoted to lieutenant. His commission had been lost. He died 19 Nov. 1834. His son, John L. Kip, represented his siblings, and they were able to have their father's rejection in 1832 overturned on 10 Jan. 1857 by Congress.

Kiper, George Frederick. Va. —. His wife and three children were granted £4 per month support in Yohogania Co., Va. 23 June 1778 while he was away in the service.

Kipple, Laurence. —. —. His application was referred to the Secretary of War.

Kirk, James. Pa. —. He was awarded a $40 gratuity and a $40 annuity in Bucks Co., Pa. 11 Mar. 1833. He died 16 June 1841.

Kirk, John. —. —. His application was referred to the Secretary of War.

Kirkendale, Samuel. N.J. Capt. He served under Col. John Cleave Sims in the Sussex County militia and was wounded through his hand. He was 48 years old and lived in Knolton. He was on the 1791 pension roll. He was on the 1813 pension list. He also appeared as Samuel Kirkendall. In 1820 he appointed Benjamin Kirkendol of Knowlton Twp., Sussex County to collect his pension.

Kirkendall, John. N.J. —. He was born in New Jersey. He took camp fever in the service with the flux or dysentery. The disease fell into his knees and left him a cripple. He realized that he was ineligible for a half-pay pension, but he applied for relief in Sussex County 13 Nov. 1801.

Kirker, John. Pa. —. He was granted relief in Jefferson County 8 Jan. 1838. He was 71 years old in 1840.

Kirkland, John. Pa. —. He was awarded a $40 gratuity and a $40 annuity in Allegheny Co., Pa. 1 Apr. 1827.

Kirkland, Reubin. S.C. —. He was on the roll in 1791.

Kirkpatrick, —. Pa. —. His widow, Nancy Kirkpatrick, received a $40 gratuity 8 May 1850 and a $40 annuity 17 Mar. 1852 in Perry County.

Kirkpatrick, John. Md. Pvt. He was pensioned 7 June 1785. He was on the 1813 pension list.

Kirkpatrick, John. Pa. —. He was granted relief.

Kirkpatrick, Moses. Pa. —. He served under Capt. Denny and Col. Watts in the militia. He was wounded in Gen. Lacey's Surprise 1 May 1778 in both of his arms and his back. He applied 18 Apr. 1778.

Kirkpatrick, Samuel. Va. Pvt. He was awarded a £1,000 gratuity and an annuity of £5 in specie. He was in Rockbridge County 4 Apr. 1787. He served under Col. Samuel McDowell in the militia and received several wounds at the battle of Guilford. He was pensioned at the rate of £12 per annum on 17 Apr. 1787 and at the rate of £15 per annum on 20 Dec. 1792. He was aged 48 in 1787. He was on the 1813 pension list. His pension was increased to $20 per annum on 25 Feb. 1818. He also appeared as Samuel Killpatrick. He died 1 Apr. 1818.

Kirkwood, James. S.C. —. He lost his life in the service. His widow, Margaret Kirkwood, was granted an annuity 2 Aug. 1785 and was a resident of Pendleton District.

Kirtland, Elizur. Conn. —. He enlisted at the age of 14 in 1781 for one year under his father, Capt. Martin Kirtland and Col. Ledyard. He was a waiter to his father at Fort Saybrook until he was discharged. He applied from Granville, Green Co., Ky. Congress rejected his claim because he was under the age of 15 when he served.

Kisby, Richard. —. —. He was pensioned 25 Apr. 1808 at the rate of $4 per month from 24 Mar. 1807.

Kitchey, Robert. Pa. Pvt. He enlisted in Apr. 1778 under Capt. Murray and Col. Miles. He was also under Col. Walter Stewart. He was from Cumberland County.

Kitchman, Salisbury. Mass. —. He served in the 14th Regiment and was paid $20.

Kittle, —. S.C. —. His widow was Mary Kittle. She was on the roll in 1791.

Kittle, Andrew. Mass. —. He served in the 3rd Regiment and was paid $20.

Kittle, John. N.Y. Pvt. He served under Col. John Cantine in the Ulster County militia and was slain 12 Aug. 178-. His widow, Sarah Kittle, received his half-pay pension.

Kitts, John. Pa. —. He was awarded a $40 gratuity in Delaware Co., Pa. 6 Apr. 1830 and a $40 gratuity and $40 annuity on 20 Feb. 1833. His widow, Catharine Kitts, was awarded a $40 gratuity and a $40 annuity on 14 Apr. 1834. She died 20 Sep. 1840.

Klein, John. Pa. Pvt. He was in Berks Co. 8 Apr. 1788. He served in Capt. Jacob Sevier's [?Sweer] Company in the Berks County militia. He was wounded in his left arm in service in Wyoming against the Insurgents. Col. Lindenmuth deposed that he was little disabled. He was wounded in state rather than in Continental service. He signed in German. He also appeared as John Kline. He received $3.33 per month. He was a cordwainer. He was also wounded in Oct. 1784 while serving under Gen. Amboy.

Kline, Conrad. Pa. —. He was awarded a $40 gratuity and a $40 annuity in Washington Co., Md. 11 Apr. 1825. He died 6 Dec. 1826.

Kline, Conrad. Pa. —. He was awarded a $40 gratuity and a $40 annuity in York Co., Pa. 14 Apr. 1834.

Kline, Jacob. Pa. —. He was pensioned 27 Mar. 1837 in Mifflin County.

Kline, John. Md. Pvt. His widow, Mary M. Kline, was pensioned at the rate of half-pay of a private in Frederick County on 12 Mar. 1834.

Kline, John. Pa. —, He was paid in Feb. 1811.

Kline, Samuel. Pa. —. He was awarded a $40 gratuity and a $40 annuity in Berks Co., Pa. 7 Feb. 1831.

Kline, William. Pa. —. He received a $40 gratuity and a $40 annuity in Fayette County 15 June 1836.

Klinedienst, Christian. Pa. He was awarded a $40 gratuity and a $40 annuity in York County 14 Apr. 1834. He was dead by July 1838.

KlineSmith, —. Pa. —. His widow, Mary KlineSmith, was granted relief in 1815. She died 17 Oct. 1818.

Klingman, Peter. Pa. —. He was awarded a $40 gratuity and a $40 annuity in Union Co., Pa. 15 Apr. 1834. He died 1 June 1848.

Klink, George. Pa. —. He was awarded a $40 gratuity and a $40 annuity in Cumberland Co., Pa. 15 Mar. 1826. He died 1 July 1827.

Klock, Adam. N.Y. Lt. He served under Col. Samuel Clyde. He was killed at Oriskany 6 Aug. 1777. His children received a half-pay pension. They included Elizabeth Klock, Jacob Klock, and Henry Klock. [The names of the others were illegible.]

Klock, Jacob. N.Y. Ens. His family was granted support 14 May 1779. He served under Col. Goose Van Schaick.

Knap, Aaron. N.Y. Pvt. He served under Col. Lewis Dubois and died in prison in captivity in Jan. 1778. His orphans, James Knapp, Thomas Knapp, Elizabeth Knapp, and Hannah Knapp, received his half-pay pension for seven years from 1782. He also appeared as Aaron Knapp.

Knap, James. N.Y. Pvt. He served in the Orange County militia under Capt. John W------- and was slain 22 July 1779. His widow, Hester Knap, received his half-pay pension. He also appeared as James Knapp.

Knap, Jonathan. N.Y. Pvt. He served in the Orange County militia under Col. John Hathorn and was wounded in battle.

Knapp, —. —. —. Congress rejected the petition of his widow, Mary Knapp, because there was no evidence on file on 4 Apr. 1840.

Knapp, —. N.Y. Pvt. He served under Col. Cortland. His family was furnished 30 pounds of flour in Nov. 1779.

Knapp, Abial. N.H. Pvt. He served under Col. Leonard Scammel in the New Hampshire Continental Line. He was wounded in his right leg at Bemis Heights on 7 Oct. 1777. He was pensioned 15 Aug. 1788. He was 46 years old. He lived in Philips Town, N.Y. 20 July 1789 and later in Ontario County. He was on the 1813 pension list.

Knapp, Abijah. Mass. Sgt. He served in the 3rd Regiment and was from Easton. He was paid $50.

Knapp, Elijah. Conn. Sgt. He served in Col. Swift's Regiment. He was wounded by a ball which passed through his right thigh in July 1781 at Jamestown, was taken prisoner by the enemy, and remained such for some months before he joined the company as an invalid. He was pensioned in Sep. 1790. He lived in Bernard's Town, Somerset Co., N.J. in 1794. He transferred to Saratoga Co., N.Y. 4 Mar. 1795. He was on the 1813 pension list.

Knapp, Jared. Conn. Sgt. He served in Col. Bradley's Regiment. He was disabled by the explosion of gunpowder in Nov. 1777. He lived in Litchfield, Conn. in 1794. He enlisted 5 Mar. 1777 and continued to the end of the war. He moved to Greene Co., N.Y. 4 Sep. 1825. He was on the 1813 pension list.

Knapp, Joseph. Conn. Pvt. He served in the Conn. militia in a company of rangers under Capt. Isaac Howe and Col. John Mead in Fairfield County. He was wounded in his left hand by a broad sword and lost four fingers. He was taken prisoner and held six weeks. On 7 May 1786 he was 28 years old. He was a weaver and lived in New York City, N.Y. in 1787. He also served under Capt. Samuel Lockwood and Col. Matthew Mead, Jesse Hait, Joseph Bush, and Capt. Isaac Howe swore to his service. He was on the 1813 pension list.

Knapp, Samuel. N.Y. Lt. He served in the Orange County militia and was slain 22 July 1779. His widow, Mehitabel Knapp, received his half-pay pension.

Knapsnyder, John. Pa. —. His heirs were awarded 200 acres of donation land 29 Mar. 1813.

Knecht, Jacob. Pa. —. He received a $40 gratuity and a $40 annuity in Northampton County 21 Mar. 1837.

Knight, Benjamin. N.H. Sgt. He served under Col. Scammel in Benjamin Stone's Company. He lost one finger of his right hand and one of his thighs was considerably weakened by wounds in July 1777 at Hubbardstown. He lived at Landaff, N.H. in 1795. He enlisted 27 Feb. 1777 for three years and was discharged Feb. 1780. He was granted one-third of a pension 20 Apr. 1796. He was on the 1813 pension list. He died 26 July 1831.

Knight, Elijah. —. Pvt. He served in Col. Brewer's Regiment. He was wounded on guard duty by a ball from a musket in the hands of a soldier in the company to which he belonged. It entered the back part of his leg at Roxbury, Mass. in 1775. He resided at Rockingham, Vt. in 1796. He was granted one-fourth of a pension 20 Apr. 1796. He was on the 1813 pension list.

Knight, Jacob. Md. Pvt. He was pensioned at the rate of half-pay of a private in Ohio. 12 Feb. 1821.

Knight, John. —. Surgeon's Mate. He received his five years' full pay commutation 15 June 1832.

Knight, John. N.H. Pvt. He served in the militia under Col. Peabody. He lost two fingers on his left hand when his gun went off accidentally while on guard duty in 1778 at Boston Neck. He lived in Northwood, N.H. in 1794. He was granted half a pension 20 Apr. 1796. He was on the 1813 pension list.

Knight, John. N.C. Capt. He served four months and eleven days which was not sufficient to qualify. Congress rejected the claim of the widow, Sarah Knight, on 6 Mar. 1840 and 30 Mar. 1848. She did not prove that her husband was the same individual alleged to have the service. Congress had earlier rejected her claim on 9 Jan. 1847 because she failed to establish his service sufficiently. She was 80 years old.

Knight, John. Pa. Pvt. He was in Philadelphia County 12 Dec. 1785. He was discharged in Jan. 1783 from the Invalids as unfit for duty being worn out in the service. He was 42 years old.

Knight, John. S.C. —. He was pensioned from Laurens District 4 Dec. 1832. He was over 80 years of age but had no family. He wanted to remove to Georgia to join his sister. He sought the equivalent of his annual pension, but he was denied that benefit. He applied for a federal pension in 1834 but was refused. He sought reinstatement 2 July 1837. He also appeared as John Night.

Knight, Jonathan. Conn. Surgeon's Mate. He died about 1831 and had not received his commutation of five years' pay. In the absence of proof that he served to the end of the war, Congress rejected the claim of the heirs on 27 Apr. 1836. They were Ann Knight, Abigail Knight, and Jonathan Knight.

Knight, Jonathan. Me. —. He was from Watertown.

Knight, Joseph. —. —. He had been pensioned under the act of 1832. Congress denied his children their claim 1 Aug. 1850.

Knight, William. Me. —. He died 11 Apr. 1831. His widow was Phebe Knight from Poland. She was paid $50 under the resolve of 1836.

Knight, William. Mass. Pvt. He served in the 7th Regiment and was from New Salem. He was paid $50.

Knighton, John. S.C. —. He served 18 months in Marion's Brigade. He was poor and blind. His officers included Capt. William Dukes, Lt. Joseph Terry, and Col. Richard Richardson. He was from Clarendon County 28 Nov. 1793.

Knittel, Michael. Pa. —. He was awarded a $40 gratuity in Berks Co., Pa. 15 Apr. 1835.

Knittle, Adam. Pa. —. He was awarded a $40 gratuity and a $40 annuity in Schuylkill County 5 Feb. 1836.

Knowland, Moses. Mass. Pvt. He was in the Invalids under Col. Nichola and Capt. Hills in the 4th Regiment. He was entirely worn out. He was 67 years old in 1786. He was on the 1813 pension list. He was from Charlton and was paid $20 by the Commonwealth. He also appeared as Moses Nowland.

Knowles, John. N.H. Pvt. He served under Col. Stickney in the militia. He was wounded by a ball shot through his body in 1777 at the battle of Bennington. He was in Capt. Stephen Dearborn's Company. He lived in Sterling, N.H. in 1794. He was granted half a pension 20 Apr. 1796. He was on the 1813 pension list. He transferred to Kennebec Co., Me. 4 Mar. 1822.

Knowles, John. N.C. Pvt. He served in the 2nd Regiment. He was wounded by the British horse at Rockfish Bridge in his right and left shoulders; his left arm and left shoulder were almost cut off. He lived in Duplin Co., N.C. in 1795. He was granted two-thirds of a pension 20 Apr. 1796. He died 15 Jan. 1804.

Knowlton, Grant. S.C. —. He was from Salem Co., Sumter District. He enlisted in 1779 under Col. Daniel Horry. He was wounded in the knee by a musket ball near Camden at Gates's defeat. He had a wife and children. He was granted $645 in arrearage of his pension on 18 Dec. 1818. His widow, Frances Knowlton, was granted his arrearage on 17 Dec. 1821 from his death on 22 Apr. 1821 and was pensioned from the same date. She was paid her annuity as late as 1834. Her brother, Stephen Evans, sought her arrearage, but his request was denied because her children were the ones who needed to do so. She died 3 Jan. 1842. Her only son, John W. Knowlton, of Clarendon County, Sumter District, was paid $110 on 18 Nov. 1845.

Knowlton, John. Mass. Pvt. He served in the Invalids under Col. Lewis Nichola and Capt. Hill. He was injured in his left leg. He was 26 years old in 1788.

Knowlton, John. Me. —. He died 18 Oct. 1798 in Kittery. His widow was Dorcas Knowlton from Eliot. She was paid $50 under the resolve of 1836.

Knowlton, Thomas. —. Lt. Col. He entered the service in 1775 and was soon appointed major of the 20th Regiment called Durkee's Regiment. He was appointed Lt. Col. 10 Aug. 1776. He was killed 16 Sep. 1776 at Harlem Heights survived by his widow and eight children. His widow died in 1808. His son, Frederick Knowlton, and others received his seven years' half-pay 22 Dec. 1837.

Knox, —. Va. —. His wife and three children were granted £3 per month support in Yohogania Co., Va. 23 May 1782.

Knox, David. Mass. —. He was paid $20.

Knox, George. N.Y. Sgt. Maj. He was appointed Sgt. Maj. Oct. 1777. On 13 July 1778 on the march from White Plains to Schoharie he was shot through his body at Albany by Richard Roach, a soldier in the same regiment. The musket ball entered the right side of his back bone and came out about two inches above his navel. He was discharged in Nov. 1779 as unfit for duty and entered the commissary department. He lived in New York City, N.Y. on 16 June 1788.

Knox, George. Pa. Pvt. He served in the 4th Pennsylvania Regiment under Col. William Butler. His rank was given as private on the 1791 pension roll. He was on the 1813 pension list.

Knox, Hugh. S.C. —. His widow, Jennet Knox, of Chester District was paid her annuity as late as 1832.

Knox, James. S.C. —. He was killed in the service. His widow, Jennet Knox, was granted an annuity 30 Mar. 1785 in Chester. There were three children in 1791.

Knox, Matthew. Pa. Lt. He was awarded 400 acres of donation land in Montgomery County on 12 Mar. 1813. He was rejected for a pension 17 Dec. 1813.

Knox, Thomas. Va. Sgt. He served in Capt. Stephen Ashby's Company under Col. James Woods and died in the service. His widow, Mary Knox, was entitled to half-pay since March. The Ohio Co., Va. court certified same 4 Oct. 1779.

Knox, William. S.C. Capt. In Feb. 1781 at Congaree Fort he had his mare shot out under him. One of the bones in his leg was dislocated. He was a private in the 6th Regiment under Sumter. One of his officers was Capt. McClure. After the battle of Hanging Rock he became a captain. He was from Chester District in 1808. He was granted the arrearage of his pension, $85.71, on 8 Dec. 1814. He died 31 Oct. 1830. His widow, Patience Knox, was pensioned at the rate of $30 per annum on 25 Nov. 1830. All of her children were married. She was paid her annuity as late as 1834.

Koch, —. Pa. —. His widow, Elizabeth Koch, received a $40 gratuity and a $40 annuity in Berks

County in 1836.

Koch, —. Pa. —. His widow, Eve Koch, was awarded a $40 gratuity and a $40 annuity in Dauphin County, Pa. 15 Apr. 1834.

Koch, Adam. Pa. Pvt. He was wounded in the battle of Brandywine in 1777 by a musket ball in the face which entered blow his right eye and passed out under his right ear. His hearing was injured. He was afterwards severely bruised by a log which rolled over his breast at the building of the fort at West Point. He lived in Berks County in 1794 and 1805. He did not give his disability or prove the time of his leaving the service in 1796. He enlisted 18 May 1777 for the war in the 9ᵗʰ Pa. Regiment under Capt. McClellan and Col. Nagle. He was awarded an annuity of $40 per annum 21 Mar. 1806 and lived in Berks County. He died 26 Apr. 1816. He also appeared as Adam Kough.

Koch, Adam. Pa. —. He was paid $300 for his donation land 14 Jan. 1823 in Somerset Co., Pa.

Koch, Christian. Pa. —. He was awarded a $40 gratuity and a $40 annuity in Lycoming Co., Pa. 25 Mar. 1831. He died 6 Oct.1832.

Koch, Johannis. N.Y. Sgt. He served in Capt. Andrew Tillebogh's Company under Col. Jacob Klock. He was wounded in his face by a musket ball on 6 Aug. 1777. He was 41 years old when he applied 15 Sep. 1786. He lived in Palatine, Montgomery Co., N.Y. i20 Aug. 1789. He died 4 Mar. 1790 or 2 Feb. 1798. He also appeared as Johannis Kough and John Kock. His captain's name also appeared as Andrew Dellenbogh. There was a Johannes Koch on the 1813 pension list.

Koch, John. Pa. —. He was awarded a $40 gratuity in York Co., Pa. 14 Apr. 1834. He was 82 years old in 1840.

Koch, John. Pa. —. He was awarded a $40 gratuity and a $40 annuity in Berks County 12 Mar. 1836.

Koch, John Michael. Pa. —. His widow, Catharine Koch, was awarded a $40 gratuity and a $40 annuity in York Co., Pa. 23 Apr. 1829.

Koch, Sebastian. Pa. —. He was awarded a $40 gratuity and a $40 annuity in Berks Co., Pa. 7 May 1832.

Koch, Severnius. N.Y. Sgt. He served in Jacob Klock's N.Y. Regiment. He was pensioned 20 Aug. 1777. He lived in New York County. He was on the 1813 pension list.

Kochenderfer, John. Pa. —. He was awarded a $40 gratuity and a $40 annuity in Lebanon Co., Pa. 6 Feb. 1835.

Kocher, Conrad. Pa. —. He served on the frontiers. He was from Northampton County.

Kocher, George. Pa. —. He was killed in Sep. 1780 in an engagement with the savages in Nescopeck Valley. His widow, Magdalena Kocher, and two small children were pensioned 26 Apr. 1781 in Westmoreland County.

Koeller, George. Pa. —. He was awarded a $40 gratuity and a $40 annuity in Westmoreland Co., Pa. 8 Apr. 1826.

Kohler, Valentine. Pa. —. He was awarded a $40 gratuity and a $40 annuity in York Co., Pa. 4 May 1832.

Kohne, Michael. Pa.—. His widow, Elizabeth Kohne, received a $40 gratuity and a $40 annuity in Berks County 17 Apr. 1854.

Koine, Dominick. Md. Pvt. He was pensioned. His widow, Mary Koine, was a resident of Harford County in 1803.

Kolb, Andrew. Pa. —. He was pensioned.

Kolb, Jehu. S.C. —. He was wounded in the knee at the battle of Eutaw. He was granted an annuity 8

Sep. 1785. He was from Cheraw. He applied for a pension 18 Nov. 1813 from Darlington District. His sons were in the service of the country. He was paid his annuity as late as 1834. He was mistakenly listed as John Kolb in some records.

Kolb, John. N.Y. Pvt. He served in the 5th N.Y. Regiment under Col. Lewis Dubois in Capt. John Johnson's Company. At Fort Montgomery in Oct. 1777 he was wounded in the back part of his head by a musket ball which fractured his skull. He was also wounded in his private parts. He had other wounds. He also served in Capt. Anthony Phelps' Company under Lt. Col. Marinus Willet. He was wounded by a musket ball through his left wrist. He lost the great toe and three other toes on his right foot due to frost bite in Jan. 1783. He was 45 years old on 24 July 1787 and was from Ulster Co. He was a breeches maker. He lived in Dutchess Co., N.Y. on 12 May 1789. He was on the 1813 pension list. He also appeared as John Kulb.

Konkle, Lawrence. Pa. —. He was awarded a $40 gratuity and a $40 annuity in Beaver Co., Pa. 15 Apr. 1835. He was dead by Nov. 1838.

Koockooyaei, Samuel. Pa. Musician. He served in the Pa. Artillery Regiment under Col. Thomas Forrest. He was discharged due to epileptic disease near the close of the war. He was awarded donation land 1 Feb. 1808.

Koons, —. Pa. —. His widow, Susannah Koons, was granted relief in Lancaster County 18 Apr. 1843.

Koons, Daniel. Pa. —. He was awarded a $40 gratuity and a $40 annuity in Center Co., Pa. 12 Apr. 1828.

Koontz, Francis. Pa. —. He had his leg amputated in hospital. He was pensioned in Lancaster County.

Koplin, John. Pa. —. He served under Col. De Haas and marched to Canada under Capt. Le Mars. He was at the taking of Fort Ann. When he returned to Pennsylvania, he was a teamster under Christopher Hart. His last tour was for three months in the militia under Capt. Read. He was from Chester County. He died 26 Aug. 1827. His widow, Susannah Koplin, was awarded a $40 gratuity and a $40 annuity in Chester County 12 Apr. 1828.

Kormony, John. Pa. —. He was awarded a $40 gratuity in Lebanon Co., Pa. 16 Feb. 1835.

Korr, Peter. Pa. —. He was awarded a $40 gratuity and a $40 annuity in Northampton Co., Pa. 19 Mar. 1824.

Koutz, Thomas. Pa. —. He was in the Flying Camp under Col. Ross in 1776 and under Capt. John Miller in 1777. He was from Lancaster County.

Koveler, Adam. Pa. —. His widow, Elizabeth Koveler, was awarded a $40 gratuity and a $40 annuity in Montgomery Co., Pa. 5 Mar. 1828.

Kramer, Johannes. —. —. His application was laid on the table.

Krebs, George. Pa. —. He was awarded a $40 gratuity and a $40 annuity in York Co., Pa. 23 Jan. 1830. He was 86 years old in 1840. He died 7 May 1842. He also appeared as George Krehs.

Krebs, Peter. Pa. —. He was awarded a $40 gratuity in York County 5 Feb. 1836. He also appeared as Peter Krepps.

Kreemer, Conrod. —. QM Sgt. He was pensioned in 1832 at $80 per annum. He sought an additional sum of $96 per annum from 10 June 1825 to 15 Jan. 1827 from Congress on 30 Jan. 1836.

Kreider, Jacob. Pa. —. He served in the Flying Camp and was taken prisoner at Fort Washington. He was released on parole in Feb. 1777. He was exchanged in May 1780. He was awarded a $40 gratuity and a $40 annuity in Northampton County on 21 Jan. 1819. He died 19 May 1832.

Kreidler, —. Pa. —. His widow, Mary Kreidler, was awarded a $40 gratuity and a $40 annuity in York Co., Pa. 14 Apr. 1834.

Kreiner, Philip. Pa. —. He received a $40 gratuity and a $40 annuity in Schuylkill County 9 Feb.

1837 He died 9 Nov. 1841. His widow, Mary Kreiner, received a $40 gratuity and a $40 annuity 21 Mar. 1860.

Kremer, John. Pa. —. He was awarded a $40 gratuity and a $40 annuity in Franklin Co., Pa. 22 Dec. 1834.

Kremer, Michael. Va. His widow, Margaret Kremer, lived in Frederick County on 1 Jan. 1786. He served in Capt. Johnstone's Company in the 10th Virginia Regiment and was wounded at the battle of Brandywine and died. She was put on the pension roll on 19 Dec. 1786 at the rate of £8 per annum. He also appeared as Michael Kreamer.

Krewson, John. Pa. —. He was awarded a $40 annuity in Philadelphia County 5 Feb. 1836. He also appeared as John Kruson.

Krewson, Simon. Pa. —. He was awarded $100 in Philadelphia Co., Pa. 3 Feb. 1824, a $60 gratuity 7 Mar. 1827, a $40 gratuity 6 Apr. 1830, and a $40 gratuity 11 Jan. 1831. He also appeared as Simon Krawson. He was 86 years old in 1840.

Krieder, —. Pa. —. His widow, Harriet Krieder, was granted support in Philadelphia County 5 Dec. 1842.

Krieder, Jacob. Pa. —. He was awarded a $40 gratuity and a $40 annuity in Philadelphia Co., Pa. in Feb. 1834.

Kroan, John. Pa. —. He was awarded a $40 gratuity and a $40 annuity in York Co., Pa. 7 May 1832. He also appeared as John Kroon.

Krone, John Andrew. Pa. Pvt. He was granted relief.

Krough, Phillip. Pa. Dragoon. He served in Van Heer's Dragoons. He was on the 1813 pension list as Philip Krugh. [The next entry may apply to the same individual.]

Krug, Philip. Pa. —. His widow, Mary Ann Krug, was awarded a $40 gratuity and a $40 annuity in Dauphin Co., Pa. 12 Apr. 1828. She died 27 Feb. 1846. [The preceding entry may be the same person.]

Kuder, Valentine. Pa. —. He was awarded a $40 annuity in Schuylkill County 5 Feb. 1836. He also appeared as Valentine Kuter.

Kuhl, Casper. Pa. Pvt. He served under Col. Cook. He was wounded in his hand. He lived in Berks Co., Pa. in 1794. He did not prove his disability and place of residence in 1796.

Kuhn, Andrew. Pa. —. He was granted relief.

Kuhn, Christian. Pa. Pvt. He served in Capt. Pike's Company under Col. Moylan. He was on the 1791 pension roll and transferred to New York 4 Mar. 1791. He was on the 1813 pension list of New Jersey. He died 23 Jan. 1823 in Montgomery County, New Jersey.

Kuhn, Jacob. Pa. —. He was awarded a $40 gratuity in Montgomery County on 31 Mar. 1812.

Kuhn, Phineas. Pa. —. He enlisted under Capt. Brunner in the 2nd Regiment. He served in the expedition to Canada. He re-enlisted and died at Valley Forge. His widow was Elizabeth Kuhn from Philadelphia County. There were three children.

Kuhns, John. Pa. —. He was awarded a $40 gratuity in Union Co., Pa. 4 May 1832.

Kunkle, —. Pa. —. His widow, Magdalena Kunckle, was awarded a $40 gratuity and a $40 annuity in York Co., Pa. 14 Feb. 1833.

Kuntz, Daniel. Pa. —. He was paid a $40 gratuity in May 1834.

Kuntz, Francis. Pa. —. He was in Lancaster Co. 19 Apr. 1786. He had his leg amputated in July at the General Hospital at French Creek. He was 55 years old. He was discharged under the name of Francis Kunt. He died 21 Apr. 1786 at the house of Martin Bard in Lancaster, Pa. He also appeared as Francis Koontz.

Kuntz, Lawrence. Pa. —. He was awarded a $40 gratuity and a $40 annuity in Mifflin Co., Pa. 11 Apr. 1825. He died 20 Feb. 1841.

Kurtes, —. Pa. —. His widow, Eve Kurtes, was awarded a $40 gratuity and a $40 annuity in Lancaster County 3 Apr. 1841 for his Revolutionary service.

Kurtz, Peter. Pa. —. He was awarded a $40 gratuity and a $40 annuity in Berks Co., Pa. 5 Mar. 1828. He died 20 Feb. 1848.

Kusick, John. Pa. Pvt. He was in Philadelphia County Sep. 1786. He served in the 2nd Pa. Regiment under Capt. William Craig and was wounded at the battle of Three Rivers in Canada. He lost his speech. He was aged 53 years.

Kuyper, Hendricus. N.J. Capt. He was in the Bergen County militia and suffered from the loss of a leg. He resided in Cumberland County. He received a half-pay pension.

Labar, Casper. Pa. —. He was granted relief.

Labar, Jacob. Pa. —. He was granted a $40 gratuity in Monroe County 16 Apr. 1838. His service was not specified.

Labar, John. S.C. Sgt. Maj. He served under Gen. Pulaski, was wounded several times, and taken prisoner. He had lived as a hair dresser for many years. He became totally deranged, and his wife had to attend him every moment or he might stray away and hurt another citizen. He was pensioned in 1796. His widow, Anna Christiana Labar, was on the roll in 1797.

Labar, Leonard. Pa. —. His widow, Elizabeth Labar, was awarded a $40 gratuity and a $40 annuity in Northampton Co., Pa. 22 Dec. 1828. She died 20 Jan. 1829.

Labaw, Charles. N.J. —. He was pensioned in Mercer County on 25 Jan. 1842 at the rate of $50 per annum.

Labo, Casper. Pa. —. He was pensioned 14 Jan. 1823.

Labon, Jacob. Pa. —. He received a $40 gratuity in Allegheny County 14 Apr. 1838, but his service was not specified.

Labonte, John Baptist. Canada. Capt. He served under Col. James Livingston from the siege of Quebec to the end of the war. Congress granted him half-pay for life 2 Mar. 1860.

Labor, John. Pa. Pvt. He lived in Philadelphia County. He may be the one on the 1813 pension list as John Lalor..

Lacey, —. S.C. —. He was killed in the service. His wife was dead. His children were granted an annuity 1 July 1785. They were Jane Lacey, Samuel Lacey, and Mary Lacey.

Lacey, Josiah. Conn. Capt. He served under Col. P. B. Bradley in the 5th Regiment. He was unable to walk or step due to rheumatism. He resided in Stratford, Conn. in 1792. He was commissioned 1 Jan. 1777 and resigned 20 July 1780..

Lackey, —. Pa. —. His widow, Mary Lackey, was awarded a $40 gratuity and a $40 annuity in Berks Co., Pa. 24 Mar. 1832.

Lackey, Robert. Pa. —. He was awarded a $40 gratuity in Perry County 6 Apr. 1833. He died 18 Dec. 1840. He was 76 years old in 1840.

Lacum, John. Pa. Pvt. He was on the 1791 pension roll.

Lacoton, George. R.I. Pvt. He resided in Providence Co., R.I.

Lacount, Samuel. Mass. Pvt. He served in Col. Samuel Johnson's Regiment in Capt. Joseph Eaton's Company. He lost his left thumb and the use of his left hand. He was 40 years old in 1786 and was pensioned by Massachusetts having removed to New Hampshire. He was pensioned 20 June 1787. He was on the 1813 pension list. He died 18 Jan. 1832 in Grafton Co., N.H.

Lacy, Elkanah. Va. —. His wife, Mary Lacy, was granted support in Halifax Co., Va. on 17 Sep.

1778.

Lacy, Titus. S.C. —. He was pensioned 14 Dec. 1824.

Ladd, Nathaniel. Mass. Pvt. He was pensioned 5 May 1810. He lived in Essex Co., Mass. He was on the 1813 pension list.

LaFayette, James. Va. —. He was pensioned in Culpeper Co. 9 Mar. 1819. He was a slave and the property of William Armistead of New Kent County and obtained the permission from his master to served under Gen. LaFayette. At the peril of his life he found means to frequent the British camp and thereby faithfully executed important commissions entrusted to him. He was emancipated by the Virginia legislature in 1786 in recognition of his Revolutionary War service. He was pensioned at the rate of $40 per annum and $60 immediate relief. He died 9 Aug. 1830.

LaGross, Francis. Mass. —. He served in the 5th Regiment and was paid $20.

Lahorn, Henry. Va. —. His wife, Sarah Lahorn, was allowed 300 pounds of pork and 6 barrels of corn for support of a family of six in Bedford Co., Va. in Nov. 1780.

Lain, —. Pa. —. His widow, Charlotte Lain, was granted relief in Allegheny County 16 Apr. 1838.

Lain, Charles. Pa. —. He was pensioned.

Laird, David. Va. —. He was away in the service. His wife, Margaret Laird, and her children were granted financial support in Botetourt Co., Va. 15 Apr. 1778.

Laird, John. Pa. —. He applied in Sussex Co., Del. 29 Dec. 1823. He served in Capt. Moore's Company of Infantry under Col. Johnson in the 6th Pa. Regiment.

Laird, John. S.C. —. His widow, Mary Laird, was a resident of Abbeville District in 1828.

Laird, Robert. —. Capt. He was put on the pension roll but died before he received any payment. He left no widow. Two of his children, William Laird and Elizabeth Laird, had supported him for many years. His other children were scattered over the world and some had wandered to Texas. He had named the two children in his will. They were from Clarke Co., Ga. Congress authorized the pension to be paid to the executor 24 Feb. 1838.

Laird, Samuel. S.C. —. When he delivered his account for wagon hire, it was not certified so it was not passed. Major Siban [?] of the Little River Regiment later certified it, and his indent for £46.17.1 ½ with interest from 1 April 1783 was approved on 18 Dec. 1792.

LaJeunesse, Prudent. —. Maj. In 1828 he stated that he was a major to the close of the war. In 1829 he stated that his only role was that of baker at West Point. In his third attempt he said he was a Canadian refugee and in 1775 collected a company of Canadian volunteers. He joined the army at Crown Point under Gen. Montgomery and was commissioned captain. He served more than a year when he became superintendent of the government bakery at West Point. This testimony discredited what he had said under oath earlier. He drew two lots in New York as a Canadian refugee. He died with no wife or descendants in any degree. Nephews, nieces, and other collateral relatives in more remote degrees some of whom were already drawing pensions on other grounds sought further relief as his heirs. Congress rejected their claim 9 Feb. 1848.

Lake, George. N.J. —. His seven surviving heirs sought a donation of land of one-quarter to one section. Congress rejected the claim 23 May 1856.

Lake, Jonathan. N.H. Corp. He served in 2nd Regiment. He was wounded in his left thigh by a musket ball on 3 July 1781 at Kingsbridge. He lived in Rindge, N.H. in 1794. He enlisted 10 Apr. 1778 for the war. He was granted half a pension 20 Apr. 1796. He was on the 1813 pension list of Vermont. He lived in Windsor Co., Vt.

Lake, Joseph. N.J. —. His daughter, Mary A. Kendle, had a large family to provide for and to educate. She furnished no evidence whatsoever. Congress rejected her claim for a pension 3 Mar. 1851.

Lake, Phineas. Conn. Pvt. He was in the Invalids Corps since he was disabled by rheumatism and was good for nothing. He was pensioned 4 Jan. 1783. He resided in Chittenden Co., Vt. He was on the 1813 pension list in Connecticut.

Lakeman, Thomas. Mass. Sgt. Maj. He served in the 5th Regiment and was paid $20.

Lakin, William. N.H. Pvt. He was from Hancock, N.H. in 1783. He served in Col. Dearborn's N.H. Regiment and was wounded in his hand and hip. He was on the 1813 pension list as William Laken.

Lalor, John. Pa. Pvt. He was on the 1791 and 1813 pension rolls.

Lamb, David. Pa. —. He was awarded a $40 gratuity and a $40 annuity in Center Co., Pa. 8 Apr. 1833. He was dead by July 1837.

Lamb, Ephraim. Va. —. His family was granted assistance in Prince Edward Co., Va. on 20 Sep. 1779 while he was away in Continental service.

Lamb, Gideon. N.C. Col. He died in the service. His heirs applied in Camden County in 1789. He was in the Continental army and died in the service. His children were William Lamb, Louisa Lamb, and Abner Lamb.

Lamb, Jacob. S.C. —. He was killed in action 28 Aug. 1781. He served under Capt. Benjamin Odom. His son, Jacob Lamb, was born 21 June 1781. His widow, Bethel Lamb, was a resident of Orangeburg District in 1795.

Lamb, Nahum. Mass. Pvt. He served in the 4th Regiment and was from Charlton. He was paid $50.

Lamb, Richard. Conn. Capt. In the building of Carlton Bridge, he suffered a violent contusion on his left side from a piece of timber. He was from Norwalk and aged 45 on 26 Nov. 1788. He was on the 1791 pension roll. He died 21 Mar. 1809.

Lambert, —. Pa. —. His widow, Dorothy Lambert, was granted relief in Berks County 14 Mar. 1835. She was dead by Dec. 1837.

Lambert, Christopher. Md. Pvt. He was pensioned in Frederick County in 1783. He was disabled by fire in Carolina. He was wounded at the battle of Frenchtown and confined to hospital for twelve months. He was on the 1813 pension list. He was pensioned at the rate of half-pay of a private in Baltimore 21 Mar. 1838. He served in the 3rd Regiment. His daughter, Sarah Cook, sought his bounty land and his invalid pension from 18 Mar. 1818 to 24 Apr. 1846. Congress denied her claim 3 Mar. 1851.

Lambert, Cornelius. N.Y. —. He enlisted in the spring of 1780 for one year and was attached to the Quartermaster Department. He was stationed at King's Ferry as a ferryman. He served five months under Col. Drake in 1776 and was on Long Island and the retreat to White Plains. In 1777 he served four months under Col. Luddington followed by one year under Col. Graham. He was 80 years old. Congress granted him a pension 3 Jan. 1832.

Lambert, David. N.Y. —. He was awarded 200 acres of bounty land 19 June 1812.

Lambert, Jacob. Pa. —. He was awarded a $40 gratuity in Berks Co., Pa. 11 June 1832. He was awarded a $40 gratuity and a $40 annuity in Berks Co., Pa. 18 Feb. 1834.

Lambert, Zacheus. Mass. Sgt. He served in the 10th Regiment and was from Middleborough. His widow, Rosanna Niles, was paid $50.

Lambright, —. Pa. —. His widow, Mary Lambright, was awarded a $40 annuity 3 Apr. 1852.

Lamme, Nathan. Va. Capt. He served in the infantry and continued in the service until after the surrender of Cornwallis in Oct. 1781. He retired as supernumerary but never resigned. Congress awarded him commutation 9 Jan. 1838.

Lammon, Francis. Mass. —. He was granted relief.

Lamont, Samuel. Mass. Pvt. He was from Bath, N.H. in 1787. He was in Col. Samuel Johnson's Regiment in Massachusetts. He lost his left thumb and the use of his left arm due to a wound. He was aged 40 in 1787.

Lampkin, John. Va. —. He was pensioned in Culpeper County on 6 Mar. 1826 at the rate of $60 per annum with immediate relief of $30. He was in the battles of Monmouth and Paulus Hook as well as several skirmishes. After his enlistment expired, he was ordered to Yorktown during the siege where he remained until the surrender. He died 26 July 1830. Administration on his estate was granted to Philagattius Roberts 16 Aug. 1830. He had served under Col. George Gibson. He had been pensioned in 1819 but dropped from the rolls when it was decided that his was state service. That decision was reversed in Jan. 1830. His widow, Mary Lampkin, sought his arrearage from Congress 7 June 1836. Congress approved same on the condition that she prove he was in indigent circumstances to be entitled under the act of 1 June 1820.

Lampman, Henry. N.Y. Pvt. He served under Col. Klock in the Montgomery County militia and was slain 6 Aug. 1777. His daughters, Elizabeth Lampman and Mary Lampman, received a half-pay pension for seven years.

Lampman, Peter. N.Y. Pvt. He served in Capt. Fox's Company under Col. Jacob Klock. He was disabled in his right leg 6 Aug. 1777. He lived in Montgomery Co., N.Y. on 1 Sep. 1788. He was on the 1813 pension list. His rank was also given as a corporal.

Lampson, William. Me. —. He died 15 Oct. 1823. His widow was Martha Lampson from Edgecomb. She was paid $50 under the resolve of 1836.

Lamson, Jonathan. Mass. Sgt. He served in the 6th Regiment and was from Vermont. He was paid $20.

Lamson, Nathan. Mass. —. He served in the 4th Regiment. He was paid $20.

Lancaster, Jesse. S.C. —. He was on the roll in 1791.

Land, —. Va. —. Mary Land was granted support in Prince Edward County 21 June 1779 while he was away in Continental service.

Land, Benjamin. S.C. —. He was taken prisoner in Mar. 1781 and died in confinement. His widow, Mary Land, was granted an annuity 26 May 1785. There were children in 1791.

Land, Ephraim. Va. Pvt. He applied in Rockingham County in Aug. 1797. He enlisted in Amelia Co., Va. and served under Col. Abraham Bluford. He was wounded in his hand at Reedy Fork in 1782 by a musket ball. He was at Hanging Rock and at Col. Washington's defeat at Santee. He was allowed £12 per annum from Mar. 1781. He was in Stokes Co., N.C. on 13 Sep. 1821. He was born 15 Oct. 1738.

Land, James. S.C. —. There were children in 1791.

Land, John. S.C. —. He was killed in Mar. 1781. His widow, Mary Land, was granted an annuity 26 May 1785.

Land, William. Va. Pvt. His wife, Elizabeth Land, was granted £50.8.3 support in Halifax Co., Va. on 17 June 1779. He died in the service, and his heirs were granted support on 16 Sep. 1779 and on 16 Nov. 1780.

Landaman, George. Va. —. While he was away in the service, his wife, Elizabeth Landaman, and children were granted support on 8 Apr. 1777, 3 Sep. 1778, and 7 Dec. 1778 in Richmond County.

Landers, Moses. S.C. —. He was enlisted by Capt. Francis Prince and was wounded in the service. He was from Greenville District when he was pensioned 21 Dec. 1804 at $22 per annum. He was granted his arrearage from 1806 on 20 Dec. 1810.

Revolutionary War Pensions

Landman, Newman. Va. Dragoon. He resided in Culpeper County. He was on the 1813 pension list. He later removed to Ohio.

Landin, —. Pa. —. His widow, Elizabeth Landin, was pensioned in Bradford County 13 Apr. 1838.

Lanenberger, George. Pa. —. He received a $40 gratuity and a $40 annuity in Columbia County in 1832. He was dead by Dec. 1837.

Lands, Andrew. Pa. —. He was pensioned.

Lane, —. Va. —. He and his brother were in Continental service. Their father, John Lane, and mother were furnished 3 barrels of corn and 100 pounds of meat in Essex Co., Va. on 21 Mar. 1780.

Lane, Caleb. Mass. Pvt. He served at the Castle and was from Abington. He was paid $50.

Lane, Cornelius. N.J. Pvt. He served in 4th Regiment of Hunterdon County militia under Col. John Taylor and was wounded prior to the battle of Monmouth on 27 June 1778 by a musket ball through his body by accident near Allentown. He was unable to support himself for three years. He was allowed half-pay for those years in Hunterdon County.

Lane, Drury. S.C. —. He was from St. Peters Parish when he was pensioned 6 Dec. 1828. He died 10 May 1830. His widow, Sarah Lane, was from St. Peter's Parish, Beaufort District when she was paid $71.66 2/3 in arrearage of his pension on 25 Nov. 1830. She was pensioned at the rate of $30 per annum on 4 Dec. 1832 and received her annuity as late as 1846.

Lane, Ephraim. Mass. Lt. Col. He served under Col. Thomas Cattender. He was disabled by a musket ball in his left arm. He was 67 years old in 1786. He was on the 1813 pension list.

Lane, George. Mass. —. He served in the 9th Regiment and was paid $20.

Lane, Gilman. Va. —. He was disabled by an illness he contracted at Portsmouth. He applied 23 Nov. 1778 in Virginia.

Lane, Job. Mass. Pvt. He served under Col. E. Brooks. He was wounded in the left side at the battle of Bunker Hill on 17 June 1775. In another account he stated that he was wounded on 19 Apr. in 1775 at Concord. He lived in Bedford, Mass. in 1792. He was in the militia. He was granted half a pension 20 Apr. 1796.

Lane, John. Pa. Pvt. He was in Philadelphia County 13 Mar. 1786. He served in the 2nd Pa. Regiment. He was disabled by a hurt and rupture by lifting a large stone at the building of Fort Putnam. He died 3 Dec. 1803.

Lane, John and **Anna Maria Lane**. Va. —. They were pensioned on 6 Feb. 1808 at the rate of $40 per annum. Anna Maria Lane in the garb and with the courage of a soldier performed extraordinary military service and received a severe wound at Germantown. They received a pension of $100 and $40 relief. He received a $40 increase on 10 Feb. 1812. He received a $40 per annum increase plus $50 immediate relief on 10 Feb. 1817. He called Sarah Lain his daughter 30 Nov. 1816. He died 14 July 1822, and administration of his estate was granted to Elijah Brown in May 1823 in Henrico County. He also appeared as John Lain.

Lane, Timothy. —. —. His application was laid on the table in Congress.

Lane, William. N.J. Lt. He was at Germantown 4 Oct. 1777. His widow, Mary (Brocaw) Lane drew his half-pay from 2 Oct. 1782.

Lanenberger, George. Pa. —. He was awarded relief in Columbia County 6 Apr. 1833.

Laney, Titus. S.C. —. He served under Col. Thompson in a scouting party to Key Wee. The Indians stole his horse. He drove a wagon with his team at the battle of Stono. He was from Lancaster District in 1824. His wife was dead; he lived with his only daughter. He was under the age of 90. He was paid his annuity as late as 1827.

Lanford, Richard. Mass. Pvt. He was in the Invalids under Capt. Ebenezer Cleveland and Col. Lewis

Nichola. He was worn out in the service. He was pensioned 1 Sep. 1782. He lived in Cape Ann, Mass. and was aged 57 in 1786. He died 2 Nov. 1789. He also appeared as Richard Langford.

Lang, —. Pa. —. His widow was Hannah Lang.

Lang, Robert. N.Y. Qr. Mr. Sgt. He served under Col. Samuel Drake in 1776 and was taken prisoner. He was disabled in his right groin by the cold. He lived in Westchester Co., N.Y. on 25 June 1788. He was on the 1813 pension list.

Langbourne, William. Va. Maj. In 1824 his heirs received a bounty land warrant for 6,224 acres for his seven years of service from Virginia. His commutation was issued to Martha Jones and others 13 Jan. 1838 by Congress.

Langenbach, Michael. Pa. —. He served in Flying Camp and was taken prisoner at Fort Washington. He was confined on the prison ship *Jersey*. He was awarded a $40 gratuity in Northampton County on 14 Mar. 1814.

Langford, Elijah. Md. Pvt. He was pensioned at the rate of half-pay of a private in Somerset County 2 Jan. 1813.

Langston, —. Va. Pvt. His widow, Sukey Langston, was awarded a £12 gratuity in King William County on 6 Nov. 1779. He was slain in the service.

Langston, John. N.C. —. His widow, Ann Langston, applied in Wayne County in Dec. 1793. He served in the militia. He was taken prisoner 17 Aug. 1781 and died in captivity. He left seven children. She was paid £40 for ten years of her pension.

Langton, —. Va. —. Lucy Langton was granted support in Prince William County in 1778.

Langworthy, Southcot. R.I. Pvt. He suffered from general disability, bodily infirmities, and asthma. He served under Col. Jeremiah Olney. He was aged 40 in 1786.

Lanham, John. Va. Pvt. He was from Prince William County. He was put on the pension list at the rate of £18 per annum on 2 Sep. 1788.

Laning, David. N.J. —. His widow, Mary Laning, was pensioned on 8 Mar. 1844 at the rate of $60 per annum.

Laning, James. N.J. —. He was pensioned in Burlington County on 20 Feb. 1838 at the rate of $60 per annum.

Lansdale, Thomas. Md. Maj. His widow, Cornelia Lansdale, was pensioned at the rate of half-pay of major 8 Mar. 1850. He served in the 4th Md. Regiment.

Lansing, Jacob John. N.Y. Deputy Muster Master. He was issued certificates for his arrears of pay and a year's advance 15 Apr. 1786.

Lapish, John. N.H. Pvt. He served under Col. Cilley in Capt. Wait's Company. He was wounded in his right arm by a musket ball on 7 Oct. 1777. He lived in Lyman, N.H. in 1795. He enlisted 17 Nov. 1776 and was on the rolls in 1780. He was granted one-fourth of a pension 20 Apr. 1796. He was on the 1813 pension list.

Lapley, Michael. Pa. —. His widow applied 28 June 1786. He was killed 26 Apr. 1779 at Freeland's Fort. He was survived by his widow and children.

Lapper, Jacob. N.Y. —. He was granted relief.

Lapsley, John. Va. Lt. He was awarded a gratuity of half-pay for life 6 Nov. 1779. He was in Botetourt County 29 July 1785 and was aged 34 years old. He entered the service in Feb. 1776 in the 7th Va. Regiment as an ensign. He was detached to Col. Morgan's Rifles under Maj. Thomas Posey in the 7th Va. Regiment in June 1777. He was wounded at Edge Hill at White Marsh in Nov. 1777. He partly recovered and reconnoitered the enemy through the Jerseys under Col. Daniel Morgan. He received a ball through his left elbow. Col. Alexander McClenachan of the 7th Va.

Regiment attested to his service. He was pensioned at the rate of half-pay for his disability on 4 Aug. 1785. He was 34 years old in 1787. His pension was continued at the rate of £40 per annum on 26 Oct. 1787.

Lard, Samuel. N.J. —. His widow, Rachel Lard, was pensioned in Cape May County on 26 Feb. 1867 at the rate of $100 per annum.

Larimore, James. N.C. —. He applied in Stokes County in 1807. He had lived in Guilford County. He served in the militia under Gen. Ashe in 1779 and was wounded in right arm which broke the bone and in his right side at the battle of Briar Creek, Ga. He served under Capt. James Shepard and Col. Archibald Little. James Stewart and John Dunlap who served with him attested to his service. He also lived in Rowan County. He was on the 1813 pension list. He also appeared as James Larremore.

Larimore, Robert. S.C. —. He entered the service before he was 16 years old. He was at Wambaw Bridge. His claim for a lost horse, saddle, bridle, halter and pistols was rejected in 1825. He served under Jonah Clarke, Capt. John Mozele, and Capt. William Alston. He sought a pension 14 Nov. 1826. He received his annuity as late as 1837 in Horry District. He also appeared as Robert Lourimore and Robert Lowrimore.

Larison, Jacob. Pa. —. His widow, Joanna Larison, was awarded a $40 gratuity in Lycoming County 28 Mar 1836. He also appeared as Jacob Larrison.

Larkin, James. Pa. Sgt. He applied in Somerset County on 15 July 1814. He served in the 4th Pa. Regiment in the Light Dragoons under Col. Stephen Moylan. In Jan. 1782 he was severely wounded in his left thigh near Bacon's Bridge in South Carolina. Felix Duffel and Thomas Littler were soldiers with him.

Larned, —. —. —. His son, Salem Larned, had his application for a pension rejected by Congress on 23 Mar. 1860 because he had furnished no proof of verification of service and no date of his father's death.

Larned, Lyls. Mass. —. He served in the 4th Regiment.

Laroach, Benvil. R.I. Sgt. He lost the use of his left arm upon falling from a sleigh in Jan. 1783 when he was in public service after clothing for the troops from Saratoga to New Windsor. He served under Col. Jeremiah Olney. He was aged 39 when he applied 29 Dec. 1785. He died 24 Dec. 1786 in Providence Co., R.I.

Larrabee, Benjamin. Mass. Pvt. He served in the 5th Regiment and was from Danvers. His widow, Ann Larrabee, was paid $50.

Larrance, Hugh. Pa. —. He was granted relief in Montgomery County.

Lash, John. Mass. —. He wrote Henry Knox on 15 Aug. 1790 inquiring about being placed on the pension roll. Secretary of War Knox told him only Congress could place his name of the roll. He instructed Lash to secure certificates from a surgeon and his commanding officer verifying his disability. He did not appear on any roll.

Lashe, Andrew. Pa. —.He received a $40 gratuity and a $40 annuity in Perry County 16 June 1836. He died 12 Apr. 1849.

Lashley, George. Md. Pvt. He was pensioned in Cecil County 12 Mar. 1836 at the half-pay of a private. His arrearage of $20.44 was paid to Granville S. Townsend for the heirs, Mary Sproul and Nancy Lashly, on 27 May 1836. He also appeared as George Lashly.

Laskey, Andrew. —. —. Congress rejected his petition because there was no evidence in the file on 4 Apr. 1840.

Laskum, John. Pa. Pvt. He was in Philadelphia County 13 Apr. 1786. He served in the 5th Pa. Regiment.

He was disabled to some degree by loss of his toes due to frost bite in the service. He was dead by 26 Aug. 1802. He also appeared as John Lauscum.

Laswell, —. Va. —. Andrew Laswell was granted assistance while he was away in the service in Loudoun County 14 Dec. 1778.

Latham, Christopher. Conn. Pvt. He served in the militia in the 1ˢᵗ Company of the 8ᵗʰ Regiment. In opposing the British troops under Gen. Arnold who landed at New London, he was wounded by a musket ball in his left arm on 6 Sep. 1781 at Fort Griswold. He served under Capt. William Latham in the Artillery. He was pensioned at Groton, Conn. on 28 Sep. 1788 at the age of 24 years. He was on the 1813 pension list.

Latham, John. Va. —. He served in the militia a short time before the surrender of Cornwallis under Capt. Ballard. He was present at Yorktown and guarded the prisoners. He was discharged at Winchester, Va. after three months. In 1782 he enlisted for two years under Capt. Fitzpatrick, Capt. Johnson, and Col. Haws. He was from Stafford Co., Va. Congress granted him a pension for six months of service on 5 Mar. 1840.

Latham, John. S.C. —. He was at the fall of Charleston and the battle of Bluford's. He was wounded in the head while out on a scouting party. He was from Lancaster District and was pensioned 30 Nov. 1824. He died 12 Oct. 1831. His executrix, Margaret Latham, sought his arrearage 17 Dec. 1831. He also appeared as John Lethem.

Latham, Jonathan. Conn. Pvt. He served in the 2ⁿᵈ Company of the 8ᵗʰ Regiment of militia. In opposing the British troops who landed at New London under Gen. Arnold 6 Sep. 1781, he was wounded in the head and body at Fort Griswold. He served under Capt. William Latham in the Artillery. Amos Prentice, Surgeon, attended him. He was pensioned 26 Sep. 1788. He was 44 years old and resided in Groton, Conn. He died in 1811.

Latham, Robert. S.C. —. He served under Col. William Bratton. He was pensioned 30 Nov. 1827. He received his annuity as late as 1829.

Latham, William. Conn. Capt. He served in the militia in opposing the British troops who landed at New London under Gen. Arnold 6 Sept. 1781. He was wounded in the thigh and hip by a bayonet at Fort Griswold. He was pensioned at Groton 26 Sep. 1788. He was 46 years old.

Lathrop, Allen. Conn. Capt. He entered the service in May 1775 under Capt. Baldwin and Col. G. Van Schaick. He was at Montreal under Capt. Roswell Beebe. He was at Bennington and Saratoga in the militia. He served from 1776 or 1777 under Col. Samuel Elmore until the regiment was dissolved, and he became supernumerary. His widow was Abigail Allen. Henrietta Barnes petitioned for the representatives 19 Jan. 1836. Congress rejected the claim for relief 23 June 1840.

Lathrop, Samuel. —. Pvt. He served in Durkee's Regiment. He was pensioned at the rate of $5 per month from 22 Sep. 1807. He was pensioned 25 Jan. 1809 in Grafton Co., N.H. He was on the 1813 pension list.

Latour, John C. —. —. His application was rejected 9 Jan. 1797.

Latta, John. S.C. —. He was wounded in his left arm 4 May 1779 in battle at Tulefinny. He was awarded an annuity 16 Mar. 1785. He was from Chester District.

Lattimore, —. Pa. —. His widow, Mary Ann Lattimore, was granted relief 21 June 1839. She died in Erie County 4 June 1841.

Lattimore, Arthur. S.C. —. There was one child in 1791.

Lattimore, George. S.C. —. He was granted an annuity 22 Nov. 1783.

Laudon, Archiblad. Pa. —. He was awarded a $40 gratuity and a $40 annuity in Cumberland County

28 Mar. 1836. He was dead by July 1842.

Lauer, Philip. Pa. Sgt. He served in Proctor's Artillery. He was wounded at the battle of Brandywine at Shadsford on 11 Sep. 1777. He was wounded in his head by a musket ball which remained lodged therein. He lived in Philadelphia, Pa. in 1794. He was granted one-fourth of a pension 20 Apr. 1796.

Laughery, —. Pa. —. His widow, Margaret Laughery, was awarded a $40 gratuity and a $40 annuity in Armstrong County 27 Mar. 1837. She was 69 years old in 1840.

Laughinghouse, John. N.C. —. He was wounded in his groin and left arm in the war. He died in Aug. 1831. His children were Joseph Laughinghouse, Edward Laughinghouse, Mary Ann Laughinghouse, and Elizabeth Laughinghouse. They were in Beaufort Co. in Nov. 1845. He was from Pitt Co., N.C.

Laughinghouse, Thomas. N.C. —. He was at Germantown. He was from Pitt Co., N.C. His wife was dead by Nov. 1845 in Beaufort Co., N.C.

Laughman, Nicholas. Pa. Pvt. He was in Montgomery County on 28 Mar.1786. He served in the Philadelphia County militia in the 2nd Company of the 6th Battalion and was wounded in the leg in an engagement with the British troops on 16 Sep. 1777 near White Horse Tavern in Chester County. He died 23 Aug. 1788.

Lauman, Philip. Pa. —. He was awarded a $40 gratuity and a $40 annuity in Beaver Co., Pa. 3 Apr. 1829.

Laurence, Joseph. Va. —. His wife was granted 20 shillings support in Henry Co., Va. 21 Oct. 1777 while he was away in the service.

Laurens, John. S.C. Col. He was killed in the service in a skirmish on the Combahee 27 Aug. 1782. His orphan daughter, Frances Eleanor Laurens, sought his seven years' half-pay in 1791. She married Francis Henderson, and they sought additional compensation 3 Apr. 1818.

Laurentz, Vandel. Md. Pvt. He served in the German Regiment under Capt. Philip Graybill, Capt. Christopher Meyers, Col. Honsegger, and Col. Weltner to 20 July 1779. He fought at Trenton, Princeton, Brandywine, Germantown, and Monmouth. His widow, Ann Laurentz, was pensioned at the rate of half-pay of a private in Baltimore 24 Mar. 1838. His daughter, Christina Graham, aged 72, was granted a pension by Congress 19 Mar. 1846. He also appeared as Wendel Laurentz.

Lauther, James. Pa. —. He served three tours in the militia. He was awarded a $40 gratuity and a $40 annuity in Franklin Co., Pa. 3 Mar. 1825. He died in 1826.

Lavarnway, Tousant. Canada. Pvt. He served under his father, Capt. Francis Lavarnway, and Col. James Livingston from 1 Nov. 1775 for two weeks. He was taken prisoner at Montreal along with Ethan Allen but escaped. He was appointed conductor of teams with the American Army to Quebec and served until the retreat. He returned home and tended the crops while his father was a prisoner. His claim for a pension under the act of 1832 was denied since he was a wagoner and not a soldier. He died 15 Mar. 1845. He had no widow. His children sought relief in 1851. They renewed their claim 7 Feb. 1856. They proved he served a half month as a private and eight months as a teamster or conductor of a team. The children were granted relief 16 Jan. 1857 and on 19 Mar. 1860.

Lavenberg, Frederick. Pa. —. He was awarded a $40 gratuity and a $40 annuity in Columbia Co., Pa. 22 Dec. 1834.

Lavender, Hugh. S.C. —. He was paid £14.3.1 plus interest for two horses lost in the war on 9 Dec. 1816.

Law, William. Md. Pvt. He was pensioned at the rate of half-pay of a private 27 Jan. 1816.

Lawley, John. Mass. Pvt. He served in the 3rd Regiment under Capt. Joseph Williams and Col. John Greaton. He was worn out by old age. He was pensioned 1 Sep. 1782. He was 57 years old in 1786. He was resided in Harvard, Mass. in 1788.

Lawrence, —. Pa. —. His widow, Eve Lawrence, was pensioned 2 Apr. 1822.

Lawrence, Abraham. N.H. Pvt. He entered the service at Prospect near Charleston under Capt. Hervey for eight months. He enlisted in Capt. Chase's Company in Col. Reed's Regiment and served in the expedition up the Lakes. He enlisted a third time a year later for a tour of three years under Capt. William Ellis and Col. Scammel. He lost his clothing at Ticonderoga on the retreat. He was at Stillwater at the reduction of Burgoyne where he was slightly wounded. He was from Winchester. On 29 Aug. 1779 he was wounded at New Town on 29 Aug. 1779. He served in the 3rd N.H. Regiment. His eyesight was impaired, and he had an ulcer in his leg. He died at Bridgeport, Vt. 13 Nov. 1837 aged 85. His application for a pension was pending at that time due to a question about the length of his service. Albert G. Whittemore, his administrator, filed a claim but was accidentally killed. On 7 Feb. 1867 his daughter, Lois Clark, submitted a memorial to Congress. She was 84. The bill failed and, although it was reintroduced in 1869, She was dead. His grand-daughter sought relief, but Congress ruled that she was ineligible on 14 Jan. 1871.

Lawrence, Daniel. Mass. —. He served in the 2nd Regiment and was from Hanover. He was paid $20.

Lawrence, Ebenezer. Mass. —. He was pensioned 7 Mar. 1805 at the rate of $90 per annum for five years on account of his son.

Lawrence, Elihu. Mass. Matross. He served in Crane's Artillery and was from Medfield. His widow, Tamar Lawrence, was paid $50.

Lawrence, Henry. S.C. Legionnaire. He served aboard the frigate *South Carolina* under Commodore Gillon. His administrator sought his payment 28 Feb. 1808.

Lawrence, John. Va. —. His wife, Mary Lawrence, was granted £25 support in Henry Co., Va. 15 Feb. 1779 while he was absent in the service.

Lawrence, Josiah. Mass. —. He served in the 8th Regiment and was from Pittsfield. He was paid $50.

Lawrence, Thomas. Mass. Fife Major. He served in the 8th Regiment and was from Pepperell. His widow, Anna Lawrence, was paid $50.

Lawrence, William. N.Y. —. He served under Col. Dubois. His family was granted assistance 27 Apr. 1779.

Lawson, —. S.C. —. His widow was Elizabeth Lawson. There were three children in 1791.

Lawson, —. Va. —. He and his brother were in Continental service. Their father, George Lawson, was furnished 4 barrels of corn and 300 pounds of pork in Charlotte Co., Va. on 6 Nov. 1780 and £1100 provisions on 5 Feb. 1781. His father had a family of six in 1780.

Lawson, Hugh. Ga. Capt. He served under Col. Twiggs in the militia. He was wounded in the right shoulder by musket ball in 1780 at Augusta. He died 20 Feb. 1802.

Lawson, John. S.C. Pilot. He was a pilot for Count d'Estaing's fleet and was taken prisoner. His wife, Mary Lawson, was awarded a gratuity in Apr. 1780.

Lawton, George. R.I. Pvt. He lost his left foot and was wounded in the wrist and hand by a cannon shot from a British ship while on duty at Fogland Ferry 10 Jan. 1777. He served under Col. John Cooke. He applied 12 Jan 1786 at the age of 25. He died 24 Dec. 1786.

Lawyer, Peter. Pa. —. He applied in Cumberland County on 13 Mar. 1813. His 19 year old son was in the U.S. Army. He also appeared as Peter Layer. He was dead by July 1837.

Lay, Lea. Conn. Capt. He was granted one-sixth of a pension 20 Apr. 1796. He was on the 1813 pension list. He died 13 Feb. 1813.

Layfield, Timothy. Del. Pvt. 1783. He was wounded in the left leg by a musket ball at the battle of Camden in South Carolina on 25 Apr. 1781. He served under Col. John Hazlet and David Hall. He was aged 35 in 1783 and lived in Sussex County. He was on the 1791 pension list.

Layman, William. Md. Lt. He was pensioned at the rate of half-pay of a lieutenant 27 Jan. 1816. His executor, Francis Valendar, was paid the amount due him at the time of his death on 12 Feb. 1842.

Layton, Robert. Va. Capt. He was pensioned in 1833 for eight months of service as a captain and sixteen months as a lieutenant. Virginia allowed him 4,000 acres of bounty land. Congress granted his children or their heirs a pension from 4 Mar. 1835 to the time of his death 8 Mar. 1838 by special act 26 May 1842.

Laytor, John. Pa. Pvt. He also appeared as John Later. He was on the 1789 pension list.

Lazier, John. Pa. —. He applied 7 Apr. 1823.

Leabrooks, Moses. Pa. —. He was granted relief in Adams County 10 Apr. 1835.

Leach, —. Pa. —. Jane Leach of Westmoreland County received relief.

Leach, Andrew. Va. Pvt. He was wounded at Germantown. He was on the 1785 pension roll. He was listed as dead in Orange Co., Va. in 1786.

Leach, James. Pa. —. He died 29 Aug. 1819.

Lead, Adam. Pa. —. He was awarded a $40 gratuity in Lancaster Co., Pa. 11 Mar. 1833.

Leader, —. Pa. —. His widow, Susanna Leader, was granted a $40 annuity in York County in Apr. 1845 for his Revolutionary service.

Leader, Frederick. Pa. —. He was awarded a $40 gratuity and a $40 annuity in York Co., Pa. 7 Apr. 1830. He died 28 Apr. 1844. He also appeared as Frederick Leeder.

Leagh, Richard. Va. —. He was on the 1785 pension list.

League, Bartholomew. Va. —. His wife, Ann League, was granted support while he was away in the service in Amelia Co., Va. 24 July 1777.

League, James. Va. —. His wife, Judith League, and children were granted support for necessaries while he was away in the service in Amelia Co., Va. 25 Mar. 1779, 28 Oct. 1779, 23 Nov. 1780, and 23 May 1782. Compare the entry under James Legg.

Leake, Henry. Md. Sgt. He was pensioned at the rate of half-pay of a sergeant in Montgomery County on 27 Jan. 1817. His arrearage of $10 was paid to James Brown in Montgomery County on 16 Feb. 1820. He also appeared as Henry Leeke.

Leaman, Henry. Pa. —. He applied 15 Feb. 1813. He enlisted in Capt. Lewis Farmer's Rifle Company under Col. Miles in Apr. 1776 for eighteen months. He then enlisted in Capt. John Cove's Company under Col. Walter Stewart. He strained himself lifting baggage on the wagons and got a rupture. He signed in German.

Leard, John. S.C. —. He served under Capt. Anderson, Capt. William McGaw, Capt. John McGaw, Patterson, Lt. James Noble, and Lt. William McClelland. He was in the Florida Expedition, the Midway Expedition, Ninety Six, and Kettle Creek. James Shank and George McFarlin served with him. He was from Abbeville District and was pensioned 4 Dec. 1828. He was about 76 years old. He received his annuity as late as 1834 and died 8 Nov. 1843. His widow, Mary Laird, was paid his arrearage. He also appeared as John Laird.

Leard, Samuel. S.C. Pvt. He served under Capt. John Anderson. He was wounded in his head on 18 Nov. 1775 at his post as a sentinel at Ninety Six. He was from Abbeville in 1802. His wife was dead, and his children had left him. He also appeared as Samuel Laird.

Learned, Benjamin. Mass. —. He served in the 3rd Regiment and was from Watertown. He was paid $20.

Learned, Ebenezer. Mass. Col. He was in the 3rd Regiment. He was ruptured in his groin by falling on a stake at Dorchester Heights in the night in March 1776. He resided in Oxford, Mass. in 1792 and 1794. He was appointed Brigadier General 24 Mar. 1778. He was granted one-fourth of a pension 20 Apr. 1796. He died 1 Apr. 1801.

Learned, Sylvanus. Mass. —. He was in the 4th Regiment. He was paid $20.

Leary, Dennis. Del. Pvt. He was ruptured in consequence of a wound he received in his groin. He applied in 1783. He was on the 1791 pension list.

Leary, Edward. Md. Pvt. He was pensioned 5 July 1812. He was on the 1813 pension list. He lived in Washington Co., Md.

Leary, William. Pa. Pvt. He was in Philadelphia County on 9 May 1787. He was in the 11th Pa. Regiment first under Col. Thomas Hartley and later under Col. Adam Hubley and received sundry wounds in his hand by a sword, in his right leg with a bayonet, and had his jaw bone broken by a bayonet at Paoli in Sep. 1777. He was 24 years old.

Leasure, Abraham. Pa. —. He was 77 years old in 1840. He was granted a $40 gratuity and a $40 annuity in Butler County 13 Apr. 1841.

Leather, John. Md. Sgt. He was pensioned at the rate of half-pay of a sergeant in Frederick County 27 Jan. 1816.

Leatherman, Michael. Pa. —. He was awarded a $40 gratuity in Philadelphia Co., Pa. 6 Apr. 1830.

L'Eaumont, Viscompte. —. —. He was a French officer and was wounded at the siege of Savannah. He was not entitled to a pension from the U.S. He was rejected 22 Mar. 1838.

Leaver, William. Mass. Pvt. He resided in Hampshire Co., Mass. He also appeared as William Laver. He was pensioned 22 Dec. 1812.

Leavitt, Nathaniel. N.H. Corp. He served under Col. James Reed. He was wounded by a musket ball which entered his breast on 17 June 1775 at Bunker Hill. He lived in Hampton, N.H. in 1794. He was in the militia. He was granted half a pension 20 Apr. 1796. He was on the 1813 pension list.

LeBert, John. Mass. Pvt. He served in the 7th Regiment under Col. John Brooks. He was disabled by an ulcerated leg. He was 37 years old in 1792. He was pensioned 31 Dec. 1782.

Lebo, Henry. Pa. —. He was awarded a $40 gratuity in Lycoming Co., Pa. 17 Feb. 1817. His widow, Sarah Lebo, was awarded a gratuity of $40 on 27 Mar. [?]1830. She died 9 July 1852.

Lebold, —. Pa. —. His widow, Christina Lebold, was granted a $40 gratuity and a $40 annuity in Montgomery County 28 Mar. 1836.

LeBosquet, John. Mass. Fifer. He served in the 8th Regiment and was from Medford. He was paid $50.

Ledbetter, —. Ga. —. Neomia Ledbetter and her five children were furnished assistance 25 Jan. 1782.

Ledyard, Isaac. —. Surgeon. He served as hospital surgeon, surgeon apothecary, assistant deputy directory, and assistant purveyor. He became assistant purveyor of the hospital department 7 Oct. 1780. He received his five years' full pay in commutation 2 Mar. 1833.

Ledyard, John. Conn. Pvt. He served in the 3rd Regiment. He was wounded on the back side of his leg and foot while on duty at West Point by the fall of a stick of timber. He had a rupture at West Point on 20 Nov. 1778 and had to wear a truss thereafter. He resided at Hartford, Conn. in 1796.

He enlisted 26 May 1777 for the war. He deserted 2 Sep. 1777, rejoined in Feb. 1778, and was discharged 11 Apr. 1781. He was granted one-third of a pension 20 Apr. 1796. He died in 1808. He was on the 1813 pension list.

Lee, —. S.C. —. His widow was Unity Lee. There was one child in 1791.

Lee, Drury. S.C. —. He was killed near Savannah in 1782. He had a thirteen year old child living. His widow was Susannah Brown from Georgetown District in 1793.

Lee, Dudley. Md. Pvt. He was pensioned at the rate of half-pay of a private 3 Jan. 1812. His widow, Margaret Lee, was pensioned at the same rate 21 Mar. 1838.

Lee, Elisha. Conn. Capt. He served in Durkee's Regiment under Simeon Thayer, Major Commandant. He was disabled at Mud Island by being wounded in the shoulder. He was pensioned 18 Feb. 1787 as a resident of Lyme, Conn. He was on the 1813 pension list. He died 15 Oct. 1815 in New London Co., Conn.

Lee, James. Pa. Pvt. He was in Philadelphia County on 30 Sep. 1785. He served in the 7th Pa. Regiment and was transferred to the Invalids. He was wounded at Paoli. He was 65 years old.

Lee, John. N.J. Pvt. He served in 2nd Regiment and lost his left leg. He was 41 years old. He was on the 1791 pension roll at the rate of $40 per annum. He died 19 Jan. 1792.

Lee, John. N.Y. Pvt. He served in Capt. McKown's Company under Col. Warner. He was killed 11 July 1780. His widow, Marvel Lee, received his seven years' half-pay pension. She was on the roll in 1783.

Lee, John. Pa. —. He also appeared as John Lies and John Leese.

Lee, John. S.C. —. He sought a pension in Dec. 1823.

Lee, Josiah. Mass. —. He served in the 5th Regiment and was from Manchester. He was paid $50.

Lee, Lay. Conn. Capt. He served in the 1st Regiment Conn. State Troops. He was wounded in his head by a broad sword which cut through his skull in 1780 at Greenwich. He lived in Lyme, Conn. in 1794.

Lee, Lewis. S.C. —. There was one child in 1791.

Lee, Parker. Md. Lt. His widow, Mary Lee, was pensioned at the rate of half-pay of a lieutenant 5 Mar. 1850. He served in the 4th Md. Regiment.

Lee, Peter. —. —. His application was rejected 9 Jan. 1797.

Lee, Richard. Pa. —. He was granted relief in Northampton County 31 Mar. 1836. His name has been incorrectly rendered as Richard See.

Lee, Richeson. Va. —. His mother, Sarah Lee, and her three children were granted £75 support in Middlesex Co., Va. on 28 June 1779 while he was away in Continental service.

Lee, Samuel. Mass. Pvt. He served in the 9th Regiment and was from Barre. He was paid $50.

Lee, Samuel. Pa. Pvt. He was on the 1813 pension list.

Lee, Simon. S.C. Capt. He was a native of America. He first served as an ensign under Capt. Coffield and Col. Abraham Shepherd. At Eutaw he was shot through one leg and shoulder. He had a large family. Thomas Batteman saw him shot and taken captive at Eutaw. He was made a prisoner at the defeat of Maj. Gen. John Ashe's defeat at Briar Creek in Georgia on 3 Mar. 1779 and was held for 12 months and 14 days. Augustine Wilson served with him. Jesse Lee knew he served under Col. Shepherd. He was from Williamsburg District when he was pensioned 19 Dec. 1809. His son, Arthur Bryan Lee, collected his pension in 1811. He was 66 years old in 1818. In 1822 at the age of 71 he sought an increase in his pension. He suffered from rheumatism. He died 4 Apr. 1829.

Lee, Solomon. Mass. —. He served in the 5th Regiment and was from Manchester. He was paid $50.

Leech, Archibald. Pa. —. He served under Capt. Joseph Irwin and Capt. James Carrahan in Col. Stewart's Regiment for about two years. He was a resident of Westmoreland County in 1814.

Leech, William. Conn. Pvt. He served under Col. S. B. Webb. He was wounded in one of his legs by the rolling of a cannon ball which caused a carious ulcer in Oct. 1778 at Newport, R.I. He resided in Litchfield, Conn. in 1794. He enlisted 28 Apr. 1777 and continued to the end of the war. He also lived in Chenango Co., N.Y. He was on the 1813 pension list in Connecticut.

Leeder, George. Pa. —. He was awarded a $40 gratuity and a $40 annuity in Montgomery Co., Pa. 14 Jan. 1835.

Leeds, —. Va. Pvt. His widow, Elizabeth Leeds, was pensioned.

Leeds, Nathan. Mass. Corp. He served in Craft's Artillery and was from Dorchester. His widow, Elizabeth Leeds, was paid $50.

Leeds, William. Conn. 1st Lt. He served in the marines. He was badly wounded by a musket ball which entered his breast and shoulder and lodged in his shoulder blade in the winter of 1777 and 1778 aboard the armed brig *Resistance* under Capt. Chew in an engagement with a British letter of marque. Capt. Chew was killed, and the command devolved upon him. He lived in New London, Conn. in 1794. He entered on board on 5 July 1777 and was wounded 4 Mar. 1778. He was granted half a pension 20 Apr. 1796. He died in 1804.

Leeland, Isaac. N.H. Pvt. He was a soldier in Capt. Blodget's Company in Col. Nathan Hale's Regiment in 1777. He was killed in Sept. 1777. He left no estate. His widow and her second husband, Joel and Mary Russell of Rindge, Cheshire County, sought his back pay and clothing on 30 May 1785. He was due £2,042.23 9/10 plus interest. It was to be paid to Elijah Grout, his administrator *de bonis non*, on 26 Apr. 1800.

Lees, James. Pa. Capt. He was in the artillery. He took all of his servants and apprentices with him into service. He was a resident of Philadelphia County.

Lefey, Shadrack. Va. —. He enlisted in Feb. 1776 under Capt. A. Mead and Col. Spotswood. He also served under Capt. Taylor and Col. Feebacker. He was discharged at Valley Forge. His third tour was in 1777 under Capt. Watts and Col. Bland to 1780. He was also under Capt. G. Fauntleroy and Col. Lee to 1781. He was at Brandywine, Germantown, Mud Island Fort, Red Bank, Hanging Rock, Guilford, Savannah, and Charleston. He was 68 years old and from Lincoln County, N.C. on 23 Oct. 1820.

Leftwich, Joel. Va. —. He enlisted in Bedford County in 1776-77 under Capt. Alexander Cummings and served to 1 Aug. 1779. He was inoculated for smallpox at Baltimore. He joined the army at Middlebrook, N.J. in the 1st Regiment under Gen. Muhlenburg. In May 1780 he entered as a substitute for Joseph Dickenson and was appointed orderly sergeant. He was a substitute for John Hook in the winter of 1781. He was at Guilford where he sprained his ankle. He was a baggage guard at Brandywine and was in the battle of Germantown. He was at Gates' defeat and was then attached to Capt. Daniel. In Feb. 1781 he was a substitute for John Hook, a merchant from Bedford County. He served under Capt. Bowan Price and Col. Charles Lynch.. He later served in the War of 1812. In 1832 he applied from Campbell Co., Va. He sought an additional pension at the rank of ensign from Congress on 25 Apr. 1840. Congress declined since he served but one day at that rank. He resided at Lynchburg was nearly 79 years old.

Legg, David. Mass. Sgt. He served in the 2nd Regiment and was from Mendon. He was paid $50.

Legg, James. Va. —. His wife was granted assistance in Amelia County 28 Oct. 1779.

L'Eglisle, Dominique. —. —. He was pensioned by the Continental Congress act of 8 Aug. 1782.

LeGrande, —. Va. —. He served in the state cavalry. His widow Pauline LeGrande died 5 Feb. 1845.

She had no children. Henry Carrington was the executor of Pauline LeGrande. Congress ruled that he had no right to her arrears.

Legrande, Claudius. Md. —. His arrearage of $31.67 was paid to Charles Croxall 9 Mar. 1832.

Leher, Peter. Me. —. He died 3 Nov. 1822. His widow was Catherine Leher from Washington. She was paid $50 under the resolve of 1836.

Lehman, —. Pa. —. His widow, Rosannah Lehman, was awarded a $40 gratuity and a $40 annuity in York Co., Pa. 20 Mar. 1834. She died 17 Dec. 1840.

Lehman, Anthony. —. —. He married 28 July 1778 and died 24 Apr. 1827. Congress granted his widow, Catharine Lehman, a pension 8 Mar. 1842. Her brother was John Arnick and her son-in-law was Henry Cramer.

Lehman, George. Pa. —. He was pensioned.

Lehman, Henry. Pa. —. He was pensioned.

Lehman, John. Pa. —. He was awarded a $40 gratuity and a $40 annuity in Lancaster County on 24 Mar. 1812. He also appeared as John Lemon.

Lehman, John. Pa. —. He was awarded a $40 gratuity and a $40 annuity in Dauphin Co., Pa. 20 Feb. 1833. He was 84 years old in 1840. He died 8 Mar. 1844.

LeHoux, Charles. S.C. —. He was a Frenchman who came to America in 1771. He was a sea captain. The English seized his vessel. He was at the last siege of Charleston and was taken prisoner. He was a resident of Charleston in 1787.

Leibley, Andrew. Pa. —. He was awarded a $40 gratuity and a $40 annuity in Lancaster County 1 Apr. 1836.

Leiby, John. Pa. Pvt. He was in Northampton County on 22 June 1786. He was in the Northampton County militia. He served under Capt. John Krum and Col. Jacob Stroud. At the house of Isaac Summong in North Wales Township he was wounded in 27 parts of his body in 1778. He was cut in each hand by a cutlass and in one of his ankles. He was 40 years old. He was on the 1813 pension list.

Leider, George. Pa. —. He was pensioned in Montgomery County 14 Jan. 1835.

Leigh, Richard. Va. —. He was being pensioned 9 Apr. 1783. He was disabled.

Leighton, —. Mass. —. His widow, Hannah Leighton, of Acton was paid $50 per annum.

Leininger, —. Pa. —. His widow, Christina Leininger, was awarded a $40 annuity 12 Jan. 1836. She died 30 July 1841.

Leininger, Peter. Pa. —. He was awarded a $40 gratuity and a $40 annuity in Berks Co., Pa. 18 Feb. 1834. He was paid to 11 Sep. 1835.

Leinscott, Theodore. Mass. —. He served in the 1st Regiment and was from Sanford. He was paid $20.

Leisicu, Abraham. Pa. —. He was granted relief in Butler County 21 June 1839.

Leister, William. Va. —. His wife, Mary Leister, was allowed £10 support in Bedford Co., Va. on 9 May 1778, £40 on 28 June 1779, and 2 barrels of corn and 100 pounds of pork on 28 Feb. 1780.

Leitch, Andrew. Va. Maj. He served in the 1st Virginia Continental Regiment. He was killed in the service on 15 Sep. 1776 at Harlem Plains. His children sought half-pay of a major for seven years from Sep. 1776 in 1791. His seven years' half-pay was to be paid to the legal representative of his widow, Margaret Leitch, 30 June 1834. The heirs were allowed interest 18 Jan. 1836. He was captain of the Prince William County Minutemen 23 Feb. 1776. He also appeared as Andrew Leach. Anthony Addison, administrator of Margaret Leitch, late of the District of Columbia, in behalf of her only heir, Sarah Addison, sought the interest on the retroactive portion of her pension, but Congress declined to do so. Sarah Addison's son was James Leitch Addison. Stephen Crowther, the son of the daughter Judith Leitch, was entitled to seven years' half-pay. Andrew Leitch's son, James F. Leitch, was born a few months after his death. Congress rejected him as a legal child and reported against any relief in 1842.

Leitch, John. Pa. Pvt. His widow, Jean Leitch, was in Westmoreland County on 10 Dec. 1792. He was in Capt. James Leech's Company of the Westmoreland County militia and was killed by the Indians in the attack on Capt. James Leech's house 26 Feb. 1779. He left eight small children. He also appeared as John Leach and John Leech.

Leitheiser, —. Pa. —. His widow, Elizabeth Leitheiser was awarded a $40 gratuity and a $40 annuity in Berks County 1 Apr. 1837. She died 27 Jan. 1860,

Leitheiser, Hartman. Pa. —. He was awarded a $78 gratuity and a $78 annuity in Berks County on 2 Apr. 1822. He died 11 Feb. 1829.

Lembert, —. Pa. —. His widow, Margaret Lembert, was awarded a $40 gratuity and a $40 annuity in Lancaster County in 1837.

Lemington, Timothy. Pa. Sgt. He was in Cumberland County on 23 Feb. 1786. He was in the 4th Battalion of the Northumberland Company militia under Col. James Murray in Capt. Taggart's Company and received 16 principal wounds in his head, body, and arms in battle with the enemy on 11 Dec. 1777 at Gulph Mill. He was 38 years old. He had a wife and eight children in 1788. He was on the 1813 pension list. He died 10 June 1823 in Armstrong County. He also appeared as Timothy Lemmonton. His widow, Mary Lemmonton, was awarded a $40 gratuity and a $40 in Armstrong Co., Pa. 17 Feb. 1827. She died 27 July 1827.

Lemmon, George. Pa. —. He was granted relief in Dauphin County 20 Mar. 1838.

Lemmon, John. Md. & Pa. —. He enlisted in the Maryland Line in 1775. He subsequently served in the Cumberland County Battalion of the Flying Camp. Later he served in the marines. He was blind in 1793. He was 76 years of age in 1821. He was from Armstrong County.

Lemmon, William. Pa. —. He was awarded a $40 gratuity and a $40 annuity in Steuben Co., N.Y. 19 Jan. 1827.

Lemon, George. Conn. —. He served in Capt. Joseph Birdsey's Company in Col. Samuel Whitney's Regiment. He was wounded in the lower part of his body on the Danbury Expedition in Apr. 1776. He was pensioned 3 Jan. 1777 in Stratford, Conn.

Lemon, John. Pa. —. He applied in Mifflin County on 9 Sep. 1816. He enlisted in 1776 in Capt. Harris's Company under Col. Cook in the 12th Pa. Regiment. He served under sundry captains of whom the last was Boush in the 9th Regiment. He was put in the hospital in Carlisle and was discharged in the fall of 1781. He served five years and four months. He was wounded at Monmouth in the head and left leg by a bayonet. His stepfather was Henry Leaf. He was 15 or 16 when the war began.

Lemon, John. Pa. —. He was from Montgomery County.

Lemon, John. Pa. —. He was granted assistance in Armstrong County 11 Apr. 1825.

Lemon, John. Va. Pvt. He was in Jefferson Co., Ky. 7 Dec. 1785. He was in Lt. Richard Clarke's Company under Col. Crockett from 9 Sept. 1779 to 8 Dec. 1781. From the latter date he was in the Illinois Regiment. Lt. R. Clarke and Major Commandant George Watts [?Walls] attested to his service. He lost an eye and suffered from other bodily disabilities. He lived at Clarksville, Ky. He was probably the John Lamon put on the pension roll on 29 Nov. 1788 at the rate of £5 per annum.

Lemon, William. Pa. —. He was granted relief in Steuben Co., N.Y. 1 Jan. 1827.l

Lemont, Thomas. Me. —. He died in Oct. 1777. His widow was Lucy Mallet from Wales, Maine. She was paid $50 under the resolve of 1836.

Lemote, George. Mass. —. He was from Hanover and was paid $20.

Lemptinck, John. N.Y. —. He was pensioned.

Lenchen, —. Pa. —. His widow as Rachel Lenchen.

Lendell, John. Mass. —. He served in the 5th Regiment and was from Manchester. His widow, Anna Lendell, was paid $50.

Lengle, —. Pa. —. His widow, Eve Lengle, was awarded a $40 gratuity in Schuylkill County in 1836.

Lenhart, Peter. Pa. —. He received a $40 gratuity and a $40 annuity in Perry County 3 Mar. 1837.

Lenhart, Philip. Pa. —. He was awarded a $40 gratuity and a $40 annuity in Cumberland Co., Pa. in Feb. 1834. He was 79 years old in 1840. He died 3 Apr. 1842.

Lenis, Jabez. —. Pvt. He served under Col. C. Burell for one year. He was wounded and beaten by the Indians when he was taken prisoner. He resided in Conn. in 1792.

Lenox, Charles. Pa. Pvt. He was on the 1813 pension list.

Lenox, Charles. Va. —. He was wounded in the knee while in Continental service. He was made a pensioner for life. He had been advanced £30 by Capt. Carr in Prince William County 4 Aug. 1779.

Lent, Hendrick. N.Y. Pvt. He served under Capt. Jonathan Hallet in the 2nd N.Y. Regiment and was slain 10 July 1778. His children, Arie Lent [?Anna Lent] and Mary Lent, received a half-pay pension.

Lent, James. N.Y. —. He enlisted for one year about 10 Apr. 1780 at Peekskill, Westchester Co., N.Y. and served under Capt. Bond, Capt. Jonathan Knapp, Col. Hughs, Maj. Kears, and Lt. Occoman and was discharged after a year. He served on Continental boats. In 1781 he again served under Col. Hughs, Maj Kears, and Lt. Occoman. He was pensioned in 1832 at the rate of $80 per annum. His pension was discontinued after two years because he was employed in boat service. Congress granted him a restoration of his pension on 24 Feb. 1836 from the time the Secretary of War discontinued it. He as 71 years old and was from Wysox, Bradford Co., Pa. in 1832.

Lentz, John. N.Y. —. His family was granted support during the war.

Leob, Casper. Pa. —. He was granted relief in Lebanon County 4 Jan. 1823.

Leonard, —. Va. —. He died in the service under the age of 21. His father, David Leonard, and mother were furnished 2 barrels of corn and 50 pounds of pork in Louisa Co., Va. on 12 Aug. 1782.

Leonard, —. Va. —. His wife, Sarah Leonard, was granted £6 support in Fauquier Co., Va. in Nov. 1776 while her husband was away in the service.

Leonard, Cuff. Mass. —. He served in the 7th Regiment and was from Raynham. He was paid $20.

Leonard, Ebenezer. Mass. Col. He was on the pension list of 1796.

Leonard, George. Pa. —. He was granted relief in Lancaster County in 1836. He was 82 years old in 1840. His widow, Catherine Leonard, received a $40 gratuity and a $40 annuity 7 Feb. 1856.

Leonard, Henry. Pa. —. He was pensioned 17 Aug. 1813.

Leonard, Henry. Va. —. He served in the militia. He lived in Washington Co., Va. and was pensioned 29 Oct. 1789.

Leonard, James. Md. Pvt. He was pensioned at the rate of half-pay of a private in Cecil County 7 Feb. 1817. He received a bounty land warrant for 50 acres as a donation 9 Mar. 1826.

Leonard, James. Pa. Pvt. He was on the 1813 pension list.

Leonard, James. Pa. —. He served one year and upwards in the rifle service. He was pensioned 19 Nov.

1831 and was from Warren Co., Ohio.

Leonard, Laughton. —. Capt. He was killed in the service. His widow, Mary Leonard, was granted an annuity 30 May 1785.

Leonard, Lot. N.J. Pvt. He served in the militia under Capt. Condict and guarded the coast between Elizabethtown and Amboy, N.J. for four months. He afterwards moved to Greene Co., Pa. In July 1777 he volunteered under Capt. Hurd against the Indians in scouting parties as a spy. He was elected captain. In May 1779 he was at Ross's Fort for five months. In 1780 he pursued the Indians to Wheeling. They had been murdering the settlers along Fish Creek. In 1781 he was unable to serve because he broke the cap of his knee while pursuing the Indians. In 1782 he was at Bell's, Jackson's, and Klein's Forts. In 1783 he was Seal's Fort for five months. He claimed 22½ months of service. Congress granted him a pension for twelve months of service 21 Mar. 1836.

Leonard, Patrick. Pa. —. He applied in Campbell Co., Ky. 4 Feb. 1817 and was in Hamilton Co., Ohio 1 June 1817. He was born in Ireland and came to America with Gen. Amherst. He continued in the British Army until the troubles began in Boston. He viewed the massacre and joined the American standard. He pursued the British in the retreat from Concord to Boston and Bunker Hill. He afterwards joined the 1ˢᵗ Pa. Regiment in Capt. Craig's Company under Col. Hand in Proctor's Artillery. He was in the battles of Bunker Hill, Long Island, Haarlem Heights, Brandywine, Germantown, Monmouth, and Stoney Point. He was in Capt. David Teigler's Company at the dreadful attack on the Block House near New York. He bore on his back Lt. Hammon who was badly wounded from the field. He was disbanded near the end of the war near Pittsburgh. He died 11 Aug. 1822.

Leonard, Robert. Pa. Pvt. He was pensioned at $40 per annum in 1797. He was in Botetourt Co., Va. on 6 Jan. 1798. He served as a soldier. He was granted relief in the amount of $40 and a pension of the same amount per annum on 5 Jan. 1798. He was in Greenbrier Co., Va., Rockbridge Co., Va. in 1802, Hardy Co., Va. in 1804, and Montgomery County in 1807. He also appeared as Robert Linnard. He transferred to Virginia in or by Sep. 1795. He was on the 1813 pension list.

Leonard, Samuel. N.J. Pvt. He served in the 3ʳᵈ N.J. Regiment. He lived in Morris Co., N.J. He was on the 1813 pension list.

Leonard, Samuel. Pa. —. He applied in Mifflin County on 1 Feb. 1813. He was in the 1ˢᵗ Pa. Regiment from 1776 to 1781 under Col. James Chambers in Capt. Michael Simpson's Company. Capt. David Davidson and Sgt. Benjamin Carson were in the service with him. He died 7 June 1817.

Lepley, Michael. Pa. Pvt. His widow, Mary Anne Lepley, was in Northumberland County 6 July 1790. He was in the Northumberland militia at Freeland's Fort under the command of Lt. Jacob Spence [or Speece]. On 26 Apr. 1779 he was out on escort when attacked by Indians. He was killed and scalped. He was 41 years old.

Lepley, Samuel. Pa. Sgt. He was on the 1791 pension roll. His name was on the 1813 pension list.

Leremon, —. S.C. —. His widow was Barbara Leremon. There were two children in 1791.

Lerhry, Johann Casper. N.Y. Pvt. He served under Col. Jacob Klock in the Montgomery County militia and was slain 10 July 1781. His widow received a half-pay pension. He also appeared as Johann Casper Lerhre.

Lescure, Abraham. Pa. —. His widow, Jane Lescure, received a $40 annuity in Armstrong County 28 Mar. 1854.

Lesene, Isaac. S.C. Cornet. He served under Col. Peter Horry. His widow, Judith Audebert, applied for his back pay from Georgetown District 16 Oct. 1793. She had two children.

Lesher, Benjamin. Pa. —. He was pensioned 27 Jan. 1837 in Armstrong County.

Lesley, John. Pa. Pvt. He was from Chester County. He was pensioned by the court of enquiry 27 Oct. 1815 and was in Virginia.

Lesley, Samuel. Pa. Sgt. He served under Capt. James Long in the 10th Pennsylvania Regiment under Col. Hartley. He was disabled by a rupture brought on fatigue at Brandywine. He was 56 years of age. He was wounded and received his half-pay pension 2 Sep. 1784. He was in Chester County in 1785. He was on the 1813 pension list but according to another record was dead by Mar. 1812.. He also appeared as Samuel Lessly.

Leslie, William. S.C. —. He was wounded in his right arm 13 Aug. 1776 by the Indians. He was granted an annuity 29 Mar. 1785.

Lessly, John. Pa. Sgt. He applied in Berkeley Co., Va. 6 Mar. 1816. He enlisted in Capt. McAllester's Company under Col. Thomas Hartley. He served three years. He also appeared as John Lesley.

Lester, Amos. Conn. Pvt. He served in the 2nd Company of the 8th Regiment of militia. He was wounded by a musket ball in his left breast at Fort Griswold on 6 Sep. 1781 in opposing the British under Gen. Arnold who had landed at New London. He was pensioned 26 Sep. 1788 at Groton, Conn. at the age of 61 years. He died in 1802.

Lesure, Gideon. Mass. Corp. He served in the 6th Regiment and was from Uxbridge. He was paid $20.

Letcher, James. S.C. —. He was killed in the service. His widow, Millicent Letcher, was granted an annuity 22 Apr. 1785.

Letford, Robert. Pa. Drummer. He was in Philadelphia County on 9 Jan. 1786. He served in the 1st Pa. Regiment. He was wounded in his right arm on 28 June 1778 at Monmouth, N. J. He was 23 years old. He also incorrectly appeared as Robert Setford.

Letson, Thomas. N.J. —. He was upwards of 92 years of age when he applied for a pension in Monmouth County 28 Dec. 1848.

Lett, —. Ga. —. Mrs. Lett of Burke County was granted assistance 15 Mar. 1782.

Letts, John. —. —. He and Jacob Slingerland called for a bill for the support of all Revolutionary soldiers by raising gratuities to full pensions on 9 May 1850. Congress declined to do so.

Letson, Thomas. N.J. —. He was pensioned in Monmouth Co. on 26 Jan. 1849 at the rate of $60 per annum.

Levacher de Van Brun, John. Md. Lt. He entered the service 10 Mar. 1777 and was furloughed 11 Dec. 1782. He sailed for Europe 4 Aug. 1782; the ship, *Favorite,* was lost at sea. Capt. Buchanan was from Baltimore. He had been promoted to ensign 10 Mar. 1777. He married 4 Sep. 1781. His widow, Ann Levacher de Van Brun, was granted a pension of £15 per annum on 12 Aug. 1789. She sought his commutation 2 July 1838. He had received bounty land from Maryland.

Levan, Isaac. Pa. —. He applied in North Carolina 20 July 1828. He enlisted at Philadelphia 3 Mar. 1775 in Capt. Lenly's Company in the Dutch Battalion under Maj. Dechart and Gen. Hays. Capt. Lenly discharged him on 3 Mar. 1778. His fellow soldiers were George Brieger, Henry Fleisher, John Messenger, Richard Stoner, Jacob Frey, and Conrad Litler. He reenlisted in the Pa. Line in Capt. Van Leer's Company. He had a third enlistment in the same unit. He was discharged 23 June 1783 by Maj. Barker for Gen. Baron Steuben.

Lever, Adam. Pa. Pvt. He applied in Washington County on 20 Apr. 1824. He enlisted in the spring of 1775 in Chester County in Benjamin Broanbacker's Company and fought at Bunker Hill, White

Plains, Long Island, and Brandywine. He was wounded three times. He also served in the 3rd Regiment of Horse. He had lived in Washington County the past twenty years. He was 72 years and 11 months old and was afflicted with rheumatism.

Leverett, Thomas. Ga. —. He served in 1779 and 1780 as a ranger guarding the frontier against the Indians and Tories. In 1780 he volunteered under Capt. John Clark, Col. Elijah Clark, and Col. Josiah Dunn for eighteen months. He was with Col. Samuel Alexander at the siege of Augusta. He was discharged in 1781. He was in the Georgia Continental Line. He married in Wilkes Co., Ga. 3 July 1789 Mary G. Griffin. He died 8 June 1834. His first wife was an aunt of Elizabeth Crawford who was 65 years of age in 1846. He received 250 acres of bounty land on 2 Feb. 1784. Congress allowed Mary Leverett a pension 20 June 1848.

Levering, Peter. Md. Corp. He was pensioned at the rate of half-pay of a corporal in Baltimore 24 Feb. 1823.

Levi, Judah. Va. Pvt. He lived in Fauquier County on 30 Jan. 1789 and was 28 years old. He served in Col. Buford's Battalion of the Southern Army for 18 months. He was made a prisoner at Col. Buford's defeat. He suffered from several wounds in the head and face and was wounded by a bayonet in his left thigh. He lost the sight in his left eye. Capt. Thomas Hard of the 6th Va. Regiment attested to his service. He was continued on the pension list at the rate of £15 per annum on 31 Jan. 1789 and on 5 June 1790. He was about 28 years old in 1789. He was on the 1813 pension list. He also appeared as Judah Levy.

Levie, Alexander. —. —. He sought a pension and his back pay, but Congress rejected his petition 24 Mar. 1818.

Levingston, Alexander. Va. —. His wife, Catherine Levingston, was granted financial support in Amelia Co., Va. 25 Mar. 1779. The widow Young was granted support for the soldier's children 23 Nov. 1780. He died in Continental service.

Levy, Abraham. Pa. Pvt. He was in Philadelphia County on 24 Sep. 1787. He served in the 4th Pa. Regiment under Col. Craig and was drafted into Capt. Rice's Company in the Artillery. He was wounded in the ankle at Valley Forge in 1781 by the overturning of a gun carriage. He continued lame thereafter. He also served in the 14th Virginia Regiment. He was 46 years old. He was dead by 27 Oct. 1801.

Levy, Judah. —. —. He was pensioned 3 Mar. 1809.

Levy, Michael. N.Y. Pvt. He served in the Montgomery County militia and died 6 Aug. 1777. His widow, Mary Elizabeth Levy, received a half-pay pension for seven years.

Lewalling, Jonathan. S.C. —. There were children in 1791.

Lewis, —. Mass. —. His widow, Mary Lewis, was paid $50.

Lewis, —. Pa. —. His widow, Sarah Lewis, was awarded a $40 annuity and a $40 gratuity in Fayette County 31 Mar. 1836.

Lewis, Abraham. Va. —. He served in the 2nd Virginia Regiment and was wounded. He was granted a pension of £8 per annum during his disability and relief in the same amount on 24 Nov. 1785.

Lewis, Ambrose. Va. Pvt. He was in Spotsylvania County on 9 May 1787 and was 26 years old when he was continued on the pension list at the rate of £8 per annum. He served in the 2nd Va. Regiment of militia and was wounded at Gen. Gates' defeat at Camden. He had a musket ball through his right thigh, two stabs of a bayonet in his left arm, and two more in his left side. One bayonet stab went through his body from the left to right side. He was taken prisoner. He was continued on the pension list on 14 Apr. 1791. He lived in Alexandria, D.C. in 1812 and in Fairfax Co., Va. in 1820. He died 26 Aug. 1833. Thomas Burns of Alexandria, D.C. was administrator of his estate.

Lewis, **Andrew**. Va. Pvt. He lived in Mason Co., Va. He was on the 1813 pension list.

Lewis, **David**. Conn. Pvt. He suffered from rheumatic disorders and lameness. He lived in Westerly, R.I. in 1794. He enlisted 23 Feb. 1777 and was discharged 11 Nov. 1781.

Lewis, **David**. S.C. —. He was granted relief.

Lewis, **Edward**. Va. Pvt. He was awarded a gratuity of £20 and a £10 annuity in Lunenburg County on 21 Nov. 1777. He was in Pittsylvania County 13 June 1787 and was 28 years old. He was in the Lunenburg County militia and was on duty in Williamsburg in 1777 when he was wounded accidentally by the bursting of a gun and lost several fingers on his right hand and the use of his hand. Capt. Edward Broadnax attested his service. He was continued on the pension list at the rate of £15 per annum on 13 June 1787. He was in Patrick County in 1792 and Franklin County in 1823.

Lewis, **George**. S.C. —. He contracted smallpox at the siege of Augusta, Ga. and lost his eyesight. He was granted a £30 gratuity in 1781. He lived in Rutherford Co., N.C. He was from Spartanburgh Dist., S.C. in 1796. In response from a petition from a number of inhabitants of Spartanburgh District, he was stricken from the roll on 14 Dec.1814. They indicated that he had 6 Negroes, 212 acres, a grist mill, a gin for cleaning cotton, livestock, a wife in good health, and no other whites in his family.

Lewis, **Henry**. N.Y. Ens. He served under Col. Vischer. He was wounded in the shoulder in action with the Indians on 6 Aug. 1777 at Oriskie. He lived in Mohawk, N.Y. when he was pensioned in Sep. 1794. He later lived in Montgomery County. He was on the 1813 pension list.

Lewis, **Isaac**. Pvt. Pa. He was in Bucks County on 13 Mar. 1786. He was wounded in the thigh on Long Island. He was 36 years old. He received a $40 gratuity and a $40 annuity. He was on the 1813 pension list. He served under Capt. Ludwig in Col. Heller's Regiment. Congress did not grant his petition for an increase 25 June 1818.

Lewis, **Jabez**. Conn. Pvt. He served under Col. Bunnel [?Burrel]. He was captured by the Indians at St. Lawrence and beaten so that he became lame from his ulcerated leg. He lived in Conn. in 1792. He was in the militia.

Lewis, **James**. Ga. Lt. He served in the Burke County militia. He was wounded in the right hip on 22 May 1779 at Daniel Howel's plantation. He resided in Burke Co., Ga. in 1796. He died in 1807.

Lewis, **James**. Pa. —. He served under Capt. James McClure and Col. William Montgomery in the Flying Camp. He was taken prisoner at Fort Washington and confined on the prison ship *Jersey* and died shortly thereafter. He was from Chester County.

Lewis, **Jehu**. Pa. —. He was awarded $200 in full satisfaction for his tract of donation land on 19 Mar. 1816. He was awarded a $40 gratuity and a $40 annuity in Bucks Co., Pa. 18 Feb.1834. He was dead by Jan. 1841.

Lewis, **John**. Mass. Pvt. He served in the 16th Regiment and was from Boston. His widow, Ann Lewis, was paid $50.

Lewis, **John**. N.H. —. He enlisted on 6 Dec. 1775 in Capt. Benjamin Titcomb's Company. He died at Trenton on 26 Dec. 1775 following the battle. His mother, Elizabeth Lewis of Portsmouth, Rockingham County, sought his 100 acre bounty and £20 further bounty on 10 June 1780.

Lewis, **John**. Pa. Sgt. He enlisted in the 11th Pa. Regiment under Col. Richard Humpton on 7 June 1777. He sought back pay for the period 1 June to 1 Nov. 1778 on 24 Feb. 1806.

Lewis, **Joseph**. Me. —. He died 9 Dec. 1834. His widow was Mehitable Lewis from Waterboro. She was paid $50 under the resolve of 1836.

Lewis, Joseph. Mass. —. He was from Marblehead and was paid $20.

Lewis, Joseph. Va. Pvt. His widow, Martha Lewis, lived in Chesterfield County on 9 Aug. 1786. He entered the service in June 1780 and died in South Carolina. His wife went with him from Petersburg, Va. to Charleston, S.C. and lived with him until after the surrender. Lt. John Cocke of Surry County deposed that he entered the service 1 Aug. 1779. He was on detachment under Col. William Heath when he died in the service. She was 50 years of age in 1786 and had no children. Rev. John Bracken of Bruton Parish married them in Apr. 1779. She was Martha Webb.

Lewis, Marsh. Mass. Pvt. He was granted relief.

Lewis, Miles. Pa. Pvt. He was on the 1789 and 1813 pension lists.

Lewis, Naboth. Conn. Pvt. He served in Col. Sheldon's Regiment. He was wounded in various parts of his body by a cutlass. The bones of his cranium were divided by it in Dec. 1777 near Philadelphia, Pa. He resided at Middleton, Conn. in 1796. He enlisted 25 Dec. 1776 for the war. He was a prisoner 8 Sep. 1778. He rejoined 13 Feb. 1779 and deserted 5 Aug. 1779. He rejoined 13 May 1780 and was promoted to corporal in 1781. He was granted two-thirds of a pension 20 Apr. 1796. He was on the 1813 pension list.

Lewis, Nathaniel. Conn. Pvt. He served in the 18th Regiment of Militia under Col. Pettibone. He was wounded by a grape shot in his right thigh which entered about the middle and towards the back part of his thigh and came out near the knee on 15 Sep. 1776 at Turtle Bay on the retreat from New York. He resided at Berkhamstead, Conn. in 1792. He resided some time in Madison Co., N.Y. He was granted one-fourth of a pension 20 Apr. 1796. He was on the 1813 pension list in Connecticut.

Lewis, Peter. Conn. Pvt. He was in the Invalids Corps and had been disabled by consumption and other infirmities. He was pensioned 15 Sep. 1782. He was aged 41 in Apr. 1787. He was a Negro. He was on the 1813 pension list. He was from Stratford.

Lewis, Robert. Conn. Capt. He served in Col. Charles Webb's Regiment. He died in the service 22 Mar. 1777 and his orphan children sought seven years' half pay from 22 Mar. 1777 on 3 Mar. 1791.

Lewis, Salathiel. Va. —. His widow, Sarah Lewis, was furnished support in Southampton County 12 Feb. 1778 and 2 barrels of corn on 10 June 1779. His orphan was Exum Lewis.

Lewis, Samuel. —. —. He received his commutation. He was to receive half-pay for life upon proof and deducting his commutation.

Lewis, Samuel. Pa. —. He was from Fayette County.

Lewis, Samuel. Pa. —. He was from Cumberland County. He was pensioned 10 Dec. 1814.

Lewis, Samuel. Pa. —. He served in the 3rd Regiment and was between 70 and 80 years of old. He was from Huntingdon County.

Lewis, Samuel. Pa. 2nd Lt. His widow, Rebecca Lewis, was in Northumberland County on 1 July 1788. He served in the 3rd Battalion in the Northumberland County militia under Col. Peter Hosterman in Capt. Mool's Company. He was killed by the Indians at his house on Shamokin Creek in 1778. His son was taken prisoner. The claim was rejected since he was not in actual service. He died 1 Feb.1825.

Lewis, Samuel. Pa. Pvt. He applied in Westmoreland County 12 Aug. 1814. He enlisted in Capt. Wendel Oury's Company. Capt. Samuel Brady took command at Pittsburgh. He was under Col. Enos McCoy. He marched to New Jersey and joined the army at Bonbrook. The regiment was ordered to Pittsburgh under the command of Col. Brodhead. He often had command of a boat carrying provisions for the use of the army on the rivers Ohio, Allegheny, and Monongalia. He was ordered to Wheeling under Lt. Benjamin Neely to bring in a load of whiskey. He was taken prisoner by the Indians in 1780, given to the British, taken to Niagara, and held until the peace in 1783. He was 67 years old. Peter Shellhammer was in the same company, Henry Slater served with him in 1776, Robert Campbell saw him at Niagara as a prisoner, and Capt. Benjamin Burd knew him as a soldier in the 3rd Pa. Regiment.

Lewis, Samuel. Vt. —. He was born in Lynn, Mass. and was brought up to the trade of a woman shoemaker. On 19 Apr. 1775 he was a volunteer solider at Lexington and was discharged in Jan. 1777. He entered on the privateer *Rising States* and took a prize. He was ordered to take her into port. On 2 Apr. of that year he was captured by the British, taken to the West Indies, Scotland, and finally to Halifax. He made his escape and returned to his family in Nov. 1781. He had been in prison for debt for four years and sought an act of insolvency 1 Oct. 1799.

Lewis, Seth. —. Maj. He served as Deputy Paymaster and attached to the Paymaster General's office in Philadelphia for more than two years. He was a member of the Society of the Cincinnati. His widow, Rhoda Lewis, aged 88, of Southington, Conn. had no other proof. Congress rejected her claim 18 Apr. 1854.

Lewis, Thomas. S.C. —. His annuity was £44.17.4 in 1787.

Lewis, Thomas. Va. —. He was disabled when a horse broke his leg. He applied in Nansemond Co., Va. 17 May 1777.

Lewis, William. Conn. Pvt. He served under Lt. Thomas Grosvenor in Capt. Wolcott's Company in the 1st Conn. Regiment. He was disabled in the breast by falling rock while working on the road. He was aged 29 years on 20 June 1786. He lived in Fredericksburg, Dutchess Co., N.Y. on 24 May 1787 and was in Albany Co., N.Y. 28 May 1789. He was on the 1813 pension list. He also appeared as William Lues.

Lewis, William. Md. Sgt. He was pensioned at the rate of half-pay of a sergeant in Washington County on 12 Feb. 1820.

Lewis, William. Md. Capt. He was pensioned at the rate of half-pay of a captain in Washington County on 25 Feb. 1826. His widow, Mary Lewis, was pensioned at the same rate 14 Mar. 1828.

Lewis, William. Va. Lt. He served in the 1st Virginia Regiment under Capt. John Fleming. He was commissioned a captain 27 Jan. 1776 and a major 12 May 1779. He was reported as supernumerary at Winchester 1 Jan. 1783. He received land and commutation after the war. Congress found no other man of his name and concluded the heirs were trying to get more than was deserved. It was also stated that he died at Yorktown 14 Nov. 1779. If so, the date of death given by the widow was wrong. His widow, Lucy Lewis, married John Marks 13 May 1780 in Albemarle County. In due course evidence revealed that he was not the major. If her husband belonged to the Continental Army, he did so as a non-com or in some staff capacity. Congress rejected the claim of the heirs 25 May 1842.

Lewizell, Nicholas. N.Y. —. He was granted relief.

Libby, Azariah. Mass. —. He was granted relief.

Libby, Harvey. Me. —. He was from Limington. He was pensioned in 1818 but stricken from the roll in 1820. His petition to be restored was rejected 2 Feb. 1825. He was paid $50 under the resolve of 1836.

Libby, Nathaniel. Me. —. He was from Limerick. He was paid $50 under the resolve of 1836.

Libengood, Jacob. —. —. He sought an increase in his pension for the wound he received in his right shoulder at Brandywine. Congress rejected his petition 7 Mar. 1844 because he failed to establish satisfactory proof. His widow, Margaret Libengood, received a $40 gratuity and a $40 annuity in Westmoreland County 12 Mar. 1860.

Libert, John. Mass. Pvt. He died 28 Aug. 1807.

Liddell, Andrew. S.C. —. He was pensioned 3 Dec. 1825. He received his annuity as late as 1833.

Liddle, Moses. S.C. Capt. He was wounded by the Indians. He was granted an annuity 4 Aug. 1785.

Liddy, Matthew. Pa. —. He was awarded a $40 gratuity and a $40 annuity in York Co., Pa. 1 Apr. 1830. He died 24 Apr. 1830.

Liebcup, Mathias. S.C. —. His house was burnt by the Tories led by Maj. William Cunningham, and all of his vouchers were consumed. Afterwards he obtained vouchers and delivered them to Mr. Arthur in Orangeburg District, and his accounts were passed at £392.19.10. His indent was to be issued to his executors, Robert Lithgow and Alexander Bell, for said amount plus interest on 18 Dec. 1792.

Ligget, Robert. Pa. —. He was awarded a $40 gratuity and a $40 annuity in Franklin Co., Pa. 3 Mar. 1829.

Light, John. Pa. Capt. He served in the militia. He was from Lancaster County.

Light, John. Pa. —. He was paid $300 for his donation land 7 Feb. 1828.

Lightfoot, —. Va. —. His wife, Mary Lightfoot, was granted relief in May 1777 in Lunenburg Co., Va.

Lightfoot, Philip. Va. Lt. He served in Harrison's Regiment of Artillery, was in the campaign of 1781 under Gen. LaFayette, was at the siege of York, and marched south under Gen. Greene. He had been allowed land bounty from Virginia. His son, Philip Lightfoot, was allowed commutation 6 Apr. 1838. His heirs sought commutation from Congress 17 June 1857.

Lightner, George. Pa. —. He was granted relief in Beaver County 21 June 1839. He also appeared as George Lightener.

Ligon, Joseph. Va. Pvt. He was pensioned in Dec. 1807. He was on the 1813 pension list. He transferred from Halifax Co., Va. to Montgomery Co., Tenn. Congress did not grant his petition for an increase 25 June 1818.

Likens, David. Pa. —. He was awarded a $40 gratuity in Delaware Co., Pa. 14 Apr. 1834. He was awarded a $40 gratuity and a $40 annuity on 10 Apr. 1835.

Likens, Elisha. Pa. —. He was awarded a $40 gratuity and a $40 annuity in Delaware County 31 Mar. 1836. This individual also appeared as Eliza Lykens. Eliza Lykins died 1 Oct. 1842.

Liles, Ephraim. S.C. —. At the age of 16 he served as a spy after the fall of Charleston. He was at Granby Fort, Black Stocks, and Fish Dam. He was wounded in his thigh at the latter. He had a family of small children. Hugh Means proved he was a soldier in 1780 and 1781. He applied for a pension in Nov. 1824. He was paid his annuity as late as 1833. He also appeared as Ephraim Lyles.

Lilley, Reuben. Mass. 1st Lt. He received commutation for five years in full in lieu of half-pay for life.

Lilly, Thomas. Mass. Pvt. He served in the 5th Regiment. He contracted diseases at Saratoga in Sept. 1777. He resided in Marblehead, Mass. in 1792. He enlisted 15 Mar. 1777 for three years.

Lincoln, Caleb. Mass. —. He served in the 3rd Artillery and was paid $20.

Lincoln, David. Mass. —. He served in the 4th Regiment and was from Taunton. He was paid $20.

Lincoln, Elijah. Conn. Sgt. He served in the 2nd Conn. Regt. under Col. Heman Swift from 1777 to the end of the war. He was wounded at Yorktown in Oct. 1781 by a musket ball through his wrist and arm. He was on the 1813 pension list.

Lincoln, Elijah. Pa. Pvt. He transferred to New Hampshire in or by Sep. 1797.

Lincoln, John. N.H. Pvt. He served under Col. Bayley. He was wounded by a musket ball shot through his right leg in Sep. 1776 at Harlem Plains. He lived in Bedford, N.H. in 1794. He served in the militia. He was granted one-fourth of a pension 20 Apr. 1796. He was on the 1813 pension list.

Lincoln, Joseph. Mass. —. He served in the 2nd Regiment and was paid $20.

Lincoln, Luther. Mass. —. He served in Crane's Artillery and was paid $20.

Lincoln, Oliver. Mass. Matross. He served in Crane's Artillery and was from Mansfield. His widow, Ruth Lincoln, was paid $50.

Lind, John. Pa. —. He was awarded a $40 gratuity and a $40 annuity in Northampton Co., Pa. 15 Mar. 1826.

Lindell, John. Mass. —. He was pensioned.

Linden, James. Va. —. His wife, Mary Linden, was allowed £15 for her support and her two children on 16 Dec. 1777. Her husband had enlisted for three years. She was allowed £45 relief as the wife of a soldier in Augusta Co., Va. 17 Nov. 1779.

Lindersmith, George. Pa. —. He applied in Lancaster County on 28 Dec. 1812. He died 8 June 1826.

Lindley, —. —. —. His widow, Abigail Lindley, had her petition for a pension rejected by Congress on 27 Mar. 1846 because they were married subsequent to 1 Jan. 1794.

Lindsay, David. Pa. —. His widow, Sarah Lindsay, was awarded a $40 gratuity and a $40 annuity in Warren Co., Pa. 6 Apr. 1830.

Lindsay, David. Va. —. His wife, Catherine Lindsay, was granted £12 support in Berkeley County on 19 May 1778. She received £25 on 18 May 1779 and £100 on 16 May 1780. There were four children.

Lindsay, John. Ga. Aide-de-camp and Major. He served in Col. Few's militia or Col. Clarke's. He lost his right hand, the bones of his right leg were shattered, and his leg shortened by wounds in Dec. 1780 at the battle of Long Cane. He lived in Wilkes Co., Ga. in 1795. He died in 1808. He also appeared as John Lindsey.

Lindsay, John. S.C. —. He died of a wound received at Tarleton's defeat. His widow, Rebecca Lindsay, was granted an annuity 4 Aug. 1785. She and her two children were granted an annuity 4 Oct. 1786. It was paid to James Lindsay. He was from Abbeville District.

Lindsay, Samuel. Pa. Lt. He served in Col. T. Bull's Battalion of Flying Camp. He was wounded in the head by the stroke of a butt end of a musket in the attack at Fort Washington, N.Y. on 16 Nov. 1776. He lost his left eye and lost his sight in the other eye. He was also wounded by a musket ball in his right leg. He lived at Nether Providence, Delaware Co., Pa. in 1794. He was a prisoner. He was died 16 Apr. 1800.

Lindsay, William. Va. —. He served under Cornet Bland from 16 June 1776 and was promoted to lieutenant 15 Mar. 1777 in Lee's Corps. He was badly wounded in Jan. 1778, was promoted to captain, but resigned in Oct. 1778 when he was incapable of serving. He never applied for a pension. His daughter, Elizabeth Lomax, was allowed a pension from 1 Oct. 1778 to 1 Sep. 1797 when he died by Congress 9 Apr. 1856.

Lindsey, David. Pa. —. His widow, Sarah Lindsey, was awarded a $40 gratuity in Warren Co., Pa. 23 Apr. 1829.

Lindsey, Ezekiel. Va. —. His wife, Eleanor Lindsey, and five children were granted £5 per month support in Yohogania Co., Va. 28 Apr. 1778.

Lindsey, James. Pa. Sgt. He served in the Flying Camp. He died of wounds in New York. His widow, Martha Lindsey, was granted a half-pay pension in Delaware County 6 Aug. 1791.

Lindsey, John. —. —. He died 10 Sep. 1838. He was due three full months of his pension. There were twelve children who were a great distance apart, and it was too expensive to get powers of attorney from them. Congress authorized that the pension be paid to the administrator 5 Mar. 1848 for the heirs.

Lindsey, John. Pa. —. He was awarded a $40 gratuity in Philadelphia, Pa. 11 June 1832.

Lindsey, John. Pa. —. He was pensioned in Delaware County 21 Feb. 1838. He was 88 years old in 1840 and died 8 Feb. 1843. He also appeared as John Lindsay.

Lindsey, Mungo. Pa. Sgt. He enlisted in Lancaster County in 1776 under Capt. Murran and Col. Miles as a rifleman. He marched to Long Island and transferred to the regiment of Col. Walter Stewart. He was discharged 1 Jan. 1778. He was 72 years old and from Center County on 29 Jan. 1824. He was also under Col. Luke Broadhead.

Lindsey, Robert. Mass. —. He served in the 4th Regiment and was paid $20.

Lindsey, Samuel. S.C. Pvt. He fought against the Cherokee under Gen. Andrew Williamson in 1775. He also served under Col. James Williams, Maj. Downs, Capt. Samuel Merrow, Lt. Gerard Smith, Lt. Col. James Lindsey, and Lt. Thomas Dugan. He was wounded slightly at Ninety Six. He was also at Hanging Rock. He suffered from palsy and had an aged, infirm wife. He had been bereft of speech for five years. Thomas McCrackin and John Enlow served with him. Col. John Speak also proved his service. He was from Newberry District and was pensioned 14 Dec. 1820. He was paid his annuity as late as 1829. John Lindsay sought the $60 arrearage due the deceased on 6 Dec. 1828. He also appeared as Samuel Lindsay.

Lindsey, William. Va. —. His wife, Mary Lindsey, and six children were granted £5 support in Yohogania Co., Va. 28 Apr. 1778.

Lindsley, Samuel. N.J. —. He served in the N.J. militia. He lived in Essex Co., N.J. He was on the 1813 pension list and died 18 June 1820.

Lindy, Jacob. Pa. —. He was awarded a $40 gratuity and a $40 annuity in Lancaster Co., Pa. 24 Mar. 1828 and 6 Apr. 1833. He was dead by Nov. 1835.

Lines, Michael. N.Y. Pvt. He served under Col. Frederick Weisenfels. He was wounded in Aug. 1782 in Ulster County. He was pensioned from 9 Aug. 1782.

Linfield, —. Mass. —. His widow was Hannah Linfield.

Lingan, Thomas. Md. Lt. He was pensioned at the rate of half-pay of a lieutenant 22 Feb. 1823. He was from Montgomery County. His widow, Janet Lingan, was pensioned at the same rate 13 Feb. 1830.

Lingenfelter, —. Pa. —. His widow, Mary Lingenfelter, was awarded a $40 annuity in York County 12 Apr. 1851 for his Revolutionary service.

Lingenfelter, George. Pa. —. He was awarded a $40 gratuity and a $40 annuity in York Co., Pa. 4 May 1832.

Lingo, James. Va. Pvt. His wife, Caty Lingo, was furnished 4 barrels of corn and 200 pounds of pork for herself and three children in Essex Co., Va. on 25 May 1781 and on 20 May 1782. His widow lived in Essex County in June 1787. He was killed at the siege of Ninety Six. Williamson Hardy saw his corpse after he was killed. He left three small children. Dr. Mace Clements saw him as a soldier at the siege and deposed that he was returned killed. She was put on the pension list at the rate of £10 per annum on 23 July 1787.

Link, Simon. Pa. —. He was awarded a $40 gratuity in Berks Co., Pa. 15 Apr. 1834. He received a $40 gratuity and a $40 annuity 5 Feb. 1836. He was 82 years old in 1840. He died 12 Mar. 1841.

Linn, David. —. —. He married in Apr. 1795. His widow was Mary Linn. Congress rejected her claim for relief 9 Apr. 1840.

Linn, Dewalt. Pa. —. He was awarded a $40 gratuity in Northumberland Co., Pa. 8 Apr. 1829 and again on 7 Feb. 1831. He was awarded a $40 gratuity and a $40 annuity on 1 Apr. 1834. He also appeared as Dewalt Lynn and David Linn.

Linn, James. Pa. —. He was awarded relief in Washington County 5 Feb. 1836.

Linn, Robert. Pa. Pvt. He was in Philadelphia County 14 Nov. 1785. He served under Capt. Vernon under Col. Wayne. He was stationed on board a schooner on Lake Champlain and had his leg accidentally broken. He was transferred from the 4th Pa. Regiment to the Invalids. He was wounded in the leg and arm. He was discharged 10 Apr. 1783. He was 55 years old.

Linn, William. Va. Col. He entered the service as a lieutenant under George Gibson in 1776. They went to New Orleans for 12,000 pounds of gunpowder which they delivered to Pittsburgh after six months. George Rogers Clark used it to take the Illinois Country. Linn was at the battle of Pequa on the Chillicothe plain. Elizabeth A. R. Linn sought relief from Congress.

Linnen, Thomas. Mass. Corp. He served in Col. Samuel McCobb's Volunteers in Capt. John Hinckley's Company. He was disabled by grape shot through the instep of his left foot. He was pensioned 8 July 1786. He was on the 1813 pension list. He transferred to Lincoln Co., Me. 4 Nov. 1826.

Linton, —. Va. —. He served in Capt. Bruin's Company in the 11th Virginia Regiment and was killed in the service. His widow, Elizabeth Linton, and child were granted £5 support in Frederick Co., Va. on 5 Nov. 1777.

Linton, Bernard. Va. Pvt. His widow, Sarah Linton, lived in Norfolk County 20 Apr. 1787, was 46 years old, and had three children aged 16, 13, and 11. He enlisted for three years 1 Mar. 1777 and died at Portsmouth 1 Feb. 1778 as attested by Lt. J. Hudson of the 2nd Va. Regiment. Capt. Thomas Bressie of the 2nd Regiment also confirmed his service. He also appeared as Barnet Lynton. His widow was put on the pension list at the rate of £8 per annum on 25 Aug. 1787.

Linton, James. Pa. —. He was pensioned 13 Apr. 1833 and resided in Baltimore, Md.

Linton, Joseph. Pa. His widow, Jane Linton of Baltimore, Md. was paid $200 for the 200 acres of donation land to which he was entitled 13 Apr. 1838. She received a $40 gratuity and a $40 annuity in 1838

Linton, Michael. Va. Pvt. He was disabled at the Waxsaws. He was on the 1785 pension roll.

Linton, William. Pa. —. He was awarded a $40 gratuity and a $40 annuity in Franklin Co., Pa. 9 Mar. 1826.

Linton, William S. —. —. Congress granted his widow, Mary Ann Linton, a pension 18 Mar. 1844.

Lintz, John. N.Y. Pvt. He served in the Montgomery County militia under Col. Peter Bellinger and was slain 6 Oct. 1780. His widow, Anna Lintz, received his half-pay pension.

Linzey, Daniel. Mass. —. He served in the 10th Regiment and was from Vermont. He was paid $20.

Lipkey, Henry. Pa. —. He applied in Cumberland County in Apr. 1818. He also appeared as Henry Lepkey. He died 18 Dec. 1821.

Lipscomb, Darius. —. —. He was pensioned when he lived in Vermont. His widow, Sarah Lipscomb, sought a pension from the time of his death. Congress denied her request 31 Jan. 1854.

Lipscombe, James. Md. Pvt. He was pensioned 4 Mar. 1789. He died in 1790.

Lisenbie, Charles. S.C. —. He was from Chesterfield District and was pensioned 23 Nov. 1829. He served under Gen. Harrington, Gen. Ludenton, Col. James Fain. He was at Beatie's Bridge on Drowning Creek and was at Wilmington, N.C. He suffered from rheumatism. He was 69 years old. Charles Hinson, aged 67, of Anson Co., N.C. had served with him as had Robert Hundley of Anson Co., N.C. He received his annuity as late as 1834.

Liske, Peter. Pa. —. His children and heirs were paid $200 for his donation land 25 Mar. 1831.

Liswell, Thomas. Mass. —. He served in the 4ᵗʰ Regiment and was paid $20.

Lithgow, William. Mass. Maj. He served in the 11ᵗʰ Regiment under Col. Ebenezer Francis. He was wounded by a musket ball in the joint of his right elbow on 19 Sep. 1777 and lost the use of one arm. He was pensioned at one-third pay 16 June 1783. He was 31 years old in 1787.

Litly, Thomas. —. —. He was pensioned 9 June 1794.

Littell, Mathias. Pa. —. He served in the 12ᵗʰ Regiment under Col. William Cook. He was from Northumberland County.

Little, —. Pa. —. His widow, Ann Little, was awarded a $40 gratuity and a $40 annuity in Adams Co., Pa. 27 Feb. 1834. She died 25 Feb. 1848.

Little, —. Pa. —. His widow, Jane Little, was pensioned in Allegheny County 21 Feb. 1838. She died 15 June 1857.

Little, Andrew. Pa. —. He served seven months under Col. Potter. He was awarded a $40 gratuity in Adams Co., Pa. 30 Mar. 1831.

Little, Henry. Pa. —. He served seven months under Col. Potter. He was 77 years old in 1826. He was awarded a $40 gratuity in Adams Co., Pa. 12 Apr. 1828 and again on 23 Mar. 1829.

Little, James. Pa. —. He was pensioned in Allegheny County 21 Feb. 1838.

Little, John. Conn. —. His widow, Sarah Little, sought a pension from Congress. There was not the slightest evidence in support of her claim so Congress rejected her claim 29 Apr. 1846. He had been pensioned in 1832, but the record indicated that his time of service was too little than what he had claimed under Capt. Slawson.

Little, John. N.Y. Capt. He served under Col. Fisher in the militia. He was wounded in the shoulder in action with the enemy under Maj. Ross at Johnstown. He lived in Johnstown, N.Y. in 1794 and later in Montgomery County. He was on the 1813 pension list.

Little, John. N.Y. Capt. He served under Col. Allison and was slain 22 July 1779 at Minnisink. His widow, Experience Little, received his half-pay pension.

Little, Luther. Mass. Midshipman. He served aboard the brigantine *Protector* under Capt. John Foster and was wounded in the head 10 May 1781. He was a captive. He was pensioned 15 Feb. 1790 at the rate of $30 per annum.

Little, Matthias. Pa. —. He applied in Northumberland County on 6 May 1813. He served in the 12ᵗʰ Pa. Regiment under Col. William Cook and was discharged at Trenton. He had an abdominal rupture. He died 7 Oct. 1821.

Little, Nathaniel. Pa. Sgt. His widow, Christiana Little, was in Lancaster County on 7 Sep. 1786. He was in the 4ᵗʰ Battalion of the Lancaster County militia in Capt. David McQueen's Company and was killed in an engagement with the British Army at Chestnut Hill in Dec. 1777. He was wounded by a musket ball on 5 Dec. and died 6 Dec. He left two children one of whom died by 6 Sep. 1789. The living child was eleven years old.

Little, Samuel. N.J. Pvt. He served in 1ˢᵗ N.J. Regiment under Capt. Daniel Little and was killed at Germantown 4 Oct. 1777. His widow, Phoebe Little, of Elizabeth Town was allowed his half-pay 10 Apr.1782.

Little, Thomas. Pa. —. He resided in Fayette County and was awarded 200 acres of donation land 22 Mar. 1813.

Little, William. Pa. —. He was pensioned.

Little, William. S.C. —. There were three children in 1791. One William Little was a soldier under Gen. Pickens. He was of Abbeville Dist., S.C. and died in 1796. His administrators were his widow Isabel Little and son James Little. In 1825 his son sought compensation for the supplies his father had furnished the military.

Littlefield, Abraham. Me. —. He died 20 July 1831. His widow was Susannah Littlefield from York. She was paid $50 under the resolve of 1836.

Littlefield, Daniel. Mass. Maj. He was from Wells, Maine and was killed by a ball from the enemy in 1779 in the expedition to Penobscot. His widow, Hannah Littlefield, married secondly ------ Eldridge who went to sea as a privateer and was never heard from again. Congress granted her a pension 18 Jan. 1837. His son, Daniel Littlefield, sought the half-pay due his father. Congress denied the claim 6 Feb. 1855 because the service was as an officer in state troops.

Livingston, Abraham. S.C. —. —. He was the Continental agent at Charleston and was taken prisoner. He died on parole in Christ Church Parish 20 Nov. 1780. Congress granted the widow of his nephew relief.

Livingston, Abraham. S.C. —. He served under Capt. Coffey, Col. Hill, Capt. Taggart, and Col. William Polk. He was severely wounded. He applied 23 Nov. 1827.

Livingston, Henry Brockholst. Lt. Col. N.Y. He was born 26 Nov. 1757 and graduated from Princeton in 1774. He entered the service as a captain in 1776, a major and aide-de-camp under Gen. Schuyler. He was at Ticonderoga and Stillwater. He retired 1 Jan. 1782. He received bounty land warrant #1117 for 450 acres in Mar. 1825. He died 18 Mar. 1823. Edward Livingston was his brother. His son, Anson Livingston, and the rest of the children sought his half-pay from Congress 23 Mar. 1860. Congress rejected the claim 11 Apr. 1860 because he had been fully paid in 1778.

Livingston, Moses. S.C. —. He served under Col. Charles S. Middleton. Benjamin Hart, James Miscampbell, William Paulding, and Sgt. George Campbell deposed regarding his service. He died before his claim could be adjusted so his brother, William Livingston, did so 23 Nov. 1819.

Lloyd, Benjamin. S.C. 2nd Lt. He served in the artillery under Col. Bateman. He was a citizen of Savannah, Georgia and sought his pay 2 Mar. 1789.

Lloyd, Edward. S.C. Lt. He was pensioned 27 Apr. 1810. He served to the end of the war. He lost an arm at Savannah. He died in 1812. Congress declined assistance to his daughter, Rebecca Frances Bailey, on 27 Mar. 1876. Her husband was Samuel Armstrong Bailey. They sought bounty land. They lived but a short distance of the public lands in Alabama and Mississippi and sought the right to receive same in either state. Congress granted them the right on 18 Apr. 1834.

Lloyd, Thomas. Md. Pvt. He was pensioned at the rate of half-pay of a private in Philadelphia, Pa. 12 Feb. 1820. His widow, Mary Lloyd, was pensioned at the same rate 9 Mar. 1846.

Lloyd, William. S.C. —. He was wounded in the service. He had a small family. He was pensioned in Sumter District 20 Dec. 1804. He died 3 Nov. 1822. His widow, Dorcas Lloyd, was granted his arrearage 3 Dec. 1822. He also appeared as William Loyd.

Lloyd, William. Va. —. His wife, Sarah Lloyd, was granted assistance in Dec. 1777 and £30 support on 8 Apr. 1779 in Caroline Co., Va. while he was away in the service. He also appeared as William Loyd.

Loaser, Jacob. Pa. Pvt. His widow, Margaret Loaser, was in Dauphin County 18 Dec. 1787. He served in Capt. Peter Berry's Company in Col. Philip Greenwalt's Battalion of the Lancaster County militia. In 1776 he was taken captive at Fort Washington and died in captivity leaving a widow and three children.

Locharty, John. N.Y. Pvt. He served in Capt. Garrit Putnam's Company under Col. Marinus Willet. He received several wounds near Johnstown on 25 Oct. 1782. He was ruptured in his groin. He was

44 years old in 1786. He lived in Montgomery Co., N.Y. on 5 May 1789. He died in May 1808. He also appeared as John Lockarty and John Lochary.

Lochman, Mathias. Pa. —. He was awarded a $40 gratuity and a $40 annuity in Montgomery Co., Pa. 18 Mar. 1834.

Lochry, Archibald. Pa. Col. He was in the volunteers from Westmoreland County who joined Gen. George Rogers Clark on 24 Aug. 1781 and went down the Ohio River and were attacked by Indians. He acted as colonel and was killed on the expedition by the Shawnee. His widow, Mary Lochry, was in Westmoreland County on 4 May 1791. She married secondly John Guthrie. His daughters were Jean Lochry born 15 April 1776 and Elizabeth Lochry born 3 May 1780. Jean Lochry married David McBride and Elizabeth Lochry married Samuel Thompson. The daughters sought bounty land, but Congress rejected their claim on 16 May 1848. They applied again 17 Apr. 1858. He also appeared as Archibald Lockry and Archibald Loughery.

Lock, Ebenezer. Mass. Corp. He served in the 15th Regiment under Col. Timothy Bigelow and Capt. Bowman. He was also under Capt. Munro. He was wounded at White Plains 3 Feb. 1780 by a musket ball in his right thigh. He was pensioned at the rate of half-pay from 1 Apr. 1780 on 17 Mar. 1784. He was 26 years old in 1786. He lived in Deering, N.H. in 1788.

Lock, Francis. N.J. Capt. He served under Col. Freylinghausen in the Somerset County militia. He was shot through the body at Elizabeth Town on 15 Sep. 1777. He married Anna McMurtrie on 3 Oct. 1772. Rev. Mr. Hanna preformed the marriage. He had four children, the youngest born 4 ½ months after he was killed. The widow and children were allowed half-pay for her widowhood and until the children arrived at the age of eight in Hunterdon County, New Jersey in 1780. She married secondly ----- Newton.

Lock, William. Pa. —. He was pensioned.

Lockart, John. Pa. —. He was awarded a $40 gratuity in Lancaster Co., Pa. 23 Apr. 1829 and again 7 Apr. 1830.

Lockart, Samuel. Pa. —. He was awarded a $40 gratuity in Lancaster, Pa. 7 Mar. 1827 and a $40 gratuity and a $40 annuity 7 Feb. 1828.

Locke, Edmund. Mass. Pvt. He served in the 4th Mass. Regiment in Capt. William Moor's Company. He was wounded in the leg by the fall of a tree. He was discharged 9 June 1783. He was pensioned at the rate of one-quarter pay on 4 June 1785.

Locke, Henry. Md. Sgt. He was pensioned at the rate of half-pay of a sergeant in Montgomery Co. on 27 Jan. 1816.

Locke, John. Va. —. He was pensioned in Rockingham County on 25 Feb. 1818 at the rate of $100 per annum and $60 immediate relief. He died 18 May 1829 and his administrator was John Ludwick.

Locke, Jonas. Mass. Pvt. He served in the 9th Regiment and was from Lexington. His widow, Deborah Locke, was paid $50.

Lockhart, John. Pa. —. He was awarded a $40 gratuity and a $40 annuity in Lancaster Co. 23 Apr. 1829.

Lockhart, Samuel. Pa. —. He was awarded a $40 gratuity and a $40 annuity 7 Feb. 1828 in Lancaster County. He died 2 Nov. 1835.

Lockheart, Charles. S.C. Pvt. He served under Col. Mahon in the Light Dragoons. John Abernathy was his administrator and sought his benefits 20 Dec. 1794.

Lockman, Mathias. Pa. —. He was granted a $40 gratuity and a $40 annuity in Montgomery County 18 Mar. 1834. He died 13 Nov. 1848.

Lockmann, Charles. S.C. Asst. Surgeon. He served 14 months in the Artillery and Hospital Department. He was taken captive and held in Virginia and Pennsylvania. He received his commutation of pay 26 Jan. 1788.

Lockmann, John. Junior Surgeon. He was in the Hospital Department for nearly five years. He was a foreigner and had very little acquaintance with the English language. He sought relief 13 Feb. 1786.

Lockry, John. Pa. —. He was on the 1789 pension list.

Locus, Valentine. N.C. Pvt. He served in the 3rd Regiment under Capt. James Emmet. He married in 1777 and died in 1812. His widow was Rachel Locus, a free woman of color aged 80 who applied in Wake Co., N.C. 24 May 1838.

Lockwood, Moses. N.Y. Gunner. He served in Capt. Samuel Lockwood's Company in Col. Lamb's 2nd Regiment of Artillery. A fellow solider struck him with an axe across his nose and corner of his eye in 1779. He was disabled by the loss of his eye sight, occasional numbness, and deafness. Capt. Henry Waring of Greenwich, Conn. testified as to his service. He was 48 years old on 28 Mar. 1788. He was a farmer and lived in Lower Salem, Westchester Co., N.Y. when he was pensioned on 21 Dec. 1787. He was on the 1813 pension list.

Lodge, Jonathan. Pa. —. His widow, Margaret Lodge, was awarded $200 in Columbia Co., Pa. 8 Feb. 1825.

Loeb, Casper. Pa. —. He was awarded a $40 gratuity and a $40 annuity in Lebanon Co., Pa. 4 Jan. 1823. His widow, Margaret Loeb, was awarded a $40 gratuity and a $40 annuity 17 Jan. 1834. He died 10 Sep. 1841.

Loehman, John. —. Surgeon. He served in a hospital in the Southern Department. He applied from Philadelphia, Pa. He lost the use of his limbs from colds and hardships while a prisoner of the British. He could not get a pension because he had not been wounded. It could not be ascertained that his infirmities were from the service. He was rejected 28 Feb. 1795 and 26 Feb. 1813.

Logan, Charles. Pa. Pvt. His widow, Hannah Logan, was in Dauphin County. He was in the 5th Battalion of the York County militia in Capt. Samuel Nelson's Company. His heirs were his widow and children.

Logan, David. Pa. —. He applied 31 May 1813 and was from Northumberland Co. He died 14 Feb. 1826. His heirs were his widow and children.

Logan, George. S.C. —. His annuity was £102 in 1787.

Logan, John. —. —. He applied in 1818 but his papers were mislaid. He was rejected in 1820. In 1832 he applied and was again suspended. Congress credited him with nine months of service and granted him a pension 10 Feb. 1836.

Logan, John. Va. —. He was wounded in the service and allowed a half-pay pension. He was in Henrico Co., Va. 8 July 1783.

Loggin, John. S.C. —. He was at the battle of King's Mountain and served under Col. Benjamin Cleveland. He was a cripple. He was nearly 86 years of age, and his wife was nearly 83. He was from Pendleton District and was pensioned 7 Dec. 1826. He received his annuity as late as 1833. He died 20 Oct. 1838. His son, Peter Loggin of Habersham Co., Ga. sought his arrearage 8 Nov. 1856.

Loghlin, George. Pa. —. He was in Lancaster County on 25 Dec. 1785.

Logue, Hugh. Pa. —. He was granted relief.

Lohn, David. Pa. —. He enlisted in 1776 under Capt. Abraham Miller in the 5th Regiment and served five years and nine months. He was from Lehigh County

Lohr, Joseph. Pa. Sgt. He applied in Frederick Co., Md. 15 Apr. 1833. He enlisted in the Pa. Line and served one year under Col. Shaw or Shay in the 3rd Regiment in Capt. Peter Skull's Company. He was taken prisoner at Fort Washington and taken to New York where he spent nine weeks in jail. He was paroled. He enlisted a second time in Capt. Connelly's Company in the 4th Pa. Regiment under Col. Butler. He thought he served three and a half years. He was also in Capt. Campbell's Company. He was 74 years old and lived with his son, John Lohr. He also appeared as Joseph Lohn.

Lollar, Daniel. Mass. Pvt. He lost several joints of his toes due to frost bite in transporting supplies on sleds to West Point in 1779 in a snow storm. He served in the 12th Regiment. He enlisted 17 Jan. 1777, was transferred to Invalids 3 Nov. 1779, and was discharged 18 Feb. 1780.

Lomax, John. Md. Pvt. He was pensioned at the rate of half-pay of a private 19 Feb. 1819.

Lomax, William. —. —. He applied in 1819 in Rowan Co., N.C. He was suspended in 1820 and restored in 1821. He was refused the arrearage. Congress authorized the arrearage 5 Mar. 1840 and 27 Aug 1842.

Lombart, —. Pa. —. His widow, Margaret Lombart, received a $40 gratuity and a $40 annuity in Lancaster County 21 Mar. 1837. She was dead by Sep. 1840.

Long, —. Va. —. Mary Long was granted £10 support in Caroline Co., Va. 9 Apr. 1778 while her sons were away in the service.

Long, —. Va. —. His wife, Dorothy Long, was granted £30 support in Caroline Co., Va. 8 Apr 1779 while he was away in the service. She lost her husband and two sons in the service. Her youngest son returned home from Georgia in a weakened state. She prayed additional relief 10 Nov. 1780.

Long, Andrew. Pa. —. He was awarded a $40 gratuity and a $40 annuity in Fayette Co., Pa. 14 Apr. 1827.

Long, Benjamin. Pa. Pvt. He served under Col. Stewart in the 2nd Regiment of Infantry. He was discharged in 1778. He was from Cumberland County.

Long, Benjamin. Pa. Pvt. He applied in Franklin County 4 June 1827. He was 69 years old and suffered from rheumatism. He enlisted in Lancaster County in 1776 in Capt. Grubbs' Company in Col. Miles' Regiment. He marched to the capes of Delaware, Amboy, New York, Long Island, White Plains, Brandywine, and Germantown. He was also commanded by Col. Butler and Col. Walter Stewart. He served in Capt. Robb's Company. He was discharged at Valley Forge 1 Jan. 1778 after twenty months of service.

Long, George. Pa. —. He was granted relief in Warren County 28 Mar. 1836. He died 11 Mar. 1854.

Long, Gideon. Pa. —. He was awarded a $40 gratuity and a $40 annuity in Greene Co., Pa. 7 Apr. 1832.

Long, Jacob. Pa. —. He received a $40 gratuity in Berks County in 1838.

Long, James. Mass. Pvt. He served in the 6th Regiment under Col. Calvin Smith and Capt. Jepeth Daniels. He was worn out in the service. He was 56 years old in 1786. He died 11 May1789.

Long, James. Pa. —. He was awarded a $40 gratuity and a $40 annuity in Crawford Co., Pa. 1 Apr. 1825. He died 6 Apr. 1830.

Long, Job. Mass. —. He served in the 2nd Regiment and was paid $20.

Long, John. Md. Pvt. He was pensioned at the rate of half-pay of a private in Harford County on 7 Feb. 1817.

Long, John. Pa. —. He was awarded a $40 gratuity in Philadelphia Co., Pa. 24 Mar. 1828.

Long, John. Va. Pvt. He served in the 6th Va. Regiment. He lived in Spotsylvania County. He was on the 1813 pension list. He died 14 Feb. 1821.

Long, Joseph. Mass. —. He served in the 6th Regiment and was from Cheshire.

Long, Joseph. Pa. —. He was granted a $40 gratuity in Indiana County in Dec. 1839.

Long, Michael. Pa. —. He was awarded a $40 gratuity in Philadelphia, Pa. 27 Feb. 1834.

Long, Nicholas. Pa. —. He was awarded a $40 gratuity and a $40 annuity in Northumberland Co., Pa. 15 Apr. 1834.

Long, Peter. Pa. —. His widow, Christina Long, received a $40 gratuity and a $40 annuity in Adams County 20 May 1855.

Long, Richard. —. —. His warrant was issued to someone he had not authorized to receive same. Congress ruled it could not regrant same on 27 Feb. 1809.

Long, Richard. Va. —. He died in the service. His widow, Bertha Long, and eight children wee granted support in Louisa Co., Va. 11 Aug. 1777.

Long, Richard. Va. —. He died in Continental service. His widow. Dorothy Long, and children were furnished £10 support on 11 Aug. 1777 in Louisa Co., Va. She had three small children and was granted support on 13 Mar. 1781. She also lost two sons in the service.

Long, Robert. N.Y. Sgt. He was ruptured in his right groin while a prisoner of war. He lived in Westchester Co., N.Y. on 6 June 1787. He died 23 June 1813.

Long, Robert. Va. Pvt. He served in the militia under Capt. Jameson and was disabled in 1775. He was deprived of the use of his limbs. He was awarded a £30 gratuity in Culpeper Co., Va. 17 May 1779.

Long, William. Md. Pvt. He was pensioned at the rate of half-pay of a private in Missouri 20 Mar. 1840.

Long, William. Pa. —. He was awarded a $40 gratuity in Delaware Co., Pa. 27 Mar. 1830 and a $40 gratuity and a $40 annuity 30 Jan. 1834.

Longenbach, Michael. Pa. —. He was awarded a $40 gratuity and a $40 annuity in Northampton Co. on 27 Mar. 1819.

Longley, Jonathan. Mass. —. He served in the 15th Regiment and was paid $20.

Longstreth, —. Pa. —. His widow, Salome Longstreth, received a $40 gratuity and a $40 annuity in Greene County 24 Mar. 1837. She was 85 years old in 1840. She died 6 May 1846.

Longstreth, Martin. Pa. —. He was awarded a $40 gratuity and a $40 annuity in Bedford County 1 Apr. 1836.

Longstreth, Philip. Pa. —. He was awarded a $40 gratuity and a $40 annuity in Greene Co., Pa. 2 Apr. 1831.

Longworthy, Southcot. R.I. Pvt. He resided in Providence Co., R.I.

Lonsdale, William. Va. —. He was disabled on the expedition against the Indians on the Ohio River under Capt. George Moffat. He was awarded a £5 annuity for four years on 13 May 1776.

Looker, William. —. —. His application was referred to the whole House 6 Jan. 1796.

Loomis, Amasa. —. —. He was in public service at Springfield, Mass. as a clerk or assistant to Col. Chevers for the space of three years. He left because he could not get his pay. He married soon after leaving the service. He died 16 Nov. 1815. His widow, Ruth Loomis, submitted no proof of his being a soldier or his appointment as officer, conductor, or assistant conductor of military stores. Congress decided that he was a mere employee and rejected her claim for a pension 14 Mar. 1848.

Loomis, Isaac. —. —. Congress awarded his widow, Sarah Loomis, the arrearage of her pension from 4 Mar. 1848 to 3 Feb. 1853 on 10 Dec. 1857.

Loomis, Isaiah. —. —. He served as a conductor of teams. His widow, Sarah Loomis, of New London, Conn. sought arrears from 4 Mar. 1848 to 3 Feb. 1853. Congress refused her 15 Dec. 1857.

Loomis, Jacob. Mass. Fifer. He served under Col. Bayley. He was disabled by fatigue and heat at the battle of Monmouth. He resided in Boston, Mass. in 1792. He enlisted 1 Apr. 1777 and was discharged 15 Apr. 1780. His widow, Union Whitney of Great Britain, was paid $50 by the Commonwealth.

Loomis, Samuel. Conn. Corp. He served in the 1st Regiment. He was wounded in the arm which had greatly weakened by a fracture of the radius in 1780 at Elizabeth Town being pursued by the enemy. He resided in Colchester, Conn. in 1792. He enlisted 28 Apr. 1777 for the war, was promoted to corporal 1 Jan. 1781, and continued to the end of the war. He was granted one-fourth of a pension 20 Apr. 1796. He was on the 1813 pension list. He died 1 Feb. 1825.

Loomis, Uriah. N.Y. —. He enlisted 1 May 1777 at Ticonderoga. He was discharged the last of Oct. or the first of Nov. Congress granted him a pension for six months of service on 18 Mar. 1844.

Looney, John. S.C. Pvt. He was wounded at the battle of Savannah on 9 Oct. 1779. He was pensioned in 1784. He was in Pendleton in 1791. Lt. Thomas Farrar of the 1st Independent Company of Capt. Benjamin Tutt proved that he was wounded. He was granted his arrearage from 1779 to 1784 and was pensioned 1 Dec. 1823. He received his annuity as late as 1833. He was on the 1813 pension list.

Lope, John. Mass. —. He served in the 2nd Regiment and was from Nantucket. He was paid $50.

Loper, —. S.C. —. His widow, Dorothy Loper, was a resident of Colleton District in 1797. She was paid as late as 1809. Her son, Missick Loper, collected her annuity in 1808, and her son, Peter Loper, did so in 1809. She also appeared as Dolly Loper.

Lorantz, Ferdinand. Md. Pvt. His widow, Elizabeth Lorantz, was pensioned at the rate of half-pay of a private in Baltimore 1 Apr. 1839.

Lord, Amos. Conn. Pvt. He served in the 6th Conn. Regiment and was wounded in his knee by the cut of an axe. He returned home to his father. He was a native of Saybrook but lived in Harwington, Conn. when at the age of 33 he was pensioned 22 Sep. 1788. He died in 1806.

Lord, Andrew. Md. Pvt. He was pensioned at the rate of half-pay of a private in Baltimore 23 Jan. 1816. His heirs received a warrant for 50 acres, and his widow, Amelia Lord, was pensioned on 12 Mar. 1828.

Lord, Daniel. Me. —. He died 15 Dec. 1833. His widow was Hannah Lord from Limerick. She was paid $50 under the resolve of 1836.

Lord, Elias. Me. —. He died 26 Nov. 1833. His widow was Elizabeth Lord from Lyman. She was paid $50 under the resolve of 1836.

Lord, George. Conn. Pvt. He was in Col. Meade's militia under Capt. Benjamin Wright. He was wounded with a cutlass in the head, neck, and back in a skirmish with the British light horse 23 May 1780 at Greenwich. He was taken prisoner. He resided at East Hartford, Conn. in 1792. He was granted half a pension 20 Apr. 1796.

Lord, Henry. Md. Pvt. He was pensioned at the rate of half-pay of a private in Dorchester County 16 Feb. 1820. His widow, Amelia Lord, was paid his arrearage of $12.44 for 3 months and 2 days at his death 23 Jan. 1839. She was pensioned at the same rate 27 Feb. 1839.

Lord, Jeremiah. Mass. Ens. He received his commutation for five years in lieu of half-pay of life. He died in 1795.

Lord, John. —. —. He served as a seaman on the ship of war, *Ranger* from Apr. or May 1779 to May 1780 and was taken at the surrender of Charleston. He was liberated the following July. His sister and devisee was Abigail Nason. Congress granted her relief 4 Jan. 1859.

Lord, William. Mass. Sgt. He served in the 15th Regiment and was from Ashby. He was paid $50.

Lorentz, —. Pa. —. His widow, Mary Lorentz, was awarded a $40 gratuity and a $40 annuity in

Northumberland Co., Pa. 27 Mar. 1824.

Lorentz, Joseph. Pa. Sgt. He enlisted under Col. Christopher Gettig and Capt. John Harris in the 12th Regiment. He was taken prisoner at Piscataway, N.J. in the spring of 1777 and carried to New York. He was exchanged and rejoined his company. Fellow soldiers who testified in his behalf were Wendle Lorentz and Samuel Auchmutty, He applied in Northumberland County on 23 June 1813. Col. Thomas Craig signed his discharge.

Lorentz, Wendel. Pa. —. He was at the battle of Piscataway 10 May 1777 where he, Joseph Lorentz, and Joseph McHard were taken prisoners and taken to New York. Sgt. Joseph Lorentz was in Capt. Chambers' Company under Col. William Cook. He was in Capt. John Harris's Company in the 12th Pa. Regiment. After he was exchanged, he rejoined his company. Samuel Auchmutty served with him. Christopher Gettig enlisted Lorentz and made him first sergeant. He died 1 July 1815. His widow, Eve Lorentz, received a $40 gratuity and a $40 annuity 2 Apr. 1822.

Loring, Joseph. Conn. Pvt. He served in Capt. Baldwin's Artificers. He was ruptured while erecting a wharf at West Point in 1778. He resided in Huntington, Conn. in 1792. He enlisted 2 Dec. 1777, was mustered, deserted Sept. 1779, and was discharged in Nov. 1779.

Loring, Joseph. Mass. Lt. He served in Col. Knox's artillery. He contracted smallpox while a prisoner in New York and had a very diseased arm in Dec. 1775. He lived in Boston, Mass. in 1792.

Lose, John. Pa. —. He was awarded a $40 gratuity in Northumberland Co., Pa. 15 Apr. 1835. The act had stated he was a resident of Northampton County. The correction was made in 1838. His name was also incorrectly rendered as John Sose.

Loss, —. Pa. —. His widow, Martha Loss, was pensioned in Chester County 21 Mar. 1833.

Lotbinier, Louis. Canada. Chaplain. He served in Col. Livingston's Regiment. He was being pensioned by the Continental Congress act of 22 Aug. 1780.

Lott, Bartholomew. N.J. —. He was pensioned in Sussex County on 10 Nov. 1837 at the rate of $60 per annum. His widow, Mary Ann Lott, was pensioned 17 Apr. 1846 at the rate of $30 per annum.

Lott, Jeremiah. Pa. —. He applied in Greenwich, Sussex Co., N.J. on 21 Mar. 1814. He served in the 1st Troop of the 4th Regiment of Light Dragoons in the Pa. Line under Capt. John Herd and Col. Stephen Moyland for six years and three months as trumpeter. Previously he had served one year under Capt. Caleb Dorsey. He was wounded in South Carolina in the thigh at Hunters Bluff at Dorchester. At Little York he received a severe wound in his right shoulder. He had a numerous family.

Lott, Joshua. S.C. —. He was from Winton. There was one child in 1791.

Lott, Nicholas. Pa. Sgt. He was pensioned 25 Apr. 1808 at the rate of $2.50 per month from 23 Jan. 1808. He was on the 1813 pension list.

Lott, Paul. Pa. —. He was pensioned.

Lott, Richard. Pa. —. His application was postponed 26 Feb. 1813.

Loud, David. Mass. Pvt. He served at the Castle and was from Braintree. He was paid $50.

Loud, William. Mass. Pvt. He served at the Castle and was from Weymouth. He was paid $50.

Louden, Archibald. Pa. —. He was granted relief 31 Mar. 1836 and died 12 Aug. 1840 in Cumberland County. He was 86 years old in 1840.

Loughrey, Jeremiah. Pa. —. He was wounded in the shoulder in defense of the state on the frontiers by Indians. He was in Westmoreland County 4 Mar. 1807. He was awarded a $40 annuity. He died 1 Jan. 1829. He also appeared as Jeremiah Lochrey.

Louks, William. N.Y. Pvt. He was wounded in his right arm by a musket ball at Oriskany on 6 Aug. 1777. He served in Capt. Christopher Fox's Company under Col. Jacob Klock. He applied 14

Sep. 1786. He also appeared as William Loucks.

Loury, Joseph. Pa. —. The act for his pension incorrectly gave his name as Alexander Loury of Armstrong County. The error was corrected 25 June 1839 by which time he was deceased so his $40 gratuity was paid to his administrators in Indiana County.

Louser, Jacob. Pa. —. He was in the militia. His heirs were his widow and children.

Louther, David. Pa. —. He was granted relief 21 Feb. 1838 in Westmoreland County. He died 18 Sep. 1840. His widow, Sarah Louther, received a $40 annuity in Westmoreland County 8 Apr. 1853. She died 2 Sep. 1854.

Love, —. Pa. —. His widow was Catherine Love. She was from Luzerne County 11 Apr. 1825.

Love, Henry. Pa. Matross. He was in Northampton County 18 Jan. 1786. He was in the Pa. Regiment of Artillery and lost his leg at the siege of York. He was transferred to the Invalids and was discharged 1 Nov. 1783. He was on the 1813 pension list.

Love, Thomas. —. Surgeon. He died in the service. Congress rejected the claim of his son, George Love, 6 Apr. 1820. The heirs were not entitled to bounty land.

Love, William. N.J. Quartermaster Sergeant. He served in the 3rd New Jersey Regiment. He received a rupture at the battle of Monmouth. He lived in Pa. in 1794. He enlisted 22 Mar. 1777 and was discharged 3 June 1779.

Lovegrove, Hampton. —. —. He entered the service in Mar. 1779 for nine months and was in Conn., Vt., and N.Y. He returned home in September having been disabled by a wound from one of his oxen in his foot. He was in the teaming service. In Aug. 1781 at the age of thirteen he enlisted for three months in the Vermont State Troops and performed camp duty. He was born in 1768. He performed first service at the direction of his master Mr. Ecles of Colchester, Conn. Congress rejected his application 28 Jan. 1837 because his three months was not sufficient. His type of service was not contemplated by the law, and he was of tender age.

Lovejoy, Abner. Mass. —. He was paid $20. He served in the 8th Regiment.

Lovejoy, Joshua. N.H. Sgt. He was in Col. James Frye's Militia Regiment. He was wounded in his right foot and ankle by two musket balls on 17 June 1775 at Bennington. He lived in Hopkinton, N.H. in 1794. He was granted half a pension 20 Apr. 1796. He was pensioned at the rate of $5 per month from 5 June 1807. He was on the 1813 pension list. He died 28 Jan. 1832.

Lovejoy, Samuel. —. —. He died in 1822. His widow, Esther Lovejoy, sought a pension. She was 84 years of age. Her husband lacked three days of having served the requisite six months. Congress granted her a pension 3 Aug. 1854.

Loveland, George. Mass. —. He served in the 1st Regiment and was from Northfield. He was paid $50.

Lovell, Benjamin. Mass. 1st Lt. He was pensioned 28 Jan. 1780 at the rate of half-pay.

Lovell, Caleb. Mass. Pvt. He served at the Castle and was from Abington. His widow, Ruth Lovell, was paid $50.

Lovell, Robert. Va. Lt. His widow, Elizabeth Lovell, lived in Northumberland County 14 Feb. 1787 and had three children to maintain. He joined the state troops with his men at Williamsburg in Apr. 1777. He was in Capt. Henry Garnett's Company of the 2nd State Troops under Col. Haynes Morgan. He died 11 Aug. 1779. His widow was continued on the pension list at the rate of £30 per annum on 31 Oct. 1787. On 8 Aug. 1791 his children were 18, 14, and 15 years of age. He also appeared as Robert Lovewell. She was continued on the list on 13 Sep. 1791.

Lovering, Isaac. Mass. —. He served in the 2nd Regiment and was paid $20.

Lovett, William. Va. —. His wife was furnished assistance in Loudoun Co., Va. on 14 Apr. 1778.

Loving, Christopher. S.C. —. He served in the 6th S.C. Regiment. He was made a prisoner at the reduction of Charleston. When he escaped, he returned to the service under Gen. Sumter until 1781. While on furlough, he was wounded by a party and lost his right hand. He had his application rejected in 1795 because he was a resident of Virginia.

Loving, John. —. —. He was granted relief.

Loving, Joseph. —. Lt. He served under Col. Knox. He was disabled by smallpox while a prisoner in New York in 1775. He resided in Mass. in 1792.

Low, —. Va. —. His wife Elizabeth Low was allowed £4 relief in Augusta County 23 August 1783.

Low, Thomas. S.C. R.I. & S.C. —. He enlisted at Bunker Hill, Massachusetts under Gen. Warren and was out under Benedict Arnold to join Ge Providence, Rhode Island and was in the battle of Bunker Hill under Gen. Joseph Warren. He was ordered out under Col. Benedict Arnold to join Gen. Montgomery to take Quebec. He was taken prisoner and held ten months before he was exchanged in New York. His enlistment was up so he entered the service again . He served as a quartermaster on the ship *Providence* under Commodore Abram Whipple. They crossed the Atlantic Ocean to France. They returned to Boston. Shortly thereafter they sailed to Charleston, South Carolina. There ship was taken in the blockade, but the seamen escaped. Gov. Rutledge ordered every man to attach himself to some corps. He petitioned to joined Pulaski's troops as sergeant major. He was at the battle of Stono after which he was promoted to ensign. He then went to the siege of Savannah where Pulaski lost his life. On the retreat to Hillsborough, North Carolina he was under Baron DeKalb. He was at Gates' defeat. He retreated and joined Gen. Greene. He was wounded at the battle of Guilford in North Carolina and taken prisoner. His horse had been killed. He was carried to Wilmington, North Carolina where he was put on a prison ship and held for six months. He served a total of eighteen months from South Carolina but received pay for only three months. He was 74 years old and had been deprived of his consort by the cold shaft of death. His family were scattered in different sections of the United States. He had been left an invalid and sought relief from South Carolina. He applied from Abbeville District 13 Sep. 1826. He had lost his discharge. He was paid $192.66 for his service in the South Carolina Continental Line on 20 Dec. 1810. John Dawkins saw him at Stono in the horse company. James Dixon and John Anderson had seen his discharge. He was from Abbeville District and was pensioned 6 Dec. 1826. He was paid as late as 1830. He also appeared as Thomas Lowe.

Lowder, Jacob. Va. —. His wife, Eleanor Lowder, was granted £8 support in Berkeley County on 21 Apr. 1778.

Lowell, Thomas. Me. —. He was from Dixmont. He was paid $50 under the resolve of 1836.

Lowell, William. N.H. Sgt. He served under Col. James Frye and Capt. William Ballard. He was wounded by a musket ball shot through his body on 17 June 1775 at Bunker Hill. He lived in Warner in 1794. He was in the militia. He was granted one-third of a pension 20 Apr. 1796.

Lowenberg, Frederick. Pa. —. He was pensioned.

Lower, Hartman. Pa. —. He applied in Philadelphia County on 15 Sep. 1824. He was 81 years old. He served under Capt. Airs, Col. Irwin, and Col. Cadwalder to the end of the war. He was at Brandywine, Germantown, Trenton, and Princeton. He was wounded in the right thigh at Germantown. The enemy killed his wife by giving her a blow on the breast with a fence rail. She had an infant at the time. He had a small plantation in Montgomery County where he lived until a few years ago. A highway robber entered his house one night, took all of his money and things of value, beat him, and left him for dead. He died 6 Oct. 1828.

Lownsbury, Samuel. Pa. —. He was awarded a $40 gratuity and a $40 annuity in Bucks County 5 Feb. 1836. He died in 1846.

Lowrie, John. Md. Pvt. He served in the 7th Regiment. He was wounded at Camden. He was pensioned in Somerset County in 1784. He also appeared as John Lowry.

Lowry, Alexander. Pa. —. He was granted a $40 gratuity 27 Mar. 1837 in Armstrong County. [Compare with Alexander Lowry in appendix.]

Lowry, Henry. S.C. —. He was pensioned 6 Dec. 1825. He received his annuity as late as 1831.

Lowry, John. Md. Pvt. He was pensioned in 1783. He was on the 1791 pension list. He was on the 1813 pension list.

Lowry, John. Md. Pvt. He was on the 1791 pension list. He was on the 1813 pension list.

Lowry, Joseph. Pa. —. He was granted relief.

Lowry, William. Va. —. He died in Continental service. His widow, Elizabeth Lowry, was granted his half-pay from 11 May 1778 in Northumberland Co., Va.

Lowther, James. Pa. —. He was granted relief in Franklin County 3 Mar. 1825. He was dead by Apr. 1836.

Loyer, Peter. Pa. —. His application was postponed 8 Mar. 1813. It was approved 3 June. He was from Cumberland Co.

Lucas, —. Va. —. His widow, Elizabeth Lucas, resided in Charlotte Co., Va. on 2 Jan. 1786.

Lucas, —. S.C. —. His widow, Winney Lucas, was a resident of Georgetown/Liberty. There were children in 1791.

Lucas, Barnabas. Mass. —. He was wounded by a musket ball in the left thigh. He resided in Mass. in 1796. He served in the 2nd Regiment. His widow, Betsey Lucas, was from Plymouth and was paid $50 by the Commonwealth.

Lucas, Basil. Md. Sgt. He was pensioned at the rate of half-pay of a sergeant 23 Jan. 1816.

Lucas, Elisha. Mass. —. He enlisted in 1780 and twelve days before the expiration of his term he was discharged in Westchester, N.Y. He was 240 miles from home. Congress allowed him travel time of 20 miles per day and granted him a pension for six months of service on 11 Feb. 1834.

Lucas, George. Pa. Sgt. He applied in Bedford County on 12 Apr. 1813. He enlisted in 1776 in Franklin County in the 6th Pa. Regiment under Col. William Erwin in Capt. Abraham Smith's Company. He was in Canada at the battle of Three Rivers and returned home. In 1777 he reenlisted in the 7th Pa. Regiment under Col. Erwin and Capt. John Alexander. He was discharged 23 Jan. 1781. He was in the battles of Monmouth and Stoney Point. He was 64 years old. He had nine children, eight of whom were still living. Three lived with him.

Lucas, Humphrey. Va. —. His wife, Elizabeth Lucas, was furnished 2 barrels of Indian corn in Charlotte Co., Va. on 2 June 1777, provisions for her and her children on 6 Oct. 1777, a peck of salt on 2 Feb. 1778, £24.14.6 on 5 Oct. 1778, £84 on 1 Feb. 1779, 3 barrels of corn, 150 pounds of pork, and ½ bushel of salt on 1 Nov. 1779, £188 on 6 Mar. 1780, 5 barrels of corn and 250 pounds of pork for her and her family of five on 6 Nov. 1780, and £995 on 5 Feb. 1781. He died in the service and his widow was entitled to his half-pay on 4 Dec. 1781.

Lucas, Isaac. Mass. —. He was from Plymouth and was paid $20.

Lucas, John. Md. Sgt. He was pensioned at the rate of half-pay of a sergeant in Anne Arundel County on 12 Feb. 1820.

Lucas, John. Md. Pvt. His widow, Rachel Lucas, was pensioned at the rate of half-pay of a private in Anne Arundel County on 6 Mar. 1832.

Lucas, Philip. Pa. —. He was awarded a $40 gratuity in Schuylkill County 28 Mar. 1836.

Lucas, Samuel. Pa. —. He received a $40 gratuity in Indiana County 22 Mar. 1813.

Lucas, Thomas. Va. —. His wife, Elizabeth Lucas, was granted £25 support in Northumberland Co., Va. on 10 May 1779 and 2 barrels of corn on 12 Aug. 1782. On the latter date she was his widow.

Lucas, William. Conn. —. He served in the 6th Connecticut Regiment under Col. Jonathan Meigs and Capt. Samuel P-------. Near Verplank's Point he was wounded twice by musket balls. One went through his body a little below the breast and the other entered his right arm. He was taken into captivity and held seventeen months. He was granted half-pay in 1780. He lived in Mass. 1789 and was 38 years old. He was on the 1813 pension list and transferred from Berkshire Co., Mass. to Tioga Co., N.Y. 4 Mar. 1827.

Lucas, William Budd. N.Y. Farrier. He served in Capt. Samuel Delaven's troop of light dragoons in the Westchester County militia under Col. Samuel Drake. He was ordered out by Jacob W. Vermillia and was cornet of the same troop in 1781. He was wounded in the head by being beaten, whipped, and thrown to the ground. He was bruised on his breast and different parts of his body. He was carried a prisoner to New York City. He was aged 53 years on 16 Mar. 1788. He lived in Pittstown, Albany Co., N.Y. on 29 Apr. 1789. He was a school master.

Luce, Abijah. Mass. Pvt. He served in the 2nd Regiment and was from Boston. His widow, Mary Luce, was paid $50.

Luce, Abner. Mass. Pvt. He served in the 1st Regiment and was from Tisbury. His widow, Amelia Luce, was paid $50.

Luce, Crosby. Mass. Gunner. He served under Gen. Henry Knox and Dimond Morton. He was disabled by the loss of his forefinger and had his right hand otherwise injured. He was 39 years old in 1789. He was on the 1813 pension list.

Luce, Joseph. Mass. —. He served in the Artillery. He was pensioned 1 Sep. 1782. He died 11 Jan. 1786.

Luce, Marvil. N.Y. —. He was pensioned.

Luckey, Andrew. Pa. —. He was pensioned 2 Apr. 1822 and died 23 Oct. 1826.

Lucus, Samuel. Pa. —. He was awarded a $40 gratuity in Indiana County on 22 Mar. 1813.

Ludden, Lemuel. Mass. Pvt. He served at Castle William and was from Boston. His widow, Elizabeth Ludden, was paid $50.

Ludeman, William. Va. Maj. He was granted £100 relief on 20 Jan. 1786.

Ludkin, Jacob. Mass. Pvt. He served in the 3rd Regiment and was from Royalston. His widow, Dorcas Forbush, was paid $50.

Ludwick, Christopher. —. —. He was pensioned by the Continental Congress in 1785.

Ludwig, —. Pa. —. His widow, Elizabeth Ludwig of Philadelphia County, received a $40 gratuity and a $40 annuity in Crawford County in 1836. She was 80 years old in 1840.

Ludwig, John Martin. Pa. Pvt. He was in Philadelphia County 14 Nov. 1785. He was transferred from the 4th Artillery Regiment to the Invalids. He was disabled by a rupture and loss of health. He was 31 years old. He was dead by Sep. 1793. He also appeared as John M. Lodwick\.

Luellin, John. Del. Pvt. He was on the 1799 pension roll. He died in Apr. 1809.

Lues, William. N.Y. —. He was granted relief.

Lufkin, Moses. Mass. Pvt. He served in the Invalids under Col. Lewis Nichola and Capt. Moses McFarland. He was entirely worn out. He was pensioned 15 Sep. 1782. He was 54 years old in 1790. The Commonwealth paid $20 to Mehitable Poland and the other children 4 May 1816.

Lum, Squire. N.J. Ens. He served under Capt. David Bates and Col. Martin and died 6 Aug. 1776 of camp sickness in New York City. He married Phebe Ward 3 Nov. 1768. His widow, Phebe Lum, married secondly David Leonard 23 Apr. 1778. She was awarded her half-pay pension during the time of her widowhood in Morris County in 1790.

Lummus, John. S.C. —. He was from Abbeville District and was pensioned 17 Dec. 1821. He was paid an annuity as late as 1825. He also appeared as John Lumus.

Lumpkin, Dickinson. —. —. Congress refused him a pension 19 July 1848. His claim was not supported by evidence.

Lunderman, —. Va. —. He and his brother were in Continental service from Charlotte Co., Va. Their mother, Sarah Lunderman, was furnished ½ bushel of salt for her and her family on 1 Dec. 1777.

Lunt, Joseph. Mass. —. He was pensioned.

Lunt, Thomas. Mass. —. He served in Nixon's Regiment and was paid $20. He was from Newburyport.

Lunt, William. R.I. Pvt. He served in the Kingston Reds. He was wounded in his head and arm by the explosion of an alarm gun before he had finished loading it at Rest Hill on 7 May 1779 in South Kingston. He lived in North Kingston, R.I. in 1794 and South Kingston, R.I. in 1795. He was granted half a pension 20 Apr. 1796. He was in the militia. He was on the 1813 pension list.

Lush, Richard. N.Y. Deputy Muster Master. He was issued certificates for his arrears of pay and a year's advance 15 Apr. 1786.

Lush, Stephen. —. —. He served as brigade major and aide-de-camp to Gen. George Clinton and was taken prisoner. He was released on parole in Feb. 1778 and discharged in Oct. 1778. He died in 1825. He married in 1781. His widow, Lydia Lush, sought a pension from Congress. She sought to qualify under the act of 1836 for a pension for life; yet, her pension under the act of 1838 entitled her for five years only. Congress rejected her claim 28 Jan. 1846.

Lusk, Nathan. S.C. Lt. He served under Capt. Joseph Lawson in the infantry and was wounded in his left arm on 28 July 1778 in the Florida Expedition in action with the Tories and Creeks. He was totally disabled in that limb. Other officers were Capt. William Strain, Capt. Joseph Pickens, Capt. Andrew Pickens, and Capt. Thomas Weems. He sought his pension for the years 1779 to 1795. He was pensioned in 1795 at the rate of $21.42 per annum. He was on the verge of 70 years of age on 24 Nov. 1819. He was granted $342.72 on 25 Dec.1820. He was late of Pendleton District but formerly of Abbeville District when in 1831 his widow, Bell Lusk, had her application rejected. She was about 70 years of age. Only one of her children, a daughter, had left her.

Lusk, Patrick. Pa. Sgt. He was in Dauphin County 21 June 1786. He served in the 2nd Pa. Regiment in Capt. John Murray's company under Col. Samuel Miles. He was wounded in the right wrist on 3 Jan. 1777 at the battle of Princeton. He was 35 years old. He was on the 1813 pension list. He died 17 Mar. 1816 in Lycoming County. He also appeared as Patrick Lush.

Lusk, Robert. S.C. —. He was formerly of Abbeville District and late of Pendleton District. He served under Capt. William Strain, Capt. Joseph Pickens, Capt. Andrew Pickens, and Capt. Thomas Weems. His widow, Bell Lusk, 70 years of age, applied 21 Oct. 1831.

Lusk, William. S.C. —. He was killed in the service on 10 Mar. 1781 and left a widow and a ten month old child. She was granted an annuity 18 Mar. 1785 as Jane Lusk for herself and her child and did so until it was twelve years old. His remarried widow, Jane Crawford, was granted an annuity for her child by her first husband on 22 Nov. 1786. She was from Abbeville District 1 Oct. 1804. She had a family of six children.

Luter, Charles. Va. —. His wife, Elizabeth Luter, was allowed two barrels of corn and 100 pounds of pork in Bedford Co., Va. on 27 Mar. 1780.

Luther, David. Pa. —. He was pensioned.

Lutterloh, Henry Emanuel. —. Com. Gen. of Forage. He sought commutation of half-pay for life. He served 24 years as a major in the Duke of Brunswick's Guards. He resigned and came to America. On 7 June 1777 he became the first Deputy Quartermaster General. He was appointed Commissary General of Forage with rank of colonel 10 May 1780 and served to the end of the war. He sought commutation of half-pay for life 20 May 1790.

Lutz, Andrew. Pa. —. He was awarded a $40 gratuity and a $40 annuity in Lebanon Co., Pa. 7 Mar. 1829.

Lutz, Henry. Pa. Pvt. He served under Capt. Hagenbush in the Flying Camp and was taken prisoner 7 Aug. 1776. He was awarded a $40 gratuity in Northampton County on 14 Mar. 1814 and a $40 gratuity and $40 annuity 28 Mar. 1822. He died 8 Nov. 1828.

Lutz, Henry. Pa. —. He applied 29 June 1819. He served in Capt. Grubbs's Company under Col. Miles. One of his name received relief in Northampton County 28 Mar. 1820. He could be identical with the preceding soldier of the same name.

Lutzmore, —. Pa. —. His widow, Mary Ann Lutzmore, was granted relief in Erie County 21 June 1839.

Lybrook, John. —. —. In the spring of 1776 he was ordered to repair to Philip Baregan's fort in Montgomery County against Indian excursions. He served seven months under Capt. John Flood. In 1777 he served five months under Capt. Christian Snidow. He served from April to October 1778 under Col. Preston and. In 1779 he was under Lt. Christian Snidow and Ens. John Chapman. He served from Mar. to 13 June 1780. He sought relief from Congress 5 Mar. 1840.

Lydson, Robey. Me. —. He died 27 May 1809. His widow was Olive Lydson from Kittery. She was paid $50 under the resolve of 1836.

Lyell, Robert. S.C. Col. He served as a captain of rangers and later as a major at the siege of Charleston. He suffered from dead palsy. He was helpless and had a small family on 15 Dec. 1791. His application was rejected.

Lyford, Nathaniel. —. —. He was unable to prove that he served the minimum of six months so Congress rejected his petition for a pension 4 May 1846.

Lyle, Charles. Va. —. His wife, Elizabeth Lyle, was granted £6 on 17 Aug. 1778 and £22.10 support on 20 Sep. 1779 in York Co., Va.

Lyles, David. S.C. —. He served under Capt. Daniel Jackson and died in the service at Charleston in 1777. His widow was Priscilla Lyles of Mecklenburg Co., N.C. 6 Dec. 1796.

Lyles, Ephraim. S.C. —. He was pensioned 30 Nov. 1824.

Lyles, James. S.C. —. He was at Black Stocks, Hanging Rock, Fish Dam, Augusta, Cowpens, Deep Creek, and Congaree Fort. In 1829 he was 85 or 86 years old. He was from Richland District when he was pensioned 25 Nov. 1830. Philip Pearson and William Cate knew him as a soldier. Ephraim Lyles stated he served under Capt. John Lyles, Maj. Frederick Gray, and Col. James Lyles. He received his annuity as late as 1834.

Lyman, Andrew. —. —. He was on the pension roll in 1836 at the rate of $20 per annum. Congress granted him an increase of $30 per annum on 7 Jan. 1837.

Lyman, Richard. N.H. Sgt. He served under Col. Prentiss in Capt. Troop's Company. He had obstructions in his liver and spleen and a general debility in consequence of wading in water in 1777 at Schuylkill. He lived in Lebanon, N.H. in 1795.

Lynch, Hugh. Md. Pvt. He was pensioned at the rate of half-pay of a private 1 Jan. 1813.

Lynch, John. Md. Corp. He was pensioned in Kent County in 1786.

Lynch, John. Md. Pvt. He was pensioned under the act of 7 June 1785. He died in 1813. He was on the 1813 pension list.

Lynch, John. S.C. —. He was killed in 1781. His widow, Margaret Lynch, was granted an annuity 10 Dec. 1784. There were children in 1791.

Lynch, Michael. Pa. —. He was awarded a $40 gratuity and a $40 annuity in Delaware Co. on 4 Apr. 1809.

Lynch, Thomas. Md. Pvt. He was pensioned at the rate of half-pay of a private 12 Mar. 1828. He was of St. Mary's County. He died 13 Nov. 1832. His arrearage was paid to his administrator, James M. K. Hammet, 8 Mar. 1833.

Lynch, William. S.C. —. At the age of 25 he volunteered in the militia. His father had been killed by the Indians when he was 11 years old. On 3 July 1776 he was wounded in his right eye by a musket ball in action with the Cherokee. He was blinded in that eye. He was stationed as Fort Seneca under Capt. Tutt. He also served under Capt. Joseph McJunkin. He was from Greenville District. His application for a pension was approved 7 Dec. 1816. He died 5 Dec. 1821. His widow, Mary Lynch, was granted his arrearage on 3 Dec. 1821. She was paid his arrearage of $45.68 on 16 Dec. 1823. He also appeared as William Linch.

Lynch, William. Va. —. He was from Brunswick County and was the father of 34 legitimate children by four wives. His fourth wife was young and healthy. Twenty-seven children were still living. He was exempt from any public and county taxes on 9 Feb. 1827.

Lyne, John. Pa. —. He was pensioned 8 Apr. 1818.

Lynn, —. Pa. —. His widow, Anna Catherine Lynn, received a $40 gratuity and a $40 annuity in Northampton County 16 June 1836.

Lynn, David. Md. Capt. His widow, Mary Lynn, was pensioned at the rate of half-pay of captain 25 Feb. 1836. He had died 11 Apr. 1835.

Lynn, Dewalt. Pa. —. He was paid a $40 gratuity 7 Feb. 1831 in Northumberland County. He was pensioned 14 Apr. 1834. He was 85 years old in 1840 and died 15 Dec. 1846.

Lynn, James. Pa. —. He was granted a $40 gratuity and a $40 annuity in Washington County 12 Feb. 1836.

Lynn, John. Md. Lt. He was wounded at Eutaw Springs 8 Sep. 1781. He was pensioned in 1785. His widow, Eleanor Lynn, was pensioned at the rate of half-pay of a lieutenant on 13 Feb. 1819. She died 23 Apr. 1824, and her daughters were paid her arrearage on 19 Jan. 1825. They were Jane Lynn and Elizabeth Lynn who married David Richardson.

Lynn, John. N.C. —. He was wounded in his hand and unable to do labor. He sought the privilege of retailing spirituous liquor with an exemption from taxes. He was granted such in Dec. 1811.

Lynn, John. Pa. Pvt. He was from Union County. He served under Capt. Gill and Col. Moylan having enlisted in Lancaster Co., Pa. On 1 Jan. 1780. in the 4th Regiment of Cavalry. He was pensioned at the age of 63 on 6 Apr. 1818. He died 28 Sep. 1847 in Union Co., Pa., and his widow, Jane Lynn, in 1854. Congress rejected her claim for a pension 29 Feb. 1848 because of the date of her marriage. Their daughter, Mary J. Lynn, was born in Union Co., Pa. 23 Nov. 1817 and was more than 78 years old when Congress granted her petition for a pension 29 Apr. 1896.

Lynn, Valentine. Md. —. He was granted relief.

Lyon, —. Pa. —. His widow, Elizabeth Lyon, was awarded a $40 gratuity and a $40 annuity in Northumberland Co., Pa. 25 Mar. 1824.

Lyon, —. Pa. —. His widow, Mary Lyon, was awarded a $40 gratuity in Butler County 14 Mar. 1842 for his Revolutionary service. She received a $40 gratuity and a $40 annuity 18 Apr. 1843. She died

2 Sep. 1843.

Lyon, Benjamin. Pa. —. He was awarded a $40 gratuity and a $40 annuity in Mifflin County on 14 Mar. 1818.

Lyon, David. Pa. Pvt. He served in Askin's Company. He was on the 1813 pension list.

Lyon, Jonathan. Mass. Pvt. He served in the 10th Regiment under Capt. Christopher Marshall and Col. Benjamin Tupper. He was disabled by the loss of his left arm above the elbow joint. He was pensioned 1 Sep. 1782. He was 27 years old in 1788. He was on the 1813 pension list of Vermont. He transferred to Addison Co., Vt. 24 Apr. 1816.

Lyon, Joseph. Conn. He enlisted in 1778 in the brigade of teams for one year. In 1780 he enlisted for a year under Capt. Hodge, Col. Sherman, and Gen. Parson. He was discharged due to the scarcity of provisions. In Apr. 1781 he enlisted in the spy boat service in Long Island sound under Capt. Brewster for a year. He renewed his enlistment to June 1782 and received a furlough. Afterwards, he was discharged. Congress granted him a pension 21 Dec. 1831.

Lyon, Joseph. Va. Pvt. He served in the 7th Virginia Regiment. His widow, Mary Lyon, was on the pension roll of 1791.

Lyon, Henry. N.J. Corp. He enlisted in the 1st Regiment under Capt. Isaac Morrison from 24 July 1777, was promoted to corporal in Mar. 1778, and died in July 1778. He married Martha Tomkin in 1773. His widow, Martha Lyon, married secondly Richard Treelease 10 May 1788. She was granted a half-pay pension from the time of her first husband's death to her remarriage in Morris County in 1790.

Lyon, Robert. Pa. —. He was awarded a $40 annuity in Northumberland County on 29 Mar. 1813. He died 19 Aug. 1823.

Lyon, William Pa. Pvt. He served in the 3rd Company of the 2nd Battalion of the Lancaster County Flying Camp under Col. Clotz. He was wounded in his leg and thigh at Fort Washington 16 Nov. 1776. He had a wife and five children and resided in Cumberland County in 1788.

Lyon, William. Va. Pvt. His widow, Mary Lyon, was in Hampshire County 11 Oct. 1785. He served in Capt. Crockett's Company in the 7th Va. Regiment. He fell at the battle of Guilford. She was pensioned at the rate of £18 per annum on 9 Jan. 1786 in Frederick County. There were six children alive on 16 Oct. 1788 in Hampshire Co., Va. In 1791 in Rockbridge County his children were William Lyon aged 15, John Lyon aged 13, twins Peter Lyon and Paul Lyon aged 10, and Ephraim Lyon age 8. Mary Lyon was in Botetourt County in 1795. He also appeared as William Lyons.

Lyons, Edward. Pa. Pvt. He died 1 May 1799.

Lyons, Michael. N.Y. Pvt. He served in Capt. Gilbert Livingstone's Company under Col. Frederick Wissenfels. While on a scouting party in Ulster County, he was wounded in his right side by a musket ball which penetrated his body. He was pensioned 11 Sep. 1786. He lived in Marbletown, Ulster Co., N.Y. 3 Sep. 1789. He was on the 1813 pension list. He died 14 Jan. 1818 in Ulster County.

Lyons, Thomas. N.Y. Lt. He served under Capt. Burrow in Col. Seth Warner's Regiment. He was wounded in his leg at Ticonderoga by savages on 2 July 1777 and was disabled by the fracture. He was 38 years old in 1786. He lived at White Hall, Washington Co., N.Y. on 2 May 1789. He was on the 1813 pension list. He also appeared as Thomas Lyon. He was probably the Lt. Thomas Lyon who died in Erie Co., Penn. 3 Sep. 1827.

Lyons, William. Pa. —. His administratrix, Hannah Shaw, was pensioned in Philadelphia on 24 June 1785.

McAdams, Alexander. Va. —. His wife, Mary McAdams, was granted 20 shillings per month for support while he was away in Continental service in Yohogania Co., Va. 26 Aug. 1778.

McAdams, John. —. —. Congress rejected the claim from his heirs for commutation on 25 July 1850 because he did not serve to the end of the war

McAllister, Andrew. S.C. Pvt. He served under Col. John Irwin on the Florida Expedition. He lost the use of one leg and arm. He was a resident of Abbeville District. He was pensioned at the rate of $21.30 per annum for life on 20 Dec. 1800. He was on the 1813 U.S. pension list. He died 1 Sep. 1831. His widow was Elizabeth McAllister of Pendleton District, and. she had four small children.

McAllister, Benjamin. —. —. —. He was never pensioned. His only surviving child, Jane McAllister, had her claim rejected by Congress 30 May 1862.

McAllister, Nathan. S.C. —. He lost his life in a skirmish with the Tories. His widow, Margaret McAllister, was awarded an annuity 8 Jan. 1785. She was a resident of Abbeville District. There was one child in 1791.

McAmis, James. Va. —. He lived in Campbell County in 1795. He was in the militia and was wounded in his right arm by the bursting of a bomb shell at the reduction of York in 1781. James Dinwiddie deposed he was present and saw it. Thomas McAmis, who was also at Yorktown, corroborated the service. He was in Greene Co., Tenn. 12 Nov. 1799 and died 30 Nov. 1822. His children were Alexander McAmis, Nancy McAmis who married William Edmiston and lived in Ohio, John McAmis, Margaret McAmis, Jane McAmis, Betsy McAmis, Eleanor McAmis, and Isabel McAmis. The latter was the only one under age at the time of her father's death, and he was between 20 and 21. He was commonly called James McCamish and James McAmish.

McAnnalty, John. Mass. —. He was paid $20. He also appeared as John McNelty.

McArthur, Neil. Mass. Pvt. He served in the 1st Regiment under Col. Joseph Vose and Capt. Miller. He was disabled by a rupture. He was 64 years old in 1788. He was on the 1813 pension list. He was paid $20 by the Commonwealth.

McBarney, Thomas. Pa. —. He was on the 1789 pension list.

McBee, Elijah. S.C. —. His children were paid 9 Dec. 1820. They were still on the roll in 1824.

McBeth, George. S.C. —. He served under Capt. John Bowie and was taken prisoner by the Tories. He was from Pendleton in 1815. He served three years in the state troops and was pensioned 7 Dec. 1819. Samuel Earle was lieutenant in the same company. He was paid as late as 1832.

McBride, —. Pa. —. His widow, Mary McBride, received a $40 annuity in Fayette County 8 May 1854.

McBride, Archibald. Del. Sgt. He was pensioned in 1783. He was on the 1791 pension list. He died 25 Apr. 1803 in Pennsylvania.

McBride, Francis. N.Y. Pvt. He served under Col. James McClaughry in the Ulster County militia and was slain 6 Oct. 1777. His children, James McBride and Jennet McBride, received a half-pay pension.

McBride, Peter. Pa. —. He was wounded. He was awarded a $40 gratuity and a $40 annuity in Somerset County on 30 Mar. 1812. He was awarded a $40 annuity in Chester County on 13 Mar. 1815. He died 31 May 1820.

McBride, Robert. Pa. —. His heirs were paid $300 for his donation land. Payment was to be made to John McMeens of Lycoming Co., Pa. 22 Mar. 1824.

McBride, William. S.C. —. He lost his life in the service. Martha McBride was granted an annuity 25 Apr. 1785. She was later Martha Speer. There were children in 1791. She sought his arrearage

11 Nov. 1826.

McBurney, Thomas. Pa. Pvt. He was on the 1813 pension list.

McCabe, Michael. Va. —. His wife, Judith McCabe, was granted £20 support in Berkeley County 18 May 1779.

McCain, Theophilus. S.C. —. He was paid an annuity of $60 per annum in 1851 [?1831].

McCain, William. —. —. He enlisted in Feb. 1776 under Capt. Dorsey or Dolsey and served eighteen months. He had several tours of duty. He died in 1808. He married 13 Jan. 1778. His widow, Charlotte McCain, had her application rejected by Congress 9 Feb. 1848 because it could not be determined how many months he served.

McCall, David. S.C. Pvt. He served under Capt. Brumfield and Gen. Rutherford in the N.C. militia. He was at Thompson's Ferry, Coosawhatchie, and Two Sisters. He then served in the S.C. State Troops under Col. William Hill and Capt. James Giles. He was at Eutaw Springs, Biggen Church, and Wahabe. He was 74 years old and had a wife. He was from York District when he was pensioned 17 Nov. 1831. He was paid his annuity as late as 1834.

McCall, James. S.C. —. He served in the militia under Gen. Pickens and was at Cowpens. He died in 1781 of smallpox. His daughter, Jennett H. McCall, was only eleven years old when her father died. She suffered from deformity of her feet since infancy. She sought relief from Congress 9 Feb. 1856. She was 86 years old.

McCall, Joseph. S.C. —. He was on the roll in 1791.

McCallister, John. Pa. —. He was awarded a $40 gratuity and a $40 annuity in Montgomery County on 30 Mar. 1822.

McCallister, Randall. N.H. Pvt. He served in Stark's Regiment. He was pensioned 13 Sep. 1808. He was on the 1813 pension list and died 23 May 1819 in Hillsborough Co., N.H.

McCamack, David. Pa. —. He received a $40 gratuity and a $40 annuity in Tioga County, N.Y.15 June 1836.

McCamant, Isaac. Pa. —. He was awarded a $40 gratuity and a $40 annuity in Mercer Co., Pa. 11 Apr. 1825.

McCann, —. Pa. —. His widow, Martha McCann, was awarded a $40 gratuity and a $40 annuity in York County in Apr. 1837. She died 25 Mar. 1845.

McCann, Michael. Md. Pvt. He was pensioned at the rate of half-pay of a private in Frederick Co. on 6 Feb. 1817.

McCannon, Christopher. Va. Sgt.-Maj. He served under Col. Campbell. He was wounded at the battle of Guilford on 15 Mar. 1781 by a musket ball which deprived him of the use of his left arm. He lived in Va. in 1794.

McCants, Thomas. S.C. —. He was at Orangeburg, Congaree Fort, and Charleston. His comrades were George Straight and David Neely. Henry Brown was with Neely at Orangeburg. John Moffet swore that he was a prisoner at the time of Huck's defeat. McCants was a soldier of John McClure who fell at Hanging Rock. James McClure was a prisoner with him. He was from Chester District when he was pensioned 7 Dec. 1825. He was being paid an annuity as late as 1830.

McCarney, John. Pa. —. He was pensioned.

McCarr, John. Pa. —. He applied 25 May 1813 in Franklin County. He served in the 3rd Pa. Regiment and was discharged at Trenton by Anthony Wayne on 16 Jan. 1781.

McCarothers, Neill. Mass. —. He served in the 1st Regiment under Capt. Willis. He was disabled by a rupture. He lived in Pittsfield, Mass. in 1788 and was 64 years old.

McCart, William. Pa. —. He was pensioned.

McCarter, Walter. S.C. —. He was wounded in his knee at Ashe's defeat at Briar Creek, Georgia. He served under Maj. Francis Ross and Capt. James Martin. He was 77 years old and had five small children. He was pensioned from York District on 3 Nov. 1829. He was paid his annuity as late as 1833.

McCarthey, Henry. Pa. —. He was awarded a $40 gratuity in Huntingdon Co., Pa. 15 Apr. 1835.

McCarthy, Daniel. N.C. Second Master. He was born in Ireland. He served as Master Mate on the Continental ship *Randolph* for a year and a half, two years on the *Notre Dame*, and then on the *Rattlesnake* which was driven ashore near Cape Henry in an engagement with the British. He served aboard the brig *Belona* under Capt. Pemberton as prize master where he lost his eyesight by the bursting of a gun in an engagement with the *Mary* of London. He was awarded a gratuity of £500 in 1780. He applied in 1789 in Craven Co., North Carolina. Both the House and Senate rejected his application. He was allowed a pension 7 Feb. 1791 and awarded an annuity 26 Mar. 1792 in South Carolina. He was from Chesterfield Co., S.C.

McCarthy, John. Pa. Matross. He was in Philadelphia County 14 Dec. 1785. He served in the 4th Regiment of Artillery under Col. Proctor. He was wounded in the belly at the battle of Green Springs, Va. in 1781. He was 64 years old. He was dead by Mar. 1793. He also appeared as John McCarty and John McCarte.

McCartney, Henry. Pa. —. He applied in Union County in 1815. He was wounded by a musket ball in his leg at the battle of Long Island. It was never extracted.

McCarty, Daniel. —. —. He sought to have his pension increased from his rank of private to that of lieutenant. Congress rejected his claim 15 Feb. 1841 because of insufficient proof.

McCarty, Daniel. Va. Pvt. He served in Buford's Detachment. He lived in Fairfax County. He was on the 1813 pension list.

McCarty, Dennis. Pa. Pvt. He was in Philadelphia County on 12 Dec. 1785. He was transferred from the 3rd Pa. Regiment to the Invalids. He was disabled by a sore leg in the service. He was 31 years old. His wife was Mary McCarty. He died 23 May 1786.

McCarty, Dennis. Pa. —. He was awarded a $40 gratuity and a $40 annuity in Fayette Co., Pa. 27 Mar. 1832.

McCarty, Dennis. Va. Pvt. He served in the 8th Virginia Regiment. He was from Frederick Co., Va. on 7 May 1783. He was being pensioned 18 June 1784.

McCarty, Jeremiah. Va. —. His wife, Margaret McCarty, was granted £4 per month for her support and her three children in Yohogania Co., Va. 30 Sep. 1779.

McCarty, John. N.Y. —. His family was granted support 18 Feb. 1779 while he was away in the service.

McCarty, John. Pa. Matross. He was on the 1789 pension list.

McCarty, Josiah. Pa. Matross. He was on the 1813 pension list. He appeared incorrectly as Isaiah McCarty.

McCarty, Josiah. Pa. Lt. He was transferred to New York in or by Sep. 1794.

McCarty, Owen. Pa. Sgt. He applied 5 June 1817. He served in Col. Proctor's Artillery Regiment. He also appeared as Owen McCarte.

McCarty, Timothy. Va. Drummer. His widow, Mary McCarty, was in York County on 19 Mar. 1787 and 51 years old. He was in a state ison regiment and died in the service. She was continued on the pension list at the rate of £7 per annum on 2 Apr. 1787. One son was 8 years old. She was in Henrico County in 1792.

McCarvey, James. Pa. —. He applied in Lancaster County. He did a tour of militia with Peter Shaeffer and Andrew Gross in the Regiment of Col. Galbraith. At Amboy, N.J. he entered the regular service in the Flying Camp under Capt. Clark. He married Catherine Thorn, daughter of Francis Thorn, before his enlistment. She was awarded a $40 gratuity and a $40 annuity in Dauphin Co., Pa. 13 Apr. 1827.

McCauley, Campbell. Va. —. He was wounded many times in Col. Buford's defeat in South Carolina. He was awarded a £300 gratuity on 9 Nov. 1780. He was pensioned in Montgomery County on 31 Dec. 1811 at the rate of $60 per annum and $60 immediate relief.

McCaw, James. S.C. —. He served under Capt. Dixon and was at the Snow Camps, Rocky Mount, Hanging Rock, and Fish Dam Ford. He was in his 65th year and had a family of small children. William McGerrity, Joseph Morrow, James McClure, and David Morrow deposed anent his service. He was from Chester District and was pensioned 12 Dec. 1826. He was receiving his annuity in 1832.

McCaw, John. S.C. —. His annuity was £1 in 1787.

McCay, Alexander. N.Y. Bombardier. He enlisted in 1777 in Capt. Andrew Moodie's Company in the 2nd N.Y. Regiment of Artillery under Col. John Lamb. He was disabled by several wounds in his body and arms at Fort Clinton one of the redoubts of Fort Montgomery on 6 Oct. 1777. He was aged 36 years on 2 July 1788. He lived in Montgomery, Ulster Co., N.Y. on 29 Apr. 1789. He was a farmer. He was on the 1813 pension list. He also appeared as Alexander McCoy.

McCay, Daniel. Va. —. His wife was granted 20 shillings per month in Yohogania Co., Va. 25 Aug. 1778 while he was away in the service.

McChan, John. Pa. —. He was pensioned.

McChesney, John. Pa. Pvt. He served in Hendrick's Rifle Company. He was wounded in his left leg on 31 Dec. 1775 in the storming of Quebec. He lived in Pa. in 1794. He was on the 1813 pension list of Virginia. He died 22 Sep. 1822.

McClain, —. —. —. His widow, Elizabeth McClain, had her petition for a pension rejected by Congress 27 Mar. 1846 because they were married subsequent to 1 Jan. 1794.

McClain, Alexander. Pa. —. His widow, Margaret McClain, was awarded a $40 gratuity and a $40 annuity in Westmoreland Co., Pa. 7 Mar. 1827. She died 18 Dec. 1843.

McClain, Alexander. Pa. —. He applied 5 Jan. 1821. He enlisted in 1776 for three years and was discharged in 1779. In the summer of 1777 he and David Davidson were mess mates and continued so for two years. He and John Wilson were discharged together. He was in the battles of Trenton and Princeton. He settled above Lancaster in 1781.

McClain, Charles. Pa. —. He applied in Center County on 17 Mar. 1814. He enlisted in Capt. Wheitzel's Company in Col. Miles' Regiment. He was wounded by buck shot in his right leg on Long Island and taken prisoner. He made his escape by swimming across the East River to New York nine hours later. He served under Col. Walter Stewart at a skirmish at King's Bridge and White Plains. Afterwards he joined the dragoons under Col. Broadhead. He was wounded in his left leg by buck shot and through the knee with a highlander bayonet in Germantown. He was discharged at Lancaster. He was 57 years old and had an aged wife. He also appeared as Charles McLean.

McClain, John. Pa. —. He was awarded a $40 gratuity and a $40 annuity in Cumberland County on 26 Mar. 1822.

McClananhan, John. Va. Pvt. He was in Norfolk County on 31 Mar. 1788. He served in the Va. Line under Lt. Col. Campbell and was wounded in his right leg. His leg was broken, crooked, ulcerated, and almost useless. He was 30 years old.

McClannahan, William. Va. Pvt. He served in Buford's Regiment and was pensioned 10 Nov. 1808. He lived in Fauquier Co., Va.

McClane, Archibald. Pa. Pvt. He was in Philadelphia County on 12 Dec. 1785. He served in the 1ˢᵗ Pa. Regiment and was wounded at Brandywine in his left arm and right thigh in 1777. He was 33 years old.

McClane, Charles. Pa. Pvt. He served in 3ʳᵈ Pa. Regiment. He was wounded in his left leg and thigh on 16 July 1779 at the battle of Stoney Point by two musket balls. He lived in Chester Co., Pa. in 1794. He enlisted 17 Feb. 1777 for the war.

McClany, Archibald. S.C. —. He escaped from the enemy in Georgia and was granted a gratuity towards defraying his expenses to North Carolina 20 Dec. 1779.

McClanning, Plato. R.I. Pvt. He lost one joint from two toes on his right foot and one joint on the big toe on the left foot by frost bite on the Oswego Expedition in Feb. 1783 under Col. Willet. He also had a rupture in his groin. He served under Col. Jeremiah Olney. He was aged 30 when he applied on 23 Feb. 1786. He resided in Providence Co., R.I. He also appeared as Plato McClannel. He was 28 years old.

McClaren, Thomas. Pa. —. He was from Westmoreland County when he was pensioned 6 Jan. 1825. He was also from Allegheny County.

McClarney, Francis. Va. —. He was granted support in Orange Co., Va. in 1778.

McClary, Andrew. N.H. Maj. He was in Col. John Stark's Regiment and was killed by a cannon ball at Bunker Hill on 17 June 1775. His widow, Elizabeth McClary, sought his seven years' half-pay in 1793.

McClary, John. Mass. Sgt. He served in Capt. Benjamin Walcot's Company under Col. Thomas Marshall. He was unfit for guard or prison duty due to lameness. He was pensioned at the rate of half-pay from 24 Dec. 1779 on 27 Apr. 1780.

McClary, Michael. N.H. —. He had command of a company on 8 Nov. 1776 but had to resign due to bad health which ruined his constitution. He was granted relief on 25 Apr. 1780.

McClean, Hugh. Md. Pvt. He served in the 1ˢᵗ Regiment. He was a resident of Kent County in 1785. He was struck from the roll in 1789 because he was able bodied. He was dead by Sep. 1796. He also appeared as Hugh McLean.

McClean, Hugh. Pa. Pvt. He was on the 1791 pension roll.

McClean, John. Pa. —. He applied in Philadelphia 13 Apr. 1822. He lived in that part of Cumberland County which became Tioga County.

McClear, John. Pa. —. He was pensioned 2 Apr. 1814. He died 2 Oct. 1821. He also appeared as John McElleer and John McElaar, *quo vide.*

McClellan, —. S.C. —. His widow, Martha McClellan, was pensioned 4 Dec. 1835.

McClellan, John. —. —. He enlisted in the artillery in 1781 and left the service in the spring of 1783 at Cape Elizabeth. Congress granted him a pension for one year of service 24 Jan. 1837.

McClellan, John. Pa. —. He was pensioned at the rate of $40 per annum 13 Aug. 1817.

McClellan, John. Pa. Lt. His heirs were from Cumberland County 22 Aug. 1787. His widow, Elizabeth McClellan, received his half-pay for four years and seven months prior to remarriage. She was Elizabeth Dickey 17 Jan. 1788. He served in the 1ˢᵗ Battalion of the Pa. troops under Capt. William Hendricks and and died on the march to Quebec 3 Nov. 1775. His only child was Priscilla McClellan who became the ward of her grandfather, John McClellan. She was Priscilla

Greer or Grier when she received $400 in lieu of 400 acres of donation land 27 Mar. 1837. She received his seven years' half-pay 22 Mar. 1838. He also appeared as John McClelland.

McClellan, John. Pa. —. He applied in Mifflin County on 20 Mar. 1813. He enlisted in Capt. John Steel's Company in the 11th Pa. Regiment in the spring of 1777 and served to Jan. 1781. He next served in Capt. King's Company under Col. Arnold and was discharged at Trenton, N.J. by Gen. Wayne. George Bush was paymaster. He was wounded in the side at Germantown. Of low stature, he was not considered adequate for field service. He also stammered in his speech. He acted as a waiter. He was with Lt. Archibald McGuire in 1777. He was blind in one eye and lived with John Jameson. He died 25 May 1831.

McClellan, Robert. Pa. Lt. He was on the 1813 pension list.

McClelland, James. Pa. —. He was awarded a $40 gratuity in Washington Co., Pa. 5 Apr. 1826 for his Revolutionary service.

McClelland, —. Pa. —. His widow, Mary McClelland, was awarded a $40 gratuity and a $40 annuity in Fayette Co., Pa. 8 Apr. 1833.

McClelland, John. Pa. Lt. Col. His widow, Martha McClelland, was in Fayette County in Dec. 1793. He served in the 4th Battalion of the Westmoreland County militia and was killed 4 June 1782 in the expedition against the Sandusky Indians. He served under Col. William Crawford. One Martha McClelland died 21 Jan. 1822.

McClelland, Samuel. Pa. —. He was awarded a $40 gratuity and a $40 annuity 1 Apr. 1823 in Lancaster County.

McClenehan, Robert. Va. —. His widow, Katey McClenehan, was on the 1785 pension roll.

McClennen, John. Va. Pvt. He served in the Continental Line in Campbell's Detachment and was disabled at Eutaw 8 Sep. 1781. He resided in Norfolk County. He was being pensioned 16 Nov. 1783. He was continued on the list at the rate of £12 per annum on 31 Mar. 1788. He was on the 1813 pension list.

McClintock, Alexander. Pa. Lt. His widow, Sarah McClintock, was in Philadelphia County 8 Mar. 1781 and later of Montgomery County. He served in the 5th Pa. Regiment under Col. Francis Johnston and was wounded several times at Brandywine on 11 Sep. 1777 and died leaving four small children. She died 25 May 1826. He also appeared as Alexander McClintick.

McClintock, William. Va. —. His application was rejected 7 June 1787. He was probably the one of the name whose representatives sought the arrearage of his pension on 15 Jan. 1789 because he was never put on the pension list.

McClintock, William. Va. Pvt. He served in Capt. Baller's Company and was badly wounded at the battle of Guilford Court House. He was in Botetourt County 10 Mar. 1784. On 10 May 1785 one William McClintock, Jr. who was wounded at Guilford Court House, was recommended for a pension in Botetourt County.

McClintock, William. Va. —. He died in the service. His widow, Alice McClintock, was pensioned at the rate of £10 per annum on 20 Dec. 1792. She was in Bath County on 28 Mar. 1794.

McClorken, Thomas. S.C. —. He served under Lt. Kennedy, Capt. Turner, and Maj. Wallace. He was in the Snowy Camp, Reedy River where 21 Tory prisoners were taken, Fort Moultrie, Purysburg, Mably's Meeting House, Little River, Fryday's Fort at Granby, Orangeburg, the skirmish at the house of James Wylie, and Stono. His father's home had been plundered by the enemy and his brother had been hung by the Tories. He was about 73 years of age. He suffered from a complaint in his stomach and bowels. James Harbison, James Graham, and John McDill served with him. He was in Chester District in 1827. His application was rejected.

McClughan, Samuel. Pa. Pvt. He was in Northumberland County 26 Sep. 1786. He was in the 1ˢᵗ Pa. Regiment in Capt. William Wilson's company. He was drafted into Capt. Parr's Company of Rifle Corps under Col. Morgan. He was wounded in the groin in Sep. 1777 at Stillwater or Saratoga. He was 32 years of age in 1786. He was on the 1813 pension list. He died 31 Mar. 1825 in Westmoreland County.

McClung, William. Pa. Pvt. His widow, Jane Martin, applied 17 Sep. 1790 in Mifflin County. He served in the Northumberland County militia in Capt. John Lytle's Company. He was killed at the surrender of Freeland's Fort 28 July 1779. His widow, Jane McClung, married David Martin 15 Oct. 1781. Martin was the guardian of Sarah McClung, Rebecca McClung, and William McClung, the minor children.

McClure, —. S.C. —. His widow was Sarah McClure from Spartanburg District in 1815.

McClure, —. S.C. —. He died at Hadrel's Point. His widow, Sarah McClure, and her child were pensioned 19 Dec. 1825 for her widowhood. She was due $148.

McClure, Charles. S.C. —. He served under Capt. Steele and was captured by Ferguson's troops. He was taken to Camden jail and held for eight months. He was held in irons, and one of his legs was dislocated. He was 67 years old, and his wife was upwards of 60 years. He was from Pendleton District when he was pensioned 3 Dec. 1819. He received one year arrearage. His widow, Martha McClure, was pensioned at the rate of $30 per annum on 23 Nov. 1829. She was paid as late as 1834.

McClure, Hugh. S.C. Capt. He was wounded. He was granted an annuity 15 Nov. 1784. His widow was Sarah McClure.

McClure, James. S.C. —. He served under Col. William Thompson and Capt. R. Winn. He lost personal property at Fort McIntosh in Georgia and sought compensation. Capt. D. McDuff gave testimony about his losses. He applied in Nov. 1821, but his claim was rejected.

McClure, John. —. —. Congress rejected the claim of his widow, Margaret McClure 2 Mar. 1857 because there was no evidence to support her claim.

McClure, John. N.J. Pvt. He was on the 1791 pension roll. He served in the 2ⁿᵈ N.J. Regiment. He lived in Bergen County. He was wounded in his right arm and was 33 years old. He was on the 1813 pension list.

McClure, Richard. N.C. —. He was in Rutherford Co., N.C. in Dec. 1832.

McClure, Samuel. S.C. —. His widow was Sarah McClure. She and one child received an pension in 1824. She was paid as late as 1855.

McCollester, Daniel. Va. —. His widow, Mary McCollester, and three children were awarded £12.6 per month in Accomack Co., Va. 24 Feb. 1778.

McCollester, John. Pa. —. He was pensioned 30 Mar. 1823.

McComb, Allen. Pa. —. He was granted relief.

McComb, John. N.J. Pvt. He served in 2ⁿᵈ N.J. Regiment. He lost the sight of his right eye by smallpox in 1777 at Short Hills. He was removed to the hospital in Mendham, was transferred to the corps of Invalids until July 1783 when he was discharged by Gen. Lincoln. He lived in Bernard's Town, N.J. in 1794. He enlisted 15 Dec. 1776 and was discharged in Oct. 1777. He was pensioned at the rate of $15 per annum.

McCon, James. Pa. Corp. He was in Philadelphia County on 19 Jan. 1786. He was in the 7ᵗʰ Pa. Regiment and was wounded at Germantown in Oct. 1777. He was 27 years old. He was on the 1791 pension list but was deceased by Sept. 1797. He also appeared as James McCoun.

McConchey, John. Pa. Pvt. He was on the 1813 pension list.

McConnally, John. Pa. He served in the 8th Regiment.

McConnally, Michael. Pa. Gunner. He was on the 1791 pension roll.

McConnel, —. Pa. —. His widow, Nancy McConnel, was granted relief in Westmoreland County 18 Apr. 1834.

McConnell, John. Pa. —. He enlisted in 1776 under Capt. Eli Myer in the 8th Regiment under Col. McCoy for three years. He was at Bonbrook. In 1778 he was ordered to Pittsburgh to guard the frontiers. He was sent down the Ohio River and built Fort McIntosh in 1778 and Fort Muskingum in 1779. He went up the Allegheny on Gen. Brodhead's campaign where the Indians attacked. The Indians were defeated and their towns and corn were burnt. He returned to Pittsburgh and was discharged. His widow, Nancy McConnell, was awarded a $40 gratuity and a $40 annuity in Westmoreland Co., Pa. 18 Mar. 1834. She died in Apr. 1846.

McConnell, Matthew. Pa. Capt. He was on the 1813 pension list.

McConnell, Samuel. Md. Sgt. He was pensioned at the rate of half-pay of a sergeant in Cecil Co. on 23 Jan. 1813.

McConnell, William. Pa. —. He was awarded a $40 gratuity and a $40 annuity in Armstrong County on 14 Mar. 1818.

McConnick, Thomas. Pa. —. He was granted relief.

McCord, Isaiah. Pa. Pvt. He served in the 1st Regiment and was wounded in his right shoulder and arm at Brandywine. He was pensioned in Philadelphia 14 Nov. 1785.

McCord, James. Pa. —. He was awarded a $40 gratuity and a $40 annuity in Mifflin Co., Pa. 1 Apr. 1834.

McCord, James. S.C. —. There were children on the list of 1793.

McCord, Josiah. Pa. Pvt. He was in Philadelphia County on 14 Nov. 1785. He served in the 1st Pa. Regiment and was wounded in his right shoulder and arm at Brandywine in 1777. He was 35 years old. He died 8 Feb. 1791.

McCord, Mark. Pa. Corp. His widow, Catherine McCord, was in Dauphin County on 6 Nov. 1792. He served in the 10th Pa. Regiment, was furloughed in Jan. 1781, and died a few weeks after. He was married in Philadelphia by Rev. McClennachan on 26 Nov. 1764. He was a tin plate maker and coppersmith.

McCorkey, Peter. Va. —. His two children were granted £2 per month support in Yohogania Co., Va. 28 Apr. 1778.

McCorkle, William. S.C. —. He was killed in action 20 Nov. 1780. His widow, Esther McCorkle, was awarded an annuity 7 Nov. 1785. Payment was made to John Gaston.

McCormack, Adam. Va. —. He was away in Continental service. His wife, Mary McCormack, and child were granted £30 support in Botetourt Co., Va. 10 Sep. 1779.

McCormack, Samuel. S.C. —. He applied in 1842. He was paid as late as 1851.

McCormick, Charles. Pa. Pvt. He served in 2nd Pa. Regiment. He was wounded in his left leg by a musket ball on 4 Oct. 1777 at Germantown. He was discharged in Jan.1778. He lived in Pa. in 1794. He was granted a full pension 20 Apr. 1796.

McCormick, George. Va. Capt. His heirs sought commutation but were rejected 29 Mar. 1838 because he had resigned in the fall of 1788.

McCormick, John. Pa. Lt. He entered the service in Oct. 1776 at Pine Creek, Pa. and served under Capt. Cook. He served until the spring of 1778 in scouting parties. Col Hunter ordered the entire force with the women and children to be removed to Fort Augusta where they arrived 7 July 1778. He returned to Big Island and brought back the cattle. He was then called back to bring the horses which the Indians had driven off. He was born in Ireland in 1750. He applied from Lycoming Co., Penn. Congress granted him a pension for two years and three months service 4 Jan. 1838.

McCormick, Thomas. Pa. ---. He was in Philadelphia County on 9 Apr. 1787. He served in the 7th Pa. Regiment. He was disabled by a rupture. He was discharged 1 Jan. 1782.

McCormick, Thomas. Va. Fife Major. He served in the 11th Regiment having enlisted in Apr. 1777. He was transferred to the Invalids in Aug. 1777. His officers were Lt. Col. Commandant Christian Febiger, Col Morgan, Col. Henry Lee, and John Bayard. He also appeared as Thomas McCracken. He was 38 years of age in 1788 and was in Pennsylvania receiving a pension.

McCormick, William. Pa. —. He applied in Mercer County on 22 Feb. 1808. He served four years in the 1st Pa. Regiment and also in the Lancaster County militia. He was taken prisoner at Paoli and spent eight months in captivity. He was awarded donation land.

McCowan, Archibald. Pa. Pvt. He was in Philadelphia County on 12 June 1786. He was in the 12th Pa. Regiment in Capt. Lincoln's Company under Col. William Cook. He was wounded in the arm 10 May 1777 at the battle of Piscataway and lost his hand. He was dead by Mar. 1794.

McCowan, John. Pa. Pvt. He was in Philadelphia County on 13 Oct. 1785. He was transferred from the 5th Pa. Regiment to the Invalids. He was wounded in the service and was discharged 10 June 1783. He was 36 years old. He was on the 1813 pension list.

McCowen, Constant. N.J. Pvt. He served in the 2nd Regiment and was disabled by a fractured leg. He was 47 years old and lived at New Castle.

McCown, John. Pa. —. He was from York County.

McCoy, Angus. Pa. —. He was awarded a $40 annuity in Washington County 5 Feb. 1836. He died 12 Jan. 1840.

McCoy, Charles. Pa. —. He was awarded a $40 gratuity and a $40 annuity in Perry Co., Pa. 11 Apr. 1825. He died 20 Mar. 1829.

McCoy, Daniel. Pa. —. He applied in Indiana County. He served in Capt. John Clark's Company under Col. Walter Stewart. He was wounded in the head at Germantown and was discharged at Valley Forge. His widow, Deborah McCoy, was awarded a $40 annuity in Indiana County on 29 Mar. 1822. She died 22 Oct. 1829.

McCoy, Ephraim. Pa. Pvt. He was pensioned 11 Aug. 1790. He was on the 1813 pension list. He died 30 June 1823 Delaware Co., Ohio. His executrix was Sarah McCoy.

McCoy, George. Va. —. He was pensioned in Rockingham County on 19 Feb. 1821 at the rate of $60 per annum. He was a free man of color and was wounded at Buford's defeat. He died 25 Dec. 1825.

McCoy, John. Md. —. Pvt. He served in the 3rd Md. Regiment and lost his leg. He was pensioned in St. Mary's County on 16 Aug. 1780. He was on the 1813 pension list.

McCoy, John. N.H. Marine. He received wounds from grape shot in his left thigh on 4 Sep. 1777 while serving aboard the Continental ship of war, *Raleigh,* under Thomas Thompson in action with the *Druid.* The shot was lodged in the bone and could not be extracted. The ship's surgeon, John Jackson, and George Jerry Osborne, Captain of the Marines, attested to his service. He was discharged 22 Apr. 1778. He was in Barrington, N.H. in 1786 and in Nottingham, N.H. in 1787. He was aged 22 in 1787. He was pensioned at the rate of $5 per month from 15 Mar. 1808. He was on the 1813 pension list.

McCoy, Kenneth. Pa. Lt. He was on the 1813 pension list.

McCoy, Neal. Pa. —. His widow, Rachel McCoy, was paid $200 in Northumberland Co., Pa. 29

Mar. 1823. She was awarded a $40 gratuity and a $40 annuity 6 Apr. 1833.

McCoy, Robert. Pa. Capt. His heirs applied 18 May 1791 in Franklin County. He served in the Cumberland County militia under Col. Abraham Smith and was killed in action at Crooked Billet 1 May 1778. His widow, Sarah McCoy, and children were due the pension.

McCoy, William. Va. —. His mother, Anne McCoy, was granted £30 support for herself and her family in Rockingham Co., Va. 22 Nov. 1779 while he was away in Continental service.

McCracken, Henry. Pa. Pvt. His widow, Mary McCracken, was in Northumberland County 28 June 1786. He was in the Northumberland County militia and was killed by Indians. He served in the 8th Company of the 1st Battalion of the militia. There were five small children.

McCracken, James. Md. Pvt. He was pensioned at the rate of half-pay of a private in Harford County on 1 Mar. 1826. His widow, Mary McCracken, was pensioned at the same rate 12 Feb. 1844. He also appeared as James McCrackin.

McCracken, John. Pa. —. He applied in Bedford County on 2 July 1814. He enlisted in Apr. 1777 in Capt. Vernon's Company in the 5th Pa. Regiment under Col. Francis Johnston. Alexander Brown served with him for three years and eight months. Both were discharged at Rareton. He was 89 years old in 1840 and died 21 June 1845.

McCracken, Joseph. N.Y. Maj. He served in the Continental Troops under Col. Van Schaick. He was wounded in his left arm below the elbow at the battle of Monmouth on 28 Jan. 1778, and it was amputated the same day. He was appointed Major of the 4th N.Y. Regiment on 28 June 1779 under Lt. Col. Regnier. He was 50 years old in Mar. 1787. He was pensioned 28 May 1787. He lived in Salem, Washington Co., N.Y. 6 July 1789. He was issued certificates for £580 on 20 Mar. 1782. He was on the 1813 pension list. He died 5 May 1825.

McCracken, William. S.C. —. He was awarded an annuity 16 Feb. 1778.

McCrackin, James. S.C. —. He served under Capt. Abraham Sessions and Capt. Joseph Lany [?]. He was at Edisto, Parker's Ferry, Santee, and Black River. He was in his 70th year. He was pensioned in Horry District on 23 Nov. 1829.

McCraven, Duncan. S.C. —. He was wounded at Wrights Bluff in 1781 and made a prisoner. He had large scars about his head from the swords of the party of dragoons in the battle. He was granted an annuity 27 Aug. 1785. He lived in Union Dist., S.C., Mecklenburg Co., N.C., and York Dist., S.C. There were three children in 1791. He died 22 May 1832 in Mecklenburg Co., N.C. His son, Adam McCraven, died ten or twelve years before him. His other two sons went west and had never been heard from. His wife was dead. His daughter had not been heard from since 1840. His daughter-in-law, Aramin McCraven, the widow of Adam, had cared for him. She had been dead many years when her children, Eveline McCraven, David O. McCraven, and Jane C. Beard, sought his arrearage. They were paid $1,349.98 in 1859.

McCraw, Francis. Va. —. He served three years and was from Buckingham County. He married 20 June 1777 in Surry Co., N.C. and died 2 June 1839. His widow was Sally McCraw. Congress rejected a pension for her 16 Apr. 1844.

McCready, Robert. Penn. Capt. He served as a private and captain. He was on the roll in 1832 and sought to be pensioned at the higher rank of an officer. Congress rejected his claim 13 Mar. 1838.

McCreary, John. Pa. —. He was awarded a $40 gratuity and a $40 annuity in Baltimore Co., Md. 7 Mar. 1829.

MvCrory, James. N.C. Ens. He served as a sergeant in the 9th Regiment from 15 Apr. 1776 to the end of the war. He was promoted to ensign 2 May 1777. Congress granted his commutation on

26 Dec. 1838.

McCrum, William. Pa. —. He served with the Associators at Trenton, Princeton, and Brandywine. He was 73 years old in 1826. He was awarded a $40 gratuity in Bucks Co., Pa. 19 Feb. 1828 and a $40 gratuity and a $40 annuity on 3 May 1831.

McCue, William. Va. Pvt. He was awarded a £20 gratuity and a £10 annuity 31 May 1777. He was in Berkeley County in Apr. 1788. He was 36 years old in 1788. He entered the service in 1775 under Capt. Hugh Stephenson, Lt. Abraham Shepherd, and Col. George Scott. He was shot through his wrist when his rifle burst on Staten Island and his left hand had to be amputated. He also appeared as William McCice.

McCulloch, —. Pa. —. His widow, Agnes McCulloch, was awarded a $40 gratuity and a $40 annuity in Beaver County in Apr. 1837. She died 23 Apr. 1844.

McCulloch, John. Pa. Capt. He applied at Philadelphia 27 Aug. 1838. He served in the artillery in the militia.

McCulloch, Joseph. Mass. —. He served in the 16th Regiment and was from Barre. He was paid $20.

McCulloch, Roger. Pa. Pvt. He was in Philadelphia County on 8 May 1786. He served in the 11th Pa. Regiment in Capt. John Coats' Company under Col. Richard Humpton and was wounded in the leg in the skirmish at Brunswick. He was 50 years old. He was dead by Sep. 1792.

McCullough, David. Pa. —. He was awarded a $40 gratuity and a $40 annuity in Lancaster Co., Pa. 5 Mar. 1828. He died 15 Nov. 1829.

McCullough, John. Pa. —. He was awarded a $40 gratuity and a $40 annuity 8 Jan. 1838 in Butler County. He was 70 years old in 1840. He died 8 Sep. 1847.

McCullough, Robert. Pa. Pvt. He was wounded in action with the savages in his left arm at Shamungo in the Western Territory. He was also wounded in the left leg at the battle of Germantown. He lived in York Co., Pa. in 1794. He died 7 Mar. 1807. His widow, Elizabeth McCullough, was awarded a $40 gratuity 24 Mar. 1817 in Lycoming County. He also appeared as Robert McCullock.

McCullough, Samuel. S.C. Pvt. He had served four and a half years in the French and Indian War. He was wounded 18 Aug. 1780 at Sumter's defeat. He received so many wounds that he could neither speak or move. He served in the 1st S.C. Regiment. He had a wife and helpless family. He was granted an annuity 16 Dec. 1784. There was one child in 1791.

McCullough, Thomas. S.C. —. He was taken prisoner at Sumter's defeat and died on board a prison ship. His widow, Rebecca McCullough, was granted an annuity 12 Nov. 1784. There were two children in 1791.

McCullough, William. S.C. —. He served in the 2nd S.C. Regiment and was killed at Savannah 9 Oct. 1779. His widow, Sarah, was granted an annuity 13 Sep. 1785. She was paid for her son 17 Aug. 1791. She was Sarah Dawson when she was paid the annuity for her son, Alexander McCullough, on 7 Aug. 1791. He also appeared as William McCulloch.

McCully, George. Pa. —. His widow, Ann McCully, received a $40 gratuity and a $40 annuity 26 Mar. 1822. She was allowed an additional $20 to the pension she was receiving on 24 Mar. 1828. She resided in Allegheny Co., Pa.

McCully, James. S.C. —. He was taken prisoner at Sumter's defeat. He drew an annuity from North Carolina. When he moved to South Carolina, he sought an annuity from that state. His widow was Rebecca McCully from York District.

McCundy, William. Pa. —. He was pensioned.

McCune, James. Pa. —. He was awarded a $40 gratuity and a $40 annuity in Northumberland Co., Pa.

19 Feb. 1823.

McCurdy, Alexander. Pa. —. He was awarded a $40 gratuity 18 Mar. 1814. He was awarded a $40 gratuity and a $40 annuity in Beaver County 11 Mar. 1815. He was dead by Mar. 1839.

McCurdy, Archibald. N.C. Lt. Congress rejected commutation for his service 7 June 1836.

McCurdy, Moses. Pa. —. His widow, Margaret McCurdy, was awarded a $40 gratuity and a $40 annuity in Lancaster Co., Pa. 12 Apr. 1828. On 3 Mar. 1829 an act was passed authorizing payment to be made to her as Margaret Hughes.

McCurdy, William. Pa. —. His widow, Mary McCurdy, was awarded a $40 gratuity and a $40 annuity in Lancaster, Pa. 21 Jan. 1823. She died 22 May 1823.

McDade, William. —. —. His application was allowed to lay on the table.

McDaniel, —. —. —. His widow, Bersheba McDaniel, sought a pension to be continued for life from Congress 9 Feb. 1848. Congress refused because she was covered by a general bill.

McDaniel, David. S.C. —. He was paid an annuity 1 June 1846.

McDaniel, Edward. S.C. —. He was wounded in his shoulder at Rocky Mount in 1780. The wound broke open four or five years later, and several pieces of bones had to be extracted under the shoulder blade and the elbow joint. He was awarded an annuity 18 May 1785. He was from Chester. He was being paid in 1821. His widow was Elizabeth McDaniel who was upwards of 62 years of age. Her youngest son had married and left home, but two daughters were still with her when she applied in Dec. 1826. In 1837 her son James McDaniel sought her pension. She was paid as late as 1846.

McDaniel, Enenias [Aeneas]. Va. Pvt. His widow, Lucy McDaniel, lived in Hanover County 13 July 1790. He served in the 4th Va. Regiment and died in the service. She was on the 1785 pension roll. She was continued on the pension list at the rate of £6 per annum on 13 July 1790. She was Lucy Lambeth on 19 Apr. 1792.

McDaniel, George. S.C. —. His application was rejected 21 Dec. 1822.

McDaniel, James. Mass. Pvt. He served in the 2nd Regiment.

McDaniel, John. Pa. —. His heirs received $200 in lieu of donation land in Apr. 1837.

McDaniel, William. Pa. —. He was taken prisoner and killed in action with the Indians 3 June 1781. His widow, Margaret McDaniel, of Cumberland County was granted a pension in 1787. There were five children. The eldest was 7, and the youngest was born after the father's death.

McDaniels, John. —. Pvt. He served for seventeen months. He was pensioned but suspended for further evidence. He married prior to rendering his service. His widow, Margaret McDaniels, died 7 Aug. 1849. Congress credited him with six months service and authorized that $452 be paid to the heirs 13 Apr. 1860.

McDaniels, John. Mass. Pvt. He served in the Invalids under Capt. Hill. He was disabled by rheumatism. He lived in Dorchester, Mass. and was 49 years old in 1786. He was paid $20 by the Commonwealth.

McDermot, Daniel. Pa. —. He was awarded a $40 gratuity and a $40 annuity in Allegheny Co., Pa. 25 Mar. 1831.

McDermot, John. Pa. Pvt. He was in Philadelphia County 8 July 1788 and was 40 years of age. He served in the 3rd Pa. Regiment in Capt. John Stake's Company. He was wounded in the right arm at Benbrook in N. J. He was on the 1813 pension list.

McDermot, Joseph. Pa. —. He was awarded a $40 gratuity and a $40 annuity in Allegheny Co., Pa. 25 Mar. 1831.

McDermot, Robert. Pa. —. He was pensioned.

McDill, John. S.C. —. He entered the service in 1777 at the age of 17 and served under Capt. Alexander Turner, Maj. Joseph Brown, Capt. John Dixon, Col. John Winn, Capt. Samuel Adams, and Col. McGriff. He was at Purysburg, Wright's Bluff, Biggen Church, Orangeburg, and Augusta. He was in his 71st year and suffered from pain in one of his thighs. One son lived with him. James Harbison, James McCaw, and William McGerrity deposed anent his service. He was pensioned from Chester District 17 Dec. 1831.

McDonald, Arthur. Pa. —. He was pensioned.

McDonald, David. S.C. —. He served under Capt. John Turner and Col. John Winn. He was at Hanging Rock, Carey's Old Field where 75 Scots and 32 wagons were captured, Sumter's defeat, Friday's Fort, Wright's Bluff, and Haddrel's Point. He was 68 or 69 years old and had two sons and a daughter with him. He was pensioned from Fairfield District on 17 Nov. 1831. James Harbison and William McGerrity served with him. He was paid as late as 1850.

McDonald, Donald. Del. Corp. He served in Capt. Jacquet's Regiment. He was wounded in the leg at Germantown on 4 Oct. 1777. He lived in New Castle Co., Del. in 1794. He enlisted in Apr. 1777 for the war and was discharged in Sep. 1778. He was granted a full pension 20 Apr. 1796. He also appeared as Daniel McDonald.

McDonald, Donald. N.Y. Pvt. & Batteauman. He was wounded by a kick from a horse, and his sight was impaired. He served in Capt. Parson's Company under Col. Goose Van Schaick. He was 71 years old in 1786. He lived in Albany, N.Y. on 21 Apr. 1789 and in 1794. He also appeared as Daniel McDonel and Daniel McDonald. He was on the 1813 pension list. He died 24 Jan. 1813.

McDonald, Edward. S.C. —. He was wounded in his shoulder at Rocky Mount. The wound later broke open. He was paid $300 on 20 Dec. 1810.

McDonald, Francis. Pa. —. He was pensioned 29 Oct. 1813.

McDonald, Godfrey. Pa. Pvt. He was in Philadelphia County on 30 Sep. 1785. He was transferred from the 3rd Pa. Regiment to the Invalids. He was disabled by a rupture and was 58 years old. He also appeared as Godfrey McDonnel.

McDonald, Henry. S.C. —. He was from Chester and was on the roll in 1791.

McDonald, James. Pa. Pvt. He was on the 1813 pension list. He died 4 Oct. 1822. His widow was Catherine McDonald.

McDonald, John. Va. —. His wife, Mary McDonald, was granted £8 support in Berkeley County on 16 Sep. 1777 and 15 Sep. 1778. He was a volunteer away in Continental service in Capt. Francis Willis' Company. She also received £30 on 17 Nov. 1779.

McDonald, Michael. —. —. He was a lieutenant in the British navy at the commencement of the war. He volunteered his service at Bunker Hill. In 1777 he enlisted as a private in Putnam's Regiment and served from 23 Mar. 1777 to 1 Jan. 1781. He also served under Col. Nixon. He abandoned the army for a cruise as a privateersman. His daughter, Elizabeth Peachy or Beachey of Kensington, Pa., sought remuneration 10 Aug. 1842, but Congress rejected her claim. It did so again 25 July 1850.

McDonald, Randall. Va. —. He made an agreement with John Magill to maintain his daughter, Ruth McDonald, while he was away in Continental service. Upon the expiration of the agreement, Magill sought assistance. He was granted a barrel of corn and 50 pounds of pork for her support for a year in Rockingham Co., Va. on 23 Oct. 1780.

McDonald, William. Pa. Pvt. His widow, Hester McDonald, was in York County on 10 Nov. 1808. He was in the Cumberland County militia in Capt. John Mateer's Company. He was killed in a skirmish at White Horse in 1777. He died at the age of 35 of wounds. He left four children. His widow was paid in May 1809 died 28 Dec. 1818.

McDougal, Hugh. R.I. Pvt. He suffered from general disability and bodily infirmities. He served under Col. Jeremiah Olney. He was aged 57 in 1786. He lived in Providence Co., R.I.

McDougal, William. Pa. Pvt. He was in Philadelphia County on 9 Jan. 1786. He was in the 5th Pa. Regiment and was wounded in his left leg at Bound Brook, N.J. 17 Apr. 1777 in action with the enemy. He was 41 years old. He also appeared as William McDugall.

McDougall, Alexander. Va. —. He was deprived of the use of his limbs by a disorder and sought relief on 3 June 1784.

McDowell, —. Pa. —. His widow, Barbara McDowell, was awarded a $40 gratuity and a $40 annuity in Bucks County in 1836. She died 1 Oct. 1838.

McDowell, —. Pa. —. His widow, Ann McDowell, was awarded a $40 gratuity and a $40 annuity in Chester County 24 Mar. 1837. She died 5 Mar. 1841.

McDowell, Andrew. Pa. —. He was pensioned under the act of 4 Mar. 1815. He was from Greene County. He received a $40 gratuity and a $40 annuity.

McDowell, James. Pa. —. He was awarded a $40 gratuity and a $40 annuity in Mifflin Co., Pa. 25 Mar. 1833.

McDowell, John. Pa. —. He enlisted in 1776 under Capt. Moses McLean of York County for one year. He went to Canada where he was in the battle of Three Rivers under Gen. Thompson. He was taken prisoner a few days later by Indians, taken to Montreal, sold to the British, and sent home on parole. He enlisted again in 1777 for three years under Capt. George Bush in the 11th Pa. Regiment under Lt. Col. Hartley. In 1779 he was under Gen. Sullivan in the campaign against the Indians. On 13 Aug. on a scouting party under Capt. Bush, he was wounded by a ball through his body. He was given an unlimited furlough by his captain. He was awarded a $40 gratuity and a $40 annuity 22 Mar. 1809. He resided in Fayette County.

McDowell, John. Va. Lt. He was an ensign in the 12th Regiment until it became the 8th when he became a lieutenant. He served from 1 Jan. 1777 to 16 Feb. 1781. He received half-pay for life 22 Dec. 1837. His legal representatives sought his commutation pay from Congress 17 Apr. 1858, but payment had already been made.

McDowell, Matthew. N.Y. —. His application was allowed to lay on the table.

McDowell, William. Pa. —. He was awarded a $40 gratuity in York County 28 Jan. 1836.

McDowell, William. S.C. —. At the age of 18 he was in the Snowy Camps. He was forced to take refuge in North Carolina and enlisted in the militia under Col. Malmoody. He received a severe wound at Stono. He was pensioned from Kershaw District on 14 Dec. 1818. He was paid as late as 1832.

McDuff, Daniel. S.C. Capt. He entered the war as a private. He was wounded and taken captive at the fall of Fort McInosh in 1777. He was exchanged and served under as 2nd Lt. under Col. Thompson in S.C. He was breveted a sergeant in 1780 and later that year he was taken captive at Ninety Six. He was literally cut to pieces with fourteen wounds. He was held at Charleston, S.C. before being taken to Kinsale, Ireland and then England where he was imprisoned from 1 Sep. 1781 to 2 July 1782 when he was exchanged. He returned to S.C. and engaged as a captain. He was given bounty land and five years' full pay. [Compare with the entry for Daniel McElduff.]

McDuff, John. N.C. Pvt. He entered the service at the age of 15 and was attached to the 3rd S.C. Regiment under Col. Thompson in 1777. He was commissioned a lieutenant and was breveted a captain. He was captured by the British in 1780 at the fall of Charleston. He went to North Carolina where he raised a company of volunteers. He was taken prisoner again at Ninety Six where he was almost cut to pieces. He received fourteen wounds. He was taken to Charleston, shipped to Ireland, and then taken to England. He was tried for rebellion and high treason. He was exchanged and sent to America. He returned to South Carolina where he raised a company and served until the British evacuated Charleston. He was on the pension roll as an invalid with the rank of 2nd lieutenant. Congress declined to grant his bounty land or commutation of half-pay 29 Dec. 1826.

McElaar, John. Pa. —. He was pensioned in Franklin County 27 Nov. 1814. He also appeared as John McElear and John McClear *quo vide.*

McElduff, Daniel. S.C. Capt. He was captured. He was a resident of Union District in 1793. He was on the 1813 pension list. He was being pensioned in 1820. He later lived in Georgia and Franklin Co., Tenn.

McElhaney, Samuel. S.C. —. William Lewis was with him at Rocky Mount and Wright's Bluff. He was from Chester District in 1826. He was pensioned as late as 1843. His application was rejected in 1844.

McElheney, Stephen. S.C. —. He was from Chester District in 1826. He was paid $68.87 ½ for property lost in the Revolutionary War on 5 Dec. 1817. He served in the 6th Regiment under Capt. George Wade, Col. Sumter, and Maj. Henderson. He fought at Charleston, Ripley's Fort, and Sullivan Ford. He had two tours in 1780 and was at Black Swamp and Jacksonsburg. He was also at Rocky Mount, King's Mountain, and Wright's Bluff. His brother was Samuel McElheney. He and James McElheney were paid $129.90 interest for services on 18 Dec. 1818. He applied 21 Nov. 1826 and was paid as late as 1834.

McElhenny, James. S.C. —. He had been paid £26.18.3 for property lost in the Revolutionary War. He produced the necessary vouchers and was paid £20.9.3 on 6 Dec. 1816. He and Samuel McElheney were paid $129.90 interest for services on 18 Dec. 1818.

McElhouse, Samuel. Pa. —. He was granted relief in Mifflin County 8 Apr. 1840.

McElnay, John. Pa. —. He enlisted in the spring of 1776 in Capt. Philip Albright's company of the 1st Regiment of Riflemen under Col. Samuel Miles to serve until 1 Jan. 1778. He was taken prisoner at Long Island in August. When he was released, he spent considerable time in hospital in Philadelphia and returned home on furlough where his enlistment expired 1 Jan. 1778. He was to be paid from the time of his imprisonment by statute of 14 Mar. 1805.

McElroy, —. Pa. —. His widow, Catharine McElroy, was granted relief in Philadelphia 23 Apr.1852.

McElroy, —. S.C. —. His widow was Jane McElroy. There were three children in 1791.

McElroy, James. Pa. —. He was awarded a $40 gratuity and a $40 annuity in Huntingdon Co., Pa. 23 Apr. 1829.

McElroy. Thomas. Pa. —. He was pensioned 4 May 1832 in Fayette County.

McEllevy, Hugh. Pa. —. He applied in Cumberland County on 4 Mar. 1813. He had drawn his bounty land from the United States and his donation land from Pennsylvania. He suffered from piles, a rupture, and rheumatism. His children were not able to support him. He also appeared as Hugh McElvanny, Hugh Elway, Hugh McElroy, and Hugh McElvary.

McElwee, James. S.C. —. He served under Capt. William Byers, Col. Thomas Neal, Maj. Francis Ross, and Lt. William Love. He was made a prisoner at Ashe's defeat. He applied in York District 1822.

McEntire, John. S.C. —. He served under Capt. Johnston and Capt. Philemon Waters. He was discharged at Orangeburg in 1782. He applied in 1812.

McEver, Angus. Pa. Pvt. He was on the 1791 pension roll. He was on the 1813 pension list. He transferred to Berkeley Co., Va.

McEwen, Archibald. Pa. —. He was pensioned.

McEwen, Henry. Pa. —. He was awarded $40 gratuity and a $40 annuity in Center County on 18 Mar. 1814. He died 1 Oct. 1825. He also appeared as Henry McEuen.

McEwen, Patrick. Va. Pvt. He served under Col. George Gibson. He was pensioned in 1818 and stricken in 1819 because his service was not Continental. He was restored in 1831 but was not paid for the interim. Congress restored him to the pension roll and authorized payment of his pension from 1819 to 1831 on 3 Mar. 1836. He was from Prince William Co., Va.

McFadden, William. Pa. —. He received a $40 gratuity and a $40 annuity 27 Feb. 1821. His widow, Rebecca McFadden, was awarded a $40 gratuity and a $40 annuity in Crawford Co., Pa. 29 Mar. 1823. He died 29 Oct. 1822. She died in or about July 1827.

McFall, Archibald. Pa. —. He was in Chester County on 31 Mar. 1807. He was in the 5th Regiment. He served seven glorious campaigns. He was wounded twice and taken prisoner. He was permitted to return. He was awarded a $40 annuity. He was dead by Feb. 1815.

McFall, James. Pa. —. He applied from Dauphin County on 2 June 1818. He enlisted in Chester County in Capt. Christopher Stewart's Company in the 5th Pa. Regiment under Col. Robert McGaw in Jan. 1776. He was taken prisoner in Nov. 1776 at Fort Washington and was exchanged three months later. He enlisted again in 1777 in Capt. Benjamin Bartholomew's Company in the 9th Pa. Regiment and was discharged at Philadelphia in Apr. 1782. He was in battle at Long Island, Fort Washington, Germantown, and Brandywine. He received four wounds, three of which were severe. He served under Maj. John Beatty.

McFall, Paul. N.Y. Pvt. He served in Col. Van Schaick's Regiment in Capt. Grigg's Company. He was disabled by sickness and was discharged from the Invalids Corps on 10 June 1783. He lived in Albany, N.Y. on 24 Apr. 1789. He was on the 1813 pension list.

McFall, Thomas. Pa. Pvt. He served in the 5th Regiment. He was wounded in his left leg by a musket ball at the capture of Fort Washington. He was taken prisoner and after 18 weeks of captivity was dismissed on parole. He lived in Pa. in 1794. He was on the 1813 pension list. He was in the Chester County poor house when he was pensioned.

McFarland, Alexander. Va. Pvt. He enlisted in 1775 at Staunton and served under Lt. Thomas Hughes and Capt. Fountain for one year in the Augusta County militia. He was on furlough in the spring of 1776. In the fall he was on the expedition against the Cherokee. He was under Col. Christian. Later he was a soldier from Nowlachuka. He lost his sight in one eye accidentally from the point of an Indian spear he had taken in the skirmish. He was in the battle of Great Bridge. He was aged 38 years in 1788. He was put on the pension list at the rate of £10 per annum on 22 Oct. 1788. He had served in Dunmore's War under Col. Andrew Lewis and was wounded at Point Pleasant in 1774.

McFarland, George. N.J. Ens. He served in the 4th Penn. Regiment and lost the use of his right hand. He was on the 1791 pension roll at the rate of $120 per annum. He was 39 years old. He died 19 Mar. 1792.

McFarland, James. Mass. —. He served in the 10th Regiment. He was paid $20. He also appeared as James McFarlin.

McFarland, John. N.J. Pvt. He served under Col. West in the Sussex County militia and was wounded in the thigh. He was 35 years old. He was on the 1791 pension roll. He later transferred to Pennsylvania. He was on the 1813 pension list.

McFarland, Moses. Mass. Capt. He served in Col. John Nixon's 4th Regiment. He was wounded in the right shoulder by a musket ball on 17 June 1775 at Bunker Hill and lost the use of his right arm. He was pensioned at the rate of half-pay on 31 Dec. 1776. He was 49 years old in 1786. He resided in Essex Co. He was granted one-third of a pension 20 Apr. 1796.

McFarland, Samuel. Pa. —. He applied in Cumberland County on 13 May 1813. He enlisted in 1776 in the 3rd Pa. Regiment under Col. Craig. He was in the battles of Brandywine, Germantown, Long Island, and Trenton. He was discharged 29 Dec. 1781 at Trenton. He was 79 years old. His wife was quite aged, and their daughter had been their mainstay for the last five or six years. He died 29 Feb. 1814.

McFarland, Solomon. Me. —. He died 3 June 1827. His widow was Deborah Scribner from Fairfield. She was paid $50 under the resolve of 1836.

McFarland, William. —. —. He lost an arm in the service and suffered from several wounds in his head producing mental derangement at times. He sought an increase in his pension 26 Jan. 1819. His request was not approved.

McFarlane, Andrew. Pa. Capt. He served in the militia and died at Monmouth in Feb 1777 from a fever which infected the camp. His widow, Margaret McFarlane, in Jan. 1778.

McFarlin, John. Va. —. His wife, Elizabeth McFarlin, was awarded assistance in Halifax Co., Va. on 17 Sep. 1778.

McFarlin, John. Va. —. He died in Continental service. His widow, Susannah McFarlin, was awarded assistance in Halifax Co., Va. on 18 May 1780.

McFarlin, Mordecai. S.C. Sgt. He served in the artillery in the Continental Army. He died in the service. His widow, Mary McFarlin, was awarded an annuity 21 May 1785. She and her son, Andrew McFarlin, were paid 15 Apr. 1791. He also appeared as Mordecai McFarland. His widow intermarried with William Lynn. In less than a year she learned that he had a wife and four children so she separated from him in 1792. He died about 1793. Her son, the editor of *The Georgetown Gazette,* died in July 1806. She suffered from rheumatism. She applied in 1815 and was paid as late as 1825.

McFarlin, Walter. Pa. —. He applied 5 Jan. 1814. He served in Capt. Andrew Porter's Artillery Company. He also appeared as Walton McFarland.

McFarron, John. Pa. —. He was killed by the Indians at Piper's Fort in 1782.

McFartridge, Daniel. Pa. —. He applied 24 Nov. 1817.

McFerrin, Andrew. S.C. —. His "memory was almost as frail as his body." He served under Capt. Benjamin Tutt. He was in Gen. Williamson's expedition against the Cherokee Indians. He was captured at Fort Rutledge in 1780 (he thought). He applied to the federal government in 1818 but could not demonstrate that his service was at Continental level. John Lummas and Col. Thomas Farrar deposed anent his service. He was pensioned from Abbeville District on 17 Dec. 1821.

McGaffy, Andrew. N.H. Lt. He was in Capt. McClary's Company in the 3rd N.H. Regiment and was wounded at the battle of Bunker Hill on 17 June 1775 by a shot from a musket which passed through the trunk of his body. At that battle he was under the command of Capt. Henry Seaborn. He was under the care of Regimental Surgeon Obadiah Williams. He served until Nov. 1778. He was aged 42 in 1787. He was on the 1813 pension list. He was from Sandwich.

McGahey, Andrew. Pa. —. Mary Baker, his former widow, was paid $200 for his donation land on 7 Apr. 1830.

McGahey, John. Pa. Corp. He was in Philadelphia County on 2 July 1787. He was in the Invalids under Capt. James McLean and had been disabled by rheumatism and other complaints. He served six years. He was 61 years old. He died 17 June 1790. He also appeared as John McGaughey. One of his name was on the 1791 and 1813 pension rolls.

McGahey, William. Pa. —. He was paid $200 for his right to donation land. He lived in Putnam Co., Ind. 12 Feb. 1829. He was granted a $40 gratuity and a $40 annuity 12 Feb. 1829.

McGahy, R. Pa. —. His widow, Mary Baker, was paid $200 for his donation land 7 Apr. 1830.

McGard, John. Pa. —. He was pensioned in Indiana County 21 Feb. 1838.

McGarity, William. S.C. —. He sought a pension in 1802. He was in the militia under Capt. McClure, Capt. Cooper, Capt. Patton, Col. Richardson, Capt. Nixon. He was in the Snowy Campaign, Kettle Creek, Stono, Rocking Mount, Hanging Rock, Fishing Creek, Fish Dam Ford, Blackstocks, Bigen Church, and Quinby Bridge. He was in his 70th year, and his wife was in her 69th. All of their children were gone from home. He was pensioned 7 Dec. 1826 in Chester District. Joseph Gaston, James Harbison, William Knox, and George Wier deposed about his service. He suffered from an enormous rupture. He was paid as late as 1834.

McGarvey, Neal. Pa. —. He applied in Beaver County on 4 Dec. 1816. He enlisted in 1777 in Capt. Hopps' Company under Col. Hartley and was discharged in 1783. He also appeared as Neal McGeary.

McGarvey, —. Pa. —. His widow, Catharine McGarvey, was granted relief in Dauphin County 13 Apr. 1827. She was dead by Mar. 1828.

McGaw, William. Pa. —. He was 88 years old in 1840. He applied 23 Mar. 1841.

McGawen, Archibald. Pa. —. He served in the 12th Regiment under Col. William Cook and Capt. Lincoln. He lost his hand from a wound received at Princeton on 12 May 1777. He was pensioned 14 Dec. 1786.

McGee, —. Pa. —. His widow, Judy McGee, was granted a $40 gratuity in Columbiana County, Ohio in 1836.

McGee, —. Pa. —. His widow, Margaret McGee, was granted relief in Venango County 11 Apr. 1825. She was later in Warren County.

McGee, Charles. Md. Pvt. He was pensioned at the rate of half-pay of a private 23 Jan. 1816.

McGee, George. Va. —. His wife, Lucy McGee, and five children were granted £1,200 support in Shenandoah Co., Va. 30 Aug. 1781.

McGee, James. Pa. —. His son, James McGee, was paid $200 for his father's right to donation land in Lancaster Co., Pa. 23 Mar. 1829.

McGee, John. Pa. —. He was from Philadelphia County.

McGee, Patrick. Pa. —. He served in Capt. Huston's Company under Col. Frederick Watts in the Flying Camp. He was taken prisoner at Fort Washington. He was liberated on parole in Jan. 1777 and was indisposed for four years. He had received no compensation for his confinement or while he lay sick. He was awarded $100 on 10 Mar. 1810.

McGee, Robert. Pa. Lt. He served in the Rifle Battalion of Philadelphia Militia. He was wounded in the neck and right shoulder at Millstone, N.J. on 20 Jan. 1777. He lived in Philadelphia Co., Pa. in 1794.

McGee, William. Md. Pvt. He was pensioned at the rate of half-pay of a private 23 Jan. 1816 in St. Mary's County. His widow, Sarah Magee, was paid his arrearage 15 Feb. 1830.

McGennis, Peter. Va. —. His wife, Elizabeth McGennis, and their two children were granted 3 barrels of corn and 150 pounds of pork in Prince William Co., Va. on 5 Sep. 1780.

McGhee, William. —. —. He drew a pension. His heirs were Mary Lovera and Frederick Greve. Congress did not grant their petition for bounty land because there was a bill pending for issuing land scrip for bounty land on 26 Apr. 1848.

McGibbon, Joseph. Del. Pvt. He lived in Sussex County. He served two years under Capt. William McKennan and was wounded and taken sick at the surrender of Gen. Cornwallis. He lost his discharge from Col. Stewart of the Pennsylvania Line. He was pensioned 11 Aug. 1790. He was on the 1813 pension list.

McGibboney, Patrick. —. —. His heirs received his commutation 13 June 1838.

McGill, John. Del. Pvt. He was pensioned in 1787. He was on the 1791 pension list. He was listed as dead on the 1796 roll.

McGill, John. Pa. Pvt. He was in Philadelphia 14 Nov. 1785. He served in the 8th Pa. Regiment and was transferred to the Invalids. He was wounded in both hands and one leg. He was 46 years old. He was awarded a $40 gratuity and a $30 annuity on 16 Jan. 1813. He was on the 1813 pension list. He died 18 May 1813.

McGill, William. Me. —. He died 9 Sep. 1828. His widow was Martha McGill from Brunswick. She was paid $50 under the resolve of 1836

McGill, William. Pa. —. He was granted a $40 gratuity and a $40 annuity in Mercer County.

McGinnis, —. Va. —. Edward McGinnis was furnished support in Loudoun County in May 1779.

McGinnis, John. Pa. —. He applied in Adams County on 24 Aug. 1811. He enlisted in 1776 after having served John Bell from the age of 7 to 21. He remained in the service to the end of war. He received 200 acres of donation land, and Col. Alexander of Carlisle applied and got a patent for 100 acres. He sold that 100 acres to John McGinnis of Carlisle. He was 71 years old in 1814.

McGinny, James. S.C. Capt. He was enlisted in Feb. 1779 by Capt. John Couterier and served sixteen months under Col. Daniel Horry. He was discharged by Capt. Lewis Ogier. He was at Stono and the storming of Savannah. Hugh Paisley served with him. He applied 12 Dec. 1822 but was rejected.

McGirk, Michael. Pa. —. He received a $40 gratuity and a $40 annuity in York County 9 Feb. 18371

McGlaughland, Robert. Pa. —. He was awarded a $40 gratuity and a $40 annuity in Adams Co., Pa. 18 Mar. 1834. He also appeared as Robert McGlaughlin.

McGlockin, George. Pa. Pvt. He was dead by Mar. 1791. He also appeared as George McLocklin.

McGluire, —. Pa. —. His widow, Barbara McGluire, was awarded a $40 gratuity and a $40 annuity in Lancaster County 1 Apr. 1836.

McGoff, John. Mass. Seaman. He was wounded. He was pensioned from 13 Mar. 1779 on 15 June 1785.

McGoven, William. Va. Pvt. He was wounded in the service. He was on the 1785 pension roll.

McGovern, James. Va. Pvt. His widow, Eleanor McGovern, and four children were granted £1,000 support in Shenandoah Co., Va. 30 Aug. 1781. She and her five children were granted a pension 24 Apr. 1783. His widow lived in Shenandoah County on 13 Nov. 1786 when she was continued on the pension list at the rate of £12 per annum. He served in the 8th Virginia Regiment and was killed at the siege of Ninety Six.

McGowan, James. S.C. —. He served in the 2nd S.C. Regiment, was wounded in the service, and was crippled. He was awarded an annuity 6 Dec. 1784.

McGowan, John. Pa. Capt. He was in Philadelphia County on 9 Jan. 1786. He was wounded at Germantown 14 Oct. 1777. He was 44 years old. He was transferred from the 4th Pa. Regiment to the Invalids. He also appeared as John McGorvan.

McGowan, John. Pa. —. He was in the Flying Camp in 1776 and then was on an active tour of duty. He lost his servant in one engagement. He settled on a donation tract believing it was vacant. It was not. He was, therefore, issued a patent for 250 acres.

McGowan, John. Pa. —. He served for four years and ten months in the 2nd Regiment in the 2nd Brigade under Gen. Wayne in the infantry. He was from York County in 1813.

McGown, Edward. Mass. Pvt. He served in the 5th Regiment and was from Sandwich. He was paid $50.

McGrath, Thomas. N.Y. Pvt. He was pensioned in 1809. He was on the 1813 pension list.

Macgraw, —. Va. —. His wife, Jemima Macgraw, was awarded £20 support in June 1776, £10 in Apr. 1779, £80 in July 1780, and 8 barrels of corn in Aug. 1781 in Fauquier Co., Va. while her husband was away in the Continental Army.

McGraw, Benjamin. S.C. Pvt. He was in the Snow Camps, Fort Moultrie, the Florida Expedition, Four Holes, Congaree Fort, and Biggins Church. He had two daughters living with him, one of whom was an invalid. His application was rejected in 1829.

McGraw, Charles. Va. —. He lived in Richmond 28 Jan. 1799. He was disabled at West Point in 1778 and was unable to labor. He was granted $60 relief on 25 Jan. 1799.

McGraw, Charles. Va. —. His wife, Sarah McGraw, was allowed £20 for her support and her child in Augusta Co., Va. 17 Feb. 1778.

McGraw, James. N.Y. & Pa. —. During the French and Indian War he served as a soldier under James Clinton in 1759. He enlisted 13 June 1777 in the 3rd N.Y. Regiment in Capt. Leonard Bleeker's Company under Col. Peter Gansevort. He was discharged in Canada. He served in Capt. John Nicholson's Company under Col. James Clinton. He later served under Capt. Thomas DeWitt, and Capt. Thomas Dorsey in a Pennsylvania Regiment. He was 58 years old on 17 Aug. 1786.

McGraw, James. Va. —. He died in Continental service at Bluford's defeat in South Carolina. His widow was Molly McGraw. Their children were John McGraw, Jonathan [?] McGraw, Isaac McGraw, and Isaiah [?] McGraw. He was from Fauquier Co., Va.

McGraw, Solomon. S.C. —. He was from Fairfield in 1794.

McGraw, William. S.C. —. He served in the French and Indian War under Capt. Charles Russell, Maj. William Thompson, and Col. James Grant. He enlisted in 1775 in Capt. Charles Keating's Company under Col. William Thompson. He was also under Capt. Thomas Woodward and Col. William Drayton. He caught cold in his left knee and never recovered. He was pensioned 30 Nov. 1827 in Edgefield District. He died 29 Sep. 1830. His widow, Esther McGraw, was pensioned 6 Dec. 1832 at the rate of $30 per annum. She resided with her son Amos McGraw. She was paid as late as 1834.

McGreay, Neal. Pa. —. He enlisted in 1777 under Capt Hopps and Col. Hartley. He was discharged in 1778. He was from Beaver County.

McGredy, William. Pa. —. He was pensioned under the act of 24 Mar. 1818. He was paid to May 1828.

McGregor, James. Pa. —. He was awarded a $40 gratuity and a $40 annuity in Mifflin Co., Pa. 18 Feb. 1834. He died 15 Mar. 1847.

McGregor, William. Pa. —. He served under Capt. Wilson in the Flying Camp and was taken prisoner at Fort Washington and died shortly after release from captivity. He was from Allegheny County.

McGuigan, Andrew. Pa. Pvt. He was in Bucks Co. 12 June 1786. He served in the 10th Pa. Regiment. He was disabled by wounds and hurts in the service and was discharged in Jan. or Feb. 1781 by Brigadier General Richard Humpton. He was dead by Mar. 1797.

McGuillen, Robert. Va. Pvt. He was on the 1791 pension list.

McGuire, —. Pa. —. His widow, Jane McGuire, was awarded a $40 gratuity and a $40 annuity in

Westmoreland Co., Pa. 29 Mar. 1824.

McGuire, Andrew. Va. Pvt. He was pensioned 21 Apr. 1783 at the rate of £8 per annum. He served under Maj. William Lewis in the Continental Army. He enlisted about 1778 and served to the end of the war in the 1ˢᵗ Va. Regiment. He was 65 years old. He was disabled by a broken left collar bone and a rupture in his left groin. He lived in Frederick Co., Va. He was on the 1813 pension list.

McGuire, Bernard. Pa. Corp. He was in Philadelphia County 13 Mar. 1786. He was in the 1ˢᵗ Pa. Regiment under Col. James Chambers in Capt. Hendrick's Company and marched with Thomas Anderson and Timothy Connor from Carlisle to Boston to Quebec in 1776. They were taken prisoner when Gen. Montgomery fell. He was wounded in the right thigh at Germantown. He was wounded again at Stony Point and on North River below Fort Lee. He was at the battle of Green Springs, Virginia. Anderson and Connor were in Westmoreland County 16 Feb. 1814. He was on the 1813 pension list. He also appeared as Barney McGuire.

McGuire, John. Pa. —. He had his leg broken by a fall from a wagon which he was loading. He was old and lame and was awarded a $40 gratuity and a $40 annuity in Bucks Co., Pa. 3 Feb. 1812.

McGuire, John. Pa. —. He applied 2 Feb. 1818.

McGuire, Michael. Md. Pvt. He was pensioned 4 Mar. 1789. He was on the 1813 pension list.

McGuire, Thomas. Del. Sgt. He was pensioned in 1784. He was on the 1791 pension list.

McGuire, Thomas. N.C. Maj. He served in the militia under Col. Lock and Col. Caldwell. He was promoted from adjutant to major. He went to Georgia to fight the Cherokee with Jacob Nichols and his company. He returned two months later. He served to the close of the war. He was from Statesville, Iredell Co., N.C. He was at Pile's defeat at the Crossroads, Ramsour's Mill, and at a skirmish at Catawba where he was made prisoner. He escaped with the loss of his horse. When Cornwallis entered Virginia, he was ordered to Wilmington where he remained to the close of the war. He died in 1799. He married in 1770. His widow was Jane McGuire but she failed to furnish any record evidence so Congress did not approve her application 19 Mar. 1844.

McGuire, William. Va. Lt. He was in Frederick County 30 Jan. 1787 and was 23 years old. He served in the 1ˢᵗ Regiment of Artillery under Col. Charles Harrison. He was wounded at Eutaw Springs and broke his right thigh. He was continued on the pension list at the rate of £60 per annum on 30 Jan. 1787. He was continued on the pension list on 27 Apr. 1791. He died 24 Nov. 1820 in Jefferson Co., Va. William C. Craighill was the administrator of his estate.

McHan, John. Pa. —. He applied at Fredericktown, Maryland 3 Sep. 1829.

McHatton, John. Pa. Capt. He enlisted in July 1776 in Pennsylvania and was commissioned as a captain in a company of volunteers. Two months later he was commissioned a captain in the Flying Camps under Col. Watts in the Pennsylvania Line. He was made a prisoner at Fort Washington and soon was made a captain in the Pennsylvania Continental Line under Col. McGaw. He was held on the prison ship, *Jersey*. He was held in prison on Long Island until about the time of the surrender of Lord Cornwallis at Yorktown. He was exchanged and returned to the army. He was detached as supernumerary. Previously he had served in the French and Indian War under Gen. Braddock, Col. Dunbar, Gen. Stanwick, Gen. Forbes, and Gen. Monkton. He was on the Bouquet Expedition. His father was a Scotchman and spelled his name McIlhatton. He removed to Kentucky in 1783. His application for commutation pay was not approved on 21 Mar. 1838 because he was in the flying camp.

McHatton, William. Pa. 1ˢᵗ Lt. He served in the 12ᵗʰ Regiment under Col. W. Cook. He returned his commutation in order to be placed on the pension roll in 1794. He was wounded in his right shoulder by a musket ball and three buck shot in 1777 at Bonhamtown. He lived in Nelson Co., Ky. in 1794. He joined the Invalids 1 July 1779. He was granted a full pension 20 Apr. 1796 in exchange for his half-pay. He died 26 Apr. 1807.

McHenry, Henry. Pa. —. He was paid $200 in Allegheny Co., Pa. 15 Mar. 1826.

McHenry, Isaac. Va. Sgt. He entered the service in Mar. 1780 under Capt. Alexander Maxwell in the Indian spies. He applied in Putnam Co., Ohio for a pension from Congress 25 Apr. 1840. He was born in Hampshire Co., Va. 27 Dec. 1763. He moved to Green Co., Ky, in 1786 and in 1807 to Pickaway Co., Ohio. Congress did not grant him a pension 25 Apr. 1840.

McHenry, John. Pa. —. He was awarded a $40 gratuity and a $40 annuity in Tioga Co., N.Y. 11 Apr. 1825.

McHenry, Thomas. Pa. —. He was awarded a $40 gratuity and a $40 annuity in Columbia Co., Pa. 27 Mar. 1824.

McHenry, William. Pa. —. He was pensioned in Indiana County 13 Apr.1838. He was 70 years old in 1840.

McHerg, John. S.C. —. He lost his life in the service. His widow Susanna McHerg, was awarded an annuity 1 Oct. 1785. Compare with John Meherg.

McIlhattan, Samuel. Pa. —. His widow, Mary McIlhattan, was awarded a $40 gratuity and a $40 annuity 30 Jan. 1834. She died 23 Apr. 1840 in Northumberland County.

McIlney, John. Pa. —. He was awarded a $40 gratuity and a $40 annuity 27 Mar. 1837 in Bedford County. He died 18 Oct. 1848.

McIlvaine, Ebenezer. Mass. Pvt. He served in Col. Reed's Regiment. He was wounded in his left arm by a musket ball which entered between the fourth and fifth ribs on his left side in Aug.1779 at Newtown. He resided in Rockingham, Vt. in 1796. He enlisted 1 Jan. 1777 for the war and was promoted to corporal in Oct. 1779. He was discharged 10 Jan. 1780. He was granted half of a pension 20 Apr. 1796. He was on the 1813 pension list of Vermont.

McIlwaine, —. Pa. —. His widow, Mary McIlwaine, was awarded a $40 gratuity and a $40 annuity in Adams Co., Pa. 15 Apr. 1834. She also appeared as Mary McIlvaine.

McInnis, Daniel. N.C. —. He served several tours in the militia from his entry into service in 1778 until he left the service in 1781. He was 78 years old in Nov. 1832. Congress declined to grant him assistance 28 Jan. 1835. He was a resident of Mississippi.

McIntire, Thomas. Pa.. Capt. He received his commutation of his half-pay 27 Mar. 1792.

McIntosh, John. Me. —. He was from Brunswick. He was paid $50 under the resolve of 1836.

McIntosh, John. Pa. Pvt. He was transferred to New York by Sep. 1792. He was on the 1813 pension list. He may have been the one of that name who died 27 Jan. 1820.

McIntosh, William. Va. Pvt. He served under Col. Campbell. He was wounded in the battle of Guilford by a musket ball in the left leg on 15 Mar. 1781. He lived in Richmond, Va. in 1794.

McIntyre, John. Pa. —. His widow, Catherine McIntyre, received a $40 gratuity and a $40 annuity in Westmoreland County 13 Apr. 1854.

McIsack, Archibald. S.C. —. His widow was Mary McIsack from Marion District when she was granted a pension 10 Dec. 1838.

McJunkin, Daniel. S.C. Lt. He applied from Union District. He was wounded in the service. He married Jane Chesney in the latter part of Nov. 1781. He was granted an annuity 18 Jan. 1785 in Greenville. He died 20 Mar. 1825. His widow, Jane McJunkin, was distressed by disease, sought his arrearage, and applied for a pension 9 Oct. 1832 at the rate of $30 per annum. She was paid as late as 1834.

McJunkin, Joseph. S.C. Maj. He was wounded in his arm in 1781. He was granted an annuity 23 Dec. 1784. He was on the 1813 pension list.

McKannon, Christopher. Va. Sgt.-Maj. He served in the Va. line and was wounded in his left arm.

McKay, Daniel. Va. —. His wife was awarded an allowance in Yohogania Co., Va. 24 Mar. 1779 while he was away in Continental service.

Mackay, John. Md. Corp. He served in the 3rd Regiment and was wounded. He was pensioned in St. Mary's County in 1785.

McKean, James. Pa. —. He was pensioned in Armstrong County 17 Mar. 1838.

McKean, Samuel. N.Y. Pvt. He served in Capt. Elihu Marshall's Company under Col. Marinus Willett. He was wounded by a musket ball in his chin which fractured his jaw bone and came out his left cheek at Turlough, Montgomery Co., N.Y. in July 1781. He was pensioned 1 Jan. 1782. He was aged 23 years on 22 June 1788 and was a carpenter in Cherry Valley, Montgomery Co., N.Y. on 25 Apr. 1789. He later lived in Otsego County. He was on the 1813 pension list. He also appeared as Samuel McKeen.

McKee, —. Pa. —. His wife, Mary McKee, was awarded a $40 gratuity and a $40 annuity in Armstrong Co., Pa. 17 Mar. 1835.

McKee, —. Pa.—. His widow, Judy McKee received a $40 gratuity and a $40 annuity in Columbiana Co., Ohio 12 Mar. 1836. She died 29 Mar. 1848.

McKee, Andrew. Pa. —. He applied in Armstrong County 6 Mar. 1813. He served in Capt. Robert Adams' Company under Col. Irwin for one year in 1777. He next enlisted in Capt. Zeigler's Company under Col. Hartley for the war. He was also under Col. Minges in the 6th Battalion and served with Matthew Orgin. They were enlisted in the 3rd Pa. Regiment under Col. George Harmer. He was paid $750 for his donation land on 21 Jan. 1823. He died 17 June 1833.

McKee, John. S.C. —. He served in the 1st Regiment and was taken prisoner 12 May 1780 at Charleston. He had a large family to support. He sought compensation 26 Nov. 1812.

McKee, Richard. Md. —. He served under Benjamin Speaker and Capt. Richard Henderson in the Maryland Infantry. He was wounded by a musket ball through his leg near Camden. He was a prisoner of war. He was a waiter to Lt. Trueman. When his unit returned to Maryland, he was sick in hospital and remained in South Carolina. He was married and had four children. He had also been wounded in his hand at Germantown. He fought at Monmouth, Morristown, Trenton, Brandywine, Fish Kill, White Plains, Eutaw, and Camden. He applied in 1806.

McKeen, Barnard. N.H. He served under Col. Baldwin in Capt. McConnell's Company. He was seized with a fever at Windsor. He had a wife and six children when he sought relief in June 1787.

McKeen, Robert. N.Y. Capt. He served under Col. Willet. He was killed by the Indians at Fort Plain 10 July 1781. His widow, Jennet McKeen, received his half-pay pension.

McKeever, Angus. Pa. Pvt. He was in Philadelphia County on 13 Feb. 1786. He served in the 3rd Pa. Regt. He was dismissed from the Invalids on account of the loss of his thumb and forefinger and another wound in his thigh from grapeshot. He was 27 years old. He was from Virginia when he was pensioned 25 Oct. 1827 by Pennsylvania.

McKelduff, Adam. S.C. —. He was deceased when David McKelduff was paid £122.4.9 in an indent with interest on 24 Jan. 1791.

McKelvy, Daniel. S.C. —. He was mortally wounded in 1781 and died under age. His father, James McKelvy, died seized of the land. One-third of the land was to go to the one Daniel McKelvy said he wanted to be his heir and whom he called cousin, Robert McKelvy. The matter had to be referred to the legislature in 1787 for action.

McKennan, William. Del. Capt. He was pensioned in 1783. He was on the 1791 pension list. He was on the 1813 pension list in Pennsylvania.

MacKene, William. Pa. —. He received a $40 gratuity and a $40 annuity in Berks County 1 Apr. 1823.

McKenney, Timothy. N.J. Pvt. He served in the 3rd Regiment. His widow Mary McKenney received a half-pay pension 23 Dec. 1783.

McKennon, William. —. —. His application was allowed to lay on the table.

McKenny, —. Va. —. His father, Rowland McKenny, was granted £10 support on 9 Apr. 1778 and £20 on 12 July 1779 in Caroline Co., Va. while he was away in the service. On 8 May 1781 Rowland McKenny had two in his family.

McKenzie, Daniel. S.C. —. He lost an eye in an explosion of powder set at Sullivan's Island. He was upwards of 70 years. He had an aged and afflicted companion. George Green saw him in the uniform of a regular soldier. He was pensioned from Williamsburg District 7 Dec. 1826. He was paid as late as 1833.

McKenzie, James. —. Seaman. He was disabled by the loss of limb in action with the British on 23 Sep. 1779. He served under Capt. John Paul Jones aboard the *Bon Homme Richard*. He was pensioned by the Continental Congress act of 15 Sep. 1783.

McKenzie, John. —. —. His application was allowed to lay on the table.

McKenzie, Joseph. Pa. —. He was pensioned in Beaver County 21 Feb. 1838.

McKeown, John. Pa. —. He applied in Dauphin County 21 Jan. 1818. He enlisted in the spring of 1776 under Capt. Mercer in the 2nd Pa. Regiment and was discharged after four years and ten months of service.

McKesson, John. N.Y. —. He was wounded. He was on the 1785 pension list.

Mackey, Eneas. Pa. Col. He died 4 Feb. 1777. His widow, Mary Mackey, was granted a half-pay pension in Westmoreland County.

Mackey, William. Pa. Capt. He served in the 9th Regiment under Col. Richard Humpton and was wounded 11 Sep. 1777 at Brandywine by a musket ball through his lungs. He applied 12 May 1788. He also appeared as William Mackay.

McKim, —. Pa. —. His widow, Hannah McKim, was awarded a $40 gratuity and a $40 annuity in Beaver County 24 Mar. 1837.

McKinley, Duncan. —. —. His application was rejected 2 Mar. 1795.

McKinley, John. Va. —. Sgt. He entered in 1776 and served under Capt. Stephen Ashby. He was commissioned a lieutenant in the 13th Regiment. He later became a captain. An Indian squaw cut off his head with an axe in June 1782. William McKinley and the other heirs sought commutation and bounty land for his rank as a captain. He had received relief for his rank of lieutenant. Congress declined any further relief on 20 Aug. 1842.

McKinney, Charles. N.Y. Sgt. He served in Capt. Jacob Hallet's Company in the 2nd N.Y. Regiment under Col. Philip Van Cortland. He was wounded at Stillwater on 19 Sep. 1777 in his right arm. He lived in Orange Co., N.Y. on 7 June 1787. He was 51 years old in Aug. 1785. He lost two joints of the fingers on his right hand and two on his left due to frost. He was on the 1813 pension list.

McKinney, Daniel. Pa. —. He entered the service at Muncey, Pa. about 1 Apr. 1779 under Capt. Berry and Col. Arthur. He was in a skirmish with the Indians while out scouting at Loyal Sock Creek. Five of his comrades were killed. He and six others were taken prisoner and carried to Lake Seneca where they remained until September when they marched to Niagara Fort under Col.

Bolton of the British army. He was sent to Oswego in 1783 and was detained until the spring of 1784 when he was sent to Montreal with other prisoners to Ticonderoga, and by boat to Skeensboro where they were given up. Congress granted him a pension 9 Jan. 1838.

McKinney, Isaac. Mass. Pvt. He served in the Mass. Line and was pensioned 29 Sep. 1789. He was on the 1813 pension list. He later lived in Cumberland Co., Maine.

McKinney, John. Pa. —. He was awarded a $40 gratuity and a $40 annuity in Bucks County on 14 Mar. 1818.

McKinney, Peter. Pa. Fifer. He applied in Butler County on 7 Apr. 1819. He served in the 8th Pa. Regiment in Capt. Clark's Company under Col. Broadhead until he was discharged at the end of the war. Simon Fletcher proved his service. He also appeared as Peter Kinney. He was 75 years old in 1840.

McKinney, Robert. Pa. Lt. He was on the 1813 pension list. He also appeared as Robert McKenna. He transferred to Pennsylvania.

McKinney, Robert. Va. Lt. He was on the 1800 pension list.

McKinney, Roger. S.C. —. He served in the 3rd S.C. Regiment and died in Charleston 1 June 1780. His widow, Elizabeth Marr, was awarded an annuity 19 May 1783. There were children.

McKinney, Samuel. S.C. —. He served under Capt. Kimble and was wounded in the leg by a bayonet at Hanging Rock. He was pensioned in 1813.

McKinnor [?], Robert. Pa. Lt. He was granted relief.

McKinsey, Daniel. Pa. Pvt. He was in Philadelphia County on 14 July 1787. He was in Capt. Willing's Company at Fort Pitt in 1777. He was at Manahuac on the Mississippi River in 1778. He was wounded in an engagement with the British troops. He had several pieces of his ribs taken out. He was 33 years old. He had a wife and four children, the youngest of whom was six weeks. He was dead by Mar. 1790.

McKinsey, Isaac. Mass. Pvt. He served in the 11th Regiment under Col. Benjamin Tupper and Capt. Thomas Tomes. He lost his left hand. He was 42 years old in 1789.

McKinsey, John. Pvt. Conn. He served under Col. Silliman. He was wounded by the stroke of a musket in his face; his arm was fractured and broken. He resided in New Haven, Conn. in 1792.

McKinsey, John. Conn. Pvt. He served under Col. Chandler. His eyesight was much impaired due to sickness. He lived in Stratford, Conn. in 1792. He enlisted 9 June 1777 and was invalided 7 Apr. 1781.

McKinsey, John. Mass. Pvt. He served in the Invalids. He was disabled by a wound in his left arm and right thigh. He was pensioned 4 Jan. 1783. He was 30 years old and resided in Boston, Mass. in 1786. He was 30 years old.

McKinsey, Moses. Md. Drummer. He was pensioned in Allegany County on 23 Jan. 1816 at the rate of half-pay of a drummer. His widow, Sarah McKinsey, was pensioned at the same rate 9 Mar. 1827.

McKinstry, John. N.Y. Capt. He served under Col. John Patterson. He was wounded in his left leg and thigh by musket balls on 20 May 1776 at the Cedars in Canada. He was made a prisoner by the Indians and received a wound in his belly and another in his breast by the blow with a muzzle and butt end of a musket. He was pensioned 18 Jan. 1787. He lived in Hudson, Columbia Co., N.Y. on 18 Apr. 1789 and in Livingston, N.Y. in 1795. He served in the militia. His rank was reported as major when he was awarded 300 acres of bounty land 11 Apr. 1808. His rate was $12 per month from 7 Dec. 1807. He was on the 1813 pension list.

McKissick, Daniel. N.C. Capt. He was wounded by a musket ball in his left arm on 20 June 1780 near Ramsour's Mill. He lived in Lincoln Co., N.C. in 1795. He served in the militia. He was alive in 1807. He served in a troop of horse in the militia from Burke County. He was on the 1813 pension list.

McKissick, James. Pa. —. He was pensioned in Indiana County 16 June 1836.

McKissick, Thomas. N.C. Pvt. He was a resident of Person County in 1802. He served in the 3rd N.C. Regiment under Col. Patton. He was wounded in the battle of Germantown on 4 Oct. 1777. John Christian served with him and swore to his service. John Atkinson who attended the doctors at Redding, Pa. where the wounded were carried also attested to his service. Isaac Hudson of Chester District, S.C. swore that he entered the service with him on 3 May 1776 under Col. Jethro Sumner and Capt. Jacob Turner. McKissick served 2 ½ years. He was on the 1813 pension list. He later lived in Giles Co., Tenn.

McKleroy, Thomas. Pa. —. He was awarded a $40 gratuity and a $40 annuity in Fayette Co., Pa. 7 May 1832.

McKnight, —. Va. —. Mary McKnight, and small children were allowed £10 as the wife of a Revolutionary soldier in Augusta Co., Va. 17 Mar. 1778.

McKnight, Charles. N.Y. Surgeon General. His administrator was John M. S. McKnight. Congress rejected the claim because the veteran had already received his commutation of five years' full pay on 19 Feb. 1836.

McKnight, Dennis. Pa. Pvt. He served in the 8th Battalion of the Chester County militia, was wounded, and taken prisoner. He was allowed an $80 gratuity and $40 annuity per annum on 26 Jan. 1807 and was a resident of Chester County. He was on the 1813 pension list. He died 3 or 4 June 1819.

McKnight, John. Del. Pvt. He served from 1776 to the conclusion of the war. He had his wrist broken in South Carolina. He was pensioned in 1784. He was on the 1791 pension list.

McKnight, Robert. —. —. He was pensioned 13 Mar. 1804.

McKnight, Robert. Pa. —. He was awarded a $40 gratuity and a $40 annuity in Washington County 12 Mar. 1836.

McKolly,—. Pa. —. Molly McKolly was awarded a $40 annuity and a $40 gratuity for his service in the Revolutionary War 21 Feb. 1822. She also appeared as Molly McColly.

McKowan, John. Pa. —. His pension commenced 15 Jan. 1818.

McKowan, Thomas. Pa. —. He was granted relief.

McKown, John. Pa. —. He was pensioned 30 Jan. 1818.

McLain, —. Pa. —. His widow, Mary McLain, was awarded a $40 gratuity and a $40 annuity in Center Co., Pa. 27 Mar. 1824.

McLain, Charles. Pa. —. He was pensioned by the court of enquiry 12 July 1814. He died 21 Dec. 1822.

McLain, John. Pa. —. He was granted relief in Tioga County 26 Mar. 1832.

McLaland, William. N.Y. Pvt. He was pensioned 3 Mar. 1809. He was on the 1813 pension list.

McLane, Moses. Del. —. He was pensioned 1 Feb. 1780.

McLanahan, William. —. —. He was pensioned 3 Mar. 1809.

McLaughlin, —. Pa. —. His widow, Elizabeth McLaughlin, was granted a $40 annuity 12 Mar. 1836.

McLaughlin, Andrew. Pa. —. He was granted relief 11 Apr. 1844 in Indiana County. He died 1 May 1846.

McLaughlin, George. Pa. Pvt. He was in Lancaster County on 7 Dec. 1785. He served in the 3rd Pa. Regiment. He was disabled, incapable of duty, and lost his eyesight. He was 30 years old. He also appeared as George McLocklin. *Vide* George McGlockin.

McLaughlin, Robert. Pa. —. He was granted a $40 gratuity and a $40 annuity in Adams County 18 Mar. 1834. He died 10 June 1840.

McLaughlin, William. Pa. He was in Washington County and received relief under the act of 18 Feb. 1839.

McLean, A. —. Col. He was attached to Col. Harry Lewis's Corps until Nov. 1782 when he retired on half-pay for life. He later found out that Col. Lee had commuted his pay and that he was not entitled to half-pay for life. He doubted that Col. Lee had that authority and was hard pressed for money. He sought his half-pay for life, but his claim was rejected in 1815.

McLean, Alexander. Pa. —. He applied in Westmoreland County on 30 Apr. 1818. He served three years from 1776 to 1779. He was 71 years old and had reared thirteen children, three of whom were in the service of the U.S. He was in Capt. Doyle's Company in the 1ˢᵗ Pa. Regiment and later in the 6ᵗʰ Pa. Regiment under Lt. Col. Harmar because Col. McGaw was a prisoner. John McDowell was surgeon. He was discharged by Col. Harmar.

McLean, Archibald. Pa. Pvt. He was on the 1791 pension roll. He was dead by Sep. 1792.

McLean, Arthur. Md. Sgt. He was pensioned in Baltimore Co. at the rate of half-pay of a sergeant 30 Jan. 1829.

McLean, James. Conn. —. He served under Capt. John Chester and Col. Wyllys in 1775. He was from Hartford County.

McLean, James. Pa. Lt. He was in Philadelphia County on 30 Nov. 1785. He contracted severe and chronic complaints in public service. He was transferred from the 10ᵗʰ Pa. Regiment to the Invalids. He was 49 years old. He also appeared as James McClean. He died 28 Oct. 1804.

McLean, John. N.Y. Sgt. He served under Capt. Andrew Moody in Col. John Lamb's artillery regiment. He was to be granted his bounty land on the condition that he proved that he was not the man of the same name who served as matross in the same unit on 10 Apr. 1804.

McLean, William. N.C. Pvt. He served in the militia and was wounded in the right elbow at Ramsour's Mill in June 1780. He was a carpenter. He died 1 Oct. 1806. He was from Rowan County. He also appeared as William McLain and William McClean.

McLenaghen, Charles. Pa. —. He was awarded a $40 gratuity and a $40 annuity in Mifflin Co. on 14 Apr. 1834.

McLenchen, —. Pa. —. His widow, Rachel McLenchen, was awarded a $40 gratuity and a $40 annuity in Erie Co., Pa. 18 Mar. 1834.

McLeod, —. Va. —. His wife, Else McLeod, was granted support in Prince Edward Co., Va. on 15 Mar. 1779 while he was away in Continental service.

McLeod, Hugh. Md. Pvt. He was pensioned 4 Mar. 1789. He was on the 1813 pension list.

McLeod, John. Pa. —. He was awarded a $40 gratuity and a $40 annuity in Butler County 30 Mar. 1822.

McLucas, John. Me. —. He died 27 Mar. 1813 in Hiram. His widow was Margaret McLucas from Waterboro. She was paid $50 under the resolve of 1836.

McLure, James. —. —. He was given leave to withdraw his application.

McMahan, John. Pa. Sgt. He was from York County 14 June 1788. He served in the 3ʳᵈ and the 4ᵗʰ Pa. Regiments. He suffered from rheumatism and a rupture. He then served as a drill sergeant and did drill duty in camp. In 1781 he got a fall on board a vessel. He had previously been a pensioner in Lancaster County.

McMahan, John. Va. —. His wife was granted relief in Pittsylvania Co., Va. on 28 Aug. 1777, 23 Jan. 1778, 26 Mar. 1778, and 25 Feb. 1779.

McMahon, Jeremiah. N.J. Pvt. He served in the 2nd Regiment. He lived in Gloucester Co., N.J. He was on the 1791 pension roll at the rate of $40 per annum.

McMahon, Peter. S.C. —. He served under Capt. John Purvis and Col. Thompson. He was from Pendleton District when he was pensioned 14 Dec. 1820 and was allowed one year arrearage. His son, William McMahon, collected the payment in 1825. He was paid as late as 1833.

McMallow, James. Pa. —. He applied 25 Sep. 1787.

McManus, Charles. S.C. Maj. He had a feeble wife. John Laney served with him. He was pensioned 2 Dec. 1824. He was paid as late as 1830.

McManus, James. Pa. —. He was from Tioga on 17 May 1787.

McManus, John. Pa. Pvt. He was in the 2nd and 3rd Regiments. He was wounded at Brandywine and afterwards at Charleston. He was in Philadelphia County 12 June 1786. He was in the 1st Pa. He was 41 years old. His daughter, Sarah McManus, was in the Girls Charity School of the university. He was dead by Mar. 1794.

McMaster, Hugh. N.Y. Pvt. He served in David McMaster's Company under Col. Frederick ---- in the militia. He was wounded in the neck at Saratoga in Oct. 1777. He lived in Washington Co., N.Y. in 1786. He was on the 1813 pension list.

McMasters, Edward. Pa. —. He was awarded a $40 gratuity and a $40 annuity in Lycoming Co., Pa. 29 Mar. 1824. He died 2 Apr. 1833. His widow, Rhoda McMasters, was awarded a $40 gratuity and a $40 annuity 15 Apr. 1834. She died 25 Nov. 1842.

McMath, Daniel. Pa. —. He enlisted in the fall of 1776 under Capt. John Brady and Col. William Cook. After the battle of Monmouth his unit was drafted into the 3rd Regiment under Col. Thomas Craig. He was discharged in 1781. He subsequently served on the frontiers. He was from Allegheny County. He was pensioned in Feb. 1813. He died 11 Mar. 1824. He also appeared as Daniel McMarth and Daniel Mitchell [sic].

McMeans, —. S.C. —. His widow was Elizabeth McMeans from Lancaster in 1793.

McMechan, John. Pa. Sgt. He was in York County 30 Nov. 1785. He served in the 3rd Pa. Rifle Regiment. He enlisted in 1776 and served first under Col. Morgan. He was out with Gen. Sullivan in 1779. He was ruptured and afflicted with rheumatic pains contracted in the service. In going south with recruits, he got a fall on board the vessel and nearly lost his life. He was 44 years old. He also appeared as John McMachen

McMeyers, Andrew. N.J. Capt. He served under Col. Matthew Ogden. He died 4 Oct. 1777 at Germantown. His widow, Mary McMeyers, sought a half-pay pension 23 Nov. 1789. His heirs were paid his seven years' half-pay of $1,680.

McMillan, Archibald. N.H. Sgt. He was from New Boston. He enlisted in May 1775 and served under Capt. William Scott and Col. John Starke. He was wounded in his right hand on 17 June 1775 at Bunker Hill. He was aged 58 in 1787.

McMillan, John. N.H. —. He was pensioned.

McMillan, William. —. Lt. He was a non-commissioned officer, was taken prisoner at Long Island, put on a prison ship, and sent to Halifax. He escaped, went to Boston, and rejoined. He was at Monmouth. In Aug. 1778 he enlisted in the Maryland Line for three years. He was commissioned a lieutenant by Gen. Smallwood in the spring of 1779. He was furloughed to visit his parents whom he had not seen in four years. He was ordered to Baltimore to recruit. He was pensioned as a private but later found proof of his grade as a lieutenant. Congress granted him a pension at the new level 10 Jan. 1832.

McMillen, Thomas. Pa. —. He was pensioned under the act of 14 Mar. 1818 in Allegheny County.

McMillen, William. Md. —. He applied as a non-commissioned officer in 1818. He sought commutation pay as a lieutenant 24 Apr. 1840. Congress rejected his claim because it was seemingly an afterthought and without foundation.

McMillin, Michael. Pa. —. He was awarded a $40 gratuity and a $40 annuity in Lancaster Co., Pa. 7 Mar. 1827.

McMillion, William. Mass. —. Drummer. He served in Revere's Regiment and was from Boston. His widow, Eliza McMillion, was paid $50.

McMinimy, William. Va. —. His wife, Catharine McMinimy, was allowed support on 28 July 1777. She was granted £14 support on 24 Nov. 1777 in Bedford Co., Va.

McMullan, Michael. Pa. Pvt. He applied in Mifflin County on 26 May 1812. Daniel Davis of the 5th Pa. Regiment proved that McMullan was in Capt. Murray's Company under Col. Walter Stewart at Brandywine 11 Sep. 1777. His deafness was due to cannon fire in different battles in Col. Proctor's Artillery. He enlisted in March 1775 in Capt. Hendrick's Company for a year and went to Quebec. He was wounded on the same day that Gen. Montgomery fell. He was discharged at Three Rivers and returned home. Three months later he enlisted in Capt. John Morrow's Company for two years. He was in the battles of Long Island, Trenton, Princeton, Brandywine, and Germantown. He was discharged in Jan. 1778 at Valley Forge. James McIlroy was in the same company.

McMullan, Thomas. Pa. —. He was pensioned under the act of 14 Mar. 1818.

McMullen, —. Pa. —. His widow, Elizabeth McMullen, was awarded a $40 gratuity 6 Apr. 1830 in Center County.

McMullen, —. Pa. —. His widow, Sarah McMullen, was awarded a $40 gratuity and a $40 annuity in Butler Co., Pa. 30 Mar. 1824.

McMullen, Archibald. N.H. —. He was wounded at Bunker Hill. He was being pensioned in 1780.

McMullen, Hugh. Pa. Pvt. He was in Philadelphia County on 12 Dec. 1785. He was in the Invalids and was discharged 1 Sep. 1782 as unfit for duty on account of the loss of his sight and other disabilities. He was 64 years old.

McMullen, John. Pa. —. He applied in Mifflin County on 23 May 1812. He enlisted 1 Mar. 1776 at Greensburgh in Capt. William Butler's Company in the Pa. Line under Col. Craig. He marched to Carlisle, Philadelphia, and to Canada. He was in the battles of Three Rivers, Short Hills in New Jersey, Brandywine, Germantown, Monmouth, and Stoney Point. He and 33 other Irishmen and many American soldiers were taken prisoners by the British at Newark. He was a prisoner nine months and ten days. He was exchanged and rejoined the same company under Capt. Thomas Butler. He marched to the south and was at the battle of Green Springs, Va. in Capt. William Henderson's Company. He was present at the taking of Cornwallis at Yorktown. Afterwards he marched to South Carolina under the command of Capt. Marshall and continued there two years. Capt. Doyle was in command at James Island. He marched back to Philadelphia and was discharged after seven years. He was awarded $40 on 20 Mar. 1812.

McMullen, John. Pa. Capt. He was awarded $150 for his expenses of being wounded under Gen. Brown on 19 Mar. 1816.

McMullen, William. Pa —. He applied in Mifflin County on 13 Apr. 1813. He enlisted at Newark, Del. in Apr. 1777 for three years and joined the regiment at Fort Mifflin. He was in the battles of Brandywine and Germantown. He served three years in Capt. H. Courtney's Company. Capt. Lt. Joseph Barker attached him to a six pound cannon in the 4th Pa. Regiment under Col. Thomas Proctor. While he was assisting in fixing the cannon, the report was so great as to cause the blood to run down his cheeks from both ears. He was also from Somerset County. He also appeared as William McMillian.

McMullin, Daniel. S.C. —. He was on the roll in 1791.

McMullin, John. Va. —. He died in the service. His father, William McMullin, was allowed his half-pay in Frederick Co., Va. in Apr. 1785.

McMullin, Michael. Pa. —. He served under Capt. Charles Morrow and Col. Miles. He was taken prisoner at Long Island. He was also under Col. Brodhead and Col. Bull. He was from Center County.

McMullin, Thomas. Pa. —. He was awarded a $40 gratuity and a $40 annuity in Northampton Co. on 14 Mar. 1818.

McMullin, Thomas. Pa. —. He was awarded $80 in Allegheny County 14 Mar. 1818.

McMullin, William. Pa. —. He was from Allegheny County.

McMurdy, John. Pa. —. He was awarded a $40 gratuity and a $40 annuity in Washington County on 26 Mar. 1813.

McMurphy, Daniel. N.H. Lt. He was from Alexandria. He was in Capt. Elliot's Company in Col. David Hobart's Regiment in Gen. Stark's Regiment. He was shot through his body at Bennington on 16 Aug. 1777. He was aged 54 in 1787.

McMurray, William. Pa. —. He served under Capt. Docherties from 1775 to 1778. He was from Allegheny County.

McMurray, William. Pa. —. He was granted relied 16 Dec. 1829.

McMurray, William. S.C. —. He lost his health and was discharged from the Continental Line due to disability. He sought assistance 30 July 1784.

McMurry, John. —. Pvt. He left the army in 1780. He married 29 Jan. 1781 and died 16 Mar. 1811. Congress granted his widow, Margaret McMurry, a pension 8 Mar. 1842.

McMurry, William. Pa. —. He was from Dauphin County.

McMurry, William. Pa. —. He applied in Pittsburgh 20 Sep. 1819. He served in the 1st Pa. Regiment in Capt. John Docker's Company from June 1775 to June 1778. Thomas Vaughan served with him in Capt. James Chambers' Company. Charles Cochran of Crawford County was with him from July 1775 to July 1776. He was discharged at Valley Forge.

McMuth, Daniel. Pa. —. He applied 29 Apr. 1811. He served nearly three years in the 3rd Pa. Regiment under Col. Thomas Craig in Capt. Isaac Buddow's [?] Company.

McNair, Archibald. Pa. —. He was awarded donation land 2 Apr. 1811.

McNalty, Michael. Pa. Gunner. He was in Philadelphia County on 9 Jan. 1786. He was in Col. Proctor's Regiment of Artillery and lost his right eye and most of the sight in his left eye. He was also ruptured. He was 50 years old. He also appeared as Michael McNulty, Michael McOnalty, and Michael McAnalty. He was on the 1813 pension list. He was granted a $40 gratuity and a $40 annuity on 20 Mar. 1812. He died 28 Dec. 1813.

McNamara, Darby. Md. —. He was pensioned at the rate of $57 per annum in lieu of his depreciation pay of $399 in Nov. 1798. He was paid £25.6.11 with interest from 1 Aug. 1780 for a depreciation certificate in Nov. 1799. He was paid £15 per annum in Nov. 1807.

McNamara, James. Pa. —. He was pensioned in 1838 and was 93 years old in 1840 in Crawford Co.

McNamara, Timothy. Va. Pvt. He was in Augusta County on 20 May 1784. He entered the service in 1777 and served to the end of the war. He received several wounds, particularly at the Waxsaws at the defeat of Buford in 1780. He had four wounds in the face, one in the shoulder, and one in the leg. Capt. Ro. Gamble deposed that McNamara was in the Va. Line to the northward.

Gamble saw him under Gen. Green at Ashley Hill in 1782. Lt. Ro. Breckinridge of the Va. Detachment deposed that McNamara was in Capt. Stoak's Company. Lt. Charles Cameron deposed that McNamara was in Capt. Syme's Company of the 10th Va. Regiment. Maj. G. [George] Nicholas of the 10th Va. Regiment also attested to his service. He was continued on the pension list at the rate of £10 per annum on 13 Jan. 1787. He also appeared as Timothy McLamare.

McNatt, Jonathan. —. —. His application for an increase in his pension was rejected 2 Mar. 1799.

McNeal, —. Pa. —. His widow, Elizabeth McNeal, was awarded a $40 gratuity and a $40 annuity in Montgomery Co., Pa. 25 Mar. 1824.

McNeal, Daniel. Pa. —. He was granted relief 29 Mar. 1822.

McNeely, James. S.C. Capt. He was wounded in several parts of his leg at Eutaw. He had a large family of females. Capt. James Brown saw him wounded. He applied in 1809.

McNeil, James. Pa. Pvt. He was on the 1813 pension list.

McNeil, John. Pa. Pvt. He was granted relief.

McNeil, Neil. N.Y. Capt. He served as first lieutenant in the militia under Capt. Samuel Hodge and Col. Yates for five months. He built and repaired Fort Ann. In May or June 1779 he was elected captain by a commission from Gov. George Clinton. Congress credited him with five months' service at the rank of lieutenant, four months and eighteen days as a captain, and nine months and eighteen days as a private on 20 Jan. 1837 and 22 Dec. 1837 when he was pensioned. He was from Herkimer County.

McNeil, William. Mass. Cooper. He served aboard the Continental ship *Alfred* under Capt. Elisha Hinman. He was wounded in the body and other parts by the blowing up of cartridges in an engagement with two English ships on 9 Mar. 1778. He was pensioned 26 Sep. 1788 in New London, Conn. at the age of 47. He was William McNeal on the 1791 roll.

McNeill, Laughlin. Pa. Lt. His widow, Ann McNeill, was in Philadelphia County on 14 Jan. 1788. He served on the galley *Effingham* in the State Navy and died 30 Mar. 1777 leaving two children. He also appeared as Laughlan McNeal. Ann McNeal died 20 Nov. 1815.

McNeill, Robert. —. Lt. —. He served in the marines on the *Boston* under Hector McNeill for a month or two. On 7 June the ship and the *Hancock* captured the British frigate *Fox*. He was appointed to command the marines on board the said prize. On 7 July 1777 the British frigate *Flora* recaptured the *Boston*. He and other marines were taken to Halifax and held prisoners until exchanged six months later. He served from 21 May 1777 to 24 Jan. 1778. He died in Savannah, Georgia in 1792. His widow died in 1808. Her children, Catharine Hall and Caroline Guzdaur or Gyzdaur, sought what their mother might have been due. Congress denied their claim 20 June 1848 and 3 Mar. 1851. His children received the final payment due him of $4,178 on 16 Jan. 1657. He also appeared as Robert McNiel.

McNeill, Samuel. Pa. —. He volunteered in Capt. Longstreth's Company at Princeton. He suffered from a violent contusion on his leg. He was awarded a $40 gratuity and a $40 annuity in Northampton County on 29 Mar. 1809. He died 8 May 1817.

McNiel, —. Pa. —. His widow, Ann McNiel, was awarded a $40 gratuity and a $40 annuity in Chester Co., Pa. 6 Apr. 1833.

McNish, Alexander. N.Y. Pvt. He was wounded by a musket ball in the neck at Saratoga in 1777. He served under Col. John Williams. He was pensioned 14 Sep. 1786. He lived at Salem, Washington Co., N.Y. 6 July 1789. He was on the 1813 pension list. He died 23 Mar. 1827.

McPherson, Dugal. Me. —. He died 11 June 1815. His widow was Mary McPherson from Madison. She was paid $50 under the resolve of 1836.

McPherson, Duncan. Va. —. His wife, Margaret McPherson, was granted £3 support in York Co., Va. on 19 May 1777.

McPherson, John. Pa. Midshipman. He was in Northumberland County on 27 June 1786. He served on the frigate *Randolph* under the command of Nicholas Biddle. He was wounded on board in action with the British ship of war, *True Briton*, in 1777. He was wounded in his groin and in his right leg. He was on the 1813 pension list. He died 9 Aug. 1827 in Union County. His administrators were John McPherson and Alexander McPherson.

McPherson, John. Pa. —. He was granted support in Tuscarawas Co., Ohio 8 Feb. 1842.

McPherson, Mark. Md. Lt. He was pensioned at the rate of half-pay of a lieutenant 23 Jan. 1816. His arrearage of $80 was paid to the attorney of Walter McPherson, the executor of the pensioner, Christian Keener, on 10 Feb. 1848.

McPowers, —. S.C. —. Elizabeth McPowers was granted the arrearage of $317.91 on 11 Dec. 1855. She also appeared as Elizabeth Powers.

McQuarters, John. S.C. Sgt. His widow was Priscilla McQuarters from Fairfield District in 1826.

McQuigg, Daniel. Me. —. He died 5 June 1816. His widow was Phebe McQuigg from Newcastle. She was paid $50 under the resolve of 1836.

McQuillan, Alexander. Pa. —. He applied in Dauphin County on 30 Jan. 1826. He was 81 years old. He marched to Reading in the summer of 1776 with the militia and enlisted in Capt. William Scull's Company in the 11th Pa. Regiment for three years. He was transferred to Capt. Jacob Weaver's Company in the 10th Pa. Regiment. He was wounded at Monmouth in June 1778. He was in the battle of Springfield. He was discharged when the Pa. Line revolted. He came to Lancaster and enlisted in the same regiment. George Dietrich of Lebanon County was with him at Valley Forge the winter of 1777 and 1778. Dietrich belonged to Maj. Grier's Company in the 10th Regiment. He saw McQuillan at Millstone, N.J. and at West Point. Abraham Riblet of Lebanon County saw him at Millstone, N.J., and they were together one winter at Valley Forge.

McQuillen, Robert. Va. Pvt. He was aged 52 years and served in the 1st Virginia Regiment. He was disabled at Charleston, S. C. He was recommended for a pension on 15 May 1783 in Powhatan Co., Va. He lived in Powhatan County in 1787. He was sometimes listed as Robert Quillen. His widow was Elizabeth McQuillen.

McQuinny, Thomas. Md. Pvt. He was pensioned at the rate of half-pay of a private 19 Feb. 1819.

McQuown, Joseph. Va. —. He was pensioned in Rockbridge County on 8 Mar. 1819 at the rate of $50 per annum. In 1777 he served in the campaign against the Indians on the Ohio River. Afterwards he volunteered and marched to the relief of Donnally's Fort and contributed to the relief of the garrison. He engaged occasionally as a militia man. He died 25 Dec. 1825. Robert White was his administrator.

McReynolds, Joseph. Va. Pvt. He served under Capt. Samuels and Lt. Col. Stephen Moore. He was wounded at Gates' defeat by a rifle ball through his ankle. He was crippled. He was from Russell Co., Va. Congress granted him a pension 4 June 1859.

McRorey, Thomas. N.C. Capt. He died in Continental service. His heirs received his pension in 1789.

McSorley, James. Pa. —. He was awarded a $40 gratuity and a $40 annuity in Westmoreland Co., Pa. 27 Feb. 1834. He died 12 Mar.1841. His surname was also incorrectly rendered as James McLorley.

McSwain, Edward. Va. —. His application was rejected on 22 Oct. 1787.

McSwain, Hugh. Pa. Marine. He was in Philadelphia County on 12 June 1786. He was in a Floating

Battery under Capt. William Brown. He was wounded in the loins by a splinter of wood occasioned by a shot from the *Augusta* ship of war on the day she was blown up on the Delaware River in Oct. 1777. He was aged 60.

McVaugh, —. Pa. —. His widow, Mary McVaugh, received a $40 gratuity and a $40 annuity in Philadelphia County 13 Apr. 1841.

McVaugh, John. Pa. —. He was awarded a $40 gratuity and a $40 annuity in Philadelphia County 5 Feb. 1836. He was 88 years old in 1840. He died 18 Jan. 1841.

McVicar, Duncan. Pa. —. He served two months under Capt. William Wilson at Potter's Fort in Penn's Valley and several tours on the frontiers. He was awarded a $40 gratuity on 1 Mar. 1811.

McWaters, John. S.C. Sgt. He served under Col. Wade Hampton, Gen. Sumter, and Capt. John McCord. He enlisted in Apr. or May of 1781 and was discharged at Orangeburg in 1782 by Col. Middleton. He was at Hanging Rock, Rocky Mount, Fish Dam Ford, and Blackstocks. He received three wounds. Lt. John Miller and John Hollis deposed about his service. He was 75 years old in 1819. He was from Fairfield District in 1826 and was 84 years of age when he sought an increase. He died 31 Aug. 1828. There was no administration on his estate because he had nothing. His widow, Priscilla McWaters, was granted one year arrearage on 17 Nov. 1831 and an annual pension of $30. She had grown grandchildren. She was paid as late as 1834.

McWeeks, Arthur. S.C. —. His application was rejected 16 Dec. 1831.

McWilliam, John. Pa. —. He served under Capt. Robert Buyers in the Lancaster County Associators at Amboy. Afterwards he was under Capt. William Scott at Trenton. He was from Armstrong Co.

McWilliams, —. Pa. —. His widow, Elizabeth McWilliams, was awarded a $40 gratuity and a $40 annuity in Clearfield Co., Pa. 8 Apr. 1826.

McWilliams, Alexander. Pa. —. He applied in Center County on 2 Apr. 1813. He served in the Pa. Line in Capt. Joseph McClelland Company from Chester County for three years under Col. Richard Butler in the 9th Regiment. He was drafted out of his company and put in the 5th Regiment under Col. Menges, a Dutchman, in Capt. John Christie's Company. He was wounded in his left arm by a bayonet in a skirmish in New Jersey. He was in the battles of Springfield, Brandywine, Monmouth, Germantown, and Stoney Point. He served five years and six months to the end of the war. Col. Richard Humpton discharged him. He was 77 years old.

McWilliams, George. Pa. —. He was granted relief in Apr. 1827 in Clearfield County.

McWilliams, George. Pa. —. He was granted relief in Westmoreland County 8 Jan. 1838. He was 69 years old in 1840. He died 5 June 1852.

McWilliams, John. Pa. —. He was being paid in 1845.

McWilliams, Robert. Pa. Pvt. His widow, Elizabeth McWilliams, was in Northumberland County 15 May 1790. He was called out in 1777 in Capt. Robert Taggart's Company of the Northumberland County militia under Col. James Murray. He was mortally wounded 12 Dec. 1777 by a musket ball at Gulph Mills. On the evening of the same day he was cut to pieces and killed by the Light Horse. He was aged 28 years. He left three children.

Maban, Matthew. S.C. —. He served under Col. James Lyles and Capt. John Lyles from 1778 to the close of the war. He was also under Col. Wallis. George Johnston, M. Littleton, Samuel Otterson, Ephraim Liles, James Kelley, Ephraim Liles, Sr., Arramanos Liles, John Steward, Thomas Dugan, and Sims Brown served with him. He was out of South Carolina between 1783 to 1790. He applied 25 Oct. 1809. He had been unable to walk without crutches for the past four or five years. The joint of his thigh and hip was entirely dislocated.

Maben, William. S.C. —. He was taken prisoner at Sumter's defeat 20 Aug. 1780 and died in confinement. His widow, Mary Maben, was granted an annuity 20 Aug. 1785. There was one child in 1791, and they was from Newberry. She also appeared as Mary Mabon.

Mace, Andrew. Mass. —. He was pensioned 15 Feb. 1806 for life from 1 May 1804 at the rate of $144 per annum.

Machemer, William. Pa. —. He served in 1779 under Capt. Joseph Hiester in the Flying Camp. He was awarded a $40 gratuity and a $40 annuity in Berks Co., Pa. 1 Apr. 1823.

Machin, Thomas. N.Y. Capt. He was pensioned 19 Mar. 1808 at the rate of $10 per month. He was on the 1813 pension list and died 3 Apr. 1816. The physician through an unintentional mistake caused him to be pensioned at the rate of $10 per month rather than the $20 to which he was entitled. His widow, Susannah Machin, sought to collect his underpaid back pension; her claim was rejected 31 Dec. 1816.

Mack, Joseph. N.H. Pvt. He served a three year enlistment in the 1st N.H. Regiment and was discharged in 1780. He was wounded in his side on 7 Oct. 1777 at Bemis Heights. He was aged 38 in 1787 and lived in Londonderry. He was on the 1813 pension list in New York.

Mack, Nehemiah. —. —. His son, John Mack, who had never been in the service, sought to receive the pension his mother would have been granted as the widow of a Revolutionary War veterans. Congress rejected his petition 3 Mar. 1882.

Mack, Nicholas. Pa. —. He was granted a $40 gratuity in Philadelphia County 14 Apr. 1838 but his military service was not specified. He was 93 years old in 1840.

Mackey, Eneas. Pa. Col. His widow, Mary Mackey, was from Westmoreland County.

Mackcy, William. Pa. Capt. He was in Lancaster County on 12 May 1788. He was dangerously wounded at Brandywine by a musket ball which passed through his lungs. He was in the 9th Pa. Regiment. There was man of his name and rank on the 1813 pension list, but he had died 4 Nov. 1812.

Mackins, Samuel. —. —. His application was referred to the Secretary of War 26 May 1794.

Macklin, John. Pa. Sgt. He applied 4 May 1787.

Mackrell, James. Va. Pvt. He was on the 1785 pension roll. He was in Orange County on 1 Jan. 1786. He served in the 1st Va. Regiment and lost his right arm in action in Georgia. He was 27 years old. His pension was continued at the rate of £18 per annum on 6 Feb. 1786. He was in Culpeper County in 1787. He died 16 Aug. 1804. He also appeared as James Mackerell.

Madden, John. Mass. —. He served in the 7th Regiment and was paid $20.

Madden, John. Mass. —. He served in the 8th Regiment and was from St. Georges. He was paid $20.

Maddox, —. Va. —. His widow, Elizabeth Maddox, was paid £44 on 1 Dec. 1779 in Culpeper Co., Va.

Maddox, Matthew. Va. Pvt. He was wounded at Camden. He was in Shenandoah County on 4 Feb. 1787.

Maddox, Wilson. Va. —. His wife, Jeanne Maddox, was awarded assistance in Goochland Co., Va. in 1777.

Madeira, —. Pa. —. His widow, Anna Madeira, received a $40 gratuity and a $40 annuity 4 Apr. 1837. She resided in Monongalia Co., Va.

Madeira, —. Pa. —. His widow, Margaretta Madeira, was pensioned in Berks County 8 Apr. 1833. She was dead by Aug. 1838.

Maden, Joseph. Pa. —. He applied 14 May 1813. He was discharged at Trenton. He also appeared as Joseph Madden.

Madera, —. Pa. —. His widow, Elizabeth Madera, was awarded a $40 gratuity and a $40 annuity in Berks Co., Pa. 14 Apr. 1834. She was dead by Jan. 1837.

Maderwell, John. Pa. Pvt. He enlisted in 1780 and served under Capt. John Alexander in the 7th Regiment under Col. Harmer[?]. He was wounded in the latter part of 1780 by a musket ball in his right arm. He was from Lancaster County.

Madison, —. Va. —. His wife, Ann Madison, was granted £80 support in Fauquier Co., Va. in Oct. 1779.

Madison, George. —. —. He was wounded by the enemy. His daughter, Mira M. Alexander, had her claim rejected by Congress 6 July 1852.

Madison, William. —. Lt. Congress awarded his widow, Nancy Madison, the arrearage of her pension from 4 Mar. 1848 to 3 Feb. 1853 on 21 Feb. 1857. She resided in Fairfield Co., Ohio.

Madison, William. Va. Gen. While a student at Hampden Sidney College, he served in the militia in 1778. He then became a lieutenant in the State Legion of Virginia. He was on recruiting service but had little success. In 1781 he volunteered in the militia cavalry. He was appointed lieutenant in the regiment of artillery under Col. Harrison. After the surrender of Cornwallis at Yorktown, he was sent home on furlough ill. He never resigned. His commutation was approved 26 Mar. 1838.

Magby, Samuel. S.C. —. He served under Col. McDonald and was deprived of the use of his limbs. James McCracken was acquainted with him in camp. He was pensioned from Horry District 23 Nov. 1830. He was stricken from the roll as a Tory on 17 Nov. 1831 in response from a petition from sundry citizens from Horry District. He also appeared as Samuel Magbee.

Magee, —. Pa. —. His widow was Margaret Magee. She was from Venango County 11 Apr. 1825.

Magoon, John. Mass. Pvt. He served for three months and ten days on his first tour. He next served eleven months under Capt. William Carpenter. No record could be found for the latter service. He served under Capt. Oliver Coney and Col. Sears from 15 Aug. to 15 Nov. 1781. Congress granted him a pension for eleven months of service 10 July 1840.

Magoon, Josiah. N.H. —. He was a resident of Nottingham in 1784. He was in Continental service in the 1st N.H. Regiment. He came down with epileptic fits and was discharged 10 Apr. 1783. He was aged 22 in 1787. He was on the 1813 pension list in Pennsylvania.

Magruder, Nathaniel B. Md. Lt. He was pensioned at the rate of half-pay of a lieutenant 23 Jan. 1816.

Magruder, Owen. S.C. —. He was granted 3,000 acres in Cheraws District in 1793. His widow might have been entitled to a pension.

Maguire, Barney. Pa. Corp. He was on the 1791 pension roll.

Maguire, John. Pa. —. He was pensioned by the act of 5 Feb. 1812.

Mahl, Frederick. —. —. His widow, Polly Mahl, had her petition for a pension rejected by Congress on 27 Mar. 1846 because they were married subsequent to 1 Jan. 1794.

Mahon, John. Va. —. He served in Col. Grayson's Regiment. He was disabled by rheumatism in the service. He applied 10 Nov. 1779. He had a wife and child. His claim was rejected.

Mahoney, Clement. Md. Pvt. He was pensioned at the rate of half-pay of a private 23 Jan. 1816.

Mahoney, Florence. Va. Pvt. He was in Buckingham County on 30 Aug. 1786 and was aged 32. He served from 15 Aug. 1779 to 1 Jan. 1782 in Capt. John Rogers's Company of State Cavalry in Col. Charles Dabney's Legion. Capt. Christopher Roane attested to his service. He was a fifer and lost his left leg. He was granted half-pay for his disability, £6 relief, and a suit of clothes on 26 Sep. 1785.

Mahoney, James. Pa. —. He applied in Montgomery County on 4 Mar. 1815. He served in the 9th Pa. Regiment from 1777 to 1783. He was discharged by Col. Josiah Harmer. Andrew Nelson was

Quarter Master Sergeant. He died 14 Aug. 1823.

Mahooney, Edward. Md. Pvt. He was pensioned at the rate of half-pay of a private 4 Jan. 1812.

Mahue, William. N.C. —. He was in Rutherford Co., N.C. in Oct. 1832. He was 72 or 73 years old.

Maiden, James. Va. —. His wife, Theodosia Maiden, was granted £30 support in Rockingham Co., Va. 23 Nov. 1779 while he was away in the service.

Maiden, Robert. Va. —. His wife, Margaret Maiden, was granted £15 on 11 Dec. 1777 and £50 on 8 Oct. 1778 in Lunenburg Co., Va.

Maidera, —. Pa. —. His widow, Margaretta Maidera, was awarded a $40 gratuity and a $40 annuity in Berks Co., Pa. 8 Apr. 1833.

Major, —. Va. Pvt. He died in Continental service 23 June 1778. His widow, Nancy Major, was awarded a £12 gratuity in King William Co., Va. 6 Nov. 1779.

Major, —. Va. Pvt. He died in Continental service 23 June 1778. His widow, Sarah Major, was awarded a £12 gratuity in King William Co., Va. 6 Nov. 1779.

Makins, Samuel. —. Matross/Mate. He served on the ship *Queen of France*. He was wounded when taking an anchor from the wharf to carry on board when one of his legs was caught between the wharf and the anchor which ruptured the bone. The accident happened on 9 Oct. 1779 in Boston. He lived in Philadelphia, Pa. in 1794.

Malbuef, Baptiste. N.Y. —. He served under Capt. Jean Baptiste la Port de la Bonte in Col. James Livingston's Regiment of Refugees from Canada to the close of the war. He was due bounty land 2 Apr. 1806.

Mallard, —. —. —. He married 6 Sep. 1792. His widow, Polly Mallard, sought private relief from Congress. Congress denied her petition on because she was covered under the act of 1848 and should apply in the regular fashion.

Malleby, Cornelius. N.J. Pvt. He served under Col. Philip Johnson, Capt. John Anderson, and Lt. George Holcomb in the New Jersey Levies. He was taken prisoner at Long Island and died in captivity 26 Dec. 1776. Grace Malleby was his widow. She was awarded his half-pay for her widowhood in Hunterdon Co., N.J. in 1780. He also appeared as Cornelius Malteby.

Malone, —. Va. —. His wife, Mary Malone, was awarded £20 support while he was away in the service in Caroline Co., Va. 12 July 1779.

Malone, John. N.Y. Pvt. He served under Col. Willett. He had his feet frozen and lost some of his toes in Feb. 1783. He lived at Connajorharrie, N.Y. in 1794.

Malone, John. Va. —. His pension application was rejected 3 Apr. 1787.

Malone, Leslie. N.Y. —. He was engaged in herding cattle for the army in Dec. 1779. He was fourteen or fifteen years of age. He was taken prisoner by the Senecca and carried to Genesse Country where he was held four years. He was carried to Cattaraugus Creek for two more years. He was ransomed by his father. He was 72 years old. Congress rejected him for a pension 14 Jan. 1837 because he was not employed in military service.

Malone, Philip. Va. —. His wife was furnished 5 bushels of corn and 100 pounds of pork in Charlotte Co., Va. on 3 Mar. 1777. Mary Malone received £217.10 provisions on 6 Mar. 1780.

Malone, Philip. Va. —. His wife, Mary Malone, was awarded assistance in Goochland Co., Va. in 1780.

Maloney, John. Pa. Sgt. He was in Lancaster County on 9 May 1787. He served in the 1st Pa. Regiment under Col. James Chambers and Capt. James Parr and was wounded in the thigh by a musket ball at Long Island in Aug. 1776. At Brandywine he was wounded by a fence rail by force from a cannon ball. He was 40 years old. He was granted a $40 gratuity and a $40 annuity on 28 Mar. 1808. He was on the 1813 pension list. He also appeared as John Malony and John Malone. He died 21 Nov. 1817.

Maloney, Michael. Pa. Pvt. He was transferred to New York 4 Mar. 1789. He was on the 1813 pension list.

Malphurs, John. S.C. —. He served in the light infantry under Col. John Baker. He was on the Florida Expedition. He served as a scout. He was in his 80th year and lived in Prince William Parish, Beaufort District. He made a claim for compensation 15 Nov. 1827. It was rejected.

Malphus, Edward. S.C. —. He enlisted in March 1779 and served under Col. Daniel Horry and John Hampton. He marched to Charleston and was taken prisoner and died of smallpox. He left a widow and four children. Three were under the age of 9. One was nine the last of May after the siege of Charleston, the next was 6, and the youngest was 3. His widow, Sarah Malpus, married (2) Adam Smith. She was Sarah Smith from Beaufort District in 1793.

Manary, Gilbert. S.C. Pvt. He served in the Little River Regiment and was taken prisoner four days after the battle of Black Stocks. He was put in Camden jail where he died. He left a widow and two children, both of whom were over 12 years of age. His widow was Jane Manary from Laurens District who was pensioned 5 Nov. 1795 from 1 Jan. 1792.

Manchester, Edward. Mass. —. He was awarded £90 which with his former grant of £5 per annum was in full for his last two years of his pension on 13 Jan. 1780. He was paid £13.10 on 20 Feb. 1781. It had been 18 months since he had last been paid.

Mandingo, Judah. —. Pvt. He was 15 years old when he entered the service as a private and as a waiter in Apr. 1782 under Capt. Dana and Lt. Thomas Pearce at Fishkill in Dutchess Co., N.Y. He was employed at the baking house. He drove cattle and drew wood. He had been rejected because he was under age and his service was that of a waiter. He died 28 Apr. 1847. His widow, Sarah Mandingo, applied for a pension but died before her claim was acted upon. They married at Watertown, Conn. 14 Jan. 1797. She died 22 Jan. 1854. His brother was Jonathan Mandingo. Congress did not allow relief to their son, Daniel Mandingo, 21 Jan. 1858.

Manerson, John. Pa. Pvt. He was in Lancaster County 25 Mar. 1786. He received sundry wounds by sword at the battle of Short Hills in 1777. He served under Col. C. Armand. He acted as sergeant. He was 57 years old. He was on the 1813 pension list. He also appeared as John Munnerson and John Mannerson.

Manley, John. —. Midshipman. He was probably the last survivor of the *Jersey* prison ship. He had no living comrades or officers to confirm his service. His sister was Ann Manley, and his brother was Dr. James R. Manley. He entered the service as a midshipman on the *Trumbull* under Capt. James Nicholson in the spring of 1781. In early July he sailed from Philadelphia but was blocked in the Delaware until 8 Aug. 1781. After putting to sea, two British cruisers, the *Iris* of 32 guns and the *General Monk* of 18 guns captured his vessel. Fifteen were killed and eleven were wounded of whom he was one. His officers were Commander James Nicholson, 1st Lt. Maltby, 2nd Lt. Richard Dal, Surgeon John Morrow, Assistant Surgeon Samuel Morrow, Midshipman David Haight of N.J., and Alexander Morrow a volunteer. They were taken to New York and confined to 30 Nov. 1781 when they were exchanged. In Oct. 1782 he entered again on the *General Washington* under Commodore Barney. They sailed for France with dispatches for Dr. Franklin. He was discharged 4 Mar. 1784. His service was two years and three months on the *Trumbull,* one year and five months on the *General Washington* of which seven months were after the war. Congress granted him a pension 19 Jan. 1848.

Manley, John. Md. Corp. His daughter. Elizabeth M. Dittoe, a widow over 80 years of age, sought 100 acres of bounty land. Congress rejected her claim 4 Apr. 1876 on the presumption that such an award would have been made sometime before a hundred years had lapsed.

Manly, John. Mass. Capt. He received several wounds and blows on his left shoulder and leg so that he lost the use of his arm and was rendered lame. His toes were contracted. He was a marine on the frigate *Hancock* in 1777.

Mann, Benjamin. Va. —. His wife, Milly Mann, and two children were furnished 3 barrels of corn and 75 pounds of bacon in Louisa Co., Va. on 8 July 1782.

Mann, David. Va. Lt. His commutation was made 13 Apr. 1792.

Mann, Elijah. Mass. —. He was pensioned.

Mann, John. Pa.—. He was 83 years old in 1840 and died 25 Aug. 1849. His widow, Mary Mann, received a $40 gratuity and a $40 annuity in Northampton County 11 Apr. 1856.

Mann, Josiah. Pa. —. He was awarded a $40 gratuity and a $40 annuity in Fayette County 28 Mar. 1836.

Mann, Justice. —. —. He was pensioned 20 Apr. 1796.

Mann, Thomas. S.C. Pvt. He was from Pickens District and was pensioned 6 Dec. 1828. He died 31 May 1834. His widow was Sarah Mann who was about 80 years of age. She was paid his arrears and pensioned. She was paid as late as 1859.

Manning, Isaac. N.J. —. He was a pensioner and died 31 Mar. 1843. He married Rosanna ----- 31 Oct. 1785. He had claimed he served three months and seven days in Somerset County at a time when tours were limited to one month in rotation of eight classes. His alleged service under Capt. Sebring and Capt. Ten Eyck was not confirmed by the rolls. His widow was from Plainfield, N.J. Congress granted her a pension from 31 Mar. 1843 at the rate of $36.66 per annum.

Manning, Phineas. Mass. —. He served in the 2nd Regiment and was from Gorham. He was paid $20.

Manning, William. S.C. —. There was a child in 1793.

Manning, William T. Mass. —. He was in the 5th Regiment and was from Beverly. He was paid $20.

Mansfield, Amos. Mass. Pvt. He served in the artillery under Col. Benjamin Simond in Capt. George King's Company and lost his right leg at White Plains. He had fallen from a wagon and broken his right leg "by reason of which the same was dessected." He was pensioned at the rate of half-pay from 7 Mar. 1777 on 11 Feb. 1779. He was from Tyringham, Mass. He was 45 years old in 1788.

Mansfield, Daniel. Conn. Pvt. He was disabled by rheumatism. He was pensioned 10 Apr. 1783. He died in 1811. He was listed as dead on the 1813 pension list.

Mansfield, John. Mass. —. He served in the 8th Regiment and was from Salisbury. He was paid $50.

Manson, John. Pa. —. He applied in Washington County on 18 Oct. 1814. He enlisted in Col. Hartley's Regiment for five years. He was discharged by Capt. Bush. He died 20 Sep. 1823. His daughter, Jennet Manson, testified that she was living at home when her father came home at different times on furlough. His widow, Elizabeth Manson, was awarded a $40 gratuity and a $40 annuity in Washington Co., Pa. 26 Dec. 1824.

Mantz, Nicholas. Pa. —. His widow, Mary Mantz, was awarded a $40 gratuity and a $40 annuity in Northumberland Co., Pa. 12 Feb. 1820..

Mantz, Peter. Md. Maj. His widow, Catharine Mantz, was pensioned at the rate of half-pay of a major 20 Feb. 1846.

Mapes, John. N.J. —. He was in Gloucester County on 14 Mar. 1837 when he was paid $100 for the six months he served under Capt. Vincent before he entered Lee's Legion of Cavalry.

Maple, William. Pa. —. He was granted relief in Greene County 21 June 1839.

Revolutionary War Pensions

Maples, Marmaduke. —. —. His application was rejected 11 Apr. 1800.

Marble, —. —. —. Congress denied his widow, Mehitable Marble, a pension 9 Feb. 1848.

Marble, —. Pa. —. His widow, Christiana Marble, was awarded a $40 gratuity and a $40 annuity in Northumberland Co., Pa. 17 Mar. 1835.

Marble, Joseph. Mass. Pvt. He served in the 15th Regiment and was from Worthington. His widow, Lydia Marble, was paid $50.

Mardick, Elisha. Va. —. His wife, Elizabeth Mardick, was awarded 6 bushels of corn in Accomack Co., Va. 28 May 1782. His widow and three children were furnished 3 barrels of corn and 150 weight of pork on 31 Jan. 1783.

Maree, —. S.C. —. His widow, Ann Maree, from Chesterfield was on the roll in 1791.

Margery, Jonathan. N.H. Pvt. He served in the 2nd Regiment in Capt. Clough's Company. He was wounded in his thigh while on a scouting party on 29 July 1777 near Fort Edward. The ball had not been removed. He lived at Hancock, N.H. in 1794. He enlisted 10 Jan. 1777 and was invalided Nov. 1779. He was granted two-thirds of a pension 20 Apr. 1796. He was on the 1813 pension list.

Marinus, William. N.Y. Corp. He served under Col. Samuel Clyde in the Montgomery County militia and was slain 6 Aug. 1777. His widow, Mary Marinus, received a half-pay pension.

Mark, John. Pa. —. He applied in Mifflin County on 25 Aug. 1813. He enlisted in the Pa. Regiment of Artillery for three years. He was in Capt. Andrew Porter's Company. He was next enlisted by Lt. Zechael Howel in Charleston in the summer of 1777 and was under Col. Lamb and Col. Proctor. He was in the battles of Brandywine, Germantown, and Monmouth and was with Gen. Sullivan against the Indians. He was discharged at Morristown, N.J. He left his discharge with his master, George McElheney, at Charleston. He signed in German. He also appeared as John Marck and John Marks.

Mark, Joseph. N.H. Pvt. He was disabled.

Marker, Frederick. Pa. —. He was awarded a $40 gratuity and a $40 annuity in Delaware Co., Pa. 27 Jan. 1835. He was dead by Dec. 1838.

Markham, Ambrose. Mass. —. He served in the 6th Regiment and was paid $20.

Markham, Anthony. N.C. —. He was born in Pasquotank Co., N.C. and died in 1819. He married Elizabeth Srall (?Hall). His daughter, Elizabeth Markham, married Exum Trueblood. She was in Pasquotank in 1833.

Markham, Ebenezer. —. —. He was a merchant in Montreal and espoused the rebel cause. He moved to New York and received 300 acres. He was sued for debt contracted back in Canada and died in 1818. His child was Catharine Lydia McLeod. Congress rejected her claim for relief 6 Mar. 1850.

Markham, Jeremiah. Conn. Sgt. He served in Col. Cook's Regiment in Capt. Joseph Blague's Company. He was wounded 19 Sep. 1777 by a musket ball which passed through his eye to the ear on the opposite side on 19 Sep. 1777 near Stillwater. He was discharged 1 Oct. 1777. He resided in Middleton, Conn. in 1796. He was granted half a pension 20 Apr. 1796. He was on the 1813 pension list. He died 27 Nov. 1827.

Markham, Stephen. N.Y. —. His wife and two children were granted support 3 Nov. 1781 in Dutchess County.

Markill, William. N.Y. Pvt. He served under Col. Samuel Clyde and was slain 6 Aug. 1777. His children, Margaret Markill, Catherine Markill, Delia Markill, Jacob Markill, Henry Markill, and John Markill, received a half-pay pension.

Markland, Edward. Md. Lt. He served as 1ˢᵗ Lt. under Capt. William Patterson on the schooner *Dolphin*. He sailed from Annapolis to Martinque where they captured a British schooner. He was put in charge of the prize. The British recaptured the vessel and sent him to New York as a prisoner. He was held for six months. He was released destitute. He was pensioned at the rate of half-pay of a lieutenant in the naval service in Baltimore 25 Feb. 1824. He died 7 Oct. 1827. He married 29 May 1790. His widow, Alice Markland, was pensioned at the same rate 30 Jan. 1839. Congress granted her a pension from 4 Sep. 2844 on 11 Apr. 1850.

Markle, Bernard. Pa. Seaman. He served aboard the *Hyder Alley* under Capt. Barney. He was wounded in the engagement with the *General Monck* 8 Apr. 1782. He was from Dauphin County. He was in Berks County on 20 Apr. 1786.

Markle, Charles. —. —. He served under Capt. Armand's Legion and was commissioned 6 Jan 1779 in the Light Dragoons. He died in Missouri in 1828. His grandson, R. B. Markle of Oregon, had his claim rejected by Congress 1 May 1876.

Markle, Charles. Va. —. Capt. His son, John Markle, had a 2,000 acre warrant which he sought to be able to locate on any U.S. lands. Congress rejected the request without satisfactory evidence of the grounds upon which the warrant was issued on 30 July 1842. He was awarded a $40 gratuity and a $40 annuity 27 Jan. 1835.

Markle, Christian. Pa. —. He served in the Flying Camp in 1776 and was a teamster under Gen. Wayne at Valley Forge. He subsequently served in the Berks County militia under Capt. Landig. He was from Northumberland County.

Markley, —. Pa. —. His widow, Catherine Markley, was awarded a $40 gratuity and a $40 annuity in Adams Co., Pa. 25 Mar. 1824.

Markley, Charles. —. Capt. He served in Armand's Corps. He was pensioned 11 Aug. 1790.

Marklin, John. Pa. Sgt. He was in Philadelphia County on 11 Sep. 1786. He served in the 6ᵗʰ Pa. Regiment under Col. William Irvine in Capt. Adams' Company and was wounded in his right heel on the St. Lawrence River on 6 June 1776. He was 38 years old.

Marks, John. Va. Capt. He served in the 14ᵗʰ and 10ᵗʰ Virginia Regiments. He married the widow of William Lewis after the war and moved to Georgia where he died. His widow, Lucy Marks, returned to Albemarle County and received his commutation of five years' full pay 22 Dec. 1837.

Marks, William. Pa. —. He was awarded a $40 gratuity and a $40 annuity in Berks County on 14 Mar. 1818.

Marnay, Louis. —. Capt. He served under Col. Moses Hazen. He died 2 Jan. 1829. He was entitled to his $80 reward. His administrator, Ezra T. Marnay, of Rouse's Point, Clinton Co., N.Y. sought the reward and bounty land for all the grandchildren. Congress rejected his claim for the latter and indicated that the bounty land should be sought in the regular manner on 10 Dec. 1857.

Marnay, Patrick. —. Pa. —. The right to his donation land became vested in John McDaniel. The land fell into New York. The heirs of McDaniel in Warren Co., Ohio were paid $200 for the 200 acres 3 Mar. 1837.

Marner, Archibald. Pa. —. He was pensioned.

Marr, John. Pa. —. He enlisted in the 3ʳᵈ Regiment in 1776. In Dec. 1780 he was absent on furlough to visit his brother in the Sussex jail in New Jersey for some misconduct when his company was discharged. He was from Columbia County. He was from Northumberland County. He also appeared as John Mars.

Marr, William. Md. Pvt. His widow, Arra Marr, was pensioned at the rate of half-pay of a private 10

Feb. 1836.

Marriner, Jeffrey. Va. Pvt. His widow, Susanna Marriner, was in Essex County in Nov. 1787. He enlisted in Nov. 1776 for three years and died in May 1777. He served in the 2nd State Regiment under Capt. Henry Garnett. His widow aged 56 had nine children, the youngest being three years, in 1787. She was put on the pension list at the rate of £8 per annum on 1 Dec. 1787. She died 1 July 1797 in Essex County.

Marrs, John. Pa. —. He was from Columbia County. He was pensioned 3 Feb. 1815.

Marsden, George. Mass. Lt. He appointed adjutant of foot under Col. James Scamman on 19 May 1775. He was commissioned 2nd Lieutenant under Capt. Darby in the 7th Regiment of Foot under Col. William Prescott. He also served as adjutant. He, therefore, served 20 months in 1775 and 1776, but 24 months were required. He married in Nov. 1775 at Mystic, Mass. He and his wife left Mystic in 1798. His widow was Wilmot Marsden. Their family register showed that their son William Marsden was born 14 June 1778 nine months before George Marsden was in service in Saratoga. Congress granted Wilmot Marsden of Oneida Co., N.Y. a pension for two years for his service as adjutant 18 Mar. 1844.

Marseilles, Garrett. N.Y. —. He served under Col. Van Schaick. His family was granted support 26 Mar. 1779.

Marsh, Allyn. Conn. Corp. He served in Col. Levi Wells' Regiment. He was wounded in the small of his back from two bullets while on duty in Dec. 1780 at Greenwich. He resided in East Hartford, Conn. in 1796. He was granted half a pension 20 Apr. 1796. He was on the 1813 pension list.

Marsh, Casper. Pa. —. He was awarded relief in Northampton County 9 Apr. 1833. He was paid to 20 Dec.

Marsh, Christopher. Pa. —. He applied 24 May 1802. He enlisted in Capt. Philip Schroeder's Company in the Pa. Line in 1781 to serve for the war. He served 22 months and was discharged at Wyoming. His petition to the U.S. in 1818 was rejected because he served in the rangers.

Marsh, Daniel. Mass. —. He served in the 1st Regiment and was paid $20.

Marsh, David. Pa. —. He was awarded a $40 gratuity and a $40 annuity in Northampton County on 28 Mar. 1820.

Marsh, Elisha. Mass. Corp. He served in Capt. John Leland's Company under Col. Ephraim Doolittle and was wounded on the heights at Charlestown on 17 June 1775. He lost the use of the joint of his left knee due to a musket ball. He was pensioned at the rate of a quarter of his pay from 31 Dec. 1775 on 26 Jan. 1778. He was 36 years old in 1787.

Marsh, Joshua. N.J. Sgt. He served in the militia in Middlesex County. He was killed 25 Sep. 1781 at Spanktown. He married Phebe Cosart. His widow was granted a pension 10 Oct. 1782 in Middlesex County.

Marsh, Lewis. Mass. —. He served in the 2nd Regiment and was paid $20.

Marsh, Noah. N.H. Pvt. He was a resident of Gilmantown when he was pensioned in 1786. He was a Continental soldier under Capt. Caleb Robinson. On 7 Oct. 1777 at Stillwater he was wounded by a ball through his hand and lost the forefinger on his right hand. All of the other fingers on that hand were rendered useless. He was aged 30 in 1787. He was on the 1813 pension list.

Marsh, Richard. N.J. —. He was a teamster attached to a foraging party under Capt. Thomas Bloomfield. Congress granted him a pension for six months of service 12 Apr. 1842. Congress rejected his petition because he was not a soldier on 13 Jan. 1843. His was civil service.

Marsh, Samuel. N.J. —. He served in the Middlesex County militia and was wounded 17 Oct. 1777. He applied 8 Dec. 1784.

Marsh, Seymour. N.Y. Pvt. He was on the 1813 pension list. He later moved to Montgomery Co., N.H. 4 Sep. 1822.

Marsh, William. N.J. —. He served under Capt. Jacob Crane and died 26 Feb. 1777. His widow, Sarah Marsh, was allowed his half-pay in Essex County 11 Apr. 1783.

Marsh, William. Mass. —. He served in the 5th Regiment. He was paid $20.

Marshalk, Cornelius. N.Y. Post Rider. He served in the Quarter Master General's Regiment of the Continental Army and died in the service. His widow, Eleanor Marshalk, had her application rejected because the law did not cover his type of service.

Marshall, —. Va. —. His wife, Ann Marshall, was granted £10 support in Caroline Co., Va. 14 May 1778.

Marshall, —. Va. —. His mother, Isabella Marshall, was granted £20 support in Caroline Co., Va. 13 May 1779 while he was away in the service.

Marshall, Benjamin. Md. —. He received a warrant for 50 acres of bounty land as a donation 9 Mar. 1826.

Marshall, Humphrey. Va. Capt. He received his full pay for five years in lieu of half-pay for life as a captain of artillery in the Virginia line on 16 Jan. 1829. In 1836 he resided in Kentucky when Congress rejected his petition for relief.

Marshall, James M. Va. Lt. He was entitled to half-pay. He served in the artillery.

Marshall, John. Md. Pvt. He was pensioned in Cecil County at the rate of half-pay of a private on 22 Mar. 1833.

Marshall, John. Pa. Capt. He was awarded a $120 gratuity and a $120 annuity in Washington Co. on 16 Mar. 1819.

Marshall, John. Va. Boatswain's Mate. He was in King and Queen County on 29 June 1786. He served on the ship *Tartar* as a midshipman and boatswain's mate. Thomas Grant, also a midshipman on board, deposed that he saw him injured by a capson bar in his breast and side and that he was incapable for duty for a considerable time. He had a wife and five children. He was put on the pension list at the rate of £6 per annum on 19 Dec. 1786. His pension was augmented to £12 on 13 July 1790. He died 17 Nov. 1814. John L. Marshall was administrator of his estate.

Marshall, John M. Va. Lt. He served in the state artillery and became supernumerary. He was entitled to half-pay for life from 6 Feb. 1784 and was paid $2,200.

Marshall, Meade. N.Y. Gunner. He enlisted 1 April 1777 and served in Capt. Samuel Lockwood's Company in the 2nd Regiment under Col. John Lamb. His feet were frozen while he was out on a detachment under Col. Samuel B. Webb on Long Island in Dec. 1777. He was discharged 12 Sep. 1779. He was aged 49 on 15 Apr. 1788. He lived in New York City, N.Y. 19 Nov. 1788. He was on the 1813 pension list.

Marshall, Richard. Va. Pvt. He was pensioned 29 Nov. 1791 at the rate of £12 per year. He was given the same amount for his relief at that time. He was in Albemarle County on 9 Jan. 1791. He served in the 6th Va. Regiment and was wounded at Camden, S.C. 25 Apr. 1781. He served under Capt. Thomas Barbee. Mary Marshall was a widow by 4 Mar. 1799.

Marshall, Robert. —. Pvt. He served in Col. Little's Regiment. He was wounded in the right thigh, the fingers of his left hand, and in the belly by a bayonet at Bunker Hill on 17 June 1775. He had a scar on his right hand. He resided in Mass. in 1796.

Marshall, Thomas. —. —. His application was rejected 16 Feb. 1798.

Marshall, William. Pa. —. He was awarded a $40 gratuity and a $40 annuity in Westmoreland Co., Pa.

7 Mar. 1827. He died 17 Nov. 1828.

Marshall, William. Pa. —. He was granted relief in Washington County 21 Feb. 1838.

Marshall, William. Va. —. He was discharged at Yorktown 15 Nov. 1783. He married Mrs. Newingham. He was very poor and in 1805 or 1806 came to live with his stepson, Henry Newingham, who supported both his stepfather and his mother until they died. Marshall left no lineal heirs. His widow was dead. Congress awarded the stepson bounty land 19 June 1840.

Marsters, Edward. Mass. —. He served in the 1ˢᵗ Regiment and was paid $20. He also appeared as Edward Masters.

Marten, Francis. —. —. He was allowed half-pay for life.

Martick, Benjamin. Mass. Pvt. He was on the 1791 pension roll.

Martin, —. —. —. Congress denied Elizabeth Martin relief 10 June 1854.

Martin, —. S.C. —. His widow, Margaret Martin, was pensioned at the rate of $22 per annum on 19 Dec. 1805.

Martin, —. S.C. —. His widow was Rachel Martin from Darlington. There were children in 1791. She died at the house of Moses Bradford who sought her arrears for his expenses in Dec. 1817.

Martin, Aaron. Mass. —. He served in the 6ᵗʰ Regiment and was from Dighton. He was paid $20.

Martin, Alexander. Va. Pvt. He was awarded a gratuity of two years' pay and an annuity of two years' pay on 22 Nov. 1781. He was in Augusta County 18 Oct. 1785 and was aged 27. He served in the militia from Rockbridge County and was wounded at Guilford, N.C. on 15 Mar. 1781. He was in Capt. Joseph Alexander's Company under Col. Samuel McDowell. A ball passed through his abdomen. He was continued at the rate of £15 per annum on 13 Nov. 1786. He moved to Pennsylvania in 1795. He was on the 1813 pension list.

Martin, Arthur. Pa. —. His heirs were paid $300 for his donation land on 11 Apr. 1825.

Martin, Balzer. Pa. —. He was awarded a $40 gratuity and a $40 annuity in Lancaster Co., Pa. 23 Jan. 1833.

Martin, Benjamin. Pa. —. He was pensioned.

Martin, Charles. Pa. Sgt. Maj. He enlisted in 1777 in the Pa. Line and in 1781 was drafted into Gen. Armstrong's Legionary Corps. He was discharged in 1783. He was awarded his bounty land 27 Mar. 1812.

Martin, Eleazer. N.H. Pvt. He was a resident of Richmond when he was pensioned in 1783. He was an enlisted soldier in Capt. Ellis's Company in the 3ʳᵈ N.H. Battalion under Col. Alexander Scammell. He was wounded on 19 Sept. 1777 near Saratoga at Bemis Heights. A ball passed through his right wrist. He had a wife and three children. He transferred to Grand Isle Co., Vt. He was on the 1813 pension list.

Martin, Eleazer. Pa. Pvt. He had been transferred to Massachusetts by 1794.

Martin, Ennals. Md. Surgeon's Mate. He was pensioned at the rate of half-pay of a surgeon's mate in Talbot County on 17 Jan. 1833. His widow, Sarah Martin, was pensioned at the same rate 11 Feb. 1835.

Martin, Ephraim. N.Y. Pvt. He served under Capt. John Wood in the Orange County militia and was slain 22 July 1779. His widow received a half-pay pension.

Martin, Francis. —. Lt. He died in 1780 in Continental service. Ellen Martin, wife of John Levake of La Cole, Huntingdon, Canada sought payment plus interest on his commutation pay 10 Dec. 1857. Congress ruled that the claim was barred, and there was no cause for action. Francis Martin had ten children: (1) Francis Martin who left no issue; (2) Joseph Martin who left four children: (a) Joseph Martin who left a daughter Josette Martin, (b) Baird Martin, (c) Alexy

Martin whose issue were James Martin, Alexander Martin, Fulgence Martin, Virginie Martin, Jane Martin, and Adalie Martin and (d) Warsis Martin deceased, who was the father of Stephen Martin, Nelson Martin, Joseph Martin, and Caroline Martin, (e) Catharine Martin who married Joseph Fayan, (f) Julia Martin who married Baptiste Polo; and (g) Ellen Martin who married John Levake; (3) Alexis Martin who died young; (4) a son who died unchristened; (5) Frances Martin who married Anve Morgette and was supposedly dead; (6) Margaret Martin who died young; (7) Mary Ann Martin who died young; (8) Catherine Martin who died young; (9) Ganerieu Martin who married Louis Valois and left no issue; and (10) Angelica Martin who died young. Francis Martin married Genevieve Boucher at Berthier, Canada 15 Feb. 1763. His widow married secondly Lt. Felix Victor 11 Feb. 1782 at Fishkill. Felix Victor was an ensign from 1 Nov. 1777, was promoted to lieutenant, and died at St. Antoine, Canada 30 Oct. 1820. His widow died 18 Dec. 1836. She was deranged in mind and did not apply for relief. Two of the sons of Francis Martin, Francis Martin and Joseph Martin, were also veterans. Francis Martin died in hospital from disease. Congress granted the grandchildren relief 12 Dec. 1856.

Martin, George. —. —. Because his widow, Elizabeth Martin, furnished no evidence for six months of service or her marriage, Congress rejected her petition 13 July 1846.

Martin, George. Pa. Pvt. He was in Northumberland County on 23 Sep. 1786. He was in the 12th Pa. Regiment under Col. William Cook in Capt. Hawkins Boone's Company and was drafted into Col. Morgan's corps. He was a shoemaker. He was wounded in his left side at Saratoga and disabled. He was 31 years old. He died 10 Mar. 1806.

Martin, George. Va. Dep. QM. He was an express rider from Charlottesville Barracks to different parts of the state for twelve months before the surrender of Cornwallis. He also acted as deputy quartermaster to press horses, cattle, and provisions for the prisoners at the barracks. His widow, Elizabeth Martin, aged 90, married him before 1782. Congress granted her a pension 12 Dec. 1856. She had been denied in Feb. 1848.

Martin, George. Va. —. His son, John Martin, was in Essex County on 10 Nov. 1787. George Martin enlisted under Henry Garnett in the 2nd State Regiment for three years. He died in the service. His son John Martin was 12 years old and was maimed by the loss of a hand. His guardian was his mother Mary Purks. She was in Caroline County in 1790. John Martin was placed on the pension roll on 6 Dec. 1787 at the rate of £6 per annum.

Martin, Henry. Md. Pvt. He was pensioned at the rate of half-pay of a private in Frederick County on 2 Feb. 1828.

Martin, Henry. Va. —. His widow, Mary Martin, was granted £15 support in Caroline Co., Va. 12 Mar. 1778.

Martin, Jacob. Md. Pvt. His widow, Margaret Martin, was pensioned at the rate of half-pay of a private in Westmoreland Co., Pa. 9 Mar. 1846.

Martin, Jacob. Pa. —. He was awarded a $40 gratuity and a $40 annuity in Montgomery Co., Pa. 5 Mar. 1828.

Martin, James. S.C. Capt. He was at Briar Creek and lost his horse, saddle, bridle, saddle bags, holsters and sword while trying to save a soldier from drowning. He was in the campaign against the Creeks where Maj. Francis Ross was killed. He was at the defeat of Capt. Huck or Hook at Williamson's. He was at Rocky Mount, Hanging Rock, Fish Dam Ford, Blackstocks, and Friday's Fort. He was in the action at Big Glades where 14 wagons of military stores were taken. He became a refugee in North Carolina and fought at Ramsour's Mill. He was 74 years old and nearly blind. He was pensioned from York District 3 Nov. 1829. Capt. James Jamieson and

William Carson were with him in several of the actions. He was receiving his annuity as late as 1833.

Martin, Jirah. Mass. —. His widow, Hannah Martin, drew a pension. Their daughter, Nancy Martin, sought a pension from 4 Mar. 1836 to 5 Mar. 1841 in right of her mother. Her mother died 17 Mar. 1843. Her father died 17 Feb. 1843. Congress ruled that she was ineligible.

Martin, John. N.J. —. In the fall of 1777 he was on a month tour of duty at Elizabeth Town under Maj. Sealy. He, Joshua Ball, and Ephraim Manning were on guard at Crane's Point and were taken prisoner and conveyed to Staten Island. They were placed in the Sugar House in New York. He took sick and died in hospital there. He married Susannah Brant 27 July 1777. His widow, Susannah Martin, married secondly George Bowlsby 1 Apr. 1788. She was entitled to a half-pay pension during her widowhood. It was awarded in Morris County in 1791.

Martin, John. Pa. Sgt. He served in the Artillery and was transferred to the Invalids. He had lost his health. He was from Philadelphia County.

Martin, John. Pa. Pvt. His widow was in Mifflin County 15 Sep. 1791. He was killed at Crooked Billet in May 1778. He was in the militia under Col. Frederick Watts. His widow, Elizabeth Martin, married ----- Thompson in July 1780. His orphans were James Martin born 27 May 1771, Mary Martin born 18 Feb. 1774, Elizabeth Martin born 14 Apr. 1776, and John Martin born 26 May 1778. Their guardians were Frederick Watts and James Taylor.

Martin, John. Va. Sgt. He lived in Caroline County. He was wounded at the siege of Ninety Six and was pensioned 27 Apr. 1810. He was on the 1813 pension list. He later removed to Wilson Co., Tennessee.

Martin, Joshua. S.C. —. There were three children in 1791.

Martin, Julius. S.C. —. He lost his eye by the accidental firing of his gun in public service. His other eye was much damaged. He was allowed a pension of £5 for one year 14 Dec. 1801.

Martin, Martin. S.C. —. He served in the 6th and 1st Regiments. He was under Col. Wade Hampton. He was taken prisoner at Charleston. He was from Richland District in 1793. He was paid $192.66 as a Revolutionary soldier in of the Continental Line of South Carolina on 20 Dec. 1810. He had a large family of children to support. He was paid his annuity as late as 1821. Another man of the same name applied about the same time. Because there were three men of the same who presented claims, their claims were submitted to Comptroller General.

Martin, Martin. S.C. —. By his attorney, John Bird, he sought his pay as a Revolutionary soldier for his service. There were two men of the same name, and the one from St. James Goose Creek had lately obtained his payment. On 16 Dec. 1816 he was to be paid $192.66 if the power of attorney was valid.

Martin, Merrick. N.J. —. He was pensioned in Middlesex County on 16 Feb. 1846 at the rate of $60 per annum. His widow, Tabitha Martin, was pensioned 29 Mar. 1855 at the rate of $60 per annum.

Martin, Nathaniel. Mass. Corp. He served in the 8th Regiment and was from New Hampshire. He was paid $20.

Martin, Patrick. Pa. —. He was awarded a $40 gratuity and a $40 annuity in Greene County on 19 Mar. 1816. He received $40 on 31 Mar. 1812.

Martin, Peter. Mass. —. He served in the 11th Regiment and was from Boston. His widow, Elizabeth Martin, was paid $20.

Martin, Peter. Pa. —. He first enlisted under Capt. Bratton in the 7th Regiment under Col. Minges. and wintered at Valley Forge. He was in battle at Monmouth, White Plains, Brandywine, and

Germantown. He served three years and nine months. He was at the taking of Cornwallis. He was awarded a $40 gratuity on 31 Mar. 1812 in Westmoreland County. His widow, Jane Martin, was awarded a $40 gratuity and a $40 annuity on 7 Mar. 1827. He died 22 May 1822. His widow died 24 Apr. 1831.

Martin, Peter. Pa. Lt. His widow, Sarah Martin, was in Philadelphia County on 4 Sep. 1791. He served in the Pa. Line and was killed in the service at Brandywine 11 Sep. 1777. His widow died 27 July 1803 and was buried in the Second Presbyterian burial ground 28 July 1803 in Philadelphia.

Martin, Philip. N.Y. Pvt. He served in Capt. Abraham Veeder's Company under Col. Frederick Fisher in the militia. He was wounded through the thigh on 6 Aug. 1777 at Oriskany and in his left arm near the elbow at Johnstown on 21 Oct. 1781. He was 34 years old in 1786. He lived in Montgomery Co., N.Y. on 29 June 1789. He was on the 1813 pension list. He also appeared as Philip Martain.

Martin, Richard. Pa. Lt. He protected the frontier settlements under Col. Thomas Hartley and was paid $200 on 20 Feb. 1818. He enlisted in the spring of 1778 in Northumberland County under Col. Samuel Hunter and Capt. John Chatham. He was elected 1st lieutenant. He built redoubt and stockade for defense against Indians. He was 74 years old and lived in Mifflin Twp., Lycoming Co., Penn. His brother was Elias Martin who was 67. He served on scouting parties for at least eight months in 1778, eight months in 1779, six months in 1780 and again in 1781, and four months in 1782. Congress granted him a pension 23 Jan. 1836.

Martin, Robert. Va. —. His wife, Peggy Martin, was granted necessaries 14 Aug. 1777 in Lunenburg Co., Va.

Martin, Salathiel. N.C. Capt. He served in the militia. He served one tour of six months and another of 12 months. He was in the battle of Guilford Courthouse. In 1780 he took a party of Tories lodged in a blockhouse on New River. He married 23 Apr. 1782. He died 6 May 1827. His widow, Mary Martin, received a pension from Congress on 14 June 1850 for six months of his service.

Martin, Simon. S.C. —. He was wounded at the battle of Eutaw. He was granted an annuity 2 Sep. 1784.

Martin, Thomas. Pa. —. He served on the frontiers under Col. Samuel Hunter from 1776 to 1778.

Martin, Thomas. Pa. —. He protected the frontier settlements under Col. Thomas Hartley and was paid $200 on 20 Feb. 1818.

Martin, William. N.Y. Pvt. He was wounded in an engagement with the enemy in his neck in June 1781 near Kingsbridge. He lived in Newburgh, N.Y. in 1794. He was on the 1813 pension list. He also appeared as William Martine.

Martin, William. Pa. —. He applied in Mifflin Company on 23 May 1812. He enlisted in 1776 in Capt. William Butler's Company in the 2nd Pa. Regiment. under Col. St. Clair and went to Canada. When St. Clair became Brigadier General and Butler rose to Major, James Christy became his captain in the 3rd Pa. Regiment under Col. Craig. He continued in the same unit for four years. He joined the horse troop under Capt. Henry Bithen and Col. Amory Marquis de la Rure, a Frenchman. He had a large family to support. He served seven years to the end of the war. He died 3 Apr. 1820.

Martin, William. S.C. Capt. He was killed in the service in Sep. 1780. His widow, Grace Martin, was awarded an annuity 2 Mar. 1785. Her annuity of 7 Sep. 1786 mentioned three children. She was from Edgefield.

Martin, William. Vt. Pvt. He served in a corps of rangers under Capt. Aldrick. He was wounded in his right arm by a cannon ball in 1777 at Lake George. He lived in Westminister, Vt.

in 1795. He was granted two-thirds of a pension 20 Apr. 1796. He was on the 1813 pension list.

Martin, William. Va. —. He served as assistant commissary. His widow, Jane Martin, sought arrearage from 4 Mar. 1848 to 3 Feb. 1853 which Congress allowed 15 Dec. 1857. She was from Harrison County.

Martin, William. Va. Pvt. His widow, Sarah Martin, lived in Monongalia County 15 Dec. 1786. He served in the 13th Va. Regiment under Capt. James Neal. She was 60 years old. She was continued on the pension list at the rate of £18 per annum on 16 Dec. 1786.

Martindale, John. Md. Fifer. He was burnt on his left hand. He served in Col. John H. Stone's Regiment. He was pensioned in Charles County in 1783.

Martine, William. N.Y. Pvt. He served under Col. James Hammon in the Westchester County militia and was wounded by a musket ball in his testicles in the attack at North Castle en route to White Plains. He had a wife and two children. He lived in Stephentown, Westchester Co., N.Y. on 1 May 1789.

Martling, Isaac. N.Y. Sgt. He served under Lt. Col. Hammond in the Westchester County militia and was slain 27 May 1779. His widow, Anne Martling, received a half-pay pension.

Marvin, Benjamin. Vt. Capt. He served under Col. Livingston. He suffered from variant complaints occasioned by fatigue which he endured in action against Gen. Burgoyne in 1777 at Bemis Heights. He lived in Alburgh, Vt. in 1795. Since his disability was not from a wound, his claim was not allowed.

Marvin, John C. —. —. He was a seaman and pensioner. He died in 1834. His widow, Clarissa Marvin, sought an increase in her pension. She presented no proof of marriage or his length or grade of service. Congress did not act on her claim 3 Mar. 1851.

Marx, —. Pa. —. His widow, Christiana Marx, was awarded a $40 gratuity in Berks Co., Pa. 6 Apr. 1833.

Mash, —. S.C. —. His widow was Selia Mash in 1793.

Mason, Aaron. Mass. Pvt. He was stricken by a fever contracted on the night of 16 June 1775 at Bunker Hill. He served under Col. Fry. He lived in Woburn, Mass. in 1792.

Mason, Ashbel. Conn. —. He served in the 5th Regiment under Capt. Chapman, Col. Heman Swift, and Col. Bradley. He was at Yorktown. He took sick and was at home on furlough. He returned near the end of the war. He asked for his $80 gratuity and 100 acres of bounty land. Congress awarded same 17 Jan. 1838.

Mason, David. Va. Lt. He served under Col. John Mason in the 11th Regiment to the end of the war. His heirs were George B. Mason and Mary R. J. Pleasants. Congress rejected their claim for commutation 28 Jan. 1836.

Mason, George. Me. —. He died 21 Apr. 1817. His widow was Susanna Hilton from Windsor. She was paid $50 under the resolve of 1836.

Mason, George. Pa. —. He was granted relief in Crawford County 1 Jan. 1840.

Mason, George. S.C. —. He was awarded an annuity 10 Aug. 1784. He lost a leg by a cannon shot in action at Fort Moultrie on 28 June 1776. He received a state pension to Mar. 1789. He sought payment from the federal government on 28 June 1803. He also appeared as George Mayson.

Mason, George. Va. —. His grand-daughter, Ann Atkinson, was the widow of Hopeful Toler who served under Capt. Henry St. George Tucker in the Virginia Militia in the War of 1812. She was an inmate of the widows home in Washington, D.C. and received a pension from Congress 3 Mar. 1879.

Mason, John. Me. —. He died 22 Oct. 1824. His widow was Lucy Mason from Falmouth. She was paid

$50 under the resolve of 1836.

Mason, Josiah. Pa. Lt. He applied 6 Feb. 1821. He served in the Pa. Line.

Mason, Peter. Va. Pvt. He was in Fayette Co., Ky. in Aug 1786 and was 30 years old. On 25 July 1780 he was on duty in a company of Kentucky militia under Capt. Hugh McGary en route to a general rendezvous on their march to the Shawnee towns. He lost the use of his left wrist by a gun shot wound from the enemy. His pension was continued at the rate of £6 per annum on 29 Nov. 1786. He was in Caroline Co., Va. in 1789. He was on the 1813 pension list.

Mason, Robert. Mass. Pvt. He served in the 8th Regiment and was from Andover. His widow, Phebe Mason, was paid $50.

Mason, Stephen. Mass. —. He served in the Artillery and was from Plymouth. He was paid $20. He also appeared as Stephens Mason.

Mason, Thomas. N.Y. Pvt. He served under Col. Philip VanCortland and was slain 7 Oct. 1781. His widow, Mary Mason, received a half-pay pension for seven years.

Massey, —. Va. —. His wife, Lettice Massey, was granted £7 support in Aug., 1776, £12 in Sep. 1778, and £40 in July 1779 in Fauquier Co., Va.

Massey, William. S.C. —. There were four children in 1791.

Massie, Thomas. Va. Maj. He served in the 6th Regiment first as a captain and then as a major. He became supernumerary when eight regiments were consolidated into two. In 1780 he was an aid to Gen. Nelson at Yorktown. Congress rejected the claim of his representatives for commutation 10 May 1836.

Masson, Joseph. N.C. Pvt. He served in the North Carolina militia and was wounded in his left hip in June 1780 at Ramsours Mill. He resided in Iredell Co., N.C. in 1796.

Master, Hugh. N.Y. Pvt. He was pensioned.

Masterson, Patrick. Va. —. He claimed two years or more of service but produced no evidence. John Kelly proved he marched to Hilltown, Va. in the spring of 1780 and met Masterson under the command of Capt. Jennings. They served until after defeat of Cornwallis. Congress approved his petition for a pension 27 Mar. 1846.

Mastick, Benjamin. Mass. Pvt. He served in Capt. Vincent Gardner's Company under Col. Eleazer Brooks. He was disabled by a musket ball through his left arm. He was pensioned at the rate of half-pay from 9 Dec. 1776 on 20 June 1777. He was again pensioned 20 Nov. 1792. He was 32 years old in 1792. He was on the 1813 pension list. He transferred to Geauga Co., Ohio 4 Mar. 1826 and died 6 June 1830.

Maston, Epherim. N.Y. —. He was pensioned.

Maston, James. N.Y. —. His family was granted support in 1779.

Maston, John. N.Y. —. He served under Col. Dubois. His wife was granted one and a half bushels of wheat on 7 June 1779 while he was away in the service.

Matheny, William. —. —. He served three years and was wounded at Brandywine. He was taken prisoner, released, and returned home. His wound kept him from returning. Congress granted him a pension 21 Dec. 1831.

Matheny, William. Va. —. His wife, Margaret Matheny, was granted support in Berkeley County on 16 Sep. 1777. He was away in Continental service the Volunteers in Capt. Francis Willis's Company. She was awarded £5 relief as his widow on 17 Sep. 1778.

Mathers, James. N.Y. Pvt. He served in Matthew Johnson's Company under Col. James McClaughrey in the Ulster County militia. He was badly wounded in his right shoulder. He was wounded in his left hand and lost it. He lived in New York City, N.Y. in June 1788. He was aged 39 years in 1786. He was on the 1813 pension list in Pennsylvania.

Mathers, John. S.C. —. He was receiving a pension in 1838 and was a resident of Spartanburgh.

Mathers, Joseph. Conn. Ens. He enlisted as a private in May 1775 in the 1st Regiment and served ten months. He was served eight months as a sergeant and six months as an ensign. He died 29 Feb. 1840 at the age of 87. His widow died in her 95th year. Congress granted his daughter a pension. She was 66 years old.

Mathews, Ether. Vt. —. He served seven years. He suffered from fatigue and sickness in the service. Two of his children died. His family consisted of a wife and four living children. His debts amounted to $500 or thereabouts. He sought to be insulated for five years from any attempts to be persecuted for debt. He applied from Woodstock 24 Aug. 1799.

Mathiot, George. —. —. He married 30 Oct. 1787 and died 4 Apr. 1840. He was awarded relief in Fayette County 20 May 1839. Congress granted his widow, Ruth Mathiot, a pension of $71 per annum on 12 Apr. 1842. One Ruth Mathiot received a $40 gratuity and a $40 annuity in Fayette Co., Pa. 3 Apr. 1841.

Mathis, Samuel. S.C. —. He was aged 16 a few months before the Declaration of Independence. He served under Capt. John Chestnut from Jan. 1781 to May 1781 where he was paroled. He was taken prisoner again in July 1781 and exchanged. His lieutenant, Henry Bates, fell at Quinby Bridge along with a third of the company. Zacheriah Canty served with him and was a prisoner. He was paid $174.80 for his Revolutionary service on 17 Dec. 1821.

Mathison, —. Pa. —. His widow, Janet Mathison, was awarded a $40 gratuity and a $40 annuity 7 Dec. 1829.

Matlock, Daniel. N.Y. —. He was pensioned.

Matson, Joseph. Conn. Pvt. He served in the militia under Col. Thaddeus Cook in Capt. Goodrich's Company. In Sept. 1777 he was wounded at Bemis Heights in New York in the ankle by a musket ball which fractured the bones. His leg was later amputated. He was pensioned 4 Sep. 1788. He lived in Glastonbury, Conn. and was 40 years old. He died in 1810.

Matson, William. Pa. —. He was granted relief.

Mattes, Peter. N.Y. —. His family was granted support 20 Feb. 1779.

Matthew, Frederick. Pa. —. He was awarded a $40 gratuity and a $40 annuity in Berks Co., Pa. 23 Apr. 1829.

Mathews, —. Va. —. He died in the Continental Army. His widow, Martha Mathews, was paid £10 in Fauquier County in Oct. 1778 and £80 in May 1780.

Mathews, Moses. S.C. Gunsmith. He supplied and repaired arms in Fairfield District. In 1780 the Tories destroyed his workshop. He died in 1806. His heirs sought $18,000. Congress rejected their claim 7 Feb. 1850.

Matthews, —. Va. —. His wife was granted £3 per month in Yohogania Co., Va. 30 Sep. 1779 while her husband was away in Continental service.

Matthews, —. Va. Matross. He died in the service. His widow, Anne Matthews, was granted relief 24 Nov. 1777.

Matthews, James. Pa. Pvt. He also appeared as James Matthias. He was on the 1791 pension roll.

Matthews, John. Md. Corp. He was pensioned 4 Mar. 1789. He was on the 1813 pension list.

Matthews, John. Va. Pvt. He was disabled in Continental service 14 June 1778.

Matthews, Owen. Va. Pvt. He served in Capt. Dickinson's Company. His widow, Anne Matthews, was awarded a £20 gratuity on 24 Nov. 1777. She was in James City County 11 June 1787. He died in the service in New York in Mar. 1777 leaving a widow and five children. She was continued on the pension list on 16 Oct. 1787 at the rate of £12 per annum. She died about 1 Oct. 1792.

Matthews, Samuel. S.C. —. He was born in Abbeville District. He served under Capt. Samuel Reid, Capt. Irwin, Capt. Patterson, and Maj. Alex Noble. Daniel Gillespie deposed that he knew he was under Capt. Dawson and Capt. J. Calhoun. He had raised a large family who were dispersed at a great distance. He suffered from acute rheumatism and swelling in his right knee and shoulder and was pensioned 23 Nov. 1829. He was paid as late as 1830.

Matthews, Samuel. Va. Col. He served in the artillery to the end of the war. His son and executor was Thomas Matthews. Congress rejected the claim for half-pay for life on 2 Jan. 1837 because he resigned his commission.

Matthews, William. N.J. Pvt. He served under Capt. Thomas Williams and Col. Philip Van Courtland in the militia. He was dangerously wounded in action on the heights back of Second River on 13 Sep. 1777. His skull was fractured. He was allowed his half-pay in Essex County in Apr. 1780.

Matthewson, Alexander. Md. Pvt. He transferred from Maryland to Pennsylvania. He died 16 Jan. 1791.

Matthewson, Constant. Pa. —. His daughter, who lived in Washington, Dutchess Co., N.Y., claimed that her father served in the Pa. Line under Col. Harris and Capt. Samuel ------ and was killed at Fort Washington.

Matthias, Hendrick. N.Y. —. He was slain 6 Aug. 1777. His widow, Barbara Matthias, received his half-pay pension.

Mattison, Benjamin. —. —. He served nine months under Capt. William Hutchins and Col. Seth Warner in 1776 and four months in 1777 under Capt. Galusha when Burgoyne was captured. One son was Elisha Mattison. His widow, Lois Mattison, of Jefferson Co., N.Y. was awarded a pension by Congress for $40 per annum on 18 Feb. 1846 retroactive to 15 Nov. 1844.

Mattis, Christian. Pa. —. He was awarded a $40 gratuity and a $40 annuity in Montgomery Co., Pa. 17 Mar. 1835.

Mattock, John. N.C. Sgt. He served under Capt. John Nelson in the 4th Regiment. He was under Col. Alexander Martin and Col. Thomas Polk. He was in Maryland and at Philadelphia. He fought at Germantown, Sandy Hook, Stony Point, and was discharged at Peramus, N.J. He was under Col. Washington at Whitsell's Mills. He was 70 years old when he applied in Rockingham Co., N.C. 27 Aug. 1823.

Mattocks, Peter. Pa. —. He was awarded a $40 gratuity and a $40 annuity in Crawford County 28 Mar. 1836.

Mattox, —. Pa. —. His widow, Margaret Mattox, was awarded a $40 annuity in Mercer Co., Pa. 1 May 1852 for his Revolutionary service.

Mattox, —. Va. —. His wife, Martha Mattox, was granted £10 support in Feb. 1778 in Fauquier Co, Va.

Mattox, Richard. Pa. —. He was awarded a $40 gratuity and a $40 annuity in Mercer Co., Pa. 15 Jan. 1829.

Maulsbarger. D. Pa. —. He was pensioned.

Maurer, Paul. Pa. —. He was awarded a $40 gratuity and a $40 annuity in Schuylkill Co., Pa. 27 Mar. 1824.

Maurer, Peter. Pa. —. He was granted a $40 gratuity and a $40 annuity in Lancaster County 12 Mar. 1836. He was 83 years old in 1840.

Maurey, Richard. Va. —. He was disabled in Continental service at Waxsaws. He was being pensioned 13 Sep. 1783.

6

Mauser, Michael. Pa. —. He was pensioned.

Maxfield, Joseph. Mass. —. He served in the 6th Regiment and was from Springfield. He was paid $20.

Maxwell, —. Pa. —. His widow, Margaret Maxwell, was awarded a $40 gratuity and a $40 annuity in Huntingdon Co., Pa. 17 Mar. 1835. She was dead by May 1837.

Maxwell, Alexander. Pa. Pvt. His heirs were in Alleghany County on 28 June 1790. He was in the militia under Capt. William Campbell and Col. Archibald Lockry and was killed in the service 24 Aug. 1781 by Indians. His widow, Elizabeth Maxwell, remarried Thomas Halfpenny on 1 Oct. 1785. His daughter, Ann Maxwell, born 30 July 1777, was the ward of Joseph Scott and was the only surviving of the four children at the time of the soldier's death.

Maxwell, Anthony. N.Y. —. His wife and two children were granted support in Dutchess County on 3 Nov. 1781.

Maxwell, Hugh. Mass. Capt. He served under Col. Prescott. He was wounded by a musket ball in his right shoulder on 17 June 1775 at Bunker Hill. He lived in Heath, Mass. in 1795. He was in the militia. He was granted one-eighth of a pension 20 Apr. 1796. His daughter, Priscilla Maxwell, sought a pension, but Congress rejected her petition 14 Mar. 1848.

Maxwell, James. Md. Corp. He was pensioned at the rate of half-pay of a corporal in Cecil Co. on 16 Nov. 1811.

Maxwell, James. Pa. —. He was in Butler County on 17 Sep. 1821. He enlisted in 1776 in Capt. Montgomery's Company under Col. McCoy in the 8th Pa. Regiment and served three years. He received bounty land warrant #10,098 for 100 acres. It was assigned to Thomas Thompson 10 Dec. 1808, and the patent was issued 4 Jan. 1810. Congress granted no relief for the bounty land warrant 14 Feb. 1835. Congress later found that the warrant was a forgery and granted relief on 11 May 1838. One of his name received a Pennsylvania pension on 6 May 1823 as a private. He was dead by Feb. 1839.

Maxwell, Robert. Pa. —. He was awarded a $40 gratuity in Huntingdon Co., Pa. 19 Feb. 1828.

Maxwell, Robert. Pa. —. He was awarded a $40 gratuity and a $40 annuity 8 Feb. 1842 for his Revolutionary service. He lived in Harrison Co., Ohio and had formerly lived in Washington Co., Ohio.

Maxwell, Thomas. Pa. —. He served in the militia under Col. John Hamilton, Lt. Col. William Dewees, Maj. Matthew Jones, and Capt. Hugh Jones. He next volunteered in a light horse company under Capt. Henry Lee and Col. Bland in N.J. Lt. Lindsay was in command when Lee was promoted. He was at Brandywine, Germantown, and Monmouth. He was with Washington on the retreat across the Delaware. He left the service in the spring of 1779. Congress granted him a pension for one year of service 30 Mar. 1838. He was from Indiana.

Maxwell, William. N.Y. Pvt. He served in the 2nd N.Y. Regiment. He was taken sick at Crown Point with smallpox and died. His widow was Harriet Foster. Her application for arrears of his back pay was rejected 16 June 1809.

May, —. Va. —. His wife, Mary May, was granted £20 support while he was in service in the state artillery in Fauquier Co., Va. in Feb. 1779.

May, James. S.C. Capt. He served in the militia and caught a disease which caused him to lose his eyesight. He had a wife and eight children when he applied in Ninety Six District 14 Dec. 1791.

May, John. —. —. Congress rejected the application of his widow, Sarah May, for a pension 9 Feb. 1848.

May, John. Va. —. His wife, Anne May, was granted £10 on 15 June 1778, £12 in York Co., Va. on 15 Feb. 1779 and £30 on 21 June 1779.

May, Oliver. Mass. Pvt. He was in the 3rd Regiment and was from Ashfield. He was paid $50.

Mayberry, Joseph. Pa. —. His widow, Nancy Mayberry, was awarded a $40 gratuity and a $40 annuity in Montgomery Co., Pa. 30 Jan. 1834. He also appeared as Joseph Maybury.

Mayberry, Thomas. Pa. Pvt. He was in Montgomery County 26 June 1786 and in Berks County 1 Oct 1787. He served in Col. Proctor's Regiment of Artillery and was wounded in the leg. His wife was mentioned 1 July 1788. He was on the 1813 pension list. He also appeared as Thomas Maybury.

Mayer, Frederick. Pa. —. He was awarded a $40 gratuity and a $40 annuity in Dauphin County in Mar. 1828.

Mayer, Hanhendrick. N.Y. Lt. He served in Capt. Henry Dieffendorph's militia. He was sick while on guard in 1776 at Stone Arabia and continued ill for some years. He lived in Connajoharrie, N.Y. in 1794. Since he was not wounded, he was ineligible for a pension.

Mayer, Jacob. Pa. —. He applied 2 Oct. 1812 in York County. He was aged 70 years. He served under Col. Wayne in Capt. James Taylor's Company for one year from Feb. 1776. He was discharged at Chester in 1777. He died on or about 3 July 1826.

Mayer, John. N.Y. —. He was granted relief.

Mayer, Leonard. Pa. —. He was granted relief in Schuylkill County 12 Mar. 1836.

Mayer, Peter. Pa. —. He was awarded a $40 gratuity and a $40 annuity in Dauphin Co., Pa. 27 Feb. 1834. He was paid to 5 Aug. 1835.

Mayes, James. Va. —. He was on the 1785 and 1803 pension lists. He also appeared as James Maze.

Mayhew, James. Mass. —. He served in Crane's Regiment and was paid $20.

Mayhew, Jonathan. Md. Pvt. He was pensioned at the rate of half-pay of a private in Washington County on 19 Feb. 1819. His widow, Eleanor L. Mayhew, was pensioned at the same rate 4 Mar. 1834. She died 12 Dec. 1837. Her son-in-law, Adam Houk, received her arrearage of $8 for 2 months and 12 days on 24 Jan. 1838. He also appeared as Jonathan Mayhugh.

Mayhew, William. Mass. —. He served in the 10th Regiment and was paid $20.

Maynard, Anthony. N.Y. —. He was a Canadian refugee. His heirs were granted his 200 acres of bounty land 11 Apr. 1808.

Maynard, John. Mass. Quartermaster Sgt. He served under Col. Jonathan Brewer. He was wounded in his leg by a musket ball on 17 June 1775 at Bunker Hill. He was also wounded in his body by a musket ball in Feb. 1780 at White Plains when acting as lieutenant in the 3rd Mass. Regiment. He lived in Framingham, Mass. in 1794. He was in the militia. He was granted one-tenth of a pension 20 Apr. 1796 at the rank of a lieutenant. He was on the 1813 pension list. He died 21 Jan. 1823 in Worcester Co., Mass.

Maynard, Joseph. Mass. —. He served in the 6th Regiment and was from Kennebeck. He was paid $20.

Maynard, Peter. Mass. —. He served in the 5th Regiment and was from Lenox. He was paid $20.

Maynard, William. Mass. Lt. He served under Col. Nixon in Capt. Thomas Drury's Company. He was wounded in his left hip on the heights of Charlestown on 17 June 1775 at the battle of Bunker Hill. He was pensioned on 16 Mar. 1780 at the rate of a quarter of his pay from 1 Jan. 1776 to 1 June 1779 when he joined the Invalids. He moved to North Carolina during the war where he married. He applied in Anson Co., N.C. in 1802. He died in Mar. or Apr. 1806.

Mayo, Stephen. Va. —. He served four tours from the fall of 1776 to Sep. 1781. He was at Brandywine and Germantown. He married Rebecca Dawson 24 Nov. 1834 in Fluvanna Co., Va. when he was 77 years old. He died 10 Mar. 1847. She was pensioned at the rate of $12 per month. Her widowed daughter was 70. Congress increased her pension to $20 per month 25 Feb. 1904.She was one of two last widows of veterans. He was from Newbern, Pulaski Co., Va.

Mays, Edward. N.J. Pvt. He served in 2nd Regiment. He was almost blind. He lived in Trenton.

Mayson, James. S.C. Lt. Col. There was no evidence that he served in the Continental Line to the end of the war or that he became supernumerary after Oct. 1780. He served to the end of the war, His indent did not identify his service. He may have belonged to the militia. Congress considered the petition of the heirs 19 July 1842.

Mayson, James Robert. S.C. —. His annuity was £4.17.2 ½ in 1787.

Mayson, Luke. S.C. Lt. He died 1 Apr. 1780.

Maze, Joseph. Va. —. He was continued on the pension list at the rate of £8 per annum on 19 June 1788. He was on the pension roll of 1798.

Maze, Thomas. Pa. Pvt. He was on the 1813 pension list. He died in Venango County 27 Mar. 1830. His widow was Mary Maze.

Maze, Thomas. S.C. —. He was wounded at the Hanging Rock. He was granted an annuity 27 Nov. 1784. He also appeared as Thomas Mayse.

Meach, Jacob. Conn. Pvt. He served in Col. John Ely's Regiment in Capt. Oliver Coit's Company. He was disabled at White Plains on 28 Oct. 1776 by cannon shot through his right arm. He was from Preston. He was pensioned 15 Nov. 1788 at the age of 32. He was on the 1813 pension list.

Meacham, Henry. Va. —. He died in Continental service in Dec. 1779. His widow, Rebeckah Meacham, was in Sussex County on 16 Mar. 1786.

Meachum, Paul. N.C. Pvt. He applied in Halifax County in 1785. He was a mulatto. In 1789 he was 40 years old and 5'8" tall. He served in the 3rd N.C. Regiment of the Continental Line and received a broken arm in the service. He was aged 36 in 1785.

Meachum, Simeon. —. —. He was pensioned but stricken in 1820. He should not have been so Congress restored his pension 8 Apr. 1834.

Mead, Andrew. Conn. Ens. He served in the Coast Guard. He was under Maj. Gen. Samuel Holden Parsons who ordered an enterprise against the British fortress in New York. He was under Lt. Samuel DeForest against the fort on White Stone on Long Island. Since the wind did not favor the expedition and after getting part of the way, they altered the plan and made an attack on the sloop, *Shuldam*, of eight guns which was a guard vessel lying on Eastchester Creek. Mead received a musket ball and four buck shot in one shoulder and a ball and five buck shot in the other shoulder. David Maltbie was a volunteer on the same expedition. He was with a small number of Continental soldiers and as many volunteers as he could collect and proceeded in small cruising boats against the British ison at White Stone. He was a volunteer in Capt. Jabez Fitch's company. He was out on an expedition under Lt. Joseph Hull and Ens. Andrew Mead. They went to New Rochelle in a heavy storm where they landed. Maltbie was given command and led the chase. They captured one of the enemy vessels and took it to Samford the next morning. DeForest and Hull arrived with an armed sloop of six guns, a gun boat, and a small coasting vessel. Andrew Mead was on board the small armed vessel and was badly wounded in his back and shoulders. They had not attacked the garrison because of the bad weather. Instead they attacked the armed vessel laying at Eastchester Creek which was guarding the British vessels and a number of Refugees who resided in the vicinity. Mead was pensioned 13 Aug. 1788 at Greenwich, Conn. at age 33. He was on the 1813 pension list. He died in 1821 in Fairfield Co., Conn.

Mead, Hugh. —. —. His application was rejected 17 Apr. 1798.

Mead, Jacob. N.Y. —. His application was rejected 3 Feb. 1800.

Mead, John. Conn. Lt. Col. He served in the militia and was bereft of all of his property. He was from Greenwich, Conn. and his heirs asked for a pension or other compensation 2 Feb. 1855. The committee of Congress ruled that it was not within their power.

Mead, Libbeus. N.Y. Sgt. He served in Capt. Samuel Lawrence's Company under Col. Samuel Drake in the Westchester County militia. He was wounded by a musket ball in his right hip at Crompo Hill. He also had other wounds from a bayonet. Capt. Abijah Gilbert deposed that he saw him the day he was wounded. He lived at Salem, Westchester Co., N.Y. on 5 May 1789. He was a laborer. He died in 1814.

Mead, Stephen. N.J. Pvt. He served under Maj. Samuel Meeker. He was wounded at the battle of Lockwancom 22 July 1779. His widow, Mary Mead, was from Sussex County.

Mead, Theophilus. Conn. —. He served in the 8th Conn. Regiment and was disabled by wounds.

Mead, Tilly. Mass. Pvt. He served in Abner Craft's Company. He was wounded in his right knee by the stroke of an ax in 1775 at Cambridge. He lived in Barre, Mass. in 1795. He was in the militia. He was granted one-fourth of a pension 20 Apr. 1796. He was on the 1813 pension list.

Meade, Everard. Va. Capt. He entered the service as captain in the spring of 1775, was promoted to major in 1777 until the fall of Charleston, and then to aide-de-camp to Gen. Lincoln. He was colonel in a legion under Brig. Gen. Alexander Spotswood, but it was never filled so he became supernumerary. He served to the end of the war. He received 5,333 ½ acres for his rank of major from Virginia 20 Feb. 1784. His five years' full pay was paid to his children 7 July 1832. Hodijah Meade and Benjamin Meade sought interest on the principal 17 Jan. 1838. He was from Amelia County. The heirs found new evidence of his being an aide-de-camp and qualified for five years' full pay at that higher grade 23 June 1854.

Meade, Richard J. Va. Capt. He served as aide-de-camp to the commander in 1777. Due to ill health in 1780 he was absent. His son, David Meade, sought his half-pay at the rank of lieutenant colonel 1 Feb. 1855.

Meadows, William. N.C. —. He served in the 6th N.C. Regiment in 1776 and died in the service. His mother, Ann Williams, had her request for a gratuity rejected in 1789.

Means, —. Va. —. William Means was furnished support in Loudoun County in May 1779.

Means, Allen. Pa. —. He was awarded a $40 gratuity in Allegheny County in 1845 for his Revolutionary service. He died 12 Sep. 1848.

Means, Hugh. Pa. Ens. He applied in Northumberland County on 4 Mar. 1827. He was in the Rangers Company in Bedford County under Capt. John McDonald in 1779 for eight months. He next served under Capt. John Boyd. On 3 June 1781 he was wounded in his left arm and taken prisoner by a party of Indians near Franks Town. He returned in 1783. He was from Mercer County. He died 12 Feb.1835.

Means, Thomas. Pa. —. He was granted 200 acres of donation lands which lay in New York in lieu of the tract granted him.

Mears, Russell. Mass. —. He served in the 3rd Regiment and was from Tewksbury. He was paid $50.

Mears, Samuel. —. —. He was pensioned 3 Mar. 1811.

Mears, William. Mass. —. He served in the 2nd Regiment and was paid $20.

Mearse, Samuel. Mass. Pvt. He served in the Mass. Line. He lived in Middlesex Co., Mass. and was pensioned 16 July 1811. He appeared on the 1813 pension list as Samuel Mears.

Meddagh, Frederick. Md. —. He was granted the privilege to hawk and peddle without a license in Nov. 1801 by virtue of being a Revolutionary War veteran. He was from Frederick County.

Medlar, Bostian. Md. Drum Maj. He was pensioned at the rate of half-pay of a drum major 23 Jan. 1816.

Meek, Abner. Pa. —. He was granted relief.

Meek, James. S.C. —. He was awarded £50 to help him on his journey to Philadelphia being discharged from hospital on 18 Nov. 1778.

Meek, James. S.C. Matross. He served in a Continental Regiment of Artillery and lost the use of his limbs in the service. He was awarded an annuity 1 July 1785.

Meek, John. Md. Pvt. He was pensioned in Frederick County on 4 Mar. 1789. He served in the 7ᵗʰ Regiment and was wounded at the battle of Guilford. He was on the 1813 pension list.

Meeker, Abraham. N.J. Pvt. He enlisted at Elizabeth Town 5 May 1776 and went to New York and then Long Island. On 5 Aug. 1776 he obtained a pass from Gen. Heard to return home on business for a day. He died eighteen days later on 23 Aug. 1776. Surgeon Robert Halstead attended him from 12 to 23 Aug. He was married to Elizabeth ----- in 1759 by Rev. Tichenor, but the church book was lost in the war. His widow received his half-pay 11 Jan. 1799.

Meeker. John. Conn. Pvt. He served in the 3ʳᵈ Conn. Regiment. He was aged and ulcerated. He was pensioned 4 Jan. 1783.

Meen, Calvin. Mass. Sgt. He served in the 4ᵗʰ Regiment and was from Greenfield. He was paid $20.

Mehaffey, Samuel. Pa. —. He was awarded a $40 gratuity and a $40 annuity in Westmoreland Co., Pa. 17 Mar. 1835.

Meherg, John. S.C. —. His widow was Susanna Meherg from Laurens District in 1786. There were two children in 1791. She also appeared as Susannah Mehergh. Compare with John McHerg.

Meise, Balzer. Pa. —. He applied in Somerset County on 1 Mar. 1819. He enlisted in the 2ⁿᵈ Pa. Regiment under Col. Walter Stewart in 1776 and was discharged in 1781. He also appeared as Baltzer Meese. He was dead by Mar. 1839.

Meisner, John. Pa. —. He was awarded a $40 gratuity and a $40 annuity in Lycoming Co., Pa. 12 Apr. 1828.

Melendy, James. Mass. Pvt. He served in the 4ᵗʰ Regiment and was from Charlton.

Mellen, David. Mass. —. He was born in Hopkinton, Mass. in 1763. He entered the service for six months under Capt. Dix and Col. James Mellen. He was discharged at West Point. He was a six-month man raised in 1780 to reenforce the Continental Army. He was paid from 4 July to 16 Dec. 1780. Congress granted him a pension even though he was short a few days from the minimum of six months on 5 Mar. 1840. He was from Hudson, N.Y.

Mellon, —. Pa. —. His widow, Susannah Mellon, was granted support 8 Apr. 1840 in Berks Co. She died 14 Mar. 1842.

Mellon, Atcheson. Pa. —. He was awarded a $40 gratuity and a $40 annuity in Lycoming County on 1 Mar. 1811. He was also covered by an act passed 24 Mar. 1817.

Melone, John. Va. Pvt. He was in Caroline County in Jan. 1787. He was disabled by rheumatism contracted in the service. He also appeared as John Malone.

Meloy, Bartholomew. Pa. —. He was awarded a $40 gratuity and a $40 annuity in Washington Co. on 29 Mar. 1813. He also appeared as Bartholomew Melony. He died 29 May 1842.

Meloy, John. Pa.—. He served five tours in the militia. He was from Mifflin County.

Meloy, William. S.C. —. In 1776 he served under Capt. Simms White and Col. Owen Roberts in the artillery. He was at Charleston, James Island, Georgetown, and Savannah. Other officers were Capt. James Mitchell, Ephraim Little, and Col. Bateman. At the siege of Charleston he was wounded in his left shoulder by a bomb shell and taken prisoner to Camden. He was forced to serve against his countrymen. He lost an eye. He escaped and fled to North Carolina. He was near 70 years old and was from Abbeville District in 1825. Robert Crawford stated that Meloy lived with him when he enlisted, and he saw him at Charleston. He was pensioned.

Melville, John. Mass. —. He served in the 1st Regiment and was paid $20.

Melvin, James. Mass. —. He was from Springfield and was paid $20.

Melvin, John. S.C. —. He died 18 Nov. 1781. His widow, Mary Melvin, was awarded an annuity 3 Feb. 1785.

Mendon, Robert. Va. Pvt. He died in Continental Service in Mar. 1777. His widow, Elizabeth Mendon, and children were awarded £12.6 per month in Accomack Co., Va.

Mengel, Adam. Pa. —. He was awarded a $40 annuity in Schuylkill County 12 Jan. 1836.

Menzies, Samuel P. —. —. Congress allowed his widow, Hannah Menzies, the arrearage of her pension from 4 Mar. 1848 to 3 Feb. 1853 on 21 Feb. 1857. She was from Kentucky.

Mercer, Hugh. Va. Brig. Gen. He died 12 Jan. 1777 at Princeton. His heirs were paid his seven years' half-pay of $5,250. His widow, Isabella Mercer, was pensioned at the rate of £150 per annum on 22 Mar. 1786. She lived in Spotsylvania County. There were five children. She died 16 Sept. 1791; George Weedon was administrator of her estate. She also appeared as Elizabeth Mercer. The son, William Mercer, was on the 1785 pension roll. The son was deaf and dumb.

Mercer, Thomas. S.C. —. He enlisted in 1777 under Col. Giles in the militia. John Saunders and James Goodson were with him in the war. He sought a pension in Nov. 1827. He was from Darlington District.

Mercer, William. Va. —. He was in Fredericksburg 5 May 1788.

Mercereau, John. N.Y. —. He was the assistant of Joshua Mercereau as assistant to deputy commissary of prisoners. In 1776 Gen. Washington sent him behind enemy lines to procure intelligence after the British took Long Island. He served more than two years as a spy until he was suspended. He transferred to the barracks at Rutland, Mass. and served as deputy commissary of prisoners under his father, Joseph Mercereau, for not less than twenty months. His brother, Joseph Mercereau, was also a deputy commissary. He filed for his pension in 1840 and the age of 83. He died 18 May 1841. His son-in-law was appointed administrator. With the death of Rev. John Caldwell, Deputy Quartermaster General, his accounts were never fully discharged. Congress rejected his petition for bounty land 14 Jan. 1820. Congress took the position that if he had been granted his pension promptly in his lifetime, he would have received 5/6th of the full pay of an officer and granted relief to his heirs 18 May 1860.

Merchant, Joseph. —. —. He was pensioned for 8 months and 24 days but appealed to Congress to be credited for 9 months and 7 days with thirteen days for going and returning from the service. Congress declined to do so 11 Apr. 1850.

Mercy, Jonathan. Mass. —. He served in the 4th Regiment and was from Norton. He was paid $20.

Meredith, William. —. Maj. He was at Stoney Point under Wayne; at Germantown and Monmouth under Washington; and at Camden under Gates. He was taken prisoner at the latter and was exchanged at the end of the war. He was pensioned. His son, William L. Meredith, sought relief, but Congress rejected his claim 25 Apr. 1854.

Meree, —. S.C. —. His widow was Ann Meree who was on the roll in 1791.

Meriwether, James. Va. Lt. He was an officer in the state cavalry on the Illinois Expedition. He was not entitled to commutation of half-pay as decided 26 Mar. 1790. He was allowed commutation of $4,504.93 and was the James Meriwether of Jefferson Co., Ky. He died intestate.

Merkel, Jacob. Pa. —. He was awarded a $40 gratuity in Berks Co., Pa. 18 Mar. 1834. He also appeared as Jacob Merkle and Jacob Menkel. He received the same 28 Mar. 1836.

Merkle, Bernard. Pa. Seaman. He was in Berks County on 3 Aug. 1802. He served aboard the warship *Hyder Alley* and was wounded by two gunshots in the knee in an engagement with the *General Monk* on 8 Apr. 1782. Capt. Joshua Barney was in command. He was 22 years old. He was pensioned at $3.33 per month.

Merkle, Christian. Pa. —. He was granted a $40 gratuity and a $40 annuity in Columbia County 29 Mar. 1824. He also appeared as Christian Merckle.

Merkle, George. Pa. —. He was awarded relief in Berks County 10 Apr. 1833. He also appeared as George Markle. He died 19 Apr. 1846.

Merrick, John. Me. —. He died 15 June 1835 at Skowhegan. His widow was Mary Merrick from Burnham. She was paid $50 under the resolve of 1836.

Merrick, William. Md. Corp. He was pensioned at the rate of half-pay of a corporal in Dorchester County on 16 Feb. 1821.

Merrifield, Abraham. —. Pvt. He served under Col. Learned. He was wounded by a musket ball which passed through his right leg at Boston light house in an expedition against the British in Aug. 1775. He resided in Bennington, Vt. in 1792.

Merrill, Asa. Mass. —. He was pensioned for three years of service in 1818, stricken in 1820, and restored. Congress refused to grant him his pension for the three and a quarter years he did not receive it on 24 Jan. 1837.

Merrill, Benjamin. Mass. Pvt. He was pensioned 23 Aug. 1786. He served under Col. James Tony and Capt. Jonathan Evans. He was disabled by a musket ball in his right knee. He was 39 years old in 1786. He was on the 1813 pension list.

Merrill, John. Me. —. He was from Lewiston. He was paid $50 under the resolve of 1836.

Merriman, Josiah. Conn. Corp. He served in 2nd Regiment of Light Dragoons in Capt. Porter's Company. He was wounded in right leg by the accidental discharge of his pistol in his holster in June 1777 on his march to Morristown. In Oct. 1777 at Frankfort he was wounded in the shoulder of his right arm by a musket ball and in his right thumb by a broadsword. He resided in Wallingford, Conn. in 1792. He enlisted 28 Dec. 1776 and continued to the end of the war. He died in 1810.

Merris, William. Pa. Pvt. He was in Philadelphia County on 10 July 1786. He lost his eye by cold and hardships in 1776. He served in the militia. He was 46 years old.

Merritt, Asa. Mass. Pvt. He lost the sight in one of his eyes due to inoculation for smallpox in 1777 at Prospect Hill. He served under Col. Greaton. He enlisted 15 Jan. 1777 and was discharged 2 Sep. 1777.

Merritt, James. S.C. —. He served under Capt. Goode, Maj. Williamson, and Col. John Williams. He served in the Cherokee Expedition, Stono, Liberty Hill, Two Sisters, Bacon Bridge, and King's Mountain. He was 74 years old and lived in Pendleton District. He suffered from an almost total loss of eyesight. William Southerland served with him. He was afflicted with rheumatism. His wife was 67 years old in 1830.

Merritt, Stephen. N.C. Capt. His name was not found on the rolls so Congress rejected the claim from the heirs for his commutation 24 Apr. 1840.

Merriwether, James. Va. —. He sought his half-pay for life in 1790. He served in the cavalry in Illinois. His claim was rejected.

Merryman, Josiah. Conn. Corp. He was granted two-thirds of a pension 20 Apr. 1796.

Merryman, Luke. Md. Pvt. His widow, Elizabeth Merryman, was pensioned at the rate of half-pay of a private 16 Mar. 1836.

Merselles, John J.. N.Y. —. He enlisted in Capt. Van Ness's Company for three years at Schenectady, N.Y. He was born there 16 July 1761. He was sent with a drove of cattle to Fort Stanwix with 28 privates under Lt. Hardenbergh, Ens. Wendell, and Col. Gansvort. His family was granted assistance on 26 Mar. 1779 while he was away in the service. He applied 19 July 1834. He also appeared as John Marselles.

Mershon, Andrew. N.J. —. He served under Col. Johnson and Capt. Benjamin VanCleve in the Flying Camp in 1776. He was killed in the battle of Long Island on 27 Aug. 1776. His children were John Mershon and Peter Mershon who were under the age of eight. They were allowed his half-pay until they became eight years old in Hunterdon Co., N.J. in 1780.

Merts, George. Pa. —. He was awarded a $40 gratuity and a $40 annuity in Westmoreland Co., Pa. 18 Mar. 1834. He also appeared as George Mertz. He died 10 Apr. 1846.

Messer, George. Pa. —. He was awarded a $40 gratuity and a $40 annuity 11 Mar. 1815.

Metlin, —. Pa. —. His widow was Sarah Metlin. She was from Union County 11 Apr. 1825. She died 13 Nov. 1831.

Metlin, Patrick. Pa. —. He was awarded a $40 gratuity and a $40 annuity in Union Co., Pa. 19 Jan. 1825. He died 6 Mar. 1825.

Mettet, James. S.C. —. He was in Pendleton District in 1829.

Metz, John. Pa. —. He applied in Schuylkill County on 25 Feb. 1813. He died 14 June 1821.

Meyer, —. Pa. —. His widow, Christiana Meyer, was awarded a pension in York County 20 Mar. 1834.

Meyer, Frederick. Pa. —. He was awarded a $40 gratuity and a $40 annuity in Dauphin Co., Pa. 5 Mar. 1828.

Meyer, Isaac. Pa. —. He was awarded a $40 gratuity and a $40 annuity in Lancaster Co., Pa. 11 Feb. 1825.

Meyer, Jacob. N.Y. Lt. He was killed at Johnson's Hall 24 Oct. 1781. A pension was paid to his survivor(s).

Meyers, Lewis. Pa. Sailor. He served aboard the galley *Hancock*. He was 39 years old and was wounded by a cannon ball from the enemy in the Delaware River in Nov. 1777. He was pensioned in Philadelphia 9 Jan. 1786.

Miatt, Peter. Va. —. His widow, Nancy Miatt, was granted £6 on 17 Aug. 1778 and £12 in York Co., Va. on 19 July 1779. He also appeared as Peter Myatt.

Michael, Jacob. Pa. —. He served from York County under Capt. Long and Maj. Swope at Amboy. He was taken prisoner. He died in 1813. Catharine Michael failed to present any evidence with her petition so Congress denied her a pension 6 Mar. 1850.

Michem, Colin. Va. —. He was from Shenandoah County and was pensioned at $80 per annum on 24 Dec. 1816.

Mick, Philip. Pa. —. He was awarded a $40 gratuity and a $40 annuity in Dauphin Co., Pa. 12 Apr. 1834.

Mickle, —. S.C. —. His widow, Jane Mickle, was on the roll in 1793.

Middagh, Ephraim. N.Y. Ens. He served under Col. Hathorne and was slain 22 July 1779 at Minnisink. His widow received his half-pay pension. She may have been Anna Middagh. [The text is difficult to interpret.]

Middaugh, John. Pa. —. He was awarded a $40 gratuity in Juniata Co., Pa. 4 May 1832. He was 81 years old in 1840.

Middleton, Basil. Va. Surgeon. He applied 22 Apr. 1790.

Middleton, Gilbert. Md. Capt. He was pensioned at the rate of half-pay of a captain in Baltimore 25 Jan. 1823. His widow, Sarah Middleton, was pensioned at the rate of half-pay of a captain in Baltimore 9 Feb. 1822.

Middleton, Samuel. Mass. —. He served in the 1st Regiment and was from Haverhill. He was paid $20.

Middleton, Theodore. Md. Lt. He entered in Apr. 1779 in 2nd Maryland Extra Regiment. He went to Annapolis, Philadelphia, shipped out of the head of Elk River to Annapolis, and marched south to Virginia into North Carolina. He was at the battle of Guilford. He became supernumerary. He sought five years' full pay but was rejected because he did not serve in the Continental Line 27 June 1838.

Mier, John. S.C. —. There were children in 1791.

Mier, Nicholas. Pa. —. He was granted a $40 gratuity and a $40 annuity in Crawford County in 1836. He died 10 June 1846.

Mignault, Basil. —. Lt. In Sep. 1775 he joined Gen. Montgomery at St. John's, Lower Canada. He was commissioned a lieutenant under Capt. Arnold and Col. Livingston. He served at Chambly, St. John's, Montreal, and Quebec. At the latter his captain was intoxicated, and two other captains were absent so he was appointed to command by Gen. Montgomery. He was on furlough to visit his sick father when he was taken prisoner and tried for assisting the Americans. He was acquitted because the British could not get witnesses. He was let out on parole but confined to parish of St. Dennis. He gave his papers to one Benway who drowned. His papers were lost. He was 73 years old in 1828. He died 20 June 1832 at Chambly and his widow on 31 Aug. 1832. His children were Stephen Mignault, Mary, Francis, Peter Mignault, John Baptiste Mignault, Lewis Mignault, Mary Ann, Basil Mignault, and Joseph Mignault. His son, Francis, died before him survived by sons Anthony and Joseph. His daughter Mary left two children Octave and Odile. His son Lewis was survived by Lewis, Basil, Joseph, Stephan, Victor, Cordelia, and Theresa Alicia. His son Francis was survived by Amilie and Alfred. The heirs claimed his arrearage from 3 Mar. 1826 to 20 June 1832. Congress approved relief for his children of Chambly, Kent Co., Lower Canada 24 Jan 1857 and on 4 Mar. 1860.

Milam, Jordan. —. —. He lived in Hickman Co., Tenn. He was 105 years old and his wife was about 80. He sought an increase in his pension. Congress denied his request 11 Apr. 1850.

Milam, William. Va. —. He served under Capt. John Brent. His wife, Margaret Milam, was furnished ½ bushel of salt, 5 bushels of corn, and 100 pounds of pork in Charlotte Co., Va. on 3 Feb. 1777. She received 300 pounds of pork, 5 barrels of corn, and beef on 2 Feb. 1778 and £8.7 provisions on 7 Sep. 1778.

Milburn, Nicholas. Md. Pvt. He was pensioned at the rate of half-pay of a private 30 Dec. 1812.

Milburn, Thomas. Va. —. His wife, Hannah Milburn, was granted support in Pittsylvania Co., Va. 27 Nov. 1777 and 26 Feb. 1778. As his widow she was given additional support on 24 Sep. 1778.

Milby, James. Va. —. He served in Col. Harrison's Regiment of Artillery. He died in the service and his widow, Elizabeth Milby, and her child about a year old were awarded a £20 gratuity on 24 Nov. 1777. She also appeared as Ellinah Milby.

Miles, —. Va. —. Ann Miles was allowed three bushels of corn valued at £15 as the wife of a soldier in the service in Augusta Co., Va. 21 Mar. 1780.

Miles, Daniel. S.C. —. There were two children in 1791.

Miles, Hardy. S.C. —. He served under Capt. John Moore. John Crossland was present when he enlisted. He applied from Fairfield District in Nov. 1813.

Miles, John. N.Y. Pvt. He was granted relief.

Miles, John. S.C. Capt. He was taken prisoner at Hanging Rock and was put to death at Camden by hanging 24 Aug. 1780. His widow, Elizabeth Miles, was awarded an annuity 24 Feb. 1786. There were three children in 1791. His son, Samuel Miles, sought a pension 5 Dec. 1844, but his application was rejected.

Miles, Joseph alias **Jacob**. Va. Pvt. He served under Capt. Richard Meade. He lost his eyesight on militia duty in 1776 at Norfolk. He was from Sussex County. He was awarded a £30 gratuity and a £50 annuity until his sight was restored on 12 May 1777. He was maintained by his two very poor brothers. He received an additional annuity of £9.6 which amounted to full pay of a soldier on 23 May 1778. He resided in Dinwiddie County on 22 Nov. 1786. He served in the 2nd Va. Regiment. Aged 32, he was disabled in the service by the firing of a cannon and was blinded. On 30 Dec. 1806 he received a $40 increase his pension. He was on the 1813 pension list. He was in Sussex County in 1814. He died Thursday night 12 Jan. 1819. John Raney was administrator of his estate.

Miles, Joshua. Md. Capt. His widow, Jane Miles, was pensioned at the rate of half-pay of a captain 2 Apr. 1836. The resolution was modified to have the payment for her natural life on 4 June 1836.

Miles, William. —. —. He married in 1806. Congress denied his widow, Sarah Miles, a pension 29 Feb. 1848.

Milford, Thomas. S.C. —. He was pensioned from Abbeville District on 6 Dec. 1828. He was paid as late as 1834. On 7 Jan. 1859 his heirs were his children Thomas B. Milford, Elenor Milford, Sarah Jones, and Polly Milford. Payment was made to Margaret Pruitt on 21 Apr. 1859.

Millan, Richard. Mass. Sgt. He served in the 10th Mass. Regiment. He had an incurable sore in his leg. He lived in Vt. in 1792. He died 24 Dec. 1817.

Millar, Samuel. Mass. —. He was from Newton and was paid $20.

Miller, —. Pa. —. His widow, Barbara Miller, was pensioned in Lancaster County 16 June 1836.

Miller, —. Pa. —. His widow, Barbara Miller, was awarded a $40 gratuity and a $40 annuity in York Co., Pa. 15 Apr. 1835. She died 4 Dec. 1840.

Miller, —. Pa. —. His widow, Catherine Miller, was awarded a $40 gratuity and a $40 annuity in Philadelphia Co., Pa. 19 Jan. 1827. She died 11 Nov. 1831.

Miller, —. Pa. —. His widow, Jane Miller, was awarded a $40 gratuity and a $40 annuity in Lancaster Co., Pa. 6 Apr. 1833.

Miller, —. Pa. —. His widow, Mary Miller, was awarded a $40 gratuity and a $40 annuity in Center Co., Pa. 21 Mar. 1833. She died 12 Sep. 1841.

Miller, —. Pa. —. His widow, Mary Miller, was awarded a $40 gratuity and a $40 annuity in Franklin County 3 Apr. 1837. She died 12 Mar. 1846.

Miller, —. Pa. —. Elizabeth Miller was pensioned 12 Feb. 1814.

Miller, —. Pa. —. His widow, Sarah Miller, was awarded a $40 gratuity and a $40 annuity in Northumberland Co., Pa. 31 Jan. 1825.

Miller, —. Pa. —. His widow, Susanna Miller, received relief in Montgomery County 10 Feb. 1841.

Miller, Andrew. Pa. —. He was awarded a $40 gratuity and a $40 annuity in York Co., Pa. 8 Apr. 1833. He was 86 years old in 1840. He died 22 Nov. 1842.

Miller, Andrew. S.C. —. He was killed in the service. His widow, Mary Miller, was granted an annuity 30 May 1785. There were children in 1793.

Miller, Anthony. Md. Pvt. He was in Philadelphia Co., Pa. 12 Dec. 1785. He served in Withers' Regiment in the Md. line. He was disabled by chronic disorders contracted in the service. He was

50 years old. His wife was alive 3 Mar. 1788. He died 1 Sep. 1789.

Miller, Charles. S.C. —. He was at Coosahatchy Bridge. He was knocked down by a limb of a tree. At Sumter's defeat he was chopped in the head and shoulder and left for dead. His skull was cut and fractured. He was from Chester District when he was pensioned 4 Dec. 1811. He was paid from the year 1790.

Miller, Christian. Pa. —. He applied in Berks County on 19 Jan. 1816. He had several small children one of whom was afflicted with a white swelling and was lame. He was disabled with rheumatism contracted when he was under Gen. Anthony Wayne. His service was not stated to have been during the Revolution. He was 85 years old in 1840. He died 30 Apr. 1845.

Miller, Conrad. Pa. Capt. He applied 4 Sep. 1838. He served in Col. Eyre's Battalion in a regiment of volunteer artillery in 1777 and 1778. He served as a lieutenant in Capt. Cowper's Company and was later made a captain.

Miller, Conrad. Pa. —. He was awarded a $40 gratuity and a $40 annuity 6 Apr. 1833 in York Co., Pa. He was paid to 4 Apr. 1835.

Miller, Daniel. N.J. —. He served under Capt. Silas Howell and Col. Wind. He died 1 Aug. 1776 at Lake George. His widow, Elizabeth Miller, was granted a half-pay pension in Morris County 19 Dec. 1781. Daniel Miller and Elizabeth Bowers were married in Nov. 1771.

Miller, Daniel. Pa. —. He was awarded a $40 gratuity and a $40 annuity in York Co., Pa. 8 Feb 1825.

Miller, Daniel. S.C. —. He was killed 28 Aug. 1781. His widow, Barbara Miller, was granted an annuity on 29 Dec. 1785.

Miller, David. Smith. Md. —. He died in the service. His widow, Rachel Miller Smith, was pensioned in Frederick County in 1783.

Miller, David. N.C. Pvt. He applied in Lincoln County in 1802. He served under Col. William Polk and was wounded at Horse Shoe. He was on the 1813 pension list.

Miller, Edward. —. —. He was pensioned 3 Mar. 1811.

Miller, Eleazer. N.J. —. His widow, Hannah Miller, was pensioned in Essex County on 18 Feb. 1847 at the rate of $50 per annum.

Miller, Francis. Pa. Sgt. His heirs, his twin daughters Isabella the wife of John Rogers and Nancy the wife of William Lawson, were awarded 250 acres of donation land on 4 Mar. 1813. The children were born a short time before their parents were married and were legally disqualified from succeeding to the land. They were declared entitled to do so.

Miller, Frederick. Pa. —. He was awarded a $40 gratuity and a $40 annuity in Montgomery Co., Pa. 16 Feb. 1835.

Miller, George. Md. Pvt. He was pensioned at the rate of half-pay of a private in Baltimore 2 Mar. 1827.

Miller, George. Pa. —. He was in Philadelphia 26 Jan. 1808. He was in a corps of artificers under Maj. Flowers when he was 15 years old.

Miller, George. Pa. —. He was awarded a $40 gratuity and a $40 annuity in Schuylkill Co., Pa. 27 Jan. 1835. He was dead by Dec. 1839.

Miller, Henry. —. —. He was blind in one eye. His sight was defective in the other eye. Congress granted him relief 30 Jan. 1852.

Miller, Henry. Pa. —. He was awarded a $40 gratuity and a $40 annuity in Franklin Co., Pa. 14 Jan. 1823.

Miller, Henry. Pa. —. He was awarded $240 in Perry Co., Pa. 29 Mar. 1824.

Miller, Henry. Pa. Gen. He left his wife and children and entered the service in York Co., Pa. as a lieutenant in the rifle corps. He had been engaged in the profession of law. He marched to Cambridge, Mass. and to Long Island where he was attached to Col. Thompson's rifle regiment. He was promoted to a captaincy at Bunker Hill in Oct. 1775. At the battle of Long Island 27 Aug. 1776 he remained with rear guard and was in the last boat to leave the island. He was commissioned major 12 Nov. 1777 effective from 28 Sep. 1776. In 1778 he became Lt. Col. of the 2nd Penn. Regiment. He was at Long Island, York Island, White Plains, Princeton, Trenton, Head of Elk, Brandywine, Germantown, and Monmouth. After the war he was commissioned Brig. Gen. of the 1st Brigade of the 2nd Division of the Penn. militia to repel the Indians. He also acted as Quartermaster General in the Whiskey Rebellion. During the War of 1812 he marched from Baltimore to the defense of Fort McHenry. His private estate was sold while he was away in the service in the Revolution. He died 5 Apr. 1824 at Carlisle, Penn. His daughter and grand-daughter, Julia Watts and Juliana W. Campbell, were poor. Congress awarded his arrearage from 18 Mar. 1818 to his death to them on 6 Mar. 1850.

Miller, Henry. S.C. —. His widow, Lydia Miller, was from Orangeburg in 1793. Her pension was later revoked because he served with the British. Philemon Waters had petitioned to correct the injustice.

Miller, Isaac. Pa. —. He was pensioned in Erie County 27 Mar. 1837. He was dead by Dec. 1839.

Miller, Jacob. N.C. —. He served in the militia from Rowan Co., N.C. for twelve months against the Tories in Orange Co., N.C. He was discharged in Aug. or Sept. 1779 after engagements with them. In 1780 he served three months as a guard in the county and pursued the Tories under Col. Bryan in the forks of the Yadkin. Capt. Cunningham reassembled the company; he served out his time in May 1781. In Aug. 1781 he was under Capt. Smith and went to Wilmington. After the defeat of Cornwallis he returned to Rowan County and was discharged He served under Capt. Hedrick. Congress granted him a pension for six months of service. Congress granted him a pension 19 Jan. 1843.

Miller, Jacob. Pa. Pvt. He was in Chester County 1 Sep. 1786. He served in the 5th Pa. Regiment and was ruptured in the service in 1778 and was transferred to the Invalids until he was discharged 6 Jan. 1783 by Gen. Washington. He was 50 years old. He died 4 Mar. 1812. There was a man of his name on the 1813 pension list.

Miller, Jacob. R.I. —. He entered the service in Apr. 1780 for one year under Capt. William Potter and Col. Christopher Green. He was discharged at Newport in Feb. 1781 due to sickness. He resided in Chenango Co., N.Y. and was pensioned by private act of Congress 10 Jan. 1832.

Miller, Jacob. Va. Pvt. He was disabled at Guilford. He served in the Bedford County militia. He applied 23 Nov. 1782. He was on the 1785 pension roll.

Miller, James. —. —. He served two years and died in 1788. His widow, Asenath Miller, married secondly John Campbell who died 25 Apr. 1833. Asenath Campbell had submitted her application for a pension. She was the widow of Campbell and not of Miller and was ineligible under the law. Congress approved a bill for her relief 5 Mar. 1840.

Miller, James. N.Y. Pvt. He served under Col. Thomas Thomas in the Westchester County militia and was slain 10 Jan. 1779. His widow, Eunice Miller, received a half-pay pension.

Miller, James. Pa. —. He was pensioned.

Miller, James. Va. —, He and his brother, **Thomas Miller**, died without issue. Their brother, John Miller, came to Perquimans Co., N.C. and died in 1822. He married Susan Humphries. The children of John Miller were James Miller and Martha Miller who married Thomas S. Stacy in

1833.

Miller, Jeremiah. N.Y. Capt. He served under Col. Henry K. Van Rensaler in the militia. He was wounded in an engagement in Montgomery County. He was a pensioner in 1787 in Columbia County.

Miller, Jeremiah. Pa. —. He was awarded a $40 gratuity and a $40 annuity in Somerset Co., Pa. 15 Apr. 1835.

Miller, Jesse. N.Y. Corp. His trustees, James W. Wilkins and Seth Marvin, were paid $242.22 with interest at 6 per cent per annum from 1 Jan. 1782 in full for his arrears of pay due on 19 June 1812.

Miller, John. —. —. He was killed by Indians in 1781 on the frontiers of New York. His children sought a pension. He was in the militia, and his service was not covered by the law.

Miller, John. N.Y. Pvt. He served under Col. Hawthorn. He received several wounds in action with the Indians at Minisink in July 1779. He lived in Warwick, N.Y. in 1794. He was on the 1813 pension list.

Miller, John. N.Y. Pvt. He served under Col. Lewis DuBois and died in captivity on or about 1 Jan. 1778. His widow, Ann Miller, received a half-pay pension.

Miller, John. Pa. —. He was awarded a $40 annuity in Lehigh County 5 Feb. 1836.

Miller, John. Pa. Capt. His widow, Margaretha Miller, was in Philadelphia County on 11 Mar. 1782. He served in the 5th Pa. Regiment under Col. Magaw and was killed 16 Nov. 1776 at York Island at the capture of Fort Washington. There were six small children.

Miller, John. Pa. Pvt. He served in the 5th Regiment. He was disabled by a rupture in 1778 and retired to the Invalids. He was 50 years old when he applied for a pension in New Jersey 1 Sep. 1786.

Miller, John. S.C. Adjutant. He served under Col. Edward Lacy. He was wounded in Feb. 1781 by a fall from his horse in making his escape. His horse brushed against a tree and dragged him in his stirrups under its belly. He lost his hat, and his gun was broken. He was forced to bind out his children. He was from Chester District and was paid $450 for his pension from 1786 to Jan. 1808 on 19 Dec. 1807. He was paid as late as 1820.

Miller, John. Va. —. His wife, Judith Miller, was granted 125 pounds of bacon and 5 barrels of corn for herself and her child in Berkeley County on 20 Aug. 1782.

Miller, John. Va. Pvt. His widow, Judith Miller, was in Orange County in Mar. 1790. He served in the 8th Va. Regiment and died of wounds in the service. She was continued on the pension list on 15 Oct. 1791. His widow married (2) ------ Burdine 4 June 1795. She lived in Rockingham County in Feb. 1796.

Miller, Johnson. Pa. —. He was granted relief and was paid in 1839.

Miller, Jonathan. N.Y. —. He was pensioned.

Miller, Joseph. Mass. Lt. He received his commutation for five years in lieu of half-pay for life.

Miller, Justus. N.Y. Pvt. He served under Col. William Livingston and was slain 23 Mar. 1777. His widow, Mary Miller, received a half-pay pension for seven years.

Miller, Marion. N.J. Pvt. He served in Somerset County militia. His widow, Mary Miller, received a half-pay pension.

Miller, Martin. Pa. —. He was awarded a $40 gratuity in Berks Co., Pa. 1 Apr. 1830 and a $40 gratuity and $40 annuity in Feb. 1834.

Miller, Matthew. N.C. —. He applied from Mecklenburg County.

Miller, Nathaniel. S.C. He served from 1776 to the close of the war. Robbed by the Tories of his whole property, he was wholly destitute and suffered from rheumatism. James Alexander, a fellow soldier, took him in and supported him. He sought a pension or pay 18 May 1819. He settled in Spartanburgh after the war. His spouse, Mary Miller, had fallen sixteen years ago and was a cripple herself.

Miller, Nelson. R.I. Drummer. He enlisted in June 1775 under Capt. Martindale and Col. Church for eight months. He was kept in service nine months. In 1776 he enlisted for a year under Capt. Peek and Col. Lippit followed by fifteen months under Col. Crary. Congress granted him a pension 3 Jan. 1832.

Miller, Nicholas. N.Y. —. He served in the militia and was killed by the Indians. His children sought half-pay but his service did not qualify.

Miller, Philip. N.Y. Pvt. He served under Capt. Rockfellow and Col. Livingston in 1776 at Greenbush for two weeks, at Fishkill for two months in the autumn, and at Fort Edward in the spring of 1777 for six weeks. He was at the taking of Burgoyne at Saratoga. In 1780 or 1781 he served six weeks at Ballston and Saratoga against the Indians. He married in July 1777 Helen Hamm. Their first child was born eighteen months later. He died in 1798. His widow, Helen Miller, aged 84 years in 1837, was from Livinston, N.Y. Congress granted her a pension 5 Mar. 1840.

Miller, Philip. Pa. —. He was awarded a $40 gratuity and a $40 annuity in York Co., Pa. 7 Mar. 1829.

Miller, Richard. —. —. His pension was rejected 9 Feb. 1807.

Miller, Robert. S.C. —. He served under Capt. Roberts and Col. Thomas. He was wounded at King's Mountain by a ball which passed through his thigh. He was from Chester District when he was pensioned 16 Dec. 1816. He died 12 Aug. 1831. His executors, his sons William Miller and Robert H. Miller, sought his arrearage. Their claim was rejected.

Miller, Samuel. Mass. —. He was from Newton.

Miller, Samuel. N.Y. Pvt. He served under Gen. McDougall. He had his leg mashed and broken in hauling a sleeper for a bridge building over Croton River by order of Gen. McDougall in Apr. 1779. He was pensioned 4 Sep. 1793. He lived in Mount Pleasant, Westchester Co., N.Y. in 1794. He was granted a full pension 20 Apr. 1796. He was on the 1813 pension list.

Miller, Samuel. Pa. Capt. He served in the 8th Regiment and was killed 8 July 1778. His widow, Jane Cruikshank was in Westmoreland County on 23 Mar. 1787. She married Andrew Cruikshank 9 May 1780. He left a widow and children Jenny Miller born 20 Oct. 1785, Dorcus Miller born 12 Nov. 1785, and Isaac Miller 10 Jan. 1786. Dorcas Miller married Joseph Russell, and Jane Miller married William Clark. He was killed by Indians 10 July 1778. Congress granted the heirs, represented by Samuel Miller, relief 2 Mar. 1860.

Miller, Samuel. Pa. —. He was pensioned in Indiana County 1 Apr. 1837.

Miller, Samuel. S.C. —. He was born in 1763 and married in 1800. He served in the Charleston Artillery under Lt. John Barry and Capt. Nesbitt. He applied to the federal government in 1825 but died before his application had been processed. His widow was Margaret Miller from Chester District in 1845. John Dill knew he served under Capt. John Turner. Juliana Kennedy and Isabella Patrick were present at their marriage.

Miller, Solomon. N.Y. —. He was slain 6 Aug. 1777. His children were granted half-pay.

Miller, Valentine. —. Pvt. He served more than three years. His proof was totally insufficient so Congress denied him a pension 13 Feb. 1849.

Miller, William. Md. Pvt. He was pensioned 4 Mar. 1789.

Miller, William. Pa. —. He was awarded a $40 gratuity and a $40 annuity in Luzerne County on 7 Mar. 1821. He died 25 Sep. 1825.

Miller, William. S.C. —. He served under Capt. Mazyck and Gen. Marion. He was at Fort Moultrie. He was pensioned from Richland District 19 Dec. 1825. He was paid in 1826.

Millett, John. —. —. Congress rejected his claim for a pension because it was not supported by proof on 24 Feb. 1847.

Milligan, Jacob. S.C. Capt. He was a meritorious naval officer at the battle of Fort Moultrie in 1776. He was sent to Philadelphia where in saluting them, a keg of powder blew up. His wrist was broken. His father gave him assistance and cared for him. He was a lieutenant on the *Prosper*. He commanded a party of seamen at Sullivan's Island. He was next on the *Action* and took spoils for the ison at Fort Moultrie. He was with Capt. Benjamin Stone when twenty-one of the company were wounded and five were killed. He was in the siege of Savannah and took the wounded to Charleston. He was taken prisoner and carried to Philadelphia in a canoe where he, Gov. Rutledge, and Capt. Anthony were exchanged. He was taken to St. Eustace and sent to England. After his release he was given command of a galley. He and his brother, John Milligan, were at Purysburg. He was granted one year annuity in 1788. His daughter, Mrs. Caroline Johnson, was pensioned at the rate of $60 per annum in appreciation of his service on 19 Dec. 1825. She was paid as late as 1834.

Milligan, Moses. S.C. —. His widow was Lucy Milligan in 1839. She was old and blind.

Milligan, Nathaniel. N.Y. Lt. He served under Col. McClaghry and was killed at Fort Montgomery 12 Oct. 1777. His son, Nathaniel Milligan, received a half-pay pension for seven years.

Milligan, Robert. N.Y. —. His family was granted support while he was away in the service 7 May 1779. He was from Dutchess County.

Milliken, James. N.Y. Capt. He served under Col. McClaghry. His orphans, William Milliken, Peter Milliken, and Susannah Milliken, received a half-pay pension. He also appeared as James Millican.

Millin, Richard. Vt. Sgt He served under Col. Marshall. He was disabled by hardships and fatigue. He lived in Windham, Vt. in 1794. He enlisted 24 Dec. 1776 and was discharged 20 Dec. 1779. He was on the 1813 pension list.

Milliner, John. N.C. Pvt. He was granted an annuity of £75 in Mecklenburg County. He served in the militia under Gen. Rutherford, Col. Mebane, Col. George Alexander, Gen. Sumter, Gen. Irwin, and Maj. Thomas Harris. He applied at the age of 84 in 1827.

Milling, Hugh. S.C. Capt. He was a lieutenant in the 6th S.C. Regiment on 15 Sep. 1778 and was a captain by 1 Nov. 1779. John Milling and Richard Nason sought his commutation but were rejected 28 Mar. 1838. In his lifetime he had stated that he had received his five years' full pay, but there was no certificate issued. While he had received bounty land from the United States, his own affidavit and those of two witnesses merely confirmed the truth of his statement. He was a deranged officer thrown out of his command and was subsequently a volunteer. On 8 Jan. 1819 he sought to locate his bounty land in Alabama Territory, but Congress ruled that he was not allowed to do so.

Milling, William. S.C. —. He served under Capt. Dixon, Col. Richardson, Col. Winn, Col. Lacy, Capt. Cooper, and Capt. Philip Walker. He was at Purysburg, Bigham Church, Fishing Creek, Coosahatchie, and Fort Reedy. He was 76 years old. Francis Wylie, James McCaw, William Morrow, William Lewis, and James McClure deposed anent his service. He had a second family of two small children. He was pensioned from Chester District 23 Nov. 1829.

Mills, —. N.J. —. His widow, Mary Mills, of Morris County was receiving a pension 10 Jan. 1793.

Mills, —. S.C. —. Margaret Mills and her children were granted an annuity in 1819, 1820, and 1821.

Mills, —. S.C. —. Mary Mills sought a pension, but her claim was rejected in 1845.

Mills, Alexander. N.Y. Pvt. He served under Col. Goose Van Schaick in Capt. Leonard Bleeker's Company. He was wounded in his right foot by a cannon at Yorktown, and his right leg was amputated. He was ruptured. He lived in New York City, N.Y. on 13 June 1788.

Mills, Cornelius G, Md. —. He was pensioned in 1811.

Mills, Daniel. N.Y. Capt. He served in the 4th Regiment under Col. James Holmes from July 1775 to his death in 22 Apr. 1776. His half-pay was due to his surviving children, Nathaniel Mills, Abby (Mills) Young, and Hannah (Mills) Broughton on 8 Mar. 1842.

Mills, Francis. Pa. Pvt. He was in Philadelphia County on 25 Sep.1787. He served in the 10th Pa. Regiment in Capt. George Kuhn's Company under Col. Adam Hubley. He was disabled by the total loss of his sight occasioned by hardships in the service. He was 48 years old. He had a wife and numerous family of helpless children. His lineal heirs were paid $300 for his donation land 9 Mar. 1826.

Mills, Joseph. Pa. —. He was awarded a $40 gratuity and a $40 annuity in Bedford Co., Pa. 23 Apr. 1829. He died 5 June 1833.

Mills, Josiah. Mass. —. He served in the 5th Regiment and was from Jay. He was paid $20.

Mills, Reuben. —. —. He served under Col. Robinson for five months and twenty-four days. Congress rejected his claim for a pension because he did not serve a minimum of six months on 8 Apr. 1846.

Mills, Samuel. Conn. Pvt. He served in Charles Burrall's Conn. Regiment in Capt. Titus Watson's Company. He was taken by smallpox in July in Canada in 1776. He was seized with bilious fever which fell into one of his legs and could not be cured. He was pensioned 13 Nov. 1788. He was on the 1813 pension list. He transferred to Chenango Co., N.Y. 4 Mar. 1824. He was the son of Capt. Samuel Mills.

Mills, Simeon. Conn. —. He went on the Canada Expedition and returned with the smallpox. He was pensioned 2 Nov. 1780 in Norfolk, Conn.

Mills, Solomon. N.Y. He served under Col. Wysenfelt. He was dropped from the roll because it was not known if his unit was on Continental establishment. Congress restored him to his pension 18 Feb. 1832.

Mills, Zachariah. Md. Pvt. He was pensioned at the rate of half-pay of a private in Anne Arundel County on 12 Feb. 1820.

Millspaugh, John. N.Y. Bombardier. He served in Capt. John Doughty's Company under Col. John Lamb in the Artillery. He was wounded in his left arm by grape shot at the battle of Germantown. He also served under Lt. John Waldron. He lived in Montgomery, Ulster Co., N.Y. on 21 May 1789. He died 19 Feb. 1810. He was on the 1813 pension list.

Millwee, William. S.C. Maj. He served in the Little River Regiment. He was in his 74th year. He was from Pendleton District and was pensioned 12 Dec. 1826. He was paid as late as 1834.

Millyard, —. Va. —. He was in the naval service. His wife, Sarah Millyard, and her four small children sought relief on 22 Oct. 1776.

Milstead, —. Va. Pvt. He died in Continental service 7 Oct. 1778. His widow was Ann Milstead. She was awarded support in Prince William Co., Va. in Sep. 1779.

Milton, Richard. —. —. His application was rejected 9 Feb. 1807.

Miner, Amos. N.Y. Orderly Sgt. He served under Col. C. Burrall. He was wounded in his left arm by an accidental discharge of a musket of one of the men with whom he was ordered on particular duty in Nov. 1776 at Mount Independence. He lived at Canaan, N.Y. in 1794. He was on the

1813 pension list. He also appeared as Amos Minor, *quo vide*, and Ames Minor.

Minitree, Paul. Md. Pvt. He was pensioned at the rate of half-pay of a private in Charles County on 19 Feb. 1819.

Minnis, John. N.C. —. He lived in Orange County. He died 20 Nov. 1836; his executor was William Minnis.

Minor, Amos. —. —. He was pensioned 7 June 1794. *Vide* Amos Miner *supra*.

Minor, Drover. Mass. Pvt. He served in the 14th Mass. Regiment under Col. Gideon Bradford and Capt. Joseph Russell. He lost both legs. He was pensioned at the rate of half-pay from the date of his discharge of 28 Sep. 1780 on 30 Apr. 1781. He was 40 years old in 1787.

Minor, Stephen. Conn. Quarter Gunner or Matross. He served in Col. Ledyard's matrosses. His left wrist was broken by accident in exercising a field piece, and his arm withered in 1779 at Fort Trumbull. He resided in New London, Conn. in 1792 and 1794. He was in the militia. He was granted half a pension 20 Apr. 1796. He was on the 1813 pension list.

Minor, Thomas. Va. Capt. He entered as a lieutenant until the enlistment of his men expired leaving him without a command. He was back in the service at Yorktown and was aide to Gen. Stephens. He received his five years' full pay commutation 30 June 1834.

Minot, Ephraim. Mass. Lt. He served under Col. Thomas Nixon and Capt. Wheeler in the 4th Regiment. He was wounded at Princeton 3 Jan. 1777 by a musket ball in his right ankle. He was pensioned at the rate of half-pay from 1 Sep. 1780, the date of his discharge, on 2 Feb. 1782. He was 45 years old in 1787.

Minthorn, Philip. N.J. Sgt. He enlisted for the war in the 1st Regiment under Col. Mathias Ogden. He died 23 Dec. 1780. His widow, Abigail Minthorn, was granted a half-pay pension in Morris County in 1782. She married secondly Charles McMillan 1 Sep. 1783.

Minthorn, William. N.J. Pvt. He served under Capt. John Holmes in the 1st Regiment. He died of wounds received before York in Virginia on 2 Nov. 1781. He married about 1771 Deborah Dodd. His widow, Deborah Minthorn, was granted a half-pay pension in Morris County in 1782.

Minton, John. Va. Pvt. His widow, Mary Minton, lived in Henrico County in 1789. He was in the 1st Va. Regiment and died in captivity in Charleston, S.C. Major William Lewis certified his service. She was put on the pension roll on 8 Jan. 1789 at the rate of £5 per annum. She was 50 years old and had no children in Jan. 1793.

Mitchard, James. Pa. Sgt. Maj. He entered the service in 1776 and was wounded at Long Island and rendered unfit for duty. When he returned to the service later, he was appointed to Sgt. Maj. by Col. Richard Butler. He was discharged after the surrender of Cornwallis. He received an allotment of land in 1805-6.

Mitchel, —. Va. —. His wife, Mary Mitchel, was granted support in Westmoreland County in Feb. 1779 and Feb. 1781.

Mitchell, —. Pa. —. His widow, Mary Mitchell, was awarded a $40 gratuity and a $40 annuity in Cumberland Co., Pa. 8 Apr. 1826.

Mitchell, —. Va. —. His wife, Mary Mitchell, was granted support in Lunenburg Co., Va. in May 1777.

Mitchell, —. Va. —. He and his brother were away in the service. Their mother, Sarah Mitchell, was granted £8 support for her and her four children on 17 Aug. 1778. She was granted £15 support in York Co., Va. 15 Feb. 1779 and £30 on 21 June 1779.

Mitchell, Abner. Mass. Pvt. He served in the 2nd Regiment and was from Shirley. His widow, Jane Mitchell, was paid $50.

Mitchell, Benjamin. Mass. Pvt. He served from Feb. to Nov. 1776 at Dyer's Point, Cape Elizabeth, Maine under Capt. Bryant Morton as a substitute for his brother, Robert Mitchell. He was rejected because his service was credited to Robert Mitchell. Congress granted him a pension 25 Jan. 1838.

Mitchell, Charles. Md. Pvt. His application was rejected.

Mitchell, Daniel. Pa. —. He was pensioned.

Mitchell, Darius. —. —. He served from 1775 to the end of the war at different times. Since his widow, Anna Mitchell, did not prove the alleged service, Congress denied her relief 8 May 1860.

Mitchell, Eliphas. Mass. —. He served in the 2nd Regiment and was paid $20.

Mitchell, James. —. —. His application was rejected 24 Apr. 1800.

Mitchell, James. Pa. —. He enlisted in the spring of 1776 under Col. Attlee. He was wounded at Long Island. He rejoined the 9th Regiment under Col. Butler and was appointed sergeant major. He was at Green Springs in 1781. He returned from the south to Pennsylvania to raise a regiment. He left the prison at Philadelphia under Col. Hampton. He was discharged due to wounds. He was 82 years old when Congress granted him a pension 3 Jan. 1832.

Mitchell, James. Pa. Sgt. Maj. He enlisted in 1776 and was wounded in his ankle at Long Island. He later was sergeant major in Col. Richard Butler's Regiment and served to the surrender of Cornwallis at Yorktown, Va. He was due donation land 10 Feb. 1807.

Mitchell, James. Pa. Sgt. He applied in Cumberland County on 3 June 1813. He died 16 Oct. 1835.

Mitchell, James. Pa. —. He was awarded a $40 gratuity and a $40 annuity in Cumberland County on 19 Mar. 1816.

Mitchell, James. S.C. Capt. He was wounded at Hanging Rock. He was in the militia. He was granted an annuity 1 Nov. 1784.

Mitchell, James. Va. —. His widow, Margaret Mitchell, was granted £15 support in Berkeley Co. on 18 Nov. 1778.

Mitchell, John. Me. —. He was from Harrington. He was paid $50 under the resolve of 1836.

Mitchell, John. Pa. —. He was awarded a $40 gratuity and a $40 annuity in Mifflin Co., Pa. 14 Apr. 1834.

Mitchell, John. Pa. Capt. He had command of the ship *Montgomery* employed in the naval defense of Pennsylvania. He was instrumental in blowing up a British ship of war.

Mitchell, John B. Pa/S.C. —. He enlisted at Philadelphia in Mar. 1776 and joined the army at Middlebrook, N.J. He was at Staten Island where he was wounded by a canon ball on the inside of his right leg and by a musket ball in his left leg below the knee. He was taken prisoner and conveyed by boat to New York, to St. Johns, Florida, and to Savannah, Ga. in 1778. He was compelled to serve under the British. At Cambridge, S.C. he was taken prisoner. Gen. Greene granted him a furlough. He made his way to Mecklenburg Co., N.C. where he taught school for nine years. He was deprived of his speech and sight. He was a minister of the gospel. He was from Edgefield District, South Carolina in 1841.

Mitchell, John. Va. —. His father and mother were granted an annual pension in Berkeley Co. on 16 Sep. 1777.

Mitchell, John. Va. —. His wife and five children were granted support in Berkeley County on 16 Sep. 1777. He was away in the service in Capt. Francis Willis's Company of Volunteers.

Mitchell, Joseph. N.Y. —. His wife and four children were granted support in Dutchess County on 3 Nov. 1781.

Mitchell, Joshua. Mass. —. He served in the 6ᵗʰ Regiment and was paid $20.

Mitchell, Reuben. Mass. Pvt. He served in the 2ⁿᵈ Regiment under Capt. Adams Bailey and Col. Ebenezer Sprout. He was disabled by a rupture. He was pensioned 3 Dec. 1787. He was 30 years old in 1788. He resided in Berkshire Co., Mass. He was on the 1813 pension list. He was from Bridgewater when he was paid $20 by the Commonwealth.

Mitchell, Robert. Me. —. He died 3 Feb. 1820. His widow was Mary Mitchell from Portland. She was paid $50 under the resolve of 1836.

Mitchell, Samuel. Conn. Pvt. He served in the 3ʳᵈ Conn. Regiment. He was disabled by rheumatism and palsy. He was pensioned 3 Jan. 1788. He was on the 1813 pension list. He died 13 Jan. 1819 in Middlesex Co., Mass.

Mitchell, Stephen. Mass. —. He served in the 13ᵗʰ Regiment and was from Newburyport. He was paid $20.

Mitchell, Theophilus. N.C. —. He died in the service. His widow was Martha Mitchell. Her application was rejected in 1787 because she did not have an affidavit from any officer.

Mitchell, Thomas. Va. —. He was pensioned in Charlotte County on 10 Feb. 1812 at the rate of $60 per annum. He served under Gen. Thomas Green at the battle of Guilford Courthouse and was shot through both of his thighs. He had resided in Charlotte County twelve years in 1818.

Mitchell, Timothy. Mass. —. He served in the 2ⁿᵈ Regiment and was from Bridgewater. He was paid $20.

Mitchell, William. Va. —. He served in Col. Dabney's Legion. He was pensioned 5 May 1785.

Mitchum, Colin. Va. —. He was in Shenandoah County 24 Jan. 1818. His only children were Sally (Mitchum) Brown and Harry Mitchum on 13 Mar. 1834.

Mitman, Charles. Pa. —. He was awarded a $40 gratuity and a $40 annuity in York Co., Pa. 14 Apr. 1827. He died 29 Oct. 1829.

Mix, Amos. Conn. Pvt. He served in Capt. Samuel Camp's Company under Col. Mead. He was wounded in May 1780 at Greenwich by a musket ball which was never extracted. He was brought home helpless about 9 July 1780. He was pensioned 17 Nov. 1780. He married in New Haven 5 Jan. 1784 and was the father of eight children by 1802. His widow, Clarinda Mix, sought a special pension, but Congress indicated that she should apply in the normal way on 29 Feb. 1848.

Mix, Eli. Conn. —. He was paid from 8 Mar. to 28 May 1781. He submitted no vouchers.

Mix, Timothy. N.Y. Lt. He was first a sergeant in the 2ⁿᵈ Regiment of Artillery on 9 Oct. 1777. He lost his right hand at Fort Montgomery. He served in Col. Lamb's Regiment under Lt. Peter Woodward and Lt. Jno. R. Throop. He served in the N.Y. Line. He was pensioned 28 Aug. 1788 in New Haven, Conn. at the age of 45. He was on the 1813 pension list. He died 11 June 1823 in New London Co., Conn.

Moak, Gerardus. N.Y. Pvt. He served under James Livingstone in Capt. Hansen's Company. He was later transferred to the Invalids Corps under Col. Nichola due to a rupture in his groin and was discharged by Gen. Washington. He lived at German Flatts, Montgomery Co., N.Y. 26 June 1789. He also appeared at Gerardus Mok(e) and Gerardus Mook. He was on the 1813 pension list.

Moast, —. Pa. —. His widow, Elizabeth Moast, was awarded a $40 gratuity and a $40 annuity in Lancaster Co., Pa. 16 Feb. 1835.

Mobb, Philip. Va. —. His wife, Sarah Mobb, and three children were furnished £8 support in Louisa Co., Va. on 11 Aug. 1777. He died in the service 13 Oct. 1778. His widow and three children were furnished £12 on 10 Aug. 1778, 4 barrels of corn and 200 pounds of pork on 11 Aug. 1780, and 150 pounds of pork and 3 barrels of corn for herself and two children on 10 Dec. 1781, and 2 barrels of corn and 50 pounds of bacon on 8 July 1782.

Modwell, John. Pa. Pvt. He was in Lancaster County 23 Oct. 1786. He served in the 7th Pa. Regiment under Col. Harmar in Capt. John Alexander's Company and was wounded by a musket ball in his right arm in 1780 near Morristown, N.J. He was 40 years old. He also appeared as John Moderwell and John Modewell. He was on the 1813 pension list.

Moffatt, Robert. Pa. Rough Rider. He was on the 1789 pension list.

Moger, Joseph. Conn. Pvt. He served three years, ten months, and sixteen days. He died in 1791. His widow, Huldah Moger, married secondly William Farlow in 1793. He deserted her nearly two years later. He reportedly died in 1811. He had not been heard from for almost forty-five years. Congress accepted that he was deceased and granted Huldah Farlow a pension 4 Jan. 1841.

Molin, —. Va. —. His father, Nicholas Molin, was granted £10 support in Caroline Co., Va. 9 Apr. 1778 and £30 11 Mar. 1779 while he was away in the service.

Moms, William. Mass. —. He was in the 10th Regiment and was from Scituate. He was paid $20.

Moncey, Ceaser. Mass. —. He served in the 4th Regiment and was from Norton.

Mona, Brian. —. —. His application was rejected.

Moncrief, Charles. Mass. Drummer. He served in Revere's Artillery and was from Boston. His widow, Hannah Yates, was paid $50.

Monday, John M. Mass. —. He served in the 3rd Regiment and was from Newbury. He was paid $20.

Monday, Thomas. Pa. Pvt. He was in Philadelphia County on 13 Mar. 1786. He was in the 6th Pa. Regiment. He was wounded at Fort Washington in his right arm and taken prisoner. He also received a rupture at West Point. He was on the 1813 pension list.

Monday, William. N.Y. Lt. He served under Col. Philip Van Courtlandt and was wounded in his leg on 19 Sep. 1777 in the engagement with Gen. Burgoyne. He was at Yorktown when he was arrested for disobedience of an order. He was tried and broke of his commission not more than two days before Lord Cornwallis surrendered. He was rejected 16 Dec. 1806.

Monderback, John. N.Y. —. His family was granted support during the war.

Mondle, George. Md. Pvt. He was pensioned at the rate of half-pay of a private in Pennsylvania 10 Feb. 1817. He also appeared as George Montle.

Moneer, Jacob. Mass. —. He served in the 7th Regiment and was paid $20. He also appeared as Jacob Mooner. He was from Charlestown.

Monk, Joseph. Va. —. He was pensioned in Dinwiddie County 25 Feb. 1818 at the rate of $100 per annum with $60 immediate relief. He was in Chesterfield County in Feb. 1818. He was wounded in the leg at Camden and was blind and helpless. His son was William Monk. Beverly T. Willis was administrator of his estate on 14 Sep. 1835.

Monks, Daniel. R.I. Pvt. He was worn out with old age, infirmities, and rheumatism. He served under Col. Jeremiah Olney. He was aged 67 in 1786. He resided in Providence Co., R.I.

Monnell, Robert. N.Y. Lt. He served under Col. McClaughrey in the Ulster County militia and was slain at Fort Montgomery 6 Oct. 1777. His widow, Isabel Monnell, received a half-pay pension

Monninger, Henry. Pa. —. He was awarded relief in Franklin County 14 Mar. 1835.

Monroe, James. Va. Lt. Col. He was commissioned in 1779 and served to Mar. 1780. He became supernumerary and continued to 3 Nov. 1783. He was born in Westmoreland Co., Va. 28 Apr. 1750 and died in New York 4 July 1831. He had enlisted as a cadet when he left William and

Mary College. He was severely wounded at Trenton and promoted to a captaincy. He was at Brandywine, Germantown, and Monmouth. His grandson and administrator, Samuel L. Gouvernear, sought his half-pay which Congress granted 16 Apr.1878. He was the fifth President of the United States.

Monrow, Barney. Md. Pvt. He served from 20 Apr. 1778 to 12 Nov. 1780. His step-daughter was Elizabeth Devinne aged 49. Congress rejected the request for bounty land on 21 Mar. 1856.

Monshomer, Sebastian. Pa. —. He applied 27 June 1829. He served in Capt. John Christy's Company in the 5th Pa. Regiment. He drew his donation land. He signed in German.

Montague, Benjamin. —. —. Benjamin Montague, heir at law, sought his pay, but Congress rejected the claim 20 Dec. 1861.

Montague, Peter. Va. —. His family was granted £8 assistance in Orange Co., Va. on 26 Mar. 1778 while he was away in the service.

Montgomery, Hugh. Del. Capt. He was captain of the brig, *Nancy*, and in 1775 sailed to the West Indies with a cargo of flour to be sold and the proceeds to be used to buy gunpowder and munitions. He sold the former at Porto Rico and at St. Croix loaded 460 barrels of gunpowder, six long one pounders, four chests of small arms, and other munitions. He converted his ship into a vessel of war and sailed for Delaware and Philadelphia. His ship was intercepted by two British ships of war. Since it was impossible to escape, he ran his ship into shallow water and commenced removing the powder and munitions onto shore. He was able to keep off the enemy's boats and with Capt. Weeks unloaded 244 barrels of powder, cannon, small arms, and other munitions. He destroyed his vessel and the rest of the cargo to keep them out of the enemy's hands by having them blown up. He transported the part of the cargo which he had saved to Philadelphia. He then went to sea in a private armed ship and was captured by the British. He became disordered and a fit of insanity leaped overboard and drown. He left a widow and a child. Congress gave Elizabeth Montgomery $5,000 on 28 Jan. 1856.

Montgomery, Hugh. Mass. Corp. He served in the 8th Regiment and was from Great Barrington.

Montgomery, James. N.Y. Guide. He served as a guide to Morgan's Riflemen.

Montgomery, James. Pa. Capt. His widow, Martha Montgomery, was in Westmoreland Co. 8 Oct. 1784. He served in the 8th Pa. Regiment. He was appointed captain 9 Aug. 1776 and died 26 Aug. 1777 in the service.

Montgomery, Richard. N.Y. Maj. Gen. He was killed at Quebec 31 Dec. 1777. His heirs were paid his seven years' half-pay of $6,972. His widow was Jennet Montgomery.

Montgomery, Robert. Pa. Pvt. He applied 14 Nov. 1788. He served in the 7th Battalion of the Cumberland County militia under Capt. Isaac Miller and Col. Frederick Watt. He was wounded 18 times in the head, hands, and arms at Crooked Billet in 1778 in an engagement with the enemy. He had a wife 50 years old and a 10 year old son. He was on the 1813 pension list.

Montgomery, Samuel. Va. —. The auditor was left to his own discretion whether to pay the heirs on 5 Jan. 1787.

Montgomery, Thomas. Pa. —. He was paid $300 for his donation land and resided in Washington Co., Ky. on 5 Mar. 1828. He was awarded a $40 gratuity 7 May 1832. His widow, Frances Montgomery received a $40 gratuity and a $40 annuity 13 May 1857.

Montle, George. Md. Pvt. He lived in Pennsylvania in 1817.

Monty, Francis. Conn. Lt. He served under Col. J. Livingston. He was wounded in his thigh by a musket ball in 1778 in R.I. He lived in Lake Champlain, N.Y. in 1794. He was commissioned 25 Nov. 1775, deranged 1 Jan. 1781, and received commutation which was not returned. He transferred from Pennsylvania 4 Sep. 1796. He died 8 Feb. 1809; yet, he was also on the 1813 pension list.

Monty, John. Canada. Warsman. He served in Gen. Hazen's Regiment. He never received his bounty money or gratuity. He was a U.S. pensioner. The Commissioner of Pensions was withholding his bounty land. His father was Francis Monty who served as a lieutenant. His father had six sons as soldiers: James Monty, Joseph Monty, Placide Monty, Amable or Abraham Monty, John Monty, and Francis Monty, Jr. all of whom were pensioned under the act of 1818. They lived in Clinton Co., N.Y. James Monty died 9 July 1819. John or Jack Monty was the only survivor of a family of nine children and 110 descendants. His claim was approved 24 Jan. 1857. Congress did so again 6 Apr. 1860.

Montz, Nicholas. Pa. —. His widow, Mary Montz, was awarded a $40 gratuity in Northumberland County on 28 Mar. 1820.

Moody, —. Va. —. His infirm father, John Moody, was furnished £30 for himself and his children in Essex Co., Va. on 25 June 1779.

Moody, Alexander. S.C. —. There were three children in 1791.

Moody, Benjamin. Mass. Pvt. He served in the 9th Regiment under Col. James Wesson and Capt. Amos Cogswell. He was disabled by an injury done to his left leg and thigh. He was 25 years old in 1788.

Moody, Blanks. Va. Pvt. He was in Pittsylvania County in May 1785. He served in the militia under Col. Peter Perkins at the battle of Guilford where he was wounded by a ball through his right shoulder. He was 30 years old on 3 Aug. 1786. He was on the 1813 pension list.

Moody, Edward. —. —. He enlisted in Sept. 1780 and served to 9 July 1781 for ten months when he left due to wounds. He was disabled for life. He married in March 1794. His widow, Fanny Moody, sought an increase in his pension for her husband having served a total of eighteen months. Congress denied her claim 6 Mar. 1850.

Moody, George. Mass. —. He served in the 2nd Regiment and was paid $20.

Moody, Isaiah. Va. —. His wife, Mary Moody, was granted support for herself and her family in Charlotte County on 6 Oct. 1777 and on 2 Feb. 1778.

Moody, Joshua. Me. —. He died 29 Dec. 1829. His widow was Rebecca Moody from Baldwin. She was paid $50 under the resolve of 1836.

Moody, Lemuel. —. —. He served seven months and twelve days in a company of sea coast guard under Capt. Joseph Pride and Col. Prince in 1780. He was stationed at Falmouth, Me. In 1781 he enlisted and served under Capt. John Reed and Col. Samuel McCobb until discharged in Dec. 1781. Congress granted him a pension 15 Feb. 1845.

Moody, Samuel. Va. Pvt. He served in the 4th Va. Regiment in Capt. Watkins's Company on Continental establishment and died in the north in the service about the close of 1776. His widow, Hannah Moody, was awarded a £20 gratuity in Surry Co., Va. 9 Dec. 1777. There were three children. She was still in Surry County in 1786. One child was 12 years old in Dec. 1786. She was put on the pension list at the rate of £6 per annum on 7 Mar. 1787. On 25 Sep. 1792 Hannah Moody had three children, one of whom was still at home and was aged 18. The children were Blanks Moody, Rebecca Moody, and Mary Moody.

Moody, Thomas. —. —. His applied for a pension in 1833, 1835, 1836, and 1853. He claimed to have resided in Irvine Co., N.C. or Tenn. but no such place existed. He resided in Alabama in 1853. John Moody stated that he went with him on his first tour of duty. The parol evidence did not provide the season, the year, or when the service was concluded. Congress deemed it was all hearsay and rejected the application of his administratrix, Temperance C. Lyle, 23 Mar. 1860.

Moody, Thomas. N.C. —. His widow, Mary Moody, applied in 1784 for her children and herself. He was at the battle of Guilford Court House and was upwards of 20 years of age.

Moody, Thomas. Va. Pvt. He was on the expedition to Tennessee against the Cherokee and was at White Oak Gales in 1776 for five months. In 1777 he served as a captain engaged as a recruiting officer for six months. In 1780 he served another six months. He was 97 years of age. He was approved for relief 16 Jan. 1857.

Moody, William. Va. —. He lived in Lexington, Rockbridge County and was pensioned 19 Jan. 1813 at the rate of $60 per annum. He was wounded at Ash Swamp near Amboy, N.Y. [sic] in his left knee and at Brandywine in his left arm and head. He died 30 Dec. 1822; his administrator was John Irvine.

Moody, William. Va. —. His wife, Catherine Moody, was granted £20 support in Berkeley County on 21 Sep. 1779. She received 7 bushels or corn and 75 pounds of pork on 16 Aug. 1780.

Mooers, Benjamin. —. Lt. & Adjt. He served in Hazen's Regiment and died in 1838. He had failed to ask for half-pay for life as an adjutant—only as a lieutenant. His heirs sought the greater amount 10 Jan. 1878. There were five heirs and one was upwards of 70 years of age. Congress granted same.

Moon, Gideon. Va. —. He was accidentally wounded in the wrist by a fellow soldier in the service. He was awarded a £10 gratuity and a £5 annuity in Mecklenburg Co., Va. 11 Nov. 1777 for three years.

Moon, Henry. Pa. —. His widow, Sarah Moon, was awarded a $40 gratuity and a $40 annuity in Allegheny Co., Pa. 5 Mar. 1828. She died 25 Nov. 1839.

Moon, Jacob. —. —. He was an officer and was killed at Guilford Court House, N.C. His son, who was about a year old, was Christopher Moon. Congress refused to grant him a special pension 28 Apr. 1848.

Moon, James. Pa. —. He applied in Washington County on 29 Apr. 1815. He served in the 1st Pa. Regiment in June 1777 under Col. James Chambers to the close of the war. Col. Josiah Harmar was in command at the end of the war. He was wounded at Green Springs, Va. He and Philip Verner were discharged at Philadelphia. He and his wife were old. He had a small family. He was dead by 10 Sep. 1823 when his brother David Moon was mentioned.

Moon, James. Pa. —. He was from Westmoreland County. He was pensioned in 1813. He was 70 years old in 1840. He died 5 Apr. 1842 in Fayette County.

Mooner, Jacob. Mass. —. He served in the 7th Regiment and was from Charleston.

Mooney, Barnet. N.Y. —. He was granted relief.

Mooney, Daniel. N.C. —. He was born in Pennsylvania and was 77 years of age. He was in Rutherford Co., N.C. in Sep. 1832.

Mooney, James. Del. Pvt. He was wounded through his left knee. He was pensioned in 1793.

Mooney, William. Md. Pvt. He was pensioned 4 Mar. 1789. He was on the 1813 pension list.

Moor, George. N.Y. Pvt. He served in Visscher's N.Y. Regiment. He lived in Herkimer Co., N.Y. He was on the 1813 pension list.

Moor, King. Mass. —. He served in the 3rd Artillery and was paid $20.

Moor, Milburn. Va. —. His widow, Catherine Moor, and two children were awarded £40 in Northampton Co., Va. on 8 Dec. 1778.

Moor, William. Pa. Sgt. His heirs were paid $250 in lieu of donation land due him 14 Mar. 1851.

He was from Lancaster County.

Moore, —. —. —. He served thirteen months. After his and his wife's deaths, his son Moren Moore found out that his father had the right to $80 per annum rather than $43.33. He sought the difference, but Congress rejected the claim because heirs were not entitled to arrears on 6 July 1854. *Vide* the entry under John Moore from North Carolina on page 574.

Moore, —. —. —. His widow, Henrietta Moore, prayed for the continuance of the pension act of 1844. Congress reported on 20 June 1848 that such an act had already been passed.

Moore, —. —. —. His widow, Roxanna Moore, had her petition for a pension to Congress rejected 27 Mar. 1846 because they were married subsequent to 1 Jan. 1794.

Moore, —. Pa. —. His widow, Hannah Moore, was awarded a $40 gratuity and a $40 annuity in Philadelphia Co., Pa. 8 Apr. 1826. She died 31 May 1826.

Moore, —. Pa.—. His widow, Magdalena Moore, received a $40 gratuity in Lebanon County 21 June 1839.

Moore, —. Va. —. His wife, Jane Moore, was granted £12 in May 1778 in Fauquier Co., Va.

Moore, —. S.C. —. His widow, Jane Moore, was pensioned 16 Dec. 1818. She had not been placed on the pension list earlier even though it had been so ordered.

Moore, —. S.C. —. His widow, Mary Moore, was on the roll from 1819 to her death 21 Nov. 1842 in Chester District. Her daughters, Nancy Moore and Sarah Moore, were paid her arrearage.

Moore, —. Va. —. His wife, Mary Moore, and three children were granted support in Westmoreland County 27 Feb. 1781.

Moore, —. Va. —. Thomas Moore was granted £40 relief while his son was away in Continental service 11 Mar. 1779 in Lunenburg Co., Va.

Moore, Ashbel. Mass. —. He had his petition for a pension by a special act of Congress rejected 4 May 1846 because his service was for 3 months and 7 days.

Moore, Benjamin. —. —. Congress denied his widow, Magdalena Moore, relief 9 Jan. 1847.

Moore, Burras. Va. —. His widow was paid £73.1.4 on 1 Dec. 1779 in Culpeper Co., Va.

Moore, Christopher. R.I. Pvt. He suffered from rheumatism and infirmity of age. He lived in Providence, R.I. in 1794.

Moore, Daniel. N.H. Capt. He served under Col. Stark. He had an incurable ulcer in his leg due to smallpox contracted in the service in 1776 in Canada. He lived in Deerfield, N.H. in 1794. He was in the militia. Since he was not wounded, he was not covered by the law.

Moore, David. N.C. —. He served under Col. Ash and Maj. Hogg. He was at the battle of Eutaw Springs. His widow received a warrant for 160 acres of bounty land and sought a pension. Congress granted his widow, Keziah Pritchett, such relief 17 Apr. 1860.

Moore, Frederick. Conn. Pvt. He was in the 1st Company of the militia. In opposing the British troops who landed at New London under Gen. Arnold on 6 Sep. 1781, he was wounded in the head and body by a bayonet at Fort Griswold. He was pensioned 26 Sep. 1788 at Groton, Conn. at the age of 26. He died in 1799. He also appeared as Frederick More.

Moore, Gideon. Va. —. He was granted a £10 gratuity and £5 per annum for three years on 2 Dec. 1777.

Moore, Hugh. Pa. Pvt. He was on the 1813 pension list. He was awarded a $40 gratuity and a $40 annuity in Washington County on 2 Apr. 1821. He died 8 Dec. 1821.

Moore, Isaac. —. —. He was pensioned in 1818 but stricken in 1830 because he had property valued at $300. Congress restored him to his pension 17 May 1832.

Moore, James. N.H. Pvt. He had a large incurable sore on the back of his right leg occasioned by a bruise or wound received in falling with a barrel of flour in Sep. 1775 on the Kennebec River.

He lived in Sharon, N.H. in 1794. He was in the militia. He was granted a full pension 20 Apr. 1796. He was on the 1813 pension list. He died 15 Dec. 1831.

Moore, James. N.C. Brig. Gen. His heirs applied in New Hanover County in 1786. He was commissioned by Congress in 1776 and died in April 1777. His widow died a few months later. Four children survived. One was in Scotland where he had been sent for an education. James Walker was the surviving executor of his will. In 1836 his surviving children were Sarah Swan and Mary Waters. They were to be paid his seven years' half-pay.

Moore, James. Pa. —. He was awarded a $40 gratuity in Beaver County 7 Apr. 1830. He was 82 years of age in 1840.

Moore, James. Pa. Corp. He was on the 1813 pension list.

Moore, James. Pa. —. He was wounded in the service. He had lived in Washington County the past twenty-nine years. .

Moore, James. Va. —. He served in Capt. Abner Crump's Company and the last of March 1778 in the service. His depreciation pay and bounty land were due his next of kin.

Moore, James. Va. —. He received bounty land warrant #4018 for 100 acres on 3 Dec. 1805 from Va. His widow, Sarah Moore, was en route to Kentucky when the warrant was destroyed by rain. It was on a pack horse. The heirs wanted scrip to locate the land elsewhere. Since they did not prove her death or their heirship, Congress rejected the claim 23 May 1850.

Moore, John. Md. Corp. He was on the 1791 pension list. He was paid $22.00 extra in Nov. 1798.

Moore, John, 2nd. Md. Pvt. He was on the 1791 pension list.

Moore, John. N.C. —. He served three years. He was allowed a pension for serving thirteen months and that was on parol evidence. He died 16 Nov. 1840. His widow, Mary Moore, applied but was denied her proof that he had served more than two years. She drew the $43.33 which her husband drew to the time of her death on 27 Oct. 1844. Congress recognized that she had not drawn a full pension and authorized a bill to pay the heirs the amount due them for his having served two years. John and Mary Moore seem to have been the parents of the Moren Moore, a son, who stated that his parents were pensioned for his father's thirteen months of service at the rate of $43.33. After his father's death, proof was found that his father should have been pensioned at the rate of $80. He sought the difference of the two, but Congress rejected his claim 6 July 1854. *Vide* the entry under — Moore on page 572.

Moore, John. Pa. —. He was on the 1789 pension list. He removed to Maryland.

Moore, John. S.C. Lt. He served in the 5th S.C. Regiment against the Indians in 1777. He sought his half-pay or five year commutation pay. His widow said he rose from major to Colonel in 1818.

Moore, John. Va. Ens. He was taken from the Line and appointed a quartermaster but did not resign his commission. He was late of Alabama. His heirs, William W. Moore, Richard W. Moore, John Moore, Martha Jordan, Mary Hummer, Margaret King, and Lucy Christian, sought his commutation. Congress rejected their claim 15 Apr. 1836.

Moore, Jonathan. Mass. Pvt. He served in the 4th Regiment and was from Haverhill. His widow, Elizabeth Moore, was paid $50.

Moore, Jonathan. Mass. Pvt. He served under Capt. Hartwell from 26 Oct. 1779 to 20 Apr. 1780 for a total of 5 months and 27 days. Congress awarded him a pension 25 Jan. 1848 for the six month minimum in the spirit rather than the letter of the law.

Moore, Mark. Va. —. His wife and children were granted assistance while he was away in the service in Amelia County 28 Oct. 1779.

Moore, Michael. S.C. —. He was wounded. He was on the roll in 1805.

Moore, Nicholas Ruxton. Md. Capt. He served two years. He married 25 Dec. 1793. He died 11 Oct. 1816. His widow, Sarah Moore, was pensioned at the rate of half-pay of a lieutenant in Baltimore 4 Mar. 1834. Her pension was adjusted to that of half-pay of a captain of cavalry 7 Feb. 1840.

Moore, Peter. Va. —. He served in Crocket's Regiment as a lieutenant. His representatives received his half-pay in 1832 in the amount of $4, 472.38. They later claimed more for his service as a captain. He had been recommended for promotion but did not actually serve a day at the higher rank. He received depreciation pay as a lieutenant in 1783 and bounty land in 1784. Virginia allowed 1,333 more acres in 1832. Congress rejected relief 1 Apr. 1842.

Moore, Ralph. Pa. —. He applied in Cumberland County on 11 Jan. 1815. He served in Col. Benjamin Flowers' Regiment of Artillery and Artificers having enlisted in 1775 at Fredericksburg where he spent one year followed by two years at Martinsburg in the armory. He enlisted at Carlisle in 1778 in Capt. Wylie's Company and served to 1781 when he was discharged. Dr. Samuel McCoskey was the regimental surgeon. He was 70 years old. He died 10 June 1818.

Moore, Reuben. Md. Pvt. He was pensioned at the rate of half-pay of a private in Dorchester County 19 Feb. 1819. His widow, Mary Moore, was pensioned at the same rate 9 Mar.1827.

Moore, Richard. Mass. Pvt. He served in the Invalids under Capt. George Hill and Col. William Shephard. His disability was a left hip put out. He was pensioned 1 Sep. 1782. He was 55 years old in 1786. He was paid $20 by the Commonwealth. He also appeared as Richard Moor.

Moore, Thomas. —. —. He served in the calvary under Col. William Washington and was at the battles of Guilford Court House, King's Mountain, and Cowpens. He was wounded in his body, thigh, and hand. He was 78 years old in 1825 in Rhea County, Tennessee when he petitioned for assistance from the state.

Moore, Thomas. Pa. Pvt. He was in Philadelphia County on 13 Mar. 1786. He was in the 1st Pa Regiment. He was disabled by a wound received in the service and transferred to the Invalids. He was discharged 1 Nov. 1783. He was on the 1813 pension list.

Moore, Thomas. Va. —. He was alive 24 Apr. 1833.

Moore, Willard. Mass. Maj. He served in Doolittle's Regiment and was wounded in action at Bunker Hill on 17 June 1775. He was from Paxton, Mass. He died of his wounds at Boston in July 1775. His widow, Elizabeth Moore, married secondly Mark Lincoln of Leominster. His children were Alpheus Moore and Willard Moore. They sought his seven years' half-pay 21 Feb. 1793. He was late of Paxton, Mass. He lived at Tolland at one time.

Moore, William. Md. Pvt. He was pensioned at the rate of half-pay of a private in Somerset County 21 Mar. 1833. His arrearage was paid to his son was Samuel T. Moore in Somerset County on 11 Feb. 1835.

Moore, William. Mass. Pvt. He served in the 4th Regiment and was from Tolland. He was paid $50.

Moore, William. N.C. Pvt. He served in 3rd Battalion. He was wounded in the articulation of the knee at Eutaw Springs, S.C. on 8 Sep. 1781. He was allowed 30 barrels of corn in 1782. He was aged 35 in 1785 when he was pensioned. He lived in Duplin Co., N.C. in 1794.

Moore, William. N.C. Capt. He applied in 1821 at the age of 88 years and was a resident of Robeson Co., N.C. His application was rejected on the grounds that his circumstances did not make his case any different from many others.

Moore, William. N.C. Sgt. He served in the Continental Army and was wounded. He was recommended for a pension of £8 from Duplin County.

Moore, William. Pa. Lt. He applied in Chester County on 3 Mar. 1818. He was wounded at Germantown and became lame. He was in Southern Army under Gen. Greene with Jacob Humphrey and Capt. W. Finney. He died 6 July 1824.

Moore, William. Pa. —. He was granted relief in Lancaster County 8 Jan. 1838. He died 12 Feb. 1844.

Moore, William. S.C. —. His annuity was £37.17.10 in 1787.

Moore, William. Va. Pvt. He was awarded a gratuity of two years' pay and an annuity of half-pay on 21 Nov. 1781. He lived in Washington County 19 Dec. 1787. He was in the battle of King's Mountain and was wounded in his arm and in his knee. He lost his leg in consequence of the wound. He was in the militia. He was continued on the pension list at the rate of £8 per annum on 1 Jan. 1788. He was continued on the list on 28 Oct. 1789 with an additional £3 per annum. He was on the 1813 pension list. On 25 Feb. 1818 his pension was increased from $60 to $120 per annum, and he was in Washington County.

Moorehouse, David. Conn. Pvt. He served in the 2nd Regiment. He suffered from rheumatism. He resided in Fairfield, Conn. in 1792. He enlisted 28 Dec. 1776 and continued to the end of the war. He also appeared as David Morehouse.

More, Mark. Va. —. His wife and children were granted financial support in Amelia Co., Va. 28 Oct. 1779.

Morehead, Charles. S.C. —. He died on board a prison ship. His widow, Margaret Morehead, was granted an annuity 20 Jan. 1786 in Chester District. She was Margaret Henderson.

Morehead, David. —. —. He was pensioned 7 June 1794.

Morehead, Joseph. Pa. Ens. He was on the 1813 pension list. He was from Indiana County. He died 7 Nov. 1844.

Moreland, Moses. Pa. —. He applied in Greene County on 19 Nov. 1825. He served under Lt. Thomas Marshall in 1777 in Lancaster County. He was under Col. Craig at Bound Brook and the skirmish at Short Hills. He was in the battles of Brandywine, Monmouth, Germantown, Yorktown, and Green Springs. He was discharged after five years of service. He had a wife. He was 88 years old in 1840.

Morer, —. Pa. —. His widow, Margaret Morer, was awarded a $40 gratuity and a $40 annuity in Montgomery Co., Pa. 15 Apr. 1835.

Morey, Ceasar. Mass. —. He served in the 4th Regiment and was from Norton. He was paid $20.

Morey, Jonathan. Mass. —. He served in the 4th Regiment and was paid $20.

Morfit, Henry P. Pa. Capt. He applied 4 Apr. 1822. He enlisted as a lieutenant at the age of 19 and was promoted at New Port when the French fleet was there. He was in the battles of Long Island, Germantown, and Brandywine. He also appeared as Henry P. Moffit and Henry P. Mafit. His commutation was allowed to his legal representatives 1 Feb. 1838 since he had been transferred from the Flying Camp to the Continental Army. His widow, Henrietta Morfit, had her petition for a pension rejected by Congress on 7 Jan. 1837 because she married him 13 Dec. 1783.

Morgan, —. Ga. —. Mrs. Elizabeth Morgan was granted assistance 10 Sep. 1782.

Morgan, —. Va. Pvt. He was killed in the service. His widow, Mary Morgan, was granted £20 support in Caroline Co., Va. 8 Apr. 1779.

Morgan, —. Va. —. His wife, Mary Morgan, was granted £12 support in Caroline Co., Va. 11 Nov. 1779.

Morgan, —. Pa. —. His widow, Susannah Morgan, was awarded a $40 gratuity and a $40 annuity in Northampton Co., Pa. 17 Jan. 1831. She died 31 Jan. 1831.

Morgan, Abel. —. Surgeon. His widow, Elizabeth Morgan, failed to show his service so Congress declined any relief 12 Apr. 1826.

Morgan, Abner. Mass. Maj. He was in the campaign to Canada in 1776 and served 11 months and 10 days from 1 Jan. 1776. At the age of about a hundred, he became of unsound mind. He died 6 Nov. 1837. He was 86 years old last April when Congress granted him a pension 19 Mar. 1832. His daughters, Marie A. Salisbury aged about 70 and Almira Morgan in her 81st year of Livingston Co., N.Y., were granted assistance by Congress 13 June 1888.

Morgan, Alexander. Va. Capt. He served in the 2nd Regiment and was commissioned at Winchester in Sep. or Oct. 1775. He was promoted to Colonel in 1777. He died in 1783. Congress rejected the claim of his heirs for commutation or half-pay 17 June 1838.

Morgan, Enoch. Pa. Lt. He applied 30 Sep. 1814. He served as paymaster from 15 Feb. 1777 to Aug. 1778 in the 6th Pa. Regiment. He was commissioned 15 Feb. 1777 and continued in that capacity until after the battle of Monmouth 28 June 1778. He was under Capt. Jacob Bower. Samuel Dean swore that he was discharged after the battle of Brandywine as supernumerary. Col. Thomas Craig of the 3rd Pa. Regiment proved that he served in the 2nd Pa. Brigade. His son, James Morgan, lived in Northampton County in 1826. His widow, Mercy Sherman of Brimfield, was allowed $50 by the Commonwealth.

Morgan, Ephraim. —. —. Congress awarded his widow, Elizabeth Morgan of Rensselaer Co., N. Y. the arrearage of her pension from 4 Mar. 1848 to 3 Feb. 1853 on 10 Dec. 1857.

Morgan, George. U.S. Col. He was the Agent for Indian Affairs and was granted payment for board and clothing for three Delaware youths in 1782.

Morgan, Israel. Mass. —. He was pensioned for life at the rate of $50 per annum 19 June 1807.

Morgan, J. Va. —. His widow, Frances Morgan, was granted £25 support in Caroline Co., Va. 12 Nov. 1778.

Morgan, James. Conn. Pvt. He served in the 1st Company of the 8th Conn. Regiment and was disabled at Fort Griswold. He was wounded in his left shoulder and sundry parts of his body by a bayonet. He served under Capt. William Latham in the Artillery and Amos Prentice, Surgeon, dressed his wounds. He was pensioned 22 Nov. 1788 at Groton, Conn. at the age of 29. He was on the 1813 pension list.

Morgan, James. Pa. —. He was pensioned.

Morgan, James. Va. Pvt. His widow, Frances Morgan, lived in James City County on 15 May 1787. He died in Continental service. He had one child 8 years old. She was continued on the pension roll at the rate of £8 per annum on 1 Dec. 1787. His son was 12 ½ years old on 14 Jan. 1793.

Morgan, John. —. Director & Physician-in-Chief of American Hospital. The children and grandchildren of his brother sought relief. Congress denied their request 6 Feb. 1854.

Morgan, John. Conn. Pvt. He served in the militia and opposed the British troops who landed at New London under Gen. Arnold on 6 Sep. 1781. He was wounded by a musket ball in the knee at Fort Griswold. He served under Capt. William Latham in the Artillery. He was pensioned 26 Sep. 1788 at Groton, Conn. at the age of 25 years. He was on the 1813 pension list.

Morgan, John. N.C. —. His widow, Rachel Morgan, was from Brunswick County.

Morgan, John. Va. Pvt. He was awarded a £300 gratuity on 6 Dec. 1780. He was awarded a gratuity of six months pay and an annuity of half-pay on 8 Dec. 1781. He lived in Spotsylvania County in Jan. 1786. He served in Capt. Stokes' Company under Col. Buford in the 2nd Va. Regiment. He received several wounds in his head. He was also quite disabled in his right hand except for his thumb and forefinger. He was wounded at Buford's defeat at the Waxsaws. In 1789 he was in Caroline County. He was on the 1813 pension list. He was seemingly identical with the John Morgan aged 34 in Henrico County when he was continued on the pension list at £18 per annum on 6 Feb. 1786.

Morgan, Jonathan. N.J. —. He was pensioned in Morris County on 15 Feb. 1837 at the rate of $60 per annum.

Morgan, Matthias. N.C. —. He enlisted and served nine months under Capt. Arthur Gatling and Col. Armstrong. He was at Stono. In 1825 he was told that he had to account for all of his property of which he may have disposed since 18 Mar. 1823. He was in Gates Co., N.C. in Aug. 1824.

Morgan, Simon. Va. Capt. He was pensioned at the rate of $20 per month from 2 Mar. 1808. He was on the 1813 pension list. He was from Fauquier Co., Va. He was wounded at the battle of Eutaw Springs on 8 Sep. 1780. He served in the 2nd Virginia Regiment.

Morgan, Thomas. Del. —. He served eight years in the Delaware Regiment and was wounded. He had a wife and several children. He was pensioned 4 Nov. 1794.

Morgan, William. Mass. Pvt. He served in Capt. John Baker's Company under Col. Israel Hutchinson. He was wounded on Long Island. He was pensioned at the rate of half-pay from 31 Dec. 1776 on 27 Jan. 1778.

Morgan, William. Mass. Mariner. He served aboard the *Warren* under E. Hinman. He was disabled by the blowing up of some cartridges at Penobscot. He received a musket ball in his right arm. He lived in Boston, Mass. in 1786 and was 30 years old.

Morgan, William. N.C. Pvt. & Sgt. He applied in Moore County in 1796. He was wounded at Stony Point. He sought relief in 1817, but the House did not approve his petition. His widow, Leah Morgan, lived in Brunswick County in 1820.

Morgan, William. Pa. Seaman. He was transferred to Virginia by 1797. He died 4 Sep. 1807. He was on the 1813 pension list.

Morgan, Zackquell. Va. Maj. He served in the Yohogania County militia. Gov. Jefferson commissioned him a colonel in 1781. He joined Col. George Rogers Clark. Congress rejected the claim submitted by Horatio Morgan for either half-pay for life or commutation on 26 Jan. 1835.

Morian, William. —. —. He served two and a half years and was wounded. He furnished no testimony to prove his statements co Congress rejected his claim 5 Mar. 1840.

Morrel, William. Pa. —. He was on the 1789 pension list.

Morrell, Joseph. N.H. Pvt. He served under Gen. Sullivan in 1776 and contracted smallpox and lost his sight on the retreat from Canada. He was aged 39 in 1787. He was from New Durham Gore. He residence was also given as Nottingham He also appeared as Joseph Morrill. He was on the 1813 pension list.

Morrell, Samuel. N.H. Pvt. He served under Col. Reed. He was wounded by a musket ball which entered his thigh and came out near his groin on 17 June 1775 at Bunker Hill. He lived in Candia, N.H. in 1794. He was in the militia. He was granted two-fifths of a pension 20 Apr. 1796. He was on the 1813 pension list. He died 7 Oct. 1834.

Morrill, Hibbard. N.H. Pvt. He lived at Northwood in 1778. He was in Capt. Nathan Sanborn's Company and was wounded on 7 Oct. 1777 at Stillwater by a ball passing through the trunk of his body.

Morrill, Samuel. Mass. Pvt. He served in the 8th Regiment and was from Amesbury. He was allowed $50. His widow was Elizabeth Morrill.

Morris, Ambrose. Va. —. His wife, Sarah Morris, was granted support in King William County in 1778.

Morris, Charles. Mass. —. He was wounded in the retreat from Quebec in 1776. His heirs received his pension at the rate of 20 shillings per month from 1 Jan. 1776 to his death on 8 Mar. 1785 on 4 July 1785.

Morris, Daniel. N.Y. Pvt. He was pensioned.

Morris, Daniel. Pa. —. He applied in Lycoming County 18 Mar. 1824. He served in the New Jersey infantry for seven months and in the militia.

Morris, George. Va. —. He entered the service in Louisa Co., Va. before he was 16 years old and served under Capt. James Watson. He guarded the Hessian prisoners at Albemarle Barracks for two or three months. His second tour was under Capt. James Cannady in 1780. He took sick near Petersburg. He rejoined the army and was in a skirmish below Richmond. He was at Green Springs under Col. John F. Mercer and was in the engagement at Sowell's Old Field near Gloucester. He served until the surrender of Cornwallis. Congress granted him a pension 5 Mar. 1840 and 8 Mar. 1842. He was from Orange Co., Va.

Morris, Jack. Va. —. His wife, Mary Morris, was granted £6 relief in Chesterfield Co., Va. on 7 Feb. 1778 while he was away in Continental service.

Morris, James. Pa. Lt. He served under Capt. Van Heer. Due to a severe fit of illness he resigned his commission in Nov. 1780. He never recovered his health. He was given a share of donation land. He resided in Philadelphia.

Morris, John. Md. —. He served in the 3rd Md. Regiment and was disabled by wounds received at the battle of Cowpens. He was pensioned in St. Mary's County in Apr. 1792 at half his monthly pay.

Morris, John. N.J. —. He served under Capt. McCarraher and Col. Deniston. He was wounded in his right shoulder at Wyoming and was unable to work for eighteen months. He sought relief 12 Oct. 1783 in Sussex County.

Morris, John. N.C. —. He was allowed £10 per annum. He was from Orange County.

Morris, John. Pa. —. He applied in Lancaster County on 22 Feb. 1808. He served in Capt. Mares' Company in the 4th Pa. Regiment under Col. William Butler to 1780. He enlisted again in Capt. Van Heer's Troop of Horse. He was awarded donation land. He was awarded a $40 gratuity and a $40 annuity on 2 Apr. 1811. He was on the 1813 pension list. On 21 June 1839 William Dawson and Edward Morris of Lancaster County, heirs at law of John Morris, deceased, were paid $200 for his tract of donation land.

Morris, John. Va. Pvt. He lived in Henrico County on 23 Feb. 1786. He served in the 1st Va. Regiment in Capt. Anderson's Company under Col. Hawes. He was wounded at Camden in his left shoulder and arm. He was 46 years old. He was on the 1813 pension list.

Morris, Jonathan. Md. Capt. He was pensioned at the rate of half-pay of captain in Washington Co., Pa. 2 Feb. 1830.

Morris, Joseph. N.J. Maj. He served under Col. Ogden in the artillery and was wounded in the head about 6 Dec. 1778 at Edgehill, Pa. and died 7 Jan. 1778. His widow was Hannah Morris who applied in Dec. 1779 in Morris Co., N.J. Joseph Morris married Mrs. Hannah Ford 12 Apr. 1759. She was granted a half-pay pension 21 Feb. 1791. His son, Jonathan F. Morris, died in 1810 and left children. The grandchildren, represented by William C. Morris, sought his seven years' half pay. Congress rejected their claim 7 Apr. 1860.

Morris, Joseph. S.C. —. He was granted $235.10 at the arrearage of his pension on 21 Dec.1804.

Morris, Lester. Va. —. He enlisted in 1775 for two years. He was attached to the Virginia Line on Continental Establishment. He was dropped from the pension roll because of his property value. He had a sickly wife, daughter, and a female slave worth $400. The value of his livestock was $77.50. Congress granted him a pension 22 Dec. 1831.

Morris, Richard G. Va. —. Congress rejected his petition for relief 29 Jan. 1822.

Morris, Thomas. Ga. Capt. He served in the artillery. He died of smallpox in Matthews Co., Va. in 1781. Congress gave his heirs seven years' half-pay 30 Jan. 1855.

Morris, William. Mass. Sgt. He served under Col. John Greaton and Capt. Joseph Williams. He was wounded in his right leg. He was pensioned 1 Sep. 1782. He was 30 years and resided in Dorchester, Mass. in 1786. He was 30 years old. He died 16 Jan. 1801.

Morris, William. Mass. —. He served in the 10th Regiment and was from Scituate. He was paid $20 on 29 May 1804.

Morris, William. N.J. —. He was born in Pennsylvania 15 July 1756 and moved to New Jersey about 1761. He was at Long Island, Trenton, and Monmouth. He served under Capt. Jonathan Phillips in the 2nd Regiment. His next tour was on the *Rambler* in privateer service. He was captured by the *Amphitrite* and carried to New York where he was confined on the prison ship *Jersey* for eighteen months. He was sent to Virginia and exchanged at Yorktown. He was nearing 76 when he applied 17 Mar. 1832.

Morris, William. Pa. Pvt. He was in Philadelphia 10 July 1786. He lost his leg by colds and hardships in 1776 when he was in militia service. He was 46 years old.

Morris, William. S.C. —. He was made a prisoner by the Tories and Indians and murdered. His widow, Eleanor Morris, was awarded an annuity 21 Apr. 1785.

Morrison, —. Pa. —. His widow, Elizabeth Morrison, was awarded a $40 gratuity and a $40 annuity in Cumberland County 21 Mar. 1837.

Morrison, —. Pa. —. His widow, Margaret Lowry Morrison, was awarded a $40 gratuity and a $40 annuity in Cumberland Co., Pa. 29 Mar. 1823. She died 27 Sep. 1823.

Morrison, —. Pa. —. His widow, Mary M. Morrison, received relief in Venango County 4 Apr. 1856.

Morrison, —. Va. —. He was killed in Continental service. His widow, Elizabeth Morrison, was paid £10 in Fauquier County in Nov. 1777 and £18 in Sep. 1779.

Morrison, —. Va. —. He died in the service. His widow, Lydia Morrison, was paid £12 in Fauquier County in Nov. 1777.

Morrison, Alexander. Pa. —. He was a wagoner under Capt. Samuel Hewitt in 1778. He was from Lancaster County.

Morrison, Alexander. N.C. Sgt. He applied in 1785. He was in Wayne and Cumberland Counties. He was in Continental service and was disabled at Eutaw Springs. He was aged 36 in 1785. He was on the 1813 pension list. His widow, Ann Morrison, applied in 1821 in Cumberland County. Nathaniel Greene signed his discharge papers.

Morrison, Daniel. Pa. —. He was awarded a $40 gratuity and a $40 annuity in Lancaster Co., Pa. 17 Mar. 1835.

Morrison, John. N.Y. Pvt. He volunteered in June 1780 and was discharged 13 Dec. He mustered at Westchester and was at West Point. Congress gave him a pension 11 Apr. 1850 even though his time of service fell short one or five days of the minimum six months. He was 84 years old and lived in New Hampshire.

Morrison, John. Pa. —. He was pensioned 27 Mar. 1821.

Morrison, Larkin. Pa. Pvt. He was in Philadelphia County on 14 Nov. 1785. He was transferred from the 5th Pa. Regiment to the Invalids. He was wounded in his right arm and was discharged 1 Nov. 1783. He was 47 years old.

Morrison, Samuel. Pa. —. He was pensioned in York County 3 Apr. 1837.

Morrison, William. Md. Pvt. He was pensioned in Charles County in 1780. He was wounded in his head and hand; he served under Col. John H. Stone. He died 31 Oct. 1806.

Morriss, William. S.C. —. He lived in Fairfield District in 1798. His application was rejected.

Morrow, Benjamin. S.C. —. His widow was Mary Morrow. There were children in 1791.

Morrow, David. S.C. Capt. He was at Purisburg, Black Swamp, Hook's defeat, and the taking of Congaree Fort. He lived in Chester District in 1826.

Morrow, James. S.C. —. He was killed by Indians. His widow, Esther Morrow, was awarded an annuity on 9 Feb. 1786. There was one child in 1791.

Morrow, John. S.C. —. He was killed 30 Nov. 1781. His widow, Mary Morrow, was granted an annuity 13 Aug. 1785. There was one child in 1791.

Morrow, Joseph. S.C. —. He was wounded in his right arm at Hanging Rock on 5 Aug. 1780. He was granted an annuity 17 Nov. 1786 in Chester. He was about 90 years old in 1828-29. He was paid as late as 1834.

Morrow, William. Pa. —. He was granted relief in Allegheny County 20 Mar. 1832.

Morse, Elijah. N.H. Pvt. He served under Col. Enoch Hale. He was afflicted with a nervous inflammatory disorder which deprived him of his reason for some time in consequence of wading the Battenkin River encumbered with floating ice in obedience to his commanding officer in Oct. 1777. He lived in New Ipswich, N.H. in 1794. Since he was not wounded, he was not covered by the law. He was pensioned at the rate of $4 per month from 6 Jan. 1808. He was on the 1813 pension list.

Morse, Jedediah. —. —. He served less than six months in Sullivan's expedition. Congress rejected his claim for a pension on 25 Jan. 1848 since he had but four months of service.

Morse, John. Mass. Sgt. He served in the 6th Mass. Regiment under Col. Thomas Nixon in Capt. Elijah Danforth's Company. He was disabled by a broken collar bone on his right shoulder. The fore and middle fingers of his right hand were injured. He was 43 years old in 1786.

Morse, Joseph. Mass. Corp. He was in the Invalids. He was disabled by the loss of his leg. He was pensioned 1 Sep. 1782. He died 26 June 1784.

Morse, Joseph. Mass. Pvt. He served under Col. Crane in Capt. Frearwill's Company. He was wounded in his body in Sep. 1777 at Brandywine. He lived in Fitzwilliam, N.H. in 1795. He enlisted 10 Apr. 1777, was a prisoner 1 July 1778, and was discharged Apr. 1780. He lived at Stoughton when he was paid $50 by the Commonwealth.

Morse, Obediah. Mass. Pvt. He served in the 2nd Regiment and was from Douglass. His widow, Joannah Morse, was paid $50.

Morse, Samuel. Mass. Soldier. He served in the 4th Regiment and was from Sherborn. He was allowed $50.

Morse, Seth. Me. —. He was from Paris. He was paid $50 under the resolve of 1836.

Mortimer, Benjamin. Conn. —. He served on the schooner, *Spy*, as second in command to carry the treaty of alliance between France and America. He was captured on the return voyage and confined in prison. He escaped and returned to America where he was employed in privateering. He was 70 years old, crippled, and destitute of property. Congress rejected his petition for a pension 2 Feb. 1820.

Morton, —. Va. Lt. He served on the schooner *Revenge* and was taken prisoner to New York. His wife, Sarah Morton, and her suckling child sought relief on 21 Nov. 1778.

Morton, Elisha. Mass. Pvt. He served in the 5th Regiment and was from Carver. His widow, Elizabeth Morton, was paid $50.

Morton, George. Pa. Pvt. His name may have been George Martin.

Morton, James. —. —. His widow was Abigail Morton. Their son, Robert Morton, for himself and the other heirs, sought the pension due her 31 Mar. 1856. Congress rejected the claim.

Morton, Thomas. N.C. —. He applied in Montgomery County in 1795. He served 18 months in the Continental Army under Capt. Thompson. He was wounded at the battle of Guilford Court House by a ball in his leg. He had a wife and three small children. He died 13 Nov. 1807.

Mosby, William. Va. Capt. He served in the 5th Regiment. After the battle of Monmouth, his unit was merged into the 1st and 9th Regiments. He returned home as supernumerary. He was appointed major and was at Camden and Yorktown. He did not resign. Congress refused commutation 2 May 1836 to the representatives.

Moscat, Robert. Pa. Rough Rider. He served in the 1st Troop of Philadelphia Light Horse. He was wounded by a fall from his horse. His horse fell on him and afterwards kicked him on 13 Jan. 1777 at Morristown. He lived in Philadelphia, Pa. in 1794.

Moseley, —. Va. Pvt. He died in Continental service in Oct. 1778. His widow, Elizabeth Moseley, was on the 1785 pension roll.

Moseley, George. Va. —. His wife, Martha Moseley, was granted £4 relief on 21 Aug. 1777 in Sussex Co., Va. while he was away in Continental service. He served in the 15th Virginia Regiment. She lived in Sussex Co., Va. on 16 Mar. 1786.

Moseley, Leonard. Va. —. He was wounded and disabled. He was being pensioned at the rate of £6 per annum on 1 Dec. 1785.

Moser, —. Pa. —. His widow, Elizabeth Moser, was awarded a $40 gratuity and a $40 annuity in Berks Co., Pa. 11 Mar. 1833.

Moser, John. Pa. —. He served in the Flying Camp from Northampton County. He was awarded a $40 gratuity and a $40 annuity in Butler Co., Pa. 31 Jan. 1832. He was 85 years old in 1840.

Mosher, —. Pa. —. His widow, Susan Mosher, of Lancaster County was granted relief 6 Apr. 1833.

Mosher, Jeremiah. Pa. —. His widow, Sarah Mosher, was awarded a $40 gratuity 4 May 1832 in Lancaster, Pa. and a $40 gratuity and $40 annuity 6 Apr. 1833.

Mosher, John. N.Y. Pvt. He served in Capt. Jonathan Purdy's Company in Col. Thomas Thomas's Regiment. William Mosher was lieutenant. He was wounded by a musket ball through the elbow of his left arm through his left side and breast in action near North Castle on 27 Apr. 1781. He lived in Westchester Co., N.Y. and was a shoemaker when he was pensioned. He was on the 1813 pension list.

Mosley, Joseph. Va. —. He was in Continental service. His wife was furnished support in Goochland Co., Va. on 21 July 1777.

Moss, Joseph. N.H. Pvt. He served under Col. Crane. He was granted two-thirds of a pension 20 Apr. 1796. He was on the 1813 pension list.

Moss, Simeon. —. Sgt. He served one year. Congress granted him a pension 22 Dec. 1837.

Moss, Sylvanus. Pa. —. He was granted relief.

Mosser, George. Pa. —. He was pensioned by the act of 11 Mar. 1815. He was from Lehigh Co. He died 19 -?- 1826.

Most, John. Pa. Pvt. He was on the 1813 pension list.

Motes, John. S.C. —. He served under Gen. Williamson in the Florida Expedition against the British, Cherokees, and Creeks. He was discharged at Augusta. In 1779 he and his father removed to Georgia and served under Capt. Beacom. He was discharged at Ebenezer. He was plowing his field when Gabe Davis, a Tory, and a party of Indians attacked. He was wounded in his shoulder and twice in his body. He could not walk for three months. He was 60 years old. He was from

Laurens District in 1822. Richard North deposed that Motes was brought to his father's house in Georgia badly wounded. Sarah North stated Motes was brought to her husband's home on a horse litter. She nursed him several months. His application was rejected.

Mothershead, Francis. S.C. —. He was from Camden District when he was pensioned 7 Dec. 1824. He was paid as late as 1826.

Motlow, —. S.C. —. His widow was Elizabeth Motlow. There was one child in 1791.

Motlow, —. S.C. —. His widow, Mary Motlow, was on the roll in 1791.

Motlow, Malachi. —. —. He was killed by the Cherokee in 1782. His daughter, Polly Ann Motlow, married Samuel Douthit. They sought relief for the loss of one Negro named Cyrus, five horses, and household furniture. Congress declined their request in 1818.

Mott, Thomas. N.Y. —. He served in the 3rd Regiment. His heirs sought bounty land. Congress rejected their claim on 22 Feb. 1843 because there was no proof of service.

Motte, Ebenezer. N.Y. —. He was granted relief.

Motte, Charles. S.C. Maj. He served in the 2nd S.C. Regiment on Continental Establishment and was killed on the lines at Savannah on 9 Oct. 1779. His widow remarried. His two orphan children sought his seven years' half-pay in 1791.

Mountjoy, John. —. Capt. He was issued bounty land warrant #2491 for 300 acres on 21 Feb. 1800.

Mountjoy, William. Va. Capt. He served in the 3rd Regiment and was brigade Quartermaster to Gen. Woodford's Regiment. He received bounty land for three years' service. Congress did not grant his heirs commutation since he did not serve to the end of the war on 10 May 1838.

Mounts, Richard. Va. —. His widow, Sarah Mounts, was granted £7 support on 7 Apr. 1778. On 5 Oct. 1779 she and her three children were granted £80 support for the last year and £7 for the remainder of the year. She was granted a pension in Frederick County 2 Nov. 1779.

Mounts, Thomas. —. —. He received his commutation.

Mour, George. N.Y. Pvt. He served under Col. Vischer. He was wounded in both shoulders in action with the Indians on 7 Aug. 1777 at Oriskie. He lived in Mohawk, N.Y. in 1794.

Mourning, Christopher. N.C. Pvt. He applied in Anson County in 1805. He served in the Anson County militia under Col. Thomas Wade. He was wounded in his right elbow and taken prisoner. William Nichols served with him in the same company. He lived in Pitt County in 1807. He was on the 1813 pension list. He also appeared as Christopher Moreing.

Mousher, John. N.Y. Pvt. He served under Lt. William Mousher under Col. Thomas Thomas. He was disabled at North Castle by a musket ball through the elbow of his left arm, left side, and breast. He lived in Bedford, Westchester Co., N.Y. on 29 Apr. 1789. He was a shoemaker and was aged 33 years on 6 Apr. 1788. He also appeared as John Mosher. He was on the 1813 pension list.

Mowris, Daniel. N.Y. Pvt. He was wounded by a musket ball in both thighs and in his scrotum at the battle of White Plains on 28 Oct. 1776. He served under Col. Rudolph Ritzma in Capt. Hardenbergh's Company in the 3rd N.Y. Regiment. Edward Lounsbery was lieutenant. He was 34 years old on 14 Feb. 1787. He was pensioned 27 June 1787. He lived in Ulster Co., N.Y. in July 1787 and later in Tompkins County. He was on the 1813 pension list.

Mowris, Samuel. N.Y. Pvt. He served in the 3rd N.Y. Regiment of militia under Col. Rudolphus Ritzma. He was wounded by a musket ball through his scrotum and both thighs. He lived in Marbletown, Ulster Co., N.Y. on 16 June 1789.

Mowry, John. R.I. Pvt. He was wounded in his left side and right arm at Paramus, N.J. on 12 Apr. 1780. He served under Col. Henry Sherburne. He was aged 23 in 1786. He died 2 Aug. 1816 in Providence Co., R.I. He was on the 1813 pension list.

Moxley, Joseph. Conn. Pvt. He served in the 2nd Company of the 8th Conn. Militia. He was wounded at Fort Griswold on 6 Sep. 1781 by a bayonet in his side and arm. He served under Capt. William Latham in the Artillery. He was pensioned 2 Dec. 1788 at Groton, Conn. at the age of 26. He was on the 1813 pension list. He died 10 Nov. 1815 in New London Co., Conn.

Moyer, —. Pa. —. His widow, Barbara Moyer, was awarded a $40 gratuity and a $40 annuity in Philadelphia Co., Pa. 14 Apr. 1834.

Moyer, Jacob. Pa. —. He was in Dauphin County 27 July 1824. He served one year in Capt. James Taylor's Company of the 4th Battalion and Regiment under Col. Anthony Wayne. He was 73 years old. He died 9 Nov. 1825 in York County.

Moyer, Jacob. N.Y. Pvt. He served under Col. Peter Bellinger in the Montgomery County militia and was slain 6 Aug. 1777. His children, Ludwick Moyer, Henry Moyer, Barbara Moyer, Elizabeth Moyer, Juliana Moyer, and Margaret Moyer, received his half-pay pension.

Moyer, Jacob. N.Y. Lt. He served under Col. Jacob Klock in the Montgomery County militia and was slain 25 Oct. 1781. His widow, Margaret Moyer, received a half–pay pension.

Moyer, John. N.Y. Pvt. He served under Col. Peter Bellinger in the Montgomery County militia and was slain 16 Sep. 1778. His widow received a half-pay pension. She was Grace Moyer. [The text was very faint.]

Moyer, Leonard. Pa. —. He received a $40 gratuity and a $40 annuity in Schuylkill County 12 Mar. 1836. He also appeared as Leonard Mayer.

Moyer, Martin. Pa. —. His widow, Mary Moyer, was awarded a $40 gratuity and a $40 annuity in York Co., Pa. 14 Apr. 1828. It was to be paid to her trustee, Jacob B. Wentz. She died 27 June 1830.

Moyer, Nicholas. Pa. —. He was awarded a $40 gratuity in Union Co., Pa. 20 Apr. 1829.

Moylan, Stephen. —. Brig. Gen. He was colonel of horse until 3 Nov. 1783. Congress did not grant his heirs commutation 24 Mar. 1836. Congress awarded them five years' full pay as a colonel 16 Apr. 1860.

Muck, Jacob. Pa. —. He was pensioned 21 Mar. 1837 in Union County. He died 30 Mar. 1851.

Mudd, —. Md. Sgt. His widow, Barbara Mudd, was paid a pension 1 Feb. 1834.

Mudd, Bennett. Md. Sgt. He was pensioned in Charles County at the rate of half-pay of a sergeant 19 Feb. 1819. His widow, Ann Mudd, was paid his arrearage of $24.17 in Feb. 1835. She was pensioned at the same rate 4 June 1836.

Mudd, Henry. Va. —. He was slain in the war. Congress declined any bounty land for Barbara Mudd and others because no proof had been found on 8 Feb. 1836.

Mudd, Jeremiah. Md. Sgt. He was pensioned in Charles County in 1783. He lost his left arm. He served under Col. John Gunby. He was on the 1813 pension list. He died 10 July 1815. His widow, Barbara Mudd, was pensioned at the rate of half-pay of a sergeant 1 Feb. 1834 in the District of Columbia. She received 100 acres of bounty land 8 Feb. 1836. She died while her application pending. Congress granted her only surviving child, Mary McCurdy, relief 25 Apr. 1840.

Muffli, John. Pa. —. He was awarded a $40 gratuity in Northampton Co., Pa. 6 Apr. 1833.

Muffley, John. Pa. —. He was awarded a $40 gratuity in Northampton Co., Pa. 1 Apr. 1834.

Mugford, John. Me. —. He was from Windham. He was paid $50 under the resolve of 1836.

Muir, Thomas. Md. Pvt. He was pensioned at the rate of half-pay of a private in Somerset County on 2 Feb. 1832. His arrearage of $9.66 was paid to Levin Ballard to be distributed to the nearest kin on 24 Jan. 1839.

Mulady, Robert. —. —. He lived in Georgia when he applied. His application was referred to the whole House.

Mulford, —. N.J. ---. He served in the 2nd Jersey Regiment. He enlisted 16 Nov. 1781 and died in Mar. 1783. His widow, Margaret Mulford, sought assistance. She had one child to maintain on 9 Dec. 1783.

Mulford, David. N.J. Lt. He served in the Cumberland County militia. His orphan was Enoch Mulford.

Mulhollen, Hugh. Pa. Sgt. He applied in Huntingdon County on 15 Feb. 1813. He entered the service in Mar. 1776 in Col. Samuel Miles' 1st Battalion of Riflemen for 1 year and nine months. He went to Long Island where he was wounded in the knee in 1776. He served three years. He served with Michael Fink in a grenadier company under Capt. Bankson and was discharged at Trenton. Henry Beal was also in the same regiment until being discharged in 1781. Mulhollen was in the battles of Trenton, Princeton, Brandwyine, Germantown, Mud Island Fort, Monmouth, Green Springs, and Yorktown. He was in the south with Gen. Greene. He was wounded four times. He had a running sore on his leg and resided with G. P. W. Butler. Joseph Findley of York County was his captain. He was discharged after seven years and eight months of service.

Mullen, —. N.C. —. His widow, Mary Mullen, applied in 1782 and had two children. He was killed at the battle of Stono. She was from Richmond County. Her eldest son was wounded in Col. Wade's defeat and could not walk except on crutches.

Mullen, Michael. Pa. —. He was wounded at Monmouth. He was in Indiana County and was awarded a $40 gratuity and a $40 annuity on 6 Feb. 1810.

Mullen, William. Pa. —. He received a $40 gratuity and a $40 annuity in Philadelphia County 1 Apr. 1836. The act was amended to grant him a $80 gratuity and a $40 annuity in Montgomery County 3 Mar. 1837.

Muller, Albert A. S.C. Aide-de-Camp. He served under Gen. Francis Marion. His only son and heir sought bounty land. Congress ruled that his was a stale demand because his father was not in the Continental army but in the militia and rejected it 20 Jan. 1848.

Muller, Jeremiah C. N.Y. Capt. He served under Col. Henry K. Van Renssalear in Gen. Robert Van Renssalear's Brigade of militia. He was disabled by a musket ball in his right shoulder in an engagement in Montgomery County on 19 Oct. 1780. He was aged 63 in 1786. He lived in Claversack, Columbia Co., N.Y. on 18 Apr. 1789. He also appeared as Jeremiah Miller. He died 15 Mar. 1811.

Mullet, George. N.J. Pvt. He was a native of New Jersey. He was in Philadelphia 6 Oct. 1788. He served in Capt. John Combs' Company in Col. David Forman's Regiment in the American Continental Army. He enlisted 20 May 1777 for one year. He received his pension of 25 shillings per month in New Jersey from 1785 until 1 Feb. 1788 when he moved from Hunterdon County to Pennsylvania. He was wounded in Germantown. He was inoculated for smallpox and lost the sight of his right eye. He was later wounded in his left eye. He was in the Invalids under Capt. James McClean. He was also on the pension roll of Pennsylvania after moving to that state. He was 47 years old. He was dead by Mar. 1790.

Mullin, John. Va. —. The father of the veteran, John Mullin, Sr., was caring for the son of the veteran. Each one was named John Mullin. He was paid £50 on 11 May 1780 in Caroline County. The father of the veteran was also furnished assistance on 9 Apr. 1778 while his son was away in the service.

Mullin, William. Pa. —. He was awarded a $40 gratuity and a $40 annuity in Philadelphia County

1 Apr. 1836.

Mullings, James. Va. Sgt. He was born 7 Nov. 1751 in King William Co., Va. and moved to Charlotte County when young. He served firstly seven or eight months, three months under Capt. Thomas Williams in 1776, and three months under Capt. Joseph French as a drafted militia in June 1779. In Jan. or Feb. 1781 he was drafted and stationed six weeks at Coles' ferry. In Apr. 1781 he was under Capt. Jameson for three months and was discharged by Lt. George Hallway. Congress granted him a pension 4 Feb. 1836. He was 84 years old.

Mulliwee, John. N.C. —. He served several tours under Gen. Rutherford, Col. Mebane, Col. George Alexander, Gen. Sumner, Gen. Irwin, Maj. Thomas Harris, and Col. Davie. He was from Mecklenburg County. He was 84 years old in 1827.

Mumford, Augustus. R.I. Adjutant. He was killed 27 Aug. 1775 by a cannon ball at Boston. His heirs were paid his seven years' half-pay of $756.

Mumford, John. S.C. Capt. He was killed in 1780. His widow, Patience Mumford, was awarded an annuity 26 Jan. 1786.

Mumford, William Green. —. Deputy Commissary General of Issues. Congress appointed him on 18 June 1777. He served to the end of the war. Congress rejected the claim of his heirs 25 June 1834 because his service was not covered by law.

Mummy, Jacob. Pa. —. He was awarded a $40 gratuity and a $40 annuity 28 Mar. 1820 in Northampton County.

Mun, Caleb. Mass. Sgt. He served in the 4th Regiment and was paid $20.

Muncey, John. N.Y. Lt. He served in the Albany County militia under Col. H. B. Whiting. He was killed at Moses kill 2 Aug. 1777. His widow, Mary Muncey, received a half-pay pension.

Munchester, Gershom. —. —. He served for three months and sought a pension. Congress denied his claim 3 Mar. 1851.

Munday, —. Va. —. His mother, Sarah Munday, was granted £20 in York Co., Va. 15 Feb. 1779.

Munday, William. Lt. —. He served under Col. Philip Van Cortlandt. He was badly wounded in one of his legs in action with the British under Gen. Burgoyne. At Yorktown he was arrested on the charge of disobedience, tried, and his commission broken. He lived in Maryland when he applied 16 Dec. 1806. His application was not accepted. He was dismissed by a general court martial after nearly five years of service. Congress granted his widow, Leah Munday, a pension 10 July 1840.

Mundin, John. N.Y. Sgt. He was in Col. James Livingston's Regiment. He was wounded in the small of his back by a splinter hurled against him by a cannon ball in Oct. 1777 at Saratoga. He was transferred to Capt. T. Wells' Company in Col. Philip Van Cortland's Regiment. He also had rheumatism. He lived in Catskill, Albany Co., N.Y. on 26 May 1789. He was aged 59 in 1786. He also appeared as John Mendon and John Munden.

Mundy, Levi. N.J. —. He was pensioned in Middlesex County on 12 Feb. 1851 at the rate of $60 per annum.

Muninger, —. Pa. His widow, Elizabeth Muninger, received a $40 gratuity and a $40 annuity in Franklin County 3 Mar. 1837. She was dead by Feb. 1839.

Munn, Asa. Mass. Pvt. He served in Capt. Timothy Child's Company under Col. Learned and lost his right leg. He was pensioned at the rate of half-pay from 5 Apr. 1777 on 20 Jan. 1779. He was 27 years old in 1786.

Munn, David. N.J. Pvt. He served in the militia for two years. He entered the service in 1776 and served three months under Capt. John Peck in Newark and Elizabethtown. He was pensioned in 1832 and suspended in 1835. He applied to Congress 19 Jan. 1843.

Munn, Justus. Conn. Pvt. He served in Col. Sheldon's Regiment. He was wounded in his left testicle while on duty in Aug. 1780 at Ridgefield. He resided at Saybrook, Conn. in 1796. He enlisted in Apr. 1777, was promoted to corporal 1 Dec. 1778, and reduced to private 22 Oct. 1781. He was granted half a pension 20 Apr. 1796. He died 27 Jan. 1807.

Munnerlyn, Loftis R. S.C. —. He served under Col. Baxter. He was from Marion District in 1826. He was paid as late as 1839. One of his annual payments was sent to Thomas Munnerlyn.

Munroe, Andrew. Mass. —. His widow, Ruth Munroe, was from Haverhill and was paid $50.

Munroe, Henry. Mass. Corp. He served in the 2nd Regiment and was from Hanson. He was paid $50.

Munroe, Hugh. Me. —. He died 22 June 1832. His widow was Naomi Munroe from Thomaston. He was paid $50 under the resolve of 1836.

Munroe, Isaac. Mass. —. He served in Baldwin's Artificers and was from Lincoln. He was paid $50.

Munroe, Josiah. N.H. Lt. He served in Col. Cilley's Regiment. His spouse, Susanna Monroe, sought his depreciation pay of $560 on 25 Feb. 1779. He was from Amherst.

Munroe, William. Mass. —. He was from Lexington and was paid $50.

Munsell, Elisha. Mass. Pvt. He served under Col. Marshall in Capt. Smith's Company. He was wounded by a ball which passed through his wrist in July or Aug. 1777 at Saratoga. He lived in Pelham, Mass. in 1795. He enlisted 2 Jan. 1777 for the war. He was on the rolls in 1780. Since his disability did not proceed from known wounds, his claim was not allowed. He was granted half a pension 20 Apr. 1796. He was on the 1813 pension list.

Munson, Josiah. N.J. —. His widow, Merriam Munson, was pensioned in Morris County on 11 Feb. 1847 at the rate of $30 per annum.

Murch, Ebenezer. —. Lt. He died in 1824. Betsey Murch and Ebenezer Murch sought relief from Congress 11 July 1856 but were not successful.

Murdock, Benjamin. Md. Lt. He was pensioned in 1817.

Murdock, John. Va. —. He died in Oct. 1778. He served in the 15th Virginia Regiment. His widow, Martha Murdock, was granted support in Brunswick County on 23 Nov. 1778, 22 Feb. 1779, and 23 Jan. 1781. She was on the 1785 pension roll. She was in Greensville County in 1786. The orphans were Abraham Murdock, John Murdock, Phoebe Murdock, and Sarah Murdock.

Murdock, Mathew. Pa. —. He was awarded a $40 gratuity and a $40 annuity in Washington County 12 Mar. 1836. He was 84 years old in 1840.

Murdock, Samuel. Pa. —. He applied in Greene County on 21 Sep. 1819. He enlisted 11 Aug. 1776 in Capt. Samuel Miller's Company under Col. McCoy and Col. Wilson. He was taken prisoner in 1777 at Bound Brook in N.J. where he had been wounded. He was carried to New York and detained two years and two months. He made his escape. He made his way back to Gen. Washington and was given $20. His enlistment had expired so he was given a pass to go home. He enlisted in Col. Broadhead's Regiment for service in the western country. He was 77 [or 70?] years old.

Murdock, Swanzey. Mass. Pvt. He served in the 5th Regiment. His widow, Deliverance Pierce of Plymouth, was paid $50.

Murdock, William. Md. Lt. He was pensioned at the rate of half-pay of a lieutenant 6 Feb. 1817. His widow, Jane Clagett, was pensioned at the same rate on 4 Mar. 1834.

Murphy, —. Pa. —. His widow, Barbara Murphy, was awarded a $40 gratuity and a $40 annuity in York County 6 Apr. 1833.

Murphy, —. Va. —. He and his brother were in Continental service. Their mother, Margaret Murphy, was furnished £5 support in Shenandoah Co., Va. on 28 May 1778.

Murphy, —. S.C. —. Mary Murphy had two husbands killed in the service. She applied on 23 Feb. 1784.

Murphy, Barney. Pa. Pvt. He served in the 9th and 5th Pa. Regiments. He was wounded at the battle of Monmouth on 28 June 1778 in the elbow of his right arm from the splinter of a carriage of a piece of artillery. He lived in Dauphin Co., Pa. in 1794. He enlisted 8 Apr. 1778. He died 10 June 1799.

Murphy, Charles. Va. —. His wife, Elizabeth Murphy, and three children were furnished 4 barrels of corn and 200 pounds of pork in Frederick Co., Va. on 7 Aug. 1781.

Murphy, Henderson. Pa. Pvt. He was in the militia and served under Capt. John Boyd. His widow was in Bedford County on 14 Aug. 1787. He was killed in an engagement with the Indians near Frankstown on 3 June 1781. He left a widow, Sarah Murphy, and seven children all under the age of 14. His daughter, Margaret Murphy, was under the age of 14 and was under the guardianship of George Smith in 1795. Sarah Murphy married (2) ----- Burns

Murphy, Henry. N.Y. Pvt. He served in Capt. Sipes's Company under Col. Samuel Clyde. He was wounded in his left right arm in the battle of Johnstown on 25 Oct. 1781. He was 21 years when he was pensioned 22 Oct. 1786. He lived in Montgomery Co., N.Y. 15 June 1789 and later in Herkimer County. He was on the 1813 pension list.

Murphy, Henry. Pa. Pvt. He served in the militia under Capt. John Boyd and was killed in action with the Indians near Frankstown 3 June 1781. His heirs were from Bedford County.

Murphy, James. Del. Sgt. He was pensioned in 1784. He was disabled by fatigues and hardships of war. He had a family and lived in Wilmington, Del. He was on the 1813 pension list.

Murphy, James. Md. Pvt. He was pensioned in Montgomery County in 1781. He lost a leg at Long Island on 27 Aug. 1776. He lived in Queen Anne's County on 22 June 1790.

Murphy, James. Pa. —. He was awarded a $40 gratuity and a $40 annuity in Warren Co., Ohio 20 Mar. 1827. He died 15 Nov. 1839.

Murphy, James. Va. Pvt. He served in the 6th Va. Regiment. He lived in Montgomery County in 1786 and was 32 years old. He later lived in Wythe County. He may be identical with the James Murphey who lost his right arm at Col. Buford's defeat and who was awarded a £500 gratuity and a full set of clothes on 15 Nov. 1780. He was on the 1813 pension list.

Murphy, John. —. —. He resided in Cayuga Co., N.Y. and sought restoration to his pension. Congress rejected his petition 14 Mar. 1846.

Murphy, John. Pa. —. He was awarded relief in Perry County 14 Mar. 1835. He was 81 years old in 1840. He died 22 Dec. 1843.

Murphy, John. Pa. —. He was awarded a $40 gratuity in Bucks County in 1814. He was awarded a $40 gratuity and a $40 annuity on 14 Mar. 1818.

Murphy, John. Pa. —. He was awarded a $40 gratuity in Baltimore Co., Md. 15 Apr. 1834.

Murphy, John. Pa. —. He was awarded a $40 annuity in Allegheny County 5 Feb. 1836.

Murphy, Martin. Va. Sgt. He lived in Spotsylvania County on 4 Apr. 1787. He enlisted in 1776 under Capt. Thomas West of Loudoun County. He acted as sergeant at the Waxsaws under Capt. Thomas Howard under Col. Buford. He received four wounds on his head, three of which nearly went through his skull. He was in the 11th Va. Regiment. He was 30 years old in 1786. His pension was continued at the rate of £18 per annum on 1 May 1786. It was continued at the same rate on 26 Sep. 1789. He was in Henrico County in Aug. 1788 and later in Wythe

County. He was on the 1813 pension list.

Murphy, Nicholas. —. —. His application was referred to the Secretary of War.

Murphy, William. Pa. —. His widow, Elizabeth Murphy, was awarded a $40 gratuity on 14 Apr. 1828 in Perry County.

Murphy, William. Pa. Pvt. He was on the 1813 pension list.

Murray, Francis. Pa. Lt. Col. He served in the 13th Penn. Regiment. He was deranged 1 Jan. 1781. His application was rejected 14 Sep. 1784. In 1793 he sought five years' full pay in lieu of half-pay for life.

Murray, James. Md. Pvt. He enlisted under Capt. Johnson in the 5th Regiment on 2 June 1778 for the war. He was killed at Camden. Nicholas Murray and the other heirs sought his back pay of $200 and bounty land. Congress rejected their claim because the evidence was too weak to allow on 12 Feb. 1841.

Murray, John. Md. Pvt. He was pensioned 4 Mar. 1789.

Murray, John. Pa. Pvt. He was on the 1813 pension list. He lived in Chester County.

Murray, Joseph. S.C. —. He was wounded at Hanging Rock. He was granted an annuity 25 Oct. 1784.

Murray, Reuben. Va. Sgt. He was drafted in 1781 and served under Capt. Morehead, Col. Churchill, and later Col. Dabney. In the fall he was drafted again and served under Col. Elias Edwards. He was at Yorktown. He was 76 years old. Congress granted him a pension for six months of service on 23 May 1838 and on 5 Mar. 1840.

Murray, Richard. Va. Pvt. He was awarded a £500 gratuity on 25 Nov. 1780. He resided in Westmoreland County on 30 Aug. 1786 and was 30 years old. He served in the 2nd Va. Regiment under Col. Richard Parker. He was wounded thrice at Col. Buford's defeat. He received a severe cut on his left wrist and head. He was on the 1813 pension list as Richard Munay [sic].

Murray, William. Pa. Corp. He was in Philadelphia County on 13 Feb. 1786. He served in the 1st Pa. Regiment in Capt. William McClellan's Company and was wounded in the left arm in an out piquet on Long Island on 27 Aug. 1776. He was wounded again in his ankle at Green Springs, Va. He was 28 years old. He died 23 Oct. 1824.

Murry, —. Pa. —. His widow, Jemima Murry, was awarded a $40 gratuity and a $40 annuity in Montgomery Co., Pa. 17 Mar. 1835. She also appeared as Jemima Murray. She died 13 May 1844.

Murry, Alexander. Mass. Pvt. He served in the 4th Regiment in Capt. Leonard's Company under Col. Henry Jackson. He was disabled by the loss of three fingers on his left hand. He was 45 years old in 1786. He was pensioned 7 Nov. 1786. He was on the 1813 pension list. He later transferred to New Hampshire. He also appeared as Alexander Murray.

Murry, Gabriel. Va. —. His widow, Sarah Murry, and two children were furnished 3 barrels of corn and 150 pounds of pork in Louisa Co., Va. on 11 Aug. 1780.

Murry, Joseph. N.J. Pvt. He served under Col. Asher Holmes and Lt. Garret Hendrickson in the Monmouth County militia. On a return home to visit his family, he was killed by three refugees near his barn 8 June 1780. He was shot and bayoneted. He married Rebeckah Morris. He left four children. His widow received a half-pay pension in July 1778.

Murtz, Conrad. Pa. —. He was granted relief. [The initial letter of his surname is uncertain.]

Musgrove, James. Va. Pvt. His wife, Sarah Musgrove, was granted £6 on 15 June 1778, £10 on 15 Feb. 1779, £20 on 21 June 1779, £12 on 21 Feb. 1780, and £80 on 18 Sep. 1780 in York County. He was dead before 18 Sep. 1780. His son, William Musgrove, was in York County on 26 Oct.

1786 and was put on the pension list at the rate of £6 per annum. James Musgrove died in Continental service. He was a native of Va. His orphan was in the care of Pinkethman Musgrove and was 12 years old. His pension was increased to £10 per annum on 27 Aug. 1791. The son had a sore leg on 17 Oct. 1796.

Mush, —. Va. Pvt. His widow, Sarah Mush, was awarded a £12 gratuity in King William Co., Va. on 6 Nov. 1779.

Musketnuss, —. Pa. —. His widow, Catharine Musketnuss, was awarded a $40 gratuity and a $40 annuity in Lancaster Co., Pa. 19 Jan. 1825.

Musketnuss, Adam. Pa. —. He died 1 Apr. 1821.

Musney, Jacob. Pa. Lt. He served in the Flying Camp. He was from Lehigh County.

Musteen, William. Va. —. His wife, Jane Musteen, was granted £7.8 support in Henry Co., Va. 19 Jan. 1778 while he was absent in the service.

Mutcheson, John. —. —. He presented no proof whatsoever. Congress rejected his claim for a pension 9 Feb. 1848.

Muzzy, Amos. —. —. He served in the Continental Army and moved to Vermont in 1787. He had a wife and six small children when he sought to be released from imprisonment for debt in Halifax, Windham Co., Vt. 3 Oct. 1794.

Myer, John. S.C. —. There were children in 1791.

Myers, —. Pa. —. His widow, Mary Myers, was awarded a $40 gratuity and a $40 annuity in Philadelphia County 31 Mar. 1836. She was dead by June 1839.

Myers, —. Pa. —. His widow, Margaret Myers, was awarded a $40 gratuity and a $40 annuity in Philadelphia Co., Pa. 23 Apr. 1829.

Myers, —. Pa. —. His widow, Barbara Myers, was awarded a $40 gratuity in York County 5 May 1841 for his Revolutionary service.

Myers, Henry. Va. —. His wife, Mary Myers, was granted 200 pounds of pork and 8 bushels of corn for her support and her three children in Berkeley County on 15 May 1781.

Myers, Jacob. Pa. Soldier. He was from Adams County in 1812.

Myers, John. —. —. His widow, Elizabeth Myers, had her petition for a pension by a special act of Congress rejected 4 May 1846 because she married subsequent to 1 Jan. 1794.

Myers, John. Pa. —. He was awarded a $40 gratuity 7 Apr. 1832 and on 14 Apr. 1834 in Perry Co., Pa.

Myers, John. Pa. —. He was awarded a $40 gratuity and a $40 annuity in York Co., Pa. 6 Apr. 1833. He was paid to Dec. 1837.

Myers, Lewis. Pa. Marine. He was in Philadelphia County on 9 Jan. 1786. He served aboard the galley *Hancock* where he was disabled by a cannon ball in the Delaware River in Nov. 1777. He was 39 years old. He also appeared as Lewis Meyers. He died 17 Mar. 1809.

Myers, Michael. N.Y. Sgt. He served in the Tryon County militia under Col. Visher and was wounded at Johnstown on 25 Oct. 1781 by a musket ball in his right thigh. He was on the 1813 pension list.

Myers, Peter. Pa. —. He was awarded a $40 gratuity and a $40 annuity in York Co., Pa. 21 Mar. 1833.

Myler, —. —. He was taken prisoner at Fort Washington and died about a month afterwards in captivity. His widow, Catharine Myler, had seven children and was very poor. Since he served in the militia, the claim was not covered by law.

Myler, William. Pa. —. His widow, Mary Myler, was awarded a $40 gratuity in Westmoreland Co. 4 May 1832.

Nadeau, Basil. —. —. He enlisted in Nov. 1776 and served under Col. Moses Hazen and Capt. Oliver. He received 200 acres of bounty land by special act of the New York legislature. He was 67 years old in 1819 and 72 years old in 1820. He was at Staten Island, Germantown, Brandywine, Brunswick, and Yorktown. He died 11 July 1841. His only living child, Francis Nadeau, of Mooers, Clinton Co., N.Y. sought his $80 reward. Francis Nadeau was 53 years old in 1852. Congress ruled that there was no claim 10 Dec. 1857.

Nagel, Philip. Pa. —. He applied in Franklin Co. 6 Feb. 1815. He was 60 years old. He knew Thomas Sullivan served under Col. Atlee in 1777 for one year. *Vide* Philip Nagle.

Nagerman, —. Pa. —. His widow was Eleanor Nagerman.

Nagle, —. Pa. —. His widow, Mary Nagle, was awarded a $40 gratuity and a $40 annuity in Lancaster Co., Pa. 19 Jan. 1827. She died 22 Sep. 1832.

Nagle, Frederick. Pa. —. He was awarded a $40 gratuity in Berks Co., Pa. 23 Apr. 1829. He was awarded a $40 gratuity and a $40 annuity in Berks Co., Pa. 8 Apr. 1833. He was paid to 11 Nov. 1834.

Nagle, Jacob. Pa. —. He was awarded a $40 gratuity and a $40 annuity 27 Mar. 1837 in Lancaster County. He died 3 Jan. 1842.

Nagle, Michael. Pa. —. His widow was Mary Nagle. She was from York County 11 Apr. 1825. She died 9 July 1825.

Nagle, Peter. —. —. His application was referred to the Secretary of War.

Nagle, Philip. Pa. —. He was pensioned 23 Feb. 1819 in Franklin County. *Vide* Philip Nagel.

Nagle, Richard. Md. Pvt. He received a $40 gratuity in Cambria County, Pa. 25 Jan. 1828. He was pensioned at the rate of half-pay of a private 14 Feb. 1828.

Nail, Nicholas. Pa. Pvt. He was in Philadelphia County on 29 Sep. 1787. He was in the 1st Pa. Regiment and was wounded at Brandywine in Sept. 1777 in his right hand. He lost the tips of two of his fingers. His wife was Elizabeth Nail. He also appeared as Nicholas Naille. He was a tailor.

Nailor, James. Ga. —. He was on the 1796 list.

Napp, Joshua. Pa. —. He was awarded a $40 gratuity and a $40 annuity in Columbiana Co., Ohio 2 Apr. 1831.

Narcross, John. Pa. Pvt. He served in Potter's Regiment. He was pensioned 17 Sep. 1780. He died 3 Aug. 1825 in Greene Co., N.Y.

Nash, Ebenezer. —. —. His application was laid on the table.

Nash, Francis. N.C. Brigadier General. An application in behalf of his child was made in 1786 in Brunswick County who was late of Orange County. He died at Germantown 4 Oct. 1777. His daughter, Sarah Nash, was his heiress. His seven years' half-pay was due to his legal representative 30 June 1834.

Nash, Joseph. —. —. His application was referred to the Secretary of War.

Nash, Michael. S.C. —. He was wounded in his head at Charleston and made a prisoner. He was from Richland District in 1806. He sought an increase in his annuity and was pensioned at the rate of $60 per annum from 17 Dec. 1816 on 2 Dec. 1819. He lived in North Carolina at that time. Daniel Doyley stated that Nash was in his company. He was paid as late as 1832.

Nash, Timothy. Mass. Bombardier. He served in Revere's Artillery and was from Weymouth. He was paid $50.

Nau, William. Va. —. He died in Continental service. His widow and children were granted £6 per month support in Yohogania Co., Va. 28 Apr. 1778.

Naugle, Christian. Pa. Corp. He was in Philadelphia County on 13 Feb. 1786. He served in the 10th Pa.

Regiment in Capt. Stake's Company. He was wounded in his left arm in the attack on Block House on the North River. He was 25 years old. He also appeared as Christian Nagle.

Naught, —. Va. —. His wife, Elizabeth Naught, was granted £15 support in Caroline Co., Va. 11 Mar. 1779 while he was away in the service.

Navel, Frederick. Pa. —. He was awarded a $40 gratuity and a $40 annuity in Franklin Co., Pa. 10 Apr. 1828.

Nayson, Nathaniel. Mass. Lt. He died in South Berwick, Me. He devised his right to bounty land to Ruth Quinby who lost the warrant. She had given the right to her daughter, Asenath Nayson who as Asenath Canney received a new one of #895 for 200 acres from Congress on 17 Apr. 1846.

Neafas, John. Pa. Corp. He was in Bucks County on 14 June 1786. He was in the Bucks County militia and was disabled by sickness occasioned by hardship. In 1777 the Bucks County militia crossed over the Schuylkill. He served under Capt. Danagh. He was taken ill and Dr. Joseph Fenton, surgeon to Col. John Lacey, advised that he should be permitted to return home. He was 44 years old. He was on the 1813 pension list. He also appeared as John Nefus and John Nefius.

Neagles, Michael. Mass. Pvt. He served in the 8th Regiment and was from Boston. He was paid $50.

Neal, —. S.C. —. He was killed in the service in 1777. His children were granted an annuity 1 July 1785. They were Elizabeth Neal, Sarah Neal, Ann Neal, Aaron Neal, Thomas Neal, and Mary Neal.

Their mother was also dead. He also appeared as Neil.

Neal, Charles. Pa. —. He was pensioned.

Neal, Hugh. S.C. —. He was taken prisoner at Sumter's defeat and died on board a prison ship. His widow, Jane Neal, was granted an annuity 25 Feb. 1785.

Neal, John. S.C. —. His children, A. G. Neal, Jesse Neal, and Elizabeth Neal, were granted relief by Congress 30 Jan. 1857. His indent was in the name of John Neil. His sister was Elizabeth Easter. He was late of Mississippi.

Neal, John. S.C. —. He was wounded in his left arm at Tarleton's defeat. He was granted an annuity 18 Jan. 1785. There were three children in 1791. They were from Union District.

Neal, Lawrence. Pa. Pvt. He was on the 1791 pension roll. He died 2 Jan. 1807.

Neal, Nicholas. Pa. Pvt. He applied 28 Sep. 1787. He was in the 1st Pa. Regiment. He was wounded at Brandywine in his right hand and lost the use of two of his fingers. His wife was mentioned 28 June 1787.

Neal, Stephen. S.C. —. He applied in 1827. It was rejected.

Neale, Henry. Md. Capt. His widow, Eleanor Neale, was pensioned at the rate of half-pay of a captain 10 Mar. 1837.

Neale, James. Md. —. He was awarded £15 relief and an annual pension of £15 in Nov. 1803.

Nealy, William. N.H. Pvt. He was in Capt. Morrill's Company in Col. Cilley's Regiment and was wounded in the eye at Bemis Heights. He was from Exeter in 1777. He was aged 47 in 1787. He also appeared as William Nalley.

Near, John. Pa. —. He was pensioned.

Needham, John. Mass. Sgt. He served in the Invalids and was paid $20.

Needham, William A. Md. Sgt. He was wounded by a musket ball which passed through his body and hand. He was pensioned Nov. 1791 in Montgomery County. He was on the 1813 pension list.

Neel, David. S.C. —. He was wounded by a shot through his shoulder and another in his knee. He received several wounds in his head by a broad sword. He suffered from a desperate blow to his head. He was occasionally deranged. He was on the roll in 1805.

Neely, —. S.C. —. His widow, Agnes Neely, was granted a $30 per annum pension on 16 Dec. 1835.

Neely, —. S.C. —. His widow, Nancy Neely, was granted a pension 11 Dec. 1835 as the widow of a Revolutionary War veteran.

Neely, Abraham. N.Y. Lieut. He served under Col. William Malcomb. He was wounded in his right thigh by a musket ball at the battle of Monmouth. He was shot through his penis, scrotum, and thigh bone. He was aged 41 years on 2 Oct.1786. He lived in New Windsor, Ulster Co., N.Y. on 6 May 1789. He was on the 1813 pension list. He died in Herkimer County on 24 Feb. 1823. He also appeared as Abraham Nealy.

Neely, David. S.C. —. He was at Congaree Fort and Orangeburg and served under Col. Lacy. He had an aged companion. He was from York District when he was pensioned 3 Dec. 1825. He also appeared as David Neily. He was paid as late as 1839.

Neely, John. S.C. Pvt. He served under Col. William Thompson. He was wounded in his face. He was granted an annuity 24 Sep. 1785. He was from Lancaster District. In 1794 he had a wife and five children. He was granted an increase 18 Dec. 1818. He was paid in 1819, 1820, and 1824 until he removed to Georgia. His pension was commuted on 25 Nov. 1830. He was to be paid for the years 1830 and 1831 and agreed to release the state from any further claim.

Neese, Peter. Pa. Pvt. His widow, Mary Neese, was in Northumberland County on 26 Nov. 1788. He served in the Northumberland County militia. In 1776 he did duty under Capt. John Clark under Col. James Potter. He was mortally wounded by a musket ball at Piscataway, N.J. and died in Jan. 1777. There were three small children. She died in Nov. 1822.

Neff, —. Pa. —. His widow, Elizabeth Neff, was awarded a $40 gratuity and a $40 annuity in Lancaster Co., Pa. 15 Apr. 1835. She died 15 Oct. 1843.

Negley, John. Pa. —. He was granted a gratuity 21 Feb. 1822.

Neickle, —. Pa. —. Samuel Power was guardian of Temperance Neickle and was paid $67.64 to Jan. 1829.

Neighbors, Benjamin. S.C. Pvt. He was from Pendleton District and was pensioned 6 Dec. 1828. He was paid as late as 1834. He also appeared as Benjamin Nabours.

Neil, Benjamin. S.C. —. He applied for a pension in 1814. He was paid an annuity in 1819, 1820, 1821, and 1825. He also appeared as Benjamin Kneal and Benjamin Neel.

Neil, Daniel. N.J. Capt. He was killed at Princeton 3 Jan. 1777. His seven years' half-pay of $1,680 was paid to his heirs. His widow, Elizabeth Neil, was allowed his half-pay in Essex County Apr. 1780.

Neil, James. Pa. —. He enlisted under Capt. James Moore and Col. Anthony Wayne in 1776. He also served under Col. Menges. He was 70 years of age. He was from Chester County.

Neil, John. Pa. His widow, Elizabeth Neil, was in Cumberland County.

Neil, John. Pa. Sgt. His widow, Susannah Neil, applied 12 Feb. 1788 in Washington County. He was in the 7th Battalion of the Cumberland County militia in Capt. John Buchanan's Company and was killed at the Crooked Billet 1 May 1778. His widow may have been the Susanna Neill paid in 1810.

Neil, Thomas. Pa. —. He was granted relief in Indiana County 18 Jan. 1838. He was 78 years old in 1840.

Neill, James. Pa. Sgt. He was pensioned 7 Mar. 1814. He died in Aug. 1828.

Neill, Samuel. Pa. —. He was granted relief.

Neilson, Joseph. Pa. —. He was awarded a $40 gratuity and a $40 annuity in Washington Co., Pa. 8 Apr.

1829.

Neilson, Robert. Pa. —. He was pensioned 28 Mar. 1814. He died in Apr. 1827. He was from Armstrong County.

Neishwender, Levi. Pa. —. He was pensioned.

Neitz, Philip. Pa. —. He was awarded a $40 gratuity Union Co., Pa. 27 Mar. 1830 and a $40 gratuity and $40 annuity 4 May 1832. He died 3 Dec. 1833.

Nell, Jacob. Pa. —. He was granted a $40 gratuity 1 Mar. 1815.

Nellis, Henry W. N.Y. Pvt. He served under Col. J. Klock. He was wounded in the breast by accident whilst acting as bugle man in exercising in 1776. He lived in Palatine, N.Y. in 1794.

Nellis, Jacob. N.Y. —. He was pensioned.

Nelson, —. —. —. Congress rejected the claim for relief from his widow, Mary Nelson, 4 Aug. 1842. She had not identified herself as the widow of the soldier whose service she claimed.

Nelson, —. Pa. —. Mary Nelson of Beaver County was pensioned 26 Aug. 1816 at the rate of $10 per month.

Nelson, Jesse. N.C. —. He applied from Beaufort County in 1805. He was in Continental service under Col. John Patten and was wounded in his right thigh by a ball and in his left shoulder by a bayonet at Stony Point. He was taken prisoner at the fall of Charleston, sent to the West Indies, and then to Nova Scotia. He also lived in Pitt Co., N.C. at one time. He died 15 July 1807.

Nelson, John. Va. Maj. He received his commutation of full pay in lieu of half-pay for life as a major of cavalry in the Virginia Line with no interest on 12 Jan. 1827.

Nelson, Joseph. Pa. —. He was pensioned.

Nelson, Roger. Md. Lt. He was on the 1813 pension list. He died 7 June 1815. His widow, Eliza Nelson, was pensioned in Frederick County at the rate of half-pay of an officer 4 Mar. 1834. She was awarded half-pay of a lieutenant from July 1815 to the time she was placed on the pension roll on 27 Mar. 1839.

Nelson, Thomas. S.C. —. He was at Purysburg, Thompson's Bluffs, Ratcliff's, Marshall's Mill, Orangeburg, Manigault's Ferry, South Edisto, Four Holes, Congaree, and Cowpens. He served under Capt. Alexander Montgomery. Thomas Huey served with him. He was from Fairfield District in 1825. He was paid as late and 1834.

Nelson, Thomas. Va. Maj. Gen. Congress rejected the claim from his heirs for commutation 2 July 1836.

Nelson, William. Pa. Pvt. He applied 22 Nov. 1788 in Westmoreland County. He served in the 13th Pa. Regiment in Capt. James Carnaghan's Company under Col. Walter Stewart and was wounded in his left knee at the battle of Long Island. He was 30 years old and had no family. He was pensioned at the rate of $5 per month from 22 Jan. 1808. He was on the 1813 pension list.

Nelson, William. Pa. Pvt. He applied in Mercer County on 6 Feb. 1815. He enlisted in the spring of 1777 for three years by Capt. Nicholson in the regiment of Col. Adam Hubley. He was also under Col. Hartley.

Nelson, William. Pa. —. His widow was Mary Nelson. The pension was paid to the guardian of his children, John Stroup, in Sep. 1828. They were from Beaver County.

Nelson, William. S.C. —. He was on the roll in 1793.

Nelson, William. S.C. —. His application was rejected 9 Dec. 1835.

Nelson, William. Va. Col. He entered as a private and was soon promoted. He was commissioned Lt. Col. in the 7th Virginia Regiment and served in 1776 and 1777. He was at Brandywine 11 Sep. 1777, Germantown 25 Oct. 1774, and tendered his resignation due to ill health. He commanded a regiment of militia in Virginia, served three years, and received a bounty land warrant for 6,000 acres from Virginia. His heirs sought his commutation but were rejected 23 Feb. 1838 because he had admitted resigning. Congress did so again 14 July 1854.

Nelson, William. Va. Capt. He was from Westmoreland County and served twelve months in the militia from 1777 to sometime in 1781. Congress granted his widow, Mary Nelson, a pension 18 Aug. 1842.

Nesbit, Alexander. Pa. —. He received a $40 gratuity and a $40 annuity 3 Apr. 1837 in Chester Co. He was 85 years old in 1840. He died 18 Dec. 1845.

Nesbit, Samuel. —. —. He was pensioned 25 Apr. 1808 at the rate of $5 per month from 18 Oct. 1807.

Nesbit, William. S.C. Pvt. He was at the Snow Camps, Rocky Mount, Hanging Rock, Camden, Big Sand Hill, and Bigam Church. He applied in Lancaster District at the age of 70 on 11 Nov. 1824. He was paid as late as 1830.

Nestell, Peter. Va. —. He was an officer and a member of the Society of the Cincinnati. His widow was Mary Nestell. Her pension was increased from $100 to $250 per annum on 13 Feb. 1845.

Nestle, George. N.Y. Pvt. He served under Col. Marinus Willet in Capt. Lawrence Gross's Company. He was wounded in his body which injured his lungs. He was 24 years old in 1787. He lived in Schenectady, Albany Co., N.Y. 14 Aug. 1789. He also appeared as George Nestel.

Nestler, Gotlieb. N.Y. Pvt. He served under Col. Vischer. He was wounded in the eye by the oversetting of a baggage wagon on a march in 1776. He lived in Palatine, N.Y. in 1794.

Nettle, John. Va. Pvt. He was being pensioned in 1785.

Nestor, John. N.J. Pvt. He served under Capt. Piatt and Col. Barber in the 1st Regiment of the Essex County militia. There was a John Nestor who served under Capt. Horton. Because the proof was not satisfactory, Congress rejected the claim of his widow, Phebe Nestor, 28 Apr. 1840.

Nettles, Abraham. Va. Sgt. He served in the 14th Regiment in Capt. Nathan Reade's Company. He was disabled by paralysis. He was awarded a £300 gratuity on 9 Nov. 1780. He was awarded one year's pay as a gratuity and an annuity of half-pay on 21 Nov. 1781. He was pensioned at half-pay for the duration of his disability on 12 Jan. 1785. He was in Greenbrier County in May 1787. He was stricken from the roll when Greenbrier County failed to comply with the law and neglected to appoint surgeons to inspect the disabilities of pensioners. He was restored 20 Dec. 1790. He was on the 1813 pension list.

Nettles, William. S.C. Capt. He was pensioned 6 Dec. 1828. He was from Camden District. He was paid as late as 1832.

Neuland, Jacob. Pa. Pvt. His widow, Catherine Neuland, lived in Dauphin County on 19 Dec. 1786. He was in the militia in Capt. James Crouch's Company and was killed at Chestnut Hill in Oct. 1777. His orphans were Mary Newland aged 5, Adam Newland aged 3, and George Newland aged 1 at the time of their father's death. He also appeared as Jacob Newland.

Nevel, Jesse. S.C. —. He enlisted at age 16 in Rutherford Co., N.C. under Capt. James Pearis. He also served under Capt. John Earle, Capt. James Miller, Capt. William Wood, and Capt. Edward Hampton. He had been afflicted with diarrhea for twenty years. His wife was four years older and had had two husbands killed by Indians. He was from Pickens District in 1831. His application was rejected.

Neviers, John. N.J. Pvt. He served under Col. Wind in the State Troops. His widow was Rachel Neviers.

Nevil, Henry. Pa. —. He was awarded a $40 gratuity and a $40 annuity in Montgomery Co., Pa. 4 May 1832.

Nevil, Reubin. Va. —. His widow, Mary Ann Nevil, and child were provided financial assistance in Aug. 1778. He had died in Continental service. She was awarded a £11 gratuity in Amherst Co., Va. 1 Dec. 1779.

Nevius, John. N.J. —. He was pensioned in Middlesex County on 24 Feb. 1837 at the rate of $80 per annum.

Nevius, Peter. N.J. Sgt. He served under Col. Taylor in the Middlesex County militia. He was wounded through his lungs 10 Jan. 1782. He was 36 years old. He was on the 1791 pension roll. He lived in Middlesex County. He was pensioned at the rate of $4 per month. He was on the 1813 pension list as Peter Nefies. He died 25 Nov. 1838 in North Brunswick Co., N.J. His children were John Nifes and Ellen Nifes.

New, Christopher. Pa. —. His widow, Elizabeth New, was awarded a $40 gratuity and a $40 annuity in York County 3 Apr. 1829. She died 11 Dec. 1833.

Newall, Barston. —. —. His widow, Sarah Newall, married secondly — Larrabee. After his death, Congress granted her a pension 25 Apr. 1854.

Newbegin, George. Me. —. He was from Parsonsfield. He was paid $50 under the resolve of 1836.

Newberry, James. Pa. —. He applied 31 May 1813 and was from Northumberland County.

Newbit, Christopher. Mass. Pvt. He served in Capt. Philip Ulmer's Company under Col. Samuel McCobb and lost his right arm by a cannon ball at Majorbigwaduce on 28 July. He was pensioned at the rate of half-pay from 28 Sep. 1779, the date of his discharge, on 20 Feb. 1781. He was 23 years old in 1786. He was on the 1813 pension list. He transferred to Kennebec Co., Me. 4 Sep. 1822. He died in Oct. 1826 or according to another record 29 Sep. 1826. His widow, Jenny Newbit, failed to produce any proof of his service, their marriage, or of his wounds so Congress rejected her claim for a pension 4 Apr. 1480.

Newbury, James. Mass. —. He was pensioned for life at the rate of $30 per annum 3 Feb. 1810.

Newcomb, Bryant. Mass. Gunner. He served in Revere's Regiment and was from Braintree. He was paid $50.

Newcomb, Reuben. N.J. Pvt. He served under Col. Potter in the Cumberland County militia. He suffered from a dislocated and ulcerated ankle. He was 36 years old. He was pensioned at the rate of $40 per annum. He died 1 Nov. 1789.

Newcomb, Samuel. Pa. —. He enlisted in Apr. 1777 in the 10th Regiment and was discharged in Jan. 1781. He was from Indiana County.

Newell, Samuel. Va. —. He was killed by Indians in 1777 while carrying dispatches to the Cherokee. He was tomahawked and scalped and died soon afterwards in the town of Chote. He had three small children. His widow, Elizabeth Newell, was awarded a £20 gratuity and a £10 annuity on 28 May 1777.

Newell, William. Pa. Orderly Sgt. He served in the Bedford County Associators in 1777. He was 77 years old in 1823.

Newen, —. Pa. —. His widow, Catherine Newen, was awarded a $40 gratuity in York, Pa. 14 Apr. 1828.

Newhall, James. Mass. Pvt. He served in Revere's Artillery and was from Lynn. He was paid $50.

Newhall, Jonas. Mass. —. His warrant was drawn 4 Feb. 1819.

Newkirk, Jacob. N.Y. Pvt. He served in Col. John Harper's N.Y. Regiment. He was pensioned 11 Aug. 1790. He was on the 1813 pension list.

Newland, Jabez. Mass. Pvt. He served in the 8th Regiment and was from Mansfield. He was paid $50.

Newland, Moses. Mass. Pvt. He was on the list of invalid pensioners who had not been paid by Benjamin Lincoln in 1790.

Newlin, Michael. Pa. —. He enlisted in 1776 in Capt. Robb's Company in Col. Stewart's Regiment. From severe colds, hardships, and fatigues he contracted rheumatism which dislocated his right hip joint. He was awarded $60 on 19 Mar. 1810.

Newman, —. —. —. His son, Abram D. Newman, sought a pension 10 May 1898. Congress rejected his petition since he was neither idiotic, deformed, or otherwise mentally or physically incapacitated.

Newman, —. Pa. —. His widow, Mary Newman, was awarded a $40 gratuity and a $40 annuity in Lycoming County 12 Mar. 1836. She died 7 July 1840.

Newman, John. Ga. Pvt. He was on the 1791 pension list. He died in 1805.

Newman, John. Ga. Sgt. He enlisted under Capt. John Moseley in the 2nd Georgia Battalion which had been on Continental establishment. He lost his right arm at Savannah on 29 Dec. 1776. He was awarded a £150 gratuity and an annuity of half-pay of a soldier on 30 May 1780 by Virginia. He was from Buckingham Co., Va. He was on the 1790, 1800, and 1813 pension lists. He later lived in Rutherford Co., Tenn.

Newman, John. Md. Sgt. He was pensioned 27 Jan. 1817 at the rate of half-pay of a sergeant. His arrearage of $15.33 was paid to William Ridgely on 30 Jan. 1830.

Newman, John. Md. Pvt. He served in the 3rd Md. Regiment and settled in Hampshire Co., Va. He died 26 July 1826.

Newman, John. Mass. —. He served in the 4th Regiment and was from Boston. He was paid $20.

Newman, Nehemiah. Pa. —. His widow, Catharine Newman, was awarded a $40 gratuity and a $40 annuity in York Co., Pa. 7 Mar. 1829.

Newman, Samuel. Mass. —. He served in the 2nd Regiment and was paid $20.

Newman, Thomas. Ga. —. He was on the 1796 list.

Newnan, John. Va. Pvt. He was on the roll in 1778. He died in 1805.

Newport, Daniel. Mass. —. He served in the 6th Regiment and was paid $20.

Newrisha, Lewis. France. —. He enlisted in 1778 and landed at Boston in 1780. He died in Nov. or Dec. 1782. Congress rejected any relief to his heirs 30 Mar. 1840.

Newton, David. N.H. Pvt. He served under Col. Jonathan Holman. He was overcome by heat in the retreat from Haarlem Heights near New York which occasioned universal weakness in all his limbs in Sep. 1776. He lived in Chesterfield, N.H. in 1794. He was in the militia.

Newton, John. Md. Pvt. He was pensioned at the rate of half-pay of a private on 7 Feb. 1818.

Neyfang, Nicholas. Pa. —. He was awarded a $40 gratuity 18 Feb. 1834 in Schuylkill Co., Pa.

Niblach, John. N.J. Pvt. He served in the 1st Jersey Regiment. He was wounded in the head at Rye, N.Y. and lost the sight of an eye and part of his skull bone on 20 Oct. 1776. He lived in Northumberland Co., Pa. in 1794.

Niblet, William. Md. Pvt. He was pensioned at the rate of half-pay of a private in Worcester County on 27 Jan. 1817.

Nichel, William. Pa. —. He was awarded a $40 gratuity in Mercer Co., Pa. 15 Apr. 1834.

Nicholas, Henry. Pa. —. His widow, Mary Magdalene Nicholas, was awarded a $40 annuity and a $40 gratuity in Philadelphia Co., Pa. 16 Feb. 1830.

Nicholas, John. Va. Capt. He was from Buckingham County. He served in the infantry of the Virginia line on state establishment from 1 Jan. 1777 to 5 June 1780 when he received his commission of Lt. Colonel in the militia for the defense of South Carolina. He continued in the service until after the siege of York. He received depreciation of his pay as a captain of infantry in the Virginia line from 5 June 1780 to 31 December 1781 and his commutation of full pay for five years in lieu of half-pay for life from 6 Mar. 1819 on 3 Feb. 1825.

Nicholas, Thomas. Pa. —. He was paid $200 in full 5 Mar. 1828. He was from Lycoming County.

Nicholas, William Pa. —. He was pensioned in Mercer County 21 Feb. 1838. He died 6 Nov. 1842.

Nicholls, James. Va. —. His wife, Ruth Nicholls, was granted 100 pounds of pork and 2 barrels of corn for her support and her child in Berkeley County on 19 Mar. 1782.

Nichols, —. —. —. He served three months and nineteen days. Congress rejected a pension to his widow, Sarah Nichols, 20 May 1850.

Nichols, —. Va. —. His widow, Elizabeth Nichols, was awarded a £63 gratuity in Charlotte Co., Va. 3 Nov. 1779.

Nichols, David. Pa. Capt. He was transferred to New York by 1809. He was on the 1813 pension list with the rank of corporal.

Nichols, Elnathan. Conn. Lt. He served in the 1st Company of the 3rd Troop of Light Horse under Gen. Arnold. He was wounded in his left arm by grape shot on 28 Apr. 1777 at Compo by the British under Gen. Tryon. He was under Capt. Samuel Blackman and Gen. Selleck Silliman. He was pensioned 20 Sep. 1787. He resided in New Town having previously lived in Stratford. He was 51 years old. He later transferred to Vermont.

Nichols, Joseph. Ga. —. He was granted $100 to enable him to be put on the pension list of the United States in Nov./Dec. 1817. He was from Putnam County. The act does not specify that his service was Revolutionary.

Nichols, Julius. S.C. —. His annuity was £21.0.6 in 1787.

Nichols, Lawrence. Pa. Pvt. He applied 9 Jan. 1788. He served in the Northampton County militia under Lt. John Wetzel and was wounded in the right side in a skirmish with disaffected persons when called upon to assist in the collection of militia fines for Allen Township. Joseph Romig, a disaffected person, was the one who wounded him. The ball entered his side at the lower ribs and shattered his hip bone. He had lameness in his knee. He was 30 years old when he applied in Philadelphia 9 Jan. 1788. He also appeared as Lawrence Neal and Lawrence Nihell.

Nichols, Levi. —. —. He entered the service in July under Capt. Reed and Col. Ray in 1780 and served three months at West Point under Gen. Arnold. Congress rejected his claim for a pension 27 Mar. 1846 and did so again 1 Aug. 1850 at which time he was 89 years old.

Nichols, Nathaniel. Me. —. He died 28 May 1836 in Augusta. His widow, Mehitable Nichols of Augusta, was paid $50 under the resolve of 1836. He also appeared as Nathaniel Nicholas.

Nichols, Thomas. Pa. —. He was awarded $200 in Lycoming Co., Pa. 5 Mar. 1828.

Nichols, Thomas. S.C. —. He was paid $192.66 as a Revolutionary soldier in the South Carolina Continental Line on 20 Dec. 1810. He had been taken prisoner at Charleston 17 May 1780. He lived in Rutherford Co., N.C.

Nichols, William. Va. —. He enlisted in Bedford Co., Va. His wife and children were furnished support in Charlotte Co., Va. on 6 Oct. 1777. His widow, Elizabeth Nichols, was furnished 8 barrels of corn, 500 pounds of pork, and 3 pecks of salt on 2 Nov. 1778. She was furnished provisions valued at £61.5 on 7 Dec. 1778. She received 7 barrels of corn on 1 Feb. 1779 and £63 provisions on 3 May 1779. His widow was awarded half-pay of her late husband who died in the service in Charlotte Co., Va. on 7 Feb. 1780.

Nicholson, Francis. Conn. Sgt. He served under Col. S. B. Webb in the 3rd Regiment. He was debilitated by smallpox, fatigue, and hardships in 1781. He resided in Glastonbury, Conn. in 1792. He enlisted 28 July 1778 and continued to the end of the war.

Nicholson, James. Pa. —. He received a $40 gratuity in Vanango County 20 Mar. 1838, but his military service was not identified.

Nicholson, John. Pa. Sgt. He served 15 Mar. 1777 to July 1783. He was wounded in his leg. He was also wounded in his head on a tour against the Indians. He was from Franklin County. He was pensioned 20 Dec. 1815 and died 1 Jan. 1821.

Nicholson, Samuel. —. —. He was commander of an armed vessel from 1776 to 1782 and took 44 British vessels. Fifteen were sloops of war or privateers and the residue were merchant vessels. He took nearly 1,000 prisoners. He was honorably acquitted in a court martial in 1782 but spent fourteen months in suspension during his arrest and trial. His daughters, Ann Temple Green, Maria Nicholson, and Elizabeth Nicholson, sought relief for the fourteen months. Congress rejected their claim 1 Aug. 1850. "The fact that this claim has been permitted to sleep for nearly one-third of a century is a strong presumptive proof that it rests upon a sandy foundation, and with no better evidence in its support, it should be permitted to sleep on undisturbed."

Nickelson, —. Pa. —. His widow, Sarah Nickelson, was awarded a $40 gratuity and a $40 annuity in Juniata County 24 Mar. 1837. She also appeared as Sarah Nicholson. She was 87 years of age in 1840. She died 30 Aug. 1843.

Nicken, Richard. Va. Seaman. He was pensioned in Lancaster County on 8 Jan. 1820 at the rate of $60 per annum with $50 immediate relief. He enlisted for three years and was a free man of color. He died 21 Feb. 1835. Daniel P. Mitchell was granted administration with the will annexed in Mar. 1835.

Nickless, John. Mass. Pvt. He served under Col. Simeon Spaulding in Capt. Pollard's Company. He was disabled by the loss of the middle finger on his right hand and a musket ball through his left thigh. He was on the 1813 pension list as John Nicknolls.

Nickols, William. Va. —. His wife, Elizabeth Nickols, was allowed £13.7.3 support in Bedford Co., Va. 24 Nov. 1777.

Nicks, William. S.C. Fifer. He was paid $192.66 as a Revolutionary soldier in the South Carolina Continental Line on 20 Dec. 1810.

Nicoll, John. S.C. Lt. He served under Capt. Andrew Berry and Col. John Thomas. He was cut to pieces in May 1781 in action with a party of Loyalists. He was 82 years of age. He was from Greenville District in 1819.

Nicolls, Simon. N.Y. Pvt. He served under Col. Nicholson. He was wounded in a wagon accident on a march in June 1776. He resided at Palestine, N.Y. He was pensioned 9 June 1794.

Niel, Daniel. —. Capt. He served in the artillery and was killed at Princeton 3 Jan. 1777. His widow married (2) Col. Hay 6 Feb. 1780. She was allowed half-pay from 3 Jan. 1777 to 6 Feb. 1780. His daughter, Maria M. Niel, married David Brooks. Congress rejected their claim for relief 15 Mar. 1842.

Niel, John. Pa. —. He was pensioned 2 Apr. 1822.

Nielsen, Robert. Pa. —. He was pensioned under the act of 28 Mar. 1818. He was from Armstrong County.

Night, —. Va. —. He was away in the service. His wife, Mary Night, was allowed £30 support in Augusta Co., Va. 21 Mar. 1780.

Niles, Robert. —. Capt. He served as captain of the schooner, *Spy*, 7 Aug. 1775. He took a number of prizes under Commodore Hopkins. In the summer of 1778 he was carrying the treaty of ratification to France. His was one of the three vessels sent with a copy. His was the only one to reach France. On the return voyage a British frigate captured and took them to the isle of Guernsey. He was taken to England and detained six months. He was exchanged and returned home. He died in 1818. His only child, Hannah F. Niles, sought five years' full-pay from Congress 3 Apr. 1856.

Nipper, James. S.C. —. He was on the roll in 1803.

Nipple, Frederick. Pa. —. He was from Mifflin County 11 Apr. 1825 and received a $40 gratuity and a $40 annuity.

Nisbet, John. S.C. —. He was at Hanging Rock and Ratcliffe's. He was 66 years old. Capt. James Huey and William Nesbet deposed anent his service. He was from Lancaster District in 1825. His application was rejected.

Nisbet, Samuel. Pa. Pvt. He was on the 1813 pension list.

Nisbett, William. S.C. Pvt. He was at the Snow Camp, Purysburg, Augusta, Rocky Mount, Hanging Rock, Camden, and Big Sand Hill. He was born in Lancaster District and was 70 years old. He was pensioned from Lancaster District on 19 Dec. 1825. He was paid as late as 1830.

Nisely, William. Va. —. His wife, Mary Nisely, and child were furnished £12 support in Frederick Co., Va. on 2 Mar. 1779.

Nithrew, Adam. Pa. —. He was awarded a $50 gratuity 19 Mar. 1816 in Lehigh County.

Nixon, Hugh Alexander. S.C. Midshipman. He served aboard the *South Carolina* under Commodore Alexander Gillon. He sought his prize money and that of his late brother, John Nixon, who was also on the same vessel, on 2 Dec. 1806.

Nixon, John. Mass. Col. Brigadier. He was wounded by a ball in his testicles at the battle of Bunker Hill on 17 June 1775 and was also disabled by sickness contracted in the service. He resided in Sudbury, Mass. in 1792 and 1794. He was in the militia. He was granted one-third of a pension 20 Apr. 1796 in Mass. He transferred to Vermont. He was on the 1813 pension list.

Nixon, John. S.C. —. He was killed by the enemy 20 Nov. 1780. His widow, Mary Nixon, was granted an annuity 17 June 1785. There were children in 1793.

Nixon, Joseph. Mass. Pvt. He served in the 6th Regiment and was from Boston. His widow, Nancy Nixon, was paid $50.

Nixon, Robert. —. —. His application was rejected 7 May 1796.

Nixon, Thomas. —. —. He was an officer. His widow, Sarah Nixon, had her petition for a pension rejected by Congress 4 Jan. 1848.

Nixon, Thomas. Mass. Quartermaster Sgt. He served in the 6th Regiment and was from Framingham. He was paid $50.

Noble, Anthony. Mass. —. He served in the 1st Regiment and was paid $20.

Noble, David. Mass. Capt. He served under Col. Patterson in Sullivan's Brigade. He died in 1776 and left three children. His wife was Ruh Noble. He was from Berkshire County, Mass. His last surviving child, Enoch Noble, died in Susquehannah Co., Pa. in 1836. His grandson, David Noble, sought seven years' half-pay. Congress rejected his claim 23 Feb. 1855 but granted same 17 Apr. 1858.

Noble, Gideon. Conn. Corp. He served under Col. C. Webb. He was ruptured in his scrotum in the battle of Monmouth. He resided in Middletown, Conn. in 1792. He enlisted 1 Mar. 1777 and was invalided Nov. 1780.

Noble, Goodman. —. —. He was pensioned in 1818 but stricken in 1820. He owned 32 acres which he had mortgaged and had three sons to support him and his wife. His farm was appraised at $300. Two of his sons had furnished him nothing. Congress granted him a pension 15 Mar. 1832.

Noble, Isaac. Mass. —. He served in the 4th Regiment. He was from Castle Island and was paid $20.

Noble, Mark. Conn. Pvt. He served in Strong's Regiment. He was pensioned 3 Feb. 1803. He was on the 1813 pension list. He lived in Middlesex County and died 29 Mar. 1823.

Noble, Mark. Mass. —. He served in the 1st Regiment and was from New York. He was paid $20.

Noble, Paul. Mass. Pvt. He served in the 1st Regiment and was from Westfield. His widow, Hannah Noble, was paid $50.

Noble, William. Pa. Sgt. His widow and children were awarded 200 acres donation land 26 Mar. 1813.

Noblet, Thomas. Pa. —. He received a $40 annuity in Philadelphia County 10 Apr. 1849. He died 30 Sep. 1851. His widow, Ann Noblet, received a $40 annuity 10 Feb. 1853.

Noel, Philip. N.J. Pvt. He was on the 1791 pension roll.

Nogle, Philip. Pa. —. His wife was Mary.

Noland, George. S.C. —. He served under Capt. John Pearson, Capt. Edward Martin, Col. Thomas Taylor, and Capt. Samuel Adams. He was at Four Holes and Stono. He was 80 years old and had no relation in the state. Burbridge Woodward served with him. He was pensioned from Fairfield District 7 Dec. 1837.

Nolff, George. Pa. —. He was awarded a $40 gratuity and a $40 annuity in Northampton Co., Pa. 30 Mar. 1824. His annuity was continued to his widow, Susannah Nolff, on 11 Jan. 1831.

Noll, Valentine. Pa. —. He was awarded a $40 gratuity in Berks Co., Pa. 10 Apr. 1835.

Nolt, Phillip. N.J. Pvt. He served in the Jersey Battalion and was wounded and ruptured. He was 58 years old and lived in Burlington.

Norcross, John. Pa. Pvt. He was in Northumberland County on 11 Jan. 1787. He was in the Northumberland County militia and was wounded by a musket ball at Piscataway on 1 Feb. 1777. The ball entered his body at his left shoulder and came out at his throat. He served under Col. James Morrow and Capt. Cookson Long. He was on the 1813 pension list.

Norcutt, Ephraim. Mass. —. He served in Revere's Regiment and was from Middleboro. He was paid $50.

Norcutt, William. Mass. —. He served in Revere's Regiment and was from Berkeley. His widow, Esther Norcutt, was paid $50.

Norcutt, Zenas. Mass. —. He served in Revere's Regiment and was from Middleboro. He was paid $50.

Norman, Joseph. Pa. —. He was granted a $40 gratuity and a $40 annuity in Philadelphia County 21 Mar. 1837.

Norris, —. —. —. His widow, Huldah Norris, had her petition for a pension rejected by Congress on 27 Mar. 1846 because they were married subsequent to 1 Jan. 1794.

Norris, James. Pa. Lt. He applied in Philadelphia County on 7 Feb. 1812. In 1776 he served as a private as a gunner under Capt. Proctor and was promoted to sergeant. He was commissioned as a lieutenant of artillery 1 Apr. 1779 under Capt. Van Heer. Due to illness he resigned his commission in Nov. 1781. He was in the battles of Brandywine, Germantown, and in the expedition against the Indians under Gen. Sullivan. He was badly hurt in both legs in coming through Neecopeck Falls on the Susquehannah River. Capt. Lt. Matthew McGuire, paymaster, proved his service. He was a carpenter and had a wife. He died 8 Jan. 1817.

Norris, John. Pa. —. He was from Lancaster County and served under Capt. Mares in the 4th Pa. Regiment under Col. William Butler. His next tour was under Capt. Van Heer to the close of the war. He received his donation land 22 Feb. 1808.

Norris, John. Pa. Lt. He was pensioned 24 Mar. 1813 at the rate of $90 pr annum.

North, Daniel. Mass. —. He served in the 6th Regiment and was from Hopkinton. He was paid $20.

North, Roger. Pa. —. He was awarded a $40 gratuity and a $40 annuity in Chester Co., Pa. 11 Apr. 1825. He died 15 Dec. 1830.

Northcutt, Terry. Va. —. His wife, Sarah Northcutt, was furnished 1 barrel of corn and 50 pounds of pork in Charlotte County on 1 Nov. 1779.

Northam, Timothy. Mass. Pvt. He served in Col. Chester's Regiment. He was wounded through his leg by a musket ball and the bones broken in 1776 near White Plains. He resided at Williamstown, Mass. in 1796. He was granted one-third of a pension 20 Apr. 1796. He was on the 1813 pension list.

Northeimer, Adam. Pa. —. He was awarded a $40 gratuity and a $40 annuity in Lancaster Co., Pa. 14 Jan. 1835. He was 81 years old in 1840.

Northeimer, Jacob. Pa. —. He was awarded a $40 gratuity and a $40 annuity in Lancaster Co., Pa. 20 Mar. 1834.

Northstern, —. Pa. —. His widow, Maria Elizabeth Northstern, was awarded a $40 gratuity and a $40 annuity in Schuylkill Co., Pa. 15 Apr. 1835. She died 3 Dec. 1845.

Norton, —. —. —. His widow, Hannah Norton, had her petition for a pension by a special act of Congress rejected 26 Apr. 1848 because she married subsequent 1 Jan. 1794.

Norton, —. —. —. The heirs of Martha Norton sought relief 24 Feb. 1847. The petition to Congress from Mary Andrews and Hunn B. Norton was rejected.

Norton, —. Pa. —. His widow was Jane Norton. She was from Philadelphia County 11 Apr. 1825.

Norton, Elnathan. Conn. Pvt. He served under Capt. C. Norton in the 10th militia. He was wounded by a musket ball which entered below his breast, broke one of his ribs, and exited his back on 4 July 1779 at New Haven. He lived in Durham, Conn. in 1792 and Southington, Conn. in 1795. He was granted one-third of a pension 20 Apr. 1796. He died in Oct. 1811. He was listed as dead on the 1813 pension list.

Norton, George. N.Y. —. He was pensioned.

Norton, Henry. N.Y. Pvt. He served under Col. Van Schaick and died 1 Dec. 1781. His widow, Margaret Norton, received a half-pay pension for seven years.

Norton, Hugh. S.C. —. He served under Francis Marion in 1781 and 1782. He was at Watboo and Wambaw. He was from Sumter District in 1828. His application was rejected.

Norton, Jacob. S.C. —. He was 78 years old and had lost the sight in one eye. He was a blacksmith. He was from Williamsburg District in 1830.

Norton, Jedediah. N.Y. Pvt. He served in the artillery. He was disabled by a rupture. He was pensioned in Conn. He died in 1807.

Norton, Nathaniel. Me. —. He died 22 Nov. 1831. His widow was Hannah Norton from Limington. She was paid $50 under the resolve of 1836.

Norton, William. Pa. —. He was granted relief.

Norwood, Daniel. S.C. —. He served under Capt. Felix Worley and Col. Thompson. He was made a prisoner at the taking of Savannah. He was put on a prison ship where he died. His widow was Phebe Norwood. She received an annuity in 1794, but her application for a pension was rejected in 1796.

Norwood, Joseph. Va. —. While he was away in the service, his mother was granted £60 support on 5 Apr. 1779 in Richmond County.

Norwood, Nathan. Mass.—. He served in the 4th Regiment and was paid $20.

Norwood, Thomas. S.C. Pvt. He was granted relief.

Nott, Philip. N.J. Pvt. He was pensioned at the rate of $60 per annum.

Nourse, James. Mass. —. He served in the 1st Regiment and was from Lynn. He was paid $20.

Nourse, William. —. —. He served on the frigate *Confederacy* as a midshipman. He was captured and held more than two years in a British prison. He was a pensioner. Congress ruled that he could not obtain any additional support on 29 Jan. 1836. Congress awarded his widow, Rebecca P. Nourse of Kentucky, the arrearage of her pension from 4 Mar. 1848 to 3 Feb. 1853 on 10 Dec. 1857.

Nowell, James. Md. Pvt. He was pensioned at the rate of half-pay of a private 2 Jan. 1813.

Nowland, Moses. Mass. Pvt. He was in the Invalids. He was worn out in the service. He was pensioned 15 Sep. 1782. *Vide* also Moses Knowland.

Noyes, Eliphalet. Mass. —. He was from Newburyport and was paid $20.

Noyes, Joseph. Mass. Lt. He served in the Mass. Line. He lived in Middlesex County. He was on the 1813 pension list.

Noyes, Simeon. Mass. Sgt. He was wounded in his right hand and lost one of his forefingers at Bemis Heights on 7 Oct. 1777. He had camp fever in 1779. He served in Johnson's militia. He lived in Salem, Mass. in 1792.

Noyes, Wadleigh. Mass. Lt. He served in the 9th Mass. Regiment under Capt. James Westover. He was promoted to lieutenant 1 Jan. 1777 and was mortally wounded at Saratoga on 7 Oct. 1777 and died 27 Oct. 1777. His widow remarried. His three children sought his seven years' half-pay in 1791. On 31 Jan. 1821 his remarried widow, Hannah Richardson, of Newbury, Mass. and her son, Moses Noyes, were unsuccessful again in prosecuting their claim. Congress awarded his heirs seven years' half-pay with interest 23 May 1856. He served as a sergeant under Capt. William Rogers from 19 Feb. 1775 to 1 Jan. 1776. He was from Newbury. He served as ensign under Capt. Ezra Badlam and Col. James Wesson.

Nuckle, —. Pa. —. Ruth Nuckle received $10 monthly from 5 Nov. 1816. She was from Beaver County, Pa.

Nugent, Arthur. Pa.—. He was granted a $40 gratuity and a $40 annuity in Indiana County 15 June 1836.

Nugent, Jacob. Va. —. He enlisted in Hanover County under Lt. White, Capt. Callowhill Minis, and Col. Richard Parker. He was taken prisoner at Charleston. He was also at Monmouth and Stoney Point. He had a 60 year old wife. He lived with his son and two daughters when he applied in Guilford Co., N.C. in Aug. 1826. He was born in Nov. 1756.

Nugent, John. Pa. Pvt. He was in Philadelphia County on 29 Sep. 1787. He was in the Pa. Regiment of Artillery under Col. Thomas Proctor. He was disabled while in service between 1775 and 1781 having incurred a weakness in his limbs and rheumatic complaint. He suffered from a total loss of hearing. He was destitute of friend or family in America. He was 42 years old.

Nunemacher, —. Pa. —. His widow, Edith Nunemacher, was granted support in Philadelphia 16 Apr. 1838. She was 79 years of age in 1840. She died 24 Aug. 1852.

Nunenmacher, James. Pa. —. He was awarded a $40 gratuity and a $40 annuity in Northampton Co., Pa. 15 Apr. 1835. He died 23 Mar. 1841.

Nunenmacher, John. Pa. He was pensioned 15 Mar. 1826. He was from Philadelphia.

Nunenmaker, Peter. Pa. —. He was awarded a $40 gratuity and a $40 annuity in Philadelphia Co., Pa. 15 Mar. 1826.

Nungesser, —. Pa. —. His widow, Catherine Nungesser, was awarded a $40 gratuity and a $40 annuity in Columbia Co., Pa. 23 Jan. 1834.

Nunnally, Alexander. Va. —. His wife, Elizabeth Nunnally, was furnished 8 barrels of corn, 200 pounds of pork, 200 pounds of beef, and ½ bushel of salt in Charlotte County on 7 Sep. 1778, £83 on 4 Oct. 1779, 150 pounds of pork and 3 barrels of corn on 6 Nov. 1780, £300 for her support and that of her children on 5 Feb. 1781.

Nunnally, Joseph. Va. —. He died in the service. His widow, Mary Nunnally, was furnished provisions valued at £163.4 in Amelia Co., Va. 25 Nov. 1779. She was granted additional support on 21 Mar. 1781. She also appeared as Mary Nunnery.

Nurse, Aaron. Mass. Pvt. He served in the 5th Regiment and was from Lynnfield. His widow, Rebecca Nurse, was paid $50.

Nurse, Caleb. Mass. Pvt. He was in the Invalids under Capt. Hill and Col. Lewis Nichola. He was worn out in the service. He was pensioned 4 Jan. 1783. He was aged 48 years and resided in Ashby, Mass. in 1788.

Nusom, Sylvanus. S.C. —. There were children in 1793.

Nute, Jotham. N.H. Sgt. He was in the 2nd Regiment. He was wounded in his left hip by a musket ball on 4 July 1781 near Kingsbridge. He lived in Rochester in 1783 and in Dover, N.H.   i n 1794. He enlisted 1 Feb. 1777 for the war. He was granted half a pension 20 Apr.1796. He was on the 1813 pension list.

Nute, Samuel. N.H. 2nd Lt. He served under Col. Enoch Poor. He was promoted from ensign to lieutenant on 1 Jan.1777. He never received any additional pay and sought the same and his depreciation on 7 Jan. 1790. He was from Rochester.

Nutter, John. N.J. —. He served in the 3rd Regiment and was disabled in the service. He applied in Jan. 1793.

Nutting, Daniel. Mass. Pvt. He served under Col. Ebenezer Bridge in Capt. Ebenezer Bancroft's Company. He was disabled by a musket ball in his left hand and the loss of his thumb. He was pensioned 27 July 1786. He was 30 years old. He was on the 1813 pension list.

Nutting, Thomas. Me. —. He was from Wilton. He was paid $50 under the resolve of 1836.

Nye, Jonathan. Me. —. He was from Fairfield. He was paid $50 under the resolve of 1836.

Nye, Joseph. Mass. —. He served in the 6th Regiment and was from Brookfield. He was paid $20.

Nye, Samuel. Pa. —. He served with the militia on the frontiers. He was from Washington County.

Oakes, John. Mass. —. He served in the 8th Regiment and was paid $20.

Oakley, Cornelius. —. —. He served from 1776 to 1783 on the Hudson River. He acted as a guide to the American Army, drew rations, had quarters at headquarters, and was in several skirmishes. He was not actually enrolled in the army but was with the army. He died 12 Jan. 1845. His widow was Sarah Oakley. Congress ruled that his service was analogous to spying and granted her a pension 5 Mar. 1840.

Oard, Robert. Va. —. His wife, Agnes Oard, was furnished 15 bushels of corn and 150 pounds of pork for the support of herself and three children in Rockbridge Co., Va. 6 Sep. 1780.

Oatman, Nicholas. —. —. He was taken prisoner by the Indians and exposed to hardships. Congress rejected his petition for a pension 27 Mar. 1846 because he was not in the service at the time.

Oatman, Peter. —. —. He was taken prisoner by the Indians and exposed to hardships. Congress rejected his petition for a pension 27 Mar. 1846 because he was not in the service at the time.

Oatman, William. —. —. He was taken prisoner by the Indians exposed to hardships. Congress rejected his petition for a pension 27 Mar. 1846 because he was not in the service at the time.

Ober, John. Md. Sgt. He was wounded at Eutaw Spring and received his half-pay 4 Apr. 1784 in Frederick County. He also appeared as John Auber.

Obert, John. N.J. Pvt. He served in the 1st Regiment. He was disabled by the loss of his upper lip and by a cold caught after inoculation for the smallpox in Canada in 1776 which affected the use of his limbs. He resided in New Brunswick, N.J. in 1792.

Oblenis, et. N.Y. Pvt. He served in Capt. Johnson's Rangers. He received a shot from one of the enemy's boats in the North River which broke his arm and two of his ribs on 17 Nov. 1777 n Bergen Co., N.J. He lived in Orange Co., N.Y. in 1794. He was on the 1813 pension list.

O'Brian, John. Pa. Pvt. He was on the 1813 pension list.

O'Brian, Philip. Pa. Pvt. He was in Philadelphia County on 30 Sep. 1785. He was transferred from the 6th Pa. Regiment to the Invalids. He was 64 years old. He was dead by Sep. 1793.

O'Briant, Jesse. S.C. —. He served under Capt. Anderson Thomas, Capt. Amos Davis, and Col. Richard Winn. He was on the Florida Expedition. He was 69 years old. William Roberts, Enoch Grubb, and Edward Vandever served in the war and deposed about his service. He was pensioned from Anderson District on 25 Nov. 1830. He was paid as late as 1834.

O'Brien, John. Me. —. He was from Cornish. He was paid $50 under the resolve of 1836.

O'Bryan, —. Va. —. His wife, Mary O'Bryan, was allowed £10 for her support and that of her small children in Augusta Co., Va. 17 Mar. 1778. Her husband was away in the service.

O'Bryan, Dennis. Md. Pvt. He was pensioned at the rate of half-pay of a private in Morgan Co., Va. 20 Feb. 1830.

O'Bryan, John. Va. —. His wife, Mildred O'Bryan, and children were awarded assistance in Charlotte Co., Va. on 7 July 1777, £4.11.6 provisions on 5 Jan. 1778, £22.10 on 5 Oct. 1778, and £89 on 1 Feb. 1779. He also appeared as John O'Bryant.

O'Connor, Michael. Md. Matross. He was pensioned at the rate of half-pay of a matross in Harford County 2 Jan. 1813.

O'Conner, Timothy. Va. Pvt. He was in Fairfax County on 17 Aug. 1786. He enlisted in the 15th Va. Regiment for three years. He was wounded by a musket ball a little above his left ankle and was taken prisoner at Brandywine on 11 Sep. 1777. He was 30 years old. He was discharged 23 July 1779 by Brigadier General William Woodford. He was in Henrico County in 1788. He was on the 1813 pension list.

Odam, Benjamin. S.C. —. He was on the roll in 1791.

Odam, Daniel. S.C. —. He was wounded 22 Dec. 1781. He was granted an annuity 13 Mar. 1786 in Orangeburg District in 1786. It was revoked in 1797. He served in the militia under Col. Hardin. He was on the 1813 pension list of Georgia. He transferred from Georgia to South Carolina 4 Mar. 1815.

Odam, Levi. S.C. —. He was wounded. He was from Marion District in 1838. His application was rejected.

Odam, Michael. S.C. —. He was killed 28 Aug. 1781. His widow, Martha Odam, was granted an annuity on 7 Dec. 1785 in Orangeburg/Winton.

Odam, Sabart. S.C. Pvt. He was wounded in the shoulder. He was granted an annuity 29 Dec. 1785 in Orangeburg/Winton. He had four children in 1797. He was on the 1813 pension list of Georgia and was from Chatham County. He also appeared as Seybert Odum.

Odam, Sion. S.C. —. His application was rejected 21 Dec. 1822.

Odell, Samuel. Mass. —. He was granted relief.

O'Ferrell, Dennis. Va. Pvt. He was in Shenandoah County 1 Mar. 1785. He served in the 11th Va. Regiment in Capt. Johnston's Company under Col. Daniel Morgan. He was wounded in the foot at Brandywine. He was 46 years old on 27 Apr. 1787 and 74 years old on 30 Sep. 1817. His pension was increased to $60 per annum on 25 Jan. 1813. He was on the 1813 pension roll. He was continued on the pension list at the rate of £8 per annum on 23 July 1787. He was continued at that rate on 14 May 1789 pension list. He died 29 Aug. 1832. Administration with the will annexed was granted to Samuel Combs.

Ogan, —. Va. —. He served in the 11th Virginia Regiment. His wife, Ann Ogan, and six children were granted £10 support in Frederick Co., Va. on 1 Aug. 1777. On 3 Aug. 1779 she and seven children were granted £30 support. He was in Col. Morgan's Regiment. She and four small children were furnished 4 barrels of corn and 200 pounds of pork on 2 Aug. 1780. She also appeared as Ann Ougan.

Ogden, Aaron. —. —. He served as an officer and sought half-pay for life 15 Dec. 1827.

Ogden, Stephen. N.J. Pvt. In 1777 he was in battle at Second River in Essex County and was wounded with a bullet in his left side. Dr. Bern Budd removed the ball from his right side. He was in the Morris County militia. He was pensioned 3 Mar. 1807 at the rate of $30 per annum in Morris County. He was 43 in 1793 and had a wife and three children.

Ogh, George. —. —. His application was rejected 7 May 1792.

Ogier, Lewis. S.C. Capt. He served under Capt. Daniel Horry in the calvary and was at Savannah. His fellow officers who proved his service in 1819 were James Kennedy 1st Lt. & Paymaster of 1st Continental Regiment; Samuel Warren of the 5th S.C. Continental Troops; J. H. Stevens Lt. & Adjutant in Calvary State Troops; M. Irvine Surgeon of Lee's Partisan Legion; Thomas Pinckney Major in the 1st Regiment S.C. Continental Troops; and William Fishburne Captain of the Troop of Horse under Col. Peter Horry. His widow was Susan Ogier in 1822. She was paid 16 Dec. 1856 her claim for his wages.

Ogle, Jacob. Va. Sgt. His widow, Mary Ogle, lived in Ohio Co., Va. 30 Oct. 1789. He was in the Ohio County militia and was killed in the service by Indians on 27 Sep. 1777. He served under Capt. Joseph Ogle. There were seven children. On 2 June 1778 she was awarded £25 support for herself and six children. She had her pension reduced to £8 per annum on 13 July 1790. She was continued on the pension list at the rate of £18 per annum on 17 Aug. 1790.

Oglivia, James. Pa. —. He was in Montgomery County on 21 Jan. 1807. He had several tours of duty in the militia. He enlisted 5 Oct. 1778 in Capt. Christie's Company in the 5th Pa. Regiment under Col. Francis Johnston. In 1780 he was put in the 2nd Battalion of Pa. troops under Col. Richard Butler. His tour of duty expired 5 Oct. 1781. He did not ask for his discharge until after the surrender of Cornwallis at Yorktown. He was awarded a $50 annuity.

O'Hara, —. Va. —. Her husband and two of her sons were killed in Col. Buford's defeat. Mary O'Hara applied in York Co., Va. 2 Dec. 1780. She was left with two children. She was granted £150 support on 11 Dec. 1780. The House, however, rejected the claim.

O'Hara, Francis. Pa. —. His heirs were paid $300 for his donation land 15 Mar. 1826. Another party had settled on the land before the patent had been issued.

O'Hara, James. Md. Pvt. He was pensioned 4 Mar. 1789. He was on the 1813 pension list.

O'Hara, James. Pa. —. He was awarded a $40 gratuity and a $40 annuity in Philadelphia 14 Mar. 1814.

O'Hara, James. Pa. —. His heirs received $300 in lieu of a donation tract 15 Mar. 1826.

O'Hara, John. Md. Pvt. He was on the 1813 pension list. His widow, Susan O'Hara, was pensioned at the rate of half-pay of a private 3 Mar. 1840.

O'Harrell, John. Va. —. He was away in Continental service. His wife, Mary O'Harrell, and two small children were granted £30 support in Botetourt County 11 Mar. 1779.

Ohine, —. N.Y. —. Susannah Ohine was granted support during the war.

Ohl, Eberhard. Pa. —. He was awarded a $40 gratuity in Schuylkill Co., Pa. on 14 Apr. 1828, on 14 Mar. 1832, and a $40 gratuity and $40 annuity 6 Apr. 1833.

Ohl, John. Pa. —. He was awarded a $40 gratuity and a $40 annuity in Northampton Co., Pa. 7 Mar. 1827. He was 82 years old in 1840. He died 17 Dec. 1843.

Ohlweiler, Charles. Pa. He was pensioned 2 Apr. 1822.

Oldham, George. N.C. —. He served under Col. William Moore and Col. Stephen Moore. He was at Cross Creek where Gen. Caswell defeated McCloud and at Gates's defeat. He was 80 years old and had a wife who was nearly as old. William Hubbard served a tour with him. Isaac Boring of Jackson Co., Ga. also served with him. He was from Pendleton District in 1830. His application was rejected.

Oldham, James. Pa. —. He was awarded a $40 gratuity in Baltimore, Md. 28 Mar. 1836.

Oldham, John. —. Capt. He married 12 Apr. 1795. Congress refused his widow, Anna Oldham, a pension 20 June 1848.

Oldis, Robert. Pa. —. He was pensioned in 1813. He died 4 Sep. 1824.

Oldner, Joshua. —. Sailing Master. He served on the *Scorpion* under Capt. Joseph Marshall. Congress rejected his claim on 26 Mar. 1858 because his whole testimony was loose.

Oldwine, Charles. Pa. He received a $40 gratuity and a $40 annuity 1 Apr. 1822.

Olinger, Jacob. Va. —. He was drafted in 1781 and served three months. He had a second tour of 20 days afterwards. Congress rejected his claim for a pension 9 Feb. 1848.

Oliver, —. Pa. —. His widow, Catharine Oliver, received a $40 gratuity in Berks County 1 Apr. 1836.

Oliver, —. Va. —. He died in the service. Two sons were in Continental service. The widow and mother, Elizabeth Oliver, was furnished 150 pounds of pork and 3 barrels of corn in Frederick Co., Va. on 1 Apr. 1783.

Oliver, —. Va. —. He died in Continental service. His widow, Sarah Oliver, and child were furnished support in Frederick Co., Va. on 9 Mar. 1780.

Oliver, May. —. —. He enlisted 1 Jan. 1776 for one year under Capt. Wilkinson and Col. Joseph Reed. His next tour was for three years under Capt. Oliver and Col. Grayton. He was 74 years old. Congress granted him a pension 3 Jan. 1832.

Oliver, William. Mass. —. He served in the 5th Regiment and was paid $20.

Oliver, William. N.J. Lt. He served in the Essex County Militia. He was wounded by a musket ball in the elbow of his right arm on 26 June 1781 at Rahway Meadow. He lived in Elizabeth, N.J. in 1795. He was pensioned at the rate of $166.66 2/3 per annum. He died 9 Jan. 1798.

Oliver, William. Va. Capt. He served in the artillery and died in Gloucester, Va. Congress rejected the claim of his heirs for half-pay because he had already received it on 10 Feb. 1836.

Ollard, Henry. Va. —. His widow, Judith Ollard, was granted £8 support in Northumberland County on 13 Oct. 1778 and £25 on 10 May 1779.

Olney, Joseph. R.I. Capt. He served aboard the *Columbus* and was promoted to 1st lieutenant. In Aug. 1777 he was appointed captain of the brig *Cabot*. On 20 Aug. 1783 he commanded the sloop *Peacock*. His daughter, Angelica Gilbert, sought his half-pay or commutation, but Congress ruled that he did not qualify to receive same on 12 Apr. 1838.

Olney, Stephen. R.I. Pvt. He was born in Rhode Island in 1752 and entered the service in Gloucester in Dec. 1775. He served under Gen. William West and Maj. Stephen Kimball as a sergeant major. He was discharged after three weeks. He was commissioned an ensign 29 May 1777, a lieutenant 23 June 1777, and a captain 11 May 1778. He served under Gen. Cornal, Gen. Spencer, and Gen. Sullivan. He was 84 years of age. He was from Warren, Penn. on 21 Mar. 1838 when Congress granted him a pension at the rank of a private.

O'Neal, Constantine. —. Pvt. His widow, Catharine O'Neal, submitted no evidence of her marriage so Congress rejected her claim for a pension 13 Feb. 1849.

O'Neal, Hamilton. Del. —. He was pensioned 4 Feb. 1783. He was on the roll in 1787.

O'Neal, John. Va. Pvt. He was in Continental service and was pensioned in Augusta County on 18 May 1784.

O'Neal. Laughlin. Pa. Lt. His wife was Anne O'Neal.

O'Neal, Timothy. Pa. —. He was awarded a $40 gratuity and a $40 annuity in Indiana County on 28 Mar. 1814. He died 28 Dec. 1816.

O'Neil, —. Pa. —. His widow, Susan O'Neil, was pensioned 20 Mar.1838 in Philadelphia.

O'Neil, John. Pa. Pvt. He received a $40 gratuity and a $40 annuity 2 Apr. 1822.

Oney, Amos. R.I. —. He enlisted at Charlestown, R.I. 16 June 1775 under Col. G. Hoxie and Capt. Roswell Smith for six months. In 1776 he served another six months under the same officers. In 1777 he served six months under Capt. Briar Lewis and Col. Noyes. His claim was suspended. He died but left no widow. Congress indefinitely postponed any action on 2 Mar. 1857 for the heirs.

O'Niel, Edward. Pa. Pvt. He was in Cumberland County on 23 Feb. 1786. He was in the 1st Pa. Regiment. He was wounded at Green Springs, Va. in action with the enemy and was thereby disabled from getting a livelihood. He was aged 29. He died 20 Mar. 1789. He also appeared as Edward O'Neal.

Onion, John B. —. —. His widow was Juliet Onion. Richard Pattison of Baltimore, Md., her administrator and one of the heirs, failed to submit proof to substantiate the claim so Congress denied the claim 23 Feb. 1855.

O'Quinn, Joseph. Md. Pvt. He was pensioned 4 Sep. 1789. He was on the 1813 pension list as Joseph O'Guin.

O'Quinn, Richard. Md. Pvt. He was pensioned 4 Mar. 1789.

Oray, Joshua. Pa. —. He was pensioned 26 June 1820.

Orcutt, David. Conn. Pvt. He enlisted in May 1775 at the age of 25 in Maj. Enos' command under Gen. Joseph Spencer. He was taken sick in August and carried to the Continental Hospital at Roxbury, Mass. By bad doctoring, he lost the use of his limbs. Dr. Church was detected as a traitor in the hospital. Ensign Noah Chapin was sick in the same hospital and did not think it was safe to be under Dr. Church's control. He obtained permission from Gen. Spencer to repair to a private house and procure doctor and hospital stores at his own expense. Orcutt served under Lt. Silas Blodget in the 3rd Company of the 2nd Regiment under Col. Wyllys. He was pensioned at Stafford, Conn. on 10 Dec. 1788. He was 25 years old. He was on the 1813 pension list. He died 15 Oct. 1818 in Tolland Co., Conn.

Orcutt, Seth. Mass. —. He served in the 10th Regiment and was from Scituate. He was paid $20.

Ord, —. Va. —. He was away in the service. His wife, Ann Ord, was allowed 5 bushels of corn valued at £75 in Augusta Co., Va. 20 June 1780.

Orem, Spedden. Md. Pvt. He was pensioned at the rate of half-pay of a private in Talbot County on 18 Feb. 1825.

Oren, Stephen. Md. Pvt. He was paid a further remuneration in Talbot County in 1825.

Organ, —. Pa. —. His widow, Catherine Organ, was granted a $40 gratuity and a $40 annuity in Westmoreland County 28 Mar. 1836.

Organ, Matthew. Pa. —. He applied in Armstrong County on 12 Mar. 1813. He served in Capt. Finney's Company of Light Infantry under Col. Harmar in the 1st Pa. Regiment. He had a wife and three small children.

608 Revolutionary War Pensions

Orme, Moses. Md. Pvt. He was pensioned at the rate of half-pay of a private in Anne Arundel County on 8 Mar. 1833.

Ormond, William. Md. Pvt. He served in the 2nd Regiment. He was wounded in the right hand by a musket ball which deprived him of the use of three of his fingers at Monmouth. He lived in Prince George's Co., Md. in 1794. He was granted one-third of a pension 20 Apr. 1796. He enlisted for three years and was discharged 13 June 1778.

Ormsly, Nathaniel. Mass. —. He was pensioned.

Orndorff, Christian. Md. Capt. He was pensioned at the rate of half-pay of a captain 19 Feb. 1819. His only surviving child, Eliza Shaffer the widow of Jonathan Shaffer or Jonathan Shafter of the District of Columbia, sought the $28 plus $200 interest that was due. Congress ruled that there was no cause for action. He also appeared as Christian Orendorff.

Orner, Michael. Pa. Pvt. He served in the 9th Pa. Regiment. He was wounded while on the bullock guard. On the day before the *Augusta*, an armed ship of war of the British, was blown up in the Delaware River. He slipped and fell, and one of the wagons went over him at Stony Point on 16 July 1779. His hip was put out of place. He enlisted 11 July 1777 and was mustered unfit for service in Mar. 1779. He lived in Philadelphia Co., Pa. in 1794. He was granted one-fourth of a pension 20 Apr. 1796.

Orr, John. N.H. Lt. He was from Bedford. He was wounded in the thigh at the battle of Bennington on 16 Aug. 1777. He served under Capt. Samuel McConnel and Col. Stickney. In 1778 he hired Capt. John Parker to bring him home in a sleigh and paid him £31.19.4. He was aged 37 in 1787. He was on the 1813 pension list. He died 23 Dec. 1822.

Orr, Robert. Pa. Capt. He was paid $750 for his services and losses in Armstrong County on 30 Mar. 1821. He commanded a company of volunteers raised in 1781 in Westmoreland Co., Pa. to join Gen. George Rogers Clark. At Wheeling they took boats. He was an Irishman by birth and settled in western Pennsylvania in 1773. He was wounded in the expedition against the Indians at the Big Miami River, and was held prisoner at Montreal until 1783. His children, Robert Orr and Chambers Orr, sought bounty land from Congress 15 Dec. 1857.

Orr, William. S.C. —. He was killed by the enemy. His widow, Mary Orr, was awarded an annuity 17 June 1785.

Orr, William. Va. Pvt. His wife, Faith Orr, and two children were furnished 3 barrels of corn and 150 pounds of pork on 2 Aug. 1780. His wife and child were furnished 100 pounds of pork and 2 barrels of corn on 1 Apr. 1783 in Frederick Co., Va. His widow was in Frederick County in Apr. 1787. He was in Buford's detachment, was taken prisoner, and died in captivity. His widow was 50 years old and had two children. She was put on the pension list at the rate of £6 per annum on 14 Apr. 1787.

Orvis, Gershom. N.Y. —. He enlisted in Apr. 1775 under Capt. Benedict at Hinsdale under Gen. Montgomery and was discharged. In June 1776 he enlisted for six months under Capt. Merriman and spent most of the time at Ticonderoga Point. In June or July 1776 he enlisted at Saratoga under Capt. Bridgeman and served until the surrender of Burgoyne. He died 9 Mar. 1824. He married 17 July 1776. Congress granted his widow, Asenath Orvis, a pension 12 Apr. 1844.

Orwig, Henry. Pa. —. He was awarded a $40 gratuity and a $40 annuity in Schuylkill Co., Pa. 1 Apr. 1829. His name may have been Henry Ornig.

Osborn, —. Ga. —. Mrs. Osborn was granted ten bushels of corn 12 Feb. 1782.

Osborn, Daniel. N.Y. —. He served under Col. Lewis Dubois. His wife, Phebe Osborn, was granted support while he was away in the service in Feb. 1779. There were three children. Her sister was Elizabeth Fowler.

Osborn, Danvers. N.Y. Pvt. He served under Col. James Hammon in the Westchester County militia and was slain 17 Dec. 1779. His sons, Robert Campbell Osborn and John Danvers Osborn, received a half-pay pension.

Osborn, Jeremiah. Conn. Sgt. He served in the 10th Artillery. He suffered from bleeding in his lungs and weakness in 1779. He resided in Weston, Conn. in 1792.

Osborn, Michael. Me. —. He died 4 Dec. 1834 at Wiscasset. His widow was Judith Osborn from Augusta. She was paid $50 under the resolve of 1836.

Osborn, Nehemiah. N.J. —. His widow, Mary Osborn, was pensioned in Essex County on 7 Mar. 1848 at the rate of $50 per annum.

Osborne, Richard. —. —. He was pensioned 3 Mar. 1815.

Osborne, William. Conn. Corp. He served in the militia in Capt. David Leavenworth's Company under Col. Samuel Canfield. He was wounded and taken prisoner at Horseneck by Maj.Barmore's party of dragoons on 8 June 1779. He was carried to Kingsbridge and exchanged. Anthony Burritt and Joseph Perry, Surgeons, attended him. He received nine wounds, three from a sword in his elbow. He also suffered from a dislocated shoulder. He was pensioned 7 Mar. 1787. He died in 1801.

Osgood, Phineas. Mass. —. He served in the 6th Regiment and was paid $20.

Osteer, —. Pa. —. His widow, Louisa Osteer, was awarded a $40 gratuity and a $40 annuity in Lancaster Co., Pa. 11 Mar. 1833.

Ostertrout, Isaac. —. —. He married in 1795 and died about forty years later. His widow, Maria Ostertrout, married secondly Oliver Hills. She was 80 years old and resided in Chautauqua Co., N.Y. Congress denied her a pension as a widow because she had a living husband on 3 Mar. 1851.

Ostrander, William. N.Y. Corp. He entered the service in 1776 for three years. In 1834 he received $600 from N.Y. in lieu of his bounty land. He died 15 Nov. 1839 in Ulster Co., N.Y. His widow was Maria Ostrander who received a pension from Congress for the period of 3 Mar. 1826 to 4 Mar. 1831.

Otis, Joseph. Conn. Pvt. He served under Col. Zebulon Butler and afterwards under Col. Webb. He was wounded by a musket ball which remained lodged in his thigh in Feb. 1781 at Morrisiana. He resided in Bransford, Conn. in 1795. He enlisted 1 Jan. 1777 for the war and was on the rolls in 1780. He was granted half a pension 20 Apr. 1796. He was on the 1813 pension list.

Otman, Nicholas. —. —. He was taken prisoner by the Indians and held in captivity for two years. Congress refused him a pension because he was not a soldier when he was taken captive on 27 Mar. 1846.

Otman, Peter. —. —. He was taken prisoner by the Indians and was held in captivity for two years. Congress refused him a pension because he was not a soldier when he was taken captive on 27 Mar. 1846.

Otman, William. —. —. He was taken prisoner by the Indians and held in captivity for two years. Congress refused him a pension because he was not a soldier when he was taken captive on 27 Mar. 1846.

Ott, —. Pa. —. His widow, Elizabeth Ott, was granted a $40 gratuity and a $40 annuity in Cumberland County 14 Mar. 1835.

Ott, Adam. Md. Lt. He was pensioned at the rate of half-pay of a lieutenant in Washington County on

22 Feb. 1822. His widow, Juliana Ott, was pensioned at the same rate 12 Mar. 1828. His arrears were paid to her 20 Feb. 1829.

Ott, Andrew. Pa. —. He was from Philadelphia when he was pensioned 22 Mar. 1825. He was 103 years of age in 1840. He died 16 Dec. 1841.

Ott, Elias. Pa. —. He was awarded a $40 gratuity and a $40 annuity in Northampton Co., Pa. 23 Apr. 1829. He died 14 Apr. 1834.

Ott, Jacob. Pa. —. He was awarded a $40 gratuity in Philadelphia Co., Pa. in Feb. 1834.

Otterson, Samuel. S.C. Capt. & Maj. He served in the militia. He was on the 1813 pension list. He moved to Greene Co., Ala. 4 Mar. 1834.

Ouland, John. Va. —. He served in the 8th Virginia Regiment. His wife, Sarah Ouland, and one child,who was troubled with fits, were furnished £20 support in Frederick Co., Va. on 4 May 1779. She and three children were furnished 3 barrels of corn and 150 pounds of pork on 1 May 1781.

Overdorff, John. Pa. —. He was awarded a $40 gratuity in Berks Co., Pa. 15 Apr. 1835. He also appeared as John Overduff.

Overlin, John. Va. —. His wife, Mary Overlin, and four children were granted £5 per month support in Yohogania Co., Va. 24 June 1778. He served in the 13th Virginia Regiment. On 27 Oct. 1779 she and her five children were awarded £15 per month.

Overly, Henry. Va. —. He lived in Wythe County. He was on the 1813 pension list. He later transferred to Missouri.

Overstreet, John. Va. Seaman. His widow, Leannah Overstreet, was in Lancaster County on 3 Apr. 1786. He served on the galley *Revenge* belonging to Va. and died in service. In 1786 his widow was aged 30. They had five children, ranging in age from 10 to 19 years. The children were aged 2 to 11 at the time of their father's death. She also appeared as Leander Overstreet.

Overstreet, John H. Va. Capt. He served as a cadet for a short time. He was commissioned 28 Nov. 1787 [sic] to serve under Robert Lawson in the militia. In Mar. 1781 he was appointed captain. He was in the battles of Brandywine and Guilford. His heirs were not awarded his commutation on 1 Feb. 1818 because his service was entirely in the militia.

Overstreet, William. Pa. Pvt. He was transferred to Virginia by 1806. He was on the 1813 pension list.

Overton, Seth. —. —. He served aboard a private vessel and was taken prisoner. Congress rejected his claim for a pension because he was not in actual service on 10 Feb. 1846.

Overturff, John. Pa. —. He was awarded a $40 gratuity and a $40 annuity in Fayette County 18 Mar. 1833.

Owen, Bailey. —. —. His widow, Polly Owen, had her petition for a pension rejected by Congress on 27 Mar. 1846 because they were married subsequent to 1 Jan. 1794.

Owen, Christopher. Pa. —. He applied in Philadelphia County on 12 Apr. 1819. He served in Capt. George Naugle's Company in the 1st Pa. Regiment of Rifle Corps to the end of the war.

Owen, Morris. Va. —. He served in the Col. Harrison's Regiment of Artillery. His widow, Ann Owen, was being pensioned 11 Dec. 1784.

Owen, Robert. Mass. —. He served in the 1st Regiment and was from Groton. He was paid $20.

Owen, Thomas. Pa. Pvt. He was in Chester County on 19 Dec. 1786. He served in the 5th Pa. Regiment in Capt. Joseph Potts's Company under Col. Francis Johnston. He was wounded in his right thigh
at Brandywine on 11 Sep. 1777 by a musket ball. He was 52 years old.

Owen, William. Mass. —. He served in the 4th Regiment and was paid $20.

Owen, William. Mass. —. He was paid $20. [second of the name]

Owens, Eleazar. N.Y. Pvt. He served under Col. James McClaghry in the Ulster County militia and was slain 22 July 1779. His son, Eleazer Owens, received a half-pay pension for seven years.

Owens, John. S.C. Capt. He was killed in action 18 Nov. 1781. His widow, Elizabeth Owens, was awarded an annuity 3 Feb. 1785 in Laurens. There were children in 1791.

Owens, Thomas. Va. Pvt. His widow, Ann Owens, was in Westmoreland County on 26 Apr. 1786. He was in the 1st Regiment of Artillery and died in the service.

Owens, Vincent. Va. —. His wife, Sarah Owens, was furnished £16 relief in Frederick Co., Va. on 2 Mar. 1779.

Owens, William. S.C. —. He was drafted in North Carolina and served under Capt. Potter, Gen. Lincoln, Capt. Richard Harrison, and Col. Joseph Taylor. He went from Salisbury to Savannah. He was at Bacon's Bridge and Stono. Raleigh Hammond and Frederick Owen served with him. He was pensioned in Lancaster District 7 Dec. 1826. He was paid as late as 1833.

Owland, Thomas. Va. —. His wife, Sarah Owland, and three children were furnished three barrels of corn and 150 pounds of pork in Frederick County 1 May 1781.

Packard, Daniel. Mass. —. He served in the 8th Regiment and was from Buckfield. He was paid $20.

Packard, James. Me. —. He was from Norway, Maine. He was paid $50 under the resolve of 1836.

Packard, Shepard. Mass. Pvt. He was pensioned 2 May 1808. He was on the 1813 pension list.

Packer, Thomas. N.H. —. He volunteered in the expedition to Rhode Island and served under Capt. John Folsom in Col. Kelley's Regiment. He was taken ill of fever and dysentery and was allowed £31.12.0 on 8 Nov. 1779.

Packwood, Joseph. Conn. Capt. He took his vessel from New London in 1775 to Hispaniola to purchase arms, field pieces, and other munitions of war. He sailed in Dec. 1775 and returned in Aug. 1776 with 12,000 pounds of powder, 14 field pieces, and 300 stand of arms. His vessel was seized; he was imprisoned, contracted a disease, and lost his vision. Congress rejected the claim of his daughter 18 Feb. 1857.

Paffenberger, John. Pa. —. He was awarded a $40 gratuity and a $40 annuity in Schuylkill Co., Pa. 11 Apr. 1825. He died 18 July 1826. He also appeared as John Pfaffenberger.

Pagan, Alexander. S.C. Capt. He was killed in action 18 Aug. 1780. His widow, Jennet Pagan, was awarded an annuity 29 Nov. 1784. She was from Chester District. There were two children in 1791. She was paid as late as 1826.

Page, Carter. Va. Capt. He served under Col. Baylor and was in the battle when defeated in 1779. He and his men transferred to other regiments. He became supernumerary. He was also captain of a volunteer calvary unit of the Virginia militia. He was paid to June 1779. Congress indicated that his claim should be presented to the court of claims on 8 Apr. 1856.

Page, Chase. Me. —. He died 4 May 1825 in Corinth. His widow was Lydia Page from Levant. She was paid $50 under the resolve of 1836.

Page, Daniel. —. —. He was pensioned in 1822, dropped in 1824, and restored in 1832. He paid William B. Kelley to prepare his pension application. Kelley demanded even more money and threatened to have his pension stopped. Kelley hung himself. A friend of Page wrote the Pension Office and found out that Page had been dropped. Congress granted him a pension 23 Dec. 1833.

Page, Stephen. —. —. He was a pensioner. He married 18 Feb. 1787. His wife, Eunice Page, suffered from his cruelty and wilful desertion for four years. She obtained a divorce in Mar. 1808 from the R. I. Supreme Court. He died 13 July 1834. Congress denied her a pension 14 June

1850.

Page, Thomas. S.C. —. His annuity was £1.10.4 in 1787.

Page, Timothy. —. —. He served under Capt. Belknap and Col. Brook and was slain at White Plains, N.Y. by a five pound shot. His brother-in-law was Jeduthan Willington aged 87. His daughter, Dorcas Wright, had her claim for compensation rejected by Congress 9 June 1838.

Page, Timothy. N.J. —. His widow, Mary Page, was pensioned in Monmouth County on 8 Mar. 1844 at the rate of $40 per annum.

Pailer, —. Va. —. His wife was granted support in Prince Edward Co., Va. on 20 July 1778 while he was away in Continental service.

Pailer, —. Va. —. He and his brother were away in Continental service. Their mother, Anne Pailer, had her claim rejected in Nov. 1779. She was from Lunenburg County.

Pain, John. N.J. Capt. He was wounded in action with a party of refugees and died about three weeks later on 25 Sep. 1781. Sgt. Joshua Marsh died on the spot. Pain's widow, Mary Pain, was awarded £12 in 1782. She was from Middlesex County.

Paine, Charles. Mass. —. He served in the 5th Regiment and was from Deerfield. He was paid $50.

Paine, Joseph. N.Y. Pvt. He served under Lt. Col. James Hammon in Capt. Israel Honeywell's Company in the Westchester County militia. He was disabled by two musket balls in his right side on 11 Jan. 1781. One remained lodged in his body. He was in Orange Co., N.Y. in 1786. He was on the 1791 pension roll.

Paine, Thomas. —. —. He was pensioned by resolution of 24 Feb. 1785 by the Continental Congress.

Painter, —. Conn. Maj. He sought his half-pay 4 Sep. 1787.

Painter, George. N.C. He was 78 years old in Rutherford Co., N.C. in July 1834.

Painter, John. Pa. Lt. He applied in Northumberland County on 13 Jan. 1819. He served in Capt. John Chatham's Company of militia in 1778 having been enrolled by Samuel Hunter, lieutenant of the Northumberland County militia. William Hoffman along with Thomas Martin, Richard Martin, and John Painter in the fall of 1778 assisted in building forts and batteries in the town of Northumberland and did service in 1779, 1780, 1781, and 1782. He served under Col. Thomas Hartley and was paid $200 on 20 Feb. 1819.

Painter, Melchior. Md. Pvt. His widow, Mary Painter, was pensioned at the rate of half-pay of a private in Washington County on 1 Apr. 1839.

Painter, Samuel. Va. —. His widow, Anne Painter, lived in Sussex County on 16 Mar. 1786.

Pallmeter, Uriah. Mass. —. He served in the 1st Regiment and was from New York. He was paid $20. He also appeared as Uriah Palmester.

Palmer, Isaac. Conn. Sgt. He served in the 3rd Regiment. He was debilitated by fits. He resided in Wethersfield, Conn. in 1792. He enlisted 21 Jan. 1777 and invalided 1 Apr. 1781.

Palmer, Jacob. Pa. —. He received a $40 gratuity and a $40 annuity in Lancaster County 27 Feb. 1821.

Palmer, Jared. Conn. Sgt. He served in the 4th Regiment in Capt. Barker's Company. He was wounded by a musket ball which passed through his right breast and the joint of his right shoulder on 14 Oct. 1781 at Yorktown. He lived in Pawlings, N.Y. in 1794. He enlisted in Oct. 1780 and was on the rolls in 1783. He was granted one-sixteenth of a pension 20 Apr. 1796. He was on the 1813 pension list.

Palmer, Joshua. S.C. Capt. He served under Col. Thomas, Col. William Wofford, and Maj. Thomas Brandon. He was on the Florida Expedition and at Stono. Joseph Hughes, William Sharp, and John Griffin served with him. He sought compensation in 1810.

Palmer, William. Va. Corp. He served in the 10th Regiment. He lost a leg in the service. He was pensioned in Orange Co., Va. He was continued on the pension roll at the rate of £15 per annum on 8 Nov. 1786. He also appeared as William Parmer.

Pangburn, Lines. N.J. Pvt. He served under Capt. Joseph Randolph in the Monmouth County militia and was shot by a party of refugees 30 Dec. 1780. His widow, Anna Pangburn, was granted a half-pay pension in Monmouth County. There were three children.

Pangburn, Nathaniel. N.J. —. He was pensioned in Monmouth County on 25 Jan. 1838 at the rate of $60 per annum.

Panniel, Joseph. Ga. Lt. Col. He was a deranged officer. He received his commutation of half-pay 27 Mar. 1792. He also appeared as Joseph Pannel.

Panum, George. Pa. —. He applied 27 May 1828.

Parchment, Peter. Va. Pvt. He lived in Ohio County in 1786. He was in the 9th Va. Regiment under Maj. Taylor. He served four years. Col. John Gibson deposed that he had his arm broken and shattered by a wound received from the Indians on the Muskingum River in Jan. 1779. He was in the 13th Va. Regiment. Capt. Benjamin Biggs also certified his service. He was pensioned at the rate of half-pay for his disability on 20 Apr. 1785. He moved to Pennsylvania in 1795. He was granted seven-eights of a pension 20 Apr. 1796 in Connecticut. He was on the 1813 pension list. One Peter Parchment was granted relief in Allegheny Co., Penn. 13 Apr. 1841.

Pardee, Chandler. Conn. Pvt. He served in Col. Sabin's Militia. He was wounded in the small of his back by a musket ball on 5 July 1779 at New Haven. He resided at East Haven, Conn. in 1794. He was on the 1813 pension list. He died in June 1833. He also appeared as Chandler Paradie.

Pardoe, James L. Pa. Bombardier. He served in the artillery.

Pardoe, Joseph. Pa. —. He was pensioned 22 June 1816 and died 17 Mar. 1820.

Pardue, Field. S.C. Maj. He served in the Mounted Riflemen under Samuel Hammond. His wound was the ultimate cause of his death. He received no compensation in his lifetime. His children, Gideon Pardue, Susan Pardue, Patsey Pardue, and Lucilla Covington sought same. The latter was the wife of Benjamin Covington. They were paid $2,440.32 in 1835.

Pardue, William. S.C. —. He served under Capt. George Hicks in North Carolina and was taken prisoner in Georgia. He was placed on a prison ship which sprang a leak so he was taken to land. He made his escape. He was in his 83rd year. His wife was old and frail. "I have nothing but the clothes on my back." Reuben Bennett deposed that they were neighbors in Warren Co., N.C. and both served. He was from Lancaster District, South Carolina when he applied for a pension in 1842. He died in May 1844. His administrator, Thomas W. Hagey, sought his arrearage.

Paris, Isaac. N.Y. Pvt. He and his son were slain at Oriska by the enemy. His widow, Catharine Paris, was awarded £30 per annum during her widowhood on 14 Feb. 1792. Their son also died in the same battle.

Parish, Oliver. Conn. —. He entered the service in 1778 for one year under Capt. David Umstead and Col. Roger Enos in the infantry. He was accidentally injured on piquet duty and became lame. He was discharged. After his recovery he served another tour of nine months as a substitute for his brother. He died 8 Aug. 1832. His children were Zenus Parish, Oliver Parish, Clinton Parish, Sally Bullis, Cynthia Dustin, Eliza Parish, and Betsey Parish. They claimed the pension due their father. He was late of Plattsburg, N.Y. In 1832 he was about 73 years old. Congress granted the heirs the amount which would have been due their father under the act of 1832 on 3 Jan. 1837. Congress postponed any further action 8 Aug. 1842.

Parish, Silas. N.Y. Pvt. He served in Swartwout's N.Y. Regiment. He was pensioned 29 May 1788. He lived in Ontario County. He was on the 1813 pension list.

Park, James. S.C. —. He was paid his annuity in 1828, 1830, 1831, 1832, and 1834.

Park, Jonathan. Conn. —. He served under Capt. Ebenezer Hitter and Col. Samuel Seldon. He died of camp distemper at Long Island in Nov. 1776 before the expiration of his enlistment. He was in service no longer than five months. He married 21 Mar. 1773 at Preston, Conn. Congress granted his widow, Anna Yarrington, a pension 25 Jan. 1848. She married John Boreman after Park died.

Park, Thomas. Conn. Capt. He served on the privateer, the *Prudence.* In Feb. 1782 he found floating and took up a quantity of sails and rigging belonging to the British man of war, *Bedford,* which had been thrown overboard in a gale. He sold them to Capt. Harding of the *Confederacy* for $800. His home in Groton was plundered and the receipt was lost. Hugh E. Fiddis was powder boy and proved that he was present when Park sold sails and rigging to Harding. Congress allowed the heirs relief 27 Dec. 1854.

Park, Thomas. Pa. Corp. He served under Col. Wyllys. He was wounded by a ball which entered his groin and passed through his left buttock. He was scouting with the militia when the engagement with the Indians occurred on 29 Mar. 1780 at Huntington. He lived in Luzerne Co., Pa. in 1794. He enlisted 15 Jan. 1777 for 3 years; he was discharged 15 Jan. 1780. He was on the 1813 pension list.

Parke, Joshua. Mass. Pvt. He served in the 7th Regiment and was from Groton. He was paid $50.

Parker, —. Pa. —. His widow, Frances Parker, was granted a $40 gratuity and a $40 annuity in Fayette County 16 June 1836.

Parker, —. Pa. —. His widow, Mary Parker, was awarded a $40 gratuity in Philadelphia Co., Pa. 6 Mar. 1833.

Parker, Abijah. Mass. —. He served in the 7th Regiment and was from Portland. He was paid $20.

Parker, Abraham. —. —. He was old and infirm and had a wife and several other dependents. His property was valued at $314. Congress granted him a pension 21 Dec. 1831.

Parker, Charles. Pa. Pvt. He applied in Armstrong County on 9 Jan. 1818. He served three years in the 8th Pa. Regiment. He was in the battles of Brandywine and Germantown. Lt. & Adjt. J. Round of the 8th Pa. Regiment, Capt. Finley, and James Barr proved his service. He was 79 years old.

Parker, George. Mass. Pvt. He was pensioned 31 July 1786 in Essex Co., Mass. He served under Col. Thomas Marshall in Capt. Christ: Marshall's Company. He was ruptured on both sides. He was 45 years old in 1786. He was on the 1813 pension list. He transferred to Conn. 4 Sep. 1818. He returned to Worcester Co., Mass. 4 Mar. 1819. He died 30 June 1822. He was paid $20 by the Commonwealth.

Parker, George. Pa. Pvt. He was in Philadelphia County on 9 Jan. 1786. He was in the 6th Pa. Regiment and was disabled by a hurt in his leg received in erecting huts on James Island, S.C. He was 24 years old.

Parker, Isaac. N.C. —. He applied in Greene County in 1814. He was wounded several times at the battle of Rockfish. William Sutton of Lenoir County, who served under Capt. Jacob Johnston, corroborated his service.

Parker, Jacob. Pa. —. He was awarded a $40 gratuity and a $40 annuity in Chester Co., Pa. 3 May 1832.

Parker, Jesse. Mass. —. He was in the 7th Regiment and was from Brookfield. He was paid $20.

Parker, Jesse. Mass. —. He was in the 6th Regiment and was from Palmer. He was paid $50.

Parker, John. Mass. Pvt. He served in the 15th Regiment and was from Gloucester. His widow, Lucy Parker, was paid $50.

Parker, John. Pa. —. His remarried widow, Hannah Foote, was awarded a $40 gratuity and a $40 annuity in Chester Co., Pa. 3 Mar. 1829.

Parker, John. S.C. —. He was wounded at Fort Augusta. He was granted an annuity 1 Sep. 1784 in Abbeville.

Parker, John. S.C. —. He enlisted at age 16 and served under Capt. Erwin. He was also under Capt. Samuel Moore and Capt. Maxwell. He was at Ninety Six, Snow Camp, Cherokee Expedition, and Florida Expedition. John Warnock was with him at Ninety Six. He was pensioned 23 Nov. 1829 and resided in Anderson District. He was paid as late as 1834.

Parker, John. Va. Pvt. He served in the 2nd Va. Regiment and was taken prisoner at the surrender of Charleston, S.C. He was wounded at Savannah above his knee and his thigh bone was fractured. After his escape from captivity he joined the troops under Col. Henry Lee at the siege of Augusta. He was pensioned on 9 Nov. 1785 and was pensioned at the rate of half-pay for his disability and given £24 relief.

Parker, Joseph. Conn. —. He volunteered in the summer in 1777 and was an artificer under Capt. Painter to Apr. 1778 when he was transferred to Capt. Mansfield's Company under Col. Meigs. He was sick in the fall of 1778 and spring of 1779. He rejoined in Mar. 1779. In Apr. 1779 he went out to get fresh provisions and was taken prisoner by a party of cowboys who carried him to King's Bridge. He was then eighteen years old. He was given the option to go to a prison ship or join the British army. He chose to join the British with the intention to desert. He did so and returned to his mother in Swanzy, N.H. in June. His elder brother, Benjamin Parker, was killed at Bemis Heights. He did not return to the service because he knew the British would have shot him if he had been recaptured. Congress granted him a pension 10 July 1840. He served as an artificer and soldier.

Parker, Joseph. N.J. Pvt. He enlisted for one year under Capt. Joseph Huddy and was killed at the Block House at Toms River 22 Mar. 1782. He was shot in the head. He married Elizabeth Welch in 1776. She applied from Monmouth County.

Parker, Joseph. N.J. —. He was paid $112 for claims not theretofore provided for in Mercer County on 14 Feb. 1844.

Parker, Joseph. Va. —. He was pensioned at the rate of $60 per annum on 8 Jan. 1803. He was in Rockingham County on 22 Apr. 1804. He had previously lived in Frederick County. He was in Shenandoah County in 1812 and was pensioned 13 Jan. 1813 at the rate of $60 per annum with $40 immediate relief. His pension was increased to $150 per annum on 6 Mar. 1833 in Frederick County. He died testate 25 May 1841, and his executor was James Cather.

Parker, Joshua. Mass. Pvt. He served with the 4th Regiment and was from Groton. He was paid $50.

Parker, Josiah. Me. —. He was from New Portland. He was paid $50 under the resolve of 1836.

Parker, Josiah. Mass. Matross. He served in Crane's Artillery and was from Boston. His widow, Susanna Parker, was paid $50.

Parker, Jotham. N.Y. Brigade Wagonmaster. He entered the service in 1776 under Capt. Watson and Gen. Huntington. He was at Ticonderoga, Crown Point, and St. Johns. He was between Peekskill and Fishkill when the British took Fort Montgomery. He served to 1781. He married at Norfolk, Conn. 30 Dec. 1779 Sarah -----. He died 19 July 1815. His widow was from Chenango Co., N.Y. on 15 Feb. 1844 when Congress granted her a pension at the rank of a captain.

Parker, Levi. Mass. Lt. He received his commutation for five years in lieu of half-pay for life. He was from Westford. He died 10 Sep. 1825.

Parker, Moses. —. Col. He was wounded and taken prisoner by the British at Bunker Hill on 17 June 1775 and died of wounds in Boston in July 1775. He left a large family of young children. His widow, Sarah Parker, sought compensation in 1793.

Parker, Richard. Pa. —. His heirs recovered a tract of donation land from Robert Hodge and Daniel Clark. Pennsylvania paid Hodge and Clark $500 on 2 Apr. 1830 for their great expense.

Parker, Samuel. —. Pvt. He served in Col. S. B. Webb's Regiment under Capt. J. Walker. He was ruptured in the belly by a fall in consequence of the wind from a cannon ball in 1778 on the expedition on Rhode Island. About two inches of the rim of his belly was shot away. He resided at Weston, Conn. in 1796. He enlisted 21 Feb. 1777 and was transferred to the Invalids.

Parker, Samuel. Mass. Pvt. He served in the 8th Regiment. His widow, Lucretia Farley, was from Pepperell and was paid $50.

Parker, William. Mass. —. He served from 4 Nov. 1777 to 3 Apr. 1778 under Capt. Cadwallader Ford and Col. Brooks and guarded prisoners at Cambridge. He next served six months as a substitute for his father, Jonas Parker, of Reading from May 1778 under Capt. Nathan Sargent. He was at Winterhill in Charlestown. He served one month as a substitute for his brother, Aaron Parker, in June 1779 under Capt. Nathan Sargent. He was pensioned in 1832 but stricken in 1840 on the grounds that the pay rolls did not show the length of service he claimed. Congress granted him a special pension 30 Mar. 1848.

Parker, William. Mass. Pvt. He served under Col. Samuel Johnson and was wounded at Still Water 13 Dec. 1777. The gun shot entered his right hip and passed out the left. He was pensioned 9 July 1784 from the time of his discharge. Her was 38 years old in 1791. He was on the 1813 pension list.

Parker, William. Mass. Pvt. He was pensioned 28 Dec. 1791. He transferred from Maine 4 Mar. 1833.

Parker, William. R.I. Pvt. He had a very bad rupture in his groin occasioned by a fall in Nov. 1777 on the march from Red Banks to Mount Holly. He was also disabled by infirmities of old age. He served under Col. Jeremiah Olney. He was aged 69 in 1786. He died 21 Feb. 1801 in Providence Co., R.I.

Parkey, Peter. N.Y. —. He was granted support during the war.

Parkhurst, Benjamin. Vt. Pvt. He served a month in the militia from Royalton, Vt. under Capt. Bush in Feb. 1777. In the fall of 1777 he served two months under Capt. Timothy Bush and Col. Joseph Marsh. In the spring of 1779 he served under Capt. Ezra Stearns, Lt. James Smalley, and Lt. Joel Marsh. He served out his term. In the spring of 1780 he served a fortnight in building Fort Bethel. When the Indians burnt Royalton, Vt., his property was destroyed. He was out in the service another fortnight. Congress granted him a pension for sixteen months of service on 23 Mar. 1836.

Parkhurst, George. —. —. He served ten months and sixteen days. He died in 1839. Congress rejected the claim 13 Apr. 1860 because no proof was submitted.

Parkhurst, George. Mass. —. He served in the 8th Regiment. He was paid $20.

Parkhurst, Jonathan. Mass. Pvt. He served in the 4th Regiment and was from Dana. He was paid $50.

Parkhurst, Moses. Mass. —. He served in the 6th Regiment and was paid $20. He also appeared as Moses Packhurst.

Parkhurst, Phineas. N.H. Fifer. He served in Capt. Joseph Parkhurst's Company of militia. He was wounded in his right side by a musket ball in 1780 at Royalton. He lived in Lebanon, N.H. in 1795. He was granted a full pension 20 Apr. 1796.

Parkinson, Abraham. Pa. —. He applied 20 Mar. 1827. He served six and a half years. Capt. Thomas Lucas, Thomas Campbell, Patrick Jack, and Joseph Baldwin were fellow soldiers and proved his service.

Parkinson, James. N.C. Lt. He died in service 26 Mar. 1778. He left a widow and one child, Rebecca Perkinson. His only heir, the daughter, applied in 1789. She was Rebecca Harris in 1790. He also appeared as James Perkinson and James Parkerson. His seven years' half-pay was due his daughter, 2 July 1836 at which time she was Rebecca Sutherland, wife of James Sutherland.

Parkman, Thomas. Mass. —. He served in the Artificers and was paid $20.

Parkman, William E. —. —. He and others sought pensions from 4 Mar. 1841 to 4 Mar. 1843 for those soldiers and their widows, who had not received or been entitled to same. Congress disagreed on 1 Aug. 1850.

Parks, Francis. Pa. —. He was pensioned 16 June 1836 in Fayette County. He died 22 Aug. 1840.

Parks, James. N.C. Pvt. He applied in Rutherford County in 1807. He served in the militia and was wounded in Aug. 1780 at Rocky Mount on the Wateree River in S.C. He served under Gen. Butler and Col. Isaacs. Israel Holt swore that he saw him a prisoner after the battle of Brown Marsh. He had a cut in his head, a broken right arm, and was disabled in his back. He was on the 1813 pension list.

Parks, John. Pa. Pvt. He was in Philadelphia County on 14 Nov. 1785. He was transferred from the 2nd Pa. Regiment to the Invalids. He was wounded in the right arm. He was discharged 1 Nov. 1783. He was 38 years old.

Parks, Jonas. N.H. Pvt. He served under Col. Bond in Capt. Smith's Company. He lost the sight of one eye, and that of the other was impaired in consequence of hardships under inoculation of smallpox in July 1777 at Hubbardstown. He lived at Charleston, N.H.

Parmelee, Thomas. Conn. Sgt. He was wounded by a musket shot in the right thigh which caused an exfoliation of the bone in Apr. 1777 at Ridgfield. He served in Col. Moseley's Regiment. He was pensioned 4 Mar. 1793. He lived in Washington, Conn. in 1794. He was in the militia. He was granted one-eighth of a pension 20 Apr. 1796. He was on the 1813 pension list as Thomas Parmelie. He transferred to Oneida Co., N.Y. 4 Sep 1826.

Parmelie, Jeremiah. Conn. Capt. He died 24 Mar. 1778. His heirs were paid his seven years' half-pay of $1,680.

Parmer, William. Va. Corp. He served in the 10th Virginia Regiment and was 30 years old on the 1787 pension roll. He was from Orange County. He lost his leg at Brandywine 11Sep. 1777. He was on the 1813 pension list. He was later transferred to Kentucky. He also appeared as William Palmer.

Parran, Thomas. Md. Surgeon. His heirs was awarded 200 acres bounty land in Allegany County on 11 Mar. 1828. His widow, Jane Parran, was pensioned at the rate of half-pay of a surgeon in Calvert County on 14 Mar. 1828. Her arrearage was paid to her legal representative 14 Jan. 1830.

Parris. Gabriel. Pa. —. He was awarded a $40 gratuity and a $40 annuity in Philadelphia 1 Apr. 1836. He died 10 May 1840.

Parris, Nathaniel. N.Y. —. He was granted relief.

Parrish, Edward. Md. Sgt. He was pensioned at the rate of half-pay of a sergeant in Baltimore County on 2 Mar. 1827. His arrearage was paid to James Nelson for his widow, Clemency Parrish, 24 Feb. 1836. She was pensioned at the same rate 16 Mar. 1836.

Parrish, Roswell. Conn. Pvt. He served in the militia in Capt. Benjamin Bacon's Company under Col.

John Douglass in New York in 1776. He was stationed at Westchester. He was lodged in a barn and slept in the loft. In his sleep he fell 12 to 14 feet and fractured his right arm. He was pensioned 5 Sep. 1787 at Canterbury, Conn. at the age of 28. He died 6 Sep.1807. He also appeared as Roswell Parish.

Parrish, Silas. N.Y. Pvt. He enlisted in 15 Feb. 1776 in Capt. Comfort Ludenton's Company in the Dutchess County militia under Col. Jacobus Swartwort. He was tripped by a fellow soldier in the same regiment in New York City and fell and broke his left ankle on 15 Mar. 1776. He was aged 36 years old on 4 July 1788. He lived in N.Y. on 4 June 1789.

Parrot, Christopher. Md. Sgt. He was pensioned at the rate of half-pay of a sergeant in 27 Jan.1817.

Parrot, Joseph. —. —. Congress awarded his widow, Anna Parrot, the arrearage of her pension from 4 Mar. 1848 to 3 Feb. 1853 on 21 Feb. 1853. She was from Clinton Co., Ohio.

Parrot, Silas. N.J. Lt. He served in the N. J. Line. He lived in Essex County. He was pensioned at the rate of $6 per month from 10 Feb. 1808. He was on the 1813 pension list and died 5 Oct. 1819.

Parry, Caleb. Pa. Lt. Col. He served under Col. Atlee and was killed in Aug. 1776 at the battle of Long Island. His widow was Elizabeth Parry from Philadelphia County.

Parry, Hildebert. Va. —. His mother, Joyce Parry, was granted £100 support in Middlesex Co.,Va. on 28 June 1779. He was the brother of John Parry. There were five children at home on 22 Feb. 1779. [Compare with Hildebert Perry.]

Parry, John. Va. —. His mother, Joyce Parry, was granted £100 support in Middlesex Co., Va. on 28 June 1779. He was the brother of Hildebert Parry. There were five children at home on 22 Feb. 1779.

Parsel, Nicholas. N.J. Pvt. He was under Capt. Isaac Reeves in Col. Philip Courtland's Regiment of the Essex County militia and was wounded in a skirmish with the enemy on 7 June 1780 at Connecticut Farms. He died 10 June 1780. His widow, Esther Parsel, sought his half-pay. She married secondly 23 Oct. 1796 ----- Bailey. He also appeared as Nicholas Passel.

Parshall, David. —. —. He enlisted in the spring of 1781 under Col. Paulding and served nine months. He had previously served in 1778 and 1779 from Northumberland Co., Pa. for fourteen months. His service amounted to two and a half years. Congress granted him relief in 1832.

Parsons, George. Pa. —. He was awarded a $40 gratuity and a $40 annuity in Dauphin Co., Pa. 20 Mar. 1834.

Parsons, Israel. —. Pvt. He served nine months and was pensioned in 1832 at the rate of $180 per annum until stricken in Sep. 1835. Congress restored him to his pension from 4 Sep. 1835 at $30 a year 5 Mar. 1840. He was from Granville, Mass.

Parsons, Nehemiah. Mass. Pvt. He served in the 11th Regiment and was from Gloucester.

Parsons, Joseph. Va. Pvt. He served in the expedition against the Indians under Capt. James Booth for 13 months. He was paid $104 on 13 Mar. 1814.

Parsons, Solomon. Mass. Pvt. He was wounded and pensioned at the rate of half-pay of a soldier from 1 Jan. 1781 on 24 June 1784. He was on the 1813 pension list. He died 11 May 1831.

Parsons, Thomas. Pa. Lt. His widow, Bathsheba Parsons, was in Philadelphia County on 3 Feb. 1781. He was in Capt. John Williams's Company in the 1st Battalion of Philadelphia County militia. He died of wounds received at Princeton in 1777. He left a young child.

Parsons, William. Md. Pvt. He served in the militia and died in the service. His widow, Mary Parsons, was pensioned in 1783 in Frederick County. There were two children.

Parsons, William. Mass. Pvt. He served in the 2nd Regiment and was from Plymouth. His widow, Abiah Parsons, was paid $50.

Parsons, William. Mass. —. He served in the 4th Regiment and was paid $20.

Parsons, William. Va. —. His wife, Rebecca Parsons, and children were awarded assistance in Charlotte Co., Va. on 7 July 1777 and £3.2 for provisions on 5 Jan. 1778.

Partain, Philemon. N.C. —. He was drafted in Orange Co., N.C. and served under Capt. William James in the Cheraw Hills. He died in July 1825. His widow, Mary Partain, was from Anderson District, South Carolina in 1831. Her application was rejected.

Partridge, Abel. Mass. —. He served in the 8th Regiment. He was paid $20.

Partridge, Amariah. Mass. —. He served in the 6th Regiment and was paid $20.

Partridge, John. Pa. —. He was awarded a $40 gratuity and a $40 annuity in Beaver Co., Pa. 14 Apr. 1834. He was 88 years old in 1844. He died 25 Dec. 1849.

Partridge, John. S.C. He served under Lt. Col. Hampton. He applied 31 Jan. 1791.

Paschke, Frederick. Capt. —. He was pensioned under the act of 24 Feb. 1785. He served in Count Pulaski's Legion from 14 Mar. 1777 to 18 May 1780. Afterwards he had an appointment in the Quartermaster's Department in the Southern Army until its dissolution 13 July 1783.

Passmore, Joseph. Mass. Sgt. He served in the 3rd Regiment under Col. John Greaton and Capt. Joseph Williams and was disabled by a broken left arm. He was pensioned 10 Apr. 1782. He was 36 years old in 1792. He was transferred to Vermont by 1790. He was on the 1813 pension list of New York.

Patch, George. Me. —. He died 15 Feb. 1816. His widow was Sarah Patch from Kittery. She was paid $50 under the resolve of 1836.

Patch, Jonathan. Mass. Pvt. He was from Shapleigh and was paid $20. He lived in York Co., Me. He was pensioned at the rate of $5 per month from 11 July 1806. He was on the 1813 pension list.

Patch, Samuel. Mass. —. He was from Shapleigh and was paid $20 by Massachusetts. He served from 25 Feb. 1777 to Dec. 1779 under Col. Brewer and Capt. Burbank. He was furloughed for forty or fifty days to accompany his wounded brother who had been injured by blowing rocks at Fort Putnam to his father's home in Shapleigh. He was thrown off his horse at Ipswich, Mass. and his shoulder was dislocated. Due to the accident he was unable to return to the service. His father, John Patch, later removed from Shapleigh to Kittery. He was listed as a deserter. Congress granted him a pension 12 Feb. 1841 at which time he lived in Maine.

Patchin, Ebenezer. Conn. Pvt. He served under Col. Isaac Sherman in the 5th Regiment in the company of Capt. S. Comstock. He lost his sight in his left eye by sickness, and his sight in his right eye was much impaired. He lived in Norwalk, Conn. in 1792. He enlisted 11 Jan. 1777 for three years and was discharged 11 Jan. 1780. Since he was not wounded in the service, his claim was not allowed.

Patrick, Jacob. —. —. He was on the roll as a pensioner and sought an increase. Congress rejected his claim 27 Mar. 1846.

Patrick, James. Mass. —. He was granted relief.

Patrick, Robert. Pa. —. He was pensioned 21 Feb. 1838 in Armstrong County. He was 68 years old in 1840. His widow, Barbara Patrick, was awarded a $40 annuity in Armstrong County in May 1850 for his Revolutionary service.

Patten, Benjamin. Mass. —. He served in Bailey's Regiment and was paid $20.

Patten, Coleman. Md. —. He served six years and was wounded in the thigh. He was 65 years old and lived in Baltimore County. He was pensioned in 1803.

Patten, John. Pa. —. He was pensioned in Bucks County 15 June 1836.

Patten, Nathaniel. Me. —. He was from Penobscot. He was paid $50 under the resolve of 1836.

Patten, Thomas. —. —. Congress declined to grant him a pension by a special act on 25 Mar. 1818 since he was covered by a law passed at the current session.

Patterson, —. N.Y. —. Mary Patterson was granted support in 1779.

Patterson, —. Pa.—. His widow, Martha Patterson, received a $40 annuity in Lawrence County 8 May 1854.

Patterson, —. Pa. —. His widow, Sarah Patterson, was 72 years old in 1840. She received a pension in Westmoreland County 1 May 1857.

Patterson, Alexander. Pa. Capt. He was in Northampton County on 27 Dec. 1800. He was wounded by the Connecticut Claimants. He had been active in opposing them from 1769 to the commencement of the Revolutionary War. He served in the war and was pensioned for said service. On 10 Feb. 1804 he was granted a $400 gratuity and a $100 annuity for life. His widow, Margaret Patterson, was awarded a $40 gratuity and a $40 annuity on 4 Jan. 1823.

Patterson, Andrew. Pa. —. He applied 7 Aug. 1820. He served in Capt. Thomas Wiley's Company under Col. Benjamin Flowers in the Corps of Artificers. He served about three years and was discharged due to a wound in his wrist. He was awarded donation land 4 Mar. 1807. He was from York County.

Patterson, Andrew. S.C. —. He served under Capt. James Brown and Francis Marion. He was in his 63rd year. He was from Williamsburg in 1826. His application was rejected.

Patterson, Arthur. Pa. Corp. He was in Philadelphia 13 Nov. 1786. He served in the 5th Pa. Regiment in Capt. Taylor's Company and was wounded in his back at Brandywine in 1777. He was 28 years old.

Patterson, Benjamin. N.Y. —. He served under Capt. Cambleton in 1776. He was granted an annuity in Pennsylvania.

Patterson, Eliza. Va. Pvt. He served in the 12th Va. Regiment. He was on the 1786 pension list.

Patterson, Francis. N.C. —. He served from the commencement of the war until 1782. He was 83 years old in Feb. 1833 and resided in Mississippi. Congress rejected him for a pension 28 Jan. 1835.

Patterson, George. S.C. —. He served under Capt. John Caldwell and Col. Thompson. He was wounded in his head at Ninety Six. He lay there for three months and had several bones taken out. While he was granted 200 acres of bounty land on Dutchman's Creek, he found that the tract was covered by an older grant made to one Dunlop. He sought payment for his loss. He was 82 years old in 1827. Maj. Uel Hill was acquainted with him at Ninety Six. Patterson was paid as late as 1829.

Patterson, James. N.C. Pvt. He died in 1808. He married in 1786. His widow, Elizabeth Patterson, failed to produce sufficient evidence to sustain her claim. Congress rejected her claim 7 Feb. 1850.

Patterson, James. Pa. —. He was pensioned in York County 15 June 1836.

Patterson, John. N.C. —. He volunteered in the militia in 1780 under Gen. Griffith Rutherford, Col. George Alexander, and Capt. Samuel Reed. He was made a prisoner at Gates's defeat. He had three wounds on his right elbow and one on his head. He could not pursue his occupation of blacksmith. He was rejected in 1808. He was from Iredell County in 1814 and was awarded $48 per annum for five years.

Patterson, John. Pa. —. He was awarded a $40 gratuity and a $40 annuity in Lancaster County 28 Mar. 1836. He was 81 years old in 1840. He died 3 Apr. 1843.

Patterson, Joseph. Mass. Sgt. He served under Major Littlefield and Capt. Coren. At Penobscot he was disabled by a musket ball which broke his right leg a little above the ankle. He was 29 years old in 1787.

Patterson, Joseph. N.H. Pvt. He served under Col. Baldwin and Capt. Emery. He was wounded by a ball which entered behind his right ear and came out his cheek. He became deaf in that ear and was constantly afflicted with pain. Whenever he would take a cold, he was subjected to painful sensations. He was wounded in 1776 at White Plains. He lived in Henniker, N.H. in 1794. He was in the militia. He was on the 1813 pension list.

Patterson, Robert. Conn. Pvt. He served in the 4th Conn. Regiment in Capt. Nathaniel Webb's Company under Col. Durkee. He was wounded in his right arm at Germantown in 1777. He was transferred to the Invalids in 1780. David Adams, Surgeon, attended him. He was pensioned at the age of 70 at Ashford, Conn. 21 Nov. 1788. He died in 1791.

Patterson, Robert. Pa. —. His wife was Jane Patterson. She was Jane Dawson when she was awarded a $40 gratuity in Juniata County in Apr. 1833.

Patterson, William. N.Y. Pvt. He served in Van Schaick's Regiment. He was pensioned 1 Jan. 1803 in Cayuga County. He was on the 1813 pension list.

Patterson, William. Pa. 2nd Lt. He served in the in the 1st Battalion of the Lancaster County militia. His widow, Elizabeth Patterson, applied 20 Apr. 1782. He served in the Flying Camp.

Pattie, William. Va. —. He enlisted in Caroline County under Capt. Mountjoy and went to Hampton under Maj. Buchamer. He served three months. A British sloop made an attempt to cut out the ship *Dragon*. In May 1781 he was under Capt. Bronaugh and was on the *Potomac* during the time Cornwallis and Tarleton were in Virginia. He enlisted in the same year under Capt. Thomas Moore. He was discharged about the time of Yorktown due to a "rising in his knee." He was subsequently in the army at Caroline court house. From 1779 to 1781 he was at the public manufactory of arms at Fredericksburg. Congress granted him a pension 20 Apr. 1836. He resided in Fauquier County.

Patton, —. Pa. —. Anna Patton was granted $20 per month 26 Aug. 1816. She was from Beaver Co.

Patton, —. Pa. —. Rebecca Patton was granted relief 21 Ma. 1837.

Patton, —. S.C. —. His widow, Janet Patton, was from Chester District.

Patton, James. N.J. Lt. He served in Meeker's Troop of Horse. He was wounded through the head and was 31 years old. He was on the 1791 and the 1813 pension lists and died 16 Nov. 1816 in Middlesex County.

Patton, James. Pa. —. He applied in Mifflin County 30 Aug. 1813. He enlisted in 1776 in Capt. John Doyle's Company from Lancaster County and served to 1780. He lost the sight in one of his eyes from a wound in his head.

Patton, John. —. Pvt. He died in 1838. His widow, Mary Patton, sought a special pension from Congress when the general pension act for widows was to expire on 4 Mar. 1848. Since such a bill had already been reported, Congress did not take action on 4 Jan. 1848.

Patton, John. Pa. —. He was pensioned in Huntingdon County 15 June 1836. His widow, Rebecca Patton, received the $40 which he had been granted but not received at his death by act of 21 Mar. 1837.

Patton, Robert. Pa. Capt. He was promoted to the rank of captain 1 Apr. 1778 and retired from the Pennsylvania Line 1 Jan. 1781. He sought five years of full pay in lieu of half-pay for life in 1794. His widow was Ann Patton. The pension was awarded to the children whose guardian was S. Powers.

Patton, Samuel. Pa. Sgt. He enlisted in 1776 under Capt. Kelly and Col. Hartley. He was detailed to Virginia. He was at Brandywine. He next served in the forage department and took sick after eighteen months. He was furloughed and returned home. Congress granted him a pension 22 Dec. 1831.

Patton, Thomas. S.C. —. He was taken prisoner by the enemy 18 Aug. 1780 and died in confinement. His widow, Jane Patton, was awarded an annuity 15 Mar. 1785 in Chester. There was one child in 1791.

Paubough, —. N.Y. —. Anna Paubough of Dutchess County was granted support 27 May 1779.

Paul, Benjamin. Pa. —. He served under Capt. Heatherland in the Flying Camp. He next served under Col. William Evans in the quartermaster's department. He was under Capt. William Eyre at Brandywine. He was awarded a $40 gratuity and a $40 annuity in Chester Co., Pa. 19 Mar. 1824.

Paul, David. Me. —. He was from Lewiston. He was paid $50 under the resolve of 1836.

Paul, Frederick. Pa. Pvt. He was in Philadelphia County on 5 Apr. 1787. He served in the 13th Pa. Regiment under Col. Walter Stewart. He was wounded at Brandywine by a musket ball in his left side which was never extracted. He was 30 years old. He was on the 1813 pension list. He also appeared as Frederick Powl.

Paul, James. Mass. Pvt. He served in the 14th Regiment and was from Shutesbury. He was paid $50.

Paul, John. Mass. Sgt. He served in Capt. Daniel Wheelwright's Company under Col. Ebenezer Francis. He was rendered incapable of service by a fall. He had a rupture. He was pensioned at the rate of half-pay from 31 Aug. 1777 on 22 Sep. 1778. He was 43 years old in 1786. He was on the 1813 pension list.

Paul, Robert. —. Sgt. He served under Col. Moses Hazen. He died intestate in 1814. His grandchildren, Philip Lamoy of Mooers, Clinton Co., N.Y., William S. Lamoy, and Margaret Goka, sought the $80 reward due their grandfather. Congress approved same 10 Dec. 1857. He had 500 acres of bounty land from New York.

Paul, Thomas. Md. Sgt. His widow, Catharine Paul, was pensioned at the rate of half-pay of a sergeant 7 Mar. 1840.

Paulden, William. S.C. —. He was born in Charleston, S.C. and served under Capt. Daniel Mazyck. He was taken prisoner at the fall of Charleston, sent to Jamestown, Va., and discharged. He applied in 1812 from Granville Co., N.C. He had never been back in South Carolina and had not received any pay. He was a shoemaker with light complexion, light hair, and was 5' 11" tall. His application was rejected in 1818.

Paulding, Ebenezer. Mass. Lt. He served under Col. Prescott and was at Bunker Hill. He served three years and died prior to 1818. His heirs sought relief, but Congress denied their claim because they submitted no proof on 31 Dec. 1845.

Paulding, John. N.Y. Pvt. He along with Isaac Van Wart and David Williams captured Maj. John Andre, the Adjutant General of the British Army, on 23 Sep. 1780 when the dangerous and traitorous conspiracy of Benedict Arnold was brought to light. On 3 November 1780 he was awarded $200 per annum in specie for life. He was old and had a large family some of whom were infants when he unsuccessfully sought an increase 13 Jan. 1817.

Paulent, Antoine. —. —. He received his half-pay for life.

Paulus, Jacob. —. —. His application was referred to the Secretary of War.

Pawling, Albert. N.Y. 2nd Lt. He joined in June 1775 and went with Col. James Clinton to Canada under Gen. Richard Montgomery. He returned to New York 22 Apr. 1776. He was appointed brigade major. In the summer of 1777 he was appointed major under Col. William Malcolm. He became supernumerary with the incorporation into Col. Spencer's force. He was at St. Johns,

Quebec, White Plains, and Monmouth. He was executor of his father's estate. He was 82 years old. Congress granted him a pension 31 Mar. 1836.

Pay, William. Mass. Pvt. He was wounded by a musket ball in his right shoulder. He served under Col. Moses Little in Capt. Benjamin Perkins' Company. He was pensioned at the rate of one-quarter pay from Jan. 1780 on 17 Mar. 1784. He was 31 years old in 1786.

Payne, Daniel. Mass. —. He was wounded in his right hand. He resided at Charlestown, Mass. in 1796.

Payne, Jacob. Va. —. He lived in Chesterfield County and was pensioned at the rate of $50 per annum on 2 Jan. 1807. He formerly lived in Greensville County.

Payne, Joseph. N.Y. Pvt. He served in Capt. Israel Honeywell's Company of militia under Col. James Hammond. He was wounded by two musket balls in his right side, one of which lodged there on 11 Jan. 1781. He was aged 29 on 22 May 1786. He lived in Orange Co., N.Y. on 20 Apr. 1789. He also appeared as Joseph Paine.

Payton, James. Pa. Pvt. He was in Philadelphia County on 30 Sep. 1785. He served in the 4th Pa. Regiment and was transferred to the Invalids. He was disabled by a fall while a prisoner. He was 66 years old.

Paytor, John. S.C. —. He was authorized to draw his pension from 1 Mar. 1808 on 19 Dec. 1809.

Peabody, Joseph. Mass. Pvt. He was wounded by a musket ball which entered his right side and passed through his body on 29 June 1777 between Fort Edward and Fort Miller. He served under Col. R. Putnam in the 5th Regiment. He lived in Haverhill, Mass. in 1792. He enlisted 15 Apr. 1777 and was discharged on 14 Apr. 1780. He was granted one-third of a pension 20 Apr. 1796. He died 20 Apr. 1798. He was on the 1813 pension list.

Peabody, Samuel. Mass. Soldier. He served in Revere's Artillery. He was from Salem and was paid $50.

Peabody, Stephen. N.H. Lt. Col. His widow, Hannah Peabody, was from Amherst and sought his depreciation pay on 7 June 1785.

Peabody, Seth. Mass. —. He was paid $20.

Peace, Jacob. N.C. —. His widow was in Stokes Co., N.C. in June 1838.

Peace, Samuel. Va. —. He served under Capt. John Winston and Col. Samuel Meredith from Mar. to Dec. 1776. In 1777 he was under Lt. Thompson, Capt. Windsor Brown, and Col. George Gibson. He was at Brandywine, Germantown, and White Marsh. He was wounded four times with a bayonet and by balls. In 1780 he was under Capt. Park Goodall and Col. Richardson at Camden. He was at the surrender of Cornwallis at Yorktown. He was 69 years old in Granville Co., N.C. 10 May 1823.

Peacock, Neal. Md. Pvt. He was pensioned at the rate of half-pay of a private 2 Jan. 1813.

Peacock, Richard. —. Lt. He was at Bunker Hill and in 1776 went with the army to New York. He was twice a prisoner. He served under Capt. Benjamin Stevenson in 1778. He had received 200 acres of bounty land in New York. Congress ruled he was due nothing else on 15 Feb. 1828.

Peak, Thomas. Mass. Sgt. He served in the 3rd Artillery and was from Boston. He was paid $20.

Peake, William. Va. QM Sgt. He was in Fairfax County 11 Aug. 1788 when he was put on the pension list at the rate of £18 per annum. He served in the Fifth Troop of the 1st Regiment of Light Dragoons. He was dangerously wounded in his head and in both arms and was made a prisoner 19 Jan. 1778 at Lee's surprise in the Stone House in Pennsylvania. Lt. Col. John Jameson certified his military service. He received the arrearage from 15 Nov. 1783 to 1 Jan. 1786 on 23 Apr. 1789. He was on the 1813 pension list. He died 16 Aug. 1816.

Pearce, Edward. R.I. Sgt. He lost his right arm in loading a field piece that went off accidentally at Warwick, R.I. in giving the alarm on 17 Apr. 1778. He served under Lt. Oliver Cory and Col.

Robert Elliott. He was aged 39 when he applied on 23 Feb. 1786. He was listed as Edward Pierce on the 1813 pension list.

Pearce, Edward. Va. —. He was in Continental service. His infant child was granted financial support in Botetourt Co., Va. 10 June 1779.

Pearce, George. Md. Pvt. He was pensioned at the rate of half-pay of a private in Warren Co., Ky. 1 Mar. 1833.

Pearce, Job. Mass. Pvt. He served in the 16th Regiment and was from Swansey. His widow, Polly Pearce, was paid $50.

Pearce, Jonathan. —. —. He enlisted 23 Jan. 1776 under Capt. Gorton and Col. Christopher Lippit and was discharged in New Jersey 18 Jan. 1777. He next served under Col. Elliott to Mar. 1778. His last tour was in 1779. He was at Haerlam Heights, White Plains, Trenton, and Princeton. Congress granted him a pension 3 Jan. 1832. He died 30 Mar. 1832 in Kent Co., R.I. His widow was Elizabeth Pearce who sought to recover his pension from 4 Mar. 1831 to 30 Mar. 1832. Congress refused her request 29 Jan. 1836.

Pearl, John. Va. Pvt. He served in the 1st Virginia Regiment and was pensioned from 6 Oct. 1779.

Pearsey, —. —. —. His widow, Anna Pearsey, did not receive a pension from Congress because she married him after 1 Jan. 1794.

Pearsey, Jonathan. —. —. His widow, Ann Pearsey, had her petition for a pension rejected by Congress 27 Mar. 1846 because they were married subsequent to 1 Jan. 1794. Congress did so again 25 Jan. 1848.

Pearson, Amos. Mass. Sgt. He served under Col. Little in the 12th Regiment. He was wounded in his right arm by a musket ball on 17 June 1775 at Bunker Hill. He lived in Newburyport, Mass. in 1792 and in Newbury, Mass. in 1795. He was in the militia. He was granted one-fifth of a pension 20 Apr. 1796. He also appeared as Amos Pierson. He was on the 1813 pension list.

Pearson, David. —. —. He was pensioned in 1818 and stricken in 1820. He had a wife. Congress granted him a pension 14 May 1832.

Pearson, Job. Mass. —. He served in the 9th Regiment. $20 was paid in favor of his children.

Pearson, Moses. Va. —. He was a minute soldier under Capt. Penn. He was disabled by illness in the service. He was awarded a £10 gratuity in Pittsylvania Co., Va. 8 Dec. 1777.

Pearson, Silas. Mass. Artificer. He was paid $20 by Massachusetts. In 1776 he served under Capt. William Rogers and Col. Samuel Johnson. In the summer of 1777 he was drafted for four months under Capt. John Noyes. He had been rejected because the twelve days for traveling home had not been counted towards his six months of service. He died 16 Mar. 1848 at the age of 91. He married 29 Nov. 1791 in West Newbury. His widow, Mary Pearson, was granted a pension by Congress 4 June 1852.

Pearson, Thomas. Pa. Lt. He was wounded in the war. He was on the 1813 pension list. He died 10 July 1826 in Jefferson Co., Kentucky. His widow was Nancy Pearson.

Pearson, Thomas. Va. —. He was pensioned in Henrico County on 12 Feb. 1813. He served under Col. Abraham Buford in South Carolina in 1780 and received sundry wounds on his head and arms. He was 62 years old. He received $60 per annum and $50 for immediate relief. He was in Bedford County in 1815 and Franklin County in 1834.

Pearson, William. Mass. Pvt. He served in the 2nd Regiment. His widow, Abial Pearson, was from Plymouth.

Peart, Edward. Pa. —. He was awarded a $40 gratuity and a $40 annuity in Philadelphia Co., Pa. 3 Feb. 1824.

Peary, Stephen. Me. —. He was from Denmark, Maine. He was paid $50 under the resolve of 1836.

Pease, —. —. —. His widow, Anna Pease, had her petition for a pension by special act of Congress rejected because she had married subsequent to 1 Jan. 1794.

Peay, —. Va. —. Thomas Peay was granted support in Prince William County in 1778.

Peck, —. N.Y. —. His wife, Hannah Peck, of New Marlborough, Ulster County was granted support 26 Apr. 1779.

Peck, Aaron. Conn. Pvt. He served in Waterbury's Regiment. He was on the 1813 pension list. He died 17 July 1833 in Fairfield Co., Conn.

Peck, Benjamin. Pa. —. He applied in Apr. 1817. He served in the 5th Pa. Regiment under Lt. William Schaffield. He died 19 Jan. 1824.

Peck, Ichabod. —. —. His widow died before she became eligible for a pension. His son, Ichabod Peck, had his claim rejected by Congress 20 Jan. 1846.

Peck, John. Pa. —. He was awarded a $40 annuity in Bedford County 5 Feb. 1836. He died 31 Dec. 1842.

Peck, Joseph. Mass. Sgt. He served in the 4th Regiment and was from Hadley. He was paid $20.

Peck, Levi. Conn. Sgt. He served in Capt. Waugh's Company under Col. Epaphras Sheldon and was wounded at Compo in the Danbury Alarm 16 Sep. 1778 by a musket ball in his shoulder or back. Lemuel Harrison was ensign. He lived in Litchfield.

Peck, Nathaniel. Mass. Pvt. He served in the Artillery and was from Holliston. He was paid $50.

Peck, Oliver. Mass. —. He served six months and upwards in the militia. Congress granted him a pension 21 Dec. 1838.

Peck, William. Pa. —. He was awarded a $40 gratuity and a $40 annuity in Lancaster Co., Pa. 7 Mar. 1827. He died 25 Feb. 1834.

Peckham, William. Mass. Pvt. He enlisted under Capt. Fletcher and Col. Ephraim Doolittle. He became sick and returned to his home where he remained two weeks. He returned to the service but his health drove him from the service. He found a substitute to serve out his tour. He served three months and eight days from 21 Apr. to 29 July 1775. Since he assigned all of his claim to his substitute, Congress refused to grant him relief 17 Feb. 1838. He was from Dana, Mass. and was about 88 years old.

Peden, Joseph. Pa. —. He was pensioned in Luzerne County 20 Mar. 1838.

Pedrick, Benjamin. Pa. —. He was pensioned 20 Mar. 1838 in Luzerne County. He died 15 Mar. 1848. He also appeared as Benjamin Patrick.

Pedrick, William. Mass. Quartermaster. He served aboard the brig *Resistance* under William Burk. He was disabled 1 May 1779. He lost all of his toes. He was 34 years in 1788. He also appeared as William Penderick.

Peebles, Aaron. Va. —. He served in the militia in 1781. He was under Baron Steuben at Petersburg against Gen. Phillips and Gen. Arnold. He was under Capt. Ruffin at Little York until Cornwallis capitulated. He was 70 years old. He applied to Congress 3 Jan. 1832.

Peebles, William. Pa. Capt. His heirs were his children John Peebles, Elizabeth Peebles, and Robert Peebles.

Peed, John. Va. —. He was accidentally wounded in militia service. His application was rejected 11 Nov. 1777.

Peek, —. N.Y. —. Hannah Peek of Ulster County was granted support 26 Apr. 1779.

Peek, Garret. N.Y. Pvt. He served in the militia under Col. Henry K. Van Rensselaer in Capt. Sharp's Company. He was wounded in his face and lost an eye on 12 Oct. 1782. He lived in

Rensselaerwyck, Albany Co., N.Y. 5 June 1789. He was on the 1813 pension list. He also appeared as Garret Peak and Garret Peck.

Peeling, Joshua. Pa. Sgt. He was in Chester County 19 Dec. 1786. He served in the 13th Pa. Regiment in Capt. Marshall's Company under Col. Walter Stewart and was wounded in his left hand by grape shot at Brandywine 11 Sep. 1777. He was 30 years old. He was on the 1813 pension list. He later lived in Lycoming County. He was awarded a $40 gratuity and a $40 annuity 6 Apr. 1833.

Peeples, John. Pa. Pvt. He was on the 1813 pension list.

Peery, John. Va. —. He was pensioned in Cabell County 19 Jan. 1813 at the rate of $60 per annum. He was severely wounded in the battle of Alamance in North Carolina by the British. He was in Tazewell County on 9 Feb. 1815.

Pegan, Archibald. Pa. —. He was awarded a $40 gratuity and a $40 annuity in Allegheny Co., Pa. 7 Mar. 1827.

Pegegram, William. Md. Pvt. He was pensioned at the rate of half-pay of a private in Anne Arundel County on 3 Jan. 1812.

Pegg, Benjamin. Pa. —. He applied in Franklin Co., Ohio 24 Dec. 1827. He was 75 years old. He served under Capt. Michael Cresap in repulsing the forces of Lord Dunmore. He enlisted 13 Aug. 1776 fourteen miles from Fort Pitt for three years in Capt. James Pickett's Company in the 8th Pa. Regiment. He served under Col. McCoy and Col. Daniel Broadhead to Sept. 1779 when he was discharged at Fort Pitt by Lt. Col. Byaird. He was in battle at Bound Brook on the Raritan River in N.J. and Brandywine. Elias Pegg served a part of the time with him. He never accepted any right to any federal bounty land. He sought 40 acres of unsold land in Ohio. Congress rejected his request because there was no law to cover it on 24 Jan. 1843.

Pegg, Elias. Pa. Pvt. He applied in Franklin Co., Ohio 3 Dec. 1828. He entered the service in Aug. 1778 in Capt. James Wright's Company in Montgomery County. He served under Gen. McIntosh at Fort McIntosh where he was discharged in Dec. 1778. He enlisted in Capt. John Finley's Company under Col. Daniel Broadhead and served to Jan. 1780. He was discharged at Pittsburgh by Col. Byaird. He was in action at Yellow Creek with the Indians. Benjamin Pegg proved his service. He had a wife and family.

Peiffer, —. Pa. —. His widow, Magdalena Peiffer, was awarded a $40 gratuity and a $40 annuity in Crawford County 3 Mar. 1837.

Peirce, Edward. R.I. Sgt. He was pensioned in 1785. He was on the 1813 pension list.

Peirhouse, Johannes. N.Y. Pvt. He served under Col. Samuel Clyde in the Montgomery County militia and was slain 11 Oct. 1780. His widow, Elizabeth Peirhouse, received a half-pay pension.

Peirson, George. Pa. Pvt. He lived in Dauphin County. He was on the 1813 pension list. He also appeared as George Peerson.

Peleng, Robert. Pa. —. He was paid $250 for his right to donation land on 8 Apr. 1833. As Robert Peling he was awarded a $40 gratuity and a $40 annuity in York County 18 Feb. 1834. He was dead by Dec. 1839.

Pelham, Joseph. N.Y. Pvt. He served under Col. Thomas Thomas in the Westchester County militia and was slain 10 June 1780. His widow, Freelove Pelham, received a half-pay pension.

Pell, Josiah. Pa. —. He was awarded a $40 gratuity and a $40 annuity in Luzerne County 1 Apr. 1836. He died in Dec. 1851. His widow, Elizabeth Pell, received a $40 annuity in Luzerne County 18 Apr. 1855.

Pelloms, Thomas. S.C. —. He was on the roll in 1793.

Pemberton, Christian. Pa. —. He applied 30 July 1822. He died 24 May 1825.

Pemberton, John. Del. Pvt. He was pensioned in 1783. He was disabled by chronic disorders brought on by the hardships of service. He had a large family of helpless children. He was on the 1791 pension list. He served under Capt. Kirkwood from Mar. 1777 to the battle of Camden in 1780. He was wounded at Germantown where he served under Col. Otho Williams. He died in 1809. He married Sarah ----- 24 Feb. 1777 in Wilmington, Del. by the chaplain of the army, Mr.. Mongtomery. He moved to Pennsylvania in 1788. His widow, Sarah Pemberton, was 86 years old when Congress granted her a pension 25 Jan. 1838.

Pembleton, Jabez. Conn. Pvt. He served in the Conn. militia. In opposing the British troops under Gen. Arnold who had landed at New London, he was wounded in his left hand by a musket ball at Fort Griswold on 6 Sep. 1781. He was under Capt. William Latham in the Artillery. Amos Prentice, Surgeon, attended him. He was pensioned 26 Sep. 1788 while a resident of Groton, Conn. at the age of 22. He was on the 1813 pension list. He transferred to Otsego Co., N.Y. from New Jersey on 4 Sep. 1826.

Pence, Peter. Pa. —. He was from Lycoming County. He was pensioned under the act of 10 Mar. 1819. He received a $40 gratuity and a $40 annuity.

Pence, William. N.J. —. He served under Capt. Bowman in the 2nd Regiment. He next served under Maj. Lee in the cavalry. He was killed in battle in the south. He had married Elizabeth Walton, about a week before he enlisted. They had a son William Pence. She married secondly Daniel Britton who was wounded at Plattsburgh and died. William Pence, Jr. died a few years ago leaving a widow and children. Elizabeth Britton suffered from rheumatism and sought a pension 11 Nov. 1843 in Mercer County.

Pendergast, William. Md. Lt. His widow, Juliet Onion, was pensioned at the rate of half-pay of a lieutenant 11 Feb. 1835.

Pendergrass, Lawrence. Pa. —. His widow, Sidney Pendergrass, applied 24 Aug. 1820. Her husband was a pensioner a short time before his death. He died 1 June 1818. She was awarded a $40 gratuity in Cumberland County on 29 Mar. 1822.

Pendergrass, Robert. Pa. —. He applied in Cumberland County 11 Apr. 1821. He served in Capt. Hays' Company under Col. William Irwine and with Hugh Sweeney marched from Carlisle 6 Apr. 1776 to Canada. He served four years. George Brown saw him at Carlisle after the revolt. Edward Pendergrass was his nephew. Sidney Pendergrass said that he was a full brother to her late husband, Lawrence Pendergrass. Mary Quigley said her brother, Robert, gave his discharge to their father, Philip Pendergrass, deceased, upon his return from the service. He died 12 July 1821. He was once in Perry County.

Pendergrass, Thomas. N.J. Pvt. He served in 1st Regiment and lost an arm. He was from Trenton, Hunterdon County, and was 39 years old. He was on the 1791 pension roll at the rate of $40 per annum.

Pendexter, Paul. Me. —. He was from Cornish. He was paid $50 under the resolve of 1836.

Pendleton, David. Conn. Pvt. He served in the 2nd Regiment. He was wounded by a musket ball in his thigh. He lived in Weston, Conn. in 1792. He enlisted 1 Apr. 1778 for the war. He died 11 Feb. 1826. He was on the 1813 pension list of New York.

Penefield, Thomas. Md. Pvt. His widow, Hester Penefield, was pensioned at the rate of half-pay of a private 20 Mar. 1835.

Penegar, Amos. Pa. Ens. He served under Capt. Rudolph and Gen. Irvine in 1777. He was at Brandywine and Germantown. He was ensign under Col. Davis in 1779.

Penley, —. —. —. His widow, Thankful Penley, sought a special pension from Congress 14 Mar. 1848. Since she married after 1794, her application was rejected.

Penn, John. Md. Pvt. He was pensioned at the rate of half-pay of a private in Charles County on 16 Feb. 1820.

Penn, Joshua. —. —. He served four months. He sought the arrears of his pension. He submitted no evidence for his claim so Congress did not act on his request on 21 Mar. 1836.

Pennel, Benjamin. Pa. —. He was granted relief.

Penney, Abraham. Me. —. He was from Smithfield. He was paid $50 under the resolve of 1836.

Pennington, —. Va. —. His wife, Sarah Pennington, was granted £12 support in Fauquier Co., Va. in May 1778 and £40 in Oct. 1779.

Pennington, Kinching. S.C. —. He first applied in Montgomery Co., N.C. in 1795. He was badly injured in the battle of Juniper Springs, S.C. His application in North Carolina was rejected on the interpretation that he needed to apply in South Carolina. He was from Camden District when he was pensioned 19 Dec. 1832. He also appeared as Kinchen Pennington. He was paid as late as 1833.

Pennirey, Thomas. Va. —. His wife, Elizabeth Pennirey, was granted £20 support in Rockingham Co., Va. 26 May 1778. She had smallpox.

Pennoyer, William. —. Pvt. He served three months under in 1779 under Capt. Eli Reed, nine months in 1780 under Capt. Eli Reed, and nine months in 1781 under Capt. Reuben Scorfield from Mar. to July when he was taken prisoner, carried to Jones's Island, and held there. His name was not on the roll of Capt. Scorfield and his service under Capt. Reed was discredited. Congress rejected his claim for a pension 25 Feb. 1846.

Pennybaker, Conrad. Va. —. His wife, Sarah Pennybaker, was granted 100 pounds of pork and 2 barrels of corn in Berkeley County on 22 Nov. 1780.

Pennybaker, Jacob. Va. —. His wife, Christiana Pennybaker, was granted £15 support in Berkeley County on 17 Nov. 1779.

Pensinger, Henry. Pa. —. He served in the 4th Regiment. He lost his leg . He was paid $600 and was awarded a $40 gratuity and a $40 annuity on 3 Mar. 1812. He also appeared as Henry Penfinger.

Pentell, John. Pa. Pvt. He was dead by Sep. 1797.

Pentecost, William. Va. Pvt. He was in Dinwiddie County on 22 Feb. 1787. He served under Col. A. Buford. His 18 month enlistment expired 25 Oct. 1780. He was wounded near the Waxhaw settlement in S.C. on 29 May 1780. He was deprived of an arm. He was 24 years old. Henry Bowyer, lieutenant and adjutant of the detachment, attested to his service. He removed to Georgia by 1790. He was on the 1813 pension list.

Penton, James. N.J. Corp. He was disabled with a broken thigh. He was on the 1791 pension roll at the rate of $40 per annum. He died 6 Nov. 1797.

Penwell, Aaron. Pa. Pvt. He was in Cumberland County on 11 Apr. 1786. He lost his left arm in action with the British near the Crooked Billet in 1778 and was taken prisoner. He served under Capt. Walter Denny and Col. Frederick Watt. He was 49 years old. He was dead by Mar. 1805. He also appeared as Aaron Pennwell.

Peoples, John. Pa. —. He was granted relief.

Pepin, Andrew. He sought relief for wounds and injuries received in the war. He had leave to withdraw his application 3 Mar. 1795.

Perdu, Fields. S.C. —. John B. Covington sought pay for the deceased for his Revolutionary War services on 18 Dec. 1835. It was referred to the Comptroller General.

Perkins, Ebenezer. Mass. Marine. He served aboard the Continental ship *Warren* under Capt. DudleySaltonstall, Commander, and was wounded at Penobscot by a musket ball entering his breast. It broke his collar bone and exited out his left elbow. He was pensioned at the rate of one-third of his pay from 13 Apr. 1780 on 20 Feb. 1781. On 30 Apr. 1781 he was pensioned from the date of 2 Sep. 1779. He was pensioned at the rate of half-pay on 1 Dec. 1779. In 1786 he lived in Plymouth Co., Mass. and was 29 years old. He later lived in Oxford Co., Me. His rate was $5 per month from 15 Sep. 1807. He was on the 1813 pension list.

Perkins, Enoch. —. —. He resided in Edgar Co., Ill. when he applied for a pension. Congress refused him on 17 June 1846 because there was no evidence of his service.

Perkins, John. Mass. Pvt. He served in the 15th Regiment and was from Topsfield. His widow, Sarah Perkins, was paid $50.

Perkins, Jonathan. N.H. Lt. He served in the N. H. Continental Line. He lived in Grafton Co., N. H. He was on the 1813 pension list.

Perkins, Obadiah. Conn. Lt. He was a fireworker in thegarr ison at Fort Griswold when he was wounded in his breast by a bayonet on 6 Sep. 1781. He lived in Groton, Conn. in 1794. The evidence of his being wounded in the actual line of duty appeared rather doubtful. He was on the 1813 pension list. He died in 1813.

Perkins, Solomon. Conn. Pvt. He served in the 2nd Company of the 8th Regiment of the militia. In opposing the British under Gen. Arnold who landed at New London, he was wounded by a musket ball through his breast and neck and sundry other wounds from a bayonet on 6 Sep. 1781 at Fort Griswold. He served under Capt. William Latham in the Artillery. Amos Prentice, Surgeon, attended him. He was 59 years old and resided at Groton, Conn. when he was pensioned 26 Sep. 1788. He died in 1810.

Perkins, Zophar. N.Y. 2nd Lt. He served in the minute men from New Marlboro Precinct, N.Y. organized in 1775 and continued for two years. He died in Feb. 1833. His son, Enoch Perkins, sought his arrearage, but Congress denied his claim 31 Jan. 1854.

Perkinson, Noel. Va. —. He enlisted in the artillery under Capt. Thomas Clay from Dinwiddie Co., Va. He was discharged after the surrender of Cornwallis. He was 60 years old, his wife was about 60, and his daughter about 22. He was in Guilford Co., N.C. in Aug. 1823.

Perrigo, Frederick. —. —. He served in the Revolutionary War and later in the War of 1812. He collected a pension of $96 per annum for service in the War of 1812. His widow, Mary Perrigo, sought an increase of her pension of $30 to $96 per annum from Congress on 20 Apr. 1860.

Perrin, John. Va. —. His wife, Mary Perrin, was allowed £15 support on 29 Sep. 1778, £40 on 28 June 1779, and £2.10 support in Bedford Co., Va. on 22 Sep. 1783.

Perrit, Peter. Conn. Capt. He was in the service in 1776 and was stationed at Fort Washington where he was made a prisoner. He had been made a captain a few days before his capture. He was exchanged 24 Nov. 1778. He gave notice that he wished to rejoin the army. He was never recalled to the service. On 9 Dec. 1778 he reapplied for his place in the army which was occupied by another. He was never reappointed. He sought his commutation. He was allowed one year's pay as a deranged officer but was denied further assistance 31 Mar. 1796.

Perry, —. Penn. —. He was an artillery officer. His widow was Margaret Perry. Their son, John Perry, for himself and the other children sought relief which Congress refused 6 Apr. 1860 because no proof of service had been submitted and no proof of identity of the father.

Perry, Benjamin. Mass. —. He served in Capt. Ashael Wheeler's Company under Col. John Reed. He was disabled by the loss of his left arm. He was 55 years old in 1786.

Perry, Caleb. Pa. Lt. His widow, Elizabeth Perry, was in Philadelphia 29 Jan. 1782. He was killed on Long Island in Aug. 1776.

Perry, Constant. Mass. Pvt. He served in the 4th Regiment and was from Seekonk. His widow, Lydia Perry, was paid $50.

Perry, Elnathan. Mass. —. He served in the 7th Regiment and was from Vermont. He was paid $50.

Perry, Hildebert Va. —. His widow, Sarah Perry, was pensioned 6 Feb. 1806 at the rate of $40 per annum. Mitchell Perry reported that she died 9 June 1813. [Compare with Hildebert Parry.]

Perry, John. Mass. Pvt. He served in the 4th Regiment under Col. Thomas Nixon and Capt. William Toogood. He was disabled by a musket ball through his right thigh. He was also wounded in his breast and under his right eye. He was pensioned in 1787. He died 30 Sep. 1807. He was paid $20 by the Commonwealth.

Perry, John. Mass. —. He served in the 8th Regiment and was from Roxbury. He was paid $20.

Perry, John. Pa. Artillery Officer. His widow was Margaret Perry. John Perry for himself and the other children sought the arrears of the pension. Congress rejected the claim 6 Apr. 1860 because no proof of service was submitted.

Perry, Joseph. Pa. —. He was pensioned 5 June 1817.

Perry, Noah. Mass. —. He served in the 5th Regiment and was paid $20.

Perry, Prince. Mass. Pvt. He served in the 16th Regiment and was from Plymouth. His widow, Deliverance Perry, was paid $50.

Perry, Simeon. N.C. —. He volunteered in North Carolina. He was pensioned 25 Nov. 1830 in South Carolina and died 22 Oct. 1831. His brother, Ezekiel Perry, sought his arrearage.

Perry, Simon. Md. Pvt. He was from Charles County in 1783. He served under Col. John H. Stone.

Perry, William. Mass. Ens. He died 10 Oct. 1777. His seven years' half-pay of $3,150 was paid to his heirs.

Perry, William. Pa. —. He served from 5 Mar. 1776 to July 1783. He was wounded and died in the service. His widow was from Philadelphia County.

Perryman, John. Pa. —. He served in the Cumberland County militia under Col William Chambers. He was wounded and died 1 May 1778. He left four daughters aged 10, 8, 4, and 2 and a son aged 6. His widow was Mary Perryman.

Peter, Philip. Pa. Pvt. He applied in Westmoreland County on 2 Oct. 1815. He served in the 1st Pa. Regiment in Capt. Parr's Company under Col. Hand in 1776 for at least a year. He was drafted into Col. Morgan's Rifle Regiment and continued to the end of the war. He was discharged at Trenton. His discharge was destroyed when his house in Buffaloe Valley in Northumberland burned. He was 68 years old. He also appeared as Philip Peterson.

Peterman, —. Pa. —. His widow, Rosanna Peterman, was awarded a $40 gratuity and a $40 annuity in Lancaster County 24 Mar. 1837. She was dead by Nov. 1838.

Peters, —. Pa. —. His widow, Rachel Peters of Philadelphia, Pa. was awarded relief 10 Apr. 1833.

Peters, —. Pa. —. His widow, Susanna Peters, was awarded a $40 gratuity in Montgomery Co., Pa. 6 Apr. 1833 and on 14 Apr. 1834.

Peters, —. Va. —. He and his brother were away in the service. Their mother, Mary Peters, was granted £45 support in York Co., Va. on 21 Feb. 1780.

Peters, Alexander. —. Doctor. He died at Fort Johnson, N.C. 26 Nov. 1802. His widow, Sarah Peters, sought a pension. Her application was not approved 5 Jan. 1803.

Peters, Anthony. Pa. —. He also appeared as Anthony Petri.

Peters, Jacob. Pa. —. He was awarded a $40 gratuity and a $40 annuity in Crawford County 28 Mar. 1836. His widow, Margaret Peters, received a $40 gratuity and a $40 annuity 17 Apr. 1854.

Peters, James. Mass. —. He served in the 6th Regiment and was from Worcester. He was paid $20.

Peters, John. N.H. —. A duplicate of bounty land warrant #1922 for 100 acres was issued to his children, John Peters and Sarah Farnum, by Congress 31 Jan. 1843.

Peters, John. S.C. —. He applied 2 Dec. 1793.

Peters, Jonathan. Mass. —. He was from Hanover and was paid $20.

Peters, Thomas. —. Pvt. Rebecca P. Stanbury and the other children sought the pensions which their father and mother would have been entitled to have received, but Congress rejected their petition 6 July 1854.

Peters, William. —. Ens. He died in 1848. His sons, James W. Peters and Martin Peters, sought their father's pension from 4 Mar. 1818 to 4 Mar. 1831. Congress denied their claim 21 July 1854.

Peterson, Gabriel. Pa. Lt. He applied in Allegheny County on 6 Feb. 1826. He served one year in the 8th Pa. Regt. He died 12 Feb. 1832.

Peterson, John. Del. Pvt. He was pensioned in 1783. He suffered from a rupture. He was single. He was on the 1791 pension list. Compare with John Petterjoh.

Peterson, John. N.Y. Soldier. He served under Col. VanCourtland in the 2nd Regiment for three years and nine months. In 1780 he saw a barge on the Hudson River approaching shore to take on board Major John Andre. He fired on the barge and prevented it from landing. He was the cause of the capture of John Andre and the discovery of the treason of Benedict Arnold. Congress rejected his claim for bounty land 13 Mar. 1838.

Peterson, John. Va. Pvt. His widow, Elizabeth Peterson, lived in Berkeley County and was pensioned at the rate of £10 per annum on 14 Dec. 1786. He served in the 12th Va. Regiment. He had a furlough to return home to his family. He accidentally broke his leg, reached home with great difficulty, and died.

Peterson, Simon. N.Y. Pvt. He served under Col. Frederick Wisenfell in the 4th N.Y. Regiment in Capt. Samuel Sacket's Company. He was wounded in his left ankle at New Town in 1779 on the Indian expedition. He lived in New York City, N.Y. in 1786. He was 32 years old on 1 Jan. 1786.

Petri, Daniel. N.Y. Pvt. He served under Col. Peter Bellinger and was slain 14 July 1782. His widow, Elizabeth Petri, received a half-pay pension.

Petri, Hans Yost. N.Y. Sgt. He served under Col. Peter Bellinger in the Montgomery County militia and died of wounds 30 Aug. 1777. His widow, Barbara Petri, received a half-pay pension.

Petri, Johannes. N.Y. Pvt. He was wounded in his shoulder and back. He was on the 1786 roll. He was 37 years old.

Petri, Marcus. N.Y. Sgt. He served under Col. Samuel Clyde and was slain 6 Aug. 1777. His orphans received his half-pay pension. They were ----- Petri, Ann Petri, and Nicholas Petri.

Petri, Richard. N.Y. Lt. He served under Col. Peter Bellinger in the Montgomery County militia. He was killed at Oriskany 6 Aug. 1777. His widow, Catharine Petri, received a half-pay pension.

Petrie, Anthony. Pa. —. He applied in Center County 6 July 1814. He enlisted in 1777 for three years in Capt. Weaver's Company in Lancaster County under Col. Naugle and Col. Hubley. He was later under Col. Humpton. He was at the battle of Monmouth and other engagements. He was discharged after four years at Trenton. He was 53 years old. He also appeared as Anthony Petre. He signed in German.

Petrie, Johannas. N.Y. Pvt. He served in Capt. Jacob Small's Company under Col. Peter Bellinger. He was wounded through the shoulder and back at the battle of Oriskany 6 Aug. 1777. He was aged 37 in 1787. He lived at Kingsland, Montgomery Co., N.Y. on 29 Sep. 1788.

Petry, Jacob. Pa. —. He was awarded a $40 gratuity and a $40 annuity in Berks County 1 Apr. 1836.

Petry, William. —. —. He sought a pension, but it was not approved on 28 Mar. 1816.

Pettee, Oliver. Me. —. He died 3 Aug. 1831. His widow was Abigail Pettee from Gouldsboro. She was paid $50 under the resolve of 1836.

Pettengell, John. N.Y. Pvt. He served under Col. Frederick Fisher in the militia and was slain 6 Aug. 1777. His children, Joseph Pettengell, Benjamin Pettengell, Philip Pettengell, and Ann Pettengell, received a half-pay pension.

Petterjoh, John. Del. Pvt. He was pensioned at the rate of $60 per annum. [Compare with John Peterson.]

Pettes, Abial. Mass. Sgt. He served in Lamb's Artillery Regiment and was from Dedham. His widow, Hannah Pettes, was paid $50.

Pettingall, Samuel. N.Y. Capt. He served under Col. Frederick Fisher. He was killed at Oriskany 6 Aug. 1777. His widow, Elizabeth Pettingall, received his half-pay pension.

Pettis, —. Va. —. His mother, Mary Pettis, was granted support in Caroline Co., Va. 8 May 1781. There were five in her household.

Pettit, George. Va. Pvt. He was awarded a £30 gratuity and an annuity of half-pay on 22 Oct. 1778. He was in Surry County on 22 Jan. 1787. He served in the 9th Va. Regiment having enlisted for two years. He was discharged 18 June 1778 by Brigadier General P. Muhlenberg. He was wounded at the battle of Germantown by sundry stabs of a bayonet in his body. He was shot in his left leg and left arm. He was 28 years old. He lost his left arm a little below the elbow. He was on the 1813 pension list.

Pettit, Isaiah. Va. —. His widow, Sarah Pettit, and two children were awarded £50 in Northampton County on 8 Dec. 1778.

Pettot, Enos. Conn. Pvt. He was pensioned 27 Apr. 1810. He was on the 1813 pension list.

Petts, David. Mass. Pvt. He served in Jackson's Regiment and was from Shirley. His widow, Nabby Petts, was paid $50.

Pettus, John. Va. —. He was in the battle of Guilford Court House and was in the company of Capt. William Dawson under Col. Nathaniel Cocke. He was wounded in the knee. He was alive 8 Oct. 1808 and was from Lunenburg Co. He served with James Anderson, Woodson Knight, and Thomas Wood.

Pettus, Samuel O. Va. Lt. He served in the infantry. His only son, Hugh M. Pettus, sought his five years' full pay plus interest 28 Dec. 1837. His petition was approved.

Pew, John. S.C. —. His annuity was £2.5.10 ½ in 1787.

Peyton, James. Pa. Pvt. He was in Philadelphia 30 Sep. 1785. He was transferred from the 4th Pa. Regiment to the Invalids. He was disabled by a fall while a prisoner of the enemy. He was 66 years old.

Peyton, James. Pa. —. He was awarded a $40 gratuity and a $40 annuity in Westmoreland Co., Pa. 23 Jan. 1830. He died 24 May 1831.

Peyton, John. Va. —. His widow was awarded £5 in Northampton Co., Va. 8 Dec. 1778.

Peyton, Thomas. Pa. Pvt. He was granted relief.

Phares, Robert. N.J. —. He was pensioned in Burlington County on 26 Feb. 1838 at the rate of $60 per annum.

Phelan, John. Md. Lt. He died 14 Sep. 1827 in Baltimore. His nephew and only heir, Nicholas Phelan, applied for bounty land but was refused in 1825.One Eliza Spinella represented herself as his daughter and obtained warrant #1121 for 200 acres on 18 Apr. 1825. It was claimed that his widow was Susan Phelan, but he was never married. The arrears of his pension was paid to Nicholas Phelan as administrator. The bounty land warrant was issued for a man of the same name or it was fraudulent. Eliza Spinella stated that her father was from Massachusetts.

Phelon, Edward. Capt. Mass. He was wounded four or five times and was crippled. He served in the 4th Mass. Regiment under Col. Henley. He was an aide-de-camp to Gen. Patterson. He was appointed a captain in the U.S. forces 30 Nov. 1783. He was from Nova Scotia and had left his family to join the Revolution. He had been disinherited by his parents.

Phelps, Alexander. Conn. Pvt. He served in the 1st Conn. Regiment in Capt. Eliphalet Holmes' Company under Col. Judd. He enlisted in June 1777 for three years. On 28 June 1778 at Monmouth he was shot in one of his legs which had to be amputated. After being wounded, he returned home but never had a discharge sent to him. Lt. Col. David F. Sill was Commandant. He was pensioned 6 Nov. 1786 at Lyme, Conn. He was on the 1813 pension list.

Phelps, Anthony. Va. —. He served twelve months in the militia under Gen. Clark. He was 92 years old. Congress granted him a pension 1 Mar. 1855.

Phelps, Bissel. —. Capt. In 1778 he was appointed Quartermaster with rank of captain in the Continental Line to raise a company of teams. He served to 1779 or 1780. He entered again in June 1781 and was with the French army at Annapolis to Sep. 1781. He furnished 21 oxen with carts, yokes, and chains for Capt. William Lindley and went to Williamsburg, Va. Congress denied him any further relief 4 Jan. 1819. He was from Vermont.

Phelps, Cornelius. —. —. He married in 1814. Congress denied his widow, Philena Phelps, relief on 14 Mar. 1848 because she married him after 1794. Congress also rejected her prayer 3 Mar. 1851. She had married him in 1814.

Phelps, Jacob. Mass. Sgt. He served in the 10th Regiment and was from Lancaster. His widow, Prudence Phelps, was paid $50.

Phelps, James. Ct. —. He served up to two years as a guard of public stores at Windsor when he was but 12 or 14 years of age. He bore important dispatches to Gen. Knox and was conductor and pilot to Gen. Washington. The law prevented anyone under 16 years of age from serving. Congress granted him a pension 5 Mar. 1840. His children were granted relief 2 Aug. 1856.

Phelps, Joel. N.J. Pvt. He served under Capt. S. Hardy. He was wounded in the body doing duty at Wyoming at Fort Jenkins on 16 June 1778. He lived in Hanover, Morris Co., N.J. in 1794. He was granted half a pension 20 Apr. 1796. He was on the 1813 pension list of New York.

Phelps, Reuben. Conn. He enlisted at Hebron for thee years. He married 9 Nov. 1776 ad died 25 Oct. 1799. Congress granted his widow, Mary Phelps, a pension for eighteen months of service on 23 Feb. 1838.

Phelps, Rufus. —. —.Congress rejected his petition for a pension due to an insufficient amount of service on 25 May 1860.

Phelps, Samuel. —. —. He married 27 July 1794. His widow, Hannah Phelps, sought an increase from $80 to $96 per year on 14 June 1850. Congress denied her claim.

Phile, Philip. Pa. Pvt. He was in Philadelphia County on 13 Oct. 1785. He was transferred from the German Regiment to the Invalids. He was worn out in the service. He got a rupture by a strain while lifting a barrel of flour. He was discharged as unfit for duty on account of old age. He was 31 years old. He was dead by Mar.1794.

Philhower, Christopher. N.J. —. He was pensioned in Hunterdon Co. on 21 Feb. 1840 at the rate of $60 per annum.

Philip, John. —. —. He sought a pension from the conclusion of the war to 10 July 1811 when his pension began. Congress rejected the claim 4 Mar. 1818.

Philips, —. Va. —. His wife, Ann Philips, was granted assistance in Loudoun County on 8 Feb. 1778.

Philips, Jacob. S.C. —. His application was rejected in 1827.

Philips, James. N.Y. Pvt. He served under Col. J. Klock. He was wounded in the leg in a battle with the Indians under Gen. Herkimer on 6 Aug. 1777 at Oriskie. He lived in Watervliet, N.Y. in 1794. He was on the 1813 pension list.

Philips, James. N.Y. Pvt. He served under Col. Volkert Veeder in the Montgomery County militia and was slain 6 Aug. 1777. His widow, Eve Philips, received a half-pay pension for seven years.

Philips, Philip. N.Y. Pvt. He was on the 1813 pension list.

Philips, Stephen. Md. Pvt. He was pensioned at the rate of half-pay of a private in Caroline County 16 Feb. 1820. He was a man of color. Jacob Charles was paid $13.33 which he had advanced to Stephen Philips 15 Feb. 1844.

Philips, Stephen. R.I. Drummer. He enlisted in Jan. 1776 under Capt. Blackmore and Col. Christopher Leppitt for one year. It was said that he deserted on 23 Oct. 1779 and never rejoined; yet, the record revealed that he was still an officer in 1780. He was home on furlough in 1779 when his wife was sick. He died in 1783. His widow, Alice Philips, married secondly John Usher. He died about 1841. Alice Usher of Gloucester, Providence Co., R.I. was allowed a pension by Congress 29 Mar. 1844.

Philips, Thomas. Conn. Pvt. His collar bone was dislocated. He was disabled by rheumatism and by being worn out in the service. He was pensioned 4 Jan 1783. He was in Fairfield County in 1787. He was on the 1791 pension roll.

Philips, Thomas. Va. Pvt. He lived in Orange County. He was on the 1813 pension list. He later removed to Indiana.

Phillipi, —. Pa. —. His widow, Susanna Phillipi, was granted assistance in Berks County 21 June 1839. She died 27 Oct. 1840.

Phillips, Anderson. Mass. Sgt. He served in the 16th Regiment and was from Boston. His widow, Mary Phillips, was paid $50.

Phillips, Ichabod. Me. —. He died 13 Oct. 1830 at Leeds. His widow was Elizabeth Ames from Canton. She was paid $50 under the resolve of 1836.

Phillips, Isaac. N.Y. —. He applied from Pennsylvania. He was pensioned and credited for six months of service. He was, in fact, entitled to be credited at least a year. He was nearly 100 years old. He was recommended for an increase 12 Dec. 1856 by Congress.

Phillips, John. Mass. —. He served in the 2nd Regiment and was paid $20.

Phillips, John. N.J. —. He was pensioned in Mercer County on 19 Feb. 1847 at the rate of $30 per annum.

Phillips, Nathaniel. Mass. —. He served in the 16th Regiment and was from Boston. He was paid $20.

Phillips, Silas. Mass. Sgt. He served in the 2nd Regiment and was from Easton. His widow, Susanna Phillips, was paid $50.

Phillips, Thomas. Pa. 1st Lt. He applied in New York 24 Mar. 1818. He was in Dearborn Co., Ind. 18 Nov. 1822. He served in the navy on the schooner *Delaware* from 12 Dec. 1776 to 17 Dec. 1777 and on the brig *Convention* from 1777 to 1778 when the fleet was discharged. He was 80 years,

3 months, and 12 days old on 18 Nov. 1822.

Phillips, Walter. N.Y. Pvt. He was born in Greenbush, N.Y. and was about 104 years old when Congress granted him a pension 16 Jan. 1835. He entered the service in 1775 under Capt. John Fisher and was transferred to batteaux service under Gen. Montgomery and sent to St. Johns, Canada. He was at Bemis Heights and Saratoga. He was wounded in a skirmish with the Hessians by the recoil of a cannon.. He returned to Albany after the capture of Burgoyne.

Phinney, Ebenezer. Me. Pvt. He served under Col. Brewer and was disabled at Bennington in 1777. He resided at Gorham, Maine. He was granted one-fourth of a pension 20 Apr. 1796.

Phinney, John. Me. —. He was from Gorham. He was paid $50 under the resolve of 1836.

Phipps, John. Mass. Sgt. He served in the 5th Regiment and was from Sherburne. His widow, Hannah Phipps, was paid $50.

Phips, Samuel. Mass. —. He served in the 2nd Regiment and was from Lisle. He was paid $20.

Phyler, Coonrod. S.C. —. He was pensioned 16 Dec. 1823.

Piatt, Daniel. N.J. Maj. He was appointed a captain 1 Dec. 1776 and was promoted to colonel 31 Jan. 1779. He was in the 1st Regiment. He died in 1780. His widow, Catharine Piatt, was granted a half-pay pension 10 Jan. 1791. His son, Robert Piatt, sought his seven years' half-pay. Congress reported that the evidence indicated that it had been paid and rejected any further relief 11 Apr. 1842.

Piatt, William. —. Capt. He served in the Revolutionary War. After the war, he reentered the service and was killed at St. Clair's defeat. His heirs sought his half-pay but were rejected since he had been paid in his lifetime 20 Mar. 1838.

Pickard, Adolph. N.Y. Pvt. He served in Col. Samuel Campbell's Regiment of militia in Capt. Nicholas Werus's Company. He was wounded in his shoulder on 6 Aug. 1677 at Oriskany. He was pensioned 22 Sep. 1786. He lived in Springfield, Montgomery Co., N.Y. on 15 June 1789. He was 25 years old in 1787. He later lived in Otsego County. He was on the 1813 pension list.

Pickard, John. N.Y. Qr. Mr. He was in Cox's Regiment. He was wounded in his left arm. He died 4 May 1783. His widow was Eva Pickard on 3 Nov. 1783.

Pickard, John. N.Y. Pvt. He was a private in the rangers in 1775, 1776, and 1777. He was an ensign in the militia in 1780 until the peace in 1783. He was born in 1757. He served under Col. Wittell at Johnstown, Gen. Herkimer at Oriskany, and Col. Brown at Stone Arabia. Congress granted him a pension at the rank of a private 23 Jan. 1836. Congress did not accept his service as an officer. He claimed a commission from Gov. Clinton in 1780. His daughter said she was nine years old at that time. He claimed to have served five years as an officer but, if so, he would have to have served two years after the peace. Because he was born in 1757, he would have been 23 years of age when he was commissioned in 1780 and would have been 14 years old when he sired his daughter.

Pickard, John Frederick. Pa. —. His widow, Margaret Pickard, was awarded a $40 gratuity and a $40 annuity in Berks Co., Pa. 7 Mar. 1827.

Pickens, —. Pa. —. His widow, Elizabeth Pickens, received relief in Lancaster County 28 Mar. 1836.

Pickens, Andrew. S.C. Pvt. He was wounded in his right knee 1 Aug. 1776 at Seneca in the Cherokee Country. He served under Robert Anderson. and had a numerous family. He was granted an annuity 20 Feb. 1786 in Abbeville. He was paid as late as 1832.

Pickens, John. S.C. Pvt. He was taken prisoner by the enemy and given into the hands of the Indians and put to death. His widow, Mary Pickens, married William Black 4 Jan. 1784. She was from Abbeville. There were children in 1793. She was pensioned 2 Dec. 1819 and paid three years back annuity. She died 22 Jan. 1826. Her executor, John B. Black of Abbeville District, S.C. sought her arrearage of $53.75 and was paid $60 in Dec. 1826.

Pickens, Joseph. S.C. Capt. He was wounded at the siege of Ninety Six in 1781 and died. His widow, Eleanor Pickens, was awarded an annuity 26 Feb. 1785 in Pendleton District.

Picker, —. Pa. —. His widow, Hannah Picker, was awarded a $40 gratuity and a $40 annuity in Bucks County for his Revolutionary service.

Pickering, James. N.J. 1st Lt. He served in the 5th Company, 3rd Battalion, Philadelphia Militia He was wounded in the head and left shoulder on 17 Apr. 1778 at Bristol, Bucks Co., Pa. His head was fractured in two places, and three pieces had to be taken out. His shoulder was laid open, and the joint was severely wounded. He was taken prisoner, put on a horse, and taken to Philadelphia by the British. He lived in Philadelphia, Pa. in 1794.

Picket, —. Pa. —. His widow, Alice Picket, was awarded a $40 gratuity and a $40 annuity in Luzerne County 1 Apr. 1836.

Picket, Thomas. Conn. Pvt. He served in the 1st Conn. Regiment. He was disabled by losing his foot which had been frozen. He died in 1804. He was on the 1813 pension list.

Picket, William. Me. —. He was from New Gloucester. He was paid $50 under the resolve of 1836.

Picket, William. S.C. Steward. He was on the *Fanny* in 1777 when captured by the British. He was taken to Mill Prison at Plymouth, England where he remained two years and seven months. He was exchanged in 1780 and sent to L'Orient, France. He and twenty-five others walked to Antwerp, Belgium and joined the *South Carolina* under Commodore Alexander Gillon at Amsterdam. In 1781 the ship sailed to Corunna, Spain, Teneriffe, Azores, and Havana, Cuba. Since he had enlisted for one year and eight months and not had not seen his family for five years, he left the ship at Havana in Feb. 1782. He sought his pay and prize money or a pension. He was 64 years old. John Morant was lieutenant aboard the ship. He was from Newburyport, Mass. in 1818. His application was rejected because the records indicated that he deserted. Michael Kalteissen, Richard Graham, and Hugh Alexander Nixon swore that he had done his duty well.

Pickets, Joseph. Mass. —. He served in the 5th Regiment. He was paid $20.

Pickett, Robert. N.J. Pvt. He was on the 1791 pension roll at the rate of $40 per annum.

Pier, Abner. Mass. Pvt. He was wounded in the leg, thigh, and shoulder. He was tomahawked in the forehead and scalped at Stone Arabia in Oct. 1780. He served under Col. J. Brown. He was granted half a pension 20 Apr. 1796. He resided in Berkshire Co., Mass. in 1796. He transferred to New York in Sept. 1799. He was on the 1813 pension list.

Pier, John Ernst. N.Y. —. He served under Col. Van Schaick. His family was granted assistance 22 May 1779 while he was away in the service.

Pierce, Abel. Mass. —. He served in the 1st Regiment and was from Weston. He was paid $20.

Pierce, Amos. N.H. Lt. He served under Col. Nichols. He was wounded by a ball in his left hand in Aug. 1777 at the battle of Bennington. He lived in Westmoreland, N.H. in 1794. After he returned home from the service, he was taken speechless. His condition persisted. About nine-tenths of the time he was in a state of delirium. The physicians did not know if his condition was due to his wound. He was granted one-fourth of a pension 20 Apr. 1796.

Pierce, Jesse. Mass. Pvt. He served in the 7th Regiment and was from Milbury. His widow, Lydia Pierce, was paid $50.

Pierce, John. Pa. Pvt. He was on the 1813 pension list.

Pierce, Josiah. Mass. —. He was paid $50.

Pierce, Levi. Conn. Pvt. He served under Col. Swift in 2nd Regiment. He lost the two middle fingers of his right hand by the shot of the enemy near Valley Forge or Croton River in Aug. 1777. He resided in Cornwall, Conn. in 1792 and in Litchfield, Conn. in 1794. He enlisted 2 Apr. 1777 and was discharged 8 Apr. 1778. He died in 1808.

Pierce, Nehemiah. N.H. Pvt. He served under Capt. Levi Spalding in Col. James Read's Regiment in 1776. George Aldrich was lieutenant. He lost his health at Ticonderoga and left the regiment 2 Oct. 1776 He had a sore on his lower jaw bone and the regimental surgeon, Solomon Harvey, took out part of it. He was aged 36 in 1787. His residence was given as Chesterfield and Westmoreland.

Pierce, Philip. Mass. Pvt. He served in the 16th Regiment and was from Dighton. His widow, Anna Pierce, was paid $50.

Pierce, Richard. Mass. Corp. He served in the 14th Regiment and was from Westport. He was paid $50.

Pierce, Silas. Mass. Lt. He served in the 8th Mass. Regiment. He was wounded by a ball in the right arm at Bemis Heights on 7 Oct. He resided at Dublin, N.H. in 1796. He was appointed lieutenant 1 Jan. 1777 and promoted to captain 15 Dec. 1779. He was granted one-half of a pension 20 Apr. 1796.

Pierce, Willard. Mass. —. He served in the Invalids and was from New Hampshire. He was paid $20.

Pierce, William. Mass. Pvt. He was in the Invalids under Capt. McFarland. He was disabled by infirmities and age. He was 65 years old and resided in Wareham, Mass. He died 23 Oct. 1805.

Pierce, William. Mass. Pvt. He served in the 1st Regiment and was from Waltham. His widow, Phebe Pierce, was paid $50.

Pierce, Zebulon. —. Artificer. Congress awarded his widow, Mary Pierce of Cortland Co., N.Y., the arrearage of her pension from 4 Mar. 1848 to 3 Feb. 1853 on 10 Dec. 1857.

Piercy, Henry. Va. Lt. He served to the close of the war and was entitled to 200 acres of bounty land. His warrant was issued in 1794 to one Paul Bentalow. His widow, Nancy Piercy, sought a duplicate warrant. Congress declined and informed her that she should seek legal action on 13 Jan. 1810.

Pierson, Amos. —. Sgt. He served under Col. Little and was wounded by a musket ball at the battle of Bunker Hill 7 June 1775. He was pensioned 9 June 1794.

Pierson, David. N.J. Pvt. He served in the 2nd Regiment and was disabled due to age and infirmity. He was 57 years old and was from Elizabeth.

Pierson, Erastus. N.J. Pvt. He served in the militia under Col. Philip Van Cortland and was at Long Island, Connecticut Springs, and Springfield. He was "... so wrecked in mind that his memory cannot recall his service or his sufferings." He lived in Essex Co. His children, Rhoda Pierson, Lydia Pierson, Caleb Pierson, and Jotham Pierson, sought to have their father pensioned. He was 83 years old in 1836. Congress did so by special act 5 Mar. 1840.

Pierson, Moses. —. —. He died in 1834 before the results of his application could be made known. His widow, Eunice Pierson, married secondly ----- Sanders. Congress on 2 Jan. 1839 granted her pension payments from 4 Mar. 1832 to his death.

Piggott, James. Pa. Capt. He was appointed 6 Apr. 1776 in Westmoreland County and resigned 22 Oct. 1777. He raised a company of volunteers under Col. George Rogers Clark and was in battle with the Indians. He built Piggott's blockhouse in St. Clair Co., Ill. He sought relief 9 June 1838.

Pike, Benjamin. Mass. Capt. He received his commutation for five years in lieu of half-pay for life.

Pike, David. Mass. Pvt. He served in the 5th Regiment and was from Phillipston. He was paid $50.

Pike, Ezra. —. Corp. He served 10 months and 7 days as a private and 2 months and 22 days as a corporal. He died 19 Apr. 1840. He married 18 Oct. 1784. Congress granted his widow,

Mary Pike, a pension 6 Mar. 1850. He had four children.

Pike, John. N.J. Pvt. He served under Capt. Joseph Horton and Col. Jaquis in the Essex County militia. His company was stationed at Short Hills in the winter of 1779 to attend the beacon of alarm gun placed on First Mountain and to fire the same in case of alarm or invasion. On 25 Feb. 1779 the enemy landed. In sounding the alarm, he was wounded and died three days later. His widow, Jemima Pike, received his half-pay in Essex County in Apr. 1781.

Pike, Samuel, Jr. Mass. Pvt. He served in the 7th Regiment and was from Sturbridge. His widow, Betsy Furbush, was paid $50.

Pike, Simeon. —. Sgt. He was killed at Bunker Hill 17 June 1775 and was under Capt. William Sawyer. He married in 1771. His widow, Mary Pike, was the mother of two children and had been a widow more than sixty-six years. One daughter was Phebe Pike. Congress granted her a pension 14 Jan. 1843.

Pike, Timothy. Mass. Corp. He served in the 6th Regiment and was from Framingham. His widow, Anne Stone, was paid $50.

Pike, Zebulon. N.J. Gen. His grand-daughter, Hannah Royce of Woodbridge Township, Middlesex County was pensioned 5 Mar. 1874 at the rate of $100 per annum. She was believed to be the nearest if not the only surviving blood relative and was near 80 years of age.

Piles, —. Va. —. His wife, Ann Piles, was allowed 18 shillings for her maintenance in Augusta County 23 August 1783.

Piles, Henry. Va. —. His wife, Susannah Piles, was allowed 1 barrel of corn and 50 pounds of pork on 28 Aug. 1781 in Bedford Co., Va.

Pillow, —. Va. —. His wife, Agnes Pillow, was granted assistance in Prince Edward Co., Va. on 20 July 1778 while he was away in Continental service.

Pilsbury, Daniel. Mass. Capt. He received his commutation for five years in lieu of half-pay for life.

Pimple, Paul. Pa. Pvt. He was in Philadelphia County 13 Mar. 1786. He served in DeHaas's Regiment and was ruptured in 1775 by lifting a barrel of flour. He was dead by Sep. 1795.

Pinckney, Charles Cotesworthy. S.C. Gen. He died in Aug 1825. He had three daughters. Maria Henrietta Pinckney who inherited one-third of Pinckney Island. She died unmarried and her interest was inherited by her sister. Her sister was Eliza Lucas Pinckney who married ----- Izard and died without issue. Her cousin inherited her share. The other sister, Harriott Pinckney, died in 1865 at the age of 91. She gave her share to Rev. C. C. Pinckney. The heirs were Rev. Charles Cotesworth Pinckney and his sisters Caroline (Pinckney) Seabrook, the wife of Archibald H. Seabrook, and Mary E. Pinckney. They were first cousins once removed of Harriott Pinckney and grandchildren of Thomas Pinckney who was the brother of Gen. Pinckney. The heirs sought the restoration of Pinckney Island which contained 2,000 acres and 500 acres of marsh by Congress on 7 Apr. 1860. The land had been forfeited for non-payment of taxes.

Pindell, Nicholas. Md. —. His arrearage was to be paid to his administrator, Gassaway Pindell, 18 Feb. 1830.

Pindell, Richard. Md. Surgeon. He was pensioned at the rate of half-pay of a surgeon in Kentucky 5 Feb. 1817.

Pinkerton, Andrew. Pa. Pvt. He was on the 1813 pension list.

Pinkerton, —. Pa. —. His widow, Catherine Pinkerton, was awarded a $40 gratuity and a $40 annuity in Allegheny County on 2 Apr. 1822.

Pinney, Isaac. —. Pvt. He served more than 9 months and applied for a pension in 1820. He was deafened at Stony Point. He had a wife aged 56 years, a daughter aged 24 who had been ill four or five years, and a son aged 16. His eldest son, aged 34, had a wife and four children with much sickness in their family for past ten years. In 1823 he sold half of his farm to his sons Dan and Johney Pinney. He and his son, Isaac Pinney, Jr., had divided their personal property. His wife was 58 years old and his daughter Betsey was 26. He had been denied a restoration to his pension because the agreements with his sons were not written contracts. His three eldest daughters were married. He was entitled to be restored 8 Apr. 1830.

Piper, James. Pa. Lt. Col. He was in the 1st Pa. Battalion of Riflemen and was taken prisoner at the battle of Long Island on 27 Aug. 1776. He died in New York City 29 Jan. 1777 in captivity. His widow, Lucinda Piper, was in Bedford County on 15 Jan. 1784. She was in Cumberland County at one time.

Piper, Robert. R.I. Pvt. He was disabled in his left shoulder at Springfield, N.J. on 23 June 1780. He lost the toes on his right foot by frost bite on the Oswego Expedition in Feb. 1783. He served under Col. Jeremiah Olney. He was 35 years old when he applied 12 Jan. 1786. He resided in Providence Co., R.I.

Pipes, Joseph. Pa. —. He was awarded a $40 gratuity and a $40 annuity in Washington Co., Pa. 7 Apr. 1830. He was 76 years old in 1840. He died 23 Feb. 1856.

Pistole, Charles. —. —. His widow, Elizabeth Pistole, sought a pension. Congress awarded her a pension even though she had not proved her marriage prior to Jan. 1794 on 12 Jan. 1848. She did not have to prove the actual date.

Pitcher, Jonathan. —. Lt. He was appointed a lieutenant in the navy by Congress 22 Dec. 1775. He was late of Pawtuxent, R.I. when his only child, Elizabeth Arnold, aged 83, sought a pension. Congress granted her a pension 22 Dec. 1851.

Pitman, —. S.C. —. His widow was Jane Pitman. There were children in 1791.

Pitman, George. Va. Sgt. He was in Lancaster County 15 Dec. 1785. He was in Blackwell's Company in the 5th Va. Regiment. He had a wife, child, and a Negro wench and child. He lost a leg at Charleston, S.C. in May 1780. Samuel J. Cabell, Lt. Col. and Deputy Adjutant General, attested to his service. He was 28 years old in 1787. He was continued on the pension roll at the rate of £12 per annum on 2 Apr. 1787. He was on the 1813 pension list. He also appeared as George Pittman.

Pitman, James. —. Lt. He served eight months and sixteen days as a private and one year and five months as a lieutenant. He was pensioned at the rank of a private and requested Congress to recognize his service as an officer. Congress accepted eight months of service as lieutenant but found no evidence for the rest of the service he claimed. Congress, therefore, recommended no increase in his pension 14 June 1850.

Pitsley, Benjamin. Mass. Pvt. He served in the 10th Regiment and was from Fairhaven. His widow, Hannah Pitsley, was paid $50.

Pittman, Matthew. N.C. Pvt. He applied in Mecklenburg County in 1807. He served in the militia and received multiple wounds in his head, neck, and elsewhere at the battle of Guilford Court House in 1781. He had a sword wound in his left arm. His sergeant, Henry Williamson, attested to his service. He was on the 1813 pension list.

Pitt, James. Va. Seaman. He was on the 1800 pension roll.

Pitts, —. Va. —. John Pitts was granted £10 support while his two sons were away in the service on 12 Feb. 1778 and £25 support in Caroline Co., Va. 11 Mar. 1779 while his three sons were away in the service.

Plane, Jacob. Md. Pvt. His widow, Catherine Plane, was pensioned at the rate of half-pay of a private in Anne Arundel County on 24 Feb. 1830.

Plaskett, Joseph. Mass. —. He served in the 7th Regiment. His widow, Tabitha Plaskett, was paid $20.

Platt, —. N.Y. —. Elizabeth Platt was granted support 3 Apr. 1779 in Ulster County.

Platt, Frederick. Conn. Pvt. He served in the Conn. militia. He was wounded by a musket ball in his thigh which passed near the bone on 19 Sep. 1777 near Stillwater. He resided at Haddam, Conn. in 1796. He was granted one-third of a pension 20 Apr. 1796.

Platt, Samuel. N.J. —. His widow, Eunice Platt, was granted relief 5 Sep. 1789.

Plumb, Jacob. Pa. —. He served in the militia in 1782 against the Indians and was wounded in the right shoulder by a musket ball and tomahawked across the nose at Piper's Fort in 1782. He was awarded a $40 gratuity and a $40 annuity on 7 Feb. 1812. He was from Somerset County. He died 18 Dec. 1817.

Plumb, Joseph. Conn. Artificer. He entered the service from Woodbury, Conn. under Lt. Thompson for three years. He was ordered to Danbury in 1778. He next served under Capt. Humphrey and Col. Return J. Meigs. His father, Isaac Plumb, hired Asahel Chittenden as a substitute for Joseph for £70 because Joseph was sick at Morristown, N.J. Chittenden's name was not on the roll. He had been rejected for a pension in 1833 on the grounds of desertion. He died in Bangor, N. Y. Congress granted the heirs a pension from 4 Mar. 1831 to the time of his death 3 Oct. 1838 on 9 Feb. 1842. Congress denied his children a special pension 19 July 1848.

Plumb, Joseph. —. —. His record indicated that he deserted 20 May 1780. There was no parol evidence to refute such so Congress denied his claim 1 Aug. 1850.

Plumb, Nathaniel. Conn. —. He served in the 1st Regiment under Col. Samuel Prentiss from 1777 to May 1778. He was wounded in his hand and was unable to serve as fifer. He hired Samuel Button for $250 as his substitute but reserved his right to bounty land. Near the end of the war he was furloughed and was discharged before it expired. Congress awarded him bounty land 17 June 1838.

Plumb, Stephen. N.Y. Pvt. He enlisted 12 Dec. 1776 in Capt. Benjamin Walker's Company under Col. Henry B. Livingstone in the 4th Regiment. He was in the 2nd Regiment under Col. Philip Van Cortland when he was wounded at the siege of Yorktown in Oct. 1781 and lost the sight in his left eye from gravel forced from the breast work by a cannon ball. He was 46 years old on 4 Nov. 1787. He lived in Westchester Co., N.Y. on 13 June 1788. He was a carpenter and joiner. He was on the 1813 pension list.

Plumline, Charles. Pa. Pvt. He was on the 1813 pension list.

Plummer, Jabez. N.H. Pvt. He was in Capt. Page's Company and in Col. Drake's Regiment and was wounded in the battle of Still Water on 7 Oct. 1777. His wife was Anna Plummer.

Plummer, John. Me. —. He was from Freedom. He was paid $50 under the resolve of 1836.

Plunket, —. —. —. Congress rejected the petition of his widow, Penelope Plunket, because there was no evidence on file 4 Apr. 1840.

Plunket, Reuben. Va. Sgt. He was in Baylor's Regiment. He lived in Caroline Co., Va. He was on the 1813 pension list.

Plunkett, Patrick. Va. —. His wife, Catherine Plunkett, was granted £20 support in Berkeley County on 18 May 1779.

Plunkett, Thomas. Va. —. He was pensioned in Rockbridge County on 8 Feb. 1817 at the rate of $60 per annum and an immediate relief of $65. He died 18 Dec. 1830. His administrator was Samuel Petigrew.

Plutt, Frederick. Conn. Pvt. He was granted relief.

Plyler, Coonrod. S.C. —. He fought at Sumter's defeat and served under Capt. Marlin. He was nearly 70 years old and had a wife and a large family. He was from Richland District in 1823. He was paid as late as 1834.

Plympton, Ebenezer. —. —. He enlisted under Capt. Wheeler and Col. Read 1 Dec. 1775 for two months. He next served five months from July 1776 and was at Ticonderoga. In 1778 he served under Capt. Maulton and Col. Poor. He was at White Plains and West Point in New York. He was 76 years old and could not walk without a crutch. Congress granted him a pension 10 Jan. 1832.

Poe, —. Md. Capt. His widow, Elizabeth Poe, was pensioned at the rate of half-pay of a captain in Baltimore on 9 Feb. 1822.

Poe, Virgil. Va. —. He had his application rejected 3 Apr. 1787. He was pensioned 16 July 1812. He was on the 1813 pension list of Kentucky. He resided in Floyd County.

Poh, John. Pa. —. He was awarded a $40 annuity and a $40 gratuity in Berks Co., Pa. 16 Feb. 1835. He died 13 Sep. 1845.

Pohe, —. Pa. —. His widow, Eve Pohe, was awarded a $40 gratuity 18 Feb. 1834.

Pointer, Levin. Del. Pvt. He was wounded in the hip at Ninety Six on 14 June 1781. He was single. He was on the 1813 pension list. He also appeared as Leven Pointer.

Poirey, —. —. Aide-de-Camp. He served as secretary and aide-de-camp to Gen. Lafayette and received a brevet from Gen. Washington. His petition for a pension was rejected by Congress 28 Mar. 1818.

Polan, Peter. Pa. —. He applied in Lancaster County on 1 Oct. 1814. He served two years in the artillery under Col. Proctor and Capt. William Brown at Mud Island Fort. He was in the battles of Trenton and Princeton. He also appeared as Peter Poland. He had lost his discharge on a journey to Carolina several years ago.

Poland, Abner. Mass. Corp. He served in the 8th Regiment and was from Ipswich. He was paid $20.

Poland, Samuel. Pa. —. He enlisted in 1776 under Capt. James Herren and Col. Moses Weson. He was wounded at Brandywine. He was 60 years old. He was awarded a $40 gratuity and a $40 annuity in Franklin County on 19 Mar. 1816.

Pole, David. —. Seaman. He was disabled and received $5 per month from 5 Mar. 1789.

Polereczsky, John S. France. Maj. He served in the Duke of Lausun's Regiment until 1783. He was at King's Mountain and led the charge on Tarleton's cavalry. His horse was shot out from beneath him. He was naturalized in 1788. He received a pension from France, but it stopped when Napoleon came to power. His share of his paternal and maternal estates were confiscated. Congress declined to grant him relief 8 Feb. 1820.

Polhemius, Joseph. Md. Pvt. He was pensioned 4 Mar. 1789. He was on the 1813 pension list.

Polhemus, John. Capt. N.J. He served in the 4th Company of the 1st N. J. Regiment. He was at the battle of Monmouth in June 1778. He served under Gen. Maxwell and was taken prisoner by the British and held until 1780 when he was paroled. He was sent to Elizabethtown where he was received by David Baldwin. He had given his son, John Pohlemus, his certificate for $1,750. His house burned and consumed the certificate. Another son was Montgomery Polhemus whose wife was Ann Pohlemus. He did not fall within any of the categories of officers due commutation and was rejected 30 Dec. 1818.

Polin, Joshua. Mass. —. He served in the 4th Regiment and was paid $20.

Pollard, Abner. Mass. Corp. He served in the 8th Regiment. He was from Ipswich.

Pollard, Andrew. Del. Pvt. He was pensioned in 1783. He was on the 1791 pension list.

Pollard, Jonathan. Mass. Pvt. He served under Col. Thomas Nixon in the 6th Regiment under Capt. Clay. He was disabled by a musket ball which broke his left leg. He was pensioned 19 Sep. 1786 and lived in Windsor, Mass. He was 27 years old in 1786. He was in New Braintree when he was allowed $20 by the Commonwealth. He transferred to Madison Co., N.Y. 4 Sep. 1804. He was on the 1813 pension list.

Pollard, Solomon. Mass. Corp. He served under Col. Nixon in Capt. Elijah Danforth's Company. He was disabled by a fever sore on his left leg. He was 28 years old in 1786. He died in Sep. 1789.

Pollock, James Smith. Pa. —. He was awarded an $80 gratuity on 27 Mar. 1819. He was from Columbia County.

Pollock, John. S.C. —. He was from Kershaw District and was pensioned at the rate of $21.30 per annum for life on 20 Dec. 1800.

Pollock, Oliver W. Va. —. He was in Washington, D.C. 2 Jan. 1813. He was in Baltimore, Md. 21 Jan. 1815, Annapolis, Fairfax Co., Md. 29 Dec. 1818, and Wilkinson Co., Miss. 21 Apr. 1823. He died there 17 Dec. 1823. Administration of his estate was granted to Herbert A. Claiborne 11 Mar. 1840 in Richmond, Va. He was pensioned at the rate of $333 1/3 per annum and was awarded $1,000 in immediate relief on 17 Feb. 1812. On 31 Mar. 1821 he received one year's pension in advance.

Polly, John. —. —. Congress awarded his widow, Phebe Polly of Otsego Co., N.Y., the arrearage of her pension from 4 Mar. 1848 to 3 Feb. 1853 on 10 Dec. 1857.

Pomeroy, Grove. Mass. —. He served in the 6th Regiment and was paid $20.

Pomeroy, Phineas. Mass. Ens. He was wounded by the bursting of a soldier's musket. He was paid £40 8 Feb. 1794.

Pomeroy, Pliny. Vt. Pvt. He served under Col. Ward in Capt. Allen's militia company. He was ruptured in his groin while carrying provisions from Roxbury to Dorchester in Jan. or Feb. 1777 near Boston. He lived in Westminster, Vt. in 1795. He was granted four-fifths of a pension 20 Apr. 1796.

Pond, Elihu. —. Pvt. He enlisted 4 June 1779 for nine months. He went from Springfield, Mass. to West Point, N.Y. He was in the 6th Regiment under Col. Nixon and was taken prisoner 3 Feb. 1780 and detained until 12 Dec. 1780. He was stricken from the roll in 1820. Congress granted him a pension 13 Mar. 1832.

Ponder, James. S.C. —. He died in the war. William Gunter served with him. His widow, Patsey Ponder, had her application denied in 1836.

Pool, Conrad. Pa. —. He served under Capt. William Scull in 1777 and was killed in action in New Jersey. He was from Berks County.

Pool, John. —. —. Congress denied his widow, Elizabeth Pool, a pension on 29 Feb. 1848 because her petition was not in proper form and signed.

Pool, Thomas. —. —. In 1780 he was employed by the Commander in Chief in procuring intelligence within enemy lines. On 7 Sep. 1780 he was seized as a spy in New York and confined in the provost prison until 24 Oct. 1782 when he was sent to Bermuda where he remained a prisoner in Castle Rock until 30 Apr. 1783 when he was sent back to New York. He was again returned to Bermuda and confined aboard the *Carolina* until 24 Aug. 1783 when he escaped until he got on board an American vessel on 9 Sep. Fellow prisoners with him included Capt. Howlet, Major Brush, Mr. Rattoon, Mr. Mulligan, Capt. Grinnell, and Capt. Congklin. He had left his horse, saddle, and bridle at Bergen, N.J. when he went to New York. Their value was $160. His wife and brother sent him money and clothing amounting between $400 and $500 which the enemy intercepted.

Poole, David. Conn. Boatswain. He served aboard the *Trumbull*. He was pensioned 11 Aug. 1790. He was on the 1813 pension list. He died 1 Jan. 1821 in New London Co., Conn.

Poole, Job. Me. —. He was from Falmouth. He was paid $50 under the resolve of 1836.

Poor, Enoch. N.H. Gen. He died 8 Sep. 1780. His widow was Martha Poor who was granted his half-pay 16 Apr. 1784. She was from Exeter.

Poor, Thomas. Va. Pvt. He was wounded in Phillip's invasion. He served in the 1st Virginia Regiment. He was pensioned 21 Jan. 1809 at the rate of $40 per annum in Goochland County. He died 18 Sep. 1837. His heirs were Edward H. Poor, Abraham Poor, Richard James, William M. Poor, James Poor, and James Brooks. Edward H. Poor was the administrator of his estate.

Pope, —. Va. —. His father, John Pope, was granted support in Westmoreland County 23 Feb. 1779.

Pope, Adam. Pa. —. He was awarded a $40 gratuity and a $40 annuity in York Co., Pa. 4 May 1832.

Pope, James. Md. Pvt. He served in the 3rd Maryland Regiment and became blind. He was pensioned 29 Aug. 1780. He was on the 1791 pension list on the 1813 list.

Pope, Samuel. —. —. His widow, Ruth Pope, had her request rejected 4 May 1846. She lived in Maine.

Popham, Benjamin. Md. Pvt. He was pensioned at the rate of half-pay of a private in Anne Arundel County on 12 Mar. 1827. His arrearage was paid to his sole legatee, Anne Busey, on 29 Mar. 1839 at which time his name was given as Benjamin Topham.

Popple, George. R.I. Sgt. He served in Col. Green's Regiment. He was wounded in his right thigh by a ball which he received in an engagement with the Hessian troops on 22 Oct. 1777 at RedBank. He resided in Hopkinton, Washington Co., R.I. in 1794. He was granted one-eighth of a pension 20 Apr. 1796. He enlisted 1 May 1777 and was discharged 1 Apr. 1780. He resided in Providence County.

Porter, Aaron. Mass. —. He was paid $50.

Porter, Asa. Mass. —. He was in the 5th Regiment and was paid $20.

Porter, Asa. Mass. —. He was in the 1st Regiment and was paid $20.

Porter, Benjamin Jones. Mass. Surgeon's Mate. He sought five years' full pay. He was commissioned by Congress 10 Apr. 1780 having previously served in that capacity in 1779 in Maine. He was disbanded in Nov. 1783. On 1 Dec. 1783 he was appointed assistant paymaster in the army. Congress approved him for relief 25 Feb. 1848.

Porter, Daniel. Va.—. He was away in the service. His wife, Mary Porter, was allowed one bushel of corn, 100 pounds of pork, and 124 pounds of beef in Augusta Co., Va. 19 Dec. 1781. She was allowed 3 bushels of corn and 100 pounds of beef on 19 Mar. 1782. There were two children.

Porter, Ephraim. Mass. —. He served in the 2nd Regiment and was from Great Barrington. He was paid $20.

Porter, Hugh. S.C. —. He was taken by Tories and murdered by the Indians. His widow, Elizabeth Porter, was awarded an annuity 21 Apr. 1786 in Abbeville.

Porter, James. N.C. Pvt. He applied in Rutherford County in 1801. He served in the Rowan County militia and was wounded by a ball through his body which broke away some of his backbone on 20 June 1780 at Ramsour's Mill. He served under Capt. William Armstrong and Ens. Richard Graham. He lived with his brother. He was on the 1813 pension list.

Porter, Joel. N.H. Pvt. He served under Col. Prescott in Capt. Lawrence's Company. He was wounded in his ankle by a musket ball on 17 June 1775 at Bunker Hill. He lived in Marlborough, N.H. in 1795. He was in the militia. He was granted one-fourth of a pension 20 Apr. 1796. He was on the 1813 pension list.

Porter, John. —. —. He served six months from June 1780. Congress granted him a pension 4 Jan. 1841.

Porter, John. Va. —. He served in the 2ⁿᵈ Regiment under Capt. Mead in 1776 and was discharged at Valley Forge in Feb. 1778. His next tour was for a year and a half as wagon conductor. He was afflicted with rheumatic pain. He was at Brandywine, Germantown, and the defeat of Col. Buford. He was 54 years old in 1808 and was dependent upon his aged parents in Louisa County for support. He was 60 years of age in 1812. He sought relief 2 Mar. 1818 from Congress.

Porter, Nathan. Md. Pvt. He was pensioned at the rate of half-pay of a private in Talbot County on 18 Feb. 1825.

Porter, Philip. S.C. Pvt. He was pensioned from Pickens District on 17 Dec. 1831. He died 8 May 1841. His widow was Mary Porter. She was paid as late as 1851.

Porter, Samuel. Pa. —. He was awarded a $40 gratuity and a $40 annuity in Center County on 7 Mar. 1821.

Porter, Samuel. Va. Pvt. He served in Capt. David Gass' Company under Col. Bowman. He was wounded in his thigh on an attack on the Shawnee towns. He sought relief on 18 Oct. 1779.

Porter, Shadrack. S.C. —. He was taken prisoner by the enemy and died in confinement. His widow, Susanna Porter, was awarded an annuity 16 June 1785.

Porter, William. Va. —. He was away in the service. His wife, Mary Porter, was allowed £360 for her support and her children in Augusta Co., Va. 15 May 1781.

Porterfield, Charles. Va. Sgt. He served under Capt. Daniel Morgan and was taken prisoner at Quebec and taken to Detroit until Dec. 1775. He next served in the 11ᵗʰ Regiment and was at Brandywine, Germantown, and Monmouth. He returned to Virginia and became Quarter-master. His regiment was cut to pieces at Buford's surprise. He fell mortally wounded at Camden and died in 1780. He left no wife or children. His brother, Robert Porterfield, received 6,000 acres of bounty land which he perfected in 1824 and received a patent in Kentucky which was in conflict with an older warrant of George Rogers Clark for the same land. He was given relief for the Virginia situation 2 Mar. 1860 by Congress.

Porterfield, George. N.C. —. He enlisted for nine months under Capt. Goodwin and Col. Thaxton in the 4ᵗʰ Regiment. He was 63 years old in Granville Co., N.C. in Feb. 1822.

Posey, Belair. —. Capt. He was in the Flying Camp and marched to New Jersey from Maryland. The payroll for his troops was stolen from his trunk. He paid them out of his own funds. His daughter, Elizabeth A. Middleton, had her claim rejected 13 Apr. 1858.

Posey, Hezekiah. S.C. Pvt. He came to South Carolina in 1772. He served under Capt. John Norwood and was severely wounded in his left shoulder and arm while guarding the baggage train at Ninety Six. John McCord saw him the day after he was wounded. James McCord saw him a few minutes before he was wounded. Mary Stephens of Henry Co., Ga. testified that he was in her father's house where his wound was dressed. He was from Lancaster District in 1793. He was on the pension list in 1793 and was continued to 1796 when he left the state. On 25 Nov. 1830 he was allowed his arrearage of £5 per annum from 1 Jan. 1797 to 1 Jan. 1817 and then $60 per annum from 1 Jan. 1817 to Jan. 1830. He was in Madison Co., Alabama when he reapplied.

Posey, Micajah. Pa. —. He was pensioned 1 Apr. 1823 in Chester County and was dead by 30 Mar. 1829. His widow, Rachel Posey, received a $40 gratuity and a $40 annuity 4 Apr. 1856.

Post, John C. N.J. —. He served under Capt. David Marinus and Col. Philip Cortlandt at Flatbush, Long Island, Fort Washington, and White Plains where he was wounded in the knee. His next tour for seven months was under Capt. John Outwater, Capt. Peter Ward, Capt. Chrystie, Capt. David Demarest, Capt. Elias Romeyn, Capt. Jeraloman, and Capt. Kidney. At Egg Harbor he was a guide to Gen. Wayne. He was severely wounded in his leg in storming Block Fort. He applied from Bergen County. He was 71 years old. He was born on 9 June.

Posters, Jacob. Pa. —. His widow applied in Ovid, N.Y. 15 Mar. 18--. He was in the Pa. Line.

Poth, Matthias. Pa. —. His widow, Feronica O. Poth, was granted a $40 gratuity in Philadelphia County 10 Apr. 1849 for his Revolutionary service.

Pott, Jacob. Pa. —. He was pensioned in Berks County 21 Mar. 1837. He died in May 1841.

Potter, Abel. —. —. He was granted relief.

Potter, Edmund. Mass. Pvt. He served under Col. Henry Jackson and Capt. John Orchard. He was debilitated in the service with rheumatism and pensioned at the rate of one-third pay of a soldier from 12 June 1783 on 1 Feb. 1785. He was aged 24 in 1788.

Potter, James. Mass. —. He served in the 6th Regiment and was from Holden. He was paid $20.

Potter, Samuel. N.H. Sgt. He served under Col. Cilley. He was wounded in his leg on 19 Sep. 1777. He lived in New Ipswich in 1784 and in Francistown, N.H. in 1794. He enlisted 15 Nov. 1776 and was invalided 1 Oct. 1778. He was granted half a pension 20 Apr. 1796. He was on the 1813 pension list.

Potter, Thaddeus. Conn. Pvt. He was drafted early in 1780 in Litchfield under Capt. Converse and Col. Swift. He contracted a violent disease from fatigue and exposure. He became lame and unfit for duty. He was discharged 9 Dec. 1780. Congress granted him a pension for six months of service 13 Feb. 1836.

Potts, George. Pa. —. He was granted relief in Fayette County 21 June 1839. He died 9 Jan. 1842.

Potts, James, Jr. N.C. Pvt. He applied in Iredell County in 1801. He served in the militia of Rowan County under Col. Francis Lock and Capt. John Laurance. He was wounded in his left ankle at Ramsour's Mill. He had a large family. He was on the 1813 pension list. He died 16 Feb. 1826. He was from Iredell County.

Potts, Jesse. —. Ass't Dep. QM Gen. He served under Col. Nicholas Long and Gen. Gates for three years. N.C. granted him 3,840 acres of bounty land as a captain. He sought commutation of five years' full pay. Congress rejected his claim 19 Jan. 1836.

Potts, John. Pa. —. He was in Lancaster County on 26 Sep. 1798. He married Eleanor Masters in 1766 or 1767. She was an indented servant to the father of Abraham Carpenter. Potts was a widower and had one child by his first wife who lived with Joel Ferree and was aged 30. In 1776 Potts marched with Abraham Carpenter under Capt. Bowman to the camp at Blazing Star, New Jersey. He was 55 years old.

Potts, Jonathan. Pa. —. He was awarded a $40 gratuity and a $40 annuity in Montgomery Co., Pa. 8 Apr. 1833. He died 22 Feb. 1840.

Potts, Joseph. Pa. Capt. He entered as a lieutenant in 1776 and was promoted at Brandywine where he was wounded by a musket ball in his thigh which broke the bone and by a thrust of a bayonet in his shoulder. He was taken prisoner 1 July 1778. He was deranged. Donation land in the amount of 500 acres was awarded to his heirs 20 Mar. 1812.

Powell, John. Md. —. He enlisted for three years under Capt. Allen. He was taken prisoner at Brandywine and placed on a prison ship and taken to Pensacola where he was held to the close of the war. He came to Huntington, Conn. He was 90 years old when Congress granted him a pension on 1 Apr. 1836.

Powell, John. Va. Sgt. He served in the 10th Va. Regiment He lived in Fairfax County on 20 Mar. 1809.

He was on the 1813 pension list. He died 5 Feb. 1824.

Powell, Lloyd. Pa. Pvt. He was in Philadelphia County on 2 July 1788. He served in the 4th Pa. Regiment and was afflicted with a complication of disorders. On the march in the night after the battle of Monmouth, he injured his kidneys by a fall upon a stone. He was discharged in June 1783. He was 67 years old. He died 6 Sep. 1804.

Powell, Nathan. N.C. —. He applied in Montgomery County in 1794 and again in 1808. He served under Col. Thomas Wade and was wounded by a ball in his left shoulder in 1781 at Betty's [i.e. Beaty's] Bridge.

Powell, Robert. Va. Capt. He served in the 3rd Regiment for somewhat more than three years. He was a major in the state line. Congress rejected the claim of the heirs for his commutation 9 June 1836.

Powell, Stephen. N.Y. Pvt. He served under Col. Van Cortland. He was injured in his left shoulder by a fall on stump which dislocated his shoulder in Apr. 1782 at Princeton, N.J. He lived in Westchester Co., N.Y. in 1794. He enlisted 1 Jan. 1777 for the war. He was on the rolls in 1782. He was granted one-sixteenth of a pension 20 Apr. 1796. He was on the 1813 pension list.

Powell, Thomas. N.Y. Pvt. He served in Capt. Hamtramack's Company in the 2nd N.Y. Regiment under Col. Philip Van Schaick. He was disabled by a rupture. He was 62 years old in 1786. He lived in Albany Co., N.Y. 2 June 1789. He was on the 1813 pension list.

Powell, Thomas. Va. —. He was in Capt. Shield's Company. His wife, Mary Powell, and two children were furnished £6 support in York Co., Va. 21 July 1777.

Powell, Thomas. Va. Surgeon. He served from 1776 to the end of the war. Congress granted his heirs commutation 21 Jan. 1839.

Powell, William. Va. —. His wife, Sarah Powell, was granted £45 support in York Co., Va. on 20 Mar. 1780.

Power, Robert. —. —. His application was laid on the table 8 Mar. 1802.

Powers, Abner. N.H. —. He enlisted 13 Feb. 1778. He sought his depreciation pay in Nov. 1792. He was from Monadnock.

Powers, Alexander. —. —. He sought commutation in lieu of half-pay, but his application was rejected because he was an officer of artillery artificers 19 Mar. 1790.

Powers, —. N.J. —. Congress did not grant a pension increase for Getty Powers.

Powers, Jesse. Md. Pvt. He was pensioned in St. Mary's County at the rate of half-pay of a private 23 Jan. 1816. His widow, Milly Powers, was pensioned at the same rate 25 Feb. 1836. Her arrearage was to be paid to Henry Fowler for the use of Clement Thompson, her legal representative, on 13 Jan. 1845.

Powers, Josiah. N.H. Pvt. He was from Westmoreland in 1786. He served in the 3rd N.H. Regiment in Capt. Ellis' Company. He became ill on the retreat from Ticonderoga. He was wounded at Stillwater 7 Oct. 1777.

Powers, Pierce. Mass. Midshipman. He lost his right arm on 24 Apr. 1778 in an engagement with the British sloop of war *Drake* in action in St. George's Channel. He served aboard the Continental ship of war *Ranger*. Ezra Green was the surgeon. He was pensioned from 23 Aug. 1778 at the rate of half-pay on 27 Feb. 1779. He lived in Rochester, N.H. in 1788. His widow was Mary Powers. She married secondly Richard Thurber.

Powers, Robert. Pa. Cornet. He died 20 Jan. 1811.

Powers, Timothy. —. Corp. He served more than two years. Congress credited him with seven months and ten days of service. He refused to accept that amount. He filed his objection but died before any action was taken. His widow was Elizabeth Powers. Congress granted her a pension for two years of service 10 Jan. 1843.. They married in 1779. He died in Albany, N.Y. 2 Apr. 1841.

Powers, William. N.H. Pvt. He served in Hubbard's Regiment. He lived in Grafton Co., N.H. He was on the 1813 pension list.

Poyas, John Ernest. S.C. Surgeon. He served in a Continental Hospital and was captured at the surrender of Charleston. In 1785 he sought relief on a equal basis as other officers.

Prator, John. S.C. —. He served in the 3rd Regiment under Col. Thompson. After two and half years he enlisted a man in his place and got his discharge. He had been wounded through his shoulder and received a broken bone in action with a party of Royalists under Col. Boyd. He was granted a five year pension and placed on the list 3 Dec. 1808. His wife was Eleanor Prator of Pendleton District. She had married him about four months after he was wounded. He removed to the western country and left her. She was 75 years old. She was pensioned at the rate of $30 per annum on 25 Nov. 1830. Her son-in-law with whom she lived at the time of her death was John Crouch. Andrew Prator of Pickens Co., Ala. stated that his father, John Prator, died at his home in Dec. 1829. John Couch, administrator of John Prater, deceased, applied for the arrearage of the pension due to the soldier since the widow had not done so on 17 Dec. 1831. She died 15 Nov. 1837.

Pratt, Benjamin. Mass. —. He served in the 2nd Regiment and was from Middleboro. His widow, Jemima Pratt, was paid $50.

Pratt, Cyrus. Mass. Pvt. He served in the 3rd Regiment and was from Needham. His widow, Deborah Pratt, was paid $50.

Pratt, Daniel. —. —. He was an officer. His son, Robert Pratt, sought the balance of seven years' half-pay. He presented no evidence so Congress rejected his claim 7 Apr. 1848.

Pratt, David. Conn. Drum Major. He served in the 3rd Regiment. He was ruptured in 1780. He resided in Glastonbury, Conn. in 1792. He enlisted 7 Oct. 1777 and continued to the end of the war.

Pratt, Elam. Me. —. He died 18 Apr. 1836. His widow was Lydia Pratt from Skowhegan. She was paid $50 under the resolve of 1836.

Pratt, Ephraim. Mass. —. He served in the 2nd Regiment and was from Carver. He was paid $20.

Pratt, George. Me. —. He was from Salem. He was paid $50 under the resolve of 1836.

Pratt, Jabez. R.I. Pvt. He suffered from old age, rheumatism, and bodily infirmities. He was wounded seven times at the battle of Monmouth on 28 June 1778. He was aged 64 in 1785.

Pratt, James. Pa. —. He applied in Philadelphia 14 Jan. 1813. He served under Capt. John Stiek [?] in the 1st Pa. Regiment. In 1781 he was transferred to the 6th Pa. Regiment. He resided in Luzerne County.

Pratt, James. Pa. —. He was awarded a $40 gratuity in Columbia Co., Pa. 3 Mar. 1829.

Pratt, James. S.C. —. He was in the 3rd Regiment under Col. William Thompson, Gen. Richardson, and Col. Lacey. He was in his 90th year and had broken his arm not long since. He was from Pendleton District when he was pensioned 14 Dec. 1820. He was allowed one year arrearage. He was last paid in 1826.

Pratt, Joseph. Mass. —. He served in the 4th Regiment and was from Norton. He was paid $20.

Pratt, Nathaniel. Mass. Pvt. He served in the 6th Regiment and was from Framingham. He was paid $50.

Pratt, Paul. Mass. Pvt. He served in the 1st Regiment and was from Weston. His widow, Abigail Pratt, was paid $50.

Pratt, Seth. Mass. —. He served in the 2nd Regiment and was paid $20.

Pratt, Thomas. —. —. He died 27 Sep. 1838. His widow was Sarah Pratt of Hawkins Co., Tenn.

Congress granted her a pension 8 Mar. 1842.

Pratt, Thomas. N.H. Pvt. He was wounded in his right arm by a musket ball which fractured the bone at the battle of Bunker Hill on 17 June 1775. He was in Capt. Reuben Dow's Company of militia under Col. William Prescott. He was discharged in June 1783. He lived in Hollis, N.H. in 1785 and in 1794. He was granted half a pension 20 Apr. 1796. There was a man of his name on the 1813 pension list in Massachusetts.

Pray, John. Mass. Capt. He served to the end of the war and received his commutation. One of his heirs, John W. Pray, had his petition rejected by Congress 7 Apr. 1858.

Pray, Jonathan. Pa. —. He was awarded a $40 gratuity and a $40 annuity in Niagara Co., New York 5 Mar. 1828.

Preble, David. Mass. —. He was paid $20.

Prentice, Valentine. Mass. —. He served in the 3rd Regiment and was from Vassalboro. He was paid $20.

Prescott, Joseph. —. Surgeon. He served from 1776 to the close of the war. He was at the general hospital of the Northern Department and was at the general hospital at Albany in 1778. He was in the campaign against the Confederated Indian tribes in 1779. In 1780 he was under Gen. Gates in the south. He was junior surgeon of the Maryland Regiment of Horse in the neighborhood of Camden. In 1781 he was director of the hospital at Cheraw Hills. He was put in charge of the hospital at Guilford. It was moved to Charlotte. He returned to the north 14 Jan. 1783. He was allowed his commutation 7 July 1838.

Prescott, Sampson. Mass. Matross. He served in the Artillery and was from Groton. His widow, Lucy Prescott, was paid $50.

Pressey, Benjamin. Mass. Pvt. He was disabled by excessive heat and exertions at the battle of Monmouth in June 1778. He served under Col. Wesson. He resided in Haverhill, Mass. in 1796. He enlisted 11 Feb. 1777 for the war, was promoted to corporal 1 Jun. 1779, transferred to the Invalids 12 Dec. 1779, and was discharged 30 Jun. 1780.

Preston, Daniel. Conn. Pvt. He served under Gen. Israel Putnam. He was wounded by ball in his right shoulder and lost the free exercise of his arm in June 1775 at Bunker Hill. He lived in Lisbon, Conn. in 1794. He was in the militia. He was granted one-third of a pension 20 Apr. 1796. He was on the 1813 pension list.

Preston, Isaac. N.J. Col. He served in the Cumberland County militia. He was seized with a violent disease 28 Feb. 1777 and died 5 Mar. No claim was made for half-pay. His heirs applied in 1797 but were rejected since their claim was one for the Untied States. The United States Congress rejected their claim and ruled the claim was one for New Jersey in Oct. 1809. His widow was Hannah Preston. One of her executors was Ephraim Newcomb. Her heirs were her children Bathsheba Newcomb the widow of Ephraim Newcomb; Elizabeth Whitaker and her husband Carl Whitaker; Hannah Foster and her husband Ezekiel Foster; and Priscilla Foster and her husband Jeremiah Foster; and her grand-daughter Elizabeth Williams daughter of Theodosia Williams (youngest child of Col. Preston).

Preston, Jonathan. N.Y. Pvt. He served in Capt. John Copp's Company under Col. Goose Van Schaick. He lost his left leg in July 1779. He was aged 40 years in 1787. He lived in Columbia Co., N.Y. in 1788 and in Albany, N.Y. on 16 June 1789. He moved to Vt. by 1806. He died 19 Aug. 1809.

Prestwood, —. S.C. —. His widow, Elizabeth Prestwood, was receiving a pension in 1793.

Prett, William. —. —. Congress rejected his petition for a pension on 4 May 1846.

Prewett, Solomon. Va. —. He entered the service in 1778 for five years or the war and served under Capt. John Nelson and Col. Josiah Parker. He was at the surrender of Lord Cornwallis and was discharged in Philadelphia. He was 86 years old and petitioned Congress to have his pension restored 21 Dec. 1838.

Prewit, John. Va. —. He was in Rockcastle Co., [Ky.] on 12 Dec. 1834. He had previously lived in Franklin Co., Va. He was a soldier in the infantry.

Prewitt, —. Va. —. His mother, Mary Prewitt, was allowed £10 support in Bedford Co., Va. on 9 May 1778.

Price, —. Va. —. He was in state service. His wife, Mary Price, and child were granted financial support in Botetourt Co., Va. 11 May 1780 and 9 Feb. 1781.

Price, —. S.C. —. His widow, Sarah Price, was a resident of Pinckney. There were two children in 1791.

Price, Abner. N.Y. Surgeon's Mate. Congress rejected the claim of his heirs for commutation 27 June 1838.

Price, Benjamin. N.J. Teamster. He proved but three months of service 10 Feb. 1836. Congress granted him a pension for six months of service from 4 Mar. 1831. He was pensioned in Hunterdon County on 4 Mar. 1844 at the rate of $60 per annum by New Jersey.

Price, Daniel. S.C. —. He died in the service. His widow, Rachel Price, was awarded an annuity 16 Nov. 1784.

Price, Francis. Va. —. While he was away in the service, his widowed mother, Elizabeth Price, was granted support in Surry Co., Va. 28 Dec. 1778. He died in the service.

Price, George. Md. Pvt. He was pensioned at the rate of half-pay of a private in Talbot County on 2 Mar. 1827. His arrearage was paid to his legal representatives 13 Mar. 1829.

Price, Henry. Pa. —. He was awarded a $40 annuity in Center County 12 Jan. 1836. He died 28 Oct. 1842.

Price, Jacob. Va. Pvt. He was in Greenbrier County in May 1786. He enlisted in Capt. Thomas Posey's Company in 1776 in the Continental Army. He was wounded in 1777 in a skirmish near Piscataway, N.J. in the regiment of Col. Morgan. He was in Botetourt County in 1787. Later he was in Greenbrier County. He was stricken from the roll when the county neglected to appoint surgeons to inspect the disabilities of the pensioners. He was restored 20 Dec. 1790. He was on the 1813 pension list.

Price, John. Va. —. He was in Continental service. His wife, Mary Price, was allowed support on 21 Nov. 1780 in Augusta Co., Va. She was allowed £300 for her support and that of her child in lieu of two barrels of corn and 100 pounds of pork.

Price, Josiah. Mass. —. He served in the 6th Regiment and was paid $20.

Price, Nehemiah. N.H. Pvt. He was from Westmoreland. He transferred to Vermont. He was on the 1813 pension list as Nehemiah Peirce. He served under Capt. Levi Spalding in 1776 and was seized with a scorbutic disorder and became unfit for duty.

Price, Samuel. N.J. Pvt. He served under Capt. William Piatt in the 1st Regiment under Col. M. Ogden in 1780 and was drowned while crossing the North River in Oct. 1780. His widow, Hannah Price, married secondly Thomas Cobb in Nov. 1783. At the time of her first husband's death, she had one child of the age of six months. The widow received a half-pay pension from 1 Nov. 1778 to 1 Nov. 1783 in Morris County.

Price, Stephen R. Md. QM Sgt. He was pensioned at the rate of half-pay of a quartermaster sergeant in Franklin Co., Ohio 24 Feb. 1830.

Price, Thomas. Pa. Sgt. He served in Col. Miles' Regiment, was wounded, and taken prisoner at Long Island. To preserve his life, he was forced to enlist with the enemy. He went to Nova Scotia and there escaped. He made his way to New England and rejoined the army. He was due donation land on 4 Apr. 1805.

Price, Thomas. Pa. —. His widow, Rosina Price, was awarded a $40 gratuity and a $30 annuity in Union County on 21 Dec. 1818.

Price, William. —. Lt. His widow, Sarah Price, was to be paid the interest due her 2 Mar. 1833.

Price, William. Va. Lt. He joined the 1ˢᵗ Regiment in the spring of 1778. He was wounded twice at Monmouth—one in his hip and the other in his leg. His 1779 term expired at Middlebrook, N.J. He was appointed lieutenant and was in the recruiting service at Richmond. He never received his commutation of half-pay. He was between 70 and 80 years old. Congress granted him his five years' full pay in commutation of his half-pay for life 29 Mar. 1830.

Prichard, Jeremiah. N.H. Lt. & Adjt. He was wounded by a ball which passed through his left shoulder and ruptured his groin in July 1777 in the expedition of Gen. Sullivan against the Indians. He served under Col. Cilley. He lived at New Ipswich, N.H. in 1792. He was commissioned 8 Nov. 1776 and resigned 5 July 1780. His rate was $13.33 1/3 per month from 6 Jan. 1808. He was on the 1813 pension list. He also appeared as Jeremiah Pritchard.

Prichard, Richard. Mass. Pvt. He was under the command of Maj. Vose at Stony Beach in Hull and was dangerously wounded in his leg. He petitioned for a pension 30 Dec. 1776 and stated that he was a soldier in Capt. Job Cushing's Company under Col. Greaton.

Priest, Job. Mass. Ens. He was ruptured in the groin while removing ordnance stores at the retreat from Canada in 1776. He served under Col. Vose. He was appointed 1 Jan. 1777 and resigned 4 Nov. 1777. He was granted one-third of a pension 20 Apr. 1796. He was on the 1813 pension list.

Priest, John. Mass. Pvt. He served in Capt. Samuel King's Company under Col. Thomas Marshall in the 10ᵗʰ Regiment. He was wounded in the retreat from Ticonderoga on 8 July 1777. He was disabled by a rupture of the groin. He was discharged 27 Feb. 1778. He was pensioned at the rate of half-pay on 2 Mar. 1778. He resided in Essex Co., Mass. He was 42 years old in 1790. He was on the 1813 pension list.

Primer, —. Pa. —. His widow, Anna Maria Primer, received a $40 gratuity and a $40 annuity in Philadelphia County 16 June 1836. She died 22 Nov. 1841.

Prince, Daniel. S.C. —. He was pensioned 23 Nov. 1829 as a Revolutionary soldier.

Prince, Edward. S.C. —. He served under Lt. Dodd, Col. Brandon, and Col. William McFair [?]. He was a nurse for the sick and wounded at the Block House. He had been in the state about 62 years and was about 78 years old. Caleb Smith and Martin Murphey served with him. He was last paid in 1834.

Prince, Henry. S.C. Pvt. He served under Gen. Pickens and was at the siege of Augusta. The enemy pillaged his home in Spartanburgh while he was away in the service. He was 76 years old. His application for compensation was rejected in 1824. His brother was Thomas Prince who was a lieutenant under Capt. John Bowie. He was wounded and taken to hospital at Charleston where he died. He sought his commutation.

Printrip, Joseph. N.Y. Lt. He served in Capt. Robert Yates' Company under Col. Frederick Fisher. He was wounded in his left thigh on 25 Oct. 1781. He was pensioned 25 Oct. 1786. He lived in Mohawk, Montgomery Co., N.Y. on 12 June 1789. He also appeared as Joseph Printop and Joseph Prentrop. He was on the 1813 pension list.

Prior, Abner. N.Y. Surgeon's Mate. He heirs sought his commutation plus interest 11 May 1838. They were approved.

Prior, Elisha. N.Y. Pvt. He was on the 1813 pension list.

Prior, Gideon. —. —. He served as a teamster in a train commanded by Col. Wadsworth under Count de Rochambeau from May to Dec. 1781. He supplied the works erected at the siege of Yorktown with ammunition. In 1782 he was aboard a privateer and was captured. He was compelled to do duty by the British to the end of the war when he was put ashore on Antigua. He was 89 years old. He did not prove his allegations. Congress rejected his claim 22 Dec. 1851. Congress ruled that if he ever could do so, the general laws would apply.

Pritchard, Jeremiah. N.H. Lt. He was granted half a pension 20 Apr. 1796.

Proby, Solomon. S.C. —. He served in the 1st S.C. Regiment. He was blown up abroad the frigate *Randolph*. His widow, Mary Proby, was granted an annuity on 10 Mar. 1785. Her annuity of 20 Sep. 1791 included payment for one child. In 1803 Sarah Evans received the annuity for her mother. She died 14 Oct. 1805, and her arrearage was paid to Sarah Gould.

Proctor, John. Va. Sgt. He was in Dinwiddie County in 1790. He enlisted for three years in the Continental Army in Feb. 1779. He joined the battalion of A. Buford in Petersburg in Aug. following. He was appointed sergeant in Capt. Mark's Company. On 29 May 1780 he was wounded six times and taken prisoner at Buford's defeat. He was discharged in 1782 at Fredericksburg. He was 33 years old. His wounds were from a bayonet and broad sword once in his left hand, another in his left arm, and two or more on his head. A bayonet also pierced one side of his left breast. He was put on the pension list at the rate of £12 per annum on 2 Apr. 1787. He was on the 1813 pension list.

Proctor, Leonard. —. —. He and his wife died in 1827. Neither was entitled to a pension at the time of death. Congress rejected the claim from the heirs 20 Feb. 1854.

Proctor, Richard. Md. Pvt. He was pensioned at the rate of half-pay of a private 6 Jan. 1813.

Proctor, William. R.I. Sgt. Maj. He was ruptured in his belly by a stick thrown at him by one Kelly because he refused to play at cudgels with him in Apr. 1779 at Warren. He lived in Mass. in 1795.

Prodo, Joseph. Pa. —. He enlisted under Capt. Turnbull in the Artillery under Col. Porter. He was 62 years old and was from Bucks County.

Proud, Charles. Pa. Matross. He was in Philadelphia County 10 Apr. 1787. He was in Col. Proctor's Regiment in Capt. James Lee 's Company. He was wounded in 1777 by a cannon carriage running over his leg during action with the enemy at Fort Mifflin. He had a brother in County Cork, Ireland. He and his wife had no children and proposed giving up his pension in return for passage for himself and his wife to Ireland. He was 55 years old. He was dead by Mar. 1791. He also appeared as Charles Prout.

Prouty, Burphy. Mass. —. He served in the 6th Regiment and was from Vermont. He was paid $20.

Provost, Daniel. Conn. Pvt. He served in Chandler's Regiment and was wounded. He was also disabled by hectic disease. He was pensioned 19 May 1792. He was on the 1813 pension list of New York. He transferred from Fairfield Co., Conn. to New York. He died 14 Dec.1832.

Provost, Jasper. N.J. —. He was pensioned in Middlesex County on 14 Feb. 1844 at the rate of $60 per annum.

Provence, George. Pa. —. He was pensioned.

Pruitt, Walter. Md. Pvt. He was pensioned at the rate of half-pay of a private in Worcester County on 9 Mar. 1827.

Puckett, Sheppey. Va. —. He died in Continental service. His mother, Mary Puckett, was granted two barrels of corn in Chesterfield Co., Va. on 7 Apr. 1780.

Pugh, —. Va. – . Sarah Pugh was granted £30 support while her son was away in Continental service in Richmond County on 7 June 1779.

Pullen, Oliver. Me. —. He was from Palermo. He was paid $50 under the resolve of 1836.

Pullin, Samuel. Pa. —. He was awarded a $80 gratuity 31 Mar. 1812.

Pullum, Zacheriah. N.C. —. He was in Rutherford Co., N.C. in Oct. 1832.

Pumroy, Benjamin. Mass. —. He was pensioned for 1775 and 1776. His pension expired in Nov. 1776.

Purcell, Henry D. Penn. Lt. He served in the infantry to the end of war. His heirs sought his five years' full pay. They were rejected 11 May 1838 because he had claimed same in his own lifetime.

Purcell, John. Pa. —. He was on the 1789 pension list.

Purcell, William. S.C. —. He was from Edgefield District when he was pensioned 30 Nov. 1827. He enlisted in 1777 under Capt. Carter and was at Golphin Fort. He was on both the Florida and Cherokee Expeditions. He was 70 years old. He was paid as late as 1832. He also appeared as William Pursell.

Purchase, Robert. —. Musician. He served more than two years and was at Long Island, Stillwater, and Saratoga. He was over 100 years old. His wife, Sarah Purchase, was also old. He never applied because there was no need. Congress approved his petition 6 Apr. 1860. His mind and memory were incapable of making a sworn application so it was necessary to apply to Congress.

Purdo, Joseph. Pa. Bombardier. He applied 24 Mar. 1814. He was enlisted at Lancaster in 1781 as a bombardier by Capt. Webster. He was in Capt. Turnbull's Artillery Company in Col. Andrew Porter's Regiment. He was discharged at Philadelphia in 1783. He was 62 years old. He also appeared as John Purdon.

Purdy, Daniel. —. —. He enlisted 1 June 1775 under Capt. Doolittle, Col. Waterbury, and Gen. Wooster for five months. He was sent to Canada under Gen. Montgomery and served more than three months. On 1 Dec. 1775 he enlisted as a drummer under Capt. Steward and Col. Drake for upwards of three months. In July 1776 he was under Col. Thomas and Gen. Clinton as a drummer for five months. He was credited with more than twelve months of service and more than ten months in the militia. Congress granted him a pension 23 Dec. 1831.

Purdy, James. Pa. —. He was awarded $80 in Mifflin Co. on 20 Mar. 1812. He was awarded $40 gratuity and a $40 annuity on 22 Mar. 1813. He served as captain and colonel of a battalion on the frontiers. One of his sons drowned in the Juniata pursuing Indians. Two other sons, a captain and a lieutenant, were killed at St. Clair's defeat.

Purdy, Jonathan. N.Y. Corp. He served under Maj. Thaddeus Crane and Capt. Ephraim Lockwood in the Westchester County militia. Isaac Keeler was lieutenant. He was disabled by a cleft in his skull. He lived in Salem, Westchester Co., N.Y. on 22 Apr. 1789. He was on the 1813 pension list.

Purdy, Solomon. N.Y. Sgt. He served in Capt. James Teller's Company in the Westchester County militia under Col. Samuel Drake. He then served under Capt. Israel Honeywell under Col. Hull. He was disabled by a pistol shot in his belly; the ball came out his right hip. He was taken prisoner in action at Morrisania on 3 and 4 March 1782. He was pensioned 2 May 1788. He was 28 years old on 11 Dec. 1787. He lived in Newburgh, Ulster Co., N.Y. on 1 June 1789 and later in Orange Co. He was on the 1813 pension list.

Purks, —. S.C. —. His widow, Joanna Purks, was from Orangeburg District. There were two children in 1791.

Purnell, John. Pa. Pvt. His widow, Sarah Ann Purnell, applied 20 Aug. 1879 in York County. He was in Capt. M. Greenwood's Company in the 16th Pa. Regiment. Her application was rejected since his name was not found on the books. One John Purnell from York received a $40 gratuity and a $40 annuity from Pennsylvania 21 July 1842.

Pursell, John. Pa. Pvt. He was in Philadelphia County on 13 Feb. 1786 and served in the 11th Pa. Regiment in Capt. Dean's Company. He was discharged from the Invalids unfit for duty on account of a wound in his shoulder received at Brandywine. He was dead by Sep. 1796. He also appeared as John Purcell.

Pursell, William. S.C. —. He enlisted in 1777 and served under Capt. Carter from Edgefield District. He was at Augusta, Ninety Six, and the Florida Expedition. He was afflicted with the dead palsy and had an aged wife. Capt. John Ryan was acquainted with him, and Joshua Hammond served with him. He applied in 1827. He was paid as late as 1832.

Purtle, John. Pa. Pvt. He was in Philadelphia County on 30 Sep. 1785. He was transferred from the 5th Pa. Regiment to the Invalids. He was wounded at Fort Washington in 1776. He was 62 years old.

Purvis, James. Va. Capt. He served in the 1st Virginia Regiment in 1775 and was appointed an ensign. He resigned in Feb. 1778. In Jan. 1779 he was appointed lieutenant in the regiment to guard the Convention prisoners. He was promoted to captain 8 Oct. 1779 until the regiment was disbanded at which time he became supernumerary. His heirs were granted his commutation 1 Mar. 1837. Congress ruled that the petition from his heirs should be presented to the court of claims 8 Apr. 1856.

Putnam, Daniel. N.H. —. He served under Col. Thomas Bedel in Capt. Easterbrook's Company. He took sick in Quebec and lost all of his clothes. He was from Cornish in 1786.

Putnam, Edward. N.Y. —. He served one month under Col. Holmes in 1775 and five months under Col. Halman in 1776. Congress granted him a pension for six months of service 25 May 1840.

Putnam, Nathan. Mass. Pvt. He was in Capt. Hutchinson's Company. He was wounded in his right arm near the shoulder by a musket ball which broke the bone on 19 Apr. 1775 at Menotomy. He resided at Danvers, Mass. in 1794. He was on the 1813 pension list.

Putney, Asa. N.H. Sgt. He applied at Henniker in 1778. He was in Capt. Bailey's Company of militia under Col. Thomas Stickney. He lost the use of his right arm by a musket ball shot through it 16 Aug. 1777 at Bennington. He had his arm broken at the battle of Loomsot on 16 Aug. 1777. He lived at Hollis, N.H. in 1794. He was granted half a pension 20 Apr. 1796. He was on the 1813 pension list.

Pyke, Abraham. Pa. Pvt. He served in Hewitt's Infantry. He was wounded in his right thigh in the engagement with Indians on 3 July 1778 in Wyoming. He lived in Luzerne, Pa. in 1794. He was on the 1813 pension list.

Pyon, Francis. N.Y. —. He served under Capt. Jean Baptiste la Port de la Bonte in Col. James Livingston's Regiment of Refugees from Canada to the close of the war. He was due bounty land 2 Apr. 1806.

Pyon, Jacques. N.Y. —. He served under Capt. Jean Baptiste la Port de la Bonte in Col. James Livingston's Regiment of Refugees from Canada to the close of the war. He was due bounty land 2 Apr. 1806.

Pyon, Joseph. N.Y. —. He served under Capt. Jean Baptiste la Port de la Bonte in Col. James Livingston's Regiment of Refugees from Canada to the close of the war. He was due bounty land 2 Apr. 1806.

Pyon, Pierre. N.Y. —. He served under Capt. Jean Baptiste la Port de la Bonte in Col. James Livingston's Regiment of Refugees from Canada to the close of the war. He was due bounty land 2 Apr. 1806.

Quarles, James. Va. Maj. He entered the service in 1775 in the 2nd Regiment and was promoted to captain in Jan. 1777. He was at Monmouth in 1778. Gov. Patrick Henry promoted him to major in Jan. 1778. He became supernumerary in 1779 and was employed in reviewing and receiving recruits. His heirs' application for his commutation was rejected 23 Dec. 1833.

Quarles, Philip. Va. —. He had received his half-pay from 6 Feb. 1781 to 22 Feb. 1804. The balance of $346.66 without interest was paid to his administrator, Robert Pollard, 22 Dec. 1837.

Quarles, Robert. Va. Ens. He died 27 July 1827. He received his commutation so Congress rejected the claim of his widow, Martha Quarles, 10 May 1836.

Quarles, Wharton. Va. Lt. & Regimental Quartermaster. He served in the 2nd Va. State Regiment. He died 22 Feb. 1804. His administrator was allowed the balance on a judgment obtained for half-pay 7 July 1838.

Quarles, William. Mass. Pvt. He served in the 15th Regiment and was from Salem. His widow, Polly Quarles, was paid $50.

Quasha, Cato. Conn. Pvt. He served in the 4th Conn. Regiment under Col. John Durkee and was wounded in the arm by a musket ball at Germantown on 4 Oct. 1777. He was pensioned at Colchester, Conn. at the age of 57 on 22 Sep. 1788. He died in 1807. He also appeared as Cato Quasher. He was a free Negro.

Quay, Hugh. Pa. Sgt. He enlisted in 1776 in the Chester County Flying Camp. He was made a prisoner on 16 Nov. 1776 at Fort Washington. He was confined in Bridewell prison in New York City. He was ultimately restored to his wife and five small children. He was sick for nine months thereafter. He was paid for three months only. He was given a $40 annuity in Chester County 4 Apr. 1809. He died 27 Mar. 1813.

Quay, James. Md. —. He was granted relief.

Queen, Marsham. Md. Pvt. He was pensioned in Charles County at the rate of half-pay of a private on 13 Mar. 1832.

Quellin, John. Del. Pvt. He was pensioned at the rate of $2.50 per month. He was on the roll in 1802.

Quick, John. N.Y. Pvt. He served in the Orange County militia under Col. William Allison in Capt. Martinus Decker's Company. He was wounded in his left arm and right wrist as well as through his belly in action with the Tories and Indians under the command of Brandt. On 11 Dec. 1787 he was 43 years old. He lived in Ulster Co., N.Y. 4 June 1789 and was a farmer. He was on the 1813 pension list.

Quig, Henry. N.J. Pvt. He served in the 3rd Regiment. His widow, Prudence Quig, received a half-pay pension.

Quigg, John. Pa. Pvt. He was in Philadelphia County on 13 Feb. 1786. He was in the 4th Regiment and was wounded in his right thigh at Monmouth. He was discharged 1 Nov. 1779 on account of his wound. He was 45 years old and had two small children.

Quigley, Edward. Pa. —. He was a wounded soldier. He was awarded a $40 gratuity and a $40 annuity in Center County on 27 Mar. 1812. He died 15 Apr. 1819.

Quigley, Samuel. Pa. —. He was awarded a $40 gratuity and a $40 annuity in Beaver Co., Pa. 15 Apr. 1835. He died 21 Apr. 1842.

Quigg, John. Pa. Pvt. He was in Philadelphia County on 13 Feb. 1786. He was in the 4th Pa. Regiment and was wounded in his right thigh at Monmouth. He was discharged 1 Nov. 1779 on account of said wound. He was 45 years old.

Quillen, Nathaniel. Pa. —. He was awarded a $40 annuity in Allegheny County 5 Feb. 1836.

Quillen, Robert. Va. Pvt. He was in Powhatan County on 8 May 1787 when he was continued on the pension list at the rate of £10 per annum. He enlisted in the 1st Va. Regiment in the spring of 1776 for the war and was discharged on account of infirmities by Col. Febiger on 10 Jan. 1780. He was taken prisoner at the surrender of Charleston. He was afflicted with dropsy and had an ulcerated leg. He was 52 years old. Maj. William Lewis certified his service. He also appeared as Robert McQuillen.

Quin, John. Pa. —. He was pensioned.

Quinby, John. N.J. Pvt. He served in the 3rd Regiment. He was wounded through the lungs. He was from Roxbury and was 42 years old. He was on the 1791 pension roll. He was pensioned in Morris Co., N.J. in 1786. He was on the 1813 pension list.

Quinlan, Joseph. Va. Surgeon. He served to the end of the war. He was wounded at Camden in 1780. His heir, Tasker C. Quinlan, sought his commutation. Congress rejected the claim 14 June 1836.

Quinn, Joseph. Md. Pvt. He was on the 1791 pension list.

Quinny, Thomas M. Md. Pvt. He was pensioned in 1819 at half-pay.

Quinton, John. —. —. He was pensioned.

Quinton, Samuel. S.C. —. He served 276 days in 1780, 1781, and 1782. There was no proof that the soldier was the person of the same name. Congress denied his claim for relief 3 Mar. 1851.

Rabb, James. S.C. —. He was to be issued his indent by act of 19 Dec. 1792 upon producing proper vouchers.

Rabel, Christopher. Pa. —. He was granted relief in Washington County 18 Apr. 1843.

Raberg, Andrew. —. —. His application was referred to the Secretary of War.

Raddon, —. Va. —. Mary Raddon was allowed £10 support as the wife of a Revolutionary soldier in Augusta Co., Va. 20 Apr. 1778.

Rader, Nicholas. Va. —. He was in Montgomery Co. 3 Nov. 1812, Rockingham Co. 1821, Wythe Co. 1823, Rockingham Co. 1825, and Augusta Co. 1835. He also appeared as Nicholas Reeder and Nicholas Reader.

Radford, John. Mass. —. He served in the 6th Regiment. He was paid $20.

Rady, Daniel. Va. Pvt. He was on the 1813 pension list.

Ragan, Richard. Va. Maj. He served under Gen. Lafayette and Col. Benjamin Harrison. He did not prove his first term but did so for his second term of three months and ten days. Congress believed that his first term was at least three months and granted him a pension 6 Feb. 1839. Congress rejected a pension for his widow, Cecilia Ragan, on 21 Apr. 1838.

Rager, Conrad. Pa. —. He was awarded relief in Fayette County in Apr. 1833. He was 85 years old in 1840. He died 6 Feb. 1844.

Rager, Michael. Pa. —. He was awarded a $40 gratuity and a $40 annuity in Cambria Co., Pa. 25 Mar. 1833. He died 19 Feb. 1840.

Ragland, Evan. Va. Pvt. He was on the 1813 pension list.

Railey, James. N.Y. Pvt. He served in Col. Courtland's Regiment in Capt. Hallet's Company. He was wounded in his right leg and lost the sight of his left eye by the flash of a howitzer in Oct. 1777 at Stillwater. He lived in Fredericktown, Dutchess Co., N.Y. on 20 Apr. 1789. He died in 1793. He also appeared as James Reyley, James Reley, James Reilly, and James Rilly.

Rainey, Peter. Va. —. He was in Essex County when he was pensioned at the rate of $60 per annum on 8 Jan. 1820. He had been wounded and disabled in the service.

Rains, —. —. —. His widow, Nancy Rains, received an increase in her pension from Congress 19 Mar. 1888. She was 96 years of age. She was the oldest pensioner at that time. Her pension was increased from $8 per month to $30 per month. Her name had been incorrectly given as Nancy Roins in Feb. 1888.

Rains, Bailey. Va. —. His wife, Hannah Rains, was allowed 2 barrels of corn and 100 pounds of pork in Bedford Co., Va. on 28 Aug. 1781 and 1 barrel of corn and 50 pounds of pork on 25 Nov. 1782. She had a family of four. He also appeared as Bailey Raines.

Ralston, —. Va. —. He was away in Continental service. His wife, Elizabeth Ralston, was granted £20 support in Botetourt Co., Va. 13 Aug. 1779.

Ralston, Andrew. Pa. —. He applied in Westmoreland County on 22 Nov. 1816. He enlisted in Capt. William Peebles' Company of Riflemen under Col. Miles in Mar. or Apr. 1776. He was discharged 1 Jan. 1778. He next served in Capt. Matthew Scott's Company under Col. Walter Stewart. He died 31 Aug. 1819.

Ralston, John. Pa. —. He was awarded a $40 gratuity and a $40 annuity in Crawford County 28 Mar. 1836. He was 80 years old in 1840. He died 14 May 1847. His widow, Margaret Ralston, was granted a $40 gratuity 8 May 1850.

Ralston, John. Va. —. He died in Continental service. His widow, Mary Ralston, and her two childrenwere granted £60 support in Botetourt Co., Va. 10 Sep. 1779. She was not a widow when she was paid 11 Aug. 1778.

Rambo, Benajiah. S.C. —. He served under Lt. Col. Samuel Hammonds. His widow, Rachel Rambo, was on the roll in 1803.

Ramey, John. Va. —. He was a pensioner and died in July 1834. He married in Mar. 1776 in Fauquier Co., Va. His widow, Edith Ramey, was given a pension by a special act of Congress 17 June 1846.

Ramsay, John. Ga. Pvt. He served under Col. James Jackson in the Light Dragoons. He was wounded in his left thigh and left arm by a broadsword on 6 July 1781 at Long Cane Mills. He lived in Columbia Co., Ga. in 1795.

Ramsay, John. Va. Surgeon. He died in the service on 4 Nov. 1776. His widow, Mary Ramsay, was pensioned at the rate of £30 per annum on 15 Dec. 1791. She was in Norfolk 24 Apr. 1792. Congress granted his children and grandchildren relief 18 Apr. 1840.

Ramsay, Thomas. S.C. Capt. He served under Maj. Dugan. He sought his back pay in 1825.

Ramsbottom, Isaac. Va. —. He served under Capt. Dickinson. He was wounded in the leg. He was awarded a £100 gratuity on 17 May 1780.

Ramsdale, James. Mass. Pvt. He served in the 3rd Regiment and was from Essex. He was paid $20.

Ramsdale, Moses. Mass. Pvt. He served in the 6th Regiment and was disabled by rheumatism and consumption. He was pensioned 1 Sep. 1782. He was on the 1813 pension list. He transferred to Jefferson Co., N.Y. 4 Mar. 1826. He also appeared as Moses Ramsell.

Ramsdell, Amos. Mass. —. He served in the 7th Regiment and was paid $20.

Ramsdell, James. Mass. —. He served in the 2nd Regiment and was from Washington. He was paid $20.

Ramsdell, Joseph. Mass. Pvt. He served in the 12th Regiment and was from East Bridgewater. His widow, Lydia Ramsdell, was paid $50.

Ramsdell, Saul. Mass. —. He served in the 6th Regiment. He was from Mendon. He was paid $20.

Ramsey, James. S.C. —. He enlisted in 1778 and served under Col. Hawthorn. He was from Lancaster District. He was pensioned 19 Dec. 1825. His administrator, William H. McMurry, sought his arrearage in 1841 following his death.

Ramsey, John. —. Pvt. He was a resident of Georgia when he applied in 1795.

Ramsey, Joseph. Va. —. He served under Col. Clarke in Illinois until 1780 when he resigned. His agents, Samuel McCamant and John H. Price, passed his claim to the U.S. Treasury for half-pay. They collected $7,658.96 and paid him $2,540. He brought suit against them in the western district court of Virginia. Ramsey was a party to the fraud even though he alleged that he was not guilty. Congress could not grant him relief on 23 June 1840.

Ramsey, Joseph Hall. S.C. Surgeon. He served in a Continental Hospital and was captured at the fall of Charleston. In 1785 he sought relief on an equal basis with other officers.

Rancier, George. N.Y. —. His family was granted support during the war.

Randall, Benjamin. Mass. —. He served in the 3rd Regiment and was from Barre. He was paid $20. He also appeared as Benjamin Randell.

Rand, Walter. Va. Pvt. He served in the infantry. He married in 1783. He removed to N.C. about 1789 and died in 1812. Congress granted his widow, Mary Rand, a pension 8 Mar. 1842.

Randall, James. Me. —. He died 15 May 1821. His widow was Mary Randall from Limington. She was paid $50 under the resolve of 1836.

Randall, John. S.C. —. He was 81 years old; his wife was 77 years old. They had 14 children and ninety odd grandchildren. Joseph Youngblood knew he was a soldier. He was from Barnwell District and was pensioned 7 Dec. 1826. He was paid as late as 1832.

Randall, Stephen. Me. —. He died 18 Sep. 1837. His widow was Elizabeth Randall from Limerick. She was paid $50 under the resolve of 1836.

Randall, William. —. —. He applied for a pension but Congress rejected his petition on 31 Dec. 1845 because of his failure to submit sufficient evidence.

Randolph, James F. Pa. —. He was awarded a $40 gratuity and a $40 annuity 27 Mar. 1837. His name may have been James Fitzrandolph. He died 2 Jan. 1844.

Randolph, Maliciah. —. —. His widow, Elizabeth Randolph, had her petition for a pension rejected by Congress on 27 Mar. 1846 because they were married subsequent to 1 Jan. 1794.

Randolph, Taylor F. Pa. —. He received a $40 gratuity in Crawford County 15 Apr. 1851. His name was probably Taylor FitzRandolph.

Randolph, Thomas F. N.J. Wagoner. Congress rejected his petition 12 Jan. 1838. He was pensioned in Essex County on 28 Feb. 1839 at the rate of $60 per annum.

Raner, John. Va. —. He stated in 1786 that he served in the Va. State Legion under Col. Charles Dabney and was discharged 24 Apr. 1783. Lt. David Mann attested to his service. His left thumb was cut off in Feb. 1780.

Raney, Peter. Va. —. He was pensioned in Essex County on 8 Jan. 1820 at the rate of $60 per annum. He also appeared as Peter Rainey. He had been wounded.

Rankin, Jesse. —. Pvt. He performed a tour of duty under Col. Crawford in the Sandusky Expedition.

Rankin, John. Mass. —. He was in the 1st Regiment and was from Lebanon. He was paid $20.

Rankin, Richard. Pa. —. His widow, Jane Rankin, applied at Sevierville, Tenn. 22 Jan. 1845. He entered the service in Cumberland Co., Pa. in 1778 in Capt. Gibson's Company and marched to Valley Forge and Philadelphia under Gen. Washington and others.

Rankin, Robert. Pa. —. He was from Mercer County. His daughter, Jane Rankin, received his donation land in 1843.

Ranney, David. Conn. Pvt. He served in the 1st Conn. Regiment in Col. Gemott's light troops. He was wounded by a fascine striking against his left knee in Oct. 1781 at Yorktown. He became a cripple. He resided at Chatham, Conn. in 1792. He enlisted 13 Nov. 1778 and was discharged 30 Nov. 1781. He was granted one-third of a pension 20 Apr. 1796. His rate was $5 per month from 5 Nov. 1807. He was on the 1813 pension list. He died 19 Apr. 1814.

Ransom, George P. Pa. —. He was awarded a $40 gratuity and a $40 annuity in Luzerne Co., Pa. 29 Mar. 1824. He was 78 years old in 1840. He died 5 Sep. 1850.

Ransom, Joseph. N.Y. Sgt. He enlisted in 1776 in Capt. Andrew Billings' Company and later in Capt. Benjamin Pelton's Company in the 3rd N.Y. Regiment under Col. Rudolphus Ritzma. He was wounded by a bomb shell in his left cheek at White Plains on 28 Oct. 1776. He had two wounds in his head and one in his left thigh above the knee. He was 45 years old on 23 Sep. 1788. He lived in New York City, N.Y. on 21 Nov. 1788. He died 9 May 1790.

Ransom, Richard. N.C. Capt. His company was raised shortly before the taking of Yorktown at Franklin, N.C. and marched to Charleston in search of Tories. He served nine months. He married 10 Oct. 1784 and died 22 July 1827. His widow, Keziah Ransom, failed to demonstrate sufficiently his service as to date and circumstances so Congress did not grant her a pension on 12 Feb. 1841.

Ransom, Samuel. Conn. Pvt. He was a native of Conn. He served in Hazen's Regiment and was wounded. He was pensioned 20 May 1783. He died in 1808.

Ransom, Samuel. —. Capt. He was killed in Wyoming 3 July 1776. Congress granted the heirs relief 28 Mar. 1850.

Rap, Jonathan. Pa. Pvt. His widow, Eliza Rap, and children were in Cumberland County on 26 Mar.1787. He served in the Cumberland County militia.

Rapelye, Joris. N.Y. —. His widow was paid an annual annuity in 1786 and 1788.

Rasburg, Frederick. N.Y. Pvt. He served in Capt. Small's Company under Col. Peter Bellinger in the militia. He was wounded in his lower jaw on 6 Aug. 1777. He was pensioned 28 Dec. 1786. He lived in Montgomery Co., N.Y. on 1 Sep. 1788. He also appeared as Frederick Rasbach. He was 37 years old in 1787. He was on the 1813 pension list.

Rasin, William B. Md. Lt. He was pensioned in Kent County at the rate of half-pay in Nov. 1804.

Rasor, Jacob. Pa. Pvt. He was on the 1813 pension list.

Ratchford, John. S.C. —. He was on the Cherokee Expedition under Capt. Ross. He was also at Charleston and Rocky Mount. At Hanging Rock he was wounded through his body by a musket ball. He was carried off the field. Six months later he was able to return to active duty. At Guilford he was taken prisoner by a party of Lord Cornwallis' army. He was paroled the next day after the battle. He was under Col. Brannum at Ninety Six and at Blackstocks. He was partially deprived of the use of his right arm. He lost his right leg a few years ago and lately lost his eye. Several of his children had died. He was pensioned 19 Dec. 1825 in York District Thomas Caswell assisted in carrying him from the field when he was wounded. James Jamieson was with him at Hanging Rock as was Robert Wilson. His son, Joseph Ratchford, was paid the $60 arrearage due his father on 30 Nov. 1827.

Ratchford, Moses. S.C. —. He was from York District in 1825.

Ratcliff, —. S.C. —. His widow was Charity Ratcliff and was on the roll in 1793.

Ratinhouever, Godfrey. N.Y. Pvt. He served under Col. Samuel Clyde in the Montgomery County militia and was slain 6 Aug. 1777. His son, Jacob Ratinhouever, received a half-pay pension. He also appeared as Godfrey Ratenhourer.

Rattenaur, Jacob. N.Y. Pvt. He served under Col. Samuel Clyde in the militia in Capt. Adam Sikes' Company. He was wounded by a musket ball in his left hip at Torlach on 10 July 1781 on the same day as Gerrard Dunckel. He lived in Montgomery Co., N.Y. on 2 June 1789. He was 28 years old in 1787. He was on the 1813 pension list. He also appeared as Jacob Raddenar.

Rau, John. Pa. —. He was awarded a $40 gratuity and a $40 annuity in Berks Co., Pa. 11 June 1832.

Raub, Henry A. Pa. —. He was awarded a $40 gratuity in Northampton County 31 Mar. 1836.

Raven, James. Mass. Pvt. He was in the 13th Regiment and was from Milton and was paid $50. He was unable to read and write. Bounty land warrant #4917 for 100 acres had been issued to him on 26 Jan. 1790. It had been assigned to John May. Congress ruled that he had no claim on 29 Dec. 1826.

Rawlings, Samuel. Md. Pvt. His widow, Ann Rawlings, was pensioned at the rate of half-pay of a private in Washington County 23 Feb. 1822.

Rawlings, Solomon. Md. Pvt. He was pensioned at the rate of half-pay of a private 19 Feb. 1819.

Rawlins, Nathan. Pa. Capt. He was on the 1813 pension list.

Rawson, Jeduthan. Mass. Ens. He received his commutation for five years in lieu of half-pay for life. He was from Mendon.

Ray, —. N.C. —. He was killed at the battle of Camden. His widow, Jemima Ray, was on the roll in 1784.

Ray, Alexander. S.C. —. He was wounded in 1781. He was granted an annuity 16 Nov. 1784.

Ray, Benjamin. Mass. Pvt. He was in the 1st Regiment and was from Shutesbury.

Ray, James. S.C. —. He was from Winton in 1791.

Ray, Joseph. Md. Pvt. He was pensioned at the rate of half-pay of a private in Montgomery County on 7 Feb. 1818.

Raymond, Benjamin. Mass. Drummer. He was in the 14th Regiment and was from Taunton.

Raymond, Isaac. Pa. —. He was awarded a $40 gratuity and a $40 annuity 9 Jan. 1818 in Montgomery County.

Raymond, Moses. Conn. Pvt. He served in Capt. Samuel Comstock's Company in Col. Samuel Whiting's Regiment and was wounded 26 Jan. 1777 at Delaney's Mills at Westchester in his left arm by a musket ball. Dr. W. Eustis attended him. He was pensioned 9 Oct. 1787 in Norwalk, Conn. He was a weaver. He had a wife and four small children. He was on the 1813 pension list.

Raymond, Phineas. —. —. He served three tours under Capt. Sparrow in 1779. He stated that he was a substitute for James Churchill whose name was on the roll but was deceased. Congress denied his claim for relief on 9 Feb. 1848. Congress declared that the widow or children of Churchill could claim relief.

Raymore, Edward. —. Sgt. He served as a corporal in the artillery under Capt. Burbeck and spent most of the time in Georgia for three years. His second tour was also for three years after which he returned home to Massachusetts. He served as a recruiting officer and marched to St. Mary's, Ga. where he served as sergeant until the expiration of his second tour. He was severely wounded in the abdomen by a falling stick of lumber while building a block house leaving him totally disabled. Congress granted him a pension 8 Aug. 1846.

Read, —. Pa. —. His widow, Elizabeth Read, was awarded a $40 gratuity and a $40 annuity in Berks Co., Pa. 10 Apr. 1835.

Read, —. Pa. —. His widow, Jane Read, was awarded a $40 gratuity in Chester Co., Pa. 11 Feb. 1834.

Read, —. Va. —. He and his brother were away in the service. Their mother, Mary Read, was granted £20 on 21 Dec. 1778 for the support of her and her other children.

Read, Edmund. Va. Capt. He served under Maj. Nelson in the Virginia State Cavalry. His widow, Pauline Le Grand, was paid a pension of $600 per annum to Mar. 1844. She died 5 Feb. 1845. She had applied for her last $300 semi-annual payment but never received it due to the fact that Congress failed to make the necessary appropriations. Congress authorized that the $300 but no more be paid to Henry Carrington, her executor, on 29 Feb. 1848. The veteran also appeared as Edmond Reid.

Read, Isaac. Mass. Pvt. He served in the 6th Regiment and was from Northfield. He was paid $50.

Read, Isaac. Va. Col. His children were being pensioned 18 June 1784. Their guardians were John Coleman and Thomas Read.

Read, Joseph. S.C. —. After the fall of Charleston, he was a refugee in North Carolina with Col. Benjamin Cleveland of Wilkes County. He had his thigh broken at King's Mountain on 7 Oct. 1780. He was taken with the wounded to Quaker Meadows where he remained twelve months. He sought an annuity in 1790. He had a wife and four children in 1795.

Read, John. Mass. Capt. He served in the 7th Regiment. He was wounded in his left leg and thigh. He was 43 years old in 1789. He also appeared as John Reed. He died in 1797.

Read, John. N.H. Pvt. He lived in Stafford Co., N.H. and was pensioned 14 July 1810.

Read, Noah. Mass. Pvt. He served at the Castle and was from Milton. He was paid $50.

Read, Thaddeus. Conn. Pvt. He served under Lt. N. Slasson and was disabled by violent pains and inflamation in the service. He resided in Norwalk, Conn. in 1792 and at Westford, Mass. in 1796 but produced no evidence of his disability at that time. He also appeared as Thaddeus Reid.

Read, William. Pa. Corp. Lt. He served more than two years as a private and corporal and six months as a lieutenant under Capt. Morgan. He married 15 Dec. 1785 Susannah -----. He died in 1798. She married secondly John Warner in 1800. He died in 1813. Congress granted her a pension for his six months of service as a lieutenant 2 May 1844. She was in her 80th year.

Reading, Henry. Md. Pvt. He was pensioned at the rate of half-pay of a private 16 Nov. 1811.

Reading, Robert. Va. Pvt. He was in Campbell County 25 Oct. 1786. He served in the 1st State Regiment. He served under Lt. Col. Samuel Hawes and was wounded at Camden, S.C. He lost his right leg. He was 26 years old. He was on the 1813 pension list. He also appeared as Robert Reeding.

Reading, Samuel. N.J. Maj. He served in the 2nd Regiment under Col. William Maxwell. He was on the expedition to Quebec in 1776 and was taken prisoner at Three Rivers. He was confined in Quebec and exchanged in 1777. He rejoined and served to the close of the war. He had a large family. He applied 30 Pct. 1789.

Reading, William. Va. Pvt. He lived in Frederick County in Nov. 1785. He served in the Continental Army under Col. Daniel Morgan in his detachment of riflemen at Saratoga. He suffered a gunshot wound in his right wrist. He was 35 years old. He was put on the pension list at the rate of £12 per annum on 21 Apr. 1788. He was on the 1813 pension list.

Readpath, John. N.C. Lt. He was killed in the battle of Germantown in 1777. His widow, Elizabeth Douglass, applied for her benefits as a widow due half-pay 4 Jan. 1792.

Ready, Isaac. Va. —. He served under Col. Charles Lynch. He was wounded in the hip at Guilford Courthouse. He applied in Bedford Co., Va. on 20 May 1782.

Ready, James. S.C. —. He was from Winton in 1791.

Ream, —. Pa. —. His widow, Barbara Ream, was awarded a $40 annuity in Lancaster County in Apr. 1845 for his Revolutionary service.

Ream, Andrew. Pa. —. He was awarded a $40 gratuity and a $40 annuity in Lancaster Co., Pa. 27 Jan. 1835. He was 84 years old in 1840. He died 13 Mar. 1845.

Ream, George. Pa. —. He was awarded a $40 gratuity and a $40 annuity in Westmoreland County

5 Feb. 1836. He also appeared as George Reem.

Ream, Henry. Pa. Lt. He served several tours in the militia. He was awarded a $40 gratuity and a $40 annuity in Lancaster Co., Pa. 1 Apr. 1834. He was 84 years old in 1840. He died 5 Oct. 1841.

Ream, John F.. Pa. —. He was awarded a $40 annuity in Center County 5 Feb. 1836.

Ream, Peter. Pa. —. He was granted relief.

Ream, William. Pa. —. He was pensioned in Mercer County and was being paid in 1831.

Reap, Michael. N.C. —. He applied in Lincoln County in 1807. He was wounded in his left hand by a sword in battle with Tarleton's Corps of Dragoons. He was taken prisoner. The Assembly struck his name off of the list of pensioners in 1807. He qualified for a federal pension. He also appeared as Michael Reep. He was rejected for reinstatement in 1810. He died 5 July 1812.

Reardon, John. S.C. —. He was wounded by the enemy 1 Apr. 1781 and lost his arm. He was granted an annuity 3 Aug. 1785 in Salem County. There were two children in 1791. He died in June 1801. His widow was Jane Reardon. She was paid as late as 1818.

Reardon, John. Va. Pvt. He was pensioned 20 Oct. 1785 at the rate of £8 per annum and £3 relief. He was in Rockbridge County on 24 Dec. 1816 when he received an increase of $50 per annum to his pension. He served under Col. Buford in Capt. Adam Wallace's Company. He was a drafted soldier for 18 months from Rockbridge County from 25 Apr. 1779 to 29 May 1780. He was wounded at the Waxsaws. He was on the 1813 pension list. He died 6 Aug. 1822. Robert White was his administrator.

Reasoner, Jacob. Va. —. His wife, Eleanor Reasoner, was granted £8 support in Berkeley County on 21 Apr. 1778. She received £80 support for herself and two children on 16 May 1780. He also appeared as Jacob Raisener. She was probably the same Eleanor Reasoner with two children granted £3.7 support in Frederick Co., Va. on 7 May 1782.

Reaves, William P. S.C. —. He was a pensioner in 1840.

Reaves, Zacheriah. N.C. —. He enlisted in 1775 under Capt. John Allen and Col. Moone. In 1776 he served under Capt. Griffith MacRee and was discharged in 1777. In 1778 he was under Capt. Cofield and Col Shepherd Miles. He was at Camden and Charleston. His wife Deborah Reaves was 57, son James Reaves was 16, and daughter Eliza Ann Reaves was 12.

Rebeck, William. N.J. Pvt. He was pensioned at the rate of $48 per annum.

Reckey, David. Pa. Pvt. He lived in Washington County.

Recok, Jacob. Pvt. He served under Capt. Isaac Reeve and Col. Philip Van Courtlandt in the Essex County militia. He was killed in a skirmish with the enemy on 7 June 1780 at Connecticut Farms. His widow, Eunice Recok, received his half-pay in Sep. 1780. He also appeared as Jacob Roeck

Red, Job. S.C. —. He was badly wounded by the Tories. His widow was Edy Red from Orangeburg in 1791. She was eighty-odd years old and was from Barnwell District in 1845. John Wise testified that her maiden name was Edy Bentley. Mrs. Elizabeth Carter of Edgefield District deposed that Job Red was brought to her mother's house where his wife Edy visited him. She was paid as late as 1857.

Red, John. S.C. —. He was on the roll in 1791.

Redden, William. Del. Sgt. He was wounded in the right shoulder at the battle of Camden on 25 Apr. 1781. He served under Col. John Hazlet and David Hall. He was married and was aged 43 in 1783. He lived in Sussex County. He died 5 Oct. 1790.

Redding, John. N.H. Pvt. He served under Col. Moses Nichols. He had a large putrefied ulcer on both his legs occasioned by a cold caught in wading a river in pursuit of the enemy in a high state of perspiration on 16 Aug. 1777 at the battle of Bennington. He lived in Surry, N.H. in 1794. He was in the militia.

Reddington, Daniel. —. —. He enlisted for nine months on three different occasions. He next was in privateering and was captured off the coast of Ireland. He was detained as a prisoner until Cornwallis was captured and exchanged. He was wounded in the service but not in battle. He had been lame ever since and had been on the pension list but had been displaced because he held too much property. Congress did not grant him a pension 22 Dec. 1831.

Reddington, Jacob. —. —. Congress said he had no claim to arrearage 16 Feb. 1836.

Redevault, George. S.C. —. He was a subordinate officer on the frigate *South Carolina*. He and John Dutville were paid $3,030 on 20 Dec. 1810.

Redfern, James. N.C. Pvt. He applied in Anson County in 1792. He served in the militia under Col. Thomas Wade and was wounded in the arm and side at Drowning Creek near Betty's Bridge. John Hill who was taken prisoner and Isaac Jackson who was with Redfern attested to his service. He was on the 1813 pension list.

Reding, Joshua. Pa. Sgt. He served under Capt. Marshall and Col. Walter Stuart in the 13th Regiment. He was wounded in his left hand by grapeshot at Brandywine 11 Sep. 1777.

Redington, Jacob. —. —. He removed to Canada and Congress granted him a pension in 1830. He died in Aug. 1843. He married Eunice ------ in 1785. She sought his pension with interest from 1820. Congress rejected her claim 8 Jan. 1844.

Redington, John. —. —. He died in 1830. He had applied in 1824 based on his own oath alone. His papers were returned to him, and he was instructed to remedy the defects. He returned the testimonies of two witnesses but did not satisfy the other defects. He married in 1811 Laura ------ She sought a pension by a special act of Congress but was rejected 27 Mar. 1846.

Redman, John. Pa. Pvt. He was in Philadelphia County on 14 Nov. 1785. He was transferred from the 3rd Pa. Regiment to the Invalids. He was wounded in the thigh and arm. He was 60 years old. He was discharged 22 Oct. 1783.He died 1 Nov. 1790.

Reed, —. Pa. —. His widow, Jane Reed, received a $40 gratuity in Chester County 11 Feb. 1834.

Reed, —. Pa. —. His widow, Mary Reed, was awarded a $40 gratuity and a $40 annuity in Adams Co., Pa. 15 Apr. 1834.

Reed, Andrew. Pa. —. He was awarded a $40 gratuity on 16 Jan. 1823 and a $40 gratuity and a $40 annuity in Chester Co., Pa. 27 Mar. 1824.

Reed, Archibald. Pa. Lt. His widow, Elizabeth Reed, was paid $600 for the right to 400 acres of donation land 29 Mar. 1824. She was from Pittsburgh.

Reed, Benjamin. Mass. Lt. He died 19 Sep. 1777. His heirs were paid his seven years' half-pay of $1,120.

Reed, Christopher. Md. Pvt. He was pensioned in Montgomery County in 1784. He moved to Virginia in 1799 and transferred back to Maryland 4 Sep. 1805. He was on the 1813 pension list.

Reed, Daniel. N.Y. —. He was awarded 200 acres bounty land on 13 Apr. 1813.

Reed, Eleazer. Mass. Pvt. He was in the 7th Regiment and was from Fitchburg. His widow, Elizabeth Reed, was paid $50.

Reed, Elijah. Mass. Fifer. He served in the 16th Regiment and was from Troy.

Reed, Elphas. Pa. —. His pension began June 1792 at the rate of $5 per month. He was paid by Pennsylvania to August 1792. From Sept. 1792 to 5 Mar. 1793 he was paid by New York. Because he collected $38.33 more than he was due, payment was stopped until he had met the eligibility.

Reed, Elphas. Mass. He was paid $30 pension for the period September 1806 to March 1807.

Reed, Isaac. N.C. —. He was wounded in the battle of Alamance. He was pensioned at the rate of £20 per annum in Craven County in 1794.

Reed, James. Mass. —. He served in the Dragoons. He was paid $20.

Reed, James. N.H. Brig. Gen. He enlisted in 1775. On the retreat from Canada at the head of Lake George, he was seized with a fever which deprived him of his sight and most of his hearing. He was a resident of Fitzwilliam when he was pensioned in 1782. He died 13 Feb. 1807. He transferred to Massachusetts.

Reed, James. Pa. —. He served about twenty months in the 4th Regiment under Col. Anthony Wayne. He was also under Capt. Thomas Church. He was at Three Rivers in Canada, Brunswick in the Jerseys, Brandywine, Iron Hill in Delaware, and Paoli. He was wounded at Paoli and Brunswick. He was 73 years old in 1824. He was from Beaver County. He was 89 years old in 1840. He died 17 Sep. 1845.

Reed, James. Pa. —. He was granted relief 17 Mar. 1838 and died 17 Oct. 1839 in Huntingdon County. His widow was Eleanor Reed who was pensioned 18 Apr. 1843.

Reed, James. S.C. —. He was granted an annuity 3 Aug. 1779.

Reed, James. S.C. —. He was wounded by the Indians in 1776. He was granted an annuity 14 May 1785. He was receiving a pension in 1791.

Reed, Jesse. Mass. —. He served in the 7th Regiment and was paid $20.

Reed, John. —. —. Congress rejected his petition for a pension because no evidence was offered to prove his case on 27 Mar. 1846.

Reed, John. N.H. Pvt. When Gen. Sullivan visited Reed's town, he met with an accident in loading the cartridge which caught fire and blew off his right hand on 26 Mar. 1777. His limb had to be amputated. While he had enlisted in Capt. Richard Wear's company a few days before, he had not joined the service. The accident prevented him from doing so. He had a wife and numerous children. He was eventually deemed being in the military and credited with service under Col. Gilman. He lived in Portsmouth, N.H. in 1792. He was on the 1813 pension list.

Reed, John. Pa. —. He was awarded a $40 gratuity and $40 annuity in Schuylkill Co., Pa. 15 Mar. 1826. He died 26 Dec. 1827.

Reed, John. Pa. —. He was awarded a $40 gratuity and a $40 annuity in Montgomery Co., Pa. in Apr. 1833.

Reed, Joseph. Pa. —. He was pensioned 27 Feb. 1821 in Washington County.

Reed, Joseph. S.C. —. He was wounded in the thigh and knee in the service on 7 Oct. 1780. He was awarded an annuity 7 May 1785 in Pendleton District. He also appeared as Joseph Reid.

Reed, Richard. S.C. —. He was pensioned 6 Dec. 1828. He was paid as late as 1833.

Reed, Samuel. Mass. Pvt. He served in 12th Regiment and was from Wendell.

Reed, Samuel. Pa. —. He served under Capt. Thomas Craig of the Flying Camp. He was taken prisoner at Fort Washington. He was from Indiana County.

Reed, Samuel. Pa. —. He was pensioned 9 Feb. 1837 in Perry County. He was dead by Dec. 1840.

Reed, Thomas. —. —. He received his commutation.

Reed, Uriah. Mass. Pvt. He was in the 16th Regiment and was from Taunton. He was paid $50.

Reed, Ward. Me. —. He was from Dixmont. He was paid $50 under the resolve of 1836.

Reed, Zacheriah. Pa. Pvt. He was on the 1813 pension list.

Reeder, Nicholas. Va. Pvt. He was wounded in the service. He was pensioned at the rate of $90 per annum on 19 Jan. 1811.

Reeder, Shadrack. Va. Corp. His wife, Susannah Reeder, was furnished assistance in Loudoun County on 15 Apr. 1777 and in Apr. 1779. He was the son of Cornelius Reeder.

Reem, George. Pa. —. He was granted relief in Juniata County 12 Feb. 1836.

Reem, John F. Pa. —. He was pensioned in Center County 5 Feb. 1836.

Reem, Nicholas. Pa. Sgt. He was granted his donation land 2 Apr. 1804. He was in Northumberland County. He enlisted in 1776 for three years or the war and served to 1778 when he was discharged due to his wounds. He also appeared as Nicholas Rheam.

Reemer, George. Pa. —. He was granted relief in York County 4 April 1833.

Reemy, Conrad. Pa. —. He was awarded a $40 gratuity and a $40 annuity in Center Co., Pa. 5 Mar. 1828.

Reepoolds [?], Elisha. Pa. Marine. He was on the pension roll of 1791.

Rees, George. Pa. —. He was awarded a $40 gratuity in Philadelphia 6 Apr. 1833. He died 29 July 1841.

Rees, Griffith. Pa. Pvt. He served in Capt. Brooke's detachment of Pa. Militia. He was wounded in the body and head in Oct. or Nov. 1777 near Darby, Chester Co., Pa. He was left for dead on the field. He lived in Upper Merion, Montgomery Co., Pa. in 1794. He was granted half a pension 20 Apr. 1796. He was on the 1813 pension list. He died 19 Mar. 1820. His administrator was his brother George Rees.

Rees, John. Pa. —. He received a $40 gratuity and a $40 annuity 5 Apr. 1841 in Philadelphia County but died a few days before the passage of the act. His widow, Mary Magdalena Rees, received the $40 gratuity 5 May 1841.

Rees, Philip. Pa.—. His widow, Catharine Rees, received a $40 gratuity and a $40 annuity in Crawford County 27 Apr. 1855.

Reese, —. Pa. —. His widow, Barbara M. Reese, was awarded a $40 gratuity and a $40 annuity in Berks Co., Pa. 14 Apr. 1834. She died 21 Aug. 1834.

Reese, David. Pa. —. He served in the 1st Regiment and died at Ashley Hill, Carolina. His mother, Susanna Reese, was granted a pension in Lancaster County. She was awarded a $40 gratuity and a $40 annuity in Philadelphia Co., Pa. 14 Apr. 1834.

Reese, Peter. Pa. —. He applied in Dauphin County on 20 May 1818. He died 2 Sep. 1824.

Reeves, Frederick. N.C. —. His widow, Elizabeth Reeves, applied in Wake County in 1824. She had formerly lived in Franklin County. He was wounded in the ankle at the battle of Eutaw Springs. He lost his leg and died from infection. They had three children. She was over 70. His brother was Richard Reeves. She was granted an annuity of $40. It became an annuity for life in 1827.

Reeves, Israel. N.Y. Pvt. He enlisted 7 Oct. 1777 in Capt. Jonathan Titus's Company under Col. Henry B. Livingstone in the 4th N.Y. Regiment. He was wounded by grape shot in his left thigh at Stillwater on 7 Oct. 1777. He was discharged 29 May 1779. He was pensioned 21 Dec. 1787. He lived in Southold, Suffolk Co., N.Y. in 1788 with his wife and three children and in Albany Co., N.Y. on 4 May 1789. He later lived in Cayuga County. He was on the 1813 pension list.

Reeves, James. N.Y. Pvt. He served in Capt. John Little's Company under Col. William Allison in the Orange County militia. He was wounded at Minisink on 22 July 1779 by a musket ball through his left arm above the elbow. He was 26 years old 24 Apr. 1787. He was pensioned 7 Apr. 1788. He lived at Minisink, Orange Co., N.Y. on 24 Apr. 1789. He was on the 1813 pension list.

Reeves, John. N.J. —. His widow, Hester Reeves, was pensioned in Camden County on 27 Feb. 1847 at the rate of $50 per annum.

Regan, —. Pa. —. His widow, Miriam Regan, was granted relief in Fayette County 3 Apr. 1841.

Reger, —. Pa. —. His widow, Anna Reger, was granted relief in Westmoreland County 10 Apr. 1849. She died 27 Apr. 1854.

Reghter, Nicholas. N.Y. Capt. He served in the militia under Col. Jacob Klock. He was wounded in his right arm by a musket ball on 20 Apr. 1779 at Stone Arabia. He was pensioned 15 Sep. 1786 and was 52 years old. He lived in Palatine, Montgomery Co., N.Y. in Oct. 1788. He was on the 1813 pension list. He died 25 Nov. 1820. He also appeared as Nicholas Richter. He was 42 years of age in 1787.

Regnaw, John. N.Y. Pvt. He was on the 1791 pension roll.

Rehern, Joseph. N.Y. Pvt. He was wounded by a musket ball in his left wrist at Bennington on 16 Aug. 1777. He served in Capt. Elijah Russell's Company under Col. John Knickerbocker. He was also under Capt. Peter Yates. He was 50 years old in 1787. He lived in Cambridge, Albany Co., N.Y. in 1787. He was on the 1813 pension list.

Rehr, Joseph. Pa. —. He was awarded a $40 gratuity in Berks Co., Pa. 16 Feb. 1835. One of his name received a $40 gratuity in Philadelphia County 12 Mar. 1836. One of the name was in Schuylkill County in the early 1840s.

Rehr, Mathias Pa. —. He was awarded a $40 gratuity and a $40 annuity in Berks Co., Pa. 8 Jan. 1827. He died 12 Dec. 1828. His widow, Catharine Rehr, was awarded a $40 gratuity and a $40 annuity 11 Mar. 1833.

Rehrer, —. Pa. —. His widow, Anna Maria Rehrer, was granted a $40 gratuity in Schuylkill Co. 26 Jan. 1835.

Rehrer, —. Pa. —. His widow, Susanna Rehrer, was awarded a $40 gratuity and a $40 annuity in Lancaster Co., Pa. 27 Jan. 1835.

Reichart, Adam. Pa. —. He was pensioned 24 Mar. 1837 in Bucks County.

Reichart, Charles. Pa. —. He was granted relief in Westmoreland County 7 Mar. 1827.

Reichenbach, Adam. Pa. —. He was awarded a $40 gratuity and a $40 annuity in Lehigh Co., Pa. 15 Apr. 1835. He was dead by July 1836.

Reid, Isaac. N.C. —. He applied from Craven County.

Reid, James. S.C.—. He was paid an annuity 3 Aug. 1779.

Reid, John. Md. —. He was paid $125 quarterly in Allegany County 2 Jan. 1813.

Reider, Adam. —. —. His application of 17 Apr. 1798 was not accepted.

Reighley, —. Pa. —. His widow, Barbara Reighley, was awarded a $40 gratuity and a $40 annuity in Cumberland Co., Pa. 15 Apr. 1835.

Reighley, William. S.C. Pvt. His widow had remarried. His son, William Reighley, being left an orphan, sought a pension from Abbeville District in 1829.

Reiley, George. Va. —. He claimed two tours of three months each. One of his tours was less than fourteen days when he was sick. His aged sister, aged 91, stated that he was drafted in 1781. His only other proof was his affidavit. Congress rejected his claim for a pension 15 Feb. 1844.

Reiley, James. Mass. —. He served in the Artillery. He was disabled by consumption. He was pensioned 1 Sep. 1782.

Reiley, Michael. Pa. —. He was awarded a $40 gratuity and a $40 annuity in York Co., Pa. 14 Apr. 1834. His daughter was Catherine Reiley.

Reilly, John. Pa. Pvt. He was on the 1813 pension list.

Reily, William. Md. Capt. He was pensioned at the rate of half-pay of a captain in the District of

Columbia 27 Jan. 1817. His widow, Barbara Reily, was pensioned at the same rate 1 Mar. 1833. He entered the service as a lieutenant 10 Dec. 1776 and became a captain 15 Oct. 1777 in the Baltimore County militia. At the end of the war he held the brevet rank of major. He died 8 July 1824. Congress granted his widow his arrearage. His administrator, John H. Reily, failed to show the right to half-pay due for the veteran's service so Congress rejected his claim 11 Feb. 1860. Heirs included John H. Reily, Susan W. Reily, and the children of Thomas Reily, deceased.

Reim, Nicholas. Pa. —. His widow, Margaret Reim, was awarded a $40 gratuity in Union County on 28 Mar. 1820.

Reiner, Martin. Pa. —. He was pensioned.

Reinhart, Frederick. Pa. —. Hid widow was Ann M. Reinhart.

Reinick, Christian. Pa. Surgeon's Mate. He served in the 1st Regiment and was killed at Paoli 21 Sep. 1777. His minor daughter, Catherine Reinick, was granted a pension in Lancaster County. Her guardian was Bernard Hubley. He also appeared as Christian Rennick.

Reischer, —. Pa. —. His widow, Christiana Reischer, was awarded a $40 gratuity and a $40 annuity in Franklin County 11 Apr. 1842 for his Revolutionary service.

Reiscker, Michael. Pa. —. He was granted relief.

Reiser, Philip. Pa. —. He was granted a $40 gratuity and a $40 annuity in Berks County 1 Apr. 1823. He also appeared as Philip Reeser.

Reisiner, John. Va. —. His wife, Eleanor Reisiner, was granted £8 support in Berkeley County on 21 Jan. 1778. He was away in Continental service.

Reist, Frederick. Pa. —. He applied in Dauphin County on 6 Aug. 1814. Capt. John Stoner enlisted him in 1776 about April. He served in Capt. John Murray's Company in the 2nd Regiment of Pa. Riflemen under Col. Daniel Broadhead. He signed in German. He also appeared as Frederick Riest. *Vide* also Frederick Rust.

Relay, Henry. Mass. Pvt. He served in Capt. John Walton's Company under Col. Brook and was wounded 28 Oct. 1776. He was pensioned at the rate of half-pay from 27 Nov. 1776 on 2 Dec. 1777. He was a fifer. He also appeared as Henry Relly.

Remel, Jacob. Pa. —.He received a $40 gratuity and a $40 annuity in Northampton County 21 Mar. 1837.

Remick, Samuel. N.H. —. He was a resident of Goffstown when he was pensioned in 1778. He was in Capt. McConnel's Company in Col. Stickney's Regiment and was wounded in both hips at the battle of Bennington in 1777. He was under a surgeon's care for four months. He was discharged without pay and was obliged to work to pay his way the 250 miles to his home. He received no compensation. He was late of Derry, N.H. His widow, Sarah Remick, had her petition rejected by Congress 18 Apr. 1860 because she should have applied in the normal way. She was dead when his daughter, Rebecca B. Remick was nearly blind and without property and aged 78 and granted a pension 8 Feb. 1878 by Congress.

Remington, Jabez. R.I. Pvt. He was on the 1788 roll. He lived in Providence Co., R.I.

Rems, William. Pa. —. He applied in Berks County on 21 Jan. 1815. He served in Capt. Stake's Company.

Renau, John. N.Y. Pvt. He was on the 1791 pension roll. He appeared as John Renan on the 1813 pension list.

Renekel, Lawrence. N.Y. Pvt. He served under Col. Peter Bellinger in the Montgomery County militia and was slain 11 Oct. 1780. His children, Lawrence Renekel, Catherine Renekel, Anna Renekel, Margaret Renekel, and Amariah [?] Renekel, received a half-pay pension for seven years.

Reniff, Charles. —. Sgt. Congress awarded his widow, Almira Reniff, the arrearage of her pension from 4 Mar. 1848 to 3 Feb. 1853 on 15 Dec. 1857. She was from Crawford Co,, Pa.

Renison, John. Pa. Ens. He was from Butler County. He enlisted in 1776 under Capt. Forbett and Col. William Irwin. He next served under Capt. Ferry and Col. Haisen. He was exchanged to the 7th Regiment under Capt. Parker, Col. Hays, and Col. Minge. He was at Paoli, Brandywine, and Three Rivers. He was in the 7th Pa. Regiment and became blind and disabled. He died 18 May 1829.

Renn, Philip. Pa. —. He was awarded a $40 gratuity and a $40 annuity in Northumberland Co., Pa. 7 Apr. 1830. He was dead by 1830. His final payment was made to Solomon Renn.

Rennel, Jacob. Pa. —. He was granted relief 21 Mar. 1837 in Northampton County. He died 25 Feb. 1842.

Renney, John. S.C. —. His administrator, Peter Oliver, was paid $1100 or such part as would pay the interest of 6% due him, Thomas Short, Jacob Schon, and David Zahl, on 20 Dec. 1810. They were marines on the *South Carolina.*

Rennison, John. Pa. Sgt. He was pensioned 23 Mar. 1819.

Renol, Christopher. Md. Pvt. He was pensioned 4 Mar. 1789.

Repley, James. Pa. —. He was granted relief.

Requa, James. N.Y. Pvt. He served in the 2nd N.Y. Regiment of Artillery under Col. John Lamb. He fell from his horse. He was in N.Y. on 13 June 1786.

Requa, John. N.Y. Pvt. He served in Capt. Gabriel Requea's Company under Col. James Hammond in the Westchester County militia. He was wounded by a musket ball in his leg on 7 Jan. 1781. He was later wounded by a two more musket balls. He was aged 2- in Nov. 1785. He was pensioned 14 June 1786. He lived in Westchester Co., N.Y. in 1787. He was on the 1813 pension list.

Resner, George. N.Y. Lt. He served under Col. Clyde in the Montgomery County militia. He was slain 6 Aug. 1777. His widow remarried 2 Dec. 1782. There was an inquiry whether she or his only orphan child was due his seven years' half-pay on 21 July 1783.

Restine, Charles. Pa. —. He was granted a $40 gratuity in Philadelphia County 23 Apr. 1829. His widow, Hannah Restine, was granted relief in Philadelphia 13 Mar. 1839.

Revell, John. N.C. —. He served in the militia and was taken prisoner near Camden. He was carried to Charleston where he died. His widow was Mary Revell who was recommended for an allowance in 1784 in Wayne County.

Rewalt, John. Pa. Capt. He served in the militia and was at Bunker Hill, Brandywine, White Plains, and the taking of the Hessians at Trenton. His last three years he served in a brigade of wagons stationed at Lebanon, Lancaster Co., Penn. He married 20 Mar. 1778 Ann ------. He died in Yates Co., N.Y. in 1822. His son, John Rewalt, settled in Illinois. Congress granted his widow, Ann Rewalt, a pension 17 Feb. 1838.

Rex, John. Pa. —. He applied at New Germantown, Hunterdon Co., N.J. 30 Oct. 1813. He served in the 3rd and 12th Pa. Regiments. On the reduction of the 12th Pa. Regiment, he was in the company under the command of Lt. Peter Smith, Quartermaster of the 3rd Pa. Regiment, until being discharged. He also appeared as John Shreck.

Rex, William. Pa. —. He was awarded a $40 gratuity and a $40 annuity in Northampton Co., Pa. 11 Apr. 1825.

Reybecker, John. Pa. Pvt. He was on the 1813 pension list.

Reyes, Daniel. Mass. —. He served in the 4th Regiment and was paid $20.

Reynolds, Arthur. Va. Pvt. He was wounded at the battle of Eutaw. He was on the 1785 pension roll. He was "struck off by consent 18 Sep. 1784."

Reynolds, Benjamin. N.Y. Pvt. He served under Col. Thaddeus Crane in Capt. Lawrence's Company in the Westchester County militia. He was wounded by a musket ball in his right arm. He lived in Westchester Co., N.Y. on 17 June 1788. He was 25 years of age on 18 Sep. 1786. He was on the 1813 pension list.

Reynolds, Daniel. —. —. He served upwards of two years. He married before 1794 and died 13 May 1832. His widow, Thankful Reynolds, sought to have his pension continued from 1 Jan. 1845 for five years. The year of their marriage was given as 1779 and 1784. The discrepancy could be due to her poor memory. The age of the eldest child would place the marriage in 1784. No record could be found in Grafton, N.H. Congress granted her a pension 13 July 1846.

Reynolds, Elisha. Pa. Marine. He was in Philadelphia County on 12 June 1786. He was disabled by one of his legs being bruised between two boats in crossing troops over to New Jersey. He was in the galley service under Capt. Nathan Boyce. He was 25 years old. He also appeared as Elisha Bennolds. He seemed to be the same person who appeared as Eleher Reynolds.

Reynolds, Elisha. R.I. Pvt. He served in Col. Dyer's militia. He was wounded by a musket ball in his left arm on 5 Aug. 1777 at Kingston. He lived in Alburg, Vt. in 1794. He was on the 1813 pension list.

Reynolds, George. Pa. —. He was awarded a $40 gratuity and a $40 annuity in Center Co., Pa. 29 Mar. 1824.

Reynolds, James. Md. Pvt. His widow, Ruth Reynolds, was pensioned at the rate of half-pay of a private 16 Mar. 1835.

Reynolds, John.. Pa. 1st Lt. His widow, Catherine Reynolds, was in Philadelphia County on 1 Mar. 1781. He served on the galley *Franklin*.

Reynolds, Jonathan. Conn. Pvt. He served in Capt. Thomas Hobby under Col. David Waterbury. He was wounded by a musket ball in his left hip at the siege of St. Johns in Canada and was discharged 10 Nov. 1775. He was from Greenwich, Conn. He had not been placed on the half-pay pension list. He lived in Lower Salem, Westmoreland Co., N.Y. on 17 Apr. 1789. He died 24 Dec. 1809. He was on the 1813 pension list as dead.

Reynolds, Robert. Md. —. He enlisted for three years in Aug. or Sep. 1776 under Capt. Thomas Bell and Col. Rawling. He was wounded and taken prisoner at Fort Washington 16 Nov. 1776. He was exchanged and sent to Philadelphia where he was discharged 11 July 1777. Congress granted him a pension 30 Dec. 1833.

Reynolds, Samuel. N.J. —. He was pensioned in Somerset County on 8 Mar. 1837 at the rate of $60 per annum.

Reynolds, Solomon. Conn. Pvt. He served in the Conn. line. He was wounded by a musket shot which entered near his left breast and was taken out near his navel. It fractured his ribs and occasioned an exfoliation. His ribs were still disunited. His wound was received in a skirmish with the British at Elizabethtown in 1780. He lived in Woodbury, Conn. in 1794. He enlisted 25 May 1777 fo the war and was discharged 29 May 1780. He was granted two-thirds of a pension 20 Apr. 1796. He was on the 1813 pension list.

Reynolds, Thomas. Mass. —. He served in the 16th Regiment and was paid $20.

Reynolds, Tobias. Md. Pvt. He was pensioned at the rate of half-pay of a private in Anne Arundel County on 7 Feb. 1818.

Reynolds, William. N.Y. Pvt. He served in the volunteers. He was wounded at the taking of Fort Montgomery and was taken prisoner 6 Oct. 1777. He served in Capt. Francis Smith's Company in Col. Jesse Woodhull's Regiment of the Orange County militia. He lived at New Cornwall, N.Y. in 1794. He was on the 1813 pension list.

Rhame, Ebenezer. S.C. —. He entered the service at the age of 16 under Col. Ervin and Gen. Horry. He was captured at the fall of Charleston. He was exchanged and rejoined the Americans. Evans Jones served with him. He was pensioned in Sumter District on 25 Nov. 1830. He was paid as late as 1834.

Rhem, John. N.C. —. He was from Craven County.

Rhine, George. Pa. —. His widow, Catherine Rhine, received a $40 annuity 18 Apr. 1853.

Rhinehart, Frederick. Pa. —. He was awarded a $40 gratuity in Cumberland Co., Pa. 6 Apr. 1833.

Rhinevault, William. —. Pvt. He married 11 Apr. 1782, but the family register appeared to have been altered. He died 16 June 1840. His children were due what his widow, Mary Rhinevault, was due from 16 June 1840 to 20 Aug. 1842 according to Congress on 24 Jan. 1843.

Rhode, Jacob. Me. —. He was from Lyman.

Rhode, Moses. Me. —. He was from Waterboro.

Rhodes, —. Va. —. His wife, Mary Rhodes, was furnished assistance in Loudon County 15 Nov. 1778 while he was away in the army.

Rhodes, Arthur. S.C. —. His application was rejected in 1822 for want of vouchers.

Rhodes, Bristol. R.I. Pvt. He lost his left leg and left hand by a cannon shot at Yorktown, Va. in Oct. 1781. He served under Col. Jeremiah Olney. He was aged 31 in 1785. He lived in Providence Co., R.I. He was on the 1813 pension list.

Rhodes, Jacob. Me. —. He was from Lyman. He was paid $50 under the resolve of 1836.

Rhodes, Jacob. Va. —. His son was furnished assistance while his father was away in the service in Loudoun County 15 Nov. 1778.

Rhodes, Mark. Pa. —. He was paid $300 for his right to donation land on 10 Apr. 1826.

Rhodes, Moses. Me. —. He was from Waterboro. He was paid $50 under the resolve of 1836.

Rhodus, John. S.C. —. He was ruptured by exertion at Fort Moultrie. He applied in 1817.

Rhodus, Nathaniel. S.C. —. He was killed in the service. His widow, Elizabeth Rhodus, was awarded an annuity 15 Dec. 1785. Salem. He also appeared as Nathaniel Rhodes. She died in Nov. 1801. Her son, John Rhodus, administrator, sought her arrearage. *Vide* also Nathaniel Rowdus.

Riblet, Abraham. Pa. —. He was pensioned in 1813. He also appeared as Abraham Rivlet.

Riblet, Christian. Pa. —. He was awarded a $40 gratuity in Union Co., Pa. 14 Mar. 1831.

Rice, —. Va. Pvt. His wife, Hannah Rice, and two children were furnished £25 in Frederick Co., Va. on 2 Mar. 1779. He died in the service 23 May 1783. She was on the 1785 pension roll.

Rice, Abijah. Mass. —. He served in the 1st Regiment and was paid $20.

Rice, Chauncey. —. —. He was born in Litchfield, Conn. 22 Apr. 1756. His father was a tavern keeper and merchant in Norfolk. He volunteered 10 May 1776 at Long Island. General Washington authorized him to select a number of men as a scouting party. He was commissioned as a captain and helped in the evacuation of New York City up the Hudson. He was at a skirmish at Harlaem Heights and was wounded in his leg by a musket ball. He was also at Trenton and Princeton. Afterwards he resided at Burlington, N.J. He resided in Northampton Co., Pa. when he sought a pension from Congress 5 Mar. 1840. Congress had no hesitation about his service as a private but insisted on some documentary testimony for his service as a captain.

Rice, Charles. N.H. Pvt. He served under Col. John Stark and Capt. Jeremiah Stiles. He was wounded by a ball which passed through his shoulder and breast on 17 June 1775 at Bunker Hill. He lived in Surry, N.H. in 1794. He was in the militia. He was granted half a pension 20 Apr. 1796. He was from Keene in 1795. He was on the 1813 pension list. He died 12 Oct. 1831.

Rice, Elijah. Conn. Pvt. He enlisted in 1775 under Capt. Ezekiel Scott. He served in 3rd Regiment. He was wounded in his right shoulder. He resided in Southington, Conn. in 1792. He enlisted 21 Apr. 1777 and was discharged 21 Apr. 1780. His bounty land warrant #6362 was issued to Richard Platt 10 Aug. 1789. His brother, Thomas Rice, died a prisoner in Quebec. His son, Amos Rice, fell at Tippecanoe. His son, Elijah Rice, was massacred in the hospital at Fort Niagara. He delivered his paperwork to Gen. Parsons; the papers were lost when Parsons drowned. Congress granted him an increase in his pension in 1816. Congress rejected his petition for back pay 5 Feb. 1818.

Rice, Elisha. Mass. Corp. He served in the 15th Mass. Regiment and was wounded on 3 Feb. 1780. He served under Col. Timothy Bigelow and Capt. Moses Roberts. He was disabled with sundry wounds on his head. His skull was broken and many pieces were taken out. He was pensioned at the rate of one-third of his pay from the time of his discharge on 5 Jan. 1781 on 19 Apr. 1781. His original certificates were mislaid or lost. He was pensioned 8 Mar. 1788. He was 31 years old. He was on the 1813 pension list.

Rice, George. Va. Capt. He was appointed 18 Jan. 1776 in the infantry in the 11th Regiment and became supernumerary 30 Sep. 1778. His heirs sought his commutation but were rejected 18 May 1838.

Rice, James. Va. —. He died about the 1st of June 1778. His wife, Hannah Rice, and two children were granted support in Loudoun County in Apr. 1781. His widow was first granted support in Fauquier County 9 Oct. 1780.

Rice, James. Va. —. He died in the service about the 1st of June 1778. His widow was Hannah Rice of Frederick Co., Va. on 7 May 1783. [Compare with — Rice with widow Hannah *supra* and with James Rice.]

Rice, James B. Va. —. He served three tours in the militia for a total of six months. He was taken sick without doing any actual service. After recovering, he returned and was excused. Congress refused to grant him a pension 25 Apr. 1840.

Rice, John. N.Y. Pvt. He served under Col. James Livingstone in the Continental Troops. He was disabled by an inguinal rupture at Bemis Heights in 1777. He lived in Montgomery Co., N.Y. on 26 June 1789. He was on the 1813 pension list.

Rice, John. Pa. —. He was awarded a $40 gratuity and a $40 annuity in Lancaster Co., Pa. 14 Apr. 1828. It was to be paid to William Rice.

Rice, Josiah. Mass. —. He served in the 6th Regiment and was from Rutland. He was paid $20.

Rice, Nahum. Mass. —. He served in the 3rd Regiment and was from Sunderland. He was paid $20.

Rice, Nathan. S.C. —. He was on the roll in 1826. He was paid as late as 1834.

Rice, Nathaniel. Va. Lt. His commutation pay was issued 3 May 1791.

Rice, Oliver. Mass. —. He served in the 9th Regiment and was from Marlborough. He was paid $20.

Rice, Philip. Va. —. He was from King William County. He, his two Negro servants Jim Top and Abraham, and his small vessel, the *Madam* or *Alice Taylor*, were pressed into service by Robert Radford and Micajah Crews shortly before Cornwallis took possession of Yorktown to transport munitions of war from Cumberland to Taylor's ferry. He was directed to go to Newcastle to load flour from Col. Simms' mill, cannon, shells, and park and to transport same to York. The British attacked, and he had to scuttle the vessel. He escaped in a skiff. He died in Bracken Co., Ky. 25 Apr. 1841. His father bought the vessel in 1781. It was lost in the service. His heirs sought relief from Congress on 25 July 1850. Congress granted same 30 Jan. 1855.

Rice, Richard [?]. Va. —. His wife, Martha Rice, was furnished support in Westmoreland County in Feb. 1779.

Rice, Simon. Mass. Pvt. He served in the 3rd Regiment and was from Charlton. His widow, Sarah Harrington, was paid $50.

Rice, Thomas. Mass. —. He was in the 10th Regiment and was paid $20.

Rice, William. Pa. Lt. He was on the 1813 pension list.

Rice, William. Va. —. He was pensioned at the rate of $60 per annum and $40 relief on 6 Feb. 1808. He was in Richmond County on 9 Feb. 1809. He died 10 Nov. 1814. His administrator was Richard Efford.

Rich, Lemuel. Conn. Pvt. He was captured and lost his toes. He was on the 1813 pension list in Vermont. He transferred to Berkshire Co., Mass.

Rich, S. N. Pa. —. This person received relief 23 Jan. 1841.

Rich, Zacheus. Mass. Sgt. He served in the 9th Regiment and was from Phillipston. He was paid $50. He was on the 1795 pension list in Connecticut.

Richard, Charles. Pa. —. He was awarded a $40 gratuity and a $40 annuity in Westmoreland Co., Pa. 7 Mar. 1827. He was 85 years old in 1840.

Richard, Jeremiah. N.H. Lt. He served in the 1st Regiment. He was wounded by a musket ball in his left shoulder on 7 Oct. 1777 at Hubbardstown. He was ruptured in his groin in the Indian expedition under Gen. John Sullivan in the summer of 1779. He lived in New Ipswich, N.H. in 1794. He was discharged 6 July 1780.

Richards, —. Va. —. His wife, Ann Richards, was furnished assistance in Loudoun County in Sep. 1780.

Richards, Daniel. Mass. Pvt. He also served on various armed vessels. He was discharged 9 May 1780. He married in 1782 and died 20 Aug. 1835. He was from Newburyport, Mass. His widow was Marcy Richards. Congress granted her pension 8 Feb. 1838.

Richards, Isaac. Conn. Pvt. He served in Capt. E. Reed's Company in the 9th Regiment of militia under Lt. Col. Stephen St. John. He was wounded by a musket ball in his left leg on 27 Apr. 1777 at Ridgefield. He lived in Norwalk, Conn. in 1792. He was granted one-third of a pension 20 Apr. 1796.

Richards, Isaac. N.Y. Pvt. He was pensioned 4 Mar. 1794. He lived in New York County. He was on the 1813 pension list.

Richards, John. S.C. —. One of his children, Betsey Richards, was paid an annuity of $60 on 21 May 1825.

Richards, John. Va. —. He was pensioned in Spotsylvania County on 3 Feb. 1819 at the rate of $60 per annum. He served three years as a marine aboard the galley *Page*.

Richards, Joseph A. R.I. Corp. He lost part of all of his toes on his left foot by frost bite on the Oswego expedition under Col. Willet in 1783; he was also wounded in the knee at the battle of Springfield on 23 June 1780. He was aged 37 when he applied on 29 Dec. 1785. He was on the 1813 pension list.

Richards, Paul. Md. Pvt. His widow, Mary Richards, was pensioned at the rate of half-pay of a private in Baltimore 24 Feb. 1823. Her arrearage was paid to her representative 13 Mar. 1828.

Richards, Philip. N.Y. Pvt. He served in Dubois's Regiment in Capt. Vanderburg's Company. In 1777 he had both his collar bones broken while carrying heavy timber at Fort Montgomery. He was discharged from the Invalids Corps 10 Apr. 1783. He lived in New Marlborough, Ulster Co., N.Y. 2 June 1789. He was a laborer. He died 27 Feb. 1790.

Richards, Richard. Mass. Pvt. He served in Capt. Job Cushing's Company under Col. John Greaton. He was wounded in the leg at Hull on 20 July 1775 and was pensioned at the half-pay from 31

Dec. 1775 on 9 Oct. 1777.

Richards, Samuel. N.J. Sgt. He enlisted in 1777 and served under Capt. David Lyon and Col. Oliver Spencer. He was killed at Brandywine on 11 Sep. 1777. He married Jemimah Genung in either Nov. or Dec. 1776. She lived three years, one month, and eleven days thereafter. Her heirs sought her half-pay pension in Morris County in 1783.

Richards, Thomas. Va. —. His wife, Anne Richards, was granted support in Loudoun County 9 Oct. 1780. His wife was also granted support in Fauquier County 9 Oct. 1780.

Richardson, Benjamin Allen. Mass. Pvt. He served in Capt. Enoch Putnam's Company under Col. Israel Hutchinson and was wounded in North River 3 Aug. 1776. A cannon ball struck him on his hip bone. He was pensioned at half-pay from 31 Dec. 1776 on 9 Oct. 1777. He was on the 1813 pension list. He died 13 Jan. 1815 in Suffolk Co., Mass.

Richardson, Charles. Md. Pvt. He was pensioned at the rate of half-pay of a private 2 Jan. 1813. His widow, Nancy Richardson, was pensioned at the same rate 16 Feb. 1820. Her arrearage was paid to Lydia Ackworth, her daughter, 9 Mar. 1846.

Richardson, Daniel. Md. Pvt. He was pensioned at the rate of half-pay of a private 3 Jan. 1812.

Richardson, Daniel. S.C. Pvt. He was severely wounded by being hacked and cut to pieces by a sword in his left arm in 1782. He served under Capt. Frederick Gragg and Col. Glenn. John Arnold deposed that he was wounded. He was from Newberry District in 1813. He was paid as late as 1826.

Richardson, David. —. —. He claimed two years of service but was allowed only seven months. His son and administrator sought the difference, but Congress rejected his claim 1 Mar. 1854.

Richardson, David.. N.C. —. He served for three years. He did not apply for a pension due to ignorance or patriotism. He died in 1842. His widow, Sarah Richardson, applied and was approved for a pension for seven months of service. She died 30 Oct. 1847. She was entitled to as much as two years of service, and her children petitioned Congress for the arrearage due them on 23 Mar. 1860.

Richardson, Ebenezer. Mass. —. He served in the 2nd Regiment and was paid $20.

Richardson, Ebenezer. Mass. —. He served in the 2nd Regiment and was paid $20. [second of the name]

Richardson, Ezekiel. Pa. —. He was in Lancaster County on 4 Feb. 1784. He served in the 3rd Pa. Regiment.

Richardson, George —. —. He was pensioned 25 Apr. 1808 at the rate of $4 per month from 10 Feb. 1808.

Richardson, Isaac. —. —. He was pensioned 9 June 1794.

Richardson, Joel. Me. —. He died 20 Feb. 1827 at Durham. His widow was Lydia Richardson from Guilford. She was paid $50 under the resolve of 1836.

Richardson, Jonas. Mass. —. He served in the 7th Regiment and was from Antrim. He was paid $20.

Richardson, Joseph. Md. Pvt. He was pensioned from 4 Mar. 1802. He was on the 1813 pension list.

Richardson, Joseph. N.H. Pvt. He served in Hale's Regiment. He lived in Stafford Co., N.H. He was on the 1813 pension list.

Richardson, Joseph. S.C. —. He served three years and nineteen days. He was wounded in 1780. He was pensioned in Darlington District 25 Nov. 1830.

Richardson, Joseph A. R.I. Corp. He died 23 Dec. 1825 in Providence Co., R.I.

Richardson, Paris. N.H. Pvt. He was from Acworth in 1783. His shoulder was dislocated in Continental service. He was in the 1st N.H. Regiment in Capt. Farwell's Company.

Richardson, Richard. S.C. Pvt. He served in 2nd Regiment. He was wounded by a musket ball which went through his breast at Drawgates when Gen. Provost marched on Charleston neck in 1779. He lived in Charleston, S.C. in 1794.

Richardson, Robert. N.Y. Sgt. He was in the 2nd N.Y. Artillery under Col. John Lamb in Capt. Gershom Mott's Company. He was wounded on 9 July 1776 by a shot from the enemy at Paul's Hook in his private parts. At White Plains on 13 Aug. 1776 he was wounded in his right shoulder. He lived in Dutchess Co., N.Y. in June 1787. He was a weaver. He was aged 63 on 21 Aug. 1785. He died in 1796.

Richardson, Seth. Mass. Pvt. He served in the 11th Regiment and was from Danvers. His widow, Hannah Richardson, was paid $50.

Richardson, Stephen. N.H. Pvt. He resided in Warner in 1783. He was in the 2nd N.H. Regiment. He suffered from deafness, and his constitution was worn out. He was aged 29 in 1787. He was on the 1813 pension list.

Richardson, Thomas. R.I. Pvt. He lived in Providence Co., R.I. in 1788.

Richardson, William. Md. Col. He served until 22 Oct. 1779 when he resigned. He was from Caroline County. His son, Joseph Richardson, had his petition for commutation rejected 22 Oct. 1779. His father resigned 22 Oct. 1779 so he was not supernumerary. Congress rejected the son's claim for half-pay on 1 Mar. 1838 in Caroline Co., Md.

Richardson, William. N.C. —. He applied in Wake County in 1805. He was in Continental service under Maj. Reddin Blount. He was wounded in his thigh by a musket ball and in his shoulder by a bayonet. A wagon ran over his leg. He died 2 Nov. 1807.

Richardson, William. S.C. —. He served under Capt. Culp and Capt. Council. He was at Black Swamp. He was discharged at Watboo. He was wounded in the head by a bayonet. He suffered from pain in his left shoulder and was in his 72nd year. He was pensioned 23 Nov. 1829 from Horry District. He was paid as late as 1843.

Richardson, William. S.C. —. His widow was Ann Richardson. Her application was rejected in 1843 in Marion District. She had eight children.

Richart, Thomas. Pa. Pvt. He was granted a full pension 20 Apr. 1796. He died 12 Aug. 1805.

Riche, William. Pa. —. He was awarded a $40 gratuity and a $40 annuity in Montgomery Co., Pa. 12 Feb. 1825. He died 3 July 1842.

Richer, John. Pa. —. He was granted relief in Dauphin County 20 May 1839. He also appeared as John Ricker.

Richey, James. Pa. —. He was granted a $40 gratuity and a $40 annuity in Fayette County 16 June 1836. He died 29 June 1843.

Richey, Robert. Pa. —. He was awarded a $40 gratuity and a $40 annuity in York Co., Pa. 6 Apr. 1833.

Richma, John. N.Y. —. He was granted relief during the war.

Richmond, —. Pa. —. Hid widow, Jane Richmond, was granted relief 19 Mar. 1816.

Richmond, Gamaliel. Mass. Sgt. He served in the 4th Regiment and was paid $20.

Richmond, James. R.I. —. He enlisted under Capt. Sawyer and Col. Elliott from 1777 to 1778. Congress granted him a pension 4 Jan. 1832.

Richmond, Nathaniel. Mass. —. He served in the 2nd Regiment and was from Herkimer. He was paid $20.

Richmond, Seth. Mass. —. He served in the 14th Regiment. His widow, Phebe Richmond, was from Raynham.

Richmond, Sigbe. R.I. Pvt. He was worn out with old age and bodily infirmities. He was aged 68 in 1786.

Richner, John. Pa. —. He was awarded relief in Northampton County 9 Apr. 1833. He was dead by July 1836.

Richter, Nicholas. N.Y. Capt. He served in Capt. Jacob Klock's Regiment. He was wounded in his right arm on 20 Apr. 1779. He was pensioned 15 Sep.1786 and was 52 years old. He died 25 Nov. 1820 in Montgomery Countny. He also appeared as Nicholas Righter. He was on the 1813 pension list.

Rickart, Thomas. Pa. Lt. He completed the application process in 1795. He died 12 Aug. 1805.

Ricker, Abraham. N.Y. Capt. He served in the 2nd N.Y. Regiment and died of excessive desertion and fatigue at Valley Forge, Pennsylvania 7 May 1778 leaving one child. His widow, Margaret Ricker, was driven from her home on Long Island by the enemy. She sought seven years' half pay in 1793. His only child was dead when his widow in her 93rd year, who was blind and helpless, received his commutation 7 Jan. 1834. He also appeared as Abraham Riker.

Ricker, Frederick. Pa. —. He was awarded a $40 gratuity and a $40 annuity in Dauphin Co., Pa. 6 Apr. 1833. He died 30 Dec. 1850.

Ricker, John. Pa. —. He was pensioned in Dauphin County 20 May 1839. He died 23 June 1849.

Ricker, Peter. Pa. —. He applied 22 Dec. 1813.

Ricker, Simeon. Me. —. He was from Lisbon.

Rickey, Robert. Pa. —.He was paid a $40 gratuity in Montgomery County in 1833.

Rider, Joseph. N.Y. Corp. He served in the Orange County militia under Col. John Hathorn and was slain 22 July 1779. His son, George Rider, received his half-pay pension.

Riddick, Josiah. Va. —. He entered the service during Gen. Matthews' invasion. He was captured and sent to New York. He was granted a gratuity of 5,000 pounds of tobacco in May 1780. It was finally approved on 25 Mar. 1782.

Riddick, Willis. Va. Col. He was the colonel of Nansemond County. The British burned his home and other buildings in 1779 as they marched from Norfolk to capture the public stores and property at Suffolk which had been removed to his cellar. His losses amounted to $8,000 to $10,000. He died testate in 1781. His heirs sought compensation for the losses with interest in the amount of $41,600. He made his will 10 Apr. 1781; it was proved 8 Apr. 1782. His executors were his son-in-law Josiah Riddick and Archibald Richardson. The witnesses were Henry Riddick, David Campbell, and Christian Parker. He named his grandson James Riddick and Edward Riddick; his children Willis Riddick, James Riddick, Elizabeth Carr, Priscilla Riddick, Ann Riddick, Teresa Riddick, and Christian Richardson; and his wife Mary Riddick. Congress did not allow the petition filed by Nathaniel Riddick, administrator *de bonis non*.

Riddle, Robert. Pa. —. He was 72 years old in 1840.

Rideout, William. Mass. Pvt. He served three years in Col. Edward Wigglesworth's Regiment in Capt. Nicholas Blaisdell's Company and lost the sight in both eyes due to smallpox. He was discharged from the Invalids and was pensioned at half-pay from 16 Feb. 1780 on 25 Apr. 1780. He was 31 years old in 1791. He was on the 1813 pension list. He transferred to Kennebec Co., Me. 4 Mar. 1818.

Rider, Benjamin. Mass. Pvt. He was in the Invalids under Capt. John Webb and Col. Lewis Nichola. He was debilitated in the service. He was pensioned 1 Sep. 1782. He was 62 years old in 1788. He was on the 1813 pension list. He also appeared as Benjamin Ryder. He lived in Greenwich when he was paid $20 by the Commonwealth.

Rider, Giles. Mass. Pvt. He served in the 6ᵗʰ Regiment and was from Enfield. He was paid $50.

Rider, Peter. Vt. Corp. He served under Col. Greaton. He lost his right eye by a wound with a musket ball in 1776 at Lake Champlain. He lived in Hartford, Vt. in 1795. He was in the militia. He died 6 Feb. 1808.

Ridgaway, Zedikiah. Del. Pvt. He was wounded in the knee at the battle of Guilford Court House on 15 Mar. 1781. He was single. He also appeared as Zedikiah Ridaway.

Ridgeway, John. S.C. Capt. He was killed 3 Sep. 1781. His widow, Charity Ridgeway, was awarded an annuity 31 Dec. 1785. Two children were under the age of twelve in 1787. There were three children in 1791. Benjamin Arnold and Ellis Cheek deposed anent his service.

Ridgeway, John. S.C. —. He fought at Cowpens, Guilford, and Yorktown. His father was killed by the Tories and left a large family. He was upwards of 70 years of age. He applied in Laurens District in 1831.

Ridley, —. Va. —. His wife, Elizabeth Ridley, was granted support in Brunswick Co., Va. on 26 July 1779 while he was away in Continental service.

Riebsom, Matthias. N.Y. Pvt. He served in the Montgomery County militia and was slain 6 Aug. 1777. His widow, Elizabeth Riebsom, received a half-pension for seven years.

Riend, Christopher. Md. Pvt. He was on the 1813 pension list. He also appeared as Christopher Reind.

Rife, Peter. N.C. —. He entered the service at Salisbury, N.C. in the spring of 1780. He was transferred to an armory as an artificer under the command of Gen. Greene at Guilford and was in various skirmishes with Tarleton. He resided in Wythe Co., Va. when he applied to Congress for a private pension bill. Congress accepted him for nine months of service on 10 Feb. 1846.

Riffle, Melchior. Pa. —. He was awarded a $40 gratuity and a $40 annuity in York Co., Pa. 20 Feb. 1832. He was 90 years old in 1840. He died 16 Apr. 1841.

Rigby, William. Md. QM Sgt. He was pensioned at the rate of half-pay of a quartermaster sergeant in Fairfield Co., Ohio. 12 Feb. 1820.

Rigsby, Jesse. N.C. —. He served under Capt. Abraham Allen in 1781 and was wounded through his body. He was two-thirds disabled. He applied for a pension from Orange Co., N.C. in May 1799.

Rigg, Benjamin. Va. Pvt. His daughter, Betsey Rigg, was in King George County and was put on the pension list on 22 Oct. 1788 at the rate of £8 per annum. She was continued on the list on 31 May 1790. He served in the 5ᵗʰ Va. Regiment and died in the service. Betsey Rigg was 9 or 10 years old and lived with her maternal grandfather, William Armstrong. Her guardian was Jesse Armstrong.

Riggs, John. S.C. —. He was wounded at Hanging Rock and died of his wounds on 30 June or 1 July 1780. Three of his sons were in the same battle. His widow, Elizabeth Riggs, was awarded an annuity 23 Dec. 1785. She applied for a pension in 1819. James Jamieson, W. Brown, and John Moffett deposed about his service.

Righter, —. Pa. —. His widow, Phoebe Righter, was awarded a $40 gratuity and a $40 annuity in Philadelphia Co. Pa. 15 Apr. 1834. She was 81 years old in 1840.

Righter, Michael. Pa. Pvt. His widow, Christine Righter, was in Chester County on 6 Apr. 1795. He served in Capt. Henry Barker's [or Baker] Company in the Chester County militia and died in captivity.

Righter, Nicholas. N.Y. Capt. He served under Col. Klock and received a half-pay pension.

Rightmyer, —. Pa. —. His widow, Elizabeth Rightmyer, was awarded a $40 gratuity and a $40 annuity in Berks County 5 Feb. 1836. She was dead by Feb. 1839.

Rightmyer, Henry. N.Y. Pvt. He served in Capt. Garrit Putnam's Company in Willet's Regiment. He was wounded in his left arm on 2 Oct. 1781. He lived in Montgomery Co., N.Y. 26 June 1789. He also appeared as Henry Rightmire and Hendrick Richtmeyer. He was on the 1813 pension list.

Rigsby, Jesse. N.C. Pvt. He applied in Orange County in 1800. He served in the militia under Capt. Abraham Allen and received a gun shot through his body in Sept. 1781 at the plantation of Lewis Kirk in Orange County in a battle with a party of Tories led by Richard Edwards. He was rejected in 1805, He was on the 1813 pension list.

Riker, Abraham. N.Y. Capt. He served in the 2nd New York Regiment and died at Valley Forge 7 May 1778 leaving a widow, Margaret Riker, and children. The enemy drove her from her house on Long Island. She sought relief 21 Feb. 1793. His seven years' half-pay was issued to his widow 30 June 1834.

Riker, John B. N.J. Surgeon. He served in the 4th Regiment. He was captured, exchanged, and deranged.

Riley, —. Va. —. His wife, Anna Riley, was granted £10 support in Fauquier Co., Va. in Feb. 1778.

Riley, Ephraim. —. —. Congress rejected his claim for a pension because there was not sufficient evidence that he was a soldier on 23 June 1854.

Riley, William. —. —. He received his commutation.

Riley, William. —. —. His widow, Barbara Riley, was granted relief by Congress 11 Feb. 1852.

Rima, Johann. N.Y. Pvt. He served under Col. Peter Bellinger in Capt. Starry's Company. He was wounded in Oct. 1780 in his right arm at New Petersburgh. He lived in Herkimer, Montgomery Co., N.Y. 6 Oct. 1789. He also appeared as John Reima.

Rimby, Jacob. Pa. —. He was pensioned in Chester County 16 June 1836.

Rine, George. Pa. —. His widow, Catharine Rine, was granted relief in Allegheny County 18 Apr. 1853.

Rinehart, —. Pa. —. His widow, Ann Mary Rinehart, was awarded a $40 gratuity in Cumberland Co., Pa. 28 Feb. 1834.

Rinehart, George Simon. Pa. —. He applied in Cumberland County on 9 Jan. 1814. In the summer of 1775 he enlisted for three years in Capt. Phillip Gribble's Company. He also served under Capt. Myres. His next enlistment was under Capt. Walker for eight months. He found a substitute and was discharged by Lt. Col. North. He was at the taking of the Hessians at Trenton, Princeton, Germantown, and divers other skirmishes. He was 70 years old. He received a $40 gratuity and a $40 annuity in Nov. 1819. He was 94 years old in 1840 in Cumberland County. He also appeared as George Simon Rhinehart.

Ring, Jonathan. Mass. —. He served in the 5th Regiment and was from Worthington. He was paid $20. He served five years and was discharged with the badge of merit. He was divested of his reason and confined in chains for the last three years. He was incapable of making a declaration of his service as required the act of 1818. His wife was Hannah Ring. Congress awarded him a pension 24 Dec. 1818.

Ring, Michael. Pa. —. He was at Brandywine, Germantown, and Stony Point. He was from Bucks County. He died 19 Sep. 1815.

Ringle, —. N.Y. —. Catherine Ringle was granted support during the war.

Rinker, —. Pa. —. His widow, Gertrude Rinker, received a $40 gratuity and a $40 annuity in Northamptonborough, Lehigh County, 3 Apr. 1837.

Rinker, Edward. Va. —. His wife was furnished assistance in Loudoun Co., Va. on 14 Apr. 1778.

Ripley, Epaphras. —. —. His heirs sought relief 23 June 1854. They did not provide sufficient evidence of his service. Congress denied them relief 23 June 1854. They were from Vermont.

Ripley, John. Conn. Maj. He entered the service as a captain 6 July 1775 under Col. Jedediah Huntington and served to 18 Dec. 1776. He was under Col. Ward from May 1776 to 15 Feb. 1777. He became supernumerary in June 1778 but was called back into the service 11 June 1779. His heirs sought five years' commutation pay from Congress 17 Apr. 1858. He died in Windham, Conn.

Ripley, Peter. Pa. Matross. He was in Philadelphia County on 10 Apr. 1787. He served in Canada. His skull was fractured by a fall from the barracks at Fishkill in endeavoring to extinguish a fire in 1779 in same. He was at Charleston, S.C. and was sent from the hospital on James Island back to Philadelphia. He was in Capt. Jones' Company of Artillery. He also suffered from many fatigues. He was aged 40. He died 10 Nov. 1804.

Ripley, William. Mass. Drummer. He was at the Castle and was from Abington. He was paid $50.

Risden, Daniel. —. —. He was receiving everything he was entitled to receive so Congress saw no need for further action 14 June 1850.

Risdon, Zadock. Md. Pvt. He was pensioned in Prince George County at the rate of half-pay of a private 24 Feb. 1830. His arrearage was paid to Benjamin Riston and Cassandra Ann King, his children, 26 Mar. 1839. He also appeared as Zadock Riston and Zadock Risden.

Risner, Issac. S.C. —. His widow, Amy Risner, and children were placed on the pension list 12 Dec. 1818. She was pensioned as late as 1858.

Ristine, Charles. Pa. —. He was awarded a $40 gratuity in Philadelphia Co., Pa. 23 Apr. 1829.

Ritchie, —. Pa. —. His widow, Sarah Ritchie, was awarded a $40 gratuity and a $40 annuity in Fayette Co., Pa. 15 Apr. 1835.

Ritchie, Abraham. Va. —. His wife and three children were granted £3 per month support 20 Oct. 1777. His wife was granted further support in Yohogania Co., Va. 27 May 1779.

Ritchie, David. Pa. Pvt. He was awarded a $40 gratuity and a $40 annuity 26 Mar. 1813. He was on the 1813 pension list. He also appeared as David Richie. He was from Washington County.

Ritchie, William. Pa. Pvt. He was in Philadelphia County on 13 Feb. 1786. He served in the State Navy under Capt. William Brown and was blinded by powder flying in his eyes from a cannon. He was discharged 27 Nov. 1777. He was 31 years old. He was on the 1813 pension list.

Ritchie, William. Pa. Ens. He applied in Montgomery County on 24 May 1814. He served in Capt. Thomas Craig's Company under Col. William Baxter and was at the surrender of Fort Washington when he and William Crawford were taken prisoners on 16 Nov. 1776. They remained prisoners two and a half years. Capt. Nathaniel Vansant of Bucks County was also made a prisoner at the same time. The latter served under Capt. Robert McGaw.

Ritchie, William. Va. —. His wife and two children were granted support in Yohogania Co., Va. 20 Oct. 1777 at the rate of £2 per month.

Ritchy, Robert. Pa. Pvt. He applied in Cumberland County on 7 Jan. 1814. He enlisted in Apr. 1776 in Capt. Murray's Company attached to the 2nd Battalion of Riflemen under Col. Miles. The unit merged with the 1st Battalion to form the Pa. State Regiment under Col. Walter Stewart. He also appeared as Robert Ritchie. He died 17 Aug. 1825.

Rittenhouse, Jacob. Pa. —. He was awarded a $40 gratuity and a $40 annuity in Luzerne Co., Pa. 15 Jan. 1829. He was 82 years old in 1840.

Ritter, Johannes. N.Y. Pvt. He served in the militia under Col. Klock in the Tryon County militia and was slain 6 Aug. 1777. His orphans, Elizabeth Ritter, Henry Ritter, Frederick Ritter, Maria Ritter, and Maria Catharine Ritter, received his half-pay pension.

Ritter, Martin. Pa. —. He was awarded a $40 gratuity and a $40 annuity in Northumberland Co., Pa. 17 Mar. 1835.

Ritz, Matthias. Pa. —. He was awarded a $40 gratuity and a $40 annuity in York Co., Pa. 20 Feb. 1833. He was paid to 24 Mar. 1835.

Roach, John. Me. —. He died 22 Aug. 1828. His widow was Abigail Roach from Wilton. She was paid $50 under the resolve of 1836.

Roach, Thomas. Mass. Sgt. He was from New York and was paid $20. He served in the Artillery.

Roach, Littleberry. N.C. —. He served under Capt. William Jones. He was drafted in Orange Co., N.C. and served three months in the Cheraw Hills in South Carolina. He was also under Capt. Nathaniel Christmas and Col. Pacely. Mary Partain swore that she saw him out in the service in Orange County. His application was rejected by South Carolina.

Roads, —. Va. —. His orphans were pensioned.

Roane, Christopher. Va. Capt. His heirs received his commutation of full-pay for five years in lieu of half-pay as captain of artillery in the Virginia Line with no interest on 11 Feb. 1828. He was from Prince George County.

Roark, —. S.C. —. Charlotte Roark had her application rejected in Dec. 1837.

Roaser [?], Martin. Pa. —. He removed to Maryland.

Robards, Caleb. N.Y. —. He served under Col. Cortlandt. His wife, Sarah Robards, was granted support in 1778 and 1779 while he was away in the service.

Robb, John. N.H. Sgt. He resided in Stoddard. He was wounded on 16 Aug. 1777 at the battle of Bennington by two balls. An ounce ball passed through his shoulder. He had a buck shot in his ear. He served in Capt. Parker's Company under Col. Nichols. He was struck off the roll i n 1780. His pension ceased 21 July 1786 when he was reported dead. On 12 Mar. 1794 it was proved that he was very much alive; he was restored to the rolls. He also appeared as John Robbe. He later moved to Vermont.

Robb, Samuel. Pa. —. He served under Capt. William Armstrong and Col. William Montgomery in the Flying Camp. He was taken prisoner at Fort Washington. After his release he was a wagon master for three years. He was awarded a $40 gratuity and a $40 annuity in Butler County on 7 Mar. 1821. He also appeared as Samuel Rabb.

Robbins, Brintal. —. —. Congress awarded his widow, Mary Robbins of Westmoreland Co., Pa. the arrearage of her pension from 4 Mar. 1848 to 3 Feb. 1853 on 21 Feb. 1857.

Robbins, Daniel. Me. —. He was from Leeds. He was paid $50 under the resolve of 1836.

Robbins, David. N.H. Pvt. He served under Col. Reid in Capt. Hind's Company. He had eruptions over his body and great debility occasioned by the violent heat of the weather at the battle of Bunker Hill on 17 June 1775. He lived in Westmoreland, N.H. in 1795.

Robbins, Ebenezer. Mass. Corp. He served in the 4th Regiment and was from Oxford. His widow, Merribah Robbins, was paid $50.

Robbins, Eliphalet. Me. —. He was from Norridgewock. He was paid $50 under the resolve of 1836.

Robbins, Jeremiah. Mass. Pvt. He served in the 7th Regiment under Col. Alden and Capt. William H. Ballard. He was disabled by a cannon ball in his left thigh. He was pensioned at the rate of one-eighth pay of a soldier from 1 Jan. 1780 on 9 July 1784. He was pensioned in 1786. He resided in Suffolk Co., Mass. He was on the 1813 pension list.

Robbins, John. Md. Pvt. He was pensioned at the rate of half-pay of a private in Montgomery Co. on 7 Feb. 1818.

Robbins, John. Mass. Pvt. He served under Col. Thomas Brattle and Capt. John Parker. He was wounded by a musket ball on 19 Apr. 1775. His jaw bone was shattered, and his right arm was rendered almost useless. He had a wife and five children. He was pensioned at the rate of £13.6.8 per annum on 5 Nov. 1776. He was pensioned at the rate of half-pay from 19 Apr. 1781. His pension was increased by £26.13.4 above his pension for the year on 5 Oct. 1779 at which time he lived in Lexington. He was pensioned at the rate of £8 from 19 Apr. 1779 to 19 Apr. 1780. He was 48 years old in 1786.

Robbins, Moses. N.J. Pvt. He was pensioned at the rate of $40 per annum.

Robbins, Samuel. Mass. Pvt. He served in the 5th Regiment and was from Middleboro. He was paid $50.

Robbins, William. Mass. Pvt. He served in the 2nd Regiment and was from Plymouth.

Robbins, William. Va. —. He died in the service in 1776. His widow, Frances Robbins, and family were granted support in Prince Edward County in 1776. She was dead by Oct. 1784 at which time there were three children.

Robbinson, Isaac. Mass. —. He served in the 2nd Regiment and was paid $20.

Robbe, John. —. —. He was pensioned 4 June 1794.

Robenold, John. Pa. —. He was awarded a $40 gratuity and a $40 annuity in Lehigh Co., Pa. 29 Mar. 1824. He also appeared as John Rebenold and John Rabenold.

Roberts, —. Va. —. His wife, Elizabeth Roberts, was granted £25 support in Caroline Co., Va. 14 Jan. 1779 while he was in the service.

Roberts, —. Va. —. He and his brother were in the service. Their mother, Ann Roberts, was furnished £20 support in Caroline Co., Va. in May 1779.

Roberts, —. Conn. Capt. He served in the militia in New York and was discharged 6 Sep. 1776 after 23 days of service due to illness. He died in Dec. 1789 by falling down a flight of stairs. His widow, Ruth Roberts, had her claim rejected.

Roberts, Abraham. S.C. —. His annuity was £1 in 1787.

Roberts, Benjamin. Va. Capt. He served in the state line and became supernumerary. He was due half-pay from 22 Apr. 1783 and received $1,415.33.

Roberts, Edward. Pa. —. He was awarded a $40 gratuity and a $40 annuity in Montgomery Co., Pa. 11 Feb. 1834. Application was made for his three children in Montgomery County 24 June 1836. He had no widow.

Roberts, Jesse. —. —. He was pensioned under the act of 1832 at the rate of $68 per annum. Congress rejected his request for an increase 9 Jan. 1847.

Roberts, John. Conn. Trumpeter. He served under Sheldon in the 2nd Dragoons. He was ruptured by a violent cold and blowing the trumpet in the service. He resided in New Hartford, Conn. in 1792. He enlisted 13 Jan. 1777 and was discharged 1 May 1779.

Roberts, John. S.C. —. He served under Capt. Daniel Morral and was wounded in a skirmish with the Tories at Bear Bluff on the Waccamaw River by a musket ball which entered below his right breast and through his body. He had a large family. He lived in All Saints Parish, Horry District. He was pensioned 10 Dec. 1794 from 1 Jan. 1792. He was paid as late as 1834.

Roberts, John. Va. Surgeon. He served as early as Jan. 1776 and was soon promoted to surgeon. He was in the 6th Regiment. He died 19 Feb. 1827. Francis Lloyd was administrator. Congress refused to grant his heirs five years' full-pay because he left the service seven months too early on 4 Apr. 1840. Congress allowed his heirs the half-pay for life to which he was entitled on 18 Jan. 1861.

Roberts, John. Va. Capt. He served in the artillery from Culpeper County. His widow, Lucy Ann Roberts, died 6 Oct. 1863. His daughter, Elizabeth (Roberts) Strother was nearly 80. Congress granted her a pension 28 Jan. 1895.

Roberts, John. Va. Maj. He served in the Virginia Line on Continental Establishment. He became a major in Mar. 1779 and served as late as Sep. 1781. He served under Col. James Wood and discharged various duties in relation to Saratoga prisoners. He never resigned. He received his five years' full pay in lieu of half-pay for life 25 May 1832. He died 30 Nov. 1843. His widow died *ca.* 1863. His daughter, Isabella V. Jett, of Washington, Rappahannock County was granted relief by Congress in 1895. She was over 70.

Roberts, Joseph. N.H. Carpenter. He resided in Somersworth in 1784. He was aged 21 on 16 July 1779. He lost an arm at Penobscot on 19 Aug. 1779. He was a carpenter aboard the *Hampden* under Titus Salter, commander. He was under the care of Ivory Hovey aboard the vessel. He lived at Berwick, Me. in 1792. He was on the 1813 pension list.

Roberts, Joseph. Pa. Pvt. His widow was in Huntingdon County 9 Sep. 1794. He served in Capt. William Philips' Company in the Bedford County Rangers militia. He was killed 16 July 1780 by Indians at a station or fort in Woodcock Valley in Bedford County. He was 40 years old. His widow, Agnes Roberts, married ----- Berry 24 Mar. 1783. His children were Ann Roberts born 23 Apr. 1767, Jemima Roberts born 17 Mar. 1773, Mary Roberts born 5 Mar. 1776, and Levi Roberts born 9 Feb. 1779. Their guardians were William Philips and Thomas Wilson on 9 Sep. 1794.

Roberts, Martin. Va. Pvt. He enlisted in Chesterfield County in the spring of 1776 under Capt. Ralph Faulkner and Col. Josiah Parker in the 5th Regiment. He was appointed forage master in 1778 with the rank of captain. He served under Timothy Pickering to the end of the war. He died 30 Oct. 1834. He had been pensioned at the level of a private because he was unable to prove his service as forage master. He married Elizabeth ----- 10 May 1777 in Kent Co., Md. She died 19 Oct. 1840. His sons found proof of their father's service among the papers of Pickering. The son, John Roberts, was then deceased. The sons sought his arrearage. James Roberts, Noah Roberts, and John Roberts were paid his $600 arrearage in 1854. They brought suit in the court of claims in 1857. When the rebellion broke out, they were unable to come north. In Dec. 1863 the case was ordered off the docket for failure to prosecute. At the close of the war the sons petitioned Congress and learned that the statute of limitation had expired. They bore faith to the Union. Congress granted them relief 16 Mar. 1878.

Roberts, Nathan. Pa. —. He was awarded a $40 gratuity and a $40 annuity in Mercer County in Apr. 1829.

Roberts, Owen. S.C. Col. He died in the service at Stono Ferry, S.C. 20 June 1779. He was in the artillery. His widow, Anne Roberts, sought seven years' half-pay from the date of his death from the general government 3 Mar. 1791. She was to receive same unless South Carolina had paid her the pension she was entitled.

Roberts, Peter. S.C. —. He was pensioned in Abbeville District 30 Nov. 1827. He was paid as late as 1834.

Roberts, Philip. S.C. —. He served under Col. Baxter and Capt. Amos Wyndham. He suffered from severe rheumatism. He was 58 years old and had a wife. His ankle was dislocated. He was pensioned in Richland District on 25 Nov. 1830. Gabriel Clements and Thomas Farmer deposed anent his service.

Roberts, Reubin. —. —. He sought relief in land from the state of Tennessee in 1827.

Roberts, Samuel. N.J. —. He served in Capt. Howell's Company of the 1st Regiment on 11 March 1777 and was returned dead 24 October. He was killed in action at Germantown. His last words were "I am a dead man." He was married to Elizabeth Bedell 8 Dec. 1766 at North Providence by Jonathan Elmer. She sought his half-pay in Essex County.

Roberts, Thomas Pa. —. His widow, Catharine Roberts, was awarded a $40 gratuity and a $40 annuity 14 Apr. 1828 in Philadelphia.

Roberts, Thomas. Pa. Sgt. He served in the 4th Regiment of Light Dragoons under Col. Stephen Moylan. He was from Lancaster County. He died 12 Oct. 1821.

Roberts, William. Md. Pvt. He was pensioned at the rate of half-pay of a private in Allegany Co. 23 Jan. 1816. His widow, Jane Roberts, was pensioned at the same rate 4 Mar. 1834. She was paid his arrearage of $1.11 on 9 Mar. 1835. Her arrearage of $9.89 for 2 months and 29 days was paid to Mary Roberts 26 Mar. 1839.

Roberts, William. Va. —. His child was granted support in Westmoreland County in Apr. 1779.

Roberts, Zacheriah. Md. Corp. He was pensioned at the rate of half-pay of a corporal on 24 Feb. 1823. Payment was to be made to Peter Levering of Baltimore.

Robertson, —. N.C. —. His widow, Jemima Robertson, applied in Warren County in 1803. Her husband died in militia service.

Robertson, Francis. R.I. Pvt. He lost the use of his arm by a fall in Nov. 1779 on duty under Col. Christopher Greene. He was aged 36 when he applied on 29 Dec. 1785. He lived in Providence Co., R.I.

Robertson, Hartwell. Va. Pvt. He served in the 4th Va. Regiment and died in the service. His widow, Lucy Robertson, was granted £42.12.6 relief on 11 Mar. 1779 in Southampton Co. She still lived in Southampton Co. 13 Nov. 1786. She had no children but did have an aged parent. He also appeared as Hartwell Robinson.

Robertson, Henry. N.C. —. He entered from Halifax Co., N.C. and served under Capt. Flewellyn and Capt. Richard Ransom of Franklin Co., N.C. He was wounded in the head at Camden and taken prisoner. He never fully recovered and died in 1789. His widow was Mary Robertson, and she married secondly Peter Robertson. They removed to South Carolina in 1796. She had two children by her first husband and four children by the second. She was from Edgefield District in 1839 and was above 73 years of age.

Robertson, Isaac. S.C. —. He was paid $192.66 as a soldier on 20 Dec. 1810.

Robertson, James. Va. Pvt. He lived in Prince William County. He was 30 years old in 1787. He served in Grayson's Regiment. He was on the 1813 pension list.

Robertson, John. N.Y. —. He was granted relief.

Robertson, Peter. N.H. Pvt. He served under Capt. Archelaus Town in 1775 and lost his right hand by a cannon ball at the battle of Bunker Hill 17 June 1775. Thomas Kitt, regimental surgeon under Col. Fry, amputated his hand. He had been in the colony but a few years. He also served under Capt. John Stark. All of his relations and friends lived in England. He was aged 42 in 1787. He was a tailor but could not provide for his family. He died 31 Jan. 1807. He also appeared as Peter Robinson. He was from Amherst.

Robertson, Robert. Mass. —. He served in the 2nd Regiment and was paid $20.

Robertson, Robert. N.J. Lt. He was wounded at Germantown 4 Oct. 1777. He was pensioned at the rate of $120 per annum.

Robertson, Robert. N.Y. Pvt. He served in Capt. Henry Dubois's Company under Col. Philip Van Cortlandt. He lost the use of his limbs due to sickness. He was 41 years old in 1786 and lived in Albany, N.Y. on 27 May 1789. He was on the 1813 pension list.

Robertson, Thomas. N.C./S.C. —. He was born in 1753 in Amherst Co., Va. He moved to Rutherford

Co., N.C. and served 14 months in S.C. He enlisted in 1776 under Felix Walker and Lt. Conyers. He marched to Charleston and was enrolled under Capt. Richardson in the 5th S.C. Regiment under Col. Isaac Huger. He was also at Savannah, Ga. He was discharged in 1777 and returned to N.C. His children were grown and gone from home. His wife was blind. His application of 18 Oct. 1830 was rejected because it was not vouchered.

Robertson, William. S.C. Capt. He served under Commodore Alexander Gillon on the *South Carolina*. He was due £150 on 29 Nov. 1794. He was from Charleston.

Robins, John. Va. Lt. He served in the 9th Regiment and in the 5th Regiment. He became supernumerary and died shortly after the termination of the war. Congress awarded his heirs his commutation 2 Jan. 1834.

Robins, Moses. N.J. Pvt. He served under Capt Huddy in the State Troops. He was wounded in the eye through the head. He was 55 years old and was from Dover, Bergen Co. He was on the 1791 pension roll.

Robinson, —. Pa. Col. His widow, Grizzel Robinson, was in Bucks County in May 1794.

Robinson, —. Va. —. His wife, Mary Robinson, was granted £12 support in Fauquier Co., Va. in Mar. 1778.

Robinson, —. Va. —. He died in Continental service. His widow, Ruth Robinson, was granted £39.5 in Brunswick Co., Va. 23 Aug. 1779.

Robinson, Andrew. N.Y. —. His wife and child were granted support on 3 Nov. 1781 in Dutchess County.

Robinson, Andrew. Pa. Lt. He served in the 11th Pa. Regiment. He sought five years' full-pay rather than half-pay for life in 1793.

Robinson, Charles. Md. Pvt. He was pensioned 4 Mar. 1789. He was on the 1813 pension list.

Robinson, Charles. Va. Pvt. He was in Ohio County 10 May 1787. He served in the 7th Va. Regiment. He was wounded in his right arm. He applied to Brigadier General William Irvine, commander of Fort Pitt, for a discharge rather than being transferred to the Invalid Corps on 27 Nov. 1782. He was 50 years old. It was also stated that he served in the 13th Va. Regiment. He was put on the pension list at the rate of £10 per annum on 16 June 1789. He was on the 1813 pension list as Charles Robertson.

Robinson, Dewalt. Pa. —. He was awarded a $40 gratuity and a $40 annuity in York Co., Pa. 23 Jan. 1833.

Robinson, Eber. —. —. He served more than seven years. He married 12 Sep. 1804. His widow, Lucinda Robinson, of Orleans Co., Vt. received her arrearage from 4 Mar. 1848 to 3 Feb. 1853 from Congress 20 Feb. 1857.

Robinson, George. Pa. Sgt. He served in the Congress Regiment. He was wounded by an accidental fall by which he dislocated his left shoulder in endeavoring to assist a sick soldier at Lancaster barracks in Mar. 1778. He was discharged as unfit for duty. He had no residence and wandered about the country begging charity. He enlisted in Jan. 1777 and was discharged 15 June 1777. He lived in Pa. in 1794. He was on the 1813 pension list.

Robinson, George. —. —. He had to leave to withdraw his application 21 Feb. 1812.

Robinson, Hugh. Pa. —. He was awarded a $40 gratuity in Perry Co., Pa. 20 Apr. 1829.

Robinson, Isaac. Mass. Fifer. He served in the 4th Regiment.

Robinson, Isaac. N.J. Pvt. He was on the 1791 pension roll at the rate of $20 per annum. He lost the sight of one eye by the stroke of a limb of a tree while cutting wood for the Jersey Brigade. He lost the sight in the other eye by inflamation of the said stroke. He applied from Sussex

County 21 June 1784. He served in the 4ᵗʰ Regiment and was 55 years old. He also appeared as Isaac Robertson.

Robinson, James. Pa. —. He was awarded a $40 gratuity and a $40 annuity in Beaver Co., Pa. 15 Apr. 1835. He received a $40 gratuity in 1840. He died 7 Aug. 1842.

Robinson, James. Pa. —. He died in Mercer County in Sep. 1843.

Robinson, James. Va. —. His family was granted support in Brunswick Co., Va. on 23 Nov. 1778 while he was away in Continental service. [Compare with the entry for the widow Ruth Robinson *supra*.]

Robinson, James. Va. Pvt. He was in Shenandoah County when he was pensioned at the rate of £8 per annum on 23 July 1787. He served in Capt. Francis Mills' Company under Col. William Grayson in the 16ᵗʰ Va. Regiment. He was wounded in his left arm and in his hip at Brandywine. His leg was broken. He was 36 years old. He moved from Bath Co., Va. to Shelby Co., Ky. before 28 Aug. 1799. He died 13 Dec. 1805, and his executors were Elizabeth Robinson, John Sawyers, and Stephen Allen, Jr.

Robinson, John. Pa. —. He was awarded $134.81 in Fayette County on 18 Mar. 1814. He was on the 1813 pension list. He also appeared as John Robison.

Robinson, John. Pa. —. His widow was alive 19 May 1838. He served under Col. Broadhead and Commissary Butcher.

Robinson, Matthew. Pa. Pvt. He was pensioned.

Robinson, Michael. Pa. —. He was awarded a $40 gratuity and a $40 annuity in Cumberland Co., Pa. 20 Mar. 1834.

Robinson, Noah. N.H. Lt. He served in the N.H. Continental Line. He lived in Stafford Co., N.H. He was on the 1813 pension list. Congress awarded his widow, Rosamond Robinson of Belknap Co., N.H. the arrearage of her pension from 4 Mar. 1848 to 3 Feb. 1853 on 21 Feb. 1857.

Robinson, Prince. Vt. Pvt. He was on the 1813 pension list. He lived in Rutland Co., Vt.

Robinson, Robert. Mass. —. He served in the 2ⁿᵈ Regiment and was from Vermont.

Robinson, Robert. N.C. Pvt. He served three months in Gen. Lillington's Brigade under Capt. Sharp and Col. Frederick Hambright, five months under Capt. William Alexander and Wagonmaster James Orr, and three months under Gen. William Davidson with his wagon and team. He applied in Mecklenburg County in 1827.

Robinson, Standly. Md. Pvt. He was pensioned in Baltimore at the rate of half-pay of a private 25 Feb. 1824.

Robinson, Stephen. Va. —. His wife, Mary Ann Robinson, was granted £10 support in Bedford County on 28 Mar. 1778.

Robinson, Stephen. Va. —. His wife, Maryan Robinson, and two children were granted support in Greenbrier County 20 Mar. 1781.

Robinson, Thomas. Pa. Capt. His wife was Mary Robinson.

Robinson, William. —. Seaman & Gunner's Mate. He served on private armed ships in 1779-80, 1781, and 1782. Congress found that there was no law under which his claim could be sustained 10 Feb. 1836.

Robinson, William. S.C. —. He was wounded by a ball through his left shoulder at Hanging Rock. He was granted an annuity 8 Jan. 1785. He served in the militia. He resided in York District. He was paid as late as 1834.

Robinson, Zophar. Conn. —. He entered the service 4 Apr. 1777 for three years at Windham, Conn. and served to 4 Feb. 1780. He enlisted again 25 Feb. 1781 under Col. Durkee for three years and was slain 3 Mar. 1782 on service as a picket guard. His widow was Charity Robinson had been insane from 1831. His son-in-law and daughter, Elias and Chloe Burnham, sought to obtain a pension for the widow by a special act of Congress. Congress ruled that the widow was covered by pension laws in effect so rejected their petition 24 May 1838.

Robison, James. Va. —. He served in the 16th Virginia Regiment and was wounded in the arm and hip. He was recommended for a pension in Frederick Co., Va. on 1 Apr. 1783. [Compare with James Robinson.]

Robison, Robert. Pa. —. His widow, Rachel Robison, of Miami Co., Ohio, received a $40 annuity 13 Apr. 1859.

Robosson, Charles. Md. 1st Lt. His widow, Rebecca Robosson, was pensioned at the rate of a first lieutenant in the army in Baltimore 27 Jan. 1839.

Roby, John. Md. Pvt. He was pensioned at the rate of half-pay of a private 23 Jan. 1816.

Roch, John P. Pa. —. He was awarded a $40 gratuity and a $40 annuity in Baltimore, Md. 31 Mar. 1836. He died in 1836.

Roche, Thomas. —. —. He was pensioned.

Rochefermois, Matthew Alexis de. France. Brig. Gen. His sole heir, Madame A. Bon Bernard, was granted his pay 19 May 1874. He had never been paid.

Rock, John. Va. —. He was away in Continental service. His wife, Mary Rock, was allowed provision for herself and her children in Augusta Co., Va. 15 Oct. 1782.

Rock, Patrick. Pa. Pvt. He was in Philadelphia County 13 Feb. 1786. He was in the 9th Pa. Regiment in Capt. McClennan's Company. He was wounded by buck shot in his thigh and rendered incapable of getting a livelihood by labor. He was discharged in 1783. He also appeared as Patrick Roch and Peter Rook.

Rockhill, William. N.J. Sgt. He served in the 4th Regiment and was disabled by a rupture. He was 53 years old. He was on the 1791 pension roll at the rate of $20 per annum. He also appeared as William Rockwell.

Rockwell, Merrit. Conn. Pvt. He was wounded in the shoulder. He was pensioned 29 Aug. 1782. He died 22 Apr. 1800.

Rockwood, Frost. Mass. —. He was from Worcester and was paid $50.

Rodamer, Christopher. Pa. —. He applied in Montgomery County on 5 Mar. 1829. He was a native of Pottstown, Pa. He enlisted in Capt. Skull's Company under Col. Craig. He was 80 years old.

Rodden, Benjamin. Va. —. His wife, Keziah Rodden, was furnished 4 barrels of corn and 200 pounds of pork in Essex Co., Va. on 25 May 1781 and on 20 May 1782.

Roddenwall, Frederick. S.C. —. He served aboard the *South Carolina*. He was paid $38.28 balance due on the portage ball 19 Oct. 1810.

Roden, —. Pa. —. His widow, Mary Roden, was granted support in Mercer County 21 July 1842.

Roderfield, William. Mass. —. He served in the 3rd Artillery and was from Philadelphia. He was paid $20.

Rodering, William. Va. —. His pension was £12 in Frederick Co., Va. in 1788.

Rodes, —. Pa. —. His widow, Catherine Rodes, was awarded a $40 gratuity and a $40 annuity in Philadelphia Co., Pa. 6 Apr. 1830.

Rodes, Mark. Pa.—. He received $300 in lieu of donation land 10 Apr. 1826. He was from Philadelphia.

Rodewalt, George F. S.C. —. He served aboard the frigate *South Carolina* as an officer. He and John Dutteile sought interest on the balances due them of 1 Dec. 1808.

Rodgers, John. S.C. Capt. He served under Col. James Williams against the Cherokee Indians in

1776 and 1777. His indent had been drawn by an imposter. He had loaned money to Gen. Williamson to buy provisions. Commissary Lusk received the money. He brought suit against Lusk but received nothing. He was 79 years old in 1819 and was from Laurens District. He was pensioned 4 Dec. 1832. He was paid as late as 1848.

Rodgers, Joseph. S.C. —. He served under Capt. Benjamin Hall. John Knight deposed about his service. He was 70 years old. He was at Gates' defeat under Capt. Weathers. He was disabled by the dead palsy. He was pensioned in Laurens District 17 Dec. 1831. He was paid as late as 1834.

Rodgers, Shadrack. S.C. —. He served under Capt. James. He was pensioned in Sumter District 25 Nov. 1830. Reuben Brown of Kershaw District served 14 months with him. He died 7 Oct. 1832. His wife was Celia Rodgers, and she died 7 Aug. 1844. His children, two daughters and a son, sought his arrearage from the time of his death to that of their mother. She died 7 Aug. 1844. They were paid in 1851.

Rodin, Frederick. Pa. —. He was granted relief 17 Jan. 1831 in Niagara Co., N.Y.

Roe, Michael. Pa. —. He was pensioned from 4 Sep. 1797 in Somerset Co., Md. He was on the 1813 pension list.

Roe, Nathaniel. N.Y. —. He was disabled. He lived in Orange Co., N.Y. on 26 June 1788.

Roe, William. S.C. —. There was one child in 1791.

Roebuck, William. Va. Pvt. His widow, Mary Roebuck, was in Culpeper County on 17 Apr. 1787. He was in the Culpeper County militia and died at the siege of York leaving a widow and five small children. He had two old Negroes and 375 acres. He died of smallpox. His wife lost her mind in grief over the death of her husband. She and her children were under the care of her father, Richard Vernon, who was 83 years old. The parents of William Roebuck lived a great distance away and were ancient. She was put on the pension list on 15 Oct. 1787 at the rate of £15 per annum. She was in Madison County in 1794. Administration on her estate was granted to Robert Thomas, Sheriff, 28 Oct. 1826.

Roemer, —. Pa. —. His widow, Elizabeth Roemer, received relief in Franklin County 18 Feb. 1839.

Roemer, Philip. Pa. —. He was awarded a $40 gratuity and a $40 annuity in Franklin Co., Pa. 9 Mar. 1825. He died 21 Aug.1832.

Roeser, Adam Frederick. Pa. —. He was awarded a $40 gratuity and a $40 annuity in Westmoreland Co., Pa. 3 Mar. 1824.

Roger, —. Pa. —. His widow, Anna Roger, was granted relief 10 Mar. 1849 in Westmoreland County. She died 27 Oct. 1854.

Rogers, —. Pa. —. His widow, Jane Rogers, was awarded a $40 gratuity and a $40 annuity in Lancaster Co., Pa. 29 Mar. 1824.

Rogers, Ahaz. S.C. —. He was from Chesterfield District in 1793. He received his annuity in 1819 and in 1824 sought an increase. He was paid as late as 1834.

Rogers, Bryant. S.C. Fifer. He served under Gen. Francis Marion and Gen. Benjamin Smith of N.C. He suffered from a paralytic stroke and had lost the use of his limbs. He was 66 years old with a wife and six children. He was from Williamsburg District and was pensioned 14 Dec. 1822. He was paid as late as 1827.

Rogers, George. Pa. —. He served under Capt. Zantzinger in the Flying Camp. He subsequently served under Capt. Clark and Col. Cunningham. He was awarded a $40 gratuity and a $40 annuity in Lancaster Co., Pa. 19 Feb. 1823. He died 14 Apr. 1823.

Rogers, Giles. S.C. Legionnaire. He served aboard the frigate *South Carolina*. His administrator,

Nathan Bowen, was paid $103.80 on 10 May 1809.

Rogers, Hezekiah. —. Maj. He entered as a captain. He left a widow, Esther Rogers, and two children. There were three grandchildren. He had served as a clerk in the War Department until he died. Congress rejected the claim of his widow for a pension 22 Jan. 1821.

Rogers, Humphrey. N.C. Pvt. He applied in Anson County in 1794. He served in the militia under Col. Thomas Wade and was wounded in his head and hand by a sword in 1781 at Betty's Bridge on Drowning Creek. John Pemberton swore he saw him in camp as a soldier and James Redfearn saw him as a prisoner of the Tories. He was on the 1813 pension list.

Rogers, Jacob. Pa. Pvt. He applied 2 Jan. 1788. He served in the 11ᵗʰ Pa. Regiment under Col. Richard Humpton. He was wounded in his back and knee at Brandywine. He was made a prisoner, his wounds were neglected, and he became disabled. He was 25 years old. He was on the 1813 pension list. He also appeared as Jacob Rogen and Jacob Rodgers. He was from Morris Co., N.J.

Rogers, Jacob. S.C. —. He served in the 11ᵗʰ Regiment. There were children in 1791.

Rogers, James. N.J. Ens. He served in the Jersey Regiment under Col. Elias Dayton and died 24 Aug. 1780 at Basking Ridge from a wound received at Springfield. He had enlisted in the brigade and served as sergeant major until promoted 1 Feb. 1779. His widow, Sarah Rogers, sought his half-pay in Essex County in Apr. 1783.

Rogers, James. Va. Pvt. He was pensioned at the rate of half-pay during his disability on 6 Oct. 1785. He was in St. George Parish in Accomack County on 21 May 1787. He served in Levin Joyner's Company in the 9ᵗʰ Va. Regiment. He enlisted in Feb. 1777 and was wounded in his right leg at Germantown 4 Oct. 1777. He was 29 years old. He was continued on the pension list at the rate of £12 per annum on 21 May 1787. He was on 1813 pension list.

Rogers, Jedediah. —. —. He had been a pensioner. His widow, Sarah Rogers, sought a pension, but Congress rejected her claim on 4 Feb. 1837 because they were married after the war.

Rogers, John. Mass. —. He served in the 3ʳᵈ Regiment and was from Plymouth. He was paid $20.

Rogers, John. Mass. —. He was from Williamsburgh and was paid $50. He served in the 9ᵗʰ Regiment.

Rogers, John. N.Y. Pvt. He served under Col. Meigs. He was wounded in his left leg by a musket ball which passed through same and cut off one of the sinews in Nov. 1779 in Hackensack, N.J. He lived in Stephentown, N.Y. in 1794. He enlisted 27 Feb. 1777 for the war. He was on the rolls in 1781. He was granted half a pension 20 Apr. 1796. He was on the 1813 pension list.

Rogers, John. Va. —. He served in the cavalry in Illinois. He sought half-pay for life in 1790, but his application was rejected. He was the son of George Rogers.

Rogers, Joseph. S.C. —. He was killed at Fishing Creek 11 Sep. 1781. His widow, Eleanor Rogers, was from Claremont County. There were seven children born 12 Oct. 1771, 6 Feb. 1774, 13 Mar. 1776, 27 Dec. 1777, twins 27 Jan. 1779, and 31 Mar. 1781. The youngest died at the age of 6 years and 11 months. By mistake Benjamin O'Neal represented that he was a Tory and killed while a prisoner of the Americans. That individual was a different person of the same name. The applicant was pensioned from 1 Apr. 1792. In 1793 she stated that she supported nine children.

Rogers, Oliver. Conn. Pvt. He served on the frigate *Confederacy* under Capt. Seth Harding. He was wounded by the accidental discharge of a musket and wholly lost the use of two fingers and his wrist. He was attended by Phineas Hyde, Surgeon Mate and Master at Arms, on board the ship. He was pensioned 18 July 1787 at Windham at the age of 39. He was on the 1813 pension list.

Rogers, Solomon. Va. —. His widow, Sarah Rogers, and two children were awarded £15 in Northampton Co., Va. That amount was increased to £50 on 8 Dec. 1778.

Rogers, Stephen. Mass. Matross & Artificer. He served in Capt. Noah Nicholas' Company under Gen. H. Knox. He was ruptured and rendered unfit for service. He was pensioned at a third of his pay from 22 Jan. 1780 on 14 Apr. 1780. He was 57 years old in 1787. He died 18 Nov. 1805.

Rogers, Thomas. Pa. —. His widow, Elizabeth Rogers, was in Chester County on 30 Sep. 1782. He was in Capt. William Peebles' Company of Riflemen and was taken prisoner on Long Island. He died in New York.

Rogers, Ulysses. Va. —. He served in the 6th Virginia Regiment. He was wounded in his thigh at Fort Mifflin during the service. He was awarded a £30 gratuity and an annuity of half-pay for six years on 17 Oct. 1778.

Rogers, William. Mass. —. He was paid $20.

Rogers, William. Md. Pvt. He was pensioned 4 Mar. 1789. He was on the 1813 pension list.

Rogers, William. Va. Capt. He served in the 4th Regiment and served seven years and eight months having served to the end of the war. He settled in Virginia 17 June 1783 and charged pay to Mar. 1781 but no longer. Congress ruled that his heirs, Sarah B. Potts and Priscilla B. Harman, were not entitled to relief on 19 May 1834. They had received bounty land from Virginia for seven years and eight months of service.

Roheson, Isaac. N.J. Pvt. He was pensioned at the rate of $20 per annum.

Rohn, Christopher. Pa. —. He was awarded a $40 gratuity and a $40 annuity in Philadelphia Co., Pa. 1 Apr. 1823.

Rohrer, —. Pa. —. His widow, Elizabeth Rohrer, was awarded a $40 gratuity and a $40 annuity in Philadelphia Co., Pa. 15 Apr. 1835. She also appeared as Elizabeth Roher. She died 4 Sep. 1841.

Rohrer, John. Pa. Pvt. He was awarded a $40 gratuity and a $40 annuity 7 Apr. 1830 in Lebanon Co., Pa.

Roke, Hugh. Va. —. His wife and children were granted support in 1779. They were from Amelia County.

Roland, —. Pa. —. His widow, Christiana Roland, was granted relief in Lebanon County 5 Apr. 1842.

Roland, Jacob. Pa. —. He was granted a $40 gratuity and a $40 annuity in Lebanon County 3 Apr. 1841.

Roland, William. Va. Pvt. His widow, Mary Roland, was in Sussex County in Dec. 1787. He served in the 15th Va. Regiment and died in the service. His widow was alive in 1789. She also appeared as Mary Rolling and Mary Rowland.

Rolf, Jeremiah. Me. —. He was from Abbot. He was paid $50 under the resolve of 1836.

Roll, Matthias. N.J. Pvt. In the spring of 1826 his bounty land warrant was delivered to his agent, John Woods, who lost warrant #1164. Congress authorized a duplicate 17 Jan. 1828.

Rolle, Robert. Md. Lt. He was pensioned in Talbot County at the rate of half-pay of a lieutenant 13 Mar. 1829.

Rollins, Aaron. —. —. His widow, Catherine Rollins alias Moody, sought her husband's back pension from 1816 to 1842. Congress refused her petition 11 Jan. 1845.

Rollins, Moses. Va. —. He was pensioned in Harrison County 19 Jan. 1813 at the rate of $60 per annum. He had been shot through the thigh at Guilford Courthouse. His pension was increased to $100 per annum on 1 Feb. 1816. He was in Wood County in 1822 and Ritchie County in 1851. He was still alive 1 Feb. 1856.

Roney, Maurice. S.C. —. He was wounded at Eutaw. He was also at Guilford. He was pensioned in Richland District 17 Dec. 1819. He died 31 Jan. 1825. His widow, Mary Roney, was pensioned at the rate of $30 per annum on 9 Dec. 1825. She was 65 years old. She also appeared as Mary Rhoney. She was paid as late as 1831. He also appeared as Morris Rone.

Rood, John. Conn. Pvt. He served in Col. Gold Selleck Silliman's Regiment in Capt. Reuben Bostwick's Company under Lt. Isaac Deforrest. and was disabled at White Plains by being wounded by a musket ball passing through his thigh on 28 Oct. 1776. He was pensioned 4 May 1787 at New Milford, Conn. at the age of 33. In 1789 he was from Brookfield. He was on the 1813 pension list. He died 4 Apr. 1827.

Roods, Edward. Va. —. His wife, Prudence Roods, was furnished support in Charlotte County 6 Sep. 1779 and 6 Mar. 1780. She had a family of five children 4 Dec. 1780 and six on 5 Mar. 1781.

Rooke, Hugh. Va. —. His wife and family were granted support in Amelia Co., Va. 22 July 1779 and 25 Nov. 1779 while he was away in Continental service. He also appeared as Hugh Roke.

Root, Abraham. Mass. —. He served in the 8th Regiment and was from New York. He was paid $20.

Rorer, —. Pa. —. His widow, Elizabeth Rorer, was granted relief in Lebanon County 8 Apr. 1840. She was dead by Aug. 1842.

Rosa, Jacobus. N.Y. Capt. He served in the militia under Col. McClaghrey. He was killed at Fort Montgomery 6 Oct. 1777. His children, Mary Rosa, Simeon Rosa, Deborah Rosa, and ----- Rosa, received his half-pay pension.

Rosburgh, John. N.J. Pvt. He was on the 1791 pension roll.

Rose, —. Va. —. Thomas Rose was granted £20 support in Caroline Co., Va. in Feb. 1779. He had two sons absent in the service.

Rose, Abner. Mass. Matross. He served under Capt. Thomas Peirce and Col. Mason. He was disabled by the bursting of a cannon which wounded him in his right foot and leg. He was pensioned 10 July 1786. He was on the 1813 pension list. He died 16 July 1829 in Hampden Co., Mass. His widow, Abigail Rose, lived at Westfield when she was paid $50 by the Commonwealth.

Rose, Alexander. Va. Capt. He served in the 6th Regiment from Mar. 1776. He served from 17 Sep. 1776 to 3 Sep. 1778. He received bounty land for 4,000 acres for three years service 11 Nov. 1785, for 666 2/3 acres for a seventh year 20 Feb. 1807, and for 444 acres for eight months on 1 Sep. 1807. He died in 1814. One of his representatives in 1836 was Ann R. Rose. Congress granted Virginia Rose and the other heirs his commutation 30 May 1860.

Rose, Benjamin. —. —. He married in 1806. His widow, Susannah Rose, had her request for a pension denied by Congress 19 Sep. 1850.

Rose, Edward. Md. Pvt. He served in the militia. He was pensioned in Frederick County in 1786. He was wounded in New Jersey.

Rose, Elijah. Mass. —. He served in the 4th Regiment and was from New York. He was paid $20.

Rose, Enoch. Mass. —. He served in the 4th Regiment and was paid $20.

Rose, James. N.Y. —. He was awarded 200 acres bounty land 19 June 1812.

Rose, James. Va. —. He was pensioned in Lee County 15 Mar. 1831 at the rate of $60 per annum with $30 immediate relief. He was in Russell County in 1838 and King George County in 1842. He died 11 Nov. 1842. Administration with the will annexed was granted to William Rowley 2 Mar. 1843.

Rose, John. —. —. Congress accepted four months of service but rejected the balance because it was rendered after the war closed. His petition for a pension was, therefore, rejected 27 Mar.1846.

Rose, John. S.C. —. He received an annuity 11 Jan. 1834.

Rose, Reuben. Va. Pvt. His wife, Patty Rose, was granted £24 support while her husband was in the service on 11 Nov. 1779. His widow lived in Caroline County 3 Apr. 1787. He died in the service. She had four children to support. She was continued on the pension roll 7 Apr. 1787 at the rate of £8 per annum and again on 27 June 1790.

Rose, Thomas. Va. —. His wife, Jean Rose, was granted £50 support 27 July 1779 in Bedford County.

Roseberry, John M. —. —.The allegations he made were not supported by proof. Congress rejected his claim for a pension 19 July 1848. He was from Mason Co.,Va. He was wounded in his side at Germantown. He received a serious injury in his shoulder in breaking down an old bridge while aiding in conveying cannon in the retreat of Greene's army after the siege of Ninety Six. Congress granted him a pension of $4 per month 13 Mar. 1850 from 13 Mar. 1844. He also appeared as John M. Rosebury.

Rosebrough, —. Pa. —. His widow, Rachel Rosebrough, was awarded a $40 gratuity and a $40 annuity in Huntingdon Co., Pa. 4 May 1832. She died 3 Aug. 1832.

Roseburg, John. Pa. Chaplain. His widow, Jean Roseburg, was in Northampton County 17 May 1788. He was in the Northampton County militia under Col. John Siegfried. He was 55 years old when he was killed at Trenton on 2 Jan. 1777. He was survived by five minor children and his widow. Her nephew was James Ralston. He also appeared as John Roseborough and she as Jane Roseborough.

Rosecrants, Alexander. Va. —. His family was provided aid in Orange Co.

Rosentelle, Jacob. Pa. —. He was awarded a $50 gratuity in Westmoreland County on 18 Mar. 1814.

Roshon, —. Pa. —. His widow, Catharine Roshon, received a $40 gratuity and a $40 annuity in Montgomery County 24 Mar. 1837.

Ross, —. Pa. —. His widow, Margaret Ross, received a $40 gratuity in Washington County 15 June 1836. She died 18 May 1847.

Ross, —. Pa. —. His widow, Martha Ross, was awarded a $40 gratuity in Chester Co., Pa. 21 Mar. 1833. She was perhaps the Martha Ross who died 26 Mar. 1848.

Ross, Adam. Mass. Corp. He served in the 5th Regiment and was from Topsfield. His widow, Elizabeth Ross, was paid $50.

Ross, Alexander. Mass. Pvt. He served in the artillery. He was pensioned 1 Sep. 1782.

Ross, Alexander. Va. Capt. He served from 17 Sep. 1776 to 3 Sep. 1778. He died ca. 1814. He received 4,000 acres of bounty land on 11 Nov. 1785 for three years of service. Bounty land warrant #1863 for 300 acres was issued 3 Mar. 1791. A warrant for 666 2/3 acres was issued 20 Feb. 1807. On 1 Sep. 1807 bounty land for 444 acres for eight additional months of service was issued. Congress granted the heir, Virginia Ross, his commutation 30 May 1860.

Ross, Andrew. N.J. Pvt. He served in Capt. David Paul's Company under Maj. Reeves. He was also reported as having served under Capt. John Cozen and Col. Bodo in the Gloucester County militia. He was sent out on a scouting party and came in wounded through his knee on 13 Nov. 1777. He applied for half-pay in Gloucester County 6 Dec. 1783. He was on the 1791 pension roll. He was 29 years old. He served in the 1st N.J. Regiment. He lived in Gloucester County. He was on the 1813 pension list and died 24 Aug. 1832. His widow was Easter Ross.

Ross, Eliakim. N.J. Sgt. He served under Capt. David Edgar in the 2nd Regiment of the Light Dragoons. He was wounded 2 July 1779 and died the next day. His widow, Mary Ross, married John Hays 4 Dec. 1780. They sought his half-pay in Essex County 4 Oct. 1785 Both were entitled to receive half-pay of corporal from 2 July 1779 to 4 Oct. 1780.

Ross, Jacob. Pa. He received a $40 gratuity in Union County in 1838 and a $40 gratuity and a $40 annuity later in the year. He died 31 Mar. 1852.

Ross, James. Pa. He was awarded a $40 gratuity and a $40 annuity in Washington County 28 Mar. 1836.

Ross, John. N.J. —. His widow, Eleanor Ross, was pensioned in Morris County on 16 Feb. 1847 at the rate of $30 per annum. She was quite possibly the widow of the John Ross of Morris Co., N.J. who received a $40 gratuity and a $40 annuity from Pennsylvania in 1840. He died 31 Dec. 1843.

Ross, John. Pa. —. He was awarded a $40 gratuity and a $40 annuity in Chester Co., Pa. 6 Apr. 1833.

Ross, John. Pa. Sailing Master. He applied 5 Jan. 1788. He served aboard the *Arnold* floating battery in the Delaware under the command of Commodore John Hazelwood. He contracted rheumatism after the retreat from Trenton and was greatly afflicted with the disorder. He was 56 years old. He was dead by Mar. 1792.

Ross, John. Va. Pvt. He was in New Kent County when he was put on the pension list at the rate of £12 per annum on 1 Apr. 1788. His pension was continued on 11 June 1790. He served in Capt. W. Armistead's Company under Lt. Dudley Digges in Maj. J. Nelson's Light Dragoons. He was wounded in his left leg and was 24 years old. His leg was amputated in 1791.

Ross, Jonathan. Pa. Pvt. His widow, Elizabeth Ross, was in Cumberland County 20 June 1792. He was in the Cumberland County militia and was killed at the Crooked Billet on 1 May 1778. He was 50 years old at the time of his death.

Ross, Joseph. Va. —. His wife, Rosanna Ross, and three children were furnished 3 barrels of corn and 150 pounds of meat in Essex Co., Va. on 15 May 1780.

Ross, Lemuel. Mass. —. He served in the 6th Regiment. He was paid $20.

Ross, Micah. Mass. Pvt. He served in the 6th Regiment and was from Boylston. His widow, Molly Rowe, was paid $50.

Ross, Samuel. —. —. He resided in Ohio when Congress denied him a pension on 23 June 1854 because his service was not rendered during the Revolutionary War.

Ross, Samuel. Mass. —. He served in the 6th Regiment. He was paid $20.

Ross, William. Mass. —. He served in the 3rd Regiment and was from Newton. He was paid $20.

Ross, William. Mass. —. He served in the 3rd Regiment and was from Ipswich. He was paid $20.

Ross, William. Pa. Capt. He was in Philadelphia 20 Nov. 1788.

Ross, William. Va. —. His wife, Mary Ross, was allowed £10 support in Bedford Co., Va. on 24 Nov. 1777.

Ross, William. Va. —. He served at least five years. He married 29 Jan. 1787 or 1789 Sarah -----. His brother was Alexander Ross. Congress rejected her claim for relief 30 Mar. 1840 and reported that she should be able to prove his identity by his bounty land.

Ross, Zephaniah. —. —. He died in Jan. 1835. His widowed daughters were upwards of 80 years of age. They were Anna Norton and Louis Foskit. One was blind and both were very infirm. Congress granted them their father's pension from 4 Mar. 1822 to 1 Jan. 1828 on 25 Feb. 1852.

Rossburgh, John. N.J. Pvt. He served in the 4th Regiment. He lost an eye and was worn out in the service. He was 65 years old and lived in Springfield. He was pensioned at the rate of $60 per annum.

Rossell, Thomas. N.Y. —. He lived in New York City and was awarded 250 acres of bounty land on the condition that he deliver the comptroller orders drawn on Gerard Bancker, deceased, treasurer of the state, for $149.03.

Rosseter, Samuel. Conn. Pvt. He served in the Conn. Line. He was ruptured by over straining himself in carrying timber for the erection of a redoubt in New York state in Aug. 1781 at Neilson's Point. He lived in Litchfield, Conn. in 1794. He enlisted 15 Jan. 1778 for the war. He was granted half a pension 20 Apr. 1796. His rate was $5 per month from 18 Jan. 1808. He was on the 1813 pension list. He died 7 Jan. 1823.

Roth, —. Pa. —. His widow, Catharine Roth, was granted a pension 20 Mar. 1838. She resided in Northampton County.

Roth, Christian. Pa. —. He served in the Flying Camp and was taken prisoner at Fort Washington. He was released on parole in Feb. 1777 and was exchanged in May 1780. He was from Northampton County.

Roth, Michael. Pa. —. He was awarded a $40 gratuity and a $40 annuity in Berks Co., Pa. 18 Mar. 1834.

Rouark, James. Md. Pvt. His widow, Julia Rouark, was pensioned at the rate of half-pay of a private 7 Mar. 1838.

Rough, Ludwick. Pa. Pvt. Bounty land warrant #404 for 100 acres was issued 4 Apr. 1808. It had been lost. Congress authorized a duplicate to his heirs, Samuel Rowe and John Rowe, on 30 Mar. 1836. On 9 Jan. 1838 the heirs were called Samuel Rough and John Rough when they were issued a replacement warrant.

Round, Amos. Mass. Pvt. He served in the 4th Regiment and was from Taunton.

Roundtree, —. S.C. —. His widow, Mary Roundtree, was from Winton in 1791.

Roundtree, Job. S.C. —. He entered the service about the age of 14. He served under Capt. Joseph Vance, Capt. Joseph Harley, and Lt. Jethro Ward. His father and eldest brother were taken prisoners at Williams' Ferry on the Savannah Rive. His father died aboard a prison ship. He was at the siege of Augusta. He was 68 years old. He was from Barnwell District in 1827. Andrew Nimmons served with him. His application was rejected.

Roundtree, Reuben. S.C. —. He was on the roll in 1791.

Roundy, Luke. Mass. Ens. He died 22 Oct. 1777. His heirs were issued his half-pay of $840.

Rouse. Casper. N.Y. —. He claimed that he was employed by Gov. Clinton to disarm Tories. His evidence was vague and indefinite. Congress rejected the claim of the heirs 25 July 1850.

Rouse, George. Va. Pvt. He served more than two years. Congress granted him a pension on 21 July 1842. He was from Mason Co., Va.

Rouse, Jacob. Pa. —. He was wounded. He was awarded a $40 gratuity and a $40 annuity in Northampton County on 6 Mar. 1812. He died 15 Sep. 1814.

Rouse, Lewis. Va. —. He was in Madison County in Apr. 1794. He was wounded in action near Petersburg in 1781. He was pensioned at the rate of £8 per annum on 20 Dec. 1792. In 1805 he was in Boone Co., Ky. and in 1812 in Campbell Co., Ky. His son was Matthews Rouse.

Rouse, Luke. Pa. —. He was granted relief 5 June 1839. He also appeared as Luke Roupe.

Roush, George. —. —. His name was not on the roll, but the name of Jacob Roush was. Congress accepted that there was an error in his forename and granted him a pension 7 Feb. 1845. He was from Mason Co., Va.

Routledge, —. Va. —. His wife, Judith Routledge, was granted support in Prince Edward Co., Va. on 16 June 1778 while he was away in Continental service.

Roux, Albert. S.C. Capt. He served in the 2nd S.C. Regiment and was wounded 9 Oct. 1779 at Savannah. He was deprived of the use of his right arm. He applied 19 Feb. 1783 for three years and two months of pay.

Row, —. Pa. —. His widow, Susannah Row, was awarded a $40 gratuity and a $40 annuity in Berks County 21 Mar. 1837. She died 5 June 1851.

Row, Benjamin. Va. —. He served in Capt. Thomas Nelson's Company. He died in the service. His widow, Frances Row, was awarded a £30 gratuity on 22 Nov. 1777. There were five small children.

Row, George. Pa. Pvt. His widow, Mary Magdelena Row, was in Northumberland Co. on 27 Sept. 1786. He served under Col. Peter Hosterman and was stationed at Foutz's Mill in Buffalo Valley when he was wounded by a musket or rifle ball near his breast from the Indians in July 1780 and died within eight hours. He was 58 years old when he died.

Row, John. Pa. —.He was granted relief 11 June 1832. He died 11 Feb. 1835.

Rowan, Benjamin. S.C. —. He enlisted in 1775 under Capt. Ezekiel Polk and Col. Thompson. He was in the Snow Campaign. He also served under Capt. James Beard, Col. Graham, Capt. James Duff, Capt. Goodman, Col. Crow, and Col. Malmody. He was at Cross Creek, Fort Moultrie, Fort McIntosh, Purysburg, Stono, the burning of Col. Hill's Iron Works, Hanging Rock, Fishing Creek, King's Mountain, Fish Dam, Blackstocks, Congaree, and Ninety Six. He was in his 75th year and had a daughter living with him. William Knox and Archibald Brown deposed anent his service. He was pensioned in Chester District 7 Dec. 1826.

Rowan, John. Pa. —. He applied in Franklin County on 15 June 1813. He served in the 3rd Pa. Regiment under Col. Richard Butler in Capt. William Wilson's Company. He enlisted in the spring of 1780 and served to the fall of 1783. He received two wounds on his right knee from gun shots and another on his left leg from a bayonet. William Magaw was surgeon in the 4th Regiment.

Rowdus, Nathaniel. S.C. —. His widow was Elizabeth Rowdus from Salem in 1786. There were two children in 1791. *Vide* also Nathaniel Rhodus.

Rowe, John. N.J. —. He married 27 Mar. 1779 in Essex Co., N.J. Susannah -----. He removed to Harrison Co., Va. and died 29 Sep. 1829. Their eldest child, Clarissa Rowe, was born 18 June 1782. Congress granted Susannah Rowe a pension 22 Mar. 1838.

Rowe, Ebenezer. Mass. Seaman. He was on the 1813 pension list. He lived in Lincoln Co., Me.

Rowell, —. S.C. —. His widow was Phebe Rowell from Marion District in 1838. Her application was rejected.

Rowell, Enoch. —. —. He died 2 Aug. 1840. His widow, Rachel Rowell, died 1 Dec. 1844 without obtaining relief. Congress declined to grant relief to the children on 14 June 1850.

Rowin, Bracey. N.C. —. He was in Rutherford Co., N.C. in Oct. 1832 and was aged about 70.

Rowland, Burwell. Va. Pvt. His widow, Susanna Rowland, was *ca.* 38 years of age and had three very infirm children, all of whom were remarkably small for their age, the eldest of whom was *ca.* 18 years old. He was in the 15th Va. Regiment and died in the service. She was in Sussex County and was put on the pension list at the rate of £8 per annum on 20 Mar. 1789. She was continued on 12 Oct 1791. She died 29 Aug. 1827; letters of administration were issued to Nathaniel Rowland in Nov. 1827. The children were named Nathaniel Rowland, Thomas Rowland, and Joseph Rowland.

Rowland, David. S.C. —. He served under Capt. Moore, Lt. Prince, and Capt. Sinkfield. He was at Stono where Lt. Prince fell and the siege of Savannah. He was 77 years old. John Swords, who w a s made a prisoner at Savannah, was with him at Stono. He was from Pendleton District andwas pensioned 19 Dec. 1825. He also appeared as David Roland. His widow, Judith Rowland, was paid his arrearage of in 1832. She was pensioned 9 Dec. 1834 at $30 per annum. She was paid as late as 1850.

Rowland, Howell. Va. Pvt. He served in the 15th Virginia Regiment in Capt. John Mallory's Company. He died in 1778. His widow, Susannah Rowland, applied from Sussex County and was 38 years old with two children, the elder a son aged about 16 years who was considered an idiot and the younger a daughter aged about 14. She was continued on the pension list at the rate of £12 per annum on 17 Nov. 1787. She was continued on the roll on 20 Mar. 1789, 29 Mar. 1790, and 12

Oct. 1791. He also appeared as Howell Rawlings.

Rowland, John. —. —. He was pensioned.

Rowland, Nathan. Va. Pvt. He was in Pittsylvania County on 14 Oct. 1786. He served in the Pittsylvania County militia and was wounded at Guilford in his left foot. He was in Col. Perkins' Regiment in Gen. Stevens' Brigade as proved by the oath of ----- Browne 24 Mar. 1781. Maj. Abraham Shelton and Col. Benjamin Lankford of the Pittsylvania County Militia also confirmed his service. Sgt. ----- Bardet, who was in the service of the King of France, certified his wounds. Rowland was 30 years old. He was on the 1813 pension list. He died 16 Feb. 1830.

Rowland, William. Va. He served in the 15th Va. Regiment and died in service. His widow, Mary Rowland, was aged *ca.* 45 years and had four children on 16 Mar. 1786 in Sussex County. In June 1791 she had three children. The eldest was *ca.* 14 years old and the youngest *ca.* 10 years old. She was continued on the pension list at the rate of £10 per annum on 20 Mar. 1789, 29 Mar. 1790, and 12 Oct. 1791.

Rowley, Aaron. Mass. Maj. He was wounded by a musket ball in his left ankle on 25 Oct. 1781. He was pensioned at the rate of one-quarter of a major from 25 Oct. 1781 on 15 Oct. 1783.

Rowntree, James. S.C. —. He was paid his annuity 18 Feb. 1829.

Rowse, Thomas. Md. Lt. He was pensioned at the rate of half-pay of a lieutenant 21 Dec. 1811.

Roy, Beverley. Va. Capt. He received the commutation.

Royall, William. Va. Capt. Bounty land was allowed on 21 Jan. 1815 by warrant #4489 for seven years and four months of service in the Continental Line. He died in 1815. His widow, Anne Royall, had her petition for a pension by a special act of Congress rejected 27 Mar. 1846. They married 4 May 1798 or 18 Nov. 1797. She claimed that her husband had received no pay, but Congress ruled that it had no authority to entertain her claim on 25 Apr. 1840. His widow, Anne Royall, and heirs received his five years' full-pay commutation 30 June 1834. Congress gave her no further compensation 18 Apr. 1854. Elizabeth Roane, a widow, was an heir 25 Apr. 1834.

Royce, Elijah. Conn. Pvt. He served in the 3rd Conn. Regiment. He was wounded by a stroke with a broad sword on his head which fell on the joint of his right shoulder in 1777. He was also wounded by grape shot in his right side in 1779 at Scotch Plains. He resided at Southington, Conn. in 1796. He enlisted 21 Apr. 1777 for three years and was discharged 21 Apr. 1780. He was granted three-fourths of a pension 20 Apr. 1796. He was on the 1813 pension list. He was 74 in 1818.

Royden, Amos. Mass. —. He served in the 3rd Regiment and was from Orange. He was paid $20.

Rozar, David. S.C. —. He was on the roll in 1793.

Rozar, Mesheck. S.C. Pvt. He was from Clarendon, Sumter District. He served under Capt. Fleming Richbourg and Col. Thomas Sumter. and was pensioned 3 Dec. 1819. He was paid as late as 1821. He also appeared as Mesheck Rosier.

Rozier, William. S.C. —. His widow was Chole Rozier from Marion District in 1838. She had lived 86 winters. Her application was rejected. He also appeared as William Rozar.

Ruark, James. Md. Pvt. His widow, Barbara Ruark, was pensioned at the rate of half-pay of a private 7 Mar. 1838. Her arrearage was paid to William Wells in Anne Arundel County on 18 Feb. 1848.

Ruble, Jesse. Va. —. He was in Frederick County on 13 Mar. 1801. He served as a volunteer militia man under William Crawford to repel the Indian invasion on the frontier in 1781 and was wounded in the shoulder. He was pensioned at the rate of $40 per annum on 31 Dec. 1799. He was in Brooke County in 1802, and Jefferson Co., Ohio in 1804.

Rucker, Angus. Va. Capt. He was from Madison County and received his commutation of full-pay for five years in lieu of half-pay as captain of infantry in the Virginia Line with no interest on 9 Jan. 1826.

Rucker, Colley. Va. —. His administrator, William Hays, sought a pension, but Congress rejected his petition 6 Apr. 1860.

Rucker, Elliott. Va. Lt. He lived in Shelby Co., Ky. when he received commutation of full pay for five years in lieu of half-pay of life with no interest on 15 Feb. 1826. He died 19 Mar. 1832.

Ruckle, George. Pa. —. He was awarded relief in Northampton County 18 Feb. 1834. He was dead by Apr. 1837.

Rudd, Jeremiah. Md. —. He was pensioned in Charles County on 13 Oct. 1789.

Rudd, John. Va. —. He served aboard the armed schooner *Liberty*. He was pensioned 21 Jan. 1809 at the rate of $50 per annum. His widow, Sarah Rudd, was in Elizabeth City County on 24 May 1810. She relinquished her right to administer his estate to Sheriff William Armistead. Ann Rudd said her husband died 25 Nov. 1809. [*n.b.* the different forenames of his wife]

Ruddeau, John. Pa. Pvt. He was in Philadelphia, Pa. 9 Jan. 1786. He was in the Invalids. He was disabled by old age and infirmities contracted in the service. He was discharged in Sep. 1782 unfit for duty. He was 55 years old. He also appeared as John Ruddow.

Ruddock, John. Mass. —. His collar bone and right leg were broken. He resided in Mass. in 1796.

Rudolph, Jacob. Pa. —. He was awarded a $40 gratuity and a $40 annuity in Butler Co. 28 Mar. 1820. He died 2 Nov. 1839.

Rudy, Jacob. Pa. —. He was awarded a $40 gratuity and a $40 annuity in York Co., Pa. 4 May 1832. He was 91 years old in 1840. He died 2 Mar. 1841.

Rue, Mathias. N.J. Pvt. He served under Capt. Hankinson in the 1st Regiment of the Monmouth County militia. Ens. John Walton and Col. Nathaniel Scudder were also his officers. He was taken prisoner at the Highlands of Neversink 13 Feb. 1777, carried to New York, and died on 28 Feb. 1777. His widow, Elizabeth Rue, gave birth to a child four and a half months later. She was granted a half-pay pension.

Ruff, Benjamin. Va. —. His wife, Sarah Ruff, was allowed £50 relief in Bedford Co., Va. on 27 Sep. 1777.

Rugg, Stephen. Mass. —. He served in the 5th Regiment and was from Templeton. His widow, Elizabeth Rugg, was paid $50.

Ruggles, Joseph. Mass. —. He was from Roxbury and was paid $20.

Ruggles, Lazarus. Conn. Lt. He was wounded in the left wrist and right hand by a cannon shot on 28 Oct. 1776 at White Plains. He lived at New Milford, Conn. in 1794.

Rumblo, Thomas. Mass. Pvt. He died 21 May 1807.

Rumery, Dominicus. Me. —. He died 27 Oct. 1835. His widow was Pamelia Rumery from Lubec. She was paid $50 under the resolve of 1836.

Rumney, William. Va. Surgeon. He served at the hospital in Alexandria to the end of the war. Congress did not grant his representatives his commutation on 15 Feb. 1836.

Rumpfield, George. Pa. —. He was pensioned in Lehigh County 27 Mar. 1837. He died in 1843.

Rumrill, Joseph. Mass. Pvt. He served under Col. Bailey and Capt. Maxwell. He was pensioned 26 May 1780. He was on the 1813 pension list. He died 30 Aug. 1822 in Middlesex Co., Mass. He also appeared as Joseph Runnell and Joseph Runwell.

Rundio, Charles. Pa. Capt. His widow, Susannah Rundio, was awarded a $40 gratuity and a $40 annuity 23 Apr. 1829. His name have also been interpreted to be Charles Rundie. She died

26 Mar. 1834.

Rundy, Jacob. Pa. —. He was granted relief in York County 4 May 1832.

Runion, Isaac. Va. —. He was pensioned in Tazewell County on 8 Jan. 1820 at the rate of $60 per annum and $60 immediate relief.

Runnals, Samuel. N.H. Pvt. He served under Col. Scammel for three years. He had never received any pay as an invalid when he sought relief on 24 Feb. 1791.

Runnels, Frederic. Ga. —. His widow, Jean Runnels, and four children were granted three years' allowance 26 Nov. 1784.

Runyan, John. Va. —. His wife, Susannah Runyan, was granted 4 barrels of corn in Bedford Co., Va. on 28 Feb. 1780.

Runyon, George. Pa. —. He applied in Franklin County on 18 Sep. 1818 to the court of inquiry.

Rupe, Nicholas. Va. —. His wife, Mary Rupe, and seven children were granted £7 support 23 Nov. 1778 in Rockingham County while he was in Continental service.

Rupp, —. Pa. —. His widow, Susan Rupp, was awarded a $40 gratuity and a $40 annuity in York Co., Pa. 18 Feb. 1834. She was dead by July 1838.

Rupp, Andrew. Pa. —. He was granted relief in Lehigh County 14 Mar. 1835.

Rush, Benjamin. Va. —. He was pensioned in Madison County on 1 Jan. 1820 at the rate of $60 per annum. He died 11 Mar. 1831.

Rush, William. Pa. —. He was awarded a $40 gratuity and a $40 annuity in Lycoming County on 19 Mar. 1816.

Rusher, Jacob. N.C. —. He enlisted in 1778 under Capt. Cowan and Maj. Armstrong in Rowan Co., N.C. He was at Stono under Col. Little of South Carolina. He applied from Rowan County in Aug. 1820 at aged 66 years.

Russ, Samuel. S.C. —. He was on the roll in 1793.

Russell, —. Va. —. His wife, Elizabeth Russell, was granted £500 in May 1781 in Fauquier Co., Va. while her husband was absent in the service. She was furnished 5 barrels of corn and 50 pounds of bacon in July 1782.

Russell, —. Va. —. His wife, Eliza Russell, was granted £500 in Fauquier County in May 1781. [second of the name on this date.]

Russell, Albert. —. —. His application of 13 Feb. 1797 was not accepted.

Russell, Alexander. Pa. —. He was awarded a $40 gratuity and a $40 annuity in Adams Co., Pa. 14 Jan. 1835. His widow was Mary Russell.

Russell, Amos. Mass. Pvt. He served in the 7th Regiment and was from Carlisle. He was paid $50.

Russell, Andrew. Va. Maj. He served in the 5th Regiment and was commissioned 12 May 1778. He was granted 5,333 acres of bounty land by Virginia for three years of service 19 Dec. 1784. His only heir in 1858 was Penelope Harrison. His heir received 300 acres of federal bounty land 2 Apr. 1846. He died 12 Jan. 1819 as a bachelor. His sister's grandchildren and great-grandchildren sought his half-pay but were rejected 27 July 1866.

Russell, Calvin. Me. —. He was from Moscow. He was paid $50 under the resolve of 1836.

Russell, Charles. Va. Capt. & Ass't QM. In a half-pay claim he was stated to have been Paymaster of the 1st Va. State Regiment. He died 27 Sep. 1795 leaving a widow and son, Elgin Russell. Congress did not allow half-pay to the heirs on 27 Jan. 1836.

Russell, Daniel. N.H. Pvt. He enlisted 5 Mar. 1777 from Rindge. He was shot through the back at the battle of Stillwater on 19 Sep. 1777. He was in hospital at Albany to 23 Oct. He served in the 2nd N.H. Regiment under Lt. James Crombie and in Capt. Samuel Blodget's Company under

Col. Hale. He was aged 32 in 1787. He was on the 1813 pension list. He was from Jaffrey and had a large family of small children. He was also a veteran of the French and Indian War.

Russell, Edward. N.J. —. He sought an act to be released from debtor prison. He served under Capt. Bloomfield and Lt. Eben Elmer in 1776. He lost his wife and all his property. He sought assistance 28 Oct. 1810.

Russell, Evan. Pa. —. He was granted a $40 gratuity and a $40 annuity by the act of 16 June 1836. The act gave his place of residence as Center County when it should have been Chester County. The correction was made 27 Jan. 1837.

Russell, James. Mass. Sgt. He served in the 10th Regiment and was from Boxford. His widow, Rebecca Russell, was paid $50.

Russell, James. N.C. Sgt. He served under Capt. Redden Blount in 1779. He was at Hillsboro and under Col. Lillington in the 10th Regiment. He transferred into the 3rd Regiment under Col. Robert Mebane. He was a prisoner of war. He was a blacksmith by trade but unable to work due to his wounds. He had two daughters who were married.

Russell, James. Pa. Pvt. He served in Capt. Potts' Company in the 5th Pa. Regiment. Afterwards he was drafted into a company of light infantry under Capt. Thomas Boude until 1 Jan. 1781. William Tennant served in the same unit.

Russell, John. —. Pvt. He served under Col. Clover in the Marine Regiment and was at Princeton, Saratoga, and Valley Forge. He transported the army across the Delaware on the eve of the battle of Trenton. His likeness was on the statute at Trenton on guard at the door on the monument. He was from Marblehead, Mass. His daughter, Hannah Lyons, 91 years of age, sought a pension. She was also the niece of James Mugford who captured the *Hope*, a British transport, but lost his life in hand to hand combat when his small vessel was surrounded by 200 men in boats. Hannah Lyons' only support was her daughter, who "...hardly earns enough to keep the wolf from the door." She received a pension from Congress 15 Feb. 1894.

Russell, John. N.J. —. He served under Lt. Elihu Chadwick. He was wounded in the hip in 1780 by a musket ball and in his shoulder. He was in Monmouth County 30 Apr. 1800.

Russell, John. Va. Lt. He served in the infantry. Hannah Russell, his executrix, and James L. Russell, Gervas E. Russell, Joshua Russell, and John B. Russell, executors, received his commutation of full-pay for five years in lieu of half-pay for life as a lieutenant of infantry in the Virginia with no interest on 13 Feb. 1826.

Russell, Joseph. Mass. —. He served in the 6th Regiment and was paid $20.

Russell, Joseph. Pa. Pvt. He was transferred to Maryland by 1803. He was on the 1813 pension list.

Russell, Oliver. Mass. Corp. He lived in Plymouth County. He was pensioned 24 Aug. 1812. He was on the 1813 pension list.

Russell, Paul. Pa. —. He was pensioned 17 Mar. 1839 in Philadelphia. He was 84 years old in 1840. He died 8 July 1843.

Russell, Philip M. Va. Surgeon's Mate. He entered in the spring of 1776 and served ten months. He took a furlough for two months and returned to the army when he was attached to another regiment, the 2nd Virginia under Gen. Lee, and served to Aug. 1780 when he quitted the service with a loss of his hearing and sight produced by an attack of camp fever. In his later years he was a mental imbecile. He died in 1830. His widow, Esther Russell, sought an increase in her pension which Congress granted 19 Jan. 1848.

Russell, Samuel. Pa. —. He was pensioned.

Russell, Samuel. Va. —. His wife, Sarah Russell, was granted support in Fauquier Co., Va. 9 Oct.

1780.

Russell, Samuel. Va. —. His wife, Sarah Russell, was granted support in Loudoun County in Nov. 1780.

Russell, Samuel L. —. Capt. His widow, Elizabeth S. Russell, received five years' half-pay. She married (2) ------- Sailly who could not support her and her family so she sought to be restored. Congress rejected her claim for relief 24 Jan. 1855.

Russell, Solomon. Mass. —. Bounty land warrant #705 for 100 acres was issued to his agent, Joshua W. Wing, who died many years ago in Mobile. Congress authorized a duplicate 21 Feb. 1846.

Russell, Solomon. Mass. —. He served in the 1st Regiment and was from Shirley. He was paid $20.

Russell, Thomas. Pa. —. He was awarded a $40 gratuity and a $40 annuity in Venango County 28 Mar. 1836.

Russell, Timothy. S.C. Surgeon. He served in the militia but received no compensation. His son, William Russell, sought same in 1828. He was from Abbeville District. He had treated John Lockbridge who had been wounded. Andrew Johnson, who had been wounded at Eutaw, died under his hands. Robert Crawford was a guard at the hospital at Ninety Six. The application was rejected.

Russell, William. N.Y. —. He served under Col. Dubois. His wife, Rachel Russell, and one child were granted support 8 June 1778 while he was away in the service. Her son was John Simson.

Russell, William. Pa. Ens. He was in York County 1 May 1786. He was in the 3rd Pa. Regiment and lost a leg at Brandywine on 11 Sep. 1777. He was 30 years old. He died 4 Mar. 1802.

Russell, William. Pa. —. He was in Beaver County on 17 Nov. 1814. He served 13 months in Col.Clay's Regiment in Capt. Thomas Robinson's Company. In his second application he was awarded a $40 gratuity 14 Mar. 1814. He was awarded a $40 gratuity and a $40 annuity in Beaver County 14 Mar. 1818. He also stated that he served under Col. Wagner.

Russwurm, William. N.C. Lt. He received his commutation 12 Jan. 1838. His son, John S. Russwurm, sought his father's commutation pay. Congress rejected the claim since it had slept for nearly fifty years on 8 Apr. 1852.

Rust, Frederick. Pa. —. He was pensioned 13 Aug. 1814. His name may have been Frederick Riest.

Rust, John. Va. Pvt. He served in the militia. He lived in Loudoun County and died 1 Oct. 1827.

Rust, Peter. Va. Pvt. He was in Frederick County in Sep. 1786. He served as a soldier in Col. Churchill's battalion of Fauquier County militia. He received three wounds at Williamsburg in Apr. 1781. He was in Capt. John Thomas Chunn's Company. He was 25 years old. One musket ball was lodged in his left hip, and another fractured his right leg. He was put on the pension list at the rate of £10 per annum on 17 Oct. 1787. He was on the 1813 pension list.

Rutgers, Henry. N.Y. Deputy Muster Master General. He was issued certificates of arrears of pay and a year's advance 15 Apr. 1786.

Rutherford, William. Pa. —. He was pensioned.

Rutledge, Joshua. Md. Lt. He was pensioned at the rate of half-pay of a lieutenant 2 Jan. 1813 in Harford County. He was stricken from the roll 23 Feb. 1822 because he was wealthy. His widow, Elizabeth Brooks, was pensioned at his rate 3 Mar. 1840. He also appeared as Joshua Rutlage.

Rutlin, Asa. S.C. —. His widow and one child were on the roll in 1791.

Ryan, —. Va. —. Jane Ryan was awarded £40 while her two sons away in Continental service on 16 Aug. 1779 in Goochland Co., Va.

Ryan, Francis. Mass. Sgt. He served in the 11th Regiment and was from Danvers. He served three years. He came home from the army in 1783 claiming to be married. He died nine years later. His widow, Mary Reed, was paid $50. Congress granted her a pension 12 Feb. 1841.

Her first husband was Barnabas McCoy.

Ryan, James. Pa. —. He enlisted 7 Nov. 1775 at the Seven Stars Tavern by Capt. Lamar of the 1st Regiment. He served five years. He was from Montgomery County. He was pensioned 26 Aug. 1816.

Ryan, Jeremiah. Conn. Pvt. He served from 1775 to 1780. He was disabled by debility of nerves. He was on the 1813 pension list.

Ryan, John. Pa. —. He was in Philadelphia County. He served in the 1st Pa. Regiment under Col. Hand and Col. Chambers. He was wounded at Miles Square in New York. He was given a $40 annuity 28 Mar. 1806. He was from Lycoming County in 1806.

Ryan, John. Pa. —. He applied 22 Jan. 1813. He served 5 ½ years at Valley Forge and lost an eye by the bursting of a gun. He was 80 years old.

Ryan, John. Va. Pvt. He was in Montgomery County 12 June 1787. He enlisted in Berkeley County in 1776 in Col. Hazen's Regiment. He was wounded by a gun shot in his left ankle and had the bone fractured. He was then discharged. He was 24 years old. In 1788 he was in Augusta County. He was continued on the pension list on 13 June 1789 at the rate of £12 per annum. He was on the 1813 pension list.

Ryan, Richard. Mass. Pvt. He served in the 1st Regiment under Col. Joseph Vose. He was disabled with a rupture and was discharged at his own request. He was pensioned 10 Jan. 1783. He was 26 years old and resided in Boston, Mass. in 1788.

Ryan, Thomas. N.Y. Pvt. He served under Col. Van Schaick and was slain 28 May 1779. His children, Thomas Ryan and Sarah Ryan, received a half-pay pension. He also appeared as Thomas Rion.

Ryan, William. Mass. Pvt. He served in the 9th Regiment and was from Boston. He was paid $20.

Rybecker, John. Pa. Pvt. He was in Philadelphia County on 25 Sep. 1787. He served in the German Regiment under Col. Ludwick Weltner. He was wounded through his hand and his shoulder by musket balls at Germantown. He was 34 years old. He was pensioned at the rate of $4 per month from 18 Apr. 1807. He was on the 1813 pension list. He died 9 Sep. 1822 in York County.

Ryers, John. Pa. —. He was awarded a $40 gratuity and a $40 annuity 4 Apr. 1831.

Ryley, James. Pa. —. He received a $40 gratuity and a $40 annuity in Trumbull Co., Ohio 14 Apr. 1827.

Rylie, John. Va. —. His wife, Mary Rylie, was granted £20 relief in Rockingham Co., Va. on 23 Aug. 1779.

Rynsel, Valentine. Pa. —. He was awarded a $40 gratuity and a $40 annuity in Butler Co., Pa. 15 Mar. 1826. He died 27 Dec. 1839.

Sabin, Elihu. Conn. Pvt. He served under Gen. Israel Putnam. He was wounded by a musket ball which passed through his right leg at the battle of Bunker Hill in June 1775. He lived in Pomfret, Conn. in 1792 and 1794. He was in the militia. He was granted half a pension 20 Apr. 1796. He was on the 1813 pension list.

Sachabaugh, Adam. Pa. —. He was pensioned in Franklin County 27 Mar. 1837.

Sacker, John. Pa. Pvt. He was in Philadelphia 12 Dec. 1785. He served in a Pa. Regiment and was transferred to the Invalids where he was discharged on 14 Sep. 1782 on account of wounds. He was 45 years old. He died 17 Jan. 1790. He also appeared as John Tacker.

Sadler, Benjamin. Va. Pvt. He served in the 9th Va. Regiment. He was taken prisoner at Germantown. He lived in Goochland County where he was pensioned at the rate of $3 per month from 1 Jan. 1803 on 25 Apr. 1808. He removed to Sumner Co., Tenn.

Sadler, Isaac. Pa. —. He received a $40 gratuity and a $40 annuity in Westmoreland County 1 Apr. 1837. He died 28 June 1843.

Sailhammer, Nicholas. Pa. —. He enlisted under Capt. Hare and later served under Capt. Coleman and Col. Proctor in the artillery. He served three and a half years. He was from Cumberland County. He was pensioned 24 Feb. 1818. He also appeared as Nicholas Sailheimer and Nicholas Sellhamer.

Sailheimer, —. Pa. —. His widow, Elizabeth Sailheimer, was awarded a $40 gratuity and a $40 annuity in Franklin Co., Pa. 30 Mar. 1824. She died 25 Sep. 1849.

Sailor, Jacob. Pa. —. He was awarded a $40 gratuity and a $40 annuity in Philadelphia, Pa. 27 Mar. 1830. He served three years. His widow, Elizabeth Sailor, had her claim rejected by Congress 17 Feb. 1846 because they were married in 1799 which was too late.

St.Clair, —. Pa. —. His widow, Isabella St. Clair, received a $40 gratuity and a $40 annuity in Northumberland County 3 Apr. 1837.

St.Clair, Arthur. Pa. Major-General. He was awarded a $200 gratuity and a $200 annuity on 4 Feb. 1813. He died 30 Aug. 1818. His daughters, Eliza Dill, Jane Jervis, and Louisa St. Clair Robb, sought money they believed was due their father. They submitted no documents to support their claim, and Congress rejected it 14 Dec. 1820. He came to America in the regiment of Highlanders under Gen. Wolfe, having enlisted as an ensign in the French and Indian War. He received a crown grant of 1,000 acres in Pennsylvania. In 1775 he was commissioned a colonel and was promoted to Brigadier General and then to Major-General. He was pensioned in 1818. Congress received a petition from the heirs again on 19 May 1856.

St.Clair, Daniel. Pa. Drum Major. He was in Northampton County on 18 Jan. 1786. He served in the 11th Va. Regiment. He lost his left hand and received other wounds in his body and head in the service. He had a certificate from Baron Steuben, Inspector General of the Army. He was on the 1813 pension list. He also appeared as David St.Clair.

St.John, James. Conn. —. He served in the 5th Conn. Regiment under Col. Philip Burr Bradley. He was left sick at Norwalk. On his way to rejoin the regiment he was attacked on the road by two persons at Salem, New York who were believed to be Tories. He was cruelly beaten and wounded over his left eye in Aug. 1779. He lost his eyesight. He was discharged at the end of his three-year enlistment. He was pensioned at Guildhall 30 July 1785. He was 24 years old.

St.John, John. —. Pvt. He served in Col. Waterbury's Regiment. He was pensioned 29 Jan. 1808 at the rate of $5 per month. He was on the 1813 pension list of New York. He lived in Saratoga County.

St.John, John. Pa. Drum Major. He was in Philadelphia County on 30 Sep. 1785. He served in the 2nd Pa. Regiment. He was disabled by a rupture and was 55 years old. He died 25 July 1791, and his widow received his final payment.

Salisbury, Henry. N.Y. —. He was ramming down the cartridge when there was an explosion which carried off his right hand when the news of the capture of Gen. Cornwallis arrived. He was from Columbia Co., N.Y. and had a large family on 10 Dec. 1788.

Sallade, Jacob. Pa. —. He was awarded a $40 gratuity and a $40 annuity in Dauphin County 31 Mar. 1836.

Salliday, —. Pa. —. He died 1 July 1824. His widow was Mary Salliday. She was in Huntingdon County 11 Apr. 1825.

Sallisbury, Pettigrew. S.C. Pvt. He was under 21 when he enlisted. He was killed at Eutaw. His father, Andrew Sallisbury, sought compensation in 1788.

Salman, Jesse. Va. Pvt. He was wounded in the battle at the Waxhaws and lost the use of both hands. He was in Cumberland Co., Va. 29 Apr. 1783. He died in Oct. 1785. He also appeared as Jesse

Salmon.

Salmon, George. S.C. —. He was on the roll in 1791.

Salmon, Henry. Va. Pvt. He was pensioned at the rate of £12 per annum on 20 Dec. 1792. He was in Princess Anne County on 19 May 1793. He received several wounds in the service and was disabled. He died 22 Oct. 1805, and William Capps was his executor.

Salmon, Joseph. Pa. Capt. He applied 4 Mar. 1807. He served in Col. James Murray's Regiment of Northumberland County militia. He was taken prisoner by Indians and detained upwards of two years in Canada. He was awarded 300 acres of donation land.

Salmon, Joseph. Pa. —. His widow, Ann Salmon, was awarded a $40 gratuity and a $40 annuity in Columbia Co., Pa. 7 Mar. 1827.

Salomon, Haym Pa. —. He was a merchant banker and made frequent loans of money. He was imprisoned in New York at the Prevost. His son, Hayn M. Salomon, sought relief from Congress 9 Aug. 1850.

Salter, Benjamin. N.J. Pvt. He served under Col. Seely in the Morris County militia. He was wounded in action in the battle of Second River on 5 Sep. 1777 and died the following day. He married Phebe Merit. She received his half-pay in Morris County in Mar. 1781. She married secondly Rufus Randle 15 Jan. 1789.

Salter, John. N.J. —. He was granted relief.

Salter, Peter. Mass. —. He served in the 6th Regiment and was from Shrewsbury. He was paid $20.

Saltonstall, Brittain. R.I. Pvt. He was aged 21 when he applied 29 Dec. 1785. He served under Col. Jeremiah Olney and was disabled by the loss of all the toes on his right foot and one joint from each of the toes on his left foot by severe frost bite on the Oswego Expedition under Col. Willett in Feb. 1783. He was on the 1813 pension list. He died 7 Aug. 1817.

Saltzman, Anthony. Pa. Sgt. His widow, Rosanna Ritchie, was in Lycoming County. He was in Capt. Thomas Wilson's Company of militia in the 4th Battalion in Northumberland County under Col. Cookson Long. He was killed by savages on 2 Jan. 1778. He was tomahawked and scalped. He left five children: George Saltzman born 23 Sep. 1768, Mary Saltzman born 25 Sep. 1770, Anthony Saltzman born 21 Sep. 1772, John Saltzman born 26 Jan. 1776, and William Saltzman born 22 Nov. 1777. His daughter Mary Saltzman married Lewis Keith. His widow married Robert Ritchie about 1779.

Sammons, Jacob. N.Y. —. He was awarded 200 acres of bounty land 19 June 1812.

Sample, Edward. Va. —. His wife, Susannah Sample, and four children were furnished 5 barrels of corn and 250 pounds of pork in Frederick Co., Va. on 5 Feb. 1782.

Sample, Ezekiel. Pa. —. He was awarded a $40 gratuity in Westmoreland Co., Pa. 3 Apr. 1829.

Sample, Nathaniel. Va. —. His wife, Susannah Sample, and four children were furnished 5 barrels of corn and 250 pounds of pork in Frederick Co., Va. on 6 Mar. 1781. He died in the service prior to 5 June 1782.

Sample, Robert. Pa. Capt. He received a patent for 500 acres of donation land. The land fell into New York, and the patent had been mislaid. He was issued a new patent for land in Pennsylvania.

Sampsel, Peter. Pa. Sgt. His widow, Catharine Sampsel, was in Berks County on 26 June 1792. He was in Capt. Stiver's Company of the Berks County militia under Gen. Lacy. He was wounded in Nov. 1777 and taken to Philadelphia where he died of his wounds. He left eight small children. His widow died 10 May 1798. He also appeared as Peter Samsel.

Sampson, —. Va. Pvt. He died in Continental service in 1778. His widow was Nancy Sampson. She was probably the Nancy Sampson who was granted support in King William County.

Sampson, Crocker. Mass. Lt. His bounty land warrant #1915 for 200 acres had been lost so Congress granted his heirs, Lucy Sampson and Rebecca Crocker the wife of Zenas Crocker, a duplicate 15 Jan. 1834. He was late of Kingston. Harriet S. Adams was named as an heir in another record.

Sampson, Luke. Md. Pvt. He served in the 1st Regiment. He was pensioned in Frederick County in 1785.

Sampson, Samuel. Mass. Pvt. He served in the 2nd Regiment and was from Middleborough. He was paid $50.

Samson, Jonathan. Mass. Sgt. He served in the 6th Regiment and was from Vermont. He was paid $20.

Samson, Moses. N.J. —. He was pensioned in Morris County on 26 Feb. 1847 at the rate of $50 per annum.

Samuel, —. Va. —. The brothers were in Continental service. Their mother, Judith Samuel, was furnished 1 barrel of corn and 50 pounds of pork in Essex Co., Va. on 21 May 1781.

Samuel, Elisha. S.C. —. There were two children in 1791.

Sanborn, Nathan. N.H. Capt. He was wounded at Bemis Heights 7 October 1777 by a shot through his arm. The musket ball lodged in his shoulder. He was in Col. Stephen Evans' militia regiment. He was aged 51 in 1787. He was on the 1813 pension list. He was from Deerfield. He also appeared as Nathan Sandborn.

Sanby, Ezekiel. Pa. —. He was paid $300 in lieu of donation land.

Sanders, —. Va. —. He died in the service. His widow, Tabitha Sanders, and two children were furnished support in Feb. 1780 and Feb. 1781. She was pensioned in 1783 in Westmoreland County.

Sanders, —. Va. —. His mother, Tabitha Sanders, was furnished support in Westmoreland County in Mar. 1782. Her husband and three sons were in the service.

Sanders, Isaac. Mass. Pvt. He served in the 10th Regiment.

Sanders, Jacob. Pa.—. He was pensioned.

Sanders, Joseph. Me. —. He died 12 Sep. 1831. His widow was Lucy Sanders from Farmington. She was paid $50 under the resolve of 1836.

Sanders, Robert. N.Y. Pvt. He was disabled by rheumatism due to sudden cold at the battle of Monmouth. He served in Capt. John Graham's Company in Col. Goose Van Schaick's Regiment. He was disabled at the battle of Monmouth and suffered from rheumatism in all of his limbs. He was 58 years old in Nov. 1786. He lived in Albany Co., N.Y. 23 June 1789. He was on the 1791 and 1813 pension lists. He also appeared as Robert Saunders.

Sanders, Thomas. Md. Pvt. He resided in Charles County in 1781. He was wounded in the hand and head at the battle of Camden on 16 Aug. 1780. He served under Col. John H. Stone. He was on the 1791 pension list. He also appeared as Thomas Saunders. He was on the 1813 pension roll.

Sanderson, —. Mass. —. Sophia Sanderson was paid $50 for the service of her husband.

Sanderson, David. N.H. —. He was under 16 when he enlisted for three months in 1776. He was at White Plains and Peekskill. He reenlisted in 1777 in the 1st Regiment under Col. Cilley. He sought bounty land. He was rejected because he was not present when his regiment was discharged. He had granted a furlough for 19 days to visit his uncle and family in Connecticut. He had a fever and could not rejoin his unit. He was discharged by his captain. Congress accepted that he was in service to the end of the war on 28 June 1836 and awarded the bounty land.

Sanderson, Moses. Vt. Pvt. He served under Col. Putnam in militia. He was wounded in the neck by a musket ball while on sentry and lost the use of his left arm in 1777 at Moses's Creek. He lived in Rockingham, Vt. in 1795. He was granted two-thirds of a pension 20 Apr. 1796. He transferred to Worcester Co., Mass. 4 Sep. 1806. He was on the 1813 pension list. He also appeared as Moses Saunderson.

Sandford, James. S.C. —. He was paid an annuity in 1831, 1832, 1833, and 1834.

Sandford, William. N.J. —. He served under Col. Van Courtland in the militia for two years and seven months. He was pensioned and died 4 Mar. 1812. His widow was pensioned and died 12 Feb. 1864. His daughter, Eliza Sandford, was born in 1816 and was a nurse. She received a pension from Congress 26 Feb. 1896 at the rate of $12 per month.

Sandidge, Joseph. Va. Pvt. He was awarded a £30 gratuity and full-pay for three years on 10 Oct. 1778. He was in Louisa County 1 May 1786 when his pension was continued at the rate of £8 per annum. He served in Capt. Towles' Company under Col. Buckner in the 6th Va. Regiment. He was wounded by a ball which broke his left arm between the shoulder and elbow at Brandywine. He was 33 or 34 years old. He also appeared as Joseph Sandridge. He was continued on the pension roll on 10 Mar. 1789. His pension was increased to £15 per annum on 14 May 1789. He was on the 1813 pension list.

Sandiford, Rowland. S.C. Legionnaire. He served aborad the frigate *South Carolina*. He was paid $123.33 on 7 June 1808.

Sands, Andrew. Pa. Sgt. He applied in Huntingdon County. He served in the 1st Pa. Regiment. The board rejected his application because "in appearance he is a robust healthy man altho he says he is afflicted with the rheumatism." He was pensioned 3 May 1814. He was 86 years old in 1840 in Huntingdon County. He died in Bedford County 20 Mar. 1848. His name has been misread as Andrew Lands.

Sandler, Jacob. Va. —. His wife, Eleanor Sandler, was granted £8 support in Berkeley County on 21 Jan. 1778. He was away in Continental service.

Sanford, —. Va. —. His mother, Easter Sanford, was furnished support in Westmoreland County 30 Mar. 1779.

Sanford, Ezekiel. Conn. Capt. He served in the 5th Regiment under Col. Philip B. Bradley and Lt. Ebenezer Olmsted of Ridgefield. He was inoculated in 1777 for smallpox and had a very bad case of the disease. He was discharged in Mar. 1778 due to lameness and a sore leg due to smallpox. He was pensioned 22 Nov. 1788 and resided in Reading, Conn. He died in 1808.

Sanford, James. S.C. —. He was pensioned 25 Nov. 1830. He was paid as late as 1834.

Sanford, Joel. Va. —. He died in the service. His widow, Jemima Sanford, and four children were furnished support in Feb. 1780 and Feb. 1781. She was pensioned in 1783.

Sanford, Zachariah. Conn. Sgt. He served in the 1st Regiment. He was disabled by diseases at North River. He resided in Hartford in 1792.

Sanger, Nathaniel. Mass. Pvt. He served in the 3rd Regiment and was from Watertown. His widow, Catherine Sanger, was paid $50.

Sansbury, John. Md. Pvt. He was a marine. His widow, Sarah Sansbury, was pensioned in Baltimore at the rate of half-pay of a private marine 7 Feb. 1840.

Sansom, John. S.C. Forage Master General. He was a prisoner of the British and taken to St. Augustine. He was transferred to Philadelphia. His widow, Mary Sansom, and three children had an annuity in 1788.

Sanson, Luke. Md. Pvt. He was in Frederick County in 1785. He served in the 1st Regiment and was wounded at Guilford Court House.

Sansum, John. S.C. —. The Tories killed him while he was riding an express. His widow, Jane Sansum, was granted an annuity 10 June 1785 in Abbeville. She was paid in 1796. He also appeared as John Sansom.

Santee, John. Pa. —. He was awarded a $40 gratuity in Northampton Co., Pa. 2 Apr. 1831 and a $40 gratuity and a $40 annuity on 7 May 1832. He died 5 Mar. 1840.

Sapp, Joseph. Del. Pvt. He was on the roll in 1787. He was wounded in the arm at the battle of Ninety Six on 14 June 1781. He was married. He was on the 1791 pension list. He died in 1797 in North Carolina.

Sapper, Jacob. N.Y. Pvt. He served under Col. Jacob Klock in the Montgomery County militia and was slain 6 Aug. 1777. John Sapper and the other children received a half-pay pension for seven years.

Sappington, Richard. Md. Surgeon. His widow, Cassandra Sappington, was pensioned at the rate of surgeon in Harford County on 7 Mar. 1844.

Sargent, James. N.C. —. He was from Rutherford Co., N.C. and was in his 80s when he applied in Rutherford Co., N.C. in Sep. 1832.

Sargent, John. Me. —. He died 23 Nov. 1801. His widow was Lydia Sargent from Frankfort. She was paid $50 under the resolve of 1836.

Sargent, William. N.Y. Pvt. He was wounded in his left leg at White Plains in 1776. He served under Col. William Malcomb. He was discharged from the Invalids Corps 5 Jan. 1783. He was 56 years old on 25 Aug. 1785. He lived in New York City, N.Y. on 13 June 1788. He died 11 Mar. 1790.

Saring, John. Pa. Pvt. He was on the 1813 pension list.

Sartine, James. N.Y. Pvt. He served under Col. Philip Van Cortlandt. He was wounded in his left arm. He lived in Albany Co., N.Y. 2 June 1789. He also appeared as James Sartain and James Certain. He died 18 Dec. 1812. He was on the 1813 pension list.

Satterlee, Richard. N.Y. —. He died in Brookhaven, Suffolk Co., N.Y. and his heirs were awarded 200 acres of bounty land 11 Apr. 1808.

Saunders, —. S.C. —. Nancy Saunders and children were from Spartanburg District in 1820. She was paid as late as 1859.

Saunders, Celey. Va. Capt. He served in the state navy. He became supernumerary in 1781 and died in 1793. His grandchildren sought his five years' full pay with interest. Congress rejected their claim 14 Jan. 1836.

Saunders, Joseph. Mass. Corp. He served in Col. Gamaliel Bradford's Regiment of Infantry in Capt. Eddy's Company. He was wounded in his left hip. He was pensioned 27 Oct. 1786. He was 36 years old. He transferred from Plymouth Co., Mass. to Kennebec Co., Me. 4 Mar. 1826. He was pensioned at the rate of $5 per month from 7 Feb. 1807. He was on the 1813 pension list. He died 12 Dec. 1831.

Saunders, Joseph. Va. Lt. He served in the artillery to the close of the war. His half-pay of $1,168.88 was paid to his administrator.

Saunders, Noah, Jr. Mass. —. He served in the Artillery in the 6th Regiment and was from Andover. He was paid $20.

Saunders, Richard. N.J. Pvt. He served in the artillery under Capt. Samuel Hugg. He died 15 Sep. 1776. He married Mary Fortune about Oct. 1764. His widow, Mary Saunders, married secondly Frederick Shinfelt 23 Mar 1778. She received a half-pay pension in Gloucester County in 1800.

Savage, Francis. Mass. —. He served in the 5th Regiment and was paid $20.

Savage, John. S.C. Pvt. He served in the 2nd Regiment under Capt. Gray. He was in St. Bartholomew Parish in 1827.

Savage, Joseph. Va. Surgeon's Mate. He served to the end of the war and received his five years' full-pay 11 May 1838. His heirs received his commutation 10 June 1854.

Savage, Nathaniel. Va. —. He was from Northampton County. His heirs received his commutation of full pay for five years in lieu of half-pay for life as a lieutenant of cavalry in the Virginia Line with no interest on 24 Jan. 1828.

Savage, Robert. S.C. Pvt. He served under Capt. Jolly, Col. William Farr, and Col. Brandon. He was 65 years old and had an aged wife and several children. He was pensioned from Union District on 4 Dec. 1823. He was paid as late as 1834.

Savels, Thomas. Mass. Sgt. He served in the 3rd Regiment and was from Medford. His widow, Miriam Savels, was paid $50.

Savidge, Philip. Va. Pvt. His widow, Mourning Savidge, was awarded a £25 gratuity in Surry Co., Va. 9 Dec. 1777. She was in Surry County on 7 Mar. 1787 when she was pensioned at the rate of £8 per annum. He served in the 4th Va. Regiment in Capt. Watkins's Company and died in the service. There were four children. In 1792 one child was in his 20th year and one in his 17th. He also appeared as Philip Savage.

Sawtell, Hezekiah. N.H. Pvt. He was pensioned 17 June 1809 in Cheshire Co., N.H. He was on the 1813 pension list.

Sawtell, Jonas. —. —. He died in 1829. His widow, Eunice Sawtell, sought his pension from 1819 to 1820. Congress rejected her petition 1 Apr. 1844.

Sawyer, —. —. Pvt. He served at least twelve months. Congress granted his widow, Esther Sawyer, a pension 9 Feb. 1843.

Sawyer, Abraham. Mass. Pvt. He served under Col. Tupper and was wounded at Hubbardstown on the retreat from Ticonderoga. He was greatly disabled in his right hand by a musket ball. He was pensioned at the rate of half-pay from Feb. 1780 on 27 Mar. 1780. He was on the 1813 pension list. He also served under Col. Ebenezer Francis and Capt. Wheelwright.

Sawyer, Azariah. —. Pvt. He served for fifteen months. He married in 1781 or 1782. He died 12 Dec. 1829. Congress granted his widow, Esther Sawyer, a pension 9 Feb. 1842. Her sister was Hannah Cunningham.

Sawyer, George. S.C. —. He was wounded in the war by being shot in the head behind his right ear. He lost all feeling in that part of his head. He was taken prisoner after the fall of Charleston but escaped and rejoined. He had a wife and one child. He was 70 years old. He was pensioned 8 Dec. 1825. He was paid as late as 1831.

Sawyer, Horace. —. —. He was pensioned 9 June 1794.

Sawyer, James. —. —. He received his commutation. He was to receive half-pay for life upon proof by deducting his commutation.

Sawyer, James. Pa. —. He was awarded a $40 gratuity in Dauphin Co., Pa. 14 Apr. 1828.

Sawyer, John. N.H. —. He enlisted in 1777 at Oxford and served under Col. Chase from 25 Sep. to Oct. After the burning of Royalton, Vt., he helped drive the enemy into Canada. He became a clergyman. He was in Capt. Jonathan Chase's Company in the militia and marched to reenforce the Continental Army on the Hudson River near Stillwater in Sep. 1777. He was 103 years old when Congress pensioned him at the lowest grade 29 May 1858.

Sawyer, Oliver. Mass. —. He was paid $20.

Sawyer, Peter. Pa. —. He was from Cumberland County.

Sawyer, Samuel. Conn. Pvt. He served in Capt. Rogers' Militia Company. He was wounded in the body by a musket ball which passed through him, broke two of his ribs, and passed through his liver on 27 Apr. 1777 at Wilton. He resided at Cornwall, Conn. in 1794. He was granted half a pension 20 Apr. 1796. He was on the 1813 pension list. He died in 1813.

Sawyers, William. S.C. Dragoon. He served in the 3rd Regiment of Light Dragoons. He was wounded in his head and three places in his right shoulder. He lost both thumbs. He was wounded on 8 Sept. 1781 at Eutaw Springs. He lived in Beaufort Dist., S.C. in 1794. He lived in Prince William Parish in 1809.

Saxton, James. —. —. His widow, Huldah Saxton, had her petition for a pension rejected by Congress 27 Mar. 1846 because they were married subsequent to 1 Jan. 1794.

Saxton, James. S.C. Pvt. He served 18 months under Gen. Sumter, Col. Polk, and Capt. Martin. He applied for a pension in 1850. His papers were mislaid, found, and then rejected. He was nearly 100 years of age. Congress approved him for relief 19 Mar. 1860.

Say, Richard. S.C. —. He was killed at Savannah. His widow, Mary Say, was granted an annuity 1 Sep. 1785. There were three children in 1791.

Sayer, James. Pa. —. He was awarded a $40 gratuity and a $40 annuity in Dauphin Co., Pa. 11 June 1832.

Sayers, —. Va. —. His wife was granted £6.6 support in Halifax Co., Va. on 16 Oct. 1777.

Sayers, George. S.C. Pvt. He served under Capt. John Wickley. He had his skull fractured and his brains laid open by the overturning of a baggage wagon. He was in hospital a considerable time. He was on the roll in 1799.

Sayler, George Michael. Pa. —. He was awarded a $40 gratuity and a $40 annuity in Somerset Co., Pa. 16 Feb. 1835. He also appeared as George Michael Saylor.

Sayre, James. N.Y. Corp. He entered the service for six months in 1775 under Capt. John Hurlbert and Col. James Clinton. He was from Southampton, Suffolk Co., N.Y. Congress granted him a pension 11 May 1838.

Scammel, Samuel Lisle. Mass. Eng. He received his commutation for five years in lieu of half-pay for life.

Scanning, David. Mass. —. He was in the 7th Regiment and was paid $20.

Scarlet, Thomas. N.C. —. He was born 20 Jan. 1763 and married Anna James in July 1779. He applied in Orange Co., N.C. in 1838.

Scelly, Hugh. Pa. Pvt. His widow, Ann Scelly, applied 14 Aug. 1783. She had married Richard Clark. Hugh Scelly served in the Bedford County militia in Capt. William Phillips' Company and was taken prisoner by the Indians 16 July 1780 in Woodcock Valley and was murdered soon after. He was survived by his widow and his daughter, Mary Scelly. Her guardian was George Buchanan; she was born 14 Aug. 1780. She was in Butler County. He also appeared as Hugh Shelly and Hugh Skelly.

Sceve, John. Ga. Pvt. He served in the 2nd Regiment. He was on the roll in 1782.

Schaefer, Peter. Pa. —. He was pensioned.

Schafer, Henry. N.Y. Sgt. He served under Col. Voorman. He was wounded in the thigh by a musket ball at an engagement with the British and Indians on 30 May 1778 at Cobuskill. He lived at Cobuskill, N.Y. in 1794. He also appeared as Hendrick Schafer.

Schafer, Peter. N.Y. Pvt. He served under Col. Voorman. He was wounded in his left arm in action with the Indians and Tories on 30 May 1778 at Cobuskill. He lived at Cobuskill, N.Y. in 1794. He

Revolutionary War Pensions

also appeared as Peter Schiffer.

Scharp, John. Pa. —. He applied in Berks County on 2 Aug. 1820. He enlisted in 1779 in Capt. Bone's Company under Col. Butler. He was in the 9th Pa. Regiment under Gen. Anthony Wayne for one year. He had been in the militia before he enlisted. He had his feet frozen in New Jersey. He was 62 years old and signed in German.

Schatz, Henry. Pa. —. He was awarded a $40 gratuity and a $40 annuity in Montgomery Co., Pa 23 Jan. 1830.

Schaum, —. Pa. —. His widow, Margaret Schaum, received a $40 gratuity and a $40 annuity in Lancaster County in 1836.

Schaum, Melchoir. Pa. —. He received a $40 gratuity and a $40 annuity in Lancaster County 12 Mar. 1836. He was dead by July 1837.

Scheetz, —. Pa. —. His widow, Catherine Scheetz, of Lehigh County was granted a pension 25 Mar. 1844. She had been incorrectly named as Christian Scheetz earlier in the act of 18 Apr. 1843.

Scheiner, Philip. Pa. Pvt. He was on the 1791 pension roll.

Schell, George. N.Y. Pvt. He served in Ganesvort's N.Y. Regiment. He was pensioned 19 Oct. 1786. He died 8 Aug. 1818 in Rensselaer County. He was on the 1813 pension list.

Schell, Johannes. N.Y. Pvt. He served under Col. Bellenger. He was wounded in his left side in action with the Indians at Oriskie. He lived in Herkimer, N.Y. in 1794.

Schillinger, James. N.J. —. He was pensioned in Cape May County on 28 Feb. 1840 at the rate of $60 per annum.

Schindle, Peter. Pa. —. He was awarded a $40 gratuity and a $40 annuity in Lancaster County 1 Apr. 1836.

Schindledecker, Michael. Pa. —. He was awarded a $40 gratuity and a $40 annuity in Mercer Co., Pa. 4 May 1832.

Schively, Jacob. Pa. —. He served for 4 years and 9 months and was wounded. He was from Montgomery County. He served in Miles' Rifles.

Schlagle, Conrad. Pa. —. He was awarded a $40 gratuity and a $40 annuity in Northampton Co., Pa. 1 Feb. 1834.

Schlater, Godfrey. Pa. —. He was awarded a $40 gratuity and a $40 annuity in Philadelphia Co., Pa. 24 Mar. 1828. His widow, Elizabeth Schlater, was awarded a $40 gratuity 3 Mar. 1829. He died 3 Dec. 1833.

Schlauck, Bernard. Pa. Pvt. He was in Philadelphia County on 17 July 1787. He was in the 1st Pa. Regiment, was wounded at Princeton 2 Jan. 1777, and lost his leg. He served under Capt. Henry Shade in the 1st Regiment. He was aged 30. He also appeared as Bernard Slough, Barnet Schlauck, and Bernard Schlough.

Schlokeman, Christopher. Pa. —. He was awarded a $40 gratuity and a $40 annuity in Berks Co., Pa. 5 Mar. 1828. He also appeared as Christopher Scholkerman.

Schlosser, Peter. Pa. —. He was pensioned in Adams County 9 Feb. 1837 and died 1 June 1841.

Schlott, Frederick. Pa. —. He was awarded a $40 gratuity and a $40 annuity in Lancaster Co., Pa. 25 Mar. 1831.

Schlotter, John. Pa. —. He was awarded a $40 gratuity and a $40 annuity in Lehigh Co., Pa. 15 Mar. 1826.

Schmick, Christian. Pa. —. He was awarded a $40 gratuity and a $40 annuity in Berks County 24 Mar. 1829.

Schmidt, Andrew. Pa. —. He was granted a $40 gratuity in York County 4 May 1832.

Schmidt, Conrad. Pa. —. He received a $40 gratuity in Montgomery County 4 May 832.

Schmuck, John. Pa.—. He was awarded a $40 gratuity and a $40 annuity in York County 31 Mar. 1836. He died 13 Dec. 1839.

Schmuck, Michael. Pa. —. He was awarded a $40 gratuity and a $40 annuity in York Co., Pa. 8 Apr. 1833.

Schmull, Peter. Pa. —. He was awarded a $40 gratuity and a $40 annuity in Montgomery Co., Pa 16 Feb. 1830.

Schnable, Joseph. Pa. —. He was awarded a $40 gratuity in Berks County 6 Apr. 1833. He also appeared as Joseph Schnavle.

Schneider, Adam. Pa. —. He was awarded a $40 annuity in Schuylkill County 5 Feb. 1836. He died 27 Dec. 1843.

Schneider, Dieter. Pa. —. He was awarded a $40 gratuity in Schuylkill Co., Pa. 23 Apr. 1829.

Schneider, Jacob. Pa. —. He was awarded a $40 gratuity in Schuylkill Co., Pa. 23 Apr. 1829 and a $40 gratuity and a $40 annuity 31 Jan. 1831.

Schneider, John. Pa. —. His wife was Elizabeth Schneider and his daughter was Catherine Snyder. According to an anonymous letter, he prevailed on his daughter to swear that she was Catherine Glenning, the sister of Charles Glenning who died intestate, and to take out letters of administration on his estate. She was to use the estate to apply to her father's needs. Charles Glenning was due pay for his service in the levies, and Catherine Glenning signed for same. No record could be found for the administration and she was dead some time before of despair and great agony of body and mind due to lock jaw. Elizabeth Schneider related that she and her old man were fishing and heard that Carlisle was after them. She was to swear that she was a sister to John Squibb. She revealed how William Campbell had been granted administration of the estate of John Squibb who had been a soldier. She got a certificate for nearly £90 plus five or six years of interest. She truly was the administrator and could not be prosecuted. The date of the application was Apr. 1787.

Schnell, Jacob. Pa. Musician. He was in Philadelphia County on 13 Oct. 1785. He was in Col. Proctor's Regiment. He was wounded at Block House on Bergen Point 21 June 1780.

Schobert, Francis. Pa. —. —. He was granted support 11 Apr. 1825 in Franklin County.

Schoeckler, Frederick. Pa. —. He received a $40 gratuity and a $40 annuity in Northampton County 15 June 1836.

Schoener, —. Pa. —. His widow, Elizabeth Schoener, was awarded a $40 gratuity and a $40 annuity in Berks County 15 June 1836. She died 18 Sep. 1840.

Schofield, Joseph L.. —. —. His children, Joseph Schofield aged 73 and Sarah N. Giese aged 68, did not have their claim approved by Congress 17 July 1886.

Schofield, William. Va. Pvt. He served in Capt. Ball's Company. He was wounded in his knee at Germantown. He was awarded a gratuity of £30 and an annuity of half-pay of a soldier for two years on 21 Oct. 1778.

Schon, Jacob. S.C. —. Peter Oliver, as administrator, was to be paid $1,100 or such part as would pay the interest on 6% due him, Thomas Short, David Zhal, and John Renney for service on the frigate *South Carolina* on 20 Dec. 1810.

Schonmaker, Frederick. N.Y. Capt. He served in the militia in 1775 and again in 1778. He enlarged and fortified his dwelling and was left in debt. He lost $50,000 worth of property in the war. He became insane about 1803 and died in 1819. He was from Ulster County. Congress denied relief 2 Feb. 1855.

Schooler, —. Va. —. His father, William Schooler, was granted £60 support in Caroline Co., Va. 14 Apr. 1780 while he was away in the service. There were two sons in the service and five in his household on 8 May 1781.

Schoonmaker, Henry. N.Y. —. He was awarded 200 acres bounty land for furnishing a man to serve in the levies in 1783 on 31 Mar. 1797.

Schrach, Andrew. Md. Pvt. He was from Baltimore in 1829. He was pensioned at the rate of half-pay of a private.

Schreiber, Frederick. Pa. —. His widow, Susanna Schreiber, was awarded a $40 gratuity and a $40 annuity in Lancaster Co., Pa. 9 Apr. 1828.

Schreiner, John. Pa. Pvt. He was on the 1791 pension roll.

Schrieder, Philip. Pa. —. He was pensioned.

Schroder, —. Pa. —. His widow, Catherine Schroder, was awarded a $40 gratuity and a $40 annuity in Philadelphia Co., Pa. 28 Feb. 1834.

Schroyer, Peter. N.Y. —. His wife and two children were granted assistance in Dutchess County 3 Nov. 1781.

Schucker, Jacob. Pa. —. He was granted a $40 gratuity and a $40 annuity 15 Apr. 1834 in Berks County. The initial act mistakenly reported him as John Schucker. The correction was made 19 Dec. 1834.

Schulenger, George. Va. Pvt. He died in Continental service 22 May 1778. His widow was Mary Schulenger.

Schultz, Johann. N.Y. —. He served in the militia until he was taken prisoner by the Tories and British in 1781. He returned home in Dec. 1783. He died in 1813. Since he was not in Continental service, Congress rejected the petition for relief from the heirs.

Schureman, Hercules. —. —. He was pensioned 3 Mar. 1805.

Schuyler, Derrick. N.Y. Lt. He received half-pay for life.

Schuyler, Nicholas. N.Y. Surgeon. He received half-pay for life. He died 24 Nov. 1824.

Schuyler, Philip. N.Y. Pvt. He served under Col. Peter Bellinger in the Montgomery County militia and was slain 6 Aug. 1777. His widow, Anna Schuyler, received a half-pay pension..

Schuyler, Philip. N.Y. Gen. His daughter, Catharine V. R. Cochram, was granted five years' half-pay by Congress 8 July 1856.

Schwanger, John. Pa. Pvt. He was in Philadelphia County on 13 Mar. 1786 He was in the Invalids and was disabled by a hurt on his hip bone. He was discharged 30 Aug. 1782. He also appeared as John Schwager.

Schwarts, Philip. Pa. —. He was granted relief in Schuylkill County in Apr. 1835.

Schwartz, Peter. Pa. —. He was granted relief 7 Mar 1821.

Schwenk, Jacob. Pa. —. He was awarded a $40 gratuity and a $40 annuity in Columbia Co., Pa. 18 Feb. 1834.

Schwoyer, Nicholas. Pa. —. He was pensioned 21 Dec. 1827 in Dauphin County.

Scisson, William. S.C. —. He was killed in Nov. 1781. His widow, Lydia Scisson, was granted an annuity 23 Aug. 1785.

Scoby, James. Pa. —. He was taken or killed at Nescopeck Valley in an engagement with the savages. His wife, Catherine Scoby, and five small children were pensioned 26 Apr. 1781 in Northampton County.

Scoffield, Pettit. Conn. Pvt. He enlisted 8 May 1775 under Col. David Waterbury. He was taken sick in the service and left at Albany on 13 Dec. 1775. He was pensioned 8 Dec. 1788. He was

43 years old and was from Sanford. He died in 1810. He also appeared as Pelet Scoffield.

Scoffield, Selah. Conn. Pvt. He served in Charles Webb's Conn. Regiment in Capt. Stephen Betts' Company. He entered the service 1 Jan. 1777. He was injured at the battle of Monmouth.He was disabled by a hernia and suffered from pains and weakness in his breast. He lived in Stamford, Conn. and was pensioned 8 Dec. 1788. He was on the 1813 pension list. He transferred to Onondaga Co., N.Y. 4 Sep. 1823.

Scofield, Neazer. He was pensioned at Gallipolis, Ohio 17 Aug. 1853 at $50 per annum.

Scoggins, —. S.C. —. His widow was Mary Ann Scoggins from Pendleton District in 1828. She was paid her annuity as late as 1833.

Scollay, John. Mass. Sgt. He served in the 6th Regiment and was from Newton. His widow, Esther Scollay, was paid $50. They were married in 1808. Congress rejected her claim for a pension 12 Jan. 1848 because of the time of their marriage.

Scoone, George. Md. Corp. He was pensioned 4 Sep. 1805. He was on the 1813 pension list.

Scotland, Thomas. Pa. Sgt. He was on the 1813 pension list.

Scott, —. Va. —. His father and mother were granted support in Fluvanna Co., Va. on 5 Oct. 1780. They received 100 pounds of pork and 2 barrels of corn. They had another son away in the service.

Scott, —. Va. —. His father and mother were granted support in Fluvanna Co., Va. on 5 Oct. 1780. They received 100 pounds of pork and 2 barrels of corn. They had another son away in the service.

Scott, Alexander. Pa. —. He was awarded a $40 gratuity and a $40 annuity in Franklin Co., Pa. 29 Mar. 1824.

Scott, Amasa. Mass. Pvt. He served under Col. Holman. He was wounded by a musket ball in his right leg in Oct. 1776 at White Plains. He lived in Belchertown, Mass. in 1795. He served in the militia. He was granted one-fourth of a pension 20 Apr. 1796. He was on the 1813 pension list. He died 16 May 1824 in Windsor Co., Vermont.

Scott, Charles. R.I. Pvt. He had a lame hip from a wound received on 29 Aug. 1778 in Rhode Island. The ball remained in his hip or thigh. The wound had broken out several times. His right leg had shortened about five inches. He served in Maj. General Sullivan's Life Guard under Capt. Aaron Mann who certified his disability. He was aged 27 on 23 Feb. 1786. He lived in Providence Co., R.I. He was on the 1813 pension list.

Scott, Christopher. Pa. —. He was awarded a $40 gratuity and a $40 annuity in Mifflin Co., Pa. 16 Feb. 1835.

Scott, David. S.C. —. He lived in Sumter District and had a large family. His neighbors petitioned that he and his descendants be freed from the tax imposed on free people of color in recognition of his military service in the Revolutionary War.

Scott, David. Va. Capt. He was in Monongalia County 14 Nov. 1784. He served in the 13th Va. Regiment under Col. Gibson and was wounded in his right arm in an engagement with the Indians at Salt Lick Towns in 1779. He was 49 years in 1786. He was on the 1813 pension list.

Scott, Edward. N.Y. Pvt. He was pensioned 11 Aug. 1790. He was on the 1813 pension list.

Scott, James. —. —. He was pensioned. He married in Oct. 1781 and died 1 Dec. 1840. His widow was Anna L. Scott. Congress declined to grant her a pension 11 Apr. 1850.

Scott, James. Md. Sgt. He was pensioned 4 Mar. 1789. He was on the 1813 pension list.

Scott, James. Md. Pvt. He was pensioned 4 Mar. 1789.

Scott, James. Md. Sgt. He was on the 1813 pension list.

Scott, James. N.Y. Pvt. He served in Capt. Wilson's Company in the Montgomery County militia under

Col. Clyde. He was disabled in both hands and in his body by wounds on 11 Nov. 1778 at Cherry Valley. He lived in Cherry Valley, Montgomery Co., N.Y. on 11 May 1789. He was on the 1813 pension list.

Scott, James. Pa. —. He came from Ireland to Mount Bethel, Pa. In 1773. In 1777 he marched to Trenton, Princeton, and New Brunswick. He drew his arms at Philadelphia. He was in Capt. Mach's Company and took a number of prisoners. He was discharged after two months. He was a minuteman under Col. Stroud in 1778. Prussian General Nepausin visited them. Congress granted him a pension for six months of service 21 Mar. 1836. He was from Sparta, N.Y.

Scott, John. Mass. —. He served in the 4th Regiment and was paid $20.

Scott, John. Pa. Pvt. He was on the 1791 pension roll. He was transferred to New Jersey by Sep. 1809. He was on the 1813 pension list.

Scott, John. Va. —. He served under Capt. Rowland Madison in the Continental Army and died in May 1778. His widow, Jean Scott, was awarded £20 in 1778 and 1779.

Scott, Joseph. Va. Capt. He was in Amelia County in 1786. He was in the 1st Va. Regiment as captain from 9 Aug. 1777. He was wounded and disabled at Germantown 4 Oct. 1777. He served from Cumberland County. Lt. Col. Samuel Hawes certified his service. In 1789 Brig. Gen. James Wood deposed that he was a captain in the 5th Va. Regiment. His son was Edward Scott. He was continued on the pension roll at full-pay on 26 Jan. 1789. In 1794 he was in Albemarle Co. He died 30 Nov. 1810 between 3 and 4 p.m. William Scott was his executor.

Scott, Moses. Ct. Pvt. He served in the 2nd Conn. Regiment. He was ruptured by a fall from a horse in 1781. He resided in New York in 1796.

Scott, Moses. S.C. —. He served under Col. William Stafford. Capt. William Mann, Lt. Joseph Lawton, Richard Bostick, and Edward Stafford were acquainted with his service. He had a large family and slender means. He was from St. Peter's Parish in 1826. His widow was Rhoda Scott. Paul [?Saul] Solomon was paid one's year pension due to Moses Scott, deceased, in the amount of $60 on 4 Dec. 1828 because he had let him have several articles from his store.

Scott, Richard. Pa. Pvt. He was pensioned at the rate of $2.50 per month from 5 Oct. 1807. He was on the 1813 pension list.

Scott, Robert. Pa. —. He was awarded a $50 gratuity and a $50 annuity in Northumberland Co., Pa. 15 Mar. 1826.

Scott, Robert. Va. —. His wife was granted £6 support in York County on 15 June 1778.

Scott, Samuel. —. —. His widow, Martha Scott, sought a pension. Since she did not prove he served sufficient time, Congress denied her claim 23 June 1854.

Scott, Samuel. —. Maj. His widow, Ann Scott, sought commutation and bounty land. The evidence upon which she had been pensioned could not be found. Congress refused to approve a private act in her behalf 20 Jan. 1846.

Scott, Samuel. Md. Pvt. He was pensioned at the rate of half-pay of a private 5 Feb. 1816. His arrearage of $14.44 was paid to Benjamin L. Gantt for the widow in Prince George's County on 21 Feb. 1834. His widow, Elizabeth Scott, was pensioned at the same rate 4 Mar. 1834. Her arrearage was paid to William Scott, one of her legal representatives, 19 Jan. 1848.

Scott, Samuel. Va. Maj. He served three years as a captain. His widow was pensioned in 1836. When the papers for his bounty land were found in 1854, time had expired to apply to Virginia. Congress approved that the heirs should have a warrant for what he had been entitled on 8 Apr. 1856.

Scott, Thomas. Pa. Pvt. He was in Philadelphia County on 8 May 1786 and in Bucks County 12 May 1787. He served in the 10th Pa. Regiment under Col. Richard Humpton. He was also in the 11th

Pa. Regiment in Capt. Stakes' Company. He was disabled by a paralytic complaint contracted by hardship in the service. He was 64 years old.

Scott, William. —. Capt. He was at Bunker Hill and Yorktown and died in 1796. His son, John Scott, supported the other orphans and sought to be restored to the pension roll from which he had been erased because he could not claim pauperism. Congress refused his claim 4 Feb. 1829.

Scott, William. —. —. He enlisted in 1776 and served three terms of three months each and another term of four months. He left the service in 1777 at the end of another term in consequence of a service injury he had received. The record indicated that he had deserted. He died 7 Nov.1838. Congress determined that his record should have read discharged rather than deserted. His widow, Susannah Scott, died 13 Feb. 1847 while her claim for a pension was pending. Her son and administrator, Thaddeus Scott, was allowed the amount of the pension his mother should have received on 19 Mar. 1860.

Scott, William. N.H. Capt. He served under Col. Cilley. He lost the use of his left hand in a great measure by a wound received from a musket ball on 19 Sep. 1777 at Bemis Heights. He was also wounded in the back by a bayonet at or near North Castle in 1778. He lived in Greenfield, Saratoga Co., N.Y. in 1794. He received commutation as major.

Scott, William. N.Y. Maj. He was on the 1813 pension list.

Scott, William. Pa. Drummer. He applied 9 Apr. 1787. He enlisted 12 July 1775 under Capt. Chambers of the 2nd Rifle Regiment. He served in the 3rd Pa. Regiment under Col. John Shea and was wounded by a musket ball through his shoulders at Fort Washington 16 Nov. 1776. He was 44 years old and lived in Crawford County. He died 19 July 1824.

Scott, William. Pa. Capt. He was on the 1791 pension roll. He died in 1797.

Scott, William. S.C. Lt. Col. He served in the 14th Regiment and was taken prisoner at the fall of Charleston in 1778. Bounty land warrant #4604 was issued to William Putnam, the assignee of Mary Scott, the wife of William Scott. His son, Joseph Scott, believed that he was entitled to a proportion of the land. He also believed that Mary Scott did not make the assignment. He sought other bounty land, but Congress refused 1 Apr. 1842.

Scouden, —. Pa. —. His widow, Sarah Scouden, received a $40 gratuity and a $40 annuity in Crawford County 3 Apr. 1837.

Scout, James. Pa. —. He served in the Associators. He was from Bucks County.

Scovell, John. Mass. Pvt. He served in Col. Latimer's Regiment in the Northern Army under Gen. Gates. He was wounded by two musket balls--one in his left armpit and the other below the arm which lodged near the shoulder blade on 9 Sept. 1777 near Stillwater. He resided at Partridgefield, Mass. in 1796. He also appeared as Jonas Scovell and Jonah Scovell.

Scovill, Jonah. —. Pvt. He was wounded at the capture of Gen. Burgoyne. He was an invalid pensioner in Mass. In 1792. His widow, Sarah Scovill, had her petition for a pension rejected by Congress on 27 Mar. 1846 because they were married subsequent to 1 Jan. 1794.

Scribner, Nathaniel. Conn. Capt. He served in Col. Luddington's militia. He was wounded by a musket ball which passed obliquely through his left arm in June 1778. He resided in Norwalk, Conn. in 1792 and in Dutchess County in 1795. He served in the militia. He was granted one-fourth of a pension 20 Apr. 1796. He died in 1799.

Scruggs, Thomas. Va. Pvt. He served in the 2nd Va. Regiment. His widow was Keziah Scruggs,

Scudder, William Smith. N.Y. Pvt. He lost two fingers and the use of both hands by being frozen in a snow storm when he went with his men to Long Island in a boat to take certain pieces of ordnance that had belonged to the enemy's shipping by order of Gen. Putnam on 3 Mar.

1778. He was granted half a pension 20 Apr. 1796. He lived in Westchester Co., N.Y. He died 7 Mar. 1804.

Scurry, John. Va. Pvt. He was pensioned at the rate of £8 from 1 Nov. 1783 on 15 Dec. 1791. He was in Charlotte County on 12 Feb. 1792. He served in the Va. Line and was wounded. In 1797 he was in Amelia County. He also appeared as John Skurry.

Scutt, William. N.Y. Pvt. He served under Capt. Philip Conyne and Col. Marinus Willett. He was drafted for nine months in Apr. 1781 and returned home. On 1 Jan. 1782 he was at a blockhouse six miles from Catskill, N.Y.. He served eight months and six days. He died 13 May 1825. He married in May 1790. His widow, Ruth Scutt, married secondly John C. Hallenback 23 Jan. 1826. He died 16 Aug. 1828. Congress granted her a pension 29 Feb. 1848.

Seabrooks, Moses. Pa. —. He was awarded a $40 gratuity in Adams Co., Pa. 10 Apr. 1835.

Seaburn, John. Md. Pvt. He was pensioned at the rate of half-pay of a private 21 Dec. 1811.

Seals, —. Pa. —. His widow, Sarah Seals, was awarded a $40 gratuity and a $40 annuity in Greene Co., Pa. 21 Mar. 1833. She died 19 Apr. 1846. Her name has been read as Sarah Scales.

Seals, James. Pa. —. He was awarded a $40 gratuity and a $40 annuity in Center Co., Pa. 24 Mar. 1832. He died 6 Nov. 1833.

Seamster, John. Va. Pvt. His wife, Margaret Seamster, was granted assistance on 17 June 1779 in Halifax Co., Va. She received £60 on 18 May 1780, £86 in May 1780, and a half barrel of corn and 15 pounds of bacon on 15 June 1780. He was awarded a gratuity of one year's pay and an annuity of half-pay on 3 Dec. 1781. He was in Halifax County in June 1786. He was a soldier in Col. Buford's Regiment and lost his right arm at Hanging Rock in Buford's defeat. He was 35 years old. He had his pension continued on 4 Nov. 1786 at the rate of £8 per annum. He also appeared as John Simster and John Seemster. He was on the 1813 pension list.

Seanning, David. Mass. —. He served in the 7th Regiment.

Searl, Joseph. Mass. Pvt. He served in the 11th Regiment and was from Danvers. His widow, Margaret Searl, was paid $50.

Searls, Samuel. Mass. —. He served in the 5th Regiment and was paid $20.

Sears, Elnathan. N.Y. Lt. He enlisted in 1776 under Capt. Milliken and Col. Paulding for two years. He enlisted in 1779 under Col. Brown and was commissioned in the spring of 1779 or 1780 at Fort Stanwix and served under Capt. Joshua Drake. He was put in command at Stone Arabia and was paid as a captain from Dec. 1782 to the summer of 1783. Congress granted him a pension at the rank of lieutenant on 4 Apr. 1840. His only daughter, Mary Miller, was very poor and quite aged in Dec. 1852. He was pensioned at the rank of sergeant. His daughter, Mary Miller, sought a pension for his having served as a lieutenant for two years. Congress rejected her claim on 23 Feb. 1855 because no record of his service as a officer had been found. She asked for an increase from Congress 23 Mar. 1860.

Sears, Isaac. —. —. He served from 1 Jan. 1776 to 1 Jan. 1777. He married in Nov. 1780 Grace Daniels and died 16 Sep. 1838. Her brother was Nehemiah Daniels. Her son was Isaac Sears. Congress granted her a pension for six months of service 9 Feb. 1842.

Sears, John. Md. Lt. His widow, Mary Sears, was pensioned at the rate of half-pay of a lieutenant 26 Jan.1828 in Harford County.

Sears, John. Mass. Pvt. He served in Nichols' Regiment and was from Amherst. His widow, Mary Sears, was paid $50.

Sears, Joseph. Va. Pvt. He was in Mecklenburg County in May 1788. He enlisted 1 May 1779 in Richard Parker's Company in the cavalry and served to Mar. 1780 as proved by the oath of Lt. Samuel Selden. He reenlisted in the 1st Va. Regiment in Mar. 1780. He was wounded at Lanneau's Ferry on 6 May 1780 as proved by Maj. J. Belfield of the Light Dragoons. He had two bad wounds, one in his knee and another in his shoulder. He lost one of his fingers. He was 26 years old. He was pensioned at the rate of £8 per annum on 10 Mar. 1785. He was continued at the same rate on 9 Jan. 1788. He was on the 1813 pension list and to Kentucky. He was 26 years old in 1788.

Seaton, William. Va. —. His wife, Elizabeth Seaton, and child were furnished £5 in Louisa Co., Va. on 11 Aug. 1777.

Seavey, —. Me. —. His widow was Elizabeth Seavey from York.

Seavey, Eliakim. Me. —. He was from York. He was paid $50 under the resolve of 1836.

Seavey, Isaac. Pa. His heirs were awarded $200 for the donation land he had not drawn on 9 Apr. 1852.

Seaward, John. N.H. Mariner. He was captured, carried to England, and confined to Mill Prison. He was worn out in the service. His father, Giles Seaward, sought compensation.

Seawell, —. N.C. —. His widow, Mary Seawell, applied in Moore County in 1805. She also appeared as Mary Sowell.

Seawright, William. S.C. Pvt. He served under Capt. Rosamond and Capt. John Norwood. He was 64 years old, had an aged partner, and four daughters. He was from Pendleton District in 1827. John Verner served with him. His application was not granted.

Seay, Jacob. Va. Pvt. He served in the 2nd Va. Regiment. He lived in Nottaway County. He was on the 1813 pension list. He died 1 Apr. 1826.

Seayers, John. Va. Lt. Col. He was killed at the battle of Germantown 4 Oct. 1777. His seven years' half-pay of $2,520 was paid to his heirs. His widow, Frances Seayers, received a £200 gratuity on 6 Dec. 1777. On 23 Oct. 1779 she received a £500 gratuity, and her three sons were to be educated at public expense. He also appeared as John Seayres and John Sears.

Sebold, Christian. Pa. —. He was pensioned in Montgomery County 31 Mar. 1836.

Sebolt, Abraham. Pa. —. He was awarded a $40 gratuity and a $40 annuity in Lebanon Co., Pa. 18 Feb. 1834.

Sebree, William. Va. —. His wife, Jane Sebree, was granted £8 support in Northumberland County on 13 Oct. 1778, £40 on 10 May 1779, 1 barrel of corn and 50 pounds of pork on 11 Apr. 1780, and 1 barrel of corn and 50 pounds of pork on 9 Jan. 1781.

Sebring, —. Pa. —. His widow, Sarah Sebring, was granted relief in Luzerne County 10 Feb. 1841 for his Revolutionary service. She died 23 Nov. 1845.

Sebryng, Peter, Jr. N.Y. —. His wife and two children were granted support in Dutchess County on 3 Nov. 1781.

Sechler, Michael. Pa. —. He was awarded a $40 gratuity and a $40 annuity in Lycoming Co., Pa. 15 Mar. 1826. He also received donation land. He was 79 years old in 1840.

Second, George. Md. Corp. He was pensioned in 1785. He was later pensioned at the rate of $54 per annum in Kent County in Nov. 1803.

See, James. N.Y. Sgt. He served under Col. James Harman. He suffered from inflamation caused by hurting his left leg by a fall out of bed in a fit of delirium when he had the smallpox in captivity in the sugar house in New York in 1779. He lived at Mount Pleasant, Westchester Co., N.Y.

Seeber, Adolph. N.Y. Ens. He served in the Tryon County militia and was killed at Oriskany 6 Aug. 1777. His son, Jacob Seeber, was granted assistance.

Seeber, Henry. N.Y. Pvt. He served in Capt. Reynier Van Yerveren's [?] Company under Col. Ebenezer

Cox. He received several wounds at Oriskany on 6 Aug. 1777. He was pensioned 25 Nov. 1786. He lived in Montgomery Co., N.Y. on 29 June 1789 and later in Herkimer County. He was on the 1813 pension list.

Seeber, Jacob William. N.Y. Capt. He served in the Tryon County militia under Lt. Col. Samuel Clyde. He was killed at Oriskany 6 Aug. 1777. His daughter, Elizabeth Seeber, was granted a half-pay pension.

Seeber, Severinus. N.Y. Lt. He served under Lt. Col. Samuel Clyde in the Tryon County militia. He was killed at Oriskany 6 Aug. 1777. His children, William Seeber and Severinus Seeber, received his half-pay pension.

Seeber, William. N.Y. Lt. Col. He served in the Tryon County militia and was killed at Oriskany 6 Aug. 1777. His children, William Seeber, ------ Seeber, Henry Seeber, Mary Seeber, Elizabeth Seeber, Catharine Seeber, and John Seeber received his half-pay pension.

Seel, John. Mass. Corp. He served in the 4th Regiment and was from Becket. He was paid $20.

Seelback, ett. N.Y. Pvt. He was pensioned 19 Oct. 1786. He lived in Montgomery County.

Seeley, Benjamin. Conn. Pvt. He served in Col. Elmore's Regiment. He was disabled by a fall from the second story of the barracks in Aug. 1776 in Albany. He resided in Litchfield, Conn. in 1794. He resided in Steuben Co., N.Y. and Tioga Co., Pa. He was on the 1813 pension list of Connecticut.

Seely, Isaac. Pa. Maj. His widow, Elizabeth Hunt, and her children received patent #2803 for 500 acres of donation land in Erie County, They were paid $750 for the tract. She died in July 1837. Their sole surviving child was Eliza Seely Vethake, the wife of Henry Vethake of Philadelphia, Pa. Congress did not grant her relief on 1 Aug. 1850.

Seely, Michael. N.Y. Pvt. He served under Col. James Livingston and was slain 11 May 1778. His widow, Elizabeth Seely, received a half-pay pension.

Seely, Silvanus. N.Y. Pvt. He served under Col. Morris Graham. He was disabled by a musket ball in his right thigh at Joseph Yong's in Philip's Manor fired by a sentry of Capt. Sybert Acker's Company. He enlisted in Mar. 1778 and was discharged 15 July following. He was pensioned 21 June 1786. He lived in Dutchess Co., N.Y. on 20 Apr. 1789. He was 35 years old in 1786. He was on the 1813 pension list.

Seely, Shadrack. N.Y. Pvt. He served in Capt. Marcus Moseman's Company under Col. Thomas Thomas. He was wounded three times in his left arm with a broadsword when Capt. Kip led the enemy incursion into Bedford 21 Nov. 1780. He was from Westchester County 4 Dec. 1788.

Seely, Thaddeus. N.Y. Pvt. He served in Capt. Marcus Moseman's Company of Westchester County militia under Col. Thomas Thomas in 1780. He was wounded in his arms and head on 21 Nov. 1780. He was a farmer. He was pensioned 4 Dec. 1788. He lived in Tompkins County. He was pensioned at the rate of $2.50 per month from 9 Jan. 1808. He was on the 1813 pension list.

Segar, Ebenezer. Mass. —. He served in Crane's Regiment and was paid $20.

Segar, Peter. N.Y. —. He served under Capt. Van Ornum and Gen. Schuyler in 1776 for three months, two months under Capt. Van Ornum and Capt. Abraham Vedder at the battle of Saratoga in 1777, nine months in the militia under Capt. Vedder and Col. Leonard Gansevoort in 1778, and six months each year as an Indian spy from 1779 to 1782. He married Mary ----- 15 June 1776. James Segar was his son. His widow was allowed a pension by Congress for six months of service from 8 Aug. 1837 on 27 Mar. 1846.

Segart, Eli. Pa. —. He was awarded a $40 gratuity and a $40 annuity in Bedford Co., Pa. 10 Apr. 1826. He also appeared as Eli Sergart.

Seider, —. Pa. —. His widow, Mary Eve Seider, was awarded a $40 gratuity in Berks Co., Pa. 14 Apr. 1834.

Seidle, Peter. Pa. —. He was awarded a $40 gratuity and a $40 annuity in Lebanon Co., Ohio 11 Apr. 1825.

Seigle, Frederick. Va. Surgeon. His daughter, Amelia Hotsenpiller, sought his seven years' half-pay. Congress granted her the same 1 Apr. 1844.

Seigle, Henry. Pa.—. He was granted relief in Northampton County 12 Feb. 1825.

Seigler, George. S.C. Pvt. He served under Col. Leroy Hammond and Capt. John Carter. He entered the service at the age of 15. He was 64 years old.. He was from Barnwell District and was pensioned 4 Dec. 1828. Peter Day and Joseph Day swore that he was a good soldier. He was paid as late as 1834. He also appeared as George Siegler.

Seitsinger, Michael. —. —. He had been rejected because he was too young to have been in the service which he claimed. Congress granted him a pension 5 Mar. 1840 for six months of service. His heirs sought $20 per year from 4 Mar. 1831 to his death. They claimed two months of service for him in 1776, two months in 1777, and two months in 1781. Congress ruled that the first tour could not have been for military duty. His second tour at the age of 14 was absurd for he could not have been drafted at that age.

Seitz, Peter. Pa. —. He was pensioned.

Selden, Samuel. Va. Lt. He was in Powhatan County 16 Dec. 1786. He was 28 years old. He served in the 1ˢᵗ Va. Regiment. He was wounded in attempting to storm the British fortification at Ninety Six, S.C. in June 1781. He lost his right arm between the shoulder and elbow. Lt. Col. Samuel Hawes certified his service. He was continued on the pension roll at the rate of half-pay on 16 Dec. 1786. He was continued on the pension list on 14 July 1791. He died after 15 June 1799. His executors were Miles Selden and Samuel Selden.

Selfridge, Robert. S.C. —. He was wounded in an expedition against the Indians. He was on the roll in 1793.

Selhamm, Nicholas. Pa. —. His pension began 24 Feb. 1818.

Sell, Philip. S.C. Pvt. He served under Capt. William Alexander and was wounded at Eutaw Springs. He applied from Mecklenburg County, N.C. He was on the roll in 1826. He was paid as late as 1833. He was told that it was necessary for him to come in person to Columbia, S.C. to collect his pension so he received no further payments. He died 1 Aug. 1843. His widow, Dorothy Sell, died in Feb. 1848. His children, Garright Sell, Solomon Sell, and Parthenia Sell of Stanley Co., N.C., sought the arrearage in 1857. They were paid $625 on 23 Jan. 1858.

Sellers, Daniel. N.C. —. He came from Scotland in 1774. He enlisted under Capt. McCrief and Col. Lamb at Wilmington. He was Brandywine, Monmouth, and Stony Point. He was at the siege of Charleston under Col. Hogan. He was wounded and held prisoner for eleven months. He was about to be put on a prison ship when a Highland captain in British service who knew his family in Scotland persuaded Sir Henry Clinton to let him go to Halifax, Nova Scotia. He remained there 56 years until last May when he came to Portsmouth, N.H. He had voluntarily left the country early in the century and was loyal by remaining in British dominions. Congress rejected his application for a pension 28 Jan. 1837.

Sellers, George. Pa. —. He served as a ranger under Capt. Shannon on tour to Wheeling and later under Capt. Leasure in guarding the frontiers.

Selser, Matthias. Va. —. He served under Capt. John Gillison. His knee was mortified. He sought his pay on 20 June 1780.

Semmes, James. Md. 2nd Lt. He was pensioned at the rate of a second lieutenant in Charles County on 2 Jan. 1813.

Semson, John. Pa. —. He enlisted in 1776 and was discharged in Sep. 1783. He was from Lancaster Co.

Septre, Frederick. Pa. —. He was pensioned in Westmoreland County 24 Mar. 1837. He was 78 years old in 1840. He died 25 Mar. 1846. His widow, Catharine Septre, was awarded a $40 annuity 11 Apr. 1848. She died 12 Nov. 1850.

Serena, Joseph. Pa. —. He was pensioned in Westmoreland County 27 Mar. 1837.

Serena, George. Pa. —. He was pensioned in Armstrong County 15 Mar. 1838. His widow, Barbara Serena was pensioned in 1852 and died 18 Mar. 1853

Sergeant, John. Vt. Corp. He served under Col. Wait. He was wounded by a musket ball which entered his right breast and came out under his right shoulder blade on 16 Oct. 1781. He was carried to Quebec where he was a prisoner for six months. He lived in Bennington, Vt. in 1792.

Sergeant, William. Pa. —. He was granted relief.

Sessions, Josias. S.C. —. He served at the early age of 12 and was under Capt. Maxwell. He fought the Tories at Bear Bluff. He was also under Capt. Prior, Capt. Joseph Long, and Capt. Mark Huggins. He was 64 years old. John Green and James McCracken served with him. He was from Horry District and was pensioned 23 Nov. 1829. He was paid as late as 1836.

Sethammer, Michael. Pa. —. He was pensioned.

Seva, John. Ga. Pvt. He was on the 1791 pension list.

Seveir, Robert. Va. —. His wife, Margaret Seveir, and three children were furnished £10 support in Frederick Co., Va. on 4 Aug. 1778 and £30 support on 3 Aug. 1779. He served in Col. Morgan's Regiment. He also appeared as Robert Savier.

Severance, Jos. Mass. —. He resided in Massachusetts in 1796.

Severson, Richard. N.Y. —. In 1775 he fought the Indians and Tories at several different times. He spent one in every three days guarding boats. In 1776 he was under Capt. Van Bergur for three months. He spent one under Lt. Brong. He paid $26 to a substitute to serve the other two months. In May 1777 he was under Capt. Van Schaick at the taking of Burgoyne. He spent five months under Capt. Houghtailing at Schoharie. In 1779 he enlisted for six months under Capt. Corwin and was out in scouting parties. Congress gave him credit for nine months as a pensioner 21 Mar. 1836.

Sevier, Robert. —. —. He was mortally wounded at King's Mountain. His widow, Keziah Sevier, died between 1800 and 1806. His sons, Valentine Sevier and Charles Sevier, had their claim rejected by Congress on 14 June 1850.

Sewall, Charles. Md. 1st Lt. He was pensioned in Charles County at the rate of half-pay of a first lieutenant 14 Feb. 1820.

Seward, —. Va. —. His wife, Frances Seward, was granted £50 relief in Brunswick Co., Va. on 28 June 1779 while he was away in Continental service. He died in Continental service. His widow was granted relief in Brunswick Co., Va. on 27 Sep. 1779 to enable her to travel to her friends in South Carolina.

Sewell, Clement. Md. Ens. He was on the 1813 pension list. He was pensioned at the rate of half-pay of an ensign in the District of Columbia 24 Feb. 1823. He entered the service in Mar. 1777 under Capt. Ford in the 1st Regiment. He was promoted the day after Brandywine. He received a severe wound in his leg at Germantown. His daughter sought five years' full pay. Congress did not allow the claim 2 Feb. 1855.

Sewell, James. Md. Pvt. He was wounded by a musket ball passing through both his thighs in Sept. 1781 at Eutaw Springs. He was in Md. in 1795. He was pensioned at the rate of a half-pay of a private 6 Feb. 1818. He was on the 1813 pension list.

Sewell, William. Md. Pvt. He was pensioned at the rate of half-pay of a private 16 Nov. 1811 in Annapolis.

Sewell, William. Md. Pvt. He was pensioned at the rate of half-pay of a private in Talbot County on 22 Feb. 1822.

Sewell, William. Md. Pvt. His widow, Rebecca Sewell, was pensioned at the rate of half-pay of a private 6 Feb. 1832.

Sexton, Aaron. Vt. Pvt. & Sgt. He served a day under Capt. Gideon Ormsby and Col. Ira Allen, four days under Capt. Thomas Bull and Col. Allen, 92 days under Capt. George Sexton and Col Ebenezer Walbridge ending in Nov. 1781, and six months under Capt. George Sexton and Maj. Gideon Bronson from 1 Apr. To 1 Oct. 1782. He died in Aug. 1782. His sister was Elizabeth Johns. His widow was Jane Sexton. Congress rejected her claim for a pension on 14 June 1850 because his third and fourth tours were actually the same one.

Seybert, —. Pa. —. His widow, Mary Seybert, was awarded a $40 gratuity and a $40 annuity in Philadelphia Co., Pa. 20 Feb. 1833. She died 13 May 1843.

Seybert, Adam. Pa. —. He died 23 Oct. 1793.

Seymour, William. Conn. Pvt. He was disabled at Fort Griswold. He resided in Hartford Co., Conn. He served in the militia. He was on the 1813 pension list.

Shackleford, —. Va. —. His widow was granted £100 support for necessaries in Halifax Co., Va. 17 Feb. 1780.

Shackleford, John. Va. Pvt. He was in Halifax County in June 1786. He served in the 1st Va. Regiment and was wounded by a ball through the elbow of his right arm at the siege of Savannah, Ga. He was 24 years old. He was continued on the pension roll at the rate of £12 per annum on 15 Nov. 1787. He removed to Georgia in or about 1793. He was on the 1813 pension list.

Shade, —. Pa. —. His widow, Mary Shade, was awarded a $40 gratuity and a $40 annuity in Cumberland Co., Pa. 27 Mar. 1824.

Shade, Henry. Pa. —. He was awarded a $40 gratuity and a $40 annuity in Northampton County on 27 Mar. 1812.

Shaefer, John. Pa. —. He was awarded a $40 gratuity in Philadelphia County 27 Jan. 1835.

Shaeffer, John. Pa. —. He applied in Dauphin County 14 Jan. 1815. He served in Capt. Smith's Company under Col. Arnold and was at Quebec when Gen. Montgomery fell. He was taken prisoner and detained for nine months. He was exchanged and later enlisted in Col. Porter's Artillery in Capt. John Brice's Company. He served two more years. Frederick Schaeffer of Baltimore, Md. proved his service on 14 May 1814.

Shafer, Christian. N.Y. —. He died in 1819. His widow was Elizabeth Shafer and his son was Henry C. Shafer from Schoharie Co., N.Y.

Shafer, Peter. Pa. —. He was awarded a $40 annuity in Lancaster County 5 Feb. 1836.

Shaffer, —. Pa. —. His widow, Barbara Shaffer, was awarded a $40 gratuity and a $40 annuity in York Co., Pa. 15 Apr. 1834

Shaffer, Adam. Pa. —. He was pensioned in 1839.in Luzerne County and was 70 years old in 1840.

Shaffer, Henry. —. —. He served twenty tours in the Virginia or Pennsylvania militia, fourteen of which he was drafted. Seven of his tours were as a substitute for his father. Congress refused him a pension 30 Mar. 1848. [There was a Henry Shaffer who was pensioned by Pennsylvania 27 Mar. 1837. He died in Allegheny County 5 Dec. 1850.]

Shaffer, Jacob. Pa. —. He was awarded a $40 gratuity and a $40 annuity in Montgomery County in 1836. He also appeared as Jacob Shefer. He was dead by Jan. 1839.

Shaffer, John. Pa. —. He was pensioned 7 Feb. 1813.

Shaffer, John. Pa. —. He was awarded a $40 gratuity in Bucks County 13 Apr. 1841 as a Revolutionary veteran.

Shaffner, George. Pa. Maj. He served in the militia. His heirs were paid $300 for his right to donation land 23 Apr. 1829.

Shaffner, Peter. —. —. His application was not accepted.

Shail, —. N.Y. —. Elizabeth Shail was granted a gratuity of a cow.

Shainer, George. Va. —. His wife, Elizabeth Shainer, and child were granted support child in Berkeley Co. 21 Aug. 1781. She received 1 barrel of corn and 100 pounds of bacon on 20 Aug. 1782.

Shaler, Joseph. —. —. His application was accepted 27 Apr. 1810.

Shall, John. Pa. —. He was granted relief in Bedford County 16 Mar. 1835.

Shally, Abraham. S.C. —. His widow was Drusilla Shally in 1786. There were three children in 1791.

Shambaugh, George. Pa. —. He was awarded a $40 gratuity and a $40 annuity in Perry Co., Pa 15 Apr. 1835.

Shandley, Jacob. Md. Pvt. He was pensioned 4 Mar. 1789. On the 1813 pension list he was Jacob Shanley.

Shane, Henry. Md. Pvt. He was pensioned at the rate of half-pay of a private in Baltimore County on 12 Mar. 1828. His arrearage was paid to his son Henry Shane 7 Feb. 1830.

Shanks, —. Va. —. His father, Conrad Shanks, was furnished assistance in Loudoun County while he was away in the service in Aug. 1779.

Shanks, James. S.C. Pvt. He served under Lt. James Noble and Lt. John McGaw. He was 14 years old when he entered the service. He was at Tugolo Old Town against the Indians and Tories. He buried the bones of a number of friends and companions murdered at Chota. His wife and a son had been sick for two years and unable to work. George McFarling and Elias Gibson served with him. He was pensioned from Abbeville District on 6 Dec. 1826. He died 5 Dec. 1828. His widow, Jane Shanks, was pensioned 23 Nov. 1829 and was paid as late as 1834. She supported two children.

Shanks, John. Md. Pvt. He was on the 1791 pension list.

Shanley, Patrick. Mass. Pvt. He was wounded in the right ankle and left arm near the wrist at Kingsbridge in 1781. He served in the 10th Regiment. He lived in Boston, Mass. in 1792.

Shannon, —. Pa. —. His widow, Elizabeth Shannon, was awarded a $40 gratuity and a $40 annuity 27 Mar. 1837. She was from Allegheny County. She was 77 years old in 1840.

Shannon, —. Pa. —. His widow, Barbara Shannon, was granted relief in Crawford Co. 13 Apr. 1841 and 18 Apr. 1843.

Shannon, George. —. —. His application was accepted 2 Aug. 1813.

Shannon, Samuel. Pa. Capt. His widow, Elizabeth Shannon, was in Westmoreland County 2 Feb. 1791. He was in the Westmoreland County militia under Col. Archibald Lockry on the expedition against the Indians in 1781 and was killed about the middle of Oct. 1781. He was tomahawked. He was 35 years old when he died and left seven children. Five were under 14 years of age at the time of his death. His widow was 50 years of age in 1795.

Shannon, William. Pa. —. He was awarded a $40 gratuity and a $40 annuity 27 Mar. 1837.

Shanon, Daniel. Pa. —. He was pensioned.

Shantz, Henry. Pa. —. He was awarded a $40 gratuity and a $40 annuity in Montgomery Co., Pa.

25 Mar. 1831. His widow, Magdalena Shantz, was awarded a $40 annuity in Montgomery Co., Pa. 21 Apr. 1852 for his Revolutionary service.

Shapley, John. —. Capt. He served on the sloop of war *Ranger* for more than twelve months. He was not covered by any law so Congress rejected his application 6 Mar. 1820.

Sharer, John. Pa. —. He was awarded a $40 gratuity and a $40 annuity in Huntingdon Co., Pa. 15 Mar. 1826.

Sharman, Abel. N.Y. Pvt. He was pensioned.

Sharman, John. Pa. —. He was pensioned.

Sharp, James. Pa. —. He served six months against the Indians. He was 82 years old in 1823 and was from Butler County.

Sharpe, John. Va. —. He was wounded in Continental service at the storming of Augusta, Ga. He was being pensioned in 1783.

Sharpent, Simon. N.Y. —. He was wounded in the back part of his head, neck, and left hand. He lived in Westchester Co., N.Y. on 12 May 1787. He also appeared as Simon Sharpanest.

Sharpless, David. Pa. —. He enlisted for three years and was taken prisoner at Brandywine. He swam the Schuylkill in an escape attempt, was shot, and killed. His widow and children were awarded his donation land 30 Mar. 1811.

Sharpless, Robert. Md. Corp. He was from Kent County in 1785. He was struck off the roll in 1789 because he was able bodied and a great drunkard.

Shartel, Jacob. Pa. Capt. He served under Col. Hartley. He was wounded by a party of Indians by a musket ball which passed through his right ear. He suffered from dizziness. He was wounded at Muncy Creek in 1778. He lived in Berks, Pa. in 1794. He was on the 1813 pension list.

Shartzer, Christopher. Pa. —. He died in Oct. 1826, and his arrearage was paid to his widow, Catharine Shartzer, in Lancaster County 27 Dec. 1826.

Shattuck, Jonas. Mass. Pvt. He served under Col. Samuel Bullard and Capt. Jewett. He was disabled due to the loss of his right leg. His pension began 4 Mar. 1790. He was on the 1813 pension list. He lived in Lincoln, Me.

Shaver, Christian. N.Y. Pvt. He served under Col. Bellinger in the Montgomery County militia and was slain 6 Aug. 1777. His widow, Anna Margaret Shaver, was granted a half-pay pension for seven years. His name may have been Christian Sharer.

Shaver, James. N.Y. Gunner. He served in the 2nd N.Y. Artillery under Col. John Lamb. He was disabled by a cannon ball in the small of his back. He lived in Wallkill, Ulster Co., N.Y. on 18 Apr. 1789. He also appeared as James Shever.

Shaver, John. Pa. Lt. He received relief in Huntingdon County 15 Mar. 1826. His widow applied 12 Aug. 1846. He served in Col. Thomas Smith's Regiment in 1776.

Shaw, Abraham. Me. —. He was from York. He was paid $50 under the resolve of 1836.

Shaw, Alexander. Pa. Sgt. Maj. He was in Philadelphia County on 13 Feb. 1786. He served in the 4th Pa. Regiment and was wounded in the attack on one of the enemy's outposts near Brunswick, N.J. in 1777. He was wounded in his hip and otherwise afflicted. He was 33 years old.

Shaw, Alexander. Pa. —. He was pensioned in Westmoreland County 1 Apr. 1837. He was dead by Dec. 1843. He died 19 May 1843.

Shaw, Archibald. Pa. —. He was awarded a $40 gratuity and a $40 annuity in Baltimore, Md. 7 Apr. 1832.

Shaw, Asa. Mass. Pvt. He served at the Castle and was from Abington. He was paid $50.

Shaw, Daniel. N.Y. Lt. He was granted relief.

Shaw, Daniel. N.C. Pvt. His widow, Lucy Shaw, applied in Cumberland County in 1783. He served in the militia under Col. Robeson of Bladen County and was wounded in the battle at Rockfish in 1781.

Shaw, Daniel. S.C. Pvt. He was killed in the service. His widow, Catherine Shaw, was granted an annuity 20 Dec. 1785. She was from Union District. There were two children in 1791.

Shaw, Ephraim. Mass. Pvt. He served in the 5th Regiment and was from Malden. He was paid $50.

Shaw, George. Mass. Pvt. He served in the 5th Regiment and was from Colrain.

Shaw, Gideon. Pa. —. He was awarded a $40 gratuity in Bucks Co., Pa. 18 Mar. 1834 and on 31 Mar. 1836.

Shaw, Jesse. Mass. Pvt. He served at the Castle and was from Weymouth. His widow, Sarah Shaw, was paid $50.

Shaw, John. Md. Sgt. Maj. He was pensioned 4 Mar. 1789.

Shaw, John. Pa. —. He was transferred to Maryland.

Shaw, John. Pa. —. He was wounded at Brandywine and was pensioned. He died 15 Nov. 1798 in Fayette County. His widow, Elizabeth Shaw, was due a pension for four years and two months. Congress granted her relief 16 Jan. 1828.

Shaw, John. S.C. —. He was pensioned 12 Dec. 1826.

Shaw, John Robert. Pa. Pvt. His application was accepted 3 Mar. 1809. He was on the 1813 pension list.

Shaw, Josiah. Mass. Pvt. He served in Burbeck's Regiment and was from Plainfield. He was paid $50.

Shaw, Nathaniel. Me. —. He was from Turner. He was paid $50 under the resolve of 1836.

Shaw, Samuel. N.Y. Lt. He served in Col. Stephen J. Schuyler's militia. He received a violent bruise in his leg while assisting his men in erecting a bridge occasioned by the sliding of a large log on 9 Oct. 1776 near Fort Ann. He lived in Stephentown, N.Y. in 1794. He was pensioned at the rate of $8 per month from 13 Feb. 1808. He was on the 1813 pension list.

Shaw, Samuel. Pa. —. He was awarded a $40 gratuity in Delaware Co., Pa. 25 Mar. 1833 and again on 1 Apr. 1834.

Shaw, Sylvanus. R.I. Capt. He was killed in the action at Red Bank on the Delaware 22 Oct. 1777. His heirs were paid his seven years' half-pay of $1,680.

Shaw, William. S.C. —. He was under Lt. George Story, Maj. Brannon, Capt. James Crawford, Capt. John Moffet, and Col. Bratton. He was at King's Mountain and skirmishes at Col. John Thomas' and two in Georgia. John Forbes saw him at Orangeburg after the fall of Charleston. He was 67 years old and had a wife, a son afflicted with fits, and two daughters. He was from York District in 1825. He was paid as late as 1834.

Shaw, William. Va. —. He died in the service. His wife and six children had their subsistence extended in Yohogania Co., Va. 25 Aug. 1778 at the rate of 20 shillings per month.

Shaw, William Va. —. His wife was granted support in Halifax Co., Va. on 17 June 1779 and on 16 Sep. 1779.

Shay, John. N.Y. Pvt. He was on the 1813 pension list.

Shaylor, Joseph. —. —. His application was laid on the table.

Shays, Daniel. Mass. Lt. He served in Col. Woodridge's Regiment. He had a rupture in his groin. He resided in Mass. in 1796. He was appointed captain 1 Jan. 1777.

Shea, —. Pa. —. His widow, Mary Shea, was awarded a $40 gratuity and a $40 annuity in Lancaster Co., Pa. 10 Apr. 1826.

Shea, Edward. Pa. —. He was granted a pension 26 Feb. 1814. He died about 1 Mar. 1814. His administrator was Joseph Blackburn.

Shea, George. Pa. —. He was granted relief.

Shead, Lemuel. Mass. —. He served in the 5th Regiment and was from Norway, Maine. He was paid $20.

Shean, Henry. Md. Pvt. He was pensioned at the rate of a private in 1828 in Baltimore County. His arrearage was paid to his son, Henry W. Shean, in 1830.

Shean, James. Md. Pvt. He was in Frederick County in 1787. He served in the 2nd Regiment. He was wounded at Monmouth.

Shearman, Thomas. Pa. —. He was awarded a $40 gratuity and a $40 annuity in Columbia Co., Pa. 11 Apr. 1825.

Shech, —. Va. —. His wife, Eve Shech, and two children were granted £18 support in Yohogania Co., Va. 27 May 1779.

Shed, Amos. Me. —. He was in Connecticut in 1796. He died 11 July 1800. His widow was Lucy Crosby from Norridgewock. She was paid $50 under the resolve of 1836.

Shee, Edward. Pa. —. He enlisted in 1776 in the militia. He went on board a marine ship under Capt. John Dill. Subsequently, he served under Col. William Butler and Capt. Thomas Campbell in the 4th Regiment. He was from Dauphin County. He died 4 May 1814. He also appeared as Edward Shea.

Sheeley, —. Pa. —. His widow, Catherine Sheeley, was awarded a $40 gratuity and a $40 annuity in York Co., Pa. 6 Mar. 1833. She was dead by July 1838.

Sheets, Jacob. Md. Pvt. His widow, Hannah Sheets, was pensioned at the rate of half-pay of a private in Frederick County on 26 Jan. 1828.

Sheets, Jacob. Pa. —. He was granted relief in Washington County 12 June 1846.

Sheets, Philip. Pa. —. He was pensioned 1 Apr. 1825 in Berks Co., Pa.

Sheffield, Deming. Mass. —. He served in the 6th Regiment and exchanged his payment for bounty land.

Sheffield, George. —. —. His widow, Mary Sheffield, did not furnish sufficient proof of her marriage and the alleged date was too late so Congress denied her relief 9 Mar. 1848.

Sheffy, —. Pa. —. His widow, Margaret Sheffy, was awarded a $40 gratuity and a $40 annuity 17 Mar. 1835 in Montgomery County..

Sheffy, Christopher. Pa. —. He was awarded a $40 gratuity and a $40 annuity in Montgomery Co., Pa. 23 Jan. 1833. He was dead by Jan. 1840.

Shehan, James. Md. Pvt. He served in the 2nd Regiment and was disabled at Monmouth. He was pensioned in Frederick County in 1783.

Shehm, William. Pa. —. He was pensioned 6 Mar. 1837 in Beaver County.

Sheib, —. Pa. —. His widow, Catharine Sheib, received relief in Philadelphia 18 Apr. 1843.

Sheifley, Jacob. Pa. —. He enlisted in 1776 in the Rifle Company under Capt. Farmer and Col. Miles. He was wounded by the stroke of a sword in the head. He was at the battle of Long Island. He re-enlisted under the same captain. He served four and a half years. He was from Montgomery County. He was awarded a $40 gratuity 30 Mar. 1812. He also appeared as Jacob Sheffley and Jacob Shivele.

Sheild, David. Mass. —. He served in the 4th Regiment. He was paid $20.

Sheiser, Henry David. Pa. —. He received a $40 gratuity and a $40 annuity in Berks County 3 Apr. 1837.

Sheit, Peter. N.Y. Pvt. He served in the Montgomery County militia under Col. Jacob Klock.

Shelby, Abraham. S.C. —. His widow, Drucilla Shelby, was granted an annuity 30 Nov. 1785. She and her children were paid an annuity 20 Jan. 1787.

Shelby, Isaac. —. Col. Congress awarded his heirs his commutation pay 15 Aug. 1856.

Shelby, William. S.C. —. He served under Capt. William Withers and Col. Daniel Horry. He applied from Marion District when he applied 29 Oct. 1828. He was paid as late as 1841.

Shelcut, Ezekiel. Pa. —. His heirs were paid $300 for the right to his donation land on 29 Mar. 1824.

Sheldon, Elijah. Conn. Pvt. He served under Col. Thaddeus Cook and was wounded on 19 Sep. 1777. He was pensioned 7 May 1778 at Suffield, Conn. He died in 1812. He was listed as dead on the 1813 pension list.

Sheldon, Jacob. Conn. —. He served under Col. Thaddeus Cook and was wounded on 19 Sep.1777. He was pensioned 7 May 1778 at Suffield, Conn.

Sheldon, Job. —. —. His bounty warrant was issued to someone he had not authorized to receive same. Congress declined to reissue him a warrant 27 Feb. 1809.

Sheldon, Joseph. —. —. He was wounded in the leg at the battle of Connecticut Farms, N.J. He resided at New Cornwall, N.Y. in 1794. He enlisted 30 May 1777 for the war.

Shell, Christian. N.Y. Pvt. He served under Col. Peter Bellinger in the Montgomery County militia and was slain 8 July 1781. His widow, Elizabeth Shell, was granted a half-pay pension for seven years.

Shell, Edward. N.Y. Pvt. He was on the 1813 pension list.

Shell, George. —. —. His application was accepted 3 Mar. 1811.

Shelley, Medah. —. —. He served four different tours for about seven weeks. He also did guard duty for the town of Guilford, Conn.. Congress rejected his petition for a pension 6 Apr. 1846.

Shelhamer, George. Pa. —. He received a $40 gratuity and a $40 annuity in Dauphin County 15 June 1836. He was dead by July 1837.

Shellhamcr, Peter. Pa. —. He was pensioned.

Shelly, —. Pa. —. His widow, Rosanna Shelly, was awarded a $40 gratuity and $40 annuity in York Co., Pa. 1 Apr. 1830. She died 29 May 1843.

Shelly, William. S.C. —. He served in Col. Horry's Regiment of Horse and Capt. William Withers. Joseph Davis deposed anent his service. He was pensioned from Marion District on 23 Nov. 1829. He was dead by 28 Aug. 1841 when Elizabeth Shelly was his administratrix.

Shelman, Henry. Pa. —. His widow, Margaret Shelman, was awarded a $40 gratuity and a $40 annuity in York Co., Pa. 10 Apr. 1827.

Shelton, —. Va. —. His mother, Sarah Shelton, was granted support in Caroline Co., Va. 8 May 1781. There were five in her household.

Shelton, John. Del. Pvt. He was pensioned in 1787. He lived in Kent County. He was on the 1813 pension list as John Skelton.

Shenfessel, —. Pa. —. His widow, Margaret Shenfessel, was pensioned in Berks County 3 Apr. 1837. She was dead by Dec. 1837.

Shepard, Edward. —. —. The only proof he furnished was his own testimony. Congress rejected his claim for a pension 19 July 1848.

Shepard, James. Mass. Lt. He was in the Dragoons.

Shepard, John. Mass. Pvt. He served in the 13th Regiment. He was from Boston, and his widow, Sally Shepard, was paid $50.

Shepard, Thomas. Mass. —. He served in Crane's Regiment and was paid $20.

Shepardson, Nathan. Mass. Pvt. He served in the 1st Regiment and was from Adams. His widow, Sarah Shepardson, was paid $50.

Shepherd, Abraham. N.Y. Lt. He served under Col. William Allison and was killed at Minisink 22 July 1779. His children, Jonathan Shepherd, James [?] Shepherd, Abraham Shepherd, Temperance Oldfield, Anna Shepherd, and Mary Shepherd, received a half-pay pension.

Shepherd, Benjamin. N.C. —. He served in the militia under Capt. James Foy. He was at Camden in 1782 and at Gates' defeat. He was wounded by a saber on the head and was blinded. He served two tours of 15 months. He also served under Captains Grant, Wood, and Mason. He was from New Hanover County. He applied in 1819.

Shepherd, George. N.J. —. He served in the militia under Capt. Abram Speer for more than six months. Congress denied his widow, Catharine Shepherd, a pension because it was based solely on parol evidence on 7 May 1860.

Shepherd, James. Conn. Pvt. He served under Gen. Putnam. He was wounded by a musket ball at Bunker Hill 19 June 1775. He lived in Ashford, Conn. in 1794. He died in 1795.

Shepherd, John. S.C. —. He was wounded on 1 Apr. 1781 and died at Congagree Fort. His widow, Mary Ann Shepherd, was granted an annuity 2 Mar. 1785.

Shepherd, John. Va. —. He was in Monroe County 9 Nov. 1799. He served in Capt. John Moore's Company of the Kanawha County militia. He was wounded in his hand and in his thigh. He was pensioned at the rate of $40 per annum on 22 Jan. 1798 in Kanawha County.

Shepherd, Thomas. Conn. Pvt. He served in Douglas' Regiment. He was wounded in his left leg by a cannon ball from a British ship in Sep. 1778 at Turtle Bay. He was pensioned 4 Sep. 1794. He resided in New Haven Co., Conn. He was granted one-fourth of a pension 20 Apr. 1796. He was on the 1813 pension list.

Shepherd, William. Me. —. He died 17 Mar. 1832. His widow was Lucy Shepherd from Jefferson. She was paid $50 under the resolve of 1836.

Shepherd, William. Va. Pvt. His orphan daughter, Anne Shepherd, was in Chesterfield County in Oct. 1787. He was in the Chesterfield County militia and died in the service. His daughter, Anne Shepherd, was 7 years old. She was put on the pension list on 9 May 1788 at the rate of £5 per annum. She was continued at the same rate on 4 Apr. 1789. Mary Hacket, his widow, of Buckingham County stated that her daughter's pension was inadequate on 14 May 1792. She was on the pension roll of 1797.

Shepherd, William. Va. Pvt. He served in the Greenbrier Co. militia. He was continued on the pension roll at the rate of £7 per annum on 11 Dec. 1787. He received $200 in lieu of his $25 per annum on 22 Dec. 1804.

Sheppard, Robert. Pa. —. He was awarded a $40 gratuity and a $40 annuity in Schuylkill Co., Pa. 23 Jan. 1833.

Sheppard, Samuel. —. —. His application was laid on the table.

Sheppard, Stephen. Mass. —. He served in the 7th Regiment and was paid $20.

Sheppard, Thomas. —. —. He was pension 9 June 1794.

Shepperd, Carlton. N.J. Capt. He served under Col. Benjamin Holmes in the Salem County militia. He was wounded at Hancock's Bridge 21 Mar. 1778. He applied 25 Aug 1778 in Salem County.

Shepton, Richard. R.I. Pvt. He lost his left arm at Prince's Bridge, N.Y. on 14 May 1781. He had several wounds received at Red Bank on 22 Oct. 1777. He served under Col. Jeremiah Olney. He was aged 31 in 1786. He died 24 June 1822 in Providence Co., R.I. He was on the 1813 pension list. He also appeared as Richard Sephton.

Sherburn, Charles. Md. —. His widow was Mary Sherburn.

Sherburn, Henry. —. —. He was granted relief in consideration of his Revolutionary disabilities.

Sherburne, John Samuel. —. —. His daughter, Julia Sherburne Horton, had her claim for a pension rejected by Congress 23 June 1854.

Sherburne, Samuel. N.H. Major. He was from Portsmouth. He lost his leg by a cannon shot on 29 Aug. 1778 on Sullivan's expedition in Rhode Island. He was aged 28 in 1787. He was on the 1813 pension list. He died 2 Aug. 1830.

Sheredine, John. Md. —. He was granted relief.

Sheredon, —. Pa. —. His widow, Mary Sheredon, was awarded a $40 gratuity and a $40 annuity in Perry Co., Pa. 1 Apr. 1825. She died 13 Oct. 1843.

Sheredon, James. Pa. Pvt. He was in Philadelphia County 13 Feb. 1786. He served in the 11th Pa. Regiment in Capt. Scott's Company and was discharged from the Invalids 11 June 1783 unfit for duty on account of a wound in his leg at Germantown. He was 54 years old. He also appeared as James Sheridan. He died 18 May 1803.

Sherer, David. Pa. —. He was stricken from the rolls in 1820 in consequence of an error but restored in 1823 without any allowance for his arrearage. Congress approved same 10 July 1840.

Sherer, James. N.Y. Gunner. He served in the 2nd N.Y. Regiment under Col. John Lamb. He was disabled by a cannon ball in the small of his back at Fort Montgomery on 6 Oct. 1777. He was discharged 5 Jan. 1783. He was born 18 Nov. 17—. He applied from Ulster Co., N.Y. 15 June 1786. He died on or about 15 Mar. 1790.

Sherman, Abiel. N.Y. Pvt. He served under Capt. Samuel Delavan in Col. Drake's Regiment. He was wounded at Fort Independence on 8 or 10 Jan. 1777 by a musket ball. He also served under Lt. Col. Thaddeus Crane and Lt. Noah Bouton. He was 43 years old on 7 Mar. 1787. He was pensioned 16 Mar. 1787. He was a cooper and lived at Salem, Westchester Co. N.Y. in 1787. He later lived in Rensselaer County. He was on the 1813 pension list. He also appeared as Abiel Shearman.

Sherman, Benjamin. Mass. Pvt. He served in the 1st Regiment and was from Brimfield. He was paid $50.

Sherman, Edward. Mass. Pvt. He served under Col. Manasah Clinton and Capt. William Gordon. He lost his right hand by a three pound shot 1 Jan. 1780. He was pensioned at the rate of one-third of a soldier from 1 Jan. 1780 on 12 Feb. 1785. He was 23 years old in 1786. He also appeared as Edward Sharman.

Sherman, Lemuel. —. Sailing master. He served aboard a galley on Lake Champlain and was taken prisoner. He was placed on the pension roll 27 Mar. 1792.

Sherman, Richard. N.H. Pvt. He enlisted in 1777 and in the retreat from Ticonderoga he was wounded in the hip. At the capture of Burgoyne he was wounded in the arm. At Susquehanna with General Sullivan, he was wounded by a ball which entered the breast and passed through the shoulder. He was in Col. Scammel's Regiment. He applied in 1782 and was discharged 5 May 1783. He was from Portsmouth. He was aged 40 in 1787. His rate was $5 per month from 8 Oct. 1807. He died in 1809.

Shertzer, —. Pa. —. His widow, Elizabeth Shertzer, was granted relief in Washington Co., Md. 25 June 1839.

Shertzer, Christopher. Pa. —. He was awarded a $40 gratuity and a $40 annuity in Lancaster, Pa. 29 Mar. 1824. He died 26 Oct. 1826. His widow, Catharine Shertzer, was granted relief 27 Dec. 1826.

Sherwood, Eliphalet. —. —. He was pensioned 3 Mar. 1809.

Sherwood, Moses. N.Y. —. He served under Col. Wysenfelt and transferred to Col. Malcolm for nine months in 1781 and 1782. He had been stricken because it was not known if his unit was

Continental. Congress granted him a pension 18 Feb. 1832.

Sherwood, Sarah. —. —. She sought relief by virtue of being wounded in escaping from a party of British in 1776. Her petition was laid on the table.

Sherwood, Thomas. Md. Pvt. He was pensioned 4 Mar. 1789. He was on the 1813 pension list.

Shethar, John S. —. —. He served from the commencement of the war until he resigned due to ill health 8 Mar. 1780. Congress did not grant commutation to his daughter, Betsey C Shethar, and the other children on 15 Feb. 1839.

Shibe, Matthias. Pa. —. He served in Capt. Roman's Company in 1776 for six months but received no pay. His widow, Catherine Shibe, was to be paid $40 on 23 Mar. 1809. She lived in Lancaster Co., Pa.

Shickler, Jacob. Pa. —. He was pensioned 25 Jan. 1815.

Shief, —. N.Y. —. His widow was granted support during the war.

Shields, Charles. Va. Pvt. He lost his right leg in Continental service. He died 15 Apr. 1784. He was on the 1785 pension roll.

Shields, James. Pa. —. He was awarded a $40 gratuity and a $40 annuity in Indiana Co. 12 Mar. 1813. He was 101 years old in 1840.

Shields, John. Pa. —. He was awarded a $40 gratuity and a $40 annuity in Armstrong County 1 Apr. 1836. His widow, Elizabeth Shields, was pensioned 24 Apr. 1857.

Shields, John. Pa. —. He was pensioned 9 Feb. 1837 in Indiana County. He died 26 Oct. 1840.

Shields, Robert. S.C. —. He served under Col. William Polk and was wounded in 1781. He was from Beaufort District in 1792.

Shields, Thomas B. S.C. —. He served under Col. William Thompson, Capt. White, and Col. Polk. He was at Stono, Ramsour's Mill, Congaree, Orangeburg Jail, Buckhead Fort, Hanging Rock, and Guilford. His sword was shot from his side. He was 66 years old. He was from Barnwell District and was pensioned 12 Dec. 1826. He was paid as late as 1829.

Shields, William. N.C. Pvt. He served under Capt. William Alexander at the taking of Orangeburg, S.C. and several other skirmishes. He applied in Mecklenburg County in 1821 at the age of 80 years. His application was rejected since his disability did not appear to be service related.

Shiffen, George. N.Y. Pvt. He served under Col. Peter Bellinger in the Montgomery County militia and was slain 1 June 1780. His widow, Catharine Shiffen, received his half-pay pension.

Shiffley, Jacob. Pa. —. He was granted a gratuity 30 Mar. 1812.

Shilling, —. Pa. —. His widow, Bedy Shilling, was granted support in Mercer County 14 Apr. 1834.

Shindle, Conrad. Pa. —. He applied in Philadelphia 4 Apr. 1794.

Shindle, Peter. Pa. —. He was pensioned 1 Apr. 1836 in Lancaster County. He also appeared as Peter Shinkle. He was 86 years old in 1840.

Shindledecker, Michael. Pa. —. He was awarded a $40 gratuity and a $40 annuity in Mercer Co., Pa. 20 Feb. 1833. He also appeared as Michael Shingledecker.

Shipes, David. S.C. Lt. He served under Capt. Burney and Capt. Murray. He was at Stono and King's Mountain. He was from Barnwell District and was pensioned 7 Dec. 1825. In 1828 Daniel Odam swore that he served with him. He was 80 years old. He drew his pension as late as 1829.

Shipman, Asahel. N.J. He served in the 1st N.J. Regiment in Capt. Silas Howell's Company under Col. William Winds. He died at Fort George of smallpox on 16 July 1776. He married Electa Riggs on 23 Nov. 1772 in Morris Town. His widow, Electa Shipman, married secondly Matthew Camfield 15 Dec. 1783. Electa Camfield sought his half-pay in Morris County on 24 Sep. 1793.

Shippen, William. Pa. Capt. His heirs were in Philadelphia County on 10 July 1786. He was in the marine service in 1776. He was in the militia artillery and was killed at Princeton on 3 Jan. 1777. He left four children, but two died before the end of the war. Jeremiah Fisher was guardian of his children, Ann Shippen and William Shippen. They were to turn 14 years of age on 18 Aug. 1788. His widow was also dead.

Shipton, Matthew. Pa. —. He was awarded a $40 gratuity and a $40 annuity in Mifflin County 12 Apr. 1834.

Shipwash, William. Va. Pvt. His widow, Elizabeth Shipwash, was in Norfolk County on 16 May 1791. He was in the militia and was killed at Great Bridge. He had been detached with a party to collect cattle for the army. She was pensioned at the rate of £10 per annum on 25 Mar.1790. She was 45 years old and had three children. His widow was in Robeson Co., N. C. in 1811, Norfolk, Va. in 1813, and in Robeson Co., N.C. in 1821. His son was William Shipwash.

Shircliff, William. Md. Lt. His widow, Melinda Shircliff, was pensioned at the rate of half-pay of a lieutenant 29 Mar. 1838. Her son, Leonard Shercliff of Allegany County, was paid her arrearage of $36.45 in 1841. She died 22 Mar. 1840.

Shires, —. Pa. —. His widow, Mary Shires, was awarded a $40 gratuity and a $40 annuity in Lycoming County 3 Mar. 1837. She was dead by Dec. 1839.

Shirley, Bennet. Md. Pvt. His widow, Susanna Shirley, was pensioned at the rate of half-pay of a private 19 Jan. 1837.

Shirley, Champanious. S.C. —. He died about the close of the war. He served under Capt. Sinckfield, Capt. Ryan, and Col. Leroy Hammond. His heirs sought compensation in 1808.

Shirley, James. Va. —. He served in the 13th Virginia Regiment and was killed in the service. His wife and child were granted £40 shillings per month in Yohogania Co., Va. 24 June 1778.

Shirley, Richard. Pa. Pvt. His widow, Rachel Gartrel, was in Huntingdon County on 13 May 1794. He was in the militia and was killed by the Indians at a station or fort in Woodcock Valley, Bedford County on 16 July 1780. He was in Capt. William Phillips' Company and was 25 years old when he died. His widow married ------- Gartrel on 11 Mar. 1783. His children were William Shirley born 12 Jan. 1780 and Margaret Shirley born 23 Dec. 1777. Their guardians were Levi Moore and William Shirley.

Shirtley, Joseph. Md. Pvt. His widow was in Prince George's County in 1778. He served under Col. Thomas Williams and was killed 4 Oct. 1777 at Germantown.

Shirts, Samuel. N.Y. Pvt. He served under Col. Van Schaick. He was awarded 200 acres of bounty land 9 Apr. 1804.

Shirtzer, Casper. Pa. —. He applied in Hagarstown, Md. 28 May 1822. He was awarded a $40 gratuity and a $40 annuity in Washington Co., Md. 1 Apr. 1823.

Shitz, John. Pa. —. He was awarded a $40 gratuity and a $40 annuity in Dauphin Co., Pa. 27 Feb. 1834.

Shitz, John. Va. —. He died in Continental service. His widow, Mary Shitz, and two children were granted £8 support in Frederick Co., Va. on 2 Dec. 1777. She received £16 on 3 Mar. 1779. She also appeared as Mary Sheets.

Shitzell, —. Pa. —. His widow, Margaret Shitzell of Philadelphia County, received a $40 gratuity and a $40 annuity 3 Apr. 1837.

Shive, Lewis. Pa. —. He was granted relief in York County 5 Apr. 1843.

Shiveler,—. Pa. —. His widow, Elizabeth Shiveler, was pensioned in Fayette County 16 June 1836.

Shively, —. Pa. —. His widow, Catharine Shively, was awarded a $40 gratuity and a $40 annuity in Montgomery Co., Pa. 8 Apr. 1833.

Shiver, Frederick. Pa. —. He was awarded a $40 gratuity and a $40 annuity in Lancaster Co. 24 Mar. 1817.

Shober, Francis. Pa. —. He also appeared as Francis Shobert. He was granted a $40 gratuity and a $40 annuity in Franklin County 11 Apr. 1825.

Shoby, John. Mass. —. He served in Crane's Artillery and was from Wiscassett. He was paid $20.

Shock, John. Pa. —. He was awarded $60 in Northampton County on 24 Mar. 1812. He was awarded a $40 gratuity and a $40 annuity on 14 Mar. 1818.

Shockey, Christian. Pa. —. He was in Somerset County on 24 Mar. 1808. He served in Capt. Samuel Hearly's Company. He was attached and drafted into Capt. George Claypool's Company in the 11th Pa. Regiment under Lt. Col. Hubley and then transferred to the 3rd Pa. Regiment under Col. Thomas Craig. He was in Capt. William Henderson's Company and Capt. John Doyle's Company to the end of the war. He was wounded in his left arm at Yorktown. He was awarded a $40 gratuity and a $40 annuity. He was on the 1813 pension list. He died 18 Apr. 1829.

Shockey, Christian. Pa. —. He was pensioned 24 Mar. 1848.

Shockiene, —. N.Y. —. Magdalen Shockiene was granted support during the war.

Shockley, David. S.C. —. His application was rejected in Dec. 1826.

Shoe, John. Pa. —. His widow, Mary Shoe, was awarded a $40 gratuity and a $40 annuity in York Co., Pa. 23 Apr. 1829. She died 16 Oct. 1831.

Shoebrook, Edward. Md. Pvt. He was pensioned 24 Feb. 1823. It was to be paid to Joseph Boon of Caroline County.

Shoebrook, Philip. Md. Pvt. He was on the 1791 pension list. He was on the 1813 pension list.

Shoemaker, Abraham. Pa. —. He was awarded a $40 gratuity and a $40 annuity in Columbia County 23 Jan. 1833. He was 81 years old in 1840.

Shoemaker, Daniel. Pa. —. He was granted relief in Tioga County, New York 15 June 1836.

Shoemaker, Peter. Pa. —. He was awarded a $40 gratuity and a $40 annuity in Chester Co., Pa. 14 Apr. 1828.

Shoemaker, Samuel. Pa. —. He received a $40 gratuity and a $40 annuity 15 June 1836. He lived in Tioga Co., N.Y.

Shoener, —. Pa. —. His widow, Elizabeth Shoener, was pensioned in Berks County 15 June 1836. She was dead by Dec. 1840.

Sholl, John. Pa. —. He was awarded a $40 gratuity and a $40 annuity in Bedford Co., Pa. 16 Feb. 1835. He died 8 Dec. 1843.

Shontel, Jacob. Pa. Capt. He was granted relief.

Shook, John. Pa. —. He served under Capt. John Arndt and Col. Kechline in the Flying Camp. He was taken prisoner at Fort Washington and confined on the prison ship, *Jersey*. He was from Northampton County. He received a $40 gratuity and a $40 annuity 10 Mar. 1818. He died 7 Dec. 1829.

Shope, Nicholas. Pa. —. He was awarded a $40 gratuity and a $40 annuity in Cumberland Co., Pa. 22 Dec. 1834.

Shoppe, Anthony. Mass. Pvt. He served in the 7th Regiment under Capt. Maynard and Col. John Brooks. He was disabled by indurated testicles. He was pensioned 31 Dec. 1782. He resided at Petersham, Mass. in 1786 and was 24 years old. He was born in Germany. He was pensioned 28 July 1786 in Norfolk Co., Mass. He was on the 1813 pension list.

Shores, Peleg. N.J. Pvt. He served in Capt. Mekers' Company under Col. William Winds in the 1st

Regiment and died at Fort George 4 Aug. 1776. He married Rachel Freeman. She received his half-pay pension in Morris County in Sep. 1781.

Short, Martin. Pa. —. He was awarded a $40 gratuity and a $40 annuity in Allegheny Co., Pa. 18 Mar. 1834. He died 20 Jan. 1840.

Short, Thomas. S.C. —. Peter Oliver was to be paid $1,100 or as such part which would pay the interest of 6% due them on the portage bill book of the frigate *South Carolina* for him, Jacob Schon, David Zhal, and John Renney on 20 Dec. 1810.

Short, William. S.C. —. His widow was on the roll in 1793.

Shortridge, Richard. N.H. Capt. He was from Portsmouth in 1785. He died in the service on 8 July 1776 at Gwynn's Island leaving a widow, Mary Shortridge, and eight children. She married John Donaldson on 9 July 1783 in Portsmouth. His heirs were paid his seven years' half-pay. She was on the pension roll of 1785. (He was mistakenly identified as Benjamin Shortridge in some records.)

Shott, Richard. —. —. His application was not approved in 1797.

Shotts, John. Md. Pvt. He was from Frederick County. He was pensioned at the rate of half-pay of a private 7 Feb. 1818.

Shoudier, —. Pa. —. His widow was Sarah Shoudier.

Shouds, Stephen. N.J. —. He was pensioned in Burlington County on 11 Mar. 1839 at the rate of $60 per annum.

Shovell, John. Md. Pvt. He was wounded at Camden. He was pensioned in Frederick County in 1789. He served in the 6th Regiment. He was on the 1813 pension list.

Shover, Francis. Pa. —. His wife was Catherine Shover.

Shraeder, —. Pa. —. His widow, Elizabeth Shraeder, was granted relief in Berks County 18 Apr. 1843.

Shrayer, George. Pa. —. His widow, Catherine Shrayer, was awarded a $40 gratuity and a $40 annuity in Berks Co., Pa. 5 Mar. 1828.

Shreader, Anthony. Pa. —. He was awarded a $40 gratuity and a $40 annuity in Berks Co., Pa. 20 Feb. 1833. He was dead by Aug. 1838.

Shreder, Philip. Pa. —. He was pensioned by the court of enquiry 13 Dec. 1813. He died 28 Mar. 1814.

Sregendaler, —. Pa. —. His widow, Juliana Sregendaler, was granted relief in Berks County 21 June 1839. The correct surname was Seigendaler.

Shriller, Joseph. Pa. —. He was granted relief.

Shriner, Christopher. S.C. Sgt. He was in Philadelphia, Pa. 9 Sep. 1785. He served in the 1st S. C. Regiment and was transferred to the Invalids. He was wounded in the right thigh at Savannah in 1777. He was 26 years old. He also appeared as Christian Schreiner. He was pensioned by Pennsylvania.

Shrite, Jacob. Pa. —. He was awarded a $40 gratuity and a $40 annuity in Dauphin Co., Pa. 14 Jan. 1830.

Shriven, Thomas. Del. Pvt. He was pensioned in 1777. He was on the 1791 pension list. He died 27 Nov. 1808. He also appeared as Thomas Shirven and Thomas Skirven.

Shriver, Frederick. Pa. —. He was pensioned under the act of 14 Feb. 1817. He was from Lancaster County.

Shroeder, Philip. Pa. Sgt. He applied 17 Dec. 1813. He died 29 Mar. 1823.

Shryock, —. Pa. —. His widow, Phoebe Shryock, was awarded a $40 gratuity and a $40 annuity in Bedford Co., Pa. 12 Feb. 1825.

Shryock, John. Md. Pvt. He was pensioned at the rate of half-pay of a private 16 Mar. 1835.

Shubert, —. Pa. —. His widow, Elizabeth Shubert, was awarded a $40 gratuity and a $40 annuity in Philadelphia Co., Pa. 25 Mar. 1824.

Shubrick, Richard. S.C. Capt. He served in the 2nd S.C. Regiment on Continental Establishment. He was appointed 15 Nov. 1776 and died 8 Nov. 1777 at Charleston harbor. His widow remarried. His two daughters sought his seven years' half-pay in 1791. One daughter, Mary Shubrick, died without issue. His other daughter, Susannah Haynes Pinckney, sought his seven years' half-pay 25 Jan. 1838. Congress rejected the claim from Roger Pinckney and Susannah Haynes Pinckney 1 Feb. 1843.

Shulenger, George. Va. —. He died in Continental service. His widow, Elizabeth Shulenger, was granted £30 support in Rockingham Co., Va. 22 Mar. 1779.

Shuler, Henry. Pa. —. He was awarded a $40 gratuity and a $40 annuity in Mifflin County on 22 Mar. 1814.

Shull, David. Pa. —. He was awarded a $40 gratuity and a $40 annuity in Bedford Co., Pa. 15 Apr. 1835.

Shull, Michael. Pa. —. He was awarded relief in Armstrong County 20 May 1839.

Shultz, George. S.C. Marine. He served under Commodore Alexander Gillon aboard the frigate *South Carolina*. Michael Spatz and John Fox, both of Reading, Pa., enlisted with him. They were taken prisoner and put on the prison ship *Jersey* near New York. His widowed mother, Juliana Shultz of Reading, Berks Co., Pa. and his administratrix, sought compensation 23 July 1804.

Shultz, John. Pa. Pvt. He was on the 1813 pension list. He lived in Berks County.

Shultz, John. Pa. —. He was awarded a $40 gratuity in Lebanon Co., Pa. 16 Feb. 1835.

Shuman, William. Pa. —. He was awarded a $40 gratuity and a $40 gratuity in Chester Co., Pa. 5 Mar. 1828.

Shumway, Jonathan. Mass. —. He served in the 5th Regiment and was from Groton. He was paid $20.

Shumway, Peter. Mass. —. He served in the 4th Regiment.

Shurley, Bennett. Md. Soldier. He was at Guilford, Camden, and Eutaw Springs. He was badly wounded at the latter. He received bounty land warrant #11706 for 100 acres on 11 Mar. 1791. The certificate had been lost. His widow was Susannah Shurley. Congress issued a new warrant 31 Jan. 1838.

Shuster, Andrew. Pa. —. He was awarded a $40 gratuity in Philadelphia, Pa. 19 Jan. 1827, 24 Mar. 1828, 3 Mar. 1829, and 31 Jan. 1831. He was awarded a $40 gratuity and a $40 annuity on 10 Feb. 1832. His final payment was made to his son in July 1836 by which time he was deceased.

Shute, John. Pa. Lt. He applied in Baltimore, Md. on 25 Nov. 1846. He served in the Pa. Artillery from 1 Apr. 1777 to 10 Mar. 1780.

Shutliff, John. N.Y. Pvt. He was on the 1791 pension roll. He was on the 1813 pension list. He also appeared as "Joseph say John Shuttlief."

Shuttlief, Joseph. —. —. He was pensioned 11 Aug. 1790.si

Sidebottom, —. Va. —. He and his brother were in Continental service. Their mother, Mary Sidebottom, was granted £3 support in Prince William Co., Va. on 5 Oct. 1778.

Sidle, George. Pa. —. He was pensioned 2 Apr. 1822. He also appeared as George Seidle. He died in York County 20 Mar. 1848.

Siegel, Henry. Pa. —. He was awarded a $40 gratuity and a $40 annuity in Northampton Co., Pa. 12 Feb. 1825.

Sigler, Jacob. Pa. —. He was awarded a $40 gratuity and a $40 annuity in Lancaster Co., Pa. 22 Feb. 1823.

Sigourney, Andrew. Mass. —. He served in Mason's Artificers and was from Oxford. He was paid

$50.

Sill, Benjamin. Pa. —. He applied for relief but died in the same legislative session. His widowed daughter, Margaret Miller, was awarded a $40 gratuity 3 Mar. 1837.

Sillaway, Reuben. Mass. —. He served in the 8ᵗʰ Regiment and was paid $20.

Silley, Benjamin. Me. —. He was from Brooks. He was paid $50 under the resolve of 1836.

Sillyman, Thomas. Pa. —. He was awarded a $40 gratuity and a $40 annuity in Northampton Co., Pa. 17 Mar. 1835. He was 84 years old in 1840. He died 29 May 1843.

Silver, Daniel. Mass. Corp. —. He served in the 1ˢᵗ Regiment and was from Haverhill. He was paid $50.

Simington, Alexander. Pa. —. He was pensioned.

Simkins, Jeremiah. N.Y. —. His children, Phebe Ludington, Isaac Simkins, Hannah Platt, Sarah Blake, and Gilbert Simkins, were awarded 200 acres of bounty land 19 June 1812.

Simms, William. N.H. —. He served in Gen. Stark's Brigade in Col. Stickney's Regiment and was wounded on 16 Aug. 1777 at the battle of Bennington.

Simmons, —. Va. —. His widow, Mary Simmons, was allowed an increase in her annuity in Albemarle Co., Va. 6 Nov. 1779. She had recently died.

Simmons, —. Md. Pvt. His widow, Sarah Simmons, was pensioned at the rate of half-pay of a private in Charles County on 4 Mar. 1834.

Simmons, Aaron. Md. Pvt. He was pensioned at the rate of half-pay of a private 19 Feb. 1819.

Simmons, Benoni. Mass. Gunner. He was on the galley *Trumbull* commanded by Capt. Seth Warner when he lost his left arm on Lake Champlain on 11 Oct. 1776. He was pensioned at the rate of half-pay from the time his wages ceased on 28 Apr. 1777. He was pensioned 6 Feb. 1784. He was aged 31 and resided in Rhode Island in 1786. He was on the 1813 pension list.

Simmons, James. Va. —. His widow, Dorcas Simmons, was granted £8 support in Northumberland County on 14 Apr. 1778 and £50 on 13 Apr. 1779. He was in the artillery.

Simmons, James. Va. —. His pension of £15 per annum was continued 18 Dec. 1788.

Simmons, Jeremiah. S.C. —. He was in the 3ʳᵈ Regiment of Militia under Col. William Thompson. He served three years and was wounded in his leg at Fort Moultrie. The wound never healed. He was also at Eutaw where he was wounded in his head by a sword. He was from Lancaster District when he was pensioned 12 Dec. 1820. He died 15 Nov. 1830. His widow, Margaret Simmons, was granted a pension 25 Nov. 1830 on the condition that her late husband's name was on the pension roll.

Simmons, William. Va. Sgt. He served in Buford's Detachment. He was being pensioned 25 Nov. 1783. He was wounded in the service.

Simmons, William. Va. Pvt. He was in Southampton County on 22 Dec. 1785. He served in the 6ᵗʰ Va. Regiment and was wounded by a ball in his left side below the ribs at Saratoga. The ball was never extracted. He was on the 1813 pension list.

Simon, —. Va. —. Ann Simon was granted £10 support while he was absent in the service in Fauquier Co., Va. in Dec. 1778.

Simonds, Daniel. Mass. Lt. He served in the 5ᵗʰ Regiment. He had a scorbutic humor in his left leg occasioned by an accidental contusion while in service. He lived in Marlborough, Vt. in 1795.

Simons, Bennet. Mass. Sgt. He served in the 7ᵗʰ Regiment and was from Plymouth. He was paid $20.

Simons, James. N.H. —. He was from Westmoreland. He suffered from extreme heat at the battle of Monmouth and lost his health. He sought relief 18 Dec. 1781.

Simons, James. S.C. Capt. He served under Col. Daniel Leroy and Gen. Pulaski. He was made a prisoner and resigned his commission to accept an appointment under Col. Wade Hampton. He was at Cowpens and Eutaw Springs. Sarah Tucker Simons was paid five years' full-pay for her husband's service as a captain in the cavalry for herself and children on 20 Dec. 1820 amounting to $3,000 plus 3% interest from 1791. She was the daughter of Tucker Harris who deposed 20 Oct. 1819.

Simons, Joseph. Mass. —. He served in Wessons's Regiment and was paid $20.

Simons, Pompe. Mass. —. He served in the 5th Artillery and was paid $20.

Simons, Robert. N.Y. —. He was a native of Great Britain and came to the colonies before the Revolutionary War. He served in Col. Lamb's Regiment until discharged at the end of the war. He was upwards of 80 years of age, and his wife was nearly 70. They were unable to maintain themselves and had no property or relatives bound to support them. The town of Harpersfield, N.Y., was at much expense in maintaining them. The treasurer was to pay $180 to the overseers of the poor which was the amount they had paid to the overseers of the poor in Aurelius, N.Y., by court order in Delaware County on appeal from an order of removal of said Robert Simons and his wife from Harpersfield to Aurelius in 1811. The private act was 12 Apr. 1813.

Simons, Simeon. S.C. —. He was taken prisoner and died in confinement in May 1781. His widow, Sophia Simons, was granted an annuity 14 Sep. 1785.

Simonton, Alexander. Pa. Sgt. He served in the Pa. Line in Col. Chambers's Regiment and was wounded at Brandywine. He was put on the list of those entitled to donation land. He was on the 1813 pension list. He died 3 July 1821 in Mercer County.

Simpson, —. Va. —. His widow, Nancy Simpson, was awarded a £12 gratuity in King William Co., Va. 6 Nov. 1779.

Simpson, —. Va. —. His wife, Alice Simpson, and family were granted £38.14 relief in Brunswick County on 25 May 1778.

Simpson, Andrew. Pa. Ens. His heirs were in Westmoreland County on 3 Aug. 1791. He served in the Westmoreland County Associators in Capt. Samuel Moorehead's Company. He was killed by the savages near Fort Kittaning 16 Mar. 1777. His child was Agnes Simpson whose guardian was Charles Campbell. His widow, Agnes Simpson, married Samuel Hale 3 Aug. 1791.

Simpson, Andrew. Pa. —. He was awarded a $40 gratuity and a $40 annuity 1 Apr. 1837 in Westmoreland County. He died 22 Aug. 1856.

Simpson, George. N.H. Matross. He served in the militia. He died in 1798.

Simpson, George. Pa. Sgt. He was pensioned.

Simpson, James. Pa. —. He was pensioned.

Simpson, John. N.H. Pvt. He served under Capt. Elisha Woodberry in Col. John Stark's Regiment and was wounded in his hand by a cannon shot on 17 June 1775 at the battle of Bunker Hill. He lost two of his fingers and part of his hand. He was from Windham in 1779. He was aged 31 in 1787. He was on the 1813 pension list. He died 18 Nov. 1824. He also appeared as John Simson. He was from North Durham Gore.

Simpson, John. S.C. Pvt. He was pensioned 30 Nov. 1827. He died 19 July 1831. His widow was Lydia Simpson from Anderson District in 1831.

Simpson, Joseph. Pa. Seaman. He was in Philadelphia County on 14 Dec. 1785. His arm had been broken in an engagement with the enemy. He served aboard the Continental sloop of war, *Reprisal*, commanded by Lambert Weeks. He was 45 years old.

Simpson, Lawrence. Md. Pvt. He was pensioned at the rate of half-pay of a private in Charles County 27 Jan. 1817. His arrearage was paid to Peter W. Crain for the widow 27 Feb. 1843.

Simpson, Nathaniel. Pa. Pvt. He enlisted for the war and died in 1782 in the service. He devised all his land to which he was entitled to his uncle who did not apply for the land until barred by the act of limitation. The tract of the 200 acres was to be granted to Lewis Brown of Mifflin County in trust for the heirs of Nathaniel Simpson 6 Mar. 1812.

Simpson, Rezin. Md. Sgt. He was pensioned at the rate of half-pay of a private 2 Jan. 1813. His rate was changed to that of half-pay of a sergeant of dragoons 23 Jan. 1816. His arrearage was paid to Robert Swan for the use of the widow, Mary Simpson, 18 Feb. 1830. She was pensioned at the rate of half-pay of a sergeant 24 Feb. 1830 in Allegany County. Her pension was to be paid of William Shaw.

Simpson, Salathiel. Va. —. His widow, Nancy Simpson, was awarded financial support from July 1777 in Accomack Co., Va. on 23 Feb. 1779.

Simpson, Simeon. Me. —. He was from Winslow. He was paid $50 under the resolve of 1836.

Simpson, Thomas. —. Capt. He was a lieutenant under Capt. Weary who died in battle with the British and Indians and the command devolved on him. He received a musket ball in his body in the last battle with Burgoyne. He still carried it. He became qualified for an invalid pension under the act of 1818. He availed himself of the benefits of 1832. His invalid pension stopped and he prayed to be reinstated to it in addition to his annuity. He received his invalid pension of $17 per month from 4 Mar 1831 to 4 Mar. 1834. His petition was before Congress on 5 Feb. 1835.

Simpson, Thomas. Md. Corp. In 1777 he lost an eye after being inoculated for smallpox. He was pensioned at the rate of half-pay of a corporal 2 Jan. 1813.

Simpson, Thomas. N.H. Capt. Lt. He was from New Hampton. He was shot in the right side of his belly on 7 Oct. 1777 at Bemis Heights. In Feb. 1778 he was wounded in his leg. He served under Col. Scammel. He lost an eye by smallpox. He was twice wounded and one musket ball remained in his body. He was aged 31 in 1787. His rate was $13.33 1/3 from 24 Dec. 1806. He was on the 1813 pension list. He was from New Hampton.

Simpson, William. Va. Pvt. He served in the 5th Regiment. He was wounded by a musket ball which entered his left side near the region of the kidneys. He was pensioned at the rate of £36 per annum on 29 Dec. 1785. He lived in Rockingham Co., N.C. in 1794. He was on the 1815 pension list.

Simpson, William. Va. —. He was from Russell County.

Sims, —. S.C. —. His widow, Charity Sims, was on the roll in 1793.

Sims, James. S.C. —. He lost a leg. He was granted an annuity 19 Feb. 1778.

Simson, —. Va. —. His wife, Sally Simson, was awarded £48.16 support in Southampton Co., Va. on 9 July 1779.

Simson, Francis. Mass. —. He was in the Invalids and was disabled by the loss of his arm. He was pensioned 1 Sep. 1782. He died 2 Dec. 1785.

Sinclair, Noah. N.H. Drummer. He was from Canterbury in 1786. He was wounded in his left hand and had both bones fractured on 14 June 1776 at St. Johns by two musket balls. He was in Capt. Morrill's Company. He was aged 31 in 1787. His rate was $3.75 per month from 8 Oct. 1807. He was on the 1813 pension list. He transferred from Maine to Coos Co., N.H. 4 Sep. 1827. He also appeared as Noah Sinkler.

Sinclear, Ebenezer. N.H. —. He served in General Poor's Brigade in Col. Cilley's Regiment under Capt. Morill. He was killed at Saratoga. He left a widow, Mary Sinclear, and three small children the eldest of whom was under 14 years of age. He owned 150 acres in Wentworth, and his widow sought to be excused from paying taxes on the tract.

Sing, John. S.C. —. He served under Capt. Charles Gause, Capt. Joseph Long, Capt. John Tomplitt,

Capt. Samuel Price, Capt. Absalom Sessions, and Capt. Fishburn. He was 78 years old and had an aged wife. Thomas Durant and Joseph King deposed anent his service. He was pensioned in All Saints Parish 12 Dec. 1826. He was paid as late as 1828.

Single, Jacob. Pa. —. He was awarded a $40 gratuity and a $40 annuity in Columbia Co., Pa. 18 Feb. 1834.

Singletary, Ithamar. N.C. Pvt. He served in the Bladen County Militia. He was wounded in several places in his back by a broadsword as he was retreating from the enemy on 6 June 1781 at Rockfish. He lived in Bladen Co., N.C. in 1795. He was on the 1813 pension list.

Singletary, Joseph. N.C. Lt. He was wounded in the left arm by the accidental discharge of a musket. His arm withered, the joint of his elbow crooked and stiffed, and his fingers contracted. He was wounded in 1776 at Wilmington. He lived in Bladen Co., N.C. in 1794. He was in the militia.

Singletary, Joseph, Jr. N.C. Pvt. He served in the Bladen County Militia. He was wounded by a broadsword in several places in his left arm and disabled in one of his legs in consequence of being trod upon by a horse on 6 June 1781 at Rockfish. He lived in Bladen Co., N.C. in 1795.

Singleton, Christopher. Va. —. He died in the service. His widow, Mary Singleton, was granted £40 relief in Mecklenburg Co., Va. 8 Mar. 1779.

Singlewood, —. Pa. —. His widow, Nancy Singlewood, received a $40 gratuity and a $40 annuity in Philadelphia County 1 Apr. 1836. *Vide infra.*

Singlewood, Stephen. Pa. —. His widow, Nancy Singlewood, was awarded a $40 gratuity and a $40 annuity in Philadelphia County 1 Apr. 1836. *Vide supra.*

Singley, George. Pa. Pvt. He entered at 15 or 16 years of age in July 1776 as a drafted militiaman from Northampton Co., Pa. He served under Capt. Kuhn and Col. Karn. He was in the flying camp at New Brunswick, N.J. under Gen. Mercer. He served a second tour of two months under Capt. Addleman at Coryell's Ferry on the Delaware and at Neshamony under Col. Cadwalder. He was also under Capt or Lt. Moyer from Dec. 1776. He served a month in 1777 and in June was a sergeant. He was discharged by Maj. Wolf. He was at Brandywine in Aug 1777 and was discharged at Germantown. In 1778 he was under Capt. Addleman and Lt. Snelling. He also spent two months scouting against the Indians on the Lehigh. He was pensioned for ten months as a sergeant and five months as a private by Congress on 18 Mar. 1844. There was a George Singley who received a $40 gratuity and a $40 annuity in Westmoreland County, Pa. 18 Apr. 1843 and who died 7 Mar. 1846.

Sisco, Jacob. N.J. —. He was pensioned in Morris County on 13 Mar. 1837 at the rate of $60 per annum.

Siscoe, Nicholas. —. Pvt. He entered the service as a substitute for his master, David Bogart, on the condition that he would have his freedom at the end of the war. He claimed several tours, but none was sustained by evidence. Congress rejected him for a private pension bill 9 Jan. 1847.

Sitter, Jacob. Pa. —. He was granted relief.

Sizemore, Ephraim. S.C. —. He was from Winton. There were children in 1791.

Sizer, Jonathan. Conn. —. He enlisted in the spring of 1778 under Col. Meigs. He was compelled to resign due to ill health in 1780. He was 73 years and suffered from "rheumatic affection." His right arm was paralyzed and he was unable to work. His wife was more than 75, and his property was valued at $868.25. His old dwelling house was in New London. Congress granted him a pension 22 Dec. 1831.

Sizler, Philip. Md. Sgt. He was pensioned at the rate of half-pay of a sergeant in Baltimore 22 Feb. 1829.

Skadin, Robert K. Pa. —. He applied in Clark Co., Ohio 1 June 1847. He volunteered in Capt. Clark's Company in Cumberland County for three months and two weeks in 1779. He then enlisted in the regular service for the war. He was in Capt. James Butler's Company under Col. Israel Putnam and Gen. Wayne. He was discharged at Philadelphia. He also appeared as Robert Kis Skaddin.

Skaggs, John. Va. Pvt. He was in Stafford County in 1783. He served in the Va. State Line. He was wounded in his right wrist. He was in Russell County in 1793, Amelia County in 1793, Green Co., Ky. in 1802, and Barren Co., Ky. in 1802

Skeggs, John. Va. Pvt. He was in Washington Co., Va. 15 Apr. 1783 where he was pensioned for being wounded at King's Mountain. His rate was £8 annually on 15 Dec. 1791.

Skell, Amos. Conn. Pvt. He served in the 13ᵗʰ Conn. Regiment. He was wounded by a musket ball which passed through the bones of his right arm in Apr. 1777 at Norwalk. He resided at Chatham, Conn. in 1796. He was granted one-third of a pension 20 Apr.1796. He was on the 1813 pension list. He transferred to Hampden Co., Mass. 4 Mar. 1826.

Skelton, James. Pa. —. He was pensioned in Crawford County 15 June 1836.

Skelton, John. Del. Pvt. He was pensioned at the rate of $36 per annum in 1791.

Skelton, Jonathan. Pa. —. He applied in Butler County on 17 Mar. 1813. He died 10 Nov. 1818.

Skiles, John. Pa. —. He received a $40 gratuity and a $40 annuity in Cumberland County 16 June 1836.

Skillings, John. Mass. Capt. He died 2 Apr. 1777. His seven years' half-pay of $1,680 was paid to his heirs.

Skillman, John. Pa. —. He was granted relief in Allegheny County. He was paid in 1843.

Skillman, Thomas. N.J. —. He served under Col. Ogden in the 1ˢᵗ Regiment. He was wounded at Short Hills with a musket ball through his thigh. He was being pensioned 30 Jan. 1802. His wife was Ursula Skillman.

Skinner, Isaac. N.Y. Pvt. He served under Col. Bellinger and was slain 2 Apr. 1782. His child, Isaac Skinner, Jr. was granted his half-pay pension.

Skinner, Jonathan. N.J. —. The Americans used his house and out buildings as a hospital for the sick and wounded. The British seized and burnt them to the ground on the retreat from Springfield. His daughter, Serepta Cleveland, sought relief from Congress 3 Mar 1859.

Skinner, Richard. N.J. Capt. He served in the Middlesex militia under Col. John Webster and was killed by the enemy in June 1779 on Long Island. His widow was Sarah Skinner. She married secondly Cornelius Baker 9 Sep. 1788. She was granted a half-pay pension 24 Jan. 1798.

Skipper, —. Va. —. His widow, Lucy Skipper, was awarded a £12 gratuity in King William Co., Va. 11 Dec. 1779.

Skipton, Matthew. Pa. —. He was awarded a $40 gratuity and a $40 annuity in Mifflin Co., Pa. 15 Apr. 1834.

Skiventon, Roger. Md. —. He was pensioned.

Skriggins, Thomas. Me. —. He was from Eliot. He was paid $50 under the resolve of 1836.

Slacht, Cornelius. Va. —. He was an eighteen-month draft. His wife and three children were furnished assistance in Loudoun County in Jan. 1782 while he was away in the service.

Slack, Joseph. N.H. Pvt. He served in Col. Read's Regiment. He was on the 1813 pension list.

Slasson, Deliverance. —. Pvt. He sought an increase in his pension. Congress rejected his claim 8 Apr. 1846 because he was receiving the amount to which he was entitled.

Slater, James. Mass. Pvt. He served in Col. Brown's Regiment. He was wounded in the head and eye by a musket ball in action with the Indians on the Mohawk in Oct. 1780. He lived in

Canaan, N.Y. in 1794 and later in Litchfield Co., Conn. He was granted half a pension 20 Apr. 1796. He was on the 1813 pension list.

Slater, John. Pa. —. He was granted relief in Greene County 21 June 1839.

Slaugh, Bernard. Pa. Pvt. He was on the 1791 pension roll. He was on the 1813 pension list.

Slaughter, Francis L. Pa. Pvt. He served in Yancey's 1ˢᵗ Regiment. He was pensioned 7 Sep. 1807. He was on the 1813 pension list. He removed to Franklin Co., Ky. 4 Mar. 1816. He died 9 Jan. 1832.

Slaughter, Philip. Va. Capt. In the fall of 1775 as a youth he marched to Williamsburg. In 1776 he enlisted as a soldier under John Jameson in a company of horse. The Committee of Safety of Culpeper County appointed him lieutenant in Capt. Gabriel Long's Company of riflemen under the command of Col. Stevenson. Part of the regiment was raised in Maryland and part in Virginia. He was in the northern campaign in New York, New Jersey, and Pennsylvania. When part of the regiment under Col. Rawlings was captured at Fort Washington, the Virginia companies were assigned to the 11ᵗʰ Virginia Regiment under Col. Daniel Morgan. Later he became captain. He acted as both captain and paymaster in 1779 and did additional duty of regimental clothier. He returned to Virginia and married. He authorized John Marshall (later Chief Justice) to resign his commission, but he never did. He received his five years' full pay in commutation of his half-pay for life 26 May 1828. He was not allowed interest at that time, but that proviso was repealed 22 Dec. 1837. His daughter, Ann Mercer Slaughter, petitioned and was allowed a pension by Congress 27 July 1892. She stated that her father was in the Culpeper County Minute Men and was the first officer to respond in Virginia. He marched to Williamsburg flying the famous flag with coiled rattlesnake painted upon its fold with the motto, "Don't tread on me." She was blind and in her 83ʳᵈ year of age.

Slaughter, William. Va. Lt. He received his commutation pay 9 Apr. 1791.

Slaven, James. N.Y. Pvt. He was disabled. He was pensioned on 1 Sep. 1782.

Slavin, John. —. —. He served three years and received a pension. He was stricken due to his property. He was 70 years old. Both he and his wife were disabled and helpless. He owned 96 acres in the Alleghany Mountains in Virginia but they were of no great value. Congress granted him a pension 21 Dec. 1831.

Slawter, Gilbert. N.Y. Pvt. He served under Col. Thomas Thomas in the Westchester County militia and was slain 12 Nov. 1778. His widow, Mary Slawter, received a half-pay pension for seven years. He also appeared as Gilbert Hawter.

Sled, William. Va. Drummer. He served in the artillery and was discharged at Yorktown. He lived eight or nine years in North Carolina, removed to South Carolina, and returned to North Carolina where he had resided eleven years when he applied 18 May 1830.

Sleeth, David W. Va. —. He served thirteen months in a company of rangers under Capt. James Booth as an Indian spy in Harrison, Lewis, and Wood Counties. When Capt. Booth was killed, Lt. Freeman took command. He was also a spy in 1780 under Capt. George Jackson. He received $104 on 1 Mar. 1832 and lived in Lewis County. He was 76 years old when Congress granted him relief 5 Mar. 1840.

Sleeth, John. Va. Sgt. He served thirteen months under Capt. James Booth in the expedition against the Indians. His son, David W. Sleeth, was paid $130 for his services on 13 Mar. 1834.

Slewman, John. Mass. Capt. He served in the artillery under Col. John Crane and was wounded in the head by a musket ball over his right eye at Germantown 4 Oct. 1777. The ball lodged in his head. He was pensioned at the rate of half-pay 8 July 1784. He was on the 1813 pension list.

He also appeared as John Sluman.

Slingerman, Jacob. —. —. He and John Letts submitted no paperwork with their petition to Congress calling for a bill for supporting surviving soldiers by raising their gratuities or granting full pensions on 9 May 1850.

Sloan, —. Pa. —. His widow, Martha Sloan, was granted a $40 gratuity and a $40 annuity in Armstrong County 13 Mar. 1839.

Sloan, Bryant. Pa. Pvt. He served in the 8th Regiment. He was wounded by a ball in his left hand on 28 June 1778 at Sullivan's Island. He enlisted 31 Jan. 1776 for two years. He was not on the rolls in Nov. 1777. He was on the 1813 pension list.

Sloan, David. Pa. Lt. He served in the 1st Regiment under Capt. Joseph Erwin and Col. Samuel Miles. He was in Capt. Peter Grubb's Company when he was killed at Long Island 27 Aug. 1776. His widow, Mary Sloan, married secondly Robert Orr 1 Apr. 1788. She was in Westmoreland County on 8 Feb. 1787. His daughter Ann Sloan was aged 11 years old on 10 Jan.1789. She married Robert Hunter who was paid $209 in full of her pension 13 Apr. 1827.

Sloan, James. Pa. His widow was Elizabeth Sloan who received a $40 gratuity and a $40 annuity 2 Apr. 1822.

Sloan, James. S.C. —. He served in Col. Middleton's Regiment under Capt. More. He received no pay. He applied from Mecklenburg Co., N.C. 29 Dec. 1786.

Sloan, John. N.C. Capt. He was killed in battle. His widow, Mary Sloan, was allowed $100 in Dec. 1833.

Sloan, John. Pa. Pvt. He was in Philadelphia County on 14 Nov. 1785. He was transferred from the 2nd Pa. Regiment to the Invalids. He was wounded in his left thigh at Green Springs, Va. He was discharged 12 Nov. 1783. He was 5'5" and had fair complexion and very gray hair. He served under Col. Richard Humpton. He was 40 years old.

Sloan, William. N.Y. Sgt. He served under Col. Herrick. He was wounded in five places in an ambuscade in Oct. 1777 at Skinesborough. He lived at Westfield, N.Y. in 1794. He was on the 1813 pension list. He died 12 July 1828 in Madison Co., N.Y.

Slocum, John. R.I. Pvt. He lost his left leg in action on 7 June 1780 at Connecticut Farms in New Jersey. He served under Col. Israel Angel. He was aged 30 when he applied 12 Jan. 1786. He was on the 1813 pension list. He died 8 Oct. 1828 in Providence Co., R.I. He married Sally Beard 19 Mar. 1783 in Providence, and she survived him

Slonecker, John. Pa. —. He was awarded a $40 gratuity and a $40 annuity in Cumberland Co., Pa. 6 Apr. 1833. He was paid to 29 Sep. 1835.

Slotterbeck, Henry. Pa. Pvt. He was in Dauphin County 17 June 1786. He was in the Lancaster County militia under Capt. Daniel Oldenbruck and Col. Philip Greenawalt. He later was under Capt. Michael Holderbaum and was wounded in his thigh in a skirmish with the British in Dec. 1777 at Chestnut Hill. His head was fractured. He was on the 1813 pension list. He died 10 Feb. 1817 in York County.

Sluthour, Anthony. Pa. —. He was awarded a $40 gratuity and a $40 annuity in York Co., Pa. 3 Mar. 1829.

Sly, Isaac. N.J. Pvt. He was pensioned at the rate of $30 per annum.

Slye, William. Md. Pvt. He was on the 1813 pension list. He later moved to Clermont Co., Ohio.

Small, Daniel. Me. —. He was from Raymond. He was pensioned in 1818 and stricken in 1820. His petition to be restored was rejected 2 Feb. 1825. He was paid $50 under the resolve of 1836.

Small, Henry. Me. —. He died 9 Nov. 1826. His widow was Elizabeth Small from Limington. She was paid $50 under the resolve of 1836.

Small, Jacob. N.Y. Capt. He served in the militia and was slain in battle at Oriskany 6 Aug. 1777. His widow, Susannah Small, was awarded £672 for seven years half-pay on 9 Apr. 1792.

Small, Jeremiah. Me. —. He was from Westbrook. He was paid $50 under the resolve of 1836.

Small, William. Va. Marine. He was on the 1800 pension roll.

Smallage, Samuel. Mass. Drummer. He served in the 8ᵗʰ Regiment and was from Boston. His widow, Elizabeth Smallage, was paid $50.

Smart, Elijah. N.H. Pvt. He enlisted in 1777 and served under Col. Cilley in the 1ˢᵗ Regiment in Capt. Nathan Hutchen's Company. He lost the use of his right foot in consequence of yellow fever in May 1778 at Valley Forge. He lived in Hopkinton, N.H. in 1794. He enlisted 7 Apr. 1777 for three years and was discharged 7 Apr. 1780.

Smart, William. N.H. Pvt. He served under Col. Stark. He was totally blind in one eye and could but just discern the light with the other occasioned by the smallpox in 1776 in Canada. He lived in Rumney, N.H. in 1795. He was in the militia and was on the 1813 pension list.

Smick, Christian. Pa. —. He was awarded a $40 gratuity and a $40 annuity in Berks Co., Pa. 24 Mar. 1828. He also appeared as Christian Schmick. He was 76 years old in 1840.

Smick, William. N.J. —. He was pensioned in Salem County on 24 Feb. 1840 at the rate of $60 per annum.

Smiley, —. Pa. —. His widow, Margaret Smiley, was awarded a $40 gratuity and a $40 annuity in Fayette County in Apr. 1837.

Smiley, Samuel. Pa. —. He was awarded a $40 gratuity and a $40 annuity in Chester County 27 Mar. 1812. He died 15 Aug. 1825.

Smith, —. —. —. His widow, Anna Smith, had per petition for a pension by a special act of Congress rejected because she married subsequent 1 Jan. 1794.

Smith, —. Pa. —. His widow, Marianna Smith, was granted a $40 gratuity and a $40 annuity in Northampton County in 1841 for his Revolutionary service.

Smith, —. Pa. —. His widow, Elizabeth Smith, was awarded a $40 gratuity and a $40 annuity in Northumberland County 28 Mar. 1836.

Smith, —. Pa. —. His widow, Margaret Smith, was granted relief in Indiana County 31 Mar. 1836. She died in or about 1841.

Smith, —. Pa. —. His widow, Margaret Smith, was awarded a $40 gratuity and a $40 annuity in Lancaster County 31 Mar. 1836.

Smith, —. Va. —. His father, Jonathan Smith, was granted £10 support in Caroline County 14 May 1778.

Smith, —. Va. —. His mother, Margaret Smith, was furnished support in Westmoreland County in Aug. 1780.

Smith, —. Va. —. His grandmother, Margaret Smith, was furnished support in Westmoreland Co. in Aug. 1780.

Smith, —. Pa. —. His widow, Agnes Smith, was awarded a $40 gratuity and a $40 annuity in York Co., Pa. 14 Apr. 1834.

Smith, —. Va. Pvt. He served in the 13ᵗʰ Virginia Regiment. His widow, Catherine Smith, was awarded £7.10 for her support and her children in Aug. 1778 in Ohio County.

Smith, —. Pa. —. His widow, Elizabeth Smith, was awarded a $40 gratuity in Montgomery Co., Pa. 26 Jan. 1835.

Smith, —. Pa. —. His widow, Rebecca Smith, was granted a $40 gratuity and a $40 annuity in Bedford County 10 Apr. 1826.

Smith, —. Pa. —. His widow, Sarah Smith, was awarded a $40 gratuity and a $40 annuity in York Co., Pa. 1 Apr. 1830.

Smith, —. S.C. —. His widow, Mary Ann Smith, was from Newberry. There were two children in 1791.

Smith, —. S.C. His widow, Sarah Smith, was recommended to receive a pension 6 Dec. 1841.

Smith, —. Va. —. Sarah Smith was granted support in King William County in 1778.

Smith, —. Va. —. William Smith was granted £2.3 support in Halifax Co., Va. 21 Aug. 1777. He had three sons in Continental service.

Smith, Aaron. Conn. Pvt. He served in the militia. He was disabled with his right knee being dislocated at White Plains on 28 Oct. 1776. The head of the tibia was out of place. He was lame. He resided at Haddam, Conn. in 1796. He was granted one-fourth of a pension 20 Apr. 1796. He was on the 1813 pension list. He died 25 Nov. 1825.

Smith, Aaron. N.H. Ens. He resided in Chesterfield in 1785. He served under Col. Timothy Beddell in Capt. Carlisle's Company. Elisha Whitcomb was lieutenant. He was ordered to Canada under Maj. Isaac Butterfield and was captured by the savages. He lost the use of his left eye and of his right arm on the return to Ticonderoga. He was wounded in the elbow. He was aged 44 in 1787. He was on the 1813 pension list. He died 6 June 1819.

Smith, Aaron. S.C. —. His widow, Elizabeth Smith, was from Fairfield District. There were children in 1791.

Smith, Aaron. S.C. Pvt. He served under Col. Taylor, Col. Hunter, Capt. Robertson, and Capt. Craig. He was a prisoner. He was pensioned 25 Nov. 1830 from Fairfield District. His name was stricken in 1836. He was between 70 and 80 years old. He was pensioned again 7 Dec. 1836. He died in 1850. His widow, Elizabeth Smith, was about 80 years old in 1850. Her claim was rejected.

Smith, Abner. —. Sgt. He enlisted for nine months under Capt. Abijah Gilbert and Gen. Clinton. He was dismissed at White Plains. He was commissioned a sergeant in the dragoons under Capt. Samuel Delavan and served as a minuteman to the end of the war. Congress granted him a pension 4 Jan. 1832.

Smith, Abraham. Pa. —. He was awarded a $40 gratuity and a $40 annuity in Mercer Co., Pa. 15 Jan. 1829. He died 20 June 1840.

Smith, Abram. N.J. Lt. He enlisted in Sussex County. He was under his brother, Capt. John Smith, for six months and was at Monmouth. He served another tour of six months. In 1780 he served under Capt. Hoover and was at his fort on the banks of the Delaware. He died in 1799. His widow, Elizabeth Smith, married secondly John Gibbs. He died in 1817. She was 95 years and lived in Thompkins Co., N.Y. when Congress granted her pension 8 Mar. 1842. Her sons were Isaac Smith and John Smith. Jacob Smith was 71 years old.

Smith, Alexander. Mass. —. He served in Crane's Artillery and was from East Sudbury. He was paid $50.

Smith, Alexander Lawson. Md. Capt. His widow, Martha Jay, was pensioned at the rate of half-pay of a captain 24 Feb. 1836. His heirs sought his half-pay from Congress, but his service was not Continental. Congress rejected their petition 12 Apr. 1842.

Smith, Ambrose. Conn. Mariner. He served in Capt. McCleave's galley. He was wounded in his right hand by a nine pound shot which fractured his middle finger in Aug. 1777 at Tappon Bay. He resided at East Haven, Conn. in 1794.

Smith, Andrew. Pa. —. He was awarded a $40 gratuity and a $40 annuity in York Co., Pa. 4 May

1832. He also appeared as Andrew Schmith.

Smith, Aquilla. Md. Pvt. He was pensioned at the rate of half-pay of a private in Kentucky 7 Mar. 1834.

Smith, Ballard. Va. Lt. He served in Col. Posey's Regiment. He made a deed of gift and devised to his mother, Frances Smith, alias Sprangle, who thought that she had a right to his computation. Her claim was rejected 22 Mar. 1838 because he had already received his five years' full pay. He died 20 March 1794.

Smith, Benjamin. Md. Pvt. He was pensioned at the rate of half-pay of a private in Kentucky 7 Feb. 1830.

Smith, Benjamin. N.Y. Pvt. He enlisted under Col. Henry Livingston in Capt. William Jackson's Company in the 4th N.Y. Regiment. He had an ulcerated ankle on his right leg at Valley Forge, Pa. in 1778. He was discharged 7 June 1783. He was pensioned 26 Feb. 1787. He lived in New Windsor, Ulster Co., N.Y. on 13 June 1788. He died 26 Mar. 1823 in Orange County. He was on the 1813 pension list.

Smith, Benjamin. S.C.—. He served under Capt. Adam Crain Jones and Maj. Andrew Pickens. He was at Seneca Old Town, Tomassy, Brasstown, Horse Creek, Cedar Island Fort, Ninety Six. He was a pilot under Gen. Williamson. He was 76 years old. He had eleven orphan grandchildren. Job Smith served with him as did David Smith of Walton Co., Ga. He was from Pendleton District in 1827. He was paid as late as 1834.

Smith, Caleb. S.C. —. He sought a pension.

Smith, Calvin. Mass. Maj. He received his commutation for five years in lieu of half-pay for life. He was from Mendon.

Smith, Charles. Me. —. He was from Belfast. He was paid $50 under the resolve of 1836.

Smith, Charles. Md. Pvt. He was pensioned at the rate of half-pay of a private 23 Jan. 1816.

Smith, Charles. Md. Pvt. He was pensioned at the rate of half-pay of a private in Talbot County 5 Mar. 1835. His arrearage of $10.00 was paid to his son, Thomas Smith, 7 Mar. 1840.

Smith, Charles. Md. Capt. His widow, Mary Smith, was pensioned at the rate of half-pay of a captain in the District of Columbia 8 Mar. 1834.

Smith, Charles. N.C. —. He was drafted in the militia from North Carolina in 1776 under Gen. Greene, Col. John Litteral, and Capt. Joseph Rossor. He was discharged in 1777 by Capt. Golston. Subsequent officers under whom he served were Maj. Cage, Capt. Joseph Rossor, Col. Henderson, Capt. John Gray, Capt. Winn, Capt. Frost, and Capt. Jacob Barnett. He was about 64 years old when he applied 4 Dec. 1828. Daniel Chitwood and John Bruster had deposed about his service when he sought a federal pension. He had been wounded at the Juniper. He was disqualified because his service was not at the Continental level. Jesse Smith, Gen. Sumter, Robert Watson of Habersham Co., Ga., and William Hodges of Madison Co., Ga. attested his service. He applied for a pension from Pendleton District, South Carolina 27 Aug. 1827. He had failed to qualify for a federal pension so he reapplied.

Smith, Charles. S.C. —. He was killed by the enemy. His children were granted an annuity 7 Sep. 1785. There was one child in 1791.

Smith, Charles. S.C. —. He served under Col. Hampton and Capt. Samuel Barnett in 1781. He died 28 Jan. 1845. His widow was Elizabeth Smith who applied for his arrearage on 13 Oct. 1847 from Cherokee Co., Ga.

Smith, Charles. S.C. —. He served under Col. Henderson, Capt. John Gray, Capt. Winn, Capt. Frost, and Lt. Gore. He served two years. He was 64 years old. He was from Richland District. He was pensioned 4 Dec. 1828 at which time he was in Hall Co., Georgia. David Chitwood of Madison

Co., Ga. served with him in 1781. He was paid as late as 1834. In 1834 he indicated that he had been wounded at the Juniper in Lexington District.

Smith, Charles. S.C. —. He was pensioned 7 Dec. 1833 with pay retroactive to 1818.

Smith, Christian. Md. Pvt. He was pensioned at the rate of half-pay of a private 23 Jan. 1816.

Smith, Christian. Pa. —. He was pensioned.

Smith, Christopher. Mass. Pvt. He served in Crane's Regiment and was from Needham. His widow, Hannah Smith, was paid $50.

Smith, Christopher. Pa. —. He applied at Mansfield 9 Sep. 1825. He served under Capt. Thomas L. Moor in Col. Johnston's Regiment. He was wounded in his right shoulder by buck shot and above the joint of his right hip by buck shot. He had lost the sight of his right eye.

Smith, Conrad. Pa. —. He was awarded a $40 gratuity and a $40 annuity in Franklin Co., Pa. 24 Mar. 1832.

Smith, Conrad. Pa. —. He was awarded a $40 gratuity and a $40 annuity in Montgomery Co., Pa. 4 May 1832.

Smith, Daniel. Md. Pvt. He was pensioned in Kent County in 1786. He was on the 1813 pension list.

Smith, Daniel. Va. —. He served in the 13th Regiment. His wife, Catherine Smith, and three children were granted support in Ohio County 3 Aug. 1778.

Smith, Daniel. Va. Pvt. He served in the 4th Sublegion under Wayne. He was on the 1813 pension list. He was in Lee County 25 Feb. 1818 when his pension was increased to $100 per annum He died 29 Aug. 1830. His widow, Sally Smith, relinquished administration of his estate to Benjamin Dickinson.

Smith, David. Md. Pvt. He was pensioned 4 Mar. 1789. He was on the 1813 pension list.

Smith, David. S.C. Pvt. He served in the cavalry for two years. Congress accepted he was identical with the man of the name who performed the service and granted a pension to his widow, Rebecca Smith, 23 May 1856.

Smith, David. Va. —. His wife and three children were granted £3 support in Yohogania Co., Va. 28 Apr. 1778. His wife and four children were granted £12 support 27 Oct. 1779. He served in the 13th Regiment.

Smith, Ebenezer. Mass. —. He served in the 8th Regiment and was from Middleton. He was paid $20.

Smith, Ebenezer. Mass. Capt. He received his commutation for five years in lieu of half-pay for life.

Smith, Edmund. Conn. Pvt. He served in Capt. Bradley's Company of Artillery. He was wounded by a musket ball which entered his right wrist and was extracted about midway between his wrist and elbow on 5 July 1779 at New Haven. He resided at New Haven, Conn. in 1794. He was granted half a pension 20 Apr. 1796. He was on the 1813 pension list. He died 8 Nov. 1831.

Smith, Edward. —. —. —. One hundred seventy-six inhabitants from Breckinridge Co., Ky. petitioned in his behalf for a pension by a special act of Congress. It was rejected 14 Mar. 1846.

Smith, Edward. Pa. —. He applied in Dauphin County on 21 May 1815. He served with Timothy Green. Before he was free, he enlisted in Capt. Makey's Company in 1778. He became lame in the service. He entered the Flying Camp in 1776 under Col. Cunningham. He returned home in 1777. It was also stated that he was enlisted by Lt. Makey.

Smith, Eleazer. S.C. —. He entered the service in Mecklenburg Co., N.C. in 1776 as a wagoner under Col. Polk and went to Charleston. He was at St. Augustine but was ordered back to Charleston. He was at Philadelphia under Gen. Washington. After Germantown he was discharged. John

Sovrence of Warren Co., Ga. deposed that he refugeed in Mecklenburg Co., N. C., and he and Smith served under Capt. James Thompson. Eleazer Smith was 75 years old and suffered from rheumatism. He was born in Pennsylvania and moved to Abbeville, S.C. in his infancy with his parents. He applied 4 Nov. 1826. He was paid as late as 1830.

Smith, Eli. Mass. Pvt. He served in the 3rd Regiment. His widow was Mary Smith of Medfield was paid $50.

Smith, Eli. Mass. —. He was put on the pension roll and then stricken. He was from Norfolk, Mass. in 1825. Congress restored him to his pension.

Smith, Elijah. Md. Pvt. He was pensioned at the rate of half-pay of a private in Baltimore 6 Feb. 1818. His widow, Priscilla Smith, was paid his arrearage Mar. 1826. She was pensioned at the same rate 1 Apr. 1839.

Smith, Eleazer. S.C. —. He was from Pendleton District and was pensioned 30 Nov. 1827.

Smith, Enoch. Mass. Pvt. He served in the 6th Regiment and was from Rutland. He was paid $20.

Smith, Ephraim. Md. Pvt. He was pensioned at the rate of half-pay of a private in Baltimore 4 Feb. 1843.

Smith, Ephraim. Mass. Pvt. He served in the 2nd Regiment and was disabled due to rheumatism &c. He was pensioned 1 Sep. 1782. He transferred to Vermont. He was on the 1813 pension list.

Smith, Ezra. Conn. Lt. He was injured by the heat of the day in the battle of Monmouth 28 June 1778. He applied in 1790.

Smith, Francis. Pa. Pvt. He was pensioned.

Smith, George. Pa. —. He was from Philadelphia County.

Smith, George. Pa. —. He served under Col. Piper and later in Capt. Boyd's Ranging Company. He was taken prisoner by the Indians in June 1781 and held in captivity until Nov. 1784. He was awarded a $40 gratuity and a $40 annuity in Bedford County on 29 Mar. 1813. He died 9 Aug. 1824. His widow, Rebecca Smith, was awarded a $40 gratuity and a $40 annuity 10 Apr. 1826.

Smith, George. S.C. —. His widow, Agnes Smith, was paid an annuity 21 Feb. 1787 in Greenville Dist.

Smith, Godfrey. N.Y. Pvt. He served in Col. Schuyler's militia. He was wounded in his right hand and wrist on 7 July 1777 at Fort Ann. He resided in Rensselaer Co., N.Y. in 1796.

Smith, Griffith. Pa. —. He was awarded a $40 gratuity and a $40 annuity in Montgomery Co., Pa. 18 Feb. 1834. He died 3 Jan. 1843.

Smith, Harry. N.C. Capt. His application was rejected in 1821.

Smith, Heber. Conn. Sgt. He served under Col. Sherman and Col. Webb. He was wounded in his thigh by a musket ball at White Plains on 28 Oct. 1776. He was subject to fits occasioned by being bled in the artery of his temple for the headache. He resided in Huntington, Conn. in 1792. He enlisted 10 Mar. 1777 and invalided 7 Apr. 1781. He served in the militia. He was granted half a pension 20 Apr. 1796. He was on the 1813 pension list. He died 4 Apr. 1818.

Smith, Henry. Mass. —. He was from Natick and enlisted 19 Apr. 1776 under Capt. Joseph Morse and Col. Samuel Bullard. He was wounded at Lexington. He next served under Capt. James Mellon and Col. Jonathan Ward for four years and eleven months. He was at Dorchester and White Plains. His daughter was Abigail Stafford. Her uncle, Thomas Bacon, was deprived of the use of his feet at White Plains and her father died of his wounds when she was only a child. On the night of 18 Apr. 1775 her grandfather, Ephraim Smith, guided troops to Lexington. He had five sons and five sons-in-law in that battle. Her uncles, John Bacon of Needham and Jonathan Smith, a minuteman, were brought home dead. The females in the household carded, spun, wove, and made clothes and sent bedding and other articles to Castle Island and Dorchester

Heights. Congress granted her a pension 25 July 1850.

Smith, Isaac. N.Y. —. He was pensioned at the rate of $80 per annum. He sought a record of his service 25 June 1855 from Wyoming County.

Smith, Israel. Mass. —. He served in the 7th Regiment and was paid $20.

Smith, Jacob. Pa. —. He was awarded a $40 gratuity and a $40 annuity in Northampton Co., Pa. 18 Feb. 1834.

Smith, James. —. —. His widow, Adah Smith, failed to prove his service and their marriage so Congress refused her pension by a private act 20 Jan. 1847. Congress did so again on 20 June 1848 when she claimed she married in 1803.

Smith, James. Md. Pvt. He was pensioned in Frederick County in 1789. He was disabled at Camden. He served in the 2nd Regiment. He may be identical with one of the three James Smiths on the 1813 pension list.

Smith, James. Md. Pvt. He was on the 1791 pension list. [second of the name]

Smith, James. Mass. —. He served in the Dragoons and was paid $20.

Smith, James. N.Y. Pvt. He served in the 4th N.Y. Regiment under Col. Frederick Weissenfells and died 30 Sep. 1779. His son was granted support according to an undated roster.

Smith, James. N.Y. Pvt. He served in Capt. Israel Honeywell's Company of the Westchester County militia under Col. Thomas Thomas. He was disabled by a musket ball in his right shoulder and several stabs of a bayonet in his right arm and the left side of his body. He was 24 years old in 1787. He lived in North Castle, Westchester Co., N.Y. 1 June 1789. He was on the 1813 pension list.

Smith, James. N.C. Pvt. He received a fourth of a pension in 1796.

Smith, James. N.C. —. He died at Stono 20 June 1779. His widowed mother, Katherine Smith, sought his back pay and a pension 29 Jan. 1780.

Smith, James. N.C. Sgt. He served under Col. Buford. He was wounded by a musket ball shot through his right thigh on 15 Mar. 1781 at the battle of Guilford. He lived in Richmond Co., N.C. in 1795. He was granted a full pension 20 Apr. 1796. He was on the 1813 pension list.

Smith, James. Pa. Pvt. He was in Philadelphia County 11 Apr. 1788. He served under Francis Johnston and Capt. Job Vernon in the 1st Pa. Regiment and was wounded by a musket ball in his face at Germantown. It went through his head. He was also wounded with a bayonet in his forehead. He was 55 years old. He lived in Lycoming County.

Smith, James. Pa. —. He applied at Carlisle, Pa. 6 July 1818. He served 13 months. He enlisted in Capt. Samuel McCune's Company in Cumberland County for six months in the latter part of 1776. In 1777 he enlisted for another six months.

Smith, James. Pa. Pvt. He served in Capt. James Murry's Company in the Flying Camp. He was taken prisoner at Fort Washington on 16 Nov. 1776 and held in confinement to Mar. 1777 when he was liberated. He reached home a month later. He was granted $100 in Lycoming County in 1807.

Smith, James. Pa. Pvt. He was transferred to Maryland by Mar. 1796.

Smith, James. Pa. —. He was awarded a $40 gratuity and a $40 annuity in Perry Co., Pa. 19 Mar. 1824.

Smith, James. Pa. —. He was awarded a $40 gratuity and a $40 annuity 31 Mar. 1836. He resided in Columbiana Co., Ohio. He died 28 May 1845 in Butler County, Pa.

Smith, James. S.C. —. He was wounded on a galley at Stono and died on 6 Feb. 1783 at Charleston. His widowed mother, Katherine Smith, sought his back pay and a pension 29 Jan. 1780. Thomas

Hall certified that he served under him.

Smith, James. S.C. —. He was pensioned in 1783 and was a resident of Charleston.

Smith, James. S.C. —. He was from Marion District and was pensioned 25 Nov. 1830. He was paid as late as 1832.

Smith, James. Va. —. He was a soldier in Continental service. His wife, Mary Smith, was granted financial support in Botetourt Co., Va. 15 Apr. 1778.

Smith, James. Va. Pvt. He applied 24 Nov. 1781. He was in Halifax Co., Va. on 15 May 1783. He was on the 1785 pension roll. He lived in North Carolina 18 Mar. 1796. He was a Continental soldier and was wounded in his right thigh by a musket ball at Guilford. [He may be identical with the James Smith from North Carolina.]

Smith, James. Va. —. His wife, Susanna Smith, was granted £25 relief in Bedford Co., Va. on 27 Sep. 1779.

Smith, Jedediah. Conn. Pvt. He served in the infantry under Maj. Wyllis under Lafayette in Va. in Col. Jamet's [?] Regiment. His constitution was ruined in action between Jamestown and Green Springs when driven through a creek by the enemy when he took a severe cold. He resided in Stafford, Conn. in 1792 and in Tolland, Conn. in 1794. He enlisted 27 May 1777 and continued to the end of the war.

Smith, Jeremiah. Mass. —. He was paid $50.

Smith, Jeremiah. N.C. —. He was a colored man and was the servant of Col. John Smith of Johnston Co., N.C. He carried expresses and served the entire war. Congress denied his claim because his type of service was not covered by law on 3 Mar. 1851.

Smith, Jesse. Mass. Pvt. He was in the 3rd Dragoons and was from Salem. He was paid $50.

Smith, Jesse. S.C. —. He served under Col. John Litteral, Capt. William Golston, and Capt. Joseph Rosser. He was at Guilford and Eutaw Springs. He was taken prisoner at Bear Creek and confined on the *Provo*. He escaped and rejoined. Charles Smith served with him. He was 68 years old in 1829. He was from Greenville District and was pensioned 25 Nov. 1830. He was paid as late as 1834. He made a successful application for a federal pension. He sought arrearage for the time between the suspension of his state and the approval of his federal pension. His claim was rejected by South Carolina.

Smith, Job. S.C. —. He fought as Savannah, Augusta, Ninety Six, and the Snow Camps. He served under Capt. Pugh, Col. Marlborough, Capt. John Wilson, Capt. Samuel Earle, and Col. Thomas Farrar. He had lived in Pendleton District for 35 years. He was 77 years old. He was pensioned from Pendleton District 19 Dec. 1825 and was paid as late as 1834.

Smith, John. —.—. He served as an officer. His son, Samuel S. Smith, was administrator of his estate. He sought his father's commutation pay but the papers had been lost. Congress considered his petition 8 Jan. 1846.

Smith, John. Conn. Lt. He served in the militia. He was wounded in the back by a musket ball on 28 Apr. 1777 at Campo. He resided at Milford, Conn. in 1794. He died 16 Feb. 1807.

Smith, John. Conn. Pvt. He served under Col. M. Willets. His feet were badly frozen on a tedious march from Oswego to Fort Rensselaer on the Mohawk River in Feb. 1783. He lost the toes of his feet. He lived in Bristol, Conn. in 1792. He was on the 1813 pension list. He died 30 Mar. 1822.

Smith, John. Me. —. He died 15 May 1824 at Isleboro. His widow was Lydia Covel from Belfast. She was paid $50 under the resolve of 1836.

Smith, John. Me. —. He died at Mt. Desert 7 June 1828. His widow was Anna Smith from Mt. Desert.

She was paid $50 under the resolve of 1836.

Smith, John. Md. Pvt. He was pensioned at the rate of half-pay of a private in Charles County on 19 Feb. 1819.

Smith, John. Md. Pvt. He was pensioned at the rate of half-pay of a private in Anne Arundel Co. on 19 Feb. 1819. Hid widow, Sarah Smith, was pensioned in Anne Arundel County on 14 Mar. 1823 and on 26 Feb. 1825..

Smith, John. Md. Corp. He was pensioned at the rate of half-pay of a corporal in Prince George's County on 24 Feb. 1823. His arrearage was paid to Richard L. Jenkins 7 Feb. 1843.

Smith, John. Mass. —. He served more than seven years. He married 12 Sep. 1805. His widow, Jane Smith of Clermont Co., Ohio sought his arrearage. Congress granted her relief 16 Feb. 1857.

Smith, John. Mass. Lt. He served under Col. Porter. He had a rupture in his left side in the scrotum in Mar. 1781. He lived in Hadley, Mass. in 1795.

Smith, John. N.H. Corp. He was in Durham and was aged 37 in 1786. He enlisted in the 2nd N.H. Regiment and was disabled by a wound in his left hip at Saratoga on 7 Oct. 1777. He died 17 Sep. 1807.

Smith, John. N.H. Sgt. He served in the 1st Regiment under Col. Scammel. He was wounded in his head by a musket ball which remained lodged therein in July 1781 near Kingsbridge. He lived in Francistown, N.H. in 1794. He enlisted 5 Apr. 1777 for the war. He was on the rolls in 1783. He was granted half a pension 20 Apr. 1796. He was on the 1813 pension list.

Smith, John. N.J. Pvt. He served in the 2nd Regiment and lost his sight. He lived at Elizabeth, Essex County and was 48 years old. He was on the 1791 pension roll at the rate of $60 per annum. He was 48 years old.

Smith, John. N.Y. Pvt. He lived in N.Y. in 1788.

Smith, John. N.Y. Sgt. He served in the 2nd N.Y. Regiment and was slain 29 Jan. 1781. His children, John Smith and Charles Smith, received a half-pay pension,.

Smith, John. N.Y. —. He served under Col Van Schaick. His family was awarded assistance in Jan. & Apr. 1779 while he was away in the service.

Smith, John. —. Pvt. He served in Col. Willet's Regiment. On his return from Oswego to Fort Rensslaer, his feet were frozen, and he lost sundry joints of his toes in Feb. 1783. He resided in Bristol, Conn. in 1796. He died 30 Mar. 1822.

Smith, John. Pa. —. He was killed at Crooked Billet 1 May 1778. His widow, Mary Smith, married ----- Blair. He left three orphan children who were granted a pension 29 May 1788.

Smith, John. Pa. —. He was awarded a $40 gratuity and a $40 annuity in Armstrong Co., Pa. 14 Apr. 1828. He died 17 Dec. 1830.

Smith, John. Pa. Pvt. He was in Chester County on 20 June 1786. He was wounded by a musket ball in his right thigh in May 1776 at Lake Champlain in an engagement with the Indians. He served in the 9th Pa. Regiment in Capt. Benjamin Davis' Company. He was 60 years old.

Smith, John. Pa. —. He was awarded a $40 gratuity in Baltimore, Md. 27 Feb. 1834. He died 17 Mar. 1848.

Smith, John. Pa. —. He was awarded a $40 gratuity and a $40 annuity in Northampton Co., Pa. 6 Apr. 1833.

Smith, John. Pa. —. He was wounded by a cannon ball in his left thigh at Brandywine 11 Sep. 1777 and was in the Invalids. He received his half-pay pension 17 June 1783.

Smith, John. Pa. Non-com. He was in Philadelphia County on 13 Oct. 1785. He was wounded by rejoicing fire held at Amboy on 4 July 1780 by the rammers of a cannon. His wife was Jane

Smith. He was 45 years old.

Smith, John. Pa. —. He was awarded a $40 gratuity and a $40 annuity in Lancaster Co., Pa. 5 Mar. 1828.

Smith, John. Pa. —. He was from Westmoreland County. He was pensioned 11 Apr. 1844 and died 23 Dec. 1857. He also appeared as John A. Smith.

Smith, John. Pa. —. He was awarded a $40 gratuity and a $40 annuity on 25 Feb. 1813. He was from Mifflin County, He died 13 July 1813.

Smith, John. Pa. —. His heirs in Mercer County were awarded $65 for his arrearage of pay on 29 Mar. 1813.

Smith, John. Pa. —. He was awarded a $40 gratuity and a $40 annuity in Cumberland Co., Pa. 20 Mar. 1834.

Smith, John. Pa. —. He applied 14 Nov. 1814.

Smith, John. Pa. —. He was awarded a $40 gratuity in Fayette County 6 Apr. 1833.

Smith, John. Pa. Capt. He served in the 11th Regiment. He was disabled by rejoicing fire held at Sunsbury on 4 July 1780. He was dead by Mar. 1792.

Smith, John. Pa. —. He was awarded a $40 gratuity and a $40 annuity in Lebanon Co., Pa. 1 Apr. 1823.

Smith, John. Pa. —. He was granted relief in York County 27 Mar. 1837.

Smith, John. R.I. Pvt. He received a broken arm in a fall near Newtown, Pennsylvania when on a march to Red Bank, N.J. in Oct. 1777. His arm was weakened and was of little use. He served under Col. Jeremiah Olney. He was aged 48 when he applied 10 Feb. 1786. He lived in Providence Co., R.I.

Smith, John. S.C. —. He served in the 3rd S.C. Regiment under Col. Thompson. Jeremiah Simmons served with him. He was discharged 9 June 1779. He was 70 years old. He had a wife and two daughters when he applied in Nov. 1823. He was pensioned 20 Dec. 1823. He was paid as late as 1834. In 1836 he was 80 years old. He died 30 Mar. 1840. His widow was Sarah Smith from Lancaster District. They married in 1778. She was almost blind. She was granted his arrearage and a pension.

Smith, John. S.C. —. His remarried widow, Barbara Glover, sought a pension. The stub indent for £97.4.5 issued to one John Smith did not prove that person was her husband. Congress denied her a pension 29 Mar. 1860.

Smith, John. S.C. Pvt. His widow was Susannah Townsend from Abbeville District in 1802.

Smith, John. Va. —. He was in Berkeley County in Apr. 1790.

Smith, John. Va. —. He was in Gloucester County on 2 July 1787.

Smith, John. Va. —. He was on the roll in 1790. He served in the 1st Va. Regiment of Foot and was wounded at Mud Island Fort in 1777. Capt. Thomas Buckner of the 5th Va. Regiment of Foot certified his service.

Smith, John. Va. —. He was wounded at Fort Mifflin 10 Nov. 1777. He was on the pension roll in 1784.

Smith, John. Va. Pvt. He applied 2 Apr. 1787. He served in the 7th Va. Regiment and was wounded by a musket ball through his hip and thigh. He was 40 years old. He was on the 1813 pension list.

Smith, John. Va. —. He served in Capt. Bruin's Company in the 11th Virginia Regiment. His wife, Lucy Smith, and child were furnished £5 support in Frederick Co., Va. on 2 Dec.1777.

Smith, John. Va. Pvt. He was in Frederick County on 16 June 1786. He served in the 8th Va. Regiment in Capt. Swearingen's Company. At Ninety Six he was wounded by a musket ball in his left arm, another in his left shoulder which lodged therein, another which passed through his left loin, and another in his right ankle. His skull was fractured. He was 40 [?49] years old. He was on the 1813 pension list.

Smith, John Kilby. Mass. Capt. He received his commutation for five years in lieu of half-pay for life. He died 7 Aug. 1842.

Smith, Jonathan. Md. Pvt. He was pensioned 4 Mar. 1789.

Smith, Jonathan. S.C. —. He entered the service at the age of 15 under Capt. Jacob Barnett and Col.. Moffit. He was wounded at Blackstocks and was taken to his father's house. He was 66 years old and had an eight year old child who was born deformed. His wife had been confined to bed for the greater part of six years. William Millwee served with his brother, Daniel Smith, at Stono where the latter was killed. Henry Smith of Franklin Co., Ga. deposed anent his service. He was from Anderson District and was pensioned 4 Dec. 1828. His spouse was Elizabeth Smith. He died 14 Sep. 1829. One Elizabeth Smith was pensioned 23 Nov. 1829. She died 14 Nov. 1862. Her administrator was Jesse R. Smith who was paid her arrearage.

Smith, Jordan. Conn. Pvt. He served in the 1st Conn. Regiment and was disabled due to old age and infirmity. He was pensioned 29 Jan. 1783. He died in 1799.

Smith, Joseph. Conn. Pvt. He died in 1807.

Smith, Joseph. Md. Pvt. He was pensioned 4 Mar. 1789. He was on the 1813 pension list.

Smith, Joseph. Md. Capt. He was pensioned at the rate of half-pay of a captain 23 Jan. 1816.

Smith, Joseph. S.C. —. His widow, Mary Ann Smith, was to be issued a corrected indent plus interest from April 1783 due her late husband on 9 Dec. 1793.

Smith, Joseph. Va. —. His wife, Susannah Smith, was granted financial aid while he was away in the service in Mecklenburg Co., Va. 11 Aug. 1777.

Smith, Josiah. Conn. Pvt. He was in the Connecticut militia on the frontier under Noadiah Hooker in Capt. Bronson's Company. He was wounded by a party of light horse while on guard duty at Sherwood's Bridge on 29 June 1779. His right arm was much perished by a cut in his elbow One of his fingers on his left hand was cut off, and he had a cut across his left arm. He was pensioned 14 Sep. 1787 and resided in Cheshire, Conn. He was pensioned at the rate of $5 per month from 29 Dec. 1807. He was on the 1813 pension list. He transferred to Ohio and back to Connecticut.

Smith, Josiah. Conn. Lt. He served in Capt. James Stoddard's Company under Lt. Col. Samuel Canfield in a Conn. Regiment. He was disabled by a musket wound in his left hand by which he lost his thumb and another in his right arm above the elbow by a broad sword on 25 May 1778 by a detachment of De Lancey's Corps. He was 37 years old when he was pensioned 30 May 1788. A farmer, he lived in Poundridge, Westchester Co., N.Y. on 17 Apr. 1789. He was on the 1813 pension list. He died 29 Nov. 1830 in New York County.

Smith, Josiah. Mass. Capt. He retired on half-pay 1 Jan. 1782.

Smith, Larkin. Va. Capt. He served in the cavalry. He was in service as a private as early as Nov. 1775 under Capt. Oliver Towles. In 1776 he was a cadet and then ensign in the 6th Battalion. He was paid as captain of cavalry to 25 Nov. 1782 and served to the end of the war. His heirs received his commutation 13 Mar. 1838.

Smith, Lawrence. Pa. Marine. He was in Philadelphia County 2 Oct. 1787. He was a soldier at New Orleans, La. under James Willing in 1778. He served on the Continental sloop *Morris* under Capt. Pickle and was wounded in the hip with a musket ball at the capture of the sloop *West Florida*. He was transferred to the Invalids in 1780. He was 66 years old. He was dead by Sep. 1797.

Smith, Leonard. N.Y. Ens. He entered the service in a company of militia in Marlborough, Ulster Co., N.Y. under Capt. Silas Purdy and Col. Thomas Palmer in Sep. 1775. He was detached to build fortifications at Fort Montgomery and continued duty to May 1776. In June he was commissioned 2nd Lt. Under Capt. Samuel Clark and served to Jan. 1777. In Mar. 1777 he was under Gen. George Clinton to raise a company of volunteers for three years. He served as captain and was discharged in 1780. He received a pension from Congress on 4 Jan. 1839. He was 76 years old and lived in Orange Co., N.Y.

Smith, Leonard. Pa. —. He was awarded a $40 gratuity and a $40 annuity 1 Apr. 1837 in Westmoreland County. He was dead by July 1838.

Smith, Matthew. Va. Capt. & Dep. Adj. Gen. He held the rank of major and was killed at Germantown. His heirs were allowed bounty land 17 July 1886.

Smith, Michael. N.J. Pvt. He was on the 1813 pension list at the rate of $60 per annum.

Smith, Moses. Conn. Pvt. He served under Col. Swift. He was injured in his back and hips by an accidental fall. He resided in Washington, Conn. in 1792.

Smith, Moses. Mass. Pvt. He served in 9th Mass. Regiment under Col. James Wesson in Capt. Thomas Migill's Company. He was disabled by the loss of his right hand at the battle of Trenton. He was pensioned in 1777. He was 30 years old in 1786. He was pensioned 17 Mar. 1786. He was on the 1813 pension list. He later transferred to Washington Co., N.Y.

Smith, Moses. N.J. Pvt. He served under Capt. Jones and Col. Philip Van Courtlandt in the Essex County militia. He was killed by a cannon ball at Elizabeth Town on 8 June 1779. His widow, Esther Smith, was granted his half-pay in Essex County in Jan. 1781.

Smith, Nathan. Conn. Sgt. He served in the 2nd Regiment of Light Dragoons in Capt. Belden's Company under Col. Elisha Sheldon and Maj. Benjamin Tallmadge. He was wounded in his right shoulder and twice in his left arm. He was taken prisoner at Pound Ridge. He was pensioned 15 May 1781.

Smith, Nathan. Va. Surgeon's Mate. He served to 15 Nov. 1783. His widow, Ann J. Smith, was allowed five years' full pay and was approved for the balance of $14.87 due her on 9 June 1838.

Smith, Nathaniel. Md. Maj. His widow, Sarah Smith, was pensioned at the rate of half-pay of a captain in Baltimore 22 Feb. 1823. She was pensioned at the new rate of half-pay of a major 9 Mar. 1827.

Smith, Nicholas. N.Y. Pvt. He served under Capt. Herter and Col. Bellinger and was slain 10 May 1779. His children, George Smith, Nicholas Smith, and Elizabeth Smith, received his half-pay pension.

Smith, Nicholas. Pa. —. He was granted relief.

Smith, Noah. Me. —. He died at Hollis 15 Oct. 1830. His widow was Comfort Smith from Hollis. She was paid $50 under the resolve of 1836.

Smith, Noah. S.C. —. He served under Capt. Love Page [?], Ward Glisson, and Gen. Livingston. He had no wife or children. He was 68 years old. He was from Williamsburg District in 1827.

Smith, Parker. —. —. He fell at the siege of Charleston, S.C. His only surviving son, John Smith, sought a pension from Congress 20 Jan. 1847. Congress rejected his petition.

Smith, Paul. S.C. —. He was allowed a pension of $21.30 per annum for life on 20 Dec. 1800. He was from Kershaw District.

Smith, Peter. Conn. Pvt. He served in the Conn. Line. He lived in Fairfield Co., Conn. He was pensioned at the rate of $4 per month from 16 July 1806. He was on the 1813 pension list.

Smith, Peter. Pa. Lt. He had been a resident of New Jersey for more than 30 years in 1814. He was awarded an $80 gratuity and an $80 annuity in 1814.

Smith, Peter. Pa. —. He was awarded a $40 gratuity and a $40 annuity in Lancaster Co., Pa. 18 Feb. 1834.

Smith, Philip. Pa. —. He was awarded a $40 gratuity and a $40 annuity in Berks Co., Pa. 10 Apr. 1835. He was dead by Aug. 1838.

Smith, Robert. Conn. Pvt. He was scalped, tomahawked, and suffered from bodily infirmities. He died in 1794.

Smith, Robert. Mass. Pvt. He served under Col. Nicholas. He had an ulcerated sore on his left leg occasioned by a wound received from a piece of timber which he was employed in drawing for use of the public works in Mar. 1780 at West Point. He lived in Barre, Mass. in 1795. He was in the militia. He was granted two-thirds of a pension 20 Apr. 1796. He was on the 1813 pension list. He died 24 Dec. 1820 in Worcester Co., Mass.

Smith, Robert. N.Y. —. His brother, Joshua Smith, enlisted in 1777 for the war. In May 1778 he took his brother's place. He rode a hundred miles to do so. His brother returned home. They were both artificers at West Point. Joshua Smith was marked as a deserter 1 Mar. 1780 but was discharged due to ill health 12 May 1781. Robert Smith answered for the name of his brother. Congress granted him a pension for twelve months of service on 7 Apr. 1836.

Smith, Robert. S.C. & Ga. He served for two years. His application for a pension was rejected. He died in 1853. He received bounty land in Georgia for his meritorious service. His widow, Mrs. Ferguson Smith, received 160 acres of bounty land from the federal government. Congress awarded her a pension 30 Mar. 1860 at which time she lived in Georgia.

Smith, Robert. Va. —. His wife, Catherine Smith, was granted £25 support in Berkeley County on 19 Aug. 1779. She received 10 bushels of corn and 44 pounds of bacon on 15 Aug. 1780.

Smith, Samuel. Conn. Pvt. He served in the 7th Conn. Regiment. He was worn out in the service. He was pensioned 15 Sep. 1782. He died in 1800.

Smith, Samuel. Pa. —. He served in the 11th Regiment under Capt. John Harris. He served in the 11th Pennsylvania Regiment and was 32 years old. He received his half-pay 17 June 1783.

Smith, Samuel. Pa. Marine. He was dead by Sep. 1800.

Smith, Samuel. Pa. Pvt. He was in Chester County 20 Dec. 1785. He was in the 11th Pa. Regiment in Capt. John Harris's Company and was wounded in his left thigh by a cannon ball. He lost both legs at Brandywine on 11 Sep. 1777. He was 32 years old.

Smith, Samuel. Pa. —. He was dead by Sep. 1800.

Smith, Samuel. Va. —. He served in the 13th Virginia Regiment. His wife Catherine Smith and three children were granted £7.10 on 3 Aug. 1778 for the next six months in Ohio Co., Va.

Smith, Simeon. Mass. —. He served in the 6th Regiment and was from New York. He was paid $20.

Smith, Simeon. N.H. —. He enlisted in 1780 for six months and served under Capt. Lawrence and Lt. Col. Henry Dearborn in the 3rd Regiment. He was discharged at Soldier's Fortune 6 Dec. 1780 by Maj. John Wait. He applied 25 Jan. 1837 from Campton, Grafton Co., N.H. Congress granted him a pension for six months of service.

Smith, Smallwood. S.C. —. He was killed in the service by a party under the command of William Cunningham. His widow, Elizabeth Smith, was granted an annuity 27 Jan. 1785. It was paid to Francis Jones.

Smith, Solomon. Mass. —. He served in the 6th Regiment and was from Worcester. He was paid $20.

Smith, Stephen. S.C. —. He served under Capt. William Kirkland. He was at Augusta in Mar. 1778. John Smith and John Crossland gave details about his service. His widow, Martha Smith, was pensioned from Fairfield District on 23 Nov. 1829. She said he died fifteen to twenty years ago.

She was between 70 and 80 years old. She was paid as late as 1834.

Smith, Studely. Mass. —. He served in the 4ᵗʰ Regiment and was paid $20.

Smith, Tarpley. Va. Capt. He was in the service in 1780 and 1781 and was paid to 15 Feb. 1781. He was not named in the Chesterfield arrangement so he must have resigned. Congress rejected the petition of his legal representative 10 June 1854. He had received 4,000 acres of bounty land 15 July 1783. On 1 June 1805 he received 333 1/3 and 333 1/3 acres for seven years as a captain.

Smith, Terrence. N.J. Pvt. He served in the 1ˢᵗ Regiment and was worn out in the service. He was 67 years old and was from Nottingham.

Smith, Theophilus. Conn. —. He served in the 8ᵗʰ Regiment and was disabled by wounds. He was pensioned 7 June 1783..

Smith, Thomas. Me. —. He was from Litchfield. He was paid $50 under the resolve of 1836.

Smith, Thomas. Md. Pvt. He was pensioned at the rate of half-pay of a private in Ohio 26 Feb. 1829.

Smith, Thomas. N.C. Pvt. He applied in Guilford Co. in 1785. He lost a leg. He was on the 1813 pension list.

Smith, Thomas. N.C. Pvt. He was pensioned 4 Mar. 1790. He removed to Greenville Dist., South Carolina 4 Mar. 1826.

Smith, Thomas. Pa. —. He served under Capt. Templeton and was taken prisoner at Fort Freeland. He was held three years and five months. He was awarded a $40 gratuity and a $40 annuity in Mifflin County on 11 Mar. 1815.

Smith, Thomas. S.C. —. He was wounded 28 June 1776. He was granted an annuity 24 Mar. 1778.

Smith, Thomas. S.C. —. There were children in 1793.

Smith, Thomas. Va. —. His wife, Catherine Smith, was granted £7 support in Berkeley County on 17 Nov. 1778. He was away in Continental service.

Smith, Thomas. Va. —. His wife, Susannah Smith, was grated support in Mecklenburg Co., Va. 11 Aug. 1777.

Smith, Valentine. Md. Pvt. He was pensioned 4 Mar. 1789. He lived in Harford County. He was on the 1813 pension list.

Smith, Valentine. Md. Pvt. He was pensioned 4 Mar. 1789. He was on the 1813 pension list. [second one of the name]

Smith, William. —. —. There was nothing specially meritorious in his service, and his heirs, William Smith, John Smith, and Sarah Meredith, did not seem in circumstances of need. Congress rejected their claim 20 May 1862.

Smith, William. —. —. His widow, Meridy Smith, of Newnan, Georgia, was 85 years of age. She was allowed an increase in her pension of $12 a month by Congress 12 Feb. 1891.

Smith, William. Del. Pvt. He was pensioned in 1787. He died 12 Oct. 1804.

Smith, William. N.C. —. He served three months in the garrison at Watauga, N.C. under Capt. John Sevier in 1776; five months under Lt.-Capt. L. Carter and Col. John Sevier in 1779; two months under Capt. Dooley and Col. Clark in 1780; seven months under Capt. V. Sevier and Col. Shelby; two months in 1781; four months under Capt. Dooley and Clark; and two months as captain under Col. Sevier. Congress granted him a pension at the rate of $10 per months 30 Dec. 1836. He resided in Tennessee.

Smith, William. Pa. Pvt. He was in Cumberland County on 21 Sep. 1786. He was transferred from the 9ᵗʰ Pa. Regiment to the Invalids. He was wounded in the service. He died 12 Sep. 1786. He came to live with Francis Irwin of Cumberland County in July 1783.

Smith, William. Pa. Drummer. He applied 3 July 1787 in Philadelphia. He was disabled by rupture and rheumatic complaint contracted in the service. He was also wounded. He died 24 Oct. 1787. He served aboard the *Congress* under Capt. Isaac Roach and afterwards on the galley *Effingham* under Capt. Hugh Montgomery. He was strained in his groin. He left a widow.

Smith, William. Pa. —. He was pensioned 7 May 1796. He was from Philadelphia County.

Smith, William. S.C. —. He entered the service in 1779 or 1780 and served under Capt. Henry Foster and Col. Leroy Hammond. He was also under Capt. Joseph Towles and Capt. Sinkfield. He was at Stono and Ninety Six. Samuel Deen and Zak S. Brown served with him. He was pensioned in Edgefield District 7 Dec. 1837. He died 17 Mar. 1848. His widow was Frances Smith. They married 2 Sep. 1784. She was in her 87th year. She was the mother of seven children, but only two sons were still alive one of whom was David Smith. Frances Smith conveyed information to the American camp on the approach of the Tories under Cunningham. She and Mrs. Butler journeyed four miles in a canoe on the Saluda River. She also protected and nursed the wounded and sick soldiers. Congress granted her a pension 31 May 1854.

Smith, William. Va. Pvt. He was pensioned on 30 Dec. 1791 at the rate of £10 per annum. He was in Culpeper County in Apr. 1792. He was wounded. In Apr. 1799 he was in Madison County.

Smith, William. Va. —. His wife, Catherine Smith, was granted £10 support in Berkeley County on 15 Sep. 1778. He was away in Continental service.

Smith, William. Va. —. His wife, Betty Smith, and children were granted 4 barrels of corn and 200 pounds of pork on 20 Apr. 1780 and again on 16 Aug. 1781 in Lancaster Co., Va. There were three small children.

Smith, William Hooker. Pa. Surgeon's Mate. He served to the end of the war. From 3 July 1779 he was surgeon at the post of Wilkesbarre in the Wyoming Valley. He was the only officer of the medical staff at the post. The garrison consisted of two companies of regulars and militia. His heirs were allowed his commutation 7 July 1838.

Smithcomb, Aquilla. Md. Capt. He served in the militia to the end of the war. He died in 1790. Congress denied any relief because no evidence had been furnished.

Smithey, Benjamin. Va. —. He was in Prince William County when he was pensioned on 26 Jan. 1804 at the rate of $60 per annum.

Smoke, Andrew. S.C. —. He was drafted in 1776. He fought at Charleston, Stono, and Orangeburg. He was from St. Bartholomew Parish, Colleton District in 1826. He was paid as late as 1835.

Smyth, —. S.C. —. His widow, Mary Smyth, was pensioned 6 Dec. 1828. She also appeared as Mary Smith.

Smyth, Thomas. Md. Maj. His widow, Anna Maria Smyth, was pensioned at the rate of half-pay of a lieutenant 18 Feb. 1830. Her pension was increased to that of half-pay of a major 25 Mar. 1836.

Snable, Joseph. Pa. —. He was granted relief in Berks County 6 Apr. 1833.

Snagg, Henry. N.Y. Pvt. He served in Gen. Knox's artillery. He was wounded in his left leg by the drag rope of a field piece at the battle of Princeton, N.J. in Oct. 1777. He lived in Orange Co., N.Y. in 1794.

Snail, Thomas. Va. —. He served as an officer in the state navy. His widow, Elizabeth Snail, was pensioned at the rate of £15 per annum on 15 Dec. 1791. His widow was in Norfolk 24 Apr. 1792. He also appeared as Thomas Snale.

Snalbacker, Daniel. N.J. Pvt. He was on the 1791 pension roll. He served in Lee's Legion and suffered from the loss of a leg. He was 30 years old. He lived in Gloucester County. He was on the 1813 pension list.

Snapp, Joseph. Pa. Pvt. He was pensioned.

Snead, —. S.C. —. His widow, Jane Snead, was pensioned 16 Dec.1818. She was paid as late as 1821.

Snead, Bowdoin. Va. Pvt. He served under Capt. Cope in the Accomack County militia about two years. His widow, Mary Snead, aged 74, had her petition for an increase from $12 to $30 per month granted by Congress 17 Mar. 1890.

Snead, Charles. Va. Capt. He served in the 8th Virginia Regiment until the spring of 1781 when he became supernumerary 22 Oct. 1780 with the reorganization of the army. He was a lieutenant from 1 Jan. 1777 to 4 July 1778 and captain from 7 July 1778 to 31 Dec. 1781. He was from Chesterfield County. His heirs were allowed half-pay 22 Dec. 1837.

Snead, Thomas. Va. —. His widow, Catherine Snead, and two children were awarded £13 in Northampton Co., Va. on 8 Dec. 1778.

Snead, William. S.C. —. He was from Kershaw in 1791.

Snedier, George. S.C. Legionnaire. He served aboard the *South Carolina* under Commodore Alexander Gillon. He was paid $20 on 12 May 1808.

Snell, Asa. Mass. —. He served in the 15th Regiment and was paid $20.

Snell, Frederick. N.Y. Pvt. His child was granted relief according to an undated roster.

Snell, George. N.Y. Sgt. He served in the Montgomery County militia under Col. Klock and was slain 6 Aug. 1777. His widow, Mary Snell, was granted a half-pay pension for seven years.

Snell, George. Pa. —. He was awarded a $40 gratuity and a $40 annuity in Berks Co., Pa. 27 Jan. 1835. He died 2 Dec. 1843. He also appeared as George Schnell.

Snell, Gilbert. Mass. Pvt. He served in the 4th Regiment and was from North Bridgewater and was paid $50.

Snell, Hans Yost. N.Y. Pvt. He served under Col. Jacob Klock in the militia in Capt. Severnius Cough's Company. He was wounded in his side and in his foot on 25 Oct. 1781. He was 37 years old when he was pensioned 15 Sep. 1786. He lived in Palatine, Montgomery Co., N.Y. on 17 June 1789. He died 28 July 1832 in Herkimer County. He was on the 1813 pension list.

Snell, Jacob. N.Y. Pvt. He served in the militia under Col. Klock and was slain 6 Aug. 1777. His orphans were Johannes Snell, Jacob Snell, Jost Snell, Sarah Snell, Catharine Snell, Elizabeth Snell, Anna Snell, and Peter Snell. They received his half-pay pension. .

Snell, Jacob. Pa. Musician. He applied 13 Oct. 1786. He was born in Philadelphia, was 24 years old, was 5'8" in height, and had black hair and a dark complexion. He was a cordwainer. He served five years under Col. Thomas Proctor in the artillery. He was wounded at the Block House on Bergen Point on 21 June 1780. He was dead by Sep. 1797. He also appeared as Jacob Shnell.

Snell, Jacob Frederick. N.Y. —. He was pensioned.

Snell, Job. R.I. Pvt. He served in Col. William Richmond's Regiment. He lost the index finger of his right hand due to long and extreme exertion in rowing a boat removing the regiment from Newport to New Haven in 1776. He first had the finger amputated and later the hand as well. He lived at Little Compton, R.I. in 1794. He was granted one-fourth of a pension 20 Apr. 1796. He was on the 1813 pension list of New York.

Snell, Joseph. N.Y. Pvt. He served under Col. Jacob Klock and was slain 6 Aug. 1777. His children, Margaret Snell and Catharine Snell, were granted a half-pay pension.

Snell, Thomas. Va. —. His widow was Elizabeth Snell from Norfolk in 1796.

Snell, William. Mass. —. He was paid £159 in full for two years of pension ending 20 Dec. 1779 on 31 Mar. 1780.

Snelling, John. Va. —. He died in Continental service. His widow, Elizabeth Snelling, was furnished £15 support on 24 Sep. 1778. His widow and three children were granted £800 support in Shenandoah County 30 Aug. 1781.

Snider, Anthony. Pa. —. He was awarded a $40 gratuity in Cumberland County 12 Jan. 1836. He also appeared as Anthony Snyder. He died 11 Nov. 1843.

Snider, George. Pa. —. His daughters, Catharine Shade and Polly Lanhar, were paid $200 for his donation land 5 May 1841. He also appeared as George Snyder. They were from Franklin Co.

Snider, John. Md. Corp. He lost a leg. He served in the Flying Camps under Capt. Adam Grosper. He was wounded at White Plains. He was pensioned in Frederick County in 1776. He was on the 1813 pension list as John Snyder.

Snook, Richard. Md. Sgt. He served in the 2nd Md. Regiment and was wounded. He was pensioned.

Snook, Richard. Pa. Pvt. He was on the 1789 pension list.

Snow, Abner. Mass. Pvt. He was pensioned 2 May 1808 at the rate of $3.75 per month from 27 Jan. 1808. He was on the 1813 pension list. He died 27 Sep. 1833.

Snow, Amos. Vt. Pvt. He served under Col. Ciley. He was deaf and worn out in service. He lived in Claremont, Vt. in 1795. He enlisted 28 Dec. 1779 and was discharged in 1782. Since he was not wounded, his claim was not allowed.

Snow, Henry. Va. —. His wife, Elizabeth Snow, was allowed 4 barrels of corn and 200 pounds of pork in Bedford Co., Va. on 27 Mar. 1780.

Snow, James. Mass. —. He served in the Sappers & Miners and was from Pepperelboro.

Snow, Jonas. —. Lt. He entered the service in 1775 for nine months. He reenlisted as a sergeant for one year and continued in the service as a lieutenant for a year. He married in 1777 and died in 1813. Congress granted his widow, Mary Snow, a pension 6 Apr. 1838.

Snow, Paul. Mass. —. He served in the Sappers & Miners and was from Wells.

Snow, Richard. Mass. —. He served in the 4th Regiment and was paid $20. He was from Rochester and was listed as dead in 1803.

Snow, Silvanus. Mass. Pvt. He served in Col. Putnam's Regiment. He was wounded in the cheek by a musket ball on 17 Jun. 1775 at Bunker Hill. He resided in Mass. in 1796. He was granted one-third of a pension 20 Apr. 1797. He was on the 1813 pension list. He died 19 Jan. 1828 in Plymouth Co., Mass.

Snowden, Jonathan. N.J. Lt. He served in the Revolutionary War in Lee's Virginia Regiment and was wounded at Guilford 15 Mar. 1781. He was pensioned 1 Jan. 1784. He lived in Cornwell, Orange Co., N.Y. When he was pensioned, the Secretary of War miscalculated the amount. He should have been allowed no arrearage before 1 Jan. 1803 except for his commutation. The Secretary of War requested a refund. He sought to be able to retain the funds, but Congress did not agree with him on 19 Jan. 1807. He died 25 Dec. 1824.

Snowden, Thomas. Pa. Sgt. He was in Montgomery County in 1808. He served in Capt. Samuel Bennezett's Company under Col. McGaw in the 5th Pa. Regiment in 1776. He was discharged from the 5th Pa. Regiment under Col. Morgan a year later. He served in the 9th Pa. Regiment under Capt. Thomas Bowen until the dissolution of the corps when he was transferred to Col. Richard Butler's Regiment. He was wounded at Monmouth, N.J. on 28 June 1778 by a musket ball which shattered his right ankle. He was also hard of hearing. He was granted a $40 annuity and a $40 gratuity 21 Mar. 1808 as amended 4 Feb. 1809. He died 16 Nov. 1813.

Snyder, —. Pa. —. His widow, Dorothy Snyder, was awarded a $40 gratuity and a $40 annuity in

Schuylkill County 31 Mar. 1836, She died 20 Apr. 1844.

Snyder, Andrew. —. —. Congress refused his heirs relief on 19 July 1848.

Snyder, Andrew. Pa. —. He was awarded a $40 gratuity and a $40 annuity in Lancaster Co., Pa. 23 Apr. 1829. He died 4 Nov. 1845.

Snyder, Dieter. Pa. —. He was awarded a $40 gratuity and a $40 annuity in Schuylkill Co., Pa. 31 Jan. 1832.

Snyder, Frederick. Pa. —. He received a $40 gratuity and a $40 annuity in Monroe County 18 Apr. 1842.

Snyder, George. Pa. —. He was awarded a $40 gratuity and a $40 annuity in Philadelphia Co., Pa. 15 Mar. 1826.

Snyder, Henry. Pa. —. He was awarded a $50 gratuity and a $40 annuity in Adams Co., Pa. 23 Jan. 1834.

Snyder, John. Pa. Pvt. He was in Philadelphia County 10 Apr. 1787. He was in the German Regiment in Capt. Hubley's Company and was wounded at Germantown in his breast and right side by a piece of rail fence splintered by a cannon ball. He was 65 years old.

Snyder, John. Pa. —. He was awarded a $40 gratuity and a $40 annuity in York County on 17 Feb. 1817. One Catherine Snyder, widow of John G. Snyder, was awarded a $40 gratuity in York County 12 Apr. 1851.

Snyder, John. Pa. —. His widow, Elizabeth Snyder, received a $40 annuity in Cumberland County 27 Apr. 1852.

Sohn, David. Pa. —. He applied in Lehigh County. He enlisted in 1775 in Capt. Abraham Miller's Company in the 1st Pa. Regiment for five years and nine months. He was discharged at Philadelphia.

Sohn, George Jacob. Pa. —. He applied in Lehigh County on 14 Sep. 1818. He enlisted in 1776 in Capt. Sealey's Company in the 5th Pa. Regiment for five years. He was discharged at Philadelphia by Col. Richard Butler.

Soliday, —. Pa. —. His widow, Mary Soliday, was granted relief in Armstrong County 11 Apr. 1825.

Solladay, John. Pa. —. He was awarded a $40 gratuity and a $40 annuity in Montgomery Co., Pa. 16 Feb. 1835. He died 19 Jan. 1842.

Sollar, Daniel. Mass. Pvt. He served in the 12th Mass. Regiment. He feet were frozen in 1779. He resided in Mass. in 1796. He enlisted 11 Feb. 1777 for three years, transferred to the Invalids 3 Nov. 1779, and was discharged 18 Feb. 1780.

Solt, David. Pa. Pvt. He applied in Adams County on 28 Sep. 1819. He served under Lt. Craig in Capt. Warner's Company in the 5th Pa. Regiment in the fall of 1775 under Col. Anthony Wayne. He was discharged at Trenton, N.J. He served four years and returned to Northampton County. He was 65 years old. He was also from Tioga County.

Sommer, —. Pa. —. His widow, Elizabeth Sommer, was awarded a $40 gratuity and a $40 annuity in Lancaster, Pa. 15 June 1836.

Sommerville, James. Md. Capt. He was pensioned in Nov. 1785 for his disability acquired in the service. His arrearage was paid to his son, James Somervell, of Prince George's County on 12 Mar. 1828.

Son, Jacob. Pa. —. He was pensioned 4 Aug. 1817.

Son, Michael. Va. —. He was away in the service in the Continental Army. His wife, Elizabeth Son, was allowed 6 bushels of corn valued at £60 in Augusta Co., Va. on 18 May 1780. She was allowed £600 for her support and that of her child on 15 May 1781. She also appeared as Elizabeth Sun.

Sonday, Adam. Pa. —. He was awarded a $40 gratuity and a $40 annuity in Center Co., Pa. 20 Feb. 1832. He died in 1855. His widow, Mary E. Sonday, received a $40 gratuity and a $40 annuity 28 Feb. 1856.

Soper, Amasa. Mass. Capt. He served in Col. Marshall's Regiment from 1 Jan. 1777 to 30 Oct. 1780. The record indicated that he resigned on that date, but it should have stated relieved. After the war he moved with his family to Vermont. He gave his papers to David Quinton to take to Philadelphia for his half-pay commutation. Quinton fell ill with smallpox and died en route. He was dependent on his two sons. They died leaving several small children. He sought his commutation. His claim was rejected 27 June 1838 because his resignation papers were not found.

Sorrall, Robert. S.C. —. He was issued an indent for £6.19.3 plus interest from 1 Apr. 1783 by act of 18 Dec. 1792.

Sose, John. Pa. —. He was pensioned.

Sott, Paul. Pa. —. He was pensioned.

Soule, Asa. Me. —. He was from Montville. He was paid $50 under the resolve of 1836.

Soult, David. Pa. —. He was pensioned.

Southall, Thomas. Va. Pvt. His widow, Elizabeth Southall, was in Northampton County on 11 Oct. 1786. He served in the 9th Va. Regiment and died in Feb. or Mar. 1777. Maj. S. Snead of the 2nd Va. Regiment attested to his service. His child was 10 years old. He also appeared as Thomas Southwell. She was continued on the pension roll 17 Nov. 1791.

Southard, Constant. Me. —. He died 19 Nov. 1826. His widow was Lucy B. Southard from Corinna. She was paid $50 under the resolve of 1836.

Southard, Henry. N.J. —. He was pensioned.

Southerland, Samuel. Va. —. He served nearly three years under Col. Charles Harrison from Aug. 1778 to 22 May 1781 when he was taken prisoner at Little York. He was paroled 6 June 1781 but not exchanged. On 16 May 1834 Congress granted his widow or children a pension of $80 per annum from 1 Mar. 1831 to the time of his decease.

Southwick, George. Mass. —. He was from Danvers and was paid $50.

Sowders, Christopher. Pa. —. He was granted relief in Philadelphia County 12 Mar. 1836.

Sowell, —. N.C. —. His widow was Mary Sowell from Moore County. She also appeared as Mary Seawell.

Soyars, James. —. —. He enlisted in 1776 and then reenlisted for the war. He served to the defeat of Col. Buford in 1780 when he was wounded and taken prisoner. He was put on the pension list for half disability. He sought the $80 bounty. Congress granted him same 20 Feb. 1829.

Spady, Thomas. Va. —. His widow, Ann Spady, was granted support in Isle of Wight County 1 Jan. 1778.

Spafford, Amos. N.H. Pvt. He served in the N.H. Continental Line. He lived in Hillsborough Co., N.H. He was on the 1813 pension list.

Spafford, Eliphalet. —. Pvt. He entered in 1780 for three years and served to the end of the war. His daughter, Lucy Strange, sought his bounty land. Congress rejected her claim 23 June 1840.

Spalding, Aaron. Md. Sgt. He was pensioned at the rate of half-pay of a sergeant 23 Jan. 1816.

Spalding, Daniel. Md. Pvt. He was pensioned at the rate of half-pay of a private in Baltimore 7 Mar. 1826. His arrearage was to be paid to Samuel Spalding of Baltimore provided he proved that he was the only surviving heir entitled to receive the same.

Spalding, Henry. Md. Pvt. He was pensioned at the rate of half-pay of a private 21 Dec. 1811.

Spalding, Josiah. Conn. Lt. He served in the militia under Col. Smith. He was wounded by a cannon ball which passed through a stone wall near which he was stationed. It forced a stone against the calf of his leg and much injured his knee and tendons on 29 Aug. 1778 in R.I. He lived in Ashford, Conn. in 1795. He served in the militia. He was granted half a pension 20 Apr. 1796. He died in 1799.

Spang, Peter. Pa. —. He was awarded a $40 gratuity and a $40 annuity in Berks Co., Pa. 14 Apr. 1828. He also appeared as Peter Spong.

Spangenberger, —. Pa. —. His widow, Elizabeth Spangenberger, was awarded a $40 gratuity and a $40 annuity in Northampton Co., Pa. 10 Apr. 1826. She died 19 Mar. 1840.

Spare, Jacob. Pa. —. He was awarded a $40 gratuity and a $40 annuity in Montgomery Co., Pa. 11 Feb. 1834. He was dead by Nov. 1843.

Sparks, Daniel. S.C. Capt. He served in the militia. He was paid for 30 out of the 140 days he served. He had suffered from a paralytic complaint for the last five years. He applied 22 Nov. 1794 from Marlborough County.

Sparks, Pearl. N.Y. Pvt. He served under Henry Difendorf in the Tryon County militia under Col. Clyde. He was wounded in his left arm by a musket ball at Oriskany 6 Aug. 1777. He was pensioned 22 Sep. 1786. He lived in Montgomery Co., N.Y. on 15 June 1789. He was on the 1813 pension list as Pearl Sharks [sic].

Sparks, Samuel. Va. —. His wife, Rebecca Sparks, and two children were furnished £35 support in Frederick Co., Va. on 5 Oct. 1779.

Sparran, William M. Pa. —. He was pensioned.

Sparry, Jacob. Pa. —. He was pensioned 11 Feb. 1834 in Montgomery County. He died 28 July 1843.

Sparry, John. Pa. —. He was awarded a $40 gratuity and a $40 annuity in Montgomery Co., Pa. 1 Feb. 1834.

Spatz, Michael. S.C. —. He engaged on the *South Carolina*, was captured, and sent to a prison ship in New York. Eleven months later he was discharged. He was pensioned under the act of 1818 but was excluded because his service was not on Continental Establishment. Congress restored him to his pension 14 May 1832. He was probably the Michael Spatz of Berks County, Pa. who was pensioned 13 Feb. 1840 and died 1 Sep. 1851. He was 78 years old in 1840.

Spaulding, Ebenezer. —. Lt. He was at the battle of Bunker Hill after which he served as a lieutenant under Col. Prescott for three years. He died before the passage of the act of 1818 so he never received a pension. His children sought a pension, but they furnished no proof. They were not covered under existing laws so Congress rejected their claim 31 Dec. 1845.

Spaulding, Ezekiel. Mass. Sgt. He served in the 7th Mass. Regiment. He was hurt loading a wagon in 1777. He enlisted 10 Feb. 1777. He resided at Georgetown, Me. in 1792. He was on the 1813 pension list as Ezekiel Spalding.

Spaulding, Henry. Md. Pvt. He was pensioned.

Spaulding, Job. Mass. Pvt. He served in the 15th Regiment and was from Chelmsford. He was paid $50.

Spaulding, John. Mass. Drummer. He served in the 16th Regiment and was from Chelmsford. He was paid $50.

Spaulding, William. N.H. Pvt. He served in Capt. Joseph Moore's Company under Col. William Prescott. He was wounded by a ball entering his arm and lodged in his wrist at the battle of Bunker Hill on 17 June 1775. He lived in Raby, N.H. in 1783 and had a numerous family. He was 55 years old in 1790 and a resident of Massachusetts.

Spear, James. Md. —. He served in the 2nd Regiment and was wounded at Monmouth. He received his half-pay pension 4 Apr. 1784 in Frederick County.

Spear, William. Pa. —. He was awarded a $40 gratuity and a $40 annuity in Butler Co., Pa. 12 Feb. 1829.

Spearing, John. Me. —. He died 9 Nov. 1831 at Hartland. His widow was Mary Spearing from Frankfort. She was paid $50 under the resolve of 1836.

Spears, John. N.C. Pvt. He was in Moore County in 1797 and Cumberland County in 1807. He served in the militia under Col. Phillip Alston in the company of Capt. Israel Folsom. He was wounded by a musket ball in the knee in a skirmish at David Alston's house. David Fanning had command of the Tories. He was on the 1813 pension list. He had a large family. He died 19 June 1828. His widow, Martha Spears, was granted a gratuity of $50 in 1833. She was paid as late as 1854 in Craven County.

Spears, Samuel. Vt. Pvt. He served under Col. Nichols in Capt. Runnell's Militia Company. He was subject to fits. His senses and memory were impaired by being wounded in the head with a musket ball in Aug. 1777 at Bennington. He lived in Cavendish, Vt. in 1795.

Specht, Adam. Pa. —. He was from Union County and received a $40 gratuity and a $40 annuity on 17 Feb. 1817.

Specht, Christian. Pa. —. He was awarded a $40 gratuity and a $40 annuity in Montgomery Co., Pa. 6 Apr. 1833. He was dead by Jan. 1838.

Spedden, Edward. Md. 2nd Lt. He was pensioned at the rate of half-pay of second lieutenant in Baltimore 12 Feb. 1820. His widow, Ann Spedden, was pensioned at the same rate 22 Feb. 1823.

Speed, James. Pa. Lt. He died in 1811.

Speed, James. Va. Lt. He served under Col. Cocke in the Va. Militia. He was wounded in his left side by a ball which destroyed two or three ribs on 15 Mar. 1781 at Guilford. He lived in Mercer Co., Ky. in 1795. He was granted a full pension 20 Apr. 1796.

Speets, Jacob. Pa. —. He was granted relief.

Speider, Jacob. Pa. Pvt. He applied 10 Sep. 1813 in Rockbridge Co., Va. He and Job Pennington were in the Pa. Line. He was awarded 200 acres of donation land 10 Mar. 1812. He also appeared as Jacob Speeder.

Speir, Samuel. Pa. —. He applied 13 Oct. 1787. He also appeared as Samuel Speer.

Spence, —. Va. —. His mother, Sarah Spence, was furnished support in Westmoreland County in Apr. 1779.

Spence, James. Pa. —. He was 71 years old in 1840 in Mercer County.

Spencer, —. Va. —. He and his three brothers were in the service. Their father, James Spencer, was furnished support in Loudoun Co., Va. on 15 Apr. 1777.

Spencer, —. Va. —. He was killed in the service. His widow, Jane Spencer, was pensioned at the rate of $60 per annum on 30 Jan. 1808. She was in Westmoreland County on 9 Dec. 1809. She died 26 Sep. 1810. William Murdock was administrator of her estate.

Spencer, —. Va. Pvt. He was killed in action near Camden. His widow, Susannah Spencer, was on the 1785 pension roll.

Spencer, David. —. —. He died in Burke Co., N.C. 18 Dec. 1843. His widow, Mary Spencer, applied in Burke County in Jan. 1844.

Spencer, John. S.C. Officer. He served aboard the *South Carolina* under Commodore Alexander Gillon and was paid 28 May 1811.

Spencer, Joseph. Va. Capt. He served in the Va. Line for early three years and retired on account of ill health. He regained his health and rejoined. He was taken prisoner. His heirs sought his bounty and commutation. Congress refused their request because they did not show if he was deranged or served to the end of the war on 31 Jan. 1849.

Spencer, Reuben. N.H. Pvt. He served under Capt. Robert Oliver in Col. James Reed's Regiment in Dec. 1775. He marched from New York to Canada and was discharged at Montreal. On 7 Feb. 1776 he accidentally fell and hit his knee on hard rock while on guard duty. He was rendered unfit for duty. He never recovered, and his left leg eventually had to be amputated. He was aged 30 in 1787. He was on the 1813 pension list. He was from Claremont in 1786. Gershom York served with him. Richard Mann was a captain.

Spencer, Thomas. Me. —. He was from Limington. He was paid $50 under the resolve of 1836.

Spencer, William. Me. —. He died 29 May 1835. His widow was Eleanor Spencer from Baldwin. She was paid $50 under the resolve of 1836.

Spengle, —. Pa. —. His widow, Susannah Spengle, was granted relief 8 Apr. 1840 in York County. She was dead by Dec. 1843. Her name may have been Susannah Spergle.

Spering, John. Pa. —. He was awarded a $40 gratuity and a $40 annuity in Philadelphia, Pa. 17 Jan. 1834.

Spera, William. Pa. Pvt. He was awarded a $40 gratuity and a $40 annuity in Lancaster County 23 Jan. 1833.

Spevis, John. N.C. —. He had his knee shattered by a musket ball in battle. He had a wife and child. [Compare with the entry under John Spears.]

Spicer, Samuel. Pa. Pvt. He applied 22 May 1787. He served in the 10th Pa. Regiment under Col. Richard Humpton and was disabled by having his wrist dislocated in 1779 while building huts for the army near Morristown, N.J. He had a wife and family. He was 40 years old. He was on the 1813 pension list.

Spicer, Samuel. Pa. —. He was awarded a $40 gratuity and a $40 annuity in York County 6 Apr. 1833.

Spiece, Balzer. Pa. —. He was awarded a $40 gratuity and a $40 annuity in Berks Co., Pa. 1 Apr. 1830.

Spiers, —. S.C. —. His widow was Sarah Spiers from Barnwell. There were children in 1791. She also appeared as Sarah Spears.

Spikeard, George. Va. —. His mother, Elizabeth Spikeard, was granted £30 relief in Rockingham Co., Va. in 24 Aug. 1779 while her son and her husband, Julius Spikeard, were away in Continental service.

Spikeard, Julius. Va. —. His wife, Elizabeth, was granted £30 relief in Rockingham Co., Va. on 24 Aug. 1779 while her husband and her son, George Spikeard, were away in Continental service. The surname also appeared as Spykeard.

Spires, Richard. Md. Pvt. He was pensioned at the rate of half-pay of a private in Brown Co., Ohio 7 Mar. 1829.

Spitfathom, John. —. Ens. He received his commutation 12 June 1838. He had been stricken from the pension roll in 1820 but restored in 1823. Congress declined to pass a law to allow him arrearage on 8 Mar. 1838.

Spohn, Peter. Pa. —. He was awarded a $40 gratuity in Berks Co., Pa. 18 Mar. 1834.

Spong, John Leonard. Pa. Pvt. He applied in Cumberland County 27 Apr. 1821. Henry Lipkey was with him at the taking of Stoney Point. He was enlisted by William Blackney, recruiting sergeant, in 1775 in Cumberland County. He went into the service in the spring and was gone about three years. He was in Capt. Bull's Company in the 6th Pa. Regiment. He was wounded in the battle of Monmouth. He was a prisoner for nine months. After nearly four years in the service, he was discharged at Trenton by Capt. Doyle. He was 67 years old. He received a $40 annuity and a $40 gratuity.

Spooner, William. Mass. Bombardier. He served in the Invalids under Capt. David Bryant and Col. John Craine. He was disabled by the loss of his right arm. He was pensioned 1 Sep. 1782. He was 41 years old and resided in Boston, Mass. in 1788. He was listed as dead on the 1813 pension list.

Spotswood, John. Va. Capt. He was in Orange County in 1787. He served in the 10th Va. Regiment of Infantry from 1 Jan. 1777 to 31 Dec. 1781. He was wounded by a musket ball which shattered his right thigh bone at Germantown 4 Oct. 1777. He was taken prisoner. He was pensioned at half-pay during his disability on 5 Nov. 1785 and granted £140 from the time of his discharge on 5 Nov. 1785. He was 35 years old in 1787. He was continued on the list of pensioners at the rate of £60 per annum on 5 Jan. 1787. He was in Stafford County on 1 Oct. 1805. His heirs sought his commutation but were rejected 29 May 1838 since he had received a pension.

Spragg, Jeremiah. Pa. —. He was granted relief in Greene County in 1857. [His service was not stated.]

Spraggins, Clark. S.C. —. He enlisted and served eighteen months under Col. Samuel Hammond. He was inoculated for smallpox and took the fever. He paid George Miller three guineas to serve out the remainder of his term. He was from Edgefield District and was pensioned 23 Nov. 1829. He was paid as late as 1831.

Sprague, Caesar. Mass. Pvt. He served in the 4th Regiment under Col. Shephard. He was wounded by a cannon which shot off his left foot. He had his left leg amputated on 28 June 1778 at Monmouth. He resided in Mass. in 1796. He enlisted 1 Jan. 1777 for the war. He joined the Invalids 10 May 1779 and was discharged 15 Apr. 1780. He was granted half a pension 20 Apr. 1796. He resided in Dudley, Mass. in 1792.

Sprague, Seth. N.Y. —. His sickly wife was granted support in Dutchess County on 3 Nov. 1781.

Spratt, Thomas. Va. —. He was pensioned in Norfolk County on 19 Mar. 1832 at the rate of $60 per annum and $30 immediate relief.

Spriggell, Joseph. Pa. —. He served under Col. Curtis Grubb and subsequently under Capt. Henry Neems and Col. Benjamin Mills. He was wounded in battle at Fort Montgomery. He was from Cumberland County.

Springer, Silvester. S.C. —. Surgeon's Mate. He sought his commutation 29 Jan. 1789.

Springer, Uriah. Pa. —. His widow, Sarah Springer, was awarded a $40 gratuity and a $40 annuity in Fayette Co., Pa. 5 Mar. 1828.

Springs, Micajah. N.C. —. He enlisted in Duplin County. He applied in Sampson County in July 1843. His wife, Letitia Springs, was 47 and his children were Dicy Springs age 17, Michael Springs age 17, Cannon Springs age 14, Pherabe Springs age 11, William Springs aged 8, and Hardy Springs age 5. He lived in Sampson County.

Springsteen, Hermanus. N.Y. —. He was disabled and was pensioned 11 June 1783. He served in Col. Dubois's and Col. Van Schaick's Regiments. His children, Magdelane Rynnis and John Springsteen, were awarded 200 acres of bounty land 13 Apr. 1813. He also appeared as Hermanus Springstead.

Sprott, —. Pa. —. His widow, Elizabeth Sprott, applied in Lawrence County 2 July 1856. Her son was Robert Sprott. She died 25 Aug. 1860.

Sprowl, James. N.J. Ens. He served in the 4th Regiment under Col. Ephraim Martin and Capt. John Forman and was killed at Short Hills 26 June 1777. His widow, Zilpha Sprowl, married secondly Nehemiah Tilton. She received a half-pay pension from 26 June 1777 to 22 Dec.

1779 on 14 Oct. 1786.

Spurr, Enoch. Me. —. He was from Otisfield. He was paid $50 under the resolve of 1836.

Spurr, John. Mass. Capt. He received his commutation for five years in lieu of half-pay for life. He died 1 Nov. 1822.

Squire, David. Conn. Sgt. He served under Lt. Isaac Burr. On 21 Mar. 1778 in ramming a shot into one of the guns in the battery at Fairfield, he lost both hands and an eye when the cartridge caught fire. He was attended by Dr. Francis Forgue. He was pensioned 7 Jan. 1779 in Fairfield, Conn. He died in 1796.

Squires, Samuel. Conn. Pvt. He served in the 2nd Conn. Regiment of Artillery and was worn out in the service. He was pensioned 28 Jan. 1783. He died in 1796.

Squires, Samuel. Conn. Commissary. He served from May 1775 to Aug. 1783. He died in 1801 at the age of 86. He married 20 July 1789. His widow, Ellen Squires, married secondly James Chapman of Fairfield. He served as a lieutenant and died 9 Sep. 1822 aged 72 years. She married thirdly Aaron Turney 9 Nov. 1829 who also served as a lieutenant and died 15 Nov. 1833 aged 82. Congress granted her a pension 9 Feb 1842. He also appeared as Samuel Squyres.

Staats, Philip. N.Y. Lt. He served in Capt. Nicholas Staats's Company under Col Henry Killian Van Rensselaer in the militia. He was wounded in the leg in July 1777. He was pensioned 15 Sep. 1786. He lived at Crawls, Rensselaerwyck, Albany Co., N.Y. on 11 July 1789. He later lived in Putnam County. He was on the 1813 pension list.

Stack, John. —. Col. He was wounded by a cannon ball at Bunker Hill in June 1775.

Stack, Richard. Pa. Fife Major. He served in the 7th Regiment. He received thirteen bayonet wounds at Paoli in Sept. 1777. Gen. Wayne was in command of the American forces. He lived in Philadelphia, Pa. in 1794. He enlisted 20 Nov. 1776 for the war. He was 39 years old and had a wife and three small children. He was one of those who took letters of administration and drew pay and depreciation of soldiers whom he swore had died intestate. He was not worth anything. Many of them appeared and proved that they were not deceased. They did so late as their certificates had drawn interest which Stark had collected as administrator. One soldier had him arrested by a local constable, but he made his escape into New Jersey. The ruling was that he was due no pension since he resided out of state.

Stackhouse, —. Pa. —. His widow, Nancy Stackhouse, was awarded a $40 gratuity and a $40 annuity in Bucks Co., Pa. 29 Mar. 1823. She died 18 Sep. 1824.

Stackhouse, Francis. Pa. —. He was awarded a $40 gratuity and a $40 annuity in Bucks Co. 4 Feb. 1813. His arrearage was paid to Joel Bailey for his funeral and burial expenses 1 Apr. 1823.

Stackhouse, John. Pa. —. His widow, Ann Stackhouse, received a $40 gratuity and a $40 annuity in Bucks County 30 Mar. 1859.

Stackhouse, John. Va. —. He was pensioned in Harrison Co., Va. 25 Feb. 1818 at the rate of $100 per annum. He was a native of Hampshire County. In 1774 near Morgantown he served six months under Capt. Zackwell Morgan against the Six Nations in Lord Dunmore's War. In the Revolutionary War he served three years in Capt. David Scott's Company in the 10th Va. Regiment. After his discharge he did duty under Gen. Clarke and was captured by the Indians and held in captivity for two years and ten months. His feet were severely frost bitten on his return from Fort McIntosh to Fort Pitt. He died 20 June 1827. His widow, Mary Stackhouse, was administratrix of his estate.

Stacy, Aaron. —. —. His widow, Nancy Stacy, applied in Burke Co., N.C. in July 1843.

Stacy, John. Mass. Corp. He served in the 7th Regiment and was from Harvard. He was paid $20.

Stacy, Simon. Va. Pvt. He served in the 15ᵗʰ Va. Regiment and died in the service. His widow, Sarah Stacy, was in Sussex County 18 Jan. 1787. She was *ca.* 35 years of age and had two children on 16 Mar. 1786. She was *ca.* 43 years of age and had a female child aged *ca.* 14 years old as well as a Negro girl about the same age in June 1791. She was continued on the pension list at the rate of £18 per annum on 18 Jan. 1787, 25 Mar. 1790, and 12 Oct.1791. She had lost the use of one of her arms by 3 May 1792.

Stadner, John. Va. Pvt. He was from Henrico County. He was continued on the pension list on 20 Feb. 1788 at the rate £12 per annum. He served in the 2ⁿᵈ Va. Detachment for 14 months and 8 days per certificate from Lt. John Hackley, Paymaster, at High Hills Santee 30 Oct. 1781. Col. Samuel Hawes deposed that he was wounded at Camden. He was wounded by a horseman's sword in his head and in his right arm. He lost two fingers on his right hand. He was 35 years old. He was on the 1813 pension list.

Stafford, James Bayard. —. Midshipman. He acted as lieutenant on the *Alliance* under Commodore Barry. He landed at Wexford and went by foot to London in disguise as an Irish laborer. A relative got him admitted to the Tower of London where he delivered an important message to the prisoner, Henry Laurens, and returned to Wexford. His daughter, Sarah Smith Stafford, sought his half-pay as a lieutenant from Congress 17 Mar. 1858.

Stafford, Joab. N.Y. Capt. He served under Col. Simmons. He was wounded in his foot and nose at the battle of Bennington 16 Aug. 1777. He lived in Herkimer, N.Y. in 1794, Since he could not obtain his arrears from Congress, he applied to Vermont in Jan. 1795. He died 21 Nov. 1801.

Stagert, Henry. Pa. —. He was granted relief in Allegheny Co. 17 Mar. 1838. He died *ante* 30 Apr. 1842.

Staggers, John. Pa. —. He was granted relief in Greene County 11 Apr. 1848.

Stahl, John. Pa. —. He served in the militia.

Stahle, —. Pa. —. His widow, Barbara Stahle, was awarded a $40 gratuity and a $40 annuity in Lancaster Co., Pa. 23 Jan. 1834.

Stahler, —. Pa. —. His widow, Eve Maria Stahler, was awarded a $40 gratuity in Northampton Co., Pa. 18 Feb. 1834 and a $40 gratuity and a $40 annuity in Columbia Co., Pa. 10 Apr. 1835. She died 24 May 1842.

Stalman, William. S.C. Legionnaire. He served aboard the *South Carolina* under Commodore Alexander Gillon. He was paid 21 Oct. 1809.

Stalnaker, Samuel. S.C. Pvt. He served under Capt. Briant, Col. Hammond, Capt. William Cain, Lt. Howard, Maj. Bowie, and Maj. Tutt. He was at Ninety Six. He also fought the Cherokee. He served about three years. He was 82 years old. Elias Gibson served with him at Augusta. He was from Abbeville District and was pensioned 4 Dec. 1828. He died 7 Mar. 1837. His widow was Elizabeth Stalnaker. She had married about twenty-six ago and was upwards of 70 years old. Her application was rejected 29 Sep. 1837.

Stam, Laurence. N.Y. Pvt. He served under Col. Jacob Klock in the Montgomery County militia and was slain 19 Oct. 1780. His widow received a half-pay pension.

Stambaugh, Peter. Pa. —. He received a $40 gratuity and a $40 annuity in Franklin County 14 Apr. 1838. He was 89 years old in 1840.

Stanaland, James. S.C. —. He served under Col. Peter Horry and Capt. Alexander Dunn. He was disabled by palsy or deadness in his feet and legs. He had an aged companion. He was born 11 Jan. 1762. He was from All Saints Parish, Horry District and was pensioned 10 Dec. 1825. He had been authorized a pension the previous year, but the act omitted his forename so he was unable to draw his pension. He was to receive the arrearage. He was paid in 1826. He was paid as late as 1835.

Standish, Nathaniel. —. —. He served nine months and was restored at the rate of $8 per month by Congress 25 May 1830.

Standley, —. Ga. —. The family of Mrs. Mary Standley was granted relief 8 Feb. 1782.

Stanford, John. Mass. —. He served in the 6th Regiment and was paid $20.

Stanford, Zacheriah. Conn. Sgt. He served in the militia. He was disabled by cold by sleeping on the wet ground. He resided in Conn. in 1792.

Stanley, —. —. —. Congress rejected the claim of his widow, Sally Stanley, 4 Apr. 1840.

Stanley, Hugh. N.C. Pvt. He was in Jones County in 1784. He was in the Jones County militia under Gen. Keonan and was wounded at Rockfish Bridge where he was chopped in the head, shoulders, and hands. He also appeared as Hugh Stanland. He was on the 1813 pension list.

Stansberry, Luke. —. —. He was on the pension roll and sought an increase. The only reasons he gave were his age and poverty. Congress rejected his application 25 Feb. 1846.

Stansill, George. N.Y. Pvt. He served in Capt. Cogh's Company under Col. Jacob Klock in the militia. He was wounded through his shoulder at Johnstown 25 Oct. 1781. He was pensioned 22 Sep. 1786. He was aged 26 in 1787. He lived in Montgomery County. He was on the 1813 pension list as George Stansel.

Stanton, Daniel. Conn. Pvt. He was disabled by a musket ball through his ankle at Fort Griswold 6 Sep. 1781. He was aged 33 years and was in Stonington in 1788. He transferred to Vermont. He was on the 1813 pension list. He died 4 Jan. 1826 in New London Co., Conn.

Stanton, Edward. —. —. His widow, Martha Stanton, received an increase in her pension from Congress 31 Mar. 1856.

Stanton, Edward. Conn. Pvt. He served in the militia as a volunteer and was disabled at New London 6 Sep. 1781 when Fort Griswold was captured. He was wounded by a musket ball through his ankle and had sundry other wounds in his head and body. He was pensioned 1 Oct. 1788. He was 25 years old and was from Stonington. He was on the 1813 pension list. He died 27 July 1832.

Stanton, John. Md. Pvt. He was pensioned at the rate of half-pay of a private 23 Feb. 1829.

Stanwood, Job. Mass. —. He was granted a pension 15 Mar. 1776.

Staples, Isaac. —. —. He was a pensioner. His widow, Esther Staples, was also a pensioner and died 4 Mar. 1856. She had applied for 160 acres of bounty land. The warrant was dated 24 Sep. 1855. The children were Abram Staples and Warner Staples. Abram Staples cared for his parents. Warner Staples renounced his claim so Congress reissued the warrant to Abram Staples on 29 May 1858.

Staples, John. Md. Pvt. He was pensioned at the rate of half-pay of a private 12 Feb. 1820.

Staples, John. Md. Sgt. He served under Capt. William Brown in the artillery. His widow, Margaret Staples, was pensioned at the rate of half-pay of a sergeant 10 Mar. 1845.

Staples, William. Me. —. He died 15 Feb. 1832. His widow was Joan Staples from Bethel. She was paid $50 under the resolve of 1836. Congress rejected her claim for a pension on 14 Mar. 1848 because she married after 1 Jan. 1790.

Stapleton, William. Pa. —. He was awarded a $40 gratuity and a $40 annuity in Chester Co., Pa. 3 Mar. 1825.

Starboard, Anthony. Me. Pvt. He lost the sight of one eye, and his other eye was much injured by smallpox about Apr. 1777. He served under Col. Rose. He resided at Pepperellborough, Me. in

1792. He enlisted 19 Jan. 1777 and was discharged 19 Jan. 1780. He was on the 1813 pension list.

Stark, Caleb. N.H. Lt. He served in the army. He received his commutation for half-pay 24 May 1828. He was at Bunker Hill in 177 and; served under Col. Cilley in 1776 and 1777. He was an ensign, lieutenant and adjutant, brigade major, and aide-de-camp to Gen. Stark. He was wounded at Stillwater 7 Oct. 1777. Congress rejected his claim for half-pay and bounty land 27 Mar. 1826 but did so on 28 Jan. 1828.

Stark, John. N.J. —. His widow, Elizabeth Stark, was pensioned in Morris County on 2 Mar. 1847 at the rate of $30 per annum.

Stark, John. Vt. Capt. He served under Col. Timothy Brownson. He was wounded by a musket ball shot through his right thigh on 16 Aug. 1777 at Bennington in opposing Burgoyne. He lived in Pawlett, Rutland Co., Vt. in 1794. He was in the militia. He was granted one-fourth of a pension 20 Apr. 1796. He died 26 Sep. 1806.

Stark, Robert. S.C. —. He served in the Cherokee Expedition. He was made a prisoner at the siege of Savannah and taken to Charleston in irons. He applied from Edgefield District 2 Feb. 1791. He was rejected because his claim was not submitted within the proper time frame.

Stark, Solomon. Conn. Pvt. He served in the militia under Col. Lattimer in Capt. Richard Hewitt's Company. He was wounded in his thigh in action with Burgoyne on 1 Sep. 1777. On 2 Oct. 1777 he was furloughed for a fortnight by Malachi Treat, Physician General of the Northern Department. He was pensioned 26 Sep. 1788. He was 30 years old and resided in Groton. He died in 1811.

Starling, Levi. Pa. —. He was awarded a $40 gratuity and a $40 annuity in Bucks Co., Pa. 18 Mar. 1834.

Starr, Daniel. —. Lt. He was a naval officer aboard the *Trumbull* and was mortally wounded 2 June 1780 in action with the British letter-of-marque *Wasp* and died 5 June 1780. He married Lucy Douglass 5 Jan. 1764. She died in 1832. One of his children was E. Thatcher. Congress allowed his heirs the seven years' half-pay plus allowance of such claims remains on 12 Dec. 1856. Congress did not grant the petition for a pension from the heirs 13 Apr. 1860.

Starr, John. Conn. Pvt. He served in the militia in the 1st Company of the 8th Regiment. He was wounded in the right arm while opposing the British under Gen. Arnold who had landed at New London on 6 Sep. 1781 at Fort Griswold. He served under Capt. William Latham in the Artillery. He was 45 years old and pensioned 26 Sep. 1788. He was on the 1813 pension list.

Starr, Thomas. Conn. Capt. He was in an alarm company. He was wounded very badly by a party of British horse in Apr. 1777 at Danbury. He resided in Danbury, Conn. in 1794. He died 21 Apr. 1806.

Starr, William. —. —. —. His widow, Eunice Starr, had her petition for a pension by a special act of Congress rejected 4 May 1846 because she had married subsequent to 1 Jan. 1794.

Starr, William. Conn. QM. He served in the militia in the 8th Conn. Regiment. In opposing the British troops under Gen. Arnold who landed at new London, he was wounded in the breast and arm on 26 Sep. 1788 at Fort Griswold. He served in a company of matrosses under Capt. William Latham. He was pensioned 26 Sep. 1788. He lived in Groton, Conn. and was 43 years old. He was on the 1813 pension list. He died 31 Dec. 1817 in New London Co., Conn.

Starratt, John. N.C. —. He applied in Lincoln County in 1800. He served in the Lincoln County militia under General Greene and lost an eye due to smallpox. He was drafted in Feb. 1781 for three months. George Cox and Capt. Samuel Caldwell served with him and swore to his service.

Starring, Valentine. N.Y. Pvt. He served under Col. Peter Bellinger in the Montgomery County militia and was slain 17 July 1782. His widow, Margaret Starring, was granted his half-pay pension.

Statleman, John. Pa. —. He applied at Germantown 30 Oct. 1818. He suffered from a rupture and was 68 years old. He applied 16 Nov. 1818. He also appeared as John Stadleman and John Stattleman.

Statzer, —. Pa. —. His widow, Elizabeth Statzer, was awarded a $40 gratuity and a $40 annuity in Berks Co., Pa. 29 Mar. 1824. She died 9 Oct. 1841.

Staver, Daniel. Pa. —, He was pensioned in Dauphin County 17 Mar. 1835.

Staves, —. Va. —. The widow, Sarah Staves, was granted £5 assistance while her two sons were away in the service in Orange Co., Va. on 26 Mar. 1778.

Stayner, Roger. Pa. Capt. He served in the 2nd Regiment and became supernumerary in consequence of being a prisoner. He had a land warrant for 300 acres on 6 June 1827. He was paid for his donation land 8 Apr. 1829. He received five years' full-pay 20 Feb. 1838.

Stead, John. Pa. Pvt. He applied in Philadelphia 13 Feb. 1786. He was in Capt. Walker's Company in the 11th Pa. Regiment under Col. Hartley. He was wounded fourteen times in the head and body at Paoli. He was discharged 6 May 1780. He had a wife and four children. He lived in Dauphin County. He was 40 years old. He was on the 1791 pension roll but was dead by May 1798. He also appeared as John Stied.

Steads, Richard. —. —. He was pensioned 9 Dec. 1807.

Steagart, —. Pa. —. His widow, Barbara Steagart, received a $40 gratuity and a $40 annuity in Allegheny County 5 Apr. 1842.

Stealey, —. Pa. —. His widow, Barbara Stealey, was granted relief in Allegheny County 11 Apr. 1844.

Stealey, William. Pa. —. He was awarded a $40 gratuity and a $40 annuity 27 Mar. 1837 in Allegheny County.

Stearns, David. Mass. —. He served under Col. Thomas Nixon and Capt. Abel Holden. He was disabled by the cut of a sword in his left hand. He was 26 years old in 1786.

Stearns, Eli. Mass. Sgt. He was in the Invalids under Capt. McGowell and Col. Lewis Nichola. He was disabled by a musket ball through his head. He was pensioned 13 Apr. 1783. He was 28 years old in 1786. He was on the 1813 pension list. He died 7 Mar. 1825 in Worcester Co., Mass. He also appeared as Eli Sterns.

Stearns, Increase. Mass. Pvt. He served in the 15th Regiment and was from Holden. His widow, Mercy Stearns, was paid $50.

Stearns, Joseph. Mass. Pvt. He served in the 16th Regiment and was from Billerica. His widow, Elizabeth Stearns, was paid $50.

Stearns, Josiah. Mass. Pvt. He served in the 16th Regiment and was from Lowell. His widow, Sarah Stearns, was paid $50.

Stearns, Nathaniel. Mass. Pvt. He served in the 6th Regiment. His widow was Azuba Saunders of Billerica.

Stearns, Stephen. Mass. —. He served in the 8th Regiment and was paid $20.

Stebbens, Samuel. Mass. —. He served in the 7th Regiment and was paid $20.

Stedham, Zacheriah. S.C. —. He served under Capt. Martin and Col. Wade Hampton and was wounded at Eutaw on 9 Sep. 1781. He received a ball in his face and lost his sight in his left eye. He had a wife and eight children. He was pensioned in 1795. He renewed his pension in 1812 and was paid as late as 1834.

Stedds, Richard. Md. Pvt. He was pensioned 4 Mar. 1789. He was on the 1813 pension list.

Steel, —. Pa. —. His widow, Mary Steel, was awarded a $40 gratuity and a $40 annuity in Franklin Co.,

Pa. 12 Apr. 1828. She died 11 Mar. 1850.

Steel, —. Va. —. His wife was Catherine Steel of Westmoreland County.

Steel, Aaron. Mass. Lt. He died 24 Nov. 1777. His seven years' half-pay of $1,120 was paid to his heirs.

Steel, Alexander. S.C. —. He was killed at Long Canes. His child was granted an annuity 10 Nov. 1786. There was one child in 1791.

Steel, Archibald. Pa. Lt. & Adjt. He was in Lancaster County on 19 Dec. 1785. He was in the 2nd Pa. Regiment in Capt. Matthew Smith's Company under Col. William Thompson. He was wounded at the storming of Quebec on 1 Oct. 1776 in the detachment under Benedict Arnold. Three of his fingers on his left hand were shot off by the enemy. He was 40 years old. He was on the 1813 pension list. He died 19 Oct. 1832 in Philadelphia County. His daughter was Jane Palmer. He had also lived in Baltimore.

Steel, James. Md.1st Lt. He married 23 July 1777 and within a fortnight was called into the service to resist the British marching from Philadelphia. He served within two months of the disbanding of the army. He was born 22 Feb. 1743/4. He suffered from two severe strokes of palsy, superannuated, and unable to speak but a few words at a time. His wife, Elizabeth Steel, of Cecil Co., Md. was about 80 years old. Their son was David Steel aged 41. Congress granted him a pension 15 Jan. 1836 for his eight months as a lieutenant.

Steel, James. N.Y. Pvt. He served under Col. Dubois. He was wounded in the breast in the taking of Fort Montgomery on 6 Oct. 1777. He lived in Goshen, N.Y. in 1794. He enlisted 2 Dec. 1776 for the war.

Steel, John. Pa. Capt. His donation tract contained 424 acres and 85 perches rather than 500 acres. He was, therefore, awarded a patent for 76 acres to be laid off on the east and west sides of said tract on 13 Apr. 1807.

Steel, John. S.C. Pvt.. He served as a horseman under Capt. William Hanna, Lt. Mason, Col. Bratton, and Col. Thompson. At the battle of Savannah on 9 Oct. 1779 he was wounded in his left shoulder by a musket ball which came out his back. It broke one of his ribs. John Smith saw him several times in hospital. He had a large family. He was from Williamsburg District and was pensioned 4 Dec. 1812. He was paid as late as 1820.

Steel, Jonas. Pa. —. He was pensioned.

Steel, Joseph. Pa. Pvt. He was on the 1789 pension list.

Steel, Philip. Pa. —. He was pensioned.

Steel, Robert. Mass. —. He served in the 4th Artillery and was paid $20.

Steel, William. N.J. —. He was drafted in the spring of 1778 at New Brunswick, N.J. In the autumn of 1779 he was ambushed by a squadron of British dragoons under Capt. Moses Guest and captured Col. Simcoe. In the winter of 1779-1780 he was in the invasion of Staten Island. In 1780 he served on the twenty gun ship *Aurora* under Capt. Sutton until it was captured by the *Iris*. He was severely wounded near his shoulder and taken prisoner to New York where he was kept eighteen weeks until discharged by the enemy. Congress granted him a pension 18 Jan. 1838.

Steel, William. S.C. —. He was in thirteen different actions including Guilford. He was a prisoner in irons on a prison ship. In due course he was taken to Great Britain and lodged in Mill Prison. He sought the favor of an appointment as waiter of customs at Charleston in room of Philip Meyer, deceased, on 18 Feb 1786.

Steele, —. Pa. —. His widow, Polly Steele, was granted relief in York County 21 Apr. 1844.

Steele, Bradford. —. —. He enlisted at the age of 16 for two months in 1776, served one month, and procured a substitute. He volunteered for six months in July 1777 on the assurance that he would not be marched out of state; yet, He was ordered to Peekskill in Westchester Co., N.Y. with 200 volunteers to attack Fort Independence. He and twelve others were taken prisoner and carried to New York where he was confined in the Sugar House Prison. He was put on the prison ship *Good Intent* and confined below for a fortnight. He was attacked with smallpox and removed to hospital. He was left almost naked in the rain. On 10 Aug. 1778 he was removed to New Jersey and exchanged. He reached home about the last of August. He was about 70 years old. He had a wife, child, and grandchild dependent upon him. Congress granted him a pension 23 Feb. 1832.

Steele, David. Va. Pvt. He served in the Augusta County militia and was wounded at the battle of Guilford Court House on 15 Mar. 1781. He was 30 years old on 21 Jan. 1789 in Augusta County. He was pensioned 11 Aug. 1790. He was on the 1813 pension list.

Steele, John. Pa. —. He was granted relief under the act of 19 Mar. 1819.

Steele, Richard. Pa. —. He was awarded a $40 gratuity and a $40 annuity in Mercer County 1 Apr. 1836. He also appeared as Richard Steel. His widow, Rebecca Steel, received $8.33 which was the proportion of the annuity due him at his death in 1838. She also was given a $40 annuity.

Steely, Silvanus. N.Y. Pvt. He served in Graham's Regiment, was pensioned 21 June 1786, and was from Dutchess County.

Steever, —. Pa. —. His widow, Elizabeth Steever, was granted relief in Northumberland County 20 May 1839. She died 8 Apr. 1840.

Steever, Daniel. Pa. —. He was awarded a $40 gratuity and a $40 annuity in Dauphin Co., Pa. 17 Mar. 1835. He died 14 Oct. 1844.

Stegal, Samuel. S.C. —. He was paid $192.66 as a Revolutionary soldier on 20 Dec. 1810.

Steger, Jacob. Pa. Pvt. He was in Dauphin County 17 June 1786. He served under Col. Philip Greenwald and Capt. Weiser. He was in the Lancaster County militia and was wounded in a skirmish with the British at Chestnut Hill in Oct. 1777. He was 40 years old. He died 8 May 1802.

Stehle, Jacob. Pa. —. He was awarded a $40 gratuity and a $40 annuity in Lancaster Co., Pa. 12 Feb. 1825.

Steinwax, Arnold. N.Y. Sgt He served under Col. Peter Bellinger in the militia and was slain 6 Aug. 1777. His children, Johannes Casper Steinwax and John Deobald Steinwax, received a half-pay pension..

Stellar, John. Pa. Pvt. —. He was on the 1789 pension list.

Stengle, —. Pa. —. His widow, Catharine Stengle, was awarded a $40 gratuity and a $40 annuity in York Co., Pa. 1 Apr. 1830. She died 9 Aug. 1842.

Stephens, Amasa. N.Y. Pvt. He served under Col. Jacob Klock and was slain 22 May 1780. His widow, Margaret Stephens, received a half-pay pension.

Stephens, Daniel. N.Y. Pvt. He served under Col. Willet in the State Troops. He was wounded through the right lobe of his lungs 25 July 1782. He lived in Montgomery Co., N.Y. on 15 June 1789. He also appeared as Daniel Stevens. He was on the 1813 pension list.

Stephens, Frederick. N.Y. Pvt. His widow was granted support according to an undated roster.

Stephens, George H. Pa. —. He applied in Philadelphia 11 June 1803. He lived with Annie Stephens, but her relationship was not indicated.

Stephens, Henry. Mass. —. He served in the Artillery and was from Boston. He was paid $20.

Stephens, John. S.C. —. His widow was Susannah Townsend of Abbeville District. On 4 Dec. 1802 she had been a widow for three years and nine months. Her children were aged 7, 3 ½, and 14 months at the time of his death.

Stephens, Joseph. Conn. Pvt. He was on the 1795 pension list. He died in 1807. He also appeared as Joseph Stevens.

Stephens, Otho. —. —. He served in the militia. Congress rejected his petition for a pension 29 Jan. 1819.

Stephens, Simeon. Mass. Sgt. He served in Capt. Stickney's Company under Col. Bridge. He was wounded on the hills of Charlestown 17 June 1775 and continued in the service until 19 May 1780. He was pensioned from the date of his discharge at the rate of one-third pay on 17 Mar. 1783.

Stephens, Smith. Va. Pvt. He was in Northumberland County 17 June 1786. He served in the 15th Va. Regiment of Foot in Capt. Edwin Hull's Company. He lost a leg. He also appeared as Smith Stevens. He was put on the pension list at the rate of £12 per annum on 17 June 1789. He received a £500 gratuity and a suit of clothes in Nov. 1780. He was on the 1813 pension list. He also appeared as Smyth Stevens.

Stephenson, Abner. Mass. —. He served in the 4th Regiment and was from Suffield. He was paid $20.

Stephenson, Abner. Mass. —. He was paid $20. [second of the name]

Stephenson, Daniel. Mass. —. He served in the 4th Regiment and was from Providence. He was paid $20.

Stephenson, David. S.C. —. He was wounded in the head and in one of his knees. His widow, Jane Stephenson, was pensioned from Anderson District 23 Nov. 1829 at the rate of $30 per annum. She was 68 years old. James Brown fought with him at Rocky Mount, Hanging Rock, and Wright's Bluff. She was paid as late as 1850.

Stephenson, David. S.C. Pvt. He served from 1776 to the close of the war. He was at Four Mile Bridge and the siege of Augusta. He was 88 years old. He was from York District in 1842.

Stephenson, James. Pa. —. He was awarded a $40 annuity in Juniata County 12 Jan. 1836.

Stephenson, John. —. —. His application was rejected 19 Jan. 1797.

Stephenson, John. Mass. —. He served in the 3rd Regiment and was from Springfield. He was paid $20.

Stephenson, John. N.Y. Pvt. He served under Col McClaghry in the Ulster County militia and died of wounds at Fort Montgomery 6 Oct. 1777. His children, Mary Stephenson, Joseph Stephenson, and Sarah Stephenson, received a half-pay pension for seven years.

Stephenson, Nathaniel. Pa. —. He applied in Butler County on 20 Nov. 1820. He enlisted 27 Sep. 1775 and served to 20 Apr. 1777 in the 6th Pa. Regiment under Col. Irwin in Capt. Rippy's Company. He also appeared as Nathaniel Stevenson.

Stephenson, William. Pa. —. He applied in Philadelphia County on 22 Apr. 1826. He enlisted 15 Aug. 1782 under Col. Miling in Capt. Zebulon Pike's Company of Light Horse. He was discharged at Lancaster. He was a cordwainer. He died 1 May 1836.

Stephenson, William. Pa. —. He was awarded a $40 gratuity and a $40 annuity in Franklin Co., Pa. 15 Apr. 1835. He was dead by July 1838.

Stern, Samuel. —. —. He was pensioned 27 Apr. 1810.

Sterner, Christian. Pa. —. He was awarded a $40 annuity in Schuylkill County 5 Feb. 1836.

Sterner, Daniel. Pa. —. He was granted relief in Northampton County 14 Mar. 1835. He was dead by Mar. 1838.

Stetson, Ebenezer. Mass. —. He served in the 14th Regiment and was from Dighton. He was paid

$50.

Stetson, Ebenezer. —. —. He served aboard the privateer *Viper*. His application of 20 Jan. 1796 was not approved since his service was not covered by law.

Stetson, Gideon. Mass. —. He served in the 2nd Regiment and was from Scituate. He was paid $20.

Sterigere, Justus. Pa. —. He was awarded a $40 gratuity and a $40 annuity in Philadelphia Co., Pa. 3 Mar. 1826.

Sterns, Samuel. Mass. Pvt. He served in the Mass. Continental Line. He lived in Sullivan Co., N.H. He was on the 1813 pension list.

Sterry, —. Pa. —. His widow, Elizabeth Catherine Sterry, was awarded a $40 gratuity and a $40 annuity in Adams Co., Pa. 14 Jan. 1835.

Steuart, —. Md. Capt. His widow, Elizabeth Steuart, was pensioned at the rate of half-pay of a captain in Queen Anne's County on 28 Feb. 1844. Her arrearage of $33.33 was paid to Woolman I. Gibson for her representatives on 8 Mar. 1850. She died 21 Feb. 1849.

Stevens, Aaron. Conn. Capt. He served in Swift's Regiment. He was pensioned at the rate of $10 per month from 24 Feb. 1808. He was on the 1813 pension list as Aaron Stephens. He died 29 Aug. 1820.

Stevens, Benjamin. Md. Pvt. He was pensioned at the rate of half-pay of a private in Somerset County on 27 Jan. 1817.

Stevens, Benjamin. N.H. Pvt. He was mustered into the service 18 July 1777 under Capt. Samuel McConnell, Col. Thomas Stickney, and Gen. Stark. He was discharged 18 Sep. 1777. He married Abigail Tilton, widow of David Tilton, 31 Jan. 1831. He died 25 Aug. 1832. She married thirdly Adoniram Paige who died in 1848. On 4 Jan. 1849 by act of the legislature she had her name changed to Abigail S. Tilton. Her son, Nathaniel D. Tilton, supported her until about 1879 when he died. She was over 90 years of age, destitute, and childless. She was recommended for a slight increase in her pension to $16 per month on 4 Apr. 1882. She was not entitled to arrearage.

Stevens, Daniel. Me. —. He died in Apr. 1796 in Thomaston. His widow was Jerusha Davenport from Hallowell. She was paid $50 under the resolve of 1836.

Stevens, Ephraim. Vt. Sgt. He was in the militia and in 1777 was carried to Canada where he was imprisoned for seven months. He was awarded $46.75 on 3 Nov. 1798. He lived in Plattsburgh, N.Y. and previously in Pittsford, Vt.

Stevens, Frances. S.C. —. There were children in 1793.

Stevens, James. —. —. Congress awarded his widow, Esther Stevens of Van Buren Co., Mich. the arrearage of her pension from 4 Mar. 1848 to 3 Feb. 1853 on 21 Feb. 1857.

Stevens, Jedutha. —. —. —. His daughter was Clarinda S. Hillman, who was the widow of Erastus Hillman, a veteran of the War of 1812. She had four sons in the Civil War. She sought an increase in her pension from $12 to $20 on 24 June 1898. She was in her 97th year.

Stevens, John. N.Y. Pvt. He served under Col. T. Clinton. He lost his sight in one eye during the siege of Quebec in 1775. He lived in Ulster Co., N.Y.

Stevens, John. N.Y. Capt. He was a hostage at the capitulation of the Cedars. He was pensioned 11 Aug. 1790.

Stevens, John. S.C. —. He was from Chesterfield in 1793. His child was receiving a pension in 1800.

Stevens, Jonah. Conn. Pvt. He was on the 1791 pension roll.

Stevens, Jonathan. Mass. Corp. He served under Col. William Prescott and Capt. Asa Lawrence. He was disabled by a musket ball in his right leg. He was pensioned 7 July 1786 in Middlesex

Co., Mass. He was 48 years old. He was on the 1813 pension list. He was from Groton when he was paid $20 by the Commonwealth. He also appeared as Jonathan Stephens.

Stevens, Josiah. Conn. Pvt. He was from Brookfield and 36 years old on 9 June 1789. He was wounded in the ankle joint in July 1779 at the burning of Fairfield. He served in the 3rd Regiment of Light Horse.

Stevens, Judah. Mass. Pvt. He was in the 8th Regiment and was from North Brookfield. His widow, Abigail Stevens, was paid $50.

Stevens, Levi. Md. Pvt. He was pensioned at the rate of half-pay of a private in Somerset County 23 Jan. 1817. His widow, Polly Stevens, was pensioned at the same rate 11 Mar. 1835. His arrearage of $28.33 for 8 months and 15 days was paid to William Stevens and David Stevens, his executors, 24 Feb. 1836. He also appeared as Levi Stephens.

Stevens, Peleg. Mass. Pvt. He served in the 7th Regiment under Col. John Brooks. He was disabled by rheumatism and being worn out. He was pensioned 1 Sep. 1782.

Stevens, Roger. Vt. Pvt. He served under Col. Cilley in Capt. Fairwell's Company. He was crippled by the cramp in his feet in service. His evidence was totally incomplete.

Stevens, Simeon. Mass. Sgt. He served under Col. Henry Jackson and Capt. Joseph Fox. He was disabled by the loss of his sight. He was 42 years old in 1788.

Stevens, Simon. Mass. Pvt. He died 18 Sep. 1789. He was on the 1791 pension roll.

Stevens, Thomas. Me. —. He was from Brooksville. He was paid $50 under the resolve of 1836.

Stevens, Thomas. Mass. —. He served in the 11th Regiment and was from Danvers. He was paid $20.

Stevens, Thomas. N.Y. —. He was pensioned.

Stevens, Vincent. Pa. —. He was awarded a $40 gratuity and a $40 annuity in Bedford Co., Pa. 15 Apr. 1835. He also appeared as Vincent Stephens.

Stevens, William Smith. S.C. Surgeon. He served in a Continental Hospital. He sought relief in 1785 on an equal basis with other officers.

Stevenson, —. —. —. His widow, Hannah Stevenson, sought a pension 20 Jan. 1847. Congress rejected her claim because she married subsequent to 1 Jan. 1794. It was actually in 1796.

Stevenson, Abner. Mass. —. He served in the 4th Regiment.

Stevenson, Alexander. —. —. He enlisted in Feb. 1776. He was at Three River, Lower Canada, and was taken prisoner. He was detained to 1783. His heirs sought relief from Congress 21 Jan. 1858.

Stevenson, George. —. Surgeon's Mate. He served to the end of the war. Congress granted his widow relief 13 Feb. 1855.

Stevenson, George. Pa. Lt. He applied in Washington County on 13 Feb. 1804. He was made a prisoner in 1779 by the Indians at West Liberty. He was tomahawked in the head, taken to Detroit, delivered to the British, and carried to Quebec. He was discharged on parole in Oct. 1782. He made his way back to Philadelphia and had been gone three years and four months. He had a large family of children. He was entitled to donation land. He removed to Knox Co., Ohio from western Virginia. He was born 13 Oct. 1755 in Franklin Co., Penn. He served under Capt. Samuel Culberson (later a colonel in the Flying Camp), 1st Lt. John Reynolds (later captain), 2nd Lt. Samuel Henry, and Ens. Reuben Galespy in Aug. 1776. He left the service 1 Nov. 1776. He was drafted a second time from Chambersburg, Pa. and marched to Amboy, N.J. where he was discharged. He then served under Capt. James McCammon as a lieutenant. He was at the battles of Trenton and Princeton. He left the service at Slabstown and reached home in Apr. 1777. He entered again in Sep. 1777 and marched to Valley Forge after Brandywine. He was at Germantown. His next tour was with 2nd Lt. James Caldwell and Ens. John Shields in 1778. He defended the frontier and was captured on an express en route to Wheeling. He was struck in the head by a tomahawk and taken to Detroit, sent to Niagara, Montreal, and Quebec where he was in irons for two years. He was let out under labor to a Frenchman for three months. He was remanded to prison for about six months before sent by ship to New York where he was liberated. He returned home in the fall of 1783. He married Catherine McComb in Jan 1783 in the Middle Spring Presbyterian Church in Cumberland Co., Penn. Rev. Robert Cooper performed the ceremony. Her sister-in-law attested to the marriage. He died 13 Sep. 1838. His widow, Catherine Stevenson, aged over 70, was pensioned in Knox Co., Ohio 16 Jan. 1845. His eldest son Thomas Stevenson was in his 54th or 55th year. Their third son George Stevenson, Jr. was 46 in 1839. Rebecca McComb was the wife of the brother of Catherine Stevenson. Congress granted the widow relief 17 June 1846.

Stevenson, Hugh. Va. Col. His widow, Nancy Stevenson, was being pensioned 27 May 1784. She was also on the roll of 1785.

Stevenson, James. Pa. —. He was awarded a $40 gratuity in Trumbull Co., Ohio 6 Apr. 1830.

Stevenson, James. Pa. —.He was granted a $40 gratuity and a $40 annuity in Juniata County 12 Jan. 1836.

Stevenson, Thomas. S.C. —. He died in the service. His widow, Margaret Stevenson, was awarded an annuity 29 Mar. 1785 in Abbeville. There were children in 1791.

Steward, Amasa. Me. —. He was from Skowhegan. He was paid $50 under the resolve of 1836.

Steward, John. Pa. —. He was awarded a $40 gratuity and a $40 annuity in Crawford Co., Pa. 25 Mar. 1831 on the condition that he had not been placed on the pension list of the United States.

Stewart, —. Va. —. His wife, Sarah Stewart, and two children were granted £3 per month in Yohogania County 26 Mar. 1778.

Stewart, —. Va. —. His mother, Mary Stewart, was granted £45 support on 21 Feb. 1780 in York Co.

Stewart, —. Va. —. His wife, Rachel Stewart, and child were furnished a barrel of corn and 50 pounds of pork in Frederick County on 6 June 1780.

Stewart, Adam. —. —. His children had their petition rejected by Congress 25 May 1860 because of proof of his service was submitted.

Stewart, Alexander. Va. —. He was wounded in the expedition against the Indians on the Ohio River under Capt. George Moffat. He was granted a £40 gratuity and a £5 annuity for five years on 13 May 1770. After his annuity expired, he was awarded a £200 gratuity on 30 May 1780.

Stewart, Alexander. Va. —. He entered the service at the age of nineteen in the fall of 1779 as an eighteen month man. He served under Capt. Boyer of Botetourt County and marched to Hillsboro, N.C. He was under Capt. Huffman at Cowpens in Jan 1781 and at Guilford in Mar. 1781. He lived in Bourbon Co., Ky. and was unable to get to court. Congress declined to grant him a pension on 21 Mar. 1836 because the evidence was too vague to entitle him to a pension.

Stewart, Archibald. Pa. —. He received a $40 gratuity and a $40 annuity in Fayette County 15 June 1836. He was 80 years old in 1840. He died 5 May 1849.

Stewart, Daniel. S.C. —. He served in the 1st S.C. Continental Regiment and was captured at Charleston. He was paid $192.66 as a soldier on 20 Dec. 1810. He also appeared as Daniel Stuard.

Stewart, David. Pa. Pvt. He was in Philadelphia County on 12 Dec. 1785. He was in the Invalids and was discharged unfit for duty on account of cancer and other complaints contracted in the service on 15 Sep. 1782. He was 48 years old. He died 17 Jan. 1791.

Stewart, Finley. N.Y. Pvt. He was a batteau man. He was wounded in his left shoulder by the enemy when landing at Fort Stanwix in Aug. 1777. He lived in Greenbush, N.Y. in 1794. One record indicated that he died 2 Feb. 1798; yet, he was on the 1813 pension list.

Stewart, George. Del. Pvt. He was wounded at the battle of Camden. He was married. He was on the 1791 pension list.

Stewart, George. Pa. Pvt. He was in Philadelphia County on 9 Jan. 1786. He was in the Invalids and had been disabled by a wound in his right thigh in the service. He was 24 years old. He died 14 Nov. 1786.

Stewart, James. Pa. —. He applied 11 Jan. 1814.

Stewart, James. Pa. —. He was awarded a $40 gratuity and a $40 annuity in Adams Co., Pa. 27 Mar. 1824.

Stewart, James. S.C. —. He was pensioned in 1827. His name was incorrectly entered into the record as John Stewart. The error was corrected at the next session 6 Dec. 1828. He died in Oct. 1829 in Chester District, S.C. His widow, Rosannah Stewart, aged 86, sought his arrearage 9 Nov. 1831.

Stewart, Joel. N.J. —. He was pensioned in Gloucester County on 21 Feb. 1844 at the rate of $50 per annum.

Stewart, John. —. Sgt. He served at least three years and part of that time was at the rank of a sergeant. Marcy Chapman went from Great Barrington, Mass. to Nobletown, N.Y. where she married the veteran 19 Sep. 1791. Her sister was Catharine Chapman. He died 28 Feb. 1810. His widow, Marcy Stewart, married secondly Curtis Olds in 1817 or 1818. He died in 1819. Congress granted her a pension 2 May 1844.

Stewart, John. N.Y. Corp. He served in Capt. Wait Hopkins's Company under Col. Seth Warner. He was disabled by a musket shot wound in his left arm on 4 July 1777 at Hulberton. He lived in Saratoga, Albany Co., N.Y. on 16 June 1789. He was on the 1813 pension list.

Stewart, John. Pa.—. He received a $40 gratuity and a $40 annuity in Adams County 1 Jan. 1824.

Stewart, John. Pa. —.He received a $40 gratuity and a $40 annuity in Crawford County 25 Mar. 1831 provided that he had not been put on the pension list of the United States.

Stewart, John. Pa. —. He was granted relief in Erie County in 1841.

Stewart, John. Pa.—. He received a $40 gratuity and a $40 annuity in Venango County 20 Mar. 1838.

Stewart, John. Pa. —. He received a $40 gratuity and a $40 annuity in Indiana County 21 June 1839. He died 19 Mar. 1843.

Stewart, John. S.C. Pvt. He served under Capt. Jacob Barnett and Col. Henry Hampton. He was wounded in the service. John Kelley served with him. He was 75 years old. He was from Kershaw District 30 Nov. 1827. Someone else impersonating him claimed that his name was incorrectly given as James Stewart in the act of the legislature. On 6 Dec. 1828 he was able to reprove his identity. He was able to prove the fraud and was restored to his pension on 25 Nov. 1830 and received his arrearage. He died about the last of Nov. 1840. Levin Stewart of Laurens District was his only surviving child, and he sought his arrearage. He stated that his father died just before the birth of the child of Lewis Perry.

Stewart, Joseph. S.C. —. He served under Capt. William Hagens, Capt. Neal Morrison, Capt. James Jack, Capt. Goodwin, Capt. Cowan, and Col. Little. He was in the Snow Camps and the Cherokee Expedition. Joshua Gorden swore that his father reared Joseph Stewart. He was from Lancaster District and was pensioned 30 Nov. 1827. He died 15 Feb. 1828. Robert Givens was administrator of his estate and was paid his arrearage of $47.50.

Stewart, Philip. Md. Lt. He served in the 3ʳᵈ Regiment under Col. Washington. He later resided in the District of Columbia.

Stewart, Ralph. Va. —. He was pensioned in Logan County on 30 Jan. 1823 at the rate of $60 per annum with $50 immediate relief. He was 73 years old. He entered the service in 1775 and served to the end of the war. He was taken prisoner twice and was wounded by a musket ball through his right shoulder. He died 18 Nov. 1835. His widow, Mary Stewart, relinquished her right of administration on 16 Aug. 1836 to Anthony Logan.

Stewart, Thomas. Pa. —. He was awarded a $40 gratuity and a $40 annuity in Franklin Co., Pa. 5 Mar. 1828.

Stewart, William. Pa. —. He was pensioned.

Steword, John. Pa. —. His widow applied 21 Dec. 1846.

Stickel, Valentine. Pa. —. He was awarded a $40 gratuity and a $40 annuity in York Co., Pa. 20 Apr. 1829.

Stickle, John. Pa. —. His widow, Elizabeth Strickle, was awarded a $50 gratuity on 13 Mar. 1817.

Stied, John. Pa. Pvt. He served in the 11ᵗʰ Regiment under Capt. Walker. He was wounded in his head, hand, and body at Paoli. He was discharged 6 May 1780 unfit for duty. He applied in Philadelphia County. He died in May 1798.

Stienrod, —. Pa. —. His widow, Rachel Stienrod, was granted relief in Greene County 21 Mar. 1840.

Stile, John. S.C. —. He left Fort Johnson to go to Savannah. He was discharged by Col. McIntosh but never received a farthing. He sought compensation 12 Nov. 1791.

Stiles, Aaron. N.J. Pvt. He was on the 1791 pension roll. He served in the 4ᵗʰ N.J. Regiment and was wounded in his left shoulder. He was 29 years old. He was on the 1813 pension list. He transferred to Delaware Co., N.Y. 4 Sep. 1826.

Stiles, Eli. Pa. Pvt. He was pensioned.

Still, Christopher. Pa. Pvt. He was in Chester County on 21 Mar. 1786. He was in the 5ᵗʰ Pa. Regiment in Capt. John Christie's Company and was wounded in the elbow joint of his right arm at Brandywine by a musket ball. He was 48 years old. His wife was mentioned 6 June 1789.

Still, John. S.C. —. He received an annuity on 5 Mar. 1821.

Still, Samuel. S.C. Pvt. He served under Capt. Fair, Capt. Daley, and Gen. Lincoln. He was at Charleston and Briar Creek. He was between 68 and 69 years of age. He was from Barnwell District in 1826. His application was rejected.

Still, William. Pa. —. He was awarded a $40 gratuity and a $40 annuity in Armstrong County 19 Feb. 1828.

Stiller, John. Pa. Pvt. He served in Capt. Nathaniel Irish's Company of Artificers. He was wounded and lost two fingers on his left hand in Mar. 1780. He lived in Philadelphia Co., Pa. in 1794. He enlisted 19 Apr. 1778 and appeared to have left the service in Sep.1780. He was on the 1813 pension list.

Stiller, Peter. N.C. —. He enlisted in 1782 for 18 months under Capt. Sharp and Col. Little. He was discharged at James Island. His son was Henry Stiller. His wife, Susannah Stiller, was 75 years, and he was 81 years old when he applied in Rowan County 19 Aug. 1831.

Stillman, John. Pa. —. He was granted relief in Allegheny County.

Stillman, Samuel. Conn. Pvt. He served in the Conn. militia. He was wounded by a musket ball below his left elbow and another which passed through his thigh on 9 Sep. 1781 at Fort Griswold. He resided in Saybrook, Conn. in 1796. He was granted half a pension 20 Apr. 1796. He was on the 1813 pension list. He died 27 Sep. 1821.

Stillwagon, —. Pa. —. His widow, Elizabeth Stillwagon, was awarded a $40 gratuity and a $40 annuity in Fayette Co., Pa. 14 Apr. 1834. She was 95 years old in 1840.

Stillwagon, Frederick. Pa. —. His widow, Margaret Stillwagon, was awarded a $40 gratuity and a $40 annuity in Montgomery Co., Pa. 8 Apr. 1829.

Stillwagon, Jacob. Pa. —. He applied in Chester County 13 May 1823. In 1776 he was in Capt. William West's Company under Col. John Shea in the 3rd Battalion in Lancaster. James Cook was his sergeant. At Fort Washington he became a prisoner on 16 Nov. 1776. The next spring he was paroled and came to Philadelphia. He then served under Col. Cadwalader. He was discharged in consequence of being lame in his right knee and ankle. His wife, Elizabeth Stillwagon aged 58, lived in Strawsburgh, Lancaster Co., Pa. Both sons were killed in the War of 1812. He was 70 years old. He died 25 Jan. 1840.

Stillwell, James. N.Y. Sgt. He was in Col. Philip Van Cortland's Regiment in Capt. Edward Lounsberry's Company and was wounded by a musket ball in his left hip and right groin at Stillwater on 19 Sep. 1777. He was pensioned 15 Aug. 1786. He lived at Marbletown, Ulster Co., N.Y. on 25 May 1789 and later in Tompkins County. He was on the 1813 pension list.

Stillwell, Obediah. N.J. Pvt. He served under Capt. Joseph Stillwell and Col. Scudder. He was made a prisoner at the Highlands and died in prison in New York 13 Apr. 1777. His widow was Mary Stillwell of Monmouth County.

Stilwell, John. N.Y. Sgt. He served under Col. Philip Van Courtland and Capt. Lounsberry in the 2nd Regiment. He received an invalid pension.

Stinchback, Aquilla. —. Capt. He served in the militia. He died about 1790. His children, Henrietta M. Stewart and Rebecca L. Weaver, furnished no evidence so Congress denied them relief 1 Aug. 1850.

Stiner, John. N.Y. Pvt. He died of wounds 15 Aug. 1781. His widow was granted support according to an undated roster.

Stinson, —. Va. —. He served in Capt. Lewis' Company of the Light Dragoons on Continental establishment. His wife, Mary Stinson, and four children were granted £10 support in Frederick Co., Va. on 7 Apr. 1778.

Stinson, William. Me. —. He died 9 Mar. 1823 at Richmond. His widow was Abiah Stinson from Litchfield. She was paid $50 under the resolve of 1836.

Stitt, David. Pa. —. He was awarded a $40 gratuity and a $40 annuity in Indiana Co., Pa. 6 Apr. 1833. He was dead by Dec. 1837.

Stitt, William. Pa. —. He was awarded a $40 gratuity and a $40 annuity in Armstrong Co., Pa. 21 Dec. 1827.

Stivers, Samuel. N.J. Pvt. He served in Capt. Richard Cox's Company in the 3rd N.J. Regiment from the spring of 1777 to his death on 1 Apr. 1778 or 5 May 1778 in a Pennsylvania hospital. His widow, Rachel Stivers, was allowed his half-pay in 1796. She was from Essex County.

Stoak, John. Mass. Pvt. He served in the 2nd Regiment under Col. Ebenezer Sprout and Capt. Lord. He was disabled by a rupture. He was pensioned 1 Sep. 1782. He lived in Chandlers River, Me. in 1788. He was 45 years old in 1791. He was on the 1813 pension list. He died 12 Jan. 1816 in Plymouth Co., Mass.

Stober, Valentine. Pa. —. He was awarded a $40 gratuity and a $40 annuity in Center Co., Pa. 17 Jan. 1834.

Stockeley, Thomas. Pa. —. He served in the 8th Regiment from Aug. 1776. He was from Washington County.

Stock, David. Pa. —. He married Elizabeth Connor 10 June 1812. Robert Blackwell, D.D. of the Protestant Episcopal Church, performed the wedding. Daniel Stock proved that he died 22 May 1816.

Stockbridge, Jonathan. Mass. —. He served in the 4th Regiment and was from Freeport. He was paid $20.

Stockbridge, Joseph. Mass. —. He was paid $20.

Stocker, Enoch. Mass. Pvt. He served under Col. Bailey and Capt. Alden. He was disabled by a musket ball in his right thigh. He was 25 years old. He was pensioned 10 Nov. 1787 in Middlesex Co., Mass. He was 25 years old. He was on the 1813 pension list.

Stocker, Samuel N.H. Pvt. He served under Col. Isaac Wyman. He suffered a violent strain in his back in consequence of carrying a plank in 1776 at Mount Independence. He lived in Hopkinton, N.H. in 1794. He was in the militia. He enlisted 16 Apr. 1777 for three years and was discharged 17 Mar. 1780. He was granted half a pension 20 Apr. 1796. He was on the 1813 pension list. He died 10 Dec. 1815.

Stocker, Seth. N.Y. —. He served under Col. Dubois. His wife, Sarah Stocker, was furnished support while he was away in the service 25 Mar. 1779.

Stodard, Hosea. Mass. Corp. He served in the 3rd Regiment and was from Boston. His widow, Lucy Stodard, was paid $20.

Stoddard, Daniel.—. —. He enlisted for three years on 7 July 1777 under Col. Samuel B. Webb. In drawing wood for the troops at Morristown, N.J. in winter quarters, he was injured when a load of wood overturned and passed over his right foot against his ankle. He was left with an incurable lameness. Congress granted him relief 23 Feb. 1836.

Stoddard, Philo. Conn. Pvt. He served in Capt. Phelps' Company under Col. Durkee. He was wounded at Germantown 4 Oct. 1777 by a ball shot through his left arm. Lt. Col. Commandant John Sumner by orders from Gen. Putnam permitted him to go to Woodbury. He was ordered to join the Invalid Corps. He was pensioned 30 April 1787. He was 28 years old. He was on the 1813 pension list of Vermont.

Stoddart, Nathan. Conn. Capt. He died 15 or 27 May 1777. His heirs were paid his seven years' half-pay of $1,680. He also appeared as Nathan Stoddard.

Stoey, —. Pa. —. Hannah Stoey of Beaver County was granted $5 per month 13 July 1813.

Stohl, —. Pa. —. His widow, Mary Stohl, was awarded a $40 gratuity and a $40 annuity in Lancaster County 31 Mar. 1836.

Stokely, Nehemiah. Pa. Capt. He served in the 8th Regiment from 1776 to 1779 when he became supernumerary. He raised a militia and served from 1 June 1779 to 4 Oct. 1779. He died in 1792. His widow, Susanna Stokely, in trust for his children was awarded donation land 27 Mar 1812. He died in 1792. She was awarded a $40 gratuity and a $40 annuity in Westmoreland County 14 Apr. 1834. She died 23 July 1834. Her children, Joseph Stokely and Polly Findly of Westmoreland County, sought relief 15 Dec. 1857. Congress ruled that their claim was barred by the statute of limitations.

Stokely, Thomas. Pa. Capt. He served in the Rangers and was granted $2,400 in commutation of his pay 23 Mar. 1818.

Stoker, John. Va. —. His wife, Mary Stoker, was furnished assistance in Loudoun Co., Va. on 11 Feb. 1777 and in Aug. 1779 while he was away in Continental service.

Stoker, William. —. —. He sought compensation for being wounded 28 Mar. 1796, but his application was not accepted.

Stokes, John. —. —. His widow, Sarah Stokes, died before she could collect her pension. Her administrator, Jonathan Shelton, of Kentucky sought the money she was due from 4 Sep. 1840 to the time of her death 2 Mar. 1842. Congress granted the children relief 11 Apr. 1850.

Stokes, John. —. —. He died in Apr. 1840. He married 2 July 1781 Sarah Hall, daughter of Henry Hall. Congress granted her a pension 19 Jan. 1848.

Stokes, John. Va. Capt. He was from Lunenburg County and was pensioned on 13 June 1787 at the rate of £72 per annum. He served in the 2nd Va. Regiment and was wounded at the defeat of Col. Buford. His right hand had to be amputated. His left hand was considerably impaired by the stroke of a broad sword on his elbow and by the loss of his forefinger. He had several cuts on his head. He was 29 years old. He was granted his commutation of half-pay from 1 May 1783 to 1 Jan. 1787 on 4 June 1789. He died in 1791. Congress ruled on 28 Jan. 1837 that his heirs no claim to commutation because he had received his half-pay to his death.

Stokes, William. Pa. —. He was pensioned.

Stoll, Andrew. Pa. —. He received a $40 gratuity and a $40 annuity 2 Apr. 1822 in Bucks County.

Stoll, Frederick. Pa. —. He was from Northampton County. He was pensioned 6 Jan. 1818.

Stone, David. Pa. —. His daughter was Ann Stone.

Stone, John. Pa. Lt. He applied 4 Oct. 1787. He served in the militia and Flying Camp. He was much afflicted with piles contracted during the service. He agreed to take the place of Lt. Gottlieb Kucher in the Lancaster Flying Camp on the condition that Kucher was to maintain him and his family if he became disabled. He was from Dauphin County.

Stone, John Hoskins. Md. Col. He was appointed captain in Jan. 1776. He was wounded severely at Germantown. He was also at White Plains, Brandywine, and Long Island. He resigned 1 Aug. 1779. He was pensioned 12 Aug. 1789. He died 5 Oct. 1804. Nathaniel Pope Causin (also reported as Nathaniel P. Cousins) and his wife Elizabeth Causin and Ann Turner sought his commutation 28 Dec. 1818, but their application was not allowed. He was appointed a captain in the Maryland Line in Jan. 1776. Congress denied the heirs bounty land on 11 Mar. 1836 because he resigned in Aug. 1779. Congress allowed his heirs half-pay from 1 Aug. 1779 to 5 Oct. 1804 on 8 Aug. 1848. His nephew was Alexander Scott.

Stone, Joseph. Mass. —. He was from Dedham and was paid $50.

Stone, Levi. Conn. —. He served seven or eight months from Mar. 1775 from Danbury. He was promised a captaincy if he would raise a company of artificers. He did so and was commissioned. He served under Maj. Wood, QM General. He worked on anchor chains strung across the Hudson River at West Point. Congress granted the heirs of Levi and Mary Stone relief 12 Dec. 1856.

Stone, Moses. S.C. —. He was pensioned 4 Dec. 1832. He was paid as late as 1834.

Stone, Samuel. Mass. —. He served in the 6th Regiment and was from Dover. He was paid $20.

Stone, Uriah. R.I. Steward. In 1785 he was from Swanzey, N.H. He was an invalid pensioner in Rhode Island until Nov. 1785 when he left that state. He lost his left arm on 22 Feb. 1777 in an engagement with the enemy near Howland's Ferry. He enlisted in 1776 aboard the galley *Spitfire*. Isaac Tyler was the ship's commander. He was on the N.H. roll in 1786. He was aged 36 in 1787. He transferred to Vermont. He was on the 1813 pension list.

Stone, William. Mass. Pvt. His name was on the list of pensioners who had not been paid by Benjamin Lincoln in 1790.

Stone, William. Pa. —. He was awarded a $40 gratuity and a $40 annuity in Chester Co., Pa. 15 Apr. 1834.

Stone, William. S.C. —. On 7 Dec. 1831 it was recommended that his application be rejected.

Stone, William. Va. —. He was pensioned in Stafford County on 3 Mar. 1824 at the rate of $60 per annum. He was wounded twice in battle. He died 3 Mar. 1829. Administration with the will annexed was granted to James Corbin on 10 Mar. 1829.

Stoneking, Jacob. Pa. —. He received a $40 gratuity and a $40 annuity in Greene County 21 Feb. 1838. He was 75 years old in 1840.

Stoner, Caspar. Pa. —. He was awarded a $40 gratuity and a $40 annuity on 13 Mar. 1817.

Stoner, John. Pa. Capt. He applied 7 May 1813. He enlisted in 1775 and went from Lancaster in Capt. Matthew Smith's Company under Lt. Michael Simpson to Boston. In 1776 he was appointed lieutenant in Col. Milen's Regiment. In 1777 he commanded a company in the 10th Regiment. After one campaign after Germantown he gave his resignation.

Stonert, Henry. N.Y. Pvt. He served under Col. Jacob Klock and was slain 1 July 1782. His widow received a half-pay pension. [Her name may have been Catharine Stonert.] He also appeared as Henry Stoner.

Stonewax, —. N.Y. —. Gertrude Stonewax was granted support during the war.

Stoops, John. Pa. —. He enlisted in Capt. Smith's Company in the 6th Battalion in Feb. 1776 under Col. Irwin and Gen. Thompson. He went to Philadelphia, took sick, and lay in hospital in Fort George until discharged by Dr. John Potts. His first lieutenant was John Allen; the second lieutenant was a brother of Col. Irwin.

Storer, —. Md. Capt. His widow, Dorothy Storer, was pensioned at the rate of half-pay of a captain in the District of Columbia 21 Mar. 1827.

Storie, Enoch. N.C. Capt. He served under Capt. Carson in the North Carolina militia. In 1779 he volunteered and served under Gen. Rutherford, Col. Loftin, and Capt. Carson. He served four or five years. He was 71 years old. He was supported by his son-in-law, Mr. Jirman [?]. He was from Barnwell District, South Carolina when he applied in 1827. His application was rejected.

Storr, Peter. S.C. —. His widow, Elizabeth Storr, was furnished meat, bread, and wood 1 Feb. 1783.

Storrs, Lemuel. —. Orderly Sgt. He served for six months in 1776 and in 1777 was assistant commissary to the end of the war under Col. Henry Champion and Jeremiah Wadsworth. He married Elizabeth Champion, daughter of Col. Henry Champion, 5 Oct. 1783. He died in 1816. Congress granted her heirs relief 12 Dec. 1856. Their son, William L. Storrs, applied for all the heirs.

Stors, Greenberry. Va. —. His wife, Jane Stors, and child were granted £2 support in Yohogania Co., Va. 27 July 1778 while he was in Continental service.

Story, Daniel. Va. —. He served twelve months in the Continental Line in 1778. His name was not on the roll. His witness claimed six months. Congress rejected his claim for a pension 7 Feb. 1850 because the evidence did not support the claim.

Story, James. Mass. Pvt. He served in the 1st Regiment and was from Gloucester. He was paid $50.

Story, Joseph. Mass. —. He served in the 8th Regiment and was from Ipswich. His widow, Mary Story, was paid $50.

Story, Nathan. Mass. Sgt. He served in the 16th Regiment and was from Essex. His widow, Elizabeth Story, was paid $50.

Story, Park. Mass. Pvt. He served in the 8th Regiment. $20 was paid to his only child, Mary Story.

Story, Thomas. Pa. —. He was killed by the Indians after he was discharged.

Stott, David. Pa. —. He was granted relief.

Stoucts, Philip. N.Y. Pvt. His widow was granted support according to an undated roster.

Stoudemire, John. S.C. —. He was pensioned in St. James Goose Creek 4 Dec. 1832. He also appeared as John Stoudmire. He was paid as late as 1842.

Stouffer, Henry. Pa. —. He was awarded a $40 gratuity and a $40 annuity in Somerset Co., Pa. 4 Jan. 1823.

Stough, —. Pa. —. His widow, Elizabeth Stough, was pensioned 1 Apr. 1836 in York County. She was dead by July 1841.

Stough, Andrew. Pa. —. He was awarded a $40 gratuity and a $40 annuity in York Co., Pa. 27 Mar. 1830.

Stout, —. N.C. Pvt. He entered the service in Randolph County about 1781 and was discharged in 1783. Congress denied his widow, Nancy Stout, a pension 9 Apr. 1860 because of the absence of any proof of his service.

Stout, Abraham. Pa. Lt. He applied 2 Mar. 1799. He died 18 July 1821 His arrearage was due his administrator, Lemuel John.

Stout, Harman. Pa. Officer. He applied 5 Sep. 1793.

Stout, John. Pa. —. Congress did not grant his request for a pension 9 Jan. 1847. He stated that he served with Jacob Foulkrod, but the latter's papers indicated that he was not in the service after 1778. Foulkrod was in the militia under Col. Moore and was never stationed in Bucks Co., Penn. Stout said in 1781 that it was rumored that the British were about to attack New York City. In actuality they had occupied the city since 1776. Militia tours in Pennsylvania were for two months and not three months as he had claimed. He also stated that the enemy returned to Philadelphia for winter quarters in 1781 but, in fact, they had not been there since 1777. There was a John Stout who was awarded a $40 annuity in Philadelphia, Pa. in 1846. He died 6 Sep. 1847. The widow of John Stout was awarded a $40 annuity 8 May 1850.

Stout, Joseph. N.J. Capt. He served in the 2nd N.J. Regiment and was killed at the battle of Brandywine on 11 Sep. 1777. His wife, Theodosia Stout, was deceased. Their daughter, Mary Stout, was born 23 Nov. 1770. She was allowed his half-pay from 11 Sep. 1777 to 3 Nov. 1778 in Hunterdon Co., N.J. in 1781.

Stout, Joseph. N.C. Pvt. He was discharged in 1783. His widow was Nancy Stout of Randolph County whom Congress rejected for a pension because there was no evidence of his service on the rolls on 9 Apr. 1860.

Stout, Samuel. N.J. Pvt. He served in the 3rd Battalion of the Middlesex County militia and was wounded in the hand 16 Oct. 1777. He was on the 1791 pension roll. He served in the 1st N.J. Regiment. He lived in Middlesex County. He was on the 1813 pension list. He died 12 Jan. 1837. His widow was Ann Stout.

Stover, Michael. Pa. —. He was awarded a $40 gratuity and a $40 annuity in Lancaster Co., Pa. 10 Apr. 1835. He died 22 Apr. 1840.

Stow, Abijah. Mass. —. He served in Hazen's Regiment and was paid $20.

Stow, Lazarus. Pa. Lt. He was granted relief.

Stow, John. Pa. Lt. He was on the 1789 pension list..

Stowe, Ebenezer. —. —. Congress rejected his petition 4 Apr. 1840 because there was no evidence on file.

Stoy, Daniel. Pa. —. He applied in Somerset County on 26 Apr. 1816. In 1775 a group of 29 found and chose him to command them. They met at Carlisle and in the election chose Robert Clagget captain, Richard Brown first lieutenant, John Halloday second lieutenant, and himself third lieutenant. Robert McKenney was at headquarters. He was a nephew of Col. William Thompson who had McKenney commissioned in Stoy's place. Stoy remained a sergeant the rest of the time. He was in New York in 1776 and was sent home as recruiting sergeant. He served one year. He was 70 years old; his wife was about 70 years old. In 1777 out of fear of the Indians, he went to the county lieutenant and was told to make a stand at the blockhouse. He paid the company of eleven men out of his own pocket for two months. He was awarded a $40 gratuity and a $40 annuity in Somerset County on 17 Feb. 1817. He also appeared as David [sic] Stoy.

Stoy, Daniel. Va. —. He was drafted in 1778. His name was not on the roll. Congress granted him a pension 22 Dec. 1840.

Straber, Peter. Pa. Pvt. He was wounded in his right arm at Trenton and was left an invalid for the rest of his life. He died in Sep. 1820. Congress rejected the claim from William Straber on 22 Jan. 1851.

Strader, John. N.J. —. He was granted relief.

Straker, Peter. Pa. Pvt. He served in the militia and was wounded in his right arm at Trenton. He died in Sep. 1820 as an invalid. His son, William Straker, sought relief for the heirs. Congress rejected the claim 22 Jan. 1851.

Strap, Jacob. Md. —. He served three years in the 1st Md. Regiment. He was captured at sea and carried to Portsmouth, Great Britain where he remained imprisoned until the peace. He lacked the means to return home until Dec. 1787. He was awarded his depreciation pay in 1788.

Strasner, John. Md. —. He served in 2nd Regiment. He applied for his half–pay in Frederick County. [He was not the same man as John Stresner.]

Stratton, David. Mass. Pvt. He served in the 6th Regiment and was paid $20.

Stratton, Thomas. N.Y. —. He enlisted in July 1776 under Col. Malcolm. He subsequently served under Col. Spencer in New Jersey and was at Monmouth. He served against the Indians on the Genesse River. He was discharged at the end of three years. He sought 100 acres of bounty land or money in lieu thereof. Congress rejected his claim on 8 Mar. 1842 because he did not serve to the end of the war.

Straw, Nicholas. Pa. —. He was awarded a $40 gratuity and a $40 annuity in Clearfield Co., Pa. 8 Feb. 1823.

Strawbaugh, Peter. Pa. —. He was pensioned.

Streads, Richard. —. —. He was pensioned 25 Apr. 1808.

Streeper, William. Pa. Pvt. He was awarded a $40 gratuity and a $40 annuity in Philadelphia Co., Pa. 16 Apr. 1827. His widow, Margaret Streeper, was awarded a $40 gratuity and a $40 annuity 14 Apr. 1828.

Streeter, John. —. Pvt. He served in Col. Hitchcock's Regiment. He was wounded in the right hand by a musket ball which entered his left thigh on 16 Sep. 1776 at Harlem Straights. He resided in Berkshire Co., Mass. in 1796. One man of the name enlisted in the 12th Mass. Regiment 10 Jul. 1779 for nine months. He was discharged 10 Sep. 1780. He reenlisted 10 Jul. 1780 for six months.

Stresner, John. Md. Pvt. He served in the 7th Regiment and applied for his half-pay in Frederick County. [He was not the same man as John Strasner.]

Streter, Benjamin. Mass. —. He served in the 4th Regiment and was paid $20.

Stribling, Clayton. S.C. —. He served several tours in South Carolina and Virginia. At Stedham's Mill he was wounded in the head by a ball and was deprived of his senses for a considerable time. It destroyed the organ of hearing in one ear. He applied from Union District in Dec. 1827. His application was rejected.

Strickland, James. Mass. Pvt. He served in the 1st Regiment and was from Palmer. He was paid $50.

Strickler, —. Pa. —. His widow, Nancy Strickler, was awarded a $40 gratuity and a $40 annuity in York Co., Pa. 18 Feb. 1834.

Strickler, Jacob. Pa. —. He applied 24 Jan. 1815. He enlisted in Capt. Jacob Humphrey's Company in the 6th Regiment under Col. Henry Becker from 10 Apr. 1777 to 1783 when he was discharged at Philadelphia. He lost the sight in one eye, and the other was much impaired.

Strickler, William. Va. Pvt. He was in Henrico County 30 Aug. 1786. He served in the Henrico County militia under Capt. Joseph Price. He was wounded in right shoulder two or three days before the surrender of the town of York. He was 23 years old. He also appeared as William Stricker. He was on the 1813 pension list.

Stricklin, Lot. —. —. He was pensioned in 1833 and stricken in 1835. He reapplied and was pensioned at the rate of $40 per annum instead of the $80 per annum he had previously received. Since he received nothing for many years, he petitioned Congress for relief and further relief for two years of service. Congress rejected his claim 28 May 1840.

Strider, Jacob. Pa. —. He was granted relief.

Strider, Philip. Md. —. He died 6 Jan. in Bedford Co., Pa. His arrearage of $12.93 was paid to M.C. Sprigg for the legal representative 6 Apr. 1841.

Stringer, John. Mass. —. He served in Crane's Artillery. He was paid $20.

Stringfield, William. N.Y. Pvt. He transferred to Philadelphia Co., Pa. He was on the 1813 pension list in Pennsylvania.

Strite, Jacob. Pa. —. He was pensioned.

Stroah, —. Pa. —. His widow was Hannah Stroah.

Stroaking, Jacob. Pa —. He was pensioned.

Strobeck, Adam. N.Y. Pvt. He served in Capt. Lawrence Gross's Company under Col. Marinus Willet. He was wounded in the arm and small of his back on 7 July 1778. He was pensioned 19 Dec. 1786. He was 23 years old. He lived in Canajoharie, Montgomery Co., N.Y. on 24 Mar. 1788 and later in Seneca County. He was on the 1813 pension list as Adam Stroback.

Strohl, —. Pa. —. His widow, Catharine Strohl, was awarded a $40 gratuity and a $40 annuity 6 Apr. 1833 in Northampton County.

Strohl, —. Pa. —. His widow, Mary Strohl, received a $40 gratuity and a $40 annuity in Lancaster County 31 Mar. 1836.

Strohl, Daniel. Pa. —. He was awarded a $40 gratuity and a $40 annuity in Northampton Co., Pa. 23 Jan. 1833. He was dead by July 1840.

Strohl, Peter. Pa. —. He was awarded a $40 gratuity and a $40 annuity in Northampton Co., Pa. 11 Apr. 1825.

Strong, John. Mass. Capt. He was with Col. Eaton at Ticonderoga in 1776. He served two tours in the militia in 1777. His brother was King Strong. He married in 1776. Congress granted his widow, Martha Strong, a pension based upon six months of service on 5 Mar. 1840. She was 84 years old in Aug. 1839.

Strong, Josiah. Conn. Pvt. He was wounded at Germantown on 4 Oct. 1777 by a musket ball through his leg which had to be amputated. He served in the 5th Conn. Regiment. He was pensioned 3 Apr. 1787 at Sharon, Conn. He was 28 years old. He was on the 1813 pension list.

Strong, Roger. —. —. He was a native of Lebanon, Conn. At the age of 13 he joined as a musician in Apr. 1775 and served to 1778. He served under Col. John Durkee and Col. Ely. He was compelled to leave the army due to lameness. He was 70 years old and destitute of property. Congress granted him a pension 23 Dec. 1831.

Stroop, John. Pa. Sgt. He was on the 1813 pension list. He died 6 Mar. 1831 in Philadelphia County. His papers were destroyed in the fire in 1814. His widow was Hannah Stroop. Congress granted her a pension 7 Jan. 1859.

Strother, Benjamin. Va. Dragoon. He served in Lee's Legion and lived in Prince William County. He was on the 1813 pension list.

Stroud, Joseph. —. —. He was pensioned.

Stroud, William. Ga. —. He was awarded $75 to enable him to be placed on the pension list of the United States in Nov./Dec. 1817. He was from Jasper County. The act did not specify that his service was Revolutionary.

Stroud, William. S.C. Pvt. He served under Col. Lacy. He and three sons enlisted in 1776 in the 6th Regiment. He was wounded by a musket ball at Congaree. It penetrated his left shoulder and lodged in his back. It was removed with considerable difficulty and pain. He was from Chester District and was pensioned 3 Dec. 1811. He was above 80 years of age. His pension was retroactive to 1806. He died 12 Dec. 1812. Hardy Stroud sought one year's annuity due his late father on 9 Dec.1813.

Stroup, —. Pa. —. His widow, Eve Stroup, was awarded relief in Venango County 5 Feb. 1836. She was 79 years old in 1840.

Struckler, Jacob. Pa. —. He enlisted under Capt. Jacob Humphrey and Col. Henry Beiker 10 Apr. 1777. He lost the sight of one of his eyes in the service. He was discharged in 1783 at Philadelphia. He was from Dauphin County.

Strunk, —. Pa. —. His widow, Mary Strunk, was awarded a $40 gratuity and a $40 annuity in Berks County in 1836.

Strunk, William. Pa. —. He was awarded a $40 gratuity and a $40 annuity in Berks Co., Pa. 5 Apr. 1830.

Strupe, Malcher [Melchoir]. Va. —. He was pensioned in Cabell County on 21 Feb. 1827 at the rate of $60 per annum and $30 immediate relief. He enlisted in 1777 and was severely wounded by the Indians. On 14 Dec. 1827 the date of his pension payment was set on 1 Dec. He died 11 June 1833. His executor was Solomon Thornburg.

Stuart, —. Md. —. His widow, Elizabeth Stuart, was on the roll in 1850.

Stuart, Alexander. Va. —. He was pensioned in Augusta County in 1794. His pension of £8 was increased by $20 in Jan. 1814. He had been wounded. He died 13 Oct. 1823 in Rockingham County. His executor was James Sims.

Stuart, George. Del. —. He was wounded in his body at Camden 25 Apr. 1781. He was married. He was pensioned in 1783.

Stuart, John. Pa. Pvt. His widow was in Westmoreland County 11 Mar. 1794. He was in the militia company of Capt. Robert Orr. He was killed by Indians 28 Aug. 1781. His widow married Robert Roseburg in Sep. 1787. His posthumous son, John Stuart, was born 3 Sep. 1781, and John Young was his guardian.

Stuart, John. Pa. Pvt. He was in Westmoreland County on 20 Mar. 1794. He served in the 11th Pa. Regiment under Col. Potter. He was wounded in his left arm at Brandywine on 11 Sep.1777. He was transferred to the Invalids. His brother died in the service. He applied for his brother's and his own pay in 1786.

Stubbs, John S. —. Lt. His heirs did not prove that he served to the end of the war or that he died in the service. Their application for commutation was rejected 23 Mar. 1838.

Stuck, —. Pa. —. His widow, Elizabeth Stuck, was awarded a $40 gratuity and a $40 annuity in 1842 for his Revolutionary service. She died in Fayette County 1 Apr. 1849.

Stucky, —. Pa. —. His widow was Anna Maria Stucky. She was from Lebanon County when she was pensioned 11 Apr. 1825.

Studer, Philip. Md. Pvt. He was pensioned at the rate of half-pay of a private 23 Jan. 1816.

Studley, Thomas. Mass. Sgt. He served in the 3rd Regiment and was from Scituate. He was paid $20.

Stull, Frederick. Pa. —. He applied in Northampton County on 20 Dec. 1817. He enlisted in 1776 in the 2nd Pa. Regiment under Col. Walter Stewart in Capt. John Pugh's Company for five years. He was discharged at Trenton 15 Jan. 1781. He signed in German.

Stump, Charles. Pa. Pvt. He was in York County on 11 June 1788. He was in Col. Miles' Regiment and was wounded in several places at the battle of Long Island in 1776. He was taken prisoner by the British. He lost the use of his fingers and his left arm. He was stabbed in the groin by a bayonet and was afflicted with a rupture. He was 45 years old. He signed in German as Carl Stump.

Stump, John. Pa. Pvt. He was in Philadelphia County on 13 Feb. 1786. He served in 3rd Pa. Regiment. He received several wounds in sundry parts of his ankles, right leg, and left side at the battle of Germantown. His wife was Rebecka Stump. He was 27 years old. He died 16 Dec. 1810.

Sturdivant, Zenas. Pa. —. He was on the 1789 pension list.

Sturges, Benjamin. Conn. Pvt. He served in Capt. Woodhull's Company commissioned to command three whale boats. He was wounded by a bayonet thrust into his left side while attempting to grapple one of the enemy's boats in Long Island Sound on 7 Dec. 1782. He lived in Fairfield, Conn. in 1795. He was granted one-sixth of a pension 20 Apr. 1796. He died 11 Dec. 1832. He was on the 1813 pension list.

Sturges, David. —. —. He was wounded.

Sturges, Joseph. Pa. —. He was awarded a $40 gratuity and a $40 annuity in Luzerne County 28 Mar. 1836.

Sturtevant, Joseph. Me. —. He died at Hebron 20 Mar. 1835. His widow was Sarah Sturtevant from Paris. She was paid $50 under the resolve of 1836.

Sturtevant, Samuel. —. —. He served as a marine on the *Providence* under Capt. Abraham Whipple and died 14 Feb. 1777. His widow was Jerusha Sturtevant. She married secondly Isaiah Ripley in Jan. 1780. Ripley died in Jan. 1827. He served eight months from Roxbury under Capt. Bradford and Col. Cotton in 1775. Jerusha Ripley had been totally blind when she applied to Congress for relief 7 Jan. 1837. Her brother was Zebedee Cushman who was 73 years old. Congress granted her a pension for her husband's thirteen months of service.

Stuston, James. Pa. —. He was pensioned.

Stutts, Casper. —. —. His widow was Anna E. Stutts in Stokes Co., N.C. in June 1838.

Styles, Henry. Pa. —. He was granted a $40 gratuity and a $40 annuity in Berks County 14 Mar. 1835. He was 84 years old in 1840. He died 19 Dec. 1845.

Styphlamyre, John. S.C. —. He was from St. James Goose Creek Parish in 1836.

Suagar, John. Pa. —. He died 22 July 1807.

Sufference, Ephraim. Mass. —. He served in the Artillery and was paid $20. He was from Amesbury. He also appeared as Ephraim Sufferson.

Sugg, Thomas. Va. Pvt. His widow, Keziah Sugg, was in Norfolk County and was pensioned at the rate of £12 per annum on 1 Oct. 1787. He was in the 2nd Va. Regiment in Capt. Thomas Bressie's Company as proved by deposition of Henry Wallace. He enlisted in Mar. 1777 and died in the fall of 1778 on 1 Dec. He had four children. One was 23 years old and an idiot, one 16 a cripple, one 20, and one 13.

Sulbach, it. N.Y. Pvt. He served in Capt. Bradpick's Company in Col. Jacob Klock's Regiment. He was wounded in his abdominal muscles on 6 Aug. 1777. In 1786 he was in Montgomery County. He was aged 39 years old in May 1789. He lived in Palatine, Westchester Co., N.Y. He was a weaver. He was on the 1813 pension list.

Sullender, Isaac. Pa. —. He was awarded a $40 gratuity and a $40 annuity in Delaware Co., Pa. 1 Feb. 1834. He was paid to 27 June 1834.

Sullivan, John. Pa. Pvt. He was in Philadelphia County on 14 Nov. 1785. He was worn down in the service and discharged 8 May 1783 from the Invalids. He was 33 years old. He was on the 1791 pension roll. He was transferred to New Jersey by Mar. 1796.

Sullivan, John. S.C. —. His widow was Mary Sullivan from Abbeville District in 1795.

Sullivan, John. S.C. Matross. He served in the 4th S.C. Continental Regiment. He served under Maj. Tutt. He was killed by Tories in Dec. 1779. He was survived by a widow and seven children. His widow was Sarah Sullivan who sought his arrearage in 1795.

Sullivan, John. S.C. —. He entered the service 1 June 1776 under Capt. Peter Bagwell and Col. Maurice Simmons. He also served under Capt. Hopson Pinckney. He was wounded at the siege of Savannah and held a prisoner at Charleston for thirteen months on a prison ship. By trade he was a saddler. He made caps and other accouterments for the troops. He was from Richland District and was pensioned 27 Nov. 1827. He was paid as late as 1832.

Sullivan, Martin. Pa. Pvt. He was in Philadelphia County on 19 Dec. 1785. He was in the Invalids. He was wounded in his back and sundry parts of his body and was discharged 25 Dec. 1782. He was 50 years old. He died 2 July 1786.

Sullivan, Owen. S.C. —. He was killed Nov 1781. His widow, Susanna Sullivan, was granted an annuity 20 Aug. 1785.

Sullivan, Patrick. Pa. —. He applied in Hamilton Co., Ohio 20 Mar. 1818. At Samuel Getty's tavern on 24 June 1775 he and about 50 others joined Capt. McDougal's Company in the 1st Volunteer Rifle Regiment of the Pa. Line under Col. Thompson. They marched to Little York and on to Boston. He served one year. At Millstone, N.J. he enlisted under Col. Hand for two years. He next served in the 2nd Pa. Regiment under Col. Walter Stewart in Capt. Bankhead's [?] Company of grenadiers. He was twice wounded--once in the leg at Germantown and the other in the groin at Yorktown. He was discharged in 1783 at Philadelphia on his return from the southward. He was 79 years old. He died 30 Mar. 1821.

Sullivan, Philip. Md. Pvt. He was wounded at the battle of Camden 16 Aug. 1780. He was in Baltimore Co., Md. in 1787. He was pensioned 4 Mar. 1789. He was on the 1813 pension list.

Sullivan, Thomas. Pa. Sgt. He applied 1 Nov. 1820 in Franklin County. In 1774 he enlisted under Abraham Dehooff for one year and nine months. He next enlisted under Capt. Clark at Mud Island for the war. He was discharged by Gen. Wayne and Col. Walter Stewart. He was wounded in the leg at the taking of Fort Washington. Simon Rhinehart of Cumberland County, Capt. P. Gribble, Nicholas Greenwalt of Franklin County (who served under Capt. Rode), Thomas Welch of Franklin County (who served under Capt. Clark), and Henry Brimm of Franklin County (who served under Capt. Weaver) were soldiers whom he knew. He died 23 Aug. 1824.

Sullivan, Thomas. Va. —. He served in the 5th Virginia Regiment. He was inoculated for smallpox and lost his eyesight. He sought relief on 26 Oct. 1778. He was awarded a gratuity of £30 and an annuity of half-pay of a soldier on 14 Nov. 1778. It was made retroactive from 2 Jan. 1778. He also appeared as Thomas Sullivant.

Sullivant, Michael. Va. —. His wife, Biddy Sullivant, was awarded assistance on 20 July 1788 and £8 on 21 June 1779 in Goochland County.

Summers, Farrell. N.Y. Corp. He served in Capt. John Doughty's Company under Col. John Lamb and was disabled in his left arm above the elbow by grape shot at the battle of Germantown on 4 Oct. 1777. He lived in Ulster Co., N.Y. on 1 June 1789. He was a farmer and was aged 28 years on 4 May 1787. He died in 1799.

Summers, George. Va. —. He married Mary Presgraves 24 Mar 1789 in Fairfax County. He died 1 Sep. 1838. Congress granted his widow, Mary Summers, a pension 9 Feb. 1842.

Summers, John. S.C. —. He served more than three years. He served in 1777 under Capt. Benjamin Tutt and was captured at Charleston. He was paroled. His first lieutenant was Thomas Farrar. He applied from Ninety Six 8 June 1818.

Summers, Simon. Va. Lt. He served in the 6th Virginia Regiment to the close of the war. By resolution of Congress he received the pay and rations of a captain. He received his five years' full pay of a captain 11 Jan. 1838. Since he was a staff officer and not an officer in the Line, Congress rejected the claim for commutation 26 Feb. 1846 from the heirs.

Summers, Solomon. Md. Drummer. He was pensioned at the rate of half-pay of a drummer in Queen Anne's County on 27 Jan. 1817.

Sumner, Samuel. Mass. —. He served in the Invalids and was paid $20.

Surage, John. Pa. —. He was pensioned.

Surrage, Isaac. —. —. He was disabled by a rupture.

Susee, Francis. Mass. —. He served in the 12th Regiment and was paid $20.

Susong, Andrew. Va. —. His wife, Barbara Susong, was granted £25 in Berkeley County on 20 Apr. 1779 and £120 on 16 May 1780.

Sutherland, George. Pa. Pvt. He was pensioned.

Sutherland, John. Pa. —. He received a $40 gratuity and a $40 annuity in Mercer County 13 Apr. 1838. He was 83 years old in 1840. He received a $40 gratuity 27 Apr. 1844 and a $40 annuity 7 Apr. 1846. The act was repealed 11 Apr. 1848. He died 27 July 1850.

Sutherling, —. S.C. —. His widow, Rachel Sutherling, was receiving a pension in 1791.

Sutphen, Samuel. N.J. —. He was pensioned in Somerset County on 10 Mar. 1836 at the rate of $50 per annum.

Sutphin, John. N.J. —. He served in the New Jersey Levies under Col. Joseph Phillips, Gen. Heard, and Capt. John Anderson. He was wounded in Sept. 1776 by a musket ball in his ankle at Fort Washington and was discharged 1 Dec. 1776. He was allowed 25 shillings per month from that date. He applied in Hunterdon Co., N.J. in 1786.

Sutton, Ephraim. Pa. Sgt. He applied in Fayette County on 18 Jan. 1822. He enlisted in Mar. 1777 at Easton in Capt. Bush's Company in the 9th Pa. Regiment under Col. Richard Butler for three years. He reenlisted in Capt. Walker's Company for the war. He also served in Capt. Christy's Company. He was discharged by Col. Richard Butler after serving upwards of five years. He sold his donation land to Col. Thomas Craig of Northampton County.

Sutton, John. Pa. —. He was awarded relief in York County 14 Mar. 1842 for his Revolutionary service.

Sutton, John. Va. Capt. He entered the service in 1776 in the 1st Regiment as commissary. He went to New York and was appointed paymaster. In 1779 he was charged with misconduct in the management of public funds. He was acquitted by Congress. He was furloughed at Petersburg due to ill health. He was taken prisoner by Tarleton in 1781. He was paroled but never resigned. He received 4,000 acres of bounty land from Virginia. Congress ruled that he was not entitled to commutation pay 19 May 1836.

Sutton, Jonathan. N.J. Lt. He was born and reared in New Jersey. He served under Gen. Washington three or four years. He was at the battles of Trenton and Princeton. He married secondly Mary Campbell 8 Aug. 1809 in York, S.C. He died 19 May 1818. She made an unsuccessful application for a federal pension. His widow was Mary Sutton who had been confined to bed for years and was from York District in 1858. She was paid as late as 1869. Daniel Seehorn aged 79, Philip Williams, Catharine Miller aged 86, and McCasland Wallace age 86 gave testimony in 1859.

Sutton, Robert. N.J. Pvt. He served under Capt. Carlisle and Col. Bowes Reed in the Burlington County militia. His widow, Mary Sutton, received a half-pay pension 30 May 1792.

Sutton, William. Pa. —. He was granted relief in Fayette County 21 June 1839.

Swachamer, Samuel. N.J. —. His widow, Margaret Swachamer, was pensioned in Morris County on 16 Feb. 1855 at the rate of $50 per annum.

Swager, —. Pa. —. His widow, Elizabeth Swager, was granted relief in Lawrence County 19 Apr. 1853.

Swager, George. Pa. —. He was awarded a $40 gratuity and a $40 annuity in Beaver County 28 Mar. 1836. He was 70 years old in 1840. He died 21 May 1846.

Swager, John. Pa. Pvt. He was on the 1791 pension roll. He died 22 July 1807.

Swain, —. Pa. —. His widow, Mary Swain, was awarded a $40 gratuity and a $40 annuity in Philadelphia Co., Pa. 6 Apr. 1830.

Swain, Charles. —. Lt. He served at least fourteen months as a private and lieutenant. He became insane and incapable of attending to business. He died within the last three or four months when Congress granted a pension 27 Jan. 1834. He died insane 11 July 1833. Congress granted his widow, Elizabeth Swain, relief for more than eighteen months of service on 17 May 1836.

Swain, Edward. Pa. Sgt. He was in Philadelphia County on 12 Dec. 1785. He enlisted for one year and was taken prisoner at Fort Washington. He was exchanged and reenlisted in the 6th Pa. Regiment. He was transferred to the Invalids by Col. Humpton. He was disabled by a wound received in the service and was 32 years old. He died 14 June 1790.

Swain, Samuel. N.J. Pvt. He was on the 1791 pension roll at the rate of $60 per annum.

Swan, James. S.C. —. He was wounded in his shoulder in action at Musgrove in Aug. 1780. He was granted an annuity 19 Jan. 1785 in Pendleton District.

Swan, John. Va. —. His wife, Susannah Swan, was granted support in Berkeley County on 16 Sep. 1777. He was in Capt. Francis Willis' Company of Volunteers.

Swan, Leonard. Md. Pvt. He was pensioned at the rate of half-pay of a private 7 Feb. 1817.

Swaney, John. N.Y. —. He was pensioned under the act of 26 Mar. 1794. He was paid in 1796 and 1799.

Swanson, John. Va. Pvt. His widow, Margaret Swanson, was granted £6 support on 14 Apr. 1778, £8 on 13 Oct. 1778, and £12 on 15 Sep. 1779 in Northumberland County. She was pensioned 2 Apr. 1787 at the rate of £10 per annum. He served in the 15th Va. Regiment under Capt. Edwin Hull. Two of their sons also died in the service. She was put on the pension roll 15 Nov. 1785.

Swaringer, John. Pa. —. He was granted relief. His surname may have been Swaringen.

Swart, Adam. —. —. His children sought relief from Congress 25 May 1860, but they offered no record of his service and were not covered by law. Their petition was rejected.

Swartwood, James. Pa. —. He received a $40 gratuity and a $40 annuity in Tioga County, N.Y. 15 June 1836.

Swartwout, Cornelius. N.Y. Pvt. He served in Capt. Abraham Cuddeback's Company under Col. James McClaughrey. He was wounded in his right hip on 13 Oct. 1778 by a musket ball and buck shot from the Indians when he was ordered out on a scout by Lt. Stewart. He was pensioned 6 Mar. 1787. He lived in Ulster Co., N.Y. on 4 May 1789 and later in Sullivan County. He was on the 1813 pension list.

Swartz, Peter. Pa. —. He was on the 1813 pension list. He was awarded a $40 gratuity and a $40 annuity in Northumberland County on 7 Mar. 1821. He also appeared as Peter Schwartz.

Swartz, Philip. Pa. —. He was awarded a $40 gratuity and a $40 annuity in Schuylkill Co., Pa. 15 Apr. 1835.

Swearingen, Samuel. Va. Pvt. He died 17 Oct. 1801. He was on the 1813 pension list.

Sweat, —. S.C. —. His widow, Lydia Sweat, was receiving a pension in 1791.

Sweat, Cicero. Mass. —. He served in the 6th Regiment. His widow was paid $20.

Sweedy, Thomas. Pa. Gunner. He served in the artillery under Col. Thomas Proctor. He was wounded by a musket ball through his right leg in action with the Indians at Newton on 29 Aug. 1779. He was wounded a second time at Bull's Ferry on the North River 1 July 1780 by a musket ball through his right thigh. The ball lodged in his left thigh. He was from Chester County.

Sweeney, Isaac. Pa. Capt. His heirs were awarded 500 acres of donation land in trust to James Sweeney 29 Mar. 1813.

Sweeney, William. Va. —. He was wounded in the service. He died in New Kent County on 25 June 1785. He was stricken from the pension list on 9 Jan. 1786 due to death. He also appeared as William Swene.

Sweeny, Hugh. Pa. —. He applied in Cumberland County in Feb. 1814. He was a pauper in the poor house. He died 13 Dec. 1823.

Sweeny, James. Pa. Pvt. He was transferred to New Jersey 4 Sep. 1795. His pension was $45 per annum. He was on the 1815 pension list.

Sweeny, Joseph. Pa. —. He was awarded a $40 gratuity and a $40 annuity in Lycoming County 1 Apr. 1836. He died 3 May 1849.

Sweet, —. S.C. —. His widow was Sarah Sweet. There were children in 1791.

Sweet, Godfrey. N.Y. Pvt. He served in Col. Henry Van Rensselaer's militia from Albany County. He was wounded in the right hand and wrist on 7 July 1777 at Fort Ann. He was pensioned in Mar. 1795 at half-pay. He resided at Stephentown, N.Y. in 1796. He was on the 1813 pension list.

Sweet, Jabez. Mass. Pvt. He served in the 15th Regiment and was from Ipswich. His widow, Hannah Sweet, was paid $50.

Swenk, —. Pa. —. His widow, Margaret Swenk, of Lancaster, Pa. was awarded a $40 gratuity and a $40 annuity for his Revolutionary service on 21 June 1839. She died 12 Apr. 1841.

Swesey, Peter. Pa. —. He was granted relief in Beaver County 21 Mar. 1840.

Swett, Joshua. Me. —. He was from Gorham. He was paid $50 under the resolve of 1836.

Swetzer, George. Pa. —. He was awarded a $40 gratuity and a $40 annuity in York Co., Pa. 1 Mar. 1833. He also appeared as George Switzer. He was 77 years old in 1840.

Swift, James. N.J. Pvt. He was 59 years old. He was on the 1791 pension roll. He served in the 3rd N.J. Regiment. He lived in Essex County. He was on the 1813 pension list.

Swift, John. N.Y. Pvt. He served in Capt. Bell's Company under Col. Philip Van Courtland. He was disabled by blindness and lameness. He lived in Canaan, Columbia Co., N.Y. on 17 Apr. 1789. He died 23 Dec. 1807.

Swilling, George. S.C. —. He served under Capt. Benjamin Tutt and Col. Huger. Matthew Barrett served with him. He was a cripple and unable to support himself. He was pensioned from

Pendleton District 30 Nov. 1824. He was paid as late as 1826. He had served 15 months. He married Martha ----- before 1 Jan. 1794. She died in Georgia. Congress ruled that she was entitled to a pension and granted the sum due her to her children 2 March 1860.

Swinney, John. N.C. Pvt. He applied in Caswell County in 1785. He was wounded in the service. He was aged 23 in 1785. He also appeared as John Swaney. He appeared as John Swenney on the 1791 list.

Swir, William. Pa. —. He was pensioned.

Swords, —. Pa. —. His widow, Jemima Swords, was awarded a $40 gratuity and a $40 annuity in Fayette County 31 Mar. 1836. She died 25 Sep. 1845.

Swords, John. S.C. —. He was born and reared in York District. He served under Lt. Montgomery in the 6th S.C. Line for three years. He was taken prisoner after two and half years at the siege of Savannah but managed to escape and rejoin the army. He was under Capt. Carson and Lt. Pickens in the militia. He was about 79 years old when he applied from Pendleton District. David Rowling served with him He was pensioned 12 Dec. 1826. He died 28 Sep. 1834. His widow, Eleanor Swords, died 3 May 1841. His heirs sought their arrearage, but they were not entitled to same.

Swoyer, Nicholas. Pa. —. He was awarded a $40 gratuity and a $40 annuity in Harrisburg, Pa. 21 Dec. 1827.

Syars, —. Va. —. His wife, Sarah Syars, was granted £10 support in Fauquier Co., Va. in June 1778 while he was absent in the service.

Sybert, Adam. Pa. Pvt. He served in the Congress Regiment. He was wounded by two musket balls in both legs at the storming of one of Cornwallis's redoubts in Virginia just before his capture. He was mustered in Hazen's Regiment, but the date of enlistment was not known. He resided in Philadelphia, Pa. in 1794.

Sybert, Charles Frederick. Va. —. He died in the service. His widow, Mary Sybert, and her one helpless child were granted £30 support in Rockingham Co., Va. 22 Mar. 1779.

Sykes, —. Va. —. Jonas Sykes was granted £10 relief while his two sons were away in Continental service 11 Dec. 1777 in Lunenburg Co., Va.

Sykes, Jesse. Va. —. He entered the service in 1781 for six months. His brother-in-law was the minister, Beverley Booth, who was the father of Daniel Booth. Congress granted Jesse Sykes a pension 17 Feb. 1835. He was from Prince George Co., Va.

Sylvious, Henry. Pa. —. He was awarded a $40 gratuity and a $40 annuity in Northampton Co., Pa. 18 Feb. 1834.

Symms, William. N.H. Pvt. He served under Capt. Peter Kimball in the militia. He was wounded by a musket ball which fractured his right arm bone on 16 Aug. 1777 in battle near Bennington. He resided at Washington, Me. in 1794. He was on the 1813 pension list. He was from Concord.

Sype, Christopher. Pa. —. He was awarded a $40 gratuity and a $40 annuity in York Co., Pa. 12 Apr. 1828.

Sype, Tobias. Pa. —. He was awarded a $40 gratuity and a $40 annuity in York County in Apr. 1833. He was dead by July 1839.

Taber, Philip. —. —. He served from June 1779 to June 1780. He sought his pension from 8 Apr. 1818 to 8 Mar. 1830, but Congress ruled that he had no claim to arrearage on 14 June 1850.

Taber, Philip. Mass. Pvt. He was on the 1813 pension list. He died 23 Jan. 1826 in Bristol Co., Mass.

Tabor, Noel. R.I. Pvt. He was on the 1791 pension roll.

Tacker, John. Pa. Pvt. He was in Philadelphia County on 12 Dec. 1785. He was in the Invalids and was discharged unfit for duty 12 Nov. 1782 on account of wounds received in the service. He was 45 years old. He also appeared as John Sacker.

Tacket, Peter. Va. —. His wife, Margaret Tacket, and three children were furnished £10 support in Frederick Co., Va. on 1 Sep. 1778. He served in the 2nd State Regiment.

Tackett, Benoni. Va. —. He died in 1777. His widow, Lydia Tackett, was in Prince George County when she was pensioned 21 Jan. 1809 at the rate of $40 per annum with $10 immediate relief. She died 10 Nov. 1821, and Elizabeth Tackett was her executrix.

Taft, Jonathan. Mass. Pvt. He served in the 2nd Regiment under Col. Ebenezer Sprout and Capt. Seth Drew. He was disabled by a fall from his horse which disabled his right shoulder. He lived in Mendon, Mass. He was pensioned 4 Jan. 1783. He was 39 years old in 1786. He was paid $20 by the Commonwealth. He was on the 1813 pension list.

Tager, Jacob. —. —. His application was not approved.

Tagert, John. Pa. —. He was awarded a $40 gratuity and a $40 annuity in Belmont Co., Ohio 11 Apr. 1825.

Taggart, Patrick. Pa. Sgt. He was in Philadelphia County on 2 July 1788. He served in the 9th Pa. Regiment and was afflicted with a rupture and a paralytic disorder contracted during service in the Continental Army while he was building huts at Morristown. He was under Caleb North. He was 30 years old. He was on the 1813 pension list. He died 15 Nov. 1825. He also appeared as Patrick Tegart.

Taggart, William. N.H. Ens. He was wounded in the shoulder on 17 Aug. 1777 at Hubbardstown in the retreat from Ticonderoga; in 1778 he lost the sight of his eye due to smallpox. He was in the 2nd Regiment. He lived in Hillsborough Co., N.H. in 1792. He was commissioned 8 Nov. 1776 and resigned 6 Feb. 1780. He was granted half a pension 20 Apr. 1796. He was on the 1813 pension list. He died in Mar. 1830.

Talbert, John. Pa. Pvt. He was pensioned.

Talbert, John. S.C. —. He was wounded. He was granted an annuity 22 Sep. 1779.

Talbot, David. Mass. —. He served in the 4th Regiment and was from Canton. He was paid $20.

Talbot, Silas. N.Y. Lt. Col. He was appointed a major in Oct. 1777. He was wounded in his left thigh, and the ball lodged in his groin. He was also wounded in his left wrist on 14 Sep. 1778 at the evacuation of Fort Mifflin on Mud Island in the Delaware River. He was promoted to Lt. Col. He was appointed to take command of the sloop *Argo*. He was wounded in battle with the British privateer, the *Dragoon*, and the brigantine, *Hannah*. He was 35 years old on 11 Feb. 1786. He lived in Johnstown, Montgomery Co., N.Y. on 6 May 1789. He was on the 1813 pension list. He died 30 June 1813.

Taler, —. Va. —. His widow, Susannah Taler, was allowed £25 for her support and that of her young children in Augusta Co., Va. 19 May 1778 as the wife of a Revolutionary soldier.

Talford, —. Va. —. He was killed in Continental service. His mother, Marianne Talford, and her five children were granted support in Prince William Co., Va. on 7 Dec. 1778.

Taliafero, Richard. Va. Capt. He was a recruiting officer in 1776 or 1777. He was with the barrack guards in 1779 and was discharged in 1781. Congress rejected a claim for half-pay 4 June 1860.

Tallman, Peleg. Mass. Yeoman. He was paid $51 as a pension for the period Sep. 1805 to Sep. 1806. He was in privateer and naval service. In June 1780 he was on the *Trumbull* under Capt. James Nicholson in the engagement with the English ship *Wait*. He acted as captain and was wounded by having his left arm shot away by the enemy's gun. He received a ball in the left side of his neck which passed through his shoulder blade and the upper part of his body. He had a third wound of grape shot in his thigh. He sought a pension as a midshipman. He was from Tiverton, R.I. He applied for relief from Congress 12 Feb. 1841.

Tallman, Samuel. R.I. Pvt. He was pensioned in 1788. He died 5 Sep. 1807 in Providence Co., R.I.

Tally, —. Va. —. His wife was granted £180 for necessaries in Halifax Co.,Va. on 21 June 1781.

Talmadge, Stephen. N.Y. —. He enlisted and served under Capt. John Davis and Col. Henry B. Livingstone in Apr. 1776 at Bridge Hampton, Suffolk Co., N.Y. for nine months. He served two months under Gen. George Clinton until discharged in Mar. 1777. He was 75 years old. Congress granted him a pension 4 Feb. 1836.

Talmage, Daniel. N.J. Pvt. He served in the Sussex County militia. He was killed in battle 22 July 1779 in Orange Co., N.Y. He married Lois Allen 21 Dec. 1766. She married secondly John Herriman. She received a half-pay pension in Sussex County 27 Nov. 1787.

Tankard, John. Va. Surgeon. He served in the Virginia Line. He died 24 Apr. 1836. His widow died 7 Feb. 1845. His heirs sought his unpaid pension in the amount of $3,083.33 from 5 Mar. 1831 to 24 Apr. 1836. Congress approved the petition from his son, John W. Tankard on his own behalf and of his siblings, Philip B.Tankard, Mary Tankard, Susan Tankard, besides several grand-children on 21 Jan. 1911.

Tannahill, James. Pa. Pvt. He was wounded in his breast on the expedition against the Sandusky Indians under Col William Crawford and Capt. Thomas Rankin in May or June 1782. David Williamson commanded the brigade. He was 40 years old in 1787. He was on the 1791 pension list. He lived in Beaver County. He was on the 1813 pension list. He also appeared as James Tannehill and James Tawnhill. He was from Washington County.

Tannehill, Adamson. Md. Capt. His widow, Agnes M. Tannehill, was pensioned at the rate of half-pay of a captain in Allegany Co., Pa. 8 Mar. 1826. She died 6 Aug. 1828.

Tanner, Jacob. Va. —. His widow, Dorothy Tanner, was in Madison County on 26 Oct. 1793. He died in the service. She was pensioned at the rate of £8 per annum and received £12 relief on 18 Dec. 1794. She was in Shenandoah County in 1807.

Tanner, John. N.H. Master's Mate. He served on the frigate *Raleigh* under Thomas Thomson as quartermaster from 26 Mar. 1777 to 1 May 1778. He served on the *Hampden* under Thomas Pickering as master's mate. He lost his left arm and was much wounded on 8 Mar. 1779. He served under Capt. Titus Salter on the same ship in July 1779 and was taken prisoner. He returned in 1780 and served on the *General Washington* under Charles Welden bound from Martinique. The ship was torn apart in a hurricane on 11 Mar. He was deprived of his health and sought relief on 1 Nov. 1797. He was from Rochester.

Tanner, Joseph. R.I. Pvt. He had a bad rupture in the groin caused by building huts at Morristown, N.J. in Dec. 1779. He served under Col. Jeremiah Olney. He was aged 30 when he applied 23 Feb. 1786. He resided in Providence Co., R.I.

Tanner, Josiah. S.C. Lt. He was wounded. He was granted an annuity 19 Jan. 1785. His annuity of 1 Feb. 1787 was for himself and three children. He was from Spartanburg District.

Tanner, William. R.I. Pvt. He was on the 1791 pension roll. He transferred to New York 4 Mar. 1793. He was on the 1813 pension list.

Tantlinger, Henry. Pa. Pvt. His heirs were in Bedford County on 14 Feb. 1786. He was in the Bedford County militia under Capt. John Boyd. He was killed in action by Indians at Frankstown 3 June 1781. He left a widow, Catherine Tantlinger, and five children. Edward Rose was appointed guardian. The son, Henry Tantlinger, was under 14. Other children were Nelly Tantlinger and John Tantlinger whose guardian was John Cessna.

Tapp, Vincent. Va. Sgt. He served in the 12ᵗʰ Va. Regiment and lived in Augusta County. He was on the 1813 pension list.

Tapp, William. Va. —. He was disabled at the battle of Guilford. He was on the 1785 pension roll.

Tappan, Michael. Me. —. He was born in Manchester, Mass. and died 5 Aug. 1831. His widow was Hannah Tappan from Gardiner. She was paid $50 under the resolve of 1836.

Tapper, William. S.C. —. He served in the Continental Line and was disabled. He was granted an annuity 21 Aug. 1786.

Tarball, William. Conn. Capt. He served in the 4ᵗʰ Conn. Regiment in Capt. John McGriegier's Company under Col. John Durkee. He was wounded at Germantown by a musket shot in his thigh. Thomas Gray was surgeon of the regiment. He was transferred to the Invalids. He was granted £60 value of confiscated lands of the estate of William Brown in lieu of a pension on 2 Oct. 1784. He was 40 years old when he was pensioned on 22 Sep. 1788. He lived in Colchester, Conn. He was on the 1813 pension list. He was a tailor. He also appeared as William Tarbell.

Tarbell, William. Mass. Pvt. He served in the 4ᵗʰ Regiment and was from Groton.

Tarbox, Solomon. Conn. Lt. He served under Col. Samuel Wyllis and died 20 Dec. 1777 in the service. His brother, Roswell Tarbox, sought a pension. Congress denied his claim 3 Mar. 1851 because collateral relatives were not so entitled.

Tarbutton, —. Md. —. He was a pensioner and died Wednesday 30 May 1781. His widow, Rachel Tarbutton, lived in Queen Anne's County. Her brother's son was Richard Ratcliffe, and her son was William Tarbutton. Rachel's brother left the state several years ago and left his child in a helpless condition. Her husband took him to raise. Her husband was pensioned to his death leaving her with four children one of whom was disabled. Richard Ratcliffe was her only means of support.

Tarr, David. Mass. —. He served in the 8ᵗʰ Regiment and was paid $20.

Tarr, David. Mass. Pvt. He served in Scammel's Regiment and was from Danvers. His widow, Abigail Tarr, was paid $50.

Tarrance, Hugh. Pa. —. He was granted a $40 gratuity as a Revolutionary soldier in Montgomery County 13 Feb. 1840.

Tash, Oxford. N.H. Pvt. He died in 1810.

Tasker, Matthew. —. —. He was from Boston, Mass. His application was unaccompanied by proof so Congress rejected his application 17 June 1846.

Tasker, Richard R.. Md. Pvt. He was pensioned at the rate of half-pay of a private in Allegany Co. on 12 Feb. 1820.

Tate, Adam. Pa. —. He was awarded a $40 gratuity and a $40 annuity in Lancaster Co., Pa. 15 Mar. 1826. His widow, Jane Tate, was awarded a $40 gratuity and a $40 annuity on 13 Apr. 1827.

Tate, Edmund. Va. Capt. He was at Cowpens, Camden, and Guilford Court House. Congress rejected the claim of his widow, Lucy Tate, for relief 8 Apr. 1856. His engagement was under civil contract.

Tate, Edward. Pa. Pvt. He was in Northumberland County on 28 Feb. 1787. He was in the militia and was wounded by a rifle ball through his body and another through his left thigh by Indians at Buffalo Township in said county on 6 May 1782 in an attempt to prevent cattle from being seized. He served under Capt. George Overmire.

Tatnel, Robert. Pa. Capt. He was granted relief.

Tatum, Thomas. S.C. Pvt. He served in Capt. Isaac Ross's Company under Col. Charles S. Middleton.

Margaret Tatum and Christopher Tatum sought his back pay. His administrator, William Paulling, was paid $1,418.78 for him and Jesse Duesto on 20 Dec. 1810.

Taylor, —. Pa. —. His widow, Mary Taylor, was awarded a $40 gratuity and a $40 annuity in Berks Co., Pa. 8 Apr. 1826.

Taylor, —. Pa. —. His widow, Mary Taylor, was awarded a $40 gratuity in York County 13 Mar. 1815.

Taylor, —. Pa. —. His widow, Elizabeth Taylor, was awarded a $40 gratuity and a $40 annuity 28 Mar. 1836. She resided in New York.

Taylor, —. S.C. —. His widow, Sarah Taylor, was on the roll in 1791.

Taylor, —. Va. —. He died in Continental service 15 Dec. 1778. His widow was Sarah Taylor.

Taylor, Andrew. S.C. Pvt. He was killed in Mar. 1780 at Guilford. His widow, Lucy Mancell, was on the roll in 1802.

Taylor, Arthur. S.C. —. He served in Capt. Robert Maxwell's Company of Rangers. He was killed in the service on 8 Dec. 1781. He left a widow who was pregnant and five small children. His widow, Selah Taylor, was from Pendleton District and was pensioned at the rate of $22 per annum on 19 Dec. 1805. She was paid $385.56 on 20 Dec. 1806. A few years later John Barrett proved that Arthur Taylor lived in Rutherford Co., N.C. at the time of the war and was killed in his house for horse stealing by Indians or an Indian trader. Leonard Clayborne and William Grant swore that he was a Tory. Millington Ledbetter, a son-in-law, testified that Celah Taylor told him that her husband had been killed by some unknown person but supposed to be an Indian trader by the name of Mahafee. Celah Taylor conspired with Thomas Haselip in exchange for half of the money.

Taylor, Asa. Conn. Pvt. He served in Capt. John Isham's Company under Col. John Chester in the Conn. Line. He was wounded in the right foot by a cannon ball at White Plains on 28 Oct. 1776. He was discharged 25 Dec. 1776. He lived in Washington Co., N.Y. on 2 May 1789. He was on the 1813 pension list. He also appeared as Asa Tyler.

Taylor, Augustus. Conn. Lt. He served under Col. Swift from 1 June 1777 to 26 July 1778 when he was appointed regimental paymaster. He was discharged 25 June 178-. He died in 1816. His widow was Huldah Taylor. Congress granted her a pension 22 Dec. 1837 from 4 Mar. 1831.

Taylor, Benjamin. Va. Pvt. He was pensioned at the rate of £15 per annum on 20 Dec. 1792. He was in Fauquier County on 26 Mar. 1793. He was in the Illinois Regiment and was disabled in an engagement with the Indians in 1781 in Kentucky.

Taylor, Benoni. R.I. —. He was on the roll in 1788.

Taylor, Charles. Va. Surgeon. He served as surgeon's mate in the 2nd Virginia Regiment under Col. Francis Taylor. In Oct. 1779 he was appointed surgeon in the regiment of guards until disbanded. His heirs were allowed commutation 12 Apr. 1836. He was not eligible for Virginia bounty land so his heirs sought same from Congress 9 Mar. 1842.

Taylor, Chase. N.H. Capt. He was from Sanborn, Stafford County in 1787. He was in Col. Stickney's Regiment and was wounded by a musket ball in the thigh which fractured his bone at the battle of Bennington on 16 Aug. 1777. Josiah Chase was the regimental surgeon. He was aged 49 in 1787. His rank was given as lieutenant on the 1791 roll. He also lost his gun and cartouch box.

Taylor, Christopher. —. Surgeon's Mate. Congress refused the heirs commutation 24 June 1834.

Taylor, Eliphalet. N.H. Pvt. He served under Col. Jackson in Capt. Keith's Company. He had a large rupture in the scrotum occasioned by rolling a large log in obedience to the command of his lieutenant in July 1778. He lived in Langdon, N.H. in 1795. He was granted one-third of a pension 20 Apr. 1796. He transferred to Suffolk Co., Mass. 4 Sep. 1802. He was on the 1813 pension list.

Taylor, Ephraim. Conn. Pvt. He lost the use of his hand. He was pensioned 1 Sep. 1782. He was on the 1791 pension roll.

Taylor, Ephraim. Mass. Pvt. He was on the 1813 pension list.

Taylor, Francis. Va. Col. He was granted half-pay for life on 4 June 1783. His regiment was to guard the convention prisoners and served until 17 June 1781 when the prisoners were removed from Winchester and he became supernumerary. Robert Taylor and the other heirs received his commutation 22 Dec. 1837.

Taylor, George. Mass. —. He served in the 7th Regiment and was paid $20.

Taylor, George. N.J. —. He was pensioned in Cumberland County on 15 Mar. 1837 at the rate of $60 per annum.

Taylor, George. Va. —. His widow, Sarah Taylor, and three small children were granted support in Cumberland Co., Va. 25 Aug. 1777. He died in Continental service.

Taylor, Henry. N.C. —. His widow, Mary Ann Taylor, applied in Brunswick County in 1797. He was in militia service.

Taylor, Isaac. —. —. His widow, Margaret Taylor of Putnam Co., Tenn. sought his arrearage on 23 Feb. 1857 from Congress.

Taylor, Jacob. Md. —. He served in the militia in 1781 and was at Yorktown. He was discharged 3 Dec. 1781. He married in Mar. 1782 Tripphany ------. He died in March 1792. His widow married secondly John Campbell in 1827, and he died in 1836. Her petition for relief was rejected by Congress 19 Jan. 1848 because the affidavits did not have the weight of evidence and there was no proof of marriage.

Taylor, James. —. —. Congress awarded his widow, Margaret Taylor, of Putnam Co., Tenn. the arrearage of her pension from 4 Mar. 1818 to 3 Feb. 1853 on 23 Feb. 1857.

Taylor, James. Mass. —. He delivered his papers to his Congressman, Mr. Bates, in 1830. Bates did not present the papers to the Secretary of War until 4 Jan. 1832. Congress granted him a pension from 18 Mar. 1830 to 4 Jan. 1832.

Taylor, James. Va. —. His wife, Elizabeth Taylor, and children were furnished 5 barrels of corn and 250 pounds of pork in Essex Co., Va. on 17 June 1782.

Taylor, James. Va. Pvt. He was in King and Queen County on 29 Nov. 1787. He was continued on the pension list at the rate of £12 per annum on 3 Dec. 1787. He was an eighteen month soldier. His arm was dislocated in the service. Thomas Coleman deposed that he thought Taylor had a discharge from Col. Davis and Capt. Crane. He was in a detachment under Col. Gaskins. Later he was in Patrick County. He was on the 1813 pension list. He later transferred to West Tennessee.

Taylor, James. Va. —. His wife, Jane Taylor, was granted £10 support in Berkeley County on 18 Nov. 1778.

Taylor, James. Va. Lt. He served as private, corporal, and sergeant from 1775 to 1778 when he was appointed lieutenant in the Virginia State Garrison under Lt. Col. Charles Porterfield. He was furloughed for six weeks in Dec. 1779 and became supernumerary when his unit was reduced by act of the legislature in 1781. He acted as brigade major under Gen. Lawson at Guilford, N.C. He was taken prisoner at Petersburg, Va. in Apr. or May 1781 and held until the surrender of Cornwallis 19 Oct. 1781. He was pensioned under the act of 1818. His heirs sought his half-pay from 5 Feb. 1781 when he became supernumerary to the time of his death 15 May 1834. Congress approved their petition 30 Mar. 1860. They were from Prince Edward Co., Va.

Taylor, Jesse. Va. Sgt. He served upwards of two years. He married in Mecklenburg Co., Va. His widow, Polly Taylor, received a pension from Congress 22 Mar. 1848.

Taylor, John. —. —. His five years' full pay commutation was paid to his heirs 30 June 1834.

Taylor, John. Md. Pvt. He was pensioned at the rate of half-pay of a private in Anne Arundel County 8 Feb. 1834. His arrearage was paid to his widow, Sidney Taylor, 8 Mar. 1836. She was pensioned at the same rate 1 Apr. 1836.

Taylor, John. Mass. Sgt. He served in the 15th Regiment under Col. Bigelow. He was ruptured in the left side in consequence of a wound and injured in his knee at West Point in May 1780 by some timber falling on him. He resided in Marlborough, Mass. in 1792 and in Boxley, Mass. in 1795. He enlisted 4 Sep. 1779 for nine months. His widow, Rebecca Taylor, was from Southborough when she was paid $50 by the Commonwealth.

Taylor, John. N.Y. Pvt. He was disabled by a musket ball in the small of his back which fractured his back bone at Closter, Bergen Co., N.J. in 1779. He served in the Orange County Regiment under Col. Hathorn in Capt. Jacob Onderdonk's Company. He lived in New York City, N.Y. on 23 June 1788. He was aged 36 years on 5 Feb. 1786. He died 10 Mar. 1809. He was, however, on the 1813 pension list.

Taylor, John. Pa. Pvt. He was in Cumberland County on 23 Feb. 1786. He served in the Cumberland County militia and received several wounds at Crooked Billet in May 1778. He was a shoemaker and was 60 years old. He was on the 1813 pension list.

Taylor, John. Pa. —. He served under Capt. Timothy Jayne in the Flying Camp and was taken prisoner at the surrender of Fort Washington 22 Dec. 1780. He was incapable of getting a livelihood and was pensioned 25 Mar. 1781 in Northampton County.

Taylor, John. Pa. —. He was awarded a $40 gratuity and a $40 annuity in Franklin Co., Pa. 7 Mar. 1829. He died 10 May 1831.

Taylor, John. S.C. —. His application was rejected 18 Dec. 1849 because he did not serve the minimum of six months.

Taylor, John. Va. Lt. He served in the infantry under Col. Francis Taylor from the commencement of the war to the spring of 1781 when he became supernumerary. He received a 200-acre bounty land warrant from the U.S. His son, John M. Taylor, received his five years' half-pay 30 June 1834.

Taylor, John Jarman. Md. Pvt. He was pensioned.

Taylor, Joseph. Pa. —. He was awarded a $40 gratuity and a $40 annuity 27 Mar. 1837 in Fayette County. He was 65 years old in 1840. He died 18 Aug. 1849.

Taylor, Joseph Spencer. R.I. Assistant Commissary of Issues. He had disorders contracted from exposure and great exertions to save public property lying on the beach at the storming of Rhode Island by Gen. Sullivan in 1778. He resided in East Greenwich, R.I. in 1794.

Taylor, Lewis. Mass. Sgt. He served in the 8th Regiment and was from Middlefield. He was paid $20.

Taylor, Matthew. Pa. Cornet. He entered the service in 1778 at Lancaster, Pa. in the cavalry. He resigned in 1780. He was pensioned in 1818 and died six months later. His widow, Mary Taylor, was 75 years old. She offered no proof of marriage or identity. Congress rejected her claim 10 Mar. 1838.

Taylor, Nathan. N.H. Lt. He served in Maj. Whitcomb's Rangers. He was pensioned at the rate of $10 per month from 19 Feb. 1808. He lived in Stafford County. He was on the 1813 pension list.

Taylor, Noah. Mass. Pvt. He served in Capt. Daniel Merrill's Company under Col. Samuel Brewer. He lost his left leg and thigh. He was awarded £30.19.5 to discharge his doctor's bill. He was pensioned at half-pay from 1 Jan. 1780 on 4 Oct. 1781. He was 27 years old in 1788. He was on the 1813 pension list. He transferred to York Co., Me. 4 Mar. 1826.

Taylor, Philip. Pa. —.His widow, Elizabeth Taylor, received a $40 gratuity and a $40 annuity 29 Mar. 1860.

Taylor, Richard. Md. Pvt. He was pensioned at the rate of half-pay of a private 23 Jan. 1816.

Taylor, Richard. Va. Capt. He was in Caroline County on 5 Jan. 1786. He was captain of the *Tartar* and was wounded in the thigh. He was pensioned 5 Jan. 1786 at the rate of half-pay. On 28 July 1789 his pension was replaced with his former allowance. He was continued on the roll on 4 Feb. 1791. On 15 Dec. 1792 his pension was increased to £120 per annum. He was in Jefferson Co., Ky. in 1795, Franklin Co., Ky. in 1811, and Oldham Co., Ky. in 1825. He died 30 Aug. 1825. Richard Taylor was administrator with the will annexed.

Taylor, Richard. Va. Lt. Col. He served in the 6th Regiment from 1 Nov. 1776 to the close of the war. He received his full settlement. Congress rejected the claim of his administrator, Nathaniel Reddick, on 29 Jan. 1855.

Taylor, Robert. Md. —. He was a wounded soldier in distress from the Southward and was paid £5 on 23 Mar. 1782.

Taylor, Robert. Va. —. His wife, Rebecca Taylor, was granted £25 support 18 May 1779.

Taylor, Samuel. Mass. Sgt. He served in the 14th Regiment and was from Yarmouth. He was paid $50.

Taylor, Samuel. N.J. Corp. He served under Col. Allison in the militia. He had an ulcerous leg occasioned by a wound from a cannon ball on 6 Oct. 1777 at Fort Montgomery. He lived in Elizabethtown, N.J. in 1795. He was pensioned at the rate of $40 per annum. He was on the 1813 pension list.

Taylor, Shubal. Mass. Pvt. He served under Col. Bradford and was disabled in the service in 1778. He was disabled by the loss of his right arm and by rheumatism. He was pensioned at half-pay from 15 May 1780 on 23 Sep. 1782. He was 23 years old in 1786. He died 24 July 1790.

Taylor, Thomas. N.J. —. His widow, Hannah Taylor, was pensioned in Monmouth County on 25 Feb. 1847 at the rate of $50 per annum.

Taylor, Thomas. Pa. —. He was pensioned 20 Mar. 1838 in Armstrong County. He was 78 years old in 1840. His widow, Martha Taylor, was awarded a $40 annuity 6 May 1850 for his Revolutionary service.

Taylor, Thomas B. Va. —. He was pensioned in Norfolk County 13 Jan. 1813 at the rate of $60 per annum and $100 immediate relief. He had been wounded and taken prisoner at Germantown. He was in great distress since his house had been blown down and all his furniture destroyed. He died 4 July 1813. Administration of his estate was granted to his son, Burton Taylor, on 5 Mar. 1814.

Taylor, Thornton. Va. Ens. He served in the Virginia Line on Continental Establishment. His five years' full pay commutation was paid to his legal representative, Woodford Taylor the administrator of his estate, 2 July 1836.

Taylor, William. Pa. —. He was pensioned in Center County 27 Mar. 1832. He was 74 years old in 1840. He died 2 Apr. 1845.

Taylor, William. Va. Maj. He was pensioned in 1818, stricken in 1820, and restored in 1824. His widow, Elizabeth Taylor, asked to be paid from 1 May 1820 to 23 Nov. 1824. Congress saw no reason to interfere and recommended that she should apply to the proper department on 11 May

1846.

Teagart, William. Pa. Pvt. He applied 22 Nov. 1788. He served in the 8th Pa. Regiment and was wounded 17 Apr. 1779 while he was loading a field piece. The gun went off, and he lost both of his arms. His left eye was much hurt. He had no family. He was at the battles of Monmouth and German-town and was under Capt. John Clark and Col. Daniel Brodhead.

Teague, Josiah. S.C. —. He was killed at Savannah in Sep. 1779. His widow, Elizabeth Teague, was from Georgetown District in 1802.

Teas, William. Va. Cornet. He served in the cavalry under Col. William Washington. He was severely wounded. He was at Guilford, Cowpens, and Eutaw Springs and served to the end of the war. His five years' full pay commutation was paid to his heirs 30 June 1834. His administrator was Charles Perrow. He married in July 1797 or 1798 and died in Mar. 1824. His widow, Sarah Teas, sought a pension. She indicated that all of his children were deceased. Congress declined to grant her a pension and urged her to apply in the normal manner 3 Mar. 1851.

Teeder, Michael. Pa. Pvt. He was in Philadelphia County 12 June 1786. He served in the 5th Pa. Regiment in Capt. Smith's Company under Col. Francis Johnston and lost the use of his feet due to the severity of the weather doing duty under Col. Morgan. He was discharged 15 Sep. 1779. He was 38 years old. He also appeared as Michael Tetter.

Teel, John. Pa. —. His heirs were paid $375 for his right to donation land in Beaver Co., Pa. 3 Mar. 1826.

Teem, Adam. S.C. —. He was one of the ten-month men. He applied 9 April 1823. He was paid as late as 1832.

Tees, John. Pa. —. His widow, Barbara Tees, was awarded a $40 gratuity and a $40 annuity in Huntingdon Co., Pa. 1 Apr. 1825.

Telker, George. Pa. Pvt. His widow, Agnes Telker, was in Philadelphia County on 11 Mar. 1782. He served in Capt. Leech's Company under Col. McVeagh in the Philadelphia County militia. He was killed at Germantown in Oct. 1777. He left one daughter. He also appeared as George Delker.

Teem, Adam. S.C. —. He was from Richland District and was pensioned 4 Dec. 1823. He was 73 years of age. He was paid as late as 1832.

Temple, —. —. —. His widow, Tabitha Temple, had her application for a pension rejected by Congress because it was wholly unsubstantiated by proof.

Temple, Ephraim. Mass. Pvt. He served in the 10th Regiment and was from Gardner. He was paid $50.

Temple, James. S.C. —. He served under Capt. John Ledbetter, Gen. Weatherford, Capt. Green, and Gen. Sumter for five years. He was wounded four times in his head, once in his neck, once in his shoulder, once in his face, and once in his arm. His arm and shoulder were useless. He had four small grandchildren and two daughters. Matthew Baley served with him. He was from Edgefield District and was pensioned 2 Dec. 1824 effective from 1 Mar. 1823. He died 7 Sep. 1829. Lewis Holmes, administrator of his estate, sought his arrearage. His widow, Rachel Temple, applied for a pension 9 Oct. 1830.

Temple, John. Va. —. He served in the 6th Virginia Regiment under Capt. Cabell. He lost an eye in Continental service. He was awarded a £30 gratuity on 20 May 1778.

Temple, Josiah. Mass. Pvt. He was pensioned 8 Apr. 1809. He lived in Suffolk Co., Mass. He was on the 1813 pension list.

Temple, Stephen. Mass. Pvt. He served in the 1st Regiment and was from Cheshire. He was paid $50.

Temple, Thomas. N.Y. Pvt. He served under Col. Philip Van Cortlandt. His widow, Elizabeth Temple, received his half-pay pension. He also appeared as Thomas Templer.

Ten Eyck, Henry. N.Y. Capt. He was pensioned 25 Apr. 1808 at the rate of $15 per month from 21 Nov. 1807. He was on the 1813 pension list.

Ten Eyck, John. N.J. Lt. He was wounded near Millstone on 15 June 1777 and died 17 June 1777. His widow, Elizabeth Ten Eyck married secondly Andrew Ten Eyck 6 Jan. 1778. She was allowed a half-pay pension for six months and twenty days in Somerset County 23 June 1785.

Tennant, Alexander. S.C. —. He served under Capt. Hugh Knox and Gen. Henderson. He was at Four Holes, Orangeburg, and Edistoe. Hugh Ross served with him. He was from Fairfield District and was pensioned 16 Dec. 1823. He also appeared as Alexander Tenant. He was paid as late as 1834. He died 8 May 1835. His widow was Martha Tennant. They were married in Ireland and came to America a few years before the Revolution. She was between 80 and 90 years old in 1840. Their eldest daughter married James Swan in 1793.

Tennant, William. Pa. —. He was enlisted into the 5th Regiment with Lt. Griffith. He was at the battles of Couches Bridge, Brandywine, Germantown, and Monmouth. He was under Gen. Wayne and Col. Stewart at Stoney Point where he was wounded. He was under Capt. Thomas Boude at the time of his discharge. He was awarded a $40 gratuity 31 Mar. 1812 in Lancaster County.

Tennis, —. N.Y. —. Mary Tennis was granted support during the war.

Tenure, Michael. N.Y. —. He served under Capt. Henrick Tenure and Col. Hays. In July 1776 two or three ships sailed up the Hudson river and anchored at Tappan. He served one week in every four guarding along the river in 1777, 1778, 1779, 1780, 1781, and to Sept. 1783. He married in 1775. He died in 1817. Congress granted his widow, Leah Tenure, a pension 12 Apr. 1842.

Terrance, Thomas. —. Pvt. He served in Col. Moseley's Regiment. He was pensioned in Mar. 1794. He transferred from Vt. 4 Mar. 1821 to Ontario Co., N.Y.

Terrel, Edmund. Va. —. His wife, Sarah Terrel, and child were furnished 2 barrels of corn and 100 pounds of pork in Essex Co., Va. on 25 Ma7 1781.

Terrel, James. S.C. Capt. He was wounded in 1780. He was granted an annuity 31 Dec. 1785. He was from Union District.

Terrel, James. S.C. —. He applied 3 June 1819. He was paid his arrearage in Dec. 1822 and lived in Franklin Co., Ga. 16 Mar. 1823.

Terrel, —. S.C. —. His widow, Elizabeth Terrel, was paid her annuity 9 June 1831.

Terry, Josiah. N.J. Pvt. He served under Capt. Nicholas Keen on the armed boat *Friendship* for the defense of the Delaware River. He was wounded in his right knee by a musket ball in Apr. 1782 and lost his leg. He was discharged 15 Dec. 1782 and given a half-pay pension for life in Cumberland County in Feb. 1783.

Terry, Stephen. Va. Pvt. He was awarded a £25 gratuity on 5 Dec. 1777. He was awarded an annuity of half-pay for six years on 19 Oct. 1778. He received a gratuity of £500 on 16 Nov. 1780. He was in Louisa County 8 Nov. 1786 and was 27 years old. He served in the 3rd Va. Regiment under Col. Marshall in Capt. Powell's Company. He was wounded in his right shoulder at Brandywine and deprived of the use of his right arm. He was put on the pension roll at the rate of £12 per annum and was continued at the same amount on 29 Jan. 1789. He was on the 1813 pension list.

Terry, Thomas. Mass. —. His warrant was issued in favor of his children 31 Jan. 1832.

Terwilleger, Mathew. N.Y. Pvt. He served in the Ulster County militia under Col. McClaghry and Col. James Hathorn. His widow, Elizabeth Terwilleger, received his half-pay pension.

Test, Francis. N.J. —. He was pensioned 10 Mar. 1832 at the rate of $60 per annum.

Teulon, Charles. S.C. —. He was a schoolmaster. His widow, Christiana Teulon, was born 20 June1756 in Limerick, Ireland and was the daughter of George and Catharine (Teulon) Patterson. Her parents moved to Kilkinney, Ireland and afterwards to Edinburgh. To avoid a press, her father enlisted in a regiment which was afterwards ordered to America. He served at the siege of Quebec. He received his bounty land and took up his abode at Charlotte, N.C. and sent for his family. His wife and two daughters, Christiana and Jennie, landed at Charleston in 1768.George Patterson met them and took them to his home in the New Acquisition. Christiana Teulon married firstly George Henderson in Mar. 1776 who served as a lieutenant in Capt. Sumter's Militia Company. He died after the Snowy Camps in 1775. He had resigned his commission some time before due to ill health. On 1 January 1779 Christiana (Teulon) Henderson married secondly Charles Teulon at Briar Creek, Georgia. The Rev. M. Lewis, a Presbyterian minister, performed the wedding. Charles Teulon was an active friend of America and was almost always out with the militia as a volunteer. He stood one tour as a draftee in the expedition against the Quarters House under Capt. McGraw. He was in the battle of Fort Moultrie in Capt. Snipe's Company and received three wounds and had a rib broken on Goat Island. At the siege of Augusta he was in a party of scouts and received a saber wound in the head. He was in a great many expeditions. Christiana Teulon stayed at the house of one Lamar where a Mrs. McCoy was living during the siege of Augusta. While at the house of one Flanagan a foraging party of British and Tories came. They charged her with being a rebel and having a husband out and knowing where they were. She denied knowing where they were. A man called Conner pushed at her with his bayonet and gave her a severe wound on the left breast. One Blaney pushed him back as he made his lunge which shorted the blow; otherwise, he might have killed her. She still had the scar of the wound and felt the pain many years after it was healed--particularly when nursing. Her husband died 12 Oct. 1812. In the latter part of his life he was a hypochondriac, and a set of swindlers got away with his land. Her two sons died young. Her daughters were married or dead. All of them were at a distance but one who was very poor. She applied 25 November 1836. She was granted a pension of $30 per annum. She later sought an increase to $60 per annum at which time she was nearing the age of 90 and was being maintained by daughter and son-in-law, Mary and William Beasly, who were very poor. She applied from Abbeville District.

Thacher, James. —. Surgeon. He served as early as 1775. In 1776 he was under Col. Asa Whitcomb and in 1778 was a full surgeon of the 1st Virginia Regiment under Col. George Gibson. He accepted the office of surgeon under Col. Henry Jackson in 1779 in Mass. He retired 1 Jan. 1783. He died 4 Mar. 1831. His heirs, Susan T. Bartlett of Cambridge, Mass. and Betsey H. Hodge of Plymouth, Mass. sought relief from Congress 18 Jan. 1859 but were not successful.

Tharp, John. Va. Pvt. He was wounded in his leg at Savannah and discharged. He was granted relief 22 June 1780. He lived in Stafford County on 5 Apr. 1787 when he was continued on the pension list at the rate of £12 per annum. He was a soldier in the 2nd Va. Regiment under Capt. Thomas Parker for 18 months in the Va. Continental Line. He was 40 years old. He was granted a $20 increase in his pension on 27 Jan. 1814. In 1823 he was in Fauquier County. He also appeared as John Thorp. He was on the 1813 pension list.

Tharp, Paul. Pa. —. He was granted relief 4 May 1832 in Fayette County. He was deceased by Nov. 1838.

Thatcher, John. Conn. Capt. He was wounded in his leg by a howitzer shell in an engagement on Lake Champlain on 11 Oct. 1776. He commanded the galley *George Washington*. He was paroled. He was from Stratford and aged 45 years on 22 Apr. 1788. He died 17 July 1805. He also appeared as John Thacher and John Tacker.

Thatcher, Nathaniel. Mass. Lt. He received his commutation for five years in lieu of half-pay for life. He was from Milton and died in Feb. 1809.

Thatcher, William. Va. Seaman. His widow, Hannah Thatcher, was in Lancaster County on 27 Apr. 1786. He died on the galley *Revenge* at the age of 24. He left a widow and children aged 2 and 5. They were 14 and 11 in 1786. She and her two children were continued on the pension roll at the rate of £8 per annum on 17 Aug. 1790. He was in the state navy. He also appeared as William Thacker.

Thayer, Abraham. Mass. Gunner. He served at the Castle and was from Braintree. His widow, Lydia Thayer, was paid $50.

Thayer, Samuel. Mass. —. He served in the 3rd Regiment and was from Bennington. He was paid $20.

Thayer, Samuel. Mass. —. He served in the Artillery and was from Randolph. His widow, Sarah Thayer, was paid $20.

Thayer, Simeon. R.I. Maj. On 28 June 1778 he lost his right eye by a cannon ball at Monmouth. He was pensioned in 1791. He resided in Pennsylvania. He died 13 Oct. 1800 in Providence Co., R.I.

Thayer, Simeon. Vt. —. He sought the arrears of his pension 12 Oct. 1795.

Thayer, Stephen. Mass. —. He served in the 9th Regiment and was from Vermont. He was paid $20.

Thayer, Stephen. Mass. —. He served in the 2nd Regiment and was from Petersham. He was paid $50.

Thayer, William. Mass. —. He sought a larger pension for the loss of his leg. He was awarded £8 for the present year to 11 January next on 30 Oct. 1781 His pension was increased by £3 per annum on 21 Jan. 1789.

Thomas, —. N.C. —. His widow was Susannah Thomas of Hillsborough. Her application was rejected in 1819.

Thomas, Adam. Pa. —. He was awarded a $40 gratuity and a $40 annuity in Adams Co., Pa. 14 Apr. 1834. He died 1 Apr. 1845.

Thomas, Alexander. Pa. Sgt. He applied 5 Jan. 1788. He was in Capt. Wilson's Company in the 6th Pa. Regiment. He was wounded in the knee at Germantown. He was 47 years old. He died 14 Feb. 1802.

Thomas, Caleb. —. —. He married 9 Jan. 1794 and died 8 Jan. 1842. Congress rejected the petition of his widow, Polly Thomas, 20 Jan. 1847.

Thomas, Elisha. N.H. Sgt. He was from New Durham in 1787. He served in Col. Thomas Tash's Regiment in Capt. John Gordon's Company. He was wounded and deprived of the use of his hand when his gun malfunctioned and split at Verplank's Point. His thumb was carried away. He was aged 40 in 1787. He was listed as dead on the 1789 pension roll.

Thomas, Israel. Mass. Pvt. He served in the 5th Regiment under Capt. Trotter and Col. Rufus Putnam. He was disabled with consumptive complaints. He was pensioned 1 Sep. 1782. He resided in Hampshire Co., Mass. He was 44 years old in 1788. He was on the 1813 pension list.

Thomas, Isaac. Mass. Pvt. He served in the 2nd Regiment and was from Pembroke. His widow, Averick Thomas, was paid $50.

Thomas, James. Pa. —. He was granted relief 8 Jan. 1838 in Chester County. He was 83 years old in 1840. He died 19 Feb. 1848.

Thomas, John. —. —. He was late of Georgia but never applied for a pension in his lifetime. His surviving children had their petition rejected by Congress 4 May 1860.

Thomas, John. Mass. Maj. Gen. He died 3 June 1776 at Chambil, and his widow, Hannah Thomas, was granted £675 for five years to 3 June 1781 on 23 Oct. 1781. She was paid his seven years' half-pay of $3,150. He died of smallpox so his heirs were not due any bounty land according to Congress on 9 June 1838.

Thomas, John. N.Y. Pvt. He served in Col. Philip Van Cortland's Regiment. He was disabled by lameness occasioned by rheumatism. He was discharged by Gen. Washington. He was aged 49 years in 1788. He lived in Kinderhook, Columbia Co., N.Y. 10 June 1789. He was on the 1813 pension list.

Thomas, John. Pa. —. He applied in Cumberland County on 20 June 1817. In 1779 he enlisted under Capt. Bradford and Col. Bradford for the war. He was in the battles of Trenton and Princeton. He was a pauper in the poor house.

Thomas, John. Va. —. He was a Continental soldier who died in the service. His widow, Hannah Thomas, was granted 2½ bushels of wheat and 30 pounds of bacon support in Mecklenburg Co., Va. 11 Nov. 1782.

Thomas, John. Va. Capt. He served in the infantry and received his five years' full-pay commutation 2 Mar. 1833.

Thomas, John. Va. Capt. He was appointed a lieutenant in the navy in June 1776. He became a captain 26 Aug. 1778 and served to the close of the war. He served aboard the galley *Protector* until it was destroyed by fire 9 June 1779 when he was transferred to the *Dragon*. He received 5,333 1/3 bounty land from Virginia. He died in 1796. His son, William Thomas, sought relief, and Congress directed him to apply to the proper department if he were entitled on 3 Mar. 1851.

Thomas, John Jarman. Md. Pvt. He was pensioned at the rate of half-pay of a private 16 Mar. 1836.

Thomas, Joseph. Md. Pvt. He was pensioned at the rate of half-pay of a private in Cecil County on 20 Feb. 1822. Payment was to be made to his trustee, Frisby Henderson.

Thomas, Joseph Merrill. N.H. Lt. He served under Col. Scammell and was killed 19 Sep. 1777 at Bemis Heights. His widow, Anna Thomas, was paid his seven years' half-pay of $1,120. She was from Nottingham.

Thomas, Mark. Va. —. His heirs received 3,333 1/3 acres of bounty land from Virginia. They sought the remaining land due them. Congress rejected their claim 2 Feb. 1843.

Thomas, Moses. N.Y. Sgt. He served under Col. McClaughry in the Ulster County militia and was slain 22 July 1779. His daughters, Sarah Thomas and Ruth Thomas, received a half-pay pension for seven years.

Thomas, Nicholas. —. —. He died in 1838. His son, Nicholas Thomas, had his application for a pension rejected by Congress 6 Feb. 1844.

Thomas, Philip. N.C. Sgt. He served in the 3rd Battalion. He was wounded in the left arm at Eutaw Springs, S.C. on 8 Sep. 1781. He lived in Duplin Co., N.C. in 1794. He was on the 1813 pension list.

Thomas, Robert. N.J. —. He was pensioned in Mercer County on 16 Feb. 1843 at the rate of $50 per annum.

Thomas, Robert. S.C. Capt. He was killed in 1781 by the enemy. His widow, Martha Thomas, was granted an annuity 6 Jan. 1785. There were children in 1791.

Thomas, Rowan. S.C. —. He was from Marion District and was pensioned 4 Dec. 1832. His widow was Ann Thomas. She was 88 years old when she applied 24 Nov. 1838. Her application was rejected.

Thomas, Stephen. N.C. Pvt. He was from Richmond County in 1785. He was in Continental service in Armstrong's Regiment and was wounded. He was aged 22 in 1785. He was on the 1813 pension list. He later removed to Montgomery Co., Tenn. He died 10 May 1825.

Thomas, Thomas. Pa. Boatswain. He was in Philadelphia County 14 Nov. 1785. He served aboard the galley *Washington*. He was wounded in his right leg and shoulder by the blowing up of the British ship of war *Augusta* in the Delaware River in 1777. He was 60 years old. He died 1Dec. 1790.

Thomas, W. Me. —. He was granted relief.

Thomas, William. Mass. Pvt. He served in the 15th Regiment under Col. Timothy Bigelow and Capt. Joshua Brown. He was disabled with weakness which settled in his left hip and side. He was 32 years old in 1789.

Thomas, William. S.C. Seaman. He served aboard the *South Carolina* under Commodore Alexander Gillon. His widow, Martha Thomas, was paid 18 Nov. 1808.

Thomas, William. Va. —. His widow, Milly Thomas, was granted £25 support in Northumberland County on 8 Feb. 1779.

Thompson, —. —. —. His widow, Mary E. Thompson, had her petition for a pension rejected by Congress 10 Feb. 1846.

Thompson, —. —. —. Congress denied his widow, Nancy Thompson, relief 3 Mar. 1851. She had married in 1809.

Thompson, —. Ga. —. Mrs. Thompson of Wilkes County was granted assistance 15 Mar. 1782. She was a widow.

Thompson, —. Pa. —. His widow, Elizabeth Thompson, received a $40 annuity in York County 12 Apr. 1851.

Thompson, —. Pa.—. His widow, Lucy Thompson, received a $40 annuity in Fayette County 6 Apr. 1852.

Thompson, — Va. —. His wife, Mary Thompson, was allowed £5 support for herself and her small children while her husband was away in the service in Augusta Co., Va. 17 Nov. 1778. She was allowed £30 on 17 Nov. 1779.

Thompson, —. Pa. —. His widow, Elizabeth Thompson, was awarded a $40 annuity in York County 12 Apr. 1851 for his Revolutionary service.

Thompson, —. Pa. —. His widow, Ruth Thompson, was awarded a $40 gratuity and a $40 annuity in Chester Co., Pa. 29 Mar. 1824.

Thompson, Alexander. —. —. Congress rejected his claim 29 Mar. 1842 because his evidence was too loose and unsatisfactory.

Thompson, Alexander. S.C. —. He enlisted for three years in 1778 under Capt. John Moore and Col. Neal. He was discharged in 1780. He was at Stono and Savannah. He applied from Mecklenburg County, N.C. 25 Aug. 1824 at the age of 68. He had a wife Rebecca and a daughter aged about 12.

Thompson, Amos. Conn. —. He enlisted and served under Capt. Reed and Col. Starr for four months and 26 days. Previously he had served a month under Capt. Griswold as a substitute for Joseph Tinney from New London. He was short three days of service so Congress granted him a pension 10 Jan. 1837.

Thompson, Barnard. Md. Pvt. He was pensioned at the rate of half-pay of private in Washington Co., Ky. 1 Mar. 1833.

Thompson, Benjamin. Me. Lt. He contracted rheumatism and bilious rhind on the retreat from Ticonderoga in 1777. He served under Col. Brewer. He was a blacksmith. He resided at Topsham, Me. in 1792. He was commissioned 6 Nov. 1776 and was supernumerary 16 Jan. 1779.

Thompson, Caesar. Mass. Pvt. He served in the 4th Regiment under Col. Shephard and Capt. Stanton. He was disabled with a rupture. He was 45 years old in 1786. He lived in Acton, Mass. in 1788. He was a Negro. He also appeared as Cesar Thomson.

Thompson, Charles. Md. Pvt. He was pensioned at the rate of half-pay of a private in St. Mary's County on 27 Jan. 1817.

Thompson, Daniel. Conn. Pvt. He served under Maj. Gen. Parsons. His feet were frozen and injured by severe traveling on the retreat of the army from New York in 1776. He lived in Montville, Conn. in 1794. He served in the militia.

Thompson, David. Mass. —. He was granted an additional £20 to his pension 25 June 1779. He was to be paid his pension 1 Feb. 1790. He also appeared as David Thomson.

Thompson, Edward. —. —. His application was referred to the Secretary of War.

Thompson, Elizabeth. N.Y. Housekeeper & Cook. She was pensioned under the act of 18 Feb. 1785 by the Continental Congress and was aged 81 years. She left New York City early in the war in the capacity of housekeeper and cook to his Excellency General George Washington. She remained in service till the war's termination. All of her property lay in houses in New York City and were burned in the fire of 1776. General Washington desired that she end her days with him in his own house, but she was too feeble to travel. She was granted $100 immediate relief and a pension of $25 per quarter. She died testate in 1788 in New York City. Daniel McCormack was her executor and received her final payment.

Thompson, Ephraim. Me. —. He was from Lyman. He was paid $50 under the resolve of 1836.

Thompson, Ezra. Mass. —. He was wounded in Rhode Island and sought a pension in 1778.

Thompson, George. Va. —. His family was granted support in Prince Edward County 17 May 1779 while he was away in Continental service.

Thompson, Henry. Pa. —. He died 21 July 1823.

Thompson, Herminus. Pa. Pvt. He was on the 1791 pension roll.

Thompson, Hezekiah. Pa. —. He was pensioned in Dauphin County 4 Apr. 1837.

Thompson, Isaac. Pa. —. He was pensioned under the act of 29 Jan. 1816. He was formerly from Mifflin County and had moved to the state of Ohio.

Thompson, Jack. Mass. —. He was paid $20.

Thompson, James. N.J. Pvt. He served in the 2nd Regiment and suffered from the loss of an eye. He was on the 1791 pension roll at the rate of $60 per annum. He was on the 1813 pension list. He also appeared as James Thomson.

Thompson, James. Pa. Col. He applied 1 Dec. 1786 in York County. He was Col. of the 1st Battalion of York County militia and was wounded in the fall of 1777 by a musket ball which entered near the top of his shoulder. He served under Gen. James Potter.

Thompson, James. Pa. —. He enlisted in 1776 in Capt. Robert Adams' Company. At Three Rivers he had a button shot off his coat. He served five weeks and three days on Lake Champlain on a gondola. He suffered much from want of food and clothes. He was in a severe skirmish with the Indians. He volunteered again under Gen. Wayne. His next tour was under Capt. Grimes and Col. Buchanan. His fourth tour was under Capt. Lemon against the Indians at Sunbury. He next volunteered under Capt. Buchanan against the insurgents in the western part of the state. He was transferred to the 8ᵗʰ Regiment. He was nearly 80 years old. His children were bound out to strangers. He was from Westmoreland County.

Thompson, James A. Pa. —. He was granted a gratuity in 1841.

Thompson, James. Va. —. He served in Capt. McGuire's Company. His wife, Esther Thompson, and two children were granted £2.10 support in Frederick Co., Va. on 4 Nov. 1777 and £25 on 1 June 1779.

Thompson, Jesse. Md. Sgt. He was pensioned at the rate of half-pay of a sergeant 1 Jan. 1813.

Thompson, Jesse. Pa. Sgt. He was in York County on 1 Dec. 1785 and was 37 years old. He was in Col. Murray's [also Murrow's] Company of Six Month Rangers. He was wounded with spears and scalped near Wyoming in 1778.

Thompson, John. Md. Pvt. He was pensioned at the rate of half-pay of a private in Kent County on 1 Jan. 1813.

Thompson, John. N.H. —. He was from Rindge. He served in Capt. Philip Thomas' Company in Col. Reed's Regiment. He was wounded on 15 June 1775 at Charlestown. He applied 7 Sep. 1776.

Thompson, John. N.C. —. He applied in Mecklenburg County in 1820. He was in militia service under Gen. Ashe and was wounded in the arm at Briar Creek. William Thompson was his brother. He died 22 Mar. 1822. His son was James Thompson. His widow, Martha Thompson, was on the pension list in 1827 and 1828 for $40 per annum and was unable to support herself.

Thompson, John. Pa. Sgt. Major. He was in Philadelphia County on 13 Oct. 1785. He was in the Invalids. He had been disabled by a cold by lying out in the winter of 1777 and 1778. He was 50 years old. He was transferred from the 2ⁿᵈ Pa. Regiment to the Invalids.

Thompson, John. Pa. Pvt. He was in Philadelphia County on 30 Sep. 1785. He was transferred from the 3ʳᵈ Pa. Regiment to the Invalids. He was wounded after he was taken prisoner at Fort Washington in 1776. He was 55 years old.

Thompson, John. Pa. Col. He was in Chester County on 2 June 1786. He was in the 1ˢᵗ Battalion, York County Militia. He was wounded in the left shoulder by a musket ball on 16 Sep. 1777 after he was taken prisoner at Fort Washington. He was 42 years old. He died 3 Oct. 1807.

Thompson, John. Pa. Gunner. He was in Philadelphia County on 12 Dec.1785. He served aboard the Continental brig *Lexington* under Capt. Henry Johnson and lost his leg in an engagement with the British cutter, *Alert*.

Thompson, John. Pa. —. His heirs were paid $270 for the right of 200 acres of donation land on 8 Apr. 1833.

Thompson, John. Pa. —. He served under Capt. Wilson in the militia. He was from Indiana County.

Thompson, John. Va. —. He was in Halifax County on 4 Jan. 1799. He was wounded in Col. Buford's defeat. He was pensioned at the rate of $50 per annum on 11 Jan. 1800. He received a $40 increase to his $60 pension on 6 Dec. 1814. He was in Campbell Co., Va. in 1815. He died 28 June 1823 in Wythe County, and Francis Thompson was administrator of his estate. His children were Francis Thompson, Rebecca Thompson, Sarah Thompson, Elizabeth Thompson, and Anne the wife of William Myers.

Thompson, John. Va. —. He was in King William County 12 Feb. 1820. His son was Yancey Thompson. He was totally blind in 1826.

Thompson, Joseph. Me. —. He was from York. He was paid $50 under the resolve of 1836.

Thompson, Nathaniel. —. —. His application of 28 Mar. 1806 was not accepted.

Thompson, Robert. Mass. —. He served in the 6ᵗʰ Regiment and was from Rutland. He was paid

$20.

Thompson, Robert. Pa. —. He received a $40 gratuity and a $40 annuity 2 Apr. 1822.

Thompson, Robert. Pa. —. His widow, Keziah Thompson, received a $40 gratuity in Dauphin County 3 Apr. 1837. Her name may have been Heziah Thompson.

Thompson, Samuel. Conn. Capt. He served under Col. Mead and was from Mansfield. He married 21 May 1788 and died in Jan. 1793. His widow, Hannah Thompson, married secondly Jesse Waldo. Congress granted her a pension 8 Mar. 1842.

Thompson, Samuel. S.C. —. He was taken prisoner in Feb. 1779 at Ashe's defeat and died in confinement. His widow, Sarah Thompson, was granted an annuity 30 Sep. 1785.

Thompson, Stephen. Va. —. His widow, Elizabeth Thompson, and child were granted support in Greenbrier Co., Va. 22 Aug. 1781. He died in the service.

Thompson, Thaddeus. Mass. Surgeon's Mate. He received his commutation for five years in lieu of half-pay for life.

Thompson, Thomas. Md. Pvt. He was pensioned at the rate of half-pay of a private in Dorchester County on 27 Jan. 1817. His widow, Mary Thompson, was pensioned at the same rate 16 Feb. 1820.

Thompson, Thomas. N.J. —. He served in the militia and died in the service in Jan. 1777 at Connecticut farms at the house of John Thompson. His widow, Abigail Thompson, sought his half-pay in Morris County on 17 Dec. 1794. Thomas Thompson married Abigail Ross 1 Dec. 1763 at the Presbyterian Church in New Providence.

Thompson, Thomas. Va. —. His wife, Elizabeth Thompson, and four children were granted £100 for necessaries in Fluvanna Co., Va. 3 June 1779. She and her five children were granted additional support on 1 June 1780. He died in the service, and his widow and four children were granted support on 7 Dec. 1780. His widow and three children were granted relief on Feb. 1782.

Thompson, William. Mass. Corp. He served in Lamb's Artillery. He was from Marblehead and was paid $50.

Thompson, William. N.Y. —. He was pensioned.

Thompson, William. N.Y. —. He was awarded 200 acres of bounty land 11 Apr. 1808. He also was pensioned.

Thompson, William. Pa. Brigadier General. He was commissioned in Mar. 1776. He died in the service on 3 Sep. 1781 as a prisoner or on parole. His eldest son was George Thompson whose widow was Mary Thompson. Gen. Thompson's widow, Catherine Thompson, applied 3 Mar. 1786. He was commissioned by Congress 1 Mar. 1776. He was captured and released from captivity. She moved to Dauphin County in 1794. She died in Dec. 1809. Her administratrix was Terissa Catherine Stern, a grand-daughter. His grandson and administrator, Robert C. Thompson, died before his claim to Congress had been acted upon. His great-grand-daughter, Fannie Thompson, was administratrix *de bonis non*.. Gen. Thompson had paid his troops out of his own pocket when they were held in captivity. He died wealthy so his heirs did not present their claim until poverty forced them to do so. His eldest son married 20 July 1786, and his wife's name was Mary. Congress approved the petition of the heirs 4 May 1876. Congress recommended that no more than the principal be allowed on 4 May 1786. Congress awarded the heirs his seven years' half-pay 15 Dec. 1857.

Thompson, William. S.C. Sgt. He served under Col. Thomas Taylor. He was a substitute for James Norman. He applied from Fairfield District 3 Dec. 1811.

Thompson, William. S.C. Col. He served in the 3rd Regiment and served from 24 July 1776 to 1783. He died 2 Nov. 1796. William E. Haskell, a grandchild, applied for the heirs for the commutation and bounty land due their grandfather on 13 Jan. 1859.

Thomson, —. S.C. —. His widow was Lucy Thomson from Spartanburg. There were four children in 1791.

Thomson, Alexander. N.J. Wagonmaster. He was from Amwell, Hunterdon County. In Oct. 1787 he sought relief. He was upwards of seventy years of age.

Thomson, Charles. S.C. —. His widow had two children in 1791.

Thomson, John. Pa. Pvt. He served in the 3rd Regiment and was transferred to the Invalids. He was from Philadelphia County.

Thomson, John. Pa. Sgt. Maj. He served in the 2nd Regiment and was transferred to the Invalids. He wad disabled by a cold by lying out in winter between 1777 and 1778.

Thomson, Michael. S.C. —. He served in the Ninety Six militia and died at Orangeburg of a wound received in May 1782 in the attack on Tories near Edisto Swamp. His widow, Martha Watson, was granted an annuity 12 June 1784..

Thorn, John. Va. —. He died in the service. His widow, Martha Thorn, and five children were granted support in Surry Co., Va. 28 Dec. 1778. Sarah Thorn was a daughter.

Thorn, Samuel. N.Y. Capt. He died in the service. Samuel Reynolds petitioned to have letters patent issued for his bounty land 18 June 1812.

Thorne, Daniel. N.Y. —. He served in Col. Lamb's artillery. His heirs, James Thorne, Stephen Thorne, Polly Tyson, Eliza Bradley, Sally Thorne, and John Thorne, were awarded his 300 acres of bounty land 13 Apr. 1813.

Thornhill, John. Va. —. His father, Samuel Thornhill, was granted £20 support in Rockingham Co., Va. while he was in Continental service on 23 Nov. 1779.

Thornhill, Thomas. Va. Pvt. He served in Col. Lee's Legion under Capt. Joseph Eggleston. He drew a pension until his death in 1838 or 1839. His daughter, Lucinda Stone, who was totally blind, was pensioned by Congress 19 Feb. 1895.

Thornton, —. Va. —. John Thornton was granted relief 9 July 1778 and 10 Dec. 1778 in Lunenburg Co., Va. while his two sons were away in Continental service.

Thornton, Harmenius. Pa. Pvt. He was in Philadelphia County on 13 July 1786. He was in the 4th Regiment of Artillery under Col. Proctor and was disabled by a hurt at Germantown by a cannon running over him. He was 40 years old.

Thornton, Henry. Va. —. His wife, Mary Thornton, was granted relief 12 June 1777, 14 Aug. 1777, and £50 on 8 Oct. 1778 in Lunenburg Co., Va.

Thornton, Jeremiah. Va. Pvt. He served in the 7th Virginia Regiment and was disabled 4 Dec. 1778.

Thornton, John. Pa. —. He applied 31 Dec. 1814 in Chester County.

Thornton, John. Pa. —. He served in the Penn. Line. He was from Dauphin County.

Thornton, John. Pa. Corp. He was a blacksmith or artificer in Capt. Ferguson's Company of Artillery under Col. Proctor. He was wounded in the heel at Camden, S.C. by a musket ball fired by the Tories. The ball had just killed a private. He served six years. He was at the taking of Cornwallis. He also served under Capt. Thomas Proctor. He enlisted 18 May 1777. He also served as a matross. He also appeared as John Thorton.

Thornton, John. Va. Col. He served in the 3rd Virginia Regiment under Col. Hugh Mercer. He entered the service 22 Feb. 1776 and was promoted to Major 20 Mar. 1777. He was appointed Lt. Col. that same year. He was at the battles of Trenton and Princeton. In 1781 Marquis Lafayette gave him as a continental officer the command of a Virginia regiment of militia. After the consolidation of the regiments, he became supernumerary. His five years' full pay commutation was paid to his administrator who was to pay one-quarter to the widow, Jane Thornton, and the rest to the persons entitled 9 Feb. 1833.

Thornton, Presley. Ga. Corp. He served under Col. Hawes in the 18 Months Men. He was wounded in the left shoulder joint on 25 Apr. 1781. He resided in Augusta, Ga. in 1796. He was on the 1813 pension list.

Thornton, Presley. —. Capt. He served in Col. George Baylor's Regiment of Light Dragoons to the end of the war. He had entered the service prior to 10 Nov. 1776. He died in 1811. His children, Francis A. Thornton and Elizabeth P. Gwin, sought his five years' full pay 4 Jan. 1838.

Thorp, Charles. —. —. He married 9 Dec. 1796. His widow, Elizabeth Thorp, had her petition for a pension rejected by Congress on 14 Mar. 1848 because she married after 1 Jan. 1794.

Thorp, Paul. Pa. —. He was awarded a $40 gratuity and a $40 annuity in Fayette Co., Pa. 4 May 1832.

Thorp, Thomas. Mass. —. He served in the 4th Regiment and was from Acton.

Thorpe, James. Va. —. He was away in the service. His widow, Elizabeth Thorpe, was allowed £5 support for herself and her children in Augusta Co., Va. 16 Mar. 1779. She was allowed provisions on 16 Sep. 1783.

Thorpe, Jonathan. Va. —. He enlisted in Augusta County in 1779 under Capt. Southey Capes and Col. Feebaker for 18 months. He was a prisoner of the British. He also served under Capt. John Kirkpatrick, Col. Webb, Maj. John Poalson, and Col. John Cropper. He applied from Surry Co., N.C. in Apr. 1825. He had two grown daughters, a wife, a son aged 10, and twin daughters aged 9.

Thracher, Charles. R.I. Pvt. He served in Capt. William White's Company under Col. John Brown and was wounded at Stoney Robby on 19 Oct. 1780. A musket ball entered his belly just below his navel and remained in him. He was pensioned 10 June 1789. He was 34 years old. He was on the 1813 pension list. He died 27 Dec. 1827 in Berkshire Co., Mass. He also appeared as Charles Trasher.

Threewits, Edward. S.C. —. He served under Capt. Maurice Murphy. He was wounded by two balls in his shoulder at Brown's Mill in Marlborough District. He lived in a sickly place on the Pee Dee so he removed to Tennessee in 1791. He was pensioned again on 17 Dec. 1819. On 14 Dec. 1822 he received arrearage of $21.42 per annum for the years 1795 to 1819. He was 58 years old in 1819.

Throp, Thomas. Mass. —. He served in the 4th Regiment and was from Acton. He was paid $20.

Throuston, John. Va. —. He served as an officer in the cavalry in the Illinois Expedition and sought his half-pay for life in 1790. His application was rejected.

Thruston, Charles Mynn. Va. Capt. He was on the 1813 pension list.

Thurston, Benjamin. N.Y. Lt. Col. He served in the Orange County militia. He was killed at Minisink 22 July 1779. His widow, Ann Thurston, received his half-pay pension.

Thurston, James. S.C. Pvt. He served under Col. James Williams. He was taken prisoner at Ninety Six. He fell ill with smallpox and was blinded. He had a wife and two helpless babes. He was from Laurens District. He was paid his arrearage of an annuity from 15 Mar. 1786 on 9 Dec. 1791. There were children in 1791.

Thurston, John. Va. —. He died in Continental service 6 Aug. 1778. His widow, Frances Thurston, and child were granted £12 support in Middlesex Co., Va. on 28 June 1779.

Thurston, Oliver. N.H. Sgt. He was wounded in the thigh near his groin in 1779 in the battle of New Town in the Indian Territory and was crippled. He was in Col. George Reid's 2nd N.H. Regiment. He was aged 43 in 1787 and was a resident of Brentwood.

Thweatt, Thomas. Va. Capt. He was in Dinwiddie County and was 38 years old. He served in the 14th Va. Regiment. He became a captain on 26 Mar. 1777 and was wounded 4 Oct. 1777 in action near Germantown. Lt. Col. Samuel Hawes attested to his service. He was 43 years old in 1786. He was put on the pension list at the rate of half-pay on 27 Jan. 1786. He was in Lunenburg County in 1787, Halifax County in 1789, and Prince Edward County in 1792. He died 15 Aug. 1811. His name was still on the 1813 pension list.

Tibbets, Stephen. Me. —. He was from Bristol. He was paid $50 under the resolve of 1836.

Tibbons, Henry. Pa. —. He applied in Adams County on 27 June 1814. Lt. John Edie in Capt. Moses McClean's Company in the 6th Pa. Regiment enlisted him in 1777 to serve one year. He was at Three Rivers when Edie was taken prisoner. He also appeared as Henry Tibbers and Henry Tibbins. His daughter, Catharine Tibbons, was paid $200 for his donation land 21 June 1839. She was from Huntingdon County.

Tichenor, John. N.J. Pvt. He served under Capt. Samuel Pierson and Col. Philip Van Cortlandt in the Essex County militia. He was badly wounded in a skirmish with the enemy on 1 Jan. 1777. He lost the use of one of his hands. He received his half-pay in Essex County in Sep. 1782. He was 39 years old. He was on the 1791 pension roll at the rate of $40 per annum. He died 27 July 1810.

Ticount, Francis. Pa. Pvt. He was in Philadelphia 11 Sep. 1786. He served in Hazen's Regiment and was wounded in his left arm at Brandywine in 1777. His wife was Catherine Ticount. He was 40 years old. He later lived in Maryland. He also appeared as Francis Tycount. He was on the 1791 pension list of Maryland. He was on the 1813 pension list in Pennsylvania. He also appeared as Francis Tiscount.

Tidd, Daniel. Mass. Bombardier. He served in Crane's Artillery. His widow, Anna Saunders, was from Holliston and was paid $50.

Tiffany, Joel. N.H. —. He enlisted at Swanzy, N.H. under Capt. Fish and Col. Shepherd 3 Dec. 1776. He was later transferred to the Invalids and deserted 6 July 1779. He was pensioned in 1833 for fourteen months of service. Congress credited him with three years and eight months service and granted him a new pension 9 Feb. 1842 after deducting the amount paid him under his former certificate.

Tignall, —. Va. Pvt. He died in the service 11 Sep. 1778. His widow, Priscilla Tignall, and her three children were awarded £30 in Accomack Co., Va. 23 Feb. 1779.

Tilden, Charles. N.H. Pvt. He served under Col. Warner in Capt. Vail's Company. He had a considerable debility of both arms occasioned by being pinioned to a bed with cords tied round his arms while in a state of insanity in 1775 in Montreal. He lived in Lebanon, N.H. in 1795. His claim was rejected since he was not wounded.

Tilden, Josiah. Vt. —. He served in Capt. John Benjamin's Company under Col. Benjamin Wait. He was awarded £5 on 19 Oct. 1793.

Tileston, Cornelius. Mass. Corp. He served in the 16th Regiment and was from Williamsburg. He was paid $50.

Tilford, Alexander. N.Y. Pvt. He served under Capt. William Tilford and Col. James McClaughrey in the Ulster County militia and was wounded in his left foot by a musket ball at Fort Montgomery on Oct. 1777. He received half-pay of a private from Oct. 1777 to Apr. 1784. He lived in Ulster

Co., N.Y. on 7 July 1788. He was aged 42 years on 14 Apr. 1786. He was on the 1791 pension roll. He also appeared Alexander Telford and Alexander Tillford. He was on the 1813 pension list.

Tillard, Edward. Md. Lt. Col. He was from Montgomery County. He was pensioned at the rate of $125 per annum in 1811. His widow, Sarah Tillard, was pensioned at the rate of half-pay of a lieutenant colonel 22 Jan. 1820. Her arrearage of $57.33 was paid to Capt. Otho Thomas of Frederick County for the benefit of the heirs 11 Feb. 1835.

Tillard, James. Md. Pvt. He lost his left arm. He served under Col. John H. Stone. He lived in Charles County on 1 Dec. 1787. He was on the 1813 pension list.

Tilley, Samuel. Mass. Sgt. He served in the 7th Regiment and was from Lee. He was paid $20.

Tillien, Henry. Pa. Pvt. He served in Capt. O'Hara's Independent Company. He was wounded by a musket or rifle ball which passed through the joint of his right arm. It produced a contusion, and his arm became stiff. He was dead by 1794.

Tillotson, Thomas. Md. Surgeon. He was pensioned at the rate of half-pay of a surgeon in Rhinebeck, N.Y. 19 Feb. 1830. He was granted a warrant for 200 acres of bounty land in Allegany County on 14 Mar. 1832.

Tilman, Daniel. Va. —. He was pensioned in Albemarle County on 2 Feb. 1819 at the rate of $100 per annum and $80 immediate relief. He was one of the first volunteers to march to Williamsburg at the commencement of the war and went to Hampton with the first volunteer company seen there. He served as ensign and lieutenant at Williamsburg under Capt. William Henry. He returned home and next served as a minuteman under Capt. Roger Thompson for one year. He was advanced to a captaincy and served between Williamsburg and Richmond. He was at Albemarle Barracks guarding British and Hessian prisoners. He was 75 years old.

Tilman, Philip. N.J. —. He enlisted in 1775 or 1776 in Sussex County and served under Capt. John Forgeinder and Col. Hooper for nine months. He was 82 years old when he applied in Lincoln County, N.C. on 25 Oct. 1826. He had no family. His brother was John Tilman.

Tilson, David. Pa. Lt. He served in the 6th Battalion of the Philadelphia Militia and died of wounds at Pottstown in Mar. 1788. His widow was Catherine Tilson who applied in Montgomery County in Aug. 1796.

Tilson, George. Pa. Pvt. He was on the 1791 pension roll. He died in May 1800.

Tilton, Peter. N.Y. —. He served under Dubois. His wife, Phebe Tilton, and three children were granted assistance 28 Apr. 1779 while he was away in the service.

Tilton, Sylvester. N.J. Pvt. He served under Col. S. Forman. He was wounded in the breast by a ball which penetrated his body in action with a party of refugees who invaded the coast of Monmouth County. He resided in Stafford Township, Monmouth Co., N.J. in 1792. He was on the 1813 pension list.

Timberlake, —. Va. —. Several brothers and their brother-in-law died in the service. Their father, Philip Timberlake, was the father of 14, aged, and in poverty. The brother-in-law was also disabled with a wife and 4 children. He prayed relief on 20 May 1783.

Timberlake, John. Va. —. His wife, Mary Timberlake, and three children were furnished £10 in Louisa Co., Va. on 12 Jan. 1778.

Timmerman, Henry. N.Y. Ens. He served under Col. Jacob Klock in Capt. House's Company. He was wounded in his left side at Oriskany on 6 Aug. 1777. He was 46 years old in 1786 and lived in Palatine, Montgomery Co., N.Y. 15 June 1789. He died 8 May 1807. He also appeared as Henry Zimmerman.

Timmerman, Jacob. N.Y. Sgt. He served under Col. Jacob Klock in the Montgomery County militia and was slain 5 Aug. 1781. His widow, Elizabeth Timmerman, received a half-pay pension.

Timmerman, Johannes. N.Y. Lt. He served under Col. Jacob Klock in the Montgomery County militia and was slain 5 Aug. 1781. His widow, Elizabeth Timmerman, received a half-pay pension.

Timothy, —. S.C. —. His widow was Ann Timothy. Her annuity was £220.18.3 in 1787.

Tingley, Edward. Pa. —. He was wounded in the war. He was granted a $40 gratuity and a $40 annuity 27 Mar. 1812.

Tingley, Lemuel. N.J. —. His widow, Martha Tingley, was pensioned in Morris County on 16 Feb. 1847 at the rate of $30 per annum.

Tinkham, Ebenezer. N.H. Pvt. He was wounded by a musket ball which entered his right shoulder, went through a joint of his neck, and came out by the collar bone in July 1779 at Penobscot. He served aboard the frigate *Warren*. He resided in Lyme, N.H. in 1795. He was granted one-third of a pension 20 Apr. 1796. He was on the 1813 pension list. He died 25 Nov. 1825.

Tinkham, Levi. Mass. He was paid $20.

Tinsley, James. S.C. —. He resided in Newberry District at the time of the war. He volunteered at the age of 15 under Col. Williams. He was also under Col. Brannon and Col. Hays. He was at Ninety Six, Guilford, and Blackstocks. He was wounded in his right arm and shoulder. He was from Richland District and was pensioned 2 Dec. 1819. He received one year arrearage.

Tinsley, James. S.C. Capt. He served under Capt. Isaac Tinsley and Col. Hays from Spartanburgh District. He was wounded and had a wife and children. He was paid from 1820 to 1832.

Tinsley, Jonathan. Pa. Pvt. He was pensioned 3 Mar. 1809. He was on the 1813 pension list.

Tinsley, Samuel. Va. Cornet. He was from Hanover County and received commutation of full pay for five years in lieu of half-pay for life as a cornet of cavalry in the Virginia Line with no interest on 2 Mar. 1827.

Tipp, —. Va. —. His widow, Mary Tipp, was on the 1785 pension roll.

Tipper, —. Pa. —. Mary Tipper, was pensioned 13 Apr. 1838 in Franklin County and died 14 Mar. 1853.

Tipper, Charles. Pa. —. He applied in Bedford County. He served one year and went to Canada. He remained in the service two months longer than his enlistment and was discharged. He was awarded a $40 gratuity and a $40 annuity on 19 Mar. 1816.

Tipper, Christopher. N.J. Pvt. He served in the 1ˢᵗ Regiment and was disabled with a rupture. He was 61 years old. He was on the 1791 pension roll at the rate of $40 per annum.

Tipton, Abraham. Va. Capt. He died in the service, but the rolls neither indicated that he died nor served to the end of the war. He was in the barracks in Albemarle County in 1780. He was killed by the Indians near the falls of the Ohio, scalped, and divested of most of his clothing. Congress rejected relief 1 Mar. 1838.

Tipton, Alexander. Va. Capt. He was killed by the Indians near the falls of the Ohio, scalped, and divested of most of his clothing in 1781. The application for his commutation was rejected 1 Mar. 1838.

Tipton, Jonathan. —. Pvt. Congress awarded his widow, Lavina Tipton of White Co., Tenn., the arrearage of her pension from 4 Mar. 1848 to 3 Feb. 1853 on 21 Feb. 1857.

Tipton, Jonathan. —. —. He volunteered in 1781 under Capt. Jonathan Tipton and served seven months under Col. Sevier of N.C. and was at Fort Watauga on the Watauga River and Denningesen's Fort. He was drafted for three months under Capt. John McNabb and Col. Williams in Burke Co. He was at King's Mountain but not in the heat of the battle. He was born in Shenandoah

Co., Va. and was 80 years old. He applied from Marshall Co., Ala. Congress denied him a pension 30 Mar. 1848 because of no proof whatsoever.

Tipton, William. Va. Pvt. He served in Parker's Regiment. He was wounded three times at Savannah. One of his wounds was in his right shoulder. He received a gratuity of £250 and a suit of clothes on 20 Nov 1780. His wife, Mary Tipton, was granted 300 pounds of pork and 6 barrels of corn for her support and their five children in Shenandoah Co., Va. 30 Mar. 1781. He was on the 1813 pension list. He later removed to Tennessee.

Tirrell, Benjamin. Mass. Matross. He served in Revere's Regiment and was from Weymouth. He was paid $50.

Tislow, George. Va. —. His wife, Mary Tislow, was furnished one barrel of corn or wheat in Charlotte County on 2 Aug. 1779 and £50 on 5 June 1780.

Titcomb, Benjamin. N.H. Lt. Col. He was on the roll in 1783. He served in Col. Reid's Regiment and was wounded in three different battles. He received an invalid pension and was from Dover.

Titlow, John. Pa. —. He served under Gen. Potter and was wounded in his foot at the battle near Yellow Springs. He was at Brandywine. He was from Bucks County.

Titter, Jacob. Pa. Pvt. He was in Philadelphia County 8 Jan. 1787. He served in the 10th Pa. Regiment under Col. Richard Humpton. He was later a blacksmith in the Artificers. He was disabled by a bruise in his breast by a horse. He was 33 years old. He also appeared as Jacob Titler.

Tobin, Samuel. Me. —. He died 29 Dec. 1834 at Buckfield. His widow was Margaret Tobin. She was paid $50 under the resolve of 1836.

Tod, John. Pa. —. He applied 18 Mar. 1820.

Todd, Daniel. Mass. Bombadier. He served in Crane's Artillery. His widow was Anna Saunders of Hollister.

Todd, Solomon. N.H. —. He was from Londonderry in 1786. He served in Capt. Ebenezer Fry's Company in 1st N.H. Regiment. He was under Gen. Sullivan in the glorious Western Expedition. He became disabled in 1776 with a hydrocel. He was discharged in 1781. Robert Hodgert was orderly sergeant, and Timothy Harrington was a fellow soldier. He had a wife and five children.

Todd, Yale. Conn. Pvt. He served in Gen. Wooster's Regiment. He was lame from an ulcerated leg due to exposure in 1776 in Canada. He resided in North Haven, Conn. in 1792.

Toey, Simon. Pa. Corp. His widow, Catherine Toey, was in Dauphin County on 24 Nov. 1786. In 1776 he served in Capt. William Brown's Company in the Lancaster County militia and was drafted into the Flying Camp. He was taken prisoner at Fort Washington. He languished on a prison ship and died 8 Dec. 1776. He left eight children or by another record nine children and a widow. He also appeared as Simon Duey and Simon Twoey. Since he was in the Flying Camp, her pension was not allowed under the act of 1 Oct. 1781. She was, however, pensioned 3 Feb. 1806 and 5 Apr. 1822.

Tolin, Elias. Va. —. His wife, Ann Tolin, and five children were furnished £10 support in Frederick Co., Va. on 15 May 1778. She and six children were furnished £35 on 7 Apr. 1779.

Toller, Jacob. N.Y. —. He served in the Montgomery County militia under Lt. Col. Samuel Clyde. He was slain 6 Aug. 1777. His children, Henry Toller, Jacob Toller, Elizabeth Toller, and Anna Toller, were granted support. He also appeared as Jacob Zoller [sic]

Tolley, William. Mass. —. He was paid $20.

Tolman, John. Mass. Pvt. He served in the militia under Col. William Heath and Capt. Robert Smith. He was disabled by a musket ball in his right shoulder. He was 33 years old. He was pensioned

18 July 1786. He was on the 1813 pension list of Vermont.

Tolman, Peleg. Mass. Carpenter's Yeoman. He served aboard the Continental frigate *Trumbull* under Capt. J. Nicholson and was wounded in an engagement with a British ship of war. He lost his left arm on 1 June 1780. He was pensioned at half-pay from 1 Oct. 1780 when his pay ceased on 19 Apr. 1781. He was pensioned 7 July 1786. He was aged 22 and resided in Boston, Mass. in 1786. He was on the 1813 pension list. He also appeared as Peleg Tallman.

Tom, Thomas. —. —. He was pensioned 9 June 1794.

Tomkins, Abel. N.J. —. He served in the militia and took sick with smallpox. He married Elizabeth Bridge 6 Dec. 1764 in Morristown. He guarded continental stores and provisions under Lt. Benjamin Pierson. He was taken from guard duty to hospital to care for Continental soldiers sick with the smallpox. The hospital was in the home of Ralph Bridge in Morris County. He died 1777. He left six children. His eldest son was Jacob Tomkins who was five years old. His widow, Elizabeth Tomkins, married secondly 16 Mar. 1783 Benjamin Prudden. She received a half-pay pension 12 Feb. 1794 in Morris County. He also appeared as Abel Tompkins.

Tomlin, Jacob. N.J. Pvt. He served under Capt. David Paul and Col. Potter. He died 4 Mar. 1777 at Somerset of illness. He married Elizabeth Franklin. His widow married secondly Jacob Collatter 9 May 1780 in Gloucester County. She was granted a half-pay pension for the period of her widowhood.

Tomlin, Jasper. Ga. —. He was wounded in Mar. 1779 while in Continental service. It may have been at Williamsburg on the Savannah River. He had enlisted in Virginia with Benjamin Dilloson and George Dameron under Capt. John Dooley. He was under Col. Mulberry. He was in the service eighteen months. He applied 29 Aug. 1803 in South Carolina.

Tomlinson, Jabez. Conn. Pvt. He served in Col. Sheldon's Dragoons. He was disabled on fatigue cutting wood by cutting off the two smallest toes on his left foot and almost cut off the next two on the same foot in Nov. 1780. He resided in New Milford, Conn. in 1794. He enlisted 23 Oct. 1780. He died in 1811. He was on the 1813 pension list.

Tomlinson, William. Pa. Pvt. He was in Philadelphia County on 14 Nov. 1785. He was transferred from the 5th Pa. Regiment to the Invalids. He was wounded in his left arm. He was discharged 1 Nov. 1783. He was 45 years old. He was on the 1813 pension list.

Tomm, Henry. Md. Pvt. He served in the German Regiment. He was wounded in his right arm in 1777 at the battle of Germantown. He lived in Md. in 1794. He mustered, was wounded in Aug. 1777, and invalided in Mar. 1779. He was on the 1813 pension list. He was from Washington County as a pensioner.

Tompkins, Abraham. —. —. Congress rejected the claim of the heirs on 8 Mar. 1882.

Tompkins, Benjamin. R.I. Marine. He was pensioned on 15 Dec. 1785 at the age of 27. He served aboard the sloop *Providence* under Capt. Hacker and was disabled by the loss of his left arm above the elbow in action with a British brig on 6 May 1779. He resided in Newport Co., R.I. He was on the 1813 pension list.

Tompkins, Christopher. —. Lt. He served in the navy for three years. He was on the galley *Henry* under his father Robert Tompkins, commander. He served as 2nd Lieutenant from 29 Jan. 1777 to 14 Jan. 1779. He was entitled to 2,666 2/3 acres of bounty land by warrant #4544. An additional warrant for 1,333 ½ acres was issued to his only daughter and sole heir, Ann D. Shirley, by warrant #6936. He died in 1789. He married in Mar. 1783. His widow, Martha Tompkins, lived in Hampton until 1785 and moved to Norfolk in July 1796. She married secondly Omnaforas Dameron 5 May 1799. She was a widow again when Congress granted her a pension 9 May 1850.

Tonder, —. Ga. —. Mrs. Lucy Tonder was granted five daily rations 10 Sep. 1782.

Toms, Thomas. Va. Pvt. He served in Capt. George Maxwell's Company of militia. He was wounded in the head being scalped in his left temple with a stroke from a hatchet which did much injury to his eye. He was disabled in two fingers on his left hand and wounded in his right hip and neck, all of which he received in 1780 at King's Mountain against Maj. Ferguson. He lived in Albemarle Co., Va. in 1794.

Tool, Richard. Va. Gunner. He served aboard the galley *Henry* and died in the service in Feb. 1778. His widow, Sarah Tool, was pensioned at the rate of £8 per annum 18 Dec. 1794. She was in York County in 1796.

Toomey, John. Md. Corp. He was pensioned at the rate of half-pay of a corporal in Queen Anne's County on 16 Feb. 1820.

Toomey, Matthew. Va. Pvt. His widow, Elizabeth Toomey, and five children were granted £5 support in Frederick Co., Va. on 6 May 1777, £10 on 7 Oct. 1778, £25 on 3 Aug. 1779, and on 5 Nov. 1782. His widow was in Frederick County when she was put on the pension list on 1 May 1786 at the rate of £12 per annum. He served in the 8th Va. Regiment and died upon his return from the Southern Expedition in S.C. She died 16 July 1806. There were several children. She also appeared as Elizabeth Toony.

Toone, Argellon. Va. —. He was pensioned in Mecklenburg County on 19 Jan. 1813 at the rate of $60 per annum. He had a wife, five daughters, and a small son.

Toops, Leonard. Pa. —. He enlisted under Capt. Hedrick in the 11th Regiment. In May 1777 and was discharged in Aug. 1783. He was from Huntingdon County and applied 2 Apr. 1814. He also appeared as Leonard Doops.

Topham, Benjamin. Md. —. His sole legatee, Ann Busey, was to be paid his arrears in 1826.

Topping, Major. Va. —. His wife, Catherine Topping, and her child were furnished one barrel of corn and 50 weight of pork in Accomack Co., Va. 31 Jan. 1783.

Torrence, Thomas. Vt. Pvt. He served in Col. Moseley's militia. He was wounded by a musket ball which entered three inches above the anus and lodged in his body on 28 Apr. 1777 at Campo or Fairfield. He lived in Bennington, Vt. in 1794 and Sandgate, Vt. in 1795. He was granted half a pension 20 Apr. 1796. He was on the 1813 pension list.

Torrey, Isaac. Mass. —. He lived in Scituate, Plymouth County and sought his pension for £45 for one year ending in June 1779 on 5 Apr. 1780.

Torrey, Joseph. —. Maj. He served in Col. Hazen's Regiment until his death in Sep. 1783. His executor was his brother. His heirs received his five years' full pay commutation 3 June 1834. They sought 6% interest 27 May 1892.

Torry, Thomas. Mass. —. His warrant for $20 was drawn in the name of his children 31 Jan. 1821.

Tousard, Louis de. Lt. Col. —. He was pensioned under the act of 27 Oct. 1778. He was promoted to lieutenant colonel by brevet for action in Rhode Island on that date and was granted an annual pension. On 30 Apr. 1794 he was paid $3,600 in lieu of his annual pension of $360. He died 18 Sep. 1821.

Toussiger, Peter. S.C. Matross. He served in the Continental Artillery of S.C. and was wounded at Stono in 1779. He was made a prisoner in 1780 and died in hospital 5 Apr. 1781. There were four young children. His widow, Elizabeth Toussiger, was receiving a pension in 1793.

Tower, Benjamin. Mass. Pvt. He was in the Invalids under Col. Lewis Nichola and was disabled due to rheumatism. He was pensioned 31 Dec. 1787. He was 49 years old in 1786. He died 13

Sep. 1806.

Tower, Benjamin. Vt. Pvt. He served under Col. Bayley in Capt. Jacob's Militia Company. He was wounded by a ball passing through his right thigh on 17 Sep. 1776 at Harlem Heights. He was pensioned in Mar. 1794. He was granted one-third of a pension 20 Apr. 1796. He lived at Westminister, Vt. in 1795. He transferred to Franklin Co., N.Y. 4 Mar. 1824. He was on the 1813 pension list. He died 10 May 1829.

Towle, Jeremiah. N.H. Corp. He was wounded at Bemis Heights on 19 Sep. 1777 by a musket ball through his arms and body. He served in Capt. Amos Emerson's Company. He was from Chester. He was aged 27 in 1787. He was on the 1813 pension list.

Towle, Samuel. Mass. —. He served under Col. James Frye in Capt. Benjamin Farnum's Company. He was disabled by a ball entering his right thigh which breached his bowels.

Towles, —. S.C. —. His widow was Martha Towles. There were three children in 1791.

Towles, Oliver. S.C. Capt. He served in 3rd S.C. Regiment. He was a prisoner for fourteen months after the fall of Charleston and was killed in 1781. His widow, Jane Towles, was receiving a pension in Newberry District in 1791. She died 21 Aug. 1826. Her son, Daniel Towles, sought her arrearage. Among the other heirs was a son Oliver Towles.

Town, Ebenezer. Mass. Ens. He died 18 Feb. 1778. His heirs were paid his seven-years' half-pay of $840.

Town, Joseph. Me. —. He was from Kennebunk. He was paid $50 under the resolve of 1836.

Townehill, James. Pa. Pvt. He served under Capt. Thomas Rankin and Col. Crawford in the militia. He was wounded in the breast with a ball on the expedition against the Sandusky Indians. He was from Westmoreland County. He was receiving a half-pay pension in 1790.

Towns, John. Va. Lt. He served in the Continental Line. His legal representatives received his commutation 11 May 1838.

Townsend, Allen. Md. Pvt. He was pensioned at the rate of half-pay of a private 27 Jan. 1817.

Townsend, Daniel. Conn. Pvt. He served in the 1st Conn. Regiment under Col. Josiah Starr. He was wounded in 1780 and lost the sight of his right eye. He had liberty to pass to Danbury to be transferred to the Invalids Corps 27 Apr. 1780 from Lt. Col. David F. Sill. He lived in Fredericksburgh, Dutchess Co., N.Y. on 20 Apr. 1789. He was a carpenter. He was aged 56 years on 11 Apr. 1787. He was on the 1813 pension list. He died 6 Jan. 1813.

Townsend, George. R.I. Pvt. He was pensioned in 1785. He lost all the toes on his right foot, and his toes on his left foot were much injured by frost bite on the Oswego Expedition in Feb. 1783. He served under Col. Jeremiah Olney. He was aged 24. He was on the 1813 pension list. He died 12 Jan. 1814 in Providence Co., R.I.

Townsend, Solomon. Conn. Pvt. He was disabled by hemorrhoidal tumors. He was pensioned 10 Apr. 1783. He was on the 1813 pension list. He died in 1813.

Townsend, Sylvanus. N.Y. Pvt. He served under Capt. Ephraim Lockwood and Col. Crane in the Westchester County militia from 1 June 1778 to the end of the war. He served at least ten months out of each year for the last four years. His daughter was Polly Townsend. He was 75 years old when Congress granted him a pension 10 Jan. 1832.

Townsend, Thomas. Md. Pvt. He was pensioned at the rate of half-pay of a private in Talbot County on 18 Feb. 1825.

Townshend, Roger. N.Y. Pvt. He served in the Orange County militia under Col. Allison and was slain 22 July 1779. His widow, Keziah Townshend, received his half-pay pension. He also appeared as Roger Townsend.

Townsley, Daniel. Mass. Pvt. He served in the 16th Regiment and was from Buckland. He was paid $50.

Townsley, Daniel. Mass. Pvt. He served in the 16th Regiment and was from Buckland. He was paid $50.

Tozar, John. —. —. He was injured in the war. His application of 28 Mar. 1806 was not accepted.

Trabue, Daniel. Va. —. He entered the service in 1776 at the age of sixteen and served a month guarding the magazine at Chesterfield. He was under Capt. Matthew Scott. In 1777 he was on a tour under James Trabue at Boonsborough, Ky. He acted as commissary and received pay as a captain. In 1779 he brought supplies on forty pack horses from Virginia and delivered them to Col. Bowman in Jan. 1780. His next tour was in the militia under Capt. Edward Morley, Col. Markam, and Col. Faulkner. He was at the battle of Petersburg. Col. Goode employed him to carry dispatches to Gen. Lafayette. He was commissioned a captain by Gov. Thomas Jefferson. In 1777, 1778, and 1779 he was at Fort Logan. His last service was of a private character and not state or continental. Congress granted him a pension for six months of service 26 Mar. 1836. He gave his age as 72 years on 31 Mar. 1832 in Adair Co., Ky.

Trabue James. Va. Subaltern & Commissary. He served in the Illinois expedition under Col. George Rogers Clark and died in 1802. He qualified for bounty land from Virginia. Congress ruled that his service did not qualify for federal bounty land on 13 Apr. 1842.

Tracey, Moses. Conn. Sgt. He was disabled by old age and being worn out. He was pensioned 4 Jan. 1783. He was on the 1813 pension list. He died in 1813.

Tracy, James. S.C. Sgt. He was from Union District in 1810. He was pensioned 21 Dec. 1822 at the rate of $60 per annum for life. He served under Captains Kilpatrick, Jamieson, Montgomery, and Jacob Barnett. He was at Rocky Mount, Hanging Rock, Blackstocks, and Eutaw. John Bird was lieutenant under Capt. Jacob Barnett. John Williams proved his service. He was paid as late as 1834.

Tracy, Solomon. —. —. He married 3 Nov. 1803. Congress denied his widow, Dolly Tracy, a pension 9 Mar. 1848 because she married him too late to qualify.

Trafton, Lemuel. Mass. —. He served under Col. Nixon and Capt. Thomas Barnes. He was disabled by the loss of his right arm. He was 33 years old in 1786.

Trainum, —. Va. —. His wife, Elizabeth Trainum, was granted £20 support in Caroline Co., Va. 14 Apr. 1780.

Trammel, Philip. S.C. —. He was wounded in the service. He was granted an annuity 14 Feb. 1786. He was from Union District.

Trammel, William. S.C. —. He was wounded in 1781 near the Broad River in South Carolina. He was receiving a pension in Greenville District in 1791. On 8 Nov. 1820 he sought the balance of his annuity. He was being paid as late as 1831.

Tranus, John. Pa. Pvt. He was on the 1791 pension list. He was a Negro.

Trask, David. Mass. Pvt. He was from Marlborough and was paid $20.

Trask, Jonathan. Mass. —. He was paid $20.

Trask, Samuel. Mass. Pvt. He served in Crane's Artillery and was from Roxbury. He was paid $50.

Trask, Samuel. Mass. —. He was from Truro and was paid $20.

Traston, Lemuel. Mass. Pvt. He served under Col. Thomas Nixon in Capt. Thomas Barnes' Company and lost his right arm on York Island 16 Sep. 1776. He was pensioned at the rate of half-pay from 31 Dec. 1776 on 4 Oct. 1777. He was 33 years old in 1786. He transferred to New Hampshire 15 June 1812. He was on the 1813 pension list as Lemuel Trafton.

Travers, Mathias. Md. —. He served six months in 1776 and again in 1777. He was under Gen. Henry Hooper and Col. Thomas Enals. In 1778 he volunteered as a captain and raised 110 men. He received his commission 24 June 1778. He guarded the eastern shore and took one schooner and one sloop and made prisoners of their crews. He was elected a captain of another company in Oct. 1779. He resigned in oct. 1780. Congress granted him a pension 3 Mar. 1836 for two years and eight months of service. He was 78 years old.

Traversie, Joseph. —. Capt. He served under Gen. Hazen. He was pensioned under the act of 8 Aug. 1782 by the Continental Congress. He died at Chazy, N.Y. in 1808. His heirs received his half-pay from 21 Oct. 1780 to 8 Mar. 1785 on 2 Mar. 1860.

Travis, —. Va. —. His mother, Mary Travis, was furnished support in Westmoreland County in Mar. 1779.

Travis, Ezekiel. N.Y. Pvt. He served in Col. James McClaughry's Regiment in Capt. Abraham Cuddeback in the militia. He was wounded in his right arm by Indians 10 June 1779. He lived in Ulster Co., N.Y. on 16 Apr. 1789. He was on the 1813 pension list.

Travis, Jacob. N.Y. Lt. He served under Sgt. Robert Graham, Capt. William Franchier, and Maj. Thaddeus Crane in the Westchester County militia. He lost his left arm by a cannon shot on the march to Danbury on 27 Apr. 1777. He requested to be exempted from serving in the Invalids Corps because he had a wife with four small children. He lived at Poundridge, Westchester Co., N.Y. in 1787. He was aged 45 years on 15 Jan. 1787. He was on the 1813 pension list. One record gave his date of death as 10 Mar. 1809.

Tray, Elijah. Vt. Sgt. He served under Col. Warner. He lost his health on the expedition to Joseph's patent in N.Y. by order of Gen. Schuyler in Apr. and May 1777. He lived in Bennington, Vt. in 1792.

Treadwell, Daniel. Conn. Pvt. He served in Bradley's Regiment. He was on the 1813 pension list. He died 15 Apr. 1822 in Fairfield Co., Conn.

Treasure, Richard. Del. Pvt. He was first pensioned in 1781. He was pensioned by South Carolina in 1785. He was wounded at the battle of Cowpens and was reported to have died. Matthew Hilford, one of his fellow soldiers, administered his estate and obtained his depreciation pay. On 10 Mar. 1786 South Carolina awarded him £10 to enable him to return to Delaware. In 1786 Richard Treasure returned to Delaware and learned what had happened. He called on Hilford who was unable to make satisfaction. Hilford fled so he brought suit against his security, Solomon Alcock. Alcock disposed of his land and assigned away the bonds given him for the purchase money to relatives in Maryland. Treasure had a wife and two children. He lost a leg. He was on the 1791 pension list. He died in 1803 in North Carolina. Richard Treasure was at one time on the pension roll of Pennsylvania.

Treat, Samuel. Mass. —. He was in the 4th Regiment. He was from Truro.

Treine, George. Pa. —. He was awarded a $40 gratuity and a $40 annuity 15 Apr. 1834. He died 7 Jan. 1843.

Trench, James. Conn. Pvt. He was on the 1795 pension list. He died in 1807.

Trench, Lemuel. Mass. —. He served in the 9th Regiment and was from Hardwick. He was paid $20.

Trent, John. N.C. Capt. He served in the Wake County militia. He received several wounds in the upper extremities and a wound in the right leg in 1780 at Turkey Creek. He resided in Augusta, Ga. in 1796.

Trent, Thomas. Va. Sgt. He served in the 15th Va. Regiment. He was awarded a gratuity of £250 in addition to his pay of a soldier on 2 Nov. 1779. He was in Chesterfield County 13 Mar. 1787 when he was continued on the pension roll at the rate of £18 per annum. He lost both arms at the battle of Monmouth as attested by Col. William Davis. He was 30 years old. He lived in Buckingham County in 1789. He was on the 1813 pension list. He died 28 June 1820.

Treine, George. Pa. —. He was awarded a $40 gratuity and a $40 annuity in Bucks Co., Pa. 15 Apr. 1834.

Trenkle, Christopher. Va. —. His wife, Elizabeth Trenkle, and two children were furnished 3 barrels of corn and 150 pounds of pork in Frederick Co., Va. on 3 Apr. 1781.

Tresner, John. Md. Pvt. He served in the 7th Regiment and was disabled at Germantown. He was pensioned in Frederick County in 1786. He also appeared as John Trisner. He was on the 1813 pension list.

Tressler, Frederick. Pa. —. His name was incorrectly given as Frederick Tressla in the act. The correction was made 21 June 1839. The war in which he served was not specified.

Tretabough, Conrad. Va. —. His wife, Mary Tretabough, and two children were furnished 3 barrels of corn and 150 pounds of pork in Frederick Co., Va. on 5 Sep. 1780.

Trexler, John. Pa. Capt. He was commissioned 10 May 1778 and marched to Wyoming.

Trewitz, Conrad. Pa. —. He applied in Union County on 16 May 1822. He enlisted 15 Aug. 1776 in Capt. Benjamin Weiser's Company in Col. Husieker's Regiment until the latter deserted to the British. Col. Weldner replaced him. He was discharged in 1781 by Gen. Muhlenberg in N.J. His messmate was Michael Yeisley. They served a year and a half together. He also appeared as Conrad Trevitz.

Trickey, John. N.H. Pvt. He was from Portsmouth in 1787. He served in Capt. Isaac Fry's Company in the 1st N. Y. Regiment. He received a fall and injured his knee and his ankle rendering him lame. John Dennett knew him from Capt. Fry's Company. He was aged 42 in 1787.

Triplet, Thomas. —. Capt. He served in the Infantry. He received his five years' full pay in commutation 2 Mar. 1833.

Triplett, —. —. —. His widow, Sarah Triplett, had her petition for a pension by a special act of Congress rejected 4 May 1846 because she married subsequent to 1 Jan. 1794.

Triplett, —. Ga. —. His widow, Mrs. Triplett, of Burke County was granted two daily rations 15 Mar. 1782.

Triplett, George. Va. Lt. He received commutation of full pay for five years in lieu of half-pay for life as lieutenant of infantry in the Virginia Line with no interest on 8 Jan. 1827.

Triplett, Hedgeman. Va. Lt. He was reared in Culpeper County. He was a private under Capt. Yancey and Col. Glen and, sergeant major under Col. Edmonds, He served to the close of the war. He received 2,666 2/3 acres of bounty land from Virginia. He sought commutation of five full years from Congress on 11 Feb. 1833.

Triplett, Peter. Va. —. He served three years. He was pensioned in Culpeper County on 12 Feb. 1828 at the rate of $60 per annum and $30 immediate relief. He had been wounded in battle.

Triplett, Thomas. Va. Capt. He served to the end of the war. His heirs received his half-pay 28 Dec. 1831. There was a fraudulent claim by a Thomas Triplett who claimed to be the lawful heir. He was arrested, tried, found guilty, and imprisoned. He died in jail. The rightful heirs obtained a judgment against him, but he was insolvent. The five years' full pay of $7,245.45 was paid to another Thomas Triplett and the rightful heirs 17 Feb. 1838.

Triplett, William. Va. —. He received his commutation.

Tripner, —. Pa. —. His widow, Mary Tripner, was awarded a $40 annuity in Philadelphia Co., Pa. 1 May 1852 for his Revolutionary service.

Tripner, George. Pa. —. He was awarded a $40 gratuity and a $40 annuity in Philadelphia Co., Pa. 22 Dec. 1834. He was paid $200 for his right to his donation land. He was 78 years old in 1840. He died 17 June 1848.

Tripp, —. Va. He was in Continental service. He marched to the northward and died in the service. His widow, Mary Tripp, was being pensioned 4 Jan. 1785.

Tripp, Jonathan. Mass. Sgt. He served in the 16th Regiment under Col. Henry Jackson and Capt. North. He was disabled by the loss of his left leg. He was 28 years old in 1788. He was on the 1791 pension roll. He died 19 Aug. 1807.

Tripp, Robert. Me. —. He was from Sanford. He was paid $50 under the resolve of 1836.

Trissler, John. Pa. —. He was granted relief in Lancaster County 24 Mar. 1837.

Tritipoe, Conrad. Va. —. His wife, Mary Tritipoe, was granted support in Loudoun County in May 1781.

Trittler, Jonathan. Pa. —. He was pensioned.

Troop, —. Va. —. His wife, Elizabeth Troop, was granted £10 support in Caroline Co., Va. 9 Apr. 1778 while her husband was in Continental service.

Trouin, Francis. —. —. His application was not accepted in 1801.

Trout, —. N.Y. —. Mary Barbara Trout was granted support while he was away in the service under Cortlandt 30 June 1778.

Trout, William. Mass. —. He was in Jackson's Regiment and was from Boston. He was paid $20.

Trow, Solomon. —. —. His application was not accepted.

Trowant, Nathan. Mass. Pvt. He served in the 10th Regiment under Col. Thomas Marshall and Capt. Amasa -----. He was wounded in his right thigh.

Trowbridge, James. Mass. —. He was served in the 12th Regiment and was from New Hampshire. He was paid $20.

Troxel, David. —. —. He claimed service in 1799 under Capt. Moses Webb for nine weeks, five weeks under Capt. Michael Harrison, and three months as a substitute for Abraham Vandeventer under Capt. James Gregg and Gen. Sevier. He was in battle with the Cherokee at Highwassee in 1780. He was drafted and served three months in Sullivan County under Sgt. Abraham Britton to guard the people planting corn. He also served three months as a substitute for William Wyreck under Ens. Elisha Cole and was promoted to sergeant. In 1838 he stated that he was about 70 years of age. If true, he was 12 in 1780. Also in 1838 he stated that he entered at the age of 17 and was born in 1773 or 1774. Congress concluded that his service was not in the Revolutionary War. It was in the Indian wars. Congress rejected his claim for relief 3 Mar. 1851.

Truck, John. Md. Sgt. He was pensioned at the rate of half-pay of a sergeant in Frederick County on 1 Mar. 1826. He was issued a warrant for 50 acres of bounty land as a donation 9 Mar. 1826. His widow, Elizabeth Trux, was pensioned at the same rate 6 Mar. 1832.

True, —. Va. —. His widow, Elizabeth True, was granted £20 support in Caroline Co., Va. 11 Mar. 1779. He was killed in the service.

True, Zebulon. Me. —. He died 4 Feb. 1830. His widow was Martha True from Temple. She was paid $50 under the resolve of 1836.

Truelove, John. N.C. —. His widow, Eleanor Truelove, applied from Chowan County in 1797. He died in the service as a militia man in 1778. She received a pension of $20 to assist in rearing the children. It ended when they were grown. In 1821 she was 74 years old and had but one child in the state and sought another pension. She was paid as late as 1827.

Trueman, John. Md. Lt. He served in the 3rd Regiment under Col. John E. Howard. He was disabled in the service before Camden on 25 Apr. 1781 and was pensioned in Nov. 1785 at the rate of half-pay of a lieutenant. He died 4 Feb. 1809. He also appeared as John Truman. He was from Anne Arundel County. Congress rejected the petition from his representatives 29 Mar.1836.

Truesdale, Samuel. N.J. —. He was granted relief.

Truett, —. S.C. —. His widow was Rhoda Truett. There was one child in 1791.

Truefant, David. Mass. Pvt. He served at the Castle and was from Weymouth. He was paid $50.

Truitt, —. S.C. —. His widow, Isbel Truitt, was receiving a pension in 1793.

Trump, George. Pa. —. He applied in Dauphin County on 19 Apr. 1826. He enlisted 25 Jan. 1775 for five years in Capt. Fisher's Company in the 4th Regiment under Col. Stewart. After Germantown he was taken sick and sent to hospital until he was discharged by Col. Thompson in the fall of 1778. He was at the battles of Germantown, Kingsbridge, Fort Washington on the Hudson, and Trenton where he was wounded in the ankle. He was 78 years and had a wife and four children living. One, a daughter, was still at home. He was born in Lebanon, Pa. Peter Moyer lay together in camp with him for two winters at Morristown, N.J. and thought Trump was in the 10th Regiment. Abraham Riblet spent two winters at Morristown with him. They were also together at West Point. He saw Trump at Valley Forge in the winter of 1777-1778. Trump signed in German.

Trusdell, Stephen. N.J. Pvt. He enlisted at the age of 18 in the militia for five months in June 1776 under Capt. John Seward. At Long Island he served under Capt Silas Beckwith and Col. Freylinghausen. He was a native of New Jersey. He was in his 80th year when he applied in Sussex County 31 Oct. 1837.

Truslow, Benjamin. Va. Pvt. He served more than two years. He was under Capt. Wallace at the siege of York in 1781 and was wounded in his eye. He was also at Cowpens. He enlisted under Lt. Thomas Victor and Capt. William Mountjoy for three years. His father was a tailor. He had previously lived in King George County but was from Stafford County when he applied. Congress granted him a pension 30 July 1842.

Trussell, Moses. N.H. Pvt. He was from Hopkinton/Dunbarton in 1786. He enlisted in Capt. Isaac Baldwin's Company in Col. Stark's Regiment in 1775. After the battle of Bunker Hill on 17 June, he endeavored to recover Captain Baldwin who was mortally wounded. He had his left hand shot off. His widowed mother came to visit him. She was dead by 10 Feb. 1781. He was aged 32 in 1787. He was on the 1813 pension list.

Trussell, Reuben. N.H. Pvt. He served in Gen. Stark's Brigade in Col. Stickney's Regiment. He was wounded at the battle of Bennington 16 Aug. 1777.

Tryer, —. Pa. —. His widow, Elizabeth Tryer, was awarded a $40 gratuity and a $40 annuity in Lancaster Co., Pa. 8 Apr. 1826. She died 2 Nov. 1829.

Tryon, Salmon. Conn. —. He served three months in the militia and spent a year as guard of British prisoners and Continental stores at Litchfield under the direction of the county sheriff. Congress rejected his claim for a pension 23 Dec. 1836.

Trytle, Jonathan. Pa. —. He applied in Franklin County on 29 Apr. 1813. He served from Nov. 1776 to Sep. 1783. He had a large family to maintain. He died 10 Mar. 1814. His brother-in-law was David Snider of Chambersburg.

Tubbs, Ananias. N.H. Pvt. He was from Swanzey in 1787. He was wounded on 16 Aug. 1777 at Bennington by a musket ball in one hip. He served in James Heaton's Company in Col. Nichols's Regiment. He was aged 45 in 1787. He was on the 1813 pension list in Vermont. James Heaton was ensign in the same company.

Tubbs, Joseph. Mass. Sgt. Maj. He served in the 14th Regiment. His widow, Eunice Winslow of Taunton, was paid $50.

Tuck, Edward. Va. Pvt. He served in the militia. He was pensioned 2 Jan. 1808. He lived in Halifax

County. He was on the 1813 pension list.

Tuck, John. —. Pvt. He was drafted and served three months under Capt. Edward King at Ninety Six. He was drafted a second time and served under Capt. Parham Booker at Cabin Point or Portsmouth. He was at Guilford and Camden His brothers were Thomas Tuck and William Tuck. He died 6 July 1822. He married 10 Nov. 1791 in Halifax County Eady Standley. His widow, Eady Tuck, had her claim for a pension rejected by Congress 9 May 1850. Congress rejected the claim of their son, John R. Tuck, 11 July 1856.

Tucker, —. —. —. His son, John R. Tucker, had his claim rejected by Congress 11 July 1856.

Tucker, Benjamin. Mass. Pvt. He served under Col. Holman and Capt. Loring Lincoln. He was disabled by a gun shell in his left arm. He was 57 years of age in 1791.

Tucker, George Mass. Pvt. He served in the 16th Regiment and was from Newburyport. His widow, Sarah Tucker, was paid $50.

Tucker, Jesse. Va. —. He served three months under Capt. Dillard and Col. Holcomb. He had enlisted for the war and did so for eight months before the war ended. His widow, Nancy King, sought a pension. Congress rejected her claim 26 Apr. 1848 unless she could confirm his service by records. Proof of her marriage was unsatisfactory because the family register was either altered or retraced. The first birth in the register was in 1798.

Tucker, John. Va. Pvt. He served thirteen months in the expedition against the Indians under Capt. James Booth. He was paid $104 on 13 Mar. 1834.

Tucker, Joseph. Mass. —. He served in the 9th Regiment and was paid $20.

Tucker, Joshua. —. —. He died in the service. His widow, Mary Tucker, did not have her application accepted on 26 Feb. 1806.

Tucker, Lemuel. Mass. —. He served in the 3rd Regiment and was paid $20.

Tucker, Lewis. N.C. —. He was wounded by the Tories and allowed a gratuity of 20 barrels of corn in 1782. He was from Randolph County.

Tucker, Samuel. Mass. Capt. He served in the navy and was disabled. He was taken prisoner at Charleston in May 1780 and exchanged in Aug. 1780. He returned and served to 1783. He received no pay from 1780 to his discharge. He was granted relief 12 Jan. 1821. He was pensioned in 1826 at the rate of $240 per annum.

Tucker, William. Va. Pvt. He received $50 relief and a pension of $40 per annum on 4 Dec. 1795. He was in Essex County on 4 Dec. 1795. He served in the State Garrison Regiment and was wounded in the leg. He resided in Caroline County in 1804.

Tucker, Zephaniah. Conn. Pvt. He entered the service in 1776 and served under Gen. Glover, Col. Timothy Bigelow, and Capt. Martin until July 1779 when he went home on furlough. He accidentally broke his shoulder and was unable to return. Two officers came looking for him as a deserter and left with the pledge of the surgeon, Dr. Waldo, that he would return if his health was restored. It never did. He married 4 Feb. 1779 and died 25 Apr. 1817. He was from Woodstock. Congress granted his widow, Huldah Tucker, a pension 30 Jan. 1838.

Tucks, —. Va. —. His wife, Rachael Tucks, was awarded £6.9.3 relief in Halifax Co., Va. on 15 Jan. 1778. His surname could have been Turk.

Tuel, William. Md. Pvt. His widow was from Prince George's County in 1778 when she was pensioned. He was killed 4 Oct. 1777 at Germantown. He served under Capt. Horatio Clagett.

Tufts, Eliakim. Mass. Pvt. He served in the 1st Regiment. His widow, Merriam Tufts, was from Littleton and was paid $50.

Tufts, Samuel. Mass. —. He served in the 10th Regiment and was paid $20.

Tugerden, William. Pa. —. He received $5 per month in 1786. He was from Westmoreland County.

Tumbling, James. Va. Pvt. He was in Norfolk County 4 Sep. 1787. He enlisted in the 1ˢᵗ State Regiment 10 Mar. 1777 and died about 18 months later as attested by Capt. William Hoffler. He left a widow, Euphan Tumbling, and three children aged 19, 16, and 11. A son was John Tumbling. She was placed on the pension list at the rate of £8 per annum on 1 Oct. 1787. The widow died between Apr. 1789 and 15 Nov. 1790. He also appeared as James Tumlin.

Tuniece, at. —. —. He received half-pay for life.

Tunkle, Christopher. Va. —. His wife, Elizabeth Tunkle, received assistance in Frederick County 3 Apr. 1781.

Tupper, Anselm. Mass. Lt. & Adj. He received his commutation for five years in lieu of half-pay for life.

Tupper, Benjamin. Mass. Maj. He received his commutation for five years in lieu of half-pay for life. He was from Chesterfield and died 1 July 1792.

Tupper, John. Mass. Sgt. He served in the 5ᵗʰ Regiment. He was from Vermont and was paid $20.

Turball, William. Conn. Corp. He served in the 4ᵗʰ Conn. Regiment and was disabled at Germantown. He was pensioned 22 Sep. 1788. He died in 1823.

Turbeville, Absolum. S.C. —. He was killed in battle in May 1782. His widow, Lucy Windham, was receiving a pension in 1802.

Turberville, George. —. —. He served as an officer. His heirs claimed his commutation. Congress rejected the claim on 3 Mar. 1836 because he did not continue in the service after 5 Dec. 1778.

Turbeville, Jonathan. N.C. —. He enlisted in Mar. 1777 in Capt. Edward Ward's Company under Col. Armstrong. He was killed in the service in May 1782 leaving a widow, Lucy Turbeville, and four small children. His father-in-law, Edward Burke, sought relief for the family.

Turk, Ephraim. Pa. —. He received a $40 gratuity and a $40 annuity in York County 21 Mar.1837.

Turk, William. Pa. Pvt. He applied 2 July 1787. He served in Capt. McCariker's Artillery Company of the Chester County militia. He was wounded in the leg with a musket ball on 4 Oct. 1777. He was 40 years old. He also appeared as William Turck.

Turlington, Charles. Va. —. His son, Peter Turlington, was awarded £13, later increased to £25, in Northampton Co., Va. on 8 Dec. 1778.

Turnal, William. Va. —. He died in the service. His daughter was awarded 30 shillings per month in Accomack Co., Va. 27 Jan. 1779.

Turner, —. Pa. —. His widow, Jane Turner, was awarded a $40 gratuity and a $40 annuity in York Co., Pa. 15 Apr. 1835.

Turner, —. Pa. —. His widow, Jane Turner, was awarded a $40 gratuity and a $40 annuity in Beaver County in June 1836. She died 10 Dec. 1840.

Turner, Charles. N.C. —. He enlisted in 1779 and served under Capt. John Bozier and Col. Pointer. He was at Briar Creek and Great Bridge. He applied at the age of 75 in Pasquotank Co, N.C. 4 Mar. 1834.

Turner, Consider. Mass. —. He served in the 5ᵗʰ Regiment and was paid $20.

Turner, David. —. —. He was a soldier in 1776 under Col. Miles. He caught cold for want of sufficient clothing. It fell into his leg. He was incapacitated from labor. Since he was 17 years, it was doubtful that he was due any special favor.

Turner, David. Me. —. He was from New Vineyard. He was paid $50 under the resolve of 1836.

Turner, Edward. Mass. Lt. He died 26 Dec. 1777. His seven years' half-pay of $2,120 was paid to his heirs.

Turner, Elisha. Mass. —. He served in the 10ᵗʰ Regiment and was from Scituate. He was paid $20.

Turner, Enoch. Conn. Pvt. He served under Col. T. Cook. He was wounded with a musket ball below his knee which fractured both bones 19 Sep. 1779. He lived in New Haven, Conn. in 1792. He was in the militia. He was granted two-thirds of a pension 20 Apr. 1796. He was on the 1813 pension list.

Turner, Ezra. Mass. —. He served at the Castle. His widow. Sarah Turner, was from Canton and was paid $50.

Turner, Hezekiah. Mass. Pvt. He served in the 5th Regiment and was from Dedham. He was paid $50.

Turner, Isaac. Me. —. He was from Durham. He was paid $50 under the resolve of 1836.

Turner, James. S.C. —. He was receiving a pension in 1791.

Turner, Jarzel. N.J. Sgt. He served in Capt. Jonas Ward's Company under Col. Oliver Spencer. He died in July 1777 in hospital near Pompton. His brother was Nathan Turner. On 2 July 1789 Samuel Turner testified that he was present at the marriage of Jarzel Turner and Sarah Holmes about thirty-four years ago. She sought his half-pay in Morris County in 1789.

Turner, John. N.Y. Pvt. He served in the 4th Regiment in Col. Moylan's Dragoons. He was wounded in his arm and leg in June 1777 near Brunswick. He lived in Philadelphia, Pa. in 1794.

Turner, John. Pa. —. He was granted a pension 21 Mar. 1837 in Allegheny County. He died 20 May 1840.

Turner, John. Pa. —. He was awarded a $40 gratuity and a $40 annuity in Beaver Co., Pa. 15 Apr. 1835.

Turner, Maltiah. N.C. Sgt. He applied in Chatham County in 1785. He was aged 28 in 1785 and lost a leg in Continental service. He was on the 1813 pension list. He died 25 May 1831.

Turner, Nathan. Mass. Sgt. He served in the 16th Regiment and was from Swansea. His widow, Mercy Turner, was paid $50.

Turner, Philip. —. Surgeon. He served as a hospital physician and surgeon and was paid his commutation of full-pay 22 Apr. 1808. His son, John Turner, of Norwich, Connecticut received the unpaid interest 22 Dec. 1837.

Turner, Robert. Me. —. He died 29 Nov. 1836. His widow was Elizabeth Turner from Belmont. She was paid $50 under the resolve of 1836.

Turner, Starbird. Me. —. He was from Rome. He was paid $50 under the resolve of 1836.

Turner, Thomas. Md. Pvt. He was pensioned at the rate of half-pay of a private in Montgomery County on 19 Feb. 1819.

Turner, Titus Jennings. N.C. —. He served in 1778 for two and a half years. He served under Maj. Bennett Crafton. He was nearly 75 years old when he applied in Wake County in 1827. If he were not pensioned, he would have to go to the poor house.

Turner, William G. Pa. —. He applied in Fayette County on 5 May 1818. He enlisted in Capt. Nehemiah Stokeley's Company in the 8th Pa. Regiment under Col. McCoy. Later he was under Brig. Gen. Daniel Broadhead. He served three years from 17 Sep. 1776 to 17 Sep. 1779. He was discharged by Col. Stephen Bayard. He also appeared as William G. Turnon. He was 86 years old in 1840. He died 27 June 1841.

Turner, Zadock. Mass. Pvt. He served in the 2nd Regiment and was from Northfield. His widow, Hannah Turner, was paid $50.

Turney, Abel. Conn. Pvt. He served as a marine in the Continental Navy under John Barry on the *Alliance*. He was wounded by a ball in his right leg from enemy. He was pensioned at the rate of $1 per month from 1 Jan. 1781. He lived in Fairfield Co., Conn. He was on the 1813 pension list in New York.

Turney, Asa. Pvt. Conn. He enlisted 1 Apr. 1777 under Capt. Andrew Wakeman at Fairfield, Conn. After his first year, he hired a substitute to take his place. In his third year he rejoined the army. Andrew Wakeman was discharged so he had no regular commander for four months. He was put under the command of wagon master, Simeon Catline, for about eight months. His application for a pension was rejected 21 Dec. 1818.

Turney, Toney. Conn. Pvt. He served in the 2nd Regiment. He was wounded in the left side of his head by a cutlass which injured the sight of his eyes. He was stabbed in the breast with a bayonet and burst in his right side by stamping on him. Barmore's corps of light horse rode over him in 1779. He was cut in his left shoulder by a cutlass near New York. He resided in Stratford, Conn. in 1792. He enlisted 14 May 1777 for the war. In 1796 it was noted that he did not appear to have been disabled in the line of duty.

Turvey, William. Pa. Pvt. His pension began in 1792.

Turvey, William. Va. Pvt. He was in Loudoun County on 3 Aug. 1786 and was 35 years old. He enlisted in the 3rd Va. Regiment for the war in 1777. He was wounded in his left arm at the Waxsaws 29 May 1780 and rendered unfit for duty. Lt. John Roney attested to his service. He was continued on the pension list at the rate of £18 per annum on 19 Feb. 1789. He was in Ohio County in 1790.

Tutt, Benjamin. S.C. Capt. He commanded an independent company to guard the frontier. He served to the end of the war. He sought the same compensation given Capt. John Bowie, Richard Tutt, Prince, Farrar, and Earle. Andrew Hamilton, William Carithers, Thomas Farrar, John Looney, and Thomas Shanklin served with him. His only heir, Catherine Tutt, married Edmond Holman. They sought his commutation 11 Nov. 1827.

Tutt, Gabriel. S.C. Lt. He came to visit his brothers, Benjamin Tutt and Richard Tutt, early in the war. He served in the 5th Regiment under Col. Isaac Huger. His unit was taken into Continental service. He was in Capt. John Moore's Company. He was taken prisoner at the fall of Charleston but violated his parole. In 1783 he returned to his parents in Culpeper Co., Va. He sought five years' full pay 23 Nov. 1825. He was 69 years old in 1826. George McBeth aged 75, Col. Samuel Hammond, John Looney, Col. Thomas Farrar aged 74, Thomas Shanklin, and Samuel Earle testified in his behalf.

Tutt, James. Va. —. He was pensioned in Bedford County on 28 Jan. 1825 at the rate of $60 per annum and $40 immediate relief. He was in Harrison County in 1826. He died 2 June 1828, and John M. Woodyard was granted administration of his estate.

Tutt, Richard. S.C. Lt. He served on Continental establishment and served until the resolution of the legislature of South Carolina placed him in state service. His widow, Betty Tutt, was awarded $1,800 plus interest of 3% from Dec. 1793 on 17 Dec. 1821. She was administratrix *c.t.a.* and was paid $3,312. His other heirs were children Mary Tutt, Henry Tutt, Eliza Mims the wife of Josiah Mims, Ann Randolph the wife of James H. Randolph, and the heirs of his deceased son John Tutt whose guardian was Elizabeth Tutt. Samuel Garner, Simon Looney of Burke Co., Ga., and Matthew Barrett served with him. The heirs were his three children Richard H. Tutt age 25, Mary Tutt aged 38, Eliza Mims aged 30, and four grandchildren Eleanor Randolph aged 7, Elizabeth Ann Randolph age 5, Frances Tutt aged 8, and Elizabeth Tutt aged 6.

Tuttle, Aaron. Conn. Pvt. He served in Col. Cook's Regiment. He was wounded by a musket ball in the foot which entered between the first and second toe and came out some distance above the great toe joint on 7 Oct. 1777 at the capture of Burgoyne. He lost one toe. He resided at Hamden,

Conn. in 1794. He was on the 1813 pension list. He was 81 years old in 1818 and died 17 May 1831.

Tuttle, Isaiah. N.J. Pvt. He served in the 2nd Regiment and lost his sight. He was 43 years old and was from Roxbury. He was on the 1791 pension roll.

Tuttle, John. Mass. Pvt. He was in the Invalids under Capt. Williams and Col. Rufus Putnam. He was worn out in the service. He was 60 years old and resided in Chelsea, Mass. in 1786.

Tuttle, Joseph. —. Pvt. He served at least one year. Congress granted him a pension 3 Mar. 1836.

Tuttle, Levi. Conn. Pvt. He lived in Fairfield Co., Conn. He was on the 1813 pension list.

Tuttle, Stephen. N.Y. —. He served under Col. Fisher and was slain 6 Aug. 1777. His children, Catharine Tuttle, Betsey Tuttle, and John [?] Tuttle, received his half-pay pension. [The text of the document is damaged. There may have been more children.] He also appeared as Stephen Tuthill.

Tuttle, Thaddeus. Conn. —. He entered the service for nine months in July 1776 under Capt. Martin. He was at the battle of Long Island and ordered to bring off the retreating American army in boats under heavy fire. He was carried home sick in Dec. 1776. He next served from Oct. 1777 to 1 May 1778. He then entered the service under Gen. Wooster and was at Danbury when the stores were destroyed. In July 1779 he was under Capt. Stephen Parker who was killed while guarding the coast. In 1780 Capt. Dayton took charge of four whale boats of ten men each to watch the movements of the enemy in the sound. He was taken prisoner by surprise and robbed of his clothing and five guineas. He served as a sergeant for nine months in a horse company. His total period of service was three years and three months. He was 79 years old. His brother, Moses Tuttle, was 85 years old. Congress granted him a pension 15 Jan. 1836.

Tutwiller, Jonathan. Md. Pvt. He was pensioned at the rate of half-pay of a private 2 Jan. 1813. His pension was increased to half-pay of a sergeant in 1815. He died 20 July 1819.

Tweed, Joseph. Pa. —. He was awarded a $40 gratuity and a $40 annuity in Lancaster Co., Pa. 29 Mar. 1824.

Tweedy, Thomas. Pa. Gunner. He was in Chester County on 12 Dec. 1785. He served in Col. Thomas Proctor's Artillery Regiment. He was wounded by a musket ball through his right leg in action with the Indians at Newton on 29 Aug. 1779. He was also wounded on 21 July 1780 by a musket ball in his right thigh which lodged in his left thigh at the battle of Block House at Bulls Ferry on the North River. He was 26 years old. He was on the 1813 pension list.

Twiggs, P. Decatur. —. —. Congress did not grant his widow relief 30 Mar. 1848.

Twiney, Toney. Conn. Pvt. He died 2 June 1810.

Twitty, —. S.C. —. His widow, Isbel Twitty, was receiving a pension in 1793.

Tydings, Kealy. Md. Sgt. He was pensioned at the rate of half-pay of a sergeant in 3 Jan. 1812.

Tyler, Abraham. Me. —. He was from Saco. He was paid $50 under the resolve of 1836.

Tyler, Asa. Conn. Pvt. He served under Capt. John Isham under Col. Chester. He was wounded in the foot at White Plains 28 Oct. 1776. He was pensioned 17 July 1787 in New York. He was aged 30 years in or about 1786.

Tyler, Benjamin. S.C. Sgt. He served under Col. Erwin and Capt. Thornley. He was wounded on the east side of the Pee Dee River in Feb. 1781 by a ball between his ribs. It came out his back. He also had large buck shot in his hip. He kept a country school. Of his seven children two were deaf and dumb. He was pensioned at the rate of $22 per annum on 21 Dec. 1804. He was pensioned again on 4 Dec. 1812. He was from St. Johns Parish, Charleston.

Tyler, Bezaleel. N.Y. Pvt. He served under Col. McClaughry in the Ulster County militia and was slain

22 July 1779. His children, John Tyler, Sarah Tyler, and Abigail Tyler, received a half-pay pension.

Tyler, Daniel. —. —. His widow, Sally Tyler, had her petition for a pension rejected by Congress 27 Mar. 1846 because they were married subsequent to 1 Jan. 1794.

Tyler, Daniel. Me. —. He was from Brownfield. He was paid $50 under the resolve of 1836.

Tyler, Ebenezer. R.I. Pvt. He served in Hitchcock's R.I. Regiment in Capt. Jeremiah Tyler's Company. He was wounded in his right shoulder. He lived in N.Y. in 1782. He was pensioned 1 Oct. 1789. He lived in Albany County and later in Rensselaer County. He was on the 1813 pension list.

Tyler, Jeremiah. Mass. Pvt. He served in the 15th Regiment and was from Lowell. He was paid $50.

Tyler, Joseph. —. Pvt. He was said to hold a Major's Commission in a regiment of Minute Men. He was wounded in the thigh by a musket ball on 16 Aug. 1777 at Bennington. He resided in Townsend, Vt. in 1796. He was on the 1813 pension list. He died 25 July 1815.

Tyler, Lewis. S.C. Capt. He was taken prisoner by the Tories and died in the *Provo*, a prison ship, in Wilmington in Sep. 1782. He froze to death. His widow, Mourning Tyler, was from Georgetown District in 1797. His children were born 15 Apr. 1772, 24 Sep. 1773, 12 Jul. 1775, 10 Mar. 1777, 24 Jan. 1780, and 14 Jan. 1782.

Tyler, Nathaniel. —. —. He received bounty land warrant #3301 for 2,666 2/3 acres 1 July 1784. He died prior to 1796. His agent neglected to locate it. The entry and survey were made out after his death. Congress ruled that his heirs were not entitled to scrip 29 Mar. 1836.

Tyrrell, Jacob. Mass. Pvt. He served in the 5th Regiment and was from New Salem. He was paid $50.

Ulmer, George. Mass. Lt. He served under Col. Joseph Prime and Capt. Archibald Mc-----. He was wounded in his left foot. He was pensioned at the rate of half-pay from 20 Nov. 1782 on 15 Mar. 1786. He was on the 1813 pension list.

Ulrich, Adam. Pa. —. He was granted a $40 gratuity and a $40 annuity in Crawford County 13 Apr. 1827.

Ulrich, George. Pa. —. He served under Capt. Michael Weaver in 1780. He was from Northumberland County.

Ulrich, John. Pa. —. He was awarded a $40 gratuity and a $40 annuity in Reading, Pa. 18 Feb. 1834. He was a paper maker.

Ulrich, John. Pa. —. He was pensioned 17 Jan. 1834 in Berks County. He died 24 Mar. 1839.

Umstadt, Abram. Pa. —. He applied 3 Oct. 1818.

Unangst, Jacob. —. He was granted a $40 gratuity in Northampton County 9 Feb. 1837. His name was incorrectly given as John Unangst. The error was corrected 4 Apr. 1837.

Uncles, Benjamin. Md. Pvt. He was pensioned at the rate of half-pay of a private in Anne Arundel County on 22 Feb. 1822. His widow, Rebecca Uncles, was pensioned at the same rate 28 Jan. 1838. Her arrearage was paid to Mrs. Sarah Earlougher 10 Mar. 1827.

Underwood, Gideon. Pa. —. He was pensioned in Luzerne County 7 May 1857.

Underwood, John. Pa. Capt. He was commissioned ensign 15 Mar. 1776. He served in the Fifth Battalion of the Lancaster Associators. He subsequently became a captain. He was awarded a $40 gratuity and a $40 annuity in Cumberland Co., Pa. 29 Mar. 1824 and paid to May 1828.

Ungerman, Nicholas. Pa. Sgt. He served under Capt. John Mearse and Col. William Butler in the 4th Regiment.. He was killed by the Indians in Sep. 1779. He left an aged mother, Elizabeth Smith, the wife of Peter Smith, of Northumberland who was granted his donation land. He also appeared as Nicholas Hungerman.

Union, John. Mass. Pvt. He served in the Continental Line. He was pensioned 5 May 1810 and lived in

Essex County. He was on the 1813 pension list.

Updegraff, —. Pa. —. His widow, Elizabeth Updegraff, was granted assistance in Lancaster County 20 May 1839. She died 25 Feb. 1846.

Updegraff, Isaac. N.J. —. He married Mary Thomas in Sussex Co., N.J. in 1778 when he came home on furlough. He returned to the service the next week. He died in Feb. 1825. His eldest son was Abraham Updegraff aged 58. The youngest of his eight children was Elizabeth Updegraff who was 42 and the wife of Thomas Alexander. Congress granted his widow, Mary Updegraff, a pension 16 Jan. 1839. She was 83 years old.

Updegrove, —. Pa. —. His widow was Mary Updegrove.

Upham, Wait. Mass. —. He served in the 12th Regiment and was paid $20.

Upjohn, James. Pa. —. He was awarded a $40 gratuity and a $40 annuity in Westmoreland Co., Pa. 18 Mar. 1834. He died 15 Oct. 1841.

Upshaw, William. S.C. —. His widow, Patience Upshaw, was receiving a pension in 1791.

Upson, Noah. Conn. Pvt. He served in the 2nd Regiment of Dragoons. He was taken sick in the line of duty; the sickness fell into his eye and produced a cataract in 1779. He lived in Woodbury, Conn. in 1794. He enlisted 15 Feb. 1778 for three years and was discharged 31 Dec. 1780.

Uptegraft, Peter. Pa. —. He was granted a $40 gratuity and a $40 annuity in Lancaster County 28 Mar. 1836. He was dead by Jan. 1840. He also appeared as Peter Updegraff.

Uran, James. Me. —. He died 11 Feb. 1824. His widow was Anna Uran from Waterboro. She was paid $50 under the resolve of 1836.

Urich, Adam. Pa. —. He was awarded a $40 gratuity and a $40 annuity in Crawford Co., Pa. 13 Apr. 1827.

Ussleton, William. Md. —. He was pensioned.

Utt, —, Pa. —. His widow, Lucretia Utt, received a $40 gratuity and a $40 annuity in Northampton County 15 June 1836. She died 14 Nov. 1859.

Utt, Elias. Pa. Pvt. He served in Col. Hartley's Regiment. He lived in Northampton County. He was on the 1813 pension list.

Utter, John. N.Y. Matross. He served in Col. Lamb's artillery. He was lame from a bruise or wound received when exercising a piece of ordnance in Dec. 1782 at West Point. He lived in Westchester Co., N.Y. in 1794. He enlisted for the war and was on the rolls in May 1783. He was pensioned 10 Aug. 1796. He was on the 1813 pension list. He died 11 June 1823 in Westchester County.

Utter, Samuel. Pa. —. He was awarded a $40 gratuity and a $40 annuity in Perry Co., Pa. 29 Mar. 1824.

Vail, Benjamin. N.Y. Capt. He served in the militia under Col. John Hathorn and was killed at Minisink 22 July 1779. His widow, Elizabeth Vail, received a half-pay pension.

Vail, —. N.Y. Pvt. He served under Capt. Woods in the Orange County militia and was slain 22 July 1779. His widow, Hannah Vail, received a half-pay pension.

Vail, Gilbert. N.Y. —. He was pensioned.

Vail, Joseph. N.Y. —. He was pensioned.

Valdenar, William. Md. —. He was from Montgomery County.

Valentine, Bernard. Pa. —. He applied 2 Jan. 1819. He enlisted in 1777 under Lt. John Steel in Capt. Sample's Company in the 10th Pa. Regiment 1st Brigade. He continued until shortly before Monmouth when he was drafted into a company of artillery under Capt. Lee attached to Col. Lamb's Regiment. He was discharged at Princeton, N.J. in 1783. He was awarded a $40 gratuity and a $40 annuity 19 Mar. 1816. He died 14 July 1831. He was granted bounty land 18 Jan. 1833. He was from Mifflin County.

Valentine, Jacob. Va. Capt. He served under Capt. Gibson. He lost the sight in one of his eyes at Valley Forge in 1778. He lived in Princess Anne Co., Va. in 1794. He was returned sick in Oct. 1777 and mustered to May 1778. He was rejected 10 Nov. 1784.

Vanaman, Samuel. Pa. —. He was pensioned.

VanAmburgh, Abraham. N.Y. —. His wife and six children were granted support on 3 Nov. 1781 in Dutchess County.

VanAnglen, John. N.J. Capt. He was pensioned 25 Apr. 1808 at the rate of $180 per annum. He died 14 Oct. 1812.

Vananken, —. Pa. —. His widow, Margaret Vananken, was granted relief in Monroe County 21 June 1839.

VanAntwerp, John. Pvt. He served under Col. Fischer. He was wounded in his left hand on 7 Aug. 1777 at Oriskie in battle with some Indians. He lived in Mohawk, N.Y. in 1794.

Vanartsdalen, Jacob. Pa. —. He was awarded a $40 gratuity and a $40 annuity in Bucks County 31 Mar. 1836.

VanBuskirk, Abram. —. —. He died in 1805. His widow, Jane VanDeen, died 3 Jan. 1838. His son, Thomas VanBuskirk, applied in 1851. Lucretia Bell, the heir of Jane VanDeen, was unsuccessful in her claim for relief from Congress 5 Apr. 1758. Abram VanBuskirk was pressed into service in 1776, 1777, and 1778 for two years and nine months. The date of his marriage was not proved, and there was no proof that his widow made application but died before she was able to perfect her proof.

VanBuskirk, Peter. —. Assistant Commissary. He was 98 years old. Congress allowed him a pension at the rate of $60 at the level of a private per annum 13 Mar. 1860.

VanBuskirk, Thomas. N.J. —. He served in 1778, 1779, and 1780 under Gen. Wayne and Baron DeKalb. He never received any payment for a span of horses, lumber wagon, forage, and grain worth $3,000. He died in 1808. His heir and executor, Peter VanBuskirk, aged 84, had his claim rejected by Congress in 1850. Another source gave his date of death as Mar. 1811. Congress authorized relief to Maryette Van Buskirk 4 Jan. 1859 for payment of supplies furnished.

VanCampen, Daniel. Pa. —. He received a $40 gratuity and a $40 annuity in Tioga County, N.Y. 15 June 1836.

VanCampen, Moses. Pa. Lt. He received his commission from Congress 8 Apr. 1780. In Feb. 1781 he was a lieutenant in Capt. Robinson's Company. He was taken prisoner by the Indians who stole his commission. His commission as ensign was lost when it was sent to Harrisburg in 1827. For his service in Boyd's Regiment, Pennsylvania awarded him 400 acres. He was awarded a $80 gratuity and a $80 annuity in Allegany County 20 Mar. 1827. He was awarded a $20 gratuity on 9 Apr. 1828. He received his commutation 29 May 1838.

Vance, George. Pa. —. He resided in Mifflin County. He was a volunteer scout in the militia against the Indians in 1781 under Capt. Walter McKinney and Col. Alexander Brown. He was to be paid £10.14.6 plus interest on 28 Mar. 1806.

Vance, John. Va. —. He was pensioned 27 Jan. 1814 at the rate of $80 per annum. He had been wounded at Germantown. He lived in Randolph County 20 Oct. 1814 and was 68 years old. He was in Pendleton County 5 Nov. 1814.

Vance, Robert. Va. Capt. He served from 1776 to the end of the war. He was commissioned in the

9th Regiment 19 Aug. 1778. He was on the rolls in 1779 and 1781. Robert Porterfield was appointed in his place 26 May 1781. Congress found that he left the service between Feb. 1781 and May 1782 due to his resignation and rejected his petition for commutation pay 12 Feb. 1841.

Vance, Thomas. N.J. —. He served from 1777 to 1780 under Col. Spencer. He was pensioned at $95 per annum. He died 22 Jan. 1837. His daughter, Mary A. Bailey, was 84 and sought a pension on her father's service. Five of her brothers fought in the War of 1812. Congress rejected her petition 28 Feb. 1891.

Vandal, Adam. N.Y. Gunner. He served under Capt. George Fleming in Col. John Lamb's 2nd N.Y. Regiment to the close of the war. He was disabled by lifting a cannon. He was 60 years old on 5 Jan. 1786. He was 68 years old on 5 Jan. 1786. He resided in New York City, N.Y. 2 June 1786.

Vandall, —. N.Y. —. Susanna Vandall was furnished one bushel of wheat 21 Apr. 1779. She also appeared as Susanna Vandoll.

Vandegrift, Benjamin. Pa. —. He was awarded a $40 gratuity and a $40 annuity in Philadelphia Co., Pa. 22 Dec. 1834. He was 81 years old in 1840. He was dead by Dec. 1843.

Vandenburg, Bartholomew. N.Y. —. He enlisted in 1779 under Col. Philip Van Courtland. He married in Beekman, Dutchess County in Oct. 1792. He died in 1797. Congress granted his widow, Eve Vandenburg, a pension 12 Apr. 1842.

Vanderbelt, David. Pa. —. He was awarded a $40 gratuity and a $40 annuity in Adams Co., Pa. 15 Apr. 1834.

Vanderburgh, James. N.Y. Pvt. He enlisted in 1775 under Col. Humphrey for nine months followed by a second enlistment of three months. He was wounded in his ankle and discharged at White Plains. He was a guard over military stores and served three years. He was discharged at Beekman, Dutchess County. Congress granted him a pension 15 Mar. 1832.

Vanderlip, Thomas. Pa. Pvt. He was granted relief.

Vandermerken, Guysbert. N.Y. Pvt. He served under Col. Lewis DuBois and was slain 17 Oct. 1779. His widow, Elizabeth Vandermerken, received a half-pay pension.

Vanderslice, Henry. Pa. —. His widow, Ann Vanderslice, was awarded a $40 gratuity and a $40 annuity in Northumberland Co., Pa. 13 Apr. 1827.

Vanderveer, Albert. —. —. He entered the service at the age of 16 and served five years. His sister was Jemima Wooley who was born about 1770. He was not in any engagement and attached to no regular troop. It amounted to no service at all. His sister was only 7 years old and could not have the recollection of the facts as would warrant. Congress rejected his claim 17 Jan. 1837. He was from Wayne Co., N.Y.

Vanderver, Edward. S.C. —. He served under Capt. Anderson Thomas, Col. Winn, Capt. Lyles, Lt. Ephraim Lyles, Capt. Pearson, and Artimus Lyles. He was from Anderson District and was pensioned 18 Dec. 1830. Mary Vandiver, the wife of George Vandiver, saw him nearing the meeting house between 1779 and 1782 and believed he was going into the service. He was 85 years old. He was a native of South Carolina and had been rejected for a federal pension in 1836. His widow, Catherine Vanderver, had her application rejected because she failed to show that she was his wife at the time the law required. He also appeared as Edward Vandiver and was pensioned 7 Dec. 1836.

VanDuzer, John C. —. —. He and twenty-five others from Chautauqua Co., N.Y. requested pensions for all widows without reference to the date of marriage. Congress denied the request 1 Aug.

1850.

VanDyke, Abraham. N.Y. —. He served on the frigate *Saratoga*. His widow, Mary VanDyke, was granted a pension.

VanDyke, —. —. —. He was killed in battle with the Indians in Delaware Co., N.Y. Congress refused his son, Lawrence VanDyke, relief on 26 Apr. 1848.

Vane, John. Md. Pvt. His widow, Lucretia Vane, was pensioned at the rate of half-pay of a private in Dorchester County on 12 Mar. 1827. She died 28 Sep. 1835, and her arrearage was paid to James Vane, one of the legal representatives, 28 Jan. 1837.

VanEps, Evert. N.Y. Sgt. He served in Capt. Fonda's militia. He was wounded in the left leg in an engagement with the British and Indians in 1777 at Oriskie. He lived in Mohawk, N.Y. in 1794.

VanEtten, Peter. N.Y. —. His wife and two children were granted support in Dutchess County on 3 Nov. 1781.

VanFliet, —. Pa. —. His widow, Susanna VanFliet, was awarded a $40 gratuity 18 Apr. 1843 in Monroe County for his Revolutionary service.

Vangarden, John. Pa. —. He was pensioned.

Vangorden, Jacob. Pa. —. He was awarded a $40 gratuity and a $40 annuity in Beaver County on 14 Mar. 1818. His widow, Mary Vangorden, married ------ Morton *ante* July 1820. William Kaines was the guardian of the daughter, Jane Vangorder. He also appeared as Jacob Vangorder.

Vangordon, Moses. Pa. —. His widow, Elsie VanGordon, received a $40 gratuity and a $40 annuity 31 Mar. 1854. She died 20 Apr. 1855.

Vangordon, Wayne. Pa. —. He was granted relief.

VanHoesen, John. N.Y. —. He was wounded. He was on the 1785 pension list.

Vanhook, —. Pa. —. His widow, Sarah Vanhook, received a $40 gratuity 6 Apr. 1833.

Vanhook, Isaac. Pa. —. He was awarded a $40 gratuity and a $40 annuity in Fayette Co., Pa. 6 Apr. 1833.

VanHook, Laurence. N.J. —. He was pensioned in Cape May County on 13 Feb. 1845 at the rate of $50 per annum.

VanHorn, Abraham. Penn. Pvt. He served in 1778 or 1779 in Proctor's Regiment. He had a second tour in 1780 and following. More than a hundred citizens signed a petition in Tyrrell Co., N.C. in support of his application. Congress granted him a pension 21 July 1842. A soldier of his name claimed bounty land in 1793.

Vanhorn, Isaiah. Pa. —. He was awarded a $40 gratuity and a $40 annuity in Indiana Co., Pa. 17 Mar. 1835. He was 80 years old in 1840. He died 27 Aug. 1844. His widow, Dorcas Vanhorn, received a $40 annuity in Indiana County 19 Mar.1853.

Vanhorn, William. Pa. —. He applied in Philadelphia County on 1 May 1819. He was 65 years old. He enlisted in 1777 in Capt. Joseph Prowell's Company under Col. Gurney in the 4th Pa. Regiment of Infantry. He served one year or more. Afterwards he enlisted in Capt. Matthew Sadler's Company for two years. He was discharged at Philadelphia. David Boggs, aged 67, was a fellow soldier in the same regiment.

VanIsdall, James. N.Y. Pvt. He served under Capt. Hamtrammack and Col. DuBois. He was slain 6 Oct. 1777. His children, ----- VanIsdall, James VanIsdall, and Richard VanIsdall, received a half-pay pension. He also appeared as James VanOsdall.

VanKleck, Peter. N.Y. Sgt. He served under Col. Van Courtland and was slain 19 Sep. 1777. His widow, Catharine VanKleck, received a half-pay pension.

Vanloving, Joseph. Pa. Pvt. He was in Philadelphia County 13 Nov. 1785. He was 55 years old. He served in the 11th Pa. Regiment. He was in the Invalids under Capt. James McLean. He was wounded at Brandywine.

Vann, —. S.C. —. His widow was Martha Vann from Pendleton in 1793. She was paid an annuity as late as 1820.

Vann, Edward. S.C. Pvt. He was born at Horn's Creek, Edgefield District, South Carolina. At the age of 16 he served in Capt. Thomas Jones' Company under Col. Leroy Hammond in the Edgefield militia. He was also in Col. Hammonds's Corps of Dragoons, Capt. John Ryan's Calvary Troop, and Col. Thomas Keys. He fought against such Tories as McGirk, Cunningham, Foster, Coffee, and Col. Williams. He mentioned the murder of George Foreman and his two sons. His father served in the Revolution for five years. He applied from Abbeville District 19 Nov. 1842. He died 26 June 1850 at the age of 92. He had eleven children. He left 229 direct descendants. His widow was Elizabeth Vann from Abbeville District in 1842. She was formerly Elizabeth Walls, daughter of John Walls who fell in battle at Camden, and had married him in 1790. She sought his arrearage and her own pension. She was still on the roll in 1861.

VanNess, et. N.Y. — He served in the militia at Fort George and Fort Edward as an orderly sergeant under Capt. Smith for eight months in 1776 and 1777. He was commissioned a lieutenant under Capt. Charles Doty and Col. Van Wart in Albany County. He died 13 Aug. 1831. He married 16 Mar. 1769. Congress granted his widow, Effe VanNess, a pension 9 Feb. 1842.

VanNort, Jacobus. N.Y. —. He was pensioned.

VanNorth, Joseph. N.Y. Pvt. He served under Col. Lewis Dubois in Capt. John Hamtramack's Company in the 5th N.Y. Regiment. He was wounded by a musket ball in his right leg on 6 Oct. 1777 at Fort Montgomery. He was struck off the rolls due to disability in Jan. 1780. He lived in Cornwell, N.Y. in 1788. He also appeared as Joseph Van Nort. He died in 1797.

VanOrman, Isaac. Pa. —. He applied in Medina Co., Ohio. in Feb. 1838. He was born in Dauphin Co., Pa. His father and sons were zealous Whigs when the Revolution came along. In 1779 the Indians fell upon them, killed, and burnt the buildings. They fled to Col. Stroud's and fortified his house. They had to harvest the crops in armed companies. Col. Zebulon Butler and Capt. Michel had command of the fort at Wilkesbarre. On 25 Apr. 1779 he agreed to go upriver to Jacob's Plains and there erected houses on the bank on the river. Till the war ended, he made sugar in the spring and corn in the autumn. In 1781 his father and Capt. Daniel Gore were selected by Col. Butler and Denison to go as scouts. They returned safely in a fortnight. There was no evidence of his service.

Vanorman, Samuel. Pa. —. He was pensioned in Monroe County 20 Mar. 1838. He also appeared as Samuel Vanaman.

Vanosten, James. —. —. Congress rejected the petition from his children, Elizabeth Johnson and Ann Hughes, for relief 8 May 1840.

VanPelt, John. N.Y. & N.J. Pvt. He was a resident of Richmond, Staten Island when he entered the service. He served in the militia for 8 ½ months under Capt. George Lane and Col. Henry Ludington prior to 10 June 1779. He was under Capt. Daniel Williams and Col. Albert Pawling prior to 26 Dec. 1781. He received two gun shot wounds. He married in Woodbridge, Middlesex Co., N.J. 17 Mar. 1784 Sarah -----. He died in Milo, Yates Co., N.Y. 22 Apr. 1828. She died 29 May 1854. Their children Rachel King, Mary Ashley, Nancy Dilks, George VanPelt, Anthony VanPelt, Sarah See, Charlotte Wagener, and James VanPelt sought relief 8 Aug. 1856.

VanRensselaer, Henry Kilian. N.Y. Lt. Col. He served in the militia under Col. Stephen J. Schuyler.

He was wounded in the thigh which fractured his thigh bone at Fort Ann on 7 July 1777. He was pensioned 15 Mar. 1788. He lived at Rensselaerwyck, Albany Co., N.Y. on 2 June 1789. He was on the 1813 pension list. The musket ball in his thigh was not removed until after his death on 9 Sep. 1816. His widow was Nancy G. VanRensselaer whom he married in Apr. 1776. In 1848 she applied for a pension claiming two years of service. Congress awarded her a pension of $600 per annum deducting $343.32 which she had been receiving 1860.

Vanscoysck, Timothy. Pa. He also appeared as Timothy Vancoyoch. He was pensioned 17 Mar. 1838 in Huntingdon County. He was 72 years old in 1840.

Vansice, John C. —. —. He was on the pension roll at the rate of $80 per annum. He sought an increase for the injury in his leg by a ball in the war. He proved his disability by two physicians, but he did not prove it was received during the war. Congress rejected his petition 4 May 1846.

VanSlyck, Harmanus. N.Y. Maj. He served under Col. Klock in the militia. He was killed at Oriskany 6 Aug. 1777. His widow, Elizabeth VanSlyck, received his half-pay pension.

VanSlyke, John. N.Y. Lt. He served under Col. Jacob Klock in the Montgomery County militia and was killed 22 July 1781. His widow, Margaret VanSlyke, received a half-pay pension. He also appeared as John VanSlike.

VanSyckle, Cornelius. N.J. —. His widow, Mary VanSyckle, was pensioned in Morris County on 7 Mar. 1848 at the rate of $50 per annum.

VanTassel, Jacob. N.Y. Lt. He served in the militia and was taken prisoner at Pine Bridge. He was detained two years and four months. The American army used his house and quarters in Greensburg, Westchester County for the officers and men. The British burned his house, barn, and out houses destroying his livestock, grain, farming utensils, and furniture in Sep. 1779. Congress rejected relief 4 Sep. 1818.

VanTassel, John. N.Y. Pvt. He served under Lt. Col. James Hammond in the Westchester County militia and was slain 27 May 1779. His children, Catharine VanTassel, John VanTassel, and Ann VanTassel, received a half-pay pension.

Vantyle, Abraham. N.J. —. His widow, Catharine Vantyle, was pensioned in Morris County on 12 Mar. 1846 at the rate of $30 per annum.

VanValkenburg, Bartholomew Jacob. —. —. He served as an officer and bounty land warrant #2255 for 200 acres was issued in his name. It was located by James Stanbury for the holder Joseph Hardy. Congress granted no relief 1 Feb. 1831.

VanValkenburg, Benjamin. —. —. He sought commutation of five years of full-pay. Congress rejected his claim 11 Apr. 1846.

VanValkenburg, Jehoakim. —. —. He was killed in the service in battle with the Indians in 1781. Lawrence VanDyke and the other heirs sought relief on 7 Feb. 1850. Congress rejected their claim 10 Feb. 1846 on the grounds that he was not in the service at the time of his death.

VanVeghten, Dirck. N.Y. Maj. He died 8 Aug. 1777 from wounds received at Oriskany. His widow, Allada VanVeghten, received a half-pay pension.

VanVoast, Gershom. N.Y. —. In the summer of 1779 he served under Capt. Gray, Col. Wemple, and Gen. Henry Glen. For more than three years he had the care of the horses at the Congress stable on the land of his father at Schenectady. He once carried mail or express to Schoharie. He drove cattle to Fort Plain and Fort Herkimer. His brother, James J. VanVoast, had the same service and deposed that Gershom entered the service at 14 years of age. He was not enlisted when he entered the service. He was recommended for a pension 12 Dec. 1856. Congress refused him a pension because the nature of his service did not entitle him to such on 25 May 1860. He also appeared as Gershom VanVorst.

VanWart, Isaac. N.Y. —. He along with John Paulding and David Williams as volunteer militia men captured Maj. John Andre, Adjutant General of the British Army, on 23 Sep. 1780 whereby the dangerous and traitorous conspiracy of Benedict Arnold became known. He was awarded $200 per annum for life on 3 Nov. 1780 by Congress. He died 23 May 1828.

VanWart, Isaac. N.Y. Lt. He married 24 Jan. 1779 while he was in the service. The Rev. Samuel Sackett performed the ceremony. He died 13 July 1840 in Pittstown, N.Y. Congress postponed indefinitely acting on the petition of his widow, Amy VanWart, for a pension on 19 Aug. 1842 because she was not a widow when the act of 1838 was passed.

VanWart, John. N.Y. Lt. He served under Lt. Col. James Hammond in the Westchester County militia 4 Mar. 1782. His children, Mary VanWart and Daniel VanWart, received a half-pay pension for seven years.

VanWart, William. N.Y. Pvt. He served under Capt. Gabriel Requa in the Westchester County militia under Col. James Hammond. He was wounded in his left shoulder with a cutlass and also above the left eye in Dec. 1779. He lived in Westchester Co., N.Y. on 12 June 1788. He was a farmer. He was 47 years old in 1786. He resided in Westchester County. He was on the 1813 pension list as William VanWard.

VanWart, William. —. —. He was on a prison ship for twelve months. He rejoined the army and served to the end of the war. He was in the Old Sugar House in New York in 1781. His brother was Isaac VanWart. His heirs sought his arrears and bounty land from Congress 20 Apr. 1854. Congress granted them the arrearage.

VanWest, John. N.Y. Lt. He was pensioned.

VanWhye, —. Pa. —. His widow, Mary VanWhye, was awarded a $40 gratuity and a $40 annuity in Pike Co., Pa. 7 Mar. 1829.

VanWyck, Philip G. —. —. He received half-pay for life.

VanZandt, John. Md. Pvt. He was pensioned 4 Mar. 1789. He died in 1790.

Vanzant, et. Pa. —. He was awarded a $40 gratuity as a Revolutionary War veteran 13 Apr.1841 in Bucks County.

Varding, Richard. Pa. Corp. He was in York County on 16 May 1786. He served in the Flying Camp in 1776 under Capt. Graff and Col. Swoop and was disabled by lameness by hardship contracted in the service. He was 65 years old. He died 27 July 1786. He also appeared as Richard Vardin.

Varick, Richard. N.Y. Col. & Deputy Muster Master General. He was granted certificates of depreciation for arrears of pay and a year's advance 10 May 1784.

Varlow, Stephen. Md. Pvt. He was pensioned at rate of half-pay of a private in Cecil County on 12 Feb. 1820.

Varnadow, —. S.C. —. His widow, Sarah Varnadow, was in Winton in 1793. She was paid a pension as late as 1834.

Varner, John. Pa. —. He received relief in Lycoming County 31 Mar. 1825.

Varner, Michael. Pa. —. He was granted relief in York County 18 Feb. 1834.

Varner, Philip. Pa. Pvt. He applied in Fayette County on 26 Nov. 1816. He was in Capt. Finney's Company under Col. Harmar in the 3rd Pa. Regiment. James Moon came round with him in the same ship from the south to Philadelphia where they were given their discharges. He died 22 July 1835.

Varner, Robert. Pa. —. He enlisted in 1776 and was wounded in his right arm at Monmouth. He was awarded a $40 gratuity and a $40 annuity in Mifflin County on 4 Apr. 1809.

Varnum, Enoch. Pa. Pvt. He served in Col. Gibson's Regiment. He was pensioned 25 Mar. 1794 in Butler County. He was on the 1813 pension list. He was 75 years old in 1840.

Varnum, John. N.H. Pvt. He served under Col. James Reed. He was wounded in one of his shoulders on 17 June 1775 at Bunker Hill. He lived in Raymond, N.H. in 1794. He served in the militia. He was granted half a pension 20 Apr. 1796.

Varrel, Samuel. Me. —. He was from Minot. He was paid $50 under the resolve of 1836.

Vasey, John. Pa. —. He was awarded a $40 gratuity and a $40 annuity in Armstrong County on 7 Mar. 1821. He died 23 Oct. 1814. He also appeared as John Veasey.

Vass, Samuel. Va. —. His wife, Ann Vass, and two children were furnished £10 support in Frederick Co., Va. on 6 Oct. 1778.

Vass, Vincent. Va. —. He was pensioned in Rockingham Co., N.C. on 18 Feb. 1828 at the rate of $60 per annum and $30 relief. He was in Henry Co., Va. 18 Feb. 1828. He was a native of Virginia. He was in Tipton Co., Tenn. in 1837 and was aged 83 on 2 June 1837. He was born 2 June 1755 in Essex Co., Va. He grew up in Spotsylvania County. He and Samuel Arnold were baptized by Rev. John Waller. He and Samuel Arnold enlisted for three years under Lt. Peter Stubblefield in Capt. John Kemp's Company in the 1st Va. Regiment under Col. George Gibson. They were not to be carried out of the state. They marched to Williamsburg and then to little York. They were ordered to go north to aid Gen. Washington. The regiment refused. There was some confusion and they were called up again. Those who were willing to go had their wages raised from $5 to $8 and were promised bounty land. He was given a furlough. His officer resigned and did not go. He was to meet at Alexandria to receive the smallpox. He joined Washington at Valley Forge and was put in Gen. Muhlenburg's Brigade. He was also under Marquis de Lafayette. The British evacuated Philadelphia, and Gen. Lee overtook them at Monmouth. Gen. Washington was not far behind. Many died due to the intense heat and fatigue in 1778. They marched toward the Hudson. Gen. Washington had Wayne to attack Stony Point. Maj. Stewart called for volunteers. He and Samuel Arnold did so on 15 July 1779. They joined Gen. Anthony Wayne's men. Col. Flurg struck the colors with his own hands. He was wounded by a musket ball in his hip and buck shot in his thigh. His mess mate Samuel Arnold was also wounded. They went to Albany Hospital where Arnold died. The doctor kept him there as an assistant. He went to Philadelphia where he was discharged by Col. George Gibson. He returned home and learned his brother had entered in Capt. Buford's Regiment and was killed. Eight months later he was drafted for three months. He served under Col. George Stubblefield and joined Gen. Gates at Rugeley's Mill. He was in battle Camden. He was discharged and went home to Granville Co., N.C. His half-brother Philip was there, and Col. Joseph Taylor owned the place. Col. Long appointed him quarter-master and commissary to the post of Harrisburg. He continued in that position to the end of the war. He moved from Rockingham Co., N.C. to Tipton Co., Tenn. His application for a federal pension in 1818 was rejected because he was in a state regiment so he applied to Virginia. Congress rejected his application for bounty land on 22 Dec. 1840 because he was not in the Continental Line. He died 8 Jan. 1858. His widow was Caty Vass. Jennings Wise was appointed administrator of his estate 12 Apr. 1858 in Richmond, Va.

Vatterly, Henry. N.Y. Pvt. He served under Lt. Col. Samuel Clyde and was slain 6 Aug. 1777. His widow, Eva Vatterly, received a half-pay pension.

Vanghan, Benjamin. —. —. He was a pensioner under the act of 1832. He claimed a pension from 1818 to 1831. Congress rejected his claim 12 Jan. 1838.

Vaughan, George. —. Pvt. He also served as a non-commissioned officer. In 1778 he was a wagon conductor. He hurt his leg against a stump in 1777 and was greatly disabled. He was destitute of proof.

Vaughan, George. Md. Lt. He was on the 1813 pension list. He lived in Baltimore County and died 2 Dec. 1820.

Vaughan, James. Va. —. While he was absent in the militia in Georgia, his wife was granted support in Mecklenburg Co., Va. 11 May 1779.

Vaughan, John. N.Y. Sgt. He served under Col. Brooks. He was wounded by a ball which passed through his body in Oct. 1777 at Bemis Heights. He lived in Hudson, Columbia Co., N.Y. in 1794. He enlisted 24 Apr. 1777 and was invalided 9 Dec. 1779. He was granted one-fourth of a pension 20 Apr. 1796. He was on the 1813 pension list.

Vaughan, Prince. R.I. Pvt. He was pensioned on 12 Jan. 1786. He lost all of his toes on his right foot and one joint from the toes on his left foot on the Oswego Expedition under Col. Willett. He served under Col. Jeremiah Olney. He was aged 22. He was on the 1813 pension list.

Vaughan, Thomas. Pa. —. He applied in Allegheny County on 16 July 1814. He served under Col. George Stevenson in the 1st Pa. Regiment.

Vaughan, Thomas. Pa. —. He was awarded 200 acres of donation land 25 Mar. 1813.

Vaughan, William. Md. Pvt. He was pensioned at the rate of half-pay of a private 2 Jan. 1813.

Vaughn, —. Pa. —. His widow, Agnes Vaughn, was awarded a $40 gratuity in Mercer Co., Pa. 31 Jan. 1832.

Vaughn, Joseph. S.C. —. He wounded in the hip by Tories. He was granted an annuity 2 Sep. 1785. There were children in 1791.

Vaughn, Lewis. Pa. Pvt. He was on the 1813 pension list.

Vaughn, Stephen. N.C. —. He was born in Edgecomb County 18 July 1765. He served fifteen months under Capt. William Kidd of Halifax County and Major Hogg. He moved from Nash County to Wake County in 1810. He was a substitute for Benjamin Tucker. He was 68 years old when he applied 21 Aug. 1832.

Vaughn, William. S.C. —. He was pensioned 30 Nov. 1827. He sought reinstatement 25 Nov. 1836.

Vaught, Godfrey. N.Y. —. He enlisted for one year at Peekskill, Westchester Co., N.Y. in Apr. 1780. He was recruited by Thomas VanPeldt. He was under Capt. Bond and subsequently under Capt. Jonathan Knapp. He was attached to Col. Hughes and Maj. Kears. His lieutenant was John Occoman. He was ordered on boats at Kings Ferry at Stony Point and Verplanck's Point on the Hudson River to transport troops and supplies for a year. He next served for nine months under Capt. Richard Sackett and Lt. Merker and 2nd Lt. Tucker in a company of rangers in a scouting party. He also served ten to fifteen stints on alarms in militia service. Congress granted him a pension on 19 Feb. 1836 for twenty-one months of service.

Vause, William. Va. Capt. He served in the 12th Virginia Regiment as a captain from 19 Feb. 1777 to 30 Nov. 1779. He became supernumerary 21 Oct. 1780. He was at the surrender of Cornwallis in Oct. 1781. His heirs had a land warrant for 666 2/3 acres for his seven years of service. His commutation was issued to his administrator *de bonis non*, Vause Fox, 4 Jan. 1838. Congress rejected the claim of his heirs for commutation on 1 Apr. 1842 because Jacob Swearingen filled his place 18 Feb. 1781. He also appeared as William Vanse.

Vawters, William. Va. 2nd Lt. He entered the service as a private in the 1st Virginia Regiment under Col. George Gibson in 1777. He continued to the battle of Germantown when the 9th Virginia Regiment was captured by the enemy. He was promoted to ensign and then lieutenant when he was deranged and made supernumerary. He died in Kentucky. His heirs received his five years' full pay in lieu of his half-pay for life 23 Dec 1831. He died in Boone Co., Ky. 27 Nov. 1823. The heirs received the unpaid portion 25 May 1832. He also appeared as William Vawter.

Veazey, Eliphalet. N.H. —. He was on the roll in 1783. He received an invalid pension.

Veazie, Joseph. Mass. Pvt. He entered the service in the spring of 1777 from Portland, Cumberland Co., Maine under Capt. Abner Lowell. Congress granted him a pension for nine months of service 24 Jan. 1837.

Vedder, Arent. N.Y. —. He died during the service. He was the natural son of Mary Kittle who for upwards of twenty years had been mentally deranged. His 450 acres of bounty land were to be vested in her son Alexander Lansing, Jr. and her sons-in-law, Philip Van Ness, Jeremiah Weeks, and William Van Vorst, on the condition that they execute a deed to the overseers of the poor of Schnectady for the maintenance and support of Mary Kittle. The private act was dated 5 Apr. 1810.

Veesey, John. Pa. —. He was granted relief 7 Mar. 1821. He died 23 Oct. 1821.

Venable, Joseph. Pa. Pvt. He was pensioned.

Venus, John. —. —. He was pensioned 25 Apr. 1808 at the rate of $2.50 per month from 11 Dec. 1807.

Vercloss, John Conrad. Pa. Matross. He was in Philadelphia 9 Apr. 1787. He served in Capt. Derrick's Company in the 4th Regiment of Artillery under Col. Thomas Proctor. He was wounded at Brandywine on 11 Sep. 1777 in his left knee by a musket ball. A gun carriage ran over his wounded knee on the same day in the afternoon. He was discharged 6 May 1779. He was 39 years old and had a wife and three children ranging in age from 7 to 4. He also appeared as John Conrad Verclass.

Verding, Richard. Pa. —. He was pensioned.

Veregerau, Peter. N.Y. Lt. He served under Col McDougall and was killed by lightning 20 Aug. 1776. His widow, Abigail Vergerau, received a half-pay pension. He also appeared as Peter Veregeran.

Verner, David. S.C. Sgt. He joined the army to guard the frontier against the Indians and Tories. He served under Capt. Robert Anderson, Capt. Pettigrew, Capt. McCall, and Capt. William Harris. He was in Florida and Georgia. He was at Ninety Six. He was nearly deaf. His younger brother, George Verner, proved he was in the service. He was from Pendleton District and was pensioned 7 Dec. 1826. He was paid as late as 1834.

Verner, John. Pa. —. He was pensioned in Luzerne County 31 Mar. 1825.

Verner, Philip. Pa. —. He was pensioned.

Vernor, —. Pa. —. His widow, Mary Vernor, was granted relief in Delaware County 17 Mar. 1839. She died 1 Mar. 1840.

Verpelia, Francis. Pa. —. His children were paid $300 for his donation land 22 Mar. 1825. They were from Lehigh County.

Verrus, John. N.Y. Pvt. He was on the 1813 pension list as John Venus. He lived in Putnam County. He died 23 Feb. 1824.

Very, William. Mass. Pvt. He served in the 5th Regiment and was from Salem. His widow, Sarah Very, was paid $50.

Vessels, James. S.C. Artist. He was taken prisoner 11 June 1780 and carried to Charleston. He was lodged in the prison ship *Provost*. He was transferred to England and held in Mill Prison until being exchanged. He returned to Philadelphia in Aug. 1782 and in November 1782 reached Ninety Six. He was from Charleston District and sought the balance of his pension on 2 Dec.

1824.

Vessels, —. S.C. —. Ridley Vessels was from Newberry District. There were two children in 1791. She died 4 July 1818. Her heirs, James Vessels, John Vessels, and Elizabeth Kelly sought her arrears 14 Nov. 1824. They were from Ninety Six District.

Vial, Samuel. Mass. Sgt. He served in the 3rd Regiment and was paid $20.

Via, William. Va. Pvt. Congress rejected his claim for a pension on 9 Jan. 1847 because the service he claimed was that of a namesake. He proved he served more than two years under Capt. Jesse Miller at Albemarle Barracks from Feb. 1779 to Feb. 1780. Congress granted him a pension 30 Mar. 1848.

Vicary, Benjamin. —. —. He was colored. He was pensioned due to disabilities.

Vice, John. —. —. Congress rejected his claim for a pension because he failed to prove six months of service on 27 Mar. 1846.

Vickery, David. Mass. Pvt. He served under Col. John Greaton and Capt. James Tisdel. He was disabled by a broken left shoulder. He was 53 years old in 1786.

Vickery, Elijah. Mass. —. He was in the 4th Artillery and was paid $20.

Vickery, John. Mass. —. He served in the 8th Regiment and was from Dighton. He was paid $20.

Victor, Felix. —. Lt. He served in Hazen's Regiment to the end of the war. He sought his commutation of half-pay. If he could prove his claims, he would be entitled to same. He appeared as sick on the rolls in Mar. 1781, and after 1 Aug. 1781 his name was absent. He died at St. Antoine, Canada 30 Oct. 1820. He married Genevieve Boucher, the widow of Francis Martin, 11 Feb. 1782 at Fishkill. She died 18 Dec. 1836 without applying for a pension due to her old age of 97 and derangement of her mind. Her first husband was Francis Martin whom she married 15 Feb. 1762 at Berthier, Canada. Martin served under Col. Livingston and marched to Canada and was commissioned lieutenant after the retreat. He died in 1780 in hospital at Fishkill. Her grandchildren sought compensation from Congress 12 Dec. 1856.

Vincent, John. N.Y. Pvt. He was pensioned 22 Mar. 1810. He was on the 1813 pension list. He died 14 Mar. 1820.

Vincent, Joseph. N.Y. Pvt. He served in Col. Lewis Dubois' Regiment. He was transferred to Samuel Pell's Company in the 2nd N.Y. under Col. Philip Van Cortland. He was wounded in his left wrist and in his head by a broadsword. He was aged 33 in 1788. He lived in Ulster Co., N.Y. on 11 June 1789. He died 14 Nov. 1805.

Vincent, Peter. Pa. —. He was awarded a $40 gratuity and a $40 annuity in Lycoming Co., Pa. 16 Jan. 1823. He died 24 July 1823.

Vinial, John. Pa. —. He was in Philadelphia County on 10 Apr. 1786. He served in Armand's Legion. He was wounded in his leg and his head. He also appeared as John Vineal.

Vining, John. Me. —. He died 27 Oct. 1837. His widow was Mary Vining from Durham. She was paid $50 under the resolve of 1836.

Vinter, Felix. —. —. He received half-pay for life.

Vinyard, —. Va. —. His widow and two children were granted support in Greenbrier Co., Va. 10 Apr. 1781.

Vinyard, John. Pa. —. He enlisted for three years and served under Capt. Mars, Col. Butler, and Gen. Wayne from 1777 to 1781. He was discharged at Princeton. He was at Monmouth and Brandywine. Congress granted him a pension 3 Jan. 1832.

Virgil, Asa. Mass. Corp. He served in the 4th Regiment. He had frequent attacks of dizziness and partial blindness from a wound in his head by a musket ball in Aug. or Sep. 1778 on Newport Island.

He lived in Hillsdale, N.Y. in 1795. He enlisted 1 Feb. 1777 for the war and was on the rolls in 1780. He was granted one-fourth of a pension 20 Apr. 1796. He was on the 1813 pension list.

Visbee, Jacob. Mass. —. He served in the 3rd Artillery. He was from Philadelphia and was paid $20.

Vogan, Samuel. Pa. —. He served under Capt. Brown in the Lancaster County Associators.

Vogelson, Aurand. Va. Capt. He was in the cavalry. His commutation was made 14 Apr. 1795.

Vols, Jost. N.Y. —. His family was granted support during the war.

VonHeer, Bartholomew. Pa. Capt. He served in the artillery. He was appointed to the command of the Marehouse Troop of Horse.

Voorhies, Minne L.. N.J. Pvt. He served under Col. Forman. He was wounded in his right knee by a musket ball in 1777 on Long Island. He lived in Middlesex Co., N.J. in 1795. He died 14 Oct. 1812.

Vosburgh, Peter I. —. Regt. QM. He received half-pay for life.

Vose, Amariah. Mass. Sgt. He was wounded in the ankle and right shoulder. He also suffered from rheumatism. He was pensioned 16 Jan. 1783. He lived in Mendon, Mass. and was 34 years old. He was from Boston and was paid $20. He was on the 1791 pension roll. He was on the 1813 pension roll. He transferred to New Haven, Conn. 4 Mar. 1826. He also appeared as Amariah Voze.

Vose, Edward. R.I. Sgt. He served in the Light Corps. He received a stroke from an oar by a prisoner trying to escape which caused an inguinal rupture in Aug. or Sept. 1779. He was in pursuit of some prisoners. He had to wear a steel truss thereafter. He served under Col. W. Barton. He lived in Newport, R.I. in 1794. He was in the militia. He was granted one-sixth of a pension 20 Apr. 1796. He was on the 1813 pension list.

Vose, Jesse. Mass. —. He was paid $20.

Vreeland, Daniel. Conn. Pvt. He enlisted 5 May 1777 under Col. Sheldon. He was discharged between 4 and 10 June 1783. He married 10 June 1783 in Reading, Conn. He died in 1829. Congress granted his widow, Betsey Vreeland, a pension 9 Feb. 1842.

Vreeland, Jacob. N.J. Lt. He served under Capt. Spier and Capt. Gerolamon from 1778 to the end of the war for as much as four months each year for a total of one year and eighteen months. He married Jane ----- in Mar. 1778. Congress awarded her a pension 10 Jan. 1857.

Vroman, Bartholomew. N.Y. —. On 9 Aug. 1780 the Indians and Tories invaded and massacred many of the inhabitants including his mother and sister. They burned his father's dwelling house.They took him and his father captive and carried them to Montreal. They were exchanged in 1781. His brother was Josias E. Vroman. He was frequently in the militia. He was from Schoharie Co., N.Y. Congress rejected his petition for a pension because he had to have been at least fifteen years old and engaged in actual service.

Vroman, Josias E. N.Y. —. On 9 Aug. 1780 the Indians and Tories under Col. Brandt attacked Vroman's land in Schoharie Co., N.Y., massacred his mother and sister, burnt his father's house, and destroyed his personal property. He was eleven years old and was taken to Montreal. In 1781 he was exchanged. Congress rejected his claim for a pension since he was not competent to bear arms on 17 Feb. 1838.

Wachter, John. Pa. Pvt. He was on the 1789 pension list.

Wachter, John. Pa. —. He was awarded a $40 gratuity and a $40 annuity in Berks Co., Pa. 16 Feb. 1835.

Waco, Joseph. —. —. He was pensioned 25 Apr. 1808.

Wadden, Thomas. Mass. —. He served in the 7th Regiment and was paid $20.

Wadden, Thomas. Mass. —. He served in the 7th Regiment and was paid $20. [second of the name]

Waddle, Robert. N.Y. Pvt. His wife, Mary Waddle, was granted support 31 May 1779 while he was away in the service. She was from Poughkeepsie. He was discharged in June 1781. He, his wife, and five children were granted support on 3 Nov. 1781 in Dutchess County. His children, William Waddle, Mary Hilleguest, Margaret Boss, Isaac Waddle, Jane Kidney, and Elsie Landers, were awarded his 200 acres of bounty land on 13 Apr. 1813.

Waddle, William. Pa. —. He served 22 months. He enlisted under Capt. Joseph Erwin in Apr. 1776. He was under Col. Brodhead and Col. Walter Stewart. He was from Westmoreland County.

Wade, —. Va. —. He and his brother were away in Continental service. His father, David Wade, was granted support in Fluvanna Co., Va. 7 May 1779.

Wade, Augustine. Md. Pvt. He served in the Maryland line and was wounded at Brandywine. He was pensioned 1 Oct. 1783. He died in 1790.

Wade, Edward. Pvt. Md. He was disabled by a wound in his left thigh and received several fractures in 1779 at Stoney Point. He resided in Bucks Co., Pa. in 1796. He enlisted 24 Apr. 1778 for three years and was omitted Oct. 1780. He was granted half a pension 20 Apr. 1796. He died 1 Aug. 1817 in Philadelphia County. He was on the 1813 pension list.

Wade, Jonathan. Mass. He served two and a half years. He married 15 June 1794. His widow, Margaret Wade, sought relief from Congress 25 Feb. 1839.

Wade, Nathan. N.J. Pvt. He served in the militia under Maj. Meekes and was killed 22 July 1779. His widow, Ammia Wade, received a half-pay pension in Sussex County in Aug. 1784.

Wade, Richard. Va. —. His wife and two children were granted £2 per month support in Yohogania Co., Va. 28 Apr. 1778.

Wadkins, —. Va. —. His father, Benjamin Wadkins, and his mother were furnished 2 barrels of corn and 100 pounds of pork in Louisa Co., Va. on 11 Aug. 1780.

Wadleigh, John. N.H. Pvt. He served in Capt. Daniel Moore's Company. At the battle of Bunker Hill he took sick. His doctor's bill was a burden and he sought compensation. He was awarded £1.16 on 31 Oct. 1775. He was from Epping.

Wadsworth, Ichabod. Conn. Capt. He served three months as a sergeant and two months as a captain. He married 22 Mar. 1771. His widow, Lydia Wadsworth, died 22 Feb. 1837 at the age of 94. The heirs sought relief. Congress rejected the claim because there was no reason for special legislation on 17 Feb. 1838. Samuel A. Wadsworth was one of the heirs.

Wafford, Absalom. S.C. —. He was paid $192.66 as a Revolutionary soldier on 20 Dec. 1810.

Waggerman, Emanuel. N.Y. Pvt. He served under Col. Gansevoort. He was wounded in his left hip by the accidental discharge of a musket in July 1777 on the Mohawk River. He lived in Montgomery Co., N.Y. in 1794. He enlisted 16 Apr. 1777 and continued to end of the war.

Waggoner, Andrew. Va. Capt. He was pensioned at the rate of $20 per month from 2 Nov. 1807. He was on the 1813 pension list. He died 27 May 1813.

Waggoner, Henry. Pa. Pvt. He was in Philadelphia County 14 July 1787. He served in the German Regiment in Capt. Hyer's Company and was wounded in the leg at Germantown in 1777. He was a native of Pennsylvania. He was 44 years old.

Waggoner, Henry. Pa. —. He was awarded a $40 gratuity and a $40 annuity in Cumberland Co. on 28 Mar. 1820.

Waggoner, Philip. Pa. —. He was awarded a $40 gratuity and a $40 annuity in York Co., Pa. 20 Feb. 1833. He also appeared as Philip Wagner. He was dead by July 1836.

Wagner, George. N.Y. Pvt. He served in Capt. Henry Diefendorft's Company under Col. Clyde.

He was wounded in his left thigh at Oriskany on 6 Aug. 1777. He lived in Montgomery Co., N.Y. on 15 June 1789. He also appeared as George Waggon and George Waggoner.

Wagner, Martin. Pa. —. He was awarded a $40 annuity in Schulykill County 5 Feb. 1836. He died 15 June 1841.

Wagnon, John Peter. Ga. Lt. His legal representative was awarded his five years' full-pay 2 Mar. 1833. He also appeared as John Peter Waynon.

Wagoner, Daniel. Pa. —. He was awarded a $40 annuity in Center County 14 Mar. 1831.

Wagoner, George. N.Y. Pvt. He served in Cox's N.Y. Regiment. He was pensioned 19 Oct. 1786. He lived in Oneida County. He was on the 1813 pension list.

Waid, Increase. —. —. He served under Capt. Saltonstall at New London and Horseneck. It was claimed that he served twelve months under Capt. Nathaniel Edwards and Col. Erastus Wolcott in 1781. His sister was Mary Woodruff. He married 30 May 1778 and died 10 Mar. 1832. His widow, Freelove Waid, applied for a pension 25 Feb. 1845 from Congress. She was 48 years old. She sought an increase in her pension. Congress reviewed his file and credited him with eight and a half months of service. Her request was rejected by Congress 9 Jan. 1847.

Waid, John. Va. Pvt. He was disabled in June 1782.

Waight, Asa. Mass. —. He served in the 8th Regiment and was from Leicester. He was paid $20.

Wainwright, Richard. S.C. Seaman. He served aboard the *South Carolina* under Commodore Alexander Gillon. He was paid 6 June 1809.

Wainwright, Samuel. Conn. Pvt. He served in Col. Elisha Sheldon's Regiment of Light Dragoons under Capt. John Webb. He served from 1777 to the end of the war. He was disabled by a fall at Fishkill. He hurt both sides of his body. He also suffered from great fatigue. He had a wife, a child, and an aged mother-in-law to support. He was troubled with a cough, rheumatism, and expectoration of pus from his lungs. He lived in Middletown, Conn. He was pensioned 4 Dec. 1788. He died in 1790.

Wair, John. Va. —. He was disabled at Eutaw Springs. He served in the cavalry. He was on the 1785 pension roll.

Waire, John. —. He served a total of 21 months between May 1776 and Feb. 1779. He died in 1826. His widow died in 1831. His children sought a pension in his rights. They were Ezekiel Waire, Mary Potter, Martha Lord, Daniel Waire, and Charles Waire. Congress rejected their claim because they submitted no evidence on 10 Feb. 1875.

Wait, Joseph. N.H. Lt. Col. He was wounded in a skirmish and died 28 Sep. 1776 at Clarendon, Vt. en route home. His seven years' half-pay of $2,520 was paid to his widow. His widow, Martha Wait, was pensioned in 1786 and resided at Claremont.

Waitneight, Jacob. Pa. —. His widow, Catharine Waitneight, was awarded a $40 gratuity in Chester County in 1848 for his Revolutionary service. He also appeared as Jacob Weighnight.

Waits, Isaac. N.C. Pvt. He was granted £15 in 1776 for loss of his arm in a fight with the Cherokee. He served in Capt. John Sevier's Company.

Waits, William. Md. Surgeon's Mate. His heirs sought five years' full pay. He was paid for serving from 1 Aug. 1780 to 15 Nov. 1783. Congress rejected their claim 22 Feb. 1843.

Waitt, Jonathan. Mass. Pvt. He served in the 8th Regiment and was from North Danvers. His widow, Elizabeth Waitt, was paid $50.

Wakefield, Gibbons. Me. —. He died 14 Mar. 1807. His widow was Nancy Wakefield from Westbrook. She was paid $50 under the resolve of 1836.

Wakelee, Jonathan. Conn. Pvt. He served in the Continental Army for nearly three years. He died 15

Dec. 1800. He married 21 Aug. 1783. His widow, Esther Wakelee, married secondly Abraham Parrott who died 5 July 1816. She lived in Bridgeport, Conn. when Congress granted her a pension 10 July 1840 and 9 Feb. 1842. He also appeared as Jonathan Wakeley.

Wakeley, John. Conn. Pvt. He served as a marine on the frigate *Alliance* in 1780 and 1781. He was wounded in his legs and returned home from Boston in 1782. He was pensioned 28 Nov. 1788. He resided in Stratford, Conn. and was 29 years old. Thomas Elwood, Lieutenant of Marines, enlisted him. John Barry was Captain of the ship. He was on the 1813 pension list as John Wakelee.

Wakeman, Gersham. —. —. He sought an increase in his pension for more than the eight months that he had been credited. Congress rejected his petition 16 Feb. 1837.

Walborn, —. Pa. —. His widow, Catharine Walborn, was pensioned in Lebanon County 26 Jan. 1835.

Walch, John. N.Y. Pvt. He died 4 Apr. 1803. One John Walsh was on the 1813 pension list.

Walcutt, Thomas. Mass. Pvt. He served in the 10th Regiment and was from Boston. He was paid $50.

Waldo, Benjamin. Mass. —. He was in the 5th Regiment and was paid $20.

Waldo, Edward. N.H. Lt. He served under Col. David Hobart. He was wounded by a ball passing through his left wrist which broke the bones on 16 Aug. 1777 at Bennington. His wrist remained dislocated. He lived at Alstead, N.H. in 1792. He was granted two-thirds of a pension 20 Apr. 1796. He was on the 1813 pension list.

Wales, Joseph. Mass. Lt. He received his commutation for five years in lieu of half-pay for life. He was from Braintree.

Wales, Nathaniel. Conn. Capt. He served under Jonathan Latimer. In the expedition against Burgoyne he suffered from extraordinary fatigue. He was a farmer. He served under Maj. Joseph Abbott and Col. Morgan. His son, Eliel Wales, was with him in the service as a waiter in 1775 and 1776. He was from Windham and aged 45 on 25 Nov. 1788. He was on the 1791 pension roll. He died in 1811.

Walhever, Abraham. N.Y. Pvt. He served under Col. Bellenger and was granted a pension 14 Sep. 1786. He died 6 Feb. 1819.

Walker, —. Pa. —. His widow, Mary Ann Walker, was granted relief in Lancaster County 11 Feb. 1825.

Walker, —. S.C. —. His widow, Magdaline Walker, was receiving a pension in 1791.

Walker, —. S.C. —. His widow, Mary Walker, had her application rejected 4 Dec. 1839.

Walker, —. Va. —. His wife, Susannah Walker, was granted £12 support in Fauquier Co., Va. in July 1778.

Walker, Alexander. Pa. —. He received a $40 gratuity and a $40 annuity in Beaver County 3 Apr. 1837. He died 31 May 1842.

Walker, Benjamin. —. Capt. He served in Colonel Bridges' Regiment and was wounded at Bunker Hill on 17 June 1775. He died in Aug. 1775. His widow, Abiel Walker, lived at Chelmsford, Mass. and sought seven years' half-pay in 1793.

Walker, Edward. Me. —. He died 5 Nov. 1832. His widow was Susan Walker from Waterboro. She was paid $50 under the resolve of 1836.

Walker, George. N.C. Capt. He served as a lieutenant in 1776 under Capt. John Hardin for three or four tours to 1779 at which time Hardin resigned and Walker was elected as his successor. He served to 1782 and was at Ramsor's Mills and Blackstock under Maj. Rutherford. He was also in battles with the Indians. He was pensioned under the act of 1832 at the rank of lieutenant and died 12 Oct. 1833. Congress allowed his heirs the difference from $230 to $480 from 4 Mar. 1831 to his death on 30 Mar. 1860.

Walker, Gideon. Vt. Lt. He lost the use of his limbs by lodging two nights on the ground in 1777 in New Jersey. He lived in Cavendish, Vt. in 1795. Since his disability was not due to wounds, his claim was not allowed.

Walker, Henry. Pa. —. He was awarded a $40 gratuity and a $40 annuity on 21 Feb. 1814. He died 9 Nov. 1820. He was from Schuylkill County.

Walker, Isaac. Mass. —. He served in the 6th Regiment and was paid $20.

Walker, John. Me. —. He died 7 May 1809. His widow was Mary Walker from Livermore. She was paid $50 under the resolve of 1836.

Walker, John. Md. Corp. He was pensioned at the rate of half-pay of corporal in Frederick County on 16 Feb. 1820. His widow, Mary Walker, was pensioned at the same rate 8 Mar. 1848.

Walker, John. Mass. —. He served in the 5th Regiment and was paid $20.

Walker, John. Mass. —. He served in the 5th Regiment. [second of the name.]

Walker, John. Mass. —. He served in the 10th Regiment and was from Boston. He was paid $20.

Walker, John. N.Y. Pvt. He served under Col. William Malcolm and was slain 31 July 1778. His widow, Catherine Walker, received a half-pay pension.

Walker, John. Pa. —. His widow, Mary Walker, was awarded a $40 gratuity and a $40 annuity 10 Feb. 1817; she was from Pike County.

Walker, John. Pa. —. He was awarded a $40 annuity and a $40 gratuity in Washington Co., Pa. 15 Mar. 1826. He died in Mar.1830.

Walker, John. S.C. —. He received an annuity in 1831 and 1832.

Walker, John. Va. —. His wife, Winny Walker, was granted 2 barrels of corn and 150 pounds of bacon on 12 Aug. 1782 in Northumberland Co., Va.

Walker, John H. —. Pvt. He served under Capt. Henry and Col. Alexander. He married 14 Mar. 1815 and died in 1836. His widow, Maria Walker, was over 90 years of age when Congress granted her arrears from 4 Mar. 1860 to 9 Mar. 1878 on 26 Apr. 1886.

Walker, Joseph. Mass. Pvt. He served in the 3rd Regiment and was from Worcester. His widow, Asenath Walker, was paid $50.

Walker, Nathaniel. N.C. —. He served in the 3rd Regiment under Col. Archibald Little and Capt. Benjamin Carter. He applied at the age of 57 in New Hanover County 14 Aug. 1821.

Walker, Robert. S.C. Lt. He was wounded in action at King's Mountain in 1780. He was granted an annuity 29 Mar. 1785. There was one child in 1791.

Walker, Thomas. Canada. —. He was being pensioned by the Continental Congress in 1785.

Walker, Thomas. S.C. —. He was from Lancaster District and later Tennessee. He was on the roll in 1829. He was on the roll as late as 1834. His son took him to Tennessee in the autumn of 1836. His arrears were paid 1 Mar. 1846. Thomas Howie had a power of attorney to collect the pension.

Walker, Timothy. Mass. —. He served in the 9th Regiment and was paid $20.

Wall, Gilbert. S.C. —. He served aboard the *South Carolina* under Commodore Alexander Gillon. His administrator, Richard Wall, received $39.31 due him on 9 Apr. 1808.

Wall, Isaac. Pa. —. His application was rejected 3 Feb. 1813.

Wall, Jesse. Pa. —. He was pensioned.

Wall, William. —. Surgeon. He served in the 1st Rifle Regiment. He was dismissed with violent rheumatism. Ten months later he applied for a pension. He was unsuccessful until 1820. He wanted to have his pension backdated to the time when he became disabled. Congress rejected his request 5 Jan. 1821.

Wall, William. Md. Pvt. He was pensioned in Dorchester County at the rate of half-pay of a private 19 Feb. 1819. His widow, Keturah Wall, was paid his arrearage of $10.78 for three months and seven days. She was pensioned at the same rate 16 Mar. 1837.

Wallace, —. Pa. —. His widow, Elizabeth Wallace, was awarded a $40 gratuity and a $40 annuity in Allegheny Co., Pa. 8 Apr. 1833. She was dead by Nov. 1837.

Wallace, —. Pa. —. His widow, Sarah Wallace, received a $40 gratuity and a $40 annuity in Allegheny County 3 Apr. 1837.

Wallace, —. S.C. —. His widow, Esther Wallace, applied 18 Jan. 1845. She was dead by 6 Dec. 1855, and her son, A. Wallace, sought her arrearage.

Wallace, Aaron [?]. Pa. —. He applied 1 May 1813.

Wallace, Alexander. Pa. —. He was from Northumberland County and served six months under Gen. LaFayette and was discharged at Providence, R.I. Congress rejected his prayer because it was unsupported by evidence on 4 Jan. 1848. He was in his 88th year. He was probably the Alexander Wallis who was awarded a $49 gratuity and a $40 annuity in Northumberland County 18 Apr. 1843.

Wallace, Andrew. Pa. Sgt. He applied 1 May 1813. He served under Col. Anthony Wayne and Lt. Col. Francis Johnston in what was afterwards called the 5th Pa. Regiment. He was discharged in 1780 or 1781. He was on the 1813 pension list. $20 was added to his annuity on 1 Apr. 1830. He was issued the patent for the 100 ½ acres where he lived in Lower Oxford Township in Chester Co., Pa. free of charge because he was a Revolutionary War veteran 1 Feb. 1834. He was dead by 22 Jan. 1835.

Wallace, Charles. Pa. —. He was awarded a $40 gratuity and a $40 annuity in Chester County on 2 Apr. 1822. He was 79 years old in 1840. He died 15 May 1842.

Wallace, Ebenezer. Vt. —. He lost his sight in a great measure to smallpox and measles with which he was afflicted while in the service. He resided in Marlborough, Vt. in 1795. Since he was not wounded, his claim was not allowed.

Wallace, Hugh. Va. Sgt. He was awarded a £30 gratuity and an annuity of full-pay on 18 May 1778. He was awarded a £250 gratuity on 10 May 1780 and an additional £400 gratuity on 10 Nov. 1780. He had a wife and six small children. He was in Lunenburg County on 12 July 1787. He served in the 6th Va. Regiment and lost his right leg and part of his thigh in 1779 at Brandywine. He was enlisted by Capt. James Johnson. He was 40 years old. He also appeared as Hugh Wallis. He had an application rejected 22 Oct. 1787. He was on the 1813 pension list.

Wallace, Jacob. N.Y. Pvt. He served under Capt. Daniel Delavan in the dragoons for five months and twenty-eight days. Congress granted him a pension 21 Mar. 1836.

Wallace, James. Pa. Sgt. Maj. He applied 18 July 1818. He served in Capt. John Ewing's Company under Col. Michael Swoop. He was under Gen. James Erwin in the Flying Camp in 1776. He was at Fort Washington where Col. Swoop was killed and was discharged 1 Jan. 1777.

Wallace, James. Pa. Pvt. He served under Col. Watts and was taken prisoner at Fort Washington.

Wallace, James. Va. —. He received his commutation.

Wallace, John. —. —. He was a pensioner. Congress declined to grant a pension to his widow, Frances Wallace, on 14 June 1850.

Wallace, John. Mass. Sgt. He served in the 2nd Regiment and was from Fairhaven. He was paid $50.

Wallace, John. Pa. —. He served under Capt. Thomas Robinson in the Rangers and was killed on Bald

Eagle Creek in 1781.

Wallace, Moses. —. —. He died in the war. His widow, Sarah Wallace, had her application rejected 31 May 1796.

Wallace, Nathaniel. N.Y. Pvt. He served under Capt. James Hadlock and Col. Yates in the 14th Albany County. He became blind. His only child, Lucy Hale, aged about 67, was in Michigan when Congress granted her $20 a month

Wallace, Thomas. Pa. Pvt. His widow, Jane Wallace, was in Chester County on 18 Dec. 1792. He served in the militia and was taken prisoner by the British after being wounded on 24 Feb. 1778 in Berks County. He died in captivity.

Wallace, Thomas. Va. Lt. He served in the 8th Virginia Regiment on Continental Establishment. He was commissioned 23 Nov. 1779 and in 1781 was ordered to take command of a company belonging to his regiment. In Mar. 1807 the U.S. issued a 366 2/3 acre bounty land warrant to his heirs. They were paid his five years' full pay commutation 30 June 1834.

Wallace, Weymouth. N.H. Pvt. He served in Capt. Henry Dearborn's Company under Col. Stark and was wounded in his right wrist at Bunker Hill on 17 June 1775. He lived at Epsom, N.H. in 1792 and 1794. He was granted half a pension 20 Apr. 1796. He was on the 1813 pension list. He also appeared as Weymouth Wallis. He was from Epsom. Michael McClary was ensign in the same company and Obadiah Williams was the regimental surgeon.

Wallace, William. —. —. Congress rejected his petition because there was no evidence on file on 4 Apr. 1840.

Wallace, William. N.H. Pvt. He was from Deerfield in 1786. He served in the 3rd N.H. Regiment in Capt. James Wedgewood's Company from 5 Mar. 1777 to 20 Mar. 1780. He received a wound through his elbow and body at Bemis Heights. He was aged 28 in 1787. He was pensioned at the rate of $8 per month from 30 Jan. 1808. He was on the 1813 pension list.

Wallace, William. N.H. Pvt. He was from Gilmanton.

Wallace, William. N.J. He enlisted in Jan. 1777 and was wounded 25 June 1780 in action with the British at Springfield.

Wallace, William. N.Y. Lt. He entered the service 6 May 1779 and resigned 17 Aug. 1779. He served in Van Weeder's Regiment. He was pensioned 8 Aug. 1808 and lived at Johnstown, Montgomery County. He was on the 1813 pension list. He died 25 Jan. 1837. His sole heir, John Wallace, sought his five years' full-pay but was rejected 9 Jan. 1838. The heirs sought his commutation on 12 Apr. 1842, but Congress rejected their claim.

Wallace, William. Pa. —. He was awarded a $40 gratuity and a $40 annuity in Juniata Co., Pa. 8 Apr. 1833.

Wallace, William. Va. —. His wife, Elizabeth Wallace, and children were granted support while he was away in the service in Mecklenburg Co., Va. 8 Sep. 1777.

Wallan, Hugh. Va. —. His wife, Mary Wallan, was granted relief 11 Dec. 1777 in Lunenburg Co., Va.

Walliger, Michael. Pa. —. He was pensioned.

Walling, John. N.J. —. He was pensioned in Bergen County on 28 Feb. 1839 at the rate of $60 per annum.

Walling, William. S.C. —. He was in the militia under Capt. William Lang in 1777 and 1778. Benjamin Mason served with him. He was from Kershaw District in 1825. His claim was rejected.

Wallingford, Samuel. N.H. Lt. He served in the marines on the Continental ship *Ranger* and fell in battle on 24 April 1778 in an engagement with the *Drake*. He left a widow, Lydia Wallingford alias Cogswell, and one child. They received his half-pay for seven years. Amos Cogswell presented her claim.

Wallington, Charles. Pa. Pvt. He was in Philadelphia 13 Mar. 1786. He served in the 5th Pa. Regiment and was stabbed in the back at Paoli. He had a wife and three children. He also appeared as Charles Warrington. He was on the 1813 pension list. He died 6 May 1819.

Wallis, George. Va. Maj. His administrator, Philip Nadenboush, received $7,144 as his half-pay.

Wallis, John. S.C. —. He served under Capt. Joseph Smith, Col. Bratton, and Col. Winn as a drafted soldier for six months. David Patton served with him. He was from York District in 1842.

Wallizer, Michael. Pa. —. He enlisted in the Penn. Line and served to the peace. He was 80 years old. He was from Columbia County. He also appeared as Michael Walliser and Michael Walliger.

Walls, —. Md. Pvt. His widow, Martha Walls, was pensioned in Prince George's County at the rate of half-pay of a private 20 Mar. 1840.

Walls, George. Va. Maj. He served under Col. Joseph Crockett in a state regiment. His commutation was $7,144.

Walls, William. Va. —. His wife, Margaret Walls, was granted £12 support in Berkeley County on 17 Mar. 1779.

Walrath, Henry A. N.Y. Sgt. He served in Capt. House's Company under Col. Samuel Clyde. He was wounded in his left arm and side at Fort Walrath on 26 May 1781. He lived in Montgomery Co., N.Y. on 15 June 1789. He died in 1792. He also appeared as Henrick Walrath.

Walrath, Nicholas. N.Y. Pvt. He served in Capt. Fox's Company in Col. Jacob Klock's Regiment. He was disabled by a wound in the elbow of his right arm on 6 Aug. 1777. He was 36 years old in 1786. He lived in Montgomery County in 1789. He was on the 1791 pension roll. He was on the 1813 pension list.

Walser, Jacob. N.Y. —. He served under Col. Van Schaick. His family was granted assistance 2 Mar. 1779 while he was away in the service.

Walsh, —. —. Capt. of Marines. He served on the expedition to Penobscot and was slain there. His widow, Anna (Hurlburt) Walsh, sought his seven years' half-pay in 1797.

Walsh, Edward. N.Y. Pvt. He was disabled by a musket ball in his left leg at Fort Washington. He lived in Westchester Co., N.Y. in May 1787.

Walsh, John. —. —. He was pensioned 3 Mar. 1809.

Walsh, Mark. Md. Pvt. He served in the 7th Md. Regiment and was wounded at Germantown in 1777. He was in Baltimore Co., Md. in 1787. He was pensioned 4 Mar. 1789. He was on the 1813 pension list.

Waltamayer, David. Pa. —. He was awarded a $40 gratuity and a $40 annuity in York Co., Pa. 18 Feb. 1834. He also appeared as David Wattamayer.

Walter, George. N.Y. Pvt. He served in Capt. Andrew Dillingbogh's Company under Col. Jacob Klock in the Montgomery County militia. He received several wounds including one in the neck on 6 Aug. 1777. He was pensioned 4 Aug. 1808. He was aged 25 years in 1787. He lived in Palatine, Montgomery Co., N.Y. 9 July 1789. His rate was $2.50 per month from 24 Feb. 1808. He also appeared as George Walters. A man of his name was on the 1813 pension list.

Walter, Henry. Pa. —. He was awarded a $40 gratuity in Lancaster Co., Pa. 27 Jan. 1835.

Walter, Jacob. N.Y. —. He served under Col. Van Schaick. His family was granted assistance while he was away in the service in Mar. 1779.

Walter, Jacob. Pa. —. He was awarded a $40 gratuity and a $40 annuity in Berks Co., Pa. 7 Mar. 1829. He was 84 years old in 1840. He died 29 Jan. 1843.

Walter, John. N.J. Pvt. He served in the 3rd N.J. Regiment under Col. Elias Dayton and was wounded at the battle of Short Hills on 20 June 1777 in his left arm. He applied for his half-pay in Gloucester County. He was 39 years old. He was on the 1791 pension roll.

Walter, John. Pa. —. He served under Capt. Brown in the Lancaster County Associators.

Walter, Michael. Pa. —. His brother, Jacob Walter, was administrator of his estate and sought his depreciation pay 19 Mar. 1804. He served in the 3rd Pa. Regiment.

Walters, Jacob. Pa. —. He was awarded a $40 gratuity and a $40 annuity in Westmoreland Co., Pa. 7 Mar. 1827.

Walthall, Henry. —. —. His widow, Elizabeth Walthall, had a pension of $24 per annum which was inadequate. She sought an increase and to be made a participant of land bounty without the usual formalities because she was too poor. She was recommended for same 12 Dec. 1856.

Waltman, Michael. Md. Pvt. He was wounded at Guilford. He served in the 1st Regiment. He was pensioned in 1784. He was on the 1813 pension list. He was pensioned at the rate of half-pay of a private in Frederick County on 18 Feb. 1825. His widow, Mary Waltman, was pensioned 16 Mar. 1840.

Walton, Benjamin. Me. —. He was from Chester. He was paid $50 under the resole of 1836.

Walton, George. Va. Pvt. He transferred to Maryland.

Walton, John. N.H. Pvt. He served under Col. James Reed. He was wounded by a musket ball shot through his neck which caused an abscess in his back. He was wounded 17 June 1775 at Bunker Hill. He lived in New Ipswich, N.H. in 1794. He was in the militia.

Walton, John. N.Y. Pvt. His widow was granted support according to an undated roster.

Walton, Josiah. N.H. Pvt. He served in Bird's Regiment. He was pensioned 22 Aug. 1794 in Hillsborough Co., N. H. He was granted one-third of a pension 20 Apr. 1796. He was on the 1813 pension list.

Walton, Thomas Rose. Va. —. His wife, Jenny Rose Walton, was allowed £50 on 27 Sep. 1779. She was granted 50 pounds of pork and 2 barrels of corn on 28 Aug. 1781 and 2 barrels of corn and 25 pounds of bacon for her family of five in Bedford Co., Va. on 23 Sep. 1782.

Walton, William. Pa. —. He was pensioned 13 Mar. 1839. He was 77 years old in 1840 in Luzerne Co.

Wamack, Jesse. Va. —. His wife, Sarah Wamack, was allowed 100 pounds of pork in Bedford Co., Va. on 22 Jan. 1781. There were nine in her family.

Wambach, Philip. Pa. —. He was awarded a $40 gratuity and a $40 annuity in York Co., Pa. 11 June 1832. He also appeared as Philip Wambaugh.

Wand, Thomas. N.Y. —. He served under Col. Thomas Thomas in the Westchester County militia. He was wounded in his left arm. He lived in Westchester Co., N.Y. on 12 June 1788.

Wandel, Adam. N.Y. —. He was pensioned.

Wandel, John. N.Y. —. He served under Col. Dubois. His wife, Susannah Wandel, and one child were granted support while he was away in the service 20 May 1779.

Wandle, David. N.Y. Pvt. He lost his right arm in the battle of Germantown 4 Oct. 1777. He served in Col. Spencer's Regiment. He was pensioned 7 July 1786. He lived in Goshen, Orange Co., N.Y. 30 May 1789 and later in Monroe County. He also appeared as David Wandell and David Wandall. He was aged 26 years on 22 Dec. 1785.

Wanoll [?], Mark B. Pa. Pvt.

Waples, Samuel. Va. Lt. He served in the 9th Regiment, was taken prisoner in 1777, and escaped. His heirs sought his commutation pay. Congress rejected their claim 25 July 1850.

Ward,—. Pa. —. His widow, Elizabeth Ward, received a $40 gratuity and a $40 annuity in Luzerne County 5 May 1855.

Ward, —. S.C. —. His widow, Susannah Ward, was paid an annuity of $30 on 24 Nov. 1829.

Ward, Abner. Mass. —. He was in the 4th Regiment and was paid $20.

Ward, Charles. —. —. He served at least two years in the Revolution. He married 13 Jan. 1783. Congress granted his widow, Mary Ward, a pension 13 Feb. 1849.

Ward, Christopher. Mass. —. He served in the 6th Regiment and was from Brimfield. He was paid $50.

Ward, Elisha. Mass. Pvt. He was pensioned 7 Nov. 1786. He served under Col. Michael Jackson and Capt. Benjamin Brown. He was disabled with a broken left leg. He was 28 years. He was on the 1813 pension list. He later transferred to Vermont. He was from Worcester when he was paid $50 by the Commonwealth.

Ward, James. S.C. Sgt. He was wounded. He was from Winton. There were four children in 1791. He was unable to work and had five children in 1814. He was paid as late as 1825.

Ward, John. N.H. Pvt. He was worn out in the service. He was 48 years old in 1785. He was from Kensington in 1786. He served in Col. Reid's Regiment. He was reported dead on the 1789 pension roll.

Ward, John W. —. —. His request for a pension was rejected 4 May 1846. He lived in Maine.

Ward, Joseph. N.Y. —. He was granted relief.

Ward, Josiah. Mass. —. He was wounded in his left leg by a musket ball. He lived in Mass. in 1795.

Ward, Kerby. Mass. Corp. He was in Capt. Seth Washburn's Company under Col. Jonathan Ward. He was wounded in battle on Charlestown heights. He lost the use of his right arm in a great degree. He was pensioned at the rate of three-eights of a soldier on 26 Jan. 1778. He was pensioned at the rate of three-eighths of the pay of a corporal on 14 Feb. 1778. He was 33 years old in 1786. He lived in Franklin Co., Mass. He was on the 1813 pension list of New York.

Ward, Stephen. N.Y. —. He lived in Westchester County. The Americans occupied his dwellings and buildings as their headquarters. In an engagement with the British, Gen. Tryon destroyed Ward's houses. His surviving son, Jonathan Ward, sought relief from Congress. Congress refused on 30 Dec. 1818.

Ward, Thomas. N.Y. Pvt. He served in Capt. Theodosius Fowler's Company in the 2nd N.Y. Regiment under Col. Philip Van Cortland. He was discharged 3 Nov. 1782 by General Washington. He lived in Albany Co., N.Y. in 1787.

Ward, Thomas. N.Y. Corp. He served in the 1st Regiment of Artillery under Col. Harrison. He was wounded in the leg by a bayonet on 18 July 1779 at Stony Point. He lived in Mamakating, N.Y. in 1795. He enlisted 6 July 1777. He was on the 1813 pension list.

Ward, Thomas. Pa. —. He was awarded a $40 gratuity and a $40 annuity in Columbia Co., Pa. 9 Mar. 1825. He was 92 years old in 1840.

Ward, William. S.C. —. His widow was Milly Ward of Greenville District. She had a child born without arms. She was pensioned in 1819. She was stricken from the pension roll 4 Dec. 1832. She was forced to live in the poor house with her son. She was later restored. She was being pensioned in 1866.

Wardell, Eliakim. N.Y. Pvt. He served under Capt. Hunt and Col. Wessenfel. His daughter, Sara A. Wardell, of Peekskill, N.Y. was born in 1823. She taught school until she was in her 70th year. She was granted a pension by Congress 12 Apr. 1904.

Warden, —. Mass. —. His widow, Rebecca Warden, was paid $50 for his service.

Warden, Barnard. —. —. He did not serve in the regular army. Congress refused him relief 23 Feb. 1820.

Wardwell, Benjamin. Mass. Pvt. He was in Chevers's Regiment and was from Springfield. His widow, Margaret Wardwell, was paid $50.

Ware, —. Va. —. His wife, Betty Ware, was granted financial support while he was away in the service in Amelia County 23 Apr. 1778.

Ware, Asa. Mass. Pvt. He served under Col. Henry Jackson and Capt. David Vanhorn. He lost his left arm at Monmouth on 28 June 1778. He was pensioned at half-pay from 13 June 1780, the time of his discharge, on 27 Feb. 1781. He was 35 years in 1786. He was on the 1813 pension list. He died 8 May 1832 in Essex Co., Mass.

Ware, David. S.C. —. He served under Col. Abel Kalb, Col. Lemuel Benton, Col. Murphy, and Maj. Stanlane. He was at Eutaw Spring in 1781. Capt. Peter Dubose attested to his service. He died 10 Aug. 1831. His widow was Elizabeth Ware of Darlington District in 1827 when she sought his arrearage.

Ware, George. S.C. —. He served under Capt. John Nixon, Col. Richardson, and Capt. Samuel Adams. He was at the Snowy Camps, Fort Moultrie, Hanging Rock, Casey's Fort, and Fishing Creek, Congaree. He was discharged at Orangeburg. William McGarrity, John Cooper, William Knox, and Alexander Walker proved his service. He applied 17 Nov. 1827 from Chester District. He also appeared as George Weir.

Ware, Francis. Md. Lt. Col. He was pensioned at the rate of half-pay of a lieutenant colonel in Nov. 1800.

Ware, Joseph. Mass. Pvt. He served in Capt. Aaron Gardner's Company under Col. Eleazer Brooks and lost his left arm by a ball from the enemy at White Plains 28 Oct. 1776. He was pensioned from 16 Nov. 1776 at half-pay on 27 Jan. 1778. He was 35 years old. He was on the 1813 pension list. He was from Walpole when he was paid $20 by the Commonwealth. He died 11 June 1833 in Middlesex Co., Mass.

Ware, William. Mass. Corp. He served in the 14th Regiment. His widow, Sarah Crossman, was of Taunton and was paid $50.

Warfield, Aaron. Mass. —. He served in the 3rd Regiment. He was paid $20.

Warfield, Joshua. Mass. Pvt. He served in the 1st Regiment and was from Heath. He was paid $50.

Warfle, Casper. Pa. —. He was awarded a $40 gratuity and a $40 annuity in Philadelphia Co., Pa. 17 Mar. 1835. He was dead by June 1839.

Waring, James. Pa. —. He was paid a gratuity on 30 Mar. 1812.

Warner, —. Pa. —. His widow, Sarah Warner, was awarded a $40 gratuity and a $40 annuity in Mercer County in Apr. 1833.

Warner, Daniel. Mass. —. He served in the 2nd Regiment and was from Richmond. He was paid $20.

Warner, Daniel. Pa. —. He was granted a $40 gratuity in Montgomery County 14 Mar. 1835.

Warner, Elias. Mass. Soldier. He served in the 3rd Regiment and was from Harvard. He was paid $50.

Warner, Jacob. Pa. —. He applied in Beaver County on 20 Nov. 1812. He enlisted in the Pa. Line in the spring of 1777 for four years. He was discharged by Col. Flowers. He was 70 years old. He received 200 acres of donation land 12 Mar. 1813.

Warner, Jonathan. Mass. Lt. He served under Col. Israel Chapin and was wounded at Saratoga on 11 Oct. 1777. He was disabled for five months. He received one-third pay from 19 Oct. 1777 to 19 Oct. 1778.

Warner, Michael. Pa. —. He was paid $200 for his right to his donation land 11 Apr. 1825. He resided in York County. He was awarded relief in York County 6 Apr. 1833. He was 78 years old in

1840. He died 22 Dec. 1845.

Warner, Peter. Pa. Pvt. He applied in Philadelphia 13 Feb. 1786. He was in Capt. Fishbourne's Company in the 4th Pa. Regiment. He was transferred to the Invalids after having been wounded in the leg and knee at Brunswick, N.J. He was 63 years old. He also appeared as Peter Werner.

Warner, Philip. Pa. Pvt. He was in Philadelphia County 13 Feb. 1786. He served in the 3rd Pa. Regiment under Maj. Tudor. He was dismissed from the Invalid Regiment unfit for duty on account of a wound received at Fort Washington on 15 Apr. 1779. He was 33 years old. He also appeared as PhilipVerner and Philip Werner. He was on the 1813 pension list.

Warner, Samuel. Mass. Pvt. He served in Col. Ashley's militia. He was ruptured in his groin by lifting heavy timber at the capture of Gen. Burgoyne in 1777. He resided in Stockbridge, Mass. in 1792 and 1796. He did not prove his wounds were the cause of his disability. He was granted half a pension 20 Apr. 1796. He was on the 1813 pension list.

Warner, Wareham. Mass. Pvt. He served in the 2nd Mass. Regiment under Col. Sprout and Capt. —. He was discharged 17 Sep. 1783 on account of a casual injury. He was pensioned at the rate of one-sixth pay of a soldier from 17 Sep. 1783 on 11 Mar. 1785. He was 46 years of age in 1790. He was on the 1813 pension list.

Warner, Zacheriah. Mass. —. He was in the 3rd Regiment and was from Springfield. He was paid $20.

Warnick, —. Pa. —. Mary Warnick was pensioned 19 Mar. 1816. She died 24 Feb. 1827.

Warnock, Charles. S.C. Pvt. He served in the militia under Capt. John Nelson and was killed by the British at Camden. His widow, Elizabeth Warnock, was paid her annuity 7 Aug. 1792. She was in Orangeburg District in 1801. She had to dispose of three of her children. Two others, who were daughters, lived with a friend and worked for their living. She had lost the use of her limbs due to rheumatic pain. She could not rise up out of her bed without help. She could not feed herself and had been so for eighteen years.

Warr, James. Va. —. He enlisted for three years. His wife, Mary Warr, was allowed £15 in Augusta Co., Va. 16 Dec. 1777. He was away in the service. There were four children.

Warren, Abijah. Me. —. He was from Paris. He was paid $50 under the resolve of 1836.

Warren, Daniel. Me. —. He was from Limerick. He was paid $50 under the resolve of 1836.

Warren, Edward. Pa. Pvt. He was in Philadelphia County on 29 Sep. 1787. He was in the 1st Pa. Regiment. He was wounded in his left hand by a musket ball in action at White Plains. He was 36 years old. He was on the 1813 pension list. He later applied in Greene Co., Ohio 19 Jan. 1824. He was in Capt. John Holliday's Company. He was discharged by Col. James Chambers. He had a wife and eight helpless children. Henry Miller was major.

Warren, Gideon. N.H. Capt. He served under Col. Thomas Lusk. He was disabled by a stroke of a cutlass at Ticonderoga while he was disarming Capt. Abiel Brown, a Tory. It almost cut off his right hand in May 1775. Ichabod Parker and Ebenezer Kellogg were present and attested to his role. He was pensioned in 1779. He lived at Hampton, Washington Co., N.Y. in 1787 and on 20 May 1789. He was 55 years old on 12 Dec. 1786. He also appeared as Gideon Waring and Gideon Warring. He was on the 1791 pension roll. He died 4 Apr. 1803.

Warren, Hugh. Va. —. His wife, Mary Warren, was granted relief in Lunenburg Co., Va. 11 Dec. 1777.

Warren, James. Mass. Lt. of Marines. He lost his right leg by a wound received in an engagement on board the frigate *Alliance* under Capt. John Barry and was discharged 1 Nov. 1781. He was pensioned 1 Nov. 1781. He was 27 years old in 1786. He was on the 1813 pension list as James

Warner [sic]. He died 5 Aug. 1821 in Plymouth Co., Mass.

Warren, John. N.C. —. His widow, Mary Warren, applied in Nash County in 1805. He was taken prisoner at the battle of Rockfish in 1781.

Warren, John. Pa. —. He was awarded a $40 gratuity and a $40 annuity in Berks Co., Pa. 30 Nov. 1829.

Warren, Joseph. Mass. Maj.-Gen. He was killed at Bunker Hill on 17 June 1775. His son, Joseph Warren, and the three youngest children were pensioned by the Continental Congress on 8 Apr. 1777 and on 11 May 1787. Their guardian was Dr. John Warren, executor of the deceased. He left two sons and two daughters. On 6 Sep. 1778 the eldest son was under the care of Rev. Mr. Payson; the eldest daughter, Elizabeth Warren, aged 12 was with a family in Boston; the second son aged 8 was living with his grandmother, and the youngest daughter, Mary Warren, aged 6 was under the care of a lady. The three younger children were to be educated at the expense of the United States until the second son was 21 and the younger daughter was 18. After that time they were to receive £1,000 to set up in some genteel profession. On 1 July 1780 the three children were to receive a pension of half-pay of major general until the youngest should be of age. His daughter Elizabeth was born 26 Mar. 1790, his son Richard in Sep. 1791, and his daughter Mary 26 Feb. 1793. Elizabeth Warren married Arnold Welles of Boston and died without issue. His daughter Mary Warren married Richard E. Newcomb of Greenfield, Mass. and died leaving one child–Joseph W. Newcomb. The latter sought relief from Congress 25 May 1842.

Warren, Neverson. Mass. Pvt. He was in the 3rd Regiment and was from Deerfield. His widow, Anna Warren, was paid $50.

Warren, Samuel. S.C. Capt. He entered as a lieutenant and was promoted. He was badly wounded, taken prisoner, exchanged, and deranged from his command due to disability from his wound. He was employed as Deputy Commissary of Prisoners. He received his commutation 7 July 1838.

Warren, Timothy. Mass. Pvt. He served in the 1st Regiment and was from Ashfield. He was paid $50.

Warren, William. Mass. Lt. He was wounded by the bursting of a shell at Breed's Hill in Charlestown on 17 June 1775. In consequence of the shock he was subject to ulcerations in his head which discharged at his ears and deprived him of the use of his eyes some part of every year since 1775. He served under Col. J. Nixon. He lived in Watertown, Mass. in 1792 and in Boston, Mass. in 1795. He was granted one-third of a pension 20 Apr. 1796. He was on the 1813 pension list. He died 29 July 1831.

Warren, William. N.Y. Sgt. He served under Col. McClaghry in the Ulster County militia and was slain at Fort Montgomery 6 Oct. 1777. His children, John Warren and Catharine Warren, received a half-pay pension for seven years.

Warriner, Aaron. Mass. —. He served in the 4th Regiment and was paid $20.

Warring, Basil. Md. Lt. His widow, Ann Warring, was pensioned at the rate of half-pay of a lieutenant 4 Mar. 1834.

Warrington, Charles. Pa. Pvt. He served in the 5th Regiment. He was stabbed with a bayonet in his back at Paoli. He was from Philadelphia County.

Warrington, William. Va. Sgt. He served under Capt. Thomas Snead from 1775 to 1777. He was then chosen as one of Washington's life guards in Mar. 1777 and was discharged in Feb. 1778. He was pensioned. Congress rejected his claim for bounty land 10 June 1842.

Wascot, Thomas. Mass. —. He served in the 10th Regiment and was from Hudson, N.Y. He was paid $20. He also appeared as Thomas Wasket and Thomas Wescott. He was later also paid $50 and was from Freetown.

Washburn, Asa. Mass. Pvt. He served in the 6th Regiment and was from Bridgewater. He was paid $50.

Washburn, Daniel. Pa. —.He received a $40 gratuity and a $40 annuity in Luzerne County 1 Apr. 1836.

Washington, William. Conn. Col. He served in the militia. He was wounded by a musket ball in his right temple which deprived him of hearing with his right ear and injured the sight in his right eye on 6 July 1779 at East Haven. He resided in New Haven, Conn. in 1794

Wasson, Joseph. N.C. Pvt. He applied in Iredell County in 1792. He was wounded in his left hip in June 1780 at Ramsours Mill. He was on the 1813 pension list.

Waterbury, John. Conn. Pvt. He served in the militia with James Waterbury. He was wounded in the spring of 1777 at Ridgefield, Conn. and lost one of his eyes. He was 69 years old and resided at Stamford, Conn. when he was pensioned 28 Nov. 1788. He died in 1804.

Waterman, Ephraim. Mass. —. He served in the 2nd Regiment and was from Duxborough. He was paid $20.

Waterman, Ephraim. Mass. —. He was paid $20. [second of the name]

Waterman, John. R.I. Lt. He died of smallpox at Valley Forge on 20 Apr. 1778. His seven years' half-pay of $1,120 was paid to his heirs.

Waterman, Joseph. Conn. Pvt. He served in Jedediah Huntingdon's Regiment. He was wounded in the attack on Stony Point and disabled with a hernia. He was pensioned 25 Nov. 1788. He was on the 1791 and 1813 pension lists. He died 9 Jan. 1834 in Madison Co., N.Y.

Waterman, Joshua. Mass. Pvt. He served in the Invalids and was disabled with several wounds. He was pensioned 1 Sep. 1783.

Waterman, William. —. Pvt. He was in Capt. Dixon's Company. He was wounded by a musket ball in the right thigh in Sep. 1776 at White Plains. He resided at Royal Town, Vt. in 1796. He was granted one-third of a pension 20 Apr. 1796. He was on the 1813 pension list.

Waters, Bordwine. S.C. Lt. He was killed 15 Sep. 1782. His widow, Elizabeth Waters, was granted an annuity 3 Sep. 1784 in Newberry District.

Waters, David. S.C. Pvt. He served under Capt. John Wilson, Capt. Hugh Wardlaw, Capt. Thomas Samuels, Capt. Samuel Moore, and Capt. Robert Maxwell. He was at Kettle Creek, the siege of Ninety Six, and served to the end of the war. Maj. John Hodges and William Bell said his particulars were true. He was from Abbeville District and was pensioned 17 Dec. 1831. He was paid as late as 1843.

Waters, Jacob. Pa. —. His widow, Eleanor Waters, was awarded a $40 gratuity and a $40 annuity in Philadelphia Co., Pa. 6 Apr. 1830.

Waters, Jacob. Pa. —. He was granted relief in Westmoreland County in Mar. 1827.

Waters, James. Pa. —. He applied 21 Mar. 1808 in Lancaster County. He served in the Pa. Line and was wounded three times. He was awarded a $40 gratuity and a $40 annuity. He died 16 Nov. 1813

Waters, John. Pa. —. He was awarded a $40 gratuity and a $40 annuity in Philadelphia Co., Pa. 3 Feb. 1824.

Waters, Jonathan. Md. Pvt. He was pensioned at the rate of half-pay of a private 19 Feb. 1819.

Waters, Joseph. Pa. Pvt. He was on the 1813 pension list.

Waters, Richard. Conn. Pvt. He resided in New Haven Co., Conn.

Waters, Richard. Md. Capt. He was pensioned at the rate of half-pay of a captain 12 Mar. 1827.

He was pensioned at the rate of half-pay of captain in Baltimore 2 Feb. 1830. His widow, Elizabeth J. Waters, was pensioned at the same rate 2 Feb. 1830.

Waters, Richard. Pa. —. He was granted relief.

Waters, Wilson. Md. Surgeon's Mate. His widow, Margaret Waters, was pensioned at the rate of half-pay of a surgeon's mate 16 Mar. 1836.

Watford, Joseph. S.C. —. He served under Col. Johnson, Gen. Caswell, Col. Sowell, and Maj. Shepherd. He was wounded in his leg. He was at Stono and Trent River. He was from Darlington District and was pensioned 17 Dec. 1831. He was paid in 1832.

Watkins, Gassaway. Md. Capt. He was pensioned in 1811. On 23 Jan. 1816 he was pensioned at the rate of half-pay of a captain. His widow, Eleanora B. Watkins, was paid her pension from 16 July 1840, the date of her husband's death, to 1 Jan. 1852. He had entered the service as a sergeant and served under Lt. Col. Smallwood. He was at Long Island, White Plains, Monmouth, Camden, and Cowpens. He was born in 1752 in Anne Arundel Co., Md. His daughter, Caroline Watkins, was pensioned by Congress 29 Apr. 1896. She was 92 years old and living with relations in Baltimore. The founder of the family in America was John Watkins who immigrated about 1660. His five other original settlers of Maryland were his great-grandfather, Capt. John Worthington, Col. Nicholas Greenberry who came in 1674, Col. Henry Ridgely, and Matthew Howard. John Watkins married Anne Gassaway, daughter of Nicholas Gassaway, *ca.* 1689. Their son, Nicholas Watkins, the second, married *ca.* 1743 Ariana Worthington, and they were the parents of the veteran. Ariana was the daughter of Thomas Worthington and grand-daughter of Capt. John Worthington who married Sarah Howard, the daughter of Matthew Howard. Thomas Worthington married 23 July 1711 Elizabeth Ridgely, daughter of Henry Ridgley and Catherine Greenberry and grand-daughter of Col. Henry Ridgley and Elizabeth Howard who married in England before immigrating and of Nicholas Greenberry. Gassaway Watkins entered the service in Jan. 1776. After the war he married (1) Sarah Jones who died a year later. He married (2) Ruth Dorsey by whom he had four sons and three daughters all of whom were dead. One of the sons died as a lieutenant in the War of 1812. He married (3) Eleanor Bowie Claggett, daughter of William Claggett who was the son of Edward and Ellen (Bowie) Claggett. The latter was the daughter of John Bowie of Prince Georges Co. Gassaway Watkins by his third wife had eight daughters and two sons. He had a plantation of 600 acres and was an original member of the Society of the Cincinnati and President of the Society at his death on 14 July 1840 in Howard Co., Md. He was 6 feet 2 inches tall. His widow died in 1871 at the age of 89. There were five living children: Priscilla Kenly the wife of George T. Kenly of Baltimore; Albina Clark a widow; Margaret O. Warfield a widow; Caroline Watkins a widow; and John S. Watkins. A grandson, Edwin Warfield, was President of the Fidelity and Deposit Company of Maryland. Gassaway Watkins had received 300 acres of bounty land in Knox Co., Ohio and 200 acres in Garrett Co.,Md. His grandsons, Edwin Warfield and John Warfield, owned the latter. He was elected President General of the Society of the Cincinnati 4 July 1839. Congress on 29 Apr. 1896 approved the petition of his daughter, Caroline Watkins.

Watkins, John. S.C. —. He was killed by Tories in 1781. His widow, Rachel Watkins, was granted an annuity 2 June 1785.

Watkins, John. S.C. —. His widow, Elizabeth Watkins, was in Claremont in 1786. She may be the Elizabeth Watkins who died 13 May 1819 whose arrearage was paid to Martha West, her daughter in 1820.

Watkins, Joseph. Va. Pvt. He was awarded a £30 gratuity and an annuity of half-pay on 26 May

1778. He was in Louisa County in June 1786. He was in the 6th Va. Regiment and was wounded at Brandywine. He lost an arm. He served under Col. Aylett in Capt. Towles' Company. He was 34 years old. He was continued on the pension list at the rate of £12 per annum on 10 Mar. 1789. He was on the 1813 pension list.

Watkins, Leonard. Md. Sgt. He was pensioned 2 Jan. 1813 at the rate of half-pay of a sergeant. His widow, Mary Watkins, was pensioned at the same rate in Montgomery County on 28 Feb. 1839.

Watkins, Robert. —. —. He was a pensioner and died in 1833. David Pugh, administrator of the estate of his widow, Hannah Watkins, sought what could have been allowed the children from 4 Mar. 1837 to her death in 1839. Congress rejected his petition in 1846.

Watkins, Seth. —. —. His widow was Abigail Watkins. They were married 22 July 1778. Congress rejected her petition 4 May 1846.

Watkins, Solomon. N.J. Pvt. He served under Capt. John Ross, Lt. Richard Cox, and Col. Elias Dayton in the 3rd Regiment. He died at Ticonderoga in Dec. 1776 or Jan. 1777. He married Elizabeth Hickman 13 Sep. 1772. His widow, Elizabeth Watkins, married secondly William Epin 24 Dec. 1781.

Watrous, Richard. Conn. Pvt. He served in the 6th Regiment under Col. R. J. Meigs. He was wounded by musket balls in his arms and hands and received several bayonet stabs in the breast and side in July 1779 at Norwalk, Conn. when the town was burned. He resided at Derby, Conn. in 1792. He enlisted 1 Apr. 1777 for three years and was discharged 29 Mar. 1780. He was granted three-fourths of a pension 20 Apr. 1796. He was on the 1813 pension list.

Wats, James. Md. Pvt. He was on the 1813 pension list as James Watts. He was pensioned at the rate of half-pay of a private in Dorchester County on 5 Feb. 1833.

Watson, —. Va. Pvt. He died in Continental service 26 Oct. 1778. His widow was Catherine Watson.

Watson, —. Va. —. Thomas Watson was granted assistance in Prince Edward County in Apr. 1777.

Watson, Abner. —. —. He did not have six months of service. He resided in Mercer Co., Ill. when Congress refused to grant him a pension by private act 14 Mar. 1846.

Watson, Benjamin. Pa. —. He was awarded a $40 gratuity and a $40 annuity in Montgomery Co., Pa. 11 Mar. 1833.

Watson, Benjamin. Va. —. He was disabled by illness on the Indian Expedition in 1776 at Long Island at Holstein and was not likely to recover. He was awarded a £20 gratuity on 3 June 1777. His father was Christopher Watson.

Watson, Christopher. Va. —. He contracted illness on the Indian expedition in 1776 and was not likely to recover. He was granted £20 relief 3 June 1777.

Watson, Guy. R.I. Pvt. He lost three joints from the toes on his right foot by frost bite on the Oswego Expedition in Feb. 1783. He served under Col. Jeremiah Olney. He was aged 33 in 1786. He was on the 1813 pension list.

Watson, James. Pa. —. He was awarded a $40 gratuity and a $40 annuity in Huntingdon Co., Pa. 16 Feb. 1835.

Watson, John. Conn. Capt. He served under Col. Benjamin Hinman. He was ordered to join a party under Samuel Elmore, Major Commandant, for the reduction of the British garrison at St. Johns in 1775. He was wounded 18 Sep. 1775 by a musket ball in the small of his back. He was disabled by a sprain in his right shoulder. He lived in Canaan, Conn. and was pensioned 4 Apr. 1787 and was 47 years old.

Watson, John. Me. —. He died in Bowdoinham 2 May 1823. His widow was Eunice Watson from Richmond. She was paid $50 under the resolve of 1836.

Watson, John. Pa. —. He applied 6 July 1809. He served in the 4th Pa. Regiment under Col. Anthony Wayne. He enlisted for one year and went to Ticonderoga in 1779. He reenlisted for three years in the winter of 1779 under Lt. Col. Caleb North in Monmouth, N.J. In collecting provisions, he was rendered incapable of duty due to harsh weather and was sent to hospital. Lt. David Marshall of the 5th Pa. Regiment proved his service. He was awarded a $40 gratuity and a $40 annuity on 30 Mar. 1811. He was from Chester County. His name has also been interpreted as John Matson.

Watson, John. S.C. —. He was taken prisoner at the defeat of Gen. Ashe at Briar Creek in 1779 and died with the enemy. His children were granted an annuity 25 Feb. 1785.

Watson, Joseph. Conn. —. He lost a leg. He was from Glastonbury 9 Feb. 1789.

Watson, Michael. —. Capt. He was in the rangers and was killed at Dean's Swamp, South Carolina. His daughter, Mary Perry, was granted relief by Congress 27 Jan. 1853.

Watson, Robert. S.C. —. He enlisted in 1781 in Col. Hampton's Regiment. Charles Smith of Hall Co., Ga. knew him in the service. His son, John Watson, had fits daily. He lived in Habersham Co., Ga. in 1829. His application was rejected.

Watson, Thomas. Del. Sgt. He was pensioned in 1778. He resided in Sussex County. He served in Casely's Company of the 16th Regiment of Artillery. He was on the 1813 pension.

Watson, Titus. Vt. He was from Poultney, Vt. He was discharged in 1781. He had a family of small children and sought an act of insolvency.

Watson, Thomas. Va. —. His family was granted support in the amount of 18 May 1778 in Prince Edward Co., Va. while he was away in Continental service.

Watson, William. Pa. Pvt. He was in Lancaster County on 10 May 1787. He first served under Col. Attlee. He was next in the 13th Pa. Regiment under Col. Stewart. He was wounded in his right thigh near the knee at Germantown in 1777 and was discharged unfit for duty. He was taken prisoner at Long Island, exchanged and was repeatedly wounded in the 13th Regiment. He was 44 years old.

Watson, William. S.C. —. His indent was to issued to his administrator, Samuel Watson, on 18 Dec. 1792.

Watt, James. Pa. Sgt. His widow, Ann Watt, was in Northumberland County on 5 Oct. 1790. He was called into the service in 1778 and was stationed at Freeland's Fort. He served in the militia under Col. James Murray, Capt. Arthur Taggart, Lt. Atkinson, Ensign Freeland, and Adjutant Steele. On 28 July 1779 he was set upon by Indians about 100 yards from the fort, tomahawked, and put to death. He was 44 years old. His son was John Watt.

Watt, James. Pa. —. He was pensioned in Center County 27 Mar. 1837. He was 85 years old in 1840. He died 24 Sep. 1843.

Watt, James. S.C. —. He served from 1775 to 1783 under Capt. Andrew Pickens, Capt. Thomas Weems, Capt. William Strain, and Col. Pickens. His widow was Jenny Watt from Anderson District in 1831. She was 72 years old, and her children had left her. Her application was rejected.

Watt, James M. Pa. —. He was granted relief in Indiana County 20 May 1839.

Watt, Samuel. Pa. —. He was awarded a $40 gratuity 31 Mar. 1812.

Watters, Jacob. Pa. —. He received a $40 gratuity and a $40 annuity in Westmoreland County 7 Mar. 1827. He also appeared as Jacob Watler.

Wattles, Mason. Mass. Capt. He received his commutation for five years in lieu of half-pay for life. He died 23 July 1819.

Watts, Aaron. Va. —. His wife, Rebeckah Watts, was given support in Bedford Co., Va. on 23 Feb. 1778. She was given £32 support on 23 Nov. 1778, £25 on 22 Feb. 1779, and £50 on 27 Sep. 1779.

Watts, William. Mass. Pvt. He served in the 7th Regiment under Col. Henry Jackson and Capt. Samuel Henley. He was disabled due to old age. He was pensioned 30 Jan. 1783. He was 57 years old and resided in Chelsea, Mass. in 1786. He was on the 1813 pension list.

Watts, William. Va. —. He was pensioned in Portsmouth, Norfolk Co. 27 Jan. 1820 at the rate of $60 per annum and $60 in immediate relief. He died 25 Jan. 1822. His widow, Ann Watts, was executrix of his will. Her securities were Samuel Watts and Abraham Watts.

Wattson, Thomas. Va. —. His widow, Katherine Wattson, was granted £30 support on 3 May 1779 in Richmond County.

Waugh, —. Va. —. His wife, Mary Waugh, was allowed £25 support for herself and her small children while her husband was away in the service in Augusta Co., Va. 17 Nov. 1778 and £20 on 17 Nov. 1779.

Waugh, George. Va. —. He was an officer in the militia. He died in 1814 and his widow in 1840. The heirs sought the pension arrears, but Congress rejected the claim 12 Jan. 1854.

Waugh, Michael. Pa. —. He received a $40 gratuity and a $40 annuity in Westmoreland County 9 Feb. 1837. He was 67 years old in 1840.

Waugh, Thaddeus. Conn. Sgt. He died in 1810.

Way, Isaac. Conn. Pvt. He served under Col. Benjamin Hinman. His daughter was Augusta Tuller, aged 96, of Bridgeport, Conn. She was pensioned at the rate of $12 per month from Congress 19 May 1896.

Way, Nicholas. Del. —. He received his half-pay pension in 1787.

Wayland, James. Conn. Pvt. He served under Col. Samuel B. Webb in Capt. Walker's Company. He had deafness in his right ear occasioned by the explosion of cannon. His body was bruised by a fall when employed in carrying mortar. Being on duty on a wet night, he caught a great cold which brought on diabetes. He lived in Stratford, Conn. in 1792. He enlisted 7 Apr. 1778 for the war and transferred to the Invalids 1 Sep. 1782. He was on the 1813 pension list. He died 29 June 1828.

Waysall, Nicholas. N.Y. Pvt. He served in the 1st New York Regiment. He had his collar bone broken by carrying timber. He was discharged by Gen. Washington. He was 46 years old when he applied 2 June 1786.

Weaber, Jacob. N.Y. Pvt. He served under Col. Bellinger in the militia and was slain 2 Sep. 1779. His children, John Weaber, Nicholas Weaber, Jacob Weaber, Michael Weaber, Peter Weaber, and Margaret Weaber, received his half-pay pension.

Weakley, Thomas. —. —. His widow, Prudence Chapel, had her petition rejected by Congress 4 Jan. 1848.

Weare, William. Conn. Pvt. He served under Col. Wyllys. He was wounded in the head, had a fractured skull, and suffered other disabilities in 1776. He lived in Hartford, Conn. in 1792. He enlisted 19 Jan. 1777 and was invalided 1 Apr. 1781.

Weatherall, Job. S.C. Legionnaire. He served aboard the *South Carolina* under Commodore Alexander Gillon. His administrator, Richard Wale, was paid $78.50 on 16 Mar. 1808.

Weatherby, William. N.J. —. His widow, Elizabeth Weatherby, was pensioned in Burlington County on 16 Feb. 1846 at the rate of $30 per annum.

Weatherford, Richard. Ga. —. He was an invalid soldier receiving a $50 per annum pension as early as 1796 and as late as 1804. In 1800 his name was incorrectly reported as Richard Rutherford.

Weaver, —. Pa. —. His widow, Maria Elizabeth Weaver, was awarded a $40 gratuity in Schuylkill Co., Pa. 15 Apr. 1835.

Weaver, Aaron. S.C. —. He was murdered by Tories. His widow, Jane Weaver, was granted an annuity 3 Feb. 1785 in Edgefield District. There were two children in 1791.

Weaver, Aaron. Va. Seaman. He was pensioned in Princess Anne County on 10 Feb. 1812 at the rate of $50 per annum and $50 immediate relief. He was wounded twice in an engagement at the mouth of York River. He died the last week of July or first week of Aug. 1819. His administrator was John B. Ogg. He was a free man of color.

Weaver, Abiel. R.I. Pvt. He lost his sight in his left eye by a bad cold taken on sentry duty at Warren in Dec. 1778. His left hand was somewhat frost bitten, and he had a lame knee due to rheumatism. He served under Col. Jeremiah Olney. He was 54 years old when he applied on 23 Feb. 1786. He resided in Providence Co., R.I.

Weaver, Adam. Pa. —. He was awarded a $40 gratuity and a $40 annuity in Westmoreland Co., Pa. 23 Jan. 1833. He was 89 years old in 1840.

Weaver, Albright. Pa. —. He was wounded in his right hand at the battle of Brunswick. He was granted a $40 gratuity and a $40 annuity. He was from Philadelphia in 1808. He died 11 May 1814.

Weaver, Anthony. Pa. —. He was awarded a $40 gratuity and a $40 annuity in Luzerne County in 1836.

Weaver, Benjamin. Va. —. His father, William Weaver, was furnished support in Westmoreland County. in Mar. 1779.

Weaver, David. N.Y. Pvt. He was pensioned 11 Aug. 1790. He was on the 1813 pension list.

Weaver, Jacob. N.Y. Pvt. He served in the militia under Col. Frederick Bellinger and Capt. Henry Horton. He resided at German Flats. He served two years and three months. Congress granted him a pension 5 Jan. 1836.

Weaver, Jacob. Pa. —. He enlisted in 1775 under Capt. Folbert and Col. Irwin. He was in both the wagon and foot departments. During the revolt in New Jersey he was transferred to the 4th Regiment under Col. Richard Butler and Capt. Andrew Irwin. He was discharged 15 Oct. 1784. He was paid $200 for his right to donation land in Adams Co., Pa. 23 Apr. 1829.

Weaver, John. Pa. —. He applied in Philadelphia County on 1 June 1812. He was a native of Pennsylvania and was 72 years old. He enlisted in Capt. Christie's Company in Col. Miles' Regiment and was discharged at Valley Forge by Col. Walter Stewart. He served a tour of six months, another of seven months, and a third tour for the war. He served more than a year in the 3rd Regiment under Col. Thomas Craig. He was discharged 3 Nov. 1783. He was in the battles of Long Island, Germantown, Trenton, Princeton, and Brandywine.

Weaver, Michael. Pa. —. He was awarded a $40 gratuity and a $40 annuity in York Co., Pa. 6 Apr. 1833.

Weaver, Samuel. —. —. Congress awarded his widow, Hannah Weaver of Wayne Co., Penn., the arrearage of her pension from 4 Mar. 1848 to 3 Feb. 1853 on 23 Feb. 1857.

Weaver, William. Pa. —. He was discharged 3 Nov. 1783. He was from Philadelphia County.

Webb, —. —. —. He died in the war. His widow, Mary Webb, had her application laid on the table 3 Mar. 1807.

Webb, Benjamin. Mass. —. He served in the 5th Regiment and was from Salem. He was paid $20.

Webb, Benjamin. Pa. —. He applied at Staunton, Va. 17 May 1838. He enlisted for the war in 1776 in Pa.

Webb, Charles. Conn. Col. He was disabled by a rupture. He resided in Stamford, Conn. in 1792. He was commissioned 1 Jan. 1777 and left the service 1 June 1778.

Webb, Constant. Conn. Sgt. He served in Col. Matthew Mead's Regiment raised at Morrisena, N.Y. He was wounded in 1779. He was taken prisoner and exchanged. He was again wounded 18 Jan. 1780 in his left arm and elbow by a cutlass. He served under Capt. Samuel Keeler. He was pensioned 3 Dec. 1788. He resided in Saybrook, Conn. He was on the 1813 pension list.

Webb, Frederick. Pa. —. He was deceased by Dec. 1791.

Webb, John. Mass. Pvt. He served at the Castle and was from Weymouth. He was paid $50.

Webb, John. Va. Capt. He received his commutation.

Webber, Benjamin. Mass. —. He was from Gloucester and was paid $50. He also appeared as Benjamin Webb.

Webber, Noah. Me. —. His widow was Nancy Webber. She was paid $50 under the resolve of 1836.

Webber, William. Mass. Pvt. He was in the 11th Regiment and was from Chelmsford. His widow, Anna Webber, was paid $50.

Weber, Henry. Pa. —. He was awarded a $40 gratuity and a $40 annuity in Lebanon County 28 Mar. 1836.

Weber, John. Pa. —. He was awarded a $40 gratuity and a $40 annuity in Lehigh County 1 Apr. 1823.

Webster, Isaac. —. Sgt. He served in Col. Warner's Regiment. He was wounded in the upper part of his arm and in the forearm on 7 July 1777 at Hubbardston. He resided at Bennington, Vt. in 1794. He enlisted 1 Mar. 1777 for three years and was in service 12 July 1779. He resided in Vt. in 1792. He was on the 1813 pension list.

Webster, John. Pa. —. He was awarded a $40 gratuity and a $40 annuity in Lehigh Co., Pa. 1 Apr. 1823.

Webster, Joshua. Mass. —. He served in the 8th Regiment and was paid $20.

Webster, William. S.C. —. He was wounded at St. Tillys. He was granted an annuity 1 Oct. 1784. He was from Newberry District.

Wedgewood, James. N.H. Lt. He was from North Hampton, Rockingham County. He served in the 3rd N.H. Regiment. He took sick and had to return home on 13 Sep. 1778. He was to remain at home until he was called for, but he never was. He sought his depreciation pay on 20 Oct. 1784.

Weed, Andrew. S.C. —. He served under Lt. Matthew Findley, Capt. Joseph Calhoun, and Col. Robert Anderson. He was at the blockhouse in Abbeville, a campaign in Georgia, and in East Tennessee against the Indians. He was 63 or 64 years old, and his wife was nearly as old. He applied 13 Nov. 1827. George Patterson, George Creswell, and James Shanks served with him. He died in Feb. 1850. His widow was Mary Weed of Abbeville District. She was paid in 1851. They were married in 178[?].

Weed, Benjamin. Conn. Pvt. He served in the 9th Conn. Militia in Capt. Silvanus Knap's Company in 1777 under Gen. Arnold. He was wounded at Ridgefield by a musket ball in his right shoulder blade which lodged in his breast on 27 Jan. He was attended by James Cogswell. He lived in Stamford, Conn. and was 38 years old when he was pensioned 24 Nov. 1788. He was on the 1813 pension list.

Weed, Elnathan. —. —. He enlisted in May 1775 under Capt. Silvanus Brown and Col. David Waterbury for nine months. He marched from New York City to Ticonderoga to Canada. He took sick at St. John's and was in hospital. He served nine months under Capt. Keeler in 1776.Congress granted him a pension 3 Jan. 1832.

Weed, Jonathan. N.Y. —. He served in Col. Marinus Willett's Regiment. His heirs were awarded 200 acres of bounty land 13 Apr. 1813.

Weed, Seth. Conn. Lt. He served in Webb's Regiment. He was wounded by a musket ball in his left leg. He was pensioned at the rate of $6 per month from 7 Oct. 1807. He was on the 1813 pension list. He was totally disabled but had his petition for an increase in his pension rejected by Congress 25 June 1818. He died 26 Dec. 1822 in Fairfield Co., Conn.

Weed, Smith. Conn. —. He was wounded in both thighs at Ridgefield 27 Apr. 1777. He was pensioned 30 Sep. 1777 at Stamford. Congress awarded his widow, Sarah Weed, the arrearage of her pension from 4 Mar. 1848 to 3 Feb. 1853 on 15 Dec. 1857. She was from Albany Co., N.Y.

Weedman, Jacob. Pa. Sgt. Maj. He was on the 1791 pension roll.

Weeks, Arthur Moore. S.C. —. He served eight or nine months in North Carolina about the time the Tories rose up on Cape Fear. He served under Capt. Adkins, Col. Alston, Col. Folsome, Capt. Hall, and Col. Johnson in the militia. He went to South Carolina and Georgia. He was discharged at Stono. He also served under Capt. Blanks, Capt. Cofield, and Col. Reed and fought at Guilford. He was discharged at Camden. He was in his 75th year and his wife was nearly as old. He had a helpless son afflicted with the fits and a daughter in 1831. He was from Barnwell District and was pensioned 4 Dec. 1832. Willoughby Wells served with him. He died in 1839. His widow was Lucretia Weeks.

Weeks, Elijah. Mass. —. He served under his father, Capt. Thomas Weeks, having enlisted 1 Jan. 1777 and was discharged 15 Jan. 1778. He subsequently served under Capt. Smith in the New York Line. He and his widow, Sarah Weeks, were pensioners. She died 29 Dec. 1853. Their daughter, Sarah C. Hurlbutt, of Chatham Valley, Tioga Co., Pa., aged 73, was granted a pension by Congress 28 Jan. 1890.

Weeks, Francis. S.C. Ens. He entered the service in 1778 and served four years. He bore the colors at Ninety Six, Briar Creek, and Eutaw Springss. He applied under the act of 1832 but died before relief was granted. His widow was Nancy Weeks. She had a land warrant for his service. She was pensioned for his service as a private. She was recommended for relief 16 Jan. 1857. He and Lt. William Coggan caught and hanged seven Tories. Congress on 5 Feb. 1860 awarded her a pension at the rate of $20 per month deducting whatever pension she had received.

Weeks, John. Mass. Pvt. He served in the 8th Regiment and was from Northfield. His widow, Susanna Weeks, was paid $20.

Weeks, Nathan. R.I. Lt. He was commissioned 17 Feb. 1777 and served under Col. Israel Angel He was killed at Monmouth, N.J. 28 June 1778. His son, John Weeks, sought the back pay of $1,216 and seven years of half-pay due his father. Congress awarded him the same 19 Feb. 1855.

Weeks, Thomas. Mass. & Conn. —. He enlisted for three years in 1777 in the dragoons. He was between 17 and 18 years of age. He was under Capt. Soaper, Capt. Marshall, Col. Marshall, and Gen. Patterson. He joined the troops in the Connecticut Line. He was at Stillwater and the surrender of Burgoyne. He was wounded in his head and leg at the battle of Plymouth. He was at White Plains, Tarrytown, Horseneck, Pine ridge, West Point, and Valley Forge. He resided in Limestone Co., Ala. Congress granted his a pension 22 Dec. 1837.

Weems, Henry. S.C. Pvt. He lost a leg in action with the Cherokee Indians in 1776. He was granted an annuity 9 Sep. 1784. He lived in Edgefield District. He was in Abbeville District in 1799. He had seven small daughters. He was on the 1813 pension list.

Weickle, —. Pa. —. His widow, Catherine Weickle, was awarded a $40 gratuity and a $40 annuity in Berks Co., Pa. 14 Feb 1833. She also appeared as Catharine Weikle. She was dead by 1843.

Weida, Michael. Pa. —. He was awarded a $40 gratuity and a $40 annuity in Berks Co., Pa. 18 Mar. 1834. He was dead by Jan. 1837.

Weidley, —. Pa. —. His widow, Rosanna Weidley, was awarded a $40 gratuity and a $40 annuity in Lancaster Co., Pa. 19 Jan. 1825.

Weidner, —. Pa. —. His widow, Susanna Weidner, was granted relief in Chester County 13 Mar. 1839.

Weidner, Peter. Pa. —. He served in 1781 and 1782.

Weidman, Jacob. Pa. Sgt. Maj. He served in the 2nd Penn. Regiment under Col. Walter Stewart. He applied 21 Jan. 1788. He was disabled by hardship, cold, and fatigue suffered in the service on the expedition to Canada. His wife was mentioned 29 Feb. 1788. There were five small children.

Weigant, John. Pa. Adjt. He served in the militia. He was from Northampton County.

Weigell, Stoffel. Pa. —. He served in Capt. Benjamin Weiser's Company under Col. Husecker. He was wounded in his ankle. He took sick at Valley Forge and was discharged. He was awarded a $40 gratuity on 27 Mar. 1812.

Weimir, Adam. Pa. —. He was awarded a $40 gratuity and a $40 annuity in Mercer Co., Pa. 10 Apr. 1835. He died 2 Jan. 1845.

Weir, —.Va. —. His widowed mother, Sarah Weir, received £20.3.6 in Halifax Co., Va. on 17 June 1779. She was furnished 3 barrels of corn, 300 pounds of pork, 150 pounds of beef, and a half bushel of salt on 21 Oct. 1779 and £15 on 17 Feb. 1780.

Weir, Edward. Mass. Pvt. He served in the 3rd Regiment under Capt. Watson. He was disabled with asthma. He lived in Woburn, Mass. in 1788 and was 24 years old.

Weir, James. N.Y. Corp. He served in the Washington County militia in Capt. Green's Company under Col. Lewis Van Woert and was disabled at Saratoga with a shoulder wound. He lived in Salem, Washington Co., N.Y. on 2 May 1789. He was aged 46 years in 1787. He also appeared as James Were, James Wire, and James Wier. He was on the 1813 pension list.

Weir, John. Pa. —. He was 81 years old in 1840. He was granted support in Greene County 21 July 1842.

Weirick, Valentine. —. Pa. Pvt. He and Emanuel Bollinger served in Capt. Matthew Smith's Company in the 1st Pa. Regiment and marched from Lancaster County to Boston and on to Quebec under Benedict Arnold. They had to support themselves seven months without compensation. He was awarded $60 on 27 Mar. 1812. He also appeared as Valentine Weinrich.

Weiser, —. Pa. —. His widow, Justina Weiser, was awarded a $40 gratuity and a $40 annuity in Dauphin Co., Pa. 25 Mar. 1833.

Weisner, —. Pa. —. His widow, Sarah Weisner, was granted relief in Chester County 11 Apr. 1848. Her name has been misinterpreted as Sarah Weimer.

Weisner, Jacob. Pa. —. He was from Chester County and was pensioned 2 Mar. 1829. His widow, Sarah Weisner, was granted a $40 annuity in Chester County 11 Apr. 1848.

Weiss, Henry. Pa. Pvt. He served in the 2nd Pa. Regiment. He was wounded in his right hand and in one of his ribs by buck shot and a bayonet in Oct. 1777 at Germantown. He also had a rupture. He was also injured by a log falling on him while he was assisting in throwing up a work to prevent an attack at White Marsh. He lived in Berks Co., Pa. in 1794.

Weissenfels, Frederick. N.Y. & Pa. Col. He had a claim to 2,000 acres of land for his service in the French and Indian War. He was at Ticonderoga and Havanna. He left the British service to serve in the American forces. He died 14 May 1806 in New Orleans. His daughter, Harriet de la Palm Baker, sought bounty land in the west to which her father might have been entitled had he remained in British service. Congress rejected her claim 23 June 1840. He was at White Plains, Monmouth, Saratoga, Trenton, and Princeton in the Revolution. Congress granted the heirs of Harriet de la Palm Baker relief 19 Mar. 1860

Weitzel, John. Pa. —. His widow and heirs were paid $200 in lieu of his donation land 18 Apr. 1843. One of the heirs was Jane White.

Weitzel, Philip. Pa. —. He served three months under Capt. Jacob Glotz and Col. Cunningham in the Flying Camp. He was awarded a $40 gratuity and a $40 annuity in Lancaster Co., Pa. 31 Jan. 1831.

Welch, —. Va. —. His wife, Elizabeth Welch, was furnished assistance in Loudoun County on 9 Nov. 1779.

Welch, David. Va. Sgt. He served under Col. Hannow. He was wounded at the battle of Monmouth by a musket ball on 28 June 1778. He lived in Henrico Co., Va. in 1794. He was granted a full pension 20 Apr. 1796.

Welch, Dennis. Mass. —. He served in the Artillery and was paid $20. He also appeared as Dennis Welsh.

Welch, James. Me. —. He was from Gray. He was paid $50 under the resolve of 1836.

Welch, John. Pa. Pvt. He served three years in Capt. John McDowell's Company in the 7th Pa. Regiment under Lt. Col. John Greer. He was wounded in his left shoulder at Germantown. He was due his donation land 14 Mar. 1806. He applied in Butler County.

Welch, John. S.C. —. He was killed in Jan. 1782. His widow, Eleanor Welch, was granted an annuity 2 Mar. 1786. There were two children in 1791. She was being paid as late as 1825.

Welch, Joshua. Va. —. His wife was granted support in Pittsylvania Co., Va. on 24 Sep. 1778.

Welch, Nathaniel. Va. Capt. His heirs received commutation of full-pay for five years in lieu of half-pay for life as captain of infantry in the Virginia Line with no interest on 6 Jan. 1827. He served in the 1st Regiment and had a land warrant which he located in Pulaksi Co., Ky. Peter Kemp located his warrant in the same location and deprived Welch of his 1,000 acres. Kemp received 400 acres 20 Mar. 1783 and Welch 400 acres 26 Apr. 1783. Congress ruled that he was not entitled to relief 26 June 1834.

Welch, Paul. Me. —. His widow was Mary Welch from York. She was paid $50 under the resolve of 1836.

Welch, Stephen. S.C. —. He served eighteen months under Capt. John Nelson, Col. Singleton, Capt. John Rogers, and Capt. Joseph Henderson. He later served two years in the calvary. James Smith knew he was a soldier. He was 68 years old. He was from Marion District and was pensioned 25 Nov. 1830. He was on the roll as late as 1834.

Welch, William. —. —. He was pensioned in 1818 and stricken in 1820. He was restored in 1828. Congress granted him arrearage from 3 Mar. 1820 to 29 May 1828.

Welchell, John. S.C. Pvt. He was from Union District and was pensioned 4 Dec. 1823. He had been wounded several times.

Welding, —. —. —. His widow, Catherine Welding, simply knew that her late husband had served in the Revolution. Her application for bounty land had been rejected, and Congress denied her a pension 6 Apr. 1860.

Welker, Daniel. Pa. —. He applied in Franklin County 29 Mar. 1813. He enlisted in Col. John Patton's Regiment in 1777 and was wounded at Ash Swamp, N.J. He was discharged in 1781. He was due his donation land on 17 Mar. 1806. He was dead by Aug. 1824. He was granted a $40 gratuity and a $40 annuity.

Wellburn, William. Va. —. He was wounded in the wrist of his left hand at the defeat of Col. Buford. He applied for relief 14 Dec. 1780.

Weller, Daniel. Pa. —. He was awarded a $40 gratuity and a $40 annuity in Franklin County on 29 Mar. 1813.

Weller, John. Pa. —. He was awarded a $40 gratuity in Lancaster Co., Pa. 12 Apr. 1828. He was awarded a $40 gratuity and a $40 annuity 1 Apr. 1830.

Wellington, Samuel. Pvt. He served in Col. Hollman's Regiment. He was wounded through his throat at White Plains in 1776. He resided at Templeton, Mass. in 1796. Congress rejected his petition for an increase 25 June 1818.

Wellman, Jacob. Mass. —. He served in the 4th Regiment and was paid $20.

Wellman, Jacob. N.H. Pvt. He served in the militia under Col. James Reed. He was wounded by a musket ball shot through his right leg on 17 June 1775 at Bunker Hill. He lived in Lyndeborough, N.H. in 1794. He was granted one-fourth of a pension 20 Apr. 1796.

Wellman, Silas. Mass. —. He served in the 4th Regiment and was paid $20.

Wellman, William. Mass. —. He served in the 1st Regiment and was paid $20. He was listed as drowned in 1801.

Wells, —. Ga. —. Mrs. Wells of Richmond County was granted six bushels on 15 Mar. 1782.

Wells, —. Md. Pvt. His widow, Martha Wells, was pensioned in Prince George's County at the rate of half-pay of a private 20 Mar. 1840.

Wells, —. Va. —. His wife, Catharine Wells, and four children were granted £8.4 support in Frederick Co., Va. on 5 Feb. 1782.

Wells, Bayze. Conn. Lt. He served under Col. Chandler. He was disabled by disease in 1777. He lived in Farmington, Conn. in 1792. He was commissioned 1 Jan. 1777 and resigned 1 Mar. 1778.

Wells, Conrad. Pa. —. He was pensioned 18 Oct. 1814. He was from Chester County.

Wells, Cuff. Ct. Pvt. He served three years and was discharged in Jan. 1783. He married Phillis ---- in May 1783. She married secondly ----- Tatton. Congress granted her a pension 8 Mar 1842. She was from Lebanon, New London Co., Ct.

Wells, James. N.Y. Pvt. He was disabled by a dislocated left elbow in Oct. 1781. He served in Capt. Spalding's Company under Col. Grosvenor. He lived in Hilldale, Columbia Co., N.Y. on 1 May 1789. He was on the 1813 pension list as James Wills [sic].

Wells, Samuel. N.H. Sgt. He served in the N.H. Line. He was on the 1813 pension list. He later moved from Grafton Co., N.H. to Orleans Co., Vt. He died 21 Nov. 1830.

Wells, Stephen. Conn. Lt. He served in Col. Whitting's militia. He was wounded in his leg by a ball 27 Apr. 1777 at Ridgefield. He resided at Stratford, Conn. in 1796. He was granted half a pension 20 Apr. 1796.

Wells, Thomas. Del. Sgt. He was pensioned in 1782. He died 21 Aug. 1804.

Wells, Thomas. Va. —. He was away in the service and his wife, Ann Wells, was allowed support in Augusta Co., Va. 18 May 1779.

Wells, William. Pa. Capt. He died 10 Mar. 1812 in the District of Columbia.

Welsh, —. —. Capt. His widow was Anna Welsh. Her husband was in the Marines and served on the expedition to Penobscot where he was slain. His widow was not entitled to half-pay since he was in the Navy. She was the executrix of her late brother, George Hurlbut, who was in Sheldon's Regiment of Light Dragoons and was wounded on duty at Tarrytown in the summer of 1781. He languished of his wounds and died 8 May 1783. She was due no benefits under her brother since he died before 3 Nov. 1783. Congress also rejected her claim 7 Feb. 1797 because marines were not covered by the law

Welsh, —. Va. —. His wife, Mary Welsh, was granted £8 support in Frederick Co., Va. on 2 Sep. 1777.

Welsh, —. Pa. —. His widow, Elizabeth Welsh, was awarded a $40 gratuity and a $40 annuity in Franklin Co., Pa. 7 Apr. 1830.

Welsh, Edward. N.Y. Pvt. He served in Capt. Bovier's Company in the 5th N.Y. Regiment under Col. Lewis Dubois. He also served in Capt. Henry Vanderburgh's Company in 2nd N.Y. Regiment. At Fort Montgomery he was wounded by a musket ball in his left leg. He was discharged 10 Apr. 1783. He lived in Mount Pleasant, Westchester Co., N.Y. on 15 Apr. 1789.

Welsh, Henry. Pa. —. He was granted relief.

Welsh, John. Pa. —. He was awarded a $40 gratuity and a $40 annuity in York Co., Pa. 14 Apr. 1834. He was dead by July 1837.

Welsh, John. Pa. —. He served in the 7th Regiment under Lt. Col. Greer and Capt. John McDonald. He was wounded at Germantown. His widow, Mary Welsh, was awarded a $40 gratuity and a $40 annuity in Butler County 5 Jan. 1832 and 15 Mar. 1838.

Welsh, John. Va. Pvt. He transferred to the District of Columbia. (One John Welch was on the 1785 pension list of Virginia, but he was a veteran of the last war.)

Welsh, Michael. Pa. Sgt. He was in Lancaster County on 7 Apr. 1786. He was wounded in the knee by a shot from the enemy on 3 Jan. 1777 at the battle of Princeton. He served in the 10th Pa. Regiment in the company of Capt. Herman Stout under Lt. Col. Adam Hubley, Jr. He received pay as per certificate from Jacob Howell, Secretary of the Board of War. He was 38 years old. His wife was Jean Welsh. He also appeared as Michael Walsh.

Welter, George. N.Y. Pvt. He was pensioned.

Wemer, Peter. Pa. —. He was receiving a pension in 1790.

Wendell, David. N.Y. Pvt. He was discharged 22 Apr. 1782 by Gen. Washington. He was pensioned in 1785. He was on the 1800 list of pensioners and on the 1813 pension list.

Wendel, John H. N.Y. —. He served under Capt. Van Schaick from 1776 to 5 Apr. 1783 when he resigned due to ill health. His children, Catharine Wendel, Maria Wendel, and Anna Wendel, of Albany, N.Y. sought his five years' full pay. Congress rejected their claim 3 Mar. 1859.

Wendt, Frederick. Pa. —. He was awarded a $40 gratuity in Union County on 26 Mar. 1822.

Wenner, —. Pa. —. His widow, Anna Maria Wenner, received a $40 gratuity and a $40 annuity in Luzerne County 3 Mar. 1837. She died 8 June 1841.

Wenner, George Nicholas. Pa. —. He was awarded a $40 gratuity in Luzerne Co., Pa. 20 Feb. 1832.

Wentling, George. Pa. Maj. He received his commission in July 1776 and joined the army in New York. He was discharged seven years later at Philadelphia. He was at Long Island, White Plains, Trenton, Princeton, Brandywine, Germantown, Stoney Point, and Yorktown. He was slightly wounded at Brandywine by a musket ball in his thigh. He applied for a pension from Lancaster Co., Penn. which Congress granted 21 Jan. 1845. One George Wentling received a $40 gratuity and a $40 annuity in Lancaster Co., Pa. 11 Apr. 1844.

Wentworth, John. Me. —. He died 27 Sep. 1827 at Belmont. His widow was Lydia Wentworth from Ellsworth. She was paid $50 under the resolve of 1836.

Wentz, John. N.C. Pvt. He applied in Mecklenburg County in 1802. He served in the militia under Capt. Conrad Hise. He received a cut from a sword in his right hand between his thumb and forefinger, a cut in his head, and a wound in his knee. He was also in Capt. Beaver's Company. Leonard Lipe who served with him attested to his service. He was on the 1813 pension list. He also appeared as John Wence. He was also in Cabarrus County.

Wentzel, John. Pa. —. He was awarded a $40 gratuity and a $40 annuity in Montgomery County in 1836. His widow and heirs received $200 in lieu of donation land 18 Apr. 1843.

Wenwood, Godfrey. —. —. He was a baker in Sept. 1775 when the country became indebted to him for the discovery, detection, and exposure of the treasonable correspondence of Dr. Church, then Director General of Hospital. The British confiscated his property. His daughters, Salley C. Wenwood and Eliza F. (Wenwood) Waldo of Newport, R.I. sought relief. Congress rejected their claim 31 Dec. 1845.

Wertman, Jacob. Pa. —. He was awarded a $40 gratuity in Schulykill County 12 Jan. 1836.

Wertz, Daniel. Pa. —. He was awarded a $40 gratuity and a $40 annuity in York County 6 Apr. 1833.

Wescott, Benjamin. Mass. —. He served in the 8th Regiment.

Wescott, Isaac. Me. —. He was from Gorham. He was paid $50 under the resolve of 1836.

Wesner, William. Pa. —. He was awarded a $40 gratuity and a $40 annuity in Berks Co., Pa. 27 Feb. 1834. He was dead by Dec. 1839.

Wesson, Isaac. N.H. —. He enlisted in 1778 and was not heard from after 1 Apr. 1779. His widow, Lucy Wesson, and children of Jaffrey sought relief on 12 Sep. 1782.

Wesson, James. Mass. Col. He was on the 1813 pension list.

West, —. S.C. —. His widow was a pensioner. His daughter, Martha West, received what was due her mother on 7 Dec. 1819.

West, Alexander. Va. Pvt. He served 13 months in a company of rangers under Capt. James Booth and received $104 on 9 Feb. 1833. He was from Lewis County.

West, Benjamin. Md. Pvt. He was pensioned at the rate of half-pay of a private in Baltimore 9 Mar. 1826.

West, Benjamin. S.C. —. He was from Greenville District and was pensioned 6 Dec. 1828. He was paid as late as 1834.

West, Benjamin. S.C. —. He was killed by the enemy. His widow, Jane West, was granted an annuity 7 June 1785 in Spartanburg District. There were children in 1791. James West, administrator, of the estate of Benjamin West, deceased, and uncle of the orphans, was to be paid the arrearage on 14 Dec. 1821. Jane West died four days before 1 Mar. 1829. Her arrearage was due to her heirs and was to be paid to her administrator or administratrix on 17 Dec. 1831. The heirs were George West, Solomon West, Rachel West, and James West.

West, Charles. Va. —. His daughter, Mary West, was in the care of Mourning Lucas in Isle of Wight Co., Va. She was paid £15 for her support on 4 June 1778 and £30 on 4 Mar. 1779.

West, Jackson. Mass. —. He enlisted in June 1778 under Capt. James Berry and Col. Poor for eight months. He died in 1797. Congress granted his widow, Anna West, a pension 19 Jan. 1837. Her son, Josiah West, of Beverly, Essex Co., Mass. was her guardian. She had been deprived of her reason more than two years ago.

West, Leonard. N.Y. Corp. He served under Col. McClaughry in the Ulster County militia and was slain 6 Oct. 1777 at Fort Montgomery. His children, John West and William West, were granted a half-pay pension.

West, Randolph. Va. —. His wife Mary West was granted support of £5 per annum in Isle of Wight County, Va. on 7 Aug. 1777.

West, Robert. S.C. —. He was twice wounded in the service. He was from All Saints Parish, Horry District and was pensioned 7 Dec. 1826. He died 29 Dec. 1827. His widow, Mary West, received the arrearage of his pension and was pensioned at the rate of $30 per annum on 23 Nov. 1829. She was 62 years old and had two sons.

West, Robert. S.C. —. He was from Pendleton District in 1828.

West, Thomas. Mass. —. At the age of 17 or 18 he enlisted for three years in 1777 and served in the dragoons under Capt. Soaper and next under Capt. Marshall. He joined the Connecticut Line under Col. Sheldon. He was at Stillwater, the surrender of Burgoyne, and Plymouth where he was wounded in his head and leg. He was also at White Plains, Tarrytown, Horseneck, Pine Bridge, and Valley Forge. Congress granted him a pension for twelve months of service on 1 Feb. 1837.

West, Thomas. Va. Capt. He was appointed in Apr. 1776 in the 10th Regiment under Gen. George Weeden. He served in Morgan's Corps and died in the service. His received 4,000 acres of bounty land 1 Apr. 1807. His cousin was Jemima West. Congress rejected the petition from the heirs 7 Mar. 1842. There were two men of the name from Virginia. One served in the 11th Regiment under Col. Daniel Morgan and was commissioned in July 1776. He was listed as dead in 1778. His heirs received bounty land 1 Apr.1807 The other Thomas West served in the 10th Regiment and was appointed 19 Feb. 1777. He was the one from whom commutation was claimed. He was paid from 1 Jan. 1777 to 1 Sep 1778. He received 5,333 1/3 aces which would have been for eight years. He was not entitled to an inch of bounty land. He did not ask for it in his lifetime. Congress rejected the petition.

Westbrook, Peter. N.J. Capt. He served under Col. Rosengratz and was killed in action with the savages 19 Apr. 1780. His widow was Lydia Westbrook who received a half-pay pension in Sussex County.

Weston, Josiah. —. —. He was involved in capturing the British schooner, *Margaretta*, Machias, Me. in June 1775. He died 29 Aug. 1828. His widow, **Hannah Weston**, was 93 years of age and had lived at Jonesborough, Washington Co., Me. for seventy years. She and her husband's sister carried about 30 pounds of powder and ball from Jonesborough to Machias (a distance of nine miles). She claimed a pension on her husband's and her own service. Congress denied her request 11 Apr. 1850.

Westphal, Nicholas Ferdinand. —. —. He was a sergeant-major in British service and deserted from Fort Edward. He took his picket of twelve men on 8 Aug. 1777 and arrived at the American camp at Stillwell with five of his men on 17 Aug. 1777. He retired and married and had three children. He was disabled in an accident. He sent his wife and two children to Hanover via Hamburg, Germany to recover his property. He applied in 1791. He received 100 acres and $336.

Wescott, Benjamin. Mass. —. He served in the 8th Regiment and was paid $20.

Wescott, Thomas. Mass. Pvt. He served in the 10th Regiment and was from Freetown.

Wethington, Peter. Pa. Capt. His widow, Eve Wethington, was in Berks County 17 July 1790. He was in 12th Battalion of Pa. Regulars under Col. William Cook and was commissioned by Congress in 1776. He died of sickness at Reading 6 May 1777. His sons-in-law were Peter Himm [?] and Augustus Stoner. His son was Martin Wethington. He also appeared as Peter Withington. Eve Wethington died 27 June 1833.

Weygandt, Jacob. Pa. —. He was awarded a $40 gratuity and a $40 annuity in Berks Co., Pa. 11 Apr. 1825.

Weygandt, John. Pa. —. He was awarded a $40 gratuity and a $40 annuity in Northampton Co.,

Pa. 29 Mar. 1824. His widow, Elizabeth Weygandt, was awarded his annuity on 7 Mar. 1829.

Whaley, Jonathan. Conn. Pvt. He served in the 3rd Regiment. He was wounded by a musket ball shot through his thigh on 6 Sep. 1781 at New London. He lived in Montville, Conn. in 1794. He served in the militia. He was granted one-fourth of a pension 20 Apr. 1796. He died 1 Sep. 1805. He was on the 1813 pension list.

Wharfield, Aaron. Mass. —. He served in the 3rd Regiment and was paid $20.

Wharton, —. Pa. —. His widow, Sarah Wharton, was awarded a $40 gratuity and a $40 annuity in Mifflin Co., Pa. 29 Mar. 1824.

Wharton, Samuel. S.C. Col. He served a tour against the Indians, a tour under Capt. William Ritchie, and one in Georgia in the winter season. He was at Ninety Six and served in the Indian expedition under Col. Killgore. His fellow soldiers included Andrew Burnside, Paul Findley, Zacheriah Bailey, and Robert McNess. He was unable to walk without assistance and was disabled by rheumatism. He applied in Laurens District and was pensioned 6 Dec. 1825.

Wharton, Samuel. Va. —. He was pensioned at the rate of $50 per annum on 3 Jan. 1804. He was in Louisa County in Feb. 1805. He died 11 Dec. 1841. His administrator was William Wharton.

Wharton, Samuel. Va. —. He served 18 months in the war under Capt. F. Colman and Col. W. Colman. His daughter, Sarah Wharton, of Washington, Rappahannock Co., Va. was granted a pension by Congress 3 Feb. 1897.

Whatley, —. —. —. He was wounded in the militia service and was an invalid pensioner. His widow, Catharine Whatley, did not state the period, grade, his officers, or state of his service so Congress rejected her pension application 18 Aug; 1842.

Whatley, Samuel. Ga. Pvt. He was pensioned in 1781. He served in 2nd Regiment. He was on the 1813 pension list.

Wheatland, Joseph. R.I. Lt. His father, Caleb Wheatland, and ten brothers held commissions in the British forces. He wad disinherited for joining the American cause. He enlisted at the age of 19 on 11 May 1775. He was a native of R.I. and served in nine campaign. He fought in every battle the Rhode Island Line did. At the capture of the *Margaretta* and two other schooners he received a saber wound in his head. He took the first flag that was ever taken from the British. They used the ship to capture Fort Howe in St. John's habor. He also volunteered in the War of 1812. He died 23 Nov. 1828 in the insane asylum in Baltimore, Md. His administratrix, Mary Berault, was granted relief by Congress. L. J. Anderson sought relief from Congress for the heirs on 31 Jan. 1854, but Congress did approve the claim. His administrator *de bonis non*, John A. Clarke, was awarded his half-pay by Congress on 16 Jan. 1872.

Wheatley, William. Md. Pvt. His widow, Rhoda Wheatley, was pensioned at the rate of half-pay of a private in Dorchester County on 13 Mar. 1832. She died 5 June 1839. Her arrearage of $7.12 ½ was paid to Esther Williss, one of the legal representatives, 25 Feb. 1840.

Wheaton, Jesse. Mass. Pvt. He served in the 16th Regiment and was from Dedham. He was paid $50.

Wheeland, —. Pa. —. His widow, Elizabeth Wheeland, was awarded a $40 gratuity and a $40 annuity in Northumberland Co., Pa. 11 Mar. 1833.

Wheeland, Michael. Pa. —. He was granted a $40 gratuity and a $40 annuity 8 Feb. 1816. He was from Northumberland County. He also appeared as Michael Weiland.

Wheelan, Edward. N.Y. Sgt. In 1777 he served in Capt. W. Butler's Company under Col. Patten. On 1 Apr. 1780 he transferred to Washington's Guard under Maj. Caleb Gibbs and afterwards under Capt. William Colfax. In July 1781 he was wounded in the foot. He was sick with rheumatism in the winter of 1782 and procured another man to serve in his stead. He was then discharged. He lived in New York City where he was a carpenter after the war. He was on the 1791 pension roll. He also appeared as Edward Whelan.

Wheeler, —. —. —. His widow, Catherine Wheeler, had her laid on the table 28 June 1790.

Wheeler, Benjamin. —. —. He applied in Orange Co., N.C. 25 Aug. 1824.

Wheeler, James. Md. Pvt. His widow was Priscilla Wheeler.

Wheeler, James. Pa. —. He was pensioned.

Wheeler, John. Mass. Pvt. He served in the 7th Regiment.

Wheeler, John. Vt. Pvt. He served under Col. L. Butler. He was afflicted with palsy occasioned by being greatly fatigued in drawing cannon in Virginia in Oct. 1781. He lived in Tinmouth, Vt. in 1794.

Wheeler, John. Va. Pvt. He was in Augusta County in 1789. He was a soldier in the Va. Line. He was disabled by several wounds. He received £8 relief and was pensioned at the same rate on 30 Dec. 1791. He was in Fauquier County in 1793.

Wheeler, Nathaniel. Md. Pvt. He was wounded at Eutaw Springs and lost his leg. He was pensioned in 1784 in Somerset County. He was on the 1813 pension list. He died 5 Nov. 1825. His widow, Mary Wheeler, was pensioned at the rate of half-pay of a private 2 Feb. 1832.

Wheeler, Phineas. Mass. —. He served in the 6th Regiment and was from Vermont. He was paid $20.

Wheeler, Plato. R.I. Pvt. He lost all his toes on the left foot and part of the toes on his right foot by frost bite on the Oswego Expedition in Feb. 1783. The sores never healed. He served under Col. Jeremiah Olney and Col. Willett. He was aged 51 when he applied 17 Feb.1786. He died 28 May 1805 in Providence Co., R.I.

Wheelock, Levi. Mass. —. He served in the 1st Regiment and was paid $20.

Whelchel, John. S.C. Pvt. He served under Capt. John Thompson and Col. Thomas Brandon. He was wounded several times at Cowpens in action with Tarleton's horsemen. He had seven cuts in his head and two in his shoulder. His skull was opened to the brains. He was 67 years old and his wife 60. Capt. Joshua Palmer, William Morehead, and William McKown were with him at Cowpens. He died 14 Mar. 1837. His daughter, Judith McAdams, of Hall Co., Ga. sought the arrears for herself and her brother, Francis Whelchel, 4 Nov. 1856.

Wherry, James. Pa. —. He was awarded a $40 gratuity and a $40 annuity in Washington Co., Pa. 18 Mar. 1834.

Whidden, James. Me. —. He was born in Penobscot and died 29 Mar. 1828 at Canaan. His widow, Sally Whidden, was paid $50 under the resolve of 1836.

Whidden, Noah. N.C. —. He served from Nash Co., N.C. under Capt. Coleman, Capt. McCotes, and Lt. Gibson in 1781. He applied from Darlington District, South Carolina in 1827. His application was rejected because he did serve from that state.

Whileber, John. N.Y. Pvt. He served under Col. Morgan. He was wounded in the right thigh by a musket ball on 7 Oct. 1777 at Bemis Heights. He lived in Otsego, N.Y. in 1794.

Whipple, Abraham. R.I. —. He served from 1775 and had command of the ship *Columbus*. He was on two expeditions to Bermuda and Providence. He was injured in a fall of more than 15 feet, especially in his ankle and knee, in action with the British frigate *Syren* at Port Judith in an attempt to save the guns and stores. He fell more than fifteen feet from the side of the vessel. He was taken prisoner at Charleston, S.C. He was crippled. He applied in Marietta, Ohio 27 Mar. 1810. Congress granted him relief 27 May 1810.

Whipple, Samuel. Mass. Sgt. He served in the 11th Regiment. His widow, Elizabeth Whipple, was from Danvers and was paid $50.

Whitaker, Benjamin. N.Y. Pvt. He served in the Orange County militia under Col. John Hathorn and was wounded on 22 July 1779.

Whitaker, Ephraim. —. Capt. He entered the service as a sergeant and was a sergeant major until the battle of Monmouth when he was appointed forage master with the rank of captain. He served to the end of the war. He was paid his five years' full-pay in commutation 30 Apr. 1834. His son, Ira Whitaker, sought interest on the said sum. Congress refused his claim 31 Jan. 1854.

Whitaker, William. Md. Pvt. His widow, Sarah Scrivner, was pensioned at the rate of half-pay of a private in Baltimore, 27 Jan. 1839.

Whitcomb, Francis. N.H. Pvt. He served under Col. Thomas Marshall. He was wounded in his left groin while on a scouting party by some Indians and Tories belonging to Gen. Burgoyne's army near Schuyler's River in Saratoga on 31 July or 1 Aug. 1777. He lived in Fitzwilliam, N.H. in 1794. He enlisted 1 Apr. 1777 for three years and was discharged 1 Apr. 1780. He was granted one-third of a pension 20 Apr. 1796. He was on the 1813 pension list.

Whitcomb, Isaac. Mass. Pvt. He served in the 5th Regiment under Col. Rufus Putnam and was disabled with rheumatism and other complaints. He was pensioned 1 Sep. 1782. He lived in Littleton, Mass. in 1788 and was 52 years old. He was reported dead on the 1813 pension list.

Whitcomb, John. Mass. —. He served in Burbeck's Artillery. His widow, Elizabeth Whitcomb, was from Randolph and was paid $50.

Whitcomb, Moses. Mass. —. He served in Burbeck's Artillery. He was from Randolph and was paid $50.

Whitcomb, Richard. Mass. —. He served under Col. Lewis Nichola and Capt. Ryles. He was disabled by rheumatism. He was 50 years old in 1786. He lived in Boston.

White, —. Pa. —. His widow, Jane White, was awarded relief in Westmoreland County 5 Feb. 1836.

White, —. Va. —. His wife, Mary White, was granted £15 support in Caroline Co., Va. 9 Apr. 1778 while he was in Continental service.

White, Alexander. Pa. —. His heirs in Cumberland County were paid $200 for his donation land 7 Mar. 1837. The heirs were James White and John Lawson.

White, Anthony Walton. Va. Col. He was one of the most wealthy men at the commencement of the war. His wife, Margaret White, had her own large fortune. All was consumed in the vicissitudes of war. She was bent under the weight of four score years and was supported by her daughter. Congress granted her relief 9 Jan. 1838. Congress granted the daughter, Eliza M. Evans, repayment with interest on 7 Apr. 1852.

White, Francis. Pa. Lt. He was on the 1813 pension list.

White, Charles. S.C. —. He was pensioned 25 Nov. 1830. He was paid as late as 1834.

White, David. —. —. He was a pensioner and died in Feb. 1831. He married 25 Nov. 1790. His first child was born 18 Sep. 1793. His widow, Hannah White, married William Wilcox in 1811. She died 11 Jan. 1856. His children, Lucy Press and Lucinda Hammond, were granted relief by Congress 16 Jan 1856. They were from New York.

White, David. Mass. —. He served in the 2nd Regiment and was paid $20.

White, Elijah. Mass. —. He served in the 2nd Regiment and was paid $20.

White, Francis. Pa. Lt. He was granted relief.

White, Hector. Pa. —. His wife, Barbara White, was awarded a $40 gratuity and a $40 annuity in York Co., Pa. 10 Apr. 1828. She died 22 Dec. 1842.

White, Henry. Pa. —. He was awarded a $40 gratuity and a $40 annuity in Lancaster Co., Pa. 15 Apr. 1835.

White, Holloway. Va. —. His widow and children were awarded £19 and later £25 in Northampton Co., Va. on 8 Dec. 1778.

White, Jacob. Pa. Capt. He entered the service in May 1777 under Capt. James Brinton and Col. John Stinson for six months. He was dismissed at Jackson's Fort. In May 1778 he was elected captain in the militia from Washington County. He rendezvoused at Fort Pitt and erected Fort McIntosh at the mouth of Big Beaver Creek on the Ohio. He then built Fort Tuscarawas on the upper forks of the Muskinghum River. He marched to the relief of Col. Gibson in Mar. 1779. He was at Mingo Bottom in Aug. 1779 and at Minor's Fort on Whitely Creek in 1780. He commanded twenty-nine men for three months at the fort on the Mungo Bottom in the fall of 1781. His son was Caleb White. Congress granted him an increase in his pension 4 Jan. 1843.

White, James. Ga. Pvt. He served in the 2nd Regiment and was maimed. He was deprived of his arm. He was pensioned in 1778. He was on the 1791 pension list.

White, James. Md. Pvt. He was pensioned in Montgomery County in 1783. He was on the 1813 pension list. He was also pensioned at the rate of half-pay of a private 24 Feb. 1823. He died 21 Oct. 1829. Arrearage of his pension was paid to Henry Harding for the use of the widow, Priscilla White, 5 Feb. 1839.

White, James. Mass. Pvt. He served under Col. Putnam in Capt. Gates' Company. He had an ulcerous sore on his right leg, the effect of smallpox when in service in June 1777. He lived in Harwich, Mass. in 1795. He enlisted 12 Apr. 1777 for three years and was discharged 12 Apr. 1780.

White, John. —. —. He died 7 July 1838 without having applied. Congress denied his children relief 4 May 1860.

White, John. Ga. Col. He served in the Ga. Line and was paid $465.64 3/4 in 1801. He served in the 4th Battalion and was wounded at the siege of Savannah in 1779 which caused his death in Nov. 1780. His widow married (2) ----- Gordon. His daughter, Catharine Proctor Hayden, sought his seven years' half-pay from Congress 3 Aug. 1852. John White was born in England of Irish parentage and was a surgeon in the British navy. He married at Barbados, Mrs. Thomasin Gay, resigned from the navy, and came to America before the Revolution. Mrs. Thomasin White submitted a memorial to Congress in 1789 but failed in her application. She petitioned the Georgia legislature for bounty in 1801; it was granted. She remarried and died in New York City in 1810. Her second husband died in Savannah, Ga. There was a fraud in the case. One John White married Margaret Ogden in 1765 and had a daughter, Susannah White, born 16 Apr. 1770. She married William Richardson. Euphema Roach gave an affidavit I Feb. 1793 purporting to have been taken in New York City. She swore that she was at the wedding of John White and Margaret Ogden in 1765 and was present at the birth of their daughter, Susannah White, on 16 Apr. 1770, who married William Richardson. Margaret (Ogden) White was deceased. She did not prove that he was the John White of Georgia. Her affidavit was found in 1850. It was base fraud. The payments to Susannah Richardson and her husband were to be applied with interest to the claimant.

White, John. N.Y. Pvt. He served under Col. Thomas Thomas in the Westchester County militia and was slain 21 Nov. 1778. His widow, Mary White, received a half-pay pension for seven years.

White, John. Pa. Maj. His son, John Moore White, sought his bounty land and seven years' half-pay. He was the only surviving child. He acted as an aid of Maj. Gen. John Sullivan at Germantown and attempted to set fire to Chew's house in order to drive out the British. He was mortally wounded by a shot and died a few days later on 4 Oct. 1777. He married Sarah Moore, daughter of Alexander Moore, of Moore's Hall or Bridgeton, in 1765 or 1766. She died 15 Oct. 1770 in her 23rd year. Of his three children, Alexander White and William White died unmarried. The veteran's wife, Sarah Moore, was the sister of the mother of Ephraim Miller. John Moore White was born 27 Sep. 1770 and received his father's half-pay. 26 Mar. 1852.

White, John. Va. Lt. He received his commutation pay so his legal representative, Israel White, had his claim rejected 4 Jan. 1838 because the veteran had received his commutation. There were two men of the name, but the other acted as paymaster after the war.

White, Jonathan. Md. Pvt. He served in the 1st Regiment. He was pensioned in Prince George's County in 1781. He was wounded at Camden on 25 Apr. 1781. He died 29 Jan. 1803.

White, Joseph. N.Y. Pvt. He served under Col. Goose Van Schaick in Capt. John Copps' Company and was disabled with a rupture due to hard labor and fatigue. He lived in Montgomery Co., N.Y. on 23 June 1787 and in Albany Co., N.Y. on 12 July 1789. He also appeared as Joseph Voit.

White, Joseph. Pa. —. He applied 6 July 1814 in Center County. He enlisted for three years in Sep. 1777 in Chester County in Capt. Moore Fountleroy's Company in the 4th Regiment under Col. Stephen Moylan. He was in the battle of Monmouth. He was discharged in Sept. 1780 at Hackensack. He was 57 years old. He had a wife and nine children, three of whom were young.

White, Joseph. Va. Pvt. He lived in Fauquier County. He was on the 1813 pension list.

White, Luther. Mass. —. He served in the 4th Regiment and was from Suffield. He was paid $20.

White, Matthew N. N.Y. Cadet. He was on the 1813 pension list as Matthew N. Whyte.

White, Moses. Mass. Capt. He served in the Canada Regiment under Col. Moses Hazen. He was disabled with a hematal. He was 31 years old when he was pensioned 7 May 1787. He was on the 1813 pension list. He died 28 May 1833. Congress granted John H. White and the other heirs relief 20 Mar. 1848.

White, Nathaniel. —. —. His widow, Rebecca White, sought an increase in her pension. She submitted no evidence so Congress rejected her petition 25 Feb. 1846.

White, Oliver. Conn. Pvt. He served in the 4th Conn. Regiment and was disabled by a rupture and was worn out in the service. He was pensioned 29 Aug. 1782. He died in 1801.

White, Philip. Conn. Pvt. He served in the 1st Regiment. He was lamed by a wound in his legs when two boats jammed on the Hudson River. He resided in Chatham, Conn. in 1792. He enlisted 28 June 1779 and continued to the end of the war.

White, Reuben. Mass. Pvt. He served in the 1st Regiment and was from Colrain. He was paid $50.

White, Richard. Md. Pvt. His widow, Margaret Lamb, was pensioned at the rate of half-pay of a private 11 Feb. 1835.

White, Robert. S.C. —. He served in the mounted infantry. He was at Fish Dam Fort on Broad River and the fall of Charleston. His officers included Capt. John Drennan, Capt. Tompkins, Capt. Kimball, and Maj. Thompson. He served to the close of the war. He was pensioned from Pendleton District 19 Dec. 1825. He was paid as late as 1834.

White, Robert. Va. Capt. He was awarded a gratuity of £100 and an annuity of full-pay of a lieutenant for life on 19 Nov. 1778. He was in Frederick County in Apr. 1786 and was 27 years old. He entered the service as a private and was commissioned a lieutenant in the 12th Virginia Regiment. He was wounded in his left thigh by a musket ball in action at the Short Hills in New Jersey 26 June 1777. He was promoted to captain in 1782 as certified by Brig. Gen. James Wood. He was continued on the pension list at half-pay on 28 Oct. 1786. He was continued at the same rank and amount on 5 Mar. 1787. He was on the 1813 pension list. He died 9 Mar. 1831. His son was John B. White. He sought five years' pay 18 May 1838. Congress awarded John B. White for the heirs the amount of the pension which had been mistakenly suspended for his father 20 Feb. 1851.

White, Samuel. Mass. Pvt. He served in the 4th Regiment and was from West Springfield. His widow, Abigail White, was paid $50.

White, Samuel B. Md. Pvt. He was pensioned in 1789 in Montgomery County. He was disabled in his body at Camden. He was aged 30 in 1789. He served in the 1st Md. Regiment. He was on the 1813 pension list. He was pensioned at the rate of half-pay of a private 7 Mar. 1826. He died 18 Jan. 1832. His widow, Sarah White, was pensioned at the same rate 6 Mar. 1832.

White, Samuel Corwin. N.Y. —. He was awarded 200 acres of bounty land on 11 Apr. 1808.

White, Simeon. R.I. Pvt. He had a knee broken when he fell on the ice at West Point in Feb. 1782 while drawing provisions for the regiment. He served under Col. Jeremiah Olney. He was aged 57 in 1785. He died 16 Dec. 1804 in Providence Co., R.I.

White, Solomon. Mass. Lt. He received his commutation for five years in lieu of half-pay for life. He was from Mendon.

White, Stephen. N.Y. Pvt. He served under Col. Hammon in the Westchester County militia and was slain 2 Dec. 1778.. His widow, Sarah White, received a half-pay pension.

White, Stephen. N.C. —. His widow, Sarah White, applied in 1784. He was killed at the battle of Monmouth.

White, Tarpley. Va. Capt. He served seven years in the infantry. His legal representative, Israel White, sought his commutation 4 Jan. 1838.

White, Thomas. Md. Pvt. He was pensioned at the rate of half-pay of a private in Baltimore 3 Feb. 1828.

White, Thomas. —. Lt. He entered the service in July 1776 under Capt. William Armstrong and Col. William Montgomery in the Flying Camp. He was a prisoner at Fort Washington. When he returned from captivity in Nov. 1776, he removed to North Carolina. He sought payment for the time he was in captivity. He had gone to Philadelphia and made application to Maj. Howell. He resided in Bond Co., Ill. when Congress dismissed his petition 8 Mar. 1822.

White, Thomas. Va. Capt. He entered the service at Leesburg, Loudoun Co., Va. as an ensign on 5 June 1777 and marched to Fredericktown, Md. where he was appointed captain in room of Capt. Thomas who was discharged for his incapacity and intemperance. He marched through York and Lancaster to Philadelphia a few days before Brandywine and fought there on 11 Sep. 1777 and at Germantown 4 Oct. 1777. He retreated with Gen. Crawford to wet encampment in Pennsylvania. He crossed the Schuylkill near Valley Forge to join Potter's Brigade near Chester, Pa. He was discharged 28 Mar. 1778. His tour was for 9 months and 23 days. He commanded a company of Virginia militia under Col. Holmes at Winchester from 4 Apr. to 1 July 1778. He was a captain near Hillsboro from 21 Sep. to 19 Oct. 1778 with Lt. Samuel Potts, Ens. John Peterson, and 60 privates. He also served from 1 Sep. to 28 Oct. 1781 when he learned of Cornwallis' defeat. He died 16 Sep. 1839 Carroll Co., Va. He married Sarah Keyes at Keyes' Ferry in Berkeley Co., Va. on 13 Oct. 1783. His daughter Elizabeth White was born 8 June 1785 and his daughter Sarah White on 17 Feb. 1787. Congress granted his widow, Sarah White, a pension 26 Apr. 1848. She was from Belmont Co., Ohio.

White, Vassel. —. —. Congress rejected his petition 27 Mar. 1818. He was covered under the law passed at the present session.

White, William. —. —. His widow, Caty White, had her petition for an increase in her pension rejected by Congress 25 Apr. 1854.

White, William. —. —. He did not serve in the regular army. Congress declined to grant him a pension by special act 23 Feb. 1820.

White, William. Conn. Pvt. He served in Capt. James Chamberlain's Light Horse Company in the expedition to R. I. in 1778 for at least one month. He served under Capt. White of Tolland in the 2nd Conn. Regiment from 29 Sep. 1779 to 15 Jan. 1780. He also served from 1 Nov. 1782 to 1 Jan. 1783. He died in 1837. He married in 1791 or 1792. His widow, Zilpha White, had been rejected because she mistakenly claimed the service of a different man of the same name. Her husband was of weak and intemperate habits and was unlikely to have communicated to her any distinct information. Congress granted her a pension 25 Jan. 1848.

White, William. Mass. —. He served in the 8th Regiment and was paid $20.

White, William. Mass. Capt. He served in the Massachusetts Line and was killed in Oct. 1781. His orphan children sought his half-pay in 1791.

White, William. N.Y. Pvt. He served in Capt. David Stowel's Company in the Cumberland County Militia under Col. William Williams. He was wounded at Saratoga on 11 Oct. 1777. He was pensioned 1 Apr. 1786. He lived in Otsego County. He was on the 1813 pension list.

White, William. S.C. Legionnaire. He served aboard the *South Carolina* under Commodore Alexander Gillon. He was paid 21 Oct. 1809.

White, William. Va. —. His widow, Agnes Cardwell, and his infant daughter received support in York County 15 June 1778 at which time he was deceased.

White, William. Va. Lt. He was on the 1791 pension roll.

Whitehead, David. N.J. —. He was pensioned in Essex County on 11 Nov. 1837 at the rate of $60 per annum.

Whitehead, Timothy. N.J. —. He served under Col. William Winds. He was killed in a skirmish at Spanktown 31 Jan. 1777 where the militia was attempting to take some field pieces from the British troops. He married Hannah Beach, daughter of Nathaniel Beach, in Dec. 1775 in Morris County. Her brother was James Beach. She married secondly Benjamin Genung 10 May 1779. Hannah Genung, sought his half-pay in Morris County 19 Mar. 1793.

Whitehead, William. N.Y. —. He was awarded 200 acres of bounty land on 11 Apr. 1808.

Whitehorn, John. N.H. Pvt. He was from Nottingham in 1786. He entered the service in 1776 and was wounded by a musket ball in the knee at Ticonderoga in Aug. 1776. He served under Capt. Samuel Johnson in Col. Wigglesworth's Regiment. James Roberts was Lieutenant Colonel. John Wingate was Regimental Surgeon at Ticonderoga. He was wounded accidentally while on duty cutting hay. He was aged 54 in 1787. His rate was $5 per month from 13 Sep. 1808. His name was also misinterpreted as John Whitehouse.

Whiteman, John. Pa. —. He served two years and ten months. He married in Philadelphia Elizabeth -----. Congress granted her a pension 30 Aug. 1842 for two years of service from 1 Jan. 1781 to 3 Nov. 1783.

Whiteman, Wollery (or **Ulrich**). Pa. Sgt. He applied in Philadelphia County on 28 Aug. 1819. He was 90 years old. He served under Gen. Braddock at his defeat at Fort Duquesne in 1755. He had no discharge because he was at home on furlough. In 1776 he enlisted in Capt. Thomas Craig's Company in the 3rd Pa. Regiment under Col. McCully. He served nearly to the end of the war. He took sick and came home on furlough.

Whitfield, William. Va. —. His wife, Mary Whitfield, was awarded £12 assistance in Goochland Co., Va. 19 Oct. 1778.

Whiting, Caleb. Mass. Pvt. He served in the 2nd Regiment. His widow, Elizabeth Whiting, was from Boston and was paid $50.

Whiting, Caleb. Mass. —. He was at Lexington on 19 Apr. 1775 and served ten days. He was also in the 3rd Worcester Regiment as 2nd Major on 15 Feb. 1776. He was captain of the 8th Company of the 3rd Regiment 10 Apr. 1778. He served on the expedition to Rhode Island 20 July to 10 Sep. 1778. He died in 1830. His son, Caleb Whiting, served under Capt. Martin and Col. Ward. He was under Lt. Col. Tyler for 1 month and 5 days from 8 Dec. 1776. He served 12 days under Capt. Knapp from 27 July 1780. He died in 1808. His daughter was Lucy Cheney who was alive when her son, T. Apoleon Cheney of New York, sought a pension on the service of his grandfather and his great-grandfather. Congress rejected his petition 23 Mar. 1860.

Whiting, Daniel. Mass. Lt. Col. He received his commutation for five years in lieu of half-pay for life. He was from Dedham and died in Oct. 1807.

Whiting, Francis. Va. Lt. He lived in Berkeley County in Apr. 1786. He served in the 1st Regiment of Light Dragoons. He was wounded 14 Apr. 1780 at Monk's Corner, S.C. He was 27 years old. He was in Frederick County 28 June 1786. He was continued on the pension list on 14 July 1791. He was in Jefferson Co., Va. in Sep. 1802. He died 21 Apr. 1818. Francis B. Whiting was his executor.

Whiting, Sampson. Me. —. He was from Denmark, Maine. He was paid $50 under the resolve of 1836.

Whiting, Samuel. Conn. Col. He served in the 4th Regiment. He suffered from rheumatism and inflamation in his eyes. He caught cold by wading a river when heated by marching and exhausted by fatigue. He had an obstruction of the urinary passage. He lost the use of his right eye in 1777 in Norwalk. He resided in Stratford, Conn. in 1792. He was in the militia.

Whiting, William. Mass. Pvt. He served in the 2nd Regiment. His widow, Mary Whiting, was from Plymouth and was paid $50.

Whitley, Michael. Pa. Capt. His widow, Martha Whitley, was in Dauphin County on 20 Dec. 1791. He was in the militia in Col. Robert Elder's Battalion, was wounded at Chestnut Hill 6 Dec. 1777, taken prisoner, and died a few days afterwards in Philadelphia. He left seven children. He died at the age of 47.

Whitlock, John. N.J. Lt. He served under Capt. Thomas Hunn. He was killed at Middle Town on 13 Feb. 1777. His widow, Lydia Whitlock, received a half-pay pension 20 Mar. 1786.

Whitlock, John. Va. Pvt. He was on the 1813 pension list.

Whitlow, John. Va. —. He died in the service in the northward in the summer of 1778. His widow, Elizabeth Whitlow, was furnished support for herself and her family in Charlotte Co., Va. 5 Apr. 1779.

Whitlow, John. Va. —. His wife, Elizabeth Whitlow, was granted relief in Halifax Co., Va. on 17 July 1777. She received £1.19 on 16 Oct. 1777 and £9 on 17 Sep. 1778.

Whitlow, William. Va. —. He died in Continental service in the northwest in the summer of 1778. His widow, Elizabeth Whitlow, was furnished 3 ½ barrels of corn, the use of a milch cow, and as much bacon as necessary for the support of her and her family until November on 3 May 1779. She received his half-pay on 2 Aug. 1779. She was awarded £47 in Charlotte Co., Va. 3 Nov. 1779.

Whitman, George. Pa. —. He was grated relief in Berks County 16 Dec. 1813.

Whitman, Jacob. Pa. —. He was pensioned in Venango County 14 Apr. 1838. He died 26 May 1841.

Whitman, Jeremiah. Mass. —. He was paid $20.

Whitman, William. Pa. Lt. He was in Reading, Berks Co., Pa. 7 Jan. 1786. He served in the 9th Pa. Regiment and was wounded at Germantown 4 Oct. 1777 by a musket ball through his body. He was 34 years old. He died 12 Oct. 1808.

Whitmarsh, Ezra. N.Y. Pvt. He was pensioned 24 Oct. 1832 at the rate of $40 per annum.

Whitmarsh, Micah. R.I. Capt. He resigned 28 Apr. 1778 and later was a captain in the militia. Congress rejected the request of the heirs for commutation and bounty land on 8 Aug. 1848 because he was in the militia.

Whitmarsh, Samuel. Mass. Matross. He served in Revere's Regiment. He was from Weymouth and was paid $50.

Whitmyer, Philip. Pa.—. He received a $40 gratuity and a $40 annuity in Lebanon County 14 Mar. 1835.

Whitmore, Enoch. Mass. —. He served in the 9th Regiment and was from Warwick. He was paid $20.

Whitney, Lemuel. Mass. Sgt. He served in Tupper's Regiment and was paid $20.

Whitney, Samuel. Conn. Corp. He was discharged 11 June 1783. He resided at New Town and was pensioned 17 Sep. 1787. He was 30 years old. He died in 1807.

Whitney, Seth. N.Y. Pvt. He was born in Danbury, Conn. in 1759. He enlisted in Oct. 1782 under Lt. Peter Nessals, Sgt. Smith, Lt. Col. Stevens, and Maj. Bowman. He was at West Point and was discharged in June 1783. Congress granted him a pension for eight months of service on 4 Jan. 1838. He lived at Delhi, Delaware Co., N.Y.

Whitt, Charles. S.C. —. He enlisted for two years under Capt. John Moore and Maj Tutt. He was at Kettle Creek. He was a shoemaker. His wife was between 40 and 50 and his stepson was to be 15 the next August. He was 74 years old when he applied in Lincoln Co., N.C. in Oct. 1824.

Whitt, Shadrach. Va. —. His widow, Mary Whitt, was in Charles City County on 29 Dec. 1792. Her husband died in the service. She was granted a pension of twelve pounds per annum.

Whittaker, Ephraim. —. —. His heirs sought interest on his commutation. Congress rejected their claim 1 Feb. 1836.

Whittemore, Joseph. Mass. Lt. He served in the 12th Regiment under Col. Moses Little and Capt. Benjamin Perkins. He was disabled by a musket ball in his left thigh. He was 54 years old in 1788. He was pensioned 30 Jan. 1788. He was on the 1813 pension list. He died 25 June 1821 in Essex Co., Mass. He also appeared as Joseph Whitmore.

Whittemore, Paul. Mass. —. He served in the 4th Regiment and was from Pepperelboro.

Whitten, Richard. Me. —. He was from Troy. He was paid $50 under the resolve of 1836.

Whittier, Moses. Mass. Sgt. He served in the 11th Regiment. His widow, Sarah Lunt, was from Rowley and was paid $50.

Whittington, Jarrat. S.C. Lt. He was on the roll in 1793.

Whittington, John. Pa. Pvt. He was wounded. He was pensioned in 1787. He transferred to Delaware in Mar. 1792. He was on the 1813 pension list.

Whittle, John Burris. S.C. —. He was mortally wounded near Cloud's Creek. His widow, Winney Whittle, applied 22 Nov. 1823 from Edgefield District. Her application was rejected.

Whittlesey, Martin. Conn. Sgt. He served under Col. Benjamin Hinman, Capt. William Cogswell, and Ens. Joseph Guthrie. He was taken with camp distemper which fell into his limbs. He was from Washington and aged 51 years on 14 Nov. 1788. He was on the 1791 pension roll. He died 29 May 1808.

Wick, John. —. —. He served in the dragoons under Col. Jacob Arnold, Col. Ford, and Col. Seely from the beginning to the end of the war. His widow, Hannah Jane Wick, sought an increase in her pension. Congress rejected her claim 9 Jan. 1847.

Wickham, Isaac. Mass. —. He served in the 11th Regiment and was from Barnstable. He was paid

$50.

Wickham, Stephen. N.Y. —. His wife and nine children were granted support in Dutchess County on 3 Nov. 1781.

Wicks, Nathan. R.I. Lt. He was killed in the battle of Monmouth 28 June 1787.

Widrig, Conrad. N.Y. —. He volunteered about the age of 15 under Capt. Henry Starling. He was one of the eleven who defended Fort Mike against a party of 200 to 300 British, Indians, and Tories. He also served in Forts Stanwix, Schuyler, Dayton House, Herkimer, Willet, and Wintaker for one year. He served two years under Sgt. Bargy and Col. Bellinger in tending the ferry across the Mohawk at Fort Plains when Col. Willet crossed over in pursuit of Maj. Ross and his party. He was discharged after three and a half years. His brother, Jacob Widrig, was with him at Fort Mick. Congress allowed him a pension for six months service 5 Mar. 1840.

Wiegell, Christopher. Pa. —. He was granted relief 27 Mar. 1812.

Wier, David. S.C. —. After the fall of Charleston he enlisted at the age of 16 and served under Capt. McClure, Capt. Samuel Adams, Col. Lacy, and Col. Williamson. He was at Congaree, Wright's Bluff, and Biggen Church near Monk's Corner. Capt. John Hollis and James Hollis served with him two months. He was 63 years old and had a wife somewhat older. He applied 13 Nov. 1827 from Fairfield District. He was paid as late as 1831.

Wier, James. N.Y. Corp. He served in the militia under Col. Lewis Van Vort and was disabled in the shoulder at Saratoga. He lived at Salem, Washington Co., N.Y. 27 Apr. 1789.

Wier, John. Pa.—. He received a $40 gratuity and a $40 annuity in Greene County 21 July 1842. He died 27 June 1845.

Wiers, James. Va. —. He was away in the service. His wife, Mary Wiers, and her children were granted £40 support in Botetourt County 10 Dec. 1779.

Wiery, Michael. Md. Pvt. His widow, Elizabeth Wiery, was pensioned at the rate of half-pay of a private in York Co., Pa. 6 Apr. 1841.

Wiger, David. Va. —. He was away in Continental service. His wife, Sarah Wiger, was granted £360 for her support and her child on 15 May 1781. She was allowed one bushel of corn, 100 pounds of pork, and 124 pounds of beef for support in Augusta Co., Va. 19 Dec. 1781.

Wigg, William Hazzard. S.C. —. He served as an officer in the militia. He hastened to the defense of Charleston. When the city capitulated in March 1780, he became a prisoner on parole. He was one of the 130 kept on the *Torbay* and the *Packhorse*. He and 39 others remained on the latter for fourteen months. The British executed his brother-in-law, Col. Hayne. They destroyed all of his property on his two plantations on Oketee River 120 miles from Charleston. When the *Packhorse* went to sea the next summer, the prisoners assaulted the crew and captured the vessel. They put into one of the ports of North Carolina. All of them returned safely to South Carolina. Wigg's Negroes had been carried to St .Augustine in Spanish Florida and sold at auction. Mr. Leavitt of Georgia bought 20 or 21 of them. Wigg went after and recovered them. After his death, Wigg's son had to pay for them in full. Wigg's brother-in-law, Thomas Hutson, died after Wigg and before Wigg's son returned from Princeton. Hutson's grandson found the paperwork of Wigg in his grandfather's papers. Congress approved relief for Wigg's losses 30 Aug. 1852.

Wiggens, Thomas. Pa. —. He was pensioned.

Wigglesmith, William. Mass. Lt. He received his commutation for five years in lieu of half-pay for life. He was from Ipswich.

Wight, John. Mass. —. He served in the 5ᵗʰ Regiment and was paid $20.

Wilborne, William. Va. Pvt. He was in Sussex Co., Va. 16 Mar. 1786. He was wounded in Buford's defeat at the Waxsaw. He lost one hand, and his other was much disabled. He was awarded a £300 gratuity 14 Dec. 1780. He was 25 years old in 1788. He was continued on the pension list at the rate of £12 per annum on 19 June 1788. He was on the 1813 pension list. He also appeared as William Wilburn and William Wilbourne.

Wilbourn, —. S.C. —. His widow, Mary Wilbourn, was from Spartanburg. There were two children in 1791.

Wilbur, George. Mass. Soldier. He served in Revere's Artillery. His widow, Mary Wilbur, was from Bridgewater and was paid $50.

Wilcox, —. Va. —. His wife, Eleanor Wilcox, was granted support in Loudoun County in Feb. 1782. Eleanor Wilcox was granted support in Fauquier Co., Va. 13 Mar. 1782.

Wilcox, Ezra. Conn. Pvt. He served in the Conn. militia in Capt. Shipman's Company under Col. Thaddeus Cook. He was wounded by a musket ball above the right knee which passed through the thigh bone to his ham from which it appeared to have been extracted at Bemis Heights on 7 Oct. 1777. He resided in Guilford, Conn. in 1796. He was granted one-fourth of a pension 20 Apr. 1796. He died 14 May 1805. He also appeared as Ezra Willcox and Ezra Wilcocks.

Wilcox, James. —. —. Congress awarded his widow, Lucretia Wilcox of Wayne Co., Michigan the arrearage of her pension from 4 Mar. 1848 to 3 Feb. 1853 on 21 Feb. 1857.

Wilcox, Joel. Conn. Pvt. He served under Col. Swift. He was disabled by measles, dysentery, and a bilious fever. He lost the use of his right leg. He resided in Killingsworth, Conn. in 1792. He enlisted 27 June 1780 for six months and was discharged 3 Dec. 1780. He was on the 1813 pension list.

Wilcox, Phineas. N.H. Pvt. He served under Col. Warner. He had smallpox in the service in Quebec which left him weak and debilitated. He lived in Newport, N.H. in 1795.

Wilcox, Robert. —. Surgeon. Esck Hopkins appointed him surgeon on the brigatine *Cabot* 11 Feb. 1776. Gov. Rodney appointed him a surgeon in the Delaware militia 5 Aug 1780. His daughter, Sophia Turner, was entitled to bounty land under the act of 3 Mar. 1855, but Congress granted her no relief 8 Apr. 1856.

Wild, Ebenezer. Mass. Sgt. He served in the 1st Regiment. His widow, Abigail Baxter, was from Cambridge and was paid $50.

Wild, Jacob. Pa. —. He was awarded a $40 gratuity and a $40 annuity in Lehigh Co., Pa. 15 Apr. 1835.

Wild, John. Mass. Gunner. He served at the Castle. His widow, Jemima Wild, was from Randolph and was paid $50.

Wilde, Richard. Del. Lt. He was wounded at Germantown and resigned his commission in Aug. 1778. He died in 1786. His daughter Elizabeth Robison, wife of James Robison, had been awarded the amount her father would have been entitled had he applied. She asked for interest for total disability from day of his resignation to the time of his death. Congress refused to grant the interest 14 Jan. 1846.

Wilder, Aaron. Conn. Pvt. He was disabled due to old age. He was pensioned 15 Sep. 1782. He was on the 1813 pension list of Vermont. He also appeared as Aaron Willdier.

Wilder, Abel. Mass. Sgt. He served in the 6th Regiment.

Wilder, James. Va. — He was issued bounty land warrant #2429 for 100 acres for his three years of service on 9 Feb. 1784. In 1802 his brother, Spencer Wilder, sold it to John Carroll who by deed transferred to John Carroll, Jr. on 21 Oct. 1831. Congress allowed scrip on said warrant should any other heir come forth on 14 Jan. 1836.

Wilder, Timothy. Mass. Pvt. He served in the 8th Regiment. His widow, Eunice Wilder, was from Sterling and was paid $50.

Wiley, Aldridge. Mass. Lt. He died 7 Oct. 1777. His seven years' half-pay of $840 was paid to his heirs.

Wiley, Ephraim. Mass. He was paid $20. He also appeared as Ephraim Whiley.

Wiley, Henry. S.C. —. He was killed by Indians. His children were granted an annuity 31 Dec. 1785.

Wiley, Isaac. Pa. —. He applied in 29 Mar. 1802 in Cumberland County. He served in the militia under Capt. Samuel Leaman and Col. Samuel Hunter in defending the frontiers of Northumberland County against the Indians. He was wounded 2 May 1782.

Wiley, John. Pa. —. He was from Cumberland County and was pensioned 29 Mar. 1802.

Wiley, Matthew. Pa. 1st Lt. He volunteered in the summer of 1776 for six months and served in the Chester Co., Pa. militia under Capt. McDowel and Col. William Montgomery. He was seized with fever after three months and was unfit for nine weeks. He was commissioned as 1st lieutenant in July 1777 and served two months. Congress granted him a pension 7 Mar. 1838 for six months of service.

Wiley, Owen. Pa. Pvt. He was in Bedford County on 1 Nov. 1783. He was in the Invalids. He was disabled in the service. He was discharged at Fort Pitt by Brigadier General William Irwin on 27 Nov. 1782.

Wiley, Robert. —. Ens. He was wounded by a musket ball which entered the back of his neck. He resided in Mass. in 1796. He was appointed 1 Jan. 1777 and discharged 14 Aug. 1778.

Wiley, Samuel. Pa. —. He was awarded a $40 gratuity and a $40 annuity in Fayette Co., Pa. 1 Mar. 1832.

Wiley, Thomas. Pa. Capt. He served in the Pennsylvania Corps of Artillery Artificers and sought commutation in lieu of his half-pay in 1790.

Wilfong, John. N.C. Pvt. He applied in Lincoln County in 1807. He was wounded in his left arm in militia duty at King's Mountain in 1780. He served under Col. Joseph McDowell of Burke County. He was on the 1813 pension list.

Wilfong, John. Pa. —. He was awarded a $40 gratuity and a $40 annuity in Montgomery Co., Pa. 23 Jan. 1834. He died 15 May 1841.

Wilheid, Frederick. Md. —. He was on the roll in 1820 and dropped. He was restored in 1823. The sheriff of Frederick Co., Md. sold his land to satisfy several executions. The money was insufficient to satisfy the amount due. Congress granted him payment for one year and eleven months from 27 Feb. 1826 rather than 29 Jan. 1828 when he was restored.

Wilhelm, —. Pa. —. His widow, Christiana Wilhelm, was awarded a $40 gratuity and a $40 annuity in York Co., Pa. 20 Feb. 1833. She died 21 Sep. 1841.

Wilhelm, Henry. Pa. Pvt. He applied in New Jersey 19 Nov. 1813. He served in Capt. Ciely's Company in the 3rd Pa. Regiment under Col. Butler. He was blind in one eye. He had drawn his donation land. He was 62 years old.

Wilkerson, Richard. Md. Pvt. He was pensioned in Anne Arundel County on 4 Mar. 1789. He was on the 1813 pension list.

Wilkerson, Thomas. Va. Pvt. His widow, Sarah Wilkerson, was in Sussex Co., Va. 16 Mar. 1787. He served in the 15th Va. Regiment and died in the service. She was aged *ca.* 35 years old and had two children on 16 Mar. 1786. She was continued on the pension list at the rate of £6 per annum on 12 Nov. 1787. She was upwards of 60 years of age in June 1791. She was continued on the pension list on 12 Oct. 1791. She also appeared as Sarah Wilkinson.

Wilkerson, Young. Md. Lt. He was pensioned at the rate of half-pay of a lieutenant in Anne Arundel County in Nov. 1810.

Wilkins, George. N.Y. Pvt. He served under Col. James McClaughry in the Ulster County militia and died of wounds 31 Jan. 1778. His widow was granted support according to an undated roster. His children received a half-pay pension.

Wilkins, Jonathan. U.S. Marine. He served in the Continental Navy on the frigate *Hague* under Capt. John Manley. He was wounded in his right leg by shot and was greatly disabled. He lived in Hillsborough, N.H. He was pensioned at the rate of $2.50 per month from 26 Mar. 1807. He was on the 1813 pension list.

Wilkins, Nathaniel. Va. Pvt. He was awarded a gratuity of £300 on 10 Nov. 1780. He was awarded a gratuity of one year's pay and an annuity of half-pay on 15 Dec. 1781. He was in Gloucester County on 2 Apr. 1787. He was in the 7th Va. Regiment. He was wounded in the service at the battle of Waxsaw and had to have his right hand amputated. He was 28 years old. He was continued on the pension list at the rate of £18 per annum on 7 June 1787. He was issued a duplicate certificate 22 June 1790.

Wilkins, Robert Bradford. N.H. Pvt. He served in Col. James Reed's Militia. He was wounded by a musket ball in his right elbow which deprived him of the use of his wrist and fingers on 7 June 1775 at Bunker Hill. He lived in Amherst, N.H. in 1794. He was granted two-thirds of a pension 20 Apr. 1796. He was on the 1813 pension list.

Wilkinson, —. Pa. —. His widow, Marcy Wilkinson, was awarded a $40 gratuity and a $40 annuity in Beaver Co., Pa. 22 Dec. 1834.

Wilkinson, David. —. Gunner. He served three years and ten days in Crane's Continental Artillery. His only surviving child, Irena Gibson, had a husband who had suffered a severe fall two years ago and was an invalid. Congress granted her a pension of $20 per month 19 May 1890. She was 82 years old. At that time there were two other daughters of Revolutionary veterans on the pension rolls.

Wilkinson, —. Va. —. He was killed or died in the service. His widow, Elizabeth Wilkinson, was granted £70 relief in Lunenburg Co., Va. 11 Feb. 1779.

Wilkinson, James. Md. Col. He was pensioned at the rate of half-pay of a colonel of dragoons 23 Jan. 1816. His widow, Catherine T. Wilkinson, sought relief on the basis of his having received a brevet rank for the capture of Burgoyne. Congress declined her request 24 Feb. 1830.

Wilkinson, Mott. —. —. He was a pensioner and sought an increase in his pension. He offered no additional evidence so Congress rejected his petition 27 Mar. 1846. Congress did so again 11 Apr. 1850.

Will, —. S.C. —. His widow, Martha Will, was paid her annuity 29 May 1834.

Will, Conrad. Pa. —. He was in Lancaster County on 12 Sep. 1814. He was in the 1st Pa. Regiment in Capt. Thomas Boude's Company. He was discharged at Philadelphia in Nov. 1783.

Willard, —. Pa. —. His widow, Sarah Willard, applied in Philadelphia 4 Sep. 1786.

Willard, Elias. N.Y. Surgeon. He was awarded 600 acres of bounty land for his service as surgeon and surgeon's mate on 19 June 1812.

Willard, Humphrey. —. —. He lived in Genessee Co., N.Y. and sought land. Congress rejected his claim 12 Feb. 1841 because there was no precedent for such.

Willard, Jacob. Pa. —. He was awarded a $40 gratuity and a $40 annuity 27 Mar. 1837 in Armstrong County.

Willard, Jonathan. N.H. Ens. He served under Col. Ciley in Capt. Farwell's Company. He was wounded in the right shoulder by a musket ball on 7 Oct. 1777 at Bemis Heights. He lived in Langdon, N.H. in 1795. He was commissioned 8 Nov. 1776 and was on the rolls in 1780. He was granted one-fourth of a pension 20 Apr. 1796. He was on the 1813 pension list.

Willard, Peter. Mass. —. He served in the 5th Regiment and was Worcester. He was paid $20. He also appeared as Peter Williard.

Willard, Samuel. Mass. —. He served in the 10th Regiment and was from South Brimfield. He was paid $20.

Willbank, Richard. S.C. —. He went to North Carolina to see his brother and turned out as a volunteer in Bute County under Capt. Benjamin Sowell. He was discharged at Wilmington three months later and returned to Union District. He served under Col. Thomas Brannon and went to Camden. He was under Lt. Burgess, Maj. William Fair, Capt. William Young. At Ninety Six he dug and made breast works. He was 70 years old and had been blind for eight years. He had a wife and two small children aged 5 and 8. He was from Pickens District and was pensioned 30 Nov. 1829. Thomas Hays served with him. Avarilla Willbank, whose late husband William Willbank was his cousin, remembered his going into service. He was paid as late as 1834.

Willbank, William. S.C. —. He married in 1773 or 1774. His widow, Abarilla Willbank, was pensioned and paid in 1849 and 1850. She died 14 Feb. 1853 in Cherokee Co., Ga. Her only surviving child, Sarah Hunnicutt, sought her arrearage in July 1854. Jesse Hunnicutt was present when she died and closed her eyes after her death.

Willett, Augustin. Pa. Capt. He served in the 1st Regiment and went to Canada in 1775-1776. He was commissioned major in the 4th Battalion of the Bucks County militia. In 1780 the governor made him a commissioner to procure provisions for the Continental Army. Congress ruled that his heirs were not entitled to commutation pay 12 Feb. 1841.

Willcutt, Thomas. Mass. Gunner. He served in Revere's Regiment. His widow, Susannah Willcutt, was from Cohasset and was paid $50.

Willey, Thomas. Pa. Capt. He served in the Corps of Artillery Artificers. He sought commutation in lieu of half-pay. It was rejected 19 Oct. 1785.

Williams, —. S.C. —. His widow was Amey Williams. There was one child in 1791.

Williams, —. Pa. —. His widow, Elizabeth Williams, was granted relief in 1810 and 1811.

Williams, —. Pa. —. His widow, Mary Williams, was granted relief in Center County 10 Apr. 1826. She was dead by Sept. 1828. Ephraim Williams was administrator of her estate.

Williams, —. Pa. —. His widow, Sarah Williams, was awarded a $40 annuity in Fayette Co., Pa. 4 May 1852 for his Revolutionary service.

Williams, —. Pa. —. His widow, Rebecca Williams, was awarded a $40 gratuity and a $40 annuity in Baltimore, Md. 31 Mar. 1836.

Williams, —. Pa. —. His widow, Susanna Williams, was pensioned in Bucks County 21 Mar. 1840. She died 5 Apr. 1845.

Williams, —. S.C. —. His widow, Sylvia Williams, was from Darlington in 1793.

Williams, —. Va. —. His father, James Williams, was granted £80 on 21 Aug. 1780 in York County.

Williams, Amariah *et ux* **Ruamah**. —. —. They were involved in a struggle with a British soldier near Plattesburg. The soldier attempted to ill treat Ruamah Williams. They delivered him to the U.S. troops. She was injured by her great exertion. Congress refused her relief 18 Dec. 1821.

Williams, Baruch. S.C. —. He was on the roll in 1793.

Williams, Benoni. Pa. —. He was pensioned in Indiana County 21 Mar. 1837.

Williams, Britton. S.C. —. He was killed 13 Jan. 1781. His widow, Elizabeth Williams, was granted an annuity 8 Dec. 1785.

Williams, Charles. Md. —. He died in the service. His widow, Elizabeth Williams, was pensioned in Frederick County in 1783.

Williams, Charles. Md. Pvt. He was pensioned at the rate of half-pay of a private 1 Jan. 1813.

Williams, Charles. Pa. —. He was awarded a $40 gratuity and a $40 annuity in Allegheny County 1 Apr. 1836.

Williams, Charles. Va. —. His wife, Elizabeth Williams, was granted support for herself and children while he was away in the service on 3 Sep. 1778 in Richmond County.

Williams, Daniel. Mass. —. He served in the 6th Regiment and was from Lynn. He was paid $20.

Williams, Daniel. N.C. Capt. He was paid for four years and two months service from 1 Apr. 1777 when he was commissioned. He served to the end of the war. His executor, Joseph Williams, sought his commutation 23 Mar. 1838.

Williams, David. Conn. Lt. He served in the 4th Regiment of the militia under Capt. George Burr and Col. Samuel Whitney. He was wounded in the right shoulder by a musket ball on 26 Apr. 1777 at Ridgefield opposing Sir William Tryon. He was pensioned 16 Aug. 1788 at Fairfield, Conn. He was 53 years old. He died in 1804.

Williams, David. N.Y. —. He along with John Paulding and Isaac Van Wart captured Major John Andre, the Adjutant General of the British Army, on 23 Sep. 1780 whereby the dangerous and traitorous conspiracy of Benedict Arnold became known. He was a volunteer militia man. He was awarded $200 per annum for life on 3 Nov. 1780 by Congress. He died 2 Aug. 1831. Congress granted his widow, Nancy Williams, a pension of $200 per annum on 3 Feb. 1843.

Williams, David. S.C. —. There was one child in 1793. He or one of the same name was paid an annuity 14 Mar. 1829.

Williams, Ebenezer. Pa. —. He was pensioned in Fayette County 27 Mar. 1837. He died 29 Dec. 1841.

Williams, Edd Payson. Mass. Maj. He died 25 May 1777. His seven years' half-pay of $2,100 was paid to his heirs.

Williams, Elijah. Mass. Corp. He served in the 4th Regiment under Col. William Shepard and Capt. Libbeus Ball. He was disabled by a musket ball through his lungs. He was 33 years old in 1790. He resided in Worcester Co., Mass. He was on the 1813 pension list. He was from West Springfield when he was paid $50 by the Commonwealth.

Williams, Elisha. Md. Capt. His widow, Harriet Williams, was pensioned in Georgetown, D.C. at the rate of half-pay of a captain 27 Feb. 1832.

Williams, Elisha. Va. Pvt. His widow, Catharine Williams, was in Shenandoah County on 26 July 1787. He was in the Culpeper County militia and died in 1777 in service in the north. She was put on the pension list at the rate of £6 per annum on 15 Aug. 1787.

Williams, Ephraim. Pa. —. He was awarded relief in Perry County 6 Apr. 1833. He was 85 years old in 1840. He died 15 Aug. 1843.

Williams, Ezekiel. Conn. Pvt. He served in Capt. Clark's Company in the Conn. Line under Col. Sage. He was disabled by sickness 19 Nov. 1776. He lived in Hillsdale, Columbia Co., N.Y. when he was pensioned 21 Nov. 1788. In Apr. 1789 he was aged 29 years. He later lived in Madison Co., N.Y. He was on the 1813 pension list.

Williams, George. Pa. —. He applied 2 Apr. 1830. He served in Col. Haskell's [?] Regiment in Capt. Paupum's [?] Company.

Williams, George. Pa. —. He was awarded a $40 gratuity and a $40 annuity in Clearfield Co., Pa.

13 Apr. 1827.

Williams, Henry. N.J. Pvt. He served in the 2nd Regiment and was wounded in his arm. He was 27 years old. He was on the 1791 pension roll. He transferred to Monongalia County, Va. He was on the 1813 pension list.

Williams, Henry. N.C. Pvt. He lived in Rowan County. He was on the 1813 pension list and died 1 July 1829.

Williams, Henry. S.C. —. His widow, Delila Williams, was pensioned 11 Dec. 1823.

Williams, Herbert. N.C. —. His widow, Judah Williams, applied in Orange County in 1805. He was in Continental service in the 1st N.C. Regiment in 1776 until his death.

Williams, Ichabod. N.Y. Pvt. He enlisted for three months in Capt. Samuel Delavan's Company of Rangers on 1 Jan. 1777. He was disabled by a wound in his left thigh on 16 Mar. 1777. He was pensioned 15 Apr. 1788. He was 31 years old on 17 May 1788. He lived in North Salem, Westchester Co., N.Y. on 29 Apr. 1789 and later in Cayuga County. He was on the 1813 pension list.

Williams, Jacob. Conn. Sgt. He enlisted as a corporal in Dec. 1776 and was promoted to first sergeant 1 June 1780. He was reduced to the ranks in 1781 and deserted 12 Nov. 1782. He took sick en route home on furlough at Stamford, Conn. He had to hire a man to take him home. He did not return to the army. Congress did not accept that he deserted at the end of the war because he had already served six years. Congress, therefore, granted his widow, Mary Williams, of East Hartford a pension 18 Apr. 1842.

Williams, Jacob. Conn. Pvt. He served in Capt. John McGrieggier's Company under Col. John Durkee. He was wounded at the battle of Monmouth in 1778 with a musket ball in his left shoulder. It came out his right shoulder. He was pensioned at Groton, Conn. 13 Nov. 1788. He was 36 years old. He was on the 1813 pension list.

Williams, James. N.C. —. He enlisted under Capt. Blount in the Continental Line. He served two years six months of which were as a prisoner. His petition was rejected 16 Feb. 1814.

Williams, James. S.C. —. He was killed at the battle of King's Mountain. His heirs had leave to take the testimony in writing of Col. Thomas Taylor, Robert Stark, Col. Samuel Hammond, and Hugh O'Neal, aged and infirm persons, to be read before the House or its committee in any future investigation of their claims against the state on 18 Dec. 1829.

Williams, James. Va. —. He was blinded in his left eye, and his vision in his right eye was sorely afflicted. He was awarded a £300 gratuity on 5 Dec. 1780. He was awarded a gratuity of six months pay and an annuity of half-pay on 15 Dec. 1781. His request for an additional gratuity was rejected on 5 June 1782.

Williams, Jarrett. Va. Lt. He served in the Illinois Regiment under Col. George R. Clark to the end of the war. He was entitled to five years' full pay plus interest in the amount of $5,061.29.

Williams, Jeremiah. S.C. —. He volunteered in 1776 and was in Capt. Wadlington's Company and fought the Cherokee Indians. He went to Virginia and was at Guilford until 1781 when he came to South Carolina. He found that his wife and four children had been plundered of their possessions. He rejoined the army. Gen. Pickens directed him to enlist a company of riflemen to join Col. Hammond's Regiment of Dragoons. George Cannemore and Abel Anderson served with him. He was from Pendleton District in 1825. His application was rejected.

Williams, John. Conn. Pvt. He lost a leg in the service. He was pensioned 1 Sep. 1782. He was dead by 26 Feb. 1790.

Williams, John. Md. Corp. He was pensioned at the rate of half-pay of a corporal in St. Mary's County on 23 Jan. 1816.

Williams, John. Md. Pvt. He was pensioned at the rate of half-pay of a private in Baltimore 3 Feb. 1828.

Williams, John. N.J. Corp. He served in the 2nd N.J. Infantry. He lived in Essex Co., N.J. He was on the 1813 pension list.

Williams, John. N.Y. —. He served under Col. Van Schaick. His family was furnished assistance 26 Mar. 1779 while he was away in the service.

Williams, John. N.Y. Pvt. He served under Col. Samuel Drake in the Westchester County militia and was slain 16 Mar. 1777. His widow, Elizabeth Williams, received his half-pay pension.

Williams, John. Pa. Pvt. He was in the 3rd Pa. Battalion and was taken prisoner at Fort Washington. He was in Capt. West's Company. He had a wife and three children.

Williams, John. Pa. Pvt. He was in Philadelphia County on 10 Apr. 1787. He served in the 10th and 11th Pa. Regiments and was wounded in the shoulder at Elizabeth Town in 1777 by the butt of a musket. He contracted deafness in the service. He was transferred to the Invalids. He was aged 50.

Williams, John. Pa. —. He was pensioned 4 Apr. 1837 in Jefferson County.

Williams, John. S.C. —. His widow was Sarah Williams in 1824. Her youngest child was 10 years of age, and her eldest was 12 years old. She was granted his arrearage and her pension.

Williams, Joseph. Md. Pvt. He was pensioned in Annapolis at the rate of half-pay of a private 25 Feb. 1824. He was issued a warrant for 50 acres of bounty land in Allegany County 21 Mar. 1833.

Williams, Joshua. Pa. Capt. He enlisted early in 1776 in the Flying Camp. He served in the 4th Pa. Regiment. In 1778 and 1779 he rendered essential service to Gen. Wayne. He was awarded $100 on 25 Feb. 1813. He was awarded an $80 gratuity and an $80 annuity in Center County on 25 Feb. 1819. He died 12 Dec. 1824. His widow, Mary Williams, was awarded a $60 gratuity and a $60 annuity 10 Apr. 1826.

Williams, Lewis. Va. Pvt. His widow, Mildred Williams, was awarded a gratuity of £25 on 9 Dec. 1777 in Surry County. She was in Surry County in June 1786. He was in the 4th Va. Regiment under Capt. Watkins and died at the beginning of 1777 leaving three children. His widow on 24 Apr. 1787 had two children with her, one aged 12 and the other aged 9. She was put on the pension list 1 Jan. 1788 at the rate of £6 per annum. She died in Nov. 1791.

Williams, Moses. S.C. —. He was wounded on the lines at Charlestown in May 1779. He was granted an annuity 25 Nov. 1785 in Chester. His widow, Martha Williams, was granted his arrearage on 3 Dec. 1821. She was pensioned 30 Nov. 1827. She was about 70 years old and had two daughters with her. James Anderson was in the same company with him. She died 10 May 1838. Her daughter and executrix, Esther Williams, sought her arrearage.

Williams, Nathan. Vt. Capt. He was from Halifax, Vt. and served in the militia. He was slain en route to Ticonderoga by a bayonet through his body. Indians scalped him. His two sons were with him. His only heir was his son, Nathan Williams, who sought his seven years' half-pay in 1837. The surviving son was 77 years old and resided in Brooklyn, Windham Co., Conn.

Williams, Osborn. Md. Lt. He was pensioned at the rate of half-pay of a lieutenant 19 Feb. 1829.

Williams, Regnal. S.C. —. He entered the service in 1775 under Col. Richardson. He was in the Snow Camps and fought under Williamson against the Cherokee Indians. He was under Col. Beard in the Florida Expedition. Lewis Hogg served with him. He was 72 years old and from Newberry District when he was pensioned 30 Nov. 1827. He was paid as late as 1830.

Williams, Robert. Pa. —. His widow, Elizabeth Williams, was in Northumberland County on 27

Sep. 1786. He was in the Northumberland County militia and was killed 12 Dec. 1777.

Williams, Robert. Va. Pvt. He was from Hampshire County 11 July 1786. He was in Capt. Isaiah Marks' Company as a recruit from Hampshire County for 18 months service in the Continental Army. He was enlisted 17 Feb. 1779 by County Lt. Abraham Hite. His time commenced 25 Apr. 1779. He was wounded on 29 May 1777 and made a prisoner at the Waxsaw by Tarleton. He was discharged at Mount Airey, Culpeper Co., Va. 13 June 1783 as attested by Col. A. Buford. He was 30 years old. While in the 11th Va. Regiment, his skull was fractured in two places, the use of his right hand had been greatly impaired, and he had been wounded a little below the breast. He was in Frederick County when he was put on the pension list on 19 Dec. 1786 at the rate of £15 per annum and was continued at the same rate on 2 Nov. 1789. He was on the 1813 pension list. He was granted a $40 increment to his pension 19 Feb. 1824. That amount was amended on 24 Feb. 1824 to be valid even if he were to receive any increase from Virginia or the federal government. He died 21 Nov. 1834 leaving no widow or children. His administrator was John Hiett.

Williams, Sanford. Conn. Pvt. He was wounded at Fort Griswold by a musket ball through his body on 6 Sep. 1781. He was from Groton and aged 24 years on 26 Sep. 1788. He was on the 1791 pension roll. He died in 1796.

Williams, Stacy. Pa. —. He enlisted under Capt. Jacob Humphrey in the 6th Regiment in the spring of 1777. He served until after the army returned from South Carolina and was discharged at Philadelphia. He was from Chester County. He was a free man of color. He was at Trenton, Germantown, Stony Point, Monmouth, and Brandywine. He was wounded at the latter by a musket ball in his right thing. He applied from Philadelphia County.

Williams, Thaddeus. Pa. Pvt. He was granted one-fourth of a pension 20 Apr. 1796.

Williams, Thomas. Conn. Pvt. He suffered from fatigue and lameness incurred by crossing the river at Valley Forge. He was from East Haddam and aged 60 years on 19 Nov. 1788. He was pensioned 10 July 1783. He was on the 1813 pension list. He died 28 Feb. 1826.

Williams, Thomas. N.Y. QM. He served in the 3rd Battalion from 21 Nov. 1776 to 30 May 1779. He was appointed a lieutenant. He married Hellitie Miller, the daughter of Cornelius Miller. Her brother was Jeremiah Miller. Williams' children and grandchildren received 2,000 acres of bounty land from New York. They sought 200 acres from Congress 10 Dec. 1857. The children were Jeremiah Williams, Thomas Williams, and Cornelius Williams. The son Cornelius Williams married Albertine ----- who married secondly ---- Young. The children of Cornelius were Thomas Williams, Cornelius Williams, Maria Williams who married Phineas Walker, Jeremiah Williams, Julia Williams, Helen Williams, and Van Ness Williams. The claim was submitted by the veteran's son, Jeremiah Williams of Claverack, Columbia Co., N.Y. on 15 Dec. 1857.

Williams, Thomas. S.C. —. He served under Col. Hill, Col. William Polk, Col. Neill, Capt. Anderson, and Capt. James Giles. He was at Charleston, Stono Ferry, and Eutaw. He had a family of ten children. There were three sons (one of whom was an idiot), two daughters, and two small grandchildren in need of support. His son, Josiah Williams, bore that responsibility. He was 72 years old. He was pensioned 30 Nov. 1827. He died in Feb. 1828. His arrearage of $60 was paid to William Wright, his administrator, on 6 Dec. 1828.

Williams, Thomas. S.C. Legionnaire. He served aboard the *South Carolina* under Commodore Alexander Gillon. He was paid $109.60 on 20 Sep. 1808.

Williams, William. N.J. Pvt. He served in the 1st Regiment and was disabled in his back and by a wound in his leg. He was 55 years old. He was on the 1791 pension roll at the rate of $60 per annum.

Williams, William, 2nd . N.J. Pvt. He served in 2nd Regiment and was wounded in the leg and suffered from old age. He was 65 years old. He was from Gloucester County. He was on the 1791 pension roll at the rate of $60 per annum.

Williams, William. Capt. N.C. He was appointed 1 Apr. 1778 and served to the end of the war. He bequeathed his commutation of five years' pay to his widow. She married secondly ------- Williamson. He made a donation of one month's pay to the Society of the Cincinnati in Pennsylvania. He received bounty land from North Carolina. His only heir and son, William W. Williams, received his commutation 6 Mar. 1838.

Williams, William. S.C. —. He was wounded at Tarleton's defeat at Cowpens by saber cuts in his body, head, and arm. He was granted an annuity 26 Mar. 1785 and was from Union District. He sought an increase in his pension, but it was rejected 14 Dec. 1814. He was 69 years old. He was paid as late as 1820.

Williamson, Julian.—. —. He was 68 years old in Smith County, Tennessee in 1825. All of his children were married. He sought compensation in bounty land.

Williamson, William. Pa. —. He was pensioned.

Williford, Jesse. Va. —. He was in Southampton County on 5 Mar. 1832. He died 12 May 1840 leaving a widow, Cherry Williford. He was pensioned at the rate of $60 per annum with $30 relief on 28 Feb. 1832.

Willin, Charles. Md. Pvt. His widow, Eleanor Robertson, was pensioned at the rate of half-pay of a private in Somerset County on 27 Feb. 1839.

Willin, Evans. Md. Pvt. His widow, Mary Easom, was pensioned at the rate of half-pay of a private in Dorchester County on 23 Feb. 1832.

Willin, Levin. Md. Pvt. He was pensioned in Somerset County at the rate of half-pay of a private 4 Feb. 1833.

Willington, Samuel. Mass. Pvt. He was granted half a pension 20 Apr. 1796. He was on the 1813 pension list. He transferred to Windham Co., Vermont 4 Sep. 1825 from Worcester Co., Mass.

Willis, —. Va. —. His mother, Mary Willis, was granted £10 support in Caroline Co., Va. 8 Oct. 1778 while he was in Continental service.

Willis, Andrew. Md. Pvt. He was pensioned in Washington County at the rate of half-pay of a private 6 Feb. 1818. His widow, Lethe Willis, was pensioned at the same rate 18 Feb. 1825.

Willis, Daniel. Md. Drummer. He was on the 1791 pension list.

Willis, George. Va. —. He was alive 3 Dec. 1795. He had been disabled by wounds received in the service. He received $60 relief 2 Jan. 1799.

Willis, James. Me. —. He died 18 July 1836. His widow was Sarah Willis from Minot. She was paid $50 under the resolve of 1836.

Willis, James. Mass. —. He served in the 7th Regiment and was paid $20.

Willis, John. Va. —. He was held as a prisoner for nearly three years on Long Island. He was granted relief in Dec. 1780.

Willis, Joseph. Mass. —. He served in the 6th Regiment.

Willis, William. —. —. He served in the summer of 1778 for more than three years. He next served in private armed vessels. He was with Capt. Decatur when several vessels including one large British transport with part of a regiment of Hessian troops with their colonel were taken. He returned to Philadelphia and engaged on the brig *Holker* for the West Indies. They took a British privateer of twelve guns. He last served as commander of the brig *Dolphin* fitted out at Edenton, N.C. They took two merchant vessels from Jamaica. Congress granted him an increase in his pension 21 July 1842. He was born in New Bedford, Mass. and resided in Monroe Co., Va.

Willis, Zacheriah. Mass. —. He served in the 3rd Regiment and was paid $20.

Willman, Jacob. N.H. Pvt. He served in Bird's Regiment. He was pensioned 22 Aug. 1794 in Hillsborough Co., N.H. He was on the 1813 pension list.

Willmarth, Ephraim. —. —. He was pensioned 9 June 1794.

Willmot, Robert. Md. Lt. He served in the state artillery in 1776 and the next year transferred to Harrison's Virginia Regiment of Artillery. He was aged, infirm, and unable to walk without crutches. He was in need of pecuniary assistance. He was pensioned in Bourbon Co., Ky. at the rate of half-pay of a lieutenant 24 Jan. 1830 He was pensioned at the new rate of a lieutenant of artillery instead of a lieutenant of a line 13 Feb. 1836. He received his five years' full-pay commutation 30 June 1834. He also appeared as Robert Wilmot.

Willoughby, Charles. Pa. —. He was awarded a $40 gratuity and a $40 annuity in Beaver Co. 27 Mar. 1819. He died 15 Mar. 1826. He also appeared as Charles Willoby.

Wills, Conrad. Pa. —. He applied in Lancaster County on 21 Apr. 1815.

Wills, Daniel. Md. Drummer. He was pensioned 4 Mar. 1789.

Wills, James. —. —. He served nine months and then reenlisted for three years. He was discharged four months before the expiration of his term. He was pensioned at the rate of $8 per month. His widow, Patty Wills, was pensioned at the rate of $9 per month. Their daughter, Rhoda Chick, born 12 June 1815, was dependent on charity and sought a pension from Congress 21 May 1896. She was in her 80th year. Congress granted the pension.

Wills, James. Me. —. He was from Belgrade. He was paid $50 under the resolve of 1836.

Wills, James. Md. Pvt. He was pensioned in Baltimore County on 7 June 1785.

Wills, John. Md. Pvt. He was on the 1791 pension list. He was on the 1813 pension list. He also appeared as Jonathan Wills.

Willson, Ebenezer. Mass. —. He enlisted in June or July 1781 in Capt. Thomas Francis' Company in Col. Tupper's Regiment. He also served under Capt. Mason Wattles, Capt. Michael G. Houdin, and Col. Sprout until Oct. or Nov. 1783 when he was discharged at West Point, N.Y.

Wilmarth, Ephraim. Vt. Sgt. He served in Col. Robinson's militia. He was wounded by a musket ball which lodged in his left shoulder blade on 28 Aug. 1777 near Bennington. He lived in Shaftesbury, Vt. in 1792. His evidence was incomplete.

Wilmarth, Samuel. Mass. Pvt. He served in the 6th Regiment and was from Worcester. He was paid $50.

Wilmot, Robert. Md. Lt. He served in the artillery in 1776. The next year he transferred to Harrison's Virginia's Regiment. He had to walk with crutches. Congress granted him five years' full pay 23 Dec. 1833.

Wilson, —. Pa. —. His widow, Prudence Wilson, was granted relief in Juniata County 5 Feb. 1836.

Wilson, —. N.Y. —. Mary Wilson was granted support for necessaries 6 May 1779.

Wilson, —. S.C. —. His widow, Elizabeth Wilson, lived in Winton, Orangeburg District in 1791.

Wilson, —. Va. —. His wife, Elizabeth Wilson, was allowed £15 for her support and her young children in Augusta Co., Va. 20 Apr. 1778 and £20 on 16 Mar. 1779. Her husband was away in the service. On 21 Mar. 1780 she was allowed three bushels of corn.

Wilson, —. Pa. —. His widow, Mary Wilson, was awarded a $40 gratuity in Philadelphia Co., Pa. 15

Apr. 1835.

Wilson, Abraham. Pa. —. He was awarded a $40 gratuity and a $40 annuity in Mifflin Co., Pa. 11 Apr. 1825.

Wilson, Allen. Pa. Lt. His widow, Martha Wilson, applied 23 Aug. 1792.

Wilson, Andrew. Pa. —. He enlisted under Capt. John Jordan and Col. Benjamin Flowers in the Regiment of Artillery and Artificers. He received a great injury by falling off a crane. He was discharged 25 Apr. 1781. He was from Lycoming County.

Wilson, Archer. Va. Pvt. He served in the 6th Virginia Regiment. He lost his left arm at Germantown. He was awarded a £30 gratuity and an annuity of full-pay of a soldier on 26 May 1778. He was on the 1785 pension roll.

Wilson, Archibald. Pa. Q.M. His widow, Mary Wilson, applied in Beaver County on 29 Nov. 1838. He served in the Pa. Line.

Wilson, Benjamin. Va. Col. In 1774 he was a lieutenant under Gov. Dunmore against the Indians. From 1781 to 1795 he was colonel of the Harrison County militia and saw active service in the Revolutionary War. He died 2 Dec. 1827. His son, Noah Wilson, died in 1863 upon a return voyage from South America. His heirs asked for the allowance of the equivalent of commutation of half-pay, but Congress rejected their petition 30 Jan. 1857. His last surviving child was Rachel Wilson of Quiet Dell, W. Va. She was a member of the DAR and had been presented with a gold spoon as the only surviving daughter. Her father had 29 children by two wives. He was born 30 Nov. 1747 in Frederick Co., Va. She sought relief from Congress 12 Feb. 1900.

Wilson, David. Md. Pvt. He was pensioned in Washington County on 16 Feb. 1820. His widow, Rachel Wilson, was pensioned at the same rate on 20 Feb. 1829.

Wilson, David. N.Y. Pvt. He served under Lt. John Van Tuyles in the Orange County militia in Capt. Benjamin Tuston's Company. He was wounded on 25 Oct. 1778 three times in his hand, arm, and breast in the right lobe of his lung. His wife was Hannah Wilson. There were five children. He was 45 years old in 1788 and lived in Orange County. He was on the 1813 pension list.

Wilson, Ephraim. Mass. Sgt. He served in the 16th Regiment. His widow, Alice Wilson, was paid $50 and lived at Amesbury.

Wilson, George. Pa. Pvt. He served under Capt. Wilson in the 1st Regiment. He was wounded by a musket ball through his left leg near Trenton 2 Jan. 1777.

Wilson, George. Pa. Lt. Col. His widow, Sabina Wilson, was in Philadelphia County on 16 Feb. 1793. He was commissioned 20 July 1776 and served in the 8th Pa. Regiment. He died in Feb. 1778 of severe sickness occasioned by fatigue in an engagement with the enemy in the service. His widow married Samuel Williams in May 1783. On 4 Feb. 1803 Joseph Darlington *et alia* sought his benefits. They requested that he be covered as if he had been slain by the enemy. Congress rejected the claim. His children were paid $1,125 for his right to donation land 20 Feb. 1826 from Pennsylvania. On 13 Apr. 1827 it was directed that the money was to be paid to William G. Hawkins of Greene Co., Pa. until it could be determined who was entitled to the value of the donation land. His heirs were William G. Wilson, Sarah Darlington, Jane Wilson, and Phebe Turney.

Wilson, George. Va. —. His wife, Sarah Wilson, was granted £12 support in Berkeley County on 16 Mar. 1778.

Wilson, Hosea. Del. Pvt. He was pensioned in 1787. He died 12 Nov. 1798. One of his name was listed on the 1813 pension list. He also appeared as Hosea Willson.

Wilson, James. —. Col. His daughter, Sarah Griffith, sought her father's half-pay. Since he served in the state troops, Congress denied her claim 6 Feb. 1855.

Wilson, James. N.C. Pvt. He applied in Lincoln County in 1800. He served from Burke County in Capt. Joseph McDowell's Company and was wounded in his left arm at Ramsour's Mill on 20 June 1780. He had a wife and several small children.

Wilson, James. Pa. —. He was wounded. He was awarded a $40 gratuity and a $40 annuity on 7 Feb. 1812.

Wilson, James. S.C. —. He was killed at Cowpens on 17 Jan. 1783 survived by his widow and three children. The Tories stole their two slaves and all their property of value. One child was 9 years old, the second was 7 years old, and the third was 5 years old. A fourth child was born the day after his death. There was one child in 1791 qualifying for an annuity. Martha Wilson intermarried with William Anderson. She later learned that he had a wife living so she separated from him. He was dead by 18 Oct. 1824 when she sought the arrearage from 1785 to 1825 in Pendleton District. She was pensioned but was not allowed any arrearage. She was more than 80 years old.

Wilson, James. S.C. —. He volunteered in the militia in 1776 and went into Continental service under Col. Robert Goodwin in Capt. William Simmons's Company. He was upwards of 80 years of age. He was from Fairfield District in 1834. His application was rejected.

Wilson, James. Va. —. He enlisted for two years in the 5th Regiment under Col. Josiah Parker. He was at Brandywine, Germantown, Monmouth, and was discharged at Valley Forge in 1778. He married 1 Sep. 1785 and died 8 Aug 1835. Congress granted his widow, Catherine Wilson, of Muskingum Co., Ohio a pension on 8 Mar. 1842 for five years from the time of his death.

Wilson, Jeremiah. Pa. Pvt. He was on the 1813 pension list.

Wilson, John. —. Lieut. He served as a private in 1777 for a month; as a private and lieutenant for 15 months in 1778; and 1 ½ months in 1782. He was 89 years of age in 1845. He received 450 acres of bounty land from Georgia. One of the children was Elias Wilson. Congress granted the children a pension 25 May 1860.

Wilson, John. Mass. —. He served in the 5th Regiment and was from Haverhill. He was paid $20.

Wilson, John. N.C. Pvt. He lived in Gates County. He was on the 1813 pension list and died 11 Aug. 1815.

Wilson, John. Pa. Pvt. His widow, Jennet Wilson, was in Cumberland County on 12 May 1789. He served in the Cumberland County militia and was wounded at Gulph Mills on 11 Dec. 1777. He was taken prisoner and died in captivity in Philadelphia.

Wilson, John. Pa. —. He was awarded a $40 gratuity and a $40 annuity in Dauphin Co., Pa. 11 June 1832.

Wilson, John. Pa. —. He was pensioned in Northumberland County 5 June 1836.

Wilson, John. S.C. —. He was wounded in the wrist 20 Nov. 1775. He was paid £70. He was not cured and was believed to be disabled on 4 Apr. 1776.

Wilson, John. Vt. Sgt. He was in Gen. Washington's lifeguard. He was wounded in his right arm by a musket ball on 27 June 1778 at Monmouth. He lived in Windsor Co., Vt. in 1795. He was discharged 11 Dec. 1778. He was granted one-third of a pension 20 Apr. 1796. He was on the 1813 pension list.

Wilson, John. Va. Lt. His orphans were in Culpeper County on 19 June 1786. He was in the 4th Va. Regiment and was killed in battle at Eutaw as certified by Capt. James Curry. His orphans were John Wilson and Francis Jeritta Wilson. Their guardian was George Eastham. They were put on the pension list 18 Oct. 1787 at the rate of $18 per annum. They were in Frederick County in 1788. They removed to Kentucky and never received any part of the pension. His seven years' half-pay plus interest was paid to his heirs 27 Feb. 1833.

Wilson, John. Va. —. He served in Capt. William Forman's militia company and was wounded in his right arm by a ball on 3 Aug. 1777. He sought relief on 21 May 1778.

Wilson, John. Va. —. He was awarded a £30 gratuity in Hampshire County 21 May 1778. He was pensioned in Randolph County 19 Jan. 1813 at the rate of $60 per annum. He was wounded at Wheeling in his right arm. His pension was increased to $100 on 1 Jan. 1818. He was in Harrison County 2 Nov. 1820.

Wilson, John G. N.Y. Pvt. He was awarded 200 acres of bounty land 13 Apr. 1813.

Wilson, Joseph. Pa. —. He was awarded a $40 gratuity and a $40 annuity in Fayette Co., Pa. 4 May 1832. He was 80 years old in 1840.

Wilson, Josiah. Pa. Sgt. He served in the 7th Pa. Regiment and was transferred to the Invalids. He rejoined his old regiment in the spring of 1780 and acted as sergeant in Capt. Montgomery's Company. When he could not march with the regiment, Col. Butler ordered him to return to the Invalids.

Wilson, Mark. Me. —. He died 23 Aug. 1804 in Jay. His widow was Olive Wilson from Canton. She was paid $50 under the resolve of 1836.

Wilson, Matthew. Pa.—. He served on the frontiers of Northumberland County and was a spy among the Indians. He was out four summers. He was pensioned under the act of 24 Mar. 1812. He was from Allegheny County.

Wilson, Matthew. Pa. —. He was pensioned 24 Mar. 1833. He died in Allegheny County on 2 Nov. 1844.

Wilson, Moore. Va. —. His wife, Charlotte Wilson, was granted support while he was away in Continental service on 5 Apr. 1779 in Richmond County.

Wilson, Peter. Conn. —. He served under Capt. Matthew Mead and Capt. Isaac How for six years starting in 1776. He was commissioned by Gov. John Trumbull 23 Dec. 1776. Congress granted him a pension 15 Feb. 1848.

Wilson, Peter. Pa. Drummer. He served in the 3rd Pa. Regiment. He received a warrant for £88.1.9 for a lost certificate and interest on 2 Feb. 1802.

Wilson, Peter. Va. —. His wife and child were granted relief in Hanover County in Sep. 1779.

Wilson, Robert. Pa. —. His widow, Sarah Wilson, was awarded a $40 gratuity and a $40 annuity in Beaver Co., Pa. 10 Apr. 1826.

Wilson, Robert. Pa. Ens. He was in Northumberland County on 27 Sep. 1786. He was in the militia and was wounded by a musket ball in his left foot on 23 Feb. 1777 at Ash Swamp in N. J. He served under Capt. Hawkins Boone and Col. Cookson Long in the 12th Regiment for four years from Oct. 1776. He was 64 years old and was from Beaver County. He later lived in Washington County. He was on the 1813 pension list. He died 1 Oct. 1824.

Wilson, Robert. S.C. Capt. He served as a lieutenant after the fall of Charleston in May 1782. He served twelve months as 1st Lt. and Capt. He was elected–not commissioned. Congress awarded him an increase in his pension for his higher rank on 1 Aug. 1850.

Wilson, Samuel. Md. Sgt. He was pensioned 4 Mar. 1789.

Wilson, Samuel. Pa. —. He was awarded a $40 gratuity and a $40 annuity in Fayette Co., Pa. 14 Apr. 1834. He was 76 years old in 1840. He died 1 July 1851.

Wilson, Theophilus. S.C. —. He substituted for his father, John Wilson, who had been drafted. He served under Col. Richard Winn, Col. Robert Goodwyn, Maj. Joseph Kirkland, William Simons, and Capt. James Craig. His father and four brothers also served. They were deceased. His brother William Wilson, also a pensioner, died in 1837. Other brothers were James Wilson, Jesse Wilson and John Wilson, Jr. He was a wagoner for two to three years. He was under age and employed by his father so his name did not appear on the rolls. He could not qualify for a federal pension. He was pensioned in 1847 from Fairfield District. He was 85 years old on 15 Dec. 1852. He died 25 June 1853. All of his children were in indigent circumstances and had large families. They sought his arrears. They were John Wilson, Swan Wilson, Naomi Kelly, Hiram Wilson, and Theophilus Wilson.

Wilson, Thomas. Del. Sgt. He received a pension.

Wilson, Thomas. N.Y. Pvt. He served in Capt. Leonard Bleeker's Company under Col. Gansvort. He was wounded in his left shoulder and arm by a musket ball at Fort Schuyler in the summer of 1777. He lived in Washington Co., N.Y. on 6 July 1789. He was aged 55 on 12 May 1786. He was on the 1813 pension list. He also appeared as Thomas Willson.

Wilson, Thomas. S.C. —. He was pensioned 6 Dec. 1828.

Wilson, Thomas. Va. —. He served against the Indians in 1780 under Gen. George R. Clark. He enlisted in 1776 under Capt. Gibson and Lt. Lynn to descend the Ohio and Mississippi Rivers to New Orleans for ammunition and military stores. Congress ruled that there was not sufficient testimony to prove the service in 1780 and his service in 1776 was not of a military character. His widow was Mary Wilson. Congress rejected her claim 8 Mar. 1844.

Wilson, Valentine. N.Y. Pvt. He died 4 July 1838. Congress granted his widow, Amy Wilson, a pension 5 Jan. 1836 from 4 Mar. 1831 to the time of his death.

Wilson, William. Conn. Pvt. He was pensioned in 1792. He was on the 1813 pension list. He died 24 May 1817.

Wilson, William. N.C. Capt. He was wounded in Feb. 1781. He was at Ramsour's, Camden, and Cowpens. He was shot through his thigh in nine different places at Cowpens when he met Tarleton's Cavalry at Second Creek. He was shot through his body by a pistol, run through his abdomen with a sword, and his head was cut in seven places. He applied in Rowan County in 1801 for a state pension. He married 5 Mar. 1785. He died 14 Aug. 1817. Congress granted his widow, Nancy Wilson, a pension 20 Apr. 1844.

Wilson, William. Pa. —. He was awarded a $40 gratuity and a $40 annuity in Allegheny Co., Pa. 27 Mar. 1827. He was 86 years old in 1840.

Wilson, William. S.C. —. He served under Capt. William Simmons and Col. Robert Goodwyn. He was a drafted militiaman in Continental service. He was on the Florida Expedition. He was 70 years old and applied from Fairfield District 23 Nov. 1831. He died 13 Sep. 1837. His widow, Mahala Wilson, had two little children.

Wilson, Willis. Va. Lt. He was in Cumberland County on 19 Jan. 1788. He served in the 11th Va. Regiment and had eight wounds in his right arm and hand and several others on his head and body. He was at Buford's defeat at Waxsaw, S.C. He was deprived of the use of his right arm and hand and had a bayonet thrust into his abdomen to the spine. He was put on the pension list at the rate of £40 per annum on 19 June 1788. His request for arrearage was postponed on 9 Dec. 1788. On 3 Mar. 1789 he was paid from 1 Jan. 1783 to 1 Jan. 1788. He was on the 1813 pension list. Congress refused him a pension 24 Feb. 1818. He died 10 Feb. 1822 and John P. Wilson was his executor. His grandsons, Willis Wilson and William W. Wilson, sought payment on 2 Feb. 1855 but Congress rejected their claim.

Wilt, Frederick. Pa. Sgt. He was in Philadelphia County on 10 Apr. 1786. He served in the 10th Regiment. He was wounded in the right leg by a bayonet, and his right wrist was fractured in Sept. 1777 near Paoli. He was transferred to the Invalids and was discharged in 1781. After the war he went on a voyage to England and left behind a wife and three children who sought some relief. He was 56 years old.

Wilt, Jacob. Pa. —. He received a state pension from Pennsylvania in 1835. Congress rejected him for a federal pension because he did not fix the length of his service on 22 Feb. 1843.

Wiltman, William. Pa. Lt. He was in Berks County on 7 Jan. 1786. He served in the 9th Regiment under Col. George Nagel. He was wounded through his body by a musket ball at Germantown on 4 Oct. 1777.

Wilton, James. N.C. —. He was murdered by John High. His widow was Angelica Wilton of Franklin County, and her small son was James Wilton. She sought the forfeitures in her distressed condition in 1786.

Wilton, James. Va. —. His wife, Betty Wilton, was furnished with provisions while he was in the Continental Army in Amherst Co., Va. in Nov. 1779.

Wimber, Thomas. Md. Pvt. He was pensioned at the rate of half-pay of a private in Worcester Co. on 3 Feb. 1828.

Wimberly, Isaac. S.C. —. There were children in 1791.

Win, John. S.C. —. He was made a prisoner at Augusta in 1780 and died on board a prison ship. His widow, Mary Win, was granted an annuity 16 Feb. 1785.

Winans, Silas. —. —. He was pensioned under the act of 1818. His remarried widow, Elizabeth Calkins, had her petition for a pension approved by Congress 13 July 1846. He was entered on the roll as having deserted. He received a furlough to visit his family, became ill, and was unable to return. William Seacraft was his commanding officer.

Winbrough, Thomas P. Md. Pvt. His widow, Leah Winbrough, was pensioned at the rate of half-pay of a private 2 Feb. 1832.

Winch, Joseph. —. Pvt. He served two and a half years. He applied in 1818 and reapplied in 1829. Congress refused to grant him a pension from 26 Mar. 1818 for twelve years and five months on 13 Jan. 1836

Winchester, Charles. Mass. —. He served in Wesson's Regiment. He was from Charlemont and was paid $20.

Winchester, Jabez. Conn. —. He served under Capt. Joshua Bottom and Col. Ely in 1779 for eight months and fourteen days. He spent nine months on a prison ship in New York harbor and was exchanged. He served one year under Capt. Dana for a year. Congress granted him a pension in 1832.

Windham, —. S.C. —. His widow was Lucy Windham. She also appeared as Lucy Wyndham. She was receiving an annuity in 1802.

Windham, Benjamin. Va. Pvt. His widow, Mary Windham, was in Southampton County on 13 Dec. 1787. He was in the State Regiment under Col. Dabney and died in Portsmouth. He left a widow and six children. Four of them were bound out, but the two girls remained with their mother. His father deprived his daughter-in-law from the land he had suffered them to occupy. She was put on the pension list at the rate of £10 per annum on 21 Apr. 1788.

Windham, Micajah. N.C. Wagonmaster. He received several wounds. He served under Capt. Daniel Williams and Michael Kenan. He was from Edgecombe County and sought permission to sell spirituous liquors free of tax. He was rejected in Dec. 1809.

Windom, John. S.C. —. He died in enemy confinement. His widow, Ann Windom, lived in Orangeburg District in 1794. She sold her annuity certificate to James Halliday.

Windon, —. Va. —. He was away in the service. His wife, Sarah Windon, was allowed £30 support in Augusta Co., Va. 15 Feb. 1780.

Wine, Jacob. Va. Pvt. He was in Frederick County in July 1786. He was in Continental service in Capt. Oldham's Company in the 1ˢᵗ Va. Regiment. He was wounded in his left leg by a musket ball at the siege of Ninety Six, S. C. It became ulcerated. He was 25 years old. He was wounded six times. He was on the 1813 pension list.

Wing, Moses. Mass. Drummer. He served in Capt. Dimond Morton's Company under Col. Henry Knox in the artillery. He was disabled by the loss of his left leg. He was pensioned at full pay from 31 Dec. 1776 on 2 July 1777. He was 27 years old in 1786. He was on the 1813 pension list. He transferred to Kennebec Co., Me. 4 Mar. 1833 from Essex Co., Mass.

Wing, Nathan. Me. —. He died 10 Apr. 1836. His widow was Love Wing from Abbot. She was paid $50 under the resolve of 1836.

Winget, Daniel. Pa. —. He was granted relief in Knox Co., Ohio 13 Apr. 1838. He also appeared as Daniel Wingret.

Wingler, Jacob. Pa. —. He was awarded a $40 gratuity in Cumberland Co., Pa. 7 Feb. 1831.

Wining, James. Pa. —. He applied in Mifflin County on 11 Jan. 1814. James Patton did duty with him. He also appeared as James Winning. He died 31 Dec. 1824.

Winn, Elisha. Va. Corp. He applied 8 Dec. 1813 from Lunenburg Co., Va. He served in the 6ᵗʰ Virginia Regiment and contracted a disease in the winter of 1777 at Valley Forge. Hugh Wallace proved that Winn was in Capt. James Johnson's Company.

Winn, John. N.Y. Pvt. He enlisted in Capt. James Black's Company in Col. Malcolm's Regiment. He later served in Col. Oliver Spencer's Regiment. He was wounded in his right knee by a musket ball on 12 June 1780 at the battle of Springfield. He lived in Ulster Co., N.Y. on 13 June 1789. He was on the 1813 pension list. He died 8 Jan. 1827 in New York County.

Winn, John. N.Y. —. He was awarded 200 acres of bounty land on 11 Apr. 1808.

Winn, John. Pa. Sgt. He applied in Franklin County on 19 Aug. 1813. He served in Capt. Andrew Irwin's Company in the 1ˢᵗ Regiment under Col. Brodhead.

Winn, Joshua. Mass. Pvt. He served under Col. Daniel Hitchcock and Capt. Kimball. He lost the use of his right arm. He was 39 years old in 1786. He lived in Essex Co., Mass. He was on the 1813 pension list.

Winn, Peter. N.Y. Soldier. Bounty land warrant #1106 was issued to his niece, Rebecca Dudley, on 15 Feb. 1825. Congress issued her a duplicate warrant 25 May 1840.

Winn, Richard. S.C. 1ˢᵗ Lt. He was commissioned in June 1775 and served under Col. Thompson and Gen. Richardson. He was at Sullivan's Island. He was sent as captain to command a company defending Fort McIntosh. The fort capitulated. He returned to Fairfield District and took command of the militia. He moved to Tennessee in 1818. His son, Samuel Winn, sought relief from Congress 5 Feb. 1859.

Winslow, Abraham. Me. —. He died 6 Feb. 1806. His widow was Elizabeth Winslow from Freeport. She was paid $50 under the resolve of 1836.

Winslow, Ezekiel. Me. —. He died 13 June 1835. His widow was Sedonah Winslow from Waldoboro. She was paid $50 under the resolve of 1836.

Winslow, John. —. —. He served more than three years as Deputy Paymaster General and captain of artillery and was attached to the Northern Department. He left the service in 1778. He married in 1782. He died 20 Nov. 1819. His widow died 12 Nov. 1836. The claim based upon his service from his heirs was rejected by Congress on 23 Feb. 1855.

Winslow, Oliver. Mass. Pvt. He served in the 1st Regiment and was from Scitutate. He was paid $50.

Winslow, William. Mass. —. He served in the 4th Regiment and was paid $20.

Winston, John. S.C. —. His widow and children were on the roll in 1793.

Winston, John. Va. Capt. He entered the service in 1776. He was with Gen. Washington while retreating through New Jersey at Trenton, Princeton, Germantown, White Plains, and Monmouth. In 1781 he returned home to visit his family when the army came to the siege of Yorktown. He died shortly after the peace. He was paid as a captain from 1 Jan. 1777 to 13 Feb. 1781 when he became supernumerary. His heirs received his commutation 19 Apr. 1835.

Winston, William B.. Va. —. He was pensioned in 1819 bjonathaut dropped from the rolls because he served under Col. George Gibson which was deemed state rather than Continental service. Congress granted him relief 5 Mar. 1840.

Winter, James. N.J. Pvt. He served under Col. Scudder in the militia. He died in prison in New York 4 Mar. 1777 having been taken prisoner at the Highlands 13 Feb. 1777. His widow, Mary Winter, was granted a pension. She was from Monmouth County.

Winter, John. Mass. Pvt. He served in the 5th Regiment and was from Ashburnham. His widow, Phebe Hawks, was paid $50.

Winter, Joseph. Me. —. He died 13 June 1832 at Carthage. His widow was Betsy Morse from Jay. She was paid $50 under the resolve of 1836.

Winter, Joshua. Mass. —. He served in the 5th Regiment and was from Boston. He was paid $20.

Winter, Timothy. —. —. His application was rejected 27 Feb. 1798.

Wire, Edward. Mass. Pvt. He served in the 3rd Regiment under Col. John Greaton and Capt. Watson. He was disabled with asthma.

Wire, James. N.Y. —. *Vide* James Wier.

Wirt, George. Pa. 1st Lt. His widow, Mary Wirt, was in Philadelphia County on 12 Feb. 1787. He served in Col. Miles' Regiment and died in captivity 14 Nov. 1778.

Wise, —. Va. —. His wife, Catharine Wise, was granted £4 support in Fauquier County in Nov. 1776 and £10 in May 1778.

Wise, —. S.C. —. His widow was Mary Wise who was on the roll in 1791.

Wise, Andrew. Pa. —. He was awarded in Lancaster County 14 Mar. 1835.

Wise, Jacob. Pa. —. He was awarded a $40 gratuity and a $40 annuity in Juniata County 31 Mar. 1836. He was 83 years old in 1840. He died 7 Aug. 1844.

Wise, Samuel. S.C. Maj. He served in the 3rd S.C. Regiment of Infantry on Continental Establishment and was killed at Savannah 9 Oct. 1779. His widow was deceased. His daughter, Jane Ann Wise, was about 14 years old at the time of his death. She married Joseph Ball. They sought his seven years' half-pay in 1791.

Wise, Thomas. S.C. —. He was paid $139.93 3/4 on 11 Dec. 1818 for a horse impressed in the service in the Revolutionary War.

Wise, Thomas. S.C. —. He was trooper under Col. Peter Horry and Capt. Richard Richardson. Hugh Paisley served with him. He was from Sumter District and was pensioned 23 Nov. 1829. He was paid as late as 1830. John Rhodus and other heirs sought his arrearage in Nov. 1832. Their claim was rejected because they presented no proof of probate or if there were other heirs.

Wiseman, George. Pa. —. He was awarded a $40 gratuity in Cumberland Co. 27 Mar. 1812. He died 27 Mar. 1826.

Wiseman, Noah. —. Lt. He died at home and not of wounds contracted in the service. Congress denied his heirs, a widow and child, a pension 13 Feb. 1849.

Wisner, Gabriel. N.Y. Pvt. He served in the militia under Col. John Hathorn and was slain 22 July 1779. His widow, Elizabeth Wisner, received a half-pay pension for seven years.

Wisener, Jacob. Pa. —. He also appeared as Jacob Wisner. He was granted relief 28 Mar. 1829 in Chester County.

Wiser, John. Pa. —. He was awarded a $40 gratuity and a $40 annuity in Cumberland Co., Pa. 13 Apr. 1827.

Wishart, Thomas. Va. Lt. He served in the 15th Regiment from Nov. 1776 to 1778 when he became supernumerary. In Apr. 1781 he was taken prisoner by the British and held in captivity until the surrender at Yorktown in Oct. 1781. Sidney Wishart and the other heirs sought his half-pay for life 20 Feb. 1830. Congress granted the same to them 14 June 1854.

Wishart, Walter. S.C. —. He was killed in 1781 or 1782 at Wright's Bluff. His widow, Elizabeth Wishart, married William Eakin. There was a child in 1793. Elizabeth Eakin applied for a pension 12 Nov. 1825 from York District. Her second husband had died about nine years earlier. John Barry confirmed her first husband's service. She had a daughter by Wishart who was upwards of fifty years of age and almost as helpless as she. He also appeared as Walter Wisher.

Wisner, Gabriel. N.Y. Pvt. His widow was granted support according to an undated roster.

Wisner, William. Pa. —. He was granted relief in Berks County 27 Feb. 1834.

Wiswall, Daniel. Mass. —. He was in the 8th Regiment and was from Dorchester. He was paid $20.

Wiswall, Enoch. Mass. —. He was paid $20.

Witham, James. Mass. —. He served in the 2nd Regiment and was paid $20.

Witham, Jedediah. Me. —. He was killed in the service 28 June 1778 at Monmouth. His widow was Hannah Spinney from Eliot. She was paid $50 under the resolve of 1836. She married (2) John Tuttle and (3) Timothy Spinney.

Witham, Jeremiah. Mass. —. He was pensioned on 17 Apr. 1777 for three years ending 7 June 1778 at £12. On 31 Mar. 1788 he was pensioned at the rate of £3 per annum. He also appeared as Jeremiah Whitam.

Withee, Zoe. Me. —. He was from Industry. He was paid $50 under the resolve of 1836.

Witherell, James. Mass. Ens. He served in the 11th Regiment. He first served as a non-commissioned officer. He became an ensign 26 Sep. 1780 and served to the end of the war. He received his commutation 25 May 1838.

Witherington, Solomon. N.C. —. He enlisted as a substitute at the age of 14 for John Dismal. He was born 4 Oct. 1761 in Lenoir Co., N.C. He served under Col. William Caswell, Capt. John Stringer, Capt. McIlvean, Lt. Thoms Shute, Ens. Blaney Harper, Sgt. Isler Kirkpatrick, and Sgt. James Conrad. He went to Augusta, Ga. and was discharged at 16 at Purrysburgh. He next substituted for Christopher Taylor. He volunteered in Aug. 1782 under Capt. Matthew Mosely and Maj. William Shepherd. He was then a substitute for Nathan Witherington under Capt. Thomas Gatlin. He applied from Craven County 25 Oct. 1832.

Withers, —. Pa.—. Sarah Withers of Bullitt County, Kentucky received $300 in lieu of donation land.

Withers, Enoch K. Va. Ens. He served from Aug. 1777 to May 1778. He was at Cowpens under Maj. Triplett. He was not in the regular army but in the militia. Congress rejected his claim for commutation on 3 Feb. 1842 because he resigned in 1778.

Witherspoon, David. S.C. Matross. He was wounded in Charleston at the battle Sullivan Island. He was granted an annuity 23 June 1785. He died 19 Aug. 1792. William Linen, who had maintained him, sought his arrearage.

Withrington, James. Mass. —. He served in the 8th Regiment. He was paid $20.

Withrighton, John. Mass. —. He served in the 3rd Regiment and was paid $20.

Withrow, Samuel. Pa. —. He was awarded a $40 gratuity and a $40 annuity in Franklin Co., Pa. 17 Mar. 1835. He also appeared as Samuel Witherow.

Witman, —. Pa. —. His widow, Ann Maria Witman,, was awarded a $40 gratuity and a $40 annuity in Berks Co., Pa. 14 Apr. 1834. She was dead by Dec. 1837.

Witman, —. Pa. —. His widow was Mary Witman. She was awarded a $40 gratuity and a $40 annuity in Northumberland Co., Pa. 13 Apr. 1827.

Witman, George. Pa. —. He applied in Berks County on 10 Oct. 1812. He enlisted in 1775 in Capt. Cluggage's Company of Riflemen under Col. Thompson and went to Boston. He marched to New York and was at Long Island in 1776. Capt. Jacob Brown was in the same regiment. He was discharged at Trenton in 1781. His widow, Mary Witman, was awarded a $40 gratuity and a $40 annuity in Berks County 13 Apr. 1827. He also appeared as George Whitman.

Witman, George. Pa. —. He was from Schuylkill County.

Witman, William. Pa. Lt. He served under Col. George Nagel. He was shot through his body by a musket ball in battle. He was taken prisoner. He signed a parole while lying wounded at Germantown to prevent his going to hospital in Philadelphia. He was left out of the army in 1779. He was 34 years old. He died 12 Oct. 1808. His widow, Catherine Witman, was awarded a $60 gratuity and a $60 annuity in Berks Co., Pa. 10 Apr. 1826.

Witmeyer, Eberhard. Pa. Sgt. He was in Berks County on 12 May 1786. He served in Capt. Jacob Bower's Company in the Battalion of Col. Becker. He was ruptured in one of his testicles at Brandywine in Sep. 1777. He was 64 years old.

Witmyer, Peter. Pa. —. He was granted relief in Lebanon County 14 Mar. 1835.

Witram, John. Pa. Pvt. He was on the 1791 pension roll.

Witrick, Michael. N.Y. —. He was granted support during the war. He also appeared as Michael Wederick.

Witson, William. Pa. —. He was pensioned.

Witt, —. Va. —. Ann Witt was allowed £15 support in Bedford Co., Va. on 27 July 1778.

Witt, Jesse. Va. Pvt. He was a drafted soldier from Bedford County. He was disabled by paralysis and was awarded a £50 gratuity on 10 Nov. 1779 in Bedford County. He was in Bedford County on 14 Aug. 1788. He was in the 14th Va. Regiment having enlisted 1 Jan. 1777 for three years in the Continental Army. Due to sickness he lost the use of his left arm and was rendered unfit for military duty as certified by Lt. Col. Commandant B. Ball and Brig. Gen. P. Muhlenburg. He was on the 1813 pension list.

Witter, Josiah. Conn. Lt. He served in the Volunteers. He was wounded by four musket balls, one of which passed through the trunk of his body and separated one of his ribs from the back bone in Mar. 1783 on Long Island. He was taken prisoner. He resided in Brooklyn in 1792. Since his certificate had been signed by commissioners James Iredell and Richard Law and not by the Clerk of the Circuit Court of the U.S., the Secretary of War refused to approve his application in 1794. He also appeared as Joseph Witter.

Wohleber, Abraham. N.Y. Pvt. He was scalped and wounded on 17 Oct. 1781. He was pensioned 14 Sep. 1786. He lived at German Flatts, Montgomery Co., N.Y. on 10 July 1789. He served in Bellenger's N.Y. Regiment in Capt. Frank's Company. He also appeared as Abraham Woleber, Abraham Wohlever, and Abraham Walhever. He was on the 1813 pension list. He died in

Columbia County, N.Y. 6 Feb. 1819.

Wohleber, Johannes. N.Y. Pvt. He served under Col. Peter Wohleber in the Montgomery County militia and was slain 6 Aug. 1777. His son, Peter Wohleber, received his half-pay pension.

Wolbarn, —. Pa. —. His widow, Catharine Wolbarn, was awarded a $40 gratuity and a $40 annuity in Lebanon Co., Pa. 27 Jan. 1835.

Wolcot, Giles. N.Y. —. He was awarded 600 acres of bounty land on 19 June 1812.

Wolcott, Benajah. Conn. —. He enlisted in the second year of the war and was at White Plains and at the capture of Cornwallis. He was born in Conn. He applied from Danbury, Huron Co., Ohio. Congress did not grant him relief.

Wolcott, William. Md. Pvt. He was pensioned in Ohio 26 Feb. 1829 at the rate of half-pay of a private.

Wolf, —. Pa. —. His widow was Susanna Wolf in Northampton County. No other data.

Wolf, Frederick —. —. He enlisted under Duke De Lauzun at Strasbourg, Alsace and came to America with the French troops with him and Count de Rochambeau. He married in 1800 and died 20 June 1837. His widow, Elizabeth Wolf, had her pension application rejected because he was an ally and not a veteran. Congress recognized his service and granted her a pension 4 May 1860. She was 80 years old. Her first husband, **Elijah Bliss**, whom she married 1 May 1792, died in 1797. He was also a veteran and fought at Monmouth and White Plains. He was wounded in the service and was a native of West Springfield, Mass. He served more than three years.

Wolf, George. Pa. —. He served three tours on the frontiers against the Indians on the Delaware north of the Blue Mountain. He was a sergeant, lieutenant, and captain. He was from Northampton County. He was awarded a $40 gratuity and a $40 annuity in Lebanon Co., Pa. 16 Feb. 1835.

Wolf, Jacob. Pa. —. He was awarded a $40 gratuity and a $40 annuity in Armstrong Co., Pa. 29 Mar. 1824.

Wolf, Michael. N.Y. Pvt. He served under Col. Van Schaick and was slain 4 June 1779. His widow, Elizabeth Wolf, received a half-pay pension. He also appeared as Michael Wolt.

Wolf, Peter. Pa. —. He was awarded a $40 gratuity and a $40 annuity in Lehigh Co., Pa. 17 Mar. 1835.

Wolfe, Christian. Pa. Pvt. He was pensioned 11 Aug. 1790.

Wolfe, George. Pa. Pvt. He was on the 1813 pension list. He moved to Washington Co., Ohio 4 Sep. 1826.

Wolfe, John. Pa. —. He entered the service as a sergeant under Capt. Andrew Geyer and Col. Matlock in a rifle company. He was at Staten Island, Amboy, New Brunswick, Newark, Trenton, Princeton, Germantown, and Monmouth. He was in encampment in Morristown in 1777 for nine months. He served in both the 3rd and 5th Regiments. Congress granted his widow, Mary Wolfe, of Northern Liberties, Philadelphia a pension 25 Apr. 1840 for nine months of service. She died 1 Feb. 1842.

Wolfe, Philip. Va. —. His wife, Elizabeth Wolfe, was granted 150 pounds of pork and 3 barrels of corn for her support and two children in Berkeley County on 16 Oct. 1781.

Wolff, John. N.Y. —. His family was granted support during the war.

Wolleber, Peter. N.Y. Sgt. He served under Maj. Copeman in the militia. He was wounded in the right thigh by a musket shot from a party of Indians on 18 July 1781 at Connajorharrie. He lived in Palatine, N.Y. when he was pensioned 9 June 1794. He also appeared as Peter Woleber.

Wood, —. N.J. —. His widow was Lydia Wood. *Vide* Benjamin Wood *infra.*

Wood, —. N.J. —. His widow was Sarah Wood.

Wood, Abel. Mass. Pvt. He served in Col. Ruggles Woodbridge's Regiment under Capt. Reubin Dickerson. He was wounded by a swivel ball from a ship through his right thigh on 17 Dec.

1775 on Lechmere's Point. He was pensioned at a quarter-pay from 1 Jan. 1776 to the time of his discharge on 29 Apr. 1782. He was 42 years old in 1792. He was on the 1813 pension list. He removed from Shuftebury, Mass. to Sudbury, Vt. He died in Rutland Co., Vt. 3 Sep. 1831. He also appeared as Abel Woods.

Wood, Benjamin. N.J. Pvt. He served under Col. Spencer and was killed 1 July 1780. His widow was Lydia Wood who received a half-pay pension 7 Aug. 1784 in Sussex County.

Wood, David. Mass. Sgt. He served in David Warner's Company under Col. Jonathan Holman. He was disabled by a gun shot in his right thigh which contracted the nerve. He received a full pension from 1 Dec. 1776 on 26 June 1777. He resided in Worcester Co., Mass. He was 36 years old in 1790. He was on the 1813 pension list. He also appeared as David Woods.

Wood, Edward. Ga. Capt. He served under Col. Samuel Elbert. He died 16 Feb. 1784 at Augusta, Ga. He received bounty land from Georgia. His brother, James Wood, administrator and heir, sought his commutation. Neither one had received any federal bounty land. Congress denied his claim 23 Jan. 1822. James Wood was from Columbia County.

Wood, George. S.C. —. He was under Col. Hammond in battle near the Blue Ridge where 300 prisoners were taken. He was also at Charleston under Col. Glover. At Window Hill he was thrown from his horse across his gun lock which caused the rim of his belly to give way. Levi Peacock served with him. He was born 4 Dec. 1740. His wife was nearly as old as he was. He applied 13 Aug. 1825 in Barnwell District and was pensioned 7 Dec. 1825. He died 10 Mar. 1826 without having received a cent of his pension. His widow, Susanna Wood, who was 70 years old, received his arrearage of $60 on 12 Dec. 1826. She was pensioned at the rate of $30 per annum. She was blind. She sought an increase in her pension 11 Nov. 1839.

Wood, Gerard. Md. Surgeon's Mate. He received half-pay for life. Congress granted his heirs relief 29 May 1858.

Wood, Hugh. Pa. Pvt. He was in Philadelphia County on 14 Nov. 1785. He was transferred from the 4th Pa. Regiment to the Invalids. He was wounded in the wrist and discharged 15 Sep. 1782. He was 33 years old.

Wood, Isaac. Mass. Pvt. He served in the 14th Regiment. His widow, Sarah Wood, was from Taunton and was paid $50.

Wood, Isaac. N.J. Pvt. He served in the 1st N.J. Regiment in Capt. William Piatt's Company. He enlisted about Mar. 1778. He died in camp at Williamsburg, Virginia 27 Sep. 1781. He was a native of Morris Town. Lt. Ephraim Darby certified his death. He married Sarah Whitenack in 1776. His widow, Sarah Wood, sought his half-pay in Morris County in July 1783.

Wood, James. S.C. —. He was killed in 1781. His widow, Mary Wood, was granted an annuity 28 Feb. 1786.

Wood, Jesse. Me. —. He was from Wilton. He was paid $50 under the resolve of 1836. He also appeared as Jesse Atwood.

Wood, Jerard. —. Surgeon's Mate. He was paid to 3 Apr. 1783. Congress granted relief to his administrator 12 Feb. 1855.

Wood, John. N.Y. Ens. He served under Col. John Hathorn in the Orange County militia. He was killed at Minisink 22 July 1779. His widow, Mary Wood, was granted a half-pay pension.

Wood, John. Pa. Pvt. He was on the 1813 pension list. He died 2 Sep. 1819 in Allegheny County. His arrearage of $71.73 was due his wife Sarah Wood, sons James Wood, John Wood, Joseph Wood, Presley Wood, Jeremiah Wood, Peter Wood, and daughters Fanny Gray, Elizabeth Mayberry, Eleanor Sprague, Rebecca Stevenson, and Sarah Woods. His widow, Sarah Woods, may be the one of the name who received a $40 gratuity and a $40 annuity in Allegheny County 31 Mar. 1836. She died 15 Apr. 1844.

Wood, John. S.C. —. He was killed 12 July 1781. His widow, Catherine Wood, was granted a pension 15 Dec. 1785.

Wood, John. Vt. In Mar. 1775 he led his company after the massacre at Westminster in securing the perpetrators. They were confined to the jail in Northampton, Mass. He expended £48.11.7. He sought relief 30 Jan. 1797 in the form of a lottery for the raising of £100. He was from Pittsford. He resided in Kingsbury, N.Y. in 1798.

Wood, Joseph. N.Y. Pvt. He served in the Ulster County militia under Col. James McClaughry and was slain at Fort Montgomery 6 Oct. 1777. His daughter, Esther Wood, was granted his half-pay pension.

Wood, Joseph. Pa. —. He was awarded relief in Mifflin County 6 Apr. 1833. He died 11 [?17] Feb. 1847.

Wood, Joseph. Pa. Lt. Col. He was in Dauphin County on 7 July 1786. He served in 2nd Pa. Regiment from the latter part of the summer of 1776 under Arthur St. Clair. He was wounded in the left leg while conducting a body of troops in boats from Crown Point to Ticonderoga. He was also wounded in his left arm at Lake Champlain. He was aged 65 years. He died in 1796.

Wood, Lemuel. Conn. Pvt. He enlisted in 1781 in an independent company in Conn. under Capt. Jabez Fitch. He was wounded by a musket ball on 14 June 1781 at King's Neck. His ribs were fractured. He was from Greenwich, Conn. He was aged 25 years on 6 Aug. 1787. He lived in North Castle, Westchester Co., N.Y. in 1787. He was on the 1813 pension list. According to one record he died 4 July 1808.

Wood, Nicholas. Mass. Pvt. He served in the 14th Regiment and was from Middleboro. His widow, Hope Wood, was paid $50.

Wood, Samuel. Mass. Pvt. He served in the 4th Regiment. He was from East Bridgewater and was paid $50.

Wood, Thomas. Me. —. He died 28 Sep. 1824. His widow was Lois Wood from Hebron. She was paid $50 under the resolve of 1836.

Wood, William. N.H. Pvt. He was from Hollis. He was wounded at Bunker Hill on 17 June 1775 by a musket ball in his arm. He served under Capt. Reuben Dow. He was aged 34 in 1787. He was on the 1813 pension list.

Wood, William. N.C. —. He served in the N.C. Continental Line and was considerably wounded and disabled. His application was rejected in 1807 for lack of vouchers.

Wood, William. Pa. —. He was awarded a $40 gratuity and a $40 annuity in Lebanon Co., Pa. 18 Feb. 1834.

Wood, William. S.C. —. He served under Capt. Dixon at Camden. He was wounded in his side at Stono and had a rib broken. He was at the siege of Savannah. He was made a prisoner at the capture of Charleston where he was wounded in the haunch. He escaped from prison. He had an old wife. He was from Lancaster District when he applied 18 Nov. 1824. He was paid as late as 1831. He was literate.

Wood, William. S.C. —. He enlisted in 1782 for three years in the Continental Line under Col. Charles Cotesworth Pinckney. He served ten months and sought his pay 29 July 1819 from Sumter District. He was illiterate. His claim was rejected.

Wood, William. Va. Pilot. He served in the state navy. He received Virginia bounty land warrants #8433, 8434, 8435, and 1841 for 2,666 1/3 acres on 22 Mar. 1837. His heirs sought scrip from Congress on 17 Feb. 1838.

Woodall, Joseph. S.C. Ens. He served under Capt. John Lindsay, Col. Beard, Lt. Thomas Lindsey, and Col. Lyles. He was on the Florida Expedition. Frederick Gray was a fellow soldier. He applied 27 Nov. 1812 from Newberry District.

Woodberry, John. S.C. —. His annuity was £45 in 1787.

Woodberry, Samuel. Mass. Marine. He served under Caleb Dodge in the militia. He was wounded at Lexington 19 Apr. 1775. A musket ball broke the bone of his right arm, and he lost the use of it. He was pensioned at half-pay from Apr. 1775 on 4 Oct. 1777. He was 68 years old in 1791.

Woodbury, Samuel. Mass. Marine. He was on the list of unpaid pensioners by Benjamin Lincoln in 1790. He was on the 1813 pension list.

Woodcock, Samuel. Conn. Sgt. He served in the 2nd Conn. Regiment. He was worn out by long sickness. He was pensioned 13 Dec. 1782. He was on the 1813 pension list. He died 22 Oct. 1833 in Litchfield Co., Conn.

Woodcock, Samuel. Mass. —. He enlisted in 1775 under Capt. Knapp and Col. Reed for eight months. He next served a year under Capt. Joseph Allen Wright and Col. Philip B. Bradley. He returned to Conn. after the taking of Cornwallis and was discharged 31 Dec. 1782. Congress rejected his claim for bounty land 25 Jan. 1832. He also appeared as Samuel Woodstock.

Woodford, William. Va. Brig. Gen. His widow, Mary Woodford, was on the pension roll of 1785.

Woodhull, Nathaniel. N.Y. Brig. Gen. He died of wounds 20 Sep. 1776. His widow, Ruth Woodhull, received his half-pay pension.

Woodman, Ephraim. Me. —. He died 23 Mar. 1828. His widow was Elizabeth Woodman from Buxton. She was paid $50 under the resolve of 1836.

Woodmancy, Joseph. Conn. Pvt. He served in the 1st Company in the 8th Regiment of militia. In opposing the British troops who landed at New London, he was wounded in the shoulder on 6 Sep. 1781 at Fort Griswold by a musket ball which took out his right eye, passed through his cheek and right shoulder, and came out his back. He served under Capt. William Latham. He resided at Groton, Conn. and was 34 years old when he was pensioned 26 Sep. 1788. He was on the 1813 pension list. He died in 1813. He also appeared as Joseph Woodmansee.

Woodruff, Isaac. Pa. —. His widow, Elizabeth Woodruff, was awarded a $40 gratuity and a $40 annuity in Northumberland Co., Pa. 7 Mar. 1829. She died 5 Sep. 1831.

Woodruff, William. Conn. Corp. He served in the 5th Regiment. He was wounded at the battle of Monmouth in 1778 and was ruptured while on special command in launching boats in 1781. He resided in Bristol, Conn. in 1792. He transferred from Vermont. He was on the 1813 pension list. He died 1 May 1813.

Woods, —. Pa. —. His widow, Sarah Woods, was awarded a $40 gratuity and a $40 annuity in Allegheny County 1 Apr. 1836.

Woods, Benjamin. —. —. There was no evidence of his service except his own statements. Congress denied him a pension 25 Apr. 1850.

Woods, Cornelius. N.J. —. He served under Capt. Archibald Shaw in the 2nd Jersey Regiment from 8 Nov. 1775 to 15 Dec. 1776. He applied in Rowan County, N.C. 20 Aug. 1818.

Woods, David. Mass. Sgt. He served under Col. Jonathan Holman and Capt. Daniel Warren. He was disabled by a gun shot wound in his right thigh which contracted the nerves. He was 36 years old in 1790.

Woods, Henry. Pa. —. He was awarded a $40 gratuity and a $40 annuity in Beaver Co., Pa. 1 Mar. 1832. He died 18 July 1842.

Woods, Hugh. —. —. Congress denied his widow a pension 29 Jan. 1850.

Woods, John. Mass. —. He served in the 6th Regiment and was paid $20.

Woods, John. Pa. Sgt. He served in the 1st Regiment and was pensioned from 21 Nov. 1782 in Cumberland County.

Woods, John. Pa. —. He applied in Allegheny County. He was wounded and disabled in the service. He had settled and made improvements on land in Pittsburgh. He was granted lots 224, 219, 198, 199, 218, 217, 200, 201, 216, 215, 202, 203, 214, 213, 204, 205, 206, 207, 212, 211, and 208. The patent was to be issued to him for no costs by statute of 20 Mar. 1810.

Woods, Samuel. Mass. Sgt. He served in the 1st Regiment under Capt. Christopher Marshall and Col. Joseph Vose. He was disabled by being infirm. He lived in Boston, Mass. in 1786 and was 46 years old.

Woods, Thomas. S.C. —. He was born in Williamsburg, S.C. When he was 12, his father moved the family to the back country. He volunteered in 1776 and served 42 months. He was under Andrew Williamson against the Cherokee. He applied from Dallas Co., Ala. 20 Apr. 1831. His application was rejected.

Woodside, John. Pa. Capt. He served as lieutenant in the Pennsylvania Line and was returned supernumerary. On 15 Apr. 1780 he was captain-lieutenant of the 1st Company of the artillery battalion of the militia. His administrator, John D. Woodside, sought his commutation. Congress rejected the claim 12 May 1836.

Woodsworth, Ziba. Conn. Pvt. He was on the 1791 pension roll. He was on the 1813 pension list of Vermont. He died 27 Nov. 1826 in Washington Co., Vt.

Woodson, Frederick. Va. Lt. & Adjt. His executor, Charles Woodson, received his commutation of full-pay for five years in lieu of half-pay for life as a lieutenant and adjutant of infantry in the Virginia Line with no interest on 21 Feb. 1826.

Woodson, Tarleton. Va. Maj. He entered the service in 1775 and was made a prisoner of the enemy 22 Aug. 1777. He was promoted to major in Col. Hazen's Regiment. He became supernumerary. He was at Norfolk, Trenton, Yorktown, and Trenton. His heir, Charles Woodson, received his commutation 17 Feb. 1838. Congress approved his son's claim 21 Feb. 1846. Congress granted further relief 24 Jan. 1901.

Woodward, Benjamin. Mass. —. He served in the 10th Regiment and was paid $20.

Woodward, Isaac. Mass. —. He served in the 6th Regiment and was from Swansey. He was paid $20.

Woodward, John. —. —. He married 5 May 1784 and died in Mar. 1839. Congress rejected a pension for his widow, Sarah Woodward, on 17 May 1842 because she was not a widow at the passage of the act.

Woodward, John. Mass. Pvt. He served in the 2nd Regiment and was from Northfield. He was paid $50.

Woodward, Joshua. —. —. He was killed in 1778 by a party of British, Indians, and Tories while he and fourteen others were trying to take wheat from a barn of a Tory residing on Lake Champlain. He served under Capt. Sawyer. His son, Amos Woodward, was in the War of 1812 and was wounded by a rifle ball in his thigh at Fort Erie under Gen. Brown in 1813. His only surviving son, Joshua Woodward, sought relief, but Congress refused his claim on 9 May 1850.

Woodward, [?Thomas]. S.C. —. His widow was Elizabeth Woodward. There were five children in 1791.

Woodward, William. Mass. —. He served in Hazen's Regiment and was paid $20.

Woodworth, —. N.Y. —. His widow was granted support during the war.

Woodworth, Azel. Conn. Pvt. He was wounded in the neck by a musket ball at the storming of Fort Griswold in Groton on 6 Sep. 1781 by the British. He lived in Groton, Conn. in 1792 and 1794. He was in the militia. He was granted one-third of a pension 20 Apr. 1796. He was on the 1813 pension list. He died 18 Dec. 1816.

Woodworth, Ezekiel. —. —. He served three years as a soldier on Continental establishment from 10 Feb. 1777 to 10 Feb. 1780. He was pensioned in 1818 and stricken in 1820 from the rolls. He conveyed his 50 acres of land to his son who was above 21 years of age in 1824. He reserved the rest of his land for himself, his wife, and a minor son. He was the surety for an old friend who died in 1827 insolvent, and he had to pay his debts. In 1829 he was 71 and his wife was 70. He was restored to his pension 6 Apr. 1830.

Woodworth, Rozual. Mass. Pvt. He served in Capt. Levi Ely's Company in Col. Brown's Mass. Regiment. He was wounded in his left arm near the shoulder joint on 19 Oct. 1780 on the Mohawk River. He was paid $2 per month from 19 Oct. 1780 to 23 Mar. 1808 after which he was paid $5 per month. He lived in the East District of Rensselaerwyck Manor, Albany Co., N.Y. when he was pensioned 25 Jan. 1788. He also appeared as Roswell Woodworth. He was on the 1813 pension list. He was pensioned at the rate of $2 per month from 19 Oct. 1780 to 23 Mar. 1808 at which time his pension became $5 per month. He sought a back pension for $5 per month plus interest from 1780 to 1808. He lived in New Lebanon, N.Y. on 5 Mar. 1822 when Congress rejected his request. He also appeared as Roswell Woolworth.

Wool, Ellis. N.Y. Pvt. He served in the militia under Col. McClaghrie. He was captured 6 Oct. 1777 and died in confinement 14 Jan 1778. His widow, Mary Wool, received his back pay.

Wool, Isaiah. N.Y. Capt. He served in Col. Lamb's Regiment of Artillery. His heirs were awarded 750 acres of bounty land on 13 Apr. 1813. Catherine Telfair was a daughter. She sought his commutation 2 Feb. 1837. It was not granted since he resigned 21 Aug. 1780. She sought bounty land on 9 June 1838, but Congress rejected her claim and on 12 Feb. 1841.

Wooleber, Dederick. N.Y. Pvt. He served under Col. Peter Bellinger. He died in the service, and a pension was paid to his children, Mary Wooleber and Nicholas Wooleber, from 6 Aug. 1781.

Woolery, Henry. Pa. —. He was awarded a $40 gratuity in Northampton County on 19 Mar. 1816. He was awarded a $40 gratuity and a $40 annuity 27 Mar. 1819. He also appeared as Henry Wollery.

Woolerod, Nicholas. N.Y. Pvt. He served under Col. Samuel Clyde and was slain 18 July 1781. His widow, Mary Woolerod, received a half-pay pension..

Woolley, Jonathan. N.H. Pvt. He was from Thomlinson, Vt. in 1787. He entered the service in 1777 in Capt. William Ellis' Company in Col. Scammel's Regiment. He was wounded in battle on 7 Oct. 1777 with General Burgoyne near Saratoga. He was on the pension list of Pennsylvania until 1792 when he was transferred to Vermont. He was on the 1813 pension list of Vermont. He would appear to be the Jonathan Woolley whose daughter, Phoebe M. Palmenter, stated that her father served under Capt. Capron in the Vermont Volunteers. If so, his widow, Anna Woolley, died *ca.* 1858. Phoebe's husband, Russell Parmenter, died in 1890. Congress granted her a pension 26 May 1896.

Woolridge, George. Va. —. His wife, Barbara Woolridge, was granted £20 relief in Rockingham Co., Va. on 23 Aug. 1779.

Wooster, David. Conn. Maj. Gen. He was mortally wounded at the invasion of Danbury by Tryon's forces 27 Apr. 1777 and died 2 May 1777. His seven years' half-pay of $5,250 was paid to his heirs. His widow was Mary Wooster.

Wootan, John. N.C. —. He was in the militia in Col. Benjamin Seawell's Regiment in 1780 and was wounded in the shoulder at Gates' defeat. He applied in 1796 and was late of Franklin Co.

Worden, Samuel. N.J. Sgt. He enlisted in the 3rd N.J. Regiment in Capt. Cox's Company 20 Feb. 1777 and died in the service in Oct. 1779. He married Elizabeth Young about 1765. His widow, Elizabeth Worden, sought his half-pay in Morris County 8 July 1790. They had seven children, five of whom were living.

Worley, Caleb. Pa. Lt. He lived in Fayette County. He was on the 1813 pension list.

Wormsley, James. —. —. He enlisted for six months but after five months was discharged. He was under Lt. Johnson and Col. Christopher Green. He received pay for the six months. Congress granted him a pension 28 Feb. 1854. He was 83 years old.

Worrell, Mark Bingley. Pa. Pvt. He was in Philadelphia County on 16 Nov. 1785. He served in the 11th Pa. Regiment. He lost his right leg at Germantown on 4 Oct. 1777.

Worrell, Nicholas. N.J. —. He served five months in the militia and five months in the state troops under Capt. Schank. He was upwards of 70 years old and was disabled with rheumatism. He applied 27 Dec. 1819 in Monmouth County.

Worstler, —. Pa. —. His widow, Mary Worstler, was awarded a $40 gratuity and a $40 annuity in Montgomery County 27 Mar. 1837.

Worthen, Isaac. —. —. He was pensioned and died 1 Mar. 1841. His widow was Judith Worthen. She received a pension for three days only. Nathan Worthen, in behalf of the heirs, sought what she should have received for five years if her application had been processed in a timely manner. Congress granted the same 2 Feb. 1855.

Worthington, William. Conn. Col. He was on the 1795 pension list. He died in 1810.

Wren, Joseph. Pa. —. He served in the Pa. Line and was wounded. He was awarded a $40 gratuity and a $40 annuity in York County on 2 Apr. 1811.

Wren, Theodoric. S.C. —. He died in the service. His brother and administrator was to be paid 19 Jan. 1791.

Wright, —. —. —. His widow, Ann O. Wright, had her petition for a pension rejected by Congress on 4 May 1846.

Wright, —. Ga. —. His widow, Elizabeth Wright, was granted three rations per day for the support of her family 22 July 1782.

Wright, —. Ga. —. Elizabeth Wright was granted four daily rations on 10 Sep. 1782.

Wright, —. Va. —. His wife, Alice Wright, was granted £15 support in Caroline Co., Va. on 11 Mar. 1779.

Wright, —. Va. —. His father, Joseph Wright, was granted £20 support in Caroline County 11 Mar. 1779. The veteran had two brothers in Continental service.

Wright, Alexander. Pa. —. He was awarded a $40 gratuity in Mercer Co., Pa. 11 Feb. 1834.

Wright, Andrew. —. —. He served three months as a driver of a public wagon, two months in 1780, and 3 months in the summer of 1781. His first service was not qualifying. He married in Nelson Co., Va. 11 Mar. 1777. His daughter Sarah S. Wright was born 25 Feb. 1779 and his daughter Jennie Wright was born 9 Jan. 1780. His son, Benjamin Wright, had a Bible with the family register. His widow, Lucy Wright, stated she married in Feb. 1780. There was no way of reconciling the conflict. One possible interpretation was she was his second wife or it raised the presumption of her legal marriage. Congress denied her a pension 29 Feb. 1848.

Wright, Edward. Md. Lt. He was pensioned in Kent County on 9 Feb. 1812 at the rate of half-pay of a lieutenant.

Wright, Henderson. Pa. Pvt. He was in Philadelphia County on 13 Feb. 1786. He was in the 9th Pa. Regiment and was wounded in his leg in a skirmish with the British on 27 Nov. 1777 near White Marsh. He was 27 years old. Jacob Irwin, Henry Crone, and Jacob Beetam proved that his disability was not received in the service but in Ireland before he came to America. He was not in the skirmish in which he claimed to have been.

Wright, Isaiah. Conn. Pvt. He served in Capt. Holmes' Company in the Conn. Regiment under Col. Durkee. He was wounded while driving oxen near Bethlehem, Pa. in Nov. 1777. He was 40 years old in 1788. He lived in Hilldale, Columbia Co., N.Y. on 11 May 1789. He was on the 1813 pension list.

Wright, Jacob. N.Y. Pvt. He served in Capt. Copman's Company under Col. Clyde. He was wounded in his left arm by a musket ball at Oriskany on 6 Aug. 1777. He lived in Montgomery Co., N.Y. 15 June 1789. He died in 1811. He was on the 1813 pension list.

Wright, Jesse. Md. Pvt. He was pensioned at the rate of half-pay of a private 2 Jan. 1813.

Wright, John. Mass. —. He was paid $20.

Wright, John. Pa. Sgt. He served in Col. Lee's Dragoons. He was wounded in the knee in a skirmish with the enemy. He lived in Mifflin Co., Pa. in 1794. He enlisted 7 Apr. 1778 for the war.

Wright, John. Pa. Sgt. He applied 24 Sep. 1787 from Philadelphia County.. He served in the 11th Pa. Regiment under Col. James Moore. He was disabled by hardships endured while in the service and contracted violent rheumatism. He was 39 years old. He was on the 1813 pension list. He died 26 Aug. 1825 in Mercer County.

Wright, John. Pa. Sgt. He applied from Philadelphia County. He was granted half a pension 20 Apr. 1796.

Wright, John. Va. —. He was in Bedford County on 27 June 1794. He was in the militia under Col. Charles Lynch. He was dangerously wounded at the battle of Guilford by a musket ball which fractured the bones of his head and occasioned an exfoliation. He had a wife and five small children. He received £15 relief and a pension of £12 per annum on 5 Dec. 1793.

Wright, John G. N.Y. Surgeon's Mate. He served in the general hospital of the Northern Department. He died in Westchester County. His administratrix and administrator, Charity Wright and Anthony Bartow, in trust for the said Charity Wright for her natural life and for the heirs, received his 500 acres of bounty land 19 June 1812.

Wright, Josiah. Mass. Pvt. He served in the 9th Regiment under Col. Henry Jackson and Capt. Joseph Fox. He was from Billerica. He lost the use of his right eye and was otherwise debilitated. He was pensioned 27 Sep. 1786. He resided in Norfolk Co., Mass. He was on the 1813 pension list.

Wright, Lewis. Pa. —. He was awarded a $40 annuity in Greene County 28 Jan. 1836. He was 87 years old in 1840. He died 24 Nov. 1845.

Wright, Nahum. Mass. Sgt. He served under Col. Brewer. He had an ulcerous sore in his right leg due to the effects of a wound from a ball in his thigh on 17 June 1775 at Bunker Hill. He lived in Medfield, Mass. in 1795. He was in the militia. He was appointed 6 Nov. 1776 and resigned 28 Oct. 1777. He was granted one-eighth of a pension 20 Apr. 1796. He was on the 1813 pension list.

Wright, Robert. Pa. —. He served under Capt. Thomas Brewer, Col. Thomas McKean, and Gen. Cadwalder in the 4th Battalion of the Philadelphia Brigade in 1776. He was awarded a $40 gratuity 24 Mar. 1828, 23 Mar. 1829, 2 Apr. 1831, 24 Mar. 1832, and 20 Feb. 1833 in Cumberland Co., Pa. He received a $40 annuity and a $40 gratuity 18 Feb. 1834. He died 6 Dec. 1845.

Wright, Samuel T. Md. Capt. His widow, Ann Wright, was pensioned at the rate of half-pay of a captain 30 Jan. 1837.

Wright, Thomas. Mass. —. He served in the 1st Regiment and was paid $20.

Wright, Thomas. Mass. —. He served in the 8th Regiment and was paid $20.

Wright, Uriah. Mass. —. He served in the 8th Regiment and was from Beverly. He was paid $50.

Wright, William. —. —. He served as commissary under Gen. Greene for not less than twelve months in 1782. He died 14 Aug. 1824. His widow, Elizabeth Wright, sought a pension. Congress denied her request 9 May 1850 because the evidence was too slight to warrant any action.

Wunder, —. Pa. —. His widow, Ann Wunder of Philadelphia County, received a $40 gratuity and a $40 annuity 16 June 1836. She died 17 Oct. 1840.

Wyatt, Cary. Va. Lt. His commutation was made 16 June 1791.

Write, David. Mass. —. He served in the 2nd Regiment and was paid $20.

Wyatt, Pittman. Va. Capt. He was wounded at Camden in Apr. 1781. He died 17 June 1801. He was from King and Queen County. The court in that county disallowed him a pension 13 May 1784.

Wyatt, Speircy. —. —. He was a pensioner for fifteen months of service. Congress found that he was not entitled to a pension for any more time of service on 19 Jan. 1836.

Wyatt, Thomas. Va. —. He served in the Halifax County militia and was disabled at Guilford. He was pensioned for two years. It had expired on the 1785 pension roll.

Wycall, Adam. Md. Pvt. His widow, Ann Martin, was pensioned at the rate of half-pay of a private in Prince George's County in 1833. He also appeared as Adam Wykall.

Wyley, Henry. S.C. —. His widow was Jane Wyley in 1786. There was one child in 1791.

Wyley, Robert. Mass. Ens. He served in the 8th Regiment. He was wounded in the head at the battle of Bemis Heights on 19 Sep. 1777. He resided in Dalton, Mass. in 1792. He was appointed 1 Jan. 1777 and left the service 14 Aug. 1778.

Wyley, Thomas. S.C. Pvt./Drummer. He served under Capt. Andrew Hamilton, Capt. Dawson, Capt. Liddle, and Gen. Pickens. He was in the Florida Expedition and at Eutaw. He was 70 years old and had a wife, two young daughters, and a son. He applied 3 Nov. 1820. He was rejected. He was from Abbeville District in 1826.

Wylie, Francis. S.C. —. He served under Capt. John Nixon in a company of volunteer militia. He was at the defeat of the Indians and Tories at Lyndie's Fort. He was also in the Snow Campaign, Mobley's Meeting House, Hook's defeat, Rocky Mount, Hanging Rock, Fish Dam Ford on Broad River, Blackstocks on Tyger River, Col. Thompson's, and Wright's Bluff. He was 77 and had an aged wife. His children were all grown and had left him save one–a son with falling fits. He was from Chester District 25 Nov. 1826. His service was corroborated by John Cooper, William McGerrity, Joseph Gaston, Joseph Morrow, and William Knox. He was paid as late as 1834.

Wylie, William. S.C. —. He was paid $128 on 18 Dec. 1818 for property lost in the war.

Wyman, Daniel. —. —. He served about 15 months. He was pensioned under the act of 1818 and was stricken from the rolls in 1820. Congress restored his pension 2 Mar. 1832.

Wyman, Dean. Mass. —. He served in the 15th Regiment and was from Fairfield. He was paid $20.

Wyman, Henry. Me. —. He was from Madison. He was paid $50 under the resolve of 1836.

Wyman, Reuben. Me. —. He was from Fairfield. He was paid $50 under the resolve of 1836.

Wyman, Seth. N.H. Pvt. He served under Col. James Frye. He was wounded by a musket ball which passed through his thigh on 17 June 1775 at Bunker Hill. He lived in Goffstown, N.H. in 1794. He was granted one-fourth of a pension 20 Apr. 1796. He was on the 1813 pension list. He died 22 June 1825.

Wyndham, —. Md. Sgt. His widow, Sarah Wyndham, was pensioned at the rate of half-pay of a sergeant in Annapolis 22 Feb. 1822. She died 5 Aug. 1841. Her arrearage of $20.83 was paid to Andrew Slicer 2 Mar. 1842.

Wynkoop, Jacobus. N.Y. —. His certificates of 18 Mar. 1777 for £480.10, 7 May 1778 for £200, and 1 Sep. 1779 for £582.3.6 were to be audited and liquidated on 14 Feb. 1783.

Yancey, Leighton. Va. Lt. He served until the close of the war. He was in the 1ˢᵗ Regiment of Light Dragoons under Col. Theodore Bland and received bounty land as a lieutenant. He had received his five years' full pay as a lieutenant. He had become entitled to the rank of captain but the treaty of peace occurred before he received his commission. His application for commutation at the rank of captain, therefore, was rejected 11 Jan. 1838.

Yancy, John. —. Pvt. He served not less than three years as a private and quartermaster. There was some doubt that he was the man of the name who was the quartermaster. He married in Dec. 1777. His widow, Elizabeth Yancy, applied under the act of 1836 but was suspended because of the question of her husband's service as a quartermaster. She died 19 Dec. 1848. Congress credited him with that service and approved $720 to be paid to her daughters, Jane C. Smith and Mary Franklin, on 25 May 1860.

Yarborough, —. S.C. —. His widow, Nancy Yarborough, was on the roll in 1791.

Yard, Isaiah. N.J. Lt. He was pensioned for his militia duty of seven years and nine months 15 Mar. 1832 at the rate of $60 per annum. He served under Capt. Clunn in the Artillery.

Yardley, John. Va. Pvt. He was on the 1813 pension list.

Yaters, John. N.J. Sgt. He served in John Cummings' Company in the 2ⁿᵈ N.J. Regiment and was killed by the refugees at Bergen on 29/30 Mar. 1782. His widow, Margaret Yaters, sought his half-pay in Essex County 24 June 1784.

Yates, George. Va. Surgeon's Mate. He served to the end of 1782. He was allowed five years' full pay 11 May 1838. Congress ruled that his heirs had no further claim 18 Jan. 1859 because he was a regimental surgeon and not a hospital mate. One of the heirs was Reuben Zimmerman.

Yates, Thomas. Md. Pvt. He was pensioned in Anne Arundel County in 1788. He was on the 1813 pension list.

Yates, William. —. Dept. Q.M Gen. He was employed in military service from 11 Apr. 1777 to 9 June 1781. His grandson-in-law, Frederick Fishback who had married his grand-daughter, Sophia, sought his commutation money. Since he did not serve to the end of the war, Congress rejected the claim 1 Aug. 1850.

Yates, William. Vt. Pvt. He served under Col. Butler. He was disabled by a ventral rupture occasioned by a piece of timber on which account he was discharged. He resided in Bennington, Vt. in 1792. He enlisted 5 May 1777 and was discharged 23 Dec. 1781.

Yeager, George. Pa. —. He was awarded a $40 gratuity and a $40 annuity in Dauphin County 1 Apr. 1836. He was 76 years old in 1840. He died 30 Sep. 1848. Margaret Yeager, widow of George Yeager, received a $40 annuity 4 May 1855.

Yeager, John. Va. Pvt. He was in Augusta County in June 1786. He was wounded in his left arm at the battle of Stillwater on 19 Sep. 1777 and lost that limb. He was in the 7ᵗʰ Va. Regiment. He was 36 years old. He was continued on the pension list on 30 Oct. 1786 at the rate of £15 per annum. He later lived in Wythe County. He was on the 1813 pension list. He died 3 Jan. 1831.

Yeager, Joshua. Va. Pvt. He served in the 8ᵗʰ Virginia Regiment and was disabled 31 May 1779.

Yearks, William. N.Y. —. He was pensioned.

Yeaton, Hopley. —. —. His plea for a federal gratuity was rejected 1 Feb. 1811. He had served as a naval officer in command of a revenue cutter in the Revolution.

Yeger, Christian. Pa. —. He was awarded a $40 gratuity and a $40 annuity in Lebanon County on 7 Mar. 1821.

Yeisly, Michael. Pa. —. He was awarded a $40 gratuity and a $40 annuity in Union County on 28 Feb. 1822.

Yentzer, John. Pa. —.The legal representatives of his widow, Mary Yentzer, received her benefits due at the time of her death in Lancaster County 3 Mar. 1837.

Yeoman, John. N.H. —. He enlisted in Mar. 1776 for five years and served under Capt. Tazewell, Col. Lilly, and Gen. Poor. He was badly wounded at Saratoga and was discharged in 1777. He was from Cabarrus County when he applied in Rowan County, N.C. 21 Aug. 1819.

Yeomans, —. N.J. —. Sarah Yeomans received a half-pay pension 16 July 1784.

Yerich, Simon. Pa. —. He was awarded a $40 gratuity in Union Co., Pa. 22 Apr. 1829.

Yerkis, Herman. Mass. —. He was in the artillery. He was paid $20 and was from Fishkill.

Yeulin, William. Me. —. He was from Skowhegan. He was paid $50 under the resolve of 1836.

Yoe, James. N.C. —. He applied in Anson County in 1806. He served under Col. Thomas Wade and was wounded by a sword in his head at Betty's Bridge on Drowning Creek. One of his brows was cut from his skull. He was left forgetful and somewhat simple. He understood that Thomas Chales, Humphrey Rogers, and James Redfearn who were wounded and disabled at the same time were receiving pensions. Humphrey Rogers and William Williams served with him. He was awarded an annuity of £10.

Yoe, Stephen. Md. Pvt. He served in the 2nd Md. Regiment. He was pensioned in Queen Anne's County on 11 Mar. 1789. He was on the 1813 pension list. He died in 1823.

Yorden, John. N.Y. Pvt. He served in Samuel Clyde's N.Y. Regiment. He was disabled on 25 Oct. 1781 with a wound in his left thigh received at Johnstown. He was pensioned 19 Oct. 1786. He lived in Montgomery County. He also appeared as John Yadan, John Yourdan, and John Jordan. He was on the 1813 pension list.

Yorden, Nicholas. N.Y. Pvt. He served in the militia under Col. Samuel Clyde in Capt. Adam Lyb's Company. He was wounded in his left hand at Trolach on 7 July 1781. He was pensioned 19 Oct. 1786. He lived in Montgomery Co., N.Y. in 1789 and later in Oswego County. He also appeared as Nicholas Yadan and Nicholas Jordan. He was on the 1813 pension list.

York, Ruggles. Mass. —. He served in the 1st Regiment. He was paid $20.

York, William. —. —. He commanded a partisan troop of horse at different times for more than a year in North and South Carolina. He was in several battles and was severely wounded. Congress ruled that his service was not under the authority of a state but as domestic police and rejected him for a pension 22 June 1840.

York, William. N.C. Capt. He served in a troop of horse from 1777 to the fall of 1781. He received a federal pension and died 14 July 1837. His widow, Ailsey York, died 7 July 1839. His son Joseph C. [or O.] York for himself and his living siblings, Margaret Lacy a widow, Letty Horse, Elizabeth Philpot a widow, and Deliah Philpot a widow, sought relief and were recommended for same 8 Aug. 1856. The bill was not passed by Congress until 23 Mar. 1860.

Yorke, —. —. —. Congress rejected the claim of his widow, Abigail Yorke, because there was no evidence on file on 4 Apr. 1840.

Yorke, Samuel. —. Lt. He served aboard the armed sloop *Sachem*. He was taken prisoner in 1777 and carried to New York. He was greatly debilitated and resigned his commission. Since he did not claim his benefits before 11 Dec. 1788, he forfeited same.

Yorke, Sawney. —. —. He was a pensioner and was last paid 4 Sep. 1824. He shipped on a vessel at Portland for Havanna on 18 Sep. 1825 but never returned. He reportedly died in Aug. 1826 but no positive proof was presented. His only child, Huldah Yorke, was the wife of Charles Plato. Congress granted her $184.

Yorkis, Hermon. Mass. —. He served in the Artillery and was from Fishkill. He was paid $20.

Yorkshimer, Adam. Pa. —. He was awarded a $40 gratuity and a $40 annuity in Columbia Co., Pa. 22 Dec. 1834.

Yorrence, Thomas. —. Pvt. He served under Col. Moseley. He was wounded by a musket ball which entered about three inches above the arms and lodged in his body. He resided in Vt. in 1792.

Yost, John. Pa. —. He was from Berks County. He also appeared as John Youse. He was pensioned 8 Dec. 1817.

Youman, Jonas. N.Y. —. He served under Col. Wysenefels in 1780 and 1781. He was pensioned in 1818 but dropped in 1831 because the unit was not considered to be Continental. Congress granted him a pension 19 Mar. 1832.

Youndt, Daniel. Pa. —. He was awarded a $40 gratuity and a $40 annuity in Armstrong Co., Pa. 14 Apr. 1834.

Young, —. Pa. —. His widow, Alice Young, was awarded a $40 gratuity and a $40 annuity in Philadelphia Co., Pa. 16 Feb. 1835.

Young, —. Pa. —. His widow, Elizabeth Young, was awarded a $40 gratuity and a $40 annuity in Berks Co., Pa. 15 Apr. 1835.

Young, —. Pa. —. His widow, Franey Young, was awarded a $40 gratuity and a $40 annuity in York Co., Pa. 11 June 1832. She died 31 May 1844.

Young, —. Mass. —. His widow, Mary Young, was paid $50.

Young, Andrew. Pa. —. He was awarded a $40 gratuity and a $40 annuity in Adams Co., Pa. 10 Apr. 1828.

Young, Andrew. S.C. Sgt. He was wounded at Ninety Six in 1775. He was from Pendleton District in 1793. He was paid the arrearage of his pension of $100 on 20 Dec. 1810. He was granted his arrearage again on 3 Dec. 1819. On 21 Dec. 1821 he was paid his arrearage of $221.32. He was on the roll as late as 1833.

Young, Benjamin. Md. Sgt. He was pensioned at the rate of half-pay of a sergeant in Baltimore County 27 Jan. 1816.

Young, Christian. Pa. —. His widow, Mary Young, was awarded a $40 gratuity and a $40 annuity in Lebanon County 1 Apr. 1823. She died 2 Apr. 1832.

Young, Felix. Pa. —. He marched to Lancaster guarding prisoners in 1781. He was from Cumberland County.

Young, Godfried. N.Y. Corp. He served in Capt. Copeman's Company under Col. Clyde. He was wounded in his private parts at Oriskany on 6 Aug. 1777. He was pensioned 22 Sep. 1786. He lived in Montgomery Co., N.Y. 15 June 1789 and later in Herkimer County. He also appeared as Godfrie Young and Gotfield Young. He was on the 1813 pension list. He died 31 July 1830.

Young, Guy. N.Y. Capt. He entered the service as a lieutenant and was promoted. He had already received his commutation so Congress rejected the claim from his daughter, Catharine Burnham, for same on 21 Jan. 1836.

Young, Henry. Pa. —. He was awarded a $40 gratuity and 200 acres of donation land on 12 Mar. 1813. He was from Washington Co., Md.

Young, Henry. Pa. —. He was awarded a $40 gratuity and a $40 annuity in Philadelphia, Pa. 18 Feb. 1834. He was 86 years old in 1840. He died 29 Oct. 1842.

Young, Hiat. Mass. —. He served in the 4th Regiment and was paid $20.

Young, James. S.C. —. He served four years in the militia. He was under Capt. Joseph Vince. He was shot nearly through his body when he was out on a scouting party on the west side of Savannah River. He had a wife and three small children. A daughter had been an idiot since infancy. He was from Barnwell District and was pensioned 9 Dec. 1825. He was paid as late as 1834.

Young, John. S.C. Sgt. He was wounded at Fort Moultrie on 28 June 1776. He was paid his annuity 16 Apr. 1785.

Young, Joseph. Mass. —. He served in the 10th Regiment. He was from Wells and was paid $20.

Young, Michael. Pa. —. He was awarded a $40 gratuity and a $40 annuity in Lancaster Co., Pa. 9 Feb. 1824.

Young, Ralph. —. —. He sought an increase in his pension from $20 per annum but offered no evidence. Congress rejected his claim 25 Feb. 1846.

Young, Robert. Pa. —. He applied 18 Mar. 1813. He had a wife. He died 19 Dec. 1824.

Young, Thomas. Pa. —. He was on the 1789 pension list.

Young, Thomas. Pa. —. He was awarded a $40 gratuity and a $40 annuity in Greene Co., Pa. 4 May 1832.

Young, Thomas. Va. Capt. He served in a state regiment under Col. Joseph Crockett and became supernumerary. He was due half-pay for life. He died 21 Apr. 1837. His half-pay amounted to $1,520.

Young, William. N.C. & S.C. —. He left North Carolina in June 1780 under Col. Sewell and landed on the Pee Dee River near Cheraw. He was there when Gen. Gates was defeated at Camden. Col. Murphy took several prisoners a few days before, and Col. Sewell took charge of them and conducted them to North Carolina. He marched from N.C. to the Waxsaw settlement to halt Cornwallis. He was under Gen. Greene at Guilford. He was under Col. Owens when he was discharged at Wilmington, N.C. in Nov. 1781. He also served under Col. Lemuel Benton. He applied in South Carolina when he was 68 years old. He had fallen on the ice the previous winter and had hurt his hip and knee. John Powell and Henry Young stated they had seen him in the service. He was from Darlington District and was pensioned 23 Nov. 1829. He was paid as late as 1831.

Young, William. Pa. Lt. He served in the Flying Camp and was held a prisoner for two years. He was from Northampton County.

Youngblood, —. S.C. —. One Mary Youngblood was on the roll in 1791. She was from Winton.

Youngblood, David. N.Y. Pvt. He served in the militia under John Van Renssalear and Lewis Van Woort. He was wounded in the shoulder and back at Bennington on 16 Aug. 1777. He lived in Montgomery Co., N.Y. 2 June 1789. He was on the 1791 pension roll. He died in Washington County in 1797.

Youngblood, Joseph. S.C. Pvt. He was pensioned from 1825 to 1834. He died 20 Feb. 1836 leaving a widow and four small children. His widow was Mary Youngblood who sought the arrearage of his pension. Her request was denied.

Younger, Joshua. Va. Pvt. He served in the 8th Virginia Regiment and was disabled. He was being pensioned 14 Aug. 1787. He was continued on the pension list at the rate of £6 per annum on 15 Aug. 1787.

Younglove, John. N.Y. Maj. He served in Lewis Van Vort's N.Y. Regiment of militia. He was pensioned 30 July 1781. He was on the 1813 pension list. He died in Washington County on 3 Feb. 1821.

Younger, Joshua. Va. Pvt. He was alive 14 Aug. 1787. He was in the 12th Va. Regiment under J. Wood. He was wounded in the thigh at Short Hills, N.J. in 1777. He was ruptured on his left side and put on the pension list in 1779. He was 34 years old. He was on the 1813 pension list.

Youngman, George. Pa. —. He was granted a $40 gratuity in Union County 28 Mar. 1836.

Youngs, John. N.J. Pvt. He served in the 2nd Regiment and suffered from rheumatism and old age. He was 59 years old and was from Amwell. He was on the 1791 pension roll at the rate of $36 per annum.

Youngs, Joseph. —. —. His son, Samuel Youngs, sought relief from Congress 30 Mar. 1826.

Youngs, Samuel. N.Y. —. He served under Col. Wysenfelt. He was stricken from the pension roll because it was not know if Wysenfelt was on Continental establishment. Congress granted him a pension 18 Feb. 1832.

Youse, John. Pa. —. He enlisted in Northumberland County in 1775 under Capt. Louden and marched to Boston. He was at Plowed Hill and several battles and skirmishes on Long Island. He was at the taking of Burgoyne, the taking of the Hessians, Trenton, and Stoney Point. He was on the center guard at Paoli. He was also at Green Springs, Va. He was wounded in his left hip at Brunswick. He was also wounded in his left thigh at the block house on York Island. His last engagement was James Island in South Carolina. He was also on the expedition against the Indians at Genesee and Sauckee. Out of the twenty-five on a scouting party, he was one of the five survivors. He applied in Berks County. His widow, Dorothy Youse, was awarded a $40 gratuity and a $40 annuity in Berks Co., Pa. 14 Apr. 1834

Zahl, David. S.C. —. He served aboard the *South Carolina*. His administrator, Peter Oliver, was paid $1,100 or such part as would pay the interest due him, Thomas Short, Jacob Schon, and John Renney on the portage bill on 20 Dec. 1810.

Zegar, Caspar. Pa. —. He was awarded a $40 gratuity and a $40 annuity in York Co., Pa. 15 Apr. 1835. He died 16 May 1840.

Zell, William. Pa. —. He was awarded a $40 gratuity and a $40 annuity in Lancaster Co., Pa. 20 Mar. 1834.

Zeller, Michael. Pa. Pvt. He and George Huber served in Capt. Deckert's Company in the 5th Pa. Regiment and were taken prisoners at the surrender of Fort Washington. They were awarded 200 acres of donation land in Dauphin Co. 31 Mar. 1807.

Zerfoss, Henry. Pa. —. He was awarded a gratuity of $80 on 29 Mar. 1813. He was awarded a $40 gratuity and a $40 annuity in Armstrong County on 2 Apr. 1821. He also appeared as Henry Zerfas.

Zettlemier, Martin. Pa. He received a $40 gratuity and a $40 annuity in Berks County 15 Apr. 1835. He died 16 May 1845.

Ziegler, Michael. Pa. —. His widow, Mary Ziegler, was awarded a $40 gratuity and a $40 annuity in York Co., Pa. 8 Apr. 1833.

Zigler, Martin. Pa. —. He was awarded a $40 gratuity and a $40 annuity in Franklin Co., Pa. 27 Mar. 1824.

Zigler, Jacob. Pa. —. He was pensioned 22 Feb. 1823 in Lancaster County. He died 20 May 1835. He also appeared as Jacob Siegler.

Zumbro, Jacob. Pa. —. He received a $40 gratuity and a $40 annuity in Chester County 16 June 1836.

Appendix: Pennsylvania Pensioners with Unidentified War Service

The text of the laws of Pennsylvania granting pensions to individuals does not always differentiate between those who served in the Revolutionary War and subsequent conflicts such as the Indian Wars. This appendix contains the names of individuals mentioned in acts which do not indicate the specific conflict.

Acker, Martin. He received a $40 annuity in Berks County in Apr. 1846. He died 26 Dec. 1846.

Adams, —. His widow, Margaret Adams, received a $40 gratuity in Berks County 12 Apr. 1845.

Adams, John. His widow, Nancy Adams, received a $40 annuity in Blair County 27 Feb. 1851.

Agnew, Robert. He received a $40 gratuity and a $40 annuity in Allegheny County in Apr. 1840.

Alexander, John. He received a $40 annuity in Butler County 21 Apr. 1846.

Allison, David. He received a $40 gratuity and a $40 annuity in Washington County 13 Apr. 1838. He died 13 Apr. 1859.

Allum, Jacob. He received a $40 gratuity in Bucks County in 1840.

Alum, Philip. He received a $40 gratuity in Bucks County 11 Apr. 1844.

Ammon, Jacob. He received a $40 gratuity and a $40 annuity in Holmes Co., Ohio 18 Apr. 1843.

Anderson, —. His widow, Mary Anderson, received a $40 gratuity and a $40 annuity in Bradford County 13 Apr. 1838. She also lived in Allegheny County.

Anderson, —. His widow, Adah Anderson, received a $40 gratuity and a $40 annuity in 1838 in Armstrong County in 1838. Addy Anderson was 70 years in 1840.

Andrews, John. He received a $40 gratuity and a $40 annuity in Warren County 20 May 1839.

Archibald, Robert. He received a $40 gratuity and a $40 annuity in Holmes Co., Ohio 18 Apr. 1843. He later removed to Henry Co., Iowa.

Armstrong, —. His widow, Mary Armstrong, received a $40 gratuity and a $40 annuity in Fayette Co. in 1838.

Armstrong, James. He received a $40 gratuity and a $40 annuity in Washington County 16 Apr. 1838. He died 12 Sep. 1853.

Arner, Martin. He received a $40 gratuity and a $40 annuity in Luzerne County 8 Apr. 1840.

Amey, Henry. He received a $40 gratuity and a $40 annuity 11 Apr. 1844 in Philadelphia.

Artis, —. His widow, Chloe Artis, received a $40 gratuity and a $40 annuity in Fayette County 5 Apr. 1841. She died 24 Nov. 1842.

Artis, Isaac. He received a $40 gratuity and a $40 annuity in Fayette County 20 May 1839. He was 82 years old in 1840. He died 8 May 1841.

Auxer, —. His widow, Catharine Auxer, received a $40 gratuity and a $40 annuity in Apr. 1838 in Lancaster County.

Babel, Christopher. He received a $40 gratuity and a $40 annuity 18 Apr. 1843 in Washington County.

Baggs, William. He received a $40 gratuity and a $40 annuity in 1838 in Allegheny County. He died 10 Mar. 1848.

Bailey, Nathaniel. He received a $40 gratuity and a $40 annuity in 1839 in York County.

Baird, —. His widow, Margaret Baird, received a $40 annuity in Washington County 12 Apr. 1851. She died 5 Dec. 1851.

Baird, Thomas. He received a $40 gratuity and a $40 annuity 21 June 1839 in Erie County. He died

21 Apr. 1852.

Baker, —. His widow, Elizabeth Baker, received a $40 gratuity and a $40 annuity in Mercer County 14 Apr. 1838. She died 1 Nov. 1841.

Baker, Richard. He received a $40 gratuity and a $40 annuity in Perry County in 1840. He died 8 Apr. 1851.

Balding, —. His widow, Elizabeth Balding, received a $40 gratuity and a $40 annuity in Crawford County 2 July 1842.

Ball, James R. He received assistance in Columbia County 17 Mar. 1838. His name may have been James R. Bell.

Balliott, —. His widow, Barbara Balliott, received a $40 gratuity in Northumberland County 12 Apr. 1851.

Baltzer, —. His widow, Mary Baltzer, received a $40 gratuity and a $40 annuity in Washington Co., Md. 2 July 1842.

Barley, James. He received a $40 gratuity and a $40 annuity 20 May 1839. He resided in Rockbridge Co., Va.

Barnes, Samuel. He received a $40 gratuity and a $40 annuity in Philadelphia 8 Feb. 1841.

Barnet, —. His widow, Margaret Barnet, received a $40 gratuity and a $40 annuity 11 Apr. 1844 in Westmoreland County. She died 11 Oct. 1854.

Barnheart, —. His widow, Catharine Barnheart, received a $40 gratuity and a $40 annuity 2 July 1842. She died 13 Oct. 1845.

Barnwell, —. His widow, Jane Barnwell, received a $40 gratuity and a $40 annuity in Pittsburgh 18 Apr. 1843.

Barr, Thomas. He received a $40 annuity in Indiana County 27 Feb. 1851. He died 24 Feb. 1859.

Barth, Stephen. He received a $40 gratuity and a $40 annuity in Lancaster County 5 Apr. 1842. He died 25 Sep. 1845.

Bathurst, —. His widow, Rebecca Bathurst, received a $40 annuity in Center County in Apr. 1846.

Battin, —. His widow, Mary Battin, received a $40 gratuity and a $40 annuity in Philadelphia County in 1840.

Baugher, Peter. He received a $40 gratuity and a $40 annuity in Allegheny County 20 May 1839.

Bay, William V. He received a $40 gratuity in Lawrence County 8 May 1850.

Beatty, —. His widow, Nancy Beatty, received a $40 gratuity and a $40 annuity in Venango County 20 Mar. 1838.

Beatty, Ebenezer. He received a $40 annuity in Butler County 15 Mar. 1847. His widow, Jane Beatty, received a $40 annuity 10 Apr. 1849. She died 19 Feb. 1850.

Beaty, John. He received a $40 gratuity and a $40 annuity in Cumberland County in 1838.

Beaty, William. He received a $40 annuity 12 Apr. 1845. He was from Westmoreland County.

Behney, —. His widow, Elizabeth Behney, received a $40 gratuity and a $40 annuity in Lebanon County 20 May 1839.

Behny, —. His widow, Anna Maria Behny, received a $40 gratuity and a $40 annuity in Lebanon County 21 June 1839. Compare with the entry under Belmey.

Bell, —. His widow, Jane Bell, received a $40 gratuity and a $40 annuity in Columbia Co. 13 Apr. 1841.

Bell, John. He received assistance in Juniata County 27 Mar. 1837. He died 27 Jan. 1842.

Bellas, —. His widow, Martha Bellas, received a $40 annuity in Franklin County 3 Apr. 1851.

Belmey, —. Pa. —. His widow, Anna Maria Belmey, was granted relief in Lebanon County 20 May 1839. Compare with entry under Behny.

Bender, —. His widow, Christiana Bender, received a $40 gratuity and a $40 annuity 17 Mar. 1838 in Philadelphia.

Bender, —. His widow, Margaret Bender, received a $40 gratuity and a $40 annuity 17 Mar. 1838 in Philadelphia.

Benedick, —. His widow, Susannah Benedick, received a $40 gratuity and a $40 annuity in York Co. 5 Apr. 1842.

Bennett, —. His widow, Mary Bennett, received a $40 gratuity and a $40 annuity in Mercer County 20 May 1839. She died 28 Jan. 1851.

Bennett, —. His widow, Sarah Bennett, received a $40 gratuity and a $40 annuity in Bucks County 20 May 1839.

Bentley, John. He received a $40 gratuity and a $40 annuity in Mercer County 20 May 1839.

Bergetresser, —. His widow, Rosannah Bergetresser, received a $40 gratuity and a $40 annuity in Perry County 13 Apr. 1841. She died 25 Sep. 1845. She also appeared as Rosannah Bergstresser.

Bergmeyer, —. His widow, Christiana Bergmeyer, received a $40 gratuity and a $40 annuity in Philadelphia 11 Apr. 1844.

Biemensderfer,—. His widow, Elizabeth Biemensderfer, received a $40 gratuity and a $40 annuity in 1838 in Lancaster County.

Bigony, —. His widow, Ann Bigony, received a $40 gratuity and a $40 annuity 17 Mar. 1838 in Philadelphia. She was 82 years of age in 1840.

Bills, Alanson. He received a $40 gratuity and a $40 annuity 18 Apr. 1843 in Indiana County.

Black, Elias. He received a $40 gratuity and a $40 annuity in Bucks County 13 Feb. 1840.

Black, Jonathan. He received a $40 gratuity and a $40 annuity in Greene County 20 May 1839.

Blair, —. His widow, Nancy Blair, received a $40 gratuity and a $40 annuity 11 Apr. 1844. She died 16 June 1844.

Blair, —. His widow, Rebecca Blair, received a $40 gratuity and a $40 annuity in Northumberland County in 1841. She died 13 Apr. 1846.

Blashford, James. He received a $40 gratuity and a $40 annuity 18 Apr. 1843 in Allegheny County.

Boggs, Robert. He received a $40 gratuity and a $40 annuity in Franklin County 15 Mar. 1838.

Boies, John. He received a $40 gratuity and a $40 annuity in Beaver County in 1838. He died 12 Sep. 1849. His widow, Nancy Boies, received a $40 annuity 19 Apr. 1853.

Bolan, George. He received a $40 annuity in Butler County 12 Apr. 1845.

Bomberger, —. His widow, Susanna Bomberger, received a $40 gratuity and a $40 annuity 20 May 1839 in Berks County. She died 2 Apr. 1844.

Boney, —. His widow, Eunice Boney, received a $40 annuity 13 Apr. 1854 in Armstrong County.

Boney, John. He received a $40 gratuity and a $40 annuity 11 Apr. 1844 in Armstrong County. He died 14 Feb. 1853.

Booker, Francis. He received a $40 gratuity and a $40 annuity in Allegheny County 18 Apr. 1843. He died 7 June 1862.

Boone, Ralph. He received a $40 gratuity and a $40 annuity in Fayette County 18 Apr. 1843.

Bosley, —. His widow, Sarah Bosley, received a $40 gratuity and a $40 annuity 5 Apr. 1842. She resided in Rockbridge Co., Va.

Boston, —. His widow, Catharine Boston, received a $40 annuity 15 Mar. 1847 in Fayette County. She died 30 May 1850.

Boston, Christian. He received a $40 gratuity and a $40 annuity in Luzerne County 20 Mar. 1838. He died 27 July 1843.

Bowers, —. His widow, Barbara Bowers, received a $40 gratuity and a $40 annuity in 1840 in Armstrong County. She died 23 Aug. 1845.

Boyer, —. His widow, Elizabeth Boyer, received a $40 gratuity and a $40 annuity 14 Mar. 1842. She died 20 Apr. 1846 in York County.

Boyer, Frederick. His widow, Margaret Boyer, received a $40 gratuity in Schuylkill County 8 May 1850.

Boyles, Charles. He received a $40 annuity in Crawford County 14 Apr. 1851.

Boyls, —. His widow, Mary Boyls, received a $40 gratuity and a $40 annuity 17 Mar. 1838 in Indiana County.

Bradley, —. His widow, Catharine Bradley, received a $40 gratuity and a $40 annuity 25 June 1839 in Lancaster County. She died 28 Oct. 1858.

Brady, —. His widow, Margaret Brady, received a $40 gratuity 8 May 1850 in Indiana County.

Brallier, Emanuel. He received a $40 gratuity and a $40 annuity in Somerset County 5 Apr. 1842.

Brannon, —. His widow, Mary Brannon, received a $40 gratuity and a $40 annuity in Allegheny County 17 Mar. 1838. She also appeared as Mary Brandon.

Brensinger, Caspar. He received a $40 gratuity and a $40 annuity 18 Apr. 1843. He also appeared as Caspar Bensinger. He died 4 June 1848.

Brewer, —. His widow, Elizabeth Brewer, received a $40 annuity in Butler County 3 Apr. 1851.

Brewer, John. He received a $40 annuity 16 Mar. 1847 in Fayette County.

Brewer, John. His widow, Mary Brewer, received a $40 annuity in Fayette County 11 Apr. 1849.

Bricker, Jacob. He received a $40 gratuity and a $40 annuity 11 Apr. 1844 in Indiana County.

Brickle, George. He received a $40 gratuity 18 Apr. 1843 in Allegheny County.

Brinker, Abraham. He received a $40 gratuity in Butler County 7 Apr. 1846.

Britton, —. His widow, Hannah Britton, received a $40 gratuity and a $40 annuity in Union County 5 Apr. 1842.

Brookhouser, Adam. He received a $40 annuity in Fayette County 16 Mar. 1847.

Brooks, —. His widow, Maria M. Brooks, received a $40 gratuity and a $40 annuity in Philadelphia 2 July 1842.

Brown, —. His widow, Jemima Brown, received a $40 gratuity in Mercer County 18 Apr. 1843.

Brown, —. His widow, Mary Brown, received a $40 gratuity and a $40 annuity in Mifflin County 21 July 1842.

Brown, James. He received a $40 gratuity and a $40 annuity in Luzerne County 30 Mar. 1838.

Brown, John. He received a $40 gratuity and a $40 annuity in Mercer County 21 Mar. 1840.

Brown, Peter. He received assistance 17 Mar. 1838. He was from Allegheny County. He died 13 June 1843.

Brown, William. He received a $40 gratuity in Beaver County 18 Apr. 1843.

Burk, John. He received a $40 annuity in York County 21 Apr. 1846. He died 26 Feb. 1852.

Burns, William. He received a $40 gratuity in Ashtabula Co., Ohio 18 Apr. 1843.

Burns, William. He received a $40 annuity in Crawford County 12 Apr. 1845 and 11 Apr. 1848.

Butler, —. His widow, Ann Butler, of Philadelphia, received a $40 gratuity and a $40 annuity in 1838.

Buzzen, —. His widow, Catherine Buzzen, received a $40 annuity in Crawford County 19 Apr. 1853.

Byers, —. His widow, Mary Byers, received a $40 annuity in Mercer County 12 Apr. 1851.

Byrod, Frederick. He received a $40 gratuity and a $40 annuity in 1838 in Dauphin County. He died 16 May 1840. He was 85 years old.

Caldwell, John. He received a $40 annuity in Portage Co., Ohio 15 Apr. 1847.

Calhoun, —. His widow, Anna Maria Calhoun, received a $40 gratuity and a $40 annuity 12 June 1840 in Centre County.

Callahan, —. His widow, Margaret Callahan, received a $40 gratuity and a $40 annuity in Westmoreland County 13 Apr. 1841.

Callan, Hugh. He received a $40 gratuity and a $40 annuity in Armstrong County 14 Apr. 1838. He died 9 Feb. 1842.

Campbell, —. His widow, Jane Campbell, received a $40 gratuity and a $40 annuity 11 Apr. 1844. She died 6 Dec. 1845 in Indiana County.

Campbell, —. His widow, Mary Campbell, received a $40 gratuity and a $40 annuity in Butler County 5 May 1841. She died 27 Apr. 1856.

Campbell, —. His widow, Mary Campbell, received a $40 gratuity and a $40 annuity in Chester County 20 May 1839.

Campbell, —. His widow, Martha Campbell, was issued a $40 gratuity and a $40 annuity in Washington County 18 Apr. 1843. She died 20 Dec. 1853.

Campbell, Alexander. He received a $40 gratuity and a $40 annuity in Butler County 21 Feb. 1838.

Campbell, James. He received a $40 gratuity 13 Mar. 1839.

Campbell, John. He received a $40 gratuity and a $40 annuity 21 Feb. 1838 in Westmoreland County.

Campbell, Robert. He received a $40 gratuity and a $40 annuity in Washington County 15 Mar. 1838. He was 87 years old in 1840.

Campbell, William. He received a $40 gratuity and a $40 annuity in Westmoreland County in 1838. He died 2 Nov. 1850.

Canely, William J. He received a $40 gratuity and a $40 annuity in Philadelphia County in 1838. He died 11 May 1841.

Cannon, Joseph. He received a $40 gratuity and a $40 annuity in Jefferson County, Ohio 5 May 1841.

Cannon, William. He received a $40 annuity in Indiana County in Apr. 1846. He died 3 July 1848.

Carle, Jacob. He received a $40 gratuity in Berks County 14 Mar. 1842.

Carlton, —. His widow, Mary Carlton, received a $40 gratuity and a $40 annuity in York Co. in 1841.

Carnagey, William —. He received a $40 gratuity and a $40 annuity in Apr. 1840. He died 16 Oct. 1841. His widow, Mary Carnagey, received a $40 gratuity and a $40 annuity in Columbiana Co., Ohio 5 Apr. 1842.

Carothers, James. He received a $40 gratuity and a $40 annuity in Carroll Co., Ohio in 1841.

Cartright, Gideon. He received a $40 gratuity and a $40 annuity in Tioga County in 1838.

Casselman, Henry. He received a $40 gratuity and a $40 annuity in Carroll Co, Ohio 8 Feb. 1842.

Casteler, —. His widow, Elizabeth Casteler, received a $40 gratuity and a $40 annuity 11 Apr. 1844. She also appeared as Elizabeth Casteder She died 11 Apr. 1844 in Union County.

Casteter, John. He received a $40 gratuity and a $40 annuity in Union County 2 July 1842. He also appeared as John Casteler. He died 1 Sep. 1843.

Cather, —. His widow, Sarah Cather, was late of Greene County and received a $40 annuity 19 Apr. 1853.

Cather. Robert. He received a $40 gratuity 18 Apr. 1843.

Cather, Robert. He received a $40 gratuity and a $40 annuity in Greene County 11 Apr. 1844.

Chambers, John. He received a $40 gratuity and a $40 annuity in Butler County in 1839.

Chick, Nathaniel. He received a $40 gratuity and a $40 annuity in Pike County 5 Apr. 1842.

Christ, Lorance. He received a $40 gratuity and a $40 annuity 25 June 1839 in Lancaster County. He died 26 Aug. 1841. He also appeared as Lawrance Christ.

Christ, Nicholas. He received a $40 gratuity and a $40 annuity in Washington County 20 May 1839.

Clark, Alexander. He received a $40 gratuity and a $40 annuity in Crawford County 5 Apr. 1842. He had a $40 gratuity in 1840.

Clawes, John. He received a $40 gratuity and a $40 annuity in Allegheny County 14Apr. 1838. He also appeared as John Claws. He died 24 June 1844.

Clawson, Keziah. This person received a $40 gratuity and a $40 annuity in Fayette County in 1838.

Clemens, Peter. He received a $40 gratuity and a $40 annuity in Union County 3 Apr. 1841.

Clift, —. His widow, Jemima Clift, received a $40 gratuity and a $40 annuity in Philadelphia County 20 Mar. 1838.

Clingman, David. He received a $40 annuity in Mercer County 11 Apr. 1849.

Cockenbaugh, John. He received a $40 gratuity and a $40 annuity in Fayette County 25 June 1839. He died 23 Feb. 1842.

Coe, —. His widow, Margaret Coe, received a $40 gratuity and a $40 annuity 8 Feb. 1841 in Allegheny County. She died 20 Sep. 1842.

Cogley, —. His widow, Catharine Cogley, received a $40 annuity in Armstrong County 21 Apr. 1846.

Cogley, James. He received a $40 gratuity and a $40 annuity in Armstrong County 13 Apr. 1841. He died 22 Oct. 1845.

Colbey, Christopher. He received a $40 gratuity and a $40 annuity in Center County 13 Mar. 1838. He died 13 Mar. 1845.

Coleman, —. Adah Coleman received a $40 gratuity and a $40 annuity in Columbia County 16 Apr. 1838 and died 15 Apr. 1840.

Coleman, Valentine. He received a $40 gratuity and a $40 annuity in York County 18 Apr. 1843.

Colestock, Jonas. He received a $40 gratuity in Fayette County in 1840.

Collins, —. His widow, Anna Collins, received a $40 gratuity and a $40 annuity in Crawford Co.. 11 Apr. 1844.

Collins, —. His widow, Leah Collins, received a $40 gratuity and a $40 annuity in Tompkins Co., N.Y. 11 Apr. 1844. She died in June 1848.

Collins, James. He received a $40 annuity 16 Mar. 1847. He died in Fayette County 10 Feb. 1852.

Colmer, William. He received a $40 gratuity and a $40 annuity 13 Mar. 1839 in Butler County. He died 23 Apr. 1845.

Coln, —. His widow, Ann Coln, received a $40 annuity in Greene County 3 Apr. 1851.

Conn, —. His widow, Elizabeth Conn, received a $40 gratuity and a $40 annuity 13 Apr. 1838 in Lancaster County.

Connelly, Thomas. He received a $40 gratuity and a $40 annuity in Greene County 16 Apr. 1840.

Conner, —. His widow, Mary Conner, received a $40 gratuity and a $40 annuity in Allegheny County 13 Apr. 1838. She was 77 years old in 1840.

Conrad, —. His widow, Mary M. Conrad, received a $40 gratuity and a $40 annuity in Crawford Co. 18 Apr. 1843. She died 5 Mar. 1851.

Conrad, John Nicholas. He received a $40 gratuity and a $40 annuity in Crawford County 20 May 1839. He died 17 Aug. 1841.

Conway, —. His widow, Esther Conway, received a $40 gratuity and a $40 annuity in Montgomery County 14 Apr. 1838.

Conway, Hugh. He received a $40 annuity in Butler County 12 Apr. 1845.

Conway, William. He received a $40 annuity 12 Apr. 1845. The act had his name incorrectly given as William Scott. The correction was made 21 Apr. 1846. He died 17 Sep. 1846.

Coock, George. He received a $40 annuity in Armstrong County 14 Apr. 1851.

Cook, —. His widow, Martha Cook, of Mercer County received a $40 annuity 19 Apr. 1853.

Cooper, John. He received a $40 gratuity and a $40 annuity in Monroe County 21 June 1839.

Corey, Benjamin F. He received a $40 annuity in Tioga County 7 Apr. 1846.

Corl, Jacob. He received a $40 gratuity in Berks County 18 Apr. 1843. He also appeared as Jacob Carl.

Correll, —. His widow, Catharine Correll, received a $40 gratuity and a $40 annuity in Columbia County in 1838.

Cosner, —. His widow, Sarah Cosner, received a $40 gratuity and a $40 annuity 20 May 1839 in Bucks County.

Cotton, William. He received a $40 gratuity and a $40 annuity in Fayette County 21 Feb. 1838. He died 20 Dec. 1842.

Cotton, William. He was pensioned in Fayette County 1 Jan. 1838. He was 98 years old in 1840.

Coulter, —. His widow, Isabella Coulter, received a $40 gratuity and a $40 annuity in Portage Co., Ohio. She died 25 Apr. 1845.

Coyle, Mark. He received a $40 gratuity and a $40 annuity in 1840 in Washington County. He died 8 Jan. 1841.

Craft, Andrew. He received a $40 gratuity and a $40 annuity in Armstrong County 21 Feb. 1838. He also appeared as Andrew Croft.

Crawford, James. He received a $40 gratuity and a $40 annuity in Beaver County in 1837.

Crawford, James. He received a $40 gratuity and a $40 annuity in Mercer County 21 Feb. 1838. He died 7 Apr. 1856 in Venango County.

Cromley, Christian. He received a $40 gratuity and a $40 annuity in Philadelphia County 16 Apr. 1838.

Cromlow, —. His widow, Ann Cromlow, received a $40 gratuity and a $40 annuity in Fayette County 11 Apr. 1844. Her name may have been Ann Cumlow.

Cromlow, —. His widow, Ann Cromlow, received a $40 gratuity in Greene County 15 Mar. 1847.

Cronemiller, Martin. He received benefits in Union County 27 Mar. 1837. He was dead by Jan. 1839.

Croushour, Henry. He received a $40 gratuity and a $40 annuity in Westmoreland County 13 Apr. 1838.

Culbertson, —. His widow, Agnes Culbertson, received a $40 gratuity and a $40 annuity in Indiana County 11 Apr. 1844.

Cummings, —. His widow, Abigail Cummings, received a $40 annuity in Northampton County 12 Apr. 1845.

Cunningham, —. His widow, Margaret Cunningham, received a $40 gratuity and a $40 annuity in Juniata County 5 May 1841. She died 2 July 1843.

Cupp, Ludwig. He received a $40 gratuity and a $40 annuity 15 Mar. 1838 in Allegheny County. He died 10 May 1841. His widow, Elizabeth Cupps, received a $40 gratuity and a $40 annuity in Allegheny County 14 Mar. 1842.

Currie, —. His widow, Sarah Currie, received a $40 gratuity and a $40 annuity in Lancaster County in 1840.

Dagon, Jacob. He received a $40 gratuity and a $40 annuity in Washington County 3 Apr. 1841.

Dailey, —. His widow, Nancy Dailey, received a $40 gratuity and a $40 annuity in Mercer County 11 Apr. 1840. She died 16 June 1844.

Danfield, John. He received a $40 gratuity and a $40 annuity in 1838 in Berks County.

Dannenhower, —. His widow, Elizabeth Dannenhower, received a $40 gratuity and a $40 annuity in Philadelphia County 11 Apr. 1844.

Dannenhower, George. Pa. —. He was pensioned in Philadelphia 1 Apr. 1836.

Darragh, —. His widow, Sarah Darragh, received a $40 gratuity and a $40 annuity in Bucks County in 1838.

Davidheiser, —. His widow, Elizabeth Davidheiser, received a $40 gratuity and a $40 annuity in Berks County in 1838.

Davidson, —. His widow, Elizabeth Davidson, received a $40 annuity in Westmoreland County 7 Apr. 1846.

Davidson, —. His widow, Sarah Davidson, received a $40 gratuity and a $40 annuity in Baltimore, Md. 18 Apr. 1841 or 1843.

Davidson, Francis. He received a $40 gratuity and a $40 annuity 11 Apr. 1844.

Davis, —. His widow, Mary Davis, received a $40 gratuity and a $40 annuity 11 Apr. 1844 in Armstrong County. She died 15 Mar. 1854 or 25 Mar. 1852.

Davis, —. His widow, Mary Magdalena Davis, received a $40 annuity in Armstrong County 10 Apr. 1849.

Davis, —. His widow, Rachel Davis, received a $40 gratuity and a $40 annuity 13 Apr. 1841 in Columbia County.

Davis, Azariah. He received a $40 gratuity and a $40 annuity in Fayette County 21 Mar. 1840.

Dawson, William. He received relief in Lancaster County 21 June 1839.

Deam, —. His widow, Catharine Deam, received a $40 gratuity 15 Mar.1838. Her name may have been Catharine Dean.

Dean, —. His widow, Jane Dean, received a $40 annuity in Crawford County 11 Apr. 1848.

Dean, Samuel. He received a $40 annuity in Fayette County 21 Apr. 1846.

Deeds, —. His widow, Catharine Deeds, received a $40 gratuity and a $40 annuity in Montgomery Co. in 1841.

Deily, —. His widow, Catharine Deily, received a $40 gratuity and a $40 annuity 8 Apr. 1840 in Lehigh County.

Dempsey, —. His widow, Mary Dempsey, received a $40 gratuity and a $40 annuity in Chester County 5 May 1841. She died 16 May 1846.

Dennis, Andrew. He received assistance in Allegheny County 27 Mar. 1837.

Deobler, Abraham. He was granted relief 14 Apr. 1836 in Lebanon County. His widow, Mary Deobler, received a $40 gratuity 8 May 1850.

Depuy, —. His widow, Catharine Depuy, received a $40 gratuity and a $40 annuity 11 Apr. 1844 in York County.

Derr, John. He received a $40 gratuity and a $40 annuity in Franklin County 18 Apr. 1843.

Dickson, Joseph. He received a $40 gratuity and a $40 annuity in Crawford County 21 Feb. 1838.

Dietrich, John. He received a $40 gratuity and a $40 annuity in Schuylkill County 13 Apr. 1841. He died 18 Aug. 1845.

Dill, Michael. He received a $40 gratuity in Allegheny County 16 Mar. 1847.

Dillinger, —. His widow, Mary Ann Dillinger, received a $40 gratuity and a $40 annuity in the District of Columbia 5 Apr 1842.

Dillon, —. His widow, Sarah Dillon, received a $40 gratuity and a $40 annuity 8 Apr. 1840 in Westmoreland County.

Dilman, —. His widow, Catharine Dilman, received a $40 gratuity and a $40 annuity in Perry Co. in 1841. She died 8 Apr. 1849.

Ditlow, —. His widow, Susannah Ditlow, received a $40 gratuity and a $40 annuity in Lehigh County 11 Apr. 1844.

Dixon, —. His widow, Eleanor Dixon, received a $40 gratuity and a $40 annuity in Fayette County 8

Apr. 1840. She died 9 [Nov.] 1849.

Dohrman, —. His widow, Mary Dohrman, received a $40 gratuity and a $40 annuity in Union County 8 Apr. 1840. She also appeared as Mary Dorman. She died 23 Sep. 1842.

Doll, —. His widow, Elizabeth Doll, received a $40 gratuity and a $40 annuity in York Co. 5 May 1841. She died 25 June 1842.

Doll, John. A new trustee was named for him 5 Mar. 1828 in Lehigh County. He died in 1843.

Donahay, James. He received a $40 gratuity in Indiana County in 1838 and a $40 gratuity and a $40 annuity 18 Apr. 1843. He died 6 Aug. 1848.

Donough, Robert. He received a $40 gratuity and a $40 annuity in Greene County 12 June 1840.

Donovan, —. His widow, Eleanor Donovan, received a $40 gratuity and a $40 annuity in York Co. 18 Apr. 1843. She died 21 Jan. 1858.

Downard, Joshua. He received a $40 gratuity and a $40 annuity in Jefferson Co., Ohio in 1841.

Downs, John. He received a $40 gratuity and a $40 annuity 8 Feb. 1841.

Doyle, —. His widow, Mary Doyle, received a $40 gratuity and a $40 annuity in Bucks County 11 Apr. 1841. She died 9 Sep. 1847.

Drake, Joseph. He received a $40 gratuity and a $40 annuity 13 Apr. 1841. He died 9 May 1852 in Monroe County.

Dreher, —. His widow, Christina Dreher, received a $40 gratuity 8 May 1850 in Schuylkill County.

Drennen, —. His widow, Martha Drennen, received a $40 gratuity and a $40 annuity in Chester County 5 Apr. 1842.

Duck, —. His widow, Elizabeth Duck, received a $40 gratuity and a $40 annuity in Dauphin County 8 Apr. 1840. She died 7 Feb. 1848.

Duff, —. His widow, Ann Duff, received a $40 gratuity and a $40 annuity in 1838 in Butler County.

Duff, John. He received a $40 annuity in Armstrong County 7 Apr. 1846.

Duffield, —. His widow, Elizabeth Duffield, received a $40 gratuity and a $40 annuity in Venango County 1 Jan. 1838. She was dead by July 1838.

Duncan, James. He received a $40 gratuity and a $40 annuity in Westmoreland County 11 Apr. 1844. He died 5 Feb. 1845. His widow, Jane Duncan, received a $40 annuity 11 Apr. 1848.

Duncan, Thomas. He received a $40 annuity in Cambria County 11 Apr. 1848. He died 21 Dec. 1848.

Eager, —. His widow, Rosanna Eager, received a $40 gratuity and a $40 annuity in Westmoreland County 5 Apr. 1842.

Eardon, —. His widow, Elizabeth Eardon, received a $40 annuity in Lancaster County 12 Apr. 1851.

Eckert, —. His widow, Elizabeth Eckert, received a $40 gratuity and a $40 annuity 11 Apr. 1844.

Edgar, —. His widow, Mary Edgar, received a $40 gratuity and a $40 annuity 11 Apr. 1844 in York Co.

Eisenhauer, —. His widow, Mary Eisenhauer, received a $40 gratuity and a $40 annuity 20 May 1839 in Berks County. She died 28 Feb. 1841.

Ellender, —. His widow, Mary Ellender, received a $40 annuity in Lehigh County 27 Feb. 1851. She died 20 Dec. 1851.

Ellender, Joseph. He received a $40 gratuity and a $40 annuity in Lehigh County 16 Apr. 1838.

English, Thomas. He received a $40 gratuity and a $40 annuity in Mercer County 18 Apr. 1843.

Erb, —. His widow, Elizabeth Erb, received a $40 gratuity and a $40 annuity in 1838 in Northampton County. She died 5 Oct. 1844.

Erdman, —. His widow, Barbara Erdman, received a $40 gratuity and a $40 annuity in Montgomery County in Apr. 1840.

Erdman, —. His widow, Susanna Erdman, received a $40 gratuity and a $40 annuity in Montgomery

County 11 Apr. 1844.

Essick, Jacob. He received a $40 gratuity and a $40 annuity in Perry County 12 June 1840. He was 81 years old.

Etter, Jacob. He received a $40 gratuity and a $40 annuity in Monroe County 13 Apr. 1841.

Everett, Joseph. He received a $40 gratuity and a $40 annuity in Armstrong County 24 Apr. 1838. He also appeared as Joseph Evert.

Ewing, Alexander. He received a $40 gratuity and a $40 annuity in Apr. 1840. He was from LaGrange Co., Indiana.

Ewing, John. He received a $40 gratuity and a $40 annuity in Indiana County 18 Jan. 1838.

Eyler, ——. His widow, Rachel Eyler, received a $40 gratuity and a $40 annuity 18 Apr. 1843 in Franklin County.

Fare, Jacob. He received a $40 gratuity and a $40 annuity in Mifflin County 14 Apr. 1838.

Farr, John. He received a $40 gratuity and a $40 annuity in Fayette County in 1839.

Feathers,——. His widow, Mary Feathers, received a $40 gratuity and a $40 annuity in Preston Co., Va. 20 Mar. 1838.

Fee, John. He served as colonel. His widow, Jane Fee, received a $40 gratuity in Huntingdon County 8 May 1850. She died 30 Sep. 1858.

Felton, ——. His widow, Rachel Felton, received a $40 gratuity and a $40 annuity in Luzerne County 10 Feb. 1841. She died 4 Nov. 1844.

Felty, ——. His widow, Rosinda Felty, received a $40 gratuity and a $40 annuity in Philadelphia County in 1838.

Felty, George. He received a $40 gratuity and a $40 annuity in Greene County in 1838. He died 22 May 1848.

Finch, Samuel. He received a $40 gratuity and a $40 annuity in Tioga County , N.Y. in 1838.

Finefrock, ——. His widow, Margaret Ann Finefrock, received a $40 gratuity in Somerset County 8 May 1850 and 12 Apr. 1851.

Finfrock, ——. His widow, Barbara Finfrock, received a $40 gratuity and a $40 annuity in Apr. 1840.

Firon, John. He received a $40 annuity in Beaver County 15 Mar. 1847.

Fiscus, ——. Pa. ——. His widow, Catharine Fiscus, was granted a $40 gratuity and a $40 annuity in Armstrong County 18 Apr. 1843. She died 29 Sep. 1845.

Fisher, ——. His widow, Magdalena Fisher, received a $40 gratuity and a $40 annuity in 1838 in Berks County. She died 23 July 1854.

Fisher, Jacob. He received a $40 gratuity and a $40 annuity in Delaware Co., Ohio 21 July 1842. He died 19 Oct. 1844.

Fisher, John. He received a $40 gratuity and a $40 annuity in Fayette County in 1841.

Fiss, ——. His widow, Catharina Fiss, received a $40 gratuity and a $40 annuity in Philadelphia County 14 Apr. 1838. She died 9 Oct. 1847.

Flanagan, Thomas. He received a $40 gratuity and a $40 annuity in Philadelphia 18 Apr. 1843. He died 24 Mar. 1855.

Fleming, John. He received a $40 gratuity and a $40 annuity in 1838. He was from Fayette County. He was 79 ½ in 1840. He died 23 Nov. 1840.

Fluck, ——. His widow, Catherine Fluck, received a $40 annuity in Bedford County 12 Apr. 1851.

Fluck, ——. His widow, Dorothy Fluck, received a $40 gratuity and a $40 annuity in Bedford County 18 Apr. 1843.

Foreman, Samuel. He received a $40 gratuity and a $40 annuity in Armstrong County 16 Apr. 1838. He died 25 Nov. 1841.

Forman, —. His widow, Esther Forman, received a $40 gratuity and a $40 annuity in Franklin County 18 Apr. 1843.

Forster, John. He received a $40 gratuity and a $40 annuity in Armstrong County 8 Apr. 1840.

Forsythe, James. He received a $40 gratuity and a $40 annuity in Allegheny County in 1840. He died 6 Apr. 1850.

Foster, —. His widow, Catharine Foster, received a $40 gratuity and a $40 annuity in Warren County 13 Apr. 1841. She died 7 Feb. 1851.

Foster, John. He received relief in Crawford County 5 May 1841.

Fox, —. His widow, Barbara Fox, received a $40 gratuity and a $40 annuity in Philadelphia County 2 July 1842. She died 18 Oct. 1851.

Frank, Abraham. He received a $40 gratuity and a $40 annuity in Fayette County 20 May 1839. He removed to Bureau Co., Ill.

Fre, —. His widow, Rebecca Fre, received a $40 annuity in Fayette County 12 Apr. 1851.

Freeman, —. His widow, Elizabeth Freeman received a $40 gratuity 8 May 1850 in Indiana County. She died 26 May 1851.

Frey, Peter. He received assistance in Chester County 15 Mar. 1838.

Fry, —. His widow, Elizabeth Fry, of Mercer County received a $40 annuity 19 Apr. 1853.

Fry, Ephraim. He received a $40 annuity 16 Mar. 1847 in Franklin County. His widow, Mary Fry, received a $40 annuity in Westmoreland County 10 Apr. 1849. She died 6 Aug. 1850.

Fry, Mathias. He received a $40 gratuity and a $40 annuity in Rockbridge County, Virginia 14 Apr. 1838. He died 14 Apr. 1850.

Fryer, —. His widow, Anna Maria Fryer, received a $40 gratuity and a $40 annuity in Montgomery County in 1838. She died 22 Oct. 1839.

Fryer, Abraham. He received a $40 gratuity and a $40 annuity 13 Mar. 1839 in Butler County. He died 2 Sep. 1856..

Fullom, —. His widow, Magdalena Fullom, received a $40 annuity in Indiana County 15 Apr. 1852.

Funk, —. His widow, Catharine Funk, received a $40 gratuity and a $40 annuity in York County 16 Apr. 1838.

Funk, Jacob. He received a $40 gratuity and a $40 annuity in Westmoreland County in 1838.

Gallaher, James. He received a $40 gratuity and a $40 annuity in Clearfield County 14 Mar. 1842.

Gallentine, —. His widow, Susannah Gallentine, received a $40 gratuity and a $40 annuity in Fayette County 16 Apr. 1838. She died 16 Dec. 1862.

Gans, —. His widow, Charlotte Gans, received a $40 gratuity and a $40 annuity in Northampton County in 1838.

Gaskill, —. His widow, Budd Gaskill, received a $40 annuity in Crawford County 19 Apr. 1853. She died 6 Feb. 1863.

Gaw, Chambers. He received a $40 gratuity and a $40 annuity in Lancaster County 14 Mar. 1842. He died 14 Oct. 1846 in Philadelphia.

Gehr, —. His widow, Catherine Gehr, received a $40 gratuity and a $40 annuity in 1839 in Crawford Co. She died 30 Sep. 1844.

Gehr, —. His widow, Henrietta Gehr, received a $40 gratuity 19 Apr. 1853 in Crawford County.

Gehr, John H. He received a $40 gratuity and a $40 annuity 18 Apr. 1843. He died in Crawford County 5 July 1852.

Gehr, Joseph. He received a $40 annuity in Crawford County 12 Apr. 1845.

Gehret, —. His widow, Christina Gehret, received a $40 annuity in Berks County 21 Apr.. 1846. She died 6 Oct. 1850.

Geissinger, John. He received assistance 17 Mar. 1838 in Huntingdon County. He died 29 Nov. 1843.

Gensel, Adam. He received a $40 gratuity and a $40 annuity in Columbia County 8 Apr. 1840.

George, David. He received a $40 annuity in Allegheny County in Apr. 1846. He died 15 June 1857.

Gettemy, —. His widow, Sarah Gettemy, received a $40 gratuity and a $40 annuity in Westmoreland County in 1837.

Gibson, —. His widow, Abigail Gibson, received a $40 annuity in Armstrong County 13 Apr. 1854.

Gibson, Gideon. He received a $40 gratuity and a $40 annuity in Armstrong County 14 Apr. 1838.

Gibson, John. He received a $40 annuity in Butler County 15 Mar. 1847.

Gideon, Jacob. He was identified as a resident of Washington, D.C. in the law of Jan. 1836. The law of 1839 corrected the place to Washington County, Pa. He received a $40 gratuity and a $40 annuity 20 May 1839.

Gilbert, —. His widow, Permelia Gilbert, received a $40 gratuity and a $40 annuity in Greene County 13 Apr. 1841.

Gilchrist, Robert. He received a $40 annuity in Westmoreland County in Apr. 1846.

Gillespie, —. His widow, Martha Gillespie, received a $40 annuity in Mercer County 3 Apr. 1851.

Gilmore, —. His widow, Elizabeth Gilmore, received a $40 gratuity and a $40 annuity in Crawford County 1 Jan. 1838. She died 27 Mar. 1844.

Glantz, John. He received a $40 gratuity and a $40 annuity in 1837 in Center County.

Glencer, —. His widow, Anna Margaret Glencer, received a $40 gratuity and a $40 annuity in 1838 in Berks County. She died 5 Nov. 1844.

Gonter, —. His widow, Elizabeth Gonter, received a $40 annuity 3 Apr. 1851 in Lancaster County.

Good, —. His widow, Catharine Good, received a $40 gratuity and a $40 annuity in Columbia County 18 Apr. 1843. She was dead by Oct. 1843.

Gooden, —. His widow, Jane Gooden, received a $40 gratuity and a $40 annuity in Greene County 16 Apr. 1838.

Gordon, Henry. He received benefits 27 Mar. 1837. He was from Mercer County.

Gordon, James. He received a $40 gratuity in Apr. 1840.

Gordon, James. He received a $40 annuity in Butler County in Apr. 1846.

Gordon, John. He received a $40 gratuity and a $40 annuity 5 Apr. 1842 in Beaver County. He died in Jan. 1859.

Gordon, John. He received a $40 gratuity and a $40 annuity in Beaver County 2 July 1842.

Gos, Abraham. He received a $40 gratuity and a $40 annuity in Clearfield County 21 Mar. 1837.

Gossler, —. His widow, Mary Gossler, received a $40 gratuity and a $40 annuity in 1840. She died 10 Aug. 1843.

Gould, Daniel. He received a $40 gratuity and a $40 annuity in Armstrong County 20 Mar. 1838. He was 69 years old in 1840.

Graff, —. His widow, Margaret Graff, received a $40 gratuity and a $40 annuity in Berks County 20 May 1839. She died 9 Nov. 1844.

Gray, —. His widow, Maria Gray, received a $40 gratuity and a $40 annuity in 1838 in Lancaster Co.

Gray, —. His widow, Mary Gray, received a $40 annuity in Westmoreland County 11 Apr. 1848.

Gray, Henry. He received a $40 gratuity and a $40 annuity in Perry County 3 April 1841. He died 8 Feb. 1843.

Gray, Martin. He received a $40 gratuity and a $40 annuity 11 Apr. 1844.

Greer, Thomas. He received a $40 gratuity and a $40 annuity in Allegheny County 13 Apr. 1838.

Gregory, John. He received a $40 gratuity and a $40 annuity in Huntingdon County 20 May 1839. He died 18 Jan. 1841.

Greinder, Martin. He received a $40 gratuity and a $40 annuity in Mercer County 20 May 1839.

Gring, —. His widow, Gerdraud Gring, received a $40 annuity in Berks County 27 Feb. 1851.

Gring, David. He received a $40 gratuity and a $40 annuity in Berks County 14 Mar. 1842.

Groscost, Jacob. He received benefits in Beaver County 27 Mar.1837.

Grove, —. His widow, Catherine Grove, received a $40 annuity in Allegheny County in Apr. 1846.

Grubbs, —. His widow, Leah Grubbs, received a $40 gratuity and a $40 annuity in Allegheny County 5 Apr. 1842.

Grubs, Jacob. He received assistance 17 Mar. 1838 in Allegheny County. He was dead by July 1840.

Gruby, —. His widow, Mary Gruby, received a $40 gratuity and a $40 annuity in Luzerne County 21 Mar. 1840.

Gunn, Alexander. He received a $40 gratuity in Washington County 11 Apr. 1844.

Gunter, John. He received a $40 annuity in Berks County 3 Apr. 1837.

Guthrie, James. He received a $40 annuity in Armstrong County 12 Apr. 1845. He died 26 Dec. 1848.

Gwinn, John. He received assistance 17 Mar. 1838 in Huntingdon County. He was dead by Dec. 1839.

Haas, —. His widow, Eve Haas, received a $40 gratuity and a $40 annuity in Northumberland County 3 Apr. 1841.

Haas, Jacob. His widow, Anne Haas, received a $40 gratuity 8 May 1850 in Philadelphia.

Hackny, —. His widow, Margaret Hackny, received a $40 gratuity in Warren County 8 May 1850.

Hage, Peter. He received a $40 gratuity and a $40 annuity in Beaver County 12 June 1840.

Hagerman, —. His widow, Eleanor Hagerman, received a $40 gratuity and a $40 annuity in Westmoreland County 21 Feb. 1837.

Haines, Samuel. He received a $40 gratuity and a $40 annuity in Lancaster County 21 July 1842.

Hall, John. He received a $40 gratuity and a $40 annuity in Berks County 2 July 1842. He died 30 Aug. 1852.

Haller, Henry. He received a $40 gratuity and a $40 annuity in 1838. He died 6 May 1838 in Armstrong County.

Hamilton, William. He received a $40 gratuity and a $40 annuity in Fayette County in 1838. He died 7 May 1849 Allegheny County

Hammer, George. He received a $40 gratuity and a $40 annuity in Armstrong County 14 Apr. 1838.

Hammon, William. He received a $40 annuity in Beaver County 12 Apr. 1845. He died 7 Oct. 1846.

Hanning, John. He received a $40 gratuity and a $40 annuity in Fayette County 16 Apr. 1838.

Hantz, John. He received assistance in Dauphin County 27 Mar. 1837.

Harbison, —. His widow, Jane Harbison, received a $40 gratuity and a $40 annuity in 1841. She was late of Chester Co., Pa. and resided in Wilmington, Del.

Harbison,—. His widow, Jane Harbison, received a $40 annuity in Butler County 13 Apr. 1854.

Harbison, John. He received a $40 gratuity and a $40 annuity 21 Feb. 1838 in Westmoreland County. He was 77 years old in 1840. He died 18 Dec. 1846.

Harlin, —. His widow, Elizabeth Harlin, received a $40 gratuity and a $40 annuity in Mercer County 2 July 1842.

Harlin, Jonathan. He received assistance 27 Mar. 1837 in Mercer County. He died 28 June 1841.

Harlinger, Martin. He received a $40 gratuity and a $40 annuity in 1838 in Bucks County. He was 78 years of age in 1840. He died 5 Nov. 1842.

Harper, —. His widow, Elizabeth Harper, received a $40 annuity in Fayette County 3 Apr. 1851 She died 10 Apr. 1852.

Harple, Lewis. He received a $40 gratuity and a $40 annuity 8 Apr. 1840 in Chester County. He was 82 years of age in 1840. He died 30 May 1842.

Harrison, William. He received a $40 gratuity and a $40 annuity in Venango County 20 Mar. 1838. He died 1 Aug. 1841.

Hartman, —. His widow, Eve Hartman, received a $40 gratuity and a $40 annuity in Perry County in 1841. She died 7 Dec. 1841.

Hartman, John. He received a $40 gratuity and a $40 annuity in Columbia County 8 Apr. 1840.

Hasson, —. His widow, Elizabeth Hasson, received a $40 gratuity and a $40 annuity in Venango County in 1838. She died 26 Oct. 1843.

Hauk, Peter. He received a $40 gratuity and a $40 annuity in Lehigh County in 1838. He died 18 Oct. 1842.

Hawk, —. His widow, Anne Hawk, received a $40 annuity in Armstrong County 7 Apr. 1846. She died 5 Oct. 1854.

Hawk, James. He received a $40 gratuity and a $40 annuity in Fayette County in 1837.

Hawn, —. His widow, Christiana Hawn, received a $40 gratuity and a $40 annuity 18 Apr. 1843 in York County.

Hayden, John. His widow, Mary Hayden, received a $40 gratuity and a $40 annuity in George Twp., Fayette County 12 May 1857.

Hays, —. His widow, Sarah Hays, received relief in Butler County 12 Apr. 1841. She died 20 Aug. 1842.

Hays, James. He received a $40 gratuity and a $40 annuity in 1840.

Heckman, —. His widow, Elizabeth Heckman, received a $40 gratuity and a $40 annuity in 1838 in Northampton County. She died 4 Mar. 1843.

Hefner, Valentine. He received a $40 gratuity and a $40 annuity in Huntingdon County in 1838. He was 84 years old in 1840. He died 4 Nov. 1849.

Heft, —. His widow, Eve Heft, received a $40 gratuity and a $40 annuity in Bucks County 18 Apr. 1843.

Hegie, Adam. He received assistance in Huntingdon County 17 Mar. 1838. He died 4 Nov. 1839.

Heim, Jacob. He received a $40 gratuity in Lebanon County in 1841.

Heimer, —. His widow, Elizabeth Heimer, received a $40 gratuity and a $40 annuity in Philadelphia County 25 June 1839.

Heimond, —. His widow, Elizabeth Heimond, received a $40 gratuity and a $40 annuity in Erie Co. 25 June 1839.

Heiney, Frederick. He received a $40 gratuity and a $40 annuity in Mifflin County 20 May 1839. He also appeared as Frederick Hiney.

Heisly, —. His widow, Mary Heisly, received a $40 gratuity and a $40 annuity 12 June 1840 in Lancaster County.

Hellem, Samuel. He received a $40 gratuity and a $40 annuity 5 Apr. 1842 in York County.

Henderson, Daniel. He received a $40 gratuity and a $40 annuity 18 Apr. 1843 in Butler County. He died 5 Aug. 1849.

Henderson, Samuel. He received a $40 gratuity and a $40 annuity 18 Jan. 1838. He died 22 Apr. 1843 in Indiana County.

Henderson, Samuel. He received a $40 gratuity and a $40 annuity 11 Apr. 1844 in Westmoreland Co.

Henwood, Elisha. This person received a $40 gratuity and a $40 annuity in Washington County 4 Apr. 1837.

Herring, —. His widow, Elizabeth Herring, received a $40 gratuity and a $40 annuity in Bedford County 13 Apr. 1841. She died 10 Apr. 1843.

Hetrick, —. His widow, Margaret Hetrick, received a $40 gratuity and a $40 annuity in Jefferson County 16 Apr. 1838. She was dead by 13 May 1842.

Heydt, —. His widow, Elizabeth Heydt, received a $40 gratuity and a $40 annuity in Berks County 20 May 1839. She died 24 Apr. 1841.

Hibler, —. His widow, Helen Elizabeth Hibler, received a $40 gratuity and a $40 annuity 14 Mar. 1842. in Northampton County. She died 2 June 1843.

Hill, —. His widow, Hannah Hill, received a $40 gratuity and a $40 annuity in Allegheny County 13 Apr. 1841. She was dead by Nov. 1841.

Hill, —. His widow, Rachel Hill, received a $40 gratuity and a $40 annuity in Lycoming County in Apr. 1840.

Hill, William. He received a $40 gratuity and a $40 annuity in Armstrong County 20 Mar. 1838. He was 69 years old in 1840. He died 19 Nov. 1855.

Hillary, Ashburn. He was pensioned 8 Apr. 1833. He was 78 years old in 1840. His widow, Eleanor Hillary, received a $40 gratuity and a $40 annuity in Fayette County 21 Apr. 1857. He also appeared as Osburn Hillary.

Hillman, John. He received assistance in Allegheny County 17 Mar. 1838. He died 22 Dec. 1848.

Himrod, —. His widow, Isabella Himrod, received a $40 gratuity and a $40 annuity in Erie County 25 June 1839. She died 27 Apr. 1841. She also appeared as Isabella Himond.

Hinish, George. He received a $40 gratuity and a $40 annuity in Bedford County 3 Apr. 1841.

Hinton, —. His widow, Martha Hinton, received a $40 gratuity and a $40 annuity 10 Feb. 1841 in Center County. She died 17 Sep. 1846.

Hite, James. He received a $40 gratuity and a $40 annuity in Juniata County 17 Mar. 1838.

Hoffman, —. His widow, Magdalena Hoffman received a $40 gratuity and a $40 annuity in Lancaster County 13 Apr. 1839.

Hoffman, John. He received a $40 gratuity in Montgomery County 12 June 1840.

Holdren, Benaiah. He received a $40 gratuity and a $40 annuity in Bucks County in 1838.

Holmes, —. His widow, Jane Holmes, received a $40 gratuity and a $40 annuity in Franklin County 8 Apr. 1840. She died 9 May 1844.

Homon, —. His widow, Christina Homon, received a $40 annuity in Berks County in Apr. 1846.

Hornier, George. He received a $40 gratuity and a $40 annuity in Apr. 1840. He was from Washington County, Maryland.

Hornsher, —. His widow, Catharine Hornsher, received a $40 gratuity and a $40 annuity in Montgomery County in 1840.

Houston, James. He received a $40 gratuity and a $40 annuity in Indiana County 20 May 1839. He died 16 Sep. 1841.

Howard, Samuel. He received a $40 gratuity and a $40 annuity in Mercer County 15 Mar. 1838.

Huberd, —. His widow, Mary Ann Huberd, received a $40 gratuity and a $40 annuity 2 July 1842. She died 9 May 1858 in Lancaster County.

Huberd, —. His widow, Elizabeth Huberd, received a $40 gratuity and a $40 annuity in Lancaster County 2 July 1842.

Hubley, —. His widow, Elizabeth Hubley, received a $40 gratuity and a $40 annuity in Mercer County in Apr. 1840. She died 12 Oct. 1842.

Hubner, —. His widow, Catharine Hubner, received a $40 gratuity and a $40 annuity in York County

21 July 1842. She died 1 Dec. 1842.

Huffman, —. His widow, Christeena Huffman, received a $40 gratuity and a $40 annuity in Westmoreland County in Apr. 1840. She died 6 May 1849.

Huffnagle, —. His widow, Catharine Huffnagle, received a $40 gratuity and a $40 annuity in Westmoreland County 16 Apr. 1838. She died 21 Feb. 1843.

Hull, David. He received a $40 annuity in Armstrong County 21 Apr. 1846. He died 20 Mar. 1848.

Hultz, Zadock. He received a $40 gratuity in Allegheny County 18 Apr. 1843.

Hum, Henry. He received a $40 gratuity and a $40 annuity in Jefferson County 13 Apr. 1838. He was 77 years old in 1840. He died 16 Apr. 18??. He also appeared as Henry Hurn.

Hummel, —. His widow, Susannah Hummel, received a $40 gratuity and a $40 annuity in Venango County 20 May 1839. She died in Clarion County 8 June 1849.

Humphrey, —. His widow, Jane Humphrey, received a $40 gratuity and a $40 annuity in Lancaster County 13 Apr. 1838.

Hunt, —. His widow, Ann Hunt, received a $40 gratuity and a $40 annuity in Fayette County 8 Apr. 1840. She died 27 July 1840.

Hunter, —. His widow, Ann Hunter, received a $40 gratuity and a $40 annuity in Westmoreland County 13 Feb. 1840. She died 27 June 1859.

Hunter, James. He received a $40 gratuity and a $40 annuity in Crawford County in 1838 and 5 Apr. 1842.

Hunter, William. He died 15 Nov. 1848. His widow, Mary Hunter, received a $40 annuity in Mercer County 10 Apr. 1849. She died 13 Dec. 1852.

Hurtz, Conrad. He received benefits in Berks County 27 Mar. 1837. He died 5 June 1846,

Huston, —. His widow, Mary Huston, received a $40 gratuity and a $40 annuity in Indiana County 11 Apr. 1844.

Huston, James. He received a $40 gratuity and a $40 annuity in Mercer County 3 Apr. 1841.

Hutchinson, —. His widow, Mary Hutchinson, received a $40 gratuity in Huntingdon County 22 Apr. 1844.

Idel, Conrad. He received a $40 gratuity and a $40 annuity in 1838 in Philadelphia. He died 12 Feb. 1840.

Inglehopt, —. His widow, Barbara Inglehopt, received a $40 gratuity and a $40 annuity in Crawford County 20Mar. 1838.

Ingraham, —. His widow, Polly Ingraham, received a $40 gratuity and a $40 annuity in Crawford County in Apr. 1840. She died 28 Apr. 1842.

Inners, —. His widow, Mary Inners, received a $40 gratuity and a $40 annuity in Apr. 1840 in York Co. She died 7 May 1849.

Irvin, Hugh. He received a $40 annuity in Westmoreland County 10 Apr. 1849.

Irwin, —. His widow, Mary Irwin, received a $40 annuity in Columbia County 15 Apr. 1851.

Jacobs, —. His widow, Dorothy Jacobs, received a $40 gratuity and a $40 annuity 11 Apr. 1844 in York County. She died 5 Aug. 1853.

Jacoby, —. His widow, Barbara Jacoby, received a $40 gratuity and a $40 annuity in Adams County in Apr. 1840. She died 5 Sep. 1843.

James, —. His widow, Margaret James, received a $40 gratuity and a $40 annuity in 1838 in Philadelphia..

Jameson, Archibald. He received a $40 gratuity and a $40 annuity in Armstrong County 25 June 1839.

Jamieson, —. His widow, Elizabeth Jamieson, received a $40 gratuity and a $40 annuity in

Westmoreland County in 1838.

Jamieson, John. He received a $40 gratuity and a $40 annuity in Indiana County 16 Apr. 1838. He was styled "Scotch."

Jefferies, —. His widow, Sarah Jefferies, received a $40 gratuity and a $40 annuity in Baltimore, Md. 14 Mar. 1842 She died 1 Oct. 1842.

Jefferies, James. He received a $40 gratuity and a $40 annuity in 1838 in Allegheny County. He died 17 Oct. 1842.

Jeffries, —. His widow, Elizabeth Jeffries, received a $40 gratuity in Gallia Co., Ohio 22 Apr. 1844.

Jellison, Ephraim. He received a $40 annuity in Westmoreland County 7 Apr. 1846.

Jennings, —. His widow, Nancy Jennings, received a $40 gratuity and a $40 annuity 5 Apr. 1842 in Philadelphia County. She died 25 May 1842.

Johnson, James. He received a $40 gratuity 21 Mar. 1840. He was from Indiana County.

Johnston, —. His widow, Anna Johnston, received a $40 gratuity and a $40 annuity in Huntingdon County 21 July 1842.

Johnston, —. His widow, Margaret Johnston, received a $40 gratuity and a $40 annuity in Westmoreland County 21 Feb. 1838.

Johnston, Joseph. He received a $40 annuity 12 Apr. 1845.

Jones, —. His widow, Mary Jones, received a $40 annuity 12 Apr. 1851. She removed to Hamilton Co., Ohio.

Jones, Thomas. He received a $40 gratuity and a $40 annuity in 1839 in York County.

Jordan, —. His widow, Elizabeth Jordan, received a $40 annuity in Mercer County 11 Apr. 1848.

Jordan, James. He received a $40 gratuity and a $40 annuity in Allegheny County 12 Mar. 1839.

Jordan, Samuel. He received a $40 gratuity in Westmoreland County 8 May 1850.

Kaufman, Henry. He received a $40 annuity in York County 12 Apr. 1845. He died 28 Dec. 1848.

Keatley, —. His widow, Esther Keatley, received a $40 gratuity and a $40 annuity in Clarion County 18 Apr. 1843.

Keefer, —. His widow, Anna Maria Keefer, received a $40 gratuity and a $40 annuity 8 Apr. 1840. She was 76 years old in 1840 in Delaware County. She died 19 Oct. 1849.

Keel, Philip. He received a $40 gratuity and a $40 annuity in Bedford County 20 Mar.1838.

Keen, —. His widow, Christiana Keen, received a $40 gratuity and a $40 annuity in Chester County 8 Apr. 1840.

Keesy, —. His widow, Elizabeth Keesy, received a $40 gratuity and a $40 annuity 8 Apr. 1840 in Montgomery County.

Keeth, Solomon. He received a $40 annuity in Washington County 11 Apr. 1848.

Keiser, Henry. He received a $40 gratuity in Montgomery County in 1840.

Keller, —. His widow, Elizabeth Keller, received a $40 gratuity and a $40 annuity in Lancaster County in 1838.

Keller, John. He received a $40 gratuity and a $40 annuity in Allegheny County 18 Apr. 1843. He died 11 Apr. 1845.

Kelly, James. He received a $40 gratuity and a $40 annuity in Indiana County in 1838.

Kelly, Patrick. He received a $40 gratuity and a $40 annuity 11 Apr. 1844.

Kenar, Adam. He received a $40 gratuity and a $40 annuity in York County 20 May 1839. He died 24 Oct. 1840.

Keppel, —. His widow, Margaret Keppel, received a $40 gratuity and a $40 annuity 5 May 1841 in Berks County.

Kepple, George. He received a $40 gratuity in Armstrong County 12 Apr. 1845.

Kerr, Hugh. He received a $40 gratuity in Mercer County 13 Apr. 1841.

Kester, John Nicholas. He received a $40 gratuity and a $40 annuity in Clinton County 3 Apr. 1841, but he died before the act was passed. He also appeared as John Nicholas Kiser. His gratuity was paid to his son, Lawrence Kester.

Kettleman, —. His widow, Susanna Kettleman, received a $40 gratuity and a $40 annuity in Berks County 20 May 1839.

Keyser, Jacob. He received a $40 gratuity and a $40 annuity 3 Apr. 1841 in Union County. He died 31 Mar. 1845.

Kilgore, —. His widow, Eleanor Kilgore, received a $40 annuity in Westmoreland County in Apr. 1846. She died 23 Dec. 1856 in Allegheny County.

Kilpatrick, —. His widow, Nancy Kilpatrick, received a $40 gratuity in Perry County 8 May 1850.

King, Jacob. He received a $40 gratuity and a $40 annuity in 1838 in Berks County. He died 22 Oct. 1849.

King, John. He received relief in Armstrong County 5 May 1841.

Kintz, —. His widow, Sebina Kintz, received a $40 gratuity and a $40 annuity 11 Apr. 1844.

Kinzer, —. His widow, Mary Ann Kinzer, received a $40 gratuity and a $40 annuity in Allegheny Co. 21 July 1842.

Kip, —. His widow, Margaret Kip, received a $40 gratuity and a $40 annuity in Juniata County 18 Apr. 1843.

Kitchen, John. He received a $40 gratuity and a $40 annuity in Center County 20 May 1839. He was 89 years old in 1840.

Kline, —. His widow, Margaret Kline, received a $40 gratuity and a $40 annuity in Northampton County in 1838.

Kline, Jacob. He received benefits in Mifflin County 27 Mar. 1837.

Klinedinst, Godfrey. He received a $40 gratuity and a $40 annuity in York County in 1838.

Kling, —. His widow, Maria Kling, received a $40 gratuity and a $40 annuity in York Co. 5 Apr. 1842.

Klippert, Ernst. He received a $40 gratuity in Starke Co., Ohio in 1841.

Knicely, John. He received a $40 gratuity and a $40 annuity 14 Mar. 1842 in Greene County. He died 2 Apr. 1845.

Knight, John. He received a $40 gratuity in Beaver County 27 Mar. 1837.

Koken, —. His widow, Mary Koken, received a $40 gratuity and a $40 annuity in Centre County 10 Feb. 1841.

Koons, —. His widow, Mary Koons, received relief in Perry County 13 Apr. 1841.

Krebs, —. His widow, Catharine Krebs, received a $40 gratuity and a $40 annuity in York County 2 July 1842.

Kreider, —. His widow, Harriet Kreider, received a $40 gratuity and a $40 annuity in Philadelphia 5 Apr. 1842.

Krewson,—. His widow, Phebe Krewson, received a $40 gratuity and a $40 annuity in Philadelphia County in 1838.

Krick, Jacob. His residence was corrected to Washington Co., Md. He was granted a $40 gratuity and a $40 annuity 20 May 1839. He died 15 Dec. 1841.

Kriss, Conrad. He received a $40 gratuity and a $40 annuity in Lycoming County 8 Apr. 1840. He was dead by June 1845.

Kuhns, —. His widow, Susanna Kuhns, received a $40 gratuity and a $40 annuity in Lancaster County

18 Apr. 1843.

Kulp, Abraham C. He received a $40 gratuity and a $40 annuity in Lycoming County 18 Apr. 1843.

Kurtz, John. He received a $40 gratuity and a $40 annuity in Lancaster County 18 Apr. 1843. He died 6 Feb. 1844.

Labar, —. His widow, Catharine Labar, received a $40 annuity in Monroe County in Apr. 1846. She died 11 Nov. 1850.

Labar, Jacob. He received a $40 gratuity in Allegheny County 16 Apr. 1838. He also appeared as Jacob Lobar.

Lackey, —. His widow, Mary Lackey, received a $40 gratuity and a $40 annuity in Perry County 18 Apr. 1843. She died 10 Aug. 1845.

Landon, —. His widow, Elizabeth Landon, received a $40 gratuity and a $40 annuity in Bradford County in 1838.

Lane, —. His widow, Lucretia Lane, received a $40 annuity in Beaver County 15 Apr. 1852. She died 22 Dec. 1857.

Lane, Samuel. He received a $40 gratuity and a $40 annuity in Beaver County in 1838. He was 73 years of age in 1840.

Latimore, —. His widow, Mary Ann Latimore, was granted a $40 gratuity and a $40 annuity in Erie County in 1838.

Laumon, Jacob. He received a $40 annuity in Montgomery Co., Md. 16 Mar. 1847.

Lazarus, —. His widow, Elizabeth Lazarus, received a $40 gratuity and a $40 annuity in Northumberland County 25 June 1839. She died 22 Nov. 1839.

Leasure, John. He received a $40 gratuity and a $40 annuity in Indiana County 18 Jan. 1838. He died 20 Dec. 1844.

Lehman, —. His widow, Catharine Lehman, received a $40 gratuity and a $40 annuity in York County in Apr. 1840. She died 24 July 1854.

Leibengood, Jacob. He received a $40 gratuity and a $40 annuity 11 Apr. 1844.

Leibley, —. His widow, Elizabeth Leibley, received a $40 gratuity and a $40 annuity in Lancaster County 8 Apr. 1840. She died 23 Nov. 1854.

Leitheiser, —. His widow, Catharine Leitheiser, received a $40 gratuity and a $40 annuity in Starke Co.., Ohio in 1840.

Leitner, —. His widow, Anna M. Leitner, received a $40 gratuity in Baltimore, Md. 12 Apr. 1845.

Leitner, Adam. He received a $40 gratuity 8 May 1850.

Lemon, —. His widow, Agnes Lemon, received a $40 annuity in New York 3 Apr. 1851,

Lemon, —. His widow, Lydia Lemon, was awarded a $40 gratuity and a $40 annuity 11 Apr. 1844 in Dauphin County. She died in 1846.

Lemon, George. He received a $40 gratuity and a $40 annuity in Dauphin County 20 Mar. 1838.

Leslie, William. He and Mary Leslie were granted a $40 gratuity and a $40 annuity in Allegheny County in 1838. She died 27 Apr. 1849. He died 30 July 1850.

Levering, —. His widow, Mary Levering, received a $40 gratuity and a $40 annuity in Philadelphia County 20 May 1839. She was 75 years of age in 1840.

Lightener, George. He received a $40 gratuity and a $40 annuity in 1839.

Lincoln, John. He received a $40 gratuity and a $40 annuity in Fayette County 15 Mar. 1838.

Lindsay, Samuel. He received a $40 gratuity and a $40 annuity in Venango County 18 Apr. 1843. He died 20 Sep. 1857.

Lingafelter, Michael. He received a $40 gratuity and a $40 annuity in York County 18 Apr. 1843.

Linn,—. His widow, Jane Linn, received a $40 gratuity and a $40 annuity in Allegheny County 21 Feb. 1838.

Linn, —. His widow, Jane Linn, received a $40 annuity in Union County 12 Apr. 1851. She removed to Clinton County.

Logan, —. His widow, Elizabeth Logan, received a $40 gratuity and a $40 annuity in Northumberland County 13 Apr. 1841. She died 6 Mar. 1844.

Long, —. His widow, Hannah Long, received a $40 gratuity and a $40 annuity in Greene County 16 Apr. 1838. She died 27 May 1850.

Long, John. He received a $40 gratuity and a $40 annuity in Allegheny County 18 Apr. 1843.

Longshore, Abner. He received a $40 gratuity and a $40 annuity in Cumberland County 12 June 1840. He died 1 Oct. 1843.

Longwell, —. His widow, Rachel Longwell, received a $40 gratuity and a $40 annuity in Mifflin County 5 Apr. 1842. She died 10 Jan. 1845.

Lord, —. His widow, Nancy Lord, received a $40 annuity in Crawford County 15 Apr. 1852.

Lott, —. His widow, Maria Lott, received a $40 gratuity and a $40 annuity in Berks County in 1838.

Lower, John. He received a $40 gratuity and a $40 annuity in Philadelphia County 20 May 1839.

Lowman, Abraham. He received a $40 gratuity and a $40 annuity 11 Apr. 1844 in Indiana County. He died 17 Nov. 1846.

Lowry, Alexander. He received a $40 gratuity 27 Mar. 1837.

Lucas, George. He received a $40 gratuity and a $40 annuity in Cambria County 8 Apr. 1840.

Lutman, —. His widow, Margaret Lutman, received a $40 gratuity and a $40 annuity in Lancaster County 13 Apr. 1838.

Lyon, William. He received a $40 gratuity and a $40 annuity in Venango County 13 Mar. 1839.

Lyon, William. He was granted a gratuity 13 Mar. 1839. His daughter, Mary Dewoody, cared for her father to his death and received a $40 gratuity 8 Apr. 1840. She was from Venango County.

McCain, James. He received a $40 gratuity and a $40 annuity in 1838.

McCall, Samuel. He received a $40 gratuity and a $40 annuity in Butler County in 1840. He was 70 years old in 1840. He died 11 Nov. 1843.

McCandles, Peter. He received a $40 gratuity in York County 8 May 1850.

McCarty, —. His widow, Letitia McCarty, received a $40 gratuity and a $40 annuity 16 Apr. 1838 in Columbia County.

McCaskey, Daniel. He received a $40 gratuity and a $40 annuity in Beaver County 15 Mar. 1838.

McClanahan, —. His widow, Elizabeth McClanahan, received a $40 gratuity and a $40 annuity 5 Apr. 1842 in Mifflin County. She died 25 Oct. 1845.

McClary, William. His widow, Jane McClary, received a $40 annuity in Washington Co. 11 Apr. 1848.

McClelland, George. He received a $40 gratuity and a $40 annuity in Fayette County 13 Apr. 1838.

McCord, George. He received a $40 gratuity and a $40 annuity in Mercer County 16 Apr. 1838.

McCormack, John. He received a $40 annuity 12 Apr. 1845. He died in 1850 in Westmoreland County.

McCormick, John. He received a $40 annuity in Adams Co., Ohio 11 Apr. 1848.

McCoy, Daniel. His widow, Ruth McCoy, received a $40 gratuity and a $40 annuity in Paradise Twp., Lancaster County 25 Mar. 1861.

McCready, Alexander. He received a $40 gratuity and a $40 annuity in Washington County 4 Apr. 1837.

McCune, —. His widow, Martha McCune, received a $40 gratuity and a $40 annuity in Franklin County in 1840. She died 28 June 1842.

McDonald, —. His widow, Sarah McDonald, received a $40 gratuity and a $40 annuity in Chester County in 1838. She died 11 Jan. 1842.

McDonald, Robert. He received a $40 gratuity and a $40 annuity in Mercer County 20 May 1839. He died 9 June 1840..

McElroy, —. His widow, Catharine McElroy, received a $40 annuity in Philadelphia 23 Apr. 1852. She died 21 May 1855.

McElroy, James. He received a $40 annuity in Westmoreland County 12 Apr. 1845. He died 8 Dec. 1847.

McEwen, —. His widow, Elizabeth McEwen, received a $40 gratuity and a $40 annuity in Center County 8 Apr. 1840.

McFerson, John. He received a $40 gratuity and a $40 annuity in Tuscaroras Co., Ohio 8 Feb. 1842.

McGary, —, His widow, Rosanna McGary, of Wayne Co., Ohio received a $40 annuity and a $40 gratuity 13 Apr. 1854.

McGlaughlin, Hosannah, He received a $40 annuity in Indiana County 11 Apr. 1848.

McGlaughlin, William. He received a $40 gratuity and a $40 annuity in Washington County in 1838.

McGreary, William. He received a $40 annuity in Butler County 15 Mar. 1847.

McGregory, William. He received a $40 gratuity and a $40 annuity in Butler County in 1838.

McGuire, Robert. He received a $40 gratuity and a $40 annuity in Westmoreland County 18 Apr. 1843. He died 6 Jan. 1850.

McIlney, John. He received a $40 gratuity and a $40 annuity in Bedford County in Apr. 1840. His act was repealed later in the year. His widow, Mary McIlney, received a $40 annuity 10 Apr. 1849.

McKin, Andrew. He was a soldier under Gen. Arthur St. Clair and was paid a $40 annuity in Butler County 10 Apr. 1849. His name may have been Andrew Kim.

McKinley, Robert. He received a $40 gratuity in Armstrong County in 1841.

McKinzey, James. He received a $40 gratuity and a $40 annuity in 1838 in Westmoreland County.

McKinzey, Joseph. He received a $40 gratuity and a $40 annuity in Beaver County in 1837.

McKinzie, —. His widow, Jane McKinzie, received a $40 gratuity and a $40 annuity in Beaver County 20 May `1839.

McLaughlin, —. His widow, Jane McLaughlin, received a $40 gratuity and a $40 annuity in Beaver County in 1838.

McManus, Joseph. He received a $40 gratuity and a $40 annuity in Starke Co., Ohio 8 Feb. 1841.

McQuillen, Garret. He received a $40 gratuity and a $40 annuity in Huntingdon County 8 Apr. 1840. His widow was Elizabeth McQuillen.

McVay, William. He received a $40 annuity in Greene County 12 Apr. 1845.

McWilliams, John. He received a $40 gratuity in Erie County 12 Apr. 1845.

Mace, Joseph. He received a $40 gratuity and a $40 annuity in Chester County 17 Mar. 1838.

Magaw, William. He received a $40 gratuity and a $40 annuity in Mercer County 16 Apr. 1838.

Maglaughlin, Andrew. He received a $40 gratuity and a $40 annuity 11 Apr. 1844.

Maning, —. His widow, Nancy Maning, received a $40 gratuity and a $40 annuity in Beaver County 20 May 1839.

Maple, William. He received a $40 gratuity and a $40 annuity 21 June 1839. He died 19 Mar. 1842 in Centre County

Marshall, —. His widow, Mary Magdalene Marshall, received a $40 annuity in Adams County 19 Apr. 1853.

Marshall, John. He received a $40 gratuity in Adams County in 1841.

Marshall, Samuel. He received a $40 annuity in Westmoreland County 12 Apr. 1845. He died 26 Apr. 1845.

Martin, —. His widow, Catharine Martin, received a $40 gratuity and a $40 annuity in Venango County in 1838. She died 1 May 1840.

Martin, —. His widow, Eve Catharine Martin, received a $40 gratuity and a $40 annuity in Lancaster County in Apr. 1840. She died 28 Apr. 1846.

Martin, —. His widow, Mary Martin, received a $40 gratuity and a $40 annuity in Lycoming County 2 July 1842.

Martin, Armand. His widow, Mary Martin, formerly of Erie Co., N.Y. received a $40 annuity in Iowa 27 Mar. 1862. They had lived in Missouri before moving to Iowa.

Martin, Arnold. He received a $40 gratuity and a $40 annuity in Erie County 13 Apr. 1841.

Mason, Philip. He received a $40 gratuity and a $40 annuity in 1838 in Beaver County.

Mathers, —. His widow, Elizabeth Mathers, received a $40 gratuity and a $40 annuity in Perry County 8 Feb. 1841.

Mathias, —. His widow, Elizabeth Mathias, received a $40 gratuity and a $40 annuity in Philadelphia County in 1838.

Mattocks, —. His widow, Jane Mattocks, received a $40 gratuity and a $40 annuity 2 July 1842 in Crawford County.

Mattocks, —. His widow, Mary Mattocks, received a $40 gratuity and a $40 annuity in Mercer County 13 Apr. 1841.

Maull, Uriah. He received assistance 17 Mar. 1838 in Allegheny County. He died 31 Mar. 1839.

May, —. His widow, Mary May, received a $40 gratuity and a $40 annuity in Fayette County 21 Mar. 1840. She died 1 Oct. 1840

Mead, —. His widow, Catharine Mead, received a $40 gratuity and a $40 annuity in Crawford County 20 May 1839.

Means, —. His widow, Rosannah Means, received a $40 gratuity and a $40 annuity in Mercer County 14 Apr. 1838.

Melarkey, Daniel. He received a $40 gratuity and a $40 annuity in Butler County 8 Apr. 1840. He was 68 years old in 1840.

Mell, —. His widow, Maria Mell, received a $40 gratuity and a $40 annuity in Berks County in 1837.

Mento, —. His widow, Elizabeth Mento, received a $40 gratuity and a $40 annuity in Crawford County 20 Mar. 1838. He died 14 Oct. 1840.

Merriman, Archibald. He received a $40 annuity in Crawford County 19 Apr. 1853.

Merriman, Frederick. He received a $40 gratuity and a $40 annuity in Allegheny Count 5 May 1841. He died 24 Feb. 1849. His widow, Mary Merryman, received a $40 gratuity and a $40 annuity 27 Mar.1855.

Messersmith, —. His widow, Susannah Messersmith, received a $40 gratuity and a $40 annuity in 1838 in Lancaster County. She died 2 Sep. 1843.

Meyers, —. His widow, Salome Meyers, received a $40 gratuity and a $40 annuity in Northampton County 13 Mar. 1839. She also appeared as Salome Myers.

Miller, —. His widow, Catharine Miller, received a $40 gratuity and a $40 annuity in Franklin County 11 Apr. 1844.

Miller, —. His widow, Charlotte Miller, received a $40 annuity in Franklin County 16 Mar. 1847. She died 16 Mar. 1847.

Miller, —. His widow, Elizabeth Miller, received a $40 gratuity and a $40 annuity in Susquehanna Co. 18 Apr. 1843.

Miller, —. His widow, Elizabeth Miller, received a $40 annuity in Berks County 12 Apr. 1845. She died 22 Aug. 1845.

Miller, —. His widow, Mary Miller, received a $40 gratuity and a $40 annuity in Cumberland County 13 Apr. 1838. She died in 1847.

Miller, —. His widow, Mary Miller, received a $40 gratuity and a $40 annuity in Lancaster County in 13 Apr. 1838. She was dead by Jan. 1842.

Miller, —. His widow, Margaret Miller, received a $40 gratuity and a $40 annuity 18 Apr. 1843 in Philadelphia.

Miller, —. His widow, Nancy Miller, received a $40 gratuity and a $40 annuity in Center County in 1840. She died 12 Sep. 1841.

Miller, Benjamin. He received a $40 annuity in Fayette County 12 Apr. 1845. He died 21 Jan. 1851.

Miller, Christian. He received a $40 gratuity and a $40 annuity 8 Apr. 1840 in York County.

Miller, George. He received a $40 annuity in Beaver County 12 Apr. 1851.

Miller, Isaac. He received benefits in Erie County 27 Mar. 1837.

Miller, Martin. He received a $40 gratuity and a $40 annuity in Franklin County 8 Feb. 1841.

Miller, Peter. He received a $40 gratuity and a $40 annuity in Lancaster County 20 Mar. 1838.

Miller, Sebastian. He received a $40 gratuity and a $40 annuity in Monroe County 14 Mar. 1842. He died 11 Nov. 1842.

Miller, William. He received a $40 gratuity and a $40 annuity 18 Apr. 1843 in Greene County. He died 9 Apr. 1843.

Mitchell, Shadrach. He received a $40 annuity in Greene County 21 Apr. 1846.

Mitman, —. His widow, Barbara Mitman, received a $40 gratuity and a $40 annuity in York County 13 Apr. 1841. She died 13 Nov. 1849.

Moore, —. His widow, Isabella Moore, received a $40 gratuity and a $40 annuity in Beaver County 2 July 1842.

Moore, James. He received a $40 gratuity and a $40 annuity in 1838.

Moore, John. He received a $40 gratuity and a $40 annuity in Greene County 14 Mar. 1842.

Moore, William. He received a $40 gratuity and a $40 annuity in Lancaster County 18 Jan. 1838.

Moorhead, James. He received a $40 gratuity and a $40 annuity in Venango County 20 May 1839.

Mooreland, William. He received a $40 gratuity and a $40 annuity in Westmoreland County 21 June 1839.

Moreland, —. His widow, Elizabeth Moreland, received a $40 gratuity and a $40 annuity 18 Apr. 1843.

Moreland, —. His widow, Rebecca Moreland, received a $40 gratuity and a $40 annuity 20 May 1857.

Morris, —. His widow, Ann Morris, received a $40 gratuity and a $40 annuity in Lancaster County in 1838. She died 28 May 1841.

Morris, Samuel. His widow, Temperance Morris, received a $40 gratuity and a $40 annuity in Fayette County 1 May 1861.

Morrison, —. His widow, Martha Morrison, received a $40 gratuity and a $40 annuity in Venango County 21 Mar. 1840.

Moshier, Henry. He received a $40 annuity in Westmoreland County 11 Apr. 1848.

Mowry, —. His widow, Mary Ann Mowry, received a $40 annuity 12 Apr. 1845. She died 5 Dec. 1848 in Westmoreland County.

Mullin, Alexander. He received a $40 gratuity in Cumberland County 8 May 1850.

Murphy, —. His widow, Ruth Murphy, received a $40 gratuity and a $40 annuity in Perry County 11 Apr. 1844.

Murphy, Jeremiah. His widow, Elizabeth Murphy, received a $40 gratuity and a $40 annuity in Armstrong County 14 Apr. 1859.

Muse, —. His widow, Margaret Muse, received a $40 annuity in Mercer County 13 Apr. 1854. She died 10 Oct. 1859.

Myer, —. His widow, Catherine Myer, received a $40 gratuity and a $40 annuity in Franklin County 21 July 1842.

Myers, —. His widow, Jane Myers, received a $40 gratuity in Allegheny County 8 May 1850. She died in May 1855.

Myers, —. His widow, Mary Myers, received a $40 gratuity and a $40 annuity in Lancaster County 11 Apr. 1844. She died 14 Nov. 1848.

Myers, John. He received a $40 gratuity and a $40 annuity 5 May 1841 in Allegheny County.

Myers, Peter. He received a $40 gratuity and a $40 annuity in Holmes Co., Ohio 21 July 1842.

Nagle, Philip. He received a $40 gratuity and a $40 annuity in Berks County 20 May 1839. He died 29 Sep. 1843.

Neel, Thomas. He received a $40 gratuity and a $40 annuity in Indiana County 18 June 1834.

Newberry, —. His widow, Sarah Newberry, received a $40 gratuity and a $40 annuity in Northumberland County 21 Mar. 1840.

Nicholas, George. He received a $40 gratuity and a $40 annuity in Bucks County 11 Apr. 1844.

Nichols, William. He received a $40 gratuity and a $40 annuity in Fayette County 13 Mar. 1839.

Nixon, —. His widow, Jane Nixon, received a $40 annuity in Apr. 1846. She died 9 July 1848 in Westmoreland County.

Noble, —. His widow, Elizabeth Noble, received a $40 annuity in Washington County 12 Apr. 1845.

Norman, Daniel. He received a $40 gratuity and a $40 annuity in Berks County 18 Apr. 1843. The title of his pension act gave his name as David Norman.

Nugent, —. His widow, Mary Nugent, received a $40 gratuity in Indiana County 18 Apr. 1843.

Null, Joseph. He received a $40 gratuity and a $40 annuity in Venango County 20 May 1839. He died 4 Sep. 1842.

Nunnemacher, —. His widow, Catharine Nunnemacher, received a $40 gratuity and a $40 annuity in Northampton County 14 Mar. 1842. She died 4 Mar. 1847.

Oliver, James. He received a $40 annuity in Indiana County 7 Apr. 1846.

Oliver, William. He received a $40 annuity in Indiana County 12 Apr. 1845. He died 17 Aug. 1845.

Orner, Martin. He received a $40 gratuity and a $40 annuity in Luzerne County 5 Apr. 1842.

Overfield, —. His widow, Elizabeth Overfield, received a $40 gratuity and a $40 annuity in Monroe County in 1838.

Overhals, —. His widow, Sarah Overhals, received a $40 gratuity in Luzerne County 3 Apr. 1841.

Overholtz, —. His widow, Sarah Overholtz, received a $40 gratuity and a $40 annuity in Luzerne Co. 18 Apr. 1843.

Overly, Christopher. He received a $40 annuity 7 Apr. 1846.

Overturff, —. His widow, Elizabeth Overturff, received a $40 gratuity and a $40 annuity in Fayette County 20 May 1839. She died 16 Sep. 1845.

Owens, John. He received a $40 gratuity in Greene County 12 Apr. 1845.

Owry, —. His widow, Mary Owry, received a $40 gratuity and a $40 annuity 18 Apr. 1843. She died 6 Sep. 1844.

Ozias, Christopher. He received a $40 gratuity and a $40 annuity in Philadelphia County 13 Mar. 1839.

Ozier, —. His widow, Mary Ozier, received a $40 annuity in Monroe County 19 Apr. 1853. She transferred to Luzerne County.

Pace, William. He received a $40 annuity in Luzerne County 15 Mar. 1847.

Pain, Robert. He received a $40 gratuity and a $40 annuity 21 Feb. 1838 in Westmoreland County. He died 29 Sep. 1843.

Painter, —. His widow, Elizabeth Painter, received a $40 gratuity and a $40 annuity 18 Apr. 1843 in Armstrong County.

Palmer, Adam. He received a $40 gratuity and a $40 annuity in Westmoreland County 13 Apr. 1838.

Palmer, Peter. He received a $40 gratuity and a $40 annuity in Indiana County 13 Mar. 1839.

Palmiteer, —. His widow, Mary Catharine Palmiteer, received a $40 gratuity and a $40 annuity in Lancaster County 11 Apr. 1841.

Parker, Richard. He received a $40 gratuity 12 Apr. 1845. His name was incorrectly given as Richard Patton. The correction was made 21 Apr. 1846.

Parris, —. His widow, Sarah Parris, received a $40 gratuity and a $40 annuity 2 July 1842 in Philadelphia. She died 28 July 1845.

Patrick, James. He received a $40 gratuity and a $40 annuity 18 Apr. 1843.

Patrick, William. He received a $40 annuity in Westmoreland County 12 Apr. 1845.

Patton, —. His widow, Sarah Patton, received a $40 gratuity and a $40 annuity in Philadelphia County 13 Apr. 1841.

Patton, Richard. He received a $40 gratuity in Greene County 12 Apr.1845.

Peadric, Benjamin. He received a $40 gratuity and a $40 annuity in Luzerne County in 1838.

Peden, Job. He received a $40 gratuity and a $40 annuity in 1838 in Indiana County.

Peden, Joseph. He received a $40 gratuity and a $40 annuity in 1838 in Washington County.

Peebles, Samuel. He received a $40 gratuity and a $40 annuity in Allegheny County 21 Feb. 1838.

Perky, Daniel. He received a $40 gratuity in Holmes Co., Ohio 15 Mar. 1847.

Phillipe, —. His widow, Susannah Phillipe, received a $40 gratuity and a $40 annuity in 1839 in Berks County.

Pierce, Job. The law of 21 June 1839 incorrectly had his name as Job Pedant of Indiana County. The correction was made in Apr. 1840. He died 9 Aug. 1842.

Piper, Robert. He received a $40 annuity 12 Apr. 1845.

Plank, —. His widow, Elizabeth Plank, received a $40 annuity in Adams County 19 Apr. 1853.

Plott, John. He received a $40 gratuity and a $40 annuity in Cambria County 13 Apr. 1838. He was 85 years old in 1840. He died 12 Feb. 1850.

Polk, James. He received a $40 gratuity and a $40 annuity in Delaware County 13 Apr. 1838. He was dead by Dec. 1839.

Pollock, Samuel. He received a $40 gratuity in Beaver County in 1840.

Pope, —. His widow, Salome Pope, received a $40 gratuity and a $40 annuity in Apr. 1840 in York County. She died 17 May 1841.

Posten, Charles. His widow, Hannah Posten, received a $40 gratuity in Monroe County in Apr. 1840.

Postens, —. His widow, Ann Postens, received a $40 gratuity and a $40 annuity in Monroe County 8 Apr. 1840.

Pott, —. His widow, Catharine Pott, received a $40 gratuity and a $40 annuity in Berks County 8 Feb. 1841. She died 10 Sep. 1854.

Potts, —. His widow, Mary Potts, received a $40 gratuity and a $40 annuity 11 Apr. 1844 in Dauphin

County. She died 25 Sep. 1844.

Potts, —. His widow, Sarah Potts, received a $40 gratuity and a $40 annuity 13 Apr. 1841 in Montgomery County.

Potts, Noah. He received a $40 annuity in Beaver County 12 Apr. 1851. He died in 1856.

Power, James. He received a $40 gratuity and a $40 annuity in Allegheny County 21 July 1842.

Powers, —. His widow, Elsy Powers, received a $40 gratuity and a $40 annuity in Allegheny County in 1838. She died 29 Oct. 1840.

Powers, George. He received a $40 gratuity and a $40 annuity in Venango County 15 Mar. 1838. He died 21 Apr. 1845.

Pratt, James. He received assistance 13 Apr. 1838.

Price, Nathaniel. He received a $40 gratuity in Bucks County 16 Mar. 1847.

Provance, Joseph Y. His widow, Rachael Provance, received a $40 gratuity and a $40 annuity in Fayette County 28 Mar. 1854.

Rager, —. His widow, Mary Rager, received a $40 annuity in Cambria County in Apr. 1846.

Rankin, David. He received a $40 gratuity and a $40 annuity in Jefferson County 10 Feb. 1841.

Ransall, —. His widow, Mary Ransall, received a $40 gratuity and a $40 annuity in 1840 in Butler County.

Rasher, —. His widow, Elizabeth Rasher, received a $40 gratuity and a $40 annuity in Armstrong County 18 Apr. 1843.

Rathfon, —. His widow, Elizabeth Rathfon, received a $40 gratuity and a $40 annuity in Lancaster County 13 Apr. 1838.

Rayborn, —. His widow, Eleanor Rayborn, received a $40 gratuity and a $40 annuity in Armstrong County 20 Mar. 1838. She also appeared as Eleanor Razborn.

Ream, —. His widow, Juliana Ream, received a $40 gratuity and a $40 annuity in Lancaster County 10 Feb. 1841. She died 22 Mar. 1841.

Ream, George. He received a $40 gratuity and a $40 annuity in Lancaster County 13 Apr. 1841.

Reden, —. His widow, Mary Reden, received a $40 gratuity and a $40 annuity in Mifflin County 21 July 1842.

Reed,—. His widow, Martha Reed, received a $40 gratuity and a $40 annuity in Allegheny County in 1838. She was dead by 27 Dec. 1842.

Reed, —. His widow, Mary Reed, received a $40 annuity in Crawford County 10 Apr. 1849. She died 14 Oct. 1850

Reed, James. He received assistance 17 Mar. 1838 in Huntingdon County. He was dead by Dec. 1840.

Rees, —. His widow, Rebecca Rees, received a $40 gratuity and a $40 annuity 5 Apr. 1842 in Philadelphia.

Regun, —. His widow, Miriam Regun, received a $40 gratuity and a $40 annuity in Fayette County 3 Apr. 1841.

Reherd, John. He received a $40 annuity in York County 7 Apr. 1846.

Reichart, —. His widow, Elizabeth Reichart, received a $40 gratuity in Bucks County 8 May 1850.

Reichart, —. His widow, Margaret Reichart, received a $40 gratuity and a $40 annuity in Bucks Co. 2 July 1842.

Reigelman, —. His widow, Magdalena Reigelman, received a $40 annuity in Berks County 21 Apr. 1846.

Reisinger, —. His widow, Catharine Reisinger, received a $40 gratuity and a $40 annuity in 1838.

Remley, Emanuel. He received a $40 annuity in Greene County 12 Apr. 1851. He was an "old soldier."

Remmel, Francis. He received a $40 annuity 12 Apr. 1845 in Westmoreland County. He died 24 Mar. 1853.

Reomer, —. His widow, Elizabeth Reomer, received a $40 gratuity and a $40 annuity in Franklin County in 1838. She died 15 May 1849.

Repine, Daniel. He received a $40 gratuity in Indiana County 15 Mar. 1847 and a $40 annuity 11 Apr. 1848. He died 31 May 1856.

Repine, James. He received a $40 gratuity and a $40 annuity in Indiana County 13 Apr. 1838.

Reyer, Jacob. His widow, Mary Reyer, received a $40 gratuity in Westmoreland County 10 Apr. 1849.

Reynolds, Benjamin. He was 79 years old in 1840. He received a $40 annuity in Bradford County 21 Apr. 1846.

Rher, Joseph. He received a $40 gratuity in Fayette County 14 Mar. 1842.

Rhorer, —. His widow, Elizabeth Rhorer, received a $40 gratuity and a $40 annuity in Lebanon Co. 8 Apr. 1840.

Rice, Christian. He received a $40 gratuity and a $40 annuity in Somerset County 20 Mar. 1838.

Rice, William. He received a $40 gratuity and a $40 annuity in Philadelphia County 13 Feb. 1840.

Richards, —. His widow, Catherine Richards, received a $40 gratuity and a $40 annuity 18 Apr. 1843. She died in Berks County 27 Aug. 1845.

Ricker, John. He received a $40 gratuity and a $40 annuity in Dauphin County 20 May 1839.

Riddle, Robert. He received a $40 gratuity and a $40 annuity in Butler County in 1838.

Riggs, Joseph. He received a $40 gratuity in Mercer County 5 Apr. 1842.

Rihn, George. He received a $40 gratuity and a $40 annuity in Allegheny County in 1837.

Rinker, Henry. He received a $40 gratuity and a $40 annuity in Northampton County 20 May 1839.

Ristine, —. His widow, Hannah Ristine, received a $40 gratuity and a $40 annuity in 1838 in Philadelphia.

Ritchie, William. He received a $40 gratuity and a $40 annuity in Allegheny County in 1840.

Ritter, —. His widow, Barbara Ritter, received a $40 gratuity and a $40 annuity in Northumberland County 11 Apr. 1840.

Robb, Samuel. He received a $40 gratuity and a $40 annuity 15 Mar. 1838 in Westmoreland County.

Robertson, Robert. He received a $40 gratuity and a $40 annuity 18 Apr. 1843. He moved from Fayette County to Ohio.

Robinson, —. His widow, Rebecca Robinson, received a $40 annuity in Beaver County in Apr. 1846.

Robison, —. His widow, Jane Robison, received a $40 gratuity and a $40 annuity in Mercer County 8 Feb. 1841. She died 15 Apr. 1843.

Robison, —. His widow, Margaret Robison, received a $40 gratuity and a $40 annuity in Allegheny County 13 Apr. 1841.

Rodes, —. His widow, Hannah Rodes, received a $40 gratuity and a $40 annuity in Mercer County 21 July 1842.

Rodgers, Michael. He received a $40 gratuity and a $40 annuity in Berks County 21 June 1839.

Rogers, James. He received a $40 gratuity and a $40 annuity in Fayette County 20 May 1839. He died 27 Dec. 1840.

Rollyer, David. He received a $40 gratuity in Crawford County in 1840.

Ross, John. He received a $40 gratuity and a $40 annuity 11 Apr. 1844.

Rowland, —. His widow, Christiana Rowland, received a $40 gratuity and a $40 annuity in Lebanon County 5 Apr. 1842. She also appeared as Christiana Roland.

Rowland, Jacob. He received a $40 gratuity and a $40 annuity in Lebanon County 3 Apr. 1841. He also appeared as Jacob Roland. He died 16 Aug. 1841.

Ruffner, Henry. He received a $40 annuity in Indiana County 11 Apr. 1848.

Ruffner, Simon. He received a $40 gratuity in Westmoreland County in 1838 and a $40 gratuity and a $40 annuity in Indiana County 18 Apr. 1843. His widow, Barbara Ruffner, received a $40 gratuity in Westmoreland County 8 May 1850.

Rundles, Hardy. He received a $40 gratuity and a $40 annuity 8 Apr. 1840 in Allegheny County. He died 22 Mar. 1842.

Russel, John. He received a $40 gratuity and a $40 annuity in 1838 in Armstrong County.

Russel, Paul. He received a $40 gratuity and a $40 annuity in Philadelphia County 17 Mar. 1838.

Rust, Henry. He received a $40 annuity in Crawford County 21 Apr. 1846. He died 23 Apr. 1851.

Rutter, George. He received a $40 annuity 15 Mar. 1847.

Sampson, Charles. He received a $40 gratuity and a $40 annuity in Venango County 20 Mar. 1838. He died 1 Dec. 1848.

Sankey, —. His widow, Catharine Sankey, received a $40 gratuity and a $40 annuity in Lancaster County 20 May 1839.

Santee, —. His widow, Maria Santee, received a $40 gratuity and a $40 annuity in Apr. 1840 in Northampton County. She died 27 Nov. 1848.

Savell, —. His widow, Mary Savell, received a $40 gratuity and a $40 annuity in Philadelphia County in 1837. She was 95 years old in 1840. She died 12 Aug. 1842.

Scause, —. His widow, Barbara Scause, received a $40 gratuity and a $40 annuity in Washington Co., Md. 5 Apr. 1842.

Schall, John. He received a $40 gratuity and a $40 annuity in Jefferson County in 1838. He died 9 Apr. 1845 in Armstrong County.

Scheetz, —. His widow, Catherine Scheetz, received a $40 gratuity and a $40 annuity in Lehigh County 18 Apr. 1843. The law had her name incorrectly as Christian Scheetz. A correction was made 25 Mar. 1844.

Schlatter, —. His widow, Anna Maria Schlatter, received a $40 gratuity and a $40 annuity in Lancaster County 20 May 1839. She died 12 Sep. 1850.

Schlotterer, —. His widow, Elizabeth Schlotterer, received a $40 gratuity and a $40 annuity in Philadelphia County in 1838.

Schmaltz, —. His widow, Elizabeth Schmaltz, received a $40 gratuity and a $40 annuity in Philadelphia County in 1838. She died 3 Jan. 1841.

Schmull, —. His widow, Juliann Schmull, received a $40 gratuity and a $40 annuity in Montgomery County 13 Apr. 1843.

Schraeder, —. His widow, Elizabeth Schraeder, received a $40 gratuity and a $40 annuity in Berks County 18 Apr. 1843.

Scott, —. Pa. His widow, Elizabeth Scott, received a $40 gratuity and a $40 annuity in Butler County 16 Apr. 1838. She was 70 years old in 1840. She died 17 Mar. 1861.

Scott, —. His widow, Sarah Scott, received a $40 gratuity and a $40 annuity in Northumberland County 20 May 1839. She was 78 years in 1840. She died 29 Dec. 1852.

Scott, Alexander. He received a $40 gratuity and a $40 annuity in Westmoreland County 14 Mar. 1842.

Scott, George. He received a $40 annuity 12 Apr. 1845.

Scott, James. He received a $40 gratuity and a $40 annuity in Armstrong County 3Apr. 1841.

Scott, John. He received a $40 gratuity and a $40 annuity in Clearfield County 18 Apr. 1843.

Sechler, —. His widow, Rebecca Sechler, received a $40 gratuity in Lycoming County 8 May 1850.

Seitzinger, —. His widow, Catharine Seitzinger, received a $40 annuity 12 Apr. 1845. She died 24 Apr. 1845 in Berks County.

Seitzinger, —. His widow, Margaret Seitzinger, received a $40 gratuity and a $40 annuity in Berks County 5 May 1841.

Seling, Henry. He received a $40 gratuity in Fayette County 14 Mar. 1842.

Semans, Henry. He received a $40 annuity in Fayette County 21 Apr. 1846.

Shaback,—. His widow, Elizabeth Shaback, received a $40 gratuity and a $40 annuity in Lancaster County 21 June 1839. She died 20 Sep. 1845.

Shade, Jacob. He received a $40 gratuity and a $40 annuity in Montgomery County in 1838. He died 23 Dec. 1840.

Shaffer, Adam. He received a $40 gratuity and a $40 annuity in Luzerne County 20 May 1839.

Shaffer, Thomas. He received assistance in Washington County 27 Mar. 1837. He was 84 years old in 1840. He died 7 Dec. 1849.

Shall, Michael. He received a $40 gratuity and a $40 annuity in Armstrong County 20 May 1839. He was 70 years old in 1840. He died 13 Mar. 1856.

Shaw, —. His widow, Catharine Shaw, received a $40 gratuity and a $40 annuity in Westmoreland Co. 11 Apr. 1844.

Sheets, Jacob. He received a $40 gratuity and a $40 annuity in Washington Co., Maryland in 1840.

Shepley, Adam. He received a $40 gratuity and a $40 annuity in Allegheny County 18 Apr. 1843.

Shields, David. He received a $40 gratuity and a $40 annuity in Armstrong County 13 Mar. 1839. He was 80 years old in 1840.

Shine, Lewis. He received a $40 gratuity and a $40 annuity in York County 5 Apr. 1842.

Shinkle, —. His widow, Catharine Shinkle, received a $40 gratuity and a $40 annuity in Philadelphia County 16 Apr. 1838.

Shockey, —. His widow, Mary Shockey, received a $40 gratuity and a $40 annuity in Lancaster County in 1848.

Shope, Jacob. He received a $40 gratuity and a $40 annuity in Dauphin County 17 Mar. 1838.

Shover, —. His widow, Catharine Shover, received a $40 gratuity and a $40 annuity in Franklin County in 1838.

Shroders, John. He received a $40 gratuity and a $40 annuity 21 June 1839 in Allegheny County. The law had his name misspelled as John Shrodes. It was corrected 13 Feb. 1840.

Shutzer, —. His widow, Elizabeth Shutzer of Washington Co., Md. received a $40 gratuity and a $40 annuity 25 June 1839.

Sideman, —. His widow, Eliza Sideman, received a $40 gratuity and a $40 annuity in Northampton County in Apr. 1840.

Siegendaler, —. His widow, Julianna Siegendaler, received a $40 gratuity and a $40 annuity in Berks County in 1839.

Siemensderfer, —. His widow, Elizabeth Siemensderfer, received a $40 gratuity and a $40 annuity in Lancaster County in 1839.

Sillyman, —. His widow, Nancy Sillyman, received a $40 gratuity and a $40 annuity in Northampton County 11 Apr. 1844. She died 8 June 1845.

Simpson, Peter. He received a $40 gratuity and a $40 annuity 11 Apr. 1844.

Simpson, Robert. He received a $40 gratuity and a $40 annuity in Armstrong County 11 Apr. 1844.

Sipes, John. He received a $40 gratuity and a $40 annuity in Armstrong County in 1838.

Skepton, —. His widow, Nancy Skepton, received a $40 gratuity and a $40 annuity 5 Apr. 1842. She died 25 Mar. 1844 in Mifflin County.

Slaback, —. His widow, Elizabeth Slaback, received a $40 gratuity and a $40 annuity in Lancaster Co.

Slater, Henry. He received a $40 gratuity in Greene County 18 Apr. 1843.

Slater, John. He received a $40 gratuity and a $40 annuity in Greene County in 1839.

Slaysman, —. His widow, Mary Slaysman, received a $40 gratuity and a $40 annuity 18 Apr. 1843. She lived in Baltimore, Md.

Sloan, —. His widow, Martha Sloan, received a $40 gratuity and a $40 annuity in Armstrong County in 1838. She died 1 Mar. 1842.

Smeltzer, Jacob. He received a $40 gratuity in Westmoreland County 3 Apr. 1841.

Smick, —. His widow, Elizabeth Smick, received a $40 annuity in Apr. 1846. She was probably the one of the name who was from Northampton County 31 Mar. 1846.

Smith, —. His widow, Ann Smith, received a $40 gratuity and a $40 annuity in Westmoreland County in 1839.

Smith, —. His widow, Mary Smith, received a $40 gratuity and a $40 annuity in Monroe County 13 Mar. 1839.

Smith, —. His widow, Mary Smith, received a $40 gratuity and a $40 annuity in Montgomery County 11 Apr. 1844.

Smith, —. His widow, Sarah Smith, received a $40 gratuity and a $40 annuity in Armstrong County 8 Apr. 1840.

Smith, John. He received benefits in Baltimore, Md. 27 Mar. 1838.

Smith, Philip. He received a $40 gratuity and a $40 annuity in Beaver County in 1840.

Smouse, George A. He received a $40 gratuity in Indiana County 11 Apr. 1844.

Snell, Philip. He received a $40 gratuity and a $40 annuity in Lancaster County 18 Apr. 1843.

Snyder, —. His widow, Barbara Snyder, received a $40 gratuity and a $40 annuity in Westmoreland County 11 Apr. 1844.

Snyder, —. His widow, Catharine Snyder, received a $40 gratuity and a $40 annuity in 1838 in Berks County.

Snyder, —. His widow, Catharine Snyder, received a $40 gratuity and a $40 annuity in Franklin County 20 May 1839. She died 12 Mar. 1841.

Snyder, —. His widow, Mary Snyder, received a $40 gratuity and a $40 annuity in Westmoreland Co. in 1838.

Snyder, Frederick. He received a $40 gratuity and a $40 annuity in Monroe County 18 Apr. 1843.

Solt, Paul. He received a $40 gratuity and a $40 annuity in Northumberland County 20 May 1839.

Souder, —. His widow, Elizabeth Souder, received a $40 gratuity in Philadelphia County 8 May 1850.

Spang, —. His widow, Margaret Spang, received a $40 gratuity and a $40 annuity in Cumberland County 11 Apr. 1844. She died 10 Mar. 1846.

Spangler, —. His widow, Sarah Spangler, received a $40 gratuity and a $40 annuity in York County 5 Apr. 1842.

Spatz, Michael. He received a $40 gratuity and a $40 annuity in Berks County 13 Feb. 1840.

Speigle, —. His widow, Susannah Speigle, received a $40 gratuity and a $40 annuity in York County 8 Apr. 1840.

Spoon, Melchior. He received a $40 gratuity and a $40 annuity in Perry County 13 Apr. 1838.

Sprott, Samuel. His widow, Eleanor Sprott, received a $40 gratuity and a $40 annuity in Lawrence County 12 Apr. 1856.

Stambaugh, Peter. He received a $40 annuity in Franklin County 16 Apr. 1838.

Stanart, —. His widow, Sarah Stanart, received a $40 gratuity and a $40 annuity in Philadelphia in 1839. She was 81 years of age in 1840. She died 14 Apr. 1843.

Statler, Jacob. He received a $40 gratuity and a $40 annuity in Greene County 18 Apr. 1843.

Steagart, —. His widow, Barbara Steagart, received a $40 gratuity and a $40 annuity in Allegheny County 5 Apr.1842.

Steager, Peter. He received a $40 gratuity and a $40 annuity in Lebanon County 13 Apr. 1838.

Stealy, Christopher. He received a $40 gratuity and a $40 annuity in Allegheny County 8 Apr. 1840.

Stedman, —. His widow, Rebecca Stedman, received a $40 gratuity and a $40 annuity in Northumberland County 18 Apr. 1843. She died 7 Oct. 1843.

Steel, —. His widow, Margaret Steel, received a $40 gratuity and a $40 annuity in Center County 20 May 1839.

Steel, —. His widow, Polly Steel, received a $40 gratuity and a $40 annuity 11 Apr. 1844. She was from York County. She died 25 May 1852.

Steel, Isaac. He received a $40 gratuity and a $40 annuity in Armstrong County 20 Mar. 1838. He was 77 years old in 1840. He died 24 Oct. 1842.

Steff, —. His widow, Elizabeth Steff, received a $40 gratuity and a $40 annuity in Berks County 8 Feb. 1841. She died 3 Sep. 1849.

Steinmetz, Jacob. He received a $40 gratuity and a $40 annuity in Allegheny County 16 Apr. 1838.

Steinrod, —. His widow, Rachel Steinrod, received a $40 gratuity and a $40 annuity in Greene County 21 Mar. 1840. She died 26 Apr. 1851.

Stetzer, Henry. He was incorrectly reported as George Stetzer. The correction was made 4 Apr. 1837. He was from Mifflin County.

Stevens, —. His widow, Elizabeth Stevens, received a $40 gratuity and a $40 annuity in Northampton County 20 May 1839. Her name may have been Elizabeth Stever. She died 8 Apr. 1840.

Stevens, Reynolds. He received a $40 gratuity in Westmoreland County 12 Apr. 1845.

Stevenson, —. His widow, Mary Stevenson, received a $40 gratuity and a $40 annuity in Butler County in 1840.

Stewart, —. His widow, Elizabeth Stewart, received a $40 gratuity and a $40 annuity in Armstrong County in 1840.

Stewart, —. His widow, Nancy Stewart, received a $40 gratuity and a $40 annuity in Beaver County 5 Apr. 1842. She died 14 Dec. 1842.

Stewart, —. His widow, Rebecca Stewart, received a $40 annuity in Union County 12 Apr. 1845.

Stewart, James. He received a $40 gratuity in Allegheny County 11 Apr. 1844.

Stewart, John. He received a $40 gratuity and a $40 annuity in Venango County in 1838.

Stillwaggoner, —. His widow, Elizabeth Stillwaggoner, received a $40 gratuity and a $40 annuity in Lancaster County 14 Mar. 1842. She also appeared as Elizabeth Stillwaggon. She may have the widow of Jacob Stillwagon.

Stivers, Daniel. He received a $40 gratuity and a $40 annuity in Fayette County 13 Apr. 1838. He died 13 Oct. 1843.

Stone, Philip. He received a $40 gratuity and a $40 annuity in Northampton County in 1838.

Stour, John. His widow received a $40 gratuity 8 May 1850. His name may have been John Stout.

Straub, Charles. He received a $40 gratuity and a $40 annuity in Union County 4 Apr. 1837.

Stroop, —. His widow, Hannah Stroop, received a $40 annuity 19 Apr.1853 in Philadelphia. She may be the Hannah Stroop who was the widow of of John Stroop.

Sturges, —. His widow, Sarah Sturges, received a $40 gratuity and a $40 annuity in Delaware County 13 Feb. 1840.

Styles, —. His widow, Catherine Styles, received a $40 annuity in Berks County 15 Apr. 1852.

Sype, —. His widow, Anna M. Sype, received a $40 gratuity and a $40 annuity in York Co. 8 Apr. 1840.

Taggart, —. His widow, Hannah Taggart, received a $40 gratuity and a $40 annuity in Philadelphia County 5 Apr. 1842. She died in Mar. 1851.

Tanner, John. He received a $40 annuity in Erie County 12 Apr. 1845.

Tar, Daniel. He received a $40 gratuity in Westmoreland County 5 May 1841. One Daniel Tarr received a $40 gratuity and a $40 annuity 18 Apr. 1843.

Taylor, —. His widow, Jane Taylor, received a $40 gratuity and a $40 annuity in Westmoreland County in 1838.

Teagart, —. His widow, Barbara Teagart, received a $40 gratuity and a $40 annuity 5 Apr. 1842.

Templeton, James. He received a $40 gratuity and a $40 annuity in Washington County 20 Mar. 1838. He died 10 Apr. 1841.

Tenant, —. His widow, Rachael Tenant of Harford Co., Md. received a $40 gratuity and a $40 annuity 8 Apr.1840.

Thomas, David. He received benefits in Delaware County 27 Mar. 1837. He was dead by July 1838.

Thomas, George. His widow, A. Magdalene Thomas, received a $40 gratuity and a $40 annuity in Lancaster, Pa. 1 Feb. 1836.

Thomas, Henry. He received a $40 gratuity and a $40 annuity. His place of residence was corrected from Allegheny County to Fayette County in 1838. He died 6 June 1839.

Thomas, William. He received a $40 gratuity and a $40 annuity in Hagerstown, Md. 2 July 1842.

Thompson, —. His widow, Tacy Thompson, received a $40 annuity in Fayette County 27 Apr. 1852. Her name had been incorrectly given as Lucy Thompson.

Thompson, Robert. He received a $40 gratuity and a $40 annuity 20 May 1839 in Fayette County.

Till, George. He received a $40 gratuity in Berks County 8 May 1850.

Tillotsen, Asahel. He received a $40 gratuity and a $40 annuity in Tioga County 20 May 1839.

Tipton, Luke. He received a $40 gratuity and a $40 annuity in Holmes Co., Ohio 18 Apr. 1843.

Toops, —. His widow, Margaret Toops, received a $40 gratuity and a $40 annuity in Dauphin County 18 Apr. 1843. She died in Mar. 1853.

Torrance, James. He received a $40 annuity in Beaver County in Apr. 1846.

Transue, Elias. His widow, Catharine Transue, received a $40 annuity in Monroe County 11 Apr. 1848.

Transue, Philip. He received a $40 gratuity and a $40 annuity in Monroe County 8 Apr. 1840. He died 20 Sep. 1843.

Trensue, —. His widow, Mary Trensue, received a $40 gratuity and a $40 annuity in Monroe County 14 Mar. 1842.

Truax, —. His widow, Sarah Truax, received a $40 gratuity and a $40 annuity in Bedford County 21 Mar. 1840. She was 78 years old.

Truax, Joseph. He received a $40 gratuity and a $40 annuity in Bedford County 20 May 1839. He died 25 June 1839.

Truby, Christopher. He received a $40 gratuity in Clarion County 18 Apr. 1843.

Truby, Michael. He received a $40 gratuity and a $40 annuity in Armstrong County 20 Mar. 1838.

Tubbs, Samuel. He received a $40 gratuity and a $40 annuity in Tioga County 20 Mar. 1838.

Tunison, —. His widow, Susanna Tunison, received a $40 gratuity and a $40 annuity in Philadelphia 18 Apr. 1843.

Vananum, Rhea. He received a $40 annuity in Greene County 15 Mar. 1847.

Vancoyock, Timothy. He received assistance 17 Mar. 1838. He died 15 May 1844 in Huntingdon Co.

Vanorman, Samuel. He received a $40 gratuity and a $40 annuity in Monroe County in 1838.

Vanzant, John. He received a $40 gratuity and a $40 annuity 16 Apr. 1838 in Fayette County. He died 31 Mar. 1853 in Allegheny County.

Varden, John. He received a $40 annuity in Allegheny County 11 Apr. 1846.

Vernon, —. His widow, Mary Vernon, received a $40 gratuity and a $40 annuity in Delaware County 17 Mar. 1838. She died 1 Mar. 1840

Vinegardner, John. He received a $40 gratuity and a $40 annuity in Allegheny County 15 Mar. 1838.

Wakefield, Thomas. He received a $40 gratuity in Indiana County 13Apr. 1838.

Walker, James. He received a $40 gratuity and a $40 annuity in 1838 in Armstrong County.

Wall, William. He received a $40 gratuity and a $40 annuity in Juniata County 5 Apr. 1842. He died 20 Mar. 1858.

Wallace, —. His widow, Abigail Wallace, received a $40 gratuity and a $40 annuity in Chester Co. 18 Apr. 1843.

Wallace, James. He received a $40 gratuity and a $40 annuity in Greene County 25 June 1839.

Walter, —. His widow, Barbara Walter, received a $40 gratuity and a $40 annuity in Lancaster County 18 Apr. 1843.

Walton, William. He received a $40 gratuity and a $40 annuity in Luzerne County 13 Mar. 1839.

Wand, —. His widow, Susannah Wand, received a $40 gratuity and a $40 annuity. She resided in Harford Co., Md. 10 Feb. 1841.

Wann, —. His widow, Ann Catharine Wann, received a $40 gratuity and a $40 annuity in Lebanon County 14 Mar. 1842.

Warren, —. His widow, Mary Warren, received a $40 gratuity and a $40 annuity in Allegheny County 30 Apr. 1855.

Warren, James. He received a $40 gratuity and a $40 annuity in Berks County 13 Apr. 1841.

Washington, John. He received a $40 gratuity and a $40 annuity in Fayette County 20 May 1839. He was 69 years old in 1840.

Watles, —. His widow, Marcy C. Watles, was awarded a $40 gratuity and a $40 annuity in Baltimore, Md. 5 Apr. 1842.

Watson, James. He received a $40 gratuity and a $40 annuity in Allegheny County 20 May 1839. He died 8 Dec. 1843.

Watson, Oliver. He received a $40 gratuity and a $40 annuity in Lancaster County 21 Mar. 1840. He died 2 Jan. 1841.

Weber, —. His widow, Ann Maria Weber, received a $40 gratuity and a $40 annuity in Lebanon County 13 Apr. 1841.

Weidner, Michael. He received a $40 gratuity and a $40 annuity in York County 5 May 1841.

Weir, —. His widow, Margaret Weir, received a $40 annuity 7 Apr. 1846.

Welsh, John. He received assistance in Butler County 15 Mar. 1838.

Welshantz, John. He received a $40 gratuity and a $40 annuity 8 Apr. 1840 in York County.

Wentz, —. His widow, Catherine Wentz, received a $40 gratuity and a $40 annuity in York County in 1839.

Wentzel, —. His widow, Elizabeth Wentzel, received a $40 gratuity and a $40 annuity in Montgomery County 8 Apr. 1840. She died 7 Feb. 1845.

Werner, Peter. He received a $40 annuity in Schuylkill County 12 Apr. 1845.

Wertz, —. His widow, Catharine Wertz, received a $40 gratuity and a $40 annuity in Berks County 13 Apr. 1841. She died 8 Nov. 1839.

Wertz, John. He received a $40 gratuity and a $40 annuity in Northumberland County in 1838.

Weygandt, —. His widow, Catharine Weygandt, received a $40 gratuity and a $40 annuity in Berks County in 1838.

White, David. He received a $40 gratuity and a $40 annuity in Allegheny County 13 Feb. 1840.

White, George. He received a $40 gratuity and a $40 annuity in Monroe County 21 Mar. 1840. He died 4 Feb. 1845.

White, Joseph. He received a $40 gratuity in Indiana County 13 Apr. 1838.

White, William. He received a $40 gratuity and a $40 annuity in Indiana County 27 Mar. 1838.

Whitehead, Thomas. He received a $40 annuity 12 Apr. 1845.

Whollery, Jacob. He received a $40 annuity in Fayette County 16 Mar. 1847.

Widaw, —. His widow, Barbara Widaw, received a $40 annuity in Adams County 19 Apr. 1853.

Widener, —. His widow, Susan Widener, received a $40 gratuity and a $40 annuity in Chester County in 1838.

Wilcox, —. His widow, Catharine Wilcox, received a $40 annuity in Fayette County 21 Apr. 1846.

Wilhelm, Frederick. He received a $40 gratuity and a $40 annuity 5 Apr. 1842. He died 22 Dec. 1842 in York County.

Wilkins, —. His widow, Eleanor E. Wilkins, received a $40 gratuity and a $40 annuity 11 Apr. 1844 in Indiana County.

Wilkins, —. His widow, Nancy Wilkins, received a $40 annuity in Jefferson County 15 Apr. 1851.

Wilkins, —. His widow, Jane Wilkins, received a $40 gratuity in Indiana County 8 May 1850.

Willard, —. His widow, Mary Willard, received a $40 gratuity and a $40 annuity in Armstrong County 22 Apr. 1857.

Williams, —. His widow, Honore Williams, received a $40 annuity in Fayette County 12 Apr. 1851.

Williams, —. His widow, Margaret Williams, received a $40 gratuity and a $40 annuity in Allegheny County in 1838. She was 70 years old in 1840.

Williams, Eli. He received a $40 gratuity and a $40 annuity in Mifflin County 15 Mar. 1838.

Williams, Robert. He received a $40 gratuity and a $40 annuity 21 Feb. 1838 in Westmoreland County.

Williamson, —. His widow, Mary Williamson, received a $40 gratuity and a $40 annuity in Mercer County 20 May 1839.

Wilson, John. He received a $40 gratuity and a $40 annuity in Armstrong County 20 May 1839.

Wilson, Thomas. He received a $40 gratuity in Westmoreland County 15 Mar. 1847.

Wilson, William. He received a $40 gratuity and a $40 annuity in Butler County 13 Mar. 1839. He died 1 Feb. 1839.

Wilson, William. He received a $40 gratuity and a $40 annuity in Allegheny County 5 Apr. 1842.

Wilt, Thomas. He received a $40 gratuity and a $40 annuity in Bedford County 13Apr. 1838. He died 8 Oct. 1842.

Wise, Martin. He received benefits 27 Mar. 1837. His widow, Elizabeth Wise, received the $140 due her late husband 10 Feb. 1853.

Wisener, Ananias. He received a $40 gratuity and a $40 annuity in 1838 in Westmoreland County.

Witman, —. His widow, Elizabeth Witman, received a $40 gratuity and a $40 annuity in Berks County 13 Feb. 1840. She died 27 Sep. 1845.

Wolf, —. His widow, Catherine E. Wolf, received a $40 gratuity and a $40 annuity in Lehigh County 13 Apr. 1839.

Wolf, —. His widow, Mary Wolf, received a $40 annuity and a $40 gratuity in Philadelphia County 17 Mar. 1838.

Wolf, John. He received a $40 gratuity and a $40 annuity in York County 8 Feb. 1842.

Woodcock, John. He received a $40 gratuity and a $40 annuity in Potter County in 1841. He died 10 Apr. 1848.

Workman, —. His widow, Jane S. Workman, received a $40 annuity in Washington County 12 Apr. 1851.

Wowert, Martin. He received a $40 gratuity and a $40 annuity in 1838. He was from Lancaster County.

Wright, Aaron. He received a $40 gratuity and a $40 annuity 8 Apr. 1840. He was 78 years old in 1840. He died 4 Mar. 1841 in Berks County.

Wurtz, Philip. His widow, Dorothy Wurtz, received a $40 annuity in Philadelphia County 10 Apr. 1849.

Yellis, Henry. He received a $40 gratuity and a $40 annuity in Montgomery County 25 June 1839.

Yerkes, George. He received a $40 gratuity in Montgomery County 17 Mar. 1838.

Yoho, Jacob. He received a $40 gratuity and a $40 annuity in 1838 in Beaver County. He died 26 July 1843.

Young, —. His widow, Jemima Young, received a $40 gratuity and a $40 annuity in 1838. She died 11 Aug. 1849 in Northampton County.

Young, —. His widow, Magdalena Young, received a $40 gratuity and a $40 annuity 18 Apr. 1843 in Berks County.

Young, John. He received a $40 gratuity in Venango County in 1840.

Young, Philip. He received a $40 annuity in Beaver County 7 Apr. 1846. He died 23 May 1847. He was 83 years old in 1840.

Youngman, —. His widow, Ann Elizabeth Youngman, received a $40 gratuity and a $40 annuity in Union County 11 Apr. 1844. She died 28 Sep. 1851.

Zeigler, Emanuel. He received a $40 gratuity and a $40 annuity in Adams County 16 Apr. 1838.

Zimmerman, —. His widow, Barbara Zimmerman, received a $40 annuity in Schuylkill County 27 Feb. 1851.

Zimmerman, —. His widow, Mary Zimmerman, received a $40 gratuity and a $40 annuity in Baltimore, Md. 18 Apr. 1843.

Zimmerman, Abraham. He was awarded a $40 gratuity and a $40 annuity in Schuylkill County 16 Apr. 1838. He was 83 years old in 1840. He died 1 May 1846.

Addenda

Allison, John. N.C. Pvt. He served in the Continental Line under Col. Archibald Lyttle and Capt. William Lyttle for nine months. He had not drawn his land warrant. He was from White County, Tennessee in 1809.

Ashe, John Baptiste. N.C. Maj. He served in the Continental Army. His great-grand-daughter, Martha B. (Ashe) Rogers sought the return of his commission signed by John Jay on 4 May 1937 by private act of Congress.

Breakbill, Peter. —. —. He had purchased land in the Highawassee. The land turned out to be a mountain unfit for cultivation. He had lost 7 head of valuable horses and about 12 head of cattle. He sought relief from Tennessee.

Cannon, Pugh. N.C. —. One of his legs had to be amputated and he was likely to lose his eye sight. He had a family of females to support and sought a pension in Maury Co., Tennessee in 1821. He also appeared as Hugh Cannon.

Capron, Seth. —. —. He received his depreciation pay and sought additional relief from Congress 24 Nov. 1837.

Chapman, —. —. —. He was at Brandywine. His son, James Chapman, was nearly 75 years old and had served at different periods of time. He was incompetent to support his family and was afflicted with rheumatism. He applied from Giles County, Tennessee 29 Nov. 1845 for relief.

Clayton, John. N.C. Lt. His realty in Monroe County, Tennessee had not more than 15 acres suitable for cultivation. He was 87 years old and sought relief to own the track in fee simple in 1825.

Draper, Simeon. —. —. He received his depreciation pay and sought further relief from Congress 24 Nov. 1837.

Gideon, Roger. N.C. —. He was at Long Cane under Gen. Clarke and in a great many skirmishes with the Tories. He lost his land in Roane County and was compelled to rent land. He sought land in the Highawassee District.

Hall, Jacob. N.J. —. He was pensioned under the act of 1818. He was wounded at the battle of Springfield 7 June 1780. Oliver Cromwell was with him at that time. Dr. Tucker extracted the ball in 1807. He was enlisted by Capt. Nathaniel Boman. He sought an increase in his pension. Congress rejected his petition 21 May 1840. *Vide* his entry on page 331.

Haskell, Samuel. —. —. He received his depreciation pay and sought further relief from Congress 24 Nov. 1783.

Humphress, Elijah. N.C. —. In Oct. 1792 he had a military warrant for 640 acres which had been located and surveyed by Sampson Williams to whom a grant was issued. He had made a search for the land and applied to Williams to show it. It could not be found. He sought a law for new warrant as in cases for land lost by prior claims. He was in Wilson County, Tennessee in Oct. 1803.

Jones, William. N.C. —. He served against the British and the Indians. He had been a Baptist minister for more than 40 years. He sought 160 acres in McMinn County. He was from Claiborne County, Tennessee in Oct. 1823.

Kenner, Howson. N.C. Surgeon. He served under Martin and Gen. Sevier in the attack on Col. Tipton. He was from Hawkins County , Tennessee in 1823. He sought remunerations.

LeJeunesse, Prudent. —. —. He first applied for a pension under the act of 1828 for service as a major. He stated that he was a baker at West Point so his application was rejected. He applied again under the act of 1832. He stated he was a Canadian refugee and joined in 1775 under Gen. Montgomery as a captain. He was in charge of the government bakery at West Point. He was again rejected. He had no wife or children. Congress rejected the claim from his nephews and nieces for relief 9 Feb. 1848.

McNabb, David. N.C. Capt. He served under Gen. Francis Marion. He sought land for the amount of his certificate plus interest. He was from Carter County, Tennessee in 1823.

Moore, Thomas. N.C. — He served three years in the horse troops under Col. Webb and Washington. He was at Guilford Court House and King's Mountain. He was wounded in his body and thigh and lost part of his hand. He sought relief in Rhea County, Tennessee at the age of 78 in 1825.

Osborn, James.—. —. He received his depreciation pay and sought further relief from Congress 24 Nov. 1837.

Scott, William. Va. —. He served in the 14th Regiment. He was captured at Charleston and died in captivity. His widow was Mary Scott and she received bounty land warrant no. 4,604 which she assigned to William Putnam. His son and heir, Joseph Scott, stated that Mary Scott did not assign the warrant. The 200 acres in the Virginia Military Tract in Ohio had been patented to John Graham 3 Feb. 1800. Congress refused the petition of Joseph Scott because he had failed to show that he had taken legal action to show the defects in the matter.

Wade, Edward. Va. Lt. He served under Nathaniel Cook in 1776 and was promoted to Captain. He died at Williamsburg 7 Mar. 1776. His sole heir, Washington Wade, sought his seven years' half-pay plus interest 21 Jan. 1840. Washington Wade's sister was the mother of Matthew Martin, aged 74 years of Bedford Co., Tenn. who testified in his behalf.

Walker, John. N.C. QM Sgt. He served two and a half years. He was unable to get a living and had been reduced to sickness. He sought relief from Tennessee in Wayne County in July 1818.

Walker, Samuel. N.J. —, His widow, Hepzeba Walker, failed to prove the length of his militia service and was rejected by Congress 21 May 1840.

Index

Because the lists of pensioners are in alphabetical order in the text, the entries in the index are those other individuals appearing in each entry. The index entries also include all persons appearing in the appendix and the addenda. The spelling is that which appears in the records so it is advisable to seek out all possible variants.

Index

Index

Index

Index

Index

Index

Index

979

Index

Index

Index

989

Index

May, Anne 549
May, John 659
May, Mary 549, 924
May, Sarah 549
Maybank, — 212
Mayberry, Elizabeth 890
Mayberry, Nancy 550
Maybre, Richard 150, 278
Maybury, Joseph 550
Maybury, Thomas 550
Mayer, Leonard 583
Mayham, — 166, 205
Mayhew, Eleanor L. 550
Mayhugh, Jonathan 550
Maylen, Stephen 403
Maynard, — 727
Mayo, Rebecca 550
Mayrant, John 264
Mayse, Thomas 551
Mayson, George 545
Mayson, James 92
Maze, James 550
Maze, Mary 551
Mazyck, — 563
Mazyck, Daniel 622
Meacham, Rebeckah 551
Mead, — 118, 567, 644, 801, 924
Mead, A. 469
Mead, Andrew 551
Mead, Catharine 924
Mead, James 8
Mead, John 31, 97, 408, 450
Mead, Mary 552
Mead, Matthew 265, 406, 450, 852, 882
Meade, — 30, 443 330, 489
Meade, Benjamin 552
Meade, David 552
Meade, E. 167
Meade, Hodijah 552
Meade, Richard 558
Meadows, Ann 552
Means, — 924
Means, Hugh 479
Means, Rosannah 924
Means, William 552
Mears, — 256
Mears, Samuel 552
Mearse, John 821

Mebane, — 563, 585
Mebane, Robert 196, 696
Meddick, — 84
Meeker, Elizabeth 553
Meeker, Samuel 552
Meekes, — 834
Meese, Baltzer 553
Meeze, Balser 317
Megan, Robert 302
Meherg, John 520
Meherg, Susanna 520, 553
Mehergh, Susanna 553
Meigs, Jonathan 494
Meigs, Return J. 30, 57, 58, 177, 193, 238, 278, 283, 284, 306, 313, 615, 640, 686, 733, 848
Mekers, — 727
Melarkey, Daniel 924
Mell, — 924
Mell, Maria 924
Mellen, James 553
Mellon, Atchison 225
Mellon, James 741
Mellon, Susannah 553
Melony, Bartholomew 553
Melvin, Mary 554
Menager, Cornelia S. 428
Menager, Maria L. 428
Mendon, Elizabeth 554
Mendon, John 585
Menges, — 531, 592
Menkel, Jacob
Mento, — 924
Mento, Elizabeth 924
Menzies, Hannah 554
Mercer, — 733
Mercer, Elizabeth 554
Mercer, Hugh 802
Mercer, Isabella 554
Mercer, John F. 578
Mercer, William 554
Mercereau, Joseph 554
Mercereau, Joshua 554
Merckle, Christian 554
Meredith, Charlotte A. 345
Meredith, Samuel 623
Meredith, Sarah 749
Meredith, William L. 554

Meree, Ann 554
Merit, Phebe 700
Merkle, Jacob 555
Merker, — 830
Meriwether, Col. 21
Meriwether, T. 16
Merrell, Peter 369
Merrick, Mary 555
Merrill, Daniel 792
Merriman, — 608
Merriman, Archibald 924
Merriman, Frederick 924
Merriman, Mary 924
Merrow, Samuel 481
Merryman, Elizabeth 556
Merryman, Mary 924
Merser, Thomas 306
Mershon, John 556
Mershon, Peter 556
Mertz, George 556
Mescotzay, — 294
Messenger, John 474
Messer, — 124
Messersmith, — 924
Messersmith, Susannah 924
Metlin, Sarah 556
Meyer, — 96
Meyer, Christiana 556
Meyer, Philip 764
Meyers, — 924
Meyers, Christopher 464
Meyers, Lewis 589
Meyers, Salome 924
Miatt, Nancy 556
Michael, Catharine 556
Michel, — 826
Mickle, Jane 556
Middagh, Anna 556
Middleton, — 308, 531, 736
Middleton, Benjamin 485
Middleton, Charles 230, 329
Middleton, Charles S. 484, 788
Middleton, Elizabeth A. 644
Middleton, Sarah 557
Miels, Charles 370
Mifflin, — 216
Migill, Thomas 747
Mignault, Alfred 557
Mignault, Amilie 557
Mignault, Anthony 557

Index

Index

Index

Index

Index

Index

Index

Index

Index

Index

Index

CPSIA information can be obtained at www.ICGtesting.com
Printed in the USA
LVOW041352170113

316021LV00004B/96/P